• Carchemish

COMMITTEE FOR TECHNICAL EDUCATION

• Nineveh

Euphrates

Tigris

• Babylon

N

• Ur

E. LOWENSTEIN

THE INTERPRETER'S BIBLE

THE INTERPRETER'S BIBLE

IN TWELVE VOLUMES

VOLUME VI

THE
INTERPRETER'S BIBLE

—

The Holy Scriptures

IN THE KING JAMES AND REVISED STANDARD VERSIONS

WITH GENERAL ARTICLES AND

INTRODUCTION, EXEGESIS, EXPOSITION

FOR EACH BOOK OF THE BIBLE

IN TWELVE VOLUMES

VOLUME

VI

דבר־אלהינו יקום לעולם

NEW YORK *Abingdon Press* NASHVILLE

975

ISBN 0-687-19212-9

Library of Congress Catalog Card Number: 51-12276

P

SET UP, PRINTED, AND BOUND BY THE
PARTHENON PRESS, AT NASHVILLE,
TENNESSEE, UNITED STATES OF AMERICA

ABBREVIATIONS AND EXPLANATIONS

ABBREVIATIONS

Canonical books and bibliographical terms are abbreviated according to common usage

Amer. Trans. — *The Bible, An American Translation*, Old Testament, ed. J. M. P. Smith
Apoc.—Apocrypha
Aq.—Aquila
ASV—American Standard Version (1901)
Barn.—Epistle of Barnabas
Clem.—Clement
C.T.—Consonantal Text
Did.—Didache
Ecclus.—Ecclesiasticus
ERV—English Revised Version (1881-85)

Exeg.—Exegesis
Expos.—Exposition
Goodspeed—*The Bible, An American Translation*, New Testament and Apocrypha, tr. Edgar J. Goodspeed
Herm. Vis., etc.—The Shepherd of Hermas: Visions, Mandates, Similitudes
Ign. Eph., etc.—Epistles of Ignatius to the Ephesians, Magnesians, Trallians, Romans, Philadelphians, Smyrnaeans, and Polycarp

KJV—King James Version (1611)
LXX—Septuagint
Macc.—Maccabees
Moffatt—*The Bible, A New Translation*, by James Moffatt
M.T.—Masoretic Text
N.T.—New Testament
O.L.—Old Latin
O.T.—Old Testament
Polyc. Phil.—Epistle of Polycarp to the Philippians
Pseudep. — Pseudepigrapha
Pss. Sol.—Psalms of Solomon

RSV—Revised Standard Version (1946-52)
Samar.—Samaritan recension
Symm.—Symmachus
Targ.—Targum
Test. Reuben, etc.—Testament of Reuben, and others of the Twelve Patriarchs
Theod.—Theodotion
Tob.—Tobit
Vulg.—Vulgate
Weymouth—*The New Testament in Modern Speech*, by Richard Francis Weymouth
Wisd. Sol.—Wisdom of Solomon

QUOTATIONS AND REFERENCES

Boldface type in Exegesis and Exposition indicates a quotation from either the King James or the Revised Standard Version of the passage under discussion. The two versions are distinguished only when attention is called to a difference between them. Readings of other versions are not in boldface type and are regularly identified.

In scripture references a letter (*a*, *b*, etc.) appended to a verse number indicates a clause within the verse; an additional Greek letter indicates a subdivision within the clause. When no book is named, the book under discussion is understood.

Arabic numbers connected by colons, as in scripture references, indicate chapters and verses in deuterocanonical and noncanonical works. For other ancient writings roman numbers indicate major divisions, arabic numbers subdivisions, these being connected by periods. For modern works a roman number and an arabic number connected by a comma indicate volume and page. Bibliographical data on a contemporary work cited by a writer may be found by consulting the first reference to the work by that writer (or the bibliography, if the writer has included one).

GREEK TRANSLITERATIONS

α = a	ε = e	ι = i	ν = n	ρ = r	φ = ph
β = b	ζ = z	κ = k	ξ = x	σ(ς) = s	χ = ch
γ = g	η = ē	λ = l	ο = o	τ = t	ψ = ps
δ = d	θ = th	μ = m	π = p	υ = u, y	ω = ō

HEBREW AND ARAMAIC TRANSLITERATIONS

I. HEBREW ALPHABET

א = ’	ה = h	ט = ṭ	מ(ם) = m	פ(ף) = p, ph	שׂ = s, sh
ב = b, bh	ו = w	י = y	נ(ן) = n	צ(ץ) = ç	ת = t, th
ג = g, gh	ז = z	כ(ך) = k, kh	ס = ş	ק = q	
ד = d, dh	ח = ḥ	ל = l	ע = ‘	ר = r	

II. MASORETIC POINTING

	Pure-long	Tone-long	Short	Composite *shewa*
	ָ = â	ָ = ā	ַ = a	ֲ = ᵃ
	ֵ = ê	ֵ = ē	ֶ = e	ֱ = ᵉ
	ִ or ִי = î		ִ = i	ֳ = ᵒ
	ֹ or וֹ = ô	ֹ = ō	ָ = o	
	וּ = û		ֻ = u	

NOTE: (*a*) The *páthah* furtive is transliterated as a *haṭeph-páthah*. (*b*) The simple *shewa*, when vocal, is transliterated ᵉ. (*c*) The tonic accent, which is indicated only when it occurs on a syllable other than the last, is transliterated by an acute accent over the vowel.

TABLE OF CONTENTS

VOLUME VI

THE BOOK OF LAMENTATIONS

THE BOOK OF EZEKIEL

THE BOOK OF DANIEL

THE BOOK OF HOSEA

THE BOOK OF JOEL

THE BOOK OF AMOS

THE BOOK OF OBADIAH

THE BOOK OF JONAH

THE BOOK OF MICAH

TABLE OF CONTENTS

THE BOOK OF NAHUM

THE BOOK OF HABAKKUK

THE BOOK OF ZEPHANIAH

THE BOOK OF HAGGAI

THE BOOK OF ZECHARIAH

CHAPTERS 1-8

CHAPTERS 9-14

THE BOOK OF MALACHI

MAPS

The Book of

LAMENTATIONS

Introduction and Exegesis by THEOPHILE J. MEEK
Exposition by WILLIAM PIERSON MERRILL

LAMENTATIONS

INTRODUCTION

Since the Old Testament is an anthology of the literature of the ancient Hebrews, it contains many different types. Among these is the elegy, well represented by the book of Lamentations, whose five chapters are five separate poems, each complete in itself.

I. Title

The book has no title in Hebrew, but like the first five books of the Old Testament, it was known by its first word, 'ěkhāh, which is an exclamatory particle, meaning "How!" By the rabbis, however, it came to be called Qînôth, "Dirges" or "Lamentations," and this is its title in the Talmud and the Septuagint. In the later Greek versions, the Syriac, and Latin versions it has the longer title, "The Lamentations of Jeremiah."

The dirge seems to have originated as a funeral spell to keep the dead in their place and protect the living from them, and its composition was in the hands of women professionals (cf. Jer. 9:17-22). In course of time, however, it came to be a genuine expression of grief over the loss of a loved one (cf. II Sam. 1:17-27). In Lamentations (cf. Amos 5:1-2; Ezek. 26:17-18) it is a poem commemorating the destruction of Jerusalem by the Babylonians in 586 b.c. and is similar to the laments which the Sumerians composed over the fall of some of their great cities, particularly Ur.[1] However, only chs. 1-2; 4 are dirges in the strict sense of the word; ch. 3 is a personal lament, ending in a prayer, and ch. 5 is a prayer.

II. Place in the Canon

In the Hebrew Bible the book is in the third division, the Writings, as the third of the five

[1] See "A Sumerian Lamentation," tr. Samuel N. Kramer, in James B. Pritchard, ed., *Ancient Near Eastern Texts Relating to the Old Testament* (Princeton: Princeton University Press, 1950), pp. 455-63.

Megilloth or Rolls, the others being the Song of Songs, Ruth, Ecclesiastes, and Esther. In the Septuagint it came to be placed in the second division, after Jeremiah, and the later versions, including the English, continued this practice. Like the other Megilloth, Lamentations is used liturgically, being read in the synagogue on the ninth of Ab, the fast day observed in commemoration of the destruction of Jerusalem. Its canonicity seems never to have been questioned.

III. Literary Form

Chs. 1-4 are alphabetic acrostics of twenty-two stanzas, one for each letter of the Hebrew alphabet in their usual order in ch. 1, but with ע and פ transposed in chs. 2-4. In chs. 1-3 the stanzas contain three lines each, with the exception of 1:7 and 2:19, which have four lines. Ch. 4 consists of two-line stanzas exclusively. In ch. 3 all three lines of each stanza begin with the same letter and each line carries a verse number (cf. Ps. 119). Ch. 5 is not an acrostic, but it contains twenty-two lines, corresponding to the number of letters in the Hebrew alphabet (cf. Pss. 33; 38; 103). It is possible that this was a first draft which the author intended later to work into an acrostic. The acrostic structure is found in Prov. 31:10-31 and rather often in the Psalter. Doubtless it was originally used because of a belief in the magic power of the acrostic, but in course of time the form became traditional, and it also functioned as an aid to memory.

IV. Metrical Structure

It was in Lamentations that metrical structure was first definitely recognized in Hebrew poetry, and it was from the name of this book that the meter of chs. 1-4 came to be called qînāh. The regular form is a line of two stichs (a distich) of irregular length, the first with

3

three feet, indicated by stresses, and the second with two feet—that is, 3+2. It used to be thought that this was the only form of the *qînāh* meter, but we know now that this dominant form has 2+3 and 2+2 as variants, and in place of the usual distich there may be an occasional tristich (e.g., 3+2+2).[2] Even a casual glance at chs. 1–4 will show that a line like 1:3*a* or 1:14*c* can be construed only as 2+3, and another like 1:1*b* or 1:19*b* as 2+2, and these are assuredly not to be taken as changes in meter, which is consistently *qînāh* throughout. Neither is the caesura to be put in an unnatural place in the 2+3 line simply to make it 3+2; and in the 2+2 line another word is not to be introduced nor is a single word in the first stich to be given two stresses to make it the regular 3+2. Since parallelism in thought is basic to Hebrew poetry, the balancing units are thought units; hence each stress unit must be a thought unit, and since part of a word cannot be a thought unit, no word can be given two stresses, despite current practice to the contrary. The only recourse, accordingly, for a 2+2 line in a 3+2 context is to take it as a variant. Another variant is the tristich, as, for example, in 1:16*a*, which is clearly to be scanned as 3+2+2. The existence of the tristich, demonstrated as long ago as 1905 by W. H. Cobb,[3] is not as generally recognized as it should be.

It may be objected that this interpretation of Hebrew meter is too elastic, but if one follows the usual rigid system, he is forced continually to do one of three things: either have more frequent changes of meter in a single poem than are found in any other literature, or give a single word two stresses, or emend the text. An elastic metrical interpretation that fits the facts is surely better than a rigid one to which the facts have to be fitted. It is to be noted that the lines in the Revised Standard Version correspond to the stichs of the Hebrew text, with the secondary stich or stichs indented.

In ch. 5, as already indicated, there is a change in literary form, and there is likewise a change in meter, from 3+2 to 3+3, which occasionally has the variant 3+2, as in 5:2, or the variant 2+2+2, as in 5:3, or even 2+2+3, as in 5:1.[4]

[2] See Theophile J. Meek, "The Structure of Hebrew Poetry," *Journal of Religion,* IX (1929), 523-50, and "The Metrical Structure of II Kings 19:20-28," *Crozer Quarterly,* XVIII (1941), 126-31; also T. H. Robinson, *The Poetry of the Old Testament* (London: Duckworth, 1947), pp. 20-46.

[3] *A Criticism of Systems of Hebrew Metre* (Oxford: Clarendon Press, 1905), p. 5 *et passim.*

[4] For these and other variants of the 3+3 see Meek, *op. cit.,* pp. 542-44.

V. Authorship, Date, and Provenance

The tradition that Jeremiah was the author of Lamentations is ancient and persistent. It manifestly had its origin in the statement in II Chr. 35:25: "So Jeremiah composed a lamentation for Josiah, and all the men and women singers speak of Josiah in their lamentations down to the present, and they made them a rite for Israel; in fact, they are written in the Lamentations." And 4:20, which evidently refers to Zedekiah, was interpreted by the Targum as referring to Josiah, an interpretation followed by all the early commentators. Hence, it is little wonder that the whole book came to be ascribed to Jeremiah and was transferred to a place in the canon immediately after his book. Not only is it called "Lamentations of Jeremiah" in most of the versions, but at the head of the Septuagint is this explicit statement: "And it came to pass, after Israel was taken captive and Jerusalem laid waste, that Jeremiah sat weeping and lamented with this lamentation over Jerusalem and said . . . ." This has every appearance of being a translation from Hebrew and apparently stood at the head of the text used by the translator. It is followed in the Syriac, Old Latin, and Vulgate, and the Targum similarly ascribes the book to Jeremiah.

It is easy to understand how the tradition arose. Lamentations, in part at least, must have been written by one who had experienced the siege and fall of Jerusalem, with all the miseries that followed; Jeremiah was such a person and was much moved by those experiences. There is much in the vocabulary and phraseology of Lamentations that is found also in Jeremiah (see Exeg.), and there is as well some likeness in general tone and temper between the two books.[5] Jeremiah was highly emotional in temperament and was often given to sorrow and lamentation, but his traditional reputation as the weeping prophet ("jeremiad" being a synonym of "dirge") rests, not on his own book, but on his professed authorship of Lamentations, and that would seem to be quite impossible despite the strength of the tradition.

For one thing, if there had been any general belief when the prophetic books were canonized that Lamentations was written by Jeremiah, it would assuredly have been included with the Prophets and not left for the Writings, which was the last portion of the Old Testament to be canonized. The fact that it was canonized so late shows that the tradition connecting it with Jeremiah was late. The Codex

[5] See, e.g., S. R. Driver, *An Introduction to the Literature of the Old Testament* (rev. ed.; New York: Charles Scribner's Sons, 1913), p. 462.

Vaticanus and certain other Greek manuscripts have the title simply as "Lamentations," as against the later "Lamentations of Jeremiah," and this must represent the original Septuagint because otherwise it would be difficult to explain the absence of Jeremiah's name from the title.

Despite the likenesses between Lamentations and the book of Jeremiah, there are certain marked differences which far outweigh the similarities. The ideas of the two books differ radically on a number of points. Lamentations has a much higher regard for kings, princes, and priests than Jeremiah ever had. Jeremiah's opinion of Zedekiah (37:17-20), his house (22:13-30), the nobles (5:4-9), and the priests (2:26-28; 20:1-5) stands in marked contrast to that expressed in Lam. 1:6; 2:2, 6, 9; 4:7, 16, 20; 5:12. Passages like 1:4, 9, 19; 2:6, 9, 20; 4:16 show a concern for the cultus that is quite foreign to Jeremiah. In 4:17 the author identifies himself with those who had expected help from Egypt, whereas Jeremiah had affirmed that such a hope was utterly vain (37:5-10). Jeremiah could hardly have written Lam. 5:7, which is a direct contradiction of Jer. 31:29-30. Neither could a man so natural, free, and unaffected as Jeremiah be the author of poetry so artificial in structure as Lamentations. The style is quite different and likewise the vocabulary. For example, Adonai (Lord), as a title of Yahweh, is used by itself fourteen times in Lam. 1–3, but only in combination with Yahweh in Jeremiah. The particle ש is never used as the relative in Jeremiah, but it appears a number of times in Lamentations (2:15, 16; 4:9; 5:18). There are also a large number of other words in Lamentations that are not found in Jeremiah; we have in the latter a more ordinary vocabulary, lacking the many *hapax legomena* and unusual words found in the former.[6] In fact, Lamentations would seem to have closer affinities with books other than Jeremiah—chs. 2 and 4 with Ezekiel, chs. 1 and 5 with Second Isaiah, and all five chapters with the Psalms.[7] This suggests that the five poems were not written by a single author at all, and that is indicated also by the difference in the alphabetic order of the stanzas, already noted, between ch. 1 and chs. 2–4, and by the difference in character, style, point of view, and historical background among the poems. Wilhelm Ru-

dolph is the one modern scholar to argue for a single author, making him a member of Zedekiah's suite that fled with the king on the fall of Jerusalem (cf. 4:19), but the likenesses among the poems, which he stresses, are to be expected from the common theme and purpose.

Chs. 2 and 4 have most in common and are generally supposed to be the work of a single author. The descriptive material is so vivid that it must have been composed at a time very close to the fall of Jerusalem by one who lived through the catastrophe and wrote while the details were still fresh in his mind. Ch. 1 is further removed from the catastrophe and is more concerned with its effect upon the city than with the catastrophe itself. This chapter should probably be dated toward the end of the Exile, when time had somewhat toned down the agony of grief. Rudolph, however, makes it the earliest of the poems, maintaining that its references point to the first capture and deportation in 597 B.C. As already noted, ch. 3 is strictly not a dirge but a personal lament, and may not be associated with the fall of Jerusalem at all. Its terms are so vague and general, in contrast with the wealth of detail in the other three chapters, that it could come from almost any time in the postexilic period. Ch. 5 is nearest in general character to ch. 3, but it is manifestly earlier. Since 5:18 shows that the temple had not yet been rebuilt and 5:7 indicates a time at least one generation after the catastrophe of 586, we may date it about 530 B.C.

The poems were put together in a single collection, not because of common authorship, but because of common theme and common use in the cultus. They came from different authors and different dates, but they were probably all composed in Palestine, although chs. 2 and 4 may be of Babylonian origin. The latter are the highest in literary merit, with ch. 1 a close second, then ch. 5, and finally ch. 3, the most artificial and least artistic of all. The poems are not the spontaneous outpouring of sorrow that we would expect from a man like Jeremiah, but a work of conscious art, with the grief restrained and measured, but poignant nevertheless, and well suited to liturgical usage. They are universally recognized as a classic of their kind.

VI. Religious Significance

The book of Lamentations was written, not simply to memorialize the tragic destruction of Jerusalem, but to interpret the meaning of God's rigorous treatment of his people, to the end that they would learn the lessons of the past and retain their faith in him in the face of

---

[6] See *ibid.*, p. 463, and the references there cited.

[7] See the exhaustive study by Max Löhr, "Der Sprachgebrauch des Buches der Klagelieder," *Zeitschrift für die alttestamentliche Wissenschaft*, XIV (1894), 31-50; "Threni III. und die jeremianische Autorschaft des Buches der Klagelieder," *ibid.*, XXIV (1904), 1-16; and "Alphabetische und alphabetisierende Lieder im Alten Testament," *ibid.*, XXV (1905), 173-98.

overwhelming disaster. There is deep sorrow over the past and some complaint, but there is also radiant hope for the future, particularly in ch. 3.

VII. Outline of Contents

I. The misery of Jerusalem (1:1-22)
II. Divine judgment upon the city (2:1-22)
III. A personal lament and prayer (3:1-66)
IV. Jerusalem in the past and in the present (4: 1-22)
V. A national prayer for mercy (5:1-22)

VIII. Selected Bibliography

BETTAN, ISRAEL. The Five Scrolls. Cincinnati: Union of American Hebrew Congregations, 1950.
BUDDE, KARL. Die fünf Megillot ("Kurzer Hand-Commentar zum Alten Testament"). Tübingen: J. C. B. Mohr, 1898.
GOTTWALD, NORMAN K. Studies in the Book of Lamentations ("Studies in Biblical Theology No. 14"). London: Student Christian Movement Press, 1954.
HALLER, MAX. Die fünf Megilloth ("Handbuch zum Alten Testament"). Tübingen: J. C. B. Mohr, 1940.
LÖHR, MAX. Die Klagelieder des Jeremia ("Handkommentar zum Alten Testament"). 2nd ed. Göttingen: Vandenhoeck & Ruprecht, 1906.
RUDOLPH, WILHELM. Die Klagelieder ("Kommentar zum Alten Testament"). Leipzig: A. Deichert, 1939.
STREANE, A. W. The Book of the Prophet Jeremiah Together with the Lamentations ("Cambridge Bible"). Cambridge: Cambridge University Press, 1913.

LAMENTATIONS

TEXT, EXEGESIS, AND EXPOSITION

1 How doth the city sit solitary, *that was* full of people! *how* is she become as a widow! she *that was* great among the nations, *and* princess among the provinces, *how* is she become tributary!

1 How lonely sits the city
    that was full of people!
How like a widow has she become,
    she that was great among the nations!
She that was a princess among the cities
    has become a vassal.

I. THE MISERY OF JERUSALEM (1:1-22)

In vss. 1-11, 17 the poet is the speaker, except in the last lines of vss. 9, 11, where Jerusalem, personified as a woman, is the speaker, as she is in vss. 12-16, 18-22. The dirge, according to rule, ends in a prayer, vss. 20-22.

1:1. The meter of the first line is 2+2+2, a variant of the 3+2; or the last two words might possibly be joined, to make the regular 3+2. The first word איכה, **how,** is used to introduce dirges, appearing again in 2:1; 4:1, and also in Isa. 1:21; Jer. 48:17. The shorter form without deictic ה is more frequent. The verb ישבה, **sits,** the perfect of experience, translated by the English present, is a common construction in Lamentations; the word is here used in the sense of "to live," "to pass one's existence" (so also in vs. 3). **The city** is of course Jerusalem, devastated by the Babylonians in 586 B.C. **Full of people:**

The Book of Lamentations.—One wonders how many ever read this book! In the old days when the Bible was read through "from cover to cover" at daily devotions, Lamentations was undoubtedly read. But how many really enjoyed it? Why should such a book be in the Bible? "Just a series of heartbroken cries," one might say. The answer may be in Paul's word, "The foolishness of God is wiser than men" (I Cor. 1:25). The Bible has a strange way of

justifying itself against the protests of those who object to this or that book, this or that statement. It is indeed so easy to be careless and blithe in the presence of human misery that we need reminders of the solemn fact that there is much in human life that calls for sorrow and penitence. Can we forget that our Lord Jesus Christ, in listing those whom he would call blessed, included "those that mourn" and the "persecuted"? One must learn to keep awake

2 She weepeth sore in the night, and her tears are on her cheeks: among all her lovers she hath none to comfort *her:* all her friends have dealt treacherously with her, they are become her enemies.

3 Judah is gone into captivity because of affliction, and because of great servitude: she dwelleth among the heathen, she findeth no rest: all her persecutors overtook her between the straits.

2 She weeps bitterly in the night,
  tears on her cheeks;
among all her lovers
  she has none to comfort her;
all her friends have dealt treacherously
    with her,
  they have become her enemies.

3 Judah has gone into exile because of affliction
  and hard servitude;
she dwells now among the nations,
  but finds no resting place;
her pursuers have all overtaken her
  in the midst of her distress.

Lit., "great of people," in the quantitative sense. The word רבתי, "great," has the helping *yôdh,* found rather often in Hebrew poetry and appearing no less than three times in this verse. The ending of course cannot be a survival of the genitive case ending, as the grammars regularly assert, because the word to which it is attached is not in the proper position to be genitive (see Theophile J. Meek, "Some Emendations in the Old Testament," *Journal of Biblical Literature,* XLVIII [1929], 165-67). The word מדינות, **cities** (so Targ. and Syriac), rather rare in Hebrew, has usually the meaning **provinces** or "districts" (so here in the LXX and Vulg.; cf. I Kings 20:14-19). In each line of this verse the contrast between stichs is what Jerusalem is now and what she used to be. The reversal of the order in the last line heightens the contrast.

2. Her lovers and **her friends** are those states that once supported Jerusalem in her revolt against Babylonia (cf. Jer. 27:3; 37:5-8). Since Jerusalem is personified as a woman, these heathen nations are personified as libertine lovers and hence fickle fair-weather lovers (so also in vs. 19).

3. In this verse the poet turns from the city to **Judah,** the nation as a whole, also personified as a woman. The first line is difficult. In order to make sense scholars usually interpret גלתה to mean, not "was deported," but **has gone into** [voluntary] **exile,** referring to the Judeans in Palestine who found the Babylonian yoke intolerable (cf. Jer. 42–43). This meaning for גלה is based on Ezek. 12:3, which gives it very questionable support, since Ezekiel there is playing the role of a deportee, not that of a voluntary exile. A frequent meaning of מן is "because of," "in consequence of," but here it has to do with the consequence instead of the cause; hence it means "to suffer." This is an unusual use of מן, but the principle involved is characteristic of the Hebrew language; e.g., the word "sin" can mean guilt as the cause of punishment or it can mean the punishment itself, which is the consequence of sin. **She dwells,** better, "she has to live," represents the same word that was translated "sits" in vs. 1 and is used in the same perfect of experience; so also the following verb, **but finds;** better, "she finds," since there is no

to the presence in the world of sorrow, pain, and misery, and to have some sense of personal responsibility in it all.

That may be a chief item in the value of such a book as this. Few lives if any can go on their way without facing experiences that challenge their faith. If God is just, kind, our God, how can such trials and sorrows come? Why should God act thus toward us, his own children? In every age there are many who find faith difficult to maintain when life is so hard

and merciless. Christian men and women, of course, have an answer which far surpasses any other, in that their leader, their Lord, the object of their faith, is one who suffered so terribly that he cried out, "My God, my God, why . . . ?" And yet out of that tragic experience came the greatest spiritual force history has known. But whenever it was that these elegies were collected and preserved, they come from a time when there was no such source of solace. We should therefore find it of no little significance to walk

4 The ways of Zion do mourn, because none come to the solemn feasts: all her gates are desolate: her priests sigh, her virgins are afflicted, and she *is* in bitterness.

5 Her adversaries are the chief, her enemies prosper; for the LORD hath afflicted her for the multitude of her transgressions: her children are gone into captivity before the enemy.

4 The roads to Zion mourn,
    for none come to the appointed feasts;
all her gates are desolate,
    her priests groan;
her maidens have been dragged away,[a]
    and she herself suffers bitterly.

5 Her foes have become the head,
    her enemies prosper,
because the LORD has made her suffer
    for the multitude of her transgressions;
her children have gone away,
    captives before the foe.

a Gk Old Latin: Heb *afflicted*

---

but in the original. The preposition בין usually means "between"; the meaning **in the midst of** (again in vs. 17) is found only in poetry (e.g., Judg. 5:16; Song of S. 2:2-3; Ezek. 19:2; 31:3). The word המצרים, "the troubles," found elsewhere only in Pss. 116:3; 118:5, should perhaps be emended to מצריה, **her distress;** better, "her troubles," with Codex Alexandrinus, some minuscules, and Arabic.

4. In the first two lines the personification is transferred from the city to the **roads and gates** of Zion, but in the last line it reverts to the city. **Zion** is strictly the hill on which the temple was built, but in Lamentations, *et al.,* e.g., Amos 6:1; Isa. 1:27; Jer. 3:14, it is used for the city as a whole. The particle מן is causal, **for none come to the appointed feasts,** or, better, "through lack of pilgrims to the feasts." The verb שוממין, **are desolate,** has a plural ending that is common in Aramaic, but is found only sporadically in the O.T.: in poetry and in the later books. The word נאנחים, **groan,** a favorite with the author of ch. 1, is found also in vss. 8, 11, and 21, but nowhere else in Lamentations. **Her maidens** are those who had an appointed part in the cultus (cf. Ps. 68:25 [Hebrew 68:26]; Jer. 31:13). The verb נוגות, "are grief-stricken," is the Niphal participle of יגה, "to grieve," with the unusual but perfectly normal *shûreq,* arising from an original *páthaḥ* plus *wāw,* which may become either *shûreq,* as here, or *ḥōlem,* which would be expected here. The RSV follows the LXX and O.L. in reading נהוגות, **have been dragged away,** but the M.T. is preferable because the parallelism is better. The fact that all the verbal forms in this verse are participles, expressing long, continuous action, intensifies the sense of misery.

5. The expression הלך שבי is found only here, with שבי not in the terminative accusative, "into exile," as regularly interpreted, but in the adverbial accusative of manner, "as exiles." In this verse Yahweh is represented in regular prophetic fashion as using a foreign people as his instrument of punishment—a punishment which was the result of sin (so also in vss. 8, 18, 20, 22).

---

for a while with those who, centuries before, had faced life at its worst and had yet seen some bits of hope and faith left them. (For information as to authorship and date the reader is referred to the Exeg. It is the unity into which the poems have been gathered that concerns us here.)

1:5-7. Personal Responsibility.—Note that the writers, all the way through, feel most deeply not their own misfortunes and calamities, bitter as they are, but the sufferings of the community. What concerns them most is the tragic state of the common life. Someone may point out the fact that in 3:1 the poet is at the center: "I am

the man that hath seen affliction by the rod of his wrath." But at most that is only a moment in the lament. And even there it is not impossible that the author was thinking of himself not so much as an individual, but rather as a representative of the community. Apart from this one passage, the thought centers steadily in the common life.

And at that point there is a touch of the Christian spirit. We are all too prone to be so occupied with our affairs as to forget that we belong to a city, a nation, a world that has its deep problems to be solved and its tragic burdens to be borne. This lament opens not with

6 And from the daughter of Zion all her beauty is departed: her princes are become like harts *that* find no pasture, and they are gone without strength before the pursuer.

7 Jerusalem remembered in the days of her affliction and of her miseries all her

6 From the daughter of Zion has departed
    all her majesty.
Her princes have become like harts
    that find no pasture;
they fled without strength
    before the pursuer.

7 Jerusalem remembers
    in the days of her affliction and bitterness[b]
all the precious things
    that were hers from days of old.

[b] Cn: Heb *wandering*

---

6. Daughter of Zion: A Hebraism very common in the O.T., with **Zion** in the appositional genitive. The verb מצאו is the perfect of experience; hence, **find. They fled** ignores the conjunction *wāw;* better, "but flee" (Amer. Trans.), with the perfect of experience parallel to the preceding verb and continuing the figure of speech. **Without strength:** Lit., "in the condition of not having strength, without strength," with the *bêth essentiae* attached to a clause whose verb "to be" is understood.

7. This verse has four lines instead of the usual three; hence most scholars delete either the second or the third as a gloss; but it is difficult to see how such a gloss came to be inserted. Probably the two lines are variant readings, giving us a conflate text. The words ימי עניה, with the first in the accusative expressing duration of time (or the direct object of זכרה, if the second line is omitted) and the second in the abstract plural, constitute a compound expression with the suffix attached to the second element, as regularly in Hebrew, but belonging to the compound as a whole (see Theophile J. Meek, "Old Testament Notes," *Journal of Biblical Literature,* LXVII [1948], 239); hence, "in her time of affliction," not **in the days of her affliction.** There is no occasion to emend מרודיה, as in the RSV; it is another abstract plural and is found elsewhere in 3:19; Isa. 58:7. It is a derivative from רדד, "to oppress," and means "oppression" here (see C. C. Torrey, *The Second Isaiah* [New York: Charles Scribner's Sons, 1928], p. 438). The next line should be translated, "All her splendor [another abstract plural], which

---

the cry "How sad is my lot!" but with the cry **How doth the city sit solitary! . . . Judah is gone into captivity.** Here is the lesson we need. How many of us are thus deeply conscious of the sorrows and ills of the common life, more concerned about them than we are about our own worries and sorrows? Something of the spirit of Jesus is in the heart of these poems.

7. Look Forward.—Almost everybody is inclined to look back and think how lovely the past was, compared with the present. The man of faith will look forward, and believe that good will come. Recall Rabbi Ben Ezra's words:

    The best is yet to be,
The last of life, for which the first was made.[1]

Even better is it to remember the answer Jesus gave to his disciples when they asked about the end of the world. He told them they would hear of wars and rumors of war, "men's hearts failing them for fear, and for looking after those things

which are coming on the earth." But he added, "When these things begin to come to pass, then look up, and lift up your heads; for your redemption draweth nigh" (Luke 21:26, 28).

7. Remembering Precious Things.—Once again, as so often in scripture—though perhaps here in a variant reading—do we come upon the

                truth the poet sings,
That a sorrow's crown of sorrow is remembering
    happier things.[2]

There is no assurance that such remembering will prove to be the "godly sorrow" that "worketh repentance." It may well be "the sorrow of the world" that "worketh death" (II Cor. 7:10). So was it here. Mercies forgotten in prosperity and remembered in the time of **affliction** have a way of yielding **bitterness.** Even when there is a wistful turning back to God, with all of the quick and answering incursions of his love, the heart that is set on its own is soon "filthy"

[1] Robert Browning, "Rabbi Ben Ezra," st. i.

[2] Tennyson, "Locksley Hall."

pleasant things that she had in the days of old, when her people fell into the hand of the enemy, and none did help her: the adversaries saw her, *and* did mock at her sabbaths.

8 Jerusalem hath grievously sinned; therefore she is removed: all that honored her despise her, because they have seen her nakedness: yea, she sigheth, and turneth backward.

9 Her filthiness is in her skirts; she remembereth not her last end; therefore she came down wonderfully: she had no comforter. O LORD, behold my affliction: for the enemy hath magnified *himself*.

When her people fell into the hand of the foe,
and there was none to help her,
the foe gloated over her,
mocking at her downfall.

8 Jerusalem sinned grievously,
therefore she became filthy;
all who honored her despise her,
for they have seen her nakedness;
yea, she herself groans,
and turns her face away.

9 Her uncleanness was in her skirts;
she took no thought of her doom;
therefore her fall is terrible,
she has no comforter.
"O LORD, behold my affliction,
for the enemy has triumphed!"

prevailed in days of old," with the temporal, and not separative, use of מן, and no **hers** in the original. The next line should be translated, "Now that her people have fallen at the hands of the adversary, with none to help her." Arnold B. Ehrlich (*Randglossen zur hebräischen Bibel* [Leipzig: J. C. Hinrichs, 1914], VII, 31) has shown that ב in ביד cannot be terminative, **into,** but must be instrumental, and the last clause must be circumstantial, with subject first and verb as participle. In the last word, לה, we have the ל of specification introducing the object (see Meek, "The Syntax of the Sentence in Hebrew," *Journal of Biblical Literature,* LXIV [1945], 12-13; Julius Lewy, "Studies in Akkadian Grammar and Onomatology," *Orientalia,* N. S. XV [1946], 415), which is common in Aramaic, but is not an Aramaism because it is found in classical Hebrew and in other Semitic languages. The RSV makes the first line of the verse refer to the present and the rest to the past, but all the verbs are in the same tense, and the whole verse has to do with present, not past, misery. **Gloated** reads more into the verb ראה, "to see," than is there. The meter of the last line is clearly 2+2.

8. Sinned grievously: Lit., "sinned a sin," an emphatic construction here. The word נידה (a *hapax legomenon*), "mockery," with the LXX, Vulg., Arabic, and Targ., is to be derived from נוד, "to mock," as the context clearly shows, and should not be confused with נדה of vs. 17, "filthy thing," as with the RSV and most translators. **Who honored her** is a participle in Hebrew (better, "who used to honor her") to express a situation that used to prevail in contrast with the present, which is expressed by the following stative perfect, **despise her. Turns her face away:** Lit., **turneth backward,** in the sense of going off by oneself in shame (cf. Isa. 42:17).

9. Her uncleanness was in her skirts: The suffix of the first word is pleonastic, meaning simply that Jerusalem, personified as a woman, was unclean because of sin. **Her doom,** for אחריתה, reads more into the word than is there; better, "her future"

again (vs. 8). If **the precious things** were the temple treasures, the memory, sadder still, is of a faith that was squandered, a pride and bulwark then, a shame and mockery now. In ch. 3 are the "spires on the world's rim."

8-9. *The Real Cause.*—Notice the clear statement that the city and nation which are suffering so grievously are but reaping the fruit of their own carelessness and sin. "The Lord hath

afflicted her for the multitude of her transgressions" (vs. 5). "Jerusalem hath grievously sinned; therefore she is become as an unclean thing" (vs. 8 ASV). Without hesitation she is compared to that ancient city which was the type of ungodliness and of divine vengeance: "For the punishment of the iniquity of the daughter of my people is greater than the punishment of the sin of Sodom" (4:6).

10 The adversary hath spread out his hand upon all her pleasant things: for she hath seen *that* the heathen entered into her sanctuary, whom thou didst command *that* they should not enter into thy congregation.

11 All her people sigh, they seek bread; they have given their pleasant things for meat to relieve the soul: see, O LORD, and consider; for I am become vile.

10 The enemy has stretched out his hands
    over all her precious things;
yea, she has seen the nations
    invade her sanctuary,
those whom thou didst forbid
    to enter thy congregation.

11 All her people groan
    as they search for bread;
they trade their treasures for food
    to revive their strength.
"Look, O LORD, and behold,
    for I am despised."

(Amer. Trans.). **Her fall is terrible:** Lit., "she has gone down astoundingly," the last word being an abstract plural noun in the adverbial accusative of manner. The verb may have the sense in which it is used in Deut. 28:43, "to decline," "to degenerate," or it may refer to the razing of the city, as used in Deut. 20:20; 28:52. The following stich is clearly circumstantial, "with none to comfort her" (Amer. Trans.), and the ל is not possessive, but the ל of specification introducing the object (so RSV in vss. 17, 21, where the same phrase appears, but is differently translated). In the last line the city herself is speaking. The conjunction כי is not causal here, but introduces a clause in the accusative, in apposition to את־עניי, **my affliction;** hence, "how the enemy has triumphed."

10. **Has stretched out his hands** is used in a hostile sense only here. **Precious things** is the same word that is translated "treasures" in vs. 11; with a slightly different pointing we had it in vs. 7 as an abstract plural, "splendor." Here it means the treasures of the temple captured by the enemy (cf. II Chr. 36:10, 19). The RSV takes כי as emphatic, **yea,** but the more usual meaning **for** is preferable. **The nations** are of course alien peoples; for their exclusion from the sanctuary see especially Ezek. 44:9. The second stichs in the last two lines are object clauses, with כי omitted, as so often in poetry. The meter of the last line is 2+3, with אשר, a deictic pronoun here like Old Akkadian *šu* (see Meek, "Some Passages Bearing on the Date of Second Isaiah," *Hebrew Union College Annual,* XXIII [1951], 178-79), constituting a foot, and likewise לך, "belonging to thee," a more emphatic construction than adding the suffix directly to the noun.

11. The verbs in the first line are participles to express long continuous action. The word נתנו, **they trade,** lit., "they give," is a perfect of experience. **Their treasures** is the *Kethîbh;* the *Qerê* is a variant reading, with partitive מן and the noun differently vocalized: "some of their treasures." The words להשיב נפש, found again in vss. 16, 19,

True it is that in the main all the tragedy of the situation is looked upon as coming from God's anger; but it is made abundantly clear that the wrath of God is upon the people because of their sins (see vss. 17-18). Notice Moffatt's translation of vs. 9:

> She never thought of what would follow,
>   and so her fall was tragic.

Over and over God is represented as ultimately responsible for these hard and tragic conditions. "Why has our God forsaken us, and brought upon his people such a terrible fate?" It is a spirit all too common when trouble comes upon us. How often the question arises, "If God is good, why does he let such things happen?" The author is in no quandary about it. There

is a poem by Rudyard Kipling which deals with this very matter. Each stanza leads to the question, from a soul in the throes of some hard experience, "Why have the gods afflicted me?" The answer comes with force at the end:

> This was none of the good Lord's pleasure;
>   For the Spirit He sets in Man is free;
> But what comes after is measure for measure
>   And not a God that afflicteth thee.
> As was the sowing so the reaping
>   Is now, and evermore shall be.
> Thou art delivered to thine own keeping.
>   Only thyself hath afflicted thee.[3]

[3] "Natural Theology," from *The Years Between.* Copyright 1919 by Rudyard Kipling. Used by permission of Mrs. George Bambridge, Methuen & Co., and Doubleday & Co.

12 ¶ *Is it* nothing to you, all ye that pass by? behold, and see if there be any sorrow like unto my sorrow, which is done unto me, wherewith the LORD hath afflicted *me* in the day of his fierce anger.

13 From above hath he sent fire into my bones, and it prevaileth against them: he hath spread a net for my feet, he hath turned me back: he hath made me desolate *and* faint all the day.

12 "Is it nothing to you,[c] all you who pass
    by?
  Look and see
if there is any sorrow like my sorrow
  which was brought upon me,
which the LORD inflicted
  on the day of his fierce anger.

13 "From on high he sent fire;
  into my bones[d] he made it descend;
he spread a net for my feet;
  he turned me back;
he has left me stunned,
  faint all the day long.

[c] Heb uncertain

[d] Gk: Heb bones and

are, lit., "to revive the spirit"; hence, "to keep themselves alive" (Amer. Trans.). The reference is to the hunger that was rampant in the city after its capture and destruction. In the last line the city herself speaks.

12. The first two words in the M.T. are difficult—"not to you." On the basis of the late Jewish expression לא עליכם they may mean "May it never happen to you!" but scarcely **Is it nothing to you?** The LXX, Symm., Targ., and Vulg. had the same C.T. as we, but they manifestly vocalized the first word as the particle *lû'* instead of the M.T. *lô'*. Ehrlich maintains that the use of this particle with the imperatives that follow is un-Hebraic, but the construction is found in at least one other place, Gen. 23:13, and the particle is clearly emphatic and exclamatory; hence, "Ho, all you who pass along the road" (Amer. Trans.). This reading has the advantage of requiring no change in the C.T. and is preferable to the usual emendation לכו לכם, "Come!" The appeal for sympathy to the wayfarers is like that to the nations in vs. 18. The expression כל־עברי דרך, **all you who pass by,** omitting דרך, "the way," appears again in 2:15, where it is more correctly translated by the RSV, "All who pass along the way."

13. The first line of the M.T. reads, "From above he hurled fire into my bones and trampled it," which does not yield a satisfactory rhythm or meaning. The difficulty is

---

It is a basic principle of all true religion that we must reap what we sow. That prophetic soul, Dwight L. Moody, once said to a group of students what one of them at least has always remembered. He said, "Never forget that 'whatsoever a man soweth, that shall he also reap.' You have got to reap what you sow. Do you ask, 'If I repent and God forgives me, then will I have to reap?' Yes, you will; nothing can change that law, that you reap what you sow. You may in surprise say, 'Well then, what good is there in repentance and forgiveness?' Ah, then God will help you in the hard work of reaping."

12. The Neglected Christ.—Doubtless all of us are familiar with the use of this outcry in Stainer's "Crucifixion," **Is it nothing to you, all ye that pass by?** It is a plea that the crucified Lord makes to everyone who calls himself a Christian; but it applies not only to the experience of the Crucifixion, it applies as well to our indifference, both to the sorrows of our Lord and to the sorrows of the world.

Years ago there was painted a picture that haunts the memory of those who have seen it. It is a scene in some public place. Christ is at the center, not on a cross, but tied by his hands with a rope to a kind of altar, head bowed, a crown of thorns on it, his body bent low in suffering. Near by is the inscription *Deo Ignoto* —"To the Unknown God." Past him is flowing, on one side and the other, a crowd of people representative of our modern life, men and women in rich dress and poor people in ragged attire; clergymen engaged in heated theological discussion; men reading newspapers, a priest intoning a prayer, a mother and her child—all sorts of people. Only one of them looks at the suffering figure of the Savior, and she but for one shocked glance. **Is it nothing to you, all ye that pass by?** What a picture of our modern life in its neglect of the Christ!

13-15. God's Ingenious Wrath.—There is no escape for the sinful city. Fire is hurled upon her from above and trampled into her very

14 The yoke of my transgressions is bound by his hand: they are wreathed, *and* come up upon my neck: he hath made my strength to fall, the Lord hath delivered me into *their* hands, *from whom* I am not able to rise up.

15 The Lord hath trodden under foot all my mighty *men* in the midst of me: he hath called an assembly against me to crush my young men: the Lord hath trodden the

14 "My transgressions were bound[e] into a yoke;
   by his hand they were fastened together;
they were set upon my neck;
   he caused my strength to fail;
the Lord gave me into the hands
   of those whom I cannot withstand.

15 "The Lord flouted all my mighty men
   in the midst of me;
he summoned an assembly against me
   to crush my young men;

[e] Cn: Heb uncertain

eased if we transpose the last two words: "From above he hurled fire, and trampled it into my bones." The last word, ירדנה, is from the root רדה, here and in Joel 3:13 (Hebrew 4:13) in its original meaning, "to trample," as indicated by its Arabic cognate. The versions all had trouble with the word; most of them derive it from ירד, "to go down," and this is the basis for the usual emendation, הורידה, **he made it descend,** which is found in some LXX MSS and is followed by the RSV. **He spread a net:** A rather frequent figure in cuneiform literature as well as in the O.T. (e.g., Ezek. 12:13; Hos. 7:12; Jer. 50:24). **He turned me back:** Lit., "backward," perhaps in the sense of tripping up with the net. **Stunned, faint** are possible translations, but **desolate** (KJV) and "miserable" (Amer. Trans.) fit the context better.

14. This verse is difficult. The RSV emends the singular נשקד to the plural נשקדו, **were bound,** but this translation is purely conjectural. For נשקד (with letter *sin*) some twenty-seven MSS, the LXX, and Vulg. read נשקד (with *shin;* Syriac, נשקדו) and for 'ol, **yoke,** the LXX and Arabic read 'al, "over" (cf. Syriac "over me"), to make the stich read, "Watch has been kept over my transgressions" (so Amer. Trans.). The word עלו may be translated "they have come up," but scarcely **they were set.** Symm. and Lucian vocalized it as "his yoke," and the Syriac as "his yokes," suggesting that we should insert על, **yoke,** before עלו; it could easily have been lost by haplography, and its presence would account for the vocalization of על in the first line as **yoke** rather than "over." If inserted, it would be in the adverbial accusative of manner, "like a yoke," and the line would be the regular 3+2, "They have come up like a yoke on my neck; it has shattered my strength," lit., "caused my strength to totter." In any case, the figure is that of bringing an animal under one's power by putting a yoke on it. Here the city's sins constitute the yoke; it was they that brought about her subjection. In place of אדני, **Lord,** in the first line, as elsewhere in the book, many MSS have the divine name יהוה, "Yahweh," which was undoubtedly the original reading, but the tendency of later scribes was to substitute אדני, since this substitution was always made in the synagogue service. This line is a clear example of the 2+3 variant because בידי cannot possibly be separated from the following clause to which it is construct. In spite of some scholars' practice, which reflects the desire to get a rigidly regular meter, it is evident that a caesura cannot separate a construct and its genitive.

15. The word מועד regularly means a religious **assembly,** but here it would seem to be used in a secular sense (cf. Lev. 23:4*b*). However, Zeph. 1:7-8 (cf. Jer. 46:10; Ezek. 39:17-30; Isa. 34:6) represents Yahweh's judgment upon Israel as a sacrificial feast,

bones. A net is spread for her feet that trips her and causes her to fall. Utterly desolate and miserable, she has been brought under the yoke and power of her own sin (vs. 14), her people crushed, the blood of their bodies like the wine of grapes (vs. 15). We talk of God's ingenious bounty: are we too soft ever to give a thought to his ingenious wrath? To read history not as genetic process but as religious drama to document them both. Never is he

virgin, the daughter of Judah, *as* in a wine-press.

16 For these *things* I weep; mine eye, mine eye runneth down with water, because the comforter that should relieve my soul is far from me: my children are desolate, because the enemy prevailed.

17 Zion spreadeth forth her hands, *and there is* none to comfort her: the Lᴏʀᴅ hath commanded concerning Jacob, *that* his adversaries *should be* round about him: Jerusalem is as a menstruous woman among them.

18 ¶ The Lᴏʀᴅ is righteous; for I have rebelled against his commandment: hear, I pray you, all people, and behold my sorrow:

the Lord has trodden as in a wine press
   the virgin daughter of Judah.

¹⁶ "For these things I weep;
   my eyes flow with tears;
for a comforter is far from me,
   one to revive my courage;
my children are desolate,
   for the enemy has prevailed."

¹⁷ Zion stretches out her hands,
   but there is none to comfort her;
the Lᴏʀᴅ has commanded against Jacob
   that his neighbors should be his foes;
Jerusalem has become
   a filthy thing among them.

¹⁸ "The Lᴏʀᴅ is in the right,
   for I have rebelled against his word;
but hear, all you peoples,
   and behold my suffering;

---

and that may also be the thought here. The verb לשבר, **to crush,** is never elsewhere found with animate beings as its object. The word גת, **as in a wine press,** is in the adverbial accusative of manner. The figure is a lurid one; the wine for the feast was the blood squeezed out of human bodies, conceived of as grapes (cf. Isa. 63:3).

16. The M.T. repeats עיני, **mine eye,** or collectively, **my eyes,** but the RSV and most scholars read only one, as in some MSS and the versions. Its deletion, however, makes the line 3+3, which is not a variant of the *qînāh* meter. As it stands, the line is 3+2+2, which is a variant, and this favors the retention of עיני, repeated for emphasis. **Flow with tears:** Lit., "go down [a participle to express long continuous action] with water."

17. In this verse the direct narration is interrupted and the poet himself is the speaker, as in vss. 1-11. **Stretches out her hands,** lit., "spreads out [a perfect of experience] with her hands," is a construction found only here. In the expression ליעקב, **concerning Jacob,** the preposition is the ל of specification rather than the ל of disadvantage. Jacob is strictly one of the names of the Northern Kingdom, but like the others, Israel and Ephraim, it is often used, as here, of the nation as a whole, whereas Judah never is (see Theophile J. Meek, *Hebrew Origins* [rev. ed.; New York: Harper & Bros., 1950], p. 46, n. 133, p. 166). The last stich of the second line may be translated as in the KJV, but the RSV is preferable. **His neighbors** are the "lovers" and "friends" of vs. 2 and the "lovers" of vs. 19 (see Exeg. on vs. 2).

18. In this verse the direct narration is resumed and Jerusalem is represented as acknowledging the justice of her punishment, but protesting against its severity. The imperative שמעו-נא is emphatic, **but hear,** with the particle נא translated as **but;** better, "yet hear." The last line is in the accusative in apposition to מכאבי, **my suffering;** hence,

---

mocked—by men or nations. His will is like a circle at the center of life: to break out and away is to break into the circle of his judgments round about it; and from that there *is* no breaking out, except into the still vaster circle of his mercy!

17-18. *Two Explanations.*—Here are two interpretations of the tragic condition of the people. The poet says:

The Lᴏʀᴅ has commanded against Jacob,
   that his neighbors should be his foes.

But Jerusalem sees deeper into the facts and exclaims:

The Lᴏʀᴅ is in the right,
   for I have rebelled against his word.

There is the cause behind the "cause."

my virgins and my young men are gone into captivity.

19 I called for my lovers, *but* they deceived me: my priests and mine elders gave up the ghost in the city, while they sought their meat to relieve their souls.

20 Behold, O LORD; for I *am* in distress: my bowels are troubled; mine heart is turned within me; for I have grievously rebelled: abroad the sword bereaveth, at home *there is* as death.

21 They have heard that I sigh; *there is* none to comfort me: all mine enemies have heard of my trouble; they are glad that thou hast done *it:* thou wilt bring the day *that* thou hast called, and they shall be like unto me.

22 Let all their wickedness come before

---

my maidens and my young men
   have gone into captivity.

19 "I called to my lovers
   but they deceived me;
my priests and elders
   perished in the city,
while they sought food
   to revive their strength.

20 "Behold, O LORD, for I am in distress,
   my soul is in tumult,
my heart is wrung within me,
   because I have been very rebellious.
In the street the sword bereaves;
   in the house it is like death.

21 "Hear*f* how I groan;
   there is none to comfort me.
All my enemies have heard of my trouble;
   they are glad that thou hast done it.
Bring thou*g* the day thou hast announced,
   and let them be as I am.

22 "Let all their evil doing come before
   thee;
and deal with them
   as thou hast dealt with me

f Gk Syr: Heb *they heard*
g Syr: Heb *thou hast brought*

---

better, "how my maidens and youths have gone into captivity." The preposition ב in בשבי, **into captivity,** is terminative and locative. It might also be taken as *bêth essentiae:* hence, the translation "have gone away as captives."

19. The word המה, **they,** is pleonastic and accordingly emphatic; hence, **but they.** The word כי is better translated "when" than **while.**

20. The RSV interprets כי as causal, but the word is better interpreted as introducing an object clause: lit., "that distress is mine"; hence, "what distress I have." **My soul:** Lit., **my bowels,** a seat of the emotions according to the Hebrews. The words בבית כמות, "in the house as death," are in an unusual order, perhaps representing poetic license. In order to get the regular sequence the LXX and Arabic transpose them. The O.L. and Syriac omit the letter ב, **as;** however, if those versions are followed the presence of the letter in the M.T. can hardly be accounted for. The line is strikingly like Deut. 32:25a.

21. The verb שמעו, **they have heard,** is vocalized by the LXX as indefinite plural imperative, while the Syriac reads singular imperative, with Yahweh as the one addressed, as in vss. 20, 22; this is followed by the RSV and most scholars. The RSV also follows the generally accepted Syriac reading in the last line, הבא את-יום, **bring thou the day,** for הבאת יום, **thou hast brought the day.** The Syriac readings in both cases are attractive, but they give a totally different meaning from the M.T., and despite their popularity there is the serious objection that **the day** is regularly the day of Yahweh's judgment upon Israel (so vs. 12) rather than upon her enemies. It would seem better to abide by the M.T., as in the Amer. Trans. The second line is a tristich, 3+2+2; or the pleonastic אתה may be dropped to make the regular 3+2.

22. Some scholars (e.g., Rudolph and Haller) interpret כי in the last line as asseverative.

thee; and do unto them, as thou hast done unto me for all my transgressions: for my sighs *are* many, and my heart *is* faint.

2 How hath the Lord covered the daughter of Zion with a cloud in his anger, *and* cast down from heaven unto the earth the beauty of Israel, and remembered not his footstool in the day of his anger!

2 The Lord hath swallowed up all the habitations of Jacob, and hath not pitied: he hath thrown down in his wrath the strongholds of the daughter of Judah; he hath brought *them* down to the ground: he hath polluted the kingdom and the princes thereof.

because of all my transgressions;
for my groans are many
and my heart is faint."

2 How the Lord in his anger
has set the daughter of Zion under a cloud!
He has cast down from heaven to earth
the splendor of Israel;
he has not remembered his footstool
in the day of his anger.

2 The Lord has destroyed without mercy
all the habitations of Jacob;
in his wrath he has broken down
the strongholds of the daughters of Judah;
he has brought down to the ground in dishonor
the kingdom and its rulers.

II. DIVINE JUDGMENT UPON THE CITY (2:1-22)

The description of the suffering of the people, the contempt of onlookers, and the rejoicing of the foe is more vivid and the lamentation less formal than in ch. 1. Like the latter, the dirge ends in a prayer (vss. 20-22) put into the mouth of the city. The poet is the speaker throughout and, in striking contrast with ch. 1, God is made the subject of almost half the sentences.

2:1. The word יעיב is regularly derived from עוב, "to becloud," but it is better derived, with Ehrlich, *et al.*, from a middle *yôdh* root which is found in Arabic and means "to disgrace." As it stands, the verb is frequentative imperfect, but the LXX reads the perfect. **The splendor of Israel** may be the temple (cf. Isa. 64:11 [Hebrew 64:10]) or the city (cf. Isa. 13:19), **cast down** like a falling star (cf. Isa 14:12) —probably the latter. **His footstool** may also be the city (cf. Isa. 66:1), but more probably the temple (cf. Ezek. 43:7; Isa. 60:13; Ps. 132:7).

2. The verb בלע, he **hath swallowed up,** meaning "to consume," "to destroy utterly," appears again in vss. 5, 8, 16. The clause לא חמל, **without mercy,** following the Amer. Trans., is in the adverbial accusative of manner, lit., "in that he did not show mercy (see Meek, "Syntax of the Sentence in Hebrew," p. 8, and articles there cited). The same construction appears again in vss. 17, 21; 3:43. The word חלל, "he has degraded" (Amer. Trans.), is taken with the preceding verb by the RSV as adverbial, **in dishonor,** but this is contrary to the accents and it spoils the parallelism. The word ממלכה, **the**

2:1-3. *Why Is Evil in God's World?*—Again the author puts upon the Lord the blame for all the evil that has come about. We may well set over against his protest a quotation from an address by Arnold J. Toynbee:

One of the deepest spiritual laws we know is the law that is proclaimed by Aeschylus in the two words "πάθει μάθος"—"It is through suffering that learning comes"—and in the New Testament in the verse "whom the Lord loveth, He chasteneth; and scourgeth every son whom He receiveth" [Heb. 12:6]. It was the premature and permanent overthrow of [the] worldly commonwealths [of Israel and Judah], and the extinction of all the political hopes which had been bound up with their existence as independent polities, that brought the religion of Judaism to birth and evoked the highest expression of its spirit in the elegy of the Suffering Servant.[4]

For all who are taking life too easily there is food for thought in this cry that comes out of a suffering age. Have we not known such periods in our modern world? And are not their consequences lingering yet through the years?

[4] *Christianity and Civilization* (Wallingford, Pa.: Pendle Hill, 1947), pp. 24-25.

3 He hath cut off in *his* fierce anger all the horn of Israel: he hath drawn back his right hand from before the enemy, and he burned against Jacob like a flaming fire, *which* devoureth round about.

4 He hath bent his bow like an enemy: he stood with his right hand as an adversary, and slew all *that were* pleasant to the eye in the tabernacle of the daughter of Zion: he poured out his fury like fire.

5 The Lord was as an enemy: he hath swallowed up Israel, he hath swallowed up all her palaces: he hath destroyed his strongholds, and hath increased in the daughter of Judah mourning and lamentation.

---

3 He has cut down in fierce anger
   all the might of Israel;
he has withdrawn from them his right
   hand
   in the face of the enemy;
he has burned like a flaming fire in Jacob,
   consuming all around.

4 He has bent his bow like an enemy,
   with his right hand set like a foe;
and he has slain all the pride of our eyes
   in the tent of the daughter of Zion;
he has poured out his fury like fire.

5 The Lord has become like an enemy,
   he has destroyed Israel;
he has destroyed all its palaces,
   laid in ruins its strongholds;
and he has multiplied in the daughter of
   Judah
   mourning and lamentation.

---

kingdom, without the first מ, is vocalized by the Syriac to read, "her kings," and by most MSS of the LXX to read "her king," i.e., King Zedekiah. However, the M.T. is quite satisfactory. The meter is clearly 2+3.

3. In this verse Yahweh is described as depriving the nation of strength, of withholding his own help, and then of taking the offensive against it (cf. Isa. 42:24-25). **The might** is, lit., **the horn,** a frequent symbol of strength in the O.T. (again in vs. 17). The second line reads, lit., "He has drawn back his right hand from the face of the enemy," which Ps. 74:11 shows must mean that Yahweh has withdrawn his help, symbolized by the **right hand,** as often in the O.T. The meter of the last line is 2+2+2; or להבה may be a variant reading of אש, to make the meter 3+2. The last stich is a relative clause, with the relative particle understood, and the verb is in the perfect of experience, "which consumes the neighborhood" (Amer. Trans.).

4. As regularly set up, this verse lacks a final stich; the best solution is to transpose כצר and ויהרג:

> He has bent his bow,
>   with his right hand set like an enemy;
> And he has slain like an adversary
>   all the notables;
> On the tents of the daughter of Zion
>   he has vented his fury like fire.

All the pride of our eyes: Lit., "all the desirable ones of the eye"; hence, "all the notables" (Amer. Trans.), the first word being the same as that used of inanimate things in 1:10-11 (cf. 1:7), "treasures." **The tent** may be the temple, but it is better taken as collective, "the tents" (Amer. Trans.), i.e., the habitations of the people of Zion. This proposal is supported by the fact that **the daughter of Zion** means the people, and vss. 1-5 have to do with the land and people, while the temple does not appear until vss. 6-7.

5. The כ here expresses identity (usually called the *kaph veritatis*; see Paul Joüon, *Grammaire de l'hébreu biblique* [Rome: Institut biblique pontifical, 1947], sec. 133g;

---

4. *God the Adversary.*—See Expos. on Job 6:4; 10:13; 16:13.

6 And he hath violently taken away his tabernacle, as *if it were of* a garden; he hath destroyed his places of the assembly: the LORD hath caused the solemn feasts and sabbaths to be forgotten in Zion, and hath despised in the indignation of his anger the king and the priest.

7 The Lord hath cast off his altar, he hath abhorred his sanctuary, he hath given up into the hand of the enemy the walls of her palaces; they have made a noise in the house of the LORD, as in the day of a solemn feast.

8 The LORD hath purposed to destroy the wall of the daughter of Zion: he hath stretched out a line, he hath not withdrawn his hand from destroying: therefore he made the rampart and the wall to lament; they languished together.

6 He has broken down his booth like that
   of a garden,
   laid in ruins the place of his appointed
      feasts;
   the LORD has brought to an end in Zion
      appointed feast and sabbath,
   and in his fierce indignation has spurned
      king and priest.

7 The Lord has scorned his altar,
   disowned his sanctuary;
   he has delivered into the hand of the
      enemy
   the walls of her palaces;
   a clamor was raised in the house of the
      LORD
   as on the day of an appointed feast.

8 The LORD determined to lay in ruins
   the wall of the daughter of Zion;
   he marked if off by the line;
   he restrained not his hand from de-
      stroying;
   he caused rampart and wall to lament,
   they languish together.

it is better to call it the asseverative *kaph;* see Robert Gordis, "The Asseverative Kaph in Ugaritic and Hebrew," *Journal of the American Oriental Society,* LXIII [1943], 176-78) — "The Lord has really become an enemy" or "has become a veritable enemy." The word ארמנותיה, **her palaces,** must be emended to "his palaces" to agree with **his strongholds** and the masculine antecedent of both, **Israel. Mourning and lamentation:** Better, "mourning and moaning" (Amer. Trans.), because this brings out the paranomasia of the original.

6. The word שכו, **his booth,** is found only here with ש in place of ס; it is parallel to מועדו, "his meeting place," and both refer to the temple, as indicated by Ps. 76:2 (Hebrew 76:3); but in the next line מועד is used in an alternative meaning, "festival." **Like that of a garden:** Better, "as in a garden," with the pregnant use of *bêth,* i.e., Yahweh destroyed his booth, the temple, as easily and with as little concern as one destroys a booth erected temporarily for shelter in a harvest field (cf. Isa. 1:8). There is no need to emend the line as most scholars do. **Has brought to an end:** Lit., "has caused to forget," hence, "has abolished" (Amer. Trans.). **King and priest** are coupled because of the participation of both in the cultus.

7. The word נאר is found only here and in Ps. 89:39 (Hebrew 89:40), and its meaning, **disowned,** is a conjecture from the context. The expression "to deliver into the hand of the enemy," and similar expressions elsewhere, always have people as their object, not inanimate things, as here. **Her palaces** are apparently Zion's **palaces.** Since the context has to do with the temple, it is strange to have the city introduced; hence most scholars regard the text as corrupt and offer various emendations, of which the simplest is to read "his palaces," i.e., the Lord's palaces attached to the temple. **A clamor was raised:** Lit., "they [indefinite] gave a shout" (cf. Ps. 74:4).

8. He marked it off by the line is a doubtful paraphrase, better translated, lit., **he hath stretched out a line,** i.e., a plummet line, to discover defects, a figure drawn from building (cf. Amos 7:7-9; II Kings 21:13; Isa. 34:11). This is a clear example of the 2+3 variant.

9 Her gates are sunk into the ground; he hath destroyed and broken her bars: her king and her princes *are* among the Gentiles: the law *is* no *more;* her prophets also find no vision from the LORD.

10 The elders of the daughter of Zion sit upon the ground, *and* keep silence: they have cast up dust upon their heads; they have girded themselves with sackcloth: the virgins of Jerusalem hang down their heads to the ground.

11 Mine eyes do fail with tears, my bowels are troubled, my liver is poured upon the earth, for the destruction of the daughter of my people; because the children and the sucklings swoon in the streets of the city.

12 They say to their mothers, Where *is*

---

9 Her gates have sunk into the ground;
  he has ruined and broken her bars;
her king and princes are among the nations;
  the law is no more,
and her prophets obtain
  no vision from the LORD.

10 The elders of the daughter of Zion
  sit on the ground in silence;
they have cast dust on their heads
  and put on sackcloth;
the maidens of Jerusalem
  have bowed their heads to the ground.

11 My eyes are spent with weeping;
  my soul is in tumult;
my heart is poured out in grief[h]
  because of the destruction of the daughter of my people,
because infants and babes faint
  in the streets of the city.

12 They cry to their mothers,
  "Where is bread and wine?"

[h] Heb *to the ground*

---

9. In the word באָרֶץ, **into the ground,** the ב is both terminative and locative. Since the line is too long metrically, one of the two synonymous verbs in the second stich must be taken as a variant reading, thus giving us a conflate text. The words אֵין תוֹרה, against the M.T. punctuation, should be taken as a new clause, "there is no instruction," with the last word referring to priestly instruction, as indicated by the context and by comparison with Jer. 18:18; Ezek. 7:26; Mal. 2:7; scarcely **the law.** Here and in the next line the author is saying that Yahweh has utterly forsaken his people and comes to them no longer through any medium (cf. Ezek. 7:26).

10. All the figures in this verse express mourning (cf. Isa. 3:26; Jer. 6:26; Ezek. 27:30). The word לאָרֶץ (again in vs. 21), **on the ground,** is, lit., "to the earth," ל bringing out the idea of flinging oneself in despair to the earth. The verbs in this line are both imperfect, but most scholars emend with the LXX and O.L. (plus the Syriac, Vulg., and Targ. for the first) to the perfect, to agree with the other verbs in the verse.

11. The last clause in the first line also appears in 1:20. **My heart,** lit., **my liver,** was regarded by the Hebrews as a seat of the emotions; for the metaphor cf. vs. 19; Ps. 62:8 (Hebrew 62:9). The word בעטף, "because of the fainting," as pointed, is the causal (not temporal) ב, plus the Niphal infinitive construct, with the syncope of ה; better pointed as Qal. **In the streets of the city:** Lit., "in the broad places of the city"; hence, "in the city squares" (Amer. Trans.).

12. The verb יאמרו is imperfect to express frequentative action; hence, "they keep

---

9-10, 14. *The Responsibility of Religious Leaders.*—Here the lamentable conditions are seen as due largely to the failure of the religious leaders (cf. 4:12-16). The **prophets** receive **no vision from the LORD;** the **elders** can do or say nothing; they **sit on the ground in silence,** with **dust upon their heads. Your prophets have** seen for you false and deceptive visions; . . . oracles false and misleading.

May not all of our leaders, religious leaders particularly, ask themselves if they are not in part at least responsible for the lack of power and wisdom among the people for whose life they have the responsibility? **No vision; silence;**

corn and wine? when they swooned as the wounded in the streets of the city, when their soul was poured out into their mothers' bosom.

13 What thing shall I take to witness for thee? what thing shall I liken to thee, O daughter of Jerusalem? what shall I equal to thee, that I may comfort thee, O virgin daughter of Zion? for thy breach *is* great like the sea: who can heal thee?

14 Thy prophets have seen vain and foolish things for thee: and they have not discovered thine iniquity, to turn away thy captivity; but have seen for thee false burdens and causes of banishment.

15 All that pass by clap *their* hands at thee; they hiss and wag their head at the

as they faint like wounded men
    in the streets of the city,
as their life is poured out
    on their mothers' bosom.

13 What can I say for you, to what compare
    you,
    O daughter of Jerusalem?
What can I liken to you, that I may com-
    fort you,
    O virgin daughter of Zion?
For vast as the sea is your ruin;
    who can restore you?

14 Your prophets have seen for you
    false and deceptive visions;
they have not exposed your iniquity
    to restore your fortunes,
but have seen for you oracles
    false and misleading.

15 All who pass along the way
    clap their hands at you;
they hiss and wag their heads
    at the daughter of Jerusalem;

---

saying" (Amer. Trans.). The noun דגן is "grain," not **bread.** The preposition אל, "to," should be על, **on,** a frequent mistake in the M.T.

13. The *Qerê* אעידך is the Hiphil of עוד, which Ehrlich shows appears again in Jer. 49:19 and has the meaning "to liken," as indicated by the Vulg.; hence, "To what can I liken you?" (Amer. Trans.), exactly parallel to the following stich. The compound vocative, "O daughter Jerusalem," is unusual; one MS and the LXX have the usual construct, **O daughter of Jerusalem,** as in the next line, **O virgin daughter of Zion.**

14. The verb חזו, **have seen,** is better rendered "have divined" (Amer. Trans.), since the root means "to see ecstatically." **False and deceptive visions:** Lit., "emptiness and whitewash"; hence, "stuff and nonsense" (Amer. Trans.), the reference being to the false or professional prophets who did not do their duty by the people but misled them (cf. Isa. 3:12; 9:15-16; Jer. 23:13; Ezek. 13:8-10), and so brought them into their misfortune. The expression להשיב שביתך is general, **to restore your fortunes,** not specific, as in the KJV and most translations. The word מדוחים, found only here, is an abstract plural noun, best translated into English by an adjective, **misleading.**

15. The verb ספקו is a perfect of experience, "they clap," i.e., in malicious delight and mockery (cf. Job 27:23; Zeph. 2:15). The word שיאמרו has the relative particle ש, in place of the more usual אשר, plus an imperfect of customary action, indefinite third person plural; hence, "which they used to call." The line is a tristich, in 2+3+3, but the last stich may be a marginal gloss from Ps. 48:2 (Hebrew 48:3), or it may be a variant reading, thus giving us a conflate text.

---

a pitiful shaking of the head, coupled with a folding of the hands; **oracles false and misleading:** what an indictment! How clearly the lines are drawn. Read I Pet. 4:17.

13. *Who Can Heal Thee?*—To ask such a question in such a context is to answer it. And

with the answer opens out that long vista through the centuries with a Cross at the end of it. Humanity will try everything else first. Men will even take the healing that God does and soften it, until of all things they least expect that to hurt! (Cf. Gen. 32:31.)

daughter of Jerusalem, *saying, Is* this the city that *men* call The perfection of beauty, The joy of the whole earth?

16 All thine enemies have opened their mouth against thee: they hiss and gnash the teeth: they say, We have swallowed *her* up: certainly this *is* the day that we looked for; we have found, we have seen *it*.

17 The LORD hath done *that* which he had devised; he hath fulfilled his word that he had commanded in the days of old: he hath thrown down, and hath not pitied: and he hath caused *thine* enemy to rejoice over thee, he hath set up the horn of thine adversaries.

18 Their heart cried unto the Lord, O wall of the daughter of Zion, let tears run down like a river day and night: give thyself no rest; let not the apple of thine eye cease.

19 Arise, cry out in the night: in the be-

"Is this the city which was called
  the perfection of beauty,
  the joy of all the earth?"

16 All your enemies
    rail against you;
  they hiss, they gnash their teeth,
    they cry: "We have destroyed her!
  Ah, this is the day we longed for;
    now we have it; we see it!"

17 The LORD has done what he purposed,
    has carried out his threat;
  as he ordained long ago,
    he has demolished without pity;
  he has made the enemy rejoice over you,
    and exalted the might of your foes.

18 Cry aloud[i] to the Lord!
    O[j] daughter of Zion!
  Let tears stream down like a torrent
    day and night!
  Give yourself no rest,
    your eyes no respite!

19 Arise, cry out in the night,
    at the beginning of the watches!
  Pour out your heart like water

[i] Cn: Heb *Their heart cried*
[j] Cn: Heb *O wall of*

15. Five MSS, Lucian, the Syriac, and Arabic have this verse after vs. 17, thus putting the ע and פ stanzas in regular order. **Rail against you:** Lit., "open their mouth against you," with this verb and the following three in the perfect of experience. **Now we have it:** Lit., we have found.

17. The clause אשר צוה is in the accusative of specification, lit., "in the matter of that which he ordained"; hence, **as he ordained** (see Meek, "Hebrew Poetic Structure as a Translation Guide," *Journal of Biblical Literature*, LIX [1940], 3).

18. The first line as it stands makes no sense; the easiest solution is to read צעקי לך, "cry out," for צעק לבם, **their heart cried,** and to read המי, "wail," for חומת, **wall;** but it is very difficult to explain how such a simple text became so corrupt. The word יומם, "by day," is one of the few adverbs in Hebrew. The word פוגת, **respite** or **rest,** found only here, is not construct, but a noun with the old feminine in *tāw.* **Your eyes:** Lit., "the daughter of your eye," i.e., the pupil of the eye according to Ps. 17:8, or perhaps the product of the eye, i.e., tears, as in Arabic (see Edward Robertson, "The Apple of the Eye in the Masoretic Text," *Journal of Theological Studies*, XXXVIII [1937], 59). The RSV makes the verb imperative, but it is jussive, as in the KJV.

19. The words לראש אשמרות, with distributive ל and not point of time (see Meek, "Old Testament Notes," pp. 236-38), mean "as the watches begin," i.e., continually

17. *The Faithfulness of God.*—Cf. I Cor. 1:9. There are times when God's faithfulness feels like a mailed fist; when the only mercy possible is judgment (see Luke 22:61; Rom. 11:22).

18-19. *A Cry for Help.*—Instead of bitterly blaming God for her wars, Israel is exhorted to turn to him for deliverance. To whom else can she go (vs. 13)? Cf. Cowper's hymn "God

ginning of the watches pour out thine heart like water before the face of the Lord: lift up thy hands toward him for the life of thy young children, that faint for hunger in the top of every street.

20 ¶ Behold, O Lord, and consider to whom thou hast done this. Shall the women eat their fruit, *and* children of a span long? shall the priest and the prophet be slain in the sanctuary of the Lord?

21 The young and the old lie on the ground in the streets: my virgins and my young men are fallen by the sword; thou hast slain *them* in the day of thine anger; thou hast killed, *and* not pitied.

22 Thou hast called as in a solemn day my terrors round about, so that in the day of the Lord's anger none escaped nor remained: those that I have swaddled and brought up hath mine enemy consumed.

before the presence of the Lord!
Lift your hands to him
  for the lives of your children,
who faint for hunger
  at the head of every street.

20 Look, O Lord, and see!
  With whom hast thou dealt thus?
Should women eat their offspring,
  the children of their tender care?
Or should priest and prophet
  be slain in the sanctuary of the Lord?

21 In the dust of the streets
  lie the young and the old;
my maidens and my young men
  have fallen by the sword;
in the day of thy anger thou hast slain
    them,
  slaughtering without mercy.

22 Thou didst invite as to the day of an appointed feast
  my terrors on every side;
and on the day of the anger of the Lord
  none escaped or survived;
those whom I dandled and reared
  my enemy destroyed.

---

through the night, which was divided by the Hebrews into three watches (cf. Judg. 7:19). Since this stanza, like 1:7, has four lines, most scholars delete the last line as a gloss based on vss. 12 and 4:1, 4, but it is probable that the M.T. represents a conflate text, with the second line a variant of the first (cf. Exeg. on 1:7).

20. This verse and the following two are put in the mouth of the city as the response to the poet's appeal in vs. 19. The two clauses beginning with אם are explanatory of כה, **thus,** with the alternative use of אם in an interrogative sentence. This verse indicates that Jerusalem was actually reduced to cannibalism in the siege of 586 (cf. 4:10; Jer. 19:9).

21. In the first line the RSV emends לארץ, **on the ground,** to the construct, **in the dust of the streets,** and puts the verb in the second stich when it belongs to the first. The word חוצות in the M.T. must be in the adverbial accusative, **in the streets. Slaughtering:** Better, lit., "thou hast slaughtered," i.e., since everything that happened was decreed by God as punishment for sin, everything was his act, even to the slaughtering of the people—the regular prophetic interpretation of history.

22. The verb תקרא is imperfect and may be interpreted as frequentative, "Thou didst keep inviting," or as an archaism preserving the early preterit, which disappeared from Hebrew prose in the course of time, but survives sporadically in poetry, **Thou didst invite** (see Meek, "The Metrical Structure of II Kings 19:20-28" *Crozer Quarterly,* XVIII [1941], 127-28). It is used here because it has the initial ת required by the acrostic scheme. The word מגורי may be derived from גור, "to sojourn" (so LXX), but comparison with the expression, "terror all around," in Jer. 6:25, *et al.,* indicates that it is better derived from גור, "to fear," with subjective suffix (so Syriac and Vulg.), "those whom I fear," i.e., "my enemies," the neighboring peoples (see Exeg. on 1:2). There is no prayer for vengeance here as there is at the end of chs. 1; 3.

3 I *AM* the man *that* hath seen affliction by the rod of his wrath.

2 He hath led me, and brought *me into* darkness, but not *into* light.

3 Surely against me is he turned; he turneth his hand *against me* all the day.

4 My flesh and my skin hath he made old; he hath broken my bones.

5 He hath builded against me, and compassed *me* with gall and travail.

6 He hath set me in dark places, as *they that be* dead of old.

7 He hath hedged me about, that I cannot get out: he hath made my chain heavy.

8 Also when I cry and shout, he shutteth out my prayer.

---

3 I am the man who has seen affliction
 under the rod of his wrath;

2 he has driven and brought me
 into darkness without any light;

3 surely against me he turns his hand
 again and again the whole day long.

4 He has made my flesh and my skin waste
 away,
 and broken my bones;

5 he has besieged and enveloped me
 with bitterness and tribulation;

6 he has made me dwell in darkness
 like the dead of long ago.

7 He has walled me about so that I cannot
 escape;
 he has put heavy chains on me;

8 though I call and cry for help,
 he shuts out my prayer;

III. A Personal Lament and Prayer (3:1-66)

As the speaker is called גבר, a **man** (vss. 1, 27, 35, 39), this poem must be a personal lament, not a dirge by or for the city, as in chs. 1; 2; 4. The author seems to have the experiences of Jeremiah in mind (cf. Jer. 38:6-13) and may in fact be playing the role of Jeremiah in the poem. The order of thought is affliction, resignation, repentance, and prayer.

3:1. The words ראה עני, "who has experienced affliction," form a relative clause with the relative particle understood, as so often in poetry. **By the rod** is preferable to **under the rod. His wrath:** God's wrath.

2. Without any light is incorrect, since this would require a circumstantial clause, with the negative אין; translate **but not into light,** if the noun is taken as in the terminative accusative, or "and not in light," if it is taken as in the adverbial accusative.

3. The Hebrew idiom ישב יהפך, lit., "he returns, he turns," expresses repeated action and the imperfect of the two verbs is frequentative; hence, "he has repeatedly turned" (Amer. Trans.) .

5. The words בנה עלי mean, lit., **he hath builded against me;** hence, "he has fenced me in" (Amer. Trans.) rather than **he has besieged . . . me. Bitterness:** Lit., **gall** (so RSV in vs. 19) , a bitter and poisonous herb, always with figurative purport.

6. This verse is a direct quotation from Ps. 143:3, with the order of the first two words changed to fit the acrostic scheme.

7. He has walled me about: I.e., as a prisoner (cf. Job 19:8) . The words הכביד נחשתי, lit., "he has made my bronze heavy," mean fetters of bronze (cf. our "irons") , and are used elsewhere with this meaning always in the dual.

8. The RSV ignores גם, **also,** "moreover," at the beginning of the verse. The word כי, **though,** is better translated "whenever," since the verbs are in the frequentative imperfect. However, שתם is in the perfect; hence, "he has ignored" in place of **he shuts out.**

---

moves in a mysterious way." What is behind the "frowning providence"? (See 3:22, 25, 31-33.)

3:1-66. *Appearance and Reality.*—This chapter opens with tragic lamenting and outcries against God for what has happened (cf. Job 6-7; 9-10; 19) . But then comes a swift turn of

feeling with vs. 21: **This I recall to my mind, therefore have I hope.** Here we sound the depth and approach the climax of this little book. The "author" may fall back indeed into the mood of questioning (vss. 42-47) ; but his soul rises to higher and nobler thoughts (vss. 55-57) : **I called**

9 He hath inclosed my ways with hewn stone; he hath made my paths crooked.

10 He *was* unto me *as* a bear lying in wait, *and as* a lion in secret places.

11 He hath turned aside my ways, and pulled me in pieces: he hath made me desolate.

12 He hath bent his bow, and set me as a mark for the arrow.

13 He hath caused the arrows of his quiver to enter into my reins.

14 I was a derision to all my people; *and* their song all the day.

15 He hath filled me with bitterness, he hath made me drunken with wormwood.

16 He hath also broken my teeth with gravel stones, he hath covered me with ashes.

17 And thou hast removed my soul far off from peace: I forgat prosperity.

18 And I said, My strength and my hope is perished from the LORD:

---

9 he has blocked my ways with hewn stones,
   he has made my paths crooked.

10 He is to me like a bear lying in wait,
   like a lion in hiding;

11 he led me off my way and tore me to pieces;
   he has made me desolate;

12 he bent his bow and set me
   as a mark for his arrow.

13 He drove into my heart
   the arrows of his quiver;

14 I have become the laughingstock of all peoples,
   the burden of their songs all day long.

15 He has filled me with bitterness,
   he has sated me with wormwood.

16 He has made my teeth grind on gravel,
   and made me cower in ashes;

17 my soul is bereft of peace,
   I have forgotten what happiness is;

18 so I say, "Gone is my glory,
   and my expectation from the LORD."

---

9. With hewn stones: A stronger obstruction than ordinary stone would make. In the last clause the crooked paths are bypaths leading to destruction rather than to help.

11. The words דרכי סורר, lit., **he hath turned aside my ways,** "he has driven me off my way," as a wild animal would.

13. Cf. Job 6:4; 16:12-13. The word כליתי is, lit., "my kidneys," a very sensitive and vital organ; hence "my vitals" (Amer. Trans.) rather than **my heart. The arrows of his quiver:** Lit., "the children of his quiver," the arrows being thought of as the offspring of the quiver—a figure that appears also in Horace (*Odes* I. 22. 3).

14. Of all peoples is the reading of many MSS, Sebhir, and the Syriac, but the M.T. has "of all my people," which is preferable. The text was changed when the poem came to be interpreted as a lament by the city rather than by an individual. **The burden of their songs** is one word in the Hebrew; better, "their taunt-song" (Amer. Trans.) ; so also in vs. 63 (cf. Jer. 20:7).

15. Wormwood: A bitter herb like gall, always with figurative purport.

16. The word גרם is found only here and in Ps. 119:20; its meaning is uncertain, but the translation of the verse in the RSV can be accepted (cf. Prov. 20:17; Matt. 7:9), except that it ignores ו, **also,** at the beginning and adds a ו, **and,** to the last clause.

17. The word תוגח can be taken as second masculine Qal with oscillation from third to second person (see Exeg. on Song of S. 1:2, 4), as in vs. 23 (so KJV), or the verb may be repointed as second person feminine Niphal, with נפשי as subject (so RSV, following Targ., Vulg., and Syriac), or it may be emended to the third person masculine Qal, with נפשי as object (so Amer. Trans., following LXX). There is little difference in meaning. The word נפשי, lit., **my soul,** is simply a Hebrew idiom for the personal pronoun

---

on thy name, O LORD . . . ; thou didst hear my plea . . . ! Thou didst come near when I called on thee; thou didst say, "Do not fear!" The answer which he hears coming from God

reminds us of Jesus' great word, "Do not fear, only believe" (Mark 5:36)—which a great student of the Bible once said has in it the heart of the Christian religion.

19 Remembering mine affliction and my misery, the wormwood and the gall.
20 My soul hath *them* still in remembrance, and is humbled in me.
21 This I recall to my mind, therefore have I hope.
22 ¶ *It is of* the LORD's mercies that we are not consumed, because his compassions fail not.
23 *They are* new every morning: great *is* thy faithfulness.
24 The LORD *is* my portion, saith my soul; therefore will I hope in him.
25 The LORD *is* good unto them that wait for him, to the soul *that* seeketh him.

19 Remember my affliction and my bitterness,[k]
the wormwood and the gall!
20 My soul continually thinks of it
and is bowed down within me.
21 But this I call to mind,
and therefore I have hope:

22 The steadfast love of the LORD never ceases,[l]
his mercies never come to an end;
23 they are new every morning;
great is thy faithfulness.
24 "The LORD is my portion," says my soul,
"therefore I will hope in him."

25 The LORD is good to those who wait for him,
to the soul that seeks him.

[k] Cn: Heb *wandering*
[l] Syr Tg: Heb *we are not cut off*

(so RSV in vss. 51, 58), used here and elsewhere for metrical reasons. **What happiness is:** Lit., **prosperity,** which is preferable, since the word has to do with physical well-being.

19. The verb זכר can be taken as imperative, **remember,** or better as the infinitive construct, "the thought of," following the Amer. Trans., or it may be repointed as a noun with the same meaning. For מרודי, **my affliction,** "my oppression," see Exeg. on 1:7.

20. The first verb has the emphatic infinitive absolute construction and its subject is נפשי, **my soul**="I"; hence, "I am indeed thinking of it" (Amer. Trans.). The reading of the *Qerê,* many MSS, Targ., Lucian, Symm., and Vulg. (followed by RSV and KJV), תשוח (from שחח, "to be bowed down"), is preferable to תשיח (from שיח, "to meditate"), which is the reading of the *Kethibh,* LXX, and O.L.

21. There is no **but** at the beginning because its inclusion would spoil the acrostic; but it is to be understood.

22. The noun חסדי, an abstract plural, "mercy," or **steadfast love,** is in the *casus pendens,* and כי introduces an object clause in apposition to זאת, "this," of vs. 21. The verb תמנו is an irregular form (cf. Num. 17:13 [Hebrew 17:28]; Jer. 44:18) for תמנו, "we cease," which makes no sense here; hence, emend to תמו, with one MS, the Targ., and Syriac, **never come to an end,** with the verb in the stative perfect.

23. In לבקרים, the ל is distributive, hence, **every morning.**

24. The words אמרה נפשי, **says my soul,** with the verb in the perfect of instantaneous action, better, "I said" (Amer. Trans.), make the line 2+2+3. In לו we have the ל of specification. The thought of this and the following verses is rather frequent in the psalms, but unusual in a lament.

25. The verb קוה here is "to wait eagerly," "to crave" rather than simply "to wait." The *Qerê* reads the plural, "to those who crave for him," the *Kethibh,* the singular, which agrees better with the context.

25-27. *Waiting on God.*—Here the poet comes to new and deep realizations, giving us a beautiful statement of the real meaning of our relationship to God our Father. We are to **seek** him, and **wait quietly for the salvation of the LORD,** knowing that **it is good for a man that he bear the yoke in his youth.** Significantly

we call a child who has been petted and coddled, and so never feels a sense of responsibility, a "spoiled child." Remember Jesus' severe judgment on one who inflicts any such injury, that it were better for him to have a great stone tied about his neck, and to be drowned in the sea (Matt. 18:6). A leading psychologist once

26 *It is* good that *a man* should both hope and quietly wait for the salvation of the Lord.

27 *It is* good for a man that he bear the yoke in his youth.

28 He sitteth alone and keepeth silence, because he hath borne *it* upon him.

29 He putteth his mouth in the dust; if so be there may be hope.

30 He giveth *his* cheek to him that smiteth him: he is filled full with reproach.

31 For the Lord will not cast off for ever:

32 But though he cause grief, yet will he have compassion according to the multitude of his mercies.

33 For he doth not afflict willingly, nor grieve the children of men.

34 To crush under his feet all the prisoners of the earth,

35 To turn aside the right of a man before the face of the Most High,

---

26 It is good that one should wait quietly
　　for the salvation of the Lord.
27 It is good for a man that he bear
　　the yoke in his youth.

28 Let him sit alone in silence
　　when he has laid it on him;
29 let him put his mouth in the dust —
　　there may yet be hope;
30 let him give his cheek to the smiter,
　　and be filled with insults.

31 For the Lord will not
　　cast off for ever,
32 but, though he cause grief, he will have compassion
　　according to the abundance of his steadfast love;
33 for he does not willingly afflict
　　or grieve the sons of men.

34 To crush under foot
　　all the prisoners of the earth,
35 to turn aside the right of a man
　　in the presence of the Most High,

---

26. The words ויחיל ודומם must be emended because there is no root חיל, "to wait," and דומם, as a noun, is impossible after *wāw*. The simplest reading and the one best fitting the context is that of the LXX, ויחל ודמם, where the first *wāw* introduces a subject clause, יחל is the Piel perfect of יחל, "to wait," and ודמם, "and he is quiet," is a clause in the adverbial accusative of manner (also in vs. 28), best reproduced in English by an adverb, **quietly.**

27. The meter is 2+3, not 3+2, as in the RSV. For the thought cf. Heb. 12:7-11.

28. Translate כי **because** or "since" (Amer. Trans.) rather than **when**; it is better also to understand God as the subject of נטל, "he has laid," "loaded" (so KJV), than to take it as indefinite (so RSV). Vss. 28-30, constituting the *yôdh*-strophe, may be taken as the continuation of vs. 27 (so Amer. Trans.), or the verb may be taken as jussive (so KJV). Since the strophes in this chapter are not always separate units and the former interpretation fits the context better, it is to be preferred.

29. The first clause is without parallel in the O.T., but it is a typically Oriental expression to indicate self-abasement. The word אולי is strictly "perhaps" (Amer. Trans.), not **yet.**

30. Cf. Isa. 50:6. The last clause is more literally "that he be sated with disgrace."

31. The line may be scanned as 2+2, but it is probable that some word such as אדם, "mankind," was lost by haplography in the second stich (cf. Targ., which has "his servants") either before or after אדני.

32. The word כי can be interpreted as **but** after the preceding negative, or as "for" (ERV), or it can be taken with the following אם as emphatic **though.**

33. The verb ענה is in the perfect of experience, **he does not . . . afflict. Willingly:** Lit., "from his heart." Better, "willfully." The verb ויגה may be the Piel of יגה, contracted from וייגה, or it may be pointed as Hiphil (cf. vs. 32). **The sons of men** is a literal translation, but **sons** here is used in its Semitic idiomatic sense, meaning "those belonging to the species, man"; hence, "mankind."

34. Not **prisoners of the earth**, but "prisoners of the land," i.e., Palestine.

36 To subvert a man in his cause, the Lord approveth not.

37 ¶ Who *is* he *that* saith, and it cometh to pass, *when* the Lord commandeth *it* not?

38 Out of the mouth of the Most High proceedeth not evil and good?

39 Wherefore doth a living man complain, a man for the punishment of his sins?

40 Let us search and try our ways, and turn again to the LORD.

41 Let us lift up our heart with *our* hands unto God in the heavens.

42 We have transgressed and have rebelled: thou hast not pardoned.

43 Thou hast covered with anger, and persecuted us: thou hast slain, thou hast not pitied.

44 Thou hast covered thyself with a cloud, that *our* prayer should not pass through.

45 Thou hast made us *as* the offscouring and refuse in the midst of the people.

---

36 to subvert a man in his cause,
  the Lord does not approve.

37 Who has commanded and it came to pass,
  unless the Lord has ordained it?

38 Is it not from the mouth of the Most
  High
  that good and evil come?

39 Why should a living man complain,
  a man, about the punishment of his
  sins?

40 Let us test and examine our ways,
  and return to the LORD!

41 Let us lift up our hearts and hands
  to God in heaven:

42 "We have transgressed and rebelled,
  and thou hast not forgiven.

43 "Thou hast wrapped thyself with anger
  and pursued us,
  slaying without pity;

44 thou hast wrapped thyself with a cloud
  so that no prayer can pass through.

45 Thou hast made us offscouring and refuse
  among the peoples.

---

36. The word אדם is always generic; hence, not **a man** but "man" (Amer. Trans.). For the thought cf. Exod. 23:6; Deut. 10:17. Some scholars follow the Targ. and interpret the last clause as a question, "Does the Lord not see?" They maintain that **approve** is not a legitimate translation of ראה, "to see," but this can perhaps be defended from the English "to countenance."

38. The abstract plural noun, הרעות, **evil,** in the sense of misfortune (cf. Amos 3:6; Isa. 45:7), is preceded by the generic article.

39. Better and more literally, "Of what can living man complain, a person because of his punishment?" The last word is, lit., **sins,** but here, as often elsewhere, the reference is to the consequences of sin in the form of **punishment.**

40. Beginning with this verse and running to the end of vs. 47, the poet identifies himself with his people.

41. For אל, "into," we should undoubtedly read על, meaning "upon" (LXX and Syriac) or "along with" (Vulg.). The expression used here is found nowhere else in Hebrew, but manifestly means wholehearted prayer on either interpretation of על.

43-44. The verb סכתה, **thou hast wrapped,** has no object expressed, but this is to be understood from vs. 44, viz., לך, **thyself,** with the ל of specification. **Anger** is compared to an impenetrable **cloud.**

45. The verb תשימנו is imperfect; hence, "thou makest us."

---

said, "If there be a sin against the Holy Spirit, it is the sin of doing anything to harm one's own or another's youth."

37-39. *Who, Unless the Lord?*—Who indeed, when all seems to go wrong and evil has power? Why should such things be in a universe created and ruled by God? Has he not allowed it? More —has he not **ordained it? Is it not from the**

mouth of the Most High that good and evil come? The problem then was even more poignant than it is now, especially for the innocent. Nothing was known of our so-called "secondary causes" (cf. Job 24:25). This much though was clear: God had made a world in which are found both good and evil, and no one was free to forget the word that the Lord had spoken to

46 All our enemies have opened their mouths against us.

47 Fear and a snare is come upon us, desolation and destruction.

48 Mine eye runneth down with rivers of water for the destruction of the daughter of my people.

49 Mine eye trickleth down, and ceaseth not, without any intermission,

50 Till the LORD look down, and behold from heaven.

51 Mine eye affecteth mine heart, because of all the daughters of my city.

52 Mine enemies chased me sore, like a bird, without cause.

53 They have cut off my life in the dungeon, and cast a stone upon me.

54 Waters flowed over mine head; *then* I said, I am cut off.

55 ¶ I called upon thy name, O LORD, out of the low dungeon.

---

46 "All our enemies
    rail against us;
47 panic and pitfall have come upon us,
    devastation and destruction;
48 my eyes flow with rivers of tears
    because of the destruction of the daughter of my people.

49 "My eyes will flow without ceasing,
    without respite,
50 until the LORD from heaven
    looks down and sees;
51 my eyes cause me grief
    at the fate of all the maidens of my city.

52 "I have been hunted like a bird
    by those who were my enemies without cause;
53 they flung me alive into the pit
    and cast stones on me;
54 water closed over my head;
    I said, 'I am lost.'

55 "I called on thy name, O LORD,
    from the depths of the pit;

---

46. This verse is identical with 2:16*a* and is probably a direct quotation here. Six MSS and the Syriac place the פ strophe (vss. 46-48) after the ע strophe (vss. 49-51), thus putting the letters in their regular order.

47. Note the assonance in פחד ופחת, **panic and pitfall,** lit., "terror and pit," appearing again in Jer. 48:43; Isa. 24:17. It is strange that the first two nouns have no article, while the last two have; this anomaly can be avoided by pointing the last two words as Niphal infinitive absolute, with no change in meaning.

48. In this verse, belonging in thought to the following strophe, the poet returns to the lament which he interrupted in vs. 40. The second stich is a duplicate of one in 2:11, and the first is almost identical with one in 1:16.

49. The verb נגרה must be in the perfect of certainty, "shall flow." The form הפגות, an abstract plural, **respite,** is found only here (but cf. פוגת, "respite," in 2:18).

51. At the fate of is a paraphrase of מן, **because of.** Many scholars transpose this verse to the beginning of the strophe and make vs. 50 the conclusion.

52. The expression צוד צדוני is emphatic (so KJV), and this is ignored by the RSV; translate "have indeed hunted me."

53. Lit., "They imperiled my life in a pit," with צמתו better pointed as Piel; hence, "they threw me into a pit to die" (Amer. Trans.), not **they flung me alive into the pit.** The verb וידו, **and cast,** is the Piel of ידה, contracted from וידדו (cf. ויגה in vs. 33).

55. From the depths of the pit: Lit., "from the pit of depth," the last word being an abstract plural.

Israel of old: "I have set before you life and death, blessing and curse; therefore choose life" (Deut. 30:19). There was forever that solemn responsibility. Man could do wrong if he chose, but God had given him the power to do right. The choice was his. So much our "author" sees, and in vss. 40-42 calls on those who have sinned and therefore are suffering to "return to the LORD," however cruelly God seems to have dealt with them (cf. vss. 34-35).

55-57. Do Not Fear.—God answers the agonized plea. And what an answer it is! Two simple words, **Fear not.** That is what the religion of Jesus says to us, "Do not fear, only

56 Thou hast heard my voice: hide not thine ear at my breathing, at my cry.

57 Thou drewest near in the day *that* I called upon thee: thou saidst, Fear not.

58 O Lord, thou hast pleaded the causes of my soul; thou hast redeemed my life.

59 O Lord, thou hast seen my wrong: judge thou my cause.

60 Thou hast seen all their vengeance *and* all their imaginations against me.

61 Thou hast heard their reproach, O Lord, *and* all their imaginations against me;

62 The lips of those that rose up against me, and their device against me all the day.

63 Behold their sitting down, and their rising up; I *am* their music.

64 ¶ Render unto them a recompense, O Lord, according to the work of their hands.

56 thou didst hear my plea, 'Do not close thine ear to my cry for help!'[m]

57 Thou didst come near when I called on thee;
Thou didst say, 'Do not fear!'

58 "Thou hast taken up my cause, O Lord, thou hast redeemed my life.

59 Thou hast seen the wrong done to me, O Lord;
judge thou my cause.

60 Thou hast seen all their vengeance, all their devices against me.

61 "Thou hast heard their taunts, O Lord, all their devices against me.

62 The lips and thoughts of my assailants are against me all the day long.

63 Behold their sitting and their rising; I am the burden of their songs.

64 "Thou wilt requite them, O Lord, according to the work of their hands.

[m] Heb uncertain

56. The verb עלם, **hide,** translated **close** by the RSV, is nowhere else used with אזן, ear, or with the preposition ל, "to," but with מן, "from." The word לרוחתי, "to my respite," makes no sense here; hence, read לצוחתי, "to my cry," with the LXX. The last word, לשועתי, "to my supplication," may be a gloss on the preceding word, but it is more likely a variant reading, thus giving us a conflate text.

57. The verb אקראך is frequentative imperfect; translate accordingly, "whenever I called on thee."

58. The meter is 2+2+2, but since the plural ריבי נפשי, **the causes of my soul,** is most unusual, we should probably read ריבי singular, **my cause.** In that case the meter would be 3+2. If ריבי plural is original, it must be an abstract plural; or the word may be singular construct with the helping *yôdh,* which is found rather often in Hebrew poetry (see examples in 1:1; also עלי in 4:5).

62. The RSV translates this verse as an independent clause and thus spoils the parallelism; it is regularly regarded as the continuation of vs. 61, further objects of **thou hast heard** (so KJV). **Lips** is a literal translation; better, "utterances" (Amer. Trans.).

63. The words שבתם וקימתם mean, lit., "during their sitting down and their rising up," i.e., "during their time of leisure and their time of work," i.e., all the time. There is nothing in the original to suggest **Behold.**

64. The imperfects here and in vss. 65-66 are regularly taken as future, but it is assuredly better to take them as precative because lamentations regularly end in a prayer. Vs. 64 reads, lit., "Mayest thou bring retribution on them, O Yahweh, according to the work of their hands," which is almost identical with Ps. 28:4*b.*

believe." "See, but do not be afraid." Paul gives this same counsel to his followers: "God hath not given us the spirit of fear; but of power, and of love, and of a sound mind" (II Tim. 1:7). Observe the confidence expressed in 5:19; see Rev. 19:6.

Yet there immediately follows a cry to God for vengeance (cf. 1:21-22). Read as a comment Matt. 18:23-35. Is failure to forgive evidence in itself that he who fails is not himself forgiven? Forgiveness, in the O.T. at its best, as well as in the N.T., is creative forgiveness.

65 Give them sorrow of heart, thy curse unto them.

66 Persecute and destroy them in anger from under the heavens of the Lord.

4 How is the gold become dim! *how* is the most fine gold changed! the stones of the sanctuary are poured out in the top of every street.

2 The precious sons of Zion, comparable to fine gold, how are they esteemed as earthen pitchers, the work of the hands of the potter!

3 Even the sea monsters draw out the breast, they give suck to their young ones: the daughter of my people *is become* cruel, like the ostriches in the wilderness.

---

65 Thou wilt give them dullness of heart;
　　thy curse will be on them.
66 Thou wilt pursue them in anger and
　　　destroy them
　　from under thy heavens, O Lord."[n]

4 How the gold has grown dim,
　　how the pure gold is changed!
The holy stones lie scattered
　　at the head of every street.

2 The precious sons of Zion,
　　worth their weight in fine gold,
how they are reckoned as earthen pots,
　　the work of a potter's hands!

3 Even the jackals give the breast
　　and suckle their young,
but the daughter of my people has become cruel,
　　like the ostriches in the wilderness.

[n] Syr Compare Gk Vg: Heb *the heavens of the* Lord

---

65. The compound מגנת־לב is found only here, but its Arabic cognate suggests the meaning "derangement of mind."

66. The expression שמי יהוה, **the heavens of the** Lord, is found only here and should probably be read with the Syriac שמיך יהוה, "thy heavens, O Lord" (Amer. Trans.).

IV. Jerusalem in the Past and in the Present (4:1-22)

This chapter is closely allied with ch. 2 and is generally regarded as having the same author. It contrasts Jerusalem's humiliation at the hands of the Babylonians with her former splendor and lays the blame upon the priests and prophets (vss. 13-16). Like ch. 2, it is the work of an eyewitness of the siege, vivid and concrete.

4:1. The verbs are imperfect to indicate the present condition of things; translate accordingly, "How the gold is dimmed, the fine gold changed!" The word ישנא, the Aramaic form of ישנה, which appears in many MSS, is better pointed as Niphal, **is changed**, parallel to the preceding Hophal, and may be a gloss on it or a variant reading, giving us a better meter, 3+2. The word טוב, usually "good," here can be either **pure** or **fine. Lie scattered** is a paraphrase of תשתפכנה, "they pour themselves out," or "are thrown out." Not **the stones of the sanctuary,** but **the holy stones,** lit., "the stones of holiness." The gold, fine gold, and sacred stones are the temple treasures, here a metaphor for Jerusalem's most precious possessions, viz., her people, the **sons of Zion,** as vs. 2 indicates.

2. The first line is in the *casus pendens.* **Worth their weight in fine gold:** Lit., "the ones weighed out against fine gold." **As earthen pots:** With the ל of norm.

3. Even contemptible beasts of prey suckle their young, but the mothers of Jerusalem under the pressure of famine became unnatural, like the ostrich, which was proverbially neglectful of its young (cf. Job 39:13-18). The Targ., LXX, and many scholars emend בת, **the daughter of,** to the plural בנות, "the women of," but the singular is better since in the O.T. the city is frequently personified as a woman. The *Kethîbh,* כי ענים, makes no sense; read as one word with the *Qerê,* **like the ostriches.**

4:1-22. *Past Glory and Present Misery.*—See Expos. on 1:7, 13-15; 2:9-10, 14. On vs. 21, cf.

Expos. on 3:55-57.

4 The tongue of the sucking child cleaveth to the roof of his mouth for thirst: the young children ask bread, *and* no man breaketh *it* unto them.

5 They that did feed delicately are desolate in the streets: they that were brought up in scarlet embrace dunghills.

6 For the punishment of the iniquity of the daughter of my people is greater than the punishment of the sin of Sodom, that was overthrown as in a moment, and no hands stayed on her.

7 Her Nazarites were purer than snow, they were whiter than milk, they were more ruddy in body than rubies, their polishing *was* of sapphire:

4 The tongue of the nursling cleaves
   to the roof of its mouth for thirst;
the children beg for food,
   but no one gives to them.

5 Those who feasted on dainties
   perish in the streets;
those who were brought up in purple
   lie on ash heaps.

6 For the chastisement[o] of the daughter of
   my people has been greater
   than the punishment[p] of Sodom,
which was overthrown in a moment,
   no hand being laid on it.[q]

7 Her princes were purer than snow,
   whiter than milk;
their bodies were more ruddy than coral,
   the beauty of their form[r] was like sapphire.[s]

[o] Or *iniquity*
[p] Or *sin*
[q] Heb uncertain
[r] Heb uncertain
[s] Heb *lapis lazuli*

4. Cf. 2:12. The first two verbs are in the perfect of experience, as in the RSV, but the last clause is circumstantial, "with none to give it to them."

5. This verse presents a striking contrast between past glory and present misery and degradation. The ל with מעדנים, **dainties,** may be the ל of specification introducing the object, or the ל of norm with an abstract plural, **delicately. Perish** is a questionable rendering of נשמו, **are desolate,** "stand aghast," a stative perfect. The reference in the last line is to those brought up in the lap of luxury, symbolized by **purple,** the color of royalty. The word חבקו is a perfect of experience, lit., **embrace,** hence, "have to take to" (Amer. Trans.), which is closer to the original than **lie. Ash heaps,** better, "refuse heaps" or **dunghills,** are still a conspicuous feature of Oriental towns and villages.

6. **For** is a questionable rendering of *wāw* consecutive; better consequential, "so" (Amer. Trans.). Hence, it is better to take the two following words for **sin** in their root meaning, as in the ERV and Amer. Trans., agreeing accordingly with Ezek. 16:47-50, rather than in the derived meaning of **punishment,** as in the KJV and RSV. In כמו־רגע the preposition can be taken as pregnant, **as in a moment,** or simply as temporal, **in a moment.** Sodom's destruction was instantaneous, in contrast wtih Jerusalem's long-drawn-out agony. The last clause is circumstantial, the verb being perfect rather than participle, since it has to do with an instantaneous act in the past. The word חלו is difficult; it is usually taken as the Qal perfect of חול, in the sense in which it is used in Jer. 23:19 (=30:23); II Sam. 3:29, "to fall whirling," "to fall in violent fashion," hence, "to be laid." The meaning would be that Sodom fell at the hand of God directly, not through human agency, as was the case with Jerusalem.

7. The word נזיריה, "her devotees," is usually translated **her princes,** but this is a questionable meaning; some scholars emend to נעריה, "her youths." The word עצם, an accusative of specification, is, lit., "in bone," but here it means **in body.** The word גזרתם, lit., "their cutting," is here apparently **their polishing,** "their luster," i.e., "their beauty of form," or simply **their form,** something cut out.

8 Their visage is blacker than a coal; they are not known in the streets: their skin cleaveth to their bones; it is withered, it is become like a stick.

9 *They that be* slain with the sword are better than *they that be* slain with hunger: for these pine away, stricken through for *want of* the fruits of the field.

10 The hands of the pitiful women have sodden their own children: they were their meat in the destruction of the daughter of my people.

11 The LORD hath accomplished his fury; he hath poured out his fierce anger, and hath kindled a fire in Zion, and it hath devoured the foundations thereof.

12 The kings of the earth, and all the inhabitants of the world, would not have believed that the adversary and the enemy should have entered into the gates of Jerusalem.

13 ¶ For the sins of her prophets, *and* the iniquities of her priests, that have shed the blood of the just in the midst of her,

8 Now their visage is blacker than soot,
　they are not recognized in the streets;
their skin has shriveled upon their bones,
　it has become as dry as wood.

9 Happier were the victims of the sword
　than the victims of hunger,
who pined away, stricken
　by want of the fruits of the field.

10 The hands of compassionate women
　have boiled their own children;
they became their food
　in the destruction of the daughter of
　　my people.

11 The LORD gave full vent to his wrath,
　he poured out his hot anger;
and he kindled a fire in Zion,
　which consumed its foundations.

12 The kings of the earth did not believe,
　or any of the inhabitants of the world,
that foe or enemy could enter
　the gates of Jerusalem.

13 This was for the sins of her prophets
　and the iniquities of her priests,
who shed in the midst of her
　the blood of the righteous.

8. The noun שׁחוֹר is, lit., "blackness"; hence, **coal** or **soot.** The verb היה, "it has become," is quite redundant after יגשׁ, **it has become . . . dry,** and its deletion makes the meter the regular 3+2 instead of the irregular 3+3. The reference here is to the wasting effects of famine resulting from the siege.

9. The word שׁהם appears again in Song of S. 6:5; it can scarcely be relative, as in the RSV, but causal, as in the KJV (see Exeg. on Song of S. 1:7). The verb יזובו, "they flow," is difficult; the usual translation **pine away** is so questionable that it is best to emend the word with Ehrlich to יזונו, the Niphal of זון, "to feed." The word מדקרים, lit., "pierced through," cannot possibly be applied to those wasting away through hunger, but to those pierced or wounded by **the sword** in battle at the time of the siege; translate accordingly, "For the former can feed, though wounded, on the fruits of the fields," as **the victims of hunger** cannot.

10. This verse, like 2:20, is a reference to cannibalism. It is better to point ברות as the noun **food,** as in Ps. 69:21 (Hebrew 69:22), rather than the Piel infinitive, "devouring."

11. The second line may be understood metaphorically as referring to **anger,** or it may refer to the actual burning of the city recorded in II Chr. 36:19.

12. The poet here represents the surrounding peoples as sharing the Jewish belief in the inviolability of Jerusalem—a belief in which he himself concurred, but against which Jeremiah vigorously protested (e.g., Jer. 27:14).

13. The KJV makes this verse the protasis of vs. 14; this sort of thing has been noted in the inferior style of ch. 3, but in chs. 2 and 4 the strophes are clearly separate, each complete in itself. The thought agrees exactly with 2:14 (see Exeg.), with which the

14 They have wandered *as* blind *men* in the streets, they have polluted themselves with blood, so that men could not touch their garments.

15 They cried unto them, Depart ye; *it is* unclean; depart, depart, touch not: when they fled away and wandered, they said among the heathen, They shall no more sojourn *there*.

16 The anger of the LORD hath divided them; he will no more regard them: they respected not the persons of the priests, they favored not the elders.

14 They wandered, blind, through the streets,
   so defiled with blood
that none could touch
   their garments.

15 "Away! Unclean!" men cried at them;
   "Away! Away! Touch not!"
So they became fugitives and wanderers;
   men said among the nations,
"They shall stay with us no longer."

16 The LORD himself has scattered them,
   he will regard them no more;
no honor was shown to the priests,
   no favor to the elders.

Targ. compares it. Since the prophets and priests by their wrong guidance were responsible for the nation's plight, they were responsible for the bloodshed and were in fact murderers of the innocent.

14. The subject of the verbs is manifestly the prophets and priests of the preceding verse. The RSV follows the general interpretation of the second line by making ב introduce a result clause, but this would be the only instance in all of Hebrew literature and is most questionable. It is better to take ב as introducing a clause that is the object of יגעו, a verb which regularly takes its object with ב; the subject of the verbs (both imperfect) would be the same as in the first line and not indefinite. Translate accordingly, "Those whom they should not, they kept touching with their clothes," i.e., they were ceremonially unclean because of the bloodshed and should not communicate their uncleanness to others, but in their heedlessness and general lack of responsibility they did.

15. The prophets and priests are here compared to lepers, and since it was the leper that had to cry **Unclean!** not the onlookers (Lev. 13:45), it is best to take קראו as having the same subject as the verbs in the preceding verse, and not indefinite, as regularly understood. In that case למו would be the ל of specification, "of themselves" (Amer. Trans.), or the reflexive ל, which is simply emphatic. The meter of the line is 2+2+3 and there is no need to delete anything, as is usually done. The second line is difficult. The word כי assuredly cannot mean so, but **when,** or, better, "because." The word נעו is found nowhere else and its meaning is quite uncertain. Most scholars would emend it to נדו on the basis of Gen. 4:12, 14, where נוע of our text also appears. In any case, the meaning and paranomasia of the Hebrew can be well reproduced by "they have become vagabonds and vagrants," just as Cain did. The verb אמרו is manifestly a perfect of experience, indefinite plural. The last stich reads, lit., "they may not add to settle as immigrants" —a Hebrew idiom meaning "they may not settle as immigrants any more," i.e., like Cain they were denied all rights, even those of an immigrant or sojourner in a foreign land. Our translation then would run as follows:

> Because they have become vagabonds and vagrants,
> people say among the nations,
> "They may not settle as immigrants any more."

16. The words פני יהוה, lit., "the face of Yahweh," can perhaps be translated **the LORD himself** on the basis of Exod. 33:14-15, but it is questionable whether חלק, "to divide," "to apportion," can be given the meaning "to scatter." Although it does seem to have a meaning akin to this in Gen. 49:7, even here it still has the idea of apportioning (cf. Num. 35:8). It would seem better to follow two MSS and the LXX, and point חלקם as a noun, "their portion," making with יהוה a clause genitive to פני; in this case

17 As for us, our eyes as yet failed for our vain help: in our watching we have watched for a nation *that* could not save *us*.

18 They hunt our steps, that we cannot go in our streets: our end is near, our days are fulfilled; for our end is come.

19 Our persecutors are swifter than the eagles of the heaven: they pursued us upon the mountains, they laid wait for us in the wilderness.

20 The breath of our nostrils, the anointed of the LORD, was taken in their pits, of whom we said, Under his shadow we shall live among the heathen.

21 ¶ Rejoice and be glad, O daughter of

17 Our eyes failed, ever watching
  vainly for help;
in our watching[t] we watched
  for a nation which could not save.

18 Men dogged our steps
  so that we could not walk in our
    streets;
our end drew near; our days were num-
    bered;
for our end had come.

19 Our pursuers were swifter
  than the vultures in the heavens;
they chased us on the mountains,
  they lay in wait for us in the wilderness.

20 The breath of our nostrils. the LORD's
    anointed,
  was taken in their pits,
he of whom we said, "Under his shadow
  we shall live among the nations."

21 Rejoice and be glad, O daughter of
    Edom,
  dweller in the land of Uz;

[t] Heb uncertain

the line would read: "The face of those whose portion was Yahweh [i.e., the priests; cf. Deut. 10:9] he no longer regards," and the expression would be parallel to that in the next line, נשא פנים, "to lift up the face," meaning "to show favor." In the latter line the verbs are indefinite plural, but they are usually emended to the singular to make Yahweh the subject. In either case they are best interpreted as in the perfect of experience, to be translated by the English present. In the last clause the M.T. has **elders** in place of an expected "prophets," which appears in some LXX codices and the O.L. but is probably not original. **Elders** is used here to emphasize the degradation of those previously honored so highly. Five MSS and the Syriac have this verse after vss. 17, thus keeping the ע and פ strophes in their regular order.

17. The RSV is a paraphrase; more literally, "Our eyes still kept straining [frequentative imperfect] after help for us that was vain," the poet identifying himself with his people who had looked so often to Egypt for help that never materialized (cf. e.g., Isa. 36:6-10; Jer. 37:5-10).

18. In our streets: Lit., "in our broad places," i.e., abroad. The second line is a tristich, 2+2+2. This verse and vss. 19-20 give a vivid description of the end of the siege.

20. In the light of II Chr. 35:25, "our breath of life," not **the breath of our nostrils** (see Exeg. on 1:7), is identified with Josiah by the Targ. and the older commentators, but Ibn Ezra rightly saw that the reference is to Zedekiah, who was captured by the Babylonians as he fled from the beleaguered city (II Kings 25:4-7). It is better to take the verb אמרנו as pluperfect, "we had said," since the hopes in Zedekiah expressed by the poet are past, not present, hopes.

21. Of all their neighbors none was so hated by the Jews as **Edom** (see Isa. 34:1-17; 63:1-6; Ezek. 35:1-15; Jer. 49:7-22; Obad. 1-21; Ps. 137:7). There was a certain satisfaction, accordingly, in the thought that her turn was coming and she would have to drink of the same cup of shameful humiliation (cf. Jer. 25:15-29; Hab. 2:15-16). Here and in

Edom, that dwellest in the land of Uz; the cup also shall pass through unto thee: thou shalt be drunken, and shalt make thyself naked.

22 ¶ The punishment of thine iniquity is accomplished, O daughter of Zion; he will no more carry thee away into captivity: he will visit thine iniquity, O daughter of Edom; he will discover thy sins.

5 Remember, O LORD, what is come upon us: consider, and behold our reproach.

2 Our inheritance is turned to strangers, our houses to aliens.

3 We are orphans and fatherless, our mothers *are* as widows.

4 We have drunken our water for money; our wood is sold unto us.

5 Our necks *are* under persecution: we labor, *and* have no rest.

---

but to you also the cup shall pass;
  you shall become drunk and strip yourself bare.

22 The punishment of your iniquity, O
  daughter of Zion, is accomplished,
  he will keep you in exile no longer;
but your iniquity, O daughter of Edom,
  he will punish,
  he will uncover your sins.

5 Remember, O LORD, what has befallen
  us;
  behold, and see our disgrace!

2 Our inheritance has been turned over to
  strangers,
  our homes to aliens.

3 We have become orphans, fatherless;
  our mothers are like widows.

4 We must pay for the water we drink,
  the wood we get must be bought.

5 With a yoke[u] on our necks we are hard
  driven;
  we are weary, we are given no rest.

[u] Symmachus: Heb lacks *with a yoke*

Gen. 36:28 (=I Chr. 1:42) **Uz** is connected with Edom, but elsewhere in the O.T. it is variously located. The *Kethîbh* יושבתי is simply the regular feminine participle יושבת of the *Qerê*, with the helping *yôdh* that is sometimes added to the construct in poetry (see Exeg. on 1:1).

22. The second stich may also be translated "never again will he exile you." The verbs in the last line are in the perfect of certainty.

V. A NATIONAL PRAYER FOR MERCY (5:1-22)

In this poem we have the nation's prayer for compassion rather than a dirge. In the Vulg. it bears the title "A prayer [*oratio*] of the prophet Jeremiah." Vs. 3 indicates that the author was living in Palestine as one of the remnant that were left there, and he dwells upon their miserable condition as ground for compassion.

5:2. The verb הפך is used again in the sense of "to turn over," "to surrender" in Isa. 60:5. Most scholars introduce a verb, נתנו, "have been given," into the second stich to make the meter 3+3, but the 3+2 meter here is simply a variant of the regular 3+3 and to emend the line is wholly unwarranted.

3. The people are described as **orphans** because their fathers were slain in battle or were carried off into exile and this made their mothers **like widows**; better, "actually widows," with the asseverative *kaph*. The poet of course is speaking in hyperbole because not all the fathers were killed or deported. The meter is 2+2+2.

4. The RSV is a paraphrase; more literally, "We get our drinking water with money; our wood must come by purchase." The poet is emphasizing the complete vassalage and degradation of the people.

5. The literal reading of the first stich, **on our necks we are hard driven** (if נרדפנו can be given this meaning, as perhaps it can), seems to make no sense. It would seem better to follow the text of Symm., which has על, yoke, before על, on (so RSV and most scholars), the absence of the former from the M.T. being easily accounted for as due to haplography. On the other hand, we could point the M.T. על, **on**, as ʿōl, **yoke**, construct

6 We have given the hand *to* the Egyptians, *and to* the Assyrians, to be satisfied with bread.	6 We have given the hand to Egypt, and to Assyria, to get bread enough.
7 Our fathers have sinned, and *are* not; and we have borne their iniquities.	7 Our fathers sinned, and are no more; and we bear their iniquities.
8 Servants have ruled over us: *there is* none that doth deliver *us* out of their hand.	8 Slaves rule over us; there is none to deliver us from their hand.
9 We gat our bread with *the peril of* our lives, because of the sword of the wilderness.	9 We get our bread at the peril of our lives, because of the sword in the wilderness.
10 Our skin was black like an oven, because of the terrible famine.	10 Our skin is hot as an oven with the burning heat of famine.
11 They ravished the women in Zion, *and* the maids in the cities of Judah.	11 Women are ravished in Zion, virgins in the towns of Judah.

to the following word, and still get the same translation, **with a yoke on our necks,** lit., "with a yoke of our neck," The last stich is better translated "we toil without any rest being given us," with the last clause in the adverbial accusative of manner.

6. Egypt and **Assyria** are manifestly used here in a geographical sense to indicate the two parts of the world (the west and the east) to which refugees might flee from their intolerable lot in Palestine. Have **given the hand to:** Paid homage to.

7. Since the fathers died with the fall of Jerusalem, it was the children who had to pay the price of their mistakes; contrast Jer. 31:27-34; Ezek. 18:1-32. In vs. 16, however, the poet does acknowledge that the present generation had some part in that sin.

8. The government officials (cf. Jer. 39:3) are called **slaves** because they were minions of the Babylonians and the poet had only scorn for them. Some may actually have been slaves because the ancients often used slaves in responsible positions (cf. "Tobiah the slave," Neh. 2:10, 19). The last clause is clearly circumstantial, "with none to deliver from their hand."

9. At the peril of: Lit., "at the price of"—the *bêth* of price. From ancient times down to the present day the raids of Bedouin bands have always been a menace to peasants living near the edge of the desert, and that menace was increased after the fall of Jerusalem by the weakness of the people and the enmity of their neighbors.

10. Here the subject is singular and the verb plural, but since disagreement between subject and predicate is sometimes found in poetry, it is not necessary to pluralize the subject, as many MSS do, or to make the verb singular with the LXX, O.L., and Vulg. **With:** Lit., "because of the presence of." The reference is to raging fever brought on by hunger.

11. The indefinite third person plural perfect, ענו, **they ravished,** may refer to conditions on the fall of the city, but it is better taken as the perfect of experience, referring to a state of affairs that is always the aftermath of invasion and conquest (so RSV); so also the perfects in vss. 12-13.

5:7. On Blaming Others.—How readily we look back and blame the faults of the past for our own ills! Of course we are forced to deal with the outcome of the sins of past days. But we need to be on guard lest we take the easy way of excusing ourselves for our conduct by laying the blame on others (cf. vs. 16). How readily we utter our passionate lament when some special sorrow comes upon us, "Who else ever had to suffer such an affliction?" There was once a woman who had ceased to attend church.

Her pastor called at her home and asked why she held herself aloof. She told him with marked indignation that some of the members had been ungracious to her and had spoken to her most unpleasantly, until she could no longer stand it. When all the details were out, she asked, "Did you ever know anyone who was worse treated?" "Yes," her pastor answered. Surprised, she wanted to know who, and he told her—"Jesus." She broke down then and they prayed together. The next Sunday saw her in her old place.

12 Princes are hanged up by their hand: the faces of elders were not honored.

13 They took the young men to grind, and the children fell under the wood.

14 The elders have ceased from the gate, the young men from their music.

15 The joy of our heart is ceased; our dance is turned into mourning.

16 The crown is fallen *from* our head: woe unto us, that we have sinned!

17 For this our heart is faint; for these *things* our eyes are dim.

18 Because of the mountain of Zion, which is desolate, the foxes walk upon it.

19 Thou, O LORD, remainest for ever; thy throne from generation to generation.

12 Princes are hung up by their hands;
   no respect is shown to the elders.

13 Young men are compelled to grind at the mill;
   and boys stagger under loads of wood.

14 The old men have quit the city gate,
   the young men their music.

15 The joy of our hearts has ceased;
   our dancing has been turned to mourning.

16 The crown has fallen from our head;
   woe to us, for we have sinned!

17 For this our heart has become sick,
   for these things our eyes have grown dim,

18 for Mount Zion which lies desolate;
   jackals prowl over it.

19 But thou, O LORD, dost reign for ever;
   thy throne endures to all generations.

---

12. The reference is not to crucifixion (so RSV), but **by their hand** means "by their power," i.e., "by them," the conquering foe.

13. The word טחון is often taken as a noun, "grinding mill," in which case this would be its only occurrence. It is accordingly better interpreted, with Symm., followed by the KJV and RSV, as infinitive construct, making the clause read, lit., "They [indefinite] carry off the young men to grind." For the indignity of grinding, the work of slaves and women, see Judg. 16:21; Isa. 47:2. The foraging for **wood** was also the work of slaves and women.

14. At **the city gate** was an open square, corresponding to the Roman forum, the place of assembly and seat of government, but now it was in Babylonian hands (cf. Jer. 39:3). **Have quit** is the same word that is translated **has ceased** in vs. 15; lit., "have ceased from the city gate."

15. Not **the joy of our hearts,** but "our joy of heart" (see Exeg. on 1:7).

16. For the fallen **crown** as a figure for the loss of statehood cf. Jer. 13:18.

17. **This** and **these** could refer back, but more likely forward, as in the RSV. The word דוה, **sick,** is better, **faint** (as in 1:13). The verb היה, "to be," is unnecessary here and its deletion would improve the meter.

18. The last clause is parallel to the preceding and must, like it, be relative ("on which jackals prowl") and not independent, as in the RSV. The statement is hyperbole, but it emphasizes the desolation of the temple mount.

19. But is omitted in the M.T., but is found in three MSS, the LXX, O.L., Syriac, Vulg., and Arabic. **Dost reign:** Lit., "dost sit," i.e., as a king, hence, "art enthroned"

19-22. Conclusion.—We shall fail to make the right use of this book if we come from the reading of it just to thank God that we have never attributed to God the ills of our life. Rather should we earnestly consider our own misuse of religion, our contentment with the thought that we have indeed come now upon better days. Rather should we search our hearts, realizing how easily we take what faith God has given us simply as a pleasant assurance of personal salvation; how lightly we turn cross and crucifix into ornaments or mere reminders of how we were "saved" by the death of our Lord. From what? His cross is a solemn presentation to us of the evil state of the world in which the greatest man who ever lived, God's own unspeakable gift to the world, after a few hard years was condemned to a cruel death. And we? Shall we come cheaply out of the struggle? We call Jesus Lord and Master. What then of the divisions of the church? What of the insistence on creeds and practices and tenets which he

20 Wherefore dost thou forget us for ever, *and* forsake us so long time?	20 Why dost thou forget us for ever, why dost thou so long forsake us?
21 Turn thou us unto thee, O Lord, and we shall be turned; renew our days as of old.	21 Restore us to thyself, O Lord, that we may be restored! Renew our days as of old!
22 But thou hast utterly rejected us; thou art very wroth against us.	22 Or hast thou utterly rejected us? Art thou exceedingly angry with us?

(Amer. Trans.). **To all generations:** Better, **from generation to generation,** with the distributive repetition of דור, **generation.** Against the changeful fortunes of men the poet sets the strength and stability of God's throne, which still continues despite the destruction of the temple and the suspension of the cultus; so he makes that the basis of his appeal for compassion in vss. 20-22 (cf. Hab. 1:12-13). The meter is 2+2+3 (a variant of the 3+3), unless we delete אתה, which could very well be omitted as unnecessary.

20. Why dost thou: Better, "Why wilt thou" (Amer. Trans.). **So long:** Lit., "to length of days," usually meaning "to an old age," but here perhaps "for life," in parallelism with **for ever** of the first stich. The thought is frequent in the psalms.

21. This is another tristich, 2+2+3, unless we omit אליך, **to thyself,** with two MSS. It is not necessary, and is omitted in the parallel passage, Jer. 31:18.

22. The RSV interprets the two stichs of the verse as questions, but to translate כי אם as **or** is quite impossible. Some scholars omit אם with six MSS, the LXX, O.L., Syriac, and Arabic. However, כי and אם appear rather often together and there is no reason why they should not be given their normal meanings, "for if," in which case the literal translation would be, "For if thou didst reject us completely, thou wouldst be angry unto much against us," i.e., "be too angry against us." Another possible translation makes vs. 22 a continuation of vs. 21: "Unless thou hadst rejected us completely, art most angry against us" (so ERV mg.), giving כי אם the meaning that it sometimes has, e.g., in Gen. 32:26 (Hebrew 32:27). No matter what translation is followed, vs. 22 sounds a somber note; not wishing to end in this fashion, the Jews in their synagogue reading always repeat vs. 21 after vs. 22, so as to end in a more pleasant strain; so also in the conclusions of Isaiah, Malachi, and Ecclesiastes.

never mentioned? Are these to be the "entrance requirements" for all who would enlist in the "school of Christ"? What of the easy religious life we lead? And in a world like ours! God be praised that the dreadful agony of this book of Lamentations is not ours; but God pity us—if his pity can reach so far—unless by his Spirit and at cost we dedicate ourselves to him anew, and to the true and full worship of his Son Jesus Christ our Lord (see Exeg. on vs. 22).

The Book of

EZEKIEL

Introduction and Exegesis by HERBERT G. MAY
Exposition by E. L. ALLEN

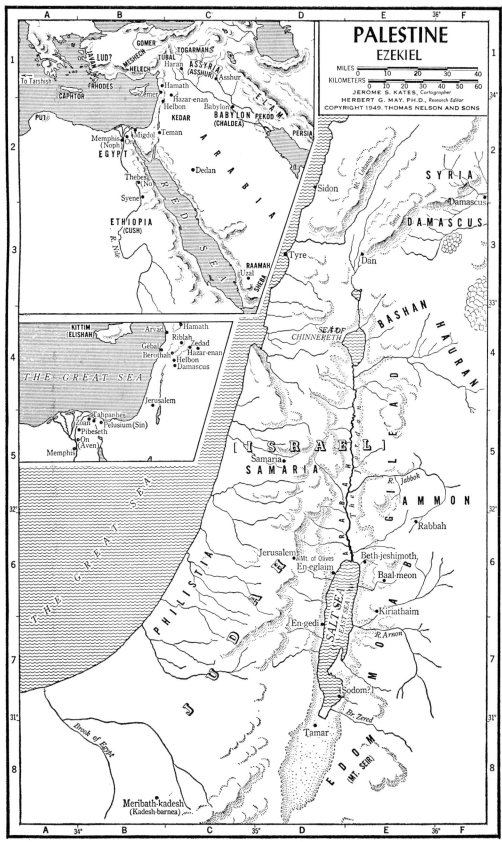

PALESTINE
EZEKIEL

MILES
KILOMETERS

JEROME S. KATES, *Cartographer*
HERBERT G. MAY, PH.D., *Research Editor*
COPYRIGHT 1949, THOMAS NELSON AND SONS

GOMER
TOGARMAH
LUD?
MESHECH
TUBAL
HELECH
ASSYRIA
(ASSHUR)
Haran
Asshur
JAVAN
RHODES
To Tarshish
Hamath
Zemer
Hazar-enan
Helbon
Babylon
ELAM
CAPHTOR
KEDAR
BABYLON
(CHALDEA)
PEKOD
PUT
Teman
PERSIA
Memphis
(Noph)
On
Migdol
EGYPT
ARABIA
Thebes
(No)
Dedan
Syene
ETHIOPIA
(CUSH)
R. Nile
RED SEA
RAAMAH
Uzal
SHEBA

KITTIM
(ELISHAH)
Arvad
Hamath
Riblah
Gebal
Zedad
Berothah
Hazar-enan
Helbon
Damascus
THE GREAT SEA
Jerusalem
Tahpanhes
Zoan
Pelusium (Sin)
Pibeseth
On
(Aven)
Memphis

SYRIA
Damascus
DAMASCUS
Sidon
Mt. Lebanon
Seir
Tyre
Dan
BASHAN
HAURAN
SEA OF
CHINNERETH
GILEAD
[ISRAEL]
Samaria
SAMARIA
R. Jabbok
AMMON
Rabbah
The Jordan
Jerusalem
Mt. of Olives
En-eglaim
Beth-jeshimoth
Baal-meon
ARABAH
MOAB
Kiriathaim
SALT SEA
(EAST SEA)
En-gedi
R. Arnon
THE GREAT SEA
PHILISTIA
J U D A H
[Sodom?]
Br. Zered
Tamar
EDOM
(MT. SEIR)
Brook of Egypt
Meribath-kadesh
(Kadesh-barnea)

40

EZEKIEL

INTRODUCTION

Ezekiel, like the books of the other prophets, has had a complex literary history. On this fact most modern biblical scholars are agreed, although there is wide variance of opinion as to the nature of that literary history. Some think the book is largely or entirely by one author, while others find in it the activity of many writers. Some think Ezekiel prophesied only in Palestine, others that he prophesied only in Babylonia, and still others that he prophesied in both Palestine and Babylonia. A few doubt that there was any such person as Ezekiel. One scholar would date Ezekiel in the reign of Manasseh in the early seventh century B.C., and another in the period after the time of Nehemiah in the last half of the fifth century. The text dates him in the first half of the sixth century. Some think he wrote mostly or entirely poetry, while others credit him with more prose than poetry. Some think he was a priest of the family of Zadok, while others question whether he was a priest. Some think him an Israelite, but others a Judean. Some characterize him as an ecstatic prophet; others deny it.

I. History of Interpretation

Much of the difference of opinion has come into biblical scholarship within modern times, but it has a hoary background. As early as the time of the formation of the canon of the Old Testament, Jewish scholars raised questions about the book of Ezekiel. To them the Torah or Law (e.g., the Pentateuch) was the norm of Scripture. But Ezekiel conflicted at a number of points with the Torah. For instance, the new moon burnt offering in 46:6 is one bullock without blemish, six lambs, and a ram. But in Num. 28:11 it is two bullocks, seven lambs, and

one ram. From the Talmud we learn that Hananiah ben Hezekiah, head of the school of Shammai, commissioned three hundred jars of oil, and, in modern idiom, he "burned the midnight oil," sitting in his upper chamber until he finally succeeded in harmonizing Ezekiel with the Pentateuch (Shabbath 13b; Hagigah 13a; Menahoth 45a). The Talmud tells us moreover that when Elijah comes (Mal. 4:5) the discrepancies between Ezekiel and the Pentateuch will be explained (Menahoth 45a). The rabbis were also bothered about the beginning of the book, which with its mysterious symbolism and imagery of the throne chariot gave rise to esoteric doctrines concerning God, and Jerome reports a Jewish regulation forbidding those under thirty years of age to read the beginning and the end of the book. The rabbis were unwilling to permit the first chapter to be read in the synagogue. There is also considerable controversy over the statement in the Talmud that "the men of the Great Synagogue wrote Ezekiel, the Twelve Prophets, Daniel, and Esther" (Baba Bathra 14b, 15a), which probably refers to a tradition of collecting and editing.[1]

The seventeenth-century philosopher Spinoza doubted that we have Ezekiel's complete writings, or that they are in the original order. Josephus,[2] the first-century Jewish historian, has reported that Ezekiel left behind him two books. In 1771 G. J. L. Vogel published at Halle a

---

[1] For Ezekiel in rabbinical tradition see Shalom Spiegel, "Ezekiel or Pseudo-Ezekiel?" *Harvard Theological Review,* XXIV (1931), 258-81; see H. H. Rowley, "The Book of Ezekiel in Modern Study," *Bulletin of the John Rylands Library,* XXXVI (1953-54), 146-90; and William A. Irwin, "Ezekiel Research Since 1943," *Vetus Testamentum,* III (1953), 54-66.

[2] *Antiquities* X. 5. 1.

book by G. L. Oeder,[3] in which these two books were identified with chs. 1–39 and chs. 40–48 respectively, and the latter was reckoned to be spurious. An anonymous author in the *Monthly Magazine and British Register* in 1798 denied the unity of the book of Ezekiel, going so far as to name Daniel as the author of chs. 25–32, and perhaps chs. 35, 38, and 39, believing the author names himself in 28:3. Anticipating some of the more recent attempts to date the book late, in 1832 Leopold Zunz published the thesis that it was unauthentic and belonged to the Persian period,[4] and some years later he maintained that it should be dated around 440-400. So also L. C. F. W. Seinecke[5] thought the book to be pseudepigraphic, written in 163, and that there was no ground to believe Ezekiel a sixth-century prophet. Hugo Winckler near the beginning of the twentieth century maintained the composite character of the book, placing most of it in the early Persian period,[6] and Richard Kraetzschmar in 1900[7] found parallel texts and doublets in the book of Ezekiel, maintaining that there were two recensions of Ezekiel, one in the first person, the other in the third person, the present book being the work of a redactor. Not all scholars agreed with such radical interpretations, and in 1892 A. B. Davidson could begin his commentary on Ezekiel in the "Cambridge Bible" with the words: "The Book of Ezekiel is simpler and more perspicuous in its arrangement than any other of the great prophetical books. It was probably committed to writing late in the prophet's life, and, unlike the prophecies of Isaiah, which were given out piecemeal, was issued in its complete form at once."[8]

Space permits only a brief outline of the more important recent criticism. Johannes Herrmann[9] concluded that the book in general came from Ezekiel, although not written at one time. Ezekiel gradually collected the results of his prophetic activity, re-editing them in the light of new circumstances. The prophecies of

promise may have been added later by the prophet, or may be considered pleas to repent. One meets also, Herrmann notes, various phenomena which can scarcely be ascribed to Ezekiel, but which belong to the editorial expansion of the book. Herrmann's sober, critical analysis marks a new stage in the criticism of the book. In contrast with this, and in sharper contrast with each other, are the opinions of Gustav Hölscher[10] and Charles C. Torrey.[11]

According to Hölscher, Ezekiel, who was essentially a poet, can be credited with less than 170 of the 1,273 verses in the book that bears his name. These comprise 21 passages, 16 of which are in poetic form. Ezekiel was carried into exile in 597, and there prophesied only oracles of doom.[12] Most of the book belongs to a redactor of the first half of the fifth century, who has given to it the systematic structure which it now has. To him belong the stereotyped formulas (such as "Then you will know that I am the LORD") ; the throne-chariot vision; the basic elements in chs. 40–48; the representation of Ezekiel's dumbness in the first part (3:26), corresponding to the oracles of doom; and the opening of his mouth in the second part (33:21-22), corresponding to the oracles of restoration. Also contributing to the impression of unity, the redactor has deliberately contrasted the vision of the idolatry in the temple in ch. 8 with the vision of the restored temple in chs. 40–42. The main part of the non-Ezekielian materials thus come from one hand, but not all. Although Hölscher uses the scissors too freely, and some of his poetry is questionable, most scholars have to their profit been greatly influenced by various aspects of his critical theories.[13]

Torrey, whose views on Second Isaiah, Ezra, and the Gospels are well known, considers Ezekiel a pseudepigraph which purports to come from the reign of Manasseh, but which was actually written in the Greek period, perhaps near the end of the third century. The original work was converted into a prophecy

[3] *Freye Untersuchung über einige Bücher des Alten Testament.*

[4] *Die gottesdienstlichen Vorträge der Juden* (Berlin: A. Asher), pp. 157-63.

[5] *Geschichte des Volkes Israel* (Göttingen: Vandenhoeck & Ruprecht, 1876-84).

[6] *Altorientalische Forschungen* (Leipzig: E. Pfeiffer, 1902), Reihe 3, Bd. I, pp. 135-55.

[7] *Das Buch Ezechiel* (Göttingen: Vandenhoeck & Ruprecht, 1907; "Handkommentar zum Alten Testament").

[8] *The Book of the Prophet Ezekiel* (Cambridge: Cambridge University Press), p. ix; see also H. A. Redpath, *The Book of the Prophet Ezekiel* (London: Methuen & Co., 1907; "Westminster Commentaries").

[9] *Ezechielstudien* (Leipzig: J. C. Hinrichs, 1908; "Beiträge zum Wissenschaft vom Alten Testament"); *Ezechiel* (Leipzig: A. Deichert, 1924; "Kommentar zum Alten Testament").

[10] *Hesekiel, der Dichter und das Buch* (Giessen: A. Töpelmann, 1924).

[11] *Pseudo-Ezekiel and the Original Prophecy* (New Haven: Yale University Press, 1930); see also "Certainly Pseudo-Ezekiel," *Journal of Biblical Literature*, LIII (1934), 291-320, in answer to Spiegel, *op. cit.*

[12] Cf. G. R. Berry, "The Composition of Ezekiel," *Journal of Biblical Literature*, LVIII (1939), 163-75: all oracles of hope and all apocalyptic passages are later than Ezekiel, a revision of the entire book being made in the third century B.C.

[13] See W. Kessler, *Die innere Einheitlichkeit des Buches Ezechiel* (Herrnhut: 1926), who criticizes Hölscher's methodology and argues for an inner unity in the larger part of the book; but without the use of the literary critical method, the identification of this unity is very subjective.

purporting to come from the Babylonian exile by a later editor. Arguing with dubious success that there was no pagan reaction to the Deuteronomic reform after the death of Josiah, he believes that the author must have drawn upon the account of the paganism which flourished in the reign of Manasseh (II Kings 21:2-16) for his knowledge of the assumed historical setting of the prophet. None of the datings by the year of the Exile is early, the original chronology extending from the thirtieth to the thirty-fifth year of the reign of Manasseh. "Multiform and pervasive" Aramaisms [14] and literary affinities with later writings cause him to conclude that the book belongs to the later period. Gog is identified with Alexander the Great. The editor who added the Babylonian setting was among those who would defend the Jewish church and its authority in the controversy with the Samaritans, and who invented the Babylonian exile to prove that the Jewish tradition had not been broken or the priesthood contaminated by foreigners with the destruction of Jerusalem in 586. Millar Burrows, when a student of Torrey, after studying the literary relations of Ezekiel, concluded that the opinion that Ezekiel is a product of the late pre-Maccabean period is not only possible but very probable.[15]

Where Torrey had argued that the book of Ezekiel was a postexilic production which placed a fictitious Ezekiel in the reign of Manasseh, James Smith[16] tried to prove that Ezekiel actually lived at the time of Manasseh; and Nils Messel[17] would show that Ezekiel really lived in the postexilic period, around 400. Smith pictured Ezekiel as a North Israelite who opposed the Jerusalem priesthood, his prophecies having been edited by a Judean to make it appear that they were delivered in Babylonia. The thirtieth year (1:1) is the thirtieth year after the destruction of Samaria, the fifth year of Manasseh. Smith asks whether it is possible that Ezekiel was the priest sent back to teach the new settlers "the law of the god of the land" (II Kings 17:27). The book contains two sets of oracles delivered by Ezekiel, one in Palestine, the other in the Diaspora, both artificially united by a redactor. Messel, on the other hand, places Ezekiel in Palestine in a

presumed period of pagan reaction which followed Nehemiah's governorship, an editor being responsible for the Babylonian background. The original call of Ezekiel is to be found in 1:2-3; 2:9–3:9; 3:14-16. The throne-chariot vision in ch. 1 is original, but it has been misplaced by the redactor from its original position before ch. 45, the "thirtieth year" showing it must come later than 40:1. The exiles to whom Ezekiel prophesied were those who had returned to Palestine.

Whereas there seems little justification for the excision of all allusion to the Exile or to the time of Nebuchadrezzar and Jehoiachin from the genuine materials in Ezekiel, there are clearly postexilic elements in the book, and these studies have sharpened the issue of a Palestinian ministry for Ezekiel. Volkmar Herntrich[18] finds the problem of the locale of Ezekiel central in interpreting the book. Ezekiel prophesied in Palestine.[19] It is simplest to assume that Ezekiel may have gone with his Jerusalem prophecies to Babylonia with one of the later companies of exiles, and death may have hindered him from collecting his prophetic oracles. It was thus left to a redactor, who gave the book its present Babylonian framework, to edit Ezekiel's oracles. This might have been done by one man or by a school. From him, or them, come ch. 1, the framework of the vision of the call in chs. 2–3, the representation of the tour through the temple in chs. 8 and 11, all of chs. 9, 10, 25–32, 35, the Babylonian setting of the fugitive bringing news of the destruction of Jerusalem in 33:21-23, and with reasonable certainty chs. 40–48, as well as other additions and expansions. Besides this, later hands have expanded and distorted the text, especially in chs. 40–48. Possibly Ezekiel wrote chs. 38–39 in Babylonia. John Battersby Harford,[20] Alfred Bertholet,[21] and I. G. Matthews[22] follow with variations in the footsteps of Herntrich.

Harford's chief contribution is his study of the divine names in Ezekiel and the meaning of the term "house of Israel." In 1897 Bertholet had published an earlier commentary,[23] but his

[14] Aramaisms in the book of Ezekiel would in themselves have little bearing on the date of the book, since one may well expect Aramaisms as early as the traditional date of Ezekiel. The amount of Aramaic influence on the vocabulary has been greatly exaggerated, as shown by C. G. Howie's careful study, *The Date and Composition of Ezekiel* (Philadelphia: Society of Biblical Literature, 1950), pp. 47-68.

[15] *The Literary Relations of Ezekiel* (New Haven: 1925).

[16] *The Book of the Prophet Ezekiel* (New York: The Macmillan Co., 1931).

[17] *Ezechielfragen* (Oslo: J. Dybwad, 1945).

[18] *Ezechielprobleme* (Giessen: A. Töpelmann, 1932).

[19] Cf. G. R. Berry, "Was Ezekiel in the Exile?" *Journal of Biblical Literature*, XLIX (1930), 83-93. Ezekiel was a prophet of doom and never in the Exile; see Berry, "Composition of Ezekiel," pp. 163-75.

[20] *Studies in the Book of Ezekiel* (Cambridge: Cambridge University Press, 1935).

[21] Alfred Bertholet and Kurt Galling, *Hesekiel* (Tübingen: J. C. B. Mohr, 1936, "Handbuch zum Alten Testament").

[22] *Ezekiel* (Philadelphia: American Baptist Publication Society, 1939; "An American Commentary on the Old Testament").

[23] *Das Buch Hesekiel* (Freiburg i. B.: J. C. B. Mohr; "Kurzer Hand-Commentar zum Alten Testament").

recent study reflects the newer viewpoints. Ezekiel prophesied first in Palestine, and his call came in the vision of the scroll in 2:9–3:3 in Jerusalem. Some of the oracles were uttered in a town of Judah other than Jerusalem (cf. 24:25-26) to which the prophet had moved during the siege of the city (see 12:3). Bertholet accepts the throne-chariot vision in ch. 1, but interprets it as Ezekiel's call to prophesy in Babylonia in the thirteenth (not thirtieth) year of the captivity. The redactor is responsible for the consistent Babylonian setting, but Ezekiel did prophesy in Babylonia a number of oracles found in chs. 1–39 and the larger part of chs. 40–48. Bertholet finds evidence of double recensions or doublets in the book, many of which are due to Ezekiel while others result from the activity of editors.[24] Kurt Galling, who is responsible for the discussion of 40–42:20; 43:10-17, has added a section (sec. 5) to the introduction, refuting the arguments given there to show that the temple plan could not belong to Ezekiel. Matthews thinks Ezekiel lived in or near Jerusalem and his ministry was to the citizens of Jerusalem and the house of Israel (e.g., Judah). We cannot know whether he was ever in Babylonia, although he may have been a member of the captivity of 581 (cf. Jer. 52:30), or may have gone to Babylonia of his own free will. It is also uncertain whether he was a native of Judah; he may have been a northerner. He was not an ecstatic prophet, for the strange visions and the dumbness are the product of the Babylonian editor. His message was in two divisions, separated by the destruction of Jerusalem in 586, the earlier being largely prophecies of doom, the later being prophecies of reconstruction. His message was ethical in character and included the doctrines of individualism and the new heart. The Babylonian editor, probably a priest, wrote around 550-500, and to him belong also the sketch of the Holy City, the laws for the priesthood and sacrifice, the throne-chariot visions, and so forth. There are still later additions from 500-400 or later, among which are most of the oracles against the foreign nations, the Gog and Magog prophecies in chs. 38–39, and additional materials in chs. 40–48. A chief criticism of Matthews is his occasional placing in different sources materials of similar ideological and literary character (see his analysis of ch. 36).

According to G. A. Cooke,[25] the book of Ezekiel is an anthology of prophetic oracles collected by editors into their present form. The general plan of the book and the dates go back to Ezekiel, though now altered by the editor or editors. There is no necessity for assuming a Palestinian audience, for to a man of Ezekiel's temperament the unseen was more vividly present than the seen, and second sight explains his knowledge of Pelatiah's death in Jerusalem (11:13). In chs. 1–24 the passages following the dates and alluding to definite occasions are genuine (e.g., chs. 1; 3–5; 8; 20; 24), as also poems embedded in the prose in chs. 15–17; 19; 21, while other passages may be original though with additions. The oracles against the foreign nations are genuine, save possibly those in ch. 25 and in 28:20-24. Chs. 38–39 are late, but not chs. 34–37. The main narrative in chs. 40–48 is genuine, though expanded by successive hands. Cooke fails to appreciate the fact that the homogeneity of the language of Ezekiel is largely the handiwork of a chief editor, but his book is one of the most thorough and important of all the commentaries.

This same failure is more especially true of W. A. Irwin's study of Ezekiel.[26] He would distinguish between genuine and spurious materials by the presence of false commentary, and by the introductory formula, "And the word of the Lord came to me, saying," which precedes the original oracle and is sometimes expanded to give the occasion for the oracle. He believes that Ezekiel's oracles were poetry, and that it is possible to recover the poetic oracle in the midst of many prose chapters. Thus in chs. 4–5 he recovers an original poem of six tristichs in 4:1-2, 9-11 and 5:1-3, with the rest of the material late commentary, or even commentary upon commentary. The commentators wrote over several centuries and in many different countries, none writing a whole chapter, for the commentaries are composite. There is no original material in chs. 9–10; 19; 39; 40–48. Irwin fails to take sufficiently into account the homogeneity of the language or the existence of poetic prose, and it is doubtful if what he isolates as poetry is always that; for example, the poems in 21:1-3, 5; 22:17-18; 22:23-24; etc. Ezekiel, he thinks, began his career about 600 and prophesied consistent criticism and warnings before 586, but went to Babylonia after the fall of Jerusalem to prophesy there the restoration of Israel and Judah. His analysis

[24] Johannes Hempel, *Die althebräische Literatur* (Potsdam: Akademische Verlagsgesellschaft Athenaion, 1930), p. 170, explains the parallel passages by presuming that the oracles of Ezekiel circulated orally among the exiles and were collected and supplemented by several hands before they took their final form, which was hardly after 515.

[25] *A Critical and Exegetical Commentary on the Book of Ezekiel* (Edinburgh: T. & T. Clark, 1936; New York: Charles Scribner's Sons, 1937; "International Critical Commentary").

[26] *The Problem of Ezekiel* (Chicago: University of Chicago Press, 1943).

makes more than 80 per cent of the book secondary, with 251 verses genuine in whole or part, but in some instances no more than a word or two.

In great contrast with the foregoing views are those of Howie. According to this scholar, chs. 1–24 constitute the unit of prophecy recorded by a scribe who took notes while Ezekiel spoke in his thirtieth year; chs. 25–32 are an appendix, and ch. 33 is a literary device which a disciple used to connect chs. 34–39 (which contain oracles collected from memory or written sources) with chs. 1–32. Chs. 40–48 existed independently and were written down after the vision. Thus Howie affirms the substantial accuracy of the traditional view of Ezekiel.

Likewise, Georg Fohrer [26a] presumes redactional work by Ezekiel himself and a considerable number of non-Ezekielian additions and glosses; he insists, however, that the major part of the book is authentic, and that the editing has not changed the essential content of the life and message of Ezekiel, but had the purpose of elucidating and expounding the prophecies of the prophet. He argues for the consistent Babylonian setting of the activity of Ezekiel, but he admits that the book is composed of many collections concerning visions, symbolic actions, and prophetic oracles, the last put together according to catchwords and content. Ezekiel used predominantly a "short-verse" poetic form which lacks the couplet or tristich arrangement usually associated with Hebrew poetry and which appears in regular strophic units. Fohrer turns what is really prose into poetry. It is particularly precarious to use this type of strophic evidence for identifying additions to the text. Fohrer's analysis of later additions to Ezekiel's writings is illustrated in the first three chapters of Ezekiel where the following secondary material is found: 1:2, 3a, 4b, 8-9, 12, 14, 17-21, 23b-25, 28aβ; 2:2b, 4aα, 6b; 3:1, 3aβ, 5b, 9bβ, 13, 15aβ, 23aβ, 25, 26b.

All this should show that the search for the truth is not easy, but there have been many positive gains in the course of all these attempts to unlock the secrets of the book of Ezekiel. In the first place, the nature of the problems involved is clearer, as well as the implications of the many suggested solutions. To understand the nature of the problems, to know what the possible solutions are, and to appreciate the implications of the various solutions for the total story of the nature and history of Hebrew religion is not a slight accomplishment. In the

second place, we can know that the history of the book has been so complicated that any solution must be considered only a probability, and we must take our choice among the probabilities. What seems a thoroughly subjective approach to one scholar may appear to be objective induction to another. Each has to do his best to understand the problems and to come to an independent opinion of their solution. The same may, of course, be said of the other books of the Old Testament, even where the problems are by no means as complicated as in the book of Ezekiel. Literary and historical criticism is not an exact science. The scholar can only be as honest as possible in considering and weighing all the facts, and must use, in so far as he is able, the best techniques of the historian and the linguist. There is one further warning: in a book as difficult as that of Ezekiel it is inevitable that biblical scholars should have been much influenced by their total conception of the development and character of Hebrew religion and history. One can see this clearly in Hölscher, Torrey, Irwin, Cooke, and others. This is not in itself a criticism, for a critic is bound to bring to his assistance in the solution of the problems of Ezekiel his knowledge of the total conspectus of the prophetic movement and other aspects of Bible history. He must try at the same time to let Ezekiel speak for itself, and not to judge it merely in the light of the other books of the prophets or of the Bible.

II. Search for the Original Book

The problem of the book is the recovery of Ezekiel's own writings. The thoroughness of the editing makes this a most difficult task. One of the most impressive aspects of the book, despite the opinion of some scholars, is its considerable homogeneity. This is seen in the repetitious phraseology and is also evidenced in ideological content at many points. The book has by no means a perfect unity, but it has been so thoroughly edited that it is easy to understand why some scholars are convinced of its relative unity, and it is somewhat difficult to appreciate a viewpoint that recognizes a multitude of editors. Despite obvious evidence of later glosses and emendations, one person was largely responsible for the present form of the book, and it is often futile to depend on literary criteria to isolate the work of Ezekiel. We shall call this main redactor of the book the editor, even though he is both author and editor. There is no reason to disagree with Hölscher's early fifth-century date for him, however much one may disagree with other details of Hölscher's exegesis.

[26a] *Die Hauptprobleme des Buches Ezechiel* (Berlin: A. Töpelmann, 1952; "Beihefte zur Zeitschrift für die alttestamentliche Wissenschaft").

The literary structure of the book and something of the character of the original prophecies may be revealed first by considering certain special passages, and then by discussing the problem of the locale of Ezekiel's prophecies.

Our first issue is the originality of the throne-chariot vision in Ezekiel, with special reference to chs. 1 and 2. Some scholars have declared the vision in ch. 1 to be composite, made up of a vision of a storm and a vision of a throne chariot, with the latter secondary. Hölscher[27] thus isolates vss. 4, 28 as the original vision, while I. G. Matthews[28] finds it in vss. 4, 5a, 22ab, 26-28a, as a poem now embedded in the throne-chariot vision.[29] They would also dissociate the throne-chariot vision from the vision of the scroll (2:8 ff.). Others would likewise distinguish between the two. Herntrich[30] finds nothing original in the vision in ch. 1, the introduction to the call of Ezekiel occurring in 3:22-23a, and the details of the call within 2:6–3:9. Messel[31] also separates the scroll and the throne-chariot vision, since he considers the latter (1:1, 4-28a) to be misplaced by the editor from its original position before ch. 45. Irwin[32] finds original neither the throne-chariot vision, the storm vision, nor the scroll vision, and thinks a number of hands responsible for the present text.

Actually, the vision of the storm, the throne chariot, and the scroll form an ideological unit, and to separate them thus is artificial and unnatural. All or none belong to Ezekiel. The concept of the glory of Yahweh belongs with the concept of the storm. The best illustration of this is Ps. 29, which may be much earlier than Ezekiel. This is a psalm of the glory of Yahweh:

Ascribe to the LORD, O heavenly beings [sons of gods],
ascribe to the LORD glory and strength (vs. 1).

Note especially in vs. 3 the words "the God of glory thunders." Or in vs. 9, "in his temple all cry, 'Glory!'" This is a ritual cry, recalling the chant of the seraphim in Isaiah's vision of the glory of Yahweh (Isa. 6). But above all we have here the imagery of the storm-god, with graphic description of the violence of the storm. Here also are the divine voice and the "many waters" (Ps. 29:3) of Ezekiel's vision (Ezek. 1:24). In

the psalm, as in Ezek. 1, is the enthroned Deity, here sitting over the flood and in his palace or temple (Ps. 29:9, 10). We perhaps can even see in the final verse of the psalm a reflection of the theme of the determination of the fates by the enthroned Deity. In Ps. 18 (=II Sam. 22) the theophany of Yahweh has many details in common with Ezek. 1 (see Exeg., ad loc.), and the throne chariot and the storm are united in the words,

He rode on a cherub, and flew;
  he came swiftly upon the wings of the wind (Ps. 18:10).

In the myth and ritual pattern the enthronement of the Deity and the determination of the fates belonged together. It was at the New Year enthronement of Yahweh that Isaiah heard fate decreed for the Judeans (Isa. 6). While the prophet Ezekiel in ch. 1 was obviously in the month of Tammuz not witnessing an enthronement ritual, it is natural that he should have associated with the enthroned Deity the scroll of fate. This is the season of the summer solstice, the descent of the sun-god from the sky, the departure or death of Tammuz, and a fitting time for the vision of a scroll covered with words of lamentation, mourning, and woe.

A presupposition in favor of the originality of the throne-chariot vision is the manner in which the vision of the departure of the glory of Yahweh in 10:1-22; 11:22-23 hangs together with the detail of the temple practices described in ch. 8. Women were weeping for the absent god Tammuz (8:14). The twenty-five men with their backs to the temple worshiping the sun in the east were lamenting the declining powers of the sun-god and his descent into the lower world as the sun was about to pass below the celestial equator, for the vision is dated on September 7. That in the popular syncretism Yahweh was also thought to have departed may be indicated in the words of the elders, "The LORD does not see us, the LORD has forsaken the land" (8:12). T. H. Gaster has correlated the rites described here with the Ugaritic mythological text of Shalem and Shahar, interpreted as an autumnal equinoctial liturgy.[33] With this milieu a vision of the departure of the glory of Yahweh is certainly ideologically thoroughly consistent.

Such a vision of the glory of Yahweh in the

---

[27] *Hezekiel, der Dichter und das Buch*, pp. 45-50.

[28] *Ezekiel*, pp. 3-7.

[29] Herrmann (*Ezechiel*, pp. xxiv, 12-16) would limit the original description of the theophany to vss. 4-5, 27-28, with vss. 6-26 added by Ezekiel himself as a result of later reflection on the earlier intuition.

[30] *Ezechielprobleme*, p. 77.

[31] *Ezechielfragen*, pp. 39-44.

[32] *Problem of Ezekiel*, pp. 223-34.

[33] "Ezekiel and the Mysteries," *Journal of Biblical Literature*, LX (1941), 289-310. See also H. G. May, "The Departure of the Glory of Yahweh," *ibid.*, LVI (1937), 309-21, and Julian Morgenstern, "The Book of the Covenant," *Hebrew Union College Annual*, V (1928), 45-81; "The Gates of Righteousness," *ibid.*, VI (1929), 1-37, etc.; cf. F. J. Hollis, "The Sun-Cult and the Temple at Jerusalem," in S. H. Hooke, ed., *Myth and Ritual* (London; Oxford University Press, 1933), pp. 87-110,

early sixth century is consonant with our knowledge of the general character of Hebrew religious culture in that period. The theme of the return of the glory of Yahweh to the temple at Jerusalem appears in Isa. 40 (see vss. 3-5, 10-11) ; it may presuppose on the part of the author a knowledge of the picture of the departure and return of the glory of Yahweh in Ezekiel. "For I will be to her a wall of fire round about, says the LORD, and I will be the glory within her" in Zech. 2:5 may imply acquaintance with the description of the entrance of the glory of Yahweh into the city and temple in Ezek. 43:1-7. Compare also Zech. 2:13 with Ezek. 43:7.[34] Isa. 6:1-3 is sufficient evidence of the existence of the complex ideology of the enthronement of the glory of Yahweh long before the time of Ezekiel. Indeed, coming perhaps from the same century as Isaiah's vision is Exod. 24:10 (from the J source), which describes the the theophany of the Deity on Mount Sinai: "And they saw the God of Israel; and there was under his feet as it were a pavement of sapphire stone, like the very heaven for clearness." In view of all this we cannot say that the vision of the glory of Yahweh in Ezekiel is not thoroughly "at home" in the sixth century, even though outside the psalms it is a concept most prominent and expressed with most detail in the P source (see, e.g., Exod. 40:34-38) .

The distinctive diction of the throne-chariot vision in Ezekiel is such that a study of literary relationships is of little help in determining its date. The "firmament" (רקיע, 1:22, 23, 25, 26) appears elsewhere only in Gen. 1 (P), Ps. 19:1, and Dan. 12:3, but Ps. 19A may be pre-exilic in date, and in Gen. 1 the word may have been in the earlier story adapted by the P author.[35] The rainbow appears only in Ezek. 1:28 and Gen. 9:13 (P), but this may be a coincidence. The cloud of the glory of Yahweh, which appears in 10:4, is a common P conception (cf. Exod. 16:10; 40:34-38; etc.), but it appears in a passage which does not harmonize with its wider context and may be editorial (see Exeg., *ad loc.;* cf. also I Kings 8:10, which is probably postexilic). It is, however, comparable to the smoke in Isa. 6:4, and consonant with the storm associations of the glory of Yahweh. The literary parallels with P are certainly no more than one might expect in view of the common priestly milieu, if Ezekiel was a Jerusalem priest. We may note the expression "touched one another" (חברת אשה אל־אחותה) in 1:9, which is elsewhere used twice of the curtains of the tabernacle in Exod. 26:3; it is missing in the

Septuagint Vaticanus, and by some considered part of a gloss (cf. Bertholet, Bewer) .

The matter of the integration of the throne-chariot vision in chs. 9-11 will be noted in connection with the discussion of the locale of Ezekiel's prophecies. We need not be astonished at the similarity of diction in the description of the throne-chariot in chs. 1-3; 8-11; 45, or even at the similarity of the other details of the visions of Ezekiel in these and other passages, even though the latest visions are dated nineteen or twenty years after the earliest ones. The parallelism of imagery and diction may be due to the fact that Ezekiel himself worked over his writings when he issued the temple description and the constitution for the restored community in chs. 40-48, or that in his later writings he deliberately imitated the style of his earlier productions. If the date in 1:1 is that of Ezekiel's own final edition of his book, some elements of the unity of diction in the book may be due to his own revision in the thirtieth year of exile, although certainly not the present over-all unity, which is due to a writer of the postexilic period. It may be presumed from the nature of the description that the vision of the prophet in chs. 40-48 is a purely literary device, as in the case of Zechariah's visions. There is no reason for doubting that a real vision experience lies behind chs. 1-3; 8-11, however much conscious literary effort may have been used in the telling of the experiences.

We conclude, then, with a presupposition in favor of the originality of the throne-chariot concept in Ezekiel, which would include by inference also its appearance in chs. 40-48. By contrast, a few comments on ch. 36 and ch. 6 will reveal something about the date and the character of the work of the editor. Ch. 36 describes the restoration of the land of Israel and the regeneration of the people. In view of its literary and ideological homogeneity, efforts to analyze it into variant sources seem to be quite subjective. It is true that there is redundancy in the chapter, but this is characteristic of the editor. As Irwin has noted,[36] 36:7-12 may well reflect the time just before Nehemiah's great work. It is doubtful that 36:1-6 reflects a different period, namely, just after 586, for the antagonism to Edom recalls the similar sentiment in fifth-century Obadiah (vss. 15-18) . Matthews [37] relates "the rest of the nations" in 36:5 to the racial groups troublesome at the time of Nehemiah. The editor's typical formula, "Then they [the nations, you, etc.] will know

---

[34] Cf. Burrows, *Literary Relations of Ezekiel,* p. 69.

[35] H. G. May, "The Creation of Light in Genesis 1₃-₅," *Journal of Biblical Literature,* LVIII (1939), 203-11.

[36] *Problem of Ezekiel,* pp. 59-60.

[37] *Ezekiel,* p. 136.

that I am the LORD," in vss. 11, 23, 36, 38, is due to the influence of Second Isaiah, as Sheldon H. Blank has pointed out.[38] In the immediate context it is not surprising to find in considerable detail (36:20-23) an echo of Second Isaiah's doctrine of "for his name's sake"; theologically consonant with this is the concept of the "new heart" in 36:26. Both conceptions reflect a doctrine of grace. The latter occurs in 18:31, within a long composition of the editor; it also appears in 11:19—a passage presupposing the Diaspora—and, as in ch. 36 (see vs. 28), in intimate association with the expression, "They shall be my people and I will be their God" (11:20), which also appears in the context of the editor in 14:11; 37:23, 28. "They shall be my people, and I will be their God" is a familiar Deuteronomic (R[D]) expression which, along with the "new heart" and "for his name's sake" doctrines, belongs in the book of Jeremiah to the fifth-century biographer.[39] In 36:36 occurs the formula "I the LORD have spoken it," which with slight variations appears fifteen times in Ezekiel as a typical editor's expression; it is combined with the formula "Then you shall know" in 6:10; 17:21, 24; 37:14.[40] The editor was much concerned with Yahweh's holy name, and the expression "to profane my holy name" in 36:20-23 occurs also in 20:39; 39:7; etc. (see xxviii on p. 51; cf. Lev. 18:21; 19:12; 20:3; 21:6; etc., in the H code).

Despite the omission of 36:23b-38 in the Scheide Papyrus of Ezekiel, these verses are certainly integral to their context, for here are some of the most typical expressions found in the book. Attempts to isolate an original Ezekiel core in the chapter are futile. To mention but a few attempts, Matthews would find it in vss. 26-28; Bertholet in vss. 1-12, 16-36; Messel, vss. 6-12; Irwin, a single tristich line with introductory formula within vss. 16-18; Hölscher, none. The presumed viewpoint of the author is the Diaspora, as we see clearly from vss. 17-20. We may conclude that Ezek. 36 is a post-Ezekiel production, reflecting a probable fifth-century origin.

In some contrast is ch. 6, where the vantage point assumed by the author is obviously before 586. Irwin isolates two original poems of different date within 6:1-5, 11-12; while Cooke considers original 6:1-4, 13-14; and Herntrich, 6:1-7. The total impression, however, is that the author is preaching for the benefit of the Diaspora (see 6:7-10). Hölscher and Eissfeldt

find the whole chapter secondary.[41] And it is curious that 6:3-6 is closely paralleled in Lev. 26:30-31; in this case we know that the author belongs to the period after 586, although he presumed to write from the time of Moses. Are there more compelling reasons to believe that in Ezek. 6 we have an original pre-exilic utterance? While we cannot arbitrarily deny that Ezekiel may not have given an oracle of doom which inspired this chapter, to recover that oracle from a chapter which possesses as much unity of thought and diction and as close parallelism with ch. 36 as this one does is a hopeless task (see further discussion in Exeg.). The consistent literary character of the chapter is illustrated in the fourfold repetition of the formula "They shall know that I am the LORD" in 6:7, 10, 13-14.

These two chapters stand in contrast with many others in which genuine materials are more easily recognizable, such as 4:1–5:17; 12:1-28; 24:15-27, with dramatic action and oracle, or 15:1–17:24; 23:1–24:14, allegorical oracles. Even in these, however, the editor's redaction is not absent, and may be prominent; but as in Jer. 18:1–19:15 or 27:1-22, where the later expansions of the dramatic action oracles can be recognized, so they may be seen in these, although not always in their sharp contours. With respect to many passages, although not all, we may agree with Mowinckel's dictum that a clean discrimination between "original" and "editorial" on the lines of literary criticism as attempted by Hölscher and Messel in Ezekiel "is certainly not possible."[42] This is not because oral tradition has grown over the original matter, but is due to the thorough integration of the work of the prophet and the editor. Ezekiel wrote both prose and poetry, and to abstract poems from a present prose passage is to take insufficient consideration of the possibility of poetic prose. Words and phrases that some scholars omitted as harmonistic glosses, trite repetitions, or intrusive phrases may quite probably be original even when they are omitted by the Septuagint, which may have omitted them for much the same reason as the modern critic.

There are four passages in the book which should be discussed together, and which raise the question of the genuineness of the doctrine of individual responsibility in Ezekiel. These are 3:17-21; 14:12-23; 18:1-32; and 33:1-20. They are closely interrelated in thought and diction, and only an impossibly subjective scholarship

---

[38] "Studies in Deutero-Isaiah," *Hebrew Union College Annual*, XV (1940), 34-41.

[39] H. G. May, "Jeremiah's Biographer," *Journal of Bible and Religion*, X (1942), 196-98.

[40] See Blank, *op. cit.*, pp. 36-38.

[41] See Otto Eissfeldt, *Einleitung in das Alte Testament* (Tübingen: J. C. B. Mohr, 1934), p. 424, rejecting 6:1-7:27 and 35:1–36:15.

[42] Sigmund Mowinckel, *Prophecy and Tradition* (Oslo: J. Dybwad, 1946), pp. 84-85.

could assume variant authorship for the four passages as they stand. Both 3:17-21 and 33:1-22 consider the responsibility of the prophet as a watchman, relating it to the ideology of individual responsibility worked out in ch. 18. The section 33:1-20 repeats considerable detail of the theory found in ch. 18, and in similar phraseology. The passage 3:17-19 is nearly identical in wording with 33:7-9, while 33:17-20 parallels 18:29-30, both posing the problem in terms of the rightness and fairness of Yahweh; the house of Israel says that the way of Yahweh is not right (e.g., fair), when actually it is their way that is not right. In all four passages there is the same succession of conditional clauses in legalistic exactness. Theological theory is here worked out with almost rabbinical exactitude, especially in ch. 18, where the problem of responsibility is traced through three generations. Each generation is strictly responsible for itself alone, and each individual is judged only in the light of what happens to be his state at a given moment.

The section 3:17-21 is one of four commissions added to the original account of the call and commissioning of Ezekiel, and at variance with the original commission in 3:4b-9, where no repentance is envisaged (see Exeg., *ad loc.*). In 18:31 the doctrine of responsibility is associated with the "new heart" doctrine, which we have found in the editor's oracle in ch. 36. But the late date of these passages is most obvious in 14:12-23, where we learn that were Noah, Daniel, and Job in the midst of a land, they would by their righteousness save only themselves. Unlike the reference to Daniel in ch. 28, this cannot be an allusion to the Danel of the Ugaritic inscriptions (see Exeg., *ad loc.*). In ch. 28 the basic imagery is mythological, in contrast with this passage. The author here refers to the popular traditions which were later to be gathered up in our present book of Daniel. We may doubt that Ezekiel would thus class with Noah and Job of patriarchal tradition his younger contemporary and fellow exile, Daniel. The preceding context (14:1-11) belongs to the editor, concerned in part with the role and the responsibility of the prophet, and associating with the house of Israel the "strangers [e.g., proselytes] that sojourn in Israel." See 14:7, which presupposes the legislation in the H code (Lev. 17:10, 13; 25:47; etc.). The same phrase is used by the editor in Ezek. 47:22. One should compare 14:12-23 with Jer. 15:1-4 and 18:1-32 with Jer. 31:29-34, which may come from the same period.[43]

While these passages may be of later date, we should not draw the conclusion that the

emphasis on the responsibility of an individual for his actions comes only in the postexilic period. It has pleased our logical, Hegelian mentality to believe that before the time of these passages in Ezekiel, and the contemporary statement in Jer. 31:29-34, the Hebrews believed in corporate responsibility, and that these passages represent an evolutionary emergent, something quite entirely new. The philosophical niceties of ch. 18 may be new, along with the unrealistic, atomistic ethics, but many of the psalms of lamentation of the individual, belonging to the pre-exilic period, disclose a strong emphasis on individual responsibility, and one can find much of it in the JE histories and at other points in the earlier literatures. While ch. 18 is in definite and deliberate opposition to the corporate responsibility doctrine that Yahweh could and would punish with death sons for the sins of their parents, this does not mean that the doctrine of corporate responsibility itself excludes a strong feeling of individual responsibility.

It is by no means necessary to assume that Ezekiel's importance is diminished by the conclusion that the doctrine of individual responsibility as elucidated in ch. 18 and the three other passages is probably not original with Ezekiel. There is much to be said for the thesis in 18:21-23 that God does not judge by his past sins a wicked man who has reformed. Somewhat less palatable is the viewpoint in 18:24 that God remembers none of the good deeds done by a righteous man who has now turned from his righteousness. It helps if we appreciate the fact that the verse is intended to be taken not by itself but with the following verses to imply that such a one should repent and return to his original goodness, and then God will judge him not in accordance with his backsliding, but rather in accordance with his new state of righteousness (see 18:30-32). The doctrine emphasizes dramatically the reality and terribleness of sin. It does not recognize sufficiently that a man is both an individual and a part of society. Men are so integrated in society that they become responsible for the sins of society, and sin is social as well as individual. The editor may have visioned a situation in which "the son shall not suffer for the iniquity of the father, nor the father suffer for the iniquity of the son" (18:20), but in the world in which we live the opposite is most often tragically true.

If we take at all seriously a study of literary relationships such as Hölscher, Burrows, and others have made, we cannot plausibly deny that much in the book is late. Cooke has also taken great care to note characteristic diction

[43] May, "Jeremiah's Biographer," p. 200.

in Ezekiel and its parallels, but he does not sufficiently draw the conclusions that seem evident from the data he presents. (For parallels to the characteristic diction of the editor, see Exeg.) Diction is, of course, not the only criterion for recognizing non-Ezekielian passages; since the editor has seemingly been quite thorough in his rewriting, it is impossible to tell in many passages just what belongs to Ezekiel, and even though the characteristic diction of the editor may be present, an Ezekielian core may be presumed on ideological grounds or because of apparent composite origin. So in 5:5-17; 7:1-27; 10:1-22; 12:21-28; 13:1-23; 17:11-21; 20:45-49; 21:1-7; 22:1-31; 23:31-35; 24:6-24; 26:1-6; 27:9b-25a, 27; 28:1-10; 29:1-5; 30:1-26; 31:10-18; 32:17-32; 33:30-33; 37:1-14; 42:13, 14; 43:6-12, 18-27; 44:1-2, 6-31; 45:10-25 there have been reasons for not denying the possibility of Ezekielian materials, even though it has seemed impossible to isolate them with any certainty. Excluding these passages, about 40 per cent of the text of Ezekiel (some five hundred verses) may be ascribed to the editor (cf. the less conservative estimates of Matthews, Herntrich, Irwin, Hölscher, et al.).

The hypothesis that the books of the prophets are the result of editing and re-editing in many different periods by many scribes who added passages and changed the text here and there is not acceptable. Neither is the "traditio-historical" approach of the Swedish school (such as that maintained by Engnell), which lays too much stress on the oral tradition and too little on literary analysis.[44] Rather, the books of the prophets, to an extent, are more like anthologies, with a single hand responsible for the book in its present form. They were prepared for the use of the postexilic community, as the Gospels were written for the early church. The editors had as definite a purpose as the editor of the Deuteronomic history (Joshua through II Kings), the P redactors of the Pentateuch, the Chronicler, or even the author(s) who wrote down the legends of Daniel. The distinctive diction and ideology which reflect the postexilic scene can be identified. In Ezekiel this diction gives to the book a real unity, and makes it necessary to treat as from a single hand what many have ascribed to numerous editors and redactors.

The following list of expressions typical of the editor is not complete, nor does it concern

[44] See the critique of this school by G. W. Andersen, "Some Aspects of the Uppsala School of Old Testament Study," *Harvard Theological Review*, XLIII (1950), 239-56; see also Geo Widengren, *Literary and Psychological Aspects of the Hebrew Prophets* (Uppsala: Lundequistska, 1948).

itself with phraseology which the editor has in common with Ezekiel. The expression is here given in the form in which it appears in the first instance.

i "as I live, says the Lord GOD"—5:11; 14:16, 18, 20; 16:48; 17:16; 18:3; 20:3; 33:11, 27; 34:8; 35:6, 11.

ii "I will bring the sword upon you"—5:17; 6:3; 11:8; 14:17; 29:8; 33:2.

iii "set your face toward"—6:2; 13:17; 20:46; 21:2 (Hebrew 21:7); 25:2; 28:21; 29:2; 35:2; 38:2.

iv "the mountains of Israel"—6:2, 3; 19:9; 33:28; 34:13, 14; 35:12; 36:1, 4, 8; 37:22; 38:8; 39:2, 4, 17.

v "the mountain height of Israel"—17:23; 20:40; 34:14.

vi "idols" (*gillûlîm*)—6:4, 5, 6, 9, 13; 8:10; 14:3, 4, 5, 6, 7; 16:36; 18:6, 12, 15; 20:8, 16, 18, 24, 31, 39; 22:7, 8, 16, 18, 24, 31, 39; 23:7, 30, 37, 39, 49; 30:13; 33:25; 36:18, 25; 37:23; 44:10, 12.

vii "I will stretch out my hand"—6:14; 14:9, 13; 16:27; 25:7, 13, 16; 30:25; 35:3.

viii "judge you according to your ways"—7:3, 8; 18:30; 24:14; 33:20; 36:19.

ix "the whole house of Israel"—11:15; 20:40; 36:10; 37:11, 16; 39:35; 45:6; 3:6(?).

x "scattered through the countries"—(with *zrh*) 6:8; 12:15; 20:23; 22:15; 29:12; 30:23, 26; 36:19; (with *hpyṣ*) 11:16, 17; 20:34, 41.

xi "disperse them among the nations"—12:15; 20:23; 22:15; 29:12; 20:23, 26; 36:19; see also 28:25; 29:13.

xii "Behold, it comes"—7:5, 6, 10; 21:7 (Hebrew 21:12); 30:9; 33:33; 39:8.

xiii "stumbling block of their iniquity"—7:19; 14:3, 4, 7; 18:30; 44:12.

xiv "proud might"—7:24; 24:21; 30:6, 18; 33:28.

xv "the countries where they have gone"—11:16; 12:16; 36:20, 21, 22.

xvi "I will gather you"—11:17; 20:34; 28:25; 29:13; 34:13; 36:24; 37:21; 39:27.

xvii "one [new] heart and . . . a new spirit"—11:19; 18:31; 36:26.

xviii "they shall be my people, and I will be their God"—11:20; 14:11; 36:28; 37:23, 27.

xix "requite their deeds upon their heads"—9:10; 11:21; 16:43; 17:19; 22:31.

xx "acting faithlessly"—14:13; 15:8; 17:20; 18:24; 20:27; 39:28.

xxi "cut off from it man and beast"—14:13, 17, 19, 21; 25:23; 29:8; see also 21:3 (Hebrew 21:8); 35:7.

xxii "bring a sword upon that land"—14:17; 33:2; cf. 6:3; 11:8.

xxiii "make the land desolate"—6:14; 15:8; 12:19, 20; 23:33; 32:15; 33:28, 29; 35:3, 7.

xxiv "bear your disgrace"—16:52, 54; 32:24, 25, 30; 34:29; 36:6, 7, 15; 39:26; 44:13.

xxv "the reproach of the nations"—34:29; 36:6, 15; see 16:52.

xxvi "restore their fortunes"—16:53; 29:14; 39: 25.

xxvii "profane my sanctuary"—7:24; 24:21; 25:3; 44:7.

xxviii "my name, that it should not be profaned" —20:9, 14, 22, 39; 36:20-23; 39:7, 25; 43:7, 8.

xxix "swore [lifted up my hand]"—20:5, 15, 23, 28, 42; 36:7; 47:14; 44:12.

xxx "manifest my holiness"—20:41; 28:22, 25; 36:23; 38:16, 23; 39:27.

xxxi "princes of Israel"—19:1; 21:12 (Hebrew 21:17) ; 22:6; 45:9.

xxxii "they shall dwell securely"—28:26; 34:28; 38:8, 11, 14; 39:26.

xxxiii "require at your hand"—3:18, 20; 33:6; 34:10.

xxxiv "your people"—13:17; 33:2, 12, 17, 30; 37:18.

xxxv "I the LORD have spoken, and I will do it" —17:24; 22:14; 36:36; 37:14.

xxxvi "I, the LORD, have spoken [it]"—5:13, 15, 17; 17:21; 21:17 (Hebrew 21:22) , 32 (Hebrew 21:37) ; 24:14; 26:14; 30:12; 34:24; cf. 23:34; 26:5; 28:10; 39:5.

xxxvii "countries"—5:5, 6; 6:8; 11:16, 17; 12:15; 15:32; 20:6, 15, 23, 32, 34; 22:4, 15; 25:7; 29:12; 30:23, 26; 32:9; 34:13; 35:10; 36:19, 24; 39:27.

xxxviii "walking in my statutes"—5:6, 7; 11:20; 18:9, 17; 20:13, 16, 18, 19; 33:15; 36:27.

xxxix "nations that are round about you"—5:7, 14, 15; 11:12; 36:4, 7.

xl "Behold, I . . . am against you"—5:8; 13:8, 20; 21:3 (Hebrew 21:8) ; 26:3; 28:22; 29:3, 10; 30:22; 34:10; 35:3; 36:9; 38:3; 39:1.

xli "detestable things"—5:11; 7:20; 11:18, 21; 20:7, 8, 30; 37:23.

xlii "in the sight of the nations"—5:8; 20:9, 14, 22, 41; 22:16; 28:25; 38:23; 39:27.

xliii "I will vent my fury upon them"—5:13; 16:24; 21:17 (Hebrew 21:22) ; 24:13.

xliv "Their ways and their doings"—14:23; 20: 43, 44; 24:14; 36:17, 19.

xlv "my sabbaths"—20:12, 13, 16, 20, 21, 24; 22:8, 26; 23:38; 44:24; 45:17; 46:3.

xlvi "bear the punishment"—4:5, 6; 14:10; 44: 10, 12.

xlvii "Then they will know that I am the LORD" —more than fifty times.

The literary parallels to these expressions are noted in the Exegesis, usually in connection with their first appearance, and they form an important part of the evidence that we are dealing with a late writer. These and other expressions illustrate the complex and numerous interrelationships among the various parts of the book of Ezekiel, and make it improbable objectively to presume a multiplicity of authors.

III. Locality of Ezekiel's Activity

One of the widely accepted hypotheses of modern biblical critics is that, contrary to the general impression given by the book, some or

even all of Ezekiel's prophetic career took place in Palestine. This is in general the viewpoint of Torrey, James Smith, Herntrich, Harford, Bertholet, Spiegel, Oesterley and Robinson, Matthews, Irwin, Pfeiffer, Messel, and others. This opinion is not entirely new, for there is a rabbinical tradition that Ezekiel's career began in Palestine (Mekhilta Bo 1b; Targ. Ezekiel 1:3) .[45] The arguments presented in 1930 by Torrey to show that Jerusalem is presumed to be the dwelling place of the prophet, and that the message was intended to be delivered in person to those for whom it was prepared, have received deserved attention. He concluded that the Babylonian setting is found only in a series of brief and easily recognized interpolations.[46] James Smith in 1931 independently came to the same conclusion regarding the scene of Ezekiel's activity, although believing Ezekiel to be a historical rather than fictitious person, living in the reign of Manasseh.[47] It was Herntrich (1931) who most effectively stated the case for the Palestinian background of Ezekiel's oracles.[48] See also Bertholet's position that Ezekiel prophesied in Jerusalem, in a town near Jerusalem, and in Babylonia. He is followed by P. Auvray.[49] These discussions have established the probability that Ezekiel's prophetic activity before 586 took place in Palestine. That the Babylonian background is purely editorial is much less probable. The arguments pro and con depend naturally on one's analysis of the genuine and secondary materials in the book. For instance, Torrey argues that if the blood of the people were on the head of the prophet in case he did not warn them, as we are told in 3:17-21, it would be folly and wretched mockery if all he did was to perform dramatic actions and utter oracles many hundreds of miles distant from those whom he was supposed to warn. But 3:17-21 is not genuine, as we have seen. In itself there is no unsurmountable difficulty in a prophet in Babylonia uttering oracles or performing dramatic scenes primarily for the benefit of people

[45] See Shalom Spiegel, "Toward Certainty in Ezekiel," *Journal of Biblical Literature*, LIV (1935), 169-70. Spiegel believes ch. 17 may have been given in Palestine, along with some of the bulk of undated oracles, in the last days of Jehoiakim or early in the reign of Zedekiah, before Ezekiel first went to Babylonia. See "When Did Ezekiel Go into Exile?" in *Sēfer Touroff* (Boston: Hebrew Teachers College, 1938), pp. 2-8, and also *Journal of Biblical Literature*, LVI (1937), 407-8.
[46] *Pseudo-Ezekiel and Original Prophecy*, pp. 24-44.
[47] *Book of the Prophet Ezekiel*, pp. 15-21.
[48] *Ezechielprobleme*.
[49] "Le problème historique du livre d'Ézéchiel," *Revue Biblique*, LV (1948), 503-19. See also P. Auvray, *Ézéchiel* (Paris: Les Éditions du Cerf, 1947), and Auvray's discussion in *Ézéchiel* (Paris: Les Éditions du Cerf, 1949; "La Sainte Bible"), pp. 13-15.

in Palestine. Presumably his words could be carried there, and prophets in Palestine often gave oracles of judgment against the foreign nations.[50] It was to proclaim the judgment of God, not to persuade to repentance, that Ezekiel was called. It must, however, be acknowledged that Ezekiel's dramatic actions would seem to have a much more natural setting in Palestine. It is true that Isaiah went barefoot and naked in Jerusalem to symbolize the coming exile of the Egyptians and Ethiopians (Isa. 20:1-6), but the oracle was primarily for the Judeans, who were trusting in Egypt's help.

It may be that the original commission of Ezekiel was to go to Palestine and to prophesy there. That Ezekiel received his call in Palestine (cf. Herntrich, Matthews, Bertholet, Auvray) necessitates too much violence to the text, especially if we credit the genuineness of the throne-chariot vision. Among the five separate commissions of Ezekiel in chs. 2–3, he seems to be told to go to the exiles with his message (3:10-11, 25-27) and also to the people of Palestine (3:4b-9). At least this is a possible meaning of the latter passage; it may be so interpreted if there is elsewhere evidence that Ezekiel did go to Palestine. The commission mentioned in 2:3b-8a should probably be interpreted according to 3:10-11 (vss. 17-21 are noncommittal). Of these commissions, the one in 3:4b-9 is most probably original (see Exeg., ad loc.). There the prophet is told to go to the "house of Israel," a term which sometimes apparently refers to the people of Judah and Jerusalem (see 4:3; 8:6; 9:9; 11:5; 12:10; 22:18; etc.), but not exclusively so.

The most obvious evidence of Ezekiel's Palestine audience is found in 11:1-13. Supposedly in a vision in Babylonia, Ezekiel saw at the east gate of the Jerusalem temple courts twenty-five men, among them a certain Pelatiah. Ezekiel prophesied against them, and as he did so, Pelatiah dropped dead. Unless we assume clairvoyance, Ezekiel must have been in Jerusalem, for Pelatiah was a real person and must have dropped dead at that time. Presumably he did so because he heard Ezekiel's prophecy. The oracle is in the second person, addressed directly to the twenty-five men (cf. vss. 3 and 11). So Ezekiel may have been in Jerusalem on September 7, 591 (8:1). Howie[51] explains this incident by presuming that 11:13 is a later addition by Ezekiel himself when he wrote down the

oracle in the thirtieth year, when by that time he knew Pelatiah had died. But he could hardly have known that Pelatiah's death occurred at the actual moment of the prophecy if he only heard of it later in Babylonia. Furthermore the narrative implies that the twenty-five elders actually heard Ezekiel prophesy, and this is best explained by Ezekiel's presence in Jerusalem. The miraculous transportation of Ezekiel by the Spirit from Babylonia to Jerusalem would then be the account of an actual journey to Jerusalem. R. H. Pfeiffer[52] points out that in 3:14-15 the transportation by the Spirit describes an actual bodily journey, and that the same may be true in 8:3; 11:24 (cf. I Kings 18:12; II Kings 2:16). "In visions of God" in 8:3 may be due to the editor. It is possible that 11:24a is Ezekiel's own account of his somewhat later return to Babylonia, with vs. 24b the addition of the editor.

Ezekiel was probably still in Palestine at the time of the beginning of the siege of the city on January 15, 588. On that very day an oracle came to him concerning the imminent destruction of the city, instructing him to write down the name of the day, for it was the day the king of Babylon had invested the city (24:1-14). Ezekiel could hardly have been aware of the beginning of the siege on the day it began if he were in Babylon, unless he were endowed with second sight. The data on the time of Ezekiel's return to Babylonia show apparent contradiction. In 24:25-27 Ezekiel is told that on the day that Jerusalem falls a fugitive will come to him with the news, and he will be no longer dumb. Presumably Ezekiel was in the vicinity of Jerusalem. In 33:21-22 we are told that the fugitive came to Ezekiel on January 8, 585, six months after the fall of the city, bringing him the news thereof, and obviously implying that the prophet was in Babylonia. A scribal error in 24:25-27 might be responsible for the discrepancy; we should read in vs. 26 "in the day [e.g., when] a fugitive will come," etc., rather than "on that day a fugitive will come," and translate in vs. 25 "in the day [e.g., when]" instead of "on the day when" (see Exeg., ad loc.).[53] In any case, since 24:25-27 presupposes exact foreknowledge of an event which happened three years later, and quite obviously interprets the dumbness symbolically as the period when Ezekiel was prophesying doom (cf. 29:21), it is to be ascribed to the editor. There is inadequate reason to deny the historicity of 33:21-22 (see Exeg., ad loc.), despite vast differences of opinion among schol-

[50] See Howie (Date and Composition of Ezekiel, pp. 5-26), who argues for the traditional view of the residence of Ezekiel; see also H. M. Orlinsky, "Where Did Ezekiel Receive the Call to Prophesy?" Bulletin of the American Schools of Oriental Research, No. 122 (April, 1951), pp. 34-36.

[51] Op. cit., pp. 82-83.

[52] Introduction to the Old Testament (New York: Harper & Bros., 1941), p. 537.

[53] See also Cooke, Ezekiel, I, 273.

ars and variant attempts to revise the date. Whatever the solution for the date, which is accepted here without change, the incident does imply the presence of Ezekiel in Babylonia after the destruction of the city in 586.

IV. Composition of Chapters 40–48

It is generally agreed that chs. 40–48 are composite in authorship, although there is wide disagreement on the issue of Ezekielian authorship. If the throne-chariot vision is original in chs. 1–3; 8–11, there would seem little justification for denying its genuineness in chs. 40–48, where it is a part of the vision of the restored temple, which also cannot be discarded *in toto*. For the larger part, the oracles of promise scattered through the writings of the earlier prophets are secondary additions. The same is true of the oracles looking forward to the return in chs. 1–39 of Ezekiel, save perhaps for the vision of the valley of dry bones in 37:1-14. Ezekiel's oracles before 586 were oracles of coming judgment. But in chs. 40–48 we have something without precedent in the books of the other prophets—a vision of the new age deliberately dated to a later period in Ezekiel's career, after a long period of silence. This makes it likely that we may have here something of Ezekiel's own writing, especially when we remember that he was a priest and a member of the family of Zadok. That such a one might revert to earlier interests is not without precedent. Besides, Ezekiel's earlier oracles had been uttered in Palestine for the Hebrews who had deserved Yahweh's judgment. Ezekiel had now been living among the exiles continuously for some thirteen years or more, and might well have desired to direct their thoughts toward a return to Palestine. Many of the exiles still centered their hopes around Jehoiachin, looking for the restoration of the political regime in Palestine very much as it had been. Ezekiel protested against this attitude, and visualized instead a theocratic community, a kingdom of God.

Ezekiel's view of the new community was even more strictly theocratic than at present appears from chs. 40–48, where a prince (נשׂיא) is found as the secular ruler of the community (44:3; 45:7-16, etc.; 46:2, 4, 8, 10, etc.; 48:21-22). The prince, as the ruler for the new age, belongs to the editor, rather than to Ezekiel. This is evident both from an analysis of the passages in which the prince of the new age appears in chs. 1–39 (see Exeg., *ad loc.*) and from a study of the structure of chs. 40–48.

Outside of chs. 40–48 we find the Davidic king mentioned in 34:23-24 and 37:24-25, in both instances associated with the new covenant and designated as a prince. Both are in typical contexts of the editor, with various forms of the formula "They will know that I am Yahweh" and "I will be their God, and they shall be my people" (34:24, 27, 30-31; 37:23, 27-28). The distinction made by Hölscher and Harford between the Davidic prince here and the prince in chs. 40–48, that the former is an ideal figure of the future and the latter an actual historical figure, the secular head of a body of people, is unjustified; the author in chs. 34 and 37 is naturally looking forward to the future, while in chs. 40–48 the prince is placed in the midst of a community which, seen in a vision, is pictured as though restored. The same figure is intended. The Davidic king or prince in chs. 34 and 37 is no literally resurrected David, but a descendant of David. Doubt of similarity of authorship of the prince concept in these two sections is dispelled by a study of the context of 37:24-25, for not only is it in the context of the restoration of both Israel and Judah, but vs. 26 contains an obvious allusion to the division of the land with the sanctuary in the center as, for instance, in 45:1-8; 47:13–48:35. There is another allusion to the king of the line of David in 29:21, attached by the editor to an oracle against Egypt. Yahweh will cause a horn to spring forth to the house of Israel. This is linked with a probable allusion to Ezekiel's dumbness, interpreted after the manner of the editor, and with the typical formula, "Then they will know that I am the LORD."

Harford, Messel, Cooke, and others are correct in thinking that 47:13–48:35, with its artificial allotment of the tribes on each side of the sacred district, falls outside the framework of the original vision. Ezekiel's vision of the New Jerusalem ends with the vision in 47:1-12. There is nothing in what follows to suggest even remotely the vision of Ezekiel. The address is not to Ezekiel, but directly to the Israelites, without even the preliminary directions, "And say to . . . the house of Israel" (44:6). It is one long oracle, beginning with "Thus says the Lord GOD." It is to the editor also that we should probably ascribe the oracles beginning with "Thus says the Lord GOD" in 45:9-17, 18-25; 46:1-15, 16-18, which, significantly enough, are concerned with the prince. Likewise 45:1-8, which describes the sacred allotment and includes the allotment of the prince, obviously is to be associated with 47:13–48:35, and comes from the same source. While in 42:20 Ezekiel made the wall of the temple area the separation between the sacred and the common, in 45:1-8 (so also 48:10-12) it is the area of 25,000 by 20,000 cubits which is "a sacred district throughout its entire extent." The same author is responsible for the appearance of the prince in 44:3, as a comparison with 46:1-2 indicates.

The prince, who is the king of the line of David, belongs to the editor's messianic eschatology, whereas Ezekiel's eschatology was theocratic. Ezekiel, indeed, is one of the founders of Hebrew theocratic eschatology, and Second Isaiah, whose ideology should be described as theocratic also (despite some attempts to force Isa. 55:3 into a messianic mold) may have been influenced by him. Whether Ezekiel ever used the word "prince" (נשיא), even to designate a contemporary ruler, cannot be determined with certainty because of the thorough redaction of the editor, but in chs. 1–39 it is so used many times in passages which most probably come from the editor (see Exeg. on 12:12; 26:16; 27:21; 38:2-3; 39:1, 18). Among others, Second Isaiah, Malachi, and the author(s) of the book of Daniel followed in the tradition of Ezekiel's theocratic eschatology.

The legislation for the ritual and priesthood of the temple in its present form in 43:18-27; 44:6-31; 45:9-25; 46:1-18 seems to belong to the secondary portions of chs. 40–48, that is, to the editor, and there are many analogies with the later literature, especially P. That Ezekiel attached some legislation to his description of the temple area is, however, at least probable, although it cannot be closely defined. The probable composite character of the legislation in 44:6-31 may suggest an original Ezekiel kernel (see Exeg., *ad loc.*), and some of the legislative details may be presupposed in the details of the temple arrangements in 40:1–42:20. Thus 42:13, referring to "the priests who approach the Lord," may imply the Zadokite as over against the Levite priests, and the verse seems to anticipate the regulations in 44:28-30. It must be noted, however, that some commentators take 42:13-14 as a later addition; Herrmann makes it a later revision by Ezekiel. A reference to the Zadokite priests appears in 40:45-46, although it may here be the editor's explanatory comment, for it seems outside the framework of the description of the temple area.

The following passages should be ascribed to Ezekiel: 40:1–43:12 (see, however, the reservations concerning 40:45-46; 42:13-14; 43:6-12); 43:13-17 (moved by the editor from after 40:17?); 46:19-24 (possibly moved from after 42:13-14?); 47:1-12 (see also Exeg. on 44:1-2, 4-5). To this perhaps may be added an uncertain element in the legislation, with the reasonable presumption that Ezekiel the Zadokite had a view of the priesthood much like that of the editor.

The imagery of Ezekiel is no more developed than one might expect in this period. It is true that in chs. 40–48 an intermediary, rather than Yahweh himself, shows Ezekiel around the temple, but this is because the situation demands the divine architect, as that in ch. 9 called for the divine scribe. Hölscher's assumption that the temple vision in chs. 40–48 and that in chs. 8–11 come from different hands[54] is adequately refuted by Messel,[55] who makes the suggestion that what Yahweh as the guide in chs. 8–11 does is inspection, while what the guide in chs. 40–48 does is work, which would hardly be fitting for the Lord. About fifty years later than the time of Ezekiel, Zechariah has many more angelic intermediaries than Ezekiel. In ch. 1 Ezekiel saw Yahweh himself seated on his throne, but in Zech. 3 an angel apparently takes the place of Yahweh as the court sits for judgment with Satan as prosecutor (cf. Job 1:6; etc.).

The theocratic community envisaged in Ezek. 40–48 centered around the temple and its priesthood. The temple was "a structure like a city" on the top of "a very high mountain" (40:2). Only the Levitical priests who were sons of Zadok could minister before Yahweh in the temple. Ezekiel himself may have belonged to the Zadokite family, although it is true that this is not specified. We only know he was the son of Buzi the priest. But if he was exiled in 597 it may have been because of his prominent position in the Jerusalem priesthood. The Deuteronomic law of Josiah's reform in 621 had in theory placed all the Levites on an equal footing. Any Levite could come to Jerusalem to minister in the name of Yahweh (Deut. 18:1-8), and the Levitical priests were "all the tribe of Levi" (Deut. 18:1). There is no suggestion that the Levites were unclean because they had served at a shrine other than Jerusalem. Events soon conspired to nullify the intentions of the Deuteronomic law. There was obviously no place for all the Levites to function at Jerusalem, and the entrenched Zadokite priesthood would have held jealously to their prerogatives, supported by more than three centuries of precedent. In the reaction which followed the death of Josiah the local sanctuaries were re-established, and the local Levitical priesthoods doubtless functioned at them, leaving Jerusalem more and more largely to the Zadokites. Jeremiah witnesses the pagan character of the practices at the local sanctuaries in this period (7:16-20; 18:15; cf. 2:20-25), and although the corruptions existed within the Jerusalem temple itself, some would have regarded the restoration of the local sanctuaries as contrary to the best insights of Hebrew reli-

[54] *Hesekiel, der Dichter und das Buch*, pp. 191-92.
[55] *Ezechielfragen*, pp. 127-28.

gion, and the Levites who served at them would have lost caste in their eyes. Jeremiah had condemned the priesthood in general, making no exception for that of Jerusalem (see Jer. 2:8, 26; 5:31; 6:13; 8:10; 14:12, 18; 23:11; etc.). In the description of the abominations in the temple in Ezek. 8 the elders are condemned, but there is no specific condemnation of the priesthood. The priests are condemned in 22:26, but there is some real question of the genuineness of the passage (see Exeg., *ad loc.*). An argument from silence may not mean too much, but we may have here a reflection of an attitude toward the Jerusalem priesthood which makes it possible for us to understand how Ezekiel might have been willing to give the Zadokites credit for being faithful to Yahweh while the Levites, the priests of the local sanctuaries, went astray, if we are to credit Ezekiel as well as the editor with this ideology. The Levites are demoted to be temple servants, unworthy to enter the inner court or offer the sacrifices on the altar. This all may help answer the query of many (cf. Hölscher, Messel, *et al.*) as to how the prophet could credit the Zadokites with not participating in paganism, in the light of his indignant criticism of the paganism in the temple in ch. 8.

The conception of the priesthood in chs. 40–48 differs not only from that of the Deuteronomic Code, but also from that of the P source. The legitimate priesthood in the latter is limited to the sons of Aaron, the distinction between the Aaronites and Levites corresponding to that between the Zadokites and Levites in the legislation of Ezekiel (see Num. 17–18). The Aaronite priesthood was probably of Israelite origin, and had secured control of the Jerusalem sanctuary after 586, when the Zadokite priests were in exile. It has been maintained that the Judean tradition down to the Exile contained no reference to Aaron as a priest associated with Moses, and that the earliest J stratum did not mention Aaron. It may be that even the E source preserves in Exod. 33:7-11 a tradition of Moses as the sole priest of Yahweh, with Joshua, not Aaron, in attendance. The prototype of the J and E histories, formulated perhaps during the united monarchy, may have ignored Aaron. In any case, the story of Aaron making the golden calf (bull) in Exod. 32 postdates Jeroboam's installation of the golden calves at Dan and Bethel (I Kings 12:25-33), and was originally written to establish a precedent for the calf images at these two sanctuaries, where the Aaronites functioned as priests.[56] The Aaronite

priesthood appears not in the Deuteronomic Code (Deut. 12:1–26:19) but in its framework, e.g., RD (10:6; cf. 9:20; 32:50), which is at this point closer to P than is Ezekiel.

It is not clear where the Holiness Code fits into the picture of the development of the priesthood. In its present form the priests are described as the sons of Aaron (see Lev. 17:2; 21:1, 17, 24; 22:2, 4, 18; 24:3-4), but this is probably due to a P redaction (cf. Lev. 24:1-4 with Exod. 27:20-21).[57] See Pfeiffer's suggestion[58] that H utilized a lost code in which the priesthood was neither Levitical, Zadokite, nor Aaronite, but was a provincial priesthood of one of the local sanctuaries desecrated by Josiah. The silence of the H code may perhaps be taken to mean that it accepted the existing status of the priesthood at Jerusalem. Since it was legislating for the Jerusalem sanctuary, early in the period of the return, it would then presume the Aaronite priesthood. The later P revisions introducing the Aaronites by name may be consistent with the intentions of the originators of the Holiness Code. Like Haggai and Zechariah, they raised no objection to the Aaronites, and Zechariah gives clear support to the priest Joshua, who was probably an Aaronite.[59]

The support of the Zadokites in Ezek. 40–48 is not in itself any necessary indication of the chronological priority of Ezekiel's legislation to H, D, or P, for although the Aaronites continued in power, there would have been strong protagonists for the Zadokites. It may be that Ezra's law, brought back from exile in the fifth century, supported the cause of the Zadokites, since Ezra himself belonged to that family. Ezra's law is now lost, or else has been much revised into our present P legislation. The editor of Ezekiel in the same century must likewise have sponsored the cause of the Zadokites as over against the Aaronites. That this division of the Zadokites and Levites may go back to Ezekiel, and may be prior to H, D, or P, is just possibly evident in the implication of 44:6-16 that formerly the Levites, theoretically at least, had enjoyed full priestly rights. Driver[60] suggests that had they not previously enjoyed such rights, the prohibitions here would

[56] See R. H. Kennett, "The Origin of the Aaronite Priesthood," *Journal of Theological Studies*, VI (1905),

161-86; T. J. Meek, "Aaronites and Zadokites," *American Journal of Semitic Languages and Literatures*, XLV (1928-29), 149-66.

[57] See J. M. P. Smith, *The Origin and History of Hebrew Law* (Chicago: University of Chicago Press, 1931), p. 72; S. R. Driver, *An Introduction to the Literature of the Old Testament* (rev. ed.; New York: Charles Scribner's Sons, 1913), pp. 47-49.

[58] *Intro. to O.T.*, p. 249.

[59] Zech. 3; see Kennett, *op. cit.*, p. 177; Meek, *op. cit.*, pp. 160-2.

[60] *Op. cit.*, pp. 139-40.

be superfluous. Ezekiel, as the other legislations do not, charges the Levites with abusing privileges formerly theirs. By contrast, P would present the menial position of the Levites to date from the time of Moses (Num. 18:1-7, and especially Num. 16:8-10). D and, presumably, H accord with the viewpoint of P. This argument is suggestive though not conclusive, and many scholars would date Ezekiel's code later than H, some later than P.[61] Most, though by no means all, of the parallels in diction between H and the book of Ezekiel are to be found in chs. 1–39, where they are due to the editor who does come after H, and who has left the imprint of his diction even in many oracles which have an Ezekielian origin, so thorough has been his redaction. This is seen in such expressions as "set your face toward" (see iii on p. 50; cf. Lev. 17:10; 20:3, 5; 26:17); "walking in my statutes" (see xxxviii on p. 51; cf. Lev. 18:3; 20:23; 26:3); "to profane my sanctuary" (see xxvii on p. 51; cf. Lev. 19:8; 21:12, 23; 22:15; etc.); "my sabbaths" (see xlv on p. 51; cf. Lev. 19:3, 30; 26:2; etc.); "bear the punishment" (see xlvi on p. 51; cf. Lev. 17:16; 19:8; 20:17, 19); "I will . . . cut him off from the midst of my people" (14:8; see also 13:9; cf. Lev. 17:10; 20:3, 5-6); "his blood shall be upon himself" (18:13; 33:5; cf. Lev. 20:9, 11-13, 16, 27); "I the LORD sanctify them" (20:12; 37:28; cf. Lev. 20:8; 21:8, 15, 23; 22:9, 16, 23); "any man of the house of Israel" (14:4, 7; Lev. 17:3, 8, 10),[62] and so forth. That Ezekiel, like the author(s) of the Holiness Code, was concerned with the concept of holiness is indubitable, but there is no need to think that he was influenced directly by H. That the editor was thus influenced is much more probable.

V. Life and Times of Ezekiel

A. Ezekiel in Exile.—In the year 597 Nebuchadrezzar king of Babylon besieged the city of Jerusalem. Eighteen-year-old King Jehoiachin, who had reigned for only three months, was forced to surrender and was carried captive to Babylonia with some 10,000 (II Kings 24:14) or perhaps only 3,023 (Jer. 52:28) of his fellow Hebrews. Mattaniah, Jehoiachin's uncle and the third son of Josiah to reign on the throne, was made king in the place of Jehoiachin, his name being changed to Zedekiah. Although Jehoiachin was now in exile, he still bore the title of king, and many hoped that he would soon return and sit again on the throne (see

Jer. 28:2-4). Ezekiel, like Jeremiah, thoroughly disagreed with the prevailing hopes for a speedy return. Upon the exile of Jehoiachin, Jeremiah had prophesied that the exile would be long, but that if the Hebrews in Judah would put their necks under the yoke of the king of Babylon they could live (ch. 27). Ezekiel was yet more pessimistic with respect to the future. His first message presaged the inevitability of the coming destruction of Jerusalem. Yahweh had deserted his city, and a future of lamentation, woe, and mourning awaited its citizens.

The judgment of Yahweh upon his rebellious people was more real to Ezekiel than the signs which pointed seemingly to the return of Jehoiachin. The people could cite the return of Manasseh from temporary exile (II Chr. 33:10-13). The Babylonians themselves seem to have anticipated his return when they took him into exile, continuing to give him his royal title. The excavations at the city of Babylon have revealed a large number of cuneiform tablets, dated around 595-570, which have to do with the distribution of oil, barley, and so forth, as rations to captives and skilled workmen. These tablets mention Yaukin king of Judah and his five sons. Yaukin (=Jehoiachin) is called "king of the land of Yahud" (=Judah). There are other Jews mentioned in these tablets, as well as people from other countries. Since rations were distributed to Jehoiachin, it has been rightly presumed that he was not at this time as yet in prison. One of the tablets mentioning Jehoiachin is dated 592.[63] Three stamped jar handles found in the excavation in Palestine, two from Kiriath-sepher and one from Beth-shemesh, bear the inscription "Belonging to Eliakim, steward of Yaukin" (=Jehoiachin). Eliakim seems to have been the steward of Jehoiachin's property in Judah while Jehoiachin was in exile and in anticipation of his return.[64] It is obvious that many people, including the Babylonians themselves, must have looked on Jehoiachin as the real king, with Zedekiah serving in much the position of a regent.

This helps explain the intensity of the expectation of a quick return from exile, and why Jeremiah found it necessary to criticize those prophets in the midst of the exiles who were

---

[61] See Burrows, Literary Relations of Ezekiel, pp. 64-68.
[62] See Driver, op. cit., pp. 49-50, 146-47. On p. 147 Driver lists a great many parallels with Lev. 26:3 ff., but none of them come from chs. 40-48. More than 90 per cent of the references in Ezekiel which have some parallel in H, listed by Burrows, come from Ezek. 1–39.

[63] See W. F. Albright, "King Joiachin in Exile," Biblical Archaeologist, V (1942), 49-55; cf. A. L. Oppenheim, "Babylonian and Assyrian Historical Texts," in J. B. Pritchard, ed., Ancient Near Eastern Texts Relating to the Old Testament (Princeton: Princeton University Press, 1950), p. 308.
[64] See W. F. Albright, "The Seal of Eliakim and the Latest Preëxilic History of Judah, with Some Observations on Ezekiel," Journal of Biblical Literature, LI (1932), 77-84.

speaking lying words in Yahweh's name (Jer. 29:15, 21-23). The archaeological data also make probable the much disputed dating system in the book of Ezekiel. Ezekiel dated his oracles by the years of the captivity, rather than by the years of the reign of Jehoiachin, because Jehoiachin was no longer on the throne. Although he may have returned for a time to prophesy in Jerusalem, he was one of the exiles, and as a member of the exilic community, where Jehoiachin still bore the title of king, he avoided dating his oracles according to the years of the reign of Zedekiah.

It would appear from Jer. 29:4-7 that the conditions within the exilic community were not altogether deplorable. The Jews did have the wherewithal to build houses, and they had vineyards to plant. Something of their normal social life could be continued. Their welfare could progress with the welfare of the country. The economic and social conditions of the exiles were not such as to cause Ezekiel concern, if we may presume this by his silence with respect to them. Some of the exiles entered into the commercial life of the country, apparently acquiring considerable wealth. When a comparatively small minority of them were to return in 538, a few heads of the families were able to make contributions of no mean amount, to judge from Ezra 2:68-69. Archaeological records from the city of Nippur in the following century disclose the names of Jews on business documents. Furthermore, there was frequent and not too difficult communication between the Jews in Babylonia and those in the homeland. Instances of this appear in Jer. 39, and Ezekiel himself may have returned to Palestine for a number of years. Although Ezekiel's oracles against Jerusalem and Judah may have been uttered in Palestine, it must be acknowledged that they could readily have been sent from Babylonia to Jerusalem. Of course the fact that the Jews were away from their native land with its rich traditions already memorized in unique literary expression would in itself make for much unhappiness. But despite Second Isaiah's criticism of the Babylonian treatment of the Jews in exile (Isa. 42:22-25; 52:2), their lot might have been much worse. This may help us understand how we find in Ezekiel no anti-Babylonian sentiment, despite the fact that he had been carried into exile. The main reason for this, however, was his belief that Babylonia was Yahweh's agent for bringing upon Judah the judgment of Yahweh for its sins.

Ezekiel may have known of the corruptions in the religious life of Jerusalem and Judah not only through personal experiences in Pales-

tine before his exile in 597, but also through the continuous reports that would have come to the exilic community after 597. From these reports he would have known that the house of Israel was still unfaithful to Yahweh, despite the judgment which had been inflicted in 597. So, much moved, Ezekiel saw in the stormcloud and lightning the vision of the throne chariot of Yahweh, and ate the scroll upon which were written the words he must preach—words of lamentation, mourning, and woe.

Ezekiel was the son of Buzi, and a priest. If we accept the tradition of his exile in 597, the probability that he belonged to the family of Zadok is increased. That members of the Zadokite priesthood would have been among "all the princes and all the mighty men of valor" exiled by Nebuchadrezzar in 597 (II Kings 24:14) is no hazardous conjecture (cf. II Kings 25:18-21). Ezekiel may be the author of the legislation in ch. 44, which restricts the priesthood to the Zadokite family.

His home among the exiles was at Tel-abib, a name which has been selected for the largest community in the Holy Land today. Tel-abib was by the river Chebar, a canal known from cuneiform sources as *nâru kabari,* which passed through the city of Nippur southeast of Babylon. During his five-year residence in Babylonia before his call, Ezekiel would have become familiar with much in the culture of the Babylonians. Certain aspects of his vision may reflect Babylonian myth and symbolism,[65] although much of Ezekiel's imagery was doubtless rooted in Hebrew culture. The great altar before the temple in 43:13-17, which reflects something of the form and symbolism of the Babylonian ziggurat or temple tower, was not necessarily, however, a new invention of Ezekiel in the light of his experiences in Babylonia, but probably goes back to the time of the construction of the temple by Solomon. Although the ultimate inspiration reflects Mesopotamian influence, the prophet himself may not have been drawing directly from his Babylonian experiences in picturing the altar.

The city of Babylon in Ezekiel's time is well known to us, thanks to the excavations which have disclosed its great fortifications, its temples and palaces, and its famous Ishtar Gate. This gate, with alternating figures of bulls and dragons in enameled brick reliefs, was dedicated to the goddess Ishtar, the consort of Marduk, and formed the entrance to the great processional street on whose enameled brick walls were depicted stalking lions. Towering above the city was the great ziggurat, built in stages

[65] See Lorenz Dürr, *Ezechiels Vision von der Erscheinung Gottes* (Münster: W. Aschendorff, 1917).

and simulating the cosmic mountain, the Tower of Babel of Genesis. It is not improbable that Ezekiel may have witnessed here in the city of Babylon the famous New Year festival with its re-enactment of the victory of Marduk over the powers of chaos at creation and the fixing of the fates.

B. Jerusalem and Judah.—If, as seems probable, Ezekiel came to Jerusalem in 591, the year following his call, he must have found the city in the midst of great tensions. King Zedekiah was following the advice of Jeremiah for the time being, and was a loyal subject of Nebuchadrezzar. But the members of the court of Zedekiah were largely and strongly anti-Babylonian, and objected to having the neck of Judah under the yoke of the king of Babylon. At the first possible moment, with the promise of help from Egypt and the encouragement of neighboring smaller nations, they would bring pressure to bear which would result in a complete break with Babylonia. There were also those who felt that their first loyalties were to exiled Jehoiachin, rather than to Zedekiah. The political situation brought complications into the religious atmosphere of the nation. Yahweh, the God of the nation, had lost prestige in the minds of many because he had not prevented his people from suffering defeat. Marduk seemed stronger than Yahweh, for Judah was vassal to Babylonia. Even as some exiles in Egypt after the fall of Jerusalem in 586 were to offer sacrifices to the queen of heaven because Yahweh had shown himself impotent (Jer. 44:16-18), so many now would have decided that they could perhaps get more help from the nature gods than from the God of a vanquished people. Likewise, the position of Judah as a vassal to Babylonia would have encouraged the adoption of aspects of the cult of the more powerful nations, even as in an earlier period Ahaz had changed the temple arrangements when a vassal to Assyria (II Kings 16:10-18). "The seat of the image of jealousy, which provokes to jealousy," which Ezekiel saw at the entrance to the temple courts, was perhaps the seat of the fertility deity Baal or Tammuz, who would have been identified with Marduk, and the women weeping for Tammuz may at the same time have been conscious of honoring Marduk, in some ways his counterpart (Ezek. 8:3, 5, 14). Over against this there were doubtless those who were stressing a return to the national Deity, Yahweh, for political reasons.

Torrey, James Smith, and others who doubt that there was any reaction against the reform of Josiah after Josiah's death at Megiddo in 608 are refuted by the evil days which fell on unfortunate Judah following Josiah's death, as well as by the positive evidence of pagan reaction. The disillusion which had come with the death of Josiah, the exile of Jehoahaz to Egypt, the more than one attack on Judah by Babylonia in the days of Jehoiakim, and the exile of Jehoiachin and his fellow Hebrews, must have been very great. Although the historian reports that "all the people" had joined in the covenant at the time of Josiah's reform (II Kings 23:3), it was, after all, a reform largely enforced by the crown and from above, and the reaction after Josiah's death is as understandable as that which came after the death of Egypt's reformer king, Akhenaton.

Economic conditions in Judah must have been difficult, now that Judah was under the necessity of paying tribute to Babylon and many of her business heads and craftsmen were in exile. All this was on top of the plundering of the treasures of the temple and palace by Nebuchadrezzar in 597. The Babylonians had not treated the Judeans as badly as they might have done, however, and were a tolerant master compared with some. Jeremiah was convinced that Judah could live under the yoke of Nebuchadrezzar (ch. 27), and even after a second revolt, and despite the added provocation, the Babylonians obviously did not follow a "scorched earth" policy (see Jer. 40:9-12). Ezekiel pictures Zedekiah as a seed of the land planted by Nebuchadrezzar in a fertile field that it might sprout and become a spreading vine (17:5-6). Some of those who were left behind were doubtless glad, and with reason, to be rid of their oppressors who had built their houses by unrighteousness and had made their neighbors serve them without pay (cf. Jer. 22:13). But the times were not normal, and despite the exile of some of the oppressive leaders, there seems to have been an increase in the number of people in a position of slavery (Jer. 34:8-12). The licentious cults may have been sought by many as an escape, while some, in their desperation, resorted even to human sacrifices (Ezek. 16:15-22).

In Jerusalem Ezekiel would have found the prophet Jeremiah. It is not strange that neither prophet mentions the other. Had not Jeremiah's biographer mentioned the prophet Uriah, who was preaching a message similar to that of Jeremiah in the reign of Jehoiakim, we would not know of the existence of such a prophet as Uriah (Jer. 26:20-23). Haggai and Zechariah, who were interested in the project of rebuilding the temple and setting up Zerubbabel as king on the throne of Judah, in their writings ignore one another. Amos and Hosea, who were contemporaries, do not refer to each other. It is more than probable that in the first years of Ezekiel's prophesying in the city of Jerusalem, Jeremiah was in a period of prophetic inactivity. There are no oracles of Jeremiah which can with assurance be placed after 597 and before 589. The date in Jer. 28:1, in the fourth year and fifth month of Zedekiah, which would be about a year before Ezekiel's call, is an intrusion, and the oracle belongs with Jer. 27 at the beginning of the reign of Zedekiah. So also the oracle in Jer. 29.

C. Chronology of Ezekiel's Oracles.—Although there are real difficulties in the determination of the chronology of Ezekiel's oracles, we can at least make some probable equation of the dates attached to some of the oracles with our present calendar. Such an equation is attempted in the list below. The first date given in each case is according to an autumnal calendar, with the year reckoned from autumn to autumn. The Hebrews were probably employing such an autumnal calendar in this period, although many scholars believe that they were using a vernal calendar. The dates in parentheses are according to the spring calendar. The equations with the modern calendar are on the basis of the tables given by R. A. Parker and W. H. Dubberstein.[66]

July 21, 592 (July 1, 593):
    fifth year, fourth month, fifth day (1:2).
Sept. 7, 591 (Sept. 17, 592):
    sixth year, sixth month, fifth day (8:1).
Sept. 1, 590 (Aug. 13, 591):
    seventh year, fifth month, tenth day (20:1).
Jan. 15, 588 (Jan. 15, 588):
    ninth year, tenth month, tenth day (24:1).
Uncertain:
    eleventh year, first day (26:1).[67]
Jan. 6, 587 (Jan. 6, 587):
    tenth year, tenth month, twelfth day (29:1).
Apr. 16, 570 (Apr. 26, 571):
    twenty-seventh year, first month, first day (29:17).
Apr. 19, 586 (Apr. 29, 587):
    eleventh year, first month, seventh day (30:20).
June 11, 586 (June 21, 587):
    eleventh year, third month, first day (31:1).
Mar. 3, 585 (Mar. 3, 585):
    twelfth year, twelfth month, first day (32:1).
Apr. 16, 585 (Apr. 27, 586):
    twelfth year, first month,[68] fifteenth day (32:17).

Jan. 8, 585 (Jan. 8, 585):
    twelfth year, tenth month, fifth day (33:21).
Apr. 17, 572 (Apr. 28, 573):
    twenty-fifth year, first month, tenth day (40:1).[69]

There are three dates out of order: those in 26:1; 29:17; 33:21. This is not surprising when one compares the chronological chaos in Jeremiah. It is rather in favor of the authenticity of these dates than otherwise, for it suggests that we may not have merely a late, schematic chronological arrangement. Some have argued that these dates are editorial addenda, or that they are by and large not to be trusted in their present form (see Zunz, Hitzig, Hölscher, Torrey, Irwin, and others). More often than not the content of the oracles is quite consonant with the dates to which they are attached. As in the case of Jeremiah, where the chronology is trustworthy with a few important exceptions, the dates should be accepted if there are no reasons in the context for rejecting them. Even if it could be shown that the wording of the chronological data in Ezekiel comes from the editor, the dates could still reflect information preserved in Ezekiel's own record of his prophecies. The chronology in Haggai and Zechariah is equally specific, and quite trustworthy, whether or not it comes from the hand of the prophet himself.[70]

That all the oracles following a date should be credited to that date is not to be presumed.[71] Thus the oracles against Moab, Edom, and Philistia in ch. 25 were obviously written after 586, and so later than the date in 24:1. The oracles in chs. 4; 5; and 7, if given in Palestine, presumably should be dated chronologically later than chs. 8–11, if the latter present Ezekiel's earliest experiences and oracles after his return to Palestine. Probably not all the oracles against Tyre in chs. 26–28 were written or uttered on the date given in 26:1; indeed, they contain considerable secondary material, and 32:17 does not appear to be attached to an original oracle. Many of the oracles, such as those in chs. 16; 19; 23, have little suggestion

that only in an autumnal calendar reckoning the date in 32:17 comes later than that in 32:1 suggests the validity of such reckoning.

---

[66] *Babylonian Chronology 626 B.C.–A.D. 45* (Chicago: University of Chicago Press, 1942), pp. 25-26.

[67] This uncertain date is perhaps after the time of the date given in 33:21, and in the twelfth (with LXX^A) rather than the eleventh year. The oracle in ch. 26 at present presumes the fall of Jerusalem, but Ezekiel did not learn about it until Jan. 8, 585, according to the data in 33:21. If we may presume that the oracle in 26:1 originally was dated in the twelfth year, the eleventh month, the first day, it would be Feb. 3, 585 (see also Exeg. on 26:1; 33:21).

[68] With LXX. The M.T. omits the month. The fact

[69] The equation of the dates in Ezekiel with our calendar in the list above is intended to help make more realistic to the general reader the chronology of the books. If the beginning of the reign of the king was reckoned from the New Year preceding the time of his accession, a still different and earlier series of dates might be achieved; cf. Jack Finegan, "The Chronology of Ezekiel," *Journal of Biblical Literature*, LXIX (1950), 61-66.

[70] See Howie, *Date and Composition of Ezekiel*, pp. 34-46, for a thorough study of the dates in Ezekiel.

[71] Cf. Eissfeldt, *Einleitung in das A.T.*, pp. 417 ff.

of specific date.[72] The date in 20:1 may originally have belonged with 20:45-49(?) or with the genuine oracles in ch. 21, if, as seems probable, the intervening materials come from the hand of the editor. We must remain uncertain of the date of many of the oracles. Ch. 7, for instance, pictures the sword without and the famine within, while he that is in the field is dying by the sword. This might have been written during the siege of Jerusalem between 588-586, but on the other hand the imagery is no more vivid than that in Jeremiah's oracles on the foe from the north, where the prophet depicts the coming disaster as though it were already present (cf. Jer. 4:19-31), and in Ezek. 7:24 the disaster is seemingly yet to come. So the siege symbolism in chs. 4–5 might or might not indicate a date between 588-586. The oracle depicting Nebuchadrezzar at the crossroads in 21:19-23 may have been uttered shortly before or after the Babylonian king started to move against Palestine in the late summer of 589. Possibly shortly before the opening of hostilities came the oracle in 17:1-21, criticizing Zedekiah for sending ambassadors to Egypt to ask for help against Babylonia.

According to our reckoning, the siege of Jerusalem lasted from January 15, 588, to July 19, 586. Within this period are dated the oracle in 24:1-14 and the oracles against Egypt in 29:1-16; 30:20-26; 31:1-18. By the time of these latter oracles the Egyptians had proved themselves unable to give effective aid against the Babylonians, although they had caused a temporary lifting of the siege (see Jer. 37:1-10). Two oracles against Egypt are dated in the year following the fall of Jerusalem (e.g., 32:1-16, 17-32), while another (29:17-20) is the latest of all Ezekiel's oracles, April 16, 570. Only one of the oracles against Tyre is dated (26:1-21), but since the Masoretic Text is probably wrong one should, with the Septuagint Alexandrinus, assign this oracle to the year following the fall of Jerusalem. The enigmatic thirtieth year in 1:1 is best taken as the latest date in the book— that is, 568-567, possibly the year Ezekiel wrote his final edition of his prophecies. We have some parallel for this in Jeremiah, who dictated an edition of his oracles nearer the beginning of his career (Jer. 36), and who wrote his "memoirs" near the end of his career, presumably after his exile in Egypt.

Whether Ezekiel or the editor has given the

dates their present form we cannot know. They are by and large reliable, or at least probable, even though, like some other elements of the introductory formulas, they might belong to the editor. The influence of the Babylonian calendar, according to which the year began in the springtime, is evident in the designation of the months. It was in the Neo-Babylonian period that the Hebrews, while still probably counting the regnal years from autumn to autumn, began to number the months from spring to spring.[73] Before this, in the pre-exilic period, the months had been named, although only the names Abib (=the first month; Exod. 13:4; 23:15; Deut. 16:1); Ziv (=the second month; I Kings 6:1); Ethanim (=the seventh month; I Kings 8:2); and Bul (=the eighth month; I Kings 6:38) have been preserved in the biblical record. In the later postexilic period the Babylonian names of the months were adopted, such as Nisan (Neh. 2:1; Esth. 3:7), Elul (Neh. 6:15), and Chislev (Zech. 7:1; Neh. 1:1).

D. Sketch of Ezekiel's Message.—Aspects of Ezekiel's message have been noted frequently in the preceding discussion. His dated prophecies extend through twenty-two years, from 592 to 570. It has been suggested that some of Ezekiel's oracles are to be dated before this period, but the evidence for this is very tenuous. Ezekiel's message to Judah and Jerusalem before the fall of the city of Jerusalem in 586 was comparable to that of the prophets who preceded him. His were words of lamentation, mourning, and woe. God's judgment was upon the sinful nation. Even though a few might escape, doom had been decreed for the rebellious house of Israel. Ezekiel's criticisms were largely directed at the same evils as those condemned by Jeremiah. It was the apostasy of the Judeans that concerned him most, and like Isaiah he protested against foreign alliances which carried with them acceptance of the paganism of the neighbors of the Hebrews. Yahweh would neither spare nor pity, for the people were stubborn and would not listen to his appeals. Because of the abominations practiced in the temple courts, the glory of Yahweh had deserted the city of Jerusalem. In Ezekiel's vision the six divine executioners, recalling the angel of destruction in II Sam. 24, had slain without mercy in the

---

[72] Cf. Eissfeldt's view (ibid., pp. 411-27) that besides two diarylike, dated collections—one containing revelations, symbolic actions, poetry, and speeches concerning Jerusalem and Israel, the other containing oracles against Tyre and Egypt—Ezekiel left other speeches and poems which were not dated, and these have been inserted by a later hand.

[73] See especially, Julian Morgenstern, "The New Year for Kings," in Bruno Schindler, ed., Gaster Anniversary Volume (London: Taylor's Foreign Press, 1936), pp. 447-51; compare also E. R. Thiele, "The Chronology of the Kings of Judah and Israel," Journal of Near Eastern Studies, III (1944), 182-83. Thiele, however, takes the dates in Ezekiel, when referring to the captivity of Jehoiachin, as a spring to spring system; see also his book, The Mysterious Numbers of the Hebrew Kings (Chicago: University of Chicago Press, 1951), pp. 157-65.

temple and the city, and Yahweh had ordered his scribe to scatter over the city blazing coals of fire from among the wheels of the throne chariot (chs. 8-11). The end had come, violence had grown up into a rod of wickedness, and Yahweh was soon to pour out his wrath and spend his anger against the people of the land (ch. 7).

Ezekiel's dramatic actions gave color and force to his message. He drew on a brick the picture of a city under siege, and he ate the rations of a city in the state of siege (ch. 4). He shaved himself with a sharp sword, and his disposal of the hair symbolized the fates awaiting the people of the city (ch. 5). To dramatize the coming exile he prepared his baggage and went out of his house through a hole dug in the wall (12:1-12). He marked out two roads and set up signposts, for the king of Babylon was at the crossroads, and his divination would lead him to take the road against Jerusalem (21:18-23). At the death of his wife, Ezekiel did not perform the usual mourning rites, and this was a sign that when Yahweh should profane his sanctuary, the people, like the prophet, deprived of the delight of their eyes, would be unable to lament or weep, but would pine away in their iniquities (24:15-24).

The allegories of Ezekiel carried the same message. The inhabitants of Jerusalem were a worthless vine, not good enough to be used as timber, or even as a peg, but only to be given over as fuel for the fire (ch. 15). Jerusalem was a faithless wife, repaying evilly the favors of Yahweh, and giving her favors to pagan gods, consorting with Assyrians and Babylonians; she must now be exposed and punished (16:1-43). Yahweh had as wives two sisters, Oholah and Oholibah, that is, Samaria and Jerusalem. Oholah played the prostitute with Assyrians, adopting their paganism; so Yahweh handed her over to them for destruction. Oholibah was more sinful than her sister, for she did not profit from knowing her sister's fate, but consorted with the Egyptians and Babylonians, and must now be destroyed by the Babylonians (23:1-35). Judah was a lioness, and one of her whelps (Jehoahaz) has been caught and carried away to Egypt, and another (Jehoiachin) to Babylon (19:1-9). Judah was a fruitful vine in a fertile vineyard, but now she is transplanted in the wilderness, and there remains no strong stem, no scepter for a ruler (19:10-14). An eagle (the king of Babylon) took away the tip of a cedar of Lebanon (Jehoiachin), and planted one of the seed of the land (Zedekiah) to grow as a vine, but it will be plucked up, getting no help from another eagle (the king of Egypt; 17:1-21). The city of Jerusalem is a caldron, the people the flesh in it, and Yahweh will kindle the fire beneath it (24:1-14). It is small wonder that it is said of Ezekiel, "Is he not a maker of parables?" (that is, allegories; 20:49). Equally vigorous are the oracles on the sword polished and sharpened for slaughter (21:1-17).

The Egyptians and Phoenicians were, with the Judeans, part of a more general struggle against the power of Nebuchadrezzar. In the first year of the siege of Jerusalem (588) Pharaoh Hophra (Apries) had come to the aid of the Judeans, resulting in the temporary lifting of the siege. About the same time Nebuchadrezzar began the siege of the city of Tyre and for thirteen years the city held out against him. It is thoroughly understandable why Ezekiel should have picked out Egypt and Tyre for the prominent attention he gives them. His oracles against Tyre contain some of his most effective poetry.[74] Tyre is a ship of state, reflecting in its construction, its crew, and its cargo the wide reaches of its commercial dealings, but it is to be sunk in the sea (ch. 27). The prince of Tyre presumes himself to be a god and as wise as Daniel, but he will die the death of the slain in the heart of the seas (28:1-10). He is the first man in the Garden of Eden, but has sinned through the greatness of his trade, and must be cast out from paradise (28:11-19). Upon Tyre from the north Yahweh is bringing Nebuchadrezzar, and Tyre will become an uninhabited bare rock, a place for the spreading of nets (26:1-18). So also Egypt to Ezekiel was the mythological dragon of chaos about to be defeated by the God of order and light (32:1-9; 29:1-5), or a glorified cedar of Lebanon, the world tree, about to topple to the land-of-no-return (ch. 31). The day of Yahweh, the day of doom, was to come upon Egypt (30:1-19). Shortly after the long siege of Tyre by Nebuchadrezzar was over, Ezekiel prophesied that Yahweh would give Egypt to Nebuchadrezzar as wages for his unprofitable campaign against Tyre (29:17-20).

We cannot say just when Ezekiel's theme first turned from judgment to promise. We may suspect that it was not until the twenty-fifth year of the Exile, in 572, when he issued the description of the new temple and the laws for the new community in chs. 40–48. We know he was prophesying still longer than this, for the oracle against Egypt in 29:17-21 is dated in 570. It was possibly within this same period that he had the vision of the valley of dry bones in 37:1-14, if this is to be considered original with

<hr>

74 Contrast Howie, *op. cit.*, p. 89, who suggests Ezekiel was a poet but not an original one, starting with well-known poetic models which he refashioned.

Ezekiel. The only date within the oracles of promise in chs. 33–39 is January 8, 585 (33:21), but one may not be certain to what oracle it was originally attached; it is now followed by an oracle of judgment. It is very doubtful whether the oracles of restoration in chs. 33–39 are genuine, other than possibly the vision of the valley of dry bones. Among the many plans which were being made for the restored community, Ezekiel advocated a theocratic community, a temple-centered society, in which the Zadokites would be given sole charge of Yahweh's sanctuary, with the Levites relegated to the position of temple servants. His ideal was an ecclesiastical community. The glory of Yahweh would return to the temple. Symbolizing the whole is the beautiful vignette in 47:1-12, picturing the stream of life flowing from the temple to bring to life even the Dead Sea. This was the new paradise, the end and purpose of history.

VI. The Editor

It is not always sufficiently realized that a biographer or a disciple who is presenting the life and message of his master has his reasons for so doing, and his presentation reflects those purposes. This is axiomatic in gospel criticism, but has received less attention than it deserves by Old Testament scholars. The author-editor of the book of Ezekiel can be roughly classed in the category of a biographer or disciple, although what he presents is not strictly a biography, and to call him a disciple would be a somewhat loose application of the term.

Something of the editor's ideas and interests have been noted in the preceding discussion. We may here outline a few of the high lights of his message. He would have his contemporaries learn the lessons of the history of the Hebrews. Israel deserved the punishment of exile which came upon it, for its behavior had been an abomination to Yahweh (6:13; 14:23; 36:16-19); it had rebelled against Yahweh's statutes and ordinances (5:5-8; 20:9-13, 16 ff.; etc.), and those in exile should recognize the sins for which Israel was exiled, loathe such behavior, and confess their abominations among the nations where they have been scattered (6:8-10; 7:16-19; 12:16). These were the sins of bloodshed and idolatry, and lewdness which involved also worship on the high places (6:3-10; 7:23; 16:44-52; 20:27-31; 22:6-12; 23:7-8; etc.). False prophets misled the people (13:1-23; 22:28), and the priests profaned Yahweh's holy things (22:26), the rulers violated their charge (22:25, 29; 34:1-10), and the sabbaths were broken (20:12, 20; 22:26; 23:38; etc.). The editor's concern was largely apostasy, although he does

have the prophetic interest in social justice and morality, stated in such terms that it recalls the Deuteronomic school (cf. 22:6-12). Like the Deuteronomist, the editor is convinced of the continuously rebellious attitude of pre-exilic Israel (2:3-8; 14:6-11; 20:1-39; 23:36-39).

But the Exile was the final punishment, and it will not occur again (5:9; cf. 44:1-3). The editor is preparing his contemporaries for the coming new age, and this best appears in his "sermons" in chs. 33–39. Both Israel and Judah will return from exile (11:17-19; 37:15-23; 47:13–48:35). None of the exiles will be left among the nations (16:53; 39:25-29). The messianic king of the line of David, the new shepherd, the prince, will be established as their head (29:21; 34:23; 37:24-28). Israel will be given a new heart and a new spirit, and Yahweh will pour out his spirit upon them and make them a new covenant, the covenant of peace (11:19; 16:59-63; 34:25-31; 36:25-27; 39:29). He will do it for his name's sake, that his name may not be profaned among the nations (20:44; 36:22-23; 39:7; cf. 20:9-26; 36:20-21). Judgment will come upon the nations around Israel, particularly Edom (35:1-15; 36:1-7), and the new age will be preceded by the destruction of the foe from the north (38:1–39:29). Prosperity and peace will be given to Israel in its land (34:11-31; 36:28-38). The pagan nations as well as Israel will come to know that Yahweh is the true God (cf. the formula, "then they will know that I am Yahweh"), and Yahweh will manifest his holiness in the sight of the Gentile nations (28:22, 25-26; 36:23; cf. 23:48).

The editor may indeed have belonged, like Ezekiel, to priestly circles, to judge from his interest in the priesthood, the sacrifices, and the festivals (see 43:1–46:24; cf. 20:40-41), and his emphasis on the law, the statutes and ordinances of Yahweh (5:5-8; 20:9-26; 36:27; etc.). But he is also interested in prophecy and the problem of the nature of prophecy (3:17-21; 14:9-10; 33:1-16), discussing at length the responsibility of the prophet and of the hearers of the prophet. We have already noted his interest in the general problem of responsibility. Since he is preparing the people for the return from exile, we may presume that his writing is largely for the benefit of the exiles who will return to participate in the new age; for this reason he refers often to those scattered among the nations and dispersed through the countries, and insists upon a recognition by them of the sins of Israel which justified the Exile. The commission in 3:10-11 is really that which the editor himself accepts. This does not, of course, necessitate that he was himself living among the exiles.

VII. Text of Ezekiel

The text is at times almost unbelievably corrupt. Resort must be made to the versions, and particularly to the Septuagint, for help in restoring the original text. Ancient translators were under obligation to their readers to make good sense despite the confusion in the Hebrew text, even as in the case of modern translators.[75] The reader will see from the margin of the Revised Standard Version how frequently appeal has been made to the versions.[76] More recently available for textual studies is papyrus Codex 967, originally containing the Septuagint text of Ezekiel along with Daniel and Esther. It is found in the Chester Beatty Papyri, which contain portions of Ezek. 11:25–17:21, and in the John H. Scheide collection of biblical papyri, containing most of Ezek. 19:12–39:29.[77] It is to be dated in the early part of the third century A.D., or possibly in the late second century. Other important codices of the Septuagint containing Ezekiel are the Codex Vaticanus (fourth century), Codex Alexandrinus (fifth century), Codex Marchalianus (sixth century), and Codex Venetus (eighth or ninth century).[77a]

Scholars often differ as to the extent to which omissions and variants in the text of the Septuagint represent the original Hebrew. Omissions may be due to the fact that the passage omitted was not in the translator's exemplar, or to copyists' errors, or at times to deliberate intention on the part of the editor in the interest of clarity or even brevity, or for other reasons. Some analogy may be found in the Chronicler's abbreviation of his Samuel-

Kings source, as in I Chr. 17:1 (cf. II Sam. 7:1-2); 17:13 (cf. II Sam. 7:14-15); 17:26 (cf. II Sam. 7:28-29); 18:2 (cf. II Sam. 8:2). F. V. Filson has shown how two large omissions in Codex 967 (e.g., Ezek. 12:26-28; 36:23b-38) may be accidental and charged to the copyist.[78] In addition, we do not always take into sufficient consideration the intentions and habits of the translators. In Jeremiah, for instance, the very vocabulary of many of the Septuagint omissions discloses them to be more probably omissions by the translator than post-Septuagint additions to the Hebrew text.[79] The same holds true for many Septuagint omissions in Ezekiel, where the literary style and thought of the omitted passage can be shown to be integral to the book. So in the case of 36:23b-38. The Septuagint translator has seemingly quite frequently omitted repetitious words and phrases in the interest of a simpler text.[80] In any case, we must take seriously the warning of H. M. Orlinsky against creating from the Septuagint a text which never existed outside the imagination.[81] It is not possible to admit that the Septuagint of Ezekiel is an absolutely faithful translation and therefore a trustworthy witness of the Hebrew text known in Alexandria in the third century B.C.[82]

One point may be briefly noted. The evidence of the Septuagint, especially as preserved in the Scheide Papyrus, suggests that the present Hebrew text reading of the divine name in the book of Ezekiel, אדני יהוה, "the Lord GOD," is an expansion of an original יהוה, "the LORD," the addition of אדני resulting from the objection to pronouncing the tetragrammaton.[83]

[75] See J. A. Montgomery, "A Modern Translation of the Hebrew Bible Compared with Ancient Versions," *Journal of Biblical Literature*, LXVI (1947), 311-14.

[76] See the important textual studies by C. H. Cornill, *Das Buch des Propheten Ezechiel* (Leipzig: J. C. Hinrichs, 1886).

[77] See F. G. Kenyon, *The Chester Beatty Biblical Papyri* (London: E. Walker, 1933, 1937); Fasciculi I, VII. A. C. Johnson, H. S. Gehman, and E. H. Kase, Jr., eds., *The John H. Scheide Biblical Papyri: Ezekiel* (Princeton: Princeton University Press, 1938). See also H. S. Gehman, "The Relations Between the Text of the John H. Scheide Papyri and That of the Other Greek MSS. of Ezekiel," *Journal of Biblical Literature*, LVII (1938), 281-87; "The Relations Between the Hebrew Text of Ezekiel and That of the John H. Scheide Papyri," *Journal of the American Oriental Society*, LVIII (1938), 92-102; J. B. Payne, "The Relationship of the Chester Beatty Papyri of Ezekiel to Codex Vaticanus," *Journal of Biblical Literature*, LXVIII (1949), 251-65; J. W. Wevers, "Evidence of the Text of the John H. Scheide Papyri for the Translation of the Status Constructus in Ezekiel," *Journal of Biblical Literature*, LXX (1951), 211-16.

[77a] Two fragments of the Hebrew text of Ezek. 4:16–5:1 (first century B.C. ?), found in Qumran Cave I, correspond to the C.T. (See D. Barthélemy and J. T. Milik, *Qumran Cave I* [Oxford: Clarendon Press, 1955; "Discoveries in the Judean Desert"], I, 68-69, Pl. XII.)

[78] "The Omission of Ezek. 12:26-28 and 36:23b-38 in Codex 967," *Journal of Biblical Literature*, LXII (1943), 27-32.

[79] See H. G. May, reviewing W. A. Irwin, *The Problem of Ezekiel*, in *Journal of Near Eastern Studies*, IV (1945), 63-64.

[80] There may be a lesson in the fact that the Dead Sea Scroll of Isaiah, while it has some minor omissions, has nothing comparable with those found in the LXX of some of the books of the O.T. See Millar Burrows, "Variant Readings in the Isaiah Manuscript," *Bulletin of the American Schools of Oriental Research*, No. 111 (Oct., 1948), p. 17. We must qualify this by more recent evidence from the Dead Sea scrolls regarding the fluidity of the Hebrew text before A.D. 70, making it impossible to assume that all variations of the LXX from the M.T. are due to the translator rather than his Hebrew *Vorlage*; see F. M. Cross, "A New Qumran Biblical Fragment Related to the Original Hebrew Underlying the Septuagint," *Bulletin of the American Schools of Oriental Research*, No. 132 (Dec., 1953), 15-25.

[81] "Current Progress and Problems in Septuagint Research," in H. R. Willoughby, ed., *The Study of the Bible Today and Tomorrow* (Chicago: University of Chicago Press, 1947), p. 154.

[82] W. O. E. Oesterley and T. H. Robinson, *An Introduction to the Books of the Old Testament* (New York: The Macmillan Co., 1934), p. 329.

[83] See Johnson, Gehman, and Kase, *John H. Scheide Biblical Papyri*, pp. 48-63; cf. Harford, *Studies in the Book of Ezekiel*, pp. 102-62.

VIII. Outline of Contents

There are four obvious main divisions in the book. The first (chs. 1–24) is composed primarily of oracles of judgment on Judah and Jerusalem. It begins with the call and commission of Ezekiel in chs. 1–3. An important unit is chs. 8–11, the vision of Ezekiel's visit to Jerusalem to witness the abominations in the temple and the departure of the glory of Yahweh. The gloom of the oracles of judgment is lifted by an occasional prophecy of restoration, as in 11:14-21; 16:53-63; 20:39-44. This section begins in 592 in the fifth year of the Exile, and ends in 588 at the beginning of the siege of Jerusalem.

The second division (chs. 25–32) consists of oracles against the foreign nations, directed chiefly at Tyre and Egypt, but with some of the neighbors of Judah included, such as Ammon, Moab, Edom, Philistia, and Sidon. This is to be compared with parallel collections of oracles against the foreign nations in the books of Jeremiah and Isaiah. The oracles are not in chronological order, and range between 587 and 570.

The third division (chs. 33–39) contains predictions of the coming restoration of Israel, with the rule of the Davidic Messiah. Yahweh will give the house of Israel a new heart and a new spirit, and will triumph over the pagan nations. Both Israel and Judah will be restored. The only date here is in 33:21—January 8, 585 —but this fact is of little help since the major part of this section contains materials of a secondary nature.

The fourth and final division (chs. 40–48) is the vision of the restored community. It is dated April 17, 572, and centers in the temple, for which the arrangements with detailed measurements are presented. It includes the laws for the priesthood and for the temple worship as well as the division of the land among the twelve tribes north and south of the sacred district and the territory of the prince and the city. The glory of Yahweh returns to the temple, and a stream of life flows from the temple to the Dead Sea.

I. Judgment on Judah and Jerusalem (1:1–24:27)
  A. Call and commission (1:1–3:27)
    1. Superscription (1:1-3)
    2. The throne-chariot vision (1:4-28)
    3. The commissions (2:1–3:27)
      a) First commission (2:1-8*a*)
      b) Eating the scroll (2:8*b*–3:3)
      c) Second commission (3:4-9)
      d) Third commission (3:10-11)
      e) Sequel (3:12-15)
      f) Fourth commission (3:16-21)
      g) Fifth commission (3:22-27)
  B. The fate of Jerusalem and the Exile (4:1–5:17)

    1. Symbol of the siege (4:1-3)
    2. Symbol of the duration of the Exile (4:4-8)
    3. Symbol of rationing restrictions (4:9-11)
    4. Symbol of unclean food (4:12-15)
    5. The rationing symbolism interpreted (4:16-17)
    6. Symbols of the fate of Jerusalem (5:1-17)
      a) The symbolic action (5:1-4)
      b) Interpretation (5:5-17)
  C. Oracle against the mountains (6:1-14)
    1. Destruction of the high places (6:1-7)
    2. The exiles will remember Yahweh (6:8-10)
    3. Israel will know Yahweh as God (6:11-14)
  D. Prophecy of the coming end (7:1-27)
  E. The visit to the temple (8:1–11:25)
    1. The vision of idolatry (8:1-18)
      a) Setting of the vision (8:1-4)
      b) The image of jealousy (8:5-6)
      c) Rites before pagan imagery (8:7-13)
      d) Worship of Tammuz (8:14-15)
      e) Worship of the sun (8:16-18)
    2. Slaughter of the guilty (9:1-11)
    3. Departure of Yahweh's glory (10:1-22)
    4. Judgment and hope (11:1-25)
      a) The wicked leaders (11:1-13)
      b) Hope for the exiles (11:14-21)
      c) Departure of Yahweh's glory (11:22-25)
  F. Symbols of the Exile and of dismay (12:1-28)
    1. The Exile (12:1-16)
    2. Fear of the people (12:17-20)
    3. The end is at hand (12:21-28)
  G. Oracles against prophets and prophetesses (13:1-23)
    1. Oracle against false prophets (13:1-16)
    2. Oracle against prophetesses (13:17-23)
  H. Judgment on idolaters and Jerusalem (14:1-23)
    1. Punishment of idolaters (14:1-11)
    2. The righteous save but themselves (14:12-23)
  J. The vine (15:1-8)
  K. The unfaithful wife (16:1-63)
    1. The foundling child (16:1-7)
    2. The maiden (16:8-14)
    3. Apostasies and alliances (16:15-34)
    4. Punishment (16:35-43)
    5. Sodom and Samaria (16:44-52)
    6. Restoration (16:53-63)
  L. The two eagles and the cedar (17:1-24)
    1. Allegory of the two eagles (17:1-10)
    2. Interpretation (17:11-21)
    3. Messianic allegory of the cedar (17:22-24)
  M. Individual responsibility (18:1-32)
    1. All souls are mine (18:1-4)
    2. The righteous man shall live (18:5-9)
    3. The wicked son of the righteous shall die (18:10-13)
    4. The righteous son of the wicked son shall live (18:14-20)
    5. The wicked man who becomes righteous shall live (18:21-24)
    6. The way of the Lord is just (18:25-29)
    7. New heart and new spirit (18:30-32)
  N. The lioness and the vine (19:1-14)
    1. Fate of Jehoahaz (19:1-4)

IX. Selected Bibliography

BERTHOLET, ALFRED, and GALLING, KURT. *Hesekiel* ("Handbuch zum Alten Testament"). Tübingen: J. C. B. Mohr, 1936.

COOKE, G. A. *A Critical and Exegetical Commentary on the Book of Ezekiel* ("International Critical Commentary"). New York: Charles Scribner's Sons, 1937.

HARFORD, JOHN BATTERSBY. *Studies in the Book of Ezekiel.* Cambridge: Cambridge University Press, 1935.

HERNTRICH, VOLKMAR. *Ezechielprobleme.* Giessen: A. Töpelmann, 1932.

HÖLSCHER, GUSTAV. *Hesekiel, der Dichter und das Buch.* Giessen: A. Töpelmann, 1924.

HOWIE, C. G. *The Date and Composition of Ezekiel.* Philadelphia: Society of Biblical Literature, 1950.

IRWIN, W. A. *The Problem of Ezekiel.* Chicago: University of Chicago Press, 1943.

MATTHEWS, I. G. *Ezekiel* ("An American Commentary on the Old Testament"). Philadelphia: American Baptist Publication Society, 1939.

TORREY, C. C. *Pseudo-Ezekiel and the Original Prophecy.* New Haven: Yale University Press, 1930.

EZEKIEL

TEXT, EXEGESIS, AND EXPOSITION

1 Now it came to pass in the thirtieth year, in the fourth *month,* in the fifth *day* of the month, as I *was* among the captives by the river of Chebar, *that* the heavens were opened, and I saw visions of God.

1 In the thirtieth year, in the fourth month, on the fifth day of the month, as I was among the exiles by the river Chebar, the heavens were opened, and I saw visions

---

I. JUDGMENT ON JUDAH AND JERUSALEM (1:1–24:27)
A. CALL AND COMMISSION (1:1–3:27)

Like Isaiah (ch. 6), Ezekiel at his call had a vision of the glory of Yahweh. The prophet was the mouthpiece of Yahweh, speaking Yahweh's words. When Yahweh called Jeremiah, he put his words in the mouth of Jeremiah (1:9; cf. 5:14), and Ezekiel ate a scroll which was given to him by Yahweh and upon which were written words of lamentation, mourning, and woe. Like the prophets before him, Ezekiel was called to proclaim the judgment of God. He received his call in Babylonia in a vision of the throne chariot of Yahweh. The call is found in ch. 1, and the commission of the prophet is in chs. 2–3. Despite the disturbed condition of the text, the vision of the throne chariot of Yahweh is one of the most impressive pictures of the glory and majesty of the Deity in the O.T., suggesting the artistry and sensitivity of a Dante by its imagery and avoidance of anthropomorphism. This is not the imagery of eroticism, to be explained in terms of Freudian psychology. C. G. Howie (*The Date and Composition of Ezekiel* [Philadelphia: Society of Biblical Literature, 1950], pp. 69-84) effectively refutes E. C. Broome's attempt so to interpret Ezekiel ("Ezekiel's Abnormal Personality," *Journal of Biblical Literature,* LXV [1946], 277-92). Something of the origin and significance of the symbolism has already been noted (see Intro., pp. 45-46). The commission in chs. 2–3 has been greatly expanded by the editor, who is perhaps responsible for 2:3*b*-8*a*; 3:10-11, 17-21.

1. SUPERSCRIPTION (1:1-3)

1:1-3. These opening words signalize the difficulties with which the book of Ezekiel bristles. The composite character of the superscription is evidenced by the dual chronological reference and the shift from first to third person. We should not try to recover a consistent third person original which would be consonant with the superscriptions to the books of the other prophets (cf. Herntrich), for the date formulas elsewhere in the book are in the first person, and we expect the same here. It is best to ascribe

---

1:1-3. *Among Displaced Persons.*—The exile is surely among the unhappiest of men. War or political conflict has uprooted him from his native soil and transplanted him to a strange land. World War I scattered thousands of downcast men and women from Tsarist Russia about the world, with little hope of ever returning to their country. The displaced persons of World War II, flotsam and jetsam of humanity, were present at every conference of foreign ministers, like Banquo's ghost at Macbeth's feast.

All about us today there are men and women who are in a very real sense uprooted and displaced. They have come from the countryside

2 In the fifth *day* of the month, which *was* the fifth year of king Jehoiachin's captivity,

3 The word of the LORD came expressly unto Ezekiel the priest, the son of Buzi, in the land of the Chaldeans by the river Chebar; and the hand of the LORD was there upon him.

of God. 2 On the fifth day of the month (it was the fifth year of the exile of King Jehoi'achin), 3 the word of the LORD came to Ezekiel the priest, the son of Buzi, in the land of the Chalde'ans by the river Chebar; and the hand of the LORD was upon him there.

---

the third person reference to Ezekiel and his situation in vss. 2-3 to the revision of an editor. If the superscription originally read somewhat as follows, it would be consistent with 8:1; 20:1; 40:1; etc.: "In the fifth year of the exile of King Jehoiachin, in the fourth month, on the fifth day of the month, as I was among the exiles by the river Chebar, the heavens were opened, and I saw visions of God, and the hand of the LORD was upon me there." A dual recension is responsible for the present form of the text. The first recension involved the addition of the reference to the **thirtieth year,** and may have been made by Ezekiel himself; the second was perhaps by the editor, who introduced the third person, the parentage of the prophet, etc., in accord with the other books of the prophets (for variant reconstructions, see W. F. Albright, "The Seal of Eliakim and the Latest Preëxilic History of Judah, with Some Observations on Ezekiel," *Journal of Biblical Literature,* LI [1932], 97 [cf. Howie, *op. cit.,* pp. 91-92]; C. C. Torrey, *Pseudo-Ezekiel and the Original Prophecy* [New Haven: Yale University Press, 1930], p. 18; Karl Budde, "Zum Eingang des Buches Ezechiel," *Journal of Biblical Literature,* L [1931], 20-41).

The thirtieth year has been taken as the thirtieth year of the reign of Manasseh, as the thirtieth year of Ezekiel's life, as the thirtieth year since the reform of King Josiah, and as a redactor's reconciliation of the prediction of the forty-year exile in Ezek. (4:6) and the seventy-year exile in Jer. 25:12. Another suggestion is to emend the text to read "in the third year," identifying the third year of Zedekiah with the fifth year of the Exile by variant calendar reckonings, while some would emend to read "in the thirteenth year," e.g., of Nebuchadrezzar. If Ezekiel had some hand in editing his book at one stage, it may represent the date of his completion of his book, three years after his last dated oracle in 27:19 (so Albright and Howie. G. R. Berry thinks it is misplaced from before 43:4; see "The Title of Ezekiel (1_{1-3})," *Journal of Biblical Literature,* LI [1932], 54-57; cf. Shalom Spiegel, "Ezekiel or Pseudo-Ezekiel?" *Harvard Theological Review,* XXIV [1931], 285-86). Even this must remain a conjecture. The date of Ezekiel's call was July 21, 592 (July 1, 593).

The river Chebar is the cuneiform *nâru kabari,* a canal which left the Euphrates above Babylon and flowed southeast, passing through Nippur and entering the Euphrates again near Erech; it is known today as Shaṭṭ en-Nîl. The expression **visions of God** signifies majestic, striking visions, and is a superlative, even as "wind of God" in Gen. 1:2 means a great or raging wind. **The exile of King Jehoiachin** began in 597. The number of the month has dropped out of vs. 2, perhaps by a scribal error. The name **Ezekiel** means "God strengthens." **The hand of the LORD was upon him** is Ezekiel's way of expressing the impact of Yahweh upon him and his vivid consciousness of Yahweh's presence (see 3:14, 22; 8:1; 33:22; 37:1; 40:1; I Kings 18:46; II Kings 3:15). Thirteen Hebrew MSS and three versions read "upon me" rather than **upon him,** and this is possibly the form in which it originally appeared in Ezekiel's superscription.

---

to the city, they have moved from one neighborhood to another, perhaps even they are strangers in a strange land. And others—a still graver misfortune—have lost touch with the faith in which they were brought up: they are rudder-

less amid the storms of life. We are called to be in some measure prophets to such people, because for us by God's mercy **the heavens** have been **opened** and we have seen what his purpose is in the confusion of the time.

4 ¶ And I looked, and, behold, a whirlwind came out of the north, a great cloud,
and a fire infolding itself, and a brightness

4 As I looked, behold, a stormy wind
came out of the north, and a great cloud,

---

2. The Throne-Chariot Vision (1:4-28)

Ezekiel witnessed a coming storm, and the sensory perceptions mingled with the vision experience to produce the spectacle of the throne chariot and the glory of Yahweh. In like manner the chant of a priestly choir, a basket of summer fruit, an almond rod, or a boiling pot might enter into a vision experience (Isa. 6:3; Amos 8:1-3; Jer. 1:11-19). Ezekiel's imagery, which is by no means as bizarre or tedious as some would judge it, is based largely on traditional Hebrew concepts, with the possibility of some more immediate Babylonian influence. The studies of Gunkel, Mowinckel, Morgenstern, Hooke, and others have illuminated the ritual and symbolism involved. The temple at Jerusalem was so oriented that at the equinoxes the rays of the rising sun could shine directly across from the Mount of Olives, through the east gate of the temple area, and into the temple to illumine the holy of holies. This was the entrance of the glory of Yahweh into the temple, the New Year enthronement of Yahweh, and it was accompanied by a complex ritual of the New Year at the autumnal equinox. Symbolizing the enthronement, the ark was carried in sacred procession and placed within the holy of holies between the two cherubim. This was the day of Yahweh. It has its analogies in non-Hebrew religions of the ancient Near East. The origin of the symbolism and ritual was to a large extent solar in character. A number of psalms were written for use in this ritual or were influenced by its symbolism (see Pss. 18; 24; 29; 110; 118; etc.). It was during such a New Year festival that Isaiah had his call (see the studies of Julian Morgenstern, "The Gates of Righteousness," *Hebrew Union College Annual*, VI [1929], 1-37; S. H. Hooke, *The Origins of Early Semitic Ritual* [London: British Academy,

---

4-28. The Glory in the Storm.—He who would find God in what threatens him and his fellows must begin by facing the storm at its fiercest. There is no revelation of God for those who flinch from their destiny. It is when he confronts the storm cloud without shrinking that the prophet sees the glory of the LORD. So the people stood trembling at the base of Sinai while Moses made his way up it and into the darkness (Exod. 20). So when Saul accepted his mission to challenge the Philistine enemy and deliver his people, "God gave him another heart" (I Sam. 10:9).

We too must learn to face our crises, whether in private life or in the great world, in the same valiant spirit. As we do so, the clouds open, they begin to glow with light, and the splendor of God is unveiled before our eyes. We see how all the forces of nature and the various aspects of human life are sustained by him, and how he is throned in majesty above them all. It is important to remember that we have in this narrative one of those forces which have made history. The writer of this chapter saw God in the disaster which had overtaken his nation, and so he was able to redeem that disaster.

For the details of the vision see Exeg. A curious commentary is provided by William Blake in *The Marriage of Heaven and Hell*,

beginning, "The Prophets Isaiah and Ezekiel dined with me, and I asked them how they dared so roundly to assert that God spoke to them; and whether they did not think at the same time that they would be misunderstood, and so be the cause of imposition."

4-28. The Ever-present God.—We can content ourselves with trying to elicit from this vision its spiritual import. The great aim of the seer is to convince his people that, though they have lost land and temple, God remains. Behind this, of course, lies the territorial conception of religion. Each people has its own god, and that god's jurisdiction is limited to the land which his people inhabit. Hence, when Ruth the Moabitess vows to follow her mother-in-law back to Canaan, she cries, "Thy people shall be my people, and thy God my God" (Ruth 1:16). On the other hand, Orpah is said to have "gone back unto her people, and unto her gods" (Ruth 1:15). For people who thought in these terms exile was a major disaster in the religious as well as in the political sphere.

We are perhaps inclined to dismiss this as so much superstition. But we should hesitate before we do so. The fact is that religion cannot live in a realm of ideas; it must body itself forth visibly in this actual world. It holds men, in part at any rate, by attachments which they

was about it, and out of the midst thereof as the color of amber, out of the midst of the fire.	with brightness round about it, and fire flashing forth continually, and in the midst of the fire, as it were gleaming bronze.

1938]; F. J. Hollis, "The Sun-Cult and the Temple at Jerusalem," in S. H. Hooke, ed., *Myth and Ritual* [London: Oxford University Press, 1933], pp. 87-110; H. G. May, "The Departure of the Glory of Yahweh," *Journal of Biblical Literature,* LVI [1937], 309-21). Entering into the throne-chariot concept are also the cherub and royal chariot motives. The cherub throne is well known from archaeological sources. On the tenth-century sarcophagus of King Hiram of Gebal the ruler is pictured seated on a throne supported by cherubs, and a Canaanite king is similarly enthroned on a twelfth-century inlay from Megiddo. The cherub was a winged lion with human head, and may be compared with the winged bull with human head from Mesopotamia (see Gordon Loud, *The Megiddo Ivories* [Chicago: University of Chicago Press, 1939], Pl. IV; W. F. Albright, "What Were the Cherubim?" *Biblical Archaeologist,* I [1938], 1-3). The chariot motive appears in the wheels in vss. 15-21. The cosmic reference is obvious from the firmament over the heads of the cherubim, with Yahweh enthroned above (cf. Isa. 40:22). There is also an association between the ark and the throne chariot. Cherubim decorated the ark, which may have been in the form of a miniature temple in which the Deity could be moved from place to place (H. G. May, "The Ark—A Miniature Temple," *American Journal of Semitic Languages and Literatures,* LII [1935-36], 215-34). By the time of the Chronicler the ark and cherubim concepts had coalesced, and we read of the "chariot of the cherubim that . . . covered the ark of the covenant of the LORD" (I Chr. 28:18). Note also the bronze stands in the Solomonic temple, with their wheels constructed like chariot wheels, and with lion, ox, and cherub decoration, suggesting the antiquity of Ezekiel's symbolism (I Kings 7:27-37).

In brief, we have here four cherubim, perhaps arranged in a square, each having four wings and four faces. Beside them are four wheels, with eyes in the rims, and in the middle of them is a flaming fire, from which lightning issues. Above them is something like a firmament, and above that the likeness of a throne upon which Yahweh sits.

4. The throne chariot emerged from a storm **out of the north,** which was the direction of the home of the gods in Canaanite mythology. So Baal-zephon, "Lord of the north," was the title of the Canaanite god who gave his name to the locality in Exod. 14:2; Num. 33:7, and the Canaanites at Ugarit pictured the deities dwelling in the interior or the height of the north (ṣrrt [mrym] ṣpn); cf. Isa. 14:13; Ps. 48:2. **Flashing continuously:** As in Exod. 9:24. A scribal gloss may account for the repetition in **out of the midst thereof . . . , out of the midst of the fire.** With חשמל, **bronze,** cf. the Akkadian *elmešu,* Egyptian ḥsmn, "bronze" (see G. R. Driver, "Ezekiel's Inaugural Vision," *Vetus Testamentum,* I [1951], 60-62; see, however, Akkadian *ešmaru,* Elamite *ismalu,* "inlay," and discussion by G. G. Cameron, *Persepolis Treasury Tablets* [Chicago: University of Chicago Press, 1948], 129-30; William A. Irwin, "HASHMAL," *Vetus Testamentum,* II [1952], 169-70.)

---

form to particular places, persons, times, and institutions. If these attachments are severed, the whole spiritual life may be imperiled.

A family that moves to a new housing development on the edge of one of our great cities may to all appearance lose its religion. Why? Because it no longer has a connection with the downtown church in which husband and wife were married and their children baptized. A man may even drop the Ten Commandments when he goes east of Suez. What we have to do is to use the local attachments to foster a spirit which is robust and independent enough

to retain its faith even when old ties have been severed. This can be done only by showing men and women an ever-present God who goes where they go and abides where they abide.

Observe how this is worked out in the vision. Nothing can impede God; when he forms a purpose he executes it without the slightest deviation (vs. 9). He has all forms of power at his disposal (vs. 10). He is free and sovereign, capable of meeting every conceivable emergency, and is unswerving in all that he does (vs. 12). The whole created universe stands ready to do his will. From whatever quarter need

5 Also out of the midst thereof *came* the likeness of four living creatures. And this *was* their appearance; they had the likeness of a man.

6 And every one had four faces, and every one had four wings.

7 And their feet *were* straight feet; and the sole of their feet *was* like the sole of a calf's foot: and they sparkled like the color of burnished brass.

8 And *they had* the hands of a man under their wings on their four sides; and they four had their faces and their wings.

9 Their wings *were* joined one to another; they turned not when they went; they went every one straight forward.

10 As for the likeness of their faces, they four had the face of a man, and the face of a lion, on the right side: and they four had the face of an ox on the left side; they four also had the face of an eagle.

5 And from the midst of it came the likeness of four living creatures. And this was their appearance: they had the form of men, 6 but each had four faces, and each of them had four wings. 7 Their legs were straight, and the soles of their feet were like the sole of a calf's foot; and they sparkled like burnished bronze. 8 Under their wings on their four sides they had human hands. And the four had their faces and their wings thus: 9 their wings touched one another; they went every one straight forward, without turning as they went. 10 As for the likeness of their faces, each had the face of a man in front;[a] the four had the face of a lion on the right side, the four had the face of an ox on the left side, and the four had the face of an eagle at the

[a] Cn: Heb lacks *in front*

5. In view of the following description, it is difficult to understand how the creatures **had the form of men.** The LXX, ὁμοίωμα ἀνθρώπου ἐπ' αὐτοῖς, "the likeness of a man was upon them," apparently refers to Yahweh. By changing אדם, **man,** to אחת, "one," it would mean that they all had the same form. Another possibility is that the reference is to their upright posture. Or vs. 5*b* may be a gloss. Presumably the four creatures faced the four corners of the earth.

6. Cf. the seraphim in Isaiah's vision (ch. 6), which were also a part of the theophany of Yahweh. A tenth-century pottery incense altar from Megiddo in the form of a miniature temple was decorated with four cherubim (H. G. May, *Material Remains of the Megiddo Cult* [Chicago: University of Chicago Press, 1935], Pl. XIII).

7. **Their legs were straight** follows the LXX, Syriac interpretation of the obscure Hebrew text. The **calf's foot** is reminiscent of the bull-bodied Assyrian *šedu* and *lamassu.* Confusing כף for כנף, the LXX has "and their feet were winged."

8. Does vs. 8*a* mean that each had four hands? **On their four sides** may mean "on the sides of the four of them." Composite winged creatures appear in Assyrian and Babylonian sculpture. Vs. 8*b* is also obscure.

9. Cf. the cherubim in the temple, whose wings touched tip to tip (I Kings 6:27).

10. **In front** and **at the back** have properly been added. The Hebrew text places the face of a man and the face of a lion on the right side. The latter part of the verse

may arise, he is there to meet it. No alteration of his plans is called for, since he is present everywhere (vss. 10-21). He is all-seeing too, and nothing escapes his observation (vs. 18). How foolish then to imagine that we have been overlooked! How preposterous to confine such a God to a single strip of the earth's surface! In Babylon as in Israel, in misfortune as in prosperity, God is with us; we have but to call upon him, and he is there to help us.

In 1453 some Benedictine monks approached Nicholas of Cusa with the request for instruction in the mystic way. He sent them a copy of

his book *De Visione Dei,* with a picture in it of a face such that, no matter where the person was who looked at it, he felt its gaze resting upon him. Our seer has given his people such a picture of God. How can we give it to our time?

5. *The Four Zoas.*—In the prophetic literature of Blake the four living creatures of this vision reappear as the Four Zoas. They are called by him Urizen, Luvah, Los, and Tharmas, and they correspond to "the Four Universes" and to "the Four Eternal Senses of Man." Modern psychological study enables us to

11 Thus *were* their faces: and their wings *were* stretched upward; two *wings* of every one *were* joined one to another, and two covered their bodies.

12 And they went every one straight forward: whither the spirit was to go, they went; *and* they turned not when they went.

13 As for the likeness of the living creatures, their appearance *was* like burning coals of fire, *and* like the appearance of lamps: it went up and down among the living creatures; and the fire was bright, and out of the fire went forth lightning.

14 And the living creatures ran and returned as the appearance of a flash of lightning.

15 ¶ Now as I beheld the living creatures, behold one wheel upon the earth by the living creatures, with his four faces.

16 The appearance of the wheels and their work *was* like unto the color of a beryl: and they four had one likeness: and their appearance and their work *was* as it were a wheel in the middle of a wheel.

back.*b* 11 Such were their faces. And their wings were spread out above; each creature had two wings, each of which touched the wing of another, while two covered their bodies. 12 And each went straight forward; wherever the spirit would go, they went, without turning as they went. 13 In the midst of*c* the living creatures there was something that looked like burning coals of fire, like torches moving to and fro among the living creatures; and the fire was bright, and out of the fire went forth lightning. 14 And the living creatures darted to and fro, like a flash of lightning.

15 Now as I looked at the living creatures, I saw a wheel upon the earth beside the living creatures, one for each of the four of them.*d* 16 As for the appearance of the wheels and their construction: their appearance was like the gleaming of a chrysolite; and the four had the same likeness, their construction being as it were a

b Cn: Heb lacks *at the back*
c Gk Old Latin: Heb *And the likeness of*
d Heb *of their faces*

is also corrupt (cf. KJV and RSV). Some believe the original text placed the face of a man and the face of a lion on the right and the face of an ox and the face of an eagle on the left of each one of the four. Cf. the four six-winged creatures, resembling respectively a lion, ox, man, and flying eagle, in Rev. 4:7. Lion, ox, and eagle symbolism associated with deities appears frequently in Near Eastern religions.

11. This verse is also corrupt. For **such were their faces** the Hebrew has only "and their faces"; the LXX and O.L. omit. Cf. the position and use of the wings of the seraphim in Isa. 6.

12. (Cf. vs. 9*b*.) The purposiveness of the Godhead may be indicated. **The spirit:** I.e., of the cherubim, which was also in the wheels (see vs. 20). This is also the spirit of the Godhead (cf. 2:2; 3:12, 24; 11:24).

13. The details are suggested by the thunderstorm and by traditional theophanic terminology (see Pss. 18:12-13; 97:4; Gen. 15:17; Exod. 19:16; 20:18). The more literal KJV translation suggests the textual difficulties. Considerable emendation is necessary to achieve a grammatical equivalent of the RSV translation, which follows the LXX.

14. The verse makes little sense in the context. The LXX translators may have omitted it for this reason.

15. See the wheels of the throne of "the ancient of days" in Dan. 7:9. In origin the wheels are those of the royal chariot or the chariot of the sun-god; cf. the chariots of the sun and the horses dedicated to the sun in the temple before Josiah's reform (II Kings 23:11). Pottery models of chariot wheels found in excavations may also belong to solar religious ideology. In apocalyptic literature these wheels, ophannim, were personified as heavenly beings (Enoch 61:10; 71:7).

16. Chrysolite or **beryl** is the Hebrew *tarshish;* some yellow, gold-colored precious stone is intended, perhaps topaz (see 10:9; 28:13; Exod. 28:20; 39:13; Dan. 10:6). The name suggests that its source was in Tarshish. **A wheel within a wheel** perhaps means that each wheel was composed of two wheels at right angles to each other (cf. vs. 17).

17 When they went, they went upon their four sides: *and* they turned not when they went.

18 As for their rings, they were so high that they were dreadful; and their rings *were* full of eyes round about them four.

19 And when the living creatures went, the wheels went by them: and when the living creatures were lifted up from the earth, the wheels were lifted up.

20 Whithersoever the spirit was to go, they went, thither *was their* spirit to go; and the wheels were lifted up over against them: for the spirit of the living creature *was* in the wheels.

21 When those went, *these* went; and when those stood, *these* stood; and when those were lifted up from the earth, the wheels were lifted up over against them: for the spirit of the living creature *was* in the wheels.

22 And the likeness of the firmament upon the heads of the living creature *was* as the color of the terrible crystal, stretched forth over their heads above.

23 And under the firmament *were* their wings straight, the one toward the other: every one had two, which covered on this side, and every one had two, which covered on that side, their bodies.

24 And when they went, I heard the noise of their wings, like the noise of great

wheel within a wheel. 17 When they went, they went in any of their four directions[e] without turning as they went. 18 The four wheels had rims and they had spokes;[f] and their rims were full of eyes round about. 19 And when the living creatures went, the wheels went beside them; and when the living creatures rose from the earth, the wheels rose. 20 Wherever the spirit would go, they went, and the wheels rose along with them; for the spirit of the living creatures was in the wheels. 21 When those went, these went; and when those stood, these stood; and when those rose from the earth, the wheels rose along with them; for the spirit of the living creatures was in the wheels.

22 Over the heads of the living creatures there was the likeness of a firmament, shining like crystal,[g] spread out above their heads. 23 And under the firmament their wings were stretched out straight, one toward another; and each creature had two wings covering its body. 24 And when they went, I heard the sound of their wings like

[e] Heb *on their four sides*
[f] Cn: Heb *uncertain*
[g] Gk Heb *awesome crystal*

---

17. Without turning: As in vss. 9, 12, this does not mean "without revolving."

18. The KJV is closer to the original, which literally begins, "And their rims, and they had height, and they had terror." With the help of the versions one might read: "And they had rims, and I looked, and behold, the rims of the four of them were full of eyes round about." Any reconstruction of the text is conjectural. The eyes symbolize the all-seeing Godhead; cf. 10:12; cf. also the "Horus eye" amulets of the Egyptians and the rhomb (=eye) on Mesopotamian cylinder seals.

21. Several commentators omit vs. 21 as a doublet or repetition of vs. 20, with some Hebrew and LXX MSS; some omit vss. 20-21 as glosses on vs. 19.

22. The symbol tends to coalesce with the thing for which it stands, and the throne chariot is at the same time the cosmos in miniature. The **firmament,** רקיע, is the sky, as in Gen. 1:6-8; etc.; Ps. 19:1. This is an illustration of mythopoeic thought (see H. and H. A. Frankfort, *et al., The Intellectual Adventure of Ancient Man* [Chicago: University of Chicago Press, 1946], pp. 10-27). The word דמות, **likeness,** may have a more concrete sense than often implied in the English translation (see Paul Humbert, *Études sur le récit du paradis et de la chute dans la Genèse* [Neuchâtel: Secrétariat de l'Université, 1940], pp. 158-66).

23. The text of vs. 23*b* is awkward, but the RSV gives the probable meaning. With vs. 23*a* cf. vss. 9, 11.

24. Great waters or **many waters** (מים רבים) in this context, as often elsewhere, refers to the waters of the great deep. Note the "many waters" in the enthronement

waters, as the voice of the Almighty, the voice of speech, as the noise of a host: when they stood, they let down their wings.

25 And there was a voice from the firmament that *was* over their heads, when they stood, *and* had let down their wings.

26 ¶ And above the firmament that *was* over their heads *was* the likeness of a throne, as the appearance of a sapphire stone: and upon the likeness of the throne *was* the likeness as the appearance of a man above upon it.

the sound of many waters, like the thunder of the Almighty, a sound of tumult like the sound of a host; when they stood still, they let down their wings. 25 And there came a voice from above the firmament over their heads; when they stood still, they let down their wings.

26 And above the firmament over their heads there was the likeness of a throne, in appearance like sapphire;[h] and seated above the likeness of a throne was a like-

[h] Heb *lapis lazuli*

psalms (Pss. 29:3; 93:4; cf. 18:16 and Dan. 7:2; Rev. 1:15; 14:2; 19:6). Cf. also Isa. 17:12-13, and the analogous imagery in the Ugaritic myth of the struggle of Baal against Prince Sea and Judge River (J. A. Montgomery, "Ras Shamra Notes IV: The Conflict of Baal and the Waters," *Journal of the American Oriental Society*, LV [1935], 270-71). **The thunder of the Almighty** is "the voice of Shaddai." Shaddai is a pre-Mosaic designation of deity, somehow related to the cuneiform *šadû*, "mountain" (cf. W. F. Albright, "The Names *Shaddai* and *Abraham*," *Journal of Biblical Literature*, LIV [1935], 180-93; H. G. May, "The Patriarchal Idea of God," *ibid.*, LX [1941], 121-23). The expression קול המלה, **a sound of tumult,** is uncertain, and is elsewhere found only in Jer. 11:16, where it is translated "the roar of a great tempest." **The voice of speech** presumes a different root, and is less probable in the context, despite some versional agreement.

25. This verse may be dittography from vs. 24. Nine Hebrew MSS and a Syriac MS omit it. It disturbs the sequence of the description.

26. Sapphire is really **lapis lazuli**, a blue stone used for inlay, beads, seals, etc. In Exod. 24:10 (J) appears a lapis lazuli construction as clear as the sky beneath the feet of Yahweh. The LXX revises the verse to accord with Exod. 24:10 at this point. With

identify the Four Zoas with the four basic psychological functions of thought, feeling, intuition, and sensation. C. G. Jung has shown how the health of the personality depends on the integration of these functions.[1]

26-28. God Like and Unlike.—All that went before did but prepare the way for this, the crowning moment. The eye of the seer, gazing steadfastly into the storm cloud, discriminates one feature after another, until the celestial chariot has taken shape before him. Now he falters as he looks still higher, where the King himself sits on his throne. Language fails him at this point, and he has to take refuge in hint, suggestion, and metaphor. Can we do otherwise in face of the higher, the spiritual world? Notice how he makes use of the word **likeness** and its equivalents again and again. It was like

[1] The following books are a useful guide to further study in this field: D. J. Sloss and J. P. R. Wallis, eds., *The Prophetic Writings of William Blake* (Oxford: Oxford University Press, 1926); W. P. Witcutt, *Blake, A Psychological Study* (London: Hollis & Carter, 1946); C. G. Jung, *The Integration of the Personality* (New York: Farrar & Rinehart, 1939); *Psychology and Religion* (New Haven: Yale University Press, 1938).

that—yet not like that—of such surpassing grandeur was it.

So all our human language breaks down before the majesty of God. We must borrow analogies from the world of our experience if we are to speak of him at all; we must transfer to him categories borrowed from personal life and personal relations. But these at the best are as arrows shot at the sun: they reach but a tiny fraction of the way to their goal and then fall back to the earth from which they were sent forth. We can almost feel, as we read these verses, a man stammering in a vain attempt to put into words what had overwhelmed him. Little wonder that under constraint of such a vision he fell prostrate on the ground.

There is something here which runs through all the work of Ezekiel. The strength this man had was derived from an encounter with a God infinitely beyond him. That is true of all the prophets, and is therefore true here, whatever view we may take of the composition of this opening chapter. There are times, to be sure, when this sense of God as other than ourselves leads the prophet to think of God as wholly

27 And I saw as the color of amber, as the appearance of fire round about within it, from the appearance of his loins even upward, and from the appearance of his loins even downward, I saw as it were the appearance of fire, and it had brightness round about.

28 As the appearance of the bow that is in the cloud in the day of rain, so *was* the appearance of the brightness round about. This *was* the appearance of the likeness of the glory of the LORD. And when I saw *it,* I fell upon my face, and I heard a voice of one that spake.

ness as it were of a human form. 27 And upward from what had the appearance of his loins I saw as it were gleaming bronze, like the appearance of fire enclosed round about; and downward from what had the appearance of his loins I saw as it were the appearance of fire, and there was brightness round about him.*i* 28 Like the appearance of the bow that is in the cloud on the day of rain, so was the appearance of the brightness round about.

Such was the appearance of the likeness of the glory of the LORD. And when I saw it, I fell upon my face, and I heard the voice of one speaking.

i Or *it*

---

likeness as it were of a human form cf. Gen. 1:26-27. Ezekiel is attempting to avoid anthropomorphisms.

27. Cf. this picture of Yahweh with that in Hab. 3:4; Ps. 97:3; Dan. 7:9-10. Ezekiel has a vivid sense of the *mysterium tremendum.* **Enclosed round about** is obscure, more literally, "having a house round about." The LXX omits it along with **the appearance of fire.**

28. The rainbow appears elsewhere only in the story of the covenant after the Flood (Gen. 9:12-17). The latter part of the verse reflects the consciousness of the weakness and unworthiness of man in the presence of God (cf. Jer. 1:6; Isa. 6:5; see also Gen. 32:30; Exod. 20:19-20; 24:11). The voice in vs. 28*b* is the voice of Yahweh.

---

terrible, and there we shall need to correct him by what we have learned from Christ. But it would be good for us could we recover something of that awe in the presence of God which was characteristic of our fathers.

A study of Luther has rightly emphasized what it calls his "Copernican revolution" in religion, when he transferred its center from man to God.[2] Does not a good deal of our modern religion need a revolution of this kind? We place man on the throne, man made in our own image, and feel secure. But it is a false security, for experience makes it clear that the Power behind the world does not wait on our desires to fulfill them. We have to reckon with a wisdom which is at times inscrutable, a purpose which crosses our own yet which we cannot evade, a claim addressed to our whole being and not to be refused.[3] To such a God our sole adequate response is in awed worship and obedient devotion.

1:28-3:27. *The Prophet's Call.*—We come now to that tense moment in Ezekiel's life when he knew himself to be a prophet. We have here the original account of his call, to which the preceding material was prefixed by the editor to whom final publication of the book was due. Ezekiel's call should be compared with those of his predecessors, particularly Isaiah and Jeremiah.

There are two possible applications of such a narrative as this. What happened to the prophet has its parallel in the experience of the preacher, both when he comes at first to his lifework and when he looks back upon it after much discouragement. But also there is something here that is true of each one of us. For we all have our vocation, that of being men and women on this earth.

1:28-2:2. *The Measure of Man.*—These verses bring out clearly that paradox in the biblical view of man which makes it immensely superior to any alternative conception. Man comes to a sense of his own greatness only after he has been humbled to the dust before the majesty of God. God, on the other hand, does not want us to obey him out of fear or cringe before him. He wants men with whom he can speak and who will stand erect before him, girt and ready to do his work. The center of our being lies outside ourselves and in God.

[2] Philip S. Watson, *Let God Be God!* (Philadelphia: Muhlenburg Press, 1948), pp. 32-38.

[3] See John Addington Symonds, "An Invocation" and Emily Brontë, "Last Lines," modern poems which convey something of this sense of the divine transcendence.

2 And he said unto me, Son of man, stand upon thy feet, and I will speak unto thee.

2 And the spirit entered into me when he spake unto me, and set me upon my feet, that I heard him that spake unto me.

3 And he said unto me, Son of man, I send thee to the children of Israel, to a rebellious nation that hath rebelled against

2 And he said to me, "Son of man, stand upon your feet, and I will speak with you." 2 And when he spoke to me, the Spirit entered into me and set me upon my feet; and I heard him speaking to me. 3 And he said to me, "Son of man, I send you to the people of Israel, to a nation*j* of rebels, who

j Syr: Heb *nations*

3. THE COMMISSIONS (2:1–3:27)

One might perhaps expect the original commission of Ezekiel to follow the eating of the scroll. Chs. 2–3 contain five separate commissions. The first one, found in 2:3*b*-8*a*, interrupts the account of the eating of the scroll. Its character is such as to suggest that it may come from the editor. In 2:4, as in 3:11 and 3:27, which are more certainly the editor's, the prophet is told to say, "Thus says the Lord GOD." In 2:5*b*, "they will know that there has been a prophet among them" recalls the editor's formula, "Then they will know that I am Yahweh," and occurs again in 33:33. This commission, along with those in 3:10-11, 17-21, and 24*b*-27, presumes some of the people may listen, in contrast with 3:4*b*-9. Richard Kraetzschmar's theory of parallel recensions (cf. also Bertholet) will hardly explain the differences between 2:3*b*-8*a* and 3:4-9. The former is redundant, and the only original touch seems to be the scorpions in vs. 6. A study of the occurrences of the term "rebellious house" does not reveal whether this expression is exclusively the editor's.

a) FIRST COMMISSION (2:1-8a)

2:1-3a. Son of man means a mortal, and is the usual term by which Yahweh addresses Ezekiel (see also Num. 23:19; Job 25:6; Ps. 8:4; etc.). The familiar Ps. 8:4 will suggest something of the connotation of the term. In Dan. 7:13 it alludes to one in human form who is the personification of the ideal Israel or the saints of the Most High. It later became a messianic designation. In Ezekiel it may belong both to the prophet and the editor, and its frequent repetition (eighty-seven times) adds to the impression

the God who made us and who calls us into his fellowship. There is no room therefore for pride, since we are not our own and Another has made us. Equally, there is no excuse for evasion of responsibility, since the Power that made the world has singled us out as those with whom he can have speech.

What is worked out thus in the story is compressed into the term **Son of man,** by which the prophet is addressed. He knows himself, that is, to be but as others are, a frail, weak mortal; nevertheless, the hand of God is upon him and he is capable of great things. Was the meaning of this term for Ezekiel in the mind of Jesus when he used it for himself? Did he too wish to emphasize his share in our common mortality and his dependence on the Father as the conditions under which he must do his work? [4]

Stand upon thy feet: We stand upon our feet before those in whom we have confidence and who trust us. **I will speak unto thee:** They

speak to us who have something to share with us, who call us in some sense into partnership. Here a man stands, awed yet fearless, because out of the splendor a voice has spoken to claim him; he knows that he is wanted and valued. So it can be argued that it is precisely those who feel themselves as nothing in God's sight who have handled the events of their time as a potter does his clay. Their strength came from their humility before him. One can name in this connection John Calvin, John Knox, William the Silent, Oliver Cromwell, and many others. [5]

The preacher especially must stand before his hearers as one who is delivered from the common human fears because he has seen a vision of which he knows himself to be unworthy. Here is a theme for an ordination service or similar occasion.

2:3-4. *A Man's Mission.*—We can imagine Ezekiel complaining that the task assigned him is too difficult. Why must he go to the rebellious

[4] See W. A. Curtis, *Jesus Christ the Teacher* (London: Oxford University Press, 1943).

[5] Cf. James Anthony Froude, *Short Studies on Great Subjects* (New York: Charles Scribner's Sons, 1868).

me: they and their fathers have transgressed against me, *even* unto this very day.

4 For *they are* impudent children and stiffhearted. I do send thee unto them; and thou shalt say unto them, Thus saith the Lord GOD.

5 And they, whether they will hear, or whether they will forbear, (for they *are* a rebellious house,) yet shall know that there hath been a prophet among them.

6 ¶ And thou, son of man, be not afraid of them, neither be afraid of their words, though briers and thorns *be* with thee, and thou dost dwell among scorpions: be not afraid of their words, nor be dismayed at their looks, though they *be* a rebellious house.

have rebelled against me; they and their fathers have transgressed against me to this very day. **4** The people also are impudent and stubborn: I send you to them; and you shall say to them, 'Thus says the Lord GOD.' **5** And whether they hear or refuse to hear (for they are a rebellious house) they will know that there has been a prophet among them. **6** And you, son of man, be not afraid of them, nor be afraid of their words, though briers and thorns are with you and you sit upon scorpions; be not afraid of their words, nor be dismayed at their looks,

---

of an over-all unity. **The Spirit entered into me:** This is Yahweh's spirit. The word occurs with similar meaning in 3:12, 14, 24; 11:1, 5, 24; 37:1; 43:5. In 11:5; 37:1 it is called "the Spirit of Yahweh" and in 11:24 "the Spirit of God." Cf. the spirit of God which inspired prophetic frenzy and prophecy in Num. 24:2; I Sam. 10:6; 19:20; I Kings 22:24; Isa. 61:1, or other activity in Judg. 3:10; 6:34; 11:29; 13:25; I Sam. 11:6; I Kings 18:12; etc. We should tentatively read vss. *2a, 8b* in sequence as, "And he said to me, 'Son of man, open your mouth,' " etc.

3b-8a. Cf. the earlier prophetic criticism of the Hebrew people for continuous apostasy, as in Amos 4:6-11; Jer. 2, and the later Deuteronomic editor in the books from Deuteronomy to II Kings; see also the Deuteronomic editor or biographer in the book of Jeremiah (25:3-7; 32:30-35; etc.) ; cf. Pss. 78; 106. The double name, **the Lord GOD,** is the result of later editing, the original text having only "the LORD," יהוה, as is now evident from the Scheide Papyrus (see Intro., p. 63). **The Lord GOD** is Adonai (my Lord) Yahweh, and the word Adonai may have been added to be read as a substitute for Yahweh, which was reckoned too sacred to be pronounced. The word κύριος, standing for Yahweh of the M.T., is found in the Scheide Papyrus seventy-six

---

and stubborn, to those who are resolved not to heed his message? It is just such a question that many a man asks himself today. Why am I sent to work here, where the people are so unreceptive, where circumstances are so adverse? There is perhaps no one who does not wish at times that life had been easier for him; merely to be a man or woman in this world is to be exposed to conflict, pain, and failure. The answer to all such questionings is that life is a campaign, not a holiday. It is precisely to the obstinate and perverse that a prophet must be sent, and precisely in adverse circumstances that we must prove our mettle. "Those who are well have no need of a physician, but those who are sick" (Mark 2:17).

Let us count it an honor when God assigns us his most difficult tasks, for, like a wise general, he sends his best officers on his most exacting enterprises. In this sense we must learn to

say "Yes" to life, and to volunteer for the battle where it is fiercest.

4-5. *The Task and Its Reward.*—Note the stages in the development of the thought: *(a)* **I do send thee unto them.** The dedicated man does not seek his own ends, but is under orders. Behind every valiant life there is this consciousness of being on an errand. *(b)* **Whether they will hear, or whether they will forbear.** There may be no guarantee of success. We are responsible only for the faithful discharge of our duty, not for men's attitude toward us. Let us be neither elated by their praise nor dismayed by their criticism, but simply steadfast in our obedience to him who has sent us. *(c)* **They . . . shall know that there hath been a prophet among them.** The day will come at last that vindicates God's faithful servant. He may not live to see it, his very name may be forgotten, but in the end men's hearts will turn

7 And thou shalt speak my words unto them, whether they will hear, or whether they will forbear: for they *are* most rebellious.

8 But thou, son of man, hear what I say unto thee; Be not thou rebellious like that rebellious house: open thy mouth, and eat that I give thee.

9 ¶ And when I looked, behold, a hand *was* sent unto me; and, lo, a roll of a book *was* therein;

for they are a rebellious house. 7 And you shall speak my words to them, whether they hear or refuse to hear; for they are a rebellious house.

8 "But you, son of man, hear what I say to you; be not rebellious like that rebellious house; open your mouth, and eat what I give you." 9 And when I looked, behold, a hand was stretched out to me, and, lo, a

---

times, while κύριος ὁ θεός, "the Lord God," occurs but six times, and may be explained as a later revision based on the changed Hebrew text. The sentiment in vs. 6 recalls Jer. 1:8, 17-19. The figure of sitting on **scorpions** is most vivid to one who has lived in Palestine.

b) Eating the Scroll (2:8b–3:3)

8b-10. The narrative continues into ch. 3, and is unfortunately interrupted by the chapter division. The prophets were called to announce the coming judgment of Yahweh. So Amos was informed at his call that the end had come for the Israelites (8:1-3), and Isaiah was to prophesy until cities were laid waste, without inhabitant (6:11-13). Jeremiah was to announce the foe from the north (1:13-19). And the **scroll** which Ezekiel was asked to eat was inscribed on both sides with **words of lamentation and mourning and woe.** Cf. the scroll in Zech. 5:1-4, symbolizing Yahweh's curse. In Rev. 10:8-11 the author is told to eat a scroll, after which he must prophesy. The scroll was of papyrus or animal skins, and is best illustrated in Jer. 36 (see also Ps. 40:7). A clay seal found at Lachish had on the back the impression of the papyrus document to which it had been attached. The seal had belonged to Gedaliah, Ezekiel's contemporary. Pottery sherds were also used for writing materials, and are best illustrated by the ostraca

---

in homage to the truth for which he stood against his time. History is full of illustrations of this, from Socrates onward. Those whom men refuse to hear in their lifetime are acclaimed by later generations as messengers of God.

9-10. The Power of the Book.—Common to most prophets is the presence in their inaugural experience of some object, often quite a commonplace one, which becomes for them a vehicle of revelation. With Amos it was a plague of locusts; with Jeremiah, a cooking pot. With Ezekiel it is something quite different, **a book.** It is as the written word that the prophetic oracle appears to him.

Here we have vividly symbolized the power of the book in history. We may select certain moments at which that power becomes peculiarly evident: (*a*) The discovery of the scroll of the law in the temple under Josiah, and the reforms which followed thereupon. Henceforth the Jews are "the people of the book." (*b*) The invention of printing and the publication of such epoch-making books as Erasmus' Greek New Testament, the translations of Luther, Tyndale, etc. (*c*) The books which

have made history or revolutionized our minds in modern times, e.g., Adam Smith's *Wealth of Nations*, Charles Darwin's *Origin of Species*, Karl Marx's *Capital*, etc.

Is it true that "the pen is mightier than the sword"?[6] Does this hold good even in the atomic age?

Today, as the result of the extension in so many countries of educational facilities, there is widespread hunger for the printed word. We speak of a reader as devouring a book, and such a description is applicable to multitudes at the present time.

Here is a message which might serve as charter to a valuable type of missionary enterprise, one which seeks to bring home to Christian people the efficacy of the printed word as an instrument of evangelization, and places the provision of Christian literature on the same level as the traditional forms of missionary activity.

2:9–3:3. The Bittersweet of Life.—The experience of the prophet continues to symbolize the common human situation. Life deals with

[6] Edward George Earle Bulmer-Lytton, *Richelieu*, Act II, scene 2.

10 And he spread it before me; and it *was* written within and without: and *there was* written therein lamentations, and mourning, and woe.

3 Moreover he said unto me, Son of man, eat that thou findest; eat this roll, and go speak unto the house of Israel.

2 So I opened my mouth, and he caused me to eat that roll.

3 And he said unto me, Son of man, cause thy belly to eat, and fill thy bowels with this roll that I give thee. Then did I eat *it;* and it was in my mouth as honey for sweetness.

written scroll was in it; 10 and he spread it before me; and it had writing on the front and on the back, and there were written on it words of lamentation and mourning and woe. 1 And he said to me, "Son of man, eat what is offered to you; eat this scroll, and go, speak to the house of Israel." 2 So I opened my mouth, and he gave me the scroll to eat. 3 And he said to me, "Son of man, eat this scroll that I give you and fill your stomach with it." Then I ate it and it was in my mouth as sweet as honey.

found at Lachish, letters written while Nebuchadrezzar's armies were attacking Judah in 599, shortly before the beginning of the siege of Jerusalem. In Ezek. 37:16 there is an allusion to writing on a wooden tablet or stick (see Harry Torczyner, *et al., The Lachish Letters* [London: Oxford University Press, 1938]; W. F. Albright, "The Oldest Hebrew Letters: The Lachish Ostraca," and "The Lachish Letters After Five Years," *Bulletin of the American Schools of Oriental Research,* No. 70 [April, 1938], pp. 11-17; No. 82 [April, 1941], pp. 18-24; J. Philip Hyatt, "The Writing of an Old Testament Book," *Biblical Archaeologist,* VI [1943], 71-80). Perhaps Ezekiel's scroll had been written at Yahweh's dictation by the divine scribe of ch. 9. The extent of the doom is hinted by the fact that the scroll was inscribed both **on the front and on the back,** for a scroll would normally have writing on one side only. It contained many **lamentations,** קנים (the masculine plural form occurs only here; perhaps read with several versions, קינה, **lamentation).** It is doubtful that the oracles were thought to be more powerful because they were written down, for nothing could be more powerful than Yahweh's word, whether written or spoken (see Jer. 23:29).

Lamentation, mourning, and woe were the tenor of Ezekiel's oracles before 586. As Hölscher says, Ezekiel was the Cassandra of the city about to be destroyed.

3:1-3. Eat what is offered to you correctly interprets the literal idiom reflected in the KJV; the LXX omits, perhaps deliberately, as tautologous. **The house of Israel** in Ezekiel may mean the exiles, the people in Judah, the Northern Kingdom, or both the Israelites and the Judeans. Here it may mean the exiles (see vss. 10-11). **Sweet as honey:** Cf. Ps. 119:103, where Yahweh's promises are "sweeter than honey to my mouth," and Ps. 19:10, where Yahweh's ordinances are "sweeter also than honey and drippings of the honeycomb." The manna from heaven tasted like wafers made with honey (Exod. 16:31; see Rev. 10:9-10). The scroll tasted **sweet** because of its divine origin.

us as God here did with him. As we look on life from without, as the destiny in store for us, how forbidding it seems! But once we have accepted it as our God-given vocation and sphere of service it becomes a source of unanticipated satisfactions. We are like the swimmer who finds the water threatening and hostile so long as he looks at it from the shore; he has only to plunge boldly in and it is a friendly element which bears him up.

The metaphor of eating is still in use among us, as in the words of the collect, "read, mark, learn, and inwardly digest." [7] It stands here for

[7] Book of Common Prayer, Second Sunday in Advent.

the process of assimilation by which we transmute an event into an experience and build the experience into our very selves. What was at first terrifying to Ezekiel becomes **sweet as honey** when he has accepted it thus. He has learned to make God's will his own, and the task from which he shrank becomes a vocation to be accepted with gratitude. So in Gethsemane Jesus anticipated the Cross and, by learning to endure it, "despising the shame" (Heb. 12:2), he turned his harsh trial into joy. We grow by this assimilation of the enforced and unwanted elements in our experience, so that they minister finally to the soul's health; and we are

4 ¶ And he said unto me, Son of man, go, get thee unto the house of Israel, and speak with my words unto them.

5 For thou *art* not sent to a people of a strange speech and of a hard language, *but* to the house of Israel;

6 Not to many people of a strange speech and of a hard language, whose words thou canst not understand. Surely, had I sent thee to them, they would have hearkened unto thee.

7 But the house of Israel will not hearken unto thee; for they will not hearken unto me: for all the house of Israel *are* impudent and hard-hearted.

4 And he said to me, "Son of man, go, get you to the house of Israel, and speak with my words to them. 5 For you are not sent to a people of foreign speech and a hard language, but to the house of Israel — 6 not to many peoples of foreign speech and a hard language, whose words you cannot understand. Surely, if I sent you to such, they would listen to you. 7 But the house of Israel will not listen to you; for they are not willing to listen to me; because all the house of Israel are of a hard forehead and

---

c) SECOND COMMISSION (3:4-9)

4. Does **go, get you to the house of Israel** mean that the prophet is to go to Jerusalem?

6. The picture of the house of Israel more stubborn than even foreigners is consonant with ch. 23, where Jerusalem is said to be more sinful than Samaria (cf. also 5:6; 16:48-52). Vs. 6b does not mean that the pagans would be converted to the worship of Yahweh as the sole Deity. Yahweh's prophets might be heard and even sent for by pagans (cf. Num. 22:1–24:25; II Kings 8:7-8; see also II Kings 5:1-6 and the oracles against the foreign nations in the early prophets). **Peoples of foreign speech and a hard language:** See Isa. 33:19; Jer. 5:15. **Surely, if** is אִם לֹא, "if not," but possibly rendered as above (see E. F. Kautzsch, *Gesenius' Hebrew Grammar*, tr. A. E. Cowley [2nd English ed.; Oxford: Clarendon Press, 1910], sec. 149*b*); the LXX, O.L., and Vulg. omit לֹא, **not.** Isaiah at his call reckoned the people so bad that they did not deserve an opportunity to repent (Isa. 6:10; cf. Jer. 7:16). The prophetic function was not so much to teach the way of salvation as to announce the judgment of Yahweh.

7. All the house of Israel are of a hard forehead and of a stubborn heart: A typical prophetic estimate. Even Second Isaiah was to describe the Hebrews as an obstinate people whose neck was an iron band and whose forehead was bronze (Isa. 48:4).

---

capable of this growth as we receive our task from God's hands, leaving him to decide how we can best serve his gracious purpose.

3:5-6. *The Rebuke of the Stranger.*—What makes the prophet's mission so hard is that he is sent to his own people, who might be expected to understand him since their whole history has prepared them to receive him. Had he been sent to one of the neighboring peoples with a language unintelligible to him, he would have had just cause for complaint. But no! They would have been more ready to hear him than Israel is ever likely to be.

There is a thought here which runs through the Bible and reaches its consummation in the sad words, "He came to his own home, and his own people received him not" (John 1:11). In the O.T. we have the story of Jonah, with its contrast between the disobedient prophet and the heathen sailors who turn to the Lord once

his will is clear. In the N.T. we have the story of the ten lepers, of whom only the Samaritan returned to give thanks (Luke 17:11-19). There is also the lament of Jesus over the cities which had not received him, when the heathen of Tyre and Sidon would surely have done so (Luke 10:13-15). The book of Acts closes with the ominous words "This salvation of God has been sent to the Gentiles; they will listen" (28:28). Jesus had already said as much when he found in the Roman centurion a faith which was missing "in Israel" (Matt. 8:10).

What a rebuke for us Christians there is in these words! At times it seems that those who are outside the church are more sensitive to certain aspects of the gospel than those who are within it. One may find among humanists a passion for justice which puts us to shame, a kindliness and fellowship on the part of the man in the street which is lacking in the man

8 Behold, I have made thy face strong against their faces, and thy forehead strong against their foreheads.

9 As an adamant harder than flint have I made thy forehead: fear them not, neither be dismayed at their looks, though they *be* a rebellious house.

10 Moreover he said unto me, Son of man, all my words that I shall speak unto thee receive in thine heart, and hear with thine ears.

11 And go, get thee to them of the captivity, unto the children of thy people, and speak unto them, and tell them, Thus saith the Lord God; whether they will hear, or whether they will forbear.

12 Then the spirit took me up, and I heard behind me a voice of a great rushing, *saying,* Blessed *be* the glory of the Lord from his place.

of a stubborn heart. 8 Behold, I have made your face hard against their faces, and your forehead hard against their foreheads. 9 Like adamant harder than flint have I made your forehead; fear them not, nor be dismayed at their looks, for they are a rebellious house." 10 Moreover he said to me, "Son of man, all my words that I shall speak to you receive in your heart, and hear with your ears. 11 And go, get you to the exiles, to your people, and say to them, 'Thus says the Lord God'; whether they hear or refuse to hear."

12 Then the Spirit lifted me up, and as the glory of the Lord arose[k] from its place, I heard behind me the sound of a great

[k] Cn: Heb *blessed be the glory of the* Lord

8-9. The prophet must be more stubborn for the truth than the people for evil (cf. Jer. 1:18). These verses express effectively the opposition between the true prophet and his people, illustrated dramatically in Amos 7:10-17; Jer. 20:7-18; 26:1-24.

d) Third Commission (3:10-11)

10-11. This probably is from the editor (see Intro., p. 52). **Your people:** A typical expression of the editor (see xxiv on p. 50; cf. Dan. 12:1). Ezekiel is ordered to go to the exiles and utter his prophecies to them (cf. vs. 27; 2:4-5).

e) Sequel (3:12-15)

Matthews (see also Herntrich) considers all of vss. 10-16a secondary, but Ezekiel may well have gone to **Tel-abib** after his commission, even though the present arrangement of the text makes it appear that in vss. 12-15 Ezekiel is obeying the command in vss. 10-11 to go to the exiles. If Ezekiel went to Jerusalem, he seems not to have gone until sometime in the year following his call and commission.

12. **The Spirit lifted me up** means that the prophet felt divine impulsion to go to **Tel-abib** (cf. 2:2; Acts 8:39). The difference between **Blessed be** and **as . . . arose** is just one letter (ברום instead of ברוך). If the M.T. is correct, we should compare the song of the seraphim in Isa. 6:3.

in the pew. If Christ were to come again today, where would he find a readier welcome, in the church or outside it?

8-9. *A Man of Adamant.*—We are naturally attracted by strength, and one of the favorite devices of evil is to suggest that the service of God is only for the weak. In our own time evil has created hard, ruthless individuals whose anti-Christian morality has been accepted by whole peoples. But there is no strength comparable with what is required of the hero of the spirit, the man called to set his conscience in opposition to the standards of his day. He must possess an indomitable courage and iron resolu-

tion. Yes, but more is needed than physical courage. A man might go gladly to the stake and yet shrink from the ridicule of his fellows. He who serves God must be prepared, should the occasion require it, to stand *contra mundum.* What makes the prophet's courage in some instances more heroic is that it is not in accordance with his temperament. There is a clear reminiscence in the words of Jeremiah at the time of his call (Jer. 1:6). A timid, sensitive youth whose nature craved for sympathy, he shrank from his vocation; yet God made him "a fortified city, an iron pillar, and bronze walls, against the whole land" (Jer. 1:18). He

13 *I heard* also the noise of the wings of the living creatures that touched one another, and the noise of the wheels over against them, and a noise of a great rushing.

14 So the spirit lifted me up, and took me away, and I went in bitterness, in the heat of my spirit; but the hand of the LORD was strong upon me.

15 ¶ Then I came to them of the captivity at Tel-abib, that dwelt by the river of Chebar, and I sat where they sat, and remained there astonished among them seven days.

earthquake; 13 it was the sound of the wings of the living creatures as they touched one another, and the sound of the wheels beside them, that sounded like a great earthquake. 14 The Spirit lifted me up and took me away, and I went in bitterness in the heat of my spirit, the hand of the LORD being strong upon me; 15 and I came to the exiles at Tel-a'bib, who dwelt by the river Chebar.[l] And I sat there overwhelmed among them seven days.

[l] Heb *Chebar, and to where they dwelt.* Another reading is *Chebar, and I sat where they sat*

13. **Touched:** Lit., "kissed." **That sounded like:** The M.T. has "and a sound of" (cf. KJV), but "and" is due to dittography. The RSV translates רעש, **earthquake**, as in Amos 1:1; Zech. 14:5, although the KJV's **rushing** is not impossible (cf. Nah. 3:2).

14. **In bitterness** (מר) has been taken as an interpretative gloss on **in the heat of my spirit**, and is omitted by the LXXᴮ and the Syriac, but it may express the prophet's reaction to the commission in vss. 4b-9, and it recalls Jeremiah's agony (20:7-10).

15. The form of the name **Tel-abib** is to be compared with Tel-melah and Tel-harsha in Babylonia, where exiles also lived (Ezra 2:59; Neh. 7:61; cf. Tel-assar in II Kings 19:12; Isa. 37:12). The Babylonian *til abûbi* refers to the low mounds containing buried cities which were believed to antedate the flood, *abûbu* meaning "deluge." On such a mound the Jews had built their town (see Albright, "Seal of Eliakim and the Latest Preëxilic History of Judah," p. 100). The Hebraized form, **Tel-abib**, would mean "Hill of young ears [of barley]." The pre-exilic month of Abib was the later first month or month of Nisan (Exod. 13:4; 34:18; Deut. 16:1; etc.). Tel-abib was probably Ezekiel's home in Babylonia, for he had a house there (vs. 24). Vs. 15b has been expanded by a gloss (see RSV mg.), e.g., ואשר המה יושבום שם, "and to where they dwelt" (or, with *Qerê*, "and I sat [ואשב] where they dwelt"), which is omitted by two Hebrew MSS and the Syriac. It may be significant that **seven days** is a period of mourning in Gen. 50:10 (cf. Job 2:13). Ezekiel was **overwhelmed** or appalled (משמים), perhaps both by the vision of the glory of Yahweh and by the nature of his commission.

who is inwardly reinforced by God can stand against the world even though he has had first of all to stand against himself.

14-15. *Vision and Sympathy.*—The vision passes, but its power remains with the seer. The ecstasy of the great hour dies away only slowly in turbulent emotion and inexplicable unrest. He carries in his heart the secret of his call, but he does not yet know how his work is to be done. One thing is clear, however: his place is with the exiles by the **river Chebar.** We may suppose that the hand of the editor has been at work here, and that he has reintroduced the divine chariot at vss. 12-13 to enable him to locate the ministry of Ezekiel in Babylon at vs. 15; vs. 14 will then belong to the original narrative of the call as it lay before the editor. However, we can for our purpose adopt the standpoint of the editor and see how he introduces Ezekiel to the exiles. He throws in his lot with them without reserve; henceforth their fortunes are to be his own.

There was enough in the prophet's circumstances to produce a conflict of feelings in his mind—the sin of Israel, who were yet his own people; the task before which he stood, and his close and awful communications with heaven. The simple feeling of bitterness and indignation which filled his mind when he newly left the presence of God became broken into a tumult of feelings when he saw the face of men. Zeal for God becomes tempered and humanized in actual service.[8]

Seven days passed before Ezekiel attained to a clear understanding of what he was meant to do. But clarity would not have come to him had he remained apart from his fellows. It was

[8] A. B. Davidson, *The Book of the Prophet Ezekiel* (Cambridge: Cambridge University Press, 1893, "Cambridge Bible"), p. 22.

16 And it came to pass at the end of seven days, that the word of the LORD came unto me, saying,

17 Son of man, I have made thee a watchman unto the house of Israel: therefore hear the word at my mouth, and give them warning from me.

18 When I say unto the wicked, Thou shalt surely die; and thou givest him not warning, nor speakest to warn the wicked from his wicked way, to save his life; the same wicked *man* shall die in his iniquity; but his blood will I require at thine hand.

19 Yet if thou warn the wicked, and he turn not from his wickedness, nor from his wicked way, he shall die in his iniquity; but thou hast delivered thy soul.

20 Again, When a righteous *man* doth turn from his righteousness, and commit iniquity, and I lay a stumblingblock before him, he shall die: because thou hast not given him warning, he shall die in his sin, and his righteousness which he hath done shall not be remembered; but his blood will I require at thine hand.

16 And at the end of seven days, the word of the LORD came to me: 17 "Son of man, I have made you a watchman for the house of Israel; whenever you hear a word from my mouth, you shall give them warning from me. 18 If I say to the wicked, 'You shall surely die,' and you give him no warning, nor speak to warn the wicked from his wicked way, in order to save his life, that wicked man shall die in his iniquity; but his blood I will require at your hand. 19 But if you warn the wicked, and he does not turn from his wickedness, or from his wicked way, he shall die in his iniquity; but you will have saved your life. 20 Again, if a righteous man turns from his righteousness and commits iniquity, and I lay a stumbling block before him, he shall die; because you have not warned him, he shall die for his sin, and his righteous deeds which he has done shall not be remembered; but his

---

f) FOURTH COMMISSION (3:16-21)

The editor's doctrine of responsibility (see 14:12-23; 18:1-32; 33:1-20; see Intro., pp. 48-49) is discussed with reference to the prophet (cf. the statement of the nature of prophecy in Deut. 18:18-22).

16. Perhaps originally **And at the end of seven days** introduced the account of Ezekiel's experience in 3:22-24.

17. For the prophet as **watchman** see 33:2-6; Jer. 6:17; Hos. 9:8; Hab. 2:1; cf. Isa. 56:10. The watchman was a most responsible figure in the security situation in Palestine (see I Sam. 14:16; II Sam. 18:24-27; II Kings 9:17-20; Isa. 21:6).

20. A man's past good deeds cannot counteract his present iniquity (see 18:24-26).

---

as he bound himself to them that the will of God for him became evident. So our doubts and uncertainties are best resolved as we enter in sympathy into the everyday life of our fellows, seeking there the heavenly guidance we so much need. The law of true life is that what we have seen in vision must be expressed in service. So Jesus turned aside from his retreat with the disciples after their return from the mission to Galilee to answer the call of the five thousand and meet their needs (Mark 6:30-44). So from the mount of transfiguration he came down into the valley to heal the epileptic lad (Mark 9: 14-29).

17-21. *My Brother's Keeper.*—The first thing that is made clear to the prophet is that he is in a position of responsibility. The sentry in the front line knows that the safety of his unit,

perhaps even of an army, turns on his individual vigilance. So Ezekiel feels.

Is not every one of us a sentry? There are moments when the future of mankind turns upon the faithfulness of some unknown and insignificant individual. So Byzantium fell in 1453 and the cross was displaced by the crescent over Eastern Europe because someone in the city had forgotten to close a door in the inner wall. "Never will mankind know all the disaster which befell it in that fateful hour when Kerkaporta was left open."[9]

On the other hand, fidelity may win untold blessings for generations to come. Monica's prayers for her scapegrace son were but the expression of such a love as any true mother

[9] Stefan Zweig, *The Tide of Fortune* (tr. Eden and Cedar Paul: New York: Viking Press, 1940), p. 59.

21 Nevertheless, if thou warn the righteous *man,* that the righteous sin not, and
he doth not sin, he shall surely live, because
he is warned; also thou hast delivered thy
soul.

22 ¶ And the hand of the LORD was there
upon me; and he said unto me, Arise, go
forth into the plain, and I will there talk
with thee.

23 Then I arose, and went forth into the
plain: and, behold, the glory of the LORD
stood there, as the glory which I saw by the
river of Chebar: and I fell on my face.

24 Then the spirit entered into me, and
set me upon my feet, and spake with me,

blood I will require at your hand. 21 Nevertheless if you warn the righteous man not
to sin, and he does not sin, he shall surely
live, because he took warning; and you will
have saved your life."

22 And the hand of the LORD was there
upon me; and he said to me, "Arise, go
forth into the plain,*m* and there I will speak
with you." 23 So I arose and went forth into
the plain;*m* and, lo, the glory of the LORD
stood there, like the glory which I had seen
by the river Chebar; and I fell on my face.
24 But the Spirit entered into me, and set

m Or *valley*

21. The M.T. is difficult, having the pronominal suffix "him" after **warn,** and the
second **the righteous** is in an awkward position. The text may originally have read
"Nevertheless, if you warn the righteous not to sin, and he sin not, the righteous will
surely live" (with LXX).

g) FIFTH COMMISSION (3:22-27)

This is a confusing passage, but the situation is in part clarified by the recognition
that the preceding section belongs to the editor. Otherwise we would have Yahweh
speaking at length to Ezekiel in his house, and then ordering him to go out of the
house to receive an oracle which ordered him to go back into the house and be dumb
for a period of time! Hölscher salvages only vs. 24*b*. Vss. 25-27, the fifth commission of
Ezekiel, seem to belong to the editor. Vs. 25 anticipates the editor's exile symbolism in
4:4-8 (see Exeg.). With vs. 27 cf. 2:4*b*-5*a*; 3:11. The dumbness of Ezekiel appears again
in 24:25-27; 33:21-22, and possibly 29:21. To be consistent with 3:17-21, the dumbness
here must be interpreted symbolically as the period when Ezekiel could not be a
reprover, e.g., a preacher of repentance, but could only utter doom. Comparison with
24:25-27 and 29:21 suggests it is the editor's viewpoint that this period lasted until after
the destruction of Jerusalem in 586. By contrast, in 33:21-22 the dumbness may be
something which comes the night before. We cannot be certain what oracle was given
to Ezekiel on the plain. The transference of this allusion to the dumbness of Ezekiel
to a period after or shortly before his return to Babylon (see Bertholet, Pfeiffer) removes
the problem of a period of dumbness lasting from 592-585, but it is a counsel of
desperation.

22. **The plain** (הבקעה) is apparently the same place as that in the vision of dry
bones (37:1). The same term is used in Gen. 11:2 to refer to the territory of the lower
Tigris-Euphrates area.

would feel; but through the conversion of
Augustine, and what came of it, they have to
be reckoned among the forces which have made
our civilization. She kept watch for the welfare
of her home, but did not know that at the same
time she was keeping watch for generations to
come. The significance of the insignificant is
something which our mass society with its over-
organization needs to learn.

24-27. *The Silence of God.*—The interpretation, and even the translation, of this passage
are attended with difficulty (see Exeg.). Here we

shall be concerned only with the silence of the
prophet as an illustration of the silence of God.
The prophet's voice is no more to be heard
in rebuke, for his hearers **are a rebellious house**
and not disposed to listen. There is an economy
in God's dealing with us; why should he send
his warning to those who have no intention of
heeding it? Since men will not hear him when
he speaks to them, he withdraws into silence.
So Amos can include among the disasters which
are to befall Israel, "a famine . . . of hearing
the words of the LORD" (Amos 8:11). So Jesus

and said unto me, Go, shut thyself within thine house.

25 But thou, O son of man, behold, they shall put bands upon thee, and shall bind thee with them, and thou shalt not go out among them:

26 And I will make thy tongue cleave to the roof of thy mouth, that thou shalt be dumb, and shalt not be to them a reprover: for they *are* a rebellious house.

27 But when I speak with thee, I will open thy mouth, and thou shalt say unto them, Thus saith the Lord GOD; He that heareth, let him hear; and he that forbeareth, let him forbear: for they *are* a rebellious house.

4 Thou also, son of man, take thee a tile, and lay it before thee, and portray upon it the city, *even* Jerusalem:

me upon my feet; and he spoke with me and said to me, "Go, shut yourself within your house. 25 And you, O son of man, behold, cords will be placed upon you, and you shall be bound with them, so that you cannot go out among the people; 26 and I will make your tongue cleave to the roof of your mouth, so that you shall be dumb and unable to reprove them; for they are a rebellious house. 27 But when I speak with you, I will open your mouth, and you shall say to them, 'Thus says the Lord GOD'; he that will hear, let him hear; and he that will refuse to hear, let him refuse; for they are a rebellious house.

4 "And you, O son of man, take a brick and lay it before you, and portray upon

---

25. **They shall put** and [they] **shall bind** (KJV) are both impersonal, and should be translated as passives with the RSV. The first can be pointed as a passive.

B. THE FATE OF JERUSALEM AND THE EXILE (4:1–5:17)

These two chapters belong together. They contain five dramatic actions, three having to do with the fate of Jerusalem, and two with the Exile. Ezekiel is told to draw on a brick a picture of Jerusalem under siege, and to set his face against it (4:1-3), to eat rationed food and water (4:9*a*, 10-11, 16-17), and to shave his hair with a sword and dispose of the hair in ways indicative of the fates of the people at the destruction of the city (5:1-17). He is instructed to lie bound for three hundred and ninety days on his left side to symbolize the years of the punishment of Israel, and for forty days on his right side to symbolize the years of the punishment of Judah (4:4-8); he is ordered to eat food cooked in an unclean manner, even as the people of Israel will eat their food unclean among the nations (4:12-15).

As some commentators have noted (cf. Hölscher, Herntrich, Messel), the symbols of the Exile are a later addition. Others (cf. Herrmann, Matthews, Cooke, Pfeiffer) credit them to Ezekiel, although to the later period and not originally associated with the symbols of the siege. They probably belong to the editor. Howie follows H. W. Hines ("The Prophet as Mystic," *American Journal of Semitic Languages and Literature*, XL [1923-24], 56, 71) in explaining 3:22–5:17 as a vision rather than a real activity, but Ezekiel is specifically instructed to carry out the dramatic action, and presumably he did, although the consummation of the action is not described. The forty-year exile in 4:6 may be compared with the forty-year exile for Egypt in 29:11. The return of both Israel and Judah is presumed, and this is the editor's theme in chs. 40–48 as well as in 37:15-28. The exile symbolism is out of context here, and 4:4-8 interrupts the sequence

---

kept silence before his judge; the time had gone by when explanation would serve any purpose, nor was Pilate disposed to listen (Matt. 27:13-14).

Does this mean that men are left without instruction? Not at all. God delegates to life itself the task of teaching those who will not receive his warnings; they must learn the lesson

of events, as these come upon them. So perhaps they will become receptive once more, and God will break his silence. With unmistakable fact to reinforce his utterance, he may convince at last. If only it is not then too late!

4:1-17. *The Cup of Suffering*.—The only way in which this chapter can be treated for expository purposes is by passing over the details,

2 And lay siege against it, and build a | it a city, even Jerusalem; 2 and put siege-
fort against it, and cast a mount against it; | works against it, and build a siege wall
set the camp also against it, and set *batter-* | against it, and cast up a mound against it;
ing rams against it round about. | set camps also against it, and plant batter-

---

from vss. 3 to vs. 9*a*, while vss. 12-15 separate the dramatic action in vss. 9*a*, 10-11 from
the interpretation in vss. 16-17. In contrast with the other dramatic actions, that in vss.
4-8 would be physically impossible to perform, and the addition of these verses reduces
to absurdity the dramatic action of rationing, which Ezekiel could hardly have performed
while lying tightly bound. The secondary character of the exile symbolism is also
shown by the editor's awkward attempt in vs. 7 to link his exile symbolism with the
siege symbolism, and in vs. 9*b* with the rationing symbolism. One of the many suggested
solutions is that vss. 4-8 originally concerned the length of the siege but was later
changed to refer to the duration of the Exile (Herntrich; cf. also Herrmann).

Jeremiah also used dramatic actions to illustrate his prophecies (13:1-11; 18:1-12;
19:1-13; 27:1-15; 32:1-15; 35:1-19; etc.; see also Isa. 8:1-4; 20:1-6). Earlier examples may
be seen in the reign of Solomon, when Ahijah tore his garment into twelve pieces
(I Kings 11:29-39), or in the reign of Ahab, when Zedekiah made himself horns of iron
(I Kings 22:11). Some may have felt that there was a power within the dramatic action
itself which helped to bring to pass the prediction involved in the oracle; cf. the Middle
Egyptian execration texts written on vessels which were then broken. For Isaiah, Jeremiah,
and Ezekiel the dramatic action was illustrative, not magical. As Ezekiel did, so would
the inhabitants of Jerusalem do, not because Ezekiel did it, but because it was the
oracle of Yahweh, the word of God, which was powerful because of him who uttered it.

1. Symbol of the Siege (4:1-3)

It would have been easy to incise on the relatively large sun-dried bricks used in
city or house walls such a picture as that described here. Pictures of Palestinian cities
under siege are known from archaeological sources. One of the most notable is the
relief of Sennacherib's army besieging the Judean city of Lachish in a campaign in the
reign of Hezekiah (see II Kings 18). It was a sculpture on the walls of the palace of
Sennacherib at Nineveh, and shows the Assyrians climbing earthen embankments or
ramparts covered with stone flagging, from which they operate their battering rams
from wheeled towers (see Ira M. Price, *The Monuments and the Old Testament* [new
ed.; Philadelphia: Judson Press, 1925], facing p. 312). In his annals Sennacherib tells
how he attacked the cities of Judah with battering rams, brought near the walls on
earth ramps, and by using mines, breaches, and sapper work (see J. B. Pritchard, ed.,
Ancient Near Eastern Texts Relating to the Old Testament [Princeton: Princeton
University Press, 1950], p. 288).

4:1. Jerusalem is syntactically awkward, and possibly an explanatory gloss.

---

often bizarre if not indeed unintelligible, and
taking it as a whole. According to the view here
set forth, we may assume that the events described, in so far as they were history, took
place during the siege of Jerusalem which
ended in 597 with overthrow and exile. The
prophet is commissioned to portray the certain
doom of the capital before the eyes of its in-
fatuated people, and to represent in his own
person now the besiegers, **thou shalt lay siege
against it** (vs. 3), and now again the besieged,
**so shalt thou bear the iniquity of the house of
Israel** (vs. 5). What he has to do is intensely
distasteful (vss. 12-15) and is not calculated to

enhance his popularity with his countrymen.
We can imagine what they said. It was sheer
madness. It was open propaganda on behalf of
the enemy, designed to produce dismay among
the civil population. No doubt Ezekiel incurred
mockery and derision. Yet, as the doom of the
city drew near, there must have been those who
remembered too late the warning he had given
and reflected that **a prophet** had been **among
them** (2:5).

For the interpretation of the various actions
described here see the Exeg. What is of importance for us is to look beyond the outward acts
to what was happening in the prophet's soul.

3 Moreover take thou unto thee an iron pan, and set it *for* a wall of iron between thee and the city: and set thy face against it, and it shall be besieged, and thou shalt lay siege against it. This *shall be* a sign to the house of Israel.

4 Lie thou also upon thy left side, and lay the iniquity of the house of Israel upon it: *according* to the number of the days that thou shalt lie upon it thou shalt bear their iniquity.

5 For I have laid upon thee the years of their iniquity, according to the number of the days, three hundred and ninety days: so shalt thou bear the iniquity of the house of Israel.

6 And when thou hast accomplished them, lie again on thy right side, and thou shalt bear the iniquity of the house of Judah forty days: I have appointed thee each day for a year.

ing rams against it round about. 3 And take an iron plate, and place it as an iron wall between you and the city; and set your face toward it, and let it be in a state of siege, and press the siege against it. This is a sign for the house of Israel.

4 "Then lie upon your left side, and I will lay the punishment of the house of Israel upon you;[n] for the number of the days that you lie upon it, you shall bear their punishment. 5 For I assign to you a number of days, three hundred and ninety days, equal to the number of the years of their punishment; so long shall you bear the punishment of the house of Israel. 6 And when you have completed these, you shall lie down a second time, but on your right side, and bear the punishment of the house of Judah; forty days I assign you, a day

[n] Cn: Heb *you shall lay . . . upon it*

3. The **iron plate** or griddle was a household utensil used in baking. The prophet could make ordinary things speak (cf. Amos' basket of summer fruit or Jeremiah's almond rod). In the P legislation the cereal offering is baked on a griddle or plate (Lev. 2:5; 7:9; etc.). Ezekiel is here in the position of Yahweh, for it is Yahweh who has decreed the siege. The **iron plate** represents the wall which Yahweh has placed between himself and the city, or else Yahweh's fortifications set up against the city, comparable to those of the enemy. The picture recalls Jer. 21:5: "I myself will fight against you with outstretched hand and strong arm, in anger, and in fury, and in great wrath."

2. SYMBOL OF THE DURATION OF THE EXILE (4:4-8)

4-8. The forty years of the exile of Judah is in round numbers, and probably refers to the period from 596 to the return in 538. It is in contrast with the seventy-year exile in Jer. 25:11-12; 29:10 (cf. Zech. 7:5). To what the three-hundred-ninety-year exile of Israel refers is unclear. Three hundred and ninety years before 538 would be roughly the time of the schism, but this makes little sense. The regnal years of the Judean kings from Rehoboam through Zedekiah, as given in I and II Kings, total three hundred and ninety-three years, and the sect which produced the so-called "Damascus Fragments" interpreted the three hundred and ninety years to refer to this period, perhaps subtracting from three hundred and ninety-three the three years of II Chron. 11:16-17 (see I. Rabinowitz, "A Reconsideration of 'Damascus' and '390 Years' in the 'Damascus' ('Zadokite') Fragments," *Journal of Biblical Literature*, LXXIII [1954], 11-35). The LXX reads "one hundred and ninety years," which might suggest a beginning point at the time of the

He was called upon to anticipate in his own person the impending fate of his people. While they were still confident and secure, he was to drink the bitter cup which was being prepared for them by their own political ineptitude. He comes before us therefore as one elected to suffering. He does not merely see what is to happen; he also feels it. He lives through in

advance what is to befall his people. We must think of him as in his Gethsemane, oppressed and burdened by something of which he alone is aware. Thus he is one of a succession of men and women upon whom the sorrow of their time has been laid by God.

Kierkegaard felt himself to be such. If men's eyes are ever to be opened, "first a poet's heart

7 Therefore thou shalt set thy face toward the siege of Jerusalem, and thine arm *shall be* uncovered, and thou shalt prophesy against it.

8 And, behold, I will lay bands upon thee, and thou shalt not turn thee from one side to another, till thou hast ended the days of thy siege.

9 ¶ Take thou also unto thee wheat, and barley, and beans, and lentils, and millet, and fitches, and put them in one vessel, and make thee bread thereof, *according* to the number of the days that thou shalt lie upon thy side; three hundred and ninety days shalt thou eat thereof.

10 And thy meat which thou shalt eat *shall be* by weight, twenty shekels a day: from time to time shalt thou eat it.

11 Thou shalt drink also water by measure, the sixth part of a hin: from time to time shalt thou drink.

for each year. 7 And you shall set your face toward the siege of Jerusalem, with your arm bared; and you shall prophesy against the city. 8 And, behold, I will put cords upon you, so that you cannot turn from one side to the other, till you have completed the days of your siege.

9 "And you, take wheat and barley, beans and lentils, millet and spelt, and put them into a single vessel, and make bread of them. During the number of days that you lie upon your side, three hundred and ninety days, you shall eat it. 10 And the food which you eat shall be by weight, twenty shekels a day; once a day you shall eat it. 11 And water you shall drink by measure, the sixth part

---

exile of Israelites by Tiglath-pileser III after the Syro-Ephraimite War of 734 (II Kings 15:29). However, if this belongs to the editor, he surely knows that Israel did not return in 538. Does he intend the **forty** years to refer to the period ending in 538, when part of Judah returned, and the **three hundred and ninety** or one hundred and ninety years to refer to a period ending considerably after this, when Israel would return at the time of the final great return of Judah? It may be that the original editor's text gave no number of days in vs. 5, and that "three hundred and ninety" is a later addition. Or it may have been three hundred and fifty days, for vs. 9 suggests that three hundred and ninety is the total number of days for lying on both sides. The natural starting point for the exile of Israel would be the fall of Samaria in 721. All is confusion. Forty years is one generation, and it has been suggested that this corresponds to the theory that sons will not expiate the sins of the fathers. Cf. the forty years in the wilderness of wandering (Num. 14:34-35).

In Hebrew idiom the **left** is the north and the **right** is the south, e.g., as one faces east. Israel is to the north and Judah to the south. The slight emendation of the RSV in vs. 4 is עליך . . . ושמתי for עליו . . . ושמת. This passage would be taken as a prophecy of hope by the postexilic Jews: they expected to return soon and to be united with Israel under the messianic king.

3. SYMBOL OF RATIONING RESTRICTIONS (4:9-11)

9-11. The food and water supply inside a besieged walled city would be severely restricted (cf. II Kings 7:1, 4; Jer. 37:21). During the siege of Jerusalem the inhabitants were forced to eat their own children (Lam. 2:20). The odd mixture of grains in one

---

must break," [1] and he was to be that poet. God chooses someone to discern in advance whither his age is moving and to experience its future catastrophe as his present grief. So Savonarola agonized over what was to come upon Italy for

[1] Alexander Dru, ed., *The Journals of Søren Kierkegaard* (New York: Oxford University Press, 1938), p. 397.

the corruption of her leaders and the fickleness of her people. John Woolman was another of these sensitive souls. Because he felt the suffering of the slave and the exploitation of the worker as though they had happened to him, he was able to be a pioneer in their deliverance.

Can we interpret the Cross in the light of such heroisms? Certainly there are passages in

12 And thou shalt eat it *as* barley cakes, and thou shalt bake it with dung that cometh out of man, in their sight.

13 And the Lord said, Even thus shall the children of Israel eat their defiled bread among the Gentiles, whither I will drive them.

14 Then said I, Ah Lord God! behold, my soul hath not been polluted: for from my youth up even till now have I not eaten of that which dieth of itself, or is torn in pieces; neither came there abominable flesh into my mouth.

15 Then he said unto me, Lo, I have given thee cow's dung for man's dung, and thou shalt prepare thy bread therewith.

16 Moreover he said unto me, Son of man, behold, I will break the staff of bread in Jerusalem: and they shall eat bread by weight, and with care; and they shall drink water by measure, and with astonishment:

17 That they may want bread and water, and be astonished one with another, and consume away for their iniquity.

of a hin; once a day you shall drink. 12 And you shall eat it as a barley cake, baking it in their sight on human dung." 13 And the Lord said, "Thus shall the people of Israel eat their bread unclean, among the nations whither I will drive them." 14 Then I said, "Ah Lord God! behold, I have never defiled myself; from my youth up till now I have never eaten what died of itself or was torn by beasts, nor has foul flesh come into my mouth." 15 Then he said to me, "See, I will let you have cow's dung instead of human dung, on which you may prepare your bread." 16 Moreover he said to me, "Son of man, behold, I will break the staff of bread in Jerusalem; they shall eat bread by weight and with fearfulness; and they shall drink water by measure and in dismay. 17 I will do this that they may lack bread and water, and look at one another in dismay, and waste away under their punishment.

batch of bread suggests the extent of the scarcity and recalls the oatmeal bread of World War I. Shekel weights are known from the excavations, and **twenty shekels** would be about eight ounces, each shekel weighing about 11:4 grams (see W. F. Albright, "The Excavation of Tell Beit Mirsim: III. The Iron Age," *Annual of the American Schools of Oriental Research,* XXI-XXII [1941-43], 76). **The sixth part of a hin** would be about one quart, the hin being estimated to be approximately 6.4 quarts.

4. Symbol of Unclean Food (4:12-15)

12-15. This passage interrupts the description of the symbolic act of rationing in vss. 9-11 and its interpretation in vss. 16-17. The uncleanliness of **human dung** appears in the legislation in Deut. 23:12-14. Hosea predicted Israel would eat unclean food in Assyria (9:3); cf. also the story of the youths refusing the king's delicacies in Dan. 1, and the modern concern in Judaism for kosher foods. In vs. 14 the reference is doubtless to the prohibition against eating meat with the blood in it, and possibly directly to the legislation in Lev. 17:11-16 (see also Deut. 12:16; Exod. 22:31; cf. Acts 10:11-16).

5. The Rationing Symbolism Interpreted (4:16-17)

16-17. For **staff of bread** see 5:16; 14:13; Ps. 105:16; cf. Isa. 3:1; cf. vs. 16 with 12:19. In time of siege the **water** supply in Jerusalem came largely from cisterns (cf. Jer. 2:13;

the Gospels which suggest that Jesus saw in advance and longed to avert the doom which his people were to bring upon themselves (Luke 13:6-9, 34-35; 19:41-44). Did he take into his own heart the desolation which he saw waiting for a world alienated from God? Was not the anguish of Gethsemane his anticipation of this world's suffering rather than of his own?

The mention of the Cross enables us to supply what is lacking in Ezekiel. He was commissioned

to **bear the iniquity of the house of Israel** (vs. 5) in the sense that its doom was symbolized by what he did and suffered. But he had no hope that any action of his might avert that doom. He was but to set it forth for all to see and then to wait until it descended. The scene is one of unrelieved gloom. Christ has brought us the assurance that sympathy and self-identification with men and women in the tragic issue of their sin may serve his redeeming purpose.

5 And thou, son of man, take thee a sharp knife, take thee a barber's razor, and cause *it* to pass upon thine head and upon thy beard: then take thee balances to weigh, and divide the *hair*.

5 "And you, O son of man, take a sharp sword; use it as a barber's razor and pass it over your head and your beard; then take balances for weighing, and divide the

38:6) and from the springs Gihon in the Kidron Valley and En-rogel below the juncture of the Kidron Valley and the Valley of Hinnom. Hezekiah's tunnel and pool had provided a way to bring the water from the spring Gihon inside the city (II Kings 20:20); cf. also the upper pool (Isa. 7:3; 36:2; II Kings 18:17).

6. Symbols of the Fate of Jerusalem (5:1-17)

In ch. 4 Ezekiel had pictured the duration and rigors of the siege; here in proper chronological order he represents the fate of the people of the city upon its destruction. The dramatic action is described in vss. 1-4; in vs. 12 is the expected interpretation of this dramatic action. The explanation given in vss. 5-17 is as a whole an interpretation of the dramatic actions in ch. 4, as well as the one in 5:1-4. Vss. 5-17 are so thoroughly in the editor's style that we cannot isolate what genuine material there might be here, with perhaps the exception of vs. 12. Some commentators (Hölscher, Herntrich, Irwin) find nothing original in vss. 3-17. Ezekiel's explanation of the dramatic action has been expanded and perhaps paraphrased. Only a few of the many typical expressions of the editor may be noted, and the parallels to them belong largely to the later literature. The plural of "land," e.g., ארצות, **countries**, vss. 5-6 (see xxxvii on p. 51) is found also six times in P, and in Jeremiah it belongs to the "biographer" (Jer. 16:15; 23:3, 8; 27:6; 28:8; 32:37; 40:11). **Walked in my statutes,** vss. 6-7 (see xxxviii on p. 51) occurs also in H, in the compiler of Kings, and in Jer. 44:10, 23. **Nations that are round about you,** vs. 7 (see xxxix on p. 51); so also Lev. 25:44. **Detestable things,** vs. 11 (see xli on p. 51). **I, the Lord, have spoken,** vss. 13, 15, 17 (see xxxvi on p. 51). **In the sight of the nations,** vs. 8 (see xlii on p. 51). **Behold, I . . . am against you,** vs. 8 (see xl on p. 51). **I will vent my fury upon them,** vs. 13 (see xliii on p. 51). **I will bring the sword upon you,** vs. 17 (see ii on p. 50). S. R. Driver (*An Introduction to the Literature of the Old Testament* [rev. ed.; New York: Charles Scribner's Sons, 1937], p. 147) has listed the striking literary parallels between the book of Ezekiel and Lev. 26, and seven of them appear in Ezek. 5.

a) The Symbolic Action (5:1-4)

5:1-4. Vss. 3-4 have sometimes been regarded as a gloss, since there would be no **hair** left after the three thirds had been disposed of (see Bertholet, Irwin, Matthews). They also modify the impression of complete destruction given in vss. 1-2, for some of the hair put in the prophet's **robe** obviously escapes. The emphasis in vss. 3-4 is not, however, on the few who escape so much as on the destruction (cf. Isa. 6:13). We cannot tell whether or not we have here the editor's modification of Ezekiel's description of the dramatic action in the light of the former's belief in the restoration (cf. 20:34-44; 36:1-15).

Ezekiel is very appropriately told to use a **sword.** The context makes the usual translation of חרב as "sword" correct here, rather than **knife**, even though the word appears in the plural in Josh. 5:2-3 in a reference to "flint knives" (חרבות צרים). Likewise **use it as a barber's razor,** sometimes considered a gloss, is more accurate than the KJV, and is in accord with the versions (Syriac, Theod., O.L.; cf. LXX). Ezekiel may be

---

He who feels in advance what is coming upon his fellows may so move their hearts that what he dreads for them will be averted by their penitence. No one knows when he will be called to such redemptive suffering, whether in the life of the community or in some intimate personal relationship. Every true parent has experienced something of this, and every true human being will count it a privilege to be called to it.

2 Thou shalt burn with fire a third part in the midst of the city, when the days of the siege are fulfilled: and thou shalt take a third part, *and* smite about it with a knife: and a third part thou shalt scatter in the wind; and I will draw out a sword after them.

3 Thou shalt also take thereof a few in number, and bind them in thy skirts.

4 Then take of them again, and cast them into the midst of the fire, and burn them in the fire; *for* thereof shall a fire come forth into all the house of Israel.

5 ¶ Thus saith the Lord GOD; This *is* Jerusalem: I have set it in the midst of the nations and countries *that are* round about her.

hair. 2 A third part you shall burn in the fire in the midst of the city, when the days of the siege are completed; and a third part you shall take and strike with the sword round about the city; and a third part you shall scatter to the wind, and I will unsheathe the sword after them. 3 And you shall take from these a small number, and bind them in the skirts of your robe. 4 And of these again you shall take some, and cast them into the fire, and burn them in the fire; from there a fire will come forth into all the house of Israel. 5 Thus says the Lord GOD: This is Jerusalem; I have set her in the center of the nations, with coun-

influenced here by the figure of speech in Isa. 7:20 (cf. II Sam. 10:4-5). Shaving the head was a sign of mourning and lamentation, and this adds to the import of the imagery (cf. Isa. 15:2; 22:12; Jer. 47:5; 48:37; Amos 8:10; Mic. 1:16; etc.). An excellent illustration of weights and balances comes from the excavations of Ugarit, where a complete set of weights was found beside the two trays of the balances (Claude F. A. Schaeffer, *The Cuneiform Texts of Ras Shamra-Ugarit* [London: British Academy, 1939], pp. 26-27, Pl. XX). **When the days of the siege are completed** is an obvious reference to ch. 4. Does a comparison with 4:8 imply that behind 4:4-8 lies a genuine oracle which referred originally to the duration of the siege? The last clause in vs. 2, **and I will unsheathe the sword after them,** is generally taken as a gloss from vs. 12, since it violates the picture by introducing an action of Yahweh within the description of the dramatic action. It may be due to the editor.

b) INTERPRETATION (5:5-17)

5. The center of the nations: In the Catholicon of the Church of the Holy Sepulchre at Jerusalem is a kind of cup holding a flattened ball which is said to be at the very

5:5. *The Center of the World.*—The geography with which the prophet works strikes us at first as incredibly naïve. For him **Jerusalem is the center** of the habitable earth, the rest of the nations being grouped around it. So the Chinese still speak of their own country as the Middle Kingdom, though they no longer imagine that outside it there are only a few barbarian peoples toward the edge of the world. So also the ancient Greeks did not doubt that the shrine of Apollo at Delphi was central. The proud claim was made for imperial Rome that all roads led to it; it was the center of a circle within whose circumference fell the whole of civilized mankind.

Ezekiel therefore was not alone in attaching so much importance to his little capital. The rabbis at a later date make the same claim for Jerusalem,[2] and in the Middle Ages it was taken

for granted, as, for example, by Dante.[3] Maps have been preserved which show Calvary as the center of the habitable earth.[4]

Is all this so much childishness, if not indeed mere arrogance? How preposterous that a tiny people like the Jews should dramatize themselves in this way, with the rest of mankind grouped around them! Is it not a Joseph's dream of measureless self-exaltation? We should look upon it rather as a piece of poetic symbolism. When an artist paints a group of people, he will normally place the more important figures in the center where they will command attention, while the rest can be assigned to less prominent positions. So in that picture-thinking which was characteristic of the Hebrews, what was decisive in significance was supposed to be

[2] G. A. Cooke, *A Critical and Historical Commentary on the Book of Ezekiel* (New York: Charles Scribner's Sons, 1937; "International Critical Commentary"), I, 58-59.

[3] *Inferno,* Canto XXXIV, l. 114.

[4] *Encyclopaedia Britannica,* 14th ed., XIV, 839-40.

6 And she hath changed my judgments into wickedness more than the nations, and my statutes more than the countries that *are* round about her: for they have refused my judgments and my statutes, they have not walked in them.

7 Therefore thus saith the Lord God; Because ye multiplied more than the nations that *are* round about you, *and* have not walked in my statutes, neither have kept my judgments, neither have done according to the judgments of the nations that *are* round about you;

8 Therefore thus saith the Lord God; Behold, I, even I, *am* against thee, and will execute judgments in the midst of thee in the sight of the nations.

tries round about her. **6** And she has wickedly rebelled against my ordinances[o] more than the nations, and against my statutes more than the countries round about her, by rejecting my ordinances and not walking in my statutes. **7** Therefore thus says the Lord God: Because you are more turbulent than the nations that are round about you, and have not walked in my statutes or kept my ordinances, but have acted[p] according to the ordinances of the nations that are round about you; **8** therefore thus says the Lord God: Behold, I, even I, am against you; and I will execute judgments in the midst of you in the sight of the nations.

[o] Or *changed my ordinances into wickedness*
[p] Another reading is *and have not acted*

---

center of the world. Jerusalem as the center of the world appears in pseudepigraphical and rabbinical literature and on medieval maps. In 38:12 the Jews in Palestine "dwell at the center [טבור] of the earth," which the LXX translates "the navel of the earth," τὸν ὀμφαλὸν τῆς γῆς. Delphi was reckoned the center of the earth: see the ὀμφαλός of Greece, the oracular center of the earth, ὀμφαλὸν γῆς θεσπιῳδόν (Euripides *Medea* 666),

---

also central in location. Jerusalem as the spiritual center of humanity was envisaged also as its geographical center. In the same way, Isaiah sees the hill on which the temple stands rising to a height above earth's loftiest mountains, because from it is to go forth direction to mankind the world over (Isa. 2:2-4).

Yet there is something wrong about this conception. We have no right to assume that to inner value there must correspond an appropriate degree of outward dignity, so that what merits our homage will necessarily be outstanding to our eyes. Jerusalem may be the spiritual center of our civilization; yet from one point of view it was only the hill-capital of an obscure people who passed as the spoil of war from one conqueror to another. We see in the Cross the pivot on which all history turns; yet at the time it was only a passing item of business in the life of a worried Roman official. We must not confuse outward appearance and inward reality; God works through men and women whom their contemporaries often hardly notice.

Other reflections suggest themselves. Unless the world is to be handed over to confusion, there must be a principle of order in it, a distinction between what is central and what peripheral. There is therefore at any period of stability a center of the world. Or rather, there are two such, a power center and a moral center. From the first, organization radiates; from the second, spiritual leadership. The two will not usually coincide. When the Romans

conquered Greece they recognized that Athens would still be supreme in culture, though they might police and govern the nations. Berlin could administer Germany, but she could never inspire it as Weimar did in the days of Goethe and Schiller. Rome herself had no such hold upon the conscience of mankind when she spoke in Caesar's name as when she did so in Christ's.

We may legitimately read the history of Israel as one of conflict between the ambition to become a power center and the call to be a moral center. For a brief period, indeed, the two did in a measure coincide, when David achieved the unity of the nation and surrounded it with subject peoples, while at the same time dedicating its life to the service of the Lord. But Second Isaiah saw that the hopes of Israel could be fulfilled worthily only in a very different sphere, and that the political leadership which David gave her was meant to be transmuted in the end into a spiritual mission to mankind (Isa. 55:3-5). Through the bitterness of defeat and exile Israel had to learn that she could not excel in both orders of greatness but must choose between them.

Nor is it only Israel which has to make such a decision. Repeatedly in the course of history a nation is forced to realize that never again will it be able to take the part it once played in international politics. More formidable rivals are in the field and its resources are too limited for it to compete any longer for a place among

9 And I will do in thee that which I have not done, and whereunto I will not do any more the like, because of all thine abominations.

10 Therefore the fathers shall eat the sons in the midst of thee, and the sons shall eat their fathers; and I will execute judgments in thee, and the whole remnant of thee will I scatter into all the winds.

11 Wherefore, *as* I live, saith the Lord GOD; Surely, because thou hast defiled my sanctuary with all thy detestable things, and with all thine abominations, therefore will I also diminish *thee;* neither shall mine eye spare, neither will I have any pity.

12 ¶ A third part of thee shall die with the pestilence, and with famine shall they be consumed in the midst of thee: and a third part shall fall by the sword round about thee; and I will scatter a third part

9 And because of all your abominations I will do with you what I have never yet done, and the like of which I will never do again. 10 Therefore fathers shall eat their sons in the midst of you, and sons shall eat their fathers; and I will execute judgments on you, and any of you who survive I will scatter to all the winds. 11 Wherefore, as I live, says the Lord GOD, surely, because you have defiled my sanctuary with all your detestable things and with all your abominations, therefore I will cut you down;*q* my eye will not spare, and I will have no pity. 12 A third part of you shall die of pestilence and be consumed with famine in the midst of you; a third part shall fall by the sword round about you; and a third part I will

q Another reading is *I will withdraw*

and the *umbilicus orbis terrarum* (Livy XXXVIII. 48. 2). "The center of the land" (Judg. 9:37) may be the name of a place so designated because it was locally thought to be the center of the earth (for discussion of this idea in the O.T. see W. H. Roscher, *Der Omphalosgedanke bei verschiedenen Völkern, besonders den Semiten* [Leipzig: Akademie d. Wissensch., 1918]). **This is Jerusalem** is a reference to 4:1, 2.

10. This may be a *post eventum* description of the horrors of the siege (cf. Deut. 28:53; Jer. 19:9; Lam. 4:10).

11. I will withdraw (RSV mg.) would perhaps be a reference to the departure of the glory of Yahweh, but such a use of the verb אגרע is not very probable (cf. Cornill); אגדע, **I will cut (you) down,** has Hebrew MSS support, also Symm., the Targ., and

the so-called great powers. At such a time it need not lose heart; surrendering power, it may consecrate itself to justice and humanity. Modern history provides us with notable instances: The rebirth of Denmark and its achievements in education and democracy dating from the loss of Schleswig-Holstein and the rise of Prussia on her frontier, is one example. We can set beside this the recovery of Turkey under Kemal Pasha, when she surrendered the Ottoman dream of empire under stress of defeat and contented herself with making a decent life possible for the highlanders of Anatolia. Who knows when our own people will be summoned to some such reinterpretation of the national mission?

It is by no means easy for a nation to abandon the position of a power center and accept that of a moral center. Often enough it must be driven thereto by sheer pressure of circumstances. Human nature being what it is, we require to be frustrated in the lower ambition before we are content with the realization of the higher. But also the call of God is needed.

Adversity in itself has no saving quality; it may indeed dishearten us and unfit us for further service: only as it is interpreted to us by the voice of God can we discern aright what we must do. No nation aspires to moral leadership; that is a greatness which is thrust upon it. It must be disciplined for it, perhaps even driven to it.

Finally, no nation can be the center of the world in this lofty sense unless it in turn has a center, groups and individuals whose loyalty is not given to it but to God. They constitute the prophetic witness which again and again reminds the nation of the divine intention for it; they rebuke it when faithless and encourage it when faithful. Shall we say that they are the church? Yes, if we remember here again that what is outwardly central may not be so inwardly, that the church as an institution may betray her mission as the nation does its, so that she too needs within her a spiritual center.

5-9. Privilege and Responsibility.—Because Jerusalem is in the center of the world, the eyes of God are upon her, as well as those of men.

into all the winds, and I will draw out a sword after them.

13 Thus shall mine anger be accomplished, and I will cause my fury to rest upon them, and I will be comforted: and they shall know that I the Lord have spoken *it* in my zeal, when I have accomplished my fury in them.

14 Moreover I will make thee waste, and a reproach among the nations that *are* round about thee, in the sight of all that pass by.

15 So it shall be a reproach and a taunt, an instruction and an astonishment unto the nations that *are* round about thee, when I shall execute judgments in thee in anger and in fury and in furious rebukes. I the Lord have spoken *it*.

16 When I shall send upon them the evil arrows of famine, which shall be for *their* destruction, *and* which I will send to destroy you: and I will increase the famine upon you, and will break your staff of bread:

17 So will I send upon you famine and evil beasts, and they shall bereave thee; and pestilence and blood shall pass through thee; and I will bring the sword upon thee. I the Lord have spoken *it*.

scatter to all the winds and will unsheathe the sword after them.

13 "Thus shall my anger spend itself, and I will vent my fury upon them and satisfy myself; and they shall know that I, the Lord, have spoken in my jealousy, when I spend my fury upon them. **14** Moreover I will make you a desolation and an object of reproach among the nations round about you and in the sight of all that pass by. **15** You shall be[r] a reproach and a taunt, a warning and a horror, to the nations round about you, when I execute judgments on you in anger and fury, and with furious chastisements — I, the Lord, have spoken — **16** when I loose against you[s] my deadly arrows of famine, arrows for destruction, which I will loose to destroy you, and when I bring more and more famine upon you, and break your staff of bread. **17** I will send famine and wild beasts against you, and they will rob you of your children; pestilence and blood shall pass through you; and I will bring the sword upon you. I, the Lord, have spoken."

[r] Gk Syr Vg Tg: Heb *And it shall be*
[s] Heb *them*

Vulg. The LXX, O.L., and Syriac apparently read אֶגְעַל, "I will loathe," i.e., "reject." The variants may be due to copyists' errors.

13. (Cf. 6:12-13.) For the exiles this contained an implicit promise; Yahweh's anger had been spent. **Satisfy myself:** E.g., get satisfaction or ease myself by taking vengeance. For the theme of Yahweh's **jealousy** see 16:38, 42; 23:25; 35:11; 36:5-6; 38:19; 39:25. Yahweh's jealousy causes him both to punish and to restore. The anthropopathy is striking, but characteristic of the Hebrew view of God. The verse also recalls Second Isaiah's doctrine that the true God is known by the fulfillment of his prophecies (Isa. 41:22-29; etc.).

14. This is in deliberate contrast with 36:34, and the editor intends it to be taken thus.

15. The multiplication of synonymous words is characteristic of the editor. The versional reading noted in the RSV mg. is והיית for והיתה.

16. Arrows for destruction is an interpretation of the text reproduced more literally in the KJV. Perhaps to simplify, the LXX omits **which I will loose to destroy you, and when I bring more and more famine upon you.**

17. Cf. Yahweh's "four sore acts of judgment, sword, famine, evil beasts, and pestilence" in the editor's discussion of individual responsibility in 14:21.

She has rejected God's will and fallen even below the level of the heathen; therefore shall her doom be unprecedented and nothing ever afterward shall equal it. To be called to moral leadership is to be placed in an exposed position and burdened with a peculiar responsibility. There are many illustrations of this truth in the Bible: "You only have I known of all

the families of the earth: therefore I will punish you for all your iniquities" (Amos 3:2). Perhaps the most searching of all such utterances for ourselves is this, "The time has come for judgment to begin with the household of God" (I Pet. 4:17). When the church seeks—as she must—to bring secular society under the judgment of God, let her not forget these words.

6 And the word of the LORD came unto me, saying,

2 Son of man, set thy face toward the mountains of Israel, and prophesy against them,

3 And say, Ye mountains of Israel, hear the word of the Lord GOD; Thus saith the Lord GOD to the mountains and to the hills, to the rivers and to the valleys; Behold, I, *even* I, will bring a sword upon you, and I will destroy your high places.

6 The word of the LORD came to me: 2 "Son of man, set your face toward the mountains of Israel, and prophesy against them, 3 and say, You mountains of Israel, hear the word of the Lord GOD! Thus says the Lord GOD to the mountains and the hills, to the ravines and the valleys: Behold, I, even I, will bring a sword upon you, and

C. ORACLE AGAINST THE MOUNTAINS (6:1-14)

Disaster is coming to the mountains of Israel because of the pagan high places upon them. The high places will be destroyed, and will be desecrated by the dead bodies of the Israelites. Those who escape in exile will remember Yahweh and realize their guilt. The Israelites will know that Yahweh is the true God when the whole land is desolate and waste and Yahweh has wreaked his fury upon them.

At the high places, where there were sacred trees, altars, and idols, and where wanton practices characterized the cult, the fertility gods of the Canaanites were worshiped and Yahweh himself was often the object of the polluted rites. Josiah's reform had wiped out these local sanctuaries, desecrating them with the dead bodies of men (II Kings 23:13-20). The reaction against the reform of Josiah resulted in the restitution of the high place cults, which apparently persisted into the postexilic period. Both R^D and H were concerned with this, probably not merely as a historical matter of the past (cf. the polemic motives of the Deuteronomic redaction of Joshua to Kings; see Lev. 18:3; 26:30). Third Isaiah criticized his contemporaries for their worship on high places (Isa. 57:3-12; see also Zech. 12:11; Mal. 2:10-11).

This chapter has already received general discussion (see Intro., p. 48). If it has a genuine kernel, its recovery seems impossible, for the chapter is replete with the editor's phraseology. Both ch. 6 and ch. 36 are prophecies to the mountains of Israel, the latter picturing the restoration on the hills of Israel.

1. DESTRUCTION OF THE HIGH PLACES (6:1-7)

The object of the address shifts from the mountains (vss. 3-5a) to the people (vss. 5b-7). Not until vss. 13-14 does the address shift back to the mountains. It would be convenient to be able to say with some scholars that only the address to the mountains is

6:1-7. *When the Half-gods Go.*—The prophet's eye sweeps over the countryside of Judah and takes in at a glance its numerous hilltops. Each of these has been consecrated by the piety of centuries. Here stand the hill places with their altars to which the peasants of the neighborhood have come on pilgrimage at the great occasions of the agricultural year, bringing their gifts of thanksgiving to the Lord of the harvest and praying for his mercies to be continued. They are associated too, in legend and folktale, with the fathers and heroes of the nation. Below them, in the valleys and by the streams, other shrines stand, each with its own associations.

That is how these high places appeared to their worshipers. To Ezekiel, however, they

present a totally different appearance. The name of the Lord may be named over them, but their worship is in fact offered to false gods. It is not merely that some have idols and that in all of them the fertility rites associated with the Baalism are practiced. They stand for a wholly erroneous view of the Lord and his relation to Israel. They are centers of a natural, not an ethical, religion; places where men hope to benefit by him, not where they are awed by his holiness and pledged to his service.

We can transfer not a little of this to our churches today. Are they centers of true or of false worship? Do they serve a denominational divinity or the Lord of the whole earth? Are they bound up with some theory of racial superiority? Do they promote some local interest?

4 And your altars shall be desolate, and your images shall be broken: and I will cast down your slain *men* before your idols.

5 And I will lay the dead carcasses of the children of Israel before their idols; and I will scatter your bones round about your altars.

6 In all your dwelling places the cities shall be laid waste, and the high places shall be desolate; that your altars may be laid waste and made desolate, and your idols may be broken and cease, and your images may be cut down, and your works may be abolished.

7 And the slain shall fall in the midst of you, and ye shall know that I *am* the LORD.

I will destroy your high places. 4 Your altars shall become desolate, and your incense altars shall be broken; and I will cast down your slain before your idols. 5 And I will lay the dead bodies of the people of Israel before their idols; and I will scatter your bones round about your altars. 6 Wherever you dwell your cities shall be waste and your high places ruined,*t* so that your altars will be waste and ruined, your idols broken and destroyed, your incense altars cut down, and your works wiped out. 7 And the slain shall fall in the midst of you, and you shall know that I am the LORD.

t Syr Vg Tg: Heb *and be made guilty*

---

genuine, but the editor's ch. 36 is addressed only to the mountains. The listing of mountains, hills, ravines, and valleys in vs. 3 occurs again in 35:8; 36:4, 6.

4. The objects known as *ḥammānîm* are not **images** (KJV) or "sun-images" (ASV), but **incense altars** (RSV). They are known from excavated sites as small limestone altars having a "horn" or projection at each corner. The identification of such incense altars is assured by the appearance of the word on a specimen found at Palmyra in Syria, and the term probably also applies to pottery incense stands found in excavations of Canaanite and Hebrew cities (see W. F. Albright, *Archaeology and the Religion of Israel* [Baltimore: Johns Hopkins Press, 1942], pp. 146, 215; Wright, " 'Sun-image' or 'Altar of Incense'?" *Biblical Archaeologist,* I [1938], 9-10). The word גלולים, *gillûlîm,* **idols,** occurs thirty-nine times in Ezekiel. Otherwise it is found only in Lev. 26:30; Jer. 50:2 (late); Deut. 29:16 (R^D), and I Kings 15:12; 21:26; II Kings 17:12; 21:11, 21; 23:24 (the Deuteronomic editor). In Ezekiel it occurs frequently in passages more obviously by the editor, and he may always be responsible for it. The root means "to roll," a derivative means "dung," and it is obviously a term of deep contempt. It is formed after the analogy of שקוצים, found in 5:11; 7:20, translated "detestable things."

5. A dead body was thought unclean, and its presence would desecrate the sanctuary (see II Kings 23:14). Vs. 5a is omitted by the LXX and is taken by some as a gloss on Lev. 26:30, but it is in context and consonant with the many parallels with Lev. 26 in chs. 5–6.

6. The reading וישמו, **and ruined,** agrees with Symm., the Syriac, Targ., Vulg.; the M.T. has ויאשמו, "and be held guilty"; the LXX omits.

Do they merely gather in folk of one particular social class? If so, wherein do they differ from these high places which the prophet denounces?

What remedy does Ezekiel suggest for such a state of things? He proposes none here; he simply foresees the course which events will take. One day the local shrines will be swept away by the tides of invasion and men will be left face to face with the truth and righteousness of God, those austere but salutary realities. There are countries in our own day in which Christians have been robbed of all trusts, in order that they might turn at last to the only sure and abiding one. How should we stand such a test? Years of ease may spoil the character of a religion, because men assimilate it to

the standards of the society about it; judgment is needed to enforce a separation between these two, so that men may learn to surrender the temporal in the assurance that the eternal remains.

7. Demonstration of God.—Here we meet for the first time the theme which, with variations, is to dominate the whole work of Ezekiel: **Ye shall know that I am the LORD.** He has a passion for the honor of the God he serves, and to this end he lays all history, particularly that of Israel, under contribution. He lives amid stirring events, for the world power of Assyria has collapsed and that of Babylon has taken its place. His nation may struggle to maintain itself in independence, but its efforts

8 ¶ Yet will I leave a remnant, that ye may have *some* that shall escape the sword among the nations, when ye shall be scattered through the countries.

9 And they that escape of you shall remember me among the nations whither they shall be carried captives, because I am broken with their whorish heart, which hath departed from me, and with their eyes, which go a whoring after their idols: and they shall loathe themselves for the evils

8 "Yet I will leave some of you alive. When you have among the nations some who escape the sword, and when you are scattered through the countries, 9 then those of you who escape will remember me among the nations where they are carried captive, when I have broken[u] their wanton heart which has departed from me, and blinded their eyes which turn wantonly after their

[u] Syr Vg Tg: Heb *I have been broken*

2. The Exiles Will Remember Yahweh (6:8-10)

The context shows that the meaning of the expression "Then they will know that I am Yahweh" is that he will be recognized as the one and only God. This follows Second Isaiah's use of the term Yahweh to mean the sole Deity (Sheldon H. Blank, "Studies in Deutero-Isaiah," *Hebrew Union College Annual*, XV [1940], 14-18, 34-41; as Blank comments, the author assumes that the reader is already acquainted with Second Isaiah's reasoning and his monotheistic construction of the name "Yahweh"). This passage is obviously written for the benefit of the Diaspora. The editor has a vivid sense of the meaning of sin and the necessity for recognition of guilt. In 20:43; 36:31 he repeats again that the Jews will remember their evil ways and loathe themselves for their iniquities and abominations (see also 12:16). In vs. 9 there may be an anticipatory allusion to the new heart doctrine (for the redemptive implications of these verses compare them with 16:59-63; 36:31-38; 39:25-29; etc.).

8. **Yet I will leave some of you alive** is omitted by the LXX, and the M.T. provides no object for the verb, but the context and the parallel with 12:16 support some such interpretation. The syntactical relationship of vss. 8-9 is not clear (cf. KJV).

9. The difference between **I am broken** and **I have broken** is one letter, e.g., נשברתי (M.T.) and שברתי (cf. Aq., Theod., Symm., Targ., Vulg.). **Wanton** and **turn wantonly**

are foredoomed to failure. Yet a little while and the conqueror's ruthless hands will toss it carelessly on the scrap heap of vanquished peoples. He refuses, however, to let such a prospect dishearten him: instead, he attains to a point of view so elevated that from it the rise and fall of empires, yes, even the defeat of his own people and the devastation of the land he loves, serve as a mighty demonstration of the God who has claimed his life and whom he knows to be supreme over all.

Ezekiel's great merit is that, more than any prophet before him, he sees Israel in a world setting. The purpose of God embraces all mankind. Amos, Isaiah, and Jeremiah, to be sure, were aware of this truth, but they did not establish, as Ezekiel does, an intimate connection between the fortunes of their people and God's work for the race. For him, what befalls Israel is in itself an argument for or against the God it serves, who is at the same time the Lord of the whole earth. By its exile he is discredited and by its restoration he is vindicated. The eyes of the nations are on this little people and in their history God himself is mirrored.

But there is one grave defect in this conception, as we see once we compare it with the use Second Isaiah makes of the same thought. Whereas for the later prophet God uses Israel's history to draw mankind to himself, for the earlier, God is known rather by the doom which befalls his people. There is a certain lack of feeling on Ezekiel's part; he seems not merely indifferent to the vast human misery which authenticates God as judge of all, but actually to rejoice in it. How different from the missionary who stretched his arms in invitation to all mankind, crying in God's name, "Look unto me, and be ye saved, all the ends of the earth: for I am God, and there is none else" (Isa. 45:22). Nevertheless, we can follow with profit the two lines of thought by which he works out his demonstration of God in history.

8-10. *Sorrow Human and Divine.*—If we are to use this passage, we must admit at the outset that the translations of both texts above are inaccurate. **I have broken their wanton heart** is preferable in vs. 9. But the mistranslation can help us to see in the stern discipline of history something of the healing sorrow of the Cross,

which they have committed in all their abominations.

10 And they shall know that I *am* the LORD, *and that* I have not said in vain that I would do this evil unto them.

11 ¶ Thus saith the Lord GOD; Smite with thine hand, and stamp with thy foot, and say, Alas for all the evil abominations of the house of Israel! for they shall fall by the sword, by the famine, and by the pestilence.

12 He that is far off shall die of the pestilence; and he that is near shall fall by the sword; and he that remaineth and is besieged shall die by the famine: thus will I accomplish my fury upon them.

13 Then shall ye know that I *am* the LORD, when their slain *men* shall be among their idols round about their altars, upon every high hill, in all the tops of the mountains, and under every green tree, and under every thick oak, the place where they did offer sweet savor to all their idols.

idols; and they will be loathsome in their own sight for the evils which they have committed, for all their abominations. **10** And they shall know that I am the LORD; I have not said in vain that I would do this evil to them."

11 Thus says the Lord GOD: "Clap your hands, and stamp your foot, and say, Alas! because of all the evil abominations of the house of Israel; for they shall fall by the sword, by famine, and by pestilence. **12** He that is far off shall die of pestilence; and he that is near shall fall by the sword; and he that is left and is preserved shall die of famine. Thus I will spend my fury upon them. **13** And you shall know that I am the LORD, when their slain lie among their idols round about their altars, upon every high hill, on all the mountaintops, under every green tree, and under every leafy oak, wherever they offered pleasing odor to all

---

refer to the licentious practices of the fertility cults, if we may judge from the associations of the Hebrew root, זנה.

3. ISRAEL WILL KNOW YAHWEH AS GOD (6:11-14)

Vss. 11-12, like vs. 8, are deliberately reminiscent of the dramatic action in chs. 4–5. Many would have looked on the defeat of the nation as a sign of the weakness of its Deity. Our author, like the earlier prophets, takes it as evidence of the power of the Hebrew God of righteousness and justice.

11. In 25:6 clapping the hands and stamping the feet accompany rejoicing with malice; mournful anger is intended here (cf. 22:14). For **alas** (אח) see 21:15 (Hebrew 21:20); some would read האח, an exclamation of exultation and malice, as in 25:3; 26:2; 36:2, but it is less appropriate here.

12. Herntrich thinks **he that is far off . . . ; and he that is near** implies that the author is in Palestine.

13. The sacred trees were probably associated with the fertility goddess (see H. G. May, "The Sacred Tree on Palestine Painted Pottery," *Journal of the American Oriental Society*, LIX [1939], 251-59). **Oak** should probably be "terebinth" (as in Hos. 4:13; etc.).

Not all will perish: some will remain, to carry into the future the salutary lessons taught them by dire calamity. They will look back on the judgment and understand why it had to be. They will see that what God did, he did with a breaking heart, driven to it by their sin. How they had hurt him by their thoughtless identification of him with the Canaanite gods, by their use in his service of means that were wholly unworthy of him, and by the attitude of mind which made of him the mere dispenser of material blessings instead of the sovereign righteousness revealed in conscience! They catch a momentary glimpse of the deep pain in the

heart of the divine Father when his human children become estranged from him. His sorrow kindles theirs, so that they turn to him in penitence. They are like the prodigal in the parable, anxious to show their contrition and eager for any opportunity to live down a shameful past.

So the gospel of God's seeking and suffering love emerges from this grim scene of devastated shrines and fallen images. It was our sin that forced such stern measures on him. The demonstration of God in catastrophe is therefore not the final one. For that we must turn to the demonstration of him in sorrow. How to link

14 So will I stretch out my hand upon them, and make the land desolate, yea, more desolate than the wilderness toward Diblath, in all their habitations: and they shall know that I *am* the LORD.

7 Moreover the word of the LORD came unto me, saying,

2 Also, thou son of man, thus saith the Lord GOD unto the land of Israel; An end,

their idols. 14 And I will stretch out my hand against them, and make the land desolate and waste, throughout all their habitations, from the wilderness to Riblah.[v] Then they will know that I am the LORD."

7 The word of the LORD came to me: 2 "And you, O son of man, thus says the

[v] Another reading is *Diblah*

The **pleasing odor** is that of the animal sacrifices, the smell of "cooking" meat (cf. Gen. 8:21; Exod. 29:18, 25, 41; Lev. 1:9; etc.).

14. I will stretch out my hand is used often by the editor (see vii on p. 50). There is little question about the correctness of **Riblah,** the letters ר and ד being easily confused in Hebrew. Riblah was a city on the Orontes River, near the northern boundary of Israel at its greatest extent at the time of David and Solomon and again at the time of Jeroboam II (I Kings 8:65; II Kings 14:25). The editor visualizes these ancient borders restored in 47:16; 48:1, and the allusion here belongs to him. **The wilderness** is that south of Palestine.

D. PROPHECY OF THE COMING END (7:1-27)

"The end has come upon my people Israel." These words from Amos 8:2 express well the theme of this chapter. Yahweh has passed judgment; the day of doom draws near. This is the equivalent of the day of Yahweh of the earlier prophets, as the LXX recognized by beginning vs. 10 with the words, "Behold, the day of the Lord!" It is called in vs. 19, "the day of the wrath of Yahweh," although in a possible gloss. **The day is near** in vs. 7 recalls Isa. 13:6; Obad. 15; Zeph. 1:7, 14; etc. Vss. 1-13 are given over primarily to the announcement of the coming disaster. The short staccato sentences, often without the usual conjunction "and," express urgency and inevitability and a suppressed excitement reminiscent of some of Jeremiah's oracles. Vss. 14-27 picture in detail the coming disaster. The chapter contains much poetic prose, and some of the verses can be scanned. Irwin finds in this chapter his longest oracle from Ezekiel, which he calls Ezekiel's best poem. Kraetzschmar, Bertholet, Matthews, and others would also try to recover the original poetic form. In contrast with Irwin, Hölscher finds nothing original in the chapter; cf. also Eissfeldt. An original may have been paraphrased and expanded by the editor, but there are here many expressions and ideas which occur with more or less frequency in more obviously late passages. Besides those already mentioned, we may note such phrases as the following: **judge you according to your ways,** vss. 3, 8 (see viii on p. 50); **Behold, it comes,** vss. 5, 6, 10 (see xii on p. 50); **stumbling block of their iniquity,** vs. 19 (see xiii on p. 50); **might,** vs. 24 (see xiv on p. 50); cf. Lev. 26:19. The editor may be responsible for the form of vss. 1-9, which are divided into two oracles (vss. 1-4 and vss. 5-9), each beginning with **Thus says the Lord GOD** and concluding with the formula, **Then you will know.** Much in vss. 8-9, 15-24 particularly sounds like the editor. The LXX has a different order in vss. 1-9, reading 1, 2, 6*a*, 7-9, 3-5*a*.

7:2. The context is against translating "the four corners of the earth," which would imply a cosmic catastrophe.

---

up the two, Ezekiel will not have seen; but we can see, we who have learned in the tragic horror of Calvary to trace the divine grief over human faithlessness and to hear in it the appeal of divine love. That sin brings suffering is the law of the universe; what saves us is that God does not merely inflict this suffering upon us,

he enters into it and shares in it himself. "God commendeth his love toward us, in that, while we were yet sinners, Christ died for us" (Rom. 5:8).

7:1-27. *Two Pictures of Doom.*—The text of this chapter has suffered considerable corruption, so that the meaning is often difficult to

the end is come upon the four corners of the land.

3 Now *is* the end *come* upon thee, and I will send mine anger upon thee, and will judge thee according to thy ways, and will recompense upon thee all thine abominations.

4 And mine eye shall not spare thee, neither will I have pity: but I will recompense thy ways upon thee, and thine abominations shall be in the midst of thee: and ye shall know that I *am* the LORD.

5 Thus saith the Lord GOD; An evil, an only evil, behold, is come.

6 An end is come, the end is come: it watcheth for thee; behold, it is come.

Lord GOD to the land of Israel: An end! The end has come upon the four corners of the land. 3 Now the end is upon you, and I will let loose my anger upon you, and will judge you according to your ways; and I will punish you for all your abominations. 4 And my eye will not spare you, nor will I have pity; but I will punish you for your ways, while your abominations are in your midst. Then you will know that I am the LORD.

5 "Thus says the Lord GOD: Disaster after disaster! Behold, it comes. 6 An end has come, the end has come; it has awak-

---

3-4. **You** and **your** refer to the land of Israel, being feminine singular pronominal forms, save in the case of **you will know,** which is masculine plural, referring to the people, which the LXX and Syriac correct to the singular. So also in vss. 5-9 the forms are feminine singular, save in vs. 7, where the masculine singular refers to the **inhabitant,** and in vs. 9, where the concluding formula is masculine plural. The editor's expansion may be responsible for the confusion. **I will let loose my anger upon you** makes the anger almost a separate entity, as Yahweh's word is sometimes likewise viewed. The parallel in Ps. 78:49 is significant at this point:

> He let loose on them his fierce anger,
> wrath, indignation, and distress,
> a company of destroying angels.

5-6. For these verses the LXX reads merely, "For thus says the Lord, 'Behold, the end has come.'" It is difficult to explain the rest as post-LXX additions. Even if the LXX used a Hebrew MS with a shorter text, which is not itself certain, it may not be as "original" at this and at comparable points as our present M.T. In vs. 5 the difference between **disaster after disaster** (with thirty MSS and Targ.) and **an evil, an only evil** is one letter, e.g., רעה אחר רעה for רעה אחת רעה. In vs. 6 **it has awakened,** *hēqîç,* forms a pun with **the end,** *haqqēç;* it is reminiscent of the pun in Amos 8:2.

---

recover. It is a grim picture of total doom descending upon the land like a hurricane which sweeps away everything in its path. The sins of the nation have already been fully enumerated; the prophet is concerned now with the terrible issue of what seemed at the time so pleasant, so natural, and so justifiable.

Ezekiel speaks in two ways of the impending catastrophe. It is at once God's judgment on the nation and the inevitable consequence of its misdeeds. There is a divine reaction against the sins of Judah, in wrath and indignation; there is also a moral order in virtue of which those sins weaken the nation, disrupt its unity, and hand it over to its enemies. Which of these descriptions are we to prefer? The answer surely is that each has its justification and each its limits.

If we are to think of God as personal we are forced to admit that he will not look on unmoved at the follies of his creatures. He will take them seriously, set himself against them, and see to it that men do not mock at truth and righteousness with impunity. If we admire in a man the flaming passion which makes him a sworn foe to any injustice, so that he says of it what Lincoln reputedly said of slavery, "If I ever get a chance to hit that thing, I'll hit it hard," [5] we cannot doubt that something of this quality is to be found in God himself. Is not the conscience of an Amos, challenging in God's name a corrupt society, evidence enough that there is in God an antagonism to all that injures human life, that the sin of man against

[5] See Benjamin P. Thomas, *Abraham Lincoln* (New York: A. A. Knopf, 1952), p. 24.

7 The morning is come unto thee, O thou that dwellest in the land: the time is come, the day of trouble *is* near, and not the sounding again of the mountains.

8 Now will I shortly pour out my fury upon thee, and accomplish mine anger upon thee: and I will judge thee according to thy ways, and will recompense thee for all thine abominations.

9 And mine eye shall not spare, neither will I have pity: I will recompense thee according to thy ways and thine abominations *that* are in the midst of thee; and ye shall know that I *am* the LORD that smiteth.

10 Behold the day, behold, it is come: the morning is gone forth; the rod hath blossomed, pride hath budded.

ened against you. Behold, it comes. 7 Your doom[w] has come to you, O inhabitant of the land; the time has come, the day is near, a day of tumult, and not of joyful shouting upon the mountains. 8 Now I will soon pour out my wrath upon you, and spend my anger against you, and judge you according to your ways; and I will punish you for all your abominations. 9 And my eye will not spare, nor will I have pity; I will punish you according to your ways, while your abominations are in your midst. Then you will know that I am the LORD, who smite.

10 "Behold, the day! Behold, it comes! Your doom[w] has come, injustice[x] has blos-

[w] The meaning of the Hebrew word is uncertain
[x] Or *the rod*

7. The meaning of הצפירה, **doom**, here and in vs. 10 is presumed from the context (cf. **morning** KJV). It occurs elsewhere only in Isa. 28:5, in the sense of diadem or crown (cf. Akkadian *ṣapāru,* "to destroy"). The end of the verse is thoroughly corrupted (cf. KJV).

9. The word מכה, "do smite," should probably be read המכה, **who smites**, with the LXX and Syriac, the present text resulting from haplography.

10. The difference between **injustice** and **rod** is one of pointing, e.g., *hammuṭṭeh* (cf. 9:9) for *hammaṭṭēh* (M.T.). If the former is correct, it is another pun (see vs. 11). Accepting the usual metrical analysis, the verse contains five lines of two beats each, but we probably have here poetic prose rather than poetry. (That which appears to be

man stirs him to act, so that he cannot allow men to build their social structure on falsehood and still be secure?

On the other hand, we must be careful not to impute to God any merely personal resentment, as though he were angry because men pay insufficient attention to him or transfer elsewhere the homage that is his due. We do well therefore to think also of the law of the universe by which, as men sow, so also will they reap. Jesus himself, with his strong sense of God as personal and as our Father, yet found it at times appropriate to speak in impersonal language, "With the judgment you pronounce you will be judged, and the measure you give will be the measure you get" (Matt. 7:2).

Can we say that certain sins inevitably bring doom upon those who are guilty of them? Sooner or later the tyrant has to face conspiracy or rebellion, the crafty schemer finds himself without a friend, the arrogant nation overshoots the mark and raises the world in arms against it. The pride of a Napoleon matches itself in vain against the snows of a Russian winter. Our sins may not be found out, but, given time, they will find us out.

Wrote W. E. Hocking:

The conception of God as Law has its right in destroying the *poverty* of my thought of personality. I confess that this word "person" has for me a harsh and rigid sound, smacking of the Roman Code. I do not love the word personality. I want whatever is accidental and arbitrary and atomic and limited and case-hardened about that conception to be persistently beaten and broken by whatever of God I can see in the living law and order of this Universe until it also has all such totality and warmth.

But I see that personality is a stronger idea than law; and has promise of mutuality and intercourse that laws, even if living, cannot afford. I see further that personality *can include law,* as law cannot include personality. . . . Until I can perfectly conceive personality, God must be for me alternately person and law.[6]

10-27. *The Three Securities.*—The life of any nation is organized as a system of defense in depth. Three lines, each with its supports and ramifications, give to the ordinary man his

[6] *The Meaning of God in Human Experience* (New Haven: Yale University Press, 1912), pp. 335-36. Used by permission.

11 Violence is risen up into a rod of wickedness: none of them *shall remain,* nor of their multitude, nor of any of theirs: neither *shall there be* wailing for them.

12 The time is come, the day draweth near: let not the buyer rejoice, nor the seller mourn: for wrath *is* upon all the multitude thereof.

13 For the seller shall not return to that which is sold, although they were yet alive: for the vision *is* touching the whole multitude thereof, *which* shall not return; neither shall any strengthen himself in the iniquity of his life.

somed, pride has budded. 11 Violence has grown up into a rod of wickedness; none of them shall remain, nor their abundance, nor their wealth; neither shall there be pre-eminence among them.*y* 12 The time has come, the day draws near. Let not the buyer rejoice, nor the seller mourn, for wrath is upon all their multitude. 13 For the seller shall not return to what he has sold, while they live. For wrath*z* is upon all their multitude; it shall not turn back; and because of his iniquity, none can maintain his life.*a*

y The Hebrew of verse 11 is uncertain
z Cn: Heb *vision*
a Heb obscure

meter may be simply an impression given by the parallelistic character of Hebrew poetry: see G. D. Young, "Ugaritic Prosody," *Journal of Near Eastern Studies,* IX [1950], 124-33.)

11. The verse seems quite unintelligible (see KJV, omitting **shall remain** and **shall there be**). There may be several dittographies. **Nor their wealth** is a desperate attempt to make sense, associating הם with המון. **Wailing** and **pre-eminence** are uncertain translations of נה, although the latter is more probable (cf. Arabic *nāha*). T. H. Gaster ("Ezekiel and the Mysteries," *Journal of Biblical Literature,* LX [1941], 299) believes that the last part of the verse is a conflation of three alternative readings, and suggests ולא נה בה, "and possesses no 'tall shoot.'"

12-13. There may be an allusion to the sale of hereditary property under compulsion for paying debts (cf. Neh. 5:3; Jer. 32:7). For the legislation for the redemption of hereditary property see Lev. 25:24-25. Reference to the year of Jubilee (Lev. 25:8-55) is dubious. Or the allusion may be to those selling to speculators at reduced prices in time of military crisis. Property would be of little value to those threatened with exile. **For wrath is upon all their multitude** is omitted by the LXX*B* in vss. 12, 14, and also in vs. 13 (with a part of the context) where חזון, **vision,** is an obvious scribal error for חרון, **wrath. It shall not turn back** may be dittography from **shall not return,** identical in the M.T. **While they live** is, lit., "and still in life their life." The last part of vs. 13 is also difficult, and might be more literally rendered, "and [as for] a man, in his sin [is] his life; they shall not strengthen themselves." All is confusion.

sense of security. The first is wealth, not that of the idle few, but that which is earned by industry and trade, the normal flow of goods from seller to buyer. In quiet times this is the basis of national life, and men expect from its development an ever-rising standard of comfort. But there are times when it is imperiled by a crisis in international relations, and for security men then have recourse to the second line of defense, to armaments. The soldier takes the place of the merchant in popular esteem, and the manhood of the nation is mobilized to maintain its interests and institutions. But suppose war threatens to end in defeat, what then? Why, then men fall back on their third line of defense, on religion. A day of prayer is proclaimed, and churches which used to be empty become full again—for that one occasion! Men become

aware that their fortunes are determined in no small measure by powers beyond their control, they search their hearts and propose to make amends for past neglect. Surely this last defense will hold, God will intervene for a people whose only hope is in him!

The situation which Ezekiel describes is one which puts all such confidence in peril. The Maginot line of Judah has been turned. One by one all these three securities have been taken from it. There is confusion in the market place. **Let not the buyer rejoice, nor the seller mourn.** There is despair in the camp. **They have blown the trumpet and have made all ready; but none goes to battle.** Fugitives take refuge in the hills, and the well-to-do townsfolk fling away their wealth, for the poor have more chance than the rich of escaping massacre. The enemy streams

14 They have blown the trumpet, even to make all ready; but none goeth to the battle: for my wrath *is* upon all the multitude thereof.

15 The sword *is* without, and the pestilence and the famine within: he that *is* in the field shall die with the sword; and he that *is* in the city, famine and pestilence shall devour him.

16 ¶ But they that escape of them shall escape, and shall be on the mountains like doves of the valleys, all of them mourning, every one for his iniquity.

17 All hands shall be feeble, and all knees shall be weak *as* water.

18 They shall also gird *themselves* with sackcloth, and horror shall cover them; and shame *shall be* upon all faces, and baldness upon all their heads.

19 They shall cast their silver in the streets, and their gold shall be removed: their silver and their gold shall not be able to deliver them in the day of the wrath of the LORD: they shall not satisfy their souls, neither fill their bowels: because it is the stumblingblock of their iniquity.

20 ¶ As for the beauty of his ornament, he set it in majesty: but they made the images of their abominations *and* of their detestable things therein: therefore have I set it far from them.

21 And I will give it into the hands of the strangers for a prey, and to the wicked of the earth for a spoil; and they shall pollute it.

14 "They have blown the trumpet and made all ready; but none goes to battle, for my wrath is upon all their multitude. 15 The sword is without, pestilence and famine are within; he that is in the field dies by the sword; and him that is in the city famine and pestilence devour. 16 And if any survivors escape, they will be on the mountains, like doves of the valleys, all of them moaning, every one over his iniquity. 17 All hands are feeble, and all knees weak as water. 18 They gird themselves with sackcloth, and horror covers them; shame is upon all faces, and baldness on all their heads. 19 They cast their silver into the streets, and their gold is like an unclean thing; their silver and gold are not able to deliver them in the day of the wrath of the LORD; they cannot satisfy their hunger or fill their stomachs with it. For it was the stumbling block of their iniquity. 20 Their[b] beautiful ornament they used for vainglory, and they made their abominable images and their detestable things of it; therefore I will make it an unclean thing to them. 21 And I will give it into the hands of foreigners for a prey, and to the wicked of the earth for a spoil; and they shall profane

[b] Syr Symmachus: Heb *Its*

14-20. For dramatic effect the doom is described as though it were already present.

18. Similar lamentation rites were used not only to lament disaster but to mourn the dead (see Isa. 15:2-3; 22:12; Amos 8:10; cf. Gen. 37:34; Deut. 14:1; Jer. 16:5-7).

19. The picture of inflated prices in time of siege in II Kings 6:25 is to be noted. Here the money is useless because there is nothing to buy. It is the **stumbling block of their iniquity** because it has been used for making idols (cf. vs. 20; Hos. 2:8). **Their silver and gold are not able to deliver them in the day of the wrath of the LORD** is duplicated in Zeph. 1:18.

20. The difference between **they used** [it] and **he set it** is only in the pointing, i.e., *sāmuhû* (with a number of versions) and *sāmāhû* (M.T.).

across the land, plundering as he goes; he is of **the wicked of the earth** and **the worst of the heathen.** Surely there is help in heaven against such foes as these! But no! The high places are surrendered to their profanation (vs. 24), the priest has no counsel to offer (vs. 26), and the prophet is dumb like the statesman (vs. 27). In

church and state alike there are agonizing problems, but there is no solution.

Nations in our own era have lived through just such experiences of utter desolation as are here described. What would Ezekiel say to them? He would say that our final trust is not in religion but in God, and that these two can be

22 My face will I turn also from them, and they shall pollute my secret *place:* for the robbers shall enter into it, and defile it.

23 ¶ Make a chain: for the land is full of bloody crimes, and the city is full of violence.

24 Wherefore I will bring the worst of the heathen, and they shall possess their houses: I will also make the pomp of the strong to cease; and their holy places shall be defiled.

25 Destruction cometh; and they shall seek peace, and *there shall be* none.

26 Mischief shall come upon mischief, and rumor shall be upon rumor; then shall they seek a vision of the prophet; but the law shall perish from the priest, and counsel from the ancients.

27 The king shall mourn, and the prince shall be clothed with desolation, and the

it. 22 I will turn my face from them, that they may profane my precious[c] place; robbers shall enter and profane it, 23 and make a desolation.[d]

"Because the land is full of bloody crimes and the city is full of violence, 24 I will bring the worst of the nations to take possession of their houses; I will put an end to their proud might, and their holy places shall be profaned. 25 When anguish comes, they will seek peace, but there shall be none. 26 Disaster comes upon disaster, rumor follows rumor; they seek a vision from the prophet, but the law perishes from the priest, and counsel from the elders. 27 The king mourns, the prince is wrapped in de-

[c] Or secret
[d] Cn: Heb make the chain

22. This verse should be contrasted with the popular view that the presence of the temple was a guarantee of security (see Jer. 7:7). **I will turn my face from them:** As a sign of disfavor (cf. I Kings 8:29). The word צפוני, **my precious place,** comes from a root meaning to hide or treasure, and thus carries the connotation of both **secret** and **precious;** it refers to the temple building, and perhaps to the holy of holies into which only properly consecrated persons could enter.

23. **Make a chain** gives little sense and can hardly refer to a symbolic action, for it is not interpreted in the context; the LXX καὶ ποιήσουσι φυρμόν, "and they shall make confusion," and the Syriac, "and they shall pass through bricks," support reading a third plural verb, and attaching it to the preceding sentence. If this is done, the rest of vs. 23 should be taken as the prodasis of vs. 24 (see RSV; contrast KJV). Some suggest "blood" rather than **bloody crimes,** omitting משפט with the LXX (cf. 9:9).

24. **The worst of the nations** here and **the wicked of the earth** in vs. 21 suggest the estimate of the Babylonians in Hab. 1:13, which raised the problem of the justice of Yahweh in Habakkuk's mind. In 28:7; 30:11; 31:12; 32:12 the Babylonians are called "the most terrible [i.e., "terrifying"] of the nations" (cf. Jer. 5:15-17; 6:22-23). **Their holy places:** I.e., the local shrines; the M.T. is pointed as a participle, *meqaddeshêhem,* "they that sanctify them," but read *miqdeshêhem.*

26. The word חזון, **vision,** really means a prophecy or oracle (as in Prov. 29:18; Isa. 1:1; Obad. 1; etc.); תורה, **law,** is without the article and is used in the broader sense of instruction, rather than the written law; see Lam. 2:9, where both these words appear. The **elders** were important in the organization of Hebrew society and acted as judges and counselors (see Deut. 19:12; 22:15; Ruth 4:4; II Sam. 5:3; 17:4; Jer. 26:17; and many references in Ezekiel).

27. Since the king is normally designated in Ezekiel as **the prince** (הנשיא; cf. 12:10, 12; 21:25 [Hebrew 21:30]) and the LXX omits **the king mourns . . . ,** and some commentators

quite different. When the defenses are broken and the enemy streams across the land, there is no institution, no system of ideas, no religious tradition which can save us. We must face what comes upon us as those whom God has called to meet him in an hour of stern destiny.

In his book on Germany's guilt, written during the humiliation which followed on defeat, Karl Jaspers, one of its leading thinkers, calls on the nation to accept what has befallen it as deserved chastisement for a terrible transgression, and by individual repentance and renewal

hands of the people of the land shall be troubled: I will do unto them after their way, and according to their deserts will I judge them; and they shall know that I *am* the LORD.

8 And it came to pass in the sixth year, in the sixth *month,* in the fifth *day* of the month, *as* I sat in mine house, and the elders of Judah sat before me, that the hand of the Lord GOD fell there upon me.

2 Then I beheld, and lo a likeness as the appearance of fire: from the appearance of his loins even downward, fire; and from his loins even upward, as the appearance of brightness, as the color of amber.

spair, and the hands of the people of the land are palsied by terror. According to their way I will do to them, and according to their own judgments I will judge them; and they shall know that I am the LORD."

8 In the sixth year, in the sixth month, on the fifth day of the month, as I sat in my house, with the elders of Judah sitting before me, the hand of the Lord GOD fell there upon me. 2 Then I beheld, and, lo, a form that had the appearance of a man;[e] below what appeared to be his loins it was fire, and above his loins it was like the appearance of brightness, like gleaming

e Gk: Heb *fire*

---

take this reference to the king to be a gloss. **The prince** is characteristic of the editor; note also the final clause in the verse.

E. The Visit to the Temple (8:1–11:25)

These four chapters belong together. They present Ezekiel's visions of the abominations in the temple (8:1-18), the slaughter of the wicked in the sanctuary and the city (9:1-11), a prophecy against certain leaders devising iniquity (11:1-13), and the departure of the glory of Yahweh (10:1-22; 11:22-23). The hand of the editor may be seen particularly in expansions in ch. 10, and he is responsible for the oracle of restoration in 11:14-21. The text is disarranged, and 11:1-13 should be placed before the destruction of all the guilty in the city (ch. 9) for in 11:1-13 the wicked are still there. Then 11:22-25 would follow after ch. 10, continuing the vision of the departure of the glory of Yahweh.

1. The Vision of Idolatry (8:1-18)

In his concern for true worship Ezekiel is in the tradition of Hosea, Micah, Isaiah, and Jeremiah. Israel was doomed because of her paganism. Vss. 1-4 are the introduction to the "vision," and vss. 5-18 describe the various idolatrous practices at the temple.

a) Setting of the Vision (8:1-4)

8:1. The date is September 7, 591 (September 17, 592). The LXX reads "in the fifth month," which many commentators accept. Some think the editor achieved the date by adding 7 days (3:16) and 390 days (4:5, 9) to the date in 1:2.

---

to make possible the winning of its soul in the hour when it has lost even its independence. He closes his appeal with the reminder that when all else passes, God remains.[7]

8:1-18. False Values.—So far our attention has been directed principally to the woes which the prophet sees to be impending over his unhappy country. We have heard much also of the sins which make this doom inevitable, more especially the idolatrous rites of the high places which are scattered about the countryside. We are now to witness a detailed exposure of the sins which have their lodging at the very center of the national life, in Jerusalem and

its temple. What is amiss with the nation is that it is corrupt at this center, that it has repudiated the God who made it a people and has replaced him by the gods of the surrounding countries. A false religion perverts its life and threatens catastrophe.

We might say today that a society is governed in the last resort by certain standards, and that when these have become corrupted, it is in mortal peril. It is organized around certain values which are for it what the fire tended by the vestal virgins was for ancient Rome; only as they are guarded can it endure and fulfill its mission. What has happened to Judah is the abandonment of these standards and the falsi-

7 Die Schuldfrage (Heidelberg: L. Schneider, 1946).

3 And he put forth the form of a hand, and took me by a lock of mine head; and the spirit lifted me up between the earth and the heaven, and brought me in the visions of God to Jerusalem, to the door of the inner gate that looketh toward the north; where *was* the seat of the image of jealousy, which provoketh to jealousy.

4 And, behold, the glory of the God of Israel *was* there, according to the vision that I saw in the plain.

bronze. 3 He put forth the form of a hand, and took me by a lock of my head; and the Spirit lifted me up between earth and heaven, and brought me in visions of God to Jerusalem, to the entrance of the gateway of the inner court that faces north, where was the seat of the image of jealousy, which provokes to jealousy. 4 And behold, the glory of the God of Israel was there, like the vision that I saw in the plain.

---

3. The being just described is Yahweh (see 1:26-27). In one of the apocryphal additions to the book of Daniel, the story of Bel and the Dragon, Habakkuk is lifted up by the hair of his head by an angel and brought from Palestine to Daniel in the den of lions, and then returned the same way. Transportation by the Spirit here may imply an actual physical journey, as it does in 3:14-15. In 40:2; 37:1, where the visions are more clearly literary forms, the interpretation must be different. **In visions of God** may be the interpretation of the editor or of Ezekiel himself. **The gateway of the inner court that faces north** may be interpreted from I Kings 7:12, which mentions a great encircling court, a court of the porch of the house (i.e., of the palace), and the inner court of the house of the Lord. The second of these is called the middle court in II Kings 20:4. The great encircling court may be the outer court in Ezek. 10:3, 5, although this is not certain (cf. II Kings 21:5). Ezekiel, with his theocratic emphasis, was to exclude the palace from the total temple complex. In his ideal temple in chs. 40–48 there were gates to the inner and outer courts on the north, east, and south. **The seat [מושב] of the image [סמל] of jealousy, which provokes to jealousy:** Albright (*Archaeology and the Religion of Israel,* pp. 165-66, 221) suggests that מושב is really the niche in the wall in which there was placed a figured slab, סמל (cf. Assyrian *sim[m]iltu*), of the type known in northern Syria, Asia Minor, and northern Mesopotamia, decorated with carved or painted cultic and mythological scenes. If סמל means an image, it may here have been the image of Tammuz (Marduk?), for it was at this gate that the women were weeping for Tammuz (vs. 14). It is curious that only the seat is mentioned. Does this mean that the image was not in its accustomed place on its throne or seat, symbolizing the absence of the deity for whom the women were weeping? The allusion to the north gate may be significant, for the Canaanite Baal was thought to dwell in the north (see Exeg. on 1:4). Cf. the image set up by Manasseh (II Kings 21:7; II Chr. 33:7, 15).

---

fication of these basic values. There is no need to wrest Ezekiel's account of the abominations in the temple unduly to see in it a series of pictures of what is wrong with us.

3-5. God and Anti-God.—In the vision God and his rival, **the image of jealousy,** confront each other. Here **the glory of the God of Israel;** there the hateful **image,** with its altar set up for public worship. We cannot take our own feeling as a guide to the horror which such a spectacle would inspire in Ezekiel. We remember how his whole soul was filled with the majesty of God, his utterly incomparable greatness, and his sole and sovereign claim upon men's allegiance. And to this God a rival is actually set up in that one place on earth which should be peculiarly sacred to him. Only when we have

done our best to recapture something of the prophet's flaming indignation at so hideous a blasphemy can we afford to enter upon a different train of thought. The glory of God prevails even in face of man's preference of another to him. Yes, it extorts homage even from those who reject it. For closer examination reveals the law which governs all such wrong preferences. The false is a hideous parody of the true; indeed, it has been able to usurp the place of the true only because it is such. So no country ever really abandons religion; what it does is to set up a religion of its own making in place of the acknowledgment of the God who made all things. Comte, for example, created in the religion of humanity a sort of caricature of Catholicism, and he prophesied that before

5 ¶ Then said he unto me, Son of man, lift up thine eyes now the way toward the north. So I lifted up mine eyes the way toward the north, and behold northward at the gate of the altar this image of jealousy in the entry.

6 He said furthermore unto me, Son of man, seest thou what they do? *even* the great abominations that the house of Israel committeth here, that I should go far off from my sanctuary? but turn thee yet again, *and* thou shalt see greater abominations.

7 ¶ And he brought me to the door of the court; and when I looked, behold a hole in the wall.

8 Then said he unto me, Son of man, dig now in the wall: and when I had digged in the wall, behold a door.

9 And he said unto me, Go in, and behold the wicked abominations that they do here.

10 So I went in and saw; and behold every form of creeping things, and abominable beasts, and all the idols of the house

5 Then he said to me, "Son of man, lift up your eyes now in the direction of the north." So I lifted up my eyes toward the north, and behold, north of the altar gate, in the entrance, was this image of jealousy.

6 And he said to me, "Son of man, do you see what they are doing, the great abominations that the house of Israel are committing here, to drive me far from my sanctuary? But you will see still greater abominations."

7 And he brought me to the door of the court; and when I looked, behold, there was a hole in the wall. 8 Then said he to me, "Son of man, dig in the wall"; and when I dug in the wall, lo, there was a door. 9 And he said to me, "Go in, and see the vile abominations that they are committing here." 10 So I went in and saw; and there, portrayed upon the wall round about, were

b) THE IMAGE OF JEALOUSY (8:5-6)

5-6. See Exeg. on vs. 3. **The altar gate** (vs. 5) may be the north gate, although the LXX, O.L., and Syriac have the eastern gate, reading המזרח for המזבח; if original, this would seem to locate the image some distance from the "seat."

c) RITES BEFORE PAGAN IMAGERY (8:7-13)

7-8. The narrative is confusing; the prophet apparently digs a hole which is already there, and it is not clear where he finds the door. The LXX omits vs. 7b and **in the wall** in both occurrences in vs. 8. Some scholars omit vss. 7b-8.

10. Albright (*ibid.*, p. 166) sees here Egyptian influence, recalling the serpent and animal figures in the Book of the Dead and late magical representations. Gaster ("Ezekiel and the Mysteries," pp. 289-310) suggests a hidden, frescoed cavern where the annual sacred marriage ceremony takes place; he would find evidence of the ritual

long he would be preaching this new gospel from the pulpit of Notre Dame, the old having surrendered to him. As many have shown, Marxism turns the biblical view of history into a political creed, with economic forces substituted for the living God, the classless society as his kingdom, and the proletariat as his chosen people. In the democratic countries patriotism sometimes claims a devotion such as in earlier ages man gave only to God. Thus in many instances **the glory of the God of Israel** is confronted by **the image of jealousy, which provoketh to jealousy.**

7-10. *Brute Force.*—Under the cult of anti-God all kinds of false values are honored as though they were genuine. The first of these is the worship of force. To this the political leader is apt to be disposed. We are shown in the scene before us the leaders of the community engaged in their secret practices with one of their number as recognized head. The symbols around which they gather are drawn from the brute creation. So we speak of force as "brute," because those who adopt it reduce themselves to a level below the human. Indeed, it is a question whether they do not fall below the beast. A cartoon that brings this out forcibly depicts an ape squatting among the topmost branches of a tree beneath which men are fighting. His sardonic comment is, "Thank God evolution missed me!" In Dan. 7 the various world empires are represented by so

of Israel, portrayed upon the wall round about.

11 And there stood before them seventy men of the ancients of the house of Israel, and in the midst of them stood Jaazaniah the son of Shaphan, with every man his censer in his hand; and a thick cloud of incense went up.

12 Then said he unto me, Son of man, hast thou seen what the ancients of the house of Israel do in the dark, every man in the chambers of his imagery? for they say, The LORD seeth us not; the LORD hath forsaken the earth.

13 ¶ He said also unto me, Turn thee yet again, *and* thou shalt see greater abominations that they do.

14 Then he brought me to the door of the gate of the LORD's house which *was* toward the north; and, behold, there sat women weeping for Tammuz.

all kinds of creeping things, and loathsome beasts, and all the idols of the house of Israel. 11 And before them stood seventy men of the elders of the house of Israel, with Ja-azani′ah the son of Shaphan standing among them. Each had his censer in his hand, and the smoke of the cloud of incense went up. 12 Then he said to me, "Son of man, have you seen what the elders of the house of Israel are doing in the dark, every man in his room*f* of pictures? For they say, 'The LORD does not see us, the LORD has forsaken the land.'" 13 He said also to me, "You will see still greater abominations which they commit."

14 Then he brought me to the entrance of the north gate of the house of the LORD; and behold, there sat women weeping for

f Gk Syr Vg Tg: Heb *rooms*

---

and even of such a cave in the Ugaritic texts. The rites take place in the dark because this is the period of the descent of the solar-vegetation deity to the land of darkness.

11. With the seventy **elders** cf. Exod. 24:1; Num. 11:16, 25. The specific naming of one of them suggests something more than a vision experience. **Each had his censer** [מקטרת] **in his hand;** cf. the "hand censers" (כף) in Num. 7:14, 20, 26; etc. The latter may possibly be illustrated by steatite objects, decorated with a hand on the base, found in excavations in Syria and Palestine (May, *Material Remains of the Megiddo Cult*, pp. 18-19, Pl. XVII).

12. Cf. Num. 33:52; Lev. 26:1, where אבן משכית means a sculptured or figured stone. The text is not clear, for they are all in one chamber, not each in his own.

d) Worship of Tammuz (8:14-15)

14-15. This god can be traced back to the Sumerians, to whom he was known as Dumuzi, the god of the subterranean ocean and shepherd deity. His consort and sister was Inanna, the Semitic Ishtar, who uttered lamentations upon his death and descended into the lower world to bring him back. When he met his death, all life on earth languished (see Maurus Witzel, *Tammuz-Liturgien und Verwandtes* [Roma: Pontificio istituto biblico, 1935]; S. H. Langdon, *Tammuz and Ishtar* [Oxford: Clarendon

---

many beasts of prey. As we should put it, they are bestial in character.

In this passage, to be sure, the men of force have a justification of their policies. They always have. They begin by dismissing as unreal, or at any rate as ineffective, all considerations of a spiritual order. **The LORD seeth us not; the LORD hath forsaken the earth.** The arguments of religion are dismissed as irrelevant in the political sphere. They belong to a man's private relations to God or to a life after this one; in this actual world they are out of place and may be discarded. A modern dramatist makes Lord Kitchener say to Queen Victoria:

"The Church has often to think and speak one way—for the sake of appearances—while the Army and the Politicians—for getting the thing done—have to think, speak, and act another way." [8]

13-14. Sensuality.—So much for the leaders of the nation. What of the mass of the people? In a society which has directed its religious enthusiasm upon something that is not God, and in which the policy of the state is exempt from criticism by conscience, where do the common folk turn for their satisfactions? They

[8] Laurence Housman, *Victoria Regina* (New York: Charles Scribner's Sons, 1937), p. 455.

15 ¶ Then said he unto me, Hast thou seen *this*, O son of man? turn thee yet again, *and* thou shalt see greater abominations than these.

16 And he brought me into the inner court of the LORD's house, and, behold, at the door of the temple of the LORD, between the porch and the altar, *were* about five and twenty men, with their backs toward the temple of the LORD, and their faces toward the east; and they worshipped the sun toward the east.

17 ¶ Then he said unto me, Hast thou seen *this*, O son of man? Is it a light thing to the house of Judah that they commit

Tammuz. 15 Then he said to me, "Have you seen this, O son of man? You will see still greater abominations than these."

16 And he brought me into the inner court of the house of the LORD; and behold, at the door of the temple of the LORD, between the porch and the altar, were about twenty-five men, with their backs to the temple of the LORD, and their faces toward the east, worshiping the sun toward the east. 17 Then he said to me, "Have you seen this, O son of man? Is it too slight a thing

---

Press, 1914]). He may be compared with the Egyptian Osiris, the Canaanite Baal, and the Syrian Adonis (see the weeping for Hadad-rimmon [=Baal] in Zech. 12:11; cf. Hos. 7:14; I Kings 18:28).

e) WORSHIP OF THE SUN (8:16-18)

The twenty-five men were lamenting as the sun was about to sink below the celestial equator, and the rite was parallel to the weeping for the god Tammuz who had descended to the lower world. These solar rites were not new to the temple courts; cf. the horses and chariots of the sun in II Kings 23:11 (H. G. May, "Some Aspects of Solar Worship at Jerusalem," *Zeitschrift für die alttestamentliche Wissenschaft*, LV [1937], 269-81).

16. **Between the porch and the altar:** See Joel 2:17, which is also concerned with lamentation rites. The orientation of the worshipers here is in contrast with that prominent in later writings, where the worshiper must face the temple (cf. I Kings 8:29, 35; Dan. 6:10).

17. The word זמורה, **branch**, appears in 15:2; Num. 13:23, as the branch of the grape vine, but more significant is Isa. 17:10, where the allusion is to the vine slips

---

turn to a riot of sexual emotion. Nowhere is this more clearly the case than in modern civilization. We are the victims of sex obsession. Anyone who doubts this has only to walk through the entertainment quarter of one of our great cities and observe the posters outside the theaters, or to open a popular magazine and glance over the advertisement pages, or to switch on the radio or television. It is not in the least surprising that we have produced a school of psychologists for whom everything human is in the last resort an affair of sex. What is surprising is that we imagine that this is the truth about human life, when it is really an exposure of our own follies.

15-16. *Aspiration.*—But is such a society then wholly corrupt? Are there none in it who are aware that the soul of man cannot live without reverence, without the acknowledgment of a wisdom and power beyond his own? Yes, there are such. They turn away alike from the grossness of the multitude and from the scheming of the men of violence; they select the highest that

is known to them and devote themselves to it. Of all the forms of religion in the ancient world, probably the worship of the **sun** was the one with most spiritual promise. At least it would have seemed so to an observer of the time. In the case of Akhenaton it led to large-scale monotheistic reforms, though the impulse out of which these sprang was not a lasting one. No other object in nature was so well calculated to purify men's thoughts and lift them beyond what is low and sordid. Does not Plato see in the sun an image of that Good which is for him the fountainhead of being and knowledge alike? [9]

But the position of these men is pathetic in the extreme. They worship with **their backs toward the temple of the LORD;** i.e., they have turned away from the historic faith which is the ultimate source of their idealism. Not a few generous spirits are in that position. They deny God for the sake of human freedom or spiritual values or something of that kind.

[9] *The Republic* VI. 508-9.

the abominations which they commit here? for they have filled the land with violence, and have returned to provoke me to anger: and, lo, they put the branch to their nose.

18 Therefore will I also deal in fury: mine eye shall not spare, neither will I have pity: and though they cry in mine ears with a loud voice, *yet* will I not hear them.

9 He cried also in mine ears with a loud voice, saying, Cause them that have charge over the city to draw near, even every man *with* his destroying weapon in his hand.

for the house of Judah to commit the abominations which they commit here, that they should fill the land with violence, and provoke me further to anger? Lo, they put the branch to their nose. **18** Therefore I will deal in wrath; my eye will not spare, nor will I have pity; and though they cry in my ears with a loud voice, I will not hear them."

9 Then he cried in my ears with a loud voice, saying, "Draw near, you executioners of the city, each with his destroying

---

of the "gardens of Adonis," planted and nourished and then allowed to die quickly to symbolize the death of the vegetation deity. In the Ugaritic myth of Shalem and Shahar, in what has been interpreted as a lament for the slain god of vegetation, it is said that "they that prune the vines now prune him," using the verb *zbr*, equivalent to the Hebrew *zmr* (Gaster, "Ezekiel and the Mysteries," p. 293; Cyrus H. Gordon, *Ugaritic Handbook* [Roma: Pontificium Biblicum, 1947], text 52, 1. 9). In a tenth-century calendar from Gezer, two successive months, the first of which would correspond to the month of Tammuz, are called the months of "vine-tending" (זמר; for the Gezer calendar, see Albright, "Palestinian Inscriptions," in Pritchard, *Ancient Near Eastern Texts,* p. 320). Whatever the more specific connotation of the rite here, זמורה belongs in this milieu. To **put the branch to** [the] **nose** has also been interpreted as an idiom meaning to harass or irritate (Robert Gordis, "The Branch to the Nose," *Journal of Theological Studies,* XXXVII [1936], 284-88).

2. Slaughter of the Guilty (9:1-11)

Although Ezekiel was perhaps actually in the temple and saw the abominations he described, he was under the impression of being guided by Yahweh himself, and he

---

While in heart and soul devoted to the service of their fellows, they repudiate the Christian tradition on which they draw for their moral fervor. Perhaps we shall part company with Ezekiel here. We shall not agree with him that this scene provides us with abominations worse than those which went before. Rather, we shall ask what it is in us who bear the Christian name which hinders men and women of such fine quality from seeing in Christ the fulfillment of their highest ideals.

One final consideration remains. Someone may suggest that so detailed a discussion of men's queer beliefs is but a waste of valuable time. It is concerned only with religious opinions, and these are a purely private affair; they have nothing to do with the social and political issues which clamor for our attention. We may well reply that today we can no longer think in such terms.

"The realistic politician no longer regards religion as a harmless indulgence of amiable sentiment; he sees that what men set up in their

inner selves to reverence is a matter of the first magnitude for their worth as citizens, workers, and fighters."[1] Little wonder therefore that when men "set up in their inner selves to reverence" such evils as we have had described to us, the result is that the land is **filled . . . with violence** (vs. 17). Where the leaders respect only force and the masses surrender to their impulses, the men of ideals are reduced to impotence. Nay, they may even, by what the French call *les trahisons des clercs,* produce specious arguments to justify the follies of their time. They have no spiritual power with which to cast out the demons from their society, since they do not stand against them in the name of the living God. They can be critical of their society, but they are not able to save it. For that God must use the prophet, the man of burning faith and moral passion.

9:1-11. Vision of Judgment.—As always hitherto, Ezekiel is concerned here with the impend-

[1] W. E. Hocking, *Living Religions and a World Faith* (New York: The Macmillan Co., 1940), p. 18.

2 And, behold, six men came from the way of the higher gate, which lieth toward the north, and every man a slaughter weapon in his hand; and one man among them *was* clothed with linen, with a writer's inkhorn by his side: and they went in, and stood beside the brazen altar.

2 And lo, six men came from the direction of the upper gate, which faces north, every man with his weapon for slaughter in his hand, and with them was a man clothed in linen, with a writing case at his side. And they went in and stood beside the bronze altar.

had seen the throne chariot at the beginning of his tour. He had heard Yahweh instruct him to utter a prophecy against the twenty-five men; he had uttered that prophecy in their hearing, and Pelatiah had dropped dead (8:1-18; 11:1-13). The vision now seemed to transcend almost completely sensory experience, as he visualized the divine agency slaughtering the wicked and saw the departure of the throne chariot.

Yahweh was king and, like a human king, had his royal chariot and throne, as well as his army of horses and chariots (II Kings 6:17; cf. Job 25:3), his commander in chief (Josh. 5:14), and his scribe (Ezek. 9:3) and official architect (40:3). The Babylonian scribe of the gods was Nebo, who at the spring New Year, at the time of the *akitu* festival, wrote upon the tablets of destiny the fates the gods had determined for the coming year. He was "the lord of the stylus" and the son of Marduk (see C. J. Gadd, "Babylonian Myth and Ritual," in Hooke, ed., *Myth and Ritual,* pp. 40-67). Ezekiel's imagery is drawn from a common Near Eastern pattern; we cannot say how directly he is influenced by the Babylonians at this point.

9:1. The **executioners of the city** who carry out Yahweh's judgment recall the angel of Yahweh who smote 70,000 at the time of David's census (II Sam. 24) and slew 185,000 in the camp of the Assyrians (II Kings 19:35; see also Exod. 12:23). The word פקדות, **executioners,** is used in II Kings 11:18 to designate the guards of the temple, also described as each having his weapon in his hand. These in Ezekiel's vision were supernatural guards.

2. They came from the north, as did the throne chariot in 1:4. The **six men** plus the **man clothed in linen** are background for the seven holy angels of Tob. 12:14; Enoch 20:1-8; etc.; Rev. 4:5; 8:1–11:19. Hebrew angels were men, and were not winged. **The upper gate** is the north gate. The **writing case,** קסת הספר, is the equivalent of the Egyptian *gsty,* the writer's kit pictured on many Egyptian reliefs and found in excavations (see Hyatt, "The Writing of an Old Testament Book," pp. 78-79). We may compare this scribe not only with Nebo, but with the Egyptian god Thoth. **Linen** was ritually clean, whereas wool, coming from an animal, might not be. It was used for priestly garments (44:17-18; Lev. 6:10; 16:4, 23; etc.), and from it the priestly ephod was made (I Sam. 2:18; II Sam. 6:14); the angels were clothed in linen (Dan. 10:5; 12:6-7; Rev. 15:6). **The bronze altar** is usually identified with the old Solomonic bronze altar (I

ing fate of his nation. He sees the catastrophe taking shape before him, especially the slaughter in the streets when resistance collapses with the flight of Zedekiah, and the Babylonian troops break in. But in this vision—for we must think of it as a visionary experience—there is no room for human intermediaries, as there is none for the long process of political folly which persuaded Judah to match itself against a power overwhelmingly superior (Babylon) and to put its trust in another power (Egypt) which was notorious for promising much and doing nothing. Ezekiel passes directly from the nation's sin to its punishment. What he sees in his vision is a divine judgment, executed by

forces which operate in the unseen, though the effect of their action is fearfully evident in the eyes of all. The divine decision to overthrow Jerusalem and stamp out its inhabitants was formed when the sins which deserved such a fate became manifest, and now the time has arrived to carry out the decree. It is in accordance with all that we have heard so far that judgment begins at the temple (vs. 6), for Judah's primary sin was the betrayal of her spiritual vocation.

But precisely because what is taking place is such a judgment of God, Ezekiel feels that it cannot be indiscriminate; it must be under control and made to serve a good end. Hence

3 And the glory of the God of Israel was gone up from the cherub, whereupon he was, to the threshold of the house. And he called to the man clothed with linen, which *had* the writer's inkhorn by his side;

4 And the Lord said unto him, Go through the midst of the city, through the midst of Jerusalem, and set a mark upon the foreheads of the men that sigh and that cry for all the abominations that be done in the midst thereof.

3 Now the glory of the God of Israel had gone up from the cherubim on which it rested to the threshold of the house; and he called to the man clothed in linen, who had the writing case at his side. 4 And the Lord said to him, "Go through the city, through Jerusalem, and put a mark upon the foreheads of the men who sigh and groan over all the abominations that are

---

Kings 8:64); Ahaz had moved it to the north side of the new great stone altar for burnt offerings which he had set up in its place and had patterned after an altar at Damascus (II Kings 16:10-16). However, II Kings 16:10-16 is obscure, and the reference there may have been to an altar of bronze which Ahaz had made in imitation of the Damascus altar, and the great altar before the temple (II Kings 16:15) may go back to the time of Solomon who used it in the dedication services of the temple (cf. I Kings 8:64). This great altar is the one mentioned in Ezek. 8:16, and served as the pattern for the altar of the restored temple in 43:13-17 (see Albright, *Archaeology and the Religion of Israel*, pp. 150-62, 161-62; for archaeological and biblical data on altars see Kurt Galling, *Biblisches Reallexikon* [Tübingen: J. C. B. Mohr, 1937; "Handbuch zum Alten Testament"], pp. 13-22).

3. Yahweh dismounts from the throne chariot, to give his orders from the threshold of the temple. **Cherub** is to be interpreted collectively with the RSV.

4. The scribe is ordered to **put a mark** upon the foreheads of those who lament the sins of the city. The book of Jeremiah gives us reason to believe that there were in Jerusalem those who did not accept the *status quo*, such as Jeremiah himself, Ebed-melech, and certain members of the house of Shaphan. The Hebrew word for **mark** is the name of the last letter of the Hebrew alphabet, *taw*, which was a cross. In Job 31:35 (see RSV) the word is used to indicate Job's signature, and may have been used as at present by the illiterate. We may also compare the sign put on Cain to prevent him from coming to harm (Gen. 4:15), and the passover blood on the doorposts and lintels which protected the inhabitants of the house (Exod. 12). The early Christians naturally interpreted this mark as the sign of the cross and as an anticipation of the Crucifixion. The cross or

---

one among the messengers of doom has a different part to play from the others. He is told to mark out for preservation the faithful element in the nation, those who have separated themselves in spirit from its evil practices. These are they **that sigh and that cry for all the abominations that be done in the midst** of the city. God's judgment will thus sift the righteous from the wicked, so that the former will be secure while the latter perish.

We can understand how Ezekiel came to think like this. Had he been in charge of the punishment of Jerusalem, he would no doubt have drawn up a list of those who did not deserve to share its fate and would have seen that they went unscathed. But does God work in this way in actual fact? When the Russian revolution swept away the old regime, did it discriminate nicely between the better and the

worse elements in the aristocracy? When Germany under allied occupation suffered for her sins against humanity, did starvation pass by those who sighed and cried for the evils of nazism? Not at all.

Amos sees more clearly how the forces work that govern history. Aware as he is of the distinction within Israel between exploiters and exploited, he does not anticipate that any notice will be taken of this in the hour of doom. The nation has sinned, and for its sin the nation will perish: that is all there is to it. But there is a higher conception of solidarity than this, one which reconciles us to the indiscriminate suffering of the just and the unjust. For it we must turn to Isa. 53 and to the Cross.

When doom falls upon a people, God's will for those who have opposed the evil in that community is not their safety but their redemption.

5 ¶ And to the others he said in mine hearing, Go ye after him through the city, and smite: let not your eye spare, neither have ye pity:

6 Slay utterly old *and* young, both maids, and little children, and women: but come not near any man upon whom *is* the mark; and begin at my sanctuary. Then they began at the ancient men which *were* before the house.

7 And he said unto them, Defile the house, and fill the courts with the slain: go ye forth. And they went forth, and slew in the city.

8 ¶ And it came to pass, while they were slaying them, and I was left, that I fell upon my face, and cried, and said, Ah Lord God! wilt thou destroy all the residue of Israel in thy pouring out of thy fury upon Jerusalem?

9 Then said he unto me, The iniquity of the house of Israel and Judah *is* exceeding great, and the land is full of blood, and the city full of perverseness: for they say, The Lord hath forsaken the earth, and the Lord seeth not.

10 And as for me also, mine eye shall not spare, neither will I have pity, *but* I will recompense their way upon their head.

11 And, behold, the man clothed with linen, which *had* the inkhorn by his side,

committed in it." 5 And to the others he said in my hearing, "Pass through the city after him, and smite; your eye shall not spare, and you shall show no pity; 6 slay old men outright, young men and maidens, little children and women, but touch no one upon whom is the mark. And begin at my sanctuary." So they began with the elders who were before the house. 7 Then he said to them, "Defile the house, and fill the courts with the slain. Go forth." So they went forth, and smote in the city. 8 And while they were smiting, and I was left alone, I fell upon my face, and cried, "Ah Lord God! wilt thou destroy all that remains of Israel in the outpouring of thy wrath upon Jerusalem?"

9 Then he said to me, "The guilt of the house of Israel and Judah is exceedingly great; the land is full of blood, and the city full of injustice; for they say, 'The Lord has forsaken the land, and the Lord does not see.' 10 As for me, my eye will not spare, nor will I have pity, but I will requite their deeds upon their heads."

11 And lo, the man clothed in linen, with the writing case at his side, brought back

---

taw is found on first-century A.D. ossuaries. The mark on the forehead appears in Rev. 7:3-4; 13:16; 14:9, 11; 20:4; 22:4.

5-6. Even **little children** were to be slain. Jonah 4:11 is in striking contrast. **The elders . . . before the house** are those who had been worshiping the sun (8:16).

8. The word ונאשאר is an obvious copyist's error; read ואשאר, **and I was left alone.** Ezekiel's exclamation is not a plea to desist but an expression of utter despair. As in 11:13, the prophet expects an affirmative answer. **All that remains of Israel:** I.e., those left in Judah after 597.

9. The reference to both Judah and Israel is traceable to the editor, consonant with his expansion in 4:4-8. **The land is full of blood** alludes to the social and economic practices which resulted in the death of the innocent (cf. ch. 22). Is this also the editor? (With vs. 9*b* cf. 8:12; with vs. 10 cf. 8:18.)

He does not take them out of the agony of their generation but calls them to enter into it with him. For he too is in it all as no mere Judge; he takes it on his heart in sympathy and fellow suffering. The true servants of God do not ask for exemption, but only that they may so accept their share in the tragic events of their time that they may be able to turn these to good, first in themselves and then in the community with which they are so closely bound. God does

indeed **set a mark upon** [their] **foreheads,** but it is in sign that he elects them to a share in his redemptive pain.

If we understand this, we can look upon the fate of Jerusalem with other eyes than those of the prophet. We know that enough men and women emerged from the catastrophe to carry on God's work. They sighed and cried for the sins of the old city, but they bore in their hearts the hope of a new one, and their children

reported the matter, saying, I have done as thou hast commanded me.

10 Then I looked, and, behold, in the firmament that was above the head of the cherubim there appeared over them as it were a sapphire stone, as the appearance of the likeness of a throne.

2 And he spake unto the man clothed with linen, and said, Go in between the wheels, *even* under the cherub, and fill thine hand with coals of fire from between the cherubim, and scatter *them* over the city. And he went in in my sight.

3 Now the cherubim stood on the right side of the house, when the man went in; and the cloud filled the inner court.

word, saying, "I have done as thou didst command me."

10 Then I looked, and behold, on the firmament that was over the heads of the cherubim there appeared above them something like a sapphire, in form resembling a throne. 2 And he said to the man clothed in linen, "Go in among the whirling wheels underneath the cherubim; fill your hands with burning coals from between the cherubim, and scatter them over the city."

And he went in before my eyes. 3 Now the cherubim were standing on the south side of the house, when the man went in;

3. Departure of Yahweh's Glory (10:1-22)

The scribe is ordered to scatter over the city burning coals taken from the midst of the cherubim; Yahweh then mounts the throne chariot, which takes off, but pauses at the east gate. The essentially genuine theme of the chapter is to be found in vss. 2, 7, 18-19. The rest may perhaps be ascribed largely to the editor, giving the reader the impression of much expansion and seemingly unnecessary repetition of details of the throne chariot already described, with some striking variants. The editor may have omitted the apparently missing account of the scribe scattering the fire over the city as he is ordered to do. It is not necessary with Hölscher, Herntrich, Matthews, Irwin, or Messel to consider the entire chapter late. The passage continues in 11:22-25.

10:1-2. The description in vs. 1 is taken from 1:26. **And he spake** and **and said** are both ויאמר, "and he said," repeated by dittography; omit the second with the LXX. The word גלגל, **whirling wheels** appears in 23:24; 26:10 in the sense of "wagons," and in Isa. 5:28; Jer. 47:3 (plural) as "wheels"; it also means "whirl" and "whirlwind" (Pss. 77:19; 83:14; Isa. 17:13). Here and in vss. 6, 13 it is no more than another name for the wheels otherwise called אופנים, and so explained in vs. 13. **Cherub** should be taken collectively as in the RSV (see 1:13-14 for the **burning coals**).

3. The **cloud** of the glory of Yahweh appears only here in Ezekiel, and is characteristic of the P source (Exod. 16:10; 24:15-18a; 40:34-38; Num. 10:34; etc.; cf. Exod. 33:7-9, which is probably also postexilic; see R. H. Pfeiffer, *Introduction to the Old Testament* [New York: Harper & Bros., 1941], p. 170; cf. also I Kings 8:10). The reference to the

returned to build it. In them the purpose of redemption was fulfilled. That was because they shared to the uttermost what came to their people. Would it have been fulfilled had they been given safety? We may well doubt it.

10:1-22. *The Withdrawal of God.*—We may well suppose that while the mass of the people turned a deaf ear to the warnings of Ezekiel and continued to the end to hope that something would turn up to avert the threatened doom, there was a more sensitive minority which shared his fearful expectations. These, however much they shuddered at his description of ruin and slaughter in the streets of the capital, carried in their hearts a far worse dread. Just because they chose God even when that carried

with it the abandonment of their people, they could not bear to think that his temple also would be involved in catastrophe. Here his dwelling place had been, and here they had met with him in worship. But once the temple was destroyed, where would they find him? The passing of the sanctuary would carry with it the withdrawal of God himself. Hence that moment which is here described, the moment in which the majesty of the divine presence quits the temple and resumes its place in the chariot of the opening vision, will have left them without hope. For God himself has gone!

We are not concerned here with the details of this chapter's composition (see Exeg.); probably the nucleus is from the prophet himself,

4 Then the glory of the LORD went up from the cherub, *and stood* over the threshold of the house; and the house was filled with the cloud, and the court was full of the brightness of the LORD's glory.

5 And the sound of the cherubim's wings was heard *even* to the outer court, as the voice of the Almighty God when he speaketh.

6 And it came to pass, *that* when he had commanded the man clothed with linen, saying, Take fire from between the wheels, from between the cherubim; then he went in, and stood beside the wheels.

7 And *one* cherub stretched forth his hand from between the cherubim unto the fire that *was* between the cherubim, and took *thereof,* and put *it* into the hands of *him that was* clothed with linen; who took *it,* and went out.

8 ¶ And there appeared in the cherubim the form of a man's hand under their wings.

and a cloud filled the inner court. 4 And the glory of the LORD went up from the cherubim to the threshold of the house; and the house was filled with the cloud, and the court was full of the brightness of the glory of the LORD. 5 And the sound of the wings of the cherubim was heard as far as the outer court, like the voice of God Almighty when he speaks.

6 And when he commanded the man clothed in linen, "Take fire from between the whirling wheels, from between the cherubim," he went in and stood beside a wheel. 7 And a cherub stretched forth his hand from between the cherubim to the fire that was between the cherubim, and took some of it, and put it into the hands of the man clothed in linen, who took it and went out. 8 The cherubim appeared to have the form of a human hand under their wings.

---

inner and outer courts (vss. 3, 5) may be made in the light of Ezekiel's vision of the restored temple in chs. 40–42. **The right side** is **the south side** as one faces east.

4. The first half of the verse repeats the action in 9:3.

5. See 1:24. **God Almighty** is El Shadday, a compound name which may be of ancient origin, like El Elyon of Gen. 14:19, El Olam of Gen. 21:33, El Berith of Judg. 9:46; etc.; cf. parallels in Canaanite nomenclature (May, "The Patriarchal Idea of God," p. 115). It occurs frequently in the P source (Gen. 17:1; 28:3; 35:11; etc.).

7. Many scholars omit **a cherub** with the LXXᴮ, reading "he stretched forth his hand," also omitting **from between the cherubim,** with the LXX, as well as the reference to the cherub giving the fire to the scribe. The verse would then read: "And he stretched forth his hand to the fire that was between the cherubim, and he took it and went out." However, the LXXᴮ probably has omitted **a cherub,** and it must be restored with the M.T. (cf. the action of one of the seraphim in Isa. 6:6, who also has hands, but who uses tongs).

8. The verse is based on 1:8, but is awkward following vs. 7. It is perhaps part of the editor's detailed description of the throne chariot or of his expansion of an original text.

---

while the section which is little more than a repetition of what we have already read in ch. 1 comes from the editor in Babylon. Our interest is in the problem of the withdrawal of God, which is with us to the present day.

We live in a society which is highly secularized. Religion has retreated from one area of life after another. Business, politics, and art have become autonomous. If religious education survives, it is as one subject among many, not as the inspiration of all learning and teaching. God does not seem to enter into the deliberations of statesmen. His name does not appear on the agenda when they meet in conference.

Science gives us a world picture in which we do not expect to find him. History tells the story of our race on the assumption that no superhuman actor is involved in it. Even within the church we often have religion but not God. We lack the vivid sense of his presence, the conviction that he is doing great things and that we have a share in them. Sermons deal with problems which arise from the apparent absence of God rather than with the joyful proclamation of his presence in our midst.

What are we to say of this withdrawal of God? Following Ezekiel, we can at least offer certain reflections.

9 And when I looked, behold the four wheels by the cherubim, one wheel by one cherub, and another wheel by another cherub: and the appearance of the wheels *was* as the color of a beryl stone.

10 And *as for* their appearances, they four had one likeness, as if a wheel had been in the midst of a wheel.

11 When they went, they went upon their four sides; they turned not as they went, but to the place whither the head looked they followed it; they turned not as they went.

12 And their whole body, and their backs, and their hands, and their wings, and the wheels, *were* full of eyes round about, *even* the wheels that they four had.

13 As for the wheels, it was cried unto them in my hearing, O wheel.

14 And every one had four faces: the first face *was* the face of a cherub, and the second face *was* the face of a man, and the third the face of a lion, and the fourth the face of an eagle.

9 And I looked, and behold, there were four wheels beside the cherubim, one beside each cherub; and the appearance of the wheels was like sparkling chrysolite. 10 And as for their appearance, the four had the same likeness, as if a wheel were within a wheel. 11 When they went, they went in any of their four directions[g] without turning as they went, but in whatever direction the front wheel faced the others followed without turning as they went. 12 And[h] their rims, and their spokes,[i] and the wheels were full of eyes round about — the wheels that the four of them had. 13 As for the wheels, they were called in my hearing the whirling wheels. 14 And every one had four faces: the first face was the face of the cherub, and the second face was the face of a man, and the third the face of a lion, and the fourth the face of an eagle.

[g] Heb *on their four sides*
[h] Gk: Heb *And their whole body and*
[i] Heb *spokes and their wings*

9-13. Vss. 9-12 are paralleled, with variations, in 1:15-18. Vss. 11-12 have been corrupted by imagery referring to the cherubim rather than to the wheels, e.g., **the head, body,** and **wings.** The context and a comparison with 1:17-18 suggest that these verses, along with vss. 9-10, were concerned with the **wheels** alone. The interpretation of **the head** as **the front wheel** is a counsel of desperation, but the translator must make sense for the reader! **Their backs,** גבהם, are properly **their rims,** as in 1:18, while ידיהם, **their hands,** may be interpreted as **spokes.** We can only omit **and their whole body** and **and their wings.** If there was an original reference to the cherubim, a quite different treatment of the text is necessary. For the creature **full of eyes** see Rev. 4:8. **The wheels that the four of them had** is another probable corruption, and we may read merely "[to] the four of them," לארבעתם, or with LXXB, "to the four wheels," לארבעת האופנים, or omit the whole as dittography. After this we are tempted to say "Amen" to the rendering of vs. 13 in the KJV, although the RSV gives the more probable translation.

14. (See 1:10.) This verse is also corrupt, and the M.T., after noting that each **had four faces,** goes on to say that the face of the first was **the face of a cherub,** and the face of the second was **the face of a man,** implying that each of these had one face! By following the Syriac and omitting **the face of** we get sense. The faces accord with 1:10, save in the order, and in the substitution of the cherub for the ox, perhaps a scribe's error. The LXXB omits the verse.

First, the withdrawal of God is never by his own will; it is we who force it upon him. It is because the temple has been filled with base objects of worship that finally there is no room in it for God. It is so with ourselves. Modern man may complain that God has abandoned his world to the operation of various impersonal forces. The fact is rather that modern man has organized his life around such forces instead of around God. We have created a society in which men are subject to economic pressure, driven by machines, and lured by meretricious entertainment—and then we ask why God does not manifest himself to us! What room have we left him in which to do so?

Second, the withdrawal of God is itself a token of his presence. The fact that a society which has falsified all its standards goes down in the end in ruin is not a sign that God has ceased to govern the world. It is an indication

15 And the cherubim were lifted up. This *is* the living creature that I saw by the river of Chebar.

16 And when the cherubim went, the wheels went by them: and when the cherubim lifted up their wings to mount up from the earth, the same wheels also turned not from beside them.

17 When they stood, *these* stood; and when they were lifted up, *these* lifted up themselves *also:* for the spirit of the living creature *was* in them.

18 Then the glory of the LORD departed from off the threshold of the house, and stood over the cherubim.

19 And the cherubim lifted up their wings, and mounted up from the earth in my sight: when they went out, the wheels also *were* beside them, and *every one* stood at the door of the east gate of the LORD's house; and the glory of the God of Israel *was* over them above.

15 And the cherubim mounted up. These were the living creatures that I saw by the river Chebar. 16 And when the cherubim went, the wheels went beside them; and when the cherubim lifted up their wings to mount up from the earth, the wheels did not turn from beside them. 17 When they stood still, these stood still, and when they mounted up, these mounted up with them; for the spirit of the living creatures*j* was in them.

18 Then the glory of the LORD went forth from the threshold of the house, and stood over the cherubim. 19 And the cherubim lifted up their wings and mounted up from the earth in my sight as they went forth, with the wheels beside them; and they stood at the door of the east gate of the house of the LORD; and the glory of the God of Israel was over them.

j Or *of life*

15. Vs. 15*a* anticipates the rising of the cherubim in vs. 19 (with vs. 15*b* cf. 3:23; 8:4; 10:20, 22).

16-17. (Cf. 1:20-21.) **The wheels did not turn from beside them** would mean that the wheels stayed with them; this translation is possible, but the Hebrew מן, **from,** sometimes loses its significance, and perhaps the meaning is as in vs. 11 (cf. Ezek. 40:7 and Francis Brown, S. R. Driver, and C. A. Briggs, eds., *A Hebrew and English Lexicon of the Old Testament* [Boston: Houghton Mifflin Co., 1906], *s.v.* מן, 4*c*).

19. **The east gate of the house of the** LORD is called "the gates of righteousness" and "the gate of the LORD" in Ps. 118:19-20, and the "ancient doors" in Ps. 24:7, 9. A Talmudic passage (Jerusalem 'Erubin V, 22*c*) gives it seven names, one of which is "sun gate," שער חריסית. Through it entered the king and the ark in the sacred processions of the New Year celebration, and through it also entered the rays of the rising sun of the equinoxes, the entrance of the glory of Yahweh into the temple (see Morgenstern, "The Gates of Righteousness," pp. 1-37). A number of scholars take vss. 18-19 as a parallel recension of 11:22-23, but both the east gate and the Mount of Olives were significant in the ritual of the entrance of the glory of Yahweh, and both may be genuine with Ezekiel. **And they stood** is, lit., "and it stood," but the subject is the cherubim, and we may read the plural verb with the LXX and Syriac, or take it as a reference to the throne chariot or the glory of Yahweh (cf. 11:23).

that he is still active, that he will not allow us to sin with impunity, and that if we insist on calling up the demons of the underworld, we need not be surprised to be torn to pieces by them. It is part of the prophetic message that when men refuse to acknowledge God in obedience to his will, they do not escape his rule of them but only ensure that it functions against them in judgment.

Third, the withdrawal of God does not mean his abandonment of the world. It means his presence in it in a new form. As we saw from

ch. 1, the editor is concerned to show that the presence which forsook the temple for its sins goes into exile with the people who had sinned within it. Those who thrust God out of their lives find him in judgment on their folly only that, beyond and through what they suffer, they may find him with them in compassion and the will to redeem. He continues with them and kindles hope in their hearts, for his purpose is one of restoration. His withdrawal now is the means to a more gracious return when they are ready to receive him.

20 This *is* the living creature that I saw under the God of Israel by the river of Chebar; and I knew that they *were* the cherubim.

21 Every one had four faces apiece, and every one four wings; and the likeness of the hands of a man *was* under their wings.

22 And the likeness of their faces *was* the same faces which I saw by the river of Chebar, their appearances and themselves: they went every one straight forward.

11 Moreover the spirit lifted me up, and brought me unto the east gate of the Lord's house, which looketh eastward: and behold at the door of the gate five and twenty men; among whom I saw Jaazaniah the son of Azur, and Pelatiah the son of Benaiah, princes of the people.

20 These were the living creatures that I saw underneath the God of Israel by the river Chebar; and I knew that they were cherubim. 21 Each had four faces, and each four wings, and underneath their wings the semblance of human hands. 22 And as for the likeness of their faces, they were the very faces whose appearance I had seen by the river Chebar. They went every one straight forward.

11 The Spirit lifted me up, and brought me to the east gate of the house of the Lord, which faces east. And behold, at the door of the gateway there were twenty-five men; and I saw among them Ja-azani′ah the son of Azzur, and Pelati′ah the son of Benai′ah, princes of

20-22. This passage is parenthetical and is probably the editor's expansion, for 11:22-25 seems to follow after 10:19. With vss. 21-22 cf 1:6, 8-9. In vs. 22 מראיהם, **whose [their] appearance[s]** is a scribal gloss, and ואותם, **and themselves**, should probably be read והמה, "and they," or possibly something like בצאתם, "as they went forth" (cf. vs. 19).

4. Judgment and Hope (11:1-25)

This chapter is in three parts. The first (vss. 1-13) continues the narrative of the tour of the temple in ch. 8, which it should follow. The second (vss. 14-21) is the editor's oracle of hope to the exiles and criticism of the people left in the land. The third (vss. 22-25) continues the narrative of the departure of the glory of Yahweh in ch. 10. While the editor's hand may be recognized in the first and third parts, they are essentially from Ezekiel. Among phrases in the second part which are characteristic of the editor are the following. "The whole house of Israel," vs. 15 (see ix on p. 50). "Scattered . . . among the countries," vss. 16-17 (see x on p. 50). "The countries where they have gone," vs. 16 (see xv on p. 50). "I will gather you," vs. 17 (see xvi on p. 50). "One heart, and . . . a new spirit," vs. 19 (see xvii on p. 50). "Walk in my statutes and keep my ordinances," vs. 20 (see xxxviii on p. 51). "They shall be my people, and I will be their God," vs. 20 (see xviii on p. 50). This covenant formula is frequent in R^D and characteristic of the biographer of Jeremiah. "Requite their deeds upon their own heads," vs. 21 (see xix on p. 50). With vss. 19-20 cf. 36:26-28.

a) The Wicked Leaders (11:1-13)

11:1. Ezekiel had been at the door of the temple (8:16), to the west of the altar, and now he was brought to the east gate, to the opposite side of the altar. The naming of **Jaazaniah the son of Azzur, and Pelatiah the son of Benaiah** gives the account a note of realism, suggesting Ezekiel was actually there. Another Jaazaniah, who was the son of Shaphan, appears in 8:11, while another contemporary Jaazaniah, the son of the Maacathite, is mentioned in II Kings 25:23; Jer. 40:8. The seal of the latter was found in the excavations at Tell en-Naṣbeh, ancient Mizpah (C. C. McCown, ed.,

11:1-13. *The Misuse of Mercy.*—The opening scene here clearly belongs with those in ch. 8. It brings to a conclusion the dreadful narrative of the abominations perpetrated in the temple. Only now a new feature is introduced, for these twenty-five men are examples of the arrogance

of which those are capable who are not humbled by catastrophe but rather emboldened by it. The first deportation under Jehoiachin lies behind them. Indeed, it made their fortunes, for it is only because so many better men have been eliminated in this way that they have arrived at

2 Then said he unto me, Son of man, these *are* the men that devise mischief, and give wicked counsel in this city:

3 Which say, *It is* not near; let us build houses: this *city is* the caldron, and we *be* the flesh.

4 ¶ Therefore prophesy against them, prophesy, O son of man.

5 And the Spirit of the Lord fell upon me, and said unto me, Speak; Thus saith the Lord; Thus have ye said, O house of Israel: for I know the things that come into your mind, *every one of* them.

6 Ye have multiplied your slain in this city, and ye have filled the streets thereof with the slain.

the people. 2 And he said to me, "Son of man, these are the men who devise iniquity and who give wicked counsel in this city; 3 who say, 'The time is not near[k] to build houses; this city is the caldron, and we are the flesh.' 4 Therefore prophesy against them, prophesy, O son of man."

5 And the Spirit of the Lord fell upon me, and he said to me, "Say, Thus says the Lord: So you think, O house of Israel; for I know the things that come into your mind. 6 You have multiplied your slain in this city, and have filled its streets with the

[k] Or *Is not the time near . . . ?*

Tell en-Naṣbeh, Archaeological and Historical Results [Berkeley and New Haven: Palestine Institute of Pacific School of Religion and The American Schools of Oriental Research, 1947], Pl. 57, No. 4).

2. Wicked counsel: Possibly an allusion to the plans for rebellion against Nebuchadrezzar and for alliance with Egypt. The princes under Zedekiah were strongly anti-Babylonian and pro-Egyptian, as we learn from the book of Jeremiah. See also the criticism of the princes in one of the letters found at Lachish (VI, ll. 5-7; cf. Albright, "The Oldest Hebrew Letters: The Lachish Ostraca," pp. 15-16).

3. The meaning of this verse is obscure. It may be an expression of insecurity (cf. vs. 8); this was no time to build houses, for the city was a caldron and the princes the flesh within it (cf. 24:3-10), and if something were not done they would be cooked within the caldron; so to save their skins they would conspire with Egypt against Babylon. However, Yahweh has said (vss. 4-12) that the real victims were those in the city slain by the leaders, and the leaders would be brought out of the caldron (i.e., the city) and delivered over to the foreigners to be slain by the sword. According to the interpretation suggested by the translation in the KJV and the RSV mg., vs. 3 is an expression of confidence and security; housing projects might be started, for the city was a caldron protecting the flesh (i.e., the leaders), while the rest of the people were but refuse. However, Yahweh has said (vss. 4-12) that the city was no source of security to them. Another suggestion comes from the LXX, rendering vs. 3*a* as הלא מקרוב נבנו הבתים, "Are not the houses recently built?" i.e., since 597—which would imply an expression of confidence. Still another suggestion is in the possible translation, "The time is not near to rebuild houses," i.e., there is going to be no destruction, and so no necessity to rebuild. This would also be understood as an expression of confidence, although implying a somewhat involved interpretation of the text. Most scholars, in one way or another, take vs. 3 as an expression of security.

6. For the oppressions within the city see ch. 22 and Jer. 34:8-16.

positions of leadership. They are the "bad figs" of Jer. 24. The very obscure expression in vs. 3 perhaps means that they pride themselves on Jerusalem's speedy recovery; the war-damaged houses have been rebuilt, and the appearance of the city is normal again. These men do not underestimate their own worth. The city exists for their sakes, as the pot is brought out only when there is cooking to be done. They have been utterly unscrupulous in maintaining their

position, so that the streets have run with the blood of their political opponents.

Pride, tyranny, murder—whence do these things come? From the abuse of that mercy which spared these men when others were led away to exile. They have no right therefore to complain when that mercy is forced in the end to arm itself against them as justice, until in another and grimmer sense they become the meat that seethes in the pot as Jerusalem goes

7 Therefore thus saith the Lord God; Your slain whom ye have laid in the midst of it, they *are* the flesh, and this *city is* the caldron: but I will bring you forth out of the midst of it.

8 Ye have feared the sword; and I will bring a sword upon you, saith the Lord God.

9 And I will bring you out of the midst thereof, and deliver you into the hands of strangers, and will execute judgments among you.

10 Ye shall fall by the sword; I will judge you in the border of Israel; and ye shall know that I *am* the Lord.

11 This *city* shall not be your caldron, neither shall ye be the flesh in the midst thereof; *but* I will judge you in the border of Israel:

12 And ye shall know that I *am* the Lord: for ye have not walked in my statutes, neither executed my judgments, but have done after the manners of the heathen that *are* round about you.

13 ¶ And it came to pass, when I prophesied, that Pelatiah the son of Benaiah died. Then fell I down upon my face, and cried with a loud voice, and said, Ah Lord God! wilt thou make a full end of the remnant of Israel?

slain. 7 Therefore thus says the Lord God: Your slain whom you have laid in the midst of it, they are the flesh, and this city is the caldron; but you shall be brought forth out of the midst of it. 8 You have feared the sword; and I will bring the sword upon you, says the Lord God. 9 And I will bring you forth out of the midst of it, and give you into the hands of foreigners, and execute judgments upon you. 10 You shall fall by the sword; I will judge you at the border of Israel; and you shall know that I am the Lord. 11 This city shall not be your caldron, nor shall you be the flesh in the midst of it; I will judge you at the border of Israel; 12 and you shall know that I am the Lord; for you have not walked in my statutes, nor executed my ordinances, but have acted according to the ordinances of the nations that are round about you."

13 And it came to pass, while I was prophesying, that Pelati'ah the son of Benai'ah died. Then I fell down upon my face, and cried with a loud voice, and said, "Ah Lord God! wilt thou make a full end of the remnant of Israel?"

7. They are the flesh can hardly mean that the slain are the real men of worth, but rather only that the oppressed and slain find the city to be their doom, while the wicked leaders will be cast out of the city to die. It is usually taken ironically; the only ones secure in the city are those already dead, but this hinges on a security interpretation of vs. 3. **You shall be brought forth** is a translation of the infinitive absolute, הוציא, and preferable to אוציא, **I will bring you forth,** following many MSS and the versions.

10-12. These verses have at least been revised by the editor, and in their present form are a *post eventum* prophecy of the judgment against Zedekiah and others at Riblah on the Orontes (II Kings 25:18-21). We should not follow the LXXᴮ in omitting vss. 11-12, for the diction and ideology are that of our editor. The translators or their MS source may have omitted a passage which adds little and repeats much (cf. 5:6; 18:9, 17; etc.).

13. It may be that when Pelatiah heard Ezekiel's prophecy he suddenly realized the enormity of his sins, and was actually frightened to death, as was Uzzah when he realized he had touched the ark of God (II Sam. 6:3-8). So also died Ananias and Sapphira when accused by Peter (Acts 5:1-10). Vs. 13*b* seems an echo of 9:8. See Intro., p. 52, for the relevance of this verse to the locale of Ezekiel's prophecies. Vs. 13*b* may be the editor's translation to his oracle in vss. 14-21 (see 20:17).

up in flame. How can men be capable of such ingratitude? But is there one of us who has not in some way misused the mercies of life? What should have awed us as undeserved deliv-

erance is dismissed as luck, or even as something we are entitled to, and the new opportunities which deliverance brings us are merely exploited for our own ends.

14 Again the word of the LORD came unto me, saying,

15 Son of man, thy brethren, *even* thy brethren, the men of thy kindred, and all the house of Israel wholly, *are* they unto whom the inhabitants of Jerusalem have said, Get you far from the LORD: unto us is this land given in possession.

16 Therefore say, Thus saith the Lord GOD; Although I have cast them far off among the heathen, and although I have scattered them among the countries, yet will I be to them as a little sanctuary in the countries where they shall come.

17 Therefore say, Thus saith the Lord GOD; I will even gather you from the people, and assemble you out of the countries

14 And the word of the LORD came to me: 15 "Son of man, your brethren, even your brethren, your fellow exiles,*l* the whole house of Israel, all of them, are those of whom the inhabitants of Jerusalem have said, 'They have gone far from the LORD; to us this land is given for a possession.' 16 Therefore say, 'Thus says the Lord GOD: Though I removed them far off among the nations, and though I scattered them among the countries, yet I have been a sanctuary to them for a while*m* in the countries where they have gone.' 17 Therefore say, 'Thus says the Lord: I will gather you from the

l Gk Syr: Heb *men of your kindred*
m Or *in small measure*

b) HOPE FOR THE EXILES (11:14-21)

This is a typical composition of the editor, to be compared with the oracles of restoration in chs. 20; 34–39. Irwin finds a genuine poem in vs. 15, but its poetic character is uncertain. Some ascribe the passage to the later period of Ezekiel's career (cf. Bertholet, Matthews), while others reckon it to be secondary (cf. Hölscher, Cooke).

15. While those who had not been carried into exile may well have reacted as described here, this verse may be taken rather as an expression of the antagonism of the exiles toward the nonexiles, comparable to that which we find in Ezra 4:1-3, and apparent in the editor's oracle in 33:24-29. See also Jer. 24, which is late (H. G. May, "Towards an Objective Approach to the Book of Jeremiah: The Biographer," *Journal of Biblical Literature,* LXI [1942], 148 ff.; "Jeremiah's Biographer," *Journal of Bible and Religion,* X [1942], 199). See also the estimate of those left in the land in II Kings 24:14.

15. Even your brethren: Omitted in five MSS and some versions, and perhaps the result of dittography. **Your fellow exiles,** with the LXX and Syriac, involves changing אנשי גאלתך, "men of your redemption," to אנשי גלותך. **They have gone far,** for **Get you far,** involves a different pointing, *rāḥaqû* for *raḥaqû*.

16. The context supports **a sanctuary to them for a while.** Yahweh himself was the sanctuary of the exiles while they could not go to the sanctuary at Jerusalem. The theological implications of this are striking. Contrast the situation at Syene in Egypt,

14-18. *Two Religions.*—Vs. 15 is evidently somewhat overloaded, but the essential point is clear. Those who are left in Palestine look with scorn upon the exiles in faraway Babylon; the ancient rights to the soil are theirs alone, and the others have lost their place in Israel's inheritance.[2] If we contrast their remarks with the oracle given to the prophet, we can see in this passage two types of religion. The first is that which in spite of defeat has maintained itself in Palestine, the other that with which the exiles must be content in a strange land. Let us glance at some of the points of difference between these.

[2] Note that the Exeg., working with a reconstructed text, would interpret differently.

First, pride stands opposed to grace. The Jews in their own land have no doubts. The temple stands and God is to be sought there as in the past. The Jews in exile have no such assurance. Yet they are not left alone, for God comes to them and himself supplies what is lacking. **I have been a sanctuary to them for a while in the countries where they have gone.** In one place the outward forms remain and are considered essential, so that those who have them refuse to recognize that those who are without them also belong to God. In the other place, just because the outward forms are lacking, God's presence is an intimate spiritual reality. Second, the past stands in contrast to the future. The Jews in Palestine have a continuous history

where ye have been scattered, and I will give you the land of Israel.

18 And they shall come thither, and they shall take away all the detestable things thereof and all the abominations thereof from thence.

19 And I will give them one heart, and I will put a new spirit within you; and I will take the stony heart out of their flesh, and will give them a heart of flesh:

20 That they may walk in my statutes, and keep mine ordinances, and do them: and they shall be my people, and I will be their God.

21 But *as for them* whose heart walketh after the heart of their detestable things and their abominations, I will recompense their way upon their own heads, saith the Lord God.

22 ¶ Then did the cherubim lift up their wings, and the wheels beside them; and the glory of the God of Israel *was* over them above.

23 And the glory of the Lord went up from the midst of the city, and stood upon the mountain which *is* on the east side of the city.

24 ¶ Afterward the spirit took me up, and brought me in a vision by the Spirit of God into Chaldea, to them of the captivity.

peoples, and assemble you out of the countries where you have been scattered, and I will give you the land of Israel.' 18 And when they come there, they will remove from it all its detestable things and all its abominations. 19 And I will give them one[n] heart, and put a new spirit within them; I will take the stony heart out of their flesh and give them a heart of flesh, 20 that they may walk in my statutes and keep my ordinances and obey them; and they shall be my people, and I will be their God. 21 But as for those[o] whose heart goes after their detestable things and their abominations, I will requite their deeds upon their own heads, says the Lord God."

22 Then the cherubim lifted up their wings, with the wheels beside them; and the glory of the God of Israel was over them. 23 And the glory of the Lord went up from the midst of the city, and stood upon the mountain which is on the east side of the city. 24 And the Spirit lifted me up and brought me in the vision by the Spirit of

[n] Another reading is *a new*

[o] Cn: Heb *To the heart of their detestable things and their abominations their heart goes*

---

where the Jews had a temple of Yahweh. **A little sanctuary** is interpreted by the Targ. and later Jewish tradition as an allusion to the synagogues.

19. A new heart (RSV mg.): With three MSS (חדש) and the Syriac, and in view of 18:31; 36:26, possibly to be preferred to **one heart**, although the latter appears in a similar context in Jer. 32:39 (cf. II Chr. 30:12), where the Syriac also reads "new." **Within them** represents MS variants and the versions; cf. **within you.**

21. But as for those ... after means changing the obviously corrupt M.T. ואל לב to ואלה אחרי.

c) Departure of Yahweh's Glory (11:22-25)

22-25. These verses should follow 10:19. The solar symbolism is obvious (cf. 43:1-4 and Isa. 60:1-3, 19-20). As the rising sun of the entrance of the glory of Yahweh rose above the Mount of Olives, so here it departs from the same point. This passage has

---

of faith and worship, but it is in Babylon that the future is to be made. Tradition is a splendid thing, but woe to us if we rely on it instead of on truth! Where men are deprived of the old defenses, they become open to new experiences. Where they cannot have recourse to the old wells, they may come upon fresh springs of living water. Third, treason stands over against fidelity. This religion which can appeal to established institutions and historic traditions

is, for all that, utterly unsound. The purifying influences must come in the end from those who have been stripped of everything save God and so have learned to know him as he is.

Note how the prophecy was fulfilled. The renewal of religion came from the few thousand exiles.

19-21. *The Gospel of Ezekiel.*—Here at last we come upon the message of hope which this harsh, stern prophet brings to a time that

So the vision that I had seen went up from me.

25 Then I spake unto them of the captivity all the things that the LORD had showed me.

12 The word of the LORD also came unto me, saying,

2 Son of man, thou dwellest in the midst of a rebellious house, which have eyes to see, and see not; they have ears to hear, and hear not: for they *are* a rebellious house.

3 Therefore, thou son of man, prepare thee stuff for removing, and remove by day in their sight; and thou shalt remove from thy place to another place in their sight: it may be they will consider, though they *be* a rebellious house.

God into Chalde'a, to the exiles. Then the vision that I had seen went up from me. **25** And I told the exiles all the things that the LORD had showed me.

12 The word of the LORD came to me: **2** "Son of man, you dwell in the midst of a rebellious house, who have eyes to see, but see not, who have ears to hear, but hear not; **3** for they are a rebellious house. Therefore, son of man, prepare for yourself an exile's baggage, and go into exile by day in their sight; you shall go like an exile from your place to another place in their sight. Perhaps they will understand,

---

influenced Zech. 14:4. Vs. 24 may be reminiscent of Ezekiel's return to Babylonia. Are vss. 24*b*-25 the addition of the editor? **In the vision by the Spirit of God** is emended by some to read "in visions of God," with 8:3.

F. SYMBOLS OF THE EXILE AND OF DISMAY (12:1-28)

In the first section of the chapter (vss. 1-16) the exile of the people and their prince is illustrated by dramatic acts. The second section (vss. 17-20) describes a dramatic action to illustrate the fearfulness of the people at the desolation of the land, perhaps with reference to the siege. In the third section (vss. 21-28) it is affirmed that the end is at hand, and the fulfillment of the predictions will not be delayed. This passage really belongs with 13:1–14:11, which is also concerned with the matter of prophecy. It is composed of two parallel statements, vss. 21-25 and 26-28.

The expansion or revision of the editor is most evident in vss. 6*b*, 12-16, 17-18. In the first symbolic action, the sign is for the house of Israel, which is to do as Ezekiel has done (vs. 11), and not for the "prince" (i.e., Zedekiah; an editorial comment; see Intro., pp. 53-54). Besides, vss. 6*b*, 12-16 are written with a knowledge of the events of 586, particularly the blinding of Zedekiah. The hand of the editor is evidenced also by the typical phraseology, such as "disperse them among the nations" (see xi on p. 50), "scatter them through the countries" (see x on p. 50), "they shall know that I am the LORD," "from the sword, from famine and pestilence," etc. (For vss. 21-28, see below.)

As Herntrich, Torrey, Harford, Messel, Pfeiffer, Bertholet, and others believe, the symbolic action here is best understood in a Palestinian background.

1. THE EXILE (12:1-16)

12:3. Prepare for yourself an exile's baggage: See Jer. 46:19. Not much could be salvaged (cf. Amos 3:12). **And go into exile,** וגלה, omitted by the LXX, may be dittography from the preceding word גולה, exile. **To another place** is taken by Bertholet to indicate that Ezekiel left Jerusalem at this time to dwell in a neighboring town, where he was at the fall of the city (cf. 24:25-26).

---

merits only judgment. There is to be a divine initiative, an act of God which will free men from their bondage and make possible that service of his will which now seems beyond them. Assuming that Ezekiel was a contemporary of Jeremiah, it is of interest to observe how

the minds of both men work along the same lines. For what we have here is a parallel to Jer. 31:31-34 with its prophecy of the new covenant. The love of God accepts the challenge of man's sin; the fact that men have been so obdurate prompts even then to a fresh effort to win

4 Then shalt thou bring forth thy stuff by day in their sight, as stuff for removing: and thou shalt go forth at even in their sight, as they that go forth into captivity.

5 Dig thou through the wall in their sight, and carry out thereby.

6 In their sight shalt thou bear *it* upon *thy* shoulders, *and* carry *it* forth in the twilight: thou shalt cover thy face, that thou see not the ground: for I have set thee *for* a sign unto the house of Israel.

7 And I did so as I was commanded: I brought forth my stuff by day, as stuff for captivity, and in the even I digged through the wall with mine hand; I brought *it* forth in the twilight, *and* I bare *it* upon *my* shoulder in their sight.

8 ¶ And in the morning came the word of the Lord unto me, saying,

9 Son of man, hath not the house of Israel, the rebellious house, said unto thee, What doest thou?

10 Say thou unto them, Thus saith the Lord God; This burden *concerneth* the prince in Jerusalem, and all the house of Israel that *are* among them.

11 Say, I *am* your sign: like as I have done, so shall it be done unto them: they shall remove *and* go into captivity.

though[p] they are a rebellious house. 4 You shall bring out your baggage by day in their sight, as baggage for exile; and you shall go forth yourself at evening in their sight, as men do who must go into exile. 5 Dig through the wall in their sight, and go[q] out through it. 6 In their sight you shall lift the baggage upon your shoulder, and carry it out in the dark; you shall cover your face, that you may not see the land, for I have made you a sign for the house of Israel."

7 And I did as I was commanded. I brought out my baggage by day, as baggage for exile, and in the evening I dug through the wall with my own hands; I went forth in the dark, carrying my outfit upon my shoulder in their sight.

8 In the morning the word of the Lord came to me: 9 "Son of man, has not the house of Israel, the rebellious house, said to you, 'What are you doing?' 10 Say to them, 'Thus says the Lord God: This oracle concerns the prince in Jerusalem and all the house of Israel who are in it.'[r] 11 Say, 'I am a sign for you: as I have done, so shall it be done to them; they shall go into

[p] Or *will see that*
[q] Gk Syr Vg Tg: Heb *bring*
[r] Heb *in the midst of them*

---

4. The trek to Babylonia would have begun in the cooler evening, after the baggage had been collected during the day (see Jer. 40:1 for the treatment of those to be exiled).

5. As a result of the seige, the walls of the house might be demolished, and one could leave through the breaches. It is uncertain whether Ezekiel has this in mind, or a secret flight in the darkness. The houses of the general populace in Palestine often had stone foundations and superstructures of mud brick. The RSV reads with the versions והוצאת for ויצאת.

6. This verse may have been revised to apply to Zedekiah's blindness. In the description of the action in vs. 7, there is no indication that Ezekiel covered his face. For illustration of captives with baggage over the shoulder see A. H. Layard, *The Monuments of Nineveh* [London: John Murray, 1849), p. 68.

7. In בקיר ביד, **through the wall with my own hands,** ביד, **with my own hands,** may be the result of dittography, and is omitted by the LXX[B], Syriac, and many commentators. Some suggest ביתד, "with a peg" (e.g., Ehrlich).

9. See 24:19; 37:18.

10-11. Vs. 10 is from the editor, who felt the need for some reference to **the prince** (see KJV and RSV mg.) in this over-all description of the significance of the oracle. Vs. 11 shows that the oracle is for the inhabitants of Jerusalem, and with vs. 10 testifies to the secondary character of the allusions to the prince. The more literal KJV shows the confusion in vs. 10 (observe that the word **concerneth** is supplied by the translators).

Zedekiah went out by night by way of the gate between the two walls, and was overtaken on the plains of Jericho and taken to Riblah, where his eyes were put out; thence he was carried in chains to Babylon (II Kings 25:4-7; Jer. 52:7-11). He did not

12 And the prince that *is* among them shall bear upon *his* shoulder in the twilight, and shall go forth: they shall dig through the wall to carry out thereby: he shall cover his face, that he see not the ground with *his* eyes.

13 My net also will I spread upon him, and he shall be taken in my snare: and I will bring him to Babylon *to* the land of the Chaldeans; yet shall he not see it, though he shall die there.

14 And I will scatter toward every wind all that *are* about him to help him, and all his bands; and I will draw out the sword after them.

15 And they shall know that I *am* the Lord, when I shall scatter them among the nations, and disperse them in the countries.

16 But I will leave a few men of them from the sword, from the famine, and from the pestilence; that they may declare all their abominations among the heathen whither they come; and they shall know that I *am* the Lord.

17 ¶ Moreover the word of the Lord came to me, saying,

18 Son of man, eat thy bread with quaking, and drink thy water with trembling and with carefulness;

exile, into captivity.' **12** And the prince who is among them shall lift his baggage upon his shoulder in the dark, and shall go forth; he*s* shall dig through the wall and go*t* out through it; he shall cover his face, that he may not see the land with his eyes. **13** And I will spread my net over him, and he shall be taken in my snare; and I will bring him to Babylon in the land of the Chalde′ans, yet he shall not see it; and he shall die there. **14** And I will scatter toward every wind all who are round about him, his helpers*u* and all his troops; and I will unsheath the sword after them. **15** And they shall know that I am the Lord, when I disperse them among the nations and scatter them through the countries. **16** But I will let a few of them escape from the sword, from famine and pestilence, that they may confess all their abominations among the nations where they go, and may know that I am the Lord."

17 Moreover the word of the Lord came to me: **18** "Son of man, eat your bread with quaking, and drink water with trembling

s Gk Syr: Heb *they*
t Gk Syr Tg: Heb *bring*
u Gk Syr Tg: Heb *his help*

dig a hole through the wall, but the editor has difficulty adapting Ezekiel's symbolic action to Zedekiah. The latter part of the verse is corrupt.

13. This verse is in imitation of 17:20, which describes Jehoiachin's exile to Babylon, and both may be reflections of 19:8-9, where the symbolism of the **net** and **snare** is thoroughly in context in the picture of the capture of the young lion, Jehoiachin. **Yet he shall not see it:** I.e., because he has been blinded.

14. This verse probably alludes to 5:2, 10, 12. **His helpers** follows the versions; the Hebrew has **his help.**

15-16. See Exeg. on 6:8-10; cf. 5:13. These verses are directed at the Diaspora by the editor.

2. Fear of the People (12:17-20)

Cf. the symbolic action in 4:9-11, 16-17. The fear of invasion was as real then as it is now (cf. Jer. 4:19-31; 6:24-26). **Carefulness** (vss. 18, 19) is here used in the KJV in its now archaic sense of "anxiety" or **fearfulness** (cf. 4:16).

19. Vs. 19*b* and vs. 20 may indicate that **the people of the land** here seems to mean the people of Judah. See 7:27, where the "people of the land" are the common people

their hearts. For the Hebrew the personality was open along all its frontiers and so could at any time be invaded from without, whether by good or by evil. Our psychology is different, and we shrink from language which would call in question human freedom. God, to be sure, does not deal with us as a potter with his clay.

But there are dealings with us in mercy which are more persuasive than any assertion of authority, and it is these which God employs to overcome our resistance. He wins our loyalty and gratitude, until we obey him not from any constraint but because it is sheer happiness to us to do his will.

19 And say unto the people of the land, Thus saith the Lord GOD of the inhabitants of Jerusalem, *and* of the land of Israel; They shall eat their bread with carefulness, and drink their water with astonishment, that her land may be desolate from all that is therein, because of the violence of all them that dwell therein.

20 And the cities that are inhabited shall be laid waste, and the land shall be desolate; and ye shall know that I *am* the LORD.

21 ¶ And the word of the LORD came unto me, saying,

22 Son of man, what *is* that proverb *that* ye have in the land of Israel, saying, The days are prolonged, and every vision faileth?

and with fearfulness; 19 and say of the people of the land, Thus says the Lord GOD concerning the inhabitants of Jerusalem in the land of Israel: They shall eat their bread with fearfulness, and drink water in dismay, because their land will be stripped of all it contains, on account of the violence of all those who dwell in it. 20 And the inhabited cities shall be laid waste, and the land shall become a desolation; and you shall know that I am the LORD."

21 And the word of the LORD came to me: 22 "Son of man, what is this proverb that you have about the land of Israel, saying, 'The days grow long, and every vision

---

(cf. II Kings 24:14). **Concerning the inhabitants of Jerusalem in the land of Israel** is omitted by some as a gloss (see Bertholet, Cooke). Bertholet would emend vs. 19*b* to the second person, but the editor's formula in vs. 20*b* cannot be used to support this correction.

3. The End Is at Hand (12:21-28)

21-28. The authorship of this passage is uncertain. It may be more purely eschatological than one might expect from Ezekiel in this period. It is, if the allusion is to the final age, the fulfillment of all prophecy. Is it the editor speaking a word of encouragement to his contemporaries who were impatient for the coming of the new age? With vs. 24 cf. 13:6-9, 23; 21:29 (Hebrew 21:34); 22:28; some think it secondary. The entire passage, notably vss. 25, 28, recalls the editor's "I the LORD have spoken, and I will do it" (see xxxv on p. 51). Cf. with this passage 33:30-33.

If there is a genuine oracle behind this passage, it has reference to the immediacy of the judgment upon the wicked in Palestine. Many people, noting the oracles of

---

12:21-28. The Prophet and His Critics.—We are apt to suppose that so outstanding and so forceful a personality as our prophet will necessarily have captured the imagination of his time. That is because we underestimate the extent to which ancient Israel was the scene of just those doubts, those secular policies, and that absorption in the moment which are characteristic of our own society. In this closing section of the chapter we see the prophet confronted by his critics and replying to the excuses they have found for rejecting his appeals. They have two arguments to bring against him, and each has won acceptance from so many that it has by now the force of a proverb.

(*a*) **The days are prolonged, and every vision faileth.** This is no wistful regret that the promised good is so slow in materializing, for Ezekiel's message has offered little hope thus far. It is rather the confident jest of men who dismiss the prophet's warnings as mere empty words. They say that enough time has elapsed

by now to put him to the test. There is evidently nothing at all in what he has said, and no need whatever to take him seriously for the future.

We need not, however, limit the meaning of their remark in that way. The problem is the old one of the seeming failure of God's truth. Why, we ask, has Christianity achieved so little though it has been in the world so long?

> When comes the promised time
> That war shall be no more,
> And lust, oppression, crime,
> Shall flee Thy face before? [3]

There are two answers to this question, one that Ezekiel gives and one that he does not. We will take the latter first.

The prophets of old often dared to forecast the shape of things to come, but their thoughts were never quite equal to the purpose of God. Sometimes they expected deliverance too soon,

[3] Lewis Hensley, "Thy Kingdom Come, O God!"

23 Tell them therefore, Thus saith the Lord GOD; I will make this proverb to cease, and they shall no more use it as a proverb in Israel; but say unto them, The days are at hand, and the effect of every vision.

24 For there shall be no more any vain vision nor flattering divination within the house of Israel.

25 For I *am* the LORD: I will speak, and the word that I shall speak shall come to pass; it shall be no more prolonged: for in your days, O rebellious house, will I say the word, and will perform it, saith the Lord GOD.

26 ¶ Again the word of the LORD came to me, saying,

comes to naught'? 23 Tell them therefore, 'Thus says the Lord GOD: I will put an end to this proverb, and they shall no more use it as a proverb in Israel.' But say to them, The days are at hand, and the fulfilment[v] of every vision. 24 For there shall be no more any false vision or flattering divination within the house of Israel. 25 But I the LORD will speak the word which I will speak, and it will be performed. It will no longer be delayed, but in your days, O rebellious house, I will speak the word and perform it, says the Lord GOD."

26 Again the word of the LORD came to

[v] Heb *word*

---

absolute destruction of Amos and others, doubted that they would ever be fulfilled, and scoffed at them. Against this background of skepticism we must also understand Jer. 1:12. The word מָשָׁל, **proverb** (vs. 23), is used in this sense in 18:2, 3; see 16:44 (cf. 14:8, "byword"), and as allegory or parable in 17:2; 20:49; 24:3. The word חָזוֹן, **vision** (vs. 27), here means "prophecy," as in 7:26; note also in vs. 23 "the word of every חָזוֹן." Cf. Amos 1:1, "The words of Amos, . . . which he saw [חָזָה]"; Mic. 1:1; Isa. 2:1. Papyrus 967 omits vss. 26-28 (see Intro., pp. 50-51).

---

before the discipline of events had made the nation ready for it. Sometimes, as in the case of Ezekiel, their stern estimate of the divine justice needed to be qualified by a more generous appreciation of the divine mercy. The witness men bear to God's truth may be refuted by events simply because God's truth is so much larger than they imagined. "My thoughts are not your thoughts, neither are your ways my ways, saith the LORD. For as the heavens are higher than the earth, so are my ways higher than your ways, and my thoughts than your thoughts." (Isa. 55:8-9.) The prophet does not mean that there is no relationship between the mind of God and the mind of man, but that we cannot conceive the generosity of the divine purpose. It is incredible from our human point of view.

The expectation of the Lord's return was cherished in the church of the first century, but was not fulfilled. Then also, no doubt, men said, **The days are prolonged, and every vision faileth.** We who look back can see that the vision failed because it was in part mistaken. Christ does not come in outward and visible form, but as a power in men's hearts; though from men's hearts, of course, he goes forth to establish his kingdom in the world in which they live. The event accords with God's purpose, but it runs counter to our conception of that purpose.

Sometimes, again, as Ezekiel urges here, the word of God goes unfulfilled because men turn from it to other and more pleasing words. Truth is not sufficiently flattering, it cannot be relied on to take vested interests under its protection, so men resort instead to vain vision and flattering divination. The society which turns from the gospel as ineffectual is all the while promoting or inventing other gospels. This society may claim that the gospel has failed, but the fact is rather that they prefer the new "gospel," because it deals more tenderly with their self-esteem and spares their favorite vices.

Like Ezekiel, we must await the future in confidence that it will vindicate what is true in our message even while it refutes what is false.

b) **The vision that he seeth is for many days to come, and he prophesieth of the times that are far off.** As we would say, the prophet's message is in the clouds; it has no relevance for the time in which we live. He speaks of what he calls the eternal issues, while we have our urgent problems of the next six months to cope with. He has fine ideals, but they can never be realized. He is a builder of utopias. Perhaps in the distant future human nature will be capable of what he is advocating, but not now.

It might give more reality to contemporary preaching if it were remembered that this criticism is constantly being directed against it. Sometimes the criticism is justified. Too often

27 Son of man, behold, *they of* the house of Israel say, The vision that he seeth *is* for many days *to come,* and he prophesieth of the times *that are* far off.

28 Therefore say unto them, Thus saith the Lord God; There shall none of my words be prolonged any more, but the word which I have spoken shall be done, saith the Lord God.

13 And the word of the Lord came unto me, saying,

2 Son of man, prophesy against the prophets of Israel that prophesy, and say

---

me: 27 "Son of man, behold, they of the house of Israel say, 'The vision that he sees is for many days hence, and he prophesies of times far off.' 28 Therefore say to them, Thus says the Lord God: None of my words will be delayed any longer, but the word which I speak will be performed, says the Lord God."

13 The word of the Lord came to me: 2 "Son of man, prophesy against the

---

G. Oracles Against Prophets and Prophetesses (13:1-23)

The oracle in vss. 1-16 is against false prophets, while in vss. 17-23 the oracle is directed against false prophetesses. The conflict between true and false prophets is dramatized for us in the incident of Micaiah the son of Imlah and the four hundred prophets in I Kings 22, and in the conflict between Jeremiah and Hananiah in Jer. 28. Amos had refused to identify himself with the prophets or the bands of prophets of his day (Amos 7:14), and Micah and Isaiah condemned the false prophets (Mic. 2:11; 3:5, 11; Isa. 9:15). Jeremiah gives much attention to them (Jer. 2:8; 5:31; 6:13-15; 8:10-12; 14:14-16; 23:9-32; 27:9-18; 29:8, 21-23). Ezek. 13:1-16 has striking parallels with Jer. 23:9-32. The false prophets misled the people, making them think that all was well when nothing was well, and were, like them, blind to the dire realities of their moral and religious state.

The composite character of this chapter is recognized by many critics. For instance, Matthews finds futile repetitions in vss. 1-16, with vs. 9 perhaps not earlier than the fourth century B.C., the text of vss. 17-23 even more confused, and only a general relationship existing between the two sections. Rothstein and Cooke find two distinct oracles combined in vss. 1-13 (cf. also Bertholet, who finds two recensions in vss. 1-16, one more probably original, and two original passages woven together in vss. 17-23). Irwin finds original poems only in vss. 3-5 and 18-19. The shifts from third to second person may suggest composite authorship, and may be due in part to the editor's expansion or revision rather than to the union of two distinct oracles. Vss. 4-5 may suggest that the city was in ruins when these words were phrased, and the latter verse may have an eschatological flavor. Vs. 9 not only looks forward to the final return, but reflects a postexilic view of the community of Israel. Vss. 22-23 (see Exeg., *ad loc.*) suggest the presence of the editor's hand, and there are a few typical phrases of his. Although we cannot neatly recover Ezekiel's original oracle, the tirade against the false prophets and prophetesses can perhaps in general be ascribed to him.

1. Oracle Against False Prophets (13:1-16)

13:2-3. See Jer. 23:16-17, where the prophets are accused of speaking visions out of their own mind. This was a particularly heinous sin, for the prophet was supposed

---

congregations are given admirable religious essays or exhortations which yet have no bearing on the problems they must face during the week. But sometimes it must be answered, as Ezekiel would have answered, that the popular estimate of what is and is not relevant cannot be accepted because that estimate is based on a very superficial judgment. God is at work all the while; men and nations are under his judg-

---

ment, and it is the prophet's and the preacher's task to remind them continually of this fact. What is today dismissed as impracticable idealism may vindicate itself tomorrow as the one policy with any promise of success. What we say may not commend itself to the present; its vindication lies with the future and with God.

13:1-7. True and False Prophecy.—The scene changes at this point, and the prophet is con-

thou unto them that prophesy out of their own hearts, Hear ye the word of the LORD;

3 Thus saith the Lord GOD; Woe unto the foolish prophets, that follow their own spirit, and have seen nothing!

4 O Israel, thy prophets are like the foxes in the deserts.

5 Ye have not gone up into the gaps, neither made up the hedge for the house of Israel to stand in the battle in the day of the LORD.

6 They have seen vanity and lying divination, saying, The LORD saith: and the LORD hath not sent them: and they have made *others* to hope that they would confirm the word.

prophets of Israel, prophesy[w] and say to those who prophesy out of their own minds: 'Hear the word of the LORD!' 3 Thus says the Lord GOD, Woe to the foolish prophets who follow their own spirit, and have seen nothing! 4 Your prophets have been like foxes among ruins, O Israel. 5 You have not gone up into the breaches, or built up a wall for the house of Israel, that it might stand in battle in the day of the LORD. 6 They have spoken falsehood and divined a lie; they say, 'Says the LORD,' when the LORD has not sent them, and yet they expect

[w] Gk: Heb *who prophesy*

to be only a medium of God's word (cf. Jer. 1:9). In vs. 2, as noted in the RSV mg., read with the LXX, הנבא for הנביאים.

5. The prophets have neither helped in time of crisis nor prepared the nation for its crisis. **In battle in the day of the LORD** refers to the time of the destruction of Jerusalem in the coming day of the Lord as predicted by Ezekiel and the earlier prophets, or, if the thought is the editor's, perhaps to the last great battle as depicted in chs. 38–39. Ezra uses the expression "a wall in Judah and Jerusalem" (9:9) to refer to spiritual defenses, and may be influenced by this passage.

6. **Divined:** This follows the suggestion of the LXX and Vulg.; the Hebrew reads "divination of a lie" (read this and the preceding verb as infinitive absolute: Cornill); cf. KJV and vs. 7. **Says the LORD** is, more literally, "an oracle of the LORD"; it is indeed the concluding formula of an oracle (cf. the parallel verse in 22:28, where the beginning formula, "Thus says the Lord GOD," is used; and see 2:4; 3:27, from the editor, as

fronted no longer by his critics but by his rivals. This contrast between genuine and spurious prophecy is one which every preacher would do well to lay to heart. There is always the possibility that he too, while convinced that it is God's word he utters, does but retail his own opinions and ideas. His people hang expectantly on his lips, but there is laid up in store for them a fearful disillusionment. The theme might be taken up at an ordination service. Then, above all, is the time for a man to search his heart and know whether he enters on his task in God's name or merely in his own.

Yet how is the line of demarcation to be drawn between truth and falsehood in this sphere? Ezekiel's answer is a simple one, but it is hardly satisfactory. The false prophet, he declares, does but utter his own thoughts, while the true prophet has a mandate from God. The false prophet sees a **vision**, yet not one that God has given; it is but the projection of his own mind. But was not this precisely the kind of accusation that Ezekiel's rivals brought against him? They thought of him as a pretender to

inspiration, passing off his own imagination as a revelation from heaven. Who is to decide between the parties to such a dispute? Being human, we must use human language and ideas. Who is to say where these correspond to God's truth and where they do not? The modern preacher too has to reckon with the possibility that he is self-deceived, that he is in his office for some ambition of his own and not at all as the messenger from God he purports to be. He can only search his own heart, keep strict watch upon his motives, and defend his conscience against all that would in any way pervert it. As he loses all thought of himself in the gospel he preaches, and in the men and women he tries to serve, he will win the assurance that, in spite of all that obtrudes from his petty self upon his work, there is enough of fidelity in him for God to use. In short, the false prophet is not to be thought of as a clearly marked individual, but as a temptation to which we are all the while exposed, a deterioration against which we must all the while be on our guard.

4-5. *Jackal and Man.*—To describe the false prophet Ezekiel has recourse to a striking con-

7 Have ye not seen a vain vision, and have ye not spoken a lying divination, whereas ye say, The LORD saith *it;* albeit I have not spoken?

8 Therefore thus saith the Lord GOD; Because ye have spoken vanity, and seen lies, therefore, behold, I *am* against you, saith the Lord GOD.

9 And mine hand shall be upon the prophets that see vanity, and that divine lies: they shall not be in the assembly of my people, neither shall they be written in the writing of the house of Israel, neither shall they enter into the land of Israel; and ye shall know that I *am* the Lord GOD.

10 ¶ Because, even because they have seduced my people, saying, Peace; and *there*

him to fulfil their word. 7 Have you not seen a delusive vision, and uttered a lying divination, whenever you have said, 'Says the LORD,' although I have not spoken?"

8 Therefore thus says the Lord GOD: "Because you have uttered delusions and seen lies, therefore behold, I am against you, says the Lord GOD. 9 My hand will be against the prophets who see delusive visions and who give lying divinations; they shall not be in the council of my people, nor be enrolled in the register of the house of Israel, nor shall they enter the land of Israel; and you shall know that I am the Lord GOD. 10 Because, yea, because they

---

also possibly here). The false prophets were victims of delusion, not deliberately falsifying, and they expected Yahweh to fulfill the oracle. As Skinner comments, the true prophet knew he had authoritative inspiration, but the false prophet could not know that he lacked it; this is the quandary of all religious belief where objective test is often lacking.

7. The latter half of the verse, beginning with **whenever,** is omitted by the LXX[B] and some commentators as a gloss on vs. 6. However, the oracular formula and the probable reflection of the frequent expression, "I the Lord have spoken it," suggest the editor.

9. We may have here the postexilic conception of the Jewish community. The penalty of exclusion from the community of Yahweh appears often in the P source (cf. Exod. 12:19; Num. 9:13; etc.) and in Ezra 10:8; Mal. 2:12 (cf. also Ezek. 14:8). **The register of the house of Israel** suggests specifically the list of returning exiles in Ezra 2, paralleled in the list of the population of Judah in Neh. 7:1-73; cf. Neh. 11:1–12:26, "the book of the genealogy of those who came up first." We should compare also the Chronicler's genealogical lists in I Chr. 1:1–8:40 and the list of returned exiles in I Chr. 9:1-44. There is an eschatological implication to this, i.e., only those so registered may participate in the new age (see also Mal. 3:16).

10. Jeremiah criticized the prophets for saying "Peace, peace," when there was no peace (6:14; 8:11), and Ezekiel may be quoting. With vs. 10*b* cf. 22:28. For **these prophets**

---

trast in images. We are introduced first to a city which has been laid in ruins. We watch a jackal leaping from stone to stone, seeking out a snug burrow amid the rubble of a house, now pouncing on a corpse which lies unburied still. It is the picture of the man who in the general overthrow is concerned solely with his own safety and advantage. He is unmoved by the catastrophe from which so few have come forth alive, himself included; he is content if he can snatch from it the necessities and pleasures of the passing day.

In the second image, the city still stands. But its walls are thronged with armed men, while the tide of a fierce attacking host beats against it. A moment more and the defenders will give

way, abandoning the city as lost. But see! A single individual leaps into the gap, sword in hand. The garrison rallies and rushes to join him. The breach is cleared, the wall rebuilt, and the city saved. So, says Ezekiel, is the man whom God sends into the world. He accepts responsibility and faces danger. That others fail in their duty is for him the best of reasons why he should be yet more faithful to his.

Think of some of the **breaches** in our society today, in personal integrity, in truthfulness, in family life, etc. It is one of the functions of the church to send forth men and women who will close these **gaps.**

8-16. *Whitewash on the Wall.*—Here we have an image from building. Some men are running

was no peace; and one built up a wall, and, lo, others daubed it with untempered *mortar:*

11 Say unto them which daub *it* with untempered *mortar,* that it shall fall: there shall be an overflowing shower; and ye, O great hailstones, shall fall; and a stormy wind shall rend *it.*

12 Lo, when the wall is fallen, shall it not be said unto you, Where *is* the daubing wherewith ye have daubed *it?*

13 Therefore thus saith the Lord God; I will even rend *it* with a stormy wind in my fury; and there shall be an overflowing shower in mine anger, and great hailstones in *my* fury to consume *it.*

14 So will I break down the wall that ye have daubed with untempered *mortar,* and bring it down to the ground, so that the foundation thereof shall be discovered, and it shall fall, and ye shall be consumed in the midst thereof: and ye shall know that I *am* the Lord.

15 Thus will I accomplish my wrath upon the wall, and upon them that have daubed it with untempered *mortar,* and will say unto you, The wall *is* no *more,* neither they that daubed it;

have misled my people, saying, 'Peace,' when there is no peace; and because, when the people build a wall, these prophets daub it with whitewash; 11 say to those who daub it with whitewash that it shall fall! There will be a deluge of rain,[x] great hailstones will fall, and a stormy wind break out; 12 and when the wall falls, will it not be said to you, 'Where is the daubing with which you daubed it?' 13 Therefore thus says the Lord God: I will make a stormy wind break out in my wrath; and there shall be a deluge of rain in my anger, and great hailstones in wrath to destroy it. 14 And I will break down the wall that you have daubed with whitewash, and bring it down to the ground, so that its foundation will be laid bare; when it falls, you shall perish in the midst of it; and you shall know that I am the Lord. 15 Thus will I spend my wrath upon the wall, and upon those who have daubed it with whitewash; and I will say to you, The wall is no more, nor those

[x] Heb *rain and you*

---

the Hebrew has והנם, "and behold them," and the LXX, Syriac, and Vulg. read "they," i.e., the prophets. **They have misled** is an Aramaism (root טעה; cf. Hebrew תעה).

11. A mud-brick wall suffers much from winter rains and hailstorms; it has to be kept in continuous state of repair. The prophets only put a veneer on the wall and did not contribute to its ability to withstand the storms. This allegorizes their affirming of peace when there was no peace. The verse is corrupt, but its sense is clear. The word ויפל, **that it shall fall,** may be dittography of תפל, **whitewash;** it is omitted by the LXX and Syriac. The address to **hailstones** (KJV) is obviously out of place; omit *weʾattēnāh,* **and ye,** for which the LXX and Vulg. read *weʾettēnāh,* "and I will give [i.e., send]."

13-14. Frequently the archaeologist finds only the stone foundations left. Beginning with the story of the Flood, the O.T. has many allusions to Yahweh's use of the elements to bring judgment (cf. 38:22; Isa. 29:6; Jer. 30:23-24; Amos 4:6-11; etc.).

15-16. Jeremiah had argued that if a prophet prophesied of **peace,** he could be known as a true prophet only when his oracle was fulfilled (28:6-9). See also Jer. 7:4

---

up a wall, for what purpose we are not told. They know that the materials are not sound and that the workmanship they have put into it is poor. That does not disturb them in the least. They have buckets of whitewash handy, which they splash all over it, so that it appears admirable, whatever it may be in reality.

Modern life provides us with as many parallels to this whitewashing as we care to employ; e.g., there is the advertiser who can make

shoddy goods so attractive that we buy them in preference to those which are of sound workmanship. There are the politicians who persuade voters to accept a candidate who has no character and will change his principles the moment it pays him to do so. There is the preacher who takes up the latest popular fancy and so prides himself on being abreast of the times that he does not stop to ask whether the times are right or wrong. All so much white-

16 *To wit,* the prophets of Israel which prophesy concerning Jerusalem, and which see visions of peace for her, and *there is* no peace, saith the Lord GOD.

17 ¶ Likewise, thou son of man, set thy face against the daughters of thy people, which prophesy out of their own heart; and prophesy thou against them,

18 And say, Thus saith the Lord GOD; Woe to the *women* that sew pillows to all armholes, and make kerchiefs upon the head of every stature to hunt souls! Will ye hunt the souls of my people, and will ye save the souls alive *that come* unto you?

who daubed it, **16** the prophets of Israel who prophesied concerning Jerusalem and saw visions of peace for her, when there was no peace, says the Lord GOD.

17 "And you, son of man, set your face against the daughters of your people, who prophesy out of their own minds; prophesy against them **18** and say, Thus says the Lord GOD: Woe to the women who sew magic bands upon all wrists, and make veils for the heads of persons of every stature, in the hunt for souls! Will you hunt down souls belonging to my people, and keep other

---

for a criticism of the attitude of unjustified optimism, which is one of the dangers of our own generation.

2. ORACLE AGAINST PROPHETESSES (13:17-23)

Miriam, the sister of Aaron and Moses (Exod. 15:20), Deborah, the judge (Judg. 4:4), and Huldah, who was consulted by Josiah (II Kings 22:14; II Chr. 34:22), were prophetesses of the pre-exilic period. The wife of Isaiah is called a prophetess (Isa. 8:3), but only as the wife of the prophet; there is analogy for this practice in the Assyrian records and in the Aramaic papyri; see E. G. Kraeling, *The Brooklyn Museum Aramaic Papyri* (New Haven: Yale University Press, 1953), p. 274. In the postexilic period there was Noadiah, a contemporary of Nehemiah (Neh. 6:14). In N.T. times we learn of Anna the prophetess (Luke 2:36), the prophesying daughters of Philip (Acts 21:9), and the false prophetess Jezebel of Thyatira (Rev. 2:20). The women denounced in Ezekiel are rather sorceresses and diviners than prophetesses. This protest against divination is consonant with true prophetic tradition (cf. Deut. 18:9-15). For prophetic prophecies against women see Amos 4:1-3; Isa. 3:16–4:1; Jer. 44:16-30 (see also W. H. Brownlee, "Exorcising the Souls from Ezekiel 13$_{17-23}$," *Journal of Biblical Literature,* LXIX [1950], 367-73, who tries to reconstruct the poetic original of vss. 17-23).

18. Sewing **bands** on the wrists and making **veils** for the heads were rites of magic whose significance escapes us. It is not clear whether these were worn by the sorceresses or by their clients (cf. vs. 20). The sorceresses are condemned for exercising a baneful influence over those who came to them for help. **Pillows** follows the versions, but כסתות is to be related to the Akkadian *kasû,* "to bind," and with the context this supports the reading **magic bands.** The words כסתות, **magic bands,** and מספחות, **veils,** occur only here. Presumably the veils covered the entire person.

---

wash daubed on a wall that the first strong wind will bring crashing down. How many of us are like that! We have a fair enough outward appearance, but inwardly what is there to it? It is the sin of hypocrisy or pretense which is castigated so severely in the Gospels, and a saying like Matt. 23:27-28 is the best commentary on this passage from Ezekiel—provided only we face the possibility that it may apply to us.

17-23. *Superstition.*—This description of the prophetesses of the time brings to our mind the part which women have played in the formation of modern cults. Here they are blamed for re-

viving those magical practices against which the higher religion in Israel had always set its face. Note that such people as these appear in a time of national crisis. They represent the kind of spurious religion in which men take refuge from a reality they do not dare to face. (Consult the Exeg. for details of their practices, such as hunting souls.) They make a living as fortunetellers, taking a fee for the good luck they bring or the ill luck they ward off. Thus they make the people their dupes. This mercenary element is by no means wanting in the modern equivalent of these prophetesses.

Ezekiel chooses the right ground on which to

19 And will ye pollute me among my people for handfuls of barley and for pieces of bread, to slay the souls that should not die, and to save the souls alive that should not live, by your lying to my people that hear *your* lies?

20 Wherefore thus saith the Lord God; Behold, I *am* against your pillows, wherewith ye there hunt the souls to make *them* fly, and I will tear them from your arms, and will let the souls go, *even* the souls that ye hunt to make *them* fly.

21 Your kerchiefs also will I tear, and deliver my people out of your hand, and they shall be no more in your hand to be hunted; and ye shall know that I *am* the Lord.

22 Because with lies ye have made the heart of the righteous sad, whom I have not made sad; and strengthened the hands of the wicked, that he should not return from his wicked way, by promising him life;

23 Therefore ye shall see no more vanity, nor divine divinations: for I will deliver my people out of your hand: and ye shall know that I *am* the Lord.

souls alive for your profit? 19 You have profaned me among my people for handfuls of barley and for pieces of bread, putting to death persons who should not die and keeping alive persons who should not live, by your lies to my people, who listen to lies.

20 "Wherefore thus says the Lord God: Behold, I am against your magic bands with which you hunt the souls,*y* and I will tear them from your arms; and I will let the souls that you hunt go free*z* like birds. 21 Your veils also I will tear off, and deliver my people out of your hand, and they shall be no more in your hand as prey; and you shall know that I am the Lord. 22 Because you have disheartened the righteous falsely, although I have not disheartened him, and you have encouraged the wicked, that he should not turn from his wicked ways to save his life; 23 therefore you shall no more see delusive visions nor practice divination; I will deliver my people out of your hand. Then you will know that I am the Lord."

y Gk Syr: Heb *souls for birds*
z Cn: Heb *the souls*

---

19. The sorceresses functioned only for profit and were willing to act for the smallest fee (cf. Mic. 3:5, 11). Some would translate "with handfuls of barley," etc., interpreting it as an allusion to divination technique.

20. With which, בם . . . אשר, is with the versions; the M.T. reads שם . . . אשר, "where." **To make them fly** (לפרחות), more literally, "for flying things," e.g., **birds,** is an Aramaism and is taken by some as a gloss, the first of its two occurrences being omitted by the LXX and Syriac. It would suggest an allusion to necromancy and the idea of the souls of the dead in the form of birds (cf. Isa. 8:19; 29:4). **Go free:** Reading אתם חפשים for את-נפשים, **the souls.**

22-23. The ideology and phraseology of vs. 22 recall the editor's discussion of responsibility in 3:16-21, and one may wonder how vs. 23 fits in with Ezekiel's predictions of the coming doom upon the people of Judah. With vs. 23 cf. vss. 6-7.

---

challenge them. What they stand for is false because it is unethical, nay, it runs counter to the plain deliverance of conscience. Here is a criterion which can be applied to those cults which compete with Christianity today. To whom, for example, does Theosophy offer its higher insights? To the pure in heart or to an intellectual elite? Does Christian Science deal with the problem of pain by showing how the dedicated will can turn it to good, or by a metaphysical theory which claims it to be unreal, quite regardless of our ethical attitude? Does not spiritualism at once appeal to the anxious and credulous and cheat them by

substituting for that eternal life which comes through unity with God in heart and mind a continuation of this present existence assured to us by table rappings and automatic writing? And what of the appeal of Hinduism to our Western world? Is it because Hinduism brings with it a moral challenge, or because it enables us to reduce the distinction between good and evil to something merely human and relative, a mistaken point of view? We must not be afraid to expose ourselves to the charge of narrow-mindedness when we insist that any religion is false which slurs over the distinction between right and wrong.

14 Then came certain of the elders of Israel unto me, and sat before me. **2** And the word of the Lord came unto me, saying,

14 Then came certain of the elders of Israel to me, and sat before me. 2 And

---

H. Judgment on Idolaters and Jerusalem (14:1-23)

The first part of the chapter (vss. 1-11) announces Yahweh's judgment on the idolaters who come to the prophet for an oracle. Yahweh himself will give the answer, apart from the prophet, obviously by means of his punishment of them (vss. 1-5). Yahweh will cut off from his people any such idolater, and if the prophet is deluded into giving an oracle for the idolater, prophet and idolater will suffer the same fate; Yahweh does this that Israel may not go astray, and Israel should repent and give up her idols (vss. 6-11). The second section (vss. 12-23) deals first with the procedure of Yahweh in passing judgment on a land; even if Noah, Daniel, and Job were in it, they should save but themselves by their righteousness (vss. 12-20). Yahweh is sending his four acts of judgment on Jerusalem, and any who may escape are but witnesses to the exiles that Yahweh was justified in destroying the city (vss. 21-23).

The chapter is a unity, and diction and thought seem to belong to the editor. Cf. such typical expressions as "stumbling block of iniquity," vss. 3, 4, 7 (see xiii on p. 50); "idols," e.g., *gillûlîm*, vss. 3-7 (see vi on p. 50); "repent and turn," vs. 6 (cf. 18:30; "You shall know that I am the Lord," vs. 8 (cf. vs. 23); the covenant formula in vs. 11; "acting faithlessly," vs. 13 (see xx on p. 50); "cut off from it man and beast," vss. 13, 17, 21 (see xxi on p. 50); "bring a sword upon that land," vs. 17 (see xxii on p. 50); "their ways and their doings," vss. 22, 23 (see xliv on p. 51). There are many analogies with R^D and H: e.g., "any man of the house of Israel" (vss. 4, 7; cf. Lev. 17:3, 10, 13; 20:2); "cut him off from the midst of my people" (vs. 8; cf. Lev. 17:10; 20:3, 5, 6); "defile themselves any more with all their transgressions" (vs. 11; cf. Lev. 18:24, 30); "acting faithlessly" (vs. 13; cf. Lev. 26:40 and in P in Josh. 22:20; Lev. 5:15); "I will set my face against" (vs. 8; cf. Lev. 17:10; 20:3, 6; 26:17). With vs. 8 cf. Deut. 28:37; Lev. 17:10; and with vs. 11b cf. Deut. 29:12; Lev. 26:12; etc. (see Gustav Hölscher, *Hezekiel, der Dichter und das Buch* [Giessen: A. Töpelmann, 1924], pp. 87-89). The theological presuppositions of the chapter are those of ch. 18—the editor's doctrine of responsibility—and with it, especially with vss. 12-23 (see Intro., p. 49), we should compare 3:17-21 and 33:1-22. The discussion of idolatry recalls also ch. 6. Commentators have taken widely variant attitudes toward the chapter. Some would ascribe part of it to Ezekiel's ministry before 586 and part to his exilic ministry (cf. Matthews, Bertholet, Pfeiffer). Hölscher thinks it all secondary, while Irwin finds an original poem in vss. 3, 6 and another in vs. 13. Herntrich thinks vss. 9-11 are an appendix to vss. 1-8, and vss. 21-23 to vss. 12-20. Bertholet finds vss. 4b-6, 7b, 11 parallel to vss. 7a, 8-10, the former with vss. 21-23 coming from the period of Ezekiel's exile. One can hardly attempt to ascribe different authorship to different parts of a composition as unified as this seems to be.

1. Punishment of Idolaters (14:1-11)

14:1. Certain of the elders of Israel are not north Israelites but representatives of the house of Israel, and here of the exiles. The phrase and setting occur again in 20:1b, before a long passage from the same hand. Contrast Ezekiel's "elders of Judah" in 8:1.

14:1-11. The God of the Lips and the Gods of the Heart.—We may begin by imagining the scene. The prophet is sitting in his house when the leading men of the community enter. He is probably in some country town, having withdrawn from Jerusalem after giving his warnings of how the siege would go. Quietly and rever-

ently the visitors take their seats on the ground before him at his request. Their whole attitude is one of deference to the man of God. Then their spokesman steps forward and reveals the errand on which they have come. There is some event—we are not told what it is—on which they would have the prophet throw light, some

3 Son of man, these men have set up their idols in their heart, and put the stumblingblock of their iniquity before their face: should I be inquired of at all by them?

4 Therefore speak unto them, and say unto them, Thus saith the Lord GOD; Every man of the house of Israel that setteth up his idols in his heart, and putteth the stumblingblock of his iniquity before his face, and cometh to the prophet; I the LORD will answer him that cometh, according to the multitude of his idols;

5 That I may take the house of Israel in their own heart, because they are all estranged from me through their idols.

6 ¶ Therefore say unto the house of Israel, Thus saith the Lord GOD; Repent, and turn *yourselves* from your idols; and turn away your faces from all your abominations.

7 For every one of the house of Israel, or of the stranger that sojourneth in Israel, which separateth himself from me, and

the word of the LORD came to me: 3 "Son of man, these men have taken their idols into their hearts, and set the stumbling block of their iniquity before their faces; should I let myself be inquired of at all by them? 4 Therefore speak to them, and say to them, Thus says the Lord GOD: Any man of the house of Israel who takes his idols into his heart and sets the stumbling block of his iniquity before his face, and yet comes to the prophet, I the LORD will answer him myself[a] because of the multitude of his idols, 5 that I may lay hold of the hearts of the house of Israel, who are all estranged from me through their idols.

6 "Therefore say to the house of Israel, Thus says the Lord GOD: Repent and turn away from your idols; and turn away your faces from all your abominations. 7 For any one of the house of Israel, or of the strangers

[a] Cn Compare Tg: Heb uncertain

We are not told the nature of the inquiry of the elders, for this is beyond the purposes of the author.

3-4. Their idols, i.e., "detestable idols," *gillûlîm,* as in 6:4-5 (see Exeg.). For idols as a **stumbling block of . . . iniquity** see also 7:19-20. These verses suggest the passion of the people for their idol worship (cf. Amos 4:4-5; Jer. 2:25). In vs. 3 correct האדרש to ההדרש, or perhaps omit as dittography from the following word, to be read *ha'iddārēsh.*

5. The words **lay hold of the hearts of the house of Israel** are probably a threat, alluding perhaps to the terror inspired by the kind of punishment envisaged in vs. 8. Possibly, however, the verse should be considered parallel to vs. 11, in which case it would suggest that the punishment is an object lesson to the house of Israel. With vs. 6 cf. 18:30*b*.

7. The strangers that sojourn in Israel may be the proselytes who were equal under the law with **any one of the house of Israel.** Cf. Lev. 17:8, 10, 13; 20:2; see also 47:22,

---

difficulty in which they need his advice. So they wait for an oracle. The prophet broods in silence till inspiration descends upon him.

When it comes, the insincerity of the men before him is mercilessly exposed. It pierces through their deferential exterior to what is in their hearts. There is nothing there but a mass of reservations and false loyalties. These men profess one allegiance with their lips while their hearts cling tenaciously to quite another. They have not the slightest intention of accepting an oracle from Ezekiel unless it chimes in with what they have already made up their minds to do.

Shall he answer them? No, for God will answer them, and that by an act. "Any man of

Israel who takes his idols to his very heart and is bent upon the sin that trips him up, and who consults a prophet, he shall get an answer from myself as heavy as all his idols" (vs. 4 Moffatt). The refusal of an oracle now is a certain indication of judgment one day in the future. God will strip these men of all their pretenses and will deal with them according to what they are, not according to what they seem to be. Is any more severe judgment possible than this?

For a parallel to this incident see the narrative in Jer. 42, where the Jewish leaders left in Palestine consult the prophet. Are they to remain or to take refuge in Egypt? Let him declare God's will and they will obey. But all

setteth up his idols in his heart, and putteth the stumblingblock of his iniquity before his face, and cometh to a prophet to inquire of him concerning me; I the LORD will answer him by myself:

8 And I will set my face against that man, and will make him a sign and a proverb, and I will cut him off from the midst of my people; and ye shall know that I *am* the LORD.

9 And if the prophet be deceived when he hath spoken a thing, I the LORD have deceived that prophet, and I will stretch out my hand upon him, and will destroy him from the midst of my people Israel.

10 And they shall bear the punishment of their iniquity: the punishment of the prophet shall be even as the punishment of him that seeketh *unto him;*

that sojourn in Israel, who separates himself from me, taking his idols into his heart and putting the stumbling block of his iniquity before his face, and yet comes to a prophet to inquire for himself of me, I the LORD will answer him myself; 8 and I will set my face against that man, I will make him a sign and a byword and cut him off from the midst of my people; and you shall know that I am the LORD. 9 And if the prophet be deceived and speak a word, I, the LORD, have deceived that prophet, and I will stretch out my hand against him, and will destroy him from the midst of my people Israel. 10 And they shall bear their punishment — the punishment of the prophet and the punishment of the inquirer shall

---

where the sojourner is mentioned with the "native born" (אזרח) ; cf. Lev. 24:22; Num. 15:15-16. The reference is less probably to the resident alien, for if the chapter is late it more probably refers to the proselyte, as in H and P; cf. the LXX ἐκ τῶν προσηλύτων τῶν προσηλυτευόντων ἐν τῷ 'Ισραὴλ (see T. J. Meek, "The Translation of *Gêr* in the Hexateuch and Its Bearing on the Documentary Hypothesis," *Journal of Biblical Literature,* XLIX [1930], 172-80; H. G. May, "Theological Universalism in the Old Testament," *Journal of Bible and Religion,* XVI [1948], 103-5) .

8. This is in the language of the Holiness Code (cf. Lev. 17:8-10; 20:3, 5-6) . Cf. the threat of excommunication in Ezra 10:8, or in the P Code in Exod. 12:15; 31:14; Num. 15:30; etc.

9-10. Under certain conditions Yahweh might even be the inspiration for a false oracle (see I Kings 22:19-23). Usually the false prophecy was regarded as the delusion

---

the while they have made up their minds what they will do, and only want an oracle to confirm their decision. See also Jas. 4:1-3 for the reason why prayer is not answered. Something in us takes sides against our prayers. Kierkegaard's discourse on purity of heart [4] should be consulted. His argument is that for purity of heart we must will one thing and that one thing must be the good. We are frustrated in the good we would do because there is something that is still nearer to our heart's desire.

How all life is poisoned by these mental reservations! Nations send their delegates to some conference, and it breaks down in spite of all the protestations of good will amid which it opened. The fact is that the delegates have been briefed twice over, first with instructions which are put on paper, then with interests, fears, and jealousies which work against all that they attempt to do. A church prays for unity, yet qualifies her petition by tacit unwillingness to con-

[4] *Purify Your Hearts,* tr. A. S. Aldworth and W. S. Ferrie (London: C. W. Daniel Co., 1937).

sider any departure from her denominational traditions; prays for revival, but on condition that it shall not be seriously disturbing. As individuals we long for a fresh beginning in the spiritual life, but cling secretly to certain old habits which are dearer still.

What is the way out of this impasse? We must recall what the prophet is always seeking to bring home to his hearers: that that religion is false which makes God an instrument of our human purposes, and that this is so even when we have taken care to attach his name in advance to those purposes. He is the God who is beyond us in majesty even while he is near to us in understanding and sympathy. The true center of life is in him, not in ourselves. We are in this world for one thing only—that we may know and do his will. If this seems harsh constraint so long as we rebel against it, it becomes sheer joy when we have once accepted it. We must therefore "let God be God," not in a general sense but in our own lives. We must search our hearts and dethrone the idols which

11 That the house of Israel may go no more astray from me, neither be polluted any more with all their transgressions; but that they may be my people, and I may be their God, saith the Lord God.

12 ¶ The word of the LORD came again to me, saying,

13 Son of man, when the land sinneth against me by trespassing grievously, then will I stretch out mine hand upon it, and will break the staff of the bread thereof, and will send famine upon it, and will cut off man and beast from it:

14 Though these three men, Noah, Daniel, and Job, were in it, they should deliver *but* their own souls by their righteousness, saith the Lord God.

be alike — 11 that the house of Israel may go no more astray from me, nor defile themselves any more with all their transgressions, but that they may be my people and I may be their God, says the Lord God."

12 And the word of the LORD came to me: 13 "Son of man, when a land sins against me by acting faithlessly, and I stretch out my hand against it, and break its staff of bread and send famine upon it, and cut off from it man and beast, 14 even if these three men, Noah, Daniel, and Job, were in it, they would deliver but their own lives by their righteousness, says the

of the prophet's own mind, as in 13:3, 7, 9, etc. Vs. 10 shows the author's concern for placing responsibility, as in 3:17-21. As Bertholet notes, we have here the viewpoint of 3:18.

2. THE RIGHTEOUS SAVE BUT THEMSELVES (14:12-23)

The legalistic and formal phraseology is consonant with the editor's discussion of responsibility in ch. 18. Yahweh's **four sore acts of judgment** (vs. 21) —e.g., **famine** (vs. 13), **wild beasts** (vs. 15), the **sword** (vs. 17), and **pestilence** (vs. 19) —form the framework of the discussion (see also 5:17; cf. Jer. 15:3-4). **Noah, Daniel, and Job** are selected because of their righteousness, and possibly also because of their role as deliverers (for Job, see Job 42:7-9). Daniel appears again in 28:3, mentioned there for his wisdom. These may be two different Daniels, however, for the context suggests that 28:3 may be an allusion to the Daniel of the north Canaanite mythological texts of Ugarit (see Exeg. on 28:3). The form of the name in Ezekiel corresponds to the Ugaritic name, i.e., דנאל, but the fact that it is here found in a postexilic passage makes probable an allusion to the Daniel of the Exile who was later to appear as the hero of the book of Daniel (this is not conclusive, however, for reflections of the Canaanite Daniel may appear even in the Book of Enoch; see Shalom Spiegel, "Noah, Daniel and Job" in *Louis Ginzberg Jubilee Volume* [New York: American Academy for Jewish Research, 1945], pp. 336-41). We may contrast the viewpoint here with that of the J author of the story of the destruction of Sodom (Gen. 18:20-33), where Yahweh is willing to save the city for the sake of ten good men that might be found in it; with both, cf. Jer. 15:1-4.

14. They would deliver but their own lives by their righteousness: Cf. 18:4; 33:12.

have their lodging there. We must unmask our own hypocrisies. But we can do that only as we put ourselves unreservedly in the hands of God, withdrawing nothing from his scrutiny. He can remake us only as we give him an entirely free hand.

> The dearest idol I have known,
>   Whate'er that idol be,
> Help me to tear it from thy throne,
>   And worship only thee.[5]

12-21. Three Just Men.—This is one of those passages from which we can learn not a little

once we have seen clearly that the gospel affirms the very thing they deny. Carried away by the certainty of the nation's so richly deserved doom, the prophet actually repudiates any possibility of atonement. In a people hopelessly corrupt like Judah, the most outstanding piety and virtue would be without influence, even on those nearest to them. It is as if, when a devastating storm has swept across a forest, three giant oaks alone rear their heads above the ruin, while even at their feet the wind has stripped the undergrowth relentlessly away in its fury. So, were the proverbial three righteous men of the past to come to life again in such a

[5] William Cowper, "O for a closer walk with God."

15 ¶ If I cause noisome beasts to pass through the land, and they spoil it, so that it be desolate, that no man may pass through because of the beasts:

16 *Though* these three men *were* in it, *as* I live, saith the Lord God, they shall deliver neither sons nor daughters; they only shall be delivered, but the land shall be desolate.

17 ¶ Or *if* I bring a sword upon that land, and say, Sword, go through the land; so that I cut off man and beast from it:

18 Though these three men *were* in it, *as* I live, saith the Lord God, they shall deliver neither sons nor daughters, but they only shall be delivered themselves.

19 ¶ Or *if* I send a pestilence into the land, and pour out my fury upon it in blood, to cut off from it man and beast:

20 Though Noah, Daniel, and Job, *were* in it, *as* I live, saith the Lord God, they shall deliver neither son nor daughter; they shall *but* deliver their own souls by their righteousness.

21 For thus saith the Lord God; How much more when I send my four sore judgments upon Jerusalem, the sword, and the famine, and the noisome beast, and the pestilence, to cut off from it man and beast?

22 ¶ Yet, behold, therein shall be left a remnant that shall be brought forth, *both* sons and daughters: behold, they shall come forth unto you, and ye shall see their way

Lord God. 15 If I cause wild beasts to pass through the land, and they ravage it, and it be made desolate, so that no man may pass through because of the beasts; 16 even if these three men were in it, as I live, says the Lord God, they would deliver neither sons nor daughters; they alone would be delivered, but the land would be desolate. 17 Or if I bring a sword upon that land, and say, Let a sword go through the land; and I cut off from it man and beast; 18 though these three men were in it, as I live, says the Lord God, they would deliver neither sons nor daughters, but they alone would be delivered. 19 Or if I send a pestilence into that land, and pour out my wrath upon it with blood, to cut off from it man and beast; 20 even if Noah, Daniel, and Job were in it, as I live, says the Lord God, they would deliver neither son nor daughter; they would deliver but their own lives by their righteousness.

21 "For thus says the Lord God: How much more when I send upon Jerusalem my four sore acts of judgment, sword, famine, evil beasts, and pestilence, to cut off from it man and beast! 22 Yet, if there should be left in it any survivors to lead

---

16. **They would deliver neither sons nor daughters:** Cf. 18:10-13. It has been presumed that this verse (see also vss. 18, 20) presupposes a narrative in which Daniel had children; so favoring identification with the Ugaritic Daniel (see *ibid.*, pp. 307-23).

21-22. The principle just formulated is applied to Jerusalem, which must certainly be destroyed. If some from Jerusalem survive and escape to the exilic community, the exiles will realize Yahweh was justified in destroying the city when they see the kind of people the survivors are. A difference in pointing (*hammôçî'îm* for *hammûçā'îm*), following the versions, is the basis for **to lead out sons and daughters** (contrast the different meaning of the KJV). Vs. 22 reflects the editor's view of the superiority of

---

day as Ezekiel sees impending, they would be powerless to mitigate its doom and able only to save themselves. There are assumptions here which we must challenge in the name of Christ.

First, no individual can thus be separated from his fellows. We live in a community and must suffer with it. So far is it from being the case that the just man is exempted from the misfortunes of his time, he feels them more poignantly than others do. Involved in the common calamity, he knows what has brought it

about and mourns the sin as well as the suffering of those with whom he is bound up.

Second, even if such exemption were offered him, the righteous man would refuse it. For to be righteous means, at least in the Christian sense of the term, not to stand apart from the evildoer, but to identify oneself with him in compassion, love, and service. Jesus came to call sinners and to bring home lost sheep. God's will for the world as we see it in him is not that the just should be spared the doom of the

and their doings: and ye shall be comforted concerning the evil that I have brought upon Jerusalem, *even* concerning all that I have brought upon it.

23 And they shall comfort you, when ye see their ways and their doings: and ye shall know that I have not done without cause all that I have done in it, saith the Lord God.

15 And the word of the Lord came unto me, saying,

2 Son of man, What is the vine tree more

out sons and daughters, when they come forth to you, and you see their ways and their doings, you will be consoled for the evil that I have brought upon Jerusalem, for all that I have brought upon it. 23 They will console you, when you see their ways and their doings; and you shall know that I have not done without cause all that I have done in it, says the Lord God."

15 And the word of the Lord came to me: 2 "Son of man, how does the

---

the first exiles (see 11:15; 33:24-29; cf. Jer. 24). There is no doctrine of the remnant here, as the more accurate RSV makes clear. The **survivors** are obviously the wicked (contrast Ezekiel's picture in ch. 9; with vs. 22 cf. 6:9-10).

23. The author would not have the house of Israel say that Yahweh's ways are not just (cf. 18:25-29; 33:17-20). He is probably meeting actual charges made by members of the postexilic community.

J. The Vine (15:1-8)

Jerusalem is useless and worthless, like the wood of the vine among the trees of the forest. We must not press the allegory too far and assume that the prophet means that the Hebrews were by nature worthless, or that other nations were much better than they. Vss. 2-5 present the allegory and vss. 6-8 its interpretation. The RSV is more probably correct in presenting the chapter as prose, although part or all of it has been considered to be poetry. Hölscher, Irwin, Cooke, and others consider vss. 2-5 to be poetry, but neither "meter" nor parallelism supports this opinion. Some think the interpretation in vss. 6-8 does not come from Ezekiel. So Hölscher, and also Irwin, who takes it as false commentary, the allegory being concerned with the nature of the vine and the interpretation with the fire; Hölscher notes how the redactor gives to Ezekiel's poetry a significance not fully coinciding with the original sense of the poem and comparing the similar technique of the N.T. evangelists. The allegory, however, seems to demand some interpretation. See the allegories in chs. 16; 17; 23; 29; etc.; cf. the two parts of the vineyard song in Isa. 5, vss. 1-6 being the allegory, and vs. 7 the interpretation. It is not surprising to find that the interpretation has been revised by the editor, even as, for instance, the interpretation of Jeremiah's parable of the potter in Jer. 18 has probably been revised. Diction characteristic of the editor appears strongly in vss. 7-8: "set my face against them," vs. 7a,c (see iii on p. 50); "and you will know that I am the Lord," vs. 7; "make the land desolate," vs. 8 (see xxiii on p. 50); "they have acted faithlessly," vs. 8 (see xx on p. 50). Vs. 6 is not an unnatural interpretation of the allegory, though the editor in vss. 7-8 seems to have slanted the interpretation in the direction of his view of the superiority of the exiles. The second person address in vs. 7 contrasts the exiles with the nonexiles (see 14:22; 33:24-29; etc.).

15:2. The figure of the vine and the vineyard was popular among the prophets (see Isa. 1:8; 3:14; 5:1-7; Hos. 10:1; Jer. 2:21; 6:9; Ezek. 17:6-7; see also Deut. 32:32;

---

unjust, but that they should share it with them, and so bring them to God (I Pet. 3:18).

15:1-8. The Wild Vine.—A concordance should be consulted to gain some idea of how often the **vine** is used in the O.T. as a symbol of Israel. A notable instance is the "Song of the Vineyard" in Isa. 5:1-7, which is drawn upon

in the N.T. (Mark 12:1-12). An examination of these various passages will show that reference is usually to the cultivated vine. Israel is precious in the sight of God and he has lavished his care upon it. But alas! It has failed so far to respond to his hopes (Luke 13:6-9), or it has been trodden down by cruel foes (Ps. 80:8-16).

than any tree, *or than* a branch which is among the trees of the forest?

3 Shall wood be taken thereof to do any work? or will *men* take a pin of it to hang any vessel thereon?

4 Behold, it is cast into the fire for fuel; the fire devoureth both the ends of it, and the midst of it is burned. Is it meet for *any* work?

5 Behold, when it was whole, it was meet for no work: how much less shall it be meet yet for *any* work, when the fire hath devoured it, and it is burned?

6 ¶ Therefore thus saith the Lord God; As the vine tree among the trees of the forest, which I have given to the fire for fuel, so will I give the inhabitants of Jerusalem.

7 And I will set my face against them; they shall go out from *one* fire, and *another* fire shall devour them; and ye shall know that I *am* the Lord, when I set my face against them.

8 And I will make the land desolate, because they have committed a trespass, saith the Lord God.

wood of the vine surpass any wood, the vine branch which is among the trees of the forest? 3 Is wood taken from it to make anything? Do men take a peg from it to hang any vessel on? 4 Lo, it is given the fire for fuel; when the fire has consumed both ends of it, and the middle of it is charred, is it useful for anything? 5 Behold, when it was whole, it was used for nothing; how much less, when the fire has consumed it and it is charred, can it ever be used for anything! 6 Therefore thus says the Lord God: Like the wood of the vine among the trees of the forest, which I have given to the fire for fuel, so will I give up the inhabitants of Jerusalem. 7 And I will set my face against them; though they escape from the fire, the fire shall yet consume them; and you will know that I am the Lord, when I set my face against them. 8 And I will make the land desolate, because they have acted faithlessly, says the Lord God."

Ps. 80:8-16, and Jotham's parable in Judg. 9:8-15). The prophet here limits his concern to **the wood of the vine,** rather than its fruit. **The vine branch,** הזמורה, is probably in apposition to **the wood of the vine,** and is better than **a branch**; the LXX[B] omits the word, and so also some scholars for the sake of the meter (Irwin, Cooke, Matthews). Less probably, by shifting the accent (*'athnaḥ*) one might read: ". . . surpass any wood of the twigs [=הזמורה?] which are on the trees of the forest" (cf. Bertholet, Gordon, *et al.*). Some omit part of the verse as a prosaic gloss, but the verse is not poetry.

4-5. Cf. Jer. 24:1-10. In part for dubious metrical reasons, **behold** (vs. 5) is sometimes omitted.

6. Cf. Isa. 6:13. Ezekiel here alludes to the coming burning of the city, mentioned already by him in 5:2; 10:2; etc.

7. Even those who manage to escape the burning of the city will yet meet their fate, as also in 5:4; 11:9; 12:14; 23:25. Contrast the RSV with the KJV, which less probably presumes an allusion to the disasters in 597 and again in 586.

8. We cannot take this verse as "an addition with priestly phrasing" (cf. Matthews), separating its authorship from that of vs. 7, in view of the close association of the

---

Here, however, the point is that the vine spoken of is the wild variety, the vine tree **among the trees of the forest;** i.e., the vine stands for Israel as a nation among other nations, and for what she may expect to be her fate when she measures herself against them in a struggle for power. Apart from her spiritual mission, Israel has no significance and no hope for survival. She has indeed nothing to contribute to the world. In the political sphere she is in no sense superior to others; she is hardly

indeed their equal. What can she do that others cannot do better? Therefore let her not be surprised if her end is ruin.

The wild vine is not Israel only. It is any nation that has lost its spiritual quality. Such a nation has ambitions but no vision, statistics but no soul. It is insistent on its rights but unaware that it has duties. As such, what future is there for it? True, if it possesses sufficient military might, it may stamp itself upon history, but only by the fear which it inspires. In the

16 Again the word of the LORD came unto me, saying,

2 Son of man, cause Jerusalem to know her abominations,

16 Again the word of the LORD came to me: 2 "Son of man, make known

---

diction and ideas of both verses in 6:14; 12:20; etc. It is difficult to speak of verses as glosses or additions in the book of Ezekiel in view of the nature of the work of the editor.

K. The Unfaithful Wife (16:1-63)

Jerusalem was a foundling child of mixed parentage. She was discovered by Yahweh and later taken by him in marriage and established in queenly estate. But she proved faithless, apostatizing at pagan shrines she built and making the Assyrians and Chaldeans her lovers (vss. 1-34). The judgment of Yahweh is now on his unfaithful wife; he will turn her over to her lovers, who will strip her of her regal ornaments and slay her (vss. 35-43). Vss. 1-43 are a complete unit, with vss. 44-63 an expansion of the original theme. In the latter Jerusalem is given an older and a younger sister, Samaria and Sodom; Jerusalem is more guilty than either and must bear her disgrace (vss. 44-52). Yet Yahweh will restore the fortunes of Samaria and Sodom and also the fortunes of Jerusalem. He will make an everlasting covenant with Jerusalem, and her sins will be forgiven (vss. 53-63).

The hand of the editor, not absent in the earlier part, is most evident in vss. 44-63. He has expanded this chapter, as he also did ch. 23, where vss. 36-49 are a comparable elaboration. The "secondary" character of these verses has been often recognized (cf. Herntrich, Bertholet, Eissfeldt, Messel). The picture of the restoration and the everlasting covenant in vss. 59-63 is typical, and dependent upon it are vss. 44-58. The change in the allegory is significant, and it is written with ch. 23 in mind. The thought, symbolism, and diction are paralleled in the late prose addition in Jer. 3:6-18, where Judah and Israel are sisters and wives of Yahweh, and Judah is the more guilty. Note the following expressions of the editor: "bear your disgrace," vss. 52, 54 (see xxiv on p. 50); "restore their fortunes," vs. 53 (see xxvi on p. 51); "shall know that I am the LORD," vs. 62. The quotation of a proverb in vs. 44 recalls 12:22-23; 18:2-3 (cf. 14:8). See also the allusion to Edom in vs. 57, and with the verse cf. 25:12-14; 36:5. Vss. 59-63 recall Lev. 26:42, 45. Some scholars would ascribe vss. 1-43 to Ezekiel's activity before 586, and vss. 44-63 to his later ministry (Cooke; cf. Matthews, Pfeiffer). Some find a poem in the chapter; so Hölscher, Cooke, and Irwin, the latter limiting the original poetic oracle to vs. 3.

Here as in ch. 23 the relation between Yahweh and his people is pictured in terms of a husband-wife relationship. This figure seems first to have been introduced by Hosea (see especially ch. 2). Jeremiah (2:1-3; 3:1-5) and Second Isaiah (50:1) make effective use of the symbolism. It is relatively rare in the O.T., perhaps because the

---

end it will fall unlamented. Nations live just in so far as they have a spiritual mission and are conscious of a purpose beyond their own which they are in the world to serve. They must submit to the discipline which such an obligation imposes, accepting its restrictions upon their freedom of action and their use of power. The wild vine must become the cultivated vine if it is to yield fruit.

16:1-63. *Two Allegories.*—This is one of those chapters which employ imagery so offensive to present-day taste that it is out of the question to read them in public. Nevertheless, there is much here to provoke reflection. There are two allegories in the chapter, that of the abandoned child (vss. 1-43) and that of the three sisters (vss. 44-63). Each is a picture of frightful, even incredible, sin; but while the first ends with unrelieved judgment, a note of hope is struck at the close of the second. Any use we may make of the themes suggested by the chapter will have to be with the utmost care, and it will be necessary to substitute our own imagery for that used by the prophet. It may be possible, however, to pick out from the context some few sentences which are richly suggestive, indeed painfully so.

1-43. *The Sin of Ingratitude.*—This allegory reminds us of the old story of King Cophetua

3 And say, Thus saith the Lord God unto Jerusalem; Thy birth and thy nativity *is* of the land of Canaan; thy father *was* an Amorite, and thy mother a Hittite.

4 And *as for* thy nativity, in the day thou wast born thy navel was not cut, neither wast thou washed in water to supple *thee;* thou wast not salted at all, nor swaddled at all.

to Jerusalem her abominations, 3 and say, Thus says the Lord God to Jerusalem: Your origin and your birth are of the land of the Canaanites; your father was an Amorite, and your mother a Hittite. 4 And as for your birth, on the day you were born your navel string was not cut, nor were you washed with water to cleanse you, nor rubbed with

---

Hebrews were conscious of the husband-wife motive in Canaanite religion and avoided it; cf. also the relative reticence in using the father-son motive in describing the relationship between Yahweh and Israel (see Exod. 4:22; Jer. 31:9, 20; Hos. 11:1). The predominant figure used to express the relationship between God and his people was that of the ruler-servant (Isa. 41:8-9; 42:1; 43:10; Jer. 20:10; 46:27-28; Ezek. 28:25; etc.; see G. Ernest Wright, *The Challenge of Israel's Faith* [Chicago: University of Chicago Press, 1944], pp. 36-48). Tradition was later to interpret the Song of Songs in terms of Yahweh as the husband (lover) of Israel. It has been plausibly presumed that Ezekiel in this chapter uses the theme of a popular story of an infant exposed at birth and found by a traveler. The birth stories of Sargon of Agade, Moses, and the twins Romulus and Remus come to mind.

1. The Foundling Child (16:1-7)

16:3. The Amorites were nomadic western Semites ("Amorite" means "Westerner") who invaded the Fertile Crescent *ca.* 2000 B.C. and soon ruled from Syria to Babylonia. The First Dynasty of Babylon, which included Hammurabi, was Amorite. In cuneiform the land of the Amorites appears as *Amurrû*. Much recent information on the Amorites is available from the excavations at Mari (see George E. Mendenhall, "Mari," *Biblical Archaeologist,* XI [1948], 1-19). The Hittites, in contrast with the "Canaanite" Amorites, were a non-Semitic ethnic group. They possessed a great empire in Asia Minor in the second millennium B.C., with its capital at the site of modern Boğazköy. For the Amorites in Canaan see Gen. 14:7; Deut. 20:17; Josh. 24:15; cf. the Amorite kingdom of Sihon in Trans-Jordan (Num. 21:21-30). For the Hittites in the patriarchal narratives and as late as the time of David and Solomon, see Gen. 23:10-20; 26:34; I Sam. 26:6; II Sam. 11:2-27; I Kings 11:1. See also the Hittites (Heth) and the Amorites in the genealogical table (Gen. 10:15-16; for the Hittites and Amorites see W. F. Albright, *From the Stone Age to Christianity* [Baltimore: Johns Hopkins Press, 1940], pp. 119-23). In thus depicting Jerusalem's origins Ezekiel obviously displays no false national pride.

4. Among the present-day Arab peasants in Palestine the midwife cuts the navel cord of the infant, rubs the child all over with salt, water, and oil, and swathes it in

---

and the beggar maid, except that the ending here is an unhappy and evil one. For the unwanted girl who becomes the rich skeik's wife takes what he gives and turns against him, abandoning herself shamelessly to others. If we are to apply this sad story to ourselves, we must ask whence the things come which we value most today. The answer is that the great nations of the modern Western world are great only in virtue of what they received, directly or indirectly, through the church. For when she gave us the gospel of Christ, she at the same time handed on to us the heritage of classical antiquity. The modern nations in their origins

were but tribes on the fringe of the Roman Empire; they became peoples as they took over the classical and Christian traditions. Who are the heroes of Europe and so, ultimately, of the Americas? They are Charlemagne, Alfred the Great, and men of that stamp. Who can measure what we owe to Augustine, Dante, and Luther, or to William the Silent and Oliver Cromwell? Where would our democracy be had it not been for John Knox, the Pilgrim Fathers, and the sturdy Independents with their church covenant? It is not Israel only that was constituted a people by the call of God. That is true also of ourselves.

5 None eye pitied thee, to do any of these unto thee, to have compassion upon thee; but thou wast cast out in the open field, to the loathing of thy person, in the day that thou wast born.

6 ¶ And when I passed by thee, and saw thee polluted in thine own blood, I said unto thee *when thou wast* in thy blood, Live; yea, I said unto thee *when thou wast* in thy blood, Live.

7 I have caused thee to multiply as the bud of the field, and thou hast increased and waxen great, and thou art come to excellent ornaments: *thy* breasts are fashioned, and thine hair is grown, whereas thou *wast* naked and bare.

8 Now when I passed by thee, and looked upon thee, behold, thy time *was* the time of love; and I spread my skirt over thee, and covered thy nakedness: yea, I sware unto thee, and entered into a covenant with thee, saith the Lord GOD, and thou becamest mine.

salt, nor swathed with bands. **5** No eye pitied you, to do any of these things to you out of compassion for you; but you were cast out on the open field, for you were abhorred, on the day that you were born.

6 "And when I passed by you, and saw you weltering in your blood, I said to you in your blood, 'Live, **7** and grow up[b] like a plant of the field.' And you grew up and became tall and arrived at full maidenhood;[c] your breasts were formed, and your hair had grown; yet you were naked and bare.

8 "When I passed by you again and looked upon you, behold, you were at the age for love; and I spread my skirt over you, and covered your nakedness: yea, I plighted my troth to you and entered into a covenant with you, says the Lord GOD,

[b] Gk Syr: Heb *I made you a myriad*
[c] Cn: Heb *ornament of ornaments*

---

clothes for seven days (see E. W. G. Masterman, "Hygiene and Disease in Palestine in Modern and in Biblical Times," *Palestine Exploration Fund Quarterly Statement for 1918,* p. 118).

The meaning of למשעי, **to cleanse you,** is uncertain; cf. Akkadian *mesû,* to wash or cleanse; it is omitted by the LXX[B] and Syriac.

6. Five MSS, the LXX, O.L., and Syriac omit **I said unto thee . . . in thy blood, Live,** which has crept into the text by dittography.

7. The RSV reads רבי for רבבה . . . . נתתיך, translated by the KJV as **I have caused thee to multiply;** the LXX retains נתתיך, **I made you** (RSV mg.) . **At full maidenhood** involves a slight change, reading בעת עדים or בעדים for בעדי עדיים; Urmia Peshitta and the LXX (πόλεις πόλεων) confused ר for ד, e.g., בעדים בערים, בער בערים.

2. THE MAIDEN (16:8-14)

8. I spread my skirt over you: An act symbolic of marriage (see Ruth 3:9; cf. Deut. 22:30). It might be a symbol of protection and also of identification with the household of the husband. David took a portion of Saul's skirt in part because he knew that he would thus be more closely identified with the kingship to which he aspired (I Sam. 24). **A covenant:** I.e., the marriage agreement and the covenant with Israel (cf. "your wife by covenant" in Mal. 2:14; see also Prov. 2:17).

And what return have we made for what we have received? Where does our sin differ from Jerusalem's? We took the liberty of the Christian man and made it the right of the few to enrich themselves at the expense of the many. We took the sacred adventure of self-government and handed it over to party bosses and caucuses. We took the Christian faith in a living God who guides history and made of it the easy assurance of material progress. So we have gone on, abandoning the true God for false

gods. When shall we learn wisdom? Or shall we continue until we bring destruction upon ourselves?

5. Only a Girl!—This verse takes us back to a society which had its own way of dealing with the problem of a surplus population. It anticipated the surplus and exposed girl babies where it seemed likely that the community would not be able to maintain them. If one reads the comedies of Menander, which reflect conditions in Greece in the fourth and third centuries B.C.,

9 Then washed I thee with water; yea, I thoroughly washed away thy blood from thee, and I anointed thee with oil.

10 I clothed thee also with broidered work, and shod thee with badgers' skin, and I girded thee about with fine linen, and I covered thee with silk.

11 I decked thee also with ornaments, and I put bracelets upon thy hands, and a chain on thy neck.

12 And I put a jewel on thy forehead, and earrings in thine ears, and a beautiful crown upon thine head.

13 Thus wast thou decked with gold and silver; and thy raiment *was of* fine linen, and silk, and broidered work; thou didst eat fine flour, and honey, and oil; and thou wast exceeding beautiful, and thou didst prosper into a kingdom.

14 And thy renown went forth among the heathen for thy beauty: for it *was* perfect through my comeliness, which I had put upon thee, saith the Lord GOD.

and you became mine. 9 Then I bathed you with water and washed off your blood from you, and anointed you with oil. 10 I clothed you also with embroidered cloth and shod you with leather, I swathed you in fine linen and covered you with silk. 11 And I decked you with ornaments, and put bracelets on your arms, and a chain on your neck. 12 And I put a ring on your nose, and earrings in your ears, and a beautiful crown upon your head. 13 Thus you were decked with gold and silver; and your raiment was of fine linen, and silk, and embroidered cloth; you ate fine flour and honey and oil. You grew exceedingly beautiful, and came to regal estate. 14 And your renown went forth among the nations because of your beauty, for it was perfect through the splendor which I had bestowed upon you, says the Lord GOD.

---

9. Your blood: Menstrual blood? Irwin notes this is not the duty of a husband, and would place the verse after vs. 6.

10. The word תחש, **leather** or **badgers' skin,** is also used for the covering of the tabernacle (Exod. 25:5; 26:14; Num. 4:6, 25; etc.). The kind of skin intended is uncertain; cf. Egyptian *ths,* leather; Arabic *ths,* dolphin.

11-13. Cf. the finery described in Isa. 3:18-24; also Hos. 2:13, and the ornaments in Gen. 24:22. As vs. 12b suggests, she wears the crown as a queen, as well as part of the bridal attire. **Fine flour** is semolina. Hosea's influence on Ezekiel is probable here (cf. Hos. 2:5, 8-9).

14. This suggests Jerusalem's splendor under Solomon.

---

one finds that the exposure of the unwanted baby is taken as a matter of course. A modern historian summarizes thus the information we have for this period.

> The general conclusion from *c.* 230 onwards seems certain: the one child family was commonest, but there was a certain desire for two sons (to allow for a death in war); families of four or five were very rare; more than one daughter was very seldom reared; and infanticide on a considerable scale, particularly of girls, is not in doubt. . . . Except among the Jews, no voice was raised against infanticide on moral grounds till under the Empire the Stoics Musonius and Epictetus spoke their minds.[6]

Adolf Deissmann reproduces from a papyrus find a letter from an Egyptian laborer, Hilarion

by name, to his wife Alis. It is "nothing but brutal advice in the main: if it is a girl you are bringing into the world, expose it." Deissmann comments:

> In the time of poor Alis frightened mothers innumerable of the lower class, who found it difficult to be motherly owing to the scarcity of daily bread, were waiting for that which to us—such is the extent of the moral conquests made by the Gospel—seems to be a thing of course. A century and a half later the Epistle to Diognetus (v. 6) boasts that Christians do not expose their children.[7]

One of the most effective ways of using such a passage as Mark 9:36-37 would be to set it against this sordid background. What a difference Christ has made!

---

[6] W. W. Tarn and G. T. Griffith, *Hellenistic Civilization* (3rd ed.; London: Edward Arnold & Co., 1952), p. 102.

[7] *Light from the Ancient East,* tr. Lionel R. M. Strachan (New York: George H. Doran Co., 1927), pp. 169-70.

15 ¶ But thou didst trust in thine own beauty, and playedst the harlot because of thy renown, and pouredst out thy fornications on every one that passed by; his it was.

16 And of thy garments thou didst take, and deckedst thy high places with divers colors, and playedst the harlot thereupon: *the like things* shall not come, neither shall it be *so*.

17 Thou hast also taken thy fair jewels of my gold and of my silver, which I had given thee, and madest to thyself images of men, and didst commit whoredom with them,

18 And tookest thy broidered garments, and coveredst them: and thou hast set mine oil and mine incense before them.

19 My meat also which I gave thee, fine flour, and oil, and honey, *wherewith* I fed thee, thou hast even set it before them for a sweet savor: and *thus* it was, saith the Lord God.

20 Moreover thou hast taken thy sons and thy daughters, whom thou hast borne unto me, and these hast thou sacrificed unto them to be devoured. *Is this* of thy whoredoms a small matter,

21 That thou hast slain my children, and delivered them to cause them to pass through *the fire* for them?

15 "But you trusted in your beauty, and played the harlot because of your renown, and lavished your harlotries on any passer-by. 16 You took some of your garments, and made for yourself gaily decked shrines, and on them played the harlot; the like has never been, nor ever shall be. 17 You also took your fair jewels of my gold and of my silver, which I had given you, and made for yourself images of men, and with them played the harlot; 18 and you took your embroidered garments to cover them, and set my oil and my incense before them. 19 Also my bread which I gave you — I fed you with fine flour and oil and honey — you set before them for a pleasing odor, says the Lord God.[d] 20 And you took your sons and your daughters, whom you had borne to me, and these you sacrificed to them to be devoured. Were your harlotries so small a matter 21 that you slaughtered my children and delivered them up as an offering by fire

[d] Syr: Heb *and it was, says the Lord* God

---

3. Apostasies and Alliances (16:15-34)

The term **harlotries** here (vss. 15, 21, 22, 25, etc.), as in Hosea and often elsewhere, carries the connotation of association with sexual rites of the Canaanitish cults; so also the verbal form in vss. 16, 17, 28 (see H. G. May, "The Fertility Cult in Hosea," *American Journal of Semitic Languages and Literature*, XLVIII [1932], 89-92). Jerusalem became as it were a sacred prostitute in the cult in which the sacred marriage was an important part of the ritual practices (see Gen. 38; Jer. 2:23-25; 3:1-5; Hos. 4:13, 14; 9:1; etc.).

15-16. The garments may have been used for curtains. **On them:** Cf. Amos 2:7-8.

17. Images of men: Phallic symbols?

18. Cf. the hangings for the Asherah woven by women in the houses of the sacred prostitutes in the temple area in II Kings 23:7 (cf. also Judg. 8:26-27; Exod. 32:2-4).

20-21. For child sacrifice see 20:26, 31; 23:37-39. See the sacrifice of Jephthah's daughter (Judg. 11:30-40), of the sons of Hiel (I Kings 16:34), of the son of the king of Moab (II Kings 3:27), and of the son of Manasseh (II Kings 21:6). See also II Kings 23:10; Jer. 7:31; 19:5-6; 32:55; Mic. 6:7, and the legislation in Deut. 12:31; 18:10; Lev.

---

21. *Child Sacrifice*.—One of the most atrocious crimes of which religion was guilty in the ancient world was that of child sacrifice. In Flaubert's *Salammbô* we are shown how a brilliant civilization, that of Carthage, was seared by this abominable practice. It was usually resorted to only as a desperate expedient, and as such

one reads of it now and again in the O.T., e.g., II Kings 16:3. The prophets revolt against it with disgust and horror; they can conceive of nothing more opposed to the mind of God.

But this appalling sacrifice of children to Moloch is not as strange to us as we at first suppose. In our own case, to be sure, the god

22 And in all thine abominations and thy whoredoms thou hast not remembered the days of thy youth, when thou wast naked and bare, *and* wast polluted in thy blood.

23 And it came to pass after all thy wickedness, (woe, woe unto thee! saith the Lord God,)

24 *That* thou hast also built unto thee an eminent place, and hast made thee a high place in every street.

25 Thou hast built thy high place at every head of the way, and hast made thy beauty to be abhorred, and hast opened thy feet to every one that passed by, and multiplied thy whoredoms.

26 Thou hast also committed fornication with the Egyptians thy neighbors, great of flesh; and hast increased thy whoredoms, to provoke me to anger.

27 Behold, therefore I have stretched out my hand over thee, and have diminished thine ordinary *food,* and delivered thee unto the will of them that hate thee, the daughters of the Philistines, which are ashamed of thy lewd way.

28 Thou hast played the whore also with the Assyrians, because thou wast unsatiable; yea, thou hast played the harlot with them, and yet couldest not be satisfied.

29 Thou hast moreover multiplied thy fornication in the land of Canaan unto Chaldea; and yet thou wast not statisfied herewith.

30 How weak is thine heart, saith the Lord God, seeing thou doest all these *things,* the work of an imperious whorish woman;

to them? **22** And in all your abominations and your harlotries you did not remember the days of your youth, when you were naked and bare, weltering in your blood.

23 "And after all your wickedness (woe, woe to you! says the Lord God), **24** you built yourself a vaulted chamber, and made yourself a lofty place in every square; **25** at the head of every street you built your lofty place and prostituted your beauty, offering yourself to any passer-by, and multiplying your harlotry. **26** You also played the harlot with the Egyptians, your lustful neighbors, multiplying your harlotry, to provoke me to anger. **27** Behold, therefore, I stretched out my hand against you, and diminished your allotted portion, and delivered you to the greed of your enemies, the daughters of the Philistines, who were ashamed of your lewd behavior. **28** You played the harlot also with the Assyrians, because you were insatiable; yea, you played the harlot with them, and still you were not satisfied. **29** You multiplied your harlotry also with the trading land of Chalde′a; and even with this you were not satisfied.

30 "How lovesick is your heart, says the Lord God, seeing you did all these things,

---

18:21; 20:2. There is possible archaeological evidence of child sacrifice (see Millar Burrows, *What Mean These Stones?* [New Haven: American Schools of Oriental Research, 1941], pp. 227-33). **As an offering by fire:** Cf. **to pass through the fire,** Hebrew העביר, "to make over or dedicate," often with באש, **by fire,** as in 20:31.

23. The words in parentheses may be a later addition.

24. The meaning of גב, **vaulted chamber,** and רמה, **a lofty place,** is uncertain. The **square** is the open place before the gate.

26-29. Like the earlier prophets, Ezekiel protests against entangling alliances because they involve association with pagan cults (cf. II Kings 16:7-18; 18:24; Isa. 7:1-25; Jer. 2:18; Hos. 8:8-14). The revolt against Babylon in 589 was undertaken with the promise

---

is called Mars. Generation after generation we cause our sons to pass through the fires of war. To save our society we cripple it by sending to their death its most eager and gallant members.

Is this so great an advance on the exploitation of youth in the industrial revolution? We have our factory laws today, but it seems as though all that has happened is that we protect our

31 In that thou buildest thine eminent place in the head of every way, and makest thine high place in every street; and hast not been as a harlot, in that thou scornest hire;

32 But as a wife that committeth adultery, which taketh strangers instead of her husband!

33 They give gifts to all whores: but thou givest thy gifts to all thy lovers, and hirest them, that they may come unto thee on every side for thy whoredom.

34 And the contrary is in thee from other women in thy whoredoms, whereas none followeth thee to commit whoredoms: and in that thou givest a reward, and no reward is given unto thee, therefore thou art contrary.

35 ¶ Wherefore, O harlot, hear the word of the LORD:

36 Thus saith the Lord GOD; Because thy filthiness was poured out, and thy nakedness discovered through thy whoredoms with thy lovers, and with all the idols of thy abominations, and by the blood of thy children, which thou didst give unto them;

37 Behold, therefore I will gather all thy lovers, with whom thou hast taken pleasure, and all them that thou hast loved, with all them that thou hast hated; I will even gather them round about against thee, and will discover thy nakedness unto them, that they may see all thy nakedness.

38 And I will judge thee, as women that break wedlock and shed blood are judged; and I will give thee blood in fury and jealousy.

the deeds of a brazen harlot; 31 building your vaulted chamber at the head of every street, and making your lofty place in every square. Yet you were not like a harlot, because you scorned hire. 32 Adulterous wife, who receives strangers instead of her husband! 33 Men give gifts to all harlots; but you gave your gifts to all your lovers, bribing them to come to you from every side for your harlotries. 34 So you were different from other women in your harlotries: none solicited you to play the harlot; and you gave hire, while no hire was given to you; therefore you were different.

35 "Wherefore, O harlot, hear the word of the LORD: 36 Thus says the Lord GOD, Because your shame was laid bare and your nakedness uncovered in your harlotries with your lovers, and because of all your idols, and because of the blood of your children that you gave to them, 37 therefore, behold, I will gather all your lovers, with whom you took pleasure, all those you loved and all those you loathed; I will gather them against you from every side, and will uncover your nakedness to them, that they may see all your nakedness. 38 And I will judge you as women who break wedlock and shed blood are judged, and bring upon

---

of Egyptian help (see Ezek. 17:15). Sennacherib tells how in 701 he diminished Hezekiah's land and gave to the kings of Ashdod, Ekron, and Gaza the cities taken from Hezekiah (see Pritchard, *Ancient Near Eastern Texts,* p. 288). As Cooke notes, there could hardly be a better commentary on Ezekiel's language. In vs. 29 **Canaan** is used adjectively and in its alternative meaning of "trader" (contrast also KJV and RSV translation of Zech. 14:21; cf. Ezek. 17:4 and Exeg. on 27:8).

31-34. The hire of the sacred prostitute was a bride price. Part of it went to the sanctuary (see Isa. 23:17-18; Mic. 1:7), and the Hebrews legislated against such a practice (Deut. 23:18; see also Hos. 2:12; 9:1; May, "Fertility Cult in Hosea," pp. 92-93).

4. PUNISHMENT (16:35-43)

36. The meaning of נחשת, **shame,** here is uncertain; elsewhere it means copper or bronze (cf. Amer. Trans., "effrontery").

38. See the law in Lev. 20:10; Deut. 22:22, and the punishment of adultery by stoning in vs. 40 (cf. Deut. 22:21-24; John 8:5-7).

39 And I will also give thee into their hand, and they shall throw down thine eminent place, and shall break down thy high places: they shall strip thee also of thy clothes, and shall take thy fair jewels, and leave thee naked and bare.

40 They shall also bring up a company against thee, and they shall stone thee with stones, and thrust thee through with their swords.

41 And they shall burn thine houses with fire, and execute judgments upon thee in the sight of many women: and I will cause thee to cease from playing the harlot, and thou also shalt give no hire any more.

42 So will I make my fury toward thee to rest, and my jealousy shall depart from thee, and I will be quiet, and will be no more angry.

43 Because thou hast not remembered the days of thy youth, but hast fretted me in all these *things;* behold, therefore I also will recompense thy way upon *thine* head, saith the Lord GOD: and thou shalt not commit this lewdness above all thine abominations.

44 ¶ Behold, every one that useth proverbs shall use *this* proverb against thee, saying, As *is* the mother, *so is* her daughter.

45 Thou *art* thy mother's daughter, that loatheth her husband and her children; and thou *art* the sister of thy sisters, which loathed their husbands and their children: your mother *was* a Hittite, and your father an Amorite.

46 And thine elder sister *is* Samaria, she and her daughters that dwell at thy left

you the blood of wrath and jealousy. 39 And I will give you into the hand of your lovers, and they shall throw down your vaulted chamber and break down your lofty places; they shall strip you of your clothes and take your fair jewels, and leave you naked and bare. 40 They shall bring up a host against you, and they shall stone you and cut you to pieces with their swords. 41 And they shall burn your houses and execute judgments upon you in the sight of many women; I will make you stop playing the harlot, and you shall also give hire no more. 42 So will I satisfy my fury on you, and my jealousy shall depart from you; I will be calm, and will no more be angry. 43 Because you have not remembered the days of your youth, but have enraged me with all these things; therefore, behold, I will requite your deeds upon your head, says the Lord GOD.

"Have you not committed lewdness in addition to all your abominations? 44 Behold, every one who uses proverbs will use this proverb about you, 'Like mother, like daughter.' 45 You are the daughter of your mother, who loathed her husband and her children; and you are the sister of your sisters, who loathed their husbands and their children. Your mother was a Hittite and your father an Amorite. 46 And your

---

42-43. Here we may have evidence of the editor's revision; note the expressions **I will satisfy my fury on you** (see xliii on p. 51) and **requite your deeds upon your head** (see xix on p. 50).

5. SODOM AND SAMARIA (16:44-52)

46. The **daughters** are the cities under the domination of **Samaria** and **Sodom** respectively (cf. the usage in Num. 21:25; 32:42; Josh. 15:45; etc.). **Left hand** and **right**

---

children in their earliest years to reserve them for sacrifices later on in life. The god of war has them if the god of wealth does not.

44-52. *The Three Sisters.*—This allegory is an O.T. treatment of the theme of pharisaism. The second sister compares herself with her elder and younger sisters and is entirely satisfied with the result. She feels herself morally superior to both, and from the fact that she

survives while they have been swept away she derives additional confidence that this estimate of herself is a sound one. God's judgment, however, is very different, for it takes account of the privileges she has received. This sister has had opportunities denied to the others, and therefore her record is worse than theirs.

Such an error is a common human one. We take for granted what has been given us, assume

hand: and thy younger sister, that dwelleth at thy right hand, *is* Sodom and her daughters.

47 Yet hast thou not walked after their ways, nor done after their abominations: but, as *if that were* a very little *thing,* thou wast corrupted more than they in all thy ways.

48 *As* I live, saith the Lord God, Sodom thy sister hath not done, she nor her daughters, as thou hast done, thou and thy daughters.

49 Behold, this was the iniquity of thy sister Sodom, pride, fulness of bread, and abundance of idleness was in her and in her daughters, neither did she strengthen the hand of the poor and needy.

50 And they were haughty, and committed abomination before me: therefore I took them away as I saw *good.*

51 Neither hath Samaria committed half of thy sins; but thou hast multiplied thine abominations more than they, and hast justified thy sisters in all thine abominations which thou hast done.

52 Thou also, which hast judged thy sisters, bear thine own shame for thy sins that thou hast committed more abominable than they: they are more righteous than thou: yea, be thou confounded also, and bear thy shame, in that thou hast justified thy sisters.

53 When I shall bring again their captivity, the captivity of Sodom and her daughters, and the captivity of Samaria and her daughters, then *will I bring again* the captivity of thy captives in the midst of them:

elder sister is Samar'ia, who lived with her daughters to the north of you; and your younger sister, who lived to the south of you, is Sodom with her daughters. **47** Yet you were not content to walk in their ways, or do according to their abominations; within a very little time you were more corrupt than they in all your ways. **48** As I live, says the Lord God, your sister Sodom and her daughters have not done as you and your daughters have done. **49** Behold, this was the guilt of your sister Sodom: she and her daughters had pride, surfeit of food, and prosperous ease, but did not aid the poor and needy. **50** They were haughty, and did abominable things before me; therefore I removed them, when I saw it. **51** Samar'ia has not committed half your sins; you have committed more abominations than they, and have made your sisters appear righteous by all the abominations which you have committed. **52** Bear your disgrace, you also, for you have made judgment favorable to your sisters; because of your sins in which you acted more abominably than they, they are more in the right than you. So be ashamed, you also, and bear your disgrace, for you have made your sisters appear righteous.

53 "I will restore their fortunes, both the fortunes of Sodom and her daughters, and the fortunes of Samar'ia and her daughters, and I will restore your own fortunes in

---

hand are properly **north** and **south,** i.e., as one faces east. Samaria had the larger territory, and so is the larger (which in Hebrew idiom means **older**) sister.

49. Cf. 22:29; see Gen. 13:13; 18:20.

6. Restoration (16:53-63)

Cf. the restoration of the pagan nations in Jer. 12:14-17; 46:26; 48:47; 49:6, 39, perhaps from the same period.

---

that the easier circumstances or the fuller knowledge we enjoy are ours by right, and then pass harsh judgments on those who do not come up to our expectations. But when each of us is judged, as will finally be the case, in the light of all the circumstances, there will be some very disconcerting revelations. "And indeed Beloved, I doubt not but that there is many a

poore sinner that now follows the ale-house, and drinking, and swearing, and whoreing, that yet may be in Heaven before thee and me!" [8]

49. The Sin of Sodom.—Sodom has become proverbial for unmentionable crime; the chap-

[8] W. Cradock, quoted in G. F. Nuttall, *The Holy Spirit in Puritan Faith and Experience* (Oxford: Basil Blackwell, 1946), p. 142.

54 That thou mayest bear thine own shame, and mayest be confounded in all that thou hast done, in that thou art a comfort unto them.

55 When thy sisters, Sodom and her daughters, shall return to their former estate, and Samaria and her daughters shall return to their former estate, then thou and thy daughters shall return to your former estate.

56 For thy sister Sodom was not mentioned by thy mouth in the day of thy pride,

57 Before thy wickedness was discovered, as at the time of *thy* reproach of the daughters of Syria, and all *that are* round about her, the daughters of the Philistines, which despise thee round about.

58 Thou hast borne thy lewdness and thine abominations, saith the LORD.

59 For thus saith the Lord GOD; I will even deal with thee as thou hast done, which hast despised the oath in breaking the covenant.

60 ¶ Nevertheless, I will remember my covenant with thee in the days of thy youth, and I will establish unto thee an everlasting covenant.

the midst of them, 54 that you may bear your disgrace and be ashamed of all that you have done, becoming a consolation to them. 55 As for your sisters, Sodom and her daughters shall return to their former estate, and Samar'ia and her daughters shall return to their former estate; and you and your daughters shall return to your former estate. 56 Was not your sister Sodom a byword in your mouth in the day of your pride, 57 before your wickedness was uncovered? Now you have become like her*e* an object of reproach for the daughters of Edom*f* and all her neighbors, and for the daughters of the Philistines, those round about who despise you. 58 You bear the penalty of your lewdness and your abominations, says the LORD.

59 "Yea, thus says the Lord GOD: I will deal with you as you have done, who have despised the oath in breaking the covenant, 60 yet I will remember my covenant with you in the days of your youth, and I will establish with you an everlasting covenant.

e Cn: Heb uncertain
f Another reading is *Aram*

57. The first RSV emendation is כמוה את עתה, **now you have become**, for the difficult כמו עת, **as at the time of.** Read אדם, **Edom,** with many MSS and the Syriac, instead of ארם, **Aram (Syria).** See Ps. 137:7-9; cf. 36:15. The Exile is presumed as an accomplished fact.

59-63. Yahweh will remember the **covenant** he made in Jerusalem's youth, i.e., at the Exodus (cf. vss. 8, 43). The **everlasting covenant** is mentioned again by the editor in 37:26 (cf. Lev. 24:8; Jer. 31:31-33). The theme of the restoration of both Israel and Judah is also characteristic of the editor; see Intro., p. 62. That Sodom should be included hints at the universalism of the author; cf. 14:7.

ter which tells of her fate is one of the most repulsive in the Bible, and later generations associated the wastelands around the Dead Sea with her condign punishment. Again and again in the O.T. the destruction of Sodom and Gomorrah is referred to as the most awful instance of divine judgment, and in the N.T. the same two cities are spoken of as hitherto unrivaled in degradation. When therefore we meet their names in a prophet like Ezekiel, who is not in the least squeamish in these matters, we are prepared to hear the whole revolting story without any concealment. But in fact the account he gives is simply of a city very much like London or New York or wherever we ourselves are living. It is just the common sin of which we read here, the sin of being full, con-

tented, and prosperous, and of forgetting that there are needy folk at our gate. It is the sin of the luxurious diners whom Amos describes (6:4-6), the sin of Haman and his king (Esth. 3:15), the sin of the rich man in the parable (Luke 16:19-31). If we are guilty in this respect, as we unquestionably are, how can we expect that it will be more tolerable for us in the Day of Judgment than for Sodom? These verses are charged with that prophetic passion for justice which is more rebuking than all the virulence of Marxist propaganda. **Pride, surfeit of food, and prosperous ease** are our portion; what have we done to **aid the poor and needy?**

59-63. *The New Covenant.*—The thoughts here remind one of Jer. 31:31-34, but there are two noticeable differences. First, while Jeremiah

61 Then thou shalt remember thy ways, and be ashamed, when thou shalt receive thy sisters, thine elder and thy younger: and I will give them unto thee for daughters, but not by thy covenant.

62 And I will establish my covenant with thee; and thou shalt know that I *am* the Lord:

63 That thou mayest remember, and be confounded, and never open thy mouth any more because of thy shame, when I am pacified toward thee for all that thou hast done, saith the Lord God.

17 And the word of the Lord came unto me, saying,

2 Son of man, put forth a riddle, and speak a parable unto the house of Israel;

61 Then you will remember your ways, and be ashamed when Iɡ take your sisters, both your elder and your younger, and give them to you as daughters, but not on account of the covenant with you. 62 I will establish my covenant with you, and you shall know that I am the Lord, 63 that you may remember and be confounded, and never open your mouth again because of your shame, when I forgive you all that you have done, says the Lord God."

17 The word of the Lord came to me: 2 "Son of man, propound a riddle, and speak an allegory to the house of Israel;

ɡ Syr: Heb *you*

L. The Two Eagles and the Cedar (17:1-24)

The chapter falls into three parts: the allegory (vss. 1-10); the interpretation of the allegory (vss. 11-21); and a supplementary allegory (vss. 22-24). The allegory represents Nebuchadrezzar king of Babylonia and Pharaoh Hophra king of Egypt as eagles, with Jehoiachin as the tip of a cedar of Lebanon and Zedekiah as the seed of the land which became a vine. Zedekiah is criticized for disloyalty to Yahweh in breaking his oath of allegiance to Nebuchadrezzar by turning to Egypt for help. Yahweh's judgment is upon Zedekiah—the east wind will strike the vine and it will wither away on the bed where it grows, Ezekiel, like Jeremiah, believed that Zedekiah should have put his neck under the yoke of the king of Babylon (see Jer. 27). Ezekiel may have written this oracle close to the time of the revolt against Babylonia in the late summer of 589, when plans for alliance with Egypt were being consummated. For the first years of his reign Zedekiah apparently had accepted Jeremiah's advice of loyalty to Nebuchadrezzar.

Some scholars find poetry in the chapter, although disagreeing as to its extent (cf. Hölscher, Irwin, L. P. Smith, Cooke, Bewer, Gordon). So much excision is necessary to get good parallelism and meter (cf. Louise Pettibone Smith, "The Eagle(s) of Ezekiel 17," *Journal of Biblical Literature,* LVIII [1939], 43-50) that we can presume no more than that we have poetic prose. Scholars also disagree as to how far beyond the first part of the chapter, if at all, the genuine materials extend. The hand of the editor has at least elaborated the interpretation of the allegory in the second part. So vs. 14 is not quite in context, and the expression **that the kingdom might be humble** is paralleled by the editor in 29:15. See also "requite upon his head" in vs. 19 (see xix on p. 50) and with

looks only for "a new covenant with the house of Israel, and with the house of Judah," Ezekiel includes within it both **Sodom** and **Samaria.** It is true that they benefit only indirectly, as necessary to the full restoration of Judah. Nevertheless there is a suggestion here that the mercy of God is for all mankind, since who need despair if Sodom may hope for reinstatement?

But, second, Ezekiel does not understand how far the mercy of God can carry those who receive it. The restoration he describes stops halfway. The scene closes with Jerusalem standing abashed before God, haunted still by shame for

her unworthy past. Never again will she dare to open her mouth. Ezekiel has not learned that forgiveness can restore freedom and joy where these had been lost, that we need not carry the burden to the end of life, but can see it drop from us at the Cross. What of the kiss for the returning prodigal, the shoes, the fatted calf? What of the father's refusal to take the lad back as a hired servant and his insistence that he must come as son? Yes, there is more in the gospel than Ezekiel could imagine.

17:1-21. *The Sanctity of Treaties.*—For the historical background to this chapter consult the Exeg. Its value for the expositor is that it

3 And say, Thus saith the Lord God; A great eagle with great wings, long-winged, full of feathers, which had divers colors, came unto Lebanon, and took the highest branch of the cedar:

4 He cropped off the top of his young twigs, and carried it into a land of traffic; he set it in a city of merchants.

5 He took also of the seed of the land, and planted it in a fruitful field; he placed *it* by great waters, *and* set it *as* a willow tree.

6 And it grew, and became a spreading vine of low stature, whose branches turned toward him, and the roots thereof were under him: so it became a vine, and brought forth branches, and shot forth sprigs.

3 say, Thus says the Lord God: A great eagle with great wings and long pinions, rich in plumage of many colors, came to Lebanon and took the top of the cedar; 4 he broke off the topmost of its young twigs and carried it to a land of trade, and set it in a city of merchants. 5 Then he took of the seed of the land and planted it in fertile soil; he placed it beside abundant waters. He set it like a willow twig, 6 and it sprouted and became a low spreading vine, and its branches turned toward him, and its roots remained where it stood. So it became a vine, and brought forth branches and put forth foliage.

I will spread my net, etc., in vs. 20 cf. 12:13; with vs. 21 cf. 12:14. The supplementary allegory in vss. 22-24, ascribed by some to the later prophecies of Ezekiel after 586 (Bertholet, Matthews), seems to belong entirely to the editor (cf. Cooke). **Mountain height of Israel** (vs. 23) is the editor's in 20:40; 34:14; and vs. 24 could not be more consistently his ideology and diction. The messianism and universalism are typical.

1. Allegory of the Two Eagles (17:1-10)

17:2. A riddle: A figurative saying which must be interpreted. The word משל, **parable,** here and in certain other contexts might be translated **allegory,** e.g., in 20:49 (Hebrew 21:5); 24:3 (cf. Isa. 14:4).

3. The word נשר, is comprehensive, including both vulture and **eagle.** In some contexts "vulture" seems more appropriate and is so translated in the RSV in Hos. 8:1; Lam. 4:19; etc. Here, as in 1:10; 10:14; Ps. 103:5; Deut. 32:11, "eagle" is more fitting. In ch. 31 the **cedar** represents Pharaoh and his multitudes, and in Isa. 14, the king of Babylon. **The top of the cedar** is Jehoiachin. The cedars of Lebanon were famed throughout the ancient world.

4. Topmost of its young twigs: Jehoiachin was eighteen years old when he was exiled. **Land of trade:** Babylonia. **City of merchants:** Babylon.

5. Seed of the land: Zedekiah. The expression מים רבים, **abundant waters,** often refers to the great abyss or primordial sea; cf. the imagery associated with the symbolism of the cosmic tree in ch. 31. The word קח, **he placed,** is obscure and possibly dittography,

---

raises in sharp and challenging fashion a question which is of the utmost importance in international relationships and one with which each generation may expect to be faced in some form.

From our point of view one of the strangest episodes in the O.T. is the opposition of Jeremiah to the last struggle of his people to maintain their independence. In the siege of Jerusalem by the Babylonians he played what seemed to many of his countrymen a traitor's part. Even to ourselves it is bound to appear in that light. Not satisfied with urging on the king a policy of surrender, he goes so far as to advise individuals to desert to the enemy and so to save

at least their own lives in the doom which impends over the city (Jer. 21:1-10). Now this passage from Ezekiel shows how a contemporary who was also a kindred spirit would have justified Jeremiah's action. He would have pointed out that Zedekiah was bound by an oath to remain loyal to his suzerain in Babylon, and that when he broke that oath he brought upon himself the divine displeasure. So doing, how could he hope to succeed?

We see at once that these prophets judged treaties and the obligations attaching to them by a standard very different from our own. It is an accepted principle of international law that every treaty between nations is qualified

7 There was also another great eagle with great wings and many feathers: and, behold, this vine did bend her roots toward him, and shot forth her branches toward him, that he might water it by the furrows of her plantation.

8 It was planted in a good soil by great waters, that it might bring forth branches, and that it might bear fruit, that it might be a goodly vine.

9 Say thou, Thus saith the Lord GOD; Shall it prosper? shall he not pull up the roots thereof, and cut off the fruit thereof, that it wither? it shall wither in all the leaves of her spring, even without great power or many people to pluck it up by the roots thereof.

7 "But there was another great eagle with great wings and much plumage; and behold, this vine bent its roots toward him, and shot forth its branches toward him that he might water it. From the bed where it was planted 8 he transplanted it[h] to good soil by abundant waters, that it might bring forth branches, and bear fruit, and become a noble vine. 9 Say, Thus says the Lord GOD: Will it thrive? Will he not pull up its roots and cut off its branches,[i] so that all its fresh sprouting leaves wither? It will not take a strong arm or many people to pull

[h] Cn: Heb *it was transplanted*
[i] Cn: Heb *fruit*

not represented in the LXX and Syriac. The term צפצפה, **a willow twig,** is of uncertain meaning.

7a. Another great eagle: Hophra. The Hebrew reads אחד, "one," but the LXX, ἕτερος, **another,** =אחר or a possible rendering of אחד. L. P. Smith and Irwin find but one eagle in the chapter. For the uncertain כפנה, **bent** (cf. Arabic *kfn,* "spin," "wrap"), perhaps read פנתה, "turned"; see, however, Aramaic כפן, "be hungry." The mixed imagery is not felicitous, but might seem more so if we knew its source; cf. a Mycenaean signet showing a tree with grapes on it (see A. J. Evans, *The Palace of Minos* [London: Macmillan & Co., 1930], Vol. III, p. 142, Fig. 93) or the imagery of Song of S. 7:7-8.

7b-8. From the bed where it was planted: Contrast the KJV. **Furrows** is certainly wrong (cf. Song of S. 5:13; 6:2). Possibly we should read, "and shoot forth its branches toward him from the bed where it was planted that he might water it. It was planted in good soil," etc. Vs. 8 would then be an allusion to vss. 5-6, and "he" in vs. 9 a reference to Nebuchadrezzar. If, as seems more probable, however, the symbolism here is that of transplanting, the reference is to the new alliance with Egypt, and "he" in the RSV vss. 8-9 is a reference to Pharaoh. Critics have much trouble with these verses, transposing, excising, etc. (cf. Bertholet, Cooke, *et al.*).

9. Its branches: Read פארתיה for פריה, **its fruit.** The M.T. יבש . . . תיבש, "utterly wither," should probably be only **wither,** omitting with the LXX תיבש as a gloss from vs. 10. The word למשאות, **to pull,** is an Aramaicized infinitive of נשא (see Howie, *Date and Composition of Ezekiel,* p. 64).

by the unwritten clause *rebus sic stantibus,* i.e., a treaty does but give legal force to the power relationships which obtain between the parties signatory to it. When therefore these power relationships have undergone serious alteration, the obligation to observe the treaty is correspondingly impaired and may be annulled outright. In particular, if our own nation should be reduced to signing away part of its right under duress, we should consider it justified in repudiating such a treaty once it felt strong enough to do so.

The man in the street, to be sure, feels there is something wrong about such arguments. At least he does so when some other nation is con-

cerned. He knows that it is to the credit of an individual if it can be said of him that he "sweareth to his own hurt, and changeth not" (Ps. 15:4). Why should the standard be different for the nation? What stability is left if we are free to repudiate unpleasant obligations under the plea that conditions are not what they were when we entered upon them? Hence the readiness with which the ordinary man rallies to defend the sanctity of treaties, because he feels that it is a matter of good faith and common honesty. What has Ezekiel to say on this vexed question?

It is important to note at the outset that the pact he has in mind here was no treaty

10 Yea, behold, *being* planted, shall it prosper? shall it not utterly wither, when the east wind toucheth it? it shall wither in the furrows where it grew.

11 ¶ Moreover the word of the LORD came unto me, saying,

12 Say now to the rebellious house, Know ye not what these *things mean?* tell *them,* Behold, the king of Babylon is come to Jerusalem, and hath taken the king thereof, and the princes thereof, and led them with him to Babylon;

13 And hath taken of the king's seed, and made a covenant with him, and hath taken an oath of him: he hath also taken the mighty of the land:

14 That the kingdom might be base, that it might not lift itself up, *but* that by keeping of his covenant it might stand.

15 But he rebelled against him in sending his ambassadors into Egypt, that they might give him horses and much people. Shall he prosper? shall he escape that doeth such *things?* or shall he break the covenant, and be delivered?

it from its roots. 10 Behold, when it is transplanted, will it thrive? Will it not utterly wither when the east wind strikes it — wither away on the bed where it grew?"

11 Then the word of the LORD came to me: 12 "Say now to the rebellious house, Do you not know what these things mean? Tell them, Behold, the king of Babylon came to Jerusalem, and took her king and her princes and brought them to him to Babylon. 13 And he took one of the seed royal and made a covenant with him, putting him under oath. (The chief men of the land he had taken away, 14 that the kingdom might be humble and not lift itself up, and that by keeping his covenant it might stand.) 15 But he rebelled against him by sending ambassadors to Egypt, that they might give him horses and a large army. Will he succeed? Can a man escape who does such things? Can he break the

---

10. The east wind: The wind from the desert is often used as a symbol of an agent of destruction (see 19:12; 27:26; Isa. 27:8; Hos. 13:15; etc.). The **east wind** here is Nebuchadrezzar.

2. INTERPRETATION (17:11-21)

13. The chief men of the land: As in II Kings 24:15.

15. Cf. Jeremiah's virulent criticism of breaking another covenant (34:8-22). As early as the Amarna period (*ca.* 1400 B.C.), the kings of Canaan were seeking horses and men from Egypt (see G. A. Barton, *Archaeology and the Bible* [Philadelphia: American Sunday School Union, 1937], pp. 442-45; Pritchard, *Ancient Near Eastern Texts,* pp. 486-90 [EA, Nos. 270, 271, 286, 288, etc.]; see also II Kings 18:23; Isa. 31:1-3). As vs. 19 implies and as we learn from II Chr. 36:13, Zedekiah made the covenant with Babylonia in the name of Yahweh.

---

freely negotiated between equals; it was one imposed by a conqueror upon a conquered people. Nevertheless the prophet considers it to be binding. He does so because he is convinced that the terms imposed by the conqueror were not contrary to justice. Nebuchadrezzar is not in his eyes a mere brutal oppressor, such as the Assyrian monarchs before him had been; he is a victor who has used his power with humanity and restraint. Zedekiah under Babylonian rule is rightly compared to **a spreading vine of low stature** (vs. 6), i.e., the monarch of a politically insignificant nation. But in many respects his situation was a not unfavorable one, and it guaranteed the essentials of a happy life for his people. The vine was planted **in fertile soil**

and **placed . . . beside abundant waters.** Zedekiah ought to have realized that his position could not possibly be improved by rebellion, that only as the nation was willing to accept Babylonian supremacy could it survive and fulfill its God-given mission.

Clearly such teaching is double-edged, imposing obligations on both parties to the making of a treaty. The obligation to respect an agreement once it has been signed must not be separated from the prior obligation to make only such an agreement as can be respected after it has been signed. If a condition imposed by superior force is to be accepted for any length of time by those subjected to it, it must be such as in the long run to commend itself to them

16 *As* I live, saith the Lord GOD, surely in the place *where* the king *dwelleth* that made him king, whose oath he despised, and whose covenant he brake, *even* with him in the midst of Babylon he shall die.

17 Neither shall Pharaoh with *his* mighty army and great company make for him in the war, by casting up mounts, and building forts, to cut off many persons:

18 Seeing he despised the oath by breaking the covenant, when, lo, he had given his hand, and hath done all these *things,* he shall not escape.

19 Therefore thus saith the Lord GOD; *As* I live, surely mine oath that he hath despised, and my covenant that he hath broken, even it will I recompense upon his own head.

20 And I will spread my net upon him, and he shall be taken in my snare, and I will bring him to Babylon, and will plead with him there for his trespass that he hath trespassed against me.

21 And all his fugitives with all his bands shall fall by the sword, and they that remain shall be scattered toward all winds: and ye shall know that I the LORD have spoken *it.*

22 ¶ Thus saith the Lord GOD; I will also take of the highest branch of the high cedar,

covenant and yet escape? 16 As I live, says the Lord GOD, surely in the place where the king dwells who made him king, whose oath he despised, and whose covenant with him he broke, in Babylon he shall die. 17 Pharaoh with his mighty army and great company will not help him in war, when mounds are cast up and siege walls built to cut off many lives. 18 Because he despised the oath and broke the covenant, because he gave his hand and yet did all these things, he shall not escape. 19 Therefore thus says the Lord GOD: As I live, surely my oath which he despised, and my covenant which he broke, I will requite upon his head. 20 I will spread my net over him, and he shall be taken in my snare, and I will bring him to Babylon and enter into judgment with him there for the treason he has committed against me. 21 And all the pick*j* of his troops shall fall by the sword, and the survivors shall be scattered to every wind; and you shall know that I, the LORD, have spoken."

22 Thus says the Lord GOD: "I myself

j Another reading is *fugitives*

---

17. For **mounds** and **siege walls** see 4:2.

18. Gave his hand: An action indicating a pledge or promise of support (see II Kings 10:15; Ezra 10:19; Prov. 6:1).

20. It has been argued that this is inaccurate, since Zedekiah was judged at Riblah, not in Babylonia, and so cannot be a prophecy *ex eventu,* but must have been written before 586. However, it does not deny the Riblah judgment, and Zedekiah was taken into Babylon, which was Yahweh's punishment, and the verse in any case is only a repetition of the judgment expressed in vs. 9.

21. The pick comes from reading מבחריו ("his choice ones," with many MSS; cf. Syriac, Targ.) for מברחו, **his fugitives.**

3. MESSIANIC ALLEGORY OF THE CEDAR (17:22-24)

The imagery and language are based in part on 31:1-9, the cosmic tree (cf. especially 31:5-6, 8; see also Dan. 4:10-12).

22. Cf. the common designation of the Messiah as the **branch** or scion. **And will set it out:** Possibly an addition, omitted by the LXX, Syriac, and one Hebrew MS.

---

as not altogether inequitable. Morality must be applied to the making of treaties and not merely brought in to guarantee them after they have been made. As long as pacts express nothing more than the power relationships of those who sign them, they will be fragile and

will offer no security. It is only as they embody some degree at least of justice that we can require that they be adhered to even at one's own cost.

22-24. *The Twig Becomes a Tree.*—It is highly probable that Jesus had this passage in

and will set *it;* I will crop off from the top of his young twigs a tender one, and will plant *it* upon a high mountain and eminent:

23 In the mountain of the height of Israel will I plant it: and it shall bring forth boughs, and bear fruit, and be a goodly cedar: and under it shall dwell all fowl of every wing; in the shadow of the branches thereof shall they dwell.

24 And all the trees of the field shall know that I the Lord have brought down the high tree, have exalted the low tree, have dried up the green tree, and have made the dry tree to flourish: I the Lord have spoken and have done *it.*

will take a sprig from the lofty top of the cedar, and will set it out; I will break off from the topmost of its young twigs a tender one, and I myself will plant it upon a high and lofty mountain; 23 on the mountain height of Israel will I plant it, that it may bring forth boughs and bear fruit, and become a noble cedar; and under it will dwell all kinds of beasts;[k] in the shade of its branches birds of every sort will nest. 24 And all the trees of the field shall know that I the Lord bring low the high tree, and make high the low tree, dry up the green tree, and make the dry tree flourish. I the Lord have spoken, and I will do it."

[k] Gk: Heb lacks *all kinds of beasts*

---

23. The mountain height: The high and lofty mountain of the preceding verse is Mount Zion (cf. 40:2; Isa. 2:2; Mic. 4:1). The addition of **beasts** with the LXX is on the theory that **birds** do not dwell beneath trees; however, the last part of the verse may interpret what is meant by birds dwelling under the tree (cf. KJV).

---

mind when he spoke the parable of the mustard seed (Mark 4:30-32). What is striking here is that God's procedure so closely resembles that of Babylon. He too works with what is small and unimportant, but for a quite different purpose. The great eagle of the opening parable wanted to keep the vine turned toward itself; i.e., Babylon's policy was to keep Judah weak so that it might never again become dangerous. God wills, however, that this tiny twig should one day grow into a tree large enough to give shelter to birds from near and far, i.e., that Judah should come to spiritual leadership of mankind.

How far is such a prophecy to be described as "messianic"? Only in the sense that it is concerned with what God will do for his people in the future. A nation disheartened by its obvious political impotence is to learn that its vocation lies in another sphere altogether. As it does so, it will look into the future with hope instead of fear, confident that the God who has designed it for a spiritual mission will provide it with the opportunity to fulfill that mission and so bring blessing to mankind. The young twig that is referred to probably has a communal rather than an individual reference; the prophet is not thinking of some king who is to arise one day, but of what Judah is to become and to do, when she has learned what God's will for her is.

24. *Man's Judgment and God's.*—Here is one of the major themes of the Bible, and it comes to expression most clearly in the Magnificat.

He has put down the mighty from their thrones,
and exalted those of low degree;
he has filled the hungry with good things,
and the rich he has sent empty away (Luke 1:52-53).

Behind that again lies the song of Hannah (I Sam. 2:1-10).

All history is a comment on this truth that the final judgment on human affairs often reverses the one which is passed by contemporaries. A monument on the banks of the Rhine at Bonn bears inscription in French: "From this point the Grand Army set out to the conquest of Russia." But beneath this is another inscription, also in French: "From this point the Russian army crossed the Rhine for the invasion of France." In "Ozymandias," Shelley tells of a ruined monument in the desert on the pedestal of which might be read the words,

"My name is Ozymandias, king of kings:
Look on my works, ye Mighty, and despair!"

He continues:

Nothing beside remains. Round the decay
Of that colossal wreck, boundless and bare
The lone and level sands stretch far away.

Yet what little influence upon ourselves such dramatic reversals of the fortunes of others seem to have. We persuade ourselves that our good fortune is forever, as though we were God, not man. But the divine judgment goes forward, whatever fantasies we may cherish,

18 The word of the Lord came unto me again, saying,

2 What mean ye, that ye use this proverb concerning the land of Israel, saying, The

18 The word of the Lord came to me again: 2 "What do you mean by repeating this proverb concerning the land

M. Individual Responsibility (18:1-32)

The quotation of a popular proverb is followed by the general statement of the principal of responsibility to be elucidated (vss. 1-4). Perhaps in reaction to the thesis that God visits the sins of fathers upon their children to the third and fourth generation (cf. Exod. 20:5), the doctrine of individual responsibility is applied to three successive generations (vss. 5-9, 10-13, 14-20). It is then applied to the repentant wicked and the backsliding righteous (vss. 21-24), followed by the declaration of Yahweh's fairness (vss. 25-29). The discussion ends with a plea for repentance (vss. 30-32).

This chapter and its theme have already received a general analysis (see Intro., p. 49). It is a part of the editor's larger concern with this subject, treated by him also in 3:16-21; 14:12-23; 33:1-20, and touched upon at other points. In so far as it is a rejection of the philosophy of corporate responsibility, it represents a new current in Hebrew thought, although individualism was always prominent in the older Hebrew religion. An Adam, a Cain, a Miriam, a David, or a Jehoiakim might as an individual be held guilty for his own sins. But there is here little suggestion of the interest in social solidarity and group responsibility found at other points in early and even in much of the later Hebrew thought. There is suggested or implicit that respect for the individual and for human personality which has been one of the major emphases of the Jewish-Christian faith, despite certain legalistic aspects of the chapter and an overemphasis on logic and theory. The author's attitude toward the problem of rewards is reminiscent of that of the proverb makers and the friends of Job. Some see in the three generations a specific allusion to Josiah, Jehoiakim, and Zedekiah, but the context does not even remotely suggest this.

Scholars disagree whether **live** and **die** in this chapter should be taken merely to suggest a long and full life and premature death, or whether they are to be interpreted in an eschatological sense (contrast Herntrich, Matthews with Herrmann, Bertholet, Cooke). Probably both meanings are involved. The former is part of the picture, for the author believed that the doctrine was already in effect (vss. 3-4), and indeed had been applicable at the destruction of Jerusalem (cf. 14:12-23) and even before (cf. 3:16-20). But the eschatological element was never at any time far from the editor's thought, and the doctrine would be in effect at the coming of the new age (see also Jer. 31:27-30). The plea to repent in vss. 30-32 is in view of the judgment to accompany the imminent new age.

18:1-32. *What Is the Prophet Trying to Say?* —There is a golden rule for the expositor, and this chapter is one of those instances when it should be brought into play. We should interpret the prophet as we would wish a similar utterance on our own part to be understood; i.e., we must not tie him down to the literal meaning of what he says, but should bear in mind that when a new idea comes into the world, the man who is commissioned to express it often has to make use of language which is quite inadequate to the task. We should be concerned therefore with what the prophet is trying to say. We could, of course, strike a

critical attitude and point out that the kind of thing he is saying here is flatly contradicted by everyday experience. We do suffer for the sins of a previous generation, and it is not possible in a moment of conversion or of backsliding to detach oneself wholly from the past. Probably the prophet was as well aware of that as we are, but he had not the psychology or the vocabulary which would enable him to express the new truth otherwise than in sharp opposition to the old.

1-20. *Human Solidarity.*—Each generation, by what it does, commits those who come after it. The people of Ezekiel's day realized that

fathers have eaten sour grapes, and the children's teeth are set on edge?

3 *As* I live, saith the Lord God, ye shall not have *occasion* any more to use this proverb in Israel.

4 Behold, all souls are mine; as the soul of the father, so also the soul of the son is mine: the soul that sinneth, it shall die.

5 ¶ But if a man be just, and do that which is lawful and right,

6 *And* hath not eaten upon the mountains, neither hath lifted up his eyes to the idols of the house of Israel, neither hath defiled his neighbor's wife, neither hath come near to a menstruous woman,

of Israel, 'The fathers have eaten sour grapes, and the children's teeth are set on edge'? 3 As I live, says the Lord God, this proverb shall no more be used by you in Israel. 4 Behold, all souls are mine; the soul of the father as well as the soul of the son is mine: the soul that sins shall die.

5 "If a man is righteous and does what is lawful and right — 6 if he does not eat upon the mountains or lift up his eyes to the idols of the house of Israel, does not defile his neighbor's wife or approach a

---

1. All Souls Are Mine (18:1-4)

18:1-4. Cf. Jer. 31:27-30; Deut. 24:16; II Kings 14:6, which may come from the same period and school of thought; contrast Lam. 5:7. **Set on edge:** Lit., "blunted" (cf. Eccl. 10:10). **Have eaten,** יאבלו, is a different tense from Jer. 31:29, אבלו, and can be translated "eat" in this context, although with little difference in meaning. The use of *néphesh,* **soul,** as "person" is common in H and P legislation (see Aubrey R. Johnson, *The Vitality of the Individual in the Thought of Ancient Israel* [Cardiff: University of Wales Press, 1949], p. 24; cf. Lev. 7:20-21, 27; 20:6; 22:3; etc.).

2. The Righteous Man Shall Live (18:5-9)

The list of sins avoided by the righteous includes both religious and moral offenses. The phraseology suggests deliberate allusion to the law, particularly to Deuteronomy and the Holiness Code (cf. Lev. 18:19-20; 19:13, 15, 26, 35-36; 20:10, 18; 25:35-37; 26:1, 30; Deut. 16:18-20; 22:24; 23:19; 24:10-13; etc.). The list of offenses, repeated here with variations three times, is paralleled by the editor in 22:6-12, and reflected at other points (33:15; etc.). For life and death as reward and punishment see Pss. 9:17; 31:17; 33:18-19; 34:12, 21; etc.

6. The expression אל ההרים, **upon the mountains** (also vss. 11, 15), should perhaps be emended to על הדם, "with the blood," with 33:25 (cf. Lev. 7:26-27; 17:14; 19:26; Deut. 12:16; etc.), or perhaps the latter should be emended to read as here. The blood is the life (cf. 17:11). **The idols,** (ה)גלולי(ם) (also vss. 10, 15), are the "detestable idols"

---

acutely. Indeed, the Deuteronomic historians had stamped it upon the minds of their people when they insisted that Jerusalem fell as punishment for the sins of Manasseh (II Kings 24:3-4). But already what devout minds had suggested in order "to justify the ways of God with man" had become an excuse for an irresponsible attitude. What was the point of doing anything at all when they were the mere victims of circumstance, paying the price of other people's folly? In the modern world, with economic crisis treading hard upon the heels of war, youth brings this charge against the older generation. Why should they foot the bill for the ineptitude of those who went before them? With our knowledge of heredity and of the influence upon persons of the environment into which they

are born and for which they are in no sense accountable, we have to face the same problem. Where, we ask, is the justice in life?

Ezekiel is not so obtuse as to deny all this; his concern is to insist that there is justice in life in spite of the appearances which are against it. If he had our vocabulary, he would probably distinguish between the natural sequence of cause and effect amid the working of which we are set and God's personal dealing with us as individuals. Each of these expresses a divine intention, but it is to the latter, not to the former, that we must look for the standards by which God's ultimate judgment upon us is passed.

By what we have called the natural sequence of cause and effect we are so bound together

7 And hath not oppressed any, *but* hath restored to the debtor his pledge, hath spoiled none by violence, hath given his bread to the hungry, and hath covered the naked with a garment;

8 He *that* hath not given forth upon usury, neither hath taken any increase, *that* hath withdrawn his hand from iniquity, hath executed true judgment between man and man,

9 Hath walked in my statutes, and hath kept my judgments, to deal truly; he *is* just, he shall surely live, saith the Lord God.

10 ¶ If he beget a son *that is* a robber, a shedder of blood, and *that* doeth the like to *any* one of these *things,*

11 And that doeth not any of those *duties,* but even hath eaten upon the mountains, and defiled his neighbor's wife,

12 Hath oppressed the poor and needy, hath spoiled by violence, hath not restored the pledge, and hath lifted up his eyes to the idols, hath committed abomination,

13 Hath given forth upon usury, and hath taken increase: shall he then live? he

woman in her time of impurity, 7 does not oppress any one, but restores to the debtor his pledge, commits no robbery, gives his bread to the hungry and covers the naked with a garment, 8 does not lend at interest or take any increase, withholds his hand from iniquity, executes true justice between man and man, 9 walks in my statutes, and is careful to observe my ordinances[l] — he is righteous, he shall surely live, says the Lord God.

10 "If he begets a son who is a robber, a shedder of blood,[m] who does none of these duties, 11 but eats upon the mountains, defiles his neighbor's wife, 12 oppresses the poor and needy, commits robbery, does not restore the pledge, lifts up his eyes to the idols, commits abomination, 13 lends at interest, and takes increase; shall he then live?

[l] Gk: Heb *has kept my ordinances, to deal truly*
[m] Heb *blood, and he does any one of these things*

of 6:4. For the law on uncleanness during menstruation see Lev. 15:19-30; 18:19; 20:18. For the attitude toward taking interest see Lev. 25:36-37; Deut. 23:19-20; Neh. 5:7, 10; Ps. 15:5; Isa. 24:2; Jer. 15:10. Usury from a foreigner was permitted. The influence of prophetic ethics is strong here.

9. And is careful to observe my ordinances: The Hebrew is, lit., "and keeps my ordinances to do truly" (see RSV mg.), but probably one should read with the LXX אתם, "them," for אמת, **truly,** presupposing the scribal error of transposition of consonants (cf. vs. 19).

3. The Wicked Son of the Righteous Shall Die (18:10-13)

The implication is that a good father does not pile up "merit" for his son.

10-11. Vs. 10*b* is difficult in the light of vs. 11*a*: "And he does, alas, any one of these" (=vs. 10*b*); "and he does none of these" (=vs. 11*a*). This hardly makes sense; a scribal gloss and some dittography may be responsible for vs. 10*b*.

13. For die the M.T. has יומת, usually "be put to death," but see Prov. 19·16, where it is also a reference to premature death; however, vss. 17, 21, 24, 28 have ימות. **His blood**

that the actions of any one person will profoundly affect many others; by what I do I can infect another with disease, prejudice his mind, or create for him an environment which will weight the scales in favor of evil. We are makers of destiny for one another, particularly within the family. Indeed, it is good that it should be so, for a world in which we lived in isolation and in which our actions affected none but ourselves would be a world in which any possibility of mutual helpfulness would be ruled out in advance. That I can sink another to hell is

the obverse of the fact that I can raise him toward heaven: I can give him an evil environment because, had I acted otherwise, I should have given him a good one. What this natural pattern secures is simply that we shall share life with each other. It is for us to decide whether we pass on a blessing or a curse.

But the ultimate design of God is to use this natural order for the discipline of our souls, and to this end he has respect for the individual as such and not merely for his place in the great current of history. With his all-discerning wis-

shall not live: he hath done all these abominations; he shall surely die; his blood shall be upon him.

14 ¶ Now, lo, *if* he beget a son, that seeth all his father's sins which he hath done, and considereth, and doeth not such like,

15 *That* hath not eaten upon the mountains, neither hath lifted up his eyes to the idols of the house of Israel, hath not defiled his neighbor's wife,

16 Neither hath oppressed any, hath not withholden the pledge, neither hath spoiled by violence, *but* hath given his bread to the hungry, and hath covered the naked with a garment,

17 *That* hath taken off his hand from the poor, *that* hath not received usury nor increase, hath executed my judgments, hath walked in my statutes; he shall not die for the iniquity of his father, he shall surely live.

18 *As for* his father, because he cruelly oppressed, spoiled his brother by violence, and did *that* which *is* not good among his people, lo, even he shall die in his iniquity.

19 ¶ Yet say ye, Why? doth not the son bear the iniquity of the father? When the son hath done that which is lawful and right, *and* hath kept all my statutes, and hath done them, he shall surely live.

He shall not live. He has done all these abominable things; he shall surely die; his blood shall be upon himself.

14 "But if this man begets a son who sees all the sins which his father has done and fears, and does not do likewise, 15 who does not eat upon the mountains or lift up his eyes to the idols of the house of Israel, does not defile his neighbor's wife, 16 does not wrong any one, exacts no pledge, commits no robbery, but gives his bread to the hungry and covers the naked with a garment, 17 withholds his hand from iniquity,[n] takes no interest or increase, observes my ordinances, and walks in my statutes; he shall not die for his father's iniquity; he shall surely live. 18 As for his father, because he practiced extortion, robbed his brother, and did what is not good among his people, behold, he shall die for his iniquity.

19 "Yet you say, 'Why should not the son suffer for the iniquity of the father?' When the son has done what is lawful and right, and has been careful to observe all

[n] Gk: Heb *the poor*

---

shall be upon him: He alone will be responsible for his death (cf. 3:18, 20; for the phrase in H see Lev. 20:9, 11, 13, 16, 27).

4. The Righteous Son of the Wicked Son Shall Live (18:14-20)

The doctrine is formulated clearly in vss. 19-20; neither son nor father will be responsible for the other's iniquity.

17. From iniquity: Read with the LXX and vs. 8 and for better sense מעול for מעני, **from the poor.**

18. The word אח, **his brother,** really means either "a brother" or "alas"; perhaps a scribal error; omitted by the LXX (cf. vs. 10); perhaps instead of גזל אח, lit., "robbed robbery of a brother," read גזל גזלה, "committed robbery" (cf. vss. 7, 12, 16).

19. Yet you say: As also vss. 25, 29, i.e., the orthodox whom the author would refute (for similar diction see 13:7; 33:17, 20; cf. Mal. 1:2, 7, 13; etc.).

---

dom he is able to detect what is hidden from us, and to see in this tangle and complexity exactly what share of responsibility must be laid at the door of each one among us. God holds no man responsible for the circumstances into which he was born, but only for the use to which he puts them subsequently. In the course of nature the son suffers for the father's sin, but for the divine vision what the son has done and what the father has done stand out clear,

separate, and distinct, so that God's verdict on each is personal and strictly according to his acts. God, we may say, cuts a straight path of personal accountability through the tangled undergrowth of social involvement and biological heredity in which we find ourselves trapped. The course of nature does not represent his final sentence; it is a preliminary discipline he imposes. From its necessary severities and entanglements he means us to appeal to the wise

20 The soul that sinneth, it shall die. The son shall not bear the iniquity of the father, neither shall the father bear the iniquity of the son: the righteousness of the righteous shall be upon him, and the wickedness of the wicked shall be upon him.

21 But if the wicked will turn from all his sins that he hath committed, and keep all my statutes, and do that which is lawful and right, he shall surely live, he shall not die.

22 All his transgressions that he hath committed, they shall not be mentioned unto him: in his righteousness that he hath done he shall live.

23 Have I any pleasure at all that the wicked should die? saith the Lord God: *and* not that he should return from his ways, and live?

24 ¶ But when the righteous turneth away from his righteousness, and committeth iniquity, *and* doeth according to all the abominations that the wicked *man* doeth, shall he live? All his righteousness that he hath done shall not be mentioned: in his trespass that he hath trespassed, and in his sin that he hath sinned, in them shall he die.

my statutes, he shall surely live. 20 The soul that sins shall die. The son shall not suffer for the iniquity of the father, nor the father suffer for the iniquity of the son; the righteousness of the righteous shall be upon himself, and the wickedness of the wicked shall be upon himself.

21 "But if a wicked man turns away from all his sins which he has committed and keeps all my statutes and does what is lawful and right, he shall surely live; he shall not die. 22 None of the transgressions which he has committed shall be remembered against him; for the righteousness which he has done he shall live. 23 Have I any pleasure in the death of the wicked, says the Lord God, and not rather that he should turn from his way and live? 24 But when a righteous man turns away from his righteousness and commits iniquity and does the same abominable things that the wicked man does, shall he live? None of the righteous deeds which he has done shall be remembered; for the treachery of which he is guilty and the sin he has committed, he shall die.

5. The Wicked Man Who Becomes Righteous Shall Live (18:21-24)

His earlier wickedness shall not be counted against the repentant man. So also the righteous man who becomes wicked shall die and not profit from his earlier righteousness. Life cannot be put into the strait jacket of this logic. Often a man's good acts are tainted with the sin of selfishness; the motives for action are often mixed, and a man is more than what he is in a particular moment of time. There is here, however, a recognition of the terribleness of sin, and the author by the end of the chapter does rise above logic to love.

24. The LXX, Syriac, and Arabic omit יעשה וחי, **does, shall he live,** and so many scholars. A comparison of this verse with 3:20 and 33:13 illustrates the intimate connection of these three passages and their single authorship (see II Pet. 2:20).

sure judgment of the love for which each one of us exists as a person with his own duty and destiny.

21-32. Freedom from the Past.—Just as Ezekiel has claimed that the individual is not merely borne along by the stream of events but has his independence and his direct relationship to God, so now he declares that the individual is never a slave to his own past. The past does not determine the future, for it has to go through the present in order to become the future, and the present is an opportunity for total transformation. The present is an instant of decision in which we are not determined by

our past, but rather work with and upon it as material given to us. This is a message of hope. But at the same time it is a solemn warning. For while life shows us that the gates of God's mercy are never closed against us and that renewal is always possible, it makes clear that no man can afford to be too confident. As Bunyan puts it, even from the gate of heaven there is a way to hell.

But in what sense is it in fact true that we can shake off the past and become quite new men? Of course there is a sense in which the past lives on and the marks which it has left on us can never be effaced. The physical weak-

25 ¶ Yet ye say, The way of the Lord is not equal. Hear now, O house of Israel; Is not my way equal? are not your ways unequal?

26 When a righteous *man* turneth away from his righteousness, and committeth iniquity, and dieth in them; for his iniquity that he hath done shall he die.

27 Again, when the wicked *man* turneth away from his wickedness that he hath committed, and doeth that which is lawful and right, he shall save his soul alive.

28 Because he considereth, and turneth away from all his transgressions that he hath committed, he shall surely live, he shall not die.

29 Yet saith the house of Israel, The way of the Lord is not equal. O house of Israel, are not my ways equal? are not your ways unequal?

30 Therefore I will judge you, O house of Israel, every one according to his ways, saith the Lord God. Repent, and turn *yourselves* from all your transgressions; so iniquity shall not be your ruin.

25 "Yet you say, 'The way of the Lord is not just.' Hear now, O house of Israel: Is my way not just? Is it not your ways that are not just? 26 When a righteous man turns away from his righteousness and commits iniquity, he shall die for it; for the iniquity which he has committed he shall die. 27 Again, when a wicked man turns away from the wickedness he has committed and does what is lawful and right, he shall save his life. 28 Because he considered and turned away from all the transgressions which he had committed, he shall surely live, he shall not die. 29 Yet the house of Israel says, 'The way of the Lord is not just.' O house of Israel, are my ways not just? Is it not your ways that are not just?

30 "Therefore I will judge you, O house of Israel, every one according to his ways, says the Lord God. Repent and turn from all your transgressions, lest iniquity be

6. The Way of the Lord Is Just (18:25-29)

The author reverts to this theme in 33:17-20. It is needless to speak of duplicate recensions; rather we have variant discussions of the same subject by the same author. Some take vss. 26-29 as a doublet of vss. 21-25 or as a later addition (cf. Kraetzschmar, Herrmann, Herntrich, Bertholet), but this is unnecessary.

26. The expression וּמֵת עֲלֵיהֶם, **and dieth in them**, should perhaps be deleted with the Syriac (LXX omits עֲלֵיהֶם); note that there is no antecedent for **them** (cf. RSV).

7. New Heart and New Spirit (18:30-32)

30-32. This is the editor at his best, and the passage is to be linked with 11:17-21; 36:24-32 (cf. Jer. 31:31-34). One both gets **a new heart** and is given it (contrast 11:19

ness induced by a course of self-indulgence remains even after penitence, but its significance has changed. Since we have been brought into a new relationship to God, we can turn to good even the heritage of years of wrongdoing. Our position might be compared to that of a writer who has had the first six chapters of a book put into his hand, with instructions to complete it as he sees best. He is not allowed to alter so much as a word in those six chapters, yet he can actually transform profoundly the first part of the narrative by what he adds to complete it; e.g., he can so write the rest of the book that the apparent hero of the opening is unmasked as the villain of the piece. Or an insignificant person who has only a sentence or two to say in the first part may turn out to have been all

the while secretly directing the course of events. It is in some such sense as this that the past is fluid and may be set in a quite new direction. God's judgment of us is therefore not determined by what we have been but by what we are, for what we are is actually decisive as to the nature of what has been. The past can be remade in the present. That indeed is the meaning of the gospel. Forgiveness does not obliterate the past, but sets it all in a new relationship to God so that we can transform it until what threatened to be a curse becomes a source of blessing.

29-32. Why Will Ye Die?—Here is a poignant passage which is always relevant. Some problem obsesses us and we arraign God for his seeming injustice. We ask why he allows this or that to

31 ¶ Cast away from you all your transgressions, whereby ye have transgressed; and make you a new heart and a new spirit: for why will ye die, O house of Israel?

32 For I have no pleasure in the death of him that dieth, saith the Lord GOD: wherefore turn *yourselves,* and live ye.

19 Moreover, take thou up a lamentation for the princes of Israel,

2 And say, What *is* thy mother? A lion-

your ruin.*ᵒ* 31 Cast away from you all the transgressions which you have committed against me, and get yourselves a new heart and a new spirit! Why will you die, O house of Israel? 32 For I have no pleasure in the death of any one, says the Lord GOD; so turn, and live."

19 And you, take up a lamentation for the princes of Israel, 2 and say:
What a lioness was your mother
among lions!

ᵒ Or *so that they shall not be a stumbling block of iniquity to you*

with vs. 31). Grace is dependent on repentance, in contrast with the theology of Second Isaiah. It is to be noted that Israel did get a new heart, as it enshrined as scripture the words of the prophets who earlier had been rejected.

N. THE LIONESS AND THE VINE (19:1-14)

Here are two laments or dirges. The first (vss. 2-9) represents the mother of Israel as a lioness. One of her whelps, to be identified with Jehoahaz, was captured and carried away to Egypt (see II Kings 23:30-34), and another, to be identified with Jehoiachin, was carried away to Babylon (see II Kings 24:8-16). The history of the period is obviously telescoped, with no reference to the intervening king Jehoiakim.

happen. The problem is thus posed at the intellectual level, and it would be solved, as we see it, by God's doing something which would satisfy us. But he replies that this is completely to misunderstand the situation. The real problem is of a moral and spiritual order, and it is one for us to face, not one for us to propound. Why have we as persons so neglected our opportunities and confused our lives? Why do those who represent us release in a moment of senselessness vast powers which may well destroy mankind one day? The great need is not for an explanation which is to be given to us, but for a complete change in our conduct. The kingdom of God is not delayed by some unaccountable dispensation of his providence, but by our reluctance to part with the sins we love even to avoid the disaster they threaten to bring upon us. When nations arm and statesmen drift toward war, or when individuals live in self-indulgence while toying with intellectual problems, the divine appeal comes to us. **Why will ye die?** That is the question which demands an answer, and the compassion of God waits for our response.

31. *The New Heart.*—We have only to set these words alongside those in 11:19-20 to be faced with a problem. What the prophet there seems to regard as beyond man's power, the remaking of the self, he here calls upon man to achieve. Does the present passage represent a

position which he later came to regard as unsatisfactory, so that he appealed from man's impotence to God's grace?

There is really no clash between the two points of view, since God's grace does not exclude man's freedom, but rather enlists it. What we call "rebirth" as something which is done to us and for us might equally be termed "repentance," as something done by us. Perhaps the best illustration is that provided by the psychoanalyst. The patient is unaware of the forces which determine his conduct and feels himself their helpless victim. He cannot arrive at an account of them, but must have one given to him from without, by the analyst. Only as he abandons his own attitude to himself for that proposed to him by the analyst can he be healed. But the latter does not force anything on the patient, he goes to work slowly and considerately; each fresh point in the explanation he offers must be accepted as convincing by the patient or it will bring him no help. And the cure, when it comes, may be described either as a deliverance which the analyst has brought to the patient or as a fresh and life-changing decision on the part of the latter. God deals with us in the same way, the **new heart** which he gives us is so given that it issues from our change of attitude to him.

19:1-14. *The Fatal Weakness in Ourselves.*— In this chapter we listen to Ezekiel as he intones

| ess: she lay down among lions, she nour- | She couched in the midst of young lions, |
| ished her whelps among young lions. | rearing her whelps. |

Despite the later tradition that he was exiled (II Chr. 36:6; Dan. 1:2), Jehoiakim died in Jerusalem (see II Kings 24:1-6) and cannot be this second whelp. The lion symbolism for the royal house of Judah is appropriate. In the blessing of Jacob, Judah is pictured as a lion's whelp (Gen. 49:9; cf. Mic. 5:8). The kings of Judah sat on a throne decorated with lions (I Kings 10:18-20). For the lion as a part of the royal symbolism cf. Prov. 19:12; 20:2; II Sam. 1:23; note the seal of Shema, servant of Jeroboam, decorated with a royal lion, found at Megiddo, and the seal of Jotham from Ezion-geber, bearing the royal lion (see Nelson Glueck, "The Third Season of Excavation at Tell el-Kheleifeh," *Bulletin of the American Schools of Oriental Research,* No. 79 [Oct., 1940], pp. 13-15; Adolf Reifenberg, *Ancient Hebrew Seals* [London: East and West Library, 1950], Figs. 1, 6; note the cherub as a winged lion with a human head); see also Rev. 5:5.

The second lament (vss. 10-14) pictures Israel as a vine whose stem became a ruler's scepter. The vine has been plucked up and is transplanted in the wilderness, and there remains no strong stem. This is a reference to the tragedy of 586, and to Zedekiah, although it has been assumed that the stem is an allusion to Jehoiachin (Cooke). The vine imagery is related to that in ch. 17; see also the vine associated with Judah in Gen. 49:11-12. On a panel from the synagogue at Dura Europos (third century A.D.) the lion and the vine symbolism is based on this chapter (Rachel Wischnitzer, *The Messianic Theme in the Paintings of the Dura Synagogue* [Chicago: University of Chicago Press, 1948], p. 92; Figs. 45, 46).

Both poems are in the so-called *qînāh* (lamentation) meter (as usually interpreted), each line a distich, with three beats in the first stich and two in the second, although, as here, with occasional variations in the meter. We should probably ascribe the same date to both poems, and this must be after the fall of Judah in 586, alluded to in the second poem. The designation of these poems as a lamentation in vs. 1 suggests a comparison with the lament against Tyre in chs. 26–28 (cf. 26:17; 27:2; 28:12) and Egypt in ch. 32 (cf. 32:2), all of which belong to the same general period. Hölscher (cf. also Herntrich) regards the second lamentation secondary, while Berry, Irwin, and Messel consider the entire chapter spurious.

1. Fate of Jehoahaz (19:1-4)

19:1. Cf. the *qînāh* over Saul and Jonathan in II Sam. 1:17-27, and over Abner in II Sam. 3:33-34; see also the dirge over Israel in Amos 5:1-2; cf. Jer. 7:29; 9:9. **The princes** are Jehoahaz, Jehoiachin, and Zedekiah, but it is probable that **the princes** is the editor's expansion, since in vss. 2 and 10 **your** is singular, not plural. The original text may have had "a lamentation over Israel." The LXX solved the difficulty by reading "prince," and some accept this, taking it to refer to Zedekiah (cf. Bertholet, Matthews).

Israel, e.g., Judah, is personified as a mother **lioness** and Jehoahaz as one of her **whelps.** We are not to take vs. 3 as an accurate description of the character and exploits of Jehoahaz, nor vss. 6-7 as indicative of the accomplishments of Jehoiachin. It is rather

a lament over three kings of Judah. They are Jehoahaz (vss. 1-4), Jehoiachin (vss. 5-9), and Zedekiah (vss. 10-14). The first two have already been led into captivity, the hard fate of the third is still perhaps in the future. For us the most important point in the section as a whole is the contrast between the extravagant language of the first two poems and the restraint, even the despondency, of the third. Hopes were raised which could never be fulfilled.

Of what folly the national sentiment of the time was capable we see at once from these descriptions of a young king coming to his throne, in the one case after his father's defeat and death in battle, and in the other case during the siege of his capital. In each instance he is represented as **a young lion** whose roaring fills the nations with dismay. No doubt there were those who consoled themselves for the disasters which had befallen their nation with fantasies of this kind. They imagined that it was

3 And she brought up one of her whelps: it became a young lion, and it learned to catch the prey; it devoured men.

4 The nations also heard of him; he was taken in their pit, and they brought him with chains unto the land of Egypt.

5 Now when she saw that she had waited, *and* her hope was lost, then she took another of her whelps, *and* made him a young lion.

6 And he went up and down among the lions, he became a young lion, and learned to catch the prey, *and* devoured men.

7 And he knew their desolate palaces, and he laid waste their cities; and the land was desolate, and the fulness thereof, by the noise of his roaring.

3 And she brought up one of her whelps;
  he became a young lion,
and he learned to catch prey;
  he devoured men.

4 The nations sounded an alarm against
  him;
  he was taken in their pit;
and they brought him with hooks
  to the land of Egypt.

5 When she saw that she was baffled,*p*
  that her hope was lost,
she took another of her whelps
  and made him a young lion.

6 He prowled among the lions;
  he became a young lion,
and he learned to catch prey;
  he devoured men.

7 And he ravaged*q* their strongholds,
  and laid waste their cities;
and the land was appalled and all who
  were in it
at the sound of his roaring.

p Heb *had waited*
q Tg: Heb *he knew*

poetic license, regal exaggeration, and lion symbolism. Both kings reigned but three months each, with no positive accomplishments to their credit as far as we know. In the lioness there is no reference to Hamutal, the mother of Jehoahaz and Zedekiah. The mother of Jehoiachin was Nehushta, and his grandmother Zebediah (II Kings 23:31; 24:8, 18).

4. It was Pharaoh Neco of Egypt who deposed Jehoahaz, putting on the throne in his place Jehoiakim, who would follow a pro-Egyptian, anti-Babylonian policy. Jeremiah had also prophesied concerning Jehoahaz (Jer. 22:10-12), as well as concerning Jehoiachin (Jer. 13:18-19; 22:24-30). **Sounded an alarm:** Read *wayyashmî'û* for *wayyishme'û*; contrast the KJV. The allusion is to the beaters. Lion hunting was a sport of Assyrian kings; cf. the hunting reliefs of Ashurbanipal (see D. D. Luckenbill, *Ancient Records of Assyria and Babylonia* [Chicago: University of Chicago Press, 1927], II, 391-92).

2. Fate of Jehoiachin (19:5-9)

5. **Had waited** is more exact, but the sense is not clear, and the translation perhaps is an attempt to interpret from the context. The subject of the verb is probably not **she** but "her hope," and if so we may read, "When she saw that her hope had waited [and] was lost." The whelp, selected by its mother, cannot be Zedekiah, who was put on the throne by a foreign power (II Kings 24:17).

7. In vs. 7a read וירע, **and he ravaged** (with Targ., Theod.; cf. LXX), for וידע, **and he knew;** no emendation of the noun אלמנותיו, "their [lit., "his"] widows," is necessary

because Judah was so dangerous a rival of the Babylonian Empire and her young monarch a potential world conqueror that the nations rose against them. So they tried to conceal from themselves the unpleasant realities of their situation: political ineptitude and military insignificance.

The third poem, however, reveals what actu-

ally happened. Judah's fault was in herself, not in her stars. It was from a twig on one of her branches that the fire shot forth which devoured her (vs. 14). Her fate was one of national suicide. She herself willed the policies which led to her undoing. The guilt lay in the first instance with the king and his advisers, for they no doubt are meant by this baleful twig,

8 Then the nations set against him on every side from the provinces, and spread their net over him: he was taken in their pit.

9 And they put him in ward in chains, and brought him to the king of Babylon: they brought him into holds, that his voice should no more be heard upon the mountains of Israel.

10 ¶ Thy mother is like a vine in thy blood, planted by the waters: she was fruitful and full of branches by reason of many waters.

11 And she had strong rods for the sceptres of them that bare rule, and her stature was exalted among the thick branches, and she appeared in her height with the multitude of her branches.

12 But she was plucked up in fury, she was cast down to the ground, and the east wind dried up her fruit: her strong rods were broken and withered; the fire consumed them.

8 Then the nations set against him
snares[r] on every side;
they spread their net over him;
he was taken in their pit.
9 With hooks they put him in a cage,
and brought him to the king of Babylon;
they brought him into custody,
that his voice should no more be heard
upon the mountains of Israel.

10 Your mother was like a vine in a vineyard[s]
transplanted by the water,
fruitful and full of branches
by reason of abundant water.
11 Its strongest stem became
a ruler's scepter;
it towered aloft
among the thick boughs;
it was seen in its height
with the mass of its branches.
12 But the vine was plucked up in fury,
cast down to the ground;
the east wind dried it up;
its fruit was stripped off,
its strong stem was withered;
the fire consumed it.

[r] Cn: Heb *from the provinces*
[s] Cn: Heb *in your blood*

to get the RSV rendering, for אלמון and ארמון coexisted as words for "gate-tower [palace]"; see Albright in Howie (*Date and Composition of Ezekiel*, p. 62).

8. Snares: Read מצודות for ממדינות, **from the provinces.**

9. See Isa. 37:29 for the hook or ring, חח, in the nose of a captive (cf. 29:4). The word סוגר, **cage,** is the Akkadian *šigāru,* used of the cage of a gazelle, dog, or lion. Ashurbanipal tells how he put a king of Arabia into such a *šigāru* (see Luckenbill, *op. cit.,* II, 314). **Into custody** is probable in this context (see on vs. 8).

3. Fate of Zedekiah (19:10-14)

10. In a vineyard: I.e., בכרם for בדמך; two MSS read כרמך, "thy vineyard." Cf. the vine planted by many waters in 17:5, 8, and the figure used in the psalm in Jer. 17:5-8 and in Ps. 1 (see Exeg. on Ezek. 31:5).

11. The M.T. has **stem, scepter,** and ruler all in the plural (cf. KJV), but we should read the singular for stem and scepter, since the third stich reads, lit., "its stature was lofty," showing reference to but one (see also the singular in vs. 12*ef,* and cf. the LXX). **Strongest:** Probably better, **strong.**

12. Cf. 17:9-10. Some read with the LXX, בדיה, "her branches," for פריה, **her fruit** (cf. 17:6, and the fact that the verb is plural).

but the people themselves were not without a share in it all.

The lesson which the prophet sought to teach his people was as salutary as it was unwelcome. We all need it today. We too readily dramatize

ourselves as noble heroes who fall victims to the jealousies of others, their rage against us being evoked solely by our admirable qualities. We need to learn that the fatal weakness is within ourselves, that just where we are confident and

13 And now she *is* planted in the wilderness, in a dry and thirsty ground.

14 And fire is gone out of a rod of her branches, *which* hath devoured her fruit, so that she hath no strong rod *to be* a sceptre to rule. This *is* a lamentation, and shall be for a lamentation.

20 And it came to pass in the seventh year, in the fifth *month*, the tenth *day* of the month, *that* certain of the elders of Israel came to inquire of the LORD, and sat before me.

13 Now it is transplanted in the wilderness, in a dry and thirsty land.

14 And fire has gone out from its stem, has consumed its branches and fruit, so that there remains in it no strong stem, no scepter for a ruler.

This is a lamentation, and has become a lamentation.

20 In the seventh year, in the fifth month, on the tenth day of the month, certain of the elders of Israel came to inquire of the LORD, and sat before me.

14. The meter and sense support the RSV in vs. 14*ab*, reading *mimmaṭṭēhā*, **from its stem**, for *mimmaṭṭēh*, "from a stem of" (=KJV), and associating **its branches** with what follows rather than with what precedes. The LXX omits **her** [its] **fruit**. The prose comment at the end of the verse may be the editor's.

O. APOSTASY AND RESTORATION OF ISRAEL (20:1-49)

In the Hebrew Bible the chapter consists only of vss. 1-44, vss. 45-49 being placed in ch. 21. This latter oracle is analogous to the one at the beginning of ch. 21. Vss. 1-44 may be taken as a unit, divided into two parts. Vss. 1-32 describe the apostasies of the house of Israel and vss. 33-44 its restoration. Yahweh instructs Ezekiel to acquaint the elders of Israel who have come for an oracle with the apostasies of themselves and their ancestors (vss. 1-4). Despite Yahweh's selection of Israel and his promises and warnings, the Hebrews in Egypt apostatized (vss. 5-8). Yahweh, for his name's sake, withheld his anger and led them into the wilderness, giving them his law, but they still rebelled (vss. 9-13). Again he withheld punishment for his name's sake and did not destroy them (vss. 14-17). Their children, the second generation, were also warned and yet rebelled, but again he restrained his hand for his name's sake, trying to teach them by warnings and even by giving them laws that were not good (vss. 18-26). When he had brought them into Canaan, they continued to offend him, so Yahweh will not be inquired of by the house of Israel (vss. 27-31). But despite Israel's past and present, Yahweh will bring Israel once more into the desert and enter into judgment with them, purging out the rebels, who may not enter into the land of Israel (vss. 32-38). In the land of Israel all the house of Israel will serve Yahweh, and their sacrifices will be accepted by him, and Israel will know that he is Yahweh when he has acted according to his grace and not according to their evil-doings (vss. 39-44).

Vss. 1-44 reflect throughout the spirit and diction of the editor. The passage is, in effect, a sermon primarily for the benefit of the Diaspora. We may see in it the reflection of Second Isaiah's doctrine of "for his name's sake" (vss. 9, 14, 22, 44; cf. Isa. 48:1-22; etc.) and the conception of the return from exile as a second exodus (vss. 34, 36; cf. Isa. 43:16-21; etc.; see also Ezek. 36:22). Both ideas appear in the late writer in Jeremiah (e.g., 14:7, 21; 16:14-15). Among the characteristic phrases and words of the editor already noted are "idols" (*gillûlîm*) in vss. 7, 8, 16, 18, 24, 31, 39 (see vi on p. 50); "scatter them among the nations and disperse them throughout the countries,"

proud the fault begins which may one day destroy us, unless we guard against it in time.

20:1-44. The Hand of God.—In the first part of this chapter (vss. 1-32) we learn what Ezekiel's theology of history was, i.e., the principles

on which God directs the course of events. It is a sad story he has to tell, a story of how privileges have been forfeited by ingratitude and how the nation which might have done so much for the world has again and again foiled

2 Then came the word of the LORD unto me, saying,

3 Son of man, speak unto the elders of Israel, and say unto them, Thus saith the Lord GOD; Are ye come to inquire of me? As I live, saith the Lord GOD, I will not be inquired of by you.

4 Wilt thou judge them, son of man, wilt thou judge *them*? cause them to know the abominations of their fathers:

5 ¶ And say unto them, Thus saith the Lord GOD; In the day when I chose Israel, and lifted up mine hand unto the seed of the house of Jacob, and made myself known unto them in the land of Egypt, when I lifted up mine hand unto them, saying, I *am* the LORD your God;

2 And the word of the LORD came to me: 3 "Son of man, speak to the elders of Israel, and say to them, Thus says the Lord GOD, Is it to inquire of me that you come? As I live, says the Lord GOD, I will not be inquired of by you. 4 Will you judge them, son of man, will you judge them? Then let them know the abominations of their fathers, 5 and say to them, Thus says the Lord GOD: On the day when I chose Israel, I swore to the seed of the house of Jacob, making myself known to them in the land of Egypt, I swore to them, saying, I am the

in vs. 23 (see x, xi on p. 50) ; "your ways and all the doings" in vs. 43 (see xliv on p. 51) , and many others. The profanation of the sabbaths in vss. 12-13, 16, 24 occurs again in 22:8, 26; 23:38, and reflects the viewpoint of H that the Exile was a punishment for failure to observe the sabbath (cf. Lev. 26:34, 43) . The plural form שבתות, "sabbaths," is largely if not entirely postexilic in its O.T. usage, occurring in H (Lev. 19:3, 30; 23:15, 38; etc.) , in Neh. (10:33) , in Isa. 56:4, in P (Exod. 31:13) , and often in Chronicles (I Chr. 23:31; etc.) . Some would excise the passages alluding to the sabbaths (cf. Hölscher, Cooke) . Cf. Ezek. 44:24; 45:17. The profanation of the name of Yahweh in vss. 9, 14, 22, 39 (see xxviii on p. 51) is another link with H (Lev. 18:21; 19:12; etc.) . Characteristic also are "lifted up my hand"="swore" in vss. 5, 15, 23, 38, 42 (see xxix on p. 51) ; cf. Ps. 106:26) ; "manifest my holiness" in vs. 41 (see xxx on p. 51) , also in H and P. There are numerous analogies with H and R[D], and with P, some of which are noted below; cf. also the later writer in Jeremiah, especially 11:1-17; 14:7-9, 20-22; 17:19-27; 32:17-44. The conception of history as a continuous series of apostasies is also marked. Ps. 106, which has a number of significant literary analogies, is almost the poetic equivalent of this prose passage in Ezekiel.

Hölscher thinks the entire chapter secondary, and Irwin finds an original poetic oracle in vs. 3 and another in vs. 47 (Hebrew 21:3) , with introductory formulas, and in vs. 49 (Hebrew 21:5) . Some date vss. 1-32 in the early period of Ezekiel's activity before 586, and vss. 33-44 in the later period of his activity (see Matthews, Bertholet, Herrmann, Pfeiffer) ; cf. Herntrich, who agrees with the first part, but takes vss. 33-44 to be secondary.

1. ORACLE TO THE ELDERS (20:1-4)

20:1-4. The date is September 1, 590 (August 13, 591) ; it may be separated by the editor from an original association with 20:45-49 (?) or the genuine oracles in ch. 21. The setting, as well as the criticism of the elders, has a close parallel in 14:1-11. With the refusal to be consulted cf. 14:3-4. **The elders of Israel** are those of the Exile. **Judge:** Pass judgment upon, as in 22:2; 23:36. The author does not indicate the nature of the inquiry, for it is important only to provide the setting for the editor's sermon.

2. APOSTASY IN EGYPT (20:5-8)

The idea of the chosen race was Mosaic in origin, although the term *bḥr*, "to choose," seems to appear first in this connection in Second Isaiah (cf. Deut. 4:37; 7:6-7; 10:15; 14:2 [R[D]]; Jer. 23:24 [late]; cf. especially Deut. 4 and Isa. 48) .

5. I am the LORD your God: This expression is found also in vss. 19, 20 and often in H (cf. the covenant formula) . The allusion may be to Exod. 3:11-17; 6:2-8, where appear

6 In the day *that* I lifted up mine hand unto them, to bring them forth of the land of Egypt into a land that I had espied for them, flowing with milk and honey, which *is* the glory of all lands:

7 Then said I unto them, Cast ye away every man the abominations of his eyes, and defile not yourselves with the idols of Egypt: I *am* the LORD your God.

8 But they rebelled against me, and would not hearken unto me: they did not every man cast away the abominations of their eyes, neither did they forsake the idols of Egypt: then I said, I will pour out my fury upon them, to accomplish my anger against them in the midst of the land of Egypt.

9 But I wrought for my name's sake, that it should not be polluted before the heathen, among whom they *were,* in whose sight I made myself known unto them, in bringing them forth out of the land of Egypt.

10 ¶ Wherefore I caused them to go forth out of the land of Egypt, and brought them into the wilderness.

LORD your God. 6 On that day I swore to them that I would bring them out of the land of Egypt into a land that I had searched out for them, a land flowing with milk and honey, the most glorious of all lands. 7 And I said to them, Cast away the detestable things your eyes feast on, every one of you, and do not defile yourselves with the idols of Egypt; I am the LORD your God. 8 But they rebelled against me and would not listen to me; they did not every man cast away the detestable things their eyes feasted on, nor did they forsake the idols of Egypt.

"Then I thought I would pour out my wrath upon them and spend my anger against them in the midst of the land of Egypt. 9 But I acted for the sake of my name, that it should not be profaned in the sight of the nations among whom they dwelt, in whose sight I made myself known to them in bringing them out of the land of Egypt. 10 So I led them out of the land of Egypt and brought them into the wilder-

---

both the swearing by uplifted **hand** and the promise to bring to a land flowing with milk and honey.

6. See vss. 15 and Exod. 3:7-8, 17; Lev. 20:24; Deut. 6:3; 11:9; 26:15; etc.

8. See Josh. 24:14 for a tradition that the Hebrews served pagan gods in Egypt, although apparently before the revelation to Moses. The apostasy in Egypt and Yahweh's intent to punish Israel there may be an invention of the Deuteronomist and a corollary of his philosophy of history.

3. APOSTASY IN THE WILDERNESS (20:9-26)

9. The important doctrine of "for my name's sake" (see also 36:22; Jer. 14:7, 21; I Sam. 12:22; I Kings 8:41; Ps. 106:8; etc.) is consonant with the expression "Then they will know that I am Yahweh" (cf. Num. 14:13-19). Second Isaiah (42:6-8; 45:6; 55:5) gives a similar reason for the return from exile, the second exodus; the return from exile will prove to the pagan nations that Yahweh is the true God.

---

the purpose of God for it. In the second part (vss. 33-34) we are shown how a divine discipline restores the nation at last to its loyalty.

9. *For My Name's Sake.*—What Ezekiel is trying to do here is to maintain intact his sense of God's majesty, his unique and sovereign claim upon man, and a discernment that God does not work as we would if we were in God's place. God, who is all-righteous and against whose righteousness men have sinned, yet acts toward them in mercy. There is a marvel here which we cannot explain; we can only recognize that God is so. We must "let God be God" in

mercy as in chastisement. So the literal meaning of the language used is not to be pressed, as though God were acting with a view to his own reputation. Ezekiel would say that the reason God forbears and forgives is to be found in him, not in us. God deals with us, not as our merits require, but as his own goodness prompts. When we pray that he will forgive "for his name's sake," we appeal to his nature as love. He is a God whose property it is to have mercy.

But perhaps there is a second thought implied in these words as they are used here. God's

11 And I gave them my statutes, and showed them my judgments, which *if* a man do, he shall even live in them.

12 Moreover also I gave them my sabbaths, to be a sign between me and them, that they might know that I *am* the LORD that sanctify them.

13 But the house of Israel rebelled against me in the wilderness: they walked not in my statutes, and they despised my judgments, which *if* a man do, he shall even live in them; and my sabbaths they greatly polluted: then I said, I would pour out my fury upon them in the wilderness, to consume them.

14 But I wrought for my name's sake, that it should not be polluted before the heathen, in whose sight I brought them out.

15 Yet also I lifted up my hand unto them in the wilderness, that I would not bring them into the land which I had given *them,* flowing with milk and honey, which *is* the glory of all lands;

16 Because they despised my judgments, and walked not in my statutes, but polluted my sabbaths: for their heart went after their idols.

17 Nevertheless mine eye spared them

ness. 11 I gave them my statutes and showed them my ordinances, by whose observance man shall live. 12 Moreover I gave them my sabbaths, as a sign between me and them, that they might know that I the LORD sanctify them. 13 But the house of Israel rebelled against me in the wilderness; they did not walk in my statutes but rejected my ordinances, by whose observance man shall live; and my sabbaths they greatly profaned.

"Then I thought I would pour out my wrath upon them in the wilderness, to make a full end of them. 14 But I acted for the sake of my name, that it should not be profaned in the sight of the nations, in whose sight I had brought them out. 15 Moreover I swore to them in the wilderness that I would not bring them into the land which I had given them, a land flowing with milk and honey, the most glorious of all lands, 16 because they rejected my ordinances and did not walk in my statutes, and profaned my sabbaths; for their heart went after their idols. 17 Nevertheless my eye spared them, and I did not destroy

---

11. Shall live appears also in vs. 21 (see vs. 25); e.g., as frequently in ch. 18; see also Lev. 18:5, of which this verse seems to be a quotation (cf. Deut. 4:40; 5:16).

12-13. See Exod. 31:13-17 (P) for the sabbath as the sign of the consecration or sanctification of Israel. There can hardly be doubt of literary dependence of one of these on the other (cf. Lev. 20:8). The later writer in Jer. 17:19-27 makes the observance of the sabbath a prerequisite of the Davidic messianic kingdom (see also 23:38; Neh. 13:17-18, and the postexilic emphasis on the sabbath illustrated in the P source, e.g., Gen. 1:1–2:4*b*). For rebellions in the wilderness see Exod. 32:1-35; Num. 11:1-3; 12:1-16; 14:1-45; 16:1-50; 21:4-9; etc.; cf. Lev. 10:1-2; only the first of these, the worship of the golden calf, was idolatry, although we may add the worship of the pagan gods at Shittim in Num. 25:1-15. See Ps. 106:6-39 for a report of the rebellions. Jer. 2:1-3 pictures the period of wanderings in the wilderness as a time of loyalty.

17. A full end: Cf. 11:13*b*; Jer. 5:18; 30:11; 46:28; Isa. 10:23.

---

mercy serves a world-embracing purpose. He deals with us in goodness, whether as individuals or as peoples, because he wills to reach his other children through us. He needed Israel as his servant among the nations, and when his purpose with her was frustrated by her sin, he sought by forgiveness to win her back to faithfulness again.

12. *The Meaning of the Sabbath.*—This verse is of value as setting in a clear light the

importance of the observance of a weekly day of worship. The day of rest has social and economic importance, and it is of no slight significance that it has been taken over by so many non-Christian countries, as it has been retained even where the Christian tradition is repudiated. But for us its religious purpose is the primary one, so that any defense of it by Christians should be in such terms.

Ezekiel describes the sabbath here as **a sign**

from destroying them, neither did I make an end of them in the wilderness.

18 But I said unto their children in the wilderness, Walk ye not in the statutes of your fathers, neither observe their judgments, nor defile yourselves with their idols:

19 I *am* the LORD your God; walk in my statutes, and keep my judgments, and do them;

20 And hallow my sabbaths; and they shall be a sign between me and you, that ye may know that I *am* the LORD your God.

21 Notwithstanding, the children rebelled against me: they walked not in my statutes, neither kept my judgments to do them, which *if* a man do, he shall even live in them; they polluted my sabbaths: then I said, I would pour out my fury upon them, to accomplish my anger against them in the wilderness.

22 Nevertheless I withdrew mine hand, and wrought for my name's sake, that it should not be polluted in the sight of the heathen, in whose sight I brought them forth.

23 I lifted up mine hand unto them also in the wilderness, that I would scatter them among the heathen, and disperse them through the countries;

24 Because they had not executed my judgments, but had despised my statutes, and had polluted my sabbaths, and their eyes were after their fathers' idols.

them or make a full end of them in the wilderness.

18 "And I said to their children in the wilderness, Do not walk in the statutes of your fathers, nor observe their ordinances, nor defile yourselves with their idols. **19** I the LORD am your God; walk in my statutes, and be careful to observe my ordinances, **20** and hallow my sabbaths that they may be a sign between me and you, that you may know that I the LORD am your God. **21** But the children rebelled against me; they did not walk in my statutes, and were not careful to observe my ordinances, by whose observance man shall live; they profaned my sabbaths.

"Then I thought I would pour out my wrath upon them and spend my anger against them in the wilderness. **22** But I withheld my hand, and acted for the sake of my name, that it should not be profaned in the sight of the nations, in whose sight I had brought them out. **23** Moreover I swore to them in the wilderness that I would scatter them among the nations and disperse them through the countries, **24** because they had not executed my ordinances, but had rejected my statutes and profaned my sabbaths, and their eyes were set on their

---

between God and his people, something which indicates the peculiar relationship obtaining between him and them. One can illustrate this idea by reference to the use of signs among ourselves, so that friends or members of the same association can recognize each other. The sign brings together people with shared interests and a common purpose; it is the pledge of mutual fidelity and commitment. So for Ezekiel, as for many other devout Jews at a later period, the sabbath compresses into a single observance the whole covenant relationship between the Lord and Israel. It brings into the life of the people an awed recognition of his claim upon them, so that they know themselves to be his and not their own. There was a great need of something of this kind after the Exile, when Israel was in danger of becoming assimilated to the surrounding nations.

Can we as Christians honestly say that we do not need anything of the kind? It is useless to

argue that God should be worshiped on seven days of the week, not on one only. That goes without saying. But it is a law of life that what can be done at any time tends never to get done at all. We need a day set apart for the recognition of God so that all days may be consecrated to him. Even in sport no proficiency can be gained except as particular times are devoted to regular practice; why should we suppose that the life of the spirit can be had on easier terms?

The experience of the mission field can be cited in support of this position. Importance there is attached to observance of the Lord's day, because it is the simplest form of witness. The man who cannot speak about his faith gives testimony to it every week when his shop remains closed or he does not go out into the fields to work. And it is often a sign that a person is losing his hold upon the faith when he grows slack in this respect.

25 Wherefore I gave them also statutes *that were* not good, and judgments whereby they should not live;

26 And I polluted them in their own gifts, in that they caused to pass through *the fire* all that openeth the womb, that I might make them desolate, to the end that they might know that I *am* the LORD.

27 ¶ Therefore, son of man, speak unto the house of Israel, and say unto them, Thus saith the Lord GOD; Yet in this your fathers have blasphemed me, in that they have committed a trespass against me.

28 *For* when I had brought them into the land, *for* the which I lifted up mine hand to give it to them, then they saw every high hill, and all the thick trees, and they offered there their sacrifices, and there they presented the provocation of their offering: there also they made their sweet savor, and poured out there their drink offerings.

29 Then I said unto them, What *is* the high place whereunto ye go? And the name thereof is called Bamah unto this day.

fathers' idols. 25 Moreover I gave them statutes that were not good and ordinances by which they could not have life; 26 and I defiled them through their very gifts in making them offer by fire all their first-born, that I might horrify them; I did it that they might know that I am the LORD.

27 "Therefore, son of man, speak to the house of Israel and say to them, Thus says the Lord GOD: In this again your fathers blasphemed me, by dealing treacherously with me. 28 For when I had brought them into the land which I swore to give them, then wherever they saw any high hill or any leafy tree, there they offered their sacrifices and presented the provocation of their offering; there they sent up their soothing odors, and there they poured out their drink offerings. 29 (I said to them, What is the high place to which you go? So its name is called

25-26. Cf. Yahweh's deliberate deception of the prophets in the Micaiah incident in I Kings 22:19-23. Jeremiah's biographer seems deliberately to deny that Yahweh gave such commands regarding human sacrifice (Jer. 7:31; 19:5). See the commands in Exod. 13:2; 22:29; 34:19, which may have been misinterpreted. **To pass through the fire:** See 16:21.

4. APOSTASIES IN CANAAN (20:27-29)

27-29. See also 6:13; 34:6; Deut. 12:2-3; Jer. 3:6; etc. **Drink offerings** (vs. 28): I.e., libations (see Gen. 35:14; Lev. 23:13, 18). In vs. 29 there is a crude or obscure attempt to explain the origin of the word במה, **high place,** perhaps as though it came from בא, "one who goes in" (in the sense of *coire cum femina,* and so with reference to the orgiastic rites at the high places? Cf. Ezek. 23:44) and מה, **what.** A number of scholars take this verse as a gloss.

25-26. *The Perversion of Religion.*—In accordance with Hebrew usage, Ezekiel tends to ascribe to God whatever happens. Here he has in mind the perversion of religion at the entry into Canaan. He describes the evil practices which the newcomers took over from the original inhabitants. Most atrocious of these was the custom of child sacrifice. He carries it back to a definite divine command, though he modifies this by saying that the command was given as punishment for previous sin.

What these verses suggest to us is the reflection, painful but necessary, that religion as such is morally neutral, that there is bad religion in the world as well as good religion, and that perhaps there are no crimes quite so ter-

rible as those which are committed when men persuade themselves that they serve God by doing them. Paul in his persecuting days and such institutions as the Inquisition are in evidence. "Religion is the last refuge of human savagery." [9]

The most powerful presentation of this truth is surely the unforgettable picture in Lucretius of Agamemnon sacrificing his daughter with his own hand. "To such a pitch of evil can religion persuade men" is the comment of the poet.[1] We can maintain the Christian cause against its critics today only as we realize that

[9] A. N. Whitehead, *Religion in the Making* (New York: The Macmillan Co., 1926), p. 37.
[1] *Of the Nature of Things* I. 101.

30 Wherefore say unto the house of Israel, Thus saith the Lord God; Are ye polluted after the manner of your fathers? and commit ye whoredom after their abominations?

31 For when ye offer your gifts, when ye make your sons to pass through the fire, ye pollute yourselves with all your idols, even unto this day: and shall I be inquired of by you, O house of Israel? *As* I live, saith the Lord God, I will not be inquired of by you.

32 And that which cometh into your mind shall not be at all, that ye say, We will be as the heathen, as the families of the countries, to serve wood and stone.

33 ¶ *As* I live, saith the Lord God, surely with a mighty hand, and with a stretched out arm, and with fury poured out, will I rule over you:

34 And I will bring you out from the people, and will gather you out of the countries wherein ye are scattered, with a mighty hand, and with a stretched out arm, and with fury poured out.

Bamah*ᵗ* to this day.) 30 Wherefore say to the house of Israel, Thus says the Lord God: Will you defile yourselves after the manner of your fathers and go astray after their detestable things? 31 When you offer your gifts and sacrifice your sons by fire, you defile yourselves with all your idols to this day. And shall I be inquired of by you, O house of Israel? As I live, says the Lord God, I will not be inquired of by you.

32 "What is in your mind shall never happen — the thought, 'Let us be like the nations, like the tribes of the countries, and worship wood and stone.'

33 "As I live, says the Lord God, surely with a mighty hand and an outstretched arm, and with wrath poured out, I will be king over you. 34 I will bring you out from the peoples and gather you out of the countries where you are scattered, with a mighty hand and an outstretched arm, and with

ᵗ That is *High Place*

---

5. Yahweh Will Not Be Inquired Of (20:30-31)

30-31. Go astray (vs. 30) is the Hebrew זנים, from the same root as "wanton" and "turn wantonly" in 6:9, and connoting the licentious sex rites.

6. Israel Will Be Purged (20:32-39)

Yahweh will not permit the assimilation of Israel to the Gentile nations (cf. 25:8-11; Jer. 10:2). The Deuteronomic diction of vs. 34 is striking (cf. Deut. 5:15; 7:19; 26:8; etc.; Jer. 21:5; 27:5; 32:21).

---

we are called on to defend not religion, or even Christianity as such, but only what in them is ethically above reproach.

32. Assimilation.—The greatest perils which the Jewish people have faced in the course of their tragic history have been from assimilation rather than from persecution. One of the sources used in I Samuel carries the temptation back to the early stages of national history. "Make us a king to judge us like all the nations" is the request (I Sam. 8:5). In the Exile there was a tendency to seek to make the lot of the Jew easier by eliminating anything which distinguished him from his fellows. Precisely the same situation faces the Jew in the modern world. Some would say that those countries in which the Jew takes on the color of the society around him, becoming "Reformed" in one and "Marxist" in another, are more dangerous than others in which anti-Semitism is rampant.

There are certain questions we should put to ourselves in this connection. First, as regards the Jew. Do we really wish assimilation to prevail? Is it really desirable that the Jewish community should be absorbed into the general life of a country by intermarriage and secularization on a large scale, including the acceptance of a purely nominal Christianity in many cases? Or has Jewry still a distinctive contribution to make? The conclusion to which we come will affect our thinking on the relations between Christians and Jews, as well as our attitude to various tendencies and groups within Jewry.

Second, what of the Christian position? Are we not exposed also to the danger of assimilation? Has the process perhaps been allowed to go too far with us already? Yet we cannot follow the example of those who react so strongly in favor of a distinctively Christian way of life that they even ignore their obligations as

35 And I will bring you into the wilderness of the people, and there will I plead with you face to face.

36 Like as I pleaded with your fathers in the wilderness of the land of Egypt, so will I plead with you, saith the Lord God.

37 And I will cause you to pass under the rod, and I will bring you into the bond of the covenant:

38 And I will purge out from among you the rebels, and them that transgress against me: I will bring them forth out of the country where they sojourn, and they shall not enter into the land of Israel: and ye shall know that I *am* the Lord.

39 As for you, O house of Israel, thus

wrath poured out; 35 and I will bring you into the wilderness of the peoples, and there I will enter into judgment with you face to face. 36 As I entered into judgment with your fathers in the wilderness of the land of Egypt, so I will enter into judgment with you, says the Lord God. 37 I will make you pass under the rod, and I will let you go in by number.*u* 38 I will purge out the rebels from among you, and those who transgress against me; I will bring them out of the land where they sojourn, but they shall not enter the land of Israel. Then you will know that I am the Lord.

39 "As for you, O house of Israel, thus

u Gk: Heb *bring you into the bond of the covenant*

---

35. The wilderness of the peoples is perhaps deliberately obscure, for the reference is to the territory between the several countries of the Diaspora and Palestine, not merely the Syrian-Arabian desert. For the return from the Exile as the second exodus see also Isa. 11:15-16; Hos. 2:14-16, from the same period.

37. Pass under the rod: As sheep, each to be counted (cf. Jer. 33:13). **By number:** Reading במספר for במסרת, **into the bond,** and omit הברית, **the covenant,** with the LXX; the latter may be dittography of the following word.

39. And hereafter also, if ye will not hearken unto me: Perhaps an apocopated oath, with the punishment not mentioned.

---

citizens. How can we strike the right balance between preservation of our Christian witness and participation in the common life about us?

35-36. *Into the Melting Pot.*—The wilderness between Egypt, Arabia, and Palestine was the breeding ground of nations. From it the nomad tribes from time to time burst forth to raid what we have come to call the Fertile Crescent, eventually often settling down in it. The conquest of western Asia and eastern Europe by the warriors of Islam provides one of the most momentous instances of this process. From one point of view it was an attempt to find an outlet for the surplus population of the Arabian peninsula. For a nation with a history behind it to go back to this state of things was, as we should say, for it to be thrown into the melting pot again. What has grown hard and rigid must become pliable once more, so that it may have the chance to take on a new form. Every now and again the most settled of civilizations has in this way to be thrown into the melting pot. Times of great upheaval, such as war and economic crisis, perform this necessary function. Only as we go through the agony involved do we become capable of the rebirth which makes it all worth while in the end.

There is also a melting pot for the individual. Each of us needs his crisis by which established habits are called in question and a possibility

is given of remaking the self. At such a time one must learn to pray:

So, wash Thou me without, within;
    Or purge with fire, if that must be—
No matter how, if only sin
    Die out in me.[2]

37-38. *Partial Deliverance.*—The language of vs. 37 reminds us of the parable of the sheep and goats, as the image employed is that of a shepherd sorting out his sheep by means of his rod. But here those who are as it were on the left hand are not sent away into everlasting punishment. They are actually brought **out of the country where they sojourn** and in so far delivered. But they do **not enter into the land of Israel,** they remain outside the final blessing of their people. Why is that? Not because of a divine sentence of judgment perhaps, but simply because there would be, as we say, no place for them there. The mere circumstance that our suffering has been ended will not bring us to new life unless we are spiritually prepared for it. And if in our suffering we have been rebellious we shall not be thus prepared.

39-44. *Revival of Religion.*—The first condition of such a revival is decision. The state of affairs in which God is only one of several alle-

[2] W. Chalmers Smith, "One thing I of the Lord desire."

saith the Lord GOD; Go ye, serve ye every one his idols, and hereafter *also,* if ye will not hearken unto me: but pollute ye my holy name no more with your gifts, and with your idols.

40 For in mine holy mountain, in the mountain of the height of Israel, saith the Lord GOD, there shall all the house of Israel, all of them in the land, serve me: there will I accept them, and there will I require your offerings, and the firstfruits of your oblations, with all your holy things.

41 I will accept you with your sweet savor, when I bring you out from the people, and gather you out of the countries wherein ye have been scattered; and I will be sanctified in you before the heathen.

42 And ye shall know that I *am* the LORD, when I shall bring you into the land of Israel, into the country *for* the which I lifted up mine hand to give it to your fathers.

43 And there shall ye remember your ways, and all your doings, wherein ye have been defiled; and ye shall loathe yourselves in your own sight for all your evils that ye have committed.

44 And ye shall know that I *am* the LORD, when I have wrought with you for my name's sake, not according to your wicked ways, nor according to your corrupt doings, O ye house of Israel, saith the Lord GOD.

says the Lord GOD: Go serve every one of you his idols, now and hereafter, if you will not listen to me; but my holy name you shall no more profane with your gifts and your idols.

40 "For on my holy mountain, the mountain height of Israel, says the Lord GOD, there all the house of Israel, all of them, shall serve me in the land; there I will accept them, and there I will require your contributions and the choicest of your gifts, with all your sacred offerings. **41** As a pleasing odor I will accept you, when I bring you out from the peoples, and gather you out of the countries where you have been scattered; and I will manifest my holiness among you in the sight of the nations. **42** And you shall know that I am the LORD, when I bring you into the land of Israel, the country which I swore to give to your fathers. **43** And there you shall remember your ways and all the doings with which you have polluted yourselves; and you shall loathe yourselves for all the evils that you have committed. **44** And you shall know that I am the LORD, when I deal with you for my name's sake, not according to your evil ways, nor according to your corrupt doings, O house of Israel, says the Lord GOD."

---

7. RESTORATION OF THE PEOPLE TO THE LAND OF ISRAEL (20:40-44)

Yahweh will accept the sacrifices of his people after the restoration. A deliberate contrast to vss. 30-31? Cf. the pictures of restoration in 11:14-21; 16:53-63; 17:22-24; 34:1–39:29.

40. Holy mountain: Cf. 28:14; Deut. 9:16, 20; 11:45; Isa. 11:9; 65:25; 56:7; Joel 2:1; 3:17; Obad. 16; etc. The word תרומתיכם, **your contributions,** is used in a number of ways in Ezekiel, sometimes referring to the "holy district" or "holy portion" set aside for the temple, priests, and Levites (45:1; 48:8-10; etc.); perhaps here, as in 44:30, it is a contribution to Yahweh set apart for the priests (see also Lev. 22:12; Num. 5:9; etc.). The term is most common in P. With ראשית, **best,** cf. 44:30, where the word is translated **the choicest;** the allusion here may be to **the firstfruits,** which presumably would be the best.

43. The verse recalls 6:9; 11:17-19; 16:61, 63; 36:31; 39:26-27.

---

giances must be ended. Men must decide for him or against him (vs. 39). On this follows a twofold change, one outward and the other inward. The prophet values the first; he rejoices to see all the house of Israel thronging the temple once more with their offerings, and

he promises that God will accept the gifts that are brought to him. But these are valueless without the keen shame and penitence that will make impossible any repetition of the past. The return to public worship is genuine only if at the same time it is a return to obedience.

45 ¶ Moreover the word of the LORD came unto me, saying,

46 Son of man, set thy face toward the south, and drop *thy word* toward the south, and prophesy against the forest of the south field;

47 And say to the forest of the south, Hear the word of the LORD; Thus saith the Lord GOD; Behold, I will kindle a fire in thee, and it shall devour every green tree in thee, and every dry tree: the flaming flame shall not be quenched, and all faces from the south to the north shall be burned therein.

48 And all flesh shall see that I the LORD have kindled it: it shall not be quenched.

49 Then said I, Ah Lord GOD! they say of me, Doth he not speak parables?

21 And the word of the LORD came unto me, saying,

2 Son of man, set thy face toward Jerusalem, and drop *thy word* toward the holy places, and prophesy against the land of Israel,

---

45[v] And the word of the LORD came to me: **46** "Son of man, set your face toward the south, preach against the south, and prophesy against the forest land in the Negeb; **47** say to the forest of the Negeb, Hear the word of the LORD: Thus says the Lord GOD, Behold, I will kindle a fire in you, and it shall devour every green tree in you and every dry tree; the blazing flame shall not be quenched, and all faces from south to north shall be scorched by it. **48** All flesh shall see that I the LORD have kindled it; it shall not be quenched." **49** Then I said, "Ah Lord GOD! they are saying of me, 'Is he not a maker of allegories?' "

21[w] The word of the LORD came to me: **2** "Son of man, set your face toward Jerusalem and preach against the sanctuaries; prophesy against the land of Israel

[v] Heb Ch 21. 1
[w] Heb Ch 21. 6

---

8. ORACLE AGAINST THE SOUTH (20:45-49=Hebrew 21:1-5)

45-49. The editor's hand is obviously discernible. As in 21:1 (Hebrew 21:6) the prophet is to **set** his **face** toward Jerusalem, and in 6:2 toward the mountains of Jerusalem, so here toward the **south**. Note the similarity between vs. 48 and 21:5; we may take vs. 48 as a variant of the familiar "then they will know" formula. The **green tree** and the **dry tree** of vs. 47 occur in 17:24. As in ch. 6, the most we can say is that if an oracle of Ezekiel lies at the basis of the present editor's composition, it is futile to try to recover it.

In vs. 46 the **south** is designated by the three words, נגב, דרום, תימנה, and refers to Judah, which is in the south from the viewpoint of the northern foe. The last of these terms, i.e., *néghebh*, cannot refer merely to the **Negeb** as the desert territory of south Palestine. The kindling of the **fire** recalls especially Isa. 10:16-19; Jer. 21:14 (cf. Deut. 32:22; Jer. 15:14; 17:4, 27). In vs. 47 שלהבת, **flaming** (lit., **flame**), is a Shaphel form and not necessarily an Aramaism (see Howie, *Date and Composition of Ezekiel*, p. 60). Note the implied universalism of vs. 48. In vs. 49 **parables,** משלים, perhaps means **allegories** (as in 17:2; 24:3); cf. the reaction of the audience of Ezekiel in 12:27; 33:32.

P. PROPHECIES ON THE SWORD (21:1-32=Hebrew 21:6-37)

There are five oracles in this chapter: (*a*) Yahweh's sword will be unsheathed and will destroy both righteous and wicked (vss. 1-7); (*b*) the song concerning the sword of Yahweh, which is polished and sharpened for slaughter (vss. 8-17); (*c*) the sword of the king of Babylon who stands at the crossroads (vss. 18-24); (*d*) the day of the

---

45-49. *Doom and Defense.*—The prophet constantly finds that his sternest denunciations can be turned aside by some ready excuse on the part of his hearers. If men do not want to understand they can always find some obscurity in what is said. So here even those over whom he sees doom hanging protest that his language is not clear enough, that he is using metaphor and image when he should say what he means. Of course they follow him quite well, but they do not propose to admit it. Behind their mockery lies an overconfidence that declines to believe anything so serious could possibly happen to *them*.

21:1-32. *Suffering for Good.*—That God makes even the wrath of man to praise him is

3 And say to the land of Israel, Thus saith the LORD; Behold, I *am* against thee, and will draw forth my sword out of his sheath, and will cut off from thee the righteous and the wicked.

4 Seeing then that I will cut off from thee the righteous and the wicked, therefore shall my sword go forth out of his sheath against all flesh from the south to the north:

5 That all flesh may know that I the LORD have drawn forth my sword out of his sheath: it shall not return any more.

6 Sigh therefore, thou son of man, with the breaking of *thy* loins; and with bitterness sigh before their eyes.

7 And it shall be, when they say unto thee, Wherefore sighest thou? that thou shalt answer, For the tidings, because it

3 and say to the land of Israel, Thus says the LORD: Behold, I am against you, and will draw forth my sword out of its sheath, and will cut off from you both righteous and wicked. 4 Because I will cut off from you both righteous and wicked, therefore my sword shall go out of its sheath against all flesh from south to north; 5 and all flesh shall know that I the LORD have drawn my sword out of its sheath; it shall not be sheathed again. 6 Sigh therefore, son of man; sigh with breaking heart and bitter grief before their eyes. 7 And when they say to you, 'Why do you sigh?' you shall say,

---

punishment of the prince of Israel has come (vss. 25-27); (e) the sword of Ammon is to be returned to its sheath, and the Ammonites are to be judged and destroyed (vss. 28-32).

The second and third of these oracles are most obviously from Ezekiel. There is fairly general agreement that the last oracle is late. It seems equally obvious in the light of our preceding discussion that the originality of the fourth oracle must be questioned. The first oracle follows the pattern of the last oracle in ch. 20. The words are largely those of the editor, although the original inspiration may have been Ezekiel. Hölscher finds only the second original, while Irwin finds four short poetic oracles in the chapter.

The third oracle suggests a date in the latter part of 589, when Nebuchadrezzar's armies took the road to make the campaign against Judah which was to result in the destruction of Jerusalem and the temple. There is no reason to ascribe the second oracle to a different period.

1. YAHWEH'S SWORD IS UNSHEATHED (21:1-7=Hebrew 21:6-12)

If there is an original oracle here, it may best be represented in vss. 3-4; Irwin finds it in vs. 3 (Hebrew vs. 8). The literary formula in vs. 7 is the question and answer style used by the late biographer in Jeremiah and the Deuteronomist (cf. Jer. 5:18-19; 16:10-13; 22:8-9; Deut. 6:20-25; 29:22-29; I Kings 9:8-9, etc.; see May, "Towards an Objective Approach to the Book of Jeremiah," pp. 144-45). Note the variation on the usual editor's formula in vs. 5, and the repetition of the last sentence of vs. 7 in 39:8.

21:2. The sanctuaries is, awkwardly, without the article in the Hebrew (מקדשים); perhaps the reference is to the high places, although it is better to read מקדשם, "their sanctuary," with four MSS, the LXX, and Syriac, as a reference to the Jerusalem temple.

3. Cut off from you both righteous and wicked seems to be in contrast with the editor's doctrine of responsibility and punishment in ch. 18, etc., and contrasts the protestation of the fairness of Yahweh (18:24-32; 33:17-20). The LXX reads "unjust" in the place of "righteous" (see Intro., pp. 48-49).

5. All flesh here means all men everywhere, in possible contrast to its use in vs. 4, where it may refer to those in Palestine, although it reflects the editor's idea of a world judgment (cf. Bertholet), and is perhaps his adaptation of Ezekiel's oracle.

7. Because it cometh could be connected with what precedes or with what follows (cf. RSV; also 7:17).

cometh: and every heart shall melt, and all hands shall be feeble, and every spirit shall faint, and all knees shall be weak *as* water: behold, it cometh, and shall be brought to pass, saith the Lord God.

8 ¶ Again the word of the LORD came unto me saying,

9 Son of man, prophesy, and say, Thus saith the LORD; Say, A sword, a sword is sharpened, and also furbished:

10 It is sharpened to make a sore slaughter; it is furbished that it may glitter: should we then make mirth? it contemneth the rod of my son, *as* every tree.

11 And he hath given it to be furbished, that it may be handled: this sword is sharpened, and it is furbished, to give it into the hand of the slayer.

12 Cry and howl, son of man; for it shall be upon my people, it *shall be* upon all the

'Because of the tidings. When it comes, every heart will melt and all hands will be feeble, every spirit will faint and all knees will be weak as water. Behold, it comes and it will be fulfilled,' " says the Lord God.

8 And the word of the LORD came to me; 9 "Son of man, prophesy and say, Thus says the Lord, Say:

A sword, a sword is sharpened
　　and also polished,
10 sharpened for slaughter,
　　polished to flash like lightning!

Or do we make mirth? You have despised the rod, my son, with everything of wood. 11 So the sword is given to be polished, that it may be handled; it is sharpened and polished to be given into the hand of the slayer. 12 Cry and wail, son of man, for it

---

2. Song of Yahweh's Sword (21:8-17 = Hebrew 21:13-22)

As most commentators agree, there can be little question but that this was originally in the form of poetry. The present irregularity of form may be due largely to the editor's elaborations and to the many corruptions. These distortions fail to hide the vigorous poetic quality of the original.

10. The word ברק, **glitter**, is more properly **lightning** (see Deut. 32:41; cf. Job 20:25). The end of the verse is palpably corrupt (see RSV); lit., "or shall we rejoice, the rod of my son despising every tree?"

11. And he hath given must rather be read as an impersonal form, since Yahweh is speaking and the third person is awkward; so RSV, which rightly interprets it as impersonal and translates it as a passive. Or read with the Vulg. "and I gave."

12. The last part of the verse is the editor's expansion, introducing the **princes of Israel,** נשיאי ישראל (see Intro., p. 54; cf. Hölscher). **They are delivered over:** Read מגרי for מגורי, **terrors** (see 35:5). For smiting the **thigh** as a sign of grief and shame, see Jer. 31:19.

---

one of the major themes of the prophets. In this chapter we are shown by three instances how he does so. There are periods in which such a passage as this has nothing to offer, but again there are periods in which it comes alive because men have to bow under the harsh discipline of events and are able to do so only as they can hope that what they suffer will serve a purpose of great and lasting good.

8-13. War.—Those lines which Rudyard Kipling wrote in 1914 echo the grim oracle of the **sword** which Ezekiel intones:

> No law except the sword,
> Unsheathed and uncontrolled.[3]

Slaughter stalks abroad in the land, yet even amid the fury and desolation of war God is at work. For the achievement of his purpose he lays under fee methods which he did not himself choose, for the simple reason that they are the only ones men put at his disposal. See the poems written by John Greenleaf Whittier during the Civil War, when he accepts the fact that the liberation of the slaves will come in a very different way from that in which he had worked to bring it.

> If, for the age to come, this hour
> Of trial hath vicarious power,
> And, blest by Thee, our present **pain**
> Be Liberty's eternal gain,
> 　　Thy will be done![4]

[3] "For All We Have and Are," from *The Years Between.* Copyright 1904, 1919 by Rudyard Kipling, reprinted by permission of Mrs. George Bambridge; Methuen & Co.; The Macmillan Co., Canada; and Doubleday & Co.

[4] "Thy Will Be Done."

princes of Israel: terrors by reason of the sword shall be upon my people: smite therefore upon *thy* thigh.

13 Because *it is* a trial, and what if *the sword* contemn even the rod? it shall be no *more,* saith the Lord God.

14 Thou therefore, son of man, prophesy, and smite *thine* hands together, and let the sword be doubled the third time, the sword of the slain: it *is* the sword of the great *men that are* slain, which entereth into their privy chambers.

15 I have set the point of the sword against all their gates, that *their* heart may faint, and *their* ruins be multiplied: ah! *it is* made bright, *it is* wrapped up for the slaughter.

16 Go thee one way or other, *either* on the right hand, *or* on the left, whithersoever thy face *is* set.

17 I will also smite mine hands together, and I will cause my fury to rest: I the Lord have said *it.*

18 ¶ The word of the Lord came unto me again, saying,

19 Also, thou son of man, appoint thee two ways, that the sword of the king of Babylon may come: both twain shall come

is against my people; it is against all the princes of Israel; they are delivered over to the sword with my people. Smite therefore upon your thigh. **13** For it will not be a testing — what could it do if you despise the rod?" says the Lord God.

14 "Prophesy therefore, son of man; clap your hands and let the sword come down twice, yea thrice, the sword for those to be slain; it is the sword for the great slaughter, which encompasses them, **15** that their hearts may melt, and many fall at all their gates. I have given the glittering sword; ah! it is made like lightning, it is polished[x] for slaughter. **16** Cut sharply to right[y] and left where your edge is directed. **17** I also will clap my hands, and I will satisfy my fury; I the Lord have spoken.

18 The word of the Lord came to me again: **19** "Son of man, mark two ways for

[x] Tg: Heb *wrapped up*
[y] Gk Syr Vg: Heb *right, set*

13. This verse is obscure, and doubtless corrupt. Note the KJV minus the words **it is, the sword,** and **more.** The translator must make some sense!

14-15. Both verses are corrupt. The word החדרת, only here, probably means **which encompasses;** the versions suggest a transposition of consonants, rendering the root חרד, and so the Amer. Trans., "bring terror"; the KJV associates it with חדר, "chamber," as a denominative verb. The word אבחת, **glittering,** occurs only here, and many assume a corruption from טבחת, **slaughter,** after the LXX, which reads παραδέδονται εἰς σφάγια ῥομφαίας, "they are given up to the slaughter of the sword"; perhaps we should read, "I have given slaughter to the sword." **Polished:** Reading מרטה with the Targ. for מעטה (see vss. 11-12 [Hebrew 15-16]).

16. The expression התאחדי, **cut sharply,** is here probably taken as a mistake for התחדי, from חדד, "be sharp," since no verb from אחד, "one," is known; cf. KJV. **Set** (RSV mg.) is due to dittography (one Hebrew MS, LXX, O.L., and Vulg. omit).

3. The Sword of the King of Babylon (21:18-24=Hebrew 21:23-29)

This is another oracle illustrated by dramatic action. The sword of Yahweh is the sword of the king of Babylon.

19. On יד, signpost, see I Sam. 15:12; II Sam. 18:18; see the "waymarks" in Jer. 31:21. The word ברא, lit., "cut out" (=make, choose) appears twice in vs. 19, due once to dittography; omit its first occurrence with the LXX[B].

18-23. *Superstition.*—We watch Nebuchadrezzar at the crossroads, with no better means of discovering the will of heaven than by casting lots. Mere chance, it would seem, decides that Judah is to be crushed first and Ammon's pun-

ishment reserved till later. The leaders of Jerusalem see clearly what is happening. The whole thing is just so much crass superstition and so does not disturb them. **To them it will seem like a false divination.** But they have not

forth out of one land: and choose thou a place, choose *it* at the head of the way to the city.

20 Appoint a way, that the sword may come to Rabbath of the Ammonites, and to Judah in Jerusalem the defensed.

21 For the king of Babylon stood at the parting of the way, at the head of the two ways, to use divination: he made *his* arrows bright, he consulted with images, he looked in the liver.

22 At his right hand was the divination for Jerusalem, to appoint captains, to open the mouth in the slaughter, to lift up the voice with shouting, to appoint *battering* rams against the gates, to cast a mount, *and* to build a fort.

23 And it shall be unto them as a false divination in their sight, to them that have sworn oaths: but he will call to remembrance the iniquity that they may be taken.

24 Therefore thus saith the Lord GOD; Because ye have made your iniquity to be remembered, in that your transgressions are discovered, so that in all your doings your sins do appear; because, *I say*, that ye are come to remembrance, ye shall be taken with the hand.

the sword of the king of Babylon to come; both of them shall come forth from the same land. And make a signpost, make it at the head of the way to a city; 20 mark a way for the sword to come to Rabbah of the Ammonites and to Judah and to[z] Jerusalem the fortified. 21 For the king of Babylon stands at the parting of the way, at the head of the two ways, to use divination; he shakes the arrows, he consults the teraphim, he looks at the liver. 22 Into his right hand comes the lot for Jerusalem,[a] to open the mouth with a cry,[b] to lift up the voice with shouting, to set battering rams against the gates, to cast up mounds, to build siege towers. 23 But to them it will seem like a false divination; they have sworn solemn oaths; but he brings their guilt to remembrance, that they may be captured.

24 "Therefore thus says the Lord GOD: Because you have made your guilt to be remembered, in that your transgressions are uncovered, so that in all your doings your sins appear — because you have come to remembrance, you shall be taken in

[z] Gk Syr: Heb *in*
[a] Heb *Jerusalem, to set battering rams*
[b] Gk: Heb *with slaughter*

---

20. **Rabbah,** capital city of the Ammonites, is modern 'Ammân, the capital of Jordan. Ammon had been in a coalition opposing Babylon at the beginning of Zedekiah's reign (Jer. 27:3), and doubtless also in 589, although earlier it had been on the side of Babylon (II Kings 24:2).

21. Divination by use of **arrows** (belomancy) was known among the Arabs also. Divination by inspecting the **liver** (hepatoscopy) has many illustrations in Mesopotamia, and may be evidenced by pottery models of sheep livers found in Palestine, comparable to those known from Mesopotamia (see Gordon Loud, *Megiddo II* [Chicago: University of Chicago Press, 1948], Vol. I, Pl. 255; Edward Chiera, *They Wrote on Clay* [ed. G. G. Cameron; Chicago: University of Chicago Press, 1938], p. 219; Morris Jastrow, Jr., *The Civilization of Babylonia and Assyria* [Philadelphia: J. B. Lippincott & Co., 1915], pp. 255-56; cf. R. H. Pfeiffer, *State Letters of Assyria* [New Haven: American Oriental Society, 1935], Nos. 335-37, pp. 229-30).

22. For the **mounds, towers,** etc., see Exeg. on 4:1-3. **With a cry:** Read with the LXX and context בצרח for ברצח (**with slaughter**); cf. Isa. 42:13.

23. For example of such **solemn oaths** see Jer. 34:8-22.

24. The LXX ἐν τούτοις, **in them,** is probably only an interpretation of the Hebrew בכף, **with the hand.**

---

insight enough to perceive that even this superstition is taken up into the purpose of God. He is overruling it for his own ends of chastisement, to bring home to his people the perjury of which they have been guilty. Similarly, Nebuchadrezzar for his part may imagine that

it is his own god who is directing his strategy; he does not know that even his folly is in the hands of the mighty God who orders his march.

24-27. *Revolution.*—War usually brings in its train social upheaval. The class which possesses power is overthrown and another climbs to its

25 ¶ And thou, profane wicked prince of Israel, whose day is come, when iniquity *shall have* an end,

26 Thus saith the Lord God; Remove the diadem, and take off the crown: this *shall not be* the same: exalt *him that is* low, and abase *him that is* high.

27 I will overturn, overturn, overturn it: and it shall be no *more,* until he come whose right it is; and I will give it *him.*

28 ¶ And thou, son of man, prophesy and say, Thus saith the Lord God concerning the Ammonites, and concerning their reproach; even say thou, The sword, the sword *is* drawn: for the slaughter *it is* furbished, to consume because of the glittering:

29 While they see vanity unto thee, while they divine a lie unto thee, to bring thee upon the necks of *them that are* slain, of the wicked, whose day is come, when their iniquity *shall have* an end.

30 Shall I cause *it* to return into his sheath? I will judge thee in the place where thou wast created, in the land of thy nativity.

them.*c* **25** And you, O unhallowed wicked one, prince of Israel, whose day has come, the time of your final punishment, **26** thus says the Lord God: Remove the turban, and take off the crown; things shall not remain as they are; exalt that which is low, and abase that which is high. **27** A ruin, ruin, ruin I will make it; there shall not be even a trace*d* of it until he comes whose right it is; and to him I will give it.

28 "And you, son of man, prophesy, and say, Thus says the Lord God concerning the Ammonites, and concerning their reproach; say, A sword, a sword is drawn for the slaughter, it is polished to glitter*e* and to flash like lightning — **29** while they see for you false visions, while they divine lies for you — to be laid on the necks of the unhallowed wicked, whose day has come, the time of their final punishment. **30** Return it to its sheath. In the place where you were created, in the land of your origin, I

c Gk: Heb *with the hand*
d Cn: Heb *not even this*
e Cn: Heb *to contain*

4. THE PRINCE OF ISRAEL (21:25-27=Hebrew 21:30-32)

The derogatory estimate of Zedekiah is reflected also by the biographer in Jeremiah (see H. G. May, "The Chronology of Jeremiah's Oracles," *Journal of Near Eastern Studies,* IV [1945], 220-21). The editor applies the same derogatory description to the Judeans in vs. 29. See also 12:10 for the editor's designation of Zedekiah as a prince, נשיא.

26. The word מצנפת, **diadem,** is more properly **turban,** as in Lev. 8:9 (cf. also Exod. 28:37; 29:6; etc.).

27. Not . . . a trace: Read גם אות לא יהיה for גם זאת לא יהיה; the Hebrew is obviously corrupted. Gen. 49:10 seems to have influenced this verse.

5. THE FATE OF THE AMMONITES (21:28-32=Hebrew 21:33-37)

Cf. the editor's oracle against the Ammonites in 25:1-7 (see also Jer. 49:1-6; Zeph. 2:8-11). As in 25:3, 6, there may be an allusion to the events at the death of Gedaliah (Jer. 40:13–41:18). Note the role of the Ammonites at the time of Nehemiah (Neh. 2:10, 19; 13:1-3, 23-27; cf. Matthews). Cf. vs. 31 with 5:13; 6:12; 7:21; 14:19; etc. These verses are considered poetry by some scholars.

28. To glitter: Read לההל for להכיל, **to consume. To flash like lightning:** Read ברק as *berōq* instead of *bārāq,* **the glittering.**

place. **Exalt that which is low, and abase that which is high** is the mandate which God gives again and again to the forces governing history. Is this merely that he may let chaos loose upon the earth? No, there is a will of God for good in it all. He will not let humanity rest content in a condition of injustice; therefore he disturbs and vexes us **until he comes whose right it is,**

until one day justice is done. It is of his mercy that he overturns our society again and again, since only so can he bring us to find our security not in any political system, but in the rule of righteousness.

28-32. *Forgotten Ammon.*—The reference here may be to events after the fall of Jerusalem in 587 B.C., when Ammon took advantage of its

31 And I will pour out mine indignation upon thee; I will blow against thee in the fire of my wrath, and deliver thee into the hand of brutish men, *and* skilful to destroy.

32 Thou shalt be for fuel to the fire; thy blood shall be in the midst of the land; thou shalt be no *more* remembered: for I the LORD have spoken *it*.

22 Moreover the word of the LORD came unto me, saying,

2 Now, thou son of man, wilt thou judge, wilt thou judge the bloody city? yea, thou shalt show her all her abominations.

will judge you. 31 And I will pour out my indignation upon you; I will blow upon you with the fire of my wrath; and I will deliver you into the hands of brutal men, skilful to destroy. 32 You shall be fuel for the fire; your blood shall be in the midst of the land; you shall be no more remembered; for I the LORD have spoken."

22 Moreover the word of the LORD came to me, saying, 2 "And you, son of man, will you judge, will you judge the bloody city? Then declare to her all her

---

31. The destroyer of Ammon is identified with the Kedemites in 25:4.

32. Cf. 25:10. The verse recalls the idea of **blood** revenge.

Q. INDICTMENT OF JERUSALEM (22:1-31)

The three oracles in this chapter begin with the phrase, "The word of the LORD came to me." The first (vss. 1-16) depicts Jerusalem as a city of blood, defiled by its idolatry and oppressions. Yahweh will scatter her among the nations, and then she will know that he is Yahweh. The second (vss. 17-22) employs the familiar prophetic figure of smelting. As silver is melted in the furnaces, so will the house of Israel be smelted within Jerusalem, will prove to be but dross, and will know that Yahweh has poured out his wrath on them. The third (vss. 23-31) indicts all classes for their sins—princes, priests, nobles, and people; Yahweh has poured out his indignation upon them and requited their way on their heads.

As usual, there is a variety of opinion regarding the authorship of these three oracles. Hölscher ascribes them all to the redactor, while Irwin finds an original oracle within vss. 3-4, another in vs. 18, and a third in vs. 24. The originality of the third oracle is questioned by Herntrich and Matthews (see also Bertholet). All three are in the literary garb of the editor, and should be compared particularly with chs. 13; 20. One hesitates to say that there is no reflection of Ezekiel's thought anywhere, although it is difficult to put one's finger on it; e.g., the smelting of the house of Israel (vss. 17-22) is a figure which would be as natural to Ezekiel as it was to Jeremiah and Isaiah (cf. Jer. 6:27-30; 9:7; Isa. 1:22), and the judgment is consonant with that prophesied by Ezekiel (see also Exeg. on vs. 30). In its present form the chapter is a three-point sermon of the editor, who is concerned that his contemporaries take warning from the fate of Jerusalem.

1. THE CITY OF BLOOD (22:1-16)

The bloodshed had been in part in human sacrifice in the worship of idols, but more especially it resulted from the violence and extortions of the leaders (see also

---

neighbor's plight to encroach on its territory and was suspected of a hand in the murder of Gedaliah. The religious leaders of Ammon offered every support and assurance of success to these enterprises (vs. 29). But history sees the roles of the two nations quite reversed. Israel has arisen spiritually victorious from her calamity, while Ammon is **no more remembered.** The fact that Ammon was spared exile does not count; she has perished in the place where she was created. Israel, uprooted though she was

from her soil, had other roots in God and so did not perish.

22:1-31. *Judgment of Jerusalem.*—In this chapter Ezekiel returns to Jerusalem, her sins, and her impending doom. The theme is by now only too familiar, but a fresh treatment of it becomes possible once we note that it is dealt with here under three heads.

1-16. *The Guilt of the City.*—Sometimes the prophet is content to pass sentence upon his nation; God will shortly arise and sweep it away.

3 Then say thou, Thus saith the Lord God; The city sheddeth blood in the midst of it, that her time may come, and maketh idols against herself to defile herself.

4 Thou art become guilty in thy blood that thou hast shed; and hast defiled thyself in thine idols which thou hast made; and thou hast caused thy days to draw near, and art come *even* unto thy years: therefore have I made thee a reproach unto the heathen, and a mocking to all countries.

5 *Those that be* near, and *those that be* far from thee, shall mock thee, *which art* infamous *and* much vexed.

6 Behold, the princes of Israel, every one were in thee to their power to shed blood.

7 In thee have they set light by father and mother: in the midst of thee have they dealt by oppression with the stranger: in thee have they vexed the fatherless and the widow.

8 Thou hast despised mine holy things, and hast profaned my sabbaths.

9 In thee are men that carry tales to shed blood: and in thee they eat upon the

abominable deeds. 3 You shall say, Thus says the Lord God: A city that sheds blood in the midst of her, that her time may come, and that makes idols to defile herself! 4 You have become guilty by the blood which you have shed, and defiled by the idols which you have made; and you have brought your day near, the appointed time*f* of your years has come. Therefore I have made you a reproach to the nations, and a mocking to all the countries. 5 Those who are near and those who are far from you will mock you, you infamous one, full of tumult.

6 "Behold, the princes of Israel in you, every one according to his power, have been bent on shedding blood. 7 Father and mother are treated with contempt in you; the sojourner suffers extortion in your midst; the fatherless and the widow are wronged in you. 8 You have despised my holy things, and profaned my sabbaths. 9 There are men in you who slander to shed

f Two Mss Gk Syr Vg Tg: Heb until

7:23; 11:6-7; 18:10; 23:37, 45; 24:6-9; 33:25; 36:18). The courts had been misused to this end; see vss. 9a, 12, and cf. the Naboth incident in I Kings 21:1-29 (cf. II Kings 21:16; Amos 2:6, 8; 5:12; etc.). For analogous ideas and diction cf. vs. 2 with 20:4, vs. 4 with 16:57, and vs. 5 with 6:12. The catalogue of sins in vss. 6-12 recalls the sins mentioned in 18:5-18, and the phraseology shows strong dependence on the Holiness Code (see Lev. 18:6-9, 17, 20; 19:3, 16, 29, 30, 33; 20:9, 10-14, 17; etc.). Note the typical formula in vss. 14b, 16b, and the familiar allusion to the Diaspora in vs. 15.

22:2. The repetition of **will you judge,** lacking in four Hebrew MSS, the **LXX,** and Syriac, may be due to dittography.

4. Idols: I.e., *gillûlim;* see 6:4, etc. Read יומך, **your day,** with the Targ. (cf. 21:25 [Hebrew 21:30]), for ימיך, **thy days.** For עד, **unto,** read עת, **appointed time,** with two Hebrew MSS (Eastern), the LXX, Syriac, Targ., and Vulg.

6. **The princes of Israel:** The Hebrew is נשיאי ישראל, as in 19:1; 21:12 (Hebrew 21:17); 45:9.

7. For the later legislation regarding attitudes toward parents see Lev. 19:3; 20:9; Deut. 5:16; 27:16. **The sojourner** may be the proselyte (see Exeg. on 14:7).

But at times he is concerned, as here, to justify the ways of God with Israel and to establish a connection, clear for all to see, between the doom which hangs over the nation and the sin with which it is rife. Here the second course is taken. In the fierce light of the divine holiness all things lie naked and open, and the prophet singles out one by one the enormities of which the capital has been guilty. The various counts in his indictment can be brought under three heads:

(a) *Personal immorality.* Men give rein to their impulses, the sanctity of family life is held in open contempt, and parental authority is repudiated.

(b) *Social injustice.* There is cruel oppression of the poor by the rich, perhaps even a reign of terror by which the ruling class suppresses all opposition to its insensate policies. There would be nothing surprising in something of that kind accompanying the last struggles of the doomed capital, and it may well be

mountains: in the midst of thee they commit lewdness.

10 In thee have they discovered their fathers' nakedness: in thee have they humbled her that was set apart for pollution.

11 And one hath committed abomination with his neighbor's wife; and another hath lewdly defiled his daughter-in-law; and another in thee hath humbled his sister, his father's daughter.

12 In thee have they taken gifts to shed blood; thou hast taken usury and increase, and thou hast greedily gained of thy neighbors by extortion, and hast forgotten me, saith the Lord God.

13 ¶ Behold, therefore I have smitten mine hand at thy dishonest gain which thou hast made, and at thy blood which hath been in the midst of thee.

14 Can thine heart endure, or can thine hands be strong, in the days that I shall deal with thee? I the Lord have spoken *it,* and will do *it.*

15 And I will scatter thee among the heathen, and disperse thee in the countries, and will consume thy filthiness out of thee.

16 And thou shalt take thine inheritance in thyself in the sight of the heathen, and thou shalt know that I *am* the Lord.

blood, and men in you who eat upon the mountains; men commit lewdness in your midst. **10** In you men uncover their fathers' nakedness; in you they humble women who are unclean in their impurity. **11** One commits abomination with his neighbor's wife; another lewdly defiles his daughter-in-law; another in you defiles his sister, his father's daughter. **12** In you men take bribes to shed blood; you take interest and increase and make gain of your neighbors by extortion; and you have forgotten me, says the Lord God.

13 "Behold, therefore, I strike my hands together at the dishonest gain which you have made, and at the blood which has been in the midst of you. **14** Can your courage endure, or can your hands be strong, in the days that I shall deal with you? I the Lord have spoken, and I will do it. **15** I will scatter you among the nations and disperse you through the countries, and I will consume your filthiness out of you. **16** And I*g* shall be profaned through you in the sight of the nations; and you shall know that I am the Lord."

g Gk Syr Vg: Heb *you*

10-11. Besides the legislation regarding sexual sins in Lev. 18:7-20; 20:10-21, cf. also Deut. 22:22-23, 30; 27:22; etc. Sexual relationships with a stepmother, a daughter-in-law, a sister, or a half sister were forbidden.

13. I strike my hands together: I.e., in anger (see 6:11; 21:14, 17).

16. The verb ונחלת is properly taken as Niphal of חלל and read **and you shall be profaned;** the KJV presumes the root נחל. Jerusalem will be its own source of profanation.

---

implied in vs. 6. Trade, which should have been organized for the benefit of the community, has served instead the purposes of private gain and shameless exploitation. That interest was taken from another member of the community in his need had always been considered a violation of the spirit of brotherhood within Israel (Deut. 23:19-20).

(*c*) *Religion.* Here we can leave out of account such things as the violation of the taboo on blood (vs. 9), and concentrate on the reproach directed against idolatry (vs. 3). It is difficult for us, of course, to appreciate the prophet on this point. We are not surprised when he tells us that injustice between man and man weakens the fabric of society and exposes

it to destruction. We can follow him when he warns us that, just because the family is the basis of the state, wrong relations between men and women are fraught with the possibility of social disintegration. But we do not see how the issue God or idols enters into our life at all.

But it does. God is one who comes into our life from beyond it and to whom we respond with reverence. An idol is something we make for ourselves and which has no value save what we give it. Men today, when they lose God, are unable to live without some object of devotion, some guide for life. They are driven therefore to provide themselves with substitutes. But because these are of our own manufacture, they fail us in our hour of sore trial. Only the God

17 And the word of the Lord came unto me, saying,

18 Son of man, the house of Israel is to me become dross: all they *are* brass, and tin, and iron, and lead, in the midst of the furnace; they are *even* the dross of silver.

19 Therefore thus saith the Lord God; Because ye are all become dross, behold, therefore I will gather you into the midst of Jerusalem.

20 *As* they gather silver, and brass, and iron, and lead, and tin, into the midst of the furnace, to blow the fire upon it, to melt *it;* so will I gather *you* in mine anger and in my fury, and I will leave *you there,* and melt you.

21 Yea, I will gather you, and blow upon you in the fire of my wrath, and ye shall be melted in the midst thereof.

22 As silver is melted in the midst of the furnace, so shall ye be melted in the midst thereof; and ye shall know that I the Lord have poured out my fury upon you.

17 And the word of the Lord came to me: **18** "Son of man, the house of Israel has become dross to me; all of them, silver[h] and bronze and tin and iron and lead in the furnace, have become dross. **19** Therefore thus says the Lord God: Because you have all become dross, therefore, behold, I will gather you into the midst of Jerusalem. **20** As men gather silver and bronze and iron and lead and tin into a furnace, to blow the fire upon it in order to melt it; so I will gather you in my anger and in my wrath, and I will put you in and melt you. **21** I will gather you and blow upon you with the fire of my wrath, and you shall be melted in the midst of it. **22** As silver is melted in a furnace, so you shall be melted in the midst of it; and you shall know that I the Lord have poured out my wrath upon you."

[h] Transposed from the end of the verse. Compare verse 20

2. The Fire of Yahweh's Wrath (22:17-22)

In contrast with Isa. 1:25-26 (late); Zech. 13:9; Mal. 3:3, the purpose is not purification but judgment. The smelting would disclose that the house of Israel was dross (cf. Isa. 1:22; Jer. 6:27-30). In vss. 17 and 19 the author anticipates the final outcome, and there is no attempt at an orderly description of the smelting (cf. vss. 20-21). The confusion may be in part due to the way in which the editor has transmitted an original oracle.

18. The RSV change in the position of **silver** may be justified, although the word may also be a gloss.

20. The Hebrew omission of **As** should perhaps be corrected with the LXX, Syriac, and Targ. by reading בקבצת.

21. The LXX and Syriac omit (for sake of clarity?) **I will gather you;** it may be the expansion of the editor, using a later (Aramaic?) vocabulary, i.e., כנס, in contrast with קבץ in vs. 19.

who made us and whose we are in life and death can provide us with the security we need, whether as individuals or as societies.

17-22. *The Lure of the City.*—Ezekiel describes conditions in the capital as the invader crosses the land and the panic-stricken population of the countryside takes refuge behind its walls. The siege which ensues will be like the flame which the metalworker employs in his refining process, and the refugees will be the alloy on which he turns it. But in this case there will be no process metal left to him at the end, only so much dross for which there is no use whatever.

Perhaps we may turn the picture to a some-

what different purpose and use it to illustrate the attraction of the city for the folk of the country districts. The most vigorous and enterprising young men and women of the villages and small towns tend to be drawn into the vortex of the great cities. Only there can they find the chance to test out the powers which surge within them and to discover their latent capabilities. What is the result of this influx of healthy elements into our overgrown and highly sophisticated urban communities? Unfortunately only too often what happens is that the new elements are dragged down to the level of the old, until it almost seems as though nothing sound remained.

23 ¶ And the word of the LORD came unto me, saying,

24 Son of man, say unto her, Thou *art* the land that is not cleansed, nor rained upon in the day of indignation.

25 *There is* a conspiracy of her prophets in the midst thereof, like a roaring lion ravening the prey: they have devoured souls; they have taken the treasure and precious things; they have made her many widows in the midst thereof.

26 Her priests have violated my law, and have profaned mine holy things: they have put no difference between the holy and profane, neither have they showed *difference* between the unclean and the clean, and have hid their eyes from my sabbaths, and I am profaned among them.

27 Her princes in the midst thereof *are* like wolves ravening the prey, to shed blood, *and* to destroy souls, to get dishonest gain.

28 And her prophets have daubed them with untempered *mortar,* seeing vanity, and divining lies unto them, saying, Thus saith the Lord GOD, when the LORD hath not spoken.

23 And the word of the LORD came to me: 24 "Son of man, say to her, You are a land that is not cleansed, or rained upon in the day of indignation. 25 Her princes[i] in the midst of her are like a roaring lion tearing the prey; they have devoured human lives; they have taken treasure and precious things; they have made many widows in the midst of her. 26 Her priests have done violence to my law and have profaned my holy things; they have made no distinction between the holy and the common, neither have they taught the difference between the unclean and the clean, and they have disregarded my sabbaths, so that I am profaned among them. 27 Her princes in the midst of her are like wolves tearing the prey, shedding blood, destroying lives to get dishonest gain. 28 And her prophets have daubed for them with whitewash, seeing false visions and divining lies for them, saying, 'Thus says the Lord GOD,'

[i] Gk: Heb *a conspiracy of her prophets*

3. INDICTMENT OF ALL CLASSES (22:23-31)

In its present form the oracle presupposes the fall of Jerusalem (vs. 31), and vss. 29-30 describe the sins of the past. Vss. 25-27 have an obviously close relationship with Zeph. 3:3-4. The authorship of the latter is uncertain; it is probably postexilic and its present context is late (see Louise Pettibone Smith and Ernest R. Lacheman, "The Authorship of the Book of Zephaniah," *Journal of Near Eastern Studies,* IX [1950], 139). With the lists of sins cf. vss. 6-13; see also 18:7, 12, 18.

24. For withholding rain as a punishment see Amos 4:7-8; Jer. 3:3; cf. I Kings 17:1. The verb מטהרה, **cleansed,** is changed by some to מטרה, and the context is read, "a land without rain or without shower"; cf. the LXX, γῆ ἡ οὐ βρεχομένη, οὐδὲ ὑετὸς ἐγένετο ἐπὶ σέ, "land that is not rained upon, nor has rain come upon you."

25. Many read with the LXX אשר נשיאיה, **her princes,** for קשר נביאיה, **a conspiracy of her prophets.** The context fits the princes rather than the prophets (for the imagery see 19:1-3). Perhaps instead of **widows** we should render "palaces" (cf. 19:7).

26. See Lev. 19:8; 20:25; 22:15; 26:34, 43; see Exeg. on 20:1-49, 12-13.

27. Note how the life (*néphesh*) of man is identifiable with the **blood** in Gen. 9:4; Lev. 17:11, 14; Deut. 12:23; etc. (see Johnson, *Vitality of the Individual in the Thought of Ancient Israel,* pp. 13-14).

28. The imagery appears in 13:10-16. With the use of the standard formula introducing an oracle in vs. 28*b* cf. that in 2:4; 3:11, 27.

23-31. *The Need of the City.*—The coming woe is thought of as a drought; to endure it the land needed to be well moistened and fertilized beforehand. But this has not been the case. Three classes have a peculiar responsibility for the nation's welfare, and by their failure have helped to bring about the catastrophe. These are the priest, the noble, and the prophet. Note that the priest's primary function is to instruct the people (vs. 26), to keep alive among them

29 The people of the land have used oppression, and exercised robbery, and have vexed the poor and needy: yea, they have oppressed the stranger wrongfully.

30 And I sought for a man among them, that should make up the hedge, and stand in the gap before me for the land, that I should not destroy it: but I found none.

31 Therefore have I poured out mine indignation upon them; I have consumed them with the fire of my wrath: their own way have I recompensed upon their heads, saith the Lord God.

23 The word of the Lord came again unto me, saying,

2 Son of man, there were two women, the daughters of one mother:

when the Lord has not spoken. **29** The people of the land have practiced extortion and committed robbery; they have oppressed the poor and needy, and have extorted from the sojourner without redress. **30** And I sought for a man among them who should build up the wall and stand in the breach before me for the land, that I should not destroy it; but I found none. **31** Therefore I have poured out my indignation upon them; I have consumed them with the fire of my wrath; their way have I requited upon their heads, says the Lord God."

23 The word of the Lord came to me: **2** "Son of man, there were two women,

---

29. The people of the land obviously does not here refer to the poorest peasants.

30. The figure of speech is that which appears also in 13:5, and refers to the prophets and others mentioned above, who might have been expected to give warnings. If, as seems less probable, the idea here is that Yahweh would have saved the city could one righteous man be found in it (cf. Jer. 5:1-6), the thought stands in violent contrast with the editor's philosophy in 14:12-23, where the righteous man can save only himself, and the idea may be credited to Ezekiel.

31*b*. Cf. 9:10; 11:21; 16:43.

R. The Unfaithful Wives of Yahweh (23:1-49)

The chapter has two main divisions. In the first (vss. 1-35), Oholah and Oholibah, representing Samaria and Jerusalem respectively, are sisters who become wives of Yahweh. Oholah, the elder, bestowed her favors on the Assyrians, and for her unfaithfulness was delivered into their hands and slain. Oholibah did not profit from this, but consorted first with the Assyrians and then with the Babylonians, and was worse than her sister. Now she also will be destroyed. The second division of the chapter (vss. 36-49) contains an indictment of both Oholah and Oholibah, who have defiled Yahweh's sanctuary, profaned his sabbaths, and offered their children as sacrifices to idols, and now must face their fate. In contrast with the first part of the chapter, pagan worship rather than foreign political alliances is condemned, and the punishment is yet to come upon Oholah. Many scholars rightly find Ezekiel's allegory within the first part only (Hölscher, Herntrich, Irwin, Bertholet, Matthews), although even this is not without evidence of the editor's expansion of Ezekiel's oracle. The editor has given the chapter an apparent unity (contrast Bertholet's arrangement of vss. 1-30 in doublets and parallels). As often, the editor would point the oracle up into a sermon for his contemporaries; the

---

the sense of right and wrong, even if that includes ritual as well as moral distinctions. This enables us to identify the three corresponding classes in our modern societies. They are the teacher, the political leader, and the religious leader. What each has done is to pervert his office to private ends when he should have accepted it humbly as a trust from God and used it under his direction. How far are these classes faithful to their appointed task among us?

Julien Benda[5] has given an answer to that question, and it is by no means one on which we can congratulate ourselves. Our need is that those to whom we look for guidance should themselves first seek it from God.

23:1-49. *Seduction of Judah*.—The imagery of this chapter reproduces that of ch. 17 and makes it equally unsuitable for public reading

[5] *The Great Betrayal*, tr. Richard Aldington (London: G. Routledge & Sons, 1928).

3 And they committed whoredoms in Egypt; they committed whoredoms in their youth: there were their breasts pressed, and there they bruised the teats of their virginity.

4 And the names of them *were* Aholah the elder, and Aholibah her sister: and they were mine, and they bare sons and daughters. Thus *were* their names; Samaria *is* Aholah, and Jerusalem Aholibah.

5 And Aholah played the harlot when she was mine; and she doted on her lovers, on the Assyrians *her* neighbors,

the daughters of one mother; 3 they played the harlot in Egypt; they played the harlot in their youth; there their breasts were pressed and their virgin bosoms handled. 4 Oho'lah was the name of the elder and Ohol'ibah the name of her sister. They became mine, and they bore sons and daughters. As for their names, Oho'lah is Samar'ia, and Ohol'ibah is Jerusalem.

5 "Oho'lah played the harlot while she was mine; and she doted on her lovers the

---

fate of Oholah and Oholibah is a warning to all women that they should not commit lewdness and is to teach that the house of Israel should know that Yahweh is God (cf. vss. 48-49). The chapter has much in common with ch. 16.

It is thought by some that in its original form the allegory was a poem. This poem has been found within vss. 1-27 (Hölscher, Cooke), or even limited to parts of vss. 2, 4, 5, 11 (Irwin).

1. INTRODUCTION (23:1-4)

23:1-4. Vs. 3 seems outside the original picture of political alliances. There is a natural transition from vs. 2 to vs. 4, and the picture of the apostasy in Egypt is characteristic of the editor (see Exeg. on 20:5-8). With vs. 3 cf. also vss. 7-8, 19-21, 27. The names **Oholah** ("She who has a tent") and **Oholibah** ("Tent in her") have some reference to the sacred tent or tabernacle, an institution not limited to the Hebrews (see H. G. May, "The Ark—A Miniature Temple," *American Journal of Semitic Languages and Literatures,* LII [1935-36], 215-34; "'Ephod' and 'Ariel,'" *ibid.,* LVI [1939], 54, 58-60). Ezekiel may use the term as an allusion to the period of the wandering in the wilderness, or because of its association with pagan practices. (See 16:15; I Sam. 2:22; cf. the name of Esau's wife Oholibamah, "Tent of the high place," in Gen. 36:18, or the Phoenician אהלבעל, "tent of Baal"; see also the tents of the gods in the Ugaritic texts, where *'ahlhm,* "their tents," is paralleled with *mšknthm,* "their tabernacles"; Gordon, *Ugaritic Handbook,* text 128, III, 1. 18.) **Samaria** was the capital of Israel, as **Jerusalem** was of Judah, and the names here stand also for Israel and Judah.

2. OHOLAH (23:5-10)

Cf. Hosea's accusation that Israel gave love gifts and hire to Assyria (Hos. 8:9-10; see 5:13; 7:11). Like Hosea and Isaiah (cf. Isa. 7:1-9), Ezekiel protested against foreign alliances as disloyalty to Yahweh. See also Ezek. 16:28-29. In the days of Jehu, Israel had capitulated to Assyria, as illustrated on the Black Obelisk of Shalmaneser III; Adad-nirari III (812-782) also claimed the land of Omri (see Barton, *Archaeology and the Bible,* pp. 459, 462; Pritchard, *Ancient Near Eastern Texts,* pp. 281-84). From the Syro-Ephraimite war and the invasion of Israel by Tiglath-pileser III (734-732) until within the reign of Hoshea Israel paid tribute to Assyria (see II Kings 15:19-29; 16:1–17:4). The editor's expansion is seen in the allusion to idolatry in Egypt in vss. 7-8 (see on vs. 3; cf. vss. 30, 38, 49). Hölscher and Cooke omit vss. 7-10 from the original poem. For diction of vss. 9-10, cf. 5:10; 11:9; 16:39, 41; 30:14, 19; etc. Though the literary garb may be the editor's, Ezekiel's oracle must have contained an allusion to the punishment of Oholah.

5-6. Some read with the versions מתחתי and translate, "faithless to me" (lit., "from under me"; cf. the LXX, Syriac, Targ., and Hos. 4:12), instead of תחתי, translated

6 *Which were* clothed with blue, captains and rulers, all of them desirable young men, horsemen riding upon horses.

7 Thus she committed her whoredoms with them, with all them *that were* the chosen men of Assyria, and with all on whom she doted: with all their idols she defiled herself.

8 Neither left she her whoredoms *brought* from Egypt: for in her youth they lay with her, and they bruised the breasts of her virginity, and poured their whoredom upon her.

9 Wherefore I have delivered her into the hand of her lovers, into the hands of the Assyrians, upon whom she doted.

10 These discovered her nakedness: they took her sons and her daughters, and slew her with the sword: and she became famous among women; for they had executed judgment upon her.

11 And when her sister Aholibah saw *this,* she was more corrupt in her inordinate love than she, and in her whoredoms more than her sister in *her* whoredoms.

12 She doted upon the Assyrians *her* neighbors, captains and rulers clothed most gorgeously, horsemen riding upon horses, all of them desirable young men.

Assyrians, **6** warriors clothed in purple, governors and commanders, all of them desirable young men, horsemen riding on horse. **7** She bestowed her harlotries upon them, the choicest men of Assyria all of them; and she defiled herself with all the idols of every one on whom she doted. **8** She did not give up her harlotry which she had practiced since her days in Egypt; for in her youth men had lain with her and handled her virgin bosom and poured out their lust upon her. **9** Therefore I delivered her into the hands of her lovers, into the hands of the Assyrians, upon whom she doted. **10** These uncovered her nakedness; they seized her sons and her daughters; and her they slew with the sword; and she became a byword among women, when judgment had been executed upon her.

11 "Her sister Ohol'ibah saw this, yet she was more corrupt than she in her doting and in her harlotry, which was worse than that of her sister. **12** She doted upon the Assyrians, governors and commanders, warriors clothed in full armor, horsemen riding on horses, all of them desirable young men.

---

while she was mine (lit., "under me"; cf. Num. 5:19) . **Her neighbors:** קרובים, i.e., "near," but to be related to late Hebrew קרב, "war" (cf. Zech. 14:3; Job 38:23; etc.) , or changed to קרדים (Assyrian *qurâdu*) , and so read **warriors**. So also vs. 12. Some on the basis of vs. 23 read קרואים, "famed." The word תכלת designates blue-**purple** or violet (cf. 27:7) .

3. OHOLIBAH (23:11-21)

Judah's alliances with Assyria are best illustrated in the reign of Ahaz (II Kings 16:7-9; Isa. 7:1–8:22). Hezekiah before the reform and revolt was loyal to Assyria (II Kings 18:1-36) , as was Manasseh after his exile by Esarhaddon (cf. II Chr. 33:10-13) . For an alliance with Babylonia in the reign of Hezekiah see II Kings 20:12-21; Isa.

---

or exposition. There is, however, one fresh feature in this sordid story which invites reflection. We are shown the two small Israelite peoples succumbing to the attractions of three countries which boasted a more advanced civilization and a more formidable military power. These are Egypt, Assyria, and Babylon. In the case of Assyria and Babylon we are told what constitutes their appeal. It is the brilliant equipment and gay carriage of their ruling class, the young army officer and the provincial governor. These are the **governors and com-** **manders, warriors clothed in full armor, horsemen riding on horses, all of them desirable young men** (vs. 12) . Such figures do not need actually to be seen to be admired. The mere prestige of Babylon and the current tales of her splendor were sufficient to seduce Judah from her original allegiance (vss. 14-16) .

There is something here which has a parallel in the modern world. Everywhere people of a simpler and more natural way of life, with their traditional moral codes and their local loyalties, are surrendering to the vice and glitter of an

13 Then I saw that she was defiled, *that* they *took* both one way,

14 And *that* she increased her whoredoms: for when she saw men portrayed upon the wall, the images of the Chaldeans portrayed with vermilion,

15 Girded with girdles upon their loins, exceeding in dyed attire upon their heads, all of them princes to look to, after the manner of the Babylonians of Chaldea, the land of their nativity:

16 And as soon as she saw them with her eyes, she doted upon them, and sent messengers unto them into Chaldea.

17 And the Babylonians came to her into the bed of love, and they defiled her with their whoredom, and she was polluted with them, and her mind was alienated from them.

18 So she discovered her whoredoms, and discovered her nakedness: then my mind was alienated from her, like as my mind was alienated from her sister.

19 Yet she multiplied her whoredoms, in calling to remembrance the days of her youth, wherein she had played the harlot in the land of Egypt.

20 For she doted upon their paramours, whose flesh *is as* the flesh of asses, and whose issue *is like* the issue of horses.

21 Thus thou calledst to remembrance the lewdness of thy youth, in bruising thy teats by the Egyptians for the paps of thy youth.

13 And I saw that she was defiled; they both took the same way. 14 But she carried her harlotry further; she saw men portrayed upon the wall, the images of the Chalde′ans portrayed in vermilion, 15 girded with belts on their loins, with flowing turbans on their heads, all of them looking like officers, a picture of Babylonians whose native land was Chalde′a. 16 When she saw them she doted upon them, and sent messengers to them in Chalde′a. 17 And the Babylonians came to her into the bed of love, and they defiled her with their lust; and after she was polluted by them, she turned from them in disgust. 18 When she carried on her harlotry so openly and flaunted her nakedness, I turned in disgust from her, as I had turned from her sister. 19 Yet she increased her harlotry, remembering the days of her youth, when she played the harlot in the land of Egypt 20 and doted upon her paramours there, whose members were like those of asses, and whose issue was like that of horses. 21 Thus you longed for the lewdness of your youth, when the Egyptians[j] handled your bosom and pressed[k] your young breasts."

[j] Two Mss: Heb *from Egypt*
[k] Cn: Heb *for the sake of*

39:1-8. Zedekiah, at Jeremiah's advice, followed a pro-Babylonian policy until the revolt in 589 (cf. Jer. 27:1-22; 29:1-3).

15. The word אזור, **girdle(s), belt(s),** is more properly "waistcloth"; cf. Isa. 5:27, where it is also part of a warrior's clothing (see Galling, *Biblisches Reallexikon,* pp. 332-33). The word סרוחי is, lit., "overhanging," i.e., **flowing. Turbans:** The KJV wrongly associates the word טבלים (cf. Akkadian *ṭublu* and Ethiopian cognate) with the root meaning "to dip," and so translates **dyed.**

16-17. Judah swung more than once from a pro-Babylonian to an anti-Babylonian policy. See Jer. 29:3 for a mission to Babylon.

19-21. Not a reference to contemporary dependence on Egypt, but to harlotry in Egypt, as in vss. 3, 7-8; contrast 16:26. The expression למען, "for the sake of," should perhaps be read למעך, "to press," hence **pressed** (RSV).

alien civilization. We are not the sisters who are seduced, we are ourselves the seducers. Our wealth, our trade, and our military display have broken in upon peoples quite unprepared to encounter such temptations. They have ac-

cepted our style of clothing, our armaments, our entertainments, and our ideas. Now it is French policy which undermines Islam with a scientific education, or British gin which spreads havoc among the peoples of the Pacific. Time

22 ¶ Therefore, O Aholibah, thus saith the Lord God; Behold, I will raise up thy lovers against thee, from whom thy mind is alienated, and I will bring them against thee on every side;

23 The Babylonians, and all the Chaldeans, Pekod, and Shoa, and Koa, *and* all the Assyrians with them: all of them desirable young men, captains and rulers, great lords and renowned, all of them riding upon horses.

24 And they shall come against thee with chariots, wagons, and wheels, and with an assembly of people, *which* shall set against thee buckler and shield and helmet round about: and I will set judgment before them, and they shall judge thee according to their judgments.

25 And I will set my jealousy against thee, and they shall deal furiously with thee: they shall take away thy nose and thine ears; and thy remnant shall fall by the sword: they shall take thy sons and thy daughters; and thy residue shall be devoured by the fire.

26 They shall also strip thee out of thy clothes, and take away thy fair jewels.

27 Thus will I make thy lewdness to cease from thee, and thy whoredom *brought* from the land of Egypt: so that thou shalt not lift up thine eyes unto them, nor remember Egypt any more.

28 For thus saith the Lord God; Behold, I will deliver thee into the hand *of them*

22 Therefore, O Ohol'ibah, thus says the Lord God: "Behold, I will rouse against you your lovers from whom you turned in disgust, and I will bring them against you from every side: 23 the Babylonians and all the Chalde'ans, Pekod and Sho'a and Ko'a, and all the Assyrians with them, desirable young men, governors and commanders all of them, officers and warriors,[l] all of them riding on horses. 24 And they shall come against you from the north[m] with chariots and wagons and a host of peoples; they shall set themselves against you on every side with buckler, shield, and helmet, and I will commit the judgment to them, and they shall judge you according to their judgments. 25 And I will direct my indignation against you, that they may deal with you in fury. They shall cut off your nose and your ears, and your survivors shall fall by the sword. They shall seize your sons and your daughters, and your survivors shall be devoured by fire. 26 They shall also strip you of your clothes and take away your fine jewels. 27 Thus I will put an end to your lewdness and your harlotry brought from the land of Egypt; so that you shall not lift up your eyes to the Egyptians or remember them any more. 28 For thus says the Lord God: Behold, I will deliver you

[l] Compare verses 6 and 12: Heb *called*
[m] Gk: The meaning of the Hebrew word is unknown

---

4. The Fate of Oholibah (23:22-35)

This is divided into four sections, each with the introductory formula, "Thus says the Lord God" (vss. 22, 28, 32, 35). Opinion varies as to how much of this is original. Vs. 24 recalls vss. 46-47 and chs. 38–39, while the harlotry in Egypt appears in vs. 27 and the idolatry motive in vs. 30. Matthews questions vss. 21, 28-30 (cf. Herntrich, Irwin).

23. Pekod, Shoa, and **Koa** are usually identified with *Puqûdu, Sutû,* and *Qutû,* Aramaean tribes east of the Tigris mentioned in cuneiform sources, but the equation with all save the first is phonetically difficult. **Warriors:** Reads consistently with vss. 6 (Hebrew vs. 6), 12, instead of the M.T. קרואים, **called,** i.e., "famed" (cf. Num. 16:2).

24. From the north: Read מצפון with the LXX for the obscure הצן; some read המון, "a multitude," and so here "a multitude of chariots," etc.

---

passes, and American films bring the lure of the West to the urban populations of the Far East. Then Russian communism arms the younger generation against its predecessors, and nation-

alism becomes the religion of the politically-minded the world over. There is, as it were, a tireless and unscrupulous export of ideas from Europe and the United States going on

whom thou hatest, into the hand *of them* from whom thy mind is alienated:

29 And they shall deal with thee hatefully, and shall take away all thy labor, and shall leave thee naked and bare: and the nakedness of thy whoredoms shall be discovered, both thy lewdness and thy whoredoms.

30 I will do these *things* unto thee, because thou hast gone a whoring after the heathen, *and* because thou art polluted with their idols.

31 Thou hast walked in the way of thy sister; therefore will I give her cup into thine hand.

32 Thus saith the Lord God; Thou shalt drink of thy sister's cup deep and large: thou shalt be laughed to scorn and had in derision; it containeth much.

33 Thou shalt be filled with drunkenness and sorrow, with the cup of astonishment and desolation, with the cup of thy sister Samaria.

34 Thou shalt even drink it and suck *it* out, and thou shalt break the sherds thereof, and pluck off thine own breasts: for I have spoken *it,* saith the Lord God.

35 Therefore thus saith the Lord God; Because thou hast forgotten me, and cast

into the hands of those whom you hate, into the hands of those from whom you turned in disgust; 29 and they shall deal with you in hatred, and take away all the fruit of your labor, and leave you naked and bare, and the nakedness of your harlotry shall be uncovered. Your lewdness and your harlotry 30 have brought this upon you, because you played the harlot with the nations, and polluted yourself with their idols. 31 You have gone the way of your sister; therefore I will give her cup into your hand. 32 Thus says the Lord God:

"You shall drink your sister's cup
which is deep and large;
you shall be laughed at and held in derision,
for it contains much;
33 you will be filled with drunkenness and sorrow.

A cup of horror and desolation,
is the cup of your sister Samar′ia;
34 you shall drink it and drain it out,
and pluck out your hair,[n]
and tear your breasts;

for I have spoken, says the Lord God. 35 Therefore thus says the Lord God: Because you have forgotten me and cast me

[n] Compare Syr: Heb *gnaw its sherds*

29-30. The RSV transfers the last part of vs. 29 to the beginning of vs. 30, which can be done since the verb at the beginning of vs. 30, translated in the KJV as **I will do,** is an infinitive absolute and can be read somewhat more literally, "Your lewdness and your harlotry have done these things to you," etc.

31-34. The cup of . . . Samaria will pass to Jerusalem. See the cup of the wrath of Yahweh in Jer. 25:15-29; 49:12-13; 51:6-7 (all late); Lam. 4:21; Isa. 51:17-23; 56:12; Zech. 12:2; Hab. 2:16; Ps. 11:6; 75:8 (Hebrew 75:9); cf. Rev. 14:20 (see May, "Jeremiah's Biographer," p. 197; see the cup of [disgrace and] scorn in the Ugaritic texts [Gordon, *Ugaritic Handbook,* text 51, III, 1. 16]). This may be the earliest biblical allusion to the cup of fate if the editor is not responsible for it (cf. Hölscher). The concluding formula in vs. 34, along with vs. 35 (cf. vss. 27, 30), belongs to the editor. Vss. 32-34 may be poetry or poetic prose.

33. Some read שברון, "breaking" (i.e., of the heart; cf. 21:6 [Hebrew 21:11]), for שכרון, **drunkenness.**

34. You shall . . . pluck out your hair: Read with the Syriac שערך תמרטי for חרשיה תגרמי, **thou shalt break the sherds thereof.**

---

all the time, a vast missionary enterprise which is making converts by the million. And to what are they converted? Only too often to the false gods of pleasure, wealth, and power that many of us would gladly expel from our own lands.

Under such circumstances a twofold responsi-

bility is laid on us as Christians. In the first place we must see to it that it is not only the worst features of our civilization which are sent abroad; we must send also, as correctives, the Christian faith and hope. That is one of the most powerful arguments for the missionary

me behind thy back, therefore bear thou also thy lewdness and thy whoredoms.

36 ¶ The LORD said moreover unto me; Son of man, wilt thou judge Aholah and Aholibah? yea, declare unto them their abominations;

37 That they have committed adultery, and blood is in their hands, and with their idols have they committed adultery, and have also caused their sons, whom they bare unto me, to pass for them through *the fire*, to devour *them*.

38 Moreover this they have done unto me: they have defiled my sanctuary in the same day, and have profaned my sabbaths.

39 For when they had slain their children to their idols, then they came the same day into my sanctuary to profane it; and, lo, thus have they done in the midst of mine house.

40 And furthermore, that ye have sent for men to come from far, unto whom a messenger *was* sent; and, lo, they came: for whom thou didst wash thyself, paintedst thy eyes, and deckedst thyself with ornaments,

41 And satest upon a stately bed, and a table prepared before it, whereupon thou hast set mine incense and mine oil.

42 And a voice of a multitude being at ease *was* with her: and with the men of the common sort *were* brought Sabeans from the wilderness, which put bracelets upon their hands, and beautiful crowns upon their heads.

behind your back, therefore bear the consequences of your lewdness and harlotry."

36 The LORD said to me: "Son of man, will you judge Oho'lah and Ohol'ibah? Then declare to them their abominable deeds. 37 For they have committed adultery, and blood is upon their hands; with their idols they have committed adultery; and they have even offered up to them for food the sons whom they had borne to me. 38 Moreover this they have done to me: they have defiled my sanctuary on the same day and profaned my sabbaths. 39 For when they had slaughtered their children in sacrifice to their idols, on the same day they came into my sanctuary to profane it. And lo, this is what they did in my house. 40 They even sent for men to come from far, to whom a messenger was sent, and lo, they came. For them you bathed yourself, painted your eyes, and decked yourself with ornaments; 41 you sat upon a stately couch, with a table spread before it on which you had placed my incense and my oil. 42 The sound of a carefree multitude was with her; and with men of the common sort drunkards[o] were brought from the wilderness; and they put bracelets upon the hands of the women, and beautiful crowns upon their heads.

[o] Heb uncertain

---

5. JUDGMENT ON OHOLAH AND OHOLIBAH (23:36-49)

Adultery: I.e., sacrifice of children to detestable idols (*gillûlîm*), defilement of the sanctuary, and profanation of the sabbath. Hölscher believes that not Samaria and Jerusalem but two individual women are depicted as warnings to the contemporaries of the author. It is strange that the punishment of Oholah is yet to come, and that she is accused of defiling the Jerusalem sanctuary. The typical phraseology and ideology of the editor will be recognized.

40-41. For the **painted** harlot see Jer. 4:30; for her **couch** see Prov. 7:16 (cf. Hos. 7:14). The use of the singular pronoun in vss. 40-42 suggests that the author temporarily is thinking of Oholibah alone.

42. Men of the common sort: More literally, "men from the multitude of men." **Drunkards** may represent the *Kethîbh* סובאים, although *Qerê* סבאים may mean **drunkards** or **Sabeans.**

---

enterprise. We simply cannot sit idly by while our false gods are being so ardently propagated and not bear witness to the true God. In the second place it is our duty to oppose ever more

strenuously the idolatries which corrupt our life at home, because the eyes of the world are upon us and what we do is taken by so many as an example to imitate.

43 Then said I unto *her that was* old in adulteries, Will they now commit whoredoms with her, and she *with them?*

44 Yet they went in unto her, as they go in unto a woman that playeth the harlot: so went they in unto Aholah and unto Aholibah, the lewd women.

45 ¶ And the righteous men, they shall judge them after the manner of adulteresses, and after the manner of women that shed blood; because they *are* adulteresses, and blood *is* in their hands.

46 For thus saith the Lord God; I will bring up a company upon them, and will give them to be removed and spoiled.

47 And the company shall stone them with stones, and dispatch them with their swords; they shall slay their sons and their daughters, and burn up their houses with fire.

48 Thus will I cause lewdness to cease out of the land, that all women may be taught not to do after your lewdness.

49 And they shall recompense your lewdness upon you, and ye shall bear the sins of your idols: and ye shall know that I *am* the Lord God.

24 Again in the ninth year, in the tenth month, in the tenth *day* of the month, the word of the Lord came unto me, saying,

43 "Then I said, Do not men now commit adultery[p] when they practice harlotry with her? 44 For they have gone in to her, as men go in to a harlot. Thus they went in to Oho'lah and to Ohol'ibah to commit lewdness.[q] 45 But righteous men shall pass judgment on them with the sentence of adulteresses, and with the sentence of women that shed blood; because they are adulteresses, and blood is upon their hands."

46 For thus says the Lord God: "Bring up a host against them, and make them an object of terror and a spoil. 47 And the host shall stone them and despatch them with their swords; they shall slay their sons and their daughters, and burn up their houses.

48 Thus will I put an end to lewdness in the land, that all women may take warning and not commit lewdness as you have done.

49 And your lewdness shall be requited upon you, and you shall bear the penalty for your sinful idolatry; and you shall know that I am the Lord God."

24 In the ninth year, in the tenth month, on the tenth day of the month, the word of the Lord came to me:

[p] Compare Gk: Heb obscure
[q] Gk: Heb *a woman of lewdness*

---

43. The text of this verse is corrupt (contrast KJV and RSV). For לבלה נאופים, "to her that is old [in] adulteries," read הלא כאלה נאפו, "have they not committed adultery like this?" (Cf. LXX.)

44. **To commit lewdness:** Read with the LXX לעשות זמה, for אשת הזמה, "women of [?] lewdness" (cf. KJV).

45. **Righteous men:** I.e., of the author's own day? Here at least the author slips out of the presumed situation of before 586.

46-47. It has been suggested that the **host** or **company** (קהל) is the Hebrew assembly, not the pagan army (cf. Hölscher, Matthews, Bertholet), but see vs. 24; 16:40. The death penalty for adultery appears in Lev. 20:10 (cf. 19:20-22; see John 8:5; Deut. 13:10).

S. The Caldron on the Fire (24:1-14)

The allegory of the caldron is composed of three parts: vss. 1-2, where the prophet is told to write down the name of the day; vss. 3-5, which contain a poetic allegorical

---

24:1-14. *Excess of Judgment?*—We can perhaps make best use of the first half of this chapter (vss. 1-14) if we look at the situation, described under the figure of a **pot** or caldron, through the eyes of the people rather than, as we are shown here, through those of the prophet. It then is seen to deal with the problem of excess of judgment.

That the pot which contains meat should be heated over the fire is something we accept as natural; it is a process necessary for the preparation of our daily food. While therefore it stands

2 Son of man, write thee the name of the day, *even* of this same day: the king of Babylon set himself against Jerusalem this same day.

3 And utter a parable unto the rebellious house, and say unto them, Thus saith the Lord GOD; Set on a pot, set *it* on, and also pour water into it:

2 "Son of man, write down the name of this day, this very day. The king of Babylon has laid siege to Jerusalem this very day. 3 And utter an allegory to the rebellious house and say to them, Thus says the Lord GOD:
Set on the pot, set it on,
    pour in water also;

---

oracle of the caldron on the fire, symbolizing the siege; vss. 6-14, a prose interpretation of the oracle, into which a new theme, the rust of the caldron, has been introduced.

The date is January 15, 588, the day of the beginning of the siege of Jerusalem (see II Kings 25:1; Jer. 52:4). This involves the problem of the scene of Ezekiel's prophetic activity. Unless he was endowed with second sight, he must have been in Palestine at the time to be able to know of the beginning of the siege on the very day it began (see Intro., pp. 52-53). The poetic oracle in vss. 3b-5 accords with this date, the imperatives suggesting the beginning of the siege. Vss. 6-14 are most difficult. The theme of the rust of the pot seems foreign to the thought in the poem. In the historical context there is, to say the least, an awkwardness in the picture of the pot being emptied and set on the fire again in an attempt to burn out its rust by reducing it to scrap. The two introductory formulas (vss. 6, 9) and the two removals of the contents of the caldron (vss. 6, 10) suggest an expansion of the original oracle. How much of vss. 6-14 belongs to Ezekiel is not clear. The removal of the flesh from the vessel has an analogy in 11:7-9, and the idea that the rust could not be removed might be consonant with Ezekiel's thought (cf. 22:18-22) if the intent were only to indicate the completeness of the coming destruction of Jerusalem. However, the text implies an eventual cleansing (vs. 13b), and the section culminates in a sentence (vs. 14) which is a mosaic of the editor's typical phraseology. The rust is the blood which Jerusalem has shed (vss. 7-8), recalling what is probably the editor's oracle in 22:2-12. The introduction of the second placing of the caldron on the fire might seem to throw the first placing of it on the fire back to 597, with vs. 6b referring to the Exile in that year, and this is certainly out of accord with the poem in vss. 3b-5 (cf. Hölscher). The rust motive may best be ascribed to the editor's expansion; this would explain the difficult sequence of thought and much of the confusion in the passage.

24:2. The name of this day, this very day: The text is awkward (cf. KJV) and there may be dittography from the end of the verse; perhaps read only "the name of this day" with the Syriac and Vulg. This became a fast day among the Hebrews (cf. Zech. 8:19).

3. Parable, allegory: See Exeg. on 17:2. The allegory recalls Jeremiah's vision of the boiling caldron (Jer. 1:13-19). The same imagery appears in Ezek. 11:3, 11, the plotters in Jerusalem calling themselves the flesh in the pot. **The pot** (הסיר) may be either of pottery or metal. When pottery, it is the wide-mouthed cooking pot known in the excavations. Here, or at least in the interpretation in vss. 6-14, it is a copper

---

for pain, the pain in question is one of which a satisfactory account can be given. It is pain which serves a purpose of discipline and purification. The nation, we would say, must endure its fiery trial that it may be rid of what has harmed it in the past and may be made fit for worthier things in the future. But Ezekiel's contemporaries seem to have felt that this explanation did not hold good in their case. Judgment was surely far in excess of what could be thus justified. Was it not as though, when the flesh

had been cooked and removed piece by piece from the pot, the cook had gone on to heap up the fire beneath it, as though bent on melting it down? But what sense could there be in such a procedure? It is the problem of a suffering which could be accepted at first perhaps as discipline, but which provoked resentment when it was prolonged till it seemed no longer to serve any useful purpose.

The prophet's reply would no doubt be that evil is so ingrained in Judah that judgment

4 Gather the pieces thereof into it, *even* every good piece, the thigh, and the shoulder; fill *it* with the choice bones.

5 Take the choice of the flock, and burn also the bones under it, *and* make it boil well, and let them seethe the bones of it therein.

6 ¶ Wherefore thus saith the Lord God; Woe to the bloody city, to the pot whose scum *is* therein, and whose scum is not gone out of it! bring it out piece by piece; let no lot fall upon it.

7 For her blood is in the midst of her; she set it upon the top of a rock; she poured it not upon the ground, to cover it with dust;

8 That it might cause fury to come up to take vengeance; I have set her blood upon the top of a rock, that it should not be covered.

---

4 put in it the pieces of flesh,
    all the good pieces, the thigh and the shoulder;
fill it with choice bones.
5 Take the choicest one of the flock,
    pile the logs[r] under it;
boil its pieces,[s]
    seethe[t] also its bones in it.
6 "Therefore thus says the Lord God: Woe to the bloody city, to the pot whose rust is in it, and whose rust has not gone out of it! Take out of it piece after piece, without making any choice.[u] 7 For the blood she has shed is still in the midst of her; she put it on the bare rock, she did not pour it upon the ground to cover it with dust. 8 To rouse my wrath, to take vengeance, I have set on the bare rock the blood she has shed, that it may not be cov-

[r] Compare verse 10: Heb *the bones*
[s] Two Mss: Heb *its boilings*
[t] Cn: Heb *its bones seethe*
[u] Heb *no lot has fallen upon it*

---

caldron (see J. L. Kelso, "Ezekiel's Parable of the Corroded Copper Caldron," *Journal of Biblical Literature,* LXIV [1945], 391-93; *The Ceramic Vocabulary of the Old Testament* [New Haven: American Schools of Oriental Research, 1948], p. 27). The use of the imperatives, addressing the prophet, might suggest that this was actually performed as an acted parable, although it may be only a dramatic figure of speech.

    4. Pieces of flesh: An interpretation of נתחיה, "its pieces." **The good pieces:** Cf. I Sam. 2:13-17.

    5. The state of the text is suggested by the contrast between the ASV and the RSV. **The logs:** Read העצים for העצמים, **the bones. Its pieces:** Read with two Hebrew MSS נתחיה for רתחיה, **its boilings,** a *hapax legomenon.* **Seethe:** Read Piel imperative singular בשל for Qal perfect plural בשלו, and take **bones** as object rather than subject.

    6. Rust: חלאה, lit., "disease." Kelso notes that modern metallurgy calls a peculiar type of corrosion "copper disease." Several commentators transpose the two parts of the verse to bring the allusion to the contents of the caldron closer to vss. 3-5, but it is the "foreign" rust which disturbs the sequence. **Bloody city** is probably a biographer's idiom (see vs. 9; 22:2).

    7-18. Cf. 22:2-12. For the uncovered **blood** see the story of Cain and Abel (Gen. 4:10-11). Vs. 8 recalls Isa. 26:21 (late). Some would read נתנה, "she has set," instead of the M.T. **I have set** in vs. 8 to accord more with vs. 7, but this is unnecessary. **Her blood** is of course **the blood she has shed,** but it is also **her blood,** since **she** is Jerusalem.

---

cannot be kept within those nice limits which would satisfy his critics. It is because they do not realize the extent of the nation's depravity that they question whether chastisement need be carried quite so far. It is as if there were **rust in the pot** which must be eradicated from it at any cost. In other words, we tend to think of sin as something detached from ourselves, so that it can be removed, we suppose, by a process which does not really touch us to the quick.

Instead we have to learn that it has its seat within us and can be removed only as the whole self is passed through the fire of pain and cleansing. The doubt which remains in Ezekiel's mind is whether even so drastic a measure will suffice. Perhaps the evil is by now so deeply embedded in the life of Judah that it will remain even amid the fire of God's judgment. **In vain I have wearied myself; its thick rust does not go out of it by fire** (vs. 12).

9 Therefore thus saith the Lord God; Woe to the bloody city! I will even make the pile for fire great.

10 Heap on wood, kindle the fire, consume the flesh, and spice it well, and let the bones be burned.

11 Then set it empty upon the coals thereof, that the brass of it may be hot, and may burn, and *that* the filthiness of it may be molten in it, *that* the scum of it may be consumed.

12 She hath wearied *herself* with lies, and her great scum went not forth out of her: her scum *shall be* in the fire.

13 In thy filthiness *is* lewdness: because I have purged thee, and thou wast not purged, thou shalt not be purged from thy filthiness any more, till I have caused my fury to rest upon thee.

14 I the Lord have spoken *it:* it shall come to pass, and I will do *it;* I will not go back, neither will I spare, neither will I repent; according to thy ways, and according to thy doings, shall they judge thee, saith the Lord God.

15 ¶ Also the word of the Lord came unto me, saying,

---

ered. 9 Therefore thus says the Lord God: Woe to the bloody city! I also will make the pile great. 10 Heap on the logs, kindle the fire, boil well the flesh, and empty out the broth,[v] and let the bones be burned up. 11 Then set it empty upon the coals, that it may become hot, and its copper may burn, that its filthiness may be melted in it, its rust consumed. 12 In vain I have wearied myself;[w] its thick rust does not go out of it by fire. 13 Its rust is your filthy lewdness. Because I would have cleansed you and you were not cleansed from your filthiness, you shall not be cleansed any more till I have satisfied my fury upon you. 14 I the Lord have spoken; it shall come to pass, I will do it; I will not go back, I will not spare, I will not repent; according to your ways and your doings I will judge you, says the Lord God."

15 Also the word of the Lord came to

[v] Compare Gk: Heb *mix the spices*
[w] Cn: Heb uncertain

9-10. Cf. vss. 5-6. With vs. 10*b* cf. vs. 6*b*; this second removal of the contents of the caldron is awkward, but is introduced here to prepare for the action in vs. 11.

12-13. In vain I have wearied myself: Read הנם נלאתי for תאנים הלאת, a corrupt dittography from the end of vs. 11; the LXX omits. The last clause in vs. 12 and the first in vs. 13 are difficult, reading "in the fire of its rust" and "in your filthiness is lewdness" (cf. KJV). The former is meaningless in the context, and the RSV has taken "in the fire" with what precedes and **its rust** with vs. 13. **Its rust** may result from dittography, "in your filthiness is lewdness" being a scribal comment. The versions offer no real help. In the last part of vs. 13, the RSV more plausibly takes **from your filthiness** with the second **cleansed** rather than the third; the KJV follows the M.T. The end of the verse may be a *posteventum* allusion to the destruction of the city in 586.

14. I will judge you is with a number of MSS (contrast KJV).

T. The Death of Ezekiel's Wife (24:15-27)

The oracle set forth here is composed of two parts: vss. 15-24, in which Ezekiel uses the death of his wife as an occasion for a dramatic action oracle, and vss. 25-27, an appendix in which the reader is told that the end of Ezekiel's "dumbness" is to come on the day of the fall of Jerusalem. The hand of the editor is most evident in the appendix, vss. 25-27.

15-27. *Public Grief and Private Sorrow.*— Here we are afforded a glimpse of a human side to the personality of the prophet which would otherwise have remained hidden from us. We see how deeply attached he was to his wife, so that the conventional signs of mourning would have been in his case the expression of a very

genuine and poignant sorrow. Yet these are not permitted to him; he must repress his grief and so make himself an object of comment to his fellows.

This incident enables us to measure to some extent the great souls who have been called by God to take part in his work of redemption.

16 Son of man, behold, I take away from thee the desire of thine eyes with a stroke: yet neither shalt thou mourn nor weep, neither shall thy tears run down.

17 Forbear to cry, make no mourning for the dead, bind the tire of thine head upon thee, and put on thy shoes upon thy feet, and cover not *thy* lips, and eat not the bread of men.

18 So I spake unto the people in the morning: and at even my wife died; and I did in the morning as I was commanded.

19 ¶ And the people said unto me, Wilt thou not tell us what these *things are* to us, that thou doest *so?*

20 Then I answered them, The word of the LORD came unto me, saying,

21 Speak unto the house of Israel, Thus saith the Lord GOD; Behold, I will profane my sanctuary, the excellency of your strength, the desire of your eyes, and that which your soul pitieth; and your sons and your daughters whom ye have left shall fall by the sword.

me: 16 "Son of man, behold, I am about to take the delight of your eyes away from you at a stroke; yet you shall not mourn or weep nor shall your tears run down. 17 Sigh, but not aloud; make no mourning for the dead. Bind on your turban, and put your shoes on your feet; do not cover your lips, nor eat the bread of mourners."ˣ 18 So I spoke to the people in the morning, and at evening my wife died. And on the next morning I did as I was commanded.

19 And the people said to me, "Will you not tell us what these things mean for us, that you are acting thus?" 20 Then I said to them, "The word of the LORD came to me: 21 'Say to the house of Israel, Thus says the Lord GOD: Behold, I will profane my sanctuary, the pride of your power, the delight of your eyes, and the desire of your soul; and your sons and your daughters whom you left behind shall fall by the

ˣ Vg Tg: Heb *men*

1. DRAMATIC ACTION ORACLE (24:15-24)

A date near the beginning of the siege is possible, although the date in vs. 1 may not apply to this oracle (cf. the oracles in Jer. 16:1-9). The editor has apparently reworded the oracle; some of his characteristic phraseology appears in vss. 21, 23, 24, e.g., "profane my sanctuary," vs. 21 (see xxvii on p. 51); "pride of your power," vs. 21 (see xiv on p. 50), see also Lev. 26:19; "pine away in your iniquities," vs. 23; cf. 4:16; 33:10; Lev. 26:39; and the final clause of vs. 24. Note also the third person allusion to Ezekiel in vs. 24.

16-17. Note the mourning rites Jeremiah is told not to observe (Jer. 16:5-7); see also II Sam. 15:30; Jer. 14:3; 22:18; 34:5; Hos. 9:4. **At a stroke** may also properly be rendered **with a stroke,** e.g., a plague or pestilence. **Bread of mourners:** Read לחם אונים with the Targ. and Vulg. (cf. Hos. 9:4) for לחם אנשים, **bread of men** (see also vs. 22).

21. And your sons and your daughters whom you left behind is from the standpoint of the exiles of 597 in Babylon; this is inconsonant with the Jerusalem locale of the oracle, and is further evidence of the editor's expansion (cf. Matthews, Herntrich). **Desire of your soul:** Read with several MSS מחמד נפשכם for מחמל נפשכם, "compassion of your soul" (=KJV).

For their concern with human needs and their identification with God's purpose they have to pay a heavy price. They are called again and again to surrender their private lives to the requirements of their public responsibility. He who must bear a nation on his heart may not indulge his individual griefs as others do; his task remains and demands all his energies. Yes, and even to ordinary men and women the summons may come to "leave the dead to bury their own dead" (Luke 9:60), while they, the living, address themselves to their duties.

But there is a consolation open to us which was denied to Ezekiel; i.e., there is a possibility of ennobling private sorrow by linking it with public griefs. Ezekiel could scarcely do this, since his outlook at the time was one of un-relieved disaster. But while it is little help to be told that what we suffer as individuals is but a small part of the universal human pain, we can so use the one as to become more sensitive to the other and more eager in its relief. We do that when we direct the emotions engendered by our own painful experience into a channel

22 And ye shall do as I have done: ye shall not cover *your* lips, nor eat the bread of men.

23 And your tires *shall be* upon your heads, and your shoes upon your feet: ye shall not mourn nor weep; but ye shall pine away for your iniquities, and mourn one toward another.

24 Thus Ezekiel is unto you a sign: according to all that he hath done shall ye do: and when this cometh, ye shall know that I *am* the Lord God.

25 Also, thou son of man, *shall it* not *be* in the day when I take from them their strength, the joy of their glory, the desire of their eyes, and that whereupon they set their minds, their sons and their daughters,

sword. **22** And you shall do as I have done; you shall not cover your lips, nor eat the bread of mourners.ˣ **23** Your turbans shall be on your heads and your shoes on your feet; you shall not mourn or weep, but you shall pine away in your iniquities and groan to one another. **24** Thus shall Ezekiel be to you a sign; according to all that he has done you shall do. When this comes, then you will know that I am the Lord God.'

25 "And you, son of man, on the day when I take from them their stronghold, their joy and glory, the delight of their eyes and their heart's desire, and also their sons

ˣ Vg Tg: Heb *men*

---

2. NEWS OF JERUSALEM'S FALL (24:25-27)

This is the editor's expansion of the preceding oracle in accord with his view of Ezekiel's "dumbness" (see 3:25-27). In 33:21-22 the fugitive came six months after the fall of the city, when Ezekiel was again back in Babylonia. As usually translated, vss. 25-27 here imply that the fugitive came on the day of the city's fall. A change of text and variant translation would reconcile the passage with 33:21-22. Translate the beginning of vs. 25, "in the day that [i.e., when] I take," etc., and vs. 26 "in the day when a fugitive will come" (reading ביום יבוא for ביום ההוא יבוא), and make both vss. 25 and 26 the protasis to vs. 27, placing a comma after vs. 26 (see Cooke). This is not entirely satisfactory, but both these verses and 33:21-22 cannot be right, and the editor does presume an exilic milieu. Less happy is the solution that places Ezekiel in Palestine within a day's journey of Jerusalem at the time of the fall of the city, for this is not the editor's viewpoint, although the symbolic "dumbness" presumed here belongs to him.

25. With **the joy of their glory** cf. "the house of my glory" in Isa. 60:7. **Their stronghold:** Cf. Dan. 11:31.

---

not of resentment against what we deem an unjust treatment of ourselves, but of pure sympathy with others and disinterested resolve on their behalf. Because we have seen for ourselves unmistakably what sorrow means, our hearts are open as never before to our fellows and what they have to suffer. There is a beautiful illustration of this in the life of Margaret Ethel MacDonald. She lost a boy at the age of five and wrote to a friend in reply to a letter of comfort:

These statistics of mortality among children have become unbearable to me. I used to be able to read them in a dull scientific sort of way, but now I seem to know the pain behind each one. It is not true that other children can make it up to you, that time heals the pain. It doesn't; it grows worse and worse. We women must work for a world where little children will not needlessly die.⁶

⁶ J. Ramsay MacDonald, *Margaret Ethel MacDonald* (New York: Thomas Seltzer, 1924), pp. 119-20.

Perhaps indeed we can go still farther and see in the action of Ezekiel at this juncture a parable of God's attitude to ourselves. When we suffer, God seems to show no sign that he cares at all; he is apparently silent and pays no heed to our cry. He is like Ezekiel when his wife died and men said to him, "How callous! Does he then not really feel the loss of her? Was his love for his wife only so much pretense after all?" They were not allowed to know that all the while he was rent inwardly by grief. They could not know what tears he had to check in order to make possible that impassive exterior which he was bidden to assume. So it is with God. Behind the divine silence a divine sorrow is concealed. His apparent indifference hides from us his yearning over our race. We can see this, now that in the Cross he has revealed himself and shown us what all the while was in his heart. He enters into all our afflictions and takes them upon himself as Jesus

26 *That* he that escapeth in that day shall come unto thee, to cause *thee* to hear *it* with *thine* ears?

27 In that day shall thy mouth be opened to him which is escaped, and thou shalt speak, and be no more dumb: and thou shalt be a sign unto them; and they shall know that I *am* the LORD.

25 The word of the LORD came again unto me, saying,

2 Son of man, set thy face against the Ammonites, and prophesy against them;

and daughters, 26 on that day a fugitive will come to you to report to you the news. 27 On that day your mouth will be opened to the fugitive, and you shall speak and be no longer dumb. So you will be a sign to them; and they will know that I am the LORD."

25 The word of the LORD came to me: 2 "Son of man, set your face toward the Ammonites, and prophesy against them.

II. ORACLES AGAINST THE FOREIGN NATIONS (25:1–32:32)
A. AMMON, MOAB, EDOM, AND PHILISTIA (25:1-17)

This chapter marks the beginning of a new section of the book (chs. 25–32), the oracles against the pagan nations. Cf. the similar collections of oracles in Isa. 13–23; Jer. 46–51. The motive behind such a collection is to be found in part in the postexilic ideology of the defeat of the pagan nations before the coming of the new age, and more specifically in the theme expressed by the editor in 36:5-7: Yahweh is in hot jealousy against the nations, including Edom, who had contempt for Israel and plundered it, and as Israel has suffered reproach, so must they. Note the reasons given here also (cf. 28:26). The position of the oracles in Ezekiel and Isaiah before oracles of restoration (cf. their position in the LXX of Jeremiah) is consonant with this. It is perhaps no coincidence that in Ezekiel there are seven nations (Ammon, Moab, Edom, Philistia, Tyre, Sidon, Egypt) to be destroyed before Israel comes into her country. The Deuteronomist in Deut. 7:1 may be reflecting a similar theme, placing the pattern for it back at the time of the first entrance of Israel into the Promised Land (see Bertholet). The collections of oracles against the pagan nations in Isaiah, Jeremiah, and Ezekiel have all been expanded. The more obvious spurious oracles in Ezekiel are those in 25:1-17 and 28:20-26. The first of the literary prophets, Amos (cf. 1:3–2:3) had uttered oracles against the pagan nations, and even these have suffered expansion (see *ad loc.*).

The pagan nations are here criticized for their behavior toward Judah after the destruction of Jerusalem in 586 B.C., a theme of the editor in 36:1-5. For references to the mistreatment of Judah by Edom see Obad. 12-14; Ps. 137:7-9; cf. the role of Ammon in the death of Gedaliah (Jer. 40:13–41:18). See also the antagonism of Tobiah the Ammonite slave to Nehemiah (Neh. 2:19; 4:3; etc.). From the same period as these oracles in Ezekiel come perhaps the oracles against Philistia, Ammon, Moab, and Edom in Jer. 47:1-7; 48:1–49:22 (see also Lam. 4:21-22). The colorless prose of these oracles against the smaller nations in ch. 25 contrasts strongly with the poetic oracles against Tyre and Egypt. Each oracle ends with the predicted recognition of Yahweh by the pagan nations, a reflection of Second Isaiah. Typical phraseology may be found in such expressions as "set your face toward," in vs. 2 (see iii on p. 50); "my sanctuary . . . profaned" in vs. 3 (see xxvii on p. 51); "stretched out my hand" in vs. 7 (see vii on p. 50), "from the peoples and . . . out of the countries" in vs. 7 (cf. 11:17; 20:34, 41; 34:13; "cut off from it man and beast" in vs. 13 (see xxi on p. 50; "make it desolate" in vs. 13 (see xxiii on p. 50); "with wrathful chastisements" in vs. 17 (cf.

---

did when he walked in the sunset among the sick in Capernaum (Matt. 8:16-17). We must not doubt this, even if the heavens give no sign of him and the earth seems void of his presence. If therefore the silent mourning of Ezekiel was for his contemporaries a fearful menace of

oncoming doom, for us it is the sign of a mercy which lies in depths to which our eyes cannot pierce.

25:1-17. *Types of Anti-Semitism.*—With this chapter we find ourselves amid the petty jealousies and foolish animosities of the small states

3 And say unto the Ammonites, Hear the word of the Lord GOD; Thus saith the Lord GOD; Because thou saidst, Aha, against my sanctuary, when it was profaned; and against the land of Israel, when it was desolate; and against the house of Judah, when they went into captivity;

4 Behold, therefore I will deliver thee to the men of the east for a possession, and they shall set their palaces in thee, and make their dwellings in thee: they shall eat thy fruit, and they shall drink thy milk.

5 And I will make Rabbah a stable for camels, and the Ammonites a couching place for flocks: and ye shall know that I am the LORD.

3 Say to the Ammonites, Hear the word of the Lord GOD: Thus says the Lord GOD, Because you said, 'Aha!' over my sanctuary when it was profaned, and over the land of Israel when it was made desolate, and over the house of Judah when it went into exile; 4 therefore I am handing you over to the people of the East for a possession, and they shall set their encampments among you and make their dwellings in your midst; they shall eat your fruit, and they shall drink your milk. 5 I will make Rabbah a pasture for camels and the cities of the Ammonites*y* a fold for flocks. Then you will know that

y Cn: Heb lacks *the cities of*

5:15); etc. Hölscher, Herntrich, and Matthews think the chapter entirely secondary, while Irwin finds original only a brief oracle in vs. 4 (contrast Bertholet, Cooke, Pfeiffer). There is some literary affinity with the genuine oracles against Egypt and Tyre, which may be due to the revision of the latter or to imitation.

1. AMMON (25:1-7)

The Ammonites and Hebrews had been in frequent conflict beginning with the period of the Judges (cf. Judg. 10:1–11:40). See the tale of the birth of Ammon and Moab in Gen. 19:30-38, told to discredit them. With the defeat of Israel by the Assyrians the Ammonites had moved westward and taken over Gad (see Jer. 49:1). Although attacking Judah in 600, they were opposed to Babylon in the reign of Zedekiah (cf. 21:19-20; Jer. 27:3).

25:4. Men of the east: The inhabitants of the desert (cf. Judg. 6:3, 33; 7:12; 8:10; I Kings 4:30; Isa. 11:14). The term טירות, **encampments,** suggests nomadic tribes, as in Gen. 25:16; Num. 31:10; etc.

5. For the reduction of the city to **a pasture** in the prophetic oracles see also Isa. 17:2; 32:14; Zeph. 2:14-15; cf. Isa. 34:13. **Rabbah:** The chief city of Ammon (see 21:20).

on and around the Palestinian seaboard. These were countries which could ill afford the luxury of strife among themselves while some great power in their neighborhood was waiting to devour them one by one. But then as now nations are seldom restrained by such long-term considerations of what is in their interest. Quarrels of the same kind have gone on all over the world, in ancient Greece and in nineteenth-century Latin America, for example. Fortunately history does not often burden us with the memory of such events; only where there is a Thucydides to immortalize them does posterity remember them. In this case what has conferred immortality on the political struggles of the ancient Near East is the fact that Israel was involved in them, now as active agent and now again as victim.

We who look back upon the varied fortunes of this people over a much longer period than that which Ezekiel could survey may well see

in this chapter some pictures of that anti-Semitism which is always with us in one form or another. Indeed, we might see here clearly set before us four principal types of anti-Semitism.

The first of these is the lowest type of all, for it is but the expression of an unreasoning malice and envy. What is said of Ammon (vss. 1-7) illustrates what the Germans call *Schadenfreude,* the spirit of ill will which finds delight in gloating over the misfortunes of another. As we have already seen in 21:18-23, Ammon was involved along with Judah in the fatuous revolt against Babylon. It was indeed an open question where Nebuchadrezzar would direct his armies first, and it was only the fortune of the lot which marked out Judah as his victim and reserved Ammon to be dealt with later. Perhaps Ammon took advantage of the respite thus granted to make peace with the conqueror. If so, we can see in this gloating over the

6 For thus saith the Lord God; Because thou hast clapped *thine* hands, and stamped with the feet, and rejoiced in heart with all thy despite against the land of Israel;

7 Behold, therefore I will stretch out mine hand upon thee, and will deliver thee for a spoil to the heathen; and I will cut thee off from the people, and I will cause thee to perish out of the countries: I will destroy thee; and thou shalt know that I *am* the Lord.

8 ¶ Thus saith the Lord God; Because that Moab and Seir do say, Behold, the house of Judah *is* like unto all the heathen;

9 Therefore, behold, I will open the side of Moab from the cities, from his cities *which are* on his frontiers, the glory of the country, Beth-jeshimoth, Baal-meon, and Kiriathaim,

I am the Lord. **6** For thus says the Lord God: Because you have clapped your hands and stamped your feet and rejoiced with all the malice within you against the land of Israel, **7** therefore, behold, I have stretched out my hand against you, and will hand you over as spoil to the nations; and I will cut you off from the peoples and will make you perish out of the countries; I will destroy you. Then you will know that I am the Lord.

8 "Thus says the Lord God: Because Moab[z] said, Behold, the house of Judah is like all the other nations, **9** therefore I will lay open the flank of Moab from the cities[a] on its frontier, the glory of the country, Beth-jesh'imoth, Ba'al-me'on, and Kiri-

[z] Gk Old Latin: Heb *Moab and Seir*
[a] Heb *cities from its cities*

---

7. Cf. Jer. 48:47; 49:6, 39, where the pagan nations are to be restored, apparently to worship Yahweh, after their destruction.

2. Moab (25:8-11)

The Hebrews first came into conflict with Moab at the time of Moses and Balak (see Num. 22-24), and their relationships are most dramatically illustrated in the wars between the dynasty of Omri and Mesha of Moab (see II Kings 3 and the Moabite stone; also *Ancient Near Eastern Texts,* pp. 320-21).

8. Seir is Edom, and its omission with the LXX and O.L. is justified by the context.

9. From his cities may be due to dittography. The border cities of Moab have been explored and described by Nelson Glueck. The eastern border fortresses formed a continuation of the line of fortresses of Edom south of the river Zered (Wadi el-Ḥesā). There was a well-planned chain of fortresses, often within sight of each other, on the hilltops at the extreme edge of the fertile areas of the Moabite plateau (see Nelson Glueck, "Explorations in Eastern Palestine, III," *Annual of the American Schools of Oriental Research,* XVIII-XIX [1937-39], 72-75; *The Other Side of the Jordan* [New Haven: American Schools of Oriental Research, 1940], pp. 134-39). **Beth-jeshimoth:** Modern Tell el-'Azeimeh, about two and one-half miles northeast of the Dead Sea. **Baal-meon:** Modern Ma'în, about nine miles east of the Dead Sea. **Kiriathaim:** Modern el-Qereiyât, about ten miles below Baal-meon. All three sites are north of the river Arnon.

---

calamity which has befallen Jerusalem part of an attempt to appease the wrath of Nebuchadrezzar while there was yet time. We all know the hideous meanness which covers up its own guilt or takes revenge for some unfavorable turn of circumstance by making a scapegoat of the Jew. This is the anti-Semitism which is due to no particular cause, but which is latent in the minds of many. It provides an outlet for the worst impulses in men, their envy and sadism.

Moab shows us a rationalistic type of anti-Semitism which refuses to see anything of

special worth in the Jewish tradition and which would reduce all nations to the same level (vss. 8-11). It works with a simple judgment: **The house of Judah is like unto all the heathen;** i.e., there are only secular and political standards by which to estimate the place of nations in history, and by these there is nothing special to distinguish the Jews. That kind of thing is said often enough in the Jewish community as well as outside. Ever since the French Revolution and the opening for the Jew of the era of emancipation, he has been in danger of surrendering his specifically religious characteristics

10 Unto the men of the east with the Ammonites, and will give them in possession, that the Ammonites may not be remembered among the nations.

11 And I will execute judgments upon Moab; and they shall know that I *am* the LORD.

12 ¶ Thus saith the Lord GOD; Because that Edom hath dealt against the house of Judah by taking vengeance, and hath greatly offended, and revenged himself upon them;

13 Therefore thus saith the Lord GOD; I will also stretch out mine hand upon Edom, and will cut off man and beast from it; and I will make it desolate from Teman; and they of Dedan shall fall by the sword.

14 And I will lay my vengeance upon Edom by the hand of my people Israel: and they shall do in Edom according to mine anger and according to my fury; and they shall know my vengeance, saith the Lord GOD.

atha'im. 10 I will give it along with the Ammonites to the people of the East as a possession, that it[b] may be remembered no more among the nations, 11 and I will execute judgments upon Moab. Then they will know that I am the LORD.

12 "Thus says the Lord GOD: Because Edom acted revengefully against the house of Judah and has grievously offended in taking vengeance upon them, 13 therefore thus says the Lord GOD, I will stretch out my hand against Edom, and cut off from it man and beast; and I will make it desolate; from Teman even to Dedan they shall fall by the sword. 14 And I will lay my vengeance upon Edom by the hand of my people Israel; and they shall do in Edom according to my anger and according to my wrath; and they shall know my vengeance, says the Lord GOD.

[b] Cn: Heb *the Ammonites*

10. The text is distorted and both allusions to **the Ammonites** may be an expansion. The omission of **and** (KJV) with the LXX and Syriac properly avoids making vs. 10*a* a part of the sentence in vs. 9.

3. EDOM (25:12-14)

Tradition carried the antagonism between Edom and the Hebrews back to the days of Jacob and Esau (cf. Gen. 25:1–33:20), and it began historically with the events of the Exodus in Num. 20:14-21. Both Malachi (1:2-5) and Obadiah reflect it in the fifth century (see also Isa. 63:1-4), and the editor reverts to the theme in 35:1-15; 36:5.

13. Teman is perhaps modern Tawīlân, not far from Sela (Petra). **Dedan** here seems to be in Edom, but its location is unknown; it is apparently different from Dedan in Arabia in 27:20; 38:13 (modern el-'Ula?).

and becoming absorbed into the society around him. There are those who would encourage this and who imagine they are helping the Jew by so doing. They would explain his whole history in political and economic terms, as Karl Marx did, and they share Marx's expectation that as the result of changes in these spheres the Jewish problem will be solved—by the elimination of all that is specifically Jewish. That, to be sure, is the kind of operation which is highly successful, but the patient dies under it. There is, however, a feature which marks the Jew off from others. His religion is not something apart from, it belongs integrally to, his national and cultural heritage. He has the mission to call men and peoples to Sinai, to speak to them of the moral law and the rule of one living and righteous God. The elimination of this mission from Jewish life would carry with it

sooner or later the disappearance of the Jewish people as such.

Then in Edom we have the distressing spectacle of an anti-Semitism which is rooted in a blood relationship (vss. 12-14). These two nations were closely akin, so closely because, so the old story ran, their ancestors were born twins (Gen. 25:21-26). Is it not often the case that animosities which arise within the family tend to be more severe than those between strangers? Presumably the explanation is that where there is so much in common, we cannot endure that there should be any difference at all. Where shall we look for the modern counterpart to this anti-Semitism of a neighboring and kindred stock? Surely to that most distressing phenomenon of ill will against the Jew on the part of the Christian. There is a tragic story here which is only too little known among us.

15 ¶ Thus saith the Lord God; Because the Philistines have dealt by revenge, and have taken vengeance with a despiteful heart, to destroy *it* for the old hatred;

16 Therefore thus saith the Lord God; Behold, I will stretch out mine hand upon the Philistines, and I will cut off the Cherethim, and destroy the remnant of the seacoast.

17 And I will execute great vengeance upon them with furious rebukes; and they shall know that I *am* the Lord, when I shall lay my vengeance upon them.

15 "Thus says the Lord God: Because the Philistines acted revengefully and took vengeance with malice of heart to destroy in never-ending enmity; 16 therefore thus says the Lord God, Behold, I will stretch out my hand against the Philistines, and I will cut off the Cher'ethites, and destroy the rest of the seacoast. 17 I will execute great vengeance upon them with wrathful chastisements. Then they will know that I am the Lord, when I lay my vengeance upon them."

4. Philistia (25:15-17)

The Philistines entered Palestine *ca.* 1200 B.C. For early conflicts with them see Judg. 3:31; 14:1–16:31; I Sam. 4:1–6:21; etc.; see also II Chr. 26:6-7, in the reign of Uzziah.

16. The Cherethites are mentioned with the Pelethites in II Sam. 8:18; 15:18; 20:7; I Kings 1:38, 44, as foreign mercenaries forming David's bodyguard. Cherethite has been taken as analogous with Cretan, and Pelethite with Philistine. Note the identification of Caphtor, the home of the Philistines (Amos 9:7; Deut. 2:23; Jer. 47:4), with Crete. The western Negeb was called the Negeb of the Cherethites (I Sam. 30:14), and here in Ezekiel and in Zeph. 2:5 Cherethites seems to be a synonym for Philistine. *Hikratti,* **cut off,** is a wordplay with *kerethim,* Cherethites (cf. Amos 9:7). Any association of the Cherethites with Keret of the Ugaritic mythological texts is now quite thoroughly discredited (see W. F. Albright, "Was the Patriarch Terah a Canaanite Moon-God?" *Bulletin of the American Schools of Oriental Research,* No. 71 [Oct., 1938], pp. 35-40; cf. also "New Canaanite Historical and Mythological Data," *ibid.,* No. 63 [Oct., 1936], pp. 23-32).

In Spain the forcible conversions which brought into existence the unhappy Marrano community are part of it.[7] Amid the Black Death, Jews "at Mainz and other German-speaking towns were burned in their hundreds or thousands by an infuriated mob in the belief that the plague was a malignant device of the Semitic race for the confusion of the Catholic creed."[8] The pogroms of the late nineteenth century in eastern Europe often synchronized with Easter, and the Jew was attacked as "the murderer of Christ." Are there any signs among us of this propaganda against the Jew in the name of Christ? If so, it is something to be repudiated with shame and horror.

Last of all, there is an anti-Semitism which attracts more attention than the other forms because it is open and violent (vss. 15-17). The Philistines appear in the O.T. as "uncircumcised"; they represent a way of life which is not that of Israel. Further, they possess military

[7] See Cecil Roth, *A Short History of the Jewish People* (rev. ed.; New York: East and West Library, 1948).

[8] H. A. L. Fisher, *A History of Europe* (London: Edward Arnold & Co., 1936), p. 319.

power far in excess of Israel's, and, until the rise of David, they are able to force their rule upon it. They have had their successors in later times, from Antiochus Epiphanes to our own day. We may be confident that our people are immune from this anti-Semitism of the sword and the concentration camp. But we need to bear in mind that it never begins in this overt way, that overt cruelty is preceded by the subtler forms of anti-Semitism mentioned above. Only when it has fully established itself thus does it throw off the mask and appear in its hideous reality.

If we now look back on the wranglings and furious hatreds of these five petty states in a tiny country, we reflect that of them all only Israel has survived. Ammon and the rest have vanished, leaving little trace behind them. Israel continues its life as a people, in virtue of its call to witness to the one God and his righteous will. This fact is a challenge to all attempts to explain history in purely naturalistic fashion. No other people has sustained such misfortune or incurred such hostility as Israel, yet it has outlived its rivals and stands today by the

26

And it came to pass in the eleventh year, in the first *day* of the month, *that* the word of the Lord came unto me, saying,

26

In the eleventh year, on the first day of the month, the word of the

---

B. Oracles Against Tyre (26:1-21)

Tyre had long been an important Phoenician city. Letters from its King Abimilki appear in the Amarna correspondence at the time when the Habiru were entering Canaan (see Pritchard, *op. cit.,* p. 484). At the time of Solomon, Hiram I of Tyre had important commercial relations with the Hebrews (see I Kings 5:1-18; 9:10-14, 26-27). Ahab took the daughter of Ethbaal king of Tyre as his queen (I Kings 16:31). At the beginning of the reign of Zedekiah, Tyre had with others sought alliance with Judah against Babylonia (Jer. 27:3), and had joined the later revolt. The siege of Tyre, which was to last thirteen years (see Josephus *Against Apion* I. 21), began perhaps in the seventeenth year of Nebuchadrezzar, in 588-587 if we read "seventeen" for "seven" in Josephus (see Albright, "The Seal of Eliakim and the Latest Preëxilic History of Judah," pp. 94-95. Less probable is the view that places the beginning of the siege in 585. Eissfeldt reconstructs Josephus to read the seventh year of Ittobaal king of Tyre, i.e., 586; see "Das Datum der Belagerung von Tyrus durch Nebukadnezar," *Forschungen und Fortschritte,* X [1934], 165; see Howie, *Date and Composition of Ezekiel,* pp. 42-43. Contrast Max Vogelstein, "Nebuchadnezzar's Reconquest of Phoenicia and Palestine and the Oracles of Ezekiel," *Hebrew Union College Annual,* Vol. XXIII, Part 2 [1950-51], pp. 197-220). The date given in vs. 1 is incomplete, and it may be that it should be dated in the twelfth year (LXXᴬ), in the first day of the eleventh month (Feb. 3, 585). The reason for accepting the twelfth year of the LXXᴬ is in part that vs. 2 implies that the oracle came after the destruction of Jerusalem in 586, and it was not until the twelfth year that Ezekiel learned about the fall of Jerusalem, according to 33:21. If, with some Hebrew and the LXX MSS and the Syriac, the eleventh year is read in 33:21, then conceivably this oracle in ch. 26 came in the first day of the eleventh month of the eleventh year. This would presume also the fall of Jerusalem in 587. Or, more likely, if the allusion to the fall of Jerusalem in vs. 2 does not form a part of the genuine material in the chapter (see below), and the date is to be attached to the original portions of the chapter, then the eleventh year could be retained, the oracle being uttered on the first day of any month of the eleventh year.

There are four main divisions or four oracles in this chapter: vss. 1-6, 7-14, 15-18, 19-21. Each oracle contains the introductory formula "Thus says the Lord God" (vss. 3, 7, 15, 19). It is difficult to say how much of the chapter is poetry and how much prose, or how much is original. Hölscher and Herntrich accept none of it; Irwin accepts only a brief poetic oracle in vs. 7. Matthews finds only vss. 7-14, 17b-18a original, while Bertholet considers vss. 3-6, 19-21 secondary, the former a parallel recension to vss. 7-14 (cf. Kraetzschmar). Torrey takes the chapter as a reference to the capture of Tyre by Alexander the Great. On the other hand, Cooke thinks it in the main the work of the prophet. The following analysis will suggest that probably vss. 2-6 are to be considered secondary, with vss. 19-21 more certainly so, while the hand of the editor may also be noted in a few phrases elsewhere.

---

tomb of those who sought to destroy it. Spiritual leadership has fallen to a people whose strength came from its faith in God.

26:1-21. Much Wealth but Little Soul.—For this description of Tyre Ezekiel employs a larger canvas and more arresting colors than would have been in place when he was concerned simply with the minor states of the Palestinian seaboard. Phoenicia was not merely a great power, it was a center of civilization to which neighboring countries were deeply indebted. In the days of David and Solomon, Israel had looked to Tyre and its sister city Sidon for building materials, skilled craftsmen, and architectural models. We may suppose that one object of the marriage which Omri negoti-

2 Son of man, because that Tyrus hath said against Jerusalem, Aha, she is broken *that was* the gates of the people; she is turned unto me; I shall be replenished, *now* she is laid waste:

3 Therefore thus saith the Lord God; Behold, I *am* against thee, O Tyrus, and will cause many nations to come up against thee, as the sea causeth his waves to come up.

4 And they shall destroy the walls of Tyrus, and break down her towers: I will also scrape her dust from her, and make her like the top of a rock.

5 It shall be *a place for* the spreading of nets in the midst of the sea: for I have spoken *it,* saith the Lord God: and it shall become a spoil to the nations.

Lord came to me: 2 "Son of man, because Tyre said concerning Jerusalem, 'Aha, the gate of the peoples is broken, it has swung open to me; I shall be replenished, now that she is laid waste,' 3 therefore thus says the Lord God: Behold, I am against you, O Tyre, and will bring up many nations against you, as the sea brings up its waves. 4 They shall destroy the walls of Tyre, and break down her towers; and I will scrape her soil from her, and make her a bare rock. 5 She shall be in the midst of the sea a place for the spreading of nets; for I have spoken, says the Lord God; and she

1. The Fate of Tyre (26:1-6)

The poetic character of this oracle may be seriously questioned. The work of the editor is apparent at a number of points. Note **behold, I am against you,** vs. 3 (see xl on p. 51); **a spoil to the nations,** vs. 5 (cf. 25:7; 34:28), **for I have spoken it,** vs. 5 (see xxxv, xxxvi on p. 51), **then they will know,** etc., vs. 6. Matthews suggests that the oracle has the tone of late Judaism, shading toward apocalypticism. With the exultation over Tyre cf. 25:3, 8, 12, 15, either in imitation of this, or by the same author. The oracle may be dependent upon that in vss. 7-14. Cf. vs. 4a with vss. 9, 12a; vss. 4b-5a with vs. 14a; vs. 5b with vs. 14b; vs. 6 with vs. 8.

26:2. The designation of Jerusalem as **the gate [doors] of the peoples** may allude to its position on a major trade route where it could impose toll on passing traders. Jerusalem is pictured as a commercial rival of **Tyre.**

3. Many nations may be a play on the expression "many waters," and recalls Isa. 17:12-13.

4-6. Tyre was located on an island about one-half mile offshore, with a section or suburb of the town on the mainland. **Her daughters on the mainland** (lit., **in the field**) are these suburbs and outlying villages. Not until the time of Alexander the Great was the sea filled in to connect the island city with the coastland, as it is today. The word סלע, **rock** (vs. 4), is a play on צור, which may be read either *çôr,* **Tyre,** or *çûr,* "rock."

ated between his heir Ahab and the Tyrian princess Jezebel was that of bringing his little kingdom into touch with Phoenician civilization and overseas trade. It was from these two cities that some of the earliest explorers set out. Phoenician traders sailed beyond the Pillars of Hercules and "followed the African coast southward from the Straits of Gibraltar as far as the confines of Liberia."[9] It was the surplus population of Phoenicia which founded in Carthage the most formidable rival Rome had ever to face.

The charge which history brings against these two great trading cities is that they had much

wealth but little soul. The story of Jezebel, especially the vivid description of the frenzy and self-mutilation of the prophets of Baal on Mount Carmel (I Kings 18:26-28) shows us how menacing a primitive religion can become when it has behind it the prestige and power of an advanced civilization.

In this chapter the one reaction of Tyre to the fall of her southern neighbor is a selfish and mercenary one. Now that Judah has gone, there will be no one to levy toll on caravans from the interior bringing goods to the coast for export (vs. 2). The pathos and tragedy of what has taken place so near her, the misery inflicted upon tens of thousands of human beings, the hopelessness of deportation and the

[9] H. G. Wells, *Outline of History* (3rd ed.; New York: The Macmillan Co., 1921), p. 163.

6 And her daughters which *are* in the field shall be slain by the sword; and they shall know that I *am* the Lord.

7 ¶ For thus saith the Lord God; Behold, I will bring upon Tyrus Nebuchadrezzar king of Babylon, a king of kings, from the north, with horses, and with chariots, and with horsemen, and companies, and much people.

8 He shall slay with the sword thy daughters in the field: and he shall make a fort against thee, and cast a mount against thee, and lift up the buckler against thee.

9 And he shall set engines of war against thy walls, and with his axes he shall break down thy towers.

10 By reason of the abundance of his horses their dust shall cover thee: thy walls shall shake at the noise of the horsemen, and of the wheels, and of the chariots, when he shall enter into thy gates, as men enter into a city wherein is made a breach.

shall become a spoil to the nations; **6** and her daughters on the mainland shall be slain by the sword. Then they will know that I am the Lord.

7 "For thus says the Lord God: Behold, I will bring upon Tyre from the north Nebuchadrez'zar king of Babylon, king of kings, with horses and chariots, and with horsemen and a host of many soldiers. **8** He will slay with the sword your daughters on the mainland; he will set up a siege wall against you, and throw up a mound against you, and raise a roof of shields against you. **9** He will direct the shock of his battering rams against your walls, and with his axes he will break down your towers. **10** His horses will be so many that their dust will cover you; your walls will shake at the noise of the horsemen and wagons and chariots, when he enters your gates as one enters a

---

2. Nebuchadrezzar to Destroy Tyre (26:7-14)

If there is poetry here, it lies in vss. 12-14. In vss. 7-11 the imagery used is that of attack of a city by land. To attack the island of Tyre with mounds and siege wall, or to enter it with chariotry as depicted here, would seem a physical impossibility. This does not necessitate the assumption that the oracle is spurious, for the prophet may be deliberately using the conventionalized symbols of siege, or referring in part to the daughters on the mainland.

7. Nebuchadrezzar is the more correct form of the name, closer to *Nabu-kudurru-usur,* as over against "Nebuchadnezzar." **From the north:** As also in Jer. 46:20. The foe from the north in Jeremiah (1:13-19; 4:5–6:26; etc.) is probably also Nebuchadrezzar and his Babylonian armies (see May, in "The Chronology of Jeremiah's Oracles," pp. 225-26). **King of kings** was a title used by the Assyrian kings, but it does not seem to have been used by Nebuchadrezzar, although ascribed to him in Dan. 2:37 (cf. also Ezra 7:12 [Artaxerxes]. The title here may be due to the editor. "And host and much people" (cf. KJV) may be a scribal gloss with 38:4, 6, 15 in mind; "and with a host of much people" (cf. RSV) follows the LXX and three Hebrew MSS.

8-9. For the instruments of offensive warfare see also 4:2; 17:17; 21:22. The **roof of shields** is deduced from the context; the Hebrew term צנה is translated as **buckler** in 23:24; 38:4; 39:9 and may refer only to the larger shield, as over against מגן, the more normal-sized shield (see Galling, *Biblisches Reallexikon,* pp. 457-58). It has also been identified with the large protecting screen depicted on Assyrian reliefs (see Hugo Gressmann, *Altorientalische Bilder zum Alten Testament* [Berlin: Walter de Gruyter & Co., 1926], Pl. LVIII, No. 132).

---

shame of defeat—these touch in her no chord of sympathy. Profits will grow; that is all that matters to Tyre. Is there no parallel in our own day to such an attitude?

But yet another thought is suggested by this chapter. It shows the clash between the trading civilization of Phoenicia on the one hand and

the armed might of Babylon on the other. We have come in our time to consider that these two factors, the economic and the military, exhaust between them the forces which determine history. And some of the most dramatic contests of all times have been those between the merchant and the warrior. We see this in the strug-

11 With the hoofs of his horses shall he tread down all thy streets: he shall slay thy people by the sword, and thy strong garrisons shall go down to the ground.

12 And they shall make a spoil of thy riches, and make a prey of thy merchandise: and they shall break down thy walls, and destroy thy pleasant houses: and they shall lay thy stones and thy timber and thy dust in the midst of the water.

13 And I will cause the noise of thy songs to cease; and the sound of thy harps shall be no more heard.

14 And I will make thee like the top of a rock: thou shalt be *a place* to spread nets upon; thou shalt be built no more: for I the LORD have spoken *it*, saith the Lord GOD.

15 ¶ Thus saith the Lord GOD to Tyrus; Shall not the isles shake at the sound of thy fall, when the wounded cry, when the slaughter is made in the midst of thee?

16 Then all the princes of the sea shall come down from their thrones, and lay away their robes, and put off their broidered garments: they shall clothe them-

city which has been breached. 11 With the hoofs of his horses he will trample all your streets; he will slay your people with the sword; and your mighty pillars will fall to the ground. 12 They will make a spoil of your riches and a prey of your merchandise; they will break down your walls and destroy your pleasant houses; your stones and timber and soil they will cast into the midst of the waters. 13 And I will stop the music of your songs, and the sound of your lyres shall be heard no more. 14 I will make you a bare rock; you shall be a place for the spreading of nets; you shall never be rebuilt; for I the LORD have spoken, says the Lord GOD.

15 "Thus says the Lord GOD to Tyre: Will not the coastlands shake at the sound of your fall, when the wounded groan, when slaughter is made in the midst of you? 16 Then all the princes of the sea will step down from their thrones, and remove their robes, and strip off their em-

---

11. Pillars, מצבות, is a possible reference to sacred pillars, such as the two before the temple at Tyre described by Herodotus (*History* II. 44. See H. G. May, "The Two Pillars Before the Temple of Solomon," *Bulletin of the American Schools of Oriental Research*, No. 88 [Dec., 1942], p. 27), although this is not certain.

13. Lyres, not **harps.**

3. LAMENTATIONS OF THE PRINCES OF THE SEA (26:15-18)

Note the parallel to this section in 27:28-36.

15-16. Presumably the reason for the dismay of the **coastlands** and the city kings is their involvement with the commercial relationships of Tyre and the dependence of their prosperity upon the city, a keystone in the economic prosperity of the coastlands. **The princes of the sea** are the city kings, and a comparison with 27:35 suggests that Ezekiel may have written "kings," the term prince (נשיא) being a favorite of the editor. With the picture here cf. that in the Ugaritic Texts, where El goes down from his throne and sits on the earth, putting ashes of grief and dust on his head and clothing himself with sackcloth (Gordon, *Ugaritic Handbook*, text 67, VI, ll. 11-17; *Ugaritic Literature* [Roma: Pontificium Institutum Biblicum, 1949], p. 42; see also Isa. 47:1-3; Jer. 48:18; Lam. 2:10). The **robes** and **embroidered garments** are perhaps trade articles. The last clause appears again in 27:35; 28:19 (cf. Lev. 26:32).

---

gle of Carthage and Rome, Sparta and Athens. It meets us again in Napoleon's scornful reference to his rival across the Channel as a "nation of shopkeepers," not to mention the Anglo-American encounter with German militarism twice within one generation. The warrior has often been the defeated party because his resources were limited in comparison with those at the disposal of the merchant. His strokes come more quickly and are fiercer, yet he lacks the staying power of his opponent.

But are these the only forces which have to be included in the historian's reckoning? What of the nation which in the person of the

selves with trembling; they shall sit upon the ground, and shall tremble at *every* moment, and be astonished at thee.

17 And they shall take up a lamentation for thee, and say to thee, How art thou destroyed, *that wast* inhabited of seafaring men, the renowned city, which wast strong in the sea, she and her inhabitants, which cause their terror *to be* on all that haunt it!

18 Now shall the isles tremble in the day of thy fall; yea, the isles that *are* in the sea shall be troubled at thy departure.

19 For thus saith the Lord GOD; When I shall make thee a desolate city, like the cities that are not inhabited; when I shall bring up the deep upon thee, and great waters shall cover thee;

broidered garments; they will clothe themselves with trembling; they will sit upon the ground and tremble every moment, and be appalled at you. **17** And they will raise a lamentation over you, and say to you,

'How you have vanished[c] from the seas,
  O city renowned,
that was mighty on the sea,
  you and your inhabitants,
who imposed your terror
  on all the mainland![d]

18 Now the isles tremble
  on the day of your fall;
yea, the isles that are in the sea
  are dismayed at your passing.'

19 "For thus says the Lord GOD: When I make you a city laid waste, like the cities that are not inhabited, when I bring up the deep over you, and the great waters

[c] Gk Old Latin Aquila: Heb *vanished, O inhabited one*
[d] Cn: Heb *her inhabitants*

17. The lamentation (*qînāh;* see Exeg. on 19:1-14) may originally have had the so-called 3+2 metrical form, but has suffered corruptions. **Of seafaring men** is really only **from the seas. Inhabited** should be omitted with the LXX. The shift in persons is not unique here in Hebrew poetry; note that **you and your** is in Hebrew **she and her,** while **imposed your terror** is "[they] imposed their terror." "Her inhabitants," יושביה, whence **that haunt it,** should perhaps be changed to יושביו, "its inhabitants," i.e., of the sea, or else to השדה ("the field," see vs. 6) or היבשה ("the dry land").

18. Isles: Read, rather, **coastlands,** as in vs. 15; the M.T. has an Aramaic plural. The latter half of the verse is purest prose and is omitted by the LXX[B]; it is perhaps the editor's expansion.

4. TYRE'S DESCENT INTO SHEOL (26:19-21)

The analogies are with the picture of Egypt in the lower world in 31:14-18; 32:17-32. The diction is prosaic and repetitious. With **a city laid waste** cf. 29:12; 30:7; with **those who go down to the Pit** cf. parallels in 31:14-18; 32:17-32; Isa. 14:19; 38:18; Pss. 88:4; 143:7; etc. The **people of old** recalls Lam. 3:6, and **primeval ruins,** Jer. 25:9; 49:13; Isa. 58:12; cf. Cooke.

19. The deep and **great waters** are synonymous terms, the latter often alluding to the waters of the *tehôm,* **the deep.** These are also the waters of the primordial abyss

prophet surveys them both and brings them under the judgment of God? Judah counted for nothing in the eyes of Tyre and Babylon, yet today Judah means more to us than both of the others together. They belong only to the past; Judah is a force in the present as well. Yes, there is a spiritual factor in history. It does not impose itself on our notice as do the economic and political factors; it works unseen and is to all appearances thwarted again and again, but in the long run it alone has might. So a contemporary philosopher writes of a later period:

In Christ, not in Caesar, did the truly creative power in the history of that age manifest itself. While contemporary historians took great pains in recounting the noisy deeds of the Caesars, they failed to notice that in a far corner of the world, among people who hardly seemed worth the attention of the educated, certain things were taking place that were of an entirely different nature and of far greater importance for the history of the world than anything they had written in their books.[1]

[1] Erich Frank, *Philosophical Understanding and Religious Truth* (London: Oxford University Press, 1945), p. 126.

20 When I shall bring thee down with them that descend into the pit, with the people of old time, and shall set thee in the low parts of the earth, in places desolate of old, with them that go down to the pit, that thou be not inhabited; and I shall set glory in the land of the living;

21 I will make thee a terror, and thou *shalt be* no *more:* though thou be sought for, yet shalt thou never be found again, saith the Lord GOD.

27 The word of the LORD came again unto me, saying,

2 Now, thou son of man, take up a lamentation for Tyrus;

3 And say unto Tyrus, O thou that art situate at the entry of the sea, *which art* a merchant of the people for many isles, Thus saith the Lord GOD; O Tyrus, thou hast said, I *am* of perfect beauty.

cover you, 20 then I will thrust you down with those who descend into the Pit, to the people of old, and I will make you to dwell in the nether world, among primeval ruins, with those who go down to the Pit, so that you will not be inhabited or have a place[e] in the land of the living. 21 I will bring you to a dreadful end, and you shall be no more; though you be sought for, you will never be found again, says the Lord GOD."

27 The word of the LORD came to me: 2 "Now you, son of man, raise a lamentation over Tyre, 3 and say to Tyre, who dwells at the entrance to the sea, merchant of the peoples on many coastlands, thus says the Lord GOD:

"O Tyre, you have said,
'I am perfect in beauty.'

[e] Gk: Heb *I will give beauty*

(cf. 19:10; Pss. 29:3; 77:19 [Hebrew 77:20]; Isa. 17:13; Hab. 3:15; see Exeg. on 1:24). Rather than conquer the chaotic waters like Yahweh or the Canaanite Baal, Tyre would be conquered by them and descend to the lower world.

20. Cf. the descent of the king of Babylon to the lower world in Isa. 14. **The Pit** is a common designation for Sheol, the place of the dead beneath the earth (cf. Job 17:16; 33:18, 24, 28, 30; Pss. 28:1; 30:3 [Hebrew 30:4]; 88:4, 6 [Hebrew 88:5, 7]; etc.

C. A LAMENTATION OVER TYRE (27:1-36)

This dirge (*qînāh*, vs. 2; cf. 19:1; 28:12; etc.), which contains a dirge within a dirge (vss. 32-36), begins with poetry which depicts Tyre as a ship made of materials from widespread lands and manned by men from a number of Phoenician cities (vss. 3b-9a). A prose section follows (vss. 9b-25a), in which the imagery of the ship is dropped for that of the city with its defenders and its extensive commercial relationships. The poetic dirge is then continued, depicting the sinking of the ship in the heart of the sea, while those on the shore raise lament at its fate (vss. 25b-36). The prose passage is generally recognized as not being a part of the original composition (Cooke, Matthews, Bertholet, Hölscher, *et al.*). In vss. 3a, 25b, and expansions in vs. 27, may perhaps be seen an attempt by the editor to integrate the prose section into the poem. In vs. 3a the description of Tyre as the **merchant of the peoples on many coastlands** anticipates the content of the prose section, and it is the city, not the ship, which dwells **at the entrance to the sea.** Vs. 25b suggests that the ship was filled with the merchandise depicted in the prose section (see also Exeg. on vs. 27).

1. CONSTRUCTION AND MANNING OF THE SHIP (27:1-9a)

27:3b. See 28:2-10, 17; cf. the boasting of Egypt in 29:3; 32:2. With the perfection in beauty here cf. 28:12; 32:19 (cf. also 31:3 and Lam. 2:15). The sin of Tyre lay in its pride (cf. Isa. 47:8-10).

27:1-36. Tyre.—What is most important in this chapter is not what it says, but what it does not say. The prophet's attitude to Tyre is somewhat different from that in ch. 26. Then he

exulted with a certain fierce satisfaction at the fall of the city. Now there is genuine grief in his voice as he intones a lament over its fallen greatness. He pays tribute to it for what it

4 Thy borders *are* in the midst of the seas, thy builders have perfected thy beauty.

5 They have made all thy *ship* boards of fir trees of Senir: they have taken cedars from Lebanon to make masts for thee.

6 *Of* the oaks of Bashan have they made thine oars; the company of the Ashurites have made thy benches *of* ivory, *brought* out of the isles of Chittim.

7 Fine linen with broidered work from Egypt was that which thou spreadest forth to be thy sail; blue and purple from the isles of Elishah was that which covered thee.

4 Your borders are in the heart of the seas;
    your builders made perfect your
    beauty.

5 They made all your planks
    of fir trees from Senir;
  they took a cedar from Lebanon
    to make a mast for you.

6 Of oaks of Bashan
    they made your oars;
  they made your deck of pines
    from the coasts of Cyprus,
    inlaid with ivory.

7 Of fine embroidered linen from Egypt
    was your sail,
    serving as your ensign;
  blue and purple from the coasts of Eli'-
    shah
    was your awning.

4-5. Cf. Ashurbanipal's description of the conquered people who "dwelt in the midst of the sea" (*qabal tam-tim a-šib;* see A. C. Piepkorn, ed., *Historical Prism Inscriptions of Ashurbanipal I* [Chicago: University of Chicago Press, 1933], pp. 30-31; cf. Pritchard, *Ancient Near Eastern Texts,* pp. 296, 297). In Deut. 3:9 **Senir** is given as the Amorite name of Mount Hermon, and Sirion as its Sidonian (i.e., Phoenician) name; cf. Song of S. 4:8, where Senir and Hermon may be different peaks of the same mountain (modern Jebel esh-Sheikh).

6. **Bashan** is in northern Trans-Jordan, east of the Sea of Chinnereth; for the **oaks of Bashan** see also Isa. 2:13; Zech. 11:2. **Your deck:** The word קרש is elsewhere used in Exod. 26:15-16, Num. 3:36, etc., to refer to the boards or frames of the tabernacle. The expression שֶׁן בַּת־אֲשֻׁרִים, "ivory, the daughter of the Ashurim," is confessedly obscure; the RSV vocalizes the latter part *bith'ashshurîm,* **of** [with] **pines,** with Targ. That there was originally some reference to ivory inlaid boards is made probable by our knowledge of "Phoenician" ivory inlay art (see R. D. Barnett, "The Nimrud Ivories and the Art of the Phoenicians," *Iraq,* II [1935], 180-210; J. W. Crowfoot and Grace M. Crowfoot, *Early Ivories from Samaria* [London: Palestine Exploration Fund, 1938]). **Chittim** is probably **Cyprus** (cf. the ancient city of Kition on the south coast of Cyprus); the name may have and certainly came to have a wider geographical association (cf. Dan. 11:30; I Macc. 1:1; 8:5). See also the Jerusalem Habakkuk Scroll, which interprets the Chaldeans in Habakkuk as the Kittim, and one of the Sectarian Scrolls which speaks of the Kittites of Assyria and the Kittites of Egypt, apparently the Seleucids and Ptolemies (W. H. Brownlee, "The Jerusalem Habakkuk Scroll," *Bulletin of the American Schools of Oriental Research,* No. 112 [Dec., 1948], pp. 8-18; H. L. Ginsberg, "The Hebrew University Scrolls from the Sectarian Cache," *ibid.,* pp. 20-21; H. H. Rowley, *The Zadokite Fragments and the Dead Sea Scrolls* [Oxford: Basil Blackwell, 1952], pp. 64-66).

7. **Elishah** (Gen. 10:4) is perhaps also Cyprus, the *Alašiya* of the Tell el-Amarna records (contrast Anton Jirku, "The Problem of Alashiya," *Palestine Exploration*

achieved. Tyre was the outstanding example in the ancient world of the organization of a society for purposes of gain. The Phoenicians were the merchant people of their time, specializing in trade and commerce. It was as if the whole world centered around them; in vss. 12-25 we see the caravans pressing toward Tyre from the interior, while ships put into her harbor with their freight of goods to be exchanged in her mart.

8 The inhabitants of Zidon and Arvad were thy mariners: thy wise *men*, O Tyrus, *that* were in thee, were thy pilots.

9 The ancients of Gebal and the wise *men* thereof were in thee thy calkers: all the ships of the sea with their mariners were in thee to occupy thy merchandise.

10 They of Persia and of Lud and of Phut were in thine army, thy men of war: they hanged the shield and helmet in thee; they set forth thy comeliness.

11 The men of Arvad with thine army *were* upon thy walls round about, and the Gammadim were in thy towers: they hanged their shields upon thy walls round about; they have made thy beauty perfect.

8 The inhabitants of Sidon and Arvad
     were your rowers;
skilled men of Zemer*f* were in you,
     they were your pilots.
9 The elders of Gebal and her skilled men
     were in you,
     caulking your seams;
all the ships of the sea with their mariners
     were in you,
     to barter for your wares.
10 "Persia and Lud and Put were in your army as your men of war; they hung the shield and helmet in you; they gave you splendor. 11 The men of Arvad and Helech*g* were upon your walls round about, and men of Gamad were in your towers; they hung their shields upon your walls round about; they made perfect your beauty.

f Compare Gen 10. 18: Heb *your skilled men, O Tyre*
g Or *and your army*

Quarterly, LXXXII [1950], 40-42, who locates *Alašiya* in northern Syria), although it has received various identifications, including Greece (Hellas) and Carthage (Elissa). The term תכלת, **blue,** means blue-purple (cf. 23:6), and ארגמן, **purple,** is red-purple. The purple suggests luxury and regal splendor (cf. Song of S. 3:10; Esth. 8:15; Dan. 5:7). The purple dye was obtained from a shellfish, the murex, and the Phoenicians were famous for the purple dye industry. From it came the name "Canaan," which means "land of the purple," and "Phoenicia," from the Greek word φοίνιξ (φοινός), meaning "purple" (see B. Maisler, "Canaan and the Canaanites," *Bulletin of the American Schools of Oriental Research,* No. 102 [Apr., 1946], pp. 7-12; see also E. A. Speiser, tr., "One Hundred New Selected Nuzi Texts," *Annual of the American Schools of Oriental Research,* XVI [1935-36], 121-22; C. F. A. Schaeffer, "Une Industrie d'Ugarit—La Pourpre," *Les Annales Archéologiques de Syrie,* I [1951], 188-92).

8-9. From north to south the cities noted here are **Arvad,** modern *Erwâd,* an island about two miles off the mainland; **Zemer,** perhaps Tell Kazel (cf. Gen. 10:18, "the Zemarites," mentioned with the Arvadites); **Gebal,** modern Jebeil (cf. I Kings 5:18), later known as Byblos; **Sidon,** modern Saidā. Zemer, צמר, is more probable here than Tyre, צור, of the M.T., for the context demands a non-Tyrian people.

2. The Mercenary Soldiers Serving Tyre (27:9b-11)

9b-11. Vs. 9b, which is probably prose, introduces the main theme (vss. 12-25a) of the passage in vss. 9b-25a. The reference to **Persia** is in itself no indication of late date for the passage, for Persian contacts with the Near East preceded the time of Ezekiel (see Albright, "The Seal of Eliakim and the Latest Preëxilic History of Judah," pp. 98-99;

But in this whole description there is no reference to any activities except those which subserve the commercial enterprises of the city. She has gained the world, it may be, but has she in the process lost her soul? She has a multitude of possessions, but what she is in herself does not appear to be worth enumerating. Of course she has her religion; what state in the ancient world had not? But her religion has no independent existence over against the gain she seeks; it has no sovereign claim upon her which might compel her to pause and reflect for what end she spends her strength.

We can see in this chapter a picture of what threatens our modern civilization. With our multifarious commercial activities, we are the

12 Tarshish *was* thy merchant by reason of the multitude of all *kind of* riches; with silver, iron, tin, and lead, they traded in thy fairs.

13 Javan, Tubal, and Meshech, they *were* thy merchants: they traded the persons of men and vessels of brass in thy market.

14 They of the house of Togarmah traded in thy fairs with horses and horsemen and mules.

15 The men of Dedan *were* thy merchants; many isles *were* the merchandise of thine hand: they brought thee *for* a present, horns of ivory and ebony.

16 Syria *was* thy merchant by reason of the multitude of the wares of thy making: they occupied in thy fairs with emeralds, purple, and broidered work, and fine linen, and coral, and agate.

12 "Tarshish trafficked with you because of your great wealth of every kind; silver, iron, tin, and lead they exchanged for your wares. 13 Javan, Tubal, and Meshech traded with you; they exchanged the persons of men and vessels of bronze for your merchandise. 14 Beth-togar'mah exchanged for your wares horses, war horses, and mules. 15 The men of Rhodes[h] traded with you; many coastlands were your own special markets, they brought you in payment ivory tusks and ebony. 16 Edom[i] trafficked with you because of your abundant goods; they exchanged for your wares emeralds, purple, embroidered work, fine linen, coral, and

[h] Gk: Heb *Dedan*
[i] Another reading is *Aram*

A. T. Olmstead, *History of the Persian Empire* [Chicago: University of Chicago Press, 1948], pp. 31-32; contrast Torrey). **Lud** (cf. Gen. 10:13) is Lydia in Asia Minor; **Put** (cf. Gen. 10:6) is most probably Cyrene, east of Libya; the LXX reads "Libyans" for "Put" in Jeremiah and Ezekiel (cf. also Josephus); it is usually identified with Punt on the Red Sea (probably Somaliland; see 38:5). **Helech** is perhaps Cilicia (cf. Akkadian *Ḥilakku*); the same consonants may be read **thine army. Gamad** (Hebrew "the Gammadim") is possibly to be located in Syria, identified with the *Kumidi* of the Tell el-Amarna letters. Some suggest reading *Gômerim* (cf. 38:6; Gen. 10:2, 3; cf. also Ugaritic *gmrm* [Howie]).

3. PLACES WITH WHICH TYRE TRADED (27:12-25a)

12-25. The list of cities is in geographical order, beginning on the extreme west and moving east to Greece and Asia Minor, then from south to north from Edom through Palestine to Damascus, and then from Arabia to Mesopotamia. **Tarshish** (vs. 12; cf. Gen. 10:4) is perhaps Tartessos in Spain or is to be located in Sardinia. A ninth-century Phoenician inscription from ancient Nora in Sardinia mentions Tarshish, perhaps the Phoenician name of Nora. The word Tarshish may mean "refinery" or "smelting plant," which helps explain the expression "ships of Tarshish" (see vs. 25), meaning "refinery fleet" (see W. F. Albright, "New Light on the Early History of Phoenician Colonization," *Bulletin of the American Schools of Oriental Research,* No. 83 [Oct., 1941], pp. 17-22). **Javan** (cf. Gen. 10:2, 4) designates to the Greeks the word corresponding to Ionia, but meaning more than the Ionians of Asia Minor. Note the reference to slave trading between the Phoenicians and Greeks in Joel 3:6. **Tubal and Meshech** (vs. 13; cf. 32:26; 38:2-3; 39:1; Gen. 10:2) appear in cuneiform sources as *Tabal* and *Mušku* on the east and west sides respectively of the Anti-Taurus range in Asia Minor; in the Persian period the two peoples are called Moschoi and Tibarenoi by Herodotus and have moved farther north, in the mountains southeast of the Black Sea. **Beth-togarmah** (vs. 14;

heirs of Tyre rather than of Babylon, traders rather than soldiers. But for what is Tyre remembered today? The commerce which brought her wealth and fame was only ephemeral after all: terrible as her fall was for her contempo-

raries, it does not even stir our blood today. And what would happen were our great modern trading cities to perish so? For the time being the disappearance of London or New York would imperil the whole fabric of our civiliza-

17 Judah, and the land of Israel, they *were* thy merchants: they traded in thy market wheat of Minnith, and Pannag, and honey, and oil, and balm.

18 Damascus *was* thy merchant in the multitude of the wares of thy making, for the multitude of all riches; in the wine of Helbon, and white wool.

19 Dan also and Javan going to and fro occupied in thy fairs: bright iron, cassia, and calamus, were in thy market.

20 Dedan *was* thy merchant in precious clothes for chariots.

21 Arabia, and all the princes of Kedar, they occupied with thee in lambs, and rams, and goats: in these *were they* thy merchants.

22 The merchants of Sheba and Raamah, they *were* thy merchants: they occupied in thy fairs with chief of all spices, and with all precious stones, and gold.

23 Haran, and Canneh, and Eden, the merchants of Sheba, Asshur, *and* Chilmad, *were* thy merchants.

agate. 17 Judah and the land of Israel traded with you; they exchanged for your merchandise wheat, olives and early figs,*j* honey, oil, and balm. 18 Damascus trafficked with you for your abundant goods, because of your great wealth of every kind; wine of Helbon, and white wool, 19 and wine*k* from Uzal they exchanged for your wares; wrought iron, cassia, and calamus were bartered for your merchandise. 20 Dedan traded with you in saddlecloths for riding. 21 Arabia and all the princes of Kedar were your favored dealers in lambs, rams, and goats; in these they trafficked with you. 22 The traders of Sheba and Ra'amah traded with you; they exchanged for your wares the best of all kinds of spices, and all precious stones, and gold. 23 Haran, Canneh, Eden,*l* Asshur, and

j Cn: Heb *wheat of minnith and pannag*
k Gk: Heb *Vedan and Javan*
l Cn: Heb *Eden the traders of Sheba*

cf. 38:6; Gen. 10:3) is usually equated with Armenia; it is identified by Delitzsch, Olmstead, and others with Til-garimmu, east of the southernmost Halys River. **Dedan** (vs. 15) is in Arabia, and is mentioned in proper context in vs. 20; **Rhodes** (Rodanim is to be read with a few MSS in Gen. 10:4; see I Chr. 1:7) with the LXX is preferable. **Edom** with about twenty-five MSS, Aq., and the Syriac is preferable to **Aram,** i.e., **Syria.** In vs. 17 the obscure חטי מנית ופנג, **wheat of Minnith** [an Ammonite town; Judg. 11:33], **and Pannag,** should perhaps be read חטים זית ופגג, **wheat, olives and early figs,** one of several suggested readings. Three MSS have ופנג. **Helbon** is modern Halbûn, thirteen miles above Damascus, famed for its wine in antiquity and mentioned in inscriptions of Nebuchadrezzar; Strabo says the kings of Persia drank only the wine of Helbon (see René Dussaud, *Topographie historique de la Syrie antique et médiévale* [Paris: P. Geuthner, 1927], pp. 285-87). The coupling of **Dan also and Javan** (vs. 19) is awkward, and the latter is certainly out of place here; the RSV reconstruction with the LXX is plausible, for יון, Javan, is an easy corruption of יין, **wine. From Uzal** (cf. Gen. 10:27) follows thirteen MSS, the LXX, and Syriac, and represents only a difference in pointing, e.g., *mē'ûzāl* for *me'ûzzāl*, **going to and fro.** Uzal is perhaps Sana, the modern capital of Yemen in southeast Arabia, while **Dedan** (vs. 20; cf. Gen. 10:7) is perhaps el-'Ula, south of Tema. **Kedar** (vs. 21) is said to be descended from Ishmael (Gen. 25:13) and was in northwest Arabia. **Sheba,** whence the famous queen came to Solomon (I Kings 10:1-13), is classified as a brother of Dedan and son of **Raamah** in Gen. 10:7 (cf. Gen. 10:28); both Sheba and Raamah were in southwest Arabia (for these names in Arabia see J. A. Montgomery, *Arabia and the Bible* [Philadelphia: University of Pennsylvania Press, 1934], pp. 30, 39-40, 58, etc.). **Haran** (vs. 23), modern Ḥarrân, in Aram-naharaim (Mesopotamia), the home of Abraham as he was en route to Canaan (Gen. 11:31-32; 12:4-5). **Canneh** is also in Mesopotamia, although its location is unknown. **Eden** (cf. II Kings 19:12; Isa. 37:12) is the Beth-eden of Amos 1:5 and *Bit-adini* of the Assyrian records, a district near Haran. **Asshur,** if it is the city rather than the country, is modern Qal'ât Sherqât,

24 These *were* thy merchants in all sorts *of things,* in blue clothes, and broidered work, and in chests of rich apparel, bound with cords, and made of cedar, among thy merchandise.

25 The ships of Tarshish did sing of thee in thy market: and thou wast replenished, and made very glorious in the midst of the seas.

26 ¶ Thy rowers have brought thee into great waters: the east wind hath broken thee in the midst of the seas.

27 Thy riches, and thy fairs, thy mer-

Chilmad traded with you. 24 These traded with you in choice garments, in clothes of blue and embroidered work, and in carpets of colored stuff, bound with cords and made secure; in these they traded with you.*m*

25 The ships of Tarshish traveled for you with your merchandise.*n*

"So you were filled and heavily laden
    in the heart of the seas.
26 Your rowers have brought you out
    into the high seas.
The east wind has wrecked you
    in the heart of the seas.
27 Your riches, your wares, your merchandise,
    your mariners and your pilots,
    your caulkers, your dealers in merchandise,

m Cn: Heb *in your market*
n Cn: Heb *your travelers your merchandise*

south of Nineveh and Calah on the west side of the Tigris. **Chilmad** is unknown. **The merchants of Sheba** in vs. 23 is out of place geographically, and is probably dittography from vs. 22.

Calamus (vs. 19) or "sweet cane" (cf. Song of S. 4:14; Isa. 43:24; Jer. 6:20) is a sweet-smelling plant used in sacrifice and as a constituent in anointing oil (cf. Exod. 30:23, קנה בשם, "aromatic cane"). **Carpets of colored stuff,** גנזי ברומים (vs. 24), is a more probable reading than the KJV; for גנזי see the Targ. Esth. 1:3, and for ברום see Akkadian *burrumu,* parti-colored, and *bermu,* variegated woven material. **Made secure** is based on an Arabic cognate rather than on the Hebrew word for **cedar. In these they traded with you:** Read בם רכליך for במרכלתך, **among thy merchandise** (cf. vss. 20, 23). **Traveled for you with your merchandise** (vs. 25*a*): Read שרות לך במערבך for שרותיך מערבך; Howie suggests plausibly שכיותיך מערבך, "your ships of merchandise" (*Date and Composition of Ezekiel,* p. 60; cf. Ugaritic *skt* "ship," Egyptian *skt[y]*).

4. SINKING OF THE SHIP (27:25*b*-36)

26. The east wind is often pictured as Yahweh's agent of destruction (cf. 17:10; 19:12; Ps. 48:7; Jer. 18:17; Hos. 13:15; Jonah 4:8; etc.).

27. And all your men of war may be the editor's expansion, referring to vss. 10-11, as also **and your dealers in merchandise** and **with all your company,** referring to vss.

tion, since the economic life of the time is to so large an extent organized around them. But after a while the place they had occupied would be taken by other cities, as they themselves have taken the place of Amsterdam and Hamburg and Venice. Ships would put into other harbors and new currencies would appear on the markets of the world. And then what would be left of us? What lasting contribution would we have made? Would not our greatest contribution perhaps be that, with all our faults, we had preserved and handed on to posterity the work of earlier ages, when men lived for

nobler ends than the mere accumulation of wealth?

    Far-called, our navies melt away;
      On dune and headland sinks the fire;
    Lo, all our pomp of yesterday
      Is one with Nineveh and Tyre!
    Judge of the Nations, spare us yet,
      Lest we forget—lest we forget![2]

[2] Rudyard Kipling, "Recessional," from *The Five Nations.* Copyright 1903, 1931 by Rudyard Kipling, reprinted by permission of Mrs. George Bambridge; Methuen & Co.; The Macmillan Co., Canada; and Doubleday & Co.

chandise, thy mariners, and thy pilots, thy calkers, and the occupiers of thy merchandise, and all thy men of war, that *are* in thee, and in all thy company which *is* in the midst of thee, shall fall into the midst of the seas in the day of thy ruin.

28 The suburbs shall shake at the sound of the cry of thy pilots.

29 And all that handle the oar, the mariners, *and* all the pilots of the sea, shall come down from their ships, they shall stand upon the land;

30 And shall cause their voice to be heard against thee, and shall cry bitterly, and shall cast up dust upon their heads, they shall wallow themselves in the ashes:

31 And they shall make themselves utterly bald for thee, and gird them with sackcloth, and they shall weep for thee with bitterness of heart *and* bitter wailing.

32 And in their wailing they shall take up a lamentation for thee, and lament over thee, *saying,* What *city is* like Tyrus, like the destroyed in the midst of the sea?

33 When thy wares went forth out of the seas, thou filledst many people; thou didst enrich the kings of the earth with the multitude of thy riches and of thy merchandise.

34 In the time *when* thou shalt be broken by the seas in the depths of the waters, thy merchandise and all thy company in the midst of thee shall fall.

35 All the inhabitants of the isles shall be astonished at thee, and their kings shall be sore afraid, they shall be troubled in *their* countenance.

36 The merchants among the people shall hiss at thee; thou shalt be a terror, and never *shalt be* any more.

and all your men of war who are in
you,
with all your company
that is in your midst,
sink into the heart of the seas
on the day of your ruin.
28 At the sound of the cry of your pilots
the countryside shakes,
29 and down from their ships
come all that handle the oar.
The mariners and all the pilots of the sea
stand on the shore
30 and wail aloud over you,
and cry bitterly.
They cast dust on their heads
and wallow in ashes;
31 they make themselves bald for you,
and gird themselves with sackcloth,
and they weep over you in bitterness of
soul,
with bitter mourning.
32 In their wailing they raise a lamentation
for you,
and lament over you:
'Who was ever destroyed[o] like Tyre
in the midst of the sea?
33 When your wares came from the seas,
you satisfied many peoples;
with your abundant wealth and merchandise
you enriched the kings of the earth.
34 Now you are wrecked by the seas,
in the depths of the waters;
your merchandise and all your crew
have sunk with you.
35 All the inhabitants of the coastlands
are appalled at you;
and their kings are horribly afraid,
their faces are convulsed.
36 The merchants among the peoples hiss
at you;
you have come to a dreadful end
and shall be no more for ever.' "

[o] Tg Vg: Heb *like silence*

12-25a. The LXX^A and Syriac omit **who are in you.** It is hopeless to reconstruct the original form of the verse.

28. The word מגרשות, **countryside,** is translated "open space" in 45:2 (RSV), and usually refers to the open land around a town, the "common land" of a city (cf. Lev. 25:34; Num. 35:2; etc.).

32. Destroyed: Read נדמה with the Syriac and Targ. for כדמה, **like silence** (?); cf. **like the destroyed.**

34. Now: Read with versions עתה for עת, **time. You are wrecked** involves only variant pointing with three MSS and versions, i.e., *nishbart* for *nishbéreth*.

28 The word of the Lord came again unto me, saying,

2 Son of man, say unto the prince of Tyrus, Thus saith the Lord God; Because

28 The word of the Lord came to me: 2 "Son of man, say to the prince of Tyre, Thus says the Lord God:

"Because your heart is proud,
  and you have said, 'I am a god,

D. Prophecies Concerning Tyre and Sidon (28:1-26)

There are four main divisions to this chapter. The first is a prophecy against the prince of Tyre, predicting for him the death of a man though he thinks himself a god (vss. 1-10). The second is an allegorical lament over the king of Tyre, depicting him as a perfect being in Eden who has sinned and has been cast out (vss. 11-19). The third is an oracle against Sidon (vss. 20-23), to be classed with the oracles in ch. 25. The chapter concludes with a prophecy of the restoration of the house of Israel and judgment on the neighboring nations (vss. 24-26). It is uncertain how much of this is prose and how much poetry. Vss. 20-26 are prose, although vss. 22-23 are sometimes taken as poetry. Vss. 1-10 are taken as prose by Kraetzschmar, Hölscher, and Cooke, while Rothstein, Matthews, Gordon, and Bertholet take them as poetry. Cooke finds vss. 11-19 "a poem of highly imaginative quality" (see also Kraetzschmar, Hölscher, Bertholet, *et al.*), while others consider it prose in whole or in part. There may have been a poetic original to what now seems considerably prosaic.

The last two sections of the chapter (vss. 20-23, 24-26) come from the editor, and there is fairly general agreement that they are not from Ezekiel. The originality of the dirge in vss. 11-19 is generally conceded (Hölscher, Cooke, Bertholet, Matthews, *et al.;* cf. also Irwin), and the oracle in vss. 1-10 somewhat less generally held to be secondary (Hölscher, Matthews, Irwin; but contrast Bertholet, Cooke).

1. Oracle Against Tyre (28:1-10)

In its present form this oracle seems to belong to the editor, but it may be based on a poem of Ezekiel and may be more than just a scribal interpretation of vss. 11-19 (cf. Hölscher, Matthews). The allusion to the proud heart in vss. 2, 5 is typical of later writings (Prov. 18:12; II Chr. 26:16; 32:25), as also the use of the word "Pit" for Sheol (vs. 8; cf. Isa. 14:15; 38:17; Prov. 28:17; etc., and its use by the editor in Ezekiel). Vs. 10 recalls 31:18; 32:18-32, from the editor (cf. also 44:7-9; Jer. 9:25-26), and the concluding formula is his. Of special note is the allusion to Daniel in vs. 3. The consonants (דנאל) here as in 14:12-23 suggest Danel of the Ugaritic Texts, although in the latter instance the allusion to Danel is less probable, as we have seen (see above, Exeg., *ad loc.*). Here the context is more favorable, since it concerns a Phoenician city, and Ugarit lay to the north of Tyre. In the Ugaritic epic Danel is pictured as one who judges the case of the widow and the fatherless, and the epic centers around his son Aqhat (see Charles Virolleaud, *La légende phénicienne de Danel* [Paris: P. Geuthner, 1936]; Gordon, *Ugaritic Literature,* pp. 84-103). The description of the wisdom of Daniel here and his knowledge of secret things does recall rather the Daniel of the tradition of the book of Daniel (cf. Dan. 1:17-20; 2:48; 4:8-9; etc.). One might of course presume that the tradition of Daniel in the book of Daniel was influenced by similar ideas in the story of the Phoenician Danel as known at the time of Ezekiel, but this is not too probable. More probable, although uncertain, would be a revision of an

---

28:1-10. The State versus God.—In the opening section of this chapter (vss. 1-10), the wealth and power, and with these the pride, of the great Phoenician trading city are represented as incarnated in the person of its **prince.** He is not to be identified with any particular ruler; he stands for what is common to and characteristic of all such monarchs of Tyre; i.e., he is what we mean by the "state." Now since, as we have seen, Tyre is nearer to our modern commercial civilization than the other nations with which these oracles are concerned,

thine heart *is* lifted up, and thou hast said, I *am* a god, I sit *in* the seat of God, in the midst of the seas; yet thou *art* a man, and not God, though thou set thine heart as the heart of God:

3 Behold, thou *art* wiser than Daniel; there is no secret that they can hide from thee:

4 With thy wisdom and with thine understanding thou hast gotten thee riches, and hast gotten gold and silver into thy treasures:

5 By thy great wisdom *and* by thy traffic hast thou increased thy riches, and thine heart is lifted up because of thy riches:

I sit in the seat of the gods,
　　in the heart of the seas,'
yet you are but a man, and no god,
　　though you consider yourself as wise
　　　　as a god —
3 you are indeed wiser than Daniel;
　　no secret is hidden from you;
4 by your wisdom and your understanding
　　you have gotten wealth for yourself,
　and have gathered gold and silver
　　into your treasuries;
5 by your great wisdom in trade
　　you have increased your wealth,
　　and your heart has become proud in
　　　　your wealth —

---

original Ezekielian allusion to Danel here in the light of the Daniel of the Hebrew tradition. Or it may be that vss. 3-4 in their entirety represent the editor's expansion, for vs. 3 seems parenthetical and vs. 4 duplicates the thought of vs. 5. To add to the confusion, we may note that even though the entire passage is late, there might be some allusion to the Phoenician Danel, since there are reflections of Ugaritic mythology in the late literature, of which Isa. 14:12-15 is but one of many possible examples (see Julian Morgenstern, "The Divine Triad in Biblical Mythology," *Journal of Biblical Literature,* LXIV [1945], 29-37).

28:2. Prince is נגיד, not the usual נשיא of the editor. The presumptuous claim to be deity as well as the fate in store recalls Isa. 14:12-15, in the late oracle against the king of Babylon. Similar is Ps. 82, where the "divine" rulers will die as men do (contrast the interpretation of Julian Morgenstern, "The Mythological Background of Psalm 82," *Hebrew Union College Annual,* XIV [1939], 29-126). The ruler of Tyre at this time was Itto-baal (Ithobal of Josephus). **The seat of the gods:** Cf. Isa. 14:13-14 where the seat of El is on the mount of assembly in the recesses of the north, and the throne of

---

we can read this section as a warning addressed to the state as we know it. The prince of Tyre claiming to be God because of his wisdom and the wealth it has brought him—this is surely neither more nor less than the state as we know it today. Does not the state succumb continually to the temptation to arrogate to itself absolute value because of its diplomacy and the world position it has achieved thereby?

The state usurps the place of God whenever it declines to recognize an authority higher than its own. It does this in several ways. First, it may require of its subjects an absolute devotion, so that they are called upon to surrender to it not their lives only, but their consciences also. Is not a claim of this kind implicit in the right which the state asserts to mobilize its citizens for war, so that at its command they must be prepared to violate the sanctity of truth and to take life?

Second, over against other states, each state claims to be judge in its own cause. True, where little is at stake it may agree to a compromise or even submit a dispute to arbitration. But usu-

ally it will insist that where its vital interests are involved—and it alone is judge as to when such a situation arises—its will is the supreme law and must be asserted with armed force against those who would challenge it. The effort to establish an international authority to which all states shall yield submission is continually frustrated by this claim.

Third, the state may be exalted by its subjects to a position of a supreme and unquestioned loyalty. It is not merely that the state confronts us with claims which God alone may make, but that we tend to ascribe to it a value and dignity which belong to him only. For an increasing number of people patriotism is their most effective religion. They may call themselves Christians or Buddhists, but in fact these loyalties do not hold them as does the loyalty to their respective countries. The maxim "My country, right or wrong" is the modern equivalent of the claim, **I am God.** It is important for us to realize that the exaltation of the state to a position of quasi divinity need not be the work of a proud monarch; it may be the false

6 Therefore thus saith the Lord GOD; Because thou hast set thine heart as the heart of God;

7 Behold, therefore I will bring strangers upon thee, the terrible of the nations: and they shall draw their swords against the beauty of thy wisdom, and they shall defile thy brightness.

8 They shall bring thee down to the pit, and thou shalt die the deaths of *them that are* slain in the midst of the seas.

9 Wilt thou yet say before him that slayeth thee, I *am* God? but thou *shalt be* a man, and no God, in the hand of him that slayeth thee.

10 Thou shalt die the deaths of the uncircumcised by the hand of strangers: for I have spoken *it,* saith the Lord GOD.

11 ¶ Moreover the word of the LORD came unto me, saying,

6 therefore thus says the Lord GOD:
"Because you consider yourself
　　as wise as a god,

7 therefore, behold, I will bring strangers
　　upon you,
　　the most terrible of the nations;
　and they shall draw their swords against
　　the beauty of your wisdom
　and defile your splendor.

8 They shall thrust you down into the Pit,
　　and you shall die the death of the slain
　　in the heart of the seas.

9 Will you still say, 'I am a god,'
　　in the presence of those who slay you,
　though you are but a man, and no god,
　　in the hands of those who wound you?

10 You shall die the death of the uncircumcised
　　by the hand of foreigners;
　　for I have spoken, says the Lord GOD."

11 Moreover the word of the LORD came

El in the Ugaritic mythology which was in the "heights of the north" (*ṣrrt ṣpn*), possibly actually identified with Jebel Aqra', north of Ugarit (see Otto Eissfeldt, *Baal Zaphon, Zeus Kasios und der Durchzug der Israeliten durchs Meer* [Halle: Niemeyer, 1932]). The island of Tyre is here pictured as the mountain of the gods.

6. The **heart** was thought to be the seat of intelligence, hence the rendering of the RSV.

7. **The most terrible of the nations** is the Babylonians, as also in 30:10-11; 32:11-12.

8. **The Pit** is Sheol, the land of the dead beneath the ground (cf. 31:14-18; 32:18-32; Isa. 14:15; etc.; see O. R. Sellers, "Israelite Belief in Immortality," *Biblical Archaeologist,* VIII [1945], 1-16; W. G. Williams, "The Conception of Life After Death in the Old Testament," *Iliff Review,* II [1945], 218-23, 258-68).

2. LAMENTATION OVER THE KING OF TYRE (28:11-19)

Forms of the Eden story, other than those preserved in Genesis, are reflected here. **Eden, the garden of God** (vs. 13; cf. 31:8-9, 16) as **the holy mountain of God** (vs. 14) is consonant with the concept of Eden as the abode of the Deity, and so an idealized or cosmic sanctuary or high place with its sacred trees and streams (see 47:1-12). Eden as the source of the rivers in Gen. 2:10-14 may presume the mountain-of-God concept, and

---

religion of a democracy which has lost God and has nowhere else to look for support and allegiance except to the nation.[3]

All this is rank blasphemy, the prophet warns us. That it is also presumptuous folly the facts themselves should teach us. The prince of Tyre has only to cry I am God for his words to be echoed back by a score of other princes, one at least of them far more powerful than he is. In other words, the state clearly is not absolute, since it is limited by the existence of numerous

[3] See on this whole subject Salo Wittmayer Baron, *Modern Nationalism and Religion* (New York: Harper & Bros., 1947).

other states, each of which demands from its subjects unconditional obedience, and each of which claims to be witness, judge, and finally executioner in its own quarrel. In that clash of sovereign states which we call war the hollowness of their arrogance and self-sufficiency is exposed. **I will bring strangers upon thee, the terrible of the nations: and they shall draw their swords against the beauty of thy wisdom, and they shall defile thy brightness.**

11-19. *The Arrogance of Man.*—Here we are transported from earth to paradise, from contemporary history to the origin of things. The sin and fall of a state on the Mediterranean

12 Son of man, take up a lamentation upon the king of Tyrus, and say unto him, Thus saith the Lord God; Thou sealest up the sum, full of wisdom, and perfect in beauty.

13 Thou hast been in Eden the garden of God; every precious stone *was* thy covering, the sardius, topaz, and the diamond, the beryl, the onyx, and the jasper, the sapphire, the emerald, and the carbuncle, and gold: the workmanship of thy tabrets and of thy pipes was prepared in thee in the day that thou wast created.

to me: 12 "Son of man, raise a lamentation over the king of Tyre, and say to him, Thus says the Lord God:

"You were the signet of perfection,[p]
full of wisdom
and perfect in beauty.
13 You were in Eden, the garden of God;
every precious stone was your covering,
carnelian, topaz, and jasper,
chrysolite, beryl, and onyx,
sapphire,[q] carbuncle, and emerald;
and wrought in gold were your settings
and your engravings.[r]
On the day that you were created
they were prepared.

[p] Heb obscure
[q] Or *lapis lazuli*
[r] Heb uncertain

recalls the Ugaritic myth that in the "heights of the north" El dwells "at the sources of the two rivers in the midst of the streams of the two deeps" (*mbk nhrm qrb apq thmtm;* see Gordon, *Ugaritic Handbook,* text 49, 1, ll. 5-6; text 51, IV, ll. 21-22; text 2 Aqht, VI, ll. 47-48; etc.). The figure is that of the first man in Eden. He was created perfect in beauty and wisdom, and dressed in the splendor of precious stones. When guilt was discovered in him, he was driven by the cherub from Eden (cf. Gen. 3:24). It is uncertain how much of the mythological figure is involved in the picture of fire coming forth from him and his reduction to ashes (vs. 18). Ezekiel here seems to have the city in mind. It is thought by some (Hölscher, Matthews) that the entire allegory concerns the city rather than the king, the reference to the king being in the editorial (?) introduction (vs. 12a), but the parallel in Isa. 14 makes the king probably original.

12. Signet: Read *ḥôtham* for *ḥôthēm* with one MS, the LXX, Syriac, Vulg.; cf. the king as signet in Jer. 22:24 (cf. Hag. 2:23). **Perfection** may be got by taking the Hebrew תכנית, "proportion," to mean "perfect proportion" (cf. Irwin, "seal of shapely design"), or by emending to תכלית.

13. With the list of precious stones cf. the twelve stones of the breastplate of the high priest in Exod. 28:17-20; 39:10-13; the LXX reads all twelve stones here, rather than the nine of the Hebrew text. For **sapphire** as **lapis lazuli** see 1:26, etc. **Your settings:** For the word תפיך as "timbrel" or "tambourine" (**tabrets**) see Ps. 81:2; Gen. 31:27; etc., but here and in Jer. 31:4 it may mean some kind of ornament. With נקביך, **your engravings,** cf. Akkadian *naqibu* (?), and Ugaritic *nqbnm,* "trappings" made of gold (*ibid.,* text IV, ll. 6, 11; text 1 Aqht, l. 54). **In thee** may be due to dittography.

coast are the reflection here below of a primal sin and fall in which the spirit of man as such is involved. Created by God in his image and destined for life with him in holiness and righteousness, man has turned from these things in insensate ambition, unwilling to belong to another, even to God, and claiming to be lord of his own life. The sovereignty of the nation is built up out of the self-will of the individuals who compose it. The mythology of this chapter describes a drama which is acted out in the soul of each one of us. Life with its happinesses and privileges is the paradise in which we are

set, but over which we aspire to rule. There is in us that which frets against the acknowledgment of the wisdom and goodness from which we derive. We want to be a law to ourselves, and so we fall from our high estate. Created to be second in the universe, man aspires to be first. But that he can never be.

Bertrand Russell describes the change which came over the European mind with the Renaissance by saying, "Man, formerly too humble, begins to think of himself as almost a God." He speaks of "the intoxication of power which invaded philosophy with Fichte, and to which

14 Thou *art* the anointed cherub that covereth; and I have set thee *so:* thou wast upon the holy mountain of God; thou hast walked up and down in the midst of the stones of fire.

15 Thou *wast* perfect in thy ways from the day that thou wast created, till iniquity was found in thee.

16 By the multitude of thy merchandise they have filled the midst of thee with violence, and thou hast sinned: therefore I will cast thee as profane out of the mountain of God: and I will destroy thee, O covering cherub, from the midst of the stones of fire.

17 Thine heart was lifted up because of thy beauty, thou hast corrupted thy wisdom by reason of thy brightness: I will cast thee to the ground, I will lay thee before kings, that they may behold thee.

18 Thou hast defiled thy sanctuaries by the multitude of thine iniquities, by the iniquity of thy traffic; therefore will I bring forth a fire from the midst of thee, it shall devour thee, and I will bring thee to ashes upon the earth in the sight of all them that behold thee.

19 All they that know thee among the people shall be astonished at thee: thou shalt be a terror, and never *shalt* thou *be* any more.

---

14 With an anointed guardian cherub I placed you;[s]
  you were on the holy mountain of God;
  in the midst of the stones of fire you walked.

15 You were blameless in your ways
  from the day you were created,
  till iniquity was found in you.

16 In the abundance of your trade
  you were filled with violence, and you sinned;
 so I cast you as a profane thing from the mountain of God,
  and the guardian cherub drove you out from the midst of the stones of fire.

17 Your heart was proud because of your beauty;
  you corrupted your wisdom for the sake of your splendor.
I cast you to the ground;
  I exposed you before kings,
  to feast their eyes on you.

18 By the multitude of your iniquities,
  in the unrighteousness of your trade
  you profaned your sanctuaries;
 so I brought forth fire from the midst of you;
  it consumed you,
 and I turned you to ashes upon the earth
  in the sight of all who saw you.

19 All who know you among the peoples
  are appalled at you;
 you have come to a dreadful end
  and shall be no more for ever."

[s] Heb uncertain

---

14. The **anointed guardian cherub** is as difficult to understand as to translate. Read *'eth,* **with,** following the LXX, Syriac for *'at,* **you. The stones of fire** may be "the precious stones," although the Akkadian *aban išâti* may mean "flint," i.e., firestone.

16. And I will destroy thee, O covering cherub follows the M.T., presuming an elided letter, but the same consonants may perhaps be translated, **and the guardian cherub drove you out,** by reading ואבדך as *we'ibbadhkhā* instead of *wā'abbedhkha.*

18. You profaned your sanctuaries is a curious criticism of a pagan king, and the LXXB, "I profaned," is little improvement. Perhaps read "my sanctuary" (cf. 7:24; 24:21; etc. [see xxvii on p. 51]).

---

modern men, whether philosophers or not, are prone." He sees in this "the greatest danger of our time." [4]

The N.T. answer to this pride is in Phil. 2:5-11, where we see the triumph of Christ over the temptation which assailed him as it does us. He accepted his place as that of one who was

in the world by God's will and for God's service, not demanding to take over the government of his life but submitting it to God. So by the hard road of the Cross he came to a place of unequaled honor.

We are too often on the side of the prince of Tyre in this matter. And what is our end? Pride brings about its own destruction. The spirit whose true home was amid the jewels around

[4] *A History of Western Philosophy* (New York: Simon & Schuster, 1945), p. 828.

20 ¶ Again the word of the LORD came unto me, saying,

21 Son of man, set thy face against Zidon, and prophesy against it,

22 And say, Thus saith the Lord GOD; Behold, I *am* against thee, O Zidon; and I will be glorified in the midst of thee: and they shall know that I *am* the LORD, when I shall have executed judgments in her, and shall be sanctified in her.

23 For I will send into her pestilence, and blood into her streets; and the wounded shall be judged in the midst of her by the sword upon her on every side; and they shall know that I *am* the LORD.

24 ¶ And there shall be no more a pricking brier unto the house of Israel, nor *any* grieving thorn of all *that are* round about them, that despised them; and they shall know that I *am* the Lord GOD.

25 Thus saith the Lord GOD; When I shall have gathered the house of Israel from the people among whom they are scattered, and shall be sanctified in them in the sight of the heathen, then shall they dwell in their land that I have given to my servant Jacob.

26 And they shall dwell safely therein, and shall build houses, and plant vineyards; yea, they shall dwell with confidence, when

20 The word of the LORD came to me:
21 "Son of man, set your face toward Sidon, and prophesy against her 22 and say, Thus says the Lord GOD:

"Behold, I am against you, O Sidon,
　　and I will manifest my glory in the
　　　midst of you.
And they shall know that I am the LORD
　　when I execute judgments in her,
　　and manifest my holiness in her;
23 for I will send pestilence into her,
　　and blood into her streets;
and the slain shall fall in the midst of her,
　　by the sword that is against her on
　　　every side.
Then they will know that I am the LORD.

24 "And for the house of Israel there shall be no more a brier to prick or a thorn to hurt them among all their neighbors who have treated them with contempt. Then they will know that I am the Lord GOD.

25 "Thus says the Lord GOD: When I gather the house of Israel from the peoples among whom they are scattered, and manifest my holiness in them in the sight of the nations, then they shall dwell in their own land which I gave to my servant Jacob. 26 And they shall dwell securely in it, and they shall build houses and plant vineyards. They shall dwell securely, when I execute

3. ORACLE AGAINST SIDON (28:20-23)

20-23. This is little more than a composite of the typical phrases of the editor. Note **set your face toward** (vs. 21); **behold, I am against you** (vs. 22); **the slain shall fall in the midst of her** (vs. 23; cf. 6:7), and the concluding formula. The revelation of Yahweh's holiness and glory with the coming new age in vss. 22-23 appears in 20:41; 36:23; 38:16; 39:13 (see Exeg. on 20:1-49).

4. RESTORATION OF THE HOUSE OF ISRAEL (28:24-26)

24. Cf. Num. 33:55; Josh. 23:13.

25-26. This is a typical allusion to the widespread Diaspora. The promise that the house of Israel will **dwell securely** in the land is a recurrent theme (cf. 34:28; 38:11, 14; 39:26); the Holiness Code promises it to those who keep Yahweh's statutes and judgments (Lev. 25:19; cf. also Jer. 23:6; 32:37; 33:16, from the late "Biographer"; see also Zech. 14:11).

the throne of God perishes at last by a fire that goes out from man himself and reduces him to ashes (vs. 18).

20-24. *The Fate of an Accomplice.*—The previous section has been concerned with Tyre, and Sidon might imagine that, as a minor associate of the proud city, she would be spared her fate. But not so. If the great ones of earth may

not escape the judgment of God, the mean ones are not secure against it. The divine righteousness deals with men according to their moral quality and not according to the figure they cut in public.

25-26. *An Unfulfilled Prophecy.*—This is one of the many O.T. prophecies that the exile to Babylon will be the last, that Israel will dwell

I have executed judgments upon all those that despise them round about them; and they shall know that I *am* the LORD their God.

29 In the tenth year, in the tenth *month,* in the twelfth *day* of the month, the word of the LORD came unto me, saying,

judgments upon all their neighbors who have treated them with contempt. Then they will know that I am the LORD their God."

29 In the tenth year, in the tenth month, on the twelfth day of the month, the word of the LORD came to me:

E. ORACLES AGAINST EGYPT (29:1-21)

1. ORACLE AGAINST PHARAOH (29:1-16)

With this chapter begins a series of seven oracles against Egypt (chs. 29–32). The chapter itself contains two of them, the earliest and the latest, according to the dates given. The first (vss. 1-16) is dated January 6, 587, and the second (vss. 17-21) April 16, 570 (April 26, 571). There may be a poem of indeterminate length in the first oracle, possibly not extending beyond vs. 5, and in it we may find Ezekiel's oracle. Pharaoh of Egypt is the mythological sea dragon, here reclining in the branches and canals of the Nile, boasting as though it were a creator-god, but Yahweh will catch it with hooks and cast it and the fish of its streams into the desert to perish. The figure is dropped in vss. 6-9*a*; Yahweh will bring a sword upon Egypt because it has been a staff of reed to Israel, and the Egyptians will know that Yahweh is God. Vss. 9*b*-16 picture the desolation of Egypt and the exile of the Egyptians for forty years, after which the Egyptians will return from exile to become the lowliest of the nations. The editor uses the phraseology of his predictions of the Exile and return of the house of Israel, and the eventual return of the Egyptians may be compared with that in Jer. 46:26 (cf. Jer. 48:47; 49:6, 39); see also the restoration of Sodom and Samaria in Ezek. 16:53 (cf. Isa. 19:16-17; 23:17-18).

The second oracle (vss. 17-21) promises Nebuchadrezzar Egypt as spoil for failure to profit from the siege of Tyre. The oracle is dated after the end of the thirteen-year siege of Tyre in 575-74 (see Exeg. on 26:1-21). To this oracle, the latest from the pen of Ezekiel, the editor has added a note in vs. 21.

Irwin finds an original oracle in vs. 3, and another in vs. 19, while Hölscher thinks Ezekiel's poetic oracle appears only within vss. 3*b*-5*a*. Matthews accredits vss. 1-3*a*, 13-16, 21 to later editors, while Bertholet picks out vss. 9*b*-16, 21 as secondary, and Cooke questions vss. 6*b*-7. According to this analysis, the editor is at work chiefly in vss. 6-16, 21.

a) THE FATE OF THE GREAT DRAGON (29:1-5)

The LXX ascribes this to the twelfth rather than the **tenth** year. Two of the oracles which follow are dated in the eleventh year (30:20; 31:1), one in the twelfth (32:1), and one in the thirty-seventh (29:17). The phraseology **set your face against** in

---

securely in her own land once she has been brought back to it. We have seen that the hopes thus raised have not been fulfilled. Why? Two reasons may be offered. First, all such promises contain an implicit condition, they presuppose that those who return will have learned their lesson and will remain faithful. Second, if security is man's natural desire, he is mistaken in thinking it God's most precious boon. God gives us something better, the power to win and maintain inward serenity even in face of dire insecurity.

29:1-16. Nature and Man.—If there is one country in the world dependent upon nature, it is surely Egypt. The Nile is the creator

of the country, for the rich soil of the delta region, from which the whole productivity of Egypt derives in the last resort, has been deposited by the river. If the melting snows on the Ethiopian mountains do not swell the Nile, Egypt must starve. Yet such is the arrogance of **Pharaoh** (who stands here for the country of which he is the head) that he declares himself the creator of the Nile, thus reversing the relation that in fact obtains between nature and man.

Here is one of the great errors of the modern world. In our urban civilization, with water and light made available by the mere turning of a faucet or switch, we are apt to forget that, at

2 Son of man, set thy face against Pharaoh king of Egypt, and prophesy against him, and against all Egypt:

3 Speak, and say, Thus saith the Lord God; Behold, I *am* against thee, Pharaoh king of Egypt, the great dragon that lieth in the midst of his rivers, which hath said, My river *is* mine own, and I have made *it* for myself.

2 "Son of man, set your face against Pharaoh king of Egypt, and prophesy against him and against all Egypt; 3 speak, and say, Thus says the Lord God:

"Behold, I am against you,
  Pharaoh king of Egypt,
the great dragon that lies
  in the midst of his streams,
that says, 'My Nile is my own;
  I made it.'*t*

t Syr Compare Gk: Heb *I have made myself*

vs. 2 (see iii on p. 50) and **Behold, I am against you** in vs. 3 (see xl on p. 51) discloses the editor.

29:2. Pharaoh king of Egypt was Apries (Pharaoh Hophra) of the Twenty-sixth Dynasty, who reigned 588-569.

3. Despite the statement of Herodotus that crocodiles were caught with hooks (*History* II. 70) and despite the importance of the crocodile in Egyptian fauna and symbolism (it was sacred to Sebek), **the great dragon** (*tannîn*, with many MSS, instead of *tannîm*) is the mythological sea monster, as also in 32:2, where Pharaoh is compared with the *tannîn* in the seas; see also Isa. 27:1, where it is identified with the leviathan, and the description of this dragon as the leviathan in Job 41, also caught with a hook (cf. Ps. 74:13-14). The Hebrews also knew it as Rahab (see Pss. 87:4; 89:10; Job 9:13; 26:12; Isa. 51:9-10). It appears as the leviathan in the Ugaritic mythological texts, the terms *tnn* and *ltn* being used (cf. *ibid.*, text *'nt,* III, 1. 37; text 67, I, 1. 1; etc.; see S. N. Kramer, *Sumerian Mythology* [Philadelphia: American Philosophical Society, 1944], pp. 76-96; Barton, *Archaeology and the Bible,* pp. 279-302; Hermann Gunkel, *Schöpfung und Chaos in Urzeit und Endzeit* [Göttingen: Vandenhoeck & Ruprecht, 1895], pp. 16-114; Pritchard, *Ancient Near Eastern Texts,* pp. 61-68, 137). It was known to the Babylonians as Tiamat, and to the Sumerians as Kur. **His streams:** I.e., the arms of the Nile in the Delta or the Nile canals (cf. Isa. 19:6; Exod. 7:19); see Isa. 44:27 and Ugaritic parallels for the rivers of *tehôm*. Despite vs. 9*b*, Ezekiel may have written here, as in the Hebrew, **I have made myself**, recalling the self-begotten sun-god of Egypt,

however many removes, we are indebted for everything to the bounty of nature. War forces this upon our consciousness as peace does not. A fortress surrenders because its water supply has been cut; in the blackout we learn how dependent we are on the moon, and so on. Marxism is scathing in its analysis of the vices of modern industrialism, but it is itself dominated by the impious spirit for which nature exists only as a storehouse of raw materials to be made up into goods. The Marxist is fully aware of the power which is exercised over man by the forces of production, but he forgets that these forces can do their work only within limits imposed by nature.

Today we imagine that we can denude the countryside of its woods or strip the soil of its life-producing qualities. Our pride is in the machines which we have made. But nature is not our slave; it is she who has made us and not we ourselves. Our increasing remoteness from nature brings into our lives an insecurity and disquiet which were not known in simpler days, while it complicates our economic problems in the attempt to solve them.

Our vast technical civilization is providing more and more powerful means to do things and less opportunity for doing anything we can enjoy—that is to say, anything satisfying for its own sake. In particular it is supplying great sources of pure energy while the civilization it creates is eating up the sources of life in the earth, in local, regional and national growths. If you have its price in your pocket it will soon be easier to get a wireless set than a cabbage, a power-station than a house, or an aeroplane than a shirt.[5]

The dependence of our highly organized societies on the ultimate simplicities of nature is a salutary reminder that equally with the men of Bible times we are in the hands of God.

[5] V. A. Demant, ed., *Our Culture: Its Christian Roots and Present Crisis* (London: Society for Promoting Christian Knowledge, 1947), p. 15.

4 But I will put hooks in thy jaws, and I will cause the fish of thy rivers to stick unto thy scales, and I will bring thee up out of the midst of thy rivers, and all the fish of thy rivers shall stick unto thy scales.

5 And I will leave thee *thrown* into the wilderness, thee and all the fish of thy rivers: thou shalt fall upon the open fields; thou shalt not be brought together, nor gathered: I have given thee for meat to the beasts of the field and to the fowls of the heaven.

6 And all the inhabitants of Egypt shall know that I *am* the LORD, because they have been a staff of reed to the house of Israel.

4 I will put hooks in your jaws,
    and make the fish of your streams stick
      to your scales;
    and I will draw you up out of the midst
      of your streams,
with all the fish of your streams
    which stick to your scales.
5 And I will cast you forth into the wilderness,
    you and all the fish of your streams;
you shall fall upon the open field,
    and not be gathered and buried.
To the beasts of the earth and to the
    birds of the air
    I have given you as food.
6 "Then all the inhabitants of Egypt shall know that I am the LORD. Because you[u] have been a staff of reed to the house

[u] Gk Syr Vg: Heb *they*

with which Pharaoh was thought to be identified. In vs. 9b, the parallelism and the Syriac and LXX are usually taken to support **I made it.**

4. The fish of your streams: Cf. the "helpers of Rahab" in Job 9:13; cf. also Ps. 74:13; Hab. 3:10-15 (see W. A. Irwin, "The Psalm of Habakkuk," *Journal of Near Eastern Studies,* I [1942], 10-40; Albright, "The Psalm of Habakkuk," in H. H. Rowley, ed., *Studies in Old Testament Prophecy* [New York: Charles Scribner's Sons, 1950], pp. 12-18). The allusion may be to the population of Egypt or to its mercenaries and allies.

5. Cf. the fate of the king of Tyre in 28:18. Jeremiah prophesied a similar fate for Jehoiakim (Jer. 22:18-19; 36:30; cf. Ezek. 32:4-5, 8; 39:4-5). Improper burial or lack of burial seems to have involved some unfortunate fate in the lower world. The last sentence may be the editor's expansion. The RSV reads תקבר, **buried,** with a number of MSS and the Targ., in the place of תקבץ, **gathered.**

b) THE SWORD IS TO COME UPON EGYPT (29:6-9*a*)

Egypt's assistance had been of no help to Judah at the time of Hezekiah (see II Kings 18:21=Isa. 36:6), nor later at the time of Zedekiah's revolt (Jer. 37:1-10), although Egypt was probably the prime instigator in both revolts. Vs. 8 is a mosaic of the editor's typical expression (see 5:17; 14:13; etc.), and the entire passage may be his.

6. Because you have been: Read יען היותך, with the LXX, Syriac, and Vulg., for יען היותם, **because they have been.** The representation of Egypt as **a staff of reed** is particularly appropriate in view of the association of reeds with Egypt (cf. Exod. 2:3, 5;

What is the punishment of those who shut their eyes to this side of life? God, we are told, is **against** the **rivers,** i.e., we are surrounded by forces which we cannot control, and they work against us when we defy them. Where the soil has eroded man can no longer live. Let the Nile withdraw her waters and Egypt's greatness shrinks to the dimensions of a tiny state. Land goes out of cultivation, cities lie waste, and the people take refuge in emigration. When better conditions return she can begin over again, but humbled and permanently reduced in status as the result of her folly. That is the fate which

overtakes us when we squander what nature gives, because in our pride we think it ours to dispose of as we will.[6]

6-7. *A Broken Reed.*—There may perhaps be some connection between this oracle and the events recorded in Jer. 37:5-21. If so, the reference to Egypt as a broken reed, an ally raising hopes not destined to be fulfilled, may belong

[6] For the O.T. view of man's relation to nature see Johannes Pedersen, *Israel, Its Life and Culture, I-II* (London: Oxford University Press, 1926), pp. 453-96; for a modern study of soil erosion in Bible lands see Walter Clay Lowdermilk, *Palestine, Land of Promise* (New York: Harper & Bros., 1944).

7 When they took hold of thee by thy hand, thou didst break, and rend all their shoulder: and when they leaned upon thee, thou brakest, and madest all their loins to be at a stand.

8 ¶ Therefore thus saith the Lord God; Behold, I will bring a sword upon thee, and cut off man and beast out of thee.

9 And the land of Egypt shall be desolate and waste; and they shall know that I *am* the Lord: because he hath said, The river *is* mine, and I have made *it*.

10 Behold, therefore I *am* against thee, and against thy rivers, and I will make the land of Egypt utterly waste *and* desolate, from the tower of Syene even unto the border of Ethiopia.

11 No foot of man shall pass through it, nor foot of beast shall pass through it, neither shall it be inhabited forty years.

12 And I will make the land of Egypt desolate in the midst of the countries *that are* desolate, and her cities among the cities *that are* laid waste shall be desolate forty

of Israel; 7 when they grasped you with the hand, you broke, and tore all their shoulders; and when they leaned upon you, you broke, and made all their loins to shake;*v*

8 therefore thus says the Lord God: Behold, I will bring a sword upon you, and will cut off from you man and beast; 9 and the land of Egypt shall be a desolation and a waste. Then they will know that I am the Lord.

"Because you*w* said, 'The Nile is mine, and I made it,' 10 therefore, behold, I am against you, and against your streams, and I will make the land of Egypt an utter waste and desolation, from Migdol to Syene, as far as the border of Ethiopia. 11 No foot of man shall pass through it, and no foot of beast shall pass through it; it shall be uninhabited forty years. 12 And I will make the land of Egypt a desolation in the midst of desolated countries; and her cities shall be a desolation forty years among

v Syr: Heb *stand*
w Gk Syr Vg: Heb *he*

Isa. 19:6). The figure here is similar to that in II Kings 18:21=Isa. 36:6, which the editor may have had before him (cf. Hölscher, Jahn, Herrmann).

7. By thy hand is obviously wrong, and the *Qerê* and many MSS read **with [by] the hand** (cf. LXX, Syriac, "by their hand"). Some read with the LXX and Syriac כף, **hand** for כתף, **shoulder. Shake:** Read המעדת with the Syriac for העמדת, transposing the consonants.

c) Desolation and Restoration (29:9*b*-16)

The lowly position of Egypt in the new age recalls also Isa. 45:14 (cf. Mic. 7:16-17).

9*b*. Because you said: Read יען אמרך for יען אמר, **because he said. I made it:** The Hebrew omits **it** but the word is understood from the context.

10. An utter waste, לחרבות חרב, may be due to dittography; read only לחרבה, "a waste," with the LXX and Syriac (?). **Migdol** (meaning **tower**) is Tell el-Heir, south of Peleusium in the extreme north of Egypt (see 30:6; Jer. 44:1; 46:14), and the same as the Migdol of the Exodus narrative (Exod. 14:2; Num. 33:7). **Syene** is at the extreme southern limit of Egypt at the First Cataract, modern Aswân (see also 30:6). These are the "Dan to Beersheba" measurements of Egypt. South of Syene was **Ethiopia.**

11. See 32:13, 15; cf. 26:20. The forty years recall the years of the punishment of Israel in the wilderness of wandering (Num. 14:33; 32:13; etc.; cf. Ps. 95:10) or the editor's forty years of the punishment of Judah in 4:6.

12. This presupposes the general punishment of the pagan nations. The fate of Judah will fall on **Egypt** (cf. vs. 12*b* with 11:16-17; 12:15; etc.).

---

to the period of disappointment that followed on the withdrawal of the relieving army sent from that country to raise the siege of Jerusalem. Or it may rebuke some earlier and equally vain expectation of speedy Egyptian intervention.

Of course it was not on this occasion only that Egypt induced Judah and other states in her neighborhood to revolt. She was in the habit of promising assistance and then abandoning her allies to their fate. Isaiah already uses the image of the dragon which looks threatening enough

years: and I will scatter the Egyptians among the nations, and will disperse them through the countries.

13 ¶ Yet thus saith the Lord God; At the end of forty years will I gather the Egyptians from the people whither they were scattered:

14 And I will bring again the captivity of Egypt, and will cause them to return *into* the land of Pathros, into the land of their habitation; and they shall be there a base kingdom.

15 It shall be the basest of the kingdoms; neither shall it exalt itself any more above the nations: for I will diminish them, that they shall no more rule over the nations.

16 And it shall be no more the confidence of the house of Israel, which bringeth *their* iniquity to remembrance, when they shall look after them: but they shall know that I *am* the Lord God.

17 ¶ And it came to pass in the seven and twentieth year, in the first *month,* in the first *day* of the month, the word of the Lord came unto me, saying,

18 Son of man, Nebuchadrezzar king of Babylon caused his army to serve a great service against Tyrus: every head *was* made

cities that are laid waste. I will scatter the Egyptians among the nations, and disperse them among the countries.

13 "For thus says the Lord God: At the end of forty years I will gather the Egyptians from the peoples among whom they were scattered; 14 and I will restore the fortunes of Egypt, and bring them back to the land of Pathros, the land of their origin; and there they shall be a lowly kingdom. 15 It shall be the most lowly of the kingdoms, and never again exalt itself above the nations; and I will make them so small that they will never again rule over the nations. 16 And it shall never again be the reliance of the house of Israel, recalling their iniquity, when they turn to them for aid. Then they will know that I am the Lord God."

17 In the twenty-seventh year, in the first month, on the first day of the month, the word of the Lord came to me: 18 "Son of man, Nebuchadrez'zar king of Babylon made his army labor hard against Tyre; every head was made bald and every shoul-

14. Pathros is Upper Egypt (cf. 30:14; Isa. 11:11; Jer. 44:1, 15). This would leave the Delta, Lower Egypt, uninhabited, and so a part of the weakness of the restored nation.

2. Egypt as Nebuchadrezzar's Wages (29:17-21)

Nebuchadrezzar did invade Egypt in the thirty-seventh year of his reign (568-567), but Egypt remained outside the Babylonian empire, although Nebuchadrezzar claimed the overthrow of the armies of Egypt. Amasis (569-525) had become king after a revolt which removed Hophra from the throne. Jeremiah had also predicted that Nebuchadrezzar would destroy Egypt (cf. Jer. 43:8-13; 44:30; 46:1-25). The date is the spring New Year.

18. The allusion may be to an attempt to fill in the sea between the mainland and the island. Cuneiform texts show Nebuchadrezzar installed a Babylonian administration in the city of Tyre. The meaning here is not that he did not capture the city, but that he got no significant spoil, perhaps because goods and men had been evacuated. (See Sydney Smith, "The Ship Tyre," *Palestine Exploration Quarterly* LXXXV [1953], p. 104.)

but can be relied on to do nothing when the time for action arrives (Isa. 30:7 Moffatt). Egypt could not afford to see Palestine and Syria securely in the hands of an alien power; on the other hand, she was not disposed to risk her armies far beyond her frontier. She therefore employed the small Palestinian states to make trouble with their overlord, whether Assyria or Babylon, by promises of help which she had no intention of fulfilling.

The image of the broken reed has passed into common speech. Clearly it has an application also to the individual. Do we ourselves raise false hopes of this kind? A man should be a staff, not a papyrus reed, so that those who lean on him can find support.

17-20. Hope Deferred.—What a vivid picture the prophet draws of labor in vain! We see the thousands of men in Nebuchadrezzar's army toiling to build the causeway which will enable

bald, and every shoulder *was* peeled: yet had he no wages, nor his army, for Tyrus for the service that he had served against it:

19 Therefore thus saith the Lord GOD; Behold, I will give the land of Egypt unto Nebuchadrezzar king of Babylon; and he shall take her multitude, and take her spoil, and take her prey; and it shall be the wages for his army.

20 I have given him the land of Egypt *for* his labor wherewith he served against it, because they wrought for me, saith the Lord GOD.

21 ¶ In that day will I cause the horn of the house of Israel to bud forth, and I will give thee the opening of the mouth in the midst of them; and they shall know that I *am* the LORD.

30 The word of the LORD came again unto me, saying,

2 Son of man, prophesy and say, Thus saith the Lord GOD; Howl ye, Woe worth the day!

der was rubbed bare; yet neither he nor his army got anything from Tyre to pay for the labor that he had performed against it.

19 Therefore thus says the Lord GOD: Behold, I will give the land of Egypt to Nebuchadrez'zar king of Babylon; and he shall carry off its wealth[x] and despoil it and plunder it; and it shall be the wages for his army. **20** I have given him the land of Egypt as his recompense for which he labored, because they worked for me, says the Lord GOD.

21 "On that day I will cause a horn to spring forth to the house of Israel, and I will open your lips among them. Then they will know that I am the LORD."

30 The word of the LORD came to me: **2** "Son of man, prophesy, and say, Thus says the Lord GOD:
"Wail, 'Alas for the day!'

[x] Or *multitude*

---

21. It is uncertain that the **horn** is the Messiah of the line of David; cf. Ps. 132:17, where it is probably not a reference to the messianic king; for the figure see also I Sam. 2:1; Jer. 48:25, which make it possible that there may be here an allusion to the restoration of the life of Israel, not to the Davidic king. It is also uncertain that vs. 21*b* is an allusion to the dumbness of Ezekiel as conceived by the editor (see 3:16; 24:26-27; 33:21, 33); contrast the positions of Cooke and Matthews on this verse, the former doubting the messianic or dumbness reference.

F. COMING DOOM OF EGYPT (30:1-26)

There are two main divisions here: (*a*) a series of four poetic oracles against Egypt in vss. 1-19, and (*b*) a prose oracle in vss. 20-26, predicting that the arms of Pharaoh will be broken. Both of these have been intensively edited, particularly the first which, like the oracles of Zephaniah, has been reinterpreted in terms of the day of Yahweh which

---

them to march out from the mainland and storm the island on which Tyre stands, protected by the sea. They have carried so many burdens on their heads that there is not one among them who is not bald in consequence. Weary of the useless toil, they shift the burden to their shoulders, and these too are so chafed that the skin begins to peel off. And what is there to show for it all at the end of the long siege? Nothing whatever.

We can enter into the experience of this frustrated army, for do we not all know what it is to spend our strength and yet achieve nothing? But there is something else to be borne in mind here. The prophet, or his disciple, has also been disappointed. Did he not in God's name bid the king of Babylon assault

Tyre, assuring him of victory? It is not merely that our efforts are often in vain. The sorer problem is that which arises when what we supposed to be the will of God turns out to have been only a mistaken expectation of our own.

What shall we do at such times? Shall we abandon hope, when hope is thus deferred? No. The prophet bids us trust that the closing of one door will bring with it the opening of another. If not Tyre, then Egypt. So Livingstone prepared to work in China, but could not go there when the time came. He went instead to Africa, and how Africa gained by this frustration of his hopes!

30:1-19. *World History as World Judgment.* —The prophet meets the events of his time

3 For the day *is* near, even the day of the LORD *is* near, a cloudy day; it shall be the time of the heathen.

4 And the sword shall come upon Egypt, and great pain shall be in Ethiopia, when the slain shall fall in Egypt, and they shall take away her multitude, and her foundations shall be broken down.

5 Ethiopia, and Libya, and Lydia, and all the mingled people, and Chub, and the men of the land that is in league, shall fall with them by the sword.

6 Thus saith the LORD; They also that uphold Egypt shall fall; and the pride of her power shall come down: from the tower of Syene shall they fall in it by the sword, saith the Lord GOD.

3 For the day is near,
  the day of the LORD is near;
it will be a day of clouds,
  a time of doom for the nations.

4 A sword shall come upon Egypt,
  and anguish shall be in Ethiopia,
when the slain fall in Egypt,
  and her wealth is carried away,
  and her foundations are torn down.

5 Ethiopia, and Put, and Lud, and all Arabia, and Libya,*y* and the people of the land that is in league, shall fall with them by the sword.

6 "Thus says the LORD:
Those who support Egypt shall fall,
  and her proud might shall come down;
from Migdol to Syene
  they shall fall within her by the sword,
says the Lord GOD.

y Gk Compare Syr Vg: Heb *Cub*

will come upon the pagan nations (see Smith and Lacheman, "Authorship of the Book of Zephaniah," pp. 137-42). Indeed, vss. 1-19 have been considered wholly secondary (see Jahns, Cooke, Hölscher, Bertholet; cf. descriptions of the day of Yahweh in Obadiah and Joel). The late eschatological character of the verses in at least their present form seems obvious. Matthews considers vss. 1-9, 13-19 late, and Irwin finds an uncertain poem within vss. 6, 13 and another in vss. 22, 24.

1. THE DAY OF YAHWEH (30:1-5)

The day will be one of darkness (clouds), involving all the Gentile nations. Cf. the *dies irae* in Zeph. 1:14-18; Joel 1:15; 2:1-2. If anything here is Ezekiel's, it is perhaps to be found in vs. 4*a* (cf. 21:1-32), although the coming sword in vs. 4*a* recalls 14:17; 33:3-4, 6; etc., and the fallen slain suggests 6:7, 13 (cf. vss. 20-22). The list in vs. 5 is reminiscent of 27:10-25*a*; it is considered by some a later prose insertion.

3. The day of the LORD was originally perhaps New Year's Day, a day of promise for Israel but interpreted by Amos as the day of Israel's doom (see Amos 5:18-20; 8:9-10). In postexilic eschatology it became the day of promise for Israel and of judgment upon the Gentiles. **Time:** Time of **doom** or fate (cf. 22:3; 35:5; Jer. 8:12; 27:7; etc.).

4. The same Hebrew word may mean **multitude** or **wealth** (cf. vs. 10).

5. Arabia: Read with Aq., Symm., the Syriac, *hāʿᵃrābh* for *hāʿérebh*, **the mingled people,** which may be a reference to foreign populations, e.g., mercenary soldiers (cf. Jer. 25:20). The context, however, seems to demand a place name. **Chub** occurs only here, and is possibly an error for Lub, i.e., **Libya** (cf. LXX). For הברית, **that is in league** (lit., "the covenant"), some read הכרתי, "the Cherithites" (cf. LXX).

2. EGYPT AND HER HELPERS (30:6-9)

Some scholars omit with the LXX the introductory formula, taking vss. 1-9 as a single oracle. The poetic character of this oracle is not certain; it may be prose. For evidence of the editor cf. vs. 7 with 29:12 and the end of vs. 9 with 7:6-7; note the usual formula in vs. 8*a*, "proud might" in vs. 18 (see xv on p. 50) and **from Migdol to Syene** in vs. 6 (cf. 29:10).

6. From Migdol to Syene: I.e., the whole extent of Egypt (see Exeg. on 29:10).

229

7 And they shall be desolate in the midst of the countries *that are* desolate, and her cities shall be in the midst of the cities *that are* wasted.

8 And they shall know that I *am* the LORD, when I have set a fire in Egypt, and *when* all her helpers shall be destroyed.

9 In that day shall messengers go forth from me in ships to make the careless Ethiopians afraid, and great pain shall come upon them, as in the day of Egypt: for, lo, it cometh.

10 Thus saith the Lord GOD; I will also make the multitude of Egypt to cease by the hand of Nebuchadrezzar king of Babylon.

11 He and his people with him, the terrible of the nations, shall be brought to destroy the land: and they shall draw their swords against Egypt, and fill the land with the slain.

12 And I will make the rivers dry, and sell the land into the hand of the wicked: and I will make the land waste, and all that is therein, by the hand of strangers: I the LORD have spoken *it*.

13 Thus saith the Lord GOD; I will also destroy the idols, and I will cause *their*

---

7 And she[z] shall be desolated in the midst of desolated countries
and her cities shall be in the midst of cities that are laid waste.

8 Then they will know that I am the LORD,
when I have set fire to Egypt,
and all her helpers are broken.

9 "On that day swift[a] messengers shall go forth from me to terrify the unsuspecting Ethiopians; and anguish shall come upon them on the day of Egypt's doom; for, lo, it comes!

10 "Thus says the Lord GOD:
I will put an end to the wealth[b] of Egypt,
by the hand of Nebuchadrez'zar king of Babylon.

11 He and his people with him, the most terrible of the nations,
shall be brought in to destroy the land;
and they shall draw their swords against Egypt,
and fill the land with the slain.

12 And I will dry up the Nile,
and will sell the land into the hand of evil men;
I will bring desolation upon the land and everything in it,
by the hand of foreigners;
I, the LORD, have spoken.

13 "Thus says the Lord GOD:
I will destroy the idols,
and put an end to the images, in Memphis;

[z] Gk: Heb *they*
[a] Gk Syr: Heb *in ships*
[b] Or *multitude*

---

9. The change from the M.T. בצים, **in ships,** to אצים, **swift,** with the LXX and Syriac, is unnecessary, although made by many scholars.

3. NEBUCHADREZZAR WILL DESTROY EGYPT (30:10-12)

An original oracle may lie behind this. With the description of the Babylonians here cf. 28:7; 31:12; 32:12, and with the picture of the land filled with slain (vs. 11) cf. 9:7; 11:6; 35:8.

12. The Nile: I.e., the arms or canals of the Nile (cf. Isa. 7:18; 19:6; etc.) **The hand of the wicked:** The Babylonians (cf. Hab. 1:12-13). Some omit the second line with the LXX.

4. YAHWEH WILL DESTROY EGYPT (30:13-19)

Memphis (Noph) is modern Mit Rahneh; **Zoan** is Ṣân el-Ḥagar; **Thebes (No)** is Karnak, Luxor; **Pelusium (Sin)** is Tell Faramâ; **On (Aven)** or Heliopolis is Tell Ḥuṣn; **Pi-beseth** is Tell Basṭa; Daphne (**Tehaphnehes,** elsewhere Tahpanhes and Tahapanes) is Tell Defenneh; and **Pathros** is Upper Egypt. **On** is pointed to be read **Aven,** meaning

images to cease out of Noph; and there shall be no more a prince of the land of Egypt: and I will put a fear in the land of Egypt.

14 And I will make Pathros desolate, and will set fire in Zoan, and will execute judgments in No.

15 And I will pour my fury upon Sin, the strength of Egypt; and I will cut off the multitude of No.

16 And I will set fire in Egypt: Sin shall have great pain, and No shall be rent asunder, and Noph *shall have* distresses daily.

17 The young men of Aven and of Pi-beseth shall fall by the sword: and these *cities* shall go into captivity.

18 At Tehaphnehes also the day shall be darkened, when I shall break there the yokes of Egypt: and the pomp of her strength shall cease in her: as for her, a cloud shall cover her, and her daughters shall go into captivity.

there shall no longer be a prince in the land of Egypt;
so I will put fear in the land of Egypt.

14 I will make Pathros a desolation,
and will set fire to Zo'an,
and will execute acts of judgment upon Thebes.

15 And I will pour my wrath upon Pelusium,
the stronghold of Egypt,
and cut off the multitude of Thebes.

16 And I will set fire to Egypt;
Pelusium shall be in great agony;
Thebes shall be breached,
and its walls broken down.*c*

17 The young man of On and Pibe'seth shall fall by the sword;
and the women shall go into captivity.

18 At Tehaph'nehes the day shall be dark,
when I break there the dominion of Egypt,
and her proud might shall come to an end;
she shall be covered by a cloud,
and her daughters shall go into captivity.

c Cn: Heb *and Memphis distresses by day*

"wickedness," "iniquity"; in Jer. 43:13 it appears as Beth-shemesh, "House of the Sun"; here Re-Harakhti the sun-god was worshiped, and here Potiphera the father-in-law of Joseph was priest (cf. Gen. 41:45, 50; 46:20). **Pi-beseth,** called in Greek Bubastis, had as its chief deity Bast, a cat-headed goddess. Memphis was the chief city of Lower Egypt and often the capital of all Egypt; its tutelary god was Ptah, and here the famed Apis bull was worshiped. Thebes in Upper Egypt was the center of the cult of the sun-god Amon and the capital of Egypt in the new kingdom and in the Twenty-fifth Dynasty.

It is dubious that vss. 15-19 are poetry. Note the editor's **idols** and **prince** in vss. 13, and **execute acts of judgment** in vss. 14, 19 (cf. 5:10; 11:9; 25:11; 28:22, 26; cf. **her proud might** in vs. 18 [see xiv on p. 50]) .

16. And its walls broken down: Read ונפרצו חומתיה for ונף צרי יומם, "and Memphis adversaries of daytime," or as KJV. Some change seems necessary.

18. Dominion is an interpretation of the more literal "bars of the yoke" (cf. **yokes**). It is used as a symbol of domination or oppression in Jer. 27:2; 28:10-11; Isa. 58:6, 9; Lev. 26:13. Some critics read מטות not *mōṭôth* but *maṭṭôth*, "rods" (scepters?) with the LXX and Vulg. (cf. Syriac) .

with the faith that God is working out his purpose in them. Can we do the same? The only alternative is some such view as that propounded by H. A. L. Fisher,[7] who finds in history contingency and accident rather than design and purpose. It is true that few of us are able to discern just how God is at work. For that a measure of prophetic insight is needed.

We are aware often that something of tremendous import is afoot, but how and where the nations are being weighed in the balances of divine justice we do not know. Even the prophet may make mistakes, as we see from Ezekiel's confessed misreading of the divine will in the siege of Tyre (29:17-20). But that there is a moral order we may be sure, so that when a great nation perishes and drags others with it to

[7] *History of Europe,* p. v.

19 Thus will I execute judgments in Egypt: and they shall know that I *am* the LORD.

20 ¶ And it came to pass in the eleventh year, in the first *month,* in the seventh *day* of the month, *that* the word of the LORD came unto me, saying,

21 Son of man, I have broken the arm of Pharaoh king of Egypt; and, lo, it shall not be bound up to be healed, to put a roller to bind it, to make it strong to hold the sword.

22 Therefore thus saith the Lord GOD; Behold, I *am* against Pharaoh king of Egypt, and will break his arms, the strong, and that which was broken; and I will cause the sword to fall out of his hand.

23 And I will scatter the Egyptians among the nations, and will disperse them through the countries.

24 And I will strengthen the arms of the king of Babylon, and put my sword in his hand: but I will break Pharaoh's arms, and he shall groan before him with the groanings of a deadly wounded *man.*

25 But I will strengthen the arms of the king of Babylon, and the arms of Pharaoh

19 Thus I will execute acts of judgment upon Egypt.
Then they will know that I am the LORD."

20 In the eleventh year, in the first month, on the seventh day of the month, the word of the LORD came to me: 21 "Son of man, I have broken the arm of Pharaoh king of Egypt; and lo, it has not been bound up, to heal it by binding it with a bandage, so that it may become strong to wield the sword. 22 Therefore thus says the Lord GOD: Behold, I am against Pharaoh king of Egypt, and will break his arms, both the strong arm and the one that was broken; and I will make the sword fall from his hand. 23 I will scatter the Egyptians among the nations, and disperse them throughout the lands. 24 And I will strengthen the arms of the king of Babylon, and put my sword in his hand: but I will break the arms of Pharaoh, and he will groan before him like a man mortally wounded. 25 I will

---

5. THE ARMS OF PHARAOH WILL BE BROKEN (30:20-26)

20-26. The arm of Pharaoh has once been broken, but both arms are now to be broken as Yahweh strengthens those of Nebuchadrezzar. The historical allusion of the former is to the recent defeat of Pharaoh Hophra near the beginning of the siege of Jerusalem in 588 (see Jer. 37:1-10). The oracle is dated April 19, 586 (April 29, 587). We may assume here an original oracle which has been much elaborated by the editor; cf. the "sword" in ch. 21, and note the editor's phraseology, particularly in vss. 23, 25-26. For the exile of Egypt (vss. 23, 26; cf. vss. 17-18), see also 29:8-16. The repetitiousness has suggested parallel recensions of a single oracle (cf. Kraetzschmar, Herrmann, Matthews), while Hölscher discerns the original poetic oracle in vs. 21. Bertholet finds a threefold repetition of the thought of the broken arm, a triple draft of the same utterance, e.g., vs. 21 and vss. 22, 25*a*, 26 and vss. 24, 23, 25*b*. The editor's elaboration and adaptation is perhaps the cause of the present state of the text.

---

their doom, those who look on should learn the lessons of righteous judgment that will not be denied.

20-26. *Ordeal by Battle.*—The Egyptian army has marched to relieve Jerusalem and the siege has been raised for the time being. But news has just reached the capital that the Egyptians have been defeated and that the reinvestment of Jerusalem may be expected at any time. Ezekiel does not taunt his countrymen with the failure of their hopes, but he assures them that what has happened so far is but the beginning, and still worse things are to come. Egypt is like a

man wounded in one **arm** and forced to drop his **sword.** Not only will there be no healing for this wound, but the other arm will soon be shattered and the warrior left helpless before his enemy. There is a sword of the Lord, and the time has come for it to be transferred definitively from Egypt to Babylon.

In what sense is battle an ordeal by which the will of God is made known? Not, to be sure, in the sense that success in war is evidence of the justice of a nation's cause. There is no reason to suppose that Babylon was morally superior to Egypt at this time. Still, we may not

shall fall down; and they shall know that I *am* the LORD, when I shall put my sword into the hand of the king of Babylon, and he shall stretch it out upon the land of Egypt.

26 And I will scatter the Egyptians among the nations, and disperse them among the countries; and they shall know that I *am* the LORD.

31 And it came to pass in the eleventh year, in the third *month,* in the first *day* of the month, *that* the word of the LORD came unto me, saying,

strengthen the arms of the king of Babylon, but the arms of Pharaoh shall fall; and they shall know that I am the LORD. When I put my sword into the hand of the king of Babylon, he shall stretch it out against the land of Egypt; 26 and I will scatter the Egyptians among the nations and disperse them throughout the countries. Then they will know that I am the LORD.''

31 In the eleventh year, in the third month, on the first day of the month,

---

G. DOWNFALL OF THE GREAT CEDAR (31:1-18)

The first part of this chapter (vss. 1-9) is Ezekiel's poem depicting Pharaoh and his multitude as a great tree of life or world tree, towering to the clouds and watered by the great deep. All the birds of the heavens rested in it, and beneath its branches all the wild animals brought forth their young, while in its shade lived all the great nations. It was envied by the trees of Eden, the garden of God. The second part (vss. 10-18) depicts in prose the coming fall of the tree, hewn down by the Babylonians, and its descent to Sheol. It is composed of two oracles, vss. 10-14 and vss. 15-18. The editor is perhaps responsible for vss. 14-18, in which the descent to Sheol is pictured. It is uncertain whether the poem originally contained the description of the fall of the tree; the present prose in vss. 10-13 may be due to the editor's handling of Ezekiel's materials. Of course Ezekiel may have depicted the descent of the tree to Sheol, but it must be acknowledged that the latter part of the chapter, vss. 14-18, seems peculiarly characteristic of the editor (see Exeg. on 32:17-32). Scholars are reminded of the descent of the king of Babylon to Sheol in Isa. 14:1-32; see the descent of Tyre in Ezek. 26:19-21. The world tree motif also appears in Isa. 14:8, along with a comparable picture of the reaction of those in Sheol (vss. 9-10). The imagery here in Ezekiel has strongly influenced Dan. 4:1-37 (see also Ezek. 17:22-24; cf. Ps. 104:16-17; Ezek. 19:10-11). A number of scholars find the original poem within the first eight or nine verses, reckoning the rest to be secondary; cf. Irwin (who thinks the poem perhaps originally referred to Babylonia), Bertholet, Hölscher. Hölscher identifies the most terrible of the nations (vs. 12) with the Persians, and finds an allusion to the Persian conquest of Egypt. Matthews finds three poems (vss. 1-9, 10-14, 15-18) all from Ezekiel, although the last is of different date and possibly to be questioned.

1. EGYPT AS THE GREAT CEDAR (31:1-9)

The terminology suggests that the symbolism has its origin in mythology (for the sacred cedar see Henri Frankfort, *Cylinder Seals* [London: Macmillan & Co., 1939], pp. 205-7; see also A. J. Wensinck, *Tree and Bird as Cosmological Symbols in Western Asia* [Amsterdam: Johannes Müller, 1921], pp. 25-35; Evans, *Palace of Minos,* III, 146-48). It is no normal tree which is described here, for the symbolism is obviously

---

suppose that there is no divine overruling of war, no moral purpose to which victory and defeat alike are made subservient in the end. There is a decision of God that power is to pass from one people to another, not because it is worthier but because a new task requires a new instrument. God uses men's ambition and cruelty just because over a large area of history

these are almost the only materials they give him to work with. But what he does with them represents something much less than his will for mankind. It is his second best. For his best we must turn from the sword to the Cross.

31:1-14. The Roots of National Life.—This section furnishes yet another illustration of man's dependence on nature. But it will be

2 Son of man, speak unto Pharaoh king of Egypt, and to his multitude; Whom art thou like in thy greatness?

3 ¶ Behold, the Assyrian *was* a cedar in Lebanon with fair branches, and with a shadowing shroud, and of a high stature; and his top was among the thick boughs.

4 The waters made him great, the deep set him up on high with her rivers running round about his plants, and sent out her little rivers unto all the trees of the field.

5 Therefore his height was exalted above all the trees of the field, and his boughs were multiplied, and his branches became long because of the multitude of waters, when he shot forth.

---

the word of the LORD came to me: 2 "Son of man, say to Pharaoh king of Egypt and to his multitude:

"Whom are you like in your greatness?
3   Behold, I will liken you to[d] a cedar in Lebanon,
with fair branches and forest shade,
     and of great height,
     its top among the clouds.[e]
4 The waters nourished it,
     the deep made it grow tall,
making its rivers flow[f]
     round the place of its planting,
sending forth its streams
     to all the trees of the forest.
5 So it towered high
     above all the trees of the forest;
its boughs grew large
     and its branches long,
     from abundant water in its shoots.

[d] Cn: Heb *Behold, Assyria*
[e] Gk: Heb *thick boughs*
[f] Gk: Heb *going*

---

cosmic. The typical Assyrian sacred tree was a cedar, and one is reminded of the two cedar trees or trunks bound with copper bands which stood on either side of the temple entrance at Sargon's capital and which, like the Jachin and Boaz pillars, doubtless had a cosmic significance (see Frankfort, *loc. cit.;* also Hugo Gressmann, *Der Messias* [Göttingen: Vandenhoeck & Ruprecht, 1929], pp. 266-67).

31:3. The expression אשור ארז, **the Assyrian was a cedar,** is due to a scribal error, and we should perhaps read אשוך לארז, **I will liken you to a cedar.** Some emend to תאשור, "a pine" (cf. Isa. 41:19; 60:13; see Ezek. 27:6), taking **cedar of Lebanon** as an explanatory gloss. The cedars of Lebanon were famous through the Near East (see 17:3; 27:5; Judg. 9:15; II Kings 19:23; Ps. 104:16; Isa. 2:13; 14:8; etc.). **And forest shade** is quite conjectural; it is best omitted with the LXX[B]. **Among the clouds:** Read עבות for עבתים (cf. LXX).

4. For the rivers of the deep (*tehôm*) see 29:3. **Making . . . flow:** Read הוליכה with the LXX for הלך.

5. The words גבהא, **towered high** (although several MSS have גבהה), and סרעפתיו, **its boughs,** are Aramaisms, but Aramaisms are understandable as early as Ezekiel; see a papyrus letter in Aramaic written to the pharaoh of Egypt contemporary with Ezekiel, perhaps from Ashkelon (H. L. Ginsberg, "An Aramaic Contemporary of the Lachish Letters," *Bulletin of the American Schools of Oriental Research,* No. 111 [Oct., 1948], pp. 24-27). The word בשלחו, **when he shot forth,** is better repointed as *bīshelāḥāw,*

---

better to see what can be learned from the new figure which it employs, that of the **cedar in Lebanon.** However imposing and however high it may grow, its life is dependent from moment to moment on the nourishment which it draws from the soil. The life of a tree is not in its branches but in its roots. The cedar here described is situated in a place where conditions are peculiarly favorable to its growth. Its error is that it takes pride in its spreading

boughs and forgets the roots from which its maintenance is drawn.

What are the roots of national life today? We can enumerate three:

(a) *Personal integrity.* A nation is like some vast commercial enterprise which can operate only because several million quite ordinary folk have invested their savings in it. When one such person draws out his share, the effect is not noticeable; but as the process continues the

6 All the fowls of heaven made their nests in his boughs, and under his branches did all the beasts of the field bring forth their young, and under his shadow dwelt all great nations.

7 Thus was he fair in his greatness, in the length of his branches: for his root was by great waters.

8 The cedars in the garden of God could not hide him: the fir trees were not like his boughs, and the chestnut trees were not like his branches; not any tree in the garden of God was like unto him in his beauty.

9 I have made him fair by the multitude of his branches; so that all the trees of Eden, that *were* in the garden of God, envied him.

10 ¶ Therefore thus saith the Lord God; Because thou hast lifted up thyself in height, and he hath shot up his top among the thick boughs, and his heart is lifted up in his height;

6 All the birds of the air
　　made their nests in its boughs;
under its branches all the beasts of the field
　　brought forth their young;
and under its shadow
　　dwelt all great nations.
7 It was beautiful in its greatness,
　　in the length of its branches;
for its roots went down
　　to abundant waters.
8 The cedars in the garden of God could
　　not rival it,
　　nor the fir trees equal its boughs;
the plane trees were as nothing
　　compared with its branches;
no tree in the garden of God
　　was like it in beauty.
9 I made it beautiful
　　in the mass of its branches,
and all the trees of Eden envied it,
　　that were in the garden of God.
10 "Therefore thus says the Lord God: Because it[g] towered high and set its top among the clouds,[h] and its heart was proud

g Syr Vg: Heb *you*
h Gk: Heb *thick boughs*

in its shoots. **Abundant water** is מים רבים, "many waters," e.g., the waters of *tehôm* (see Exeg. on 1:24; 19:10; see also vs. 7 below).

6. This is a picture of the prosperity of Egypt. See Georg Steindorf and Keith C. Seele, *When Egypt Ruled the East* (Chicago: University of Chicago Press, 1947).

8-9. These verses suggest variant details of the Garden of Eden myth (see 28:11-19). The first person, Yahweh speaking, in vs. 9a is unexpected, and **I made it beautiful** is omitted by some with the LXX.

2. Its Fall and Descent to Sheol (31:10-18)

The pride of Egypt, apart from any other sin, would have been sufficient reason for her downfall (cf. vss. 10-11; see 28:1-5; 29:3; 32:2; Dan. 4:30). There are two oracles here, each with its introductory formula: vss. 10-14, 15-18. We may suspect that Ezekiel's prophecy of the judgment on Egypt lies largely behind the former, with the latter more purely the work of the editor. The RSV correctly takes the verbs in vss. 11-12, 15-17 as prophetic perfects, translating as futures; Matthews reads them as perfects, and thinks that the fall of Egypt has already taken place.

10. **It** (with Syriac, Vulg.) is required for the English reader although **thou** is probably original (see vss. 2b-3). **Clouds:** As in vs. 3 (see Exeg.).

result is that one day the business has to go into liquidation. So a nation cannot continue indefinitely unless it can draw upon a store of honesty, truthfulness, and public spirit which is renewed from generation to generation.

(*b*) *Family life.* A modern nation with its high degree of organization and its economic planning simply cannot maintain stability if it allows the impulses of its people to run riot in the sphere of sexual relations. Only a sound family life, in which it is possible to learn the great lesson of obedience and self-discipline on the one hand and the unselfish exercise of authority on the other hand, can provide an

11 I have therefore delivered him into the hand of the mighty one of the heathen; he shall surely deal with him: I have driven him out for his wickedness.

12 And strangers, the terrible of the nations, have cut him off, and have left him: upon the mountains and in all the valleys his branches are fallen, and his boughs are broken by all the rivers of the land; and all the people of the earth are gone down from his shadow, and have left him.

13 Upon his ruin shall all the fowls of the heaven remain, and all the beasts of the field shall be upon his branches:

14 To the end that none of all the trees by the waters exalt themselves for their height, neither shoot up their top among the thick boughs, neither their trees stand up in their height, all that drink water: for they are all delivered unto death, to the nether parts of the earth, in the midst of the children of men, with them that go down to the pit.

15 Thus saith the Lord God; In the day when he went down to the grave I caused a mourning: I covered the deep for him,

of its height, 11 I will give it into the hand of a mighty one of the nations; he shall surely deal with it as its wickedness deserves. I have cast it out. 12 Foreigners, the most terrible of the nations, will cut it down and leave it. On the mountains and in all the valleys its branches will fall, and its boughs will lie broken in all the watercourses of the land; and all the peoples of the earth will go from its shadow and leave it. 13 Upon its ruin will dwell all the birds of the air, and upon its branches will be all the beasts of the field. 14 All this is in order that no trees by the waters may grow to lofty height or set their tops among the clouds,[h] and that no trees that drink water may reach up to them in height; for they are all given over to death, to the nether world among mortal men, with those who go down to the Pit.

15 "Thus says the Lord God: When it

[h] Gk: Heb *thick boughs*

11. The **heathen** chief is Nebuchadrezzar. The latter part of the verse is apparently corrupt. With a number of MSS we might read "because of its wickedness," which could be taken either with the preceding or the following. To "drive out" the tree hardly fits the following context, but suggests expulsion from Eden.

12. **The most terrible of the nations:** As 28:7; 30:11; 32:11-12. Cf. the fate of the dragon in 29:5; 32:4-5. The catastrophe is in proportion to the size of the tree, as the **branches** lie broken in all the valleys and on the mountains.

14. The downfall of Egypt is to serve as a warning to other nations. Vs. 14b seems to be a *non sequitur,* for how can the trees grow at all if they are dead? It is here that the editor begins his theme of the underworld. Vs. 14a may also be his, reflecting the theme of the nations restricted in power in the new age (see Exeg. on 29:9b-16). **Clouds:** See Exeg. on vs. 3. For the final phrase, **with those who go down to the Pit,** see 26:20; 28:8; 32:18, 24, 25, 29, 30.

15. The world of nature will mourn at the downfall of Egypt. **I covered** is obviously a gloss; omit with the LXX. **Clothe . . . in gloom:** Lit., "darken," but the verb is used of

adequate basis for national life. On this whole subject Lenin gave some very sound advice,[8] and the Russian Communists, after some preliminary experimentation, found it necessary to follow him.

(c) *Reverence for the rule of God.* Without a sense of the limitations which attend upon all human life, as in the case of so many em-

pires in the past, a nation becomes arrogant, harsh in its treatment of others, and unrestrained in its ambitions, so that in the end it brings about its own ruin. The possession of power needs to be curbed continually by the consciousness that one is accountable to the divine tribunal for the use to which one puts that power.

15-18. *The Inevitable Hour.*—The descent of a nation to the grave is something more than

[8] Klara Zetkin, *Reminiscences of Lenin* (New York: International Publishers, 1934), pp. 41-64.

and I restrained the floods thereof, and the great waters were stayed: and I caused Lebanon to mourn for him, and all the trees of the field fainted for him.

16 I made the nations to shake at the sound of his fall, when I cast him down to hell with them that descend into the pit: and all the trees of Eden, the choice and best of Lebanon, all that drink water, shall be comforted in the nether parts of the earth.

17 They also went down into hell with him, unto *them that be* slain with the sword; and *they that were* his arm, *that* dwelt under his shadow in the midst of the heathen.

18 ¶ To whom art thou thus like in glory and in greatness among the trees of Eden? yet shalt thou be brought down with the trees of Eden unto the nether parts of the

goes down to Sheol I will make the deep mourn for[i] it, and restrain its rivers, and many waters shall be stopped; I will clothe Lebanon in gloom for it, and all the trees of the field shall faint because of it. 16 I will make the nations quake at the sound of its fall, when I cast it down to Sheol with those who go down to the Pit; and all the trees of Eden, the choice and best of Lebanon, all that drink water, will be comforted in the nether world. 17 They also shall go down to Sheol with it, to those who are slain by the sword; yea, those who dwelt under its shadow among the nations shall perish.[j] 18 Whom are you thus like in glory and in greatness among the trees of Eden? You shall be brought down with the trees of Eden to the nether world; you shall lie

[i] Gk: Heb *mourn for, I have covered*
[j] Compare Gk: Heb obscure

mourning (cf. Jer. 8:21; Job 5:11; etc.). **Sheol,** the name of the underworld, is a word of uncertain meaning, the most probable but still dubious meaning being "place of inquiry," e.g., of divination by means of consulting the dead (necromancy). All the dead, king and servant alike, were there (cf. Job 3:17-19).

16. Comforted in the nether world: Perhaps as in Isa. 14:9-11. **The choice and best of Lebanon** seems awkward in the Hebrew, but may be due to the influence of Isa. 14:8 (cf. also Ezek. 31:8-9). This reflects some myth of the descent of the trees of Eden to Sheol after the fall of man. Cf. the tradition in Enoch 25:4-6 that the tree of life was transplanted from Eden to a high mountain of God in the northwest to be moved later to the temple for the righteous.

17. The general downfall of the nations. Note the editor's phraseology here and in vs. 18 (cf. 32:20-32). The last half of the verse is obscure; lit., "and his arm they dwelt in his shadow among nations." The RSV apparently reads וגועו ישבי, **those who dwelt . . . shall perish,** for זרעו ישבו, "his arm they dwelt" (cf. LXX).

18. In greatness: Read בכה for ככה, **thus. Among the uncircumcised:** The unclean pagans (cf. 28:10; 32:21; etc.).

a bold flight of the poetic imagination. The work of the archaeologist is the best evidence that nations do thus perish, buried with all their civilization under some other nation which, with its civilization, takes their place. The death of nations in the past is a constant warning to those which are alive in the present.

A preacher sometimes asks an individual if he has taken into his reckoning the inescapable fact of death. When we pass the barrier which separates the next life from this, all that we take with us will have to be shown for examination. We shall have to leave behind all that we possess. Only what we actually are can be taken into the beyond. Therefore we should

begin now to prize character and to set our hearts not on what is temporal, but on what is eternal.

But who has dared to ask his nation to face the fact that it too will die? If this possibility confronts it, should not the nation too set its house in order while there is still time? When we have passed into history as a people, what will remain of us to posterity? Will it be said of us that we bequeathed to those who came after us a high sense of duty, respect for human personality, and an ideal of justice tempered with magnanimity? When the world mourns for our passing, for what exactly will it sorrow? For the loss of so imposing a spectacle as that which our power provided? Or because our

earth: thou shalt lie in the midst of the uncircumcised with *them that be* slain by the
sword. This *is* Pharaoh and all his multitude, saith the Lord GOD.

32 And it came to pass in the twelfth
year, in the twelfth month, in the first
day of the month, *that* the word of the LORD
came unto me, saying,

2 Son of man, take up a lamentation for
Pharaoh king of Egypt, and say unto him,
Thou art like a young lion of the nations,

among the uncircumcised, with those who
are slain by the sword.

"This is Pharaoh and all his multitude,
says the Lord GOD."

32 In the twelfth year, in the twelfth
month, on the first day of the month,
the word of the LORD came to me: 2 "Son of
man, raise a lamentation over Pharaoh king
of Egypt, and say to him:

"You consider yourself a lion among the
nations,

H. LAMENTATIONS OVER PHARAOH AND EGYPT (32:1-32)

The first of the two oracles in this chapter is a dirge over Pharaoh, who is pictured
as a dragon about to be captured and destroyed by Yahweh (vss. 1-16). It is dated
March 3, 585.

Ezekiel's original utterance seems to be in the poem in vss. 1-8. The second oracle
is a lamentation over the Egyptians, who are to go to the lower world, where are Assyria,
Elam, Meshech, Tubal, Edom, and the Sidonians (vss. 17-32). It is dated April 16, 585
(April 27, 586). It is most tiresome prose, with the dubious exception of vss. 18*b*-19, and
seems to come from the hand of the editor; at least it is difficult to discover an original
oracle here. Whatever oracle Ezekiel may have uttered at this date seems to be lost to us. In
view of the apparent dependability of the other dates, it is preferable to accept this
one, and to presume that the editor has failed to preserve the oracle uttered by Ezekiel
on this occasion, at least in identifiable form. In support of our preference for an
autumnal calendar it is worth noting that it is only in such a calendar that the twelfth
month of the twelfth year (vs. 1) would precede the first month of the twelfth year (vs.
17). This of course assumes the correctness of the reconstruction of vs. 17. Both these
oracles come after that in 33:21-33, and after the fall of Jerusalem, and so presumably
after Ezekiel's return to Babylonia. The original oracle in the first part is sometimes
limited to vs. 2 (Hölscher, Irwin; cf. Cooke), or to vss. 1-8 (Bertholet), while in the
second part vss. 29-32 are taken as a later addition, since Edom and Phoenicia could
not rank with the other great nations mentioned (see Jahn, Hölscher, Cooke, Matthews,
Bertholet, *et al.*). Here Irwin finds the original oracle within vss. 18-19, 21. In the
Scheide Papyrus vss. 24*b*-26 are omitted through homoeoteleuton.

1. LAMENT OVER PHARAOH (32:1-16)

Pharaoh proudly considers himself a **lion** among nations, when he is but a *tannin*
(*tannim*), a **dragon** (see Exeg. on 29:3). The contrast between the symbol of the
proud lion and the dragon of chaos is striking. Many commentators deny any allusion
to a dragon here, and interpret the *tannin* as a crocodile, but we have found the same type
of mythological terminology in Ezekiel, and this is no ordinary animal (cf. vss. 4-8),
as the tree in the preceding chapter was no ordinary cedar. Here is the sea monster,
caught by a net as was Tiamat at the hands of Marduk. The lion often was associated
with royalty in the ancient Near East, including Egypt, and Hebrew analogies have been
noted (see Exeg. on 19:1-14). The royal sphinx was a lion-bodied creature. The **rivers**
of **vs. 2** are the rivers of *tehôm* (see 31:4), here symbolically used of the Nile branches.
It is uncertain how much of vss. 9-16 is poetry. For the larger part they represent the
editor's prose expansion and depict the exile of Egypt (see vs. 9; cf. 29:8-16; 30:23-26),
with the oft-repeated purpose that they may know that Yahweh is God. In its present
form the verses seem concerned with the land of Egypt rather than Pharaoh, although
of course Pharaoh was in a sense the land of Egypt.

32:2. You consider yourself could also be translated "You are destroyed," but the
parallelism suggests the former, although the Niphal is unique with this meaning. Some

and thou *art* as a whale in the seas: and thou camest forth with thy rivers, and troubledst the waters with thy feet, and fouledst their rivers.

3 Thus saith the Lord GOD; I will therefore spread out my net over thee with a company of many people; and they shall bring thee up in my net.

4 Then will I leave thee upon the land, I will cast thee forth upon the open field, and will cause all the fowls of the heaven to remain upon thee, and I will fill the beasts of the whole earth with thee.

5 And I will lay thy flesh upon the mountains, and fill the valleys with thy height.

6 I will also water with thy blood the land wherein thou swimmest, *even* to the mountains; and the rivers shall be full of thee.

7 And when I shall put thee out, I will cover the heaven, and make the stars thereof dark; I will cover the sun with a cloud, and the moon shall not give her light.

8 All the bright lights of heaven will I make dark over thee, and set darkness upon thy land, saith the Lord GOD.

but you are like a dragon in the seas;
you burst forth in your rivers,
  trouble the waters with your feet,
  and foul their rivers.

3 Thus says the Lord GOD:
  I will throw my net over you
  with a host of many peoples;
  and I[k] will haul you up in my dragnet.

4 And I will cast you on the ground,
  on the open field I will fling you,
 and will cause all the birds of the air to
   settle on you,
  and I will gorge the beasts of the whole
   earth with you.

5 I will strew your flesh upon the mountains,
  and fill the valleys with your carcass.[l]

6 I will drench the land even to the mountains
  with your flowing blood;
  and the watercourses will be full of
   you.

7 When I blot you out, I will cover the heavens,
  and make their stars dark;
 I will cover the sun with a cloud,
  and the moon shall not give its light.

8 All the bright lights of heaven
  will I make dark over you,
  and put darkness upon your land,
                    says the Lord GOD.

[k] Gk Vg: Heb *they*
[l] Symmachus Syr Vg: Heb *your height*

ignore the nature of the symbolism of the **rivers** of the deep by emending בנהרותיך, **in your rivers**, to בנחרותיך, "in your nostrils," although this is consonant with the picture of the sea dragon in Job 41:10. The latter part of the verse perhaps indicates the blind, uncontrolled, and destructive power of Pharaoh.

3. With a host of many peoples is obscure and is deleted by a number of scholars; as a gloss or original it may refer to the Babylonian agents of Yahweh who are to defeat Egypt, or to the allies of Egypt who are also to be caught (cf. vss. 9-10; 23:24). **I will haul you up:** The first person, with the LXX and Vulg., seems demanded by the context, unless **they** may refer to the Babylonians.

4. The dragon is cast out of its natural element to perish (cf. 29:5).

5. Carcass: Read with Symm., the Syriac, and Vulg., רמתך, lit., "your worm," for רמותך, **thy height.**

6. The first two lines are perhaps glossed or corrupted; lit., "I will water [the] land [of] your overflow from your blood to the mountains."

7-8. The destruction of the dragon of chaos was associated with the day of Yahweh, and it is not surprising that the symbolism has something in common with such passages

moral leadership and our unselfish championship of the common good will be sorely missed when statesmen meet in council? Whether we shall live or die as a people we do not know. It is possible for us so to order our life that if we perish all will regret our going.

9 I will also vex the hearts of many people, when I shall bring thy destruction among the nations, into the countries which thou hast not known.

10 Yea, I will make many people amazed at thee, and their kings shall be horribly afraid for thee, when I shall brandish my sword before them; and they shall tremble at *every* moment, every man for his own life, in the day of thy fall.

11 ¶ For thus saith the Lord GOD; The sword of the king of Babylon shall come upon thee.

12 By the swords of the mighty will I cause thy multitude to fall, the terrible of the nations, all of them: and they shall spoil the pomp of Egypt, and all the multitude thereof shall be destroyed.

13 I will destroy also all the beasts thereof from beside the great waters; neither shall the foot of man trouble them any more, nor the hoofs of beasts trouble them.

14 Then will I make their waters deep, and cause their rivers to run like oil, saith the Lord GOD.

15 When I shall make the land of Egypt desolate, and the country shall be destitute of that whereof it was full, when I shall smite all them that dwell therein, then shall they know that I *am* the LORD.

16 This *is* the lamentation wherewith they shall lament her: the daughters of the nations shall lament her: they shall lament for her, *even* for Egypt, and for all her multitude, saith the Lord GOD.

9 "I will trouble the hearts of many peoples, when I carry you captive[m] among the nations, into the countries which you have not known. 10 I will make many peoples appalled at you, and their kings shall shudder because of you, when I brandish my sword before them; they shall tremble every moment, every one for his own life, on the day of your downfall. 11 For thus says the Lord GOD: The sword of the king of Babylon shall come upon you. 12 I will cause your multitude to fall by the swords of mighty ones, all of them most terrible among the nations.

"They shall bring to nought the pride of Egypt,
and all its multitude shall perish.
13 I will destroy all its beasts
from beside many waters;
and no foot of man shall trouble them
any more,
nor shall the hoofs of beasts trouble
them.
14 Then I will make their waters clear,
and cause their rivers to run like oil,
says the Lord GOD.
15 When I make the land of Egypt desolate
and when the land is stripped of all
that fills it,
when I smite all who dwell in it,
then they will know that I am the
LORD.
16 This is a lamentation which shall be chanted; the daughters of the nations shall chant it; over Egypt, and over all her multitude, shall they chant it, says the Lord GOD."

[m] Gk: Heb *bring your destruction*

as Isa. 13:10; 60:19; Joel 2:2; 3:15; Amos 5:20; 8:9; etc. This association with the day of Yahweh substantiates the identification of *tannîn* as the dragon. The detail here suggests the realm of mythology, later caught up in Hebrew eschatology.

9. Instead of שְׁבְרֵךְ, **thy [your] destruction,** the LXX reads שְׁבִיךְ, "your captivity"; hence the RSV. The conclusion of the verse shows that there must be a reference to captivity (cf. Jer. 15:14; 22:28; etc.).

10-12. Note the **sword** motif again (see 30:25). Yahweh's sword recalls the bronze images of Baal wielding a sword, found in the excavations, as well as the many references to the sword of the Lord in the O.T. (cf. Lev. 26:33; Josh. 5:13; Judg. 8:20; Ps. 7:12; Isa. 34:6; 66:16; Jer. 12:12; 47:6; etc.). Hölscher thinks the redactor is referring to the conquest of Egypt by Cambyses II in 525.

13-14. A dramatic picture of uninhabited Egypt, recalling 29:10-11. Note it is here **all its beasts,** not the one beast of vss. 2*b*.

16. Cf. the conclusion of the dirge in 19:14. There were professional women mourners (see especially II Sam. 1:24; Jer. 9:17-18; 49:3; cf. Ezek. 8:14).

17 ¶ It came to pass also in the twelfth year, in the fifteenth *day* of the month, *that* the word of the LORD came unto me, saying,

18 Son of man, wail for the multitude of Egypt, and cast them down, *even* her, and the daughters of the famous nations, unto the nether parts of the earth, with them that go down into the pit.

19 Whom dost thou pass in beauty? go down, and be thou laid with the uncircumcised.

20 They shall fall in the midst of *them that are* slain by the sword: she is delivered to the sword: draw her and all her multitudes.

17 In the twelfth year, in the first month,[n] on the fifteenth day of the month, the word of the LORD came to me: 18 "Son of man, wail over the multitude of Egypt, and send them down, her and the daughters of majestic nations, to the nether world, to those who have gone down to the Pit:
19 'Whom do you surpass in beauty?
      Go down, and be laid with the uncircumcised.'
20 They shall fall amid those who are slain by the sword,[o] and with her shall lie all her

[n] Gk: Heb lacks *in the first month*
[o] Gk Syr: Heb *sword, the sword is delivered*

2. EGYPT GOES DOWN TO THE NETHER WORLD (32:17-32)

There seems to be some suggestion of a difference of position of those in **the nether world,** although certainly not the idea of punishment and reward. Seemingly the uncircumcised are separated from the circumcised, as also perhaps those slain by the sword, and so without benefit of proper burial rites and accouterments. Perhaps it is presumed that people are gathered there by nations. The dead are inactive, lying on their beds. The inhabitants of the nether world are called רפאים, "Rephaim," "shades"; see Isa. 14:9, from which it would appear that there kings sit on their thrones and something of their pomp is preserved. Here it would appear that the warriors, with proper burial (cf. vs. 27), have a position of honor. See, however, Job 10:21-22, which describes Sheol as a land of darkness and gloom, where the weary are at rest, and Job 3:17-19, as a place where prisoners are released from their taskmasters and the slave is free from his master. The abode of the dead is here called Sheol, the Pit, the tomb, and the nether world.

Assyria (cf. 27:23), **Meshech,** and **Tubal** (27:13; 38:2-3; 39:1) appear in the editor's writings at other points. **Elam** appears in a late oracle in Jer. 49:34-39 (cf. also Jer. 25:25; Isa. 11:11). Meshech and Tubal are to the editor "the foe from the north," and Assyria appears here because of her historic rivalry with Egypt. That the editor should have included **Edom** is understandable (see also 25:12-14; 35:1-15; Jer. 49:7-22; Obad. 8; etc.). With the **Sidonians** cf. the oracle in 28:20-23. The term "Sidonians" designates the southern Phoenicians, as it does in the Ugaritic texts (see Gordon, *Ugaritic Handbook,* text Krt, ll. 199, 202; cf. Deut. 3:9; Josh. 13:4; I Kings 5:6; etc.).

17. The LXX **first month** is most probable. Some would supply "the twelfth month" in view of vs. 1, but that is unnecessary. A number of MSS and the Syriac read "eleventh year," but this also is unnecessary.

18. Vss. 18*b*-19 are a dirge to be sung by the prophet and **the daughters of majestic nations.** The lament acts as an incantation or chant to send the Egyptians to the lower world.

19. Cf. 28:7-9. Egypt boasted of an illusory grandeur.

20. The latter part of the verse is hopelessly corrupt, as the RSV mg. suggests.

32:17-32. *Vision of Hades.*—This passage is one of the most powerful in the whole book, though we cannot appreciate its force until we have made the effort to enter into the thought world out of which it springs. The underworld or Sheol is assimilated in the prophet's mind to the graves above ground. "Sheol is the entirety into which all graves are merged. . . . All graves

have certain common characteristics constituting the nature of the grave, and that is Sheol."[9] To that land of the dead we go down exactly as we were in this world. Further, not only are individuals there; nations also are among its inhabitants. The king is in Sheol with his crown, and the warrior with his sword. But there seems

[9] Pedersen, *Israel, Its Life and Culture, I-II,* p. 462.

21 The strong among the mighty shall speak to him out of the midst of hell with them that help him: they are gone down, they lie uncircumcised, slain by the sword.

22 Asshur *is* there and all her company: his graves *are* about him: all of them slain, fallen by the sword:

23 Whose graves are set in the sides of the pit, and her company is round about her grave; all of them slain, fallen by the sword, which caused terror in the land of the living.

24 There *is* Elam and all her multitude round about her grave; all of them slain, fallen by the sword, which are gone down uncircumcised into the nether parts of the earth, which caused their terror in the land of the living; yet have they borne their shame with them that go down to the pit.

25 They have set her a bed in the midst of the slain with all her multitude: her graves *are* round about him: all of them uncircumcised, slain by the sword: though their terror was caused in the land of the living, yet have they borne their shame with them that go down to the pit: he is put in the midst of *them that be* slain.

26 There *is* Meshech, Tubal, and all her multitude: her grave *are* round about him: all of them uncircumcised, slain by the sword, though they caused their terror in the land of the living.

multitudes.*p* 21 The mighty chiefs shall speak of them, with their helpers, out of the midst of Sheol: 'They have come down, they lie still, the uncircumcised, slain by the sword.'

22 "Assyria is there, and all her company, their graves round about her, all of them slain, fallen by the sword; 23 whose graves are set in the uttermost parts of the Pit, and her company is round about her grave; all of them slain, fallen by the sword, who spread terror in the land of the living.

24 "Elam is there, and all her multitude about her grave; all of them slain, fallen by the sword, who went down uncircumcised into the nether world, who spread terror in the land of the living, and they bear their shame with those who go down to the Pit. 25 They have made her a bed among the slain with all her multitude, their graves round about her, all of them uncircumcised, slain by the sword; for terror of them was spread in the land of the living, and they bear their shame with those who go down to the Pit; they are placed among the slain.

26 "Meshech and Tubal are there, and all their multitude, their graves round about them, all of them uncircumcised, slain by the sword; for they spread terror

p Gk: Heb *they have drawn her away and all her multitudes*

---

21. This is also obscure. Some follow the LXX and place vs. 19 after vs. 21*a* as the speech of the mighty chiefs. **The mighty chiefs** are perhaps the kings of the great nations (cf. 31:11).

22. His graves are about him is also obscure; we would expect **round about her grave** as in vs. 24. It is better to omit with the LXX than to emend, for it is superfluous in view of the occurrence of its parallel in vs. 23, although the latter is considered by some a marginal correction of vs. 22.

24-25. Elam was an ancient nation, important in the Near East, and often the enemy of Assyria. It was a province within the Persian Empire, and its capital city Shushan (Susa) was a capital of that empire (see Neh. 1:1; Dan. 8:2).

---

to be a class distinction among the dead, for the dishonored nations of whom the prophet speaks do not mingle with the proud heroes of old (vs. 27).

We may picture to ourselves a vast pit, heaped with slain, in which the slain preserve some sort of shadowy existence and even a vague consciousness of what is happening on the earth they have left. As we stand beside this pit, Pharaoh and his slaughtered legions approach the edge and begin their descent into

the dim interior. As they do so, there is a movement among the shadows, and bloodless figures rise to address a ghostly welcome to the new arrivals. Room, room for the conqueror who has now met his match! Our eyes become able bit by bit to pierce through the darkness, until we can make out the heaps of corpses where they lie rotting in their shame. One after another we pass in review the kings who made the earth tremble at their names, the armies which marched at the prompting of their ambi-

27 And they shall not lie with the mighty *that are* fallen of the uncircumcised, which are gone down to hell with their weapons of war: and they have laid their swords under their heads, but their iniquities shall be upon their bones, though *they were* the terror of the mighty in the land of the living.

28 Yea, thou shalt be broken in the midst of the uncircumcised, and shalt lie with *them that are* slain with the sword.

29 There *is* Edom, her kings, and all her princes, which with their might are laid by *them that were* slain by the sword: they shall lie with the uncircumcised, and with them that go down to the pit.

30 There *be* the princes of the north, all of them, and all the Zidonians, which are gone down with the slain; with their terror they are ashamed of their might; and they lie uncircumcised with *them that be* slain by the sword, and bear their shame with them that go down to the pit.

31 Pharaoh shall see them, and shall be comforted over all his multitude, *even* Pharaoh and all his army slain by the sword, saith the Lord GOD.

32 For I have caused my terror in the land of the living: and he shall be laid in the land of the living. 27 And they do not lie with the fallen mighty men of old*q* who went down to Sheol with their weapons of war, whose swords were laid under their heads, and whose shields*r* are upon their bones; for the terror of the mighty men was in the land of the living. 28 So you shall be broken and lie among the uncircumcised, with those who are slain by the sword.

29 "Edom is there, her kings and all her princes, who for all their might are laid with those who are slain by the sword; they lie with the uncircumcised, with those who go down to the Pit.

30 "The princes of the north are there, all of them, and all the Sido'nians, who have gone down in shame with the slain, for all the terror which they caused by their might; they lie uncircumcised with those who are slain by the sword, and bear their shame with those who go down to the Pit.

31 "When Pharaoh sees them, he will comfort himself for all his multitude, Pharaoh and all his army, slain by the sword, says the Lord GOD. 32 For he*s* spread terror in the land of the living; therefore he

q Gk Old Latin: Heb *of the uncircumcised*
r Cn: Heb *iniquities*
s Cn: Heb *I*

---

27. The negative **not** should possibly be omitted with the LXX and Syriac, unless we are to presume that certain fallen heroes of old, because they were properly buried and placed in their tombs, had a more favorable position in Sheol, perhaps not so far down (cf. vs. 23). **Of old:** Read with the LXX, O.L., Arabic, מעולם for מערלים, **of the uncircumcised,** an obvious corruption. **Shields:** Read צנותם for עונתם, **iniquities.**

30. The princes of the north are presumably the rulers of the countries north of Palestine, including Phoenicia. Note the RSV's different arrangement of the words, taking **caused by [of] their might** with **terror** rather than **ashamed.** The Hebrew is obscure.

32. The C.T. has "I gave his terror [*Qerê*, "my terror"]," and obviously the subject should be **he** (cf. the following verb).

---

tion, and the common soldiers who died in a quarrel which meant nothing to them. Here in this pit all the so-called greatness of the past is stored up—in decay! How ineffectual it all seems now! They that take the sword have indeed perished by the sword. The historian may write as he will of this or that "brilliant victory"; we see that military glory is as ineffectual as it is sordid. Yes, but there is one thing it can achieve better than anything else, and that is death. Left to itself, it would turn the earth into one vast burial ground.

But who is this standing by our side as we look on? It is the prophet. There is one people that has not gone down to the pit, but remains alive where the other peoples of the ancient world have perished. What is the secret of the Jews' survival? They have had no military might, nor have they sought after world power as others have done. Precisely for this reason they stand today where so many others have fallen. Their history has been one of frequent failure, even of betrayal of their ideals; nevertheless those ideals have given that history a vitality which derives from no other source. Since they began to be a people they have felt the hand of the living God upon them and known that they were in the world as in some

the midst of the uncircumcised with *them that are* slain with the sword, *even* Pharaoh and all his multitude, saith the Lord God.

33 Again the word of the Lord came unto me, saying,

2 Son of man, speak to the children of thy people, and say unto them, When I

shall be laid among the uncircumcised, with those who are slain by the sword, Pharaoh and all his multitude, says the Lord God."

33 The word of the Lord came to me: 2 "Son of man, speak to your people

---

III. Restoration of Israel (33:1–39:29)

A. Oracles on Responsibility, etc. (33:1-33)

Ch. 33 marks the beginning of a new section of the book (chs. 33–39), largely prophecies of restoration belonging to the editor, with very little which can be accredited with plausibility to Ezekiel.

The first part of ch. 33 deals with the responsibility of the prophet as watchman (vss. 1-9) and the responsibility of the individual and the fairness of Yahweh's ways (vss. 10-20). The latter part of the chapter depicts the coming of the fugitive to Ezekiel with the news of the fall of Jerusalem (vss. 21-22); to this two oracles are attached, one apparently condemning those left in the land of Israel and predicting its desolation (vss. 23-29), the other describing the reaction of the people to Ezekiel, as he is to them a singer of love songs and they do not obey his words (vss. 30-33).

If there is an editor of the book, his handiwork surely appears in the first major division (vss. 1-20; see Intro., pp. 51-52). It is of one piece with 3:16-21, which is also concerned with the prophet as watchman, and with 14:12-23; 18:5-32, where the problem of individual responsibility receives elucidation. Some scholars recognize that vss. 1-20 belong chronologically with 3:16-21, although they ascribe both passages to Ezekiel in the early period of his ministry (Matthews; cf. Herntrich) or in the later period (cf. Cooke, Kraetzschmar). The second half of the chapter is not as easily interpreted, although it also has already received considerable comment. Our interpretation of the dumbness of Ezekiel as an actual temporary dumbness is in contrast with the editor's interpretation as a symbolic dumbness (see Exeg. on 3:26-27; 24:25-27). The oracles attached to this incident are also difficult to interpret. The first (vss. 23-29), which has a parallel in 11:14-21 where it is associated with the editor's new heart doctrine, criticizes those left behind in Palestine, implying that they are not worthy to inherit the promise made to Abraham and recalling the oracle of the good and bad figs in Jer. 24, which may come from the same period. The claim for the possession of Palestine in 11:15 is on the part of those left in Palestine after 597, and here, by association with the date in vs. 21, it would be on the part of those left after 586. Actually the same persons are intended, i.e., those in Palestine at the time of the editor who could not claim exilic ancestry (cf. Exeg. on 11:14-21). The editor reflects his Palestinian situation in the phrase **these waste places** in vs. 24. Just what oracle Ezekiel uttered on January 8, 585 (vs. 21) we do not know, unless it is found in vss. 30-33, although this may be questioned (Howie recognizes that vss. 21-22 have no connection with what precedes or follows, but by placing them at the end of ch. 24, he interrupts the chronological sequence [cf. 24:1; 26:1], and a considerable time lapse exists between 24:1-27 and

---

sense his servant. Israel does not go down to the pit but stands and calls mankind before the judgment seat of a righteous God. Could we wish for a more convincing picture of the impotence of what the world calls power and the might of those spiritual forces in which it is still so reluctant to put its trust?

33:1-9. Pastor and People.—The parallel to this in 3:16-21 was dealt with as a picture of

the responsibility which each one of us bears for his fellows. We can read this passage in a more restricted sense, as a call to the prophet to accept the labor and burden of the "cure of souls." As a pastor, he becomes an example to us who are pastors today.

In time of war men choose a sentry to mount guard on their behalf; but there are perils of peace which they do not take equally to heart,

bring the sword upon a land, if the people of the land take a man of their coasts, and set him for their watchman:

3 If when he seeth the sword come upon the land, he blow the trumpet, and warn the people;

4 Then whosoever heareth the sound of the trumpet, and taketh not warning; if the sword come, and take him away, his blood shall be upon his own head.

5 He heard the sound of the trumpet, and took not warning; his blood shall be upon him. But he that taketh warning shall deliver his soul.

6 But if the watchman see the sword come, and blow not the trumpet, and the people be not warned; if the sword come, and take *any* person from among them, he is taken away in his iniquity; but his blood will I require at the watchman's hand.

7 ¶ So thou, O son of man, I have set thee a watchman unto the house of Israel;

and say to them, If I bring the sword upon a land, and the people of the land take a man from among them, and make him their watchman; 3 and if he sees the sword coming upon the land and blows the trumpet and warns the people; 4 then if any one who hears the sound of the trumpet does not take warning, and the sword comes and takes him away, his blood shall be upon his own head. 5 He heard the sound of the trumpet, and did not take warning; his blood shall be upon himself. But if he had taken warning, he would have saved his life. 6 But if the watchman sees the sword coming and does not blow the trumpet, so that the people are not warned, and the sword comes, and takes any one of them; that man is taken away in his iniquity, but his blood I will require at the watchman's hand.

7 "So you, son of man, I have made a

33:21-22; see Exeg. below). Scholars differ widely in their interpretation of the chapter, some taking all or nearly all to be original (see Cooke, Matthews), while others consider much due to redaction or editing (see Bertholet, Irwin), and Hölscher considers it all secondary. Irwin finds four separate poetic oracles here in vss. 7-9, vss. 10-11, vss. 23-24, 27, and vss. 30-32. The homogeneity of the language in vss. 1-20 and its similarity to the parallel passages noted in the preceding and following comments refute any theory of parallel recensions (contrast Bertholet) or multiple redactions as an explanation of the present form of the text.

1. The Prophet as Watchman (33:1-9)

The prophet has the responsibility to announce, the wicked to listen and obey. The watchman who does not announce the word of Yahweh is accountable for the death of the wicked (cf. 3:16-21). Vss. 1-6 present the responsibility of the watchman; vss. 7-9 apply the principle to the prophet (for the prophet as watchman see Isa. 21:6; 56:10; Jer. 6:17; Hab. 2:1).

33:2-3. For the **sword** motif in vss. 2-4, 6 cf. 32:30-32; 21:1-32. For the **watchman** see II Sam. 18:25; II Kings 9:17-18; Isa. 21:6, 11; 62:6; Jer. 51:12; for the **trumpet** of the watchman see Neh. 4:19-20 (cf. Isa. 18:3; Jer. 4:5).

4. For bloodguiltiness see 3:18, 20; 1:13 (cf. 22:12-13; 36:18; etc.). See especially Gen. 4:10; 37:26.

5. Perhaps read Hiphil הזהיר, for Niphal נזהר, and translate, "He who gave warning has saved his life."

6. Note the legalistic mind, which would include all possible cases. Even though the wicked are **not warned**, they are punished for their iniquity. Ignorance is no excuse, for lack of knowledge is itself a sin (cf. Hos. 4:1, 6).

---

and against these the pastor is appointed by God to keep watch. The details of the passage may be neglected in favor of its general drift. It serves as a warning to us not to neglect the individual in the mass. The modern minister

is in danger of being absorbed in the running of congregational and outside activities. He needs to bear in mind that his most effective work for God is done in the sphere of personal relationships, and that he should let the "cure of

therefore thou shalt hear the word at my mouth, and warn them from me.

8 When I say unto the wicked, O wicked *man,* thou shalt surely die; if thou dost not speak to warn the wicked from his way, that wicked *man* shall die in his iniquity; but his blood will I require at thine hand.

9 Nevertheless, if thou warn the wicked of his way to turn from it; if he do not turn from his way, he shall die in his iniquity; but thou hast delivered thy soul.

10 Therefore, O thou son of man, speak unto the house of Israel; Thus ye speak, saying, If our transgressions and our sins *be* upon us, and we pine away in them, how should we then live?

11 Say unto them, *As* I live, saith the Lord God, I have no pleasure in the death of the wicked; but that the wicked turn from his way and live: turn ye, turn ye from your evil ways; for why will ye die, O house of Israel?

12 Therefore, thou son of man, say unto the children of thy people, The righteousness of the righteous shall not deliver him in the day of his transgression: as for the wickedness of the wicked, he shall not fall

watchman for the house of Israel; whenever you hear a word from my mouth, you shall give them warning from me. **8** If I say to the wicked, O wicked man, you shall surely die, and you do not speak to warn the wicked to turn from his way, that wicked man shall die in his iniquity, but his blood I will require at your hand. **9** But if you warn the wicked to turn from his way, and he does not turn from his way; he shall die in his iniquity, but you will have saved your life.

10 "And you, son of man, say to the house of Israel, Thus have you said: 'Our transgressions and our sins are upon us, and we waste away because of them; how then can we live?' **11** Say to them, As I live, says the Lord God, I have no pleasure in the death of the wicked, but that the wicked turn from his way and live; turn back, turn back from your evil ways; for why will you die, O house of Israel? **12** And you, son of man, say to your people, The righteousness of the righteous shall not deliver him when

---

8. O wicked man is possibly the result of dittography and is omitted by one MS, the LXX, and Syriac (see also vs. 14; 3:18). Death here is probably premature death, the punishment of the wicked, as over against the long life of the righteous (see Exeg. on 18:1-32).

2. New Oracle on Individual Responsibility (33:10-20)

It is quite obvious that vs. 10 does not represent the attitude of the people of Ezekiel's time, but is in part a rhetorical question, asked that an opportunity for an answer may be made. This is a sermon for the exiles. The editor does not hold his contemporaries responsible for the wickedness which brought about the Exile, and he presents a theory which puts the onus of guilt and repentance upon the individual rather than the nation. God is not God of mercy, but of justice, unless there is mercy in his willingness to forget the past wickedness of the repentant sinner, although this is presented as a matter of fairness rather than mercy. God is willing to forgive the repentant sinner, but this is balanced by the warning that if a good man sins no merit shall accrue to him because of his previous goodness; he shall die in his sin. Note here that the prophetic function is primarily the call to repentance rather than the announcement of the judgment of God. This passage has much in common with 18:21-23; cf. vs. 11 with 18:23; vs. 13 with 18:24; vss. 14-15 with 18:21-22; vss. 17-20 with 18:25-30.

12. This is the general statement, vss. 13-26 being an explanation in detail.

---

souls" rank first among the many claims which are pressed upon him. He has to remember, too, that such a use of his time will not necessarily meet with the approval of his people, that the perils against which he seeks to warn men and

women may not seem perils at all to them. But as he derives his office from God, so also he receives from God the standards with which he works, and his responsibility is first to God and then to his people.

thereby in the day that he turneth from his wickedness; neither shall the righteous be able to live for his *righteousness* in the day that he sinneth.

13 When I shall say to the righteous, *that* he shall surely live; if he trust to his own righteousness, and commit iniquity, all his righteousnesses shall not be remembered; but for his iniquity that he hath committed, he shall die for it.

14 Again, when I say unto the wicked, Thou shalt surely die; if he turn from his sin, and do that which is lawful and right;

15 *If* the wicked restore the pledge, give again that he had robbed, walk in the statutes of life, without committing iniquity; he shall surely live, he shall not die.

16 None of his sins that he hath committed shall be mentioned unto him: he hath done that which is lawful and right; he shall surely live.

17 ¶ Yet the children of thy people say, The way of the Lord is not equal: but as for them, their way is not equal.

18 When the righteous turneth from his righteousness, and committeth iniquity, he shall even die thereby.

19 But if the wicked turn from his wickedness, and do that which is lawful and right, he shall live thereby.

20 ¶ Yet ye say, The way of the Lord is not equal. O ye house of Israel, I will judge you every one after his ways.

21 ¶ And it came to pass in the twelfth year of our captivity, in the tenth *month,* in the fifth *day* of the month, *that* one that

he transgresses; and as for the wickedness of the wicked, he shall not fall by it when he turns from his wickedness; and the righteous shall not be able to live by his righteousness[t] when he sins. 13 Though I say to the righteous that he shall surely live, yet if he trusts in his righteousness and commits iniquity, none of his righteous deeds shall be remembered; but in the iniquity that he has committed he shall die. 14 Again, though I say to the wicked, 'You shall surely die,' yet if he turns from his sin and does what is lawful and right, 15 if the wicked restores the pledge, gives back what he had taken by robbery, and walks in the statutes of life, committing no iniquity; he shall surely live, he shall not die. 16 None of the sins that he has committed shall be remembered against him; he has done what is lawful and right, he shall surely live.

17 "Yet your people say, 'The way of the Lord is not just'; when it is their own way that is not just. 18 When the righteous turns from his righteousness, and commits iniquity, he shall die for it. 19 And when the wicked turns from his wickedness, and does what is lawful and right, he shall live by it. 20 Yet you say, 'The way of the Lord is not just.' O house of Israel, I will judge each of you according to his ways."

21 In the twelfth year of our exile, in the tenth month, on the fifth day of the

[t] Heb *by it*

---

15. Statutes of life: Statutes "by whose observance man shall live" (20:11; see 20:13; cf. Lev. 18:5).

3. The Fugitive Brings News of Jerusalem's Fall (33:21-22)

21-22. Eight MSS., the LXX[MSS], and Syriac read "in the eleventh year," and some scholars accept this (cf. Albright, Howie), assuming that **the twelfth year** would make the fugitive arrive a year and a half after the fall of the city, which took place in the

---

21-22. *The Crisis Comes.*—On the difficulty which the date here given presents, as well as on the whole problem of Ezekiel's dumbness, see the Exeg. In what follows we shall assume that the news reached Ezekiel on the very day of the capital's fall to the Babylonian army. Ezekiel was at the time not far away in the Judean countryside and would no doubt be kept informed from time to time of how the siege was going. It is not difficult to imagine

how the certainty grew upon him that the city could not hold out much longer, until one evening the premonition of doom had become so strong as to throw him into a trance. Incapable of speech and stricken with sorrow, he sat brooding, until the fugitive broke in with the dreadful, if by no means unexpected, news. Still the prophet sat there, gripped by sorrow for his people and the plight of those who at that moment were perishing perhaps in the

had escaped out of Jerusalem came unto me, saying, The city is smitten.

22 Now the hand of the LORD was upon me in the evening, afore he that was escaped came; and had opened my mouth, until he came to me in the morning; and my mouth was opened, and I was no more dumb.

23 Then the word of the LORD came unto me, saying,

24 Son of man, they that inhabit those wastes of the land of Israel speak, saying, Abraham was one, and he inherited the land: but we *are* many; the land is given us for inheritance.

25 Wherefore say unto them, Thus saith the Lord GOD; Ye eat with the blood, and

month, a man who had escaped from Jerusalem came to me and said, "The city has fallen." 22 Now the hand of the LORD had been upon me the evening before the fugitive came; and he had opened my mouth by the time the man came to me in the morning; so my mouth was opened, and I was no longer dumb.

23 The word of the LORD came to me: 24 "Son of man, the inhabitants of these waste places in the land of Israel keep saying, 'Abraham was only one man, yet he got possession of the land; but we are many; the land is surely given us to possess.' 25 Therefore say to them, Thus says the Lord GOD: You eat flesh with the blood,

fourth month of the eleventh year. However, using the autumnal reckoning, **the tenth month** of the twelfth year would be less than six months after the fourth month of the eleventh year, and this again substantiates our use of the autumnal reckoning. The time here is then January 8, 585. Even nearly six months seems a long time for such news to reach Babylonia; it took Ezra only 108 days to make the trip with a considerable company (see Ezra 8:31; 7:9). See J. A. Bewer's ingenious solution by transposing two words and reading the eleventh year, the fifth month, on the tenth day of the month ("Das Datum in Hes 33²¹," *Zeitschrift für die alttestamentliche Wissenschaft,* LIV [1936], 114-15). Of course if 24:26-27 is interpreted to mean that the fugitive came on the day of the fall of the city, the chronological data here would have to be disregarded (cf. Herntrich, Bertholet, Hölscher, Harford, etc.). We must either presume that the incident described here is historical and that Ezekiel's dumbness came upon him the evening before (see vs. 22), or ascribe the passage in its entirety to the editor.

4. PRESUMPTION AND PUNISHMENT OF THOSE LEFT IN JUDAH (33:23-29)

Curiously, the pre-exilic prophets do not refer to the promise made to Abraham, but rather to the election at the time of the Exodus. So the references to Abraham are late in Isa. 29:22; Mic. 7:20 (cf. also Isa. 63:16; Deut. 1:8; 6:10; 30:20). Many of the expressions in this passage have been encountered before; with the sins in vss. 25-27 cf. 18:6, 10-12. Vs. 27 has three of the four deadly judgments of 14:21. Cf. vs. 28 with 14:15.

25. It is suggested that instead of **with the blood,** על הדם, we should read "on the mountains," על ההרים, as some would read in 18:6.

fallen city. But as day dawned the trance was dispelled, speech returned to him, and he stood forth to bring guidance to those around him.

We need to complete the picture by imagining the effect of the news on Ezekiel's neighbors. They had been confident to the last, unable to grasp either the magnitude of the Babylonian power or the moral deterioration which had preceded and invited political catastrophe. Now, however, they were reduced to despair. Ezekiel, on the other hand, was free to speak. Once the crisis had actually come, he knew what he must say. He had foreseen the worst and reckoned with it before God; what was inconceivable to his fellows had long been anticipated

by him. And, stunned as he was by the news, he was prepared to meet it as they were not.

The Christian's position in the world today ought to be like that of the prophet. He is forced to be silent while others parade their confidence, for he knows that we live in a moral order and must reap what we have sown. Yet when events work out as he foresaw and bring disaster, he alone has a word from God to speak to men's needs and distress.

23-29. *False Confidence.*—Here is an O.T. comment related to Matt. 3:9. Ezekiel is addressing the survivors of the catastrophe of 587, perhaps even the followers of Ishmael, fresh from the murder of Gedaliah (Jer. 41). In spite of

lift up your eyes toward your idols, and shed blood: and shall ye possess the land?

26 Ye stand upon your sword, ye work abomination, and ye defile every one his neighbor's wife: and shall ye possess the land?

27 Say thou thus unto them, Thus saith the Lord GOD; *As* I live, surely they that *are* in the wastes shall fall by the sword, and him that *is* in the open field will I give to the beasts to be devoured, and they that *be* in the forts and in the caves shall die of the pestilence.

28 For I will lay the land most desolate, and the pomp of her strength shall cease; and the mountains of Israel shall be desolate, that none shall pass through.

29 Then shall they know that I *am* the LORD, when I have laid the land most desolate, because of all their abominations which they have committed.

30 ¶ Also, thou son of man, the children of thy people still are talking against thee by the walls and in the doors of the houses, and speak one to another, every one to his brother, saying, Come, I pray you, and hear what is the word that cometh forth from the LORD.

and lift up your eyes to your idols, and shed blood; shall you then possess the land? 26 You resort to the sword, you commit abominations and each of you defiles his neighbor's wife; shall you then possess the land? 27 Say this to them, Thus says the Lord GOD: As I live, surely those who are in the waste places shall fall by the sword; and him that is in the open field I will give to the beasts to be devoured; and those who are in strongholds and in caves shall die by pestilence. 28 And I will make the land a desolation and a waste; and her proud might shall come to an end; and the mountains of Israel shall be so desolate that none will pass through. 29 Then they will know that I am the LORD, when I have made the land a desolation and a waste because of all their abominations which they have committed.

30 "As for you, son of man, your people who talk together about you by the walls and at the doors of the houses, say to one another, each to his brother, 'Come, and hear what the word is that comes forth from

---

26. Ye stand upon your sword is interpreted by the RSV; the suggestion that we read חרבתיכם, "your waste places," instead of חרבכם, **your sword,** is attractive.

28. Her proud might: As elsewhere by the editor (see xiv on p. 50).

5. EZEKIEL REGARDED ONLY AS A SINGER OF LOVE SONGS (33:30-33)

The picture of Ezekiel consulted for an oracle occurs in 20:1, 3 and is presumed in other places where the elders sit before Ezekiel, as in 8:1; 14:1. It is uncertain whether this passage comes from the editor or Ezekiel, but the editor seems responsible for it, at least in its present form. The conclusion is the editor's (vs. 33; cf. 2:5). It would seem here also that the presumed function of the prophet is that of one who calls to repentance. Hölscher and others are possibly though not certainly right in regarding this oracle as an introduction to the oracles of promise in chs. 34–39.

30. One to another seems tautologous and is omitted by some scholars. **One,** חד, is an Aramaic form.

---

the depopulation of the land, they are secure in their descent from Abraham and do not doubt that the promises made to him will be fulfilled in them. They will be the posterity that was to be as the sand of the sea. **Abraham was one, and he inherited the land: but we are many; the land is given us for inheritance.** The most important part of the whole matter, that they should do as Abraham did if they are to bear his name, simply does not enter into their minds. Here is an instance of that living

on the past and on other people's qualities to which we are only too prone.

30-33. A Popular Preacher.—The general impression we get from this book is that Ezekiel was by no means popular with his countrymen, and we can see good reason why that should be so. But to judge by this passage, he was, at one time at any rate, in a position to command a ready hearing. People flocked to him. He was actually a popular preacher. The passage therefore may well serve as a warning to anyone

31 And they come unto thee as the people cometh, and they sit before thee *as* my people, and they hear thy words, but they will not do them: for with their mouth they show much love, *but* their heart goeth after their covetousness.

32 And, lo, thou *art* unto them as a very lovely song of one that hath a pleasant voice, and can play well on an instrument: for they hear thy words, but they do them not.

33 And when this cometh to pass, (lo, it will come,) then shall they know that a prophet hath been among them.

34 And the word of the LORD came unto me, saying,

2 Son of man, prophesy against the shepherds of Israel, prophesy, and say unto

the LORD.' 31 And they come to you as people come, and they sit before you as my people, and they hear what you say but they will not do it; for with their lips they show much love, but their heart is set on their gain. 32 And, lo, you are to them like one who sings love songs[u] with a beautiful voice and plays well on an instrument, for they hear what you say, but they will not do it. 33 When this comes — and come it will! — then they will know that a prophet has been among them."

34 The word of the LORD came to me: 2 "Son of man, prophesy against the

[u] Cn: Heb *like a love song*

31. The latter part of the verse is obscure, reading "for loves in their mouths they are doing," etc., which might be interpreted as in the RSV and the KJV, but perhaps we should read כזבים, "lies," for עגבים, "loves," and consider "they are doing" a gloss.

32. Like one who sings love songs: Read כשר עגבים, for כשיר עגבים, "as a song of love," i.e., **a love song,** which may be taken without emendation as a pregnant expression. The allusion to singing may be pertinent in part because the prophet chanted his oracle. Music sometimes may have accompanied the prophetic oracle (cf. I Sam. 10:5; II Kings 3:15).

B. THE SHEPHERDS OF ISRAEL AND THEIR SHEEP (34:1-31)

The shepherds of Israel have not been good shepherds, and their flock is scattered; so Yahweh's judgment is against the shepherds (vss. 1-10). He will search for his sheep and rescue them, returning them to the mountains of Israel and acting as their good shepherd (vss. 11-16). But Yahweh is also judge over the sheep, and he will judge

today who is in that position. A preacher has a reputation and it is not uncommon for one of his hearers to invite another to go along with him to hear Mr. So-and-So. He will be sure of a treat if he does. That was how people spoke of Ezekiel, but he was not satisfied. Why?

In the first place, he has an audience, not a congregation. People come merely to listen to him. They are not a group of men and women bound together in allegiance to God's word. In the second place, they listen to him but do not really attend. Their thoughts are elsewhere most of the time. Listening to a sermon is a mere interlude in a life devoted to selfish ends and is not allowed to interfere with their pursuit. In the third place, the hearers enjoy an entertainment; they have no serious purpose. For them the prophet is simply a man who enables them to pass the time pleasantly. They admire his diction, his force of speech, his intensity of conviction, etc., but it does not occur to them to lay to heart what he says. How could

any preacher worthy of the name be content with such a state of things?

Yet is not this very much the attitude which multitudes take toward the Christian gospel in our own day? They do not doubt that it is eminently beautiful, that it can furnish a rich symbolism for literature and the arts, that it is an invaluable source of comfort in hours of trouble. But as something to act upon—ah! that is a different matter. The theme is worked out fully in Samuel Butler's *Erewhon*, where the musical banks issue a currency which no one would dream of using in a business transaction. The words of our passage are taken also by Thomas Chalmers as the text of one of his most famous sermons.[1]

34:1-10. The Use and Abuse of Power.—The nomad origins of the nation provide an urban

[1] *A Series of Discourses on the Christian Revelation Viewed in Connection with Modern Astronomy,* Discourse VII, "On the Slender Influence of Mere Taste and Sensibility in Matters of Religion."

them, Thus saith the Lord GOD unto the shepherds; Woe *be* to the shepherds of Israel that do feed themselves! should not the shepherds feed the flocks?

3 Ye eat the fat, and ye clothe you with the wool, ye kill them that are fed: *but* ye feed not the flock.

4 The diseased have ye not strengthened, neither have ye healed that which was sick, neither have ye bound up *that which was* broken, neither have ye brought again that which was driven away, neither have ye sought that which was lost; but with force and with cruelty have ye ruled them.

shepherds of Israel, prophesy, and say to them, even to the shepherds, Thus says the Lord GOD: Ho, shepherds of Israel who have been feeding yourselves! Should not shepherds feed the sheep? 3 You eat the fat, you clothe yourselves with the wool, you slaughter the fatlings; but you do not feed the sheep. 4 The weak you have not strengthened, the sick you have not healed, the crippled you have not bound up, the strayed you have not brought back, the lost you have not sought, and with force and

---

between one sheep and another (vss. 17-22). He will set over them one shepherd, even David (vss. 23-24), and make a covenant of peace with them, giving prosperity to the land and security to the sheep (vss. 25-31).

As the prophet is a watchman, so the rulers of the people are called its shepherds (see Jer. 10:21; 23:1-4; 25:34-38; 50:6; 51:23; Mic. 5:5; Zech. 10:2-3; 11:3-8; I Kings 22:17; etc.). For Yahweh as the good shepherd see Isa. 40:11; Jer. 31:10; Pss. 23:1; 80:1; 95:7; etc. The messianic king as the shepherd occurs in a passage of comparable date and content in Jer. 23:4, and again in Ezek. 37:24. Note also the characterization of Cyrus as Yahweh's shepherd in Isa. 44:28. Analogies for both king and god as shepherd occur in other literatures of the Near East (see G. Ernest Wright, "The Good Shepherd," *Biblical Archaeologist,* II [1939], 44-48).

The closest analogies of the passage are postexilic in date (see Jer. 23:1-6; 31:9-10; Zech. 11:4-17; 13:7; cf. Pss. 80:1; 95:7; etc.). The diction and ideology, with the picture of the Davidic Messiah and the doctrine of the new covenant, point to the editor as most probable author. A few parallels in diction may be noted: "As I live, says the Lord GOD" in vs. 8 (see i on p. 50); "Behold, I am against" in vs. 10 (see xl on p. 51); "I will require . . . at their hand" in vs. 10 (see xxxiii on p. 51); "mountains of Israel" in vs. 13 (see iv on p. 50); "mountain heights of Israel" in vs. 14 (see v on p. 50); "they shall dwell securely" in vs. 28 (see xxxii on p. 51; see Lev. 25:18-19); "the reproach of the nations" in vs. 29 (see xxv on p. 50). Note also the analogies between vss. 25-26 and Lev. 26:4, 6; between vs. 28 and Lev. 26:5-6 (cf. also Lev. 26:13). With vss. 26-30 cf. 36:8-12. Cooke considers vss. 17-31 supplementary (cf. also Steuernagel, Jahn, Hölscher, Matthews). Hölscher finds nothing original, and Irwin isolates as Ezekiel's oracle of doom a single tristich line in vs. 2. Most scholars question the unity of authorship of the passage, but this is inconsonant with the literary analogies throughout Ezekiel and the homogeneity of the thought and diction within the chapter.

1. JUDGMENT UPON THE SHEPHERDS (34:1-10)

34:2. Even to the shepherds: Omitted by the LXX^A, while the LXX^B and Vulg. omits **to them,** but the omissions are probably for simplification; the Hebrew authors at times wrote awkward Hebrew. Vss. 2-4 represent the true prophetic attitude toward wicked rulers (cf. Jer. 22:13-17; Hos. 1:4; 7:7; I Sam. 8:1-22).

---

prophet with his symbolism; the leader is the shepherd of his people. But unfortunately he is often a bad shepherd rather than a good one. The difference between these two is that the good shepherd is concerned for the welfare of his flock, while the bad shepherd thinks of

them only as so many opportunities for his own gain. Power and leadership there must be in any society, but they must be tempered by a sense of responsibility. The prophet requires of the leader not merely a general oversight of the interests of the community, but a patient and

5 And they were scattered, because *there is* no shepherd: and they became meat to all the beasts of the field, when they were scattered.

6 My sheep wandered through all the mountains, and upon every high hill: yea, my flock was scattered upon all the face of the earth, and none did search or seek *after them.*

7 ¶ Therefore, ye shepherds, hear the word of the LORD;

8 *As* I live, saith the Lord GOD, surely because my flock became a prey, and my flock became meat to every beast of the field, because *there was* no shepherd, neither did my shepherds search for my flock, but the shepherds fed themselves, and fed not my flock;

9 Therefore, O ye shepherds, hear the word of the LORD;

10 Thus saith the Lord GOD; Behold, I *am* against the shepherds; and I will require my flock at their hand, and cause them to cease from feeding the flock; neither shall the shepherds feed themselves any more; for I will deliver my flock from their mouth, that they may not be meat for them.

11 ¶ For thus saith the Lord GOD; Behold, I, *even* I, will both search my sheep, and seek them out.

harshness you have ruled them. 5 So they were scattered, because there was no shepherd; and they became food for all the wild beasts. 6 My sheep were scattered, they wandered over all the mountains and on every high hill; my sheep were scattered over all the face of the earth, with none to search or seek for them.

7 "Therefore, you shepherds, hear the word of the LORD: 8 As I live, says the Lord GOD, because my sheep have become a prey, and my sheep have become food for all the wild beasts, since there was no shepherd; and because my shepherds have not searched for my sheep, but the shepherds have fed themselves, and have not fed my sheep; 9 therefore, you shepherds, hear the word of the LORD: 10 Thus says the Lord GOD, Behold, I am against the shepherds; and I will require my sheep at their hand, and put a stop to their feeding the sheep; no longer shall the shepherds feed themselves. I will rescue my sheep from their mouths, that they may not be food for them.

11 "For thus says the Lord GOD: Behold, I, I myself will search for my sheep,

---

5. And they were scattered is omitted by the Syriac; it is possibly dittography from the beginning of the verse, but is perhaps best connected with the following verse, as in the RSV and with the LXX.

6. Wandered, ישגו, should be וישגו with the Syriac, to have the proper verbal form, or else is to be omitted with the LXX.

8. The **wild beasts** are the nations exploiting Judah, particularly the Babylonians, and perhaps, for the editor, Persia.

10. The sheep: Hebrew **sheep,** but perhaps with the LXX and Syriac, "my sheep."

2. YAHWEH AS THE GOOD SHEPHERD (34:11-16)

See John 10:1-18; Heb. 13:20; I Pet. 2:25; 5:4 (cf. Matt. 10:6; 25:32; etc.).

---

devoted care for individuals according to their needs. He must be like the shepherd in the parable of Jesus, whose heart is with the one animal that has strayed from the flock (Luke 15:4-7). In modern language, the just state is not merely one in which a careful balance of claims and counterclaims is preserved; it is one in which the rights of those who can put forward no such claims are respected and maintained. Without that humane element in government, self-interest asserts itself at the expense of the common good, and the community lacks

the cohesion which would enable it to meet its enemies. Betrayal from within delivers it up to attack from without.

11-16. The Good Shepherd.—Here God himself appears in the role of the faithful **shepherd,** taking over the duties neglected by the faithless shepherds he has been forced to dispossess. He begins by collecting the poor scattered sheep and then goes on to feed and protect them. As we should say, when a community has fallen victim to spurious leadership genuine leadership can be restored only by the widespread

12 As a shepherd seeketh out his flock in the day that he is among his sheep *that are* scattered; so will I seek out my sheep, and will deliver them out of all places where they have been scattered in the cloudy and dark day.

13 And I will bring them out from the people, and gather them from the countries, and will bring them to their own land, and feed them upon the mountains of Israel by the rivers, and in all the inhabited places of the country.

14 I will feed them in a good pasture, and upon the high mountains of Israel shall their fold be: there shall they lie in a good fold, and *in* a fat pasture shall they feed upon the mountains of Israel.

15 I will feed my flock, and I will cause them to lie down, saith the Lord God.

16 I will seek that which was lost, and bring again that which was driven away, and will bind up *that which was* broken, and will strengthen that which was sick: but I will destroy the fat and the strong; I will feed them with judgment.

17 And *as for* you, O my flock, thus saith the Lord God; Behold, I judge between cattle and cattle, between the rams and the he goats.

and will seek them out. 12 As a shepherd seeks out his flock when some of his sheep[v] have been scattered abroad, so will I seek out my sheep; and I will rescue them from all places where they have been scattered on a day of clouds and thick darkness. 13 And I will bring them out from the peoples, and gather them from the countries, and will bring them into their own land; and I will feed them on the mountains of Israel, by the fountains, and in all the inhabited places of the country. 14 I will feed them with good pasture, and upon the mountain heights of Israel shall be their pasture; there they shall lie down in good grazing land, and on fat pasture they shall feed on the mountains of Israel. 15 I myself will be the shepherd of my sheep, and I will make them lie down, says the Lord God. 16 I will seek the lost, and I will bring back the strayed, and I will bind up the crippled, and I will strengthen the weak, and the fat and the strong I will watch over;[w] I will feed them in justice.

17 "As for you, my flock, thus says the Lord God: Behold, I judge between sheep

v Cn: Heb *when he is among his sheep*
w Gk Syr Vg: Heb *destroy*

12. **When some of his sheep:** Read היות, "being," with one MS (cf. LXX) for היותו, "his being," and מתוך, "from among" [some of] for בתוך, among. Some read only "when his flock is scattered," i.e., ביום היות צאנו נפרשות. A slight error in the Masoretic pointing results in "separated" for **scattered abroad** (cf. 17:21). **Clouds and thick darkness:** See Ps. 97:2; Joel 2:2; Zeph. 1:15.

16. **I will watch over:** Read אשמר with the LXX, Syriac, and Vulg. for אשמיד, **I will destroy.** Yahweh is God of both the strong and the weak.

3. Judgment Between Sheep and Sheep (34:17-22)

Cf. the N.T. picture of the separation between the sheep and the goats in Matt. 25:31-32. Vss. 17-18 provide effective representation of exploitation by men so selfish that they deliberately despoil what they cannot use lest others might be able to have it. This judgment between sheep and sheep may seem inconsonant with the doctrine of grace in 36:22-32, but see Exeg. on that passage. It is consonant with the general picture of individual responsibility in chs. 14; 18. Cooke, noting that the threat of judgment does not occur again in these chapters, considers vss. 17 ff. a later addition (cf. also Matthews, Hölscher, *et al.*). Another but not clear possibility is that the judgment here is between

recognition that each individual is of value in the sight of God, and that those are most dear to him who can least press their claims upon their fellows. There must be a general sense that what is right takes precedence of what is expedient, and that the ruler must render ac-

count to God for the exercise of the power entrusted to him.

17-22. Exploiters and Exploited.—In this section quite a modern note is struck. The prophet speaks in terms of class conflict. The "haves" and the "have-nots" were to be found

18 *Seemeth it* a small thing unto you to have eaten up the good pasture, but ye must tread down with your feet the residue of your pastures? and to have drunk of the deep waters, but ye must foul the residue with your feet?

19 And *as for* my flock, they eat that which ye have trodden with your feet; and they drink that which ye have fouled with your feet.

20 ¶ Therefore thus saith the Lord God unto them; Behold, I, *even* I, will judge between the fat cattle and between the lean cattle.

21 Because ye have thrust with side and with shoulder, and pushed all the diseased with your horns, till ye have scattered them abroad;

22 Therefore will I save my flock, and they shall no more be a prey; and I will judge between cattle and cattle.

23 And I will set up one shepherd over them, and he shall feed them, *even* my servant David; he shall feed them, and he shall be their shepherd.

and sheep, rams and he-goats. **18** Is it not enough for you to feed on the good pasture, that you must tread down with your feet the rest of your pasture; and to drink of clear water, that you must foul the rest with your feet? **19** And must my sheep eat what you have trodden with your feet, and drink what you have fouled with your feet?

20 "Therefore, thus says the Lord God to them: Behold, I, I myself will judge between the fat sheep and the lean sheep. **21** Because you push with side and shoulder, and thrust at all the weak with your horns, till you have scattered them abroad, **22** I will save my flock, they shall no longer be a prey; and I will judge between sheep and sheep. **23** And I will set up over them one shepherd, my servant David, and he shall feed them: he shall feed them and be their

---

the Israelite and the pagan sheep, for the oppressor sheep here are set in contrast with **my sheep** and **my flock,** and they have scattered Yahweh's sheep abroad and made them a prey. The terms are those used of the Exile by the editor; the rams and he-goats appear in 39:18 in connection with the pagan nations (see, however, Zech. 13:7-9).

17. Some scholars suggest that **rams and he-goats** are a gloss, since otherwise the judgment is only among the **sheep.**

20. The fat sheep are those who have special economic privileges or else the oppressor nations. Instead of בריה, "food," read בריאה, **fat.**

21. See Zech. 1:18-21, where the **horns** are those who have dispersed Judah.

4. The Messianic King as the New Shepherd (34:23-24)

The editor as usual designates the king as נשיא, **prince** (cf. 37:25; 44:3; 46:2, 4, 8; etc.). He is described also as **my servant,** even as David himself is designated in II Sam. 3:18; 7:5; II Kings 8:19; etc. (R^D); Ps. 89:3, 20; see also the superscriptions of Pss. 18; 36. There is not an allusion here to the resurrection of the historic David, although the passage has been so interpreted (see also 37:24; Hos. 3:5). This figure is the "one head" of Hos. 1:11 (Hebrew 2:2), not a king who will live forever, but the restorer of the

---

in the Judah of his day. There are those in the community who enrich themselves at the expense of their fellows, robbing them of all that makes life worth while (vs. 18). And there are others who have to be content with what is left to them, sorry as that may often be (vs. 19). But God himself will enter the lists as champion of the exploited section of the community. That indeed is one of the glories of biblical religion, and it goes back to the day when the Lord made himself known to Moses as about to vindicate

the slaves. He had heard their bitter cry in Egypt and would come down to set them free (Exod. 3:7-8). Ezekiel here shows himself a worthy successor of the prophets before him, Elijah and Amos, who had put the poor under the special protection of God. But how is this divine deliverance to be effected? The answer comes in the next verses.

23-31. *The Messianic Hope.*—The writer looks forward to a time when God will intervene by raising up a man to restore peace and

24 And I the LORD will be their God, and my servant David a prince among them; I the LORD have spoken *it*.	shepherd. 24 And I, the LORD, will be their God, and my servant David shall be prince among them; I, the LORD, have spoken.
25 And I will make with them a covenant of peace, and will cause the evil beasts to cease out of the land: and they shall dwell safely in the wilderness, and sleep in the woods.	25 "I will make with them a covenant of peace and banish wild beasts from the land, so that they may dwell securely in the wilderness and sleep in the woods. 26 And I will make them and the places round about my hill a blessing; and I will send down the showers in their season; they shall be showers of blessing. 27 And the trees of the field shall yield their fruit, and the earth shall yield its increase, and they shall be secure in their land; and they shall know that I am the LORD, when I break the bars of their yoke, and deliver them from the hand of those who enslaved them. 28 They shall no more be a prey to the nations, nor shall the beasts of the land devour them; they shall dwell securely, and none shall
26 And I will make them and the places round about my hill a blessing; and I will cause the shower to come down in his season; there shall be showers of blessing.	
27 And the tree of the field shall yield her fruit, and the earth shall yield her increase, and they shall be safe in their land, and shall know that I *am* the LORD, when I have broken the bands of their yoke, and delivered them out of the hand of those that served themselves of them.	

dynasty. Probably such a phrase as "prince for ever" in 37:25 (cf. also Isa. 9:5-6) is kingly terminology, not a reference to eternal life on this earth, for this is a much later conception (cf. Dan. 12:2) and not characteristic of the O.T. Messiah (cf. Jer. 23:5-6; 33:14-17, 26).

23. He shall feed [shepherd] **them** is tautologous, particularly in the Hebrew, and is omitted by some with the **LXX: feed** and "shepherd" are the same Hebrew verb.

24. A variation of the covenant promise (see 11:20; 37:27; etc.).

5. THE COVENANT OF PEACE (34:25-31)

This belongs to the same general period as Lev. 26:6, where Yahweh promises peace and the riddance of wild beasts (see also Hos. 2:18; Isa. 11:7-8; 65:25). For the **covenant of peace** see 37:26; Isa. 54:10 (see Wright, *Challenge of Israel's Faith,* p. 77).

26. My hill: Mount Zion, the temple hill. **The showers in their season** are the former (autumnal) rains and the latter (spring) rains (see Lev. 26:4; Deut. 11:14; 28:12; Jer. 5:24; Hos. 6:3; etc.).

27. Cf. the pictures of the productivity of nature in the new age in Hos. 2:22; Joel 3:18; Amos 9:13-14; Zech. 8:12; etc. There may be here also a reflection of Jer. 27:1–28:17 in vs. 27*b*.

justice in the land. He will end strife and division, and in a united nation a life of security and happiness will again be possible for all. The roots of this hope lie far back in the past. Indeed, we can trace them to ancient Egypt. J. H. Breasted assigns to the period of political weakness *ca.* 2500 B.C. the yearning for social justice and for a strong ruler who will curb the rapacity of petty officials and so ensure to every man his rights.[2]

We can distinguish two elements in the form taken here by this hope of an ideal ruler, one which we may well accept, another which we cannot. On the one hand, God works through a man who holds office and accepts public responsibility; i.e., the sphere of political action

does not lie outside the kingdom of God. Rather can it provide the instruments and agents through which that kingdom is in some measure established among us. The God of the Bible is the God who hears a cry and sends a man. But it is an error to suppose that God will use only the instruments accredited by the past. Of course the writer anticipates that he will choose a scion of the legitimate dynasty and set up again the throne of David. But when the Good Shepherd comes at last, he does not base his claims on royal descent nor does he mount a throne. He is not concerned to restore the vanished glories of the brief but splendid empire over which David and Solomon ruled. He comes rather to discharge the duties of the good shepherd, to heal the sick, bind up the injured, and lead home the wanderers (vs. 4).

[2] *The Dawn of Conscience* (New York: Charles Scribner's Sons, 1933), pp. 198-206.

28 And they shall no more be a prey to the heathen, neither shall the beast of the land devour them; but they shall dwell safely, and none shall make *them* afraid.

29 And I will raise up for them a plant of renown, and they shall be no more consumed with hunger in the land, neither bear the shame of the heathen any more.

30 Thus shall they know that I the LORD their God *am* with them, and *that* they, *even* the house of Israel, *are* my people, saith the Lord GOD.

31 And ye my flock, the flock of my pasture, *are* men, *and* I *am* your God, saith the Lord GOD.

35 Moreover the word of the LORD came unto me, saying,

2 Son of man, set thy face against mount Seir, and prophesy against it,

make them afraid. 29 And I will provide for them prosperous[x] plantations so that they shall no more be consumed with hunger in the land, and no longer suffer the reproach of the nations. 30 And they shall know that I, the LORD their God, am with them, and that they, the house of Israel, are my people, says the Lord GOD. 31 And you are my sheep, the sheep of my pasture,[y] and I am your God, says the Lord GOD."

35 The word of the LORD came to me: 2 "Son of man, set your face against

[x] Gk Syr Old Latin: Heb *for renown*
[y] Gk Old Latin: Heb *pasture you are men*

---

29. The M.T. reads "plantations for a name"; some read with the LXX, L[h], Syriac, "plantations of peace," i.e., מטע שלם for מטע לשם, requiring only a transposition of consonants, and so the RSV.

31. You are men (RSV mg.) is perhaps a gloss, added by a theologically-minded scribe. Some versions omit **men.**

C. ORACLE AGAINST MOUNT SEIR (35:1-15)

This oracle (cf. also 25:12-14) belongs to the same general period as Obadiah and the oracles concerned with Edom in Isa. 34:1-17; Jer. 49:7-22; Mal. 1:2-5 (cf. Ps. 137:7-9). This oracle is in deliberate contrast with the oracle concerning the mountains of Israel in ch. 36 (cf. 36:5). As in Obadiah, the destruction of Edom is to be part of the destruction of the pagan nations and a prelude to the restoration of Israel. Chs. 35–36 have much in common with ch. 6. These oracles against Edom reflect the intensity of the hatred of Edom in the fifth century. Edom here is to be laid waste and made desolate because of her continuous enmity to Israel. When judgment comes, Edom will learn that Yahweh is God; this theme is reiterated (vss. 9, 11-12, 15). This is neither a great oracle nor the editor at his best. The phraseology is tiresomely familiar. With vs. 2 cf. 6:2; 25:2; with vs. 3, 5:8; 6:14; with vs. 4, 12:20; with vs. 5, 25:12, 15; 21:25 (Hebrew 30), 29 (Hebrew 34); with vs. 6, 11:8; 22:4; with vs. 7, 14:13, 17, 19; 25:13; etc.; with vs. 8, 6:3; 31:17-18; 32:20-32; 36:6; etc.; with vs. 11, 20:5, 9; with vs. 12, 15:4; 33:24; 36:4; etc. A long list of the editor's phraseology could be made here. A number of scholars correctly see this as a non-Ezekielian production (see Hölscher, Jahn, Herrmann [*Ezechielstudien*], Herntrich, Matthews). Bertholet recovers as more probable vss. 1-6, 8*b*, 12-13, 15, while Irwin finds a single distich line of poetry in vs. 3.

35:1-3. Cf. the beginning of the oracle in ch. 6 (see also 25:2). **Mount Seir** occurs as the name of Edom, the highlands east of Arabah, primarily in the later sources (cf.

He accomplishes all this by means which no one recognized as royal till he made them peculiarly his own by his teaching, his cross, and his resurrection. For God fulfills himself as we need, not as we expect.

35:1-15. *Might and Right.*—The sin of Edom was that it took advantage of Judah's defeat in war to push its own claims to territory. After

the fall of Jerusalem a considerable area of the country lay desolate, and the Edomites pressed in to occupy and settle, asserting their sovereignty over the land thus acquired. They were prompted in this by the traditional hostility between the two peoples, what vs. 5 calls their **perpetual enmity.** The prophecy of Obadiah is directed against this state of things.

3 And say unto it, Thus saith the Lord God; Behold, O mount Seir, I *am* against thee, and I will stretch out mine hand against thee, and I will make thee most desolate.

4 I will lay thy cities waste, and thou shalt be desolate, and thou shalt know that I *am* the Lord.

5 Because thou hast had a perpetual hatred, and hast shed *the blood of* the children of Israel by the force of the sword in the time of their calamity, in the time *that their* iniquity *had* an end:

6 Therefore, *as* I live, saith the Lord God, I will prepare thee unto blood, and blood shall pursue thee: since thou hast not hated blood, even blood shall pursue thee.

7 Thus will I make mount Seir most desolate, and cut off from it him that passeth out and him that returneth.

8 And I will fill his mountains with his slain *men:* in thy hills, and in thy valleys,

Mount Se'ir, and prophesy against it, 3 and say to it, Thus says the Lord God: Behold, I am against you, Mount Se'ir, and I will stretch out my hand against you, and I will make you a desolation and a waste. 4 I will lay your cities waste, and you shall become a desolation; and you shall know that I am the Lord. 5 Because you cherished perpetual enmity, and gave over the people of Israel to the power of the sword at the time of their calamity, at the time of their final punishment; 6 therefore, as I live, says the Lord God, I will prepare you for blood, and blood shall pursue you; because you are guilty of blood,ᶻ therefore blood shall pursue you. 7 I will make Mount Se'ir a waste and a desolation; and I will cut off from it all who come and go. 8 And I will fill your mountains with the slain; on your

ᶻ Gk: Heb *you have hated blood*

Gen. 36:8-9 [P]; Deut. 1:2; 2:1, 5; I Chr. 4:42; etc.). Note the biblical explanation of the name in Gen. 25:25.

5. The enmity between the Edomites and the Hebrews was traced back to the days of Jacob (cf. Gen. 25; etc.), hence **perpetual enmity** here. Looking at it more objectively, we can hardly say that the Edomites were alone responsible for the bad feeling between the two nations. David conquered Edom, and its mineral resources and commercial resources were exploited by Solomon, who used Edomite slave labor (see II Sam. 8:13-14; I Kings 9:26-28; Glueck, *Other Side of the Jordan,* pp. 50-113). The enmity had its beginning in the period of wandering through the wilderness (see Num. 20:14-21). **The time of their calamity** was perhaps the time of disaster to Judah and Jerusalem in 586; Obad. 10-14 must refer to the same event. It has been suggested that the reference is to an Edomite destruction of Jerusalem in the early fifth century (see Neh. 1:3), but the description of it as **their final punishment** suggests that the allusion is to 586, and the author is promising that there will be no more destruction and exile (cf. Isa. 40:2).

6. The blood revenge was perhaps more urgent in view of the presumed kinship between Edom and Judah (see Mal. 1:2). The verse is corrupt. **And blood shall pursue you,** in its first occurrence, is perhaps due to dittography, and **I will prepare you for blood** is scribal comment—a *ki* clause; both are omitted by the LXX. **You are guilty of blood:** Read לדם אשמת for דם שנאת, **you have hated blood.** It has been suggested that there is a wordplay on Edom and blood (Hebrew דם, אדם).

8. Cf. the picture in 39:4-5.

There was, however, one obstacle in the way of Edom's aggressive policy—the divine claim to the land of Israel. This goes back, of course, to the close connection which existed for the Semites between the god and the land, so that even when the people had been driven from it, it still remained his by right. We see that from the account in II Kings 17 of how, after the depopulation of northern Israel, "the God of the land" continued to assert his rights and avenged himself on the Assyrian colonists for their neglect of him. But something more speaks to us out of this passage as we read it today.

Edom represents the arrogance of might, while Judah has only justice on her side. What Edom considers merely the nominal claim of an ineffectual god is in reality the outraged law of humanity which interposes between aggression

and in all thy rivers, shall they fall that are slain with the sword.

9 I will make thee perpetual desolations, and thy cities shall not return: and ye shall know that I *am* the LORD.

10 Because thou hast said, These two nations and these two countries shall be mine, and we will possess it; whereas the LORD was there:

11 Therefore, *as* I live, saith the Lord GOD, I will even do according to thine anger, and according to thine envy, which thou hast used out of thy hatred against them; and I will make myself known among them, when I have judged thee.

12 And thou shalt know that I *am* the LORD, *and that* I have heard all thy blasphemies which thou hast spoken against the mountains of Israel, saying, They are laid desolate, they are given us to consume.

13 Thus with your mouth ye have boasted against me, and have multiplied your words against me: I have heard *them*.

14 Thus saith the Lord GOD; When the whole earth rejoiceth, I will make thee desolate.

15 As thou didst rejoice at the inheritance of the house of Israel, because it was

hills and in your valleys and in all your ravines those slain with the sword shall fall.

9 I will make you a perpetual desolation, and your cities shall not be inhabited. Then you will know that I am the LORD.

10 "Because you said, 'These two nations and these two countries shall be mine, and we will take possession of them,' — although the LORD was there — **11** therefore, as I live, says the Lord GOD, I will deal with you according to the anger and envy which you showed because of your hatred against them; and I will make myself known among you,[a] when I judge you. **12** And you shall know that I, the LORD, have heard all the revilings which you uttered against the mountains of Israel, saying, 'They are laid desolate, they are given us to devour.' **13** And you magnified yourselves against me with your mouth, and multiplied your words against me; I heard it. **14** Thus says the Lord GOD: For the rejoicing of the whole earth I will make you desolate. **15** As you rejoiced over the inheritance of the

[a] Gk: Heb *them*

---

9. This is in contrast to the treatment to be accorded Egypt (29:13-16).

10. These two nations: Israel and Judah. The continued presence of Yahweh in Palestine is taken as a guarantee of the right of Yahweh's people, now in exile, to the land, an unusual form of Israel's historic claim to the land, if the text is correct. There may be some doubt of this in the light of the current view that Yahweh had forsaken the land at the time of the Exile, and since the editor gives the new city of Jerusalem the name "The LORD is there" (48:35), i.e., after having been away. Some would emend to "and the Lord heard," instead of **although the LORD was there,** which involves reading שמע for שם היה (cf. vss. 12-13).

11. Reading **among you** with the LXX is obviously preferable to the M.T. **among them.**

13. And have multiplied your words against me is omitted by some scholars with the LXX as a gloss on the preceding verse; the verb is perhaps an Aramaic loan word.

14. The text is probably corrupt, and it is suggested that vs. 15a, omitted by the LXX, is a scribal emendation of the verse.

15. The LXX has "and you shall know," etc., which better suits the context, but the editor may just be careless here with the oft-repeated formula.

---

and its victims. The fact that **the LORD was there** (vs. 10) means that, impotent though the inhabitants were to resist the invader, there was still a moral power which forbade his entry. It is true that the records of history are full of occasions on which the stronger has imposed his will on the weaker, breaking down in scorn all moral barriers in his path. Yet outraged right

has again and again taken to itself might in the course of time. Conquests are never permanent; what the victor grasps today he will be compelled to resign tomorrow, when the fate which he meted out to the vanquished is meted out to him in return. Sooner or later Edom will learn that he who seemed but the tribal god of Israel was in fact the Lord of the whole earth.

desolate, so will I do unto thee: thou shalt be desolate, O mount Seir, and all Idumea, *even* all of it: and they shall know that I *am* the LORD.

36 Also, thou son of man, prophesy unto the mountains of Israel, and say, Ye mountains of Israel, hear the word of the LORD:

house of Israel, because it was desolate, so I will deal with you; you shall be desolate, Mount Se'ir, and all Edom, all of it. Then they will know that I am the LORD.

36 "And you, son of man, prophesy to the mountains of Israel, and say, O mountains of Israel, hear the word of the

---

D. RESTORATION OF THE MOUNTAINS AND THE PEOPLE OF ISRAEL (36:1-38)

The first part of the chapter is an oracle addressed to the mountains of Israel (vss. 1-15), and the second part a series of oracles concerning the house of Israel, in part addressed to Israel and in part in the third person (vss. 16-38). Vss. 1-15 are in deliberate contrast with 35:1-15, the oracle against Mount Esau. Because the enemy has rejoiced at the downfall of the mountains of Israel and claimed them as a possession, he must suffer for it (vss. 1-7), but the mountains of Israel will again be fruitful and the cities be inhabited (vss. 8-15). Vss. 16-38 contain three oracles introduced by vss. 16-21. In the introduction the sins of the house of Israel, its punishment by exile, and the resultant profanation of the name of Yahweh among the nations are noted. Not for the sake of the house of Israel, but for his own name's sake will Yahweh restore the house of Israel and give them a new heart and a new spirit (vss. 22-32). The cities will be rebuilt and inhabited and the desert land tilled, and the nations will know that Yahweh has done it (vss. 33-36). The population will increase like the flocks at Jerusalem for the great festivals, and the house of Israel will know that Yahweh is God (vss. 37-38).

This chapter has already been discussed in some detail (see Intro., pp. 47-48). The editor's doctrine of grace, with Israel to be forgiven by Yahweh "for his name's sake" and given a new heart and a new spirit, is not inconsonant with the doctrine of individual responsibility held so strictly at other points. The author is here concerned with the house of Israel in relation to the Gentile nations and the return to Palestine. Yahweh had judged the house of Israel in accordance with their deeds and conduct by sending them into exile. His name has been profaned as a result of the attitude of the pagan nations toward them and the sinning of the house of Israel in exile. Yahweh will cleanse them from all their uncleanness, not because they deserve it, but for the sake of his name. Then they will remember their evil ways and loathe themselves for their abominable deeds. Thus repenting and having turned from their evil ways, they will fall under the category of those who, in ch. 18, etc., are judged by their present goodness and not held responsible for their past wickedness. Presumably, although in general there would be repentance, in particular some would not repent, and they would come under the judgment noted in 34:17-22; 18:1-32; etc. The editor's logic may be not all that a theologian might desire, but it is the logic of Jer. 31:27-34, where the strict doctrine of individual responsibility is also linked with the new heart doctrine and new covenant ideology, from a source which stresses, as does our editor, the doctrine of "for his name's sake" (see May, "Jeremiah's Biographer," pp. 195-200.). This latter doctrine, revealing the influence of Second Isaiah, we have already encountered in 20:9, 14, 22, 44. See Cooke for numerous parallels between the diction of this chapter and other parts of the book. W. A. Irwin (*The Problem of Ezekiel* [Chicago: University of Chicago Press, 1943], p. 59) says that vss. 7-12 must surely come from the period immediately before Nehemiah's great work; this is actually the place where the entire chapter

---

Thus many a powerful nation learns that what it dismissed at the time as so much empty talk of justice and human rights was in fact the invocation of a moral order which in the end crushes those who defy it.

36:1-15. *Love Thou Thy Land.*—Here we see something of the prophet's impassioned love for the land of his birth. It is not merely that he is attached to its traditions and takes pride in its history; he dwells with love on the various

2 Thus saith the Lord God; Because the enemy hath said against you, Aha, even the ancient high places are ours in possession:

3 Therefore prophesy and say, Thus saith the Lord God; Because they have made *you* desolate, and swallowed you up on every side, that ye might be a possession unto the residue of the heathen, and ye are taken up in the lips of talkers, and *are* an infamy of the people:

4 Therefore, ye mountains of Israel, hear the word of the Lord God; Thus saith the Lord God to the mountains and to the hills, to the rivers and to the valleys, to the desolate wastes and to the cities that are forsaken, which became a prey and derision to the residue of the heathen that *are* round about;

5 Therefore thus saith the Lord God; Surely in the fire of my jealousy have I spoken against the residue of the heathen, and against all Idumea, which have appointed my land into their possession with the joy of all *their* heart, with despiteful minds, to cast it out for a prey.

Lord. 2 Thus says the Lord God: Because the enemy said of you, 'Aha!' and, 'The ancient heights have become our possession,' 3 therefore prophesy, and say, Thus says the Lord God: Because, yea, because they made you desolate, and crushed you from all sides, so that you became the possession of the rest of the nations, and you became the talk and evil gossip of the people; 4 therefore, O mountains of Israel, hear the word of the Lord God: Thus says the Lord God to the mountains and the hills, the ravines and the valleys, the desolate wastes and the deserted cities, which have become a prey and derision to the rest of the nations round about; 5 therefore thus says the Lord God: I speak in my hot jealousy against the rest of the nations, and against all Edom, who gave my land to themselves as a possession with wholehearted joy and utter contempt, that they

should be located, and is in the time of our editor. In the Scheide Papyrus of Ezekiel (see Intro., pp. 48, 63) the chapter ends with vs. 23a.

Scholars differ widely in their interpretation. Irwin finds a tristich line within vss. 17-18. Matthews seems certain only about vss. 26-28; Cooke thinks the solution that the primary form of vss. 1-15 consisted of vss. 1, 2, 4abβ, 6bβ "as good as any," while vss. 33-36 and 37-38 appear to be supplementary in the last section; cf. Hölscher's analysis, although he takes none of the passage as Ezekiel's. Bertholet largely accredits the chapter to Ezekiel (save vss. 13-14, 37-38), finding two parallel compositions of Ezekiel in the first part of the chapter.

1. Judgment on the Gentile Nations (36:1-7)

Apparently the rest of the nations (vss. 4-5) plus Edom comprise the nations round about Judah (vs. 7).

36:2-3. Cf. the exultation of the pagan nations in 25:2, 8; 26:2 (cf. 25:10). The word במות, **heights,** is usually translated **high places;** but cf. Num. 21:28; Deut. 32:13; Amos 4:13; Mic. 3:12 (=Jer. 26:18); etc. Some suggest emending to שממות, "desolations," with the LXX (cf. 35:9). Matthews suggests that **the rest of the nations** are those petty neighboring groups troublesome at the time of Nehemiah (cf. Ezra 9:1; Neh. 2:19; 4:1-3; 13:23). **Crushed:** Another possible meaning is "trampled down" (cf. Amos 2:7).

5. That they might possess it: Read למורשת for למען מגרשה, **to cast it out,** with one MS. The word מגרשה represents an Aramaic infinitive form (see 17:9). Without emendation, the object **it** (i.e., the land) would stand here for the population of the land.

features of the familiar landscape, with its hills and valleys and streams. As he saw them in earlier days they were scarred with the high places which were witnesses to the national apostasy. He was called to denounce them as such (ch. 6) and we should probably read the

words in the present passage as intended to balance those. As he looks now upon the Judean scene he sees everywhere the desolation which shows how completely his premonitions have been fulfilled. But the earth is still so dear to him that he cannot believe that it will lie

6 Prophesy therefore concerning the land of Israel, and say unto the mountains and to the hills, to the rivers and to the valleys, Thus saith the Lord God; Behold, I have spoken in my jealousy and in my fury, because ye have borne the shame of the heathen:

7 Therefore thus saith the Lord God; I have lifted up mine hand, Surely the heathen that *are* about you, they shall bear their shame.

8 ¶ But ye, O mountains of Israel, ye shall shoot forth your branches, and yield your fruit to my people of Israel; for they are at hand to come.

9 For, behold, I *am* for you, and I will turn unto you, and ye shall be tilled and sown:

10 And I will multiply men upon you, all the house of Israel, *even* all of it: and the cities shall be inhabited, and the wastes shall be builded:

11 And I will multiply upon you man and beast; and they shall increase and bring fruit: and I will settle you after your old estates, and will do better *unto you* than at your beginnings: and ye shall know that I *am* the Lord.

12 Yea, I will cause men to walk upon you, *even* my people Israel; and they shall

might possess[b] it and plunder it. **6** Therefore prophesy concerning the land of Israel, and say to the mountains and hills, to the ravines and valleys, Thus says the Lord God: Behold, I speak in my jealous wrath, because you have suffered the reproach of the nation; **7** therefore thus says the Lord God: I swear that the nations that are round about you shall themselves suffer reproach.

8 "But you, O mountains of Israel, shall shoot forth your branches, and yield your fruit to my people Israel; for they will soon come home. **9** For, behold, I am for you, and I will turn to you, and you shall be tilled and sown; **10** and I will multiply men upon you, the whole house of Israel, all of it; the cities shall be inhabited and the waste places rebuilt; **11** and I will multiply upon you man and beast; and they shall increase and be fruitful; and I will cause you to be inhabited as in your former times, and will do more good to you than ever before. Then you will know that I am the Lord. **12** Yea, I will let men walk upon you,

[b] One Ms: Heb *drive out*

---

7. To swear by the uplifted hand (KJV) appears also in 20:5. The spirit is more that of Nahum than of the author of the book of Jonah; see also Mal. 1:2-5, where the desolation of Edom is a large part of the proof that Yahweh loves Jacob.

2. Restoration of the Mountains of Israel (36:8-15)

The mountains, the hill country, really stand for all the land.

10. Some scholars take this verse as secondary (see Herrmann, Hölscher, Cooke) because vs. 10*b* does not fit the mountain imagery, but we should not overestimate the editor's style. **The whole house of Israel, all of it,** includes both Israel and Judah. With the verse cf. vss. 37-38 (see Zech. 2:4).

11. At your beginnings is perhaps a reference to the time of the Exodus, as in Hos. 11:1-4; Jer. 2:1-3, 6-7; etc.

12*b*-14. Note the striking figure of the mountains bereaving the house of Israel, perhaps through famine caused by drought. There is a certain justification for such

---

untilled for long, and it is inconceivable to him that the cities should remain indefinitely uninhabited. There is such a thing as love of the country which gave one birth and whose landscapes have been familiar since childhood. For nature also has her share in the purpose of God, and the country in which a people lives is one of the factors which condition its character and enter into the making of its history.

The land becomes thus part almost of the people itself.

We learn from this passage: (*a*) Not to despair for the present plight of the land we love, but to have faith in its future. It was never meant to lie waste, but rather to maintain men and women to do God's work. (*b*) Not to be ashamed of a land which seems poor and barren and has little to offer (vs. 13). Even

possess thee, and thou shalt be their inheritance, and thou shalt no more henceforth bereave them *of men*.

13 Thus saith the Lord God; Because they say unto you, Thou *land* devourest up men, and hast bereaved thy nations;

14 Therefore thou shalt devour men no more, neither bereave thy nations any more, saith the Lord God.

15 Neither will I cause *men* to hear in thee the shame of the heathen any more, neither shalt thou bear the reproach of the people any more, neither shalt thou cause thy nations to fall any more, saith the Lord God.

16 ¶ Moreover the word of the Lord came unto me, saying,

17 Son of man, when the house of Israel dwelt in their own land, they defiled it by their own way and by their doings: their way was before me as the uncleanness of a removed woman.

18 Wherefore I poured my fury upon them for the blood that they had shed upon the land, and for their idols *wherewith* they had polluted it:

19 And I scattered them among the heathen, and they were dispersed through

even my people Israel; and they shall possess you, and you shall be their inheritance, and you shall no longer bereave them of children. 13 Thus says the Lord God: Because men say to you, 'You devour men, and you bereave your nation of children,' 14 therefore you shall no longer devour men and no longer bereave your nation of children, says the Lord God; 15 and I will not let you hear any more the reproach of the nations, and you shall no longer bear the disgrace of the peoples and no longer cause your nation to stumble, says the Lord God."

16 The word of the Lord came to me: 17 "Son of man, when the house of Israel dwelt in their own land, they defiled it by their ways and their doings; their conduct before me was like the uncleanness of a woman in her impurity. 18 So I poured out my wrath upon them for the blood which they had shed in the land, for the idols with which they had defiled it. 19 I scattered them among the nations, and they were dis-

---

personification of the mountains of Israel, for the land and climate did play a role, albeit not the determinative one, in the history of Palestine (see George Adam Smith, *The Historical Geography of the Holy Land* [25th ed.; London: Hodder & Stoughton, 1931], pp. 45-102; cf. Num. 13:32).

14. **Bereave:** Read with Hebrew mg. and versions תשכלי for תכשלי, "cause to stumble"; the same should obviously be read for **cause . . . to stumble** in vs. 15.

3. The House of Israel Punished for Its Wrongdoing (36:16-21)

The prosperity of Israel was associated with the prestige of Yahweh because of the attitude of the nations toward a defeated Israel.

17. See also 18:6 for allusion to **uncleanness** due to menstruation. The very land was defiled by the sins of the people.

18. The **idols** (see also vs. 25) are the *gillûlîm,* "detestable idols" of 6:4, etc.

---

an unbeautiful and poverty-stricken country can command the devotion of her children. (c) To love our country not so much for what she has been as for what she may yet become (vss. 14-15). Her future is in the hands of God—and in our own.

16-32. Hallowed Be Thy Name.—From the point of view of a Babylonian the defeat of Judah and the exile of its people were ample demonstration of the bankruptcy of its God. He had clearly proved himself unable to protect his people, and as such was quite discredited.

A modern would say that the disasters which had befallen Israel showed that its religion was without foundation; the ancient mind was able, in a manner which is incomprehensible to us, to conceive of the possibility that a god might exist, though events had demonstrated that he could not meet the needs of his worshippers. They thought of him as our fathers did of Napoleon after Waterloo: he was a ruler so discredited by defeat that it was foolish for his subjects to continue loyal to him.[3]

[3] E. L. Allen, *Prophet and Nation* (London: Nisbet & Co., 1947), pp. 109-10.

the countries: according to their way and according to their doings I judged them.

20 And when they entered unto the heathen, whither they went, they profaned my holy name, when they said to them, These *are* the people of the LORD, and are gone forth out of his land.

21 ¶ But I had pity for mine holy name, which the house of Israel had profaned among the heathen, whither they went.

22 Therefore say unto the house of Israel, Thus saith the Lord GOD; I do not *this* for your sakes, O house of Israel, but for mine holy name's sake, which ye have profaned among the heathen, whither ye went.

23 And I will sanctify my great name, which was profaned among the heathen, which ye have profaned in the midst of them; and the heathen shall know that I *am* the LORD, saith the Lord GOD, when I shall be sanctified in you before their eyes.

24 For I will take you from among the heathen, and gather you out of all countries, and will bring you into your own land.

persed through the countries; in accordance with their conduct and their deeds I judged them. 20 But when they came to the nations, wherever they came, they profaned my holy name, in that men said of them, 'These are the people of the LORD, and yet they had to go out of his land.' 21 But I had concern for my holy name, which the house of Israel caused to be profaned among the nations to which they came.

22 "Therefore say to the house of Israel, Thus says the Lord GOD: It is not for your sake, O house of Israel, that I am about to act, but for the sake of my holy name, which you have profaned among the nations to which you came. 23 And I will vindicate the holiness of my great name, which has been profaned among the nations, and which you have profaned among them; and the nations will know that I am the LORD, says the Lord GOD, when through you I vindicate my holiness before their eyes. 24 For I will take you from the nations, and gather you from all the countries, and bring

---

20. For the profanation of Yahweh's name see 20:9, etc. (see xxviii on p. 51; cf. Lev. 18:21; 19:12; 20:3; etc.). **The people of the LORD:** See Exod. 6:7; Lev. 20:24, 26; Deut. 4:20; 7:6; etc. In P the theocratic community is designated the congregation or assembly of Yahweh (see Num. 16:3; 20:4; 27:17; 31:16; etc.; see also the Chronicler).

4. RESTORATION OF ISRAEL (36:22-32)

Yahweh, for the sake of his name which the house of Israel profaned among the nations, will vindicate his holiness and return the Israelites to their land, giving them a new heart and a new spirit. The land will produce abundance, and the house of Israel will loathe itself for its abominable deeds. The passage ends with a plea to the house of Israel to recognize its evil conduct. The editor properly is not concerned with the glorification of Israel but with the glorification of Yahweh.

23. **Vindicate** and **sanctify** are both involved in the meaning of the Hebrew root in this context, for the sanctification of the name is a form of vindication, as the return of Israel makes manifest to the nations the holiness of Yahweh. The verse recalls Mal. 1:11.

How should we state this problem today? It is urged that Christianity has been tried and found wanting. Surely it is discredited, men say, by the fact that it has proved impotent to prevent world wars among the peoples who have lived for centuries under its influence. What can we say in answer to such challenges?

One reply is that what lies behind our misfortunes may not be God's impotence but his righteousness. It is the truth rather than the falsehood of Christianity that is demonstrated by the disasters which overtake us when we pursue our own ends rather than a common

good. When those who take the sword perish by the sword, when men reap as they have sown, it is we who are discredited thereby, not the book which all along contained these solemn warnings.

Another reply is less severe than this. It is that God's purpose is still incomplete, and it is not for us to judge it until we see to the end. He has a purpose of redemption, and the discipline of our present suffering is needed if this is to be fulfilled. When our sins find us out, it is not because he delights to punish, but because only so can we be brought to realize

25 ¶ Then will I sprinkle clean water upon you, and ye shall be clean: from all your filthiness, and from all your idols, will I cleanse you.

26 A new heart also will I give you, and a new spirit will I put within you: and I will take away the stony heart out of your flesh, and I will give you a heart of flesh.

27 And I will put my Spirit within you, and cause you to walk in my statutes, and ye shall keep my judgments, and do *them*.

28 And ye shall dwell in the land that I gave to your fathers; and ye shall be my people, and I will be your God.

29 I will also save you from all your uncleannesses: and I will call for the corn, and will increase it, and lay no famine upon you.

30 And I will multiply the fruit of the tree, and the increase of the field, that ye shall receive no more reproach of famine among the heathen.

31 Then shall ye remember your own evil ways, and your doings that *were* not good, and shall loathe yourselves in your own sight for your iniquities and for your abominations.

you into your own land. 25 I will sprinkle clean water upon you, and you shall be clean from all your uncleannesses, and from all your idols I will cleanse you. 26 A new heart I will give you, and a new spirit I will put within you; and I will take out of your flesh the heart of stone and give you a heart of flesh. 27 And I will put my spirit within you, and cause you to walk in my statutes and be careful to observe my ordinances. 28 You shall dwell in the land which I gave to your fathers; and you shall be my people, and I will be your God. 29 And I will deliver you from all your uncleannesses; and I will summon the grain and make it abundant and lay no famine upon you. 30 I will make the fruit of the tree and the increase of the field abundant, that you may never again suffer the disgrace of famine among the nations. 31 Then you will remember your evil ways, and your deeds that were not good; and you will loathe yourselves for your iniquities and your

25. Sprinkling with **water** for purposes of ritual cleansing probably provides the imagery here (cf. the ritual sprinkling with blood in Exod. 24:6; Lev. 17:6; Num. 18:17; etc., and the ritual washings with water in Exod. 30:17-21; Lev. 14:52; Num. 19:17-19).

26. For the new heart and new spirit concept see Exeg. on 18:30-32 (cf. 11:19). New things, new songs, new names, a new heaven, and a new earth appear in Hebrew eschatology (see Isa. 42:9-10; 43:19; 48:6; 62:2; 65:17; 66:22; Jer. 3:17; 31:22; 33:16; Ps. 96:1; etc.; cf. II Pet. 3:13; Rev. 5:9; 21:1, 5; etc.).

27. The suffering servant, Israel, in Second Isaiah is endowed with Yahweh's **spirit** (Isa. 42:1), and Yahweh would pour out his spirit on the seed of Jacob-Israel (Isa. 44:3). It is not surprising to find here further influences of Second Isaiah (see 39:29; also Joel 2:28-29). The idea of possession by the spirit of God has a long history (see Gen. 41:38; Exod. 31:3; I Sam. 10:10; 11:6; etc.; and Matt. 12:18; Acts 2:17-18). Note especially the possession of the spirit in prophecy (cf. Num. 11:17, 25; I Sam. 10:10; etc.), and the spirit that entered Ezekiel (2:2; 3:24; 8:3; see Otto J. Baab, *The Theology of the Old Testament* [New York and Nashville: Abingdon-Cokesbury Press, 1949], pp. 39-41).

the heinousness of our sin and to repudiate it for new obedience. This means, of course, that the final evidence that God is indeed in Jesus Christ and his gospel is accessible only to those who respond in the end to his appeal. The ways of God with us will remain inexplicable always if we halt him halfway, just as a surgical operation seems sheer cruelty to those who come in about the middle of it and do not wait to see the beneficent purpose behind it fully worked out.

25-32. *The New Covenant.*—The prophet takes up again the theme already touched upon in 11:19-21. He has in view a new relationship between the people and their God, bonds which will unite them more closely than the covenant at Sinai could do. They have never really learned to be faithful to him, but instead of punishing them he will give them a fresh start. He will begin with forgiveness, the obliteration of the past and the grant of a hopeful future. God himself will take the initiative and wean

32 Not for your sakes do I *this,* saith the Lord GOD, be it known unto you: be ashamed and confounded for your own ways, O house of Israel.

33 Thus saith the Lord GOD; In the day that I shall have cleansed you from all your iniquities I will also cause *you* to dwell in the cities, and the wastes shall be builded.

34 And the desolate land shall be tilled, whereas it lay desolate in the sight of all that passed by.

35 And they shall say, This land that was desolate is become like the garden of Eden; and the waste and desolate and ruined cities *are become* fenced, *and* are inhabited.

36 Then the heathen that are left round about you shall know that I the LORD build the ruined *places, and* plant that that was desolate: I the LORD have spoken *it,* and I will do *it.*

37 Thus saith the Lord GOD; I will yet *for* this be inquired of by the house of Israel, to do *it* for them; I will increase them with men like a flock.

abominable deeds. **32** It is not for your sake that I will act, says the Lord GOD; let that be known to you. Be ashamed and confounded for your ways, O house of Israel.

33 "Thus says the Lord GOD: On the day that I cleanse you from all your iniquities, I will cause the cities to be inhabited, and the waste places shall be rebuilt. **34** And the land that was desolate shall be tilled, instead of being the desolation that it was in the sight of all who passed by. **35** And they will say, 'This land that was desolate has become like the garden of Eden; and the waste and desolate and ruined cities are now inhabited and fortified.' **36** Then the nations that are left round about you shall know that I, the LORD, have rebuilt the ruined places, and replanted that which was desolate; I, the LORD, have spoken, and I will do it.

37 "Thus says the Lord GOD: This also I will let the house of Israel ask me to do for them: to increase their men like a flock.

5. THE CITIES AND WASTE PLACES RESTORED (36:33-36)

33-36. The nations will know that the restoration is the work of Yahweh. The comment of the **nations** in vs. 35 is in contrast with that in vs. 20. The movement of history is from Eden to Eden (see vs. 38), and it is Yahweh, not man, who brings history to its consummation. This looks forward to a new age within history, not beyond history (contrast Daniel). Vs. 34*b* seems a deliberate allusion to 5:14.

6. THE INCREASED POPULATION (36:37-38)

37-38. The passage reverts to the **flock** symbolism of ch. 34. Yahweh's willingness to let himself be inquired of recalls 14:3; 20:3, 31, where Yahweh would not let himself be inquired of. This is deliberate contrast and a part of the literary unity of the book; those who would take vss. 33-36 and vss. 37-38 as supplementary additions fail to see

the people from their unworthy allegiances. Forgiveness will lead on to rebirth; men will face the future in a wholly new temper, in gratitude and obedience. The old obduracy and self-will will be replaced by an understanding of God's will and an eager desire to do it. This in turn will make possible the glad, free loyalty of love which surpasses all mere obedience to commands. It is the conversion of a nation that is described, but how is that possible except as the individuals of which it is composed are won for God?

Finally, the ground of all this is in God, not in ourselves (vss. 22, 32). It is the very heart of the gospel that God does not receive us for any worthiness on our part. His own goodness

prompts him to do so, and it is the recognition that he has dealt with us otherwise than as we deserve which enables us to become as worthy as it is possible for us to be.

33-38. *Restoration.*—This is one of the many passages in the Bible which speak in promise to us when we are disheartened by some experience of loss and failure. Man so often spends his strength in destruction that it is good to be assured that God spends his energies on rebuilding what has been broken down.

There are probably many ancient buildings of which the same story is told as of Tintern Abbey. It was allowed to fall into ruins, so that the people of the village near by, wanting to build their houses, had no scruple about taking

38 As the holy flock, as the flock of Jerusalem in her solemn feasts; so shall the
waste cities be filled with flocks of men: and
they shall know that I *am* the LORD.

37 The hand of the LORD was upon me,
and carried me out in the Spirit of
the LORD, and set me down in the midst
of the valley which *was* full of bones,

38 Like the flock for sacrifices,[c] like the flock
at Jerusalem during her appointed feasts,
so shall the waste cities be filled with flocks
of men. Then they will know that I am the
LORD."

37 The hand of the LORD was upon me,
and he brought me out by the Spirit
of the LORD, and set me down in the midst

[c] Heb *flock of holy things*

---

the book as a whole. For the increase of population see Isa. 49:19; 54:1-3; Zech. 2:4
(Hebrew 2:8).

E. VISION OF THE VALLEY OF DRY BONES (37:1-14)

The vision here described is one of the best-known parts of the book. The dry
bones symbolize the Israelites in exile. Yahweh's query, **Can these bones live?** (vs. 3),
doubtless reflects a question often on the tongues of the exiles. The oracle promises
the resurrection of the nation. When the prophet prophesied, the bones came together
and breath entered the corpses, and they became a great living host. The author may
be suggesting that the prophesying of the return will in some sense effect the return.
The original authorship of the vision is uncertain. The phraseology of vss. 6, 13-14 is
the editor's, and the **whole house of Israel** in vs. 11, if it designates the union of the
two kingdoms (cf. 36:10), is his. If the vision is but an illustration of the editor's statement
at other points that Yahweh will put his spirit in Israel and give it a new spirit (36:27;
39:29; cf. 37:5-6, 14), it may belong in its entirety to the editor, but this is not certain.
The setting suggests a return of those exiled into Babylon, rather than the general
Diaspora "scattered among the nations," and there remains the possibility that the editor
has transmitted and transformed a vision of Ezekiel, in which the wind (see Exeg. on
vs. 9) entered the dead bodies.

Bertholet, assigning the chapter to Ezekiel's Babylonian period after the fall of
Jerusalem, thinks the vision originally was linked to 3:24a as a part of the oracle in the
valley (plain).

The location of the valley is apparently the same as that in 3:23, and **the hand of
the LORD** (vs. 1) is deliberately parallel to 3:22, setting this oracle over against 3:22-24,
as ch. 36 is set over against ch. 6, or ch. 40 over against chs. 1; 8–10. The first time the
prophet was in the valley it was to receive an oracle of doom, but here it is to receive
an oracle of hope. The oracle does not imply belief in the general resurrection of the dead,
in contrast with Isa. 26:19; Dan. 12:1-3. It refers to the resurrection of the community of

---

stones from it as material. But a time came
when love of the old shrine led to a reversal
of the process. As the cottages one by one became uninhabitable, the precious pieces were
rescued and restored to their places, so that
parts of the abbey began to rise again in beauty.
So we make havoc of God's workmanship, but
with the failure of our foolish enterprises he is
able to recover what was thus lost, and to
restore something of the lineaments of his fair
world.

But notice vs. 37, "I will also let Israel ask
this from me and have it done for them"
(Moffatt). God does not impose his gracious
purpose on us, but waits until we ourselves
desire it of him. We sometimes hear it argued
that if God is really eager to bless us, he will

give us now what we need and not wait till we
ask him. But is that so? Surely God is never
concerned merely to give us things, but only
in and through what he gives us to train us to
be his children, true men and women. He can
adequately bless us only when we ourselves are
ready and eager for his blessing. Thus some
of us discover for the first time what it really
means to relish our food—because we come to
it hungry. It is as simple as that.

37:1-14. *Life from the Dead.*—The opening
section of this chapter is among the most important in the whole Bible, and the preacher
will turn to it again and again, so rich in
suggestion and inspiration is it. We have here
one of those instances in which what seemed at
the time only a wild flight of imagination has

2 And caused me to pass by them round about: and, behold, *there were* very many in the open valley; and, lo, *they were* very dry.

of the valley;[d] it was full of bones. 2 And he led me round among them; and behold, there were very many upon the valley;[d]

[d] Or *plain*

Israel, i.e., to its return to Palestine. Some scholars locate the plain in the vicinity of Jerusalem (see Matthews, Herntrich, Harford), but the symbolism demands Babylonia, i.e., resurrection from exile. It has been suggested that a comparison of vs. 1 with 40:1 shows that a date originally stood at the beginning of the chapter. The influence of this vision appears in Rev. 11. For a dramatic pictorial presentation of the vision see the third-century A.D. panel among the frescoes of the synagogue at Dura-Europos on the Euphrates (Wischnitzer, *The Messianic Theme in the Paintings of the Dura Synagogue,* pp. 39-46, Figs. 16, 18, 19; see also Isaiah Sonne, "The Paintings of the Dura Synagogue," *Hebrew Union College Annual,* XX [1947], 324-42, who finds the wars of Gog and Magog [cf. Ezek. 38–39] also depicted on the frescoes).

37:1-2. The figure may be that of a deserted battlefield, the many **bones** representing the extent of the disaster which has overtaken the house of Israel, and their very dry state (vs. 2), the author's opinion of the condition of the exiles. There is something more here than mere resuscitation of the newly dead (cf. I Kings 17:19-24; II Kings 4:18-37; 13:20-21).

---

been amply substantiated by the course of events. We stand at a point at which the power of God actually breaks into history and gives it a new direction.

If we take the view that Ezekiel was in Judah during the last struggle against Babylon, there is nothing to prevent our thinking of this **valley** of **dry bones** as an actual battlefield. On this very spot ineffectual resistance had been offered to the invader and the nation's hopes had been dashed. Now, as the prophet looks out over the scene, with disinterred bones scattered about the valley, it brings home to him the desperate situation of his people. Incidentally, one must bear in mind that the bones counted for more in the ancient world than they do with us. "If the bones are strong and firm, then the soul is strong; it manifests itself just as well in them as in the heart or any other vital organ. Therefore the bones are the soul." [4]

Accordingly, there is here a message of hope for those who have lost all grounds for hope. Not merely does the vision promise that the life of the nation will be renewed in spite of defeat and exile; it shows us the nation as an army of the living God. From the disasters of the present it will come forth with a closer unity, a more resolute purpose, and greater aptitude for the part which God intends it to play in his purposes.

Who among us has not stood at some time or other by the grave of his hopes? Who has not faced a situation in which any possibility of recovery seemed to be ruled out in advance? At such times we can appreciate the message

[4] Pedersen, *Israel, Its Life and Culture, I-II,* p. 172.

of this vision. It speaks to us of a God who can achieve the impossible. For is not that what is meant by raising the dead to life again? But how does the recovery come about? The first requirement is that the prophet himself should face the situation at its worst in the name of God. Notice that he is no mere spectator of the miracle, he is the agent through whom the transformation is effected. He is called to **prophesy to these bones** that they may **hear the word of the LORD** (vs. 4). He must speak the word where there is none to hear, for it will create hearers for itself. Even after the nation has to all appearances perished, he must continue as before to teach and to warn. He may not abandon his mission because there seems no hope of success. For his fidelity alone can release the powers which will bring new life to the people.

That is what actually happened. Because men like Ezekiel clung to their faith and continued their work, the renewal of the nation was possible. The vision of the prophet served to bring about its own fulfillment. Israel did rise from the grave of exile, it did stand on its feet again, **an exceeding great army** at God's service. This is one of the marvels of history, and it is something on which we can fall back in any time of individual or national disheartenment. There is with God the possibility of life from the dead.

1-14. The Spirit.—The passage has another value as well. It is one of the most instructive in the Bible for any consideration of the doctrine of the Spirit.

The Spirit lies beyond all that can be seen and measured. Its most apt symbol is the wind

3 And he said unto me, Son of man, can these bones live? And I answered, O Lord God, thou knowest.

4 Again he said unto me, Prophesy upon these bones, and say unto them, O ye dry bones, hear the word of the Lord.

5 Thus saith the Lord God unto these bones; Behold, I will cause breath to enter into you, and ye shall live:

6 And I will lay sinews upon you, and will bring up flesh upon you, and cover you with skin, and put breath in you, and ye shall live; and ye shall know that I *am* the Lord.

7 So I prophesied as I was commanded: and as I prophesied, there was a noise, and behold a shaking, and the bones came together, bone to his bone.

8 And when I beheld, lo, the sinews and the flesh came up upon them, and the skin covered them above: but *there was* no breath in them.

9 Then said he unto me, Prophesy unto the wind, prophesy, son of man, and say to the wind, Thus saith the Lord God; Come from the four winds, O breath, and breathe upon these slain, that they may live.

and lo, they were very dry. 3 And he said to me, "Son of man, can these bones live?" And I answered, "O Lord God, thou knowest." 4 Again he said to me, "Prophesy to these bones, and say to them, O dry bones, hear the word of the Lord. 5 Thus says the Lord God to these bones: Behold, I will cause breath[e] to enter you, and you shall live. 6 And I will lay sinews upon you, and will cause flesh to come upon you, and cover you with skin, and put breath[e] in you, and you shall live; and you shall know that I am the Lord."

7 So I prophesied as I was commanded; and as I prophesied, there was a noise, and behold, a rattling; and the bones came together, bone to its bone. 8 And as I looked, there were sinews on them, and flesh had come upon them, and skin had covered them; but there was no breath in them. 9 Then he said to me, "Prophesy to the breath, prophesy, son of man, and say to the breath,[f] Thus says the Lord God: Come from the four winds, O breath,[f] and breathe

[e] Or *spirit*

[f] Or *wind* or *spirit*

5-6. The word רוח, wind, **spirit**, or **breath**, occurs twice here and appears also in vss. 8-10, 14. It is difficult to know how to translate it. Fortunately the Hebrews did not have to! In vs. 9 it is clearly associated with the four winds (רוחות) of the heavens, and it becomes the breath which makes the difference between a lifeless body and a living being (cf. רוח חיים, "breath of life," in Gen. 6:17; 7:22). Vs. 14 interprets it as the Spirit of Yahweh. Is this the editor's interpretation of Ezekiel's imagery?

7. I was commanded: Hebrew צויתי, but three MSS, the LXX, O.L., Syriac, and Vulg. read צוני, "he commanded me," and so some scholars. The **noise** and **rattling** **(shaking)** may be that of the bones as they come together, or less probably of an earthquake which accompanied the miracle.

9. Wind is probably better than **breath**, for the wind has not as yet become breath. One suspects that in this context **the four winds** does not mean merely the four sides of the earth (see 42:20; Dan. 8:8; 11:4), but refers more definitely to the winds (cf. Jer. 49:36; Zech. 2:6 [Hebrew 2:10]; 6:5).

---

which is astir all about us but which is all the while invisible. We must never estimate a situation merely by those factors in it which can be brought under observation. The actual is but an excerpt from a much larger whole which includes within it all the wealth of the possible. The wise man recognizes the existence in human affairs of the imponderable and the incalculable. These may seem at first sight merely so much accident and chance, but a deeper discernment sees in them the signs of a creative and revolutionizing power which

emanates from God himself. K. S. Latourette[5] finds a law in operation in Christian history according to which periods of advance and retreat alternate. There are times when the church goes forward conquering, times also when it is driven back and forced to take up a defensive position. We can see, however, that after each fresh recession the advance which follows is greater than on the previous occasion. But there is a further law, that the forces which

[5] *The Unquenchable Light* (New York: Harper & Bros., 1941).

10 So I prophesied as he commanded me, and the breath came into them, and they lived, and stood up upon their feet, an exceeding great army.

11 ¶ Then he said unto me, Son of man, these bones are the whole house of Israel: behold, they say, Our bones are dried, and our hope is lost: we are cut off for our parts.

12 Therefore prophesy and say unto them, Thus saith the Lord GOD; Behold, O my people, I will open your graves, and cause you to come up out of your graves, and bring you into the land of Israel.

13 And ye shall know that I *am* the LORD, when I have opened your graves, O my people, and brought you up out of your graves,

14 And shall put my Spirit in you, and ye shall live, and I shall place you in your own land: then shall ye know that I the LORD have spoken *it,* and performed *it,* saith the LORD.

upon these slain, that they may live." 10 So I prophesied as he commanded me, and the breath came into them, and they lived, and stood upon their feet, an exceedingly great host.

11 Then he said to me, "Son of man, these bones are the whole house of Israel. Behold, they say, 'Our bones are dried up, and our hope is lost; we are clean cut off.' 12 Therefore prophesy, and say to them, Thus says the Lord GOD: Behold, I will open your graves, and raise you from your graves, O my people; and I will bring you home into the land of Israel. 13 And you shall know that I am the LORD, when I open your graves, and raise you from your graves, O my people. 14 And I will put my Spirit within you, and you shall live, and I will place you in your own land; then you shall know that I, the LORD, have spoken, and I have done it, says the LORD."

---

11. Hope is lost: As in Ezekiel's allegory in 19:5 (cf. the modern Zionist song, עוד לא אבדה תקותנו, "We still have not lost our hope," and Jer. 31:17). By revising the word division of the last clause we get נגזר נולנו, "our thread [i.e., of life] is cut off" (cf. Felix Perles, "נול=‛Gewebe' im Alten Testament," *Orientalische Literatur Zeitung,* XII [1909], 251-52; T. H. Gaster in *The Standard Dictionary of Folklore, Mythology, and Legend* [New York: Funk & Wagnalls, 1950], p. 988).

12-13. The reference to resurrection from the tombs **(graves),** as against that of bones exposed in the valley, introduces a new figure, and some consider it a later addition. Is the editor responsible? (See Bertholet, Herntrich, Hölscher, etc.)

---

make for renewal after a period of setback always gather in some part of the world to which no one at the time thinks of looking. If this is so, we must learn to live not by what can be seen and measured, but by that which, however insignificant in the present, will determine the future.

The Spirit stands for vitality. We see this in the N.T. very clearly, where the Spirit brings to the youthful church its throbbing life, its unbounded energy, and its indomitable hope. A mere handful of men and women went out into the Roman world with the message of Christ crucified yet Lord of all, not doubting that he would prevail. The Spirit was in them as the power to do mighty works, so that John could even claim that their works surpassed those which the Lord himself did while among men (John 14:12).

Ezekiel goes back for his imagery to the creation story of Gen. 2:7, though it should be noted that the word for **breath** there is not the one which he employs here. The Spirit is in

man as the breath of life which comes from God. A man is said to be "inspired" or "possessed" by the Spirit when he is lifted beyond his normal self and becomes for the time being the instrument of a power not his own. He is enabled to do what at any other time would have been quite beyond him. So the Spirit brings to us the power to act for God, to make history, to change the face of things.

The Spirit is not ours to command, but is given when we are faithful. Like the wind, the Spirit blows as it will. It is its own master and not subject to control by us. Who can say when the power will come upon a man to make of him a hero? Or the sudden inspiration which leaves him a poet? If today we wait for some fresh invasion of the Spirit, we know that no planning or organization on our part will decide how it is to come. An Augustine hears a voice over the garden wall, a Wesley feels his heart "strangely warmed," a Carey hangs a map on his wall, and tremendous things follow. We do not know how it is.

15 ¶ The word of the LORD came again unto me, saying,

16 Moreover, thou son of man, take thee one stick, and write upon it, For Judah, and for the children of Israel his companions: then take another stick, and write upon it, For Joseph, the stick of Ephraim, and *for* all the house of Israel his companions:

17 And join them one to another into one stick; and they shall become one in thine hand.

18 ¶ And when the children of thy people shall speak unto thee, saying, Wilt thou not show us what thou *meanest* by these?

19 Say unto them, Thus saith the Lord GOD; Behold, I will take the stick of Joseph, which *is* in the hand of Ephraim, and the tribes of Israel his fellows, and will put them with him, *even* with the stick of Judah, and make them one stick, and they shall be one in mine hand.

15 The word of the LORD came to me:
16 "Son of man, take a stick and write on it, 'For Judah, and the children of Israel associated with him'; then take another stick and write upon it, 'For Joseph (the stick of E'phraim) and all the house of Israel associated with him'; 17 and join them together into one stick, that they may become one in your hand. 18 And when your people say to you, 'Will you not show us what you mean by these?' 19 say to them, Thus says the Lord GOD: Behold, I am about to take the stick of Joseph (which is in the hand of E'phraim) and the tribes of Israel associated with him; and I will join[g] with it the stick of Judah, and make them one stick, that they may be one in my

[g] Heb *join them*

F. ORACLE OF THE TWO STICKS (37:15-28)

The very nature of the symbolism of the dramatic action in the oracle of the two sticks (vss. 15-28) implies the editor's theme of the restoration of Israel and Judah under Yahweh's servant, the Davidic Messiah. The prophet is told to take two sticks, write on one **Judah, and the children of Israel associated with him,** and on the other, **Joseph . . . and all the house of Israel associated with him,** and join them together. See the editor's use of the dramatic action motive in his revision of ch. 5. The symbolism may be compared with that in Zech. 11:7-14, where two rods are named "Grace" and "Union."

Most commentators assign the passage, save for a few expansions, to Ezekiel. Contrast Hölscher and Irwin, the latter finding, however, an original poetic oracle within vss. 16-17, 21-22.

16. Perhaps only [To] **Judah** and [To] **Joseph** were written on the sticks. **The stick of Ephraim** seems to be an explanatory gloss, and perhaps also the somewhat unparallel expressions **and the children of Israel associated with him,** as well as **and all the house of Israel associated with him.** The form of the inscriptions corresponds to that found in the excavations on seals and seal impressions (see also Isa. 44:5). It has been suggested that a wooden tablet may be intended here, rather than a stick (Hebrew עֵץ, "wood").

18. Cf. 24:19.

19. **(Which is in the hand of Ephraim) and the tribes of Israel associated with him** may be secondary (cf. vs. 16). The tribes associated with Ephraim are the other nine

---

But we are not therefore to wait inert for something to turn up. Like Ezekiel, we are to be faithful to our present tasks, even though there is little prospect of success. Had he not obeyed the inner voice which bade him address those bones, there would have been no wind of the Spirit, no **exceeding great army** astir in the valley. The world is vaster, richer, more wonderful than we imagine; therefore let us be faithful to our present task. There are no

limits to what God may do; at any moment he may break in and transform our present situation; therefore let us serve him according to our knowledge, leaving it to him whether he will continue the discipline of failure or transform our frustration into his marvelous success.

15-28. *The Hope of Unity.*—The modern world longs for unity, yet remains divided. Therein it resembles Israel of old. The union of north and south lasted through only two

20 ¶ And the sticks whereon thou writest shall be in thine hand before their eyes.

21 And say unto them, Thus saith the Lord God; Behold, I will take the children of Israel from among the heathen, whither they be gone, and will gather them on every side, and bring them into their own land:

22 And I will make them one nation in the land upon the mountains of Israel; and one king shall be king to them all: and they shall be no more two nations, neither shall they be divided into two kingdoms any more at all:

23 Neither shall they defile themselves any more with their idols, nor with their detestable things, nor with any of their transgressions: but I will save them out of all their dwelling places, wherein they have sinned, and will cleanse them: so shall they be my people, and I will be their God.

24 And David my servant *shall be* king over them; and they all shall have one shepherd: they shall also walk in my judgments, and observe my statutes, and do them.

25 And they shall dwell in the land that I have given unto Jacob my servant, wherein your fathers have dwelt; and they shall dwell therein, *even* they, and their children, and their children's children for ever: and my servant David *shall be* their prince for ever.

hand. **20** When the sticks on which you write are in your hand before their eyes, **21** then say to them, Thus says the Lord God: Behold, I will take the people of Israel from the nations among which they have gone, and will gather them from all sides, and bring them to their own land; **22** and I will make them one nation in the land, upon the mountains of Israel; and one king shall be king over them all; and they shall be no longer two nations, and no longer divided into two kingdoms. **23** They shall not defile themselves any more with their idols and their detestable things, or with any of their transgressions; but I will save them from all the backslidings in which they have sinned, and will cleanse them; and they shall be my people, and I will be their God.

24 "My servant David shall be king over them; and they shall all have one shepherd. They shall follow my ordinances and be careful to observe my statutes. **25** They shall dwell in the land where your fathers dwelt that I gave to my servant Jacob; they and their children and their children's children shall dwell there for ever; and David my

---

tribes of the Northern Kingdom (cf. I Kings 11:31). There were two Joseph tribes, Ephraim and Manasseh (see Gen. 41:51-52), but "house of Joseph" or "Joseph" may be used of the Northern Kingdom (see 47:13; Amos 5:15; Obad. 18). **In my hand** appears in the LXX as "in the hand of Judah," perhaps expressing the bias of the translators. In the similar phrase in vs. 17 it is "your hand," i.e., the hand of the prophet, but here Yahweh is to perform the same action by actually uniting the two peoples.

22. The second occurrence here of **king** (לְמֶלֶךְ) may be dittography of **over them all** (לְכֻלָּם); it is omitted by one MS, the LXX, and Syriac.

23. For the **idols** and **detestable things** see 5:11; 6:5; etc.

24. Cf. 34:23-24.

25. Cf. 28:25.

---

reigns; there were deep-seated differences between the two parts of the nation and they decided to go their separate ways. But the prophet cannot abandon the hope that God will bring them together again one day under a common loyalty to the ancient dynasty of David. The discipline of history will reconcile at last those who have been kept apart so long by jealousy and mistrust.

Note that the unity of the nation is to come about by the restoration of the divine presence

in the sanctuary. **My tabernacle also shall be with them; yea, I will be their God, and they shall be my people.** So our Western world goes back to an earlier unity in the heritage of classical antiquity and the Christian faith. Can we hope to recover that unity without a return to those sources? Granted that there must be some form of political organization to express and maintain the unity of the nations, must there not be also a common recognition of God? If that seems beyond us as yet, let us reflect that

26 Moreover I will make a covenant of peace with them; it shall be an everlasting covenant with them: and I will place them, and multiply them, and will set my sanctuary in the midst of them for evermore.

27 My tabernacle also shall be with them: yea, I will be their God, and they shall be my people.

28 And the heathen shall know that I the Lord do sanctify Israel, when my sanctuary shall be in the midst of them for evermore.

38 And the word of the Lord came unto me, saying,

2 Son of man, set thy face against Gog, the land of Magog, the chief prince of

servant shall be their prince for ever. 26 I will make a covenant of peace with them; it shall be an everlasting covenant with them; and I will bless[h] them and multiply them, and will set my sanctuary in the midst of them for evermore. 27 My dwelling place shall be with them; and I will be their God, and they shall be my people. 28 Then the nations will know that I the Lord sanctify Israel, when my sanctuary is in the midst of them for evermore."

38 The word of the Lord came to me: 2 "Son of man, set your face toward

[h] Tg: Heb give

26. Cf. 34:25. The **sanctuary in the midst** is schematically presented in 45:1-8; 47:13–48:35. Cf. the phraseology and ideology of Lev. 26:11. The Targ., **bless** (see RSV), is probably interpretative, and we may perhaps omit **and I will give them** (cf. KJV) with the LXX and Syriac.

28. This is the editor's common formula, here so worded that it might be taken at the same time as an introduction to the picture of the restored temple in chs. 40–48.

G. The Gog and Magog Oracles (38:1–39:29)

These two chapters contain seven divisions, each introduced by a **thus says the Lord God** formula (38:3-9, 10-13, 14-16, 17-23; 39:1-16, 17-24, 25-29). The author describes how Yahweh is bringing from the north Gog of the land of Magog, chief prince of Meshech and Tubal, and those associated with him. They will come against the house of Israel, now living securely in Palestine. When Gog comes against Israel, Yahweh's wrath and jealousy will be aroused, and with the world of nature quaking at his theophany he will summon terrors against Gog and his hordes, destroying them with torrential rains, hailstones, fire, and sulphur. They will fall on the mountains of Israel and will be given to the birds and beasts to be devoured, as a sacrificial feast prepared by Yahweh. The discarded weapons will be so many that they will serve as fuel for seven years, and it will take seven months to collect the bones of the dead to bury them in the valley of Hamon-gog in Trans-Jordan. This is being done that Yahweh may vindicate his holiness, and that the nations may know that Israel was punished for its sins and his name will not be profaned. It is the fulfillment of the earlier prophets' oracles on the foe from the north. So the house of Israel will know that Yahweh is their God and he will pour out on them his spirit and never again hide his face from them.

The text does not read as smoothly as this summary might indicate. It contains reiteration of the same themes and even seeming inconsistencies. Despite this we may question the attempts to analyze the oracle into parallel recensions (cf. Kraetzschmar, Toy, Gressmann, Rothstein, Bertholet, Steuernagel, etc.). We have seen this repetitious style before, and can recognize the hand of the editor throughout. That in 38:4-7, 16; 39:2-3 Yahweh brings Gog against Israel, while in 38:10-13 Gog devises the attack on

what the Bible means by a common recognition of God is not the conversion of all peoples to one religion, but the acknowledgment by all of justice and humanity. Can there be any permanent unity without this reverence for the universal moral law? We may well doubt it.

38:1-23. Barbarians Without and Within.— We need not concern ourselves here with the origins of the grandiose if bizarre vision which fills chs. 38–39, nor with the various identifications which have been suggested for the central figure, Gog. The chapters should be treated as

Israel as an evil scheme, does not necessarily imply two authors, for it is Yahweh who puts the scheme in Gog's mind, and man may be held responsible even for what Yahweh instigates (cf. II Sam. 24:1-25 and I Sam. 3:25). It is held that there are two recountings of the fate of Gog's hordes, one in 39:3-4, 17-20, the other in 38:18-23; 39:8-16, but it is understandable that in this type of literature the fate might be pictured in variant terms, and actually the pictures are supplementary rather than mutually inconsistent. That these two chapters do not belong to Ezekiel is recognized by a number of scholars, although some find possible original material in 39:25-29 (see Matthews, Bertholet, Cooke, Pfeiffer, *et al.*). Herntrich ascribes them to Ezekiel's exilic ministry. Irwin finds an original oracle consisting of a single tristich line in 38:3*b*-4, plus the usual introductory formula. In the Scheide Papyri these two chapters follow ch. 36.

The editor thinks of this prophecy as the fulfillment of the oracles on the foe from the north by the earlier prophets (38:17; 39:8). He probably has particularly in mind the oracles of Jeremiah, as in Jer. 4:5–6:26, etc., and indeed at times shows the influence of Jeremiah's diction (see also Zeph. 1:14-18; cf. Joel 2:20; Zech. 6:8; cf. the imagery of 38:9 with Jer. 4:13; of 38:11 with Jer. 49:31). Presumably the editor assumes that the vision in chs. 40–48 pictures the situation to prevail after the destruction of the forces of Gog.

That the author knew clearly who Gog and Magog were is not certain. Irwin is right that he never intended Gog to be taken in its literal historical sense, whatever that was. Magog, associated with Tubal and Meshech, appears in the table of nations in Gen. 10:2 (also I Chr. 1:5); note also Togarmah in Gen. 10:3 (also I Chr. 1:6). We have already encountered Tubal and Meshech, the Assyrian *Tabal* and *Mušku* in 27:13; 32:26, and likewise Beth-togarmah, Assyrian *Til-garimmu* (see Exeg. on 27:14), peoples of Asia Minor, and so fitting to stand for the foe from the north. To the same territory belongs Gomer, Assyrian *Gimirrai*, Greek "Cimmerians," who had moved from above the Black Sea to the region of Cappadocia in Asia Minor (see Gen. 10:2-3; I Chr. 1:6). The association with Gen. 10 has no certain bearing on the date of the author, since some materials in Gen. 10 are of early origin. It has been suggested that Gog is a distant reflection of the name of Gyges king of Lydia, who defeated Midas and was the founder of the dynasty of which Croesus was the last king. Gyges is called Gûgu in the records of Ashurbanipal, where he is described as "king of Lydia, a district of the other side of the sea, a distant place" in a passage in which the Cimmerians are also mentioned (see Luckenbill, *Ancient Records of Assyria and Babylonia*, II, 297-98). Another suggestion is that we should look to mythology for the origin of Gog, but no clear source is known, although the elements of the ideology of the cosmological conflict between the god of light and the forces of darkness and chaos are involved in these chapters, as in other similar pictures of the final assault on Israel or Jerusalem and the last great battle of the nations (see Isa. 29:5-8; 63:1-6; 66:15-19; Joel 2:28-32 [Hebrew 3:1-5]; 3:15-16 [Hebrew 4:15-16]; Zech. 12:1–14:21; Obad. 15-16; etc.). The identification of Magog is even more uncertain, and it may be an artificial formation, e.g., referring to the land of Gog. Josephus (*Antiquities* I. 6. 1) identifies Magog with the Scythians. Gog has been identified by scholars with the king of Babylon, Alexander the Great, and even Antiochus Eupator (162 B.C.). (For studies of this problem see J. L. Myres, "Gog and the Danger from the North, in Ezekiel," *Palestine Exploration Fund Quarterly Statement for 1932*, pp. 213-19; G. R. Berry, "The Date of Ezekiel 38₁–39₂₀," *Journal of Biblical Literature*, XLI [1922], 224-32; W. F. Albright, "Contributions to Biblical Archaeology," *ibid.*, XLIII [1924], 378-85: Gog=Gaga=Gašga, of the Cuneiform Texts.) See Rev. 20:7-10 for the influence of these chapters, where it is Satan who musters the forces of Gog and Magog.

1. Introduction (38:1-2)

38:1-2. The land of Magog is best taken as the territory belonging to Gog (RSV) rather than in apposition to Gog (KJV). The LXX and Syriac take it as "against

Meshech and Tubal, and prophesy against him,

3 And say, Thus saith the Lord God; Behold, I *am* against thee, O Gog, the chief prince of Meshech and Tubal:

4 And I will turn thee back, and put hooks into thy jaws, and I will bring thee forth, and all thine army, horses and horsemen, all of them clothed with all sorts *of armor, even* a great company *with* bucklers and shields, all of them handling swords:

5 Persia, Ethiopia, and Libya with them; all of them with shield and helmet:

6 Gomer, and all his bands; the house of Togarmah of the north quarters, and all his bands: *and* many people with thee.

7 Be thou prepared, and prepare for thyself, thou, and all thy company that are assembled unto thee, and be thou a guard unto them.

8 ¶ After many days thou shalt be visited: in the latter years thou shalt come into the land *that is* brought back from the sword, *and is* gathered out of many people, against the mountains of Israel, which have been always waste: but it is brought forth out of the nations, and they shall dwell safely all of them.

Gog, of the land of Magog, the chief prince of Meshech and Tubal, and prophesy against him 3 and say, Thus says the Lord God: Behold, I am against you, O Gog, chief prince of Meshech and Tubal; 4 and I will turn you about, and put hooks into your jaws, and I will bring you forth, and all your army, horses and horsemen, all of them clothed in full armor, a great company, all of them with buckler and shield, wielding swords; 5 Persia, Cush, and Put are with them, all of them with shield and helmet; 6 Gomer and all his hordes; Beth-togar′mah from the uttermost parts of the north with all his hordes — many peoples are with you.

7 "Be ready and keep ready, you and all the hosts that are assembled about you, and be a guard for them. 8 After many days you will be mustered; in the latter years you will go against the land that is restored from war, the land where people were gathered from many nations upon the mountains of Israel, which had been a continual waste; its people were brought out from the nations and now dwell securely, all of them.

Gog and [against] the land of Magog." By a simple redivision of the letters it may be read "to the land of Magog" (ארצה מגוג). Some take it as a gloss. **Prince** is the editor's נשיא, and **chief** may be in apposition or a gloss, the latter being more probable (see vs. 3; 39:1). Note the editor's phraseology at the beginning of vs. 2 and in vs. 3a.

2. Gog and His Hordes (38:3-9)

4-5. Because of the cosmological nature of the conflict, the imagery of the capture of the dragon may be used here deliberately (see 29:4, but cf. also 19:4, 9). The M.T. has no **with;** so also at the end of vs. 5. Some wonder whether vs. 5 may not be a gloss or scribal expansion, since none of these nations are from the north (see, however, 27:10).

8. In the latter years: The meaning is the same as "in the latter days" of vs. 16 (Jer. 30:24; 48:47; 49:39; Hos. 3:5; etc.), i.e., just before the new age and the restoration of the Davidic dynasty. Vs. 8b is the typical editor's picture of the restored people and mountains of Israel (see 34:13; 36:1-38; etc.). **Brought back from the sword,** i.e., after being punished by the sword, is understandable in the light of ch. 21, etc. Some translate "restored from desolation," reading מחרב as *mēḥŏrebh* instead of *mēḥérebh,* **from the sword.**

an elaborate piece of symbolism, an attempt to portray some of the ultimate problems of human life with the help of figures and incidents borrowed from the repertoire of mythology. C. H. Dodd has a useful discussion of eschatology as symbolism;[6] the purpose which

governs all history is expressed in the form of a story of what will happen at the end of history. The inner meaning of all events is seen by the apocalyptist as the final event in the series which makes up human history.

Let us attempt then to interpret this vision. To begin, we notice that, before Gog puts in an appearance, Israel has been restored to its

[6] *The Apostolic Preaching and Its Developments* (Chicago: Willett Clark & Co., 1937), pp. 135-67.

9 Thou shalt ascend and come like a storm, thou shalt be like a cloud to cover the land, thou, and all thy bands, and many people with thee.

10 Thus saith the Lord GOD; It shall also come to pass, *that* at the same time shall things come into thy mind, and thou shalt think an evil thought:

11 And thou shalt say, I will go up to the land of unwalled villages; I will go to them that are at rest, that dwell safely, all of them dwelling without walls, and having neither bars nor gates,

12 To take a spoil, and to take a prey; to turn thine hand upon the desolate places *that are now* inhabited, and upon the people *that are* gathered out of the nations, which have gotten cattle and goods, that dwell in the midst of the land.

13 Sheba, and Dedan, and the merchants of Tarshish, with all the young lions thereof, shall say unto thee, Art thou come to take a spoil? hast thou gathered thy company to take a prey? to carry away silver and gold, to take away cattle and goods, to take a great spoil?

14 ¶ Therefore, son of man, prophesy and say unto Gog, Thus saith the Lord GOD; In that day when my people of Israel dwelleth safely, shalt thou not know *it?*

9 You will advance, coming on like a storm, you will be like a cloud covering the land, you and all your hordes, and many peoples with you.

10 "Thus says the Lord GOD: On that day thoughts will come into your mind, and you will devise an evil scheme 11 and say, 'I will go up against the land of unwalled villages; I will fall upon the quiet people who dwell securely, all of them dwelling without walls, and having no bars or gates'; 12 to seize spoil and carry off plunder; to assail the waste places which are now inhabited, and the people who were gathered from the nations, who have gotten cattle and goods, who dwell at the center of the earth. 13 Sheba and Dedan and the merchants of Tarshish and all its villages will say to you, 'Have you come to seize spoil? Have you assembled your hosts to carry off plunder, to carry away silver and gold, to take away cattle and goods, to seize great spoil?'

14 "Therefore, son of man, prophesy, and say to Gog, Thus says the Lord GOD: On that day when my people Israel are dwelling securely, you will bestir yourself[i]

[i] Gk: Heb *you will know*

---

3. GOG'S PLOT (38:10-13)

11. See Zech. 2:4 (Hebrew 2:8). The unwalled cities suggest a date before the work of Nehemiah.

12. The center [navel] **of the earth:** Cf. Exeg. on 5:5.

13. For **Sheba, Dedan,** and **Tarshish** see 27:12, 20, 22. The KJV of vs. 13*a* translates the Hebrew literally (cf. RSV). **Its traders:** Read רגליה, or סחריה, or כנעניה for כפריה, **the young lions thereof,** which could be repointed to read **its villages,** with the LXX and Syriac.

4. GOG TO COME AGAINST ISRAEL (38:14-16)

Yahweh will vindicate his holiness through Gog. There is much repetition of earlier ideas, and only by the end of vs. 16 does the editor make progress.

14. You will bestir yourself: Read תער with the LXX for תדע, "you will know" (cf. KJV).

---

own land. More than that, its condition is one of complete security. The people no longer need to crowd behind the walls of the capital for protection; they can dwell scattered about the land in unwalled villages. They have returned home enriched with cattle and goods. Divine judgments have eliminated all their enemies and they dwell **in the midst of the land** (vs. 12), in the center of a world at peace. The seer's

vision, to be sure, is restricted to his own country, but it is evident that the security which prevails there presupposes a state of things in which the ancient problem of humanity has been solved and the nations learn war no more.

We notice next that the hosts marshaled behind Gog are not drawn from the countries historically hostile to Israel, nor indeed from the civilized world at all. They are barbarians

15 And thou shalt come from thy place out of the north parts, thou, and many people with thee, all of them riding upon horses, a great company, and a mighty army:

16 And thou shalt come up against my people of Israel, as a cloud to cover the land; it shall be in the latter days, and I will bring thee against my land, that the heathen may know me, when I shall be sanctified in thee, O Gog, before their eyes.

17 Thus saith the Lord GOD; *Art* thou he of whom I have spoken in old time by my servants the prophets of Israel, which prophesied in those days *many* years, that I would bring thee against them?

18 And it shall come to pass at the same time when Gog shall come against the land of Israel, saith the Lord GOD, *that* my fury shall come up in my face.

15 and come from your place out of the uttermost parts of the north, you and many peoples with you, all of them riding on horses, a great host, a mighty army; 16 you will come up against my people Israel, like a cloud covering the land. In the latter days I will bring you against my land, that the nations may know me, when through you, O Gog, I vindicate my holiness before their eyes.

17 "Thus says the Lord GOD: Are you he of whom I spoke in former days by my servants the prophets of Israel, who in those days prophesied for years that I would bring you against them? 18 But on that day, when Gog shall come against the land of Israel, says the Lord GOD, my wrath will be

---

5. DESTRUCTION OF GOG'S FORCES (38:17-23)

So will Yahweh reveal his greatness and holiness and the nations know that he is the Lord. The catastrophes of nature, frequent in poetic theophanies (see Pss. 18:7-15; 29:1-11; 68:7-9; Isa. 6:4; Hab. 3:3-6; Exod. 15:1-27; Judg. 5:4-5), became a common motive in Hebrew eschatology (see Isa. 17:12-14; 30:27-33; 64:1-4; Zeph. 1:14-18; Joel 2:28-32; Hag. 2:21; Zech. 14:3-4; etc.).

17. The interrogative prefix ה may be due to dittography, and perhaps we should read with the LXX, O.L., and Vulg., "You are he." **In old time** shows that the author is living a considerable time after Jeremiah; this is important for the date of the editor. **Years** may be an interpretative gloss meaning "long ago," or may be read with the LXX, "and years."

18-19. My wrath will be roused is, more literally, "my wrath will come up in my anger [nostrils, face]," and it is perhaps best to connect "in my anger" with vs. 19, and

---

from beyond all known territory, men of strange races inured to war and athirst for plunder, robber bands which break in upon the settled population **to carry away silver and gold, to take away cattle and goods, to seize great spoil** (vs. 13). No doubt the seer is drawing upon the tradition, perhaps even upon the memory, of such irruptions in the past. What he has in mind is some last and crowning threat from the barbarian beyond the frontier.

It is possible now to begin our interpretation. We are shown here the limits set to the extension of civilization and the rationalization of human life. Even should scientific techniques be developed to their maximum extent, and every square inch of the earth's surface be exploited in an era of unexampled prosperity; even should long-standing animosities be resolved in peace and a just, ordered society be created—insecurity will not for all that be banished. Who is to guarantee that the frontiers

will not one day be violated by the dark, fierce powers which lurk beyond them? Even should we civilize every human being on the face of the earth, who will defend us against the barbarian in the soul? It seems indeed as though the very rationalization of life does violence to certain primitive instincts, so that these take their first opportunity to break forth and work havoc with our neat systems.

Writing in 1780 as a child of the Age of Reason, Edward Gibbon expressed his confidence in the future:

Cannon and fortifications now form an impregnable barrier against the Tartar horse; and Europe is secure from any future irruption of Barbarians; since, before they can conquer, they must cease to be barbarous. Their gradual advances in the science of war would always be accompanied, as we may learn from the example of Russia, with a proportionable improvement in the arts of peace and civil policy; and they themselves must deserve a

19 For in my jealousy *and* in the fire of my wrath have I spoken, Surely in that day there shall be a great shaking in the land of Israel;

20 So that the fishes of the sea, and the fowls of the heaven, and the beasts of the field, and all creeping things that creep upon the earth, and all the men that *are* upon the face of the earth, shall shake at my presence, and the mountains shall be thrown down, and the steep places shall fall, and every wall shall fall to the ground.

21 And I will call for a sword against him throughout all my mountains, saith

roused. 19 For in my jealousy and in my blazing wrath I declare, On that day there shall be a great shaking in the land of Israel; 20 the fish of the sea, and the birds of the air, and the beasts of the field, and all creeping things that creep on the ground, and all the men that are upon the face of the earth, shall quake at my presence, and the mountains shall be thrown down, and the cliffs shall fall, and every wall shall tumble to the ground. 21 I will summon

---

read, "In my anger and in my jealousy, in my blazing wrath," etc. Note the earthquake in the picture of the last days in Isa. 24:18-20; 29:6; Joel 3:16; Hag. 2:6-7, 21; Zech. 14:5; etc. Earthquakes are not uncommon in Palestine; cf. the earthquake of 1837 which overthrew the walls of Tiberias and killed large numbers in the Galilee district (see Edward Robinson, *Biblical Researches in Palestine, Mount Sinai, and Arabia Petraea* [New York: J. Leavitt, 1841], III, 253-56), the more recent earthquake violence in 1927 (see account in "Notes and News," *Palestine Exploration Fund Quarterly Statement for 1927*, pp. 170-71), or the evidence of earthquake damage in the excavations at Jericho.

20. This recalls Gen. 1:25-26, etc., but the phraseology is older than P (see Ps. 8:6-8; Jer. 4:23-26).

21. "I will summon against him to [for] all my mountains a sword" is perhaps best interpreted by the KJV, and the frequency of the **sword** motive in the editor would

---

place among the polished nations whom they subdue. . . . It may safely be presumed, that no people, unless the face of nature is changed, will relapse into their original barbarism.[7]

In the next century another historian expressed himself in equally optimistic terms:

Amid the complications and elaborations of civilisation, the deranging influence of passion, whether for good or for evil, becomes continually less, and interest becomes more and more the guiding influence, not perhaps of individuals, but of communities. In proportion to the commercial and industrial advancement of a nation, its interests become favourable to peace, and the love of war is in consequence diminished. When therefore the different states of Europe are closely interwoven by commercial interests, when the classes who represent those interests have become the guiding power of the state, and when they are fully penetrated with the truth that war in any quarter is detrimental to their prosperity, a guarantee for the peace of Europe will have been attained, if not perfect, at least far stronger than any which either religion or philanthropy has yet realised.[8]

[7] *The Decline and Fall of the Roman Empire*, "General Observations on the Fall of the Roman Empire in the West," following ch. xxxviii.

[8] W. E. H. Lecky, *History of the Rise and Influence of the Spirit of Rationalism in Europe* (New York: D. Appleton & Co., 1866) II, 340-41.

But unfortunately, when the barbarian from beyond the frontier has been tamed, a still deadlier foe remains. He is the barbarian within the soul.

Think of the colossal brutality, cruelty and mendacity which is now allowed to spread itself over the civilized world. Do you really believe that a handful of unprincipled place-hunters and corrupters of men would have succeeded in letting loose all this latent evil, if the millions of their followers were not also guilty?[9]

Germany and Japan did not lie outside our scientific civilization; they were among its leading representatives. Theirs was the scientific barbarism which is the most terrible of all barbarisms, and its roots were in the secret places of the soul. There lurk the sadisms and cruelties which wrecked our peace.

In the vision, therefore, the forces of unreason and brutality marshal to overthrow what has been done in the name of reason and humanity. But they do not prevail. That is what turns this vision of a lowering storm into noonday brightness. How is the victory conceivable? The answer is that beyond the neat arrange-

[9] Sigmund Freud, *Introductory Lectures on Psychoanalysis* (tr. Joan Riviere; London: George Allen & Unwin, 1922), p. 122.

the Lord God: every man's sword shall be against his brother.

22 And I will plead against him with pestilence and with blood; and I will rain upon him, and upon his bands, and upon the many people that *are* with him, an overflowing rain, and great hailstones, fire, and brimstone.

23 Thus will I magnify myself, and sanctify myself; and I will be known in the eyes of many nations, and they shall know that I *am* the Lord.

39 Therefore, thou son of man, prophesy against Gog, and say, Thus saith the Lord God; Behold, I *am* against

every kind of terror[j] against Gog,[k] says the Lord God; every man's sword will be against his brother. **22** With pestilence and bloodshed I will enter into judgment with him; and I will rain upon him and his hordes and the many peoples that are with him, torrential rains and hailstones, fire and brimstone. **23** So I will show my greatness and my holiness and make myself known in the eyes of many nations. Then they will know that I am the Lord.

39 "And you, son of man, prophesy against Gog, and say, Thus says the

[j] Gk: Heb *a sword to all my mountains*
[k] Heb *him*

suggest keeping the present text, although חרדה, **terror,** with the LXX, for הרי חרב, "my mountains a sword," makes better sense, the corruption being due largely to dittography and confusion of letters.

22. Pestilence and bloodshed reflect the editor's earlier judgment on Israel and Sidon in 5:17; 28:23. The destruction of Sodom and Gomorrah may be part of the inspiration for this picture (see Gen. 19:24).

23. See especially 36:22-23.

6. Destruction and Burial of Gog's Hordes (39:1-16)

As Yahweh was responsible for bringing the foe from the north in Jeremiah's oracles, so also here, albeit this time to destroy the foe rather than Israel. The fact that Yahweh brought the foe shows how thoroughly the control of history was in his hands. **The mountains of Israel** (vs. 2) links this with ch. 36 (cf. 38:8).

39:1. Chief prince of Meshech: See Exeg. on 38:1-2.

ments and ordered systems in which we put our trust, there are two sets of forces, one from beneath, the other from above. If there are passions in man strong enough to shatter society, there is also a Spirit of God which can take possession of him and exorcise these demons. There are inspirations which can counter our worst impulses, as there is a love which can prevail even against cruelty. In spite of everything "it is the mystic souls who draw and will continue to draw civilized societies in their wake." [1]

If we discount the Spanish extravagance in his words, we can see the force of Miguel de Unamuno's demand: "Madness, genuine madness, is with us a crying need, and a possible cure for this pest of common sense which has inhibited the individual sense of each one of us." [2] There is such a thing as "the stumbling-block of the cross" (Gal. 5:11). There is a fool-

[1] Henri L. Bergson, *The Two Sources of Morality and Religion* (tr. R. A. Audra and C. Brereton; New York: Henry Holt & Co., 1935), p. 75.

[2] *The Life of Don Quixote and Sancho*, tr. Homer P. Earle (New York: A. A. Knopf, 1927), p. 97.

ishness of God" which "is wiser than men," and a "weakness of God" which "is stronger than men" (I Cor. 1:25).

Always therefore we confront the menace of the barbarian within our souls. Yet we need not unduly fear if we bear in mind that there are resources in God beyond what we can measure. There are good passions as well as bad ones; that was what our fathers implied when they spoke of angels as combating demons and putting them to flight. When some are about to wreck the world with their shameless depravity, God quickens others to the heroic virtues by which we are saved. "Where sin increased, grace abounded all the more" (Rom. 5:20).

39:1-29. A Summons to Renounce War.—We may take this chapter as a picture of a world once for all delivered from the menace of war. It is even assumed here that the evils that lurk in men's souls have been cast out. Armaments remain only as fuel for a peace-loving people (vss. 9-10), scrupulously careful to eliminate from their midst the last faint trace of bloodshedding (vss. 14-15). The consummation

thee, O Gog, the chief prince of Meshech and Tubal:

2 And I will turn thee back, and leave but the sixth part of thee, and will cause thee to come up from the north parts, and will bring thee upon the mountains of Israel:

3 And I will smite thy bow out of thy left hand, and will cause thine arrows to fall out of thy right hand.

4 Thou shalt fall upon the mountains of Israel, thou, and all thy bands, and the people that *is* with thee: I will give thee unto the ravenous birds of every sort, and *to* the beasts of the field, to be devoured.

5 Thou shalt fall upon the open field: for I have spoken *it*, saith the Lord God.

6 And I will send a fire on Magog, and among them that dwell carelessly in the isles: and they shall know that I *am* the Lord.

7 So will I make my holy name known in the midst of my people Israel; and I will not *let them* pollute my holy name any more: and the heathen shall know that I *am* the Lord, the Holy One in Israel.

8 ¶ Behold, it is come, and it is done, saith the Lord God; this *is* the day whereof I have spoken.

9 And they that dwell in the cities of Israel shall go forth, and shall set on fire and burn the weapons, both the shields and the bucklers, the bows and the arrows, and the handstaves, and the spears, and they shall burn them with fire seven years:

10 So that they shall take no wood out of the field, neither cut down *any* out of

Lord God: Behold, I am against you, O Gog, chief prince of Meshech and Tubal; 2 and I will turn you about and drive you forward, and bring you up from the uttermost parts of the north, and lead you against the mountains of Israel; 3 then I will strike your bow from your left hand, and will make your arrows drop out of your right hand. 4 You shall fall upon the mountains of Israel, you and all your hordes and the peoples that are with you; I will give you to birds of prey of every sort and to the wild beasts to be devoured. 5 You shall fall in the open field; for I have spoken, says the Lord God. 6 I will send fire on Magog and on those who dwell securely in the coastlands; and they shall know that I am the Lord.

7 "And my holy name I will make known in the midst of my people Israel; and I will not let my holy name be profaned any more; and the nations shall know that I am the Lord, the Holy One in Israel. 8 Behold, it is coming and it will be brought about, says the Lord God. That is the day of which I have spoken.

9 "Then those who dwell in the cities of Israel will go forth and make fires of the weapons and burn them, shields and bucklers, bows and arrows, handpikes and spears, and they will make fires of them for seven years; 10 so that they will not need to take wood out of the field or cut down any out

4-5. Note the common phrase, **I have spoken it** (see xxxvi on p. 51). Cf. the fate of the dragon in 29:5.

7. The Holy One in Israel should perhaps be changed with eight MSS and several versions to "the Holy One of Israel." **My holy name be profaned** (see xxviii on p. 51): The name Yahweh was to be considered so sacred by the later Hebrews that they did not pronounce it.

8. Cf. 21:7. This is **the day** of Yahweh.

9-10. Handpikes: Lit., "staff of hand," found only here; cf. the staff used in journeying or riding in Gen. 32:10; Exod. 12:11; Num. 22:27. The meaning must be that the weapons shall be for fuel, as expressed in the RSV. **For seven years:** Cf. **for seven months** in vs. 12.

is reached in a world festival that celebrates the end of all military pomp (vss. 17-24).

We need hardly ask whether the prophet means us to take him literally. As if he looked forward to a banquet at which horses and chariots, **with mighty men, and with all men**

of war would be served up as the courses! No, he is painting on a broad canvas and with colors rather crudely mixed, but the picture is designed to show the hopes which sustain him. The outward event he describes should be taken as symbolizing an inner change.

the forests; for they shall burn the weapons with fire: and they shall spoil those that spoiled them, and rob those that robbed them, saith the Lord GOD.

11 ¶ And it shall come to pass in that day, *that* I will give unto Gog a place there of graves in Israel, the valley of the passengers on the east of the sea; and it shall stop the *noses* of the passengers: and there shall they bury Gog and all his multitude: and they shall call *it,* The valley of Hamon-gog.

12 And seven months shall the house of Israel be burying of them, that they may cleanse the land.

13 Yea, all the people of the land shall bury *them;* and it shall be to them a renown the day that I shall be glorified, saith the Lord GOD.

14 And they shall sever out men of continual employment, passing through the land, to bury with the passengers those that remain upon the face of the earth, to cleanse it: after the end of seven months shall they search.

15 And the passengers *that* pass through the land, when *any* seeth a man's bone, then shall he set up a sign by it, till the buriers have buried it in the valley of Hamon-gog.

of the forests, for they will make their fires of the weapons; they will despoil those who despoiled them, and plunder those who plundered them, says the Lord GOD.

11 "On that day I will give to Gog a place for burial in Israel, the Valley of the Travelers[l] east of the sea; it will block the travelers, for there Gog and all his multitude will be buried; it will be called the Valley of Hamon-gog.[m] 12 For seven months the house of Israel will be burying them, in order to cleanse the land. 13 All the people of the land will bury them; and it will redound to their honor on the day that I show my glory, says the Lord GOD. 14 They will set apart men to pass through the land continually and bury[n] those remaining upon the face of the land, so as to cleanse it; at the end of seven months they will make their search. 15 And when these pass through the land and any one sees a man's bone, then he shall set up a sign by it, till the buriers have buried it in the Valley of

[l] Or *Abarim*
[m] That is *the multitude of Gog*
[n] Gk Syr: Heb *bury the travelers*

11. **A place there:** With one MS, the LXX, and Vulg. read שם as *shem,* "name," instead of *shām,* **there,** and so "a place bearing his name," or, more probably, "a place of renown" (cf. RSV). **The Valley of the Travelers** is repointed by some as **the Valley of Abarim** (reading *hā'abhārîm* for *hā'ōbherîm*), with the Coptic Version, an allusion to a valley in the mountains of Abarim, which included Mount Nebo, north of the river Nahaliel (Wadi Zerqā Mā'în; see Num. 27:12; 33:47-48; Deut. 32:49). **The sea** is the Dead Sea. The dead are to be buried across the Jordan outside Palestine to cleanse the land of pollution by corpses (see vs. 14). Some emend to read, "and they shall stop up the valley," for **it will block the travelers,** and so to mean that access to the polluted burial area will be impossible (cf. LXX, Syriac).

14. **Pass through** has the same derivation as **travelers** in vs. 11 and here (RSV mg.). The same root appears twice at the beginning of vs. 15 (see KJV). The LXX and Syriac omit **the travelers.**

15. The word for **sign** appears in II Kings 23:17 as a tomb monument (cf. Jer. 31:21, a waymark or guidepost).

There is here a summons to the total renunciation of war. As we have seen, against the barbarian in the soul only heroic measures are of any avail (Expos. on 38:1-23). The brute in us can be cast out only by that which is of God. Only total devotion to peace can cope with the will to power which pits nation against nation. A people therefore throws its armaments on the scrap heap and purges itself of every

taint of militarism. Once it has had the courage to do so, a new day dawns for the world. The curtain falls on a festival of universal peace.

In his *Interpretation of History* Paul Tillich works out this thought in philosophical language. He shows how the state is always characterized by the exercise of power, while the church is called to renounce any claim to power and to rely wholly on persuasion. Then he asks

16 And also the name of the city *shall be* Hamonah. Thus shall they cleanse the land.

17 ¶ And, thou son of man, thus saith the Lord GOD; Speak unto every feathered fowl, and to every beast of the field, Assemble yourselves, and come; gather yourselves on every side to my sacrifice that I do sacrifice for you, *even* a great sacrifice upon the mountains of Israel, that ye may eat flesh, and drink blood.

18 Ye shall eat the flesh of the mighty, and drink the blood of the princes of the earth, of rams, of lambs, and of goats, of bullocks, all of them fatlings of Bashan.

19 And ye shall eat fat till ye be full, and drink blood till ye be drunken, of my sacrifice which I have sacrificed for you.

20 Thus ye shall be filled at my table with horses and chariots, with mighty men, and with all men of war, saith the Lord GOD.

21 And I will set my glory among the heathen, and all the heathen shall see my judgment that I have executed, and my hand that I have laid upon them.

22 So the house of Israel shall know that I *am* the LORD their God from that day and forward.

23 ¶ And the heathen shall know that the house of Israel went into captivity for their iniquity: because they trespassed against me, therefore hid I my face from

Hamon-gog. **16** (A city Hamo'nah*°* is there also.) Thus shall they cleanse the land.

17 "As for you, son of man, thus says the Lord GOD: Speak to the birds of every sort and to all beasts of the field, 'Assemble and come, gather from all sides to the sacrificial feast which I am preparing for you, a great sacrificial feast upon the mountains of Israel, and you shall eat flesh and drink blood. **18** You shall eat the flesh of the mighty, and drink the blood of the princes of the earth — of rams, of lambs, and of goats, of bulls, all of them fatlings of Bashan. **19** And you shall eat fat till you are filled, and drink blood till you are drunk, at the sacrificial feast which I am preparing for you. **20** And you shall be filled at my table with horses and riders, with mighty men and all kinds of warriors,' says the Lord GOD.

21 "And I will set my glory among the nations; and all the nations shall see my judgment which I have executed, and my hand which I have laid on them. **22** The house of Israel shall know that I am the LORD their God, from that day forward. **23** And the nations shall know that the house of Israel went into captivity for their iniquity, because they dealt so treacherously

° That is *Multitude*

16a. The KJV follows the M.T. pointing, but the relation to the context is dubious— the **name** of what **city?** The RSV reads *shām*, **there,** for *shem*, **name,** and in this form it might be a glossator's comment. No such city is mentioned elsewhere.

7. GOG'S HORDES AND HORSES AT YAHWEH'S SACRIFICIAL FEAST (39:17-24)

Yahweh will set his glory among the nations, who will know that Israel was punished for its iniquity. The new introductory formula relieves the inconsistency of placing the devouring of the bodies after the burial described in the preceding verses. The picture of carnage recalls the almost orgiastic picture in Isa. 63:1-6. The theme is taken up in Rev. 19:17-21. The day of Yahweh as a day of sacrifice appears in Zeph. 1:1-9. Cf. the gory sacrifice in Edom in Isa. 34:6-7; see also Jer. 46:10, and cf. the scene of Anat's battle against the men of the East in the Ugaritic texts (Gordon, *Ugaritic Literature,* pp. 17-18). This is not the keenest theological insight of the editor! Vss. 21-24 emphasize the knowledge theme so common to the editor.

18. The hordes of Gog seem here to comprise all the Gentile nations. **Bashan,** in northern Trans-Jordan, was noted for its cattle (Amos 4:1; cf. Deut. 32:14; Ps. 22:12).

20. Chariots, for *rékhebh,* does not suit the context, and we can translate as "chariot horses" (cf. II Sam. 8:4; I Chr. 18:4) or "riders" (cf. Isa. 21:7; 22:6), or repoint as *rōkhēbh,* "riders."

23. The nations, knowing now the reason for the Exile, will not react as they did according to 36:20, and so the name of Yahweh will not be profaned.

them, and gave them into the hand of their enemies; so fell they all by the sword.

24 According to their uncleanness and according to their transgressions have I done unto them, and hid my face from them.

25 Therefore thus saith the Lord GoD; Now will I bring again the captivity of Jacob, and have mercy upon the whole house of Israel, and will be jealous for my holy name;

26 After that they have borne their shame, and all their trespasses whereby they have trespassed against me, when they dwelt safely in their land, and none made *them* afraid.

27 When I have brought them again from the people, and gathered them out of their enemies' lands, and am sanctified in them in the sight of many nations;

28 Then shall they know that I *am* the LORD their God, which caused them to be led into captivity among the heathen: but I have gathered them unto their own land, and have left none of them any more there.

29 Neither will I hide my face any more from them: for I have poured out my Spirit upon the house of Israel, saith the Lord GoD.

40 In the five and twentieth year of our captivity, in the beginning of the year, in the tenth *day* of the month, in the

with me that I hid my face from them and gave them into the hand of their adversaries, and they all fell by the sword. 24 I dealt with them according to their uncleanness and their transgressions, and hid my face from them.

25 "Therefore thus says the Lord GoD: Now I will restore the fortunes of Jacob, and have mercy upon the whole house of Israel; and I will be jealous for my holy name. 26 They shall forget their shame, and all the treachery they have practiced against me, when they dwell securely in their land with none to make them afraid, 27 when I have brought them back from the peoples and gathered them from their enemies' lands, and through them have vindicated my holiness in the sight of many nations. 28 Then they shall know that I am the LORD their God because I sent them into exile among the nations, and then gathered them into their own land. I will leave none of them remaining among the nations any more; 29 and I will not hide my face any more from them, when I pour out my Spirit upon the house of Israel, says the Lord GoD."

40 In the twenty-fifth year of our exile, at the beginning of the year, on the

---

8. Restoration of the Fortunes of Jacob (39:25-29)

25. The whole house of Israel: Israel and Judah. For **restore the fortunes** see 16:53; 29:14. Note that this is really the doctrine of "for his name's sake."

26. Translate "They shall bear their shame" (cf. KJV) as in the M.T. rather than **They shall forget their shame,** which reads the letter *shin* for *sin*. With vs. 26*b* cf. 34:28.

29. Cf. 37:14.

IV. Vision of the Restored Community (40:1–48:35)

These nine chapters comprise the final section of the book of Ezekiel, related to chs. 33–39, and yet standing apart as a distinct unit because of their concern with the

---

whether it is possible for a nation as such to renounce power. He answers that this could take place only were a nation found willing to die as state and be reborn as church, i.e., "only if in an unexpected historical moment it is seized as a whole by the transcendental idea and for its sake renounces power." He goes on to say, "Such an event would be one of the great turning points of history; it would perhaps create 'mankind.' " [3]

[3] New York: Charles Scribner's Sons, 1936, pp. 199-200.

Or we may quote from a book written at the time of the Versailles Treaty: "The precedents all mean war; only the great departure from all precedents can in the long run mean peace." [4]

40:1–43:27. *The Vision of the Temple.*—On the vexed question of the composition of chs. 40–48 see the Exeg. It will be assumed here that the groundwork of these final chapters is from a disciple of Ezekiel who lived in the Exile and

[4] J. L. Garvin, *The Economic Foundations of Peace* (London: Macmillan & Co., 1919), p. 574.

fourteenth year after that the city was smitten, in the selfsame day the hand of the LORD was upon me, and brought me thither.

tenth day of the month, in the fourteenth year after the city was conquered, on that very day, the hand of the LORD was upon

temple and its ritual. The passage 40:1–42:20 describes the detail of the arrangements of the temple area as witnessed by Ezekiel in a vision in which the divine architect acts as guide. The section 43:1-5 depicts the return of the glory of Yahweh, while in 43:6-27 Yahweh speaks from the inner sanctuary and gives instructions for the making of the altar and its consecration. Ch. 44 is concerned with the proper ministry in the sanctuary, granting full priestly rights only to the priests of the family of Zadok, with the Levites as temple servants and foreigners proscribed from such service. The description of the allotment of the land begins in 45:1-9, anticipating the more detailed account in 47:13–48:35. In 45:10–46:18 there are regulations for weights and measures, the contributions of the princes, the sacrifices at the stated feasts and the new moon and sabbaths, etc. In 46:19-24 the survey of the temple area continues; this is concluded with the vignette of the sacred stream flowing from the temple in 47:1-12. For a general analysis of the authorship of this section see the Intro., pp. 53-56, and Exeg. below.

A. THE TEMPLE ARRANGEMENTS: OUTER AND INNER COURTS (40:1-49)

The prophet is transported to the temple mount from Babylon, and a heavenly guide conducts him on a tour from point to point in the temple area, measuring off the various gates, walls, and chambers of the courts. The tour begins at the eastern gate and leads eventually into the inner court. The chapter ends with the beginning of the description of the temple itself, which is continued in ch. 41.

1. EZEKIEL AT THE TEMPLE MOUNT (40:1-5)

The date is April 17, 572 (April 28, 573), and the transport parallels that in ch. 8, which was also "in visions of God" (see Exeg. on 8:3; 11:22-25), but which may reflect an actual visit. Here we have no real vision, but rather the literary form of a vision, as

was confident that his people would soon be restored to their land. It is clear that the whole section is not from one hand, that there is a good deal of patchwork about it. But we shall be content to speak of "the seer" when the author of any part is referred to.

We need not doubt that the kernel of the section is a transcript of an actual vision on the part of the seer, which can be dated in 573, in accordance with 40:1-4. Of course the various details, the measurements, etc., were worked out subsequently. But the symmetry and general pattern of the sanctuary will belong to the original experience. Fresh and living at the first, it was reduced to mathematical precision in the act of committing it to writing. This draft was then amplified by various later hands, who may be held responsible in particular for the various scraps of legislation which lie scattered about chs. 40–48. Here we have something like a blueprint for reconstruction. Thus, while ch. 40 begins with a tour of the temple under angelic guidance, ch. 43 ends with elaborate ritual prescriptions.

Again, the vision will probably draw upon the seer's recollections of Solomon's temple

from the days when it still stood. Memories blend with hopes and create a condition of trance in which what was active in his waking moments now takes shape before him in symbolic forms.

The seer, we may suppose, has been brooding over the possibility of a fresh beginning in the life of his people. Convinced as he is that return to Palestine will come in God's time, his heart is set on something much more important than even that. He wants the severed bond between God and Israel to be restored. The divine presence forsook the land because of sin (11:23); what hope is there that it will return? If it returns, it will do so when the appointed hour comes, since God's majesty is not for us to command. Yet Israel need not remain passive; let the people make themselves ready in purity and dedication for what the future will bring.

We must not think of the seer as interested only in the temple as a ritualist and sacerdotalist of the most narrow sort. We should give his vision a more generous interpretation. The temple which he sees symbolizes for him a state of things in which the whole life of the restored community is dedicated to the Lord. As we read

2 In the visions of God brought he me into the land of Israel, and set me upon a very high mountain, by which *was* as the frame of a city on the south.

3 And he brought me thither, and, behold, *there was* a man, whose appearance *was* like the appearance of brass, with a line of flax in his hand, and a measuring reed; and he stood in the gate.

4 And the man said unto me, Son of man, behold with thine eyes, and hear with thine ears, and set thine heart upon all that I shall show thee; for to the intent that I might show *them* unto thee *art* thou brought hither: declare all that thou seest to the house of Israel.

me, 2 and brought me in the visions of God into the land of Israel, and set me down upon a very high mountain, on which was a structure like a city opposite me.*p* 3 When he brought me there, behold, there was a man, whose appearance was like bronze, with a line of flax and a measuring reed in his hand; and he was standing in the gateway. 4 And the man said to me, "Son of man, look with your eyes, and hear with your ears, and set your mind upon all that I shall show you, for you were brought here in order that I might show it to you; declare all that you see to the house of Israel."

p Gk: Heb *on the south*

---

also probably in Zechariah. The phrase **at the beginning of the year** (vs. 1) should probably be read "in the first month" (בראשון for בראש השנה) as in the LXX and to accord with the usual formula. **The tenth day of the month** may be after the analogy of the tenth day of the seventh month, the day of Atonement, apparently considered a New Year's Day in Lev. 25:9 (see Julian Morgenstern, "The Three Calendars of Ancient Israel," and "Supplementary Studies in the Calendars of Ancient Israel," *Hebrew Union College Annual,* I [1924], 22-28; X [1935], 8, 29). According to the P source, the tenth day of the first month was the day the Hebrews entered the Promised Land (Josh. 4:19; for another association see Exod. 12:3). The author is using the symbolism of the New Year's Day, for on this day the glory of Yahweh enters the temple (43:1-5), recalling Exod. 40:1-38 (P), where the glory of Yahweh fills the tent of meeting at its erection and dedication on the first day of the first month.

40:2. The **very high mountain** is Mount Zion, as in Ps. 48:2; Isa. 2:2; Mic. 4:1; Zech. 14:10, considered elevated beyond actual height to suggest its significance. Actually the Mount of Olives towers above the sacred area by about three hundred feet. **Opposite me:** Read מנגד with the LXX for the less probable מנגב, **on the south.** The sacred area with its gates, walls, and buildings resembled a city plan.

3. This may be the architect of the heavenly courts (see Zech. 2:1-2; cf. the divine scribe in Ezek. 9:1-11). His appearance **like bronze** indicates his supernatural character (cf. 1:4, 7, 27; Dan. 10:6). Cf. the imagery in Rev. 21:10-27, where the transport to the high mountain, the angel with the measuring rod, and the measuring of the city of Jerusalem are influenced by this passage.

---

through these final chapters we are struck by the fact that the temple stands empty, waiting for the divine presence to enter and hallow it again. When God returns everything falls into its place, the purpose of the great construction is realized, and the new name of the city reveals its character: "The LORD is there" (48:35).

40:1-4. *He Came to a City.*—J. B. Priestley's play *They Came to a City* gives expression to the widespread desire in our time for a more satisfying form of community life, one in which artificial distinctions will be banished, honest work will be prized, and man will serve his fellow man in freedom and joy. Our seer wants a city in which the life of his people will be

renewed; in his vision such a city spreads out before his eyes. It is all blurred and obscure at first, but as it takes on clearer outline he sees that it is rather a temple than a city. Is he disappointed? No, for he is well aware that a city is made not only by the materials of which it is composed, but even more by the spiritual values which it cherishes. It is not merely that our modern town planning does not often give due place to the needs of a new area for worship. Something more than church buildings is involved. Can we really hope for a worthier and healthier common life unless it gathers around reverence for all that is high and holy?

5 And behold a wall on the outside of the house round about, and in the man's hand a measuring reed of six cubits *long* by the cubit and a handbreadth: so he measured the breadth of the building, one reed; and the height, one reed.

6 ¶ Then came he unto the gate which looketh toward the east, and went up the stairs thereof, and measured the threshold of the gate, *which was* one reed broad; and the other threshold *of the gate, which was* one reed broad.

7 And *every* little chamber *was* one reed long, and one reed broad; and between the little chambers *were* five cubits; and the threshold of the gate by the porch of the gate within *was* one reed.

5 And behold, there was a wall all around the outside of the temple area, and the length of the measuring reed in the man's hand was six long cubits, each being a cubit and a handbreath in length; so he measured the thickness of the wall, one reed; and the height, one reed. 6 Then he went into the gateway facing east, going up its steps, and measured the threshold of the gate, one reed deep;*q* 7 and the side rooms one reed long, and one reed broad; and the space between the side rooms, five cubits; and the threshold of the gate by the vestibule of the gate at the inner end, one reed.

q Heb *deep, and one threshold, one reed deep*

---

5. The reed six cubits long would have measured about ten feet four inches, the long cubit being 20.679 inches, while the shorter or more ordinary cubit was about 17½ inches (see Galling, *Biblisches Reallexikon,* p. 367). The equal height and thickness of the wall surrounding the temple area are probably not without significance, as also the fact that the temple area and the inner court formed perfect squares. The great thickness of the wall is in part to emphasize the separation between the secular and the sacred (cf. 42:20).

2. The East Gate of the Outer Court (40:6-16)

For something of the significance of this gate in the ritual of the temple, see Morgenstern, "The Gates of Righteousness," pp. 1-37. The general plan of the gate has significant parallels in excavated city gates, especially the Solomonic period gate at Megiddo, with three recessed chambers on each side of the passageway (see Loud, *Megiddo II,* Vol. I, Pl. 6; Vol. II, p. 48, Fig. 105; an important discussion of the east gate is that by Howie, *Date and Composition of Ezekiel,* pp. 43-46, and "The East Gate of Ezekiel's Temple Enclosure and the Solomonic Gateway of Megiddo," *Bulletin of the American Schools of Oriental Research,* No. 117 [Feb., 1950], pp 13-19).

6. There were seven steps to the two other gates of the outer court (see vss. 22, 26), indicating that the whole temple area was on a terrace or platform. The LXX has seven steps for this east gate also, and this may be original. The gate has two thresholds, this one at the entrance corresponding to the thickness of the wall around the area. The second threshold, before the entrance into the vestibule of the gate, is mentioned in vs. 7. **And one threshold, one reed deep** (RSV mg.) is here obviously scribal dittography (note the "keepers of the threshold" in II Kings 12:9; 22:4; II Chr. 34:9; Jer. 35:4; etc.).

7. Crossing the threshold at the entrance of the gate, one went along the passageway with the three guardrooms or recessed chambers on either side, and then came to the

---

5. The Divine Standard.—The seer's guide, who is to initiate him into the plan of the temple, has a yardstick of uncommon length. In more than one country of the ancient East there were two measures, the longer of which went by the name of "royal." So the guide brings to the work a divine standard. The new community is to base its life from the very beginning on God's will. It is not sufficient that it should build part of the temple to its own

specifications and leave him to crown it; the work must be begun, continued, and finished under his direction. The trouble with us often is that we bring God in only when the work is finished and we find it going not so well as we had expected; his job is to put everything right for us! Why not bring him in as architect at the very outset of the enterprise?

40:5–42:20. *The Plan of Life.*—The plan to which the temple is rebuilt will symbolize those

8 He measured also the porch of the gate within, one reed.

9 Then measured he the porch of the gate, eight cubits; and the posts thereof, two cubits; and the porch of the gate *was* inward.

10 And the little chambers of the gate eastward *were* three on this side, and three on that side; they three *were* of one measure: and the posts had one measure on this side and on that side.

11 And he measured the breadth of the entry of the gate, ten cubits; *and* the length of the gate, thirteen cubits.

12 The space also before the little chambers *was* one cubit *on this side,* and the space *was* one cubit on that side: and the little chambers *were* six cubits on this side, and six cubits on that side.

13 He measured then the gate from the roof of *one* little chamber to the roof of another: the breadth *was* five and twenty cubits, door against door.

8 Then he measured the vestibule of the gateway, eight cubits; **9** and its jambs, two cubits; and the vestibule of the gate was at the inner end. **10** And there were three side rooms on either side of the east gate; the three were of the same size; and the jambs on either side were of the same size. **11** Then he measured the breadth of the opening of the gateway, ten cubits; and the breadth of the gateway, thirteen cubits. **12** There was a barrier before the side rooms, one cubit on either side; and the side rooms were six cubits on either side. **13** Then he measured the gate from the back[r] of the one side room to the back[r] of the other, a breadth of five

[r] Compare Gk: Heb *roof*

threshold which led into the vestibule of the gate. From the vestibule one stepped into the outer court. Howie (*op. cit.,* p. 111) believes there was no vestibule at the inner end and leaves the meaning of vs. 7*b* obscure, omitting as dittography a reference to it in vs. 9*b*.

8-10. The dittography in vs. 8 is obvious; the **eight cubits** are the depth of the vestibule, its breadth being given in the emended text of vs. 14 as twenty cubits. The **jambs** belong to the opening of the vestibule into the court, the opening itself measuring ten cubits from jamb to jamb (vs. 11).

11-12. The breadth of the gateway, not its **length** (contrast KJV), was thirteen cubits; we should perhaps read דרך, "passageway," for ארך, **length.** If so, this is the distance from the jambs of the side chambers on one side to the jambs of the side chambers on the opposite side; then the side chambers must have projected beyond their jambs, the projection possibly being the גבול or **barrier** of vs. 12. This גבול has been variously interpreted; the reference may be to the raised pavement of the side chambers, one cubit high, that pavement in the first pair of side chambers being narrower than in the others, set back one and one half cubits to permit space for the door sockets and for the door of the gate to swing back; the passageway at this point would thus be wider than through the rest of the gate, the thirteen cubits of vs. 11 (see Galling in Bertholet and Galling, *Hesekiel,* pp. 136-39). Howie takes the thirteen cubits as the measurements of the breadth of the inner vestibule, adjoining an outer vestibule; in this case we should read רהב, breadth (cf. LXX, τὸ εὖρος).

13. The over-all width of the gate was twenty-five cubits, and its length, given in vs. 15, fifty cubits. The Hebrew גג, roof, is difficult to understand, and we should perhaps emend to גו, **back;** the LXX reads τοῦ τοίχου, "wall." The doors at the back of each side chamber would open on the pavement of the outer court.

features which the seer most desires to see in the life of the restored community. There are three points which particularly call for attention.

(*a*) *Holiness.* The whole structure of the temple is intended to impress upon those who

worship there that they are a holy people, that they belong to God. This is brought about in two ways. First, by separation. Special rooms are provided in which to lay up **the most holy things,** and the priests are required to change their clothing when they go out among the

14 He made also posts of threescore cubits, even unto the post of the court round about the gate.

15 And from the face of the gate of the entrance unto the face of the porch of the inner gate *were* fifty cubits.

16 And *there were* narrow windows to the little chambers, and to their posts within the gate round about, and likewise to the arches: and windows *were* round about inward: and upon *each* post *were* palm trees.

17 Then brought he me into the outward court, and, lo, *there were* chambers, and a pavement made for the court round about: thirty chambers *were* upon the pavement.

18 And the pavement by the side of the gates over against the length of the gates *was* the lower pavement.

19 Then he measured the breadth from the forefront of the lower gate unto the forefront of the inner court without, a hundred cubits eastward and northward.

20 ¶ And the gate of the outward court that looked toward the north, he measured the length thereof, and the breadth thereof.

and twenty cubits, from door to door. 14 He measured also the vestibule, twenty cubits; and round about the vestibule of the gateway was the court.[s] 15 From the front of the gate at the entrance to the end of the inner vestibule of the gate was fifty cubits. 16 And the gateway had windows round about, narrowing inward into their jambs in the side rooms, and likewise the vestibule had windows round about inside, and on the jambs were palm trees.

17 Then he brought me into the outer court; and behold, there were chambers and a pavement, round about the court; thirty chambers fronted on the pavement. 18 And the pavement ran along the side of the gates, corresponding to the length of the gates; this was the lower pavement. 19 Then he measured the distance from the inner front of[t] the lower gate to the outer front of the inner court, a hundred cubits.

20 Then he went before me to the north, and behold, there was a gate[u] which faced toward the north, belonging to the outer court. He measured its length and its

[s] Compare Gk: Heb *and he made the jambs sixty cubits, and to the jamb of the court was the gateway round about*
[t] Compare Gk: Heb *from before*
[u] Gk: Heb *on the east and on the north. And the gate*

14. The verse is hopelessly corrupt. The emended text of the RSV, based partly on the LXX, at least makes sense and provides a missing measurement. Howie finds here the over-all measurements of the outer gate (outer vestibule) twenty cubits wide.

16. See I Kings 6:4 where חלוני שקפים אטמים may best be translated "windows with recessed frames"; the text here refers to the same kind of windows, חלונות אטמות, **windows . . . narrowing inwards,** which are illustrated on ivory plaques found in excavations and called in the Talmud "Tyrian windows." The palm tree decoration, noted also on Solomon's temple, was a common decorative motif in the Near East (see G. Ernest Wright, "Solomon's Temple Resurrected," *Biblical Archaeologist,* IV [1941], 26-27).

3. The Thirty Chambers Around the Court (40:17-19)

17-19. The size or disposition of the thirty chambers is not given. They would have been for the use of the people and the Levites who worshiped in the outer court. The pavement around the outer court extended the length of the gate from the walls, i.e., fifty cubits. It is called **the lower pavement** as over against the pavement in the inner court, which was at a higher level (cf. II Chr. 7:3). So also the gates of the outer court were the "lower" gates. The outer court was a hundred cubits deep, measuring from the inner face of the gates of the outer court to the outer face of the gates of the inner court (cf. vss. 23, 27). In vs. 19 some read "gate" for **court** with the LXX, although the latter is understandable.

4. The North and South Gates of the Outer Court (40:20-27)

These measurements accord with those of the east gate. The *Qerê* אילמיו, "its vestibules," in vss. 21, 22, 24-26 might be taken to support the idea of two vestibules (cf. also vss. 29 ff.).

21 And the little chambers thereof *were* three on this side and three on that side; and the posts thereof and the arches thereof were after the measure of the first gate: the length thereof *was* fifty cubits, and the breadth five and twenty cubits.

22 And their windows, and their arches, and their palm trees, *were* after the measure of the gate that looketh toward the east; and they went up unto it by seven steps; and the arches thereof *were* before them.

23 And the gate of the inner court *was* over against the gate toward the north, and toward the east; and he measured from gate to gate a hundred cubits.

24 ¶ After that he brought me toward the south, and behold a gate toward the south: and he measured the posts thereof, and the arches thereof, according to these measures.

25 And *there were* windows in it and in the arches thereof round about, like those windows: the length *was* fifty cubits, and the breadth five and twenty cubits.

26 And *there were* seven steps to go up to it, and the arches thereof *were* before them: and it had palm trees, one on this side, and another on that side, upon the posts thereof.

27 And *there was* a gate in the inner court toward the south: and he measured from gate to gate toward the south a hundred cubits.

28 And he brought me to the inner court by the south gate: and he measured the south gate according to these measures;

29 And the little chambers thereof, and the posts thereof, and the arches thereof, according to these measures: and *there were* windows in it and in the arches thereof round about: *it was* fifty cubits long, and five and twenty cubits broad.

30 And the arches round about *were* five and twenty cubits long, and five cubits broad.

breadth. 21 Its side rooms, three on either side, and its jambs and its vestibule were of the same size as those of the first gate; its length was fifty cubits, and its breadth twenty-five cubits. 22 And its windows, its vestibule, and its palm trees were of the same size as those of the gate which faced toward the east; and seven steps led up to it; and its vestibule was on the inside. 23 And opposite the gate on the north, as on the east, was a gate to the inner court; and he measured from gate to gate, a hundred cubits.

24 And he led me toward the south, and behold, there was a gate on the south; and he measured its jambs and its vestibule; they had the same size as the others. 25 And there were windows round about in it and in its vestibule, like the windows of the others; its length was fifty cubits, and its breadth twenty-five cubits. 26 And there were seven steps leading up to it, and its vestibule was on the inside; and it had palm trees on its jambs, one on either side. 27 And there was a gate on the south of the inner court; and he measured from gate to gate toward the south, a hundred cubits.

28 Then he brought me to the inner court by the south gate, and he measured the south gate; it was of the same size as the others. 29 Its side rooms, its jambs, and its vestibule were of the same size as the others; and there were windows round about in it and in its vestibule; its length was fifty cubits, and its breadth twenty-five cubits. 30 And there were vestibules round about, twenty-five cubits long and five cubits

---

20. The words הקדים והצפון, **eastward and northward,** are meaningless, and the RSV reads ויקדם צפונה, **he went before me to the north;** cf. the LXX καὶ εἰσήγαγέν με, "and he brought me" (=ויוליכני). Instead of **and the gate** read **and behold, there was a gate.**

5. THE THREE GATES OF THE INNER COURT (40:28-37)

28-37. These gates correspond in position and arrangements with those of the outer court, save that they were reached by eight steps instead of seven, and the vestibule, facing the outer court, was at the opposite end. Vs. 30 is meaningless in the context and is

31 And the arches thereof *were* toward the outer court; and palm trees *were* upon the posts thereof: and the going up to it *had* eight steps.

32 ¶ And he brought me into the inner court toward the east: and he measured the gate according to these measures.

33 And the little chambers thereof, and the posts thereof, and the arches thereof, *were* according to these measures: and *there were* windows therein and in the arches thereof round about: *it was* fifty cubits long, and five and twenty cubits broad.

34 And the arches thereof *were* toward the outward court; and palm trees *were* upon the posts thereof, on this side, and on that side: and the going up to it *had* eight steps.

35 ¶ And he brought me to the north gate, and measured *it* according to these measures;

36 The little chambers thereof, the posts thereof, and the arches thereof, and the windows to it round about: the length *was* fifty cubits, and the breadth five and twenty cubits.

37 And the posts thereof *were* toward the outer court; and palm trees *were* upon the posts thereof, on this side, and on that side: and the going up to it *had* eight steps.

38 And the chambers and the entries thereof *were* by the posts of the gates, where they washed the burnt offering.

39 ¶ And in the porch of the gate *were* two tables on this side, and two tables on that side, to slay thereon the burnt offering and the sin offering and the trespass offering.

broad. 31 Its vestibule faced the outer court, and palm trees were on its jambs, and its stairway had eight steps.

32 Then he brought me to the inner court on the east side, and he measured the gate; it was of the same size as the others. 33 Its side rooms, its jambs, and its vestibule were of the same size as the others; and there were windows round about in it and in its vestibule; its length was fifty cubits, and its breadth twenty-five cubits. 34 Its vestibule faced the outer court, and it had palm trees on its jambs, one on either side; and its stairway had eight steps.

35 Then he brought me to the north gate, and he measured it; it had the same size as the others. 36 Its side rooms, its jambs, and its vestibule were of the same size as the others;[v] and it had windows round about; its length was fifty cubits, and its breadth twenty-five cubits. 37 Its vestibule[w] faced the outer court, and it had palm trees on its jambs, one on either side; and its stairway had eight steps.

38 There was a chamber with its door in the vestibule of the gate,[x] where the burnt offering was to be washed. 39 And in the vestibule of the gate were two tables on either side, on which the burnt offering and the sin offering and the guilt offering

[v] One Ms Compare verses 29 and 33; Heb lacks *were of the same size as the others*
[w] Gk Vg Compare verses 26, 31, 34: Heb *jambs*
[x] Cn: Heb *at the jambs of the gates*

omitted by several Hebrew MSS and the LXX; it may be due to dittography. Vs. 36 originally read as vss. 29, 33 (see RSV mg.). In vs. 37 read **Its vestibule** as in vss. 31, 34 for "its jambs" (cf. KJV) with the LXX and Vulg.; i.e., ואלמו for ואילו.

6. Sacrifice at the North or East Gate of the Inner Court (40:38-43)

38-43. The text does not clearly identify the gate. The position of the altar and the description of the practice in 46:1-2 suggest the east gate (so Cornill, Galling, Cooke, *et al.*), but the north gate has just been described and there is a possible allusion to it in vs. 40, although vs. 40a is corrupt and obscure. The editor's prince uses the east

people. Second, by graduation. The worshiper must go up from the outer court to the inner, while the central shrine again is elevated even above that. No one could worship in such a building without receiving the vivid impression of something beyond the human which is to be

approached with awe and reverence. Each step a man takes brings him nearer to the central mystery. In this respect the seer's vision departs considerably from the ground plan of Solomon's temple, so that we can be sure he is expressing something to which he attaches the utmost

40 And at the side without, as one goeth up to the entry of the north gate, *were* two tables; and on the other side, which *was* at the porch of the gate, *were* two tables.

41 Four tables *were* on this side, and four tables on that side, by the side of the gate; eight tables, whereupon they slew *their sacrifices.*

42 And the four tables *were* of hewn stone for the burnt offering, of a cubit and a half long, and a cubit and a half broad, and one cubit high: whereupon also they laid the instruments wherewith they slew the burnt offering and the sacrifice.

43 And within *were* hooks, a hand broad, fastened round about: and upon the tables *was* the flesh of the offering.

44 ¶ And without the inner gate *were* the chambers of the singers in the inner court, which *was* at the side of the north gate; and their prospect *was* toward the south: one at the side of the east gate *having* the prospect toward the north.

45 And he said unto me, This chamber, whose prospect *is* toward the south, *is* for the priests, the keepers of the charge of the house.

46 And the chamber whose prospect *is* toward the north *is* for the priests, the keepers of the charge of the altar: these *are* the sons of Zadok among the sons of Levi, which come near to the LORD to minister unto him.

47 So he measured the court, a hundred cubits long, and a hundred cubits broad, foursquare; and the altar *that was* before the house.

were to be slaughtered. 40 And on the outside of the vestibule[y] at the entrance of the north gate were two tables; and on the other side of the vestibule of the gate were two tables. 41 Four tables were on the inside, and four tables on the outside of the side of the gate, eight tables, on which the sacrifices were to be slaughtered. 42 And there were also four tables of hewn stone for the burnt offering, a cubit and a half long, and a cubit and a half broad, and one cubit high, on which the instruments were to be laid with which the burnt offerings and the sacrifices were slaughtered. 43 And hooks, a handbreadth long, were fastened round about within. And on the tables the flesh of the offering was to be laid.

44 Then he brought me from without into the inner court, and behold, there were two chambers[z] in the inner court, one[a] at the side of the north gate facing south, the other at the side of the south[b] gate facing north. 45 And he said to me, This chamber which faces south is for the priests who have charge of the temple, 46 and the chamber which faces north is for the priests who have charge of the altar; these are the sons of Zadok, who alone among the sons of Levi may come near to the LORD to minister to him. 47 And he measured the court, a hundred cubits long, and a hundred cubits broad, foursquare; and the altar was in front of the temple.

[y] Cn: Heb *to him who goes up*
[z] Gk: Heb *and from without to the inner gate were chambers for singers*
[a] Gk: Heb *which*
[b] Gk: Heb *last*

---

gate at the time of his sacrifices in 46:1-8, but Ezekiel associates the sacrifices of the priests with a "kitchen" not far from the north gate in 46:19-20. In vs. 38 substitute באילם השער, **in the vestibule of the gate** for the impossible באילים השערים, **at the jambs of the gates** (cf. KJV). For the burnt offerings, sin offerings, and guilt offerings see Lev. 1:1–7:38. Vs. 43 is very obscure, and the translation of השפתים as **hooks** (see Targ.) is by no means certain; many read with the versions שפתם, "their edge," i.e., of the table.

7. TWO CHAMBERS ON THE NORTH AND SOUTH (40:44-47)

44-47. The RSV emendation of vs. 44 with the LXX is generally accepted by scholars (reading ויקרבני מחוצה אל־החצר הפנימית והנה לשכות שתים), the M.T. being obviously inconsistent in the context, since the chambers were to be used by priests, not singers. The word הדרום, **south,** with the LXX for הקדים, **east,** is an obvious correction of an easy corruption. For the Zadokite priests see 43:19; 44:15-16. The anticipatory allusion to the Zadokites in vs. 46 may be secondary (see Hölscher, Cooke, Herrmann, Bertholet), and if so, is by the editor. The court around the altar and before the temple was a perfect square.

48 ¶ And he brought me to the porch of the house, and measured *each* post of the porch, five cubits on this side, and five cubits on that side: and the breadth of the gate *was* three cubits on this side, and three cubits on that side.

49 The length of the porch *was* twenty cubits, and the breadth eleven cubits; and *he brought me* by the steps whereby they went up to it: and *there were* pillars by the posts, one on this side, and another on that side.

41 Afterward he brought me to the temple, and measured the posts, six cubits broad on the one side, and six cubits broad on the other side, *which was the* breadth of the tabernacle.

48 Then he brought me to the vestibule of the temple and measured the jambs of the vestibule, five cubits on either side; and the breadth of the gate was fourteen cubits; and the sidewalls of the gate were three cubits[c] on either side. 49 The length of the vestibule was twenty cubits, and the breadth twelve[d] cubits; and ten steps led up[e] to it; and there were pillars beside the jambs on either side.

41 Then he brought me to the nave, and measured the jambs; on each side six cubits was the breadth of the jambs.[f]

[c] Gk: Heb *and the breadth of the gate was three cubits*
[d] Gk: Heb *eleven*
[e] Gk: Heb *and by steps which went up*
[f] Compare Gk: Heb *tent*

---

8. VESTIBULE OF THE TEMPLE (40:48-49)

48-49. As the inner court was higher above the outer court than the outer court above the territory outside, so the temple platform was higher above the inner court than the inner court above the outer court. The significance of this is obvious. The **pillars** here are usually interpreted to be within the entrance, beside the jambs of the vestibule, but the fact that no measurements of them are given has been taken to mean that they were before the vestibule (Galling), and so correspond to the free-standing pillars of Solomon's temple. Note also that the width of the entrance ignores their presence there (vs. 48; for the pillars of the Solomonic temple see W. F. Albright, "Two Cressets from Marisa and the Pillars of Jachin and Boaz," *Bulletin of the American Schools of Oriental Research,* No. 85 [Feb., 1942], pp. 18-27; R. B. Y. Scott, "The Pillars Jachin and Boaz," *Journal of Biblical Literature,* LVIII [1939], 143-49; May, "The Two Pillars Before the Temple of Solomon," pp. 19-27). The emendations of the RSV are demanded by the context. In vs. 48 we must add ארבע עשרה אמה וכתפות השער, which has been omitted by homoeoteleuton. In vs. 49 read שתי עשרה, **twelve,** with the LXX for עשתי עשרה, **eleven,** to have the total measurements come out correctly. The corresponding measurement in I Kings 6:3 is ten cubits. Also in vs. 49 read עשר, **ten,** for אשר, "which."

B. NAVE, INNER ROOM, AND OTHER APPOINTMENTS (41:1-26)

The general plan of the temple, with its threefold division of vestibule, nave, and inner room, has parallels in the ancient Near East, e.g., the eighth-century temple found at Hattina (Tell Tainat) in Syria, and the palace-temples of Sargon from his capital at Dur-Sharrukin (Khorsabad; Gordon Loud, *et al., Khorsabad* [Chicago: University of Chicago Press, 1936], I, 80-128; for general discussions see especially Carl Watzinger, *Denkmäler Palästinas* [Leipzig: J. C. Hinrichs, 1933], I, 88-95; Wright, "Solomon's Temple Resurrected," pp. 17-31; "The Temple in Palestine-Syria," *Biblical Archaeologist,* VII [1944], 65-77; Paul L. Garber, "Reconstructing Solomon's Temple," *ibid.,* XIV [1951], 2-24). This type was of Phoenician or Syrian origin, and we recall that it was Phoenician

---

importance. Not only is the holy separated from the profane, but there are degrees within the former. The innermost shrine is holiest of all, so that the seer does not dare to enter it himself, but waits outside to receive the report of his guide. So in every community there should be some one thing which is sacred above all else, some ultimate loyalty which is dearer even than life.

(*b*) *Consecration.* It is noticeable, however, that what occupies the center of the building is not the inner shrine but the altar. Further,

2 And the breadth of the door *was* ten cubits; and the sides of the door *were* five cubits on the one side, and five cubits on the other side: and he measured the length thereof, forty cubits, and the breadth, twenty cubits.

3 Then went he inward, and measured the post of the door, two cubits; and the door, six cubits; and the breadth of the door, seven cubits.

4 So he measured the length thereof, twenty cubits; and the breadth, twenty

2 And the breadth of the entrance was ten cubits; and the sidewalls of the entrance were five cubits on either side; and he measured the length of the nave forty cubits, and its breadth, twenty cubits. 3 Then he went into the inner room and measured the jambs of the entrance, two cubits; and the breadth of the entrance, six cubits; and the sidewalls*g* of the entrance, seven cubits. 4 And he measured the length of the room, twenty cubits, and its breadth, twenty cu-

g Gk: Heb *breadth*

---

workmen who built the temple for Solomon. Temple structures are known in Palestine from as early as Neolithic Jericho; they are particularly well illustrated in the Late Bronze Period (1550-1200) at such places as Shechem, Lachish, Beth-shan, and Megiddo. The temple was the palace of the king-god, and the inner room his throne room.

There are so many instances of obscurities and corruptions in this chapter that space permits only a few of the many comments that should be made.

1. Nave of the Temple (41:1-4)

41:1. *Hêkhāl,* **nave,** is a word of ultimate Sumerian origin (*egal,* Akkad. *ekallu*) and means **temple** or **palace,** here applied to the main room of the temple. The vestibule measured 20 by 12 cubits, i.e., about 35½ by 20½ feet (40:49), the nave 20 by 40 cubits, i.e., about 35½ by 71 feet, and the inner room 20 by 20 cubits, i.e., about 35½ by 35½ feet. I Kings 6:20 describes the inner room as a cube, 20 cubits in height. In the Solomonic temple the inner room was on a podium, raised above the rest of the temple, as illustrated in Canaanite temples at Beth-shan or in the temples at Khorsabad (cf. Kurt Galling, "Das Allerheiligste in Salomos Tempel, ein Christlicher 'Thoraschrein,' " *Journal of the Palestine Oriental Society,* XII [1932] 43-46). Instead of רחב האהל, **the breadth of the tabernacle,** read רחב האיל, **the breadth of the jambs,** although this may be a scribal addition, and is omitted by the LXX and one Hebrew MS.

3. The inner room is called the *debhir* in Kings and Chronicles (I Kings 6:5, 16, 19; etc.; II Chr. 4:20; 8:6, 8; etc.), and is usually translated "oracle," from the Hebrew *dābhar,* "to speak," but this has been questioned; the word is plausibly associated with the Arabic *dbr,* "back," i.e., the rear room. The progressively narrow entrance of the vestibule, nave, and **inner room** provide significant symbolism. Ezekiel enters the nave, but he does not follow the divine guide into the inner room. According to the P legislation, only the high priest could enter the inner room and he only on the day of Atonement (Lev. 16:1-34), although Ezekiel does not specify such a regulation. For ורחב, **and the breadth,** read with the LXX, וכתפות, **and the sidewalls,** for the measurements can fit only this reading (cf. emended text of 40:48). The **sidewalls** are the walls on each side of the entrance, the jamb measurements giving their breadth. The very narrow walls here (two cubits; contrast vs. 1; 40:48, the jambs of the entrance to the vestibule and nave) are necessary to keep the over-all proportions of the temple, in view of the fact that the vestibule is here twelve cubits broad, rather than the ten in I Kings 6:3.

4. The most holy place: "The holy of holies," a name given to the inner room of the temple in I Kings 6:1-8:66; II Chr. 3:1-5:14, and of the tabernacle in Exod. 26:31-37.

---

there is only one altar, although in the old temple there were several. Thus the seer finds room at the heart of the restored community both for the presence of God and for the consecration to him of the national life. All is so designed as to lead up to that high moment

when we stand facing the shrine in which the divine glory has taken up its abode, there to offer ourselves to God. The climax of the common life is in this act of dedication.

(c) *Unity.* Wherever possible, the building and its parts are planned in the form of a

cubits, before the temple: and he said unto me, This *is* the most holy *place*.

5 After he measured the wall of the house, six cubits; and the breadth of *every* side chamber, four cubits, round about the house on every side.

6 And the side chambers *were* three, one over another, and thirty in order; and they entered into the wall which *was* of the house for the side chambers round about, that they might have hold, but they had not hold in the wall of the house.

7 And *there was* an enlarging, and a winding about still upward to the side chambers: for the winding about of the house went still upward round about the house: therefore the breadth of the house *was still* upward, and so increased *from* the lowest *chamber* to the highest by the midst.

bits, beyond the nave. And he said to me, This is the most holy place.

5 Then he measured the wall of the temple, six cubits thick; and the breadth of the side chambers, four cubits, round about the temple. 6 And the side chambers were in three stories, one over another, thirty in each story. There were offsets[h] all around the wall of the temple to serve as supports for the side chambers, so that they should not be supported by the wall of the temple. 7 And the side chambers became broader as they rose[i] from story to story, corresponding to the enlargement of the offset[j] from story to story round about the temple; on the side of the temple a stairway led upward, and thus one went up from the lowest story to the top story

[h] Gk Compare 1 Kings 6. 6: Heb *they entered*
[i] Cn: Heb *it was surrounded*
[j] Gk: Heb *for the encompassing of the temple*

2. SIDE CHAMBERS (41:5-11)

These chambers or vaults appear also in I Kings 6:5-10 (cf. the analogies in the Khorsabad temples). They went around three sides of the temple, and were in three stories, with thirty chambers in each story. All had the same length. In I Kings 6:6 the breadth is given as five, six, and seven cubits respectively for the three stories. Here the lower chambers are four cubits broad (vs. 5), and the upper two stories probably five and six cubits respectively. The breadth of the outer wall, here five cubits (vs. 9), in Solomon's temple would have been four. The entrance into the side chambers was by a doorway on the north and on the south side of the temple, and the stairway to get to the upper floor was probably at this point (vs. 7). The purpose of these side chambers is not given, but they were probably for the paraphernalia of the temple service and for holding the gifts to the temple, e.g., "the treasures of the house of the Lord" mentioned in I Kings 14:26; 15:15; II Kings 14:14; etc. Leroy Waterman has argued that the building was originally built by Solomon as a royal treasury and only later used as a temple, but the architectural form is that of a temple (see "The Damaged 'Blueprints' of the Temple of Solomon," *Journal of Near Eastern Studies,* II [1943], 284-94; "The Treasuries of Solomon's Private Chapel," *ibid.,* VI [1947], 161-63).

5. The inner wall was six cubits thick at the base, and so probably five cubits thick opposite the second story, and four cubits opposite the third story.

6. Offsets: Read ומגרעות with the LXX (cf. I Kings 6:6) for ובאות, **and they entered.** The verse is obscure, although the RSV gives the intended sense; contrast the fairly literal KJV. This structural formation is to keep the side chambers from infringing on the greater sanctity of the walls of the nave and inner room.

7. This verse is also very obscure and doubtless corrupt; contrast the KJV with the RSV. Read ונספה, "and increased" (RSV **as they rose** [?]) for ונסבה, "and it went round about"; cf. KJV **and there was . . . a winding about.** Read with the LXX, כמוסף מהקיר, "corresponding to the increase from the wall," i.e., the **enlargement of the offset** (RSV), for כי מוסב הבית, **for the winding about of the house. On the side of the temple a stairway led upward:** The RSV apparently reads אל כתף הבית לולים יעלו למעלה, adapted from I Kings 9:8, instead of על כן רחב לבית למעלה, **therefore the breadth of the house . . . upward.** A satisfactory reconstruction is difficult. For **and thus** (וכן) read "and from" (ומן) with one MS, the LXX, and Syriac, i.e., "and from the lowest story one went up to the top story," etc.

8 I saw also the height of the house round about: the foundations of the side chambers *were* a full reed of six great cubits.

9 The thickness of the wall, which *was* for the side chamber without, *was* five cubits: and *that* which *was* left *was* the place of the side chambers that *were* within.

10 And between the chambers *was* the wideness of twenty cubits round about the house on every side.

11 And the doors of the side chambers *were* toward *the place that was* left, one door toward the north, and another door toward the south: and the breadth of the place that was left *was* five cubits round about.

12 Now the building that *was* before the separate place at the end toward the west *was* seventy cubits broad; and the wall of the building *was* five cubits thick round about, and the length thereof ninety cubits.

13 So he measured the house, a hundred cubits long; and the separate place, and the building, with the walls thereof, a hundred cubits long;

14 Also the breadth of the face of the house, and of the separate place toward the east, a hundred cubits.

through the middle story. 8 I saw also that the temple had a raised platform round about; the foundations of the side chambers measured a full reed of six long cubits. 9 The thickness of the outer wall of the side chambers was five cubits; and the part of the platform which was left free was five cubits.[k] Between the platform[l] of the temple and the 10 chambers of the court was a breadth of twenty cubits round about the temple on every side. 11 And the doors of the side chambers opened on the part of the platform that was left free, one door toward the north, and another door toward the south; and the breadth of the part that was left free was five cubits round about.

12 The building that was facing the temple yard on the west side was seventy cubits broad; and the wall of the building was five cubits thick round about, and its length ninety cubits.

13 Then he measured the temple, a hundred cubits long; and the yard and the building with its walls, a hundred cubits long; 14 also the breadth of the east front of the temple and the yard, a hundred cubits.

[k] Syr: Heb lacks *five cubits*
[l] Cn: Heb *house of the side chambers*

---

8. The temple was on a platform or podium six cubits high, i.e., about ten feet. For *gŏbhah* (with *mappîq*), **height, raised platform,** some suggest *gabbāh*, interpreted as "pavement," i.e., the space on the platform left free beyond the outer wall. The RSV changes (א)מלוא, **full,** to ימדו (?), and translates **measured.** On אצילה, translated **long,** see 40:5 (cf. 13:18 where אצילי ידים means "wrists" or "elbow"; see also Jer. 38:12). Is it a technical architectural term, or does it refer to the carpenter's square? (Cf. Galling, *Biblisches Reallexikon*, pp. 283, 285.)

9. The Syriac addition of **five cubits** fits the situation (cf. "the pavement" in Exeg. on vs. 8). This is repeated at the end of vs. 11. **Between the platform:** Read בין הגבה for בית צלעות, **place** [house] **of the side chambers,** and connecting with vs. 10.

10. This breadth of twenty cubits belongs to the temple yard mentioned in vs. 12. Some would transpose vss. 10 and 11, since vs. 11 is still concerned with the side chambers and platform.

3. The Structure West of the Temple (41:12)

12. The function of this structure is not explained. It may have been an open court, since an area this size could hardly be roofed without pillars. It may have been the stalls (פרורים of II Kings 23:11=פרבר of I Chr. 26:18) for the sacred horses which, with the chariots, were removed by Josiah; these passages show that there was in the Solomonic and postexilic temple an entrance at this point (see discussion by Galling).

4. Measurements of the Temple and Yard (41:13-15a)

The temple was one hundred cubits long, including the side chambers and outer wall. The yard behind the temple plus the building behind the temple (vs. 13*b*) measured

15 And he measured the length of the building over against the separate place which *was* behind it, and the galleries thereof on the one side and on the other side, a hundred cubits, with the inner temple, and the porches of the court;

16 The doorposts, and the narrow windows, and the galleries round about on their three stories, over against the door, ceiled with wood round about, and from the ground up to the windows, and the windows *were* covered;

17 To that above the door, even unto the inner house, and without, and by all the wall round about within and without, by measure.

18 And *it was* made with cherubim and palm trees, so that a palm tree *was* between a cherub and a cherub; and *every* cherub had two faces;

19 So that the face of a man *was* toward the palm tree on the one side, and the face of a young lion toward the palm tree on the other side: *it was* made through all the house round about.

15 Then he measured the length of the building facing the yard which was at the west and its walls[m] on either side, a hundred cubits.

The nave of the temple and the inner room and the outer[n] vestibule 16 were paneled[o] and round about all three had windows with recessed[p] frames. Over against the threshold the temple was paneled with wood round about, from the floor up to the windows (now the windows were covered), 17 to the space above the door, even to the inner room, and on the outside. And on all the walls round about in the inner room and the nave were carved likenesses[q] 18 of cherubim and palm trees, a palm tree between cherub and cherub. Every cherub had two faces: 19 the face of a man toward the palm tree on the one side, and the face of a young lion toward the palm tree on the other side. They were carved on the whole temple round about;

[m] Cn: The meaning of the Hebrew term is unknown
[n] Gk: Heb *of the court*
[o] Gk: Heb *the thresholds*
[p] Cn Compare Gk 1 Kings 6. 4: The meaning of the Hebrew term is unknown
[q] Cn: Heb *measures and carved*

one hundred cubits. The line measured in vs. 14 is also the west side of the inner court (40:47).

15a. And its walls: Read וקירותיה for ואתוקיהא, which has been given an Aramaic suffix.

5. DETAILS OF THE TEMPLE DECORATION (41:15b-26)

15b. The M.T. has "the inner nave" (cf. KJV), but read "the nave and the inner [room]"; cf. LXX; see RSV. **The outer:** Read החיצון after the LXX for החצר, **the court.**

16. Paneled: Read with the LXX ספנים for הספים, "the thresholds" (cf. KJV). We should read והשקופים (cf. LXX) for the uncertain והאתיקים, **galleries,** and interpret here as in I Kings 6:4, **windows with recessed frames** (see Exeg. on 40:16 for this type of window). If we retain the less probable KJV arrangement of the text, the reference is perhaps to windows around the three divisions of the temple (see I Kings 6:5). Neither the arrangement nor the sense of the verse is clear. The expression עץ שחיף, **paneled with wood,** may be right, but some would read the letter *shin* instead of *sin,* and interpret as "shahiph wood," after the cuneiform *iṣ siḥpi,* a black wood, here used for paneling (cf. G. R. Driver, "Notes on Hebrew Lexicography," *Journal of Theological Studies,* XXIII [1922], 409).

17-18. Carved likenesses: Read דמות עשוים for the meaningless מדות ועשוי, **measures and carved** (RSV mg.). For these decorative motifs in the temple of Solomon see I Kings 6:29 (cf. I Kings 7:29, 36). Archaeological illustrations of these motifs appear particu-

square. The seer of Patmos carries the symbolism a stage farther when he throws his new Jerusalem into the form of a cube (Rev. 21:16). In each case what is meant is harmony; the city constitutes a unity because all within it accords

with the divine purpose which it is meant to serve. There is to be no discord in the national life, but a perfect balance of all elements. The people are to be at one with each other because they are first of all at one with God.

20 From the ground unto above the door *were* cherubim and palm trees made, and *on* the wall of the temple.

21 The posts of the temple *were* squared, *and* the face of the sanctuary; the appearance *of the one* as the appearance *of the other.*

22 The altar of wood *was* three cubits high, and the length thereof two cubits; and the corners thereof, and the length thereof, and the walls thereof, *were* of wood: and he said unto me, This *is* the table that *is* before the LORD.

23 And the temple and the sanctuary had two doors.

24 And the doors had two leaves *apiece,* two turning leaves; two *leaves* for the one door, and two leaves for the other *door.*

25 And *there were* made on them, on the doors of the temple, cherubim and palm trees, like as *were* made upon the walls; and *there were* thick planks upon the face of the porch without.

26 And *there were* narrow windows and palm trees on the one side and on the other side, on the sides of the porch, and *upon* the side chambers of the house, and thick planks.

20 from the floor to above the door cherubim and palm trees were carved on the wall.[r]

21 The doorposts of the nave were squared; and in front of the holy place was something resembling 22 an altar of wood, three cubits high, two cubits long, and two cubits broad;[s] its corners, its base,[t] and its walls were of wood. He said to me, "This is the table which is before the LORD." 23 The nave and the holy place had each a double door. 24 The doors had two leaves apiece, two swinging leaves for each door. 25 And on the doors of the nave were carved cherubim and palm trees, such as were carved on the walls; and there was a canopy of wood in front of the vestibule outside. 26 And there were recessed windows and palm trees on either side, on the sidewalls of the vestibule.[u]

[r] Cn Compare verse 25: Heb *and the wall*
[s] Gk: Heb lacks *two cubits broad*
[t] Gk: Heb *length*
[u] Cn: Heb *vestibule, and the side chambers of the temple and the canopies*

larly in ivory inlays, such as those from Samaria (see Wright, "Solomon's Temple Resurrected," Figs. 5-6). With the cherubim in vs. 19 cf. those in 1:10.

20. On the wall: Read with vs. 25 לקיר for וקיר, **and the wall** (cf. KJV). **Of the temple** is marked in the M.T. as dubious; it is best omitted.

21-22. The **table** of the bread of the Presence was to be at the entrance to the inner room. The KJV suggests the meaningless character of the present text. The breadth of the **table** or altar must be supplied with the LXX, i.e., **two cubits broad,** and also with the LXX must be read ואדנו, **and its base,** for וארכו, **and its length.** The table of the bread of the Presence, made of cedar and overlaid with gold, appears in I Kings 6:20; see also Exod. 25:23-30 (made of acacia wood overlaid with gold); cf. Lev. 24:5-9; etc. The altar in front of the entrance to the inner room is known in excavated Canaanite temples (see Alan Rowe, *Topography and History of Beth-shan* [Philadelphia: University of Pennsylvania Press, 1930], Pl. 56, No. 2; see also Schaeffer, *Cuneiform Texts of Ras Shamra-Ugarit,* Pl. XXVII, Fig. 2, for a relief from Canaanite Ugarit showing what is apparently a ritual scene with a table upon which are, so it seems, loaves of bread arranged in two lots (cf. Lev. 24:5-9; II Chr. 29:18).

23-24. The text is not clear, but the rendering **double door** for **two doors** helps give the meaning. The text uses דלתות, **doors,** in the sense of "leaves," rather than צלעים (cf. I Kings 6:34). The doors would swing on posts set in sockets.

25. The word עב, **canopy,** is uncertain; the versions suggest "beams" (cf. KJV; see I Kings 7:6). The canopy would perhaps be formed by projecting beams.

26. The **recessed windows** and palm tree decorations were on the **sidewalls of the vestibule** (see vs. 3). The latter part of the verse makes no sense and is generally omitted by scholars as a gloss, perhaps by a scribe who would interpret עב in vs. 25.

42 Then he brought me forth into the outer court, the way toward the north: and he brought me into the chamber that *was* over against the separate place, and which *was* before the building toward the north.

2 Before the length of a hundred cubits *was* the north door, and the breadth *was* fifty cubits.

3 Over against the twenty *cubits* which *were* for the inner court, and over against the pavement which *was* for the outer court, *was* gallery against gallery in three *stories*.

4 And before the chambers *was* a walk of ten cubits breadth inward, a way of one cubit; and their doors toward the north.

42 Then he led me out into the inner[v] court, toward the north, and he brought me to the chambers which were opposite the temple yard and opposite the building on the north. 2 The length of the building which was on the north side[w] was[x] a hundred cubits, and the breadth fifty cubits. 3 Adjoining the twenty cubits which belonged to the inner court, and facing the pavement which belonged to the outer court, was gallery[y] against gallery[y] in three stories. 4 And before the chambers was a passage inward, ten cubits wide and a hundred cubits long,[z] and their doors were on

[v] Gk: Heb *outer*
[w] Gk: Heb *door*
[x] Gk: Heb *before the length*
[y] The meaning of the Hebrew word is unknown
[z] Gk Syr: Heb *a way of one cubit*

C. The Priests' Chambers (42:1-20)

In vss. 1-14 are described the priests' chambers in the area between the temple yard (see 41:12) and the outer court, to the north and south of the temple. There the priests store their share from the sacrifices, and eat their meals. There also they deposit, before they go out into the less sacred outer court, the garments in which they minister. Only the chambers on the north are described in detail, for those on the south have corresponding arrangements. The detailed description of the chambers on the north is most obscure and the text is obviously corrupt. They may have formed two structures, the southern section lying alongside the temple yard measuring 100 by 20 cubits, and the northern section facing the outer court 50 by 20 cubits, with a passageway 10 cubits wide between, the chambers within these structures arranged in three stories. Or they may have formed a single structure with the chambers in three rows but at different levels; the row facing the outer court is thus one half as long as the other two rows, and the passageway just outside this row, protected from the outer court by a barricade.

In vss. 15-20 the over-all measurements of the temple area are given as 500 cubits square, i.e., 861.625 feet on each side.

1. Chambers to the North of the Temple Yard (42:1-10a)

42:1. The context supports the LXX הפנימית, **inner,** rather than the M.T. החיצונה, **outer. Opposite the building on the north:** I.e., opposite the north wall of the temple area (cf. 40:5), and so adjoining the outer court (vs. 8), although the text may be corrupt and we should perhaps omit **opposite the building.**

2. The RSV deletes אל פני, **before,** with the LXX, and reads פאת, **side,** for פתח, **door,** an obvious corruption.

3. The twenty cubits are perhaps the width of the yard (see 41:10). **In three stories:** Some translate "in the third story." The phrase may also mean that the rooms were arranged in three rows on the slope which led down in three descending terraces to the outer court from the temple yard (Galling; cf. Richter).

4. Inward may be retained, although omitted by the LXX and Syriac, if the **passage** separated the chambers into two structures, and so the doors were on the north side of the longer structure, opening into the passageway. Galling interprets both the passageway and the doors to be on the north side of that part of the chambers which faced the outer court (vss. 7-8). **A hundred cubits long:** Reading ארך מאה אמה with the LXX and Syriac for דרך אמה אחת, **a way of one cubit,** a probable error, although Galling reads "and a wall [וגדר] for [דרך] of one cubit," i.e., the wall of vs. 7.

5 Now the upper chambers *were* shorter: for the galleries were higher than these, than the lower, and than the middlemost of the building.

6 For they *were* in three *stories,* but had not pillars as the pillars of the courts: therefore *the building* was straitened more than the lowest and the middlemost from the ground.

7 And the wall that *was* without over against the chambers, toward the outer court on the forepart of the chambers, the length thereof *was* fifty cubits.

8 For the length of the chambers that *were* in the outer court *was* fifty cubits: and, lo, before the temple *were* a hundred cubits.

9 And from under these chambers *was* the entry on the east side, as one goeth into them from the outer court.

10 The chambers *were* in the thickness of the wall of the court toward the east, over against the separate place, and over against the building.

11 And the way before them *was* like the appearance of the chambers which *were* toward the north, as long as they, *and* as broad as they: and all their goings out *were* both according to their fashions, and according to their doors.

12 And according to the doors of the chambers that *were* toward the south *was* a door in the head of the way, *even* the way

the north. 5 Now the upper chambers were narrower, for the galleries[y] took more away from them than from the lower and middle chambers in the building. 6 For they were in three stories, and they had no pillars like the pillars of the outer[a] court; hence the upper chambers were set back from the ground more than the lower and the middle ones. 7 And there was a wall outside parallel to the chambers, toward the outer court, opposite the chambers, fifty cubits long. 8 For the chambers on the outer court were fifty cubits long, while those opposite the temple were a hundred cubits long. 9 Below these chambers was an entrance on the east side, as one enters them from the outer court, 10 where the outside wall begins.[b]

On the south[c] also, opposite the yard and opposite the building, there were chambers 11 with a passage in front of them; they were similar to the chambers on the north, of the same length and breadth, with the same exits[d] and arrangements and doors. 12 And below the south chambers was an entrance on the east side, where one enters

[y] The meaning of the Hebrew word is unknown
[a] Gk: Heb lacks *outer*
[b] Cn Compare Gk: Heb *in the breadth of the wall of the court*
[c] Gk: Heb *east*
[d] Heb *and all their exits*

6. Read החיצונה, **the outer,** supplying the word **court,** for the M.T. החצרות, **the courts,** another probable textual corruption (cf. LXX τῶν ἐξωτέρων, "the outer ones"). Just what is intended by **pillars of the outer court** is not clear, possibly the expression designates the pillars belonging to the rooms on the pavement, although they were one-storied and hardly in need of columns for roof supports. The phrase may be a scribal addition referring to a later portico arrangement.

7. This **wall,** perhaps better translated as "fence" or "party wall" (גדר), **fifty cubits** long, may have been an eastward extension of the fifty-cubits-long wall of the chambers adjoining the outer court, the party wall plus the wall of the chambers equaling the hundred-cubits length of the chambers on the inner court. Galling takes it as a barricade parallel to and outside of the fifty-cubit wall of the chambers on the court, with the passageway of vs. 4 between the two.

9-10*a.* See the KJV for a more literal rendering of the last part of the verse; the RSV reads with the LXX בראש, lit., "at the head" (cf. **begins** for ברחב, **in the breadth** [thickness], and הגדר החיצון, **outside wall,** for גדר החצר, **wall of the court.**

2. CORRESPONDING CHAMBERS TO THE SOUTH OF THE TEMPLE YARD (42:10*b*-12)

10*b.* The RSV reads with the LXX הדרום, **the south,** for הקדים, **the east.**

11. Read וכמוצאיהן, lit., "and like their exits" (hence RSV) for וכל־מוצאיהן, **and all their exits** (RSV mg.).

12. The M.T. is very obscure, but the meaning should correspond to vss. 9-10.

directly before the wall toward the east, as one entereth into them.

13 ¶ Then said he unto me, The north chambers *and* the south chambers, which *are* before the separate place, they *be* holy chambers, where the priests that approach unto the Lord shall eat the most holy things: there shall they lay the most holy things, and the meat offering, and the sin offering, and the trespass offering; for the place *is* holy.

14 When the priests enter therein, then shall they not go out of the holy *place* into the outer court, but there they shall lay their garments wherein they minister; for they *are* holy; and shall put on other garments, and shall approach to *those things* which *are* for the people.

15 Now when he had made an end of measuring the inner house, he brought me forth toward the gate whose prospect *is* toward the east, and measured it round about.

16 He measured the east side with the measuring reed, five hundred reeds, with the measuring reed round about.

17 He measured the north side, five hundred reeds, with the measuring reed round about.

18 He measured the south side, five hundred reeds, with the measuring reed.

19 ¶ He turned about to the west side, *and* measured five hundred reeds, with the measuring reed.

20 He measured it by the four sides: it had a wall round about, five hundred *reeds* long, and five hundred broad, to make a

the passage, and opposite there was a dividing wall.[e]

13 Then he said to me, "The north chambers and the south chambers opposite the yard are the holy chambers, where the priests who approach the Lord shall eat the most holy offerings; there they shall put the most holy offerings — the cereal offering, the sin offering, and the guilt offering, for the place is holy. 14 When the priests enter the holy place, they shall not go out of it into the outer court without laying there the garments in which they minister, for these are holy; they shall put on other garments before they go near to that which is for the people."

15 Now when he had finished measuring the interior of the temple area, he led me out by the gate which faced east, and measured the temple area round about. 16 He measured the east side with the measuring reed, five hundred cubits by the measuring reed. 17 Then he turned and measured[f] the north side, five hundred cubits by the measuring reed. 18 Then he turned and measured[f] the south side, five hundred cubits by the measuring reed. 19 Then he turned to the west side and measured, five hundred cubits by the measuring reed. 20 He measured it on the four sides. It had a wall around it, five hundred cubits long and five

[e] Cn: Heb *And according to the entrances of the chambers that were toward the south was an entrance at the head of the way, the way before the dividing wall toward the east as one enters them*

[f] Gk: Heb *measuring reed round about. He measured*

---

3. Use of the Chambers (42:13-14)

13-14. The priests who approach the Lord are the Zadokite priests. For the priestly portions of the sacrifices see 44:28-31; Lev. 2:1-10; 6:25-26; 7:7-10; 10:12-15; Num. 18:8-19; also I Sam. 2:12-17.

4. Over-All Measurements of the Temple Area (42:15-20)

16. The Hebrew has here and in vss. 17-19 **five hundred reeds**, but קנים, **reeds**, should be omitted with the LXX, and **cubits** understood. The C.T. of vs. 16 actually has "five cubits of reeds," but the *Qerê* is **five hundred reeds. Round about**, סביב, is meaningless; it is a corruption of וסבב, **then he turned** (see LXX; so also in vs. 17; cf. vs. 19).

20. The prophet Ezekiel makes the wall of the temple area the division between the sacred and the secular. The later writer reckons the sacred portion of the land to be an area 25,000 by 20,000 cubits, and designates a half section of this, within which is the sanctuary, "a most sacred place" (cf. 45:3-4, 2; 48:10-12).

separation between the sanctuary and the profane place.

43 Afterward he brought me to the gate, *even* the gate that looketh toward the east:

2 And, behold, the glory of the God of Israel came from the way of the east: and

hundred cubits broad, to make a separation between the holy and the common.

43 Afterward he brought me to the gate, the gate facing east. 2 And behold, the glory of the God of Israel came

---

D. The Altar of Burnt Offering (43:1-27)

Twenty years earlier Ezekiel had had a vision of the departure of the glory of Yahweh (10:1-22; 11:22-23). Now he pictures its return (vss. 1-5), and the enthroned Deity directs the prophet to describe to the people the temple arrangements and laws (vss. 6-12). The latter part of the chapter gives the direction for the construction of the great altar of burnt offerings before the temple (vss. 13-17) and the regulations for its consecration (vss. 18-27). Vss. 13-27 are thought to be secondary by several scholars (cf. Herrmann, Hölscher, Matthews, Cooke, *et al.*), and vss. 18-27 seem to reflect the influence of P (cf. Bertholet and Exeg. below) or to be closely related to it. The transition between vs. 12 and vs. 13 is abrupt. It is curious that the description of the altar is postponed to this point. One would have expected it to have been given earlier through being measured by the divine guide (cf. Galling). Did it originally stand after 40:47? Other parts of the description of the temple are certainly displaced. The editor (?) may be responsible for its present form and position, associating it here with the regulations for the consecration of the altar, which would have been out of place in chs. 40–42 and which belong to the later portions of chs. 40–48. The editor's hand is not absent from vss. 6-11. Something of the difficulties of interpretation may be seen in the oft noted fact that 43:1-11 and 44:4-5 contain parallel pictures of the glory of Yahweh in the temple and directions to tell cultic ordinances and laws. It has also been suggested that 43:1 cannot be the original introduction to the chapter, since according to 42:15 Ezekiel is already at the east gate.

1. Return of the Glory of Yahweh (43:1-5)

The return of the glory of Yahweh to the temple is reflected often in the psalms and in other parts of O.T. literature (see the studies of Mowinckel, Morgenstern, *et al.*). The glory of Yahweh could be thought to be above the throne chariot rather than integral with it (cf. 1:28; 20:4, 18; 11:22), and it has been thought that only the glory of Yahweh, without the throne chariot, appears in this vision (cf. Bertholet), but **the sound of many waters** in vs. 2 suggests the noise of the cherubim (cf. 1:24).

43:1. Omit שער, **gate** (=even the gate), with the versions, repeated by dittography. **Facing:** With one MS read פניו, "its face," as in vs. 4; 40:6 instead of פנה.

2. For the **many waters** see 1:24; 19:10; 31:4; etc. (cf. Rev. 1:15; 14:2; 17:1; 19:6). **The earth shone with his glory** reflects the solar symbolism in the concept of the glory of Yahweh (see also Isa. 60:1-3; Deut. 33:2; Isa. 24:23; Hab. 3:3-4; cf. Luke 2:9; see H. G. May, "The Creation of Light in Genesis 1₃₋₅," *Journal of Biblical Literature*, LVIII [1939], 209-11).

43:1-5. God Returns.—So a renewed and dedicated Israel stands waiting for God. And he returns in just that majesty with which he had formerly left the city. Here the writer has understood something which is at the heart of the gospel. The God who redeems us is not another than the God who once judged us; it is he who once forsook us for our disloyalty, but who still loves us enough to win us

back for himself. The sole guarantee that our deliverance, when it comes, will be final is that it is undertaken by the God who has known us at our worst and has not been sparing in his condemnation of us. The glory which now comes to pervade the temple is one with the glory which once entered the city to destroy it (vs. 3). In this there is an assurance that the sin of city and temple has been reckoned

his voice *was* like a noise of many waters: and the earth shined with his glory.

3 And *it was* according to the appearance of the vision which I saw, *even* according to the vision that I saw when I came to destroy the city: and the visions *were* like the vision that I saw by the river Chebar; and I fell upon my face.

4 And the glory of the LORD came into the house by the way of the gate whose prospect *is* toward the east.

5 So the spirit took me up, and brought me into the inner court; and, behold, the glory of the LORD filled the house.

6 And I heard *him* speaking unto me out of the house; and the man stood by me.

from the east; and the sound of his coming was like the sound of many waters; and the earth shone with his glory. 3 And[g] the vision I saw was like the vision which I had seen when he came to destroy the city, and[h] like the vision which I had seen by the river Chebar; and I fell upon my face. 4 As the glory of the LORD entered the temple by the gate facing east, 5 the Spirit lifted me up, and brought me into the inner court; and behold, the glory of the LORD filled the temple.

6 While the man was standing beside me, I heard one speaking to me out of the

[g] Gk: Heb *And like the vision*
[h] Syr: Heb *and the visions*

---

3. Like the vision (RSV mg.) is dittography from a little farther on in the verse; it is omitted by the LXX. **The visions** is likewise due to dittography, although the LXX appears to have read ומראה המרכבה, "and the vision of the chariot," for ומראות כמראות, "and visions like the visions" (cf. KJV). **When he came** follows six MSS, Theod., and the Vulg.; contrast **when I came.**

4. For the significance of the east gate see Exeg. on 40:6-16 and references cited there.

5. Cf. the glory of Yahweh filling the temple in Isa. 6:1-3; I Kings 8:11; II Chr. 5:14 (cf. Isa. 4:5); for the glory of Yahweh filling the tabernacle, see Exod. 40:34-38; Lev. 9:23.

2. YAHWEH SPEAKS FROM THE INNER SANCTUARY (43:6-12)

The most holy place or *debhir* was the throne room of Yahweh's palace, and there were his throne and his footstool (vs. 7). Numerous reliefs from the ancient Near East picture the king and king-god with throne and footstool. Cf. the viewpoint of P, and contrast that in Solomon's prayer at the dedication of the temple in I Kings 8:27 (R^D), where it is affirmed that the temple cannot really contain Yahweh (see also Isa. 66:1; Morgenstern, "The Book of the Covenant," *Hebrew Union College Annual*, V [1928], 72-81). The presence of Yahweh in the temple necessitates and emphasizes the distinction between the sacredness of the temple area as over against the profane territory outside, and the palace can no longer be essentially a part of the temple complex as in the pre-exilic period (see I Kings 6:1-10; 7:1-12; cf. II Kings 12:20; 20:8; see the suggested reconstruction of palace and temple in Galling, *Biblisches Reallexikon*, pp. 411-12; for the arrangements at Sargon's capital at Khorsabad, or the temple immediately adjoining the palace at Tell Tainat, see references cited in Exeg. on 41:26; cf. also the shrine in the home of the community leader [?] in Judg. 17). In the pre-exilic period the king was a very real head of the cultus, and the temple had something of the character of a royal chapel (see Amos 7:13). Before Hezekiah the tombs of the kings are said to have been

---

with and forgiven, so that there is nothing more to fear.

We may pause here to reflect once more on that theme of the sovereignty and majesty of God which governs the thinking behind this book. We saw it first as the awesome and inexpressible splendor which humbled the prophet to the dust and at the same time summoned him to service. As such, it was meant to be the background of all his work. Then we saw it

hovering over the city in judgment on her sins, and in the end forsaking the city because she could no longer provide a dwelling place for such holiness. Again and again it vindicated itself in the storming of cities, the ruin of shrines, and the devastation of whole countries. Exiled peoples on earth and the hopeless legions of the dead were witnesses to its might. But now the majesty and holiness of God take on their final form in blessing and restoration.

7 ¶ And he said unto me, Son of man, the place of my throne, and the place of the soles of my feet, where I will dwell in the midst of the children of Israel for ever, and my holy name, shall the house of Israel no more defile, *neither* they, nor their kings, by their whoredom, nor by the carcasses of their kings in their high places.

8 In their setting of their threshold by my thresholds, and their post by my posts, and the wall between me and them, they have even defiled my holy name by their abominations that they have committed: wherefore I have consumed them in mine anger.

9 Now let them put away their whoredom, and the carcasses of their kings, far from me, and I will dwell in the midst of them for ever.

temple; 7 and he said to me, "Son of man, this is the place of my throne and the place of the soles of my feet, where I will dwell in the midst of the people of Israel for ever. And the house of Israel shall no more defile my holy name, neither they, nor their kings, by their harlotry, and by the dead bodies[i] of their kings, 8 by setting their threshold by my threshold and their doorposts beside my doorposts, with only a wall between me and them. They have defiled my holy name by their abominations which they have committed, so I have consumed them in my anger. 9 Now let them put away their idolatry and the dead bodies[i] of their kings far from me, and I will dwell in their midst for ever.

[i] Or *the monuments*

"in the city of David" (I Kings 2:10; 11:43; 14:31; etc.), but not those of the later kings; Manasseh was buried "in the garden of his house," apparently close by the palace (II Kings 21:18), and Amon was buried in the same place (II Kings 21:26). Josiah was buried "in his own tomb" (II Kings 23:30).

Phraseology and ideology in vss. 7-9 at points recall those of the editor, who may be responsible at least for the present wording (cf. the profanation of the name of Yahweh in vs. 7 [see xxviii on p. 51]; for analogies in diction and ideas see 16:54; 18:10-12; 23:37-39; 33:26; 36:26-27; 37:26-28).

7-9. Jerusalem itself is designated the throne of Yahweh in Jer. 3:17; 14:21 (late). **Harlotry:** As in 23:27, a reference to licentious pagan rites; so also vs. 9 (KJV). The word במותם should be read, not *bāmôthām,* **in their high places,** but, with twenty MSS, *bemôthām,* "When they died" (?), though it is perhaps the result of corrupt dittography of the following word. Possibly we should read "by the steles of their kings at their high places," rendering *pgr* as monument or stele as in Ugaritic (see David Neiman, *"PGR: A Canaanite Cult-Object in the Old Testament," Journal of Biblical Literature,* LXVII [1948], 55-60; see also Lev. 26:30, and read, "the monuments of your idols," i.e., "your idolatrous monuments").

Their threshold and **their doorposts** have been interpreted as those of the tombs of the kings, which were possibly constructed to simulate a house (cf. Isa. 14:18; Job 17:13; see W. C. Graham and H. G. May, *Culture and Conscience* [Chicago: University of Chicago Press, 1936], pp. 287-89). Note that usually the tombs were placed outside the city wall because of the uncleanness of a dead body (yet cf. I Sam. 25:1; I Kings 2:34).

And he is as marvelous, as sovereign, and as awe-inspiring in the mercy he shows as ever he was in the judgment he exercised.

7-9. Church and State.—The new design for the temple implies nothing short of a revolution in the relations between church and state, to use modern language. In the older building the temple was subordinated to the palace, as is shown by the fact that Solomon took thirteen years to erect the latter and devoted only seven years to the former (I Kings 6:38–7:1). The temple seems indeed to have been enclosed

within the same court as the palace and to have been separated from it by a single wall merely (I Kings 7:12). Furthermore, it was the practice to inter the royal dead within the sacred precincts, presumably to secure for them a share in its holiness. All this is now to be altered, and the temple is to be an independent building standing entirely in its own grounds.

In Solomon's time the temple was more a royal sanctuary than a national one. The king appointed the priest who was in charge of it (I Kings 2:27, 35), and at a later time even

10 ¶ Thou son of man, show the house to the house of Israel, that they may be ashamed of their iniquities: and let them measure the pattern.

11 And if they be ashamed of all that they have done, show them the form of the house, and the fashion thereof, and the goings out thereof, and the comings in thereof, and all the forms thereof, and all the ordinances thereof, and all the forms thereof, and all the laws thereof: and write *it* in their sight, that they may keep the whole form thereof, and all the ordinances thereof, and do them.

12 This *is* the law of the house; Upon the top of the mountain the whole limit thereof round about *shall be* most holy. Behold, this *is* the law of the house.

13 ¶ And these *are* the measures of the altar after the cubits: The cubit *is* a cubit and a handbreadth; even the bottom *shall be* a cubit, and the breadth a cubit, and the border thereof by the edge thereof round

10 "And you, son of man, describe to the house of Israel the temple and its appearance and plan,*j* that they may be ashamed of their iniquities. 11 And if they are ashamed of all that they have done, portray*k* the temple, its arrangement, its exits and its entrances, and its whole form; and make known to them all its ordinances and all its laws; and write down in their sight, so that they may observe and perform all its laws*l* and all its ordinances. 12 This is the law of the temple: the whole territory round about upon the top of the mountain shall be most holy. Behold, this is the law of the temple.

13 "These are the dimensions of the altar by cubits (the cubit being a cubit and a

j Gk: Heb *the temple that they may measure the pattern*
k Gk: Heb *the form of*
l Gk: Heb *its whole form*

---

10. Vss. 10-12 may originally have come after 42:20, and may have been expanded by the editor in vss. 10*b* and 11*a*, the original speaker being the divine guide. **And its appearance and plan** reads ומראהו ותכניתו with the LXX, O.L., for ומדד את תכנית (see RSV mg.), a probable corruption.

11. Portray: Read וצרת with the LXX for צורת, **the form of.** The second occurrence of **and all the forms thereof** is a corruption of the following **all its laws** (i.e., צורתו for ותורתו), while **the whole form thereof** is a similar corruption (see 44:5).

12. See 42:20. If this means that the territory round about the temple is included in the "holy of holies," the verse belongs to the later writer, but it may refer to the temple area alone. Some delete as dittography **This is the law of the temple.**

3. The Altar of Burnt Offering (43:13-17)

Albright has maintained that this altar reflects Mesopotamian cosmic ideas; the lowest stage of the altar is called *ḥêq hā'āreç*, "the bosom of the earth" (see vs. 14), while the summit of the altar is called *har'êl* or *'ari'êl*, a word derived from the Akkadian *Arallu* or *Arallû*, which has the dual meaning of "underworld" and "mountain of the gods," the cosmic mountain. Like the Mesopotamian temple tower, the *ziggurat* ("mountain peak"), this altar is built in stages, and like it decorated with horns. Albright

---

changes in the ritual followed within it could be brought about by royal fiat (II Kings 16:10-18). The abuses of Manasseh's reign and the reforms of Josiah's were both rendered possible only by this accepted principle of royal control. Our seer therefore stands forth as the champion of a new principle, that of spiritual independence.

In what respects is the church today a mere annex of the state, a convenience for certain national purposes, a Valhalla for the distinguished dead, royal or otherwise? There are churches in Great Britain which give the im-

pression, from the memorial tablets on their walls, that there are just two ways of serving God worth mentioning, one in the church, the other in the armed forces. How is the principle of spiritual independence in danger in our day, and under what new forms should we reassert it?

10-11. *Vision and Reality.*—It is always a crucial moment when a vision has to be translated into an actual achievement. The difficulty is enhanced by the fact that normally it is one type of man who has the vision and another who must act upon it. The practical man tends to dismiss the seer as a mere dreamer, and the

about *shall be* a span; and this *shall be* the higher place of the altar.

14 And from the bottom *upon* the ground *even* to the lower settle *shall be* two cubits, and the breadth one cubit; and from the lesser settle *even* to the greater settle *shall be* four cubits, and the breadth *one* cubit.

15 So the altar *shall be* four cubits; and from the altar and upward *shall be* four horns.

16 And the altar *shall be* twelve *cubits* long, twelve broad, square in the four squares thereof.

handbreadth) : its base shall be one cubit high,[m] and one cubit broad, with a rim of one span around its edge. 14 And this shall be the height of the altar: from the base on the ground to the lower ledge, two cubits, with a breadth of one cubit; and from the smaller ledge to the larger ledge, four cubits, with a breadth of one cubit; 15 and the altar hearth, four cubits; and from the altar hearth projecting upward, four horns, one cubit high.[n] 16 The altar hearth shall be square, twelve cubits long by twelve broad.

[m] Gk: Heb lacks *high*

[n] Gk: Heb lacks *one cubit high*

---

concludes that the altar with its symbolism is derived from Phoenicia, going back to older Canaanite borrowings from Mesopotamia ("The Babylonian Temple-tower and the Altar of Burnt-offering," *Journal of Biblical Literature,* XXXIX [1920], 137-42; *Archaeology and Religion of Israel,* pp. 150-52) . The altar had a base eighteen cubits square extending one cubit beyond the lower ledge or stage. The lower ledge itself was sixteen cubits square and two cubits high. The stage above this, the upper ledge, was fourteen cubits square and four cubits high. Above this was the upper stage, the topmost section of the altar, the *har'êl* or *'ari'ēl,* twelve cubits square and four cubits high. From each of its four corners rose a "horn" one cubit high. The total height of the altar, presuming the base to be one cubit high and counting the horns, was twelve cubits, or about 20.68 feet. Excluding the horns and base, the height was ten cubits, corresponding to that given in II Chr. 4:1 for the altar of bronze, which, however, was twenty cubits square. Around the base was a rim or "boundary" half a cubit high and a span broad, perhaps to catch the blood or, if the base was at the pavement level, to set the base off from the pavement (see Albright) . The top of the altar was reached by steps on the east side. The material of the altar is not given, but it may have been stone (or possibly bronze?) . See the earlier legislation in Exod. 20:24-26, prohibiting the use of hewn stone or of steps in the altar.

13-14. Base: חיק, lit., "bosom"; in vs. 14*a,* חיק הארץ, "bosom of the earth." The word recalls the Akkadian name of the foundation platform of the royal palace and of the temple tower of Marduk in Babylon, *irat erṣiti* or *irat kigalli,* "bosom of the earth, bosom of the underworld," in inscriptions of Nebuchadrezzar (Albright, *Archaeology and the Religion of Israel,* p. 152) . It is unnecessary to emend with Toy, Rothstein, *et al.,* to מראש החיק, "from the top of the base." **Its base shall be one cubit high:** With the LXX, read חיקה אמה גבה for חיק האמה, "bosom of the cubit" (!) . The word גב, **higher place** (?) , should probably be read גבה, **height,** with the LXX, and connected with vs. 14, although גב has been taken as the name of the lowest section of the altar, below the lower ledge (see Galling) .

15. The translation **altar hearth,** based on an Arabic etymology, is not to be preferred; the first time the word is written ההראל, which may be translated "the 'mount of God,' " and the second time is to be read (see also vs. 16*a*) האריאל, "the Ariel" (see Exeg. above) . The word ההראל, "the 'mount of God,' " represents the original form (see May, " 'Ephod' and 'Ariel,' " p. 69) . The height of the **horns** is taken from the LXX.

---

seer to brand the practical man as a compromiser. But life requires both. We must establish in space and time what we have seen by an insight into the eternal.

It may encourage us in so doing to reflect that men were found to act upon this vision. No

doubt they made many mistakes, hardening its poetical symbolism into rules and regulations—perhaps indeed the seer himself was in part responsible that this happened. But they did help to make a new community which kept the faith as it had not done in the past. The Jews

17 And the settle *shall be* fourteen *cubits* long and fourteen broad in the four squares thereof; and the border about it *shall be* half a cubit; and the bottom thereof *shall be* a cubit about; and his stairs shall look toward the east.

18 ¶ And he said unto me, Son of man, thus saith the Lord God; These *are* the ordinances of the altar in the day when they shall make it, to offer burnt offerings thereon, and to sprinkle blood thereon.

19 And thou shalt give to the priests the Levites that be of the seed of Zadok, which approach unto me, to minister unto me, saith the Lord God, a young bullock for a sin offering.

20 And thou shalt take of the blood thereof, and put *it* on the four horns of it, and on the four corners of the settle, and upon the border round about: thus shalt thou cleanse and purge it.

21 Thou shalt take the bullock also of the sin offering, and he shall burn it in the

17 The ledge also shall be square, fourteen cubits long by fourteen broad, with a rim around it half a cubit broad, and its base one cubit round about. The steps of the altar shall face east."

18 And he said to me, "Son of man, thus says the Lord God: These are the ordinances for the altar: On the day when it is erected for offering burnt offerings upon it and for throwing blood against it, 19 you shall give to the Levitical priests of the family of Zadok, who draw near to me to minister to me, says the Lord God, a bull for a sin offering. 20 And you shall take some of its blood, and put it on the four horns of the altar, and on the four corners of the ledge, and upon the rim round about; thus you shall cleanse the altar and make atonement for it. 21 You shall also take the bull of the sin offering, and it shall

---

Horned altars are known from the excavations, the horns being projections at the four corners (see May, *Material Remains of the Megiddo Cult,* pp. 12-13, Pl. XII).

17. The first part of the verse describes the upper ledge, fourteen cubits square (see vs. 14); there was probably originally a reference also to the lower ledge, sixteen cubits square, for the latter part of the verse is concerned with the base (so Kraetzschmar, Rothstein, Bertholet, *et al.*). The **rim,** which was on the base, "surrounded" the lower ledge, and the absence of the reference to the lower ledge makes the rim appear to go around the upper ledge. Perhaps read הסבב, "surrounding," rather than סביב, **around** (cf. LXX). The rim was half a cubit high and a span broad (see vs. 13; cf. Galling).

4. Regulations for Consecrating the Altar (43:18-27)

These were for the purpose of removing any uncleanness, so that the altar might possess the sanctity necessary for its use and lose its "secular" nature. The shift from second person singular to third person plural has been taken as an indication of the composite nature of this passage. The oracular formulas "Thus says the Lord" (vs. 18) and "Says the Lord" (vss. 19, 27) are characteristic of the editor's work in chs. 40-48 (cf. 45:9, 18; 47:13, 23; etc.). The style recalls that of P in Exod. 29:36-37, where Moses is addressed and told to spend seven days making atonement for the altar (see also Lev. 8:14-15; Exod. 40:1-38; see Herrmann, Bertholet, Cooke, *et al.*).

18. The **blood** was dashed against the altar from a bowl (see Exod. 24:6 [JE]; Lev. 17:6 [H]; Exod. 29:16, 20; Num. 18:17 [P]; II Kings 16:13, 15).

19. The Levitical priests of the family of Zadok are in contrast with the Levites (cf. 44:5-31).

20. See Exod. 29:12; Lev. 8:14 (P). The **blood** on the **corners** and the **rim** consecrated all inside that area, making it holy. **Horns of the altar:** So the LXX and Syriac, interpreting the Hebrew **the four horns of it.**

21. So also the flesh of the sin offering is burnt "outside the camp" in Exod. 29:14; Lev. 8:17; 9:11; 16:27. **The appointed place belonging to the temple,** מפקד הבית, is mentioned by this name only here. Neh. 3:31 mentions שער המפקד, the Gate of Hammiphkad ("the Muster" or "the Appointed Place"), which, however, cannot be located with

appointed place of the house, without the sanctuary.

22 And on the second day thou shalt offer a kid of the goats without blemish for a sin offering; and they shall cleanse the altar, as they did cleanse it with the bullock.

23 When thou hast made an end of cleansing it, thou shalt offer a young bullock without blemish, and a ram out of the flock without blemish.

24 And thou shalt offer them before the LORD, and the priests shall cast salt upon them, and they shall offer them up for a burnt offering unto the LORD.

25 Seven days shalt thou prepare every day a goat for a sin offering: they shall also prepare a young bullock, and a ram out of the flock, without blemish.

26 Seven days shall they purge the altar and purify it; and they shall consecrate themselves.

27 And when these days are expired, it shall be, that upon the eighth day, and so forward, the priests shall make your burnt offerings upon the altar, and your peace offerings; and I will accept you, saith the Lord GOD.

44 Then he brought me back the way of the gate of the outward sanctuary which looketh toward the east; and it was shut.

be burnt in the appointed place belonging to the temple, outside the sacred area. 22 And on the second day you shall offer a he-goat without blemish for a sin offering; and the altar shall be cleansed, as it was cleansed with the bull. 23 When you have finished cleansing it, you shall offer a bull without blemish and a ram from the flock without blemish. 24 You shall present them before the LORD, and the priests shall sprinkle salt upon them and offer them up as a burnt offering to the LORD. 25 For seven days you shall provide daily a goat for a sin offering; also a bull and a ram from the flock, without blemish, shall be provided. 26 Seven days shall they make atonement for the altar and purify it, and so consecrate it. 27 And when they have completed these days, then from the eighth day onward the priests shall offer upon the altar your burnt offerings and your peace offerings; and I will accept you, says the Lord GOD."

44 Then he brought me back to the outer gate of the sanctuary, which

certainty, but may have belonged to the temple or palace rather than to the outer city wall (see Millar Burrows, "Nehemiah 3:1-32 as a Source for the Topography of Ancient Jerusalem," *Annual of the American Schools of Oriental Research,* XIV [1933-34] 120-21).

23-27. The types of sacrifice noted here are the sin offering (חטאת), the burnt offering (עלה), and the peace offering (שלם). The latter appears several times in Ugaritic literature. It is a comprehensive term for the sacrifice of animals, of which parts only were burned on the altar, the rest being eaten in the common meal. The entire animal was burned in a burnt offering (see George Buchanan Gray, *Sacrifice in the Old Testament* [Oxford: Clarendon Press, 1925], pp. 5-7, 64-66, etc.). With this passage cf. Deut. 27:1-7.

24. For **salt** in sacrifice see Lev. 2:13; Mark 9:49.

26. Consecrate it: Lit., "fill its hands" (cf. the Assyrian *umalli qâti;* see Judg. 17:5, 12). The original literal significance of the expression is obviously forgotten here.

E. ORDINANCES CONCERNING MINISTERS IN THE SANCTUARY (44:1-31)

The prophet is shown the closed east gate of the outer court, through which no one may enter, although the prince may sit in it to eat bread before Yahweh (vss. 1-3).

returned from exile, they built the temple and waited for the glory of God to return. And when we read the psalms which were sung in that temple, with their poignant confession of sin, their heartfelt appeal to God, and their

quiet trust in his mercy, can we doubt that the glory did return?

44:1-3. *The State Before God.*—Is this a piece of legislation or part of the original vision? If the latter, there is something very striking about

Back in the inner court, the prophet is given instructions regarding those who may minister before Yahweh. Foreigners may not act as servants in charge of the sanctuary or enter the sanctuary (vss. 6-9), but the Levites shall take their place as temple servants, demoted from the priesthood because of their contacts with idolatry (vss. 10-14). Only the Levitical priests, the Zadokites, are to have full priestly standing and enter the inner court or temple (vss. 15-16). Ordinances for the Zadokites are given, regulations regarding their garments, shaving, drinking wine, marriage, teaching and judging functions, observance of the laws for feasts and sabbaths, defilement by contact with a dead person, the priestly share of the sacrifices, and eating anything which dies of itself (vss. 17-31).

Certainty in the analysis of the authorship of this chapter is more difficult than usual. We have noted how 43:1-11 is paralleled in 44:4-5. The allusion to the prince in vs. 3 is from the editor (cf. 46:1-8; see on 12:12; 34:24; 37:25; etc.). In 43:1-5 the prophet was apparently brought from the east gate directly to the inner court. If the circuitous route here via the north gate is to avoid using the east gate of the inner court, in the light of the regulations in 46:1, the editor may be responsible for it. Possibly 43:1 ff. does not presume a closed east gate (see Hölscher). In 47:2, however, the prophet is also brought via the north gate. It is more or less generally agreed that the legislation in vss. 6-31 is composite (Herrmann, Sellin, Matthews, Cooke, Bertholet, et al.), and despite general evidence of what has been called the editor's phraseology, there may be a kernel here which we should ascribe to Ezekiel, although it is difficult to delineate. A hint of this is suggested in the fact that vss. 28-30 presume no inheritance for the priests, in contrast with the very definite inheritance ascribed to them by the editor in 45:1-5; 48:10; etc. So the legislation for the contribution to the priests in 44:30, which may be in conflict with the legislation for the contributions to the prince (see 45:13-16), may derive ultimately from an original Ezekiel legislation. A number of scholars suggest variant sources here. It would seem reasonable that Ezekiel presented some regulations for his elaborate temple, very possibly laws in which the Zadokites alone were the true priests as here. The argument that Ezekiel would never give to the Zadokites the clean slate presumed here, in view of the picture of corruptions in the temple courts in ch. 8 (Hölscher), may be countered by the presumption of a changed attitude on the part of the prophet in his later years; or it may be that the Zadokites were not primarily responsible for those corruptions, and we may believe that the Zadokite priesthood under Hilkiah had taken a not insignificant part in the Deuteronomic reform (II Kings 22:11-14; 23:4, 24). The chambers in which the priests were to put their robes (42:13-14 [by Ezekiel?]) seem to presuppose legislation like that in 44:19, which is also consonant with 46:20.

The zigzag sequence of movements of the prophet in 42:15; 43:1, 5; 44:1, 4 suggests to scholars disarrangements of the text (cf. Hölscher, Matthews, Cooke). Questions are raised in particular about the secondary character of the series of personal regulations in vss. 20-31.

1. The Closed Outer East Gate (44:1-3)

After Yahweh's entrance had hallowed the gate, the entrance of a mortal would have desecrated it or made a mortal taboo. The closed gates also perhaps stood as a symbol of the fact that Yahweh would never again leave the temple (cf. 43:7); i.e., there would be no further destruction of the temple or city, for the new age had arrived. Also it may suggest that never again could the east gate be used in connection with the pagan rites of the worship of the sun earlier mentioned in 8:16-18. The east gate of the

---

it. The seer has watched the glory of the Lord entering the temple by the eastern gate, with the brilliance of the sunrise and the majesty of the ocean at its height (43:2). When it has passed through, the gate swings to behind it, closed by no mortal hand. And closed it must

remain. But as the seer continues to look, he sees a solitary figure threading his way through the outer court and entering the vestibule of the great gate which has been thus forever hallowed. There he sits and worships "alone with the alone," the nearest that one who is not a con-

2 Then said the Lord unto me; This gate shall be shut, it shall not be opened, and no man shall enter in by it; because the Lord the God of Israel hath entered in by it, therefore it shall be shut.

3 *It is* for the prince; the prince, he shall sit in it to eat bread before the Lord; he shall enter by the way of the porch of *that* gate, and shall go out by the way of the same.

4 ¶ Then brought he me the way of the north gate before the house: and I looked, and, behold, the glory of the Lord filled the house of the Lord: and I fell upon my face.

5 And the Lord said unto me, Son of man, mark well, and behold with thine eyes, and hear with thine ears all that I say unto thee concerning all the ordinances of the house of the Lord, and all the laws thereof; and mark well the entering in of the house, with every going forth of the sanctuary.

6 And thou shalt say to the rebellious, *even* to the house of Israel, Thus saith the Lord God; O ye house of Israel, let it suffice you of all your abominations,

faces east; and it was shut. 2 And he*o* said to me, "This gate shall remain shut; it shall not be opened, and no one shall enter by it; for the Lord, the God of Israel, has entered by it; therefore it shall remain shut. 3 Only the prince may sit in it to eat bread before the Lord; he shall enter by way of the vestibule of the gate, and shall go out by the same way."

4 Then he brought me by way of the north gate to the front of the temple; and I looked, and behold, the glory of the Lord filled the temple of the Lord; and I fell upon my face. 5 And the Lord said to me, "Son of man, mark well, see with your eyes, and hear with your ears all that I shall tell you concerning all the ordinances of the temple of the Lord and all its laws; and mark well those who may be admitted to*p* the temple and all those who are to be excluded from the sanctuary. 6 And say to the rebellious house,*q* to the house of Israel, Thus says the Lord God: O house of Israel, let there be an end to all your abomina-

o Cn: Heb *the* Lord
p Cn: Heb *the entrance of*
q Gk: Heb lacks *house*

sacred area (Ḥaram esh-Sherif) in Jerusalem, the so-called "Golden Gate," is walled up so the entrance is impossible.

44:2. The Lord in vs. 2*a* is inconsonant with vs. 2*b*, and perhaps best omitted with the RSV. The speaker is the divine guide.

3. Whereas the present text might possibly be interpreted **only the prince,** it is doubtless corrupt (cf. KJV); the second **prince,** which in Hebrew is without the article, is due to dittography and is omitted by the Syriac and LXX. The initial את, sign of the accusative, is best emended to אך, **only. Eat bread:** In the sacrificial meal.

2. The Prophet Is Brought Before the Temple (44:4-5)

4-5. North gate: According to 46:1 the east gate is closed on weekdays. **Those who may be admitted:** Read מובאי for מבוא, **entrance. Those who are to be excluded:** Repoint מוצאי from *môçā'ê,* "exits" (cf. KJV), to *mûçā'ê;* see 43:11 where "entrances" and "exits" are consonant with the context.

3. Proscription of Foreigners (44:6-9)

These **foreigners** set to keep charge of the sanctuary (vs. 8) recall the temple slaves said to be descendants of the Gibeonites (Josh. 9:23), as well as those selected from the Midianites and "given" to the Levites in Num. 31:30, 47 (P); see also the Nethinim

secrated person can come to the presence of God. Who is he? He is **the prince,** the civil head of the community.

The picture thus sketched unites the state's independence of priestly control with its dependence on the divine authority. Even in the sphere of religion the state has its place and its rights, for it too is the servant of God as

truly as the church, albeit in a very different way. It is directly under God without needing any church as its intermediary. We must resist at once any form of clericalism and any claim that the state is above the moral law.

5-31. *The Consecration of the Community.*— This passage can be understood only as we bear in mind what priesthood means in the O.T.

7 In that ye have brought *into my sanctuary* strangers, uncircumcised in heart, and uncircumcised in flesh, to be in my sanctuary, to pollute it, *even* my house, when ye offer my bread, the fat and the blood, and they have broken my covenant because of all your abominations.

8 And ye have not kept the charge of mine holy things: but ye have set keepers of my charge in my sanctuary for yourselves.

9 ¶ Thus saith the Lord GOD; No stranger, uncircumcised in heart, nor uncircumcised in flesh, shall enter into my sanctuary, of any stranger that *is* among the children of Israel.

10 And the Levites that are gone away far from me, when Israel went astray, which went astray away from me after their idols; they shall even bear their iniquity.

11 Yet they shall be ministers in my sanctuary, *having* charge at the gates of the house, and ministering to the house: they

tions, **7** in admitting foreigners, uncircumcised in heart and flesh, to be in my sanctuary, profaning it,[r] when you offer to me my food, the fat and the blood. You[s] have broken my covenant, with all your abominations. **8** And you have not kept charge of my holy things; but you have set foreigners to keep my charge in my sanctuary.

9 "Therefore[t] thus says the Lord GOD: No foreigner, uncircumcised in heart and flesh, of all the foreigners who are among the people of Israel, shall enter my sanctuary. **10** But the Levites who went far from me, going astray from me after their idols when Israel went astray, shall bear their punishment. **11** They shall be ministers in my sanctuary, having oversight at the gates

[r] Gk: Heb *it my temple*
[s] Gk Syr Vg: Heb *they*
[t] Gk: Heb *for you*

("given ones") of the Chronicler, whose family names are listed in Ezra 2:43-54; Neh. 7:46-56, perhaps descendants of captives, as Ezra 8:20 may imply in asserting that David and his princes gave the Nethinim for the service of the Levites; cf. "the sons of Solomon's servants" as temple servants (Ezra 2:55-58; Neh. 7:57-60). See also the foreign temple guards, the Carites (II Kings 11:4-8; cf. Neh. 13:1-8). The Nethinim have been compared with the Babylonian order of temple servants known as *shirku*, meaning "given one" (see R. P. Dougherty, *The Shirkûtu of Babylonian Deities* [New Haven: Yale University Press, 1923], pp. 90-91).

In Herod's temple a ritual wall separated the outer court, the court of the Gentiles, from the inner courts, and inscriptions in Greek and Latin forbade a Gentile to pass beyond it on pain of death. A complete inscription in Greek and a fragment of another have been recovered (see J. H. Iliffe, "The ΘΑΝΑΤΟΣ Inscription from Herod's Temple," *Quarterly of the Department of Antiquities in Palestine*, VI [1936-37], 1-3).

7. For idea of **the uncircumcised in heart** see Jer. 4:4 (late); 9:26 (late); Deut. 10:16; 30:6 (R[D]); Lev. 26:41 (H); note also uncircumcised lips in Exod. 6:12, 30 (P) and uncircumcised ears in Jer. 6:10. For legislation regarding the food, the fat, and the blood, see Lev. 3:9-17 (P); cf. Gen. 9:4 (P), this passage recalling the former. Morgenstern argues for the period of Ezra as the date of this legislation against foreigners (see "Two Prophecies from 520-516 B.C.," *Hebrew Union College Annual*, XXII [1949], 422; cf. also Hölscher).

8-9. Emend לכם, **for yourselves**, to לכן, **therefore**.

4. THE LEVITES' SERVICE IN THE SANCTUARY (44:10-14)

10-14. The **Levites** rather than the foreigners are to serve as ministers in the sanctuary, to act as gatekeepers, to kill the sacrificial animals, and to wait on the people

The priest is not one who stands between man and God. He is one who makes possible man's approach to God. His worship is not a substitute for that of the people; rather does he worship in a representative capacity. He does not maintain the barrier of holiness between man and God—that is there in any case. He enables man to enter into God's presence in spite of this barrier. Hence we must not suppose that behind these strict regulations for the priesthood lies a national life given over to secularism and satisfied with an official and

shall slay the burnt offering and the sacrifice for the people, and they shall stand before them to minister unto them.

12 Because they ministered unto them before their idols, and caused the house of Israel to fall into iniquity; therefore have I lifted up mine hand against them, saith the Lord God, and they shall bear their iniquity.

13 And they shall not come near unto me, to do the office of a priest unto me, nor to come near to any of my holy things, in the most holy *place:* but they shall bear their shame, and their abominations which they have committed.

14 But I will make them keepers of the charge of the house, for all the service thereof, and for all that shall be done therein.

15 ¶ But the priests the Levites, the sons of Zadok, that kept the charge of my sanctuary when the children of Israel went astray from me, they shall come near to me to minister unto me, and they shall stand before me to offer unto me the fat and the blood, saith the Lord God:

of the temple, and serving in the temple; they shall slay the burnt offering and the sacrifice for the people, and they shall attend on the people, to serve them. **12** Because they ministered to them before their idols and became a stumbling block of iniquity to the house of Israel, therefore I have sworn concerning them, says the Lord God, that they shall bear their punishment. **13** They shall not come near to me, to serve me as priest, nor come near any of my sacred things and the things that are most sacred; but they shall bear their shame, because of the abominations which they have committed. **14** Yet I will appoint them to keep charge of the temple, to do all its service and all that is to be done in it.

15 "But the Levitical priests, the sons of Zadok, who kept the charge of my sanctuary when the people of Israel went astray from me, shall come near to me to minister to me; and they shall attend on me to offer me the fat and the blood, says the Lord

---

in the outer court. Much of the phraseology here recalls the editor. So **idols**, *gillûlîm* (vss. 10, 12; see 14:1-11 with much similar phraseology; cf. also 48:11); **bear their punishment** in vss. 10, 12 (see 4:4; 14:10; cf. Lev. 10:17; 16:22; Num. 30:15; Isa. 53:11); **serving in the temple** in vs. 11 (see 45:5; 46:24); **stumbling block of iniquity** in vs. 12 (see xiii on p. 50); "sworn with uplifted hand" in vs. 12 (see xxix on p. 51); **abominations which they have committed** in vs. 13 (see 33:29; 43:8). Because of parallel expressions in Num. 3:1-4:49 (P), it has been suggested that vss. 12-14 are a later expansion of vss. 9-16 (Cooke).

5. REGULATIONS FOR THE ZADOKITES (44:15-31)

The Zadokites alone may minister to Yahweh as the recognized priesthood. They were descended from Zadok, who suddenly appears as a fellow priest of Abiathar at the time of David (II Sam. 8:17; 15:24 ff.); by backing Solomon as successor of David he became the chief priest, while Abiathar was banished to Anathoth (see I Kings 1:8; 2:26-27, 35). It has been suggested that Zadok was actually a Jebusite priest of Jerusalem before David's capture of that city (H. H. Rowley, "Zadok and Nehushtan," *Journal of*

---

vicarious piety. The consecration of the priesthood is to be taken as symbolizing and expressing the consecration of the entire community from which it is drawn and in whose name it appears before God. As the first fruits of harvest were presented at the altar in token that all belonged to God, so the priest's peculiar "holiness" meant that the nation knew itself called to be holy too.

The rules laid down fall into three groups and they represent three phases of this conse-

cration of the community in the persons of its priestly representatives:

(*a*) *The will to repudiate the sin of the past* (vss. 6-9). That which is alien to the true life of the community is henceforth to be cast out from it. In particular, there must be no class engaged merely in routine and technical activities for which no personal qualifications are requisite. The seemingly harsh rule of vs. 9 has to be taken in its context. It is not the expression of a narrow nationalism or of religious

16 They shall enter into my sanctuary, and they shall come near to my table, to minister unto me, and they shall keep my charge.

17 ¶ And it shall come to pass, *that* when they enter in at the gates of the inner court, they shall be clothed with linen garments; and no wool shall come upon them, while they minister in the gates of the inner court, and within.

18 They shall have linen bonnets upon their heads, and shall have linen breeches upon their loins; they shall not gird *themselves* with any thing that causeth sweat.

19 And when they go forth into the outer court, *even* into the outer court to the people, they shall put off their garments wherein they ministered, and lay them in the holy chambers, and they shall put on other garments; and they shall not sanctify the people with their garments.

20 Neither shall they shave their heads, nor suffer their locks to grow long; they shall only poll their heads.

21 Neither shall any priest drink wine, when they enter into the inner court.

GOD; 16 they shall enter my sanctuary, and they shall approach my table, to minister to me, and they shall keep my charge. 17 When they enter the gates of the inner court, they shall wear linen garments; they shall have nothing of wool on them, while they minister at the gates of the inner court, and within. 18 They shall have linen turbans upon their heads, and linen breeches upon their loins; they shall not gird themselves with anything that causes sweat. 19 And when they go out into the outer court to the people, they shall put off the garments in which they have been ministering, and lay them in the holy chambers; and they shall put on other garments, lest they communicate holiness to the people with their garments. 20 They shall not shave their heads or let their locks grow long; they shall only trim the hair of their heads. 21 No priest shall drink wine, when

Biblical Literature, LVIII [1939], 113-41). Later legislation gave the Zadokites an ultimate Aaronite origin through Eleazar (I Chr. 6:50-53; 24:31). The Deuteronomic law had intended that the Levites should serve alongside the Zadokites as priests.

16. Approach my table: Perhaps the table of the bread of the Presence, which was before the inner sanctuary, although it has been taken to refer to the altar; **my table** is used symbolically in 39:20 of the table of the sacrificial feast, apparently the common meal sacrifice (cf. Mal. 1:7, 12; see Cooke).

17. For **linen garments** see Exeg. on 9:2. For the legislation on linen garments for priests see Lev. 6:10; 16:4, 23; cf. Exod. 28:6, 42; 39:27-29 (P uses בד for linen [שש, fine linen] rather than פשתים, as here). Wool might be unclean, and the law forbade making garments of mixed wool and linen (cf. Deut. 22:11; Lev. 19:19).

19. The communication of holiness to the people here may be contrasted with the viewpoint in Hag. 2:10-12. The repetition of **into the outer court** (cf. KJV) is an obvious instance of scribal dittography and is omitted in some MSS and the versions.

20. Note the regulation for the Nazarite in Num. 6:1-21 (cf. I Sam. 1:11). The law for the priests appears in Lev. 21:5, coupled with prohibition against self-laceration (cf. Deut. 14:1, 2).

21. Cf. Lev. 10:9, where the regulation is accompanied by a threat of death to those breaking it, and is associated with the distinction between the sacred and the common,

bigotry, but a summons to the seer's countrymen to take upon themselves the whole responsibility of the temple cultus and not to delegate part of it to outsiders. The seer thus rejects the kind of society with which we are only too familiar, one in which there is a "submerged tenth" which performs menial duties but is excluded from the rights of full membership in

the community. So vs. 8 is a call to accept the responsibility of a direct relationship to God. "You have not done your sacred duties to me yourselves" (Moffatt). The seer is by no means the sacerdotalist we took him to be.

(*b*) *The will to bear the shame of the past* (vss. 10-14). The Levites must be content with a subordinate position among the temple clergy

22 Neither shall they take for their wives a widow, nor her that is put away: but they shall take maidens of the seed of the house of Israel, or a widow that had a priest before.

23 And they shall teach my people *the difference* between the holy and profane, and cause them to discern between the unclean and the clean.

24 And in controversy they shall stand in judgment; *and* they shall judge it according to my judgments: and they shall keep my laws and my statutes in all mine assemblies; and they shall hallow my sabbaths.

25 And they shall come at no dead person to defile themselves: but for father, or for mother, or for son, or for daughter, for brother, or for sister that hath had no husband, they may defile themselves.

26 And after he is cleansed, they shall reckon unto him seven days.

27 And in the day that he goeth into the sanctuary, unto the inner court, to minister in the sanctuary, he shall offer his sin offering, saith the Lord God.

he enters the inner court. 22 They shall not marry a widow, or a divorced woman, but only a virgin of the stock of the house of Israel, or a widow who is the widow of a priest. 23 They shall teach my people the difference between the holy and the common, and show them how to distinguish between the unclean and the clean. 24 In a controversy they shall act as judges, and they shall judge it according to my judgments. They shall keep my laws and my statutes in all my appointed feasts, and they shall keep my sabbaths holy. 25 They shall not defile themselves by going near to a dead person; however, for father or mother, for son or daughter, for brother or unmarried sister they may defile themselves. 26 After he is defiled,[u] he shall count for himself seven days, and then he shall be clean.[v] 27 And on the day that he goes into the holy place, into the inner court, to minister in the holy place, he shall offer his sin offering, says the Lord God.

[u] Syr: Heb *cleansed*
[v] Syr: Heb lacks *and then he shall be clean*

the clean and the unclean (cf. also vs. 23 with Lev. 10:10-11). Obvious literary dependence is involved.

22. See Lev. 21:7, 12, where nothing is mentioned about the priest marrying the widow of a priest, and where a separate legislation is made for the "priest who is chief among his brethren" (vss. 10-15), a distinction not known in Ezekiel.

24. This regulation discloses the ultimate theocratic character of the community; cf. the earlier pictures of the elders as judges, although the priests doubtless had certain functions as judges, particularly in religious matters; note the role of the priests and elders in Deut. 21:1-5 (vs. 5*b* is a later expansion, enlarging the function of the priests as judges). For **sabbaths** see Exeg. on 20:1-49 (cf. 45:17).

25-27. See also Lev. 21:1-3. Any dead person was unclean, and even the bread of mourning, eaten during the days of mourning, was unclean (see Hos. 9:4; cf. Jer. 16:5, 7). Legislation for purification of the Israelite or proselyte who has had contact with a dead body appears in Num. 19:11-22 (cf. Num. 31:19). Reading **defiled** with the Syriac in vs. 26 for **cleansed** brings it into accord with P's legislation for the members of the community, but if the M.T. here is retained, it would suggest a total of fourteen days' cleansing for the priests, i.e., seven days' extension after the usual cleansing. The Syriac

because of their disloyalty in the days before the Exile. The past can be repudiated only in part; there is always much in it which remains with us and which we have simply to live down. So the prodigal son when he came home asked only to be a servant working for a wage, in order that he might thus make some compensation for the wrong he had done to his father. If we have erred in the past, the mark of what we did may remain upon us to the end of our days. If that is the case, there is no need to

repine. Let us be content to take the lowly place which is left to us and to make it a place of honorable service.

(*c*) *The will to lift up the present to God in utter consecration* (vss. 15-31). **The sons of Zadok** stand at the head of the temple hierarchy. Their whole life is therefore to be vowed to that purity which will enable them to bring to God the worship of their nation. They dedicate themselves on behalf of their fellows, so that the humblest worshiper will

28 And it shall be unto them for an in-heritance; I *am* their inheritance: and ye shall give them no possession in Israel; I *am* their possession.

29 They shall eat the meat offering, and the sin offering, and the trespass offering; and every dedicated thing in Israel shall be theirs.

30 And the first of all the firstfruits of all *things,* and every oblation of all, of every *sort* of your oblations, shall be the priest's: ye shall also give unto the priest the first of your dough, that he may cause the bless-ing to rest in thine house.

31 The priests shall not eat of any thing

28 "They shall have no[w] inheritance; I am their inheritance: and you shall give them no possession in Israel; I am their pos-session. 29 They shall eat the cereal offering, the sin offering, and the guilt offering; and every devoted thing in Israel shall be theirs. 30 And the first of all the first fruits of all kinds, and every offering of all kinds from all your offerings, shall belong to the priests; you shall also give to the priests the first of your coarse meal, that a blessing may rest on your house. 31 The priests shall

[w] Vg: Heb *as an*

addition at the end of vs. 26—**and then he shall be clean**—clarifies its meaning. The singular **he, his** in vss. 26-27 might indicate a later expansion (cf. Bertholet, Herrmann, *et al.*). The oracular formula **says the Lord GoD** in vs. 27 seems to be characteristic of the editor in chs. 40–48 (cf. 43:27; 45:9, 15; 47:23; 48:29). Note **to minister in the holy place** in P (Exod. 28:43; 29:30; 35:19; Num. 4:12; etc.; with these verses cf. Num. 19:11-22; 31:19).

28-31. We may compare the Deuteronomic affirmation that the Levites have **no inheritance,** illustrated in the allotment narrative in Josh. 13:14, 33; 18:7, and the P legislation regarding the Aaronites and Levites in Num. 18:20-32; etc.

28. For the necessary emendation as in the RSV read ולא תהיה להם נחלה (with Vulg.).

29. The priests' share in the sacrifices is legislated in Lev. 2:3-10; 6:14-18; Num. 18:8-32; Lev. 7:1-38 (see Millar Burrows, *The Literary Relations of Ezekiel* [New Haven: Yale University Press, 1925], pp. 53-54). **Every devoted thing** (cf. Lev. 7:28; Num. 18:14; Ezra 10:7): I.e., things devoted to Yahweh under especially stringent conditions, including fields, men, beasts, and perhaps other possessions (Lev. 27:28; cf. Josh. 6:17, 19). Contrast the informal procedures for the priests' portions in I Sam. 2:12-17.

30. See **the first of all the first fruits** legislation in Exod. 23:19 (E); 34:26 (J). **The first** may perhaps be interpreted as "the best," as in 20:40, where there may be an allusion to the first fruits, and where the contributions also appear. In Deut. 18:4 the first fruits of grain, wine, oil, and fleece are set aside for the Levitical priests who have no inheritance (cf. Deut. 26:1-11, with its litany for bringing the first fruits of the ground; see also Num. 18:12-13 [P] and its context). In contrast with P, the legislation here makes no provision for the Levites (cf. Num. 18:25-32). For **the first of your coarse meal** see Num. 15:20-21.

31. See Lev. 7:24, addressed to all the Israelites.

feel that there is a sense in which he partici-pates in what is done by the priest on his behalf. The scrupulous care with which the priest de-fends himself against any contact or relationship which might hinder his approach to God sym-bolizes the watchful obedience which ought to characterize the life of the nation day by day. Ritual holiness on the part of the priest stands for, and helps to promote, ethical holiness on the part of the people.

The words **I am their inheritance . . . ; I am their possession** (vs. 28) have a wider reference than to the priests. The land is the symbol and

guarantee of security. Israel has never enjoyed that security for more than a time. Its only sure possession has been in its faith. The rabbis spoke of the law as a "portable fatherland." Wherever the Jew went, he carried the law with him and, having that, he could be at home. In this the Jew reflects the universal human situation. "For here we have no lasting city, but we seek the city which is to come" (Heb. 13:14). In this Abraham is our pattern, because "he looked forward to the city which has foun-dations, whose builder and maker is God" (Heb. 11:10). In the last resort it is true of us

that is dead of itself, or torn, whether it be
fowl or beast.

45 Moreover, when ye shall divide by lot the land for inheritance, ye shall offer an oblation unto the Lord, a holy portion of the land: the length *shall be* the length of five and twenty thousand *reeds,*

not eat of anything, whether bird or beast, that has died of itself or is torn.

45 "When you allot the land as a possession, you shall set apart for the

---

F. The Sacred District and Its Environs (45:1-25)

The allotment of the land, begun here (vss. 1-9), is concluded in 47:13–48:35. The sacred district measures 25,000 by 20,000 cubits, and it is divided into two equal areas, 25,000 by 10,000 cubits, the one to the north for the Levites and the one to the south for the Zadokite priests. Within the latter is a square of 500 cubits for the temple area, around which is an open space 50 cubits deep. South of the sacred district and adjoining it is a section 25,000 by 5,000 cubits, the common land for the city of Jerusalem, within which is the city itself, 4,500 cubits square, surrounded by an open space 250 cubits deep (cf. 48:16-17). The above allotments make a perfect square of 25,000 cubits (i.e., about 8.3 miles) to the east and west of which lies the land of the prince, presumably reaching to the Jordan on the east and to the Mediterranean on the west. This whole area is again described in 48:8-22. Ch. 45 continues with regulations regarding weights and measures (vss. 10-12), the contributions to the prince (vss. 13-17), and certain festivals of the calendar year (vss. 18-25).

The allotment of the land belongs to the editor, and it falls outside the vision framework in chs. 40–48, as do the legislative portions in 45:9-25; 46:1-18. The address is no longer to the prophet, but for the larger part is in the second person plural, with a formal "Thus says the Lord God" oracular introduction as in 45:9, 18; 46:1, 16; 47:13. The editor's prince occurs prominently. Whether anything of Ezekiel's legislative code has been preserved here must remain a matter of conjecture. Hölscher, Matthews, Cooke, Irwin, and others find nothing of Ezekiel here (contrast Herrmann, Bertholet).

1. The Sacred District and the Property of the City and the Prince (45:1-9)

The parallel and more complete account in 48:8-22 is not, as some commentators think, of different authorship. The author is here concerned only with the heart of the allotment; he later repeats and elaborates when giving the total allotment of the land, including the tribal territories. We should by this time be used to such repetitiousness on the part of the editor. The sacred district is called תרומה, **oblation**, the same word used to describe an **offering** to the prince in vss. 13, 16, or to Yahweh set apart for the priests in 44:30 (cf. Lev. 22:12; Num. 5:9; etc.). It means a part lifted or taken from the whole. The allotment of territory to the priests and Levites here may be compared with the allotment to the Levites of towns listed in Josh. 21:1-42 (P); I Chr. 6:1-81 (see also Lev. 25:33-34; Num. 35:1-8). While found at present no earlier than in P, Albright cogently maintains that the list of Levitical towns goes back in its original form to the

---

also that our inheritance and possession, our final home, and our final security are in God.

45:1–46:24. Sacrifices.—The main topic of these two chapters is that of the sacrificial system. We have happily passed beyond the stage at which it was thought necessary to allegorize each detail of such ritual regulations as are given here, seeing in them so many types of the sacrifice of Christ. All the same, there is something we can learn from the sections in question.

We can single out the points at which the

seer would revise the traditional system, as these will show the new ideas which he wishes to infuse into the worship of the temple. First, in his scheme for the great annual feasts (45:21-25) he seems determined to get away from the old agricultural associations. He passes over Pentecost altogether and concentrates upon Passover and Tabernacles. There is a distinct suggestion of austerity in his treatment of these festivals; they are no longer to be the joyful occasions they were in the past. Instead, they are burdened with a sense of the nation's sin

and the breadth *shall be* ten thousand. This *shall be* holy in all the borders thereof round about.

2 Of this there shall be for the sanctuary five hundred *in length,* with five hundred *in breadth,* square round about; and fifty cubits round about for the suburbs thereof.

3 And of this measure shalt thou measure the length of five and twenty thousand, and the breadth of ten thousand: and in it shall be the sanctuary *and* the most holy *place.*

4 The holy *portion* of the land shall be for the priests the ministers of the sanctuary, which shall come near to minister unto the LORD: and it shall be a place for their houses, and a holy place for the sanctuary.

LORD a portion of the land as a holy district, twenty-five thousand cubits long and twenty[x] thousand cubits broad; it shall be holy throughout its whole extent. 2 Of this a square plot of five hundred by five hundred cubits shall be for the sanctuary, with fifty cubits for an open space around it. 3 And in the holy district you shall measure off a section twenty-five thousand cubits long and ten thousand broad, in which shall be the sanctuary, the most holy place. 4 It shall be the holy portion of the land; it shall be for the priests, who minister in the sanctuary and approach the LORD to minister to him; and it shall be a place for their houses and

[x] Gk: Heb *ten*

---

tenth century in the reign of David or Solomon ("The List of Levitic Cities," *Louis Ginzberg Jubilee Volume,* pp. 49-73). At the time of Joshua the land was apportioned by lots (Josh. 14:2; 18:11; 19:1; etc.), but here it is by the direct word of Yahweh.

45:1. Twenty with the LXX, instead of the M.T. **ten,** is required by the context. Omit the second **length** with four MSS, the Syriac, and Vulg. (cf. LXX).

2. There is no suggestion of such an **open space** around the temple in 42:20, where the wall of the temple area separates the sacred and the common. Here even the territory outside the open space is sacred. Vs. 2 is out of place; it belongs after vs. 4, for the sanctuary is in the midst of the priests' portion (see Cornill, Bertholet, *et al.*).

3. Thou: Emended to plural in the RSV (cf. vss. 1, 6). For the temple as **the most holy place** see 43:12; however, the LXX and Syriac omit **the sanctuary,** and perhaps the original text designated the priests' portion as the most sacred place, as in 48:12 (see also vs. 4*a*).

4. And a holy place [lit., "sanctuary"] **for the sanctuary:** This is possibly corrupt; some read "and for the pasture lands [ולמגרש; LXX, Targ.] for cattle [למקנה]" (see Bertholet, Cooke, Bewer; cf. Josh. 14:4; 21:2).

---

and are to be opportunities for an earnest reckoning with God in repentance and atonement. It is an effort on his part to get away from a nature religion, for which God is the giver of good harvests, to a religion of conscience, in which God is moral authority and judge.

Second, the seer has learned in exile that religion must be built into the daily life of the community, not just reserved for certain special occasions (46:13-15). By the institution of the daily sacrifice he seeks to stamp upon the mind of his people that their contact with God needs to be renewed afresh each day. He made provision thus for a solemn act of worship each morning in the temple, which at a later stage was supplemented by another in the afternoon.

Third, the purpose of sacrifice throughout is to make atonement, to renew a broken relationship between Israel and the Lord. The Exile had brought with it a clear understanding that the Lord was not a national ally merely, nor

was Israel his favorite. The relationship between the two was an ethical one and might at any time be gravely imperiled by sin on Israel's part. Hence the need for constant watchfulness and for elaborate preparations which would counteract any defection on the nation's side and would close the breach between the nation and the Lord before it became too wide. The sacrificial system bears witness to the fact that the problem of sin and its forgiveness was the one uppermost in the minds of men like our author. And these, we must remember, were the men who gave Judaism the shape it has continued to bear ever since.

But obviously there are some grave defects in this system, even as thus revised. Access to God is indirect, since the common people can draw near to him only in the person of some official representative, be he priest or prince. They stand and look on while these offer worship on their behalf (46:1-3). Also, while there

5 And the five and twenty thousand of length, and ten thousand of breadth, shall also the Levites, the ministers of the house, have for themselves, for a possession for twenty chambers.

6 ¶ And ye shall appoint the possession of the city five thousand broad, and five and twenty thousand long, over against the oblation of the holy *portion:* it shall be for the whole house of Israel.

7 ¶ And *a portion shall be* for the prince on the one side and on the other side of the oblation of the holy *portion,* and of the possession of the city, before the oblation of the holy *portion,* and before the possession of the city, from the west side westward, and from the east side eastward: and the length *shall be* over against one of the portions, from the west border unto the east border.

8 In the land shall be his possession in Israel: and my princes shall no more oppress my people; and *the rest of* the land shall they give to the house of Israel according to their tribes.

9 ¶ Thus saith the Lord GOD; Let it suffice you, O princes of Israel: remove violence and spoil, and execute judgment and

a holy place for the sanctuary. 5 Another section, twenty-five thousand cubits long and ten thousand cubits broad, shall be for the Levites who minister at the temple, as their possession for cities to live in.*y*

6 "Alongside the portion set apart as the holy district you shall assign for the possession of the city an area five thousand cubits broad, and five and twenty thousand cubits long; it shall belong to the whole house of Israel.

7 "And to the prince shall belong the land on both sides of the holy district and the property of the city, alongside the holy district and the property of the city, on the west and on the east, corresponding in length to one of the tribal portions, and extending from the western to the eastern boundary of the land. 8 It is to be his property in Israel. And my princes shall no more oppress my people; but they shall let the house of Israel have the land according to their tribes.

9 "Thus says the Lord GOD: Enough, O princes of Israel! Put away violence and oppression, and execute justice and right-

y Gk: Heb *twenty chambers*

5. Cities to live in: Read עָרִים לָשֶׁבֶת with the LXX for עֶשְׂרִים לִשְׁכֹת, **twenty chambers.** If the emended reading is correct, it suggests a possibly deliberate variation of the older allotment of Levitical cities now reflected in the P source, where the same expression occurs in Num. 35:2; Josh. 14:4.

8-9. In [lit., "to"] **the land** is properly transferred with the LXX to end of vs. 7 (so RSV). The fact that the prince has his own property and so his own chief source of

is no notion that "the blood of bulls and goats" (Heb. 9:13) can of itself remove sin, the penitence of the worshiper and the mercy of the divine forgiveness are not given the prominence they deserve, but seem to be taken more or less for granted. The foreground is occupied by an elaborate system of animal sacrifice and ritual laws.

Sacrifice of this kind is impermanent in its results. The act of cleansing the sanctuary or making **atonement for the temple** has to be renewed every six months (every twelve months in the later law), so that one goes away from the ceremony knowing that no more has been gained than a temporary relief, and that in a short time all will have to be done over again (45:18-20).

It is also inadequate, since it only covers sins of inadvertence. Atonement is made **for every one that erreth, and for him that is simple**

(45:20). The writer perhaps assumes that in the restored community there will be no heinous sins, but only occasional involuntary offenses against the regulations which protect the holiness of the sanctuary. Or it may be he is more realistic than that, and supposes that those who sin willfully will forfeit the mercy of God and so be cast out from the community. But can we be satisfied with a provision for sin which deliberately refrains from dealing with its worst cases?

All this leads up to the final point that in a conscientious worshiper such a system might well produce anxiety and distress of mind. Was his offense to be classed as involuntary after all, or should it be brought under the head of what is beyond pardon? Even when the atoning ceremony had been completed, what guarantee was there that some slight inadvertence had not vitiated the whole procedure? We can

justice, take away your exactions from my people, saith the Lord God.

10 Ye shall have just balances, and a just ephah, and a just bath.

11 The ephah and the bath shall be of one measure, that the bath may contain the tenth part of a homer, and the ephah the tenth part of a homer: the measure thereof shall be after the homer.

12 And the shekel *shall be* twenty gerahs: twenty shekels, five and twenty shekels, fifteen shekels, shall be your maneh.

eousness; cease your evictions of my people, says the Lord God.

10 "You shall have just balances, a just ephah, and a just bath. **11** The ephah and the bath shall be of the same measure, the bath containing one tenth of a homer, and the ephah one tenth of a homer; the homer shall be the standard measure. **12** The shekel shall be twenty gerahs; five shekels shall be five shekels, and ten shekels shall be ten shekels, and your mina shall be fifty shekels.[z]

[z] Gk: Heb *twenty shekels, twenty-five shekels, fifteen shekels shall be your mina*

income further guarantees the theocratic character of the community. Bitter experience lies behind the injunctions in vss. 8b-9. **Princes:** The successive rulers of the restored Davidic line.

2. Regulations for Weights and Measures (45:10-12)

10-12. The address, as in vss. 13 ff., is to the people. Vs. 10 begins a new paragraph; cf. the concluding formula at the end of vs. 9. For other legislation regarding weights and measures see Lev. 19:35-37; Deut. 25:13-16. The **bath** may be archaeologically determined to have been about 5¾ gallons (22 liters) from a study of jar remains marked "bath" and "royal bath" from Tell Beit Mirsim and Tell en-Naṣbeh respectively (Albright, "Excavation of Tell Beit Mirsim," pp. 58-59; McCown, *Tell en-Naṣbeh,* pp. 260-61; see also the jars from the royal potteries, with the handles stamped with the royal seal and with a capacity of two baths in David Diringer, "The Royal Jar-Handle Stamps of Ancient Judah," *Biblical Archaeologist,* XII [1949], 70-86; see Angelo Segré, "A Documentary Analysis of Ancient Palestinian Units of Measure," *Journal of Biblical Literature,* LXIV [1945], 357-75). The **ephah** is the equivalent in dry measure. The **homer** liquid measure would be about 57½ gallons (cf. Vol. I, p. 155). For a jar of this size see McCown, *op. cit.,* p. 260, and H. G. May's review in *Journal of Religion,* XXVIII (1948), 134. For the ratio of one to ten in vs. 11 see Isa. 5:10. It is difficult to determine archaeologically the exact weight of the **shekel;** the variations may be due to different local standards and to the relative inaccuracy of ancient scales compared with modern ones. In general the shekel seems to have weighed between 11.15 and 12.25 grams. A "royal" shekel from Gezer weighs 11.14 grams, and a series of eight-shekel weights from Lachish have an average unit of value of 11.389 grams (0.402 oz.). This is at least the approximate value of the shekel (see David Diringer, "The Early Hebrew Weights Found at Lachish," *Palestine Exploration Quarterly,* LXXIV [1942], 82-103; Galling, *Biblisches Reallexikon,* pp. 185-88; G. A. Barrois, "La métrologie dans la Bible," *Revue Biblique,* XLI [1932], 50-76; Hildegard Lewy, "Assyro-Babylonian and Israelite Measures of Capacity and Rates of Seeding," *Journal of the American Oriental Society,* LXIV [1944], 65-73). Coinage seems to have appeared in Palestine in the latter half of the fifth century and in the following century (see E. L. Sukenik, "Paralipomena Palaes-

imagine a man tormented by doubts and fears of this kind, until what was meant to bring him an assurance of God's grace served only to plunge him into a morass of doubt and uncertainty. These are just those agonies of conscience which Luther suffered and to which all are exposed who seek the ground of their

acceptance with God in the punctilious discharge of a set of religious obligations. They can find peace only as they turn away from this to the undeserved mercy of God.

45:9-12; 46:16-18. *Prince and People.*—Amid this strange world of sacrificial regulations we come upon two passages which reveal an interest

13 This *is* the oblation that ye shall offer; the sixth part of an ephah of a homer of wheat, and ye shall give the sixth part of an ephah of a homer of barley:

14 Concerning the ordinance of oil, the bath of oil, *ye shall offer* the tenth part of a bath out of the cor, *which is* a homer of ten baths; for ten baths *are* a homer:

15 And one lamb out of the flock, out of two hundred, out of the fat pastures of Israel; for a meat offering, and for a burnt offering, and for peace offerings, to make reconciliation for them, saith the Lord GOD.

16 All the people of the land shall give this oblation for the prince in Israel.

17 And it shall be the prince's part *to give* burnt offerings, and meat offerings, and drink offerings, in the feasts, and in the new moons, and in the sabbaths, in all solemnities of the house of Israel: he shall prepare the sin offering, and the meat offering, and the burnt offering, and the peace offer-

13 "This is the offering which you shall make: one sixth of an ephah from each homer of wheat, and one sixth of an ephah from each homer of barley, 14 and as the fixed portion of oil,[a] one tenth of a bath from each cor[b] (the cor, like the homer, contains ten baths); 15 and one sheep from every flock of two hundred, from the families[c] of Israel. This is the offering for cereal offerings, burnt offerings, and peace offerings, to make atonement for them, says the Lord GOD. 16 All the people of the land shall give[d] this offering to the prince in Israel. 17 It shall be the prince's duty to furnish the burnt offerings, cereal offerings, and drink offerings, at the feasts, the new moons, and the sabbaths, all the appointed feasts of the house of Israel: he shall provide the sin offerings, cereal offerings, burnt

[a] Cn: Heb *oil, the bath the oil*
[b] Vg: Heb *homer*
[c] Gk: Heb *watering places*
[d] Gk Compare Syr: Heb *shall be to*

tinensia," *Journal of the Palestine Oriental Society*, XIV [1934], 178-82; A. Reifenberg, "A Hebrew Shekel of the Fifth Century B.C.," *Palestine Exploration Quarterly*, LXXV [1943], 100-4). The gerah is here one twentieth of a shekel; cf. the Akkadian *gerû*, one twenty-fourth of a shekel. The M.T. of vs. 12*b* would add up to make a **mina** of 60 shekels (20+25+10+5), as in Assyria and Babylonia, although the **LXX fifty shekels** accords with the Palestinian mina, which is known at Ugarit in the fourteenth century.

3. CONTRIBUTIONS TO THE PRINCE (45:13-17)

Also, the prince shall provide the burnt offerings, cereal offerings, libations, peace offerings, and sin offerings at the festivals. The text is at points obviously corrupt. Some presume that we have more than one source by positing that in vss. 13-15 the contribution is to be given to the priest, but in vss. 16-17, to the prince. The prince plays an important part in the cultus, perhaps here a dim reflection of the earlier period when the king made sacrifices and was in effect the head of the cultus, as priest-king. Note II Chr. 30:24; 35:7 where Hezekiah and Josiah provide the offerings.

13. And ye shall give the sixth: The verb ושׁשׁיתם is denominative, but awkward, as the KJV shows, and is best emended with the versions to ושׁשׁית, **and one sixth.** One sixtieth of the grain and one hundredth of the oil are prescribed.

14. The bath the oil is an obvious gloss. Several interpretations of the end of the verse are possible, but one can perhaps best omit with the LXX the first "ten baths [are] a homer" (=which is a homer of ten baths) as dittography. The RSV represents a conflation in translation (lit., "ten baths a homer for ten baths a cor"), reading הכר, **the cor,** for חמר, **homer,** with the Vulg.

15: Families: Read משׁפחות with the LXX for משׁקה, **watering places** (=fat pastures); the Syriac omits.

16. The M.T. has "the people the land," although seven MSS (cf. vs. 22; 46:3) have **the people of the land;** the LXX omits **of the land. Shall give,** יהיו אל (lit., **shall be to**), is perhaps corrupt and should be read יתנו את, "must [shall] give," with the LXX (cf. Syriac).

17. Drink offerings: Better rendered "libations" (cf. 20:28; Gen. 35:14; Num. 15:5). For these feasts see Hos. 2:11.

ings, to make reconciliation for the house of Israel.

18 Thus saith the Lord God; In the first *month,* in the first *day* of the month, thou shalt take a young bullock without blemish, and cleanse the sanctuary:

19 And the priest shall take of the blood of the sin offering, and put *it* upon the posts of the house, and upon the four corners of the settle of the altar, and upon the posts of the gate of the inner court.

20 And so thou shalt do the seventh *day* of the month for every one that erreth, and for *him that is* simple: so shall ye reconcile the house.

21 In the first *month,* in the fourteenth day of the month, ye shall have the passover, a feast of seven days; unleavened bread shall be eaten.

offerings, and peace offerings, to make atonement for the house of Israel.

18 "Thus says the Lord God: In the first month, on the first day of the month, you shall take a young bull without blemish, and cleanse the sanctuary. **19** The priest shall take some of the blood of the sin offering and put it on the doorposts of the temple, the four corners of the ledge of the altar, and the posts of the gate of the inner court. **20** You shall do the same on the seventh day of the month for any one who has sinned through error or ignorance; so you shall make atonement for the temple.

21 "In the first month, on the fourteenth day of the month, you shall celebrate the feast of the passover, and for seven days

---

4. Regulations for the Feasts of the First and Seventh Months (45:18-25)

The third great annual feast, the feast of first fruits or weeks, is not mentioned (see Exod. 23:14-17 [E]; 34:22-24 [J]; Deut. 16:1-16 [D]). The first and seventh months marked the halves of the religious calendar. For the P legislation of the first month see Exod. 12:1-20. As in Deut. 16:1-8, 13-15, the regulations for the Passover and feast of Booths concern the central sanctuary. Note also the sacrificial animals of the Passover here in Deut. 16:2, and contrast Exod. 12:3.

18. Cf. the bullock sin offering at the installation rites of the Aaronite priests on the first seven days of the first month in Exod. 29:35-37; cf. Exod. 40:1-15 (P). **Thou shalt take:** The second person singular in vss. 18-20 is direct address to the prince (cf. vs. 22). This sudden shift does not necessarily imply a later expansion, for otherwise the verses are consonant with the context, although they are regarded as secondary by Bertholet, Cooke, Hölscher, Morgenstern. It does indicate how completely the editor has dropped the vision setting (cf. also 46:13-15).

20. The M.T. reads בשבעת בחדש, but five MSS have בשבעה לחדש, the more usual idiom for **on the seventh day of the month;** however, most scholars accept the LXX reading, "in the seventh month on the first [day] of the month," for a purification of the sanctuary each six months seems probable. Contrast the later annual purification on the day of Atonement (Lev. 16:33; see discussion by Morgenstern, "Supplementary Studies in the Calendar of Ancient Israel," pp. 106-7). **Sinned through error or ignorance:** Cf. Num. 15:22-31; Lev. 4:1–5:19.

21. The origins of **the passover** are obscure. It was apparently not mentioned in the earliest legislation, e.g., in Exod. 23:14-17, or, originally, in Exod. 34:18, 22-24 (cf. Exod. 34:25 with 23:18). In Deut. 16:1 it is dated on the first of the month of Abib (=first month in Ezekiel or Nisan in the later calendar). Some would read in Ezekiel "on the fifteenth day of the month" (cf. Smend, Hölscher, J. M. P. Smith) after the analogy of vs. 25, the later P calendar designating **the fourteenth day of the month** (Exod. 12:6; Lev. 23:5; Num. 28:16; see H. G. May, "The Relation of the Passover to the Festival

---

in those social problems with which we ourselves are so concerned. Holiness covers even such matters as standard weights and measures!

As the first of these two passages stands, it insists on strict honesty on the part of the gov-

ernment when it is collecting its revenue; e.g., there must be no debasing of the currency. But it is possible that the verses which deal with weights and measures are independent of the injunction to the princes in 45:9. In that case

22 And upon that day shall the prince prepare for himself and for all the people of the land a bullock *for* a sin offering.

23 And seven days of the feast he shall prepare a burnt offering to the LORD, seven bullocks and seven rams without blemish daily the seven days; and a kid of the goats daily *for* a sin offering.

24 And he shall prepare a meat offering of an ephah for a bullock, and an ephah for a ram, and a hin of oil for an ephah.

25 In the seventh *month,* in the fifteenth day of the month, shall he do the like in the feast of the seven days, according to the sin offering, according to the burnt offering, and according to the meat offering, and according to the oil.

unleavened bread shall be eaten. 22 On that day the prince shall provide for himself and all the people of the land a young bull for a sin offering. 23 And on the seven days of the festival he shall provide as a burnt offering to the LORD seven young bulls and seven rams without blemish, on each of the seven days; and a he-goat daily for a sin offering. 24 And he shall provide as a cereal offering an ephah for each bull, an ephah for each ram, and a hin of oil to each ephah. 25 In the seventh month, on the fifteenth day of the month and for the seven days of the feast, he shall make the same provision for sin offerings, burnt offerings, and cereal offerings, and for the oil.

---

of Unleavened Cakes," *Journal of Biblical Literature,* LV [1936], 65-82; the literature of these festivals is too vast to be noted here, but see especially Morgenstern, "The Calendar of Ezekiel 45:18-25," *Hebrew Union College Annual,* XXI [1948], 493-96; etc.). The M.T. has "a feast of weeks of days," perhaps a scribal attempt to smuggle in the feast of Weeks, but it is better to read with many MSS and versions, **a feast of seven days,** i.e., שבעת for שבעות; it may be that the word **feast** originally preceded **the passover.** Unleavened Bread (Mazzoth) is an agricultural festival, the Passover a pastoral one.

24. According to Josephus, six hins are one bath. Segré estimates the biblical hin as 5¼ liters, about 5½ quarts. For oil with cereal offerings see 46:14; Num. 15:6, 9; and for cereal offering with animal offerings see Num. 15:4; 28:20; note the proportions in each case.

25. The feast of Tabernacles or Booths (Succoth) is called the feast of Ingathering in Exod. 23:16; 34:22, where it is placed "at the year's end." See also Lev. 23:33-36 (P), where it is designated as the feast of Booths, and is an eight-day festival (cf. also Num. 29:12-38). Although related to P, this legislation is earlier, as shown by the fact that there is no reference to an eighth day (cf. also Deut. 16:15 [D]). Note that the day of Atonement is apparently also not known to the author, and Morgenstern is perhaps right in suggesting that the religious calendar here represents an early stage in the evolution of P. Although some scholars doubt that it is the work of Ezra and his associates, it may well belong to the century of Ezra. See also Neh. 8:14-18; Zech 14:16 for references to the feast of Booths (cf. Deut. 16:13, 16; 31:10). Morgenstern suggests that the name Succoth was not yet known to the author in Ezekiel and is a later substitution in the D legislation (see "Supplementary Studies in the Calendars of Ancient Israel," pp. 61-62; "The Chanukkah Festival and the Calendar of Ancient Israel," *Hebrew Union College Annual,* XXI [1948], 493-96).

---

the seer is calling for honesty in business. In Amos 8:5-6 we see the kind of malpractice against which the seer is here protesting.

It is one of the great merits of the O.T. that it brings moral standards to bear upon commerce and trade. We need to reflect on the extent to which our elaborate modern system of trade is in fact based on moral considerations. What would become of all the credit transactions with which we are familiar if a man's word and bond could no longer be relied upon? True,

the law is available in the last resort to enforce the discharge of obligations thus undertaken, but if the law had to be called in for more than a minority of transactions, the system would break down. It is only because certain moral qualities are diffused throughout the business community that we can continue delivering goods one day, sending the bill for them a month later, and receiving payment a month after that from someone whom we have never seen.

46 Thus saith the Lord God; The gate of the inner court that looketh toward the east shall be shut the six working days; but on the sabbath it shall be opened, and in the day of the new moon it shall be opened.

2 And the prince shall enter by the way of the porch of *that* gate without, and shall stand by the post of the gate, and the priests shall prepare his burnt offering and his peace offerings, and he shall worship at the threshold of the gate: then he shall go forth; but the gate shall not be shut until the evening.

3 Likewise the people of the land shall worship at the door of this gate before the Lord in the sabbaths and in the new moons.

46 "Thus says the Lord God: The gate of the inner court that faces east shall be shut on the six working days; but on the sabbath day it shall be opened and on the day of the new moon it shall be opened.

2 The prince shall enter by the vestibule of the gate from without, and shall take his stand by the post of the gate. The priests shall offer his burnt offering and his peace offerings, and he shall worship at the threshold of the gate. Then he shall go out, but the gate shall not be shut until evening.

3 The people of the land shall worship at the entrance of that gate before the Lord on the sabbaths and on the new moons.

G. Further Regulations (46:1-24)

The larger part of the chapter continues ritual specifications (vss. 1-18), and the chapter concludes with a reversion to the theme of the prophet's tour of the temple area (vss. 19-24). Vss. 1-8 are concerned with the new moon and sabbath sacrifices of the prince, who worships at the vestibule of the east gate of the inner court. Vss. 9-10 depict the arrangement for the entrance and exit of the people and the prince. In vss. 11-15 the offerings at the feasts and the appointed festivals and the daily sacrifice are specified. Vss. 16-18 concern the matter of inheritance and gifts given by the prince. Vss. 19-20 provide a place where the priests may boil the animal offerings and bake the cereal offerings, while vss. 21-24 describe the kitchens in the outer court for the common meal sacrifices of the people.

In the opinion of some scholars the regulations in vss. 1-18 have been disarranged and are composite in authorship (see, e.g., Herrmann, Hölscher, Cooke, *et al.*). We cannot, however, be certain that the legislative matters were ever arranged here as logically as some would presume, as, for instance, when they would place vss. 16-19 after 45:8. More probable is the ascription of vss. 19-24 to different authorship from the rest of the chapter, and to the prophet Ezekiel. The reversion to the temple tour is most abrupt. It is clearly not in its present order, since in 44:4 the prophet was left in front of the temple, but in 46:19 he is brought from the outer court through the entrance beside the north gate. Possibly vss. 19-24 belong after 42:13-14, where the north chambers of the priests are mentioned, although this is not certain.

1. The Prince's Offerings on the New Moon and Sabbath (46:1-8)

46:1-8. Like the east gate of the outer court, that of the inner court also had special significance. It was to be opened only on the sabbath and the new moon, the latter, of course, being the first day of the month. Cf. Nehemiah's orders to close the gates of Jerusalem on the sabbath (Neh. 13:19-22). The increasing emphasis on the sabbath in the postexilic period is notable. The prince, entering from the outer court into the

In the second passage (46:16-18) we see that holiness is opposed to class privilege. The assumption is that the land on which Israel will settle at the return is the Lord's. Since land is the source of all wealth under such conditions as are here envisaged, it follows that all the wealth of the nation is his. The prince is allowed the share of that wealth which he needs to enable him to maintain a dignity in accordance with his rank, but he must not encroach on what belongs to his people. If he endows his sons, it must be at his own expense, not at that of the community. Further, the interests of his family call for protection; his land may

4 And the burnt offering that the prince shall offer unto the LORD in the sabbath day *shall be* six lambs without blemish, and a ram without blemish.

5 And the meat offering *shall be* an ephah for a ram, and the meat offering for the lambs as he shall be able to give, and a hin of oil to an ephah.

6 And in the day of the new moon *it shall be* a young bullock without blemish, and six lambs, and a ram: they shall be without blemish.

7 And he shall prepare a meat offering, an ephah for a bullock, and an ephah for a ram, and for the lambs according as his hand shall attain unto, and a hin of oil to an ephah.

8 And when the prince shall enter, he shall go in by the way of the porch of *that* gate, and he shall go forth by the way thereof.

9 ¶ But when the people of the land shall come before the LORD in the solemn feasts, he that entereth in by the way of the north gate to worship shall go out by the way of the south gate; and he that entereth by the way of the south gate shall go forth by the way of the north gate: he shall not return by the way of the gate whereby he came in, but shall go forth over against it.

10 And the prince in the midst of them, when they go in, shall go in; and when they go forth, shall go forth.

4 The burnt offering that the prince offers to the LORD on the sabbath day shall be six lambs without blemish and a ram without blemish; 5 and the cereal offering with the ram shall be an ephah, and the cereal offering with the lambs shall be as much as he is able, together with a hin of oil to each ephah. 6 On the day of the new moon he shall offer a young bull without blemish, and six lambs and a ram, which shall be without blemish; 7 as a cereal offering he shall provide an ephah with the bull and an ephah with the ram, and with the lambs as much as he is able, together with a hin of oil to each ephah. 8 When the prince enters, he shall go in by the vestibule of the gate, and he shall go out by the same way.

9 "When the people of the land come before the LORD at the appointed feasts, he who enters by the north gate to worship shall go out by the south gate; and he who enters by the south gate shall go out by the north gate: no one shall return by way of the gate by which he entered, but each shall go out straight ahead. 10 When they go in, the prince shall go in with them; and when they go out, he shall go out.

---

vestibule, passes the length of the gate to the doorpost at the exit into the inner court, but he cannot enter the inner court itself. From this vantage point he can see the great altar before the temple, on which his sacrifices would be made. See the ritual of the anointing of the doorposts of this gate in 45:19; cf. the position of the king "by the pillar" in II Kings 11:14. Note other possible allusions to sacrifice arrangements at this east gate in 40:38-43, but see also 46:19-20. The people worship in the outer court before this east gate.

In contrast with these regulations for the sacrifice offered by the prince on the sabbath (vss. 4-5), the P legislation (see Exod. 29:38-39; Num. 28:3-4, 9-10) for the sabbath sacrifices calls for two lambs, two tenths of an ephah of flour mixed with oil as a cereal offering, and libations, plus the regular burnt offering and its libation. So also the new moon sacrifices (vss. 6-7) differ from those in Num. 28:11-15, where two bullocks, a ram, seven lambs, along with three tenths of an ephah of fine flour mixed with oil for each bullock and two tenths of an ephah of fine flour for the ram and one tenth for each lamb are prescribed.

2. Arrangements for Entering and Leaving the Temple (46:9-10)

9-10. The appointed feasts (see 45:17-25; cf. Lev. 23:4-44) brought multitudes to Jerusalem (cf. II Chr. 30:13; Ezra 10:1), and it was necessary to bring order into the

11 And in the feast and in the solemnities the meat offering shall be an ephah to a bullock, and an ephah to a ram, and to the lambs as he is able to give, and a hin of oil to an ephah.

12 Now when the prince shall prepare a voluntary burnt offering or peace offerings voluntarily unto the LORD, *one* shall then open him the gate that looketh toward the east, and he shall prepare his burnt offering and his peace offerings, as he did on the sabbath day: then he shall go forth; and after his going forth *one* shall shut the gate.

13 Thou shalt daily prepare a burnt offering unto the LORD *of* a lamb of the first year without blemish: thou shalt prepare it every morning.

14 And thou shalt prepare a meat offering for it every morning, the sixth part of an ephah, and the third part of a hin of oil, to temper with the fine flour; a meat

11 "At the feasts and the appointed seasons the cereal offering with a young bull shall be an ephah, and with a ram an ephah, and with the lambs as much as one is able to give, together with a hin of oil to an ephah. 12 When the prince provides a freewill offering, either a burnt offering or peace offerings as a freewill offering to the LORD, the gate facing east shall be opened for him; and he shall offer his burnt offering or his peace offerings as he does on the sabbath day. Then he shall go out, and after he has gone out the gate shall be shut.

13 "He shall provide a lamb a year old without blemish for a burnt offering to the LORD daily; morning by morning he shall provide it. 14 And he shall provide a cereal offering with it morning by morning, one sixth of an ephah, and one third of a hin

---

procession of the crowds. At the end of vs. 10 the Hebrew has "they shall go out" (cf. KJV), but it is better to read with many MSS and versions **he shall go out** (cf. also the conclusion of vs. 9).

3. REGULATIONS FOR SACRIFICE (46:11-15)

12. This verse qualifies the data in vs. 1, for here the east gate may be opened on a weekday for the prince to make a **freewill offering**; it is not, however, necessarily contradictory (contrast Hölscher, Bertholet, Cooke, *et al.*). The freewill offering (see Lev. 7:16; 22:18-23; Num. 15:3; Deut. 12:6; 16:10; 23:23; cf. Amos 4:5) is adequately described by its name; it represents gifts presented out of benevolence or on the impulse of the giver, not a sacrifice given in fulfillment of an obligation or vow. The continual burnt offering of a lamb a year old with its cereal offering (one sixth of an ephah) mixed with oil (one third of a hin), presented each morning, differs from the P legislation (Exod. 29:38-42; Num. 28:3-8), where there is both a morning and evening sacrifice of a yearling lamb, with a tenth of an ephah of fine flour and a fourth of a hin of oil, plus a libation of a fourth of a hin of wine. Cf. the burnt offering in the morning and the cereal offering in the evening in II Kings 16:15, and the evening burnt offerings in I Kings 18:29, 36; see also II Kings 3:20. For the continual offerings see also Ezra 3:5; Neh. 10:33; Dan. 8:11-13; 11:31; 12:11.

13-14. Thou: Read **He** with the versions, and in the first and last instance with some Hebrew MSS, although in 45:18-20 there is a parallel direct address to the prince with a sudden shift from the third person. **Flour** or **fine flour:** סלת, i.e., semolina, wheat without husk or bran. **The ordinance for the continual burnt offering:** Read חקת עולת תמיד for חקות עולם תמיד, lit., **perpetual ordinances continually;** some MSS have the singular "ordinance," and the correct reading is suggested in part by vs. 15*b*.

---

not be alienated from it, though temporary concessions are permitted as rewards for services rendered.

The principle which is here asserted is that God's will is for social stability, for the preservation of the family generation by generation, for

a contented people secure in the enjoyment of their possessions and fearing no man's violence. Where one man exercises authority he must employ it within the limits laid down by the law, for the general good, not for his own aggrandizement. A society in which men are

offering continually by a perpetual ordinance unto the Lord.

15 Thus shall they prepare the lamb, and the meat offering, and the oil, every morning *for* a continual burnt offering.

16 ¶ Thus saith the Lord God; If the prince give a gift unto any of his sons, the inheritance thereof shall be his sons'; it *shall be* their possession by inheritance.

17 But if he give a gift of his inheritance to one of his servants, then it shall be his to the year of liberty; after, it shall return to the prince: but his inheritance shall be his sons' for them.

18 Moreover the prince shall not take of the people's inheritance by oppression, to thrust them out of their possession; *but* he shall give his sons inheritance out of his own possession; that my people be not scattered every man from his possession.

19 ¶ After he brought me through the entry, which *was* at the side of the gate, into the holy chambers of the priests, which looked toward the north: and, behold, there *was* a place on the two sides westward.

20 Then said he unto me, This *is* the place where the priests shall boil the trespass offering and the sin offering, where they shall bake the meat offering; that they bear *them* not out into the outer court, to sanctify the people.

of oil to moisten the flour, as a cereal offering to the Lord; this is the ordinance for the continual burnt offering.[e] **15** Thus the lamb and the meal offering and the oil shall be provided, morning by morning, for a continual burnt offering.

16 "Thus says the Lord God: If the prince makes a gift to any of his sons out of[f] his inheritance, it shall belong to his sons, it is their property by inheritance. **17** But if he makes a gift out of his inheritance to one of his servants, it shall be his to the year of liberty; then it shall revert to the prince; only his sons may keep a gift from his inheritance. **18** The prince shall not take any of the inheritance of the people, thrusting them out of their property; he shall give his sons their inheritance out of his own property, so that none of my people shall be dispossessed of his property."

19 Then he brought me through the entrance, which was at the side of the gate, to the north row of the holy chambers for the priests; and there I saw a place at the extreme western end of them. **20** And he said to me, "This is the place where the priests shall boil the guilt offering and the sin offering, and where they shall bake the cereal offering, in order not to bring them out into the outer court and so communicate holiness to the people."

[e] Cn: Heb *perpetual ordinances continually*
[f] Gk: Heb *it is his inheritance*

---

4. Gifts and Inheritances from the Prince's Property (46:16-18)

The prescription that gifts given by the prince must be from **his** [own] **inheritance** reflects the prophetic protest against extortion, an emphasis on the limited character of monarchy, and a desire to keep intact forever the tribal territories. Since the land really belonged to Yahweh it could not be disposed of in perpetuity, and the people were only resident aliens or serfs under Yahweh, as is explicitly affirmed in Lev. 25:23 (P). To keep the prince's property intact, a gift from it to a person other than a son of the prince must be returned on the year of jubilee. The year of jubilee is known only in the later legislation (see Lev. 25:8-17 [H and P]), and the chronology of the editor, as well as the use of the term "year of liberty" (שנת הדרור; cf. Lev. 25:10), makes probable a reference here to the year of jubilee rather than to the sabbatical year, in connection with which there is no allusion to the release of land (contrast Bertholet; cf. Jer. 34:14).

17. The last clause is as difficult grammatically in Hebrew as in the KJV; emend נחלתו בניו, "his inheritance his sons," to נחלת בניו, "the inheritance of his sons," with the LXX and Syriac.

5. Cooking Arrangements in the Temple (46:19-24)

19-20. The prophet visits the place where the priests boil the guilt and sin offering and bake the cereal offering at the west end of the north row of sacred chambers for the

21 Then he brought me forth into the outer court, and caused me to pass by the four corners of the court; and, behold, in every corner of the court *there was* a court.

22 In the four corners of the court *there were* courts joined of forty *cubits* long and thirty broad: these four corners *were* of one measure.

23 And *there was* a row *of building* round about in them, round about them four, and *it was* made with boiling places under the rows round about.

24 Then said he unto me, These *are* the places of them that boil, where the ministers of the house shall boil the sacrifice of the people.

47 Afterward he brought me again unto the door of the house; and, behold, waters issued out from under the

21 Then he brought me forth to the outer court, and led me to the four corners of the court; and in each corner of the court there was a court — 22 in the four corners of the court were small*g* courts, forty cubits long and thirty broad; the four were of the same size. 23 On the inside, around each of the four courts was a row of masonry, with hearths made at the bottom of the rows round about. 24 Then he said to me, "These are the kitchens where those who minister at the temple shall boil the sacrifices of the people."

47 Then he brought me back to the door of the temple; and behold,

g Gk Syr Vg: The meaning of the Hebrew word is uncertain

priests (see 42:1-14). According to 42:13, the priests were to eat the most sacred offerings in the priests' chambers both to the north and the south of the yard; we may perhaps presume a similar place for preparing the offerings west of the south row of chambers, as well as here west of the north row. This is not certain, however, since the north side may have had a special function (cf. Exeg. on 40:38-43). **Communicate holiness to the people:** See 44:19 (cf. 42:14). For **the entrance, which was at the side of the gate** see 42:9.

21-24. The kitchens in the corners of the outer court, in contrast with the arrangements in the preceding two verses, were for the sacrifices of the people of the land, the laity, who were served by **those who minister at the temple,** i.e., the Levites, if, as is probable, this accorded with Ezekiel's view of the role of the Levites (cf. the picture in I Sam. 2:12-17).

22. Small courts: Read חצרות קטנות with the LXX, and so probably the Vulg. *atriola,* for the difficult חצרות קטרות, "enclosed [?] courts" (cf. KJV), or possibly "secluded [or "unroofed"] courts."

H. THE RIVER WHICH FLOWS FROM THE TEMPLE (47:1-23)

In vss. 1-12 the prophet culminates his description of the sacred area with a picture of the sacred stream which has its source beneath the threshold of the temple and flows south of the altar and the east gate down to the Dead Sea. Although unfed by tributaries, the stream grows deeper as it proceeds, being unfordable four thousand cubits from the sacred area. It turns fresh the waters of the Dead Sea, and it nourishes evergreen, everbearing trees on its banks. The latter part of the chapter (vss. 13-23) introduces the allotment of the land to the twelve tribes, indicating the boundaries of the land, and specifying the place of the proselyte. If our interpretation of the structure of the book is correct, the first part of the chapter belongs to Ezekiel, while the latter part, in

uprooted from the land and have no sure possessions of their own, so that they are at the mercy of those who employ or govern them— such a society, our seer would say, sins against the divine holiness which should have its dwelling in the midst.

47:1-23. Return of the Divine Presence.—The seer is with his guide again, who in inspired

imagination reveals to him what it will be like to live in a land renewed by the return to it of the divine presence. The symbolism of the first half of the chapter is clear; from the rebuilt temple a new and vitalizing impulse goes forth into the whole life of the community.

1-12. The Water of Life.—We have seen how the altar stands at the center of the temple as

threshold of the house eastward: for the forefront of the house *stood toward* the east, and the waters came down from under, from the right side of the house, at the south *side* of the altar.

2 Then brought he me out of the way of the gate northward, and led me about the way without unto the outer gate by the way that looketh eastward; and, behold, there ran out waters on the right side.

water was issuing from below the threshold of the temple toward the east (for the temple faced east); and the water was flowing down from below the south end of the threshold of the temple, south of the altar.

2 Then he brought me out by way of the north gate, and led me round on the outside to the outer gate, that faces toward the east;[h] and the water was coming out on the south side.

[h] Heb obscure

---

which the vision motif is absent, belongs to the editor. A number of scholars believe that 43:12 concludes Ezekiel's picture of the temple (see Cooke, Steuernagel, Herrmann).

1. The Sacred River (47:1-12)

The new age is a new creation and properly has its paradise, with its sacred river and trees. Like the paradise in Genesis, the picture here is ultimately based on the motif of the sanctuary with its sacred trees and stream. As paradise is the source of the rivers which water the earth, so here Jerusalem, the abode of the glory of Yahweh, is the mount of God (cf. 28:12-19). So also the hill of the gods, Mount Saphon, in the recesses of the north (cf. Ps. 48:2), was at the *mbk nhrm*, "the sources of the rivers" (cf. Gordon, *Ugaritic Handbook*, text 49, I, l. 5; 51, IV, l. 21; etc.). See Zech. 14:8, where the sacred stream from Jerusalem divides and flows both toward the Mediterranean and toward the Dead Sea (cf. also Zech. 13:1), and Joel 3:18, where the stream from the temple waters the valley of Shittim. In Rev. 22 the river of life issues from the throne of God and of the Lamb. See also Enoch 26:2-3 and Ps. 46:4. The sacred rock at the sanctuary at Jerusalem is said in Arabic tradition to be from paradise, and it is affirmed that all sweet waters issue from the rock, there to divide and flow to all parts of the world (see Ibn al-Firkah in "The Book of Arousing Souls," and Abu 'l-Fida in "The Book of Inciting Desire," translated in C. D. Matthews, *Palestine, Mohammedan Holy Land* [New Haven: Yale University Press, 1949], pp. 29, 63, 118). It is dubious that the Pool of Siloam, the Spring Gihon, or the Waters of Shiloah (cf. Isa. 8:6) are a prominent element in the symbolism here, if at all, although it may be in part suggested by the Kidron Valley, "the Brook Kidron" (נחל קדרון), which is east of Jerusalem and reaches the Dead Sea below En-eglaim. Note that here also it is called נחל, a "wadi" (vss. 5 ff.). However, the geography is more mythological than terrestrial. The stream is doubtless thought to receive its waters from the *tehôm*, "the deep" (cf. 17:8; 19:10; 31:4, and Gordon, *loc. cit.*). Note also the "sea of bronze" before the temple (I Kings 7:23, etc.) and the Mesopotamian representations of the deity with flowing streams (see May, "The Sacred Tree on Palestine Painted Pottery," pp. 253-54).

47:1. It is not clear from whence the prophet is brought back, since the order of the preceding text is uncertain. **From the . . . side:** מכתף, but read with some Hebrew MSS, מפתן, **threshold,** as earlier in the verse, a plausible scribal error; perhaps also read תימנה, "southward," for הימנית, **south,** and so translate: "from under [see KJV] the threshold of the temple southward" (cf. Targ.). This presents a clearer picture, for the waters issuing from the threshold could hardly have flowed south of the temple, although the RSV interpretation **south end of the threshold** is not impossible.

2. See Exeg. on 44:1-3. **By the way that looketh eastward** is hardly correct, for it is the gate that faces eastward; the text is probably corrupt, and דרך, **way,** may have been transposed from its original position after הפונה, **faces** (see RSV). **Coming out:** The Hebrew is a denominative verb from a noun meaning "flask," and so may mean "to come out" as from a flask, intending to suggest that the stream is a small one; some would translate "trickle."

3 And when the man that had the line in his hand went forth eastward, he measured a thousand cubits, and he brought me through the waters; the waters *were* to the ankles.

4 Again he measured a thousand, and brought me through the waters; the waters *were* to the knees. Again he measured a thousand, and brought me through; the waters *were* to the loins.

5 Afterward he measured a thousand; *and it was* a river that I could not pass over: for the waters were risen, waters to swim in, a river that could not be passed over.

6 ¶ And he said unto me, Son of man, hast thou seen *this?* Then he brought me, and caused me to return to the brink of the river.

7 Now when I had returned, behold, at the bank of the river *were* very many trees on the one side and on the other.

8 Then said he unto me, These waters issue out toward the east country, and go down into the desert, and go into the sea: *which being* brought forth into the sea, the waters shall be healed.

9 And it shall come to pass, *that* every thing that liveth, which moveth, whithersoever the rivers shall come, shall live: and there shall be a very great multitude of fish, because these waters shall come thither: for they shall be healed; and every thing shall live whither the river cometh.

3 Going on eastward with a line in his hand, the man measured a thousand cubits, and then led me through the water; and it was ankle-deep. 4 Again he measured a thousand, and led me through the water; and it was knee-deep. Again he measured a thousand, and led me through the water; and it was up to the loins. 5 Again he measured a thousand, and it was a river that I could not pass through, for the water had risen; it was deep enough to swim in, a river that could not be passed through. 6 And he said to me, "Son of man, have you seen this?"

Then he led me back along the bank of the river. 7 As I went back, I saw upon the bank of the river very many trees on the one side and on the other. 8 And he said to me, "This water flows toward the eastern region and goes down into the Arabah; and when it enters the stagnant waters of the sea,[i] the water will become fresh. 9 And wherever the river[j] goes every living creature which swarms will live, and there will be very many fish; for this water goes there, that the waters of the sea[k] may become fresh; so everything will live where the river

[i] Compare Syr: Heb *into the sea to the sea those that were made to issue forth*
[j] Gk Syr Vg Tg: Heb *two rivers*
[k] Compare Syr: Heb lacks *the waters of the sea*

4. In vs. 4*b* **through the water** is read with twelve Hebrew MSS, the Syriac, Targ., and Vulg. (cf. KJV).

6. **Along** is read with some Hebrew MSS.

8. The **Arabah** is the depression in which lie the Jordan and the Dead Sea; the term also may include the continuance of the depression south of the Dead Sea, modern Wadi el-ʿArabah. The Dead Sea was called the Sea of the Arabah. **Stagnant waters of the sea:** Read with the LXX and Syriac, המים, waters, for הימה, "to the sea," repeated by dittography and confusion; read with the Syriac המבאשים, lit., "stinking," or else החמוציים, "sour," for חמוצאים, brought forth, although neither is too happy a description of the Dead Sea. **Become fresh:** Lit., **shall be healed.**

9. The meaning of this verse is fairly clear, although the text is corrupt and repetitious. The diction recalls that in Gen. 1, perhaps in an earlier form, and suggests something of the new creation ideology that is involved. **Rivers:** In Hebrew, **two rivers,**

the place at which the life of the nation is offered up to God in utter consecration by the men who are set apart to act for it in this solemn manner. Now we see how what happens at the altar radiates over the whole land. In the old days there had been a stream flowing from the temple hill, "the waters of Shiloah that go softly" (Isa. 8:6). But this was little more than a brook and it had no fertilizing effect on the country around Jerusalem. Now, however, the stream is to possess miraculous qualities and will leave nothing untouched by its healing powers. We should do well to let our minds dwell for a moment on this piece of symbolism.

10 And it shall come to pass, *that* the fishers shall stand upon it from En-gedi even unto En-eglaim; they shall be a *place* to spread forth nets; their fish shall be according to their kinds, as the fish of the great sea, exceeding many.

11 But the miry places thereof and the marshes thereof shall not be healed; they shall be given to salt.

12 And by the river upon the bank thereof, on this side and on that side, shall grow all trees for meat, whose leaf shall not fade, neither shall the fruit thereof be consumed: it shall bring forth new fruit according to his months, because their waters they issued out of the sanctuary: and the fruit thereof shall be for meat, and the leaf thereof for medicine.

goes. 10 Fishermen will stand beside the sea; from En-ge'di to En-eg'laim it will be a place for the spreading of nets; its fish will be of very many kinds, like the fish of the Great Sea. 11 But its swamps and marshes will not become fresh; they are to be left for salt. 12 And on the banks, on both sides of the river, there will grow all kinds of trees for food. Their leaves will not wither nor their fruit fail, but they will bear fresh fruit every month, because the water for them flows from the sanctuary. Their fruit will be for food, and their leaves for healing."

---

but with the versions read **river**; the corruption may be due to the influence of Zech. 14:8. The insertion of **the waters of the sea** is necessary for the sense. The last clause, **so everything will live where the river goes,** should perhaps be omitted with the Syriac.

10. En-gedi is modern Tell ej-Jurn near 'Ain Jidi on the west shore of the Dead Sea; the name means "the spring of the goat." En-eglaim ("the spring of the calf") is perhaps at modern 'Ain Feshkha, about two miles south of the Khirbet Qumran area where an Essene community center has been excavated and significant manuscript finds have been made (see Millar Burrows, *The Dead Sea Scrolls of St. Mark's Monastery* [New Haven: American Schools of Oriental Research, 1950], Vol. I; J. C. Trever, "The Discovery of the Scrolls," *Biblical Archaeologist,* XI [1948], 46-57; R. P. R. de Vaux, "La grott des manuscrits hébreux," *Revue Biblique,* LVI [1949], 586-609; "Fouille au Khirbet Qumrân," *ibid.,* LX [1953], 83-106; Rowley, *The Zadokite Fragments and the Dead Sea Scrolls*). **A place for the spreading of nets:** See 26:5, 14.

11. Note the modern exploitation of the Dead Sea for its mineral salts (see the description of the Dead Sea, called usually in the O.T. the Salt Sea, in G. A. Smith, *Historical Geography of the Holy Land,* pp. 499-516).

12. Cf. the figure in Ps. 1:3. The center and source of health and prosperity for the community is **the sanctuary.**

Is there an altar in our nation, our home, our personal life, which is thus a center of renewal?

Experience, however, suggests that an initial impulse is not enough. There is often difficulty in maintaining it. How many revivals of religion have been like a stream which runs ever more shallow as it goes on its way, to lose itself in some barren waste in the end! The economist has his law of decreasing returns and there seems to be a similar tendency in the spiritual life. Only too often the creative impulse dies down, inspiration is replaced by routine, and instead of the breath of God's creative spirit we have an organization which struggles to keep going. The seer trusts that such will not be the case with Israel, that with the passage of time the stream of spiritual life will flow deeper and broader, the work of God once begun will go on

from triumph to triumph. What is happening in our own case? Is the stream deepening or growing shallower as time advances?

But the supreme achievement of this renewed spiritual life has yet to be mentioned. It will be able to redeem the waste places of the nation's history. The Salt Sea will teem with fish again; i.e., nothing is beyond the reach of God's grace as it will come to Israel in the new day. Where God is at work there is no hopeless situation, no group of people who are beyond redemption, no heritage from an unhappy past which need condemn us to a future delivered over to despair. Again we have the message of the gospel as we had it in ch. 37. It is the glory of God that he can achieve the impossible, giving life to the dead.

13 ¶ Thus saith the Lord God; This *shall be* the border, whereby ye shall inherit the land according to the twelve tribes of Israel: Joseph *shall have two* portions.

13 Thus says the Lord God: "These are the boundaries by which you shall divide the land for inheritance among the twelve tribes of Israel. Joseph shall have two por-

---

2. Boundaries of the Land (47:13-20)

This section was foreshadowed earlier in ch. 46, and is anticipated particularly by the editor in 37:15-28, especially vss. 26-28. The land is to be divided equally among the twelve tribes, with Ephraim and Manasseh given two portions, since they really represent two tribes. Only the territory in western Palestine is involved, the Trans-Jordan tribes being given territory in western Palestine. The northern limits apparently reach the borders presumed at the time of David, extending to the entrance to Hamath (see II Sam. 8:5-12), and at the time of Jeroboam II (II Kings 14:25; Amos 6:14). The boundary in general is that described in Num. 34:1-12; the report here in Ezekiel is perhaps based on the same tradition or source from which P drew in Numbers. Quite uncertain of location are **Hazer-hatticon** and **Sibraim** (=Sepharvaim). **Hethlon** has been identified with Heitela, to the east of Tripoli (see F. M. Abel, *Géographie de la Palestine* [Paris: J. Gabalda, 1933], I, 302). Hamath is modern Hamā, and "the entrance to Hamath" was probably in the territory of Riblah and Kadesh on the Orontes River (see G. E. Wright and F. V. Filson, eds., *The Westminster Historical Atlas to Bible* [Philadelphia: Westminster Press, 1945], p. 47), to judge from the most probable location of Zedad (at Ṣadâd) and Hazar-enon (=Hazar-enan, at Qaryatein), and the possible association of Hethlon with Heitela. The northern boundary, however, has been placed by some scholars much to the south of this, with Hethlon at 'Adlun and the entrance of Hamath in the valley between Mount Hermon and Mount Lebanon or in the north end of

---

13-23. *Concentration.*—The artificial location of the tribes in the new era is again to be understood as symbolism. Israel is to learn to accept her limitations and withdraw within them, that she may concentrate there on that service of God to which she is called.

Henceforth there is to be no exposed frontier and no unnecessary contact with the heathen world. Israel will abandon the country across the Jordan and concentrate within the area between that river and the Mediterranean Sea. The policy is definitely one of withdrawal upon interior lines, and carries with it the definitive abandonment of the hopes which no doubt were still cherished in certain circles, i.e., the hope that the frontiers of the nation would one day be restored to those of David and Solomon. The dedicated community must renounce all dreams of this kind. Imperial greatness is not for it, and it should not be anxious even for the satisfaction of its legitimate claims to territory.

Within these frontiers the nation puts itself into the hands of God without reserve, that he may give it what shape he will. The fact that the country is cut up into a number of rectangles, without regard for historical frontiers, reminds one of Solomon's organization of twelve districts as administrative areas (I Kings 4:7-20). That was the act of a despot indifferent to local loyal-

ties, if he did not in fact aim at their suppression in the interests of his centralized efficiency. Here the meaning of the arrangement is quite different. The new Israel will be content to be dealt with as God may see best; it will not demand that he respect earlier boundaries or preserve tribal dignities. Let him be free to make of the nation what he will.

There is a lesson for us all in this. In our discussions of Christian unity is not everything often vitiated from the outset by the fact that we are determined to preserve our distinctive traditions and our old associations? Is there any hope of union until we, as it were, put the map of the church before God and let him redraw it as he will, whether he respects existing rights or overrules them? Our seer no doubt found it easy to make such a surrender because the calamity of the Exile had deprived the old frontiers of their significance and made a fresh start possible. Must we wait for such constraint of circumstance?

If the new Israel is to be concentrated, it is not for all that to be exclusive. The **stranger** may take up his residence and even be admitted to citizenship and ownership of land, finding his place within one of the tribes. This leads on to our next topic.

13-23. *The Two Strategies.*—If we set chs. 40–48 beside Isa. 40–55, we can say that, while

14 And ye shall inherit it, one as well as another: *concerning* the which I lifted up mine hand to give it unto your fathers: and this land shall fall unto you for inheritance.

15 And this *shall be* the border of the land toward the north side, from the great sea, the way of Hethlon, as men go to Zedad;

16 Hamath, Berothah, Sibraim, which *is* between the border of Damascus and the border of Hamath: Hazar-hatticon, which *is* by the coast of Hauran.

17 And the border from the sea shall be Hazar-enan, the border of Damascus, and the north northward, and the border of Hamath. And *this is* the north side.

tions. 14 And you shall divide it equally; I swore to give it to your fathers, and this land shall fall to you as your inheritance.

15 "This shall be the boundary of the land: On the north side, from the Great Sea by way of Hethlon to the entrance of Hamath, and on to Zedad,*l* 16 Bero'thah, Sib'raim (which lies on the border between Damascus and of Hamath), as far as Hazer-hatticon, which is on the border of Hauran. 17 So the boundary shall run from the sea to Hazar-e'non, which is on the northern border of Damascus, with the border of Hamath to the north.*m* This shall be the north side.

l Gk: Heb *the entrance of Zedad, Hamath*
m Heb obscure

Golan, and Hazar-enon near the sources of the Jordan or in northern Trans-Jordan or in the territory west of el-Leja, in the neighborhood of eṣ-Ṣanamen, Sheikh Miskin, or el-Ḥarra (for discussion, see Abel, *op. cit.*, I, 302-4; Martin Noth, "Studien zu den historisch-geographischen Dokumenten des Joshuabuches," *Zeitschrift des deutschen Palästina-vereins,* LVIII [1935], 240-48). Berothah is modern Bereitân, and Hazezon-tamar perhaps 'Ain el-'Arûs south of the Dead Sea. Meribath-kadesh (=Kadesh-barnea) is perhaps at 'Ain Qedeis, while the Brook of Egypt is Wadi el-'Arish. The **Great Sea** is the Mediterranean. From north to south, accepting the more northerly boundary, the distance measures some 280 miles. The kingdom of David and Solomon extended farther south, to the Gulf of Aqabah or the Red Sea.

13. For **this** the Hebrew has גה, an error for זה, which correctly appears in some MSS, the LXX, Vulg., and Targ. By haplography the Hebrew has "[a] border" rather than **the border.** The final clause, יוסף חבלים, lit., "Joseph portions," should be read with the Targ. and Vulg., ליוסף חבלים, "to Joseph two portions"; "to" has been omitted by haplography.

14. I swore, i.e., with uplifted **hand** (see Exeg. on 20:5; etc.).

15-16. The Hebrew has "to the entrance of Zedad, Hamath, Berethah," etc., but it is better to transpose Hamath and read, with the LXX, **to the entrance of Hamath, . . . to Zedad, Berothah.** Num. 34:7 has Mount Hor for Hethlon. Hazer-hatticon is emended by some to Hazer-enon with the LXX, but the latter is too far north to be on the border of **Hauran.** (Or is the Hauran reference an error? Contrast Noth, *loc. cit.*) Hauran is the plateau south of the Pharpar River, roughly equivalent to Bashan. **Berothah** is the Berothai of II Sam. 8:8. For **Sibraim**=Sepharvaim see II Kings 17:24; 18:34.

17. The confusion in this verse is illustrated by the unintelligible KJV. Haplography has resulted in "and a border from the sea shall be," but it is better read with eleven MSS **and the border from the sea shall be. Which is on the northern border of Damascus . . . :** Lit., "the border of Damascus and north to the north, and the border of Hamath and [ואת] the northern side" [*sic*]; for וצפון, "and north," read צפונה, "northward." The

---

for the first the remnant is saved, for the other its mission is to save.[5] Each of the prophets sees his people reduced to a mere fraction of what they had once been, and gladly bids them surrender political power that they may devote themselves to their spiritual mission. But while

[5] T. W. Manson, *The Teaching of Jesus* (Cambridge: Cambridge University Press, 1931), pp. 178-81.

Ezekiel desires above all to preserve his people from contamination by the heathen world, Second Isaiah would have them venture all on a mission to the heathen. Probably, as thus worded, the antithesis is too sharp, but it does set before us the two strategies between which the church still has to choose. Of course there is a place for each. There are times which call

18 And the east side ye shall measure from Hauran, and from Damascus, and from Gilead, and from the land of Israel *by* Jordan, from the border unto the east sea. And *this is* the east side.

19 And the south side southward, from Tamar *even* to the waters of strife *in* Kadesh, the river to the great sea. And *this is* the south side southward.

20 The west side also *shall be* the great sea from the border, till a man come over against Hamath. This *is* the west side.

21 So shall ye divide this land unto you according to the tribes of Israel.

22 ¶ And it shall come to pass, *that* ye shall divide it by lot for an inheritance unto you, and to the strangers that sojourn among you, which shall beget children among you: and they shall be unto you as born in the country among the children of Israel; they shall have inheritance with you among the tribes of Israel.

23 And it shall come to pass, *that* in what tribe the stranger sojourneth, there shall ye

18 "On the east side, the boundary shall run from Hazar-e'non[n] between Hauran and Damascus;[m] along the Jordan between Gilead and the land of Israel; to the eastern sea and as far as Tamar.[o] This shall be the east side.

19 "On the south side, it shall run from Tamar as far as the waters of Meribath-ka'desh, thence along the Brook of Egypt to the Great Sea. This shall be the south side.

20 "On the west side, the Great Sea shall be the boundary to a point opposite the entrance of Hamath. This shall be the west side.

21 "So you shall divide this land among you according to the tribes of Israel. 22 You shall allot it as an inheritance for yourselves and for the aliens who reside among you and have begotten children among you. They shall be to you as native-born sons of Israel; with you they shall be allotted an inheritance among the tribes of Israel. 23 In whatever tribe the alien resides, there you

[m] Heb obscure
[n] Cn: Heb lacks *Hazar-enon*
[o] Compare Syr: Heb *you shall measure*

LXX[B] omits the reference to Hamath; the territory of Hamath adjoined the northern boundary (cf. 48:1). **Damascus** was thus within the territory claimed for Israel here. Instead of ואת, read זאת, **this shall be,** with a number of MSS and the Syriac.

18. The starting point was probably originally given, and may be inserted as **Hazar-enon.** The line of the eastern boundary ran between Hauran and Damascus; the verse should not be emended with some to read that it was Hazar-enon which lay between Hauran and Damascus (see vs. 17). **The eastern sea** is the Dead Sea. **As far as Tamar:** Read with the Syriac תמרה for תמדו, **ye shall measure. This shall be:** Read זאת for ואת, as in vs. 17*b*.

19. See Num. 34:3-5. **Meribath-kadesh:** See Num. 27:14 (cf. "waters of Meribah," Num. 20:13; Deut. 33:8; Pss. 81:7; 106:32; etc.). For the south border see also Ezek. 48:28.

3. PLACE OF THE PROSELYTE IN RESTORED ISRAEL (47:21-23)

21-23. The proselyte is to be equal to the native born, as also in the H and P sources (see Lev. 16:29; 17:15; 19:34; 24:16, 22; Num. 15:29, 30; etc.). The *gērim* are most probably proselytes here and in the later sources, and the LXX so interprets them here (see May, "Theological Universalism in the O.T.," p. 101; Meek, "The Translation of *Gēr* in the Hexateuch," pp. 172-80). Some suggest that these verses are a later addition (see, however, Exeg. on 14:7; 22:7).

for concentration, defense, and withdrawal upon interior lines. But this can never be accepted as a permanent state of things; it is preparatory to a fresh advance at the earliest opportunity. The Christian morality is an adventure of redemption, not a counsel of safety.[6]

[6] E. L. Allen, *Thou Must Venture* (London: Nisbet & Co., 1942), pp. 97-102.

Returning for a moment to vss. 22-23, we observe that while the new Israel of this vision is not exclusive, it is not missionary. It is hospitable to those from outside who come to throw in their lot with it, but it does not go forth to win them. In a passage which has often been quoted, a Jewish scholar points out that it is precisely here that the gospel of Jesus

give *him* his inheritance, saith the Lord God.

48 Now these *are* the names of the tribes. From the north end to the coast of the way of Hethlon, as one goeth to Hamath, Hazar-enan, the border of Damascus northward, to the coast of Hamath; for these are his sides east *and* west; a *portion for* Dan.

2 And by the border of Dan, from the east side unto the west side, a *portion for* Asher.

3 And by the border of Asher, from the east side even unto the west side, a *portion for* Naphtali.

4 And by the border of Naphtali, from the east side unto the west side, a *portion for* Manasseh.

shall assign him his inheritance, says the Lord God.

48 "These are the names of the tribes: Beginning at the northern border, from the sea by way*p* of Hethlon to the entrance of Hamath, as far as Hazar-e'non (which is on the northern border of Damascus over against Hamath), and*q* extending from the east side to the west,*r* Dan, one portion. 2 Adjoining the territory of Dan, from the east side to the west, Asher, one portion. 3 Adjoining the territory of Asher, from the east side to the west, Naph'tali, one portion. 4 Adjoining the territory of Naph'tali, from the east side to the west,

p Compare 47. 15: Heb *by the side of the way*
q Cn: Heb *and they shall be his*
r Gk Compare verses 2-8: Heb *the east side the west*

J. Allotment of the Tribal Territories (48:1-35)

This final chapter of the book presents a blueprint of the allotment of the land. The tribes are arranged north and south of the area which includes the square of 25,000 cubits and the property of the prince on each side of the square, extending to the Jordan and the Mediterranean. Vss. 1-7 give the location of the seven tribes north of this area, vss. 8-22 describe the area itself, and vss. 23-29 locate the five tribes south of the area. Vss. 30-35 describe the twelve gates of the city, which are named after the twelve tribes, and give the over-all measurements of the city.

The tribes are apparently given territories of equal width, all lines running east and west with an exactness that ignores natural geographical features. From north to south, north of the sacred portion, the order of the tribes is Dan, Asher, Naphtali, Manasseh, Ephraim, Reuben, and Judah; the southern tribes are Benjamin, Simeon, Issachar, Zebulun, and Gad. Levi, of course, has no inheritance. The Trans-Jordan tribes are placed in western Palestine, and there is discernible only a rough resemblance to the original position of the tribes. Judah and Benjamin are given places of importance on either side of the sacred portion and city property. It is perhaps significant that the sons of Rachel and Leah are placed closest to the sacred portion, four on each side: Manasseh and Ephraim (i.e., Joseph [Rachel]), Reuben (Leah), and Judah (Leah) to the north, and Benjamin (Rachel), Simeon (Leah), Issachar (Leah), and Zebulun (Leah) to the south. The first and second sons of Leah are placed north and south respectively of Judah and Benjamin (see Gen. 29:32-33). The concubine tribes are placed farthest away from the sacred area, i.e., Dan (Bilhah), Asher (Zilpah), and Naphtali (Bilhah) on the north, and Gad (Zilpah) on the south, none closer than fifth place to the sacred portion. Some scholars consider vss. 9-22 a later addition and a duplication of the materials in 45:1-8 (but see Exeg. on 45:1-9).

1. Tribes North of the Sacred Portion and City Property (48:1-7)

Reuben was originally a Trans-Jordan tribe, and the Trans-Jordan half tribe of Manasseh is ignored. Dan (after its migration), Asher, and Naphtali were the three most northerly tribes, but they were separated from Manasseh and Ephraim by Zebulun and Issachar, while Benjamin came in between Ephraim and Judah. The restoration of Israel as well as Judah is a characteristic concept of the editor.

48:1. The state of the verse is suggested by the unintelligible rendering of the KJV. The grammatical and syntactical relationship of the various parts of the verse is not clear. **From the sea:** Read with 47:15, מן הים for אל יד, "to the side of" (=**to the coast of**),

5 And by the border of Manasseh, from the east side unto the west side, a *portion for* Ephraim.

6 And by the border of Ephraim, from the east side even unto the west side, a *portion for* Reuben.

7 And by the border of Reuben, from the east side unto the west side, a *portion for* Judah.

8 ¶ And by the border of Judah, from the east side unto the west side, shall be the offering which ye shall offer of five and twenty thousand *reeds in* breadth, and *in* length as one of the *other* parts, from the east side unto the west side: and the sanctuary shall be in the midst of it.

9 The oblation that ye shall offer unto the LORD *shall be* of five and twenty thousand in length, and of ten thousand in breadth.

10 And for them, *even* for the priests, shall be *this* holy oblation; toward the north five and twenty thousand *in length,* and toward the west ten thousand in breadth, and toward the east ten thousand in breadth, and toward the south five and twenty thousand in length: and the sanc-

Manas'seh, one portion. 5 Adjoining the territory of Manas'seh, from the east side to the west, E'phraim, one portion. 6 Adjoining the territory of E'phraim, from the east side to the west, Reuben, one portion. 7 Adjoining the territory of Reuben, from the east side to the west, Judah, one portion.

8 "Adjoining the territory of Judah, from the east side to the west, shall be the portion which you shall set apart, twenty-five thousand cubits in breadth, and in length equal to one of the tribal portions, from the east side to the west, with the sanctuary in the midst of it. 9 The portion which you shall set apart for the LORD shall be twenty-five thousand cubits in length, and twenty[s] thousand in breadth. 10 These shall be the allotments of the holy portion: the priests shall have an allotment measuring twenty-five thousand cubits on the northern side, ten thousand cubits in breadth on the western side, ten thousand in breadth on the eastern side, and twenty-

[s] Compare 45. 1: Heb *ten*

which is probably a corruption by dittography from later in the verse (Cornill, Bertholet). **As far as Hazar-enon:** See 47:17. **From the east side to the west:** Read מפאת קדימה ועד פאת ימה after the analogy of vss. 3 ff. (cf. LXX) for פאת קדים הים, **the east side the west.** This is preceded by the corrupted text, **and they shall be his** (RSV mg.) ; perhaps emend to read "and he [i.e., Dan] shall have," reading with the LXX והיה for והיו; the phrase may be a gloss.

2. SPECIAL TERRITORY FOR PRIESTS, LEVITES, CITY, AND PRINCE (48:8-22)

With this section cf. 45:1-8.

8. The portion includes the territory of the priests, the territory of the Levites, and the property of the city, altogether making a square of 25,000 cubits; it includes also the prince's territory which lies east and west of this square (see Exeg. on 45:1-9) . **Reeds** is obviously wrong; read **cubits**; the Hebrew gives only the numbers.

9. The length is measured from east to west, and the breadth from north to south; the breadth here must be revised from **ten thousand** to **twenty-five thousand,** to accord with vs. 8, or better, if the term "sacred portion" here is used to include only the priests' and Levites' territory (see vss. 14, 18, 21-22), read "twenty thousand" with the LXX of 45:1 (see also 48:13) .

surpasses the best that contemporary Judaism could attain. The rabbis, to be sure, were ready to welcome the sinner when he repented; they did not consider it their duty, as Jesus did, to seek out the sinner and win him to a better mind.[7]

[7] C. G. Montefiore, *The Synoptic Gospels* (2nd ed.; London: Macmillan & Co., 1927), I, 54-56.

48:8-15. *Sacred and Profane.*—Notice the contrast between the territory connected with the temple, which as such is sacred and inalienable, and the site of the city, which is profane or secular. This raises at once the question of the distinction between these two spheres of life.

That the distinction is a real one we cannot doubt. Direct concentration upon God is one

tuary of the Lord shall be in the midst thereof.

11 *It shall be* for the priests that are sanctified of the sons of Zadok; which have kept my charge, which went not astray when the children of Israel went astray, as the Levites went astray.

12 And *this* oblation of the land that is offered shall be unto them a thing most holy by the border of the Levites.

13 And over against the border of the priests, the Levites *shall have* five and twenty thousand in length, and ten thousand in breadth: all the length *shall be* five and twenty thousand, and the breadth ten thousand.

14 And they shall not sell of it, neither exchange, nor alienate the firstfruits of the land: for *it is* holy unto the Lord.

15 ¶ And the five thousand, that are left in the breadth over against the five and twenty thousand, shall be a profane *place* for the city, for dwelling, and for suburbs: and the city shall be in the midst thereof.

16 And these *shall be* the measures thereof; the north side four thousand and five hundred, and the south side four thou-

five thousand in length on the southern side, with the sanctuary of the Lord in the midst of it. **11** This shall be for the consecrated priests, the sons[t] of Zadok, who kept my charge, who did not go astray when the people of Israel went astray, as the Levites did. **12** And it shall belong to them as a special portion from the holy portion of the land, a most holy place, adjoining the territory of the Levites. **13** And alongside the territory of the priests, the Levites shall have an allotment twenty-five thousand cubits in length and ten thousand in breadth. The whole length shall be twenty-five thousand cubits and the breadth twenty[u] thousand. **14** They shall not sell or exchange any of it; they shall not alienate this choice portion of the land, for it is holy to the Lord.

15 "The remainder, five thousand cubits in breadth and twenty-five thousand in length, shall be for ordinary use for the city, for dwellings and for open country. In the midst of it shall be the city; **16** and these shall be its dimensions: the north side four thousand five hundred cubits, the

[t] One Ms Gk: Heb *of the sons*
[u] Gk: Heb *ten*

---

11. Consecrated (=**sanctified**): The Hebrew has the singular adjective, but the מ (=**of**) of the plural ending is wrongly attached to the following word; read the plural with the LXX, Syriac, and Targ. See 44:10 for the status of the Levites.

13. The Hebrew has והלוים, "and the Levites," but read with the LXX and Vulg., וללוים, [and] **the Levites shall have. Ten thousand** (second occurrence): The context demands **twenty thousand** with the LXX (cf. vs. 9).

14. Exchange and **alienate** should probably be plural impersonal rather than singular; i.e., read with the Vulg. and Syriac, ימרו for ימר, and with the Syriac יעבירו for יעבור. **Sell** is plural.

15. Ordinary use: חל, lit., **profane,** as opposed to קדש, "sacred" (see 22:26; 42:20; 44:23), and here profane in distinction from the "sacred portion" of 25,000 by 20,000 cubits. **Open country:** The open space on all sides of the city, 250 cubits deep (cf. vs. 17); cf. the open space about the temple in 45:2; the term (מגרש) is used in P to refer to the common land around the Levitical cities (Num. 35:2-7; Josh. 14:4; etc.; see Exeg. on Ezek. 27:28).

16. The dimensions of the city, including the open country around it, are just ten times the size of the sanctuary, and so about 1.6 miles on each side, or about 6.5 miles in circumference (see 42:20). The Hebrew text repeats the second **five** by dittography.

---

thing; the devotion of our energies to work in the world is another. So here the temple and the city are assigned to different though fairly neighboring areas. When we pray, we begin by putting out of our minds the engagements and preoccupations of the day; the spirit needs withdrawal and detachment if it is to remain pure.

Further, the daring suggestion in this vision that the city should be moved southward to make room for the sanctuary contains a profound truth. The political life of the nation must be subordinated to its spiritual loyalties.

But if the distinction is a real one, it must not be made absolute. That would be tantamount to dividing life into two areas, each with

sand and five hundred, and on the east side four thousand and five hundred, and the west side four thousand and five hundred.

17 And the suburbs of the city shall be toward the north two hundred and fifty, and toward the south two hundred and fifty, and toward the east two hundred and fifty, and toward the west two hundred and fifty.

18 And the residue in length over against the oblation of the holy *portion shall be* ten thousand eastward, and ten thousand westward: and it shall be over against the oblation of the holy *portion;* and the increase thereof shall be for food unto them that serve the city.

19 And they that serve the city shall serve it out of all the tribes of Israel.

20 All the oblation *shall be* five and twenty thousand by five and twenty thousand: ye shall offer the holy oblation foursquare, with the possession of the city.

21 ¶ And the residue *shall be* for the prince, on the one side and on the other of the holy oblation, and of the possession of the city, over against the five and twenty thousand of the oblation toward the east border, and westward over against the five and twenty thousand toward the west border, over against the portions for the

south side four thousand five hundred, the east side four thousand five hundred, and the west side four thousand five hundred.

17 And the city shall have open land: on the north two hundred and fifty cubits, on the south two hundred and fifty, on the east two hundred and fifty, and on the west two hundred and fifty. 18 The remainder of the length alongside the holy portion shall be ten thousand cubits to the east, and ten thousand to the west, and it shall be alongside the holy portion. Its produce shall be food for the workers of the city. 19 And the workers of the city, from all the tribes of Israel, shall till it. 20 The whole portion which you shall set apart shall be twenty-five thousand cubits square, that is, the holy portion together with the property of the city.

21 "What remains on both sides of the holy portion and of the property of the city shall belong to the prince. Extending from the twenty-five thousand cubits of the holy portion to the east border, and westward from the twenty-five thousand cubits to the

---

18-19. The territory **ten thousand cubits to the east, and ten thousand to the west** of the city and its open land will serve to supply the city with food; it will be tilled by the workers of the city drawn from all the tribes of Israel. Perhaps the result of dittography or a marginal note, the Hebrew adds rather unnecessarily, "and it shall be alongside the sacred portion."

20. The KJV has a very obscure translation. The Hebrew reads "a fourth," but the sense demands רבועה (cf. 43:16) or מרבעת (cf. 40:47; 45:2), **square** (cf. LXX).

21-22. The portions for the prince (vs. 21) makes little sense (cf. RSV); the portions referred to are the tribal portions, i.e., those of Judah and Benjamin (see vs. 22*b*). Perhaps we should transpose יהיה, "it shall be," from vs. 22*a* and read, "it shall be for [i.e., "belong to"; cf. ASV] the prince." The last part of vs. 21 should go with vs. 22. The

---

its own standards of conduct. There must be constant intercourse between the two, a relation of giving and receiving. Nor may we identify the sacred with the church, leaving everything else profane. The church is shot through with human imperfections and selfish ambitions, while secular society is meant to be dedicated to God and his will. Therefore each must learn from the other. Therefore also the service of God is accomplished through them both; in neither perfectly, yet wholly absent from neither.

The answer we are seeking is to be found in that principle of alternation to which W. E. Hocking has called attention.[8] There must be a rhythm of worship and work, so that what is gained in the one is continuously being wrought into the fabric of the other.

19. *Community.*—Moffatt's translation is suggestive: the land "shall serve to support workers in the city, and shall be cultivated by the workers in the city, belonging to all the clans of Israel." The city is to become the

[8] *Meaning of God in Human Experience,* pp. 405-27.

prince: and it shall be the holy oblation; and the sanctuary of the house *shall be* in the midst thereof.

22 Moreover, from the possession of the Levites, and from the possession of the city, *being* in the midst *of that* which is the prince's, between the border of Judah and the border of Benjamin, shall be for the prince.

23 As for the rest of the tribes, from the east side unto the west side, Benjamin *shall have* a *portion.*

24 And by the border of Benjamin, from the east side unto the west side, Simeon *shall have* a *portion.*

25 And by the border of Simeon, from the east side unto the west side, Issachar a *portion.*

26 And by the border of Issachar, from the east side unto the west side, Zebulun a *portion.*

27 And by the border of Zebulun, from the east side unto the west side, Gad a *portion.*

28 And by the border of Gad, at the south side southward, the border shall be even from Tamar *unto* the waters of strife *in* Kadesh, *and* to the river toward the great sea.

29 This *is* the land which ye shall divide by lot unto the tribes of Israel for inheritance, and these *are* their portions, saith the Lord God.

30 ¶ And these *are* the goings out of the

west border, parallel to the tribal portions, it shall belong to the prince. The holy portion with the sanctuary of the temple in its midst, 22 and the property of the city,[v] shall be in the midst of that which belongs to the prince. The portion of the prince shall lie between the territory of Judah and the territory of Benjamin.

23 "As for the rest of the tribes: from the east side to the west, Benjamin, one portion. 24 Adjoining the territory of Benjamin, from the east side to the west, Simeon, one portion. 25 Adjoining the territory of Simeon, from the east side to the west, Is'sachar, one portion. 26 Adjoining the territory of Is'sachar, from the east side to the west, Zeb'ulun, one portion. 27 Adjoining the territory of Zeb'ulun, from the east side to the west, Gad, one portion. 28 And adjoining the territory of Gad to the south, the boundary shall run from Tamar to the waters of Meribath-ka'desh, thence along the Brook of Egypt to the Great Sea. 29 This is the land which you shall allot as an inheritance among the tribes of Israel, and these are their several portions, says the Lord God.

30 "These shall be the exits of the city:

[v] Cn: Heb *and from the property of the Levites and from the property of the city*

---

territory between Judah and Benjamin includes the sacred portion with the sanctuary in its midst and the property of the city (see vs. 21*a*; cf. vs. 8), plus that which belongs to the prince, and the text should be so reconstructed. Since **the property of the Levites** (cf. KJV) is a part of the sacred portion, it should perhaps be omitted here. To make sense, **from** must be omitted. In the light of these comments, vss. 21*b*-22 will read as in the RSV.

3. Tribes South of the Sacred Portion and City Property (48:23-29)

Gad was a Trans-Jordan tribe. **Issachar** and **Zebulun** were in northern Palestine.

28. Along the Brook of Egypt: The Hebrew has "along [to] the brook," but the Brook of Egypt is obviously intended (cf. 47:19).

4. The City of Jerusalem (48:30-35)

The measurements of the city were given earlier in vs. 16, but for one who knows the habits of the editor, this is no sign that we have here a different source. There are

---

center of a genuine and all-inclusive community, the expression of a common purpose. No tribe can claim it as its own; it belongs to all, and all go forth from it to work the common

land. What better hope could we have for our own society than something of this kind?

30-35. The City of God.—Jerusalem is rebuilt as the city of God, ancient animosities forgotten,

city on the north side, four thousand and five hundred measures.

31 And the gates of the city *shall be* after the names of the tribes of Israel: three gates northward; one gate of Reuben, one gate of Judah, one gate of Levi.

32 And at the east side four thousand and five hundred: and three gates; and one gate of Joseph, one gate of Benjamin, one gate of Dan.

33 And at the south side four thousand and five hundred measures: and three gates; one gate of Simeon, one gate of Issachar, one gate of Zebulun.

On the north side, which is to be four thousand five hundred cubits by measure, 31 three gates, the gate of Reuben, the gate of Judah, and the gate of Levi, the gates of the city being named after the tribes of Israel. 32 On the east side, which is to be four thousand five hundred cubits, three gates, the gate of Joseph, the gate of Benjamin, and the gate of Dan. 33 On the south side, which is to be four thousand five hundred cubits by measure, three gates, the gate of Simeon, the gate of Is'sachar, and the

---

three gates on each side of the city. On the north side the gates are named after the two tribes to the north, Judah and Reuben, and after Levi. All three are sons of Leah (see Gen. 29:32-34). The north gate of the city in the pre-exilic and postexilic period was called the Gate of Benjamin (see Jer. 37:13; 38:7; Zech. 14:10; cf. the upper Benjamin Gate of the house of the Lord, Jer. 20:2; cf. the modern Damascus Gate in the north wall of Jerusalem). On the south are the gates of Simeon, Issachar, and Zebulun, the three tribes located in this order south of the sacred portion, although Benjamin intervened between them and the sacred allotment; all three, like those represented by the northern gate, are sons of Leah (Gen. 29:33; 30:18-20). The gates on the east are Joseph, Benjamin, and Dan, the first two sons of Rachel and the last the son of Rachel's slave-maid Bilhah (Gen. 30:23-24; 36:16-18; 30:6). The gates on the west are named after Gad, Asher (sons of Zilpah) and Naphtali (son of Bilhah), all "concubine" tribes (Gen. 30:7-13). One gate is named after Joseph, although Joseph had been given two tribal portions; this is done to make room for Levi among the twelve, and it does not imply variant authorship. We may compare the twelve gates of the new Jerusalem, named after the twelve tribes and complemented by twelve foundation stones of the city wall named after the twelve disciples, in Rev. 21:12-14.

32. Probably מדה, "by measure," is omitted after **cubits** and it may be inserted with the LXX and Syriac; cf. vss. 30, 33, although most scholars unnecessarily emend these verses to get exact repetition of the formulas.

---

equal recognition being given to all the tribes. Each has a gate named after it. The symmetry of the plan symbolizes the harmony of purpose in which the inhabitants live. But the secret of this harmony lies in the fact that the Lord is there, the divine presence orders and unifies all that goes on within its walls. The seer means by these words that the Lord has come back; he who was driven out by the people's sin, forced to abandon his temple because of the abominations perpetrated in it and his city because of its social injustices, has now returned. He has done so at once because he is gracious and so restores his people to their own land; and because they are penitent and having learned the lesson only the suffering of exile could teach, now offer to him a dedicated common life. So a divided nation with a tragic history is renewed and drawn together again, with God at its very center.

Note some of the differences between the new Jerusalem of our seer and that of Rev. 21–22. (*a*) There it is made more clear than here that the new Jerusalem is God's gift to men. (*b*) In Rev. 21 there is no temple, while here the temple is central. (*c*) There the new Jerusalem is open to receive the nations of mankind, whereas here is nothing more than the admission to civic rights of the alien settled in the land.

On this whole theme see the argument of Bergson[9] on the distinction between the "closed" and the "open" society, the latter being that city of God whose gates are open to all and whose law is love.

But the significance of these final words of Ezekiel can only be fully understood as we bear in mind what the word "God" has meant

[9] *Two Sources of Morality and Religion, passim.*

34 At the west side four thousand and five hundred, *with* their three gates; one gate of Gad, one gate of Asher, one gate of Naphtali.

35 *It was* round about eighteen thousand *measures:* and the name of the city from *that* day *shall be,* The LORD *is* there.

gate of Zeb'ulun. 34 On the west side, which is to be four thousand five hundred cubits, three gates,[w] the gate of Gad, the gate of Asher, and the gate of Naph'tali. 35 The circumference of the city shall be eighteen thousand cubits. And the name of the city henceforth shall be, The LORD is there."

[w] One Ms Gk Syr: Heb *their gates three*

34. **Their . . . gates,** שעריהם, should be emended with one MS, the LXX, and Syriac to שערים, **gates.**

35. The new name indicates the new status of the city. For the new name given to Jerusalem in the new age see the contemporary biographer of Jeremiah in Jer. 3:17 (cf. also Zech. 8:3; Isa. 1:26; 60:14; 62:2; see May, "Jeremiah's Biographer," p. 198; cf. the ideology in II Kings 23:27) . **The name of the city is Yahweh-shammah, The LORD is there.**

throughout the book. This is no easy divine presence which makes itself at home among men. Where the God who is "a consuming fire" (Heb. 12:29) comes to dwell, what is paltry and superficial can no longer be tolerated. Where the absolute divine holiness enters in, "who may abide the day of his coming?" (Mal. 3:2.) The final mercy of God is not anything that can be taken for granted. Our response to it will be in reverence as well as in gratitude.

The Book of

DANIEL

Introduction and Exegesis by ARTHUR JEFFERY
Exposition by GERALD KENNEDY

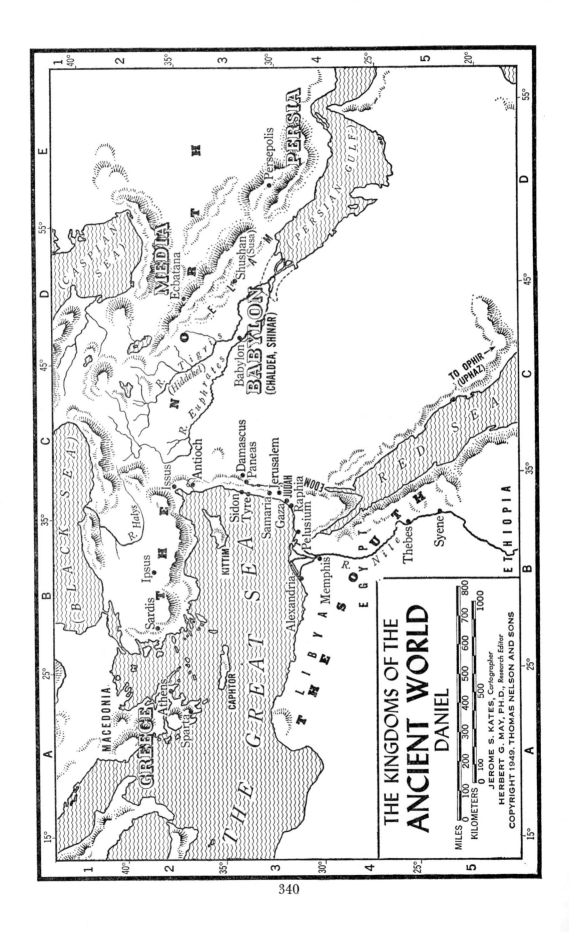

THE KINGDOMS OF THE
ANCIENT WORLD
DANIEL

JEROME S. KATES, *Cartographer*
HERBERT G. MAY, PH.D., *Research Editor*
COPYRIGHT 1949, THOMAS NELSON AND SONS

MILES 0   100   200   300   400   500   600   700   800
KILOMETERS 0   100   200   300   400   500   600   700   800   1000

DANIEL

INTRODUCTION

When Alexander the Great died untimely at Babylon in 323 B.C., the consequent partition of his empire was fraught with momentous consequences for the peoples of the Near East. During the two preceding centuries these peoples had felt the strong attraction of Greek culture, but Alexander was so ardent a Hellenizer that his eastern conquests marked a new era in which Greek culture and Greek institutions came to be important factors in all Oriental communities dwelling between the Nile and the Indus.

I. Historical Background

A. The Hellenization of the Orient.—Wherever he went Alexander founded Greek settlements, each of which attracted further settlers, set up Greek institutions, and became a center of Greek life. This in turn encouraged the flow of trade, in which Orientals were quick to see advantages to themselves. The result was not only an intermingling of peoples, but much interchange of ideas and a wide extension of the use of Greek as an international language.

Four kingdoms finally emerged from the confusion after the death of Alexander: those of the Seleucids of Syria, of the Ptolemies of Egypt, of Lysimachus in Thrace, and of Cassander in Macedonia. Both the Ptolemies and the Seleucids set themselves with energy and perseverance to the furthering of Alexander's project for the Hellenization of the Orient. It was Ptolemy Soter (323-283 B.C.) who founded at Alexandria the museum and the library where he gathered a notable band of men of learning. His rival, Seleucus Nicator (312-280 B.C.), estab-lished centers of Greek culture in almost every province under his government, and under his successors the "school" at Antioch became a serious rival to that at Alexandria.

This Hellenization was welcomed in many circles among the local populations in the Orient, particularly by those eager to cultivate Greek for cultural and not primarily for practical reasons, and who labored to model community life on the Greek pattern. These were advocates of assimilation, who adopted Greek dress and customs, studied Greek philosophy, read Greek literature, and preferred to use the Greek language as their medium for cultural expression. Such groups favored the organization of municipal affairs in the Greek fashion, and desired to be as much as possible at one with their Greek neighbors. By other groups, however, this process of Hellenization was resisted both on nationalistic and religious grounds.

The Jews were not unaffected by this ferment. There were considerable communities of them in all four of the kingdoms which succeeded Alexander, and for the Jews of the Dispersion Greek quickly came to be the normal language for cultural expression. It was to meet their needs that a version of the Old Testament was produced. From them came religious writings such as the Wisdom of Solomon, I Esdras, II Maccabees,[1] written in Greek for a Greek-reading public, the same public, indeed, as that addressed by Philo and Josephus. Alexander himself had come down through Phoenicia on his way to Egypt, and there was a tale that he

[1] See Vol. I, pp. 406-8, 396-97, 417-19.

had visited Jerusalem. It would seem that he treated the Jews favorably, and under the Ptolemies, who came to control Palestine and Phoenicia, they received as benevolent treatment as they enjoyed in Egypt, Ptolemy III (246-221 B.C.) even coming to Jerusalem to present a thank offering at the temple in accordance with Jewish usage. Nor, indeed, when the Seleucids came to control, would there seem to have been any particular reason for their being evilly entreated. The little temple-state which centered at Jerusalem was but one of many such to be found in various parts of the Seleucid Empire, and its people, like theirs, felt the fascination of the Greek world around them. Greek names became fashionable, young men desired to join in the Greek games, Greek fashions in dress and adornment were popular, so that Hecataeus of Abdera, writing about 300 B.C., remarks that "the Jews had greatly altered many of the ordinances of their forefathers." Under the Ptolemies Greek had come almost to rival Aramaic as the common language of Palestine. The tales telling of the translation of the biblical writings into Greek picture the work as having been done by pious Greek-speaking rabbis of Palestine brought to Egypt for the purpose. The grandson of Ben Sirach who translated Ecclesiasticus into Greek was a native of Palestine.[2]

There were not wanting Jews who resisted this movement toward assimilation and Hellenization, feeling that though there was much in the "Greek wisdom" that was admirable, there was danger that it might destroy other values still more precious. These included the "godly ones," the Hasidim, men who preferred to walk in the old paths and who resisted what was contrary to traditional belief and practice. Such appear often enough in the pages of the Old Testament, but it was now that they developed into a kind of community within the community. In earlier days the "godly" seem to have had their strength in the poorer classes, and on the whole the strength of the movement of resistance against Hellenization again lay in the humbler classes who, on the one hand, were less capable of understanding the attraction of Greek ways, and on the other were actually less in contact with its world. It would be a mistake, however, to think that the resistance movement was confined to the lower classes, for among the aristocracy and the wealthy there were also lovers of the old ways. It would likewise be an error to set both parties in too sharp opposition. The situation might well have developed as quietly and calmly in Palestine as in Egypt had it not been for changes in the political situation.

[2] See Vol. I, p. 408.

B. Ptolemies and Seleucids in Palestine.—

After his victory at Gaza in 312 B.C., Ptolemy had conquered all the coastal lands as far north as Sidon, and is said to have taken Jerusalem. Though he was presently driven out of Syria by Antigonus, he moved in after the Battle of Ipsus in 301 B.C. to possess Coele-Syria, which then included Palestine. As Ptolemy had not taken part in that battle, the victors had allotted Coele-Syria to Seleucus, but when Ptolemy moved in to take possession, Seleucus, for the sake of peace, made no move to oust him. The Seleucids, however, continued to feel that that area was rightly theirs, so that for the next hundred years there was a struggle between Ptolemies and Seleucids for its possession. The most determined efforts to gain control of it were those by Antiochus the Great in 221, 219, and 218, all of which failed. After the death of Ptolemy IV in 203, Antiochus had a better opportunity, which this time was crowned with success in 198 B.C. at the Battle of Paneas near the sources of the Jordan. In that year Palestine came definitely under Seleucid control. Antiochus the Great was an even more ardent Hellenizer than his predecessors, a fact which led the Hellenizing party at Jerusalem to seek to profit by his victory. Josephus says that the triumphant Antiochus entered Jerusalem, where he was received with rejoicing and obtained bountiful replenishments for his army.

C. Divided Loyalties in Jerusalem.—

The change in overlords, however, seems to have widened the rift between two of the chief families in Jerusalem, the Oniads and the Tobiads, the former, who held the high priestly office, championing the cause of the defeated Ptolemies, and the latter, who held the chief financial office, supporting Antiochus and his successors.

In 175 B.C. Antiochus IV Epiphanes succeeded his brother Seleucus IV as ruler of the Seleucid Empire. Shortly after his succession the Hellenizing party in Jerusalem asked permission to erect a gymnasium on the Greek pattern in their city. This is the matter referred to in I Macc. 1:11-15: "In those days there arose from Israel lawless men who persuaded many, saying: 'Let us go and make a treaty with the heathen round about us, for ever since we came to be separated from them, many misfortunes have befallen us.' Now the saying seemed good in their eyes, and some of the people, moved with eagerness, went to the king, and he gave them authorization to introduce heathen customs. So they built a gymnasium in Jerusalem in heathen fashion, made themselves uncircumcised, disowned the holy covenant, allied themselves with the heathen and set themselves to do evil."

The high priest Onias III happened to be

away at the time, so his brother Jason, who was pro-Syrian, made Antiochus a money offer for the high priestly office, and was appointed. From the point of view of Antiochus there was nothing wrong about this. To him that was but one of the many offices held under him in his empire, to which he was at liberty to appoint anyone he chose, and it was a recognized custom for a candidate for such an office to make a money gift for consideration. To religious-minded Jews, however, the matter was quite different. To them the office was not in the king's gift, and though Jason was of the high priestly family, they could not recognize an appointment made in this way, and they maintained their allegiance to Onias. In spite of their bitter resentment, however, there was no outward revolt. Jason was a convinced assimilationist: he sent representatives to the quinquennial games at Tyre in honor of Heracles, with an offering of three hundred drachmas of silver to pay for a sacrifice to the god. Jason enjoyed office for not more than three years at the most. An outsider named Menelaus coveted the post, offered Antiochus a sum considerably higher than that paid by Jason, and was granted the appointment. Jason fled and Menelaus, to secure his position, engineered the assassination of Onias. Then to recoup himself for his outlay, he seems to have entered into a plot with his brother Lysimachus to steal and dispose of some of the temple vessels. To the populace this was the last straw. Jason's presence in the holy office had been an affront, but this Menelaus was an outrage, and such an attempt to lay hands on the sacred vessels was more than could be borne. There were riots in the city under cover of which Jason, knowing how occupied Antiochus was with his campaign in Egypt, re-entered the city and drove out Menelaus (169/170). Antiochus, however, returned, reinstated Menelaus and, as a punishment for the people's impudence in rising against his appointee, plundered the temple. The people refused to be quieted and would not accept Menelaus. This is the story related in II Macc. 4 5.

D. The Desecration of Jerusalem.—Antiochus' reaction was swift and drastic, and from his point of view perfectly justifiable. He was the ruler, so his will was law. Menelaus was his choice and therefore, in Greek eyes, as much under divine appointment as the Jews held Onias to have been. The trouble arose from the fact that Jerusalem was one of the little temple-states where fanatic loyalty to the local deity was, as usual, causing difficulties. The solution was to enforce Hellenization there as he had enforced it elsewhere and thereby thoroughly discredit the local deity. His army

from the Egyptian campaign was brought in and allowed to plunder the city and slaughter at will. Then the city walls were razed, a Syrian garrison installed in the city, and Antiochus was ready to deal with the religious aspect of the case. The writer of I Macc. 1:41-63 tells the story: "Accordingly the king wrote to his whole kingdom that they should all become one people, each one giving up his own customs. Now all the heathen gave assent to the king's word, and many from Israel accepted his form of worship and sacrificed to the idols and profaned the sabbath. The king also sent dispatches by the hand of messengers to Jerusalem and to the cities of Judah, bidding them follow customs foreign to the land, stop the whole burnt offerings and sacrifices and drink offerings at the sanctuary, profane the sabbaths and feasts, and defile the holy place and the holy people, to build altars and sacred precincts and idol shrines, sacrifice swine and unclean animals, leave their sons uncircumcised, and pollute their souls with every unclean and profane thing, that thus they might forget the law and change all the ordinances. Anyone who would not do according to the king's word was to be put to death. In such words as these did he write to all his kingdom, and set overseers over all the people, giving command to the cities of Judah, that city by city they should offer sacrifice. Now many of the people joined themselves to them, everyone, indeed, who was willing to forsake the law, and they did evil in the land, forcing Israel into hiding-places, into every place of refuge they had. Then on the fifteenth day of Kislev, in the one hundred and forty-fifth year [i.e., 168 B.C.] he set up an abomination of desolation on the altar of sacrifice, and in the cities of Judah round about they set up altars, and at the doors of houses and in the public squares they burned incense, and the books of the law, such as they found, they tore up and burned with fire. Moreover, wheresoever they found a book of the covenant with anyone, or if anyone was found complying with the law, the king's judgment was for his death. By their force did they compel in Israel those who were found month by month in the cities, and by the twenty-fifth of the month they were sacrificing on the altar, that is on the altar of sacrifice. Also, the women who had had their children circumcised did they put to death in accordance with the decree, hanging the infants around their necks, together with their families and those who had circumcised them. Yet many in Israel stood firm, resolving in themselves not to eat anything unclean, choosing rather to die that they might not be defiled by such foods and might not profane the holy covenant, and they did die."

E. The Maccabean Revolt.—The result of these measures was the outbreak of the Maccabean Wars. Some Jews had submitted. Many more became passive resisters who went to death rather than submit. The material for active revolt, however, was there, and it was kindled at the village of Modein. There when the king's officers appeared to enforce the decree the local priest Mattathias refused to submit, and when an assimilationist Jew advanced to offer the heathen sacrifice Mattathias slew him on the altar, slew likewise the king's officer, and broke down the heathen altar that had been set up. From that moment the revolt was an actuality. Mattathias and his sons fled to the hill country where they were joined by sympathizers from all classes among the people. Their activities were at first directed against the assimilationists. They killed many of these, pulled down their heathen altars, removed as far as possible all visible signs of their Hellenization, and circumcised their sons wherever they found them. This inevitably brought them in conflict with the royal troops. At first they were badly worsted, but when Mattathias died in 166/165 and the movement came under the direction of his sons, particularly under Judas Maccabaeus, it met with amazing success. In 165 they won remarkable victories over the royal troops and were able to retake Jerusalem, all save the citadel. On the fifteenth of Kislev, the very day on which three years before swine's flesh had been offered on a pagan altar set up on the altar of sacrifice, they were able to cleanse and purify the temple and have a service of rededication.

But when the first excitement had spent itself, many began to take sober account of the situation. So far the revolt had been unbelievably successful, but what would the future hold? Men's sympathies were with the leaders of the revolt, but what did those leaders know of the real strength of Antiochus' empire? When he set himself in earnest to deal with the situation in Judea, could their puny forces continue to be victorious against the might he could assemble? In face of the vengeance he was sure to seek what hope was there for the future?

II. Origin of the Book

It was at a moment when many of the people, in the reaction following the exaltation that had been produced by the Maccabean victories, had begun to have misgivings and look with grave anxiety at what the future might hold, that the book of Daniel, which had been written under the persecutions of Antiochus Epiphanes, found a ready audience. Its message could counter the growing anxiety and incipient de-

spair, maintain enthusiasm for the national cause, encourage loyalty to God and to the ordinances of the law, keep bright men's hope in a future that could be even more wonderful than the past. Fairly early in the days of persecution the writer had seen the need for this, and to provide such a message he had used a particular literary vehicle—the allegory. He pictured to his audience a Jew living with his companions in an age long past, where they yet faced a situation similar to that which pious Jews were at the moment facing, living under a powerful monarch who sought to assimilate them to their heathen environment and bring to nought their religion. But this man and his companions were loyal to God, faithful in observing the law, and God saw them safely through their trials. Even when that king and his court exercised all their might against them, when pious observing Jews were thrown into a fiery furnace or into a den of lions, God saved them; and it was the mighty kings and their courtiers who came to ignominy, and had to acknowledge the God of the Jews, instead of Jews having to accept the gods of the heathen. From such a story the people could take heart, for what God had done he could again do, and as he had humbled Nebuchadrezzar and Belshazzar, so he could deal with Antiochus and his supporters. For further encouragement the writer added to his allegory a series of dreams and visions in which he set forth an interpretation of the historical background of their present struggle, and under symbols and images gave a forecast of the future.

For his story he used the figure of Daniel, a man with a symbolic name, "God hath given decision." An ancient Semite worthy of this name is twice referred to in Ezekiel, in 14:14, "Though these three men, Noah, Daniel, and Job, were in it, they should deliver but their own souls by their righteousness" (cf. vs. 20), and 28:3, "Behold, thou art wiser than Daniel; there is no secret that they can hide from thee." In both of these passages the name is actually Danel, which is the name of the ancient Canaanitish worthy whose legend now appears among the texts from Ras Shamra. It would seem that there was in circulation some Jewish Danel legend, which had as its setting the Babylonian captivity, and which included several popular motifs illustrating divine intervention on behalf of the righteous and the ultimate triumph of those who maintained loyalty to the observance of the law. This story (or stories) the writer retold for his contemporaries in such a way that to an outsider it would appear just a story, but one in which his audience would clearly see the figure of their present oppressor, would readily recognize the meaning of the symbols and signs of the visions, and catch the message of encouragement and inspiration it was intended to convey. To reach his audience effectively he wrote in Aramaic. In the book as we have it, 2:4b–7:28 are still in Aramaic, but 1:1–2:4a and 8:1–12:13 are in Hebrew. The Hebrew portion bears every evidence of having been translated from Aramaic, and why the book has come down partly in Aramaic and partly in Hebrew is a puzzle which scholarship has not yet solved.

III. Literary Genre

From both Egypt and Mesopotamia we have evidence for the use of the allegory as a genre of religious literature in which interpretations of historical events and forecasts of the future are put forth under the name of some ancient worthy and said to have been hidden till the appropriate time for their appearance had arrived. The book of Daniel is thus a true apocryph (cf. 12:4: "Thou, O Daniel, shut up the words, and seal the book, even to the time of the end"). In compositions of this kind the historical details given are only a framework for the religious message, and were not intended to give historical information. The instruction in such a book is religious, not historical; so that the only details that need to be historically accurate and precise are those which concern the contemporary situation for which the message is relevant. The picture of events in the past needs only to conform to popular conceptions about that past, and its picture of events in the future will conform to men's hopes of the way events will shape themselves in that future. We should thus be widely astray did we insist on regarding all the statements made about historical persons and events as statements which must be historically true and somehow justified as such to the modern reader, or insist on finding precise fulfillments of the events referred to in the prophetic visions.

To illustrate, let us imagine a present-day Arab tribal sheik holding forth to his tribal group with a message most pertinent to their contemporary situation, involved as that is with British and American interests, and saying: "When the first Elizabeth had been reigning ten years over the English and her rival Philip, who in reality was her husband, was ruling over Spain, the ships of the English set forth from the north of England and rediscovered America, which, as we know, had earlier been discovered by the Arabs, who had made nought of it. They were followed there closely by the ships of Spain. There was much rivalry between them and strife over its riches and wonders, till they said: 'Let us be wise. America is two. Let the English take the north and the people of Spain the south.' It was so, and the people of Spain were content, but the ships of the English, ever restless, came also to the lands of Islam. Then too, following them, came their progeny who had waxed mighty in America." To the sheik's audience that was an intelligible setting for the religious message he was going to give them about their contemporary situation. They knew about the great queen who had ruled over England and whose ships went exploring. They knew the legend about the Arabs having discovered America before Columbus. They knew about the Spanish-speaking people in South America, and that the Americans who in recent days had come to the Orient, and were so important a factor in their contemporary situation, spoke English like the British, whom the Arabs had known much earlier. To point out to them that it was not in the tenth year of Elizabeth that America was discovered; that Philip was not married to her, but to her predecessor Mary; that it was not the English, but an Italian, who discovered America; that the English used to set sail from the south, not from the north; that the division into Spanish-speaking and English-speaking America was not by arrangement, would mean nothing to them. Such details are unimportant. The important thing for them is that their sheik's message should come in a framework familiar and significant. Similarly to stress in our study of the book of Daniel that the capture of Jerusalem, i.e., in the third year of Jehoiakim, i.e., in 606 B.C., but in 597 under Jehoiachin; that Nebuchadnezzar should be spelled Nebuchadrezzar, that Belshazzar was not his son, but the son of Nabonidus, and was never king; that there is confusion in its order of the Persian kings and a foreshortening of their history; that "satrap" was not a Babylonian title, and so on, is to fasten on unessentials. These matters were doubtless part of the popular story framework which the writer was using for his message. Sometimes we can see why in these stories there is what we call a historical blunder, and had we more documents from the period we could probably explain them all. When we read today al-Biruni's account of the origin of the Septuagint, we know exactly why he calls Cyrus "Bahman's governor of Babel," why he says that the Samaritan Pentateuch is called "Alamassasiyya," why he states that Ptolemy had thirty-six translations in his hands, why he says that the Jews complained that they had made the translation under compulsion and had been forced to introduce confusions into the text. All these could be called "historical blunders," but we can account for each of these blunders from our knowledge of al-Biruni's sources. Similarly, it is very probable that the "historical blunders" in the book of Daniel would be equally intelligible if we had adequate material from that period available to us.

IV. Structure

The book falls into two clearly distinct parts: (a) a collection of stories about Daniel and his friends, chs. 1–6; (b) a collection of visions seen by Daniel, chs. 7–12. This division does not correspond with the difference in language, though most of the Aramaic material is in the first section and most of the Hebrew in the second. There are some who insist that we must distinguish two authors, one who put together the material in the first section somewhere between the middle and the end of the third century B.C., and another who added to this the second section between 168 and 165 B.C. There seems no compelling reason, however, for such dual authorship, and a great many little things link the two parts together as a unity. Nevertheless it may well be that certain material used in the first section had been in circulation in writing before the author of this book took it and adapted it for his own purpose.

A. The Stories.—The inevitable triumph of those faithful to the religion of Yahweh and the confusion of their enemies is illustrated in the first part.

Chapter 1. Daniel and His Friends at Nebuchadrezzar's Court. After Nebuchadrezzar's deportation of Jewish captives to Babylon some were selected to be trained for court service. These were given Babylonian names and placed under an official to be cared for and instructed. Daniel and his friends refused to eat the palace food since that would have involved violation of Jewish dietary regulations. Their refusal restricted them to a diet of vegetables and water, but nevertheless they so thrived that they proved healthier than any others. As a reward for their faithfulness God gave them the gift of "wisdom," in which they showed themselves superior to the professional court sages.

Chapter 2. Nebuchadrezzar's Dream. Nebuchadrezzar dreamed a dream but could not recall it. The court sages proved unable to tell the monarch his dream, so orders went out for their destruction. When the executioner came for Daniel and his friends, who were counted among the sages, Daniel asked for a delay. After prayer the matter was revealed to Daniel, who told the monarch his dream and its interpretation. For this he was made chief of the guild of sages and governor of Babylon, with power to appoint his friends, while the king acknowledged his God.

Chapter 3. The Golden Idol and the Fiery Furnace. Nebuchadrezzar set up at Dura a huge golden idol, to whose dedication all the officials of the kingdom were summoned, that they might bow down and worship the idol under threat of the fiery furnace. All did so except Daniel's three companions. The king was displeased, but they explained that they could not bow down to an idol, and if the threatened punishment must fall on them, their God would be able to deliver them. The enraged monarch ordered the furnace to be heated seven times hotter than usual and had them cast into it, but to his amazement he saw them walking therein unhurt, in company with a celestial being. This caused him to acknowledge their God and threaten any in his kingdom who should dare to speak against the Deity.

Chapter 4. Nebuchadrezzar's Madness. Nebuchadrezzar dreamed of a huge tree which a celestial being cut down, leaving only a stump. Daniel interpreted this to mean that the tree symbolized the king who would become insane and for seven years live like a beast of the fields. A year later, while the king was boasting of his greatness, he did go mad and had to live like an animal. When he recovered, he praised Daniel's God and his throne was restored to him.

Chapter 5. Belshazzar's Feast. Nebuchadrezzar's successor Belshazzar held a great feast for which he brought out the sacred vessels which Nebuchadrezzar had plundered from the temple in Jerusalem. When the banquet was at its height, a ghostly hand wrote a mysterious message on the wall. Since the wise men could not interpret this, Daniel was called in and read in the message the doom of the kingdom. Belshazzar honored Daniel, but that night he was slain and Darius the Mede captured Babylon.

Chapter 6. Daniel in the Lions' Den. Daniel was given high office by the Median conqueror but jealous officials planned his disgrace. They persuaded the monarch to issue a decree that for a month none should make any petition save to the king. Then they caught Daniel making his daily petition to God and accused him to the king. The king saw through their treachery, and yet reluctantly ordered Daniel to be cast to the lions; but when he saw that he was unharmed, he ordered his accusers to be cast to the lions, and bade all to reverence Daniel's God.

Though no specific reference to Antiochus Epiphanes is given in these stories, no audience of that age could fail to see how the adventures of Daniel and his friends held a message for Jews suffering under Antiochus.

B. The Visions.—Events of current history are pictured under symbols and figures looking forward to the setting up of the kingdom of God.

Chapter 7. In the First Year of Belshazzar. From the sea emerge four beasts, a lion with eagle's wings, a bear with three ribs in its mouth, a four-headed four-winged leopard, and a ten-horned beast with iron teeth. Three horns of this latter beast are presently rooted up by a little horn which sprouts human eyes and a mouth speaking great things. Divine judgment is passed on these beasts, the fourth being destroyed and the others having their dominion taken away. Thereupon a celestial being in human form appears on clouds of heaven and is given everlasting dominion. Daniel interpreted the beasts as representing the Babylonian, Median, Persian, and Seleucid empires. The ten horns are Seleucid kings and pretenders, while the little horn is Antiochus Epiphanes, whose "time and times and half a time" represent the years 168 to 165, after which the kingdom is to pass to the messianic king.

Chapter 8. In the Third Year of Belshazzar. In the palace area at Susa, Daniel sees a vision of a two-horned ram with uneven horns butting to west and north and south, with no beast being able to resist him, until a one-horned he-goat attacks him, overthrows him, and breaks his horns. The he-goat's horn is also broken but in its place come up four horns, out of one of which sprouts a little horn whose power spreads southward and eastward. In its pride this little horn exalts itself even against the celestial hosts, desecrates Yahweh's sanctuary, and for three years and two months interrupts the daily sacrifice. Gabriel tells Daniel the meaning of the vision. The ram is the Medo-Persian kingdom, the he-goat is the Greek kingdom, its horn being Alexander the Great. The four horns which succeed the broken horn are the kingdoms of the Diadochi. The little horn is Antiochus Epiphanes, who proscribed the temple services at Jerusalem between 168 and 165 B.C.

Chapter 9. In the First Year of Darius. Daniel ponders the words of Jeremiah about the seventy years of Jerusalem's desolation. In prayer he makes confession of the national sin and pleads for the end of the desolation. Gabriel then appears, having been sent in response to his prayer, to explain that the seventy years are seventy weeks of years, which fall into three periods of seven weeks, sixty-two weeks, and one week, in which last week will be the great abomination.

Though there is foreshortening, the reference here seems to be to the 49 years from Zedekiah (586) to Joshua the high priest (538), the presumed 435 years between Joshua and the assassination of Onias III in 171, and the period between the death of Onias and the establishment of God's kingdom (171-164), during which Antiochus would set up the abomination in the temple.

Chapters 10–12. In the Third Year of Cyrus. Daniel has been mourning and fasting. While he is walking by the river an angel appears and announces that he has come to reveal the future.

1. Three more kings of the Persians are yet to come, the last of whom will fight against the Greeks (11:2).

    The dynasty is foreshortened but probably Darius I, Xerxes, and Artaxerxes are meant.

2. A mighty king will arise whose dominion will be very great, but it will be divided among four not of his posterity (11:3-4).

    Alexander the Great and the Diadochi who followed him.

3. The strong king of the south and the even stronger king of the north (11:5).

    Ptolemy in Egypt and Seleucus in Syria and Mesopotamia.

4. A daughter of the king of the south will come to the king of the north but neither she nor he will stand (11:6).

    Berenice, daughter of Ptolemy II, was married to Antiochus II, but Laodice, Antiochus' divorced wife, arranged the assassination of Antiochus, Berenice, and the latter's son.

5. An army from the south will invade the north and carry away captive their gods and the princes (11:7-9).

    Ptolemy III, to avenge his sister Berenice, invaded Syria, overcame Seleucus II, the son of Laodice, and brought back much booty.

6. The sons of the king of the north will be stirred up, and one of them will march as far as the fortresses of the south (11:10).

    Seleucus III and Antiochus III.

7. The king of the south will come out in wrath and defeat him, but will not benefit from his victory (11:11-12).

    Ptolemy IV defeated Antiochus III at Raphia, but failed to follow up his victory.

8. The king of the north will return and be victorious in Palestine (11:13-16).

    Antiochus III, taking advantage of the weakness of Egypt, wrested Palestine from Ptolemy V.

9. He will give him his daughter, but it will not advantage him (11:17).

    Antiochus married his daughter Cleopatra to Ptolemy V, but this did not lead to the success he had hoped from it.

10. When he turns to the isles, he will be stopped by a commander and hurled back (11:18).

When Antiochus III attempted to conquer Asia Minor and Greece, he was defeated at Magnesia in 190 by a Roman commander.

11. He will turn to his own strongholds but will stumble and fall (11:19).

Returning from Magnesia, he plundered a temple at Elymais but was attacked by the people and killed in 187.

12. A tax raiser will succeed him but will shortly be destroyed, and not in battle (11:20).

Seleucus IV, who labored to replenish the treasury, was assassinated in 175.

13. He will be succeeded by a contemptible fellow who will gain the throne by dissimulation (11:21).

Antiochus IV Epiphanes, the brother of Seleucus, pushed aside the latter's son Demetrius, who should have succeeded.

14. Under him the prince of the covenant will be broken (11:22-24).

Onias III, the high priest, was assassinated in 171.

15. He will move against the king of the south with a large army and will bring back great booty (11:25-27).

Antiochus' expedition against Egypt in 170 was successful.

16. On his return he will set himself against the holy covenant (11:28).

It was after his Egyptian campaign that Antiochus began his campaign to destroy Judaism.

17. He will move again to attack the south, but this time "ships of Kittim" will intervene (11:29-30).

His Egyptian campaign of 168 was halted by the Romans.

18. In his chagrin he will vent his spleen on the Jews, coming to an agreement with the assimilationists, garrisoning the temple area, abolishing the daily sacrifices, and setting up the abomination (11:31).

His general Apollonius captured Jerusalem on a sabbath and introduced a Syrian garrison. In December, 168, by decree of Antiochus, the practices of the Jewish religion were forbidden and the temple was made a shrine of Zeus Olympius.

19. His actions will gain the assimilationists, but the godly will resist and will suffer persecution. They will receive a little help, but even among the helpers some will be unreliable (11:32-35).

The division between the Hellenizers and the Hasidim now became acute and the Maccabean revolt started, though at first their cause was hindered by the severity of Judas.

20. The king will magnify himself above the gods, and himself give honor not to the gods of his fathers but to a strange god (11:36-39).

Antiochus took titles of divinity and plundered many local temples. He himself honored a non-Syrian deity, Zeus Olympius.

21. The king of the south will attack, but the king of the north will come whirling down and conquer Libya, Egypt, and Ethiopia (11:40-43).

Ptolemy Philometor will make another attempt, but Antiochus will overwhelm him and gain control not only over him but also over his allies in Libya and Ethiopia.

22. Tidings from the north will make him return. He will pitch his tents between Jerusalem and the Mediterranean, and will there perish (11:44-45).

Nos. 21-22 are predictions. Antiochus actually met his death at Tabae in Persia in 164.

23. Then will come a period of great tribulation, which will usher in the resurrection and the age of bliss for the righteous (12: 1-13).

There is a certain artistic structure in the book. The stories and the visions follow the same progress of history, as the author conceived it, in parallel sequences: (a) Nebuchadrezzar, Belshazzar, Darius, Cyrus; (b) Belshazzar, Darius, Cyrus. Moreover, the Aramaic sections form a scheme, as it were, of three concentric circles: chs. 2 and 7 deal with the passing of the four empires; chs. 3 and 6 with God's miraculous deliverances; chs. 4 and 5 with how he brings low arrogant and ungodly princes.

V. Composition and Date

The text has not been transmitted without interpolations. The book apparently ended at 12:8, but as the prediction given there was not fulfilled, two later passages have been added with fresh calculations as to when the end would be. In 9:4-15 the prayer is so different in style and even in thought that it is commonly considered to be an interpolation, though it may possibly be an older prayer which the writer himself incorporated as appropriate at that point in the story. In the Greek versions there are still other interpolations. Not only are there some additional verses about the fiery furnace, but there are three long pieces containing the story of Bel and the Dragon, the Prayer of Azarias and the Song of the Three

Children, and the History of Susanna. There is nothing corresponding to these in the Masoretic Text, and in English Bibles they are given in the Apocrypha.

In the English Bible the book of Daniel comes among the Prophets, as it does in the Greek and Latin Bibles. Were our criterion subject matter, this is where the book belongs (cf. Matt. 24:15). In the Hebrew Bible, however, it comes not among the Prophets but in the third section among the Hagiographa. Even in that section it is placed late—among the latest writings within the canon. Both internal and external evidence supports this position.

A. Internal Evidence.— (a) The fact that parts of it are in Aramaic places it in the same group as Ezra-Nehemiah and suggests that it comes from the period when Aramaic was the language most familiar to the Jews. The kind of Aramaic used in the book, however, cannot be pressed as evidence for a particular date, for it is that type of Aramaic which grew up for official use in the chancelleries and came to be widely used in the ancient Near East.[3]

(b) The Hebrew of the book is late, resembling that of Ecclesiastes, Esther, and Chronicles.

(c) There are a number of Persian loan words in the book, of a kind which suggests that it was written after the Persian Empire had long been a matter of ancient history and words of Persian origin had become naturalized in the language. Moreover, there are some loan words from Greek, three of which—קיתרס= κίθαρις, פסנתרין or פסנטרין=ψαλτήριον, and סומפניה=συμφωνία—have a history within Greek which shows that they could hardly have come into Oriental languages until that spread of Greek culture which followed the campaigns of Alexander the Great.

(d) The use of the word kasdîm (Chaldeans), not in the proper ethnic sense which it has, for example, in Jeremiah, but to mean a caste of wise men, points to a time when the word was commonly used for a class of priestly astrologers, diviners, or magicians, a sense the word has in the pages of Strabo or Diodorus Siculus, who wrote in the first century B.C.

(e) The emphasis throughout the book on the observance of ritual prescriptions of the law on matters of diet, prayer, fasting, and the like, points to a late date. With this agrees much of the teaching of the book on such matters as angels, the resurrection of the dead, and so forth.

(f) The writer's knowledge of history is excellent for the period after the rise of the kingdoms which succeeded Alexander, but is quite defective for the Persian and Babylonian periods. This is understandable if he was contemporary with the latest events he records.

B. External Evidence.— (a) Ben Sirach, writing about 190 B.C., in his famous catalogue of the great men of Israel (Ecclus. 44:1–50:24) brings the list down to his own day, yet though he mentions the twelve prophets, Zerubbabel, Joshua, and Nehemiah, he makes no mention of Daniel.

(b) Since the book knows Jeremiah as a prophet, it must be later than the period of Jeremiah's activity. There are no traces, however, of later books of the Old Testament having influenced it. Daniel is mentioned as a prophet in Matt. 24:15, and it is possible that there are traces of its stories in Heb. 11:33-34.

(c) The earliest allusion to the book seems to be that in Sibylline Oracles 3:397-400, written about 140 B.C., where a reference to the ten horns and the one which grows beside recalls Dan. 7:7-8. This reference, however, need not mean more than that the symbolism of ten horns was used for the Seleucids in the second century B.C. Similarly, the allusion to the "abomination of desolation" in I Macc. 1:54 does not necessarily mean more than that this was a name used in Jewish circles for Antiochus' altar to Zeus.

(d) Clearer indications of a knowledge of the book are the references in I Macc. 2:59 ff. to the companions who were saved from the fiery furnace and to Daniel who was saved from the lions, and a passage in Baruch 1:15–3:3 which has resemblances to the prayer in Dan. 9:4 ff.

I Maccabees would seem to have been written about 125 B.C., and the early part of Baruch perhaps as early as 150 B.C. In neither case is it quite certain that the writers used the book of Daniel, for their material might have come to them from the sources used by the writer of Daniel rather than from his book.

C. Conclusion.—The position the book of Daniel has in the Hebrew Bible is what might be expected in the case of a book written during the Maccabean struggles, but not in the case of a book written in the sixth century B.C. during the Babylonian captivity. That it belonged to the period of Antiochus Epiphanes was recognized by the Neoplatonist Porphyry in the third century A.D., who showed that the events recorded in ch. 11 were concerned with the Seleucids and Ptolemies and the persecution of the Jews under Antiochus IV. Earlier still, Josephus[4] had recognized that the king who forbade the daily sacrifices was Antiochus Epiphanes, though Josephus thought that Daniel, living generations before in Babylon, had foreseen these things that were to come to

---

[3] See Franz Rosenthal, *Die aramaistische Forschung* (Leiden: E. J. Brill, 1939), pp. 66-71.

[4] *Antiquities* X. 11. 7.

pass. He even thought that some of the things foreseen by Daniel had reference to the still later sufferings of the Jews under the Romans. Among the older commentators the generally accepted theory was that the book was written by a prophet Daniel, who lived under Nebuchadrezzar and his successors, experienced the events narrated in the stories, and predicted the things set forth in the dreams and visions. Usually these predictions were considered to reach down only as far as Antiochus Epiphanes, though some followed Josephus in seeing predictions also of events in the Roman period, while a few even saw in them a forecast of European history down to the setting up of the papal power, the "little horn" being Pope Innocent III and a hint of the Inquisition. The Babylonian setting and predictive character are still maintained by most Roman Catholic commentators and find favor with a diminishing number of Protestant writers. The more natural understanding of the book is to place it in the time of Antiochus Epiphanes, and to interpret it as apocalyptic.

VI. Apocalyptic

As such, Daniel is the first great book in the class to which belong such notable writings as Enoch, the Testaments of the Twelve Patriarchs, the Assumption of Moses, II Esdras, the Apocalypse of Baruch (II Baruch), and the Ascension of Isaiah.[5] Such books were the product of a peculiar spiritual temper and were the vehicles of a peculiar spiritual message. The permanent value and relevance of the message they convey is abundantly evident in our own times.[6]

The teaching of the book is characteristic of this class of writing which comes from an age when prophecy has ceased. The old-time prophet came forward with his message in the name of the Lord, keenly alive to the circumstances and needs of the times, and directing to the contemporary scene the message that his vivid experience of contact with the Lord had given him. Because of his experience he could see with startling clarity the realities of the current situation, realities to which the people in general were blind. Because of it he could hear the word of the Lord to which the people were deaf, and so with a desperate sense of

urgency he strove to shock them to an awareness of things as they are in God's sight. He rebuked their sins. He called them to repentance. He interpreted to them the meaning of their present situation. He exhorted them, comforted them, encouraged them as need may be, and ever spoke to them with the authority born of his experience and his sense of mission. The apocalyptist, however, speaks with no such accent of authority, and has no such impact on his generation. He is rather the adapter, along one special line, of the messages of the older prophets. He sees his people in affliction and under persecution so that the burden of his message is to console them and to help them stand firm under their trials. He sees the contemporary scene but wants to have his people look beyond it to the glorious future in which they will be freed from their tribulations and the ancient predictions of wonderful triumph will be fulfilled. He emphasizes present faithfulness in religion and stresses such matters as the strict fulfillment of various ritual prescriptions, since that would be evidence of faithfulness. Thus ritual righteousness seems almost to weigh more with him than moral righteousness. If the people are really obeying faithfully the religious law, the promised redemption cannot be long delayed, and so the apocalyptists in general regard the redemption as near at hand. With redemption will come the kingdom of God. The older prophets had preached of a kingdom in which, after his judgment on the enemies of his people God would supersede the kingdoms of this world by a reign of righteousness. As a rule they thought of this as a continuation of the life of the present world. There would be a thorough "housecleaning" for this world, a purgation in which Israel also would be purged of its unworthy members, after which God would set up an ideal kingdom of peace, happiness, and righteousness, in which prosperity would abound and all peoples would be incorporated into, or at least be subject to, the people of God. The later prophets tended to shift the divine intervention to a final judgment and to interpret the kingdom as something beyond this world. In apocalyptic this eschatological interpretation dominates the whole concept of the kingdom, and with the shift in emphasis comes a development in importance of the idea of resurrection. The wicked who have died ought not to escape judgment, and the righteous who have died ought not to be deprived of the joy of the coming of the kingdom, so the idea of a general resurrection for final judgment takes a prominent place in the picture of the end.

[5] See Vol. I, pp. 427-30, 421-22, 430-31, 398-401, 431-32, 423-24.

[6] See such books as Aage Bentzen, *Danielsbogens aktualitet* (Copenhagen: 1938); A. H. Edelkoort, *De prediking van het Boek Daniël* (Wageningen: 1947), and Werner Kessler, *Zwischen Gott und Weltmacht: Der Prophet Daniel* (Stuttgart: Calwer, 1950).

VII. Theology

The theology of the book of Daniel stands in a midway position. It is more eschatological in its view of the judgment and the coming kingdom than the earlier prophets, but the shift has not yet been made from the expectation of an earthly kingdom to that of a purely spiritual kingdom. The writer of Daniel apparently expects the ideal kingdom to come soon after the fall of Antiochus Epiphanes and to be established on this earth. In his thought of the resurrection he has advanced beyond Hosea and Ezekiel, whose expectation was only for a rising of all Israel as a righteous nation, and beyond Isaiah 24:1–27:13, where it is only the pious individuals of the nation who will rise, for he teaches that both wicked and righteous will be raised. Yet he has not gone so far as to envisage a resurrection of all men such as we have in the New Testament and some of the apocalyptists. A similar midway position appears in his account of the angels. Here angels have personal names and function as patrons of the nations, which is a great advance over the angelology of earlier writings, where they appear only as anonymous messengers of God and have little personal character of their own, yet it is still far from the elaborate angelology and demonology of such a book as Enoch.

The teaching as to God and man is much the same as that of the earlier prophets, though one notices certain modifications. This writer shares the tendency to remove God from the close association with human affairs he has in the thought of prophets and psalmists. Thus he pictures God as ruling the world, at least in part, through angelic powers, who exercise such liberty and independence that in ch. 10 they are represented as being able to act contrary to the divine will. In the writer's teaching on man a deterministic note is evident. All things work out according to a plan already determined. Occasional glimpses of this plan may be gained by those possessed of vision, and they can catch these glimpses of things soon to come to pass only because the happening of such things is decreed and inevitable. Nebuchadrezzar's madness was something that had been decreed, and the "watchers" were going to see that the decree was carried out. The period of the abomination of desolation was fixed beforehand at three and a half years. Perhaps this determinism is at the root of the oft-noted fact that, save in the interpolated prayer in 9:4-15, neither Daniel nor his friends show any consciousness of personal sin or unworthiness. On the other hand, this may be due to the writer's emphasis throughout on ritual righteousness. Since Daniel and his friends are to be models of such righteousness—which consists in strict observance of the law, keeping dietary regulations, observing set times of prayer and correct postures therein, being watchful to avoid any semblance of association of any other object of worship with God, and so on—it might have seemed out of place to have these men who illustrate why sin is condemned in others confessing sin in themselves. It is perhaps hypercritical to object that the writer who has Daniel and his friends express so clearly their convictions that obeisance must be made to none save God, nevertheless pictures the king doing obeisance to Daniel without any such rebuke as Paul and Barnabas voiced to the priest and the people at Lystra (Acts 14:8-18).

One point of particular interest is that in the writer's account of the coming of the kingdom of God he sees it as the culmination of a succession of world empires. This suggests that he has caught the conception that history is a whole. The history of a little country such as Palestine is not fully significant in itself but finds its true significance in its connection with the great empires within whose sphere it lay. Yet even those great empires have their full significance only when seen in connection with the history of the peoples who preceded them and who will come after them. As history unrolls, as empire succeeds empire on the stage of time, each plays its part in a whole of history in which God's eternal purpose is developing. There are hints of such a conception of world history in the Prophets but it is in this book of Daniel that it becomes explicit and gives a foregleam of the world view of the New Testament.

VIII. Text

For the interpretation of the book of Daniel we have to depend almost exclusively on the Masoretic Text. There is no Targum to Daniel. The Greek translation in the Septuagint is paraphrastic, as it is in the case of other late books in the Hagiographa, so that at an early date its place was commonly taken in Greek manuscripts by a more literal version which goes under the name of Theodotion. There are traces of what is called a pre-Theodotion version, but the one commonly found seems to have come into existence about A.D. 180. Jerome knew that all available manuscripts of the Greek Bible contained Theodotion's version of Daniel, though he does not know why, and very little was known about the older Septuagint version till a manuscript of it was discovered in the Chigi Library in Italy. The available Syro-Hexaplar text is mainly useful for helping to restore Origen's Septuagint text. The Lucianic text presents a few useful readings. Both the Syriac and the Latin are representative of the Hebrew-Aramaic text, but the other versions are dependent on the Septuagint. The evidence from the versions is summarized in the commentaries of J. A. Montgomery and R. H. Charles listed in the bibliography.

Between 3:23 and 3:24 the LXX and its dependents have the long passage known as the Song of the Three Children, recounting legendary details of their experiences in the fire, and the song they sang as they walked among the blazing coals.[7]

In the Septuagint, the Syro-Hexaplar, and the Vulgate, ch. 13 is the History of Susanna. In Theodotion it comes at the beginning of the

book, being so placed because it concerns an incident from Daniel's youth in Babylon before he was taken to the court to be trained as a page. The story is intended to illustrate how God watches over the innocent and will not allow evildoers to prevail against them. Possibly the writer also had in mind the idea of illustrating the name Daniel (see Exeg. on 1:6).[8]

In the Greek versions and the Vulgate, ch. 14 is the History of the Destruction of Bel and the Dragon. Its title in the Septuagint reads "From the Prophecy of Habakkuk, son of Joshua, of the tribe of Levi," that is, it was considered to come from some writing attributed to the prophet Habakkuk. It recounts an incident that happened in Babylon not long after Cyrus the Persian acceded.[9]

[7] See Vol. I, pp. 412-13. See also W. O. E. Oesterley, *An Introduction to the Books of the Apocrypha* (New York: The Macmillan Co., 1935), pp. 272-79; C. C. Torrey, *The Apocryphal Literature* (New Haven: Yale University Press, 1945), pp. 54-57; and Josephus Linder, *Commentarius in Librum Daniel* (Paris: P. Lethielleux, 1939), pp. 99-108, 193-210).

[8] See Vol. I, pp. 413-14. See also Walter Baumgartner, "Susanna, die Geschichte einer Legende," and "Der weise Knabe und die des Ehebruchs beschuldigte Frau," *Archiv für Religionswissenschaft,* XXIV (1926), 259-80, XXVII (1929), 187-88; and Linder, *op. cit.,* pp. 495-520.

[9] See Vol. I, pp. 414-15. See also Linder, *op. cit.,* pp. 521-38.

IX. Chronological Table *

B.C.	
625-605	Nabopolassar ruling independently at Babylon after the Medes have destroyed the Assyrian Empire
605	Nebuchadrezzar's victory over the Egyptians at Carchemish (Jer. 46:2)
605-562	Nebuchadrezzar king of Babylonia
602	Jehoiakim's rebellion against Nebuchadrezzar
597	Nebuchadrezzar takes Jerusalem. Jehoiachin taken captive to Babylon along with the temple vessels (II Kings 24:10-16)
587	Fall of Jerusalem. Captivity of Zedekiah (II Kings 25)
562-560	Awel-Marduk successor to his father Nebuchadrezzar. He is the Evil-merodach of II Kings 25:27
560-556	Reign of Nergal-shar-uṣur, brother-in-law of Awel-Marduk
559	Cyrus becomes king of Anshan
556	Lābāshi Marduk, son of Nergal-shar-uṣur reigns for nine months
556-539	Nabū-na'id, son of Nabū-balāṭsu-iqbi, reigns as king over Babylonia. His son Belshazzar is governor for his father at Babylon
ca. 550	Cyrus of Anshan overthrows the Median Empire
539	Cyrus takes Babylon and captures Nabū-na'id. Return of the Jews under Zerubbabel
539-530	Cyrus reigns as king over Babylonia
530-522	Reign of Cambyses, son of Cyrus
522	Episode of Gaumata (Pseudo-Smerdis)
521-486	Reign of Darius I Hystaspis
486-465	Reign of Xerxes. He is the Ahasuerus of the book of Esther
465-423	Reign of Artaxerxes I
458	Return of the Jews under Ezra
423-404	Reign of Darius II Nothus
404-359	Reign of Artaxerxes II Mnemon
359-338	Reign of Artaxerxes III Ochus
336-331	Reign of Darius III Codomannus
333	Alexander the Great overthrows the Persian Empire
332	Alexander conquers Palestine
323	Death of Alexander

SELEUCIDS		PTOLEMIES	
312-281	Seleucus I Nicator	322-285	Ptolemy I Soter
301	Struggle between Ptolemy I and Antigonus for Palestine		
281-261	Antiochus I Soter	285-246	Ptolemy II Philadelphus

* Cf. chronological tables in Vol. I, pp. 146-49; minor discrepancies in the tables show that not all dates can be conclusively determined.

X. Outline of Contents

XI. Selected Bibliography

COMMENTARIES

BEEK, M. A. *Das Danielbuch.* Leiden: J. Ginsberg, 1935.

BEHRMANN, GEORG. *Das Buch Daniel* ("Handkommentar zum Alten Testament"). Göttingen: Vandenhoeck & Ruprecht, 1894.

BENTZEN, AAGE. *Daniel* ("Handbuch zum Alten Testament"). 2nd ed.; Tübingen: J. C. B. Mohr, 1952.

BEVAN, A. A. *A Short Commentary on the Book of Daniel.* Cambridge: Cambridge University Press, 1892.

CHARLES, R. H. *A Critical and Exegetical Commentary on the Book of Daniel.* Oxford: The Clarendon Press, 1929.

DRIVER, S. R. *The Book of Daniel* ("Cambridge Bible"). Cambridge: Cambridge University Press, 1922.

GINSBERG, H. L. *Studies in Daniel.* New York: Jewish Theological Seminary of America, 1948.

KAMPHAUSEN, A. H. H. "The Book of Daniel," in *The Sacred Books of the Old Testament* ("Polychrome Edition"), ed. Paul Haupt. Leipzig: J. C. Hinrichs, 1896.

KESSLER, WERNER. *Zwischen Gott und Weltmacht: Der Prophet Daniel.* Stuttgart: Calwer, 1950.

LINDER, JOSEPHUS. *Commentarius in Librum Daniel.* Paris: P. Lethielleux, 1939.

MARTI, KARL. "Daniel," in *Die Heilige Schrift des Alten Testament,* ed. E. F. Kautzsch and Alfred Bertholet. 4th ed. Tübingen: J. C. B. Mohr, 1923. Vol. II, pp. 456-90.

MONTGOMERY, J. A. *A Critical and Exegetical Commentary on the Book of Daniel* ("International Critical Commentary"). New York: Charles Scribner's Sons, 1927.

OBBINK, H. D. *Daniël.* Groningen: J. B. Wolters, 1932.

PRINCE, J. D. *A Critical Commentary on the Book of Daniel.* New York: Lemcke & Buechner, 1899.

SPECIAL STUDIES

BICKERMANN, ELIAS. *Der Gott der Makkabäer.* Berlin: Schocken, 1937.

DOUGHERTY, R. P. *Nabonidus and Belshazzar.* New Haven: Yale University Press, 1929.

JUNKER, HUBERT. *Untersuchungen über literarische und exegetische Probleme des Buches Daniel.* Bonn: Peter Hanstein, 1932.

KOLBE, WALTHER. *Beiträge zur syrischen und jüdischen Geschichte.* Stuttgart: W. Kohlhammer, 1926.

KUHL, CURT. *Die drei Männer im Feuer.* Giessen: A. Töpelmann, 1930.

ROWLEY, H. H. *Darius the Mede and the Four World Empires of the Book of Daniel.* Cardiff: University of Wales Press Board, 1935.

VOLZ, PAUL. *Die Eschatologie der jüdischen Gemeinde im neutestamentlichen Zeitalter.* Tübingen: J. C. B. Mohr, 1934.

ZIMMERMAN, FRANK. "The Aramaic Origin of Daniel 8–12." *Journal of Biblical Literature,* LVII (1938), 255-72.

———. "Some Verses in Daniel in the Light of a Translation Hypothesis." *Journal of Biblical Literature,* LVIII (1939), 349-54.

DANIEL

TEXT, EXEGESIS, AND EXPOSITION

The Book of Daniel.*—Some Christian preachers and teachers have been willing to surrender the apocalyptic books to the sects that profess to see in them a mechanical foretelling of history. In the popular mind, to take a text from Daniel or Revelation is to label oneself of the apocalyptic persuasion. Yet the books which have been favorites of those striving to set the dates of the Day of Judgment, and have been the source of so many futile and ridiculous attempts to interpret contemporary events, also contain insight and inspiration for all Christians.

It is a sad thing that, in a day when we have more information available about the Scriptures than ever before, we have so many Bible illiterates. The fault lies with those who know the facts but keep their information to themselves, as if it were dangerous or immoral. We who have found that the critical approach to the Bible makes it shine with increased brilliance and increases our faith in it, ought to invite others to make this same approach. For every one who is disturbed, there will be a hundred who will be grateful for establishing their faith on a firm foundation and expanding their religious horizons.

What the Book Is.—There are several ways in which one might introduce thoughtful people to Daniel. One could emphasize the two main points: What the book is not; and what the book is. Under the first it could be pointed out that the *date* of the book is most important, but *dates* used within the book are not. Once we have accepted the second century B.C. as the time of writing rather than the seventh century B.C., we have a book that is religiously significant. Then we are able to see how the author uses dates in the seventh century not as a historian, but as a writer desiring to give his story a setting. They are a literary device.

The book is not magical foretelling. It deals with a contemporary situation, which removes it from the realm of superstitious magic to the realm of faith. This means that Daniel is not an old writing now outgrown. For the idea of a me-

* Pp. 355-58 include the expositor's introduction. Text and Exegesis begin on p. 359. Editors.

chanical closed system of history makes the idea of freedom a mockery. But using an ancient story to illustrate a spiritual truth to one's contemporaries is another matter.

Turn to the other side and stress the positive value of the book. It lies primarily in the fact that Daniel has a message. Those who have spent their time and energy in vainly trying to figure out dates and magical numbers have neglected the heart of this writing. Daniel has something to say of moral and religious import. Like the prophets, he is proclaiming a faith. He is not talking primarily about signs which came to him and are unavailable to anyone else. He is not fundamentally in conflict with Jesus' word spoken much later: "Why doth this generation seek after a sign? verily I say unto you, There shall no sign be given unto this generation." (Mark 8:12.) There have been many who have misunderstood Daniel and twisted his message because they have not comprehended what he was trying to do.

The book is written for a time like ours. In the days when some believed in an evolutionary, optimistic creed, the apocalyptic books seemed foreign and hopelessly outgrown. The events of the twentieth century have made many understand why they were included in the canon. Days of testing and hammering are days of temptation. Then men wonder what it will matter if they should seek safety rather than risk their lives. Then we need a word to encourage us to hold steady. Daniel is a call to devotion. It is a challenge to faithfulness. It is an attempt to stop the falling away of God's people.

The fear of the future loomed large in the minds of the people to whom Daniel wrote. For the time being they were free, through the heroic efforts of their great leaders. But they were surrounded by mighty enemies, and the nightmare of tomorrow haunted their minds. The book counsels living a day at a time and trusting the future to God. The threat then was not atomic bombs, yet the power of big empires to crush Israel out of existence was real enough. God's word through Daniel to that day and to ours is one of faith and patience. Be confident, he is saying, and live nobly today.

Tomorrow is in the hands of a just and righteous God. He will not desert his people, and he will vindicate them against their enemies.

The Faith of Daniel.—Another introduction of a general nature could be built around the faith of Daniel. It is helpful if people can see that the biblical books are written by men who had made certain commitments of faith. Whether we are talking about one of the Gospels' portraits of Jesus or one of the historical books of the O.T., people need to understand that what a man believes colors his whole viewpoint. Daniel is written by a man who believed certain things about God.

For one thing, the writer assumes that God has a plan. In this the book is true to the great theme of Hebrew religion. Daniel uses ancient stories and visions as his media, but he uses them to say what the Bible is always saying: Life has a purpose. Men do not believe in a purpose for themselves for very long when they lose the sense of a purpose in the mind of God. It is remarkable that great ideas do not necessarily come from large or powerful peoples. The world thinks very little about most of the ancient empires of the past, but it cannot forget the small nation at the east end of the Mediterranean Sea, or Athens. And the thing which made Israel and Greece great far beyond their size and wealth was the vision of purposes in which they participated and of which they became a part. The vision of a divine purpose gave Daniel the basis for hope and an authority for his plea to have courage.

It is a world plan in the mind of God. No nation is left out, and all nations are to be judged. The hatred for the tyrant does not blind the author to the reality of moral values in the societies of the heathen. God is not a mere tribal deity vindicating his own people. There is the implication that Israel has a world mission.

It is a moral plan. The apocalyptic books visioned a power greater than armies and mighty empires. It was righteousness which at the end of the day should stand as power. Every act and every policy had to face the strict examination of God, and a terrible punishment awaited immoral power. Over against the pride of her enemies Israel put the retribution which would fall upon them from a holy God. The big battalions were not the decisive factors.

Daniel had faith in the kingdom of God. He thought it would come in the near future. But it was to be more than a purified earthly kingdom; Daniel approached the N.T. conception. He believed in a future, and he was sure that the righteous always have a tomorrow. He was doing for his people what some of the great leaders of the Renaissance did for their genera-

tion; i.e., he looked back into the past for his vision of the future. He is saying that, since certain things happened once long ago, we may believe that they will happen for us today and perhaps again tomorrow. The kingdom would be the gift of God. Not for Daniel was it a matter of human achievement. Humanity must do its part by being faithful, but the accomplishment was to be God's.

Absolute Loyalty.—There is at least one other great theme which the book of Daniel suggests, and this is especially relevant to our time. It is its insistence on absolute loyalty. We have been reluctant to talk about an absolute anything, and have more and more let the idea of the necessity of compromise color our attitudes. This is not new. Kierkegaard was aware of the same tendency in his time, and he warned how easy it is to let the absolutes of life be eaten away. We have seen after World War II how collaborators were treated when an enemy was driven out. Yet they were people who simply assumed it was best to get along with those in power rather than stubbornly refuse to yield. It was a general philosophy of the times, and we should not be too surprised that under the strain of danger not everybody proved to be heroic.

Until one has given his allegiance to God he is the victim of his own worst self. Daniel's appeal was to nothing less than loyalty to God himself. He was speaking to a people with a long heritage of teaching about an austere, jealous, holy God. It had proved in other times to be the only safety in the hour of danger. It was the only thing that could preserve them and maintain their culture. There is therefore no hesitation or compromise in Daniel's appeal. He goes directly to the heart of the matter. When God wills it, the man or nation who yields to his will finds power for the present and a glorious reward for the future.

This is the only way in which God deals with men. He will not adjust to our timid desires. There is a sense in which it is all or nothing when God speaks. As John Knox writes:

With a ring on my finger which would support a man and his family for a year I confront the poor man "at my door." I know what my duty ultimately is; my problem arises out of my unwillingness—or my inability, if you like—to do that duty. God says: . . . "Give to him that asketh thee, and from him that would borrow of thee turn not thou away" (Matthew 5:42) . . . . But I answer: "God, I cannot do that; thou seest that I cannot do that; and since I cannot, wilt thou not tell me what to do *short* of that?" But God does not again reply. He has nothing more to say.[1]

[1] H. P. Van Dusen, ed., *The Christian Answer* (New York: Charles Scribner's Sons, 1945), p. 168.

There is a story about a man who was given a physical examination by his doctor. It was discovered that he was in a serious condition. "Now the best thing you can do," he was warned, "is to give up drinking, smoking, and carousing." After a moment's thought the man asked, "What is the next best thing?" The writer of the book of Daniel was aware that "the next best thing" was useless. His people were facing a situation where it had to be an absolute loyalty to God or they were lost. It is the situation we face today.

As we develop Daniel's theme of God's demand for absolute loyalty, let us point out in the first place the worship of relativism. The worship of a comfortable reasonableness has blinded us to the true nature of our religion. H. G. Wells said of Jesus:

He was like some terrible moral huntsman digging mankind out of the snug burrows in which they had lived hitherto. In the white blaze of this kingdom of his there was to be no property, no privilege, no pride and precedence; no motive indeed and no reward but love. . . . For to take him seriously was to enter upon a strange and alarming life, to abandon habits, to control instincts and impulses, to essay an incredible happiness. . . .
Is it any wonder that to this day this Galilean is too much for our small hearts? [2]

In a lesser way Daniel was a moral huntsman digging his generation out of their smugness and fear.

The great religious word of our day has been "tolerance." We would rather be called immoral than be labeled intolerant. But most of what we have called tolerance is nothing more than indifference. The businessman who finds it easy to counsel tolerance in church matters does not find it so easy in economic matters, because they affect his profits. Nor does our vaunted spirit of tolerance seem to operate very well when our special privilege is being challenged. The easygoing attitude characteristic of so much of our religion is in reality a sign of our sickness, not of our progress.

This adjustment to evil, rather than standing out against it, is characteristic of our personal behavior. The worst thing that can happen, apparently, is to be thought different from the majority. The unforgivable social sin seems to be a sense of personal integrity. Whatever the crowd is doing or wants to do, we must do. Whatever constitutes the group's idea of a good time must be accepted by each member.

This is the pressure which careless social drinking puts upon people. The unanswerable argument for many a person is that "everyone is doing it." Even church members, who have been brought up in a tradition of total abstinence, throw their influence too readily on the side of cocktail parties. Sometimes they seek to justify it on other grounds, but usually they admit they are going along rather than embarrass their host or their friends.

In such an atmosphere as this the moral and political life of a people is never safe. For once the idea can be promoted that "everybody is doing it," then principles will be denied. This provides the perfect setting for the witch hunters and the demagogues. A society stands on the integrity of citizens who have wisdom enough to penetrate the disguise of bigotry, and then call it by name. But if our idea is to get along with whoever is talking the loudest and threatening the most, then we are as sand when it comes to building a democracy upon us.

Relativism splits men. A contemporary wrote of Andrew Carnegie:

There are two Andrew Carnegies. . . . There is the business man, ruthless, hard as his own pig-iron, who is the maker of millions, and there is the philanthropist, filled with the abstract love of humanity, who is the spender of millions. Neither has any dealings with the other. Each has an atmosphere and a hemisphere of his own. . . . There is no conscious conflict between the two. There is no conflict because they never meet.[3]

This has been altogether too characteristic of the kind of successful men our way of life has been producing. We keep our ethics in one narrow little area, while we deny them in another area, and we know it not.

It is easy to see how far we have gone along the road of relativism when we think of our Puritan fathers. Their narrow interpretation of duty and morality is often the subject of satire. We are not in sympathy with their strictness. But it made them great; and, in the meantime, without great principles which guided them, we move from crisis to crisis. It was against this soft, wavering spirit that Daniel spoke. He was on the side of the Puritans. Looking back on the crises of history, we know that men like the author of Daniel were right when they demanded loyalty to God rather than adjustment to the threats of men.

In the second place, we should note the failure of relativism. If this way of life had succeeded and made people content, there would be little point in speaking against it. Daniel would then be of historical interest only. But this way has not worked, either in terms of personal satisfaction or in creating the good society. To make a deal with the enemies of

[2] *The Outline of History* (New York: The Macmillan Co., 1926), I, 327.

[3] A. G. Gardiner, *The Pillars of Society* (New York: Dodd, Mead & Co., 1914), p. 91.

freedom is always a temptation. To save his people from yielding to this temptation Daniel wrote his book. It became a part of our Bible because it kept men on their feet in times of pressure.

We have had many illustrations of what happens to those who cannot see the issue and stand on the side of human dignity. It is probably true that many well-meaning people in Germany, when they became Nazis, did not consciously decide to do the unspeakable things which were done to the Jews. They may have resolved to go along with the party, but to draw the line at torture and persecution. But Nazism became a torrent that could not be controlled. The timid, harmless people were carried away as with a flood. Only those who from the beginning saw what was happening, and decided to be martyrs if necessary, were able to fight effectively against Nazism. The only men of any value to God are the men who have pledged to him an absolute devotion.

One can see much in the face of a man as the years pass by. Something happens to the features of the relativist: a slackness, a weakness, a futility seems to stamp itself on them. But the man who has stood unflinchingly for great principles shows an increasing firmness, a nobility and a majesty in his face as time goes by. A Jewish friend has devoted his life to championing every man who suffers from discrimination, regardless of race or station. No one ever doubted which side he would be on, and he has dedicated his legal talents and his time to the struggle for civil liberties. One cannot see him without thinking, "What a wonderful face." Yet he is not what Hollywood would call handsome. His features are not perfect and regular. But an absolute loyalty has made him great, and it has made him good.

In the third place, the book of Daniel says to us that God demands heroic obedience. It is an obedience that affects our whole life. It is not enough to be obedient for an hour one day a week, or with one part of our lives. He will be content with nothing less than our whole lives. E. Stanley Jones tells of a man speaking eloquently of the self-sacrifice of India's new leaders. Then he stole an electric-light bulb from a train.[4] It is too easy for us to expound the necessities of sacrifice and then steal what we want.

God's demand for obedience does not promise an immediate reward or an immediate safety. God's enemies make promises which he will not make. To betray him will give certain rewards now, but obedience to God seems to promise nothing but suffering and disgrace. We

[4] *Mahatma Gandhi* (New York and Nashville: Abingdon-Cokesbury Press, 1948), p. 131.

have tried desperately therefore to serve him without making it too difficult for ourselves. The modern heresies use the Christian vocabularies but leave out the Cross. The men who fall away are those who have no faith in the promises of God's spokesmen.

Yet, as the book of Daniel proclaims, the man who overcomes shall be glad for his decision. Though God seems to tarry, he will not delay forever. And to the man who has endured there shall be given a crown. Even in the midst of the difficulties there is a kind of joy which the worldling can never comprehend. It grows out of the consciousness of fulfilling one's best impulse and being aligned with the One who controls the future. A Napoleon of the business world was showing a group of visitors through his plant. He announced modestly: "We are a great happy family here. We never do anything until we have a unanimous vote." One of his associates was heard to murmur, "And heaven help the man who is not unanimous." God is not like that. He does not hold his anger forever, nor yet is he a soft, futile grandfather. The man who follows his own way of compromise will pay for it, and the man who is obedient to the heavenly vision will be exalted.

In the fourth and last place, Daniel emphasizes the importance of religious exercises and ritual to keep men on the right path. The book has been criticized for putting too much emphasis on this side of religion. Perhaps it does. Certainly it is a mistake to regard ritual as a substitute for righteousness. It is possible for a man to be ritually pure and ethically unclean. We want nothing of the pharisee who goes through the motions but has lost the spirit.

But we are in danger of underestimating the significance of religious exercises. This is particularly true of Protestants, and it has become one of our greatest weaknesses. In the name of being religious in the open air, there are many nominal Christians who would qualify better as sun-worshipers. In the name of being free, and superior to more regular attendants at church, we tend to neglect the exercises by which our spiritual life is kept strong and spiritual glow is maintained. The religious person who never goes near a church is like the man who professes to love music but never goes to a concert.

No one would wish to insist that church attendance invariably results in the production of saints. Unfortunately such is not the case. But there is something about church attendance and participation in church work which produces vital Christianity. The joining in the formal services produces habits which in turn hold men steady when they face the storm. Church attendance gives God a chance to help his chil-

1 In the third year of the reign of Jehoia-kim king of Judah came Nebuchadnez-zar king of Babylon unto Jerusalem, and besieged it.	1 In the third year of the reign of Jehoi'-akim king of Judah, Nebuchadnez'zar king of Babylon came to Jerusalem and

I. Six Stories of Daniel and His Friends (1:1–6:28)

The background of all six stories is the court at Babylon. Four of them are set in the reign of Nebuchadrezzar (chs. 1–4); one in the days of Belshazzar, who was governor of Babylon under Nabonidus, the last king of the Neo-Babylonian Empire (ch. 5); and one in the days of the Persian conqueror of Babylon, who is here called Darius the Mede (ch. 6). All six emphasize the point that Jewish captives rose to high positions in the heathen court, and all preach the same message of faithfulness to God and to the prescriptions of the law. This God is greater than any human potentate, and not only will he bestow wisdom on and highly reward those who serve him faithfully, at the same time confounding their enemies, but he will also make such people his instruments for bringing the heathen to acknowledge his sovereignty.

All the stories belong to the genre of Oriental court tales, but they are also in the hagiographical tradition, full of miracles and what to us are glaring improbabilities. All this, however, is but a literary device for picturing an ideal of Jewish piety. Such stories were meant not to teach their audience history, but to encourage religious people to maintain loyalty to their faith and to endure under trials. The story is merely the literary medium for the message. Others had used the medium of verse, in song or psalm, or the medium of the prophetic oracle, or narrative, or gnomic wisdom. This writer uses the story, and just as the writer who chose verse had to conform to the conventions of that medium, so this writer has to conform to the conventions of his form. Therefore it

dren. To hear the ancient words of the Scriptures read, to sing the great hymns, to join in prayer, to listen to the Word expounded, all combine to give men power for the testing of their faith. A psychologist implied that church-going is a good thing precisely because it is not pleasant. We would not go along with that, but we would agree with his other conclusion that churchmen come through difficult times better than other men.

Giving to something which we believe in has spiritual implications for our lives. Learning to love our religious heritage is best accomplished through participation in the church. There is a picture which those who have seen it cannot forget, a picture of two old Jews fleeing from a burning city, their eyes staring in horror. They have seen things too terrible to describe. But in their hands they carry the scrolls of the Torah, as if these were their most valuable possession. These they must save. The artist has understood truly the history of Judaism. It has been customs, holy observances, attendance at the synagogue, which have held together and made Israel stronger than its persecutors. Perhaps the book of Daniel knows something we have not learned. Perhaps when a people's life is in danger, it is their religious customs and habits which save them.

It is true that George Whitefield was a more eloquent preacher than John Wesley. Yet in terms of the lasting quality of their work there is no comparison. Wesley began a work that extended and grew after his death because he had given it certain organizational forms. He organized class meetings where people met regularly and went through certain routine procedures. They formed habits of self-analysis and confession. The inspiration of the movement's beginning did not pass away.

Protestantism cannot take the Roman Catholic position in regard to the church, viz., that the Roman Church is the one divinely appointed vehicle of salvation, nor can we believe in the automatic virtue of church attendance; we must never equate the church with the kingdom. But we shall do well to heed the wisdom of Daniel. Our religious observances cannot be neglected without harm coming to us and to our generation. In the hour of crisis we act in harmony with all our previous behavior. If Daniel at times goes too far in the direction of dependence on ritual righteousness, we have gone too far away from it.

1:1-21. *Faithfulness in Exile.*—There are verses and phrases in the book which contain in themselves great ideas. But there are times when it is wise to use a larger section for exposition. The early part of Daniel has a series of inspiring stories which represent units of moral teaching and are easily divided into important insights, unified by a common theme.

is important for the interpreter to distinguish carefully between what is message and what is merely framework, the *décor* of the literary form being used to convey the message.

In these stories the representation of the heathen court at Babylon is relatively favorable. The kings act in ways that are reprehensible and so suffer punishment at God's hand, but they are not pictured as intolerable oppressors of the Jews, or as monsters of iniquity. Also in the stories there is no expression of that intense hatred which is so marked in the second section of the book. For this reason some have thought that the stories were written considerably earlier than the visions and come from an age when the persecution of the Jews had not become acute.

On the other hand, there are so many little points indicative of a single author for the whole twelve chapters that we must conclude that the writer of the visions, living during the latter days of Antiochus Epiphanes, prefaced his visions by a series of stories which would lead up to them. For these he selected a number of tales of a type familiar to his audience, which pictured a situation in a far country in earlier days, but in which, as the story unfolded, the audience would immediately catch the relevance of their present situation under Antiochus. The figures of Nebuchadrezzar, Belshazzar, Darius, as they appear in these stories, are not meant to be representations of the oppressor Antiochus. They are meant to be themselves, but the story of what happened under these earlier rulers has a message relevant to Jews suffering under the tyranny of Antiochus.

It is possible that some form of each of these stories was already in circulation and was merely adapted by the writer for his book. Little inconsistencies in the representations, as well as the absence of Daniel from ch. 3, suggest that the basic stories once existed as independent units. Note also that chs. 2 and 4, and then chs. 3 and 6 (to which add Bel and the Dragon), are variations on the same motif. Yet ch. 5 looks back to ch. 4, and although ch. 2 deals only with Daniel it is conscious of the friends, so that though originally independent, the stories have been put together with some artistry to form a cycle whose common message is that of the importance of faithfulness to the Jewish religion.

A. Introduction of Daniel and His Friends to the Court (1:1-21)

This chapter is in Hebrew and is a general introduction to the stories given in Aramaic in chs. 2-6, and indeed to the whole book, since the visions of chs. 7-12 assume the presence of Daniel at court.

1. Prologue (1:1-7)

1:1. Part of the framework of stories of this genre is precise indication of place and date. Neither of these may be important for the actual message of the story but they give verisimilitude. Since they are but a literary device, strict historical accuracy

---

In ch. 1 Daniel and his friends have been carried away into a strange land. Life is always doing that to us, and men were never more aware of it than they are today. The stability of a way of life which our fathers assumed they could depend on has disappeared. The mood of our time is one of facing unknown, untried, and uncertain ways. We have been carried away by our science into a wonderful Oriental court, but one that is full of danger. The comparatively simple life of the last century now seems to us as home must have seemed to the Jews caught in the luxurious life of Babylon.

It has tragically come true that millions of our brethren are in physical exile. There has never

been a period when so many people wandered homeless and afraid, looking in vain for a nation to open its doors and give them refuge. The terrible sin of war is nowhere more apparent than in the plight of "displaced persons." Any man who has been for a time in a country where he had no friends and had great difficulty in understanding the language will know how to sympathize with the homeless millions of our day. We shall understand some of the deep thoughts of the O.T. only when we realize that it is the book of a people who knew what it was to be conquered and exiled.

Young people who go from the country and the small towns to the cities find themselves

in such particulars is not important, for they are there to provide a setting for the story, not to give historical information. In this case the date was probably already in the original story of which the writer is making use. Jehoiakim reigned from 608 to 597 B.C., so that the **third year** of his reign would be 606. Nebuchadrezzar did not become king until 605, i.e., in Jehoiakim's fourth year (Jer. 25:1), and it was not until some four years later that he subdued Jehoiakim, making him tributary for three years (II Kings 24:1), and still later in 597, after Jehoiakim's death, that he besieged Jerusalem (II Kings 24:10-15).

The date at the head of this chapter results from a combination of II Kings 24:1-2 with II Chr. 36:5-8. Jeremiah's references to the fourth and fifth years of Jehoiakim (25:1, 9 ff.; 36:9, 29) and his elegy in ch. 22 know nothing of this king having fallen into the hands of Nebuchadrezzar in the third year of his reign. We know from II Kings 24 that Jehoiakim did later become subject to Nebuchadrezzar for three years and then rebelled, bringing on himself attacks from surrounding peoples subject to the king of Babylon. After his death, however, when his son Jehoiachin was reigning, Nebuchadrezzar came and carried off both king and people. Yet there was a tradition of an attack on Jerusalem in the reign of Jehoiakim which we find recorded in II Chr. 36:6-7 and, apparently in another form, in Alexander Polyhistor. The date **in the third year of the**

---

exiled, even as did Daniel. To be thrown suddenly into the maelstrom of a big city is to be cut loose from safety and protection. There is no protection in a time like that except through character and faith. The young person with a memory of spiritual exercises cannot be as lost as the one without such memories. When we are cut adrift from home it is easy to do foolish things that will wreck us and store up tragedy ahead.

But the whole process of living is a continual going into strange countries. No wise parent ever tries to obstruct this process for his children. School is a strange country; marriage is an exile from the land of extreme individuality. There is hardly an experience which means growth that does not carry us away from the safe boundaries of the familiar into a place where the landmarks are not known. We are pilgrims on the face of the earth, as all our fathers were. Life is saying to us constantly, as God said to Abraham: "Get thee out of thy country, and from thy kindred, and from thy father's house, unto the land that I will show thee" (Gen. 12:1). But a religious faith is our protection in all these experiences of exile. Faith means being guided by eternal principles which cut deeper than our moods. The man whose court of last appeal is the way he happens to feel has no protection in exile, for he will often feel homesick and desperate. He will do the thing which tomorrow he will regret. There is no safety for the man who lacks loyalties more profound than the passing impulse. The only protection for Daniel and his friends must be a standard of life which they recognize is valid in Babylonia as well as in Judah.

The dietary laws of Judaism meant more to the Jews than they would to us. It was almost as bad as idolatry for an orthodox Jew to eat food that was not kosher. If this seems foolish to us, let us look behind the custom to its deeper implication. It was a sign of loyalty to God. Like so many things we do, it was a symbol of something profound and important. A Westerner made fun of a Chinese burial custom by asking an old Chinese gentleman when he thought the dead would come up to eat the food he left at the grave. The old man smiled and answered, "About the same time your dead come up to smell the flowers you have placed on the grave." Our lives are enriched by the impractical things we do which symbolize feelings and beliefs too deep to be stated in any other way than by symbols. The practical man who would have disregarded the dietary laws and adjusted himself to doing what was easiest would have suffered a spiritual loss in the process.

The body was something to respect, according to the Hebrew faith. It was a part of the heritage which made Paul write: "Know ye not that your body is the temple of the Holy Ghost which is in you, which ye have of God, and ye are not your own? For ye are bought with a price: therefore glorify God in your body" (I Cor. 6:19-20). Our religion is not willing to put that terrible barrier between the body and the spirit which was characteristic of so much Oriental thought. We shall not find in the Bible the pessimistic assumption that the only way to be spiritual is to despise the physical, neglect the body, and mortify the flesh. The Hebrew-Christian tradition is one of looking at the physical things as the creations of God. It means that we must see all life as a unity. It means that immorality and vice are wrong because they are the desecrating of a temple. We

reign of Jehoiakim was apparently reached by someone who was following the account in II Chronicles, but with an eye on II Kings 24 assumed that the three years mentioned were three years dating from the commencement of Jehoiakim's reign, and then made the further assumption that the "bands of Chaldeans" mentioned in Kings were a regular army under Nebuchadrezzar. A possible motive for dating the captivity as the third year of Jehoiakim is that it would provide a more exact fulfillment of the seventy years prophesied as the duration of the exile (Jer. 25:11 ff.; II Chr. 36:21).

The historical accuracy of this dating was of no particular importance to the writer, for dates are part of the *décor*, not statements of historical fact (cf. vss. 1, 5, 18 with 2:1).

Nebuchadnezzar: In his own inscriptions he is named Nabū-kudurri-uṣur, which is given correctly as Nebuchadrezzar in Jeremiah and Ezekiel. The later form with *n* for *r* has crept into II Kings and occasionally into Jeremiah, and is usual in such writings as Ezra, Chronicles, and Esther. It is the only form found in Daniel, and is unknown outside the Jewish tradition and writings dependent on it.

Nebuchadrezzar succeeded his father Nabopolassar in 605 B.C. and was the most important of the kings of the Neo-Babylonian Empire. Though his name appears in these stories, many believe that the figure covered by his name is really that of Nabonidus (Nabū-nā'id), the last of the Neo-Babylonian kings and father of that Belshazzar who was governor of Babylon at the time it was conquered by the Persians under Cyrus. Many of the details of these stories do not fit the historical Nebuchadrezzar but do fit admirably with what we know of Nabonidus. It was Nabonidus, not Nebuchadrezzar, who had the reputation for appointing foreigners to high positions in the realm. The command to slaughter the wise men would fit well with Nabonidus' quarrel with the priesthood. The strange dreams that demanded interpretation resemble those which Nabonidus records in his inscriptions. The account of the colossal image would reflect

---

cannot make our religion something entirely otherworldly, for it is rooted in a point of view which affects every human behavior pattern.

Religious faith is something which demands risk. Daniel took his courage in his hands when he insisted that he should be allowed to follow the commands of his faith. One of England's leading theologians has commented that vast numbers of people have ceased to believe in the relevance of Christianity because in their experience it no longer made any heroic demands. The very nature of faith demands courage, and the kind of belief which is compromised at the first sign of danger is not really belief. It is mere words; for the thing we really believe, we live. It might be a healthy though disturbing experience to ask ourselves when was the last time we risked anything for our religion. Too many of us have not even been willing to inconvenience ourselves slightly for the sake of bearing testimony for our faith.

It is usually true that men are at their best under extreme testing, but they easily fall away under a myriad of little annoyances which destroy their courage. The temptation must have come to Daniel to say that this was not very important, and he would wait until a more significant issue was brought before him. But when he has to face death later on, he has been prepared for that by being faithful in the less

important decisions. A fallen tree on Long's Peak, Colo., was found to be over four centuries old. It was a seedling when Columbus landed at San Salvador. It had been struck fourteen times by lightning. For over four hundred years it had withstood avalanches, tempests, and ice. It fell because it could not withstand an attack of beetles, each one so small it could be crushed between the fingers of a man's hand. It is a parable. Men are destroyed by the little things too. Begin with the realization that a man's faith has to be lived in every circumstance and must be defended against encroachment, even when it seems to be a harmless compromise.

Finally it may be pointed out that the test of a man's faith is always that it makes a difference. The average man is not so much opposed to religion as he is unaware of its relevance. He sees churchmen who are no different from anyone else. He deals with men who claim to be religious men, and he is not aware of any quality in them which he does not find in his godless friends. He comes to the conclusion that if people enjoy church work and like to participate in worship services, that is all very well. But he cannot see that he will lose anything if he declines. Religion that does not make a noticeable difference or impart some unique style to living cannot be convincing to others.

2 And the Lord gave Jehoiakim king of Judah into his hand, with part of the vessels of the house of God: which he carried into the land of Shinar to the house of his god; and he brought the vessels into the treasure house of his god.

besieged it. 2 And the Lord gave Jehoi'akim king of Judah into his hand, with some of the vessels of the house of God; and he brought them to the land of Shinar, to the house of his god, and placed the vessels in

---

the affair of the statue of Sin in the temple Ehulḫul, which Nabonidus rebuilt. The king's madness would reflect the demon possession of Nabonidus referred to in the Persian Verse Account (see Sidney Smith, tr., *Babylonian Historical Texts* [London: Methuen & Co., 1924]), and his departure to live among desert animals might be a reference to the years that Nabonidus spent at Taima in the Arabian Desert.

2. The Lord: Adonai, though some MSS read Yahweh. Possibly the original reading was the more usual Elohim. **Gave . . . into his hand:** Cf. Judg. 3:10; 20:28; II Kings 21:14; Jer. 20:4; 21:7. The expression implies that Nebuchadrezzar took complete possession of the city and its ruler. **Some,** not all, the utensils of the temple were taken away. The **vessels of the house of God** were the vessels used in the temple service, which, like those used in many of the pagan temples in the ancient Near East, were commonly made of precious metals, and so were prize booty for a conqueror. II Kings 24:12-16 relates how at the sack of the city under Johoiachin in 597 the sacred vessels were taken (cf. II Chr. 36:10), but some were left or those taken were replaced, for at the second sack of the city under Zedekiah in 586, sacred vessels were again carried away (II Kings 25:13-17; cf. II Chr. 36:18; Jer. 27:19-20).

The **house of God:** So again in 5:3. In the books of Kings the temple is normally referred to as "the house of Yahweh," but in later writers this becomes "the house of Elohim," which revives an earlier name (cf. Judg. 17:5; 18:31, where the shrine at Shiloh is called the house of Elohim). In Daniel, Elohim with the article is used for the true God of Israel as opposed to the false gods of the heathen. The author, like most late writers in the O.T., tends to avoid the use of the name Yahweh.

Brought them: Grammatically the pronoun **them** ought to refer to the vessels, but since their disposition is presently explained, **them** must refer to the prisoners. They would not normally be taken to a temple, but **the house of his god** may refer to the land of Babylon. In ancient days each land was regarded as the special house of its

---

Daniel is not afraid to say: "Try your servants for ten days, letting us have vegetables to eat, and water to drink; then compare our appearance with the appearance of the youths who eat of the king's delicacies, and deal with your servants in accordance with what you see" (vss. 12-14 Amer. Trans.). "Try," "compare," and "see" are the words men would like to hear when we are preaching our way of life. We are all pragmatists in that we are never convinced so completely as when we can see that something has obviously changed a situation. The steward needed no further argument when **at the end of ten days it was seen that they were better in appearance and fatter in flesh than all the youths who ate the king's rich food** (vs. 15). Remember Jesus' test: "Ye shall know them by their fruits. Do men gather grapes of thorns, or figs of thistles? Even so every good tree bringeth forth good fruit; but a corrupt tree bringeth forth evil fruit. A good tree cannot bring forth evil fruit, neither can a corrupt tree bring

forth good fruit. Every tree that bringeth not forth good fruit is hewn down, and cast into the fire. Wherefore by their fruits ye shall know them" (Matt. 7:16-20).

The story says that not only were Daniel and his friends better to look at, but they were also more intelligent and more discerning. It is true that the man who has some firm place to stand has the advantage over the man who must depend upon the situation of the moment for his decision. The power of discrimination is created by a unified view of living. One has to have some framework through which he views the contemporary scene. We need a "frame of reference." The man with no faith or no philosophy of life is not as interesting a companion as the man who has come to certain definite conclusions about truth and values. The conversations to be remembered with greatest pleasure are the ones with men whose lives have been devoted to purposes which have commanded all their minds and energies. Faith

3 ¶ And the king spake unto Ashpenaz the master of his eunuchs, that he should bring *certain* of the children of Israel, and of the king's seed, and of the princes;

the treasury of his god. 3 Then the king commanded Ash'penaz, his chief eunuch, to bring some of the people of Israel, both of the royal family and of the nobility,

deity, so that in Hos. 8:1; 9:15 Palestine is the "house of Yahweh," and thus, as Assyria was the "house of Assur," Babylonia would be the "house" of Nebuchadrezzar's god. This seems to be how the passage was understood by the LXX.

Land of Shinar is an archaism. It is the name for Babylonia used in Gen. 10:10; 11:2; 14:9; Isa. 11:11; Zech. 5:11. Perhaps the choice of this name was because in Genesis it is the land of the archrebel Nimrod and of the Tower of Babel, and so would symbolize the powers in rebellion against God.

His god: Lit., "his gods," but though plural in form it is singular in meaning. From 4:8 we learn that Nebuchadrezzar's god was Bel, i.e., Marduk, the city-god of Babylon and at that time head of the pantheon (cf. Isa. 46:1; Jer. 50:2; 51:44; Bel and the Dragon).

The treasury of his god: Part of a temple complex in the ancient world was the treasury in which was stored the wealth of the temple as well as supplies of cultic implements and vessels for the temple services. It was standard practice for conquering armies to plunder such treasuries, and the obvious place in which to store precious things plundered from other temples was the treasury of the conqueror's own temple. It was also an honor to a deity to have the furnishings of other gods assembled at his shrine. I Kings 7:51 mentions the treasury of the Jerusalem temple, and the cuneiform inscriptions frequently mention the *bīt niṣirti* in connection with temples in Mesopotamia and elsewhere. II Chr. 36:7 refers to the event mentioned here, and in Ezra 1:7; 5:14 there is reference to the restoration to the Jews of such vessels as Nebuchadrezzar had taken to Babylon.

3. From among the captive youths the king would choose pages for his service. It was customary for a ruler to have as pages in his court youths from the various states subject to him, not only to have them as hostages but to train them to be loyal vassals. The custom continued into Hellenistic and Roman times and in a modified form survived as late as the Turkish sultan's court at Constantinople.

Ashpenaz: LXX, Ἀβιεσδρί. No satisfactory explanation of the name has yet been suggested. It may be a corrupt form of some Mesopotamian or Iranian name, or it may have been coined to supply a name for the **eunuch**.

His chief eunuch: Lit., **master of his eunuchs**. The title is ambiguous. Originally it meant the domestic official who was in charge of the eunuchs around the monarch's person and also was overseer of the royal harem. In later times it was used to designate a high official at the court, whose title came from the fact that he was nominal head of the corps of eunuchs, but who had numerous other duties and need not himself be a eunuch. If it is used here in the narrower sense of keeper of the royal harem, then the man was probably himself a eunuch. It was part of the duties of such an official to train

stimulates our personalities and brings out our best qualities.

Strength of life is not possible without testings. Arnold J. Toynbee has made much of the effect that blows, defeats, persecutions, and exiles have had on the development of nations and individuals. Great civilizations have not grown out of easy environments or out of luxurious conditions. The historical examples of this are numerous and striking. It is true of men. It is amazing how many writers have become great under the most adverse circum-

stances. Henry James did his best work under the irritating conditions of American life, which he hated. England was too smooth and pleasant to inspire his creative faculties.

If the purpose of life is to make us great rather than comfortable, we shall do well not to rebel against the adverse circumstances under which we must live and work. It may be that only thus can we enter our heritage.

3-4. *Then the King Gave Orders.*—These young foreigners were trained to understand the culture of Babylon, while also they were

4 Children in whom *was* no blemish, but well-favored, and skilful in all wisdom, and cunning in knowledge, and understanding science, and such as *had* ability in them to stand in the king's palace, and whom they might teach the learning and the tongue of the Chaldeans.

4 youths without blemish, handsome and skilful in all wisdom, endowed with knowledge, understanding learning, and competent to serve in the king's palace, and to teach them the letters and language of the

---

the youths who were to serve as royal pages (see George Rawlinson, *The Five Great Monarchies of the Ancient Eastern World* (2nd ed.; New York: Dodd Mead & Co., 1870-71) I, 496-98; III, 221-23). Potiphar in the Joseph story was a eunuch. The youths chosen for duty as pages were sometimes made eunuchs, and on the ground that this verse points to the fulfillment of the prophecy in Isa. 39:7, earlier exegetes, both Jewish and Christian, held that Daniel and his friends were so treated. This, however, does not necessarily follow from the writer's statement here.

Some have thought that the king's command involved three classes, viz., some Israelites, some of the numerous children of the royal family, and some of the children of the Babylonian nobility. Both the LXX and Theod. understood the passage thus, but as the story is concerned with the Jewish captives the command probably refers solely to them, the youths being chosen from the Israelitish royal family and from the sons of the nobility who had been brought as captives. Vss. 2, 6 both speak of **Judah,** but the word Israelite is used here in the late sense it has in the Chronicler to cover all Jews of whatever tribal affiliation. We are not to think that it here indicates specifically that non-Judahites were included among those introduced at the court.

Royal family: Lit., "seed royal," which would cover families connected with the royal house as well as the king's children (see II Kings 25:25; Jer. 41:1).

The nobility: *Partemîm* is a word used only in Daniel and Esther (cf. Esth. 1:3; 6:9). Symm. and Peshitta translate "Parthians," making a guess at the meaning of an unfamiliar word. It is a title of Iranian origin (cf. Old Persian *martiyā fratamā,* "foremost men," used in the Behistun inscriptions).

4. The king would naturally want the finest children chosen, so the instruction is that they are to be free from any physical defect, handsome in appearance, and of superior intelligence. **Blemish:** That this means physical defect is clear from the use of the word in Lev. 21:17. **Handsome:** "Good to look at," as in the description of Rebekah in Gen. 24:16; 26:7, whence the KJV **well-favored.** They were to be "intelligent in all wisdom, those who possess knowledge, those who understand exact learning." Behrmann notes that it is a stylistic peculiarity of this writer to pile up synonyms so that any endeavor to make subtle distinctions between these expressions or have them refer to different types of intellectual ability would be pointless.

To serve: Lit., to stand. So at the end of vss. 5, 19 **to stand before the king.** It is an expression commonly used in connection with court service. (In I Sam. 16:21 the youthful David is sent to stand before Saul; in I Kings 12.6 Rehoboam consults the elder courtiers who had stood before Solomon; cf. I Kings 10:8.) Also in Dan. 7:10 the angelic attendants stand before the divine presence. The writer means his audience to understand that these youths are to be trained as members of the corps of court pages called *sōmatophylakēs* in I Esdras 3:4.

Palace: *Hêkhal* in the O.T. is generally a temple, but, like the Akkadian *ēkallu,* it can be used for a royal palace. **To teach them:** If they were to serve effectively, it was necessary for these foreign youths to learn the Babylonian language, and to learn it correctly so as to be familiar with all the elegancies of phraseology customary in court ceremonial. The court language under Nebuchadrezzar was that form of Akkadian known as Neo-Babylonian. We gather from Jer. 5:15 that the Babylonian language was unintelligible to Jews, so the audience would quite understand that this was something that would have to be acquired at the court.

5 And the king appointed them a daily provision of the king's meat, and of the wine which he drank: so nourishing them three years, that at the end thereof they might stand before the king.

Chalde'ans. 5 The king assigned them a daily portion of the rich food which the king ate, and of the wine which he drank. They were to be educated for three years, and at the end of that time they were to

---

Some think that by the **letters and language of the Chaldeans** the writer means not just the Babylonian language of the day and the cuneiform characters in which it was written, but the highly specialized lore of the Chaldean wise men. This is unlikely, but in any case the purpose of the writer is to indicate that these youths were to perfect themselves in the Babylonian wisdom of that day, much as Moses was instructed in all the wisdom of the Egyptians (Acts 7:22).

Letters: Lit., "book," whence Aq. βιβλίον, but here and in the parallel vs. 17 the word seems to mean, as in Isa. 29:11-12, "writing" in the sense of "literature"; so the LXX and Theod. render γράμματα.

Chaldeans (*Kasdîm;* Χαλδαῖοι) : The name derives from the *Kaldu,* a people who begin to appear in southern Babylonia as early as 1100 B.C., and who are mentioned frequently in the inscriptions from 880 onward. In 761 B.C. under Merodach Baladan they achieved a temporary conquest of Babylon, and in 625 under Nebuchadrezzar's father Nabopolassar they succeeded in establishing a Chaldean dynasty which lasted until the Persian conquest. The people continued to maintain their identity long after the dynasty had fallen, for Strabo (*Geography* XVI. 1. 6) records a group of them still living in a district along the Persian Gulf called by their name. The primary significance of the word is thus ethnic and in Job 1:17 and in the prophets (Isa. 13:19; Jer. 21:9; Ezek. 23:14; Hab. 1:6) the word refers to this ethnic group. So in Gen. 11:28 the city of Ur is called "Ur of the Kasdim." Chaldean is used in Daniel in this ethnic sense in 5:30; 9:1; and perhaps 3:8.

Its secondary sense is that of a name for a class of professional wise men. It has this meaning here and in 2:2, 4-5, 10; 4:7 (M.T. 4:4) ; 5:7, 11; perhaps in 3:8; but nowhere else in the O.T., and there is no evidence of its use in this sense in the inscriptions. It is used as a technical term in Herodotus (*History* I. 181, 183) ; in Strabo it refers to a class of Babylonian wise men particularly interested in astronomy. So Diodorus Siculus (II. 29-31) knows of Chaldeans as a caste of priestly magicians and soothsayers who preserved a kind of traditional lore, while Pliny (*Natural History* VI. 30) mentions three cities he had heard of as still famous for Chaldean lore. The well-known Chaldean Oracles derive their name from this sense of the word. Such a secondary meaning, of course, would only arise when the Chaldean Empire was a thing of the past.

Those who think the word means "wise men" refer to vs. 20, where the king finds that these youths at the end of their training are much superior to the wise men of his court—which suggests that their training had been in professional lore—and to the fact that in ch. 2 we find them in virtue of their court education considered as belonging to the wise men and so under the same condemnation.

5. Royal pages live on the royal bounty, so they are assigned a daily ration of **food** and drink from the royal table. Athenaeus (*Deipnosophists* IV. 26) mentions that the attendants of the Persian king all received provision from the royal table, and such a daily portion for captive royalty at Babylon is mentioned in Jer. 52:34. The word used for the food ration, *pathbagh,* five times in this chapter and in 11:26, is peculiar to Daniel in the O.T. The Masoretes treat it as though it consisted of two Hebrew words,

---

held as vassals. But it was a two-way passage. If they were influenced by the court, they too had a tremendous influence on their captors. We have seen in our time the tendency after war to take over our enemies' gods of militarism,

racial hatred, and racial pride. The master of the slave is bound to him and shares his destiny.

5. *Three Years' Training.*—Here is a fine text on religious education. Ancient peoples seemed to give more heed to the importance of educa-

6 Now among these were of the children of Judah, Daniel, Hananiah, Mishael, and Azariah:

7 Unto whom the prince of the eunuchs gave names: for he gave unto Daniel *the name* of Belteshazzar; and to Hananiah, of

stand before the king. 6 Among these were Daniel, Hanani'ah, Mish'a-el, and Azari'ah of the tribe of Judah. 7 And the chief of the eunuchs gave them names: Daniel he called Belteshaz'zar, Hanani'ah he called Shad-

---

path, "a portion," and *bagh*, "food." This is folk etymology, for the word is Iranian; from Iranian it was borrowed into Syriac to mean the kind of dainty food found at the tables of princes, and into Greek where it is used of a special repast said to have been served to Persian kings. Montgomery thinks the mention of royal **wine** also indicates that the writer was thinking of Persian custom (cf. Esth. 1:7).

The length of their training is set at **three years.** No such three-year period in the Babylonian system is known, but it is reminiscent of the three periods into which Greek writers say a youth's education was divided among the Persians (see Plato *Alcibiades* I. 121; Xenophon *Cyropaedia* I. 2).

Educated: The word is that used in Isa. 1:2; II Kings 10:6, and corresponds rather with our "bringing up" than with the older translation "nourish." When their training was complete they were to **stand before the king.** This is the point to which the story has been leading. Not only were these Jewish youths to live in a heathen land, but they were to live at the court in the very center of ungodliness, where unclean food such as the heathen eat was to be their daily ration from the king's own table, where they would be set to learn heathenish wisdom, given heathen names, and to crown all, be made attendants on the king who in his person summed up all that this heathenism meant. Having made this point, the writer is ready to name his heroes and complete his prologue.

6-7. All the youths are said to be from **the tribe of Judah,** i.e., from the tribe which had come to be preferred among the twelve. Rabbinical tradition, following Josephus (*Antiquities* X. 10. 1), assumes that they all were of the royal family of Zedekiah. This is only a surmise, but it has been followed by some Christian commentators. That they were four may have no special significance, or it may be a stylistic link with the other fours in the book—four kingdoms, four metals, four winds, four beasts, etc.—and be a symbolic number which Hubert Junker (*Untersuchungen über literarische und exegetische Probleme des Buches Daniel* [Bonn: Peter Hanstein, 1932], p. 18) thinks is schematic in the O.T. Since all four names are found among those mentioned in the book of Nehemiah, Behrmann thinks that the writer, setting his story in the period of the Exile, chose names known to have been used at that time.

Daniel, "El has judged," occurs as the name of one of David's sons (I Chr. 3:1), and of a Levite who was a contemporary of Ezra (Ezra 8:2; Neh. 10:6). In Ezek. 14:14, 20; 28:3 it occurs as the name of a sage of the patriarchal period. The name occurs also in the old Semitic inscriptions, and appears as an angel name in Enoch 69:2. It is possible that an ancient legend of Danel (see Charles Virolleaud, *La légende phénicienne de Danel* [Paris: P. Geuthner, 1936]; Bonaventura Mariani, *Danel, il Patriarca sapiente* [Rome: Pontificium Athenaeum Antonianum, 1945]) may have influenced the writer as he drew the picture of the hero of his book.

Hananiah, "Yah has been gracious," is a name that occurs frequently in the O.T. and was the name of a contemporary of Ezra (Neh. 10:23). **Mishael,** "Who is what El is?" also is the name of a cousin of Moses (Exod. 6:22; Lev. 10:4), and of a contemporary

---

tion in the field of religion. What kind of training should a child have if he is to stand before God?

7. New Names.—The ancient custom was to give those who were commencing a new station

in life a new name. Saul became Paul when he changed from a persecutor to a follower. It was a way of emphasizing the change from the old way to the new status. It was an affirmation that a man could change, and it is thoroughly in

Shadrach; and to Mishael, of Meshach; and to Azariah, of Abed-nego. 8 ¶ But Daniel purposed in his heart that he would not defile himself with the portion of the king's meat, nor with the wine which he drank: therefore he requested of the prince of the eunuchs that he might not defile himself.	rach, Mish'a-el he called Meshach, and Azari'ah he called Abed'nego. 8 But Daniel resolved that he would not defile himself with the king's rich food, or with the wine which he drank; therefore he asked the chief of the eunuchs to allow him

of Ezra (Neh. 8:4). **Azariah,** "Yah has helped," is a fairly common name in the O.T., and occurs as the name of a contemporary of Ezra (Neh. 10:2).

The chief eunuch—who here bears the title *sar,* **prince,** whereas in vs. 3 he was *rabh,* "great," the two titles being apparently synonymous—gave them new names. The motive was partly to have familiar names by which to address them, the same motive which today leads Europeans living in Oriental countries to change the names of house servants to something more pronounceable than the native names. Partly, however, it was from a sense of the auspiciousness of a new name with which to commence a new career. It was not uncommon in the ancient world for persons commencing life in a new position to be given new names. When Joseph entered Pharaoh's service, he was given a new name (Gen. 41:45). When Saul of Tarsus entered Christian service, his name was changed to Paul (Acts 13:9). Hadassah bore the name Esther at the Persian court (Esth. 2:7). When Eliakim was raised to the throne, his suzerain changed his name to Jehoiakim (II Kings 23:34), as Nebuchadrezzar changed that of Mattaniah to Zedekiah (II Kings 24:17). Curt Kuhl (*Die drei Männer im Feuer* [Giessen: A. Töpelmann, 1930], p. 24) gives instances of the same practice from secular sources.

It has been pointed out that here the change of name in each instance served to obliterate the name of the Jewish God, whereas each of the new names would seem to be associated with the name of a heathen deity. The writer may have been making a point of this, and perhaps is hitting at the readiness with which the Hellenizers were changing good Jewish names to foreign names.

Belteshazzar is the Akkadian *Balāṭsu-uṣur,* "may he protect his life." The Masoretes have pointed the word so as to suggest that it contains the name *Bēl* and thus agrees with 4:8 (M.T. 4:5), which states that this name contains the name of Nebuchadrezzar's god. **Shadrach, Meshach,** and **Abednego** are all corrupted forms. The latter is almost certainly corrupted from some such name as Abdi-nabu, "servant of Nebo," and the others seem to have some connection with the name Marduk, though they have not yet been satisfactorily explained.

2. The Trial of the Faithful (1:8-16)

8. The friends decide to risk the king's wrath rather than risk defilement from nonkosher food. **Daniel resolved:** Lit., "laid upon his heart," i.e., **purposed** to himself (see Isa. 57:1, 11; 42:25; 47:7; Mal. 2:2). **Defile himself:** Expose himself to ceremonial uncleanness. This was not religious asceticism. The youths do not refuse the king's food because it is dainty but because it might contain something by the eating of which they would, according to Jewish law, become ceremonially defiled. There would be no danger of this if they kept to a vegetarian diet (for the dietary regulation see Lev. 20:24-26).

There is ample evidence that pious Jews generally made an effort to carry out the dietary regulations when living in a non-Jewish environment (Judith 12:1-4; Tob. 1:10-11; IV Macc. 5:3, 14, 27; Josephus *Life* 3; Jubilees 22:16). When Antiochus Epiphanes was endeavoring to press his program of Hellenizing the Jews, many came to feel that loyalty to these dietary regulations was of supreme importance, and I Macc. 1:62-63 even suggests that the eating of unlawful food seemed as serious a crime as idolatry (see also I Macc. 1:47-48; II Macc. 6:18 ff.; 7:1).

9 Now God had brought Daniel into favor and tender love with the prince of the eunuchs.

10 And the prince of the eunuchs said unto Daniel, I fear my lord the king, who hath appointed your meat and your drink: for why should he see your faces worse liking than the children which *are* of your sort? then shall ye make *me* endanger my head to the king.

11 Then said Daniel to Melzar, whom the prince of the eunuchs had set over Daniel, Hananiah, Mishael, and Azariah,

12 Prove thy servants, I beseech thee, ten days; and let them give us pulse to eat, and water to drink.

13 Then let our countenances be looked upon before thee, and the countenance of the children that eat of the portion of the king's meat: and as thou seest, deal with thy servants.

not to defile himself. **9** And God gave Daniel favor and compassion in the sight of the chief of the eunuchs; **10** and the chief of the eunuchs said to Daniel, "I fear lest my lord the king, who appointed your food and your drink, should see that you were in poorer condition than the youths who are of your own age. So you would endanger my head with the king." **11** Then Daniel said to the steward whom the chief of the eunuchs had appointed over Daniel, Hana-ni'ah, Mish'a-el, and Azari'ah; **12** "Test your servants for ten days; let us be given vegetables to eat and water to drink. **13** Then let our appearance and the appearance of the youths who eat the king's rich food be observed by you, and according to what you see deal with your serv-

---

9. Montgomery notes how Jewish story loves to represent its heroes as on good terms with officialdom, e.g., Joseph in Egypt, Esther at the court of Ahasuerus, Ezra at that of Artaxerxes. So here "God set Daniel for kindness and compassion before" the chief of the eunuchs.

10. Their preceptor feared that poorer fare such as they proposed would result in unhealthiness which, as visible in their faces, would bring on him the monarch's displeasure. Since this official was responsible for carrying out the king's orders, he could expect punishment should anything go wrong by reason of his failure to carry out instructions. **Poorer condition:** Lit., "your faces sorrowful looking" (see Matt. 6:16, where a dejected look is associated with fasting). In vs. 15 it is again their faces which are noted, this time as better looking than those of the others. **Of your own age:** Lit., "as your generation." *Gîl* is a late word. **Endanger my head:** Lit., "make guilty my head." He does not fear decapitation, as many of the older interpreters assumed, but knows the fault would be visited on him, his **head** standing for his person (see I Chr. 10:9).

11-16. Having failed to influence the chief, Daniel turns to a minor official and begs a ten-day trial. A minor official might risk some deviation from the royal command without fear of discovery. This works out so successfully that the youths are able to continue their restricted diet. **Steward:** The word *melçar* occurs only here in the O.T. and has been variously interpreted. Josephus and the Greek translators took it as a personal name, and this has its modern supporters. The article, however, suggests that it is a title, not a name. Some have thought of the Persian title "Master of the Cellar," but it is perhaps best explained from the Semitic root *nçr*, which would give the meaning "guard" or "warden."

The **ten days** may be only a round number (cf. vs. 20 and 7:7, along with Gen. 24:55; 31:7; Amos 5:3; Hag. 2:16; Zech. 8:23). Bentzen notes, however, that ten days is a favorite number in descriptions of the trials of saints. **Vegetables:** The Hebrew words

---

harmony with Christianity's belief in conversion and renewal. It is also a warning against an indiscriminate use of labels. Men tend to live up to their names, or down to them. Remember the prophet's word: "But now thus saith the

LORD that created thee, O Jacob, and he that formed thee, O Israel: Fear not, for I have redeemed thee; I have called thee by thy name; thou art mine" (Isa. 43:1). The Fourth Gospel was aware of the change that is wrought by a

14 So he consented to them in this matter, and proved them ten days.

15 And at the end of ten days their countenances appeared fairer and fatter in flesh than all the children which did eat the portion of the king's meat.

16 Thus Melzar took away the portion of their meat, and the wine that they should drink; and gave them pulse.

17 ¶ As for these four children, God gave them knowledge and skill in all learning and wisdom: and Daniel had understanding in all visions and dreams.

18 Now at the end of the days that the king had said he should bring them in, then

ants." 14 So he hearkened to them in this matter, and tested them for ten days. 15 At the end of ten days it was seen that they were better in appearance and fatter in flesh than all the youths who ate the king's rich food. 16 So the steward took away their rich food and the wine they were to drink, and gave them vegetables.

17 As for these four youths, God gave them learning and skill in all letters and wisdom; and Daniel had understanding in all visions and dreams. 18 At the end of the time, when the king had commanded that

---

in vss. 12, 16 are not the same, but apparently mean the same thing. Some take "according as thou seest" to mean "as thou seest us," but others "as thou seest fit."

At the end of the ten days not only were their faces brighter but their bodies fatter than those of the other youths. The **fatter in flesh** refers to them as a whole, not to their faces. It is the phrase used of the kine in Pharaoh's dream (Gen. 41:2, 18). The point is not that a diet of vegetables and water was in itself healthier and more beneficial than food from the royal table, but that in spite of such poor fare which might have been expected to leave them thin and ill favored, God honored their loyalty by bringing about an unexpected result. So in Test. Joseph 3:4, Joseph in spite of his fasting looked to the Egyptians like one who had been living well, for those who fast for God's sake receive beauty as a reward.

Took away does not necessarily imply, as is often assumed, that as a result of Daniel's experiment the steward made all the other youth in training adopt the same diet. It may mean only that the four friends were allowed to continue their vegetarian and water diet for the three years.

3. Epilogue (1:17-21)

17. There is no suggestion here that the vegetarian diet made the youths mentally more alert than those who ate meat and drank wine. To physical perfections God added mental perfections. These were a gift from God as a reward for faithfulness, in accord with the teaching of such passages as Ps. 37; Ezek. 18; 33. All four mastered the learning of the Babylonian court, as Joseph and Moses had mastered that of Egypt, but to Daniel was given the extra endowment of skill in the interpretation of visions and dreams. Such skill was highly prized in the ancient world. It constituted an important part of the Chaldean wisdom (Diodorus Siculus II. 29. 3), as it had of the Sumerians long before, and as it continues to among the Muslim Arabs. In Egypt, Joseph was given similar skill in dream interpretation.

The mention of Daniel's special gift is doubtless to prepare the audience for the skill he is to exhibit in this matter in ch. 2. Daniel is notably differentiated from his companions in the matter of special endowment and more favored treatment, yet he never receives the power of prophecy. The writer lived in an age when it was recognized that prophecy had ceased, and the sages of Israel were engaged in studying and interpreting the messages of the prophets who had appeared in former times (cf. 9:2; Ecclus. 39:1). Thus the highest praise the writer could bestow upon his hero was to recognize him as the recipient of and interpreter of visions.

18-20. At the end of the three years of training all the youths were brought in for personal inspection by the king. In inspecting them he discovered that not only were Daniel and his friends the best of the group, but were distinguished in learning, so that after they took up their duties in attendance on him there was no matter in which they

the prince of the eunuchs brought them in before Nebuchadnezzar.

19 And the king communed with them; and among them all was found none like Daniel, Hananiah, Mishael, and Azariah: therefore stood they before the king.

20 And in all matters of wisdom *and* understanding, that the king inquired of them, he found them ten times better than all the magicians *and* astrologers that *were* in all his realm.

21 And Daniel continued *even* unto the first year of king Cyrus.

they should be brought in, the chief of the eunuchs brought them in before Nebuchad-nez'zar. 19 And the king spoke with them, and among them all none was found like Daniel, Hanani'ah, Mish'a-el, and Azari'ah; therefore they stood before the king. 20 And in every matter of wisdom and understanding concerning which the king inquired of them, he found them ten times better than all the magicians and enchanters that were in all his kingdom. 21 And Daniel continued until the first year of King Cyrus.

---

did not show more ability than the professional wise men at his court. This is the conventional story ending we often find later in such stories as the Pahlavi tale of Chosroes and his page Chusharzuk.

Inquired of them: It was the custom of kings in the ancient world to consult the celestial powers through the skills of their professional wise men before undertaking any matter of importance. The meaning here is thus probably such professional consultation in which the king found that the answers the youths gave on matters under consultation were better than those of any of the wise men at his court.

Ten times better: Lit., "ten hands than" (cf. "hand" used in this sense in Gen. 43:34).

Magicians: *Ḥarṭummîm,* a word which recurs in chs. 2; 4; and 5 and is used for magicians in Gen. 41 and Exod. 7–9. It is probably an Egyptian word meaning a person skilled in the use of hieroglyphs, and thence in the derived sense "magician." It is used here merely as a familiar name for a particular class of wise men (cf. 4:9 [M.T. 4:6]; 5:11).

Enchanters: *'Ashshāphîm,* a word found only in Daniel in the O.T. It is the Akkadian *ašipu,* "exorcist" (see Morris Jastrow, Jr., *Die Religion Babyloniens und Assyriens* [Giessen: A. Töpelmann, 1905-12], I, 286). The writer is using the word here without reference to its original meaning and merely as a familiar name for a class of wise men. The book throughout reflects a consciousness of the importance that wise men had in an Oriental court.

21. And Daniel continued: He continued at Babylon till the first year of **Cyrus** (539/538 B.C.), some seventy years after he had been carried there captive. Some have thought the verse means that he died in that year, which would be in contradiction with 10:1, though such a contradiction in a writing of this kind is not serious. Others suggest that some words have dropped from the text, perhaps "at the gate of the king" as in 2:49, meaning that he served the court throughout the Neo-Babylonian period, through the assumed Median period, and into the Persian period, when he had a change of office. Others think the meaning is that he saw the return of the exiles who went back to Palestine in the first year of Cyrus (II Chr. 36:22-23). The writer, however, seems to have no interest in the return, which he mentions but incidentally in 9:25. Indeed, it is remarkable how little his book has to say about the great and momentous events of

---

new name: "Henceforth I call you not servants; for the servant knoweth not what his lord doeth: but I have called you friends" (John 15:15).

21. *And Daniel Continued.*—The stories which follow will show us how this was no mere flash of courage. It was simply an illustration of the underlying character of Daniel. This business of being religious is a matter of continuance. One thinks of Jesus' word: "No

man, having put his hand to the plow, and looking back, is fit for the kingdom of God" (Luke 9:62). Or there is Paul's affirmation: "Brethren, I count not myself to have apprehended: but this one thing I do, forgetting those things which are behind, and reaching forth unto those things which are before, I press toward the mark for the prize of the high calling of God in Christ Jesus" (Phil. 3:13-14).

2 And in the second year of the reign of Nebuchadnezzar, Nebuchadnezzar dreamed dreams, wherewith his spirit was troubled, and his sleep brake from him.

2 In the second year of the reign of Nebuchadnez′zar, Nebuchadnez′zar had dreams; and his spirit was troubled, and

---

the days of Nebuchadrezzar and Cyrus. Events which must have been of the greatest interest to every Jew he passes over as of no moment. This in such contrast with the detailed information on contemporary events given by Jeremiah and Ezekiel, and with the detailed information he himself provides for the period of the Diadochi, that the only explanation is that he was himself living under the Diadochi and merely using the setting of the Babylonian court as a literary device.

Some think that vss. 20-21 are a dislocation and really belong after 2:48a. The inconsistencies are not entirely removed by this change, however, and it must be remembered that to a writer of apocalyptic many little things which to us seem inconsistencies would have appeared unimportant.

Cyrus: The Old Persian *Kūruš,* which appears in Akkadian as *Ku-ra-aš,* and in Greek as Κῦρος.

B. NEBUCHADREZZAR'S DREAM (2:1-49)

The parallels with the Joseph story in Gen. 41 are obvious, and the correspondences in phraseology striking, so that while this is in no sense an imitation of the Joseph story, the writer certainly had that in mind. Perhaps he also had in mind the tales of Nabonidus' opposition to the priests of Marduk and his abnormal interest in dreams and their interpretation.

The lessons this chapter would teach are: (a) The worthlessness of all human wisdom in comparison with that which is conferred by God. (b) A theory of the develop-

---

2:1-49. _Two Kinds of Wisdom._—The story of the king's dream, his unreasonable demand for a description of it and an interpretation, the ability of Daniel to describe and interpret the dream, and the king's rewarding of Daniel, constitute a story in which are implied certain great truths that are as vital and significant for the twentieth century as they were for the second century B.C.

For one thing, Daniel is pointing out the limitations of human wisdom. **The magicians, the enchanters, the sorcerers, and the Chaldeans** represent the sophisticates of any generation. They were the ones who were supposed to have plumbed the depths of human wisdom. They were the experts. But as always happens sooner or later, there arise problems with which the experts cannot deal. We are faced with mysteries and with longings to know things human wisdom cannot tell us. Our frustration at this lack of knowledge causes us to do mad things. Much of the blind fanaticism of men is caused by their sense of frustration. In a desperate attempt to find what we seek, we try to use coercion and threats, as if we could force our limited philosophies to tell us what we want to know. There is a curious parallel between what Nebuchadnezzar did and what Hitler did. In the latter days of the Third Reich, the *Führer* seemed to lose his sense of judgment. Men

whose pride has made them think they know all that is important face destruction because of the failure of their science.

One of the characteristics of our time is a growing disillusionment with our knowledge. When we compare the optimism of the first part of the twentieth century with the pessimism of today, we are aware of how much we were the victims of oversimplification. At one time everything seemed definable. We needed to increase production, raise our physical standards of living, make goods available, and presto! the good life would be a reality. There is a vast number of people who have not even yet seen through this false picture. They still assume that to hurry faster on the path we are following will take us where we want to go. Our education will save us if we make the system bigger.

In the day when we have increased our power a million times we have not increased our spiritual controls. Automobile manufacturers were wiser. They knew they could not build cars with greatly increased speed and power until they learned how to increase the braking power as well. After brakes became almost as big as the wheels themselves, they seemed to be at the end of the possibility until someone had the revolutionary idea of putting brakes on all four wheels. But in the moral realm we

ment of history according to which a series of world ages leads up to the founding of the eternal kingdom of God, which is the consummation of history. (c) How God humbles the proudest kings and makes them acknowledge him. This chapter has the previous one in mind. There it was said that none of the court wise men could compare with Daniel and his friends; this chapter proves it. There the emphasis was on faithfulness to those elements of religion which concern private living; here is the complementary emphasis on faithfulness to religion in one's public duties. There the relevance to contemporary life was a message to encourage faithfulness to the law by the strict observance of its prescriptions; here it is to encourage the people to hold fast the national hope of a coming kingdom of God, since they are living under the last of those human empires which pass away, and are very near the coming of God's kingdom which will never pass away.

The kernel of the chapter is vss. 31-45, the fall of the four world empires before the kingdom of God, all the rest being framework; cf. ch. 7, where the four empires appear again under the symbolism of beasts. There have been many attempts to identify the four empires, all of which are amply discussed by H. H. Rowley in *Darius the Mede*

---

have not even put our best efforts forth in developing controls. The fear of our time is the nightmare of unlimited might and limited character. The "Chaldeans" are all good enough when we are dealing with matters within the limits of their knowledge. But when we are facing matters beyond our sciences, then we need to find a man who has access to the Most High.

Human wisdom has a tendency to miss the essential things. We are too much impressed with our cleverness and our spectacular accomplishments. We are far advanced when it comes to the development of means, but we are still in the jungle in terms of goals. We are gods in power but apes in nature. We dismiss with a nod the religious insights of the saints. We bow before the man with a test tube. Yet the test tube, and all that it stands for, is our destruction without the more profound wisdom of the saint, which comes from God.

Soon or late we must face the essential questions of life. The king had to know about his vision and the future. We have to know about our own nature and our destiny. The essential thing is not that we should be wise about atoms, but wise about the moral law. Life is not to be by-passed forever. We may quiet the real questions which demand answers by being busy with secondary things. But at last we are cornered, and then we have to face matters stranger and more decisive than anything dreamed of in our philosophies.

This sense of values is always a gift of God. That is why plain men so often have that sense, and intelligent, gifted men lack it. There is always needed the judgment of people who live close to the unchanging, simple principles of life. The sophisticates will despise these folk, and in the name of freedom throw aside their precepts. But disaster awaits the genera-

tion that puts first things last. We must have some understanding of the way things are. We have to realize that we cannot play fast and loose with ultimate realities. We are in need of being guided by the humble who have not tried to manipulate life into serving them, but have sat at the feet of the One who tells them how they may find life.

The wisdom for living is a gift of God, says Daniel. It is more important that a man should be devout than that he should be clever. We may not put as much confidence in divining the meaning of dreams as he did, but his understanding that when human ability fails divine guidance is forthcoming for the righteous is eternally valid. One of the great contributions of Israel to the world was her understanding of the relationship between wisdom and God. It is summed up in an oft-quoted verse: "The fear of the LORD is the beginning of wisdom" (Ps. 111:10) .

Second, the story implies that God has a plan beyond history. The great religions usually put God entirely outside human affairs and historical processes, or else they make him a victim of the world and confined within it. It was one of the greatest of the Hebrew contributions to understand the concern of God in ordinary affairs, and yet to see him uncaptured by the historical processes. The idea of history divided up into certain world ages is no longer convincing to most scholars. But the underlying assumptions back of this particular theory are true to the Christian understanding of history.

Christianity is the only great religion which takes history seriously. To many faiths history is nothing more than an embarrassment. Such religious experience would escape from the contamination of ordinary affairs, and think of its god as removed from historical processes. But for the O.T., God was at work in history, and

and the Four World Empires in the Book of Daniel (Cardiff: University of Wales Press Board, 1935). The only satisfactory theory is that they represent the Babylonian, Median, Persian, and Macedonian-Greek empires. Behind the chapter lies an ancient theory of world ages, a theory which appears in a variety of forms in the literature of the Orient. One form was the cyclic theory, according to which each cycle was given a good send-off by the Divine and so begins with a golden age, but it gets progressively worse until the Divine has to intervene and bring that cycle to a close in some awful cataclysm, and then start off a new cycle with a new golden age. The notion that there were four stages in each cycle doubtless derives from the fact that there are four seasons in a normal year between the flourishing beauty of spring and the deadness of winter, which precedes another spring. The ancient Hindus knew that each "day of Brahma" fell into four *kalpas,* each successively more degenerate than its predecessor. The Buddhist doctrine of world ages is not appreciably different, and the Zoroastrian doctrine in the Bundahish is of four world periods of three thousand years each. In Hesiod's *Works and Days* (109-201) they are symbolized by metals—gold, silver, brass, and iron (cf. Ovid *Metamorphoses* I. 89-150). The four world powers of this chapter thus fit into a well-known scheme of world history, which makes the division more or less conventional, the fact that

the prophets found in him the clue to the interpretation of historical events. Daniel is not truly a prophet, because when he wrote it was assumed that prophecy had ceased. Nevertheless his historical assumptions are colored by prophetic insights.

The belief in God's plan meant purpose in life and significance in human striving. There was no endless-cycle theory, and there was no attempt to escape from the wheel of experience. All life meant something because it was being directed and there was to be a consummation of history. The development of the idea of personal immortality was never a substitute for the doctrine of God's purpose in history. It was not assumed that a plan meant the end of human freedom. Far from it. It was an encouragement to each man to know that his striving was not in vain.

God is the Lord of history. Daniel is saying that "this is our Father's world." This is the trumpet call to each man, and it saves us from whining self-pity. George Thomas wrote a book in which he told something of his life and his point of view. Son of a London dustman, and crippled by a progressive muscular atrophy, he wrote:

I have not found life a great adventure, but mostly an unbearable trial, and the only thing I know for certain is that I have to go on. I have often thought of giving up the struggle, but as long as I can do anything at all, I must do it. And so it comes about that I enjoy most things, even the fight! [5]

Such an attitude makes one ashamed of his own complaining and proud to be a brother of such a man. This kind of living is produced by the

[5] *My Mind a Kingdom* (New York: E. P. Dutton & Co., 1938), p. 253.

experience that tells us God is in this thing too. Because it means something, we have to go on and do our duty. If life meant nothing one way or the other, we could never feel obligated to play our part.

In the third place, Daniel is saying that God humbles the proud. There runs through the whole book this emphasis on God's control of human affairs and on the relatively short-lived triumph of the proud. The king is in the position of power, but it is the captive Daniel who is in control of the king. The book is telling of the limitations of physical might and the foolishness of those who take pride in force. This unredeemed pride, Daniel seems to be saying, can go only so far. When it seems to be strongest, it is really weakest.

The Jews needed that word when this book was written. Their victory had been a matter of sheer heroism and desperation. Yet the future was anything but secure. Now when the defeated pride of their powerful enemies reasserted itself, what chance would they have? The answer is one that is born out of the faith of Daniel in God. His way is the way of humility, and he uses the weak things to confound the mighty. Many years later this thought was phrased by Paul: "Because the foolishness of God is wiser than men; and the weakness of God is stronger than men" (I Cor. 1:25).

We need that lesson in our time. It is a strange and disheartening fact that we who can see pride in our enemies cannot see it in ourselves. We had no difficulty in recognizing the pride of Hitler or Tojo. But when the United States decides to settle international problems on a unilateral basis, we think that is different. The recalcitrance of others may be apparent to us, but we have no ability to see that quality in ourselves. As a matter of experience, no

there are four powers being more important to the artistic structure than to agreement with actual history; i.e., four is a symbolic rather than a historical number (see Junker, *Untersuchungen*, pp. 9, 18) .

The particular form of the four-empire theory in this chapter seems to derive from a conception of history current at the writer's time, according to which the Assyrian Empire had been inherited by the Medes, and the Median Empire by the Persians. When Alexander conquered Darius III, he added a fourth to the series. The policy of Hellenization pursued by Alexander and his successors so disturbed some groups in Oriental lands that there grew up a fierce longing for the rise of a fifth Oriental empire which would overthrow the Greeks and stem the tide of Hellenization. (J. S. Swain, "The Theory of the Four Monarchies Opposition Under the Roman Empire," *Classical Philology*, XXXV [1940], 1-21, suggested that this form of the theory was current in Persia in Achaemenid days, and H. L. Ginsberg, *Studies in Daniel* [New York: Jewish Theological Seminary of America, 1948], p. 5, follows this view.) In any case, what the author of Daniel has done is to substitute the Neo-Babylonian Empire for the Assyrian, and for the fifth empire, the national hope of a coming kingdom of God. This leads him into one confusion, in that while the Median Empire did succeed the Assyrian it did not succeed the Neo-Babylonian, so that in this book a place has to be given to the Median Empire (hence Darius the Mede) , between the fall of the last Neo-Babylonian king and the reign of Cyrus the Persian, whereas according to the inscriptions Cyrus succeeded immediately the last Babylonian king, and there is no such historical person as Darius the Mede.

1. Prologue (2:1-13)

2:1. The story is dated **in the second year** of Nebuchadrezzar. Since the time of Josephus great ingenuity has been exercised to explain how Daniel could have been

nation without a vital sense of God's judgment can escape the sin of pride. For only as we hold all our actions under his divine scrutiny can we have eyes to see our fatal weakness. The need for repentance seems to be apparent to only a few. How easy it will be for a nation with as much power as we have to take our place with all the empires of the past which have been brought down into the dust by their pride!

It is a good thing for each man to remember that God does not send understanding to the proud. There is something which rises up as a barrier when a man puts himself above his brothers and his God. It is well that this should be remembered by every man who is successful and has been put into a position of power. Such a man should recall Jesus' admonition: "Unto whomsoever much is given, of him shall be much required: and to whom men have committed much, of him will they ask the more" (Luke 12:48) .

One night on a railroad ferry the crowd was pushing forward to get off the boat as it pulled into the slip at Hoboken. One man was slouched in a corner in a drunken sleep, but no one paid any attention to him, though several glanced at him curiously and disgustedly. Then one aged man went over and shook the man awake. "Hoboken!" he shouted in his ear. The people

turned and recognized the man who had done the kindly deed as Thomas A. Edison. It was a sign of his greatness that he was not too proud to help a sleeping drunk.

Finally, this chapter suggests that only those of pure lives have visions of God. Jesus said: "Blessed are the pure in heart: for they shall see God" (Matt. 5:8) . There are many people who would like to have the vision of God, but they will not pay anything for it. Now and again they have a vague longing for something which the saint seems to possess. Sometimes in the hour of terrible stress they cry out for light and strength. Then when nothing much seems to happen, they conclude that all this religious talk is just dreaming. It never seems to enter their minds that God's entrance into the human heart must always wait for an open door. They seem to be unaware that a revelation is dependent not only upon the giver, but also upon the receiver.

The same man who knows that if he is to comprehend mathematics he must study seems to be ignorant that the spiritual life demands preparation also. We spend time in learning the laws of science, but we assume that the moral law and the spiritual law ought to require no study. The world is full of Christians who know more about the operation of their

2 Then the king commanded to call the magicians, and the astrologers, and the sorcerers, and the Chaldeans, for to show the king his dreams. So they came and stood before the king.

his sleep left him. 2 Then the king commanded that the magicians, the enchanters, the sorcerers, and the Chalde′ans be summoned, to tell the king his dreams. So they

---

active in an official capacity in the second year of the king when ch. 1 had stated that it was not till after three years of training in that monarch's court that he was introduced to Nebuchadrezzar. The precise dating, however, is merely a literary device which belongs to the framework of the story and the inconsistency which strikes us would have meant nothing to the writer or his contemporaries.

Had dreams: Lit., **dreamed dreams.** The importance of dreams was widely recognized in the ancient world. Pharaoh's dream in the Joseph story, Abimelech's dream in Gen. 20:3, the Midianite soldier's dream in Judg. 7:13-15, or Paul's dream of the man from Macedonia, can be illustrated by numerous parallels from Mesopotamian, Egyptian, Iranian, Indian, Greek, and Latin literature. For Mesopotamia in particular Jastrow (*op. cit.*, II, 954 ff.) has gathered examples from the time of Gudea in the twenty-fourth century B.C. down to Nabonidus, the last Neo-Babylonian king.

His spirit was troubled: So in vs. 3. The same word is used in Gen. 41:8 of Pharaoh being likewise troubled by dreams. In Ps. 77:4 the psalmist is so troubled and agitated that he cannot speak. In Judg. 13:25 the same verb is used of the spirit of Yahweh "moving" the youthful Samson.

"His sleep was finished for him": The same verb is used in 8:27 for Daniel being "overcome." **Sleep** here may possibly mean dream. The dream troubled him, yet when he awoke he could not recall it. The usual interpretation, however, is that the disturbing dream awakened him and he could not sleep again.

2. Consequently he summoned the wise men whose business it was to deal with such supernatural matters as perplexing dreams. Four groups of wise men are mentioned

---

automobile than they do of the operation of the law of God's love. Of such as these are the ones who want a sign. Like the king, they call for an expert to tell them what they want to know. But some things are not available to anything except moral and spiritual purity.

We shall be wrong if we minimize the part that physical purity plays in this ability to see God. The body has its effect on the spirit, and while poets may have exaggerated it, still the body helps the soul even as the soul helps the body. The abuse of the physical equipment bestowed upon us by God is a moral matter. The nervously-exhausted, stimulant-soaked man is no fit receiver for the spirit of God. That is why we have what we call "a social gospel." It means that, as Christians, we are concerned with the physical condition and environment of each man. The gospel's word is like that of a poor Englishman who said: "What's the use of belonging to an empire on which the sun never sets, if one has to live in an alley on which the sun never rises?" Because we honor the body as the temple of the Holy Spirit, we are concerned about the physical affairs of all men.

To be a fit receiver for the vision of spiritual realities, a certain austerity of life is demanded.

The luxury of the court or of wealth is not conducive to spiritual training. The custom of fasting, connected with certain religious festivals and holy days, is based upon this understanding. It is a good thing to be physically strong, but it is a sad thing when our bodies master us and appetites become determinative in all our decisions. Daniel saw the vision and comprehended it, and Daniel also refused to eat of the king's food.

All of this will take care of itself if we are dedicated to the highest. The kind of life that sees no farther than eating and drinking will have no sense of the eternal breaking into the temporal order. It is written in the nature of things that our bodies will serve us best when they are dedicated to something beyond the pleasure they can afford us. First of all, let us decide what goals are worthy of us. If to know God and hear him speak is ultimate, then everything fits into its proper place. If we are thereby denied some things which our contemporaries value highly, still we shall receive the treasures of heaven.

2:1. A Troubled Spirit.—Although he was the king, he was a mortal man with intimations of things which power could not satisfy. How

3 And the king said unto them, I have
dreamed a dream, and my spirit was
troubled to know the dream.

4 Then spake the Chaldeans to the king
in Syriac, O king, live for ever: tell thy
servants the dream, and we will show the
interpretation.

came in and stood before the king. 3 And
the king said to them, "I had a dream, and
my spirit is troubled to know the dream."

4 Then the Chalde'ans said to the king,[a]
"O king, live for ever! Tell your servants
the dream, and we will show the interpreta-

[a] Heb adds *in Aramaic,* indicating that the text from this
point to the end of chapter 7 is in Aramaic

---

here. **Magicians** and **enchanters** are the same as in 1:20, but now we meet the **sorcerers,**
mekhashshephim, i.e., those who mutter charms or incantations. The word is used in
Exod. 7:11. It is of Mesopotamian origin, the *kesheph* of Isa. 47:9, 12 and the *kashshaph*
of Jer. 27:9 being equivalents of the Akkadian *kišpu* and *kaššapu.* **Chaldeans** is used
here in its technical meaning for a caste of wise men.

The enumeration of these four groups is probably intended to mean that the
whole corps of wise men was summoned. It would be a mistake to attempt to find some
special significance in the names and the order in which they are mentioned, for examination of the passages in which these various classes are mentioned shows that the writer
uses the names vaguely. That different classes are mentioned may show that tradition
still survived that there had been various classes of priestly diviners in ancient Babylon,
but the writer's use of the names shows that he was no more conscious of their technical
significance than we are that "necromancer" technically means "a diviner by corpses."
Behrmann reminds us that it is the style of this writer to make lists (cf. the list of
officials in 3:2-3; of musical instruments in 3:4-5; of garments in 3:21).

It may seem an inconsistency that the king should summon the whole corps of
wise men when he already knew that he had at the court these Jewish youths who were
ten times more skillful in these matters than the others. It is a convention of this
literary form, however, that the man with God-given wisdom should appear only when
those with man's wisdom have proved themselves incompetent. So in spite of 1:20,
there must be a summoning of the wise men and a demonstration of the futility of
human wisdom.

4. The **Chaldeans** answered. This does not mean that they alone answered while the
other groups were silent. Here the writer is using the word Chaldean to mean the whole
corps of wise men, as in vss. 5, 10, and as he uses "magicians" to cover all the groups in
4:9. To this writer the titles were interchangeable. The expression **in Aramaic** of the M.T.
is a gloss introductory to the Aramaic portion which begins with the next word, and does
not mean that the language of the wise men in Babylon was Aramaic.

O king, live for ever! So in 3:9; 5:10; 6:6, 21; cf. I Kings 1:31; Neh. 2:3. It corresponds
to *šarru lū dār* which, as a form of greeting, was in use among the Assyrians and continued
in one form or another down to Sassanian times. **Interpretation:** *Pishrā',* from a verb
whose primary significance seems to refer to the disentangling of knotted yarn. Its
cognate is used in the inscriptions for the unriddling of dreams. The wise men make
the reasonable request that the king give them the data of the dream imagery so that they
may consult their books and work out the interpretation. Oneiromancy was an elaborate
science among the ancients, and portions of ancient dream books in cuneiform still

---

many times we find that successful men have
troubled spirits. Against fundamental human
longings and needs, there is no defense. At last
we come back to the realization that we are
made for God, and he troubles us until we let
him find us.

4. Modern "Chaldeans."—Our first reaction
to this incident is that it belongs to a superstitious past that is now ended. How naïve to

think so. Fortunetelling is big business today.
Around every city are "the Chaldeans," who for
a price will reveal the future. Every bookstand
is full of magazines purporting to tell about tomorrow on the basis of a horoscope. Do not
think that no one buys such things. In the most
scientific age the world has known, these occult
mysteries flourish, though every intelligent man
knows that it is magical nonsense. But we are

5 The king answered and said to the Chaldeans, The thing is gone from me: if ye will not make known unto me the dream, with the interpretation thereof, ye shall be cut in pieces, and your houses shall be made a dunghill.

6 But if ye show the dream, and the interpretation thereof, ye shall receive of me gifts and rewards and great honor: therefore show me the dream, and the interpretation thereof.

7 They answered again and said, Let the king tell his servants the dream, and we will show the interpretation of it.

tion." 5 The king answered the Chalde'ans, "The word from me is sure: if you do not make known to me the dream and its interpretation, you shall be torn limb from limb, and your houses shall be laid in ruins. 6 But if you show the dream and its interpretation, you shall receive from me gifts and rewards and great honor. Therefore show me the dream and its interpretation." 7 They answered a second time, "Let the king tell his servants the dream, and we

---

survive, giving detailed instructions as to how various elements in a dream were to be interpreted (see S. H. Langdon, "A Babylonian Tablet on the Interpretation of Dreams," *Museum Journal,* VII [1917], 116-22).

5-6. The king resolves to test his wise men. **Sure:** '*Azdā*' is an Iranian word; cf. the Old Persian *azdā,* "known," "certain" (R. G. Kent, *Old Persian* [New Haven: American Oriental Society, 1950], p. 173). It occurs in the Aramaic papyri. Some, however, think it means **gone,** from the Aramaic verb '*azadh,* "to go forth."

It may be that the king had really forgotten the dream and demanded that the wise men recall the details for him and give the interpretation. It is generally taken, however, to be a testing of the wise men. It was a simple matter to look up some dream books, but if they could tell him what he had dreamed, then he would know that they really had some occult powers and he could place some confidence in their interpretation. Bevan mentions a parallel which tells how an ancient king of Yemen had done this same thing with his courtiers.

Should they fail, their punishment would be not mere dismissal, but they would be dismembered and their houses destroyed (so in 3:29). Such a penalty involving destruction of person and property was nothing uncommon at Oriental courts (cf. II Kings 10:27; Ezra 6:11; II Macc. 1:16). On the other hand, it is a stylistic matter in these stories of court life to represent a ruler as going to extremes in visiting his wrath on those with whom he is displeased (cf. 3:11; 6:24). The phrase for dismemberment is "ye shall be made limbs," *haddām,* being derived from the Iranian word meaning "piece," "portion," **limb,** "member" (on dismemberment as a punishment see Josephus *Antiquities* XV. 8. 4). **Laid in ruins:** The older translations had **be made a dunghill,** i.e., become nothing more than a common privy, a form of disgrace which can be illustrated in the Orient from ancient to modern times. In later Jewish Aramaic the verb נול has the meaning "to defile," "to disgrace," but here perhaps it is the cognate of the Akkadian *nabālu,* "to destroy."

On the other hand, a successful performance of their duties would be recognized by the granting of honors. It is stylistic with this writer to pile up synonyms—**gifts, rewards, honor.** *Nebhizbāh,* "reward" (again in 5:17), is possibly a Persian word.

7-9. The wise men again ask for information on which they may base their interpretation, but the king accuses them of trying to temporize.

---

frightened, and we turn to anyone who has nerve enough to promise us information. It does not work, however, and like the king of Babylon we listen and are not comforted.

6. What Do We Want?—We need more than an answer to the question of how to get what we want. We need someone to tell us what we

want. There is no value in building a philosophy until we have defined the nature of man. The king had some vague notion that he needed something more profound than the Chaldeans could furnish. In our time we pay rewards to men who can tell us how to get what our modern philosophy has assumed we want. But the

8 The king answered and said, I know of certainty that ye would gain the time, because ye see the thing is gone from me.

9 But if ye will not make known unto me the dream, *there is but* one decree for you: for ye have prepared lying and corrupt words to speak before me, till the time be changed: therefore tell me the dream, and I shall know that ye can show me the interpretation thereof.

10 ¶ The Chaldeans answered before the king, and said, There is not a man upon the earth that can show the king's matter: therefore *there is* no king, lord, nor ruler, *that* asked such things at any magician, or astrologer, or Chaldean.

11 And *it is* a rare thing that the king requireth, and there is none other that can show it before the king, except the gods, whose dwelling is not with flesh.

12 For this cause the king was angry and very furious, and commanded to destroy all the wise *men* of Babylon.

will show its interpretation." **8** The king answered, "I know with certainty that you are trying to gain time, because you see that the word from me is sure **9** that if you do not make the dream known to me, there is but one sentence for you. You have agreed to speak lying and corrupt words before me till the times change. Therefore tell me the dream, and I shall know that you can show me its interpretation." **10** The Chalde'ans answered the king, "There is not a man on earth who can meet the king's demand; for no great and powerful king has asked such a thing of any magician or enchanter or Chalde'an. **11** The thing that the king asks is difficult, and none can show it to the king except the gods, whose dwelling is not with flesh."

12 Because of this the king was angry and very furious, and commanded that all

---

To gain time: Lit., "to buy time." The apostle's words in Eph. 5:16; Col. 4:5 are probably taken from the LXX of this passage. The king suggests they are thinking that, given a little more time, the monarch's attention may be distracted by something else. Time is something precious they would buy.

One sentence for you: Lit., "your decree is one." It is the same word as in vs. 13, derived from the Old Persian *data,* "a judicial sentence." If they do not satisfy the king, judgment on them is inevitable. "For a lying and corrupt word have ye concerted to say before me": The expression is one of courtly language, for it is a matter of respect to speak **before** the king, not to the king.

10-11. Now the wise men protest that the king is being unreasonable and is asking an unheard-of thing, expecting human beings to know what only the gods could know. The point the writer is making is that they are confessing that their wisdom is human and limited, whereas what will be made available to Daniel will be superhuman and not under limitations.

No great and powerful king: Some would translate **no king, lord, nor ruler,** as though three different classes were being mentioned. It is possible that this is a reminiscence of the Assyrian title "great kings," which survived into the Persian period. **Difficult.** Lit., "weighty." **Except the gods:** The form is plural and may be meant as such, but possibly it is meant to be taken as God in the singular. The LXX has ἄγγελος, which is a possible interpretation of the word. The probabilities are that the writer thought of these men as polytheists who believed in numerous gods inhabiting celestial places, where they could know many things about which men could not know.

12-13. Their reply enrages the king, who orders the destruction of the whole corps of wise men, a corps which, according to 1:20, includes Daniel and his friends.

---

tragedy is that after we get those things we are still empty. We ask for someone to tell us what the human dream is, and what it means. There is a parallel between the king of Babylon and the kings of success. In both cases they learn soon or late that a man of God is what they

seek. We become like the Highlander who walked miles to see a minister. When he asked why he had to see this particular man, he replied, "He knows God. He can help me."

11. *A Difficult Question.*—All important questions are difficult. Like the Chaldeans, we urge

13 And the decree went forth that the wise *men* should be slain; and they sought Daniel and his fellows to be slain.

14 ¶ Then Daniel answered with counsel and wisdom to Arioch the captain of the king's guard, which was gone forth to slay the wise *men* of Babylon:

the wise men of Babylon be destroyed. 13 So the decree went forth that the wise men were to be slain, and they sought Daniel and his companions, to slay them. 14 Then Daniel replied with prudence and discretion to Ar'i-och, the captain of the king's guard, who had gone out to slay the wise

---

Wise men: The word occurs eleven times in Daniel as a general term for the court sages, and twice (vs. 27; 5:15) as a name for one class of such. In the ancient Near East these priestly diviners, soothsayers, etc., formed a kind of caste, so the audience would have understood perfectly how the king was determined to get rid of the whole body of them. **Decree:** The same word was used for judicial sentence in vs. 9.

2. DANIEL THE INTERPRETER (2:14-45)

a) THE KING'S DECREE AND ITS CONSEQUENCES (2:14-19)

Daniel now appears as the ideal sage. He goes first to the officer appointed to execute the decree to get direct information, and then to the king to beg an opportunity to save the reputation of his caste. When this is granted he summons his friends to prayer, in response to which God reveals the matter to him. Obviously Daniel and his friends were not there when the sages were first summoned. No special reason for this absence need be sought. It is a literary device to heighten the effectiveness of the story. A real difficulty lies in the unceremonious way in which Daniel enters to the king, for no position of extraordinary favor would permit of such a thing in an Oriental court. Perhaps we are to understand that an interview had been arranged or perhaps, in the light of vss. 25-26, that Daniel sent to ask for a chance without actually going before the king.

Some would see significance in the statement that the secret was made known to Daniel not in a dream but in a vision, a higher form of spiritual experience than a dream, to show that a saint of God is on a higher plane than a pagan, even though that pagan is a king. **Dream** and **vision,** however, are used in this book in a way that suggests that to the writer they are synonymous. In vs. 28 Daniel refers to the king's dream as a vision (cf. Isa. 29:7).

14. The carrying out of the sentence was entrusted to the **captain of the king's guard.** This title is used in II Kings 25:8 (cf. Jer. 39:9; 52:12 ff.) of a Babylonian official, and in Gen. 37:36 (cf. 39:1 ff.) of an Egyptian official. Literally it is "chief of the executioners." Since a secondary meaning of the root is "to cook," the LXX here and in the passage in Genesis translates it "chief cook," a rendering preserved in Jubilees 34:11; 39:2. The old titles chief butcher, chief baker, head over the king's basket, etc., had by Neo-Babylonian times come to be purely honorific, much as the modern Knight of the Garter. Again in 3:20 it is the king's bodyguard which is responsible for carrying out his commands, so that their leader was necessarily a man of considerable authority (cf. vs. 15). When the guards came for the Jewish youths, Daniel answered "politely and tactfully." The word for tact or discretion, lit., "taste," is used elsewhere for the discreet answer (e.g., Prov. 26:16) or the tact of Abigail in averting David's vengeance (I Sam. 25:33). As Bentzen remarks, it denotes the art of finding the right word at the right time, an art which Job 12:20 says God sometimes takes away.

Arioch occurs in Gen. 14:1 as the name of a king of Ellasar, and in Judith 1:6 as the name of the king of Elymais. No such name has been found in the Neo-Babylonian texts, but it may be the Sumerian *Ēri-aku,* "servant of the moon [deity]." In vs. 15

---

one another and ourselves to be reasonable. But men being what they are, their questions cannot be confined to the earth. This ultimately

is the rock over which humanism stumbles. It may say all it likes about human values being enough. The truth is that they are not enough.

15 He answered and said to Arioch the king's captain, Why *is* the decree *so* hasty from the king? Then Arioch made the thing known to Daniel.

16 Then Daniel went in, and desired of the king that he would give him time, and that he would show the king the interpretation.

17 Then Daniel went to his house, and made the thing known to Hananiah, Mishael, and Azariah, his companions:

18 That they would desire mercies of the God of heaven concerning this secret; that Daniel and his fellows should not perish with the rest of the wise *men* of Babylon.

19 ¶ Then was the secret revealed unto Daniel in a night vision. Then Daniel blessed the God of heaven.

20 Daniel answered and said, Blessed be the name of God for ever and ever: for wisdom and might are his:

men of Babylon; 15 he said to Ar'i-och, the king's captain, "Why is the decree of the king so severe?" Then Ar'i-och made the matter known to Daniel. 16 And Daniel went in and besought the king to appoint him a time, that he might show to the king the interpretation.

17 Then Daniel went to his house and made the matter known to Hanani'ah, Mish'a-el, and Azari'ah, his companions, 18 and told them to seek mercy of the God of heaven concerning this mystery, so that Daniel and his companions might not perish with the rest of the wise men of Babylon. 19 Then the mystery was revealed to Daniel in a vision of the night. Then Daniel blessed the God of heaven. 20 Daniel said:

"Blessed be the name of God for ever and ever,
  to whom belong wisdom and might.

---

he is called the king's *shallîṭâ'*, i.e., one having command or authority. Some wish to take it there as a vocative, as Theod. does, i.e., "O Shallîṭâ' of the king, why . . . ?"

15-16. Daniel asks, **Why is the decree . . . so severe?** The idea that this meant **hasty** seems to derive from its use in 3:22. The root, however, denotes harshness or stiffness, so "harsh" here and "strict" in 3:22 are appropriate. Montgomery nevertheless defends the rendering **hasty** or "peremptory." **To appoint him a time** may mean that he asked for an appointed time at which he would come with the interpretation, or that he asked for a respite that he might seek to discover the matter. Those who favor the former interpretation point out that the king had already expressed his dissatisfaction with sages who sought to temporize. Others think that the writer would emphasize Daniel's calm assurance and trust in God, who would surely make the matter known if he had time to consult him.

17-19. "To seek mercies from before the God of heaven" is to pray for the divine compassion. The LXX adds here that they were bidden to fast, fasting being an important ally when a revelation is being sought (see 10:3). **God of heaven** is the Jewish equivalent of the Canaanitish *Ba'al šāmēm,* and was the title used by the Persians for the God of the Jews. Montgomery suggests that it later fell out of use because it resembled too closely the Greek title Zeus Ouranios. It occurs four times in this chapter. **Mystery,** *rāzā',* is from the Iranian *rāz,* secret, and outside this chapter occurs only in 4:9 (M.T. 4:6). **Vision of the night:** So God spoke to Jacob in a night vision (Gen. 46:2), and Job knows how God may so speak with men (33:14-15). Though the secret is now revealed to Daniel, it is not yet revealed to the audience but is reserved to heighten the effect of the story.

b) DANIEL'S HYMN OF PRAISE (2:20-23)

20-23. As is appropriate, Daniel now returns thanks. This passage is in verse, four stanzas of alternating tristichs and tetrastichs which, according to the classification of Hermann Gunkel and Joachim Begrich (*Einleitung in die Psalmen* [Göttingen: Vandenhoeck & Ruprecht, 1933; "Göttinger Handbuch zum Alten Testament"], pp. 265-92), would be a hymn. It is a hymn of praise to the power and wisdom of God (cf.

21 And he changeth the times and the seasons: he removeth kings, and setteth up kings: he giveth wisdom unto the wise, and knowledge to them that know understanding:

22 He revealeth the deep and secret things: he knoweth what *is* in the darkness, and the light dwelleth with him.

23 I thank thee, and praise thee, O thou God of my fathers, who hast given me wisdom and might, and hast made known unto me now what we desired of thee: for thou hast *now* made known unto us the king's matter.

24 ¶ Therefore Daniel went in unto Arioch, whom the king had ordained to

21 He changes times and seasons;
　　he removes kings and sets up kings;
　he gives wisdom to the wise
　　and knowledge to those who have understanding;

22 he reveals deep and mysterious things;
　　he knows what is in the darkness,
　　and the light dwells with him.

23 To thee, O God of my fathers,
　　I give thanks and praise,
　for thou hast given me wisdom and strength,
　　and hast now made known to me what we asked of thee,
　for thou hast made known to us the king's matter."

24 Therefore Daniel went in to Ar'i-och, whom the king had appointed to destroy

---

I Cor. 1:24). God's power is revealed in the manner in which he intervenes in nature and history. His wisdom is glimpsed in the wisdom and knowledge which he grants to his servants. He reveals deep secret things which no man could know, and since light is with him the darkness hides nothing. In this present case thanks are due him since he has given Daniel both strength and wisdom.

This seems to be an original composition of the writer, though its wording has reminiscences of Ps. 41:13; Job 12:12-13; Neh. 9:5; Esth. 1:13. That it gives thanks to God before the issue is settled instead of after Daniel has declared the dream is a problem that would occur only to a modern reader.

Blessed be the name: This beginning closely resembles Ps. 41:13 (M.T. 41:14). **The name of God** stands for the being of God: so God swears by his name (Jer. 44:26); his name dwells in the sanctuary (II Sam. 7:13); it is excellent in all the earth (Ps. 8:1); he exalts the servant who knows his name (Ps. 91:14); his name was in the angel who led Israel through the wilderness (Exod. 23:21). **For ever and ever:** Lit., "from eternity to eternity" (cf. Pss. 41:13; 90:2; 103:17).

For the idea that **kings** owe their sovereignty to God see Isa. 44:28; 45:1; Jer. 25:9; 27:6. It is clearly expressed in the Achaemenid inscriptions where Darius and Xerxes constantly assert that their rule is by the grace of Ormazd. Nebuchadrezzar's dream in ch. 4 is to teach this lesson. **To the wise** here may mean wise men in the technical sense of vs. 14, but the expression is more likely being used in a general sense. For the **deep and mysterious things** see Job 12:22; I Cor. 2:7, 10. The phrase **God of my fathers** occurs in Deut. 1:21; 26:7; *et al.;* II Chr. 20:6.

As in vs. 20, God has conferred **wisdom and strength** on Daniel, who associates his companions with himself in this hymn. They all prayed, but to him was given the revelation which in turn made things plain to them all.

c) Interpretation of the Dream (2:24-45)

24-28. Aware now of the dream and its interpretation, Daniel bids Arioch stay the execution and take him to the king. To the king's inquiry Daniel answers that

---

We can but ask questions which to our human advisers seem too difficult.

22. Light in Darkness.—The thanksgiving of Daniel for the revelation of God is a lesson we need to learn. Nothing is hidden from God, and when men want **light**, they must go to him. One

thinks of Ps. 139:12: "The darkness hideth not from thee; but the night shineth as the day: the darkness and the light are both alike to thee." Daniel's thanksgiving bears testimony to the spirit of religion, which is always one of gratefulness for gifts far beyond our deserving.

destroy the wise *men* of Babylon: he went and said thus unto him; Destroy not the wise *men* of Babylon: bring me in before the king, and I will show unto the king the interpretation.

25 Then Arioch brought in Daniel before the king in haste, and said thus unto him, I have found a man of the captives of Judah, that will make known unto the king the interpretation.

26 The king answered and said to Daniel, whose name *was* Belteshazzar, Art thou able to make known unto me the dream which I have seen, and the interpretation thereof?

the wise men of Babylon; he went and said thus to him, "Do not destroy the wise men of Babylon; bring me in before the king, and I will show the king the interpretation."

25 Then Ar'i-och brought in Daniel before the king in haste, and said thus to him: "I have found among the exiles from Judah a man who can make known to the king the interpretation." 26 The king said to Daniel, whose name was Belteshaz'zar, "Are you able to make known to me the dream that I have seen and its interpretation?"

---

though the professional techniques of the wise men have failed, the God of heaven has revealed this dream whose purport was to show what was going to happen till the end of time.

That Daniel should approach Arioch with the request for an audience was in accordance with Oriental court etiquette, and would suggest that vs. 16 does not mean that Daniel went in unceremoniously to the king. Esth. 4:11 states correctly that none might enter the king's presence without being summoned, and this custom under the Persian kings (Herodotus *History* III. 140) carried on earlier Babylonian custom.

Arioch "hastened," going with the **haste** of excitement. The usual meaning of this root is "dismay" or "perplexity" (cf. 5:9), but it is used in Hebrew for "to be hasty," e.g., in Prov. 28:22 for the eager hastening after wealth, a sense it has here in 6:19 (M.T. 6:20). Arioch's statement that he has **found a man** seems to assume that the king knew nothing about Daniel, though from 1:19 he should have been well known to him. Inconsistencies of this kind, however, are characteristic of apocalyptic writings (W. O. E. Oesterley, *II Esdras* [London: Methuen & Co., 1933; "Westminster Commentaries"], p. xii). **Among the exiles:** Lit., "among the children of the captivity." **From Judah:** *Yᵃhûdh* could be a collective, "the Jews," but most interpreters follow the versions in taking it to mean the land.

Some suspect that the words **whose name was Belteshazzar** are a gloss inserted to link this story with that in ch. 1; see, however, 4:9, where the king addresses Daniel by his Babylonian name.

To the king's inquiry Daniel admits that so difficult a matter is beyond the abilities of even professional wise men, but God, who knows all matters, can where necessary reveal them. Bentzen suggests that the writer had in mind such passages as Isa. 47:12 ff., which speak derisively of the so-called wisdom of the Babylonian sages, and is here emphasizing the fact that Israel's God alone can confer real wisdom, and for this reason Israel's faith always triumphs over heathen might.

A new group of wise men appears here, viz., the *gāzerîn*, i.e., **astrologers** or prognosticators, from גזר "to cut," then "to determine," and so "those who determine the signification of events." The word occurs again in 4:7 (M.T. 4:4); 5:7, 11. Charles thinks the reference is to those who drew up celestial charts and horoscopes (see Isa. 47:13). The art of the astrologer was much practiced in ancient Mesopotamia (A. E.

---

25. *I Have Found a Man.*—This is the search that matters. We have found many secrets of nature, but we have not **found a man** to measure up to them. The good news for the king is that there is a man among the exiles who can help him. The times in the past when great movements began through the work of one man indicate that God's plans all have to wait until he can say, **I have found a man.** So often it has been true that the man was **among the exiles.** God has a strange way of choosing his instruments from the disinherited and the re-

27 Daniel answered in the presence of the king, and said, The secret which the king hath demanded cannot the wise *men*, the astrologers, the magicians, the soothsayers, show unto the king;

28 But there is a God in heaven that revealeth secrets, and maketh known to the king Nebuchadnezzar what shall be in the latter days. Thy dream, and the visions of thy head upon thy bed, are these;

29 As for thee, O king, thy thoughts came *into thy mind* upon thy bed, what should come to pass hereafter: and he that revealeth secrets maketh known to thee what shall come to pass.

27 Daniel answered the king, "No wise man, enchanters, magicians, or astrologers can show to the king the mystery which the king has asked, 28 but there is a God in heaven who reveals mysteries, and he has made known to King Nebuchadnez'zar what will be in the latter days. Your dream and the visions of your head as you lay in bed are these: 29 To you, O king, as you lay in bed came thoughts of what would be hereafter, and he who reveals mysteries

Thierens, *Astrology in Mesopotamian Culture* [Leiden: E. J. Brill, 1935]). Symm., however, translates it θύτας, and the Vulg. has *aruspices,* showing that they took the "cutting" to refer to the inspection of the entrails of sacrificial animals; these would then be practitioners of the art of hepatoscopy (cf. Ezek. 21:21).

A God in heaven: In vs. 11 the sages had declared that only gods whose dwelling was not with flesh could reveal such matters; so now Daniel, like Joseph in Gen. 40:8; 41:16, ascribes his knowledge of the matter to God in heaven. Montgomery thinks that this emphasis on the God in heaven, as against man-made gods and deified men, is the main theme of the book. Perhaps the writer is also making a point against the popular delight in dream interpretation. That this was common in Israel as well as among their neighbors is evident from the polemic against it in Jer. 23:25 ff.; 29:8; so the writer here insists that the interpretation of such things is with God, not with the directions of dream books.

In the latter days: Driver has shown that the meaning of this phrase in the O.T. is relative to the point of view of the writer. From Jacob's point of view in Gen. 49:1 it means the end of the period of Israel's occupation of Canaan. From the point of view of Balaam in Num. 24:14 it means the end of the independence of Moab and Edom. In Deut. 4:30 it means the end of Israel's apostasy. Most often, however, the phrase is used eschatologically to mean the end of the present age, the last days before the kingdom of God commences a new age (cf. Isa. 2:2; Jer. 23:20; Ezek. 38:16; *et al.;* II Tim. 3:1; II Pet. 3:3; II Esdras 13:18; II Baruch 10:3; 25:1). From vss. 44-45 it is clear that this is the meaning here.

The visions of thy head upon thy bed: So again in 4:5, 10, 13; 7:1, 15. Charles claims that this is a non-Semitic idiom (cf. the true Semitic idiom in Jer. 23:16), since it uses **head** where we expect "heart" (cf. vs. 30; 7:28).

29-30. "Thy thoughts upon thy bed mounted up." The king had been lying in bed pondering over the future when there came a dream whose purpose was to uncover some of that future to him. Like Joseph in Gen. 41:16, Daniel disclaims any skill of his own. The vision was given by God that its significance might also be made known by God.

jected. The whole Hebrew-Christian revelation is a testimony that he finds great things among the exiles.

28, 30. *The Revelation Is from God.*—There is a God in heaven who reveals mysteries, . . . that you may know the thoughts of your mind. These two phrases brought together reveal one of the insights of Hebrew religion. God reveals **secrets** that men may understand themselves

and their needs. How quickly Israel outgrew the idea of a God who worked magic to startle people, and of prophets who revealed in order to impress men with their power. God's revelations were for the service of his children, and his spirit illuminates our minds and our hearts. Daniel wants the king to understand this. The revelation is from God, and the purpose of it is that men may know themselves.

30 But as for me, this secret is not revealed to me for *any* wisdom that I have more than any living, but for *their* sakes that shall make known the interpretation to the king, and that thou mightest know the thoughts of thy heart.

31 ¶ Thou, O king, sawest, and behold a great image. This great image, whose brightness *was* excellent, stood before thee; and the form thereof *was* terrible.

32 This image's head *was* of fine gold, his breast and his arms of silver, his belly and his thighs of brass,

33 His legs of iron, his feet part of iron and part of clay.

made known to you what is to be. 30 But as for me, not because of any wisdom that I have more than all the living has this mystery been revealed to me, but in order that the interpretation may be made known to the king, and that you may know the thoughts of your mind.

31 "You saw, O king, and behold, a great image. This image, mighty and of exceeding brightness, stood before you, and its appearance was frightening. 32 The head of this image was of fine gold, its breast and arms of silver, its belly and thighs of bronze, 33 its legs of iron, its feet partly of

---

The thoughts of your mind: Lit., **of thy heart,** the heart being the seat of the intelligence (Jer. 5:23-24; Hos. 7:11).

31. The text as it stands is untranslatable. C. C. Torrey ("Notes on the Aramaic Part of Daniel," *Transactions of the Connecticut Academy of Arts and Sciences,* XV [1909], 257-58), by transposing שגיא to a place after רב, where it can be treated as an adverb, makes good sense: "And thou, O king, sawest, and behold an image—that image was very great and its splendor extraordinary—standing before thee."

The great **image** may have been suggested by the colossal figures so common in the art of the ancient Near East. There were, however, also literary prototypes in which the world was represented by huge symbolical figures (see Richard Reitzenstein, *Studien zum antiken Synkretismus aus Iran und Griechenland* [Leipzig: B. G. Teubner, 1926], pp. 91, 97, 137). **Brightness:** *Ziw,* "splendor," seems to be derived from the Akkadian *zimu,* **appearance,** "expression of countenance," but came into Aramaic through the Midde Persian *ziwu.* It has the meaning of "splendor" again in 4:36 (Hebrew 4:33), but in 5:6, 9; 7:28 it is used of the open countenance. Here apparently it refers to the sheen of polished metal. Junker (*Untersuchungen,* p. 21, n. 1) quotes parallels for the use of the word to describe the brightness of images of the gods. Its **appearance** or aspect would strike terror. The word רו is from ראה, related to the root, "to see." It occurs again in 3:25 of the aspect of the being who walked with the friends in the fiery furnace.

32. The metal symbolism for world ages occurs not only in Hesiod but also in ancient Indian literature. Hermann Gunkel (*Genesis* [4th ed.; Göttingen: Vandenhoeck & Ruprecht, 1917; "Göttinger Handkommentar zum Alten Testament"], p. 266) suggests that it may ultimately be of Babylonian origin. The five sections of the image are arranged in a descending scale of values from gold to potsherds, in accordance with a theory of the descending dignity of the members from head to feet. The descent is in value, not in strength, for the fourth kingdom is represented as stronger than its predecessors, as indeed iron is much stronger than gold. No actual image, of course, would have been made of metals in this fashion.

Fine gold: So in Gen. 2:12. **Its breast:** Lit., "its two breasts"; the word is a dual, and the two breasts here mean the chest. **Bronze:** *Naḥāsh* is properly copper, but as this was most commonly used in an alloy with tin the resultant metal was bronze.

33. Its legs: The lower leg as distinct from the upper leg, the latter being here translated as **thighs. Clay:** *Ḥeṣaph* is properly "potsherd," the Greek ὀστράκινον. The writer means that the feet represent shoddy craftsmanship as compared with the rest of the image, being put together of iron and tilework, which might look fine but would not prove very substantial. Maybe he was thinking of iron mixed in with potsherds as the material used for the feet, or perhaps he meant they were constructed partly of iron, partly of potsherds. The fact that in the Zoroastrian Bahman Yasht 1:3, we find

34 Thou sawest till that a stone was cut out without hands, which smote the image upon his feet *that were* of iron and clay, and brake them to pieces.

35 Then was the iron, the clay, the brass, the silver, and the gold, broken to pieces together, and became like the chaff of the summer threshingfloors; and the wind carried them away, that no place was found for them: and the stone that smote the image became a great mountain, and filled the whole earth.

iron and partly of clay. 34 As you looked, a stone was cut out by no human hand, and it smote the image on its feet of iron and clay, and broke them in pieces; 35 then the iron, the clay, the bronze, the silver, and the gold, all together were broken in pieces, and became like the chaff of the summer threshing floors; and the wind carried them away, so that not a trace of them could be found. But the stone that struck the image became a great mountain and filled the whole earth.

---

a similar series of metals, the last of which is iron mixed with earth, has no bearing on this passage, for that writing is of the fourteenth century A.D., and apparently uses material from this book.

34. The **stone** which brought down the mighty image was quarried "not by hands" (so in vs. 45), i.e., **by no human hand.** Some of the versions here add "from a mountain," but this has probably crept in from vs. 45, read in the light of vs. 35. The sense of the passage requires us to think of the stone as being mysteriously quarried from some neighboring mountain by divine agency. In 8:25 Antiochus falls "without hand," i.e., by divine agency. Driver compares Job 34:20; Lam. 4:6. That the stone is not hewn by hands is probably meant to contrast with the image which was made by hands. It was inevitable that this stone should come to be interpreted messianically, for it is here parallel to the heavenly man in 7:13. In II Esdras 13:6 the man from the sea, who is a messianic figure, quarries out a stone mountain on which he stands.

The blow smites the feet which, since they are composite, are the most vulnerable part of the image, but with the amazing result that the whole image in its fall is broken into such tiny fragments that the wind can blow them away. This, however, is in a dream. Such breaking in pieces is a common picture in descriptions of the judgment of God (cf. Isa. 41:15-16; Jer. 51:20-23; Mic. 4:13). Again the contrast is between the huge image of man's construction and the swiftly moving small stone of God's hewing, which comes suddenly without warning, no one knowing whence or how, and works destruction.

35. In the Near East **summer threshing floors** are in the open air on exposed spots where, as the ears are tossed, the wind will carry away the husks while the grain falls. The word *'ûr* means both the husks and what we call **chaff.** This figure is not uncommon in scripture (cf. Hos. 13:3; Ps. 35:5; Job 21:18; Isa. 41:15-16; Matt. 3:12). The word used here for threshing floor, *'iddar,* like the corresponding Arabic *andar,* seems to be a non-Semitic word. The fragments disappeared so completely that **no trace of them could be found.** So Ps. 103:16; Job 7:10; 8:18; 20:9; Rev. 20:11. The finality of "not a trace was left" is characteristic of apocalyptic.

The small stone which was quarried from the mountain now becomes itself **a great mountain** so big that it fills **the whole earth.** To the writer and his contemporaries the

---

34. *Feet of Clay.*—The man who decides to accept this dream and its interpretation literally will have no dearth of possible interpretations. For the rest of us it may be well to note the symbolism of the kingdom with the clay feet. Every kingdom has feet of clay, and every life has its vulnerable spot. The only protection is to recognize that this is so, and to reach out for strength beyond ourselves. It is when men and nations forget their feet of clay that they go

wrong. Their downfall is like being struck by a rock **cut out by no human hand.** Daniel is aware that there is a moral realm which determines the rise and fall of human affairs. It is his way of saying what Deborah said: "The stars in their courses fought against Sisera" (Judg. 5:20).

35-36. *God's New Kingdom.*—The new **kingdom** begins as a destruction of the old, but it finally becomes universal. Daniel is saying that

36 ¶ This *is* the dream; and we will tell the interpretation thereof before the king.

37 Thou, O king, *art* a king of kings: for the God of heaven hath given thee a kingdom, power, and strength, and glory.

38 And wheresoever the children of men dwell, the beasts of the field and the fowls of the heaven hath he given into thine hand, and hath made thee ruler over them all. Thou *art* this head of gold.

39 And after thee shall arise another kingdom inferior to thee, and another third

36 "This was the dream; now we will tell the king its interpretation. 37 You, O king, the king of kings, to whom the God of heaven has given the kingdom, the power, and the might, and the glory, 38 and into whose hand he has given, wherever they dwell, the sons of men, the beasts of the field, and the birds of the air, making you rule over them all — you are the head of gold. 39 After you shall arise another king-

---

earth was flat and was surrounded by the circumambient ocean, and they were familiar with the conception of the world-mountain which was the navel of the earth. The writer here is describing that world-mountain swelling until it alone occupies the earth space, so that all the inhabitants of the earth will have to find their habitation on its slopes. Around it, of course, will still be the ocean, and over it the heavenly vault. This image serves to emphasize the universality of the kingdom of God. A mountain as a symbol of the messianic kindgom occurs in Ezek. 17:22-24. Note that it is an earthly kingdom, not a spiritual kingdom in some celestial sphere.

36. The reason Daniel uses the word **we** in introducing the interpretation may be, as Behrmann thinks, that he wishes to associate his friends therein, since they had shared with him in the prayers; or it may be merely a deferential plural of humility. It can hardly mean "God and I will now interpret."

37. King of kings was the form of address for the Persian kings (cf. Ezra 7:12, which agrees closely with the style of address in the Achaemenid inscriptions). From this Persian usage it came to be adopted by the petty kings of Armenia and surrounding kingdoms, and in a modified form came to be used by the Seleucids. The title *šar šarrani* is used in Akkadian, but seems never to have become a customary way of addressing Babylonian kings. In Ezek. 26:7 it is used of Nebuchadrezzar, but Isa. 36:4 has the more usual form of address.

Everything in the text after **king of kings** down to the end of vs. 38*a* is a parenthesis, after which vs. 38*b*, **thou art this head of gold,** picks up the main sentence again. This parenthesis may be a late interpolation (cf. 7:14).

In insisting that it is God who grants kings their sovereignty (cf. vs. 21) Daniel is only telling Nebuchadrezzar what Jeremiah had already stated plainly (Jer. 25:9; 27:6; 28:14). It was what Second Isaiah told Cyrus (Isa. 44:28 ff.), and, as Behrmann notes, it is what the early Christians told the Roman emperors (Tertullian *Apology* 30).

Might: Some insist that the word means "riches." It occurs again in 4:30; cf. Prov. 27:24. **Glory:** Perhaps "honor" would translate the word more accurately.

38. The mention of **beasts of the field** would suggest that the writer had in mind Jer. 27:6; 28:14. It means wild animals rather than domestic beasts (cf. Isa. 56:9; Deut. 7:22; Job 40:20). The LXX here adds "and the fishes of the sea." Some commentators have referred to the delight of ancient monarchs in collecting menageries of strange birds and beasts and even fish; here the expression seems an attempt to emphasize the wide sovereignty of Nebuchadrezzar, who ruled over all creatures on earth. Achaemenid kings claimed such universal sovereignty, and in this they were but following the example of earlier kings in Mesopotamia. **Thou art this head of gold:** The king stands for the kingdom (cf. vs. 44; 7:17, 24).

39. After you: Lit., "in thy place." **Shall arise:** Lit., "shall stand," as in vs. 44, where the same verb is used of the kingdom of God standing forever. No hint is given as to the identity of this second standing kingdom, but there can be no doubt that the Median kingdom is meant. In the writer's view of history Darius the Mede succeeded

kingdom of brass, which shall bear rule over all the earth.

40 And the fourth kingdom shall be strong as iron: forasmuch as iron breaketh in pieces and subdueth all *things:* and as iron that breaketh all these, shall it break in pieces and bruise.

41 And whereas thou sawest the feet and toes, part of potters' clay, and part of iron, the kingdom shall be divided; but there shall be in it of the strength of the iron, forasmuch as thou sawest the iron mixed with miry clay.

42 And *as* the toes of the feet *were* part of iron, and part of clay, *so* the kingdom shall be partly strong, and partly broken.

dom inferior to you, and yet a third kingdom of bronze, which shall rule over all the earth. 40 And there shall be a fourth kingdom, strong as iron, because iron breaks to pieces and shatters all things; and like iron which crushes, it shall break and crush all these. 41 And as you saw the feet and toes partly of potter's clay and partly of iron, it shall be a divided kingdom; but some of the firmness of iron shall be in it, just as you saw iron mixed with the miry clay. 42 And as the toes of the feet were partly iron and partly clay, so the kingdom shall be partly

---

Belshazzar at the fall of Babylon (5:31; 9:1; 11:1) and was in turn succeeded by Cyrus the Persian (6:28; 10:1). In 8:3 the Median kingdom is rated as inferior to the Persian.

The Medes, a people speaking an Iranian language, lived in the mountainous country to the southwest of the Caspian Sea. From the time of Shalmaneser III (858-824 B.C.) their name occurs in Assyrian inscriptions. Herodotus (*History* I. 96-130) tells of four of their kings between 699 and 550, the third of whom, Cyaxares, in 612 defeated the Mesopotamian armies and destroyed the Assyrian capital at Nineveh. The fourth king, Astyages, was betrayed in 550 by his own troops into the hands of Cyrus the Persian, one of his vassals, who in 538 became king over the united Medo-Persian Kingdom. This is one reason for that close connection of Medes and Persians in chs. 5-6. Some insist that we should not think here of any historical kingdoms in particular, arguing that the four is merely literary, a play on the numeral for wholeness, like the four horns in Zech. 1:18 or the title of Assyrian monarchs, "King of All the Four Regions." This, however, is unlikely. The **third kingdom** is doubtless that of the Persians, founded by Cyrus. Its kings claimed to rule over the whole earth, a claim reflected in the O.T. in Ezra 1:2; Esth. 1:1.

40. The fourth kingdom, **strong as iron,** is Alexander's empire. As in ch. 5, the writer hurries over the other three in order to give a fuller description of the one which was of more interest to his audience. He stresses its great strength (cf. 7:19), how it crushes all who oppose it (cf. 7:23), how it will be divided (cf. 7:24), and how it will vainly strive to hold together by forming marriage ties.

There is some confusion of the text in this verse, which in the versions is shorter, though they differ among themselves. The simplest emendation is that of Marti, who deletes the words **like iron which crushes.**

All these: Perhaps "all things" or "the whole earth" (cf. 7:23). The words can hardly mean all the previous kingdoms, unless we are to think of the Babylonian and Median as in some sense still surviving in the Persian Empire and so also broken and shattered by Alexander when he conquered Persia (see Ginsberg, *Studies,* pp. 5-8, who thinks that the Seleucid Empire in a way carried on the Babylonian, and the little kingdoms of Atropatene and Persis similarly carried on the Median and Persian Empires).

41-42. The **toes,** also in vs. 42, were not mentioned in the dream. As the toes are ten, it is easy to connect them with the ten horns of 7:24. Many modern scholars, however, take them as a secondary element interpolated here.

The "potsherds" of vs. 33 are here called "potsherds of a potter," and a little later "potsherds of clay." Montgomery suggests that פחר here means not a "potter" but **potter's clay,** so that it would be "potsherds of potter's clay," which fits better with the later *ṭînā',* the normal word for **clay** or loam.

43 And whereas thou sawest iron mixed with miry clay, they shall mingle themselves with the seed of men: but they shall not cleave one to another, even as iron is not mixed with clay.

44 And in the days of these kings shall the God of heaven set up a kingdom, which shall never be destroyed: and the kingdom shall not be left to other people, *but* it shall break in pieces and consume all these kingdoms, and it shall stand for ever.

strong and partly brittle. 43 As you saw the iron mixed with miry clay, so they will mix with one another in marriage,[b] but they will not hold together, just as iron does not mix with clay. 44 And in the days of those kings the God of heaven will set up a kingdom which shall never be destroyed, nor shall its sovereignty be left to another people. It shall break in pieces all these kingdoms and bring them to an end, and it shall

[b] Aram *by the seed of men*

It shall be a divided kingdom is generally taken to be a reference to the dividing up of Alexander's empire; since there are two legs, these would be the two great kingdoms of the Seleucids and Ptolemies. But *pelighāh* means "composite" rather than **divided,** i.e., it is **partly strong** and partly weak, partly having the strength, i.e., the **firmness** of iron, and partly the **brittle** character of clay pottery work. Behrmann thinks it best to follow the theory that the iron symbolizes the continuing might of the Seleucids, while the potsherds denote the feebler kingdom of the Ptolemies.

43. They may refer to the kings of this last kingdom, or perhaps to the peoples of the kingdoms. "Their mingling shall be with the seed of men" is usually taken to refer to intermarriage (cf. Jer. 31:27). Should **they** refer to the kings, then the intermarriages would be those between the Seleucids and the Ptolemies which are dealt with in 11:6, 17. If **they** refers to the peoples, it must mean the attempts made by Alexander and his successors to promote intermarriage among their peoples in the Orient. This was not very successful, however, and was particularly abhorrent to pious Jews.

44. In the days of those kings: While the Diadochi are still reigning. In 7:25-27; 11:45–12:3 we have a more precise account of how the kingdom of God is to be set up at the fall of Antiochus Epiphanes. Ginsberg *(ibid.,* pp. 6-7) points the word to read "kingdoms," not **kings,** and thinks that it means the four kingdoms of the great image. This is hardly likely for the natural implication is that the author is referring to the iron and potsherd mixture on which the stone falls, and that represents the kingdoms of the Diadochi.

Previous kingdoms had been destroyed either by internal corruption or by a conqueror from without, but this new kingdom **shall never be destroyed,** for it is to **stand for ever.** Nor shall the "sovereignty be passed on." Some prefer to read with the versions **its sovereignty.** If with the M.T. we read "the sovereignty," the reference is probably to the hope for a fifth Oriental monarchy which would rise to overthrow the Hellenizing power. The writer would thus be saying that the new kingdom would not be just another sovereignty in the hands of some national group, but in the hands of God. The reading **its sovereignty** assumes that the sovereignty in the coming kingdom will be in the hands of the people, i.e., Israel, and will never pass from them to the hands of any others. This would agree with 7:27, and would dispose of the argument that the chapter does not think of Israel in connection with the coming kingdom.

The kingdom of God is to come in with some violence, for it will **break in pieces** (cf. vss. 34, 35) and finally end **all these kingdoms,** i.e., all the various parts of the last composite kingdom. Ginsberg *(ibid.,* p. 6), however, with his eye on vs. 45, wants it to

this kingdom of God is not to be just another kingdom, but is to consummate the whole historical process. The idea of growth from small beginnings is in harmony with Jesus' picture of the grain of mustard seed. The kingdom is a

destructive agency. It challenges every empire, and it judges all policies and programs. It is the obstacle standing over against ambitions of power-worshiping tyrants. But it is not only destructive. It is to fill the earth and to be

45 Forasmuch as thou sawest that the stone was cut out of the mountain without hands, and that it brake in pieces the iron, the brass, the clay, the silver, and the gold; the great God hath made known to the king what shall come to pass hereafter: and the dream *is* certain, and the interpretation thereof sure.

46 ¶ Then the king Nebuchadnezzar fell upon his face, and worshipped Daniel, and

stand for ever; 45 just as you saw that a stone was cut from a mountain by no human hand, and that it broke in pieces the iron, the bronze, the clay, the silver, and the gold. A great God has made known to the king what shall be hereafter. The dream is certain, and its interpretation sure."

46 Then King Nebuchadnez'zar fell

---

mean the kingdoms of gold, silver, bronze, and iron, which must thus be thought of as still existing in some form at the time the final kingdom is set up. Neither in this chapter nor in ch. 7, however, is this the natural meaning of the passage. Some have thought that the writer expected the Jews to bring in the kingdom by military victories over the heathen nations (cf. Matt. 11:12), but that is against the tenor of the book.

Its standing **for ever** is the universality of the kingdom in time (so 7:14), just as the mountain filling the earth was its universality in space. The term **for ever** lifts the kingdom out of time into eternity. The world periods have ended and the timeless kingdom which has no ending is to be introduced. Each of those world periods was succeeded by another, but this kingdom will have no successors. It grew out of the stone (vs. 35) and will have the endurance of mountain rock. This development introduces a note on the origin of the stone.

45. It was quarried **from a mountain,** lit., **the mountain,** though there is no need to think the writer had any special mountain in mind, much less that he meant Mount Zion. Apparently good stones for the ballistae were quarried from special rock masses in the mountains, and the writer was thinking of such a stone, only one God-hewn not man-hewn. Some consider the words **from a mountain** an interpolation here.

The wise men had declared that only the gods could know such matters; so now Daniel says that **the great God** has indeed revealed it. The noun has no article here, whence the RSV translation **a great God,** Daniel making a concession to the king's polytheism by saying that one of these great gods referred to by the wise men has granted the revelation. It means, however, **the great God,** i.e., the God of Israel. Linguistic parallels for the omission of the article are many.

Like Pharaoh's dream in Gen. 41:28, this dream has reference to the future. Daniel closes in true apocalyptic style with a solemn affirmation of the truth of what he says. This is found again in 8:26 (cf. 10:1; 11:2), and with it we may compare Rev. 19:9; 21:5; 22:6.

In the preceding verses we have had the writer's message to his contemporaries. They were suffering grievously under the domination of a hostile and oppressive world power, whose strength seemed like iron that broke and crushed all in its way. But let them take heart. This is the last of the world powers, and has already overreached itself and become weak. Its end is near. It will pass away as other world powers have, but when it falls, its place will be taken not by another temporal power but by the eternal kingdom which God himself will set up. In Mal. 2:17 we read how the pious in Israel had been asking, "Where is the God of justice?" This is the answer. The world powers are about to end. These are the last days. The kingdom of God is on its way and will come in without human assistance.

2. The Epilogue (2:46-49)

The message to the audience has been given. Now the story which was the vehicle for the message must be drawn to an appropriate conclusion. The elements are familiar. The heathen king humbles himself before the pious Israelite, confesses the superiority of Israel's God, and largely rewards the heroes of the story (cf. Gen. 41:37 ff.; Esth. 10:3).

commanded that they should offer an oblation and sweet odors unto him.

47 The king answered unto Daniel, and
said, Of a truth *it is,* that your God *is* a
God of gods, and a Lord of kings, and a
revealer of secrets, seeing thou couldest
reveal this secret.

48 Then the king made Daniel a great
man, and gave him many great gifts, and
made him ruler over the whole province of

upon his face, and did homage to Daniel,
and commanded that an offering and incense be offered up to him. 47 The king said
to Daniel, "Truly, your God is God of gods
and Lord of kings, and a revealer of mysteries, for you have been able to reveal this
mystery." 48 Then the king gave Daniel
high honors and many great gifts, and made

The rewarding of course is a fulfillment of the promise in vs. 6 and parallels that in
1:15-21, though the writer may also have in mind the fulfillment of such prophecies as
Isa. 61:5-9. As these verses are but part of the literary framework, details should not be
pressed to yield any special significance.

46. Neither the fact that the monarch **fell upon his face** in reverence nor his doing
homage implies that he paid divine worship to Daniel, but that he ordered offerings of
minḥāh and *niḥōḥin* does imply this. It was an Oriental custom to fall on one's face
in reverence before a person, as Abigail does (I Sam. 25:23), or the woman of Tekoa
(II Sam. 14:4), or Mephibosheth (II Sam. 9:6); and of course one did the same before
the Most High. So also one may do obeisance (*seghadh,* "to do homage") to a human
being or to God. The *minḥāh,* **oblation,** and *niḥōḥin,* **sweet odors,** however, are technical
terms connected with the offering of sacrifices to a deity. **Offering** (*minḥāh*) is used in
9:21 for the evening sacrifice which Antiochus abolished. It can mean a "gift" or a
"present," such as Jacob's present to Esau (Gen. 33:10), or the tribute paid to a suzerain
(II Kings 17:4), or the bread and drink offering of Lev. 2:1; 6:14 (M.T. 6:7), but
here its association with *niḥōḥin* shows that it is to be taken as in Isa. 1:13 or Gen. 4:3,
in the sense of a sacrificial offering in an act of worship. **Incense:** *Niḥōḥin,* lit., "pleasant-
ness," "agreeableness"; but here as in Ezra 6:10 the word is used eliptically for **sweet odors,**
the technical expression for the offering of **incense** in worship (Ezek. 6:13), though it
may be used for the offering of other kinds of sacrifice and oblation.

Daniel's acceptance of this homage is to be understood as the writer's device for
having his audience see in the heathen king at the feet of Daniel a symbol of the Gentile
nations being humbled before Israel, thus fulfilling such prophecies as Isa. 49:7, 23;
52:15; 60:14. One may also recall the tale told in Josephus (*Antiquities* XI. 8. 5) about
Alexander the Great.

47. God of gods and Lord of kings may be a reference to the style of address used
by Babylonian kings, and later by the Persian kings, to their gods. Marduk is addressed
as "Lord of lords" or "Lord of gods," and Xerxes in his inscriptions addresses Ormazd
as "a great God, greatest of the gods." On the other hand, **God of gods** is a normal
Semitic idiom for the superlative. It is used again in 11:36 as equivalent to "the Most
High God," and in Deut. 10:17 Yahweh is called "God of gods and Lord of lords" (cf.
Ps. 136:2-3; Enoch 9:4). Ginsberg (*ibid.,* p. 66) would vocalize the word for **kings** as
mulkin or *molkin* instead of *malkin,* and take it as an Aramaic rendering of the "Lord
of kingships" used in the protocols of the Lagides in Egypt. If this is so, the monarch's
statement that the God of Israel alone is **God of gods** may be a gibe at the claims to
divine honors made by Seleucid kings, and that Yahweh alone is "Lord of kingdoms,"
a similar gibe at claims made by the Ptolemies.

That the king confesses Yahweh as **a revealer of mysteries** picks up the words used
by Daniel in vss. 22, 28 (cf. Job 12:22; I Cor. 4:5).

48. Gave Daniel high honors: Lit., "Made Daniel great and placed him in authority
over" the whole province of Babylon. It was no uncommon thing in the ancient Near
East for foreigners to come to posts of importance in the realm, and the writer could
assume that the stories of Joseph in Egypt and Mordecai in Persia would be familiar

Babylon, and chief of the governors over all the wise *men* of Babylon.

49 Then Daniel requested of the king, and he set Shadrach, Meshach, and Abednego, over the affairs of the province of Babylon: but Daniel *sat* in the gate of the king.

3 Nebuchadnezzar the king made an image of gold, whose height *was* threescore cubits, *and* the breadth thereof six

him ruler over the whole province of Babylon, and chief prefect over all the wise men of Babylon. **49** Daniel made request of the king, and he appointed Shadrach, Meshach, and Abed′nego over the affairs of the province of Babylon; but Daniel remained at the king's court.

3 King Nebuchadnez′zar made an image of gold, whose height was sixty cubits

to his readers, Kuhl (*Die drei Männer*, p. 23, n. 2) has collected from Jewish legend similar stories of Jews who came to high honor under foreign princes. Daniel's main office, however, was to be **chief prefect over all the wise men** of the land. The phrase is "chief of the prefects," the idea apparently being that there was a prefect over each class of wise men, while Daniel was prefect of prefects. The word *ṣeghan* is from the Akkadian *šaknu*, "governor." It occurs again in 3:2 in the list of court officials. In Babylonia a *šaknu* was the governor of a district or city, but in Hebrew the word seems to have acquired a more general sense (cf. Neh. 2:16; 12:40; Ezek. 23:6). In 4:9 (M.T. 4:6); 5:11 Daniel is referred to as the chief of the magicians, meaning apparently the office conferred on him here.

Earlier commentators were much exercised to explain, first, how a pious observing Jew could accept such a position as head of the corps of magicians, astrologers, and soothsayers, and, second, how a ruler could have imposed a foreigner as head of such closed castes as these were—a different matter from appointing a man to a political post. The stories of Joseph and Moses, however, show that in hagiography one must not expect any close reckoning of historical probabilities. These details are appropriate as framework for the story, and that is their justification.

49. The friends who shared in the prayer are not forgotten. The office to which they are now appointed is apparently meant to suggest something more important than the position granted them in 1:19, though what precisely is meant here is not clear. Some suggest that as Daniel was to be at **the gate of the king** he would remain in the city, while the three friends would go on circuit in the provinces. *'Abhîdhtā'* is, lit., "service," but in this context the word would mean public administration. It occurs again in 3:12.

At the king's court: Lit., **in the gate of the king.** So in Esth. 2:19, 21 Mordecai is at the king's gate, and in the Elephantine papyri Ahiqar is "set at the gate of the palace." It was a Persian custom for important officials to sit **in the gate.** There is also a title "Director of the Palace Gate," applied to certain senior officials at Hammurabi's court. As the gate was originally the entrance to the king's audience chamber, this was where the chief officials might be expected to sit awaiting his call. Later the name came to be used for the king's chancellery, so the LXX translates it ἐν τῇ βασιλικῇ αὐλῇ. This usage survived in the name of Sublime Porte for the Turkish chancellery.

C. THE THREE CONFESSORS IN THE FIERY FURNACE (3:1-30)

This story illustrates how martyrdom is preferable to apostasy. Nebuchadrezzar sets up a colossal image and summons all his officials to come to its dedication, at which all must worship the image under penalty of punishment. Daniel's three companions,

established forever. Daniel is saying that all kings reign by the grace of God, and all nations live only by his will.

3:1-30. Continuing Faithfulness.—The end of ch. 2 intimates that everything is now all right, and the success and prosperity of Daniel and

his friends are assured. It is like so many popular novels—"they lived happily ever after." It is somewhat of a shock, therefore, to discover that almost immediately the faithful Jews are in trouble again. One would think that by this time the king would have had such an apprecia-

being now provincial officials, are summoned with the others at the king's command. However, they avoid taking part in idolatrous worship and, when accused before the monarch, boldly accept the consequences of refusal to compromise in a matter that touches their religion. They are cast into the furnace but are miraculously delivered, so that the king admits the superiority of their God, and raises them to higher honor.

Under the Hellenizing kings there was constant danger of Jews being seduced from their national religion. At times groups were under considerable pressure to conform to the religion of their rulers. This story is a rebuke to conformists. True Israelites should choose death rather than associate themselves with heathen idolatry. It was also a lesson in loyalty. When so many were taking the easy way of conformity, or were succumbing to the lure of heathen ways, the loyalty of these three youths, living not at home in Palestine but far away amid the temptations of a foreign court, is held up as an example of true piety.

The writer is apparently using a tale that was in existence in his day, but which he has worked over to fit into his six stories. Daniel does not appear, but by the names of its heroes it is linked up with the preceding chapters. The underlying story is a variation

---

tion for these men that nothing would be allowed to threaten them further. But pride is greater than the king's compassion, and he will kill rather than allow exceptions to his edict. This is true to human experience.

We may note that there is no permanent victory here. One of our greatest blunders is the assumption that a static kind of perfection is possible. The world demands growth, and just when we believe we have walled ourselves in safely, an earthquake breaks down the walls. We think we have established an order of society in which we can be comfortable. We brand all those who want a change as radicals. But social affairs are always held in a delicate balance, and always will be until justice is established. Even then it would have to be a dynamic justice if it were to last.

The moral life of man illustrates this same principle. Substitute temptation and evil for the king, and you have a parable of what happens to the good man. If he assumes for a moment that at last he has arrived, then something brings him crashing down into ruin. The accomplishing of one moral act is good enough in its place, but it is not good enough to last a lifetime. Morality is a quest. It is a persistent spirit. It is not something that is achieved in one act, but it is a continuous pursuit of a goal. Many a man goes down before the sense of satisfaction which comes to him when he has achieved a moral victory.

Anyone who has fought for decency in a community knows that there can be no relaxation and no final victory. The reforming of our common life is always before us. Once we relax and assume that the job has been done, there creep back into power the forces which are never dead but only frightened temporarily. Every invasion of the territory of evil makes its enmity more bitter. How quickly can a people

have its moral life undermined! People do not know what is happening to them. They remember great heroes of the past, and vast moral accomplishments of yesterday. But the sudden reversal of those trends comes as a terrible surprise to many men.

The religious life knows no resting place on earth. One of the great things about Daniel's friends is their taking the next test in their stride. There is no crying out against life or God. If they are to be tested again, so be it. Apparently they had not assumed that all their troubles were over when Daniel became the king's favorite. This is not always true of us. We feel that in one great act we can become religious, and that will be enough. Not so! The tests are for the purpose of strengthening for the more difficult ones ahead. Real religion is a continuing way.

In the second place, here we have illustrated a faith that disregards consequences. The story of the three Jews asserting that God can save them from the fiery furnace and then adding, **But if not, be it known to you, O king, that we will not serve your gods or worship the golden image which you have set up** (vs. 18), is one of the high points of the O.T. For here is proclaimed a faith in a God who may not always make things comfortable for his followers.

This is an utter denial of the kind of religion which flourished in that ancient world. A god was supposed to support and vindicate his people. One chose the god that could do the most for him, and one changed his allegiance when it was obvious that there was a more powerful and benevolent god to be found. But here is announced a new idea of God. He may not always save us from the fiery furnace, or heal us, or make us prosperous. He will allow his Son to go to the Cross, and he heals the world by the stripes that are laid on his people. The

cubits: he set it up in the plain of Dura, in the province of Babylon.

and its breadth six cubits. He set it up on the plain of Dura, in the province of Baby-

on the theme of divine rescue from the flames, with perhaps some reminiscence of a folk tale connected with the last Neo-Babylonian king, Nabonidus. Also the writer seems to be conscious that he is illustrating such passages as Isa. 43:2; Ps. 66:12, and is thus linking up his example of piety with the prophetic promises to Israel.

Since Nebuchadrezzar is not represented here as an anti-Semitic ruler, the hostility shown being only an incident and not a systematic persecution of the Jews, it is suggested that the original story must have arisen at a time when the Jews were living in relatively harmonious relations with the world power of the day.

1. Prologue (3:1-6)

a) Nebuchadrezzar Sets Up an Image (3:1-6)

3:1. The LXX dates this chapter as the others had been dated, setting the event in the eighteenth year of Nebuchadrezzar and suggesting a reason for the erection of the image. These additions seem to be afterthoughts, perhaps drawn from the fact that it was in Nebuchadrezzar's eighteenth year that he finally devastated Jerusalem.

shallow religion that operates only when prosperity abounds is a far cry from the religion Daniel is proclaiming.

Our modern mood has been especially vulnerable to the success type of religion. It is amazing to note the number of books by business leaders who assume that a religion is to be judged only in terms of its ability to make a man successful. We are surrounded with modern heresies which use the Christian vocabularies but deny the heart of the Christian revelation centered in the Crucifixion. Their word is, "We will not bow down if our God saves us. But if he does not, we will try another god." For so many of us God becomes something to serve us and to use. But for Daniel faith is committing oneself to a way regardless of where it takes one. Faith is to accept God's will for us regardless of the result.

There are times when religion may become "the opium of the people." But that is only when it has lost its way and divorced itself from God. Such religion is sick. The history of Jews and Christians does not suggest an opiate philosophy. The Hebrew-Christian religion is a call to heroism and a provocation to undertake the difficult enterprise in the name of God. We have not been found by him until we can say, "Even if this does not make me comfortable, still I will be loyal to God." Remember Kirsopp Lake's definition of faith: "Faith is not belief in spite of evidence; it is life in scorn of consequence." [6]

But we should not lose sight of the deep truth that religion has its rewards. They may not be apparent immediately. In comparison

the advantages of evil are too easily seen. Evil offers certain rewards immediately, while goodness demands that we shall have faith in deeper satisfactions. The life of the faithful man is a continuous reaping of the profound, satisfying, spiritual gifts of God. The life of the betrayer is a long series of regrets and tragedies for having believed that the advantage of evil would be more than temporary and without remorse. That power of character which is the desire of every man, though sometimes hidden and unrecognized, is the gift God gives men who are faithful. The long years bring to such men the wonderful reward of an increasing spiritual strength and dignity.

Best of all, there is the sense of going on a safe path, which a complete commitment to God brings. The religious man does not know what the morrow will bring forth any more than the pagan, but he knows a security that the other may never experience. Life becomes a pilgrimage, and to follow the inner promptings of God is "safer than a known way." Bunyan had this in mind as he wrote *The Pilgrim's Progress*. In a few words he sums up what faith and action mean:

Then said Evangelist, pointing with his finger over a very wide field, "Do you see yonder Wicket-gate?" The man said, "No." Then said the other, "Do you see yonder shining light?" He said, "I think I do." Then said Evangelist, "Keep that light in your eye, and go up directly thereto." [7]

It is this sense of purpose that is one of God's great gifts to his loyal ones.

1. An Image of Gold.—This verse has a more contemporary ring than it could have had in the years before Hitler's rise. The tyrant ever

[6] Quoted by Halford E. Luccock, *In the Minister's Workshop* (New York and Nashville: Abingdon-Cokesbury Press, 1944), p. 179.

[7] Ch. i.

2 Then Nebuchadnezzar the king sent to gather together the princes, the governors, and the captains, the judges, the treasurers, the counselors, the sheriffs, and all the rulers of the provinces, to come to the dedication of the image which Nebuchadnezzar the king had set up.

lon. 2 Then King Nebuchadnez'zar sent to assemble the satraps, the prefects, and the governors, the counselors, the treasurers, the justices, the magistrates, and all the officials of the provinces to come to the dedication of the image which King Nebu-

Made an image: It was a common thing for ancient potentates to set up colossal images, sometimes images of deities, sometimes of themselves. The word *çelēm* might be used for either. Earlier commentators favored the idea that it was an image of the monarch himself, the worship of which was intended by Nebuchadrezzar to be a bond of unity in his empire, much as Caesar worship was later in the Roman Empire. The phrasing of vss. 12, 14, 18, however, suggests that it was a new statue of the king's favorite deity. It has been suggested that the dream in ch. 2 gave Nebuchadrezzar the idea of erecting this great image, but it seems quite certain that this feature belongs to the original story.

The image was **of gold.** There seems to be no cuneiform evidence for a statue of gold, though Herodotus (*History* I. 183) mentions two huge golden statues in Babylon of which he had heard. Since Antiochus Epiphanes had set up at Daphne a golden image to Apollo (Ammianus Marcellinus *Roman History* XXII. 13. 1), an audience in the Maccabean period would doubtless have been reminded of that. It is not necessary to think of the image being of solid gold. In Exodus the altar is called "an altar of gold," though actually it was only overlaid with gold (Exod. 30:3). So huge a statue as this would probably have been of wood plated with gold. There is no particular significance in its measurements **sixty cubits** by **six,** which, calculating the cubit as eighteen inches, would make it ninety by nine feet, quite out of proportion. These measurements are merely to suggest hugeness.

Set it up: Lit., "he caused it to stand," the expression used in inscriptions from Palmyra and the Hauran for setting up images. It was set up in the *biq'āh* **of Dura.** A *biq'āh* is a low **plain** between two ranges of mountains. The site of this particular Dura has not been identified. It is a not uncommon name, and we cannot suppose that every site whose name would have been familiar to an audience then can be identified today. No special significance is to be attached to the place in which it was set up, for such details are merely part of the framework of the story. Dura could be from the Akkadian *dūru,* "circuit," whence the LXX τοῦ περιβόλου.

2. Sent to assemble: For the dedication. Such a festival of dedication was customary. We remember the dedication of Solomon's Temple, and there are still extant portions of liturgies for such dedications in Mesopotamia. Special messengers were usually sent to summon those expected to attend. The common people would come as they desired, but it was correct procedure for all prominent officials to be present.

The writer now proceeds to list the officials who were summoned. He was following well-known precedent in listing them in this way. Sargon in his inscription and Esarhaddon in his Zinjirli inscription give very similar lists. The titles here are mostly Persian and were possibly taken from some official list by a writer who, not familiar with Iranian speech, has deformed some of the names. The Neo-Babylonian inscriptions show no evidence of Persian titles having been borne by officials under Nebuchadrezzar. It was at the time the Persians took over Babylon and overhauled the entire official organization that Iranian titles may have begun to come into use.

seeks to make all men bow down before something he has made. It may be a golden image, or a racial theory, or a dream of national grandeur, or military might. They are all alike in that they are created by men and that they seek to

usurp the place of God. The egocentric man has his idols before which he insists that others must bow down. They must recognize his gifts, or his power, or his position of special privilege. The days of idolatry are never over, and the

3 Then the princes, the governors, and captains, the judges, the treasurers, the counselors, the sheriffs, and all the rulers of the provinces, were gathered together unto the dedication of the image that Nebuchadnezzar the king had set up; and they stood before the image that Nebuchadnezzar had set up.

3 Then the satraps, the prefects, and the governors, the counselors, the treasurers, the justices, the magistrates, and all the officials of the provinces, were assembled for the dedication of the image that King Nebuchadnez'zar had set up; and they stood before the image that chadnez'zar had set up.

Satraps occurs also in Ezra 8:36; Esth. 3:12; 8:9; 9:3. It is from the Old Persian *xšaθrapāvan*, which in Akkadian became *satar-pānu,* and in Greek ἐξαιθράπης, then σατράπης, and the Latin *satrapes.* The division of the empire into satrapies was the work of Darius I (521-495 B.C.).

Prefects: Cf. 2:48; 6:7 (Hebrew 6:8). In Ezra and Nehemiah the same word is used as the title of certain functionaries at Jerusalem. The office seems to have been much the same as that of a satrap, so some have thought that here it is merely a Semitic gloss to the Iranian word. The *šaknūti* are the third group in the list on Esarhaddon's inscription.

Governors occurs in the singular in Ezra 5:14. It is the Akkadian *paḥatu,* abbreviated from *bēl paḥāti,* "lord of a district." The Hebrew פחה is used (a) for an Assyrian captain; (b) for a Babylonian officer; (c) for the governor of a Persian province; and (d) in a quite general sense. It occurs also in the Aramaic papyri. The *paḥāti* are the second group in Esarhaddon's list.

Counselors: The title אדרגזר is apparently from an Iranian *handarza,* "counselor," plus *kāra,* "the people." It was a title which continued into Sassanian times.

Treasurers: The word גדבריא here is apparently a variant spelling of the גזבריא of Ezra 7:21, from the Old Persian *ganjabara,* "protector of the treasure," the γαζοφύλακες of Josephus. In vss. 24, 27 and 6:7 (Hebrew 6:8), however, we have הדבריא "counselors," and some think the word here is merely a scribal error which should be corrected to agree with vss. 24, 27. Others hold that it arose by dittography from the following word and should be deleted, since the LXX both here and at vs. 3 has seven classes, not eight.

Justices: The word דתבר is from the Old Persian *dāta bara,* "law bearer" or "law guardian," the Akkadian derivative of which occurs in inscriptions from Nippur of the reigns of Artaxerxes I and Darius II.

Magistrates: The term תפתיא is apparently a deformation of some Persian title ending in *-pat,* "chief." It seems to occur in Egyptian Aramaic in the form תיפתיא for some military or palace official.

And all the officials of the provinces probably covers all the officials of lesser rank. This detail so reminiscent of legal phraseology is characteristic of royal inscriptions from Sumerian to Seleucid days in which monarchs delight to list the officials under them, the towns they have conquered, the booty they have brought home, the buildings they have erected or repaired, etc. Perhaps in these lists the writer is making sly mockery of this, though a love of lists seems to be characteristic of his own style. The word used for **officials** is *shilṭôn,* which, like the later sultan, meant persons vested with authority. They are summoned to the **dedication,** *ḥanukkāh,* a word still used for the Hanukkah festival of modern Jews.

3-4. The assembled multitude **stood before the image,** that being the correct attitude at the beginning of such a dedication, while a **herald proclaimed aloud,** lit., "called with might," as in 4:14; 5:7 (cf. Isa. 40:9; Jonah 3:8; Rev. 18:2). The **herald** was a familiar figure in the ancient Oriental court. The word *kârôzâ'* used here recalls the Greek κῆρυξ, and many consider it a borrowing from the Greek, though there is some doubt whether the Greek word itself may not be of Oriental origin.

The expression **peoples, nations, and languages** occurs again in vss. 7, 29; 4:1; 5:19; 6:25; 7:14, and is imitated in the book of Revelation. Again it reflects the style of official proclamations. It is usually assumed that there was a huge crowd at the dedication, but

4 Then a herald cried aloud, To you it is commanded, O people, nations, and languages,

5 *That* at what time ye hear the sound of the cornet, flute, harp, sackbut, psaltery, dulcimer, and all kinds of music, ye fall down and worship the golden image that Nebuchadnezzar the king hath set up:

6 And whoso falleth not down and worshippeth shall the same hour be cast into the midst of a burning fiery furnace.

Nebuchadnez'zar had set up. 4 And the herald proclaimed aloud, "You are commanded, O peoples, nations, and languages, 5 that when you hear the sound of the horn, pipe, lyre, trigon, harp, bagpipe, and every kind of music, you are to fall down and worship the golden image that King Nebuchadnez'zar has set up; 6 and whoever does not fall down and worship shall immediately be cast into a burning fiery furnace."

some think of a gathering of officials only. As such officials represented in their official capacity the various groups in the empire, all these peoples, nations, and tongues could be thought of as doing obeisance in the persons of their representatives. The fact that in Judith 3:8 Nebuchadrezzar is pictured as a monarch who set himself to destroy all other religions that he alone might be worshiped makes it possible that the writer was assuming his audience would see the parallel between all this and the policies of their own oppressor Antiochus (cf. 11:36).

5. Music was to give the signal for the high point of the dedication. This was not only that all assembled might know the precise moment when they must do obeisance but also because in ancient days it was customary to have musical accompaniment to such public ceremonials. That a list is given of the musical instruments may be in accordance with the writer's style, or it may be in imitation of Babylonian official style. No special significance need be attached to the number of instruments, or to the order in which they are mentioned, as though the writer had in mind a special kind of orchestra. Nor are we to see anything significant in the "international" character of the instruments, as though the orchestra were meant to represent the racial composition of the empire. Kuhl (*Die drei Männer*, pp. 13-14) has collected examples of such fondness for enumerating the musical instruments used on special occasions. It is clearly a stylistic convention. **Horn:** *Qarnā'* is the "ram's horn" of Josh. 6:5, and is the equivalent of the Hebrew *shôphār*, "trumpet," of Exod. 19:16. **Pipe:** *Mashrôqîthâ'* from a root "to hiss," "to whistle" (cf. Isa. 5:26). This is probably an old Canaanitish word, though some think it is from the Greek σῦριγξ. **Lyre:** *Qîthrôs* is the Greek κίθαρις, a stringed instrument whose sounding board is below the strings; i.e., the lyre or zither. **Trigon:** *Ṣabbekhâ* is the Greek σαμβύκη, though this word itself is apparently of Oriental origin. It is described as a small triangular instrument with four strings, used particularly for music provided at banquets. **Harp:** *Peṣanterîn* is the Greek ψαλτήριον, **psaltery**. It is a triangular instrument whose sounding board is above the strings. **Bagpipe:** *Sûmpônyāh* is the Greek συμφωνία, said to be a wind instrument composed of a goatskin bag with two reed pipes, one for filling the bag with wind from the mouth, the other pierced with holes for the fingers to provide various notes. Those who insist that the bagpipe was unknown at this time suggest that it was some kind of drum. **And every kind of music:** A phrase apparently intended to include music from other instruments than those mentioned. *Zēn*, **kind**, is the Middle Persian *zan* from the Old Persian *zana*. (On these musical instruments see Curt Sachs, *The History of Musical Instruments* [New York: W. W. Norton, 1940]; Eino Kolari, *Musikinstrumente und ihre Verwendung im Alten Testament* [Helsinki: 1947].)

6. **Fall down and worship:** The two verbs are those used in 2:46 for Nebuchadrezzar's falling down and doing obeisance to Daniel. **Immediately:** Lit., "at that moment."

madness of putting the idol in God's place is ever with us. All we do is to refine the idol, but the bowing down before it is the same crude thing which the king commanded the Jewish exiles to do.

4-5. *Fall Down and Worship.*—The idol commands; God entreats. The false religion does not hesitate to use force, and it believes that in the power of external compulsion there is the sign of its victory. Secret police or "thought

7 Therefore at that time, when all the people heard the sound of the cornet, flute, harp, sackbut, psaltery, and all kinds of music, all the people, the nations, and the languages, fell down *and* worshipped the golden image that Nebuchadnezzar the king had set up.

8 ¶ Wherefore at that time certain Chaldeans came near, and accused the Jews.

7 Therefore, as soon as all the peoples heard the sound of the horn, pipe, lyre, trigon, harp, bagpipe, and every kind of music, all the peoples, nations, and languages fell down and worshiped the golden image which King Nebuchadnez'zar had set up.

8 Therefore at that time certain Chalde'-ans came forward and maliciously accused

---

Sha'tā' indicates a short space of time. It occurs again in vs. 15 and in 4:19, 33 (M.T. 4:16, 30); 5:5, always with the meaning "moment," though often rendered **hour.**

The punishment for those who do not conform is to be burned alive by being cast into "the midst of a kiln fire-kindled." *'Attûn* seems to be a pre-Semitic autochthonous word for the local kilns, beehive kilns which are fed from the top but have an opening in the side. This would explain how the attendants who took the confessors up to cast them in were killed by the flames from the superheated kiln, and how when the flames had died down, the king could look in from the side and see the figures walking about.

Punishment by burning was well known in the ancient Near East. It is mentioned in the Code of Hammurabi 25, 110, 157, though in Mesopotamia it seems to have been reserved for certain classes of offenses. Herodotus (*History* I. 86) records its use by Cyrus and by the Scythians (*ibid.* IV. 69), and Diodorus Siculus (I. 59. 1-4; 77. 8) mentions its use among the Egyptians. (In the O.T. there is reference to punishment by burning in Gen. 38:24; Lev. 21:9; Josh. 7:15, 25; Jer. 29:22; cf. Jubilees 20:4; 30:7; 41:19, 25. That it was practiced in Seleucid times is suggested by II Macc. 7:3 ff.; IV Macc. 18:20.)

b) THE WORSHIP OF THE IMAGE (3:7)

7. In the enumeration of the instruments in this verse the **bagpipe** is missing in the M.T. It is found in some MSS, however, and in most of the MSS of Theod. so that some editors would restore it here.

2. TRIAL OF THE CONFESSORS (3:8-23)
a) THE ACCUSATION (3:8-12)

8. In such an assembly of provincial officers it would be noticed that the Jewish youths did not conform to the monarch's command, and so **certain Chaldeans** laid complaint against them. It is usually assumed that this word here means the caste of wise men, since they would be the most jealous of these foreigners who had been forced on them as colleagues. However, it may well be used here in its ethnic sense to mean that certain officials of Chaldean nationality laid information against them. The fact that it was a "malicious" accusation does not weigh in favor of either meaning against the other, nor does the wording of vs. 12. That the accusation was against **the Jews** does not mean that it was directed against all the Jews in the Exile. The accusation was against the three, the offense in their case being aggravated by the fact that they were government officials who ought to have been obedient to their sovereign.

Maliciously accused: Lit., "and they ate their pieces." So in 6:24. This idiom for "to accuse" is commonly used in Aramaic and parallels the "ate their flesh" used in the *Qur'ān* (Sūra 49:12), and the *akālu karṣi* of the Amarna letters (cf. Ps. 27:2). The audience would appreciate the situation so characteristic of Oriental courts at all periods

---

control" methods are cited as a proof of the terrible power of the tyrant to enforce his way on men. Yet these things are not signs of power, but confessions of weakness. Men cannot be forced to give their loyalty or their faithfulness. These must be free gifts, or they are useless.

God's way is the way of persuasion. He seems to let himself be flouted by the impious. But true religion depends on love, not force. Against faith, the force of the idol proves to be weak and ineffectual. In the things that really matter, men cannot be commanded or compelled.

9 They spake and said to the king Nebuchadnezzar, O king, live for ever.

10 Thou, O king, hast made a decree, that every man that shall hear the sound of the cornet, flute, harp, sackbut, psaltery, and dulcimer, and all kinds of music, shall fall down and worship the golden image:

11 And whoso falleth not down and worshippeth, *that* he should be cast into the midst of a burning fiery furnace.

12 There are certain Jews whom thou hast set over the affairs of the province of Babylon, Shadrach, Meshach, and Abed-nego; these men, O king, have not regarded thee: they serve not thy gods, nor worship the golden image which thou hast set up.

13 ¶ Then Nebuchadnezzar in *his* rage and fury commanded to bring Shadrach, Meshach, and Abed-nego. Then they brought these men before the king.

14 Nebuchadnezzar spake and said unto them, *Is it* true, O Shadrach, Meshach, and Abed-nego? do not ye serve my gods, nor

the Jews. 9 They said to King Nebuchadnez'zar, "O king, live for ever! 10 You, O king, have made a decree, that every man who hears the sound of the horn, pipe, lyre, trigon, harp, bagpipe, and every kind of music, shall fall down and worship the golden image; 11 and whoever does not fall down and worship shall be cast into a burning fiery furnace. 12 There are certain Jews whom you have appointed over the affairs of the province of Babylon: Shadrach, Meshach, and Abed'nego. These men, O king, pay no heed to you; they do not serve your gods or worship the golden image which you have set up."

13 Then Nebuchadnez'zar in furious rage commanded that Shadrach, Meshach, and Abed'nego be brought. Then they brought these men before the king. 14 Nebuchadnez'zar said to them, "Is it true, O

where one faction is constantly endeavoring to overthrow another by malicious accusation. The informer was so characteristic a figure at the court that he continually appears in Oriental story, and it is at least curious that the accusations brought by informers are generally concerned with some matter of lese majesty. That the informers should repeat the king's statement word for word is a stylistic nicety common in Oriental tales.

10. Made a decree: The same phrase is used in this sense in the Aramaic papyri. In vs. 12 and in 6:13 (M.T. 6:14), however, it is used to mean "pay heed," and in 2:14 *ṭeʿēm* was rendered "discretion."

12. Why Daniel is not mentioned here greatly exercised the older commentators. It may be that as Daniel is to have a story to himself in ch. 6 he was deliberately omitted here. Perhaps he was thought of as having some specially high office which relieved him from the necessity of appearing at the dedication. Bevan suggests that he is missing because he would have spoiled the story; had he been present, it would have been necessary to have him come and rescue his friends, which would have made the divine deliverance less spectacular. The answer probably is that in the original story there were but three characters and the three friends fitted admirably.

Serve: The root פלח is properly "to till the ground," hence "to labor," to **serve,** and in the derived sense of serving the gods, "to worship." For **worship** the verb "to do obeisance" is again used. It is noticeable how the accusation against the three corresponds with that made against Daniel in 6:13. Charles thinks that in this verse there is direct allusion to affairs under Antiochus Epiphanes, whom those who joined the Maccabees were "setting at nought."

b) THE AUDIENCE (3:13-15)

13-15. In furious rage: Lit., "in rage and hot wrath" (cf. vs. 19). The matter might seem to us nothing about which to be irritated, but the fury of potentates was a stock feature in stories of this type (cf. Esth. 1:12; 7:7; Tob. 1:18; Judith 5:2; II Macc. 4:38; 7:3, and for secular examples Herodotus *op. cit.* VII. 39; Plutarch *Solon* 27). However, the king does not punish on hearsay. He has the men brought in that he may hear from them himself. In vs. 5 the heralds proclaimed the command; in vs. 10 the accusers repeat

worship the golden image which I have set up?

15 Now if ye be ready that at what time ye hear the sound of the cornet, flute, harp, sackbut, psaltery, and dulcimer, and all kinds of music, ye fall down and worship the image which I have made; *well:* but if ye worship not, ye shall be cast the same hour into the midst of a burning fiery furnace; and who *is* that God that shall deliver you out of my hands?

16 Shadrach, Meshach, and Abed-nego, answered and said to the king, O Nebuchadnezzar, we *are* not careful to answer thee in this matter.

Shadrach, Meshach, and Abed'nego, that you do not serve my gods or worship the golden image which I have set up? 15 Now if you are ready when you hear the sound of the horn, pipe, lyre, trigon, harp, bagpipe, and every kind of music, to fall down and worship the image which I have made, well and good; but if you do not worship, you shall immediately be cast into a burning fiery furnace; and who is the god that will deliver you out of my hands?"

16 Shadrach, Meshach, and Abed'nego answered the king, "O Nebuchadnez'zar, we have no need to answer you in this mat-

---

it word for word, and in vs. 15 the king again repeats it word for word. To this threefold repetition with rising emphasis there are numerous literary parallels. It is also a characteristic of the martyr legends that the confessors are brought in and allowed to make their confession before the ruler himself.

Is it true? This is most probably the meaning, though some prefer to translate: "Is it that you are making mock of me?" or "Is it certain?" or "Is it of set purpose?" The LXX has Διὰ τί; Theod. has εἰ ἀληθῶς.

15. Who is the god? A highly characteristic Aramaic phrase meaning "What sort of a god is there who can . . . ?" The challenge here has often been compared with that of Sennacherib and Rabshakeh in Isa. 36:19-20; 37:10-12, and the answer of the confessors with that of the brethren in II Macc. 7. Similarly Cyrus, when he was going to burn the Lydian youths, placed the pious king Croesus on the pile with them to see if any deity would intervene to save them (Herodotus *op. cit.* I. 86).

Deliver: The usual verb is dropped here in favor of a form derived from the Akkadian. This verb is used again in vss. 17, 28 and in 6:14, 16, 20, 27 (M.T. 6:15, 17, 21, 28) to mean "release," "rescue." The king's question is purely rhetorical and should not be interpreted as deliberate defiance of Yahweh. Its literary purpose is to provide an opportunity for the confessors to bear witness by presenting them with the cue word **god**.

c) THE DEFENSE (3:16-18)

16. We have no need to answer: This is a matter for God, and he will answer with deeds, not words. This type of reply is characteristic of the martyr legends (cf. Acts 4:19; 5:29, and the examples collected by Kuhl [*op. cit.*, p. 30]). There is a certain pride such as appears again in Daniel's answer to the king in 5:17, a pride growing out of a consciousness that as servants of God they are superior to any earthly potentate and so

---

15. *Who Can Deliver You?*—Here is the voice of the materialist. One cannot but think of the scene at the Crucifixion: "And they that passed by railed on him, wagging their heads, and saying, Ah, thou that destroyest the temple, and buildest it in three days, save thyself, and come down from the cross. Likewise also the chief priests mocking said among themselves with the scribes, He saved others; himself he cannot save. Let Christ the King of Israel descend now from the cross, that we may see and believe. And they that were crucified with him reviled him." (Mark 15:29-32.) We never learn. The unseen

allies of the human spirit seem so far away, and material power so real and so immediate. We repeat over and over again the lie that God is always on the side of force. But our victories will not stay won. With complete control over a man's life, we cannot conquer his spirit. Some One is always delivering our spiritual leaders out of the hands of their enemies. The hands of power are never quite adequate to control the essential things or to clinch our triumphs.

16. *No Need to Answer.*—Great living does not need an oral defense, and a constant desire to quibble is the sign of a small mind and a

17 If it be *so*, our God whom we serve is able to deliver us from the burning fiery furnace, and he will deliver *us* out of thine hand, O king.

18 But if not, be it known unto thee, O king, that we will not serve thy gods, nor worship the golden image which thou hast set up.

19 ¶ Then was Nebuchadnezzar full of fury, and the form of his visage was changed against Shadrach, Meshach, and Abed-nego: *therefore* he spake, and commanded that they should heat the furnace one seven times more than it was wont to be heated.

20 And he commanded the most mighty men that *were* in his army to bind Shadrach, Meshach, and Abed-nego, *and* to cast *them* into the burning fiery furnace.

21 Then these men were bound in their coats, their hose, and their hats, and their *other* garments, and were cast into the midst of the burning fiery furnace.

ter. **17** If it be so, our God whom we serve is able to deliver us from the burning fiery furnace; and he will deliver us out of your hand, O king.[c] **18** But if not, be it known to you, O king, that we will not serve your gods or worship the golden image which you have set up."

19 Then Nebuchadnez'zar was full of fury, and the expression of his face was changed against Shadrach, Meshach, and Abed'nego. He ordered the furnace heated seven times more than it was wont to be heated. **20** And he ordered certain mighty men of his army to bind Shadrach, Meshach, and Abed'nego, and to cast them into the burning fiery furnace. **21** Then these men were bound in their mantles,[d] their tunics,[d] their hats, and their other garments, and they were cast into the burning fiery fur-

[c] Or Behold, our God . . . king. Or If our God is able to deliver us, he will deliver us from the burning fiery furnace and out of your hand, O king.
[d] The meaning of the Aramaic word is uncertain

have need of neither his clemency nor his gifts. **In this matter:** Lit., "a word concerning this." For the construction see I Kings 12:6, 9, 16. *Pithgām* is an Iranian word which occurs also in Ezra, Esther, and Ecclesiastes.

17. The construction of this verse is difficult. Perhaps the best translation is: "If the God whom we serve is, he is able to deliver us from the fiery furnace, and from thy hand he will deliver." The confessors are pinning their hope on faith being justified. They believe that idols are vain and that there is but one true God. If that is so and he is, he can deliver them (Isa. 43:2; Ps. 66:12); but even if it should prove not so, yet will they not worship the king's idol. It is noticeable that they say the **God whom we serve** but do not mention his name. Here as in the book of Esther we are in a period when reverence for the personal name of God forbids that name being spoken.

d) The Sentence and Its Execution (3:19-23)

19. To forestall any attempt at rescue the angry king proceeds to take excessive precautions for the execution of the punishment decreed. There was to be an unusually large fire in the kiln, the most powerful men among the soldiers were to be in charge, and the victims were to be bound before being thrown in. **Fury:** The "hot wrath" of vs. 13. "And the image of his face was altered against," i.e., his face was distorted with anger. *Çelēm*, "image," is the same word used in vs. 1 for the great image. The word **seven** merely represents a stylistic nicety and need not be pressed literally.

20. The powerful men were doubtless the stalwarts from the king's own bodyguard, whose duty it normally was to see to the carrying out of executions (see 2:14).

21. It was customary to strip criminals before execution, their garments being the perquisite of the executioners (see Matt. 27:35; Ps. 22:18). Casting them in clothed may be meant to suggest that this was a peculiarly effective way of preventing their escape.

little spirit. Nor are men convinced by such procedure. The Jewish heroes are saying that this is no time to argue the matter. They have made up their minds, and action will be their reply to the king. The deeper things of faith can never be said except by our living. One of

the students of a professor with whom many disagreed said once of him: "Whatever we may think of his theology, it has made him a great man." He had no need to answer criticisms with words. His life was answer enough. There is a story about Hugh Price Hughes being chal-

22 Therefore because the king's commandment was urgent, and the furnace exceeding hot, the flame of the fire slew those men that took up Shadrach, Meshach, and Abed-nego.

23 And these three men, Shadrach, Meshach, and Abed-nego, fell down bound into the midst of the burning fiery furnace.

24 Then Nebuchadnezzar the king was astonished, and rose up in haste, *and* spake, and said unto his counselors, Did not we cast three men bound into the midst of the fire? They answered and said unto the king, True, O king.

nace. 22 Because the king's order was strict and the furnace very hot, the flame of the fire slew those men who took up Shadrach, Meshach, and Abed'nego. 23 And these three men, Shadrach, Meshach, and Abed'nego, fell bound into the burning fiery furnace.

24 Then King Nebuchadnez'zar was astonished and rose up in haste. He said to his counselors, "Did we not cast three men bound into the fire?" They answered the

It is more likely, however, that the detail was intended to heighten the miraculousness of their deliverance, since clothing is highly inflammable. In early Christian art the confessors are commonly represented as naked in the fire.

There is still dispute as to the meaning of the various words used here for the clothing. Behrmann suggests that the three articles mentioned were meant to represent the three items which Herodotus (*op. cit.* I. 195) says were the characteristic Babylonian garments. It is possible that the three garments mentioned as in addition to **their other garments** were articles of official attire, i.e., they had come to the assembly in court dress. The words are discussed by S. A. Cook ("The Articles of Dress in Dan. III.21," *Journal of Philology,* XXVI [1899], 306-13) and by H. S. Nyberg ("Ein iranisches Wort im Buche Daniel," *Le Monde Oriental,* XXV [1931], 178-204).

Mantles: The Peshitta, Theod., Aq., Symm. all translate "trousers." *Ṣarbāl* is apparently an Iranian word. **Tunics:** The LXX and Theod. translate "turbans." Some think the word means trousers. It apparently is also Iranian. **Hats:** *Karbelāh* is the Akkadian *karballatu,* "helmet," "bonnet." **And their other garments:** Lit., "and their clothes." If the three articles specifically mentioned belong to the special court dress, then this refers to the normal **garments** over which the court dress would be worn. As the first pair of words is Iranian and the second pair Semitic, Nyberg suggests that the latter are meant as translations of the Iranian words.

22. Strict: The same word was translated "severe" in 2:15. The attendants had to carry the victims up to drop them in from the top, and because of the added fuel the flames were pouring out so that the attendants were burned to death before they could get down. Similarly, in the Abraham legend the flames gushed out and burned up those round about (Pseudo-Philo *Liber Antiquitatum Biblicarum* VI. 16-18). It is characteristic of the martyr legends that the tormentors of the righteous suffer the very penalty they proposed for their victims. So in 6:24 Daniel's accusers are those whom the lions devour, and in Esth. 7:10 Haman is hanged on the gallows he prepared for Mordecai. In some of the versions there are legendary exaggerations telling how the attendants poured naphtha, pitch, and tow on the fuel, how the flames leaped to fantastic heights, etc., but these are obviously later additions.

3. Epilogue (3:24-30)

a) The Angelic Protection (3:24-25)

24. When the flames died down, the king came to have a look and was **astonished**—the verb contains the suggestion of a very real fear (see 4:5, 19 [M.T. 4:2, 16]; 5:6)—by what he saw. It is not clear whether any save the king saw this portentous thing. That he **rose up** does not necessarily mean that he had been sitting on his royal chair to watch the proceedings. It may mean that he rose up from the stooping position he had taken in order to look in at the floor of the kiln. **In haste** is the same word used in 2:25

25 He answered and said, Lo, I see four men loose, walking in the midst of the fire, and they have no hurt; and the form of the fourth is like the Son of God.

26 ¶ Then Nebuchadnezzar came near to the mouth of the burning fiery furnace, *and* spake, and said, Shadrach, Meshach, and Abed-nego, ye servants of the most high God, come forth, and come *hither*. Then Shadrach, Meshach, and Abed-nego, came forth of the midst of the fire.

king, "True, O king." 25 He answered, "But I see four men loose, walking in the midst of the fire, and they are not hurt; and the appearance of the fourth is like a son of the gods."

26 Then Nebuchadnez'zar came near to the door of the burning fiery furnace and said, "Shadrach, Meshach, and Abed'nego, servants of the Most High God, come forth, and come here!" Then Shadrach, Meshach, and Abed'nego came out from the fire.

---

of Arioch's bringing Daniel in before the king. **Counselors:** *Haddâbhār,* a word which occurs again in vs. 27 and in 4:36 (M.T. 4:33) ; 6:7 (M.T. 6:8) but nowhere else in the O.T. It is probably a Persian title.

25. Loose: Whether we are to understand that the fire burned their bonds but not their clothes, or whether their angelic companion loosed them to walk with him, is not clear. In martyr legends it is not uncommon to find that the fetters of themselves fall from the martyrs (see Kuhl, *op. cit.,* p. 44). **Walking in the midst:** Once the flames had died down, the floor of the kiln would be covered with glowing coals and anyone walking over them could be seen from the front opening. The detail that they were walking "quite unharmed" is characteristic of martyr legends, where also when the faithful are in grave peril their rescue is likely to be at the hands of some special messenger from God. Here and at 6:22 it is an angel, as it was in the Hagar story (Gen. 21:17 ff.) and in the Isaac story (Gen. 22:11). Kuhl (*ibid.,* pp. 40-42) assembles nonbiblical examples. **Not hurt:** Lit., "and there is no harm to them." **Appearance:** As in 2:31.

It was the king who asked, "Who is the god that will deliver you?" (vs. 15), and that same king now says of the fourth figure that his form **is like a son of the gods,** i.e., an angel, a celestial being, a divinity, such as were commonly called "sons of the gods." Biblical examples are in Gen. 6:2; Job 1:6. That it was an angel appears from vs. 28. Some have seen in the phrase **son of the gods** a reference to a special class of Babylonian deity, but actually the Canaanite parallels are closer; e.g., in Ugaritic texts we find these sons of the deities. It was perhaps inevitable that Christian exegesis should see in the fourth figure a preincarnation appearance of the Redeemer. The writer, however, did not intend to suggest anything other than that it was an angel from God.

b) The Deliverance (3:26-27)

26. The king drew nearer **the door** of the kiln. The translation **mouth** is preferred by those who regard the furnace as a pit whose only opening was from above. If, however, it was a kiln fed from above but with an opening in front or at the side, from which the contents were withdrawn, then "gate" or **door,** the literal meaning of the Aramaic, is better. It would be through this door that the confessors heard the king's call and came forth.

The Most High God: This expression occurs again in 4:2; 5:18, 21. It is the equivalent of the Hebrew *ēl ʿelyōn*=θεὸς ὕψιστος, which must be a very ancient Canaanitish name for a supreme deity, for Philo of Byblos states that the Phoenicians revered Ἐλιοῦν καλούμενος Ὕψιστος.

---

lenged to a debate by the freethinker Charles Bradlaugh. Hughes suggested that each should find a hundred men who would testify how their lives had been redeemed by their faith. There is no better argument than that. The

saint has **no need to answer.** He needs only to live.

25. *I See Four Men.*—Note that it was not until the commitment had been made that the **fourth** figure was visible. There is a spiritual

27 And the princes, governors, and captains, and the king's counselors, being gathered together, saw these men, upon whose bodies the fire had no power, nor was a hair of their head singed, neither were their coats changed, nor the smell of fire had passed on them.

28 *Then* Nebuchadnezzar spake, and said, Blessed *be* the God of Shadrach, Meshach, and Abed-nego, who hath sent his angel, and delivered his servants that trusted in him, and have changed the king's word, and yielded their bodies, that they might not serve nor worship any god, except their own God.

27 And the satraps, the governors, and the king's counselors gathered together and saw that the fire had not had any power over the bodies of those men; the hair of their heads was not singed, their mantles[d] were not harmed, and no smell of fire had come upon them. 28 Nebuchadnez'zar said, "Blessed be the God of Shadrach, Meshach, and Abed'nego, who has sent his angel and delivered his servants, who trusted in him, and set at nought the king's command, and yielded up their bodies rather than serve and worship any god except their own God.

[d] The meaning of the Aramaic word is uncertain

---

27. The dignitaries of the court assemble to witness the miracle. In vs. 2 eight classes were enumerated, but here only four—the **satraps, prefects, governors,** and royal **counselors.** This latter is the word used in vs. 24, but it does not occur in vs. 2. **The fire had not had any power:** This is referred to in Heb. 11:34. It is the kind of detail that occurs in the martyr stories (cf. Pseudo-Philo, *op. cit.,* VI. 16-18; Kuhl, *op. cit.,* p. 45). There is conscious artistry in the mounting intensity as the description proceeds. Not only were their bodies not burned, but their loose hair was not singed, the heat had not damaged their clothing, and though they had been in the midst of burning fuel, there was not even the smell of burning on them. **Harmed:** The verb is "to change," "to alter," another form of which is used of the monarch's face being distorted by rage (vs. 19; 5:9), and in 4:16 (M.T. 4:13) is used of the changing of the heart. Here it does not necessarily refer to the color of the garment but probably means that none of the usual effects of fire on cloth had occurred.

The ṣarbāl is the only article of clothing mentioned here, perhaps because one garment is meant to stand for the whole, or maybe because the audience would understand that the ṣarbāl was made from some especially light and inflammable material, so the miracle was that not even such a garment suffered from the fire.

Smell: The same word in Hebrew is used for the sweet savor of sacrificial offerings, and in Song of Songs for the smell of ointment.

c) God's Exaltation (3:28-30)

28. The king now sings a little doxology in praise of the God of the confessors. His **Blessed be** is the same beginning as was made by the queen of Sheba in I Kings 10:9, and by Huram king of Tyre in II Chr. 2:12, when they witnessed God's power. **Sent his angel** would seem to indicate that at that day there were conventionally recognized forms in which an angel might be expected to appear, so that a man would know that it was an angel, not a human being. The writer, however, may merely have been assuming in his audience acquaintance with biblical stories in which angels are said to have been sent (e.g., Gen. 16:7-11; 24:7; Exod. 3:2; 23:20, 23; 32:34; Num. 20:16). **Set at nought:** Lit., **changed,** "altered." It is the same verb as in vs. 27, a secondary meaning of which is "to contradict," "to disobey," i.e., to alter to its opposite and so to frustrate (cf. Ezra 6:11). **The king's command:** Lit., **the king's word,** i.e., the word which he had pronounced in his decree.

---

truth in this. We say, "Show me that I shall win and then I shall risk it." But there is no answer. Yet when we have decided to go God's way, the angel of the Lord stands beside us to

strengthen and comfort us. It is this unseen power that upsets the plans of despots. The reality of the unseen Companion is never doubted by those who go his way, but he is

29 Therefore I make a decree, That every people, nation, and language, which speak any thing amiss against the God of Shadrach, Meshach, and Abed-nego, shall be cut in pieces, and their houses shall be made a dunghill; because there is no other God that can deliver after this sort.

30 Then the king promoted Shadrach, Meshach, and Abed-nego, in the province of Babylon.

4 Nebuchadnezzar the king, unto all people, nations, and languages, that dwell in all the earth; Peace be multiplied unto you.

29 Therefore I make a decree: Any people, nation, or language that speaks anything against the God of Shadrach, Meshach, and Abed'nego shall be torn limb from limb, and their houses laid in ruins; for there is no other god who is able to deliver in this way." 30 Then the king promoted Shadrach, Meshach, and Abed'nego in the province of Babylon.

4 ᵉ King Nebuchadnez'zar to all peoples, nations, and languages, that dwell in all the earth: Peace be multiplied to you!

ᵉ Aram Ch 3. 31

---

29. Under Antiochus Epiphanes the Jewish religion had ceased to be a *religio licita*, and decrees had been issued with the intention of preventing its practice (I Macc. 1:41-50). The people would thus appreciate the full significance of this account of how God's intervention on behalf of those who had been loyal to him was instrumental in securing for their religion the status of *religio licita* throughout the empire. Nebuchadrezzar does not become a convert to the Jewish religion, but he grants it full rights in his realm, and threatens with punishment any who would interfere with its free practice. It is curious that the threat made against **any people, nation, or language** is one that could be visited only on individuals. Bentzen is doubtless right in thinking that it means "anyone, no matter what his national or linguistic affiliation may be."

The Aramaic שׁלה, **anything,** is a puzzle. It may be interpreted as "word" or "thing," "blasphemy," "something lax or remiss," "slander," "abuse." Nevertheless the meaning is clear. The same punishment is decreed as in 2:5.

30. Promoted: Lit., "caused to prosper." Since they already had high posts, Driver suggests that the meaning here is that the king favored them in various ways in the fulfilling of their duties.

D. NEBUCHADREZZAR'S MADNESS (4:1-37)

In the printed text of the M.T. vss. 1-3 are still part of ch. 3, but the ancient tradition of the pericopes rightly makes them the beginning of a new chapter.

The story is in the form of an epistle. The fact that Nebuchadrezzar's conduct here does not correspond with that depicted in ch. 3, suggests that originally it was an independent story which the writer has taken and adapted to his plan. The picture of the friendly relations between the monarch and the sage may again point to the original story having arisen in a period when there was little active hostility toward the Jews.

Language and style make it certain that this is not an epistle taken from some ancient document but a piece that has been worked up and put in the mouth of Nebuchadrezzar by the author of the preceding and the succeeding chapters. In fact, in vss. 28-33 (M.T. vss. 25-30) the writer slips into the third person, though presently he returns to the first person. He tells of a dream, of Daniel's interpretation thereof, and

---

never found until the decision has been made to endure whatever sacrifices God demands.

29. There Is No Other God.—There is no creed to live by like that of Christians. Other ways of life promise much, and for a time seem capable of satisfying our needs. But the optimistic creeds all dissolve when the day of testing comes. Our faith begins with the worst. It is able to hold us steady under the most adverse

conditions because it centers in a God who trains us to be strong. The king knew that his god could not do for him what the God of the Jews had done for them. When Disraeli was asked what proof he had of God, he answered, "The Jews." Their whole history is a testimony of the power of their God.

4:1-37. The Peril of Pride.—An edict describing the reason for his seven years' madness is

how the dream was fulfilled. Its purpose is to teach how helpless even the greatest heathen power is when the God of Israel intervenes. To Jews suffering under Antiochus here was a story of how even Nebuchadrezzar, mightiest of all monarchs, was reduced by God's intervention to the level of the beasts and forced to confess that sovereignty and dominion belong to Israel's God. Why then should men fear Antiochus Epiphanes? Him also God could humble and force to confess his supremacy.

There is no historical confirmation for a seven-year interregnum during the reign of Nebuchadrezzar, nor is there any tradition that he suffered from such madness as is depicted here. Some have therefore thought that here Nebuchadrezzar stands for Nabonidus, the last Neo-Babylonian king, who was away from the capital for several years living in the deserts. Others have remembered the curious fragment from Abydenus preserved in Eusebius (*Preparation for the Gospel* IX. 41), which tells how Nebuchadrezzar one day fell into an ecstasy on the roof of his palace and prophesied the end of his dynasty at the hands of a Persian mule, helped by the son of a Median woman. Elements from such court tales may have entered into the composition of the original story on which this chapter is based, as indeed have elements from Oriental mythology such as the world tree or the number seven. Some of the motifs found here appear also in the story of the Babylonian Job (see W. O. E. Oesterley's review of Charles, *The Book of Daniel* in *Church Quarterly Review*, X [1930], 120-29). It is thus clear that we are not to think of history here but of story, a story used as the vehicle for a message the writer had for his contemporaries.

1. Prologue (4:1-9)

a) The King's Letter (4:1-3=M.T. 3:31-33)

4:1. Charles argues, with the support of some evidence from the LXX, that this verse is displaced and ought to come at the end of the chapter. Cf. the opening words with those of Darius in 6:25. **Peoples, nations, and languages:** As at 3:4; etc. Such a

---

issued by King Nebuchadrezzar. The meaning of the whole affair is that pride must be punished. Daniel was suggesting that God would stand only so much from power-mad rulers, and it was a subtle way of warning Antiochus, who was sometimes referred to as a "madman."

Daniel is suggesting that pride is madness. It is the loss of a sense of perspective. It is putting oneself in the place of God, and it happens to men who have cut themselves off from reality. They begin to think they can do anything they desire. The limitations of human power no longer seem real to them, and they decide that they can manipulate man and nature to suit their own convenience. It is this loss of discrimination that brings them to their ultimate downfall. In the sudden panic which envelops them when at last they see themselves thwarted, they lose their judgment. Pride always overextends itself.

We have seen this repeatedly illustrated in history. Despotic power is self-destructive because there is no check-and-balance system to keep it in line with things as they are. Pride creates a dream world, or a mad world. Fantasies are mistaken for realities. Life finally takes a terrible revenge on the proud man or nation.

William James used to say to his students in psychology, "Be willing to have it so. . . ."

Acceptance of what has happened is the first step in overcoming the consequences of any misfortune." But those who are ruled by pride are not "willing to have it so." They break themselves against the unyielding, inevitable nature of things. Madness is always a retreat from reality, and that is the nature of pride.

The other side of this picture is that humility is sanity. The king is restored when he has recognized his sin and repented of it. His healing is possible when he can say, **Now I, Nebuchadnezzar, praise and extol and honor the King of heaven** (vs. 37). Now he is able to take his proper place in the scheme of things and stop playing as if he were the Deity.

Christians have learned the great words of humility spoken by Jesus. The theme runs through all of his teaching. "Blessed are the meek," he says, "for they shall inherit the earth" (Matt. 5:5). He weaves the theme into his parables, and we know the stories. But it is as difficult for us to practice the virtue as it was for his contemporaries. There is no trait we so admire in our friends and none so difficult to practice in our own lives. We despise pride when it appears in the actions and attitudes of others, but we cannot control it in ourselves. Even when the king had been warned, he could not resist saying, **Is not this great**

| 2 I thought it good to show the signs and wonders that the high God hath wrought toward me. | 2 It has seemed good to me to show the signs and wonders that the Most High God has wrought toward me. |

claim to universal sovereignty was a pleasant conceit of ancient monarchs, though it must be remembered that "the whole earth" did not mean to them what it does to us. When Mesopotamian rulers claim to be "king of the four quarters," it means nothing more than that they are king over all the countries worth being king over (cf. Jer. 25:26). The audience was probably familiar with the statement about Nebuchadrezzar in Jer. 27:6-7.

Like most ancient letters this begins with mention of the sender, the recipients, greeting of peace, and a statement of the subject of the letter. Some MSS have the word שְׁלַח, "he sent," i.e., "King Nebuchadrezzar sent to all nations. . . ." The formula for the peace greeting is found in the Aramaic papyri and in Ezra 5:7.

2. Seemed good: The same word is translated "be acceptable" in vs. 27 (M.T. vs. 24), and "it pleased" in 6:1 (M.T. 6:2). **To show** is the same verb used in 2:4 for declaring the interpretation of a dream. **Signs and wonders:** So in 6:27. The corresponding Hebrew phrase occurs in Deut. 4:34; 6:22; Isa. 8:18 (cf. Ecclus. 36:6; Mark 13:22; Rom. 15:19; Josephus *Jewish War,* Preface, 11). **The Most High God:** As in 3:26. **Toward me:** Lit., "with me."

Babylon, which I have built by my mighty power as a royal residence and for the glory of my majesty? (Vs. 30.)

There is in humanity a fear of the sanity of humility. We are like the Gadarenes who begged Jesus to leave them after he had healed the madman. They seemed to be saying to him that they preferred their insanity to his sanity. Yet the peace of mind for which we seek so diligently always eludes us until we dare be humble. Much of the nervous disorder of our time is due to self-centeredness and to an excessive sensitiveness to fancied slights. Those who deal with disordered lives and strained spirits agree that humility is health.

Only a religious experience can keep us humble. We can hardly escape comparing our best with our neighbor's worst. According to a survey, most Americans think this would be a good world if others were as good as they are. In that attitude we have the clue to what is wrong with us. What a strange thing it is that the worse we are, the more satisfied with ourselves we are; while the better we are, the more we feel our need for forgiveness and redemption. The sinner is sure he is a better man than most, while the saint feels utterly unworthy to be called good.

Then we may draw out of this story the point that we ought to learn from our suffering. The king was healed when he had seen the truth that God was teaching him. It is possible to go through experiences as disastrous as his and not learn a thing from them. As a matter of fact, the tragedy of many a life is its inability to learn from experience. A man may go on doing the same thing over and over again, even when it brings him nothing but failure. It would seem that a little humble self-searching would open a man's eyes to his mistakes. But too many of us have developed the evil habit of assuming that everything wrong is somebody else's fault. Many a person's epitaph might read: "He could have been saved if he had learned from his experiences."

Suffering is not inevitably redeeming. There are times when it does not cleanse at all. There are times when it is destructive and embittering. The fault lies not in the experience, but in the human reaction. We discover that often the fault was our own, and the tragedy might have been avoided. We perceive sometimes that there was nothing much we could have done about it. But even then the experience will not be without value if we can learn sympathy and resignation.

Dale Carnegie [8] tells of the difference between some trees on his Missouri farm and the trees of the northern woods. His farm trees grew rapidly but were destroyed by an ice storm that broke their limbs. The spruce and pine of Canadian woods bend before the storm and bow their branches. They have learned how to cooperate with the inevitable. Men need that wisdom too. If we are humble enough to learn, God will teach us from every experience we have.

2. Signs and Wonders from God.—When God has done something for us, it is no time to keep silence. What we have discovered of God's ways

[8] *How to Stop Worrying and Start Living* (New York: Simon & Schuster, 1948), p. 73.

3 How great *are* his signs! and how mighty *are* his wonders! his kingdom *is* an everlasting kingdom, and his dominion *is* from generation to generation.

4 ¶ I Nebuchadnezzar was at rest in mine house, and flourishing in my palace:

5 I saw a dream which made me afraid, and the thoughts upon my bed and the visions of my head troubled me.

6 Therefore made I a decree to bring in all the wise *men* of Babylon before me, that they might make known unto me the interpretation of the dream.

3 How great are his signs,
    how mighty his wonders!
His kingdom is an everlasting kingdom,
    and his dominion is from generation to
    generation.

4*f* I, Nebuchadnez'zar, was at ease in my house and prospering in my palace. 5 I had a dream which made me afraid; as I lay in bed the fancies and the visions of my head alarmed me. 6 Therefore I made a decree that all the wise men of Babylon should be brought before me, that they might make known to me the interpretation

f Aram Ch 4. 1

---

3. The succeeding lines are metrical, a hymn or paean of praise (cf. Ps. 145:5, 13).

b) THE INCAPACITY OF THE WISE MEN AND THE SUCCESS OF DANIEL
(4:4-9=M.T. 4:1-6)

4. The LXX appends a date, viz., the eighteenth year of Nebuchadrezzar—clearly a later addition. To accentuate the importance of the dream the king describes how his pleasant, carefree life was disturbed by the uneasiness caused by it. *Shelēh* is properly **at rest,** "secure." In Jer. 49:31 the desert dwellers with their camels are said to be "carefree," and in Ps. 73:12 the wicked are "at ease" (cf. Ps. 30:6), but in Ps. 122:7 the word refers to the prosperous ease of holy Jerusalem. *Ra'nān,* **prospering,** seems to occur nowhere else in Aramaic. It may be a borrowing from the Hebrew word used properly of a tree and then figuratively of persons, as in Ps. 92:14 (M.T. 92:15). The reference is to the greenness of the tree and so gives the sense of "prosperous." The word is used both for the prosperity of the wicked, as in Ps. 37:35, or that of the pious, as in Ps. 52:8 (M.T. 52:10). Both meanings seem to be combined here to indicate the state of Nebuchadrezzar, perhaps with the thought in mind that such excessive contentment in itself foreshadows trouble (cf. Deut. 8:11-14). It may be doubted whether any distinction is meant between **house** and **palace,** the latter being the same word used in 1:4.

5. "A dream I saw and it made me afraid, and phantoms upon my bed and visions of my head troubled me." **Fancies:** *Harhōrîn* occurs only here in the O.T. and is of uncertain derivation. Here it must mean troubled fancies or phantom thoughts. **Visions of my head:** As in 2:28, and again in vss. 10, 13; 7:1, 15. **Alarmed:** The word is translated "astonished" in 3:24. It occurs again in vs. 19 (M.T. vs. 16); 5:6, 9-10; 7:15, 28, always of trouble of mind because of disturbing thoughts.

6. The court sages are sent for, since it is their business to interpret such dreams. One might have expected the king after his experience in ch. 2 to have summoned Daniel first, especially as he is now chief over these wise men. The convention of such a story, however, is to bring Daniel in only after the sages have demonstrated their incapacity. **A decree** is issued (cf. 3:29) to bring the wise men to the court, just as they had been summoned in 2:2. **Wise men** is used as a general term to cover all the classes who are mentioned in detail in vs. 7.

---

of dealing with men we ought to proclaim to our brethren. Our fathers were aware of their commission to testify to their religious experiences. Every Christian has this same obligation. Men have been saved many times by a simple word spoken sincerely.

4-5. *A Frightening Dream.*—There is no defense against a dream. The intimations that all

is not well with us keep breaking in at the most inopportune moments. There is something about guilt that pounces on us when we are **at ease.** We can keep busy for a time and forget the thing that is wrong, but when we relax it is there to make us **afraid.** The way the thing we know is wrong haunts us is one of the terrible characteristics of evil.

7 Then came in the magicians, the astrologers, the Chaldeans, and the soothsayers: and I told the dream before them; but they did not make known unto me the interpretation thereof.

8 ¶ But at the last Daniel came in before me, whose name *was* Belteshazzar, according to the name of my god, and in whom *is* the spirit of the holy gods: and before him I told the dream, *saying,*

9 O Belteshazzar, master of the magicians, because I know that the spirit of the holy gods *is* in thee, and no secret troubleth thee, tell me the visions of my dream that I have seen, and the interpretation thereof.

10 Thus *were* the visions of mine head in my bed; I saw, and behold a tree in the midst of the earth, and the height thereof *was* great.

of the dream. **7** Then the magicians, the enchanters, the Chalde'ans, and the astrologers came in; and I told them the dream, but they could not make known to me its interpretation. **8** At last Daniel came in before me — he who was named Belteshaz'zar after the name of my god, and in whom is the spirit of the holy gods[g] — and I told him the dream, saying, **9** "O Belteshaz'zar, chief of the magicians, because I know that the spirit of the holy gods[g] is in you and that no mystery is difficult for you, here is[h] the dream which I saw; tell me its interpretation. **10** The visions of my head as I lay in bed were these: I saw, and behold, a tree in the midst of the earth; and its height

[g] Or *Spirit of the holy God*
[h] Cn: Aram *visions of*

---

7. Magicians, enchanters, Chaldeans as in 2:2; **astrologers** as in 2:27. There is no particular significance in the order in which they are mentioned or in the fact that the sorcerers of 2:2 are not included here.

8. Finally Daniel comes in. Doubtless the order for the others had included him, but he comes in later just when their failure has become evident. The king recognizes him as he enters and addresses him by his court name, **Belteshazzar** (cf. 1:7). The king's interpretation of this name makes its first syllable Bēl, the title of Marduk, chief deity of Babylon. This is folk etymology unless we are to assume that *Balāṭsu-uṣur* is contracted from *Bēl-balāṭsu-uṣur.*

It was because of the events in 2:27-45 that Nebuchadrezzar knew that in Daniel was **the spirit of the holy gods** (cf. vs. 18 [M.T. vs. 15]; 5:11). Though the expression **holy gods,** which occurs in the Eshmunazar inscription, is plural, vs. 34 (M.T. vs. 31) clearly shows that the king is using it with a singular meaning (cf. Josh. 24:19 and the phrase used by Pharaoh of Joseph in Gen. 41:38). It is still quite uncertain what would have been understood by **spirit** in this connection.

9. Chief of the magicians: Cf. 2:48; 5:11. Magicians would seem to be a title that could cover all the various classes of wise men. **No mystery:** As in 2:19. **Is too difficult for you:** The word אנס occurs only here and in Esth. 1:8. It means "to compel," then "to incommode," so "no secret matter incommodes you." The phrase is curiously like that in Ezek. 28:3, which refers to the ancient sage Danel. "The visions of my dream which I saw, and its interpretation, tell." This phrase **visions of my dream** occurs nowhere else in Daniel and the translators of the versions did not understand it; many editors therefore emend the text to secure a smoother expression and avoid having the king bid Daniel tell both the dream and its interpretation as he had done in 2:5.

2. The Dream and Its Interpretation (4:10-27)
a) The King Tells His Dream (4:10-17=M.T. 4:7-14)

10. The king proceeds to tell his vision. "And the vision of my head upon my bed, I saw." Vss. 10-12 (M.T. vss. 7-9) are metrical, though why the monarch should commence the description in verse and then continue in prose is not clear, unless perhaps the verse part is a quotation which would have been recognized by the audience.

The imagery of the dream corresponds to Ezek. 31:3-14, a passage in which the king of Assyria is compared to a cedar in whose branches birds of heaven have made their nests, under which beasts brought forth their young, in whose shadow great

11 The tree grew, and was strong, and the height thereof reached unto heaven, and the sight thereof to the end of all the earth:

12 The leaves thereof *were* fair, and the fruit thereof much, and in it *was* meat for all: the beasts of the field had shadow under it, and the fowls of the heaven dwelt in the boughs thereof, and all flesh was fed of it.

13 I saw in the visions of my head upon my bed, and, behold, a watcher and a holy one came down from heaven;

14 He cried aloud, and said thus, Hew down the tree, and cut off his branches, shake off his leaves, and scatter his fruit: let the beasts get away from under it, and the fowls from his branches:

was great. 11 The tree grew and became strong, and its top reached to heaven, and it was visible to the end of the whole earth.

12 Its leaves were fair and its fruit abundant, and in it was food for all. The beasts of the field found shade under it, and the birds of the air dwelt in its branches, and all flesh was fed from it.

13 "I saw in the visions of my head as I lay in bed, and behold, a watcher, a holy one, came down from heaven. 14 He cried aloud and said thus, 'Hew down the tree and cut off its branches, strip off its leaves and scatter its fruit; let the beasts flee from under it and the birds from its branches.

---

nations dwelt; yet though it was so great it was destroyed (see also Ezek. 17:22 ff.; 19:10 ff.). Commentators also recall Herodotus *History* VII. 19 (where Xerxes saw himself crowned with the shoot of an olive tree whose branches covered the earth) and I. 108 (which records the dream of Astyages). More to the point, however, is the fact that in one of Nebuchadrezzar's building inscriptions Babylon is referred to as a great spreading tree. The tree symbolizes the Babylonian Empire, which extended over many lands, protected many peoples, and whose prosperity served to support varied classes of men. The tree as a figure for men is familiar in the O.T. (cf. Ps. 1:3; 37:35; Jer. 17:8). With this, however, must be remembered the ancient Oriental conception of the world tree, which was commonly conceived of as being on the navel of the earth, and so **in the midst of the earth.** In those days the earth was thought of as a disk, with the heavens as an upturned bowl above it; thus the tree is pictured as growing in the center of the land mass of this disk and extending upwards until its top touched the vault of heaven, in which case, of course, it would be visible from any point along the edge of the land mass. Some have thought the meaning is that the branches spread out until on every side they reached the horizon. This is rather difficult to picture, though the LXX τὸ κύτος αὐτοῦ seems to derive from some such idea.

11. To the end of the whole earth: The Hebrew equivalents are of frequent occurrence (cf. Deut. 33:17; Job 28:24; Pss. 22:27; 48:10). The expression may mean the edges of the land mass where the circumambient ocean begins, or perhaps the edge of the disk where the arch of the heavenly vault begins to rise all around.

12. Leaves: Foliage. So in vs. 14. The Hebrew cognate is used in Ps. 104:12 for the birds singing amid the foliage (KJV "branches"). **In it was food for all:** So vs. 21. *Māzôn* is from זון, "to feed," and is used in Gen. 45:23 for the "provision" sent by Joseph from Egypt to his father. **And all flesh was fed from it** is a poetic exaggeration but is suggestive of the empire's dependence on Babylon for its sustenance.

13. A watcher, a holy one: Not two figures but one, **a watcher** who was **a holy one.** So again in vss. 17, 23. The word עיר is connected with the root meaning "wakefulness," whence Theod. ἐγρήγορος, and the Vulg. *vigilant*. In later angelology the "watchers" became a special class of angel, but in this passage, which seems to be the earliest to use the word, it is probably only a special name for "angel." The epithet **holy** is often applied to angels (e.g., Matt. 25:31), but it has no necessary moral connotation, meaning rather that by their celestial nature they are beings apart.

14. "Calling with strength, and thus did he say." "With strength" means aloud, as in 3:4; 5:7. To whom the angel called is not mentioned. Some think that men on

15 Nevertheless, leave the stump of his roots in the earth, even with a band of iron and brass, in the tender grass of the field; and let it be wet with the dew of heaven, and *let* his portion *be* with the beasts in the grass of the earth:

16 Let his heart be changed from man's, and let a beast's heart be given unto him; and let seven times pass over him.

17 This matter *is* by the decree of the watchers, and the demand by the word of the holy ones: to the intent that the living may know that the Most High ruleth in the kingdom of men, and giveth it to whomsoever he will, and setteth up over it the basest of men.

15 But leave the stump of its roots in the earth, bound with a band of iron and bronze, amid the tender grass of the field. Let him be wet with the dew of heaven; let his lot be with the beasts in the grass of the earth; 16 let his mind be changed from a man's, and let a beast's mind be given to him; and let seven times pass over him. 17 The sentence is by the decree of the watchers, the decision by the word of the holy ones, to the end that the living may know that the Most High rules the kingdom of men, and gives it to whom he will,

---

earth were being summoned to carry out the judgment on the tree. Others think the angel must have had an angelic band with him, for vs. 17 suggests that there were other angels present. Still others judge that the writer means his audience to feel that the judgment is carried out by celestial operations which it is not for men to see or know. The words of the watcher seem to fall into metrical form. **Flee:** The verb applies to both the **birds** and the **beasts**. From the same root comes the word used in Gen. 4:12 for Cain's being a "wanderer" in the earth.

15. The leaving of a **stump** in the ground would seem to suggest that there is hope of restoration. That it was to be **bound with a band of iron and bronze** suggests to our minds the metal bands placed around stumps to prevent splitting, but there is no evidence that such a technique was practiced in ancient times. Bentzen thinks the writer has here forgotten his tree image and is thinking only of the king's throne, which is to be made secure for him (see vs. 26), even though for a while he is afflicted. Since iron and bronze are mentioned in such passages as Deut. 28:48; Jer. 1:18; Mic. 4:13 as symbols of severity, some think that here the words signify the rigor of the sentence passed on the monarch. It would seem to have some reference to his experiences during the years of his affliction, and was probably much clearer to the audience then than it is now to us. The being amid the grass of the fields and wet with the dew refers apparently to the stump. Then the thought shifts to the deranged king who is like an animal eating the herbage of the fields along with the other animals, having no longer a man's reasoning power but the mentality of a beast. In vs. 23 the phrase "in the herbage of the earth" is omitted, and some editors would omit it here.

His lot: *Ḥᵃlaq* is "to divide," as in the dividing of the spoil (Josh. 22:8) so that each has his **lot** or **portion**. The king's lot is for a time to be found not among men but among the animals. This lot may refer to his fortune in life, or perhaps to his portion of nourishment as an animal.

16. Mind: Lit., **heart**, as usual (cf. 2:30). **Be changed:** A verb used in Akkadian for mental derangement (for the Hebrew verb see I Sam. 21:14). **Seven times:** So in vss. 23, 25, 32. The meaning probably is seven years, as the LXX and Josephus (*Antiquities* X. 10. 6) take it, for עדן is used for years in 7:25. The number **seven** is merely conventional, meaning no more than "several."

17. The **watchers** are here assumed to be a sort of heavenly council. We find this idea in Job 1:6, 12; 2:1, 7; Ps. 89:6-7; Jer. 23:18. It is found, indeed, much earlier in Babylonian documents and is later assumed in the Qur'ān. In later Judaism it developed into a theory of a consultant council without whose advice the Almighty did nothing (Sanhedrin 38*b*), and which could even thwart and oppose him (Sanhedrin 94*a*). There may be a further reflection of this in ch. 10.

411

18 This dream I king Nebuchadnezzar have seen. Now thou, O Belteshazzar, declare the interpretation thereof, forasmuch as all the wise *men* of my kingdom are not able to make known unto me the interpretation: but thou *art* able; for the spirit of the holy gods *is* in thee.

19 ¶ Then Daniel, whose name *was* Belteshazzar, was astonished for one hour, and his thoughts troubled him. The king spake, and said, Belteshazzar, let not the dream,

and sets over it the lowliest of men.' 18 This dream I, King Nebuchadnez'zar, saw. And you, O Belteshaz'zar, declare the interpretation, because all the wise men of my kingdom are not able to make known to me the interpretation, but you are able, for the spirit of the holy gods[i] is in you."

19 Then Daniel, whose name was Belteshaz'zar, was dismayed for a long time, and his thoughts alarmed him. The king said,

[i] Or *Spirit of the holy God*

Decree: *Gezērāh*, from גזר, "to decide," "to determine," whence the word for those determiners of fates called "astrologers" in vs. 7; 2:27. Thus it is by what the watchers have determined that the sentence has been passed. In vs. 24 the decree is that of the Most High, who of course is the ultimate authority for it. Behrmann thinks that the distinction between the two verses is deliberate. Here in the mouth of a heathen it is the decree of the watchers; there in the mouth of Daniel it is that of the Most High.

Sentence: Lit., "word" or "matter." It is the *pithgāmā'* of 3:16 (cf. Esth. 1:20). **Decision** is properly "petition" or "command," in which sense the word occurs in the Aramaic papyri, but here it must have the meaning of sentence or decision. The purpose of the whole matter is now disclosed. This curious humiliation of the mighty king is to demonstrate to all creatures that the real ruler of the world is the God of Israel, by whose appointment kings rule. This passage reflects the teaching of Isa. 10; 14; 47; a teaching that had already been mentioned in 2:21. Though here the humiliation is said to be intended to teach all creatures the lesson, in vs. 25 it is that the king may learn. Bentzen thinks that as the message in ch. 2 was directed against polytheism, the message here is against the Oriental custom of human potentates claiming divine honors, a conspicuous case being Antiochus Epiphanes. The encouragement such a message would give to Jews suffering under Antiochus is obvious.

Lowliest of men: Some see here an allusion to the fact that the last rulers of the Neo-Babylonian Empire were men of lowly origin. The exaltation of the lowly at God's hands is a common theme of scripture, as we are reminded by I Cor. 1:28, and there is no need to look for any special reference here.

b) THE KING CALLS ON DANIEL TO INTERPRET (4:18=M.T. 4:15)

18. The king is still writing his epistle. We are to understand that the dream has already been told to the assembled wise men, and then told again to Daniel with a special appeal to him. The audience would see that the appeal here is based on Daniel's former success in interpreting the dream of the composite image.

c) DANIEL GIVES THE INTERPRETATION (4:19-27=M.T. 4:16-24)

19. When Daniel heard the dream and realized its significance, he was at first embarrassed, for it is not a pleasant thing to offer to a powerful ruler an inauspicious prediction. History has many examples of courtiers who have deliberately falsified news rather than give bad tidings to a potentate. Seeing his trouble, the king encouraged him to speak, so he spoke the truth about the matter, though with a preliminary word to avert any evil results from its inauspiciousness.

"Perplexed for a moment": The older versions say **for one hour** but, as in 3:6, the word means rather a moment. **Dismayed:** The root meaning of שׁמם is apparently the

---

19. *Speak the Truth!*—It was a terrible thing to have to tell the king that the dream meant doom for him. Daniel must have been tempted to speak in generalities, or deliberately to lie

about it. How would the king react? What good would it do to upset things by telling the truth? Why not apply the interpretation to the king's enemies and receive his further rewards? But

or the interpretation thereof, trouble thee. Belteshazzar answered and said, My lord, the dream *be* to them that hate thee, and the interpretation thereof to thine enemies.

20 The tree that thou sawest, which grew, and was strong, whose height reached unto the heaven, and the sight thereof to all the earth;

21 Whose leaves *were* fair, and the fruit thereof much, and in it *was* meat for all; under which the beasts of the field dwelt, and upon whose branches the fowls of the heaven had their habitation:

22 It *is* thou, O king, that art grown and become strong: for thy greatness is grown, and reacheth unto heaven, and thy dominion to the end of the earth.

23 And whereas the king saw a watcher and a holy one coming down from heaven, and saying, Hew the tree down, and destroy it; yet leave the stump of the roots thereof in the earth, even with a band of iron and brass, in the tender grass of the field; and let it be wet with the dew of heaven, and *let* his portion *be* with the beasts of the field, till seven times pass over him;

24 This *is* the interpretation, O king, and this *is* the decree of the Most High, which is come upon my lord the king:

"Belteshaz'zar, let not the dream or the interpretation alarm you." Belteshaz'zar answered, "My lord, may the dream be for those who hate you and its interpretation for your enemies! 20 The tree you saw, which grew and became strong, so that its top reached to heaven, and it was visible to the end of the whole earth; 21 whose leaves were fair and its fruit abundant, and in which was food for all; under which beasts of the field found shade, and in whose branches the birds of the air dwelt — 22 it is you, O king, who have grown and become strong. Your greatness has grown and reaches to heaven, and your dominion to the ends of the earth. 23 And whereas the king saw a watcher, a holy one, coming down from heaven and saying, 'Hew down the tree and destroy it, but leave the stump of its roots in the earth, bound with a band of iron and bronze, in the tender grass of the field; and let him be wet with the dew of heaven; and let his lot be with the beasts of the field, till seven times pass over him'; 24 this is the interpretation, O king: It is a decree of the Most High, which has come

---

silence of desolation (cf. Isa. 33:8; 49:8; Ezek. 36:35-36), and so it can mean profound astonishment (Lev. 26:32; Jer. 18:16). The sense of desolation appears in the use of one form of the word in 8:13, the famous "abomination of desolation," and some think that here Daniel was so appalled at the significance of the dream that he was in the silence of stupefaction. It need mean no more, however, than the silence of embarrassment or perplexity.

Alarmed him: The same verb is in vs. 5. The king uses the same word when he notices Daniel's embarrassment and kindly endeavors to assure him, bidding him not to be alarmed by what he sees in the dream. It may have been oversight on the writer's part, or a literary artifice, that he here drops from the first person to the third, picking up the first person again in vs. 34. There is a parallel to this case of the king speaking of himself as the king in Ezra 7:14-15.

Formulas for averting evil are still in common use throughout the Near East before uttering inauspicious words. Daniel cannot escape the task of expounding the dream, but he prefaces its unpleasantness by a wish that the predictions may be fulfilled not on the king but on his enemies. That he addresses the king as **My lord** is merely the courtesy of a courtier; no other significance should be read into it. **Those who hate you:** Your enemies within the realm. **Your enemies:** Your rivals without the realm.

20. Daniel recapitulates the matter of the dream. The small variations in wording from what we have in vss. 10-17 are not meant to be significant.

22. The LXX appends to this verse a long addition which seems to refer to the situation in Maccabean times.

24. A decree of the Most High: See vs. 17. The word for **Most High** is the same as in 3:26.

413

25 That they shall drive thee from men, and thy dwelling shall be with the beasts of the field, and they shall make thee to eat grass as oxen, and they shall wet thee with the dew of heaven, and seven times shall pass over thee, till thou know that the Most High ruleth in the kingdom of men, and giveth it to whomsoever he will.

26 And whereas they commanded to leave the stump of the tree roots; thy kingdom shall be sure unto thee, after that thou shalt have known that the heavens do rule.

upon my lord the king, 25 that you shall be driven from among men, and your dwelling shall be with the beasts of the field; you shall be made to eat grass like an ox, and you shall be wet with the dew of heaven, and seven times shall pass over you, till you know that the Most High rules the kingdom of men, and gives it to whom he will. 26 And as it was commanded to leave the stump of the roots of the tree, your kingdom shall be sure for you from the time that you know that Heaven rules.

25. You shall be driven: Lit., "they will be driving thee." The meaning of vss. 15-16 is now explained. The king is to be driven out as men drive out beasts. He is to dwell in the open, as do the animals, and like them feed on herbage. This does not mean that he will be turned into a beast but that in the affliction of his madness he will act like a beast and be treated as such. The writer apparently had in mind some such phenomenon as *insania zoantropia.* To ancient thought there was little difference between a person so afflicted and a real beast. **Like an ox:** Lit., as oxen; so in vss. 32, 33.

When the monarch has learned from this punishment that true sovereignty belongs solely to God (so vs. 32), his kingdom will be restored to him (vs. 36). The king's words in 2:47 would suggest that he had already learned this lesson, but as this learning is the moral of the story, it must be emphasized here. It is clear that in the sources used by the writer Nebuchadrezzar had already become a symbolic figure incarnating for Jews of the Hellenistic age the forces of heathen might arrayed against God. Some of these heathen potentates carried on the ancient tradition of claiming divine rights, but even where these were not formally claimed, the monarch's despotic power, his assumption that his will was law and that his word might not be questioned, was to a pious Jew a denial of the unique supremacy of God and an assumption of sovereignty that was God's alone. To judge Nebuchadrezzar by his own inscriptions, he was the last person to need to learn that the Most High ruled in the kingdom of men and gave to whom he would. Judith 3:8, however, is clear evidence that in the Hellenistic period he was popularly regarded as one of the potentates who had set himself up as a god to whom divine honor ought to be paid, and who sought to destroy other religions that he might increase the number of his own worshipers. He was thus to a Maccabean audience a prototype of the infamous Antiochus. Moreover, he would be remembered by Jews not as the great builder who succeeded Nabopolassar, but as the "enemy" who had destroyed their holy city, plundered their temple, and carried away a goodly part of their people into captivity (II Kings 24-25).

26. It was commanded: Lit., **they commanded,** i.e., the watchers of vs. 17, though idiomatically the verb could be passive. **Sure:** *Qayyāmā',* "standing firm," i.e., secure, steadfast, and so abiding (cf. Aboth 1:18). In 6:26 (M.T. 6:27) it is used as an epithet of God, i.e., he who abides steadfast, is enduring. **That Heaven rules:** In vs. 25 it is the Most High who rules, as it is in vs. 32; thus **Heaven** here stands for God (cf. vss. 31, 34). This usage is unknown elsewhere in the O.T. but it is common in later writings (cf. I Macc. 3:18, 19; II Macc. 9:21; Aboth 1:3; 2:2; and the N.T. expression, ἡ βασιλεία τῶν

the God of Daniel expected him to speak his message to the king. The implications are plain enough. Do we dare speak the truth to people? Do we love them enough to have the prophet's scorn of compromise? Amos learned how unpopular a prophet of doom can be. But he never hesitated to announce that the day of the Lord

would be darkness, not light. Jeremiah took his life in his hands and cursed the day he was born, but he spoke the bitter truth. So did Daniel.

25. God Rules!—This is the word of hope for our madness. We must learn that **the Most High rules** over all the earth, and that kings are

27 Wherefore, O king, let my counsel be acceptable unto thee, and break off thy sins by righteousness, and thine iniquities by showing mercy to the poor; if it may be a lengthening of thy tranquillity.

28 ¶ All this came upon the king Nebuchadnezzar.

29 At the end of twelve months he walked in the palace of the kingdom of Babylon.

30 The king spake, and said, Is not this great Babylon, that I have built for the house of the kingdom by the might of my power, and for the honor of my majesty?

27 Therefore, O king, let my counsel be acceptable to you; break off your sins by practicing righteousness, and your iniquities by showing mercy to the oppressed, that there may perhaps be a lengthening of your tranquillity."

28 All this came upon King Nebuchadnez'zar. 29 At the end of twelve months he was walking on the roof of the royal palace of Babylon, 30 and the king said, "Is not this great Babylon, which I have built by my mighty power as a royal residence and

---

οὐρανῶν, "the kingdom of heaven," which is equivalent to "kingdom of God"). Both Behrmann and Marti, however, refer to vs. 17 and think that **Heaven** means the celestial powers who made the decree.

27. The purpose of the **counsel** is not clear. Charles notes that the counsel agrees with that of Ecclus. 3:30-31; Tob. 4:7-11; but if the decree concerning the king's affliction has been passed, that affliction must come to be, as indeed vs. 33 says it has. Montgomery suggests that there was a year of grace, so the meaning would be that if in that year the king repented and did good works, the doom might be averted.

Break off: *Peraq* is normally "to redeem," whence the λύτρωσαι of the LXX. In Hebrew the word has this meaning in Lam. 5:8; Ps. 136:24. The figure, however, is that of breaking a yoke from the neck (Gen. 27:40), so that **break off** is suitable here. **By practicing righteousness:** Lit., **by righteousness,** i.e., by deeds of righteousness, good works. This verse states unequivocally the doctrine of the meritoriousness of works. The Greek versions have here ἐν ἐλεημοσύναις, "by almsgiving," interpreting it from a late meaning of the word. This has been followed by many Roman Catholic and some Protestant expositors. Charles has an excellent note on the word. **To the oppressed:** Perhaps **to the poor** (cf. Prov. 14:21). "If haply there may be a lengthening to your prosperity"; cf. "at ease" in vs. 4.

3. Epilogue: The Fulfillment of the Dream (4:28-37)
a) The King's Madness (4:28-33=M.T. 4:25-30)

29. On the roof of the royal palace: Lit., **in the palace of the kingdom,** i.e., the royal residence (cf. vs. 30), and though no **roof** is mentioned in the original, the roof was the ordinary place for the king to walk. From it he could gaze out over his city (cf. II Sam. 11:2). It is here that the resemblance to the passage from Abydenus is very close.

30. Great Babylon: The language of this verse resembles somewhat that of the great building inscriptions and may have been intended to imitate them. Nebuchadrezzar was a great builder who appears to have been prouder of his building operations than of his military expeditions. Rev. 14:8; 16:19; 18:2 witness to the endurance of the epithet **great** associated with Babylon. **By my mighty power:** *Ḥiṣnî* may mean "my wealth," as Behrmann suggests at 2:37.

---

no exceptions when it comes to his justice. This is a lesson in stewardship. The king does not own his kingdom, but administers it for God. When King James VI of Scotland was prating about his rights, Andrew Melville plucked him by the robe and said, "Thou God's silly vassal, there are two kingdoms in Scotland, and two kings: King James and King Christ Jesus; of whose kingdom King James is neither Lord nor Head, but subject." [9] So Melville echoed the central note that had been sounded in Daniel's word to the king of Babylon, viz., sovereignty of God.

27. Break Off Your Sins.—There is only one answer to the judgment. Repent! There was

[9] Quoted by Scherer, *Plight of Freedom*, p. 126.

31 While the word *was* in the king's mouth, there fell a voice from heaven, *saying,* O king Nebuchadnezzar, to thee it is spoken; The kingdom is departed from thee.

32 And they shall drive thee from men, and thy dwelling *shall be* with the beasts of the field: they shall make thee to eat grass as oxen, and seven times shall pass over thee, until thou know that the Most High ruleth in the kingdom of men, and giveth it to whomsoever he will.

33 The same hour was the thing fulfilled upon Nebuchadnezzar: and he was driven from men, and did eat grass as oxen, and his body was wet with the dew of heaven, till his hairs were grown like eagles' *feathers,* and his nails like birds' *claws.*

34 And at the end of the days I Nebuchadnezzar lifted up mine eyes unto heaven, and mine understanding returned unto me, and I blessed the Most High, and I praised

for the glory of my majesty?" 31 While the words were still in the king's mouth, there fell a voice from heaven, "O King Nebuchadnez'zar, to you it is spoken: The kingdom has departed from you, 32 and you shall be driven from among men, and your dwelling shall be with the beasts of the field; and you shall be made to eat grass like an ox; and seven times shall pass over you, until you have learned that the Most High rules the kingdom of men and gives it to whom he will." 33 Immediately the word was fulfilled upon Nebuchadnez'zar. He was driven from among men, and ate grass like an ox, and his body was wet with the dew of heaven till his hair grew as long as eagles' feathers, and his nails were like birds' claws.

34 At the end of the days I, Nebuchadnez'zar, lifted my eyes to heaven, and my reason returned to me, and I blessed the Most High, and praised and honored him who lives for ever;

---

31. There fell a voice from heaven: Cf. Isa. 9:8; Test. Levi 18:6; II Baruch 13:1; Matt. 3:17. **To you it is spoken:** Lit., "to thee are [we] speaking," i.e., the celestial watchers who are responsible for the decree.

33. Immediately: As in 3:6, "in that moment." **The word was fulfilled:** Lit., "the word came to an end." The **word** is that of vss. 31-32. **Till his hair grew:** Some think we are to understand that under his affliction the king would neglect all care of his person, letting his hair and **nails** grow at will. Others see a reference to elements in mythological accounts of men developing birdlike characteristics.

b) THE KING'S HUMBLING (4:34-35=M.T. 4:31-32)

The LXX has here a quite different text with a considerable passage not found in the M.T.

34. At the end of the days: The end of the seven "times" of vss. 16, 23, 25, 32. **Lifted my eyes:** Charles suggests a conscious contrast here with "looking down" as a symbol of the evil living which makes a man unwilling to look up to heaven (cf. Susanna 9). Thus the king's looking up to heaven would be a sign of his return to the ways of righteousness, and thereat he was restored. Beven calls attention to a parallel with the frenzied Agaue, in the *Bacchae* of Euripides, who also regained reason by looking heavenward, and who also in their period of frenzy had been in some sort assimilated to animals.

Blessed the Most High: Man's blessing God means expressing gratitude to God, acknowledging his dependence on God's blessing (see Deut. 8:10; Judg. 5:9; Ps. 103:20-22; I Chr. 29:20). **Him who lives for ever:** Cf. 12:7; Ecclus. 18:1; Enoch 5:1; Rev. 4:9-10; 10:6. That he is the "living" God is declared again in 6:26. **For his dominion:** From

---

nothing external that would work. There had to be a change of heart.

34. *A Parable for Today.*—One thinks of the prodigal son who returned to his father's house "when he came to himself." Surely here is a parable of our time. It would not be difficult

to make a case for the insanity of our way of life. The way we move toward destruction indicates that we have lost our reason. When a people can spend billions for destruction but haggle over niggardly budgets for the welfare of its citizens, that is madness. Or if we should

and honored him that liveth for ever, whose dominion *is* an everlasting dominion, and his kingdom *is* from generation to generation:

35 And all the inhabitants of the earth *are* reputed as nothing: and he doeth according to his will in the army of heaven, and *among* the inhabitants of the earth: and none can stay his hand, or say unto him, What doest thou?

36 At the same time my reason returned unto me; and for the glory of my kingdom, mine honor and brightness returned unto me; and my counselors and my lords sought unto me; and I was established in my kingdom, and excellent majesty was added unto me.

for his dominion is an everlasting dominion,
  and his kingdom endures from generation to generation;
35 all the inhabitants of the earth are accounted as nothing;
  and he does according to his will in the host of heaven
  and among the inhabitants of the earth;
and none can stay his hand
  or say to him, "What doest thou?"
36 At the same time my reason returned to me; and for the glory of my kingdom, my majesty and splendor returned to me. My counselors and my lords sought me, and I was established in my kingdom, and still

---

here to the end of vs. 35 is a doxology framed in much the same words as Ps. 145:13, a psalm which had been used in vs. 3.

35. Accounted as nothing: So Theod. ὡς οὐδέν. The text presents difficulties, but see parallel in Isa. 40:17. Our translation depends on לה being taken as a substantive, "nought" or "nothingness." There seems no analogy for this, however, either in Hebrew or in Aramaic (not even Job 6:21). Some therefore want to interpret it "as persons of no account," or "abide under his care," or "are as sun motes." There is possibly some textual corruption.

The host of heaven may be the stars (Deut. 4:19; Jer. 33:22), or angels (I Kings 22:19; Luke 2:13), or since there was an ancient idea that stars were angelic beings (Enoch 18:14-16; Rev. 9:1), it may include both. In any case, the reference is to things celestial as opposed to things terrestrial, and since the contrast is with the **inhabitants of the earth,** the reference must be to the inhabitants of heavenly places. **Stay his hand:** Lit., "strike on his hand," an idiom meaning "to interfere with." It derives from the act of knocking away a hand that is stretched out to do something. Montgomery, however, sees here some symbolic legal action. **Or say to him, "What doest thou?"** Cf. Eccl. 8:4; Job 9:12; Isa. 45:9.

The reference in this verse may be, as Charles thinks, to the judgment of God, since the judgment of human potentates may be averted or subject to appeal, but when God judges there is no appeal, nor is there any escaping the execution of his judgment.

c) The King's Recovery and Confession (4:36-37=M.T. 4:33-34)

36. My reason: The same word is in vs. 34. **My splendor:** The same word is used in 2:31 for the sheen of the great image, and occurs again in 5:6, 9; 7:28 for brightness of countenance. Here it probably refers to vs. 33, which tells how the king under his affliction neglected his appearance. Others think it refers to his royal splendor. During his affliction his throne had necessarily been vacant, but now that he is restored the royal splendor is restored to the court, and the court officials now begin again to present themselves as in normal times.

My counselors: The same word is used in 3:24, 27. Here it means in particular the ministers of state. **My lords:** Courtiers, a word which occurs again in 5:1 ff. for the

---

observe our own standard of values, we should be driven to the conclusion that we prefer our insanity to God's reason. There seems to be some inescapable fascination which insanity has for us. If we are told enough times that non-

sense makes sense—or better, that it is a more sophisticated wisdom—we will believe it. And the form of the insanity is always a denial of the supremacy of God. But when we come to ourselves, or when our reason returns to us,

37 Now I Nebuchadnezzar praise and extol and honor the King of heaven, all whose works *are* truth, and his ways judgment: and those that walk in pride he is able to abase.

5 Belshazzar the king made a great feast to a thousand of his lords, and drank wine before the thousand.

more greatness was added to me. 37 Now I, Nebuchadnez'zar, praise and extol and honor the King of heaven; for all his works are right and his ways are just; and those who walk in pride he is able to abase.

5 King Belshaz'zar made a great feast for a thousand of his lords, and drank wine in front of the thousand.

---

courtiers of Belshazzar, and in 6:17 for those of Darius. It may be meant as a translation of the Iranian word for the body under the chiliarch at the Persian court, or it may be meant to represent the *rabûti*, "princes," of the Babylonian court. **In my kingdom:** Lit., "over my kingdom." That **still more greatness was added** is a characteristic touch of the Oriental tale (cf. Job 42:10-17).

37. Nebuchadrezzar closes his letter not with the usual epistolary ending—which may have been dropped by a later editor of the story—but with a little doxology. **Extol:** or "exalt," from a verb "to make high," then "to celebrate." The corresponding Hebrew verb occurs in the psalms. **King of heaven:** Cf. "Lord of heaven" in 5:23. It is a pagan title (cf. "Queen of heaven" in Jer. 7:18). Some think that Nebuchadrezzar is here represented as identifying the Jewish God with his own god, Marduk. God is called **king**, however, in Pss. 47:2 ff.; 48:2; Mal. 1:14, and in later texts is given this very title (cf. I Esdras 4:46; III Macc. 2:2).

Right: *Qeshôṭ* normally means **truth** (cf. 2:47), "truly." Truth and justice are combined here as in Ps. 111:7. **He is able to abase** doubtless refers to Nebuchadrezzar's pride in vs. 30. The humbling of pride is a common biblical theme (cf. Prov. 16:18; Ps. 18:27; 101:5; Jer. 49:16; Acts 12:20 ff.; and one may refer to Ezek. 17:24, which is peculiarly pertinent to Nebuchadrezzar's dream).

E. Belshazzar's Feast (5:1-31)

This story tells of the end of the Neo-Babylonian kingdom and the lesson therein for pious Jews. Nebuchadrezzar has passed away and has been succeeded by Belshazzar, who, like his predecessor, flouts the God of Israel and is punished. Nebuchadrezzar had sinned by idolatry and pride. To these Belshazzar adds the crime of using for his pleasures the sacred vessels taken from the temple at Jerusalem. A mysterious message announces his

---

then we can praise God. Running all through this chapter is the great theme: pride is madness but humility is sanity.

5:1-31. The Suddenness of Doom.—This chapter goes on to the next generation and tells what happened to Nebuchadrezzar's "son" Belshazzar. It is one of the most dramatic stories in the Bible. If with imagination we can describe this scene, there will be no bored listeners. The literalist may have his way with the handwriting on the wall if he desires. But he who sees this chapter as a dramatic myth leading us into the heart of spiritual and moral truth will have the better of it—as usual. More significant than a single miraculous incident happening a long time ago is the insight of how God works through the moral law, then and always.

The striking thing at the beginning of the story is the unawareness of imminent tragedy and disaster on the part of the king and his

lords. One moment they are feasting and drinking as if they had forever to enjoy their kingdom. But in vs. 30 we read: **That very night Belshazzar the Chaldean king was slain.** It is the suddenness of the ending, and the contrast between the feast and the disaster, that sharpen the drama. It was later than they thought.

Our first impulse is to reject this sudden destruction as being melodramatic. Yet a careful reading of history will indicate that Daniel saw the thing realistically. The drift of societies to destruction is so imperceptible that they are at the brink before they know it. People do not seem to know how far they have drifted. "It can't happen here" is a universal superstition and the prelude to inevitable failure. How necessary it is for the United States to be aware of this just when she is the most powerful nation in the world and is in danger of assuming that power is the answer to all problems! The denial of civil liberties here, or the overriding

doom. Daniel is brought in and interprets the message. That very night Babylon falls. The message is much the same as that of the previous chapter. The Jews could do little against these proud Gentile tyrants who made mock of their religion, scoffed at their God, and wanted to make free with their temple treasures. God, however, could do something about it and he would bring down these haughty tyrants.

The story assumes a knowledge of chs. 1 and 4, and in its present form is clearly from the hand of the writer of those chapters. Like them, however, it seems to be the working over of an earlier narrative. There may well have been in circulation popular tales about the last days of Chaldean Babylon and the coming of the Persians, one of which the writer has adapted for his present purpose.

In many details the story does not conform to what we know from contemporary sources about the last days of the Neo-Babylonian kingdom. It makes Belshazzar the son of Nebuchadrezzar and his immediate successor. Nebuchadrezzar, however, was succeeded by his son Awel-Marduk (the Evil-merodach of II Kings 25:27-30), he by Nergalsharusur, he by Labashi-Marduk, and he by Nabū-na'id (Nabonidus), in whose seventeenth year Babylon was taken by the armies of Cyrus. Nabonidus was no blood relation of Nebuchadrezzar; his son Bēl-shar-uṣur was the ruler in charge of Babylon during his father's absence at Taima in Arabia, but he was never king, and in contemporary inscriptions appears usually as "the king's son." The conqueror of Babylon is here named **Darius the Mede.** This derives from the writer's four-empire theory, which demands a Median between the Babylonian and the Persian empires, though no such Darius is known to history. Whether this Darius already appeared in the story on which the writer based this chapter, or was introduced by the writer himself, we cannot say. His source was in many respects a good one, having many details which show acquaintance with life at an ancient Oriental court, though they give no conclusive evidence for the date of the source. The story seems to regard the Persian conquest of Babylon as something

---

of minority rights there, can prepare the frame of mind which makes fascism or communism possible. People do not deliberately choose to plunge over the abyss. They edge toward it little by little, and until they are over they are not aware of their danger. The final disaster always seems like a sudden, unexpected affair. Until the very last moment they are feasting without any awareness that the enemy stands at the gate.

The student of history is impressed with the potency of factors invisible. It is never the obvious things which are the real enemy. Before there is a split in the political life, there is always a schism in the spiritual life. To all outward appearance things seem to be the same as always. But there has been a disastrous retreat from ideals and a substitution of policies for principles. Coercion has been more and more necessary to keep things in line. But the unity of a society must depend on trust and a common loyalty to commonly accepted values. Without that inner strength the enemy has little opposition.

This is true of us individually. We see a man go down with a suddenness that is almost unbelievable. How did it happen? How could he do such a thing? The answer is that it was not as sudden as it appeared. It had been happening a long time. The outward appearance had not betrayed it to any except his most intimate

friends, but the inside of the cup was "full of extortion and excess." To vary the figure, the tree that withstands the avalanche may fall at last under the attack of termites, though they cannot be seen. Or we may be like Samson, our strength gone and we know it not.

There is about all of us a feeling of self-satisfaction that makes us unable to discern the signs of the times. We are like Clarence Day's father:

There was one kind of depression that afflicted Mother which Father was free from: he never once had any moments of feeling "unworthy." This was a puzzle to Mother, and it made her look at Father with a mixture of awe and annoyance. Other people went to church to be made better, she told him. Why didn't he? He replied in astonishment that he had no need to be better—he was all right as he was.[1]

The man unaware of his own need or his own "unworthiness" is also unaware of the proximity of disaster. Along with our prayers to be saved from sudden death, we should have prayers to be saved from that sudden defeat which was a long time in preparation and which might have been prevented if we had had eyes to see.

But Belshazzar was given a warning. So are we all. God gives us his signals when we are

[1] *God and My Father* (New York: Knopf, 1936), p. 14.

already long past, yet gives no suggestion that the persecution of the Jews had become acute; the original would therefore have to be dated before the period of Antiochus Epiphanes. But these historical details are only part of the framework of the story. They provided an appropriate setting that was intelligible to the contemporary audience and the fact that they do not agree with actual history was of no importance then and is of none now, for the story was not written to teach history but a religious lesson from which the audience could draw encouragement.

1. Prologue (5:1-4)

5:1. King Belshazzar: *Bēl-shar-uṣur,* "O Bel, protect the king," is a late Babylonian name. The Greek versions confuse it with that of Belteshazzar. The writer evidently regards him as having been a king in the fullest sense, since he speaks of documents being dated from the year of his accession (7:1; 8:1). From the inscriptions, however, it is clear that he never ruled, since though he was present in Babylon the annual New Year's festival could not be held because the real king, his father, was away in Taima. A text published by Sidney Smith (*Babylonian Historical Texts,* p. 87) does show, however, that his father had invested him with a certain kingly dignity, so that there may well have been popular tales in which he figured as king and which would explain the use of that title here.

Made a great feast: There is no date at the beginning of this chapter, but from vss. 30-31 it is clear that the occasion was on the eve of the fall of Babylon in 538 B.C. If we suppose Daniel to have been a youth of sixteen when he was brought into captivity in 605 B.C., he would at this time have been eighty-three years of age, though it is unlikely that the writer would have thought of making this calculation. By calling it **a great feast** he probably meant his audience to understand that it was a state banquet.

Contemporary inscriptions make it clear that Babylon was captured without a blow and that Nabonidus was presently taken prisoner. Cyrus' own inscription suggests that

---

approaching danger, and no man goes to his doom unwarned. This can be made something cheap and ridiculous. Opening the Bible at random and expecting to find a verse for the day's guidance or for the solution of a problem is sheer superstition. There are people who think that God has nothing better to do than tell them about matters which should be settled on the basis of their own common sense. After all, God gave us minds capable of discrimination and judgment. Perhaps he guides us no less when we use our minds to the best of our ability than when we see a vision in the sky. The signals of God are not always spectacular, but they are always, in the deepest sense, miraculous.

One of those warnings is sickness, both physical and spiritual. The body gets sick because something is wrong, not always something which is our fault. But often sickness comes to tell us that unless we change our way of life, we shall die. Always it is a warning of the necessity to change our mode of living. Men have sometimes found a sickness a blessing in disguise because they experience some things which had been previously hidden from them.

Spiritual sickness is a warning. Life ought to be full of promise. There ought to be in it the quality of victory. If it lacks those things and

becomes dull, flat, and unprofitable, then God is warning us that we are not living according to his laws. The usual reaction is to assume that something is fundamentally wrong with life, and there spring up the philosophies of despair and defeat. We can be saved if we will comprehend that spiritual staleness is like a storm signal on the coast—we had better seek a shelter.

Strangely enough, psychoanalysis reveals that all men are abnormal in one way or another. We all have splits in our personalities which could cut us off from useful life and send us to institutions if we allowed them to become too wide. Christian theology calls this original sin. When we understand ourselves, we are warned of our need for the healing touch of the Great Physician. It is the province of religion, and one of its greatest gifts, to make us aware that "there is no health in us." This realization keeps us from trying vainly to heal ourselves. It sends us to God.

The noisy life that is afraid of quietness ought to be a warning of a coming failure. There is always a temptation to substitute doing for being, to feast and carouse rather than to regard the state of our souls. A nation that has worshiped the go-getter had better be careful lest senseless activity become an opiate to pre-

2 Belshazzar, while he tasted the wine, commanded to bring the golden and silver vessels which his father Nebuchadnezzar had taken out of the temple which *was* in Jerusalem; that the king and his princes, his wives and his concubines, might drink therein.

2 Belshaz'zar, when he tasted the wine, commanded that the vessels of gold and of silver which Nebuchadnez'zar his father had taken out of the temple in Jerusalem be brought, that the king and his lords, his wives, and his concubines might drink from

---

the populace welcomed him with joy. There was a later tradition, however, that the city was taken by a night attack while the inhabitants were celebrating a feast. This tradition has left traces both in Herodotus (*History* I. 191) and Xenophon (*Cyropaedia* VII. 5. 15-31), and was doubtless in the story utilized in this chapter. It may have arisen from a transference to the capture of the city of events really belonging to the New Year's festival of 539, which Nabonidus seems to have celebrated in the city with the usual rites and with plentiful distribution of wine to the troops. *Leḥem* is, lit., "food," but the word is used in the sense of **feast** in Eccl. 10:19 and in the Hebrew text of Ecclus. 34:23. **His lords:** His courtiers, as in 4:36.

The great feasts given by Oriental potentates were notorious for their extravagance. Esth. 1 tells of one at the Persian court, and the classical authors relate many details of such extravagance. A feast, of course, was a special occasion. Normally a king in the ancient Near East would have eaten alone, or at most with a few chosen companions, but at a state banquet it might well be that he would have to give the signals for the drinking, somewhat after the fashion of the "ruler of the feast" in John 2:9. In such a case, **in front of the thousand** might mean that the ruler sat at a raised table facing the guests so as to be visible to all. Some would take **before** as temporal on the ground that as a matter of court etiquette the king would have to drink first. It is possible, however, that the writer is thinking only of emphasizing the dissolute habits of the king and the bad example he was setting his court.

2. When he tasted the wine: This is the only place in biblical Aramaic where the verb is used in its literal sense of "to taste food or drink." It probably means that, when the time came for the drinking to start, Belshazzar sent for the sacred vessels. The wine

---

vent thought. Healthy life is content with the simplicities; as a matter of fact, it prefers the simplicities to the hectic excitement of constant running about looking for something new.

Life cannot be always happy and easy. But when it is lived within the will of God, it always has meaning. It is not the fact of tragedy that defeats us, but the haunting fear that life means nothing ultimately. As Kierkegaard wrote: "But from the Christian point of view there are two kinds of disorder. The one is rioting, exterior hubbub. The other is the stillness of death, dissolution, and this perhaps is the most dangerous." [2] It is that inner dissolution which invades the soul where human pride has been substituted for God's rule. The feasting and the mad pursuit of thrills are signs of a sick generation. They reveal the spiritual emptiness, and are a warning of a coming disaster.

The story shows further that there is not as much time as we think. We are all committed to

an evolutionary hypothesis which has assumed millions of years for the working out of human plans. We have believed that things would develop automatically and gradually. The revelation of the age of the earth and the comparative briefness of the human story has given us an exaggerated idea of time. If it took a million years or so to accomplish some slight change in the physical organisms, why should we get excited about doing something immediately?

This spirit set us quite out of tune with the apocalyptic literature. Daniel and Revelation appeared to be books of an outgrown situation and an outgrown point of view. They were too much aware of sudden upsets and the need for immediate decision. On the part of many a modern biblical scholar there was an effort to play up all that seemed to support the evolutionary hypothesis, and an attempt to minimize all that suggested specific, sudden acts of God. The kingdom of God was understood as growing like a plant or spreading like leaven, as indeed it does. But the other side of the picture which portrayed the kingdom as a kind of

---

[2] *For Self-Examination and Judge for Yourselves*, tr. Walter Lowrie (Princeton: Princeton University Press, 1944), p. 45.

would be passed around after the main business of eating was over. Most interpreters take the verse to mean "when the wine began to taste," i.e., under the influence of wine, so that it was a drunken man's caprice that made Belshazzar call for the sacred vessels. Others think that as the king found on tasting that this wine was particularly good, he thought there should be some especially excellent cups from which to drink it. In the Babylonian Talmud (Megillah 11b) there is a curious notion that Belshazzar gave the order because of a calculation he had made. He knew the prophecy of Jeremiah that the Exile would last seventy years, and he calculated that, as Nebuchadrezzar had reigned forty-five years, Evil-merodach twenty-three years, and he himself had been reigning two years, the seventy years of prophecy were now up. The prophecy had not been fulfilled, the Jews had not gone back, and as the prophecy was a failure and the Jews would never return, there was no further purpose in storing the sacred vessels, which might just as well be brought out and put to use. This was a wrong calculation, of course, because he began to count his seventy years at the accession of Nebuchadrezzar.

The nature of the vessels may be gathered from the description in Ezra 1:7-11. Their coming to Babylon had been mentioned in 1:2, so that the audience would know whence Belshazzar had them brought. An audience in Maccabean times would inevitably be reminded of the outrage of the year 170 B.C. (I Macc. 1:20-24).

His father: The writer regards Belshazzar as the son and successor of Nebuchadrezzar (vss. 2, 11, 13, 18, 22). Josephus (*Antiquities* X. 11. 4) calls him his ἔγγονος, and it is true that by Oriental usage a grandson might be called a son. The various theories suggested to show how in any one of eight ways Belshazzar could have been regarded as the "son" of Nebuchadrezzar are all unsatisfactory, and it is simplest to suppose that this relationship was assumed in the narrative the writer was using as the basis for his story.

His wives and his concubines appear again in vs. 23 and are part of the *décor* of the story. It was not customary in the ancient East for women to appear at feasts, though

---

catastrophic experience, was dismissed as a later addition and a false interpretation. Or else it was assumed that the writers editorialized. But it has been shown that one point of view is as firmly embedded in the gospel tradition as the other. Only a presupposition on the part of a modern writer can explain this free and easy treatment of the Scriptures.

Gradualism can become a curse to the religious man. It justifies saying that nothing should be done that will cause controversy. It cautions against haste. All very good, unless it becomes an excuse for taking the easy way always, and never facing up to a moral issue. It is sad to see religious institutions condoning pagan practices in the name of gradualness. Sometimes an honest survey will reveal that at the rate the institution is moving, the Christian thing will not be done for another million years. It is well for Christians to learn that they do not have forever when it comes to cutting out the malignant attitudes of society. For those attitudes may even now be weakening the structure of our civilization and hastening the day of its fall.

Our life is full of crises. There are not only days like a thousand years, but there are moments when our whole future is at stake. God will not hold his anger forever. Sometimes it is this very night when our soul is required. This is one of the real differences between a philosophy and our religion. The philosophy is more concerned with the contemplation of principles. Our faith is aware of the need for decisive action now. The philosopher is likely to assume that there is no hurry, while the religious man may hear the foe marching on the city. We are nearer judgment than we think, but the man who cannot hear the tick of God's clock does not know it. Paganism destroys this time sense. It is careless in its attitude toward the present.

There is a story about a church member who regarded the collection plate with a stony stare. The deacon paused, holding it before the embarrassed man. "I can't give anything, Deacon," said the church member. "Right now I owe too many bills." "Now, Arthur," said the deacon, "you owe the Lord more than you do anyone else." "That is true," was the reply, "but the Lord is not pressing me like those other chaps." It is too easy to assume that God and his demands can be put off because he will not press us. That is not true. He is not a soft old man to be put off with promises which we do not take seriously. Daniel is saying to every man that God is not mocked, and repentance is not something to be postponed.

3 Then they brought the golden vessels that were taken out of the temple of the house of God which *was* at Jerusalem; and the king and his princes, his wives and his concubines, drank in them.

4 They drank wine, and praised the gods of gold, and of silver, of brass, of iron, of wood, and of stone.

them. **3** Then they brought in the golden and silver vessels*j* which had been taken out of the temple, the house of God in Jerusalem; and the king and his lords, his wives, and his concubines drank from them.

4 They drank wine, and praised the gods of gold and silver, bronze, iron, wood, and stone.

j Gk Theodotion Vg: Aram *golden vessels*

Herodotus (*op. cit.* V. 18) witnesses to it in Persia, and Quintus Curtius (*History of Alexander* V. 1. 38) to its occurrence at Babylon in the time of Alexander. Vashti was summoned to appear at a feast in Esth. 1:11, but that was regarded by her as something unusual. The LXX translator omits all mention of the women here and in vs. 23, though perhaps this was in the interest of decorum. *Sheghāl* for "wife" or "consort" is used in Neh. 2:6 for the wife of the Persian king, and in Ps. 45:9 for the queen of some Israelite prince. In later Hebrew it lost its honorable meaning. *Leḥēnāh* is the Akkadian *la-aḥ-na-tu,* "a vessel" (cf. σκεῦος in I Thess. 4:4). In Song of S. 6:8 queens and concubines are mentioned together (cf. I Kings 11:3).

3. That the M.T. mentions only the **golden** vessels in this verse is doubtless due to a scribal error. Theod., the Peshitta, and the Vulg. all have the **silver** as well, just as in vs. 2. **Out of the temple, the house of God** seems tautologous, and some editors delete **temple,** while others delete **house of God.** Both mean the same thing, for there is no suggestion here that the temple was only one part of **the house of God in Jerusalem.**

4. The feast was not necessarily a religious feast. Even at a state banquet it would be customary to pour a libation to the local deities, with appropriate words of praise to each as named. This detail, of course, heightens the crime of Belshazzar (see Aage Bentzen, *Daniel* [Tübingen: J. C. B. Mohr, 1952; "Handbuch zum Alten Testament"], p. 47).

Note finally that material power is no obstacle to God. In every day of great empires there comes a time when many people begin to doubt that anything can oppose that massed power except greater power. Daniel, however, is of the opinion that "the bigger they come, the harder they fall." The downfall of such mighty empires is usually more decisive and complete than that of smaller states. The moving fingers of judgment do not take into consideration size and resources. The only question is whether, being weighed in the balance, they are found wanting or worthy.

It is a needed lesson always. Too many people have accepted the idea that God cannot penetrate "iron curtains" and that he is at a serious disadvantage when it comes to dealing with atom bombs. We look back with nostalgia to the time when power problems were not so obviously out of hand. This is nothing less than a confession that we have lost faith in God's ability to deal with these problems. But once we have yielded to this fear, then we become useless to him.

As long as there is a small group of people in any society capable of being instruments in the hands of God, mighty transformations can be accomplished. H. G. Wells confessed:

I am building my expectation of a new phase in human affairs upon the belief that there is a profoundly serious minority in the mass of our generally indifferent species. I cannot understand the existence of any of the great religions, I cannot explain any fine and grave constructive process in history, unless there is such a serious minority amidst our confusions. They are the salt of the earth, these people capable of devotion and of living lives for remote and mighty ends.[3]

In these great minorities lies all our hope, for they are usable by God. Sometimes they are expendable, and by their sacrifices the divine plans go forward. It is such groups as Wells mentions that God uses to confound the might of tyranny. When the time has arrived there is nothing to prevent the overthrow of the forces which stand in his way, no matter how strong they appear to be.

4. *Profaning the Sacred.*—This blasphemy consists in using the **vessels** of the temple for a

[3] *Democracy Under Revision* (London: Hogarth Press, 1927), p. 42.

5 ¶ In the same hour came forth fingers of a man's hand, and wrote over against the candlestick upon the plaster of the wall of the king's palace: and the king saw the part of the hand that wrote.

6 Then the king's countenance was changed, and his thoughts troubled him, so that the joints of his loins were loosed, and his knees smote one against another.

5 Immediately the fingers of a man's hand appeared and wrote on the plaster of the wall of the king's palace, opposite the lampstand; and the king saw the hand as it wrote. 6 Then the king's color changed, and his thoughts alarmed him; his limbs gave way, and his knees knocked together.

No particular significance is intended by the number or order of the various materials from which the idols were made. These are normal materials from which idols were fashioned in the ancient world, save that iron is a little unusual. The writer is simply indulging his penchant for lists of things, as noted in chs. 2 and 3.

2. The Handwriting on the Wall (5:5-28)

a) A Hand Writes Words of Doom (5:5-6)

5. Immediately: Lit., "at that moment," as in 3:6; 4:33. Yahweh's response to the affront was immediate. As a sign of the king's doom, ghostly fingers appeared and wrote a message on the wall. This motif is not uncommon in Oriental tales. If the king were sitting on a dais, the **lampstand** would probably have been set near him, so that it was on the white wall illumined by the candelabrum, well within the monarch's vision, that the hand wrote. Robert Koldewey's excavations at Babylon have uncovered just such a large banqueting hall with walls of white **plaster**. There must have been many of them. (See Robert Koldewey, *Das wieder erstehende Babylon* [Leipzig: Hinrichs, 1913], p. 103.)

Nebhrashtā' is a lamp or a candelabrum, perhaps a Semitic word derived from the root ברר, "to be clear, bright," though some think it is an Iranian word cognate with the Greek λαμπάς. **Saw the hand as it wrote:** Lit., "saw the palm of the hand which wrote." *Paṣ* is used both of the palm of the hand and the sole of the foot, but since, as Obbink remarks, one cannot see the palm of a hand which is writing, it must here mean **the part of the hand** to which the fingers are attached.

6. Then the king's color changed: Lit., "the king, his brightness was changed upon him" (see vs. 9). *Ziw* is the "brightness" or "splendor" of 2:31, a word used in 4:36 of the **countenance** of Nebuchadrezzar, and in 7:28 of that of Daniel. **Was changed,** as in 3:19, occurs again in vss. 9-10; 7:28. It is the verb used in Job 14:20 of the changing of the face in death.

His thoughts alarmed him: The same verb expressive of alarm was used in 4:5, 19 and occurs again here in the queen mother's speech in vs. 10. **Thoughts:** As in 2:29-30; 4:19. It occurs again in vs. 10; 7:28. The Hebrew equivalent in Eccl. 1:17; 2:22; 4:16 is commonly translated "vexation," so that we are to think of anxious thought.

His limbs gave way: Lit., **The joints of his loins were loosed.** *Qeṭar* is properly a "knot" (see vs. 12) and *ḥarçā'* is the lower part of the back, i.e., the **loins.** The phrase is found in Targ. Jon. on Gen. 50:11, and is used in Hebrew to express panic fear in Ps. 69:23; Nah. 2:10. Charles compares the Homeric αὐτοῦ λύτο γούνατα (*Odyssey* IV. 703; *Iliad* XXI. 114). By the distress of his mind his body had been so affected that it could no longer stand steady, the knots that held it tight, as it were, have become loose. **His knees knocked together:** Cf. Ovid (*Metamorphoses* II. 180), *genua intremuere timore*. In Nah. 2:10 this is associated with the loosening of the loins.

drunken orgy. The loss of the sense of sacred things is always one of the signs of moral decay. We tend to refine the process in our time, but the ultimate spirit is the same. We allow our holy days like Christmas and Easter to be commercialized. We assume that the only worthy goal is profit, and we sacrifice everything to serve that end. Perhaps the loss of respect for the sacred things of other men is the inevitable sign of our own inner betrayals.

7 The king cried aloud to bring in the astrologers, the Chaldeans, and the soothsayers. *And* the king spake, and said to the wise *men* of Babylon, Whosoever shall read this writing, and show me the interpretation thereof, shall be clothed with scarlet, and *have* a chain of gold about his neck, and shall be the third ruler in the kingdom.

7 The king cried aloud to bring in the enchanters, the Chalde′ans, and the astrologers. The king said to the wise men of Babylon, "Whoever reads this writing, and shows me its interpretation, shall be clothed with purple, and have a chain of gold about his neck, and shall be the third ruler in the

---

b) THE COURT SAGES CAN MAKE NOTHING OF IT (5:7-9)

7. As another effect of the distress the king **cried aloud,** lit., "called with strength," the same phrase used in 3:4 of the herald proclaiming and in 4:14 of the calling of the angel.

There is no special significance in the fact that only three classes of wise men are mentioned here, for they are meant to cover the whole corps of court sages (cf. 2:2, 12). The LXX adds "magicians," and as they appear in vs. 11 this word may have dropped out here by oversight.

This writing: Since the ghostly writing has to be both read and interpreted, and in vs. 17 Daniel undertakes to read the writing and give the interpretation, some think that the **writing** here and in vss. 15-16 must be taken in the technical meaning of "script." Had the writing been in the usual style, it is argued, the wise men could have read it even if they failed to catch its meaning, but this **writing** was something srange which they could not even read. Some have thought that since it was a ghostly hand, it was in some ghostly script no wise man had ever seen before, and in favor of this interpretation point to the reward offered by the king. The solution in vs. 25, however, apparently depends on the writing having been in Aramaic, though it may have been Aramaic written in some strange way or in unfamiliar characters. It is simplest to assume that the writing itself was intelligible to the wise men, i.e., they could read the characters, but could make no intelligible sense out of them to convey a message to the monarch. The detail of the reward may have been suggested by Gen. 41:42-43, where Pharaoh in his delight at the interpretation of the dream clothes Joseph in fine linen, hangs a golden chain about his neck, and makes him ride in the second chariot.

Purple: The word is often and with some justification translated **scarlet.** It was a sign of royal dignity among the Persians (Esth. 8:15; I Esdras 3:6; Xenophon *Anabasis* I. 5. 8), the Medes (Xenophon *Cyropaedia* I. 3. 2; II. 4. 6), certain Greeks (*Iliad* IV. 141-45), the Seleucids (I Macc. 10:20; 14:43 ff.; II Macc. 4:38), and the Midianites (Judg. 8:26), whence it came to be regarded as the symbol of royalty (Herodotus, *op. cit.,* III. 20; Song of S. 3:10; Matt. 27:28; I Macc. 8:14; 10:62, 64). It probably is not a Semitic word but is borrowed from some pre-Semitic people on the Mediterranean coast among whom was the original seat of the production of this red-purple dye from the local shellfish (see Pliny *Natural History* IX. 60-62).

The **chain of gold** was another sign of princely dignity, as in Gen. 41:42. For its use in this sense see Adolf Erman, *Life in Ancient Egypt* (tr. H. M. Tirard; London: Macmillan & Co., 1894), pp. 118-20, 208; for Persia see Xenophon *Anabasis* I. 5. 8; Herodotus, *loc. cit.;* and for Galatia, Polybius *Histories* II. 31. Xenophon (*Cyropaedia* VIII. 5. 18) would suggest that such gold chains could be worn only if presented by the king, so that they are in the nature of a modern "decoration." The word for **chain** is derived from some Iranian source.

Third ruler: Lit., "and third in the kingdom shall he rule," a phrase which has given rise to much discussion. Obviously it is parallel to Joseph's being set to ride in the second chariot, but there is no certainty what תלתי here and תלתא in vss. 16, 29 mean, save that the words must have some relation to the root for "three." Some take the phrase to mean "a third part," others "every third day," some "third in rank," and others "one

8 Then came in all the king's wise *men:* but they could not read the writing, nor make known to the king the interpretation thereof.

9 Then was king Belshazzar greatly troubled, and his countenance was changed in him, and his lords were astonished.

10 ¶ *Now* the queen, by reason of the words of the king and his lords, came into the banquet house: *and* the queen spake and said, O king, live for ever: let not thy thoughts trouble thee, nor let thy countenance be changed:

11 There is a man in thy kingdom, in whom *is* the spirit of the holy gods; and in

kingdom." **8** Then all the king's wise men came in, but they could not read the writing or make known to the king the interpretation. **9** Then King Belshaz'zar was greatly alarmed, and his color changed; and his lords were perplexed.

10 The queen, because of the words of the king and his lords, came into the banqueting hall; and the queen said, "O king, live for ever! Let not your thoughts alarm you or your color change. **11** There is in

---

of three." Since in 6:2 we have reference to three presidents, of whom Daniel was one, it has seemed to many that the promise here is of a place in this triumvirate (cf. I Esdras 3:9). There was, however, a Babylonian official title *šalšu*. The monarch was head of the army, the chief officer was the one "on his right," the second officer the one "on his left," and the third officer was the adjutant, the *šalšu rakbu*. This would explain the Aramaic form and may be the office meant here.

8. Came in: In vs. 7 the king speaks of the wise men as though they were already present, yet here they are said to come in. Perhaps the writer thought of the monarch addressing them first outside the hall and then bringing them into a place from which they could see the writing. There is really no need to puzzle why they could not read the writing, for that is part of the framework of the story. The pagan wise men must fail so that the man of God may step in and succeed. We find this in Gen. 41:8, where the Egyptian wise men first fail to interpret Pharaoh's dream, and it occurred in 2:3-12, where Nebuchadrezzar's court sages failed.

9. Greatly alarmed: The same verb is used in vs. 6 and in 4:5, 19, only here in the intensive. There was room for alarm when professional wise men were unable to interpret the ghostly writing. This must point to something portentous, and uncertainty as to what it signified could but add to the king's agitation, so that "his brightness was changed upon him," as in vs. 6. His courtiers were also affected, being **perplexed,** lit., "thrown into confusion."

c) The Queen Mother's Suggestion (5:10-17)

10. The noise of voices from the banqueting hall, different from the usual sounds of revelry, brought the queen mother to discover what was wrong. The LXX has the king summon her, but the M.T. conveys the idea that the sounds were loud enough to penetrate the women's quarters and cause alarm there. The text has only **queen,** which some have thought refers to his chief consort. Usually, however, it is taken to mean the queen mother, first because vs. 2 speaks of the wives as being already there, and second because in vs. 11 she speaks to him of his father in a way that suggests a mother speaking to a son rather than a wife to her husband. Since the writer regards Belshazzar as the son of Nebuchadrezzar, this would be Nebuchadrezzar's wife, who would doubtless be regarded with respect by the courtiers.

11. The words **a man in whom is the spirit of the holy gods** clearly link this chapter with ch. 4. Perhaps the writer means that the queen mother is repeating the words of

---

11. *Spiritual Leader.*—This man may be neglected when things go well, but in the day of trouble and uncertainty he is the man we need and seek. The minister ought to be such

a man. Blessed is that church whose leader is called upon when men are frightened and lost. When war comes, we turn to spiritual leaders. When our prosperity is gone, we want a voice

the days of thy father light and understanding and wisdom, like the wisdom of the gods, was found in him; whom the king Nebuchadnezzar thy father, the king, *I say,* thy father, made master of the magicians, astrologers, Chaldeans, *and* soothsayers;

12 Forasmuch as an excellent spirit, and knowledge, and understanding, interpreting of dreams, and showing of hard sentences, and dissolving of doubts, were found in the same Daniel, whom the king named Belteshazzar: now let Daniel be called, and he will show the interpretation.

your kingdom a man in whom is the spirit of the holy gods.[k] In the days of your father light and understanding and wisdom, like the wisdom of the gods, were found in him, and King Nebuchadnez'zar, your father, made him chief of the magicians, enchanters, Chalde'ans, and astrologers,[l] 12 because an excellent spirit, knowledge, and understanding to interpret dreams, explain riddles, and solve problems were found in this Daniel, whom the king named Belteshaz'zar. Now let Daniel be called, and he will show the interpretation."

[k] Or *Spirit of the holy God*
[l] Aram repeats *the king your father*

Nebuchadrezzar. Some have remarked that she speaks as a polytheist, but here, as in 4:8, though **gods** is plural in form, the sense is singular (cf. RSV mg.). Three things were found in him, **light** or illumination, **understanding** or intelligence, and a **wisdom** that was like the divine wisdom, this latter being a close parallel to what is said of David in II Sam. 14:20. It is probable that the writer means these three words to be taken in connection with the three mentioned in vs. 12 (cf. also 1:17). It was because of these qualities that Daniel had been appointed as chief of the sages (cf. 2:48; 4:9). No significance other than literary artifice is to be seen in the number of groups of sages mentioned here or in the order in which they are named.

At the end of this verse the M.T. has **the king your father** (RSV mg.), but the words are not in the Greek or the Syriac version, nor are they in Josephus; they are probably to be regarded as a scribal addition.

12. Daniel's three special skills are enumerated as dream interpretation, riddle solving, and spell breaking, his **excellent spirit** giving him his skill in oneiromancy, his **knowledge** enabling him to solve riddles, and his **understanding** serving to break talismans. These three qualities must be associated with those in vs. 11.

Excellent spirit: So in 6:3. *Yattir* means "exceeding," "surpassing," and could well be translated by our prefix super-. It is used of the superbrightness of the image in 2:31, of the superheating of the kiln in 3:22, of the supergreatness of what was restored to Nebuchadrezzar in 4:36, of the superwisdom of Daniel in vs. 14 below, and of the superstrength and superdreadfulness of the beast in 7:7, 19. Some would have it refer here to his pre-eminent abilities in general. Others, looking ahead to 6:4 (M.T. 6:5), think that his excellent spirit is to be explained as his faithfulness, diligence, and good conduct. It seems most likely that the writer is associating it with those skills immediately to be mentioned and with the **light** of vs. 11. **Knowledge** is the word used in 2:21 for the knowledge that God gives to those who have understanding, and in 4:34, 36 for the king's reason which he lost and which was restored to him. **Understanding:** The same word is in vss. 11, 14. Some think that this word alone is to be taken with the three skills that follow, i.e., he had (*a*) ability, (*b*) knowledge, (*c*) understanding of oneiromancy, riddle solving, and talisman breaking.

To interpret dreams: In the M.T. the word is pointed as a participle, but to point it as an infinitive is a necessary correction. Daniel's skill in oneiromancy was the subject of chs. 2 and 4. There were dream books available, but without discernment on the part of the diviner their instructions were not of much use. It is Daniel's insight, as that of Joseph in Gen. 40–41, that is the source of his skill. **Explain riddles:** *'Ahidhāh* is a thing closed in and concealed. It is the equivalent of the Hebrew word used for "riddle" in

13 Then was Daniel brought in before the king. *And* the king spake and said unto Daniel, *Art* thou that Daniel, which *art* of the children of the captivity of Judah, whom the king my father brought out of Jewry?

14 I have even heard of thee, that the spirit of the gods *is* in thee, and *that* light

13 Then Daniel was brought in before the king. The king said to Daniel, "You are that Daniel, one of the exiles of Judah, whom the king my father brought from Judah. 14 I have heard of you that the spirit

---

Num. 12:8, for a "hard question" in I Kings 10:1, for a "problem" in Ps. 49:4. The word for **solve** is that used in 2:5; *et al.,* for "declaring" the interpretation of a dream. It corresponds with the Hebrew phrase in Judg. 14:14. Oriental literature is full of stories of such "hard sayings" being put in obscure, enigmatic language and then being unriddled by some clever person. In the O.T. we have Samson's riddle in Judg. 14:14, or the hard questions put by the queen of Sheba to Solomon (I Kings 10:2-3). The fame of the riddle solver is sung in Ecclus. 39. **Solve problems:** Lit., "unloose knots." So in vs. 16. *Qeṭar* is the word that was used in vs. 6 for the fastenings of the joints. In Ezek. 46:22 the verb is used for the "knotting" (joining) of corners in building construction. In later texts the word is used of magical knots, spells, talismans, etc., so that "to loose knots" became a technical term in the vocabulary of the magician's art, referring to the rites of spell breaking and exorcism. In Enoch 8:3 we read of "resolving of enchantments" (cf. 95:4); in Luke 13:16, of the loosing of the woman knotted up by Satan for eighteen years; and in the *Qur'ān,* Sūra 113:4, Muhammad seeks relief from the women who blow upon knots. The Syrian church fathers knew of "knots" as a special form of sorcery. All these are the descendants of the "knotting" of ancient Mesopotamian magic for whose "loosing" there were elaborate techniques. The third skill of Daniel was that by his wisdom he was able to loose any binding knot that even the most skilled magician might tie. Other interpreters reject this suggestion of a magical reference and insist that all that is meant is that he had ability in resolving difficulties.

That the queen mother mentions Daniel's court name also links this chapter with 1:7; 4:8. Here it is said that the king had given him his court name, whereas in 1:7 it was the chief eunuch who gave the names. Since this is merely a detail of the *décor* of the story, there is no need to discuss whether the king may not have chosen names which he gave to the chief eunuch to bestow.

13. Daniel is now **brought in.** Some commentators have sought reasons why he had not come with the corps of wise men when they were summoned, since he was the head of that group. They suggest that as he was now an old man, he might have been excused, or that as the chief, he would not necessarily have had to obey a general summons. It is part of the literary structure of such a story, however, that the man with heavenly wisdom does not appear until the men with human wisdom have been shown up as incapable. Daniel's absence at the beginning is a device to make his appearance later more effective.

You are that Daniel: Belshazzar speaks as though Daniel were quite unknown to him, though from 8:27, which concerns Belshazzar's third year, one would judge that the Daniel who was then "busied about the king's service" would have been well known to him by the last year of his reign. Again, however, this is a detail of the setting of the story where one must not look for consistency. Some make this a question, **Art thou that Daniel?** which is perhaps the better interpretation. **Of the exiles of Judah:** Lit., **which art of the children of the captivity of Judah** (as in 2:25).

14. Belshazzar's words **I have heard of you** may refer to what the queen mother has just said, since he goes on to repeat her words, or it may mean that he is saying he has not met Daniel personally though he has heard of his reputation. The M.T. omits

and understanding and excellent wisdom is found in thee.

15 And now the wise *men,* the astrologers, have been brought in before me, that they should read this writing, and make known unto me the interpretation thereof: but they could not show the interpretation of the thing:

16 And I have heard of thee, that thou canst make interpretations, and dissolve doubts: now if thou canst read the writing, and make known to me the interpretation thereof, thou shalt be clothed with scarlet, and *have* a chain of gold about thy neck, and shalt be the third ruler in the kingdom.

17 ¶ Then Daniel answered and said before the king, Let thy gifts be to thyself, and give thy rewards to another; yet I will read the writing unto the king and make known to him the interpretation.

of the holy gods[k] is in you, and that light and understanding and excellent wisdom are found in you. **15** Now the wise men, the enchanters, have been brought in before me to read this writing and make known to me its interpretation; but they could not show the interpretation of the matter. **16** But I have heard that you can give interpretations and solve problems. Now if you can read the writing and make known to me its interpretation, you shall be clothed with purple, and have a chain of gold about your neck, and shall be the third ruler in the kingdom." **17** Then Daniel answered before the king, "Let your gifts be for yourself, and give your rewards to another; nevertheless I will read the writing to the king and make

[k] Or *Spirit of the holy God*

---

holy before **gods,** but as it is found in some MSS, and is in the Syriac and some Greek texts, several editors restore it here to harmonize with vs. 11.

15. The **wise men** and **enchanters** alone are mentioned, but they stand for all the groups previously spoken of.

17. Daniel's reply reads as though it were spoken rudely and discourteously. It was deliberately phrased thus by the writer whose audience would appreciate to the full the manner in which a pious hero of Israel answers a heathen monarch. This detail is characteristic of the martyr legends whose heroes answer back to mighty potentates and preach them sermons.

The gifts and rewards refer to 2:6, where Nebuchadrezzar promises the same for an interpretation of his dream. Perhaps the story stresses that Daniel refuses the gifts but is willing to put his skill at the service of the monarch. It is, however, merely a rhetorical refusal, for in vs. 29 we find him accepting what the king had promised.

d) DANIEL'S SERMON TO THE KING (5:18-25)

The sermon in vss. 18-24 contrasts the greatness of Nebuchadrezzar with the indignity of his fall, pointing out the cause and its cure, and then condemning Belshazzar for not having learned from the experience of his father. Had he taken warning, he would have avoided that same pride and arrogance and the stupid service of idols which now bring on his own doom.

---

to tell us about God. The foundation of the state and the hope of a people is the **man in whom is the Spirit of the holy God.**

17. *Power Has No Answers.*—Let your gifts be for yourself. The rudeness of the reply heightens the dramatic contrast between the religious man and the heathen king. It also reveals that one of the greatest difficulties for the worshiper of power is to free himself from the belief that it is the answer to every problem. Belshazzar is frightened, but he assumes that he can get the information he wants by offering another what

he himself accepts as of supreme value. "If you will tell me what I want to know," he is saying, "I will give you what every man wants most." Daniel's rebuke is to show how he utterly despises the things the king worships. There are other values and other standards. One can hear the innuendo that salvation is possible only when men are disillusioned enough with their material playthings and their idols. The man of God is set free from bondage to such trinkets. His power rises from his independence. Of such as Daniel is God's saving remnant.

18 O thou king, the most high God gave Nebuchadnezzar thy father a kingdom, and majesty, and glory, and honor:

19 And for the majesty that he gave him, all people, nations, and languages, trembled and feared before him: whom he would he slew; and whom he would he kept alive; and whom he would he set up; and whom he would he put down.

20 But when his heart was lifted up, and his mind hardened in pride, he was deposed from his kingly throne, and they took his glory from him:

21 And he was driven from the sons of men; and his heart was made like the beasts, and his dwelling *was* with the wild asses: they fed him with grass like oxen, and his body was wet with the dew of heaven; till he knew that the most high God ruled in the kingdom of men, and *that* he appointeth over it whomsoever he will.

22 And thou his son, O Belshazzar, hast not humbled thine heart, though thou knewest all this;

known to him the interpretation. 18 O king, the Most High God gave Nebuchadnez'zar your father kingship and greatness and glory and majesty; 19 and because of the greatness that he gave him, all peoples, nations, and languages trembled and feared before him; whom he would he slew, and whom he would he kept alive; whom he would he raised up, and whom he would he put down. 20 But when his heart was lifted up and his spirit was hardened so that he dealt proudly, he was deposed from his kingly throne, and his glory was taken from him; 21 he was driven from among men, and his mind was made like that of a beast, and his dwelling was with the wild asses; he was fed grass like an ox, and his body was wet with the dew of heaven, until he knew that the Most High God rules the kingdom of men, and sets over it whom he will. 22 And you his son, Belshaz'zar, have not humbled your heart, though you knew all

---

18. O king: The M.T. reads "Thou, O king," "thou" being a *nominativus pendens* picked up in the pronoun of **thy father** and fulfilled in vs. 22 **thou his son. Kingship, greatness, glory,** and **majesty** are all words from 4:22, 36.

19. All peoples, nations, and languages, as in 3:4, "were trembling in fear before him." There is probably some ancient formula reflected in vss. 18-19, for the Cyrus Cylinder (ll. 11-12) uses language closely resembling what we have in these verses. **Whom he would he slew,** etc., is the language used throughout Oriental story of the typical Oriental despot acting tyrannously and irresponsibly as though he could never be brought to account. The expression used here has parallels in I Sam. 2:7; Ps. 75:7; Ecclus. 7:11; Tob. 4:19.

Heart and **spirit** here both mean "mind" viewed under two aspects. **Was lifted up:** The same expression occurs in Deut. 8:14; Ezek. 31:10; Hos. 13:6; Jer. 48:29, and we find it used of Ptolemy in 11:12. "And his spirit was hardened to act proudly": This is the same notion as the hardening of Pharaoh's heart in Exodus and the plea of the psalmist, "Harden not your heart" (Ps. 95:8; cf. Deut. 2:30; I Sam. 6:6; Acts 19:9). The hardening of the neck in such passages as II Kings 17:14; II Chr. 30:8; Jer. 7:26 means much the same thing. This verse goes a little farther than anything said in ch. 4. Deposing Belshazzar from his throne and depriving him of his glory are an interpretation of 4:31. **Glory** doubtless means the splendor of his royal estate, as in vs. 18 (see 2:37; 4:36; 7:14).

21. In 4:25, 32 the king's dwelling was with "the wild beasts," i.e., the animals of the open country as opposed to domestic animals, but here he is said more specifically to have dwelt among **the wild asses,** whose haunts are far from the dwellings of men (see Job 39:5-9). Some MSS have "flocks" instead of **wild asses** (i.e., עדריא instead of ערדיא), which suits the words that follow but is probably an emendation made to harmonize with the eating of **grass** like **oxen.**

22. Have not humbled your heart: The opposite of that hardening of the heart which indicates pride and presumption. The same verb is used in vs. 19, in **whom he would he put down** (i.e., he humbled or abased them, as in 4:37, which tells how God

23 But hast lifted up thyself against the Lord of heaven; and they have brought the vessels of his house before thee, and thou and thy lords, thy wives and thy concubines, have drunk wine in them; and thou hast praised the gods of silver, and gold, of brass, iron, wood, and stone, which see not, nor hear, nor know: and the God is whose hand thy breath *is,* and whose *are* all thy ways, hast thou not glorified:

24 Then was the part of the hand sent from him; and this writing was written.

25 ¶ And this *is* the writing that was written, MENE, MENE, TEKEL, UPHARSIN.

this, 23 but you have lifted up yourself against the Lord of heaven; and the vessels of his house have been brought in before you, and you and your lords, your wives, and your concubines have drunk wine from them; and you have praised the gods of silver and gold, of bronze, iron, wood, and stone, which do not see or hear or know, but the God in whose hand is your breath, and whose are all your ways, you have not honored.

24 "Then from his presence the hand was sent, and this writing was inscribed. 25 And this is the writing that was inscribed:

is able to abase those who walk in pride). It is used again in 7:24 for the "laying low" of three kings.

23. Belshazzar's sin was apparently fourfold: (*a*) he exalted himself **against the Lord of heaven;** (*b*) he committed sacrilege by using consecrated **vessels;** (*c*) he worshiped idols; (*d*) he failed to honor the one living God. Others make his sin but twofold: (*a*) sacrilege, whereby he affronted the Lord, (*b*) idolatry, which was an insult to God. **Lord of heaven:** Cf. 2:18, 37, 44.

No significance should be attached to the fact that **silver** is here mentioned before **gold,** contrary to vss. 2, 4. Theod. and the Peshitta mention gold first here also but they are probably harmonizing with vs. 4. **Which do not see or hear or know** is the traditional gibe at the unreasonableness of idolatry (see Deut. 4:28; Pss. 115:4-8; 135:16-17; Rev. 9:20). **In whose hand is your breath:** Perhaps "your soul" (cf. Job 12:10). *Neshāmāh* may mean the physical breath as in Gen. 2:7; Ps. 18:15 (M.T. 18:16); Job 37:10, but may also mean the soul (spirit) as in Prov. 20:27; Job 32:8. It is still common among Arabs to swear "By him in whose hand is the life [soul] of So and So." **Whose are all your ways: Ways** probably means "destinies" (cf. Jer. 10:23; Prov. 20:24; Ps. 37:5). Behrmann notes that it is a word particularly beloved of the wisdom literature, and refers to the ὅδος of Thucydides (*Peloponnesian War* III. 64) and the N.T.

24. The ghostly hand is here referred to its source. It came forth **from his presence.** As in vs. 5, it is the *paṣ* of a hand that does the writing. **Inscribed:** Recorded. In 6:9 ff. this word refers to the signing of a decree, and in 10:21 to what is recorded in scripture. The cognate verb in Arabic is used for the art of copying exemplars of the *Qur'ān.* In vs. 25 it is used for "written."

25. The solution of the writing lies in the fact that in Aramaic unpointed words may vary in meaning in accordance with how they are pointed. The ghostly hand wrote the words unpointed. By pointing them one way or another, intelligible words could be made out of each of them, but the problem was to read them as a meaningful whole and interpret this with relevance to the situation. MENE, MENE, TEKEL, and PARSIN gives us three different words with the connective particle U (and). PARSIN is the dual or plural of *peres,* so the three words in unvowelled script would be *mn' tql prs* (so in the explanation in vss. 26-28). On the surface these must be weights, for *mn'* is the mina, *tql* the shekel, and *prs* the half mina; thus we have "a mina, a shekel and two half minas."

The M.T. repeats MENE, but the LXX, Theod., Vulg., Josephus, and Jerome all agree that there were but three words, and inasmuch as only these three are considered in the explanation in vss. 26-28, many editors delete the first MENE. On the other hand,

23. *No Life Without God.*—We are reminded of Paul's word to the Athenians regarding God in whom "we live, and move, and have our being" (Acts 17:28). Daniel was proclaiming that without God we cannot live. Our souls, our breath, our bodies are in his keeping and

26 This *is* the interpretation of the thing: MENE; God hath numbered thy kingdom, and finished it.

27 TEKEL; Thou art weighed in the balances, and art found wanting.

MENE, MENE, TEKEL, and PARSIN. 26 This is the interpretation of the matter: MENE, God has numbered the days of your kingdom and brought it to an end; 27 TEKEL, you have been weighed in the balances and

---

Hans Bauer ("Menetekel," *Vierter deutscher Münzforschertag zu Halle/s* [1925], pp. 27-30) thinks that our PARSIN means that in the original it read *mn' tql prṣ prṣ*.

Whatever the original text may have been, it is clear that these words were symbolic, probably expressing some popular judgment on political matters in symbols which would be recognized immediately by the audience, though at this distance we can only guess at the significance. The usual interpretation is that it refers to Nebuchadrezzar who was worth a mina, Belshazzar who was worth no more than a shekel, and the Medes and the Persians who were worth half a mina each. Others prefer to make the reference wholly to Babylonian potentates. E. G. Kraeling ("The Handwriting on the Wall," *Journal of Biblical Literature,* LXIII [1944], 11-18) supports the M.T. and makes the reference to the successors of Nebuchadrezzar. Of these there were five, so that the first MENE means Evil-merodach, the second MENE is Neriglissar, both of whom are valued at a mina. TEKEL is the boy-king Labashi-Marduk, who reigned only eight months and so was worth only a shekel, the sixtieth part of a mina. The dual PARSIN represents Nabonidus and his son Belshazzar, each valued at a half mina. Ginsberg (*Studies,* p. 25) also thinks they were Neo-Babylonian kings but, accepting the shorter text, identifies them with the only three of these rulers known to the Jews of the Hellenistic and Roman periods, viz., Nebuchadrezzar, Evil-merodach, and Belshazzar. Charles notes that we have evidence for weights used to represent persons in the ancient Near East and therefore such symbolism here is quite possible.

e) THE RIDDLE UNRIDDLED (5:26-28)

26. The point of the interpretation is that though the words would normally be taken to mean weights and could symbolize some popular political judgment, they could also be pointed to spell out a message of relevance to local circumstances. There is a verb מנה, "to number," so that *mn'* could be pointed to suggest the meaning "numbered," i.e., God has numbered his days. There is also a verb תקל, "to weigh," and *tql* could be pointed to suggest "weighed," i.e., God has weighed him and found him lacking. And there is a verb פרס, "to divide," so that *prṣ* could be pointed to suggest "divided," i.e., God has divided the kingdom. Moreover, since *prṣ* could also be pointed to mean "Persians," it can refer to the giving of the kingdom to the Persians; indeed, Bauer's suggestion allows him to give Daniel's interpretation as "He has numbered! He has weighed! He has divided! The Persians!" Examples of this type of interpretation are well known. We find them even in the Bible. There is one in Jer. 1:11, where a word is pointed to mean an almond tree, but in the next verse, in order to make a point for the prophet's imagery, the same word is pointed to mean "watching." There is another in Amos 8:1-2, where a word is first pointed to mean "summer fruit" and then to mean "end."

Brought it to an end: Since the verb has the sense of "to complete," "to finish," the meaning is that the kingdom has been allowed its full measure of time and then brought to an end. But the verb also has the meaning of "to hand over," and is used in Ezra 7:19 for "to deliver"; some suggest that meaning here, i.e., God has handed the kingdom over to some more worthy successor.

27. The notion of human conduct being weighed in scales is very old and is beautifully illustrated in the ancient Egyptian judgment scenes where the deceased

---

subject to his will. Over against God there is the stupid worship of the idols and our praise of gods **which do not see or hear or know.**

27. *Weighed and Found Wanting.*—The biblical understanding of the justice of God is here given a picturesque expression. It represents the

28 PERES; Thy kingdom is divided, and given to the Medes and Persians.

29 Then commanded Belshazzar, and they clothed Daniel with scarlet, and *put* a chain of gold about his neck, and made a proclamation concerning him, that he should be the third ruler in the kingdom.

30 ¶ In that night was Belshazzar the king of the Chaldeans slain.

31 And Darius the Median took the kingdom, *being* about threescore and two years old.

found wanting; 28 PERES, your kingdom is divided and given to the Medes and Persians."

29 Then Belshaz'zar commanded, and Daniel was clothed with purple, a chain of gold was put about his neck, and proclamation was made concerning him, that he should be the third ruler in the kingdom.

30 That very night Belshaz'zar the Chalde'an king was slain. 31 And Darius the Mede received the kingdom, being about sixty-two years old.

---

stands before the balance while the recording is being made. Such biblical passages as Job 6:2-3; 31:6; Prov. 24:12; Ps. 62:9 reflect the idea (cf. also Pss. Sol. 5:6; Enoch 41:1; 61:8 and the *Qur'ān, Sūra* 21:48).

28. Divided: Some have raised the objection that the **kingdom** was not divided but was taken as a whole by the conquering Persians. *Peraṣ,* however, also means "to break," and the sense may be that it was broken off, i.e., was divided from one dynasty and given to another.

Medes are referred to in II Kings 17:6; Ezra 6:2, and in the Prophets. Medes and Persians are mentioned together here and in ch. 6 because the Jews, like the Greeks, regarded these two Iranian peoples as closely associated. Greek writers dealing with the struggles of their people with the Persians under Darius and his successors write indifferently τὰ Περσικά or τὰ Μηδικά, as though they meant the same thing.

3. EPILOGUE (5:29-31)

a) THE KING REWARDS DANIEL (5:29)

29. Belshazzar fulfills his promise and gives Daniel the rewards. That he shows complete unconcern with regard to the stern indictment of the man of God and to the dreadful message that has just been interpreted to him is characteristic of this story type. Some have suggested that in granting such honor to Daniel, Belshazzar was seeking to escape from the doom that had been pronounced. However, since no honor is mentioned save that promised to any of the sages, the king is merely fulfilling his word, as royalty must. **Proclamation was made:** Lit., "they heralded concerning him."

b) THE SIGN IS FULFILLED BY THE FALL OF BABYLON (5:30-31 = M.T. 5:30—6:1)

30. That very night, i.e., the same night on which the feast had been held assumes that Babylon was taken by a night attack, a tradition which, we have seen, is found also in Herodotus and Xenophon. Bentzen notes that the audience was meant to see in this the fulfillment of the prophecies in Isa. 21:1-10; Jer. 51:39, 57.

The Chaldean king: This is merely a statement that he was king of the Chaldeans, and the fact that the Neo-Babylonians never call themselves "king of the Kaldu" is irrelevant here. The phrase **king of the Chaldeans** occurs in II Chr. 36:17 and is used here in its true ethnic sense.

31. This verse belongs to ch. 5. It is, however, obviously a postscript, and in the M.T. is 6:1. **Darius the Mede:** Rowley (*Darius the Mede and the Four World Empires*) gives a summary of the discussion over this figure up to 1935 (for more recent discussion see Ginsberg, *op. cit.,* p. 15; Josephus Linder, *Commentarius in Librum Daniel* [Paris: P. Lethielleux, 1939], pp. 271-81). Attempts have been made to identify him with Cyaxares II, the uncle of Cyrus, with Cyrus himself, with Gobryas, the general who actually took Babylon and for a while governed it, with Cambyses the son of Cyrus, and with Astyages the last Median king. All these proposed identifications come to wreck on the facts that in this book Darius is (*a*) a Mede, 5:31; (*b*) son of Xerxes, 9:1; (*c*)

6 It pleased Darius to set over the kingdom a hundred and twenty princes, which should be over the whole kingdom;

6 It pleased Darius to set over the kingdom a hundred and twenty satraps, to be

---

the immediate predecessor of Cyrus, 6:28; 10:1. He is thus a figure of story, not of history, and there is no difficulty in seeing how in these folk tales the figure of Cyrus, who took Babylon in 538 B.C., came to be confused with that of Darius I, who captured it in 520. The four-empire theory demanded a Median Empire before the Persian, and prophecy had foretold the overthrow of Babylon by the Medes (Isa. 13:17; 21:2; Jer. 51:11, 28), so we have the shadowy figure of **Darius the Mede** succeeding Belshazzar. It is quite possible that reminiscences of both Gobyras and Cambyses may have gone into the formation of this figure.

Darius: *Daryâwesh,* a form which occurs in the Aramaic papyri, is the Old Persian *Dārayavauš,* a Persian, not a Median name. Darius I Hystaspis is mentioned in Ezra 4:5 ff., and Darius II Nothus (or Darius III Codomannus) in Neh. 12:22, but the Darius of this book is distinguished from them as Darius Medus. **Received the kingdom:** Since the text does not say "was made king," some have suggested that this means he was only a kind of regent for Cyrus, as Gobryas was until Cyrus entered Babylon. There can be no doubt, however, that the writer regards Darius as a real king. He is called "king," not viceroy or ruler; he exercises all the prerogatives of royalty and acts as paramount chief, appointing ministers, setting up satrapies, issuing edicts, pronouncing death sentences, making announcements to peoples, nations, and tongues, just as Nebuchadrezzar had done, and is succeeded by Cyrus. As to the phrase **received the kingdom,** both the LXX and Theod. render it παρέλαβεν τὴν βασιλείαν, which is the phrase the LXX uses of Cyrus in 6:28 and in the account of the accession of Antiochus and then of his son in II Macc. 4:7; 10:11. It is used here of the saints receiving the kingdom in 7:18, and so would seem to have been the popular formula in Aramaic.

Being about sixty-two years old: This mention of a man's age is unique in the book. Charles thinks that this was about the age of Gobryas. Some consider it a hint to explain why the Median Empire was of such short duration. Others hold that it refers to the age of Daniel. The LXX omits the note altogether.

F. Daniel in the Lions' Den (6:1-28)

This story belongs to the same type as that in ch. 3, having its connections on the one hand with the court histories, which tell tales of court intrigues, and on the other with the martyr legends, which recount the miraculous deliverance of those saintly folk who refuse to compromise in matters of religion, and the punishment of their enemies. In a sense it is a continuation and counterpart of ch. 3. There the three friends went through trial and taught the negative lesson of abstaining from heathen idolatry; here Daniel goes through trial to teach the positive lesson of faithfulness in performing one's religious duties. The parallels between the two stories are noteworthy. There the three confessors remained loyal, though that involved disobedience to Nebuchadrezzar's command; here Daniel does the same, though it means disobeying an edict of Darius. There the enemies of the confessors secured their condemnation; here the enemies of Daniel succeed in having him condemned. There it was the jealousy of the court sages at work; here it is the jealousy of court officials. There an angel from the Lord saved the confessors in the fire; here an angel comes to the pit to shut the mouths of the lions. There the fire killed those who threw the confessors into the kiln; here the lions devour the enemies of Daniel. There Nebuchadrezzar sang a doxology to the God of the

---

foundation of Israel's faith. God could not be flouted, and the people who for the time being were going through persecution and suffering could be certain that justice would be done to them and their enemies. God is concerned with human affairs. He cares enough to apply his standards to them.

6:1-28. No Compromising Dedication.—Here is another story illustrating spiritual lessons for all time. To treat it literally is both foolish

confessors; here Darius breaks into verse in praise of Daniel's God. There the result of the conspiracy was the further advancement of the three; here the result is the further prosperity of Daniel. Also in both stories the monarch's decree is concerned with punishment for all who do not conform on a detail of religious practice. Not only is the motif of the two stories the same, but careful reading reveals a number of verbal correspondences.

The lesson of this story is that of loyalty to God's prescriptions of religion. He will honor those who observe them faithfully. Religion consists not only in public observances but also in private devotions. In captivity the Jews had little opportunity for the public performance of cult observances, and private, personal religion therefore became the more important. Powerful potentates, or groups within the state, might endeavor to interfere with this private religion as well as with public cult performances. Antiochus Epiphanes had done this very thing (I Macc. 1:42; II Macc. 6:6). Yet God can intervene to aid those who wish to remain faithful to their religion, and he can humble mighty rulers.

As in the previous stories, the details of the narrative are but the writer's literary décor. He is not teaching history, he is presenting a religious message, so that the details of his literary framework are not meant to be taken literally. Thus it is beside the point to argue that no Achaemenid known to history would have been so foolish as to issue such an edict as Darius is pictured issuing here, or to urge the improbability of any such monarch breaking out into poetry in praise of the God of Israel. It is equally beside the point to assemble travelers' tales about recently fed lions doing no harm to a human being at their mercy, though if hungry ready to devour anything within reach. These

and blind. The details are not important, but the great ideas are. The question is raised: What shall a man give in exchange for his integrity? To what extent is compromise ever justified? Does it pay to trim our sails to the prevailing winds? Or is religion the dedication of one's life to the Eternal, without fear of the immediate consequences? Daniel believed certain things were true, and he answered such questions as these with a story which has been a favorite of young and old.

For one thing, the story indicates that religious faith is the bulwark against tryanny. It is important to note that the main issues of life do not change. The secondary circumstances are different, but the ultimate decisions each generation is called upon to make are the same. Daniel had to face an edict of Darius that put the king above God. The author of the book was facing the threat of the Seleucids. We are always facing an arrogant nationalism that threatens to usurp the place of God. It was the French Revolution, in the name of democracy and freedom, that instituted universal military conscription. The issues parade under different names, but they are still the same as Daniel faced.

What is the relationship of the church to the state? What is the relationship of the individual to his government? These are never easy questions to decide, and no final solution is ever found. Always there is an uneasy tension between church and state, with no clear dividing line. The one sure thing we know is that the state is not God, and man's allegiance is first of all to God. Much of the nationalism of modern times is more in the nature of a return to ancient doctrines of the divine right of rulers. It becomes another religion, and for many an empty man his only religion. If there is no real inner faith and experience, men turn to totalitarianism; or if they cannot stand that, they will search for a mild, mystical Buddhism. Only the man with an understanding of God's jealousy will be able to see the issue clearly and then decide it correctly.

It all comes back finally to our understanding of ourselves and our relationship to God. Man has to be put in his proper place and setting. It makes no difference if the man is a king or a slave, still he must be subject to the will of God. The independence of Daniel was the author's way of saying that men who worshiped God were subject to no other power, but were truly free men. The spirit of the book of Daniel is the spirit of the people who swore allegiance to their kings in Aragon: "We, who are as good as you, swear to you, who are not better than we, to accept you as our king and sovereign lord, provided that you observe all our liberties and laws; but if not, then not." [4]

The story of Daniel and the lion's den also emphasizes that religious loyalty will be interpreted as bigotry by pagans. No generation

[4] D. R. Davies, *Secular Illusion or Christian Realism?* (New York: The Macmillan Co., 1949), p. 7.

matters belong to the framework of the story, and the lions' den here, like the kiln of ch. 3, has value as setting for the story, not as literal fact.

In the Chester Beatty papyri this and the following story come after ch. 8. Such an arrangement cannot be original and would seem to be an attempt to place the stories in a more strictly chronological order. Chs. 1–4 deal with Nebuchadrezzar, chs. 5; 7–8 with Belshazzar, and chs. 6 and 9 with Darius.

Here as in the previous stories the writer seems to be using a source. G. A. Barton ("The Story of Ahikar and the Book of Daniel," *American Journal of Semitic Languages and Literature*, XVI [1899-1900], 242-47) pointed out resemblances to the Ahiqar story, and this has now been re-emphasized by Ginsberg (*op. cit.*, p. 27), who calls attention also to the Mordecai story in Esther. The heathen king is here pictured in an even more favorable light than in ch. 3, and there is no hint of any general persecution of the Jews, so that the original story may have come from a time early in the Persian period.

1. Prologue (6:1-3=M.T. 6:2-4)

6:1. The setting is provided by the fact that a change of dynasty meant overhauling the machinery of government by the appointment of new officials. The change is here described as the division of the Persian Empire into satrapies with a high official over each, together with the appointment of three presiding officers to whom the satraps report. Nothing is said of the three friends who in ch. 3 held high posts in the provincial government, but Daniel is made one of the three presidents.

Such a division of the country into satrapies was made by Darius I (522-485 B.C.). Herodotus (*History* III. 89-94) tells us that Darius created only some 20 satrapies, and in his own inscriptions we have reference to 21, 23, and 29 satrapies in the empire. Jewish tradition, however, said that the division was into some 120 satrapies (Esth.

---

should understand this better than ours. We have not realized that substituting indifference for conviction and calling it progress is always the sign of paganism. It is typically the attitude of the secularist who has lost the truth that the world and men belong to God. Religion in such a scheme is a matter of convenience and a means to an end. To suggest that religion is the first and last reality, without which men fade into the category of things, seems narrow and ridiculous to pagans.

One of the signs that we have lost our loyalty to God is our extreme fear of being called bigoted. We would much rather be called wicked than intolerant. It is an embarrassment to be told that our God is a jealous God. Yet it was this clear understanding of God's nature that made the Jew rise to the heights of religious insight. One never can understand the best characteristics of Judaism if he does not understand its recognition of loyalty as a top virtue. We have tended to water down this whole emphasis in the Bible and to substitute a vague theory of evolutionary progress which has tolerance as its final goal.

This has resulted in a loss of the sense of the absoluteness of right and wrong. It is a sad thing to hear religious people advocate being reasonable in adjusting our lives to the social environment, as if social disapproval is more to be feared than God's judgment. In too many

circles it has become popular to give up important principles in the name of being civilized. The man who sacrifices gain for righteousness is regarded as a strange fellow, never quite sane and certainly not practical.

Yet if we look back to our past we discover that, in the days of crisis at least, it has been the Daniels who have preserved humanity's chief treasures. It is only after the years have passed that they are regarded as heroes and saviors. They received the sneers and arrogant insults of the multitudes during their lifetimes. But where would the race be without them? Try to imagine a world in which no one chose death for God's sake. Once we have understood what we owe to the hated and persecuted minorities, we shall be less willing to cast a stone at the brave men of our time who put principles before profit. It is not true that the easygoing men of compromise have been the chief benefactors of the race. Let us sing again the old Sunday-school song "Dare to Be a Daniel."

Abraham Lincoln once made a speech [5] against the advice of his friends. As a result, he was defeated in his race for the senate in 1858. But he said: "If it is decreed that I go down because of this speech, then let me go down linked to the truth." By such decisions as this do we know we are the children of God. When we are called fools for taking the narrow way

[5] "Speech upon the Right of Election."

2 And over these three persidents; of whom Daniel *was* first: that the princes might give accounts unto them, and the king should have no damage.

throughout the whole kingdom; 2 and over them three presidents, of whom Daniel was one, to whom these satraps should give account, so that the king might suffer no

---

1:1; 8:9; Additions to Esth. 2:1; 5:1; I Esdras 3:2). Josephus (*Antiquities* X. 11. 4) says 360, assuming that each of the three presidents was over 120 satrapies. From Cyrus' annalistic tablet we know that he appointed his general Gobryas to be governor of Babylon, and this Gobryas set up subgovernors; it may be that some tradition about this is what is embodied in the story here. The large number 120 may perhaps be explained by assuming that the Jews used the word satrap in a wider sense than it had in official Persian usage.

2. Over them: Lit., "higher than they," the opposite to "lower than thou" in 2:39. **Three presidents:** *Ṣārakh* is not used elsewhere in the O.T., but in the Targ. it translates the Hebrew *shôṭēr*, "officer," "administrator." It is from the Iranian *sarak*, "chief." The notion of the three presidents may be the writer's own, or it may represent his understanding of some ancient tradition about certain chief officers of the Persian administration, or he may have found it in his source. We have no certain knowledge that it was Persian custom to appoint three chief ministers in this way. It may be a reflection of the fact that there were three high dignitaries in each satrapy, viz., the satrap himself, his *karanos* or military chief, and his secretary, each of whom seems to have had some independence (Herodotus, *op. cit.*, III. 128). That the audience would see nothing unusual in a Jew being appointed to high official position under the Persians is clear from the stories of Ezra and Nehemiah. Kuhl (*Die drei Männer*, p. 63) assembles other material about non-Persians attaining such positions under them.

Account: In Ezra 4:21; 6:14; 7:13 this word is used as equivalent to "decree" or "commandment," and in Ezra 5:5 for "matter," "account." **Loss:** So in Esth. 7:4, "loss" or "damage." Bentzen suggests that the sentence may mean "that the king may not be troubled," i.e., these officials would carry the burden of state to relieve the king. The usual interpretation, however, is that they watched over the finances of the empire.

---

instead of the wide one, we join the fellowship of the redeemed.

Yet there is something else which should be said. Men secretly admire those who have convictions. It is not always apparent at the time, but deep in the hearts of all men there is the inescapable feeling that we ought to stand for some things no matter what they cost. The king was caught in his own foolish decree, and his sorrow was due partly to his knowledge that Daniel was a judgment upon him. So he fasted and sorrowed for Daniel, but most of all—it may be—he was ashamed of himself.

Much of the satirical wit of men who have no faith is a vain attempt to cover up their sense of inner poverty. They laugh at the men who stand for their convictions and risk something for the maintenance of their integrity. But their laughter is hollow. Betrayal always pretends to despise loyalty. It always tries to imply that faithfulness is stupidity. But at the end of the day there is admiration for the men of conviction.

One of the most prominent business leaders in his community and one of the wealthiest men

in the state came one day to call on a young minister. Every now and again he had a nervous breakdown and had to leave all his obligations for several weeks. Telling about it, he said he was afraid the periods were becoming more intense and more frequent. He was frightened. Then he referred to his father. "My dad," he said, "had something I do not have. He had faith and serenity even when he had problems. I'd give anything if I had what he had." He went on to say that of course he found it necessary to drink and smoke, which his father never did. He was doing many things which his father would have regarded as wrong. "But," he said, "they are not really wrong, are they?"

You could hardly find a better illustration of the spirit of men who want power and peace of mind without the necessary moral and spiritual convictions. But the time comes when they think with nostalgia of men who paid the price for mastery of life. What they formerly despised they now see with clear eyes as of ultimate value. At last they know that all their boasted superiority over simple devotion to God and the moral law was pretense. They have always

3 Then this Daniel was preferred above the presidents and princes, because an excellent spirit *was* in him; and the king thought to set him over the whole realm.

4 ¶ Then the presidents and princes sought to find occasion against Daniel concerning the kingdom; but they could find none occasion nor fault; forasmuch as he *was* faithful, neither was there any error or fault found in him.

loss. 3 Then this Daniel became distinguished above all the other presidents and satraps, because an excellent spirit was in him; and the king planned to set him over the whole kingdom. 4 Then the presidents and the satraps sought to find a ground for complaint against Daniel with regard to the kingdom; but they could find no ground for complaint or any fault, because he was faithful, and no error or fault was

---

3. In the king's eyes Daniel "was distinguishing himself above" the other court officials. This was because of that **excellent spirit** mentioned also in 5:12. The monarch was minded to appoint him grand vizier (prime minister) over the whole empire. The LXX adds, "and he prospered in the king's business which he carried out." A supreme official of this kind is known from later times, but there is no evidence for his existence in the Achaemenid era.

2. THE TESTING OF THE MAN OF GOD (6:4-24)
a) THE JEALOUSY OF DANIEL'S FELLOW OFFICERS (6:4-9=M.T. 6:5-10)

4. Such favor from the king naturally aroused the jealousy of other officials, so that a characteristic court intrigue develops. Some weak spot in the armor of the king's favorite must be found where one sudden thrust may bring him down. There is no need to think that the enmity was particularly stirred by Daniel's being of another race and religion. The writer makes no suggestion that it was because he was a Jew that they sought his overthrow. The audience would understand perfectly that the mere fact that he was on a pinnacle of favor was sufficient to start a conspiracy for his fall.

Ground for complaint: *'Illāh* is the technical word for a ground for legal indictment. **With regard to the kingdom:** Lit., "from the side of the kingdom." Their first attempt was directed toward finding something remiss in the carrying out of Daniel's official

---

secretly longed for what they were unwilling to achieve.

Life does not let us live in the fool's paradise of compromise very long. It turns us out into the terrible deserts of meaningless futility. It forces us to face our poverty when we are without principles. When King Albert I of Belgium refused passage to the Germans in 1941, even when his country was promised immunity, he said that Belgium had been "cornered into heroism." We are so constituted that until we are playing heroic parts, we are unable to keep our hearts in peace. We throw our Daniels into the lions' den because they represent our own best selves which in our madness we would kill.

Finally, let us note the importance of regular worship. The story says that the signing of the decree made no difference to Daniel, for **he went to his house where he had windows in his upper chamber open toward Jerusalem; and he got down upon his knees three times a day and prayed and gave thanks before his God, as he had done previously** (vs. 10). It would have been easy, and some would say natural, to

dispense with those devotions when they meant death.

It has been said that our day is too crowded to allow time for private devotions. It is argued with eloquence that, while people in former times had leisure, we do not have time for anything but work and pleasure. The modern family, we are told, cannot be expected to have family worship. The individual caught up in the rush of our civilization does not have time enough to relax, let alone time enough to pray. Thus do we find many reasons why we must not be expected to maintain our devotional life. Even among Christian people those who have regular periods of prayer and meditation may be a very small minority. Ministers become a part of this process and in the name of organizing and directing church activities let private devotions get crowded out of their lives.

One of the most distressing things about us is our inability to see the relationship between cause and effect. It never seems to dawn upon us that our tensions and our fears spring out of our lack of quiet worship. We blame the rush for the neglect of worship, but the rushing

5 Then said these men, We shall not find any occasion against this Daniel, except we find *it* against him concerning the law of his God.

found in him. 5 Then these men said, "We shall not find any ground for complaint against this Daniel unless we find it in connection with the law of his God."

---

duties which they could build up into a charge against his loyalty or integrity. In this they failed, for his faithfulness to his sovereign and his devotion to his duties were such that no defect could be found. **Fault:** *Sheḥithāh,* "corrupt deed," is from the verb "to corrupt," and was used in 2:9 for the "lying and corrupt word" which Nebuchadrezzar accused the wise men of having prepared for his ear. **Error:** *Shālû* is "remissness"; see 3:29 where the *Qerê* uses it of Nebuchadrezzar's threat against anyone who spoke anything remiss against the God of the confessors. It is used in Ezra 4:22; 6:9 of slackness or negligence in carrying out official orders. Some editors regard this last sentence as a gloss since it is repetitious and is omitted by both the LXX and Theod.

5. Since no fault could be found in Daniel's official life, the plotters turn to his private life. Here they found a possible point of attack in his religion. **Law of his God:** *Dāth* is the Iranian word used in vs. 8 for **the law of the Medes and the Persians;** it was used in 2:9 for the judicial sentence promulgated by Nebuchadrezzar. Here it translates the Hebrew *tôrāh,* the law as a code of religious precepts (cf. 7:25), a sense it has in Ezra 7:12, 14, though it is used here in the meaning of "religion," the significance *tôrāh* was given at a time when the law had come to constitute the chief element in religion.

---

is itself a result of that neglect. The disease which makes us unhealthy is regarded as a valid reason for failing to do the things which will restore us to health. It is a vicious circle, and until we can be saved from our blindness we shall lack the power to put this first thing first.

If we would live true to our heritage as sons of God, there is no way other than keeping close to the Father. That means living in his presence and taking the time to listen to his voice. It is the mark of a very foolish generation when it talks about not having time for this essential practice. We should do well to surrender our lust for success and free ourselves from the pressure of ceaseless activity. We cannot give up our devotions and expect to find ourselves adequate for living. We shall do our work better and we shall not be nervously exhausted at the end of the day if we are wise enough to preserve some moments for worship. Daniel knew that in the ordeal ahead he must have the power of God, and it was no time to neglect the method he had found which released that power to him.

It is a great mistake to think that we can drift along and then be ready to meet the crisis when it comes. Not so! The crisis simply reveals the kind of persons we are. It uncovers our strength and our weakness. The man who has faithfully followed the disciplines of worship is prepared, and the man who has denied those disciplines is poor and unprepared. The saint is a disciplined person. The hero has been faithful in the small things. We ought to take to heart this ancient book's insight that men have to be strong within before they can per-

form the mighty act. Though we are not always in a position to withdraw for our devotions, we can learn how to be like Brother Lawrence in his kitchen, or Pippa in her factory. The main thing is that there should be called to our aid the habit of regular worship. It becomes less and less a burden and more and more a joy. It is like the growth of an appreciation for music. Time changes it from duty to privilege.

A group of tourists in the Highlands saw a rare plant over the side of a cliff. There was no way to approach it either from the top or the bottom. Then they saw a boy in a field helping his father keep the sheep. They asked him to let them lower him over the cliff on a rope, but he hesitated. They promised him a liberal reward, and finally he said he would do it under one condition. "I will do it," he said, "if my father holds the rope." Men are kept steady when they know the Father is holding them steady. But such knowledge comes only to men who take time to become conscious of this reality. We need to understand again the central significance of living in the presence of God through our daily private devotions.

5. By Their Fruits.—This approach is characteristic of many people. Since there is nothing in a man's outward actions which is wrong, throw suspicion on him by questioning his beliefs and his sacred customs. How easy it is to cast aspersions on the man who is a part of a persecuted minority. We label every man with whom we disagree a partisan of our opponents, and in the name of patriotism we seek to discredit him. We should remember Jesus' admoni-

6 Then these presidents and princes assembled together to the king, and said thus unto him, King Darius, live for ever.

7 All the presidents of the kingdom, the governors, and the princes, the counselors, and the captains, have consulted together to establish a royal statute, and to make a firm decree, that whosoever shall ask a peti-

6 Then these presidents and satraps came by agreement[m] to the king and said to him, "O King Darius, live for ever! 7 All the presidents of the kingdom, the prefects and the satraps, the counselors and the governors are agreed that the king should estab-

[m] Or *thronging*

---

6. Having come to an agreement among themselves, the conspirators approach the monarch. The verb used here occurs also at vss. 11, 15 and means "to make a tumult," so that many think of these officials in their eager animosity bursting tumultuously into the royal presence. No Oriental audience, however, would ever believe that courtiers would rush tumultuously into the presence of a king, and Bentzen would therefore translate "hastened." The versions had difficulty with the verb. It can mean "to keep watch on," so that in all these passages a meaning **came by agreement**, i.e., came in accordance with a conspiracy they had formed, is suitable (see J. A. Montgomery, *A Critical and Exegetical Commentary on the Book of Daniel* [New York: Charles Scribner's Sons, 1927; "International Critical Commentary"], pp. 272-73) .

Live for ever: The same formula occurs in 2:4. Daniel also uses it in addressing the king in vs. 21.

7. It was the two other presidents and the satraps who came before the monarch, but they claim to speak in the name of all classes of government officials. Why the king did not notice that Daniel was not present we are not told, but the audience would understand that for the purposes of the story the king must not notice this until later so that he may assume that Daniel must have been party to the request. The LXX makes the two presidential colleagues of Daniel alone conspire against him, and so in vs. 24 has only these two punished. Since Josephus agrees with the M.T., it is clear that the LXX text here is secondary, its translator having apparently felt the difficulty of so general a conspiracy even in an Oriental court, and so modified it.

That the king should establish an ordinance: If we follow the Masoretic accentuation, this must be the meaning. The word order, however, is unnatural, and some render "to establish a royal statute" (so Theod.) , or, since the courtiers had no authority to establish statutes, some take the verb as virtually passive, "that a statute be established," i.e., that they ask the king to issue such an ordinance.

Enforce: From the verb "to strike." The word might be rendered "to put into effect." **Interdict:** From the verb "to bind" (cf. the Hebrew word used in Num. 30:3) . The king was to decree something that would be binding on all his subjects. Here as in vs. 9 the writer seems to be imitating the legalistic phraseology of royal rescripts.

The substance of the **decree** was that for one month the king alone should be treated as God. From early times in Mesopotamia kings had been called "divine" and had worship offered them, a custom which became notorious in the Hellenistic age. Even so, the king was only one divinity among many, so that acts of worship to him need not interfere with a subject's offerings and petitions to his local god or gods. The point of this decree was that for a whole month no other god was to be approached with any petition whatever. For that month the king alone was to be the divinity from whom men sought the blessing and bounty they needed. On the ground that the text reads **to any god or man**, some have thought that it was a prohibition of any request at all, but this

---

tion that we should judge men as we judge trees, on the basis of their fruits. The right life is more important than the right label. The public, however, is often willing to choose the label over the reality.

7. Usurping God's Place.—Here is the pagan attempt to make the king equal to God. This sin takes different forms, but it does not die. Whenever men get power, they are tempted to take the place of God. Only the religious man

tion of any God or man for thirty days, save of thee, O king, he shall be cast into the den of lions.

8 Now, O king, establish the decree, and sign the writing, that it be not changed, according to the law of the Medes and Persians, which altereth not.

lish an ordinance and enforce an interdict, that whoever makes petition to any god or man for thirty days, except to you, O king, shall be cast into the den of lions. 8 Now, O king, establish the interdict and sign the document, so that it cannot be changed, according to the law of the Medes and the Persians, which cannot be revoked."

would be absurd, and the whole point of the story is that the petition is something that concerns the religious life. The ordinance was not that they could not ask for ordinary help, but that no religious petition could be made to any god or deified man save to the king alone. The LXX and Josephus omit **or man**, both here and at vs. 12. Behrmann thinks that the addition **or man** is an example of hyperbole, comparable to that in Jonah 3:8, where the wearing of sackcloth is prescribed for "man and beast."

There is nothing inherently absurd in the idea of such a decree. An ancient Sumerian king might well have issued one, and Linder (*Commentarius,* p. 285, n. 2) quotes an account of how a Japanese emperor at the end of the sixteenth century issued a somewhat similar edict. The difficulty is that such an action is so out of keeping with what we know of the Persian kings. We are here, however, in the realm of story, not of history. It was also part of the story technique that the king should accede to the request of his courtiers and put it into effect without consulting the one minister who was so distinguished that he had thought of appointing him as supreme minister. Had Daniel been brought in and discovered the conspiracy, the story could not have moved on to its dramatic climax to teach the lesson for which it was being used. There was a tradition abroad that the Iranians of that day worshiped their kings, for it is mentioned in Quintus Curtius (*History of Alexander* VIII. 5. 11), and the audience would have seen nothing peculiar in the wording of the decree.

Petition: *Bâ'û* is "request" or "prayer," from the verb "to seek."

Save that **thirty days** would be a month, no particular significance should be attributed to this number, which is merely a detail of the framework.

Den of lions: Ancient monarchs were fond of menageries, and we have a number of inscriptional references to beasts procured for their collections. This was so well known that taking and caging a lion to bring it to Babylon is used as a prophetic image in Ezek. 19:1-9. The word for **den** here and at vss. 12, 16 corresponds to the Hebrew *gēbh,* "cistern," of Jer. 14:3, and the Arabic *jubb,* the Qur'ānic word for the "pit" into which Joseph was cast. From vs. 17 we see that its mouth could be covered by a stone, and from vs. 23 that Daniel had to be taken up out of it, so that what the writer had in mind is a cistern such as those still to be found all over Syria and Palestine—fairly capacious pits with a bottle top which can easily be covered by a large stone. Such pits are often used for the storage of other things than water, and on occasion could serve as a temporary prison. That lions would be kept in such a pit, however, would only occur to a writer unfamiliar with lions outside the pages of literature.

8-9. The king is asked to do two things—to authorize an ordinance and then officially to sign the written form in which the ordinance would be issued. So in vs. 9 **the document and interdict** mean the written document and the ordinance therein set forth. **Establish:** Lit., "cause to stand." **Sign:** The same verb in 5:24 meant "inscribed" and in 5:25 "written," but in this chapter it is used always of signing decrees. It does not necessarily mean what we mean by signing a letter, but rather that the king has the matter committed to writing and attaches his royal seal in proof of its authority. **Document:** Lit., **writing.** The same word was used for the writing on the wall in 5:7 ff.

According to the law of the Medes and the Persians: So in vss. 12, 15. This need mean no more than that it was generally known that the Medes and the Persians followed much the same code of laws. After the Median soldiery had handed over

9 Wherefore king Darius signed the writing and the decree.

10 ¶ Now when Daniel knew that the writing was signed, he went into his house; and, his windows being open in his chamber toward Jerusalem, he kneeled upon his knees three times a day, and prayed, and gave thanks before his God, as he did aforetime.

9 Therefore King Darius signed the document and interdict.

10 When Daniel knew that the document had been signed, he went to his house where he had windows in his upper chamber open toward Jerusalem; and he got down upon his knees three times a day and prayed and gave thanks before his God, as

---

Astyages to Cyrus in 550 B.C., Cyrus did become in fact ruler over both Medes and Persians, and the important place Median officers had in his army may have favored the idea that from Cyrus onward we have a Medo-Persian combination. The book of Esther is evidence that the Jews regarded them as very closely connected. C. C. Torrey ("Medes and Persians," *Journal of the American Oriental Society*, LXVI [1946], 1-15) suggests that the Medes are mentioned first because the writer regarded the Medes as the senior partner. Behrmann had noted the anachronism of this expression's being used here under "Darius the Mede," before Cyrus the Persian had appeared. The writer of course was conscious that Cyrus had appeared in 1:21, and the audience may remember this, but here the words are in the mouth of courtiers under a monarch who, in the historical scheme of the writer, reigned before Cyrus. If, however, all that is meant is that the Medes and the Persians were known to follow a common code of laws, this is not necessarily an anachronism.

That their law was unbreakable is a matter mentioned in Esth. 1:19; 8:8. Diodorus Siculus (XVII. 30) tells a tale of how Darius III repented of his sentence on Charidemos and acknowledged that he had erred in the matter, but could do nothing about it for the king's word had gone forth and could not be broken. Herodotus (*History* V. 25) tells of Sisamnes, one of the royal judges, who for a bribe caused a miscarriage of justice. Cambyses had him flayed alive and the seat of justice upholstered with his skin on which his son who was appointed to succeed him had to sit. The word used here for **law** is the Iranian word used in 2:9 and consistently in Esther for the Persian law.

b) THE PLOT AGAINST DANIEL (6:10-15=M.T. 6:11-16)

10. One's first impression is that as soon as Daniel heard of the edict he went deliberately into his house to disobey it, thus showing his contempt for such human ordinances. It is more likely, however, that the writer meant that though Daniel heard the decree, he nevertheless continued his usual custom of performing thrice daily his private devotions.

He went to his house where he had windows in his upper chamber open: Lit., "He went up to his house. Now he had in his roof chamber windows opening." A roof chamber is a small room, such as was built for Elisha by the Shunamite (II Kings 4:10), constructed on the flat roof of an Oriental house (cf. Acts 10:9, ἐπὶ τὸ δῶμα). It provided a cool and secluded place, and as such was commonly used for mourning, or for prayer and devotions (cf. Isa. 22:1; Ps. 102:7; I Kings 17:19; II Kings 1:2; Judith 8:5; Acts 1:13; 9:37, 39). Charles thinks rather that it was a little chamber over the gateway or on the wall, reached by an independent stairway. The window was latticed (Prov. 7:6; II Kings 1:2), as opposed to the closed window (Ezek. 41:26). In Daniel's roof chamber one

---

is able to keep clear the recognition that the powerful as well as the weak stand under the judgment of God.

10. *A Center for Life.*—This picture of a man who kept his **windows . . . open toward**

Jerusalem is full of significant symbolism. How important it is to have a center for life, especially when one is in a strange land. With his mind centered on the holy temple of his God, Daniel could keep the things near at hand in

11 Then these men assembled, and found Daniel praying and making supplication before his God.

12 Then they came near, and spake before the king concerning the king's decree; Hast thou not signed a decree, that every man that shall ask a *petition* of any God or man within thirty days, save of thee, O king, shall be cast into the den of lions? The king answered and said, The thing *is* true, ac-

he had done previously. 11 Then these men came by agreement[m] and found Daniel making petition and supplication before his God. 12 Then they came near and said before the king, concerning the interdict, "O king! Did you not sign an interdict, that any man who makes petition to any god or man within thirty days except to you, O king, shall be cast into the den of lions?" The king answered, "The thing

[m] Or *thronging*

window stood open **toward Jerusalem,** and as he stood before it he would be facing in the right direction for prayer. In Tob. 3:11 Sarah prays thus at her window.

In Sifre 71*b* there is an injunction that Jews living abroad must turn toward the land of Israel in prayer, those in the land of Israel toward Jerusalem, and those in Jerusalem toward the temple. The Mishnah is aware of the custom, for Berakhoth 4:5-6 mentions the case of those traveling who find it impossible to keep their bodies turned toward the holy spot, and directs that in such situations they should so turn in their hearts. There was scriptural basis for the custom (cf. I Kings 8:35, 38, 44, 48; Pss. 5:7; 138:2; I Esdras 4:58). Such orientation in prayer was an ancient custom in the Near East. Ezek. 8:16 mentions an early practice of turning toward the east in prayer, and Muslims still turn to face the shrine at Mecca.

Berakhoth 4:1 mentions the **three** prayer times as early morning, afternoon, and sunset. In Ps. 55:17 we have "evening," "morning," "noonday," but that does not necessarily mean fixed hours for prayer, for Ps. 119:164 says seven times a day, and I Chr. 23:30 mentions only two prayer times. Some have inferred from the statement in Acts 2:15; 3:1; 10:3, 9, 30 that the third, sixth, and ninth hours were the three fixed hours for prayer, but this cannot be pressed; and of course none of this is evidence for what the custom would have been in Daniel's day. In 9:21 we find him praying at the time of the evening oblation, and as this fits later practice it is often assumed that he must have prayed regularly at the three times later customary among the Jews.

Upon his knees: Kneeling as a posture for prayer is mentioned in I Kings 8:54; II Chr. 6:13; Ezra 9:5; and such N.T. passages as Luke 22:41; Acts 9:40; 20:36; 21:5 probably represent contemporary Jewish usage. In later times it was more usual to stand while praying. This is referred to in Matt. 6:5; Mark 11:25, though our Lord preserved the custom of kneeling in private prayer (Luke 22:41). **Before his God,** instead of "to his God," is regarded as a kind of courtly circumlocution.

11. Came by agreement: As in vs. 6. This verb has also the meaning "to keep watch," and Charles therefore translates it here, "Then these men kept watch and found Daniel." It occurs again in vs. 15, where it must mean "came by collusion." **Praying:** In vs. 10 the verb used for praying is צלי, as in Ezra 6:10, but here it is בעא, "to request," "to make petition," the very thing men were forbidden to do.

12. The conspirators are careful to refresh the king's mind with regard to the details of the interdict before springing their accusation against his favorite. This is in accordance

their proper perspective. Until we have our true home clearly visualized, we can too easily wander into the wasteland. The injunction that Jews in foreign lands should turn toward their homeland daily as they prayed has many possibilities for our meditation. Where is our homeland? How long has it been since we turned in

that direction? What is more important than facing in that direction constantly?

12. *Admitting Our Mistakes.*—The king was not the first or the last man to be caught in his own decree. Men ought to be wary in proclaiming unchangeable opinions, especially when they concern other people. There is a

cording to the law of the Medes and Persians, which altereth not.

13 Then answered they and said before the king, That Daniel, which is of the children of the captivity of Judah, regardeth not thee, O king, nor the decree that thou hast signed, but maketh his petition three times a day.

14 Then the king, when he heard these words, was sore displeased with himself, and set his heart on Daniel to deliver him: and he labored till the going down of the sun to deliver him.

15 Then these men assembled unto the king, and said unto the king, Know, O king, that the law of the Medes and Persians is, That no decree nor statute which the king establisheth may be changed.

16 Then the king commanded, and they brought Daniel, and cast him into the den of lions. Now the king spake and said unto Daniel, Thy God whom thou servest continually, he will deliver thee.

17 And a stone was brought, and laid upon the mouth of the den; and the king sealed it with his own signet, and with the

stands fast, according to the law of the Medes and Persians, which cannot be revoked." 13 Then they answered before the king, "That Daniel, who is one of the exiles from Judah, pays no heed to you, O king, or the interdict you have signed, but makes his petition three times a day."

14 Then the king, when he heard these words, was much distressed, and set his mind to deliver Daniel; and he labored till the sun went down to rescue him. 15 Then these men came by agreement[m] to the king, and said to the king, "Know, O king, that it is a law of the Medes and Persians that no interdict or ordinance which the king establishes can be changed."

16 Then the king commanded, and Daniel was brought and cast into the den of lions. The king said to Daniel, "May your God, whom you serve continually, deliver you!" 17 And a stone was brought and laid upon the mouth of the den, and the king

[m] Or thronging

---

with the pattern of court stories. They catch the king by his own decree, as Herodias' daughter caught Herod.

13. One of the exiles from Judah takes up the phrase used in 2:25 and again in 5:13. The latter is what is probably in the writer's mind here. **Pays no heed to you:** As in 3:12, a meaning peculiar to these two passages. The versions are at a loss to understand it. **Makes his petition:** The accusation is not that he says his prayers, but that he makes petition to his God.

14. The king saw through the conspiracy and would rescue Daniel, but though he worked on the problem until sundown he found no way out, and when the conspirators returned in the evening, he was compelled to sacrifice Daniel, though expressing a pious hope for his deliverance.

Much distressed: Lit., "very bad was it to him" (cf. Jonah 4:1; Neh. 2:10; 13:8). The opposite appears in vs. 23. **Set his mind:** The phrase occurs in Hebrew in I Sam. 9:20; cf. "set his heart." **He labored:** Lit., "he was bestirring himself," from a root meaning "to set in motion." Some suggest that the idea is that of an animal struggling to free itself from a net in which it is caught.

15. It might seem to flavor somewhat of insolence for the conspirators to remind the king of the inviolability of the law, but this is to heighten the dramatic effect of the story. Some have remarked on the abruptness with which they speak to the monarch, using no polite formulas with which to introduce their speech. It may be doubted if the writer meant to convey this impression. He is merely emphasizing the helplessness of the king, who would have saved Daniel if he could, but was rendered impotent by the very nature of his own laws.

c) Daniel's Trial and Delivery (6:16-23=M.T. 6:17-24)

17. A single large **stone** was put over the opening. This would effectively prevent anything from forcing its way out, and yet would let in air and a certain amount of

signet of his lords; that the purpose might not be changed concerning Daniel.

18 ¶ Then the king went to his palace, and passed the night fasting: neither were instruments of music brought before him: and his sleep went from him.

19 Then the king arose very early in the morning, and went in haste unto the den of lions.

sealed it with his own signet and with the signet of his lords, that nothing might be changed concerning Daniel. 18 Then the king went to his palace, and spent the night fasting; no diversions were brought to him, and sleep fled from him.

19 Then, at break of day, the king arose and went in haste to the den of lions.

---

light. A cord or cloth band across this stone could be fastened on either side with sticky clay and would take the impression of the seals of the king and of his lords. Herodotus (op. cit., I. 195) mentions the Babylonian custom of attaching seals, a custom which continued among the Persians. Esth. 3:12 and 8:8, 10 refer to sealing at the Persian court, and Herodotus (ibid., III. 128) mentions the seal of Darius affixed to documents. In I Kings 21:8 Jezebel made free with the king's seal. In Esther the sealing is done by the seal ring of the monarch.

His lords: The same word as in 4:36; 5:1 ff., so also "his courtiers." That nothing might be changed: The purpose of the KJV comes from the fact that the original sense of צבו had to do with "will" or purpose, but here it is used in the later meaning of "matter." The reason for casting a man to the lions was that he should be devoured. Should his friends come and rescue him, or throw some more attractive food to the lions, that would change the situation; the stone was therefore set that nothing might be changed.

18. The distress of the monarch is such that when he has seen Daniel cast to the lions he retires to his palace with no interest in food or in his usual evening diversions and cannot even sleep. Fasting: The word is ṭewâth, "foodless," not the usual çôm, which is used in 9:3 and is the regular word for fasting as a religious act. So we are to think not of the king fasting in penitence for having allowed the conspirators to destroy Daniel, but that in his distress of mind he could not eat.

Diversions: The word דחון is not used elsewhere in the O.T. and its meaning is unknown. Theod. and the Peshitta take it to mean "food." The LXX evidently thought it was something indecorous and omitted it. Saadia thought it meant "dancing girls." The medieval Jewish commentators generally render it by instruments of music or "musicians." Many modern editors emend the word to לחנן, "concubines," since these are usually present at an Oriental court and it would be a normal thing for a monarch to spend his evening among them. That these diversions had to be brought in rather suggests that the reference is to persons who were to provide amusement. Sleep fled from him: The same idiom is used in 2:1 for Nebuchadrezzar's sleep leaving him. So also in Esth. 6:1 the king could not sleep. The monarch's sleeplessness is a stock element in these court stories.

19. The dramatic effect is heightened by the picture of the king hastening eagerly to the den as soon as it was light next morning. The normal expectation would be that a man thrown to the lions would be torn to pieces within a few minutes of his being dropped into the pit, but the audience had heard the king expressing in vs. 16 a pious hope that Daniel's God might deliver him, and they know he will discover that God has done so. At break of day: Lit., "at dawn with the first light." The two words have practically the same meaning, and many modern editors delete one or the other as a gloss. The second word, however, may be taken as a closer defining of the first. In haste: The same word was used in 2:25 of Arioch hastening with Daniel to Nebuchadrezzar,

---

foolish consistency bolstered up by pride and stubbornness that does great harm to men. It is a fine thing to be able to say, "I made a mistake.

I was to blame and I repent." Let us be unchanging in our loyalty to God, but willing to admit that our human wisdom is limited. There

20 And when he came to the den, he cried with a lamentable voice unto Daniel: *and* the king spake and said to Daniel, O Daniel, servant of the living God, is thy God, whom thou servest continually, able to deliver thee from the lions?

21 Then said Daniel unto the king, O king, live for ever.

22 My God hath sent his angel, and hath shut the lions' mouths, that they have not hurt me: forasmuch as before him innocency was found in me; and also before thee, O king, have I done no hurt.

23 Then was the king exceeding glad for him, and commanded that they should take Daniel up out of the den. So Daniel was taken up out of the den, and no manner of hurt was found upon him, because he believed in his God.

20 When he came near to the den where Daniel was, he cried out in a tone of anguish and said to Daniel, "O Daniel, servant of the living God, has your God, whom you serve continually, been able to deliver you from the lions?" 21 Then Daniel said to the king, "O king, live for ever! 22 My God sent his angel and shut the lions' mouths, and they have not hurt me, because I was found blameless before him; and also before you, O king, I have done no wrong." 23 Then the king was exceedingly glad, and commanded that Daniel be taken up out of the den. So Daniel was taken up out of the den, and no kind of hurt was found upon him, because he had trusted in his God.

---

and in 3:24 of the haste of the king when he witnessed the miracle of the kiln. High officials in the Orient move with pompous slowness as a sign of dignity, so that **haste** on the part of someone so highly placed is an element of dramatic effect in the story.

20. Where Daniel was: The M.T. has "to Daniel." If this is the ל of possession, and means "Daniel's den," the translation must then be **where Daniel was.** More often, however, ל is taken with the following verb "to call"; the translation would thus be "to Daniel he called." **In a tone of anguish:** The monarch's anxiety shows itself in the tone of his voice. The Greek versions interpreted it as "loud" and the Vulg. as "tearful." The word '*açîbh* is from the root "to bind," and so gives the sense of tightness or pain.

In calling Daniel a **servant of the living God** the king is using a Jewish, not an Iranian, expression. The phrase occurs in Deut. 5:26; Josh. 3:10; Ps. 42:2 (cf. Matt. 26:63; Acts 14:15; I Thess. 1:9).

21. From the darkness of the pit Daniel "spoke with the king," addressing him in the customary courtly style, **O king, live for ever** (cf. vs. 6; 2:4). This is deliberate, for the writer is contrasting with the haste and anxiety of the king the calmness and self-possession of the man of God who even in the lions' den can remember to use the official phrases of polite address when speaking to the king.

22. My God takes up "thy God" of vss. 16, 20. **Sent his angel:** In 3:28 he had also sent his angel to aid the three confessors. The shutting of the mouths of lions was a well-known element in the martyr histories. It is referred to in Heb. 11:33, which may have had this incident in mind, as I Macc. 2:60 certainly had. The grounds for Daniel's deliverance are two: (*a*) he was "clean," i.e., legally innocent (see Ps. 51:7; Job 25:4) and so **blameless** before God; and (*b*) he had committed no "crime" against the king. His loyalty to God had not suffered from any remissness that would have made him blameworthy, nor his loyalty to the king from any evil deed or wrongdoing.

23. The king was exceedingly glad: The phrase expresses the opposite of "much distressed" in vs. 14. At the king's command the seals are broken, the stone removed, and Daniel taken up (probably by a rope). Then it was seen that "no harm was found

---

are many times when holding to a decision is not wisdom but stupidity. That is why the gospel makes such a point of humility.

20-22. *Has God Delivered You?*—This is the oft-repeated question of the worldling. Can

God save men and can we testify to that divine act of his? The men without faith finally yield to their sense of futility, but there is always the inner longing to believe. They seek the man who has put God to the test. They want desper-

24 ¶ And the king commanded, and they brought those men which had accused Daniel, and they cast *them* into the den of lions, them, their children, and their wives; and the lions had the mastery of them, and brake all their bones in pieces or ever they came at the bottom of the den.

25 ¶ Then king Darius wrote unto all people, nations, and languages, that dwell in all the earth; Peace be multiplied unto you.

24 And the king commanded, and those men who had accused Daniel were brought and cast into the den of lions — they, their children, and their wives; and before they reached the bottom of the den the lions overpowered them and broke all their bones in pieces.

25 Then King Darius wrote to all the peoples, nations, and languages that dwell in all the earth: "Peace be multiplied to

---

on him." The parallel is of course with the three confessors who came out unharmed from the kiln, but Bentzen suggests the writer may also have had in mind to give body to such passages as Ps. 57:4-6; 91:15.

d) THE PUNISHMENT OF DANIEL'S ENEMIES (6:24=M.T. 6:25)

24. The conspirators suffer the fate they had planned for Daniel, as Haman was hanged on the gallows he had prepared for Mordecai. Kuhl (*Die drei Männer*, p. 76) points out that this was a favorite notion of ancient justice. The picture here is of the conspirators being thrown into the pit and the hungry lions devouring them before they even hit the bottom. If this is to be taken literally, we must think of a gradual feeding of them to the lions over a period of many months, for the conspirators of vs. 4 made up a considerable body, and with their wives and families would have provided food for a goodly number of lions for a long time. It was possibly with this in mind that the LXX translator limited the conspirators to the two fellow presidents. The writer, however, in making his point here characteristically ignored the question of the actual numbers involved. The ravenousness of the lions is a literary device intended to show that their not devouring Daniel was not because they were not hungry but because of divine intervention.

Accused: The same phrase was used in 3:8. That their wives and children should suffer with them was in accordance with the ideas of the ancient world, which emphasized the solidarity of the family (cf. Josh. 7:24-25; II Sam. 14:5 ff.; 21:5-9). So in Esther we read of Haman's sons being hanged along with him. Herodotus (*op. cit.* III. 119) gives a similar example (and see Justin *History of the World* XXI. 4; Ammianus Marcellinus *Roman History* XXIII. 6. 81). **Overpowered them:** Lit., "had the rule over them" or **had the mastery of them.** The same verb is used in 3:27 to say that the fire had no mastery over the bodies of the confessors.

3. EPILOGUE (6:25-28)
a) DARIUS' RECOGNITION OF DANIEL'S GOD (6:25-27=M.T. 6:26-28)

25. Just as Nebuchadrezzar in ch. 3 was moved by the miracle to make a decree in which he acknowledged the greatness of the God of the Jews and called on all his subjects to respect him, so Darius moved by this miracle does the same. Indeed, the details of his decree follow closely the pattern of 3:29 ff., using words and phrases already met with in 2:44; 4:1-3; 5:19.

Decree: As in 3:10, 29; 4:6. **Peoples, nations, and languages:** As in 3:4, 29; 4:1; *et al.* **That dwell in all the earth** is an exaggeration, for the Persian Empire did not embrace the whole world even of that day, but it is in the style of the inscriptions of the Achaemenid kings. The same phrase was used in 4:1.

---

ately to hear someone testify that religion works. The only answer is the testimony of the man who has found God faithful to his promises. Our

time voices that cry of the king day and night. Can he save us? He is our last chance. Wanted: Men who can say to the frightened people of

26 I make a decree, That in every dominion of my kingdom men tremble and fear before the God of Daniel: for he *is* the living God, and steadfast for ever, and his kingdom *that* which shall not be destroyed, and his dominion *shall be even* unto the end.

27 He delivereth and rescueth, and he worketh signs and wonders in heaven and in earth, who hath delivered Daniel from the power of the lions.

28 So this Daniel prospered in the reign of Darius, and in the reign of Cyrus the Persian.

you. 26 I make a decree, that in all my royal dominion men tremble and fear before God of Daniel,
for he is the living God,
    enduring for ever;
his kingdom shall never be destroyed,
    and his dominion shall be to the end.
27 He delivers and rescues,
    he works signs and wonders
    in heaven and on earth,
he who has saved Daniel
    from the power of the lions."

28 So this Daniel prospered during the reign of Darius and the reign of Cyrus the Persian.

---

26. In all my royal dominion: Lit., **in every dominion of my kingdom.** *Sholṭân* is used again in 7:27 for **dominion,** but here it must mean the various sections of the empire, and perhaps is intended to be a translation of σατραπεία. Some, with an eye on 4:3 and the second occurrence of the word in this verse where it has the abstract meaning of "rule," would translate "in all the dominion of my kingdom." **Tremble and fear:** The same words are used in 5:19 of the people in trembling and fear before Nebuchadrezzar.

The last half of this verse and all of vs. 27 are in poetry—a little hymn sung by Darius.
The living God: As in vs. 20. **Enduring for ever:** See 4:34, "him who lives for ever." The word קים occurs in 4:26 where Nebuchadrezzar is told that his realm is "assured" to him.

His kingdom may contain a hint of the coming kingdom of God, which 2:44 had said could never be destroyed but would endure forever. However, it may merely mean "sovereignty," so that the two half verses say the same thing (see also 4:3, 34; 7:14, 27). **Unto the end:** As in 7:26.

27. In vs. 14 the king had set his heart to deliver Daniel but had not succeeded. Here he acknowledges that it is God who saves (cf. vs. 16; 3:28-29 with reference to the confessors' deliverance from the fire).

Signs and wonders: As in 4:2. **Power:** Lit., "hand." The "hand" of the lion is mentioned in I Sam. 17:37, and the word is used in this sense of power in Ps. 22:20, "power of the dog"; Ps. 49:15, "power of Sheol"; Prov. 18:21, "power of the tongue."

b) DANIEL'S FURTHER PROSPERITY (6:28=M.T. 6:29)

28. The prosperous official life of Daniel continued on through the reign of Darius and into that of Cyrus. The LXX has an addition: "And king Darius was gathered to his fathers and Cyrus the Persian received his kingdom." This final verse links the chapter with 1:21 and 10:1.

---

today, **My God sent his angel and shut the lions' mouths.**

26. *The King's Decree.*—What a sad thing it is for a man to see a miracle and then totally misunderstand it. What a tragic matter it is when our worldly blindness cannot be removed. This **decree** was as foolish as the one which sent Daniel to the lions' den. If you cannot fight against God with force, neither can you fight for him with force. It is the method which **is wrong.** The king and his modern descendants

seem to assume that it is only a matter of directing power in the right direction. Not so! It is a matter of choosing a different way and losing our confidence in what power can do. "Not by might, nor by power, but by my Spirit, saith the LORD of hosts" (Zech. 4:6).

27. *He Saves and Rescues.*—There is a long period of time between Daniel and Jesus, who came "to seek and to save that which was lost" (Luke 19:10). But the same God revealed himself through both men. One of the interesting

7 In the first year of Belshazzar king of Babylon, Daniel had a dream and visions

7 In the first year of Belshaz'zar king of Babylon, Daniel had a dream and vi-

II. A DREAM AND THREE VISIONS (7:1–12:13)

These are dated—the dream in the first year of Belshazzar, and the three visions in the third year of Belshazzar, the first year of Darius, and the third year of Cyrus.

The background is still the court at Babylon where Daniel is an official, though now in his latter years. That no vision is dated during the reign of Nebuchadrezzar is perhaps because Nebuchadrezzar's own dream contains the same general prediction as that in these visions. Daniel is the hero of this section as he was of the first, but with a difference. In the stories he had been the interpreter of visions and signs; here it is he himself who is the recipient of the dreams and visions. Apart from certain connecting verses which speak of him in the third person, he is the narrator in these chapters.

There is also a difference in form, though the general message is the same. In the stories pious Jews of the Maccabean age were being encouraged to remain loyal to their religion by narratives picturing to them fellow Jews in difficult situations under heathen rulers in another age. In the visions the problem is their present distress under Antiochus Epiphanes, and the message for their encouragement looks not back but forward to the end of the present age and the coming of the never-ending kingdom of God. This had been part of the message of the stories (cf. 2:44), but now the Jews are to take courage from the revelation that the age in which they are living is the last age, the age of the great tribulation which immediately precedes and ushers in the kingdom of God. There the saints will no longer suffer but will reign, will no longer be in subjection but will have their enemies serving them. The stories had told of God's intervention on behalf of his servants; now the final intervention is at hand. The stories had shown how futile was the power of even the mightiest kingdoms when opposed to God; now men must see that the days of the heathen powers are over, the course of their history has run, and in days so few that they can be numbered God's own kingdom will be established. The visions all have the same horizon. They all lead history up to the same point, to the great tribulation which precedes the end. As the writer is keeping the same court background he had used for the stories, the visions take the form of predictions in which the course of history toward this end is unfolded.

The visions fill out the historical sketch that had been given in ch. 2. For the stories the writer took over tales which were doubtless familiar to his readers and adapted them to convey his message, suggesting the conditions of his own age as he developed the story, but always careful to preserve the background of that earlier day in which his story was set. So in the visions he uses traditional material with which his readers were well acquainted, but molds it to his purpose of showing how history is moving on to its destined fulfillment in the coming of that kingdom which is beyond history. The visions are literary visions, not reports of actual visions; for no actual vision

things for the Christian is to note how God used whatever instruments he could find to reveal his desire to save men. What Jesus reveals supremely, Daniel shows us darkly through a glass. God is the God of love and the God of power. He is able to save men, and he is willing to pursue them with tenderness and persistence.

7:1-28. The Revealing Vision.—In the first part of the book of Daniel the message is presented by stories which were familiar to the people of the time. In the second part visions are the medium used. Except for the fact that the visions look more toward the future than to the past, the message is essentially the same.

It is still a trumpet call to loyalty. It is an affirmation that history is in God's hands. Underneath all the imagery there is the unmistakable sign of a great religious experience. This is the important thing. Whatever form our message may take, the seat of its authority must always be in a personal experience of God. The author had more than a hearsay knowledge of God. This is much more important to see than vainly to regard the visions as mechanical foretellings of the future.

1. He Wrote Down the Dream.—It is always a good thing to make a record of our dreams. They fade too easily and they are too soon for-

of his head upon his bed: then he wrote the dream, *and* told the sum of the matters. | sions of his head as he lay in his bed. Then he wrote down the dream, and told the sum

---

could contain so much accurate historical material so carefully arranged, or such a mass of traditional motif worked up in the way it is here. Details of chs. 8; 10, however, seem to show that the writer did know the experience of ecstasy, and one cannot doubt that his message came to him out of some profound experience of his own. It was because the community heard in his book the note of authentic religious experience that it gained its place in the canon. In our day we can still hear that voice speaking with the authentic accent of religious authority, and that is its author's claim to a place in the prophetic succession. Whatever his own experience may have been, he is here using the vision-dream medium in a literary way to embody the message he has for his contemporaries and the insight his experience has given him into the inner meaning of history.

Daniel is not called a prophet in these chapters, but their literary form at times closely resembles that of the prophetic writings, especially those of Ezekiel and Jeremiah. Like the prophets he dates his visions, though this matter of dating may carry over from the stories; for unlike the visions of the prophets, whose dates were concerned with contemporary events, these visions have nothing to do with Babylon and the dates serve merely to maintain the convention that Daniel was in the court at Babylon. It is noticeable that throughout the messages are regarded as something that is to be written, not spoken. Visions such as these belong to a literary type well known in the writer's time, a type used in the book of Zechariah in the O.T., in Revelation in the N.T., and in such books as Enoch and II Esdras (see Vol. I, pp. 427-30, 398-401).

It was a convention for symbolic figures to appear in such visions. Into the composition of the figures went various elements from the mythology which was current in popular thought, so that in interpretation details of such figures are not to be pressed. Certain features in these symbolic figures may be meant to suggest something to the readers, but others may have no significance beyond the fact that they are conventional features in the popular representation of that figure. Favorite figures were composite beasts, which, however weird they may seem, were familiar enough from their constant use in the decorative art of the ancient East.

That the visions belong to a section by themselves is clear from 7:1, which breaks the chronological order followed in the stories and takes us back to the time when Belshazzar was just beginning to reign. The visions are closely connected, and their composition must fall between the beginning of the persecution in 167 B.C. and the cleansing and rededication of the temple in 164. Since this rededication is not mentioned we must assume that it had not yet taken place.

A. The Vision of the Four Beasts (7:1-28)

This chapter differs from the others in this section by being in the form of a dream, a fact which links it with ch. 2, whose basic idea, the four-empire theory, appears again here with the same outcome, viz., a divine intervention to overthrow the fourth empire, that God's everlasting kingdom may be set up on earth. The four empires here symbolized as beasts are the same four there symbolized by metals. Here also is a descent in value from the eagle-winged lion through bear and leopard to a nameless monster, just as there was one from gold to iron. Conflict was there because of the iron mixed with ceramics in the feet, and here among the horns of the fourth beast. There the overthrow was by a celestially cut stone, here by a man sent from heaven. In both, the kingdom which succeeds the others is God's everlasting kingdom. Yet though the empires are

---

gotten. If we could learn how to keep our dreams ever before us, how different our lives would be. The vast gulf between what we be- | come and what we once dreamed of being would not develop if we **wrote down the dream.** Great living is to a large extent harnessing the

the same, there is some difference in treatment. Here attention is focused on the little horn, the last king of the fourth empire, who makes war upon the saints, but here also it is said plainly that in the kingdom which will not pass away, it is the pious in Israel who will have prominence.

How far the writer was using material he found already in circulation has been much debated. The number four obviously belongs to popular thought. The figures of the beasts, though they could have been derived from O.T. imagery, remind us constantly of the mythological beasts of Mesopotamia, just as the winds blowing upon the great sea recall the cosmological myths, while the figure of the Ancient of Days is curiously reminiscent of the *mlk 'ab šnm* in the Ugaritic enthronement myth. It is not necessary, however, to think of any particular source from which the writer was drawing, for elements of Mesopotamian, Canaanitish, and Iranian mythology were part of the thought world of his day, just as elements of Teutonic, Celtic, and classical mythology are part of ours today without our being at all conscious of the fact.

Modern scholars have been inclined to see two apocalypses run together in this dream. Thus Ginsberg (*Studies,* pp. 16-18) sees vss. 1-7, 9-10, 11*b,* 12-19, 20*a,* 23-24*a,* 26-28 forming one document composed before the desecration of the temple, or perhaps at the beginning of the religious persecution in 167 B.C., while he considers vss. 8, 11*a,* 20*b*-22, 24*b,* 25 as forming another document which has close relationship to chs. 8–12. This removes the little horn from the earlier apocalypse.

However this may be, the Maccabean author has woven the material into such a form that it presents an eschatological representation of Yahweh's enthronement; he connects it with the theory of world periods, and pictures the transference of world dominion to the Jewish people under the Son of man.

1. Prologue (7:1)

7:1. This is merely a connecting verse linking the section with the previous series of stories. These are not the words of Daniel but of someone who knew of Daniel's dream, who speaks of Daniel in the third person, dates the dream for the readers, and suggests that this account is based on a written record of the dream going back to Daniel himself (cf. 10:1). This is a common feature in apocalyptic (cf. Enoch 1:1, 3; 92:1; II Baruch 1:1; 78:1; Test. Reuben 1:1).

The first year of Belshazzar would be 554 B.C., i.e., the third year of the reign of his father Nabonidus, when the rule of Babylon was officially entrusted to him. We know from 8:1 that the writer regarded Belshazzar as having reigned at least three years before the downfall of Babylon, but it is doubtful whether he intended any special significance to be attached to the dating either here or in 8:1. In 5:30 Belshazzar was "king of the Chaldeans," while here he is **king of Babylon,** two titles which apparently mean the same thing, for Theod. has here Χαλδαίων.

"Saw a dream and visions of his head upon his bed." So in 4:5 Nebuchadrezzar "saw a dream." In view of 4:9 Montgomery translates "had a dream-vision (cf. 4:10, 13 and vs. 15 below, which shows that it is one of the idioms linking the two parts of the book). Some think **and** here is explicative, "he saw a dream, that is, visions of his head." The detail that **he wrote down the dream** is to indicate that he followed the practice of other seers and put his vision into writing (cf. Isa. 30:8; Hab. 2:2; Rev. 1:19; Enoch 33:3, 4; II Esdras 14:42).

"A summary of matters he told," i.e., he gave the essential import of the dream, but not every detail. For the idiom see Ps. 119:160. Theod. omits the phrase and in this he is followed by some modern editors. Others think it is a gloss meaning that the introductory part is ended and the account by Daniel himself now begins.

---

power of our dreams, rather than allowing them to be dissipated in vague longings and easy forgettings. When God gives a vision, write it down. When you have seen how things ought to be, make a record of it. There is no other assurance that we can be saved from making

2 Daniel spake and said, I saw in my vision by night, and, behold, the four winds of the heaven strove upon the great sea.

3 And four great beasts came up from the sea, diverse one from another.

of the matter. 2 Daniel said, "I saw in my vision by night, and behold, the four winds of heaven were stirring up the great sea.

3 And four great beasts came up out of the

2. Daniel's Vision (7:2-27)
a) The Vision (7:2-14)

2. Many editors omit the opening words of the M.T. **Daniel said,** since such an opening seems unnecessary, is ignored by Hippolytus and Jerome in their commentaries, and is omitted by the LXX, Theod., and Vulg.

"I was looking in my vision with the night." The phrase "I was looking" is used as a literary device to introduce the various scenes in the dream: vs. 2, the scene of the beasts from the sea; vs. 7, the scene of the fourth beast with the ten horns; vs. 9, the scene of the setting of the judgment seat; vs. 11, the scene of the execution of judgment on the beasts; vs. 13, the scene of the Coming One. In vs. 21, however, the phrase comes in the middle of the interpretation to introduce the scene of the little horn making war on the saints, a fact which suggests some dislocation of the text.

The figures which follow are not purely mythological, but one must always remember that those to whom this writing was addressed were familiar with the popular mythology and would be quick to recognize points of resemblance between these and mythological figures, resemblances which would have been more meaningful to them than they are to us. The Babylonian creation epic tells how from the fuming of primeval waters came a brood of fearsome monsters to engage in battle with the gods. Some form of that story would seem to have influenced the formation of the figures in this dream.

The **four winds of heaven,** i.e., one wind from each of the four quarters, resemble the four winds of the creation epic. These four are referred to in Zech. 2:6; 6:5 (cf. Ezek. 37:9), while in Enoch 18:2 the four winds bear the firmament and in II Esdras 13:5 the multitude is gathered from the four winds of heaven, i.e., from the four quarters, as here and in 8:8; 11:4.

In the O.T. **the great sea** is normally the Mediterranean (Num. 34:6; Josh. 1:4; 15:47), but here, rather than a geographical sea it is the circumambient ocean which in the old mythology goes all around and underneath the earth and is the antipodes of heaven. This is the Nammu of the Sumerians, the Tiamat of Babylonians, the waters and the deep of Gen. 1:2, the great deep of Gen. 7:11; Amos 7:4; Isa. 51:10, which the biblical writers regard as cosmically the opposite of the heaven above (Gen. 7:11; 8:2; 49:25; Exod. 20:4; Job 28:14), with whose monsters Yahweh had earlier to deal (Ps. 74:13 ff.). By an obvious analogy the **sea** came to symbolize the nations of the earth (Isa. 17:12-13; Jer. 6:23), and the readers would understand how the beasts from the sea stood for nations emerging one after another from the turmoil of the peoples (cf. Rev. 17:15). In vs. 17, when the beasts have become kingdoms, they are said to arise out of the earth. That the wind should move the waters to produce the beasts would also be familiar. In Gen. 1 the spirit moves on the face of the waters, and the Phoenicians, according to Philo of Byblos, taught that the world was born of the wind and the deep, a notion that has survived in Arabic creation tales. In II Esdras 13:2-3 similar winds stir up the sea so that a portentous figure arises from the water.

Were stirring up: Were agitating. The Hebrew word is used in Mic. 4:10 of the pains of a woman in travail (cf. Job 38:8).

3. In ancient thought the **sea** was a seat of evil and the home of fearsome monsters (Gen. 1:21; Amos 9:3; Ps. 104:25-26) and was thus the appropriate place from which

our lives merely good-intentioned. These ephemeral visions can be the most real things we know—or they can be the most useless.

3. Four Modern Beasts.—The picture of the beasts coming up out of the sea to destroy is one which we can appreciate. For up out of the

4 The first *was* like a lion, and had eagle's wings: I beheld till the wings thereof were plucked, and it was lifted up from the earth, and made stand upon the feet as a man, and a man's heart was given to it.

4 The first was like a lion and had eagles' wings. Then as I looked its wings were plucked off, and it was lifted up from the ground and made to stand upon two feet like a man; and the

---

the **beasts** should emerge (cf. Isa. 27:1; Enoch 60:7; II Baruch 29:4; II Esdras 6:49, 50; 11:1; 12:11). To picture heathen powers as ravening beasts was also conventional. Indeed, symbolizing nations by beasts continues with us today. In the O.T. we have such animal symbolism in Ezek. 17; 19; 29; 32; Ps. 68:30, and it is even more common in later writings (cf. Enoch 85–90; Pss. Sol. 2:29).

That the **beasts** are **four** is in accordance with the four-empire theory. Interwoven with this, however, may be the thought that each wind produces a beast. Ginsberg (*ibid.*, p. 70, n. 36) notes that the Babylonian Empire might have been regarded as originating in the south of Babylonia, the Median in the north, the Persian in the east, and the Greek in the west. Junker (*Untersuchungen*, p. 18) again regards the four as merely symbolic of completeness.

They were **different.** Their diversity parallels that of the metals in ch. 2, and they come in a descending order, not of strength but of value. Junker (*ibid.*, p. 22) suggests that the criterion for their evaluation was their opposition to the people of true religion: those kingdoms which persecuted the Jews were of little value, however powerful they might be, while those which were tolerant were of high worth.

The various theories as to the identification of the beasts may be seen in detail in Rowley, *Darius the Mede.* The best theory is that they represent, as in ch. 2, the Babylonian, Median, Persian, and Greek-Macedonian empires. Since the four, however, all appear out of the sea at the same time, and are all judged in the same moment, Hugo Gressmann (*Der Messias* [Göttingen: Vandenhoeck & Ruprecht, 1929], p. 366) has argued that they must be powers which were contemporary with one another, and so would interpret them as the four kingdoms of the Diadochi who succeeded Alexander. To accept this would be to discard the four-empire theory, which seems fundamental to the book.

4. The lion-eagle, or winged **lion,** representing the Babylonian Empire, is composed of the noblest of beasts and the noblest of birds, just as in 2:32 the empire was symbolized by gold, the noblest of metals. The great winged lions of Mesopotamian temples and palaces probably originally suggested this as an appropriate symbol for the Babylonian Empire. In Jer. 4:7; 49:19; 50:17 Nebuchadrezzar himself is compared to a lion, and his armies to eagles in Jer. 49:22; Ezek. 17:3; Hab. 1:8, which for Jewish contemporaries would make this symbol even more appropriate. When it is made to stand upright **like a man,** we are again reminded of the representations in Mesopotamian glyptic art of upstanding animals who seem to be pictured as acting like men.

Driver insists that *neshar* is the griffin-vulture, not the eagle, and this may be ornithologically correct, but the translation "eagle" gives far better the idea that was in the writer's mind.

It is difficult to say what we are to understand by the seer watching till **its wings were plucked off** and it was **made to stand upon two feet like a man.** This may contain some reference that was perfectly intelligible to an audience then but is lost to us. Some think it means the curbing of the proud might of the Neo-Babylonian Empire, which under Nebuchadrezzar looked as though it could soar at will over the civilized

---

sea of our secularism we saw emerge the beasts of fascism, communism, hatred, racial pride. There seem to be times like that in human experience. Something stirs the sea, and evils too horrible to contemplate come out and stalk

the earth. There is no human defense against them. There is hope only when we know that those beasts are always waiting for their chance to come forth, and we must depend on God to keep them in check.

5 And behold another beast, a second, like to a bear, and it raised up itself on one side, and *it had* three ribs in the mouth of it between the teeth of it: and they said thus unto it, Arise, devour much flesh.

6 After this I beheld, and lo another, like a leopard, which had upon the back of it four wings of a fowl; the beast had also four heads; and dominion was given to it.

mind of a man was given to it. 5 And behold, another beast, a second one, like a bear. It was raised up on one side; it had three ribs in its mouth between its teeth; and it was told, 'Arise, devour much flesh.'

6 After this I looked, and lo, another, like a leopard, with four wings of a bird on its back; and the beast had four heads; and do-

---

world but was shorn of this power by Cyrus, who plucked off one after another the "feathers" of the empire until he was ready to take Babylon itself. In this connection Montgomery refers to Isa. 14:13; Obad. 4. Being shorn of wings so that it could not fly, reduced to walking awkwardly on two legs instead of bounding along on four, having a man's timid heart instead of the fearless heart of a beast, would represent the reduction of the Babylonian Empire to the feeble state it was in when it fell.

Verbal similarities to the account of Nebuchadrezzar's experiences in ch. 2 make others think that the giving of **a man's heart** must be interpreted as indicating an improvement in condition. This is in accord with ancient symbolism, and it is possible that Nebuchadrezzar is regarded as personifying the whole Neo-Babylonian Empire; the reference here may therefore be to his malady during which the empire was shorn of its power, but when he was restored it was a much more humane and a relatively worthy empire. It is of course historically true that during the latter years of his reign Nebuchadrezzar occupied himself more with the arts of peace than with those of war.

5. And behold, another beast, a second one, like a bear: The bear (cf. Prov. 17:12; 28:15; Isa. 11:7; 59:11; Lam. 3:10; Hos. 13:8; Amos 5:19; I Sam. 17:34 ff.) ranks inferior to the **lion,** just as silver is inferior to gold, and is said to be the most formidable beast of prey, after the lion, to be met with in Palestine. The bear does not play much part in Oriental symbolism (though it occurs occasionally on seals), and we do not know whether in this writer's day there may have been something that suggested the appropriateness of the bear as a symbol for the Medes.

The animal here is pictured as **raised up on one side.** Doubtless what this meant was clear to the audience but we are left to conjecture. According to some, the bear was moving lopsided to symbolize an empire unstable and unbalanced as compared with the Babylonian. According to others it was set to one side and played no part in history, or it was rearing itself up to strike. Still others hold that the animal is rising from crouching posture. By reading the word שטר with the letter *shin* one can understand it to mean "dominion"; i.e., only one ruler, Darius, was raised up for this kingdom. Unfortunately the verb used here has no meaning that would fit this attractive suggestion. The **three ribs . . . between its teeth** may be a detail introduced to indicate the ferocity of the Medes, a matter mentioned in Isa. 13:17-18, *et al.* Unless they were the ribs of some very small animal, three would be rather much for a normal mouth, but three may be a round number symbolical of ravenousness. In Amos 3:12 we have the image of the shepherd recovering portions of a victim from the mouth of a lion. Some suggest that the ribs are heraldic and represent the three provinces or areas which the Medes conquered. Others hold that they symbolize three quarters of the habitable world.

That the bear is bidden **Arise, devour much flesh** is probably reminiscent of passages such as Isa. 13:17-18; Jer. 51:11, 28, which tell of the savage destructiveness of the Medes. That bears actually eat flesh is suggested by I Sam. 17:34 and is vouched for by Aristotle (*History of Animals* VIII. 5).

6. The third beast resembled a four-winged, four-headed **leopard** and symbolized the Persian Empire. This animal is mentioned in the O.T. in Song of S. 4:8; Isa. 11:6; Jer. 5:6; 13:23; Hos. 13:7; Hab. 1:8, and figures of it occur in the glyptic art of Mesopotamia and Persia. Here, however, it is a heraldic beast, like the winged lion.

7 After this I saw in the night visions, and behold a fourth beast, dreadful and terrible, and strong exceedingly; and it had great iron teeth: it devoured and brake in pieces, and stamped the residue with the feet of it: and it *was* diverse from all the beasts that *were* before it; and it had ten horns.

minion was given to it. **7** After this I saw in the night visions, and behold, a fourth beast, terrible and dreadful and exceedingly strong; and it had great iron teeth; it devoured and broke in pieces, and stamped the residue with its feet. It was different from all the beasts that were before it; and

---

The **wings** may be meant to suggest the swiftness with which the Persians extended their empire, but it is more likely that they are to be taken with the **four heads** and symbolize the same thing. Some think these represent the Achaemenid claim to rule over the four quarters of the habitable world. Others, with more justification, think of the names of the four Persian kings familiar to the Jews, viz., Cyrus, Xerxes, Artaxerxes, and Darius (cf. 11:2; see Rowley, *op. cit.,* pp. 141, 155 ff.; Ginsberg, *op. cit.,* pp. 19, 72, n. 52). That the four appear together here, whereas kings succeed one another, is no more against this explanation than that presently ten horns appear together, though the ten kings must have succeeded one another.

The **four** of course may be merely a symbolic number. It has been suggested that there is a number symbolism running through this chapter, e.g., the symbolic number of the first beast is two, so he has two wings and stands on two feet. The number of the second beast is three, so he is lopsided, going on three legs, and has three ribs in his mouth. The number of the third beast is four, so he has four wings and four heads. The number of the fourth beast is five, so he is described by five attributes and has ten (5X2) horns.

That **dominion was given to it** is but saying in other words what was said of the third kingdom in 2:39, that it should rule over all the earth.

7-8. The **fourth beast** is a monster of no zoological classification. The others could be said to be "like" or "in the form of" some known animal, but this monster cannot be classified. The **horns**, the **iron teeth**, and the trampling **feet** suggest the heraldic dragon. The writer may have had in mind the monstrous *ṣirušśu* of Babylonian mythology. The material from Ugarit, on the other hand, suggests that it may be based on the old Canaanitish conception of leviathan, a description of which has survived also in Apollodorus (*The Library* I. 6. 3). It symbolizes the Greek Empire of Alexander's successors. The **iron teeth** correspond to the iron feet of 2:40, for the teeth "devoured and crushed," as those feet "broke and shattered." Bevan remarks that Alexander's empire, with its policy of Hellenization, would have appeared to the Jews of those days as something very different from the civilizing agency it appears to us. It was in fact very different from the beasts which went before it, and to those who were suffering from its Hellenizing policy it must have seemed **terrible and dreadful and exceedingly strong** as it **stamped the residue with its feet.** The Babylonian and Persian empires had interfered little with the local customs and religions of the areas they conquered, but the Greeks attempted to transform them, and were often ruthless in the measures they adopted. That this beast represented the Greek Empire was recognized as early as the Sibylline Oracles (3:388-400).

Terrible and dreadful: By a slight change in reading some make it "powerful" rather than **terrible. Great iron teeth:** Hippolytus in his commentary adds here, "and its claws of bronze," as in vs. 19, and some modern editors think these words have dropped from the text and should be restored.

The beast's three activities here and in vss. 19, 23 are to devour, crush, trample, i.e., devour with its jaws and teeth of iron, crush with its forefeet—or perhaps, if a dragon, with its tail—and trample with its hind feet. The phrases are biblical. "To devour," i.e., to destroy by eating, is used in Ps. 79:7; Jer. 10:25; Zech. 12:6; "to crush," in the sense of reducing to very small **pieces**, is used in Exod. 32:20; Mic. 4:13; Isa.

8 I considered the horns, and, behold, there came up among them another little horn, before whom there were three of the first horns plucked up by the roots: and, behold, in this horn *were* eyes like the eyes of man, and a mouth speaking great things.

9 ¶ I beheld till the thrones were cast down, and the Ancient of days did sit, whose garment *was* white as snow, and the hair of his head like the pure wool: his

it had ten horns. 8 I considered the horns, and behold, there came up among them another horn, a little one, before which three of the first horns were plucked up by the roots; and behold, in this horn were eyes like the eyes of a man, and a mouth speaking great things. 9 As I looked,

thrones were placed
and one that was ancient of days took his seat;
his raiment was white as snow,
and the hair of his head like pure wool;

28:28; 41:15; "to trample," as a draft animal tramples, is used in Job 39:15; Isa. 25:10; Hos. 10:11; Hab. 3:12. These activities are meant to correspond with those in connection with the other image in 2:40.

The **ten horns** recalls the ten toes of the image in 2:41-42. The animal horn occurs as a figure in the O.T. in Deut. 33:17; Pss. 75:4 ff.; 132:17; Ezek. 29:21; Zech. 1:18. In Daniel horns always represent kings or dynasties of that empire symbolized by the beast whose horns they are. They here refer to the ten kings who came in succession to Alexander. A many-horned beast would not have seemed strange to the readers. The human-headed centaurs pictured at Persepolis have twelve horns apiece, and horns appear on coins as emblems of the Seleucid kings. There is an account of attempts to identify the ten in Rowley (*op. cit.*, pp. 98-108) and more recent suggestions in H. W. Obbink (*Daniel* [Groningen: J. B. Wolters, 1932], p. 105), Bentzen (*Daniel*, p. 65), and Linder (*Commentarius*, pp. 322-28). Some have included Alexander in the series and others have excluded him. Some have insisted that all must be Seleucids, while others have included those Ptolemies who were important for Palestinian affairs. The Sibylline Oracles (3:381-400) are clear evidence that within a decade or two after this book came into circulation, the horns were interpreted as referring to individuals in the Seleucid succession. Doubtless to the writer's contemporaries it was obvious who the ten were, but it is unlikely that we can ever be certain that any selection we make will be correct.

The horns apparently fix the dreamer's attention. As he looks at them he sees sprouting among them a little horn which, to make place for itself, uproots three of the other horns. This horn is peculiar in that it has human **eyes** and a human **mouth**.

The little horn here, as in 8:9, is Antiochus Epiphanes, on whom attention is now focused since he impersonates the whole ferocious activity of the beast. Some see in the word **little** a hint that he was the younger son who normally would have had no chance of succeeding to the throne. Doubtless we are to understand the proud **eyes** as in Isa. 2:11; Ps. 101:5, and the proud **mouth** as in Ps. 12:3; Obad. 12. The way in which Antiochus spoke presumptuously against God is referred to in 11:36 (cf. I Macc. 1:24), and recalls what is said of Sennacherib in Isa. 37:23.

Antiochus Epiphanes had no right to the throne, but gained it by usurpation. He certainly may be regarded as having displaced his brother Seleucus Philopator and his nephew Demetrius who was next in succession, and he got rid of his rival Heliodorus, but whether these three or others are meant by the horns he uprooted we cannot know for certain. The books mentioned above also deal with the question of the identification of these three.

The LXX adds here, "and he made war upon the saints," a phrase which some editors would restore on the ground of vss. 21, 25 (cf. Rev. 11:7; 12:17; 19:19).

9. From the sea with its spawn of monsters representing lower things the dreamer lifts his gaze to the celestial sphere. There, in contrast to the wind-tossed sea and its portentous beasts which cause turmoil on earth, he sees the orderliness of the setting of

throne *was like* the fiery flame, *and* his wheels *as* burning fire.	his throne was fiery flames, its wheels were burning fire.

the judgment scene and the calm dignity of celestial beings appearing in human form. The reason he shifted his gaze is told in vs. 11. It was because of the loud-mouthed utterances of the little horn. The point seems to be that as he kept on contemplating the little horn, he realized that this could only be the final depravity which immediately precedes the end; so he looked up and saw that preparations for the grand assize were already in hand.

The picture of such a grand assize figures so largely in later eschatology that it is noteworthy how many of the forensic elements mentioned here became standard patterns for the eschatology: the judgment is set; the Judge comes down to occupy the judgment seat; the members of the divine court take places around him; the record books are brought out and opened; judgment is given according to works; the judgment is executed.

Some have suggested that this picture has drawn largely on Mesopotamian material, while others have thought of an Iranian source, and more recently Ugaritic material has raised the question of a Canaanite origin. It is not impossible that elements from all three sources have gone into the formation of various details of the picture, but for the conception of a grand assize at which the nations are to be judged by God the writer seems to have drawn in the main from O.T. material. In Joel 3:2 ff. we read how Yahweh will judge the nations, a subject that is the burden also of Pss. 50; 72; and in I Kings 22:19 there is a glimpse of God seated on his throne, around which are the celestial hosts. That man's deeds are the substance of judgment is an oft-repeated theme, and that there were record books of those deeds is referred to in Isa. 65:6; Mal. 3:16 (cf. Ps. 56:8; Jer. 17:1).

That **thrones were placed** is doubtless because with the Judge sit the assessors. These thrones are mentioned in Ps. 122:5, and here in 4:17 we have the celestial court partaking in the judgment. In the Egyptian Book of the Dead the assessors are pictured sitting above when the soul is led before the seated Judge. At the Babylonian New Year festival, when in the temple of Esagila the fates are settled, the gods who have previously been standing before the king of gods have their seats arranged for them. In the Gospels our Lord speaks of the twelve disciples sitting on twelve thrones, sharing with him in the judgment (cf. I Cor. 6:2-3; Rev. 4:4; 20:4), and in Enoch 47:3, when the books are opened, God's counselors are with him at the judgment. Ginsberg (*op. cit.,* p. 71, n. 39) refers also to the great celestial tribunal of the rabbis, which included associate judges.

One that was ancient of days: In vs. 22 "the ancient one," i.e., one who has lived a great number of years. In Ugaritic texts El is called "king, father of years." It has been objected that no pious Jew would think of representing the Deity as an old man, so this must be the Persian Ormazd, who appears as the great judge in Persian religion. Others have thought it is some figure from an ancient Mesopotamian judgment scene, or perhaps one of the watchers of 4:17. That Yahweh himself might be seen sitting in the form of a man on his throne was an idea familiar to a Jewish audience (Ezek. 1:26; 43:6-7; Isa. 6:1), and that he was **one . . . ancient of days** could not have seemed strange to people acquainted with Job 36:26; Ps. 102:24 ff.; Isa. 41:4; or Ps. 90. Junker (*Untersuchungen,* p. 52) remarks that the phrase indicates that he has been living a long time but does not mean that he was thought of as decrepit. The whiteness of his **hair** does not mean the gray of old age but, like the whiteness of his garment, refers to the purity and resplendent brightness of things belonging to the realm of light. Behrmann suggests that he is the "ancient one" as compared with the "new gods" (Judg. 5:8; Deut. 32:17).

The beasts emerge from within our own hearts. Many a man has been forced to confess a tendency to evil in his life that has destroyed his self-confidence. We know that within us	there are jealousy, selfish ambition, lust, and hatred, which emerge whenever we turn from God. No man is any good until he has been able to see the terrible possibilities of the beasts

10 A fiery stream issued and came forth from before him: thousand thousands ministered unto him, and ten thousand times ten thousand stood before him: the judgment was set, and the books were opened.

10 A stream of fire issued
    and came forth from before him;
a thousand thousands served him,
    and ten thousand times ten thousand
      stood before him;
the court sat in judgment,
    and the books were opened.

Took his seat refers to his taking the judge's place on the judgment seat. That God himself would be the judge and not some delegated being appears from Pss. 50:1-6 (which even mentions the fire going before him); 96:13; 98:9; Enoch 47:3; 90:20.

That **his raiment was white as snow**, i.e., of dazzling brightness, is what is commonly said of the raiment of celestial beings (cf. Matt. 28:3). The **snow** symbolism is used in Isa. 1:18; Ps. 51:7. His hair was "like unspotted wool." The **wool** image is used in Isa. 1:18.

The **throne** which was the judgment seat was also a chariot which moved on wheels. Such a chariot appears in Ezek. 1:15; 10:2; Enoch 14:18. That it was a fiery throne is in accordance with biblical symbolism, which often mentions the surrounding fire when God appears (Pss. 50:3; 97:3; Deut. 4:24; cf. Gen. 15:17; Exod. 3:2; Num. 16:35; Enoch 14:22). **Fiery flames**: Lit., "flame of fire," as in 3:22. In pagan religion such sun-gods as Apollo, Helios, Mithra, *et al.*, all had their blazing chariots.

10. The **stream of fire** apparently derives from the idea that fire always accompanies a theophany (Ps. 50:3; Deut. 9:3). In the development of eschatological doctrine this became associated with certain Iranian ideas of a fiery river, so that such a river is pictured flowing before the throne. Thus we should perhaps translate here "from before it" rather than **from before him**. Streams of fire appear also in the vision in Enoch 14:19. In one sense the river marks the boundary of the throne area, so that none can draw nearer without passing through it. The righteous as they pass through are purified of their remaining dross, but the wicked are consumed in it. This may be the meaning of the beast's body being given over to be burned in vs. 11.

The **thousand thousands** who **served him** are the celestial attendants who carry out the various tasks involved in the judgment. It is generally thought that the even greater number who **stood before him** are also the celestial hosts. This may be, but it is possible that they are those who are to be judged, for one of the awesome scenes of the Last Day is the gathering of all creatures to stand in silence before the throne awaiting the commencement of the assizes (for the phrase see Deut. 33:2; Enoch 1:9; Jude 14-15; Ps. 68:17). The myriad myriads merely means some number beyond count. Celestial attendants around the heavenly throne are mentioned in I Kings 22:19; Rev. 4:4; 5:11.

The **court sat in judgment**: Lit., "the judgment sat," but as *dinā'* here seems to mean "those who judge," just as *ṣôdh*, "deliberation," is used for "those who deliberate" in Jer. 23:18; Ps. 89:7 (M.T. 89:8), we get the rendering **court**, i.e., those to whom the judgment has been committed. In both ancient Egyptian and Iranian religion there was the idea of a heavenly court, and both at Babylon and at Ugarit we find the notion of celestial beings assembled for judgment. It was for some such group that the thrones in vs. 9 were placed.

The **books were opened**: In Babylonian texts we find references to the tablet of good deeds and the tablet of sins, and read of a king begging "let the tablet of my sins

within his own heart, and has resolved by the power of God to keep them chained.

10. God Is from Everlasting to Everlasting.— The dreamer looks up to the heavens and sees something which overshadows the evil beasts and the sea. He sees calmness and inevitable

judgment. The beasts rule for a while and seem invincible, but all the time they are watched by the One who is bringing them to destruction. They have to answer for all their sin when the book is opened. It is God's world. His kingdom is from everlasting to everlasting, and he

11 I beheld then, because of the voice of the great words which the horn spake: I beheld *even* till the beast was slain, and his body destroyed, and given to the burning flame.

12 As concerning the rest of the beasts, they had their dominion taken away: yet their lives were prolonged for a season and time.

11 I looked then because of the sound of the great words which the horn was speaking. And as I looked, the beast was slain, and its body destroyed and given over to be burned with fire. 12 As for the rest of the beasts, their dominion was taken away, but their lives were prolonged for a season and a

---

be broken." In Ps. 56:8; Isa. 65:6; Mal. 3:16 we read of such a record of man's doings available for scrutiny (cf. Jubilees 30:22; Enoch 81:4; 89:61-64; 98:7-8; 104:7; Ascension of Isaiah 9:22; Pirke Aboth 2:1). If even human potentates kept a record of good and evil things they had against their subjects (Esth. 6:1), why should not the sovereign of all? Then what more natural than that these records should be produced and examined at the grand assize? (See II Esdras 6:20; Rev. 20:12; II Baruch 24:1; Enoch 47:3; 90:20.) Some have suggested that here it is in particular the deeds of the four empires that are brought out for examination.

11. Great words: Blasphemies, words which exceed what any man, however exalted he may be, has any right to pronounce. The utterance of such blasphemies was evidence that the measure of iniquity must be full and the final judgment near. In this expectancy the dreamer continues looking and actually sees judgment executed on the four beasts. The blasphemies of the little horn involve the destruction of the whole empire, whose measure of guilt comes to its full in him (see 8:23). It may seem strange that all the Diadochi should be considered as falling when the Seleucids fell, but in Oriental eyes it was the Seleucids who were Alexander's successors and in a quite special way represented the continuance of those policies for which he stood (see C. C. Torrey, " 'Yāwān' and 'Hellas' as Designations of the Seleucid Empire," *Journal of the American Oriental Society,* XXV [1904], 302-11).

How **the beast was slain** we are not told, but having been slain its **body** was **given over to be burned with fire** (cf. Rev. 19:20-21, where the beast is cast into the lake of fire whereas the others are killed with the sword). Since the body of the beast represents the structure and organization of the empire, we are to understand that the whole Greek Empire was completely abolished. Perhaps some popular legend concerning the death of Antiochus Epiphanes is embodied here, but the detail should not be pressed. Obviously an empire cannot be given over to the fire, though the mangled body of a beast can. Just as fire can consume the mangled corpse and leave nothing but ashes, this great empire which had so grievously oppressed the Jews would be so destroyed that, as empire, there would be nothing of it left.

The burning of the corpses of executed criminals is mentioned in Josh. 7:25, and is known from several areas of the ancient Near East (cf. Isa. 30:33; Ezek. 39:6). Earlier commentators saw here a casting into hell, but though this fire of punishment is mentioned in Enoch (cf. 10:6; 18:11; 21:7-10; 90:24-27) and is suggested by Rev. 19:20; 20:10, 14, it is doubtful if that was in the writer's mind here.

12. The rest of the beasts were not destroyed but **had their dominion taken away.** The other three were Oriental empires, not intruders from the West; they had been

---

rules constantly. How important it was for Daniel to share this vision with his fearful contemporaries! They could see the beasts clearly enough, but not many of them could see the Ancient One, who "shall neither slumber nor sleep." Today we have no difficulty in seeing the beasts and in hearing their boasts. But we

need men who can look above to the calm of God's everlasting kingdom. The beasts will have their day, but it will be a relatively short one.

11. *Gone in a Moment.*—How sudden is the downfall of evil! Apparently so strong and invincible, it is hollow inside. Its destruction is nearly always more sudden than anyone had

13 I saw in the night visions, and, behold, *one* like the Son of man came with the clouds of heaven, and came to the Ancient | time. 13 I saw in the night visions, and behold, with the clouds of heaven there came one like a son of man,

---

relatively friendly to the Jews and so were not to be annihilated. Their existence was to be **prolonged for a season and a time,** that they might be incorporated in the coming kingdom of God in which their existence as national entities would finally cease. As the whole of the great image in ch. 2 continued standing until the stone smashed the feet, when the whole came tumbling down and was reduced to dust, so here the former empires are thought of as still existing in the Seleucid period. On the assumption that the first, second, and third empires had long since ceased to exist, some interpreters seek to take **the rest** as referring to the various horns of the fourth beast. This is not what the text says, and in any case is of little help, for those other horns would also for the most part have already passed away. There is really no difficulty about the first three still existing along with the fourth. Just as the former kingdoms of Saxony and Bavaria continued on in the German Empire, though they no longer had their former independence, so in a real sense Babylonia, Media, and Persia were still existing entities, fully conscious of their individuality, even though but part of the Greek Empire. There is thus no need to hunt for some small principalities such as Atropatian Media and Persis, which were more or less independent and so could be regarded as residual Median and Persian empires still existing under the Seleucids (see Ginsberg, *op. cit.,* pp. 7, 66, n. 10). The point the writer is making is that the Hellenizers in the Orient will be utterly destroyed and the Orient will be rid of them. The others, however, will not thereby get back their independence but will continue as national entities until the kingdom of God absorbs them.

But their lives were prolonged: Lit., "but a lengthening of being was granted to them." For this "lengthening" see 4:27, where Nebuchadrezzar's prosperity is "prolonged." **For a season and a time:** The same two words were used in 2:21. Some think this means an unspecified time, but it may mean until the moment decreed for the setting up of the final everlasting kingdom.

13. The vision in the dream changes—perhaps a sudden change, as is often the case in dreams—and looking up to heaven, Daniel sees the arrangements being made to have the judgment followed by the eternal kingdom. The old order has been judged; now the new era begins. The figure who symbolizes the new era is in human form, in contrast to the former kingdoms which were symbolized by beasts. He comes from heaven, the place of orderliness, purity, and peace, whereas the beasts came from the sea, the place of turbulence, chaos, and evil. The writer seems less interested in who this figure is than in what he accomplishes, apparently assuming that his readers will understand the identity of the figure.

Vss. 13-14 are metrical, and are apparently the writer's own composition, not pieces he is quoting from some source. These verses are introduced much as vss. 9-10. The scene is arranged with some care. The figure is seen coming **with the clouds.** Then the direction of his goal is noticed: he is moving toward **the Ancient of Days.** When he arrives he is formally presented, as befits court procedure. After his presentation, the Ancient of Days gives him the kingdom. That the figure came **with the clouds of heaven** should not be overstressed. In Ps. 104:3 Yahweh uses the clouds as his chariot (cf. Isa. 19:1; Ps. 18:10; Matt. 26:64; Rev. 1:7), and in II Esdras 13:3 the one like a man "flew with the clouds of heaven." The writer is thus using a well-known image for the method of transportation adopted by celestial beings. The clouds of heaven with their gentle, noiseless motion are being contrasted with the tumultuous waves of the wind-tossed sea of vs. 2. The LXX reads "on the clouds," which some modern editors prefer.

One like a son of man need denote no more than a figure in human form. In apocalyptic men are symbolized by beasts, but celestial beings by the human form (cf. Enoch 89–90). So here we are to think of a celestial being in contrast to the terrestrial

of days, and they brought him near before him.

14 And there was given him dominion, and glory, and a kingdom, that all people, nations, and languages, should serve him: his dominion *is* an everlasting dominion, which shall not pass away, and his kingdom *that* which shall not be destroyed.

and he came to the Ancient of Days
and was presented before him.
14 And to him was given dominion
and glory and kingdom,
that all peoples, nations, and languages
should serve him;
his dominion is an everlasting dominion,
which shall not pass away,
and his kingdom one
that shall not be destroyed.

nature of the beasts. Since each beast represented both a king and a kingdom, this figure also represents a king and a kingdom. In vs. 22 it is the saints who are to possess the kingdom, and this figure symbolizes the kingdom of the saints of God just as the lion symbolized the Babylonian and the bear the Median. As the beasts represented not peoples but kingdoms, not Babylonians but Babylonia, or its king Nebuchadrezzar, who as king could also represent the kingdom (cf. 2:39), so here the figure represents not the saints but the kingdom of the saints, and the king who inaugurates that kingdom, the messianic king. This is the connection between **son of man** and messianic king.

In the N.T. and in Enoch 45–57 the son of man is an individual whose office is to be interpreted messianically. A similar interpretation appears in the Talmud (Sanhedrin 98*a*) and was almost universal in the early church. It is often urged against the figure's being interpreted messianically here that the book of Daniel does not know a personal messianic king. Yet while it is true that this figure does embody the kingdom of the "saints of the Most High" who appear in vss. 18-27—i.e., Israel as the people of God—we may well raise the question whether he does not also represent the messianic king. In this book we find that king and kingdom interchange (cf. vs. 17; 2:37 ff.; 8:21), and there is no a priori reason why this figure may not represent both the saints as a body and the Saint of saints as an individual. It is clear that he is subordinate to the Ancient of Days, to whom he is presented and from whom he receives the kingdom. The figure here is parallel to the stone in 2:34, which is an individual stone when it smashes the image but later becomes the mountain which is the kingdom. Here as an individual he receives the kingdom which in vs. 27 becomes the kingdom of the saints. In Zoroastrian, Christian, Samaritan, and Muslim eschatology also it is an individual messianic figure who ushers in the kingdom of righteousness.

And was presented before him: Lit., **and they brought him near before him.** Who did the presenting is not told, but presumably it was some attendant celestial beings among those standing by the throne. This is how the LXX understood the passage. It may, however, have been certain angelic attendants of his own who came with him in the clouds. Such presentation was a detail of court etiquette which the audience would appreciate. Hempel has suggested that in this presentation the writer also had in mind the ancient Semitic ritual for the "Proclamation of a King." Since in place of the old heathen world empires a new kingdom of God is to be inaugurated, it would be seemly for the new king to be "proclaimed" in accordance with ancient ceremonial usages. On the other hand, Ernest Herzfeld (*Zoroaster and His World* [Princeton: Princeton University Press, 1947], II, 833) compares the Achaemenid ceremonial in which the heir to the throne is led into the presence for his investiture, a ceremonial Herzfeld thinks was also in the mind of the writer of Enoch 69:27, who has the son of man similarly introduced to his rule. Herzfeld therefore insists that the title **son of man** means heir.

14. The **dominion and glory and kingdom** make this verse sound like the protocol of a document from some royal chancellery. We have something similar, however, in 2:37; 5:18, and heaping up words is a characteristic of the writer. The words used for the description of the kingdom resemble those used of Nebuchadrezzar's great

15 ¶ I Daniel was grieved in my spirit in the midst of *my* body, and the visions of my head troubled me.

16 I came near unto one of them that stood by, and asked him the truth of all this. So he told me, and made me know the interpretation of the things.

15 "As for me, Daniel, my spirit within me was anxious and the visions of my head alarmed me. 16 I approached one of those who stood there and asked him the truth concerning all this. So he told me, and made known to me the interpretation of the

kingdom (cf. 4:22; 5:18), and the **peoples, nations, and languages** whom Nebuchadrezzar (3:4; 5:19) and Darius (6:25) considered to be under their command now come to place themselves under God's command. The verb *pelaḥ* is that used in 3:12-18; 6:16, 20 (M.T. 6:17, 21) for serving in the sense of worshiping or being obedient to a deity, whether the gods of the heathen or Israel's God. If the son of man is a messianic figure, this connects with the idea of a great conversion of the Gentiles in the last days. Such passages as Isa. 2:2 ff.; 49:6; Zech. 8:21 ff.; 14:9, 16-21 show a belief in the final turning of the Gentiles to Israel's religion, and in Enoch 10:21; 90:30; Pss. Sol. 17:31 ff.; II Esdras 13:32 ff. we have even more definitely the son of man during the last days causing the Gentiles to embrace the true religion (cf. Sibylline Oracles 3:616 ff., 710 ff.; 5:493 ff.; Matt. 24:14). Similarly, in Zoroastrian, Samaritan, Mandaean, and Muslim eschatology the conversion of all peoples is a result of the Messiah's appearing.

Already in 2:44 it had been stated that the coming kingdom would replace the earthly heathen kingdoms and would endure forever. So in 4:3; 6:26, and here, it **shall not pass away.** It is noticeable that this kingdom is given an everlastingness otherwise predicable only of God.

b) THE SEER'S DISTRESS (7:15-16)

15. That the dream is being used as a literary medium appears from the fact that now the seer asks one of the figures in the dream the meaning thereof. In the stories it was the heathen kings who were perplexed and Daniel who gave the interpretations. Here it is Daniel who has the dream, and another interprets. This does not mean that though Daniel was famous for his skill in these matters, there were certain classes of vision which were beyond even his skill and could be interpreted only by celestial beings. Neither are we to conclude that Daniel is now so old his skill is failing him. That another does the interpreting is a literary device. If it is Daniel who dreams, it must be a balancing figure who does the interpreting.

My spirit within me: Lit., "within the sheath," or, with a very slight change in the pointing, "within its sheath." *Nidhneh* is from the Iranian *nidāna*, "vessel" or "receptacle." The word occurs in I Chr. 21:27, and is used in the Targ. for a scabbard. The sheath of the soul is doubtless the **body.** Some would emend the text to read, "My spirit, because of this, was anxious." **Anxious:** A verb used only here in the O.T., in Syriac means "to be sorrowful, distressed," whence **grieved.** It denotes the opposite of being in a happy, contented, expansive spirit. Perplexity on account of the dream caused anxiety. **Alarmed:** The same word is used in 4:5 (M.T. 4:2) where the dream alarmed Nebuchadrezzar.

16. Possibly the writer is suggesting that the seer's distress of mind was such that he summoned up courage to address one of the celestial beings present at the judgment scene. The judgment of course is in the future, this being a vision of things that are going to happen, and the dreamer is in the present; yet the dreamer in the present asks a question of one who is participating in a scene that has not yet come to pass. This belongs to the literary form of apocalyptic. Since there were myriads present, the writer may have conceived of some of the attendants standing relatively near the place from which the seer was watching. He must mean one of the angels, for he uses a technical term, "a standing one," the term for court attendants. Since in ch. 8 the interpreter is Gabriel, some have thought that Gabriel is meant here. **The truth:** *Yaççibhā',* a word

17 These great beasts, which are four, *are* four kings, *which* shall arise out of the earth.

18 But the saints of the Most High shall take the kingdom, and possess the kingdom for ever, even for ever and ever.

things. 17 'These four great beasts are four kings who shall arise out of the earth. 18 But the saints of the Most High shall receive the kingdom, and possess the kingdom for ever, for ever and ever.'

---

that was translated "true" in 3:24, and "stands" in 6:12 (M.T. 6:13), is rendered "certain" in 2:45. Montgomery translates here, "to ask him the surety concerning this" (cf. vs. 19).

"So he answered me and the explanation of the matter he made me know." It is a point of some interest that the interpreter is an angel. In the visions of the earlier prophets it was God himself who spoke (Amos 7–8; Isa. 6; Jer. 1), but in later writings the office of interpreter is discharged by the angel (Zech. 1:7–6:8) as here in Daniel, Enoch, Jubilees, Testaments of the Twelve Patriarchs, II Baruch, and II Esdras. In Ezekiel, which belongs to the period of transition, we have both God and an angel discharging this office.

c) The Vision Interpreted (7:17-27)

17. The interpreter gives but a summary explanation. **These great beasts, which are four, are four kings.** Since "king" stands for "kingdom," the meaning is "four empires." This is clear from vs. 23; cf. 8:20-21, which recalls that in 2:38 Nebuchadrezzar was the head of gold. The king as head of the kingdom typified the kingdom. The beasts **arise out of the earth** here, whereas in vs. 3 they came out of the sea. The LXX reads, "who shall be destroyed from the earth." Charles accepts this as the original, pointing out that not only is the traditional idea that they arise from the sea, not the earth (Rev. 13:1; II Esdras 11:1; 12:10-12), but the interpreter is speaking of something yet to happen; whereas even if we put the seer in the court of Belshazzar, the Babylonian Empire is not something that is going to arise but something that had arisen long since and is now approaching its end. If we accept the M.T., the contradiction, which probably was the source of the change in the LXX, is not important, for all the writer is doing is making the point that the beasts originated in this lower world while the coming kingdom is from above.

18. The son of man who received the kingdom in vs. 14 has now become **the saints of the Most High,** just as the little stone became a mountain. Ginsberg notes that it is consistently "saints," not **the saints.** The word used for **saints** in this chapter and in 8:24 is not the usual O.T. word but "holy ones," the Hebrew form of which we find in Pss. 16:3; 34:9 (M.T. 34:10). To find the origin of this we need go no farther afield than the use of "holy" in connection with the people of Israel in Exod. 19:6; Deut. 7:6. If Israel is ideally to be "the holy people," then they are the "holy ones," i.e., the saints, who indeed are called "the holy people" in 12:7.

The Most High: Here and in vss. 22, 25, 27 we have the curious עליונין, which is the Canaanitish *'elyôn* with an Aramaic plural ending, the so-called plural of majesty. The Aramaic עליא occurs in 3:26, and in this chapter along with עליונין in vs. 25. The occurrence of both forms in vs. 25 makes it clear that the phrase **saints of the Most High** was a technical expression, possibly one in use among the godly in Maccabean days.

They are to **receive the kingdom,** the same verb being used in 5:31 (M.T. 6:1) of Darius receiving the kingdom; the thought is that they are to come to supreme authority

---

thought possible. One day it is shouting about lasting a thousand years; the next it is dead.

18. *The Reward of the Godly.*—In the face of the triumph of power Daniel says that the saints will outlast all their enemies. The world was made for them and they shall receive it in

due season. The saints therefore must not become impatient. The Ancient of Days is on their side, and the universe is their inheritance. This great message of faith is more significant than any tortuous interpretation of the book which is used vainly to explain contemporary events.

19 Then I would know the truth of the fourth beast, which was diverse from all the others, exceeding dreadful, whose teeth *were of* iron, and his nails *of* brass; *which* devoured, brake in pieces, and stamped the residue with his feet;

20 And of the ten horns that *were* in his head, and *of* the other which came up, and before whom three fell; even *of* that horn that had eyes, and a mouth that spake very great things, whose look *was* more stout than his fellows.

21 I beheld, and the same horn made war with the saints, and prevailed against them;

22 Until the Ancient of days came, and judgment was given to the saints of the Most High; and the time came that the saints possessed the kingdom.

19 "Then I desired to know the truth concerning the fourth beast, which was different from all the rest, exceedingly terrible, with its teeth of iron and claws of bronze; and which devoured and broke in pieces, and stamped the residue with its feet; 20 and concerning the ten horns that were on its head, and the other horn which came up and before which three of them fell, the horn which had eyes and a mouth that spoke great things, and which seemed greater than its fellows. 21 As I looked, this horn made war with the saints, and prevailed over them, 22 until the Ancient of Days came, and judgment was given for the saints of the Most High, and the time came when the saints received the kingdom.

---

among the nations. The kingdom of God is thus an earthly community, but one divinely organized and under the rule of the saints. They are also to **possess** it, the verb being that regularly used of holding property.

19. To concentrate attention on the particular interest of the writer, viz., the Macedonian-Greek Empire, the seer is made to question again with special reference **to the fourth beast.** He desires to "make sure" (again the word for "certain," "sure" of vs. 16). So he is given a further installment of the vision, followed by the explanation both of what he had seen at first of this fourth beast and what has appeared in this fresh installment. The description of the fourth beast is repeated from vss. 7-9, though the wording is slightly different, and there is the added detail, **claws of bronze.** The word for **claws** is the same as was used in 4:33 (M.T. 4:30) for Nebuchadrezzar's **nails** becoming like a bird's claws.

20. The seer's more particular inquiry is about the horns and the little horn which blasphemes and which seems to be greater and more important than the others. The description still follows vss. 7-8. The little horn, however, is no longer called "little," for Daniel sees that its appearance **seemed greater than its fellows** (cf. 8:9). *Ḥezwā',* from the verb "to see," was used in this meaning of "vision" in 2:19, and here would therefore mean that the "look" of the horn was that it seemed to be **greater.**

21. In the supplementary vision, or enlarged detail of one fragment of the vision, this horn (i.e., Antiochus Epiphanes) makes war on the saints and is successful in his campaign (cf. 8:9-12, 24-25; Rev. 11:7; 13:7). Historically the reference is to the persecution which Antiochus launched against the righteous observers of the law (I Macc. 1:24-52; 2:7-13; II Macc. 5:21-27). Eschatologically, however, the reference is to the great conflict which breaks out in the last days, when the forces of evil gather to themselves their strength for one last effort to stamp out the righteous and are so successful that only a remnant remains when God finally intervenes and brings evil to an end.

It is not necessary to conclude from the expression **made war** that the Maccabean wars were already in progress and were in the mind of the writer, for the persecutions of Antiochus would justify the use of the word here.

22. God himself has to intervene in the conflict and save his people in order to bring in the kingdom. The **Ancient of Days came:** He intervened personally in the conflict, and **judgment was given for the saints.** Many editors think that something has dropped from the text here, and would emend to read, "the court sat in judgment and

23 Thus he said, The fourth beast shall be the fourth kingdom upon earth, which shall be diverse from all kingdoms, and shall devour the whole earth, and shall tread it down, and break it in pieces.

24 And the ten horns out of this kingdom *are* ten kings *that* shall arise: and another shall rise after them; and he shall be diverse from the first, and he shall subdue three kings.

23 "Thus he said: 'As for the fourth beast,
there shall be a fourth kingdom on earth,
    which shall be different from all the kingdoms,
and it shall devour the whole earth,
    and trample it down, and break it to pieces.
24 As for the ten horns,
    out of this kingdom
        ten kings shall arise,
        and another shall arise after them;
he shall be different from the former ones,
    and shall put down three kings.

---

dominion was given to the saints of the Most High." The word *dīnā'*, however, can mean "sentence," "verdict," and, although in vss. 10, 26 it means the tribunal which sits, it could mean here that as a result of God's intervention the verdict was for the saints. It is possible of course that this coming of the Ancient of Days refers to vs. 10; the meaning would then be that the conflict continued to go badly for the godly until the Last Day itself arrived and Yahweh appeared for final judgment (cf. vs. 26).

Finally the seer saw the moment arrive when the saints took possession of the kingdom. In vs. 18 the promise was that they should receive the kingdom, and now that appointed time had arrived. The notion of an "allotted span" figures largely in eschatology. Man's life has its allotted span. The existence of social groupings and institutions has its allotted span. The world itself has an allotted span. So the statement here would reflect the idea that God had allotted a specified period during which the heathen powers should be allowed to dominate, after which, at a specified moment, the kingdom of God would come to replace them (cf. Luke 21:8). Thus *zimnā'* here may mean "term." **Received:** The same verb is translated "possess" in vs. 18. They take possession of their own property.

23. The interpreter now goes back to the original vision, dealing more particularly with the **fourth kingdom** and its development up to the contemporary situation. Vss. 23-27 are metrical. They seem to be the author's own, not a quotation from some older source. He follows to some extent the wording of vs. 19 ff.

Different: The same verb occurs in vss. 7, 19. That it should **devour the whole earth** is a rhetorical exaggeration, but well expresses the vast extent of Alexander's empire; cf. the phrase used of he Persian Empire in 2:39, and note how in 4:1 Nebuchadrezzar sends his epistle to "all peoples," where the "all" is not to be taken literally but regarded as an attempt to emphasize the extent of his rule.

24. He shall be different: The difference between this eleventh horn and the previous **ten** is apparently a reference to the statement in vss. 8, 20, distinguishing it by its eyes and mouth, which are meant to symbolize its overweening pride and presumptuousness. The **three kings** whom he will **put down** are presumably those who in vs. 20 are said to fall, and in vs. 8 to be uprooted. Porphyry the Neoplatonist suggested that they are Artaxias of Armenia and Ptolemy VI and Ptolemy VII of Egypt, all of whom were defeated by Antiochus Epiphanes; Ginsberg (*Studies*, p. 22) would revive this view. It is based on the assumption that the writer here has in mind something quite other than Antiochus' supplanting his predecessors in priority for kingship; these are three contemporary kings whom he did lay low. The verb means "to humble," "to abase," and was used in 4:37; 5:19, 22. The idea here is biblical (cf. Isa. 25:12; 26:5).

25 And he shall speak *great* words against the Most High, and shall wear out the saints of the Most High, and think to change times and laws: and they shall be given into his hand until a time and times and the dividing of time.

25 He shall speak words against the Most High,
and shall wear out the saints of the Most High,
and shall think to change the times and the law;
and they shall be given into his hand
for a time, two times, and half a time.

---

25. Vss. 8, 20 had said only that his mouth "uttered proud boasts." Here this is expanded to **he shall speak words against the Most High** (cf. 11:36). The reference is to Antiochus' attitude of contempt toward the God of Israel. That he **shall wear out the saints** expresses the results of his measures of persecution which the godly endured until their patience was worn out and they could endure no longer. The verb is that for wearing out a garment. Some think it means no more than "afflict," but such persecution as is detailed in the succeeding verses was well calculated to wear down the opposition of the godly. Driver compares the Targ. to Isa. 3:15, "the faces of the poor ye wear away."

"And shall think to change seasons and law": Cf. 11:37. The reference is to Antiochus' interference with the religious cults of his empire (I Macc. 1:41-42), and in particular with the religious life of the Jews. From I Macc. 1:44-49 we learn how he sent officers to suppress the daily sacrifices and offerings at the temple, to prohibit sabbath observance and the keeping of the periodical feasts, and to compel the people to do a number of things contrary to the law.

Think: The verb is "to hope," and then "to think" with expectancy that it may happen, so perhaps we might translate, "shall plan to change." **Times:** As in 2:21; 6:10, 13. The word probably refers to such religious observances as were appointed to be observed at fixed times, though some think it means the great seasonal festivals (Isa. 1:14; 33:20). The **law** is the Mosaic law. *Dāth* is used here as in 6:5 (M.T. 6:6); Ezra 7:12, 14. Bentzen, however, believes that here it has the more general meaning of "religion," which it has in later rabbinical writings.

The persecution was still in progress when this chapter was written. The great question in men's minds was when it would end and the triumph of the saints begin. So a prediction is made that the godly must endure for three and a half years, though whether this is meant as a precise measurement of time or as an indefinite expression (it is the half of seven) is uncertain. They are to be **given into his hand.** The word "saints" does not appear in the M.T. but is inferred from the earlier part of the verse, though some think it is not the saints but the religious customs which Antiochus will be allowed to control for a limited period. To **be given into** [the] **hand** of anyone means to be put under that person's control. In Gen. 9:2 animal life is given into the hand of Noah's progeny. In Gen. 14:20 Melchizedek tells Abraham that his enemies are given into his hand. It is thus that the Lord is said to deliver "out of the hand" (Judg. 2:16, 18; I Sam. 12:10).

A time, two times, and half a time is our first acquaintance with apocalyptic numerology. The word used here is not *zimnā'* but *'iddān*, as in 4:16 ff., a word which stands for "year." The three and a half years here agrees with 12:7 and the half week-year of 9:27, and roughly approximates the 2,300 evenings and mornings of 8:14; it was therefore inevitable that later readers would interpret the prediction as meaning a definite period of time. It is thus interpreted in Rev. 11:2; 12:14; 13:5 and by Josephus (*Jewish War*, Preface, 7).

There are various points from which one could begin calculating the three and a half years, but perhaps the most satisfactory is the legation of Apollonius *ca.* June, 168 B.C. (I Macc. 1:20, 29); in this case the three and a half years was not a bad prediction, for the rededication of the temple was in December, 165 B.C. Others, however, argue

26 But the judgment shall sit, and they shall take away his dominion, to consume and to destroy *it* unto the end. 27 And the kingdom and dominion, and the greatness of the kingdom under the whole heaven, shall be given to the people of the saints of the Most High, whose kingdom *is* an everlasting kingdom, and all dominions shall serve and obey him. 28 Hitherto *is* the end of the matter. As	26 But the court shall sit in judgment, and his dominion shall be taken away, to be consumed and destroyed to the end. 27 And the kingdom and the dominion and the greatness of the kingdoms under the whole heaven shall be given to the people of the saints of the Most High; their kingdom shall be an everlasting kingdom, and all dominions shall serve and obey them.' 28 "Here is the end of the matter. As for

that three-year predictions were a convention, and so prefer to think only of an indefinite period—half a sabbatic lustrum, a short but indefinite time.

26. When that time has run out, **the court** which the seer had beheld in vs. 10 will **sit in judgment,** and the things seen there will be fulfilled. A final end will be made to the **dominion** of the little horn. The M.T. reads **his dominion,** but the LXX, Theod., and Vulg. read "the dominion," which many prefer since it is the fourth beast that is to be utterly destroyed and we should expect to read that the entire dominion of the fourth kingdom will be taken away rather than just one part of it. However, the Seleucid power commonly stood for the whole succession of the Diadochi. **To the end:** The same expression occurs in 6:26.

27. The succeeding kingdom, the kingdom of God ruled over by his saints, will be (*a*) heir to the authority, dominion, and greatness of all the kingdoms under heaven; (*b*) an everlasting kingdom; and (*c*) a universal kingdom embracing all mankind. The saints of course are the righteous Jews. Not all mankind will be Jews, but all other groups finding a place in the coming kingdom will be subservient to the Jews and will obey them. **Under the whole heaven** assumes that this kingdom will be much greater than even the greatest of the previous kingdoms. This is probably meant to be taken literally, not as a rhetorical exaggeration such as the **whole earth** in vs. 23. The phrase occurs again in 9:12, and may be derived from its use in Deut. 2:25; 4:19; *et al.* That the new kingdom **shall be given** to the righteous agrees with the general thought of eschatology. Nobody can win it; it is God's gift. **Their kingdom:** The pronoun is singular, and the reference may be to the messianic figure to whom the kingdom was given in vs. 14, and so "his kingdom." It is more likely, however, that it refers to the rule of **the people of the saints,** which 2:44 had said was to be **everlasting.** So the other **dominions shall serve and obey him,** if we insist on the pronoun which is again singular. The verb **serve** is that used in vs. 14, which can mean "worship," but is generally taken to mean here that all mankind will be subservient to the ruling **saints.**

3. Epilogue (7:28)

28. Here is the end of the matter: Cf. Jer. 51:64; Eccl. 12:13. **End:** As in vs. 26 (cf. 12:6). **Matter:** Lit., "word," which probably is meant to include both the vision and the explanation given by the angel.

---

27. *The Ultimate Triumph.*—The last kingdom of the saints will be universal, taking in all men. The ultimate triumph is to have a redemptive quality. It is to affect all men and restore the right relationship between them and God. This is the difference between the victory of the saints and the victory of the sinners. The saints win something for all men, and their triumph is in the nature of an atonement.

28. *Enough Light.*—Daniel has not found final answers to everything. There is still much

for me Daniel, my cogitations much troubled me, and my countenance changed in me: but I kept the matter in my heart.

8 In the third year of the reign of king Belshazzar a vision appeared unto me, *even unto* me Daniel, after that which appeared unto me at the first.

me, Daniel, my thoughts greatly alarmed me, and my color changed; but I kept the matter in my mind."

8 In the third year of the reign of King Belshaz'zar a vision appeared to me, Daniel, after that which appeared to me

---

The seer's thoughts still **alarmed** him, as they did in vs. 15, even though he has had the interpretation. This anxiety is reflected in his **countenance**, as had been the case with Belshazzar in 5:6-9. Behrmann compares the prophetic fear in Hab. 3:16; Isa. 21:3 ff. "And the word [matter] in my heart did I guard [keep]": Cf. Gen. 37:11; Luke 2:19; Test. Levi 6:2; 8:19.

It is difficult to resist the impression that this last verse has the coming chapters in mind. The writer might have ended with vs. 27, but he has yet other visions he wishes to include in his book and so has Daniel make a suggestion that his mind is not entirely satisfied. Thus the readers will be in expectancy of what is coming in the next chapters. Since his setting for the visions was the Babylonian court, it is easy to suggest that such revelations of things to come seemed obscure, even when explained, and needed further elucidation (cf. 8:27; 12:8-13).

B. The Vision of the Ram and the He-Goat (8:1-27)

This vision may be regarded as an elaboration and expansion of certain features of the dream in ch. 7, which it seems intended to succeed and supplement. Here the vision framework becomes artificial as the writer proceeds with his account of Antiochus Epiphanes. The Babylonian Empire does not appear save in the setting, and the Medo-Persian appears only to introduce the Macedonian, which itself is here only to introduce the little horn, so that from vs. 9 onward attention is concentrated on Antiochus and his misdeeds.

The vision proper is of a battle between a ram and a he-goat, where the writer seems to be using an older source, though not necessarily a written one. Its animal symbolism is curiously like the zodiacal symbolism of the Persian period, derived from an older Mesopotamian astrological geography. We possess a document from the Persian period in which each country is placed under a zodiacal sign, Persia appearing under the Ram and Syria under Capricorn (see Franz Cumont, "La plus ancienne géographie astrologique," *Klio,* IX [1909], 263-73).

The purpose of the chapter is on the one hand to make clear some matters that had been dealt with rather cryptically in ch. 7, and on the other, to renew the assurance that the end is at hand. With Antiochus the cup of iniquity is surely full. This is the final episode in the great tribulation which precedes the end. God will intervene and the man of sin will be destroyed. With this chapter there is a return to Hebrew.

1. Prologue (8:1-2)

8:1. The vision is dated **in the third year . . . of Belshazzar,** i.e., in 552 b.c., two years later than the vision in ch. 7. This dating serves to maintain continuity with the rest of the book, but otherwise the court setting plays no part. That this chapter is meant as a continuation of ch. 7 is suggested by the concluding phrase of this verse. Particulariza-

---

that remains in the realm of mystery. But he has received enough light to live by, and he is willing to hold firmly to what he has been able to see. It is the questing spirit of faith that we see here. A religious experience does not settle

all our problems nor does it remove all our questions. But it gives us the essential clues, and we know that the quest is meaningful. We have discerned the signs which keep us confident and unafraid.

2 And I saw in a vision; and it came to pass, when I saw, that I *was* at Shushan *in* the palace, which *is* in the province of Elam; and I saw in a vision, and I was by the river of Ulai.

at the first. 2 And I saw in the vision; and when I saw, I was in Susa the capital, which is in the province of Elam; and I saw in the

---

tion of time and place is stylistic and intended to add verisimilitude to the account (cf. 10:4; Ezek. 1:1; 8:1-3; 11:1; Acts 10:9 ff.). Bentzen thinks the writer may have been influenced here by Ezekiel.

At the first: Cf. 9:21. Perhaps the best rendering would be "previously" or "afore-time." The word is used in this sense in Isa. 1:26; Gen. 13:3.

2. "And I saw in the vision, and it came to pass in my seeing that I was in Shushan the fortress." In the previous dream the seer was apparently in Babylon, but now he is carried away in vision to another part of the world, his body being in Babylon while his spirit is in **Susa,** the chief city of Elam. This is not an uncommon phenomenon. Ezekiel was carried away in his vision and found himself in Israel (40:1-3). Josephus, however, knew a tradition that Daniel as an important official had built himself a palace at Susa and was in residence there when the vision came. There may have been some point in the vision's being seen at Susa which would have been caught by the writer's contemporaries but is lost to us. Some suggest that as Susa was long the principal residence of the Persian kings after Darius Hystaspis, it would have been a most suitable spot for a vision of the rise and fall of the Persian power.

Shushan is the Hebrew name for Susa. It is mentioned in Neh. 1:1, and often in the book of Esther, as an official residence of the Persian kings. Like most ancient cities it had an acropolis, yet the reference in this verse seems to be not to the acropolis but to the city as a whole, which in ancient days was regarded as itself a fortress (Herodotus *History* V. 49; Polybius *Histories* V. 48. 14). Thus in the O.T. it is regularly called "Susa the fortress" (Neh. 1:1; Esth. 1:2, 5; 2:3, 5). From Esth. 3:15 it is clear that at that time a distinction was made between the acropolis citadel and the city itself. *Bîrāh,* the **palace,** is "citadel," "fortress," and Akkadian *bîrtu.* It occurs also in Neh. 2:8; 7:2; Ezra 6:2; I Chr. 29:1, 19.

Since the earlier Susa with its citadel was destroyed by Ashurbanipal in 640 B.C., the biblical references are to the later restored city which owed its greatness to Darius Hystaspis. Here the audience is meant to think of it as it was when a center of Persian power, though in the third year of Belshazzar it would have been little but ruins.

In the province of Elam: "Elam the province"—as in Ezra 6:2, "Media the province"— would mean for a courtier at Babylon that Elam was a province of the Babylonian Empire. It could hardly have been such in the third year of Belshazzar, for Cyrus had long since severed that eastern area from Babylonian control. The writer is thinking of the period when Elam was the fairest province of the Persian Empire. Montgomery suggests that we need not take the word here in its political sense but merely as a geographical indication of area.

The seer further defines the site of the vision by saying that the place in Elam where he saw it was "at the Ulai gate." **Ulai** is doubtless the Akkadian *Ulaa,* the name of a **river** in the vicinity of Susa known to the classical writers as Eulaeus, on which Pliny and Arrian say Susa lay. The gates of Oriental cities are commonly named from some local characteristic, and the writer here doubtless means that gate of Susa which faced the Ulai, or through which traffic from the Ulai customarily came. The artificial Ulai canal from the Choaspes which passed quite near Susa is probably meant here.

The word אוּבָל, which occurs only here in the O.T., is commonly translated "stream" or **river** on the assumption that it is a phonetic variation of יוּבָל, which occurs in Jer. 17:8. The fact, however, that in vss. 3, 6, we have אֻבָל makes it clear that the word is a miswriting of אֲבוּל, which is the Akkadian *abullu,* "city gate."

469

3 Then I lifted up mine eyes, and saw, and, behold, there stood before the river a ram which had *two* horns: and the *two* horns *were* high; but one *was* higher than the other, and the higher came up last.

4 I saw the ram pushing westward, and northward, and southward; so that no beasts might stand before him, neither *was there any* that could deliver out of his hand; but he did according to his will, and became great.

vision, and I was at the river U'lai. ³ I raised my eyes and saw, and behold, a ram standing on the bank of the river. It had two horns; and both horns were high, but one was higher than the other, and the higher one came up last. ⁴ I saw the ram charging westward and northward and southward; no beast could stand before him, and there was no one who could rescue from his power; he did as he pleased and magnified himself.

2. The Vision (8:3-25)
a) The Battle Between the Ram and the He-Goat (8:3-8)

3. If we have understood correctly the position of the Ulai gate, the seer would have been looking toward the northeast. There he sees a two-horned **ram**, symbolizing the Medo-Persian Empire, whose charging to the north, to the west, to the south, nothing was able to stop, until it came right down to the gate at Susa. The **two horns** represent the component parts, the Medes and the Persians, the latter rising later but presently exceeding the former in might.

To lift one's eyes in a dream really means no more than "to look," but it adds a vivid touch. So in 10:5 the seer raises his eyes and sees, as Jacob does in his dream in Gen. 31:10, and the prophet in Zech. 1:18; 2:1. The **ram** was a symbol of power and dominion, and in Phoenician was used as a figure for a despot. **Horn** is a symbol of strength (cf. I Kings 22:11; Amos 6:13; Zech. 1:18; Ps. 75:4), and is used as such here, not as in ch. 7 to represent a king.

4. Charging: From the verb "to thrust" or "to push," which in the Piel becomes "to gore." Since this is a ram, perhaps we had better say "butting" (cf. 11:40). The verb is used of animals in Exod. 21:28 and so could be used of nations symbolized as animals (see Deut. 33:17; Ps. 44:5). The image well represents what must have been the impression made in the Orient first by the Median Empire, which went so far as to subdue the once all-powerful Assyria, and then by the extraordinary success of Cyrus. That the ram did not charge eastward need be no surprise. The Achaemenids did, in fact, conquer eastward as far as India, and the LXX adds "eastward" to the text here, but these eastern conquests were of no interest to the readers, even if the writer knew of them. The addition in the LXX was doubtless an afterthought inserted in the interests of completeness. That none **could stand before him** is what is said also of the he-goat in vs. 7 and of the conqueror in 11:16 (for the idiom see Judg. 2:14; II Kings 10:4).

"And there was no deliverer from his hand." Cf. the equivalent phrase in vs. 7. The particular reference here may possibly be to the cities of Asia Minor which had felt the heavy hand of Persian government. As a consequence, **he did as he pleased**, lit., "according to his inclination" (so 11:3, 36; cf. Esth. 9:5). *Rāçôn* may mean no more than "good pleasure," but it can have the meaning of willfulness or caprice. **And magnified**

8:4. Not the Last Word.—This description of tyranny strikes a responsive note in contemporary minds. It seems that when the tyrant goes on the march there is nothing to stop him, and all men must let him do as he pleases. We remember the beginning of World War II. Hitler was keeping his time schedule precisely and could seemingly conquer any nation he desired. It looked as if he represented "the wave

of the future." No one could have blamed England or any other nation if surrender had been accepted as the only choice. We know how this description of the Medes must have seemed accurate and unmistakable to the first readers of Daniel.

In 1906 Wilhelm II of Germany and Nicholas II, Czar of Russia, met on a ship off the coast of Finland. They were making plans for the

5 And as I was considering, behold, a he goat came from the west on the face of the whole earth, and touched not the ground: and the goat *had* a notable horn between his eyes.

6 And he came to the ram that had *two* horns, which I had seen standing before the river, and ran unto him in the fury of his power.

7 And I saw him come close unto the ram, and he was moved with choler against him, and smote the ram, and brake his two horns: and there was no power in the ram to stand before him, but he cast him down to the ground, and stamped upon him: and

5 As I was considering, behold, a he-goat came from the west across the face of the whole earth, without touching the ground; and the goat had a conspicuous horn between his eyes. 6 He came to the ram with the two horns, which I had seen standing on the bank of the river, and he ran at him in his mighty wrath. 7 I saw him come close to the ram, and he was enraged against him and struck the ram and broke his two horns; and the ram had no power to stand before him, but he cast him down to the ground

himself: Lit., "and he acted big" (cf. vss. 8, 11, 25; see Jer. 48:26, 42). The word is used of God in a good sense, but more commonly in the O.T. it is used in a bad sense with a suggestion of arrogance and insolence (see Lam. 1:9; Zeph. 2:10; Ps. 35:26).

5. The vision of the might of the ram kept the seer astonished; while he was taking stock of all this, his attention was caught by the extraordinary speed with which a **he-goat** with a single **horn** was approaching from the west to attack. The he-goat represents Alexander, the speed of whose conquests in the East from the day he crossed the Hellespont in 334 B.C., to the midsummer of 323 when he died of fever in Babylon, was phenomenal.

Considering: Observing, paying attention. Cf. the Aramaic equivalent in 7:8 and the use of the word in Isa. 57:1. **He-goat:** Lit., "a buck of the goats," the proud leader of the herd being an obvious figure for the leader of a people. The choice of the he-goat as symbolic of the Macedonian-Greek Empire may have derived from the fact that the zodiacal sign Capricorn was in use as the sign for the Seleucids in Syria. Religious Jews would also remember how in Ezek. 34:17; Zech. 10:3 a contrast is drawn between the rough goat and the feebler sheep. That this was a one-horned goat, a unicorn in goat form, would not have seemed strange at that day, for in the glyptic art of the ancient Near East there are numerous representations of animals with a single horn springing from the middle of the forehead.

That Alexander moved **across the face of the whole earth** is said also in I Macc. 1:3, and though hyperbole, this expresses a sense of the vast extent of his conquests, just as **without touching the ground** suggests the almost incredible rapidity of the marches which made his armies seem to fly rather than to march. Charles recalls Isa. 41:3, which says of the swift march of Cyrus that "with his feet he treads not the road" (cf. Homer *Iliad* XX. 226-29).

A conspicuous horn: In vss. 8, 21 this is called a "great horn," but Ginsberg (*Studies,* p. 81, n. 29) thinks that the underlying Aramaic ought to be rendered here, as at 7:20, by "stout." From vs. 21 we see that this great horn represents Alexander himself, who is the "mighty king" of 11:3.

6. In his mighty wrath: Lit., **in the fury of his power.** *Ḥēmāh* is properly "heat" but is used also to express the heat of **fury.**

7. Broke his two horns: Perhaps the commentators are right in thinking that the writer had in mind the battles of Issus (333 B.C.) and Arbela (331 B.C.), though the

future. They were cousins, and called each other Willie and Nicky. Germany was the most powerful nation in Europe, and Russia had un-

limited resources. No wonder that, when the notes were published later, it was seen that those two men had said, "The next generation is ours."

there was none that could deliver the ram out of his hand.	and trampled upon him; and there was no one who could rescue the ram from his power. 8 Then the he-goat magnified himself exceedingly; but when he was strong, the great horn was broken, and instead of it there came up four conspicuous horns toward the four winds of heaven.
8 Therefore the he goat waxed very great: and when he was strong, the great horn was broken; and for it came up four notable ones toward the four winds of heaven.	

verse may merely reflect the confused general tradition concerning the disastrous defeats inflicted by Alexander on Darius III, rendering the Persian Empire as defenseless before him as other nations had been before it.

He was enraged against him: This is the "moved with anger" of 11:11, a Hithpael from *mārar,* "to be bitter," which occurs only in Daniel in the O.T. but is common in later Hebrew in the sense of "to be exasperated," and then "to be maddened, enraged."

Trampled: *Rāmas* is used in II Kings 14:9 of a beast treading down its enemy (cf. Isa. 63:3), and represents an Aramaic *rephas,* which is used in this sense in 7:7, 19. **No one who could rescue:** Lit., "there was no deliverer," as was said in vs. 4 of those whom the ram was overthrowing.

8. Tersely in vision symbolism the seer tells of the early death of Alexander and the rise of the Diadochi (cf. 11:3, 4). After defeating the Persians, Alexander overran their territories and pushed down into India. He indeed "made himself exceedingly great," but at the height of his greatness, when only thirty-two (or thirty-three) years of age, he was stricken down. Since he left no heir the succession was disputed among his generals, and after the Battle of Ipsus in 301 was divided into several kingdoms, among which the four greatest were (*a*) Macedonia and Greece under Cassander; (*b*) Asia Minor, including Thrace, Bithynia, Pontus, and Paphlagonia under Lysimachus; (*c*) Syria, Babylonia, and the east as far as the Indus under Seleucus; (*d*) Egypt under Ptolemy Lagus.

Magnified himself: The verb is the same as in vs. 4, though here it means not that the Greeks "acted big," but that by the victories of Alexander they had become a powerful factor in the life of the Orient. Alexander diligently planted Greek colonies in the Orient, which as centers of Greek life exercised a profound influence on their environment. This is the "great dominion" of 11:3.

Came up four conspicuous horns: Lit., "four conspicuous ones came up." **Conspicuous** is the same word as in vs. 5, but is apparently a textual corruption here. By a very small emendation it becomes "others," which is what the LXX read: "Four others came up." Ginsberg again would render "four stout ones." Since there were actually more than four divisions after Ipsus in 301, the number possibly comes from a stylistic preference for fours, or depends on the four-empire theory, the four old being replaced by four new. Only four out of the many divisions after Ipsus, however, were of any importance, and these do roughly represent the four quarters—Asia Minor in the north, Egypt in the south, Mesopotamia in the east, and Macedonia in the west. **The four winds of heaven** in 7:2 referred to the four cardinal points, and that the expression means the same here is clear from the parallel in 11:4 (see Jer. 49:36; Ezek. 42:20).

Many times the human race faces an evil power that for the time being does as it pleases and waxes great. But this is not the last word.

8. *The Sudden Tide.*—This is a reference to the death of Alexander while still young, with the whole world before him to conquer. This book brings out the point time and time again—at the very height of its power, tyranny

suddenly crashes. This is a part of Daniel's philosophy of history. The tide can turn suddenly, and the righteous may expect sudden deliverance. There are miracles of redemption which take place. We may be suspicious of the idea of sudden conversion, but it happens. Just as God throws down the tyrant when he seems invincible, so he enters into the human

9 And out of one of them came forth a little horn, which waxed exceeding great, toward the south, and toward the east, and toward the pleasant *land*.

10 And it waxed great, *even* to the host of heaven; and it cast down *some* of the host and of the stars to the ground, and stamped upon them.

9 Out of one of them came forth a little horn, which grew exceedingly great toward the south, toward the east, and toward the glorious land. 10 It grew great, even to the host of heaven; and some of the host of the stars it cast down to the ground, and

---

b) The Little Horn and Its Iniquities (8:9-12)

9. The vision now narrows down to an account of Antiochus Epiphanes. He is **a little horn** as in 7:8, but once on the throne he quickly **waxed exceeding great,** manifesting his military power particularly in campaigns against Egypt in the **south** and against Persia in the **east,** and becoming involved, to the sorrow of the Jews, in Palestinian affairs. He is **out of one of them** because he was of Seleucid stock, though not the direct heir to the throne (cf. I Macc. 1:10, "there sprang from them a sinful shoot named Antiochus Epiphanes"). **A little horn:** Lit., "one horn out of smallness." This could mean "one small horn," but the phrase is awkward and seems to be the result of textual corruption. A slight emendation, which is supported by the Greek versions, would give "another horn, a little one," the Hebrew equivalent of the Aramaic in 7:8, and is doubtless the original text. Josephus (*Antiquities* X. 11. 7) also reads "another lesser horn." The littleness probably refers to Antiochus' humble beginnings, when as the younger son he had no prospect of succeeding to the throne. **Exceeding:** *Yéther* is the cognate of the Aramaic word used in 3:22; 7:7, 19. **Grew . . . great:** The same verb occurs in vs. 8, but here again it could well mean "he acted big," and in that case we have a commentary on "exceedingly" in 11:22-24. On the other hand, it may refer only to the increase in his power.

Toward the south doubtless refers to Antiochus' Egyptian campaigns, further details of which are given in ch. 11 (cf. I Macc. 1:18). **Toward the east:** From the standpoint of a writer living in Palestine, for to a seer standing in Susa, Antiochus' campaigns against Persia could hardly be said to be toward the east. The reference is doubtless to the campaign of the last year of his life (see I Macc. 3:31, 37; 6:1-4). **Toward the glorious land:** Palestine, which in Ezek. 20:6, 15 is "the glory of all lands," in Zech. 7:14, "the pleasant land" and in Enoch 89:40, "a pleasant and glorious land" (see Jer. 3:19; Mal. 3:12). The M.T. has merely "and toward the glory," which many editors consider an interpolation derived from 11:16.

10. Not satisfied with the conquests which gave him control of earthly matters, Antiochus ventured to interfere in heavenly matters, desiring to control the religious life of men as well as their political life. I Macc. 1:41-42 hints at his measures for enforcing religious uniformity throughout his empire, which meant interference with the cult practices of many groups. The writer of I Maccabees gives some details of what this meant in the case of the Jews, and had we the writings of other religious groups, the tale would probably have been much the same. In Dan. 11:36-39 we read of some of his religious innovations. This aspect of his wickedness is here described as "acting big" against the host of heaven, even to pulling down some of the **stars** and trampling upon them, which recalls the statement in II Macc. 9:10 that he had "thought he could

---

heart and suddenly overthrows the rule of sin. The world and human life are to be seen in the light of crisis.

9. *Toward the Glorious Land.*—What a fine description of home! The writer is talking

about his own country and he thinks of it as a place of glory. What makes a land worthy of the designation **glorious?** We have tended to make it a matter of military conquest, but Palestine was glorious for something more sig-

11 Yea, he magnified *himself* even to the prince of the host, and by him the daily *sacrifice* was taken away, and the place of his sanctuary was cast down.

12 And a host was given *him* against the daily *sacrifice* by reason of transgression,

---

trampled upon them. 11 It magnified itself, even up to the Prince of the host; and the continual burnt offering was taken away from him, and the place of his sanctuary was overthrown. 12 And the host was given over to it together with the continual burnt

---

touch the stars of heaven" (cf. Rev. 12:4). The notion of a man thus "acting big" in regard to heaven became a characteristic element in later eschatology, where the Antichrist is pictured as so behaving. It has a biblical basis in such passages as Isa. 14:13-14; Job 20:6 (Behrmann compares Herodotus *History* III. 64).

The host of heaven is that of the heavenly bodies (cf. Gen. 2:1; Deut. 4:19; 17:3; II Kings 21:3; etc.). Since astral worship was deeply rooted in the ancient Near East, it was an easy step to use the phrase for the celestial divinities of the heathen (Isa. 24:21; Enoch 80:1), who were regarded as the rulers of the world. Thus the reference must be to the attacks Antiochus made on the various religions of his realm, some of which he cast down and even trampled upon, as we see in 11:36 ff. (see G. F. Moore, "Daniel viii. 9-14," *Journal of Biblical Literature*, XV [1896], 194-95).

Trampled: The same appears in vs. 7. His trampling was not only on human matters but upon divine (cf. Isa. 10:6).

11-12. The text here is notoriously difficult, and it seems certain there is some corruption. Various attempts at emendation have been made (see R. H. Charles, *A Critical and Exegetical Commentary on the Book of Daniel* [Oxford: Clarendon Press, 1929], pp. 204-9; Ginsberg, *op. cit.*, pp. 49-52). The versions obviously did not know what to make of the text.

The verses refer to Antiochus' attack on the Jewish religion stating that he did four things: (*a*) he flouted their God; (*b*) he abolished the daily sacrifices to Yahweh; (*c*) he desecrated the sanctuary by offering a profane sacrifice on the altar; and (*d*) he placed hindrances in the way of practicing true religion. He "was insolent" even in regard to Yahweh, who is the **Prince of the host** (cf. vs. 25). *Sar* is the normal word for **prince**, "chief," the Hebrew equivalent of the Akkadian *šarru*, "king." In the theophany of Josh. 5:13-15 the celestial visitant describes himself as "prince of Yahweh's host," and here in 10:13, 20; 12:1 the word is used for the angelic princes, so that some see in this passage not God himself but the angel in charge of the heavenly hosts. If the reference is to God, then this is the only place in the O.T. where *sar* is so used.

The continual burnt offering: The *tāmîdh* or daily burnt offering of Exod. 29:38 ff.; Num. 28:3 ff. Elsewhere in the O.T. it is called '*ôlath hattāmîdh*, even in Neh. 10:33, but in the four places in Daniel where it occurs it is simply *hattāmîdh*, as in the Mishnah, an abbreviation which is late usage. **Taken away from him** can only mean from God, who was thus deprived of the daily worship embodied in the sacrificial offering. Others render "he abolished," i.e., Antiochus abolished the sacrifices, as we read in I Macc. 1:45— a matter which is referred to again in Dan. 11:31.

Was overthrown: Antiochus seems not to have destroyed the temple building, though he plundered the treasury, and in the struggles the temple fabric must have suffered considerable damage, for the Maccabean victors found its courts overgrown,

---

nificant than that. It was the land of the chosen people, the book, the law. Its glory was the luster put upon a nation whose God is the Lord.

12. Heart and Ethics Centered in God.—Here is a description of Antiochus' blasphemies in the temple. Note that when worship becomes

---

paganized, truth is cast down. It is characteristic of false religion to glorify the lie. Until our hearts are centered on God and our ethics are rooted in him, we do not stay with the truth. Wrong always depends on falsehood, and freedom is obtained when truth is respected. Our

and it cast down the truth to the ground; and it practised, and prospered.

13 ¶ Then I heard one saint speaking, and another saint said unto that certain *saint* which spake, How long *shall be* the vision *concerning* the daily *sacrifice,* and the transgression of desolation, to give both the sanctuary and the host to be trodden under foot?

offering through transgression;[n] and truth was cast down to the ground, and the horn acted and prospered. 13 Then I heard a holy one speaking; and another holy one said to the one that spoke, "For how long is the vision concerning the continual burnt offering, the transgression that makes desolate, and the giving over of the sanctuary and

[n] Heb obscure

---

its gates burned, and some of its chambers in ruins. Thus they are described as "building" as well as cleansing and restoring (I Macc. 4:38-48). By "overthrowing," however, may have been meant defilement by unbelievers (cf. I Macc. 1:37; 3:45; II Macc. 6:3 ff.; 8:2, a matter referred to again in Dan. 11:31).

12. The M.T. reads "and a host will be given upon the daily offering in iniquity." The LXX has "and profane sacrifices were offered on (the altar of) the daily offering." *Çābhā',* **host,** could possibly mean "temple service" (Num. 4:23; 8:24), and על could mean "instead of," so that we could derive from the M.T. the meaning "an iniquitous kind of worship will be offered instead of the daily offering." Others take **host** in its natural sense of "army" and suppose it means "wicked warfare was undertaken against the daily offering," meaning the attack referred to in I Macc. 1:44-45, whereby Antiochus prohibited the daily offering. More radical emendations of the text will of course make possible yet other interpretations of the words, but in any case the reference is to his interference with the temple services, and with this interference was connected the famous "abomination of desolation" (9:27), the offering of a pagan sacrifice on the altar.

Truth here means the true religion, as "thy truth" in 9:13 (cf. Pss. 25:5, 10; 43:3; Mal. 2:6). True religion, as Daniel and the three confessors had exemplified, consisted in faithful observance of the law, so that by the success of Antiochus in carrying through his measures, truth had been **cast down to the ground** (cf. the connection between torah and truth in Ps. 119:142, 151, 160 and Paul's words in Rom. 2:20). If we read the verb as active, "he [or it, i.e., the horn] cast down," the reference is more directly to those measures of Antiochus described in I Macc. 1:45-51; II Macc. 6:6-11.

And the horn acted and prospered: Cf. vs. 24; 11:28. It carried into effect its plans against the Jewish religion and was successful, so successful that II Macc. 6:6 says a man could not keep the sabbath, or celebrate the festivals of his forefathers, or admit that he was a Jew at all.

c) THE CELESTIAL PREDICTION (8:13-14)

13-14. Ginsberg (*op. cit.,* p. 32) regards these verses as an interpolation, vs. 15 picking up the vision again where vs. 12 left it, while these verses are concerned not with a vision but with an audition. Vs. 26a, however, certainly refers to this passage, and so on this theory would have to be excised also as an interpolation. If we accept the text as it stands, then as part of his vision the seer hears a heavenly conversation. One celestial being asks another how long the state of pollution of the sanctuary would last, and the answer is 1,150 days. The burning question for contemporary Jews was how long the cessation of the sacrifices would last, and since the answer could hardly be seen in a vision, the obvious way to convey it to the audience was to change to an audition. We meet with the notion of listening in on heavenly conversation as a means of gaining information about things yet to come in Zech. 1:12 ff. There also the question is **How long?**

Holy one: An angel as in 4:13. A certain holy one spoke and a certain holy one answered, and it was the answering one who asked, **How long?** We have no hint as to what the first angel was saying that would have elicited the inquiry of the second, but the question obviously assumes acquaintance with the content of vss. 10-12. The use

14 And he said unto me, Unto two thousand and three hundred days; then shall the sanctuary be cleansed.

14 And he said to him,[p] "For two thousand and three hundred evenings and mornings; then the sanctuary shall be restored to its rightful state."

[o] Heb obscure
[p] Theodotion Gk Syr Vg: Heb *me*

---

of **holy one (saint)** for angel is common in the O.T. (cf. Deut. 33:2; Ps. 89:5, 7; Zech. 14:5) . **The one that spoke:** *Palmôni* occurs nowhere outside this verse. The Greek and Syriac translators did not understand it, so simply transliterated it as though it were a proper name. The Vulg. has *alteri nescio qui*. It would seem to be a contraction of the two words used in Ruth 4:1; I Sam. 21:2; II Kings 6:8, which mean "a certain unnamed one." Perhaps the audience would have recognized the reference to a particular angelic pair. Aq. regards it as an angel name *Palmoni*, whence we find it used in the Apostolic Constitutions VII. 35 as one of the names of God.

In our text the angel's question is unintelligible. On the basis of the LXX, Bevan emends it to read, "For how long is the vision to be, while the daily sacrifice is taken away and the iniquity set up—from the time when he shall tread down the sanctuary and the service?" However we choose to emend the text, the purport seems to be: How long is this intolerable situation to last? This **how long?** became a standard element in apocalyptic (cf. 12:6; II Esdras 6:59; Rev. 6:10) , but it had already had a long history, for the "How long?" (עד־מתי) of Pss. 6:3; 80:4; 90:13; Isa. 6:11; Hab. 2:6 is the very phrase *adi mati* which occurs repeatedly in the Babylonian psalms.

The words *tāmîdh*, "daily offering," and *pesha'*, "iniquity," are from vs. 12, but here *pesha'* seems to be connected with the following word *shômēm*, "that which appalls," and so to be connected in thought with the *shiqqûç meshômēm* of 11:31 and the *shiqqûç shômēm* of 12:11, i.e., the "abomination of desolation" familiar from the Gospels (Matt. 24:15; Mark 13:14) . If this is so, then the reference is to the heathen worship Antiochus offered in the temple (I Macc. 1:54; II Macc. 6:5) .

Sanctuary and host: *Qôdhesh* and *çābhā'* are also found at the end of vs. 11 and the beginning of vs. 12. The former doubtless means the sanctuary and the latter may mean "temple service," though some think it refers to the army of the Jews. It may of course mean the host of heaven as in vs. 10, and so indicate that Antiochus trampled on the Jewish sanctuary as he had already trampled on the pagan religions of the land. **Trampled:** As in vss. 7, 10 (cf. I Macc. 3:45, 51; 4:60; Luke 21:24) .

14. And he said to him: The M.T. reads **to me,** but Theod., LXX, Peshitta, and Vulg. all assume the reading **to him. Two thousand and three hundred evenings and mornings** is a computation similar to that in 7:25. Evening is mentioned first because by Jewish time reckoning the day began with the evening (cf. Gen. 1:5; Neh. 13:19) . So in vs. 26 it is "the vision of the evenings and the mornings." The reference is to the daily sacrifice which was offered each morning and evening (Exod. 29:38-42; I Esdras 5:50). We are to understand that 2,300 sacrifices would be omitted before the end could come, i.e., it would come after 1,150 days. This is some months less than the three and a half years of 7:25; 12:7. Since the starting point for the computation may be different from that of 7:25, whereas the end in both cases is the same, it is clearly the same prediction as to the time of the end. The calendar in use in the Maccabean age was not the same as ours, and there are various possibilities of the time between date and date; but from data in I Maccabees, the actual number of days between the defilement of the altar in 168 B.C. and its rededication in 165 was, on any calculation, somewhat less than 1,150 days.

Some take "evening and morning" as signifying one whole day, and so would move the *terminus a quo* farther back than the date in 168 when the pagan altar was set up

15 ¶ And it came to pass, when I, *even* I Daniel, had seen the vision, and sought for the meaning, then, behold, there stood before me as the appearance of a man.

16 And I heard a man's voice between *the banks of* Ulai, which called, and said, Gabriel, make this *man* to understand the vision.

15 When I, Daniel, had seen the vision, I sought to understand it; and behold, there stood before me one having the appearance of a man. 16 And I heard a man's voice between the banks of the U'lai, and it called, "Gabriel, make this man understand the

---

in the sanctuary, or would make the *terminus ad quem* later than the rededication in 165. This interpretation is much less likely than that the words mean 1,150 days. In any case, it is clear that the author is writing after the abomination has been set up and before the cleansing and rededication. His computation would thus seem to refer to this particular item in the persecution and so would be shorter than other computations which refer to the persecution as a whole. This is a genuine prediction intended to encourage the audience.

Be restored: Lit., "be justified." If we hold to the M.T., the meaning is that so long as the temple continued polluted it lay under condemnation, but when **cleansed** and **restored,** would justify itself for use again as a place where sacrifices could be offered. The Hebrew of this passage, however, is hardly tolerable, and the Greek καθαρισθήσεται indicates that the translators understood it to mean **cleansed.** Ginsberg (*op. cit.,* p. 42) shows how the Hebrew might have arisen from an Aramaic ירכי, "shall be cleansed."

d) The Interpretation (8:15-25)

15. As in ch. 7, it is a celestial being who gives the interpretation which Daniel is to record for posterity. This latter point is dictated by the framework of the visions. It is still in vision that the explanation is given, not after the seer wakes up. In ch. 7 he himself approached a celestial being to ask for the interpretation. Here the initiative is on the other side. One of the angels, noticing the seer's perplexity, summons Gabriel to reveal the meaning of all that Daniel has seen. Unless we are to excise vs. 26a, the vision to be explained includes the audition of vss. 13-14.

The celestial being in human form appears suddenly at a distance and then draws near (vs. 17). **One having the appearance of a man** is not the same phrase as "one in human form" in 7:13, nor is it quite the same as the words with similar meaning used in 10:16, 18. It was a usual thing for celestial beings to take human form when they were appearing to men. This is assumed in the story of Jacob in Gen. 32:24-32; in that of Manoah and his wife in Judg. 13; of Gideon in Judg. 6:11 ff.; and in other O.T. stories; in the annunciation story in Luke 1; in the account of Raphael in Tobit, and in the account of the fallen angels in Enoch. Similarly, in Zoroastrian story Verethragna appears as a noble youth of fifteen, and Anahita as a young maiden of noble birth.

The word used here for **man** is *gébher,* chosen apparently because it is the first element in the name Gabriel, and so hints that it was this angel. In 9:21 the more usual word for man is used. The phrase **as the appearance of,** used here and in 10:18, is characteristic of apocalyptic. It is used in Ezek. 1:13-14, 26; *et al.,* and generally in this type of literature. So in the Apocalypse of Abraham 10, the angel appeared to Abraham as "the likeness of a man."

16. Between the banks of the Ulai: Lit., "between the Ulai." The seer is indicating that he is still at Susa in the same position as at vs. 2. Others interpret the phrase as meaning that he is giving not his own position but the point from which the voice came. Since in 12:6 we again have a celestial being "above the waters of the stream," they suggest that the writer wishes his audience to think of a voice coming from somewhere above the waters, **between the banks of the Ulai.** The **voice** was that of a celestial being. but he spoke in intelligible words such as human beings use—an accommodation to

17 So he came near where I stood: and when he came, I was afraid, and fell upon my face: but he said unto me, Understand, O son of man: for at the time of the end *shall be* the vision.

vision." 17 So he came near where I stood; and when he came, I was frightened and fell upon my face. But he said to me, "Understand, O son of man, that the vision is for the time of the end."

---

the seer who could not have understood anything had the celestial being spoken in some celestial tongue. We may note that the angels who appeared at the ascension of Jesus were called ἄνδρες in Acts 1:10 because they appeared in human form and spoke in human language. Whose voice it was that called to Gabriel is not revealed. As in Ezek. 1:28, it is just a **voice.**

Gabriel: This is the first occurrence in the O.T. of a personal name for an angel. It is possible that he is meant, though not named, in 7:16. He appears again in 9:21 to reveal to the seer the significance of the seventy weeks, and in Luke 1 he is the messenger to announce the birth first of John and then of Jesus. In Luke 1:19 he describes himself as one who stands continually in the presence of God. In Enoch he is one of the four (or seven) archangels. Later Jewish writings saw him as the celestial being who had at various times in O.T. story appeared among men. His name means "El's man" ("Man of God"), El being the ancient Canaanitish word for God and *gabr* being "man." Others interpret as "El Is My Champion" or "El Has Shown Himself Valiant."

The vision: *Mar'eh*, from the verb "to see." Ginsberg (*op. cit.,* p. 55) claims that in this book it translates the Aramaic *'aḥwāya'*, and so means "oracle," not vision. *'Aḥwāya'*, however, could mean something set forth to be seen.

17-18. At the appearance of the angel the seer is so terrified that he falls down before him and has to be raised up and reassured by the angel. This rather counts against Gabriel being the one whom the seer approached in 7:16. The angel draws near from the place where he had first appeared.

Frightened: Falling on the face at the approach of an angel is a common feature in accounts of celestial appearances (see Josh. 5:14; Ezek. 1:28; 3:23; 43:3; Rev. 1:17; Enoch 14:14, 24; II Esdras 10:29 ff.; Apocalypse of Abraham 10). In part this was an Oriental mark of respect (Gen. 50:18; Ruth 2:10; I Sam. 25:23; II Sam. 9:6), but partly it was a desire to hide the face from so awesome a being (Gen. 17:3; Exod. 3:6; Lev. 9:24; Judg. 13:20; Matt. 17:6). **O son of man** has nothing to do with the messianic title "Son of man." It is used constantly in Ezekiel when the prophet is addressed (cf. Ezek. 2:1).

The angel begins his interpretation by orienting the vision. It concerns **the time of the end,** and the problem is what *'eth qēç* means. *Qēç* is used in the O.T. for Israel's "end," when God will appear in judgment (cf. Amos 8:2; Ezek. 7:2-3, 6; 21:25, 29 [M.T. 21:30, 34]; 35:5), while in Hab. 2:3 we have the parallel phrase "for the vision is for the appointed time, and it hastens toward the end." Thus it seems to be what we call the last days, the "latter days" of 2:28, and the "end of days" of 10:14, the phrase which the prophets use to indicate the end of the present age of world history (Jer. 48:47; 49:39; Ezek. 38:16; Hos. 3:5). The reference, as Junker (*Untersuchungen,* p. 76) insists, is eschatological. The "end" is the finish of the present system of things, which makes way for the entrance of a new era. To the writer the reign of Antiochus Epiphanes was the final crisis, the ultimate expression of wickedness, the filling up of the measure of iniquity, so the end was near and God's new day about to dawn. Thus the "end"— while it was the end of Antiochus and his reign and the end of the empire he represented, that fourth beast of ch. 7—was also the end of an age, the "appointed time of the end" of vs. 19. Charles insists, and Montgomery denies, that it has the further meaning of the end of time and the beginning of eternity. When we put together the use of the expression in vss. 17, 19, and its use in 9:26; 11:35, 40; 12:4, 9, 13, and the promise of a coming everlasting kingdom in 7:14, 18, 22, 27, which is to succeed immediately these "last days,"

18 Now as he was speaking with me, I was in a deep sleep on my face toward the ground: but he touched me, and set me upright.

19 And he said, Behold, I will make thee know what shall be in the last end of the indignation: for at the time appointed the end *shall be*.

20 The ram which thou sawest having *two* horns *are* the kings of Media and Persia.

18 As he was speaking to me, I fell into a deep sleep with my face to the ground; but he touched me and set me on my feet. 19 He said, "Behold, I will make known to you what shall be at the latter end of the indignation; for it pertains to the appointed time of the end. 20 As for the ram which you saw with the two horns, these are the

---

it is difficult to resist the impression that the expression does mean the end of time and the beginning of eternity. Certainly the later literature took this to be the meaning (see II Baruch 29:8; 59:4).

18. The seer had already fallen on his face at the approach of Gabriel; now at these first words his terror so increased that he could bear no more and swooned away (cf. 10:9). It is only at the touch of the angel that he regains consciousness.

Nirdam means "to fall asleep." It is used for a **deep sleep** in Judg. 4:21; Jonah 1:5; Prov. 10:5, while in Ps. 76:6 (M.T. 76:7) it is used of the sleep of death. A noun from the root is used in Gen. 2:21 for the unconsciousness into which the Lord put Adam in order to take his rib; in I Sam. 26:12 for the sleep of Saul's guards; and in Isa. 29:10; Prov. 19:15 as symbolic of insensibility (cf. Gen. 15:12; Job 4:13; 33:15). Thus "swoon" would be an adequate rendering here and in 10:9. Fainting at the close approach of a celestial being and reviving at his touch are mentioned in Rev. 1:17; Enoch 60:3-4; II Esdras 5:14-15; Apocalypse of Abraham 10.

Set me on my feet: Lit., "caused me to stand upon my standing" (cf. 10:11). This curious idiom is peculiar to late prose in the O.T. (cf. Neh. 13:11; II Chr. 30:16; 34:31). Notice how Ezekiel who had fallen on his face had to stand on his feet to hear the message (Ezek. 1:28; 2:1-2).

19. The interpretation begins with a statement that re-emphasizes, by stating more fully, the angel's first words in vs. 17, viz., that the vision concerns things which are to take place in "the last days of wrath." This is further amplified in 11:36. The last days of wrath mean on the one hand the last days of the oppression of the Jews, and on the other, the last days of the great tribulation (elsewhere called "the birth pangs of the Messiah") which immediately precede the end.

Indignation: *Za'am,* "anger," "wrath," "rage." Except in Hos. 7:16, the word is used in the O.T. only of the wrath of God. In the writings of the prophets it became a technical term for the indignation of Yahweh expressed against men for their sinfulness (Isa. 10:5; 26:20; Jer. 10:10; 15:17; Lam. 2:6; Ezek. 21:31 [M.T. 21:36]; 22:31; Nah. 1:6; Zeph. 3:8). Because of this wrath the Jews were subject to Gentile nations, but someday the period of wrath would be ended and a truly righteous Israel would enter into the inheritance of God's kingdom. So Isa. 10:25 says, "For yet a little while and the indignation shall be accomplished." To this writer the full cup of God's indignation had been reached in the subjection to Antiochus Epiphanes, who will continue to prosper "until the time of wrath is at an end" (11:36). Then the new kingdom will come and the saints will enter on their promised heritage. That others also recognized these days of Antiochus as the "days of wrath" appears from I Macc. 1:64, "And there came exceeding great wrath upon Israel."

To the appointed time of the end: Here *mô'ēdh qēç* means the same as *'eth qēç* in vs. 17. *Mô'ēdh* is used again in 11:27, 29, 35 for the "time appointed," i.e., the eschatological "end."

20. The two-horned **ram** is the empire of the Medes and Persians. The **kings** here are clearly kingdoms (cf. 7:17, where the four empires are called four kings; see also

21 And the rough goat *is* the king of Grecia: and the great horn that *is* between his eyes *is* the first king.

22 Now that being broken, whereas four stood up for it, four kingdoms shall stand up out of the nation, but not in his power.

23 And in the latter time of their kingdom, when the transgressors are come to the full, a king of fierce countenance, and understanding dark sentences, shall stand up.

kings of Media and Persia. 21 And the he-goat^q is the king of Greece; and the great horn between his eyes is the first king. 22 As for the horn that was broken, in place of which four others arose, four kingdoms shall arise from his^r nation, but not with his power. 23 And at the latter end of their rule, when the transgressors have reached their full measure, a king of bold countenance, one who understands riddles, shall

^q Or *shaggy he-goat*
^r Theodotion Gk Vg: Heb *the*

Ginsberg, *Studies,* p. 77, n. 16). Rowley (*Darius the Mede,* pp. 140, 148 ff.) is right in insisting on the duality here, Medes and Persians, against Charles Boutflower's desire to have it a unity, i.e., Medo-Persians.

21. The hairy **he-goat** is the kingdom **(king) of Greece.** *Yāwān,* which occurs again in 10:20; 11:2, is the name for Greece in the Pentateuch and the Prophets (cf. Gen. 10:2; Isa. 66:19). Torrey ("'Yāwān' and 'Hellas'") argues that it means not European Greece but the Greek Empire in the Orient and in particular the Seleucid kingdom.

The **he-goat,** in vs. 5 called "a buck of the goats," is here "the buck, the hairy one." It is generally held that the second word is an addition explanatory of the first, which it glosses by the more common word for **goat.** Theod., LXX, and Vulg. all read here precisely as in vs. 5. The **first king** is Alexander the Great.

22. Since Alexander has no particular interest for the writer in this connection, he passes on to the four main kingdoms which succeeded him. **As for the horn that was broken:** Lit., "and the broken one," a rather awkward expression which may be due to the fact that it is a translation from Aramaic (see Ginsberg, *op. cit.,* p. 42). The word **broken** fits curiously well the actual situation of Alexander's death in 323. **Arise:** Lit., **stand.** So in vs. 23 and often in ch. 11 the writer prefers עמד to the more usual verb קם. It seems to be nothing more than a stylistic preference. **From his nation:** The M.T. has **from the nation** but the Greek translators read **his,** i.e., Alexander's, and the following **his power** seems to make the emendation necessary. **But not with his power:** Cf. 11:4, "nor shall it equal the domain which he ruled." Though the kingdoms of the Diadochi carried on Alexander's rule and strove to further his policies, they were far from having his power.

23. Of the **four** others which he had mentioned in vs. 22, the writer is interested only in the Seleucids, and among the Seleucids only in the contemporary ruler Antiochus Epiphanes. So he hastens to the **latter end of their rule.** Antiochus Epiphanes was Antiochus IV; actually their line goes on to an Antiochus XIII, but for this writer the fall of Antiochus Epiphanes would involve the fall of all the Diadochi, whose Hellenic empire was to be utterly destroyed (7:11), since in this ruler its measure of iniquity became full. As early as Gen. 15:16 we meet with this idea of a measure of iniquity filling up (cf. Matt. 23:32; I Thess. 2:16; II Macc. 6:14).

Full measure: Lit., "when the sinners fill up their measure." The older commentators differed as to whether the sinners here were the ungodly Hellenizing Jews or the heathen oppressors, the **measure** in either case having to be **full** before the appointed time could come. The LXX, Peshitta, and Vulg., however, all support the reading "sins" instead of "sinners," understanding it as the iniquities of the Seleucids. "There shall stand a king hard of face and skilled in intrigues" is a succinct characterization of Antiochus IV. "Hard of face": I.e., insolent, and so of **bold countenance** (for the expression see Deut. 28:50). The verb is used in Prov. 7:13 of the harlot, and in Eccl. 8:1 of the wicked man, both of whom harden their faces. The shameless insolence of Antiochus Epiphanes was notorious (Polybius *Histories* XXVI). *Ḥîdhôth* is the plural of a word used for "riddle"

24 And his power shall be mighty, but not by his own power: and he shall destroy wonderfully, and shall prosper, and practise, and shall destroy the mighty and the holy people.

25 And through his policy also he shall cause craft to prosper in his hand; and he

arise. 24 His power shall be great,[s] and he shall cause fearful destruction, and shall succeed in what he does, and destroy mighty men and the people of the saints. 25 By his cunning he shall make deceit prosper under

[s] Theodotion and Beatty papyrus of Gk: Heb repeats *but not with his power* from verse 22

---

in Judg. 14:12, and for "dark saying" in Ps. 49:4; 78:2, the Aramaic form of which was used in 5:12. Some think that the meaning here is that Antiochus was an adept at double talk (I Macc. 1:30), and so, being skilled in the use of ambiguous language (cf. 11:27, 32), he is well described as a master of intrigue. Others think it was not so much his words as his deeds, for he was constantly guilty of double-dealing (cf. 11:23). In either case he was an adept at trickery (vs. 25).

24. Such a ruler was able, for a while at least, to attain great power, and to accomplish a great deal of what he purposed. **His power shall be great:** *'Āçam* is "to be powerful, mighty." This was true of the early part of his reign. **But not by his own power** seems to have crept in from vs. 22, and many editors delete it from the text. It is missing from some MSS of Theod. and from the Chester Beatty papyrus of the LXX. Behrmann thinks the words are original here and crept into vs. 22 by mistake. If we accept them here, there is some uncertainty as to the reference. Some read **but not with his power,** i.e., not with Alexander's power, which would make the passage parallel to vs. 22. Others render **not with his** [Yahweh's] **power,** i.e., not by divine favor did Antiochus become mighty. Others prefer "not by his own power," i.e., it was not by reason of his intrigues or any greatness of his own, but his power was by special provision of God, that he might be the one to bring the measure of iniquity to the full and so bring on the determined end. Others translate "not by his strength," i.e., his greatness is not from the prowess of a great king but from low intrigues unworthy of a king.

His power, however, shall be seen not in what he builds up, but in what he destroys, "for marvelously shall he destroy." For this expression see Job 37:5. The word *niphlā'ôth* designates things singular, wonderful, or even monstrous. The reference would be to the **fearful destruction** caused by the armies of Antiochus, not only during the massacre at Jerusalem (I Macc. 1:24, 31; II Macc. 5:11-14) but also in the course of the campaigns throughout the land. The doings of Antiochus are again called "wonders" in 12:6. Some are suspicious of the verb **destroy** here and, comparing with 11:36, would emend the text to read, "and monstrous things shall he utter," referring the thought to the blasphemies mentioned in 7:20. Others, comparing 11:24-25, would emend to read, "and presumptuous things shall he devise." The verb, however, is used thrice in vss. 24-25 so that there seems to be deliberate emphasis on the king's destructiveness. "And in all this he shall be successful" repeats the statement of vs. 12.

Destroy mighty men and the people of the saints: The usual interpretation is that the **mighty men** are political opponents, whereas the **saints** are the Jews. Others think that the former means the upper classes, among whom it was natural that such a usurper would have many enemies. If so, 11:22 ff. may refer to this same matter. **Saints** here, as in 7:25, means the godly among the Jews, and his "destroying" them here parallels his "wearing them out" there.

25. The M.T. becomes difficult here, whereas the LXX makes excellent sense; many editors therefore emend the text in accordance with the LXX, linking the beginning

---

history seems to say that whenever men depart from God it is only a question of time until they are willing to substitute the lie for the truth. Only when God is the center of our lives can we know the truth about ourselves and life.

25. *Eternal Vigilance.*—The advantage the enslaving ruler has is the laxity and blindness on the part of too many people. Antiochus had soothed the people with promises, but when they had relaxed their vigilance he fastened his

shall magnify *himself* in his heart, and by peace shall destroy many: he shall also stand up against the Prince of princes; but he shall be broken without hand.

his hand, and in his own mind he shall magnify himself. Without warning he shall destroy many; and he shall even rise up against the Prince of princes; but, by no

---

of this verse with the end of vs. 24, and translating, "And against the saints went forth his cunning." Then **he shall make** begins a new sentence. Taking the M.T. as it stands, however, perhaps we can obtain reasonable sense. **Cunning:** *Sēkhel,* "intelligence," which normally has a good meaning, seems here to have a bad sense and should be taken rather as astuteness or cunning. **Deceit:** *Mirmāh* is **craft,** "fraud." It is used in Gen. 27:35 of the guile whereby Jacob obtained his brother's birthright; in Amos 8:5, of the fraudulent balance; and in Mic. 6:11, of false weights. The deceit of Antiochus is mentioned also in 11:23, and a contemporary audience would probably have known a great deal more than we do of occasions when the underhand dealings and deceitful ways of Antiochus had been successful.

In his own mind he shall magnify himself is usually taken to mean that the success of his scheming and intriguing engendered in him an arrogance which presently made him overreach himself. Literally it is "and in his heart he shall think big" (cf. vss. 4, 8, 11), and may be a reference to certain grandiose plans which Antiochus thought he might put into effect after his craft and intrigue had given him a strong position. The clause **without warning he shall destroy many** seems to refer to the incident when in 168 B.C. his tax collector Apollonius came to Jerusalem and with peaceable words quieted the apprehensions of the people, but then suddenly fell on them and massacred a great number (I Macc. 1:29-30; II Macc. 5:23-26). Elsewhere in the O.T. *shalwāh* means **peace,** "security," so some render here "in their security" or "in time of peace." The word occurs again, however, in 11:21, 24, where the LXX has ἐξάπινα, which suggests that here also it must mean "unawares," a late meaning of the word.

Antiochus' final act of iniquity in which he overreached himself is that "he stands up against the Prince of princes," i.e., against God. **Prince of princes** here parallels the "Prince of the host" in vs. 11. The construction is the same as the more familiar "King of kings," or "Lord of lords," or "holy of holies," all expressing a superlative, and the meaning here is "the princeliest of all." The princes of whom God is the princeliest are the angelic chiefs (cf. 10:20; 12:1). The reference is the same as that in 11:36, where we have further details of Antiochus' self-deification which openly flouted the uniqueness of God. For this he will be struck down, not by any human hand but by God. Behrmann thinks that the reference is not to some sudden death but that, when it comes and in whatever form it comes, his death will be the divine nemesis.

Broken is used in the O.T. for the destruction of a kingdom (Jer. 48:4), of an army (II Chr. 14:13), and of individuals (Jer. 17:18). It was said of the horn in vs. 8, and is said of Ptolemy Philometor in 11:26. **Without hand:** As in 2:34. Probably the phrase "with none to help him" in 11:45 refers to his end being due to divine intervention against which no human help could avail. For the idea that Antiochus IV was struck down by the hand of God see II Macc. 9:5, Polybius (*op. cit.* XXXI. 9), Josephus (*Antiquities* XII. 9. 1). Polybius says he died suddenly of madness at Tabae in Persia in 164 B.C., only a few months after the Maccabees had rededicated the temple, and this mental disorder may well have suggested the idea of a divine stroke. According to I Macc. 6:8 ff., he died of melancholia during the Parthian campaign, which again might suggest an affliction caused by higher powers, and according to II Macc. 9, from the colic, a form of affliction which Josephus (*Antiquities* XIX. 8. 2) says the Jews of that day regarded as a particular punishment from God.

---

chains on them. Religious men are often the only ones who are not off-guard, and they have the courage to warn against what will happen.

Note the phrase **by no human hand, he shall be broken.** Victor Hugo in *Les Misérables* said that Napoleon fell because "he embarrassed

26 And the vision of the evening and the morning which was told *is* true: wherefore shut thou up the vision; for it *shall be* for many days.

27 And I Daniel fainted, and was sick *certain* days; afterward I rose up, and did the king's business; and I was astonished at the vision, but none understood *it*.

human hand, he shall be broken. 26 The vision of the evenings and the mornings which has been told is true; but seal up the vision, for it pertains to many days hence."

27 And I, Daniel, was overcome and lay sick for some days; then I rose and went about the king's business; but I was appalled by the vision and did not understand it.

3. Epilogue (8:26-27)

26. The angel concludes his explanation by a solemn affirmation that the vision is a **true** one and no mere fantasy of a dream world, and then instructs the seer to conceal it. The reference to vs. 14 is obvious, and editors who delete that must delete this. Similar solemn affirmations occur again in 10:1; 11:2; 12:7, with which cf. Rev. 19:9; 21:5; 22:6, 8. Such affirmations were doubtless for the reassurance of the audience.

"And thou, do thou conceal the vision." Cf. 12:4, 9. The framework had set the revelation in the third year of Belshazzar in Babylon, but the subject is what will happen in Palestine under Antiochus Epiphanes; therefore the seer is to write it and conceal it until the time comes for these things to be fulfilled. This will explain to the audience why they had never heard of these prophecies, and it will hearten them the more that the message is conveyed to them in the form of a prediction from earlier days. These things they are suffering had been foreseen, but the end was also foreseen, and with it their deliverance. The same idea of revelations given not for contemporary society but to be put aside and kept for future generations is found in Enoch 1:2; II Enoch 33:9-11; 35:3; II Esdras 14:46.

"For it is for many days," i.e., it refers to a distant age (see Ezek. 12:27). The idea had already been suggested in vss. 17, 19, and occurs again in 10:14; 12:9.

27. To finish off the framework of the vision artistically this last verse brings us back again to Babylon. The vision experience had been too much for the seer, so he had need to repose a while before taking up again his court duties. Even when back at duty he continues to marvel at the substance of the vision.

Was overcome: Lit., "I came to an end," i.e., was exhausted, at the end of his strength (cf. 2:1; Mic. 2:4). Yet the verb is a puzzle, for it normally means "to wail," "to lament." Because the LXX omits it, some think it is merely a dittograph. Ginsberg (*Studies*, pp. 58-59) suggests it is a mistranslation of an Aramaic "I was dazed." In 7:28 the dream had so upset Daniel that his health was impaired, and here again he **lay sick for some days.** So in II Esdras 5:14 the seer is in physical distress because of the dream-vision.

The king's business is apparently a court expression (cf. Esth. 9:3). The audience is doubtless meant to infer from it that Daniel was still occupying the high office to which he had been appointed in 2:48. **Appalled:** The same verb occurs in 4:19. In the light of 12:8 "and there was no one who understood" means not that Daniel told the vision and no one understood it, but that it was incomprehensible to anyone living in Babylon

God." Daniel believes that God's patience with man's impiety has a limit. He is advising that men should not despair because of the success of evildoers. They will fall victim to the divine judgment.

27. The Mystery of God.—This is a refreshing bit of humility. It is too bad that some interpreters of the book could not have shared in it. Our generation, with its rationalism, needs to

regain a sense of the mystery of God and his ways. We have had a cocksureness which is itself a sign we have only dimly comprehended the nature of God. In our science, our psychology, our economic theories, we have shown a dogmatic certainty that totally disregards the mystery of the human spirit, to say nothing about the mystery of God. It would be healthy if we would confess to God how little we understand.

9 In the first year of Darius the son of Ahasuerus, of the seed of the Medes, which was made king over the realm of the Chaldeans;

9 In the first year of Darius the son of Ahasu-e'rus, by birth a Mede, who became king over the realm of the Chalde'ans

---

as Daniel was, even after the angel had given the interpretation. Others think that the reason for its being kept secret was what was not understood, still others that no one understood why he had fallen sick. Bentzen suggests that it is a device to hold the attention of the audience by hinting that things are not yet understood, but more detailed information on these matters will be given in succeeding chapters.

C. THE PROPHECY OF THE SEVENTY WEEKS (9:1-27)

The purpose of this chapter is to elaborate on the prediction given in chs. 7–8 of the rapidly approaching end. It too is dated, but the dating has no significance for the substance of the vision. The vision differs from those which have preceded in that it contains no symbolic beasts, nor does the writer draw upon elements of popular mythology, unless the figures of Gabriel and the messianic prince are based on such. Here he takes as the vehicle of his message a prophecy of Jeremiah.

The scheme of the previous chapters is preserved. There is a vision, though this time it consists only in the seer's seeing the angel coming swiftly to him. The explanation given by the angel is not of symbolic figures but of the inner meaning of a prediction. Here prophecy, which itself was a kind of vision, takes the place of the dream material, and the function of the explanation is to relate the prophecy to the contemporary scene for the writer's audience.

As part of his introduction the writer uses a long prayer which is written in much better Hebrew than the rest of the book, and which has such close resemblances to the prayers in Neh. 1; 9; Baruch 1; 3, that it seems probable it was a prayer already in circulation at that day. It is noticeable that it uses the name Yahweh, which is avoided in other parts of the book, borrows phrases from Solomon's consecration prayer in I Kings 8 (=II Chr. 6) and other prayers known to us, and is written from the standpoint of one living in Palestine, not, as Daniel was in the framework of these chapters, in Babylon. Many of its phrases, however, were appropriate to a devout Jew living in captivity in Babylon, so that the writer could use it without much adaptation.

1. PROLOGUE (9:1-19)
a) THE SETTING OF THE VISION (9:1-3)

9:1. The vision is dated **in the first year of Darius,** i.e., by this writer's chronology the year after the fall of Babylon, and so in 538 B.C. Driver notes the appropriateness of this dating, for the year after the conquest would be the time when pious Jews in Babylon might be expected to be remembering the promises of Jeremiah (25:12-14; 29:10-14) and thinking about the possibility of return. **Darius** here is clearly the same who appeared in 5:31 as the successor to Belshazzar as king in Babylon. There he was simply Darius the Mede, but here we are told more explicitly that he was of Median race and was the son of Xerxes.

Ahasuerus: As in Esther and Ezra. This is a Persian, not a Median name. No Xerxes known to history had a son named Darius, but Darius I (521-485 B.C.) was the father of Xerxes I (485-465). Torrey ("Medes and Persians," pp. 7-8) has again raised the possibility that here it may be meant for Cyaxares, the Median king, who was the father of Astyages and whose granddaughter was the wife of Nebuchadrezzar, and who along with Nebuchadrezzar's father Nabopolassar overthrew Nineveh in 612 B.C.

By birth a Mede: Lit., of the seed of the Medes. **Seed** comes to mean "progeny" and then "family" or "race." So Mordecai in Esth. 6:13 was "of the seed of the Jews," and Hadad in I Kings 11:14 was "of the king's seed of Edom." **Became king:** Lit., **was made king.** This has been taken to indicate that Darius had only some subsidiary,

2 In the first year of his reign, I Daniel understood by books the number of the years, whereof the word of the LORD came to Jeremiah the prophet, that he would accomplish seventy years in the desolations of Jerusalem.

3 ¶ And I set my face unto the Lord God, to seek by prayer and supplications, with fasting, and sackcloth, and ashes:

— 2 in the first year of his reign, I, Daniel, perceived in the books the number of years which, according to the word of the LORD to Jeremiah the prophet, must pass before the end of the desolations of Jerusalem, namely, seventy years.

3 Then I turned my face to the Lord God, seeking him by prayer and supplications with fasting and sackcloth and ashes.

---

subordinate kingly position, a conclusion which is thought to be supported by the expression used in 5:31. This, however, is quite erroneous. **Chaldeans** has here its ethnic sense, pointing back to 5:30.

2. The cause of the vision and the reason for which the writer has some details to add to the message of the previous chapter are that he had been meditating on earlier prophecies, during which he had come upon Jeremiah's prophecy concerning the seventy years of Jerusalem's desolation. Such meditation induced acts of contrition and prayers of supplication which in their turn brought on a vision. Some think he had been reading the Law and had come upon Lev. 26, where the mention of the desolated land enjoying its sabbaths while its people are in the land of their enemies reminded him of predictions of Jeremiah, and in a flash of vision gave him the clue to the mystery of their unfulfillment. It seems more natural, however, to think that while reading a scroll containing prophecies by Jeremiah he had in a moment of illumination seen their connection with Lev. 26.

Perceived: *Bin* can mean "to understand," "to comprehend," in which sense it is used in 12:8. It may also mean "to give heed," and then "to perceive," "to observe," as in Job 9:11; Ps. 58:9. **The books** do not necessarily indicate a canonized collection, but those writings of a religious nature which would feed the piety of religious Jews, and which may have included many things not later contained in the collection that was officially canonized as scripture.

Prophets spoke forth the **word of the LORD** which came to them; this prediction was Yahweh's word **to Jeremiah.** This is the only place where the writer uses the name Yahweh, save where he is quoting, and some would therefore excise it or change it to Elohim. However, the phrase here may be quoted. The passages usually thought of are Jer. 25:11-12; 29:10, as we have them in our collection. That the seventy years of those predictions had exercised the minds of earnest folk is clear from II Chr. 36:21-22, which regards the decree of the first year of Cyrus as a fulfillment, though less than fifty years had then elapsed since the destruction of Jerusalem. **Desolations:** A word often employed to describe the state of a devastated land after the armies of an enemy have passed (cf. Lev. 26:31, 33; Isa. 49:19; Jer. 44:22; Ezek. 36:34; Mal. 1:4; I Macc. 1:39).

3. Not understanding the significance of the seventy years during which, the prophet said, Jerusalem must lie desolate, our writer sets himself to the appropriate spiritual exercises preparatory to seeking a revelation on the matter. **I turned:** Lit., **I set my face** (so in 10:15; cf. 11:17; for the expression see II Chr. 20:3). The setting of the face possibly contains a reference to correct orientation in prayer. **Seeking him by prayer:** Lit., "to seek prayer," which may mean to apply oneself to **prayer** and **supplication** (Zeph. 2:3) as a means of obtaining a revelation. Bentzen, however, suggests that prayer does not come naturally but has to be sought. This verb *biqqēsh,* however, is used of

---

9:3. *The Source of All Wisdom.*—Because of his lack of understanding, Daniel turns to the source of all wisdom. But he does not approach God effortlessly. He comes before the throne with fasting, in sackcloth and ashes. This is a judgment on our tendency to approach

God easily and carelessly. Much of our praying is no more than vaguely wishing God would do something for us. Prayer has its disciplines, and the more serious our need the more agonizing must be our prayer. Our Lord prayed in such a manner that the sweat fell from his face

4 And I prayed unto the Lord my God, and made my confession, and said, O Lord, the great and dreadful God, keeping the covenant and mercy to them that love him, and to them that keep his commandments;

5 We have sinned, and have committed iniquity, and have done wickedly, and have rebelled, even by departing from thy precepts and from thy judgments:

4 I prayed to the Lord my God and made confession, saying, "O Lord, the great and terrible God, who keepest covenant and steadfast love with those who love him and keep his commandments, 5 we have sinned and done wrong and acted wickedly and rebelled, turning aside from thy command-

---

making inquiry at an oracle, and so suggests turning to prayer as a means of obtaining spiritual enlightenment.

Fasting was early regarded as a discipline preparatory to the receiving of revelations. It is mentioned again in 10:2-3, and is found in Exod. 34:28; Deut. 9:9, 18; Esth. 4:16 and, among later writings, in II Esdras 5:13, 20; 6:35; 12:51; II Baruch 5:7; 9:2; Test. Reuben 1:10; Herm. Vis. 2:3. In the Ascension of Isaiah 2:10, 11 we find ascetic preparation for the reception of a vision. **Sackcloth and ashes** were the traditional signs of mourning (Esth. 4:1-3), and so were appropriate accompaniments to an act of contrition (cf. Isa. 58:5; Jonah 3:5-6; Matt. 11:21).

b) Daniel's Prayer (9:4-19)

4. A few connecting words introduce the prayer (vss. 4-19), which is a mosaic of phrases seemingly drawn from the liturgies used at that day. That it is to be accompanied by **confession** indicates that it is a penitential prayer, a type for which we have abundant literary evidence from the ancient Near East (cf. vs. 20; Neh. 1:6). The religious duty of confession of sin is laid down in Lev. 5:5; 16:21; 26:40 (cf. Ezra 10:1; Neh. 9:2). In this prayer there is remarkable outspokenness in dealing with the sins and shortcomings of the nation.

O Lord: The M.T. reads "And I said, Ah, now Lord." The interjection אָנָּא is a strong expression of entreaty. Vulg. *obsecro* (cf. Neh. 1:5, 11; Isa. 38:3). **The great and terrible . . . commandments** agrees in wording with Neh. 1:5 (cf. Neh. 9:32), which itself draws on Deut. 7:9, 21 (but cf. Exod. 20:6). **Terrible:** "Awful," i.e., he whose presence induces in men a sense of awe and terror (Deut. 10:17; Judg. 13:6; Ps. 47:2; Joel 2:11). "He who guards both covenant and kindness": I.e., he who observes the provisions of his side of the covenant between himself and his people, and goes far beyond the letter of the covenant in maintaining an attitude of lovingkindness toward those who love him and on their side keep the commandments. Both *berîth*, **covenant**, and *miçwôth*, **commandments**, are used here in their technical sense as that would be understood by a Jewish audience.

5. **Sinned, . . . done wrong, . . . acted wickedly** all agree with the wording of I Kings 8:47, and **turning aside** with that of Deut. 17:20. This piling up of terms is in liturgical style and suits the manner of this writer. **Commandments and ordinances** are again technical terms. A commandment is what is laid down as legislation; an ordinance is literally a judgment, a legal decision given in a case which then becomes binding in law. Here perhaps the distinction is that the commandments are on matters concerning the civil law, and the ordinances on matters concerning the moral law.

---

like drops of blood (Luke 22:44). It takes great endeavor to break through our veneer of hypocrisy and egotism. The saints did not obtain their joy without paying a price. They learned how to concentrate spiritually and to open their hearts to the spirit of God. Daniel was praying for knowledge that would help him serve his people. He had lost himself in

his desire to speak some word of hope to the persecuted ones of his time. Until we can see beyond our own situation, it is not possible for God to fulfill our desires.

4. *God's Nature.*—It was Israel's glory to keep clear the terribleness of God and at the same time to recognize his love and kindness. When either of these things is lost, we lose our under-

6 Neither have we hearkened unto thy servants the prophets, which spake in thy name to our kings, our princes, and our fathers, and to all the people of the land.

7 O Lord, righteousness *belongeth* unto thee, but unto us confusion of faces, as at this day; to the men of Judah, and to the inhabitants of Jerusalem, and unto all Israel, *that are* near, and *that are* far off, through all the countries whither thou hast driven them, because of their trespass that they have trespassed against thee.

8 O Lord, to us *belongeth* confusion of face, to our kings, to our princes, and to our fathers, because we have sinned against thee.

9 To the Lord our God *belong* mercies and forgivenesses, though we have rebelled against him;

ments and ordinances; 6 we have not listened to thy servants the prophets, who spoke in thy name to our kings, our princes, and our fathers, and to all the people of the land. 7 To thee, O Lord, belongs righteousness, but to us confusion of face, as at this day, to the men of Judah, to the inhabitants of Jerusalem, and to all Israel, those that are near and those that are far away, and in all the lands to which thou hast driven them, because of the treachery which they have committed against thee. 8 To us, O Lord, belongs confusion of face, to our kings, to our princes, and to our fathers, because we have sinned against thee. 9 To the Lord our God belong mercy and forgiveness; because we have

6. **The prophets** had been sent with God's message to the people, but the people too frequently had not hearkened to them (see Neh. 9:32, 34, and along with it, Jer. 26:5; 29:19; 35:15; 44:21; Baruch 1:16). As to the descending order of classes in the social scale here, see Jer. 1:18; 44:21. The order is royal house, princely houses, family houses, commoners. Charles notes how the list excludes priests and prophets from the unfaithful, which is in strange contrast with Jer. 14:14; Neh. 6:14; 9:34.

7-8. Cf. Baruch 1:15, 17. It is now evident that God was in the right (cf. vs. 14) and the people in the wrong. **Righteousness** is here the technical word for legal righteousness. **Confusion of face** is an idiom for shame or disgrace (cf. Jer. 7:19; Ps. 44:15; II Chr. 32:21; Ezra 9:7). There is a physical sense in the expression which is comparable to our "loss of face" before others, and is reflected in Ps. 69:7; Jer. 51:51. Included in this disgrace are the menfolk of Judah in general and the citizens of the capital in particular, as well as members of the nation living abroad (for the phraseology see Jer. 4:4; 16:15; 23:3, 8; 32:32, 37; II Kings 23:2; Isa. 57:19; Baruch 1:15). The scattering of the people is because Yahweh has **driven them** on account of their **treachery** toward him, lit., "because of their faithlessness wherewith they have acted faithlessly with thee"; מעל is used twice, first as a noun, then as a verb. The idea of **treachery** is more prominent in this word than that of **trespass** (for the expression see Lev. 26:40; Ezek. 17:20; 18:24; I Chr. 10:13).

9-10. Since rebelliousness has put the people in the wrong their only hope is in the compassion of Yahweh. They are thrown on his mercy.

standing of God's nature. Terrible in his wrath and judgment, but tender and kind in his concern for repentant men, is our God. A narrow dogmatism which takes delight in dwelling on God's wrath goes too far in one direction, while the soft, Christian heresies of our time tend to make him sentimental and futile. The Bible keeps the two extremes in a healing tension.

6. *Prayer of Confession.*—We have not listened to thy servants the prophets. Nor have we. And we come out at the same place. How long before we learn that the prophetic demand for justice and righteousness on the part of the

powerful is not only for the sake of the weak, but for the sake of the powerful themselves? The tendency is to blame everything but our own unwillingness to heed the word of the prophet. This prayer is a model for our own situation. **We have not listened,** and we have gone astray. There can be no hope until our generation can pray Daniel's prayer of confession. Then, and then only, will we learn what we must do to be saved.

8. *Confusion of Face.*—One thinks of the confusion of tongues in the Genesis story. In both instances men are confused when they

10 Neither have we obeyed the voice of the LORD our God, to walk in his laws, which he set before us by his servants the prophets.

11 Yea, all Israel have transgressed thy law, even by departing, that they might not obey thy voice; therefore the curse is poured upon us, and the oath that *is* written in the law of Moses the servant of God, because we have sinned against him.

12 And he hath confirmed his words, which he spake against us, and against our judges that judged us, by bringing upon us

rebelled against him, 10 and have not obeyed the voice of the LORD our God by following his laws, which he set before us by his servants the prophets. 11 All Israel has transgressed thy law and turned aside, refusing to obey thy voice. And the curse and oath which are written in the law of Moses the servant of God have been poured out upon us, because we have sinned against him. 12 He has confirmed his words, which he spoke against us and against our rulers

---

Mercy: Lit., **mercies;** cf. Pss. 25:6; 40:11, but our word "compassion" perhaps expresses it more happily. **Forgiveness:** Lit., **forgivenesses;** so in Neh. 9:17 (cf. Ps. 130:4). **Obeyed:** Lit., "hearkened to," as in Exod. 15:26; 19:5; Deut. 4:30; Jer. 3:13. This whole phrase occurs almost word for word in Jer. 26:4-5 (cf. Baruch 1:18; 2:10). The same verb was translated **listened** in vs. 6. **To walk in his laws:** Cf. Jer. 26:4; 44:10, 23; Neh. 9:13. The expression "the law which I set before you" occurs in Deut. 4:8; 11:32; Jer. 9:13; 26:4; 44:10. Note that in this verse the **laws** are said to be set before men by God's **servants the prophets,** not by **Moses,** whose **law** is mentioned in vs. 11. **Laws** in the plural may mean "teachings" or "instructions" rather than law in the technical sense.

11. Since the whole people is under condemnation, there has been poured out **on them as a people** the curse the Mosaic law threatened as the wages of sin. The law they **transgressed** was set before them by the prophets, but when the prophets spoke they **turned aside** (as in vs. 5) so as not to hear the Lord's **voice** (Jer. 18:10; 42:13). "So there has been poured out upon us the curse and the oath": For the phrase see Num. 5:21; Neh. 10:29. This **curse** is doubtless the body of imprecations detailed in Lev. 26:14-22; Deut. 28:15-45. That it should be **poured out** (cf. vs. 27, where destruction is "poured out") was familiar imagery; cf. in the O.T. Jer. 42:18; 44:6; II Chr. 12:7; 34:21, 25; Rev. 16:1; and the Zinjirli inscriptions, where we read "Let Hadad pour out his wrath upon him." Anyone who has listened to fluent Oriental cursing can understand how this image arose. The curse **that is written** is mentioned in Deut. 29:20 (cf. Baruch 1:20). **In the law of Moses** assumes that a code of Mosaic law was in existence when this prayer was written. The expression is used in Josh. 8:31; 23:6; I Kings 2:3, and also in the N.T. Likewise the description of Moses as **the servant of God** follows older usage.

12. The present state of affairs is only what might have been expected. The consequence of sin and disobedience had been fully set forth in God's words spoken through the prophets, and what happened was merely the fulfillment of those words. **Confirmed:** Lit., "caused to stand" (for the expression see Neh. 9:8; Deut. 9:5). God **confirmed his words,** caused them to stand firm, so that what he said did not fail (with this cf. I Kings 8:20; Baruch 2:1-2).

Our rulers who ruled us: Lit., **our judges that judged us.** In Baruch this is taken to mean those mentioned in the book of Judges and to refer to the period before there had been any kings, when Israel was ruled by judges; but the word is probably being used here in a general sense to cover all the classes or rulers mentioned in vss. 6, 8.

---

defy or ignore God. Daniel has no doubt that the confused state of the world and of his people is due to spiritual causes. Order can be re-established by God alone.

11-12. *Because We Have Sinned.*—It is well to remember that if God did not punish sin,

he would be guilty of broken promises just the same as if he failed to protect the righteous. These two sides of his law are easily separated. We are quite willing to be rewarded for our virtue, but we tend to feel badly used if we are punished for our sin. The moral law demands

a great evil: for under the whole heaven hath not been done as hath been done upon Jerusalem.

13 As *it is* written in the law of Moses, all this evil is come upon us: yet made we not our prayer before the LORD our God, that we might turn from our iniquities, and understand thy truth.

14 Therefore hath the LORD watched upon the evil, and brought it upon us: for the LORD our God *is* righteous in all his works which he doeth: for we obeyed not his voice.

who ruled us, by bringing upon us a great calamity; for under the whole heaven there has not been done the like of what has been done against Jerusalem. 13 As it is written in the law of Moses, all this calamity has come upon us, yet we have not entreated the favor of the LORD our God, turning from our iniquities and giving heed to thy truth. 14 Therefore the LORD has kept ready the calamity and has brought it upon us; for the LORD our God is righteous in all the works which he has done, and we

---

Shôphēṭ both in Hebrew and Phoenician sometimes means "ruler" rather than the narrower office of "judge."

Great calamity: Lit., **great evil** (so Jer. 35:17; 36:31). It is doubtless hyperbole to state that this calamity is "such that there has not been done beneath all the heavens as has been done at Jerusalem," but it was a natural exaggeration. To us the atrocities committed by the soldiery of Antiochus Epiphanes at Jerusalem seem a small thing compared with what we know of outrages committed in other parts of the ancient world, but to Jews, to whom Jerusalem was the symbol of all that was holy, the treatment meted out to that city seemed without parallel. There is a reflection of this in I Macc. 1:39-40; 2:7-12. **Under the whole heaven** is the same expression as the Aramaic of 7:27 (cf. Deut. 2:25; 4:19; Job 28:24).

13. Even such calamity had not taught the people to repent and turn to seek God. **As it is written** doubtless refers to such passages as Deut. 28:15; 30:1 (for the expression see I Kings 2:3; II Chr. 23:18; 35:12). This curious sense of the inevitability of that which "is written" has been continuous in the Near East since early times.

Entreated the favor: Lit., "sweetened the face," whence the meaning "to flatter" in Job 11:19; Prov. 19:6; Ps. 45:12, where it is a case of flattering someone in order to obtain a favor. It is used of seeking the favor of God in Exod. 32:11; II Kings 13:4; Ps. 119:58. With the passage here cf. Baruch 2:8. The face as a synonym for personality is of ancient use in the Near East. The Akkadian *panū* is used in this sense in the royal inscriptions, and it is of frequent use in the O.T. (e.g., Ps. 34:16; Exod. 33:14; Isa. 63:9 (where "angel of the presence" is actually "angel of the face"), and in the *Qur'ān* (where "the face," i.e., of Allah, is a common expression).

Giving heed to thy truth: The verb means "to gaze at," "to contemplate," and in the Hiphil "to pay attention to." Here, however, it is used with the preposition ב, so some render "to become wise through thy truth," others, "to deal wisely through thy truth," or "to have insight into thy faithfulness," or "to have discernment in thy truth." There is thus doubt as to the true meaning of both verb and noun. **Truth** in 8:12 meant much the same as "religion," and since the verb certainly means "to discern" or **understand** in vs. 25, many think that the more natural meaning here is that men should turn from their iniquities and come to an understanding of true religion. The root meaning of אמת, however, is "faithfulness," so others would have it mean that men are to come to an understanding of Yahweh's faithfulness and realize that what he promises he will perform. In 11:33, 35; 12:3, 10 the verb is taken by many to mean "to deal wisely," and they suppose the meaning here to be that men are to turn from iniquity and through true religion learn to act wisely.

14. The calamity is partly the result of the people's wrongdoing, partly the consequence of their perverseness, for had they turned and sought his favor it might have been avoided. God is not to be mocked. Since men were perverse, he executed his judgment, and in doing so he acted rightly. **Kept ready:** "Was watchful over," "was vigilant"

15 And now, O Lord our God, that hast brought thy people forth out of the land of Egypt with a mighty hand, and hast gotten thee renown, as at this day; we have sinned, we have done wickedly.

16 ¶ O Lord, according to all thy righteousness, I beseech thee, let thine anger and thy fury be turned away from thy city Jerusalem, thy holy mountain: because for our sins, and for the iniquities of our fathers, Jerusalem and thy people *are become* a reproach to all *that are* about us.

17 Now therefore, O our God, hear the prayer of thy servant, and his supplications, and cause thy face to shine upon thy sanctuary that is desolate, for the Lord's sake.

have not obeyed his voice. 15 And now, O Lord our God, who didst bring thy people out of the land of Egypt with a mighty hand, and hast made thee a name, as at this day, we have sinned, we have done wickedly. 16 O Lord, according to all thy righteous acts, let thy anger and thy wrath turn away from thy city Jerusalem, thy holy hill; because for our sins, and for the iniquities of our fathers, Jerusalem and thy people have become a byword among all who are round about us. 17 Now therefore, O our God, hearken to the prayer of thy servant and to his supplications, and for thy own sake, O Lord,[t] cause thy face to shine upon

[t] Theodotion Vg Compare Syr: Heb *for the Lord's sake*

(cf. Jer. 1:12; 31:28; 44:27; Baruch 2:9). He forgot not the evil that was threatened as a consequence of sin. That **God is righteous in all his works** is the message of Jer. 12:1; Ezra 9:15; Lam. 1:18 (cf. Neh. 9:8, 33).

15. The confession in the name of the people being ended, the seer begins his supplication by recalling Yahweh's signal aid to his people in bringing them out of the Egyptian bondage and making them his people (cf. Baruch 2:11-19). **With a mighty hand:** Cf. Jer. 32:21, a passage which recalls Deut. 6:21. **And hast made thee a name:** Cf. Isa. 63:12, 14; II Sam. 7:23; Jer. 32:20; Neh. 9:10; Baruch 2:11. **As at this day:** I.e., thy renown is still with us in memory of all thou hast done for thy people (cf. Ps. 44:1 ff.). Bevan notes how much this recollection of God's acts in past days, particularly his deliverance of the people from Egypt, contributed toward arousing the enthusiasm of the Jews for the Maccabean revolt.

16. Central in the writer's thought in this supplication is the holy city. It is the navel of the earth and should be the glory thereof, but by reason of the sins of the people it is a thing of mockery to the nations round about.

Thy righteous acts: Lit., **thy righteousnesses,** i.e., all those righteous acts, those mighty works God has wrought for his people to vindicate his cause (cf. Judg. 5:11; I Sam. 12:7; Mic. 6:5; Ps. 103:6). Some suggest that here it means "thy charity" in the strict sense, whence Theod., ἐλεημοσύνη.

Thy city: So again in vss. 19, 24. In Isa. 45:13 Yahweh calls it "my city." **Thy holy hill:** So again in vs. 20; Pss. 2:6; 15:1; 43:3. This **mountain** of the Lord was the navel of the earth on which Yahweh's sanctuary stood (Ps. 48:2) and will stand again on the last day (Isa. 2:2 ff.; 27:13; 66:20; Obad. 21; Mic. 4:7; Rev. 14:1). With **our sins** and the **iniquities of our fathers** cf. Neh. 9:2. **A byword:** *Ḥerpāh* is an object of **reproach** or shame (cf. Pss. 44:13; 79:4; II Sam. 13:13). It occurs again in 11:18, where it is translated "insolence," and in 12:2, where it is rendered "shame." The writer from his position in Palestine is thinking of how the treatment the Jews had received at the hands of Antiochus had drawn forth jeers and taunts from the neighboring peoples of Edom and Ammon (see I Macc. 5:1-8). This matter is alluded to again in 11:41.

17. Within the city the writer thinks particularly of the **sanctuary,** which was the center of the cult. **Hearken:** Reminiscent of I Kings 8:28; Neh. 1:6, 11 (cf. Baruch 2:14). The **prayer of thy servant** recalls the stories of Abraham in Gen. 18 and Moses in Exod. 32, where Yahweh was willing to hearken to the prayer of a devoted servant (cf. Jas. 5:16). **Cause thy face to shine upon** goes back to Num. 6:25 (cf. Pss. 67:1; 80:3; 119:135). It is the same type of idiomatic expression as the sweetening of the face in vs. 13. **Thy sanctuary, which is desolate:** So Lam. 5:18; I Macc. 4:38. This is not the word

18 O my God, incline thine ear, and hear; open thine eyes, and behold our desolations, and the city which is called by thy name: for we do not present our supplications before thee for our righteousnesses, but for thy great mercies.

19 O Lord, hear; O Lord, forgive; O Lord, hearken and do; defer not, for thine own sake, O my God: for thy city and thy people are called by thy name.

20 ¶ And while I was speaking, and praying, and confessing my sin and the sin of my people Israel, and presenting my supplication before the Lord my God for the holy mountain of my God;

thy sanctuary, which is desolate. 18 O my God, incline thy ear and hear; open thy eyes and behold our desolations, and the city which is called by thy name; for we do not present our supplications before thee on the ground of our righteousness, but on the ground of thy great mercy. 19 O Lord, hear; O Lord, forgive; O Lord, give heed and act; delay not, for thy own sake, O my God, because thy city and thy people are called by thy name."

20 While I was speaking and praying, confessing my sin and the sin of my people Israel, and presenting my supplication before the Lord my God for the holy hill of

---

for desolate which we had in vs. 2, but *shāmēm,* the word that is used in Lam. 5:18; many therefore think it was used here deliberately to hint at the "abomination of desolation" of vs. 27; 8:13; 11:31; 12:11.

For thy own sake, O Lord: This translation follows Theod. and the Vulg.; the M.T. has **for the Lord's sake.** The expression recurs in vs. 19. Many editors treat this as a gloss which should be deleted. The LXX reads "for thy servants' sake" (cf. Isa. 63:17). For the phrase see Isa. 37:35; 43:25; 48:11; Jer. 14:7; Ezek. 20:9.

18-19. The opening words are almost identical with those of II Kings 19:16 (cf. Baruch 2:16). **Hear** is the "hearken" of vs. 17 and the "listened" of vs. 6. **Desolations** is from the same root as the word in vs. 17. It occurs again in vs. 26 and is used in the same sense in Isa. 49:19; 61:4. **Which is called by thy name:** Lit., "over which thy name has been called." So in vs. 19. The implication is that God has conquered it and made it his own. The same idea appears in II Sam. 12:28; Jer. 25:29; Amos 9:12, and is one that appears early in the Near East. The expression is used of the people of Israel as God's people (Deut. 28:10; Isa. 63:19; Jer. 14:9), and of the temple as peculiarly his (I Kings 8:43; 9:7; Jer. 7:10, 14, 30; Deut. 12:5). At the root of it is the idea of using the personal name to indicate possession (cf. Isa. 4:1).

Present our supplications: Lit., "causing our supplications to fall." So in vs. 20. The idiom occurs in Jer. 36:7; 37:20; 38:26; 42:2, 9 (cf. Baruch 2:19). Some think that this idiom arises from the fact that in an Oriental land a petitioner falls down before the potentate to whom the petition is being made. The petition here is presented not on the ground that men have any rights but **on the ground of thy great mercy** (cf. II Sam. 24:14; Ps. 119:156). The expression here is similar to that in Neh. 9:19, 27, 31.

Vs. 19 has often been compared with Ps. 51:1, the O.T. *Kyrie eleison.* The phraseology of the opening words is parallel to that in I Kings 8. **Give heed** or "attend" is a word often used in the psalms.

2. The Vision (9:20-27)

a) The Coming of Gabriel (9:20-23)

20. This is a connecting verse. Vs. 21 could follow naturally after vs. 3 but the insertion of the prayer necessitated the connecting vs. 4 at the beginning and this verse at the conclusion. It is a summary of the content of the prayer.

---

both, and a God of justice must be both Judge and Father. Actually it would destroy the whole order of the universe if God ever failed to fulfill his word of punishment on sin.

18. *No Bargaining with God.*—Not on human acts do we build our hope, but on God's acts. The bargaining spirit of much religion is here repudiated. We are now in the presence of the

21 Yea, while I *was* speaking in prayer, even the man Gabriel, whom I had seen in the vision at the beginning, being caused to fly swiftly, touched me about the time of the evening oblation.

22 And he informed *me*, and talked with me, and said, O Daniel, I am now come forth to give thee skill and understanding.

23 At the beginning of thy supplications the commandment came forth, and I am come to show *thee;* for thou *art* greatly beloved: therefore understand the matter, and consider the vision.

my God; 21 while I was speaking in prayer, the man Gabriel, whom I had seen in the vision at the first, came to me in swift flight at the time of the evening sacrifice. 22 He came[u] and he said to me, "O Daniel, I have now come out to give you wisdom and understanding. 23 At the beginning of your supplications a word went forth, and I have come to tell it to you, for you are greatly beloved; therefore consider the word and understand the vision.

[u] Gk Syr: Heb *made to understand*

21. The acts of contrition and prayer bring on the vision. The same angel who had appeared in ch. 8 appears again to explain the prophecy of the seventy years. **The man Gabriel:** He is called a man because he had appeared in 8:15 in human form. "In the vision previously": The same expression was used in 8:1. **Came to me:** Lit., "was making his way to me." In 8:7; 12:12 *nāgha'* has the meaning "to come near" (cf. Jonah 3:6; Job 4:5). In 8:18; 10:16, however, it means "to touch," which Theod. and some modern interpreters take as the meaning here.

In swift flight: This is probably the best solution of the puzzling מֻעָף בִּיעָף. Theod., Peshitta, and Vulg. all render by "flying," taking מֻעָף to be from the root עוּף, **to fly.** Yet angels in the O.T. do not usually fly. In fact Gen. 28:12 seems to assume that they do not have wings. Moreover this explanation makes the succeeding word בִּיעָף even more difficult. Others therefore take מֻעָף to be from a root יָעַף, "to hasten," so the phrase would mean "making his way to me, being caused to hasten with haste." However this root יָעַף does not normally mean "to hasten," but "to be weary"; some connect the phrase with Daniel, making him say that he had earlier seen the angel when "exhausted with an exhaustion," referring either to his swoon in 8:17-18 or perhaps to his present state of weariness after all this prayer and fasting. To refer the phrase thus to Daniel does not fit very well, and angels of course do not get weary, so the most probable solution is that there is textual corruption here and the versions were correct in understanding it that Gabriel came in swift flight from heaven. Since in Enoch 61 angels appear with wings, the figures of the seraphim and the cherubim had wings, and there is abundant pictorial evidence from the ancient Near East of supernatural beings with wings, it might well be that at the time of this writer angels were popularly thought of as winged (see Rev. 14:6).

At the time of the evening sacrifice is a detail to particularize the vision, just as in 8:2 the place of it is particularized. The reference is to the evening oblation (II Kings 16:15; Ezra 9:4-5), one of the hours of prayer noticed in 6:10. It was probably the writer's purpose to call the attention of the audience to this matter of the abolition of the daily sacrifices.

22-23. The angel explains the reason for his visit. **He came and he said to me** follows the LXX and Peshitta. The M.T. reads, "and he instructed and spoke with me and said." **To give you wisdom and understanding:** Lit., "to teach thee insight,"

doctrine that men must be saved by faith. This is the contradiction of humanism, which seems to believe that religion is only a human affair. We can have no confidence in our actions until they are undergirded by what God has done.

23. *Knowledge and Love.*—We will not do violence to the spirit of the book of Daniel if we

suggest that there is a close relationship between knowledge and love. Only one who has great love for God is able to learn of him, and only because we are loved of him are we given visions of truth. The plain man who has a deep love for God and men can see through to the central meanings of events, while his more

24 Seventy weeks are determined upon thy people and upon thy holy city, to finish the transgression, and to make an end of sins, and to make reconciliation for iniq-

24 "Seventy weeks of years are decreed concerning your people and your holy city, to finish the transgression, to put an end

---

i.c, he was to open the seer's **understanding.** From the "books" Daniel had seen (vs. 2) there was a prophecy about seventy years of desolation. Now he was to be given insight that he might understand the true significance of these words hitherto not understood.

Angels do not come of their own accord; they are "messengers" who are sent, and Gabriel was sent because Daniel's prayer had been heard and God had commanded Gabriel to go and explain matters to him. No sooner had the seer begun his petition than God responded.

A word went forth: Viz., God's command to Gabriel to take the revelation to Daniel. The words are the Hebrew equivalent of the Aramaic in 2:13. The expression is used of human commands in Esth. 7:8 and of the divine word in Isa. 45:23; 55:11. Some think the **word** is the divine declaration in vss. 24-27, but that matter was not determined in answer to any prayer; it was something long since settled in the counsel and foreknowledge of God. Just when the hour of the end would strike was something hidden from angels as well as from men (Matt. 24:36), but the seer will be given a hint of it, so the angel says **I have come to tell. To you** is not in the M.T., though it is found in some MSS and is needed for the text which underlies the versions.

Greatly beloved: Cf. 10:11, 19. The word is a passive participle, used elsewhere in the O.T. only for things longed for, desired, coveted, the reference being to human desire, not to God, save in Ps. 68:16. Yet it may mean an object of affection and so indicate here that Daniel was precious in God's sight. **Consider** and **understand** are two forms of the same verb. The seer is bidden to "heed" the word that will be spoken to him and to "give heed" to the **vision.**

b) THE EXPLANATION OF THE SEVENTY WEEKS (9:24-27)

24. The angel's revelation is given metrically. Its substance is that the **seventy weeks** are to be understood as seventy hebdomads or **weeks of years;** i.e., they represent 490 years, the conclusion of which will see the coming of the end.

Seventy weeks of years: Lit., **seventy weeks,** which the sequel shows means **weeks of years.** The Greeks and Romans had a similar idea of a ἑβδομάς or week-year (Aristotle *Politics* VII. 16; Gellius *Attic Nights* III. 10). It is commonly thought that the writer derived this from Lev. 25:2; 26:18-35. The emphasis on the seven times that Israel was to be punished might well have suggested that it would last seven times Jeremiah's seventy years, and this would connect easily with the sabbatical year of Lev. 25. Indeed, the way was prepared for this by the manner in which in II Chr. 36:21 the seventy years of Jeremiah are calculated as starting with the destruction of Jerusalem in 586 and fulfilled under Cyrus, so that further destruction must mean that a yet further date is to be awaited. Some think that the seventy hebdomads should be calculated from the date of the prophecy, i.e., from the first year of Darius, but others think it is merely a round number, the writer not meaning to give any definite prediction.

Are decreed: Have been determined. The seventy hebdomads are an allotted span, and when they have been completed various things will happen. The verb is used in this way only in Daniel in the O.T. but frequently in later Jewish literature. **Concerning your people and your holy city** might suggest that the writer had in view merely the freeing of the people from Seleucid control and the restoration of the city and temple. Junker (*Untersuchungen,* p. 73) is doubtless right, however, in insisting that the writer has in view the final consummation. The antithetic arrangement of the details suggests this, for the six matters of the decree are stylistically arranged as three assertions about the removal of evil and three statements about the benefits to be brought by the coming of the ideal time.

uity, and to bring in everlasting righteousness, and to seal up the vision and prophecy,
and to anoint the Most Holy.

25 Know therefore and understand, *that*
from the going forth of the commandment
to restore and to build Jerusalem, unto the

to sin, and to atone for iniquity, to bring
in everlasting righteousness, to seal both
vision and prophet, and to anoint a most
holy place.*v* 25 Know therefore and understand that from the going forth of the word

v Or *thing* or *one*

To finish the transgression: To bring the profanation to an end (cf. 8:23). *Pésha'*
is **sin** or wickedness and so **transgression.** The narrower reference is to the heathen cult
set up in the temple by Antiochus (I Macc. 1:54; II Macc. 6:5), but the wider reference
is to the whole outrage on true religion. **To put an end to sin:** Lit., "to seal up sins" or,
with the *Qerê,* "to abolish sins." For sealing up sin see Job 14:17, and cf. Deut. 32:34.
If sealing sins means reserving them for punishment, this was precisely what would
happen at the grand assizes at the end of time. **To atone for iniquity:** *'Āwôn* is the
word used for iniquity in vss. 13, 16, referring to the iniquities of the people. *Kipper*
is a technical legal term with reference to atonement for sin. From a root meaning
"to cover" it acquires the sense of "to absolve," "to cancel" in a legal fashion. These are
the three negative elements in the decree: (*a*) the bringing to an end this flouting of
God and interfering with the cult; (*b*) the dealing with sin so that its reign ends; (*c*)
the wiping out of the old score that had been piled up by iniquity. To balance these
are three positive elements.

To bring in everlasting righteousness: This expression is without parallel in the
O.T. Driver suggests that it sums up in one phrase the teaching of such passages as
Isa. 4:3 ff.; 32:16-17; 33:24. *Çédheq* is again a legalistic term. Vs. 7 said that righteousness
belongs to God alone, and the righteousness of God can come only as a gift (as Paul
taught in Romans), so men are assured that in the messianic kingdom such an eternal
righteousness will be God's gift to men. **To seal both vision and prophet:** To seal a
vision or a prophet is to ratify or confirm the message (see John 3:33; 6:27, and Paul
calling his converts the seal of his apostleship in I Cor. 9:2). This common metaphor
is derived from the ancient custom of attaching a seal to a document in attestation of
its genuineness (cf. I Kings 21:8; Jer. 32:10-11). The coming messianic kingdom will
be the ratification of all the visions of seers and prophecies of prophets in which its
coming was foretold. Some take the meaning as "to seal up" in the sense of "to stop,"
just as above we had a sealing of sin; i.e., once the kingdom has come the era of prophecy
will be at an end, for all has been fulfilled and no further visions or prophecies will be
necessary. In either case the writer is probably playing on the use of the word in his
positive and negative lists. **To anoint a most holy place:** Lit., "and to anoint a holy of
holies." To anoint is to consecrate. The expression is used of the altar and of various
objects used in cult ceremonies (Exod. 29:36; 30:26-28; 40:9-15; Lev. 8:10-12), but
it is also used of persons, such as the king (II Sam. 5:17), the high priest (Num. 35:25),
the prophet (Isa. 61:1), the priest (Exod. 30:30; Lev. 16:32). A "holy of holies" is of
course a most holy place, for which reason the tent of meeting, the temple, the altar, all
bear this name in the O.T. (Exod. 29–30; 38; Ezek. 43:12). The narrower reference here
is to the cleansing and rededication of the temple that had been polluted and perhaps,
as Obbink urges, to the altar in particular. The wider reference is to the new temple of
the messianic kingdom (Isa. 60:7; Ezek. 40:2 ff.; Hag. 2:1-9). The early Christian
interpreters usually took this phrase to mean **to anoint the Most Holy,** i.e., the Messiah,
a view held also by some medieval Jewish commentators. It refers, however, to a **place,**
not a person.

25-27. The events of the seventy hebdomads are now specified. They fall into three
periods of seven, sixty-two, and one. In these verses the versions depart widely from
the M.T. Some have been inclined to follow them rather than the M.T., but in spite
of its difficulties, the M.T. is on the whole to be preferred. (*a*) The first seven weeks
begin with the proclamation of God and the coming of an anointed prince. (*b*) The

Messiah the Prince, *shall be* seven weeks, and threescore and two weeks: the street shall be built again, and the wall, even in troublous times.

to restore and build Jerusalem to the coming of an anointed one, a prince, there shall be seven weeks. Then for sixty-two weeks it shall be built again with squares and moat,

---

next sixty-two are occupied with the building of the city. (*c*) The last week is the time of the catastrophe: An anointed one shall be cut off; an army shall come and destroy city and sanctuary, while war desolates all; the enemy leaders shall make a covenant with some; for half the week the appointed sacrifices shall be suspended and an abomination take their place; finally the leaders shall be destroyed. The revelation is preceded by a solemn adjuration.

The **word** here is that spoken by God to Jeremiah (30:18; 31:38). The dates would suggest either 604 B.C. or 596 B.C. as the starting point for the calculation, but the writer clearly means to start from 586 B.C., the date of the destruction of the temple, so perhaps he is referring to some prophecy of Jeremiah which we no longer have in our collection. For the **going forth of the word** see Isa. 55:11. The same expression as was used in vs. 23 (cf. 2:13).

Montgomery notes that here we have an instance of the double interpretation of a prophecy. The prediction of Jeremiah is regarded as having been partially fulfilled through the restoration of the temple by those who returned under Cyrus, and still to be fulfilled in the coming restoration at the end. In the first restoration the fabric of the temple had been restored, but the promised era of felicity had not dawned, and there must be a further fulfillment yet to come.

To restore and build Jerusalem: So a little later **it shall be built again** is, lit., "it shall be restored and built." The verb for **to restore** is that used for bringing people back, not for the establishment of things, and is the verb used in the O.T. for the restoring of the exiles. A very small emendation would result in the verb "to people," and this is preferred by many editors (cf. Isa. 44:26; Jer. 30:18; Ezek. 36:10-11, 33). After the treatment the city had received at the hands of Antiochus, it would be necessary to repeople it before commencing to rebuild, as indeed had been the case in the days of Nehemiah. Another suggested emendation would make the text correspond with what apparently was read by the Peshitta and Vulg., viz., "to build again," i.e., "to return to the building of."

To the coming of an anointed one, a prince: Lit., "unto an anointed one, a Prince." Here there are two technical terms. The word *māshîaḥ,* "he who has been anointed," is used in the O.T. for leaders of the people who were initiated into their office by a ceremonial anointing with oil, just as the cult accessories were consecrated to their sacerdotal use by being so anointed. Figuratively the word could be used of those whom God employed for carrying out his purposes even though they had not been ceremonially anointed by the hands of men, for they had been, as it were, anointed by God himself. *Nāghîdh* means "one who goes in front," and is used for **prince,** "leader," "commander," "overseer" (cf. I Sam. 10:1; Ezek. 28:2; Jer. 20:1; I Chr. 13:1; II Chr. 11:11; 31:12).

There have been many theories as to the identity of this **prince.** Some take him to be Cyrus, who in Isa. 45:1 is the Lord's anointed, and who was the prince who allowed the exiles to go home. Others prefer the Zerubbabel of Hag. 1–2; Zech. 4, who in a special sense was the prince of the return. As early as Eusebius we find record of an idea that the reference must be to the line of Jewish high priests, and many therefore identify him with Joshua ben Jozadak, the contemporary of Zerubbabel, under whom the cult was re-established in Jerusalem in 538 B.C. (see Ezra 2:2; 3:2; Hag. 1:1 ff.; Zech. 3:1), and from whose day down to the time of Antiochus there did not cease to be a *nāghîdh māshîaḥ* in Jerusalem. Since, however, it is our word **Messiah,** it was inevitable that earlier Christian commentators should see in this **anointed one** a reference to the coming of Jesus, an interpretation which still has its ardent supporters, but which could hardly have been in the writer's mind.

26 And after threescore and two weeks shall Messiah be cut off, but not for himself: and the people of the prince that shall come shall destroy the city and the sanc-

but in a troubled time. 26 And after the sixty-two weeks, an anointed one shall be cut off, and shall have nothing; and the people of the prince who is to come shall

---

Seven weeks: Seven hebdomads are to elapse between the issue of the command and the arrival of the prince. The reading "seven and sixty-two weeks" as a single numeral goes against the Masoretic punctuation but is preferred by some. The arrival of the prince initiates the rebuilding program. The rebuilt city will continue inhabited, with its markets and streets functioning normally, for **sixty-two** hebdomads. It is little use to calculate mathematically from these figures by our modern datings, for the Jews in this period were hazy about dates and we have no means of knowing what year the writer would have considered that from which to calculate the sixty-two. Bentzen suggests that he gives this figure because he had in mind the period of the Aaronic princes.

With squares and moat: The versions did not know what to make of these two words, and their renderings are merely guesses. They all take both words with what precedes about the building of the city. Some modern editors, however, wish to take the first with what precedes and the second with what follows. The word רחוב is from a root meaning "wide," "spacious," and is fairly rendered by the πλατεῖα of Theod. Every Oriental city had such open spaces in which markets were held on certain days. They are mentioned in the O.T. in Jer. 5:1; Song of S. 3:2; Nah. 2:4. The word חרוץ, from a root "to cut," is normally a "ditch," though it could be **moat** or "trench," a meaning which it has in the Zakir inscription. Some would therefore take it here as "city moat," though it is not clear what evidence there is for a moat having ever formed part of the defenses of Jerusalem. Montgomery suggests that it is the great cut in the natural rock along the northern wall of the city, which was part of its defenses, and might have come under this name. Theod. has τεῖχος, "wall," and a possible emendation of the Hebrew would give this meaning. An even slighter emendation would give the word "streets," which would agree with the reading underlying the Peshitta, and has the advantage that "broad places" and "streets" are mentioned together elsewhere. In any case, the writer means that the city will be built, both its inner and its outer portions, to function as a normal city.

But in a troubled time: Lit., "and in the straitness of the times." In the M.T. this is part of the previous sentence, and so taken would mean that the rebuilt city would function even through **troublous times.** But it may be looking ahead and thus mean that the city will continue even in the distress of the great tribulation that precedes the end. The word צוק is peculiar. The LXX and Peshitta evidently read it קץ, and many editors so emend the text, whereby "at the end of the times" goes more naturally with what follows than with what goes before.

26. The passing of the **sixty-two** hebdomads brings us into the last days which precede the end. These last days occupy one hebdomad which many take as 171-164 B.C., since the events which the writer mentions all fall within these dates.

An anointed one shall be cut off: The verb is used to denote the cutting off by death (Exod. 12:15, 19; Num. 9:13; Ps. 37:28, 38), though conceivably the cutting off might mean deposition from office. The **anointed one** here must be someone other than the one mentioned in vs. 25, since sixty-two hebdomads have intervened. There is a further reference to him in 11:22. The audience doubtless understood who was meant, but we are left to conjecture. Some think it means a king, and have suggested Seleucus Philopator, who died in 175 B.C. The more common opinion, however, is that it refers to the cutting off of the legitimate line of high priests. In this case there are three possibilities: first, the cutting off of the regular succession by the elevation of Jason in 175 (II Macc. 4:7-10); second, the interruption caused by the installation of Menelaus in 172 (II Macc. 4:23-29); and third, the murder of the legitimate high priest Onias III, ca. 170 (II Macc. 4:33-38). The probabilities are that it refers to Onias, whose unjust

tuary; and the end thereof *shall be* with a flood, and unto the end of the war desolations are determined.

destroy the city and the sanctuary. Its[w] end shall come with a flood, and to the end there shall be war; desolations are decreed.

[w] Or *his*

---

deposition and murder deeply affected the people. This, however, is only the narrower meaning of the writer. To him these days are the last days, the days of the great tribulation preceding the end, and prophecies concerning that great tribulation had foretold how the leader of the people would be cut off (Hos. 3:4; Zech. 13:7-9).

And shall have nothing: Lit., "and there is nothing to him." What this means no one knows for sure, and it is possible that something has dropped from the text. The words have been variously interpreted: **but not for himself,** i.e., he shall die vicariously; "though there was nothing against him," i.e., there was no reason for his being cut off (cf. Theod., "and that without judgment"); "and he shall have no one," i.e., there will be no true successor; "and he shall cease to be," so LXX, "and shall be no more"; "and he shall be no longer remembered," a reminiscence of Ezek. 21:32. Others emend the text to read "though guiltless" or "without a helper." The Peshitta seems to refer the phrase to the city of Jerusalem, "and she [i.e., the city] shall have him not." The RSV, **and shall have nothing,** renders the words fairly literally and perhaps means that with his death the true high priestly office came to an end. There may also be some wider reference. One type of exegesis has always found in the passage a reference to the death of Jesus, though this could not have been what the writer meant his audience to understand.

The people of the prince who is to come: This is the word *nāghîdh,* but **the prince** here is distinguished from the previous one in vs. 25 because he is one **who is to come.** Since the first *nāghîdh* seems to refer to a priestly ruler some insist that the reference must be the same here (cf. 11:22). This, however, would necessitate changing *'am,* **people,** to *'im,* "with," and make the sentence mean that city and sanctuary will be destroyed along with the anointed high priest. Of course they were not, and in any case it is awkward to connect this with the earlier part of the verse. A *nāghîdh* can be a secular leader quite as well as a priestly leader, and the natural meaning is that the word refers to some hostile prince whose coming will be disastrous to city and sanctuary. Some have looked on this as a prophecy of the destruction later wrought by the Romans, but most probably it is a reference to the armies of Antiochus who fired the city gates, dismantled many of the fortifications, and damaged seriously both city and sanctuary (I Macc. 1:31-38; 3:45). The use of the word **people** for troops is normal (cf. Judg. 7:1; 9:48; II Sam. 10:13).

Shall destroy may be meant in a physical sense of smashing and destroying, but the verb can be used also, as it often is in the O.T., to mean "to corrupt," and here it may mean "he shall desecrate," referring to the behavior of the troops in the holy city (I Macc. 2:11-12; II Macc. 6:4-5). **Its end shall come:** Perhaps **his end,** the reference being to the death of Antiochus during his Persian campaign. Or if the prince is Jason, the reference would be to his miserable end (II Macc. 5:7-10). Some translate **its end,** referring to the city and sanctuary; others think that **end** means the end of all things and render "the end shall come."

With a flood: Cf. 11:22. If we read **his end,** the meaning is that he is swept away by the flood of divine judgment (cf. Nah. 1:8; Jer. 47:2 and the image of the overflowing in Isa. 8:8; 10:22). If we read **its end,** the meaning may be that the devastation of the Seleucid armies was as though a flood had overwhelmed the city (I Macc. 1:37-40; 2:8-13). If it is **the end,** then the war of Antiochus against the saints (7:21) is conceived of as part of the great tribulation, one of whose horrors is this flood of evil.

And to the end: To the end of the last hebdomad and the moment of the final consummation. This is the *qēç* of 8:17, 19. **There shall be war:** In later eschatology much was made of the great war which was part of the great tribulation. This is familiar to

27 And he shall confirm the covenant with many for one week: and in the midst of the week he shall cause the sacrifice and the oblation to cease, and for the overspreading of abominations he shall make *it* desolate, even until the consummation, and that determined shall be poured upon the desolate.

27 And he shall make a strong covenant with many for one week; and for half of the week he shall cause sacrifice and offering to cease; and upon the wing of abominations shall come one who makes desolate, until the decreed end is poured out on the desolator."

---

us from the popular conception of Armageddon, but has roots far back in the idea that all the bestial forces of evil and chaos which at the beginning fought against the introduction of orderliness at creation will make one last concerted effort at the end of time to prevent the coming of the new creation.

Desolations are decreed: Lit., "a sentence of desolations" (cf. Isa. 10:22; 28:22). *Neḥerāçāh,* which occurs again in 11:36, is from a root "to cut," and means something **decreed, determined,** "decided," hence a "sentence" that has been determined and will be carried out. **Desolations:** The same word occurs in vs. 18.

27. The final week (as two half weeks) refers to the years 171-164 B.C. **He shall make a strong covenant with many:** *Berîth* is the technical legal word for **covenant.** He would be Antiochus; **many,** the Hellenizing Jews who were apostate from Yahweh's covenant but made a covenant with the ruler (I Macc. 1:11-15). The verb is difficult. Some translate "he shall make burdensome the covenant for many," understanding it to mean that the persecutions will be so severe that the keeping of Yahweh's covenant will be burdensome to the faithful. Some emend the text to read "he will abolish the covenant for many," or "the covenant will be annulled for many," i.e., there will be a general apostasy such as later eschatology holds will be characteristic of the last days. Charles renders, "and a stringent statute shall be issued against the many," i.e., against the majority of Jews. What that statute is he thinks is explained in what now follows. The simplest explanation, however, is to refer it to the covenant of Antiochus with the Hellenizing Jews (cf. 11:30).

Half of the week: For three and a half years there will be, by command of Antiochus, cessation of sacrifice and obligation. This is the matter referred to in 8:11; and again in 11:31. It is described in I Macc. 1:54 ff. The words **sacrifice and offering** include all the different forms of cult sacrifice (I Sam. 2:29; 3:14; Ps. 40:6). From I Macc. 1:54; 4:52 ff. we gather that temple services were suspended from the fifteenth of Kislev, 168 B.C., to the twenty-fifth of Kislev, 165, which is near enough to the three and a half years. The figure is the same as in 7:25; 12:7, but it is difficult to see how all three passages can be made to refer to the same period, and perhaps each was three and a half years reckoned from a different point of time.

And upon the wing of abominations: As "on the wing" seems strange here, it is commonly emended to "and instead thereof," a phrase which occurs in 11:20, 21, 38. This would make the verse mean that, instead of the offering and sacrifice which were ordained, there would be offered the **abominations** of heathen sacrifice. This same meaning is obtained by emending the text to read "in their place." If we preserve the M.T., some suggest that the **wing** may be a wing of the temple, or the name of some structure within the temple. The LXX and Theod. have ἐπὶ τὸ ἱερόν, and the Vulg.,

---

sophisticated and learned brothers completely miss the truth. Over against the popular assumption that love is blind should be set the religious truth that love leads us into the inner meanings of human experience.

27. *An Appalling Abomination.*—This is the idol set up in the temple—a common theme throughout the whole Bible. Idols have a terrible fascination for men. We want to put something of our own creation in the place of God. This is the clue to the whole tragedy of humanity. It puts in the holy place the abomination of desolation, with the consequence that **the decreed end is poured out on the desolator.**

10 In the third year of Cyrus king of Persia a thing was revealed unto | **10** In the third year of Cyrus king of Persia a word was revealed to Daniel,

---

in templo. Since the Syrian *Ba'al Shāmēm,* which seems to be the origin of the "appalling abomination" of this book, is commonly pictured on monuments as an eagle, it may be that **wing** is correct, the reference being not to the temple but to some winged figure which had been set up therein. So we might translate, "and the wing of an appalling abomination shall rise up until . . . ."

Abominations: *Shiqqûçîm,* from the root "to be abominable," used as an opprobrious designation for idols in I Kings 11:7; II Kings 23:13; II Chr. 15:8; II Macc. 6:2, refers to the deed of Antiochus when he set up in the temple an image of the deity he called Zeus Olympius, which was not that Greek deity but a Hellenized variation of the ancient Canaanitish "God of Heaven." The common name for the latter was *Ba'al Shāmēm,* and it has been suggested that the *shiqqûç shômēm* of Daniel is a deliberate distortion of this name.

Shall come one who makes desolate: The M.T. has only "he who [or that which] makes desolate," which is usually taken as an adjective to the preceding word (read as a singular as in 11:31; 12:11; cf. 8:13), which gives "appalling abomination" (the "abomination of desolation" of Matt. 24:15) and suits the *shômēm* of 8:13; 12:11. If it is "one who desolates," it must refer to Antiochus himself.

"Until ruin and sentence are poured out upon that which [or him who] desolates." "Ruin and sentence" are quoted from Isa. 10:23; 28:22 (on "sentence" see vs. 26). Some would emend *'adh* to *'ōdh,* so as to read, "and afterwards ruin and sentence." On the pouring out see Exeg. on vs. 11. If the reading is "one who desolates," the reference must be to Antiochus and the sentence of his end which is soon to be fulfilled. Some object that it cannot refer to a person; in that case "that which" will refer to the abomination of desolation, or perhaps to the desolating distress under which the faithful had been groaning. Others would emend the text to read, "upon him that set them up," i.e., on Antiochus. In any case, the point of the message is that this goes on only so long as God allows. A limit has been set, and when that limit has been reached, destruction will inevitably come.

D. THE VISION OF THE LAST DAYS (10:1–12:13)

Chs. 10–12 are really only one vision: ch. 10 is the prologue; ch. 11, the vision and its interpretation; and ch. 12, the epilogue. Its somewhat unwieldly length doubtless suggested the division into three parts, but the division is artificial, for there is no real break in the sense after either 10:21 or 11:45.

The vision is dated, but again the date is merely part of the framework, intended to connect it with the other chapters, but having no significance for the material here presented. It differs from those in chs. 7–8 in that any direct description is missing. We gather that it was an astounding visual perception of a great warfare in heavenly places, and from the interpretation we learn that it was revealed to the seer that struggles among the nations here on earth are but the counterpart of struggles among their angelic patrons in the heavens, events here being determined by the pattern of events above. The details of this vision, however, are not given. After spiritual preparation accompanied by ascetic practices, the seer has a second vision in which an angel expounds the meaning of the things he has seen and tells of things which are to be.

The message of ch. 10 is precisely the same as that of those which have preceded it. Certain relevant portions of the history of the Diadochi are given in order to lead up to Antiochus Epiphanes. His reign and his relations with the Jews are then dealt with in more detail than in the earlier chapters. The connection of all this with the doings of the celestial powers is brought out, to prepare for the announcement that the climax is at hand, when the kingdoms of this world will be brought to an end by the advent of the kingdom of God, the kingdom which is eternal and so is beyond history.

Daniel, whose name was called Belteshazzar; and the thing *was* true, but the time appointed *was* long: and he understood the thing, and had understanding of the vision.

who was named Belteshaz'zar. And the word was true, and it was a great conflict. And he understood the word and had understanding of the vision.

---

1. PROLOGUE (10:1-21)
a) CHRONOLOGICAL SETTING (10:1)

10:1. The date is given as **the third year of Cyrus,** i.e., the third year after he took Babylon, and so 536/535 B.C. However, since the writer calculates a reign of Darius the Mede between Belshazzar son of Nabonidus and Cyrus we cannot say what date he would have regarded as the third of Cyrus. Vs. 1 is by the redactor, for Daniel begins to speak in the first person in vs. 2. This is the latest date the writer gives in connection with Daniel's life. Assuming him to have been a youth of sixteen when brought into captivity in 605 B.C., he would now, on our reckoning, be a man of eighty-six. Neither the writer nor his audience, however, would ever have made such a calculation or been interested in the matter. One has the impression that they were expected to think of the seer at each of his appearances as in the fullness of his strength. The literary sense of the LXX translator was struck, however, by the fact that in 1:21 we have the statement that Daniel continued to the first year of Cyrus, which he took to refer to the time of the seer's death, and so altered the text to "in the first year." The statement in 1:21 may mean only that Daniel continued in office until the first year of Cyrus and then retired; but even if it does mean that he died then, such small discrepancies in the framework are common in apocalyptic writing and of no significance. The verse implies that Daniel had not returned to Palestine with the exiles who went back home, for here **in the third year of Cyrus** he is still in Mesopotamia.

Cyrus is here called **king of Persia.** This may be merely a statement of fact, for he was king of Persia, but if it is meant as an official title it is an anachronism in the mouth of Daniel. The title **king of Persia** was Hellenistic usage and not the usage of the Achaemenid kings at this time (see Arthur Christensen, "Die Iranier" in *Kulturgeschichte des alten Orients* III. 1 [München: C. H. Beck 'sche Verlagsbuchhandlung, 1933], p. 253).

A word: In 4:33 (M.T. 4:30) the Aramaic equivalent was used for the "sentence" (KJV "thing") that was fulfilled on Nebuchadrezzar, and in 9:23 of a "word" (KJV "matter") to which Daniel was to give heed. Thus this is the "word of the divine oracle," a divine pronouncement. The wording of this verse seems to have 9:23 in mind.

To call the seer by his Babylonian name links this final vision to the earlier part of the book and was probably deliberately done to that end.

The word was true, and it was a great conflict: Lit., "and the word is truth and a great host." This phrase has been translated in many ways. The LXX has "the vision and the word are true." **True** is *'emeth,* as in 8:26, where the vision of the evenings and mornings is asserted to have been true. The word was true with the absolute truth of God's pronouncements and so was part of the inevitability of things. The noun *dābhār,* of course, can mean a "matter" or **thing,** and so refer to the substance of the vision, i.e., "the matter which I saw in the vision was true." The word *çābhā'* means "host," and in its primary sense refers to military matters, whence comes the idea that it has to do with **a great conflict.** In Isa. 40:2; Job 7:1 it is used metaphorically of toil and sorrow, and it is used in connection with temple service in Num. 4:23 ff.; 8:24-25. Thus it is an ambiguous word which may refer to some charge or obligation of service laid on Daniel as a result of his vision, or it may refer to the stress and strain felt at the onset of a revelation, or it may mean some great host of angels involved in this matter. If we refer it to the context of the vision, it would seem to be concerned with the great warfare in heaven whose pattern is reproduced in conflicts on earth. Since the writer is interested in the last days, this is the most likely interpretation, for the **great conflict** is characteristic of the last days (Matt. 24:6).

2 In those days I Daniel was mourning three full weeks.

3 I ate no pleasant bread, neither came flesh nor wine in my mouth, neither did I anoint myself at all, till three whole weeks were fulfilled.

4 And in the four and twentieth day of the first month, as I was by the side of the great river, which is Hiddekel;

2 In those days I, Daniel, was mourning for three weeks. 3 I ate no delicacies, no meat or wine entered my mouth, nor did I anoint myself at all, for the full three weeks. 4 On the twenty-fourth day of the first month, as I was standing on the bank of the

---

He understood: The verbal form here is peculiar. It may be an imperative, but most interpreters take it as a form of the perfect. He "gave heed" to the word. In 8:27 the same verb is rendered "understand," in 9:2 "perceived," in 12:8 "understand," but "give heed" would fit all these passages.

Vision: The word is *mar'eh,* and Ginsberg again translates "oracle." Charles notes that in apocalyptic vision is the conventional term for the content of a message, and we do not have to think of everything therein as acually seen.

b) THE PREPARATION FOR A REVELATION (10:2-9)

2-3. The seer has had his vision, has given it heed and understood it, but its significance can be given only by revelation. From vs. 12 we learn that he set himself to obtain such a revelation, preparing himself by ascetic practices such as those mentioned in 9:3. **In those days** presumably means those of the third year of Cyrus, but as it is introduction to the "I" section, the meaning should not be pressed. **Mourning:** Earlier expositors discussed whether this was mourning for the sins of the people as in 9:5 (cf. Ezra 10:6), or mourning because of the dreadful things that were going to happen. Mourning, however, is a synonym for fasting (Matt. 9:14-15) and here refers to the ascetic practices of vs. 3, which in vs. 12 are called a "humbling." The writer has in mind much the same spiritual preparation as was mentioned in 9:3 (see also Ascension of Isaiah 2:11 ff.; II Esdras 9:26-27; II Baruch 12:5; 21:1; 47:2).

Three weeks: Lit., "three weeks days." For the expression (KJV **full**) see Gen. 41:1; Deut. 21:13; II Sam. 13:23; 14:28; Jer. 28:3, 11. Possibly there is no special significance in the number of weeks. It was not a complete fast, but a diet of bread and water, as it were. He ate no "bread of daintiness," which is the opposite of that "bread of affliction" mentioned in Deut. 16:3. **Flesh** and **wine** were indications of luxurious living. Anointing with unguents was also a luxurious practice, and so was omitted from the daily delights during mourning (II Sam. 14:2; Judith 10:3), its resumption being a sign that the period of mourning was ended (II Sam. 12:20; Isa. 61:3). The verse assumes that Daniel was accustomed to use meat and wine, but for these three weeks of special abstinence he gave them up. There is no need, however, to labor this as inconsistent with 1:8 ff., where it is said that Daniel and his friends ate only vegetable food at the court so as to avoid risk of possible defilement from ritually unclean meat. This detail is merely part of the *décor.* The point is that the revelation was preceded by a period of ascetic abstinence and mention is therefore made of those things from which a man in his position would be likely to abstain.

At all in English represents the infinitive absolute of the Hebrew. Ginsberg (*Studies,* p. 60) may be right in thinking that the underlying Aramaic read, "neither did I anoint myself with oil."

4. That the date and place of the vision are given with such exactitude is part of the convention of apocalyptic and need not bear any special significance. The **first month** would be that which is called "Abib" in Deut. 16:1 and "Nisan" in Neh. 2:1; Esth. 3:7. If **the twenty-fourth day** is supposed to mark the end of the seer's fast, then his period of fasting would have included the Passover festival on the fourteenth, that of Unleavened Bread from the fifteenth to the twenty-first, and so the days when according to Deut.

5 Then I lifted up mine eyes, and looked, and behold a certain man clothed in linen, whose loins *were* girded with fine gold of Uphaz:

6 His body also *was* like the beryl, and his face as the appearance of lightning, and his eyes as lamps of fire, and his arms

great river, that is, the Tigris, 5 I lifted up my eyes and looked, and behold, a man clothed in linen, whose loins were girded with gold of Uphaz. 6 His body was like beryl, his face like the appearance of light-

---

16:3 the "bread of affliction" should be eaten. **Standing** is an interpretation, for the text merely says **I was.** In 8:1-3 Daniel was taken in spirit to the Ulai, but here it would seem that he was actually present in body at the river bank. **On the bank:** Lit., "on the hand," which may mean merely **by the side of. The great river** would normally mean the Euphrates (Gen. 15:18; Josh. 1:4), but here is doubtless the "stream" of 12:5-7. It is rather curious that these angelic visions are associated with water in chs. 8; 10; 12. Zoroaster is said to have received the vision of Ormazd on the bank of the Daitya (Dinkart 7:3, 31; 8:60; 9:23; Zatsparam 21:4, 8-9), and Enoch had his vision by the waters at Dan (Enoch 13:7 ff.).

That is, the Tigris: Lit., **which is Hiddekel** (cf. Gen. 2:14). This seems to be an early gloss. Babylon is on the Euphrates, which is where Daniel might be expected to be, not on the Tigris, some fifty miles away. The Peshitta has "Euphrates" here, but both the LXX and Theod. have **Tigris,** so it must belong to the early form of the story.

5. Here as in 8:3 the seer lifted up his eyes to look. **A man:** Not human, but an angel in human form. This is generally taken to be the Gabriel of 8:15-16, an identification favored by a comparison of what is said here in vss. 11, 13-14, 21 with 8:15-16; 9:21 ff. Charles notes, however, that he is never named in this chapter, but is like the nameless angel who appears in the Testaments of the Twelve Patriarchs, some personage of pre-eminent dignity among the celestials. The description given here seems to transcend that given of Gabriel in the earlier chapters, and his appearance had a graver effect on the seer than that of Gabriel had, which suggests some supernatural being superior to Gabriel and Michael and carefully distinguished by the writer from them. Early Christian commentators saw in this figure the Messiah Jesus.

The description of him has many reminiscences of the figures in Ezek. 1; 9–10. His clothing resembles that of a high priest (Lev. 6:10; Exod. 28:39; cf. I Sam. 2:18; 22:18), which apparently means that he is a celestial high priest (see Rev. 1:13; 15:6). The celestial visitant in Ezek. 9:2-3, 11; 10:2, 6-7 wore fine linen. Perhaps what is meant is the ancient ritual loincloth, for the word used is a special development from a root meaning "part," "portion." Charles suggests that the **linen** garment is meant to suggest the angelic body of light (Ps. 104:2; Mark 16:5). Around his waist was a girdle of gold. Such girdles are familiar from figures in the art of the ancient Near East, where the girdles are often ornamented with precious stones. The angel in Rev. 1:13 has such a girdle. **Gold of Uphaz:** The phrase occurs in Jer. 10:9; it would seem on the surface to mean gold from a place named Uphaz, but since no such place is known, some have conjectured that the text should read "Ophir," famous for its gold, a word used as here with כתם (Job 28:16; Ps. 45:9; Isa. 13:12). Others emend אופז to ופז, i.e., "and fine gold" (פז, from the verb "to purify," being mentioned in Lam. 4:2; Song of S. 5:11 as a specially refined gold), or to מופז, "finest gold," as in I Kings 10:18.

6. Body: *Gewiyyāh* is the word used in Ezek. 1:11, 23 of the bodies of the cherubim. This verse calls attention to "the man's" body as vs. 5 had to his clothing. Some have suggested that the writer had in mind those transparent garments, often represented on Egyptian wall-paintings, through which the limbs can be seen. This may be so, but it does not necessarily follow from the description. The body here as in Rev. 1:13 may refer to those parts which would not normally be covered by a garment.

Beryl: *Tarshísh,* Aq., Χρυσόλιθος, the chrysolite or topaz, called Tarshish because it was thought to have been originally brought thence. Pliny *Natural History* XXXVIII.

and his feet like in color to polished brass, and the voice of his words like the voice of a multitude.

7 And I Daniel alone saw the vision: for the men that were with me saw not the vision; but a great quaking fell upon them, so that they fled to hide themselves.

8 Therefore I was left alone, and saw this great vision, and there remained no strength in me: for my comeliness was

ning, his eyes like flaming torches, his arms and legs like the gleam of burnished bronze, and the sound of his words like the noise of a multitude. 7 And I, Daniel, alone saw the vision, for the men who were with me did not see the vision, but a great trembling fell upon them, and they fled to hide themselves. 8 So I was left alone and saw this

---

32. It is the word used in Ezek. 1:16; 28:13 (cf. Exod. 28:20; Song of S. 5:14; Josephus *Antiquities* III. 7. 5). Beryl is a modern identification of the stone.

His face like the appearance of lightning: Cf. Ezek. 1:13; Rev. 1:16. This does not mean that his face was sending out lightning flashes, but that it was so resplendent that to look at it was like looking at the brightness of lightning. The various words for gleaming, blazing, glistening in this description are meant to suggest to the audience the brightness of this celestial being.

"His eyes like flames of fire": Cf. Ezek. 1:13; II Enoch 1:5; 42:1; Rev. 1:14; 19:12. *Lappîdh* may be a "flame," as when Yahweh spoke at Sinai (Exod. 20:18), or a "torch," as in Abraham's vision in Gen. 15:17, or Samson's firebrands in Judg. 15:4. Such torches of fire are **flaming torches.** The gleaming of **burnished bronze** describes the feet of the throne-bearers in Ezek. 1:7 (cf. Rev. 1:15; 2:18). *Margelôth* means the place where the feet stand and not the **legs,** but it must have been transferred in meaning to the body, for in Rev. 1:15, which is based on this passage, we have οἱ πόδες αὐτοῦ. So in Ruth 3:4 we translate "uncover his feet," where it is, lit., "the place of his feet." **Gleam** is, lit., "an eye," but can mean the gleam of an eye. **Burnished** or **polished** is a meaning derived from the context, for what קלל means here is obscure. The writer is apparently giving the traditional understanding of Ezek. 1:7, which Rev. 1:15 takes to mean "refined by fire." The ancient versions here give it as meaning "shining."

The voice of his words is **like the voice** of a deep roaring (cf. Isa. 13:4; 33:3; Ezek. 1:24). At first the angel's speech seemed not articulate but a rolling, reverberating sound, and only as the seer became used to it did he distinguish words. *Hāmôn* is used of any deep sound, of the noise of the sea (Isa. 60:5; Jer. 51:16, 42), of heavy rain (I Kings 18:41), of the rumbling of the bowels (Isa. 63:15), of chariots (Jer. 47:3), of the deep murmur of a crowded city (Job 39:7; Isa. 32:14), or the rumbling of a host of moving cattle (Jer. 49:32). Rev. 1:15 takes it to mean the noise of waters, and in the Apocalypse of Abraham 18 we have "a voice like the roaring of the sea." The meaning **multitude** is derived, for the word itself has to do with sound.

7. As with Saul on the way to Damascus, it was the seer alone who saw the vision, though his companions were affected by the manifestation of the supernatural. Saul's companions were dumbfounded and fell to the earth. Here the seer's companions are seized with trembling and seek refuge in flight. **Trembling:** The same word is used for the trembling of the old man Isaac when he discovered how Jacob had deceived him over the blessing for the firstborn (Gen. 27:33), and for the trembling of the army at the exploits of Jonathan and his armor-bearer (I Sam. 14:15).

8-9. The effect on the seer himself is more profound than had been that of the appearance of Gabriel in 8:16-18, yet the result of the experience was that the confused

---

10:7. *Spiritual Perceptions.*—It is most astounding that in a group of men one only will see the vision and the others will not. When Saul was on the road to Damascus, he alone had his life changed. The voice of God

speaking to Jesus was only thunder to the by-standers. How unequal we are when it comes to spiritual perceptions! The world has been too much under the control of men without spiritual vision. The world has listened too little

turned in me into corruption, and I retained no strength.

9 Yet heard I the voice of his words: and when I heard the voice of his words, then was I in a deep sleep on my face, and my face toward the ground.

10 ¶ And, behold, a hand touched me, which set me upon my knees and *upon* the palms of my hands.

great vision, and no strength was left in me; my radiant appearance was fearfully changed, and I retained no strength. 9 Then I heard the sound of his words; and when I heard the sound of his words, I fell on my face in a deep sleep with my face to the ground.

10 And behold, a hand touched me and set me trembling on my hands and knees.

---

noise of the angel's speech changes to articulate sounds. **Vision** must mean here the vision of the angelic presence which the seer alone could see. **No strength was left in me:** So in I Sam. 28:20, where King Saul is similarly affected by the appearance of Samuel's ghost, though there it is said expressly that his previous fasting was partly responsible for his weakness. **My comeliness was turned in me into corruption:** In Hab. 3:16 there is a similar description of the physical effects of the coming of a divine revelation (cf. II Esdras 5:14).

Radiant appearance: *Hôdh* is **comeliness,** "splendor," but is not used elsewhere of the countenance. In 5:9 Belshazzar's "splendor," i.e., his *zîw,* brightness of countenance, was changed by his distress of mind as Daniel's was by similar distress in 7:28, and it is possible that this *hôdh* is merely a translation of an Aramaic *zîw.* **Was fearfully changed:** Lit., **was turned in me into corruption. Corruption** is used abstractly as in Ezek. 21:31; II Chr. 20:23. The root is that "marred" used in Isa. 52:14, "his visage was marred more than any man." As in 7:28, it refers to the sudden pallor induced by fear, which robs the countenance of its accustomed brightness.

Retained no strength: A late idiom found in Daniel and Chronicles. It occurs again in vs. 16; 11:6. Some scholars consider it a gloss which has crept in here from vs. 16. Others would also delete the beginning of vs. 9, **then I heard the sound of his words,** arguing that these words are merely a variant of those that follow. This judgment would be supported by the LXX, but Theod. has both sentences. According to still other students these words represent two variant attempts in Hebrew to render the underlying Aramaic. They may, however, be taken quite naturally. In vs. 6 the angelic voice was just a great rumbling sound, but now the seer distinguishes individual sounds and recognizes that they make up articulate speech, but when he realizes that these words are being spoken to him he is further overcome and falls into a swoon.

Sound again is "voice," as in vs. 6. "And as for me, I was senseless on my face." The Peshitta, Theod., and Vulg. all omit "and as for me," while the LXX omits the connecting "and" but has "as for me." *Rādham* is to lie **in a deep sleep,** "to be stunned," "to be stupefied." So in 8:18, the seer became unconscious when the angel spoke to him (cf. Rev. 1:17; Saul's falling to the ground in Acts 9:4; and the experience of the prophet in Ezek. 1:28; 2:1; Enoch 14:24).

c) THE COLLOQUY WITH THE ANGEL (10:10-21)

10-11. The seer is restored by a touch of the angel and encouraged to hearken to the message the angel has for him. It is simplest to understand that this is some angelic being who stretches out a hand to him, half raises him, and then goes on to speak to him. Some think it is another person who does this, just as in 8:16 another called and bade Gabriel explain the vision. Some suggest that in vss. 5-6 Gabriel appeared in his angelic form, which was more than the seer could bear, so here (and in vss. 16, 18) he

---

to the men who heard the voice and saw the vision.

Men do not see what they are not looking for. They do not see what they are unprepared

to see. Vision is dependent on preparation. It is the pure in heart who see God. There need to be a quiet spirit and periods of being alone. We will do well to be wary of asserting that

11 And he said unto me, O Daniel, a man greatly beloved, understand the words that I speak unto thee, and stand upright: for unto thee am I now sent. And when he had spoken this word unto me, I stood trembling.

12 Then said he unto me, Fear not, Daniel: for from the first day that thou didst set thine heart to understand, and to chasten thyself before thy God, thy words were heard, and I am come for thy words.

13 But the prince of the kingdom of Persia withstood me one and twenty days: but, lo, Michael, one of the chief princes,

11 And he said to me, "O Daniel, man greatly beloved, give heed to the words that I speak to you, and stand upright, for now I have been sent to you." While he was speaking this word to me, I sood up trembling. 12 Then he said to me, "Fear not, Daniel, for from the first day that you set your mind to understand and humbled yourself before your God, your words have been heard, and I have come because of your words. 13 The prince of the kingdom of Persia withstood me twenty-one days;

---

appears in a human form, aids him with a human hand, and speaks to him in intelligible human words. Others think that Gabriel is meant here and in vss. 16, 18, but that the celestial figure in vss. 5-6 is someone else. Many deny that Gabriel is meant at all, for, had he been, he would have been mentioned by name. Rev. 1:17 understood that it was the same celestial being who touched and restored him. In 8:18 Gabriel had to touch him to set him upright, and in 9:21, touched him to reassure him before giving him the message. In II Esdras 5:15 the angel held the seer, comforted him, and set him on his feet. Here, however, the angel only half raises him, "and he caused me to shake upon my knees and the palms of my hands," i.e., the angelic hand shook him into an unsteady position on all fours, from which he himself could rise to an upright position.

The seer is addressed as **greatly beloved,** this having been said of him in 9:23. **Stand upright:** Lit., "stand upon thy standing" (see 8:18; also Ezek. 2:1, where the prophet is raised and set upon his feet to hear the message; cf. II Esdras 5:15; Enoch 14:25). The fact that the angel says he has been **sent** with the message that he is to speak and to which the seer is to **give heed** supports the idea that this is Gabriel. **Trembling:** This is not the word used in vs. 7, but it occurs in Ezra 10:9 (cf. Ps. 104:32; Job 4:14; Isa. 33:14; Enoch 14:24).

12. It was the seer's desire to understand the vision that had brought this revelation. No sooner had he manifested such a desire by setting about spiritual preparation for the reception of a revelation than there was divine response to his desire and the angel was sent. So in Luke 1:11 ff. the angel was sent in response to Zechariah's prayer.

To **set** the **mind** is a late idiom found elsewhere in the O.T. only in Ecclesiastes and Chronicles. A somewhat different idiom to express the same thing is used in 1:8, and it seems very likely that both translate the Aramaic שום בל with an infinitive which we have in 6:14 (M.T. 6:15). **Humbled yourself:** Undertook various forms of self-mortification during the fast (cf. Ezra 8:21). The verb is commonly translated "to afflict" and is used in particular for fasting as an affliction of the soul, so that it gave rise to a technical term for fasting. As in 9:3, self-mortification was a spiritual preparation. **Your words:** His petitions. Behrmann would emend to "because of your words," a very small change in the Hebrew, it is true, but one that seems hardly necessary.

13. The angel excuses his delay by giving the seer a little glimpse of the happenings at the heavenly court. On **the first day** that Daniel had set himself to seek a revelation the command had been given the angel to bring him such a revelation. That first day,

---

because we do not see what other men see, they must be lying. Perhaps we too might have the vision if we were ready for it.

12. Seek in Humility.—Until our ruling passion is to know God and his truth, we cannot

learn much about him. What greater purpose is there for a man than to learn of God? We set our minds to attain, but not many set their minds to understand. But if a man makes that his goal, he may believe the promise of Jesus:

came to help me; and I remained there with the kings of Persia. | but Michael, one of the chief princes, came to help me, so I left him there with the

---

however, was now three weeks ago, and the angel explains that for twenty-one days he had been hindered from coming by the opposition of the angel patron of Persia; he had been finally able to get away only because Michael, the patron angel of the Jews, had come to his assistance.

Princes: As in "the Prince of the host" in 8:11. From early times in Mesopotamia each city-state, while harboring the cults of many deities, yet had its own tutelary deity who was the particular object of worship in the cult of that city-state, and who necessarily had the interests of that city-state under his or her peculiar care. Much the same situation was found in early Egypt, and at a later date in other areas of the Near East. With the growth of the great Empires there came to be one city deity who was in a special way the god of that empire, as Amon-Re became for Egypt with the supremacy of Thebes, Ashur for Assyria with the supremacy of its empire, and Marduk for Babylonia with the supremacy of Babylon. In later monotheistic thought this survived in the notion that under the one Lord there were angelic patrons of the various nations to whom was committed the task of ruling various departments concerned with mundane affairs. In this way many defects evident in the running of worldly affairs could be attributed to the limitations of angelic wisdom and not laid to the charge of the Almighty. Under such a scheme the patron angels of the nations would be responsible for the affairs of their particular national groups.

Some see this idea already present in such passages as Isa. 24:21; Ps. 82, but it does not come to clear expression earlier than these last chapters of Daniel. Here the writer takes it for granted that the idea is familiar to his audience, and it must therefore have already become familiar to the Jews. Only a little later we find it widely recognized (Ecclus. 17:17; Jubilees 15:31-32; Enoch 89:59). The usual theory was that each of the seventy nations mentioned in Gen. 10 had its patron angel who represented its interests at the heavenly court and directed its affairs on earth. It will be remembered that Origen (*Commentary on John's Gospel* XIII. 58) says some of these patron angels were converted at the sight of Jesus, which explains the rapid spread of Christianity among their national groups.

The patron angel of Persia in the later angelology was Dubbiel. **Withstood:** What the controversy was between this angel and Dubbiel we are not told. Some have thought that the patron of Persia was trying to hinder the proclamation of the message the angel was bringing to the seer. In vss. 20-21, however, the angel says he must return to the conflict where Michael was carrying on for him until his return; thus, though the conflict did hinder him for twenty-one days from bringing the message, it would seem in itself to have been something apart from the message. It seems also that he expects to be involved presently with the patron angel of Greece, with only Michael to help him. Since in ch. 11 the writer gives an account of the Persian Empire and the coming to power of the Greek Empire and the relationship of the Jews thereto, it is possible that he means his audience to understand that this present angel was an angel of higher authority than the patron angels and was continually having trouble with them in the execution of his duties, since each of them was always wanting to push the interests of his nation. Michael, the patron of the Jews, was here willing to help him because he was engaged on some matter which concerned them. This would link the controversy in one way with the message to Daniel, since that message had to do with the bringing

---

"Ask, and it shall be given you; seek, and ye shall find; knock, and it shall be opened unto you" (Matt. 7:7). The seeking must be in humility. This is a universal law of learning; | and science, no less than religion, is aware that pride is a barrier to knowing. Thomas Huxley said that one had to sit before a fact like a little child.

14 Now I am come to make thee understand what shall befall thy people in the
latter days: for yet the vision *is* for *many*
days.

prince of the kingdom of Persia[x] **14** and
came to make you understand what is to
befall your people in the latter days. For
the vision is for days yet to come."

[x] Theodotion Compare Gk: Heb *I was left there with the
kings of Persia*

---

to an end all these national powers and the setting up of the final kingdom in which
all the nations would be subject to the Jews.

Michael, as we see from vs. 21; 12:1, was the patron angel of the Jews. This is the
earliest literary reference to Michael, who is here called **one of the chief princes.** He
appears as one of the four archangels in Enoch 9:1; 71:9, and as one of the seven in
Enoch 20:5. In Jude 9 he is the angel who contends with Satan, and in Rev. 12:7 he leads
his forces against those of the dragon.

So I left him there: The text here is difficult. The M.T. reads "and I was left there
up against the kings of Persia." The simplest solution is to take the connecting particle
ו as introducing a circumstantial clause and render "seeing that I was left there," i.e.,
Michael came to his help because he was left alone to struggle with the angel who
represented the interests of the kings of Persia. Many, however, dislike this interpretation.
Some construe the verb as "I was delayed," which was why he did not come earlier.
Others translate the verb with the following preposition as "I overcame," i.e., he got
the upper hand over the kings of Persia. Others render "I was superfluous there," i.e.,
when Michael came there was no need of him, so he was free to come to the seer. The
LXX and Theod. render the verb as a transitive and insert "him," i.e., "I left him
[Michael] there while I came to you." This makes good sense but requires emendation
of the text. Ginsberg (*Studies,* p. 60) suggests that the translator mistook an Aramaic
דנה for אנה and so made it "I remained" instead of "the latter remained," i.e., Michael
remained there while he came to the seer with the message. Both the LXX and Theod.
assume a שר in the text, i.e., **with the prince,** and some editors insert it. In any case the
angel is understood, for it was not any earthly kings but the angel who represented them
who was engaged in the contest. **Kings of Persia** here means the Persian dynasty representing the power of the Persian Empire. Theod. has **the kingdom of Persia,** but the
reading **kings** is supported by what follows in 11:2.

14. The revelation concerns the future of the Jewish people and the end. It was
to make the seer **understand** that the angel was sent in 8:16 (cf. 9:22-23). The writer is
using this word almost as a technical term for the interpretation of the hidden meaning
of things. Note his use of the verb in vss. 11-12; 1:17; 8:23; 9:2; 12:10; and the noun
in vs. 1; 8:15; 9:22. The message has to do with events leading up to the end, as the
message to Nebuchadrezzar in 2:28 had been. For the expression used here see Gen. 49:1.
The reference is actually to the days of Antiochus IV, but in the writer's view these are
the last days.

"Since there is yet a vision for the days": I.e., there is still one more vision regarding
the days before the end. Some take this to mean "for the vision is still for [these] days,"
i.e., for the days just mentioned. Others render, "for the vision is to continue for [many]
days," i.e., the time of the vision will cover quite a period yet to come. In 8:26 the vision
was also for **many days,** the reference being to the end of things, and that is doubtless
what is meant here.

---

14. *Prophetic Insight.*—If this is to be interpreted mechanically and literally, then it has
no deep meaning for us. The time and the
occasion are long since past. But if it can be
regarded as God's willingness to give his prophets insights into the meaning of history and the
working out of moral laws, then God says to

religious leaders of all nations and in all generations that he will help them understand
what **is to befall** [their] **people.** The most realistic thinking is always within the religious
framework, because only in that setting are we
aware of all the factors. The nation which denies religion is facing its future blindly.

15 And when he had spoken such words unto me, I set my face toward the ground, and I became dumb.

16 And, behold, *one* like the similitude of the sons of men touched my lips: then I opened my mouth, and spake, and said unto him that stood before me, O my lord, by the vision my sorrows are turned upon me, and I have retained no strength.

17 For how can the servant of this my lord talk with this my lord? for as for me, straightway there remained no strength in me, neither is there breath left in me.

15 When he had spoken to me according to these words, I turned my face toward the ground and was dumb. 16 And behold, one in the likeness of the sons of men touched my lips; then I opened my mouth and spoke. I said to him who stood before me, "O my lord, by reason of the vision pains have come upon me, and I retain no strength. 17 How can my lord's servant talk with my lord? For now no strength remains in me, and no breath is left in me."

15-19. Again the seer is overcome by the speaking of the angel, so that he has to be touched once more and reassured before he is ready to hear the actual words of revelation. This repetition of the seer's distress and the angel's reassurance was merely to signify to the audience the exceeding importance of the message contained in the revelation. **I turned my face toward the ground** does not necessarily mean that the seer fell prostrate as at 8:17, but that in his distress he was unable to look up, and so fixed his eyes on the ground and remained silent (cf. Enoch 14:25). It was this anguish that made him **dumb.**

"And behold, one in form like the sons of Adam": Cf. vs. 18, "one with the appearance of a man" and 7:13. It was an angel in human form, but we are not told who. Some think it is a new arrival from the celestial hosts, but most expositors take it to be the same angel who had appeared in vs. 10 and who appears again in vs. 19, whether Gabriel or not. Those who take it to be a different angel generally regard vss. 16-18 as referring to him. The LXX reads "as the likeness of a man's hand," assuming יד in the text, which some editors would restore and render, "then something in the form of a man's hand touched my lips." If a ghostly hand could write on the wall, there is no reason why one should not touch lips. In this case the gesture would be something different from that aiming at strengthening in vs. 18. Apparently the touching of the **lips** was to restore the seer's power of speech. In Isa. 6:7 a hot coal touches the prophet's lips to inspire him to deliver his message. It is curious that again the writer refuses to identify the angelic figure, using an indefinite phrase "he who was standing in front of me."

O my lord is merely a respectful form of address to the august celestial visitor. Those who see the Christ in this figure suggest that this form of address proves the correctness of their identification, but in I Sam. 1:15, 26 Hannah uses it as a respectful form of address to Eli, and in I Sam. 22:12 Ahimelech uses it with King Saul.

The seer's first words are to excuse himself for his state of distress and seeming impoliteness. This vision has been more than flesh and blood could stand. "My pangs have turned upon me." He is using the imagery of the pangs of childbirth (cf. I Sam. 4:19; Isa. 13:8). Çîr is from the verb "to writhe," "to twist," and so is a vivid image of the distress into which the vision had cast Daniel. In Isa. 21:3 there is a similar comparison with reference to the strange excitement of the physical body brought about by the phenomena of revelation. **I retain no strength** is repeated from vs. 8. Yet it is not alone the vision that troubles him. It is also the presence of the angel, for how can so mean a servant of the Lord talk with so great a one as his Lord? **This,** which the KJV has endeavored to keep, is a particle of emphasis, repeated here, it is true, but since it has

17. *Real Religious Experience.*—The turning of God into a glorified greeter is a part of our loss of the sense of his holiness. Isaiah in the temple felt a sense of his own unworthiness.

The kind of Christian who knows all the answers to the vexing questions of theology is the man who has never seen God in all his glory. For that is the most humbling experience. Real

18 Then there came again and touched me *one* like the appearance of a man, and he strengthencd me,

19 And said, O man greatly beloved, fear not: peace *be* unto thee; be strong, yea, be strong. And when he had spoken untu me, I was strengthened, and said, Let my lord speak; for thou hast strengthened me.

20 Then said he, Knowest thou wherefore I come unto thee? and now will I re-

18 Again one having the appearance of a man touched me and strengthened me. **19** And he said, "O man greatly beloved, fear not, peace be with you; be strong and of good courage." And when he spoke to me, I was strengthened and said, "Let my lord speak, for you have strengthened me." **20** Then he said, "Do you know why I have

---

no equivalent in English, it is best omitted from translation. In the presence of so awesome a being a man's strength seems to leave him, his breath becomes short, and he feels paralyzed.

For now: Lit., "and as for me now." The word מעתה is normally "from now on," "henceforth," so Theod. ἀπὸ τὸ νῦν, but that does not make much sense here. Bevan emends to "from terror," a word used of supernatural alarm in Isa. 21:4; Job 6:4. Ehrlich's suggestion that it is the argumentative "now" avoids emendation and makes good sense. **Remains:** Lit., "stands" (cf. Josh. 2:11; and the statement about the queen of Sheba in I Kings 10:5).

Once more the seer is **touched** by the angel who is in the **appearance of a man.** The expression here is different from that used in vs. 16, but resembles 8:15, save that here we have אדם instead of גבר. Ezekiel in his vision saw things having the "appearance" of earthly things (Ezek. 1:13-14; 8:2; 10:1; cf. what Raphael says in Tob. 12:19). **And strengthened me:** The verb is used both for physical strengthening (Ps. 147:13; Ezek. 30:24; 34:4; Hos. 7:15) and for moral or spiritual strengthening, or as we should say, "encouraging" (Deut. 1:38; 3:28; II Sam. 11:25; Isa. 41:7).

As in vs. 11, the angel addresses the seer as **man greatly beloved,** referring without doubt to 9:23. Those who distinguish between the angels allot these words to the angel of vss. 11-14 rather than to the one of vss. 16-18. **Fear not** repeats vs. 12. It was apparently regarded as a customary expression used by celestial visitants to allay the natural terror of men at their approach. It is used with Abraham in Gen. 15:1; Hagar in Gen. 21:17; Isaac in Gen. 26:24; Moses in Num. 21:34; Zechariah in Luke 1:13; and Mary in Luke 1:30.

The greeting of **peace** appears here in the form in which it has continued to be customary in the Near East down to the present day. Its formal epistolary usage had appeared in 4:1; 6:25, and the angel uses it now because it is the customary formula of greeting among men (cf. Judg. 6:23; 19:20; Gen. 43:23; I Sam. 25:6). It is curious that the writer, having used the formula customary at the beginning of a letter, follows it by the formula used for closing a letter, **be strong and of good courage** (cf. Deut. 31:7, 23; also the ἔρρωσο καὶ ὑγίαινε of Greek writers, which appears as ἔρρωσθε in Acts 15:29; II Macc. 11:21). The M.T. has "be strong, yea, be strong," but the reading of the LXX, Theod., and Peshitta suggests emendation to the more usual formula, which occurs in Josh. i:6-7, 9, 18; I Chr. 22:13; 28:20; Deut. 31:7, 23.

At the encouraging words of the angel the seer took heart. He **was strengthened,** and having been so strengthened (cf. vs. 18), he felt able to hear what the angel had to communicate.

20. Do you know why? This is a rhetorical question since in vs. 14 he had already told the seer why he had come. Charles seeks to avoid the weakness of the question by

---

religious experience takes away our fear and worry, but it does not make us familiar with holy things. It gives us a sense of awe.

19. *You Have Strengthened Me.*—It is strange and wonderful that God makes us aware of our own weakness and our own unworthiness. Yet

it is God who gives us strength. The difficulty of realizing that it is in God that we move and have our being makes us vainly try to be adequate in our own might.

20. *God's Promise.*—Our God struggles. Our God works. He is no aristocrat retired from the

turn to fight with the prince of Persia: and when I am gone forth, lo, the prince of Grecia shall come.

21 But I will show thee that which is noted in the Scripture of truth: and *there is* none that holdeth with me in these things, but Michael your prince.

come to you? But now I will return **to fight** against the prince of Persia; and when I am through with him, lo, the prince of Greece will come. 21 But I will tell you what is inscribed in the book of truth: there is none who contends by my side against these except Michael, your prince.

---

dropping the interrogative particle and reading, "Thou knowest why I have come to thee." Ginsberg (*op. cit.,* p. 47) suggests that the translator mistook the Aramaic particle הא, "Lo," for an interrogative particle, whereas the original was "Lo, thou knowest why." If we keep the M.T. we must understand this question as intended to awaken anew the interest of the seer in the explanation now to be given. Bentzen compares the similar rhetorical question of the elders in Rev. 7:13.

From here on to the introductory verse of ch. 11 the text is in a tangle, and has exercised the ingenuity of various editors. If the arrangement of the RSV is adopted the following comment may be offered: The angel explains the haste with which he must give the revelation as due to the fact that he must return to Michael, whom he has left carrying on the warfare in heaven (vs. 13). How this warfare was understood is vividly illustrated by the passage in II Macc. 5:1-4. Some early commentators, not recognizing the popular mythological background of this account of warfare in heaven, which is illustrated in Isa. 24:21, treated the conflict as a legal one, a process being argued out by adversaries before God. That the conflict with the angel of Persia is soon to be complicated by the appearance of the patron angel of Greece is clear, but the exact rendering is not sure. The M.T. has "I am going forth, and lo, the prince of Greece has come." This may mean "I go forth to fight the patron angel of Persia, expecting to have to deal with him alone, when lo, the patron angel of Greece appears and has to be dealt with also." This follows the sense of יצא in such passages as Judg. 9:29; II Sam. 11:1; II Kings 9:21. But the verb also has the sense of "to be free from," "to be done with," as in I Sam. 14:41; Eccl. 7:18, and others take it to mean "as soon as I am free from the conflict with the patron of Persia, the patron of Greece will be there and will have to be resisted." This has in its favor the historical situation that as soon as the Persian supremacy was ended, that of Greece arose. The angel of Persia is thus "going off" that the angel of Greece may "come on" (cf. II Kings 11:5, 7). Ginsberg (*ibid.,* pp. 60-61) thinks that an Aramaic דנה was misread as אנה, and that the original had "when this one leaves [i.e., the angel of Persia] the patron of Greece comes."

21. Though his return to the contest in heaven is urgent, the angel will remain long enough to reveal to the seer the matters that have been settled in the book of decrees (cf. 8:19; 9:23). **Tell:** The same verb was used in 2:2 for Nebuchadrezzar's request that the wise men tell him the dream.

The book of truth: I.e., the book of decrees, in which have been set down all the divine decrees as to events yet to happen (cf. Ps. 139:16). These *dupšūnāti,* or tablets of fate, appear early in the religious history of Mesopotamia and in later times were associated with the events of the Babylonian New Year festival. In the Talmud (Rosh ha-Shanah 16*b*) we read how on New Year's Day the books were opened and fates recorded. These tablets and the book are frequently mentioned in Jubilees and the Testaments of the Twelve Patriarchs; and in the prayer of Joseph preserved in Origen *Philocalia* xxiii, 15 we read, "For I have read in the tablets of heaven all that shall befall you and your sons."

Who contends by my side: Lit., "who is helping me." **Against these:** Presumably against the patron angels of the nations who are pushing the interests of their groups and who have to be resisted in the interests of the general plan.

Michael is your prince because he is the patron angel of the Jewish nation (cf. vs. 13; 12:1). It is for this reason that in Jude 9 he disputes with the devil over the body of

11 Also I in the first year of Darius the Mede, *even* I, stood to confirm and to strengthen him.

2 And now will I show thee the truth. Behold, there shall stand up yet three kings in Persia; and the fourth shall be far richer

11 And as for me, in the first year of Darius the Mede, I stood up to confirm and strengthen him.

2 "And now I will show you the truth. Behold, three more kings shall arise in

---

Moses, which the devil was claiming on the ground that he had killed an Egyptian and was a murderer. In Assumption of Moses 10:2 he appears as the angel who at the end of the world avenges Israel on their enemies. In Enoch 20:5 he is one of the archangels who is set over the "best part of mankind," i.e., the Jews. That Israel had a special guardian angel was deduced from such passages as Exod. 14:19; Num. 20:16; Zech. 12:8.

2. THE INTERPRETATION OF THE VISION (11:1–12:4)

Ch. 10 having given the prologue, ch. 11 contains the interpretation of the vision referred to in 10:1 but not described. From the interpretation it appears that, like the dream of ch. 7 and the vision of ch. 8, this vision concerned the kingdoms which follow successively until we arrive at the rule of Antiochus Epiphanes, whose iniquities are part of the great tribulation which precedes the end. In ch. 8 the Babylonian Empire had been passed over, and the Median and Persian given but scant mention, in order that attention might be concentrated on the Greek Empire. Here Media drops out, save for the date in vs. 1, and Persia serves but to introduce Greece, whose history as an Oriental power is given in greater detail than before.

To suit the general scheme of the book the seer is pictured as still in Babylon, now at the beginning of the period of Persian occupation. In the form of a prediction of events to come, the writer gives a sketch of history from Cyrus to Antiochus IV as that was popularly understood by the audience. After Cyrus, he says, there will be three more kings, the last of whom, i.e., the fourth in succession, will be very rich and will make war on Greece. A great ruler will make Greece supreme, but at his death that kingdom will be divided. From then on the seer is concerned with the struggles between two of the successors of this great king, the king of the north and the king of the south, until finally a usurper in the north overcomes the south and then sets up that abomination of desolation which signifies that the end is at hand.

a) PREDECESSORS OF THE DIADOCHI (11:1-4)

11:1. And as for me, in the first year of Darius the Mede: This seems to be an interpolation inserted in order to give a date to this chapter after it had been cut off from the material of ch. 10. The versions have this note of date, but the LXX and Theod. have "Cyrus" instead of **Darius.** If we accept the M.T. we have the curious phenomenon of an angel dating events by the regnal years of an earthly monarch. This has nothing to do with the date of Daniel's vision, which is still in the third year of Cyrus.

I stood up to confirm and strengthen him: The text, lit., "my standing to be a strengthening and a protection to him," is awkward. Ginsberg (*op. cit.*, p. 46), working back to an underlying Aramaic, would read: "And I since the first year of Darius the Mede have been standing as a strengthener and fortifier for him."

2a. And now I will show you the truth would seem to be a continuation of the insertion to provide a proper beginning to what is now a new section.

---

conflicts of men. **Now I will return to fight** is his word. We are engaged in battle. We are in the army of God. Passiveness may have a place in some religions, but not in ours. **Now I will return to fight** could well be taken as a motto for the battle of life.

11:1-13. *The Delusion of Power.*—These verses tell in symbolic terms of the struggles of kings and empires. Each raises armies and waxes strong. Each assumes that what others have failed to do it can succeed in doing. If a few more thousand men can be killed, or if this

than *they* all: and by his strength through his riches he shall stir up all against the realm of Grecia.

3 And a mighty king shall stand up, that shall rule with great dominion, and do according to his will.

Persia; and a fourth shall be far richer than all of them; and when he has become strong through his riches, he shall stir up all against the kingdom of Greece. 3 Then a mighty king shall arise, who shall rule with great dominion and do according to

---

Three more kings: I.e., of the Persian Empire, which is being mentioned in order to lead up to the Greek Empire. The three who actually succeeded Cyrus were Cambyses (530-522 B.C.), the usurper Gaumata (Pseudo-Smerdis) (522-521), and Darius I (521-486) or, if we pass over Gaumata, then Cambyses, Darius I, and Xerxes I (486-465). Since Xerxes figured largely in the wars with Greece, this would seem to suit very well the last clause of the verse. On the ground that Orientals knew little or nothing of these wars of Xerxes with Greece, and that the name *Yāwān* is used for Asiatic Greece rather than for Hellas, both Torrey and Montgomery think that we must confine ourselves to the four Persian kings mentioned in the Bible, viz., Cyrus, Xerxes, Artaxerxes, and Darius III Codomannus. The more common view, however, is that the four in this writer's mind were Cyrus, Darius I, Xerxes I, and Artaxerxes, though he seems to have thought that Artaxerxes reigned before Xerxes. This view has been championed by Obbink and Bentzen. Behrmann again suggests that four is but a symbolic number and should not be pressed literally.

"And the fourth shall enrich himself riches greater than all." If the reference is to Xerxes I, one needs but refer to Herodotus (*History* VII. 20 ff.) for a description of his great wealth, the tale of which is reflected also in the book of Esther. If it means Darius III, it must derive from some legend no longer available to us.

When he has become strong: The expression "to wax strong" is used of Rehoboam in II Chr. 12:1, and of Uzziah in II Chr. 26:16. **He shall stir up:** As in vs. 25, from the verb "to arouse," "to excite" (cf. Isa. 13:17). **Against** is a problem, for את does not have this meaning (but cf. Jer. 38:5). The versions seem to have had our text but they do not help with the problem of את. Keil suggested long ago that it is the normal particle את, used here to suggest the goal of attainment, whence the Vulg. *adversum* and our **against.** Some think the original text read, "he shall stir up all," and that the phrase about **the kingdom of Greece** is a gloss by someone who took the reference as to the campaigns of Xerxes. Torrey (" 'Yāwān' and 'Hellas,' " pp. 310-11) emends it to read, "The prince of all will raise up the kingdom of Greece," i.e., after the fourth Persian king that empire will be replaced by the rise of Greek dominion in the Orient.

The kingdom of Greece: Theod. has "kingdoms." If the reference is to the Greece of the days of Xerxes, Theod. is nearer the truth, for at that time Greece was no kingdom in the Oriental sense but a number of independent states. But if the writer is thinking of the Seleucid kingdom in Asia as representing Greece, then the singular is correct.

3-4. These verses concern Alexander and the rise of the Diadochi.

A mighty king: The word *gibbôr* means a mighty man of valor and is used of warriors in Samuel and Kings, so that perhaps "warlike" or "valiant" or Driver's "warrior king" would best express the meaning. In Isa. 9:6 the messianic king is described as *'ēl gibbôr.* The reference here is to Alexander the Great, who was the he-goat with the great horn in 8:5-8, 21. **Great dominion** expresses the sense of the magnitude of Alexander's empire. Montgomery's "rule with a great rule" attempts to preserve the wordplay in the original.

And do according to his will: Cf. vss. 16, 36; 8:4. Older commentators quote the words of Quintus Curtius (*History of Alexander* X. 5. 35), "By favor of this fortune he seemed to the peoples to be able to do whatever he pleased." This detail reflects the impression made on Oriental minds by the irresistible progress of Alexander. **And when he has arisen:** Many editors emend the text to agree with 8:8 and render, "and when he has become strong," i.e., at the height of his power he was struck down. A corruption of the text could easily have come from the עמד of vs. 3, but on the other

4 And when he shall stand up, his kingdom shall be broken, and shall be divided toward the four winds of heaven; and not to his posterity, nor according to his dominion which he ruled: for his kingdom shall be plucked up, even for others besides those.

5 ¶ And the king of the south shall be strong, and *one* of his princes; and he shall be strong above him, and have dominion; his dominion *shall be* a great dominion.

his will. 4 And when he has arisen, his kingdom shall be broken and divided toward the four winds of heaven, but not to his posterity, nor according to the dominion with which he ruled; for his kingdom shall be plucked up and go to others besides these.

5 "Then the king of the south shall be strong, but one of his princes shall be stronger than he and his dominion shall be

---

hand, it is not impossible that the writer is playing with the various shades of meaning this verb may have, and so has deliberately used **arisen** here. If we accept the M.T., the meaning would be that hardly had he risen to his full height when he was brought down.

Shall be broken: Cf. 8:8. **And divided:** *Ḥāçāh* is "to split," "to disperse" (see 12:7; Zech. 2:6). This dispersion to **the four winds of heaven** had already been mentioned in 8:8 in reference to the successors of Alexander. **Four** may be merely a symbolic number, or it may contain a reference to the four larger kingdoms which arose on the ruins of Alexander's empire, viz., those of Lysimachus, Cassander, Seleucus, and Ptolemy.

But not to his posterity: If we accept the M.T., the meaning must be that the kingdom did not descend to Alexander's heirs. There were three such heirs, each of whom was a pawn in the struggle for power after Alexander's death; but his dull-witted half brother Philip was done away with in 317, Alexander, his son by Roxana, in 311, and the boy Herakles, his reputed son by his mistress Barsine, in 309. So none of them succeeded to his kingdom. The LXX, however, assumes a text "but not with his power," which is supported by what follows and agrees with 8:22. The same text probably underlies the Peshitta, "but not as his sword," and was perhaps the original reading. The word *'aḥarîth* means the last part of anything but is used of **posterity** in Ps. 109:13.

"Nor as his rule which he ruled" is the same wordplay as in vs. 3. As had been hinted in 8:22, the rule of Alexander's successors was but a feeble thing compared with his. **Plucked up:** As a tree is uprooted (cf. Mic. 5:14; Ezek. 19:12). The verb is used of uprooting cities in Ps. 9:6, of nations in Deut. 29:28; I Kings 14:15; Jer. 1:10; 12:17.

And go to others besides these: Lit., "and to others apart from these." The question is who are meant by **these,** for on that depends the translation of מלבד. Some think they are the four chief generals who set up kingdoms after Alexander, and so "others besides them" will mean the other minor dynasties that arose in Armenia, Cappadocia, and elsewhere, which also in some measure carried on the succession of Alexander's empire. In this case מלבד means "in addition to." Others take **these** to mean Alexander's **posterity,** so that **others** refers to Alexander's generals who divided the empire among them to the exclusion of his posterity. Here מלבד will mean "apart from." Charles suggests that the word renders the Aramaic בר מן, "irrespective of."

b) History of the Earlier Ptolemies and Seleucids (11:5-20)

These verses are concerned with the Seleucids and Ptolemies who preceded Antiochus Epiphanes. The other groups are passed over as they had little significance for events in Palestine, whereas from 301 B.C., when Ptolemy I began his struggle with Antigonus for possession of Palestine, until 198 B.C., when, after the Battle of Paneas, Palestine came

---

particular enemy can be destroyed, then its rule will be finally established. Larger armies, more terror, greater ruthlessness, are the methods to use. Yet all of this is a kind of madness which has taken hold of the nations. None of them

get what they want, and none of them establish a permanent rule. Daniel in his vision saw the transitoriness of political, tyrannical kingdoms. When they thought they were safe, something went wrong. And so it is with us. Victory raises

6 And in the end of years they shall join themselves together; for the king's daughter of the south shall come to the king of the	a great dominion. 6 After some years they shall make an alliance, and the daughter of the king of the south shall come to the

definitely under the Seleucids, it was the bone of contention between the Greeks in Egypt and those in Syria. For the greater part of this period the Ptolemies dominated it.

In the settlement at Triparadisus in 321 B.C. Syria had been assigned to Laomedon. Ptolemy, however, got possession of it the next year, but was driven out by Antigonus in 315. He recovered the southern territory in 312 after the Battle of Gaza, but had to relinquish it to Antigonus again in 311. It was after the complete defeat of Antigonus at Ipsus in 301 that Ptolemy gained effective control of Coele-Syria and Phoenicia. His possession, however, was disputed. Seleucus claimed that part of the agreement after the Battle of Ipsus was that the whole of Syria should be his. Ptolemy on the other hand claimed that he joined the coalition against Antigonus only on the understanding that he should be given Coele-Syria and Phoenicia. Seleucus at that moment was in no position to dispute it, but it remained a bone of contention, and the Seleucids, who thought they had a right to it, never lost an opportunity of trying to obtain it, until finally they succeeded in 198, from which date it remained in Syrian possession.

5. The **king of the south** is here Ptolemy I Soter, one of the ablest and clearly the most foresighted of Alexander's generals. He had distinguished himself in the Indian campaigns, and at Alexander's death chose Egypt as his sphere. He was a Macedonian, son of Lagos, whence the dynasty is often called that of the Lagidae. He ruled Egypt as satrap from 322 to 305, when he assumed the title of king. His becoming **strong** may refer to the fact that for a great part of the third century B.C. it was the Ptolemies who dominated Palestine. *Néghebh* in the O.T. generally refers to the southern part of Judea, but it is used here as in 8:9 for Egypt, in contradistinction to Syria, which was to the north. In Isa. 30:6 it is used for Egypt.

One of his princes: If we follow the Masoretic accentuation, this goes with what precedes, i.e, the king of the south and one of his generals will be strong. Then comes as another sentence, "but he [i.e., the general] will become stronger than he." It is usual, however, to follow the versions and to omit the second *wāw* so as to make an independent sentence. Some have taken **his** to mean Alexander, but it more likely refers to Ptolemy. In fact the phrase alludes to Seleucus Nicator who had been a companion of Ptolemy during the eastern campaigns and at the convention at Triparadisus had been given the satrapy of Babylon. When beset by Antigonus he had fled to Egypt, where Ptolemy had given him a military command and helped him recover his satrapy. The writer is thus justified in calling him one of the generals of Ptolemy. When restored to his rule, he rapidly extended his control both to the east and to the west, so that ultimately he ruled over a kingdom much more extensive than that of the Ptolemies. In this sense he became **stronger than he.**

The word for "general" here is *sar,* which was translated "prince" in 8:11, 25; 9:6, 8; 10:13, 20, but "chief" in ch. 1 for the chief of the eunuchs. It is used as a military title in Gen. 26:26; Num. 31:14; Deut. 20:9; etc.

"And shall rule, a great ruling shall his ruling be." There is a play here on *māshāl, mimshāl,* and *memshéleth,* all from the root "to rule." The reference is to the extension of power after the Battle of Ipsus in 301 B.C., where Antigonus was defeated and Seleucus had the way clear to extend his power until he controlled all from Phrygia and Cappadocia in the west to the Indus in the east. Arrian (*Anabasis* VII. 22. 5) can thus call him "the most regal and the one who ruled the greatest extent of territory after Alexander." In the ancient Near East his fame was so great that it provided a starting point for a new system of dating, that of the Seleucid era (cf. I Macc. 1:10).

6. This verse deals with the unfortunate attempt at a marriage alliance between the Seleucids and the Ptolemies. **After some years:** The date referred to is *ca.* 250 B.C. when, with a view to ending the war between the two peoples, Ptolemy II Philadelphus

north to make an agreement: but she shall not retain the power of the arm; neither shall he stand, nor his arm: but she shall be given up, and they that brought her, and he that begat her, and he that strengthened her in *these* times.

king of[y] the north to make peace; but she shall not retain the strength of her arm, and he and his offspring shall not endure; but she shall be given up, and her attendants, her child, and he who got possession of her.

[y] Or *supported*

---

gave his daughter Berenice in marriage to Antiochus II Theos. Among the conditions of the **alliance** was a provision that Antiochus divorce his wife Laodice and bar her two sons Seleucus and Antiochus from the succession, so that any son borne by Berenice would succeed to the throne. Laodice, however, seems to have held the monarch's affection in spite of the wealth and prestige brought him by Berenice, so that after two years he was living with her again. His sudden death was attributed to Laodice's revenge for the slight put upon her. Soon afterward she was able to secure the death of the infant son of Berenice and then of Berenice herself, with many of her attendants, and thus to bring her own sons back into the succession. **Some years** therefore covers the period from 312 B.C., when Seleucus regained his throne and began to extend his power, until 250 or 249, when this marriage alliance was arranged.

Come to is the regular expression for a bride going to the home of her husband (see Josh. 15:18; Judg. 12:9). **The north** here means Syria, for in 300 B.C. Seleucus had established his capital at Antioch.

To make peace: *Mêshārîm* is "evenness," "uprightness," "equity" (cf. Ps. 98:9; I Chr. 29:17; Prov. 1:3). It is the "bring to terms" of vs. 17, and some translate here **to make an** [equitable] **agreement.** The LXX and Theod. have συνθήκας. From the meaning of "evenness" can come that of "concord," and so **peace.**

But she shall not retain the power of the arm: זרוע is, lit., "the lower arm," but is used metaphorically for **power, strength,** as in vss. 15, 22, 31. Some think it means that Berenice will not be able to maintain the political support for her father which he expected from this alliance. The meaning is more likely, however, that she will not prevail against Laodice. **Not retain the power** is the same expression as in 10:8, 16, which refers to the seer's losing his strength. **Neither shall he stand, nor his arm:** Some take this to mean that not only will Berenice fail, but Ptolemy Philadelphus himself and his other support (his army) will also fail. Others would take the first pronoun as neuter, "and it shall not stand," i.e., the hope he had placed in Berenice. It and all his other supports will prove ineffectual. Most modern editors emend the text from *zerō'ô* to *zar'ô* (the reading assumed by Theod., Symm., and the Vulg.), which would mean **offspring,** not **arm,** and would be a reference to the murder of Berenice's infant son.

She shall be given up: The M.T. has only **she shall be given,** and possibly "to death" or some such phrase has dropped from the text or should be understood. Charles emends to "she shall be rooted up" (cf. vs. 4 and the same metaphor in vs. 7). In any case, the verse seems to refer to the death of Berenice at the hands of Laodice. **And her attendants:** Lit., "she and those who brought her," the reference being in all probability to the Egyptian attendants who accompanied her when she came as a bride, many of whom perished with her when Laodice arranged for her removal. Others think the reference is to those who arranged for her marriage, viz., her father Ptolemy, who presently died, and her husband Antiochus, who was poisoned. Some, however, think it means only her husband, the plural being the plural of majesty.

---

more problems than it solves. Dependence on these physical forces may lead any nation to the abyss.

When we are tempted to go through that same endless cycle of killing and destruction again, we had better read over these chapters in Daniel. It has all gone on before, and we know how it failed to achieve what men wanted. Let our faith be in something else. Let us pray for vision of a way that will lead us all to peace

7 But out of a branch of her roots shall *one* stand up in his estate, which shall come with an army, and shall enter into the fortress of the king of the north, and shall deal against them, and shall prevail:

7 "In those times a branch[z] from her roots shall arise in his place; he shall come against the army and enter the fortress of the king of the north, and he shall deal with

[z] Gk: Heb *from a branch*

Her child abandons the Masoretic pointing, for the text can mean only **he that begat her,** i.e., her father Ptolemy Philadelphus. He did die about this time, though not through any plotting of Laodice. Some have suggested that in the popular mind his death may have been connected with these events and ascribed to Laodice's plotting, but most editors accept the emendation to **her child,** which makes the reference to the murder of her infant. The Peshitta and Vulg. presuppose a text "her sons," while the LXX omits the word. **And he who got possession of her:** Lit., **and he that strengthened her in these times.** Some refer this to her father Ptolemy, taking it and the previous word as but two descriptive epithets for him, "he who begot her and he who strengthened her." Others refer it to her brother Ptolemy III Euergetes, who came to her assistance. Generally it is referred to her husband Antiochus, who was considered to have been a victim of Laodice's revenge. Charles claims that this form of the verb means "to obtain," as in vs. 21, so "he who obtained her" would be her husband. Ginsberg (*Studies,* p. 47) suggests that it is a mistaken translation of the Aramaic וגברה, "and her husband," for גבר can have the meaning "to strengthen."

7. In those times: In the M.T. this is part of the previous verse (cf. KJV), but there is general agreement among editors to transpose it so that it comes after the *wāw* at the beginning of vs. 7, or if the ו is emended to י then before it.

Vss. 7-9 deal with Ptolemy III Euergetes and Seleucus II Callinicus. To avenge the murder of Berenice, his sister, Ptolemy III invaded the Seleucid area, seized Seleucia so as to control the port of Antioch, and overran apparently a good deal of Syria and Babylonia. Had he not been called home to deal with a serious insurrection in Egypt he might well have conquered the whole Seleucid kingdom. As it was, he brought back to Egypt immense booty. Two years later Seleucus, son of Laodice, made the counterblow and attempted to invade Egypt, meeting with a disastrous defeat from which he was able to extricate but a handful of troops with whom he retreated northward.

A branch from her roots shall arise: Lit., "and there shall arise from the offshoots of her roots." The LXX makes it probable that the original text read "an offspring from her roots." *Nēçer* is a "sprout," a "shoot," hence "offspring," "descendant" (cf. Isa. 11:1). The reference is to Berenice's brother who was of the same stock and who had succeeded his father as ruler in Egypt. **In his place:** His obviously refers to the king of the south, thus meaning that Ptolemy Euergetes succeeded Ptolemy Philadelphus. The LXX has "like unto him," meaning that the new Ptolemy would follow the policies of his father with regard to Syria.

He shall come against the army interprets אל as meaning על, **against,** taking the passage to refer to Ptolemy's advance against the Seleucid army. The word אל, however, means "unto," and some take the construction to mean "unto his own army," i.e., he placed himself at the head of his troops, or "unto power," meaning he will come to power in Egypt. Others emend the text to read, "and he shall bring an army against them," which suits admirably what follows. Montgomery emends *ḥáyil* to *ḥil* so that it reads, "he shall come to the outworks and enter the fortress."

Fortress: *Mā'ôz* is a "refuge," a "place of protection," then a **fortress** or "strong city." Some think the reference is to Antioch, but the word is usually taken to mean Seleucia, the fortified city on the Mediterranean, which Polybius tells us was taken by Ptolemy

---

and security. Gladstone said that the task of the statesman is to see which way God Almighty is going to move in the next fifty years. That is

the task for the present. It is the particular task of the religious leaders and the religious fellowship.

8 And shall also carry captives into Egypt their gods, with their princes, *and* with their precious vessels of silver and of gold; and he shall continue *more* years than the king of the north.

9 So the king of the south shall come into *his* kingdom, and shall return into his own land.

10 But his sons shall be stirred up, and shall assemble a multitude of great forces: and *one* shall certainly come, and overflow, and pass through: then shall he return, and be stirred up, *even* to his fortress.

them and shall prevail. 8 He shall also carry off to Egypt their gods with their molten images and with their precious vessels of silver and of gold; and for some years he shall refrain from attacking the king of the north. 9 Then the latter shall come into the realm of the king of the south but shall return into his own land.

10 "His sons shall wage war and assemble a multitude of great forces, which shall come on and overflow and pass through, and again shall carry the war as far as his

in this campaign and remained for many years under Egyptian control. This is the Seleucia of Acts 13:4. On Montgomery's interpretation the "outworks" would be Seleucia and the **fortress** Antioch.

Having taken the strongholds, Ptolemy will deal with the people as seems good to him. **With them** would seem to mean the Syrians in general, not merely the people in the fortress (for the expression see Jer. 18:23; Neh. 9:24). **Shall prevail**: Lit., "shall show himself strong," or "shall act valiantly" (cf. vs. 32).

8. Why Ptolemy so suddenly returned is not mentioned and may not have been known to the writer, though he knows the story of the immense booty that was brought back. To carry off the **gods** of a conquered people was common custom in the ancient Near East. It is referred to in Jer. 48:7; 49:3. The Canopus decree mentions in particular that Ptolemy brought back a number of images of Egyptian gods which Cambyses had carried off after conquering Egypt in 525 B.C.—the reason for which the Egyptians conferred on this Ptolemy the title Euergetes.

Their gods: Their idols; the reference must be to images of the Syrian deities as well as those Egyptian images Ptolemy brought back. The **molten images** may be intended to particularize idols made of molten metal poured into molds. Numerous molds for the making of such images have been recovered by excavations in the Near East.

With their precious vessels: Lit., "and the vessels of their desire," i.e., costly things (for the expression see Hos. 13:15; II Chr. 32:27; 36:10). Jerome quotes from Porphyry the statement that he brought back as booty 2,500 precious vessels. Doubtless some of these were temple furniture from Syrian temples which he took, much as Nebuchadrezzar took those from the temple in Jerusalem (II Kings 25:13-17).

"And he, years shall he stand from the king of the north" is usually taken to mean that he will be satisfied with this victory and for some years refrain from further attack on the Seleucids. This interpretation takes 'āmadh as meaning "to stand away from," i.e., **refrain from**, a meaning it has in Gen. 29:35; II Kings 4:6. Theod. reads, "he shall continue stronger than," and some interpreters think that *min* is best taken as a comparative, "he shall continue to live some years longer than." Ginsberg (*loc. cit.*) suggests that הוא, **he,** is a mistake for the Aramaic הא, "lo," and that both **years** and "from the king" are mistakes, the original having read, "and behold, the king of the north shall arise a second time." This then links smoothly with vs. 9.

9. Then the latter shall come into: Lit., "and he shall come into." "He" must be the king of the north, so that the reference will be to the campaign Seleucus II began in 242 B.C. in an attempt to invade Egypt, which however developed so disastrously that Seleucus returned to Antioch in 240 with only a fragment of his army (see Justin *History of the World* XXVII. 2).

10-19. These verses deal for the most part with the reign of Antiochus III the Great. The elder son of Seleucus II succeeded him in 227 B.C. as Seleucus III Ceraunus, but in 223 he was murdered during a campaign in Asia Minor and his brother Antiochus

11 And the king of the south shall be moved with choler, and shall come forth and fight with him, *even* with the king of the north: and he shall set forth a great multitude; but the multitude shall be given into his hand.

11 Then the king of the south, moved with anger, shall come out and fight with the king of the north; and he shall raise a great multitude, but it shall be given

succeeded. Not long after his succession Antiochus III attacked Palestine. In two campaigns he defeated the armies of Ptolemy IV Philopator and conquered a considerable part of the country. In 217, however, the tide turned and Ptolemy won a decisive victory at Raphia, whereby Egypt regained control of Palestine. When Ptolemy IV died mysteriously in 203 B.C., and was succeeded by his infant son Ptolemy V Epiphanes, Antiochus was able again to venture against Egyptian forces, defeated the general Scopas at Banias, besieged him in Sidon, entered Jerusalem, and neutralized Egypt by marrying his daughter Cleopatra to the youthful Ptolemy. Attempting to extend his power to the west, he was defeated disastrously at Thermopylae in 191 and at Magnesia in 190, and in 187/186 lost his life while attempting to recoup his fortunes by plundering a temple at Elymais.

10. His sons: The *Kethîbh* reads "and his son," which is followed by the LXX. If we read a singular, the reference must be Antiochus III, but if we read a plural with *Qerê*, it will be Seleucus and Antiochus. Seleucus, however, at no time made war on Egypt, though his expedition into Asia Minor in 223 might have been regarded as preliminary to an attack on the Ptolemies, and sufficient to justify the prediction **shall wage war and assemble a multitude of great forces.** The real attack on Egypt was by Antiochus III, and it is best to refer this verse to him. The verbs are plurals and so agree with the *Qerê*. If we accept the *Kethîbh*, they must be emended to singulars. *Hithgāreh* is "to stir oneself up," as in vs. 25, but has the implication of being **stirred up** for combat.

"And it shall come onward, and shall sweep away, and shall overflow." "It" is the great multitude of forces previously mentioned which will sweep everything before it as it overflows the land (cf. Isa. 8:8). Some translate "he" and refer to Antiochus himself, for in the early part of his campaign he was generally successful against the Egyptian forces. The verb *shāṭaph* is used of rinsing in Lev. 15:11-12, of washing away defilement in Ezek. 16:9; I Kings 22:38, but generally of the overwhelming flood of water that sweeps everything in its path, as in Pss. 69:2; 124:4; Isa. 28:2; 30:28. It is used again of armies in vss. 22, 26, 40.

"And it [or he] shall return and they shall make war even unto his fortress." If we read with the *Qerê*, which is assumed by both the LXX and Theod., it will be "he shall return" and "he shall make war." Some take the reference to be to the fact that the army of Antiochus moved northward to winter at Ptolemais (Polybius *Histories* V. 66), and set out campaigning again in the spring. It is more likely, however, that the **return** refers to Antiochus' returning again to the attack. Whose **fortress** is meant is uncertain. Some think it was Antiochus' fortress at Gaza, Driver even suggesting that there is a wordplay on עזה (Gaza) and מעזה (fortress). Others think it means Ptolemy's fortress at Raphia. That he is to **carry the war,** lit., "stir himself up," suggests that the latter is correct. Still others have thought that the reference is to Pelusium, which in Ezek. 30:15 is called the "fortress of Egypt," but Antiochus seems not to have reached so far south in this campaign. Ginsberg (*loc. cit.*) would restore an underlying Aramaic text to read, "and he [Antiochus] shall fight back to his [Ptolemy's] stronghold." If we preserve the *Kethîbh* "they shall make war," it will mean the resumption of hostilities by both sides.

11. The **king of the south** here is Ptolemy Philopator. *Hithmarmar* is "to be exasperated," **moved with choler,** a late word which in 8:7 was used of Alexander and was translated "he was enraged." Actually, it was his general Nicolaus who led the Egyptian armies up through Palestine (Polybius *op. cit.* V. 68-69). **With the king of the north:** The M.T. reads "with him, with the king of the north," which Charles considers

12 *And* when he hath taken away the multitude, his heart shall be lifted up; and he shall cast down *many* ten thousands: but he shall not be strengthened *by it.*

13 For the king of the north shall return, and shall set forth a multitude greater than the former, and shall certainly come after certain years with a great army and with much riches.

into his hand. 12 And when the multitude is taken, his heart shall be exalted, and he shall cast down tens of thousands, but he shall not prevail. 13 For the king of the north shall again raise a multitude, greater than the former; and after some years[a] he shall come on with a great army and abundant supplies.

[a] Heb *at the end of the times years*

---

an Aramaism meaning "with this same king of the north." Some, however, would delete **king of the north** as an explanatory gloss inserted to make clear who was meant by **him.**

And he shall raise a great multitude, but it shall be given into his hand. Some take this to mean that Ptolemy will raise a large army of which he will personally take charge. "To be given into the hand of," however, normally means "to be defeated by" (cf. I Kings 20:28). Hence, Antiochus probably raised a great army which was then defeated by Ptolemy. This fits with vs. 13.

12. And when the multitude is taken: Lit., "and the multitude will be swept away." The verb נשא in this sense of being routed occurs in 2:35, where the wind sweeps away the chaff from the threshing floor (cf. Isa. 40:24; 41:16; 57:13; Job 32:22). The reference would then be to the defeat of Antiochus at Raphia in 217 B.C. Some take the **multitude** to be the army of Ptolemy, and so translate "and the multitude shall stand up," i.e., to fight, the verb having this meaning in Isa. 33:10.

His heart shall be exalted: Reading with *Qerê*, Ptolemy's heart will be exalted at the victory (cf. the Aramaic of 5:20; note Deut. 8:14; 17:20). The LXX, Theod., and Vulg. read also with *Qerê* ירום instead of the *Kethîbh* ירום. Polybius (*ibid.* V. 86) records that Antiochus lost nearly ten thousand infantry at Raphia, besides three hundred cavalry and four thousand prisoners, so "myriads" is justified. **But he shall not prevail:** Lit., "but he shall not show himself strong," or, perhaps better, "he shall not be bold." Ptolemy, instead of following up his victory and pursuing Antiochus, was content to occupy Coele-Syria and make peace with the Seleucids (*ibid.* V. 87).

13. Antiochus retrieved his reputation by successful campaigns in Persia and Asia Minor, as a result of which he was able to build up his power. When in 205 Ptolemy IV died and was succeeded by the infant Ptolemy V, Antiochus made an alliance with Philip of Macedon to make a joint attack on Egypt, whose possessions they would then divide. The Egyptian armies were under the command of Scopas who, after fluctuating fortunes, was by 200 B.C. in possession of Judea, but in 198 was crushed by Antiochus at Banias and had to take refuge in Sidon, where he was besieged and forced to surrender. Antiochus then invaded Phoenicia and captured Gaza (*ibid.* XV. 20; XVI. 18; Josephus *Antiquities* XII. 3. 3).

And after some years: Lit., at the end of times years. To avoid so awkward a phrase some delete **times** as a gloss that has crept in from vs. 14. Others delete **years** as the insertion of a scribe who had his mind on vs. 6. Some separate the two and construe **years** with the following verb, i.e., "and at the end of times he will for some years come repeatedly." This, however, would be an abnormal construction. Montgomery suggests that **some years** is meant to indicate the sixteen years between Raphia and Gaza. Others think it is the twelve years between Raphia and the end of the Persian campaigns. **He shall come on:** Charles prefers to read בו for בוא, with the LXX and some MSS, and to translate "and he shall attack him." **And abundant supplies:** *Rekhûsh* means "goods and chattels." In vs. 24 it is translated "goods," and in vs. 28 "riches," but here it seems to mean impedimenta, the normal camp baggage and equipage of war, as in Gen. 14:11-12; II Chr. 21:14. Since *rékhesh* means a "horse," Montgomery suggests that the writer may have been playing with this word to recall the tales about the quantity of elephants and baggage animals Antiochus brought back from his eastern campaigns.

14 And in those times there shall many stand up against the king of the south: also the robbers of thy people shall exalt themselves to establish the vision; but they shall fall.

15 So the king of the north shall come, and cast up a mount, and take the most fenced cities: and the arms of the south shall not withstand, neither his chosen people, neither *shall there be any* strength to withstand.

14 "In those times many shall rise against the king of the south; and the men of violence among your own people shall lift themselves up in order to fulfil the vision; but they shall fail. 15 Then the king of the north shall come and throw up siegeworks, and take a well-fortified city. And the forces of the south shall not stand, or even his picked troops, for there shall be no

14. It seems best to take the **many** who **shall rise against** Ptolemy to mean the insurrections which broke out in Egypt while Ptolemy V was a child, insurrections directed primarily against the regent Agathocles, who had been chief minister of Ptolemy IV, but who took advantage of the minority of the new monarch to act oppressively toward the people (Polybius *op. cit.* XV. 25. 34). Others think it refers to the alliances made by Antiochus, such as that with Philip of Macedon, to secure assistance for his projected attack on Egypt. There is no reason why the reference should not be to both.

Men of violence among your own people: Lit., "sons of the violent among thy people." The most probable interpretation is that this refers to the Jews who at this time joined themselves to Antiochus (Josephus *Antiquities* XII. 3. 3-4), and whose action was an important factor in bringing the whole country under the domination of the Seleucids. Some have pressed the word **violence** with the thought that it refers to some flaming up of a messianic hope at this time seeking to throw off heathen domination. Others have pressed the word "sons," thinking that these must be the family of the Tobiads who had secured the high priesthood and were robbing the people. Kamphausen suggests that the reference is not to any family in particular but to the whole class of tax contractors and their adherents. *Pāraç* is "to break through," so *pāriç* could mean a robber, as in Jer. 7:11.

In order to fulfil the vision: Lit., "to cause the vision to stand"; i.e., the siding of some Jewish groups with Antiochus was necessary in order that the divine predictions in the vision might be fulfilled. What the reference here is we do not know. Some have thought those who "rose up" regarded their action as fulfilling some ancient prophecy. It would seem rather to mean that unwittingly by their action they are fulfilling a prediction in this vision of Daniel. **But they shall fail:** Not fail to fulfill the prediction, but fail in the purpose of their uprising. This failure may be a reference to the measures taken by Scopas in Palestine, for Polybius (*ibid.* XVI. 39. 1) records that he subdued "the nation of the Jews," a phrase which suggests that there had been some kind of anti-Egyptian uprising among them which had to be put down. The verb used here is "to stumble," a verb which is used in both a literal (Prov. 4:12) and a moral sense (Hos. 5:5).

15. Some regard vs. 14 as a parenthesis, so that vs. 15 takes up the thread of vs. 13 and carries on the narrative from where it stopped there. Others regard this verse as referring to a later and quite different campaign. As the struggle between the two countries went on for years, there would doubtless have been many episodes in it which would have seemed striking to contemporary observers. Most probably the reference here is to the siege of Sidon in 198 B.C. *Ṣôlelāh* is a "mound" or "rampart," and so

14. **Traitors.**—Long before the terms "fifth column" and "quisling" entered our vocabularies, the things they describe existed. Traitors exist in every nation and in every organization.

The church knows them. They are the worst enemies of all. For the sake of personal profit they stand ready to betray their people and make a deal with the enemy. Their true nature

16 But he that cometh against him shall do according to his own will, and none shall stand before him: and he shall stand in the glorious land, which by his hand shall be consumed.

17 He shall also set his face to enter with the strength of his whole kingdom, and upright ones with him; thus shall he do: and

16 But he who comes against him shall do according to his own will, and none shall stand before him; and he shall stand in the glorious land, and all of it shall be in his power. 17 He shall set his face to come with the strength of his whole kingdom, and he shall bring terms

---

siegeworks. **Throw up:** Lit., "pour out." The expression, however, is used of the construction of earthworks, supposedly from the fact that in building them the workmen pour the earth out from their wicker baskets (cf. II Sam. 20:15; Isa. 37:33; Ezek. 17:17; 26:8). **A well-fortified city:** Lit., "a city of fortifications" (cf. vs. 24; I Sam. 6:18; II Kings 3:19; 10:2). This description would suit Sidon.

Forces: *Zerôaʿ* is an "arm" of the body, but is used in this chapter as a military term. **Even his picked troops:** Lit., **his chosen people,** taking **his** to refer to Ptolemy. The word is used in Exod. 15:4 for Pharaoh's chosen captains, in Jer. 48:15 for the picked youth of Moab, in Ezek. 23:7 for the picked men of Assyria. Those who **shall not stand** are taken by Driver to be Scopas and his troops shut up in Sidon and the forces sent from Egypt to relieve him, but which also fell before Antiochus.

16. He who comes against him: Antiochus coming against Ptolemy V. He will **do according to his own will,** as in vs. 3, since there is no longer any army in the field capable of opposing him. Thus Palestine will fall into his power. It was his by 197 B.C.

The glorious land, as in 8:9, is a name for Palestine. **And all of it:** This rendering depends on a reading *kullāh,* but the text has *kālāh,* "destruction," whence the KJV **shall be consumed.** If it is "destruction," the meaning is that Antiochus is there with the forces of destruction under his hand, forces that will presently do much damage. The emendation is preferable.

17. He shall set his face to come: Antiochus, after his successes in Syria, will turn toward Egypt. For "to set the face" in the sense of "to direct oneself toward" see Gen. 31:21; II Kings 12:17; Jer. 42:15, 17. **With the strength of his whole kingdom:** Antiochus will assemble his whole strength for this attack on Egypt. Actually he seems not to have launched any attack on Egypt proper, but his campaigns against the coastal cities of Cilicia, Lycia, and Caria, which were in Egyptian possession, were all directed toward weakening Egyptian power (Livy XXXIII. 19. 6-11). Some think that the **kingdom** meant is that of Ptolemy and so render, "to come against the might of his whole kingdom," i.e., having defeated the Egyptian armies outside Egypt, Antiochus will now come down to face the Egyptian might in its own land.

And he shall bring terms of peace: The text is confused. The M.T. reads, "and upright ones with him and he shall make." The LXX has "and covenants with him shall he make," which probably represents an older text underlying also Theod. and the Vulg. "With him" probably means Ptolemy, for Antiochus gave up his plan of campaign in order to make peace with the Egyptians in 197, a peace which was sealed by betrothing his daughter Cleopatra to Ptolemy. **He shall give him the daughter of women:** Cleopatra went to Egypt in 194/193 B.C. to be Ptolemy's wife, being the first Cleopatra in Egyptian history. **Daughter of women** is a peculiar expression which seems to depend on some underlying Aramaic idiom.

To destroy the kingdom: The M.T. has no word for **kingdom,** only a pronoun. Some translate this pronoun "him," making it refer to Ptolemy and assuming that Antiochus' object in giving Cleopatra to him was to bring him down. This makes sense

---

is not disclosed until the crisis arrives. But the crisis has not created them. It has only revealed them.

16. *The Glorious Land.*—Men of violence sometimes succeed in occupying holy territory, but they never possess it. **The glorious land is**

he shall give him the daughter of women, corrupting her: but she shall not stand *on his side,* neither be for him.

18 After this shall he turn his face unto the isles, and shall take many: but a prince for his own behalf shall cause the reproach offered by him to cease; without his own reproach he shall cause *it* to turn upon him.

19 Then he shall turn his face toward the fort of his own land: but he shall stumble and fall, and not be found.

of peace[b] and perform them. He shall give him the daughter of women to destroy the kingdom;[c] but it shall not stand or be to his advantage. 18 Afterward he shall turn his face to the coastlands, and shall take many of them; but a commander shall put an end to his insolence; indeed[d] he shall turn his insolence back upon him. 19 Then he shall turn his face back toward the fortresses of his own land; but he shall stumble and fall, and shall not be found.

[b] Heb *her* or *it*
[c] Gk: Heb *upright ones*
[d] Heb obscure

and agrees with what follows, for his scheme did not work out as he had planned. The pronoun, however, is feminine, and some render **to destroy her,** i.e., Cleopatra (so KJV **corrupting her**), which makes no sense. It can be referred to the kingdom, **to destroy it,** Antiochus' purpose in the alliance being to destroy Egyptian independence by bringing the country under his control. Bevan omits the pronoun altogether, rendering the words "to wreak ruin." "But it shall not stand, nor to him shall it be." Antiochus' scheme came to nothing, for Cleopatra settled down happily in Egypt, championed her husband's cause and encouraged the Egyptian alliance with Rome, which proved fatal to the plans of Antiochus (for the expression see Isa. 7:7).

18-19. Thinking that he had secured Egypt without having to waste his forces, Antiochus turned his attention to the west. In 196 B.C. he forced the more important towns in Asia Minor to submit, crossed the Hellespont and captured the Thracian Chersonese, so that in 192 he was able actually to invade Greece proper. This brought him into conflict with the Romans, who defeated him at Thermopylae in 191 and drove him out of Europe. The following year they decided to drive him out of Asia Minor and inflicted on him a disastrous defeat at Magnesia, which not only humiliated but completely ruined him (Livy XXXVIII. 39-44).

He shall turn his face to the coastlands: He is Antiochus and the reference is to the expeditions by land and sea which he set in motion in 197 B.C. to bring under his control the coastlands of Asia Minor. The word *'iyyîm* is, lit., **isles,** but may be used for coastal lands (cf. Isa. 66:19; Ezek. 27:7; Zeph. 2:11). The LXX apparently read *yām,* "sea," which might merely mean "westward." **Take many** is generally considered to refer to the coastlands or the chief cities, but some think it may refer to the prisoners taken on this campaign. There is no **of them** in the M.T., which merely says **and shall take many.**

But a commander shall put an end to his insolence: The text is confused. The M.T. reads, "But a commander shall bring to an end his reproach to him, except his reproach shall he repay him." Various emendations have been proposed. The translation above simply omits the last clause, following those editors who treat it as a gloss. The text before the LXX translator, however, contained these words. It seems to mean that a commander will first end this affront of Antiochus and then turn the affront on him. The **commander** must be that Lucius Cornelius Scipio, who in 190 crushed Antiochus at Magnesia, robbed him of the fruits of his western campaign, and forced him to submit to humiliating conditions of peace. *Qāçîn* is properly a "magistrate," from *qāçāh,* "to pronounce judicial sentence," but it is used of a military officer in Josh. 10:24; Judg. 11:6, 11. Montgomery remarks on the neatness of this choice of a word to designate the Roman consul who was both magistrate and military commander.

Insolence: *Ḥerpāh* is **reproach,** "insult," "affront." The persistent attacks of Antiochus on the coasts of Asia Minor were an affront to Roman authority and had to be dealt with severely. Possibly the word covers something more serious, for we read that

20 Then shall stand up in his estate a raiser of taxes *in* the glory of the kingdom: but within few days he shall be destroyed, neither in anger, nor in battle.

20 "Then shall arise in his place one who shall send an exactor of tribute through the glory of the kingdom; but within a few days he shall be broken, neither in anger

---

Antiochus had made bold to tell the Romans that his doings in the east were no more their concern than their doings in the west were his (Livy XXXIII. 40. 1-2; Polybius *op. cit.* XVIII. 51. 1-2). The defeat at Magnesia repaid that affront. On the basis of the LXX Bevan would emend to read, "he shall requite his insults sevenfold."

Toward the fortresses of his own land refers to Antiochus' retreat across the Taurus to his own territories. It is not necessary to think that the writer had any special place in mind, the point being that he who had been so busy robbing the strongholds of other lands now finds himself reduced to robbing those in his own territories. It was in an attempt to plunder the temple of Bel at Elymais that he stumbled and died. For the indemnity he had to pay see Polybius (*ibid.* XXI. 14. 7) and Livy (XXXVII. 45. 14); for his end while seeking funds with which to pay it see Justin (*History of the World* XXXII. 2) and Diodorus Siculus (XXIX. 15).

The words used here to describe his end are drawn from Ps. 37:36; Job 20:8. **Stumble:** The same verb is translated "shall fail" in vs. 14. **Shall not be found:** As in I Sam. 10:21; Jer. 50:20.

20. Antiochus III was succeeded by his son Seleucus IV Philopator (187-175 B.C.), whose reign is summarized in this verse. He was an unpopular ruler whose reign was inglorious (Appian *Roman History* XI. 10. 60). Even had he been a great king, his rule would have been inglorious, for his preoccupation was necessarily the paying off of the indemnity imposed on his father.

In his place: So in vss. 21, 38. This phrase is used in Daniel as practically the equivalent of our "instead of."

"One who shall cause an exactor to pass through the glory of the kingdom": This is usually taken to refer to the mission of Heliodorus, the finance minister, who was sent to see if the rumor of great wealth stored in the temple at Jerusalem was true, and if so, to seize it for the king's treasury (II Macc. 3:1-40). Heliodorus was prevented from taking it, the story says, by supernatural intervention. In this case the **glory of the kingdom** would be Judea, or Jerusalem, or perhaps Palestine as a whole (cf. vs. 16). However, **glory of the kingdom** stands for "royal glory" or "royal splendor," and some therefore deny any particular association with Judea and refer it to the mission of the finance minister throughout the Seleucid kingdom to raise funds for fulfilling the royal obligation in the matter of the tribute. Such an exactor would of course have visited Palestine annually on his rounds and so would have been well known. Bevan transposes *ma'abhir* and *nôghês,* making Seleucus himself the exactor and suggesting that it was his avarice that was the ruination of the "royal splendor." Frank Zimmermann ("The Aramaic Origin of Daniel 8–12," *Journal of Biblical Literature,* LVII [1938], 265) suggested that behind the awkward Hebrew of this passage there was a simple Aramaic sentence, "and in his place shall stand one deprived of dominion, glory, and sovereignty." This makes it a simple description of the inglorious reign of Seleucus IV and removes all reference to the exactor. It has some support from the Peshitta. **Exactor:** *Nôghês* (Zech. 9:8) is the word used for the taskmasters in Exod. 3:7. From I Macc. 1:29 we know that Antiochus Epiphanes later had such an officer.

But within a few days he shall be broken does not necessarily mean that he will be killed, but only that he will be ruined. It is generally taken to refer to the death of Seleucus, who was the victim of a conspiracy hatched by his foster brother Heliodorus, who was at the same time his finance minister (Appian *op. cit.* XI. 8. 45). Others think it is merely a reference to the sudden and inexplicable collapse of the power of Seleucus. **Broken** is used of a person brought to ruin (cf. Prov. 6:15; Jer. 14:17; 22:20). Those who think Seleucus is one of the horns of 7:8 suggest that **broken** is used here in remembrance

21 And in his estate shall stand up a vile person, to whom they shall not give the honor of the kingdom: but he shall come in peaceably, and obtain the kingdom by flatteries.

21 In his place shall arise a contemptible person to whom royal majesty has not been given; he shall come in without warning and obtain the kingdom

nor in battle.

---

of what was said there (see also 8:8, 25, and the use of the verb in this chapter in vss. 4, 22, 26).

"But not in wrath and not in war," i.e., neither by open violence **nor in battle.** *'Appayim* is the dual of *'aph,* "nose," and since the nose was the organ thought to be associated with **anger,** the dual has that meaning, as in Prov. 14:29; 15:18; 30:33. Graetz emends to באנפים, "in battle array," as in Ezek. 17:21; 38:6, 9, but such an emendation is scarcely justifiable. Behrmann keeps the present text but thinks the word is being used, like the Aramaic באנפין, to mean "openly," i.e., he was not killed openly in a battle but was the victim of a conspiracy. At the time he died his brother Antiochus was on his way back to the East from Rome, and some suspect the writer had in mind rumors that Antiochus, who succeeded him, was not innocent of the conspiracy whereby he met his end.

c) The Doings of Antiochus Epiphanes (11:21-45)

21-45. This section describes the reign of Antiochus Epiphanes (175-164 B.C.) and the enormities committed under him. He was the younger son of Antiochus the Great, and when his father in 190 made submission to the Romans he was taken to Rome as a hostage. He remained there fourteen years, during which time the Romans, as he himself admits, treated him as royalty, not as a prisoner. Then, for some reason that is not clear, there was an exchange whereby Demetrius the eldest son of Seleucus was sent to replace him as hostage. Antiochus was at Athens on his way home when he heard the news that his brother was dead and Heliodorus was attempting to take over the kingship under pretense of a regency for the younger son of Seleucus. Antiochus hastened to Antioch, where, aided by Eumenes king of Pergamum and Attalus his brother, he was able to thwart Heliodorus and seize the power for himself.

21. A contemptible person: *Nibhzeh* is from *bāzāh,* "to despise" (see Ps. 15:4). This of course is a Jewish judgment on him, like the "sinful shoot" of I Macc. 1:10 and the "little horn" of Dan. 7:8; 8:9. Secular historians have varied in their estimates of his character. Some think that the word **contemptible** is used here, like the "Epimanes" mentioned by Polybius (*op. cit.* XXVI. 1. 1), as a deliberate challenge to the title "Epiphanes," insisting that he was a contemptible man, not a manifest god. **To whom royal majesty has not been given:** Lit., "nor did they set upon him the honor of a kingdom." For the expression see Num. 27:20, where it is used of the appointment of Joshua, and I Chr. 29:25, of Solomon. **They** must refer to the people in general. In the eyes of the people Antiochus, as the younger son, had never been considered as a possible successor to his father, and when Seleucus was murdered, it was his son Demetrius who in their eyes would be the rightful heir to the throne.

We do not know the whole story of Heliodorus' conspiracy. From the point of view of the common people Antiochus came in suddenly and unexpectedly. The death of Seleucus Philopator was quite unexpected, and before the populace knew what was happening, Antiochus had appeared and secured the throne while men were off their guard. *Shalwāh* is "carelessness," and so **without warning** means when folk were careless or unheeding. The word occurs again in vs. 24 and was used in 8:25 of Antiochus' sudden

---

never home to them. It is home only to the spiritually minded.

21. *Forgetting God's Royal Honor.*—Let us be entirely allegorical. What is a man without the royal honor bestowed upon him? He is the victim of terrible tendencies and desires. The glory of the man is like the worth of a coin, not intrinsic but created by the royal superscription.

22 And with the arms of a flood shall they be overflown from before him, and shall be broken; yea, also the prince of the covenant.

23 And after the league *made* with him he shall work deceitfully: for he shall come up, and shall become strong with a small people.

flatteries. 22 Armies shall be utterly swept away before him and broken, and the prince of the covenant also. 23 And from the time that an alliance is made with him he shall act deceitfully; and he shall become strong with a small people. Without warning

---

attack on the unsuspecting people of Jerusalem. Since it commonly means "security" or "peace," Charles would translate "in time of security."

Having seized the royal dignity, Antiochus proceeded to secure his position **by flatteries.** The word *ḥallûq* means, lit., "smooth," and so *ḥalaqlaq,* "smooth cunning," while the feminine plural suggests guileful, treacherous, flattering words. The word is used in Ps. 35:6; Jer. 23:12 to mean "slippery places"; 8:23 refers to him as adept in trickeries and intrigue. It is possible that **flatteries** refers to the conspiracy whereby he was able to come in and seize the throne, but it is more likely that it refers to his actions after he had taken possession. An extant inscription reveals how he persuaded the council and people of Antioch to pass a vote of thanks to the Pergamenes for the help Eumenes and Attalus had given him. **Obtain** is, lit., "to seize with a strong hold," from a root "to be strong," i.e., he made secure his position in the kingdom.

22. Not all his difficulties, however, could be resolved by smooth speech and intrigue. Heliodorus and other domestic enemies championing the cause of claimants who had a more legitimate title to the throne than he had needed to be dealt with by force, and dissident elements in Syria had to be suppressed. Thus it is more likely that this verse concerns events of the years 175-170 in Syria than that it refers to Antiochus' campaign against Egypt.

Armies shall be utterly swept away before him: Lit., "and the arms of the flood shall be flood-swept from before him." **Arms** is the same word as in vs. 15 and occurs again in vs. 31. The flood-sweeping image was used in 9:26 and occurs in this chapter in vss. 10, 26, 40 (cf. Isa. 8:8; 28:15, 18; Jer. 47:2). Since **arms of a flood** is awkward, Bevan reads השטף not according to the Masoretic vocalization, *hashshéṭeph,* but *hashshāṭōph,* and translates, "and forces shall be utterly overwhelmed before him." This emendation has had wide acceptance. Theod. read *hashshōṭēph,* "of him that swept down," making it refer to one particular enemy, perhaps Heliodorus.

And broken: As in vs. 20. The expression is used of an army in II Chr. 14:13. In the text as we have it this must refer to the armies. Marti emends the text to have it go with **prince of the covenant,** i.e., the armies of his opponents shall be swept away and the prince of the covenant broken. The **prince** would seem to refer to Onias III, whom Antiochus removed from office in 175 and who was murdered in 170. He is the "anointed one" of 9:26 (cf. II Macc. 4:7-10, 33-36). *Nāghidh* is a title used for the high priest. *Berith* means the **covenant** of God with Israel. It is used here and in vs. 32 without the article. Theod. had recognized that the reference was to Onias, but this was thought by many earlier commentators to be an anachronism, and so, as *nekhidh berith* could be rendered "confederate prince," they thought the reference might be to Ptolemy Philometor. This is possible but not probable.

23. The various allusions in this verse are quite uncertain. "And from the uniting unto him." *Ḥābher* is an "associate," "companion," and *hithhabber* is "to join in association with" as in a **league** or **alliance** (cf. vs. 6; II Chr. 20:35, 37). **With him** is most probably with Antiochus, though some think it means with the prince of the covenant; in that case the reference would be to the arrangement with Jason, whom Antiochus had appointed in the place of Onias. Driver thinks it is Antiochus' insincere alliance with Ptolemy. The reference may be to his alliance with the Pergamenes, who helped him to attain his throne. Montgomery translates, "and by confederacy [of others]

24 He shall enter peaceably even upon the fattest places of the province; and he shall do *that* which his fathers have not done, nor his fathers' fathers; he shall scatter among them the prey, and spoil, and riches: *yea,* and he shall forecast his devices against the strongholds, even for a time.

24 he shall come into the richest parts[e] of the province; and he shall do what neither his fathers nor his fathers' fathers have done, scattering among them plunder, spoil, and goods. He shall devise plans against

[e] Or *among the richest men*

---

with him." **He shall act deceitfully:** "He shall work deceit," a reference to Antiochus' way of overreaching his friends, a conspicuous case being that of Jason. There may be a reference to this in 9:26. *Mirmāh* is "fraud," "deceit," "falsehood," and is the word translated "deceit" in 8:25.

The meaning of **he shall become strong** is much disputed. Those who interpret these verses as dealing with the Egyptian campaign translate, "he shall go up," i.e., he will go up the Nile. *'Ālāh* can mean "to take the field," as in Isa. 21:2, but here it is much more likely that it means "to mount up," i.e., to rise to power. **With a small people:** Some render "with a few men." The word גוי here seems to be used in the sense of עם, which may reflect an underlying Aramaic text. The allusion is apparently to the relatively small following Antiochus had when he first attained to power. Montgomery translates, "with a small nation," taking the reference to be to the much smaller kingdom he ruled as compared with his father.

Without warning: Or, on the other interpretation, "in time of security," as in vss. 21 (cf. 8:25). In the M.T. this is the first word of vs. 24, though it suits better here if we take this verse to mean that before men were aware of what he was doing, Antiochus with his few supporters had established himself on the throne.

24. He shall come into the richest parts of the province: The **province** seems to be Palestine. *Mishmān* means "fatness," and it is probable that the plural here, "fatnesses," means the fattest parts of the province (cf. Gen. 27:39). Ewald thought it meant Galilee in particular. Those who hold the Egyptian theory refer it to the **fattest** provinces of Egypt. Bevan would render "fat ones," i.e., warriors (Ps. 78:31; Isa. 10:16), and, as בא with the preposition ב can mean "to attack" (as in vs. 30), would translate, "and by stealth he will attack the mightiest men of [each] province," which, he points out, would agree with 8:25. Others take the word to mean the richer inhabitants of Palestine, the Jewish Hellenizers, and translate, **among the richest men;** in that case the **scattering among them** of bounty was something the earlier Seleucids had not done.

Plunder, spoil, and goods: These words remind one of the many references to the plundering activities of Antiochus (I Macc. 1:19; 3:31; Polybius *op. cit.* XXXI. 9. 1). The generosity of Antiochus in distributing lavishly to those about him is also often mentioned (I Macc. 3:30; Livy XLI. 20; Polybius *op. cit.* XXVI. 1. 8-11; Josephus *Antiquities* XII. 7. 2). Montgomery suggests that his excess over his fathers was in this matter of plundering and distributing the booty rather than in his generosity to the Jewish leaders.

"And against strongholds shall he devise his devices." He has not yet started but is making plans for reducing the **strongholds.** What fortresses the writer had in mind was doubtless obvious to his audience. Modern interpreters generally refer this to the Egyptian campaign, which is the subject of vs. 25 (see I Macc. 1:16, 19; Livy XLV. 11).

Strongholds: The word is translated "fortress" in vs. 39; it is from a root "to cut off," then "to make inaccessible," whence it comes to be used for "to fortify" (cf. vs. 15; Isa. 27:10). **But only for a time:** Lit., "but until a time," as in vs. 35. **Only** is an interpretation. Theod. has ἕως καιροῦ, i.e., for the limited time God has appointed for these things (cf. vs. 27). Let men take courage, for God has fixed a limit beyond which Antiochus and his partisans may not go. They may think that their plans are well laid, and imagine that nothing can resist them: God knows better.

25 And he shall stir up his power and his courage against the king of the south with a great army; and the king of the south shall be stirred up to battle with a very great and mighty army; but he shall not stand: for they shall forecast devices against him.

strongholds, but only for a time. 25 And he shall stir up his power and his courage against the king of the south with a great army; and the king of the south shall wage war with an exceedingly great and mighty army; but he shall not stand, for plots shall

---

25-28. See I Macc. 1:20. Cleopatra queen of Egypt was a sister of Seleucus IV and Antiochus IV, and when Seleucus was murdered, there seems to have been a party in Syria which supported the claim of her son Ptolemy VI Philometor to succeed to the throne there and thus unite the Seleucid and Ptolemaic empires as a measure to stem the growing influence of Rome in the eastern Mediterranean. When Cleopatra died in 172 B.C., both her sons Philometor and Physcon were minors, and though the former was on the throne, the real power was in the hands of his guardians, the eunuch Eulaeus and the Syrian Lenaeus. They seem to have persuaded Philometor that he had only to venture a bold stroke to recover Syria and Palestine for Egypt. Antiochus got word of this and moved forces down into Phoenicia, visiting Jerusalem on the way, where he was received by Jason (II Macc. 4:21-22). He sent an embassy to Rome to justify his action, claiming that he held these provinces by inheritance from his father and was being unjustly attacked by Egypt. But Egypt also sent an embassy to Rome to complain that these provinces had been wrongly wrested from her and now Antiochus was preparing to attack Egypt itself. In 169 Antiochus captured the key border city of Pelusium and entered Egypt. The two guardians saw they could offer no effective resistance to him and so advised Ptolemy to flee to Samothrace. He did so, but was captured by his uncle on the way and taken into "protective custody." Pretending to be acting in his nephew's interests, Antiochus now proceeded to occupy the greater part of Egypt, but was unable to take Alexandria, where the Egyptian nobles had set up Physcon as king. A combination of circumstances demanded Antiochus' return from Egypt, one of them being troubles in Jerusalem. Rumors had got abroad that Antiochus had been killed during the Egyptian campaign, on the strength of which Jason, who had been superseded by Menelaus, attempted to reinstate himself, thereby causing considerable disturbance in Jerusalem. Possibly Antiochus misjudged the situation, taking it as much more serious than it was, but he came to Jerusalem, joined forces with the Hellenizing Jews, massacred many of the inhabitants, and entered the sanctuary whose treasury he plundered (I Macc. 1:20-24; II Macc. 5:11-17; Josephus *Jewish War* I. 1. 1; *Antiquities* XII. 5. 3). During his absence Cleopatra, the sister of Philometor and Physcon, succeeded in reconciling them, an arrangement being worked out whereby they were to reign conjointly. This reconciliation having greatly enraged Antiochus, in the summer of 168 he set out on his second Egyptian expedition. The Egyptian embassies to Rome, however, had borne fruit, and as he moved toward Alexandria, he was met by Popilius Laenas at the head of Roman delegates and ordered to evacuate Egypt by a certain day. It was in the ill-temper that followed on this repulse that he vented his spleen on the non-Hellenizing Jews and desecrated the Jerusalem temple in 167.

25. Antiochus **shall stir up his power and his courage:** Lit., "his might and his heart." The use of the word "heart" for courage is normal (Gen. 42:28; Josh. 5:1; 14:8). "Might" is generally thought to mean the resources of his kingdom in men and treasure necessary for the campaign, but Montgomery suggests that it is used here in a spiritual sense as in Job 36:5; Mic. 3:8, and parallels courage; i.e., he braced himself for the effort of the campaign. Then comes the statement that his army was a **great army.** I Macc. 1:17 describes it as a "strong force," recounting that besides infantry there were cavalry, an elephant corps, and war chariots, while a fleet assisted them by sea.

King of the south here means the kingdom of Egypt, the king standing for the kingdom. Ptolemy Philometor was still only in his teens, but as he represented the king-

26 Yea, they that feed of the portion of his meat shall destroy him, and his army shall overflow: and many shall fall down slain.

27 And both these kings' hearts *shall be* to do mischief, and they shall speak lies at one table; but it shall not prosper: for yet the end *shall be* at the time appointed.

26 Even those who eat his rich food shall be his undoing; his army shall be swept away, and many shall fall down slain. 27 And as for the two kings, their minds shall be bent on mischief; they shall speak lies at the same table, but to no avail; for the end is yet to be at the

---

dom, he is assumed to be the leader of the Egyptian armies. How large these were is not recorded in secular sources, and some have estimated that the statement in this verse as to his "great and exceedingly powerful army" is somewhat exaggerated. In any case, it was not able to withstand the Syrians. His defeat was perhaps due to treachery on the part of some of his own people who ventured "to devise against him devices" (cf. vs. 26). To what this refers is uncertain. There is some suspicion that the border city Pelusium was betrayed to Antiochus. **Devised:** The same verb occurs in vs. 24, and **plots** here is the same word as "plans" there.

26. Those who eat his rich food: His courtiers, as in II Sam. 9:7, 10; 19:28; I Kings 2:7. **Food** is the same Iranian word as was used in 1:5. **Shall be his undoing:** Lit., "shall break him"; the same word is in vss. 20, 22. These courtiers may be those who "devised devices" against him in vs. 25, though it is generally considered that the reference here is to his guardians whose ill advice first brought him into conflict with his uncle and then to the mistaken flight which let him fall into his uncle's hands (Polybius *op. cit.* XXVIII. 21; Diodorus Siculus XXX. 17).

His army shall be swept away involves the reading of not *yishtôph* but *yishshāṭēph*, as in vs. 22, for the **army** must surely be that of Philometor, and the reference to the defeat at Mount Casius. "Sweep away" uses again the flood image of Isa. 8:8, as noted in vs. 10. The slaughter was great. I Macc. 1:18 seems to be based on the Greek of this passage. **Slain,** from "to be pierced" or "perforated," vividly calls to mind the prowess of the Syrian bowmen.

27. The two kings are Antiochus and Ptolemy Philometor, who was living in his uncle's custody. The Hebrew here, "and the two of them, the kings," is hardly tolerable and seems to be merely an awkward rendering of the Aramaic "both kings" (Ginsberg, *Studies,* p. 61). When Physcon was crowned at Alexandria, Philometor was theoretically in alliance with his uncle against the usurping younger brother, so Antiochus, according to Livy (XLV. 11. 1), kept up the pretense that all he did in Egypt was in the interests of his nephew. Yet this writer suggests that Philometor, though so young, was merely feigning gratitude and regard for his uncle while plotting against him. Montgomery makes the point that in Oriental eyes this was the more disgraceful, as they were eating **at the same table** where by the laws of hospitality friendship should be genuine.

Their minds shall be bent on mischief: Lit., "their hearts are at wickedness." *Mērā‘* is from the verb "to be evil." **But to no avail** may mean that Antiochus' scheme to reinstate Philometor and rule through him did **not prosper,** since he was unable to take Alexandria and drive out Physcon. Or it may mean that his attempt to subdue all Egypt after having captured its king did not succeed (see vs. 30). It is more likely, however, that we should connect this clause with the words that follow and interpret it as meaning that all his plans connected with the Egyptian campaign will prove unavailing because the end is at hand. This involves taking **for the end is yet to be at the time appointed** as

---

We have seen what men can do and what they can become when they lose the sense of the royal honor God has bestowed upon them.

26. Loyalty.—There is no guarantee that the good man will always have loyalty from those

he has served. Consider Jesus! There are enough thanklessness and lack of appreciation in all men, heaven knows. But the evil man can trust no one, for he has established no basis of trust. It is only a matter of holding men by gifts and

28 Then shall he return into his land with great riches; and his heart *shall be* against the holy covenant; and he shall do *exploits,* and return to his own land.

29 At the time appointed he shall return, and come toward the south; but it shall not be as the former, or as the latter.

30 ¶ For the ships of Chittim shall come against him: therefore he shall be grieved, and return, and have indignation against the holy covenant: so shall he do; he shall even return, and have intelligence with them that forsake the holy covenant.

time appointed. 28 And he shall return to his land with great substance, but his heart shall be set against the holy covenant. And he shall work his will, and return to his own land.

29 "At the time appointed he shall return and come into the south; but it shall not be this time as it was before. 30 For ships of Kittim shall come against him, and he shall be afraid and withdraw, and shall turn back and be enraged and take action against the holy covenant. He shall turn back and give heed to those who forsake

---

eschatological. Others take the phrase to mean that the end of this matter will not be settled in Egypt but in another place. Others think it means that only a certain limited time has been allotted for Antiochus' domination of Egypt and the plans will avail nothing because the time is so limited. Others hold that it is the end of Egypt that is predicted. Let not Antiochus think his campaign will finish Egypt. His campaign will avail nought, for the end of Egypt is to be **at the time appointed** yet to come, not at the hands of Antiochus. Charles thinks the end possibly means the end of Antiochus' own life. It is difficult, however, to separate the wording here from that of vs. 35; 12:4, and the probabilities are that the reference is not to the end of the war, or of Antiochus, but to "the End."

28. On his return from the first expedition Antiochus brought back much booty. **With great substance** is the "plunder of the land of Egypt" of I Macc. 1:19 (see also Sibylline Oracles 3:614 ff.). *Rekhûsh* is goods and chattels, as in vs. 24. In vs. 13 it means implements of war. **His heart shall be set against the holy covenant** must refer to his appearance at Jerusalem to reinstate his nominee Menelaus and drive out Jason. To Antiochus this was not a matter of any holy covenant but a question whether his royal authority was to be observed. He did, however, massacre many Jews, and he did enter the sanctuary and plunder the treasury, which may well have seemed to indicate to pious Jews that the ruler's heart was **set against the holy covenant** (II Macc. 5:5-21; I Macc. 1:20-24, 29-36). **Holy covenant** here, like the διαθήκη ἁγία of I Macc. 1:15, 63, means the Jewish religion. **He shall work his will:** Lit., he shall do, as in vs. 30. It is reminiscent of 8:12, 24. The reference is apparently to the punishment inflicted on Jerusalem for the affair of Jason. Not only was the temple robbed but a garrison was stationed in the city.

29. The second Egyptian campaign started by a march to **the south. Return and come into:** Perhaps the use of *mô'ēdh* suggests that the time of this second campaign was something decreed by God. "But not as the former time shall be the latter time": The first Egyptian expedition, in spite of all that it failed to accomplish, had been a great success for Antiochus, who returned from it laden with spoil and full of honor. From the second expedition he not only gained nothing but was sent back home like a whipped schoolboy (Polybius *op. cit.* XXIX. 23-27; Livy XLIV. 19. 6-11).

30. This second expedition comes to a sudden stop **for ships of Kittim shall come against him.** On the surface this would suggest a fleet of ships from Cyprus. From the secular historians we know that in response to the appeal from Egypt, Rome sent Popilius Laenas with a suite to intervene and force Antiochus to leave Egypt, but we have no hint that they needed more than one ship to bring them from Rome (Polybius *loc. cit.;* Appian *Roman History* XI. 11. 66; Livy XLV. 12; Velleius Paterculus *Compendium of Roman History* I. 10). It is possible that they arrived in Alexandria in a group of ships from Cyprus or of Cypriote origin. It is more likely, however, that the word **Kittim** is used here as a dramatic device to suggest the fulfillment of the

31 And arms shall stand on his part, and they shall pollute the sanctuary of strength, and shall take away the daily *sacrifice*, and they shall place the abomination that maketh desolate.

the holy covenant. 31 Forces from him shall appear and profane the temple and fortress, and shall take away the continual burnt offering. And they shall set up the abomina-

---

prophecy in Num. 24:21-24. Ginsberg (*op. cit.*, p. 78, note *a*) shows in detail how that passage could be understood by the audience as fitting this contemporary situation.

Kittim means properly Cyprus or the inhabitants thereof (Gen. 10:4; Isa. 23:1, 12), but in the Prophets (cf. Jer. 2:10; Ezek. 27:6) it is used more loosely to include the islands and coastlands of the Mediterranean, and later came to be a name applied to Macedonia (I Macc. 1:1; 8:5; Jubilees 24:28-29). That it could also mean Romans appears from the fact that the LXX here has Ῥωμαῖοι and the Vulg. *Trieres et Romani.* So Onkelos on Num. 24:24 renders it by רומאי. Some urge that as proper names are usually avoided in this book, we should emend it to read "envoys from the west" or "those who came out of the west."

And he shall be afraid: Some translators prefer "disheartened" (cf. Ps. 109:16, "broken in heart"). The LXX has "and shall threaten him," making the subject the Romans. The story in Polybius by its "deeply hurt" curiously confirms the M.T. "And he shall turn back and be wroth against holy covenant, and shall do [his will], and shall return and have regard unto those who forsake holy covenant": Some regard the latter half of this passage as a scribal insertion, and so delete it. It is possible, however, that the first **return** refers to the coming of Antiochus into Judea from Egypt, and the second, his return from Judea to Antioch. Others take the first *weshābh* as adverbial, and translate, "he shall again be wroth," so that there is only one return. In either case the reference is to the beginning of the great persecution after the second attack on Jerusalem in 167. Whether Antiochus himself entered the city this time, or whether what was done was by officers acting under his command, is not clear. It is usually assumed that in his rage at being thwarted in Egypt he needed to work off his anger on someone, and as the refractoriness of the Jews happened to be brought to his attention just at that moment they were the ones on whom he turned. There may, however, have been something more important than just working off his rage. This may have been part of his general policy of Hellenization, a policy the more urgent now that it was necessary to stem the Parthian expansion westward. To favor the Hellenizers at Jerusalem and deal harshly with those who opposed Hellenization was clearly an advisable policy.

Zā'am is "to be irritated," "to be angry," and then "to punish." **Holy covenant** again means the Jewish religion. **Shall he do:** Again as in vs. 28. "Have regard": *Bîn* here has the sense of **give heed**, "pay attention to," as in vs. 37; Job 31:1. Even after his return to Antioch, Antiochus seems to have kept in communication with the Jewish Hellenizers, those who "forsook holy covenant" (I Macc. 1:15; cf. II Macc. 4:7-17; Assumption of Moses 8:1-5).

31. Now the particular offenses of Antiochus are detailed (see II Macc. 5:25; I Macc. 1:29). The points which especially interest the writer are: his turning the temple of Yahweh into a heathen temple; his suspension of the daily offering (cf. 8:11; 9:27); his setting up the abomination of desolation (cf. 8:13; 9:27; 12:11); his establishing a strong place in the old city of David; his increasing the number of apostates; his self-deification to the prejudice of other deities; his introduction of a foreign god with his adherents; his blaspheming Israel's God; his abandonment of the god of his fathers.

Forces from him shall appear: Lit., **shall stand.** The simplest explanation is that this means that Seleucid troops will be sent to carry out his orders in Jerusalem. Some, however, think it means "shall remain," i.e., when he goes north, they will remain to garrison the city. Others think that in accordance with the use of the verb in vss. 15, 25, we must render "shall prevail," i.e., nothing the Jews can do will be able to resist them. Since these forces are said to be **from him,** some have thought the writer meant to

32 And such as do wickedly against the covenant shall he corrupt by flatteries: but the people that do know their God shall be strong, and do *exploits*.

tion that makes desolate. 32 He shall seduce with flattery those who violate the covenant; but the people who know their God shall

---

indicate that Antiochus himself was not present, but that these were forces such as those raised for him by Apollonius (I Macc. 1:29; II Macc. 5:24), who did all the damage in Jerusalem. **From him,** however, may quite well mean "at his instance," the forces being set in motion while he was in the city.

And profane the temple and fortress: Cf. 8:11. **Fortress** is here in apposition to **temple.** At this period the temple area was fortified so that it was a stronghold in the technical sense; see I Chr. 29:1, 19, where the temple is called "the fortress" (KJV "palace"). Others think that here the holy place and the fortifications are two different things. In Neh. 2:8; 7:2 we seem to have a fortress near the temple and such fortifications are mentioned in the account of the rebuilding under the Maccabees (I Macc. 4:60; 6:7).

Miqdāsh is "holy place," but here must mean the whole temple complex. It is the word used in 8:11; 9:17. *Ḥillēl* means "to defile," "to desecrate," "to make common," hence **pollute, profane** (cf. I Macc. 1:37). This pollution may refer not merely to the fact that the soldiery entered the temple precincts and broke down some of the fortifications, but in particular to the fact that Apollonius, who commanded them, strengthened the citadel which overlooked the temple and stationed there a garrison of lawless fellows (I Macc. 1:34; II Macc. 5:24). **Fortress:** Lit., "the strength," is the word used in vss. 7, 10, 19 and again in vs. 39 for "stronghold." Some editors emend it here from המעוז to המעון, "dwelling places" as a more suitable word in apposition to "holy places." Ginsberg (*op. cit.,* pp. 45-49) thinks there was a misreading of an Aramaic word and so suggests that the original text read, "and shall profane sanctuary and saints," which is precisely what I Macc. 1:46 says.

Not content with polluting the place by their presence, the troops abolished the daily cult sacrifice and in its place set up a cult center of their own. As the verbs are plural, we should understand that it is the forces which are doing these things (for the abolition of the *tāmidh* see 8:11, 13; 9:27; 12:11). I Macc. 1:45 ff. enumerates the various rites and customs which Antiochus, in pursuance of his policy of Hellenization, declared forbidden. Negative measures prohibiting the practice of the old religion, however, were not enough; there must be positive substitution of something Hellenistic to take its place. So within the temple there was set up an altar to Zeus Olympius (II Macc. 6:2). This was the "abomination of desolation" of 8:13; 9:27; 12:11. Cf. I Macc. 1:34; 4:42, 47. From I Macc. 1:59 it seems that the new altar was set up on the place of the ancient altar of sacrifice.

Abomination: *Shiqqūç* here and in 12:11 is clearly what was referred to in 8:13; 9:27, viz., the altar to *Ba'al Shāmēm* set up in the temple. Charles thinks that the reference was first to the heathen altar and then to the statue of Zeus Olympius which, according to Taanith 4:6, was **set up** beside it. On *Ba'al Shāmēm* see Philo of Byblos (according to Eusebius *Preparation for the Gospel* I. 10) and Mark Lidzbarski (*Ephemeris für semitische Epigraphik* [Giessen: J. Ricker, 1902], I, 243-60).

32. "And those who bring guilt upon covenant shall he seduce by flattering words" (cf. 9:5; 12:10). The reference is apparently to the apostates mentioned in the last

---

advantages. At last even those who have been his copartners turn against him. This is the terrible judgment meted out to the tyrant. Even those who eat his food only wait for the opportune moment to destroy him.

32. The People Shall Stand Firm.—The great obstacle to all paganism is the people who know their God. Their society does not always appre-

ciate them or even recognize them. But they represent the creative minority which restores society, and they stand against the degraders of the human spirit. The secret of their power is their knowledge of God. It is amazing how iron is put into the spirit of all kinds of humble folk who know God. It surprises the intellectuals and the hoodlums alike. That is why the so-

33 And they that understand among the people shall instruct many: yet they shall fall by the sword, and by flame, by captivity, and by spoil, *many* days.

stand firm and take action. 33 And those among the people who are wise shall make many understand, though they shall fall by sword and flame, by captivity and plunder,

---

clause of vs. 30. Some render, "those who sin against the covenant," others, "those who condemn [or renounce] the covenant." The word רשע is "to be wicked," and the Hiphil is "to put to the worse"; so here, "those whose actions put religion to shame." **Seduce:** *Ḥānēph* is an impious hypocritical person (Job 13:16; 17:8; Isa. 9:17; 33:14), and the Hiphil of the verb is "to seduce," i.e., to make a person impious or hypocritical. By specious promises Antiochus persuaded the Jews who were favorable to Hellenism to renounce openly their religion, and in seeking to make such persons his tools he seduced them and made apostates of them.

Flattery here is the "flattering words" of vs. 21, though others would translate "by treacherous means." Driver points to the flattering promises held out to Mattathias in I Macc. 2:18. True believers, however, will remain loyal Jews and will not be moved either by specious promises of flattering words or by the bitterness of persecution. Since they **know their God** they will **stand firm.**

"A people, those who know its [i.e., the people's] God": For the construction see Ps. 95:10; Ezek. 3:5. The Hebrew *'am* could perhaps be rendered by "company." This elect company of those **who know their God** by experience is set over against the body of apostates who are prepared to renounce their ancestral faith. Charles sees the writer making a subtle point here. Those who accepted that to which Antiochus was endeavoring to seduce them would become members of a religious group where Antiochus himself claimed deity. People who really knew God would naturally resist association with such a religion.

"Shall hold fast and shall do": So I Macc. 1:62, "many in Israel were fully resolved and exerted their strength," i.e., they showed firmness and constancy in face of the new situation. There were of course many martyrdoms which provided a basis for the legends in III Maccabees and IV Maccabees. *Ḥāzaq* is "to be strong," and is used for firmness of purpose in being faithful to religion in I Chr. 28:7; II Chr. 35:2; Deut. 12:23. The absolute use of "and do" has already been met with in 8:12, 24; 9:19; and vss. 28, 30 below. The meaning here seems to be that as the king had acted to further his ends, so they would act to resist him.

33. There were many pious folk who were greatly disturbed by the actions of Antiochus Epiphanes, but being simple people they were at a loss what to do about it, and many indeed were in danger of being led astray by the perplexities of the situation. It was thus incumbent on the educated in the community to take the lead in organizing resistance against Hellenization.

Wise: *Maskîlîm,* as in vs. 35; 12:3, 10. It is the word used in 1:4 for "apt in all learning." Some think that it means the teachers of the people (cf. 9:22), but it probably refers to the leaders of the resistance movement, who in I Macc. 2:42; 7:13; II Macc. 14:6 are called the Hasidim.

They will **make many understand.** In the parallel passage in 12:10 it is they themselves who "shall understand." Both by teaching and example they will make clear to the common people the path they should follow. Bentzen suggests that "understanding" here means something more profound. They will make clear to their contemporaries that the sufferings through which they are passing are a punishment from God (II Macc. 7:18, 32, 38), and thus a means of national purification (cf. vs. 35).

The early attempts at resistance were not very successful, and many were lost in the struggle (I Macc. 1:60, 63; 2:31-38; 3:41; 5:13; II Macc. 6:10, 11, 18 ff.). These are the matters referred to in Heb. 11:36-38. Who **they** are that **shall fall** is not clear, for it might refer to the **many** just mentioned, though more probably it means "the wise," many of whom will fall early in the struggle. The verb is "to stumble," as in vss. 14, 19,

34 Now when they shall fall, they shall be helped with a little help: but many shall cleave to them with flatteries.

35 And *some* of them of understanding shall fall, to try them, and to purge, and

for some days. 34 When they fall, they shall receive a little help. And many shall join themselves to them with flattery; 35 and some of those who are wise shall fall, to

---

and some have thought the meaning is that because of the **flame, sword,** etc., many who at first were prepared to resist will give way.

For some days: The early days of the resistance movement. Four types of death under persecution are mentioned, not because these were the only four, or were the most important, but because it is stylistic with this writer to use fours: **By sword** [I Macc. 2:9, 38] **and flame** [II Macc. 6:11; 7:3 ff.], **by captivity** [I Macc. 3:41] **and plunder** [I Macc. 1:31].

34. Just when things seemed to be going badly with the resistance movement it received the encouragement it needed. "And while they are falling they shall be assisted a little assistance" seems to refer to the first minor successes of the Maccabean party under Mattathias and his son Judas (I Macc. 2:15-28, 42-48; 3:11-12, 23-26; 4:12-15). Some think it is called a **little help** because it consisted of victories won by the arm of man, whereas in the writer's eyes deliverance comes not from man's efforts but from the Lord (3:17). The very success of the Maccabean uprising, while it did alleviate the situation, brought new perils of its own in that it attracted many whose motives were far from pure and tended to foster hopes that deliverance would come through human prowess rather than by divine intervention (see 2:34; 8:25).

Join themselves: *Lāwāh* is **to cleave,** "to adhere" (see Isa. 14:1; 56:3, 6; Jer. 50:5; Zech. 2:11). **To them** must mean to "the wise." **With flattery:** Insincerely. The word is used for **flatteries** or "smooth sayings" in vs. 21. There are many references to the ruthless measures Judas used against the Hellenizers (I Macc. 2:44; 3:5-8; 6:19-24; 9:23), and such severity caused many to join his party out of sheer terror, but such forced adherents would not be sincere. Behrmann emends the words to "in levity," the suggestion being that many who had no real interest in the cause would join it when success had begun to attend it.

35. Apparently the death of so many pious leaders raised questions in the minds of the people. If the cause were God's, why did he allow so many of his loyal people to perish in the persecution? Was not their death a judgment on them? The answer is that their death is part of the divine plan, and is for the purification of the community. It is a testing of the community to see if their faith will stand firm. It is a purging of the community, for the unworthy will take flight and fall away. It is a purifying of the community, for the blood of the martyrs will make it a finer community. Doubtless the writer was thinking about individuals who would have been well known to his audience and called to mind by this statement. The **wise** are those of vs. 33.

"To purge among them and cleanse": **Them** refers not to the martyrs, who by martyrdom are purged of sins and imperfections, nor to the **wise,** whose ranks are purged by losing some in death, but must refer to the **many,** or the resistance party at large, who are being disciplined and perfected by this loss of some of their leaders. *Çāraph* is used of smelting and refining metals in Pss. 12:6 (M.T. 12:7); 66:10; Jer. 6:29; Mal. 3:2-3, and so comes to mean "to purge," as in Isa. 1:25; Zech. 13:9; Ps. 26:2. *Bārar* is used of polishing metal to remove impurities that have tarnished it (Isa. 49:2; Jer. 51:11), and then in a spiritual sense, as in Ezek. 20:38; Isa. 52:11; Ps. 18:26. **And to make them white:** וללבן is a peculiar form. It is generally thought to be a contraction of the Hiphil infinitive, and so "to cause to be white." It is omitted in the LXX, and some think it may be a late gloss. Montgomery compares Rev. 3:18, which combined gold purified in the fire with white clothing. The three verbs occur again in 12:10.

This disciplining process of losing the leaders is to go on **until the time of the end.** Later eschatology made much of this final purifying of the community which was

to make *them* white, *even* to the time of the end: because *it is* yet for a time appointed.

36 And the king shall do according to his will; and he shall exalt himself, and magnify himself above every god, and shall speak marvelous things against the God of gods, and shall prosper till the indignation be accomplished: for that that is determined shall be done.

refine and to cleanse them*f* and to make them white, until the time of the end, for it is yet for the time appointed.

36 "And the king shall do according to his will; he shall exalt himself and magnify himself above every god, and shall speak astonishing things against the God of gods. He shall prosper till the indignation is accomplished; for what is determined shall

f Gk: Heb *among them*

---

necessary before the advent of the final kingdom. It is the same time of the end as in vs. 27; 8:17 (cf. vs. 40; 12:4). **For it is yet for the time appointed:** Cf. vs. 27, and for the phrase see the Hebrew of Ecclus. 36:8. Some time has yet to elapse before the consummation.

36. Having described the vigorous measures of Antiochus against the Jews and their result, the writer now commences his account of the king's measures elsewhere. That he should "do as he pleases" was nothing extraordinary. The same was said of Alexander in vs. 3 and of Antiochus the Great in vs. 16 (cf. also 8:4). But this king is to **exalt himself and magnify himself above every god,** i.e., he will assume to himself a position superior to all the deities worshiped throughout his empire. This sentence does not imply that the writer believed in the existence of gods other than Yahweh. He knew of various cults and of worship rendered to various deities throughout the Seleucid Empire, and he is merely seeking to show what a marvel of impiety Antiochus was. The secular historians, however, do not seem to have been struck by any particular impiety in Antiochus. On the contrary, both Pliny and Polybius remark on the honor he paid the gods, and it is a matter of record that he contributed lavishly to the shrines at Athens and Delos. To an Oriental writer, however, things may have looked somewhat different. He bore the title "Epiphanes," which practically meant "god manifest," assumed the title "Theos" on his coins, and seems to have progressively added divine symbols to them, and to have approximated his portrait to that of Zeus Olympius. Moreover, his contempt for other religions in the Orient, and his plundering of their temples as though their wealth belonged to him, may have favored this notion that he was setting himself **above every god.**

The **God of gods** against whom he spoke "monstrous things" was the God of Israel (cf. Isa. 37:23). In 5:23 Belshazzar had been guilty of the sin of exalting himself against the God of Israel. We do not know of any particular words of blasphemy uttered by Antiochus against the Jewish God, but in his anger at the happenings in Jerusalem in defiance of his authority he may well have uttered blasphemous words which would still be remembered by this writer's audience. In I Macc. 1:24 we read that after despoiling the temple in 169 B.C. he went away and "spoke great presumptuousness." On the other hand, the "monstrous things" may be his ordinances suppressing the daily sacrifice—which God had commanded should be observed continually—and the various religious practices through which the Jews expressed their devotion to God. The expression used here for **God of gods** is the equivalent of the Aramaic expression in 2:47, but is not the usual Jewish phrase used in Deut. 10:17; Ps. 136:2; *et al.* Some think the reason for this is that here the writer is looking at things from Antiochus' point of view, as in 2:47 he was looking from that of Nebuchadrezzar, and so uses a form of words which would be natural in the mouth of a heathen potentate rather than the expression which would have been used by a Jew.

Astonishing things: Cf. the mouth speaking great things of 7:8, and note 7:25; 8:24. It was Antiochus' lack of reverence for the God of Zion that particularly distressed the Jews, for it was in strange contrast to the attitude of other heathen potentates from Cyrus to Antiochus the Great. Yet his success in carrying through his measures against

37 Neither shall he regard the God of his fathers, nor the desire of women, nor regard any god: for he shall magnify himself above all.

38 But in his estate shall he honor the God of forces: and a god whom his fathers

be done. 37 He shall give no heed to the gods of his fathers, or to the one beloved by women; he shall not give heed to any other god, for he shall magnify himself above all. 38 He shall honor the god of

---

the religion of Israel, they are assured, has a limit. The decree has been issued. There is a limit to the "time of wrath," and when that is reached, his success will end.

Indignation: Za'am is "wrath"; the LXX and Theod. have ἡ ὀργή, which suggests that this is derived from Isa. 10:25. As in 8:19, the **indignation** is regarded as part of the great tribulation which precedes "the end." **For what is determined shall be done:** Lit., "for a sentence has been executed." Neḥerāçāh is something "decided," "decreed," hence a "sentence." It is used in 9:26-27 for matters which have been determined in connection with the last days, and in Isa. 10:23; 28:22 for what Yahweh has decreed shall come to pass. The emphasis is that a sentence which has been passed in celestial places must be executed without fail.

37-39. Ginsberg (*Studies,* p. 44) regards these verses as explicative of vs. 36. There we were told that Antiochus (a) magnified himself above every god; (b) spoke blasphemy against Yahweh; (c) will carry through his designs until the appointed time is reached. In these verses we are told (a) how he plays fast and loose with other deities, thinking himself superior to them; (b) how he offends the God of Israel (this depends on Ginsberg's interpretation of the "god of fortresses"); (c) how for a while he carries through his plans unhindered. Yet it does not necessarily follow that these verses are a later gloss, for it may well be a stylistic device to amplify here what was stated somewhat summarily in vs. 36.

37. The **gods of his fathers** to which he shows no regard were not necessarily the deities particularly reverenced by his own family, but rather the deities officially worshiped in the Seleucid Empire. We do not know what particular acts of Antiochus were regarded as showing disrespect for the official cults of the empire. Charles thinks we have an example of what is meant in the fact that on his coins the image of Apollo was replaced by that of Zeus Olympius. I Macc. 1:41-42 records his efforts at suppressing local religious usages in the interests of uniformity, and this may have been regarded as departing from the ways of his fathers and having no regard for deities to whom they showed regard.

Nor the desire of women: In all probability, the reference is to the god Tammuz-Adonis, whose cult was then popular among women as it had been from ancient times (cf. Ezek. 8:14). Hippolytus (*Refutation* V. 9) records that Adonis was called "the thrice-desired." The statement **he shall not give heed to any other god** might seem to be contradicted by the known fact that Antiochus made considerable contributions to certain shrines and even helped with the building of temples to other gods (Livy XLI. 20. 8-9; XLII. 6. 8, 11). Moreover, in vs. 38 he is said to honor a certain **god of fortresses.** It may be urged, however, that while he looked on these as sharing divinity, he regarded them as inferior to himself, for he would **magnify himself above all.** It has been noted that while the claim of a ruler to divine honors was nothing new in the ancient Near East, Antiochus seems to have taken his divinity more seriously than most. It has already been noted how his portrait on his coins approximates more and more that of Zeus (see Exeg. on vs. 36).

38. "But to the god of fortresses instead shall he give honor" may well be a reference to some event which would be remembered by the audience but to which we have no

---

called new orders always begin with an attack on the church. They know their enemy.

38. The God of Fortresses.—What an appropriate description of our time! Our real

confidence is given to **the god of fortresses,** of bombs, of armies. After we create these things, we deify them. Only of the one God can it be said, "A mighty fortress is our God." A message

knew not shall he honor with gold, and silver, and with precious stones, and pleasant things.

39 Thus shall he do in the most strongholds with a strange god, whom he shall acknowledge *and* increase with glory: and he shall cause them to rule over many, and shall divide the land for gain.

fortresses instead of these; a god whom his fathers did not know he shall honor with gold and silver, with precious stones and costly gifts. **39** He shall deal with the strongest fortresses by the help of a foreign god; those who acknowledge him he shall magnify with honor. He shall make them rulers over many and shall divide the land for a price.

---

clue. The usual interpretation is that it refers to Zeus Olympius as equivalent to Jupiter Capitolinus, for whom Antiochus had begun to erect a temple at Antioch (Livy XLI. 20. 9). Some, however, think that **god of fortresses** is merely an epithet of the god of war. Hitzig, by reading מעז ים, "stronghold of the sea," took it to mean the Tyrian god Melkarth. Bevan thinks it refers to the goddess Roma with her mural crown. The Peshitta avoids the difficulty by reading "a mighty god." The expression על-כנו is generally taken to mean "instead thereof" (cf. vss. 7, 20-21), i.e., instead of all the Oriental deities mentioned in vs. 37. On the ground that in this case we should expect the pronoun to be plural, not singular, some have held that we must think of this god as being honored "on his pedestal," כנו being "his stand," the writer thinking of a definite image on a pedestal. The singular pronoun, however, may refer to **all** (vs. 37) and so be grammatically singular though plural in meaning. The **god whom his fathers did not know** probably refers to the same deity, for the detail as to the precious metals and stones fits the accounts of the temple he was erecting at Antioch. Seleucid coins show that Zeus Olympius was known to the predecessors of Antiochus Epiphanes, but Charles thinks that the combining of him with Jupiter Capitolinus was something new. **Costly gifts:** From the verb "to desire," and so "things greatly desired," a word used in Gen. 27:15 of the goodly raiment that Rebekah took, in II Chr. 20:25 of precious jewels, and here in vs. 43 of the precious things of Egypt.

Ginsberg (*op. cit.,* pp. 43-45) thinks that in this verse we have a mistranslation of an Aramaic original. The Jews, he says, would have cared nothing for his honoring Jupiter Capitolinus or any other such deity. What worried them was his disrespect toward the God of Zion, which must be what is meant here. So he reconstructs an original text, "the God of the saints shall he despise and a god whom his fathers knew not shall he honor on his stand," i.e., on the altar of the Jerusalem temple.

39. The M.T. here does not make sense. It reads, "and he shall do to the fortifications of strongholds with a strange god," and no manipulation of the words as they are seems to make anything intelligible out of it. There is general agreement that עם, *'im,* **with,** should be emended to *'am,* "people," in which case we could translate, "and he shall procure for the strongest fortresses the people of a strange god," referring to the fact that Antiochus settled at Jerusalem and in the fortresses of Judea foreigners who worshiped strange gods (I Macc. 1:33; 3:36, 45). The word עם is used in this sense of people of another god in Num. 21:29 (people of Chemosh), and though "to procure" is an uncommon meaning for *'āsāh,* it does have this sense in I Sam. 8:16. Bentzen suggests that we should see here not merely a reference to political measures designed to control the country by foreign garrisons, but to a religious measure which sought to strengthen the cult of Zeus Olympius by bringing in non-Jewish garrisons who would favor this cult and win adherents. "Fortifications of strongholds," however, is still an awkward expression, and some would repoint the word "fortifications" to make it read "defenders," while Theod. and the Vulg. treat the word **strongholds** as a place name. Ginsberg (*ibid.*) feels that we have the same mistranslation as in vs. 31, and he would restore an underlying text, "and he shall bring as guards of the saints people of a strange god." **Foreign god:** *Nēkhār* is the normal O.T. word used in connection with "strange gods" (Deut. 32:12; Josh. 24:20, 23; Judg. 10:16; Mal. 2:11; *et al.*).

40 And at the time of the end shall the king of the south push at him: and the king of the north shall come against him like a whirlwind, with chariots, and with horsemen, and with many ships; and he shall enter into the countries, and shall overflow and pass over.

40 "At the time of the end the king of the south shall attack^g him; but the king of the north shall rush upon him like a whirlwind, with chariots and horsemen, and with many ships; and he shall come into countries and shall overflow and pass

^g Heb thrust at

The syntax of the clause is uncertain. The KJV takes it to mean that those who recognize the foreign god will be the recipients of honor from him. This would mean that Antiochus had had some success in winning adherents and bestowed honor on such as recognized his new cult. Driver translates, "he whom he recognizes will increase glory," i.e., his favorites will become honored in the land. It is better, however, to take Antiochus as the subject of both verbs. He will use his royal prestige to bestow honor where he will, those who gain his favor will be appointed to high office, and on them will be settled the lands he takes from the godly (see II Macc. 7:24).

Acknowledge: The *Kethîbh* is *hikkîr* and the *Qerê yakkîr,* but they mean much the same thing, viz., "to take notice of," as in II Sam. 3:36; Ruth 2:10. How Antiochus made those who pleased him **rulers over many** is well illustrated by the cases of Jason and Menelaus (II Macc. 4:8-10, 24). Doubtless many other instances would have been familiar to a contemporary audience.

"And the land shall he portion out as wages" is doubtless a reference to his bestowing lands on favorites. *Bimeḥîr* is **for a price** (cf. II Sam. 24:24; I Kings 10:28; Ps. 44:12 [M.T. 44:13]), and some translate **for gain,** thinking that it refers to lands being sold by Antiochus to gain money to replenish his treasury.

40-45. This section contains a prediction of events leading up to the end. With vs. 39 the writer has brought history up to his own day. Now he commences to predict what he foresees the events will be during the short period still to elapse before the final consummation. These verses, therefore, are pure prediction. So far we have had *vaticinia ex eventu,* but now we enter upon prediction proper. That the two should be mingled in a single document is not strange. Similar examples will be found in the Sibylline Oracles, in the Demotic Chronicle, and in the Oracles of Hystaspes. Some deny that there is any prediction here, claiming that in these verses we are still dealing with history, either with events in the reign of Antiochus subsequent to 168/167 B.C., or with a kind of recapitulation of events from 171 B.C. to the death of Antiochus. It is extremely difficult, however, to connect the details of these verses with actual happenings, whereas if they are the writer's expectation of what would occur they are intelligible. Behrmann points out that the author's expectations are all based on O.T. ideas which he has applied to matters relevant to him and his audience.

The writer expects a new venture against Egypt, in which Antiochus will be successful where previously he had failed. As before, he will be called away by rumors of troubles at home just as he was reaping the fruits of his victory, but on his way home, as he is once more approaching the Holy City with sinister purpose, he will meet his end. Obviously the writer is anticipating the future in terms of the various elements in the situation apparent in his own day which seemed to be pointing to a new war with Egypt that would surpass in frightfulness the previous campaigns, would extend to conquer the Libyans and Ethiopians, and would seriously affect the Jews, but whose disasters Edom, Moab, and Ammon, the enemies of the Jews, would escape. There may have been contemporary events familiar to the audience which would have made this forecast seem highly probable.

40. At the time of the end: As the date of the final consummation draws on (cf. 8:17; 12:4, 9). These are the last days. The period spoken of in vss. 27, 35 has come to its close and the final events are hastening on. The **king of the south** must be Ptolemy Philometor who, the writer thinks, will again invite disaster by provoking a war with

41 He shall enter also into the glorious land, and many *countries* shall be overthrown: but these shall escape out of his hand, *even* Edom, and Moab, and the chief of the children of Ammon.

42 He shall stretch forth his hand also upon the countries: and the land of Egypt shall not escape.

through. 41 He shall come into the glorious land. And tens of thousands shall fall, but these shall be delivered out of his hand: Edom and Moab and the main part of the Ammonites. 42 He shall stretch out his hand against the countries, and the land of Egypt

---

his uncle. No such attack is known to history. **Attack:** Lit., "shall exchange thrusts with him." The verb is that used in 8:4 in the Piel for the charging or butting of the ram. Antiochus' reply to the provocation will be an attack of **whirlwind** swiftness, "he will storm against him."

The attack is conceived of as by land and sea. The reason for this may be that Alexandria was his trouble in previous campaigns, so that he may have been expected to make a determined attack upon it this time by both land and sea. **Chariots and horsemen** are mentioned together almost as a technical term with reference to armaments (Exod. 14:17, 28; Josh. 24:6; I Sam. 8:11; I Kings 1:5; Isa. 22:6; Ezek. 26:7). "And he shall come into the lands and sweep away and overflow": The **countries** would be those between him and Egypt which he overflows as he passes along with his armies. The verbs "sweep along" and **overflow** were used in vs. 10, the image coming from Isa. 8:8. The LXX and Peshitta omit these verbs and read "land" in the singular, as does Theod.

41. As he moves southward the Holy Land will again feel the weight of his troops. It is the **glorious land** as in vs. 16; 8:9. **Tens of thousands shall fall:** This translation depends on a change of pointing in the text. It was so read by Symm., but the M.T. has "many" in the feminine plural, which suggests "many lands," i.e., those of vs. 40. For "myriads" see vs. 12 and cf. Neh. 7:71. **Fall** is again the "stumble" of vss. 14, 19, 33, 35, and means here, as there, that they, i.e., the lands, will be ruined by the invading army, or if we read "myriads," that the people will be killed in the conflict.

"But these shall escape from his hand, Edom and Moab and the chief of the Ammonites": This is a puzzle. Charles asks why the Edomites and Ammonites, who were enemies of the Jews and who, according to I Macc. 4:61; 5:1-8, were on the side of Antiochus, should be spoken of as being delivered out of his hand, and why the Moabites should appear here when as a people they had long since disappeared from history. It may be, however, that all the writer wishes to say is that this invasion will cause devastation between the Jordan and the coast, whereas the lands to the east of the Jordan, the lands associated with the names **Edom, Moab,** and **Ammon,** will escape. As the passage is reminiscent of the prophetic writings where Moab commonly appears along with Ammon, there is point to the suggestion that these words do not mean countries at all; but inasmuch as they were names of groups hostile to the Jews (II Chr. 20:1-2; Ps. 83:6-7), they are meant to represent the apostate Jews who, as Hellenizers, will not suffer from the invasion. It is also possible that there is some local allusion which would have been clear to the audience but which escapes us.

Main part: If we keep the M.T. the expression must mean the principal part of Ammon (cf. Num. 24:20; Jer. 49:35; Amos 6:1). The Peshitta, by a slight emendation, reads "remnant," and as "remnant of Edom" occurs in Amos 9:12, "remnant of the Philistines" in Amos 1:8, "remnant of Ashdod" in Jer. 25:20, some think it the more likely word here.

42. To **stretch out** [the] **hand** in the meaning "to seize hold" of something is a familiar usage (cf. Exod. 22:8, 11; Deut. 25:11; II Sam. 15:5; Esth. 8:7). "And the land of Egypt shall not be for deliverance," i.e., this time there will be no Roman intervention to save **Egypt** from his hand. The LXX read, "and in the land of Egypt not one shall escape."

43 But he shall have power over the treasures of gold and of silver, and over all the precious things of Egypt: and the Libyans and the Ethiopians *shall be* at his steps.

44 But tidings out of the east and out of the north shall trouble him: therefore he shall go forth with great fury to destroy, and utterly to make away many.

45 And he shall plant the tabernacles of his palace between the seas in the glorious

shall not escape. 43 He shall become ruler of the treasures of gold and of silver, and all the precious things of Egypt; and the Libyans and the Ethiopians shall follow in his train. 44 But tidings from the east and the north shall alarm him, and he shall go forth with great fury to exterminate and utterly destroy many. 45 And he shall pitch his palatial tents between the sea and the

---

43. In ancient days **Egypt** had a name for being a land where fabulous treasures were hidden. Antiochus had taken away great plunder on his first expedition (vs. 28), but this time, the writer suggests, even the hidden treasures of **gold** and **silver, the precious things** long concealed, will be hunted out and plundered.

Treasures: *Mikhmannîm,* "hidden things," occurs only here in the O.T. **Precious things:** Lit., "objects of desire," as in vs. 38. "And Lubim and Kushim in his train." *Lûbhîm* means the **Libyans,** who dwelt to the west of Egypt, and the *Kûshîm* are the **Ethiopians,** whose habitat was to the south. They represent Cyrenaica and Ethiopia, which were regarded as the traditional limits of the Egyptian Empire; so this sentence means that Antiochus' conquest of Egypt will be complete, and these people who formerly followed the king of Egypt will not follow him.

44. His campaign, however, will be disturbed as before (vs. 28) by news which will cause him to retreat eastward and northward out of Egypt in order to deal with threatened trouble. **Tidings:** Rumors, lit., "things heard." The word is used for the rumors which forced Sennacherib to withdraw from Palestine (II Kings 19:7) and for the "tidings" that came to David (II Sam. 13:30) and to Joab (I Kings 2:28). **Alarm him:** The Aramaic form of this verb was used in chs. 4–5; 7 for the troubles of mind caused by visions sent from God. Some frightening rumor would come to him.

Since it is a historical fact that the last months of Antiochus' life were spent in a campaign against the Parthians and the kingdom of Armenia, it is by no means impossible that the writer and his audience knew of troubles in the north which they anticipated would surely demand an expedition to settle them. Charles, however, thinks that the writer anticipates Antiochus' hearing during this expected Egyptian expedition of the Jewish successes in recovering Jerusalem, which will make him hurry back to Palestine. But he will perish on his way. Alarm engenders heat, so he will go north **with great fury,** lit., "heat," the Aramaic equivalent of which was used in 3:13, 19 of Nebuchadrezzar's furious rage.

The two verbs **destroy** and **exterminate** mean the same thing. They occur in the reverse order in II Chr. 20:23. The second verb is *ḥāram,* "to put under a ban," "to devote," which would involve destruction. Originally it had a peculiarly religious sense, being used in the O.T. for the ban placed on persons or things hostile to the people's religion (as in Exod. 22:20; Lev. 27:29; Deut. 3:6; 20:17; I Sam. 15:3-20). Here, however, it is merely a synonym for **destroy.** Cf. Vulg., *conterat et interficiat.*

45. The end of the tyrant. In the Holy Land, making his way toward Mount Zion, which he wishes once more to violate, Antiochus will be destroyed, meeting his end, with poetic justice, at the very scene of his worst offenses.

"And he will set up the tents of his palace," i.e., **pitch his palatial tents.** The word

---

which every great nation needs to heed is the contrast between **the god of fortresses** and the God who is himself the mighty defense of all who trust in him.

45. *The Defeat of the Wicked.*—When evil finally goes down, it is with the terrible feeling that there is literally nothing to help and no one to care. The suffering of the good man is a

holy mountain; yet he shall come to his end, and none shall help him.

12 And at that time shall Michael stand up, the great prince which standeth for the children of thy people: and there

glorious holy mountain; yet he shall come to his end, with none to help him.

12 "At that time shall arise Michael, the great prince who has charge of

---

'appédhen is the Old Persian apadāna, "armory," "treasury," which was borrowed also into Akkadian and Syriac to mean **palace**. Here it means his headquarters. The LXX renders it τότε; i.e., the translator mistook אפדן for the Aramaic אדין. Theod., Aq., and the Vulg. all took it as a place name, which gives us the source of Porphyry's account of how Antiochus pitched his camp at a place called Apedno.

Pitch: Lit., **plant**, used in this sense only here in the O.T. **Sea** here is **seas**, which can only mean the Mediterranean (as in Judg. 5:17; Deut. 33:19). **The glorious holy mountain:** Mount Zion (cf. Ps. 48:1-2). **Glorious** is as in vss. 16, 41. This would mean that Antiochus will set up his headquarters somewhere between Jerusalem and the sea. As it is known that he died in Persia, some have sought to interpret the **sea** as the Caspian and the **holy mountain** as the temple of Nanai at Elymais, but this is not possible. It was common eschatological expectation that the enemy of Israel would come to destruction in the proximity of Jerusalem (Ezek. 38:14-16; 39:2-4; Joel 3:2; Zech. 14:2 ff.; Enoch 90:13-19; 56:6-7; Rev. 20:9). Bentzen suggests that the writer had in mind the fulfillment of the prophecy in Isa. 10:31 ff.

Both in ch. 7 and in ch. 10 the idea had been suggested that judgment had long since been passed in heaven on Antiochus. Now the time has run out and that sentence is executed. He comes **to his end,** and no one can do anything to help ward it off. The expectation is that some sudden destruction will cut him off while he is encamped in Palestine. In 8:25 it was said that his end would be by no human hand, and the writer is doubtless here thinking of some act of divine intervention. In Jewish eyes the worst offenses of Antiochus had been perpetrated in Palestine, and it was appropriate that he should be cut off there. Actually he died at Tabae in Persia in the winter of 165/164 B.C., having been driven there by the infuriated people of Elymais, whose temple he had attempted to plunder (Polybius *Histories* XXXI. 9; I Macc. 3:31-37; 6:1-16; II Macc. 9:1-2). Some early commentators suggested that there was a break between the first part of this verse and the second, the first telling how he encamped in Palestine, and the second, by a leap ahead, telling how he died in Persia. This is not impossible, but is unlikely. The book seems to have been finished while Antiochus was still alive and the temple not yet purified and rededicated. The writer had no knowledge of where Antiochus would die, but he anticipated that it would be in Palestine immediately before the final consummation.

d) End of the Tribulation and the Resurrection (12:1-4)

With the death of Antiochus Epiphanes the final consummation begins, and in view of the imminence of the end, Michael, the patron angel of the Jews, bestirs himself. The great tribulation now really becomes great in the final spasms of agony of a dying world period, the "birth pangs of the Messiah," but it ends with the general resurrection, the great separation of the blessed from the damned, and the coming of the kingdom of the saints. Here the vision ends (vss. 1-4) and the seer is bidden to seal the book.

---

redeeming experience, because he knows that God too is suffering with him. There is in our life something that says we are not alone when we have been defeated in a good cause. But the empty horror of the defeat of the wicked is almost too terrible to imagine. That is why righteousness can endure many defeats and rise

again. The evil man is finished when he has run out of victories.

12:1. A Time of Trouble.—Arnold J. Toynbee has made this phrase descriptive of recurring experiences in the lives of people. It is a period in which the creativity of a way of life has ended. The decline may be arrested for a

shall be a time of trouble, such as never was since there was a nation *even* to that same time: and at that time thy people shall be delivered, every one that shall be found written in the book.

your people. And there shall be a time of trouble, such as never has been since there was a nation till that time; but at that time your people shall be delivered, every one whose name shall be found written in the

---

This was the end of the original apocalypse, but to it have been added three supplements (vss. 5-13): (*a*) Daniel sees in a vision two angels by the stream. He inquires of them how long it will be until the end, and is told that the tribulation will last three and a half more years. When he asks for further explanation, he is bidden to depart. (*b*) Another calculation of the duration of the abomination makes it 1,290 days. (*c*) A final calculation makes it 1,335 days. It is possible that vs. 13 belongs after vs. 4 and was the end of the original book, the supplements having been inserted between vs. 4 and vs. 13.

Though the break at 11:45 is a conventional chapter division, Charles commends its sound judgment, for while ch. 11 dealt with human history already past or about to be realized, ch. 12 passes from temporal to eternal things. Vss. 1-3 are metrical.

12:1. At that time: The time of the overthrow of Antiochus. There is no reason to suppose that the writer here jumps from the contemporary scene to some distant future. He is going to speak of the final consummation which comes at the end of time, but he regards the last days as beginning immediately after the death of Antiochus. Bentzen thinks that **at that time** refers to 11:40, the starting of the war being the commencement of the great tribulation, the signal, as it were, for **Michael** to make preparation for the end. Since the end will usher in the reign of the saints, it is the patron angel of the Jewish people who will naturally be active in the events leading up to it. **Has charge of:** Lit., **standeth for,** in the sense of protecting (Esth. 8:11; 9:16). The same verb in 8:25; 11:15 meant "to withstand." **Your people:** Lit., **the children of thy people,** which here would seem to mean the Jewish nation as a whole.

There shall be a time of trouble: The great tribulation. Because no details of the tribulation are given here, some refer to 11:44. One common feature in descriptions of the great tribulation, however, is the great war when the Gentile nations assemble for a final assault on Jerusalem and its righteous inhabitants (Zech. 14:2 ff.; Enoch 90:16; Rev. 16:14; 19:19). That the great tribulation should be **a time of trouble, such as never has been,** is characteristic of descriptions of the last times (Jer. 30:7; Mark 13:19; Rev. 16:18; Assumption of Moses 8:1). Possibly the phrase is derived from Joel 2:2.

Those who are to **be delivered,** though they are called **thy people,** are a narrower group than **thy people** over whom Michael is guardian, for here it is not the whole Jewish people but only the true Israel, those who had remained faithful observers of the law throughout the persecutions and who are **found written in the book.** The "deliverance" is the "ending of the profanation" promised in 9:24, while the people to be delivered are the saints of 7:18, 27, who are to inherit the new kingdom.

In the Persian Empire it had been customary to keep a register of citizens, and in the O.T. there appears the idea of a register of the members of the theocratic community on earth, from which for cause a name might be blotted out (Exod. 32:32 ff.; Ps. 69:28; Isa. 4:3; cf. Mal. 3:16; Ezek. 13:9; Phil. 4:3; Rev. 3:5; Enoch 104:1; 108:3; Jubilees 30:20 ff.). So here the idea is that those who had been faithful, and thus proved that they

---

time; but unless the deadly disease is cured, the end is assured. The time of trouble is a warning that something is radically wrong. In such a time do we live. It is the time when the spiritual foundations of a civilization are weakened, and force and materialism are vainly substituted for them.

But no man is utterly at the mercy of his environment and his society. God does not let his people fall the victims of evil in ultimate defeat. He knows what each man has done and what each man is. Our judge is not the king or the majority, but God. It is the certainty that the issues of our individual destinies are not

2 And many of them that sleep in the dust of the earth shall awake, some to everlasting life, and some to shame *and* everlasting contempt.

book. 2 And many of those who sleep in the dust of the earth shall awake, some to everlasting life, and some to shame and everlasting contempt. 3 And those who are wise

---

belonged to the saints of God, had been recorded as members of the new kingdom. Such would have to be delivered from the great tribulation that they might inherit the kingdom. Perhaps we have also here the idea that the names of the faithful in previous generations have likewise been recorded so that they too may share in the blessed life of the coming kingdom. The **book** mentioned here is not necessarily the "books" of 7:10, for there the reference may be not to the citizen register of the new kingdom but to the register of good and evil deeds.

2. With the deliverance comes the resurrection. Here for the first time in the O.T. we have clear mention of a resurrection of the wicked as well as of the righteous. In Hosea and Ezekiel it is a national, not an individual, resurrection that is prominent, and when emphasis comes to fall on individual resurrection, this is limited to righteous Israelites and denied to others, as in Isa. 24–27; Ezek. 37:11. A germ of the larger idea is sometimes discerned in Isa. 53:10 ff.; 26:19; Eccl. 3:18-22, and some find intimations of it in Pss. 17; 39; 49; 73. It had not yet, however, become explicit. Even in this verse the resurrection is not general, for it is only **many** who will rise. It is impossible to say with certainty what groups this writer included. Some think he was still limiting the resurrection to Israelites, some think even to those among them, whether observing Jews or Hellenizers, who had died during the reign of Antiochus, for in Enoch 22 we have the notion that God would raise only the pre-eminently good and the pre-eminently bad. Others suggest that the **many** should not be pressed, and that the writer did mean a general resurrection.

That death is a **sleep in the dust of the earth,** where the dead rest in their graves until roused for the resurrection, was a common idea (Enoch 91:10; 92:3; Athenagoras *Plea for Christians* XII; Philo *Biblical Antiquities* III. 10; XIX. 13). **Sleep** as an image for death is familiar from Jer. 51:39, 57; John 11:11; Acts 7:60; I Thess. 5:10. From the dust men were created and to dust they return, so dust as the dwelling of the departed is used as early as the Mesopotamian epics and is an O.T. image (Ps. 22:29; Job 20:11). **Dust of the earth** here, however, is a peculiar expression, "soil of dust" or "land of dust," which some think means nothing more than the grave, but others take to be a descriptive name for Sheol. **Shall awake** is a natural concomitant of sleep.

Following the resurrection comes the great separation, familiar to us from the symbolism of dividing the sheep from the goats or the companions of the right hand from those of the left (Matt. 25:32-33). The actual judgment is not mentioned here, but is assumed. Those who rise face the record of their deeds (7:10; cf. Rev. 20:12; Enoch 90:20-27; II Baruch 24:1). That is the basis on which they will be separated. Who the two groups are here depends of course on who were the groups that were raised. If we think of a general resurrection, then the separation is of the righteous from the wicked, those who will enter the kingdom from those who will be condemned. Those who insist on **many** hold that the two groups are those of the martyrs and the archsinners, or whatever two contrasting groups are, on their theory, to be raised.

From the separation they go on to their reward. **Some to everlasting life,** but **some to shame and everlasting contempt. Everlasting life** occurs only here in the O.T. A

---

to be decided by other men that makes the religious man confident and invulnerable.

2. Men Do Not Die.—This is one of the earliest references to life after death in the O.T., and it is one of the more highly developed insights. The doctrine of immortality and resur-

rection finally has to break through into the consciousness of men. It is like a sea beating at the dikes of human insensitiveness and fear. At last it forces a breach and floods into the human spirit. Men do not die, and God has made us for eternity.

3 And they that be wise shall shine as the brightness of the firmament; and they that turn many to righteousness, as the stars for ever and ever.

4 But thou, O Daniel, shut up the words, and seal the book, *even* to the time of the

shall shine like the brightness of the firmament; and those who turn many to righteousness, like the stars for ever and ever.
4 But you, Daniel, shut up the words, and seal the book, until the time of the end.

---

somewhat similar expression is used in Ps. 133:3, but there it seems to mean only the perpetual existence of Israel (cf. Ecclus. 37:25; 44:13). It is, however, a common enough expression in apocalyptic (Pss. Sol. 3:16; Enoch 15:4, 6; IV Macc. 14:5; II Enoch 50:2; 65:10), whence it came into the rabbinical writings (cf. Targ. to Lev. 18:5; Deut. 33:6; Ezek. 20:13).

Everlasting: Without any ending since the kingdom promised to the saints in 2:44; 7:14, 27 was unending (cf. Rev. 11:15; 22:5). **Shame:** Lit., "reproaches," as in 9:16, where it was translated "byword," and 11:18, where it was translated "insolence" (cf. Jer. 23:40; 24:9; 29:18; 42:18). Some think the word was not part of the original text but is a gloss explanatory of **contempt,** which is, lit., "aversion," "abhorrence." These words say nothing of the actual punishment of the wicked but suggest it. The wicked enter a mode of existence that makes them a byword to the dwellers in the kingdom; though objects of abhorrence, we are not told what their situation actually is. Perhaps the writer could assume that his audience would know what it would be. The wording of the verse is consistent with the idea that they were annihilated, or with the teaching that they went to an eternal punishment (cf. Matt. 25:46; John 5:29).

3. When those who inherit the kingdom enter into their inheritance all receive their reward, but there are certain groups who are remarkable even in this state of bliss. Two such groups are mentioned here. The first is that of the **wise** who in 11:33, 35 were called leaders among the faithful. As then they were distinguished among their fellows, so in the kingdom they will be distinguished by their **brightness.** What is meant by their shining **like the brightness of the firmament** is not clear. The use of the word *zōhar* for **brightness** or "splendor" occurs in Ezek. 8:2, and there is a somewhat similar expression for the brightness of the sky in Exod. 24:10. The LXX has "as the luminaries of heaven," and in Matt. 13:43; Enoch 39:7; 104:2; II Esdras 7:97, 125 we have this notion of the blessed as luminaries, an idea possibly derived from contemporary astral theology. In this verse they only shine **like** the stars, but the expression may have come from the same source.

The second group is that of "the justifiers of the many." The **many** apparently means the multitude of common people (Esth. 4:3; Aboda Zara 1:7). "Those who justify," here as in Isa. 53:11, seems to mean not those who technically justify in the legal sense but those who **turn many to righteousness** by their precept and example. They too are to shine brightly **like the stars** (Wisd. Sol. 3:7; Enoch 39:7; cf. 43:1-4). Some think that this clause is merely saying in other words what was said in the first clause, so that only one group is meant, those who **turn many to righteousness** being the aforementioned **wise.** The LXX certainly understood the verse to refer to two classes, for it interprets the first as those who have deep insight and are the teachers of the people, while the second are those who receive the teaching and hold it fast.

4. In the vision the seer is bidden to seal up the words. This suggests an author who has been writing an account, not a seer who has been seeing a vision. The readers may have been meant to understand it as in 8:26. As the vision and the message close, the angel

---

There is no doctrine of universal salvation here. Judgment will extend beyond death. One can hardly escape the conclusion that it is possible permanently to damage a human soul. One cannot help asking if some spirits would be

worth preserving on any basis. Daniel is quite clear. There is **everlasting life,** but there are also **shame and everlasting contempt.**

4. *Standing for Real Values.*—This is an apt description of the rootless and faithless ones.

end: many shall run to and fro, and knowledge shall be increased.	Many shall run to and fro, and knowledge shall increase."

bids the seer to conceal them until the time is ripe for their disclosure. This book, however, is apocalyptic, and its writer is very conscious of the written form. In 7:1 there is a reference to the writing of visions. The writer's literary framework is the court at Babylon, and there must be an explanation somewhere why these matters revealed there were not known to earlier generations. The explanation is that they were written down and sealed up until the time of the end drew near, when they were to be made available to the faithful that they might understand the significance of the events amid which they were living (cf. II Esdras 14:44 ff.; Enoch 1:2; Rev. 22:10).

To shut up the words and to seal the book apparently mean the same thing. The question is whether the injunction concerns the whole book or only this last vision. The probabilities are that it means all the material so far given, for there seems no sufficient reason for thinking that only the last vision should be sealed (cf. vs. 9; 8:26). *Sātham* is "to stop up," "to close" (cf. II Kings 3:19, 25; II Chr. 32:3, 30; Neh. 4:7 [M.T. 4:1]), and then in a derived sense, "to keep secret" (cf. vs. 9; Ezek. 28:3); some therefore translate "hide the words," i.e., keep them secret and hidden. The sealing of the book would serve this end, for the thought is of a scroll which, after it had been rolled up and had a seal affixed, could not be opened and read without the seal's being broken (Isa. 29:11). The same word for seal was used in 9:24 and in the Aramaic of 6:17 (M.T. 6:18).

Until the time of the end refers to the framework of the book. Daniel is in the court at Babylon at the beginning of the Persian period. The visions concern the period of Antiochus Epiphanes, the "time of the end" of 8:19, 26; 11:35. The critic may ask what good the visions would be if they were to be sealed up until the time to which they refer has arrived, but this statement is intended to answer the natural query of the writer's audience as to why they had heard nothing about these writings before, and the critic's question would not have occurred to them (see Isa. 29:11-12, 18-19). In Rev. 22:10 the seer is admonished not to seal up the vision, for the time was already at hand. It is not unusual to read that apocryphal books are to be concealed in some secret place until an appropriate time (II Esdras 12:37; Assumption of Moses 1:17-18).

Many shall run to and fro: *Shūṭ* is "to rove," "to move about," and *shôṭēṭ* is used in Amos 8:12; Jer. 5:1; Zech. 4:10; II Chr. 16:9 in the sense of rapid movement to and fro, which suggests that we should translate here in that sense. But what would that mean? Some think it suggests perplexity at the strangeness of such a book of visions whose significance none could see. Others think it means "perusing," that men's eyes will run to and fro rapidly as they eagerly read this strange document. But how could it cause perplexity if it were sealed up so that no one could read it? Are we to assume that this refers to what will happen after it has been opened and read? Others think we are to take the words literally, and that the reference is to days of commotion, turmoil, and rushing around, so that it were best for the book to be hidden in some place of safety. To this end Bevan emends דעת, knowledge, to רעת, "evils," "calamities," and has the phrase refer to the upheavals and commotions connected with the latter days of Antiochus Epiphanes (cf. I Macc. 1:9). Montgomery translates, "many shall run to and fro that knowledge may increase," thinking that the writer is alluding to Amos 8:12, a passage which pictures men rushing about trying to find the word of Yahweh but finding it not. Perhaps the writer means that the stress of those times will cause many to run about seeking some explanation of the events in the midst of which they live, but for

Having no deep convictions and no tested beliefs, they run about after every new fad and promise. This is not to suggest that the religious man is set in a stationary place. He is not a	reactionary saying "No" to every progressive movement. But the man of faith always stands for the real values. He has a base of operations and a framework for judgment. He spots the

5 ¶ Then I Daniel looked, and, behold, there stood other two, and one on this side of the bank of the river, and the other on that side of the bank of the river.

6 And *one* said to the man clothed in linen, which *was* upon the waters of the river, How long *shall it be* to the end of these wonders?

7 And I heard the man clothed in linen, which *was* upon the waters of the river, when he held up his right hand and his left hand unto heaven, and sware by him that liveth for ever, that *it shall be* for a time, times, and a half; and when he shall have accomplished to scatter the power of the holy people, all these *things* shall be finished.

5 Then I Daniel looked, and behold, two others stood, one on this bank of the stream and one on that bank of the stream. 6 And I[h] said to the man clothed in linen, who was above the waters of the stream, "How long shall it be till the end of these wonders?" 7 The man clothed in linen, who was above the waters of the stream, raised his right hand and his left hand toward heaven; and I heard him swear by him who lives for ever that it would be for a time, two times, and half a time; and that when the shattering of the power of the holy people comes to an end all these things would

[h] Gk Vg: Heb *he*

---

those who receive this message concerning the last days, their significance will become progressively clear. Bentzen compares II Thess. 2:10-12.

3. Epilogue (12:5-13)

5-9. Some regard these verses as a later addition from another hand. Others hold that they are from the same writer who in 7:25 and 8:14 had given calculations as to the date when the end would come and who desired to round out the last vision with a similar calculation. Some regard the verses not as a supplement but as an integral part of the whole passage.

The **two others** must be two angels other than the angel of 10:5, who has been telling Daniel about the vision. The reason for there being **two** is the oath in vs. 7, since for any such oath two witnesses were necessary (Deut. 19:15). Bentzen refers to 8:13-16, thinking the writer's idea is that an oath by one angel witnessed by two others and heard by Daniel as a third witness must be an ironclad oath. Apparently the two stood on either **bank of the river,** which must be the same as that in 10:4, the stream beside which the seer was when the vision came. Here, however, it is not the usual word for river, which was used in 10:4, but יְאֹר, which in the O.T. usually means the Nile. It is used in Isa. 33:21, however, for watercourses (cf. Job 28:10), and in later Hebrew is a general word for river.

6. And I said follows the LXX καὶ εἶπα, with which the Vulg. and some MSS of Theod. agree. The M.T. has **he said,** i.e., one of the angels just mentioned. The word is addressed to the angel who has all along been speaking to Daniel. This is evident from the facts that his white clothes (cf. 10:5) are mentioned and that as in 8:16 he stands somewhere above the stream.

"Until when is the end of the wonders?" *Pelā'ôth,* **wonders,** "marvels" (cf. Isa. 29:14; Pss. 77:11, 14; 78:12). The Niphal participle was used in 11:36 of the boastings of Antiochus (cf. 8:24). The reference here is to the wondrous events which have been foreshadowed in the vision (cf. 11:31-36; 12:1).

7. The angelic being answers, swearing a solemn oath to establish the certainty of the matter. The repetition of detail as to the angel's clothing and the place where he stood is stylistic and is not meant to have any other significance. To raise the **right hand** in an oath is a custom mentioned in Gen. 14:22; Deut. 32:40; Rev. 10:5, but why both hands should be raised is not clear, unless the gesture was meant to give greater emphasis to the oath. It is an angel who swears in Rev. 10:5-6, where the oath is also "by him who lives for ever" (cf. the formula in Judg. 8:19; Deut. 32:40).

"A time, times and a half" would mean three and a half years (7:25; 8:14). There is no clear indication as to the date from which the three and a half years are to be

8 And I heard, but I understood not: then said I, O my Lord, what *shall be* the end of these *things?*

9 And he said, Go thy way, Daniel: for the words *are* closed up and sealed till the time of the end.

be accomplished. **8** I heard, but I did not understand. Then I said, "O my lord, what shall be the issue of these things?" **9** He said, "Go your way, Daniel, for the words are shut up and sealed until the time of the end.

---

reckoned. The calculation in vs. 11 begins at December, 167 B.C., when the daily sacrifice was suppressed, and it may be that this is the case here, though some think the writer is calculating from the mission of Apollonius in 168.

The conclusion of the verse is a puzzle. The M.T. reads, "and as the completion of the dispersion of the hand of the holy people shall be completed all these things." Some take this to mean, "when they shall cease to break in pieces [or to scatter] the power of the holy people," or "when the scattering of a portion of the holy people shall come to an end," i.e., when the Jews are no longer dispersed abroad but shall be gathered together from exile and assembled as one people in the Holy Land, then will come the end of the tribulation and entrance into the final kingdom. The verb *nāphaç* means "to disperse," as in Isa. 11:12. Its usual meaning is "to dash to pieces," and some think that it refers to the persecutions under Antiochus; hence the rendering "when they finish shattering the power of the holy people," i.e., when the ultimate stage of the great tribulation is reached, the final consummation may be expected. *Yadh,* "a hand," meaning **power,** is a common idiom (Num. 31:49; Josh. 8:20; II Sam. 18:2).

Bevan would emend the text to read, "and when the power of the Shatterer of the holy people should come to an end." The shatterer would be Antiochus, and the reference would be to 7:25, where it is said that the people will be given into his hand for a time and times and half a time. This emendation has won much acceptance, for it makes the point that the message to the audience is the encouraging one that this Antiochus is to be the last oppressor before the great deliverance.

8. If we take this verse as part of the first supplement, the point is that the seer heard the reply of the angel but did not fully understand it. He therefore asks for a fuller explanation, but is rebuffed. Some, however, think it is the beginning of the second interpolation. Since the first calculation was expressed obscurely, or perhaps because it had proved incorrect, another attempt was made to calculate, and this is introduced by representing the seer as not satisfied with the angelic statement and seeking to have a closer definition of the time of the end.

Did not understand: The verb is translated **understand** in 8:27, "perceived" in 9:2, and "understood" in 10:1. Perhaps "gave heed" would best suit all these passages. The seer heard, but he did not heed particularly, and so became conscious that further questioning was necessary. He addresses the angel as **my Lord,** as in 10:16. **What shall be the issue of these things?** This seems a foolish question, since he has already been told, so the Peshitta and Vulg. have "what shall be after these things?" and the LXX, "what is the interpretation of these things?" If this is introducing a fresh attempt at a calculation of the time of the end, it is understandable. *'Aḥarîth* is "latter end," and since in earlier passages we had *qēç* for **end,** some would take the word here to mean "closing stages," and make the question one for further information than has yet been given. Charles and Ginsberg, however, note that if the underlying Aramaic were אחוית, "explanation," the translator might have misread it and so produced our text.

9. The seer is reminded that the revelation has been **closed** and **sealed,** and no further revelation can be given. If this is part of the first supplement, or part of the

---

insincere and the pretentious. He has been given an eternal measurement and an everlasting standard.

9. *The Words Are Sealed.*—Daniel seems to desire an exact answer and a precise date. The angel indicates that one must go his way in

10 Many shall be purified, and made white, and tried; but the wicked shall do wickedly: and none of the wicked shall understand; but the wise shall understand.	10 Many shall purify themselves, and make themselves white, and be refined; but the wicked shall do wickedly; and none of the wicked shall understand; but those who are

original chapter before the supplements begin, it would seem to mean that the angel is telling Daniel that for him in his position at the court in Babylon it is of no importance whether he understands the significance of the visions. They refer not to his day but to the future, and he has done his part in seeing and recording them. They are now finished and sealed, and in due time will be intelligible to those for whom they are meant.

The words **shut up** and **sealed** are from vs. 4 but Ginsberg (*Studies*, p. 31) suggests that here they have lost their literal sense and mean "obscure and mysterious," i.e., the visions will remain enigmatical **until the time of the end,** when their meaning will become clear. The words may, however, be meant here in the same sense as in vs. 4. In this verse the writer employs again the usual expression for the "last days."

10. The last days are days when the righteous, through the trials of the great tribulation, are **purified** and made ready for their coming heritage, but they are also days when **the wicked** are given opportunity to fill up the measure of their wickedness and exult in the final hours of their evil-doing. Vs. 1 had already spoken of this increase of wickedness in the last times, and 11:35 had mentioned that these days were for the refining of the **wise.**

The **many** are generally considered to be only Israelites, and some think only the martyrs among them. It is possible, however, that the writer means to include righteous non-Israelites also. They shall be "cleansed and whitened and refined," as in 11:35, where the same root verbs are used. The idea of a great separation into two groups on the basis of their deeds is found in Rev. 22:11.

None of the wicked shall understand: Some take this to mean that none of the wicked will act with understanding, but, given over to blindness of heart, they will plunge into wickedness without thought of consequences. Others, relating the words to vs. 8, think the meaning is that as Daniel did not understand the significance of the visions, so when they are revealed the wicked likewise will not understand, whereas the **wise shall understand** and take warning. It seems more likely, however, that the writer means that the wicked will not have any true understanding of the events amid which they are living, and never glimpse the divine plan that is inexorably being worked out to its fulfillment, whereas the righteous will have true understanding.

Those who are wise: The same word was used in vs. 3; 11:33, 35 for the leaders of the people, and it may refer to them here. More likely, however, the word here has the general meaning of "all who possess wisdom." There may have been many simple folk with no claim to count among the leaders, who nevertheless could see clearly the significance of events and were among those purified and refined by the experiences of their day. **Wise** in this sense of understanding the ways of God occurs in II Chr. 30:22; Prov. 15:24; Amos 5:13. In II Esdras 14:46 the reserved revelations are to be delivered "to the wise among the people."

faith, for the precise details cannot be known. They are **sealed** in the book **until the time of the end.** There are so many things our curiosity would like to have answered. But they are not essential. **The time of the end** is not an essential. But that a man should be faithful in the face of persecution is essential. That he should follow the straight way of loyalty is the important thing. God often says to us, "What is that to thee? follow thou me" (John 21:22).

10. *The Wise Shall Understand.*—The evil ones are enslaved. Unable to be free, they create a false illusion of freedom by pretending that their slavery is freedom. One of the main characteristics of wickedness is its power of pretense. It forces all its theories to an adjustment with slavery. The wicked can never understand because they begin with the wrong assumptions. Until they are destroyed they never quite understand what has gone wrong and

11 And from the time *that* the daily *sacrifice* shall be taken away, and the abomination that maketh desolate set up, *there shall be* a thousand two hundred and ninety days.

12 Blessed *is* he that waiteth, and cometh to the thousand three hundred and five and thirty days.

13 But go thou thy way till the end *be:* for thou shalt rest, and stand in thy lot at the end of the days.

wise shall understand. 11 And from the time that the continual burnt offering is taken away, and the abomination that makes desolate is set up, there shall be a thousand two hundred and ninety days. 12 Blessed is he who waits and comes to the thousand three hundred and thirty-five days. 13 But go your way till the end; and you shall rest, and shall stand in your allotted place at the end of the days."

11-12. Here are two fresh calculations of the date of the end. There may be doubt as to whether vss. 5-10 or vss. 8-10 are interpolations, but vss. 11-12 certainly are. Since Gunkel's work in 1895 it has been generally accepted that they are two successive glosses intended to prolong the term of 1,150 days given in 8:14 as the time which is to elapse from the abolition of the daily sacrifice until the cleansing of the sanctuary. Apparently the 1,150 days had passed, and what had been expected had not happened, so vs. 11 prolongs the period to 1,290 days, and vs. 12 to 1,335 days. Both reckonings start from the abolition of the *tāmîdh* (8:11; 9:27; 11:31), which was followed by the setting up of the abomination of desolation (8:13).

A thousand two hundred and ninety days would be forty-three months of thirty days, whereas three and a half years would be forty-two such months (i.e., 1,260 days; cf. Rev. 11:3; 12:6), so this is one month more. **The thousand three hundred and thirty-five** days would be forty-five days, or one and a half such months, longer. This figure 1,335 occurs again in Ascension of Isaiah 4:12, but perhaps that passage took it from here.

It is noticeable that nothing is said about what is to happen at the end of the 1,290 days. It is generally assumed that the reference is to the cleansing of the temple for reconsecration, an event which occurred in 164 B.C. (I Macc. 4:52). Some, however, think that the reference is to the death of Antiochus Epiphanes, and that the next number 1,335 refers to the rededication of the temple which was expected to take place after Antiochus met his end. Others suggest that the 1,335 days may refer to the end of time and the beginning of eternity, or that it will be 1,290 days to the great deliverance and then 45 more days to the setting up of the reign of righteousness. The most likely theory, however, is that they are two fresh attempts to predict the ending of the period of persecution.

Blessed is he who waits: Perhaps a reminiscence of Isa. 30:18 (cf. Jas. 1:12; Pss. Sol. 18:7).

13. This verse may have come originally after vs. 4, or some think after vs. 8. It is a final word of assurance to the seer, who is not to feel that he has no place in the wondrous kingdom to which all the visions he has recorded point. Obviously the verse cannot mean that Daniel will continue living until the final consummation, so some

what has been happening to them. But those who have sat at the feet of righteousness and learned of goodness are given the power to understand.

12. *Waiting on God.*—Patience is never a popular virtue and it is never easy to practice. Many a man who can stand up against the spectacular danger and the exciting crisis fails utterly when it is a matter of being faithful when no trumpets are blowing. Yet life is very much like warfare, in that much of it must be

spent in waiting. For every moment of high endeavor there are a hundred demands to hold steady when it does not seem worth while. As one grows older, one comes to the conclusion that more lives are destroyed by impatience than by any other weakness. We cannot wait and be faithful. We desert the cause. We give up all we have accomplished because we are bored. Yet often we can see—when it is too late —that the victory was almost ours if we had but known it. Daniel was saying that the rewards

suggest that **the end** here is the end of Daniel's life, the seer being told that he will complete his allotted span and then **rest** in the grave, but with assurance that he will share in the resurrection at the end. The wording, however, suggests that **the end** is eschatological. The seer is being told to go his way, the way all flesh will go until the end comes. The LXX and Theod. omit **till the end,** and a number of modern editors therefore delete it as an interpolation.

Rest is generally taken to mean rest in the grave, as in Isa. 57:2, or in Sheol, as in Job 3:17. The saints are said to "rest" in Wisd. Sol. 4:7; Rev. 14:13; II Esdras 7:95. The LXX has here an insertion which seems to mean that the seer is assured that in the flesh he will see and share in the new kingdom to be founded on earth.

"And thou shalt stand at thy lot": *Gôrāl* is a voting stone, then a **lot,** "portion," "share." It is used in a spiritual sense in Pss. 16:5; 125:3; Prov. 1:14; Jer. 13:25 (cf. Acts 26:18; Col. 1:12). Some think the reference is to the honorable position Daniel will continue to have at the court until the end of his days. **At the end of the days,** however, can hardly be other than eschatological, and the meaning must be that he is being assured that when the last days merge into the coming kingdom he will have his **allotted place** or portion therein.

---

of God come to the men who can wait. He was writing to urge faithfulness. It is one of the most necessary traits, and the great victories are won by the men who have it.

13. *Going On to the End.*—The main thing is go on to **the end** and see the job through. It will not be easy. This is the time of testing, but there will come the time of **rest.** Then at last Daniel is assured that he shall stand in his **allotted place.** Nothing can prevent that or interfere with that divine plan. Each man has been promised such a place. Neither tyrants nor persecutions can deflect a man from that future. His own will come to him. The kingdom is forever, and the loyal citizen of the kingdom will have his honored place reserved.

The Book of

HOSEA

Introduction and Exegesis by JOHN MAUCHLINE
Exposition by HAROLD COOKE PHILLIPS

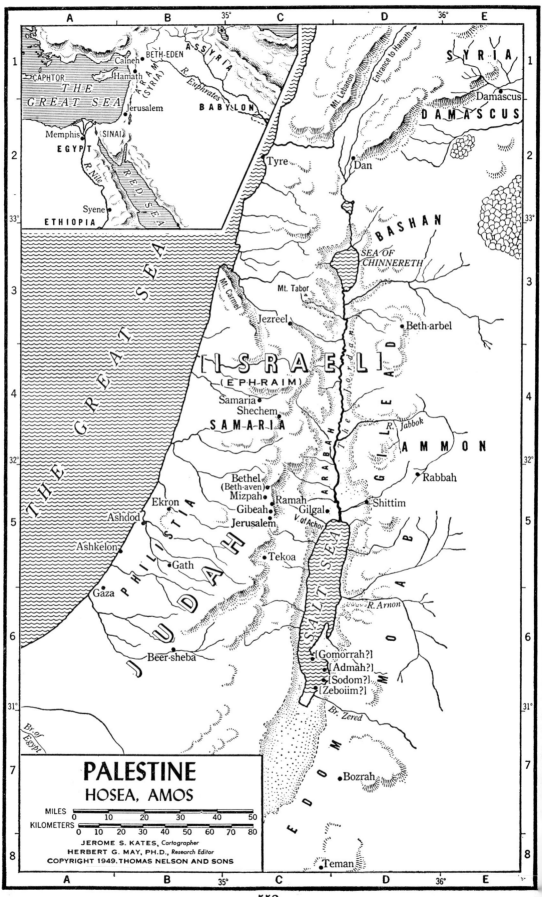

PALESTINE
HOSEA, AMOS

MILES
0 10 20 30 40 50

KILOMETERS
0 10 20 30 40 50 60 70 80

JEROME S. KATES, *Cartographer*
HERBERT G. MAY, PH.D., *Research Editor*
COPYRIGHT 1949. THOMAS NELSON AND SONS

HOSEA

INTRODUCTION

Hosea was one of the four great Israelite prophets of the eighth century B.C. of whose prophetic activity we have some knowledge and of whose utterances a collection has been preserved. Of Hosea's personal and domestic life some details are known. His father was a certain Beeri, but there is no justification for identifying him with the Reubenite prince mentioned in I Chr. 5:6; his birthplace is not named. His wife was Gomer, daughter of, or belonging to, Diblaim; she is described as a "woman of harlotries" (1:2). They had three children, Jezreel, Not pitied, and Not my people (1:4, 6, 9).

The name of Hosea's firstborn proves that he began his prophetic career before the end of the house of Jehu, that is, before the end of the reign of Jeroboam II in 746 B.C. As is indicated in the Exegesis, the superscription in 1:1b has relevance to a section of the present book, possibly chs. 1–3, while the other part of the superscription, contained in 1:1a, with its reference to the reigns of Uzziah, Jotham, Ahaz, and Hezekiah, is due to a later Judaistic editing, according to which the reference in 1:7 was taken to be to the deliverance of Judah in the time of Sennacherib's invasion in 701 B.C. (On this Judaistic editing see pp. 563-64.)

I. The Book of Hosea

It is now generally accepted that the prophetical books of the Old Testament are composed of rhythmic utterances, biographical prose, and autobiographical prose. In Hosea the second type is illustrated in ch. 1; the third type in ch. 3. Even a rapid survey of the book as a whole makes it plain that it is composed of two main sections, chs. 1–3 and chs. 4–14. But there are advantages in taking ch. 14 also by itself. It is therefore proposed, for the purposes of this Introduction, to take the book in these three parts; and inasmuch as it is always a sound principle, where there is controversy, to examine first what is not in dispute, that its evidence may be analyzed and valued, and only after that what is controversial, it seems wise to reserve consideration of chs. 1–3 until the last because of the much-discussed problem of interpretation which is involved in them.

Amos, preaching a little earlier than Hosea in the same century, had proclaimed the day of the Lord, a day of inescapable judgment by God upon human sinfulness. Israel, God's people, had been trained for its God-appointed task by prophet, priest, and Nazirite, had been disciplined by sword, famine, and pestilence, but had refused to learn. Amos had pleaded with them and for them; he had called them to repentance but they would not listen. They persisted in their evil ways; they disrupted the community of Israel by their injustice, their oppression, and their exploitation; they manifested their utter lack of any sense of social responsibility by their selfish indulgence and their dilettante ways. But they could not hope to do all this with impunity. There was a reign of law in the spiritual world as well as in the natural world. Therefore the doom of evildoers was ineluctable, and the penalties upon Israel would be severer than upon the neighboring peoples because Israel had enjoyed greater privileges of tradition and training. In calling upon the people to seek good and not evil, Amos did hold out the hope that the Lord of Hosts might be gracious to the remnant of Joseph (5:15); but if the people should remain unresponsive, he had no other word to speak to them than one of doom.

A. Sermons and Addresses (4:1–13:16).—The words of Hosea are not unlike those of Amos. He condemns social evils, the crimes which men in community commit against their fellow men to satisfy their own greed, or lust for power, or sheer selfish indulgence (4:2). "Israel has spurned the good" (8:3); there is a lack of moral restraint, and a persistent refusal to honor moral obligations (7:1-2; 10:4; 12:7-8). Time after time Hosea sums up the situation by saying that a harlot spirit has led the people astray (4:12; 5:4; 9:1); a lying and deceitful spirit has them now in thrall (10:2; 12:7). But this was not a recent development; it had a long history, going back indeed to the earliest days of Israel's history, to Baal-peor, to Gibeah and to Gilgal (9:9-10, 15; 10:9). In other words, if it was during the wilderness period that the Lord called his people and bound them to him with cords of love, it was immediately after that period that the corruption set in and it had not been eradicated since. Sometimes as Hosea reflected upon such inveterate sinfulness he was inclined to believe that the main cause of it was the ignorance of the people; they had no knowledge of the moral law or of the demands of God. "My people are destroyed for lack of knowledge" (4:6; cf. 4:1, 11, 14; 5:4; 6:6). For this ignorance the priests had a large share of the responsibility. Their function was not merely to direct the people's worship and to offer sacrifice; it was also to teach and to instruct, and in the exercise of that office they had lamentably failed (4:4-8; 5:1-2; 8:11-12; contrast 6:3; Isa. 11:2; Hab. 2:14). But the people themselves had been guilty of a stubborn rebelliousness which refused to be disciplined or rebuked (4:16-17). They had occasional qualms of conscience and a momentary purpose to repent and to turn from the evil of their ways (6:1-4); but the mood passed as a morning cloud, without effecting any change in their life. The results of this long-continued unfaithfulness were twofold: on the one hand, their deeds no longer permit them to return to their God, and on the other, even if they were now to seek to return, the Lord would not be found because he has withdrawn from them (5:4, 6, 15). As H. Wheeler Robinson says:

It [sin] creates its own penalties, alienating the good which might have brought deliverance from it, hardening itself to worse and worse deeds which dispense with even the poor excuse of its own beginning. Sooner or later, it finds the universe arrayed against it; for sin is the challenge to the whole of things by the individual man, which is the sheerest and uttermost folly.[1]

1. Israel and the Fertility Cults.—Israel had become conformed to her cultural environment. Disregarding the ethical demands of the Lord's service, she served the local Baals, bringing in due season the appropriate offerings that the fertility of the fields and the increase of the flocks might be assured (2:13; 11:2). She worshiped at many altars whose number had been increased by the prosperity of the reign of Jeroboam II (4:13; 10:1-2; 8:11). She loved sacrifice (8:13). There were those who believed that in such sacrificial worship they were rendering a service acceptable to the Lord (5:6; 8:2), but Hosea described the altars as occasions for sinning (8:11). Such people practiced a fertility cult, with the usual Canaanite accompaniments of images, maççēbhôth and 'ashērîm (3:4); special regard was paid to the calf of Samaria (8:5-6; 10:5-7). In addition to the religious apostasy which was represented by this worship for the people who were united in covenant love with the Lord, it had its physical excesses. There were the revels of the great agricultural festivals (7:14), the drinking (4:11), and the sexual indulgence. The last was in origin a representation of the divine marriage, and not only had its fertility value but was the way, however crude the practice may seem to us, by which, in the primitive days before the conception of a spiritual fellowship had dawned, it was sought to maintain fellowship with God. No one will dispute that in the myth and ritual pattern of the ancient Near East the representation of a divine marriage had a definite place. It has, for instance, been argued that the practice of living in booths at the autumn festival in Israel was not simply a convenient mode of life during the vintage season but had symbolic value; the green boughs with which the booths were constructed betoken a fertility rite. S. H. Hooke expresses the commonly accepted view when he says that the booth represented the sacred grove where the divine marriage took place.[2] The fact also

---

[1] Two Hebrew Prophets (London: Lutterworth Press, 1948), pp. 27-28.

[2] The Origins of Early Semitic Ritual (London: British Academy, 1938; cf. his Myth and Ritual (London: Oxford University Press, 1933), and the Ras Shamra documents entitled The Death of Aleyan; The Birth of the Gracious and Beautiful Gods; The Marriage of King Keret. See C. H. Gordon, Ugaritic Literature (Roma: Pontificium Institutum Biblicum, 1949), pp. 84-85.

that cult prostitutes are mentioned several times in the O.T. (cf. I Kings 14:24; 15:12; 22:46; II Kings 23:7) shows that Israel had not remained unaffected in this particular. The prophets had endeavored to purify the thoughts of the Israelites from the crude conception of divine fellowship which was represented by the immoral rites of the fertility cults, but the immoral rites continued to be practiced by many who were quite unaware of their original purpose. All this sinfulness, Hosea asserts, has caused in the world a general malaise; it has had cosmic repercussions. Even the birds and the beasts have become affected by it (2:18; 4:3). More uncompromisingly than any of his contemporary fellow prophets, Hosea condemns idolatry. He disparages images as the work of men's hands; if, therefore, they are thus inferior to their maker, man, they are utterly unable to help, let alone to save, man. Even the greatest image of them all, the calf image of Bethel, will at the last be carried away like splinters of wood upon the surface of the waves. On the other hand, the Lord lives and gives life, and beside him there is no savior. At this point Hosea anticipates the teaching of the Second Isaiah (cf. Hos. 8:4-6; 10:5-7; 13:2-3; 6:2; 13:4).

2. Political Instability and Intrigue.—Hosea emphasizes Israel's unfaithfulness toward the Lord, not only as it is exemplified in her service of the Baals, but as represented by her political intrigues and dynastic instability, and by the quest for security through reliance upon foreign alliances. Doubtless many of the political leaders of that time were acutely aware that Israel could not hope to stand in her own strength against the aggressive might of Assyria or Egypt, and it seemed to them the policy dictated by responsible statemanship to seek a protective alliance with one or other of these great powers. But the religious implications of such alliances were seriously menacing for a people trained by her prophets for a standard of life and conduct spiritually purer and morally more austere than that of the surrounding nations. In the days of Ahab and Jezebel the Northern Kingdom had had experience of the harmful effects in the religious sphere of an alliance which seemed politically advisable and economically advantageous. Hosea had no desire to see the worship of foreign deities established again in Samaria; the seductions from the service of the Lord which were already active in the land were difficult enough to combat without anything being added to them. Beyond that, help from Assyria or Egypt might meet the needs of a temporary emergency; in the long run it would be pernicious, for neither of these powers had the least interest in Israel and her welfare. If,

however, the people remained faithful to their Lord, he would supply their need and be their protector, for he was bound to them by the cords of covenant love. That would in no sense guarantee them freedom from molestation owing to the aggressive actions of great powers, but it would mean that they would not be politically extinguished; to believe otherwise would be to distrust the overruling providence of God. Therefore Hosea said to his people that it was folly for them to put their trust for salvation in foreign alliance (5:13; 7:11; 8:9); nor was it wise to put any trust in armies and chariots (10:13). If Ephraim persisted in mixing herself among the peoples, she would in the end be absorbed by them and would lose any distinctive life of her own (7:8; 8:8). It was a policy which would bring an increasing sense of frustration and disillusionment.

The political instability which manifested itself in the desire to seek foreign alliance was also illustrated in unrest and intrigue at home (7:3-7). Hosea was severe in his criticism of the political unrest which followed upon the end of the reign of Jeroboam, when no king reigned securely and most reigned briefly. The prophet spoke of the trouble of Israel as going back to Gibeah and Gilgal (9:9, 15; 10:9); he probably referred not only to the spiritual apostasy which had its origin there, but also to the institution of the monarchy. But it must be noted that it was to political usurpation and hereditary monarchy that he was opposed; he believed in the charismatic principle. His desire was for God-chosen leaders whose way of action would be in accordance with God's will and whose conduct would be praiseworthy (8:4, 10; cf. Deut. 17:14-16).

According to H. S. Nyberg,[3] the crisis in Israel of which Hosea speaks was wholly religious. The reference to "king" and "princes" is not to the political leaders, but to the god Melek (or Malik) and the lower deities who were members of the heavenly court. When it is said that Israel had made Meleks, the meaning is not that they had set up rulers over them, but that they were rendering service to the city gods, the Meleks, of the land. It was when these Meleks were seen to be powerless to help or to save, and the people for pride or for shame were unwilling to return to the Lord, that they turned for help to Assyria and Egypt. Nyberg admits that in 7:4 the term "princes" does refer to political rulers; and it must be recognized that, if Hosea had wished to speak of political rulers, he would have used the terms *mélekh* and *sārîm* (cf. Jer. 2:26). The strongest support

[3] *Studien zum Hoseabuche* (Uppsala: Almqvist & Wiksells, 1935).

555

for Nyberg's theory might seem to come from such a passage as 10:3-7, in which the words "Samaria's king shall perish like a chip on the face of the waters" might be explained as referring to the image of the Melek that would be destroyed as an insubstantial thing. But a more likely interpretation of 10:7 is that the Israelites, in the period following upon the death of Jeroboam, became utterly disillusioned about their political rulers and also lost faith in Yahweh, their God, so that, in effect, the only king they continued to recognize was the calf image of Bethel; and this, said Hosea, would be carried away as a mere trifle. The evidence of 10:15 is even less helpful for Nyberg's theory. Vs. 14 speaks of war and destruction, so that a statement in vs. 15 that the reigning king will go down in the tumult is quite in order. But to make a reference to the god Melek fit the context, Nyberg has to regard vss. 13b-14 as breaking the connection of thought between vs. 13a and vs. 15. Again, 7:3-7 is an important passage; unfortunately the text is in a very bad condition and any reconstruction must have an element of uncertainty. Nyberg considers the whole reference to be to religious unfaithfulness. He quotes with aptness the passage of Judg. 5:19-21 as likewise speaking of the Meleks of Canaan and of the princes of the heavenly court, the stars that in their courses fought from heaven against Sisera; [4] and he draws attention to a section of the Babylonian Epic [5] in which, as here, the lesser gods are described as eating and drinking. But plausible as Nyberg's case is at this point, it seems to be confronted with serious difficulties. Is it likely that Hosea would have spoken of the princes of the heavenly court as being overwhelmed with wine? Could he have spoken of men as devouring such rulers? It seems much less strained to take the passage as referring to political intrigue, in which the king was ready to enter into conspiracy with men who played him false, and plotters were consumed with passion for power, hatching their plans in secret until the chosen day when they blazed forth in destructive energy. Again, when in 8:4 the Lord says of his people:

> They made kings, but not through me.
> They set up princes, but without my knowledge,

the meaning can hardly be that they rendered service to the Meleks and the Sarim without the Lord's knowing it. Hosea could not make such a statement. But the words can easily and significantly mean that they appointed rulers who were not of the Lord's choice, and who in consequence were bound to be failures. Such passages as 5:1, 10; 13:10-11 also seem to demand a political reference. The only passage of importance which remains is 3:4. It is true that the terms used in this verse are religious, with the possible exception of the first two; so that when Nyberg interprets "king" and "princes" as having reference to deities, he seems to have the context in his favor. But here is the vital question: Is this verse speaking of legitimate things which are to be denied to the returning Israel for a period which is described as "many days," or of illegitimate things which must be prohibited? If the former line of interpretation is followed it cannot be maintained that Hosea, who censured his people so often for religious unfaithfulness, could speak of a revival of the worship of Meleks and of the Sarim as legitimate in Israel. If the latter line is followed, it is very difficult to see why the prophet should have said that Israel would be denied them for many days and not permanently. It seems to be necessary to regard the things mentioned as legitimate; Israel would be emancipated from them after a period in which their lack would show their ineffectiveness.

In summing up this survey of Nyberg's theory, one may say that most if not all of the passages which he quotes appear to speak of political unrest and intrigue, and to warrant the view that the sins of Israel in Hosea's day were religious unfaithfulness, political instability, and trust in foreign alliances. Hosea adjudged such conduct to be a violation of the covenant. As against Nyberg's line of interpretation, it must not be forgotten that Hosea's first child was named Jezreel (cf. Jer. 2:8, in a chapter much influenced by Hosea).

3. Covenant Love.—It should next be noted that, whereas Amos spoke of the people's sinfulness in terms of failure to fulfill God's demand for righteousness, Hosea spoke of it in terms of the breaking of a bond or covenant. For him the fundamental fact was that Israel was bound to God by *ḥeṣedh,* "covenant love." It may be that the root idea of the Hebrew word is "zeal"; [6] and even if the word has that quality

[4] Cf. John Gray, "The Desert God 'Atar in the Literature and Religion of Canaan," *Journal of Near Eastern Studies,* VIII (1949), 72-83, where a strong argument is advanced for the identification of Shaḥar-Shalem, Attar and Melek as an astral deity whose cult was practiced chiefly at Jerusalem (cf. the king's dale, the king's gardens, and the human sacrifice to "Molech" in the valley of the sons of Hinnom).

[5] Tablet III, ll. 130-38; see J. B. Pritchard, ed., *Ancient Near Eastern Texts Relating to the Old Testament* (Princeton: Princeton University Press, 1950), pp. 65-66.

[6] N. H. Snaith, *The Distinctive Ideas of the Old Testament* (Philadelphia: Westminster Press, 1946), pp. 122-23.

of ambivalence which is not uncommon in Semitic linguistic usage, so that it can mean "zeal" (for a thing) as well as "jealousy" (against a person or a thing), it is the idea of zeal which predominates. *Ḥésedh* can be found only where there is a contractual relationship, where two parties are bound together by obligations which must be honored with steadfast zeal and patience.[7] Into such a relationship of *hésedh* Yahweh entered with his people at Sinai; the people's sin, therefore, lay in their failure to honor their obligations. It was in the wilderness that Yahweh found them and bound them to himself (9:10; 13:4-5). There he tenderly nurtured them, preparing them step by step for fuller and fuller responsibilities, that they might be made fit to bear the full yoke of his service (10:11-12; 11:3-4). But they had cast off the yoke and broken the covenant; they had lost their trust in Yahweh and had become yoked to idols; some might continue to serve him formally, but they had ceased to serve him from the heart (4:17; 5:7; 9:10; 7:14). Hosea does seem to exalt the nomadic ideal (11:3-4; 12:9; cf. 2:15; 3:4). The words of Paul Humbert are substantially true:

The whole civilization of Canaan was poles apart from the nomadism of former days. . . . The atmosphere of joy (9:1; cf. 2:13 . . .), the surfeit of material goods (13:6), the fields, the orchards, the vineyards (2:7, 10, 14; 4:11; 7:14; 9:1, 2; 10:1), the superstitious practices (4:12) . . . , the wealth (12:9), the palaces and the fortified cities (8:14), the professional armies (10:13), the politics (5:13; 7:8-11; 8:10; 10:4; 12:2; 13:10), everything that is basic in the life of Canaan, turns Israel away from Yahweh.[8]

4. Hosea and the Autumn Festival.—There is a line of approach to much of Hosea's teaching in this section which may help to explain its categories and to give new significance to its distinctive emphases. Wellhausen, speaking of 9:1-6, said that these words were spoken by Hosea on the occasion of a great festival when there was a large concourse of people (cf. Exeg.). It may very well be true that the same may be said of not a few other passages in chs. 4-13. And if any festival deserved the title of "feast of the LORD" (9:5), it was the festival of Ingathering, which marked the end of the agricultural year. It was celebrated at the close

[7] Cf. W. F. Lofthouse, "Hen and Ḥesed in the Old Testament," *Zeitschrift für die alttestamentliche Wissenschaft*, LI (1933), 29-35.

[8] "La logique de la perspective nomade chez Osée et l'unité d'Osee 2, 4-22," in Karl Budde, ed., *Karl Marti zum siebsigsten Geburtstage* (Giessen: A. Töpelmann, 1925; "Beihefte zur Zeitschrift für die alttestamentliche Wissenschaft"), p. 161.

of the vintage season and, in consequence, was a time of joyfulness and merriment, of conviviality and drinking. And inasmuch as it was celebrated by great assemblies of people at such places as Jerusalem, Samaria, and Bethel, and the freely flowing wine loosened restraints and unleashed passions and unbridled ambitions, it was a time when popular movements of rebellion were liable to come to a head and to break forth in fury.[9]

But the fact that the autumn festival occurred at the turn of the year (cf. Exod. 23:16; 34:22) entailed that the celebration of the New Year was associated with it. So it came about that at this season the people not only looked back upon the closing year with thankful hearts for the benefits they had received, but they looked forward to the new year. The summer heat was almost over; the time of the former rains was drawing near, and inevitably their thoughts were directed to that vital rain which was the condition of the country's fruitfulness and which was the essential precursor of nature's revival (cf. Zech. 14:16-17). All this was reflected in the celebration of the New Year festival. The study of this festival has been pursued with renewed interest in recent years on the basis not only of the evidence which is believed to be contained in a group of the Psalms, but also of the analogous and contributory evidence to be found in the ritual of the Babylonian *akitu* festival, and that which is given in the Ras Shamra documents concerning similar celebrations in Syria.[10] It cannot, of course, be argued that as the festival was celebrated in Babylonia or Syria, so it must have been celebrated in Israel. A common ritual pattern may have been widespread in the ancient Near East, but that pattern may have been modified considerably in Israel in terms of her distinctive traditions and different religious outlook. At any rate, the main theme of the great autumn festival in Israel seems to have been Yahweh, the king (cf. Pss. 24:7-10; 48:2; 93:1; 95:3; 149:2); and the following notes or motifs of the festival may be regarded

[9] Cf. N. H. Snaith, *The Jewish New Year Festival* (London: Society for Promoting Christian Knowledge, 1947), pp. 75-76.

[10] Cf. Sigmund Mowinckel, *Psalmenstudien*, "Das Thronbesteigungsfest Jawäs und der Ursprung der Eschatologie" (Kristiania: Jacob Dybwad, 1922); Hans Schmidt, *Die Thronfahrt Jahves am Fest der Jahreswende in alten Israel* (Tübingen: J. C. B. Mohr, 1927; "Sammlung Gemeinverstandlicher Vorträge," no. 122); Ivan Engnell, *Studies in Divine Kingship in the Ancient Near East* (Uppsala: Almqvist & Wiksells, 1943); John Gray, "Canaanite Kingship in Theory and Practice," *Vetus Testamentum* II (1952), 193-220; S. H. Hooke, ed., *Myth and Ritual*, and *The Labyrinth* (London: Society for Promoting Christian Knowledge, 1935); Snaith, *The Jewish New Year Festival.*

as well authenticated and generally accepted by modern investigators:

(*a*) Yahweh as power. There is evidence that a narrative of the creation was read, and there took place a dramatic representation of the primeval struggle between Yahweh and *tehôm*, "the great deep" (cf. Pss. 18:14-16; 29:10; 33:6-7; 46:2-3; 89:9-10; 93:3-4). Since Yahweh was the victor in that struggle, he rules the waters of the great deep and so controls the rain that falls upon the earth.

(*b*) Yahweh as judge (cf. Pss. 33:8-10; 68:2, 5-6; 149:4-9). He gives strength and help to the obedient and the humble, and he overthrows the wicked and the rebellious.

(*c*) Yahweh as savior and giver of victory to his people over their enemies (cf. Pss. 33:16-17; 46:5-9; 48:5-7; 68:20-23). There is some evidence that this truth concerning Yahweh was represented on a morning of the festival (cf. Pss. 46:5; 110:3); if that was so, we may have in this circumstance an explanation of the significance of the statement in 10:15 that in the morning the king of Israel will be cut off.

(*d*) Yahweh as the rain giver (cf. Pss. 65:9; 68:9; 104:13-14) and as the source of the earth's fruitfulness, the giver and reviver of life (cf. Pss. 48:14; 68:19-20; 96:1; 149:1).

The part played in this ritual by Israel's king is not clear. Pss. 48:12-14; 68:24-26; 118:25-27 seem to support the view that there took place a procession moving to the temple; even if this was part of the festival celebration at Jerusalem, there is no evidence that there was a similar practice at Samaria or Bethel. However, that is not a vital matter for our present inquiry. The king must have taken part in the festival in a dual capacity. He was, on the one hand, the adopted son and the anointed servant of Yahweh, and thus answerable to him for his rule (cf. Pss. 2:6-7; 89:34-37); and, on the other hand, he was the representative of his people. Thus the king was judged not only in respect of his own personal faithfulness to the covenant, but in respect of the faithfulness of his people. If the king at this time bound himself in loyalty and faithfulness to the Lord's service, then he was renewed in his earthly rule as the anointed of Yahweh, he was promised victory over all his enemies by the power of Yahweh indwelling in him, and he and his people were given the precious gift of rain and the renewal of life that came with it.

How well much of Hosea's teaching fits in with the ritual of this autumn festival! As the preceding section of the Introduction shows, the people had rejected Yahweh as king to serve the Baals, and in particular to pay respect to the calf of Samaria. Therefore they would be denied the joy of Yahweh's festival (9:1; 2:11). They had failed to keep covenant with Yahweh; there was therefore fitness in the punishment that the rain would be withheld from them and the fruits of the field would be denied them (8:7; 9:2, 11, 14, 16); they would be denied even human offspring (9:11-12, 16). The idols they had served would be revealed in all their ineffectiveness and would be destroyed; the calf of Samaria itself would be carried off. Again, some of the people had used the festival occasions to work out their plots and their intrigues (8:4), deceiving the king and enticing the princes and inflaming them with wine so that their senses were dulled (7:3-7); and many had put their trust in Assyria and Egypt for security, not acknowledging that to Yahweh belonged the victory and that he was able to make them triumph over all their enemies. Furthermore, it must be admitted that in such a cultic context as has just been outlined, the reference in 13:13 to the unrealized possibility of Israel's rebirth and renewal attains to richer significance.

5. The Coming Retribution.—For all this manifold unfaithfulness of Ephraim punishment must come. Sometimes Hosea describes it as a sudden calamity like the deadly attack of a lion (5:14; 13:7-8); sometimes he likens it to a slow corruption such as moth and dry rot would suggest (5:12); at other times he speaks of disaster sudden and devastating. One question remains: Did Hosea regard the punishment of which he speaks in chs. 4–13 as not only inevitable but also as final? There are many references to the pleading of the Lord with his people and to his patience with them (7:1, 13; 8:6; 11:4, 7-9; 12:10). Once a return to the wilderness is spoken of, which would be remedial as well as punitive (12:9). In 11:10-11 we read how, when Yahweh utters a call like a lion, his people will rush back in fear and perturbation and be restored to their own homes; 13:13 tells of the possibility of a new beginning that existed for sinful Israel, an opportunity which they failed to use. Greatest of all, 11:8-9 describes Yahweh's yearning for his people; justice demands their punishment and their destruction; but he is God, not man. Here we have an expression of the love of God which goes far beyond the range of covenant love and is willing to give to the uttermost. And yet, in spite of these words of mercy and promise of good, it must be admitted that in chs. 4–13 words of threat and doom predominate. That doom is often declared to be destroying and obliterating. "Compassion is hid from my eyes" (13:14).

6. A Written Law in Hosea's Day?—The question has often been asked whether there was in use in Hosea's day a written torah or law, setting forth the demands of the Lord's service, or more specifically, whether the Ten Commandments had by that time been formulated. The answer to such questions is not easy. The mention in 6:1; 8:1 of the Lord's commandment and of his torah can refer to oral instruction quite as easily as to a written document. On the other hand, the meaning of 8:12 might appear to be that, even if God's law were to be written down more fully and more explicitly than ever it had been before, it would be, and would remain, strange to the people. If this interpretation can be sustained, then presumably some form of written law existed. Some scholars are prepared to go much further, finding in 13:4 a clear reference to the First Commandment, in 13:2 to the Second, and in 4:2 to the Sixth, Seventh, Eighth, and Ninth. The possibility of such reference, almost of quotation, cannot be denied; but neither can it be affirmed. All we can say with assurance is that from the book of Hosea it is obvious that there was in instructional use, in oral or in written form, a body of religious teaching, or torah, which in expression was closely related to part of the Ten Commandments.

B. The Epilogue (14:1-9).—In 14:2-3 the iniquity of Israel is described as it is in the preceding section—the offering of sacrifice, the worship of idols, and the making of foreign alliances. The call is addressed to Israel to acknowledge the folly and futility of all these and to return to the Lord in repentance. Such a call is not unknown in chs. 4–13, but in this final chapter there is an atmosphere of expectation. It seems to be assumed that Israel cannot resist the call, and so there follows a description of the Lord's healing and renewing work among his repentant people. They will become strongly rooted in him and will be gloriously fruitful; under his care they will attain to that abundant life which they had sought, but never found, in their service of the Baals. The decisive word of God to his people is, "It is I who answer and look after you" (14:8). It may be said of ch. 14, therefore, that whereas most of what it has to say can be paralleled in chs. 4–13, yet there is in it an unmistakable atmosphere of hope, and an expectation of Israel's return and renewal. There are no reasons in terms of language, style, or ideas, for denying ch. 14 to the prophet, and its atmosphere of hope is to be remembered when we pass to the study of the much debated chs. 1–3.

C. The Prophet in His Home (1:1–3:5).—It will be wise to examine the contents of chs. 1–3 in several distinct sections:

(a) In 2:2-13 Israel is entreated to return to the Lord from her unfaithful conduct and erring ways. If she does not repent she will suffer unmerciful punishment. Ignorance may have induced her to go in pursuit of her lovers; but if she persists in face of the warnings that have been given her, she will find herself utterly frustrated. She will be denied her corn and wine and oil, her wool and her flax, and all the joy of her festive season will be done away. In this section the parallels with chs. 4–13 are obvious; it might have been incorporated in these chapters.

(b) At once we are in an atmosphere of hope (2:14-23). The parallel is now with ch. 14 rather than with chs. 4–13. The old relationship between the Lord and his people is about to be re-established in the wilderness where it had its beginning (cf. 12:9). All vestiges of Baal worship will be cleansed from the life of Israel and the covenant will be renewed, not only between the Lord and his people, but with all living creatures (cf. 4:3). It is as if the penalties not only of Israel's sinfulness, but of man's fall, were to be done away. Then when Israel has been betrothed to the Lord in faithfulness, he will secure for her all the fruits of the earth, for they are his to give. So Israel will obtain mercy and become once more God's people.

(c) Reference should be made to the Exegesis for a consideration of the detailed problems of interpretation involved in 1:10–2:1. It speaks of the blessing of Israel, their unification under one leader, and their restoration. The fact that it is in prose is no reason why it should be regarded as a later addition to the book, and the thought forms which it employs strongly support its authenticity. It may be taken in close association with 2:14-23. One important feature has, however, still to be explained—why the element of hope is so prominent in ch. 2 when it is far from prominent in chs. 4–13, although it is found clearly in ch. 14.

(d) Hosea is instructed by God to marry a "woman of harlotries" (1:1-9). The whole land is described as guilty of harlotry. Hosea marries Gomer and three children are born of the marriage. The name of the first, Jezreel, proclaims the fall of the house of Jehu; that of the second, Not pitied, indicates that divine punishment is about to fall not only upon the royal house, but upon all the people; that of the third, Not my people, declares that the covenant between the Lord and his people has been broken.

(e) In form 3:1-5 might appear as an *Ich-bericht* in contrast with the *Er-bericht* of ch. 1. But the two narratives are not parallel. Ch. 1 gives an account of Hosea's family without giving any hint of broken marital relationship between him and Gomer, either at that time or thereafter, while ch. 3 describes Hosea's love for a harlot, his redemption of her, and the discipline he laid upon her. In addition, the use of the word "again" in 3:1 seems to demand that ch. 3 be interpreted as a sequel to ch. 1, however it may be related to it. In 3:5 it is said that Israel is restored to the service of the Lord.

II. Hosea's Marriage

It is now necessary to consider the circumstances of Hosea's marriage, his subsequent domestic experiences, and their influence upon his preaching categories. We should note that Hosea became convinced of his call to be a prophet before his marriage (cf. 1:2). Therefore if, for example, 2:2-13 is a sample of his preaching in the early part of his career, it probably indicates that he spoke of Israel's unfaithfulness before any domestic tragedy of his own concentrated his attention upon that way of thought. Various theories have been propounded concerning Hosea's marriage and domestic experiences:

A. Allegorical Interpretation.—It has been maintained that Hosea's marriage should be understood allegorically. This is Albin van Hoonacker's view, for instance.[11] He says that ch. 1 represents the faithfulness of Yahweh's wife and ch. 3 her reconciliation to him. In answer to the criticism that, if the marriage narrative is to be understood allegorically, it is remarkable that the name of Hosea's wife has no significance, van Hoonacker finds refuge in the hypothesis that it may have had a significance for the people of Hosea's own day which is now lost to us. Likewise Hugo Gressmann says:

Hosea's act [in marrying Gomer] does not belong to the category of acts really fulfilled, but to that of literary devices, of which one may say only that the events they relate might have been fulfilled. The oriental listener, with his lively imagination, knows quite well how the prophet wishes to be understood.[12]

He compares the literary device which is here represented by the marriage of Hosea with the narrative in Jer. 13 of the burial of a soiled loincloth in a cleft of rock by the Euphrates

and its subsequent recovery by the prophet, which he interprets similarly. But it is extremely difficult to see what Hosea hoped to achieve by the use of such a literary device. Without it he could declare to Ephraim in forceful words that punishment was coming upon her for all her unfaithfulness; by the use of the figure of marriage with a "woman of harlotries" he could do nothing more.

B. Literal Interpretation.—It has been held that Hosea married a harlot who had, according to some interpreters, already borne illegitimate children and who proved unfaithful to Hosea, in that it is said only of the first child after their marriage that she bore it to him. This theory, with certain variations, has had many supporters,[13] and sometimes it is advocated that ch. 3 refers to events before the marriage and ch. 1 is the record of the marriage and its sequel, so that the unfaithfulness from which Hosea attempted to redeem his wife had not been unfaithfulness to him. A form of this theory has more recently been advocated by T. H. Robinson.[14] He holds that, according to the narrative of ch. 1, as according to that of ch. 3, Gomer had led a shameful life. She was probably a temple prostitute, so that the period of seclusion which was prescribed for her was "in order that the atmosphere of the numinous that attached to her as a temple prostitute should be dispelled." Whether or not Gomer was faithful after her marriage with Hosea he regards as an open question. This interpretation, however, discounts the use of the word "again" in 3:1, dismissing it as a redactional addition; and—although this is not a decisive argument—it thus removes the parallelism of the relationship between Hosea and Gomer with that between Yahweh and Israel. In connection with the latter Robinson asserts that no close connection need be looked for.

C. "Harlot": A Proleptic Use.—Probably the most common theory concerning Hosea's marriage is that which submits that the term "harlot" is used proleptically in 1:2. It is argued that Gomer's unfaithfulness did not manifest itself until some time after the marriage. When it did happen, Hosea recognized it not as a sudden and inexplicable fall from grace, but as an expression of a fundamentally corrupt nature. Not a few who take this view make much of the fact that in 1:2 Gomer is described

[11] *Les douze petits prophètes* (Paris: J. Gabalda, 1908; "Études bibliques").

[12] *Die Älteste Geschichtschreibung und Prophetie Israels* (2nd ed.; Göttingen: Vandenhoeck & Ruprecht, 1921; "Die Schriften des Altentestaments in Auswahl"), pp. 369-70.

[13] Cf. William R. Harper, *A Critical and Exegetical Commentary on Amos and Hosea* (New York: Charles Scribner's Sons, 1910; "International Critical Commentary"), p. 208.

[14] *Die zwölf kleinen Propheten Hosea bis Micha* (Tübingen: J. C. B. Mohr, 1936; "Handbuch zum Alten Testament"), pp. 16-17.

not by the usual word for a harlot (זונה), but by the term "woman of harlotries" (אשת זנונים). So A. B. Ehrlich says that she was "a woman with an inclination to harlotry."[15] Hans Schmidt[16] takes the unusual line that Hosea's second and third children were originally named "Pitied" and "My people," but that after the bitter disappointment which the prophet experienced, he renamed them Not pitied and Not my people. It is sometimes maintained by the advocates of this theory that it was after the birth of the first child that Hosea came to suspect unfaithfulness on his wife's part.

This theory may appear clever, but it cannot be dismissed as R. H. Pfeiffer has done by calling it "pure sleight of hand."[17] If Hosea did marry a woman who was faithful for a season and then left him to seek her lovers, and if ch. 3 is to be interpreted as the redemption of his wife from slavery, then that does form a parallel to the Israel which had been wooed by the Lord in the wilderness, had kept covenant only for a brief period, and then had gone in pursuit of the Baals. If Hosea under the compulsion of love was constrained to redeem his erring wife, how much more must the Lord yearn to restore his erring people to the old covenant relationship!

D. An Apologia for Gomer.—Pfeiffer has put forward an apologia for Gomer. According to him, her character has been slandered. She was a woman of "wifely virtue," and all the trouble has been caused by the identification with Gomer of the woman mentioned in ch. 3. Pfeiffer rejects this identification, but his own interpretation of 3:1-4 is not easily to be maintained. "By an act of kindness to a wretched prostitute, Hosea symbolises God, in his abiding love, endeavoring to redeem his wicked people."[18] It is true that the act of redemption of such a woman might represent to some degree the Lord's redemption of sinful Israel. But what could be represented in this way which could not be represented more fittingly in Hosea's relationship with his wife, a "woman of harlotries"? And how could Hosea, a married man, represent this love relationship with another woman in such a way as to symbolize the Lord's love for Israel?

[15] *Randglossen zur hebräischen Bibel* (Leipzig: J. C. Hinrichs, 1912), V, 163-64.

[16] Cf. "Die Ehe des Hosea," *Zeitschrift für die alttestamentliche Wissenschaft*, XLII (1924), 245-72.

[17] *Introduction to the Old Testament* (New York: Harper & Bros., 1941), p. 568.

[18] *Ibid.*, p. 570; cf. Fück, "Hosea Kapitel 3," *Zeitschrift für die alttestamentliche Wissenschaft*, XXXIX (1921), 283-90; and L. W. Batten, "Hosea's Message and Marriage," *Journal of Biblical Literature*, XLVIII (1929), 257-73.

E. Covenant Love: Kept, Lost, and Renewed.—The following line of interpretation has something in common with the third set forth above, but with important modifications. The main points of contention are clearly in ch. 3. Quite a few scholars regard the word "again" in vs. 1 as an editorial expansion inserted to make ch. 3 a sequel to ch. 1, whereas originally it was a narrative parallel to that of ch. 1, though couched in autobiographical as opposed to biographical terms. But these two passages are by no means parallel. If the first (ch. 1) refers to a marriage, which remained unbroken, with a woman who had a spirit of unfaithfulness in her in precisely the same sense as all Israel had, then it is impossible to see how Hosea recognized God's guiding hand in his conjugal experience; it had no significance at all for his preaching. But if it refers to a marriage which was a happy fellowship until it was ruined by the outbreak of Gomer's harlot spirit, then we can understand how Hosea, reflecting upon his own domestic experience, could recognize in it a type of the Lord's broken fellowship with his bride Israel. Again, we should note that the second narrative (ch. 3) speaks of loving, not of marrying, a harlot, and of redeeming and disciplining her. Now if the reference is simply to the fact that Hosea married a *qedhēshāh*, put her into isolation for a period and then presumably lived with her as husband with wife, that likewise had no significance for his preaching and there seems no reason why it should ever have been recorded; the same would be true if the woman were regarded as a second wife (cf. Deut. 21: 15-17). But if it is to be interpreted in some way as a type of the Lord's experience with Israel it must be remembered that, according to Hosea's teaching, the covenant relationship was established between the Lord and his people in the wilderness; only after that did the unfaithfulness manifest itself and suffer punishment. Hosea once speaks of redemption for Israel (13:14); but the important point is that the redemption is subsequent to the unfaithfulness and the unfaithfulness is subsequent to the marriage espousals. These are reasons therefore why ch. 3 should be regarded not as a parallel narrative to ch. 1, but as a sequel to it; and they are not the only reasons. And if it is asked why in that case ch. 3 is autobiographical while ch. 1 is biographical, it may be replied that Hosea's marriage and the names of his children and the significance of these names were all known to his disciples, whereas ch. 3 describes an intimate experience of which only the fact of the restoration of Gomer may have been known to others.

It must not be forgotten that the word "again" stands in the text of 3:1 as it has been preserved for us. There are no valid reasons for dispensing with that word; according to all the available evidence it forms part of the original text. How it is to be understood is examined in the Exegesis. It should be construed with what follows rather than with what precedes, and it should be understood in the sense of continuance rather than of repetition of an action, that is, the translation of the relevant phrase should be "Go on loving," not "Go again, love." Taken in this way the words are an instruction to Hosea to go on loving his wife Gomer in spite of all her unfaithfulness. As Martin Buber says:

that a particular person should be bound to love another particular person in utter concreteness, is there such a thing as this? The word can only be spoken to one who already loves. He loves, he still loves the faithless one, he cannot suppress this love, but he does not want it, for he feels himself degraded by it. . . . Into this state of soul God's word descends, "Continue loving, thou art allowed to love her, thou must love her; even so do I love Israel." [19]

But there is another point of great importance which is commonly neglected. We have already noted that in chs. 4–13 few words of hope are spoken concerning Israel's future, little expectation is shown that Israel will ever repent and return to the Lord. On the other hand, there is a very great difference in chs. 14 and 2. What can have caused this change of outlook? There is no reason for regarding the hopeful passages in these chapters as later additions (see Exeg.). Something must have happened to bring about the change. The only explanation which is available is that the prophet's hope for Israel was nurtured in his experience of his attitude to his own erring wife. He found himself compelled by the power of the love within him to go on loving her in spite of the fact that by her conduct she had forfeited any title to that love, and he was restless and unsatisfied until he had brought her back. So, he had the insight to see, must the Lord love Israel, "though they turn to other gods and love cakes of raisins" (3:1).

In terms of all these considerations, therefore, the interpretation of Hosea's marriage and subsequent domestic experiences which seems to be indicated by the evidence is as follows: Hosea believed that it was God's will for him that he should marry Gomer, and 1:2 makes it clear that when Gomer is described as a "woman of harlotries," the reference is to

spiritual unfaithfulness, the harlot spirit within her. Secondly, it must be recognized that the names of Hosea's second and third children should not be understood as giving evidence of conjugal unfaithfulness on Gomer's part; the names have reference to Israel as a whole. In other words, there is no sign in ch. 1 that Gomer is anything other than a faithful wife. Thereafter the transition to the beginning of ch. 3 is admittedly sudden. If Hosea is now instructed by God to redeem his wife, we are left to infer that a separation must have taken place. It is a notable fact that there is no explicit statement that Gomer did forsake her husband; but it is probable that in 2:2a, 4-5a we have part of the missing narrative concerning Hosea's dismissal of his wife (see Exeg., ad loc.).

The next stage in Hosea's experience seems clear. He was tormented by his separation from Gomer, he felt maimed and incomplete, and he realized that however little Gomer might deserve his love (but cf. 4:14), yet she retained it to an undiminished degree, and he was constrained even against his own judgment to attempt to restore the old marriage relationship. The mystery of the compulsive power of his own love for Gomer made Hosea reflect upon the love of God for erring Israel. It was thereon that he founded his message of hope for his people; and that explains why the note of hope is not found uniformly in his utterances. It was possibly late in appearing; it emerged as the result of his own spiritual travail. But if Gomer did not deserve such merciful treatment as Hosea felt constrained to give her, no more did Israel merit the mercy and love of God. Her redemption from sin and shame was an act of God's grace and of his love that would not let her go (cf. 11:8). According to this view, it was not Hosea's domestic experiences which were the prevenient cause, under God, of his call to be a prophet. He must have exercised his prophetic office for several years before reflection upon his own intimate experiences at home began to influence his message. H. Wheeler Robinson is undoubtedly right when he says:

There is certainly a depth of personal emotion in this book [of Hosea] which can be paralleled nowhere else save in the greater prophet so like Hosea—Jeremiah—who knew the sorrows of a lonely and threatened life, as Hosea did those of an unhappy marriage. [20]

The judgment upon Israel's unfaithfulness was uncanceled; the judgment upon her political instability was not in the least recalled; what had been spoken had been spoken. But a new

[19] The Prophetic Faith (New York: The Macmillan Co., 1949), p. 113.

[20] Op. cit., p. 18.

and a deeper note was now sounded which had its origin, not in man's deserts, but in God's loving nature and redemptive purpose (cf. Isa. 43:25). When in spite of all man's need for condemnation and destruction, Hosea told of the wonderful love of God that would not let man go, he attained to the most distinctive notes in his teaching and proclaimed a truth which was to receive its full expression in the life and teaching of Jesus Christ. Hubert Cunliffe-Jones is right when he says:

We may read the record of the prophet Hosea and hear from him directly a true word of the love of God. But we live in the light of the Cross of Christ, and it is unthinkable that we shall read the message of Hosea without it speaking to us Christians of the meaning of the Cross of Christ in which the meaning of the love of God has been fully acted out. The message of Hosea, taken seriously in its historical context, has gained a new dimension of depth because of the Cross of Christ.[21]

III. Date of the Prophet's Activity

The fact that Hosea proclaimed the fall of the house of Jehu warrants the conclusion that he began his prophetic activity before the death of Jeroboam II (746 B.C.; cf. 1:1b). Again, such verses as 5:1; 7:3-7; 9:15; 13:10-11 give us adequate reason for concluding that Hosea continued into the troubled times after the death of Jeroboam, when there were great dynastic instability and endless political intrigue at home as well as attempts at alliance with foreign powers. It was only after 745 B.C. that Assyria rose again to power and struck fear into the hearts of the little peoples of the west. It is probable that in 5:8-10, 13 we have references to the confused situation in Palestine during the Syro-Ephraimitic War of 735-734, but there is no evidence that Hosea continued after that date; 1:1a is a later addition to the book (see Exeg., ad loc.).

IV. Structure and Literary Form

Chs. 4–13 form the main section of the book and contain the major portion of the prophet's teaching. Possibly these chapters, with or without ch. 14, circulated for a time separately from chs. 1–3. The section 1:2-9 must belong to the period subsequent to the birth of Hosea's third child, and may therefore be later in date than much of chs. 4–13. On the other hand, 2:2-13 is congruous with the teaching found in the main section. The messages of hope for the future of Israel found in 1:10–2:1; 2:14-23 must be referred to a later phase of the prophet's activity, in particular to the period following upon the restoration of Hosea's wife

to her home. Harper regards these passages which speak hopefully of Israel as later additions to the book, on the ground that they "are entirely inconsistent with Hosea's point of view, and directly contradict the representations which are fundamental in his preaching."[22] But if such a charge of inconsistency had been made against Hosea personally, he would have replied that his own experience with regard to Gomer and the reflections which it had provoked within him enabled him to learn more of the wonder of God's love for man and of the triumph of mercy and love over judgment.

The question of the so-called Judaistic revision of the book must now be discussed. The extreme form of this theory asserts that all the references to Judah are due to later editing, because Hosea addressed the people of the Northern Kingdom. The only way to answer such a theory is to examine the relevant passages. The Exegesis must be consulted for a detailed statement in each particular case; here the attempt will be made to indicate the conclusion which seems to be warranted by that detailed study. We should note at the beginning that only a few of the references to Judah are commendatory or favorable (1:7, 11; 3:5; 4:15; 11:12); two may be regarded as neutral (1:1; 10:11); the remainder, which constitute the majority, are unfavorable and some are severely critical. Therefore if these passages were added later by an editor or editors, they were not intended as a whole to redound to the greater glory of Judah.

The second point to note is that the alleged additions are not all of the same type. Sometimes the name Judah has been substituted for Israel or Ephraim (12:2); sometimes it is for one reason or another an obvious addition in the context in which it stands (4:15; 10:11); sometimes it occurs in an added clause (5:5; cf. the mention of the house of David in 3:5). Again, 6:11 and 8:14 may be considered together; the references to Judah there seem to be aimed at counteracting any attitude of complacency in that kingdom. But in 6:11 the second half of the verse should be taken closely with 7:1. If that is done, 6:11a becomes rhythmically superfluous and, since its use of the figure of the harvest does not fit its context, it may be regarded as an addition. There is much dispute about the authenticity of 8:14, since it is so clearly written in the style of Amos; but if it is difficult to understand how Hosea could have written this verse in the style of his near contemporary, it is no less difficult to understand why an editorial addition should have been written in that style. But that apart, the

---

[21] *The Authority of the Biblical Revelation* (London: James Clarke & Co., 1945), pp. 40-41.

[22] *Amos and Hosea*, pp. clix-clxi.

clause which contains the mention of Judah seems rhythmically superfluous, and for that reason additional, even within the verse which itself may be additional. The decision with regard to 1:7 and 1:1 is not difficult. The former was added after the deliverance of Jerusalem in 701 B.C., and the editorial title in 1:1a was prefixed to chs. 1-3 (or to the whole book) in terms of 1:7. The case of 11:12 is complicated by the fact that the text of the second half of the verse is very uncertain. If it originally contained words which were unfavorable to Judah it may be authentic. But as it stands, since it commends Judah, it is either a later addition or a later editorial revision of an originally unfavorable reference. There is a cluster of references to Judah in ch. 5, viz., vss. 10, 12, 13, 14. Since vss. 8, 9 describe the effects of a foreign invasion, it is quite possible that the princes of Judah took advantage of the resulting condition of insecurity and social disturbance to do some land grabbing on their own account with the result that the wrath of the prophet is directed at Judah no less than at Israel. In this way the references to Judah may be regarded as incorporated within verses which are genuine. In vss. 13-14 the position is different. The middle part of vs. 13 mentions overtures to Assyria on the part of Ephraim only; that supports the view that the name Judah has been substituted for an original Israel in both vs. 13 and vs. 14. But on the other hand it may be contended that the middle portion of vs. 13 should read:

> Then Ephraim went to Assyria,
> and Judah sent to the great king.

If that emendation were to be sustained, the references to Judah in vs. 13 and vs. 14 would be in order. In the case of these two verses, therefore, the authenticity of the Judah references must be regarded as an open question. Finally, there seems to be no reason at all for the deletion of the references to Judah in 1:11; 6:4. There is no difficulty in believing that Hosea, even if his words were commonly directed to Ephraim, sometimes had the sister kingdom of Judah in mind; at a later date Ezekiel, among the exiled Jews in Babylon, was to envisage the restoration of the whole, reunited people.

The sum of the matter is that although there is ample evidence in the book of Hosea of later Judaistic revision, yet there are references to Judah which must be regarded as original and genuine. Apart from this Judaistic revision, other evidences of editorial activity have been discovered by at least one scholar. R. E. Wolfe

traces the editorial work of those whom he designates as the early scribes, the later scribes, the anti-idol polemist, the anti-high-place editor, the late exilic editor (who introduced the sections expressive of hope and redemption) and the eschatologist.[23] Such a treatment of the book reduces the genuine work of Hosea to very small dimensions. It is based upon ill-founded assumptions of what Hosea could or could not have written. Such a theory of editing eliminates as editorial expansions those passages in the book which would serve as a refutation of the theory.

As for other passages which have sometimes been regarded as later additions, the argument for the authenticity of 1:10-2:1 and for 2:14-23 is set forth in the Exegesis. The difficulty of deciding concerning the Amos-styled 8:14 has already been mentioned. The final phrase of 14:3 may be additional; 12:4-6, 12 is probably from an external source, but when these verses were incorporated in the book of Hosea it seems impossible to determine. Also, 3:5, the concluding verse of chs. 1-3, and 14:9, the concluding verse of the whole book, are almost certainly editorial additions; the latter gives a commendatory ending to the book and is in the style of Hebrew gnomic literature. One other point may be mentioned: the use in the book of the term Beth-aven in place of Bethel (cf. 4:15; 5:8; 10:5; cf. the use in 10:8 of Aven alone) has seemed to some scholars to be due to the work of a Deuteronomic editor; but that must remain a very disputable proposition in view of Hosea's attitude to the worship of idols and of the fact that Amos also designates Bethel in this way (Amos 5:5).

V. Text and the Versions

The text of the book is in a very bad condition and, as the Exegesis shows, there are many places where the restoration of the text cannot be accomplished with the aid of the versions and resort has to be made to conjectural emendation. The Septuagint and Syriac versions seem to be derived from a Hebrew text which was substantially similar to the Masoretic Text. It is from the Septuagint that our greatest help comes in restoring the Hebrew. It has occasionally additional phrases (2:14; 8:13; 13:13), but the most common reason for the variation in reading between the Septuagint and the Masoretic Text is the difference of vocalization of the same Consonantal Text. In particular, we must note the difference in the occurrence of vocalic *wāw* and *yôdh*, a difference so notable as to warrant the conclusion that the manu-

[23] "The Editing of the Book of the Twelve," *Zeitschrift für die alttestamentliche Wissenschaft,* LIII (1935), 90-129.

scripts which the Septuagint translators used did not contain such *matres lectionis*. Take these examples, in which the first word or phrase gives the Masoretic Text and the second the Hebrew which must have been before the translators, if the *matres lectionis* were written: ‏5:4, כתך :כתכי‎; 6:9, עבר :עברו‎; 6:7, עבדו :עבר‎; ‏8:6, כשבבים :כי שבבים‎; 10:2, חלק :חלקו‎; 10:5, ‏11:4, מרומי :מרים‎; 10:10, באותי :באתי‎; שכן :שכני‎; 12:2, יובל :יובילו‎; 13:9, שחתך :שחתיך‎; 13:15, ‏וייבש :וייבוש or יובוש :וייבש‎; etc.

Again, there are differences of reading which are due to simple transposition of certain letters: 5:11, ‏עשוק :עושק‎; 5:11, ‏רוצץ רצוץ :ואני‎; 6:3, ‏נשא אשנא :נשא אישנא‎; 1:6, ‏יורה :ירוה‎; ואין ‏13:10, 14, רכבך :רבכב‎; איה :אהי.

There are examples of different word division: 5:2, ‏ושחטה שטים :ושחת השטים‎; 6:3, ‏משפטיך‎; 6:5, ‏כשחרנו כן נמצאו :כשחר נכון מוצאו‎; 11:2, ‏מפני הם :מפניהם‎; ‏משפטי כאור :אור.

And finally, there are cases of confusion of certain pairs of letters: ‏ר‎ and ‏ד‎: 4:18, ‏סד :סר‎; 2:14, ‏ידעם :ירעם‎; 9:2, ‏יתגודדו :יתגוררו‎; 7:14, ‏לעד :ליער‎; (cf. 12:2, ‏שדים‎: orig. prob. ‏שורים‎); 13:5, ‏ידעתיך :רעיתיך‎. ‏א‎ and ‏ד‎: 12:2, ‏שד :שוא‎. ‏ו‎ and ‏ד‎: 10:12, ‏דעת :ועת‎. ‏כ‎ and ‏ד‎: 5:8, ‏אחריך :אחריד‎. ‏פ‎ and ‏ת‎: 4:10, ‏יפרצו :יתרצו‎. ‏שׁ‎ (*shîn*) ‏שׂ‎ (*sîn*): 12:12, ‏שרים :שרים‎; 8:10, ‏משא :משה‎. ‏צ‎ and ‏שׁ‎: 5:11, ‏צו :שרים‎. ‏ע‎ and ‏שׁ‎: 8:1, ‏שופר :עפר.

VI. *Outline of Contents*

VII. Selected Bibliography

BROWN, S. L. *The Book of Hosea* ("Westminster Commentary") . London: Methuen & Co., 1932.

HARPER, WILLIAM R. *A Critical and Exegetical Commentary on Amos and Hosea* ("International Critical Commentary") . New York: Charles Scribner's Sons, 1910.

LINDBLOM, JOHANNES. *Hosea literarisch untersucht* ("Acta Academiae Åboensis"). Åbo: Åbo Akademi, 1928.

NYBERG, H. S. *Studien zum Hoseabuche*. Uppsala: Almqvist & Wiksells, 1935.

ROBINSON, H. WHEELER. *Two Hebrew Prophets*. London: Lutterworth Press, 1948.

ROBINSON, T. H. *Die zwölf kleinen Propheten Hosea bis Micha* ("Handbuch zum Alten Testament"). Tübingen: J. C. B. Mohr, 1936.

SELLIN, ERNST. *Das Zwölfprophetenbuch* ("Kommentar zum Alten Testament"). 2nd ed. Leipzig: A. Deichert, 1929.

SMITH, GEORGE ADAM. *The Book of the Twelve Prophets*. Rev. ed. New York: Harper & Bros., 1928. Vol. I.

SNAITH, NORMAN H. *Mercy and Sacrifice*. London: Student Christian Movement Press, 1953.

WEISER, ARTUR. *Das Buch der zwölf kleinen Propheten* ("Das Alte Testament Deutsch"). Göttingen: Vandenhoeck & Ruprecht, 1949. Vol. I.

HOSEA

TEXT, EXEGESIS, AND EXPOSITION

1 The word of the LORD that came unto Hosea, the son of Beeri, in the days of

1 The word of the LORD that came to Hose'a the son of Be-e'ri, in the days of

I. HOSEA'S DOMESTIC EXPERIENCES AND THEIR EFFECT (1:1–3:5)
A. HOSEA'S WIFE AND CHILDREN (1:1-9)
1. SUPERSCRIPTION (1:1)

1:1. The word of the LORD: It is asserted at the beginning that what Hosea had to say to his contemporaries was not a matter of surmise, or an expression of his own opinion, or simply the fruit of his own reflection upon the human situation as he saw it. It was a word from God. That was what gave authority to the prophet's preaching and urgency to his demands. Here there is presented to us, on the one hand, the God who reveals

1:1. *The Word of the Lord.*—This is the preacher's theme and authority. His message is grounded in objective reality. The gospel is not man's word to God, but God's word to man. "But I certify you brethren," wrote Paul, "that the gospel which was preached of me is not after man. For I neither received it of man, neither was I taught it, but by the revelation of Jesus Christ." (Gal. 1:11-12.) This is what differentiates the Christian preacher from all the other "preachers" of our day: he is not just voicing his opinions about this, that, or the other but he has a message given him to deliver.

He shapes, interprets, presents the message as best suits his understanding, insight, and ability. But the word he speaks is not his word. It is **the word of the LORD.**

It is true that the preacher may, and at times does, mistake ecclesiastical bigotry, prejudice, pride, or self-interest for **the word of the LORD;** but this no more permanently annuls or discredits the objective nature of his message than does some false hypothesis in science invalidate the objective nature of scientific truth. We never doubt the objective nature of truth in our dealings with the physical world. Scientific

Uzziah, Jotham, Ahaz, *and* Hezekiah, kings of Judah, and in the days of Jeroboam the son of Joash, king of Israel.	Uzzi'ah, Jotham, Ahaz, and Hezeki'ah, kings of Judah, and in the days of Jerobo'am the son of Jo'ash, king of Israel.

himself and enters into communication with his chosen servants, and who is thus the author of genuine prophetic activity; and, on the other hand, the human recipient, who is aware that a word from God demands action, and from that action there is no escape for the man who would have a quiet mind and an untroubled conscience (cf. Jer. 20:9). The words of H. Wheeler Robinson are relevant: "It is in the prophetic consciousness and its continuance in personal religion that there is found the ultimate sanctuary . . . in which the ancient Scriptures are still transformed into His living oracles" (*Inspiration and Revelation in the Old Testament* [Oxford: Clarendon Press, 1946], p. 198).

The name **Hosea** is not a usual form of personal name in Hebrew, being a Hiphil infinitive absolute, with the meaning "to save" or "to deliver." It was the name of Joshua before Moses renamed him (Num. 13:16), and it was also the name of the last ruler of the Northern Kingdom (II Kings 15:30). Of Hosea's father **Beeri** ["My Well"] nothing is known; there is no ground for identifying him with Beerah, the Reubenite prince mentioned in I Chr. 5:6. It is notable that Hosea's birthplace is not specified.

The period of Hosea's prophetic activity is doubly defined. **In the days of Jeroboam the son of Joash, king of Israel** means within the period 786-746 B.C. On the other hand, the expression **in the days of Uzziah, Jotham, Ahaz, and Hezekiah, kings of Judah,** does not indicate a period coterminous with the other, for Uzziah died *ca.* 740 B.C., and Hezekiah began his reign *ca.* 715 (cf. W. F. Albright, "The Chronology of the Divided Monarchy of Israel," *Bulletin of the American Schools of Oriental Research,* No. 100 [Dec., 1945], pp. 21-22, who gives these dates as 742 and 715; cf. also Edwin R. Thiele, "The Chronology of the Kings of Judah and Israel," *Journal of Near Eastern Studies,* III [1944], 176-77, who gives them as 740 and 716). It is probable that the original text contained the reference to the reign of Jeroboam only, and had relevance to a portion of the present book which for a time circulated separately from the rest—some scholars would specify chs. 1–3. The reference to the **kings of Judah** is probably due to a later Judaistic revision of the book (cf. Intro.), being added by an editor who considered 1:7 to refer to the deliverance of Jerusalem in the time of Sennacherib's invasion in 701 B.C. There is evidence in the book that Hosea continued his prophetic activity after the death of Jeroboam, but none that he continued later than the Syro-Ephraimitic War of 735-734 B.C.

law is but a description of what in nature is "given." The Christian maintains that spiritual truth is just as objective. It is no mere feeling "fond and fugitive," no human invention or discovery. The gospel is God's word, God's revelation, grounded in objective reality.

This "Word was made flesh, and dwelt among us" (John 1:14). In Christ the Christian gospel finds its complete objectification; for as Emerson said, the name of Christ was not written but plowed into history.

Martin Luther refused to equate the Bible with the word of God. Had you asked him how then one distinguishes the word of God in the Bible from the word of man, he would have replied, "By the spirit of Christ. Whatever in the Bible is not in harmony with the spirit of Christ is not the word of God." This would be a very good rule for the preacher to follow.

1. God Speaks Through Individuals.—It is ultimately to the individual that God speaks. "Adam, . . . Where art thou?" (Gen. 3:9.) Even when he speaks to the group, as he does, he does so through the individual. Even when he speaks in nature and in events, as he does, he speaks through the individual. Always through some man God speaks to men. Abraham, Moses, Joshua, David, Samuel, Solomon, and many others were each his mouthpiece. It is not so easy perhaps to retain that emphasis in the modern world. The forces at work are so vast that one might almost think Tennyson right when he said: "The individual withers, and the world is more and more." [1] Mighty movements are sweeping the nations. At first sight they make the individual seem like a pygmy—they dwarf him. Yet at the heart of

[1] "Locksley Hall."

2 The beginning of the word of the Lord by Hosea. And the Lord said to Hosea, Go, take unto thee a wife of whoredoms and children of whoredoms: for the land hath committed great whoredom, *departing* from the Lord.

2 When the Lord first spoke through Hose'a, the Lord said to Hose'a, "Go, take to yourself a wife of harlotry and have children of harlotry, for the land commits great

---

2. Hosea's Marriage (1:2-9)

a) Gomer, a Woman of Harlotries (1:2-3)

2. The beginning of the word of the Lord: This rendering construes the Hebrew word דבר as a noun; so the LXX ἀρχὴ λόγου Κυρίου. The M.T., which points דבר as a verbal form (infinitive construct Piel), means, lit., "the beginning of the Lord's speaking." There is no essential difference between the two renderings. The preposition before the prophet's name can bear two meanings: (a) "To Hosea." In view of Num. 12:6, 8; Hab. 2:1 this must be regarded as possible; the Targ. supports it. (b) **By Hosea** or **through Hosea.** In this case Hosea is the prophetic agent through whom God's word is mediated to his people. The second meaning is preferable, but since a prophet had to receive a word before he could proclaim it to others, the difference between the two renderings is merely one of emphasis.

The instruction which Hosea believed he had been given by God was to marry a harlot and to have children of harlotry. Various lines of interpretation have been followed: (a) Hosea, in unquestioning obedience to what he believed to be God's command, married a known harlot and had children by her. (b) A distinction is made between the ordinary Hebrew word for harlot (זונה) and the term which is used here (אשת זנונים, i.e., "woman of harlotries," **wife of whoredoms**), and on that ground it is maintained that the woman whom Hosea married was faithful to him for a period but thereafter the harlot spirit within her expressed itself. (c) The term harlot should be understood of spiritual unfaithfulness, and an allegorical interpretation of the marriage adopted.

The term **harlotry** is often used in the O.T., not of marital unfaithfulness, but of spiritual unfaithfulness. The basic idea was that the god was the owner of the land and fertilized the mother earth. But in Israel the concept of marital union was used of Yahweh and his people. This was a development of the covenant idea which enshrined the truth that the relationship between Yahweh and his people was one of intimate

---

every demonic movement which exalts race or state or class, and regards the individual as relatively inconsequential, is an individual. Thus totalitarianism denies in fact what it asserts in theory. What would Nazism have been without Hitler, Fascism without Mussolini, Communism without Stalin? It is only as ideas or ideals move out of the realm of abstraction and become operative in individuals that they have meaning for life. World-shaking events, far from dwarfing the individual, only re-emphasize his importance. It is still to some Hosea, whether prophet or pagan, that the word comes, whether of God or devil.

2b. God's Voice in Tragedy.—What a strange word! Needless to say, this passage has provoked much discussion. Is it parable or fact? Perchance the best scholarship would agree that Hosea did not marry a harlot but a good woman who later became one. Hosea married a harlot

in the sense in which a woman whose husband later commits murder might say she married a murderer. The important fact here, however, is that Hosea heard God's word through a hard and tragic experience. It came to him in the form of personal grief, disappointment, and sorrow.

We should be grateful that we can hear the word of the Lord in the tragic, for there is something tragic about man's lot. There is a dark skein woven through the texture of his life. We spend wantonly of our blood and treasure to rid the world of dictatorship, and presto, we are confronted with another dictator of equal if not worse designs. That is tragic. "The whole creation groaneth and travaileth in pain together until now" (Rom. 8:22). But if the creation, then the created—men like Hosea. Had Hosea been a blackguard, we should have said, "Well, he got what was com-

3 So he went and took Gomer the daughter of Diblaim; which conceived, and bare him a son.

4 And the LORD said unto him, Call his name Jezreel; for yet a little *while,* and I will avenge the blood of Jezreel upon the house of Jehu, and will cause to cease the kingdom of the house of Israel.

harlotry by forsaking the LORD." **3** So he went and took Gomer the daughter of Dibla'im, and she conceived and bore him a son.

4 And the LORD said to him, "Call his name Jezreel; for yet a little while, and I will punish the house of Jehu for the blood of Jezreel, and I will put an end to the

---

fellowship and love. Thus when Israel forsook Yahweh to serve Baal, she was charged by the prophets with breaking the covenant and committing adultery or harlotry. In this way the prophets took a common concept from the fertility cults and, in consequence, from popular ways of thought, and filled it with new content, giving it a purely spiritual meaning.

3. The attempt to find significance in the name of Hosea's wife, **Gomer,** daughter of Diblaim, has not been successful. Gomer could mean "completion"; Jerome considers the name to mean *consummata, perfecta;* and the medieval Jewish commentator Ibn Ezra, who follows the allegorical line of interpretation, defines the name Gomer as signifying "complete in harlotry." On the other hand, Wilhelm Nowack makes a good point when he says that if the name Gomer had had significance, Hosea himself would have declared it (*Die kleinen Propheten* [3rd ed.; Göttingen: Vandenhoeck & Ruprecht, 1922; "Handkommentar zum Alten Testament"], *ad loc.*). **Diblaim,** which may be a plural or a dual form, has sometimes been taken to mean "figcakes" (cf. 3:1; I Sam. 25:18; *et al.*). It has been suggested that the name "daughter of a couple of figcakes" meant one who could be got cheaply, a common harlot; that we must regard as very doubtful. Otherwise "daughter of figcakes" might mean simply "worshiper of Baal." On the other hand, it is just possible that the name may be a place name (cf. Num. 33:46-47; Jer. 48:22).

b) THE FIRST CHILD, JEZREEL (1:4-5)

4-5. Three children were born to Hosea in the course of five or six years (cf. vs. 8; a child was not weaned until he was between two and three years old). The fact that only the first-born is said specifically to have been born to Hosea has induced certain commentators to hold that the other two were conceived out of wedlock; but there is no warrant for such a view when we consider the extreme brevity of the narrative in ch. 1. The name of the first child is **Jezreel** (lit., "Yahweh sows"). The view of Rashi that the name refers to the exile of Israel and to their being sown or scattered among the Gentiles is farfetched. There may be a play upon the words **Jezreel** and **Israel,** but the message which the prophet intended to convey by the use of the name is quite clear. It was at Jezreel that the house of Jehu had been established upon the throne of Israel

---

ing to him." Yet this is just what he did not get. He deserved good, but evil befell him. While it is true that sin invariably brings suffering, it is not true that all suffering is the result of sin. Hosea's was not.

Some try to explain evil by explaining it away, and some by attributing it all to God and saying he willed it. "Is it because I have sinned that I am suffering like this?" a good man, dying of cancer, once asked his minister, with a voice of infinite pathos. How many dark pages does the book of life contain! It will not do to say that God deliberately planned and wrote these pages; for while that procedure

might help us to explain the fact of suffering, it would make God a problem. Better have suffering a mystery than besmirch the character of God. Though it may be hard to explain the suffering of the world with a good God, would it not, as B. H. Streeter suggested, be harder to account for the goodness of the world with an evil God or no God at all?

What can we say to someone like Hosea, to whom life brings unmerited and crushing misfortune? We may say that there is no satisfactory explanation for such happenings. "My God, my God, why . . . ?" (Matt. 27:46.) No answer was given. Harry Emerson Fosdick once ob-

5 And it shall come to pass at that day, that I will break the bow of Israel in the valley of Jezreel.

6 ¶ And she conceived again, and bare a daughter. And *God* said unto him, Call

kingdom of the house of Israel. 5 And on that day, I will break the bow of Israel in the valley of Jezreel."

6 She conceived again and bore a daugh-

---

by bloodshed (II Kings 10:11). Elisha had apparently commended the deed (II Kings 9:7) as a fit punishment of the house of Ahab for the blood shed by Jezebel. But Hosea condemns the sanguinary Jehu and declares that his house—and with it the kingdom of Israel—will be destroyed at Jezreel. The name Jezreel, as borne by Hosea's child, was at once a reminder of the bloodshed for which punishment was about to come and a prophecy of the fact that it was to be at Jezreel that the punishment would fall. (For a difficult view of the significance of the name, cf. Herbert G. May, "An Interpretation of the Names of Hosea's Children," *Journal of Biblical Literature,* LV [1936], 285-91.) This prophecy was not literally fulfilled. It is true that Jeroboam's son Zechariah was murdered in the Plain of Jezreel (II Kings 15:10), but **the bow of Israel,** i.e., Israel's strength, was not broken then; the Northern Kingdom lasted for twenty years more. It has been noted as an interesting fact that though Hosea himself survived the death of Zechariah, and saw that his prophecy concerning the house of Jehu was not fulfilled, yet neither he, nor his disciple-successors to whom we owe the preservation of the record, revised it to bring it more fully into consonance with the actual course of history. In other words, they were not troubled by the problem of unfulfilled prediction. They doubtless argued that although events did not turn out precisely as the prophet had predicted, yet the substance of his message remained; punishment was in store for the rebellious kingdom and in due time it would come. It was only the occasion of that punishment which Hosea had failed to distinguish.

Jezreel itself was strongly placed at the western end of Mount Gilboa, overlooking the **valley of Jezreel,** which separated Galilee and Samaria, and was a notable battle-ground. Megiddo, commanding the famous pass over the Carmel Ridge, was at the other end of the valley; the name "Armageddon" is derived from the Hebrew words *har meghiddô,* i.e., hill of Megiddo.

c) THE SECOND CHILD, NOT PITIED (1:6-7)

6. The name of Hosea's second child, **Not pitied,** seems to go further in its implications for Israel than the first. The first speaks of judgment to come; this affirms that

---

served that Jesus did not say, "I have explained the world," but, "I have overcome the world" (John 16:33). It is one thing to hear the word of the Lord in affliction, and another to say that God willed such affliction. "It is not the will of your Father . . . that one of these little ones should perish" (Matt. 18:14).

> Yet, in the maddening maze of things,
> And tossed by storm and flood,
> To one fixed trust my spirit clings;
> I know that God is good! [2]

To those who like Hosea meet what seem unmerited misfortunes, we can say, moreover, "Try to do what Hosea did." He made his tragedy a source of spiritual illumination. He did not say, "Why did God have to do this to me?" Rather he said, "This is what we are all

[2] John Greenleaf Whittier, "The Eternal Goodness," st. xi.

the time doing to God. Just as my wife has been unfaithful to me, so has Israel been to God." His domestic tragedy opened a door to a new spiritual truth. Hosea made the poignancy of his own grief a doorway to the discovery of religion's deepest truth—God's unmerited mercy and forgiving love. The very experience of tragedy that makes some people lose God led Hosea to find him more fully, to discover the deepest truth about his nature. This is how his grief became his gospel.

Remember that the word of the Lord came to Jesus on the Cross. The message and meaning of that Cross is that in the suffering of the Man of Nazareth God himself suffered. The Cross is not a revelation of what God inflicts on man, but of what God took upon himself. The Cross reveals not a cruel God who maliciously sends evil upon us, but a loving God who in Christ suffers for us and with us. Hosea, therefore, in

her name Lo-ruhamah: for I will no more have mercy upon the house of Israel; but I will utterly take them away.

7 But I will have mercy upon the house of Judah, and will save them by the LORD

---

ter. And the LORD said to him, "Call her name Not pitied, for I will no more have pity on the house of Israel, to forgive them at all. **7** But I will have pity on the house of Judah, and I will deliver them by the

---

God's pity is now exhausted and that nothing can turn away that judgment. We are reminded of Amos 8:2, where, after speaking of the neglected disciplinary judgments of God, Amos adds this word from Yahweh: "I will forgive them no more."

But I will utterly take them away: The fact that the word rendered here as **them** is a dative in the original Hebrew makes the KJV translation open to question, but in view of an apparent similarity of usage in 10:1, it may be possible. The same question must be raised against the translation in the LXX (ἀντιτασσόμενος ἀντιτάξομαι, i.e., "I will surely become their enemy"), which incidentally must have read אשׂא אשׂא for the M.T. אשׂא אשׂא. On the whole, the rendering given in the RSV is to be upheld: lit., "that I should at all forgive them." The verb in the Hebrew means "lift up," and that can signify (a) carry, carry away, remove; (b) carry, bear, endure; (c) lift up the face of a suppliant, i.e., forgive his fault and grant his request.

7. That this verse is out of place is clear for two reasons: (a) the promise of mercy which it conveys is foreign to a passage which tells of judgment to come and says specifically that the Lord will have no mercy; (b) vss. 2-9 deal with the Northern Kingdom of Israel, so that this mention of **Judah** is against the context, as is the method by which the merciful deliverance of Judah is to be accomplished. Various suggestions have been made for reading the verse in a different context, e.g., Albin van Hoonacker (*Les douze petits prophètes* [Paris: J. Gabalda, 1908; "Études bibliques"], pp. 30-31)

---

seeing his suffering as a symbol of God's redemptive grace, anticipated by many centuries the word of God in Christ.

6b-7a. Judgment and Mercy.—These antithetical statements suggest the judgment and mercy of God. Judgment springs from justice, mercy from love. It is not always easy to keep these two attributes in balance. Perhaps it is fair to say that speaking generally the O.T. emphasizes the judgment of God, who for the most part is conceived of as king, ruler, judge, while the N.T. emphasizes his love and thinks of him more as a father. This does not mean that the O.T. is unmindful of God's mercy or the N.T. of his judgment. Our fathers were more aware of the judgment than of the mercy. Jonathan Edwards' view of God has been called "Sultanic":

The God that holds you over the pit of hell, much as one holds a spider or some loathsome insect over the fire, abhors you . . . ; his wrath towards you burns like fire; . . . you are ten thousand times so abominable in his eyes, as the most hateful and venomous serpent is in ours.[3]

If Hosea's God was capable of being a lion, ours too often tends to be a mild-mannered lamb. But it is unrealistic to close our eyes to the sterner aspects of Providence. To think of

God as an indulgent grandfather who, never mind what we do, pats us on the back and lets us off with no suffering to himself, to our fellows, or to us, is unrealistic. God sometimes says, "I will no more have mercy. You have made your bed, now you must lie on it." "They have sown the wind, and they shall reap the whirlwind" (8:7). "If in our eagerness to make God amiable we forget that he is a God of Justice, we surrender a cornerstone of our faith."[4]

God's judgment, however, differs from man's in this—that its purpose is never vindictive but always redemptive. It has nothing to do with any feeling of revenge, or any desire "to get even." There is a severity that springs from tyranny and aims at our destruction. There is also a severity that springs from holy love and aims at our redemption. Such is the severity of God. "See now that I, even I, am he, . . . I kill, and I make alive; I wound, and I heal" (Deut. 32:39). Like physical pain, which is nature's warning to make us seek a physician, so the suffering that is due to our sin is God's way of calling us back to the Shepherd and Bishop of our souls.

In the cross of Christ both judgment and mercy stand clearly revealed. The Cross is a revelation of God's love; to reject it is to incur

---

[3] Quoted by Willard L. Sperry, *Religion in America* (New York: The Macmillan Co., 1946), p. 144.

[4] Georgia Harkness, *The Faith by Which the Church Lives* (New York: Abingdon Press, 1940), p. 150.

their God, and will not save them by bow, nor by sword, nor by battle, by horses, nor by horsemen.

8 ¶ Now when she had weaned Lo-ruhamah, she conceived, and bare a son.

9 Then said *God,* Call his name Loammi: for ye *are* not my people, and I will not be your *God.*

LORD their God; I will not deliver them by bow, nor by sword, nor by war, nor by horses, nor by horsemen."

8 When she had weaned Not pitied, she conceived and bore a son. 9 And the LORD said, "Call his name Not my people, for you are not my people and I am not your God."[a]

[a] Gk: Heb *I will not be yours*

proposes to take it at the end of ch. 2, while S. L. Brown (*The Book of Hosea* [London: Methuen & Co., 1932; "Westminster Commentary"], pp. 8-9), who advocates the view that ch. 3 should be taken immediately after 1:2-9, proposes to read vs. 7 between 3:5 and 1:10. But such contexts are in no need of expansion, and indeed show no evidence whatever that originally they gave accommodation to the erring verse. Modern scholars are right in agreeing with Julius Wellhausen's description of the verse as "a Judaistic insertion" (*Die kleinen Propheten* [3rd ed.; Berlin: Georg Reimer, 1898], *ad loc.*). The occasion of the insertion of the verse was probably the notable survival of Jerusalem at the time of Sennacherib's invasion of Palestine in 701 B.C.

d) THE THIRD CHILD, NOT MY PEOPLE (1:8-9)

The name of Hosea's third child affirms the solemn fact that the bond between Yahweh and his people has been broken. Israel has now forfeited the privileges which it had so flagrantly neglected. We should note that in Hosea's message to his contemporaries, as evidenced by the names of his children, there is no hope for the future; there is but the intimation of judgment moving to finality.

9. **I am not your God:** This is the preferable rendering and it is supported by some MSS of the LXX as well as by 2:23. The M.T., as it stands, means "for I am not

judgment. "Behold, your house is left unto you desolate" (Matt. 23:38). Any man of spiritual insight will not fail to see that the root cause of the desolation that so often seems to cover the earth, as the waters cover the sea, comes from man's rejection of God. "So speak ye, and so do, as they that shall be judged by the law of liberty" (Jas. 2:12). We are at liberty to reject the love of God, but never at liberty to escape the judgment which falls on that rejection. We are free to sin, but never to escape the wages of sin, which is death. But the Cross stands in history not only as a reminder that to sin against love is to incur judgment. It is primarily the revelation of God's mercy. "God so loved the world, that he gave . . ." (John 3:16). "Greater love hath no man than this" (John 15:13). "We love him, because he first loved us" (I John 4:19). From this love we cannot escape. If we reject it as mercy, we confront it as judgment. But it is as mercy that it speaks its deepest and truest word.

7b. Salvation, but Not by the Sword.—Here are made clear the two types of salvation—God's and man's: **I . . . will not save them by bow, nor by sword, nor by battle, by horses, nor by horsemen.** These are the methods man

relies on. The bow and the sword were the formidable symbols of destruction known to Hosea's world. Men turned to them for defense and deliverance, though they now belong to the "horse and buggy days." Our engines of destruction have gone as far beyond such implements as a blockbuster or an atomic bomb has gone beyond David's slingshot. Yet the amazing fact is that this increase in the effectiveness of his firing power has not brought man an increased feeling of security, but on the contrary has made his life vastly more precarious and insecure than it was in Hosea's day. What greater proof could there be that man's deliverance does not lie in his own strength, but in some frankly acknowledged and accepted limitation which leads him to seek the security that God offers, in which is his real defense? His true defense lies in accepting and exploring the moral and spiritual realities which God has put about him. His **bow** and **sword** will not furnish him security or salvation; for as these weapons of his grow in magnitude and power, so grow his danger and the possibility of his destruction.

9. God's Repudiation of His Own.—Our relationship to God may be nominal or real.

10 ¶ Yet the number of the children of Israel shall be as the sand of the sea, which cannot be measured nor numbered; and it shall come to pass, *that* in the place where it

10[b] Yet the number of the people of Israel shall be like the sand of the sea, which can be neither measured nor num-

[b] Heb Ch 2. 1

yours," and that is supported by the main LXX evidence (ἐγὼ οὐκ εἰμὶ ὑμῶν). Artur Weiser has suggested that this is a weakening of the original text: "This judgment, which overthrows the very foundation of Old Testament religion, sounded unendurable to later generations and was weakened into the M.T. reading 'I will not be yours'" (*Das Buch der zwölf kleinen Propheten* [Göttingen: Vandenhoeck & Ruprecht, 1949; "Das Alte Testament Deutsch"], *ad loc.*).

B. RESTORATION AND RENEWAL (1:10–2:1=Hebrew 2:1-3)

Although these verses are printed in the RSV as prose, it is very probable that they were originally in rhythmic form, and indeed Adolf Allwohn (*Die Ehe des propheten Hosea in psychoanalytischer Beleuchtung* [Giessen: A. Töpelmann, 1926; "Beihefte zur Zeitschrift für die alttestamentliche Wissenschaft"], pp. 15-17) has made a plausible attempt to restore that form. The question of their authenticity has been seriously raised, but before examining that problem, let us see what the verses have to say.

10. It is clearly assumed in this verse that the rupture between Yahweh and his people has been healed. The old fellowship has been restored. Those who were formerly named "Not my people" have been received back again and are now called **Sons of the**

Nominally we are a Christian nation. We inscribe God's name on our coins, sing of him in our national anthem, pray to him in our national assemblies. Yet as we contemplate our life in which secularism has robbed us of so many of our sanctities, a life in many respects more pagan than Christian, could not God say to us as he did to Israel, **You are not my people and I am not your God?** These words do not mean that God was "fed up" with Israel. They are a statement of fact. Israel had so paganized her life as to create a condition in which the spiritual affinity between herself and God was broken. The possibility of restoration was open to her, as it is to us.

10a. The Bounty of God.—The text suggests the immeasurable bounty of God. There is nothing stingy or calculating about his dealings with men. The starry heavens, ever expanding as we increase the size of our telescopes, symbolize his vast designs. The good earth, with its productivity, rivers, lakes, seas, that contain and supply more than we can ever use or even need, are other symbols. Even our physical bodies point to the same truth. The surgeon removes this or that, sometimes a considerable portion, and yet physical life goes on. The Creator has given us a greater endowment than we need for our normal activities—we have reserves for the unexpected.

When we move from the physical to the moral and spiritual realm, the bounty of God is equally evident if not more so. This is the testimony of the saints and seers who have

known God, not merely known about him. "He will abundantly pardon" (Isa. 55:7). He forgives till seventy times seven: "He hath not dealt with us after our sins; nor rewarded us according to our iniquities" (Ps. 103:10). He is "plenteous in mercy" (Ps. 86:15). He spoke to Jonah "the second time" (Jonah 3:1), gave him another chance, and often gives us many more than that. His mercies are new every morning and fresh every evening. He is "able to do exceeding abundantly above all that we ask or think" (Eph. 3:20).

These are but a few of the testimonies of those who have known God. That their witness is true becomes clear when we think of Christ, who emphasized and revealed this aspect of God's character. In his coming God "spared not his own Son" (Rom. 8:32), gave the best he had. Christ urged us to go the second mile. He replaced the exact and calculating ethic, the sort of slot-machine ethic in which you get out just what you put in, no more, no less— "eye for eye, tooth for tooth" (Exod. 21:24)— with a more bounteous ethic. He replaced duty with love, and love never asks whether it has done enough but what more it may do. "Love those that love you, befriend those that befriend you." Christ revealed a God who was not like that. "Love your enemies, bless them that curse you, do good to them that hate you, and pray for them which despitefully use you" (Matt. 5:44). "If ye love them which love you, what reward have ye? . . . What do ye more than others?" (Matt. 5:46-47.) "When ye shall

was said unto them, Ye *are* not my people, *there* it shall be said unto them, *Ye are* the sons of the living God.

11 Then shall the children of Judah and the children of Israel be gathered together, and appoint themselves one head, and they shall come up out of the land: for great *shall be* the day of Jezreel.

bered; and in the place where it was said to them, "You are not my people," it shall be said to them, "Sons of the living God."

11 And the people of Judah and the people of Israel shall be gathered together, and they shall appoint for themselves one head; and they shall go up from the land, for great shall be the day of Jezreel.

living God. Second Isaiah contrasts Yahweh, living and active, with the dumb idols who are impotent; here Hosea speaks in much the same way of the living God (cf. 6:2; 13:14). With a living God man may enter into fellowship; with an active God he may find salvation. The return of Yahweh's favor upon his people is evidenced by the fact that they will greatly increase—a manifest token of blessing. It is probable that the words **in the place where** should be regarded not as having local reference, but as equivalent to "whereas."

11. Three propositions are stated in this verse: (*a*) the reproach of the divided kingdom will be removed (cf. 5:13-14; 6:4-6); (*b*) Judah and Israel will be united under a single head—that rendering of the Hebrew is preferable to the other which has been proposed by some scholars: "and they shall make themselves into one company" (cf. Judg. 7:16; I Sam. 11:11; Job 1:17 for such a use of the Hebrew word ראש); (*c*) **and they shall go up from the land;** so must be translated the final phrase of the first half of the verse as it stands in the M.T. (on the meaning of the phrase see Exeg. on 2:1).

have done all those things which are commanded you, say, We are unprofitable servants: we have done that which was our duty to do" (Luke 17:10). "He went a little further" (Matt. 26:39).

Oh, the little more, and how much it is!
And the little less, and what worlds away![5]

10b. Denial and Affirmation.—It was in the place where they denied God that Israel would later reaffirm him. The very experience in which a man loses God is the one in which he often finds him. It is to the place at which we left the road that we must return if we would find the way again. The place of our transgression thus becomes the locus of our new spiritual orientation. The repentant prodigal retraces his steps. The place where formerly he had said, "Give me the portion of goods that falleth to me" (Luke 15:12) is the very place to which he came saying, "Father, I have sinned against heaven, and before thee, and am no more worthy" (Luke 15:18-19). He re-established the broken ties and restored the lost relationships on the very road where he had broken them. The wounded oyster mends its shell with a pearl. So men through the grace of God can transform weight into wings, tragedy into triumph. The experience that seemed freighted with disaster can become the place of liberation and enrichment.

[5] Robert Browning, "By the Fire-side," st. xxxix.

"Take up thy bed, and walk," said Jesus to the paralytic (John 5:11). The thing that bore him, he now bore. There may be certain evils upon which we have become as dependent as the paralytic on his couch. We seem helpless or passive in their presence. Great is their grip upon us. We take them lying down. These very enemies, however, when conquered by the grace of God, become the occasion of our greatest triumphs. We invariably win our most significant victories where we fight our hardest battles. "Peter, you are impulsive, weak, undependable, but Peter, you are going to become a rock. The very quality which made people say, 'There is a man you cannot count on,' will be transformed into the stuff of martyrdom." "When I am weak, then am I strong" (II Cor. 12:10). **In the place where it was said . . . , Ye are not . . . , there it shall be said . . . , Ye are.** The victory, however, is not ours. The power that transforms weakness to strength, fear to faith, that makes even our besetting sin an occasion for triumph, is of God. "It is God which worketh in you" (Phil. 2:13).

This truth may be seen from another angle. When Paul at the end of his missionary journeys made his speech from the castle steps in Jerusalem, the audience listened sympathetically and approvingly until he mentioned the word "Gentile." "They gave him audience up to this word, and then lifted up their voices, and said, 'Away with such a fellow from the earth: for it is not fit that he should live'"

2 Say ye unto your brethren, Ammi; and to your sisters, Ruhamah.

2 [c] Say to your brother,[d] "My people," and to your sister,[e] "She has obtained pity."

[c] Heb Ch 2. 3
[d] Gk: Heb brothers
[e] Gk Vg: Heb sisters

2:1. This verse concludes the section 1:10–2:1. **Say to your brother, "My people"** [in contrast with the name "Not my people" in 1:9], **and to your sister, "She has obtained mercy** [or "Pitied," in contrast with the name "Not Pitied" in 1:6]." The singulars of **your brother** and **your sister** are to be accepted. Now the only person to whom the instruction in this verse could have been given was Jezreel, Hosea's first-born, so that there is very good reason for reading that name as a vocative at the beginning of this verse.

Most scholars take the view that this passage belongs to the exilic period and looks forward with hope to a return of the scattered Jews to their own land. That being so, they contend that the passage is not an authentic utterance of the prophet Hosea. Let us examine the matter briefly:

(a) Note that the promises which are here made concerning the new day are intimately articulated with the penalties which Hosea declares to be the main aspects of the punishment about to befall the people. The great increase of population now promised corresponds to the threatened penalty of loss of children (cf. 9:11-16), the return "from the land" (or "from the lands") to the penalty of being taken as captive to Assyria and Egypt (cf. 8:8-10; 9:3, 6, 17; 10:5; 11:11), and the unity of the people under one leader to the former dynastic troubles and political intrigues (cf. 7:3-7; 8:4, 10). The term "living God" is not found in the utterances of Hosea, but of the activity of a living God among his people he speaks more than once (12:10, 13; 13:4-5); and the passage by reason of its reinterpretation of "Jezreel" is closely knit with ch. 1. Thus we can say that the thought forms of the passage strongly support its authenticity; the reference to a return from foreign lands gives no warrant whatever for an exilic date in view of Hosea's threat of captivity for his sinful people in Assyria and Egypt. The punishment thus threatened is not canceled; that would be to flout God's justice. But it will not mean an utter end of Israel; there will be a return and the opening of a new day.

(b) The clause in vs. 11 **and they shall go up from the land** has caused much discussion; they shall go up whither, and from which land? Van Hoonacker (op. cit., pp. 31-32) suggests "go up from the land of Palestine" because of the lack of room there in consequence of the increase of population; but go up whither? Ernst Sellin suggests "go up from Palestine into the wilderness" and so connects the passage in

(Acts 22:22). For Paul, the orthodox Jew, the word "Gentile" was a dam behind which the waters of Judaism backed up and became self-contained, if not stagnant. For Paul, the Christian, the word "Gentile" became a sluice through which the waters of Christianity flowed out across the Mediterranean world. The very barrier where it was said, "Thus far and no farther," became the avenue through which the gospel swept to the uttermost parts of the earth. Christ can transform our dead-end streets into avenues of life. One of the church fathers said that he changed our sunset into sunrise.

2:1-4. The Warnings of God.—Hosea continues here and in the following verses the parable of the unfaithful wife. The wayward

wife is Israel, the aggrieved **husband** is Yahweh, the **children** are the individual Israelites, who are urged to **plead with your mother.** S. L. Brown thinks "expostulate" would better express Hosea's meaning. "It is the language of a wrathful and exasperated husband." [6] This appears in the vividness of Hosea's style. Israel will be subjected to the punishment and humiliation reserved for the unfaithful wife in the Hebrew society of his day. Not only will she be left **naked** (Ezek. 16:39) but she will be stoned to death (Ezek. 16:40). The punishment will be meted out not only to her but to her children. To these too God will be merci-

[6] The Book of Hosea (London: Methuen & Co., 1932; "Westminster Commentaries"), p. 13. Used by permission.

2 Plead with your mother, plead; for she *is* not my wife, neither *am* I her husband: let her therefore put away her whoredoms out of her sight, and her adulteries from between her breasts;

2 "Plead with your mother, plead — for she is not my wife, and I am not her husband — that she put away her harlotry from her face, and her adultery from between her breasts;

thought with 2:14-15 (*Das Zwölfprophetenbuch* [2nd ed.; Leipzig: A. Deichert, 1929; "Kommentar zum Alten Testament"], *ad loc.*). But surely the day of cleansing and of renewed covenant making in the wilderness must precede the time of renewed blessing and prosperity and be the condition of its coming. In all the circumstances, it seems necessary to read "they shall go up from the lands," and that is to be interpreted in the terms of Hosea's own teaching as indicated above, not made an argument for an exilic date for the passage.

(*c*) **Jezreel** had been the name for a day of judgment upon Israel; now it signifies the day of Yahweh's sowing, and from that sowing there will come a great and glorious increase. There is just a possibility that there has been haplography of the name in this passage; in addition to standing, as it does now, at the end of 1:11, it may have stood originally also at the beginning of 2:1 as a vocative, giving direction for the address in the following words.

(*d*) Those scholars who are prepared to accept the passage as authentic wish to remove it from its present context. Some insert it at the end of ch. 2, while those who read ch. 3 immediately after 1:2-9 read it after ch. 3. But such proposals disregard a very important feature of prophetic utterances as we have them, viz., that they are seldom arranged in anything like a chronological order. The utterances are brief and fragmentary, and any one may have little or no close connection with that which precedes or follows. It is indubitably true that in Hosea's ministry 2:2-13, if not 2:2-23, must have been uttered before 1:10–2:1; but not for that reason need 1:10–2:1 be transferred from its present context to another part of the book.

C. Repentance and Rebetrothal (2:2-23=Hebrew 2:4-25)
1. Unfaithfulness Born of Ignorance (2:2-8=Hebrew 2:4-10)

The names of Hosea's children had made plain the separation and the break in covenant relationship which had developed between Yahweh and his wife Israel on account of her persistent unfaithfulness. This section describes the yearning of Yahweh after "his wife"; he must win her back from the error of her ways. By her separation from him she is receiving the just reward of her deeds; but God thinks in terms not of justice alone, but of mercy and restitution. Therefore this section begins with the word **Plead**. That word has commonly a forensic sense and is used of a counsel presenting

less. Hosea thought that the sins of the mother would be visited on the children. To be a member of a family or group was willy-nilly to share in and suffer for the evils of any member of it. So when Saul's slaughter of the Gibeonites was thought to have been responsible for a devastating famine, two of Saul's sons and five of his grandsons, though entirely innocent, were put to death (II Sam. 21:1-14). God was regarded as "a jealous God" who visited "the iniquity of the fathers upon the children unto the third and fourth generation" (Exod. 20:5). Ezekiel was one of the champions of individual responsibility. He taught that God deals with

individuals one by one, each one receiving the recompense of his deeds. "What mean ye, that ye use this proverb concerning the land of Israel, saying, The fathers have eaten sour grapes, and the children's teeth are set on edge? As I live, saith the Lord God, . . . the soul that sinneth, it shall die" (Ezek. 18:2-4).

Vss. 1-4 sound a stern note of warning. God threatens Israel with the dire consequences that will follow her prolonged and determined resistance to his will. She will be turned into **a wilderness, . . . a dry land.** We are more wont to stress the promises of God than the warnings of God; we are more familiar with his

3 Lest I strip her naked, and set her as in the day that she was born, and make her as a wilderness, and set her like a dry land, and slay her with thirst.

3 lest I strip her naked
  and make her as in the day she was born,
and make her like a wilderness,
  and set her like a parched land,
  and slay her with thirst.

---

a case. The Israelites who are willing to respond to the summons are urged to plead with their mother, to present Yahweh's case to her, and to expostulate with her. The idea of individual Israelites expostulating with their mother, as if mother Israel had an existence independent of her children, is easy to understand and is in line with the terms which Hosea has been using. The purpose of the pleading is defined in the final part of vs. 2:

that she put away her harlotry from her face,
and her adultery from between her breasts.

The first phrase might simply mean that she should put away her harlotry from before her, i.e., that she should abandon it; but the parallel rather suggests that both phrases refer to some mark of the harlot. That being so, the reference must be either to her brazen face and exposed breasts, or to her painted face and ornamented breasts. While Jer. 3:3 and Prov. 7:13 would give support to the former of these interpretations, the latter is more fitting here. The children are to beseech their mother to lay aside the ornaments and seductions of her adulterous traffic and to cease from her adultery.

The intervening clauses in vs. 2, **for she is not my wife, neither am I her husband,** break the close connection of the preceding and the succeeding portions of the verse and introduce the formula of dismissal into the midst of the call to Israel's children to plead with their mother to return. Sellin should be followed in his suggestion that, since a statement concerning Hosea's dismissal of his wife would have been expected in the text, this parenthetical clause should be regarded as a fragment of such a statement, and with it vs. 4 should be associated (*op. cit., ad loc.;* cf. Julius A. Bewer, "The Story of Hosea's Marriage," *American Journal of Semitic Languages and Literatures,* XXII [1905-6], 120-30).

3. There is still hope that mother Israel will respond to the pleading and return to her husband; but the penalties which she will suffer if she does not return are outlined. She will be openly disgraced and put to shame, will be deprived of all beauty and comeliness, will be made like a parched land, bare, unfruitful and desolate, and will in the end perish with thirst. Sometimes death by burning is specified in the O.T. as the penalty for harlotry (Gen. 38:24; Lev. 21:9), but more often it is death by stoning, and for this purpose the guilty woman was stripped naked (cf. Deut. 22:21; Ezek. 16:38-40). Curt Kuhl has drawn attention to the fact that the dismissal of a divorced wife naked is a practice mentioned in a cuneiform tablet from Ḥana and in another from Nuzi in northern Mesopotamia, both tablets belonging to the middle of the second millennium B.C.; and C. H. Gordon quotes another Nuzi tablet in which it is the

---

mercy than with his judgment, with his love than with his wrath. This is no doubt as it should be, for God is love and his mercy is everlasting. "He hath not dealt with us after our sins; nor rewarded us according to our iniquities" (Ps. 103:10). Are we not apt, however, to emphasize the mercy of God, his promises, to the neglect of the judgment, the warnings? Yet there they stand like danger signals on the pages of Holy Writ. The Bible is like an instrument of many keys. There are "sharps" and "minors" on the keyboard, and should they not at times be struck, the Bible would not voice its full-bodied message. It was characteristic of the prophets that while they were not unmindful of God's love and mercy, they did not overlook his judgment. They did not allow his promises to the faithful to obscure his warnings to the faithless. They could, as we shall often see in the book of Hosea, portray the God of love as one who at times appears as a roaring lion or a ferocious wild beast. Such

4 And I will not have mercy upon her children; for they *be* the children of whoredoms.

5 For their mother hath played the harlot: she that conceived them hath done shamefully; for she said, I will go after my lovers, that give *me* my bread and my water, my wool and my flax, mine oil and my drink.

4 Upon her children also I will have no pity,
    because they are children of harlotry.
5 For their mother has played the harlot;
    she that conceived them has acted shamefully.
For she said, 'I will go after my lovers,
    who give me my bread and my water,
    my wool and my flax, my oil and my drink.'

---

children who are called upon to strip their mother naked when she is dismissed for adultery (cf. "Neue Dokumente zum Verständnis von Hosea 2₄₋₁₅," *Zeitschrift für die alttestamentliche Wissenschaft,* LII [1934], 102-9; and "Hos. 2₄₋₅ in the Light of New Semitic Inscriptions," *ibid.,* LIV [1936], 277-80) . The figure of a wilderness, dry, bare, and without attraction, is very fitting for one who had decked herself with her ornaments and had lived luxuriously.

4. This verse adds nothing to what has already been said. Some scholars (e.g., Nowack and Harper) delete it as a gloss. But it must be noted that vs. 5*a* presumes the precedence of vs. 4; otherwise the third plural **their** and **them** in vs. 5*a* would have no reference. Therefore vss. 4, 5*a* must be taken together, and there is much to be said in support of the contention that they should be taken together with vs. 2*aβ* as forming a part of the missing narrative which told of Hosea's dismissal of his wife.

5. If vs. 5*a* is treated as suggested above, vs. 5*b* follows easily upon vs. 3. It describes how Israel went willfully after her lovers, the Baals, in the belief that it was they who provided her with the fruits of the earth. The service of the Baals, the owners and lords of the land, was a fertility cult. Its high days were the great agricultural festivals, when offerings of firstfruits and the firstlings of the flocks were made to the Baals in order that the increase might be received; or thank offerings were given for benefits enjoyed. But from ancient times there had been associated with this fertility cult certain rites which had their origin in the conception of a divine marriage, of which the sexual intercourse of worshipers with the so-called "sacred men" and "sacred women" of the Canaanite sanctuaries was regarded as representative. Weiser (*Das Buch der zwölf kleinen Propheten, ad loc.*) sums up the service of the Baals very well in these words: "The deity is regarded here simply as the guarantor of material blessings; the whole religious life operates on the basis of a mechanical *do-ut-des* relationship and, owing to the sexual fertility rites which are imitative of the procreative activity of the Godhead, it is brought down into the oppressive atmosphere of a sheer sensualism which has nothing to do with the high

---

symbols when used are not the marks of a weird imagination or a disordered mind. They are rather the honest expression of men who faced the actualities of life and the realities of history without benefit of rose-colored glasses. Perhaps if in reading our Bibles we underscored the warnings of God as we do his promises, and memorized them as we do the "comfortable words," perhaps if we detected and heeded the danger signals as readily as we do the green lights, we should not love God less but fear him more, not in the sense of being afraid of him, but in the sense of understanding, with awe in our hearts, the moral nature of the universe in which he has placed us to work out our destiny.

5. *The Peril of False Objectives.*—If the unexamined life is not livable, no more is the unattached life. The direction of every life is determined by what it "goes after." We all go after something. **I will go after my lovers, who give me my bread and my water, my wool and my flax, mine oil and my drink.** Who are these **lovers** and what do they give? Their gifts, be it noted, all lie on the physical level—**wool, water, flax, oil, drink.** Our **lovers** may be our amazing scientific know-how, our commercial prowess, our standard of living, our go-getter spirit, etc. To such we attribute our achievement—"Mine own hand hath saved me" (Judg. 7:2) . No one need belittle the importance of our material needs, but it is nevertheless true

6 ¶ Therefore, behold, I will hedge up thy ways with thorns, and make a wall, that she shall not find her paths.

6 Therefore I will hedge up her[f] way with
   thorns;
and I will build a wall against her,
   so that she cannot find her paths.

[f] Gk Syr: Heb your

earnestness and the deep inwardness of a spiritual religion which is aware of an indebtedness to God which is raised far above everything that is merely earthly." Hosea therefore denounces the Israelites for resorting to this fertility cult. In so far as their service was consciously directed to the Baals, it was done in ignorance, for it was not to the Baals that they owed the increase of their fields or their flocks; and in so far as they were seeking to render his service to Yahweh, they must know that it was a service which was wholly unacceptable to him. The service which he demanded of his people was altogether different.

6. This verse, like vss. 9, 14 following, begins with **therefore;** each of the sections thus introduced strikes a different note. Vss. 6-8 speak of the frustration and subsequent enlightenment and repentance of the erring wife; vss. 9-13 describe the punishment which will be meted out for her unfaithfulness; and vss. 14-23 tell how the bond between Yahweh and his wife will be renewed on a pure basis and they will be betrothed again. It is at once clear that, as far as logical order is concerned, the order of these sections should be vss. 9-13, 6-8, 14-23, with the exception that vs. 8 should be read together with, and as the conclusion of, vss. 2-5.

Vs. 6 describes how Yahweh will induce in Israel a sense of frustration. She will be thwarted in her pursuit of the Baals and she will find her way blocked by obstacles.

that material needs, even when completely and adequately met, do not satisfy man. "I shall be satisfied, when I awake, with thy likeness" (Ps. 17:15).

6. Sin Brings Frustration.—Sin invariably leads to a blind alley, a dead-end street. The broad road and wide gate of which Jesus speaks lures because it promises a full, happy, and rich life. So it seems when with gay spirits and light heart we set foot upon it. It is as though we were starting upon a high adventure in abundant living. That is why "many there be which go in thereat" (Matt. 7:13). But sooner or later we encounter a **hedge** running straight across it, in the hard and piercing realities of which we are ensnared. There is no way around. The same truth is found in Job. "Why is light given to a man whose way is hid, and whom God hath hedged in?" (Job 3:23) What had been a shelter turns into a hindrance. "He hath fenced up my way that I cannot pass, and he hath set darkness in my paths" (Job 19:8). The picture is not that of a traveler who has lost his way, but of one who thinks he knows where he is going yet finds the road blocked by some insuperable barrier. One is up against it.

"Man proposes, but God disposes."[7] In all our plans there is the unforeseen and unforeseeable, the unpredictable. Any course of action counter to God's will eventually leads to

[7] Thomas à Kempis The Imitation of Christ I. 19.

an impasse. Our world comes often to such an impasse, as though God had called a halt on us. The road is blocked because the destination we have in view and the motive and spirit of our journey are alike opposed to the purposes of God. He has sent One to be "the way," and when our chosen path ignores his proffered light and spurns his direction, we are up against it. The universe is moral. To work with it is to find the way; against it we are lost. To continue our course in spite of everything is to kick against the pricks. The wounds are deep and often fatal. "O Lord, I know that the way of man is not in himself: it is not in man that walketh to direct his steps" (Jer. 10:23).

Frustration comes not only to groups but to individuals. Often we bring it upon ourselves through our lack of wisdom, courage, or discipline. Psychologists tell us that many if not most nervous disorders or breakdowns come from unresolved moral problems. Not all of them, however, are self-induced. Sometimes they grow, as we might say, out of circumstances that are beyond our control—disappointments, hope deferred, unrequited love. These are but some of the obstacles thrown down in front of us to block our advance. The greatest of saints, Paul, spoke of "a thorn in the flesh, the messenger of Satan to buffet me" (II Cor. 12:7). Living is dangerous business. Few if any escape its hazards and perils.

7 And she shall follow after her lovers, but she shall not overtake them; and she	7 She shall pursue her lovers,
	    but not overtake them;
	and she shall seek them,
	    but shall not find them.

It is doubtful if Hosea, when he used these words, was thinking of anything specific in his people's experience. Rather he was saying that God could not remain aloof and inactive. He would block the way of Israel's desires, would make it difficult, if not impossible, for her to enjoy her sinful ways, and would make her dissatisfied with her conduct.

7. It is made plain that Israel will not easily be turned from her erring; she will not soon admit a sense of disappointment. Rather **she shall pursue her lovers, . . . and she shall seek them.** Thus Hosea indicates the power of Israel's wayward passion and the stubbornness of her unbelief. How often penitence very tardily follows upon disillusionment and failure! To declare their error to such a people has not infrequently the effect

Christ came to help remove the thorns; or if not to remove them, to give us, as he did Paul, power to live with them and make them goads or incentives to worthier living. "I besought the Lord thrice, that it might depart from me. And he said unto me, My grace is sufficient for thee: for my strength is made perfect in weakness." (II Cor. 12:8-9.) If Christ can help us here, it is because he knew the thorns firsthand. He wore them. His road was blocked by a cross, undeserved and unmerited. If ever there was a picture of a frustrated life, it was that of our Lord on the first Good Friday. How could he find his way through and beyond all this? Yet the very cross which seemed to block his advance was to become in the providence of God a way, straight and narrow, but open, and leading to life abundant, joyous, eternal. This is because Good Friday was transfigured in the light of Easter morning. Those who share "the fellowship of his sufferings" will come to know also "the power of his resurrection" (Phil. 3:10). To one whose heart is fixed on God no thorn hedge, not even a crown of thorns, will bring defeat or death. Christ by his victory gives us the assurance that the thorn-beset road to the far country can be transformed into the open road back to the Father's house, and the hardships that seem like millstones can become steppingstones to a victorious life. "Behold, I have set before thee an open door, and no man can shut it" (Rev. 3:8). "I can do all things through Christ which strengtheneth me" (Phil. 4:13). "We are more than conquerors through him that loved us" (Rom. 8:37). The man who said that knew.

7a. Sin Brings Futility.—We pursue but miss, seek but never find. We do not get what we go after. We seek happiness, but get sorrow; fulfillment, but find frustration; satisfaction, but find remorse; life, but find death. In the story of the Fall we read: "When the woman saw that the tree was good for food, and that it was pleasant to the eyes, and a tree to be desired to make one wise, she took of the fruit thereof, and did eat" (Gen. 3:6). Every one of these promises led to futility. This profound "myth" expresses in quaint ways an eternal truth. The woman (a man wrote this story!) was seeking food. But she did not get food—"Thorns also and thistles shall it bring forth to thee" (Gen. 3:18). "It was pleasant to the eyes"—good to look at! Yet it did not produce beauty but ugliness, so much so that they hid themselves, they did not want to be seen. "A tree to be desired to make one wise." They were seeking wisdom and found not wisdom but disillusionment. So Israel pursues but misses, seeks and never finds. The futility of sin!

In pursuing her lovers, turning her energies toward objects that seemed real but proved vain and elusive, Israel was really expressing her hunger for God. One never finds life in the far country, the quest is sterile. But the urge that sends one upon that journey may really be the quest for fuller life. "He hath set eternity in their heart" (Eccl. 3:11 ASV). There is in man's heart a hunger for the Eternal. But it cannot be satisfied on the animal level, for we are men, not beasts. Our personalities cry out for bread. Sin offers a stone. The impulse that sends a man into the far country is God-given, but the far country is a mirage, an illusion. The husks will not do. The futility of sin therefore lies not in seeking satisfaction and fulfillment, but in seeking it where it cannot be found.

There are many things we are seeking today and are not finding, not because the impulse that makes us seek is wrong, but because the impulse is directed to wrong objects. "Seek peace, and pursue it" (Ps. 34:14). But we have not found peace any more than did Israel find her lovers. For peace is not found in the pre-

| shall seek them, but shall not find *them:* then shall she say, I will go and return to my first husband; for then *was it* better with me than now.

8 For she did not know that I gave her corn, and wine, and oil, and multiplied her | Then she shall say, 'I will go
  and return to my first husband,
  for it was better with me then than
  now.'
8 And she did not know
  that it was I who gave her
  the grain, the wine, and the oil, |

---

of making more stubborn their hearts and making their ears more dull and unresponsive than they were before (cf. Isa. 6:9-10). It is notable that it is only the slowly dawning sense of bafflement and frustration which produces in Israel the resolve to return to Yahweh. There is no word of penitence or contrition for the evil of her doings, no evidence of a chastened mood; there is only the self-regarding reflection: "I will go back to my former husband, for I was better off then than I am now" (cf. the attitude of the returning prodigal son, Luke 15:17).

8. This verse (see Exeg. on vs. 6) should be taken closely after vs. 5. It says that Israel's service of the Baals was conditioned by her ignorance of Yahweh. She was quite unaware of the scope of his rule and of his provision for her needs. Hosea is not the only prophet who speaks of his people's profound ignorance in this way (cf. Isa. 5:13; Jer. 10:14; contrast Isa. 11:9; Hab. 2:14). Hosea declares that Yahweh provides not only **the grain, the wine, and the oil,** i.e., the staple products of Palestine, but also the **silver** and the **gold.** These were not native to the country but must have been derived from commercial activity. On the Black Obelisk of Shalmaneser III of Assyria (859-825

---

ponderance of power. "Who desires peace, let him prepare for war" [1] is a plausible half-truth that has deluded men for generations. The futility of our search to date must indicate that we are not seeking in the right way. "Seek, and ye shall find" (Matt. 7:7), but not until we seek in God's way. Even worthy ends sought in unworthy ways result in futility.

7b. Then Shall She Return.—"Man's extremity is God's opportunity." [2] Man often has to learn the hard way. Think of the road by which Israel had to come. It led through ignorance, privation, desolation, sorrow, frustration, futility. It took all that to bring her to her senses. It took all that to bring the prodigal to himself. "When he came to himself, he said, How many hired servants of my father's have bread enough and to spare, and I perish with hunger!" (Luke 15:17.) **I will . . . return to my first husband; for then was it better with me than now.** This truth, which lies at the heart of the Christian message, is verified not alone in the realm of abstract ideas or speculative thought but in the laboratory of life and human experience. The rules made by opportunism and expediency will not work in God's universe. The universe is not built for the success of evil or the evildoer. "I have learned from experience," we say. Experience is a hard teacher, but some of us seem to learn no other way. Then—after we have

drunk the dregs from life's cup and found its bitterness—**then** we leave the false gods, the lesser loyalties, and return to the Shepherd and Bishop of our souls. **Then** we discover that sin does not pay, often after we are spent and have not much to offer but wasted years and a broken life.

We do receive forgiveness. He will receive us even as did the father the prodigal son. **I will go,** and on the road back we shall find him coming toward us. For he is "slow to anger, and plenteous in mercy" (Ps. 103:8). "O the depth of the riches both of the wisdom and knowledge of God!" (Rom. 11:33.)

8. She Did Not Know.—For a fuller discussion of the relationship between sin and ignorance see Expos. on 4:1-3. In this passage Hosea is reminding us that Israel failed to recognize God as her true benefactor. She went after her lovers because she regarded them as the source of her blessings, "My lovers, that give me my bread and my water, my wool and my flax, mine oil and my drink" (vs. 5). **She did not know that I gave her corn, and wine, and oil.**

So Israel goes after her lovers, the Baalim, whom she mistakenly regards as the source of her blessings, and ignores her true Benefactor. Is not one major cause of sin man's failure to recognize his creaturehood, his dependence upon and hence obligation to God as creator and sustainer? Man acts as though he were owner rather than steward, landlord rather than

---

[1] Vegetius *Military Institutions* III. Prologue.

[2] John Flavel, *A Faithful and Ancient Account of Some Late and Wonderful Sea Deliverances.*

| silver and gold, *which* they prepared for Baal. | and who lavished upon her silver and gold which they used for Ba'al. |

B.C.) it is recorded that Jehu had to pay Assyria considerable tribute of silver and gold, while Sennacherib (704-682 B.C.) claims to have taken from Jerusalem, among other things, thirty talents of gold and eight hundred talents of silver (cf. R. W. Rogers, ed., *Cuneiform Parallels to the Old Testament* [2nd ed.; New York: Abingdon Press, 1926], pp. 304, 344). It seems clear that the use of gold in Israel dates back to Solomon's time; it was presumably imported through his maritime port of Ezion Geber.

In the second half of vs. 8 it will be noted that the KJV and the RSV introduce the subordinate clause in different places. In the original Hebrew the relative is not expressed, so that both renderings are possible. The final phrase may be translated as "they offered to Baal" or **they used for Baal** (cf. 8:4). The most common use of silver and gold in this connection was in overlaying images (cf. Jer. 10:4; Isa. 40:19; etc.).

---

tenant. We sing, "Praise God from whom all blessings flow," or say with the apostle James, "Every good gift . . . is from above" (Jas. 1:17), or with Paul, "What hast thou that thou didst not receive?" (I Cor. 4:7), "We are debtors" (Rom. 8:12); but we do not live as though we really believed this Christian insight. The fact that the graces of gratitude and humility are so singularly lacking is evidence of our failure to recognize God as the true source of our blessings. Pride and arrogance and the delusion of self-sufficiency are more authentic marks of our age than gratitude, and they ill befit our creaturehood. This failure to recognize our dependence upon and indebtedness to God, apart from whom we could not live at all, reveals the true nature of human sin. Paul speaks of those "who changed the truth of God into a lie, and worshipped and served the creature more than the Creator, who is blessed for ever" (Rom. 1:25).

What lies behind this evil attitude? Was it in part due to ignorance—Israel "did not know"? Ignorance may not be a completely adequate explanation. The main root of sin is the perversity and stubbornness of the human will; but ignorance does account for much. "If I am to judge by myself," said an eighteenth-century Frenchman, "man is a stupid animal." [3] And never so stupid, one may add, as when he deals with moral and spiritual realities. Our immaturity is appalling. **She did not know.** Why did she not know? Perhaps because there is something of deception in the very nature of sin. The devil "is a liar and the father of lies" (John 8:44). Sin never is what it seems to be— it wears a false face. "Satan fashioneth himself into an angel of light" (II Cor. 11:14 ASV).

The deception of sin is evident in much of the technique of modern advertising, which often builds up unworthy people or unworthy products and gives them a place of prominence in our thinking which in no sense they merit. The cheap, tawdry, and positively harmful can be so dressed as to "look like a million," when its true worth may be nearer ten cents. Compare a full-page liquor advertisement in all its glamour and appeal; then see the men who stagger out of a tavern, or the drunken driver who menaces the highways, or the broken homes, or the mounting tide of juvenile delinquency, to all of which liquor is a major contributing cause. Now look at the advertisement again and realize that "the devil is a liar, and the father of it" (John 8:44).

Sometimes, like Israel, we do not know not only because sin deceives, but also because man's conscience by its very nature tends to act as a *post eventum*. It turns on us most fiercely after, rather than before or during, our transgression of the moral law. "It is characteristic of sin," said Felix Adler, "that the fuller knowledge that the harmful deed is sinful *comes after the act.*" [4] "Whenever I am about to commit any folly," says Bucklaw in Scott's *Bride of Lammermoor,* "he [the devil] persuades me it is the most necessary, gallant, gentlemanlike thing on earth, and I am up to saddlegirths in the bog before I see that the ground is soft." [5] That is indeed "His Infernal Majesty's invariable strategy!" [6] He keeps us from seeing that the ground is soft until we are properly stuck. However, no matter what the reason for our deception, whether it springs from the nature of sin or from our nature, or from both, the fact is that stupidity or folly lies back of many of our misdeeds.

[4] *An Ethical Philosophy of Life* (New York: D. Appleton & Co., 1918), p. 172.

[5] Ch. v.

[6] *Ibid.*

[3] Quoted by Irving Babbitt, *Rousseau and Romanticism* (Boston: Houghton Mifflin Co., 1919), pp. 366-67.

9 Therefore will I return, and take away my corn in the time thereof, and my wine in the season thereof, and will recover my wool and my flax *given* to cover her nakedness.

10 And now will I discover her lewdness in the sight of her lovers, and none shall deliver her out of mine hand.

9 Therefore I will take back
  my grain in its time,
  and my wine in its season;
and I will take away my wool and my flax,
  which were to cover her nakedness.
10 Now I will uncover her lewdness
  in the sight of her lovers,
  and no one shall rescue her out of my hand.

2. The Punishment Fits the Crime (2:9-13=Hebrew 2:11-15)

9. Yahweh proposes to teach Israel that her service of the Baals is both misguided and futile; by disciplinary punishment he will reinforce the pleading that has been addressed to her to return. He will deprive her of the necessities of life in food and clothing. It will, of course, not be at once apparent to Israel that it is Yahweh who is denying her this essential provision; what will be apparent will be that her service of the Baals is not securing it; and in due course that service will be abandoned because it will no longer be producing the expected benefits. **I will take away:** I.e., *either* I will deprive (cf. Arabic *naṣala* IV) or despoil Israel of wool and flax since she does not deserve them, *or* I will rescue or deliver these benefits from her because, in her ignorance of their source and in ingratitude, she is using them unworthily.

10. When Israel is deprived of her food and clothing she will have nothing to offer upon the altars of the Baals, and so her shame and stubborn willfulness will be revealed. When that happens, her lot will be a hapless one, for the Baals will not be able to give her any help.

9-10. *Sin Brings Poverty.*—Israel because of her sin will be deprived of her means of livelihood: her **corn, wine, wool,** and **flax.** To say that sin always reduces one to poverty, that the poor are the sinners and the rich the saints, would be nonsense. When the psalmist wrote, "I have been young, and now am old; yet have I not seen the righteous forsaken, nor his seed begging bread" (Ps. 37:25), he must have been speaking from a limited knowledge of the facts or he must have been looking at life through rose-colored glasses. If it is true that some of the greatest sufferers have been the greatest saints, it is none the less true that sainthood has often gone hand in hand with dire economic need.

Having said this, however, it cannot be denied that in many instances sin is a root cause of economic hardship both individually and collectively. Many a prosperous prodigal in the far country has found that "wilful waste brings woeful want."[7] Multitudes have been reduced to dire economic straits by extravagant self-indulgence, which is sin; by debilitating habits like gambling, which is morally indefensible; by living beyond their incomes in order to "keep up with the Joneses," which is stupid. There is a connection between sin and poverty. It might be said, however, that far from causing

[7] Thomas Fuller, *Gnomologia,* No. 5755.

poverty, dishonest, unchristian, and shady practices are profitable to those who indulge them. Did not the psalmist complain about the wicked who prosper and spread their leaves like a green bay tree? Quite so. But is not such conduct the world over a main cause of the poverty that comes to others? Is not the selfish spirit of a Dives in part responsible for the misery of a Lazarus? Does not the man who pulls down his barns and builds greater, with no concern whatever beyond himself—"my barn," "my soul," "my goods"—help to make harder the lot of the underprivileged? Is there not a connection between the wealth of the landowners and the poverty of the sharecroppers? The selfish use and abuse of economic privilege has been the source of economic hardship to numberless souls.

Our failure to bring our industrial life under the control of moral to say nothing of Christian principles was largely responsible for the appeal and spread of communism. In this sense communism may be regarded as God's judgment upon us for our disregard of the economic condition of the masses, the plight of the poor. It is true that as practiced, communism did not keep its promise with the underprivileged. But it offered hope, and a drowning man will catch at a straw. Its appeal, especially in backward countries, lay in the fact that it was

| 11 I will also cause all her mirth to cease, her feast days, her new moons, and her sabbaths, and all her solemn feasts. | 11 And I will put an end to all her mirth, her feasts, her new moons, her sabbaths, and all her appointed feasts. |

11. The agricultural festivals had been Israel's joyful occasions. Now all that will cease. The term **feasts** renders a Hebrew word indicating festivals at which dancing had a place. The celebration of the **new moons** demonstrates the fact that the festivals of the Israelite calendar were originally nomad festivals, hence the emphasis upon the phases of the moon. Since the nomad travels by night, the moon is more in his thoughts than the sun. There is evidence that the sabbath was in the first instance a moon festival (cf. Amos 8:5; Isa. 1:13; Ezek. 46:3; II Kings 4:23). It was celebrated in ancient Babylon as a day of propitiation, a day of peace of heart for the gods; in Israel emphasis was laid upon cessation from work on the sabbath. Such cessation from work could never have been observed by a nomadic community with flocks and herds, but must have been a regulation formulated at a later agricultural stage. The **appointed feasts** were the great festival occasions, in particular, Unleavened Bread, Weeks, and Tabernacles, but new moons and other lesser occasions were doubtless also included.

understood as "the promise of a society in which all imperialistic exploitation will be a thing of the past."[8] The labor movement corrected many of the abuses of economic life and improved considerably the lot of the working man. For all this fair-minded people are thankful. But the labor movement, largely because of its inadequate leadership, itself created new problems. It often exhibited unreasonable, greedy, and highhanded policies which were detrimental to public good, and when unchecked, brought damage to itself. All this only shows that selfishness and greed are the sole possession of no single class. "The love of money is the root of all evil" (I Tim. 6:10), and its roots are to a greater or less extent in all our hearts. G. K. Studdert-Kennedy said: "If any man says to me that he has no love of money, I immediately begin to wonder whether he is a madman, a millionaire, or a tramp, those being the only types of people I can imagine saying it with anything like sincerity."[9] Most of us belong to none of these three categories. That is why we are all involved.

It is probably true that there is more dire human poverty and need in the modern world than in any previous age. The **corn, wine, wool,** and **flax** have been taken from humanity with a vengeance. This tragic condition is due to one main source—human sin. We speak of the economic causes of war, but strictly speaking the decisions that lead to war are never ultimately economic ones. When the United States decided to send the sinews of war to Japan in her aggression against China, the decision was not an economic decision; it was a moral de-

cision involving economics. And it will stand as one of the most immoral, stupid, and wicked in history. For it we have paid and continue to pay. The ultimate cause of war is man's violation of the moral laws of God—sin, in any of its myriad forms. "From whence come wars and fightings among you? come they not hence, even of your lusts that war in your members?" (Jas. 4:1.) Repentance, not pride; humility, not arrogance, is the only defensible attitude in a world like this, especially on the part of the privileged and prosperous.

11, 13. Sin Brings Drabness.—Man's betrayal of God always means first of all the betrayal of himself.

> For of all sad words of tongue or pen,
> The saddest are these: "It might have been!"[1]

The contrast between what we are and what by God's grace we might have been is often sad indeed. Rousseau regarded man as nothing more or less than a child of nature, and nature as innately good and beautiful. He made instinct the unerring guide to life. By identifying conscience with the emotions he destroyed that in man which, though not a perfect guide, when destroyed, leaves him wholly in darkness: "If . . . the light that is in thee be darkness, how great is that darkness!" (Matt. 6:23.) Those who followed their instincts Rousseau regarded as beautiful souls. He writes: "As for Julie, who never had any other guide but her heart, . . . she gives herself up to it without scruple, and to do right, has only to do all that it asks of her."[2] It is not necessary to add that this philosophy produced a literature of disillusionment, despair, and disgust. The gaiety grasped at turned to gloom, and the

[8] John C. Bennett, *Christianity and Communism* (New York: Association Press, 1948), p. 20.

[9] *The Wicket-Gate* (London: Hodder & Stoughton, 1923), p. 154.

[1] Whittier, "Maud Muller," st. liii.

[2] See Babbitt, *Rousseau and Romanticism*, p. 132.

12 And I will destroy her vines and her fig trees, whereof she hath said, These *are* my rewards that my lovers have given me: and I will make them a forest, and the beasts of the field shall eat them.

12 And I will lay waste her vines and her
    fig trees,
  of which she said,
'These are my hire,
  which my lovers have given me.'
I will make them a forest,
  and the beasts of the field shall devour
    them.

---

12. This verse seems to be repetitive, but it illustrates the fact that Israel is being taught her lesson so thoroughly that she cannot have any excuse for neglecting it. What vs. 10 terms her stubborn folly is now fully exposed. The thought of vs. 12 is closely associated with that of vs. 9. The Hebrew word *'ethnāh,* which is used here, probably means "love reward," and there is an assonance between it and the preceding word for fig tree, *te'ēnāh.* That Yahweh should make Israel's **vines** and **fig trees** into a forest is a strange and unexpected figure. If it is original, we must understand, as William R. Harper does (*A Critical and Exegetical Commentary on Amos and Hosea* [New York: Charles Scribner's Sons, 1910; "International Critical Commentary"], p. 231), that **forest** here signifies "not the dignified and stately forest . . . , but the inaccessible brushwood." It is of interest, however, that the LXX reads εἰς μαρτύριον, which means that the Hebrew text before the translators was לעד instead of the M.T. ליער. The LXX text gives excellent sense by describing the devastation of the vines and fig trees wrought by the beasts of the field as a "witness" of Yahweh's discipline and correction. At the end of the verse the LXX adds καὶ τὰ πετεινὰ τοῦ οὐρανοῦ καὶ τὰ ἑρπετὰ τῆς γῆς.

---

beauty to ashes—which was what Israel discovered long ago, as Hosea taught, by decking **herself with her earrings, and her jewels,** running **after her lovers,** and forgetting God. Disillusionment and disgust are still the fruits of sin and always will be. Joseph Wood Krutch comments upon the characters described by Huxley and Hemingway as follows:

In a generally devaluated world they are eagerly endeavoring to get what they can in the pursuit of satisfactions which are sufficiently instinctive to retain inevitably a modicum of animal pleasure, but they cannot transmute that simple animal pleasure into anything else. They themselves not infrequently share the contempt with which their creator regards them, and nothing could be less seductive, because nothing could be less glamorous, than the description of the debaucheries born of nothing except a sense of the emptiness of life.[3]

The gaiety of sin is real. There is pleasure in sin, but it is short-lived. It is the sort of pleasure that comes from a narcotic—effective while it lasts, but soon to wear off; and if persisted in, calling for ever larger doses at more frequent intervals. It is the sort of pleasure that comes from intoxication. "Drink is the shortest way out of Manchester," but suddenly you are back in Manchester again, less able to cope with its problem than before your "escape." It is

[3] *The Modern Temple* (New York: Harcourt, Brace & Co., 1929), p. 99.

here that sin's deception is most complete. Its lure lies in its promise of happiness. But the mirth soon comes to an end. The author of Heb. 11:25 speaks wisely of those who "enjoy the pleasures of sin for a season." And it is a short season. Man is so created that he never finds lasting pleasure in the violation of his personality. Lust springs up readily and as quickly cools, while love continues and grows as life matures.

12. Sin Brings Destruction.—Israel's **vines and her fig trees** will be laid waste and turned into brushwood, the wild beasts will devour them. This ancient picture of the destruction evil brings has been given an incredibly vast modern setting. Two world wars in the first half of the twentieth century should speak so loudly of the destructive nature of sin as to make arguments about it seem superfluous and wholly unnecessary. Our world has indeed been laid waste, its devastation unprecedented. Its choicest treasures have been turned into brushwood and worse—into rubble; indeed, into oblivion. They have "gone up in smoke," as we say. **The beasts of the field shall eat them.** Wild beasts, once the most dread symbol of ferocity, are as harmless house pets compared with our modern implements of destruction.

If one does not in some sense hold God responsible for the destruction, individually and socially, which sin creates, then one admits that God is not in full control of his world—an ob-

13 And I will visit upon her the days of Baalim, wherein she burned incense to them, and she decked herself with her earrings and her jewels, and she went after her lovers, and forgat me, saith the LORD.

14 ¶ Therefore, behold, I will allure her, and bring her into the wilderness, and speak comfortably unto her.

13 And I will punish her for the feast days of the Ba'als
when she burned incense to them
and decked herself with her ring and jewelry,
and went after her lovers,
and forgot me, says the LORD.
14 "Therefore, behold, I will allure her,
and bring her into the wilderness,
and speak tenderly to her.

---

13. Israel will be punished for all the festivals of the Baals which she has kept, when she decked herself in all her festival finery and ornaments and became so absorbed in the cultivation of her lovers that she wholly forgot Yahweh.

It seems clear that this whole passage, vss. 2-13, is dealing not with Hosea's wife and her faithless conduct and her pursuit of her lovers, but with erring Israel and her service of the Baals. But while the children of such a mother must indeed suffer for her sins, Hosea makes his appeal to these children to turn their mother from her shameful career.

3. RESTORATION AND REBETROTHAL (2:14-23=Hebrew 2:16-25)

This section is composed of three subsections. Vss. 14-15 describe Yahweh's persuasion of Israel to return to the attitude of trust and covenant love which characterized the wilderness period, and Israel responds; vss. 16-20 tell how all traces of Baal worship will be eliminated from her life, the new covenant will embrace the whole of God's creation, and he and Israel will be betrothed again; vss. 21-23 say that all the bounties of the earth will come to Israel, not as rewards to which she is entitled in respect of her service, but as gracious gifts of a loving God who is ever mindful of the needs of his people.

It should be kept in mind that the transition from the punishment threatened in vss. 9-13 to the promises of a new day, which are contained in the verses before us, is provided by vss. 6-7, where it is said that Israel has so far responded to Yahweh's disciplinary treatment of her that she is resolved to return to him if for no other reason than her own selfish good.

a) INVITATION AND RESPONSE (2:14-15=Hebrew 2:16-17)

14-15. This verse speaks not of what Israel will do as a result of her chastening, but of what Yahweh will do for her. The time has now come for him to win his bride

---

server rather than creator and ruler. It must be made clear, however, that to hold God responsible for the wages of sin is not to say that he desires or plans it. "It is not the will of your Father . . . that one of these little ones should perish" (Matt. 18:14). From God comes our destruction in the sense that he has created a universe that is law abiding, and its laws cannot be broken with impunity. It is not foolproof. "Our world is closed in by a groundwork of moral necessities that we cannot disregard without breaking our head against a wall."[4] Man is free to do as he pleases, but not to escape the consequences of his choice. Moreover, the eye of faith sees in the very **forest** and **beasts**, not symbols of vindictiveness, but God's

[4] Gregory Vlastos, "God of Wrath," *Christian Century,* LII (1935), 539.

messengers of love to inspire repentance and bring redemption. "I kill, and I make alive; I wound, and I heal" (Deut. 32:39).

14. *Finding God in Unlikely Places.*—Here the mood of Hosea changes from severity to tenderness, from judgment to mercy. And mercy is the deeper truth. God now will speak comfortably unto her, "speak to her heart" (Moffatt). In any event, the **wilderness** seems an unlikely place in which to find strength or comfort. For one thing, it is an uncultivated, uninhabited, barren region—from our human point of view a strange setting for the divine comfort. If we wanted to speak words of comfort to someone, would we choose such desolate surroundings? Yet God often does that. His choicest revelations have come in unlikely places.

again, and he will do it as he did at the first. **Therefore . . . I will allure her, and bring her into the wilderness, and speak comfortably unto her.** The Hebrew verb which is rendered here as **allure** is often used in a bad sense, viz., "seduce" or "entice," but it is used here in a good sense. It may be that Hosea, who idealized the wilderness period in Israel's early history, actually thought of the people as being taken out of Palestine into the wilderness, that in such a place of treasured memories the reunion of Yahweh and his people might take place. But on the other hand he may have meant by the use of the figure a time of austerity, a time when life would be reduced to its simplicities, and Israel, her eyes unclouded by the deceptive façade of the works of man and her appetites undisturbed by the bounties of nature, might have the quietness of spirit and the inclination of heart to listen to Yahweh's words to her. These words will not now be words of condemnation, but of comfort, spoken to the heart (cf. Isa. 40:1; Ruth 2:13). Israel had gone away from her husband because she believed that it was to the Baals that she owed the fruits of the earth. In the wilderness she will be taught the truth, for there the Baals have no power.

And there I will give her her vineyards
and make the Valley of Achor a door of hope.

The deepest insights of the O.T. did not come from the era of Solomon's reign, when Israel was prosperous and flourishing. They came out of the wilderness of Sinai, with its privations and insecurity, from the Exile and captivity. Even as the stars shine brightest when the night is darkest, so out of experiences that seem dark and dismal God often speaks to the heart. This is true also of the N.T. The most precious truths of Christianity did not come to the church when she was at ease. "Woe to them that are at ease in Zion" (Amos 6:1). Nothing significant comes to or from the church that is at ease, whether in Zion or anywhere else. The Christian faith came out of persecution, imprisonment, hardships—out of the shadow of a cross. It is an amazing fact that the Sermon on the Mount, the ethical insights of which are still so far ahead of us that we have hardly begun to catch up with them, was preached in the shadow of Nero's throne. Out of the darkness of a pagan empire came the light of the world.

It is no coincidence then that God should **allure** Israel to the wilderness to speak to her heart. We begin to understand why, when he wanted to deliver the Israelites, he did not lead them to Canaan by the direct route but "through the way of the wilderness" (Exod. 13:18), a forty-year journey of hard, barren, and desolate experiences. The lap of luxury is often too comfortable a state from which to be aroused by the divine summons. "Jeshurun waxed fat, and kicked" (Deut. 32:15). Good for him that he kicked! We should not have been surprised to read that "Jeshurun waxed fat, and slept." God does more for us and through us when the waters are stirred than when they are stagnant.

The **wilderness** is not only a barren place, but a lonely place. We crowd the parks, but there are no crowds in the wilderness. Perhaps God chose to speak to Israel in the wilderness because there she would be alone. The soul needs solitude to hear his voice. "He withdrew himself into the wilderness, and prayed" (Luke 5:16). There are two sides to the Christian life, the solitary and the social, being alone and being together. Both are important. Great experiences come to Christians in fellowship. The church was born in such a fellowship. "When the day of Pentecost had come, they were all together in one place" (Acts 2:1). On any given Sunday morning, barring Easter, less than a half of all Protestant Christians are together. No wonder Protestantism limps. As our foolish and false ecclesiastical barriers are broken down, and our togetherness becomes more horizontal and less perpendicular, this wider fellowship will stimulate and enrich. Never mind how much wood there is, we cannot start a fire until we bring the sticks together. "One loving spirit sets another on fire," said Ambrose.

Having said all this, however, it must be said also that the soul which does not know solitude can hardly know the God whom Jesus revealed. "Enter into thy closet, and when thou hast shut thy door, pray to thy Father which is in secret" (Matt. 6:6). It is no accident that we read of Jesus' withdrawing himself. A soul without solitude would be like a family that is never alone, but entertains and stages parties morning, noon, and night, seven days a week. "Company is good even to the grave." Yet it is necessary at times to shut the door. Even that is no guarantee of being alone. Turn a button and presto the world you have just shut out is

15 And I will give her her vineyards from thence, and the valley of Achor for a door of hope: and she shall sing there, as in the days of her youth, and as in the day when she came up out of the land of Egypt.

15 And there I will give her her vineyards,
and make the Valley of Achor a door of hope.
And there she shall answer as in the days of her youth,
as at the time when she came out of the land of Egypt.

The words Hosea uses here make it plain that he was no Rechabite. The time in the wilderness was to be for the cleansing and renewal of Israel but the wilderness was not to be a place of permanent retreat. "Back to your tents, O Israel"; yes, but for a time and for a purpose.

The Hebrew משם may mean **there** (RSV) or **from thence** (KJV); the latter is the more likely in the present context. Some scholars would emend ו משם to ושמתי ("I will make"), but that disturbs the rhythmic balance of the line. Emendation as suggested by G. R. Driver has much to commend it (cf. "Notes and Studies," *Journal of Theological Studies,* XXXIX [1938], 155). He proposes that the original text read, for משם, a place name such as משמה or שממה, each signifying a desolate place:

> And I will give her her vineyards in Meshammah,
> and the valley of Achor as a door of hope.

In the valley of Achor Israel had had a distressful experience during their entrance into Palestine (cf. Josh. 7:25-26; Isa. 65:10); now that place of unhappy memory will be **a door of hope** on this new day. And Yahweh will have the joy of seeing Israel making

---

in again, as the radio shouts its presence; turn another one and you not only hear it but see it through television. If it was ever true it is now—"The world is too much with us." Said a poor woman in a tenement: "I throw my apron over my head when I want solitude; it is all that I can get."[5] Life is crowded. It moves fast and furiously. But man needs to be alone. "Religion is what the individual does with his own solitariness. If you are never solitary you are never religious."[6]

We are wont to associate solitariness with rampant individualism. "I love to be alone," said the individualist Thoreau. "I never found the companion that was so companionable as solitude."[1] In a Christian sense, however, solitude is not selfish individualism. When God speaks to us in the solitude of the wilderness, as he did to Jesus in the temptation, it is that we may be fitted to take his message to the multitude. He spoke to Moses in the lonely recesses of Mount Horeb, and Moses became the founder of a great nation; to Elijah in a mountain cave, and Elijah became a towering statesman prophet; to John the Baptist in the desert, and John started a reform movement

[5] Robert R. Wicks, *The Reason for Living* (New York: Charles Scribner's Sons, 1934), p. 227.
[6] A. N. Whitehead, *Religion in the Making* (New York: The Macmillan Co., 1926), p. 16.
[1] *Walden,* "Solitude."

in Judea. All these great souls and others like them were lured into the wilderness of solitude. God spoke to each of them alone. But what he said to them, though personal, was not private. It is still in the solitude that God speaks to the heart.

15. A Door of Hope.—If a wilderness is a strange place to find comfort, surely a **valley** is an equally strange place to find hope. We are wont to associate hope with the hilltops, where wide horizons beckon, where the view is unobstructed and the very elevation tends to uplift the spirit. Yet Hosea says that down in the **valley,** where it is dark and maybe dank, and impinging walls shut off the view of everything save the sky above, there God puts **a door of hope.**

Notice that the prophet does not say, "When you are in the vale of trouble, cheer up, you will soon get out of it; it will not be long now, presently you will be on the hilltop and you can hope again." This is not what is meant at all. He says, "Right there and now, while you are in the vale of trouble, that very vale will be transformed into your door of hope. Hope will spring out of the very experience that seems most hopeless." The students of Charles Sylvester Horn were quite disappointed once when they saw his garden. They had heard him speak of it as the place whence came most of his inspiring thoughts. Yet how unpretentious

16 And it shall be at that day, saith the LORD, *that* thou shalt call me Ishi; and shalt call me no more Baali.

17 For I will take away the names of Baalim out of her mouth, and they shall no more be remembered by their name.

18 And in that day will I make a covenant for them with the beasts of the field, and with the fowls of heaven, and *with* the creeping things of the ground: and I will

16 "And in that day, says the LORD, you will call me, 'My husband,' and no longer will you call me, 'My Ba'al.' 17 For I will remove the names of the Ba'als from her mouth, and they shall be mentioned by name no more. 18 And I will make for you*g* a covenant on that day with the beasts of the field,

g Heb *them*

---

response to his wooing of her; her heart will be won over again. The Hebrew verb which is rendered here as **answer** can have several meanings, e.g., "suffer" (not suitable here), **sing,** and, in terms of the Arabic *rhana,* "stay," or (most interestingly and certainly appositely) "be satisfied with one's husband"; but it is doubtful if any of these is an improvement upon **answer** (cf. Israel Eitan, "Biblical Studies," *Hebrew Union College Annual,* XIV [1939], 1).

b) CLEANSING AND REBETROTHAL (2:16-20=Hebrew 2:18-22)

16. Here Israel is addressed in the second person singular, spoken of in the third person singular and again in the third person plural, and finally addressed in the second person singular. Such extreme fluidity of reference is unlikely to have been original. Either we should regard vss. 16, 17, 18 and vss. 19-20 as originally separate fragments, or we should follow the RSV and read **you** for **them** in vs. 18, or accept the third person singular of the LXX in vs. 16, and thus harmonize it with vss. 17-18. In vs. 16 it is said that in the new day Israel will not use the seductive term Baal for Yahweh, but will use the term which can cause no confusion of thought and has no corrupting associations, **Ishi,** i.e., **My husband.** In other words, every token and remnant of Baal worship will be removed.

17. The purpose of this verse is to drive home the significance of what is said in vs. 16. That is no reason for regarding it as a gloss. A prophet of ancient Israel, no less than a modern preacher, may make use of repetition in order to drive a lesson home; and this in the eyes of Hosea was a most important lesson.

18-20. These verses are regarded by some authorities as a later addition to the book, but there does not seem to be adequate reason for such a judgment. The ideas expressed have their counterpart in other parts of the book whose authenticity is not called in question; e.g., 4:3 speaks of a corruption which has affected not only human beings but the rest of creation, a teaching in line with that of a cosmic fall. That he who often

---

it actually seemed! "Why, Doctor," said one of the boys, "surely this is not the garden where all your inspiring thoughts come." "Oh, yes," he replied. "But it is so small," the student protested. "Yes," said the professor, pointing to the sky, "but look how high it is." The **valley,** never mind how deep or dark, is arched by the sky. It is high, and in that dimension if we but knew lies our main ground for **hope.** Our world is wide but flat; it lacks altitude, heights. It was Henry Drummond who said that when the outlook is bad we should try the uplook. And in the providence of God the deepest **valley** gives an uplook.

16. *My Husband, My Baal.*—In that day. What day? The day of Israel's renewed fellow-

ship with God. How one thinks of God depends on one's inner attitude. The God of the rebellious or defiant is not the God of the penitent. The antithesis between **my husband** and **my Baal** marks the difference between Israel penitent and Israel defiant. The nature of truth is such that its discovery depends on the attitude of the seeker. This change from **my Baal** to **my husband** does not indicate a change in the nature of God; it indicates a change in the nature of man.

17-18a. *God's Covenant with Man and Nature.*—It is good to be reminded of our kinship with the animal world. The domestication of animals marked a real step in the civilizing of man. Some of us are wont to lavish on animals

break the bow and the sword and the battle out of the earth, and will make them to lie down safely.

19 And I will betroth thee unto me for ever; yea, I will betroth thee unto me in righteousness, and in judgment, and in loving-kindness, and in mercies.

the birds of the air, and the creeping things of the ground; and I will abolish[h] the bow, the sword, and war from the land; and I will make you lie down in safety. 19 And I will betroth you to me for ever; I will betroth you to me in righteousness and in justice, in steadfast love, and in mercy.

[h] Heb break

---

bewailed the political intrigues and strifes of his day should now, in this new day for Israel, look forward to the cessation of strife and warfare is surely not unexpected. And that one who had spoken of Israel's broken covenant with Yahweh (cf. 4:1-2) should look forward to a rebetrothal is surely the form which his hopes were bound to take.

18. The renewal of the covenant between Yahweh and his bride Israel is represented as a new creation (cf. 13:13) in which the strifes and the combativeness of the former order have no longer any place. There are several passages in the O.T. which give expression to the belief that the enmity of **the beasts of the field** toward man is a penalty of man's fall, and that in the day of man's restoration and reconciliation to God that combativeness will cease and the beasts will live together in a covenant of peace (cf. Lev. 26:6; Num. 22:21-30; Isa. 11:6-9; 65:25; Ezek. 34:25; Job 5:23). Wars also will cease so that Israel will be enabled to live securely (cf. Isa. 2:4; 9:4-5; Zech. 9:10; Ps. 46:9). That will be a manifest sign of God's blessing.

19-20. Israel must be raised to the fullness of the true relationship with her God; there must be developed that fellowship, not degradingly physical as that with the Baals had been, but spiritually pure and elevating, by which Israel will be made in the full sense the people of God. This new betrothal of Israel by Yahweh has several notes. It will be **for ever**; it will not be a fragile bond, easily broken, but will remain steady and unshaken. Again, it will be **in righteousness and in justice, in steadfast love, and in**

---

more love and care than we bestow upon our fellow men. Surely this is wrong. Yet we must admit that no small part of our pleasure as human beings derives from our relationship with the animal world. Francis of Assisi referred to the birds as his "little brothers," and felt the compassion of God reaching out to them. In both O.T. and N.T. nature is regarded as sacramental. When the prophets visualized the redeemed earth, they pictured it as one in which even the wild beasts would lose their ferocity (Isa. 11:6-7, 9). Paul links man with the world of nature when he says that "the whole creation groaneth and travaileth in pain together until now, . . . waiting for the adoption, to wit, the redemption of our body" (Rom. 8:22-23). Not only wild animals need taming, but wild men also. You can keep wild animals in a zoo—fence them in. The fact that man is free makes immeasurably more difficult the problem of his untamed, rebellious spirit. "Harnessing the cave man" is our biggest problem.

18b. Security in Disarmament.—What a strange statement! The way to be secure is to get rid of our munitions, wipe them out. We say, "To be secure we must increase muni-

tions." Could we be mistaken? To have a stockpile of atomic bombs potentially capable of destroying every major city in the world is not to have security. The truth seems to be that man's insecurity increases with the destructive power of his armaments.

It may be questioned whether in any imperfect world, with power-hungry dictators on the loose, any peace-loving nation could find security in wiping out its defenses. Yet the prophet's insight is valid as applied to the total human scene. No nation is now secure by arming itself to the teeth, since its power incites some other nation to greater power. The balance of power seldom balances. Man's real hope for peace lies in collective security, which seeks to eliminate the armament race by making force an agent of law.

Hosea's insight that real security lies not in having munitions but in getting rid of them is valid. But his principle must be applied to all nations. Munitions must be wiped out, not from one nation but from all nations, if security is our aim. There is no security in armaments. That lesson history teaches with tragic reiteration. Armaments breed fear and distrust, not confidence and good will. They arouse suspicion

20 I will even betroth thee unto me in faithfulness: and thou shalt know the LORD.

20 I will betroth you to me in faithfulness; and you shall know the LORD.

mercy. (For an exposition of the meaning of these terms, cf. Norman H. Snaith, *The Distinctive Ideas of the Old Testament* [Philadelphia: Westminster Press, 1946], especially pp. 140-44, and *Mercy and Sacrifice* [London: Student Christian Movement Press, 1953], pp. 70 ff.) These are all great words. **Righteousness** and **justice** are words much used by Amos; they speak of the consistent dealings of God, who is no respecter of persons and never acts arbitrarily or unjustly, and of the demands and obligations of God's service which are laid upon man. But that is not all. If it were all, Israel could never be restored. The divine qualities of mercy and love, which must be the means of redeeming Israel, would not now cease their redemptive work. God's mercies would never fail; the covenant love which must exist between husband and wife if they are to live together in happiness and peace would hold together in willing bond Yahweh and his wife Israel. Third, the betrothal will be **in faithfulness.** That means it will remain steadfast and immovable (cf., e.g., "hold fast my covenant" [Isa. 56:4, 6]). It is particularly notable that these verses finish with the words **and thou shalt know the LORD.** In the former days Israel had not really known Yahweh; hence her service of the Baals. Now she will know him and that will be the ground of her spiritual assurance and peace (cf. Job 19:25; II Tim. 1:12). Martin Buber says truly: "This last word, 'knowing,' is in the book of Hosea the proper concept of reciprocity in the relationship between God and the people. 'To know' here does not signify the perception of an object by a subject, but the intimate contact of the two partners of a two-sided occurrence" (*The Prophetic Faith* [New York: The Macmillan Co., 1949], p. 115).

on the part of those against whom they might be used, and a desire to use them on the part of those who possess them. "Not by might, nor by power, but by my Spirit, saith the LORD of hosts" (Zech. 4:6). In love, not force; in good will, not fear; in justice, not oppression; in righteousness, not licentiousness; in short, in God, not man, lies human security.

When our Lord made his triumphal entry into Jerusalem, Matthew records that the people cried out in the words of the prophet: "Behold thy King cometh unto thee, meek" (Matt. 21:5). A meek king! Christ placed his trust in spiritual rather than in material power. This king who approached Jerusalem in triumph was armed, but not with the weapons of this world. While Israel's rulers relied on the power of the sword, Jesus relied on the power of the spirit. Once as the crisis deepened the impetuous Peter drew the sword, but Christ told him to put it away. The very nature of the kingdom he was about to establish was such that it could not be defended or maintained by brute force. It was a spiritual kingdom and so had to be brought by spiritual means. Christ aimed not to conquer men but to win them; not to overpower but to persuade; not to enslave but to liberate. His kingdom would have no visible, earthly capital or center. It would lay claim to all capitals. Its real seat would be in men's hearts. Those who try to conquer the earth

have their day and cease to be. The conqueror is conquered. The earth belongs to the Schweitzers, Grenfells, Booths. Our Tojos, Mussolinis, Hitlers, and other tyrants have had their reward!

20. God: Husband and Father.—Hosea employs two figures in describing the compassion of God for man: the divine Husband and the divine Father. Such symbols as applied to deity are anthropomorphic. Yet how could finite man represent the Infinite but by symbols taken from his own experience? We know, as Isaiah says, that God's ways are not our ways, nor his thoughts our thoughts. Even so we must think of him in terms meaningful to us. Herein lies the significance of the Incarnation, the Eternal taking the form of our human flesh.

Our most valued symbol for God is not the divine Husband but the divine Father. Only once does Paul use the metaphor of the divine Husband (II Cor. 11:2), and theologians seldom if ever employ it. The figure of God as a divine Husband was not original with Hosea. It was common practice in all Semitic religions to express the union of God with his land or people through the figure of marriage. Invariably, however, the union was conceived of in purely physical terms, and so led to sensuous and immoral rites. Hosea rescued this figure from its debasing connotations and gave it a wholly moral and spiritual meaning. The relationship is to be wholly moral and ethical.

21 And it shall come to pass in that day, I will hear, saith the LORD, I will hear the heavens, and they shall hear the earth;

22 And the earth shall hear the corn, and the wine, and the oil; and they shall hear Jezreel.

21 "And in that day, says the LORD,
I will answer the heavens
and they shall answer the earth;
22 and the earth shall answer the grain, the wine, and the oil,
and they shall answer Jezreel;*

*That is *God sows*

---

c) FAVOR AND BLESSING (2:21-23=Hebrew 2:23-25)

21-23. These verses speak of material blessings and are therefore in striking contrast with the verses which precede. For that reason their authenticity has been called in question by some scholars. But there is no difficulty in accepting them as genuine. It is true that by adding these verses, Hosea does not lift us to the height of the great protestation of Habakkuk: "Though the fig tree do not blossom, nor fruit be on the vines, . . . yet I will rejoice in the LORD, I will joy in the God of my salvation" (Hab. 3:17-18). Nevertheless Hosea does put the spiritual blessings first; and if he proceeds to mention the material blessings, he is but expressing in this regard the common view of his time, and indeed of a much later time than his, that the good may expect material blessings as a token of God's favor.

Whether, however, we adopt Hosea's metaphor of the divine Husband or of the divine Father, compassion is at the heart of it. And compassion must not be thought of in terms of sentimentalism. God is love, but his love is holy and we are sinful. He is infinite and we are finite. He is from everlasting to everlasting, while we spend our years as a tale that is told. These metaphors, therefore, of tenderness, love, and compassion must not obscure the thought of reverence and humility which befit our creaturehood (see Expos. on 4:1-3).

21-22a. God's Compassion Enfolds Nature.— God's compassion reaches not only to man and the animal world, but also to the inanimate world, with its grain, new wine, and oil. Man should never forget his kinship with nature. The divine Father is nature's creator and ruler. Hosea profoundly loved nature. Here he differed from Amos, his slightly earlier contemporary. Not that Amos, with his emphasis on the righteousness of God, was oblivious to the love of God. Yet there is a tenderness in the one, reaching out from man through the animal world and even to the inanimate world, which is not found in the other. Hosea's work abounds in references to nature—to the rain, the morning cloud, the early dew, to grapes, the fig tree, the olive tree, the odors of Lebanon, the corn, the vine, the grain, the fir tree. "The Book of Amos, when it would praise God's works, looks to the stars. But the poetry of Hosea clings about his native soil like its trailing vines."[2] It is noteworthy that one who had an experi-

ence which seemed to deny the significance of love should have become so evangelistic a prophet of the compassion of God, the divine Husband and Father, whose love touches not only man but the animal world and the inanimate. It is as though his experience were prophetic of the experience of the Master, who through his cross teaches the same lesson. He was a greater poet than Hosea and his life a perfect poem. With bold strokes he too sketched those areas of life which Hosea sees God encompassing, the human, animal, and inanimate, and like Hosea, he claimed them for God. He never doubted God's love for man. God, like the shepherd, leaves the ninety and nine and seeks the one who has gone astray and is now lost. He saw the compassion of God reaching to the animal creation; he declared that not one sparrow "will fall to the ground unless your Father wills it" (Matt. 10:29 Moffatt). His parables spoke eloquently of God's care for nature—"Even Solomon in all his glory was not arrayed like one of these" (Matt. 6:29).

For so the whole round earth is every way
Bound by gold chains about the feet of God.[3]

22b-23. Sowing and Reaping.—In his parable of the wicked husbandman Jesus represents God as planting a vineyard, "My Father is the husbandman" (John 15:1). Is not every great harvest a planting of the Lord? Sometimes the planting may seem small, no bigger than the grain of mustard seed. "But when it is sown, it groweth up" (Mark 4:32). Whatever God sows will grow, provided *we* give it a chance.

[2] George Adam Smith, *The Book of the Twelve Prophets* (rev. ed.; New York: Harper & Bros., 1928), I, 241.

[3] Tennyson, "Morte d'Arthur."

23 And I will sow her unto me in the earth; and I will have mercy upon her that had not obtained mercy; and I will say to *them which were* not my people, Thou *art* my people; and they shall say, *Thou art my God.*

3 Then said the LORD unto me, Go yet, love a woman beloved of *her* friend, yet

23 and I will sow him[j] for myself in the land.
And I will have pity on Not pitied,
  and I will say to Not my people, 'You are my people';
  and he shall say, 'Thou art my God.' "

3 And the LORD said to me, "Go again, love a woman who is beloved of a para-

[j] Cn: Heb *her*

The order of nature and the way of fertility are in this manner, says Hosea. The seed sown in the earth, and the plants which grow there, call upon the earth for those vital juices which are the condition of their life, and the earth does not withhold her benefits. But the earth in turn is dependent upon the heavens for the sun and the rain, and the heavens do not fail to make response to the call of the earth. It is God who rules in the heavens, and according to his beneficent purposes the sun and the rain do not fail. Thus Israel for her food and drink must look to God, and she can do that in the confidence that he will make response. In that new day the name **Jezreel,** by which Israel had been named in the time of her unfaithfulness, will no longer be a name of judgment but of promise, and will sum up the whole work of nature's provision for man's need by its declaration that **God sows** (cf. 1:10–2:1). On Israel that had been named **Not pitied** God now **will have pity,** and to those who had been called **Not my people** he will say **You are my people;** and Israel will make response and say, **Thou art my God.** The initiative in all this saving and redemptive work is with God; except he act in his mercy and love, nothing can happen. But when he does so act, man must make response in willing obedience if the saving and redemptive work is to be complete. God may draw man to himself by the cords of love, but these cords will in the end be broken if man does not respond to their pull and approach God.

D. THE REDEMPTION OF THE ADULTEROUS WIFE (3:1-5)

3:1. And the LORD said to me is an example of an *Ich-bericht* as distinct from the *Er-bericht* of 1:2-9. It might suggest that we have here simply a variant of the earlier passage; but before such a conclusion can be drawn, it is necessary to examine the significance of the words addressed to Hosea: **Go again, love a woman.** There are

---

His seed is indigenous to every soil. The forces of the universe are on its side. Sometimes we do some generous or noble deed that seems unlike us. "The Lord put it in my heart to do that," we say. God sows. Too often, however, the seed falls on stony soil. It has no chance to take root and grow. If God sows, should he not reap? If we really believed that the desire, the strength, the opportunities for honest, creative work, whatever its nature, were gifts from God, "that giveth to all men liberally, and upbraideth not" (Jas. 1:5), would we not give God the glory and realize his claim on the harvest?

3:1. The Love of God: Agapē.—In discussing vss. 1-2 we shall be considering not only the heart of this chapter but the heart of Hosea's message, which is God's love toward those who are not worthy of it. Gripped by this truth, the prophet brought back to his home his wayward wife. She was not worthy of his love, but no more was Israel worthy of God's love. Israel

went after other gods, as did Gomer after other men. Here then is an opportunity to consider the nature of divine love. Of all the qualities we attribute to God—omniscience, omnipresence, omnipotence—none is so basic and meaningful as love: "God is love" (I John 4:8). There is a great difference, however, between divine love and human love. Hosea discovered it; Christ revealed it; the church must preach it.

The difference is seen when we recall that in English we have only one word for love, and we use this for all objects. Thus we might say, "I love my friend," "I love music," "I love God." In the Greek, however, there are three different words. Two of them concern us now. One is *erōs*, a word which never occurs in the N.T., though constantly used in classical Greek; the other is *agapē*, a word which is never used in classical Greek, but is used almost exclusively in the N.T. In classical Greek, if one should say, "I love you," he would use the word *erōs*,

two views concerning the syntax of the Hebrew word עוֹד here: (a) We may conjoin it with the preceding words, as, e.g., A. B. Ehrlich (*Randglossen zur hebräischen Bibel* [Leipzig: J. C. Hinrichs, 1912], V, 170-71) and R. H. Pfeiffer (*Introduction to the Old Testament* [New York: Harper & Bros., 1941], p. 567) have done, and translate thus: "And the Lord said to me again: Go, love a woman. . . ." This would imply that the woman referred to was not Gomer, but another woman. According to Pfeiffer the instruction given to the prophet in this instance should be understood symbolically, and Gomer is to be regarded as a wife who preserved complete conjugal fidelity, the adultery mentioned of her in 1:2 signifying spiritual unfaithfulness to Yahweh (cf. L. W. Batten, "Hosea's Message and Marriage," *Journal of Biblical Literature,* XLVIII [1929], 257-73; Fück, "Hosea Kapital 3," *Zeitschrift für die alttestamentliche Wissenschaft,* XXXIX [1921], 283-90). (b) The Masoretes, by accenting אֵלַי with *rebhîa* and אִשָּׁה with *zāqēph qāṭôn,* clearly indicated that a minor pause falls at אֵלַי, and that has the effect of conjoining עוֹד with the following words. This syntactical treatment is supported by the ancient versions, is accepted by the majority of modern scholars, and should be followed.

But there are two possible renderings of עוֹד when it is construed in this way. Since it may indicate the continuance or the repetition of an action, we may translate the first phrase of the address to Hosea as "Go on loving a woman" or **Go again, love a woman.** According to the former of these translations the woman is quite certainly the Gomer of ch. 1, and this chapter introduces a sequel to 1:2-9; that it is an *Ich-bericht* may be explained as due to the fact that the intimate experience which it recounts was known only to the prophet himself, whereas the names of his children and the significance of the names would be known to all his disciples. The latter translation could mean that another woman was now involved, but such a view is untenable in face of the comparison which is made with Yahweh's love for erring Israel. We should therefore

---

designating the love of natural affection, human love. But in the N.T., if one should say, "I love you," he would use *agapē,* symbol of the divine love. It is the divine love that Hosea discovered and Christ made known.

Mark Rutherford writes: "In the love of a woman to the man who is of no account God has provided us with a true testimony of what is in His own heart."[4] Yet there is a quality in the love of God which is not found in human love, romantic love, even at its best. Human love is evoked because of something lovable to us, though maybe not to another, in the object of our affection. Rutherford says again, "If I were to think that my wife's devotion to me is nothing more than the simple expression of a necessity to love somebody, that there is nothing in me which justifies such devotion, I should be miserable."[5] That is perfectly natural and quite human. Hosea, however, discovered a deeper truth which Christ gave his life to reveal and amplify, viz., that divine love is evoked without any merit in the loved object. Something "in me . . . justifies . . . devotion." But that is precisely what differentiates Christian love, *agapē* love, from *erōs,* human love. Nothing "in me" justifies it. The word "love"

[4] William Hale White, *Mark Rutherford's Deliverance* (London: T. Fisher Unwin, n.d.), p. 109.
[5] *Ibid.,* p. 108.

is like an old ship in which Christ put a new cargo. We might say that when Judaism sent that old ship into port everyone knew its cargo was consigned to a certain few, those who merited it, the righteous. "The mercy of the Lord is from everlasting to everlasting upon them that fear him, and his righteousness unto children's children; to such as keep his covenant, and to those that remember his commandments to do them" (Ps. 103:17-18). The love of God was thus limited to those who feared him and remembered his commandments, to those who merited it. If the Jews by and large limited God's love to those who were morally qualified, the Greeks thought the divine love belonged to those who were intellectually qualified. But whom does God love? To this question Aristotle replies:

He who lives according to reason is the special object of God's love. For if the gods, as is commonly believed, take thought for our human affairs, we must rationally conclude that they take most pleasure in that which is best and most nearly related to themselves, that is, in our reason. . . . It is clear that this is most of all the case with the wise man. Therefore it is he who is most loved by the god.[6]

So, according to the Greeks, when the ship came into port, its cargo was consigned to the

[6] *Nichomachean Ethics* X. 8. 13.

an adulteress, according to the love of the
LORD toward the children of Israel, who
look to other gods, and love flagons of wine.

mour and is an adulteress; even as the
LORD loves the people of Israel, though they
turn to other gods and love cakes of raisins."

---

take the force of the words to be: "Go again, in spite of all that has happened, love your
wife, though she is a woman who is loved of a paramour and adulterous. You know
that your love for her is undiminished; only your love can help her now and save her.
Go again and love her."

In the description of the woman which follows there are two points to be noted.
The LXX ἀγαπῶσαν shows that the translators understood the participle as active,
not passive, and the Syriac supports this. Since the woman is condemned for her willful
erring and is not represented as a weak creature who was led astray, the ancient versions
may be correct in their interpretation. Nowack makes the interesting suggestion that the
Masoretes pointed the participle passive "either to show that she was no longer able to
love, all love having gone out of her, or in order to absolve the woman" (*Die kleinen
Propheten, ad loc.*). But if the passive is read, we should not follow the KJV, **beloved
of her friend, yet an adulteress** (since in such a context the Hebrew term רֵעַ would
normally signify not husband but paramour), but consider the two phrases as parallel,
i.e., as in the RSV, **beloved of a paramour and . . . an adulteress.** A. Douglas Tushingham
has recently developed the view that the term "beloved of a paramour" had specific
cultic references (cf. "A Reconsideration of Hosea, Chapters 1-3," *Journal of Near
Eastern Studies,* XII [1953], 150-59).

Cakes of raisins, mentioned here as being used in the service of the Baals, were
characteristic of the autumn vintage festival, being made of pressed grapes and fine
meal. They are mentioned in Isa. 16:7 in connection with Moab, and in Jer. 7:18 as
used by worshipers of the queen of heaven; on one festive occasion David distributed
such cakes to the people (II Sam. 6:19). O. C. Whitehouse (*Isaiah* [New York: Oxford
University Press, 1905; "New-Century Bible"], Vol. I, p. 212, n. 5) draws attention to
an interesting parallel from ancient Cyprus. Even if אֲהֻבִי is in the construct state, it

---

wise, those who were intellectually qualified.
But Christ gave a new meaning to that old
word. He made love available not just for the
righteous—"I am not come to call the righteous,
but sinners to repentance" (Matt. 9:13); not
just for the wise—"I praise thee, Father, . . .
for hiding all this from the wise and learned
and revealing it to the simple-minded" (Matt.
11:25 Moffatt); but for all mankind irrespective
of their intellectual, moral, or social condition.
When now the old ship pulled into port, not
only the righteous and the wise would crowd
the docks with expectant heart. There would
come also the lame, the halt, the blind, the
sick, the sinful. Here was something for them
also, in a sense especially for them—not because they merited it, but because God is love.

Neither the Hebrew nor the Greek mind
could understand Christian love, and that is
why they could not understand the Cross. "We
preach Christ crucified," said Paul, "unto the
Jews a stumblingblock, and unto the Greeks
foolishness" (I Cor. 1:23). The Cross was a
stumbling block to the Jews because it made
shipwreck of their self-righteous pride. It shattered the old legalistic, mercenary conception

of God's love as being limited to the righteous.
The Cross was foolishness to the Greeks because it made havoc of their intellectual pride,
which limited the interest of God to the wise.
But the love of the Cross, *agapē* love, was not
limited to those who merited or deserved it.
The love of the Cross was voiced by Paul: "For
scarcely for a righteous man will one die: yet
peradventure for a good man some would even
dare to die. But God commendeth his love
toward us, in that, while we were yet sinners,
Christ died for us" (Rom. 5:7-8).

This is the gospel of Hosea. **Go, . . . love a
woman, . . . an adulteress.** Hosea could not do
that with human love. For what could have
been lovable in such a person? In taking back
his wife he was manifesting the love of God
toward the children of Israel. This is what
gives a truly evangelical note to Hosea's prophecy. He was the first to discover that the divine
love goes out to us not because we are worthy
of it but because God is love, so that when we
say that God loves man, we are not told what
man is like but what God is like. And this is
the message that Christ, who died on the Cross
for sinful men, proclaims.

2 So I bought her to me for fifteen *pieces* of silver, and *for* a homer of barley, and a half homer of barley:	2 So I bought her for fifteen shekels of silver

should be taken as a parallel participle to the absolute פנים: there is nothing to support Sellin's view that it is the gods who love the raisin cakes (*Das Zwölfprophetenbuch, ad loc.*).

2. So I bought her: Why Hosea had to buy back his wife is not clear. If she had returned to her parents' house there would have been no need for Hosea to buy her back. (For the view that the verb used signifies "to acquire legal possession" by means of a payment, see A. Douglas Tushingham, *op. cit.*) The money must have been paid either to the paramour for the loss of his mistress, or, if Gomer was now a slave, to the master in whose service she was. The price paid was **fifteen shekels of silver and a homer and a lethech of barley.** The term **lethech** is unknown. The LXX νέβελ οἴνου renders a different but no more intelligible Hebrew text (נבל שכר). There is a tradition (cf. Midrash Shebuoth 6³; Talmud Shebuoth 43ᵃ) that the lethech was a measure equal to **a half homer.** Why part of the price was paid in cash and part in kind is not indicated. If the **barley** represented the maintenance of the woman for a certain period, then it could not, as Klostermann suggested, have reference to the period of the woman's separation before full married status was restored, but must have been paid to the paramour or to the master, as the case might be (cf. *ibid.*, p. 48). There has of course been a common tendency to think of Gomer as redeemed from slavery because of a line of argument based upon II Kings 7:18; Exod. 21:32. According to the former of these verses, barley was sold during a period of severe stringency in ninth-century Samaria at half a shekel per seah. Presumably prices at that time were abnormally high owing to the prevailing conditions, and if the normal price of barley had been a third of a shekel per seah, that would have meant ten shekels per homer; the total price which Hosea paid for Gomer must have been, according to this calculation, thirty shekels. And since Exod. 21:32 gives that as the amount of compensation to be

"Love your enemies," said he (Luke 6:27). It cannot be done with human love, for human love is evoked by that which is lovable in the loved object, and there is nothing lovable in one's enemies. But to love one's enemies is not impossible with the divine love. In this love there is nothing sentimental. Divine love is understanding, redeeming, creative. It is a fixed disposition of resolute good will. "On earth peace, good will toward men" (Luke 2:14). There never can be peace on earth until we show the divine *agapē* toward men. "He that dwelleth in love dwelleth in God, and God in him" (I John 4:16). "If ye love them which love you, what reward have ye? . . . What do ye more than others?" (Matt. 5:46-47.) There must be in our hearts something of the spirit of the generous-minded sower who with lavish hand casts his seed not only on good ground, from which he is certain to obtain a good return, but among thorns, on the shallow soil, and on the hard places whence no rich harvest comes in return. For this is the love of God, the God who makes his sun to shine on the evil and on the good, and sends his rain on the just and on the unjust. It is our faith

that this love—the outgoing, unmerited love of God, who "is kind unto the unthankful and to the evil" (Luke 6:35)—still undergirds our life and the life of our world. Herein is our greatest and surest ground for hope.

2. *Love that Redeems.*—Gomer had become a slave, a concubine. She had voluntarily sold herself. Hosea voluntarily bought her back at the price of a slave. This is *agapē*, the love that seeks not its own, that takes no account of evil, that "bears all things, believes all things, hopes all things"—redemptive love (I Cor. 13). No doubt many men since have acted as did Hosea, taken back the unfaithful. One wonders, however, whether their motive has been redemptive. Not unless with their love for the sinner goes a hatred of the sin. In taking back Gomer, Hosea was not "being a good sport," not saying, "I will forgive and forget," not thinking, "Well, I have had my fling, why should she not have had hers?" Hosea's act becomes meaningful when one recalls the kind of man he was, a gentle, sensitive soul of unquestioned integrity, whose personal life had not been smirched or weakened by moral compromise. Sin appears trivial only when the

3 And I said unto her, Thou shalt abide for me many days; thou shalt not play the harlot, and thou shalt not be for *another* man: so *will* I also *be* for thee.

4 For the children of Israel shall abide many days without a king, and without a prince, and without a sacrifice, and with-

and a homer and a lethech of barley. 3 And I said to her, "You must dwell as mine for many days; you shall not play the harlot, or belong to another man; so will I also be to you." 4 For the children of Israel shall

---

paid to the owner for the killing of a slave, it has been concluded that such an amount was a slave's market value and that it was the price which Hosea paid.

3. There is to be a time of separation and discipline for the returned Gomer. The RSV does not quite give the meaning of the original by its translation **You must dwell as mine for many days.** It was undoubtedly Hosea's desire and hope that his wife would now be his constantly. The KJV, by using the word **abide** in place of **dwell,** comes nearer to the meaning, but the full force of the original may be rendered, "For many days you must live [continently] as mine." The purpose of this discipline was that the fever of her passions might die down and she might regain quietness of spirit. The final phrase in the verse, **so will I also be to you,** must mean, in view of the translation of the phrase immediately preceding it, "I also will not be unfaithful to you, nor belong to another woman." But Hosea's constancy to his wife had never been in question. We should therefore regard the force of the negative of the first clause as having effect in the second also, and read: "You shall not have marital relationship, nor will I be a husband to you." This is the meaning arrived at by those who insert לא אלך before the final and not dissimilar אליך.

4. A period of isolation and deprivation for Israel will be prescribed as in the case of the returning Gomer. Israel will be denied **king** and **prince, sacrifice** and sacred **pillar, ephod** and **teraphim.** The specification of king and prince in this context, in which the reference is predominantly to worship and sacred objects, is notable, and some scholars regard it as additional. But no reason can be suggested why a later editor should have added the words, whereas we know how much Hosea felt that the intrigues of kings and princes had turned the minds of the people from their heavenly king. In view of the parallelism between the discipline of unfaithful Gomer and that of unfaithful Israel, we must assume that the things to be denied Israel for **many days** were legitimate aids

---

light within has become darkness. It had not for Hosea. This gives meaning to his act and makes his love redemptive. Is this why our love often lacks redemptive power?

3. *Time for Reflection.*—The prodigal wife, who now is brought back, is told that she must remain for many days in seclusion. During this period she is not only to cease her adulterous ways but must have nothing to do even with her husband. She had been following one course and now is about to start another. To do this is never easy. To do it impulsively, on the spur of the moment, without time for reflection, is often futile. The **many days** of seclusion and restraint would give Gomer time to consider what she had done and what she was now preparing to do.

This insight might be applied to conversion in general. The high-pressure type of evangelism has fallen into disrepute. Unquestionably much good came out of it. Some people were won to Christ by this method who probably

could not have been won in any other way. One of its weaknesses, however, was that it led people to make decisions in the heat of emotional excitement. Some who "hit the sawdust trail" bounced right off again. To be sure, there is such a thing as striking while the iron is hot. Nor can we say that all those who have taken **many days** for reflection have remained faithful. None the less, one cannot escape the conclusion that by whatever method one changes one's course, whether under the pressure of emotional excitement or more deliberately, much would be gained if more people took time, as Gomer was asked to do, to consider the issues involved. "This man began to build, and was not able to finish" (Luke 14:30). He had not counted the cost.

4-5a. *Deprivation the Road to Appreciation.* —As Gomer would be in seclusion, denied contact with men, even with her husband, so now **Israel shall abide many days without a king.** Would this period of deprivation make

out an image, and without an ephod, and *without* teraphim:	dwell many days without king or prince, without sacrifice or pillar, without ephod

which were temporarily prohibited. Hosea often condemns the intrigues and corruption of kings and princes, but he did not regard such rulers as essentially evil. T. H. Robinson (*Die zwölf kleinen Propheten Hosea bis Micha* [Tübingen: J. C. B. Mohr, 1936; "Handbuch zum Alten Testament"], p. 16) very relevantly quotes Gen. 28:18, 22; 31:13; Exod. 24:4 to show the popular favor in which the sacred pillar was held, according to the evidence of the E document, the document of the Northern Kingdom. It may be that after the expiration of the time of prohibition, king and prince, sacrifice and sacred pillar, ephod and teraphim were to be restored to their former place in the community; but in view of Hosea's exaltation of the wilderness ideal, it is more likely that he believed that the time of probation would make plain to Israel the uselessness and unfitness of such aids, and they would abandon them.

The **pillar**, or *maççēbhāh* as it was termed, was a standing stone. It was originally regarded as an abode of deity and was to be found, together with a wooden stump or *'ashērāh*, beside the Canaanite altars. For that reason the instruction was given that they should be destroyed (Exod. 34:13; 23:24; Deut. 7:5; 12:3) and it was enacted that none should be erected (Deut. 16:22; Lev. 26:1). Occasionally, however, they seem to have served as memorials (cf. Gen. 31:45; 35:20; II Sam. 18:18), and the one mentioned in Isa. 19:19, erected to Yahweh on the border of Egypt, should probably be understood in this way (see Millar Burrows, *What Mean These Stones?* [New Haven: American Schools of Oriental Research, 1941], pp. 210-12).

The **ephod** was commonly a vestment worn by gods and their priests in the ancient Near East. Burrows describes it as "a tight sleeveless garment" (cf. *ibid.*, p. 216; H. Thiersch, "Ependytes und Ephod," *Zeitschrift für die alttestamentliche Wissenschaft*, LIII [1935], 180-85); it may have had pockets containing stones of divination. In addition, it was sometimes a portable object, probably an image (I Sam. 23:6, 9; 30:7; *et al.*).

The **teraphim** were images; they performed the function and held the place of household gods. W. F. Albright (*From the Stone Age to Christianity* [Baltimore: Johns Hopkins Press, 1940], p. 238) has suggested that the word means "vile things," while Sellin ("Zu Efod und Terafim," *Zeitschrift für die alttestamentliche Wissenschaft*, LV [1937], 296-98), connecting the word with the Arabic verb *raffa*, "to sparkle," thinks that it signified a garment adorned with precious stones. The passage I Sam. 19:13-16 is commonly quoted to support the view that the teraphim must sometimes have been in human form, but that view is not unquestioned today (cf. W. F. Albright, *Archaeology and the Religion of Israel* [Baltimore: Johns Hopkins Press, 1942], p. 114). The fact that they were consulted tends to prove that they were a relic of ancestor worship (cf. Ezek. 21:21; Zech. 10:2). A text from Nuzi in northern Mesopotamia has now made it clear that when Rachel took with her from Harran the teraphim of her father's house, she thereby secured for her husband the title to the family property (cf. E. A. Speiser,

them value their faith the more? Just as the **many days** of seclusion would help Gomer as she started a new life, so would **many days** of deprivation, doing without the familiar and treasured symbols of her civic and religious life, heighten Israel's appreciation of them.

Few reactions are more deadly than taking things for granted. This evil attitude pervades both our civic and religious life. When our liberties are threatened, we fight for them; the thought of being without them arouses us to action. Yet ordinarily how we take them for granted! As a rule less than half the qualified

voters in a city go to the polls. If, as has actually been the case with so many millions, we were deprived of this privilege; if we were compelled to live **many days** without a free press or free speech, without the booths where we can fearlessly express our political preferences, with what heightened appreciation would we undertake our civic responsibilities!

The same is true of our Christian privileges. About one third of our Protestant Christians participate actively in the work of the church. The greatest obstacle to Christianity is not to be found in those who aggressively oppose it.

5 Afterward shall the children of Israel return, and seek the LORD their God, and David their king; and shall fear the LORD and his goodness in the latter days.

4 Hear the word of the LORD, ye children of Israel. for the LORD hath a controversy with the inhabitants of the land, be-

or teraphim. 5 Afterward the children of Israel shall return and seek the LORD their God, and David their king; and they shall come in fear to the LORD and to his goodness in the latter days.

4 Hear the word of the LORD, O people of Israel;

for the LORD has a controversy with the inhabitants of the land.

Mesopotamian Origins [Philadelphia: University of Pennsylvania Press, 1930], p. 162, n. 127).

5. Israel will once more worship the Lord in truth and sincerity; the old relationship will be restored. The phrase **and David their king** is an obvious interpolation in this context and should be deleted as a later editorial addition. Most scholars would delete what follows also, principally on the ground that the phrase **in the latter days** is characteristic of later prophecy and has eschatological significance. On the other hand, it may simply mean "in later days," i.e., after the period of separation and restraint is finished. God in his love had sought and redeemed Israel; now Israel will seek the Lord. They will know the goodness of the Lord as they had never known it before; therefore **they shall come in fear to the LORD and to his goodness in the latter** [or "later"] **days.**

II. ISRAEL'S UNFAITHFULNESS TO YAHWEH (4:1–13:16)

A. SPIRITUAL UNFAITHFULNESS (4:1–7:7)

1. EPHRAIM IS JOINED TO IDOLS (4:1-19)

a) THE LORD'S CONTROVERSY WITH HIS PEOPLE (4:1-3)

4:1. The LORD has a controversy with his people (cf. Isa. 3:13; Jer. 2:9; 25:31). We are at once reminded of 2:2 in which the Israelites are called upon to have a controversy, i.e., to plead, with their mother. The grounds for the Lord's controversy or expostulation with his people are set forth in uncompromising terms:

Its greatest enemy is not the sword of opposition aimed at its heart, but the millstone of inertia and indifference hung about its neck.

5b. Fearing the Goodness of God.—Strange that they should fear the **goodness** of God. Understandably, we fear the man who opposes us with a sword, but why a God who presents us with a cross? Why fear love, especially "the love . . . which passeth knowledge"? (Eph. 3:19.) Yet the scriptures assure us that "the fear of the LORD is the beginning of wisdom" (Ps. 111:10). "Fear God, and keep his commandments" (Eccl. 12:13). To fear God is not to be afraid of him as one would fear a tyrant. This fear has torment. It is rather to stand in awe of him, to bow reverently before his majesty and holiness. "Perfect love casteth out fear" (I John 4:18), but not the fear of awe and reverence. Such qualities are inevitable so long as man recognizes his finiteness and creaturehood. Goodness places a man under much heavier obligation than evil. Had the father of the prodigal been hard or cruel, the far country would have lost much of its torment.

But to sin against love, to answer goodness with evil—that for any sensitive soul is a heavy burden. Let any man recall the mercies of God in his own life and ask whether such blessings, mostly unmerited, do not place him under heavy obligation. To sin against love—any honest man may well fear that.

Paul speaks of a "weight of glory" (II Cor. 4:17), as though the glory that comes to one is a burden. It is. The greater the glory the heavier the obligation of trying to measure up. We fear the goodness of God because a good God requires goodness of us. "What doth the LORD require of thee" (Mic. 6:8)—offerings of silver and gold? No. Regular attendance at worship? No. These are secondary. They are expressions of, not substitutes for, God's primary requirement. That requirement is a life which emulates goodness—"to do justly, . . . love mercy, and to walk humbly" (Mic. 6:8). If the truth be told, a good God is more to be feared than an evil one.

4:1-3. God's Controversy with Man.—Into the details of this tragic picture we need not go.

cause *there is* no truth, nor mercy, nor knowledge of God in the land.	There is no faithfulness or kindness, and no knowledge of God in the land;

There is no faithfulness or kindness,
and no knowledge of God in the land.

Faithfulness: The word in the original signifies **truth**, but truth not merely in the sense of uttering what is right, but also of doing what is right. Its full sense therefore is more adequately given by such a term as **faithfulness** or "fidelity" or "steadfastness." It signifies an attitude which is stable and dependable and manifests a highly developed sense of obligation (cf. 2:20). **Kindness** is in popular usage a feeble word and generally connotes a mild kind of considerateness and regard for others. But the word rendered here as **kindness** is a strong word, meaning "covenant love," the living bond of relationship and fellowship between two who have accepted obligations in a spirit of trust and good will (cf. 2:19). Weiser's words are worth noting: "The fact that Hosea sets in the first place truth and love, the very things which in 2:21 f. and other passages he promises as the gifts of God for the new covenant, shows how God's grace corresponds to his demands" (*Das Buch der zwölf kleinen Propheten*, I, 28). **No knowledge of God in the land** may signify that there is an ignorance of God's law, so that what is needed is instruction. That is indeed meant, and also something more, viz., the disregard of God's

But its main message and meaning are clear enough. The controversy of God with his people centered about their moral condition. Here was a nation that had collapsed morally. There was no truth, no mercy; instead, **lying, killing, stealing.** It is significant that the prophet's primary concern was not the economic or political condition of his people but their moral condition. He would have us understand that the moral breakdown of a nation is the primary source of its collapse, since it usually precedes and causes economic or political decay.

We can see more clearly the truth of this if we think of the individual rather than of the nation. When a man goes to pieces, it is the moral part of him that goes first. Loss of character is more to be feared than the loss of any other possession. The prodigal's greatest loss in the far country was not his material belongings but his character. "Fear not them which kill the body, but are not able to kill the soul" (Matt. 10:28). This moral decay always starts within. It is the inwardness of sin that creates the problem for man. It ushers in a process of decay which no material factor can stop—nothing but moral and spiritual regeneration.

So it is with a nation. One may almost risk the statement that the ultimate cause of the decline and final collapse of every nation or civilization has been moral and spiritual rather than material. No nation that is morally rotten can permanently endure. Morality bears the same relationship to a nation's life which the heart bears to the human body. When the heart stops we die, never mind how well we may look, how luxurious or prosperous our surroundings. Morality is the heartbeat of a nation's life. When instead of truth and mercy there are lying, stealing, and killing, then does **the land mourn, and . . . languish.**

Certain tendencies in the national life indicate the weakening of moral fiber. The Federal Bureau of Investigation places the annual crime bill of the United States at between five and seven billion dollars. The gambling racket is vitiating the morals of millions of people. In 1944, when American soldiers and sailors were fighting for freedom, paid admissions to race tracks reached two million dollars, and one billion was wagered through pari-mutuel machines. Add to this two billion in illegal bets placed over telephones and in stores. "The money involved in these gambling transactions each year is more than a hundred times greater than the sum contributed by all the Christians of the West for the expansion of the missionary movement around the world."[7] Gambling is not confined to race tracks. It is becoming a national disease. It develops in us the pernicious habit of wanting something for nothing. And the church has not escaped. Even there, in certain instances, gambling seems to be in good and regular standing. "The man who gambles and wins is a thief; the man who gambles and loses is a fool. Now take your choice." So the matter was once put by a popular evangelist.

If our moral fiber is being weakened by gambling, it is being softened by liquor. Through the pressure of advertising and the

[7] Walter W. Van Kirk, *A Christian Global Strategy* (Chicago: Willett, Clark & Co., 1945), p. 54.

| 2 By swearing, and lying, and killing, and stealing, and committing adultery, they break out, and blood toucheth blood. | 2 there is swearing, lying, killing, stealing, and committing adultery;
 they break all bounds and murder follows murder. |

law and the refusal to honor the obligations of it, an attitude of willful neglect. It is probably worthy of note that Hosea here speaks of **knowledge of God,** not knowledge of Yahweh, the God of Israel. He thereby implies that what is lacking is not only the religious vitality and devotion that might have been expected in a chosen and trained people like Israel, but the fundamental religious consciousness which might be expected in any people that had reflected at all upon human life and destiny (cf. 2:20).

2. Having dealt with the basic sinful attitude of the people, Hosea in this verse proceeds to specify the ways in which that attitude most commonly expresses itself. **Swearing** must signify "false swearing," for the taking of oaths was never prohibited in Israel; indeed, the first two terms may be taken together by zeugma and rendered as "false swearing." The fact that transgression of the Sixth, Seventh, Eighth, and Ninth Commandments seems to be specified here gives some support for the view that by Hosea's

---

tyranny of social customs liquor tightens increasingly its stranglehold. "Here in the U. S. only tuberculosis and syphilis claim more victims than alcoholism."[8] Moffatt translates vs. 11, "Liquor and lust deprive them of their wits." Much of our moral degeneration and corruption, personal and social, is connected with such national vices as gambling and alcohol. Who can measure the extent of the moral breakdown occasioned by such excesses? Should we not be more concerned about the deflation of moral values than about the inflation of material ones? Might it not turn out that our economic problems go back to our moral condition?

What caused Israel's moral deterioration? Hosea's answer is disarmingly simple. He says this moral decay springs from the religious illiteracy of his people. They do not know God. **There is no truth, nor mercy, nor knowledge of God in the land.** This is the **controversy** of God with his people. All this deterioration has come about because men do not know God. "My people are destroyed for lack of knowledge" (vs. 6). We of the modern world are very close to the prophet in his emphasis on knowledge, yet very far from him. We stand with him in our emphasis on knowledge as essential. We agree with him that ignorance is a great enemy. Yet while we agree with Hosea in his emphasis on the importance of knowledge, we differ radically with him as to what it is essential to know, and how such knowledge is to be obtained. When Hosea spoke of knowledge, he meant first of all **knowledge of God.** Such knowledge was to him the first item on the agenda of education; he put that ahead of

all else. In this secular society of ours we reverse the agenda. What he put first we put last—if at all. Who is right? Surely the most sanguine believer in education must now realize that it has not achieved what we had hoped for. It is not bringing security, peace, or well-being.

Knowledge to us is intellectual, and is quite largely the knowledge of things. Surely we now see its inadequacy. If Paul, speaking of secularized knowledge, could say it "puffeth up" (I Cor. 8:1), we might say it "blows us up." Atomic fission, the latest child of knowledge, threatens to make the blowing up well-nigh complete. Is it not clear now that secular knowledge without divine wisdom, the **knowledge of God,** is woefully inadequate and incomplete, if not positively harmful?

When Hosea spoke of knowledge, he meant the **knowledge of God,** and this knowledge, while it involves the intellect, is not primarily intellectual. The key to the prophet's meaning is found in Gen. 4:1, "And Adam knew Eve his wife." **Knowledge of God** is intimate communion with the God in whom we live and move and have our being. Such knowledge is more than belief. It is easy glibly to say, "I believe in God," and it is remarkable how little difference such belief often can and does make to our life. Quite possibly the world's worst tyrants, criminals, gangsters, and crooks believe in God. Indeed, James went so far once as to say, "The devils also believe, and tremble" (Jas. 2:19). Belief without action, faith without works, is dead. Paul believed in God, but more than that, he could say, "I know whom I have believed" (II Tim. 1:12).

We must distinguish then between intellectual knowledge and experiential knowledge of God. Many among us may know more about

| 3 Therefore shall the land mourn, and | 3 Therefore the land mourns,
　　and all who dwell in it languish,
　　and also the beasts of the field, |

time the Decalogue may have been formulated and recognized as a standard of conduct. The reference to "the law of your God" in vs. 6 would give additional support to it (cf. Intro., p. 559). It is indisputable that vs. 2 would be improved if the final verb, which is metrically superfluous, were removed to the second half of vs. 3, where a stress is missing; in that case וגוע would be read for נגע, and the final part of vs. 3 would then be, "and even the fish of the sea are gathered away and expire."

3. Some scholars have seen in the first part of this verse evidence of the fact that the land had been suffering from drought and from the resultant famine (note that G. R. Driver correlates the Hebrew אבל with the Akkadian *abālu*="to be dry"; cf. Bruno

God theoretically than some of the saints. Knowing about God is one thing, knowing God, something else. There is a difference between being religiously sophisticated and being religious.

The **knowledge of God** of which Hosea speaks, because it was not theoretical, could not be obtained simply by man's effort (see Expos. on 4:6). As George Adam Smith writes: "It is knowledge, not as an effort of, so much as an effect upon, the mind. It is not *to know* so as to see the fact of, but *to know* so as to feel the force of; knowledge, not as acquisition but as impression."[1] Such knowledge comes from the knowing self, not simply the knowing mind. It involves the disciplining of the life, the submission of the will—"If any man will do his will, he shall know" (John 7:17). Such knowledge comes from walking in the light, not just talking about it. "Blessed are the pure in heart: for they shall see God" (Matt. 5:8). One can think of many avenues by which the soul of man may be brought into fellowship with God: nature, the great literature of devotion, the life of some saintly soul, meditation and prayer, listening to the still small voice—"Be still, and know" (Ps. 46:10)—service to our fellow men in the spirit of him who "came not to be ministered unto, but to minister" (Matt. 20:28), giving ourselves for God's sake with abandon to some great cause, espousing some great if unpopular truth, even if such commitment brings upon us criticism, personal loss, or harm. The cause of truth, never mind how unpopular, is always God's business. Supremely, however, we come to know God through his fullest revelation, the life of Christ our Lord. "Have I been so long time with you, and yet hast thou not known me, Philip?" (John 14:9.)

How are we to come to know God? "I am the way," said the Master (John 14:6). When one confronts Christ, learns his teaching, meditates on his matchless character, partakes of his spirit, and can in some small way say with Paul,

[1] *The Twelve Prophets*, I, 351.

"Christ liveth in me" (Gal. 2:20), he knows God. "No man hath seen God at any time; the only begotten Son . . . hath declared him" (John 1:18). It is the knowledge of Christ that brings to one his fullest knowledge of God. When Christ lives in us, we know God. The lack of this knowledge was in Hosea's thinking the root cause of Israel's trouble. All her political difficulties sprang from her moral collapse, which in turn grew out of her ignorance of God. The **lying, killing, stealing, adultery**—all these evils of which the prophet speaks—sprang from the fact that there was **no truth, nor mercy, nor knowledge of God.**

Why does morality need a religion based on the **knowledge of God** for its support? For one thing, religion gives to the moral law a cosmic significance. We may break a man-made law and get away with it. But a knowledge of God will convince one that man never "gets away with it" when he breaks a moral law. The reason for this is that the moral law transcends man. It speaks to his conscience, and conscience speaks always in the imperative mood. To remove the divine imperative from conscience as did Rousseau, by equating it with the instincts, is completely to destroy morality, or more accurately, ourselves; for man cannot destroy morality, though he can destroy himself in the attempt. Christianity gives to morality both a winsome and a compelling character. When we do what is right, we feel we have done that which goes beyond ourselves—we strike a cosmic chord. "There is joy in the presence of the angels of God over one sinner that repenteth" (Luke 15:10). Conversely, to disregard our moral insights, fall short of our best, is not only to feel the pressure of an accusing conscience but to suffer the sense of God's disfavor. The knowledge of God personalizes morality, gives to morality a compelling character which it could not otherwise possess.

There is, however, another reason why we believe morality will not endure without a

every one that dwelleth therein shall languish, with the beasts of the field, and with the fowls of heaven; yea, the fishes of the sea also shall be taken away.

4 Yet let no man strive, nor reprove another: for thy people *are* as they that strive with the priest.

and the birds of the air;
and even the fish of the sea are taken away.

4 Yet let no one contend,
and let none accuse,
for with you is my contention, O priest.[k]

[k] Cn: Heb uncertain

Schindler, ed., *Gaster Anniversary Volume* [London: Taylor's Foreign Press, 1936], p. 74). But the second part of the verse, and in particular the final clause, shows that the prophet is rather describing the wide range of the corruption that has laid hold upon God's world. The **beasts,** the **birds,** and the **fish** of the sea are all suffering the penalties of a fallen creation and a world tainted with sin (cf. Jer. 12:4; Joel 1:10-12, 18-20; Isa. 24:3-7; *et al.;* for nature's reviving with man's return to favor with God cf. 2:18).

b) A CORRUPT PRIESTHOOD AND A CORRUPT PEOPLE (4:4-15)

4. This verse serves as a vinculum between vss. 1-3 and vss. 5 ff., by its continuance of the idea of a controversy and by its specific designation of the priests as the party with whom in particular God has his controversy. **Yet let no one contend,** and its parallel phrase immediately following, may mean "It is God who has the controversy with his people; therefore let no man enter into it." Or they may mean "Let not anyone contend or make complaint, because the people are not really to blame." The sequel seems to support the latter interpretation, advocated by Karl Budde (cf. "Zu Text und Auslegung des Buches Hosea," *Journal of Biblical Literature,* XLV [1926], 284), who proposes that the verbs should be read as passives (ירב and יוכח). The final phrase of the verse—lit., "your people are like those who contend with the priest"—cannot be in its original form. The emendations which have been proposed by modern scholars do

---

knowledge of God. Such knowledge not only personalizes ethical and moral reality but eternalizes it, gives to it the assurance of permanence. Man needs that assurance. The path of moral reality is not an easy one. It is straight, narrow, and often steep. Those who choose the straight way accept the disciplines it demands, and those disciplines are not easy. But if man is willing to submit to them even when desire and inclination pull hard in the opposite direction, it is because he feels that "the stars in their courses" fight on his side, that the universe supports, sustains, and will at last vindicate the values he cherishes and defends. "To preach morality," said Schopenhauer, "is easy; to find a foundation for morality is hard."[2] The Christian believes God is its foundation, for only this belief gives the quality of permanence to moral values; and without that, morality will lose much of its significance. If the time should come when man believes that his values are mere bubbles on the surface of reality—beautiful, to be sure, but airy, insubstantial, and destined to break and disappear—he will

not, nor perchance should he be expected to, accept the challenge in toil and sacrifice which they demand of him. When, however, he feels that he is a laborer together with God, that God, who cannot be ultimately defeated, sustains and supports not only him but the realities he loves more than his life, then the whole struggle assumes a different face. In the brave words of John Baillie:

I am not fighting alone, against impossible odds, for a fantastically hopeless cause, and with the paralysing suspicion in my heart that it cannot really matter whether I win or lose. . . . Nay, rather it is Reality's own battle that I am fighting, and the stars in their course are fighting with me and the very Force that moves them is on my side. . . . And it is the only battle that matters in all the world, and the prize is the only prize that will endure.[3]

4-5. The Corruption of the Priests.—One indication of Israel's widespread moral deterioration was the corruption of the priesthood. In this and the opening verses of ch. 5 Hosea

---

[2] Quoted by W. Macneile Dixon, *The Human Situation* (New York: Longmans, Green & Co., 1937), p. 281.

[3] *The Interpretation of Religion* (New York: Charles Scribner's Sons, 1928), p. 326.

| 5 Therefore shalt thou fall in the day, and the prophet also shall fall with thee in the night, and I will destroy thy mother. | 5 You shall stumble by day, the prophet also shall stumble with you by night; and I will destroy your mother. |

not agree in detail, but they are very similar in sense. That represented by the RSV, **for with you is my contention, O priest** (עמך ריבי הכהן), is accepted by many scholars. Some read "for my people is like you, O priest" (עמי כמוך הכהן), while others again suggest a somewhat longer text, "for my people are like their idol-priest, my children are like their priest" (עמי ככמר ובני ככהן). Thus the transition is made from the people to the priests, who are the subject of the verses immediately following.

5. This may be taken as referring to the disabling penalty which will come upon the priest and the prophet, in that they will **stumble** as blind men; but it seems more suitable in the context to take the Hebrew imperfects of the original text as iterative in force: "You stumble time after time [or continually] by day, the prophet also stumbles with you by night." In this way it is the failure of the priest and the prophet which is described. They were the leaders from whom the people expected guidance and from whom they had a right to expect it; but inasmuch as they stumbled in their own way, they were completely unfit to aid others. The prophets mentioned here in association with the priests were the cultic prophets attached to the sanctuaries (cf. Aubrey R. Johnson, *The Cultic Prophet in Ancient Israel* [Cardiff: University of Wales Press, 1944]; Alfred O. Haldar, *Associations of Cult Prophets Among the Ancient Semites* [Uppsala: Almquist & Wiksells, 1945]). The reference of the term **your mother** has been much disputed. That it should be to Aaron, the source of the Israelite priesthood, would be suitable on general grounds, but would be a strange and not readily intelligible use of the term. Rather we should find the value of the term in 2:4, where Israel is thus addressed. But it is

excoriates the priests, who had become blind leaders of the blind.

But none protests, no man complains,
for my people are no better than their priestlings
(Moffatt).

Instead of being sources of illumination, the light in them had become darkness, so that they themselves stumbled "by broad daylight." The real sources of illumination are inner; when the light within becomes darkness, no external light can help. The depths to which the religious leaders of Hosea's day had sunk is seen not only in their shameless indulgence in evil, but also in the fact that they encouraged their people to sin. This they did because the sin offerings increased with the sins of the people and so did the wealth of the clergy. In short, the priests made money out of the moral misdeeds of mankind.

This incredible situation has had shocking parallels in the history of the Christian church. Something like that was happening when Luther broke with Rome. The sale of indulgences was an indication not only of the errors of the laity; more so, of the moral decadence of the clergy, who filled the coffers of the church and no doubt their own pockets also by capitalizing on human vice. "You have been a snare at Mizpah, and a net spread upon Tabor" (5:1). A snare, a net, a pit—imagine using such symbols to describe the relationship of the clergy to their people!

Bright in 1843, speaking at Durham of the attitude of the Church clergy to the Corn Laws, said, "It is a misfortune that by a law made by the Parliament of the country, this body of men, especially appointed to take charge of the flock, should, instead of being the shepherds, appear to all men's eyes as the shearers; and that their enormous influence should, in almost all the parishes of England, be bound up in the conservation of the most odious enactment which was ever recorded upon the statute-book." Cobden, a loyal Churchman, wrote to Bright in 1842, "The Church clergy are almost to a man guilty of causing the present distress by upholding the Corn Law, they having themselves an interest in the high price of bread." [4]

So in Hosea's day also (see vss. 7-8).

One may well wonder what produced this appalling collapse of the religious leaders of Hosea's time. The answer is not hard to find. Religion had become formal and ceremonial rather than moral and spiritual. Whenever

[4] George M. Trevelyan, *The Life of John Bright* (London: Constable & Co., 1913; Boston: Houghton Mifflin Co., 1914), p. 48, n. 1. Used by permission.

6 ¶ My people are destroyed for lack of knowledge: because thou hast rejected

6 My people are destroyed for lack of knowledge;
because you have rejected knowledge,

---

unexpected that Yahweh should here proclaim the destruction of the people at the very instant when he is causing to be proclaimed the culpability of the people's leaders. The final clause should be understood as referring to the priests, whatever may have been its precise original form. The simplest way is to read the verbal form as second singular masculine in place of first singular, and to translate, "and you are destroying your mother," i.e., "your people." These words should be taken closely with those which follow. Mother Israel is being destroyed by her priests, but she is also God's people; therefore their failure is a failure not only before men, but before God (cf. H. W. Robinson, *Inspiration and Revelation in the O.T.*, p. 201, for the view that the primary function of the priest was to teach).

6. The priests have failed to fulfill their duty of instructing the people; therefore they will be deprived of their office, as will their children after them. **The law** covers the priestly oracle and the prophetic; the Hebrew word *tôrāh* means teaching or guidance, and is especially used of the religious instruction given to men by God's chosen servants.

---

religion exalts the ceremonial above the ethical, one of two evils inevitably results. Religion becomes irrelevant and veers toward a condition of ecclesiastical dry rot, harmless and innocuous but useless; like the salt that has lost its savor, it is not poisonous, but good for nothing except to be cast out. This is the best one can say for it. The other evil is that, like the house swept and garnished, the formal but fruitless religious life may become the hunting ground of evil forces. This is what it had become in Hosea's time and has on occasion become since. In Jesus' day the ceremonialism of Pharisaism harbored the evils of pride and hypocrisy; much of religion had become a cloak for human sin. It was a pious fraud. When men forget the intellectual and moral disciplines of religion and allow it to degenerate into the meticulous performance of certain rites, or the vain repetition of rituals out of which moral reality has fled, some other "reality," sinister and degenerate, is likely to appear. No wonder Hosea excoriated the priests!

6. *The Knowledge of God.*—Hosea complained that his people were **destroyed for lack of knowledge.** Surely that accusation could not be made against us! We are well informed. We fight illiteracy as though it were a plague, and ignorance as we should some dread disease. To be sure, there is much land which is yet to be possessed, especially among the Negroes, whose per capita allowance for education compares most unfavorably with that of their white neighbors. None the less, our magnificent schools and impressive college campuses speak eloquently of our eagerness for knowledge.

Despite all this, however, Hosea would say to us precisely what he said to his people, **My**

people are destroyed for lack of knowledge, because what the prophet meant by knowledge is not what we mean by it (see Expos. on 4:1-3). Knowledge for us comes well-nigh meaning secularized knowledge, while for the prophet it meant primarily religious knowledge—the knowledge of God, his works, and his ways. **My people are destroyed for lack of knowledge; because you have rejected knowledge, . . . you have forgotten the law of your God.** Hosea is not alone in this emphasis. He voices here a characteristic prophetic insight. "Ezra had set his heart upon studying the law of God, upon obeying it, and upon teaching its rules and regulations in Israel" (Ezra 7:10 Moffatt). His own intellectual (studying) and moral (obeying) preparation preceded his attempt to teach. No effective or lasting religious teaching is possible apart from that procedure.

The knowledge of God to Hosea therefore is "not so much the acquisition as the impression of facts, an impression which masters not only a man's thoughts but his heart and will." [5] It is therefore not abstract or theoretical but personal knowledge, the knowledge of experience—"I know whom I have believed" (II Tim. 1:12). Here are two marks of the knowledge of God as Hosea understands it. It is not abstract or theoretical knowledge about, but first-hand knowledge of. It is not attained simply or even primarily by man's effort, but by God's grace. Man does not so much discover this knowledge as does God reveal it, "for it requires God Himself to speak, and discipline to chasten." [6]

The modern man believes that education is

[5] George Adam Smith, *The Twelve Prophets*, I, 353.
[6] *Ibid.*

knowledge, I will also reject thee, that thou shalt be no priest to me: seeing thou hast forgotten the law of thy God, I will also forget thy children.	I reject you from being a priest to me. And since you have forgotten the law of your God, I also will forget your children.
7 As they were increased, so they sinned against me: *therefore* will I change their glory into shame.	7 The more they increased, the more they sinned against me; I will change their glory into shame.
8 They eat up the sin of my people, and they set their heart on their iniquity.	8 They feed on the sin of my people; they are greedy for their iniquity.

7-8. These verses are not addressed to the priests but continue the description of them. The reference to the increase of the priesthood may imply that this utterance of Hosea had its original setting in the prosperous days of Jeroboam II. **I will change their glory into shame** is a threat of punishment to come. But the Targ. and Syriac support the third plural reading in the verb "they change their glory into shame." That is a description of priestly delinquency and is more in keeping with the following verse. Vs. 8 may mean that the priests **feed** upon **sin** in the direct sense that they receive their portion of the people's offerings (cf. Lev. 6:18, 29; 7:6), so that the more sinful the people are, the greater is the priests' portion. On the other hand, the words may have the less specific meaning that the priests have an appetite for human guilt and gloat over **iniquity.**

the answer to his problems—secularized, factual, scientific education. H. G. Wells said that civilization is a race between education and catastrophe. It should be clearly evident now to every impartial observer that secularized education cannot stave off catastrophe. Why not? For one thing, secularized education deals with facts; it too largely ignores meanings. Facts are one thing, facts adequately interpreted are another. Without the knowledge of God, of truth, our education is like spokes without a hub. It is fragmentary, it hangs at loose ends, it lacks meaning; or rather, its meaning lies largely in the materialistic realm. Too many think of education as that which better fits us to make money. It prepares us for making a living, but not for living a life. Such education cannot stave off catastrophe. It takes more than secularized knowledge to do that.

But secularized knowledge cannot save us because it rests on the assumption that if man knows the right, he will do it. The assumption is baseless. One does not reach the goals of life as a motorist obediently follows the route marked out for his direction. In the realm of living we often get lost, not because we do not know the way but because we do not want to follow it. "This is the way, walk ye in it" (Isa. 30:21). But something holds us back. The trouble lies not in our minds but in our wills. "But I see another law in my members, warring against the law of my mind, and bringing me into captivity to the law of sin" (Rom. 7:23). This inner conflict between knowing and doing, between desire and duty, is the very heart of the

human problem. Secularized education makes little or no attempt to face that problem. It gives us information about everything except ourselves; and when it does give us that, often we are regarded as though we were glorified guinea pigs in some scientific laboratory. Secularized education is too largely a veneer. It fails to take knowledge of the deepest truth about man: that he has or rather is an immortal soul.

If one doubts the truth of this statement, let him consider the deepest shadows that lie across the face of the earth: they have not been cast by the darkness of ignorance but, paradoxically enough, by the light of knowledge. The way is dark and insecure not because humanity does not know enough, but because it knows too much! An education that incredibly increases man's power but gives him no instruction as to how he can wisely and creatively use power, that makes him master of nature but does not teach him the secret of self-mastery, is incapable of staving off catastrophe. Catastrophe overtakes a civilization not because it lacks intelligence but because it lacks integrity. So with the individual. For want of this knowledge, according to Hosea, God says, **My people are destroyed.**

6b. Israel as Priest.—In the providence of God one people, Israel, was chosen for the salvation of all men. There was no church, called out from the nation; the nation itself was the bearer of salvation. But when the nation proved inadequate through its infidelity, God's method became one of "progressive re-

9 And there shall be, like people, like priest: and I will punish them for their ways, and reward them their doings.

9 And it shall be like people, like priest; I will punish them for their ways, and requite them for their deeds.

9. The translation of the first phrase in the KJV is unintelligible, while that in the RSV is expressed in unidiomatic English. The meaning is that the people are becoming like their priests, so that the verb should be rendered not as a future but as a progressive. If the phrase is taken in this way, it describes the effect upon the people of the failure of the priests to exercise their teaching function. Only in vs. 9b is the consequent punishment spoken of, and that is continued in vs. 10.

duction." He turned from the nation to the "remnant." "The remnant shall return, even the remnant of Jacob, unto the mighty God" (Isa. 10:21). This may be regarded as the beginning of the church, an "Israel within an Israel." The true Israel became quantitatively smaller, but qualitatively greater. A further reduction appears in Second Isaiah, where the remnant is reduced to one man, the servant of Yahweh (Isa. 42:1-4). Suffering is the mark of this servant, who vicariously bears the sins of his people. In Daniel he becomes "the Son of man," who represents "the people of the saints" (Dan. 7:13-14). The Christian faith asserts that this One was Jesus Christ, whose life so perfectly portrays the character of the suffering servant. It is through this One that the remnant, the nation, and, as we believe, mankind, will be redeemed. Thus the redemptive history unfolds itself in the principle of "progressive reduction: . . . People of Israel—remnant of Israel—the One, Christ." [7] How does this historic function of Judaism fit into the picture of political Zionism?

9. Like People, Like Priest.—Hosea means that the priests and people shall share alike— "but priests shall fare like people" (Moffatt). There will be no moral and spiritual equivalent of the 10 per cent ministerial discount. Religious officialdom will in no way escape the judgment which God will impose on priests and people alike for the sins in which they were alike involved.

There is, however, another possible interpretation suggested by E. B. Pusey:

Priest and people were alike in sin. Yea, they are wont, if bad, to foment each other's sin. The bad priest copies the sins which he should reprove, and excuses himself by the frailty of our common nature. The people, acutely enough, detect the worldliness or self-indulgence of the priests, and shelter themselves under his example. [8]

That the minister influences and molds his congregation is an obvious and generally accepted fact; that the congregation in turn can well-nigh make or break a minister is a fact not so generally recognized but equally true. The road between the clergy and laity is by no means a one-way street. The traffic moves in both directions—**like people, like priest.** If influences go out from pulpit to pew, they just as surely flow from pew to pulpit. This is especially true of Protestantism. In Roman Catholicism the road between clergy and laity is quite largely a one-way street. The authoritarianism of the priest tends to create submission and obedience in the people and so deprives them of the give and take to which the more democratic and freedom-loving spirit of Protestantism exposes the minister. The relationship in Protestantism is reciprocal—as the minister preaches to his people, so do the people by their attitudes and actions preach to the minister. **Like people, like priest.**

When George Matheson began his ministry in Innellan, Scotland, he said to his congregation:

In you I recognize the subjects of my future study. It is said by them of old time that the minister is the teacher of the people; I think that in all which is worthy to be known the people are the teachers of the minister. . . . I come to find in your cares that power which is perfect through suffering; to gain in your experience that wisdom which grows in favour alike with God and man; and if in long time to come my maturing mind shall give back to you the fruits you lent it—if the bread you shall have cast on the waters shall return to you after many days—I will deem that . . . my ministry in Innellan shall not have proved in vain. [9]

After nineteen years of service, in response to a gift presented by the church, he said, "It is I, this night, that should be the donor and you who should be the receivers." [1]

"He did not many mighty works there be-

[7] Oscar Cullmann, *Christ and Time* (tr. F. V. Filson; Philadelphia: Westminster Press, 1950), p. 116.

[8] *The Minor Prophets* (New York: Funk & Wagnalls, 1885), I, 50.

[9] Donald Macmillan, *The Life of George Matheson* (London: Hodder & Stoughton, 1907), p. 98. Used by permission.

[1] *Ibid.,* p. 202.

10 For they shall eat, and not have enough: they shall commit whoredom, and shall not increase: because they have left off to take heed to the Lord.

11 Whoredom and wine and new wine take away the heart.

10 They shall eat, but not be satisfied;
    they shall play the harlot, but not
        multiply;
because they have forsaken the Lord
    to cherish harlotry.

11 Wine and new wine
    take away the understanding.

10. The punishment mentioned in this verse is related to the forms in which the wayward spirit has expressed itself in the people's lives. They will continue to take part in the festivals of the Baal cult, they will eat and drink to the full; but instead of having a sense of satiety, they will remain quite unsatisfied. They will continue to indulge in the immoral practices at the Canaanite sanctuaries, and the penalty will be that they will be denied the fruit of legitimate marital intercourse, they will not have the blessing of children. Understood thus, the verse has none of the difficulty in it which commentators often find. There seems no need to emend יפרצו to יתרצו, and to translate "and they will not be satisfied" in place of **but not multiply**. The rhythmic form of the second part of the verse suggests that the first word of vs. 11 should be conjoined with vs. 10, so that the final phrase of vs. 10 would read: "because they have forsaken the Lord to observe harlotry."

11. Vss. 11-13a describe the excesses which were committed by the people on the festival days at the Baal shrines. Physical indulgence of one kind and another takes away all discretion and understanding.

cause of their unbelief" (Matt. 13:58). Even our Lord could not escape the influence of those he sought to serve. John Henry Jowett served Carr's Lane Chapel in Birmingham, England, for fifteen years and became world renowned. In 1911 he accepted a call to the Fifth Avenue Presbyterian Church in New York. A member of the American church attended service at Carr's Lane and inquired of one of the members: "What are you going to do about a worthy successor to Dr. Jowett?" He received this reply: "We are not worried. You know, Carr's Lane makes its preachers."[2] Some churches make them; other churches break them. Indifference, inertia, pettiness, fussiness, take the life out of a man. You cannot, as one has said, put an iceberg in the pew and then ask the minister to resign because he will not perspire! It is unquestionably true that if we had better ministers, we should have better churches. It is equally true that a more responsive and interested laity would go a long way in producing a more effective ministry. Moses needs the Aarons who hold up his hands. **Like people, like priest.**

10. *The Man of Sin.*—Herein lies sin's major curse: It is insatiable. **They shall eat, but not be satisfied.** One eats but is never satisfied; drinks, but his thirst remains. Every evil indulged but whets the appetite. Each successive

portion must be increased, for desire increases as satisfaction eludes it, until if one persists he is devoured by that which he devours. This is hell! The illicit satisfaction of an instinct does not bring satisfaction to the self, for man's real nature, unlike animal nature, is not revealed on the level of the instinctive. There is much of the animal in man, but man is not an animal. Animal nature and human nature are two different things. "I shall be satisfied, when I awake, with thy likeness" (Ps. 17:15).

Not only does satisfaction elude the sinner but also creativeness—**they shall play the harlot, but not multiply.** The life force is diverted from its true purpose. Instead of being used creatively for increasing life, it spends itself for naught. Consider the many ways in which we **play the harlot.** How many billions have been spent in cutthroat competition, selfishly conceived, which has deprived society of the more fruitful results of the co-operative spirit; in war, which does **not multiply,** leaves us no gain but, on the contrary, woefully impoverishes us. "Wherefore do ye spend money for that which is not bread? and your labor for that which satisfieth not?" (Isa. 55:2.)

11. *Liquor and Lust.*—These are twin evils in that one often leads to the other. Drunkenness played an integral part in the Canaanite worship to which Israel had succumbed. The vine was a natural feature of the agricultural community, and bore some special relation to

² Hampton Adams, *You and Your Minister* (St. Louis: Bethany Press, 1940), pp. 38-39.

12 ¶ My people ask counsel at their stocks, and their staff declareth unto them: for the spirit of whoredoms hath caused

12 My people inquire of a thing of wood, and their staff gives them oracles.
For a spirit of harlotry has led them astray,

12. Vs. 11 might seem to imply that it was only because the people had lost all sense of discretion that they were induced to resort to superstitious practices; but the second half of this verse gives a more radical cause for their error. They are possessed of a harlot spirit, have come under the dominance of a malignant influence, and have willfully left God and his service. Now they practice rhabdomancy, seeking guidance from dead **wood** rather than from the living God, from **staff** and teraphim rather than from the inspired religious leaders.

the gods of tillage, the Baals, the form of whose worship Israel had now transferred to Yahweh. Amos had opposed the use of liquor "on grounds of traditional religious conventionality." [3] Hosea, on the contrary, does so on purely moral grounds. He argues that liquor destroys men's capacity to think clearly, breaks down their resistance to evil. It so beclouds the mind that one becomes morally stupid, incapable after a while of thinking straight. **Harlotry . . . and new wine take away the understanding.**

Liquor, like the leopard, has not changed its spots. The refinements of the cocktail hour and all the social éclat with which high-pressure advertising has bedecked the liquor traffic have not altered in the slightest the moral problems that inhere in it. Liquor and lust deprive men not alone of their **understanding,** but of their money. Public education costs the United States in round numbers $15 per pupil per year; drink, $46 per person per year, and $89 per year for every person over eighteen years of age. Liquor deprives men of their independence. The drink habit is in many social circles a mark of sophistication. People adopt the pattern merely because they do not have the courage to be different. Liquor deprives men of their courage. It is an escape from reality. Said a habitual drinker to his friend: "Drink is the shortest way out of Manchester." Liquor has deprived multitudes of their character. Drink removes the inhibitions which are the normal safeguards against the coarser and more vulgar sins. It deadens the higher centers. It inspires one with a false confidence and makes havoc of the modesties and restraints which mark the self-respecting. Liquor deprives men of their homes. Consider the number of broken homes that are due to drunkenness. This evil is still with us. The cocktail hour may be more refined than the old saloon, but the leopard has not changed his spots.

[3] T. H. Robinson, *Prophecy and the Prophets in Ancient Israel* (New York: Charles Scribner's Sons, 1923), p. 82.

12. *Israel Turns to Idolatry.*—And **my people** have done this: "My own people . . . 'The tenderness of the word . . . aggravates both the stupidity and the ingratitude of Israel.' " [4] When the Israelites gave up the worship of the true God, they filled the void with the worship of false ones—the Baals. That is what men invariably do. No religion would be better than a bad religion, but there is no such thing as "no religion." Every man has some sort of religion, for "man is incurably religious." "Whom . . . ye ignorantly worship, him declare I unto you" (Acts 17:23) . Hitler renounced the Christian God, but not gods. He filled with Woden and Thor the throne left empty by the God in Christ. For the gospel of brotherhood he substituted the gospel of Nordic supremacy; for the ethic of love, the ethic of power. Communists are supposed to be antireligious. Say rather they are anti-Christian. They are fanatically religious. They do not believe in the Christian God, but believe in a god they surely do. Is it not true to say that in a real sense a man's god is whatever is for him the sum total of reality? The Communists' god is therefore the proletariat; their Bible, *Das Kapital;* their shrine, Lenin's tomb; their kingdom of god, the conquest of the world by force; their cross, the hammer and sickle.

My people inquire of a thing of wood, and their staff gives them oracles.

The **wood** and the **staff** have their modern counterparts.

There is another aspect of Israel's idolatry which has significance for our time. Israel believed in Yahweh, but she worshiped him at the shrines built for the Baals and with the ritual used for the Baals. Theoretically she did not believe in idols, but actually she did. While she gave lip service to Yahweh, she actually took over the whole pagan Canaanitish cultus with its immorality and lewdness. "They wor-

[4] S. L. Brown, p. 44, quoting Pusey, *Minor Prophets,* I, 51.

them to err, and they have gone a whoring from under their God.	and they have left their God to play the harlot.
13 They sacrifice upon the tops of the mountains, and burn incense upon the hills, under oaks and poplars and elms, because the shadow thereof *is* good: therefore your	13 They sacrifice on the tops of the mountains, and make offerings upon the hills, under oak, poplar, and terebinth, because their shade is good.

13-14. The people have returned to the old benighted ways of sacrificing upon every high hill and under every green tree. It is as if all the work of the genuine prophets had become undone. Vs. 13*b*, together with vs. 14, speaks of the consequences of all this unfaithfulness. Daughters commit harlotry and brides commit adultery. It is possible to regard the first two phrases of vs. 14 as interrogative; H. S. Nyberg (*Studien zum*

shipped the Eternal and they also served their own gods" (II Kings 17:33 Moffatt). Now our real god is not the God we worship, but the gods we serve. Israel, while giving lip service to Yahweh, in actual practice patterned her life after the Baals and became like them. Here was a good example of the difference between profession and practice, theology and religion, faith and works. "This people draw near me with their mouth, and with their lips do honor me, but have removed their heart far from me" (Isa. 29:13).

Does the same situation exist today? Is there any difference between the God we worship and the gods we serve? Does a refined type of idolatry permeate our worship? The God we worship revealed himself in One of humble birth who had not where to lay his head, who taught that "a man's life consisteth not in the abundance of the things which he possesseth" (Luke 12:15). In a word, Jesus urged that we "seek . . . first the kingdom of God, and his righteousness" (Matt. 6:33). Such is the God in whom we believe. But are we worshiping this God at Canaanitish shrines? While we give lip service to the God of Jesus, is our life being patterned after the gods of this world? How do we measure the worth of a man? By the service he renders his fellow men or by the size of the fortune he leaves? Is one of our gods perchance "success"? And who is the successful man? Do we measure him by the Sermon on the Mount, or by the success stories of some magazine that tells of his rise to fame and fortune from a five-dollar-a-week start to a millionaire? Do we judge a man by what he is—his character—or by what he has? As we think of our youth growing up, are we concerned that they "grow in grace, and in the knowledge of our Lord and Saviour" (II Pet. 3:18), or are we concerned that they grow in wealth, position, power? Is it possible that in some instances the church itself falls prey to the standards of the world,

that the simplicity and sincerity of Christ are forgotten in the church's hunger for worldly prestige and power? One is not necessarily condemning worldly success as such. Many successful men possess an admirable sense of values and a laudable spirit of stewardship. One is only saying that to make mammon the standard by which we measure man is to betray one of the profoundest truths of God's revelation (Luke 12:19-20).

The God whom Jesus reveals is the universal Father who "hath made of one blood all nations of men for to dwell on all the face of the earth" (Acts 17:26). Paul, inspired by this vision of God in Christ, cut Christianity loose from the racial, cultural, and religious particularisms of Judaism and made it a universal faith. He spoke of Christ who is "our peace" and "hath broken down the middle wall of partition between us" (Eph. 2:14), in whom "there is neither Greek nor Jew, . . . Barbarian, Scythian, bond nor free" (Col. 3:11).

Such is the God we worship, the universal Father of all mankind. But are we worshiping this God at a Canaanitish shrine? Is this the God we really believe in? How do we reconcile this God with "Jim Crow" practices, policies of segregation, economic discrimination against men of different color, the prejudice and pride which induces wholly unchristian, to say nothing of unscientific, ideas of racial superiority, the stubborn and stupid policies of isolationism for which we paid in World War II? A singular illustration of this truth is seen in our attitude to the state. "Nationalism, man's other religion" is a familiar phrase. The God in whom we believe claims primary allegiance: "Thou shalt have no other gods before me" (Exod. 20:3). Yet in our age multitudes have given to the state the place which belongs to God alone. "We ought to obey God rather than men," said Peter (Acts 5:29); but many who do that, like conscientious objectors,

daughters shall commit whoredom, and your spouses shall commit adultery.

14 I will not punish your daughters when they commit whoredom, nor your spouses when they commit adultery: for themselves are separated with whores, and they sacrifice with harlots: therefore the people *that* doth not understand shall fall.

15 ¶ Though thou, Israel, play the harlot, *yet* let not Judah offend; and come not

Therefore your daughters play the harlot,
and your brides commit adultery.
14 I will not punish your daughters when
they play the harlot,
nor your brides when they commit
adultery;
for the men themselves go aside with harlots,
and sacrifice with cult prostitutes,
and a people without understanding shall
come to ruin.

15 Though you play the harlot, O Israel,
let not Judah become guilty.
Enter not into Gilgal,

Hoseabuche [Uppsala: Almqvist & Wiksells, 1935], p. 29), quotes in support 7:13; 11:5. But the next part of the verse admits the rendering of them in the RSV as possible, and indeed as essential, if כי at the opening of the next part is rendered as **for.** The penalties for unfaithfulness on the part of women were very severe; but here the women are exculpated because they have been brought up in an atmosphere of unfaithfulness and broken vows. The practice of sexual intercourse at the Baal sanctuaries typified in its original intent the divine marriage, and was doubtless practiced as a rite to ensure human fertility. By Hosea's day that original significance was forgotten; the practice now represented a grossly physical indulgence (cf. Deut. 23:18). **A people without understanding shall come to ruin** sums up the preceding section. Those who have no knowledge of Yahweh and his ways are easily lured into false worship and superstitious practices and **come to ruin.**

15. Some scholars would read the first word of this verse, with the LXX, as עם rather than אם, would attach עם זנה to the end of vs. 14, would delete **Judah** as a later insertion, and would translate:

A people without understanding
come to ruin with a harlot.
You, O Israel, be not guilty [תאשם],
enter not into Gilgal.

If taken in this way, vs. 15 must be regarded as a separate fragment, with no integral connection with what immediately precedes it. To swear **As the LORD lives** was quite legitimate (cf. Jer. 38:16), unless the phrase is used with reference to an abuse of the

---

must pay the price of imprisonment. Not only so, but nationalism with its exaggerated particularisms, its eagerness to condemn the wrong in other countries which it condones in its own, its false pride which puts a halo of self-righteousness and sanctity about its nation's policies —is not all this a denial of the God we worship? Is it possible that even ecclesiasticism may become a fetish? "By their fruits ye shall know them," said the Master (Matt. 7:20). Do we not constantly make conformity to ecclesiastical practice a measure of the Christian life rather than the ethical and moral standards revealed by God through Christ?

**My people inquire of a thing of wood,
and their staff gives them oracles.**

Our God does not have to be a thing of wood. The image may be made not only out of something material but out of thoughts or ideals which represent our inadequate ideas of reality. "It is just as much idolatry to worship God according to a false mental image as by means of a false metal image." [5]

13b-14. *The Double Standard.*—I will not punish your daughters when they play the

[5] William Temple, *Christian Faith and Life* (New York: The Macmillan Co., 1931), p. 24.

ye unto Gilgal, neither go ye up to Beth-aven, nor swear, The LORD liveth.	nor go up to Beth-a'ven, and swear not, "As the LORD lives."
16 For Israel slideth back as a backsliding heifer: now the LORD will feed them as a lamb in a large place.	16 Like a stubborn heifer, Israel is stubborn; can the LORD now feed them like a lamb in a broad pasture?

Lord's name in transgression of the Third Commandment. Apart from this possibility, the name of a sanctuary might have been expected, corresponding to **Gilgal** and **Beth-aven.** Amos 5:5; 8:14 might suggest the reading "by Beer-sheba." For **Beth-aven,** i.e., "house of idolatry," as a condemnatory name of Bethel, cf. 5:8; 10:5; Amos 5:5. It must indeed be added that the similarity between the second half of the verse and the verses in the book of Amos which have been cited casts doubt upon the authenticity of the whole verse. The mode of interpretation which is given in the RSV is much less likely than the one which has just been set forth, because it maintains the phrase "let not Judah be guilty" in a verse which otherwise uses the second person of address to Israel, so that the reference to Judah is quite undeveloped.

c) ISRAEL, A STUBBORN HEIFER (4:16)

16. If the emended text of vs. 15 is accepted (see Exeg.), there is a connection in thought between it and the present verse. Israel has not responded to the pleading to turn from vain ways of worship; the reason now is given. It is not a wayward spirit which is mentioned, but a **stubborn** spirit. The people have proved not amenable to instruction and discipline; therefore it is not to be expected that Yahweh can now tend them as a docile **lamb.** The second part of the verse cannot be taken as a promise for the future; the RSV is right in construing it as a question, expecting the answer "No."

harlot. . . . Why not? Because the men **themselves go aside with harlots.** Hosea was the first prophet to attack the double standard. "This is an astonishing point of view to be found seven hundred and fifty years before Christ. What would a Greek have thought of it, or a Roman, or a mediaeval knight, or a Victorian squire?" [6] They would not have understood it. Hosea's statement is reminiscent of Jesus' treatment of the woman taken in adultery. Moses in the law commanded that such should be stoned, but Jesus said, "He that is without sin among you, let him first cast a stone at her" (John 8:7). Familiar as he was with the book of Hosea, perhaps he thought of Hosea's revolutionary stand when he made that statement.

In the liberation of womanhood, political, economic, social, is there any single factor that has had as much influence as the gospel of Jesus? He who immortalized the widow's mite, the woman with the box of ointment, the cottage of Bethany with its two sisters, Mary and Martha; he who spoke some of his noblest and profoundest words to an outcast woman at a well in Samaria has done more to liberate and

[6] Edith Hamilton, *The Prophets of Israel* (New York: W. W. Norton & Co., 1936), p. 80.

redeem womanhood from servility, inferiority, and injustice than any other in history.

16. *Israel a Stubborn Heifer.*—A good case may be made out for the claim that Hosea was a peasant living on the land. No stranger to the farm could possibly have used so effectively the numerous metaphors of the soil as does Hosea (see 2:6; 6:4; 10:11; 12:11; *et al.*). Anyone familiar with farm life will not miss his symbol of the **heifer.** In opposition to the **stubborn,** restive **heifer** (not **backsliding**), unwilling to be led, darting off hither and yon without rhyme or reason, as if possessed by some evil spirit, Hosea paints the picture of peace and tranquillity—a **lamb in a broad pasture,** fed by the Eternal. It is a picture of peace as opposed to turmoil, the peace that comes from the submission of one's will to a higher and wiser will, as distinguished from the self-assertive and aggressive attitude which often mistakes activity for progress and opinion for knowledge. The very helplessness of the lamb is the source of its strength. Could the lamb speak, it would admit that it was not wise enough to find its way or strong enough to defend itself against the lurking enemies of its life. A sheep without a shepherd is in a precarious position. The prophet seems to imply

17 Ephraim *is* joined to idols: let him alone.

| 17 E'phraim is joined to idols, let him alone.

d) IDOLATRY OF EPHRAIM AND ITS EFFECTS (4:17-19)

17. Ephraim is thirled to idols, bound to their service by indissoluble bonds, so that there is no cure. Therefore **let him alone.** The reading of חבר, according to the testimony of the LXX μέτοχος, in place of the passive participle form of the M.T., which is not elsewhere found, makes no material difference to the sense. But note that חבור can mean "bewitched" as well as "bound"; both suit the context very well. The RSV indicates that the text of vs. 18 is very uncertain. The KJV rendering of the first phrase is without warrant. The only meaning that can be extracted from the M.T. is: "When their drinking carousal is ended, they give themselves to harlotry." But with a slight emendation of the Hebrew (סר סבאים for סר סבאם), we get the rendering of the RSV, which is commonly accepted by modern scholars. One point remains, however; the rhythmical form of vss. 17-18, so far as it can be ascertained, is against the line division of the RSV. Rather it would suggest that vs. 17 should read:

> Ephraim is joined to idols;
> leave him with his band of drunkards.

The reference in the **band of drunkards** would of course be to the drinking excesses which took place at the Baal festivals.

that man's well-being and safety, like that of the sheep, lie not in himself—"O Lord, I know that the way of man is not in himself: it is not in man that walketh to direct his steps" (Jer. 10:23). The tragedy of man springs from the fact that through arrogance and overconfidence in his ability and wisdom he often refuses to admit his innate limitations. He acts as though he were not in need of a shepherd. He thinks he knows the way and so gets lost. He is like a restive heifer, self-assertive, stubborn, the victim of fleeting moods, and so ill-equipped to meet the realities of life.

Yet it must not be thought that a life submitted to God, seeking to follow his leading and to be sustained by his grace, is sheltered and unadventurous, free from hazards or immune to harm. Nothing could be farther from the truth. The symbol of our faith is the Cross. The Christian way is marked by blood, tears, and sweat. The greatest saints have often met the death of martyrs. Peace is not stagnation. Christianity offers not freedom from danger but freedom in danger, not freedom from pain but the power to transmute pain into joy—"for the joy that was set before him" (Heb. 12:2) Jesus bore the cross. God does not shield us from battle but fights with us. Even though Christ was led like a lamb to the slaughter, his death was "swallowed up in victory."

17. Let Him Alone.—Sometimes that is all one can do with Ephraim. It is possible to become so much the slave of sin as to be impervious alike to reason, the appeal to decency, and the stirrings of the better self. One can become so coarse that the finer influences roll off like water from a duck's back; so hardened that the capacity to respond to the choicest values is no longer there. "He that is unjust, let him be unjust still: and he which is filthy, let him be filthy still" (Rev. 22:11). Sometimes Ephraim has to learn the hard way. His will is set, his mind is made up, he is stubborn and determined. The idols to which he is bound, however, need not all be symbols of degeneracy. Many Ephraims are quite respectable and moral. They may be wedded to some half-baked religious idea or some half-truth. Half-truths are more difficult to deal with than falsehoods. The element of truth gives them a hold on the mind. Some people who are indissolubly wedded to them never give them up. It is just no use trying to change their opinion. They know what is what, and that is that! **Let him alone.**

Two observations, however, must be made. Hosea was not admonishing us to be quitters when the task is unproductive or even seems hopeless. The result is not in our hands. Our responsibility is the planting and watering. Paul may plant, Apollos water, but God gives the increase. The other observation is that it is God who says **let him alone,** and God never gives us up. "How can I give you up, O Ephraim! How can I hand you over, O Israel! . . . My heart recoils within me, my compassion grows warm and tender" (11:8).

18 Their drink is sour: they have committed whoredom continually: her rulers *with* shame do love, Give ye.

19 The wind hath bound her up in her wings, and they shall be ashamed because of their sacrifices.

18 A band[l] of drunkards, they give themselves to harlotry;
they love shame more than their glory.[m]

19 A wind has wrapped them[n] in its wings,
and they shall be ashamed because of their altars.[o]

[l] Cn: Heb uncertain
[m] Cn Compare Gk: Heb of this line uncertain
[n] Heb *her*
[o] Gk Syr: Heb *sacrifices*

18. If the phrase **A band of drunkards** is transferred to vs. 17, as suggested above, vs. 18*a* then appears to be short, while vs. 18*b* has one stress more than normal. Again, vs. 18*b* is very difficult. The rendering given in the KJV is barely intelligible and unsuitable in the context. There is general agreement among scholars that מגאנם (cf. LXX ἐκ φρυάγματος αὐτῆς) should be read in place of מגניה. If for אהבו הבו we read the very similar אהב אהבו (or אהבהבו), we get the rendering of the RSV:

> . . . they give themselves to harlotry;
> **they love shame more than their glory,**

i.e., they love Baal more than the Lord.

19. Note that in the KJV the third person singular feminine objective **her** is followed by the third plural **they** and **their.** Van Hoonacker (*Les douze petits prophètes,* p. 53) has suggested the rendering: "When the wind has wrapped it [i.e., their shame, the golden calf] in its wings, then they will be ashamed of their altars." That **altars** rather than **sacrifices** should be read (מזבחותם for זבחותם) is now generally agreed; but otherwise Van Hoonacker's rendering is doubtful. It is possible to argue that the third person feminine singular is a consequence of the erroneous text "her leaders" in vs. 18, and thus to read the third person plural throughout, as in the RSV. The faithless people will be swept away, presumably by the tempestuous assault of some foreign invader. In that day they will recognize the folly of their ways and at last become ashamed of their altars. Weiser (*Das Buch der zwölf kleinen Propheten, ad loc.*) sees a *double-entendre* in the use of the Hebrew word רוח here, suggesting at once **wind** and "spirit," the latter being the harlot spirit which Hosea mentions several times. On the other hand, the devastating wind (רוח), when its work comes to be understood as determined and directed by the Lord, will make the people think of the spirit of the Lord (רוח יהוה). It seems better to regard צרר as a prophetic perfect and to link the first part of the line more closely with the second: "A wind will wrap them up in its wings."

18*b*. *Moral Blindness.*—It seems incredible that men could lose so completely their sense of values that they love shame more than glory. Here evil shows its most tragic guise. Like an acid it eats away the sense of right or truth. It turns the light within into darkness. It made the Israelites **love shame more than their glory,** i.e., love Baal more than the Lord. Has God any modern rivals? We are too intelligent now to worship idols, but an idol may be not only a "metal image" but a "mental image." Do we love power more than the Lord? Money more than the Lord? Liberty more than the Lord? In and of themselves these things are not evil, but they become so when given the place which belongs to God alone. Money made into a god corrupts and impoverishes (see Luke 12:17-21). Power becomes a Frankenstein which terrorizes and destroys, and even liberty disappears in license. This is what happens when we love Baal more than the Lord.

19. *The Acid Test.*—**A wind has wrapped them in its wings** is a poetic metaphor (cf. Ps. 18:10). It is used here to depict the violence of the conqueror who will sweep Israel into exile. When swept into exile, **they shall be ashamed because of their altars,** i.e., they will discover how inadequate their pagan rites have been (cf. 10:6). This is always the acid test. The true nature of our pagan deities is never so clearly seen as in a crisis. They cannot keep the storm from enveloping us in its **wings, or**

5 Hear ye this, O priests; and hearken, ye house of Israel; and give ye ear, O house of the king; for judgment *is* toward you, because ye have been a snare on Mizpah, and a net spread upon Tabor.

2 And the revolters are profound to make slaughter, though I *have been* a rebuker of them all.

5 Hear this, O priests!
  Give heed, O house of Israel!
Hearken, O house of the king!
  For the judgment pertains to you;
for you have been a snare at Mizpah,
  and a net spread upon Tabor.
2 And they have made deep the pit*p* of Shittim;
  but I will chastise all of them.

p Cn: Heb uncertain

2. Treachery of Ephraim (5:1-7)

a) An Indictment of the Leaders of Israel (5:1-2)

5:1. In ch. 4 the address was to the priests and the people. The reference here made to the royal house is a new development. The likelihood is that the people addressed were three classes in the community who had responsibilities of leadership in it and had failed to honor these responsibilities. The **priests** and the royal house are two of these classes; the **house of Israel** cannot be the other. It seems clear that in place of the word **house** we should read "prophets" (נביאי) or "princes" (שרי) of Israel. **For the judgment pertains to you:** There may be a deliberate case of *double-entendre* here. The exercise of judgment was a prerogative of the king; but God's judgment (or sentence) was to be upon the king's house also. The second part of the verse may be a condemnation of the activities of the priests in particular. The seductive Baal worship had been established at **Mizpah** and **Tabor,** so that these places had become a **snare** and a trap to Israel, causing their downfall and ruin. **Mizpah** is probably to be identified with the sanctuary of that name on the east side of the Jordan (cf. Judg. 10:17; 11:11, 29, 34), not with the town in Benjamin associated with Samuel. **Tabor,** at the east end of the plain of Jezreel, was the scene of the mustering of Israel's army under Barak and Deborah (cf. Judg. 4:6), and the only possible reference to worship there is in Deut. 33:19, where unfortunately the text is very uncertain. On the other hand, it was a high hill and that fact makes it quite possible that it was a cultic center.

2. This verse is uncertain of text and meaning. The rendering of the first part as given in the KJV has no sense at all. The Hebrew word translated **revolters** is from a

offer strength or hope when calamity strikes (see Ps. 46:1).

5:1-2. *The Impartiality of God's Judgments.* —These verses continue the subject matter of ch. 4. To the priests whom he condemned the prophet now adds the royal house, the king; **the judgment pertains to you,** he says—to the priests and the king's men; those who habitually passed judgment on others will now themselves be judged. They will not escape the judgment of God. Why? Because they have been **a snare . . . and a net.** The very ones who because of their position and privilege should have had an increased sense of social responsibility have become the occasion of social disaster.

Two emphases might be made here. One is on the impartiality of God's judgments. God has no favorites. The fact that a man is a priest or a king does not shield him—**the judgment pertains to you.** This is one of the many instances in which his ways are not our ways.

In our dealings with each other there is often one kind of justice for the rich and another for the poor. The privileged and powerful are often treated with a consideration and kindness denied the underprivileged (Jas. 2:1-4). Not so the Almighty. His balances are never tipped in favor of the great or distinguished.

It is not for nothing that we have come to associate rewards and punishments with the Christian religion. In another day the joys of heaven and torments of hell were strong incentives to the righteous, and deterrents to the wicked. Granted that this has been overdone. One has much sympathy for the Saracen woman who would be seen walking with a torch in one hand and a jug of water in the other, symbolic of her desire to burn up heaven and extinguish the fires of hell so that men would do good for the love of God. Yet we cannot altogether discard the truth behind these ideas, especially behind the idea of punishment. Someone has said that there may be a heaven but there must

3 I know Ephraim, and Israel is not hid from me: for now, O Ephraim, thou committest whoredom, *and* Israel is defiled.

3 I know E'phraim,
and Israel is not hid from me;
for now, O E'phraim, you have played
the harlot,
Israel is defiled.

---

root (שׁוּט) which means "to swerve" or "to fall away," so that the noun used here (שׁטים) may mean **revolters** or "acts of revolt." Thus the translation might be: (a) "revolters have gone deep in slaughter"; or (b) "through slaughter they have sunk deep in evil deeds." Neither seems at all apposite in the context, and there is much to be said for the emendation of which the RSV gives a translation (שׁחת השׁטים): **They have made deep the pit of Shittim.** Shittim may signify the sanctuary of Baal Peor, which was close to it (cf. Num. 25:1; Josh. 2:1; 3:1). We must infer that this sanctuary, like those at Mizpah and Tabor, had been a snare and a delusion in Israel's religious life (a **pit** being a common form of trap for capturing animals).

To make the reference in the three places named to the three sanctuaries there may give adequate cause for judgment to be pronounced against the priests, but takes no account of the other two classes mentioned in vs. 1 as being under judgment. It is therefore possible that the mention of these three place names suggested to the prophet's hearers occasions of political intrigue and criminal entanglement of which no information has come down to us.

The second half of the verse can bear more than one translation. The Hebrew usage of pronoun and participle which is exemplified here may signify future development (so RSV: **But I will chastise all of them**); it may also express a continuing circumstance (thus: "Though I have been [and continue to be] correction to them all"). Some scholars propose a very simple emendation (אין for אני) and so translate: "They have no correction" (mûṣār), or "no instructor" (meyaṣṣēr), or "no [moral] restraint" (môṣēr). The last would mean that they indulge themselves in licentious ways and have no scruples. But there seems no necessity for that emendation. The LXX has παιδευτής (i.e., מיסר).

b) A Brood of Strange Children (5:3-7)

3. The rendering given in the RSV seems a very formal way of saying that Israel has been faithless; the repetition of the vocative, **O Ephraim,** is very stiff. Another rendering, which incidentally requires no textual emendation, is much more suitable:

I have known Ephraim [of old],
and Israel has not been hidden from me;
But now, O Ephraim, you have played the harlot,
and Israel has become defiled.

---

be a hell. Such a statement is not the mark of a vindictive or vengeful spirit. It is merely the desire on the part of the morally sensitive that fair play and justice shall prevail for all, not for the privileged alone. One can accept more readily the thought that the good receive no future rewards—for in a real sense goodness is its own reward—than that those who are a **snare . . . and a net,** playing havoc on their fellows, should permanently escape judgment because of the protection of position, power, and privilege. The injustices of our "justice" cry to high heaven for remedy. If one could not feel that many of the books we close will somehow sometime be opened again, one's faith in the decency or moral integrity of the

universe would be permanently shaken. There is nothing whatever vindictive in this.

The other emphasis is that not only is God's judgment impartially meted out to clergy and laymen, kings and commoners alike, but that from those more privileged he expects more. Not only does he not minimize or excuse the evils of the privileged, but on the contrary, he expects from them a greater harvest of good works. "Unto whomsoever much is given, of him shall be much required" (Luke 12:48). It sometimes seems unfortunate or even unfair that society will take in its stride the moral lapses of a layman yet raise such furor over the comparable lapses of a clergyman. In a sense, however, this is as it should be. The

4 They will not frame their doings to turn unto their God: for the spirit of whoredoms *is* in the midst of them, and they have not known the LORD.

5 And the pride of Israel doth testify to his face: therefore shall Israel and Ephraim

4 Their deeds do not permit them
    to return to their God.
For the spirit of harlotry is within them,
    and they know not the LORD.

5 The pride of Israel testifies to his face,

4. Return to God is now impossible for Israel. They have so long been unfaithful to him that they have ceased to know him, so that they have no urge or sense of need to return. But it is also true that if they had the inclination to return, they would not be able, for they are now completely in the bondage of sin (cf. Ps. 95:8; Isa. 55:6; Jer. 18:13-16).

5. The RSV is doubtless right in reading **Ephraim** in place of the M.T. **Israel and Ephraim** in the second half line. The third portion of the verse, with its unexpected mention of **Judah,** lies outside the metrical scheme and should be regarded as an

very regard and confidence which "the cloth" bestows puts its wearer under a heavier responsibility than would otherwise exist. Increased privilege means increased responsibility. This is why the **snare** and the **net** of the privileged are more socially disastrous and morally inexcusable than they otherwise would be.

4. Hindrances to Our Knowledge of God.—There are many hindrances to man's knowledge of God. Some are kept from God by a devastating emotional experience which they are unable to reconcile with a good, wise, or loving Father. Others are hindered by some intellectual difficulty. "The problem of God" is a phrase one sometimes hears. Still others do not know the Eternal because they love the darkness rather than the light. The pure in heart see God, and we are not pure. Hosea seems to hint at another common cause of man's neglect of God. **Their deeds do not permit them to return to their God.** What did he mean by **deeds?** Was he referring to their conduct, their way of life, the habits they had acquired, the objects to which they had given their loyalties?

It is evident that there are certain habits of thought or conduct wholly incompatible with one's knowledge of God. This is why renunciation is at the heart of the Christian religion. "Know ye not, that to whom ye yield yourselves servants to obey, his servants ye are to whom ye obey; whether of sin unto death, or of obedience unto righteousness?" (Rom. 6:16.) The opinion of one, never mind how brilliant or capable, whose ways are evil is worth little as far as Christian truth goes. The organ of Christian knowledge is not just the mind; it is the life. If Paul knew while the folk on Mars' Hill did not, it was not because they were intellectually stupid and he bright. Obedience is the pathway to the knowledge of Chris-

tian truth. "If any man will do his will, he shall know of the doctrine" (John 7:17). When our **deeds** are at variance with the will of God and deny his rightful lordship of our lives, we cannot know him. With the "harlot" spirit, the spirit of rebellion, indulgence, waywardness, we cannot understand God, never mind how learned or clever we may be.

The **deeds** that keep a man from God are not necessarily evil in themselves. Many of us are kept from knowing God because we are too completely occupied with the affairs of the world. "The world is too much with us"; we are "careful and troubled about many things" (Luke 10:41). How often have we heard it said, "I just have no time for the church." Our days are full, our life is crowded like the inn—there is literally no room. We need not think that the inn at Bethlehem was full of gangsters. They were no doubt respectable men, good people; but the good was the enemy of the best. "Take time to be holy." We have no time. Our life is one endless round of activity with little or no time for meditation, worship, or prayer. We could no more know God that way than we could know the treasures of art by driving past the museum in a car and taking furtive glances in its direction.

Here then are two ways in which our **deeds** keep us from knowing the Eternal. (a) They may be qualitatively incompatible with the nature of the God we seek to understand. (b) They may be not qualitatively but quantitatively an obstacle. Our lives may resemble a bargain counter at the rush hour—they are cluttered up. The goodly pearl was bought when the merchant was willing to part with those of lesser value.

5. The Interrelatedness of Life.—Judah may not have been as guilty as Israel in her self-righteous complacency. Hosea says as much (1:6-7; 4:15). Yet she would share in the same

fall in their iniquity; Judah also shall fall with them.

6 They shall go with their flocks and with their herds to seek the LORD; but they shall not find *him;* he hath withdrawn himself from them.

E'phraim*q* shall stumble in his guilt;
Judah also shall stumble with them.
6 With their flocks and herds they shall go
to seek the LORD,
but they will not find him;
he has withdrawn from them.

q Heb *Israel and Ephraim*

---

addition. Israel's **pride** is his own condemnation. When man believes that he can work out his own salvation, that he can rule his own environment for his own purposes, then he comes to have a false sense of power which induces in him a feeling of pride and presumption that leaves no room for that spirit of humility and creaturely dependence with which man fitly approaches the God who is his creator and his Savior. The Greeks recognized the heinousness of this sin, which they called ὕβρις; the Hebrews knew it no less.

6. Note the emphatic order of the words. Some at least of the Israelites **seek the LORD,** but with a service which is altogether unacceptable. He desires mercy, not sacrifice. It is useless to seek his favor by rendering to him gifts that befit the Baals. Therefore **he has withdrawn from them.** That does not necessarily mean that they can under no circumstances find him. "You will seek me and find me, when you seek me with all your heart" (Jer. 29:13; cf. Isa. 55:7; Prov. 2:1-5).

---

deterioration and destruction that was justly to be the lot of her northern neighbor.

We can understand the fall of Israel. For all her pride, which itself testified against her, she was morally corrupt, and so reaped what she sowed; but why should Israel's guilt cause **Judah** to **stumble** too? If the guilty alone experienced the tragedies of guilt, how very different would history be! But willy-nilly the guilt of the guilty involves the relatively innocent as well. The despicable action of the tyrant who holds innocent people as hostages, tortures or slays them for crimes of which they are not guilty, does not unfairly symbolize one aspect of reality. The innocent are more often than not involved. Hitler fell. He deserved to fall. But not only did Hitler fall; in falling he took Germany with him. And Germany in falling dragged down Europe with her.

Is it the fact that we cannot seem to confine evil to its proper locale, isolate or quarantine it as we do some infectious disease, that makes sin such a cruel reality? This dark nature of sin becomes less somber when we remember that we confront here a law of life—shall we call it the law of human solidarity? It is an indication of the fellowship which is God's will for man. And it works both ways. If we are not disturbed because God makes his sun to shine on the evil and on the good, perhaps we ought not to be so upset if he sends his storms on the just as well as on the unjust. Moreover, is there one of us who because of the law of human solidarity does not receive blessings far beyond his merits? We "have a goodly heritage" (Ps.

16:6). If we enjoy freedom of speech, press, and worship, it is because others have purchased our freedom with their blood. There is hardly a value we prize, a spiritual possession we cherish, but has come to us from others. If then it is true that because of this law we cannot confine the evil of the evildoer to himself alone, it is equally true that for the same reason the finest blessings of life are made available for us. The talents of artists, the discoveries of scientists, the sacrifices of saints, the exploits of heroes, the deeds of the daring: in all these we share. "We are debtors" (Rom. 8:12).

The greatest example of mutuality or solidarity is found in our Lord. "I have need to be baptized of thee, and comest thou to me?" (Matt. 3:14.) It was because Jesus wanted to identify himself with sinning humanity that he submitted to baptism at the hand of John. He acted as though he were somehow involved in the sins of his people. As Jesus faced his cross Pilate asked, "Why, what evil hath he done?" (Matt. 27:23.) None. He suffered, the just for the unjust. But if he, though innocent of sin, yet bore the cruelty of sin and experienced a death he did not deserve, it is also true that because the principle works both ways, from his triumph have come to us, unworthy though we be, the greatest blessings we have. "With his stripes we are healed" (Isa. 53:5).

6. *The Limitations of the Ceremonial.*—The Eternal could say to the Israelites and to us what Paul said to the church at Corinth, "I seek not yours, but you" (II Cor. 12:14). God is no Oriental monarch who may be appeased

7 They have dealt treacherously against the LORD; for they have begotten strange children: now shall a month devour them with their portions.

8 Blow ye the cornet in Gibeah, *and* the trumpet in Ramah: cry aloud *at* Beth-aven, after thee, O Benjamin.

---

7 They have dealt faithlessly with the LORD;
    for they have borne alien children.
    Now the new moon shall devour them
    with their fields.

8 Blow the horn in Gib′e-ah,
    the trumpet in Ramah.
    Sound the alarm at Beth-a′ven;
    tremble,[r] O Benjamin!

[r] Cn Compare Gk: Heb *after you*

---

7. Strange children are not the offspring of mixed marriages but are children who have never been trained to know the Lord, and consequently are strangers to him. The **new moon** was a festival occasion, so that there may be poetic justice in the destruction of the wayward Israelites at such a time. Less likely and less fitly the words may mean: "The [next] new moon will devour, . . ."; that would signify that a speedy doom was in store for the Israelites. Various emendations have been proposed, such as "now a destroyer [משחית] will devour their fields" or "now their fields will be destroyed by the sirocco" (יאכלו מחרישית); but the original, with its reference to the **new moon** and the **fields,** is a fit form of sentence for a people who had been lured away from the Lord and his service by the attractive and seductive rites of the Canaanite agricultural festivals.

3. WARFARE BETWEEN EPHRAIM AND JUDAH (5:8–6:6)

a) YAHWEH AS A DEVOURING LION (5:8-14)

8. This verse and the next one should be taken together. They describe an occasion when Ephraim was threatened with invasion and the alarm was sounded so that all available forces might be mustered to meet the emergency. The towns mentioned in vs. 8 were in Benjamin, near Jerusalem. **Gibeah** and **Ramah** were on hilltops, eminently suitable for giving a warning; Bethel was not so placed (for the name **Beth-aven** cf. Exeg.

---

or cajoled by our gifts, whether large or small, many or few. We cannot buy his favor with **flocks and herds,** any more than with stocks or dividends. "The sacrifices of God are a broken spirit: a broken and a contrite heart, O God, thou wilt not despise" (Ps. 51:17).

The **flocks and herds** with which the Israelites went in search of the Eternal were intended for sacrificial offerings. Hosea assured them, however, that despite these offerings by which they sought the Eternal's favor, they would **not find him; he hath withdrawn himself from them.** This fact reminds us that God is found not through outward forms of worship, not through ceremonial performances as such, but through moral sincerity. All churches, especially of those communions that are ecclesiastically minded, have to guard constantly against the danger of allowing the ceremonial to obscure the moral in worship. True worship should include both. But while worship can exist without ceremonial accouterments, it cannot really exist without sincerity. Indeed, it is of the greatest significance that some of the profoundest insights of Judaism did not come out of the era of Solo-

mon's reign, when Israel was at the peak of her national glory, but from the austerities of the Exile. God revealed himself most to his people when the ceremonial, ritualistic features of their religious life were most in abeyance. The very lack of the ecclesiastical trappings drove them into closer touch with reality, with God. All this but confirms what Jesus said: "Neither in this mountain, nor yet at Jerusalem, . . . God is a Spirit: and they that worship him must worship him in spirit and in truth" (John 4:21, 24).

This is not to speak against ritual or ceremony as such. It is only to say that at best the symbols of worship are but means to an end. When they become an end in themselves, they defeat the very purpose they are designed to achieve. Paul speaks of those who have the form of religion but will have nothing to do with it as a force (II Tim. 3:5). But form without force, like faith without works, like knowledge without love, can be but sounding brass and clanging cymbal.

7-12. *Three Lessons from History.*—In these six verses the prophet reiterates the theme

9 Ephraim shall be desolate in the day of rebuke: among the tribes of Israel have I made known that which shall surely be.

10 The princes of Judah were like them that remove the bound: *therefore* I will pour out my wrath upon them like water.

11 Ephraim *is* oppressed *and* broken in judgment, because he willingly walked after the commandment.

9 E′phraim shall become a desolation
in the day of punishment;
among the tribes of Israel
I declare what is sure.

10 The princes of Judah have become
like those who remove the landmark;
upon them I will pour out
my wrath like water.

11 E′phraim is oppressed, crushed in judgment,
because he was determined to go after vanity.[s]

[s] Gk: Heb *a command*

on 4:15), but a summons from there would be heard in the countryside that slopes from it down to the Jordan Valley. The **horn** was a ram's horn, while the **trumpet** was elongated in shape and was made of metal. The final phrase of the verse means, lit., **After you, O Benjamin.** That is an abbreviated phrase; it might signify "the enemy is after you, Benjamin," i.e., look to yourself; but in the light of Judg. 5:14, it may have been a well-known battle cry: "[We follow] after you, Benjamin." Such a battle cry on the lips of the people who rallied to Benjamin's help would be in order, but it is not likely to have been used by Hosea himself. There is therefore much to be said for the emendation which is represented by the RSV, **tremble, O Benjamin** (reading חרד for אחריך); otherwise read the very similar החרידו, and render the phrase as "terrify Benjamin," or אחריד.

9. The words **I declare what is sure** probably do not mean that the Lord is speaking through Hosea things which are sure, but that the vicissitudes of human history make known the sure, immutable decrees of God and his rule of human affairs. Man can reject God and neglect his commandments, but he cannot escape the resultant penalties.

10. Vss. 10-12 and vss. 13-14 appear to be parallel stanzas; each begins with a description of a crime committed by Judah or Ephraim and proceeds to indicate the penalty which will follow. The previous references to Judah in the book of Hosea have obviously been later insertions, but there is no reason for so regarding this one. The **princes of Judah** are charged with removing landmarks, i.e., boundary stones. This may mean that the disturbed national situation caused by the threat of invasion gave to unscrupulous land-grabbers an unusually favorable opportunity for their operations; it also means that Judah, no less than Ephraim, was deserving of punishment.

11. The passives in 11a make it a statement of penalty for Ephraim; but the second phrase, which may be rendered "crushed as to his right," seems unsuitable in the context, which is dealing not with Ephraim's rights but with his deserts. Therefore it is better to follow the LXX and to read the verbs as actives, descriptive of Ephraim's wickedness, i.e., "Ephraim oppresses, perverting judgment." **Because he willingly walked**

which seems to be the prevailing note of the second section of his book (chs. 4–14). This theme has three features. First, that Israel's difficulty is moral, faithlessness—**they have dealt faithlessly with the LORD; . . . have become like those who remove the landmark,** a particularly low type of misdoing; the landmarks were under the protection of religion (Deut. 19:14; 27:17; Prov. 22:28; 23:10). Second, that because of her moral lapses she will experience evil days, in this particular instance invasion—**Ephraim shall become a desolation.**

Third, that the resultant tragedies are the direct act of a God who punishes the evildoer—**I am like a moth to Ephraim, and like dry rot to the house of Judah.** In the main history vindicates these insights; so the morally sensitive will feel. But in the main the secular mind does not accept them, and that is largely the crux of the human problem.

The diagnosis of every dying civilization, like the post-mortem of every dead one, reveals the truth of Hosea's insights (see Expos. on 2:6; 4:1-5; 9:11-12).

12 Therefore *will* I *be* unto Ephraim as a moth, and to the house of Judah as rottenness.

13 When Ephraim saw his sickness, and Judah *saw* his wound, then went Ephraim to the Assyrian, and sent to king Jareb: yet could he not heal you, nor cure you of your wound.

12 Therefore I am like a moth to E'phraim,
　and like dry rot to the house of Judah.

13 When E'phraim saw his sickness,
　and Judah his wound,
　then E'phraim went to Assyria,
　and sent to the great king.[t]
　But he is not able to cure you
　or heal your wound.

[t] Cn: Heb *a king that will contend*

---

after the commandment is not a crime: nor can an escape be found by making the reference to a commandment other than the Lord's. The LXX should be followed (ὀπίσω τῶν ματαίων), so that שוא is read for צו, hence the RSV rendering. (But cf. G. R. Driver, "Supposed Arabisms in the Old Testament," *Journal of Biblical Literature,* LV [1936], 105-6.) The perfect הלך must surely be read as the infinitive construct *halōkh.*

12. Now it is clear that whoever the invading enemy may be, and however much Judah and Ephraim may war together and injure each other, it is the Lord who overrules it all. He does his work quietly and secretly, and for a time it may be quite unregarded of men. The figures of **moth** and **dry rot** plainly suggest a gradual process of corruption and decay; but if עש is rendered as "pus" rather than as **moth** (so G. R. Driver, "Difficult Words in the Hebrew Prophets," in H. H. Rowley, ed., *Studies in Old Testament Prophecy* [Edinburgh: T. & T. Clark, 1950], pp. 66-67) the two terms "pus" and "rottenness" will then signify suppurating wounds and sores.

13. Ephraim and Judah awake to a realization of the desperate situation in which they find themselves. Urgent action is needed; security must be sought in some quarter, or at least relief must be found. So they resort to Assyria for help; the result is political subjugation and the burden of tribute payment. The temporary need may thus be met, but there is no cure along this line; there are indeed only further burdens.

The name **king Jareb** has caused discussion. The term may be a nickname, as George Adam Smith has submitted, "King Pick-Quarrel" or "King Pretender" (*The Book of the Twelve Prophets* [rev. ed.; New York: Harper & Bros., 1928], I, 282), and may have been used of a king of Assyria; but most scholars are agreed that we should read not מלך ירב but מלכי רב, i.e., **great king.** It appears that *šarru rabū* was a title used commonly by Assyrian kings, so that the one used here may be regarded as its equivalent (cf. 10:6; cf. G. R. Driver, "Studies in the Vocabulary of the Old Testament. VIII," *Journal of Theological Studies,* XXXVI [1935], 295-96). The translation of the final phrase **nor cure you of your wound** should be accepted; a slight change in vocalization is required in the M.T. (*yaghheh* for *yighheh*). In the second portion of the verse parallelism would suggest the reading (supported by some scholars) :

Then Ephraim went to Assyria,
and Judah sent to the great king.

13-15. *Palliatives versus Remedies.*—This is proof positive of the foregoing observation concerning Israel's moral obtuseness. Had they realized the real cause of their trouble, Assyria would have been the last direction in which they would have turned. Ephraim and Judah in turning to Assyria were manifesting an all too common human weakness, viz., that of seeking palliatives rather than remedies. This was due to their faulty diagnosis of their own condition, which in turn revealed either their unwill-ingness or their inability to face the facts. The first thing the Christian religion offers to man is a correct diagnosis of his ills, and surely that is the initial step on the road to any genuine recovery. Correct diagnosis is essential. Christianity is sometimes accused of being an "escape from reality." As a matter of fact no other diagnosis of man's sickness comes so near to reality as that which Christianity proclaims. It has the insight and courage to trace man's troubles to the moral and spiritual rootage

14 For I *will be* unto Ephraim as a lion, and as a young lion to the house of Judah: I, *even* I, will tear and go away; I will take away, and none shall rescue *him*.

15 ¶ I will go *and* return to my place, till they acknowledge their offense, and seek my face: in their affliction they will seek me early.

14 For I will be like a lion to E'phraim,
　　and like a young lion to the house of
　　　Judah.
I, even I, will rend and go away,
　　I will carry off, and none shall rescue.

15 I will return again to my place,
　　until they acknowledge their guilt and
　　　seek my face,
　　and in their distress they seek me, say-
　　　ing,

---

14. The reason why these overtures to Assyria were of no avail is that the real opponent of Ephraim and Judah was no human being and the crisis from which they suffered was no mere political crisis. It was the Lord himself who was contending with his people. He has been as a raging **lion** who does not spare and from whom there is no deliverance.

What is the historical occasion to which vss. 8-14 refer? We seek in vain for a crisis caused by a foreign invader when both Judah and Ephraim appealed to Assyria for help; but it is possible that Hosea is here surveying the conduct of Judah and Ephraim over a period of years. That being so, Ephraim's overtures to Assyria may signify Menahem's action in 738 b.c. (cf. II Kings 15:19), while Judah made direct appeal to Assyria for help during the threat to Jerusalem when the confederate kings, Pekah of Ephraim and Rezin of Syria, sought to force Ahaz of Judah to join them in revolt against Assyria (cf. Isa. 7). The invasion referred to in vs. 8, therefore, may be that of the two confederate kings when they moved southward to threaten their kinsmen of Judah. The coming of the Assyrians in response to Judah's call must have caused the hasty withdrawal of the invaders, and the princes of Judah may have taken advantage of the resultant situation of confusion to work depredation and havoc upon Ephraim (vs. 10). Thus both Judah and Ephraim had been guilty of internecine strife and of putting reliance for security upon foreign alliance. Their punishment will come not from Assyria, but from the Lord.

b) Israel's Shallow Repentance (5:15–6:3)

15. This verse, together with 6:1-3, forms a minor section within 5:8–6:6. The Lord has administered disciplinary punishment to his people; he now returns to his place (cf. Ezek. 8:12; 10:19; 11:23). The next move must be with those who have broken covenant with him (cf. 5:6). The M.T. יאשמו is legitimately rendered in the RSV as **until they acknowledge their guilt**, giving a sense which is suitable in the context. But it is interesting that the LXX has ἀφανισθῶσιν, which suggests the closely

---

whence most of them surely spring, and it asserts that nothing save genuine repentance, resulting in an inner change of heart, a new birth, can effect a cure. Ephraim had neither the wit nor the courage to see that; hence when Ephraim saw his decay, he went to Assyria instead of to God. But Assyria could not cure him.

We too are like Ephraim in this. The history of international relations is replete with examples. Nation after nation turns to some Assyria today, or takes up arms against some Assyria tomorrow—not from any settled prin-

ciple of action, but purely for reasons of political or material expediency. And history abundantly proves the utter stupidity and tragedy of that policy. For inevitably the root cause of our international conflicts is moral. They spring from injustice or greed or short-sighted selfishness. The disease cannot be cured by running to Assyria, for Assyria is suffering from the same ailment. The blind cannot lead the blind. The disease can be cured only as Ephraim and Assyria both turn away from the shortsighted policies of expediency and opportunism and face up to moral realities by adopt-

6 Come, and let us return unto the Lord: for he hath torn, and he will heal us; he hath smitten, and he will bind us up.

6 "Come, let us return to the Lord; for he has torn, that he may heal us; he has stricken, and he will bind us up.

---

similar reading יְשַׁמּוּ, if indeed it may not be an alternative rendering of the M.T. (cf. G. R. Driver on שׁמם=אשׁשׁ, in Schindler, ed., *Gaster Anniversary Volume*, pp. 73-78). The meaning thus given "until they are appalled and seek my face" seems to provide a better parallel to the following phrase than the RSV rendering. There is much to be said for reversing the order of the last two phrases of the verse and reading:

> I will return again to my place
> until they acknowledge their guilt (or "until they are appalled").
> When trouble comes upon them, they will seek me betimes,
> they will seek my face.

The addition of the word "saying" in the RSV is in order in so far as it indicates that the opening verses of ch. 6 contain the words with which these people return to the Lord, but it is misleading in that it gives the impression that these words are genuine and sincere. It will be seen, when we come to examine them, that there is more reason for regarding them as a complacent and facile expression of penitence which has no depth of experience to give it real worth. It is better therefore to omit the word, to regard 6:1-3 as an example of interjected direct speech, and to determine the tone of these verses from their contents and from the context in which they stand.

6:1-3. These verses are closely related to the final section of ch. 5. God's people Israel has greatly suffered. They have found no help in foreign alliance. Their punishment has been ordained of God and is therefore ineluctable. No one can deliver them out of his hand. At last they recognize their desperate plight and resolve to return to their God.

---

ing some principle of action which transcends politics. International organizations can succeed only as the nations discard their self-righteous spirit and as each admits its share in the sin and guilt which corrupt the world. This is the only diagnosis of our situation that is true or adequate. In so far as we are able to face reality we shall have taken the initial step in some genuine repentance which will lead us not to Assyria, who cannot heal, but to God, in whose truth lies our salvation.

I will return again to my place, until they acknowledge their guilt and seek my face.

This picture of God withdrawing himself and then returning to his own place is not at all in line with our thought of him. The psalmist speaks of God as one from whose presence we cannot escape, "If I make my bed in hell, behold, thou art there" (Ps. 139:8). Jesus portrayed God as one who leaves the ninety and nine that are safe in the fold and goes out after the one that has gone astray, searching "until he find it" (Luke 15:4). Apparently, then, Hosea does not mean that God withdraws to his own place in the sense that he becomes inaccessible or remote. This could never be true

of him in whom "we live, and move, and have our being" (Acts 17:28). Yet there is a truth here. It is not that God becomes remote or inaccessible, but that in our dealings with him there comes a time when the next move, so to speak, is up to us—**until they acknowledge their guilt and seek my face.** It is not so much that God withdraws himself from us as that our sin separates us from him; but even then, never so far but that if we call in our distress, he will hear, "for he will abundantly pardon" (Isa. 55:7).

6:1-2. *True and False Repentance.*—It is a pity that these two verses cannot be taken at their face value. They are supposed to be the expression of repentant hearts. The words surely seem to be, but the spirit is lacking. George Adam Smith refers to them as a "too facile repentance," [7] S. L. Brown as "a hasty resolution which is not carried into effect," [8] T. K. Cheyne as "a hasty resolution, from which a full and free confession of sin was fatally absent." [9] The prophet here describes a people who regarded the Almighty as though he were

[7] *The Twelve Prophets,* I, 283.
[8] *Hosea,* p. 56.
[9] *The Book of Hosea* (Cambridge: Cambridge University Press, 1913; "Cambridge Bible"), p. 78.

2 After two days will he revive us: in the third day he will raise us up, and we shall live in his sight.	2 After two days he will revive us; on the third day he will raise us up, that we may live before him.

Vss. 1-3 describe the attitude in which they return. The words **Come, let us return** make plain the fact that the decision to return had to be made by the people themselves; they had to resolve to do it. If they had not so resolved, any hope of restoration and renewal would have been vain. The remainder of the verse should be taken as it is in the RSV. It is a confident assertion that God's punishment is never intended to be merely penal, but always to be disciplinary and remedial; it is part of his activity as Savior. Vs. 1 may be taken therefore as a sincere utterance, showing, indeed, no evidence of repentance or sorrow, but manifesting at least a straight purpose to return to God. But the expression of confident hope in vs. 1 gives place to an attitude of easy complacency in vs. 2. The restoration and revival are to be speedy and without trouble; in two or three days all will be well again. Therein is revealed the shallowness of the popular religious attitude. There is no sense of awe before God, no sense of the loss of an intimate relationship which can only gradually be restored, no searching sense of guilt before divine

an indulgent grandfather who, never mind what we do, pats us on the back and gives us candy as he easily lets us off. **He hath torn, and he will heal us.** In a couple of days **will he revive us,** to live under his care, and then we can go right on doing what we have been doing. There is no adequate recognition here of the consequences which follow in the wake of human sin. Hence there is no genuine spirit of repentance. For as we shall see, repentance involves the recognition of the tragic consequences of evil. But Ephraim was seemingly unconscious of this. "Strangers have devoured his strength, and he knoweth it not" (7:9).

Hosea seems to have genuine doubts not alone of Israel's desire for repentance but of her capacity for it. The marks of true repentance were missing. What were those marks as Hosea understood them? They were the ones with which the gospel confronts us. No wonder that Hosea is quoted oftener by N.T. writers than any other of the minor prophets. "More than thirty direct or indirect quotations from the book of Hosea may be found in the gospels and the epistles."[1] In the depth and clarity of his spiritual insight this prophet comes nearer to evangelical Christianity than any other in the O.T.

Hosea may be styled the first preacher of repentance, yet so thoroughly did he deal with this subject of eternal interest to the human heart, that between him and ourselves almost no teacher has increased the insight with which it has been examined, or the passion with which it ought to be enforced.[2]

What are the steps in genuine repentance as Hosea sees them? One surely is man's consciousness of his sin. That is the starting point. Without it repentance is impossible. Israel was not really conscious of her sin. That is why she was not capable of true repentance. "Father, I have sinned," said the prodigal (Luke 15:18). The amazing fact about that statement is not that the prodigal made it but that he meant it. It is easy to repeat the prayer "Have mercy upon us, miserable offenders." We are offenders all right; but not many of us are miserable. There is a type of sin which does make us feel miserable. The kind the prodigal indulged, the coarse vulgar sin which leaves some ugly mark on our life, gives a poignant prick to our conscience, and if persisted in, may even reduce us to poverty, disease, disgrace, if not death. This sort of sin makes one know he is a sinner, assuming that prolonged indulgence has not so deadened the conscience as to render it incapable of knowing light from darkness, good from evil. There is, however, a respectable type of sin often condoned by society, or at least not condemned by it, which works havoc on the individual. Strangely enough this was the type that evoked the greatest condemnation from Jesus. "All the deepest sins in the nature of most of us are sins that we have not discovered at all."[3] Charles Kingsley must have been aware of them, for when once he was asked what kind of character he disliked most, he immediately replied, "My own."[4] The "miserable sinner" is not only he whose vulgar sin brings misery to

[3] Temple, *Christian Faith and Life*, p. 61.
[4] Harry Emerson Fosdick, in *The Speaker's Bible*, ed. James Hastings, *et al.* (Aberdeen: Speaker's Bible Offices, 1938), Matthew, I, 41.

[1] Raymond Calkins, *The Modern Message of the Minor Prophets* (New York: Harper & Bros., 1947), p. 51.
[2] George Adam Smith, *op. cit.*, I, 360.

law and the need for spiritual cleansing. There is nothing but the easy assumption that God is ready at any time to receive with alacrity those who return to him.

There is in vss. 1-2 a certain confusion of metaphor. The rending as by a lion, mentioned in 5:14, is taken up responsively in vs. 1. The fact that thereafter the people are thought of as returning to God indicates that the rending meant their injury and their agony but not their death. On the other hand, the words in vs. 2 **he will revive us** seem to speak of a revival after death. But it must be remembered that a calamity such as the Babylonian exile could be regarded as the death of a people (cf. Ezek. 37); and Deut. 30:15-20 speaks of the choice that lies before a man as that between the way of life and the way of death. To be restored to the Lord's presence could therefore readily be likened to a renewal of life.

---

himself and others. He may also be one who in church circles would be regarded "in good and regular standing." This the N.T. makes plain. Whatever the nature of our sins, without any willingness to say and mean, "I have sinned," no real repentance is possible since none is deemed necessary. Israel, according to Hosea, was unwilling to confess her sin. So are many of us.

Strange as it may sound to the ears of this modern age, long tickled by the amiable idiocies of evolution popularly misinterpreted, this generation's deepest need is not these dithyrambic songs about inevitable progress, but a fresh sense of personal and social sin.[5]

But a sense of sin is impossible apart from some true vision of God. Sin is missing the mark, but if there is no mark, how can we know when we miss it? And if there is a mark, who sets it? If man has made the laws of conduct, there is no reason why man cannot break them with impunity, and surely no need for remorse or grief in disregarding them. Without a sense of God there can be no sense of sin. "Misery alone never led either man or nation to repentance."[6]

The character of our age proves this: few others in history have borne more tragic marks of human sin, and few others have been less conscious of sin. This lost sense of sin springs from our lost sense of God. So did Israel's. "My people are destroyed for lack of knowledge" (4:6). It was the knowledge of God of which Hosea was thinking. "There is no truth, nor mercy, nor knowledge of God in the land" (4:1). If misery alone were enough to make man repent, our generation the world around would be on its knees. But repentance comes only when human misery and tragedy are seen in the light of that which transcends the human scene—God's will and purpose. It takes more than the push of the far country, it takes the pull of the Father's house to effect genuine

repentance. If I know I have sinned, it is because I see my life in the light of God's holiness. I know I am not worthy when I view my life in the light of the perfect life. "Depart from me; for I am a sinful man, O Lord" (Luke 5:8). I become convinced that the road I am taking is a wrong road when I know there is a right one. "Against thee, thee only, have I sinned, and done this evil in thy sight," cried the Psalmist (Ps. 51:4). It is only as we recover our vision of God, his love, his grace, his holy purposes for our lives, that repentance is possible.

Repentance, however, as Hosea conceived it and the gospel proclaims it, involves another factor, viz., returning to God. It "is a turning back upon one's self, a retracing of one's footsteps. . . . It is a coming back and a coming home."[7] One is reminded here again of the close parallel of Hosea's idea of repentance with the N.T. idea. "I will arise and go to my father," said the prodigal (Luke 15:18). This, you see, is a genuine *metanoia*, a change of mind, which means a change of direction. "Gypsy" Smith used to say that the difference between conversion and repentance is the difference between waking up and getting up—there is a difference!—"I will arise and go." Sometimes remorse or regret wakes us up, makes us aware of the fact that we have sinned. We are quite unhappy about our condition. But unhappiness is not repentance. There is a "sorrow of the world," as Paul said, which "worketh death." But that must be distinguished from "godly sorrow [which] worketh repentance to salvation" (II Cor. 7:10). Genuine repentance therefore involves an act of the will, "I will arise and go" back to the God from whom my evil has separated me.

Was Israel capable of such repentance? That seems to be the doubt with which Hosea wrestles. Israel had lost her sense of sin because she had lost her knowledge of God; and so she had lost her desire to change her mind and the direction of her life.

---

[5] *Ibid.*, p. 39.
[6] George Adam Smith, *op. cit.*, I, 365.

[7] *Ibid.*, I, 363.

3 Then shall we know, *if* we follow on to know the LORD: his going forth is prepared as the morning; and he shall come unto us as the rain, as the latter *and* former rain unto the earth.

3 Let us know, let us press on to know the LORD;

    his going forth is sure as the dawn;

he will come to us as the showers,

    as the spring rains that water the earth."

---

3. Then shall we know does not give the intention of the original. The syntax is this: **Come, let us return to the LORD** [and] **let us know.** What was wrong with the people was that they had no knowledge of the Lord and his ways (5:4); now they will know him. Indeed, more than that is to be said. They are now aware that knowledge of God comes to men gradually, and it must be persistently pursued and zealously sought. **His going forth** [to help] **is sure as the dawn.** That is a good rendering of the original and is a very fitting figure from nature, especially in view of the fact that another common figure from nature immediately follows. It is not to be wondered at, however, that the Hebrew word for **dawn** (שחר) should recall to mind the verb "to seek" (שחר), which is used at the close of ch. 5; and when we notice that the LXX has εὑρήσομεν αὐτον (reading for the M.T. מוצאו the very similar נמצאנו), we can appreciate the attractiveness of the proposed rendering כשחרנו כן נמצאנו, "as soon as we seek him, we shall find him." It must be admitted that this also gives most fitting and excellent sense. The suggestion has sometimes been made that the final part of vs. 5 should be read as the conclusion of the first part of vs. 3 in this way:

> His coming forth is sure as the dawn,
>   and his commandment is as a light which comes forth.

However, the mention of God's judgment or of his commandment at this point, when the thought is of God's gracious favor and readiness to forgive, is quite inapposite. The final part of vs. 5 fits in well at the place where it is (see Exeg.). **He will come to us as the showers** is a figure which has little significance in some countries but is rich in meaning for the people of Palestine, where the fertility of the country is wholly dependent upon the rainfall. Rain there is the condition of life and fruitfulness; so will the Lord be to his returning people. The final phrase of the verse is, lit., "as the spring rain the early rain to the earth." The LXX has πρόιμος καὶ ὄψιμος τῇ γῇ; therefore we may take the phrase in either of two ways: (*a*) we may follow the LXX, which requires minor adjustments in the M.T., and translate, "as the spring rain and the early winter rain to the earth" (an unusual order of reference indeed); or (*b*) reading ירוה for יורה, we get the

---

3a. Pressing On to Know.—The insight is a valid one. We know as we **press on to know.** There is a marked difference between knowing about God and knowing God. It is comparable to the difference between reading about love and falling in love. The first is abstract knowledge, the second firsthand; not knowledge about, but of. To be sure, we need to know about God. Spiritual illiteracy is one of the major problems in dealing with the "educated." Nevertheless, religion begins in a firsthand experience of God—not knowledge about but knowledge of (see John 9:25; Expos. on 4:1-3, 6).

We know God when we **press on to know.** "I am the way" (John 14:6); "If any man will do his will, he shall know" (John 7:17). We need theoretical knowledge about the great truths of our religion; but in the long last only as our knowledge becomes flesh, through following on, walking in the way, obeying the commands, living the life, only so does it work its perfect work in us. This knowledge of the true God sometimes comes to a man suddenly through some deep and revealing experience such as Paul had on the Damascus road. But even such an experience lacks completeness. We know as we **press on to know the LORD.** "Grow in grace, and in the knowledge of our Lord and Saviour Jesus Christ" (II Pet. 3:18). "I press toward the mark" (Phil. 3:14). Such knowledge is never fully acquired. No knowledge ever is. At best we "know in part" (I Cor. 13:9). This is surely true of our knowledge of the Eternal. "'We cannot really speak of God,' says Eckhardt, 'when we would speak of Him we do but stammer.' 'We are like young chil-

4 ¶ O Ephraim, what shall I do unto thee? O Judah, what shall I do unto thee? for your goodness *is* as a morning cloud, and as the early dew it goeth away.

5 Therefore have I hewed *them* by the prophets; I have slain them by the words of my mouth: and thy judgments *are as* the light *that* goeth forth.

4 What shall I do with you, O E'phraim?
What shall I do with you, O Judah?
Your love is like a morning cloud,
like the dew that goes early away.
5 Therefore I have hewn them by the prophets,
I have slain them by the words of my mouth,
and my judgment goes forth as the light.*u*

u Gk Syr: Heb *thy judgment goes forth*

---

rendering given in the RSV. The early winter rain, termed in the KJV the **former rain,** normally fell in December and softened the hard surface of the ground, which had been baked during the long summer, and made plowing possible. The **spring rains,** termed in the KJV the **latter rain,** fell in late March or early April and were essential for filling the heads of the growing crops.

c) MERCY, NOT SACRIFICE (6:4-6)

4. These verses express the Lord's response to Israel's show of penitence and contrite return to his service. The first words make it quite plain that Israel's act is not accepted as genuine and sincere, but as an empty formality and as a self-regarding move. **What shall I do with you, O Ephraim?** The RSV is a truer rendering than that proposed by Harper (*Amos and Hosea,* p. 284) and Brown (*The Book of Hosea,* p. 56): "What can I make of you, Ephraim?" The Hebrew has, lit., "for you," which is a *dativus commodi;* the meaning therefore is, "What can I do for you [now], Ephraim?" The Lord had done everything possible in the way of training his people; now there was nothing more which he could do. What was the use of continuing to make endeavors to redeem a people whose love was a transient thing **like a morning cloud** that vanishes quickly before the rising sun, or like the morning **dew?**

5. It is possible to take this verse as a historical statement; so the KJV and the RSV. That would mean that the people's love had always been weak, and the chastisement they had received at the hands of the prophets had made no difference to them. Some scholars have felt the second phrase, **I have slain them by the words of my mouth,** to be an unusually harsh expression and have emended the whole line to read:

Therefore, I have hewed them [tablets of] stone [אבנים for נביאים]
and taught them by the words of my mouth [הוריתים for הרגתים].

---

dren learning to speak,' exclaims Luther, 'and can use only half words and quarter words.'"[8] Finite man can never fully comprehend God; but he can apprehend him, and through Christ our Lord come to know his nature and his purpose. Not, to be sure, in all its vastness. To do that one would have to be God! But in Christ, God incarnate, we know all we need to know for our salvation—"I know whom I have believed" (II Tim. 1:12).

4. Goodness as a Morning Cloud.—The implication is that there is nothing God can do with a people so fickle, changeable, and unstable. The **morning cloud** refers to "one of those dense masses of night-vapour, which the

westerly winds of summer bear from the Mediterranean Sea, and which more than supply the place of dew."[9] The figure is that of transitoriness. The **morning cloud** is unstable. You look, and it is there; you look again, and it is gone. It cannot stand the heat of the sun. This picture will recall Jesus' parable in which he speaks of the shallow soil. The seed springs readily because it has no depth of earth, but no sooner does it spring than it withers. Like the **morning cloud** it passes away. The Christian religion, on the contrary, places the emphasis on steadfastness and unswerving loyalty. "Be thou faithful unto death, and I will give thee a crown of life" (Rev. 2:10). "He that endureth to the end shall be saved"

[8] James S. Stewart, *A Man in Christ* (New York: Harper & Bros.), p. 81.

[9] Cheyne, *Hosea,* pp. 78-79.

6 For I desired mercy, and not sacrifice; and the knowledge of God more than burnt offerings.

6 For I desire steadfast love and not sacrifice,

the knowledge of God, rather than burnt offerings.

That gives excellent sense (cf. Exod. 31:18), although we have no reason for supposing that it is what Hosea said. But while retaining the M.T., there is much to be said for construing the perfects as prophetic perfects and so translating the line:

> Therefore, I will hew them by the prophets,
> I will slay them by the words of my mouth,
> and my judgment will go forth as light.

Taken in this way, vs. 5 pronounces judgment upon the people, and it will be noted that the final part of the verse now fits in perfectly where it stands. The second phrase illustrates the Hebrew idea that the spoken word was imbued with the power of the person who uttered it and had power to fulfill itself (cf. Isa. 55:11).

6. The first word should be "assuredly" instead of **for. More than burnt offerings** or **rather than burnt offerings:** It is not necessary to conclude that Hosea regarded sacrifice as having no value whatsoever as an act of worship. What is meant is that sacrifice as an expression of a living faith in the Lord may be a genuine religious act, but the Lord's delight is in the true knowledge of the demands of his service and in the cultivation of that love which is his will for his people. It should be noted in passing that whereas Samuel is reported to have called for obedience, not sacrifice, from Saul, Hosea's demand is for **love** (cf. I Sam. 15:22).

(Matt. 10:22). "No man, having put his hand to the plow, and looking back, is fit for the kingdom of God" (Luke 9:62).

What is it that produces this transitory, unstable, undependable attitude? The difficulty may be partly temperamental. Sometimes, like the Athenians, we are anxious to tell and hear some new thing. We change our ideas as rapidly as our styles. Like hummingbirds we flit from flower to flower, living on flavors rather than food. We would rather sample each new dish that comes along than eat a substantial meal from any one. We always go to hear every new preacher who arrives in town, until we get used to his voice; then we have heard enough of him and turn to fresher pastures. We take up things quickly and drop them as quickly; but while they retain our interest we go all out for them. Behavioristic psychology or the philosophy of instrumentalism will so sweep the country that one might think wisdom was born with John Watson or John Dewey; except that presently some new "prophet" will appear, some new voice will be heard, and then we start all over again. That there is likely to be some truth in all of them no one will deny; but only *some* truth.

This spirit of fickleness may be due, however, not only to temperament but also to our failure to look before we leap. We join the church because it is the thing to do, and that is the end of it. "This man began to build, and was not able to finish" (Luke 14:30) because he had not counted the cost. He did not see what was involved. So we begin on the straight and narrow way; but as soon as its disciplines are made clear and its demands evident, we give up. We had not thought of that.

Fickleness may also be due to selfishness. A goodness that soon passes away is one that was conceived in terms of privilege rather than responsibility. "We have forsaken all, and followed thee; what shall we have therefore?" (Matt. 19:27.) What are we going to get for this? The good life does not measure its rewards in terms of the acquisition of material things—"Your reward shall be great, and ye shall be the children of the Highest" (Luke 6:35). Being, not possessing, is the aim of the good life; sharing responsibilities, not just enjoying privileges, is its purpose. "The fruit of the Spirit is love, joy, peace, long-suffering, gentleness, goodness, faith, meekness, temperance" (Gal. 5:22-23). Such qualities have meaning in themselves. The good life needs and seeks no further reward than the fruits of goodness. Herein lies its deepest satisfaction. The type of goodness that finds rewards in itself will not be transient as the **morning cloud.** It will endure.

6. What Doth the Lord Require?—Our Lord quotes this passage from Hosea twice—Matt. 9:13; 12:7. Other prophets have voiced the same truth (Amos 5:21-24; Isa. 1:11, 14-15; Mic. 6:6, 8). When Hosea pleads for **love and**

7 But they like men have transgressed
the covenant: there have they dealt treacherously against me.
8 Gilead *is* a city of them that work iniquity, *and is* polluted with blood.

7 But at[v] Adam they transgressed the covenant;
there they dealt faithlessly with me.
8 Gilead is a city of evildoers,
tracked with blood.

[v] Cn: Heb *like*

4. A Record of Villainy and Apostasy (6:7–7:2)
a) Murder and Robbery (6:7-9)

When we examine vss. 7-9, a problem of interpretation at once arises. Do these verses describe the murderous violence of the Gileadites (cf. vs. 8*b*), or the perverse and iniquitous behavior of the priests (cf. vs. 9*a*), or both? In the Hebrew vs. 7 opens with an emphatic pronoun which has no clear reference. There are two possibilities: either vs. 8 should be read before vs. 7, so that these two verses together refer to the Gileadites, or it must be recognized that a verse or a portion of a verse before vs. 7 has been lost, and that loss has involved in its train the loss of the reference of the pronoun in vs. 7.

7. The first part, as it stands in the M.T., may be translated in several ways, e.g., "like Adam they transgressed the covenant," or "like human beings they transgressed the covenant." But neither of these gives meaning to the following word **there**; even if we suggest "then" for **there** (cf. Arabic *thumma*), the difficulty is not solved. But we may consider **Adam** as a place name, and read "at [i.e., ב for כ] Adam." In this case Adam would be understood to be the well-known ford of the Jordan (cf. Josh. 3:16); people going from Gilead to Shechem would normally cross the river there. Sellin, indeed, finds a wordplay in the use of עברו, which signified both "crossing" the ford and "transgressing" the covenant (*Gilgal* [Leipzig: Deichertsche Verlagsbuchandlung Werner Scholl, 1917], p. 35). Of the precise historical event which is referred to here, we have no information.

8. Once again the event (or events) which Hosea had in mind escapes us.

**Gilead is a city of evildoers,
tracked with blood.**

This is a serious charge. The slightly emended text for the final phrase (עקביהם דם— "bloody are their tracks"), which is supported by van Hoonacker (*Les douze petits*

not sacrifice, and the knowledge of God more than burnt offerings, he is but running true to the prophetic tradition. It is here that the priestly and the prophetic collide, so to speak, or at least are set in opposition to each other. One confronts here the whole program of the relationship between ecclesiasticism and religion, between ritualism and righteousness, between symbol and substance; in short, between priestly and prophetic emphasis.

The priestly aspect of religion has its values: beautiful architecture, symbols, color, ritual, ceremony. These help when rightly used to induce the spirit of worship, and to enrich and enhance its meaning. But the priestly approach has its perils also. Too often it becomes an end in itself, obscures rather than reveals God. Men become more concerned about the meticulous performance of ecclesiastical rites than about facing the moral and ethical realities. John Wesley said that they practiced fastidiousness

at Oxford and called it righteousness (cf. Matt. 23:23). If the church down the ages had been as concerned about the establishment of righteousness and justice as about the ceremonial and ecclesiastical aspects of religion, "the promise of his coming" (II Pet. 3:4) would be much nearer to fulfillment than it now is.

Few interests so obscure one's vision as an overpreoccupation with niceties of ecclesiastical procedure. This has often led the church to make a mountain out of a molehill, and so to lose sight of the moral and ethical obstacles that block the coming of the kingdom. But ever and again is heard the word of the prophet —mercy, not sacrifice; knowledge of God, not burnt offerings. It is a summons to the primary emphasis of the Christian religion: contact with moral and spiritual reality.

7-11a. People Make Places.—It is places, not so much people, of which the prophet is thinking: **At Adam they transgressed the covenant;**

9 And as troops of robbers wait for a man, *so* the company of priests murder in the way by consent: for they commit lewdness.

9 As robbers lie in wait[w] for a man,
   so the priests are banded together;[x]
they murder on the way to Shechem,
   yea, they commit villainy.

[w] Cn: Heb uncertain
[x] Syr: Heb *a company*

prophètes, p. 65), Sellin (*Das Zwölfprophetenbuch, ad loc.*), and Procksch (in Rudolf Kittel, ed., *Biblia Hebraica* [3rd ed., A. Alt and O. Eissfeldt; Stuttgart: Priv. Württ Bibelanstalt, 1937], *ad loc.*), makes no real difference.

9. There are two ways in which the first line of this verse may be construed: (*a*) we may regard וכחכי as equivalent to וכחכות, and read the verbal form יחברו in place of the nominal form חבר, arriving at the translation given in the RSV; or (*b*) we may read the participial form וכמחכי and retain the noun חבר, translating:

As bandits who lie in wait for a man,
   so is the confederacy of priests.

The words **they murder on the way to Shechem** (cf. Judg. 9:25) have caused discussion. The order of the words in the Hebrew is strange; G. R. Driver ("Notes and Studies," p. 156) has suggested that דרכו should be read in place of דרך and the phrase translated, "they sally forth, they murder at Shechem." Otherwise דרך should be transposed before שכמה. But that is not all. The **priests** are severely censured in the book of Hosea for gross negligence and for dishonoring their office, but they are never charged with murder. It may be contended that the reference is to spiritual murder; but whereas spiritual death is a well-known form of speech in the O.T., spiritual murder is not. The difficulty is easily resolved if we read vs. 9*b* before vs. 9*a*, in which case vss. 7-8, 9*b* are all taken as referring to the violent activities of the men of Gilead, while vs. 9*a* and vs. 10 would refer to the priests. Whether the men of Gilead committed the villainy in hostile raids upon Shechem, or when they were ostensibly on pilgrimage to the shrine there, is not clear. But the priests themselves are not free from guilt; they **are banded together** like a band of plunderers and behave wickedly against the worshipers who come to their shrines.

. . . **Gilead is a city of evildoers. . . . they murder on the way to Shechem.** Each of these towns seems to be defiled "with a sin from which it is unable to free itself. . . . It is clear that in these verses Hosea is thinking of the sinful deeds with which some of the principal towns of Israel have been branded from ancient times down to his own day."[1] He seems almost to suggest that whether the inhabitants change or not, the towns will retain the ancient evils which have stained their history through the centuries. Places acquire character and sometimes become personified. So Sodom and Gomorrah suggest a character, as does Babylon. Jesus spoke of Jerusalem as the place that "killest the prophets" (Matt. 23:37). So modern cities like Monte Carlo or Reno bring certain qualities to mind.

There are two observations to be made. One is that even in the worst city there are good people, and they keep it from complete moral deterioration and decay. Ten righteous

[1] S. L. Brown, *Hosea*, p. 61.

men could save Sodom. The forces of righteousness within a city as a rule go unnoticed and unsung. Evil makes headlines and the front page; good seldom does. "Asses bray but gentlemen speak low." Yet the good works like leaven, and but for its pervasive influence morally speaking we should go completely to the dogs.

The second observation is that the character of a city can be changed by changing the character of its people. In no other way can it be changed. "Gilead is a gang of villains" (Moffatt). But this is not Gilead's fault. It is all right to personalize places provided we remember that persons give places their character and not vice versa. Bethlehem was an obscure place, and Nazareth, if we may trust Philip's judgment, a not too good one, yet they play a well-nigh unique role in our thinking. Personality gives character to places. This truth too often eludes us. We want our cities to be big numerically. But are we as concerned about the character of the citizens? Do we realize that the very size of our cities over which we gloat

10 I have seen a horrible thing in the house of Israel: there *is* the whoredom of Ephraim, Israel is defiled.

11 Also, O Judah, he hath set a harvest for thee, when I returned the captivity of my people.

7 When I would have healed Israel, then the iniquity of Ephraim was discovered,

10 In the house of Israel I have seen a horrible thing;

E'phraim's harlotry is there, Israel is defiled.

11 For you also, O Judah, a harvest is appointed.

When I would restore the fortunes of my people,

7 1 when I would heal Israel,
the corruption of E'phraim is revealed,
and the wicked deeds of Samar'ia;

---

b) A Sickness Beyond Cure (6:10–7:2)

10. It is assumed that this verse, like vs. 9a, refers to the priests. Presumably the terms **Ephraim** and **Israel** in vs. 10b are identical in connotation; but if **the house of Israel** is identical with both, has the verse any meaning at all, and has the adverb **there** any reference? None, unless we understand **house** to mean shrine or temple, in which case the verse speaks of Bethel and describes the faithless ministry of the priests there.

11. It will be noticed that the RSV sets a space between the two lines of this verse, thus suggesting that they are not connected; that is so. The second line should be taken together with 7:1-2. The first line refers to a **harvest,** good or evil, for Judah. If this line is genuine, it is impossible to believe it was a joyful harvest that was appointed for Judah; the mention of a bitter harvest for Judah may have been inserted here lest Judah should be tempted to imagine that she was immune from the severe strictures that had been passed upon her sister kingdom. On the other hand, the line is rhythmically superfluous and the figure of a harvest is suddenly introduced, so that the line may be a later addition by a Judaistic reviser.

7:1-2. These verses form the conclusion of the section 6:7–7:2, and, in particular, 6:11b should be taken in close association with them thus:

> **When I would restore the fortunes of my people,**
> **when I would heal Israel.**

Whenever the Lord attempts to cure the hurt of his people, he discovers how deep-seated the trouble is and how hopeless any attempt at cure must be. The second half of the

---

has created some of the most appalling evils from which we suffer? We are wont to speak disparagingly of "small town stuff" as though the small town were a modern anachronism hardly worthy of consideration. It is none the less true, however, that some of the greatest names in our history are associated with small towns. To be sure, the small town has its provincialisms—which incidentally the metropolis does not escape—and its limitations; but one hazards the opinion that the small towns are the bulwark of a country, for in them character still counts, people are still individuals, what the individual does matters, he has not been lost in the crowd, caught in the shuffle, or dwarfed by the skyscrapers. It may still be true that from our Bethlehems come the forces that will help redeem our Jerusalems.

7:1. *Because of Their Unbelief.*—All God's relationships with man are marked by the spirit of mutuality. "He did not many mighty works . . . because of their unbelief" (Matt. 13:58). So Hosea hears God say:

> **When I would heal Israel,**
> **the corruption of Ephraim is revealed.**

(Ephraim and Israel are synonymous terms.) The healing forces of God cannot operate on the unrepentant. Consciously to cherish iniquity is to put an impassable barrier in the stream of God's grace.

That there are healing forces in nature is an incontrovertible fact. No sooner has the storm spent its fury than the battered and broken trees are coaxed back to life by the gentle ministry of sun, rain, and soil. Any damage to

and the wickedness of Samaria: for they commit falsehood; and the thief cometh in, *and* the troop of robbers spoileth without.

2 And they consider not in their hearts *that* I remember all their wickedness: now their own doings have beset them about; they are before my face.

for they deal falsely,
    the thief breaks in,
    and the bandits raid without.

2 But they do not consider
    that I remember all their evil works.
Now their deeds encompass them,
    they are before my face.

---

verse makes that plain. It is possible that, after the words **for they deal falsely,** a half line has been lost which contained a parallel statement. Thieves break into houses, so no man is safe in his own home; and troops of bandits range abroad and work pillage, so there is neither personal safety nor social security.

2. These evildoers live for the moment; their only end is their own selfish enjoyment and indulgence. They never reflect that they will have to give an account of their conduct; they never consider the fact that God does not forget their wickedness. **Now their deeds encompass them** may mean that these deeds are like an enveloping host from which there is no escape, or like a company of witnesses which unite in testifying against them. But parallelism might suggest the reading "encompass me" (סבבוני); in this way the deeds would be thought of as surrounding God and crying out for vengeance.

---

our bodies meets the quick response of the organism. The doctor never heals us, nature does. The doctor sets up the conditions which are most favorable for nature to do its work. His part is exceedingly important, indispensable; but the actual healing is nature's role.

There is healing, too, for minds that grow weary and depressed. Fatigue starts in the mind. More often than not it is the mind that communicates the sense of weariness to the body. But not only bodies and minds need healing— souls do also. "He restoreth my soul," said the psalmist. But no soul can be healed or restored that does not acknowledge its guilt and seek forgiveness. Israel (Ephraim) did not.

Forgiveness is not a one-way street. It is the restoration of a broken relationship. The road between my brother and me has had a washout. A chasm separates us. The chasm is too broad to be bridged from one side. Never mind how far I stretch my hand, I cannot reach my brother unless he extends his also. There is mutuality. This is true of the relationship between God and the soul. Forgiveness is impossible without repentance. It costs not only the forgiver but the forgiven. It costs the forgiver the willingness to forget the wrong done; it costs the forgiven the willingness to assume the spirit of humility, contrition, penitence—the willingness to make amends and take a new road. If it is not easy to forgive, neither is it easy to seek forgiveness.

2. *Man's Need for Reflection.*—Anything like genuine repentance is impossible without a consciousness of sin, and it is doubtful whether one can be sin-conscious who is not God-conscious. This was Hosea's indictment of his people. They were not conscious of their sins: **They do not consider.** Perhaps we could say that they no longer felt the pricks of conscience. Sin perhaps has no more tragic consequence than that in the long last it makes one insensible to the fact that he is a sinner. The sound which when first heard "scared us out of our wits," when heard again and again no longer frightens us. We may even sleep through it. Conscience is God's monitor within the soul. But like a violin string constantly plucked and never tightened, it may become incapable of sounding the right note. If the still small voice goes unheeded, it will at length become unheard. Israel never reflects. Just as one who over a long period of time has been afflicted with ill health literally forgets what it means to feel well, so one to whom evil has become habitual is no longer lured by the vision of purity or moved by the appeal of honor or inspired by the challenge of truth. The light within has become darkness. This is sin's most dismal, damning effect on personality.

And it comes about as one loses one's sense of God. Sin is not just a wrong done by one to another. It transcends the human plane. No one would minimize or make light of sin's disastrous effect on human beings, yet it involves more than the human. Sin is missing the mark, but that mark was not made by man, nor can it be erased by him. The mark is set by God. Sin therefore has not only personal or social but cosmic meaning. "Against thee, thee only, have I sinned, and done this evil in thy sight" (Ps. 51:4). Only as one sees his actions related not alone to himself or his fellows but to his God can their full import be assessed.

3 They make the king glad with their wickedness, and the princes with their lies.

4 They *are* all adulterers, as an oven heated by the baker, *who* ceaseth from raising after he hath kneaded the dough, until it be leavened.

³ By their wickedness they make the king glad,
and the princes by their treachery.
⁴ They are all adulterers;
they are like a heated oven,
whose baker ceases to stir the fire,
from the kneading of the dough until
it is leavened.

---

5. Revelry and Intrigue (7:3-7)

3. The LXX reads the plural "kings" instead of the singular of the M.T., but the singular should be retained in view of the use in vs. 5. The people who are referred to as thus taking part in intrigue and subversive activity are probably the wicked described in the preceding verses. These plotters rejoice the heart of the king and the princes; that does not mean that the rulers find pleasure and advantage in the conditions of political instability and insecurity induced by such subversive activity, but rather that the plotters maintain cordial relations with their rulers, so that they may not be suspect of disloyalty, and may thus be free to continue their intrigues without impediment. Not a few scholars would read ימשחו for ישמחו and translate, "In their wickedness they anoint kings"; but even if kings set up by a faction within the state might be anointed by them, princes would not be similarly anointed.

4. The text here is very uncertain and every scholar has his own way of emending it; but it is remarkable that when we analyze the proposed emendations the differences among them are slight, so that there is substantial agreement as to the general meaning of the verse. **They are all adulterers:** If this is retained as the original reading, it must be regarded as relating not to physical adultery, but to the circumstance that the people have become faithless and disloyal, untrue to their promises and their obligations. A slight emendation is to be commended (אנפים for מנאפים) and so the translation "all of them are enraged," which fits the dominant figure of these verses. A grammatical error and considerations of rhythmic form suggest minor alterations in the next few words (תנור בער הם אפהו for תנור בערה מאפה) and the result is the translation given in the RSV. The comparison of the plotters to **a heated oven** is easy to understand; they burn with passion to consume and destroy. But there follows the use of the figure of

---

In sinning we do not just break a law, we wound a heart.

The prophet suggests the need of reflection. **They do not consider.** Reflection is a lost art on the part of many. We are activists. We are driven. We must be on the move, on the go. It does not make so much difference where we go, or what we do, provided we keep busy. Could we sit still long enough to reflect, appraise the significance of what we are doing, we should be spared much lost motion. "Think? How do I know what I think till I hear what I say?" This remark of a young woman exaggerates, but not too much, the modern temper. No wonder we are such a ready market for quacks and sycophants. A mind without reflection is shallow if not empty. A diet of facts without reflection is like food without digestion. It leaves us unnourished. If one considers his life, its meaning, the forces which are keeping him from the realization of his selfhood, the

faith by which he is sustained, he is more likely to understand the nature of his soul's relationship with God and the "besetting sins" that mar that relationship.

3-7. An Oven Heated.—This is a "very difficult passage," and in referring to it George Adam Smith writes:

The text is corrupt, and we have no means of determining what events are intended. . . . The disorder and licentiousness of the people are favoured in high places; the throne is guilty. . . . A king surrounded by loose, unscrupulous nobles: adultery, drunkenness, conspiracies, assassinations: every man striking for himself; none appealing in truth to God.²

Difficult though the text may be, it reveals clearly the corruption of the age. It is widespread and total; the nobility and the common people alike are caught in its snare. Evil can

² *The Twelve Prophets*, I, 287-88.

5 In the day of our king, the princes have made *him* sick with bottles of wine; he stretched out his hand with scorners.

6 For they have made ready their heart like an oven, while they lie in wait: their baker sleepeth all the night; in the morning it burneth as a flaming fire.

5 On the day of our king the princes
    became sick with the heat of wine;
    he stretched out his hand with mockers.
6 For like an oven their hearts burn[v] with
    intrigue;
    all night their anger smolders;
    in the morning it blazes like a flaming
    fire.

[v] Gk Syr: Heb *brought near*

---

the **baker** who ceases to fan his fire from the time of the kneading of the dough until the bread is leavened, a figure which suggests the control of the fire. The significance of this figure may be found in one of the following interpretations: (*a*) since the interval is short between the kneading of the dough and the leavening of the bread, it is thus indicated that the plotters are so inflamed with their evil passions and their lust for power that the only occasions when they are not actively fanning the fire is when they are preparing new schemes which are not yet ready for cooking; or (*b*) just as a baker controls his fire lest it should burn his bread when the time comes for baking it, so these plotters are clever enough to control their passions, so that their plans are not ruined by excessive zeal or by overmastering lusts. It is probably the second which receives support in vs. 6.

5. The plotters entertain the king and the princes in order to give the impression that all is well and that cordial relations continue. The king joins unsuspectingly in the festivities, entirely unaware that he is associating with hypocrites and dissemblers; the princes respond so well to the treatment that they become thoroughly intoxicated and lose any sense of discretion and judgment they ever possessed. Thus a situation is prepared in which the plot can be carried out with the least trouble and the greatest expectation of success. **The day of our king** must mean the anniversary of his enthronement or his birthday; in any case it was a day of festivities (cf. Intro., p. 558).

6. Once more we return to the figure of the heated oven. The first part of the verse is, lit., "For they bring near like an oven their heart by their intrigue." That obviously is a defective text. The simplest solution of the difficulties is to read אפהם, *'ōphēhem,* "their baker," as *'appehem,* **their anger,** transposing two words, and translating thus:

> He stretched out his hand with mockers,
>   but they approached [him] with their intrigue;
> all night their anger smolders,
>   their heart is like an oven;
> in the morning it blazes up
>   like a flaming fire.

---

move in like some flame, increasing in volume and intensity until it sweeps all before it. Such was the condition Hosea described. The people and their priests, the rulers and their subjects, are alike involved. There could be no finer insight into the self-destructive nature of evil than this, that "the more evil succeeds, the more it fails." It acts upon the individual or society like a burning infection which, appearing first in one area of the body, if unchecked, spreads through the whole system; then death ensues.

They are like a heated oven. Because of his references to baking, the suggestion has been made that Hosea may have been a **baker** by

trade. At any rate, what an apt figure this: the sinful heart like an oven, now hot with passion's eager glow, now smoldering, its energies spent, its lusts satisfied, but only temporarily, for **in the morning it blazes like a flaming fire.** The heated oven may well symbolize the kind of pleasures so widely sought—the pleasures of the senses. Such pleasure is measured by the intensity of its thrills, hilarity, or sensual excitements. People frequent certain places to find escape from boredom or to give their jaded lives a thrill. Such pleasures, however, are momentary. They bring temporary satisfaction, the while the desire smolders and soon glows again. One is not condemning the legitimate and

| 7 They are all hot as an oven, and have devoured their judges; all their kings are fallen: *there is* none among them that calleth unto me. | 7 All of them are hot as an oven, and they devour their rulers. All their kings have fallen; and none of them calls upon me. |
| 8 Ephraim, he hath mixed himself among the people; Ephraim is a cake not turned. | 8 E'phraim mixes himself with the peoples; E'phraim is a cake not turned. |

Or, accepting a proposal made by Theodor H. Gaster (cf. "Short Notes," *Vetus Testamentum*, IV, 1 [Jan., 1954], 78-79), we may derive לצצים from the Arabic *lāṣa* IV, "to decoy or deceive," and render the first two lines as:

He stretched out his hand with imposters,
and they approached [him] with their intrigue.

In other words, the plotters await a suitable occasion; their passions are held in check like a smoldering fire until their plans are fully matured and the whole situation is favorable; then their passions blaze out and they do their nefarious work.

7. Here the effect of the intrigue is made plain; it has resulted in open revolution which has overwhelmed the reigning dynasty. The implication is that this was not an isolated occurrence; the prophet lived through a period of great dynastic instability. Yet, it is said, no one took the situation seriously; no one came to the conclusion that there was something "rotten in the state of Denmark." No one called upon God, interceding for his favor. They counted their distresses not as penalties but as political vicissitudes which could not be avoided and, in consequence, must be endured.

The kingdom of Judah, which remained faithful to the house of David, had few dynastic troubles, but it was different with the kingdom of Israel. Dynastic changes were frequent there after the death of Jeroboam II, and not seldom the aspirant to the throne waded through blood to the fulfillment of his ambitions. Zechariah, Shallum, Menahem, and Pekahiah reigned respectively for six months, one month, eight years, and two years. Probably the passage belongs to the close of this very troubled period.

B. Political Unfaithfulness and Instability (7:8–10:15)

1. An Indictment of Ephraim (7:8-16)

a) Ephraim's Trust in Foreign Alliances (7:8-12)

It is possible to take the whole section (vss. 8-16) in three strophes, as is done in the RSV, but since vss. 8-12 deal with Ephraim's foreign alliances and vss. 13-16 with her unfaithfulness to the Lord and her service of Baal, it seems preferable to take these as the main sections.

8. The verb translated **mixes himself** is used in Exod. 29:2 of the act of mixing oil with the dough of sacrificial cakes. The significance of the use of the figure in this context

wholesome pleasures of the senses. But when they are made an end in themselves and are pursued in betrayal of our moral insights, they lead to disillusionment and disgust. Man never finds himself in his animal hours. His durable satisfactions spring from the disciplines of the mind and spirit.

8a. In the World but Not of the World.— **Ephraim mixes himself with the peoples.** Well, why not? But there are two ways of mixing. One is so to mix that others mold you as does the potter the clay, impose their ways upon you until their standards become the norm of

your conduct. The other way is so to mix that you mold them. Instead of their dragging you down, they lift you to a higher plane. It was the former method to which Israel fell victim. Unfortunately, as a result of her contact, Israel succumbed to her neighbors' weaknesses. This was in the prophet's view most tragic, for God intended his people to be different. To them was committed a peculiar mission. They were to be the bearers to other nations of the message of the eternal God. Instead of that, however, they adopted the idolatrous and pagan ways of their contemporaries. This was because

is that Ephraim, which was called to be a distinctive people, has become mixed among neighboring peoples so that her own identity has been lost and she has become like one ingredient in a composite cultural context. If she were as leaven in the lump, the result might be good; but it is implied that she has no such important part to play, for she has been submerged in the mass. **Ephraim is a cake not turned:** A cake not turned in the baking is baked on one side only, while the other remains unfit for use. If the

---

they themselves were not sufficiently grounded in the faith. They lengthened their cords without strengthening their stakes.

The problem is still with us. It is the problem of being in the world and yet not of the world, of yielding to the perfectly proper human impulse to be friendly and sociable, the while retaining the differences which separate us from evil (cf. John 17:15). If there had been no differences between Israel and the Canaanites there would have been no problem. So also if there are no differences between a Christian and a non-Christian. The problem arises when we seek to retain our Christian principles the while we expose ourselves to the forces of an unchristian environment.

The church has at times undertaken to run away, as in the monastic movements of the early and later Christian centuries. Men tried to retain their Christian character by escaping to the monasteries. No such method ever has proved effective or ever will. Isolation does not seem to be God's way, either spiritually or politically. The monasteries developed some of the very evils from which men and women sought shelter. Man can isolate himself from evil only as he isolates himself from himself. Evil ultimately is within the soul.

But even if refusing to mix were a solution of the problem, it would not be a Christian solution. Christ did not say we should run away and leave the common life of mankind to stew in its own juice. Rather he said, "Go ye into all the world" (Mark 16:15). He mixed with the people, people whom many of his self-righteous contemporaries avoided. But in the mixing they did not drag him down; he lifted them up. The rich young ruler did not make him mercenary. Zacchaeus did not make him a grafter; he made Zacchaeus an honest man. He talked to the woman at the well. She did not pull him down to her level; he lifted her up. If we have his spirit, **the people** will not secularize us; we will help to Christianize them. If we do not make the world better, the world will make us worse (see Expos. on 8:8-10).

8b. The Danger of Being Half-Baked.— Again Hosea resorts to the metaphor of the baker. "The cake referred to is the flat, round cake of the East which is baked on hot stones." [3]

[3] S. L. Brown, *Hosea*, p. 67.

There was much in Israel to suggest the unturned scone to Hosea. The extremes of poverty and wealth might have suggested it—some very rich, others very poor. A type of religion that concerned itself well-nigh exclusively with ecclesiastical matters on the one hand while on the other it ignored the application of the religious spirit to the affairs of daily life, fitted the metaphor. Or Hosea may have had in mind Israel's politics which were marked by the alternatives of intense interest and lethargy. Again, he may very well have thought of Israel's immature culture, which tended to superficiality. [4]

Modern examples of this immature, one-sided emphasis are not so far to seek. Our education tends to be one-sided. Often it is education for making a living rather than for living a life. We are informed without being enlightened, possess a vast store of knowledge, factual and scientific, but are without an adequate understanding of truth, which is more important than fact. College and university should produce cultured people, or people who have some appreciation of our cultural heritage. Instead, note the one-sided emphasis on the "practical" which dominates so much of modern education. Macaulay is authority for the statement that nine tenths of the evils that afflict the human race come from a union of high intelligence and low desire. "To teach facts without meanings is worse than teaching notes without music. To cultivate the mind without purpose, so that it yields no sustenance, is worse than intensive farming that yields no food." [5] But that is what modern education does for the most part. It is **a cake not turned**—one-sided. Knowledge that leaves out God leaves out too much. He is to knowledge what the hub is to a wheel. Without him the spokes of information we acquire, never mind how many or far-reaching, remain formless and fragmentary; worse, they take on demonic power. Increase of knowledge has brought increase of danger because increase of power. It has produced a sort of Frankenstein, a monster, potentially able to wreck our civilization. There is no control for atomic power save moral power, and our one-sided educational emphasis does not even attempt to pro-

[4] See George Adam Smith, *op. cit.*, I, 294.
[5] George A. Buttrick, *Prayer* (New York and Nashville: Abingdon-Cokesbury Press, 1942), p. 278.

9 Strangers have devoured his strength, and he knoweth *it* not: yea, gray hairs are here and there upon him, yet he knoweth not.

9 Aliens devour his strength, and he knows it not; gray hairs are sprinkled upon him, and he knows it not.

---

figure is understood in that sense, the meaning of its application to Ephraim is that there are inconsistencies in her life—political, moral, and spiritual. She was meant to serve the Lord with heart and soul and mind and strength, but she is not so unified in her service; there is a serious lack of integration in all her activities; she is not wholly redeemed. But on the other hand, a cake which is not turned and is left upon the fire is burned. From that point of view the meaning of the words in the text may be taken to signify that Ephraim by her association with foreign influences has been corrupted and ruined.

9. Strangers may refer to those foreign peoples, especially Assyrians, who had worked havoc in the Northern Kingdom, and by the exaction of tribute were exhausting

---

duce this. "Ye shall know the truth," said Jesus (John 8:32) ; not simply the facts. Facts are like the scaffolding, truth the building. "The materialistic motives which have understandably dominated the country and education . . . will not do for the new epoch which we are now entering. . . . We must inspire our students to aspire." [6]

The one-sidedness of our life appears too in the interests to which we give our time and thought. We are go-getters. We are activists. We go from morning to night, and far into the night. Our lives are like trees so crowded together that they cannot spread their limbs. There is little breathing space about us. The old hymn says, "Take time to be holy." Our activities give us little time for meditation or prayer. Time for meditation is regarded as time wasted, but "no soul is idle that is touching God." We are like people who travel but never stop to think where they are going—only that they must go, and at ever-increasing speeds. The activist side of our nature is overdeveloped, the meditative side neglected. We are overdone on one side and raw on the other, like **a cake not turned.** Even the sabbath, which the accumulated wisdom of the race has set aside for the cultivation of spiritual values and the nurture of the soul, is for multitudes of people just another day. Our souls fare no better on Sunday than they do through the rest of the week. Perhaps this is why our life lacks stability. We lack stability because we lack roots. We are like surface plants, responding quickly to the changes of our environment, easily uprooted— now blooming, now drooping. There is no adequate reserve. We follow the largest crowd, we must be popular. We pick up the latest fad,

we must be in style. We repeat the current slogan, we must be up-to-date. "Want of thoroughness and equable effort was Israel's besetting sin, and it told on every side of their life. How better describe a half-fed people, a half-cultured society, a half-lived religion, a half-hearted policy, than by a half-baked bannock?" [7]

Perhaps the most impressive evidence of our half-baked civilization may be seen in the old story of Moses and Aaron. When God summoned Moses to the leadership of Israel, he demurred by saying that he was not eloquent. God reminded him that Aaron was; Aaron could speak well and he, Moses, might use him as his mouthpiece, tell him what to say (Exod. 4:10-16) . We are an age of Aarons. We speak well and fluently but are not saying much. We are technically overdeveloped but are morally babes in the woods. With our airplanes we can write on the sky, but what we write is not worth reading. We can send our voice around the globe, speak to the uttermost parts of the earth; we can "tell the world"—but for the most part we do not tell it much. The stuff that rides the air waves would be better left unsent. We have speed without direction, power without divine purpose. We are overstuffed mechanically, underfed spiritually.

9-10. When the Light Becomes Darkness.— This is perhaps the greatest penalty evil exacts: it makes us incapable of appreciating our true condition and so forestalls the possibility of change. Israel was losing—if she had not lost— the capacity to repent, largely because she had lost her sense of sin. Repentance is turning around, returning to God. **They do not return to the LORD their God.** And they did not because they were unaware of their real condition. They did not sense the waste and decay sin had wrought in them. "Father, I have sinned against

[6] William Edwards Stevenson, president of Oberlin College, from his address before the Cleveland chapter of Phi Beta Kappa, May 12, 1949.

[7] George Adam Smith, *The Twelve Prophets*, I, 294.

10 And the pride of Israel testifieth to his face: and they do not return to the LORD their God, nor seek him for all this.

11 ¶ Ephraim also is like a silly dove without heart: they call to Egypt, they go to Assyria.

10 The pride of Israel witnesses against him;
yet they do not return to the LORD their God,
nor seek him, for all this.

11 E'phraim is like a dove,
silly and without sense,
calling to Egypt, going to Assyria.

---

her economic strength. Even more fitly the reference may be taken to the peoples mentioned in the preceding verse, those who consume her moral and spiritual strength. The corruption has been a gradual and therefore an imperceptible process, and Ephraim has remained unaware of what was happening. Now she is becoming old as a people; gone long since are the days of the wilderness when she was a child being trained to walk.

10. Judgment is entered against Ephraim, and once more it is her pride which is condemned (cf. 5:5). That pride is born of, and at the same time nourishes, a sense of self-sufficiency, so that those who have it are unwilling to listen to any advice or warning; they imagine that no evil can befall them; or that, if evil does befall them, they will be able to save themselves by their own energies and their own wisdom.

11. Ephraim, despising the help of her own God who can be trusted and whose resources are sufficient for any human need, turns with a childish trust to Egypt and Assyria, fondly imagining that they will be able and willing to succor her. It is implied in the words used here that there were a pro-Egyptian party and a pro-Assyrian party in the politics of Ephraim in Hosea's day.

---

heaven, and before thee" (Luke 15:18). This awareness of his real condition was the initial step in the prodigal's homeward journey. Israel did not appreciate the effect of sin upon her life.

Aliens devour his strength,
and he knows it not;
gray hairs are sprinkled upon him,
and he knows it not.

Hence, **they do not return to the LORD their God.**

One of the paradoxes of our time is that while few ages have borne more tragic evidence of sin, few ages have been less conscious of it. We know our strength has been devoured. We are conscious of the marks of waste and decay. Over vast sections of the earth this is written too clearly to be doubted. But one wonders whether we understand the moral and spiritual implications of our condition. Is that the meaning of "the unpardonable sin"? Many sensitive souls have tortured themselves with the fear that they have committed it. Such self-inflicted torture is groundless. For one thing is sure: he who thinks he has committed it has not, since his very concern reveals his awareness of evil and his desire for repentance and forgiveness. As long as that desire is present no sin is unpardonable, for there is no sin that God will not forgive when one sincerely seeks forgiveness.

The unpardonable sin is not any one specific evil act but the general condition of moral blindness or spiritual insensitivity which overtakes a soul in whom the light has become darkness (Luke 11:35-36). In such a soul the power of moral discrimination has died. One calls good evil, and evil good. Even when, like Israel, **aliens devour his strength, and he knows it not; gray hairs are sprinkled upon him,** yet he still thinks he is in the bloom of youth. He cannot distinguish between strength and weakness, good and evil, life and death. The unpardonable sin is the verdict on a soul that no longer seeks pardon because it does not know its need. It has lost its capacity of moral discernment. The unpardonable sin is therefore not a reflection on God's nature but a revelation of our own.

11-13. New Words, Old Truths.—The picture is one of stupidity in the extreme. The **dove,** proverbially simple, is shown as flying from the hawk only to be snared by the fowler. The whole passage refers particularly to Israel's foreign policy—**calling to Egypt, going to Assyria.** That policy was one of expediency and opportunism, now pro-Egyptian, now pro-Assyrian, "a policy of hesitation and indecision, of reliance on 'balance of power,' rather than on Jahveh."[1]

All this has a familiar ring. It is the old story,

[1] S. L. Brown, *Hosea,* p. 68.

12 When they shall go, I will spread my net upon them; I will bring them down as the fowls of the heaven; I will chastise them, as their congregation hath heard.

13 Woe unto them! for they have fled from me: destruction unto them! because they have transgressed against me: though I have redeemed them, yet they have spoken lies against me.

12 As they go, I will spread over them my net;
I will bring them down like birds of the air;
I will chastise them for their wicked deeds.[z]

13 Woe to them, for they have strayed from me!
Destruction to them, for they have rebelled against me!
I would redeem them,
but they speak lies against me.

[z] Cn: Heb *according to the report to their congregation*

12. The first half of the verse is clear in meaning and obviously continues the figure of vs. 11. The statement that God will ensnare Ephraim when she flies off like **a silly dove** to Egypt or Assyria, is probably to be understood as the direct, Hebrew way of saying that such foreign alliances will prove to be entangling snares for Ephraim and will in the end be the death of her. The second half of the verse means, lit., **I will chastise them according to the report to their congregation.** These words, if they have any meaning at all, must mean that it is God's purpose to chastise his people in the way that had been proclaimed time after time to the congregation, i.e., to Israel. The fact that the LXX has τῆς θλιψέως αὐτῶν, however, and so must have read רעתם or צרתם in place of עדתם, has suggested the reading: "I will chastise them by the fullness [בשבע] of their distress," i.e., by overwhelming distress. Marti translates the final phrase simply as "because of their evil" (על־רעתם); so the RSV (cf. *Das Dodekapropheton* [Tübingen: J. C. B. Mohr, 1904; "Kurzer Hand-Commentar zum Alten Testament"], p. 62). But none of these renderings continues the figure of birdcatching; that is why the rendering advocated by Nyberg (*Studien zum Hoseabuche,* pp. 56-57) and Weiser (*Das Buch der zwölf kleinen Propheten, ad loc.*) is attractive, even if it is not without linguistic difficulty, "I will capture them when I hear the noise of their wings" (cf. Judg. 14:8).

b) Ephraim's Unfaithfulness to the Lord (7:13-16)

13. The first part of the verse, while it reads like an imprecation, is nonetheless an assertion of the inevitable result of Ephraim's conduct. The second part is analogous to vs. 1, speaking of the Lord's continuing purpose to save, and of the continuing obstacles which frustrate that purpose. The rendering of the RSV is preferable to that of the KJV, but another one is possible, viz.:

Am I to redeem them
when they speak lies against me?

the sordid game of "diplomacy" or "politics," high-sounding words used to cover up selfishness, greed, intrigue, and even treachery. Israel no doubt thought she was being shrewd, smart, and clever in her uprincipled opportunistic policies. Actually she was playing the role of **a silly dove.** In a moral universe expediency and opportunism, which lead us now here, now there, are shortsighted and ultimately prove self-defeating. They provide neither security nor peace. History proves this with monotonous reiteration. Nations must put their relationship on a moral basis, substitute for selfish and shortsighted principles other principles applicable to all nations and universally binding on the great and small powers alike. Any other policy leads to the fowler's net, God's net (vs. 12), in which those who violate the principles of his moral order are inevitably ensnared. **Destruction to them, for they have rebelled against me!**

Modern man is often loath to see or accept the truth when presented in theological language, yet will recognize and respond to it

| 14 And they have not cried unto me with their heart, when they howled upon their beds: they assemble themselves for corn and wine, *and* they rebel against me. | 14 They do not cry to me from the heart, but they wail upon their beds; for grain and wine they gash themselves, they rebel against me. |

14. If the Hebrew text is followed in the first part, we should understand the wailing **upon their beds** to refer not to any superstitious nonsense which they utter during the night watches (yet cf. Ps. 149:5), but to their cries at the prayer places beside the altars of which Sellin speaks (*Das Zwölfprophetenbuch, ad loc.*; cf. II Sam. 12:16, 21; Pss. 4:4; 63:6; 149:5). If that interpretation can be sustained, it is the same as that arrived at by adopting the reading עַל־מִזְבְּחוֹתָם, i.e., "beside their altars." **They assemble themselves for corn and wine** (KJV) sounds weak and can mean only that their resort to these places of worship is for the purpose of ensuring their corn and wine. Another possible rendering of the original would be "for corn and wine they

---

when presented in different terminology. If being called a sinner leaves him cold, perhaps being called **silly** might touch a live nerve. He likes to be considered quite wise and smart. This is a mark of his sophistication. If then it can be shown how his actions or policies, individual or social, which betray or violate moral principles are really **silly**, since in the long last they defeat their own ends, a dent might be made in his consciousness. Many would shy away from the word "confession"—that sounds too "religious." Yet they crowd the office of a psychiatrist and confess to their heart's content. It is reassuring that so many of the great theological words of our religion, which unfortunately preachers have been neglecting, are reappearing in psychological guise—a different plumage, but the same old bird! What better indication could there be of their enduring truth?

14. *A Lesson in Prayer.*—To the mature the essence of prayer is communion with God. We value God not primarily for what he gives us but for what he is and means to us. "It is thee and not thy gift we crave." The spiritually mature do not test the validity of prayer by the degree to which it brings them what they want. Beyond their dearest desire is the longing to do the will of God. "Thy will be done," not "My wish be granted," is the spirit of true prayer, since we know that in "his will is our peace." [2] How different this picture Hosea gives us. Prayer to his people was only a long series of petitions for material blessings—**grain and wine**. They regarded God as though he were a sort of cosmic grocer whom one calls up whenever the larder is low; when the order was not filled they became disgusted and resentful even to the point of hostility; **they rebel against me.**

This primitive idea of prayer still widely

prevails not only among primitive peoples but among the civilized. For too many prayer means primarily, if not almost exclusively, asking favors of God, and its meaning or validity is measured by the degree to which such favors are granted. When through prayer we get what we want, especially if our wants are of the material variety—**grain and wine**—then we regard prayer as real and valuable. That there are valid material needs for which we may rightly pray is no doubt true. Jesus prayed, "Give us this day our daily bread" (Matt. 6:11). He said, "Ask, and ye shall receive" (John 16:24). Yet as we think of what prayer meant to him, and to saintly souls down the ages, we realize that crying for material gifts was as far removed from the heart of it as the nagging of a spoiled child begging for more candy is from the friendship of a grown-up soul.

The **grain and wine** approach to prayer applies of course to more important matters than material benefits; sometimes to the safety of a loved one exposed to danger, or the recovery of a dear one from sickness. How natural and right for us to pray that those we love be protected in life's hazardous undertakings or restored to health. But to suppose that if our prayers go unanswered, if our loved ones are worsted in danger or succumb to disease, prayer is unreal or God cruel, is surely to misjudge the truth. Yet much of modern skepticism about prayer springs from just such a source. Faith Baldwin tells of a girl whose pilot fiancé was killed in action. She is reported as saying: "I went to church every day and prayed. I prayed every night and almost every waking hour. But he was killed. I shall never pray again nor enter a church." [3] Surely such a reaction reveals an immature if not naïve religious faith. It forgets

[2] Dante, *Paradise*, Canto III.

[3] Cited in Georgia Harkness, *Prayer and the Common Life* (New York and Nashville: Abingdon-Cokesbury Press, 1948), p. 17.

15 Though I have bound *and* strengthened their arms, yet do they imagine mischief against me.	15 Although I trained and strengthened their arms, yet they devise evil against me.

become excited." That would refer to the frenzied excesses which sometimes took place at the altars. In the same realm of thought is the rendering of the RSV which follows the LXX in reading יתגודדו **(they gash themselves)** for יתגוררו. The gashings referred to are the bodily lacerations which took place during the ecstatic manifestations which were a characteristic of Canaanite worship.

15. On rhythmic grounds, as well as on the evidence of the LXX, the verb **trained** (יסרתי) should be regarded as additional. The Lord did not call Israel to his service

that once in the grim shadows of Gethsemane a man prayed, "Father, if it be possible, let this cup pass from me"; but realizing that he might be called upon to drink it, added, "nevertheless, not as I will, but as thou wilt" (Matt. 26:39). We sometimes forget that there are two answers to prayer—"Yes" and "No." We must learn to recognize "No" as an answer and understand that sometimes God's "No" may by his grace become the source of life's purification, enrichment, and enduring power. What seems stark tragedy may be the occasion for triumph. Even the road that leads to death may become the portal to eternal life. So it was with the man who accepted God's will in Gethsemane. Let us then learn to say, "Thy will be done." And let us remember that "the disciple is not above his master, nor the servant above his lord" (Matt. 10:24).

But Hosea reveals here another widespread weakness in the act of prayer. Not only the **grain and wine** motive but a lack of sincerity: **They do not cry to me from the heart.** The prayer was on their lips, but their life was not behind it. Such prayers are earth-bound, they do not rise. They are like a bird with broken wings, they cannot soar. The danger of this attitude is not that the prayer on our lips may be unanswered, but that the prayer in our heart may be answered!

> Prayer is the soul's sincere desire,
> Uttered or unexpressed.[4]

Whatever the prayer on our lips may be, our real prayer is "the soul's sincere desire," and to that there usually is an answer. "He gave them their request; but sent leanness into their soul" (Ps. 106:15). We are not told what they asked for with their lips, but we know what they received—"the soul's sincere desire." Words without sincerity are but "vain repetitions." As John Bunyan wisely said: "In prayer it is

better to have a heart without words than words without a heart." [5] Shakespeare's Hamlet voiced the same truth:

> My words fly up, my thoughts remain below:
> Words without thoughts never to heaven go.[6]

Our greatest difficulty in prayer is not intellectual but moral, a lack of sincerity. Our words say one thing, our lives another. A small child had developed an unwholesome predilection for green apples. Her mother, after repeated but fruitless admonitions, advised her to pray about it. She did. But that very night after the child had said her prayers, her mother in fixing her pillows discovered three green apples safely hidden beneath them. Most of us are as naïve as the child. We pray for deliverance from our besetting sins, the while we make sure that the path to repeated indulgence is kept open and easily accessible. The world prays for peace, making sure however that the stock pile of atomic bombs under its pillow is increasing. Since actions speak louder than words, the prayer of our life is answered—how effectively this broken, embittered, and insecure world testifies. We pray for brotherhood and cherish prejudices which make brotherhood impossible; we pray for forgiveness and are unwilling to forgive. We pray "thy kingdom come," yet cherish the illusion that we belong to a superior race, that our country is God's country, forgetting the sizable claims the devil has staked off in it. Some maintain that one religion is as good as another and so missionary work is unnecessary, the while they believe that Christ is the Savior of the world.

15-16. ***Don't Bite the Hand That Feeds You.***—Here is a familiar saying. But just this policy was in substance part of Israel's sin as Hosea diagnosed it. God **strengthened their arms** and they used this strength not to glorify

---

[4] James Montgomery, "What Is Prayer?"

[5] Francis R. Bellamy, ed., *We Hold These Truths* (New York: Grosset & Dunlap, 1942), p. 14.

[6] Act III, scene 3.

16 They return, *but* not to the Most High: they are like a deceitful bow: their princes shall fall by the sword for the rage of their tongue: this *shall be* their derision in the land of Egypt.

16 They turn to Ba'al;[a]
    they are like a treacherous bow,
  their princes shall fall by the sword
    because of the insolence of their tongue.
This shall be their derision in the land
    of Egypt.

[a] Cn: Heb uncertain

and then leave them to make the best of it; he trained them and endeavored to fit them for the work he had committed to them (cf. Amos 2:9-11). But they **devise evil** and work wickedness against their fellow men, and so against God. Otherwise the second clause may mean that they think evil thoughts concerning God and misrepresent him.

16. The text of the first part of the verse is corrupt. The translation "they return, but not [to him who is] on high" reads more into the text than is there. The LXX has "they return to nothing" (reading עַל־לֹא for לֹא עַל). Nyberg (*op. cit.,* pp. 58-60) gives the meaning as "they turn away to 'Al" and interprets 'Al as a divine name, 'Al being the God of the whole earth, as distinct from the Meleks of the cities; he quotes in his support Isa. 59:18; 63:7; I Sam. 2:10 (cf. also Hos. 11:7). But in the absence of more evidence for the use of the name 'Al in this sense, Nyberg's interpretation must remain highly questionable; in addition, such a reference to 'Al here would be very sudden and unexpected. The reading which has the support of most modern scholars is that given in the RSV. Israel is likened to **a treacherous bow,** in that they were trained to shoot straight toward the Lord but have turned aside to Baal. **Their princes shall fall** not only because of all the intrigue which is rife, but because they have a serious responsibility for the people's failure. The fact that they will thus fall and perish will make them objects of ridicule to Egypt, upon whom they relied so much for help. Peoples like Assyria and Egypt may on occasion give help to Israel, but that action is dictated by their own interests and their own advantage. Thus they are able to take a detached delight in the destruction of Israel's puny seekers after power.

him but to **devise evil against** him. They were **like a treacherous bow,** a bow which causes the arrow to miss. The arrow, expected to go in one direction, goes in another.

The evil revealed in these verses is of a peculiarly despicable sort. It is treachery, and unfortunately not uncommon. A pedestrian on the highway begs a ride, and no sooner has he accepted the motorist's hospitality than he draws a revolver, robs him of his money, his car, and should there be the slightest show of resistance, his life. The principle involved has many and varied applications. After World War I many Norwegian families opened their homes to German children whom they cared for as though they were their own. It will always remain one of the most despicable facts of history that those very children, grown to manhood, became Hitler's allies when he invaded Norway and so betrayed the very people who had been their benefactors.

But why is not all sin treachery? In a sense it is. If we believe that God is the author and giver of life, if the food we eat, the very air we breathe, are gifts from him, if God is he apart from whom we could not live at all, then it follows that any act contrary to his will and purpose is an act of treachery, since the very strength of body or mind which enables us to sin derives from him. Yet not all sin is treachery, since not all sin is motivated by treacherous intent. The nature of one's sin is revealed not only in the act but in the motive. Judas' sin, if we accept the customary explanation of his deed, was one of treachery. Peter's sin in denying Christ was not treachery. It was lack of courage. There was nothing deliberately sinister about it. Perhaps in his thrice-repeated "Lord, thou knowest all things; thou knowest that I love thee" (John 21:17), he was thinking of his previous denials. Hosea suggests that Israel's sin was not the result of a momentary weakness or fickleness. She knew what she was doing when she turned to Baal. She was like a deceitful bow, pointing in one direction yet hurling the arrow in another. This is sin of the deepest dye. No wonder **this shall be their derision in the land of Egypt.** The Egyptians, their one-time enemies, to whom they had turned for help against Assyria, will not only make fun of them but rejoice in their destruction.

8 *Set* the trumpet to thy mouth. *He shall come* as an eagle against the house of

8 Set the trumpet to your lips,
   for[b] a vulture is over the house of the
   Lord,

   [b] Cn: Heb *as*

2. Israel Under Sentence of Death (8:1-14)
a) War's Alarm (8:1-3)

8:1. Vss. 1-3 form the opening strophe. The alarm must be sounded; the danger is imminent. Except in the case of vs. 1*b*, there is a staccato effect about these verses, so that some scholars incline to believe that vs. 1*b* may not belong to the present context. "To your lips the horn!" (For this rendering as "lips" of the Hebrew noun *hēkh* which is normally rendered as "gums" or "palate," cf. H. S. Nyberg, "Das textkritische Problem des Alten Testaments am Hoseabuche demonstriert," *Zeitschrift für die alttestamentliche Wissenschaft,* LIII [1934], 248-49.) There is in this command the brevity of urgency. The following part may be rendered: "Like a vulture [the enemy swoops] upon the Lord's house," i.e., upon Palestine; or reading כי for כ, we get the rendering given in the RSV. The **vulture** in either case refers to the Assyrian who is about to descend upon the land; as a carrion bird, he will be in at the death (for the use of the figure of an eagle with reference to Nebuchadrezzar cf. Jer. 49:22; Ezek. 17:3). An interesting suggestion has

---

8:1. *Set the Trumpet to Your Lips.*—The **trumpet** is a widely used O.T. symbol. Amos employs it (2:2); so does Jeremiah (6:1); and Ezekiel (33:3-6). The N.T. also uses it (I Cor. 14:8). These are but a few of many references. It was sometimes used for encouragement, having much the same effect on warriors that a rousing college yell has on the team putting up a game fight. It would hearten them, put new spirit in them—a note often sadly lacking among us. Too often the mood of dreariness and dullness marks our efforts. **Set the trumpet to your lips.** Not to proclaim a lot of sentimental nonsense about man's automatically getting better and better, but as a witness to our faith in the reality of a God who, despite human sin, is still the ruler, and whose purposes stand firm even in the most chaotic and disordered days. Christianity cannot lose its confidence in ultimate victory without losing its radiant, dynamic quality. "We are more than conquerors" (Rom. 8:37).

Hosea, however, uses the trumpet here as a symbol neither of encouragement nor of triumph, but of warning. And he is not the only prophet who thus uses it. Ezekiel does too. "But if the watchman see the sword come, and blow not the trumpet, and the people be not warned" (Ezek. 33:6). So too Hosea:

Set the trumpet to your lips,
for a vulture is over the house of the Lord.

He means the land of northern Israel. The danger is intensified by the figure of the **eagle.** The vulture has a fondness for carrion. So Job, referring to this very eagle, writes: "Her young ones also suck up blood: and where the slain

are, there is she" (Job 39:30). Hosea therefore is emphasizing the corruption, impurities, the moral and spiritual decay, that have taken hold of his land. No wonder he says, **Set the trumpet to your lips.** The eagle was known for its swiftness of movement—"as swift as the eagle flieth" (Deut. 28:49). So swiftly, suggests Hosea, will the Assyrian invaders pounce down upon a decadent and demoralized people.

When that note of urgency is missing, something vital goes out with it. We speak soft and polite words to mild-mannered, respectable folk about some matter which seems of no great concern. Little wonder what we say has no power. It is not in keeping with the spirit of our gospel. It will never arouse or transform mankind. "Choose you this day whom ye will serve" (Josh. 24:15); "If the Lord be God, follow him: but if Baal, then follow him" (I Kings 18:21); "The time is fulfilled, and the kingdom of God is at hand: repent ye, and believe the gospel" (Mark 1:15); "Now is the accepted time; . . . now is the day of salvation" (II Cor. 6:2). For those who rightly see the matter the gospel makes the difference between life and death—"Why will ye die, O house of Israel?" (Ezek. 18:31.) Richard Baxter preached as "a dying man to dying men."[7] The fact that our fathers thought of hell as a place of fire and brimstone and visualized lost men in eternal flames no doubt added the touch of urgency to their effort. They sought to snatch brands from the burning. Yet only the hopelessly superficial can doubt that the wages of sin is still death, and that tragedy and suffering are still the lot of the individual or the age that,

[7] "Love Breathing Thanks and Praise," Part II.

the LORD, because they have transgressed my covenant, and trespassed against my law.	because they have broken my covenant, and transgressed my law.
2 Israel shall cry unto me, My God, we know thee.	2 To me they cry, My God, we Israel know thee.
3 Israel hath cast off *the thing that is* good: the enemy shall pursue him.	3 Israel has spurned the good; the enemy shall pursue him.

been made by Tur Sinai, who correlates the Hebrew term נשר with the Arabic verb *nashara*, "to publish," "to announce," and so reads כנשר with the meaning: "Set the horn to your lips, like a herald [making a proclamation] against the house of the LORD" (Harry Torczyner, "Dunkle Bibelstellen," in Karl Budde, ed., *Karl Marti zum siebsigsten Geburtstage* [Giessen: A. Töpelmann, 1925; "Beihefte zur Zeitschrift für die alttestamentliche Wissenschaft"], pp. 277-78) .

In vs. 1*b* the sins of disloyalty and disobedience are specified as the causes of Israel's destruction. That is certainly what Hosea taught; but nevertheless these words, as they come in here, seem to hold up the onward sweep of a short passage of tremendous urgency.

2. The order of the words is significant. **To me they cry;** that is just what they had refused to do. But once again man's extremity is God's opportunity. In their dire need they turn to God whom they have ceased to know. But in spite of that they claim vociferously that they do know him. "My God, we know thee, we Israel." It is true that the order of the words here is not usual, and a change would give a smoother form of speech, "We know thee, God of Israel." But the M.T. is truer to the urgency of the situation; it makes the words come in gasps; and people who speak in gasps do not have ordered utterance.

3. This verse expresses the divine response and the divine sentence. To reject or to spurn the good is to reject God (cf. Amos 5:4, 6, 14) . A fit comment is given upon these

like Israel of old, forsakes the law of the Lord. The eagle still hovers over such an age. He hovers over ours. **Set the trumpet to your lips.**

1*b*-2. *The Broken Covenant.*—It is the same old story. Isaiah voiced it: "Wherefore the Lord said, Forasmuch as this people draw near me with their mouth, and with their lips do honor me, but have removed their heart far from me" (29:13) . Jeremiah voiced it: "They have forsaken the covenant of the LORD their God, and worshipped other gods, and served them" (22:9) . Here too they transgress the covenant and trespass against the law; yet they say **My God, we Israel know thee.** The gap between profession and practice, between pious words and godly living, is still considerable. Jesus faced it. There were those who professed to know and worship him, but their lives were quite at variance with their words. "Why call ye me, Lord, Lord, and do not the things which I say?" (Luke 6:46; cf. Matt. 7:20-21.) It is not so much in the realm of the ecclesiastical as in the realm of the moral and spiritual that the sincerity of one's quest for God and one's knowledge of him is seen. **My God, we Israel know thee.** But they did not. God is not known in a vacuum.

3. *The Neglect of the Good Brings Evil.*—A man or nation is free to turn from the right path. The choice is ours. God does not make it for us. He has indeed beset us within and without with much to help us choose wisely: conscience, Christian ideals, ennobling friendships, the church with its teachings, prayer, worship. No one ever spurns the good without some knowledge that the choice is a violation of a sacred trust. Yet though we are free to spurn the good, we are never free to escape the consequences of our choice. **The enemy shall pursue him.** Evil consequences follow. And the greater the good we spurn, the greater the evil that pursues. The evil results must not be regarded as vindictive; they are rather consequential. They indicate that we do not inhabit a fool's paradise in which we can sow tares and reap wheat, but we live in a moral, law-abiding universe in which we reap as we sow.

The choice of the good is not an easy one. "Good things are hard." No one ever achieves integrity of character or purity of life without conscious and continued effort. It is only through the disciplining of self that life is won. The choice of the broad way is easy—"as easy as falling off a log," and as significant. It gets one nowhere. Worse than that, it gets one into all sorts of trouble. It leads at last to "the far country," and that is no pleasure resort. "The way of transgressors is hard" (Prov. 13:15) . **The enemy shall pursue him.**

4 They have set up kings, but not by me: they have made princes, and I knew *it* not: of their silver and their gold have they made them idols, that they may be cut off.

4 They made kings, but not through me.
They set up princes, but without my
knowledge.
With their silver and gold they made
idols
for their own destruction.

---

verses by R. F. Horton: "The words of religion will not be accepted for the deeds; though the deeds may be for the words" (*The Minor Prophets* [Edinburgh: T. C. & E. C. Jack, n. d.; "Century Bible"], I, 45) .

b) EPHRAIM, POLITICALLY DISTRAUGHT AND SPIRITUALLY BEMUSED (8:4-14)

(1) THE FATE OF THE CALF OF SAMARIA (8:4-7)

4. In Judah there had been dynastic stability since the days of King David. But as Horton reminds us, "During 253 years Israel had eighteen kings from ten different

---

Why is it that men spurn the good and so easily turn to the evil? Why is it that a child if left to himself would grow up in ignorance and never go to school? Why does one growing into maturity find it so much harder to do right than to do wrong? Why is the temptation to do wrong so much stronger than the inclination to do right? Why are we tempted to steal but not to be honest? Does the fact that evil comes as temptation while goodness comes as obligation mean that goodness is organic to the self and evil a trespasser? But if the self was made for goodness, why do we spurn the good? Why does the devil have more attraction for us than God our creator in whose image we are made?

Such questions raise a prior question. What is the goal of man's life? Growth. A little colt shortly after birth scampers all over the lot and is able to take care of himself. A baby passes through months of helplessness. Cries and tears are his frequent companions. As he matures cries give way to sighs, and tears to grief that is often too deep for tears. Why is man's road a longer, rougher, and steeper one than that the animal takes? Because man is an immortal soul. He must grow spiritually. The poet said that the world is a vale of soul making. But growth is inseparable from effort. This is true physically. We have to creep before we walk, but if we never straightened up, we could never walk. And walking means falling, the possibility of bumps and pain. If you tied the right arm of a growing child, or of an adult for that matter, to his side for a prolonged period, his arm would waste and weaken. Keep it there indefinitely and it would be lost as surely as though it had been amputated—"the atrophy of disuse." Effort is the path to bodily development, no less to the development of the soul. Though man was made for the good, if the good could be achieved without effort the soul would be deprived of struggle and so could not grow.

The good then would become an enemy of the best and so defeat its own purpose. Jesus himself was tempted, learned through the things he suffered, and knew the agony of Gethsemane.

4. *Politics Must Be Redeemed.*—The **kings** and **princes** enthroned without God's consent and approval did not come to much. They did not last. Hosea, although he was one of the most spiritually minded of the prophets, is regarded as one of the most politically minded also. He saw very clearly the connection between the moral condition of his people and their political fortunes and misfortunes. He saw that "moral decay means political decay."

It is one of the major tragedies of our time that we do not see this. We still talk glibly about preaching the gospel and leaving politics alone, as though the church belongs to God and the state to the devil. The Roman Catholic Church knows better. It has much concern for the state, though perhaps less Christian than ecclesiastical. Pope Pius XII said that the "separation of religion and life, the church and the world, [is] contrary to the Christian Catholic idea." It is equally contrary to the Protestant idea. But there is a world of difference between the Roman Catholic and the Protestant idea as to how the church should influence the state. Speaking broadly, the Roman Catholic Church thinks the relationship should be organic, while the Protestant church thinks it should be functional. The Roman church thinks that the church as an institution should exert authoritarian control over government. But **kings** made by politically ambitious ecclesiastics hungry for worldly power could hardly win God's approval. **They have made princes, and I knew it not.** The Roman church, for all practical purposes, identifies itself with the kingdom of God. Protestantism does not attempt to do any such thing, and so does not believe in the organic control of the state by the church. Rather it

5 ¶ Thy calf, O Samaria, hath cast *thee* off; mine anger is kindled against them: how long *will it be* ere they attain to innocency?

5 I have[c] spurned your calf, O Samar'ia.
My anger burns against them.
How long will it be

[c] Heb *He has*

---

families, and no family came to a close save by violent death. The rapid succession of usurpers in the closing years was only the final plunge of a disastrous career" (*ibid.*). The form of the accusation made against Ephraim here shows that the prophet laments that the charismatic election of kings had given way to intrigue and power politics which had the seeds of strife and corruption in them. Now men made their kings and they made their gods in a vain attempt to regulate all things in heaven and earth. The statement

> With their silver and gold they made idols
> for their own destruction

has a very paradoxical sound. The people did not intend their own destruction when they made the idols; but inasmuch as that has been the consequence of their action it is said to have been the intention of it also, even if they could not see it.

5. Vss. 5-7 follow vs. 4 in dealing with the subject of idolatry. The first clause of vs. 5, as it stands, must mean either "your calf has cast you off [or "spurned you"], O Samaria," or "He has cast off your calf, O Samaria." The KJV follows the first line; in the second, "he" is a third person singular of indefinite reference. The LXX read the verb as

---

believes that the gospel the church preaches should, like leaven, work within the lump. In one instance control is external and legal; in the other, inner, moral, and spiritual.

But how to bring our age to see, as Hosea saw, the vital connection between morality and politics is a major problem. Even as the political chaos and disorder of his day were due to his people's failure to recognize and submit to God's rightful rule over their political destinies, so with ours. The public still too largely regards Christianity as though it were a fragile plant, and the church a sort of hothouse that shields it from wind and weather. The result is that not only are vast areas of life divorced from God's control, but we do not even realize that his guidance should be sought. The chaotic and desperate political situations which so frequently exist should help us realize that the nations are held fast within his righteous rule, and that to spurn it is the greatest folly.

4b. The Threat of Self-Destruction.—Silver and gold were among the most precious possessions of the Israelites. These they used for their own destruction. Such a procedure seems even more shocking than suicide. Taking one's life does not involve the loss of silver and gold; that is left intact. As far as material waste is concerned, the procedure is quite inexpensive—a bullet from a revolver or a gallon of gasoline in the tank with the motor running and the garage doors shut. Israel, however, not only destroyed herself but did so with her silver and gold. Did she know what she was doing?

And do we? For are we not doing much the same thing? With their marvelous knowledge and scientific know-how they made atomic bombs for their own destruction; with their incredible wealth they made superdreadnoughts and supersonic planes for their own destruction; with their talent for organization they converted a peaceful world into an armed camp for their own destruction. "They" does not apply exclusively to any one nation but to mankind. Is there any greater tragedy than that man should use his choicest gifts of mind, talent, and resource to destroy himself? Of course Israel thought she was bettering herself, defending herself, when she diverted her treasures to idolatry. So does modern man, and that is the most tragic aspect of his predicament. Does it mean that the light within us has become darkness? And if so, where can the smoking torches be rekindled?

5-6. Three Types of Idolatry.—From artificial, man-made kings Hosea now turns to artificial, man-made gods. He was the first prophet to attack idolatry in any thoroughgoing way, or to denounce the use of images in worship. Elijah prophesied against the worship of Baal, so did Elisha; but neither of them objected to the use of pagan symbols, pagan rites and practices in the worship of Yahweh. So long as one worshiped him, the forms mattered little. Hosea saw, and wisely, that the form in this instance mattered greatly, and he was the first to see it. For though one may say that he worships the Lord, if the kind of worship is

6 For from Israel *was* it also: the workman made it; therefore it *is* not God: but
the calf of Samaria shall be broken in
pieces.

till they are pure **6** in Israel?*d*

A workman made it;
    it is not God.
The calf of Samar'ia
    shall be broken to pieces.*e*

d Gk: Heb *for from Israel*
e Or *shall go up in flames*

an imperative. There is much to be said for the emendation of the verb to the first
person, i.e., "I spurn your calf, O Samaria"; it is in keeping with what immediately
follows, and has the additional advantage of being a counterblast to vs. 3*a*. **My anger
burns against them** means against the people of Samaria who are taken as representative
of the Northern Kingdom.

If we take now the remainder of vs. 5 together with vs. 6*a*, considerable differences
will be noticed between the KJV and the RSV. **From Israel was it** also will not stand;
even the form **from Israel was it** (i.e., deleting the connective) is not a felicitous way

not in keeping with the nature of that Lord,
then one really is not worshiping the Lord
at all.

The **calf** which Hosea denounced was set up
in the reign of Jeroboam. The reason for his
having made it is very revealing. "Whereupon
the king took counsel, and made two calves of
gold, and said unto them, It is too much for you
to go to Jerusalem: behold thy gods, O Israel,
which brought thee up out of the land of
Egypt" (I Kings 12:28). Too much trouble to
go up to Jerusalem; so much easier to make
some gods of your own and worship them
instead! Yes, but that sort of god is not God
at all. **The calf of Samaria shall be broken
in pieces.**

There are at least three types of idolatry.
One might be called simon-pure. It grows out of
ignorance. Men make an idol and bow down to
it because they do not know the true God.
Paul refers to this type of idolatry in his
speech on Mars' Hill (Acts 17:22-23). Isaiah
of the Exile mentions it too (Isa. 40:19-20).
These gods are impotent. "They bear him
[their god] upon the shoulder" (Isa. 46:7).
"Thus they changed their glory into the similitude of an ox that eateth grass" (Ps. 106:20).
These artificial gods, however, do testify to the
real and genuine human need of cosmic companionship and support.

There is another type of idolatry. The Nazis
and the Communists have furnished perfect
examples. This type is compounded of ignorance plus egotism. God is, after all, that in
which, if not in whom, we think we find the
answer to life's meaning, the key to what life is
all about. When the atheistic Communist finds
that key in "the dictatorship of the proletariat,"
he fashions his own god. Even as the prophet
voices his confidence in the Lord by saying

that "the stars in their courses fought against
Sisera" (Judg. 5:20), so does many a jingoist
seem to believe there is a cosmic principle in
the universe that supports his cause. Such
"faith" may be little more than human arrogance and egotism, its only god an enlarged
edition of the ego. "It is just as much idolatry
to worship God according to a false mental
image as by means of a false metal image." [8]

We may yet distinguish a third type of
idolatry. It is not based on ignorance—we know
the golden calf is not God. It is not an expression of the human pride and arrogance which
leads a man to deny the one true God and place
on the throne some enlarged edition of himself
as a substitute. It is what one might call "practical atheism." We know an idol is an idol, and
we know there is a power in the universe
greater than ourselves, our class, our race, or
our nation. We give that power nominal allegiance, yet our whole life is geared to a scale
of values that denies its existence. "They feared
the Lord, and served their own gods" (II Kings
17:33). There is too often a real difference
between the God we worship and the gods we
serve. But the gods we serve are those in which
we really believe, for they direct the course of
our lives and by them we pattern our conduct.
The most cursory examination of our civilization will show that the goals for which we strive
are vastly more in keeping with "the God of
this world" than with the God and Father of
our Lord Jesus Christ. We worship the God of
Jesus; but we serve our own gods. This too is a
type of idolatry. It is practical atheism.

5*b*. *Purity of Life*.—Purity is not generally
regarded as one of the greatest virtues. Paul
mentioned faith, hope, and love as the three
cardinal ones. While he omitted purity from

[8] Temple, *Christian Faith and Life*, p. 24.

of saying that Samaria's calf was a man-made thing. But that very thought may be kept by observing the rhythm of the verses, as the RSV has done, with the words **from Israel** emended to "house of Israel" or "children of Israel":

> How long will they be incapable of innocency,
>   the house of Israel?
> That thing—a craftsman made it,
>   no God is it.

Hosea condemns idols as Second Isaiah was to do with such power in his day, as man-made products, impotent to do either good or evil (cf. Isa. 41:22-24; 44:9-11, 17-20; 45:20-21; also Jer. 10:2-5). E. L. Allen (*Prophet and Nation* [London: James Nisbet & Co., 1947], pp. 47-48) says of this verse: "Hosea concentrates all his conviction of the gulf which separates the divine from the human, his contempt for all that pretends in any way

the list, his own struggle to achieve it as he wrestled with the lust of the flesh and sought to bring his bodily passions under the control of Christ's spirit leaves us in no doubt as to the importance he attached to it. At first sight purity might seem weak or immature. We connect it with innocence, "the innocence of childhood." Adam and Eve lived in innocence until the "knowledge" that comes with maturity led to their sin. Yet we should be far from the truth should we regard purity as being incompatible with adulthood. Without this quality life is badly stained, marred, and even loses its creative power. Why should it matter **how long it would be till they are pure in Israel?** Was it because without purity certain doors would be forever closed, certain truths undiscovered?

Purity of heart may be regarded as singleness of purpose. Søren Kierkegaard expresses this truth in the phrase, "Purity of heart is to will one thing." [9] "One thing I do," said Paul (Phil. 3:13). Every life, unless it accepts a fragmentary, disconnected existence, needs a center around which, like some magnet, its otherwise wayward and scattered impulses and desires may be held together. "Strait is the gate, and narrow is the way, which leadeth unto life" (Matt. 7:14). The scientist in search of a truth hews to the line. Broad is the road that leads to no discovery, but the path to the finding of truth is straight and narrow. Jesus told his hearers to seek first the kingdom of God and his righteousness. Loyalty to this idea would lead men to discover the greatest of all truth, the truth about themselves, since no man knows himself until he knows God as his creator and redeemer. Yet all the while motives other than the pure love of God lured the disciples away as they do us. Two of them wanted to know who would have the chief seats in the kingdom. Many movements have been launched on the high plane of disinterestedness only to be wrecked or at least changed by the intrusion of

motives far removed from the original idea. Even the Salvation Army, that most single-minded of institutions, did not escape this peril. As the army grew and spread there came differences of opinion and struggle for preferment, so much so that on her deathbed Catherine Booth, the wife of General Booth, could say to her daughter: "Kate, why is it that God can't keep a thing pure for more than one generation?" [1]

To have purity of heart, however, is not only to achieve singleness of purpose but to possess unconquerable power.

> My good blade carves the casques of men,
>   My tough lance thrusteth sure,
> My strength is as the strength of ten,
>   Because my heart is pure.[2]

It takes courage to die for the truth, but it takes purity of heart to know the truth for which one should die. Behind the courage of the martyr is the insight of the saint. And if the saint, whom we do not usually associate with physical strength, gives such astonishing evidences of bravery, as history abundantly proves, this is because he is sustained by the power of truth. Moral courage is of a rarer and higher quality than physical courage, and in the case of the martyr inspires physical courage. "Here I stand. I can do no other; so help me, God." [3] Luther's words are in substance the testimony of all those who have hazarded or given life for the truth. It was in Jesus that this courage which springs from purity of heart reached its highest peak. History gives no clearer example of that singleness of purpose which is the source of all triumphant loyalty.

This brings us to the point. "Blessed are the pure in heart: for they shall see God" (Matt. 5:8). There is a type of truth that can be

[1] Willard L. Sperry, *Strangers and Pilgrims* (Boston: Little Brown & Co., 1939), p. 56.
[2] Tennyson, "Sir Galahad."
[3] See Roland Bainton, *Here I Stand* (New York and Nashville: Abingdon-Cokesbury Press, 1950), p. 185.

[9] *Purity of Heart* (New York: Harper & Bros., 1938), title page.

7 For they have sown the wind, and they shall reap the whirlwind: it hath no stalk: the bud shall yield no meal: if so be it yield, the strangers shall swallow it up.

7 For they sow the wind,
  and they shall reap the whirlwind.
The standing grain has no heads,
  it shall yield no meal;
if it were to yield,
  aliens would devour it.

---

to the majesty of Yahweh while being only man-made. The god he worships is an imageless god, one, that is to say, who is beyond expression in any form borrowed from the material world. What alone communicates him to men is the obedience which responds to his revealed will, the love which answers to his covenant-love." The rendering of the second half of vs. 6, as given in the KJV and the RSV, is to be sustained; the final word in the Hebrew, although not found elsewhere in the O.T., is known in postbiblical Hebrew and means "splinters," being from a verbal root, known in Arabic, meaning "to cut." The wicked are sometimes described as the chaff which the wind drives on (cf. Ps. 1:4); here an equally disparaging figure is used of Samaria's idol, which will be **broken to pieces.**

7. "Whatsoever a man soweth, that shall he also reap" (Gal. 6:7; cf. II Cor. 9:6; Ps. 126:6). Here Hosea speaks of those who sow barren, useless seed; they will reap

---

known and loved without purity of heart, in the sense in which we now use the word. Conceivably a man may be a good scientist and not be a good man. The natural man may discover natural truth. But the natural man, as Paul said, cannot discern the things of the spirit; they must be spiritually discerned.

The highest wisdom is established, not on reason alone, not on those worldly sciences, physics, history, chemistry, and the like, on which intellectual knowledge stumbles. The highest wisdom is one. The highest wisdom has one science, the science of the All, the universal science which explains all creation, and the place which man occupies in it. In order to absorb this science, it is absolutely essential to purify and renovate the inner man, and, therefore, before one can know it one must believe and accomplish perfection. And to attain this end, our souls must be filled with that Divine light which is called conscience.[4]

When one sees God, the moral values one discovers through a conscience illumined by God's spirit assume cosmic meaning. One then regards such values not as man-made conventions but as divine compulsions. "The Son of man must . . ." (Mark 8:31).

7. *The Cumulative Power of Evil.*—The figure of sowing and reaping was often on the lips of Jesus. Hosea uses it here to describe the consequences of Israel's evil. They are real and cumulative. That we reap what we sow is proof of the material and moral trustworthiness of the universe. We do not gather grapes of thorns or figs of thistles (cf. Gal. 6:7-8). We are often amazed when evil days come upon us. In a

moral universe it would be more amazing if they did not.

We not only **reap** what we **sow** qualitatively but quantitatively. "He which soweth sparingly shall reap also sparingly; and he which soweth bountifully shall reap also bountifully" (II Cor. 9:6). To **sow the wind** and **reap the whirlwind** is a vivid way of saying that the weakness and unprofitableness of Israel's ways can have but one end—a very tempest of ruin.

The other figure is equally vivid. Israel has no standing corn. **The standing grain has no heads,** i.e., it does not grow. It is runted and scrubby. And even if it does grow, the result would be just as profitless, for if [the grain] **were to yield, aliens would devour it.** The point Hosea is trying to make by use of this metaphor of sowing and reaping is that "Israel's policy will never be successful from the worldly point of view, and any wealth which he may acquire will be seized by other nations." [5]

We sometimes say of some calamity that it has come upon us as "a bolt from the blue," suddenly and unexpectedly. But in a moral universe there are no bolts from the blue in the sense that the catastrophes which befall are uncaused or should not have been expected. In the physical universe the bolts from the blue, though they come with a suddenness that startles, are not haphazard or fortuitous. Lightnings, hurricanes, storms, and droughts are all the result of natural causes. So too are social catastrophes. No doubt the Russian revolution that swept the czars out of power and turned that country upside down must have seemed like a bolt from the blue to the privileged. Yet

---

[4] Leo Tolstoy, *War and Peace*, Part V, ch. ii.

[5] S. L. Brown, *Hosea*, p. 73.

8 Israel is swallowed up: now shall they be among the Gentiles as a vessel wherein *is* no pleasure.

9 For they are gone up to Assyria, a wild ass alone by himself: Ephraim hath hired lovers.

8 Israel is swallowed up;
    already they are among the nations
    as a useless vessel.
9 For they have gone up to Assyria,
    a wild ass wandering alone;
    E'phraim has hired lovers.

---

not only disappointment and utter want, but distress and trouble; **they sow the wind, and . . . reap the whirlwind.** The rest of the verse continues the agricultural metaphor. Any grain stocks which do rise as the result of such sowing will have nothing at the head and will yield no food; if perchance a few stocks contrive to give a yield, **strangers shall swallow it up;** even that small comfort will be denied Israel. The picture is of utter frustration.

(2) Israel Swallowed Up Among the Nations (8:8-10)

8. Vss. 8-10 turn to the subject of Israel's foreign alliances. Vs. 7 said that strangers would swallow up the little food that the Israelites might have contrived to get. But that is not the whole truth concerning Israel's plight; **Israel** herself will be **swallowed up.** Everything distinctive in her way of life is gone; she is now a useless, profitless vessel among the nations (cf. 7:8). It is in this manner that the verse should be interpreted; there is no occasion to read into it a reference to the Exile.

9. In seeking alliance with one of the great powers, Israel is like a stubborn **wild ass** that goes its own way; it will not be tamed or trained and will inevitably fall into disaster. The final phrase in the verse may be original: lit., "Ephraim gave love gifts," or, with

---

if they had realized the implications of living in a moral universe, they would not have been too surprised. For when the privileged abuse their privilege, when the wealthy misuse their wealth, when the socially prominent lose sympathy for the socially "outcast" and grow in aloofness and indifference rather than in understanding and concern, when the powerful, whether in the church or out of it, use their power to further their own selfish ambitions and to protect their own entrenched prerogatives, trouble lies ahead. Continued and prolonged abuse sets the stage for a day of reckoning. That day is often long delayed—"God does not pay at the end of every week, but he pays." [6] And though it may come suddenly, it should not be regarded as uncaused. There is a cumulative quality in evil. You **sow** it to the **wind** and reap it in **the whirlwind.** The evil habits we form at first have no more hold upon us than the force of a mild or gentle breeze— we can move against it with freedom; its pressure is light. But give those habits time to grow through repeated indulgence and presently we awaken to the sobering truth that the **wind**, imperceptibly perhaps, has become **the whirlwind.** We cannot now move freely. We cannot resist its pressure. Whenever a man says, "I am going to stop that" and fails to do so, he but increases the hold of evil upon him and makes more difficult his conquest of it. The time to

[6] Anne of Austria. To Cardinal Mazarin.

stop is now, before the **wind** becomes **the whirlwind.**

However, the symbol of **the whirlwind** may be thought of not only in terms of intensity but of outreach: the seeds of evil not only produce plants that grow in strength but in propagating power. The seeds of evil are blown to unaffected areas and produce crops far afield. If one would ponder the far-reaching effects of an evil deed, he would be less likely to commit it. Our acts, be they good or evil, like a pebble dropped on the surface of a pool, reach out in ever-widening circles. The seeds we sow are alive. Our acts are not static but dynamic. Life is not a mechanism but an organism. The principle of growth inheres in it. If the wheat grows, so do the tares; moreover, the tares do not need the nurture required by the wheat, they do not have to be cultivated. When at the close of World War I, the United States crawled back into a fictitious and fanciful isolationism and refused to help establish government by law, which is the only substitute for international anarchy, could she have realized that she was in no small measure helping to set the stage, as she unquestionably was, for the tragic drama of World War II, she might have thought twice. Was she sowing **the wind**, and has she reaped the whirlwind?

8-10. Counting for Nothing.—They are among the nations as a useless vessel. "They count for nothing . . .," (Moffatt). Neither use-

10 Yea, though they have hired among the nations, now will I gather them, and they shall sorrow a little for the burden of the king of princes.

10 Though they hire allies among the nations,
    I will soon gather them up.
And they shall cease*f* for a little while
    from anointing*g* king and princes.

f Gk: Heb *begin*
g Gk: Heb *burden*

---

a slight change in the vocalization, **Ephraim has hired lovers.** But the unexpected mention of Ephraim when the subject has already been defined, as well as the argument from parallelism, has suggested the reading, מצרימה נתנו וגו, "And to Egypt they have given love gifts."

10. Though they hire allies among the nations: Driver has proposed the translation, "Though they go bargaining among the nations" (reading *yathnû;* see "Notes and Studies," p. 158). That fits the context in general, but the use of התנו in vs. 9 supports the more usual line of interpretation. The literal rendering, "Though they give love gifts among the nations," is adequately represented by the RSV. The next part **I will soon gather them up** cannot refer to the ingathering after the Babylonian exile, though the LXX must have understood the words in that sense. If the verb is retained as it is in the M.T., the words must mean that even if they make overtures to the nations, the Lord will gather them for his disciplinary purposes; they will not escape. Many scholars, however, emend the text to אפיצם, "I will scatter them," or אנפצם, "I will shatter them." The meaning of the second part of the verse is uncertain because the main verb in it can be construed in several ways. **And they shall begin** does not fit the context at all; "And they shall grieve" is possible, but surely if the people felt the burden of their own king and princes, it would not be a temporary distress. Again, it has been suggested that the burden which the people will feel will be the tribute imposed by **the king of princes;** but it is extremely doubtful whether this title was used of an Assyrian king; surely "king of kings" would be required. Nor is it easy to accept Nyberg's contention (*Studien zum Hoseabuche,* pp. 64-65) that the terms "king" and "princes," as they are used in the book of Hosea, are to be understood as divine names. But Driver (*loc. cit.*) has suggested that the verb ויחלו may be pointed as *wiḥallû* and translated, **and they shall cease;** otherwise we may read ויחדלו with the same meaning. The rendering in the RSV, arrived at by reading משח for משא, is very suitable in the context, but the reference to the **anointing** of princes is open to question. Surely, in view of all that Hosea has to say about intrigues and rebellions within the kingdom of Israel, the rendering

> And they shall cease for a little while
> from the burden of king and princes

has much to commend it. When Ephraim is scattered among the nations, political intrigues will perforce stop awhile.

---

ful nor ornamental. Why? Because **they have gone up to Assyria, a wild ass wandering alone.** It is much easier to be an echo of the world's voice than to be the voice of God to the world; but then, instead of being leaven, we become part of the dough; spiritually we count for nothing.

To be in the world, yet not of it, is difficult. The church has tried to solve the problem by a policy of isolationism, e.g., monasticism. This is not the N.T. way. The church has tried legislation. The Roman Catholic Church does this with a fair degree of success. "Every phase of contemporary activity, . . . economic, political, or social, falls within the purview of the church." [7] But it was the limitations of legalism that made Paul break with Judaism. He said the law was weak, might even give occasion to sin; at best it was only our schoolmaster to bring us to Christ. Christianity finds its true nature not in isolation or in legislation, but in association. Such association, however, necessitates on the part of the Christian an inner

[7] William Adams Brown, *The Church Catholic and Protestant* (New York: Charles Scribner's Sons, 1935), p. 163.

11 Because Ephraim hath made many altars to sin, altars shall be unto him to sin.

12 I have written to him the great things of my law, *but* they were counted as a strange thing.

11 Because E'phraim has multiplied altars for sinning,
    they have become to him altars for sinning.

12 Were I to write for him my laws by ten thousands,
    they would be regarded as a strange thing.

---

(3) Ephraim's Many Altars and Many Cities (8:11-14)

11. In view of the fact that the line is exceptionally long, most scholars delete the second occurrence of the words **altars for sinning** and read:

> Though Ephraim has made many altars,
>   they have become a sin to them [i.e., to Ephraim].

Nyberg (*op. cit.*, p. 65) makes the interesting and feasible suggestion that we have here not an otiose repetition of two words, but a characteristic wordplay:

> Though Ephraim has made many altars to take away sin [lit., "to unsin"],
>   yet they have become for them altars for sinning.

That is to say, these altars were never capable of the purpose for which they were erected; they have been as snares and delusions, so that what were expected to take away sin have become occasions for sin and a religious offense.

12. **The great things of my law:** The KJV cannot be accepted as a rendering of a doubtful Hebrew text. Two possibilities lie before the translator: **Were I to write for him my laws by ten thousands** or "Though I write for him the multitude of my laws."

---

power which will enable him to influence society for good rather than to succumb to its evil power (see Expos. on 7:8a). "I live; yet not I, but Christ liveth in me" (Gal. 2:20). With this inner guide Paul voyaged far beyond the traditional landmarks of his day. He mixed freely with people; but they did not change him, he changed them. They did not pull him down, he lifted them up. This was because, as he said, "Christ liveth in me." The power of Christ is still available. The leaven of his spirit can still change us and make us his instruments in helping to change others.

11-12. *Not How Many but What Sort.*—The best when perverted invariably becomes the worst. **Altars** are the symbols of man in quest of life's supreme good—his quest of God; yet when used with wrong motives and for wrong ends, they become occasions for man's **sin.** And since the altars at best are viewed as a means by which through worship man can overcome his sin, when perverted they involve him most deeply in iniquity. When one is betrayed by the very object that should have been his guide, then his confusion becomes worse confounded. "If . . . the light that is in thee be darkness, how great is that darkness!" (Matt.

6:23.) Love is the source of man's greatest blessing and, for that very reason, of his deepest tragedies. There is an old saying that the best thing becomes the worst thing when the thing goes bad.

We may approach this passage from another point of view. Israel multiplied altars, but having more altars is no guarantee of possessing more religion. The Christian test is not how many altars but what sort—not quantitative but qualitative. Multiplying altars was of itself no more an indication of the increase of the religious life among the Israelites than is the multiplying of churches among Christians. The fact that there are ten struggling churches in a little town that cannot support more than two is not an indication of the health of Christianity but of its sickness. There is no word but sin for the overlapping, duplication, competition, and rivalries that grow out of our sectarian interests. Not by the multiplying of altars but by the increase of Christian charity, by a new understanding of "what is vital" in religion (Phil. 1:10 Moffatt), by a renewed interest in the kingdom of God, and by an honest effort to put that before our ecclesiastical loyalties, will God be best served.

13 They sacrifice flesh *for* the sacrifices of mine offerings, and eat *it; but* the LORD accepteth them not; now will he remember their iniquity, and visit their sins: they shall return to Egypt.

13 They love sacrifice;[h]
  they sacrifice flesh and eat it;
  but the LORD has no delight in them.
Now he will remember their iniquity,
  and punish their sins;
  they shall return to Egypt.

[h] Cn: Heb uncertain

Either of these gives excellent sense. But even if the Lord so instructed his people, they would count such instruction strange and unintelligible, so far have they gone from him and so little do they now know him. The likening of God's laws to **a strange thing** (כמו זר; i.e., strange to Israel) is thus more apposite than the likening of them to a detestable thing (כמוזר), as T. H. Robinson has suggested (*Die zwölf kleinen Propheten,* p. 32).

13. The first part of this verse is sometimes translated, "They may sacrifice my own sacrificial gifts and eat flesh." That demands the transposition of the connective, but the sense is suitable. It says again that the people may offer all manner of gifts upon an altar, but that is not the worship which is acceptable to the Lord. The RSV follows the line of emendation favored by many scholars (זבח אהבו); the meaning thus obtained is not substantially different from that of the unemended text. The verse asserts that not only has the Lord no delight in the vain worship which his people offer, but he will punish them for their unfaithfulness. The threatened return of Israel to Egypt is like an annulling of all the redemptive work which had been done for and in Israel. Now they must return to the place of bondage from which in a former day they were gloriously

The same principle applies not only to the multiplying of altars but of members. There are two facts concerning which there is no doubt. One is that Christianity made a tremendous impact upon the life of the first-century world. It made the difference between B.C. and A.D. The second equally important fact is that this impact was made not because the Christians were numerically superior to the pagans, for they were not. They were a veritable handful. Nor was it made because the Christians were by worldly standards impressive. Measured by such standards they were ordinary, average folk. They made a unique impress on the first-century world for one reason only: under God they were different. The key to Christian effectiveness is not in numbers, whether few or many. The story is told of an old preacher who said he had had a great revival in his church. When asked how many members he had added, he said, "We did not add any, but we dropped a hundred." Multiplying numbers does not necessarily result in more Christianity. One would have to ask what sort of members they are—just an echo of the world's voice or the voice of God to the world? Are they dough or leaven? This is why statistical methods applied to the church, though necessary and inevitable, are misleading. They are misleading because what one is trying to measure in Christianity cannot be measured. It is imponderable, a matter of spirit, attitude, motive, life.

Perhaps the first step in evangelizing the world is the evangelization of the church. Perhaps the first step in getting many members is to get better members. Maybe before we seek to add new members to the church we should try to add new life to the members we already have. A church full of clinkers cannot set the world on fire, never mind how numerous the clinkers are. Only live coals give off heat. "Physician, heal thyself" (Luke 4:23). The Protestant church will have to be converted before it can convert the world. The early church turned the world upside down.

13a. The Surrender of the Self.—The Christian religion makes the most exacting demand that can be made—it asks for the surrender of the self. The fact that the Israelites so largely made the sacrificing of some external object, animal or vegetable, a substitute for the inner moral and ethical disciplines of religion was the evil against which the prophets constantly inveighed (cf. Amos 5:21-24). No offering we make to God can take the place of the giving of self.

Sacrifice is a part of the history of all religions. It was regarded as a means of winning the favor of the "gods." Its development may be clearly traced in Hebrew history. Not only did the Hebrews try to win God's favor by offering animals, but even human sacrifice was practiced (Gen. 22:9-10). However, as men's religious ideas became more mature, the abuses

| 14 For Israel hath forgotten his Maker, and buildeth temples; and Judah hath multiplied fenced cities: but I will send a fire upon his cities, and it shall devour the palaces thereof. | 14 For Israel has forgotten his Maker, and built palaces; and Judah has multiplied fortified cities; but I will send a fire upon his cities, and it shall devour his strongholds. |

delivered. It is interesting that the LXX adds another half line, parallel with the one concerning the return to Egypt, "And among the Assyrians they will eat unclean food." It may be that this half line was introduced here erroneously from 9:3.

14. The authenticity of this verse has been much disputed. Especially in the second half of the verse the resemblance to the style of the prophet Amos is very notable; this has persuaded some scholars to regard the verse as an addition (cf. 4:15). Furthermore, note that the third person singular feminine suffix in the final word "her strongholds"

---

of this method of worship became clear. Such worship divorced religion from life, piety from practice. Religion became the outward performance of certain rites unrelated to moral and ethical reality. No wonder Amos could cry, "I hate, I despise your feast days" (5:21). In the N.T. sacrifice takes on a spiritual meaning. God gave himself to us in Christ, and asked of us the giving of ourselves to him. "I seek not yours, but you" (II Cor. 12:14). "I beseech you therefore, brethren, by the mercies of God, that ye present your bodies a living sacrifice, holy, acceptable unto God, which is your reasonable service" (Rom. 12:1). For this there is no substitute.

14a. What Is Vital in Christianity.—One can have God without **temples** (cf. John 4:21), but temples without God are meaningless. One can have a home without an electric dishwasher, a vacuum cleaner, or an automobile. One cannot, however, have a home without love, understanding, and good will; these are basic. Sometimes when the true values are lacking, we compensate by buying new furniture or maybe moving into a new house. But these are never adequate substitutes. No more can substitutes serve us in religion.

It was over this very matter that Jesus clashed with the Pharisees. They did not have a sense of what is vital in religion. They were sticklers for certain forms and practices. They measured a man, religiously speaking, by his meticulous performance of certain rites, his strict observance of religious laws and taboos. There were religious laws about food, things clean and unclean, about the sabbath, about fasting, about the temple and the conduct of worship; so many of them that Jesus said they were a grievous burden on men's backs. The most serious aspect of these regulations was that they diverted men's attention from the essential matters.

Jesus had a completely different standard for evaluating the religious condition of men.

He judged people not by their outward observance of any religious rite but by the inner quality of their life, their spirit. So he told the Pharisees that in their emphasis on outward forms they strained out a gnat and swallowed a camel; that they tithed mint, anise, and cummin and omitted the weightier matters; that they made broad their phylacteries, as though it mattered, broad or narrow; that they could not distinguish between the gift and the altar that sanctified it, the gold and the temple that sanctified the gift; that religiously speaking they were like whited sepulchers, outwardly beautiful but full of corruption within.

Indeed, Jesus went further than that. How honest and courageous he was! He made an outcast Samaritan the hero of one of his best-loved stories, and two church people, the priest and the Levite who had observed all the outward forms, the villains. Why? Because the Samaritan had the spirit of love, good will, neighborliness, compassion, within him, while the others did not. He commended most highly another outcast, a Roman centurion, because though he was a stranger to the religious forms and ceremonies of Judaism, he had faith, while Israel did not. **Israel hath forgotten his Maker, and buildeth temples.**

Suppose the Protestant church could put the moral, ethical, and spiritual implications involved in the love and service of God ahead of its emphasis on **temples**, the forms of worship, the kind of baptism, the type of ordination, its attitude to the Communion—would not most of the obstacles to Protestant unity disappear? In the vital matters Protestant Christians are one; indeed, all Christians are. At the surface of the sea there are islands and continents separated by vast and dreary stretches of water; but in the deep there are no islands or continents: the world is one, part of an unbroken formation. So it is in the Christian religion. The problem of church unity is not how to achieve unity but how to express

9 Rejoice not, O Israel, for joy, as *other* people: for thou hast gone a whoring from thy God, thou hast loved a reward upon every cornfloor.

9 Rejoice not, O Israel!
Exult not[i] like the peoples;
for you have played the harlot, forsaking
your God.
You have loved a harlot's hire
upon all threshing floors.

[i] Gk: Heb *to exultation*

has no reference; therefore the conclusion seems unavoidable that the second half of the verse at least is not genuine. Whether the first half belongs to Hosea is a much more open question; the mention of **palaces** and **fortified cities** is not in his style, so far as we know it, but that is not determinative. This certainly can be said; even if the verse comes to us from Hosea, it does not belong to the present context, because vs. 13 makes a fitting close to the passage.

3. Ephraim's Idolatry and Its Punishment (9:1-17)
a) The Penalties of Exile for Ephraim (9:1-6)

9:1. Wellhausen may very well be right when he suggests that these words of Hosea were spoken by him on the occasion of a great festival when the people were gathered together in large numbers (cf. Intro., p. 557). He adds: "The cult is altogether Dionysiac, as the Greeks would describe it, heathenish, as Hosea would describe it" (*Die kleinen Propheten,* p. 122). Hosea's first word, therefore, must have sounded arresting in the ears of his hearers. The original text, as it stands, must be rendered:

Rejoice not, O Israel,
exultingly like the peoples.

There is claimed to be a parallel to the use of אל־גיל ("exultingly") in Job 3:22, but its use there is even more doubtful than here. The LXX reading μηδὲ εὐφραίνου supports the text אל־תגל, i.e., **exult not** (so RSV). The words **like the peoples** mean like the peoples who have not had Israel's religious training and who engage in idolatrous practices; in particular, of course, it is the Canaanites who are intended, with their fertility cult and its immoral rites. The second half of the verse expounds the significance of the reference. In truth, Israel had rejoiced like the peoples, had come to love the harlot's hire which Baal gave her, made merry at every threshing floor, and so had been unfaithful to God.

it. In the deep things, the things that are vital, we are one. It is only at the surface that we are separated. We shall express our unity, not uniformity, when we put the emphasis where Jesus put it—"By their fruits ye shall know them" (Matt. 7:20). We shall have unity when we realize that those who know God as revealed in Christ and are trying to live in communion with him, never mind through what church or ecclesiastical form or no form, are actually in fellowship with us.

9:1-3. *The Land of the Lord.*—The prophet discusses in this chapter the sorrows of the Exile. Israel has **played the harlot.** She has turned from the Lord to the Baalim. She has thought the material blessings she received were the result of her worship at the shrines of the nature gods; and she has been given her hire—corn, wine, and oil, "These are my rewards, that

my lovers have given me" (2:12). But for that apostasy she will pay.

Threshing floor and winevat shall not feed them, and the new wine shall fail them.

The punishment is to be still greater: **They shall not remain in the land of the LORD; but . . . shall return to Egypt,** the place of enslavement. Every life made captive by sin is in Egypt. "O wretched man that I am! Who shall deliver me . . . ?" (Rom. 7:24.)

In Hosea's time a god was thought of as being attached to the land. Yahweh was Israel's God. Whoever left Israel left his God behind. When David was driven out of Israel, he had to serve other gods, "for they have driven me out this day from abiding in the inheritance of the LORD, saying, Go, serve other gods" (I Sam. 26:19). So Naaman the Syrian, after he

2 The floor and the winepress shall not feed them, and the new wine shall fail in her.

3 They shall not dwell in the Lord's land; but Ephraim shall return to Egypt, and they shall eat unclean *things* in Assyria.

4 They shall not offer wine *offerings* to the Lord, neither shall they be pleasing unto him: their sacrifices *shall be* unto them as the bread of mourners; all that eat thereof shall be polluted: for their bread for their soul shall not come into the house of the Lord.

2 Threshing floor and winevat shall not feed them,
  and the new wine shall fail them.

3 They shall not remain in the land of the Lord;
  but E'phraim shall return to Egypt,
  and they shall eat unclean food in Assyria.

4 They shall not pour libations of wine to the Lord;
  and they shall not please him with their sacrifices.
  Their bread*j* shall be like mourners' bread;
  all who eat of it shall be defiled;
  for their bread shall be for their hunger only;
  it shall not come to the house of the Lord.

j Cn: Heb *to them*

2. Some scholars would follow the LXX ἔγνω and read ידעם for ירעם and so translate the first half of the verse, "Threshing floor and winevat will not know [or care for] them." Others would relate the verb ירעם to the noun רעה, "friend," and so translate:

> Threshing floor and winevat will not befriend them,
> and the new wine will play them false [בם for בה].

But these renderings are not to be preferred to that given in the RSV. The people had served Baal in the hope that by this service they would ensure for themselves the fruits of the fields; it is these fruits which will fail them, so that the worthlessness of Baal service will be made manifest.

3. Hosea has already stated that the Lord has forsaken his land because of his people's unfaithfulness (cf. 5:15); nevertheless, it is still his land. Now it is declared that Israel is no longer fit to continue living in that land. They will be removed to Egypt, the place of their former bondage (cf. 8:13), and to Assyria, where they will be unable to keep their joyful festivals, and unconsecrated food will be their portion.

4. The accentuation of the M.T. indicates the division into the phrases which are given in the KJV, but the rhythmic form of the lines dictates that the word זבחיהם, **their sacrifices**, should be construed with what goes before rather than with what follows (so

had been healed of his leprosy by Elisha, as he set out from Palestine, took some earth with him, because he wished to worship Elisha's God (II Kings 5:17). One calls to mind also the story of Jonah, who thought that by going across the sea he could escape the presence of Yahweh (Jonah 1:3). To leave the Lord's land therefore was to forfeit the Lord's blessing. More than that, the country to which one went was regarded as unclean: **and they shall eat unclean food in Assyria.**

But the idea, as in the case of the Exile, has a symbolic as well as a literal application. There is a **land of the Lord** from which like

some garden of Eden we may be expelled, and so be deprived of the lovingkindness and tender mercy which otherwise would be ours. The "far country" of the prodigal is not a geographical location; it is a spiritual condition. We may be in that far country even though we live next door to a church and are members of it. To live **in the land of the Lord** is to live in harmony with his purposes and in obedience to his laws.

4. *The Spiritual Quality of Worship.*—This verse, like the preceding ones, has a literal as well as a symbolic meaning. It was customary as a part of the ritual of worship to make wine

5 What will ye do in the solemn day, and in the day of the feast of the LORD?

5 What will you do on the day of appointed festival,
and on the day of the feast of the LORD?

RSV). If vs. 4 is to be taken together with vs. 3, the statement that Israel will not please the Lord with their offerings in the lands to which they are removed is strange and out of keeping with Hosea's teaching. Read, therefore, יערכו for the similar יערבו and translate, "And they will not set in order their sacrifices to him"; or relate the use of ערב here to the South Arabic *'rb*—"to offer" (gifts to God), and translate, "And they will not offer their sacrifices to him" (see G. R. Driver in Rowley, ed., *Studies in Old Testament Prophecy*, pp. 64-65). "Something like mourners' bread will be theirs," the literal rendering of the next part of the verse, is intelligible, but the slightly emended form given in the RSV (לחמם for להם) gives a smoother rendering. A dead body within a house made everything in it unclean (cf. Num. 19:14; for funeral customs cf. Jer. 16:7). Such would be their bread in the lands of their exile and they would be made unclean by it. Thus those who had been careful to fulfill all the ritual demands of their cult will no longer be able to prosecute that cult; there will be no more altar offerings, for all their food will be unclean and will be fit only for the satisfaction of their hunger. Those who had emphasized in their worship physical needs would now have left to them only physical satisfactions.

5. This verse is an example of interjected direct speech (cf. W. B. Stevenson, "A Neglected Literary Usage," *Transactions of the Glasgow University Oriental Society*, VI [1934], 14-21). It is in the form of a rhetorical question. For the exiled Israelites the great festivals will be no more, and all the joy of them will be as a thing of the past.

---

offerings to the Lord. A part of the wine was poured out as a libation, and the rest drunk by the worshiper. Hosea says that in exile

They shall not pour libations of wine to the LORD;
and they shall not please him with their sacrifices,

because in another land, and therefore, as it was thought, under the aegis of some other god, the wine would be unacceptable to Yahweh—it would be unclean (yet see Exeg.). The reasoning was wrong yet the insight was right. Our offerings are often unacceptable to God, as were those of the Israelites; but not for the reason given here: not because we offer them in the wrong place, but in the wrong spirit. The distinction was clearly pointed out by Jesus himself. It was this very matter that so concerned the woman of Samaria. "Our fathers worshipped in this mountain; and ye say, that in Jerusalem is the place where men ought to worship. Jesus saith unto her, . . . The hour cometh, and now is, when the true worshippers shall worship the Father in spirit and in truth: for the Father seeketh such to worship him." (John 4:20-21, 23.)

Not a wrong country but a wrong spirit—that is what makes worship unacceptable to God. Worship is "worthship." It is giving to God his due. "Give unto the LORD the glory due unto his name" (Ps. 29:2). The heart of the worshiper, however, is sometimes so out of tune or so occupied with the visible, material symbols

as to be insensible to the spiritual realities which alone give worship its meaning.

Their bread shall be for their hunger only, unconsecrated bread. Might it be that sometimes even in the Communion we may be so bound by our senses as to fail to see the spiritual meaning of the symbols we use? The Roman Catholic Church, in attempting to spiritualize the elements, overspiritualizes them and so woefully materializes them. The bread becomes, through the miracle of transubstantiation, the actual body of Christ. This in effect materializes rather than spiritualizes the sacrament. The Protestant on the contrary often sees only bread—the material—**for their hunger only.** The true worshiper sees the bread as a visible symbol of Christ's sacrifice, and in partaking of it prays to be possessed by his life-giving Spirit. It is bread offered to the Lord, and by him used to our salvation.

5-6. *A Picture of Spiritual Desolation.*—The **appointed festival,** a time of joy and gladness, will be no more. For Israel will be in exile: **They are going to Assyria; Egypt shall gather them.** So desolate and forlorn will they be that there will be

nettles covering the rare silver idols,
thorns springing in your shrines (Moffatt).

Hosea was a child of his age. He seemed unable to distinguish between religion itself and the "apparatus of worship." Consequently "he

6 For, lo, they are gone because of destruction: Egypt shall gather them up, Memphis shall bury them: the pleasant *places* for their silver, nettles shall possess them: thorns *shall be* in their tabernacles.

7 The days of visitation are come, the days of recompense are come; Israel shall know *it:* the prophet *is* a fool, the spiritual

---

6 For behold, they are going to Assyria;[k]
    Egypt shall gather them,
    Memphis shall bury them.
Nettles shall possess their precious things
    of silver;
    thorns shall be in their tents.

7 The days of punishment have come,
    the days of recompense have come;
    Israel shall know it.
The prophet is a fool,
    the man of the spirit is mad,

[k] Cn: Heb *from destruction*

---

6. The very lands in which the Israelites had put their trust for safety and succor in time of need are the ones which will be responsible for their removal and burial (cf. Jer. 13:21). As for the possessions which they must leave behind them, their silver treasures and their idols, these will have no attractiveness for anyone. **Nettles** will cast their covering mantle over them and sing their requiem, and **thorns** will be the undisputed tenants of their forsaken dwellings. It is a picture of desolation. The first part of the verse is, lit., "Indeed, they will go from ruin." That is a possible text and would mean that they would go forth from a country which had been ruined. But parallelism has suggested the reading which is given in the RSV and which most modern scholars accept (אשור for משד). **The pleasant places for their silver, nettles shall possess them** has no meaning; either מחמדי כספם should be read, or the M.T. should be regarded as having that value, so that the satisfactory rendering of the RSV is obtained (cf. Nyberg, *op. cit.*, pp. 68-69). **Memphis** ("Moph" in the original) was the capital city of Lower Egypt.

b) THE DEPTH OF ISRAEL'S CORRUPTION (9:7-9)

7. The syntactical construction of this verse is very uncertain. We must take the main part to be:

> The days of punishment have come,
>   the days of recompense have come;
> because of your great iniquity
>   and great hatred.

---

seems to regard the suspension of sacrifice during the exile as equivalent to a *moratorium* in religion."[8] In this he was mistaken. Amos saw differently. He saw the paraphernalia of worship as actually an obstacle to true religion (Amos 5:21-24). At any rate, Hosea's position in identifying the sacred festival with religion (assuming that he does so) is but another indication of the difference noted in the Expos. on vs. 4.

7a. The Day of Recompense.—Such days always come. They come as surely as the dawn, though often not as swiftly. There is no escaping God's judgments. The verdict of human experience, individual and social, testifies to that. The moral deteriorioration of the individual, the chaos, confusion, and insecurity of society, its bleeding wounds, its staggering ills

[8] S. L. Brown, *Hosea*, p. 79.

that cry to heaven, are they not often the inevitable result of a course of action displeasing to God and at variance with his will and purpose? It must be repeated, however, that this "punishment" is never vindictive. In God's dealing with man there is never any spite or revenge. The evil days which come are the inevitable results that obtain when in a moral universe men play tricks with the moral laws of God. "Whoso breaketh a hedge, a serpent shall bite him" (Eccl. 10:8). We cannot go around breaking the laws of God without being hurt.

7b. Are Inspired Men Insane?—So some people in Israel thought. So some in Palestine in the time of Christ thought (cf. Mark 3:21). So some said about Paul (Acts 26:24). When in 1789 William Carey announced his intention to go as a missionary to India, the East India

man *is* mad, for the multitude of thine iniquity, and the great hatred.	because of your great iniquity and great hatred.
8 The watchman of Ephraim *was* with my God: *but* the prophet *is* a snare of a	8 The prophet is the watchman of E'phraim, the people of my God,

The perfect verbs **have come** would be more fittingly rendered as prophetic perfects, relating to what is yet to come. **Israel shall know it,** i.e., the time of her chastisement will bring to Israel a degree of discernment; they will recognize the disciplinary nature of their experiences. The remaining two clauses of the verse,

> The prophet is a fool,
> the man of the spirit is mad,

are not bound with the verse as a whole. It is another example of interjected direct speech, in which the popular estimate of the religious leaders is expressed. These leaders are openly disparaged and ridiculed, in order to bring their words into contempt and to allay the public conscience. If the belief can be encouraged that they are suffering from illusions and hallucinations, they will be disregarded.

8. The interpretation of the first part of the verse is uncertain. "Ephraim was a watchman with my God" pictures Ephraim as a spy keeping watch upon God. But the rhythm of the line unites the following word **prophet** with the first half; thus two renderings are possible: "The prophet is Ephraim's watchman with ['im] my God, or

> The prophet is the watchman of Ephraim,
> the people ['am] of my God.

Company said that his scheme was the craziest one ever conceived by "a moon-struck fanatic." [1] Albert Schweitzer was another quite fit to be certified. These all repeat Israel's taunt:

> The prophet is a fool,
> the man of the spirit is mad.

This is always the verdict of the "practical" man, the "hardheaded" businessman who deals in "realities." To such folk the man of vision, inspired by lofty principles that transcend the opportunistic policies of the calculating and the shrewd, is insane. The burden of proof surely rests with those who hold this point of view. The weight of the argument is all on the other side. The world is for the most part in the hands of practical, hardheaded men. Such men quite largely dictate its policies—economic, political, international. And what a world!

It *may* be said that the methods of the idealist, inspired by his vision of justice, righteousness, and truth, will not work in this world. It *must* be said that the methods of the practical man do not work. At least we have tried them, and would we say that they bring the results we want? The tragic failure of our "practical" policies is writ large in the history of our age. Economic depression following hard upon World War I, that followed by World War

II, and that by a period of uncertainty, insecurity, chaos, and suffering unprecedented in its scope and staggering in its effect, threatening still further disaster—all this condemns to folly our naïve faith in the wisdom of the so-called "practical man." It ill befits him to point his finger at the man of vision and mouth his accustomed verdict, he **is a fool.** The shoe is actually on the other foot. It is the practical, the calculating, the opportunistic who are insane. They are blind. They fail to understand that God has laid the foundations of the world in righteousness and justice, and that no policy that violates his eternal principles can work. The natural man does not understand these things. He cannot—"For they are foolishness unto him: neither can he know them, because they are spiritually discerned" (I Cor. 2:14).

8a. God's Watchman.—What more important role could a man play? God's watchman looks out for God's interests, and therefore for man's best interests also. For man's best interests are always in line with God's will. The watchman's work is peculiarly important when darkness falls. For it is then that evil prowls. Evil thrives in darkness more than in the light. "Men loved darkness rather than light, because their deeds were evil" (John 3:19). It was at night "while men slept," that the "enemy came and sowed tares among the wheat" (Matt. 13:25). It was

[1] See Stanley High, *The Church in Politics* (New York: Harper & Bros., 1930), p. 105.

fowler in all his ways, *and* hatred in the house of his God.	yet a fowler's snare is on all his ways, and hatred in the house of his God.

This describes the prophetic function (cf. Ezek. 3:17; Isa. 56:10), in contrast to the popular judgment which has just been passed upon him, and in contrast to the treatment which is meted out to him (described in the rest of the verse). As men later were to try to catch Jesus in his words in order to discredit him, so they attempted to trap the prophet and prosecuted their hostility against him even into the house of God. Weiser (*Das Buch der zwölf kleinen Propheten, ad loc.*) remarks: "This constant threat of danger

the very darkness of the days through which Israel passed that aroused the watchman of God.

The prophet is in a sense peculiar to Israel. Rome had her administrators, and Roman law is a part of the heritage of our Western civilization. Greece had her philosophers, and their influence on our thinking has been somewhat more than considerable. But Israel had her prophets. They have bequeathed us more than all the others. For in a certain sense the prophet combines the practical interest of the administrator with the speculative interest of the philosopher. Like the philosopher, the prophet is a man of insight, even though his insight may be voiced without the labored or reasoned arguments of the philosopher. Yet unlike the philosopher, his insights do not end in abstract speculation, but are always ethically relevant. Given him from above, by him brought to earth, they sometimes take the form of denunciation. When Jesus pronounced his woes upon Chorazin, Bethsaida, and Capernaum (Matt. 11:21-24), he was in line with the prophetic emphasis (Amos 1–2). Sometimes the word of the prophet was one of warning. With his clearer vision he saw the inevitable results of evil tendencies before they were apprehended by the darkened minds of his contemporaries (Ezek. 33:4-5). Again the prophet's word was sometimes voiced in skepticism. This is the significance of the brief but most important book of Habakkuk, whose author may be regarded as the skeptic among the prophets. He was the first prophet to question not the ways of man but the ways of God (Hab. 1:2-3). His skepticism ends in one of the most magnificent statements of faith in all literature [2] (Hab. 3:17-18; see Expos. on vs. 8b below).

8b. Men's Hostility to God's Messenger.— "Men are hostile to him!" (Moffatt.) So hostile as to evoke the lament of Jesus: "O Jerusalem, . . . that killest the prophets, and stonest them which are sent unto thee" (Matt. 23:37). And no wonder men are hostile. God's watchman is seldom popular. He aims not to please people but to serve them; not to give them what they want but what they need.

[2] See Calkins, *Modern Message of Minor Prophets*, pp. 88-89.

Men are hostile to him because he views life objectively, *sub specie aeternitatis*. He looks at truth without the rose-colored glasses of prejudice or the bias of some subjective interest. The primary concern of God's watchman is always the truth, and truth is seldom popular. "Ye shall know the truth, and the truth shall make you free" (John 8:32). But sometimes the truth makes us angry. Once when the kings of Judah and Israel, Jehoshaphat and Ahab, conspired to make war against Syria, they inquired of the prophets whether the expedition would be successful. The "prophets" they consulted were "yes" men and prophesied that all would go well. But there was one prophet, Micaiah by name, whose opinion Ahab, the king of Israel, particularly wanted. "I hate him," said Ahab, "for he doth not prophesy good concerning me, but evil" (I Kings 22:8). A messenger therefore was sent to Micaiah and said to him: "Behold now, the words of the prophets declare good unto the king; . . . let thy word . . . be like the word of one of them, and speak that which is good. And Micaiah said, As the LORD liveth, what the LORD saith unto me, that will I speak." (I Kings 22:13-14.) His aim was not to please but to serve. His first loyalty was to truth as he saw it.

Yet men want truth. "He calleth to me out of Seir [Edom], Watchman, what of the night?" (Isa. 21:11.) But why did one call out of Edom? As a part of ancient Arabia, no doubt Edom had necromancers and wizards aplenty. Yet when the men of Edom sought the truth about the future they did not consult the secular mind of their countrymen; they went to the prophet of God, who would tell the truth without fear or favor.

The secular mind does not see life from a true perspective. It has too many blind spots: "The god of this world hath blinded the minds of them which believe not" (II Cor. 4:4). The secular mind is fundamentally selfish. It has too many axes to grind. It identifies truth with expediency, and the real with what at the moment seems most convenient, profitable, or favorable. If we want to know the truth about ourselves or our world we must somehow transcend ourselves and our world, and that is what

9 They have deeply corrupted *themselves,* as in the days of Gibeah: *therefore* he will remember their iniquity, he will visit their sins.	9 They have deeply corrupted themselves
	    as in the days of Gib′e·ah:
	he will remember their iniquity,
	    he will punish their sins.

and of the hostility of men belongs to the prophet's calling; it is no wonder that a Jeremiah in the hour of his call trembled before the load which God was preparing to lay upon his young shoulders."

9. This opposition to the prophet which the people are manifesting is the same in spirit and character as that which they manifested of old at **Gibeah.** It is a faithless, wayward spirit. The place name Gibeah may refer to the sin of the Benjaminites there (Judg. 19), or to the institution of the monarchy under Saul (cf. I Sam. 10:26); both represent acts of sinfulness against the Lord (cf. 10:9). The final sentence of vs. 9 seems quite tame in this context and may properly belong to 8:13, where it is also found.

---

man of and by himself is unable to do. But the prophet, God's watchman, does that in a peculiar way. One is not saying that the prophet is always right, but the true prophet is always honest. He is a man of courage. He speaks the truth, and for that reason

> **A fowler's snare is on all his ways,**
> **and hatred in the house of his God.**

It frequently happens, however, that he who arouses the hostility of one generation evokes the adulation of another. One generation kills the prophet and the next will, as Jesus saw, garnish his tomb. The martyrs of one age become the heroes of another; the stake at which they were burned becomes holy ground, the cross to which they were nailed a symbol of highest reverence. Why is this? Why does history so often reverse verdicts?

For one thing, the true prophet is always ahead of his time. His vision is unclouded by the subjectivisms of fear, pride, and prejudice which darken our minds. He therefore sees further into reality than his contemporaries. With our naked eyes we can see but a relatively small number of stars. Men once thought that the heavens they saw were all there was to see. So men think the "truth" they see is all the truth there is. The prophet, like the modern astronomer, has fuller and clearer vision. He penetrates more deeply into reality. He does not create the truth; he discovers it and proclaims it. But because they cannot see, men do not believe him—they do not have his vision. The truth of many of Jesus' teachings is not yet seen; he is still centuries ahead of us. The prophet is not visionary; our sight is bad. We are looking at the heavens with our eyes, the prophet is aided by a telescope. "Having eyes, see ye not?" (Mark 8:18.) If later generations therefore revere the men whom earlier generations have killed, it is because later generations see the truth more clearly than the prophet's

contemporaries did. Is this what we mean by the perspective of history?

Not only so, but the hostility of one age becomes adulation in another because later generations have a detachment not possible in the tenseness and heat of conflict. Our opposition to truth is not nearly so intense when we explore the battlefields of old conflicts as when we are ourselves engaged in some current struggle. The hostility to prophetic truth springs from the fact that prophetic truth is never confined to the field of abstraction. It is never speculation in the realm of ideas; it is not metaphysical. It is, as we say, down-to-earth truth, life-centered truth. It bears down on our racial pride, our economic practices, our social customs, our national policies. It reaches us where we live. Actually, then, our opposition to truth is not so much opposition to truth as such, but to truth as it disturbs us, upsets, threatens the *status quo.* "He stirreth up the people" (Luke 23:5). The Sadducees were not greatly concerned about Jesus' religious ideas. Their hostility was aroused when the truth reached the temple treasury. Herein lies perhaps the greatest difference between the priestly and the prophetic approach to truth. What difference does it make to life whether one is sprinkled or immersed, is ordained by a bishop, a presbytery, or a congregation? The prophet is concerned with the "weightier matters" (Matt. 23:23), so weighty that they bear down on us and try to force us out of one position into another. This makes us angry.

As we explore the battlefields on which Jesus fought we acclaim the truth he defended: his attitude to the Samaritans; his opposition to the selfish use of money—Dives and the rich fool; his emphasis on world brotherhood—the kingdom of God, not the kingdom of Israel. But how are these same truths and others like them faring on the fields of current conflicts? How are we treating the modern Samaritans? What

10 I found Israel like grapes in the wilderness; I saw your fathers as the first ripe

10 Like grapes in the wilderness,
  I found Israel.
Like the first fruit on the fig tree,
  in its first season,
  I saw your fathers.

---

c) THE HARLOT SPIRIT AND ITS SOURCE IN BAAL-PEOR (9:10-17)

10. The two parts of this verse are contrasted. The Lord had found Israel at the beginning **like grapes** in the wilderness, as a welcome and unique pleasure, as something which gave him a peculiar delight. The same idea is expressed when the Israelites of that time are likened to **the first fruit on the fig tree.** Such was the pure and joyful fellowship between the Lord and his people in the wilderness days (cf. Jer. 2:2-3), but very soon Israel fell under the influence of the nature cult at Baal-peor, before ever they crossed the Jordan to enter into their inheritance. At Baal-peor the harlot spirit appeared in Israel and it continued to manifest itself up to Hosea's own day (for what happened at Baal-peor cf. Num. 23:28 ff.; 25:18; 31:16). Later scribes substituted *bôsheth* (**shame**) for **Baal,** in condemnation of Baal and all that such a name stood for (cf. the use of the names Ishbosheth and Mephibosheth for Ishbaal and Mephibaal, II Sam. 2:8; 9:6; *et al.*).

---

do we think of economic imperialism, of one hundred per cent national sovereignty? We acclaim truth when detached from it. We garnish the tombs of the prophets. Can we defend truth when we are personally involved? And even condemned by it?

10a. Unfulfilled Promises, Unrealized Hopes. —The text suggests the pleasure and promise that Israel first brought Yahweh. The **wilderness** is a barren place where nothing fruitful grows. Occasionally, however, the traveler may unexpectedly come upon a vine with **grapes** on it. In a wilderness of paganism, Israel was like that. Or **like the first fruit on the fig tree.** The fig tree's harvest is usually late. The first ripe figs were a great delicacy, noted for their sweetness.[3] So Israel at first brought delight to Yahweh. She was full of promise. But the delight was of short duration. The promise was not fulfilled. Life holds no greater or more satisfying surprise than that which obtains when results exceed our reasonable expectations: when the underdog walks off the field with a decisive victory; when the handicapped through his unconquerable spirit, pluck, determination, and most of all, the grace of God, gets the better of his "thorn in the flesh"; when in some political or social struggle the odds that seemed stacked against the triumph of truth and righteousness are somehow overcome and the right wins. These are among life's most thrilling surprises. On the contrary, there are no disappointments more doleful and distressing than those which result when justified expectations or hopes are never realized, when the promise of some great harvest is blighted like blossoms by an early frost.

[3] S. L. Brown, *Hosea*, p. 82.

For of all sad words of tongue or pen,
The saddest are these: "It might have been!"[4]

Why is it that so many lives, like Israel's, give promise of such great performance but never come through? Why do so many good beginnings fall short of fulfillment; why so many men of whom it can be said: "As he rose like a rocket, he fell like the stick"?[5] Sometimes Israel's promise is unfulfilled because she does not bring to her native endowment the necessary effort. It is not how many talents one has but the intelligent effort and disciplined industry with which one develops them and the wisdom with which one employs them that count. A student who is naturally brilliant and with commensurate effort could lead his class, yet slides through with only a passing grade, has failed even though he passes. "Unto whomsoever much is given, of him shall be much required" (Luke 12:48). Sometimes, too, when Israel knows she is good, the knowledge goes to her head and she ends up by not being good for much. Some young preachers of great promise have failed because of well-meaning but unhealthful adulation and praise which led them to think they had arrived when they had barely started. A good start is a great advantage if one realizes that the race is not won in the first lap. We take off our hats to the man who comes from behind and wins—the last lap counts. A promising start sometimes makes us forget that the goal is still ahead, incentive dies and effort is relaxed. "The race is not to the swift, nor the battle to the strong" (Eccl. 9:11). The man who has been given little but makes the most

[4] Whittier, "Maud Muller," st. liii.
[5] Thomas Paine, "Letter Addressed to the Addressers on the Late Proclamation." Referring to Edmund Burke-

in the fig tree at her first time: *but* they went to Baal-peor, and separated themselves unto *that* shame; and *their* abominations were according as they loved.

11 *As for* Ephraim, their glory shall fly away like a bird, from the birth, and from the womb, and from the conception.

But they came to Ba'al-pe'or,
and consecrated themselves to Ba'al,[l]
and became detestable like the thing they loved.

11 E'phraim's glory shall fly away like a bird —
no birth, no pregnancy, no conception!

[l] Heb *shame*

The final part of the verse may be taken in either of two ways: **and became detestable like the thing they loved,** i.e., the corrupt worship in which they engaged eventually corrupted their whole lives; or we may recognize that the word **Ephraim** at the beginning of vs. 11 belongs rhythmically to this verse and by a very minor emendation arrive at the translation, "and Ephraim became as lovers of idols." The important point is that the apostasy at Baal-peor is not described as a temporary lapse, but as the expression of a definite attitude and a definite commitment; they **consecrated themselves to Baal.**

11. The result will be Israel's ruin, the departure of their glory. They had committed themselves in service to a fertility cult; the penalty is the fitting one that they will be

of what God has given him will not disappoint his Creator. The man who has been given much but buries his talents has played false with life.

But Hosea gives us a reason other than those mentioned for Israel's failure, viz., that she turned her energies in the wrong direction, i.e., toward Baal (vs. 10*b*). To use what we have for unhallowed ends, to give our loyalty and devotion to unworthy objects, to "spend money for that which is not bread, and . . . labor for that which satisfieth not" (Isa. 55:2) is even worse than tying up the talent in a napkin and burying it. Not to use the talent at all is better than to use it for an evil purpose. The educated crook who lies awake nights planning some devilish deed which he intends to spring on his fellows, the ruler or dictator who in his immaturity is beguiled by delusions of grandeur and world conquest—what could not such talented people do if their gifts of leadership were channeled in the right direction, attached to socially constructive ends!

10*b*. *You Are What You Love.*—The people forsook Yahweh for Baal. The loyalty that belonged to the Eternal they gave the pagan deity. And they **became detestable like the thing they loved.** Nothing so determines character as that to which man gives his loyalty, especially his religious loyalty; for when taken seriously no loyalty is so determinative, none goes quite so deep. We sometimes say that the issue lies between religion and secularism, i.e., between religion and irreligion. It may be more true to say that the issue lies between the right religion and the wrong religion. Secularism itself is a "religion." One might venture the assertion that "no religion," if such a condition were possible, would be preferable to "bad religion." The fact that some of man's greatest

sins have been committed in the name of religion is proof of this statement. When man makes God in his own image, as he is often wont to do, his God is little more than an enlarged edition of himself. His God is self-love sanctified. That man's religion is vain; more than vain, positively harmful. He becomes as loathsome as the things he loves.

Whatever affects the emotional life of man affects man most deeply. Men are molded most effectively by what enters not their heads but their hearts. What men know affects them, but what men love transforms or disfigures them. The driving power of human life has always been and will always be the emotions. Herein lies the fallacy of the statement that civilization is a race between education and catastrophe. Secular education concerns itself almost exclusively with the mind. It imparts information. It may well leave untouched the feelings, emotions, will—the driving power. It is as though one were taught the chemical composition of a gasoline and oil, and even how engines are constructed, and then were put behind the wheel of a high-powered car on a busy thoroughfare without ever having had a single lesson in how to steer or stop. To leave the emotions untrained is to fail to educate in the area where education is most necessary. They "became as loathsome as the thing they loved" (Moffatt). They could have become as beautiful, noble, fine, and wholesome as the object of their devotion. Israel's early promise was unfulfilled because she gave her heart to what was corrupt.

11-12. *The Lord Will Give Glory.*—The bird's flight is unpredictable, sudden, swift. So the glory of man is of and by itself an unstable quantity. On the tomb of Emperor Frederick

12 Though they bring up their children, yet will I bereave them, *that there shall* not *be* a man *left:* yea, woe also to them when I depart from them!
 13 Ephraim, as I saw Tyrus, *is* planted
	12 Even if they bring up children,
	    I will bereave them till none is left.
	 Woe to them
	    when I depart from them!
	 13 E′phraim's sons, as I have seen, are destined for a prey;[m]

[m] Cn Compare Gk: Heb uncertain

childless. The greatest possible calamity is in store for them—their extinction as a people (cf. Amos 1:6, 9). Every Israelite feared that he might die childless and that his name might be cut off in Israel, so that he would cease to have any part in the living community; hence the regulations for Levirate marriage. But now the prospect is that Israel herself will be cut off.

16. There is much to be said for the view that vs. 16 should be read immediately after vs. 11, not only because it unites so fitly the two figures of fruit-bearing tree and fruitful people, which are used in vss. 10-11, but because it breaks the connection between vs. 15 and vs. 17. If vs. 16 is taken here, the translation must be:

> Ephraim is stricken,
>   their root is dried up,
>   they shall bear no fruit.

From being a pleasant and fruitful vine they will become a dry and withered tree, fit for nothing and producing nothing. If perchance any children should be born, they will perish (vs. 16b); if any should be brought up, they will die (vs. 12b); if any contrive to survive, they will be killed by the sword (vs. 13); and any who remain then will become wanderers among the nations (vs. 17). In this formally tautologous fashion the prophet declares that what confronts Israel is complete extinction.

12. One point only warrants remark. According as we read the verbal form in the last phrase with a *sîn* or *shîn*, we get the meaning **when I depart from them** or "when I look away from them" respectively. The general sense in both cases is the same; the Lord will depart from his people.

13. The KJV makes an attempt to translate the Hebrew of the first part as it stands, but the translation cannot be sustained for several reasons: the word for **planted** in

the Great in Sans Souci, Potsdam, are inscribed the words *Sic transit gloria mundi,* which an American tourist rendered, "Here today, gone tomorrow."

Those who strive for the glory of this world and seek to win the acclaim of men pay much to obtain little. Man's true glory lies not in man. It is a reflected glory. It springs from his desire to glorify God (I Cor. 1:31). "The paths of glory lead but to the grave."[6] Such is the glory that is earthborn. It is of the earth earthy, and like the body returns to the dust whence it came. The only lasting glory for man is that which he does not seek for himself. It comes as a result of seeking first the kingdom of God and his righteousness. It is the glory of a character disciplined by denial; a spirit inspired by noble ideals; a life lived in brotherly love and illumined by hope and faith. This glory does not end with the grave—it passes through death to

[6] Thomas Gray, "Elegy Written in a Country Churchyard."

life eternal. **Ephraim's glory shall fly away like a bird.** But "the LORD will give grace and glory" (Ps. 84:11). And that glory is as eternal as the Eternal himself.

The glory Israel would lose, however, would be of an even more serious nature. Israel through her sin would deprive herself of the creative forces of life (vss. 11a, 12). "The corruption that is through lust" is widespread and deep. Moral degeneracy poisons the waters of life at their source. Hosea was the first moralist "who traced the effects of national licentiousness in a diminishing population, or who exposed the delusion of libertine men that they themselves may resort to vice, yet keep their womankind chaste. Hosea appears to have been the first to do this."[7]

13. *The Tragedy and Futility of War.*—For Ephraim we could read the United States, Great Britain, or any other nation. The burden of the nation's sins often falls upon its youth—

[7] George Adam Smith, *The Twelve Prophets,* I, 308.

in a pleasant place: but Ephraim shall bring forth his children to the murderer.

14 Give them, O LORD: what wilt thou give? give them a miscarrying womb and dry breasts.

E'phraim must lead forth his sons to
   slaughter.
14 Give them, O LORD —
   what wilt thou give?
  Give them a miscarrying womb
   and dry breasts.

---

the original is feminine in gender and there is no feminine noun to which it can be related; the word rendered **pleasant place** means simply "pasture" or "habitation" and the reference to Tyre in this context has no significance. The LXX gives us some help; instead of "for Tyre" (לצור) it read εἰς θήραν, i.e., **for a prey** (לציד), and for the final words it has παρέστησαν τὰ τέκνα αὐτῶν (שתו בניה). There are therefore two possibilities: (a) following the LXX as above, and disregarding its omission of the clause **as I saw,** we get the rendering of the RSV; or (b) following the LXX as above, but making a small emendation in the M.T., we may get the rendering:

> Ephraim I see as a guilty man [כאשם],
> his children are given for a prey.

14. Give them, O LORD: These words sound like the beginning of an interrupted prayer. Did the prophet intend to pray for mercy for his people, or was he but calling upon God to give them their deserts? As a prophet obedient to the word of God, he must call for judgment upon his people. But they are his people, his own kith and kin; therefore he cannot without an acute sense of pain call for such judgment (cf. Jer. 13:17; *et al.*). The obedience of the prophet prevails: **Give them a miscarrying womb and dry breasts,** i.e., deny them that for which they wooed Baal.

---

the most guiltless. War is the supreme example. Wars are instigated or stumbled into by the shortsightedness, blunders, stupidities, and willful sins of "the old men," or at any rate, adults; but they are fought by youth. It is the sons who are led forth to slaughter. And always the choicest of these. They go first. Mars is an exacting god. He demands the choicest of the flock, "without blemish and without spot" (I Pet. 1:19). Those who are led to slaughter are never the physically or mentally marred. The standards of physical fitness laid down by the insatiable god of war are so exacting that only the best can qualify. Mars demands, too, minds that are alert and quick. Through rigid tests the slightest trace of the imbecile or moron is detected. The sons who are led to the slaughter are the fittest in the land.

And the reasons that lead them there are often invalid. Most wars could have been avoided by forthrightness, honesty, or some sane and realistic understanding of their incredible cost and disillusioning futility. Winston Churchill in *The Gathering Storm* says that the most tragic part of World War II was that it could have been avoided.

If the sacrifice of our sons achieved the ends envisioned, their slaughter, though an incalculable loss, would seem less tragic. But the ends are seldom if ever reached. Herein lies one of the most distressing and disillusioning aspects

of war: we sacrifice so much, we receive so little. Through "victory" we achieve our immediate goal, but seem to miss our ultimate one. In World War I, the immediate aim was the defeat of Kaiser Wilhelm and his marching armies so as to "make the world safe for democracy." We achieved that immediate aim. We did defeat the kaiser and so stopped the hosts of aggression. But we lost our ultimate aim. We did not make the world safe for democracy. Rather we created the climate for dictatorship. The direct result of dethroning the kaiser was the enthroning of Hitler, and our last state was worse than our first. The world as a result of World War I was made less safe for democracy than it had ever been before.

The same observation might be made about World War II. Hitler was a tyrant bent on world domination. The freedom of the world was most certainly at stake. We had to stop Hitler, our immediate aim, and defend freedom, our ultimate aim. President Roosevelt was specific about this. He delineated four freedoms: freedom of speech, freedom of worship, freedom from want, freedom from fear. These were our long-range objectives. At a cost to the world in material and spiritual values too great ever to be tabulated, we achieved our immediate goal. We stopped Hitler. We chased his *Luftwaffe* from the skies and converted his cities into rubble heaps incomparably greater

15 All their wickedness *is* in Gilgal: for there I hated them: for the wickedness of their doings I will drive them out of mine house, I will love them no more: all their princes *are* revolters.	15 Every evil of theirs is in Gilgal; there I began to hate them. Because of the wickedness of their deeds I will drive them out of my house. I will love them no more; all their princes are rebels.

15. Vs. 10 traced the origin of Israel's apostasy to Baal-peor; here it is said that all their evil-doing goes back to **Gilgal.** The place had a double significance. It was a sanctuary where Baal worship had been practiced (cf. 4:15; 12:11), and it was the place where according to one tradition Saul had been publicly acclaimed king of Israel (I Sam.

than he ever made of England's. We buried his menacing submarines in the bottom of the sea and outwitted their sinister designs. We stopped the mighty march of his armies, turned them back upon themselves in disorder, demoralization, defeat, and death. We "won." But only our immediate objective. We lost our ultimate aim. For in the defeat of Hitler we created the climate out of which dictators grow. There were more of them loose within ten years than there were on September 1, 1939, when World War II was set off. For millions the four freedoms were less secure than when we fought to guarantee their existence. We won the war only in the sense that we achieved our immediate objective, the defeat of Hitler. But we really lost. How was it with freedom? Freedom of speech—less of that than before we fought to defend it. Freedom of worship—less of that too. It was gone entirely from the postwar Communist-dominated countries. Freedom from want—let the underfed and starving millions of men, women, and children whose hungry faces and haunting cries disturbed our dreams answer that. Freedom from fear—perhaps that was the most ironic of all. Was there any country in the world at the midcentury in which fear did not lift its ugly head? It stood like a high mountain in the path. Wherever men looked, there it was. Fear dictated the policies of the nations, and policies that grow out of fear are always negative. They never can advance life on its way. They are unhealthy and unwholesome.

Ephraim must lead forth his sons to slaughter, to a slaughter that is largely futile. In gaining its immediate objective, war creates conditions that make the ultimate realization of those objectives difficult if not impossible. For every problem it solves it creates many new ones, some of vaster complexity. The path that leads temporarily out of the woods plunges ultimately into a thicket of deeper, darker, and more bewildering proportions.

15b. Deeds, Not Creeds, the Test?—God did not say, "Because of the piety of their words I will keep them in my house." He might have said that, for unquestionably their words were

pious. It is one of the paradoxes of religion that we can and do combine pious words with impure deeds, a sacred phraseology with a secularized way of life. It is always, however, by our deeds, not by our words, that God judges us. "What doth the LORD require of thee, but to do justly, and to love mercy, and to walk humbly with thy God?" (Mic. 6:8.)

In the life and teachings of Jesus this emphasis on deeds becomes very clear. "Why call ye me, Lord, Lord, and do not the things which I say?" (Luke 6:46.) "By their fruits ye shall know them" (Matt. 7:20). His test of discipleship was deeds, not words. It was the discrepancy between the religious phraseology of the Pharisees, who "for a pretense make long prayer" (Matt. 23:14), and their unethical conduct that made him accuse them of hypocrisy. He told the story of two men: one who said he would not work in the vineyard but did; the other who said he would but did not. "Whether of them twain did the will of his father?" he asked. The question answered itself. "They say unto him, The first." (Matt. 21:31.) Because though the first was wrong in his words, he was right in his deeds, while with the second the situation was reversed. **Because of the wickedness of their deeds . . . .**

In placing the emphasis on fruitfulness Jesus used the symbol of the vine. He found no pleasure in a barren life any more than in a barren tree. His judgment of people was not theoretical but practical. He judged men not by their profession but by their performance; not by beliefs but by behavior; not by labels but by life. This method was at variance with the practices of his contemporaries, who had everybody labeled, catalogued, and pigeonholed—"Samaritan," "centurion," "publican," "sinner"—and judged them accordingly. While of a Roman centurion who bore the wrong religious label Jesus said, "I have not found so great faith, no, not in Israel" (Matt. 8:10). Not labels, life!

Nothing short of a revolution would occur in the Christian church were we to lay more of our emphasis on deeds, not creeds, on the fruit

16 Ephraim is smitten, their root is dried up, they shall bear no fruit: yea, though they bring forth, yet will I slay *even* the beloved *fruit* of their womb.

17 My God will cast them away, because they did not hearken unto him: and they shall be wanderers among the nations.

| |
16 E'phraim is stricken,
  their root is dried up,
  they shall bear no fruit.
Even though they bring forth,
  I will slay their beloved children.
17 My God will cast them off,
  because they have not hearkened to him;
  they shall be wanderers among the nations.

11:15; cf. Hos. 7:3-4; 8:4). Hosea in this way probably intended to say that the two besetting sins of Israel—worshiping Baal and putting trust in kings and princes—had their origin in very early times. In punishment Israel is to be driven out of Palestine and cut off from Yahweh's love; it is again the figure of a faithless wife being driven out of her husband's home. The final phrase has an assonance in the original, **All their princes** [*sārîm*] **are rebels** [*sōrerîm*]. Various efforts have been made to get a comparable effect in English, e.g., "All their rulers are unruly" (Box) ; "All their nobles are rebels" (George Adam Smith) ; "All their princes are prancers" (Horton) , but none is satisfactory.

16. See Exeg. on p. 664.

17. My God may be a significant phrase; the faithless people could no longer claim him as their God. They are to be finally and irrevocably cast off because of their disobedience and their failure to respond to their God. The curse of Cain will be upon them; they will be without help and without succor, and every man's hand will be against them.

---

of the life, not on the words of the lips. How long would the so-called Fundamentalist-Modernist controversy have lasted? What would have happened to our denominational barriers? Might God say to some within the church, as through Hosea he said to the Israelites, **I will drive them out of my house,** and to others on the outside say, "Come, ye blessed of my Father" (Matt. 25:34) ?

16. No Roots, No Fruits.—Hosea compares Ephraim to a tree. Because Ephraim was "withered at the root" (Moffatt) , she was blighted, her leaves unhealthy, her trunk undernourished, her branches fruitless. Trees for the most part die not from the branches down but from the roots up. When the roots are **dried up,** the tree is blighted. In the parable of the barren fig tree the vinedresser said: "Let it alone this year also, till I shall dig about it, . . . and if it bear fruit, well: and if not, then after that thou shalt cut it down" (Luke 13:8-9). The casual observer is concerned about the fruits; but the vinedresser knows, no roots, no fruits.

What is true of trees is equally true of individuals or nations. Here, too, neglect of the roots is disastrous. Elton Trueblood forcefully develops this thesis. He finds that the great values of our culture, its choicest fruits, are historically rooted in the Christian faith. Man's significance does not lie in himself but rather in his relationship to God.

The impotence of contemporary moralism arises from the fact that "we are trying to maintain a political valuation of man which had roots in a religious understanding of him, when that religious understanding has been forgotten." [8]

Our civilization is therefore a "cut-flower civilization." But

beautiful as cut flowers may be, and much as we may use our ingenuity to keep them looking fresh for a while, they will eventually die, and they die because they are severed from their sustaining roots. We are trying to maintain the dignity of the individual apart from the deep faith that every man is made in God's image and is therefore precious in God's eyes. Certainly we cannot maintain this." [1]

To use another figure, such a generation may be regarded as men of the afterglow. The sinking sun leaves its splendor on the horizon, but as the sun sinks out of sight, the glow fades from the sky. Even so a culture may shine in the reflected glory of those whose faith was rooted in God. How long will the glow continue if contact with Reality is lost?

17. Without God, a Troubled Wanderer.—Goethe said that without God man is a

[8] *The Predicament of Modern Man* (New York: Harper & Bros., 1944), p. 58, with quotation from William Paton, *The Church and the New Order* (London: Student Christian Movement Press, 1941), p. 152.

[1] Trueblood, *op. cit.,* pp. 59-60.

10 Israel *is* an empty vine, he bringeth forth fruit unto himself: according to the multitude of his fruit he hath increased

10 Israel is a luxuriant vine that yields its fruit. The more his fruit increased the more altars he built;

4. THE FATE OF ISRAEL'S KING, THE CALF OF BETHEL (10:1-8)

10:1. The fact that the verb whose participle is translated here as **luxuriant** means "to empty" and the grammatical inaccuracy that it is masculine in form, although it is related to the feminine noun for "vine," have induced Sellin, *et al.*, to render the phrase as "Israel has emptied [i.e., has harvested] her vine." That might mean that Israel had enjoyed bountiful vintage seasons, but why should the vine alone be mentioned? What of the corn? On the other hand, the figure used in 9:10, 16 favors the translation

troubled wanderer upon a darkened earth. One cannot say that faith in God removes all doubt from the face of life and solves its mystery. But one can say that without God man's life is ultimately an enigma without an answer, a locked door without a key, an isolated episode in a vast drama that has no plot, no purpose, no ultimate meaning. Without faith in God man begins at no beginning, works to no end. He is a wanderer—a troubled wanderer.

When man is cast off, separated from God, this does not mean that he may not intelligently pursue his immediate ends, but he cannot find lasting satisfaction or meaning in the immediate unrelated to the ultimate. Suppose one is standing on top of a very high building, looking down at the streets below. He sees individuals and automobiles hurrying along. Each man has a definite goal. But whither is the traffic as a whole tending? If the group is going nowhere, then despite the fact that the individual may have some immediately intelligent objective, ultimately he goes nowhere. It has been said that three quarters of life is intelligible and one quarter unintelligible, and that the wise man will develop the habit of not looking around the corner. But that is just the kind of advice that the wise man is unable to take. "He hath set eternity in their heart" (Eccl. 3:11 ASV). Man is finite but he is unable to accept his finitude—the image of God is upon him.

> Man hath all that Nature hath, but *more*,
> And in that more lie all his hopes of good.[2]

Man may make money the end of life. But he knows the meaning of life is not there. For even as he pulls down his barns and builds greater the summons comes, as come it does and will, "This night thy soul shall be required of thee" (Luke 12:20).

Man may act as though pleasure were the end of life; as though he were little more than an animal. "Let us eat, drink, and be merry," he may say. But the very gratification of his

[2] Matthew Arnold, "To an Independent Preacher."

passions, if kept on the animal level, leaves a nasty taste in his mouth. The pleasures turn to ashes in his hands. Disillusionment and disgust are the end of that path. The lot of a wanderer in some far country awaits those who in selfishly seeking the immediate pleasures betray some eternal truth.

Man may make the quest of power, glory, or fame the all-consuming passion of his life. But such a quest does not suffice. For how uncertain is his life, how insecure his popularity, how fleeting its glory: "The wind passeth over it, and it is gone" (Ps. 103:16). It is only as upon his immediate interests there shines the light of that which transcends time, it is only as he sees himself in the light of God's ultimate wisdom, purpose, and love, to which he can relate himself in obedience and faith, that life becomes meaningful and in a real sense livable.

> Ah, to know not, while with friends I sit,
>   And while the purple joy is passed about,
> Whether 'tis ampler day divinelier lit,
>   Or homeless night without?

> And whether, stepping forth, my soul shall see
>   New prospects, or fall sheer, a blinded thing!
> *There* is, O grave, thy hourly victory,
>   And there, O death, thy sting.[3]

These and similar ultimate issues remain unanswered and unanswerable when man is "cast off," separated from God. He then becomes, like Israel, a wanderer **among the nations.** When he loses God, it is not God who is lost; he is.

10:1. *The Economic Factor in Religion.*— Israel was outwardly prosperous, and when a nation is prosperous the institutions of religion naturally feel the effect. The church is always affected by and reflects the economic condition of the age or nation. The more prosperity, **the more altars he built.** Great building programs, a mark of material growth and expansion, go along with the age of prosperity. It is then too

[3] J. A. Robertson, *Concerning the Soul* (London: James Clarke & Co.; New York: George H. Doran Co., 1921), p. 135. Used by permission.

the altars; according to the goodness of his land they have made goodly images.

2 Their heart is divided; now shall they be found faulty: he shall break down their altars, he shall spoil their images.

---

as his country improved
  he improved his pillars.
2 Their heart is false;
  now they must bear their guilt.
The Lord[n] will break down their altars,
  and destroy their pillars.

[n] Heb *he*

---

given in the RSV, in which the vine may be thought of as emptying its strength to bear fruit, so that the rendering **luxuriant** may be sustained; the masculine form of the word may be due to the attraction of the following word "Israel."

The richer and the more prosperous Israel became, and the more she enjoyed the bounties of nature, the more **altars** she built and the more elaborately she carved the sacred **pillars,** thus paying due service to the bountiful giver. In so far as this service was directed toward the Lord it was unacceptable service; his will was love rather than sacrifice (for the sacred pillars cf. Exeg. on 3:4). The second clause in the verse, **that yields its fruit,** is arrived at by a simple emendation. The original means "fruit it places for itself." By the change of one consonant (ישגה for ישוה) we get the sense given in the RSV. The LXX has εὐθηνῶν (Hebrew נאוה), which would give the fitting sense, "comely is its fruit."

2. Their heart is false (*ḥālaq*) and **Their heart is divided** (*ḥullaq*) are two renderings of the same C.T. with different vocalizations. Both are possible; the falseness of heart would be in forsaking the Lord for Baal, while the divided heart would signify the heart divided in loyalty between the Lord and Baal. Therefore a fit punishment will befall the people; their altars and sacred pillars will be broken down. **Now they must bear their guilt** is equivalent to saying that now they must bear the punishment of their guilt. At this point the LXX has ἀφανισθήσονται, i.e., "they shall be desolated"; that may indicate the Hebrew reading ישמו, but it may also be a variant rendering of the M.T. יאשמו (cf. G. R. Driver, in Schindler, ed., *Gaster Anniversary Volume,* p. 76).

---

that mortgages of long standing are paid. By the same token, in periods of depression the church is compelled to retrench. It may even be fair to say that, economically speaking, the church is the last institution to feel the wave of prosperity and the first to feel the wave of adversity. Is the life of the church destined in every generation to be the tardy beneficiary of a rising market and the prompt victim of its decline? Should this be true, it would be a sad commentary on our estimate of the importance of religion.

> **The more his fruit increased
> the more altars he built.**

But is the building always wise? And are the altars always necessary? Does denominational rivalry play too large a part? Must we not always distinguish beween the houses made with hands and the "building of God" that is eternal?

2. Using Christian Measurements.—One would have supposed that if Israel increased his altars, if

> **as his country improved
> he improved his pillars** (vs. 1),

then religion was really flourishing. But just here religion differs from secularized pursuits. The growth of a city is judged, in the public mind at least, by its numerical increase. If it has fifty thousand more inhabitants this year than last, it is growing. It is in a healthy state. The strength of a commercial enterprise is measured by the volume of its business. If a concern does a million dollars more business this year than last, then it is flourishing. In the area of religion, however, we cannot apply such standards of judgment; religion is not that sort of commodity. In fact, religion is not a commodity at all. It is a spirit.

We sometimes say of a person, "He is a big man." What do we mean? Physically he may be quite unimpressive—as was Paul, if tradition may be trusted. The greatness of his soul is the measure of his true stature. We do and must apply material standards to the religious life. Yet it must be said again and again that because the roots of the Christian religion are by their very nature anchored in the realm of the imponderables and intangibles, material standards, though necessary, are more often than not inadequate. The ultimate measure in the Christian religion is qualitative not quantitative;

| 3 For now they shall say, We have no king, because we feared not the Lord; what then should a king do to us? | 3 For now they will say:
"We have no king,
for we fear not the Lord,
and a king, what could he do for us?" |

3-4. These verses have caused much discussion. It has been maintained that they break the connection between vs. 2 and vs. 5 because they seem to assume that the threatened judgment has fallen. Rather ought it to be said that they describe the state of perplexity and resourcelessness which prevailed just before the judgment took place, the judgment which is referred to as captivity in vss. 5-6. The translation of vs. 3 should be in these terms:

> For now they will say:
> "We have no king,
> for we fear not the Lord,
> and a[n earthly] king, what could he do for us?"

The people had lost faith in the Lord, so that he was no longer their king; they had forsaken him for Baal. On the other hand, they had no confidence in any earthly king or ruler. They had had for years experience of unstable political conditions. There had been a dismal succession of rulers who played at foreign alliances abroad and at power politics at home and who did not rule in virtue of any charismatic gift which they possessed (cf. 8:4; 7:7). What could such a ruler do but **utter mere words**, make empty

---

the question is not how many but what sort. Despite the fact therefore that the altars were increased and the pillars improved,

> the Lord will break down their altars,
> and destroy their pillars.

Why? Because **their heart is false (divided).** "Search me, O God, and know my heart," cried the psalmist (Ps. 139:23). Purity of motive, loyalty to truth; in a word, Christlikeness of spirit—that is the measure of a church's life. Numerical strength and large budgets are significant when they express the Christlike spirit. They are never an adequate substitute for it.

3. The People's Responsibility for Government.—The truth of these profound words is writ large in Israel's history. But why Israel's history? *All* history down to the present time. Indeed, contemporary history has spelled out this truth in larger letters than Hosea's age could shape; for modern man through his amazing scientific techniques, used for destructive purposes, has made sin more tragic and tragedy vastly more poignant.

A king, what could he do for us?—or a president? It does not make much difference what we call our leader.

> Ah, if men have no reverence for the Eternal,
> what is the good of a king? (Moffatt.)

The king of Israel's day had more power than his modern counterpart. We say today that the king reigns but does not rule. In olden times, however, he ruled. Nothing opposed his will.

His people had no protection or defense against his evil designs. They were at his mercy. A bad king therefore could bring suffering and hardship on his subjects. That is why the Magna Carta, wrested from the hands of King John, is regarded as a great forward step in man's struggle for life and liberty. It gave the people protection, it curbed the power of the crown. In Hosea's day the political fortunes of the people were quite largely out of their hands. Yet even so, Hosea felt that in the people, not in the ruler, lay the key to the situation.

A president would be even less significant, for a democracy is "government of the people, by the people, for the people." In a democracy the people rule. They cannot wholly blame their leaders for the waste, inefficiency, and corruption which so often plague them. They put men in office and turn men out. They decide whether this or that policy will be followed. They get in the long run no better government than they deserve.

Democracy is no magic word. Even at its worst it is better than dictatorship at its best; for democracy safeguards human freedom. Yet abusing the privileges and neglecting the responsibilities of liberty can make democracy as bad a form of government as one would care to have. It was Voltaire who remarked that he would rather be eaten by a lion than devoured by a thousand rats.

How can reverence for the Eternal affect the condition of the people and so their political fortunes? In at least two ways: For one thing,

4 They have spoken words, swearing falsely in making a covenant: thus judgment springeth up as hemlock in the furrows of the field.

4 They utter mere words;
　with empty oaths they make covenants;
　so judgment springs up like poisonous weeds
　　in the furrows of the field.

---

protestations, and enter into alliances and compacts? That would be his technique, and of that technique they had had more than their fill. Its only result was that judgment, which in a well-ordered state is wholesome and free from taint, had become like a **poisonous** weed, pervasive and deadly. Thus vs. 4a is made to refer to the king; the verbs in the original are not defined as to person or number.

---

reverence for the Eternal carries with it some sense of responsibility. "Unto whomsover much is given, of him shall be much required" (Luke 12:48), and surely the privilege of freedom is a "much." Yet how many seem to forget this. About half of the qualified voters in the United States go to the polls. This lethargy seems to affect primarily the better citizens. How many first-rate men have been defeated because decent folk would not take the trouble to "get out and vote." Good people, who politically speaking are good for nothing, constitute one of the great liabilities of a democracy. It was while the good man slept that the enemy came and sowed tares among the wheat. The forces of greed, graft, corruption—which never sleep—can always count on the indifference and inertia of decent people. So do the best, unwittingly perchance, become allies of the worst.

Reverence for the Eternal, moreover, brings with it not only some adequate sense of responsibility, but in addition some deep loyalty to the moral values which are the foundation of government. A child cannot take care of himself; he is immature. People who are morally and spiritually immature, who lack integrity and honesty, are not really fit to take care of themselves politically, not fit to govern themselves. Freedom, without some sense of the values which derive from reverence for God, becomes an opportunity for the worst sort of demagoguery, chicanery, corruption, graft, greed.

What good is a king or a president if the people have no sense of responsibility; if honor, honesty, integrity, decency, are lacking? It is not how many people a city has that makes the city great, but what sort of people. Ten righteous men would have saved Sodom. The foundations of society are moral and spiritual and cannot be established or safeguarded simply by those in authority. The foundations can be made secure only as the people safeguard them.

4. Words Without Truth.—If proof were needed of the timelessness of truth, these words would furnish it. The Bible has been referred to as "old stuff." Its message, so some maintain, is hardly for so modern and up-to-date an age as ours. Ministers who neglect it in their pulpit work, and unfortunately there are such, say they find it too far removed from the needs and problems that harass modern man to be relevant or helpful. Such chatter does not harm the Bible, which like an anvil has worn out many hammers. But it does certainly reveal the lack of perspective, of historic sense—shall we say the shallowness and brittle superficiality?—to which men sometimes succumb.

This text speaks of **mere words, empty oaths,** which proceed from the seat of governments, and yield nothing. So does one meet in the Bible, from beginning to end, both the timelessness and timeliness of truth. Truth is neither new nor old. Truth is eternal. Without it all political arrangements, all treaties, are a sham and an emptiness. They are binding so long as their commitments do not run counter to some selfish aim, some imperialistic design, some ulterior consideration of the nations concerned. When they do, "diplomacy" is always available to get us out of them, unless we have the forthrightness to say, as did Kaiser Wilhelm II, that a treaty is a "scrap of paper"—**mere words.** Without reverence for the Eternal, which results in an appreciation of and loyalty to the eternal principles of truth, righteousness, and justice, no contract—personal, social, international—endures. Like a structure that lacks cement or steel reinforcement, it crumbles under pressure. Like the house built on sand, it falls under strain.

History teaches this with monotonous repetition. The League of Nations, though not perfect, was, on paper, capable of shifting the gears from war to peace. But the League proved to be a "scrap of paper." The Kellogg Pact? **Mere words.** The Atlantic Charter? **Mere words.** The United Nations Charter? It is our best hope for peace. It could shift the gears from war to law. Said his brother to Lord Robert Cecil, "Will your League work?" Lord Robert replied, "Hugh, does a spade work?" The United Nations Charter, like the League of Nations or the Kellogg Pact, is a spade. **It**

5 The inhabitants of Samaria shall fear because of the calves of Beth-aven: for the people thereof shall mourn over it, and the priests thereof *that* rejoiced on it, for the glory thereof, because it is departed from it.

5 The inhabitants of Samar'ia tremble
    for the calf[o] of Beth-a'ven.
Its people shall mourn for it,
    and its idolatrous priests shall wail[p]
        over it,
    over its glory which has departed from
        it.

[o] Gk Syr: Heb *calves*
[p] Cn: Heb *exult*

5. The LXX and Syriac give support for the emendations which have been adopted in the first part of this verse to get the rendering given in the RSV (עגל for the plural עגלות; שכן emended to שכני). The verse reveals the significant fact that, when the people had lost faith in the Lord and in their rulers, their whole interest centered in the **calf of Beth-aven**; in the most amazing way they put their trust for their welfare in it. But even that trust was now shaken; they trembled for their idol now; danger was threatening and they had no confidence that they would be delivered. The second part of vs. 5 is, lit.:

> Its people shall mourn over it,
>   its idol-priests for it;
> they shall exult over its glory,
>   because it has gone from it into exile.

In the second line a verb probably has been lost (e.g., יחילו) and the verb **exult** in the next half line is obviously an error, even though it is supported by the versions. Most scholars are agreed that we should read a verb like **wail** (ויליל), and translate thus:

> Its people shall mourn for it,
>   its idol-priests shall be distressed over it;
> they shall wail for its glory,
>   because it has gone from it into exile.

cannot work of itself. Spades without builders are useless. And builders without reverence for truth, loyalty to principle, honesty and integrity of motive, are not builders but bunglers. What such builders erect is not plumb, not "on the square," but lopsided, off center, crooked, ugly, and weak—the structure tumbles. Man's trouble does not come from lack of intelligence but from lack of integrity. Without moral and spiritual integrity, no relationship, no arrangement, no agreement is adequate or enduring. Paul speaks of "a house not made with hands, eternal in the heavens" (II Cor. 5:1). Our political house, made with hands and nothing more, will be neither secure nor enduring. For our hands are not clean. Our voice is the voice of Jacob speaking sweet and pleasant words—**mere words**—but our hands are the hands of Esau. They are hands that spoil and plunder and kill, they are red with blood. "He that hath clean hands, and a pure heart" (Ps. 24:4)—only a pure heart can make our hands clean, a heart in which there is reverence for the Eternal. The psalmist prayed, "Establish thou the work of our hands upon us" (Ps. 90:17). The work of our hands is established when they are guided by a purpose that transcends us, something "eternal in the heavens."

So judgment springs up like poisonous weeds. Our generation knows the truth of those words. Our fields have been full of poisonous weeds. This particular weed is referred to as "a root that beareth gall and wormwood" (Deut. 29:18). Amos refers to it when he says, "Ye have turned judgment into gall, and the fruit of righteousness into hemlock" (6:12). We have tasted of the cup. Multitudes have had to gulp it down.

5-6. The Impotence of Idols.—Hardly could one find a more graphic description of the characteristic marks of a false religion than that given in these two verses. No wonder Hosea is regarded as one of the truly great religious geniuses of all time. Only a soul pure and passionate could see truth so clearly and voice it so vividly as does this man. In these two verses he describes the nature of the false gods to which Israel had turned, and how these gods affected the nature and character of the people who worshiped them.

> The citizens of Samaria bemoan
> the Calf of Beth-Aven (Moffatt).

6 It shall be also carried unto Assyria *for* a present to king Jareb: Ephraim shall receive shame, and Israel shall be ashamed of his own counsel.

7 *As for* Samaria, her king is cut off as the foam upon the water.

6 Yea, the thing itself shall be carried to Assyria,
   as tribute to the great king.*q*
E'phraim shall be put to shame,
   and Israel shall be ashamed of his idol.*r*

7 Samar'ia's king shall perish,
   like a chip on the face of the waters.

q Cn: Heb *a king that will contend*
r Cn: Heb *counsel*

6. The **idol** in which Ephraim trusted will be carried to Assyria as a spoil of war. Thus Ephraim will be put to shame. The repetition of the fact of Ephraim's shame in the second part of the verse may very well be for emphasis. It is interesting, however, to note that the LXX has ἐν δόματι, and so presumably read במנה for בשנה. If we read מנתו, we get as the first part of vs. 6*b*: "Ephraim will meet his fate." The next part is, lit., **Israel shall be ashamed of his counsel**, i.e., will be ashamed of the evil counsel he has followed. The rendering of the RSV, which is preferable in terms of vs. 7, depends upon the change of one consonant (עצבו for עצתו). For **the great king** cf. the Exeg. on 5:13.

7. If the view can be sustained that it is to a **chip** or "splinter of wood" rather than to **foam** that the dethroned king is likened, that is an additional reason for taking the term **king** to refer to the idol which has just been mentioned (cf. vs. 3). In that idol of Bethel the people had put their trust; now they realize that it is a trivial, worthless thing, having no more stability or value than a splinter of wood tossed about upon the surface of the waves. The words **Samaria, her king** stand asyndetically in the original; a very simple change gives the smooth reading of the RSV (מלך שמרון).

They grieve for their god. He is the source of their sorrow. And "the worshippers groan" (Moffatt). That to the prophet was a caricature of true religion. God should be the source of joy—"the joy of the LORD is your strength" (Neh. 8:10). "Rejoice in the Lord always: and again I say, Rejoice" (Phil. 4:4). Sometimes the sad, languid faces of those who profess Christianity must make onlookers wonder whether the gospel they profess is good news or bad. One would think that they were worshiping some impotent man-made **calf of Beth-aven** instead of the living God who "is able to do exceeding abundantly above all that we ask or think" (Eph. 3:20). What a picture—the priestlings (little priests) trembling before a god whose glory has departed!

But that is not all, **The thing itself shall be carried to Assyria, . . . Israel shall be ashamed of his idol.** No wonder, for the idol is so weak and helpless it has to be carried, and to Assyria as tribute. Poor little god! In an unforgettable passage Isaiah paints a similar and even more vivid picture of the impotence and inconsequence of idols. He pokes fun at the pagans who, when they flee from the enemy through the streets of Babylon, have to carry their idols. "They are a burden to the weary beast" (Isa. 46:1). So many "baggage bales for beasts' backs": such are your gods, O Israel. In contrast Isaiah

turns exultantly to Yahweh, who speaks of Israel as those who "are borne" and "are carried." "And even to your old age I am he: . . . I have made, and I will bear; even I will carry, and will deliver you" (Isa. 46:3-4). How often our life belies our faith! Sometimes we seem so depressed and burdened that one might almost think we were returning from God's funeral! And one wonders again whether our God is **the calf of Beth-aven,** a helpless man-made god whittled out of wood, or the eternal God who is our refuge and strength, to whom belong power and might. "Cast thy burden upon the LORD, and he shall sustain thee" (Ps. 55:22). Thee, not it!

7. *How Are the Mighty Fallen.*—The puppet kings share the same fate as the puppet gods. Even as the puppet gods vanish, so do the puppet kings—**chip on the . . . waters** (yet see Exeg.). What a striking picture! It suggests the extreme in insecurity and instability, a little chip bobbing up and down, subject to the impact of the slightest ripple, the gentlest wind. Should the storm break, it will be tossed mercilessly to and fro until it is finally engulfed and lost in the water's vast and deep recesses. History is full of such puppet rulers. In the heyday of their power they seemed like giant, ocean-going vessels plowing their way sturdily through the stormiest seas, no wind or wave

8 The high places also of Aven, the sin of Israel, shall be destroyed: the thorn and the thistle shall come up on their altars; and they shall say to the mountains, Cover us; and to the hills, Fall on us.

9 O Israel, thou hast sinned from the days of Gibeah: there they stood: the battle in Gibeah against the children of iniquity did not overtake them.

8 The high places of Aven, the sin of Israel,
shall be destroyed.
Thorn and thistle shall grow up
on their altars;
and they shall say to the mountains,
Cover us,
and to the hills, Fall upon us.

9 From the days of Gib′e-ah, you have
sinned, O Israel;
there they have continued.
Shall not war overtake them in Gib′-
e-ah?

---

8. It is notable that Bethel is named, not Beth-aven (cf. vs. 5), but simply **Aven** ("wickedness"), as if all wickedness were concentrated there. Ephraim's places of worship will fall into disuse; they will be utterly discredited. And the Israelites themselves will suffer from such a bitter sense of disillusionment and frustration that they will be utterly ashamed and will feel like calling upon the mountains and the hills to cover them.

5. How Ephraim Kicked Over the Traces (10:9-15)

9. Hosea asserts time after time his conviction that Ephraim's sinfulness goes far back in her history. Sometimes he traces it to Baal-peor (9:10), sometimes to Gilgal (9:15); here to **Gibeah** (cf. 9:9). The reference may be to the beginning of the monarchy

---

strong enough or big enough to stop them. One recalls Kaiser Wilhelm, Hitler, Mussolini, Tojo. It seemed as though the race were to the swift and the battle to the strong as these men pushed relentlessly toward their goals. But what has become of them?

> Samaria's king shall perish,
> like a chip on the face of the waters.

There is something inherently insecure about those who, in defiance of conscience and the laws of God, plunge headlong on their way. "How are the mighty fallen!" (II Sam. 1:19.) What was launched as a giant ocean liner ends its journey as **a chip on the face of the waters:** the mighty kaiser chopping wood at Doorn, der Führer ending his own life in the chancellery, Mussolini shaking before a firing squad in the village of Dongo, the mighty Tojo standing on the gallows at Sugam Prison, Tokyo. "The wind passeth over it, and it is gone" (Ps. 103:16). One recounts the facts not to suggest that these men alone were guilty. Perchance equally guilty were the shortsighted, immoral, unbrotherly, and just plain stupid policies which helped so largely to produce them, and in which all were involved.

8. The Wages of Sin Is Death.—This is a bleak picture. Hosea was a sensitive soul. The very quality in him that produced the tender and beautiful passages found in his work could

go in reverse, so to speak, and paint gloom in its darkest hue. Those who are most sensitive to beauty react most violently to ugliness. It is the saints who know that they are sinners; the sinners as a rule do not. The picture Hosea gives us here is therefore one of complete spiritual desolation. Pusey[4] makes the suggestive comment that in only one other instance are the words **thorn** and **thistle** combined (Gen. 3:18), where the ground is cursed because of Adam's sin. Here they occur where the land is made desolate because of **the sin of Israel.**

The desolation, however, will be confined not only to the sanctuaries; it will involve worshipers also, who will call **to the mountains . . . and to the hills** around the sanctuaries to **fall** on them and **cover** them. Some things are to be feared more than death—"I would rather die than do that," we sometimes say. Is it a mark of cowardice or a tribute to the innate decency of the human spirit that there are times when man would rather be completely blotted out and buried in oblivion than face the disgrace occasioned by his sin? In calling on the hills and mountains to fall on them, the Israelites were voicing a cry of despair which became proverbial in N.T. times (Luke 23:30; Rev. 6:16; 9:6).

9-15. Whatsoever a Man Soweth.—A fine summary of these verses by S. L. Brown might

4 *Minor Prophets,* I, 102.

10 *It is* in my desire that I should chastise them; and the people shall be gathered against them, when they shall bind themselves in their two furrows.

11 And Ephraim *is as* a heifer *that is* taught, *and* loveth to tread out *the corn;*

---

10 I will come[s] against the wayward people
  to chastise them;
and nations shall be gathered against them
  when they are chastised[t] for their double iniquity.

11 E'phraim was a trained heifer
  that loved to thresh,
  and I spared her fair neck;

[s] Cn Compare Gk: Heb *in my desire*
[t] Gk: Heb *bound*

---

under Saul of Gibeah (I Sam. 9:16), although his election is said to have taken place at Mizpah or at Gilgal (I Sam. 10:17 ff.; 11:15); alternatively, and more likely, the reference may be to the crime of the Benjaminites and to the dire punishment which in due course overtook them (Judg. 19). **There they have continued** must mean that Israel since Gibeah has continued in the same moral condition. There is fitness in the declaration that the people who so egregiously sinned at Gibeah will suffer the disciplinary punishment of war at that place; and since Gibeah was in the extreme south of Ephraim, an enemy invading from the north and reaching this locality, must have traversed the whole country.

10. The RSV is doubtless correct, for syntactical and rhythmic reasons, in attaching the final words of vs. 9 to vs. 10. The word which stands in the original at the beginning of vs. 10 may be translated as "when I will" or "in my anger." Such a translation would demand the deletion of the connective immediately following. On the other hand, with some support from the LXX, we may read the verbal form (באתי, **I will come**) in place of באותי, and thus arrive at the translation given by the RSV. The final part of the verse is heavy; we may adopt the rendering given in the RSV in which באסרם, **when they shall bind** or **are bound,** is emended to ביסרם, **when they are chastised,** or is regarded as being a variant of it; otherwise read ליסרם, i.e., "in order to chastise them for their double iniquity."

Various attempts have been made to give meaning to the words **their double iniquity** (עונתם *Qerê*). The two golden calves of Bethel and Dan cannot be intended, if for no other reason than that Hosea refers to the one at Bethel only. In view of the fact that the name of Gibeah reminded the people of Saul and the monarchy as much as of the crime of the ancient Benjaminites, the reference probably applies to the two sins of spiritual unfaithfulness and political plotting and planning, of which Hosea so often speaks; vs. 3 would support such an interpretation.

11. Ephraim is described as a docile **heifer** which had willingly submitted to training and had taken pleasure in the easy and congenial task of treading out the grain

---

well precede the exposition of the individual texts.

Israel has been sinning since the days of Gibeah, and Jahveh is about to gather the nations against him. He has been like a heifer engaged in the pleasant and easy task of treading out the corn, but now he must undergo the discipline of the yoke. Ruin might have been averted by right conduct, kindness and repentance, but since Israel has ploughed wickedness, he shall reap injustice, and the tumult of war shall bring destruction on land, fortunes, and king.[5]

[5] *Hosea,* p. 91.

11. The Hard Yoke of Sin.—What Hosea is saying is that sin greatly increases the burden of life. Israel, when obedient to God and anxious to do his will, was like a heifer on the threshing floor. The work was not burdensome; moreover, it carried with it certain compensations. Animals thus employed were allowed to eat as much as they liked, "Thou shalt not muzzle the ox when he treadeth out the corn" (Deut. 25:4). But because of her apostasy her burden will now be increased.

This insight that sin makes life more difficult, increases its burden, hardships, and sorrow, con-

but I passed over upon her fair neck: I will make Ephraim to ride; Judah shall plow, *and* Jacob shall break his clods.	but I will put E'phraim to the yoke, Judah must plow, Jacob must harrow for himself.

(cf. Deut. 25:4). **And I spared her fair neck** is a legitimate rendering of the original text (for this meaning of the verb עבר, cf. Amos 7:8; 8:2); but the emphatic beginning of that phrase (ואני) and the absence of any adversative at the beginning of the next make it much more likely that the adversative effect begins here. For that reason the translation should be "But I put the yoke upon her fair neck" (העברתי על על'), i.e., Ephraim had to submit to heavy labor and wearying toil, plowing and harrowing. It is in accordance with Hebrew usage (cf. Ps. 8:6-7) that the next words should be made subsidiary to the ones just quoted, thus:

> But I put the yoke
> upon her fair neck,
> yoking Ephraim to plow
> and making Jacob harrow for himself.

The name **Judah**, which appears in the M.T., should be deleted as metrically superfluous.

fronts us in the first and earliest story of the Bible, the story of creation. The factual details of that story we may question, but how impressive are its truths! The facts are but the temporary media for the conveying of its timeless insights. One of those insights is that sin makes life immeasurably harder than God intended it to be. Before his "fall" man lived a happy life in surroundings that were beautiful, but sin changed all that. As a result, runs the tale, came sorrow, the pain of childbirth; came unproductive soil, thorns, and thistles; came the exhaustion of hard labor; came even death itself. The author no doubt oversimplifies the problem. But the truth he seeks to express cannot well be overemphasized, viz., that through sin man aggravates and complicates his mortal life, makes his lot harder, like the **heifer** that once fared well on the threshing floor but now must bend her **neck** to the **yoke**.

This fact sheds light on the problem of evil. Much of human suffering seems unreasonable and inexplicable—"the mystery of iniquity" (II Thess. 2:7). But about a considerable portion of suffering there is no mystery at all: it is the result of sin. There is no mystery about the man who once enjoyed the privileges of sonship and now experiences the humiliating hardships of a swineherd in the far country. There is no mystery about Israel, the trained heifer, laboring now under a heavy, galling yoke. In each instance the changed status results from a wrong choice. To say that God should not have made a universe in which wrong choices are possible is to say that he should not have made a universe in which the achievement of character is possible. Instead of making men,

he should have made automatons. Our actions would then be as predetermined, predictable, and controlled as the puppets at a Punch-and-Judy show. But we should not be men.

Israel was free to disobey God. So are we. But Israel was not able to escape the inevitable and far-reaching results of such disobedience. Neither are we. Those results are invariably tragic. The bitter yoke under which man now suffers is self-imposed, and is contrary to the will of God, who intends that life should be rich and meaningful. Jesus said: "Take my yoke upon you, and learn of me. . . . For my yoke is easy, and my burden is light" (Matt. 11:29-30). The yoke of sin always seems more pleasant, but only *seems*—"At the last it biteth like a serpent, and stingeth like an adder" (Prov. 23:32).

This is not to suggest that the way of obedience and discipleship is effortless or easy. The Christian religion has been criticized as being an escape from reality, as though it lured men into some fool's paradise, as though it developed weaklings fed on false hopes, incapable of facing life's contingencies with courage and strength. Literally nothing could be further from the truth. The symbol of our faith is a cross. Surely the "saints, apostles, prophets, martyrs," if they were expecting an easy time, must have been quite disillusioned. The difference between Israel the **trained heifer,** obedient to the divine direction, and Israel that now must bend to **the yoke** and **harrow for himself,** is that in the first instance the effort was not wasted effort. Sin is waste. It exacts much and gives nothing in return. It makes us **plow in** fields so stony that they produce nothing good.

12 Sow to yourselves in righteousness, reap in mercy; break up your fallow ground: for *it is* time to seek the LORD, till he come and rain righteousness upon you.

12 Sow for yourselves righteousness,
reap the fruit[u] of steadfast love;
break up your fallow ground,
for it is the time to seek the LORD,
that he may come and rain salvation
upon you.

[u] Gk: Heb *according to*

---

12. This verse is not to be interpreted as an appeal by Hosea to his contemporaries to turn from evil, but as the instructions which were given to (the heifer) Ephraim in the early days. The first part is readily intelligible, and the text is improved by adopting, with the support of the LXX, the reading **the fruit of steadfast love** (פרי for פי). The demand is not only for all the work of righteousness and love, but for the dedication of the whole field of Ephraim's life to the Lord's service (for the figure of breaking up the **fallow** or hitherto uncultivated ground cf. Jer. 4:3). **Break up your fallow ground: for it is time to seek the LORD** is a much more suitable sense than that presupposed by the LXX translation: "Light for yourselves a lamp of knowledge, that you may seek the LORD" (ניר ועת for נר דעת), although some support for the LXX may be found in vs. 13. In any case the clause **for it is time to seek the LORD** is parenthetical, the following one being in direct relation to the imperatives that precede, thus: **Sow, . . . reap, . . . break up, . . . till he come and rain righteousness upon you.** Thus Ephraim is

---

It leads to blind streets that get us nowhere. Christ's **yoke** is easy in that linked to him we find the way. The way may be narrow and steep, but it is the right way. Moreover, Christ's **yoke** not only demands strength but gives it. The **yoke** of sin depletes us, and that is all. Sin takes and takes, but never gives. Christ's **yoke** inspires and empowers. To be in tune with the Infinite is to receive not only a worth-while task, but strength for the doing of it. "I can do all things through Christ which strengtheneth me" (Phil. 4:13). The kind of plowing and harrowing that Jacob did **for himself,** and so by himself, was not only barren, unproductive of life's choicest values, but exhausting. Has Jacob been at it again? What has modern man to show for all his "blood, toil, tears, and sweat"? Would he have escaped economic and moral exhaustion and confusion had he been more willing to follow the divine direction, to be linked wth the divine power?

12. There Is Time to Seek the Lord.—Coming as it does between vs. 11 and vs. 13, this verse is like a ray of sunlight through a cloudy sky. Vs. 11 describes the heavy yoke that her sin imposes on Israel, and vs. 13 enlarges and elaborates the grim results of continued disobedience. But here is a word of hope and comfort, a final appeal to turn before it is too late, a warm and winsome invitation to seek God while he may yet be found, and to do his work while it is yet day (yet see Exeg.).

Quite apart from the particular insights of this text, just the fact that like a lighthouse it

points the course men may yet take, would they reach harbor and home, is of immeasurable importance. The words indicate the boundless love, mercy, and patience of God, who always offers another chance—and yet another. Israel has sinned. God's repeated calls have gone unheeded. She is moving onward to destruction, like a boat drifting down some Niagara, headed for the rapids; then the plunge which nothing can avert. But there is yet time to turn the boat around and breast the stream: **It is the time to seek the LORD.** And so God comes again with his plea to repentance:

> **Sow for yourselves righteousness,**
> **reap the fruit of steadfast love.**

How black would be man's lot but for the merciful providence of God! "And the word of the LORD came unto Jonah the second time" (Jonah 3:1). It had gone unheeded the first time, and Jonah had missed what might well be considered the greatest privilege that had ever come to a man of his race, the privilege of being the first missionary to take the knowledge of Yahweh to a people who had never heard of him. But "the word of the LORD came unto Jonah the second time." Herein lies the wonder of the grace of God. He gives us another chance, and another, and yet another. His mercy "is from everlasting to everlasting" (Ps. 103:17). It "endureth for ever" (Ps. 106:1).

Yet though it endures forever, it can be so spurned that in reality its healing and redeeming ministry is nullified—and worse! For re-

13 Ye have plowed wickedness, ye have reaped iniquity; ye have eaten the fruit of lies: because thou didst trust in thy way, in the multitude of thy mighty men.

13 You have plowed iniquity,
you have reaped injustice,
you have eaten the fruit of lies.
Because you have trusted in your chariots[v]
and in the multitude of your warriors,

[v] Gk: Heb *way*

commanded to continue with her work until the Lord sends his rain and gives the increase (cf. I Cor. 3:6). The verb translated "sends his rain" could have the meaning "teach," and this would support the LXX text in vs. 12a. But as we have interpreted the verses, the agricultural metaphor is maintained throughout, and that seems preferable.

13. The instructions given to Ephraim were not obeyed. The Hebrew expresses that fact as a positive statement, **You have plowed iniquity,** etc., while the LXX uses a rhetorical question, "Why did you . . . ?" In the second half of the verse the original Hebrew has "because you [singular] have trusted in your own way and in the multitude of your warriors," thus making the first portion refer to Israel's willful unfaithfulness in the sight of the Lord. On the other hand, the LXX text (ἐν τοῖς ἅρμασίν σου) supports the translation **in your chariots** (RSV); this provides an excellent parallel to **the multitude of your warriors** in the succeeding half line and makes the whole of vs. 13b a fitting prelude to vs. 14.

demption is a two-way street: God's approach, man's response, **that he may come and rain salvation upon you.** But that rain can be comparable to the water on a duck's back. It can roll off and become a devastating flood. "O Jerusalem, . . . how often would I, . . . and ye would not!" (Matt. 23:37.) When men will not, God seems powerless to change the situation.

Forgiveness is an extended hand. It may be clasped. Ignored, it becomes the wrath of God. Forgiveness is a knock at the door. The knock may be heeded—the latch is within, the door will not be forced—or ignored. Whereupon it turns into the knock of judgment.

Forgiveness is therefore costly business both to the forgiver and the forgiven. "Father, forgive them" (Luke 23:34). Did he? We do not know. Our uncertainty lies not in God's attitude but in man's response. God cannot forgive the unrepentant. Forgiveness means that the forgiven acknowledges the wrong done and sincerely desires to right it. Without repentance forgiveness has no meaning at all. **Break up your fallow ground, . . . that he may come and rain salvation upon you.** To break up the old habits, to leave the old road so long traveled, to turn around and go in an opposite direction —that is not easy. But without such change of mind God cannot forgive. Not because he may not want to, but because forgiveness without repentance would be morally and spiritually impossible. A man cannot be in the far country and in the father's house at the same time. Only as he turns his back on the far country and sets his face on the homeward road can he

receive or appreciate God's forgiving love. There is still time to do this, Israel—**time to seek the Lord.** Will you? Or else!

13. *Plow Wickedness, Reap Iniquity.*— Strange that Israel should have done this! Yet how often we do the same. Granted the sun and the rain, two conditions go to the making of a good harvest: good soil and good seed. In the physical world we observe these matters with great care. We do not put good seed in poor or unprepared soil, nor poor seed in good soil —not if we can help it. We know that good seed and good soil make a good harvest.

Oddly enough, in the moral and spiritual realm we show the most amazing disregard of this simple principle. We give little thought either to soil or seed. Instead of righteousness we sow wickedness and have "reaped disaster; you had to eat the harvest of your lies" (Moffatt). It is a bitter, barren harvest. We know its taste. Yet in seeming indifference to the inevitable results of our sowing we keep on, hoping vainly that poor seed and poor soil will combine to bring us the good we want, and are unwilling to help produce.

"The falseness of an opinion is not for us any objection to it. The question is, how far an opinion is life-furthering, life-preserving, species-preserving, perhaps species-rearing."[6] How can one as well educated and as able as Nietzsche be such a moral and spiritual ignoramus? What a combination of intellectual

[6] Nietzsche, quoted by William Ernest Hocking, *Types of Philosophy* (New York: Charles Scribner's Sons, 1929), p. 145.

14 Therefore shall a tumult arise among thy people, and all thy fortresses shall be spoiled, as Shalman spoiled Beth-arbel in the day of battle: the mother was dashed in pieces upon *her* children.

14 therefore the tumult of war shall arise
   among your people,
   and all your fortresses shall be de-
      stroyed,
as Shalman destroyed Beth-ar′bel on the
      day of battle;
   mothers were dashed in pieces with
      their children.

---

14. The general sense as given in the KJV and RSV is to be sustained. It is based upon certain minor adjustments of the Hebrew text (קם for קאם; יושדו for יושר). But the final phrase should probably be taken as referring to the day of war's tumult, and therefore translated as "mothers will be dashed in pieces." Less likely, the reference may be taken to be to the day of **Beth-arbel**; in that case the translation should be: [when] **mothers were dashed.** The **Shalman** mentioned is probably neither Shalmaneser IV of Assyria, whose invasion west of Jordan was not important, nor Shalmaneser V, who died before the actual fall of Samaria in 721 B.C., but a certain Salamanu of Moab, who invaded Gilead during the eighth century; Hosea is referring to an event which would be

---

astuteness and moral immaturity if not imbecility! What better proof of the inadequacy of secular education to get us out of our trouble? How could Nietzsche believe that a false idea could ever be life-furthering or life-preserving? How can a corrupt tree bring forth good fruit? "Do men gather grapes of thorns, or figs of thistles?" (Matt. 7:16.) One might as well put disease germs in the blood stream and expect them to be "life-furthering" and "life-preserving" as to sow wickedness and injustice and expect social health and well-being to result.

14-15. *If You Want Peace, Prepare for War (?).*—These two verses give a specific instance of the general principle in vs. 13. If you cannot sow wickedness and reap anything but disaster, no more can you trust in chariots and warriors, sow and promote the war spirit, and reap anything but war with all its ghastly train: **The tumult of war shall arise among your people, . . . your fortresses shall be destroyed, . . . mothers . . . dashed in pieces with their children.**

"If you want peace, prepare for war." That is the familiar slogan. It is a dangerous half-truth. If preparing for war, trusting in chariots and warriors, were the way to have peace, then we should inhabit a peaceful world. For this has been and still is our prevailing philosophy. But it has never brought peace—and never will—not in a moral universe. It is both psychologically and morally impossible to get peace by preparing for war.

It is psychologically impossible. By what sort of intellectual tour de force can a man bend all his energies in one direction and then suddenly find himself at a destination quite the opposite from that envisaged by his interests

and efforts? This is precisely the dilemma of those who talk peace the while they prepare for war. Their words are of peace but their actions are for war. "The voice is Jacob's voice, but the hands are the hands of Esau" (Gen. 27:22). The reason they get war, not peace, is that their actions bring results which words divorced from actions cannot bring. Actions indicate sincerity. Moreover, as in the case of war, they show where our real trust lies: not in good will, friendship, justice, or righteousness, but in **chariots** and **warriors,** jet planes and atomic bombs. "Prepare ye the way of the LORD" (Isa. 40:3). It is psychologically impossible to prepare the way of evil and expect the Lord to come marching on it. If men prepare the way for evil, they get evil; they get what they get ready for. To prepare for war is to keep war in the forefront of their minds and hearts. Their actions and attitudes are geared toward it. How can peace come in an atmosphere so saturated with the war psychology and the war spirit?

But to get peace by preparing for war is not only psychologically impossible, it is also morally impossible. It is another way of saying that the way to get a good harvest—peace—is by sowing the seeds that produce a bad harvest—war. How in a moral universe can humanity spend millions, billions, on preparation for war and expect that policy to bring peace? Bismarck said, "The stronger we are the more improbable is war." Germany under the kaiser was strong. War resulted. Germany under Hitler was strong. War resulted. Japan under Hirohito and Tojo was strong. War resulted. Can it be just a coincidence that the nations which in the twentieth century from a military point of view were the strongest were also the ones

15 So shall Bethel do unto you because of your great wickedness: in a morning shall the king of Israel utterly be cut off.

11 When Israel *was* a child, then I loved him, and called my son out of Egypt.

---

15 Thus it shall be done to you, O house of Israel,[w]
    because of your great wickedness.
In the storm[x] the king of Israel
    shall be utterly cut off.

11 When Israel was a child, I loved him,
    and out of Egypt I called my son.

[w] Gk: Heb *O Bethel*
[x] Cn: Heb *dawn*

---

fresh in the popular memory (cf. Eberhard Schrader, *Die Keilinschriften und das Alte Testament,* ed. H. Zimmern & H. Winckler [2nd ed.; Berlin: Reuther & Reichard, 1902], p. 441). If that view can be upheld, then Arbela is not the city on the Euphrates, or that west of the Jordan in Galilee (cf. I Macc. 9:2; *et al.*), but the city of that name east of the Jordan near Pella. The suggestion that, on the basis of the LXX text (ἐκ τοῦ οἴκου Ἰεροβααλ), we should adopt the translation "as Shallum destroyed the house of Jeroboam" is not to be accepted. If that had been the original, it is incredible that the present obscure text could ever have arisen; rather the LXX translation should be regarded as an attempted reading of a text which by that time had ceased to be intelligible.

15. There is no doubt that the LXX is correct in reading **house of Israel** for **Bethel.** The meaning of the king's death at **dawn** (so M.T.) is very difficult to explain. It can scarcely indicate sudden death merely; Hebrew had other and less ambiguous ways of saying that. It might signify "at the dawn or beginning of his reign," before he had had time to prove himself (but cf. Intro., p. 556). Many scholars propose that we should read **in the storm** [בשער for בשחר] **the king of Israel shall be utterly cut off** (so RSV).

C. The Love of God (11:1-11)
1. Training of the Child Israel (11:1-4)

11:1. It was during the wilderness period that Israel became God's people; at that time he began to set his love upon them (cf. 9:10). This is not the steadfast love of

---

that started aggressive wars and went down in defeat?

At the close of the World War, Major General F. B. Maurice of the British General Staff declared: "When I entered the British army I believed that the way to have peace was to be prepared for war. I now believe that if you prepare for war, you get war." . . . Sir John Simon . . . writes: "The proposition that the peace of the world is to be secured by preparing for war is no longer believed by anybody. . . . A distracted mankind may feel that armaments are inevitable. But as an instrument for world peace we know that they are useless."[7]

The proposition that if you want something good you must prepare for something bad, that if you desire a good result you must set up conditions that predict a bad result, is a psychological and moral impossibility. Ah, Israel,

**Because you have trusted in your chariots
    and in the multitude of your warriors,
therefore the tumult of war shall arise among your
    people,**

[7] Harold C. Phillips, *Sails and Anchors* (Philadelphia: Judson Press, 1934), p. 94.

**and all your fortresses shall be destroyed, . . .
mothers . . . dashed in pieces with their children.**

We shall not succeed better than Israel in this matter.

Now, to be sure, one is not saying that in a world that is an armed camp a nation should not look to its defenses. If robbers are about, it is unwise to leave the doors unlocked. We must think, however, in world terms; for there is no other way in which we can think. If the great powers prepare for war, war will be the sure result. The only way to have peace is to reduce armaments—on a world scale. Just so long as we trust in our **chariots** and **warriors,** just so long will **the tumult of war . . . arise among . . . people,** and **mothers . . .** [be] **dashed in pieces with their children.** "If thou hadst known . . . the things which belong unto thy peace! but now they are hid from thine eyes" (Luke 19:42).

11:1. The Nature of God's Love.—This chapter contains some of the most tender and heartwarming passages in the book. They re-emphasize the fact that Hosea is indeed the

God of which Hosea often speaks, but what has been termed "election love" (cf. Snaith, *Distinctive Ideas of the O.T.*, pp. 131-42). Then Israel was a child, i.e., young and inexperienced, and requiring training (cf. Ezek. 20:5-6). **Out of Egypt I called my son** is one rendering of the Hebrew (cf. Matt. 2:15); another, favored by George Adam Smith, is "from Egypt I called him to be my son," called him to a great and honorable office and responsibility (*Book of Twelve Prophets*, I, 316). Note the importance of the words **I called my son.** For the prophets of ancient Israel history was not simply a series of events determined by unforeseen contingencies and eventualities, or directed by the plannings and devisings of men. It was a course of events overruled by the sovereign purpose of God; men may hinder the fulfillment of that purpose, and they may by their obstinate sinfulness delay it, but they cannot finally obstruct it (cf. Herbert Butterfield, *Christianity and History* [London: G. Bell & Sons, 1949] and *History and Human Relations* [London: Collins, 1951]; Reinhold Niebuhr, *Faith and History* [New York: Charles Scribner's Sons, 1949]; Christopher R. North, *The Old Testament Interpretation of History* [London: Epworth Press, 1946]). In a particular sense Israel was called to be an agent of the divine purpose. It is notable that whereas Hosea, in

prophet of love, a fact which neither the severity of his outbursts nor the grimness of his predictions must be allowed to obscure. Hosea, as we have seen, sometimes uses the figure of husband and wife to describe the relationship of God to his people. He also, as in this verse, employs the father and son metaphor.

The fact that God chose Israel as the object of his peculiar concern, the vehicle of his providence, the agent of his purpose and will, throws light upon the nature of divine love. From the human angle there were other nations that seemed more likely choices, more available for so singular a purpose as that of being God's chosen vessel. Egypt, with "the wonder of the world's art in his dreamy eyes," Assyria, "grasping the promise of the world's power," Phoenicia, "the promise of the world's wealth"—from the human angle any one of these three would have seemed a more hopeful or promising choice than Israel. Yet God chose Israel— "the puny and despised captive of one of them, a people without a country, without a history, and, if appearances be true, still devoid of the rudiments of civilization—a child people and a slave." No wonder George Adam Smith concludes that this must "ever remain the supreme romance of history."[8] It confirms the word of the prophet Isaiah: "For my thoughts are not your thoughts, neither are your ways my ways, saith the LORD" (Isa. 55:8).

Why did God choose so unimpressive and seemingly so inadequate a people for the fulfillment of his purpose? Perhaps for two reasons. One lies in the nature of man; the other in the nature of God. As to the first, the nature of man, the very marks which from our viewpoint would seem to have made Israel's neighbors more likely choices—art, power, wealth—may

have made them less likely for God's purposes. Human achievement in whatever field tends to induce human pride, and pride is perchance the greatest single hindrance to the realization of God's purposes in man. "The proud he knoweth afar off" (Ps. 138:6). This of course does not in any sense mean that God cannot use the prosperous, the powerful, the privileged. For he can and does. In every age, as in our own, among his followers have been and are those whom the world calls great. For the great can be humble. Indeed, whatever else the truly great may be, humble they surely are. Humility is the inevitable ingredient of all true greatness. Perhaps then it was not that Israel's neighbors were relatively great, but that their greatness had gone to their heads that made them unavailable. If "not many mighty, not many noble" (I Cor. 1:26) were called, it was not because they were mighty and noble, but because their attainments had made them so proud as to make it impossible for God to reach them. The human vessel can be so full of pride or self-righteousness, in short, of self, that there is no room for God. Perhaps that is why a puny people, a despised, enslaved people, offered God a better chance.

But if there was that in the nature of man which led God to choose Israel, there was too that in the nature of God which may in part account for his choice. God is love, but divine love is not like human love. The word for love in classical Greek, the Greek of Plato, is *erōs*. It is romantic love, human love. *Erōs* is not found in the N.T. The word there used is *agapē*. There are many differences between the two words. Perhaps the main one is that *erōs* love, the love of desire, never mind how beautiful, is ultimately selfish. When, humanly speaking, we love someone, it is because for one reason or another the object of our love reveals

[8] *The Twelve Prophets*, I, 317.

681

2 *As* they called them, so they went from them: they sacrificed unto Baalim, and burned incense to graven images.	2 The more I*y* called them, the more they went from me;*z* they kept sacrificing to the Ba'als, and burning incense to idols.

y Gk: Heb *they*
z Gk: Heb *them*

terms of his own domestic experience, speaks usually of Israel as the wife of Yahweh, here he uses the term **son** for the young people of the early days.

2. As they called them, so they went from them has no meaning owing to the uncertain reference of the personal pronouns. To say that the meaning is "As the prophets called Israel, so Israel went away from them" is not so much to translate the words as to extract a meaning from them. The LXX at once enables us to regain the original: καθὼς κατεκάλεσα αὐτούς, οὕτως ἀπῴχοντο ἐκ προσώπου μου. Thus the rendering given in the RSV is sustained (כדרי קראי להם כן הלכו מפני הם ל'). The second half of the verse makes it plain that it was in the service of **the Baals** that the Israelites went away from Yahweh.

traits that are lovable, something in the loved object appeals to us. That is why, no matter how unselfish our love may be, all human love is to a degree a form of self-love (for fuller comment see Expos. on 3:1-21). The love of God for man, however, is of a wholly different kind. God loves us not because we are lovable but because he is love. "Peradventure for a good man some would even dare to die. But God commendeth his love toward us, in that, while we were yet sinners, Christ died for us" (Rom. 5:7-8).

While therefore we might have chosen another nation as the object of our love, because that nation possessed some peculiar quality or endowment—art, power, wealth—which seemed significant or appealing to us, God's love is prompted not by the nature of the loved object but by his own nature. God is love. "The Lord did not set his love upon you, nor choose you, because ye were more in number than any people; for ye were the fewest of all people; but because the Lord loved you" (Deut. 7:7-8a). He loved you because he loved you. Is not that a strange explanation? Yes, but in it lies the true nature of God's love. He loves not from any utilitarian motive, but because he is love.

1b. The Call of God.—In **Egypt** they were slaves. God's call was to deliverance—freedom, individual and national selfhood. Egypt is not merely geographical; it is spiritual. It is not a location but a condition. Egypt may well symbolize our enslavement, not perchance to Pharaoh's will, but to our own sinful will and way: to desires born of selfishness, to evil habits that once could have been broken but now have bound us in chains too heavy to be snapped; to customs or behavior patterns that are trivial and senseless if not positively wrong and harmful. Such is Egypt—a symbol of our bondage to sin (see Expos. on 9:1-3).

2. The Nature of Christian Freedom.—If Pharaoh had called them while they were in Egypt, they would have come because they would have had to. Pharaoh now no longer controlled them, yet they were still bound. For freedom from Pharaoh's yoke did not bring freedom from sin. Jesus came "to preach deliverance to the captives, . . . to set at liberty them that are bruised" (Luke 4:18). But release from physical slavery, great as that may be, is not the door to Christian freedom. The two types of freedom were voiced by Paul. "I was freeborn," he said to the chief captain as he sought the privileges due his Roman citizenship (Acts 22:28). But he also spoke of "the liberty wherewith Christ hath made us free" (Gal. 5:1). One may be born free politically, but Christian liberty, the liberty wherewith Christ makes us free, is an achievement through discipline. God called the Israelites out of Egypt, gave them political freedom, but

> The more I called them,
> the more they went from me.

Their freedom became the occasion of a deeper enslavement. We might well consider these two kinds of bondage: bondage to Pharaoh and bondage to sin.

The liberty of which we are all conscious is deliverance from the bondage to Pharaoh. The Statue of Liberty in New York harbor personifies American social and political freedom. It symbolizes freedom from Egypt. And it is a priceless heritage. If like Paul we are born free, it is because others have paid the price "with a great sum" (Acts 22:28). A designer at work was asked, "How long have you been learning to do that?" He replied, "Six hundred years, for so long ago did the first of us begin to design, and we have been at it ever

3 I taught Ephraim also to go, taking them by their arms; but they knew not that I healed them.

3 Yet it was I who taught E'phraim to walk,
I took them up in my[a] arms;
but they did not know that I healed them.

[a] Gk Syr Vg: Heb *his*

3. In spite of this early evidence of his people's wayward spirit, the Lord did not lose patience with them or think of giving them up. As a loving father trains his child to walk, and lifts him and carries him when he grows weary and tired, so the Lord did with his people. In the translation **taking them by their arms** (KJV), which on general grounds seems excellent as a description of the action of a parent training his child to take his first hesitant steps, the preposition **by** is open to serious criticism; the Hebrew word signifies "upon." The Targ., Syriac, and to some extent the LXX support the text represented by the RSV: **I took them up in my arms.** The figure is of a father carrying his child. The authenticity of the final part of the verse has been questioned, but it fits

since." [1] So if we were asked how long we have been enjoying this freedom, we could answer: "For hundreds of years—from the time the light of freedom first glowed in the human heart, from the death of Stephen, the first Christian martyr, to the death of those liquidated by modern tyrants. Every soldier dying on the remotest battlefields in resistance to tyranny has contributed to our liberty." In this sense we are all debtors.

But freedom from Egypt's yoke, important as it is, is not Christian freedom. Interestingly enough, the men who wrote the N.T. did not enjoy political freedom. There was no statue of liberty at the entrance to the harbor at Caesarea, yet few passages of the N.T. are more stirring than those written about freedom by the man who set sail from that harbor, a prisoner: "Stand fast therefore in the liberty wherewith Christ hath made us free" (Gal. 5:1). It is obvious that political freedom without Christian freedom, inner freedom, involves us in disastrous evils. We rejoice in democracy, yet without the disciplines of Christian freedom democracy becomes dismal, corrupt, wasteful, and inefficient. We boast of freedom of the press, yet this very freedom often is used to mislead, pollute, and poison the public mind. We are free to do what we like and go where we will, but this often leads to the destruction of personality through undisciplined indulgence and incredible folly. The freedom from Egypt which is not followed by discipline and restraint becomes the source of our greatest problems and perils.

But the more Yahweh **called them, the more they went from** him. They were free to do that, and so are we; but to disobey and disregard the call of God to the self is to lose an inner freedom which cannot be inherited. A father may bequeath his material possessions to his son,

but not his character. That each must win for himself through the temptations with which he struggles, the choices he makes, the disciplines he assumes. Inner freedom cannot be achieved by proxy. The secret of winning it lies strangely enough in being made captive, in finding a master. The man who is free in a Christian sense is he who is most completely enslaved by Christ. For the secret of Christian freedom lies in self-mastery, and we achieve self-mastery as we are mastered by that which is greater than self. "Ye call me Master and Lord: and ye say well; for so I am" (John 13:13).

A man who rejoices in the freedom democracy brings and thinks he is free to do as he likes is a most dangerous enemy of liberty. Nothing destroys liberty more quickly than a thoughtless and irresponsible enjoyment of it. The force that keeps democracy today from complete deterioration is the leaven of those who have character, whose greed, avarice, and lust have been tamed, who are mastered by something greater than their undisciplined egos. Great as is our debt to those who have freed us from Egypt's bondage, greater still is our debt to him who through his Cross and Resurrection has come to set us free from the law of sin and death. This is the liberty that is freedom. "If the Son . . . shall make you free, ye shall be free indeed" (John 8:36).

3-4. The Harness of Love.—We may understand better the action of the nation if we think of the individual. The individual often recapitulates the life of the group. Every individual begins life in helplessness, which gives way to initiative. The individual learns to walk, to act for himself. Yet he is still under parental control. Though he walks, he is **led**, "with a harness of love" (Moffatt). Finally there comes the period of maturity when he moves out of the harness and is free to follow the direction in which he has been guided, the habits he has

[1] Hastings, ed., *Speaker's Bible*, Acts, II, 124.

4 I drew them with cords of a man, with bands of love: and I was to them as they that take off the yoke on their jaws, and I laid meat unto them.

4 I led them with cords of compassion,[b]
  with the bands of love,
and I became to them as one
  who eases the yoke on their jaws,
    and I bent down to them and fed them.

[b] Heb *man*

in with the figure of child training which Hosea here employs. Marti (*Das Dodeka-propheton*, p. 86), however, may well be right in suggesting that a half line has been lost. He thinks that the line may originally have been like this:

> They did not know that I carried them,
> and healed them from their sicknesses.

In spite of the many evidences of God's love for his people, they were so blind and obtuse that they did not recognize his care and failed to trace the footprints of his ways.

4. In the first part of the verse the figure of child training may be continued. The Lord is said to have drawn Ephraim to himself with the **cords of a man** (i.e., **with cords of compassion**) and **with the bands of love,** that they might be joined to him in close fellowship. On the other hand, it may be thought that the figure used is that of handling a domestic animal, e.g., a heifer (cf. 10:11). Interpreted in this way the words would

formed, or, as Israel, to abuse his freedom, make it an occasion for waywardness: "Heeding not my care for them, they broke away from me" (Moffatt).

This third period, when we are too old to be told what to do but not morally mature or wise enough to choose the right way ourselves, is the most dangerous one for the individual or the nation. It has been truly said that a man's worst difficulties begin when he is free to do as he likes. Our greatest bondage comes out of our misuse or abuse of the freedoms of maturity.

Every parent will realize the force of the "harness of love." Here in the last analysis is the only possible parental control as childhood passes into maturity. It certainly seems frail and precarious, yet it is God's method too. It bears no relationship to the master-slave, ruler-subject relationship of Jesus' day. The master held his slave or the emperor his subject not with a harness of love but with external authority; the grip of authoritarian or tyrannical power which through force, fear, intimidation, and coercion molded and directed the fortunes and destinies of men's lives.

Now hear Christ: "Come unto me" (Matt. 11:28); "Follow me" (Matt. 19:21). There were no threats added. He imposed no dire consequences as the penalty for man's disobedience. His commands were invitations, "If any man will come after me, let him . . ." (Matt. 16:24); and if men would not obey, he would not compel them. The hold of Christ on man is not that of a vise which applies external pressure, but that of a magnet by which men are

drawn and held. "And I, if I be lifted up, . . . will draw all men unto me" (John 12:32). A harness of love: that is God's method of control.

Why? If God wants men to do right, why does he not compel them? If God wants us to walk the way of righteousness, why did he not so fence us in that we could never go astray? If he wants us to obey and serve him, why did he not use something stronger than a harness of love? Why did he not spare the world and man all the stupidities, mistakes, and tragedies that are the result of man's freedom from divine coercion? Why, in short, is the mark of God's control a cross, the symbol of love, rather than a sword, the symbol of coercion? Why a harness of love rather than one of steel?

The harness of love safeguards human freedom. It offers control without coercion. By it one is not compelled but impelled. The Christian religion is based on the relationship between the human soul and God. But if the soul were coerced, if it were so bound that it could not possibly break away, then its attachment would not really be expressive of itself; it would lack the genuineness and sincerity without which religion means little or nothing. Moreover, if man were not free, he could not be held responsible for his actions, and without responsibility there could be no genuine religion. While they were slaves in Egypt the Israelites did not break away from Pharaoh because they could not. They were held in a harness of steel. Their attachment to Pharaoh revealed nothing of their true selves, they were not free to express those selves. When, however, they exchanged Egypt for Canaan, bondage

signify that Ephraim was not as a wild heifer that had to be controlled by heavy ropes, but was a docile animal that responded to gentle and considerate treatment. The next part of the verse is, lit., "and I became to them as those who take off the yoke upon their jaws." There are several points to be noted here. The awkwardness of the comparison may be mitigated by reading, in terms of the Syriac and LXX, a singular participle, i.e., "I became to them as one who takes off." It is true that the yoke was laid upon the shoulders, not upon the jaws, but a translation such as that given in the RSV may be adopted, with the meaning that in some way or other the weight of the yoke was eased upon the head of the animal and it was given freedom to eat, an example of kindly and considerate treatment. Contrast this with the treatment of the unfaithful people as that is expressed in the rendering of vs. 7b (RSV). Joseph Reider's proposed translation (cf. "Etymological Studies in Biblical Hebrew," *Vetus Testamentum,* II. 2 [April, 1952], 121) "and I was to them as foam of the sea which caresses (כמר ים עלעל) their cheeks" uses a figure which no Israelite writer would ever have used; but his correlation of the following verbal form אוכיל with the Arabic verb *wakala,* "to trust," yields the fitting translation "and gently I began to place confidence in him." But in view of the fact that this part of vs. 4 appears to be rhythmically overloaded, many scholars regard the words **on their jaws** as additional, and for **yoke** they read "child" (עולל for על) and so translate:

> And I became to them as a guardian [lit., "a rearer of a child"]
> and I inclined to them and fed them.

In this way the figure of child training is continued and a very fitting sense is gained. The final pronoun **them** is obtained by taking the negative from the beginning of the next verse where it is quite out of order and by reading it here as "for him," i.e., לו for לא.

---

for freedom, the harness of steel for that of love, they were free to break away and did. But they had ceased to be pawns and had become people. The risks are great and the consequences often too tragic for words, but without freedom the relationship between the self and God would be meaningless. Take away from a son his right to say to his father, "Give me the portion of goods that falleth to me" (Luke 15:12), and a son's devotion to his father would have little or no significance. The fact that one does right would mean nothing at all were not the possibility of doing wrong a live option. Remove this option and one's choice of the right would be no more momentous than the rolling of a stone from the top of a hill to the bottom. There is nothing momentous in that. There is no place else for the stone to go, nothing else for it to do. The fact that it rolls down tells us nothing about the stone, but everything about the force of gravity that holds it in tow. Not so with the cords of love. As we are poised, should something shake us loose, the cords of love are strong enough to hold us should we yield to their gentle pressure; but they are not strong enough to hold us against our will.

Moreover, no other attachment is so strong as the harness of love. Here indeed we confront a paradox. The cords of love may be easily broken, but when we submit to their hold upon

us, they are vastly stronger than steel. From one point of view love is frail. From another it is the strongest force on earth. This double truth the Cross symbolizes. It testifies to the precarious and perilous nature of God's control over man. It shows that man is free to reject the love of God. It shows that the sin in man's heart can lead him to reject every overture of reason, persuasion, honor, or even decency. For the Cross is man's attempt to defeat the will of God and destroy his holy purposes. It resulted from man's rejection of God's love. Love seemed powerless to prevent it. In that sense love was weak and ineffective.

Yet the love of the Cross is unquestionably the most powerful, enduring, unconquerable force in the world. When we sing

> In the cross of Christ I glory,
> Towering o'er the wrecks of time,[2]

we are expressing poetically a historic fact; as also when we sing:

> O where are kings and empires now,
> Of old that went and came?
> But, Lord, thy church is praying yet,
> A thousand years the same.[3]

When night fell on Calvary's hill, everyone was certain he was watching the end of Jesus

[2] John Bowring.
[3] A. Cleveland Coxe.

5 ¶ He shall not return into the land of Egypt, but the Assyrian shall be his king, because they refused to return.

6 And the sword shall abide on his cities, and shall consume his branches, and devour *them,* because of their own counsels.

---

5 They shall return to the land of Egypt,
    and Assyria shall be their king,
    because they have refused to return to
      me.
6 The sword shall rage against their cities,
    consume the bars of their gates,
    and devour them in their fortresses.*c*

c Cn: Heb *counsels*

---

2. ISRAEL'S INDOCILITY (11:5-7)

5. With this verse there is a sudden change of tone. The tender words of loving care are terminated and punishment is threatened. We must understand, as the connecting link between the two sections, what Hosea says elsewhere about Ephraim's failure to remain faithful to her Lord. The phrase **because they have refused to return to me** gives the reason for the punishment which is now spoken of, but that phrase is almost certainly not original in this context; it has all the marks of an explanatory gloss. Here, as elsewhere, Hosea speaks of both **Egypt** and **Assyria** as the instruments by whom the punishment of Ephraim is to be accomplished.

6. "The sword shall whirl through their cities" is a graphic way of saying that war will sweep through them with swift onset and irresistible drive. **And shall consume his branches** is at first sight a strange expression. It doubtless does not refer to the suburbs of the cities, because the cities of Ephraim in those days were very small in extent and

---

and his cause, the end of something that had scarcely begun. But Christianity embodied a force with which the untutored world did not reckon, could not reckon—the undying, deathless power of God's love. "God is love" (I John 4:8). That love was incarnate in Jesus; and that love proved stronger than death. "It was not possible that he should be holden of it" (Acts 2:24). If the symbol of Christ's kingdom had been a sword, his kingdom would not have lasted; we might not have heard of it. Kingdoms founded on coercion, fear, intimidation, and maintained by force, do not last. But the kingdom of our Lord and of his Christ, into which men come voluntarily, and to which they are bound by no external pressure or coercion save the love and loyalty of their own souls, that kingdom stands. It stands because no motive is as great as the motive of love. "The love of Christ constraineth us" (II Cor. 5:14). "The greatest of these is love" (I Cor. 13:13).

It is here that one sees the insecurity of all nations that think their security lies in steel rather than in good will. It is too bad humanity cannot learn a lesson from the animals. The most insecure animals in the world are the most ferocious, the most heavily armed. If you should find a snake coiled on your porch some day, you would kill it. If you should find a harmless dog there wagging its tail, you would feed it. The ferocious animals kill each other and are hunted by man. They awaken fear and invite attack. Not so the domesticated ones. We do not kill them, we pet them. They are

bound to us with cords of love. Therein lies their security.

One is not condemning any nation for seeking to defend itself. One is only regretting that man is still so stupid, so uncivilized. One is wishing that we could domesticate ourselves as we have domesticated our animals; that we should cease being like wild beasts, living behind iron cages, or possessing such power that we have to keep it a darkly guarded secret. We do not want anyone to know the striking power of our jet-propelled paws, or the biting power of our atomic teeth. But all this breeds the spirit of fear and distrust, intimidation and resentment. That is why the harness of steel is so much weaker than the harness of love. No nation or civilization built on force or fear has lasted, does last, or can last. Love is the only power that can endure.

5-7. The Ideal and the Actual.—Hosea suddenly changes his mood from tenderness to severity. This is "one of those swift revulsions of feeling, which we have learned to expect in Hosea. His insight again overtakes his love. The people will not respond to the goodness of their God; it is impossible to work upon minds so fickle. Discipline is what they need."[4]

All of us are familiar with the experience. As we contemplate the love and goodness of God, envision the kind of life and world that would be ours had we the wisdom and faith to follow the principles that make for justice and righteousness, we are lifted up. But it is not

[4] George Adam Smith, *The Twelve Prophets,* I, 323.

7 And my people are bent to backsliding from me: though they called them to the Most High, none at all would exalt *him*.

7 My people are bent on turning away from me;[d]
so they are appointed to the yoke,
and none shall remove it.

[d] The meaning of the Hebrew is uncertain

had nothing to be compared even remotely with the suburbs of a modern city. It remains a possibility that the term could mean wooden beams, hence the **bars** of city **gates** (so RSV). Nyberg (*Studien zum Hoseabuche,* p. 87), on the basis of the use of the word in Isa. 44:25; Jer. 50:36; 48:30, suggests the meaning "priests" (lit., "idle talkers," "praters"); that is a possible interpretation.

And devour them, because of their own counsels fits the context. Nyberg (see above) retains it so, and if the reference of the preceding part of the verse is to the people in general, not to the priests, the meaning would be that all the evil had come upon them because the people were so ill-advised as to forsake the Lord. The RSV, with modern scholarship generally, depends upon an emended text (מצודתיו for מעצותיהם).

7. Lit., "Now my people is suspended to my turning," i.e., to turning away from me. If that was intended to signify that the people were bent upon turning away from God, it was a very poor way of saying it. The versions give no help; therefore emendation must be uncertain. Most scholars read "My people have wearied themselves [נלאה ב'] with turning away from me" or "My people have wearied me [הלאני ב'] with turning away from me." The next part of the verse is even more perplexing: "Though they call to [him who is on] high, none at all will exalt him" (or "lift him up"). Not only has that no meaning, but it does violence at several points to the Hebrew. Nyberg (*ibid.,* p. 90) considers that vss. 8-9 refer to the people's service of the war god 'Al (cf. 7:16). He may affirm that the description of 'Al as the Holy One of Israel is readily intelligible in terms of the history of religion, but that is beside the point. The real question is, Would Hosea ever have used such an expression? The answer must be No. The LXX καὶ ὁ θεὸς ἐπὶ τὰ τίμια αὐτοῦ θυμωθήσεται, καὶ οὐ μὴ ὑψώσῃ αὐτόν gives the excellent sense:

And God is angry with his precious ones,
and will not exalt them (or will not rear them).

"good for us to be here" (Matt. 17:4) indefinitely. Such moments of ecstasy may provide an escape from the sad and sobering facts that beset us. Suddenly we are called back by the fearful and grim actualities of life. From some mount of transfiguration we descend to the tortured realities that lie within its shadow.

How to keep the balance between the ideal and the actual is a constant problem. There is always the temptation to live in an ivory tower and view life through rose-colored glasses. This is particularly true of churches located in exclusive neighborhoods and made up of relatively privileged people. The priest who "passed by on the other side" (Luke 10:31) may have thought himself too respectable to be involved with a man lying by the wayside "wounded" and "half dead." Or perchance the kind of religion he espoused was in many respects class-conscious, prideful, and inhuman; it would not allow him to face such a grim reality. The ugly fact might have destroyed his illusion of "sweetness and light." Hosea was not that kind. He

had moments when he was lifted up by a contemplation of God's love and mercy; but they were kept in balance by his realization of man's stubbornness and stupidity. The tide of his feeling had its ebb and flow, the ideal was kept in touch with the actual, God's goodness and man's sin. There is nothing inconsistent about it. He can speak of a God who took Israel up in his arms, "led them with cords of compassion, with the bands of love, . . . bent down to them and fed them" (vss. 3-4), and follow that with the picture of a God who shall drive the Israelites as exiles into Assyria, send **the sword,** which

shall rage against their cities,
consume the bars of their gates,
and devour them in their fortresses.

Jesus was familiar with the writings of Hosea. In his teaching too we have this double emphasis. Hardly could we have a more tender picture of the fatherhood of God than that given in the latter part of Matt. 6. Yet Jesus

8 How shall I give thee up, Ephraim? *how* shall I deliver thee, Israel? how shall I make thee as Admah? *how* shall I set thee as Zeboim? mine heart is turned within me, my repentings are kindled together.

8 How can I give you up, O E'phraim!
How can I hand you over, O Israel!
How can I make you like Admah!
How can I treat you like Zeboi'im!
My heart recoils within me,
   my compassion grows warm and tender.

That presupposes a Hebrew text which is not very different from the M.T. (ואל על־יקרן יחרה ולא ירוממהו). Not a few scholars would read in the first part, ואל־בעל יקראו והוא וגו, "But they kept calling to Baal, but he could not lift them up." The RSV is arrived at by reading the word על as ʿōl (**yoke**) rather than ʿal (M.T.); this also gives excellent sense and provides a notable contrast to what is said in vs. 4.

3. I Am God and Not Man (11:8-9)

8. This verse brings another sharp change. We must presume that the prophet thinks of the punishment as having fallen. Could that be the end? The people could do no more; they deserved their fate. But could God do nothing more? Was he resourceless to meet the situation which had arisen? Vs. 8 begins with a cry of anguish and dereliction. How can the Lord give up his children? Can he let them be destroyed utterly, like **Admah** and **Zeboiim**, cities of the plain that perished with Sodom and Gomorrah? (Cf. Deut. 29:23; Jer. 49:18.) "My heart is turned upon me" (or **within me**) means an emotional tumult, a turmoil of feelings. The holiness and righteousness of God demand that the unfaithful Ephraim must be punished; but has God's love nothing more that it

---

could picture Dives in eternal torment (Luke 16:23), tell the self-righteous of his day that they would not escape the damnation of hell (Matt. 23:33), and predict, as he looked at Jerusalem, the center of his people's religious life, that there was not a stone in its buildings that would not be thrown down (Matt. 24:2).

We see the love of God in the beauty of the world, the goodness, often unmerited, that follows all our days, the kindness and consideration of friends but for whom life would be drab and cheerless. We must learn too to see the love of God in our exiles, in the **sword** that devours us, in the **yoke** that often galls, which **none shall remove**. Such grim actualities do not represent the will of God—God wills us good; they are the inevitable concomitant of his righteous judgments. The disciplines they entail, the tragedies they produce, are the inescapable result of our disregard of the moral and ethical realities that are the foundation of his throne. A religion that sees God only in the sunshine but not in the shadows, only in blessings but not in woes, only in prosperity but not in tragedy, is not the Christian religion. The symbol of Christianity is a cross; a cross which symbolizes the meeting of the ideal and the actual, God's love with man's sin, and so becomes the gateway of man's redemption. For God suffers with us in our exiles, and through his redemptive love can bring healing and health in our tragedy. That is the message of the gospel.

8-9. *For I Am God and Not Man.*—This is indeed a great passage. Its theme is the theme of Hosea, viz., the unmerited love and mercy of God. He voices it now in words of rare beauty and rich tenderness.

Admah and **Zeboiim** are two of the five cities of the plain (Gen. 14:2; Deut. 29:23; Jer. 49:18). They are mentioned as having been overthrown. Tradition, however, must have had it that they shared the same fate as Sodom and Gomorrah.[5] God assures Israel therefore that they will not reap the harvest of complete destruction and decay which they deserve. And that for one reason: **I am God and not man**.

These words are the key to vss. 8-9. "My thoughts are not your thoughts, neither are your ways my ways, saith the LORD" (Isa. 55:8). We are in constant danger of attributing to the Almighty most of the limitations that inhere in us; creating God in our image. A student of religion once remarked, "In the beginning God created man in his image, and man has been returning the compliment ever since."[6]

The Ethiop gods have Ethiop lips,
  Bronze cheeks and woolly hair;
The Grecian gods are like the Greeks,
  As keen-eyed, cold and fair.[7]

[5] See S. L. Brown, *Hosea*, p. 102.
[6] See Alfred Turner, "The Teaching of Religion To-day," *Hibbert Journal*, XXXIII (1935), 398.
[7] Walter Bagehot, "The Ignorance of Man," *Literary Studies* (New York: Longmans, Green & Co., 1895), III, 187.

| 9 I will not execute the fierceness of mine anger, I will not return to destroy Ephraim: | 9 I will not execute my fierce anger, I will not again destroy E'phraim; |

can do? Even if God must punish, that does not imply that he has ceased to love, for his disposition to love is continuing and indestructible. And so the next phrase follows, **my compassion grows warm and tender.** That is an excellent rendering of the original (for other examples of the rare use of the verb found here cf. Gen. 43:30; I Kings 3:26).

9. Marti cannot agree that this verse should be taken as a promise of mercy for Ephraim. He maintains that holiness that does not demand punishment has no ethical content at all. God is greatly distressed; nevertheless, loving Ephraim as he does, he must punish her. Therefore Marti (*op. cit.*, pp. 89-90) translates in this way:

> Must I not execute the heat of my anger?
> Must I not turn and destroy Ephraim?
> [Yes, I must], for I am God, not man. . . .

It is true that the penalties of God's judgment upon men are inescapable; the prophet does not deny that punishment nor does he try to explain it away. God must punish for his righteousness' sake, but he cannot cease to love; and love is always redemptive and forgiving, full of patience and inexhaustible of hope. Ephraim deserves no mercy; he has broken covenant love. But God, under the compulsion of his infinite

---

It is evident, as one reads certain passages of the Bible, that men at times have justified their unethical conduct by attributing to God the vices of their own nature. Deeds of hate, revenge, war, have been sanctified by assuming that such deeds but reflect the will and nature of God. Yahweh is referred to as a God of battles: "Be thou valiant for me, and fight the Lord's battles" (I Sam. 18:17); who "teacheth my hands to war, and my fingers to fight" (Ps. 144:1). The imprecatory psalms reveal the same error: "Happy shall he be, that taketh and dasheth thy little ones against the stones" (Ps. 137:9). In all of this we forget that **I am God and not man.**

That men should forget was in a real sense inevitable. It is impossible for Christianity to avoid the accusation of anthropomorphism. A man must think of the highest in terms of the highest that he knows. Xenophanes said that if animals had the power of making pictures, they would paint their gods as animals. Harry Emerson Fosdick, commenting on this, says, "Good for the animals!" For as he argues, "An animal thinking of God in terms of the best animal he could imagine would be closer to the truth than an animal thinking that there was nothing here except dynamic dust going it blind."[8] The trouble, however, is that man at times thinks of God not in terms of the best that is in him— the unselfish, tender, gracious elements of personality—but of the worst—the tyrannical, proud, cruel. The result is that his God, instead of acting as a corrective to the evils of his na-

ture, becomes his ally in the execution of his imperfect if not positively wicked designs.

So R. W. Livingstone observed that a Greek who wished to be drunk made Dionysus his patron; if he wanted to be vicious, he turned to the Aphrodite Pandemos; if he wanted to be a thief, Hermes would help him. If on the other hand he had a passion for purity, there was the worship of Artemis. These gods were but the shadows of the men who made them, "called into existence to patronize the actions of their creator, to utter the words which he put into their mouth, to smile to order on his faults and virtues with benignant and unfaltering complaisance."[9]

The danger of equating God with ourselves, of forgetting that we are man and not God, is one which as Christians we should not find hard to avoid. For the Christian believes that in Christ God has taken our flesh to show at one and the same time his identification with man, "in all things . . . made like unto his brethren" (Heb. 2:17); yet his otherness from man in One who is "the brightness of [God's] glory, and the express image of his person" (Heb. 1:3), in whose nature and spirit "dwelleth all the fulness of the Godhead bodily" (Col. 2:9). As Irenaeus said, "He was made what we are, that He might make us what He is Himself."[1]

It is as we remember that the Eternal is **God and not man** that we can understand the amazing patience, forbearance, forgiveness, and com-

[8] "Christ, Champion of Personality," *The Church Monthly*, II (1928), 242.

[9] F. C. Hoggarth, "The Sceptic's Salute," *Christian Century*, XLV (1928), 1196.

[1] *Against Heresies*, Bk. V, Preface.

for I *am* God, and not man; the Holy One in the midst of thee: and I will not enter into the city.

for I am God and not man,
  the Holy One in your midst,
  and I will not come to destroy.[e]

[e] Cn: Heb *into the city*

love (to use an anthropomorphic mode of expression) or, more truly, manifesting the depth of his love, goes far beyond the limits of covenant obligation; he acts in pure grace, for he is God, not man. So Weiser (*Das Buch der zwölf kleinen Propheten*, p. 69) can write: "By no other of the Old Testament witnesses is the tender intimacy and the triumphant power of the love of God so deeply comprehended and so fully expressed as by Hosea." The verse therefore should be read as in the RSV. The last phrase in the KJV, **I will not enter into the city,** has no meaning. But by assuming that there has been haplography of one letter in the Hebrew, we may render **I will not come to destroy** (so RSV, reading אבוא אבער) .

passion that these verses reveal. That after repeated rebuffs, rejections, denials, and betrayals God could still say, **How can I give you up, O Ephraim!** . . . **my compassion grows warm and tender,** proves that

> . . . the heart of the Eternal
> Is most wonderfully kind.[2]

9b. The Majesty of God.—Too often in the affairs of men majesty is a concomitant of tyranny—the great are the powerful, and the powerful exercise their power in bestriding "the narrow world like a Colossus."[3] Majesty or greatness in the secular sense suggests overlordship. A remoteness from the majority of one's fellows, exclusiveness, superiority, pomp and pride. So often have the great used the humble as steppingstones to power. Multitudes have been trampled and slain to gratify man's insatiable lust for power, to satisfy his greed, enhance his glory. History bears convincing proof of this fact. The pride of man knows no bounds. He counts not the cost to others in achieving his selfish, egotistic ends.

Perhaps in no other particular do God's ways differ so greatly from man's as in the concept of majesty, of greatness.

> "I am among you, the Majestic One,
> no mortal man to slay" (Moffatt).

In Christ, God has revealed a new concept of greatness. "Ye know that the princes of the Gentiles exercise dominion over them, and they that are great exercise authority upon them. But it shall not be so among you: but whosoever will be great among you, let him be your minister; and whosoever will be chief among you, let him be your servant: even as the Son of man came not to be ministered unto, but to

[2] Frederick W. Faber, "There's a wideness in God's mercy."

[3] Shakespeare, *Julius Caesar*, Act I, scene 2.

minister, and to give his life a ransom for many" (Matt. 20:25-28). In Christ, God has revealed a new type of greatness—a majesty bereft of pomp, pride, and tyranny, the greatness of humility. And this is the only kind that endures. Such greatness wins men, it does not wound them; serves them, but does not slay them. "A bruised reed shall he not break, and smoking flax shall he not quench" (Matt. 12:20).

The funeral of Louis XIV was held in Notre Dame, Paris. The cathedral was decorated with utmost lavishness. In attendance was as distinguished a gathering of nobility and royalty as perchance ever assembled there. The body of the king was arrayed in rich adornment as if death itself could not rob that royal form of its majestic grandeur. The preacher ascended the pulpit. The sophisticated, men of nobility and power, who had come from far and wide, awaited the great eulogy which such an occasion demanded. But instead they heard something else, something that must have chilled even as it startled them. For the preacher spoke four words that shocked his hearers—the truth does shock—and these were words of truth. Said he: "Only God is great."[4] Christ said it long ago. "Thine is the kingdom, and the power, and the glory" (Matt. 6:13).

If men did not recognize God when he came in human form, it was because they had grown so accustomed to the human concept of greatness that they could not recognize the genuine article. For God came not in royal splendor. Mary and Joseph were simple folk. Christ was born not in a palace but in a manger. God came not in the trappings of outward pomp and power but as a little child—"Unto you is born . . . a Saviour, which is Christ the Lord" (Luke 2:11). This sounds like a contradiction.

[4] See Lynn Harold Hough, *The Christian Criticism of Life* (New York and Nashville: Abingdon-Cokesbury Press, 1941), pp. 184-85.

10 They shall walk after the LORD: he shall roar like a lion: when he shall roar, then the children shall tremble from the west.	10 They shall go after the LORD, he will roar like a lion; yea, he will roar, and his sons shall come trembling from the west;
11 They shall tremble as a bird out of Egypt, and as a dove out of the land of Assyria: and I will place them in their houses, saith the LORD.	11 they shall come eagerly like birds from Egypt, and like doves from the land of Assyria; and I will return them to their homes, says the LORD.

4. ISRAEL GATHERED HOME (11:10-11)

10. It has been argued by several scholars that vss. 10-11 are a late interpolation belonging to the time of the Exile in the sixth century B.C. But if that were so, surely Babylon, not **Assyria**, would be mentioned. The verses are undoubtedly difficult, but they are even more difficult as an exilic interpolation than as a genuine utterance of Hosea (for a similar problem of interpretation, cf., e.g., Mic. 4:6-7; 5:5-6). The first clause, "after the LORD they go" (or "will go"), does not fit in where it stands, for the preceding verses have maintained the opposite; thus vss. 10-11 may have to be regarded as quite independent of these preceding verses. Again, a lion's roar, where it is spoken of symbolically in the O.T., normally signifies danger and hostile attack; it is an aggressive figure. But so interpreted it is not suitable in this context. On the other hand, there is no reason why the lion's roar should not be regarded as a summoning call to his mate or to his young. That would suit here, and parallelism might suggest the following order:

> The LORD will roar like a lion,
>> yea, he will roar;
> His sons will come tremblingly [or hurriedly] from the west,
>> and they will go after the LORD.

The term **the west** is unusual for Hosea; it may mean the coastlands, the isles of the sea; the next line is more in accord with the prophet's teaching when it speaks of return from Egypt and Assyria. Ephraim had been compared by Hosea to a simple, trustful dove that went off to Assyria and Egypt (cf. 7:11). Now like a dove, she will return home, as a bird to her nest. The figure of the returning bird may be intended to illustrate the homing instinct that responds to the Lord's call, though it must be admitted that to use the figure of birds returning home in response to a lion's roar is not a good effort. "And I will cause them to dwell in their own homes" (or following the LXX ἀποκαταστήσω, "I will return them to their own homes"; so RSV) is a thought which has great relevance in connection with chs. 1–3.

A savior serves, a lord is served. A savior offers service, a lord demands it. But that is the mystery of the Incarnation: the lordship of saviorhood, the greatness of humility; the majesty of service, God born in a stable—"the Majestic One, no mortal man to slay."

10-11. _Responding to the Call of God._— Once more we confront the sudden change of mood. Hosea's mood veers like the weather on a blustery March day, sunshine follows clouds, and clouds follow sunshine in rapid succession. So different is the tone of vss. 10-11 from vss. 8-9 that George Adam Smith inclines to view them as an interpolation added during the Exile. Other commentators share a similar view. Yet this is not Hosea's first reference to God as a **lion**. We have noted his use of the metaphor earlier (5:14). Nor is it his last. It occurs again in 13:7. So, too, he had already referred to Ephraim as **a dove** (7:11).

However, the sense in which Hosea uses the figures of the lion and the dove in these verses is different. In 5:14 the lion is ferocious and destructive. He attacks and destroys. Now his roar is thought of as a clarion call inviting the exiles home. At its sound **his sons shall come trembling from the west.** A different use too is made of the metaphor of the dove. In 7:11

12 Ephraim compasseth me about with lies, and the house of Israel with deceit: but Judah yet ruleth with God, and is faithful with the saints.

12ƒ E′phraim has encompassed me with lies, and the house of Israel with deceit; but Judah is still known byᵍ God, and is faithful to the Holy One.

ƒ Heb Ch 12. 1
ᵍ Cn Compare Gk: Heb *roams with*

D. EPHRAIM'S WICKEDNESS AND DOOM (11:12–13:16)
1. THE FUNDAMENTAL FALSEHOOD OF EPHRAIM (11:12–12:1=Hebrew 12:1-2)

12. The meaning of the first part of the verse is plain. Israel surrounds God with lies and deceit. She commits so many deceitful acts that they are like a host of witnesses before God's presence testifying against her. Hosea's emphasis upon the falsehood of his people reminds us at once of Jeremiah's characterization of the fundamental sin of his day as deceit (Jer. 7:4, 8; 8:8; 9:5, 8; 17:9; *et al.*). The second part of the verse is difficult because of uncertainty of text and resultant difficulty of interpretation. **Judah yet ruleth with God, and is faithful with the saints** is obviously commendatory of Judah. The same is true if, following the LXX νῦν ἔγνω αὐτοὺς ὁ θεός, we read עד ירע עם אל and translate, **but Judah is still known by God;** or if the evidence of the Syriac is adopted for the second phrase and the translation is given, "A people holy and faithful" (עם קדוש ומאמין); or if in that same phrase we regard קדושים as a plural of majesty and translate as in the RSV, **and is faithful to the Holy One.** But the context is against any such laudatory judgments; it is clear that the text must have undergone revision, at a time later than Hosea, by a Judaistic redactor.

The participle רד may have the meaning **ruleth,** which would presume a root רוד parallel in use to רדה (cf. Jer. 2:31); but the meaning **roams** is also possible. If this translation is accepted, two lines of interpretation open up:

> Judah is still wayward with God,
> and with a Holy One who is faithful.

In this case קדושים is taken as a plural of majesty.

> Judah is still wayward with God,
> and is faithful with sacred prostitutes.

The translation "sacred prostitutes" is arrived at by reading קדושים as קדשים.

Both of these renderings are critical of Judah's conduct and, so far, fit the context. Taken in either of these ways the verse may stand. It must, however, remain an open question whether this verse, even when couched in condemnatory terms, had originally reference to Judah, or gained that reference only by a later Judaistic revision and had its first reference to Israel.

Ephraim is a silly dove without brains. It is Ephraim's stupidity that is stressed. But now the dove is a symbol of speed. Ephraim **shall come eagerly [hurriedly] like birds from Egypt, and like doves from the land of Assyria.**

The change in the use of these metaphors in describing God's purpose and Israel's response is suggestive. The roar of the lion no longer strikes terror in the heart, but is like a gracious invitation calling men back to life. So God calls men to return. In like manner man is no longer the silly dove that flies about aimlessly; he eagerly wings his way home. Is Hosea suggesting that in the providence of God

the very experiences in which we felt his judgment become the avenues of his mercy; that the tragic results of sin for which we paid in suffering, disillusionment, remorse, can become by God's grace the open door through which the soul seeks its Savior; that the husks and swine of the far country, where God's moral laws worked on us in severe, lionlike fashion, can become his voice pleading with us to return to the shepherd and bishop of our souls? "Where sin abounded, grace did much more abound" (Rom. 5:20). But is Hosea justified in thinking that men on their part will cease playing the role of the silly dove and will

12 Ephraim feedeth on wind, and followeth after the east wind: he daily increaseth lies and desolation; and they do make a covenant with the Assyrians, and oil is carried into Egypt.

12 E′phraim herds the wind,
and pursues the east wind all day long;
they multiply falsehood and violence;
they make a bargain with Assyria,
and oil is carried to Egypt.

12:1. This verse should be taken in close association with 11:12. In 8:7 the figure is of sowing the wind and reaping the whirlwind; here it is that of herding the **wind** and pursuing the **east wind.** It is true that the two verbs used here are not good parallels, yet "herding" may be a form of pursuit. The meaning of the verse is not in doubt. Ephraim is ready, as we would say, to go on any wild-goose chase, to go after any empty and useless end, and in particular to pursue foreign alliances. Since the **east wind** was destructive and blighting in its effects, it is declared in this way that such practices are not only useless and unprofitable, but positively harmful and dangerous. The LXX has μάταια, which means that the LXX translators had before them שׁוא ("vanity" or "idols") in place of the M.T. שׁוד (violence); that also gives excellent sense. In the second half of the verse the prophet returns to speak of the folly of Ephraim's foreign alliances. **Oil** was and is one of the main products of Palestine; and the oil which is said to have been taken to Egypt may have been a rendering of tribute or a gift to maintain a friendly alliance, or, but much less likely, a commercial transaction.

return . . . to their homes, re-establish their rightful relationship with the Most High? Such at any rate was his hope.

12:1. Feeding on Wind.—In referring to ch. 12, George Adam Smith writes, "In no part even of the Book of Hosea does the text bristle with more problems."[5] The technical problems, however, need not obscure the values which Hosea's graphic language reveals, e.g., his statement **Ephraim feedeth on wind.** Not a very substantial diet—one that inflates without nourishing, fills yet leaves us empty. Unlike food that sustains the body, **wind** does not have to be cultivated. It is free and may be obtained without money or price. But one who lives on it does not live long. He starves to death. It is essential for respiration, but its food value is nil.

It was particularly of Ephraim's international policies that Hosea was thinking when he used this metaphor. Like the **wind,** they were unstable. His relations with Assyria and Egypt were utterly false and faithless—**he daily increaseth lies and desolation; and they do make a covenant with the Assyrians, and oil is carried into Egypt.** More than once Hosea warned against the insecurity of this policy, motivated, as it was, wholly by opportunism and quite devoid of loyalty to God and devotion to eternal principles. Ephraim was as one who "hunts a sirocco" (Moffatt)—chasing something that lured but was so elusive as to defy capture. For Assyria was wholly incapable of meeting Ephraim's deepest need, as was Egypt.

"When Ephraim saw his sickness, . . . then went Ephraim to the Assyrian, . . . yet could he not heal you, nor cure you of your wound" (5:13). Our international life is still as unpredictable and unsettled as that of Ephraim, and for the same reason. We make alliances now with Assyria, and concessions now to Egypt; we often cross and double-cross each other, jockeying for position, seeking to win by stealth what is not ours by right, following phantoms that lure but lead nowhere, grasping at that which seems secure but often is no more so than the proverbial will-o'-the-wisp. The well-nigh incredible expenditures that the nations make for military purposes are supposed to make us strong. Actually they make us weak. A world that spends its life and substance on purposes of destruction is an impoverished world. The more effective and numerous its weapons, the more impoverished and endangered it is. Physical force may be an accurate measure of animal prowess but not of human progress. For man is not an animal, but a child of God. In the redemption of his soul, not in the enlargement of his body, does his hope lie. Ephraim but sealed his own doom in turning to his powerful neighbors. He but **feedeth on wind** and hunts the sirocco. Man's strength lies not in man alone, as he seeks through craftiness or diplomacy to improve his position, but in God.

In other ways too do men feed on **wind,** individuals as well as nations. Our contemporary life provides an abundant diet of that airy article. By some quirk of our nature the frothy, superficial, sensational, and bizarre has

[5] *The Twelve Prophets,* I, 327.

2 The Lord hath also a controversy with Judah, and will punish Jacob according to his ways; according to his doings will he recompense him. **3** ¶ He took his brother by the heel in	**2** The Lord has an indictment against Judah, and will punish Jacob according to his ways, and requite him according to his deeds. **3** In the womb he took his brother by the heel,

2. A Judgment upon Jacob (12:2-6=Hebrew 12:3-7)

2. The KJV seems to say that because the Lord has a controversy with Judah he is about to punish Jacob; in addition, vs. 3 has a play upon the names Jacob and Israel, but quite disregards Judah. The conclusion therefore seems clear: in place of **Judah** in vs. 2 should be read Israel. The statement that the Lord has a **controversy** with his people reminds us at once of 4:1, where the same word is used. This verse makes it very plain that God's judgment falls upon a man not for any ritual error or ceremonial failure but for the evil of his doings. Among primitive peoples morality and religion are often quite unconnected. The moral code which is honored is the standard of conduct demanded by the community for the welfare of its members; it is therefore a social demand. The religious practices and observances are aimed at securing personal safety, the increase of the fields and the flocks, success in war, and other benefits which man knows he cannot secure by his own unaided efforts, either because he has not the strength, the skill, or the wisdom which are necessary, or because he believes that these benefits are in the power of a supernatural being to bestow. One of the greatest contributions of the Hebrew prophets was their teaching that the Lord has no delight in the service of rams and lambs fitly offered to a nature or a fertility deity, but he demands truth, righteousness, and love between man and man. Thus did they proclaim the religious sanction and, under the guidance of the spirit of God, formulate moral demands far beyond anything which was required by the popular social consciousness of their times.

3. Lit., **In the womb he took his brother by the heel.** The root עקב in Hebrew means "to overreach," "to supplant." In Gen. 25:26 Jacob is said to have received his name

---

a strange fascination for us, and of this there is no lack. Now as always the superficial is available and in abundance. **Wind** never needs to be rationed. We are diet-conscious—"Have you had your vitamins today?" Indeed, a slogan has it, "You are what you eat." If this slogan is true biologically, it is even more true spiritually. "As he thinketh in his heart, so is he" (Prov. 23:7). And our thoughts unquestionably are often no deeper or more stable than the impressions that come through ear and eye. By means of our amazing scientific technique the vendors of the cheap, if not the vulgar, have been provided with vastly enlarged opportunities for dispensing their wares. Ephraim can gratify his tastes today as never before. Look at the newsstands in any large city. Recreation, humor, levity are all necessary; we need relaxation: but to feed on these is like living on dessert without ever having a balanced meal. To feed on **wind** is to be incapable of understanding, let alone helping to solve, the great moral problems of our generation. These will not be solved by trickery, craftiness, cleverness, but by moral discernment and spiritual power. "I have meat to

eat that ye know not of" (John 4:32). Jesus also referred to himself as "the bread of life" (John 6:35). Meat, bread—not **wind.**

Our running to and fro, in tense and tireless effort, following the broad way which leads to disillusionment, heeding the loudest voices which often say nothing significant: these are but evidences of our deep hunger which the world cannot satisfy.

> From the best bliss that earth imparts,
> We turn unfilled to thee again.[6]

If man is essentially an animal, and the deepest truth about him is his biological endowment, then his quest of the sensational, of that which excites and stimulates, is not amiss. Once, however, we assume that he has a soul, or is a soul, the tragedy and futility of his pursuits become evident.

3-4a. Striving with God.—Hosea looks to the past in an effort to find the basis of Ephraim's present conduct. He suggests that Israel's deceptive character was "inborn and ineradica-

[6] "Jesus, thou Joy of loving hearts." Ascribed to Bernard of Clairvaux.

the womb, and by his strength he had power with God:	and in his manhood he strove with God,
4 Yea, he had power over the angel, and prevailed: he wept, and made supplication	4 He strove with the angel and prevailed, he wept and sought his favor.

because he took his brother by the heel (עָקַב). The fact that the Genesis narrative states that this took place at the birth of the twins, whereas Hosea says that it happened in the womb, cannot in itself be taken as evidence that Hosea is here using a source different from that in Genesis. According to Gen. 32:28, Jacob was renamed "Israel" because "he persevered with God and prevailed" (שָׂרָה="to persevere"). The wordplay thus made with the names Jacob and Israel introduces the next group of verses in which a difficult problem of interpretation is involved. Vs. 2 undoubtedly makes one expect that a statement of Jacob's wicked deeds will follow. Now the act of taking his brother by the heel and so supplanting him may be regarded as an act of guile and craft which is to be condemned as showing the crafty spirit at work in Jacob even from birth; but we must remember that the Semites were inclined to regard such craft more indulgently, if not indeed more approvingly, than we are accustomed to do. Again, the act of contending with God, of persevering in spiritual contest with him, is often commended as praiseworthy, and not, as the present context seems to require, an act of presumption against God.

4-6. With these verses the problem of interpretation becomes even more acute. (Cf. Th. C. Vriezen, "La tradition de Jacob dans Osée XII," *Oudtestamentische Studiën*, ed. P. A. H. De Boer [Leiden: E. J. Brill, 1942], I, 64-78.) To say that the significance of vs. 4a is that even the great patriarch Jacob had to entreat the

ble." Even in birth Jacob tried to get the better of his brother—**he took his brother by the heel.** But Jacob had good points as well, which his descendants lacked. He was a faithful lover (Gen. 28:2 ff.).

And in his manhood he strove with God,
He strove with the angel and prevailed,
he wept and sought his favor.

He showed himself penitent.

The story of Jacob striving with God at Penuel is gripping (Gen. 32:24-30). It is significant that the contest occurred when "Jacob was left alone." God and the human soul are the two ultimate realities. Fellowship is essential in life—"one loving spirit sets another on fire." A solitary Christian who like some Robinson Crusoe makes his way by dint of his own ingenuity, resourcefulness, and courage would be no Christian at all. The Christian character grows in relationships; fellowship is its truest nature. Yet while the Christian life is not solitary, some of its profoundest experiences come when like Jacob we are left alone. Despite its rich and rewarding companionships, life is essentially a lonely journey. Our friends may go with us to the water's edge, but at last we must launch out by ourselves with nothing but their fond adieus and prayers for God's blessing on the way. The soul and God stand face to face at last.

What is the nature of this encounter which brings a conscientious soul face to face with God? Sometimes one strives with God as one faces a great decision. Men have known afar off the fellowship of Christ's suffering as in some Gethsemane they have sought to find the will of God; or, having found it, to bear and do it. Perhaps they have striven with God when like Job they have been the innocent victims of a seemingly cruel fate which, like some oncoming wave, has engulfed and crushed them. "Hath God forgotten to be gracious?" they have asked (Ps. 77:9). "My God, why . . . ?" (Mark 15:34.) That question "Why?" coming out of the deep, rich soil of a people's faith has been a veritable front line where men have striven. In the contest some have been overcome—"Curse God, and die" (Job 2:9)—while others have dug in, yea more, marched forward with dauntless courage and unconquerable faith. "Though he slay me, yet will I maintain my cause to his face" (Job 13:15).

Men have striven with God when they have confronted some great moral issue, when the small but compelling voice of conscience has spoken to their souls, and the haunting sense of "ought" has run headlong into the wall of desire, only to discover that there is a gentle yet relentless persistence about the moral sense. It follows us like our shadow. We seek to escape it by pretending that it really does not matter what we do—let us eat, drink, and be merry. In this we but deceive ourselves. For we cannot escape this struggle within the soul between duty and desire, between God's ought

unto him: he found him *in* Bethel, and there he spake with us;
5 Even the LORD God of hosts; the LORD *is* his memorial.

He met God at Bethel,
   and there God spoke with him[h] —
5 the LORD the God of hosts,
   the LORD is his name:

[h] Gk Syr: Heb *us*

---

mercy and favor of God is not satisfying; it shows that he came under the same spiritual necessities as any other man, but to entreat God in this way cannot possibly be called sin and cannot be regarded as punishable (cf. vs. 2). Indeed the prophets endeavored often to bring their hearers to just such an attitude of contrition that they might entreat God's favor and mercy. Vs. 4b has its continuation in vs. 6. **He [Jacob] met God at Bethel,** or "God met him at Bethel" (the pronouns are indefinite), refers to a divine encounter in which Jacob was exhorted to practice covenant love and justice. That does not imply that Jacob was a heinous sinner; God's demand of any man is just that which was made of Jacob. Reviewing these verses we cannot say that they form a consistent statement of Jacob's sins and shortcomings, such as might give substance to the indictment against Israel which is mentioned in vs. 2. If the purpose of this section was to show that Israel's evil went back even to the time of the patriarchs (cf. Isa. 43:27), and that Jacob himself was guilty of deceit and guile even from birth, the purpose is not served by the statements that are made about Jacob. Guile and presumption are charged against him, but spiritual persistence and contrition are credited to him. It may be part of the purpose of the section to show that, in spite of repentance after his early sinfulness, Jacob returned later to his evil way (cf. vss. 7 ff.). But when we take into account the fact that Hosea commonly traces the sinfulness of Israel back to the wilderness period of their history or to the time of their early settlement in Palestine, the conclusion seems natural that vss. 4-6 at least have been inserted in the book from another source. Since the course of events in Jacob's life as

---

and man's wish. "Whither shall I go from thy Spirit? or whither shall I flee from thy presence?" (Ps. 139:7.) "Jacob was left alone; and there wrestled a man with him until the breaking of the day" (Gen. 32:24).

In Hebrew folklore Jacob was supposed to have overcome his divine protagonist. The wise redactor who adapted the story had a keener insight. He knew that when a man strives with God, sets his will in opposition to the will of God, shakes his fist at God, so to speak, and walks away thinking he has won, he is a greater fool than the man who does not believe in God at all. For it is more sensible to believe that no God exists than to suppose that man could win against him. Finite man is no match for the infinite God. He cannot win; the last word is always with God. The only way a man can win in his encounter with God is by submission and surrender.

> Imprison me within thy arms,
> And strong shall be my hand.[7]

This Jacob realized: **He wept and sought his favor,** and so prevailed. Humility and penitence are man's surest weapons as he strives with the Eternal. Pride and self-will bring sure defeat.

[7] George Matheson, "Make me a captive, Lord." Used by permission of McClure, Naismith, Brody & Co.

Man is victorious only as he works with the Eternal. "In his will is our peace"[8] and our progress. "And as he passed over Penuel the sun rose upon him" (Gen. 32:31). The sun rose upon him—a new day dawned for him. Whatever future there is for man lies in that light.

4b. Meeting God.—The scene **at Bethel** (Gen. 28:10-22) confirms or illustrates the experience at Penuel. **At Bethel** Jacob, in a submissive and reflective mood, received a vision of the transcendent God. He was surprised by it. His surprise sprang from the fact that Bethel was beyond the boundaries of his native land. How then came Yahweh there? He was awed by the vision, which awakened reverence and Godly fear. To Jacob at Bethel came a revelation of the majesty and greatness of God, and as befits one in the presence of such a Reality, he was humbled, expectant, receptive.

One seldom reads the story of Bethel but that there comes to mind another story which stands in striking contrast—the Tower of Babel. God is the center of the first, man of the second. "Surely the LORD is in this place; and I knew it not" (Gen. 28:16). But at Babel the Lord was not in the place and everyone knew it. The building of that tower was a completely human

[8] Dante, *Paradise*, Canto III.

| 6 Therefore turn thou to thy God: keep mercy and judgment, and wait on thy God continually. | 6 "So you, by the help of your God, return, hold fast to love and justice, and wait continually for your God." |

indicated in these verses seems to be different from that of the Genesis narrative, it is possible that the author was dependent upon an oral source.

Vs. 5 is obviously parenthetical, breaking the close connection between vs. 4 and vs. 6. It defines the Lord as **God of hosts.** The term may go back to early mythological ideas in which Yahweh, the God of Israel, may have been thought of as aided by a host of angels, as an earthly king is supported by his armies. But it seems fairly clear that the earliest use of the term in the records of ancient Israel gives it reference to national armies (cf. I Sam. 17:45). The God of hosts was the God of the armies of Israel, and the use of the name may have been associated with the use of the ark of the covenant as a palladium in battle. It was at a later stage that the term came to have reference to the heavenly hosts (James Hastings, ed., *Dictionary of the Bible* [New York: Charles Scribner's Sons, 1909], V, 637*b*; cf. B. N. Wambacq, *L'épithète divine Jahve Seba'ôt* [Paris: Desclée de Brouwer, 1947]). **The Lord is his name** or **The Lord is his memorial** probably refers to the meaning of the term "Yahweh," which is commonly rendered as **Lord** (for the significance of the term see Exeg. on 1:1).

enterprise from start to finish. "Go to, let us build us a city, and a tower, . . . and let us make us a name" (Gen. 11:4). Here was an undertaking in which man was to be the sole agent. There was not the slightest suggestion of any need for guidance or help on the part of the builders. Not only was their spirit that of utter self-confidence, but their purpose was one of complete selfishness—"let us make us a name." Any enterprise thus undertaken and pursued is doomed; nothing good can ultimately come of it. It assumes that we are landlords rather than tenants, owners rather than stewards. It therefore shuts us off from the truly creative and life-sustaining forces which only the spirit of dependence, humility, and unselfishness can unlock. The project at Babel ended in confusion.

The grim turmoil of our world is but added proof of the futility of every undertaking conceived in pride and carried out for narrowly selfish aims. The wisdom we need is not acquired through an increase of knowledge; it comes through a change of attitude and spirit. Our knowledge has made us masters of nature, but it has not given us self-mastery, without which we live in constant peril of each other. It has enabled us to find our way through the pathless seas and trackless air, but is unable to lead us to the peace and true security without which our life is imperiled. If we are not masters of ourselves, it is because we have not found that which masters us. We are strangers to the Bethel experience. The key to man's life does not lie in the material realm, in his ability to build atomic bombs, or jet planes, or towers that reach the skies, but in moral and spiritual reality. And moral values become obligatory and compelling only as man realizes that they are not of his own making, that he did not invent them, and that therefore they cannot be treated as though they were merely fulfilling a utilitarian purpose. When morality bows to utility, it ends in futility. But this realization does not come to minds inflamed by pride or hearts corroded by selfishness. It comes of the wisdom from above, and is acquired by those who know themselves to be but men, and do not think of themselves more highly than they ought to think. It comes to some Jacob in a meditative and receptive mood. Only what God has revealed can keep from destruction what men have achieved. Our civilization needs not more towers reaching up to the skies, but more ladders reaching down to the earth. We cannot lift ourselves by our bootstraps. A new vision of reality, of God—his nature, purpose, and will as revealed to us in Christ—is our hope. Bethel is the only antidote to Babel.

6. The Initiative Is with God.—In our dealing with the Eternal the initiative is always with him, not with us. "We love . . . because he first loved us" (I John 4:19). Israel is to return **by the help of . . . God.** Man takes the initiative when he strays from God, but when he returns it is in response to the call of God. This is another way of saying that when he strays, he does so in response to self-assertiveness, self-will; when, however, he returns, the self has assumed a new attitude or is motivated by a new spirit. But this new attitude or spirit must obviously be different from the one in obedience to which he went astray. It must now be the self in contact with that which is other than the self. It was said of the prodigal that "when he came to himself, he said, . . . I will

7 ¶ *He is* a merchant, the balances of deceit *are* in his hand: he loveth to oppress.

7 A trader, in whose hands are false balances,
he loves to oppress.

---

3. EPHRAIM, CRAFTY TRADER AND INVETERATE SINNER (12:7-14 = Hebrew 12:8-15)

a) EPHRAIM'S CONFIDENCE IN HIS WEALTH (12:7-9 = Hebrew 12:8-10)

7. This verse would follow excellently after vs. 2, and that would be an argument for regarding as additional not only vss. 4-6, but vs. 3 also, in spite of the wordplay it contains upon the names Jacob and Israel. **Trader,** arrived at by regarding the term "Canaan" as signifying a Canaanite and so a trader, gives the exact flavor. It is a condemnation of illicit practices; but there is in it also something of the protest of the austerity of the wilderness against the corrupt ways of a commercialized civilization.

---

arise and go to my father" (Luke 15:17-18). But this impulse which made him willing to go back on himself, to retrace his steps, must have come to him from a source outside himself. Certainly it must have come from other than the kind of self in response to which he set forth to the far country. If it is said that it was the self that initiated the return, but the better self, then we should still have to ask what it was that awakened the better self, loosed it from its captivity to the lower self and so set it free to assert its nature and seek the homeward way. And we should still have to say with Hosea that it was accomplished **by the help of . . . God.**

The individual who comes to himself does so in response to that which comes to him, arrests his attention, wins his consent, and inspires his will to act. In the case of the prodigal it was a consideration of his father's house compared with the poverty and privation to which he was reduced. "How many hired servants of my father's have bread enough and to spare, and I perish with hunger!" (Luke 15:17.) What was this reflection but the voice of God speaking to his better self, trying to bring him to his senses, to the place where he would be willing to say, "I will arise and go to my father"? Sometimes God speaks to us through the appeal of beauty.

> A presence that disturbs me with the joy
> Of elevated thoughts; a sense sublime
> Of something far more deeply interfused,
> Whose dwelling is the light of setting suns,
> And the round ocean and the living air,
> And the blue sky, and in the mind of man:
> A motion and a spirit, that impels
> All thinking things, all objects of all thought,
> And rolls through all things.[1]

He may speak to us through the memory of some dear friend who had faith in us, believed the best about us, and whom we cannot fail or

[1] Wordsworth, "Lines Written a Few Miles Above Tintern Abbey."

deceive. He may reach us through the prayers of a Christian mother, or a devoted soul whose love for us persists despite our folly, or through the ministry of one of his chosen vessels. In humble and quiet ways many have done for the wayward what Ambrose did for Augustine. But by whatever way the manifold grace of God may reach us, when the wayward returns to God, he does so in response to God's gracious mercy. We return **by the help of . . . God,** who is always beforehand with our soul. The initiative is with him. The response is with us.

The genuineness of our response is measured in terms of its ethical results:

> **Hold fast to love and justice,**
> **and wait continually for your God.**

Moffatt translates the passage:

> Dwell in your tents,
> ever be kind and just,
> and in your God put your unfailing trust.

The genuineness of the return is never measured by emotional reactions but by changed ethical conduct. It has too often happened that men have been emotionally moved in their religious experience, but their emotional reactions have had no connection with their wills, and so no appreciable bearing on their conduct. They have blown off steam; but the steam that is blown off never drives anything—it escapes. The prophets insisted that the valid marks of repentance were to be looked for in the realm of changed ethical relationships. It was in the ethical realm that one's religious life would be judged. Hosea, in urging men to **hold fast to love and justice,** was being true to the prophetic insight (Mic. 6:8). Jesus was being true to the prophetic tradition when he asked, "Why call ye me, Lord, Lord, and do not the things which I say?" (Luke 6:46.) "By their fruits ye shall know them" (Matt. 7:20).

7. False Balances.—This is a familiar and typical picture of life lived on a purely materialistic basis, with a purely materialistic philoso-

8 And Ephraim said, Yet I am become rich, I have found me out substance: *in* all

8 E′phraim has said, "Ah, but I am rich,
I have gained wealth for myself";

Amos (8:5) speaks of the false balances of merchants, as does Micah (6:10-11). **He loves to oppress** is possible, although the verb **oppress** is not a parallel to using **false balances.** It is notable that by changing the order of two consonants in Hebrew we get the meaning "he loves to play crooked" (עָקַשׁ for עָשַׁק).

8. This verse contains Ephraim's rejoinder. He has become rich and has amassed wealth for himself. If therefore he has thus prospered, he argues, he has been manifestly blessed, so that the charge of deceit against him is refuted by the evidence of his own material success. The second part, **in all my labors they shall find none iniquity in me that were sin,** has fitting sense, saying, as it does, that the sins of Ephraim have not been

---

phy. There is no sense of honor or honesty; the aim is to "get ahead," to get rich, and any means that further that end are employed, even to using **false balances.** Such practices of course work hardship on others, particularly the poor, who can least afford to be victimized.

We speak often of "Christianizing the social order." This, we know, can be done only by Christianizing men. Only Christian men can create a Christian social order. We speak of creating a community of nations. But we cannot legislate such a community into existence. There can be no community of nations, or of anything, unless the spirit of community is in the hearts of people. Law can regulate a community but cannot create it. Whether we are thinking of the social order or of the world order, man is the measure of it. As long as in his **hands are false balances,** he cannot create a true order anywhere. And the only way to get the false balances out of his hands is by removing falseness from his heart. "Out of the heart proceed evil thoughts, murders, adulteries, fornications, thefts, false witness" (Matt. 15:19); and, we may add, false balances. This is another way of saying that all genuine changes in the outer world result from changes in the inner world. As one thinks of the appalling harm that is done in society by trickery, deception, misrepresentation, lies, etc., one realizes what a revolution would occur could we make the social order moral, if not Christian. But can we? Meanwhile there is no doubt that many of the false balances have been in the hands of "Christian" men. Is this because Christianity has not been interpreted clearly enough in terms of moral and ethical reality? Have we kept God too much in a vacuum and failed to interpret loyalty and obedience to him in terms of the practice of "love and justice" (12:6)? To be Christian surely involves more than being ethical or moral. But if our Christian faith is not interpreted in terms of moral and ethical reality, then, though in some vague sense we feel we are "religious," our reli-

gion will fall far short. It will certainly not be the religion that Jesus lived and taught. To have in our hands **false balances** while our lips prate about truth, is to be ignorant of the A B C's of Christianity.

8a. Wealth for Myself.—To Ephraim the goal of life was to be rich. To have wealth was to have the best life offers. It mattered not how the wealth was acquired:

Swindler! he loves to practise fraud,
with false scales in his hand (vs. 7 Moffatt).

The main thing was to acquire wealth.

That we should want to acquire money is natural and in a sense right. It is true, as Jesus pointed out, that man does not live by bread alone; but it is also true that without bread, man does not live at all. We have physical needs which only money can meet; moreover, there is the need of security against sickness, old age, or other contingencies to which flesh is heir. Money therefore as a means of meeting human need, supplying our reasonable wants, or contributing to worthy or charitable causes, is not to be ignored. Like Ephraim, however, we miss the way when that which should be regarded as a means to an end becomes an end in itself, when that which should furnish a livelihood becomes our very life, when to acquire it we surrender our character, our health, and indeed life itself. The "almighty dollar" is not a misnomer. We give to it the concentration and devotion which rightly belong only to the Almighty.

The reasons why men make the acquisition of wealth the be-all and end-all of existence seem clear enough. The acquisitive instinct is a powerful one. The baby grabs for its rattle and holds it tenaciously. "This is mine" or "No, it's mine" is the cause of many childhood quarrels. Besides, never finding in riches the satisfaction we seek, we falsely assume that what little wealth fails to give, great wealth will accomplish; hence the hunger for wealth, as with lust, increases as it is indulged. It grows by what it

my labors they shall find none iniquity in me that *were* sin.

but all his riches can never offset[i] the guilt he has incurred.

[i] Cn Compare Gk: Heb obscure

---

serious. He may have been guilty of occasional misdemeanors, but not of sin which merits harsh punishment. The difficulty of the phrase **iniquity . . . that were sin,** however, has persuaded most scholars to follow the line of the LXX and to translate:

All his gains will not be sufficient [כל־יגיעיו לא־ימצאו־לו] for the guilt he has incurred [ḥāṭā'].

That is the sense of the RSV. The word rendered here as "gains" means in the first instance "toils" or **labors,** and secondarily "payment for labor" or "the fruit of labor," i.e., profits or gains. The second half of the verse should be understood as a rejoinder to the first part, signifying that not all Ephraim's wealth can possibly **offset** his **guilt.**

---

feeds on. The more we have, the more we want; the more we acquire, the more we desire. "If riches increase, set not your heart upon them" (Ps. 62:10) is wise advice; but it goes unheeded for the most part. The bigger barn surely will bring what the smaller one did not.

Of course it does. It brings an increase of prestige. A man with wealth has entree to the seats of privilege. It brings too an increase of power. "Money talks"—and what it says is usually listened to.

**Ephraim has said, "Ah, but I am rich,
I have gained wealth for myself,"**

and so he gained for himself prestige, position, power.

Admitting all this, one who accepts the Christian faith can yet understand why Jesus characterized as a fool the man who sought the meaning of life in riches. From the Christian point of view, to make riches the chief end of man is the height of folly. Christianity teaches that the choicest values are not material but spiritual. "A good name is rather to be chosen than great riches" (Prov. 22:1). When to acquire riches, however, man resorts to practices of dishonesty and fraud, "with false scales in his hand" (vs. 7 Moffatt), he surrenders in the process of gaining wealth that which is more valuable than gold—his character. "What shall it profit a man, if he shall gain the whole world, and lose his own soul?" (Mark 8:36.) Spiritual values are not airy, insubstantial phantoms. They are life's deepest realities. Nor can they always be divorced from what we call the material. The cup of water given in the spirit of Christ is transformed. The box of ointment broken does not cease to be material, but it assumes a meaning far beyond any that its market price can indicate.

Christianity emphasizes too the neighbor. The neighbor makes Ephraim's act an evil one. **Ah, but I am rich, I have gained wealth for myself.** One reason why "the love of money is the root of all evil" (I Tim. 6:10) is that the love of money increases the love of self. From the Christian point of view the increase of wealth should mean the increase of social responsibility. Generally, however, it means the increase of selfishness, until like some Dives we cannot see the need even at our door. With Ephraim to gain wealth for oneself is to be poor indeed. The abundant life Jesus revealed was not a sea with an intake but no outlet and therefore dead. He speaks of the man who "layeth up treasure for himself, and is not rich toward God" (Luke 12:21). Mammon is God's greatest rival.

Making wealth the goal of life, moreover, is from the Christian point of view the greatest folly because it fails us at the very moment when our need is greatest. There is poignancy in the words of Jesus: "Thou fool, this night thy soul shall be required of thee: then whose shall those things be, which thou hast provided?" (Luke 12:20.) One who dies very rich in this world's goods, but very poor in his discovery and experience of those eternal values which neither moth nor rust doth corrupt nor thieves break through and steal, is a pauper. "You can't take it with you!" The poverty of the soul that seeks its satisfaction in material possessions and so knows not God, the one enduring source of its life, is the most tragic poverty. **I have gained wealth for myself.** Therefore, "Soul, thou hast much goods laid up for many years; take thine ease" (Luke 12:19). You fool, this night God knocks at your door and summons you to his presence. "We brought nothing into this world, and it is certain we can carry nothing out" (I Tim. 6:7).

8b. The Guilt Incurred.—"I have gained wealth for myself," Ephraim said, and no doubt thought he had gained it *by* himself. His material success was due of course to his own energy, ingenuity, and skill. He could pat him-

9 And I *that am* the Lord thy God from the land of Egypt will yet make thee to dwell in tabernacles, as in the days of the solemn feast.

10 I have also spoken by the prophets, and I have multiplied visions, and used similitudes, by the ministry of the prophets.

9 I am the Lord your God
   from the land of Egypt;
I will again make you dwell in tents,
   as in the days of the appointed feast.

10 I spoke to the prophets;
   it was I who multiplied visions,
   and through the prophets gave parables.

---

9. According to Hosea, it was in the wilderness that Yahweh chose Israel to be his people (cf. 13:4-5). "I will again make you dwell in tents, as in the day of solemn assembly" has reference presumably to the assembly of ancient Israel at Sinai, so that the Israelites are to be made to live as they did in their days in the wilderness. But how is the verse to be understood? Does it speak of restoration or punishment? It may speak of both, but the context puts emphasis upon punishment. The Israelites are to be removed from the seductions of the nature cults which flourish in an agricultural community and from the political intrigues and foreign alliances which characterize a constituted state; and they are to be taken into the simplicities and austerities of the wilderness that they may be cleansed in thought and action. It is true of course that, thus cleansed, they will be made fit again for the Lord's service, and the possibility of restoration will be opened up; but that will be the consequence of the wilderness discipline, not the purpose of it.

b) The Work of the Prophets for Ephraim (12:10-14=Hebrew 12:11-15)

10. If vs. 9 is taken as has been suggested above, then vs. 10 will be regarded as a historical statement of what the Lord has done for his people. He did not leave them

---

self on the back. Then whence his guilt? "None of us liveth to himself" (Rom. 14:7). How many lives were blighted, impoverished, crushed in his mad quest for gain? Gold from the mines of Africa, but at what cost in human life! Cotton from the South, but the sharecroppers, what of them?

> But all his riches can never offset
> the guilt he has incurred.

Not even though he makes donations to charity.

9b. *Warning or Promise?*—Perhaps both. Israel had once dwelt in tents, but now lived no longer the nomad's life. The prophet warns, however, that their civilization will be destroyed and they shall return to the days of old. This will be the price of their denial of God. Yet even in this dark picture there is a promise. The destruction will not be complete. A remnant will remain—impoverished, disillusioned, but the seed plot from which the Eternal will try again. "For the Israelites shall remain for many a day without king or chief, without sacrifice or sacred stone, without ephod or oracle; after that, the Israelites shall turn to seek the Eternal their God once more" (3:4 Moffatt).

Does some such prospect await us? Is our civilization doomed? Will anything be left from

an atomic war, should we bring one upon ourselves? Shall we too return to our tents? Albert Einstein was once asked if he knew what weapons would be used in World War III. He replied: "I do not know. But I can tell you what the weapons of World War Four will be—stone clubs!" [2] Is Arnold Toynbee's prophecy right? He says: "If mankind is going to run amok with atom bombs, I personally should look to the Negrito Pygmies of Central Africa to salvage some fraction of [our] present heritage." [3] We may have to return to our tents!

10-14. *The Warnings of God.*—God had warned Israel of their impending doom, but the warning went unheeded. If men were only as quick to heed the warnings that come from the spiritual realm as they are to heed those that come from the physical! When a thermometer under the tongue shows a temperature above normal, we do not need to be urged to consult a doctor. Pain, loss of appetite or weight, whatever warning nature gives, arouses us to action. We usually note her danger signals and take precautionary measures. So all of life is full of warnings: a foghorn at sea, signs along

[2] David A. MacLennan, *No Coward Soul* (New York: Oxford University Press, 1948), p. 200.

[3] *Civilization on Trial* (New York: Oxford University Press, 1948), p. 162.

11 *Is there* iniquity *in* Gilead? surely they are vanity: they sacrifice bullocks in Gilgal; yea, their altars *are* as heaps in the furrows of the fields.	11 If there is iniquity in Gilead they shall surely come to nought; if in Gilgal they sacrifice bulls, their altars also shall be like stone heaps on the furrows of the field.

unhelped and unsuccored; he was a constant aid to them by the word he gave to his prophets and by the visions in which he made his will known.

11. This verse, as it is translated in both KJV and RSV, raises questions. Can Hosea be addressing his contemporaries in these words? Surely he says many times that they have been, and continue to be, guilty of false worship and spiritual adultery against their God. Therefore the words **if there is iniquity in Gilead** are quite unrealistic from Hosea's point of view. There was for him no question about the prevalence of iniquity among the people whom he addressed. Hosea therefore refers here to the sin of Gilead and Gilgal in the early days of Israel's history. In that case we must read "with" or "by" in place of **if** (i.e., עם for אם) and render the verse:

> In Gilead there was iniquity,
> yea, they became vain;
> in Gilgal they sacrificed to demons:
> so their altars became as heaps
> on the furrows of the field.

According to T. H. Robinson (*Die zwölf kleinen Propheten*, pp. 47-48), the final part means that their altars were as numerous as the stone heaps in the furrows of the field; the context, however, suggests that the altars were broken down and made to look like heaps of stones; such ruin will overtake Ephraim, and there will be no escape from it. There is in the verse a wordplay upon the names **Gilead** ("heap of testimony") and **Gilgal** ("circle of stones" or "place where stones have been rolled together in a heap") and the word for **heaps,** which is in the Hebrew *gallīm*. **In Gilgal they sacrifice bulls:** Probably read "to demons" (לשדים for שרים). The LXX text ἄρχοντες argues for the reading "to satyrs" (לשרים); but existing evidence indicates that this meaning of the Hebrew word was late in its appearance and may not have been in use in Hosea's time.

the highway that guide the motorist, a notice from the bank that an account is overdrawn. Such warnings we as a rule take seriously. And if we ignore them, as we sometimes do, we know we cannot escape the consequences.

The warnings of God, however, we tend to treat lightly. Through the word of the prophet, **visions, parables,** God had sought to arrest Israel's attention. But to no avail. Why do all these go unheeded? Is it because we are unaware of them, because of some spiritual blind spot; has something gone wrong with the receiving set of our spiritual natures so that we are unable to tune in? Jesus said of his contemporaries that they could predict the weather but could not read the signs of the times. They were spiritually obtuse. "If they hear not Moses and the prophets, neither will they be persuaded, though one rose from the dead" (Luke 16:31). He spoke of those who have eyes but see not, ears but cannot hear. Why? Can it be that our refusal is due to our stubbornness and

pride rather than to our inability? "There are none so blind as those who will not see." "How often would I, . . . and ye would not!" (Matt. 23:37.) They could, but would not.

One thing is certain: failure to hear and see does not shield us from the impending doom. The handwriting on the wall may go unheeded, but the results of its message do not go unfelt.

> Ephraim has provoked me bitterly;
> so I will crush him suddenly,
> repaying him for his insults (vs. 14 Moffatt).

Perhaps the most tragic aspect of human tragedy is that its spiritual implications go unapprehended. Wars are due to economics; as though the foundations of the universe rested on Wall Street. Economics are effect, not cause. Wars are due to moral decisions or immoral ones, which often involve economics. We see the political, economic, or social implications of our calamities, but fail to see them as an expression of the divine judgment. Is that

12 And Jacob fled into the country of Syria, and Israel served for a wife, and for a wife he kept *sheep*.

13 And by a prophet the LORD brought Israel out of Egypt, and by a prophet was he preserved.

14 Ephraim provoked *him* to anger most bitterly: therefore shall he leave his blood upon him, and his reproach shall his Lord return unto him.

13 When Ephraim spake trembling, he exalted himself in Israel; but when he offended in Baal, he died.

12 (Jacob fled to the land of Aram,
there Israel did service for a wife,
and for a wife he herded sheep.)

13 By a prophet the LORD brought Israel up from Egypt,
and by a prophet he was preserved.

14 E'phraim has given bitter provocation;
so his LORD will leave his bloodguilt upon him,
and will turn back upon him his reproaches.

13 When E'phraim spoke, men trembled;
he was exalted in Israel;
but he incurred guilt through Ba'al and died.

---

12. This verse is within parentheses in the RSV, indicating that it is not in place where it stands; it is obviously out of its context. It should be associated with vss. 4-6, and for that reason, in accordance with the conclusions reached above, should be regarded as an addition.

13-14. These verses may be taken in conjunction. They are not a sequel to what has gone before; they are but a repetition of what Hosea has already said but does not tire of saying. Vs. 13 asserts that the deliverance of Israel from Egypt was not simply one of the contingencies of history or something that the Israelites had achieved by their own strength or skill. It was an act of God and the agent of it was **a prophet,** Moses, who also was their keeper and preserver in the wilderness. Vs. 14 tells again how Israel refused to listen to God's servants and offered bitter provocation; the sense might be improved by reading "Ephraim gave him [the prophet] bitter provocation" (הכעיסו אפרים בת'). Probably a half line has been lost after this; certainly the rhythmic form would suggest so. The exact significance of the **bloodguilt** mentioned in the second part of the verse is not clear. Sellin takes it as evidence that Moses died a martyr's death, since he is obviously the prophet referred to, and he seeks additional support for this view in the opening verse of the next chapter (cf. "Hosea und das Martyrium des Mose," *Zeitschrift für die alttestamentliche Wissenschaft,* XLVI [1928], 26-33). But as far as this verse is concerned, **his bloodguilt** can as easily mean Ephraim's bloodguilt, and may refer to Ephraim's violence against the Lord's prophets or to their joining in Molech worship with its attendant human sacrifice (cf. II Kings 17:17).

4. THE INESCAPABLE DOOM OF INIQUITOUS EPHRAIM (13:1-11)

a) EPHRAIM'S IDOLS (13:1-3)

13:1. Trembling and **men trembled** represent different renderings of a noun whose syntactical relation with the rest of the verse is open to question. In the RSV the subject

---

why we seem to learn so little from them, as evidenced by their repeated occurrence? "Blessed are the meek: for they shall inherit the earth" (Matt. 5:5). Not conquer it; nobody will conquer it for long. Every conqueror is conquered. The meek inherit it because they are the teachable; they learn. But in the realm of moral realities we do not seem to learn. We have learned how to make wars more destructive, but not how to abolish them, because to make them more destructive we have only to deal with physical forces. To bring peace we have to confront moral forces. And with these we are inept, partly because we do not take them seriously. We regard them with patronizing disdain. But we err grievously. "On whomsoever it shall fall, it will grind him to powder" (Matt. 21:44).

13:1a. The Awe that Springs from Reverence.
—There is a kind of awe induced by the display

of the verbs in the second and third lines is presumably **Ephraim.** With regard to such an interpretation two observations may be offered: (*a*) a distinction is thus made between Ephraim and Israel, the former term being used to signify the tribe by itself, not the whole people; that such a use is not impossible, however unexpected it may be in face of Hosea's normal use of the term, can be seen from vs. 15; (*b*) at the beginning of the second phrase there stands in the original Hebrew an emphatic pronoun, a use which normally indicates that the subject of that part is to be distinguished from that of the part immediately preceding. If we give this evidence its due weight, the pronoun in the second part of the verse must refer not to Ephraim, but to the prophet mentioned in 12:14 or to the Lord. Sellin (*ibid.*, pp. 31-32) adopts the former of these interpretations and suggests the rendering:

> When Ephraim spoke contentiously [ריבות for רתת],
> he [the prophet] bore it for Israel;
> but when he [Israel] was guilty of Baal-worship,
> he [the prophet] died.

That rendering assumes certain slight emendations: "contentiously" is based upon the LXX δικαιώματα; "for Israel" in place of **in Israel** demands the change of one consonant (ל for ב); and Sellin uses this verse in conjunction with 12:14 to support his view that Moses, the prophet referred to, died a martyr's death.

But it is easier to make the pronoun in the second phrase of the verse refer to the Lord, in which case the translation may be:

> When Ephraim spoke tremblingly [or "stammeringly," as a child]
> then he [the LORD] was exalted in Israel;
> but when he [Ephraim] incurred guilt through Baal,
> he died.

---

of physical grandeur and power: panzer divisions sweep with incredible precision and speed across the battlefield, squadrons of bombing planes fill the sky on their mission of destruction. Tyranny—the irresponsible power of the dictator, whose cunning and fiendish fancies go unopposed by his subdued subjects—sometimes induces awe. It has been said that in a dictatorship a man can talk against the government, but only to himself, and then under his breath. Fear rules men's hearts. But such awe is like "the grass of the field, which to-day is, and to-morrow is cast into the oven" (Matt. 6:30). The dictator who once strutted is hung up by his heels, and the panzer divisions are a doleful memory. The awe that Ephraim had once induced was of another kind. It was the awe that springs from respect. **Men trembled** because he was worthy of their esteem. **He was exalted in Israel,** not by birth but by character. If there is no royal road to geometry, there is no royal road to a princely character. It is won by discipline and denial.

In Proverbs we read, "The fear of the LORD is the beginning of wisdom" (9:10); but to fear the Lord is not to be afraid of him. It is to stand in awe of him. "Put off thy shoes from off thy feet; for the place whereon thou standest is holy ground" (Exod. 3:5). So Moses was awed by the presence of God. "Depart from me; for I am a sinful man, O Lord" (Luke 5:8). So Peter was awed in the presence of Jesus.

Something like that had been true of Ephraim. When he spoke, men were in awe. His words were more than words, they were the agents and ministers of his life's rich experience. They were not counterfeit words, "sounding brass, or a tinkling cymbal" (I Cor. 13:1), but genuine—they rang true. "The people were astonished at his doctrine: for he taught them as one having authority, and not as the scribes" (Matt. 7:28-29). (Yet see Exeg.)

1b. Who Are the Dead?—The throne of character can never be usurped or conquered. It is lost only by being relinquished. Ephraim lost his position of respect and regard because he surrendered voluntarily the sanctuary of his soul to pagan influences. He worshiped Baal. The inner springs became polluted and, like poison in the bloodstream, produced death—**he died.** To be sure, his body was not placed in a casket. No hearse bore him to his grave. But **he died**—morally, spiritually, politically.

To the secular mind death means the death of the body. In the biblical tradition death has had another connotation—the death of the soul.

2 And now they sin more and more, and have made them molten images of their silver, *and* idols according to their own understanding, all of it the work of the craftsmen: they say of them, Let the men that sacrifice kiss the calves.

2 And now they sin more and more,
    and make for themselves molten images,
idols skilfully made of their silver,
    all of them the work of craftsmen.
Sacrifice to these, they say.*j*
    Men kiss calves!

j Gk: Heb *to these they say sacrifices of*

Such a reading gives excellent sense and is probably the best that can be made of a very difficult text. The meaning clearly is that Ephraim, in his young days, when he spoke tremblingly or hesitantly, honored and served the Lord, so that the Lord was exalted; but when he fell into the worship of Baal he incurred guilt and, in the spiritual sense, died. Incidentally, it may be noted that this translation gives the term Ephraim a connotation similar to that of Israel, which is Hosea's common practice.

2. The signs of Israel's spiritual death are now defined. **They sin more and more, and make for themselves molten images.** Thus they have chosen the way of death. The rhythm of the verse shows that the words **of their silver** should be taken with what follows. Lit., "Idols of their silver according to their understanding"; they make images according to their own ideas and worship these. The LXX has κατ' εἰκόνα, which suggests the Hebrew כתבנית for כתבונם, and the translation "of their silver according to the form [כתבנית] of idols" or "idols of silver according to their own plan [כתבניתם]." But such translations are not to be preferred to that derived directly from the M.T. In the final part of the verse, **they say of them, Let the men that sacrifice kiss the calves** disregards the rhythmic balance of the line and gives a very questionable translation. The Hebrew

---

In the opening chapters of Genesis the distinction is found: "But of the tree of the knowledge of good and evil, thou shalt not eat of it: for in the day that thou eatest thereof thou shalt surely die" (Gen. 2:17). "Stolen waters are sweet, and bread eaten in secret is pleasant. But he knoweth not that the dead are there; and that her guests are in the depths of hell" (Prov. 9:17-18). "But she that liveth in pleasure is dead while she liveth" (I Tim. 5:6). "Millions now living will never die" was the widely advertised subject of a popular evangelist; to which someone replied, "Millions now living are dead already." Could we but know, this is the death most to be feared—the living death. Herein lies the heart of the gospel message: "The wages of sin is death; but the gift of God is eternal life through Jesus Christ our Lord" (Rom. 6:23). "For as in Adam all die, even so in Christ shall all be made alive" (I Cor. 15:22).

To the natural man who cannot discern the things of the spirit this is foolishness. It is the foolishness of the gospel, wherein lies life's deepest wisdom. The death of a civilization—and many have died—invariably stems from its spiritual deterioration and decay. When man loses his soul, like Ephraim he is dead. He has severed the connection that keeps his finite life in touch with the infinite God. He then seeks to act as though he were infinite. He becomes the victim of vain hopes, foolish pride, and baseless

fears. For he has killed that within him wherein alone can be found the unique mark of his manhood—his fellowship with God. It was to restore this fellowship that Christ came. He came to bring through his cross pardon and redemption. "To be carnally minded is death; but to be spiritually minded is life and peace" (Rom. 8:6). **When he offended in Baal, he died.** It is from this death that the gospel offers salvation here and hereafter.

2-3. *The Transient Nature of Evil.*—In ch. 13 Hosea repeats many of the prophecies of earlier chapters. He "sums up all that has gone before: Israel's early promise and Jahveh's tender care; Israel's forgetfulness and declension to idolatry; the weakness of the kings and the stupidity of the people; the inevitability of the coming doom." [4] For Israel's idolatry see Expos. on 4:17; 8:5-6; 10:5-6. **Therefore they shall be like the morning mist:** See Expos. on 6:4. To these figures of clouds and dew Hosea adds two others: **The chaff that swirls from the threshing floor** and **smoke from a window.** The figure of the chaff is often used in prophecy (cf. Isa. 17:13; 41:15-16). One recalls too the familiar word of the psalmist who compares the ungodly to "the chaff which the wind driveth away" (Ps. 1:4). Hosea's figure of **smoke from a window** is not found elsewhere. In these vivid metaphors he reveals his poetic insights. He

[4] S. L. Brown, *Hosea*, p. 111.

3 Therefore they shall be as the morning cloud, and as the early dew that passeth away, as the chaff *that* is driven with the whirlwind out of the floor, and as the smoke out of the chimney.

4 Yet I *am* the LORD thy God from the land of Egypt, and thou shalt know no god but me: for *there is* no saviour beside me.

3 Therefore they shall be like the morning mist
　　or like the dew that goes early away,
　like the chaff that swirls from the threshing floor
　　or like smoke from a window.

4 I am the LORD your God
　　from the land of Egypt;
　you know no God but me,
　　and besides me there is no savior.

---

is, lit., "sacrificers of men." If that refers to human sacrifice, it is out of place here. Therefore follow the RSV, and construe the final clause as an incredulous exclamation. The prophet finds it impossible to believe that men can stoop so low as to worship what their own hands have made.

3. The subject of this verse is not explicitly stated: it may be the worshipers of idols or the idols themselves; both will soon pass away and be as if they had never been. **The morning mist** and **the dew** are used in the O.T. as symbols of the transient and the temporary (cf. 6:4); **the chaff** is a figure for something which has no stability and is easily driven off (cf. Ps. 1:4); and **smoke** represents that which vanishes away, that which is insubstantial and fugitive (cf. Isa. 51:6; Pss. 68:2; 102:3). The **window** was probably a lattice window in the roof, serving as an outlet for the smoke which curled upward; it is much less likely that a wall window (a distinct word in Hebrew) was intended.

b) YAHWEH, THE SHEPHERD OF EPHRAIM (13:4-6)

4. Once more Hosea emphasizes the Lord's care of his people Israel from the land of Egypt; in the presence of the evidences of such care Israel ought never to have been guilty of rebelliousness and sin against God. For the first part of the verse cf. 12:9. **You know no God but me** is the simple truth according to the mind of Hosea. The Israelites had indeed paid service to others, yet they were not gods; they were but the fabric of men's hands, things that had no power to act or to save; **besides me there is no savior.** Since God alone is savior, he alone is worthy to be worshiped; he alone merits man's

---

thinks in pictures. By the piling up of figures, **cloud, dew, chaff,** and **smoke,** he seeks to drive home the fickle, insecure, unstable, transient character of all idolatry. What could be more transient than **smoke?** As it belches out from the chimney one might think it would obliterate the sky, but soon it is gone. Evil always gives the impression of permanence, but in no respect is its deceptive nature more clearly revealed. For evil has within itself the seeds of its own destruction. When Ephraim turned away from God and to an idolatry which was but the adoration of his own finiteness and sin—for that is what idolatry essentially is—he just as surely started his undoing as if he had taken poison into his system. He then became like **the chaff** which the wind drives away, **like smoke from a window.** "I have seen the wicked in great power, and spreading himself like a green bay tree" (Ps. 37:35). "Until I went into the sanctuary of God; then understood I their end"

(Ps. 73:17). The man of faith believes, yea, knows that while goodness and truth may seem no match for evil when the latter rides high, still the race is not to the swift, nor the battle to the strong. Evil wins battles but cannot win the war. Time is on the side of truth. Truth is not smoke that vanishes, it is the rock amid the sinking sand.

4b. God the Only Savior.—The literal meaning of the phrase is that in Israel's deliverance from Egypt no other God had intervened in their behalf. It was by the help of the Eternal that they had won their freedom and established themselves in the Promised Land. There was no other savior.

Yet the words may also be taken at their face value. **I am the LORD your God . . . , and besides me there is no savior.** This is the message of our religion: man needs salvation, and there is no salvation for man apart from the one true God who spoke by the prophets and has re-

5 ¶ I did know thee in the wilderness, in the land of great drought.

6 According to their pasture, so were they filled; they were filled, and their heart was exalted; therefore have they forgotten me.

5 It was I who knew you in the wilderness,
in the land of drought;
6 but when they had fed[k] to the full,
they were filled, and their heart was
lifted up;
therefore they forgot me.

[k] Cn: Heb according to their pasture

service. At this point Hosea anticipates the teaching of Second Isaiah (cf. 43:3, 11; 44:6, 8; 45:18, 21). The LXX has a small section which is not found in the Hebrew, viz., στερεῶν τὸν οὐρανὸν καὶ κτίζων γῆν, οὗ αἱ χεῖρες ἔκτισαν πᾶσαν τὴν στρατείαν τοῦ οὐρανοῦ, καὶ οὐ παρέδειξά σοι αὐτὰ τοῦ πορεύεσθαι ὀπίσω αὐτῶν. καὶ ἐγὼ ἀνήγαγόν σε; i.e., "[I am the Lord your God] who established the heaven and created the earth, whose hands created all the host of heaven, and I did not show them to you in order that you might follow after them. And I brought you up [from the land of Egypt]."

5. I did know thee in the wilderness reminds us of the great saying of Amos: "You only have I known of all the families of the earth" (3:2). In neither case is it factual knowledge which is intended, not knowledge about Israel, but intimate and personal fellowship with Israel, like the intimate relationship between husband and wife. The LXX has ἐποίμαινόν σε, so that רעיתיך, "I shepherded you," must have been read for the M.T. ידעתיך. The main argument that can be adduced in favor of it is the use in vs. 6 of the figure of feeding and becoming satiated.

6. The first word in the Hebrew is very doubtful; it means **according to their pasture,** the word **pasture** here signifying a place of pasture, not the act of pasturing. We may read a related form, such as כרעותם or כרעיתם or כמו רעיתים; but the significance of the verse is not in doubt. The RSV expresses it suitably, though an even better translation might be:

As they fed [or "as I fed them"], they became satiated,
and they became exalted with pride.

vealed himself most fully in his Son. That man needs salvation is a fact. He probably would not admit it; but the well-nigh frantic ways in which he runs hither and yon in quest of he knows not what, the almost pathetic trust he places in his scientific achievements—which the more superficial have come to regard as a sort of messiah—all point to his need of salvation. But the salvation he thus seeks he will never find. He wants a salvation that will do something for him rather than to him and in him and with him. He wants salvation on his own terms. He wants to be saved in his sins, not from them. He seeks a deliverance that can be achieved with a minimum of effort. He often fails to see the difference between the scientific inventions which have created a revolution in his physical world and the nature of the moral and spiritual forces which are needed to revolutionize his life. He acts as if someday someone might invent a sort of spiritual elevator that could lift him into a better order at the pressing of a button. Herein lies the constant temptation to idolatry. The idol is the work of man's hands, the projection of his own nature, so to speak. He bows down to it physically, yet it too is as

finite as he is and lays upon him no demands more difficult than he is able to bear. His heart is not humbled nor is his will submitted to a superior will. The very agent therefore by which he seeks salvation from sin involves him more deeply in sin.

And now they sin more and more,
and make for themselves molten images (vs. 2).

This is why there is no other savior than the eternal God. He is love, but holy love, a love in the presence of which man knows himself to be a sinner. He speaks to the inner life. If there is no other savior, it is because there is no other God who so mercilessly reveals man to himself. He understands our thoughts afar off, and has set our secret sins in the light of his countenance (Ps. 90:8). Yet in that is seen his greatest mercy. This is the mystery of the Cross, where his judgment on man's sin appears in the light of his self-giving love for man's redemption.

5-6. The Danger of Prosperity.—This is the familiar story of man's ingratitude. It recurs time and again in the Bible, like the theme of a symphony. Men turn to God in adversity.

| 7 Therefore I will be unto them as a lion: as a leopard by the way will I observe *them:* | 7 So I will be to them like a lion, like a leopard I will lurk beside the way. |

The response of the Israelites to the Lord's shepherding of them and caring for them ought to have been thankfulness expressed in obedience to him and the keeping of covenant with him who so graciously and generously kept covenant with them. Instead they were as heedless and thankless as people who get an ample provision are always liable to be. This pride is not the ὕβρις of those who rise up in rebellion against God and assert themselves against their Creator, but the pride of those who regard their provision and their privileges as inalienable and of right.

c) YAHWEH, THE DESTROYER OF EPHRAIM (13:7-8)

7-8. The people in their pride have forgotten God; they have ceased to believe that they have any need of him, and they take no heed of the fact that they are accountable to him. Therefore God will cease to be a protecting, guardian shepherd and will become

That is as natural as looking toward the light in a darkened room or seeking shelter in storm. "God is our refuge and strength, a very present help in trouble" (Ps. 46:1). "The eternal God is thy refuge, and underneath are the everlasting arms" (Deut. 33:27). So in the **wilderness** experiences of life, **in the land of drought,** men have sought and found in the Eternal strength for the day and courage for the road. But if on the one hand the Bible reveals man's dependence on God in adversity, it just as clearly recounts his vaunted independence of God in prosperity. **When they had fed to the full, . . . they forgot me.** So the humility of adversity hardens into pride, "that poverty of soul turned inside out,"[5] and the spirit of dependence, of waiting upon God, seeking his blessings and grace, to forgetfulness—**they forgot me.**

Has not this same spirit persisted until now? The Pilgrim Fathers were exposed to certain hazards and hardships of which we know little or nothing. They too, like the Israelites, knew firsthand the severities of nature, the struggle to explore and develop a country wild and even hostile. They too knew **the land of drought.** We do not. Our mastery of nature by our mechanical devices has lifted from us heavy burdens under which our fathers bowed. Their luxuries have become our necessities, and of our luxuries they never dreamed. But was God perchance more real to them than to us? We continue the Thanksgiving Day service which they instituted. But does it mean to us what it did to them?

When they had fed to the full, . . . they forgot me. Their material benefits obscured their spiritual need. What went to their stomachs went also to their heads. They filled themselves—they were "well fixed" materially—then

[5] Nels Ferré, *Pillars of Faith* (New York: Harper & Bros., 1948), p. 20.

they grew proud. No doubt because they regarded their benefits as the result of their unaided energy or ingenuity, they congratulated themselves. Perhaps too because those who are "well fixed" materially so easily succumb to selfishness, and selfishness begets pride. The proud man is "stuck on himself," there is no other place small enough to hold him! **They forgot me.** Why not? Why remember God when you have all you need, perhaps all you want? When your barns are so stuffed that you have to pull them down and build greater? God is necessary when you are in need or in trouble; when you get bogged down he is a convenient tow car to pull you out—you remember him then! But when you get to "rolling" again, with the tank full, and hitting on all eight, and "chewing up" the miles at a great clip, of what use is God? Are you not getting on very well without him? Why not forget him?

The author of the Revelation writes to the church at Laodicea: "Thou sayest, I am rich, and increased with goods, and have need of nothing; and knowest not that thou are wretched, and miserable, and poor, and blind, and naked" (Rev. 3:17). If man is nothing but a physical mechanism to be fed adequately, housed comfortably, and brought to live lavishly, that is one thing. But the moment we posit a soul, a spiritual nature, an image of God that is hardly ever completely erased, though often defaced, then material measurements of man's progress become inadequate. Then we understand that when he forgets God, he forgets his real self. For his physical being is no more his real self than his clothes are. "Thou fool, this night thy soul shall be required of thee: then whose shall those things be, which thou hast provided?" (Luke 12:20.)

7-8. *The Perversion of the Best Brings the Worst.*—Hosea is the prophet of love, but of

8 I will meet them as a bear *that is* bereaved *of her whelps,* and will rend the caul of their heart, and there will I devour them like a lion: the wild beast shall tear them.

8 I will fall upon them like a bear robbed
     of her cubs,
   I will tear open their breast,
   and there I will devour them like a lion,
     as a wild beast would rend them.

---

to his people as a ravening, destroying beast of prey attacking to kill. The ferocity of **lion** and **leopard** were well known, and a **bear robbed of her cubs** is a particularly dangerous creature. The word in the original for **I will lurk** or "I will watch" is a weak one for the purpose, but it is confirmed by the verses, even if it is otherwise translated in them. **The caul of their heart** is the enclosure of their heart, i.e., their ribs or their **breast;** the latter is the better rendering.

As the second half of vs. 8 stands, there is not uniformity of subject:

> And there I will devour them like a lion,
> and the wild beasts will rend them.

---

holy love. And holy love betrayed brings evil to the betrayer. Only thus can we understand the terror that lurks behind these vivid symbols the prophet uses: **lion, leopard, bear,** and **wild beast.** It is hard to associate the eternal Lover of our souls with such metaphors. They have appeared before (see Expos. on 11:10-11). The one comment to be made here is that the very God who might have been their Savior now becomes their destroyer; the very forces which potentially might have brought health and healing now bring terror and tragedy.

The perversion of the best is always the worst. Human love can in some fashion help to save a man. When its obligations are met, its call heeded, it becomes the source of rich and enduring blessings. But when love is perverted into lust, it becomes the source of some of life's deepest woes. The lion of lust has devoured many a life. Disillusionment, disgust, and stark tragedy are the marks of its footsteps.

> Love comforteth like sunshine after rain,
> But Lust's effect is tempest after sun;
> Love's gentle spring doth always fresh remain,
> Lust's winter comes ere summer half be done;
>   Love surfeits not, Lust like a glutton dies;
>   Love is all truth, Lust full of forged lies! [6]

Freedom can be a major source of human welfare. Without it man is not man. "Give me liberty, or give me death!" No wonder millions rally to its defense. Without freedom to choose between duty and desire, between right and wrong, the right choice would quite lose its meaning. It would be silly to become infuriated at a traffic light that turns red as we approach it, or to thank it for staying green when we are late for an appointment. The traffic light can do no other. It is an automaton at the mercy of laws which it can do nothing but

obey. It has no choice. Man has. And from this fact spring most of his worst problems and perils. The very liberty which when used with discipline and responsibility is the key to his manhood, when betrayed and perverted into license becomes like a veritable **bear robbed of her cubs.** What is potentially the best becomes actually the worst. Unquestionably the greatest evils of life today spring from our abuse of liberty. That which could be man's "savior" becomes his destroyer.

The **lion, bear,** and **wild beast** of which the prophet speaks are therefore not foreign assailants imported by the Almighty to disturb our domestic tranquillity. They are in every man; of tremendous value when their native power is directed to worthy ends, of frightening ferocity when unleashed and left to run their course unchecked by reason, conscience, and supremely by the grace and power of God.

The good and evil in man are strangely intermingled. The saint is made of the same raw material as the sinner. Power may be used constructively in the service of mankind—"We then that are strong ought to bear the infirmities of the weak" (Rom. 15:1)—or it may be used destructively. The impulse that sends the tyrant sweeping like some prairie fire across the earth, lies side by side with that which sends our missionaries to wage war against ignorance, sin, and disease. Napoleon and Pasteur were Frenchmen both; but one used his power to destroy mankind, the other to save mankind from disease. The destroyer is always a perverted "savior," the "savior" a potential destroyer.

Who decides? What determines that "no lion shall be there, nor any ravenous beast shall go up thereon" (Isa. 35:9)? What decrees that **a leopard . . . will lurk beside the way?** What is it that perverts the potentially good in man to the

[6] Shakespeare, *Venus and Adonis.*

9 ¶ O Israel, thou hast destroyed thyself; but in me *is* thine help.	9 I will destroy you, O Israel; who[l] can help you?

[l] Gk Syr: Heb *for in me*

The RSV gets over the difficulty in a way that the Hebrew will not tolerate. The choice seems to lie between:

> And there I will devour them like a lion,
> and like a wild beast I will rend them [אבקעם]

or

> And there dogs will devour them [ואכלם שם כלבים]
> and the beasts of the field will rend them.

In none of the renderings given has the word **there** any special reference. Indeed, in each case "then" (Arabic *thumma*) rather than "there" would be the suitable adverb.

d) WHERE NOW IS YOUR KING? (13:9-11)

9. Lit., "It [the wild beast or beasts just referred to] has destroyed [or "will destroy"] you, O Israel; but in me is your helper." The LXX has τῇ διαφθορᾷ σου, Ἰσραήλ, τίς βοηθήσει; therefore read:

> שחתיך ישראל מי בעזרך
> If I destroy you, O Israel,
> who will be your helper?

Since the idols they have worshiped are altogether impotent, there can be no escape from the destruction threatened by God.

---

actually evil? Sin! "I see another law in my members, warring against the law of my mind, and bringing me into captivity to the law of sin" (Rom. 7:23). "When I would do good, evil is present with me" (Rom. 7:21). But sin is selfishness. It is the ego that forgets its finiteness and creaturehood, and in defiance of reason and conscience usurps the place which belongs to God alone. So it comes about that God who could be the Savior becomes the destroyer. Actually, however, it is man who destroys himself; for the **wild beast** is not imposed from without, it comes from within—"For out of the heart proceed evil thoughts" (Matt. 15:19).

The wild beasts are once more at hand. Their angry roars are often heard. The chains that hold them are none too strong, and are taut. There is tension between the powers that be. Should the chains break, with resultant calamity, we can say that God has destroyed us only in the sense that he has so made us that we are able to destroy ourselves.

9-11. Man's Salvation Is Not in Himself.— One of the criticisms frequently made of religion is that it is "old stuff." Here we are, modern folk living in a modern world with its modern ideas, techniques, and needs; yet we are asked to go back to a tiny country hardly bigger than a good-sized county of an American state to heed the message of One who, judged by our modern scientific methods and techniques, was wholly uninformed. What shall we answer to this charge? The best answer is to plead guilty. Admit the charge. But may not the very admission be significant? Might it not prove that religion is not some artificial contraption arbitrarily imposed from without but is organically related to the needs and destinies of men? If after all these centuries the religious sense is still with us, that must mean it is in us, part of our very being.

Religion is "old stuff." The earliest architecture was religious—the temple. So too was the earliest poetry—the hymn. The first drama was religious drama—festival, pageantry, ritual; as were the first science, magic, astrology, and priestly therapeutics. "All law was religious law. All social custom was religious custom." Moreover, "all government was originally theocratic. The ruler was either himself the high priest or was ruled by the high priest."[7] What else is it but history's testimony that man cannot take over on his own? **Give me a king and princes:** The reference here and in vs. 11 is most

[7] Abba Hillel Silver, *Religion in a Changing World* (New York: Richard R. Smith, 1930), pp. 29-30.

10 I will be thy king: where *is any other* that may save thee in all thy cities? and thy judges of whom thou saidst, Give me a king and princes?

10 Where[m] now is your king, to save you;
  where are all[n] your princes,[o] to defend you[p] —
those of whom you said,
  "Give me a king and princes"?

[m] Gk Syr Vg: Heb *I will be*
[n] Cn: Heb *in all*
[o] Cn: Heb *cities*
[p] Cn Compare Gk: Heb *and your judges*

10. The rendering given in the RSV should be followed; the KJV disregards rhythmic form and is obscure. There is no doubt that the verse began with the interrogative **where** (איה for אהי), and it may be reasonably concluded that the second interrogative introduced the second part of the line (as in RSV). The emendation of **cities** to **princes** (שריך for עריך) is suggested by the second half of the verse; **and thy judges** (KJV) is emended to "that they may judge you" (ישפטך for ושפטיך), which may mean either **to defend you** (RSV) or "that they may exercise authority over you." The rest of the verse is a reassertion of Hosea's criticism of Israel's political aspirations and political vagaries. When Israel in the first instance asked for a king, it was for the purpose of defense against their enemies; but kings and princes had proved an agent in the seduction of Israel from the trust they should have had in their God; therefore they will be removed; and beyond that, they would be resourceless to ward off the blows that were about to fall upon Israel.

likely not to the choice of Saul but to "the self-chosen dynasties of the Northern Kingdom, which experience had proved to be a failure." [8] At any rate, whether these puppet kings for which they asked were regarded as being chosen by God or not, the truth is that they had failed miserably. Why?

Ah, if men have no reverence for the Eternal, what is the good of a king? (10:3 Moffatt.)

Where is your king now to save you? (13:10 Moffatt.)

Life eagerly turns to some way of possible deliverance. Modern man has sought, still seeks, salvation in education in general and in science in particular. He assumes that his greatest enemy is ignorance, that the trouble lies in his mind; that could he but know better, he would do better. Schools outnumber anything that Horace Mann ever dreamed, while juvenile delinquency has been on the increase and the yearly crime bill rises to alarming proportions. "Where now is your education to save you?"

The same question may be put to science. How enamored are we of it! How much it has done for us that we could not have done for ourselves without its aid! With how much more speed and ease does it now enable us to do that which before its advent was done only by hard toil and endless labor! Every housewife pays her tribute as she starts the vacuum cleaner, the dishwasher, or some other of the gadgets that have been provided as helps, meet for us. To the average man science has brought the power of a thousand slaves. It has enlarged our eyes through the telescope, our ears through the radio. It has incredibly increased the power of our hands and arms through machines. It has given us the wings of a bird and made our feet incredibly swift. Yet has it brought peace, happiness, security, salvation? Can it be that in our "messiah" lies the danger of our destruction? "Where now is your science to save you?"

Our salvation does not lie in political arrangements as such. The Israelites thought their puppet kings held the secret of their deliverance. No more than do politically minded presidents or powerful dictators. Man's salvation does not lie in anything that man by himself creates, sets up, invents, or discovers—for the simple reason that man's primary need is salvation from himself. The evil that destroys his life is not some force foreign to his nature that invades from without; rather it is a power that erupts from within. However one may account for the presence of evil in man, it is quite impossible to deny the fact of it. The sin in him takes many forms: pride, greed, lust, cruelty, all the qualities which when added up produce what Paul calls "the body of this death" (Rom. 7:24).

If education does not save us, it is not the fault of education, which merely enhances our ability to express ourselves without necessarily changing the selves that we express. This is why an educated crook is vastly more of a hazard

[8] S. L. Brown, *Hosea*, p. 114.

11 I gave thee a king in mine anger, and took *him* away in my wrath.

12 The iniquity of Ephraim *is* bound up; his sin *is* hid.

11 I have given you kings in my anger, and I have taken them away in my wrath.

12 The iniquity of E'phraim is bound up, his sin is kept in store.

---

11. From the form of the Hebrew verbs it is plain that the words do not refer to the establishment of Jeroboam as the first king of Israel after Solomon's death, or to that of Saul as the first king of Israel, or to the removal of Hoshea or another at the time of the kingdom's decline and fall. Rather the reference is to the numerous dynastic changes in Hosea's own days. Since the verbs should be regarded as iteratives, the fitting translation would be:

> I have given you kings in my anger,
> and I have taken them away in my wrath.

5. The Possibility of Revival for Ephraim (13:12-14)

12. Nothing of the evil that Ephraim had done will be forgotten; it **is kept in store** against the day of reckoning. The idea here expressed is that of a book of remembrance in which the deeds of men are recorded and out of which they will eventually be judged (cf. Dan. 7:10; Rev. 20:12).

---

to society than the crook whose wit allows him to do nothing more than steal chickens.

If science does not save us, that is no fault of science. For science is wholly neutral. It deserves neither blame nor praise. It would be just as foolish to blame the revolver for the death of a murdered man as it would be to praise the surgeon's knife for the life of a patient. Science is nothing more or less than a tool. It can be used to save man only as man himself is saved; otherwise its uses are diabolical.

If politics cannot save us, that is no fault of politics. Politics is nothing more or less than what politicians make it. If an unprincipled man enters politics, there is nothing in politics as such to change him. Politics only gives him a wider scope for graft and greed. That is why some international political organization, though the best hope of man in his effort to bring order out of the chaotic condition of his life, cannot of itself achieve its goal. Organizations cannot unite people who have not the will to unity in their hearts. Unity is not mechanical but spiritual. Differences in culture, race, or language are no bar to unity if the spirit of unity is present. At Pentecost the Galileans began to speak in many different languages. But this diversity did not increase divisions; it merely enlarged and enriched the sense of unity experienced by the group. If differences are no bar to unity, then conversely, outward similarities are no guarantee of it. On the plains of Shinar the people, all of whom spoke the same language, which was regarded

as a mark of solidarity and strength, began to build a tower. But the end was Babel. Despite their similarity, the end was confusion of tongues. The causes of unity and discord are within. **Where now is your king [politics], to save you?** (Vs. 10.) Man needs salvation from self. An unregenerate self is not redeemed by education, science, or politics; rather it may use these as agents to further its evil ends. It is as impossible for a man to save himself from himself or by himself as to lift himself by his bootstraps. Man's salvation is in God. **Where now is your king, to save you?** Nowhere. The king also needs to be saved. "Besides me there is no savior" (vs. 4*b*).

12. The Stored-Up Sin.—It is a terrifying thought that one's **sin is kept in store.** A passage in Job is even more explicit: "My transgression is sealed up in a bag, and thou sewest up mine iniquity" (Job 14:17). How one wishes that the bag in which our sins are sewed up had large holes in it so that they could slip through, or that the storehouse of our iniquity would be broken into, robbed, and left empty! For this is one of the paradoxes of sin: we enjoy it as an experience but despise it as a memory. Many sins are pleasant to commit but as the writer of Proverbs said about overindulgence in wine, "At the last it biteth like a serpent, and stingeth like an adder" (23:32).

Why is it that God has so ordered the universe that our sins are **kept in store?** We do not knowingly store up bad or worthless articles. The strongboxes in banks contain our valuables, the possessions we treasure. We do not know-

| 13 The sorrows of a travailing woman shall come upon him: he *is* an unwise son; for he should not stay long in *the place of* the breaking forth of children. | 13 The pangs of childbirth come for him, but he is an unwise son; for now he does not present himself at the mouth of the womb. |

13. This verse introduces a very unexpected figure. Ephraim is often described in Hosea as an unfaithful wife, once as a son (11:1); but here it is likened to a child about to come to the birth. Such a thought must be connected with the description of the nation as spiritually dead (vs. 1). This verse therefore makes the notable assertion that there might have been a spiritual revival for it, a rebirth, a new beginning. Nothing is to be gained by seeking to discover the occasion of such a possibility of revival. Hosea taught that even though Ephraim had so seriously sinned, yet it could find life anew; but in the event Ephraim was as an infant that had not the strength to come to the birth. The verse speaks therefore not only of the patience, but also of the boundless grace of God who was willing that such a faithless child should find new life. The Hebrew of the second part of the verse cannot be in order, but emendation is simple; we may read with the RSV, **for now [כעת] he does not present himself at the mouth of the womb**

ingly store up that which brings pain, evil, distress. Perhaps if we could enjoy the pleasures of sin without the painful aftereffects, we should never want to cease from sinning. Surely the difficulties and hardships that result from our violation of the laws and disregard of the love of God should be a deterrent. Does the Roman Catholic confessional with its offer of forgiveness through penance and by the priest tend to remove too easily the **store** of sin and so encourage its commission? The sin that is **kept in store** as a buried complex can be removed, but not simply by the psychiatrist. His help is unquestionably beneficent as far as it goes. But the forgiveness we seek is beyond the power of man to bestow, whether he is priest or psychiatrist. For both priest and psychiatrist as men need forgiveness, as does the penitent who seeks it at their hands. In all our evil ultimately God is involved—"Against thee, thee only, have I sinned," said the Psalmist (51:4). He continues: "There is forgiveness with thee, that thou mayest be feared" (130:4). The clean heart and right spirit are the gifts of God to the truly penitent.

13. Human Stupidity the Obstacle to Man's Deliverance.—In this vivid picture Hosea describes Ephraim's dilemma. "His sin is kept in store" (vs. 12) because he will not face the possibility of a new birth. He is like "a senseless babe" (Moffatt) who makes impossible its own delivery. So Ephraim assumes an attitude, adopts a spirit, that makes it impossible for the cleansing, renewing, re-creating power of God to operate. The part that man plays in working out his salvation is relatively small but indispensable. It is said that only 5 per cent of the energy expended in producing a crop of wheat comes from man. The other 95 per cent is nature taking advantage of the chance the

farmer gives it. In our dealings with the physical universe we have made amazing progress. This is because we have learned the secret—the submission of our will to the will of nature, not the imposing of our will upon nature. A scientific law is a description of the way nature works, not of the way man thinks nature ought to work. "Sit down before the fact as a little child, be prepared to give up every preconceived notion, follow humbly wherever and to whatever nature leads, or you shall learn nothing." [1] The new world that science has wrought has been made possible because man has adopted the right attitude toward nature. He has thus been able to release her latent powers, to unlock her secrets, and so to make available her great resources of power. From the standpoint of science man is not like a senseless babe who makes impossible his emergence into a new and larger life.

But in the realm of the spirit? Here there is a new world possible, too, through a new birth. Here too are resources of power, available to transform the spiritual deserts and make them, no less than the material ones, to "rejoice, and blossom as the rose" (Isa. 35:1). But here also there is a secret, the same one the scientist uses—the submission of our will to the will of God. "One grain of sand can clog delicate mechanism, and one cherished grudge unconfessed can spoil a prayer." [2] And one besetting sin indulged can, like a senseless babe, keep the flowing tide of God's grace from the soul and make impossible the soul's rebirth.

The new world of science without the new birth of man makes human life today more

[1] Thomas Huxley, quoted by Harry Emerson Fosdick, *The Meaning of Faith* (New York: Association Press, 1917), p. 159.
[2] Buttrick, *Prayer*, p. 210.

14 I will ransom them from the power of the grave; I will redeem them from death: O death, I will be thy plagues; O grave, I will be thy destruction: repentance shall be hid from mine eyes.

14 Shall I ransom them from the power of Sheol?
     Shall I redeem them from Death?
     O Death, where*q* are your plagues?
     O Sheol, where*q* is your destruction?
     Compassion is hid from my eyes.

q Gk Syr: Heb *I will be*

(lit., "at the [place of the] breaking forth of children"), or "for in his time [כעתו] he does not present himself. . . ."

14. The key to the interpretation of this verse must be found in its last phrase: **Compassion is hid from my eyes.** Surely these words must mean that God can show no more mercy; Ephraim must pay the penalty. The interpretation of the rest of the verse must be in keeping with that; therefore it is necessary to accept the rendering of the RSV, which makes the first part of the verse into interrogative clauses, expecting a negative answer. It is notable that in order to retain these clauses as promising redemption, Sellin has to translate נחם in the final clause as "grudge," and Weiser has to render it as "vengeance." Ephraim cannot now be saved; he is spiritually dead, beyond the power of recovery. In the second part of the verse the KJV is unintelligible, but it is based upon the M.T. as it has come down to us. The LXX comes to our aid and the emendation required is very simple (איה for אהי in both its occurrences); and there is no doubt that the force of

> **O Death, where are your plagues?**
> **O Sheol, where is your destruction?** (cf. I Cor. 15:15)

is

> Come with your plagues, O Death.
> Come with your destruction, O Sheol.

It has sometimes been suggested that the final part of the verse should be read in close conjunction with the opening of vs. 15, thus:

> Compassion is hidden from my eyes,
> because Ephraim causes separation among brethren.

But in view of what is said in the preceding verses, that seems a very feeble reason for the cessation of God's compassion; and in addition, such a translation of vs. 15a, based upon a textual emendation, misses the wordplay on the name Ephraim.

fraught with danger than ever. The assumption that science can save us is now quite largely an exploded myth; the belief that man, natural man, can save himself is an unwarranted hope. The assurance that man, co-operating with God, following the way God has revealed, accepting his proffered salvation, can be born anew is our only sure ground for hope. "Work out your own salvation, . . . for it is God which worketh in you" (Phil. 2:12-13).

14. Israel's Hopeless Plight.—Perhaps nowhere does Hosea's picture of the doom which awaits an unrepentant Israel seem any darker than in this verse. His words sound like the tolling of a bell over a nation that is hopelessly lost. Israel by its folly "lies in the way of its own redemption, . . . Shall God then step in

and work a deliverance on the brink of death? Nay, let Death and Sheol have their way." [3]

Paul apparently took a more optimistic view of this verse. From it he drew his great war cry uttered in defiance of death: "O death, where is thy sting? O grave, where is thy victory?" (I Cor. 15:55.) As spoken by Hosea, however, the words breathed not defiance but defeat: **Compassion is hid from my eyes.**

This is not a challenge to Death and Sheol, made by one who knows that their *plagues* and *pestilence* can do no harm, since Jahveh is about to deliver Ephraim, but a command to Death and Sheol to do their worst="Hither with thy plagues, O Death, with thy pestilence, O Sheol!" [4]

[3] George Adam Smith, *The Twelve Prophets*, I, 334.
[4] S. L. Brown, *Hosea*, p. 115.

15 ¶ Though he be fruitful among *his* brethren, an east wind shall come, the wind of the LORD shall come up from the wilderness, and his spring shall become dry, and his fountain shall be dried up: he shall spoil the treasure of all pleasant vessels.

16 Samaria shall become desolate; for she hath rebelled against her God: they shall fall by the sword: their infants shall be dashed in pieces, and their women with child shall be ripped up.

15 Though he may flourish as the reed plant,[r]
the east wind, the wind of the LORD, shall come,
rising from the wilderness;
and his fountain shall dry up,
his spring shall be parched;
it shall strip his treasury
of every precious thing.
16[s] Samar'ia shall bear her guilt,
because she has rebelled against her God;
they shall fall by the sword,
their little ones shall be dashed in pieces,
and their pregnant women ripped open.

[r] Cn: Heb *among brothers*
[s] Heb Ch 14. 1

---

6. EPHRAIM'S DOOM (13:15-16=Hebrew 13:15–14:1)

15. The rendering "although he flourish among his brethren" gives the name Ephraim a narrower connotation (cf. vs. 1) than is normally found in Hosea; for that reason the RSV rendering is preferable (כאחו for the M.T. בן אחים). The **east wind** in Palestine is desolating and destructive. The flow of the verse is greatly improved if the east wind is retained as the subject throughout, thus:

> And it will dry up his fountain
> and parch his spring;
> it will strip his treasury
> of every pleasant thing.

The east wind referred to is not actually the wind of the desert but the Assyrian invader who will be the instrument of the Lord's anger. The LXX has "he will strip his land" (i.e., ארצו for אוצר) ; but there is no advantage in that.

16. Samaria shall bear her guilt is very fitting sense; it is also possible to translate as "Samaria shall be desolated" (i.e., ישׁם=יאשׁם: LXX, ἀφανισθήσεται; cf. 10:2). The nature of the disaster which is described as being in store is one which will destroy not only the guilty people, but also the rising generation and even children before they come to birth (cf. 10:14; Amos 1:13; II Kings 15:16). It appears therefore to be a message of doom unlit by any ray of hope.

15-16. The Ultimate Doom.—Were there any doubt as to the meaning of vs. 14, the two verses that conclude the chapter would dispel such doubt. Hosea, this prophet of love, whose spirit could be as gentle as a child's, could paint as despairing and dismal a picture of the tragedy of sin as the sternest of the prophets. What more desolate future could a nation confront than the one portrayed here? Israel shall wither away. He may seem as flourishing and luxuriant as a reed plant in the water, but a wind, **the wind of the LORD,** coming from the east—Assyria—will dry him up; not only his plants but the very fountains and springs from which they grow **shall be parched.** The desolation will not be temporary, so that next year new plants can be set out—for the very springs will go dry. The source of fertility will be destroyed. Israel's wealth and costly treasures will also be removed, that which she most values. But Hosea does not stop there. Not only will her agriculture be destroyed, the plants and springs; not alone her commercial power, her wealth and costly treasures; but human life also: **They shall fall by the sword: their infants shall be dashed in pieces, and their women with child shall be ripped up.** Here is a picture of complete destruction and disaster.

14 O Israel, return unto the Lord thy God; for thou hast fallen by thine iniquity.

14 Return, O Israel, to the Lord your God,
for you have stumbled because of your iniquity.

III. Call to Repentance and Promise of Forgiveness and Renewal (14:1-9)
A. Take with You Words (14:1-3=Hebrew 14:2-4)

The words in 13:14 have a sound of finality about them: "Compassion is hid from my eyes." It appeared that nothing could ransom Ephraim from Sheol, nothing redeem them from death. Now there is a sudden change. Some scholars regard it as unexpected, and they are driven to the conclusion that this final chapter is not from the prophet Hosea. Yet, 11:8-9 and 13:13, for example, are not without hope for Ephraim, not indeed in terms of Ephraim's reform, but in terms of God's love; and 2:15-23 comes to mind with its promise of restoration and renewal. The alternations between declarations of punishment dire and inevitable, and promises of mercy and renewal, cannot be explained as evidence of the prophet's changing moods; that is to underrate the problem. Whether this chapter is regarded as authentic or not must depend in large measure upon the interpretation we are persuaded to put upon chs. 1-3 (see Intro., pp. 559-60).

14:1. Israel had been guilty of turning away from God, of what the KJV calls "backsliding" (vs. 4). That is an unfortunate description, suggesting accidental slips

Is it overdrawn? Can man's continued and determined resistance to reason, conscience, and love—the voice of God to his soul—lead to his ultimate annihilation? Are they who predict the well-nigh complete destruction of man through his abuse and misuse of power, are they true prophets of doom? Time will tell.

14:1. Where Do We Go from Here?—That question is asked when one has reached the end of a course, or a point in his course at which further movement in the same direction seems unwise or futile. This experience comes to individuals as it does to groups. It may be induced by conditions or circumstances that have become unbearable or intolerable, by some moral or spiritual crisis in which we are involved. Under such circumstances a change becomes imperative.

The same experience comes also to groups. Nations often encounter crises in their careers which necessitate drastic changes of policy or procedure. Under such circumstances there are doctors aplenty with their prescriptions—political, economic, social. The Christian religion too has an answer. Israel had now reached a crisis in its history, and the question might well have been asked, "Where do we go from here?" The prophet, as though he were answering that question, said: **O Israel, return unto the Lord thy God; for thou hast fallen by thine iniquity.** His answer rings the bell on human responsibility. "You have gone away, now you must come back." In a crisis the spirit of fatalism crops up. We tend to assume that we are in the hands of some cruel fate which has decreed our downfall, and that we are quite

impotent to avert it. We act as though we were on some sort of cosmic escalator which willy-nilly is taking us down to our destruction. Hosea's word refutes that. The prophet insists that man is a responsible being. He may work out his own salvation, or his own destruction, but in either case it is he who works it out. Man is responsible; the choice is his. C. S. Lewis says there are ultimately two kinds of people in the world. There are those who say to God, "Thy will be done," and there are those to whom God says, "Thy will be done." **O Israel, return unto the Lord thy God; for thou hast fallen by thine iniquity.** It is not fate that has brought you to this condition. It is your own evil choices that have done so. You do not need to fall headlong over the precipice. You can stop. You can return to the Lord your God. Israel, you are morally responsible.

Equally penetrating is Hosea's insight into human inadequacy. The trouble with you, Israel, is that somewhere along the way you got smart and thought you could go it alone; you wanted to run your own show; but the truth is that you are not able to. Therefore, **return unto the Lord thy God.** "O Lord, I know that the way of man is not in himself: it is not in man that walketh to direct his steps" (Jer. 10:23). You are not wise enough, O Israel, or strong enough, or good enough. Recognize your finiteness, your limitations, your creaturehood. *Man's Own Show* was the title of a once popular best seller. Most people would no doubt agree that if there were a cosmic censor, he would often be justified in closing the show. It is such a grim and nasty one.

2 Take with you words, and turn to the Lord: say unto him, Take away all iniquity,

2 Take with you words
and return to the Lord;
say to him,
"Take away all iniquity;
accept that which is good

---

in the course of a purposeful attempt to reach the goal. The sins of which Israel had been guilty were not such slips; they were rather a willful turning of the back upon the goal of all their true endeavoring and true service, and a turning aside to Baal. Now the invitation comes again to return and to find the right path (cf. 12:6). The statement that Israel had **stumbled** because of their **iniquity** seems very weak; surely we must regard the verb as indicating at least the ruin which is the consequence of the stumbling. The verse affirms that Israel's sufferings and ruin had been occasioned not by their political misfortunes but by their sin. They must therefore return to him against whom they have sinned, in order that the old relationship may be restored. If any situation is to be remedied, there is no use attacking with a hopeful therapeutic what are only symptoms of the trouble; the radical cause must be tackled. **Return, O Israel, to the Lord your God.**

2. **Take with you words:** I.e., do not take with you lambs and rams for sacrificial offerings, as you have been wont to do for Baal, but take words. Now that might mean

---

The command to return is not winsome. It is a command. The theological equivalent is repent. Dwight L. Moody once said that the best definition of repentance he ever heard was given by a soldier. Someone asked him how he was converted. He replied, "The Lord said to me, Halt! Attention! Rightabout-face! March!" [5] The "about-face" is the difficult part. A motorist who discovers himself on a wrong road hates to be told that he must drive back ten miles to get on the right one. The trip back seems such a waste of time and gasoline. We hate to double back on our tracks. We feel that if we keep going in the same direction, but at an accelerated speed, we shall be more likely to arrive. This is one of the deceptions of sin. We have prayed for peace. Everybody agrees that peace is a desired goal, but we have thought that the road which leads to peace was called "preparation for war." This has not brought peace and never can. We ought to turn around and go in another direction; instead, we think that if we accelerate our speed, get faster planes, bigger aircraft carriers, deadlier bombs, and speed up the production of such implements, we shall arrive. There is no reason to believe that we shall. Going faster in a wrong direction simply takes us farther from the desired goal. **Return**—that is the answer.

Surely one reason for believing in God is that we know we live in a universe in which we cannot at long last achieve right results by wrong methods, right destinations by wrong roads. In a moral universe not all roads lead

to Rome. The universe is run in accordance with certain moral principles. If its ultimate nature were blind force and omnipotent matter going it mad, wrong roads might conceivably lead to right destinations. The prodigal who takes a certain road reaches a certain end, and it is impossible for him to reach any other, just as impossible as it is for the prodigal world. **O Israel, return unto the Lord thy God.**

Man finds it hard to return, not only because he hates to admit that he is on the wrong road, but also because he hates to admit that his presence on such a road is due to something wrong in himself, not in somebody else. **Thou hast fallen by thine iniquity.** One of the baffling facts about evil is that as it increases its hold upon man, man's consciousness of its presence in him decreases. Our own age illustrates this. The evidences of sin in our world were never more grim and tragic than now, while the sense of sin was probably never so weak. Iniquity is disharmony. It is being out of tune with the will and purpose of God. Disharmony in our family relationships is due to sin, as is disharmony in our world. But the ultimate source of the trouble is neither in the family nor in the world but in us. Israel will return to God when each Israelite is conscious of his iniquity. Jesus came to show us the way back to God, which is the only way forward. When the prodigal returned, his father ran out to meet him and embraced him. Jesus said that such a returning prodigal would make even the angels in heaven rejoice.

2-3a. Confession.—Genuine repentance is always followed by confession. Without confession the "return to God" becomes spuri-

[5] Stanley I. Stuber and Thomas Curtis Clark, eds., *Treasury of the Christian Faith* (New York: Association Press, 1949), p. 576.

and receive *us* graciously: so will we render
the calves of our lips.

and we will render
the fruit[t] of our lips.

[t] Gk Syr: Heb *bulls*

"take with you mere words," make a profession of penitence, even if your heart knows nothing of it; but the context is against such an interpretation. The meaning must be "take with you words of penitence and acknowledge that the Lord is God indeed." That this is the meaning is confirmed by the remainder of the verse. Weiser (*Das Buch der zwölf kleinen Propheten, ad loc.*) makes the interesting comment: "That the prophet here adopts the form of a liturgical approach shows that he knew, and approved, a Yahweh cult which rested upon a foundation quite different from the material, sacrificial form which grew out of Canaanite roots, and which he opposed. It is the cult in which the central position is held by the Word (God's Word and Prayer)." Concerning the words **return to the Lord,** Martin Buber says: "Hosea sees himself as the prophet of the turning. . . . Hosea has and pronounces a divine promise, the like of which we never hear in Amos, 'I will heal their turnings away' (14.5,EV4). This saying Jeremiah (3.14,22) is to develop to a perfect dialogue: 'Return, O children that turn away, I will heal your turnings away' so YHVH expresses the reciprocal movement, and the people reply: 'Behold us, we have come to Thee.' " (*Prophetic Faith,* pp. 123-24.) **Take away all iniquity** is somewhat stronger than the original Hebrew which does not have an imperative (as in the case of the following verb), but an imperfect form which expresses a desire or a request. The word for **all** is in Hebrew a prosthetic, unaccented form, and is here separated from its related noun **iniquity** by a verbal form. In

---

ous. The proof that our "return" represents a genuine ethical and spiritual experience rather than a vague and pious gesture is measured by our willingness to confess our faults and make a new start. **Take with you words.** We should say, "Take deeds," for actions speak louder than words. "Talk is cheap," we say. In Hosea's time worship had become almost inarticulate—a "dead routine of the legal sacrifices." [6] People followed a religious routine from which all meaning had gone. Religion had become a cut-and-dried performance, barren and bare. The prophet therefore urges a confession which would come voluntarily from the heart.

The Reformation confronted a comparable situation. The reformers "had to grapple with the same mechanical worship of their time," [7] and like Hosea, they said to the people, "Speak out."

So in place of the frozen ritualism of the Church there broke forth from all lands of the Reformation, as though it were birds in spring, a burst of hymns and prayer, with the clear notes of the Gospel in the common tongue. [8]

Of course words may be little more than vain repetition, as Jesus warned; but they may also be, as Hosea hoped, sincere expressions of a penitent spirit. In any event, confession is a

[6] George Adam Smith, *The Twelve Prophets,* I, 369.
[7] *Ibid.*
[8] *Ibid.*

valid and indispensable experience in one's return to God.

"Confession is good for the soul." Indeed it seems to be an essential part of the healing process, for the first step on the road to health is the acknowledgment that one is sick. The sick are never well until they admit their sickness. The best doctor cannot help us unless we know something is wrong with us and are willing to seek his help. The same is true of the Physician of souls. He can do no more for us than the physician of our bodies until we acknowledge our condition. "Father, I have sinned against heaven, and before thee" (Luke 15:18). That was the proof that the prodigal had really returned.

It is no wonder then that in the Christian religion confession is the gateway to spiritual health and healing. Says James: "Confess your faults one to another, and pray one for another, that ye may be healed" (5:16). So Hosea points out the specific sins to which Israel had succumbed: their dependence on man rather than on God—**Assyria shall not save us.**

It is an interesting fact that many of the religious ideas which modern man throws away with one hand he turns around and picks up with the other. Confession is a case in point. Many modern folk profess to have rejected the idea theologically, but they have picked it up psychologically. We do not confess our sins to God, but—as James advises—to one another, that we "may be healed." If anybody would dis-

3 Asshur shall not save us; we will not ride upon horses: neither will we say any	**3** Assyria shall not save us, we will not ride upon horses;

addition, the rhythm of the line would suggest that the word for **all** should be read in the first half line, which would make the use of the word here more notable still. Some scholars have felt these difficulties so acutely that they argue for the reading:

Say to him, all of you [כלכם],
"Take away iniquity."

But that seems hardly necessary; probably we should consider that the unusual order was employed in order to emphasize the word **all. Accept that which is good** (RSV) should be construed as part of the people's plea to God, so that these words are to be taken closely with those which precede. The plea made to God is thus twofold: he is entreated to remove all iniquity and guilt, and to receive the good service which Israel will now render him. **Receive us graciously** (KJV) is dependent upon interpreting the word for **good** as an adverb meaning "well."

So will we render the calves of our lips is an illegitimate translation of the original which is, lit., "And we will render calves our lips." Since these two nouns appear to be in apposition, the simplest translation would appear to be, "So will we render our lips as [our] calves," i.e., we will render as our sacrificial offerings our lips, our words, our praise, our acknowledgments. That is satisfactory sense; the rendering given in the RSV, which also is very suitable, is based upon a slight emendation of the Hebrew (פרים for פרי).

3. The two besetting sins of Israel had been their trust for safety in foreign alliances and their service of the fertility Baals. These sins will be abandoned by repentant Israel. They will now realize that Egypt and Assyria cannot, and have no desire to, save them, and the Baals have no kingdom to claim their regard. This is the beginning of spiritual

cover how widespread is this practice of confession to one another, let him try to make an appointment with a reputable psychiatrist, or let him consider how many trained ministers have turned psychiatrists. But a psychiatrist is not always necessary. Often a trusted friend may do as well.

The Arabs have a very beautiful description of friendship. "A friend," they say, "is one to whom one may pour out all the content of one's heart, chaff and grain together, knowing that the gentlest of hands will take and sift it, keep what is worth keeping, and with the breath of kindness blow the rest away." [9]

The psychological value of this kind of confession is too well known to be argued. It offers relief and healing. Our life is something like the sea, only in reverse. The sea, as has often been suggested, has all its unrest on the surface, where it churns and tosses. But as you explore the depths you find unbroken calm. Human life seems the reverse of that. Many a life on the surface seems calm and unruffled, as though everything were under control. But beneath are tumult, unrest, disquiet. Confession is an at-

tempt to bring the tumult to the surface where it may be met and dealt with. The griefs, the sorrows, the sins that we repress, push back and down, try to keep out of the area of the conscious mind, become after awhile like a boil. The only thing to do with a boil is to have it lanced, to let the poisonous matter run out. There is no other way of healing. If some thorn or splinter is embedded in our flesh, we have it pulled out. To leave it there is to court disaster. So some hidden grudge, the desire for revenge, the burden of remorse for some unconfessed sin, becomes like a splinter in the flesh. It must be pulled out through confession.

Give sorrow words: the grief that does not speak
Whispers the o'er-fraught heart and bids it break.[1]

As Weatherhead has said: "Suppressed sin, like suppressed steam, is dangerous. Confession is the safety-valve. To change the figure again, confession makes the skeleton in the cupboard no longer a thing to be feared, but a mere museum specimen." [2]

Herein lies the appeal of the Roman Catholic Church to multitudes of people—the confessional. Unfortunately, as practiced by that

[9] Leslie D. Weatherhead, *Psychology in Service of the Soul* (New York: The Macmillan Co., 1930), p. 92.

[1] Shakespeare, *Macbeth*, Act IV, scene 3.
[2] *Op. cit.*, p. 88.

| more to the work of our hands, *Ye are our* gods: for in thee the fatherless findeth mercy. | and we will say no more, 'Our God,' to the work of our hands. In thee the orphan finds mercy." |

revival for Israel (cf. 13:13). **We will not ride upon horses** is not to be taken as a reference to trade relations with Egypt, but to the trust Israel had been tempted to place in the horses and chariots of the great powers whose help they had sought. **In thee the orphan finds mercy** does not give an accurate impression of the Hebrew, which begins with a relative for which there is no antecedent in the preceding phrase. The words may therefore be regarded as a later addition, or the suggestion of Harper (*Amos and Hosea*, p. 412) may be adopted—that they should be read at the end of vs. 2. In the latter case it is probable that we should read the phrase as "in whom the upright finds mercy" (תמים for יתום).

church, it leaves much to be desired. Weatherhead writes:

> Our Roman Catholic friends have spoilt the idea of confession for us by making it habitual when it ought to be occasional, by enforcing it when it ought to be spontaneous and voluntary, and by making it, or allowing it to be made, a substitute for real penitence, and thus bringing about a light and loose way of thinking about sin.[3]

Some of the reformers, in order to avoid the obvious weaknesses of the confessional as practiced by the Roman Catholic Church, went to the other extreme and threw out the baby with the bath.

While one need not question the psychological, therapeutic value of confession, of taking the lid off the boiling waters, of lancing the boil, and so bringing relief, can one really stop there? When one has consulted his psychiatrist, his minister, his priest, his friend, is that the end? Is confession, which is psychologically valid, also theologically sound? Can man by himself alone or with the help of man alone

> . . . minister to a mind diseased,
> Pluck from the memory a rooted sorrow,
> Raze out the written troubles of the brain
> And with some sweet oblivious antidote
> Cleanse the stuff'd bosom of that perilous stuff
> Which weighs upon the heart?[4]

Christianity says "No." The prophet says "No." The prophet says, "Return unto the Lord thy God" (vs. 1). The apostle too says "No"; for after urging that we confess our faults to one another he adds, "Pray one for another, that ye may be healed" (Jas. 5:16). Whereupon God comes into the picture. One is not seeking here to put man's part in opposition to God's part. This is not an "either-or" approach, but a "both-and." For the laws of that healing, whether physical or mental, which comes from

human help are God's laws. Therefore the inadequacy of keeping confession purely on a human plane—to one another—is obvious.

What are we seeking when we confess our sins? Forgiveness. We have a hurt conscience that needs healing; but how can we seek forgiveness at the hands of mortal man when the very thing we ask from him is the thing he himself needs? He stands with us in the same condemnation. There is profound insight in the ancient Jewish day of Atonement. On this particular day the high priest, who ordinarily would appear in his priestly robes, would lay them aside and appear as a needy suppliant.

> He brought a "sin offering," first for himself and the priesthood, and then for the people. . . . No *man* can say, "I forgive you." He can say only, "I forgive you, as I ought, within the measure of my power." If any leader, even the high priest, should shout, "I hereby cleanse your conscience of dead works," we would answer at least silently, "Who, then, will cleanse you?"[5]

Moreover, the inadequacy of human forgiveness alone becomes clearly evident when we consider our corporate sins. Armistice Day reminds us of this. Surely this is a day for penitence. Were we penitent, to whom should we confess—just to one another? Here if anywhere we are conscious with Emerson of the silent Third Partner in all our transactions. In our corporate sins man is not just sinning against man, hurting himself. He is rather sinning against the creative life that inheres in the universe, against God, destroying the pattern of beauty and goodness and truth which God has envisioned for man. "Return to God and confess to him," says the prophet. The fact that after the experience of two world wars with their incredible horror we began talking excitedly and planning feverishly for a third proves our seemingly complete lack of penitence. And without penitence there can be

---

[3] *Ibid.*, p. 82.
[4] Shakespeare, *op. cit.*, Act V, scene 3.

[5] Buttrick, *Prayer*, p. 212.

4 ¶ I will heal their backsliding, I will love them freely: for mine anger is turned away from him.

5 I will be as the dew unto Israel: he shall grow as the lily, and cast forth his roots as Lebanon.

4 I will heal their faithlessness;
  I will love them freely,
    for my anger has turned from them.
5 I will be as the dew to Israel;
  he shall blossom as the lily,
    he shall strike root as the poplar;[u]

[u] Cn: Heb *Lebanon*

B. THE LORD'S RESPONSE (14:4-8=Hebrew 14:5-9)

These verses contain the Lord's response to Israel's penitent cry. Israel had to make the first move; the first step in redemption had to be their return to the Lord from whom they had strayed so seriously. But when they manifested their willingness to return, the Lord was ready to receive and save them in order that the bondage of sin might be broken. Therefore the first word is of healing.

4. Faithlessness is like a disease (cf. Isa. 1:6); healing is therefore required. If Israel can be healed of this disease, the harlot spirit that formerly possessed them will be conquered and they will be cleansed of all their evil. Thereafter comes the great promise, **I will love them freely.** This is not a love which is the reward of any merit on Israel's part; it is the expression of God's grace and of that alone; it is a freewill gift on his part. Nevertheless, Israel cannot receive this love without the precedent experience of penitence; but this outpouring of the love of God will confirm and fulfill the healing work and complete the spiritual renewal of his people.

5. In 13:3 **the dew** is mentioned as type of things transitory and passing; here it is that which refreshes and renews life. The lilies of the field, or anemones, grow profusely

---

no healing. The psychiatrist who works with the laws of God can bring us help. The trusted friend to whom we unburden our heart can bring relief. But psychiatrist and friend are alike fellow mortals, human beings like us. In the long last the soul confronts God, in whom alone are adequate forgiveness and healing. "I will arise and go to my father, and will say unto him, Father, I have sinned against heaven, and before thee" (Luke 15:18). In this, if genuine, are pardon and peace.

4. The Healing Forces of God.—After repentance and confession come forgiveness, restoration, healing. The healing does not remove the scars—they remain—but it removes the hurt, the sense of guilt.

> Wounded, yet healed; sin-laden yet forgiven;
> And sure Thy goodness is my only heaven.[6]

The healing powers are ever present. If the body is hurt, nature rushes all her resources to the damaged spot—the white corpuscles to prevent infection, the clotting mechanism of the blood, but for which we would bleed to death. But the soul needs healing as much as does the body. Its wounds are not always visible to our eyes; they are always visible to the eyes of God. The fact that the wounds of the soul are not external and publicly seen makes the sickness

[6] Stopford A. Brooke, "Immortal Love, within whose righteous will," st. iv. Used by permission of Miss Honor Brooke.

of the soul more serious than that of the body. The body itself bears this out. Wounds on the surface, while they are bloody and may appear grave, are for the most part not nearly so damaging as diseases that attack some organ within. Outwardly a man may seem healthy; until one day perhaps an operation discloses some hidden ailment, unseen and undetected, that may cost him his life. No one sees the sin-sick soul except as the damaging effects of the sin manifest themselves in the deterioration of character.

All healing forces work slowly. Those that are destructive make the front page. They are spectacular. The devastation wrought on Hiroshima by the atomic bomb was immediate and vivid. A tree produced by nature in a hundred years can be felled in a hundred minutes, with a thundering roar through the silent forest. The healing forces, like growth, are silent, gradual, unspectacular, and vastly more significant. The most tragic effect of evil is that it can destroy so quickly what man co-operating with God has built up, often through a long, slow process. In twenty-four hours of reckless living one may lose the results of years of training and disciplined effort. But God is on the side of the redemptive forces. He works in us and with us. "Who forgiveth all thine iniquities; who healeth all thy diseases" (Ps. 103:3).

5a. God the Refresher and Beautifier of Life.
—In this verse, which reveals the prophet's love

| 6 His branches shall spread, and his beauty shall be as the olive tree, and his smell as Lebanon. | 6 his shoots shall spread out; his beauty shall be like the olive, and his fragrance like Lebanon. |

in Palestine, and the comparison refers to the rich profusion of their growth as well as to their beauty. **And cast forth his roots as Lebanon** is doubtful. The Hebrews could speak of a mountain as deeply rooted (cf. Job 28:9), but the figure required here is one of living growth and vigorous vitality, so the comparison to a mountain is not likely. For that reason the rendering in the RSV should be followed; the change it necessitates in the original is small (לבנה for לבנון).

6. This verse continues the figure of the living tree which will rise up in strength and beauty. **His shoots shall spread out** in vigorous life. The beauty of the **olive tree** is well known; the profusion of its slender leaves gives it a most attractive appearance.

of nature, Hosea continues his discussion of God's benefactions to a repentant Israel. The picture, in the presence of life's tragic actualities, may seem illusory or utopian. Yet if the tormented boy at the foot of the Mount of Transfiguration represents reality, the beauty and wonder on the mountaintop are no less real; more real, we maintain, because more in line with the nature, purpose, and will of God as revealed in Christ, who came to bring abundant life. The impulse that enables man to trace the rainbow through the rain, to preach the kingdom of God in the midst of a pagan world, to envision the city of God when the world is tottering, is a God-given impulse. Should man lose his vision, hope would die, and with the death of hope the very purpose in living. So Hosea, seeing clearly the actualities of his age, looks beyond to the possibilities, from present evil to future good; in a word, from man to God, from sin to redemptive grace.

He sees a redeemed earth. He pictures it through symbols taken from the nature he loved—God **will be as the dew to Israel.** The word **dew** is used to suggest not transitoriness, as it does in 6:4 or 13:3, but the kindly provision whereby vegetation is protected from drying winds or rainless days. So God will be the source of Israel's refreshment.

As torrents in summer,
Half dried in their channels
Suddenly rise, though the
Sky is still cloudless,
For rain has been falling
Far off at their fountains;

So hearts that are fainting
Grow full to o'erflowing,
And they that behold it
Marvel, and know not
That God at their fountains
Far off has been raining! [7]

[7] Longfellow, *Tales of a Wayside Inn*, "The Nun of Nidaros."

Israel will **blossom as the lily.** The lily in Palestine is not only beautiful but profuse. Life as we know it today is too often a drab and ugly affair. Sin takes the bloom from us. In a certain sense sin is another word for ugliness. Greed disfigures our highway with ugly signs, pollutes our rivers, denudes our forests. Thoughtless or careless selfishness is responsible for most forest fires which each year convert lovely areas into scorched and barren wastes. The slums of our cities, marked by congestion and uncleanness within and without, are ugly blotches on our civilization. The expression of bitterness, greed, lust, or revenge, which sometimes marks the human face, is contrary to the will and purpose of God, who loves beauty. "They looked unto him, and were lightened: and their faces were not ashamed" (Ps. 34:5). Beauty is of the very nature of the Eternal. The God who created sunsets and flowers and bright-colored birds, the star-studded skies and silver-crested waves, the human form with all its graceful movements, and the face of a saint at prayer, made life to be beautiful. "And let the beauty of the LORD our God be upon us" (Ps. 90:17).

5b. Rooted and Grounded.—Israel will be well anchored—rooted. He will not be like the seed in the parable, cast in shallow soil where there is not much depth of earth; the seed that sends up leaves quickly and as quickly withers away. His roots will go down and find nourishment deep in the earth, and so remain green when the surface plants wither and die. "And he shall be like a tree planted by the rivers of water, . . . his leaf also shall not wither" (Ps. 1:3).

6a. The Hospitality of God.—"The birds of the air come and lodge in the branches thereof" (Matt. 13:32). "Many shall come from the east and west, and shall sit down with Abraham, and Isaac, and Jacob" (Matt. 8:11). "The leaves of the tree were for the healing of the nations" (Rev. 22:2). These and similar pas-

7 They that dwell under his shadow shall return; they shall revive *as* the corn, and grow as the vine: the scent thereof *shall be* as the wine of Lebanon.

7 They shall return and dwell beneath my[v] shadow,
    they shall flourish as a garden;[w]
they shall blossom as the vine,
    their fragrance shall be like the wine of Lebanon.

[v] Heb *his*
[w] Cn: Heb *they shall grow grain*

The fragrance of **Lebanon** was derived from the coniferous trees, especially the cedars, and from the aromatic plants to be found there (cf. Song of S. 4:11; Ecclus. 39:14). There seems no need at all to accept the proposal of Ehrlich that we should read "incense" instead of Lebanon (לבנה for לבנון; *Randglossen zur hebräischen Bibel,* V, 211).

7. Once again the figures used are such as to indicate growth and vitality. The KJV gives a literal rendering of the first phrase, but it is not clear who they are who shall return and dwell under Israel's shadow. It seems necessary to make a slight emendation in the Hebrew (וישבו for ישבי, and בצלי for בצלו) and read, **They** [Israel] **shall return and dwell beneath my shadow;** i.e., they shall once more dwell beneath the Lord's shadow, under his protecting care; the old order will be resumed; the old relationship will be restored. The following phrase is, lit., **they shall grow grain;** and if the next verb is read as a causative, we get the parallel saying "they will make the vine to flourish." These two phrases taken thus would signify that the restored people would enjoy the fruits of the land, the very fruits which they had tried to secure for themselves by their service of Baal. It is more likely that the words were more general in their description of Israel's prosperity and welfare; by a slight emendation, therefore, we may read "they shall flourish like the corn" (כדגן) or **as a garden** (כגן), in which case the next phrase may follow as in the RSV, **they shall blossom as the vine;** but rhythmic form demands a line division as follows:

> They shall blossom as the vine whose fragrance
> shall be like that of the wine of Lebanon.

Alternatively we may, as Procksch suggests in Kittel's *Biblia Hebraica,* consider that the Hebrew word זכרו is a corruption of a place name, so the original form of the lines was:

> They shall blossom as the vine of . . .
> and as the wine of Lebanon.

The weakness of that suggestion lies in the fact that to blossom like the vine is a fitting figure, but to blossom like wine is not.

It is notable that Israel, which had fallen away from faithfulness to the Lord through the seductions of nature worship as exemplified in the service of the Baals, is now promised

---

sages suggest the **shoots . . . spread out,** offering a resting place for the winged creatures, and shade for man and beast.

> There's a wideness in God's mercy,
>   Like the wideness of the sea;
> There's a kindness in his justice,
>   Which is more than liberty.
>
> .   .   .   .   .   .
>
> For the love of God is broader
>   Than the measure of man's mind,
> And the heart of the Eternal
>   Is most wonderfully kind.[8]

[8] Frederick William Faber.

7a. Times of Renewal.—This is reminiscent of the word of Isaiah: "And a man shall be as a hiding place from the wind, and a covert from the tempest; as rivers of water in a dry place, as the shadow of a great rock in a weary land" (Isa. 32:2). The great rock casts its shadow on the sun-baked desert, and beneath it the tired traveler wearied by his journey rests. So the psalmist: "He that dwelleth in the secret place of the most High shall abide under the shadow of the Almighty" (Ps. 91:1).

In the Christian sense, however, there is more than physical renewal suggested here. In his in-

8 Ephraim *shall say*, What have I to do any more with idols? I have heard *him,* and observed him: I *am* like a green fir tree. From me is thy fruit found.

9 Who *is* wise, and he shall understand these *things?* prudent, and he shall know

8 O E′phraim, what have I to do with idols?
  it is I who answer and look after you.ˣ
I am like an evergreen cypress,
  from me comes your fruit.

9 Whoever is wise, let him understand these
    things;
  whoever is discerning, let him know
    them;

ˣ Heb *him*

a newness of life and strength described under figures drawn from nature, such as the stability and beauty of a tree, the attractiveness of a garden, and the bountiful vitality of corn and wine. It must have been a highly significant way of saying that the Lord would fulfill all their need.

8. In the first part of the verse both the KJV and RSV express the same sense in different ways. The suggestion has been made that this verse is antiphonal in form, thus:

EPHRAIM: "What have I to do with idols?"
GOD: "I answer him and I will watch over him."
EPHRAIM: "I am like an evergreen cypress."
GOD: "From me your fruit comes."

There are other examples of antiphonal address in Hebrew literature without any specific indication of change of speaker (e.g., Isa. 40:6-8); and since the speakers in the preceding verses are God and Israel, the antiphonal structure of this final verse may be considered as difficult but possible. The alternative is to do as has been done in the RSV, which has been compelled to make two alterations in pronominal usage; but it is doubtful if the figure of an evergreen cypress would be applied to God. **It is I who answer and look after him** (RSV mg.) is a good rendering, in which the verbs are taken as present, to indicate the Lord's unchanging purposes. "I have answered him and I will look after him" is also possible and fits the context; and many scholars, by a slight adjustment of the text, get the rendering: "It was I who afflicted him, but I will restore him" (עניתיו ואשובבנו), or "I am his Anath and his Asherah" (ענתו ואשרתו).

C. POSTSCRIPT (14:9=Hebrew 14:10)

9. This verse is manifestly written in the style of the Hebrew gnomic literature and is commonly regarded as a later addition to the book, to point the moral and to give an admonition. It is difficult to believe that it comes to us from the prophet himself. It calls for reflection upon the teaching of the book that its lessons may be learned. It

vitation to the weary Jesus said, "Come unto me, . . . and I will give . . . rest unto your souls" (Matt. 11:28-29). This is the rest that comes from a new awareness of God, his love, his power—the God who is able to do exceeding abundantly. We are kept from being weary in well-doing when we remember that we are laborers with God. It is God who works in us, to will and to do (cf. Phil. 2:13).

9. The Conclusion of the Matter.—This verse is an epilogue (see Exeg.). It points the moral of the entire book. Hosea again and again has shown that man lives in a moral universe, that God governs through his righteous laws which cannot be broken with impunity. **The ways of**

the LORD are right, . . . transgressors stumble in them. The final appeal is to the **wise,** the men of sense: **Whoever is wise, let him understand these things.** The wise are not merely the "educated." Wisdom is a rarer possession than knowledge. It does not come just from books. Amazing how spiritually insensible and morally dull many educated folk are! Jesus said his contemporaries could predict the weather, master the visible, material aspects of reality, but could not understand the signs of the times, the invisible and imponderable (cf. Matt. 16:3).

What can we not "predict" today? We can read nature like a book. We have unveiled her hidden secrets. Of what real use is our knowl-

| them? for the ways of the Lord *are* right, and the just shall walk in them: but the transgressors shall fall therein. | for the ways of the Lord are right, and the upright walk in them, but transgressors stumble in them. |

finishes with the protestation that **the ways of the Lord are right.** The word **right** means straight, undeviating, free from deceit and guile. The ways of the Lord are described as straight because, his demands being constant and his actions and decrees free from arbitrary vacillations, the ways in which those who are obedient to him must go are straight and undeviating; but the unrighteous, who are not obedient to his demands, **stumble in them** (cf. vs. 1; Ps. 19:8; Prov. 4:11-12; Jer. 31:9; *et al.*).

edge if we do not know what to do with it? No wonder the book of Hosea closes with an appeal to the wise, for only the wise, those who use not merely sight but insight, are able to comprehend moral reality and to understand that in the things not seen and eternal lies the key to man's salvation. For the eternal verities are guaranteed by the reality of God, who deals justly with all. **The upright walk in them, but transgressors stumble.** In God is our hope. May he who "also is wise" (Isa. 31:2) make us wise!

The Book of
JOEL

Introduction and Exegesis by JOHN A. THOMPSON
Exposition by NORMAN F. LANGFORD

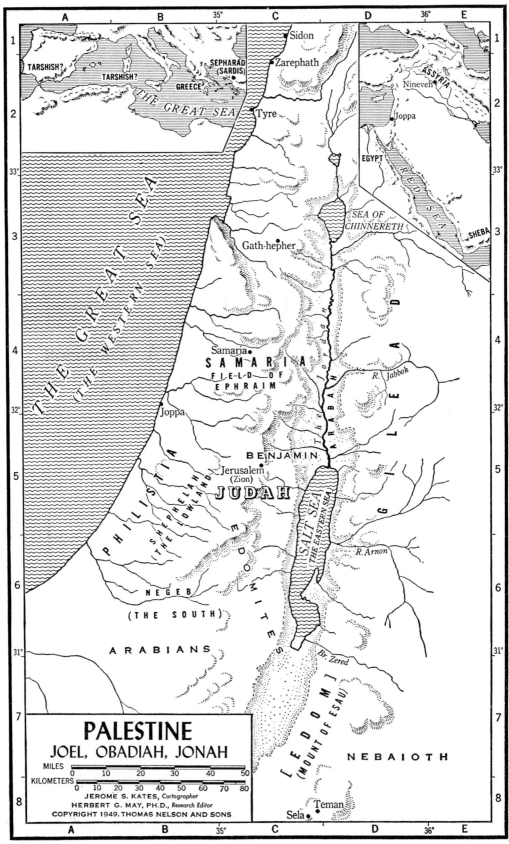

A B 35° C D 36° E

1 TARSHISH? TARSHISH? SEPHARAD (SARDIS) GREECE Sidon Zarephath Nineveh ASSYRIA 1

THE GREAT SEA Tyre Joppa 2

33° EGYPT RED SEA 33°

THE GREAT SEA (THE WESTERN SEA) SEA OF CHINNERETH SHEBA 3

Gath-hepher 3

4 Samaria SAMARIA FIELD OF EPHRAIM R. Jabbok GILEAD 4

32° Joppa The Jordan 32°

BENJAMIN 5

5 Jerusalem (Zion) JUDAH PHILISTIA SHEPHELAH (THE LOWLAND) EDOMITES SALT SEA (THE EASTERN SEA) R. Arnon 5

6 NEGEB (THE SOUTH) Br. Zered 6

31° ARABIANS 31°

7 [EDOM] (MOUNT OF ESAU) NEBAIOTH 7

PALESTINE
JOEL, OBADIAH, JONAH

MILES 0 10 20 30 40 50
KILOMETERS 0 10 20 30 40 50 60 70 80

JEROME S. KATES, *Cartographer*
HERBERT G. MAY, PH.D., *Research Editor*
COPYRIGHT 1949. THOMAS NELSON AND SONS

8 Sela Teman 8

A B 35° C D 36° E

JOEL

INTRODUCTION

Twelve other men in the Old Testament from the time of Samuel to Nehemiah have the name Joel, "Yahweh is God." The name of the prophet's father in the Masoretic Text, "Pethuel," is found only here, and perhaps for this reason the Septuagint and Peshitta read "Bethuel" (cf. Gen. 22:22-23).

I. Author

Extrabiblical traditions about Joel are few and untrustworthy; the only reliable information about him is what can be inferred from his book. Pseudo-Epiphanius in *The Lives of the Prophets* states that Joel's original home was in the territory of Reuben, perhaps on the basis of I Chr. 5:4. The geographical references in the prophecy itself indicate a knowledge of Judah, and particularly of Jerusalem, where Joel was evidently living when he described the locust attack on the city (2:7-9). According to the political and religious conditions indicated, the prophet delivered this message about 400 B.C. Though he attributes great importance to the temple worship, he was probably not one of the priests, from whom he seems to distinguish himself by addressing them objectively (1:13; 2:17). Joel could well be called a "temple-prophet." [1]

II. Occasion and Summary

The occasion of the prophecy is an unparalleled locust plague, which Joel sees as a judgment from God and as a warning and symbol of the final day of the Lord. The title (1:1) claims divine inspiration and gives the name of the prophet and his father.

The book itself may be divided into two main parts: 1:1–2:27, dealing with the present; and 2:28–3:21, with the future.

Part One (1:1–2:27) describes a locust plague and drought, calls the people to repentance, and promises the removal of the locusts and the restoration of fertility. An unprecedented calamity has resulted from successive waves of locusts (1:2-4). Since food and the means of sacrifice are destroyed, all classes of people are called to mourn (1:5-12). The priests are exhorted to summon the people to the temple for a national repentance (1:13-14). This calamity

[1] A. S. Kapelrud, *Joel Studies* (Uppsala: Almqvist & Wiksells, 1948), pp. 176, 177, 185.

is a warning of the approaching day of the Lord (1:15). As food and water are cut off by a drought, the prophet and even the animals cry to God for relief (1:16-20). The alarm must be sounded to warn of the approach of the day of the Lord (2:1-2a). The locust host is like fire in its devastation (2:2b-3). They attack the city of Jerusalem like an army (2:4-9). This plague is a foretaste of the day of the Lord and, like it, is a divine judgment (2:10-11). The people are called upon to return, not only formally but spiritually, to a gracious God (2:12-14). All classes of people are to be summoned and led by the priests in prayer for the removal of the national calamity (2:15-17). The Lord promises the removal of the locusts, plentiful rains, and abundant food for man and beast as proofs of his presence and favor (2:18-27).

Part Two (2:28–3:21) predicts the outpouring of the spirit, the signs of the day of the Lord, the deliverance of the faithful in Jerusalem, the judgment of the nations, and the blessings of Judah. God's spirit will be poured out on all ages and classes of his people (2:28-29). Wars and astronomical disturbances will warn of the coming of the final day of the Lord (2:30-31). The faithful in Jerusalem will be delivered (2:32). The exiles from Judah will be restored (3:1), but the pagan nations will be gathered and judged for their cruelties to God's people (3:2-3). The plundering and enslaving by Tyre, Sidon, and Philistia will be requited to them (3:4-8). The pagans are assembled for the final battle with the hosts of heaven (3:9-11). The Lord and his angels will execute judgment on the heathen amid the darkening of the heavenly bodies and the shaking of earth and sky (3:12-16a). The Israelites, however, will be protected by their Lord, who henceforth will preserve his holy city from violation (3:16b-17). Judah will be blessed with abundant fertility (3:18), but Egypt and Edom will be desolated because of their aggressions against Judah (3:19). Judah and Jerusalem will remain forever; the innocent Israelite blood will be vindicated; and the Lord will dwell in Zion (3:20-21).

III. Style

A. Rhythms.—The book of Joel, like most of the Hebrew prophetic literature, is rhythmic. Even passages not printed as verse in the Revised Standard Version (2:30–3:8) have the meter and parallelism of poetry. The usual Hebrew rhythms, the hexameter (3 + 3) and the pentameter (3 + 2), are the most frequent. Joel is skillful in substituting other meters for desired effects: for example, a succession of two-stress phrases for items in descriptions (1:4, 9b-11a, 19-20; 2:9) and the same meter for a series of commands (1:14;

2:15b-16; 3:9-13), and four-stress phrases for a solemn indictment (3:4-6).

B. Concrete Details.—One of the reasons for Joel's power in description is his specification of concrete details. This is particularly noteworthy as he lists the plants and classes of people and animals affected by the locusts and drought (ch. 1). Other examples are found in the picture of renewed fertility (2:19-26). He uses the same method of specifying groups to express the universality of the national repentance (2:16-17) and of the outpouring of the spirit (2:28-29). The reasons for and the methods of judgment are clarified by citing the examples of Tyre, Sidon, and Philistia (3:4-8) and of Egypt and Edom (3:19).

C. Similes and Metaphors.—Another element in the effectiveness of Joel's descriptions is his use of apt similes and metaphors. The locusts are called a "nation" (1:6), a "people" (2:2, 5), an "army" (2:11, 25). Their teeth are those of a "lion" (1:6). Their destructiveness is like that of "fire" (2:3). They look like "horses" (2:4); they sound like "chariots," "fire," or an "army drawn up for battle" (2:5). They march and attack the city "like warriors" (2:7). The rent heart (2:13) is a striking metaphor for inward repentance. The last judgment is a "harvest" or a vintage (3:13).

D. Repetition.—For so short a book there is an unusual number of studied repetitions of words and ideas. The most obvious use of repetition is for emphasis: for example, in ch. 1 repetitions and synonyms express the greatness of the suffering and the completeness of the destruction of the produce. The size and character of the locust swarm are emphasized by reiterating the unparalleled nature of the plague (1:2-3; 2:2), by the synonyms "nation" (1:6) and "people" (2:2, 5), in every case with the adjective "strong," and by the two uses of "army" (2:11, 25) each time with "great." Contrast is heightened by using the same words in describing the destruction of all produce (1:4-20) and the restoration of fertility (2:19-25). Another use of repetition is to show succession: for example, of generations (1:3) or of locust swarms (1:4). Irony is sometimes expressed by repetition, as of "recompense" (3:4, 7), "arouse" and "bestir themselves" (same Hebrew root) and "come up" (3:9, 12). Climax is achieved by the repeated references to the day of the Lord leading up to its final coming (1:15; 2:1, 11, 31; 3:14). Joel thrice repeats a characteristic phrase or idea in closing a section (1:20, cf. 1:19; 2:27, cf. 2:26; 3:21, cf. 3:17).

E. Correspondence.—Another characteristic of Joel's literary art is the drawing of parallels between corresponding or similar things. The most elaborate correspondence is between the locusts (chs. 1–2) and the pagan nations (ch. 3). Both these groups "come up" (1:6; 3:9, 12) against the Lord's land (1:6; 3:2); both ravage the land and the people (1:4–2:11; 3:2-8, 19). The locust plague is a judgment, and therefore both a warning and an aspect of the day of the Lord (1:15; 2:1, 2, 10); the corresponding judgment of the pagan nations is the final day of the Lord (2:13-16, 19). The way of deliverance from the locusts is repentance (1:13-14; 2:12-17), and in the final day of the Lord salvation is for those who call on the name of God (2:32). The blessings which follow these deliverances are also similar: abundant fertility (2:19, 22-24; 3:18); the vindication of God's people (2:19, 26-27; 3:17, 21); and God's presence in their midst (2:27; 3:21). By means of these correspondences Joel achieves symmetry and unity.

F. Contrast.—Joel uses contrasts to sharpen an effect. The devastation by locusts and drought and the resulting sorrow of men and beasts (1:4-20) are contrasted with the restoration of fertility and the resulting gladness (2:19-25). In the second main section (2:28–3:21) the judgments on the heathen nations are a foil to the blessings of God's people.

G. Alliteration.—Examples of alliteration are pointed out in the Exegesis on 1:7, 10, 15, all in the section dealing with the locust plague.

H. Change of Person.—Like other Hebrew prophets, Joel frequently shifts the persons of verbs and pronouns. His references to God are occasionally in the second person (1:19; 3:11*b*), but usually either in the third or in the first person as the direct words of God. Such changes of person reveal how closely the prophet identified his words with the word of God. Vividness is enhanced by shifting from third-person descriptions of the locust plague and of the final judgment to second-person commands (1:5, 8, 11, 13-14; 2:12, 13, 15-17; 3:9-13).

IV. Parallels in Other Old Testament Books

A remarkable number of the phrases and ideas of Joel have close parallels in other Old Testament books.[2]

The following are parallels in both thought and word: (*a*) "alas for the day" (1:15 = Ezek. 30:2); (*b*) "for the day of the LORD is near" (1:15 = Isa. 13:6; Ezek. 30:3; Obad. 15; Zeph. 1:7); (*c*) "as destruction from the Almighty" (1:15 = Isa. 13:6); (*d*) "it is near, a day of darkness and gloom, a day of clouds and thick darkness" (2:2 = Zeph. 1:14-15); (*e*) 2:3*b* is a reversal of Isa. 51:3; Ezek. 36:35; (*f*) "are in anguish, all faces grow pale" (2:6 = Nah. 2:10,

the only other place where the latter verb is used); (*g*) the catalogue of God's mercies (2:13 = Exod. 34:6; Jonah 4:2); (*h*) "who knows whether he will not turn and repent" (2:14 = Jonah 3:9); (*j*) "why should they say among the peoples, Where is their God?" (2:17 = Ps. 79:10); (*k*) "rejoice, for the LORD has done great things" (2:21, a reversal of the order of ideas in Ps. 126:3); (*l*) "I, the LORD, am your God and there is none else" (2:27 = Isa. 45:5, 6, 18); (*m*) "I will pour out my spirit" (2:28 = Ezek. 39:29); (*n*) "before the great and terrible day of the LORD comes" (2:31, and in part 2:11 = Mal. 4:5); (*o*) "for in Mount Zion . . . there shall be those that escape" (2:32 = Obad. 17); (*p*) "in those days and at that time" (3:1 = Jer. 33:15; 50: 4, 20); (*q*) "I will gather all the nations" (3:2 = Isa. 66:18; Zech. 14:2); (*r*) "I will return your recompense upon your own head" (3:4 = Obad. 15); (*s*) "for the LORD has spoken" (3:8 = Obad. 18); (*t*) 3:10*a* is the reverse of Isa. 2:4; Mic. 4:3; (*u*) "the LORD roars from Zion, and utters his voice from Jerusalem" (3:16 = Amos 1:2); (*v*) "you shall know that I am the LORD your God" (3:17 = Ezek. 36:11); (*w*) "the mountains shall drip sweet wine, and the hills shall flow with milk" (3:18 = Amos 9:13).

Parallels to some of Joel's ideas and imagery, though not in the same words, are also found: (*a*) a trumpet warning of the coming judgment (2:1 = Isa. 27:13; Zeph. 1:16); (*b*) darkening of the heavenly bodies in the day of the Lord (2:10, 31; 3:15 = Isa. 13:10; Ezek. 32:7); (*c*) imagery of grain harvest for judgment (3:13 = Isa. 17:5); (*d*) imagery of vintage for judgment (3:13 = Isa. 63:3); (*e*) life-giving waters flowing from Jerusalem (3:18 = Ezek. 47:1-12; Zech. 14:8).

Whenever the literary relationships can be determined, it seems that Joel is the one who quotes or is influenced by parallels in other prophets. (*a*) In 2:32 Joel himself indicates that he is quoting Obad. 17 by the phrase "As the LORD has said." (*b*) In several cases the similar phrases are integral parts of larger contexts in the other prophets, but only parenthetical theological interpretations in Joel:

1:15 = Isa. 13:6
2:2 = Zeph. 1:15
2:10 = Isa. 13:16

(*c*) In some verses Joel combines phrases from different prophetic passages:

1:15 = Ezek. 30:2-3; Zeph. 1:7; Isa. 13:6
2:10 = Isa. 13:13, 10
2:11 = Isa. 30:30; Mal. 3:2; 4:5
3:16 = Amos 1:2; Isa. 13:13; Ps. 61:3
3:17 = Ezek. 36:11; Isa. 52:1

---

[2] Cf. G. B. Gray, "The Parallel Passages in 'Joel' in Their Bearing on the Question of Date," *The Expositor*, VIII (1893), 208-25.

(*d*) Some of the parallels consist of phrases which are characteristic of other prophets and are therefore probably quoted. Notable examples are: "I, the LORD, am your God and there is none else" (2:27), a characteristic phrase of Deutero-Isaiah; "and you shall know that I am the LORD your God" (3:17), variations of which occur over fifty times in Ezekiel. (*e*) In two cases Joel gives the reverse of ideas each of which is found elsewhere twice and therefore probably in the original form:

2:3; cf. Isa. 51:3; Ezek. 36:35
3:10; cf. Isa. 2:4; Mic. 4:3

Several conclusions might be drawn from a survey of these parallels and the establishment of Joel as the borrower in some cases. Joel's borrowings are chiefly from the other prophetic books and consist mainly in eschatological phrases and concepts. It follows that his vivid description of the locust plague and drought is largely original, according to present evidence. Though Joel borrows widely, yet he skillfully weaves these quotations and his original material into a unified whole. In many cases he probably used common phrases and concepts without any thought of direct borrowing. The established quotations help to date Joel as one of the latest of the prophets.

V. Date

Proposals for the date of Joel vary from the tenth to the second centuries B.C. No time is given in the heading or directly stated in the book.

A. For a Postexilic Date.—A postexilic date for Joel was first proposed by Wilhelm Vatke in 1835 and is held by most recent commentators.

1. International Situation.—Since neither Assyria nor Babylon is referred to, the date is probably after the fall of Babylon in 539 B.C., for the prophets of the Assyrian and Chaldean periods regularly mention the contemporary world power. Because the Greeks are mentioned (3:6), but not yet as a world power, the prophecy must fall before Alexander's conquests (336-323 B.C.). Since no reference is made to Persia, as in Malachi, the time is probably during the period of benevolent Persian administration before the revolts in Syria and their bloody suppression about 345 B.C. The mention of Sidon as yet to be judged (3:4) also argues for a time preceding 345 B.C., when Artaxerxes III destroyed the city and sold its inhabitants into slavery (Diodorus Siculus XIV. 45).

2. Political Condition of Judah.—(*a*) Judah and Jerusalem have been taken into captivity (3:1), their people have been scattered, and the land divided (3:2). These conditions necessitate a date after the capture of Jerusalem by the Chaldeans in 587 B.C. (*b*) Some of the Israelites have returned to Judah and have rebuilt Jerusalem and the temple (1:2–2:27). (*c*) In keeping with a postexilic date, no king of Judah is mentioned (1:13; 2:17). (*d*) Priests (1:13; 2:17) and elders (1:2, 14; 2:17) are the leaders of the people, as in the time of Ezra and Nehemiah. (*e*) The people of God are in Judah (3:1, 6), and the Northern Kingdom is not mentioned. Israel, before the Exile the name of the Northern Kingdom, has become a synonym for Judah (3:1-2). (*f*) The mention of the "wall" of Jerusalem (2:9) may indicate a date after Nehemiah, who reconstructed the city wall in 444 B.C.

3. Religious Condition of Judah.—The religious life of the people centers in the temple at Jerusalem. There is no mention of the local high places or of the idolatry which the preexilic prophets condemn.

4. Postexilic Words.[3]—Some of Joel's words and phrases characteristic of the postexilic period are: "ministers" as a title of the priests (1:9, 13; 2:17; cf. II Chr. 29:11; Ezra 8:17; Isa. 61:6; Jer. 33:21-22; Ezek. 45:4); "weapons" (2:8; cf. II Chr. 23:10; Neh. 4:17, 23; Job 33:18; 36:12); "rear" (2:20; cf. II Chr. 20:16; Eccl. 3:11; 7:2; 12:13); the pronoun "I" is always 'anî (2:27 [twice]; 3:10, 17), which preponderates in later books, not 'ānōkhî, the usual form in earlier writings.

5. Postexilic Ideas.— (*a*) Like other postexilic prophets, and in contrast to pre-exilic prophets, Joel regards the sacrifices as extremely important (1:9, 13; 2:14). (*b*) Joel makes only a general call to repentance (1:13-14; 2:12-17), without denouncing specific social or religious sins as do the pre-exilic prophets. (*c*) Joel regards the nations only as objects of punishment and reserves all God's future blessings for Israel, a particularism which became more marked after the captivity (Ezra, Nehemiah). (*d*) Joel's eschatology is also postexilic, for it clearly shows the influence of the exilic prophet Ezekiel and of fifth-century Malachi.

6. Quotations of Postexilic Prophets.—It has been shown that Joel 2:32 quotes Obad. 17 and that Joel 2:11, 31 are derived in part from Mal. 3:2; 4:5. Malachi and Obadiah come from about the middle of the fifth century, and allowing sufficient time for these books to be accepted would place Joel about 400 B.C.

B. For a Pre-Exilic Date.—The position of Joel as the second of the minor prophets in the Hebrew canon is held by some to indicate an early date. But the order of these books is only generally chronological, and in the Septuagint

---

[3] Cf. H. Holzinger, "Sprachcharakter und Abfassungszeit des Buches Joel," *Zeitschrift für die alttestamentliche Wissenschaft*, IX (1889), 89-131.

Joel is the fourth of the minor prophets. In 1831 K. A. Credner argued with plausibility that the internal evidence favored a date during the minority of King Joash (later ninth century B.C.), and this dating was accepted by many in the nineteenth century. But the data cited by Credner agree as well or better with a postexilic date, which is demanded by the references to the captivity (3:1-2). Against J. W. Rothstein's proposal (1896) that 1:1–2:27 is pre-exilic and 2:28–3:21 is postexilic are the indications of a postexilic date in the first part of the book also. A. S. Kapelrud suggests a date about 600 B.C., chiefly on the basis of parallels with Jeremiah, but similarities to post-exilic prophets are more striking.

VI. Unity and Critical Analyses

The question of the unity of the book of Joel is raised by its clear division into two main sections, 1:2–2:27, dealing with the locust plague and drought in the present, and 2:28–3:21, concerning the final day of the Lord in the future.

A. Indications of Unity.— (a) All the extant Hebrew manuscripts and ancient versions give Joel as a unit. (b) The elaborate correspondences between the section on the locusts and the section on the pagan enemies knit the book together into a symmetrical whole. (c) Several distinctive features of style are found in both the main divisions, notably the borrowings from other prophets and the repetitions of important phrases. (d) The repeated references to the day of the Lord in the first part (1:15; 2:1, 11) prepare for the climax of its final coming in the second part. (e) As pointed out by R. H. Pfeiffer,[4] many other prophets of the Old Testament furnish parallels to Joel's combination of a concern for the present with an apocalyptic hope for the future. Several prophets like Joel see in a present or approaching national catastrophe a sample of the future world judgment (Isa. 13; Obadiah; Zeph. 1; Mark 13 and parallels). (f) A final indication of unity is the uniform historical background throughout the book.

B. Critical Analyses.—The first to question the unity of Joel was Maurice Vernes (1872), who assigned 1:1–2:27 and 2:28–3:21 to two different authors. Julius A. Bewer (1911) gives an elaborate analysis in which he attributes all the references to the day of the Lord to a later apocalyptist. T. H. Robinson (1938) concludes that most of 1:1–2:27 is from Joel, and in 2:28–3:21 he finds several fragments from unknown authors, with 3:9-14 as the original kernel of this section. Behind each of these analyses is the assumption that the same author could not have

described both the locust plague and the day of the Lord. In the light of the many prophetic passages interweaving the contemporary with the eschatological (see indication e in the preceding paragraph), the arguments for the division of the book lose much of their force.

VII. Interpretation of the Locusts

The locusts described in chs. 1–2 have been interpreted literally of locusts in the present, allegorically of historical invasions, apocalyptically of supernatural creatures of the end time, or as a combination of the literal and one of the other views.[5]

A. Literal Interpretation.—The simplest interpretation of the locusts is as literal insects which are compared to an invading army and are sometimes described with poetic hyperbole. An authority on locusts and their control writes: "Joel's description of a locust invasion has never been surpassed for its dramatic picturesqueness combined with amazing accuracy of detail."[6] The literal interpretation is held by many modern commentators (e.g., George Adam Smith, Wilhelm Nowack, G. W. Wade, Ernst Sellin [in the second edition of his work]).

B. Allegorical-Historical Interpretation.—On the margin of the Greek Codex Marchalianus (Q) of the sixth century the words for locust in 2:25 are identified with the Egyptians, Babylonians, Assyrians, and Greeks. Similar but varied interpretations of the locust plague as an allegory of historical human invasions are given by the Targum, patristic commentators, and even some modern expositors, for example, E. B. Pusey (1860). Against this view is the fact that both the destruction (ch. 1) and the restoration (2:22-25) are limited to plant life. Furthermore, the express comparison of the locusts to a human army (2:4-5, 7) makes it impossible that they are symbols of human soldiers; a thing is not compared with itself. The same arguments hold against combining the literal interpretation of ch. 1 with an allegorical interpretation of ch. 2 (as is done by Calvin).

C. Apocalyptic Interpretation.—According to Adalbert Merx (1877), Joel's locusts are supernatural apocalyptic creatures in ch. 1 and symbols of the invading armies of the end times in ch. 2. Similarly, Albin van Hoonacker (1908) held that these locusts were not real but types of the future catastrophe of the day of the Lord. Such futuristic interpretations do not do justice to the present outlook of the description, for example, "before our eyes" (1:16).

---

[4] *Introduction to the Old Testament* (New York: Harper & Bros., 1941), p. 575.

[5] Cf. J. A. Thompson, "Joel's Locusts in the Light of Near Eastern Parallels," *Journal of Near Eastern Studies,* XIV (1955), 52-55.

[6] B. P. Uvarov, "The Locust Plague," *Annual Report of the Board of Regents of the Smithsonian Institution,* 1944, p. 331.

Several scholars have tried to combine the literal and apocalyptic interpretations of the locusts. The original Joel, according to Bewer, was describing literal locusts, but a later editor interpreted them as eschatological armies and agents of judgment. R. H. Pfeiffer [7] sees literal insects in ch. 1, but apocalyptic creatures in some elements of ch. 2. It is true that some eschatological phrases are used of the judgments inflicted by the locusts, but the locusts themselves in ch. 2 can still be interpreted as literal insects, pictured with vivid comparisons and poetic exaggerations.

VIII. Leading Ideas

A. Judgment and Blessing Through Nature. —Not only does Joel describe nature with accuracy, vividness, and sympathy, but he also interprets natural processes as the working out of God's moral purposes. In the locust plague and drought he sees God's judgment; conversely, the removal of the locusts and the restoration of fertility he regards with joy as signs of God's favor. From Joel's personalistic Hebrew world view some of the distinctions of Greek logical thought lose their sharpness: the "natural" is the manifestation of the "supernatural"; animate and even inanimate nature are the instruments of and share in man's judgments and his blessings.

B. Necessity of Repentance. —Man's only escape from God's judgment, according to Joel, lies in true repentance, by which man becomes receptive to divine mercy. The call to general repentance is twice repeated by Joel (1:13-14; 2:12-17), the second time with greater detail. Joel urges a solemn assembly of all the people, fasting, and prayer in the temple led by the priests. He recognizes, however, that these outward forms are not in themselves true repentance, and he stresses inner contrition and spiritual return to God (2:13).

C. Salvation by Grace Through Faith. —On the day of judgment, promises Joel (2:32), those Jerusalemites who call on the name of the Lord shall be saved. This principle of salvation by faith is applied by Paul to all people regardless of race, time, or place (Rom. 10:13). In such calling upon God the prophet sees the human response to God's gracious calling of men (2:32). God's calling, limited by Joel to Israelites who survive the woes of the end time, is enlarged by Peter in his pentecostal sermon (Acts 2:39) to include all nations.

D. Importance of Formal Worship. —Like other postexilic prophets (Haggai, Zechariah, Malachi) Joel regards the regular performance of worship as extremely important. To him one of the most distressing effects of the locust

[7] Op. cit., p. 574.

plague and drought is the cessation of sacrifice because of the lack of materials (1:9, 16). Renewed fertility is counted as a blessing first of all because it will again make possible sacrificial worship (2:14). The prophet honors the priests as the ministers of the Lord (1:9, 13; 2:17) and assigns to them the leadership in the national repentance (1:9, 13-14: 2:17). The temple at Jerusalem is the house of God and the unquestioned center of national worship (1:9, 13-14; 2:17). Such emphasis on ceremonies is in contrast with the pre-exilic prophets, who condemn ritualism which lacks ethical and spiritual content (e.g., Jer. 7). At the same time Joel perceives that the essence of true religion is not in outward rites but in inner attitudes (2:13).

E. Israelite Particularism. —Since Joel was an Israelite, and since a locust plague in Judah was the occasion of his prophecy, it is not surprising that his interest in the first section (1:2–2:27) centers in his own people and their afflictions. The Lord is Israel's God (1:13-14; 2:13-14, 17, 23, 26-27); Israel is his people (2:17-18); and their land is his land (1:6). In this section foreign nations are mentioned only as scorners of Israel (2:17, 19).

In the second section of the book (2:28–3:21) Israelite particularism is even more marked. The outpouring of the spirit is for "your sons" and "your daughters," that is, for Israel (2:28). The only ones who escape from final condemnation are Israelites in Mount Zion (2:32; 3:16). Other nations are referred to only as objects of God's wrath because of their mistreatment of Israel (3:2-8, 19). The blessings of the future are reserved for the inhabitants of Judah and Jerusalem (3:16-18, 20-21), which will never again be violated by foreigners (3:17). Joel expresses none of the universalism which regards other nations as the objects of God's care (Amos 9:7) or foresees all nations as joining in Israel's faith and in her blessings in the kingdom of God (Isa. 2:2-4; 19:18-25; Zech. 14:16). Joel's exclusiveness, however, is not merely national, but also ethical and spiritual, and so of permanent significance. Not all Israel shall be saved, but only the remnant who are faithful to God (2:32). The nations are punished not because they are non-Israelites, but because they have sinned against their fellow men, and so against God. Such particularism, narrow as it seems to us, played an important part in the preservation of Israel's identity and Israel's faith during the testing years of foreign domination after the Exile. Joel's exclusiveness was perhaps a necessary stage in the preparation for the inclusiveness of the New Testament.

F. God's Goals in History. —When Joel's symbols are rightly understood his eschatology also presents elements of enduring value, particularly a conviction of God's moral purpose in human history. Joel gives almost a compendium of Old Testament eschatology, lacking only the Messiah, the resurrection, and the inclusion of the nations in the kingdom of glory.

1. The Day of the Lord.[8]—Joel's most common term for the time of judgment is "the day of the LORD" (1:15; 2:1, 11, 31; 3:14). This "day" is "near" (1:15; 2:1), that is, surely approaching, as "part of the purpose of God, . . . pressing on to its fulfillment." [9] One aspect of the day of the Lord is the contemporary locust plague (1:15; 2:1, 2, 10-11). This partial and passing judgment is only a forewarning of the universal and final day of the Lord (3:14-18), in which the nations will be judged and Israel will be blessed. Such a concept implies a God who guides history through successive crises toward his appointed goals. Similarly the New Testament "day of the Lord Jesus" (II Cor. 1:14) is ever approaching (Heb. 10:25), unites the warning of judgment and the hope of blessing, and consummates God's purpose for men.

2. Outpouring of the Spirit.—The outpouring of the Spirit of God (2:28-29) is placed by Joel in the indefinite future at the beginning of the section dealing with the end times. This gift of the Spirit is for the Israelites, but among them is distributed without distinctions of sex, age, or social rank. The recipients of the Spirit are enabled to envision God's will and to prophesy God's message. Moses wished for just such a nationwide influence of God's Spirit (Num. 11:29). Other prophets also look forward to an outpouring of the Spirit in messianic times (Isa. 32:15; 44:3; Ezek. 39:29). On the day of Pentecost (Acts 2) Peter proclaimed the beginning of the dispensation of the spiritual relationship to God which was foretold by Joel, but which went beyond the bounds of national Israel to include all believers in Christ.

3. Final Judgment of the Nations.—The final judgment of the nations is dramatically described in ch. 3. The summoning of all the nations of the earth (3:2) indicates the universality of the Lord's moral rule. As in Matt. 25:31-46, the nations are judged according to their treatment of their fellow men (3:2-6, 19). The Lord's ultimate victory over the forces of evil is implied (3:15-16). The New Testament accounts of the Last Judgment are based on these same principles and even borrow some of Joel's vivid imagery (e.g., Rev. 14:14-20).

4. Blessings of Israel.—In contrast to the condemnation and destruction of the nations, the day of the Lord brings deliverance and prosperity to Israel. In the final cataclysm the Israelites who pray to the Lord will be delivered (2:32; 3:16). The holy city, Jerusalem, will be forever safe from further violation by pagans (3:17). The supernatural fertility of Judah and the fountain of waters flowing from the temple (3:18) are interpreted as symbols of spiritual blessing in Ezek. 47:1-12; Rev. 22:1-2. As the source of all these blessings, the Lord will dwell in the midst of glorified Zion forever (3:21). According to the New Testament hope, the New Jerusalem in which God dwells will include the redeemed and faithful from every nation (Rev. 21:24-27), in contrast to Joel, who limits the blessed to the Jews.

G. The Abiding Message of Joel.—When the reader transcends Joel's national particularism, he discovers in the book truths which influenced the New Testament and have continuing validity. Joel maintains a balance between the outward and inward elements of religion. God reveals himself, according to Joel, not only in his powerful and moral control of nature and history, but also through his spirit within. On man's side of religion formal worship is given due importance, but inner repentance and faith are stressed as man's primary obligations. In the ultimate kingdom of glory the outward environment will be cleansed and perfected, but the central feature is the presence of God in the midst of his faithful people.

Perhaps the most significant contribution of Joel is his promise of the outpouring of God's spirit on all believers. In fulfillment of this promise the truest Christian experience of God since Pentecost has been primarily spiritual and personal rather than formal and priestly.

IX. Text

The Hebrew text of Joel is well preserved. Except for 1:17-18; 3:11, the Septuagint, Peshitta, and Vulgate present only minor variations from the Masoretic Text and from each other.

X. Chapter Divisions [10]

The Masoretes divided the book into two sections, 1:1–2:27 and 2:28–3:21. Stephen Langton (d. 1228) introduced the present Old Testament chapters of the Vulgate, which were followed by the first Rabbinic Bible, edited by Felix Pratensis (1517), and by most editions in other languages, including the English. The second Rabbinic Bible, edited by Jacob ben

---

[8] Cf. W. W. Cannon, " 'The Day of the Lord' in Joel," *Church Quarterly Review*, CIII (1926), 32-63.

[9] H. Wheeler Robinson, *Inspiration and Revelation in the Old Testament* (Oxford: Clarendon Press, 1946), p. 137.

[10] Cf. E. Nestle, "Miscellen. 1. Zur Kapiteleinteilung in Joel," *Zeitschrift für die alttestamentliche Wissenschaft.* XXIV (1904), 122-27.

Ḥayyim (1526), and most Hebrew editions since that time make four chapters, so that Hebrew 3:1-5 = English 2:28-32; Hebrew 4:1-21 = English 3:1-21.

XI. Outline of Contents

I. A locust plague and a drought and their removal (1:1–2:27)
 A. Title (1:1)
 B. Universal mourning for the locust plague and drought (1:2-20)
 C. The locust attack as a warning of the day of the Lord (2:1-11)
 D. A call to national repentance (2:12-17)
 E. Promises of removal of locusts and restoration of fertility (2:18-27)
II. Future blessings of Israel and judgment of the nations (2:28–3:21)
 A. Outpouring of the Spirit (2:28-29)
 B. Signs of the day of the Lord and deliverance of the faithful (2:30-32)
 C. God's purpose to judge the oppressors of Israel (3:1-3)
 D. Sins and punishment of Tyre, Sidon, and Philistia (3:4-8)
 E. The nations summoned to the final battle (3:9-11)
 F. The last judgment (3:12-16a)
 G. The blessings of Judah (3:16b-21)

XII. Selected Bibliography

BEWER, JULIUS A. *A Critical and Exegetical Commentary on Obadiah and Joel* ("International Critical Commentary"). New York: Charles Scribner's Sons, 1911.

CALKINS, RAYMOND. *The Modern Message of the Minor Prophets*. New York: Harper & Bros., 1947.

DRIVER, S. R. *The Books of Joel and Amos* ("The Cambridge Bible"). Cambridge: Cambridge University Press, 1934.

KAPELRUD, A. S. *Joel Studies*. Uppsala: Almqvist & Wiksells, 1948.

NOWACK, W. *Die kleinen Propheten* ("Handkommenter zum Alten Testament"). 3rd ed. Göttingen: Vandenhoeck & Ruprecht, 1922.

ROBINSON, T. H. *Die zwölf kleinen Propheten, Hosea bis Micha* ("Handbuch zum Alten Testament"). Tübingen: J. C. B. Mohr, 1938.

SELLIN, ERNST. *Das Zwölfprophetenbuch* ("Kommenter zum Alten Testament"). 2nd and 3rd ed. Leipzig: A. Deichert, 1929. Vol. I.

SMITH, GEORGE ADAM. *The Book of the Twelve Prophets*. Rev. ed. New York: Harper & Bros., 1928.

VAN HOONACKER, ALBIN. *Les douze petits prophètes* "Études Bibliques"). Paris: J. Gabalda, 1908.

WADE, G. W. *The Books of the Prophets*, Micah, Obadiah, Joel, and Jonah ("Westminster Commentaries"). London: Methuen & Co., 1925.

JOEL

TEXT, EXEGESIS, AND EXPOSITION

1 The word of the Lord that came to Joel the son of Pethuel.

1 The word of the Lord that came to Joel, the son of Pethu'el:

I. A Locust Plague and a Drought and Their Removal (1:1–2:27)
A. Title (1:1)

1:1. The word of the Lord that came to . . . : An introduction to several Hebrew prophetic books (Hos. 1:1; Mic. 1:1; Zeph. 1:1), indicating the divine source of the message. On the names **Joel** and **Pethuel**, see Intro., p. 727.

1:1-3. The Present Distress.—Except in unusually tranquil and optimistic times, every generation tends to think that its troubles exceed anything humanity has known before. It is easy to capitalize on this fact in order to discredit the so-called "prophets of gloom" and discount their warnings. How often ruin has been predicted, and yet mankind still survives! How often the end of the world has been foretold, and yet the world is still here!

Joel, however, does not shrink from painting the calamity of his day in the darkest colors possible. He begins by implying that the present visitation of locusts has no precedent, and is unlikely to be paralleled in the future. The devastation is such that it cannot be surpassed. This is more than a rhetorical flourish meant to command attention; and it is not to be understood as the extravagance of a habitual pessimist. For the point is not really whether the

2 Hear this, ye old men, and give ear, all ye inhabitants of the land. Hath this been in your days, or even in the days of your fathers?

3 Tell ye your children of it, and *let* your children *tell* their children, and their children another generation.

4 That which the palmerworm hath left hath the locust eaten; and that which the locust hath left hath the cankerworm eaten; and that which the cankerworm hath left hath the caterpillar eaten.

2 Hear this, you aged men,
  give ear, all inhabitants of the land!
Has such a thing happened in your days,
  or in the days of your fathers?

3 Tell your children of it,
  and lct your children tell their children,
  and their children another generation.

4 What the cutting locust left,
  the swarming locust has eaten.
What the swarming locust left,
  the hopping locust has eaten,
and what the hopping locust left,
  the destroying locust has eaten.

B. Universal Mourning for the Locust Plague and Drought (1:2-20)

2. The prophet gains attention by direct address. The verbs **hear, give ear** show that what follows was originally an oral sermon or series of sermons. In the second half of the verse the rhetorical question, which assumes a negative answer, is addressed especially to the **aged men** and implies that the event is unparalleled in the present or preceding generations.

3-4. The command to "recount" (S. R. Driver, *The Books of Joel and Amos* [Cambridge: Cambridge University Press, 1934; "The Cambridge Bible"], p. 37) the story to succeeding generations shows the memorable nature of the calamity. In both vss. 3 and 4 effective use is made of anadiplosis, the repetition of the last word in one clause at the beginning of the next clause, to convey the succession of generations in vs. 3 and of swarms upon swarms of locusts in vs. 4.

Of the nine O.T. Hebrew words for locust, four are found in vs. 4: *gāzām,* **cutting locust;** *'arbeh,* **swarming locust** or "destroying locust" (so, comparing Akkadian *aribu,* Ovid R. Sellers, "Stages of Locust in Joel," *American Journal of Semitic Languages and Literatures,* LII [1936], 82) ; *yéleq,* **hopping locust;** and *ḥāṣil,* **destroying locust.** (See Exeg. on 2:25.) These names probably indicate four stages of locust life. The first stage observed by the prophet was the *gāzām,* perhaps including the fourth and fifth larval forms, the latter of which molts and becomes the *'arbeh,* the adult, flying locust. The females of the *'arbeh* deposit eggs, from which hatch the *yéleq,* the first larval form, which develops in the *ḥāṣil,* perhaps the second and third larval forms. The Arabic has names for each of the six forms of the locust. For a comprehensive description of the desert locust (*Schistocerca gregaria,* Forsk.) see B. P. Uvarov, *Locusts and Grasshoppers* (London: Imperial Institute of Entomology, 1928) , pp. 250-61.

---

plague in Joel's time was the worst that his country ever suffered. Suffering cannot be measured by statistics. Calamities cannot be compared in any but the most superficial manner. The trouble of the moment is the one that men have to reckon with, and it cannot be brushed aside by reference to troubles of other days. Wherever suffering and evil exist, there is a situation which demands to be faced in its full gravity.

The Scriptures recognize with complete seriousness the reality of evil. The gulf between despair and faith is not crossed by ignoring the somber facts of human life. It is crossed only when the troubles of humanity are first seen as the consequence of man's fall. (See Expos. on vss. 14-20.) The sufferings of the world must be recognized as acts of divine judgment. For then the avenue of repentance may be opened up, whereby healing is to be found. Our cure must come from the hand that has smitten us. Such is the theme of Joel.

4-13. *The Universal Distress.*—As the vivid narrative of the locust plague moves on, a striking fact emerges. No one, no sector of society, is immune from the calamity. The **drunkards**—who may be taken as the irresponsible element in the community—feel the effects

5 Awake, ye drunkards, and weep; and howl, all ye drinkers of wine, because of the new wine; for it is cut off from your mouth.

6 For a nation is come up upon my land, strong, and without number, whose teeth *are* the teeth of a lion, and he hath the cheek teeth of a great lion.

7 He hath laid my vine waste, and barked my fig tree: he hath made it clean bare, and cast *it* away; the branches thereof are made white.

---

5 Awake, you drunkards, and weep;
   and wail, all you drinkers of wine,
because of the sweet wine,
   for it is cut off from your mouth.

6 For a nation has come up against my
   land,
   powerful and without number;
   its teeth are lions' teeth,
   and it has the fangs of a lioness.
7 It has laid waste my vines,
   and splintered my fig trees;
it has stripped off their bark and thrown
   it down;
   their branches are made white.

---

5. The **drunkards** are called upon to **awake** from the sleep of intoxication. The intemperate are mentioned first probably because they are the first to complain when supplies are reduced. Wine doubled in price in Palestine during the locust plague of 1915 (John D. Whiting, "Jerusalem's Locust Plague," *National Geographic Magazine*, XXVIII [1915], 543). The **sweet wine** was newly pressed and only partially fermented (cf. 3:18).

6. The locusts are called **a nation**, as in 2:2 (cf. Prov. 30:25-28), because of their organization. **My land,** i.e., the Lord's, as in 3:2. The locust swarm is called **strong,** as in 2:2, 5, 11, because of its multitude and ability to destroy vegetation. The number of locusts in a plague is usually in the millions; it was estimated that there were 24,420 billions in a swarm observed over the Red Sea (quoted by Driver, *op. cit.,* p. 40). The teeth of the locust, by an exaggerated metaphor called **lions' teeth,** are edged like a saw to enable it to gnaw through even the bark of trees.

7. **Vines** and **fig trees** are the most common fruit plants of Palestine and are frequently mentioned in this order in the Bible, e.g., Hos. 2:12. Photographs taken in Palestine in 1915 show vines and fig trees stripped of leaves and bark by locusts (Whiting, *op. cit.,* Figs. on pp. 520, 524, 525). During such plagues some fig trees are **splintered,** as the locusts gnaw off small limbs, strewing shreds of bark on the ground. Alliteration is used at the beginning of both lines of the verse: *sām . . . leshammāh,* **it has laid waste;** and *hāsōph hᵃsāphāh,* **it has stripped off.**

---

of the blight, for the **wine is cut off** (vs. 5). They are accordingly exhorted to rouse themselves, to **awake** to reality. Here is an area of life where sin quickly falls under judgment. Disasters that disturb the natural order fall heavily upon those who depend on luxury. For the intemperate to find themselves without wine; for the rich to find themselves without money, or with money that has become worthless; for the powerful to find themselves suddenly deprived of power: such are the violent readjustments to which men must accommodate themselves, if they can, when some national calamity fundamentally disrupts the social order.

Thus far it would seem that poetic justice is done. But the impact of disaster is not confined to the ranks of those who seem to deserve it. The legitimate occupations of men are similarly disrupted.

Be confounded, O tillers of the soil,
   wail, O vinedressers,
.   .   .   .   .   .   ᶜ
The vine withers,
   the fig tree languishes.
.   .   .   .
and gladness fails
   from the sons of men.

There is no distinction of persons in these acts of judgment that fall upon humankind. The respectable suffer along with the overtly guilty. The simple folk perish with the sophisticated. Every person is called upon to share in the collective chastisement of nations, and individuals cannot plead exemption. It is of the very nature of the judgment that all should come under it.

Moreover, even the worship of God is adversely affected (vss. 9, 13); i.e., the church is forced to identify itself with the nation in the

8 ¶ Lament like a virgin girded with sackcloth for the husband of her youth.

9 The meat offering and the drink offering is cut off from the house of the LORD; the priests, the LORD's ministers, mourn.

10 The field is wasted, the land mourneth; for the corn is wasted: the new wine is dried up, the oil languisheth.

11 Be ye ashamed, O ye husbandmen;

---

8 Lament like a virgin girded with sack-
     cloth
   for the bridegroom of her youth.
9 The cereal offering and the drink offer-
     ing are cut off
   from the house of the LORD.
   The priests mourn,
     the ministers of the LORD.
10 The fields are laid waste,
     the ground mourns;
   because the grain is destroyed,
     the wine fails,
     the oil languishes.

11 Be confounded, O tillers of the soil,
     wail, O vinedressers,

---

8. The whole nation is called to **lament** as bitterly as a girl who mourns the death of her betrothed. Once a man was betrothed to a woman, he was regarded in some respects as her **husband** under Hebrew law (Deut. 22:23-24; Matt. 1:19). Wearing **sackcloth** was the usual sign of mourning (vs. 13; Amos 8:10).

9. The daily sacrifice of two lambs accompanied by the **cereal offering** and the "libation" of olive oil and wine (Exod. 29:38-42; Num. 28:3-8) was the symbol and expression of fellowship between the Lord and his people (cf. 2:14). Regular temple worship was evidently very important to Joel and his contemporaries (vs. 13; 2:17). Another postexilic prophet, Malachi, also stresses the proper performance of sacrifice (Mal. 1:7-14). Pious Jews were horrified by the stopping of sacrifice in Jerusalem by Antiochus Epiphanes in 168 B.C. (I Macc. 1:20-64) and again by the Roman siege in A.D. 70 (Josephus *Jewish Wars* VI. 2. 1).

10-12. In these verses the prevailing meter, previously 3+3 and 3+2, changes to slow two-stress phrases which give solemnity to this account of destruction.

10. The fields are laid waste, *shuddadh sādheh,* is an example of double alliteration, and **destroyed** is also *shuddadh.* To the desolated **ground** is attributed the human feeling of mourning, as in Isa. 33:9. **Grain, wine** and olive **oil,** the chief agricultural products of Palestine, are frequently mentioned in this order (Deut. 7:13). An observer of a locust plague in Lebanon in 1845 writes. "I saw under my own eye not only a large vineyard loaded with young grapes, but whole fields of corn disappear as if by magic" (W. M. Thomson, *The Land and the Book* [London: Thomas Nelson & Sons, 1901], p. 418). In 1915 the olive trees around Jerusalem were the last major crop to be attacked by the locusts, but were stripped of every leaf and berry and even of the tender bark (Whiting, *op. cit.,* pp. 541, 543, Fig., p. 534). The frequent use of the verb *yābhēsh,* "to dry up," or "to wither" (vss. 10, 12, 17, 20) indicates that the locust plague took place during a severe drought, as is often the case (Uvarov, *op. cit.,* p. 146).

11. The "farmers" (Amer. Trans.) are the next class called to mourn the loss of crops. *Hōbhîsh,* **be confounded,** is a pun, being almost identical with *hôbhîsh,* "is dried up" (vs. 10).

---

time of judgment. If a calamity is really meaningful as a judgment of God, then the church too must bear its share of the general chastisement. There is no segment of the population, even though it be the church, that is free from implication in the guilt of all. There is no island of holiness that can plead to be passed

by. What everyone must suffer, the church also must suffer: confessing not only the sin of others, but its own sin as an integral part of all the rest. The church must weep along with the drunkard. The church must acknowledge that in war, or revolution, or depression, or any other calamity that is to be interpreted as a

howl, O ye vinedressers, for the wheat and for the barley; because the harvest of the field is perished.

12 The vine is dried up, and the fig tree languisheth; the pomegranate tree, the palm tree also, and the apple tree, *even* all the trees of the field, are withered: because joy is withered away from the sons of men.

13 Gird yourselves, and lament, ye priests: howl, ye ministers of the altar: come, lie all night in sackcloth, ye ministers of my God: for the meat offering and the drink offering is withholden from the house of your God.

14 ¶ Sanctify ye a fast, call a solemn assembly, gather the elders *and* all the inhabitants of the land *into* the house of the LORD your God, and cry unto the LORD,

---

for the wheat and the barley;
    because the harvest of the field has perished.

12 The vine withers,
    the fig tree languishes.
Pomegranate, palm, and apple,
    all the trees of the field are withered;
and gladness fails
    from the sons of men.

13 Gird on sackcloth and lament, O priests,
    wail, O ministers of the altar.
Go in, pass the night in sackcloth,
    O ministers of my God!
Because cereal offering and drink offering
    are withheld from the house of your God.

14 Sanctify a fast,
    call a solemn assembly.
Gather the elders
    and all the inhabitants of the land
to the house of the LORD your God;
    and cry to the LORD.

---

12. The repetition of verbs already used above to express desolation adds to the mournful effect of this verse. The **apple** is not so common in Palestine as the other fruits mentioned. The conjunction *kî* in the last clause does not give a reason, **because,** but is the asseverative *kî,* "yea" (Julius A. Bewer, *A Critical and Exegetical Commentary on Obadiah and Joel* [New York: Charles Scribner's Sons, 1911; "International Critical Commentary"], p. 84) .

13. The **priests,** from whom the prophet seems to distinguish himself, are summoned to **lament,** and then the reason is given, the reverse order of ideas from the similar vs. 9. The verbs **gird on sackcloth, lament,** and **wail** are found in the same order in Jer. 4:8. The priests are to **go in** to the sanctuary and spend the night in supplication, as did David (II Sam. 12:16) . The personal relation of the prophet to God is expressed by **my God.** Joel's God is also the priests' **your God.** The thought of this verse is expanded in 2:15-17.

14. Sanctify: I.e., institute with religious rites, here of **a fast,** as in 2:15; in 2:16 of an assembly; in 3:9 of war. Fasting was a sign of national penitence (I Sam. 7:6) . Although it is probably not meant that literally **all the inhabitants of the land** (cf. vs. 2) should gather in the temple, yet the phrase implies a small population living near Jerusalem, as was the case after the return from the Exile. The verse reaches a climax in **cry to the LORD,** the purpose of the preceding preparations. Like Amos (4:6-9) , Joel

---

divine judging act, it is entirely involved in whatever sin or failure provoked the crisis. Instead of merely berating alcoholics, and harlots, and moneygrubbers, and communists, and unscrupulous politicians, the church must bear the sin of each and all upon its heart. For when the judgment comes, in the time of men's distress, it must share the common lot (see I Pet. 4:17) .

14-20. *Man's Sin and the World's Disorder.*— Applicable as Joel's thought of judgment may be to social evils, it is not obvious to the modern reader how it applies to a natural calamity. Had the prophet only taken the plague of locusts as a kind of metaphor to describe God's judgment, or even as a reminder of God's overruling power, the difficulty would disappear. But it is evident that he regarded

15 Alas for the day! for the day of the LORD *is* at hand, and as a destruction from the Almighty shall it come.

16 Is not the meat cut off before our eyes, *yea,* joy and gladness from the house of our God?

---

15 Alas for the day!
    For the day of the LORD is near,
        and as destruction from the Almighty
            it comes.
16 Is not the food cut off
        before our eyes,
    joy and gladness
        from the house of our God?

---

regards natural calamities as divine warnings which should lead to national repentance. Intercession to an Assyrian deity for the removal of locusts is pictured in glazed tiles found at Assur and coming from the time of Sargon II (722-705 B.C.; Jack Finegan, *Light from the Ancient Past* [Princeton: Princeton University Press, 1946], pp. 175-76, Fig. 76).

15. The prophet sees the locusts and the drought as warnings of the coming of **the day** (2:2), or **the day of the LORD** (2:1, 11, 31; 3:14; see Intro., pp. 733-34). Here Joel uses the phrase, as does Amos (5:18, 20), of the time of God's judgment on Israel. **Alas for the day!** is almost identical with a phrase in Ezek. 30:2. **The day of the LORD is near** (2:1; 3:14; Ezek. 30:3; Zeph. 1:7, 14), i.e., certainly approaching. **As destruction from the Almighty it comes:** The first two words, *keshōdh mishshadday,* contain a double alliteration which some have tried to express in English, e.g., "as destruction from the Destroyer" (Moffatt), and "as an overpowering from the Overpowerer" (Driver). That Shaddai was commonly derived from *shādhadh,* "deal violently with," is evident not only from this passage and its parallel in Isa. 13:6, but also from the most common LXX rendering, *pantokratōr,* "omnipotent" (here *talaipōria,* "affliction"), and the usual Vulg. *omnipotens,* "omnipotent" (here *potens,* "mighty"). This etymology and these ancient translations have led to the traditional English rendering **Almighty.** For proposed origins of this name, see A. S. Kapelrud, *Joel Studies* (Uppsala: Almqvist & Wiksells, 1948), pp. 59-63.

16-18. The prophet further describes the desolation wrought by locusts and drought as the reason for the warning in vs. 15 and the appeal to God in vss. 19-20.

16. The phrase translated **before our eyes** is emphasized by its position at the beginning of the sentence in Hebrew. The people witness the devastation but are helpless to halt it. **Joy and gladness** in the sanctuary were associated particularly with the peace offerings (Deut. 12:7), the presentation of firstfruits (Deut. 26:10), the feast of Weeks (Deut. 16:11), and the feast of Tabernacles (Deut. 16:14-15). During an agricultural calamity such celebrations would be impossible.

---

the plague not only as a foretaste of God's great day of wrath, but as an act of God sent to bring the nation to repentance. This is made abundantly clear when he calls upon the people to fast and assemble together, with the implication that by so doing the visitation will be turned away (vss. 14-15).

It is of course true that Joel does not identify the plague with **the day of the LORD.** Rather it serves as a warning of something more fundamental, of which the locusts are a sign. The plague draws attention sharply to the fact that there is a God with whom the nation has to reckon. Nevertheless it is also true that Joel considers the plague a direct act of God. To the modern mind, nature is a neutral force, observing its own laws, bestowing its blessings or bringing its curses without regard to specific

cases of human sin. How is this to be reconciled with the biblical view that natural disasters represent the intervention of God?

We shall perhaps best understand this problem by recognizing natural calamities as indications of disorder in the created world. Man was made to have dominion over lesser creatures (Gen. 1:26). Man was to stand at the apex of a good and ordered world. With the entrance of human sin, the created order was disrupted. Man's authority over the creatures of the world was shaken; and those very things that should have served him may now destroy him. His life becomes painful, fragile, and precarious. Such is the biblical perspective.

The focal point of all our problems in the biblical view is human sin. Our distress, even to death itself, springs from what we have be-

17 The seed is rotten under their clods,
the garners are laid desolate, the barns are
broken down; for the corn is withered.

18 How do the beasts groan! the herds of
cattle are perplexed, because they have no
pasture; yea, the flocks of sheep are made
desolate.

19 O Lord, to thee will I cry: for the fire
hath devoured the pastures of the wilderness, and the flame hath burned all the
trees of the field.

20 The beasts of the field cry also unto
thee: for the rivers of waters are dried up,
and the fire hath devoured the pastures of
the wilderness.

17 The seed shrivels under the clods,[a]
    the storehouses are desolate;
the granaries are ruined
    because the grain has failed.
18 How the beasts groan!
    The herds of cattle are perplexed
because there is no pasture for them;
    even the flocks of sheep are dismayed.

19 Unto thee, O Lord, I cry.
For fire has devoured
    the pastures of the wilderness,
and flame has burned
    all the trees of the field.
20 Even the wild beasts cry to thee
    because the water brooks are dried up,
and fire has devoured
    the pastures of the wilderness.

[a] Heb uncertain

---

17. Three of the words translated, **The seed shrivels under the clods,** occur only here in the O.T., but cognate languages and the context point to these meanings. For the last word Driver and Bewer prefer "shovels," though **clods** makes better sense. A resident of Palestine reports that during a drought in the Jordan Valley the rain was not sufficient to enable the grain to sprout, the seeds literally shriveled under the clods, and the land looked like a desert (Thomson, *op. cit.,* p. 395). The quite different LXX text of this clause, "The heifers leap at their stalls," has been the basis for several unconvincing emendations. The **garners** lie **desolate,** in disuse because the drought and the locusts have destroyed the crops which would normally be stored in them.

18. The herds of cattle wander in perplexity seeking water and pasture (cf. I Kings 18:5). Even the sheep and goats, which do not need so much water nor such rich pasturage, "suffer punishment" (ASV mg.). According to the Hebrew view, the creation is so interrelated that the earth, plants, and animals must share the punishment of sinful man (Gen. 3:17-18; Zeph. 1:2-3; Jer. 12:4). The LXX translation, "are desolated," requires only a slight emendation, *nāshammû* for M.T. *ne'eshāmû,* and is followed by the KJV and the RSV.

19. The prophet now joins the many groups he has called upon to mourn in himself beseeching God for the stricken land. **Fire** and **flame** are common metaphors for severe drought and heat (Jer. 9:10 and probably Amos 7:4). **Wilderness,** *midhbār,* is etymolog- ically "a place for herding," pasture land unenclosed and uncultivated, in the western United States, the range.

20. The chorus of petition is completed when to the people, the priests, the domestic animals, and the prophet are added **even the wild beasts** as suppliants to God. With vivid

---

come. In all our distresses, whether natural or social in character, it is therefore appropriate that we turn toward God in repentance. It is our suitable recognition of our responsibility for the basic ills of the world. We are not victims. We have called down upon ourselves whatever troubles either society or nature im- poses. We do right, then, to see in even natural calamities the hand of God. It is not a case of specific evils following upon specific sins. Ex- amples of that can doubtless be cited—forests

burned through human carelessness, land de- stroyed by human greed. But beyond such instances it remains true at all times that we are justly susceptible to the vengeance of nat- ural forces, simply because we have plunged ourselves into a fallen world. Thus the apparent vagaries of nature actually are signs pointing to God's moral order.

In an unusual and poignant way Joel drives home the guiltiness of man: by underscoring the pathos of the lower animals. **How do the**

<table>
<tr><td>

2 Blow ye the trumpet in Zion, and sound an alarm in my holy mountain: let all the inhabitants of the land tremble: for the day of the LORD cometh, for *it is* nigh at hand;

2 A day of darkness and of gloominess, a day of clouds and of thick darkness, as the morning spread upon the mountains: a great people and a strong; there hath not been ever the like, neither shall be any more after it, *even* to the years of many generations.

</td><td>

2 Blow the trumpet in Zion;
  sound the alarm on my holy moun-
    tain!
Let all the inhabitants of the land trem-
    ble,
  for the day of the LORD is coming, it is
    near,
2 a day of darkness and gloom,
  a day of clouds and thick darkness!
Like blackness there is spread upon the
    mountains
  a great and powerful people;
their like has never been from of old,
  nor will be again after them
  through the years of all generations.

</td></tr>
</table>

personification they are said to long for relief from God (cf. Ps. 104:21). The climax of Jeremiah's description of the effects of a drought is also the suffering of the wild animals (Jer. 14:5-6). Most of the "stream beds" (cf. 3:18) of Palestine dry up in the absence of rain. The repetition of the last clause (cf. vs. 19) emphasizes the main theme of vss. 17-20, the burning drought.

C. THE LOCUST ATTACK AS A WARNING OF THE DAY OF THE LORD (2:1-11)

While ch. 1 stresses the destruction caused by the locusts, this section gives greater attention to the description of the locusts themselves. In ch. 1 the suffering is chiefly agricultural and pastoral; now the city is attacked, the usual succession of events in a locust plague. The eschatological warning already sounded in 1:15 is several times repeated (2:1, 2, 10, 11).

2:1. "Blow the horn in Zion" is probably addressed to the priests, as is the same command in vs. 15. "Horn" (Driver) is better than **trumpet,** since the *shôphār* was made from the curved horn of a ram or a bull. The warning blast in Jerusalem would be relayed to other towns till all would hear and **tremble.** The danger in this case is the oncoming **day of the LORD,** of which the locust plague was a foretaste. Both rhythm and sense favor taking the last two Hebrew words of vs. 1 with vs. 2, "Yea near is . . ." (so Peshitta, Amer. Trans., and O. Procksch in Rudolf Kittel, ed., *Biblia Hebraica* [3rd ed.; Stuttgart: Priv. Württ. Bibelanstalt, 1937], p. 912).

2. The same four synonyms are used to emphasize the **darkness** of the day of the Lord in Zeph. 1:15, a longer description, from which Joel quotes only two phrases. Since the time of Amos 5:18, **darkness** had been a symbol of the destructive aspect of the day of God's judgment. The Hebrew consonants שחר are vocalized *sháhar,* "dawn," in the M.T. and so interpreted in all the ancient versions, but the preceding emphasis on darkness and actual descriptions support the vocalization *shehōr,* **blackness.** The plague of locusts in Egypt is said to have darkened the land (Exod. 10:15). Of an incursion of locusts in Lebanon it was written, "The whole face of the mountain was black with

<table>
<tr><td>

beasts groan! . . . The beasts of the field cry also unto thee (vss. 18, 20). These creatures, innocent of sin, share in the general suffering. Man's sin has brought woe to all creation. It is reminiscent of the pathetic phrase with which Jonah ends: "and also much cattle."

2:1-11. *The Meaning of Calamity.*—This passage, like ch. 1, excites historical and literary interest. Historically it commands attention as a document emerging from a time of national

</td><td>

disaster, and affords an insight into the sufferings endured on more than one occasion in Eastern countries by reason of locust plagues. From the literary standpoint the passage is remarkable for its graphic description and powerful imagery.

A similar preoccupation with the details of human suffering is abundantly expressed in modern literature. In a variety of styles, ranging from the banal to the brilliant, the lurid facts

</td></tr>
</table>

3 A fire devoureth before them; and behind them a flame burneth: the land *is* as the garden of Eden before them, and behind them a desolate wilderness; yea, and nothing shall escape them.

4 The appearance of them *is* as the appearance of horses; and as horsemen, so shall they run.

5 Like the noise of chariots on the tops of mountains shall they leap, like the noise of a flame of fire that devoureth the stubble, as a strong people set in battle array.

3 Fire devours before them,
     and behind them a flame burns.
  The land is like the garden of Eden before them,
     but after them a desolate wilderness,
     and nothing escapes them.

4 Their appearance is like the appearance of horses,
     and like war horses they run.
5 As with the rumbling of chariots,
     they leap on the tops of the mountains,
  like the crackling of a flame of fire
     devouring the stubble,
  like a powerful army
     drawn up for battle.

them (Thomson, *op. cit.*, p. 417). C. S. Jarvis describes the advance of locust hoppers in Sinai as "a slow but steady inundation by a black flood" (*Three Deserts* [London: John Murray, 1936], p. 223). **Powerful people:** See Exeg. on 1:6. The unparalleled character of the plague, already implied in 1:2-3, is expressed in words reminiscent of the description of the locust plague of Egypt (Exod. 10:14).

3. The metaphor of **fire,** already used for drought in 1:19, is equally apt for the destruction caused by locusts. "Bamboo groves have been stripped of their leaves and left standing like saplings after a rapid bush fire, and grass has been devoured so that the bare ground appeared as if burned" (quoted in George Adam Smith, *The Book of the Twelve Prophets* [rev. ed.; New York: Harper & Bros., 1928], II, 394). The transformation of a fertile Eden into a desolate wilderness is the reverse of the process described in Isa. 51:3; Ezek. 36:35. **Nothing escapes them** is literally true of all green vegetable matter in the path of a locust horde.

4. The resemblance of the locust, particularly its head, to a miniature horse has induced a German name for locust, *Heupferd,* and the Italian *cavaletta.* Parallelism favors **war horses** (RSV) rather than **horsemen** (KJV). The speed and orderly advance of a locust army make this an apt simile. The leaping of a horse is compared with that of a locust in Job 39:20. In Rev. 9:7, which is clearly based on this passage, the supernatural locusts of the end time are also compared with war horses.

5. The comparison between the sound of locusts' wings and **the rumbling of chariots** is also used of the eschatological locusts of Rev. 9:9. Observers have likened the sound to "the falling of a heavy shower on a distant forest" (Thomson, *op. cit.*, p. 417), and to "the distant rumble of waves" (Whiting, "Jerusalem's Locust Plague," p. 513). Since these locusts approached from the north (vs. 20), to a dweller in Jerusalem the first wave would appear **on the tops of the mountains,** Mount Scopus and the Mount of Olives. As the locusts approach, the sound becomes sharper, **like the crackling** of blazing **stubble,**

of war, crime, disease, storm, and accident are again and again set down on paper. Such material furnishes the stuff of routine newspaper reporting, and the framework of genuinely great novels. Studies of the psychological effects of calamity have actually been made by scientists.

This interest, like the writing designed to gratify it, is often more morbid than humane. Yet from the biblical point of view one can certainly not be contemptuous of a concern for the

actualities of human affliction. The Bible too is concerned with what happens on the plane of history, and permits itself no retreat into a realm of abstract ideas. It confronts the human situation just as it is, taking with complete seriousness the ills and sorrows of mankind.

Yet the Bible, unlike the larger part of good or bad modern literature, does not content itself with setting forth the sordid story. Its theme is not the tragedy of human life. Its theme is judgment and grace—the judgment

6 Before their face the people shall be much pained: all faces shall gather blackness.

7 They shall run like mighty men; they shall climb the wall like men of war; and they shall march every one on his ways, and they shall not break their ranks:

8 Neither shall one thrust another; they shall walk every one in his path: and *when* they fall upon the sword, they shall not be wounded.

6 Before them peoples are in anguish,
    all faces grow pale.
7 Like warriors they charge,
    like soldiers they scale the wall.
They march each on his way,
    they do not swerve[b] from their paths.
8 They do not jostle one another,
    each marches in his path;
they burst through the weapons
    and are not halted.

[b] Gk Syr Vg: Heb *take a pledge*

which in Palestine is usually burned off after the harvest. The sound of flying locusts at close quarters has been compared to "the rattle of hail or the crackling of bush on fire" (Smith, *op. cit.,* II, 391). A large locust swarm resembles **a powerful army** (cf. vs. 2; 1:6) in its regular ranks and coherent regiments (Prov. 30:27). The reverse comparison of human invaders to locusts is found in Israelite (Judg. 6:5; 7:12; Jer. 46:23; 51:27; Nah. 3:16-17), Ugaritic (H. L. Ginsberg, *Legend of King Keret* [New Haven: American Schools of Oriental Research, 1946], pp. 16, 18, 38), Egyptian (L. Keimer, "Pendeloques en forme d'insectes faisant partie de colliers égyptiens," *Annales du Service des Antiquités de l'Egypte,* XXXIII [1933], 107-11), and Assyrian sources (W. E. Staples, *An Inscribed Scaraboid from Megiddo* [Chicago: University of Chicago Press, 1931], p. 62).

6. Before them peoples are in anguish: An observer of the 1928 locust plague in Palestine reports that the effect on the people "can only be really understood and appreciated by those who have witnessed the terrible spectacle of the all-devastating and relentless advance of immense swarms of young crawling locusts and the spirit of hopelessness and helplessness imbued thereby" (G. E. Bodkin, *The Locust Invasion of Palestine During 1928,* Government of Palestine, Department of Agriculture and Forests, Agricultural Leaflets, Ser. 1, Insect and Animal Pests, No. 7, p. 2). The LXX, Peshitta, and Vulg. support **all faces gather blackness;** the same clause describes a reaction of terror in Nah. 2:10.

7. Like soldiers they scale the wall: The locusts in dense masses swarmed up the walls of Jerusalem in 1915 (Whiting, *op. cit.,* p. 526, Fig., p. 517). The mention of the city **wall** may indicate a date after the rebuilding of the wall under Nehemiah in 444 B.C. The last verb in the verse is interpreted by the LXX, Peshitta, and Vulg. as "turn aside," or **swerve.** This translation requires a very slight emendation, *ye'abbethûn* (Driver), of the M.T. *ye'abbeṭûn,* "they lend on pledge," which does not suit the context.

8. Each marches in his path: Likewise, the locusts approaching Jerusalem in 1915 were compared to "numberless troops marching on parade" (*ibid.,* p. 525). **They burst through the weapons** vainly used to halt them. W. T. Thomson describes vain attempts to check locusts in Lebanon in 1845: "We dug trenches, and kindled fires, and beat and burned to death 'heaps upon heaps,' but the effort was utterly useless. Wave after wave rolled up the mountain-side, and poured over rocks, walls, ditches and hedges, those behind covering up and bridging over the masses already killed" (*op. cit.,* p. 417; cf. Whiting, *op. cit.,* pp. 535-38).

and the grace of God. For this reason it is entirely futile to try to understand the Bible merely "as literature." Joel is a poet only secondarily; primarily he is a prophet. He leaves us not with an eloquent poem inspired by a plague of locusts, but with an intimation that the Lord is at hand. He depicts calamity not as a thing in itself, not as a symptom of the vanity or frailty of life, but as a warning that bids us fear him who judges sin. Calamity has a theological meaning.

The Lord utters his voice before his army.

Zion's assailant is not nature but the Lord of nature. A personal will is behind the disaster. Were it not so, man would indeed stand

9 They shall run to and fro in the city; they shall run upon the wall, they shall climb up upon the houses; they shall enter in at the windows like a thief.	9 They leap upon the city, they run upon the walls; they climb up into the houses, they enter through the windows like a thief.
10 The earth shall quake before them; the heavens shall tremble: the sun and the moon shall be dark, and the stars shall withdraw their shining:	10 The earth quakes before them, the heavens tremble. The sun and the moon are darkened, and the stars withdraw their shining.
11 And the LORD shall utter his voice before his army: for his camp is very great: for *he is* strong that executeth his word: for the day of the LORD *is* great and very terrible; and who can abide it?	11 The LORD utters his voice before his army, for his host is exceedingly great; he that executes his word is powerful. For the day of the LORD is great and very terrible; who can endure it?

9. The first half of the verse is similar to vs. 7a. Isa. 33:4 compares to locusts human attackers rushing (same verb as here) upon the spoil. As in the eighth plague of Egypt (Exod. 10:6), the locusts **climb up into the houses,** and **enter through the windows,** which of course were without glass. In Jerusalem in 1915 they crawled up the walls of houses, squeezed through the cracks of doors or windows, and swarmed into the rooms (Whiting, *op. cit.,* p. 533, Fig. on p. 528).

10-11. These verses give a theological and eschatological interpretation of the locust invasion. Some elements are drawn from the stock descriptions of the day of the Lord and are here transferred by analogy to the locust plague because it too is a divine visitation and a precursor of that final judgment.

10. The quaking of the earth is often associated with manifestations of divine power and judgment (3:16; Pss. 18:7; 77:18; Isa. 13:13; Nah. 1:5; Hab. 3:6), as are also the trembling of the heavens (3:16; Isa. 13:13) and the darkening of the heavenly bodies (vs. 31; 3:15; Isa. 13:10; Ezek. 32:7; Matt. 24:29). Some of these features are also partially true of actual locust plagues. Of the quaking of the earth it is reported that the hopping locusts were so thick in Palestine in 1915 that "it seemed as if the entire surface of the ground moved, producing a most curious effect upon one's vision and causing dizziness" (*ibid.,* p. 523; cf. Thomson, *op. cit.,* p. 416). **The sun** is sometimes **darkened** by dense flights of locusts (Whiting, *op. cit.,* p. 513; Smith, *op. cit.,* II, 391-92).

11. The **voice** of the Lord is elsewhere connected with judgment (3:16; Isa. 30:30) and is sometimes a metaphor for thunder (Pss. 18:13; 68:33), as in the similar Ugaritic "Baal utters his voice" (J. H. Patton, *Canaanite Parallels in the Book of Psalms* [Baltimore: Johns Hopkins Press, 1944], p. 25). According to tradition Mohammed called locusts "the army of God" (al-Damīrī, *Kitāb ḥayāt al-ḥayawān al-kubrā* [Cairo: 1861], I, 261). The particle *kî,* here twice translated **for,** is better rendered "truly" or "indeed" in this context. "That which executes his [God's] word" is the locust army. The same phrase is used of the wind which fulfills God's purpose (Ps. 148:8). **The day of the LORD is great and very terrible:** Also found, except for **very,** in vs. 31; Mal. 4:5. **Who can endure it?** A similar question is asked about the day of the Lord in Mal. 3:2. This rhetor-

forth merely as the helpless victim of blind fate, and tragic events would be meaningless except in so far as they could be rationalized in a philosophy of despair. Seen as an act of God, the calamity becomes intelligible and even edifying. Hereby man is given notice of the seriousness of his situation before God. Thus did	Jesus interpret a disaster with which his contemporaries were familiar: "Or those eighteen, upon whom the tower in Siloam fell, and slew them, think ye that they were sinners above all men that dwelt in Jerusalem? I tell you, Nay: but, except ye repent, ye shall all likewise perish" (Luke 13:4-5).

12 ¶ Therefore also now, saith the LORD, turn ye *even* to me with all your heart, and with fasting, and with weeping, and with mourning:	12 "Yet even now," says the LORD, "return to me with all your heart, with fasting, with weeping, and with mourning;

12 ¶ Therefore also now, saith the LORD, turn ye *even* to me with all your heart, and with fasting, and with weeping, and with mourning:

13 And rend your heart, and not your garments, and turn unto the LORD your God: for he *is* gracious and merciful, slow to anger, and of great kindness, and repenteth him of the evil.

14 Who knoweth *if* he will return and repent, and leave a blessing behind him; *even* a meat offering and a drink offering unto the LORD your God?

12 "Yet even now," says the LORD,
"return to me with all your heart,
with fasting, with weeping, and with
mourning;
13 and rend your hearts and not your
garments."
Return to the LORD, your God,
for he is gracious and merciful,
slow to anger, and abounding in steadfast
love,
and repents of evil.
14 Who knows whether he will not turn and
repent,
and leave a blessing behind him,
a cereal offering and a drink offering
for the LORD, your God?

ical question, expecting the answer, "No one," is a fitting close to the foregoing account of the suffering of plants, animals, and people of both country (ch. 1) and city (2:1-9).

D. A Call to National Repentance (2:12-17)

This passage is appropriately used for the Epistle on Ash Wednesday in the Book of Common Prayer.

12. The prophets interpreted calamities as moral judgments and as admonitions to **return** to God (Amos 4:6-9). The **heart** in Hebrew psychology is not only the seat of the affections but even more of the will. **Fasting, weeping,** and **mourning** were the usual expressions of repentance (1:9, 13-14). In 2:12–3:21 the direct words of God in the first person alternate with the words of the prophet referring to God in the third person (see Intro., p. 731).

13. This great appeal is given a musical setting in Mendelssohn's *Elijah.* **And not your garments** does not absolutely forbid this common sign of grief (Gen. 37:29, 34), but rather emphasizes that God's primary requirement from sinners is "a broken and a contrite heart" (Ps. 51:17). The same catalogue of God's mercies is found in Jonah 4:2, and both passages go back to God's own declaration of his character to Moses on Mount Sinai (Exod. 34:6). The Lord is ever "relenting of evil" (Amer. Trans.): when sinners return to God, his attitude toward them also changes, and in compassion he revokes the threatened judgment (Jer. 26:3, 13, 19; Jonah 3:10).

14. As man turns to God (vss. 12-13), God turns to man (Jonah 3:9). Joel expresses the hope that after visiting his people in mercy, God may **leave a blessing behind him** as he returns to heaven. Grain and wine for food were regarded as blessings from God

12-17. *The Double Repentance.*—Because the assailant is not nature or fate, there is possibility of deliverance. Man may respond to the calamity with repentance, and God may graciously remove the affliction. Man is dealing with One who knows how to show mercy. Indeed, the very fact that God's judgment was given this visible form endows the act of repentance with hopefulness. The warning is itself an act of mercy, summoning man to repent lest a worse thing come upon him. And of course it is this "worse thing" that gives point to the prophet's message. A natural catastrophe could be endured stoically if it had no further significance beyond itself. Men would simply be brave, not repentant, in the face of a fortuitous affliction. The really alarming aspect of the disaster is that the present distress is not the end but only the beginning of the matter. It is a herald of God's vastly more serious day of reckoning (see vs. 11). But since this day of reckoning is announced, man may go forth to meet it in repentance.

At this point a difficulty emerges. If a calamity is thus interpreted, it would seem appropriate to call upon men to repent. But the word

15 ¶ Blow the trumpet in Zion, sanctify a fast, call a solemn assembly:	15 Blow the trumpet in Zion; sanctify a fast; call a solemn assembly;
16 Gather the people, sanctify the congregation, assemble the elders, gather the children, and those that suck the breasts: let the bridegroom go forth of his chamber, and the bride out of her closet.	16 gather the people. Sanctify the congregation; assemble the elders; gather the children, even nursing infants. Let the bridegroom leave his room, and the bride her chamber.
17 Let the priests, the ministers of the Lord, weep between the porch and the altar, and let them say, Spare thy people, O Lord, and give not thine heritage to reproach, that the heathen should rule over them: wherefore should they say among the people, Where *is* their God?	17 Between the vestibule and the altar let the priests, the ministers of the Lord, weep and say, "Spare thy people, O Lord, and make not thy heritage a reproach, a byword among the nations. Why should they say among the peoples, 'Where is their God?' "

(Deut. 7:13), and here the prophet emphasizes their religious use as the means of sacrificial worship (1:9, 13).

15. The expression "Blow the horn in Zion" is identical with the first phrase of vs. 1, although there the horn gives a warning and here it summons to national repentance. The second half of the verse is identical with 1:14a.

16. An expansion of 1:14b. The age rather than the official capacity of **elders** is emphasized by the contrast with **children**. As in the description of universal suffering in ch. 1, the nationwide character of the call to repentance is conveyed by specifying the groups involved. According to Deut. 24:5, a newly-wedded groom was exempted from military and other civic duties for a year, but here both **bridegroom** and **bride** are summoned from the very nuptial **chamber**. Similarly, in a Ugaritic text, "the newly wedded bridegroom" is the climax of those called to war (Ginsberg, *Legend of King Keret,* pp. 16, 18, 38).

17. Finally, as the religious representatives of the people, the **priests** are called upon to weep and intercede with God (cf. 1:9, 13). They are to stand between the **porch** (I Kings 6:3) and the brazen **altar** of burnt offering (II Chr. 4:1), i.e., within the inner court of the priests (II Chr. 4:9). Zerubbabel's temple probably followed the model of Solomon's, though on a less magnificent scale (Hag. 2:3). The basis of the appeal, as in the intercession of Moses (Deut. 9:26, 29), is that Israel is the Lord's special **people** and **heritage. That the heathen should rule over them** is a possible rendering and is found in the ancient versions. Since the context speaks not of foreign domination but of locusts

repent is twice applied not to man's action or attitude, but to God's (vss. 13, 14). In what sense shall we understand God as repenting? We do not dispose of the difficulty simply by taking this expression as a metaphorical way of saying—with the change of a single letter in English—that God relents. For we are still presented with a picture of a God who turns back on his course, who appears to change his mind and abandon his original intentions.

Here one can only say that there is no strictly logical way in which to describe God's mercy. To think of God under the aspect of remorse-

less eternal law would manifestly not answer to the biblical message. Yet when we attempt to see how it is that God's justice turns into pardon, we are forced back—in thought, if not in word—upon just such anthropomorphisms as Joel frankly employs. In the face of this mystery we shall do well not to cavil at scriptural language. For whatever the logical problems involved, the very essence of the gospel rests on the assurance that "we have not a high priest which cannot be touched with the feeling of our infirmities" (Heb. 4:15). We believe that man does not repent in vain; and

18 ¶ Then will the Lord be jealous for his land, and pity his people.

19 Yea, the Lord will answer and say unto his people, Behold, I will send you corn, and wine, and oil, and ye shall be satisfied therewith: and I will no more make you a reproach among the heathen:

20 But I will remove far off from you the northern *army,* and will drive him into a land barren and desolate, with his face toward the east sea, and his hinder part toward the utmost sea, and his stink shall come up, and his ill savor shall come up, because he hath done great things.

18 Then the Lord became jealous for his land,
and had pity on his people.

19 The Lord answered and said to his people,
"Behold, I am sending to you
grain, wine, and oil,
and you will be satisfied;
and I will no more make you
a reproach among the nations.

20 "I will remove the northerner far from you,
and drive him into a parched and desolate land,
his front into the eastern sea,
and his rear into the western sea;
the stench and foul smell of him will rise,
for he has done great things.

and drought, most modern commentators favor "that the nations should use a byword against them" (ASV mg.). The latter translation is supported by vs. 19c and by Jer. 24:9; Ps. 44:13-14, where "reproach" and "byword" are also used together. Israel resented becoming an object of scorn as a result of this national calamity, not only for her own sake, but also because the pagan nations might express doubt of the existence or the power of Israel's God with the taunting words, **Where is their God?** (Mic. 7:10; Ps. 79:10).

E. Promises of Removal of Locusts and Restoration of Fertility (2:18-27)

18. Evidently the prophet's repeated appeals were heeded, and the people truly repented. **The Lord became jealous** [or "zealous"] **for his land** (Zech. 1:14; 8:2). The verbs in this verse and the first two verbs in vs. 19 are rightly translated as pasts (RSV), not futures (KJV).

19. **The Lord answered,** probably through his prophet. **Grain, wine, and oil,** the basic agricultural products of the land, had been cut off by the locusts and the drought (1:10). **A reproach among the nations** echoes the wording of the prayer in vs. 17c.

20. The most obvious interpretation of **the northerner** is "coming from the north" as the locusts did to Jerusalem in 1915. This literal interpretation is strengthened by the mention below of geographical features in the other three principal directions. Since Israel's historic (Jer. 13:20) and eschatological (Ezek. 38:6, 15) enemies are from the north, some commentators consider this a term for invaders of the end time (cf. long excursus in Kapelrud, *Joel Studies,* pp. 93-108). God **will drive** away the locusts, presumably by winds, as in Exod. 10:19. **The parched and desolate land** is the desert

that implies a turning away of God's anger, a divine repentance.

18-27. *The Form of God's Favor.*—The book now, so to speak, goes into reverse motion. Vss. 18-19 are closely connected with vs. 17. God has proved responsive to the plea that Israel has become **a byword among the nations** (vs. 17). His jealousy is aroused, so that he rehabilitates the stricken land. This, which again seems rather anthropomorphic, actually establishes a point of immense importance. In the whole sweep of the biblical perspective

God's mercy is not represented as springing merely from a general disposition toward tenderheartedness. Rather it is seen as the expression of his faithfulness. God's love is manifested in the keeping of his promises to his people. It is because **the Lord became jealous for his land** that he **had pity on his people.** Faith thus rests upon a more secure foundation than any generalized conception or philosophy of divine love. Faith confesses that "if we believe not, yet he abideth faithful: he cannot deny himself" (II Tim. 2:13).

21 ¶ Fear not, O land; be glad and rejoice: for the Lord will do great things.

22 Be not afraid, ye beasts of the field: for the pastures of the wilderness do spring, for the tree beareth her fruit, the fig tree and the vine do yield their strength.

23 Be glad then, ye children of Zion, and rejoice in the Lord your God: for he hath given you the former rain moderately, and he will cause to come down for you the rain, the former rain, and the latter rain in the first *month*.

---

21 "Fear not, O land;
    be glad and rejoice,
    for the Lord has done great things!
22 Fear not, you beasts of the field,
    for the pastures of the wilderness are
        green;
    the tree bears its fruit,
    the fig tree and vine give their full
        yield.

23 "Be glad, O sons of Zion,
    and rejoice in the Lord, your God;
    for he has given the early rain for your
        vindication,
    he has poured down for you abundant
        rain,
    the early and the latter rain, as before.

---

area to the south of Judah. **His front** is the "van" (Driver) of the locust army. **The eastern sea** is the Dead Sea (Ezek. 47:18), and **the western sea** is the Mediterranean (Deut. 11:24). Jerome, in his commentary on Joel, reports that while he was in Palestine in the early fifth century A.D., locusts were blown into these same two seas. Heaps of drowned locusts were washed onto the seashores, and he blames a pestilence on the stench from the putrefying bodies. Similarly, in 1915 many locusts perished in the Dead Sea, and the smell from decaying masses of the insects was "so putrid and vile as to be almost unbearable" (Whiting, *op. cit.*, p. 544). **For he has done great things** (cf. vs. 21) in destruction.

21-23. These verses rise to a climax as the land, the beasts, and the people are successively addressed. Evidently the locusts were removed, according to the preceding promise, and fertility is restored by abundant rain.

21. The **land,** which mourned in 1:10, is urged not to **fear,** but rather to **be glad and rejoice,** as was impossible during the locust plague and drought (1:12, 16). **The Lord has done great things** (cf. Ps. 126:2-3) in restoration, in contrast to the locusts of whose ravages the same words are used in vs. 20.

22. Here and in vs. 23, animals, fruits, and people are mentioned in the reverse order from ch. 1. The grazing animals, which were distressed by lack of forage and water (1:18, 20), are assured of green pasturage. In 1:7, 12 the trees and vines were eaten by locusts or withered by drought, but now fruit trees and grape vines **give their full yield.** The Tanis stele of Pharaoh Tarharga (688-663) praises the gods for protecting a field from locusts so that it has an abundant harvest (Keimer, "Pendeloques en forme d'insectes faisant partie de colliers égyptiens," p. 107).

23. The **sons of Zion** are not only the Jerusalemites but, as indicated by the parallelism in Ps. 149:2, all Jews resident in Palestine. Instead of mourning as in 1:5, 8, 11-12, the people are called upon to **rejoice.** The means whereby the drought is overcome and

---

God's renewed favor to his people takes the form of reversing the conditions of the blight. Just as Joel has dwelt upon the actual circumstances of the distress, so now he elaborates the details of the restoration. Relief from the tribulation is not sought or found merely in a spiritualized philosophy of life. An actual return of material abundance is envisaged.

This insistence upon material blessings is very marked in the O.T., and only the faint-

hearted expositor will fail to do justice to it. The point is not, of course, that prosperity automatically accompanies righteousness in succeeding periods of history. The point is rather that God has regard for the real needs and wants of men, that he takes his creatures seriously just as he made them. He knows the reality of hunger and thirst, and all the normal desires of flesh and blood. He does not give a stone in place of bread, under the guise of

24 And the floors shall be full of wheat, and the vats shall overflow with wine and oil.

25 And I will restore to you the years that the locust hath eaten, the cankerworm, and the caterpillar, and the palmerworm, my great army which I sent among you.

26 And ye shall eat in plenty, and be satisfied, and praise the name of the LORD

24 "The threshing floors shall be full of grain,
the vats shall overflow with wine and oil.

25 I will restore to you the years
which the swarming locust has eaten,
the hopper, the destroyer, and the cutter,
my great army, which I sent among you.

26 "You shall eat in plenty and be satisfied,
and praise the name of the LORD your God,
who has dealt wondrously with you.

---

fertility is restored is abundant and regular **rain.** The meaning of *hammôreh liçedhāqāh,* "the autumn rain for vindication," has been much disputed. *Môreh* may mean either (*a*) "autumn rain" (similarly KJV, RSV, Driver, Robinson), as below in this same verse and in Ps. 84:6; or (*b*) "teacher" (similarly Targ., Vulg., Amer. Trans., Nowack, Sellin), but the context deals with physical, not spiritual, blessings. The basic meaning of *çedhāqāh* is "that which measures up to an established norm," "righteousness," but it also has the derived meaning of God's **vindication** (Bewer) of those who are righteous. In this sense it is often parallel to and practically synonymous with God's "salvation" (e.g., Isa. 45:8). This translation is supported by Hos. 10:12; Isa. 45:8, in both of which God's "vindication" comes down figuratively, as in this passage the rain is poured down literally. Other meanings proposed for *liçedhāqāh,* **moderately** (KJV), "in just measure" (ASV, George Adam Smith, Robinson), or "for prosperity" (Francis Brown, S. R. Driver, and C. A. Briggs, eds., *A Hebrew and English Lexicon of the Old Testament* [Boston: Houghton Mifflin & Co., 1906], p. 842) fail to do justice to the ethical root of the word or to its associations with divine deliverance. The rains on which agriculture in Palestine depends (Deut. 11:14) are the "autumn rain" of October-November, just before the time of planting, and the "spring rain" of March-April, when the crops are maturing. *Bārī'shôn* (M.T.) has been interpreted **in the first month** and "at the first" in contrast to "afterward" (vs. 28; Driver). Some Hebrew MSS, the LXX, Peshitta, and Vulg. read *kārī'shôn,* **as before,** i.e., before the drought (cf. Isa. 1:26), which makes better sense.

24. The famine of 1:10-12, 17 will be replaced in every particular by plenty. To this day in Palestine grain is piled up on outdoor **threshing floors,** as in Ruth 3:7. The **vats** were hewn out of rock to catch the wine or olive oil from the higher presses.

25. **Years** implies that the locusts had ravaged the land for several seasons. The same four stages of locust are given as in 1:4, though the first name there is the last here. Israel Aharoni (*Haarbeh* [Jaffa: 1919], p. 21) suggests that 1:4 gives the historical order of the stages which attacked Judah in Joel's day, while this verse gives a more logical order beginning with the adult. **My great army:** Cf. vs. 11.

26. God's **people,** who were ashamed by the locust plague and drought (1:11), and who prayed that the pagans might not use a byword against them (vs. 17), **shall never again be put to shame.**

---

substituting something spiritual for something carnal (see Luke 11:11). In the perfection of redemption full justice will be done to the happiness of man, and nothing good that God has created will then be lacking.

At the same time, even as the plague of locusts was not the day of the Lord but rather a warning of it, so the fulfillment of creaturely

wants is to be understood as the sign of God's presence. The passage here concludes with the assurance that the people will know God in their midst (vs. 27). The Giver bestows not only material gifts, but the gifts of himself. He who knows the difference between bread and a stone has also said that "man shall not live by bread alone" (Matt. 4:4). And even as the cry

your God, that hath dealt wondrously with you: and my people shall never be ashamed.

27 And ye shall know that I *am* in the midst of Israel, and *that* I *am* the LORD your God, and none else: and my people shall never be ashamed.

28 ¶ And it shall come to pass afterward, *that* I will pour out my Spirit upon all flesh; and your sons and your daughters shall prophesy, your old men shall dream dreams, your young men shall see visions:

29 And also upon the servants and upon the handmaids in those days will I pour out my Spirit.

And my people shall never again be put to shame.

27 You shall know that I am in the midst of Israel,
   and that I, the LORD, am your God and there is none else.
   And my people shall never again be put to shame.

28c "And it shall come to pass afterward,
   that I will pour out my spirit on all flesh;
   your sons and your daughters shall prophesy,
   your old men shall dream dreams,
   and your young men shall see visions.
29 Even upon the menservants and maidservants
   in those days, I will pour out my spirit.

c Heb Ch 3. 1

---

27. Because of these blessings Israel will realize that the Lord is in their **midst** as deliverer (3:17, 21; Deut. 7:21), that he is their **God** (3:17; often in Ezekiel and Deutero-Isaiah), and that there is **none else,** a statement of monotheism characteristic of Deutero-Isaiah (Isa. 45:5-6, 18). This is an effective answer to the taunt in vs. 17, "Where is their God?" The verse and the section close with a reassuring repetition of the promise of vs. 26*b*.

II. Future Blessings of Israel and Judgment of the Nations (2:28–3:21)
A. Outpouring of the Spirit (2:28-29)

28-29. Afterward, i.e., after the bestowment of the physical blessings mentioned above, at some indefinite time in the future. The imagery of pouring out (Ezek. 39:29; Isa. 32:15) may be reminiscent of the giving of abundant rain (vs. 23). One of the chief functions of God's Spirit is to illumine for prophecy, whether ecstatic utterance (I Sam. 10:6, 10) or the proclamation of God's message of instruction, warning, or prediction (II Chr. 20:14; 24:20). God here promises the fulfillment of Moses' wish that all the Lord's people might be prophets by the influence of the Spirit (Num. 11:29). **All flesh** could mean all mankind, as in Isa. 40:5, but the following possessives, **your sons and your daughters,** etc., show that the phrase here means all Israel. Previously the spirit of prophecy had been limited to a chosen few, but under this new dispensation God's revelation will come to both male and female, to both old and young, and even to the servant class. In his pentecostal sermon Peter said of the outpouring of the Spirit on that occasion, "This is what was spoken by the prophet Joel" (Acts 2:16), and he quoted

---

of the people was that they were reproached with having been deserted by their God, so their satisfaction will be in their uninterrupted communion with him.

28-32. *The Gift of the Spirit.*—The use which Peter made of this passage on the day of Pentecost (Acts 2:16-21) transfers our center of interest to the N.T. Yet in order to understand more clearly the relevance of the passage as Peter used it, we do well to inquire what it says in its own right. Four points emerge conspicuously. In the first place, the gift of the

Spirit enables its recipients to discern and declare the will of God; i.e., it is the gift of prophecy. Second, it is conceived as being bestowed upon the people of Israel without differentiation of age, sex, or class. Third, it belongs to the culminating time of history, as is indicated by the portents mentioned here. Finally, salvation comes through calling upon **the name of the LORD,** i.e., faith in Israel's God brings deliverance from judgment.

The significance of the passage in the light of Pentecost is thus extremely rich. Peter was

30 And I will show wonders in the heavens and in the earth, blood, and fire, and pillars of smoke.

31 The sun shall be turned into darkness, and the moon into blood, before the great and the terrible day of the LORD come.

32 And it shall come to pass, *that* whosoever shall call on the name of the LORD shall be delivered: for in mount Zion and in Jerusalem shall be deliverance, as the LORD hath said, and in the remnant whom the LORD shall call.

30 "And I will give portents in the heavens and on the earth, blood and fire and columns of smoke. **31** The sun shall be turned to darkness, and the moon to blood, before the great and terrible day of the LORD comes. **32** And it shall come to pass that all who call upon the name of the LORD shall be delivered; for in Mount Zion and in Jerusalem there shall be those who escape, as the LORD has said, and among the survivors shall be those whom the LORD calls.

(Acts 2:17-21) the whole passage, Joel 2:28-32. Peter, however, goes beyond Joel in extending the promise of the Spirit even to non-Israelite believers (Acts 2:39). In the light of the N.T. fulfillment, Joel's prediction of spiritual illumination for all God's people is perhaps his most important religious contribution.

B. SIGNS OF THE DAY OF THE LORD AND DELIVERANCE OF THE FAITHFUL (2:30-32)

These verses are also rhythmic and are rightly printed as poetry in Moffatt and the Amer. Trans. The time relative to the foregoing is not stated.

30. A portent is an extraordinary event, here foreboding God's judgment. Though the **earth** is mentioned second, its **portents** are listed first (chiasmus). **Blood and fire and columns of smoke** are the common accompaniments of wars, which precede the end in N.T. eschatology also (Mark 13:7-8). Vss. 30-31 are also quoted in Acts 2:19-20, but are not applied by Peter.

31. The heavenly portents are also mentioned in vs. 10; 3:15. **The sun shall be turned to darkness, and the moon to blood,** i.e., shall become blood-red in color. Such phenomena, which may be caused by eclipses or by clouds of dust, are harbingers of judgment not only in the O.T. (Isa. 13:10), but also in the N.T. (Mark 13:24; Rev. 6:12). **Before the great and terrible day of the LORD comes** equals Mal. 4:5; cf. Joel 2:11.

32. To **call upon the name of the LORD** means to invoke him in worship (Gen. 4:26). This is the way of escape from the locusts (vss. 12-17), as well as from the final judgment. Peter uses the first clause of this verse as an appeal for faith and spiritual salvation on

---

not haphazardly quoting a prophecy which had merely a general or superficial relevance to the pentecostal preaching. When the Holy Spirit came upon the church, men's mouths were opened to utter the word of the Lord; and the gift of this prophetic proclamation fell upon persons old and young, upon the rich and the poor, upon men and women. This event accompanied the beginning of the new age, the day of the Messiah's reign, thus bringing to a close the former ages and pointing on to the culmination of God's work in history when Christ should overcome all his enemies. Moreover, Pentecost was the time for urging men to call upon the name of the Lord—Israel's Lord indeed, though Israel had rejected him—so that they might be saved "from this untoward generation" (Acts 2:40).

The Christian interpretation of this passage does not of course rest upon the mechanical fulfillment of certain details specified by the

prophet. It added no validity to the preaching of Pentecost that an appropriate O.T. passage, with a striking correspondence to the occasion, could be quoted. For it is not the O.T. which lends authority to the N.T.; rather, the N.T. gives authority to the O.T. As Origen says:

The inspired character of the prophetic writings and the spirituality of the law of Moses shone out when Jesus came. Clear proofs of the inspiration of the Old Testament could not well be given before the Christ had come. Till then the law and the prophets were open to a suspicion of not being truly divine: it was the coming of Jesus that set them in a plain light as records made by the grace of heaven.[1]

What Joel foresaw was that in the fullness of time God would scatter the knowledge of himself among his people. His word would come alive in the words of men; and then under the

[1] *On First Principles* IV. 1. 6.

3 For, behold, in those days, and in that time, when I shall bring again the captivity of Judah and Jerusalem,

2 I will also gather all nations, and will bring them down into the valley of Jehoshaphat, and will plead with them there for my people and *for* my heritage Israel, whom they have scattered among the nations, and parted my land.

3 *d* "For behold, in those days and at that time, when I restore the fortunes of Judah and Jerusalem, 2 I will gather all the nations and bring them down to the valley of Jehosh′aphat, and I will enter into judgment with them there, on account of my people and my heritage Israel, because they have scattered them among the nations, and have divided up my land,

d Heb Ch 4. 1

---

the day of Pentecost (Acts 2:21). Paul also quotes this promise in Rom. 10:13, where he applies the principle of salvation by faith to all people of all ages, though Joel's outlook is limited to Israelites on the day of the Lord. **For in Mount Zion . . . there shall be those who escape** is expressly quoted by Joel from Obad. 17 with the formula **as the LORD has said.** It is implied that not all Israelites but only the true believers shall be saved. The **survivors** are those Israelites who remain after the final wars and afflictions (3:1-21; Zech. 13:8-9). **Those whom the LORD calls**—i.e., to blessing, as in Isa. 51:2—is also quoted in Peter's pentecostal sermon (Acts 2:39). Divine election is thus the complement of human faith in this deliverance.

C. GOD'S PURPOSE TO JUDGE THE OPPRESSORS OF ISRAEL (3:1-3)

These verses are rightly printed as poetry by O. Procksch in Kittel, *Biblia Hebraica* (pp. 914-15) and in the English translation of the Jewish Publication Society.

3:1. For: What follows tells how the deliverance of the faithful (2:32) will be accomplished. As in Jer. 33:15; 50:4, 20, **in those days and at that time** refers to the period of Israel's restoration. The clause translated "I shall bring back the captivity" (ASV and similarly the ancient versions and KJV) has in some contexts the more general sense of **restore the fortunes** (RSV). Even after the returns of the sixth and fifth centuries, many Jews still remained in exile.

2. God **will gather all the nations,** as in Zeph. 3:8. **The valley of Jehoshaphat** occurs only in this chapter of the Bible; the analogy of the symbolic name in vs. 14 indicates that the prophet chose this name also because of its meaning, "Yahweh has judged." Here as in vs. 12 the name is used with a form of the verb *shāphaṭ,* "to judge." Jewish (Enoch 53:1), Christian, and Moslem traditions have localized the scene of the Last Judgment in the valley of Kidron, between Jerusalem and the Mount of Olives (Edward

---

impact of the Spirit many would turn to God for the saving of their souls. Toward such a culmination God's saving work in Israel was moving. How true this prophecy was, men could not anticipate until they were confronted by the apostolic preaching. They could not know in advance that God would shake the world by the crucifixion of a Carpenter; and that fishermen who had become wiser than rabbis would proclaim their faith to such purpose that nothing would ever be the same again. In a thoroughly unexpected manner God fulfilled the expectations of Israel. Joel became surprisingly appropriate under circumstances that no one would have associated with the fulfillment of his prophecy. Thus did God preserve his freedom to interpret his own word; conferring new and unimagined meaning upon the words of a man who, without knowing the historical day

of Jesus of Nazareth, was gifted with the vision of such things as could come true only in the day of Christ.

3:1-8. Israel Avenged.—It is unnecessarily squeamish to shrink from the terminology of vengeance which appears here, as in so many other portions of the Bible. The manner of God's judgment is not, to be sure, determined by the imagery of warfare; in the light of the entire biblical message one cannot conceive this difficult theme simply in terms of vindictiveness or the principle of "an eye for an eye." But that the world is full of evils which cry out for vengeance is clear from the Scriptures, and indeed from any record of human history. The God who plans to avenge the sufferings of his people is not, as is sometimes implied, an "immoral" God; rather he is One who is determined to vindicate his own moral order. It

3 And they have cast lots for my people; and have given a boy for a harlot, and sold a girl for wine, that they might drink.

4 Yea, and what have ye to do with me, O Tyre, and Zidon, and all the coasts of Palestine? will ye render me a recompense? and if ye recompense me, swiftly *and* speedily will I return your recompense upon your own head;

3 and have cast lots for my people, and have given a boy for a harlot, and have sold a girl for wine, and have drunk it.

4 "What are you to me, O Tyre and Sidon, and all the regions of Philistia? Are you paying me back for something? If you are paying me back, I will requite your deed upon your own head swiftly and speedily.

Robinson, *Biblical Researches in Palestine, Mount Sinai and Arabia Petrea* [Boston: Crocker & Brewster, 1841], I, 396; Guy LeStrange, *Palestine Under the Moslems* [London: A. P. Watt, 1890], p. 162). With this valley the name Jehoshaphat has been associated, at least since the time of Eusebius, early fourth century A.D. (*Onomasticon*, s.v. Κοιλας, Coelas), perhaps on the basis of this passage in Joel. There God **will enter into judgment with them** on behalf of his people and inheritance (2:17). **Israel** in Joel is interchangeable with Judah (vs. 1), indicating a date long after the fall of the Northern Kingdom. The pagans' first crime against humanity is that they have **scattered** God's **people,** implying that the conquest and deportations by the Chaldeans (Jer. 52:28-30) had already taken place. Moreover, God's **land,** the land of Israel, has been divided among the conquerors.

3. The pagans have shown no consideration for the captives, not even for the children, whom they have sold to revel with wine and women. Obad. 11 also records that the Chaldeans divided the spoil of Jerusalem by lot. **For a harlot:** The Peshitta correctly interprets "for the hire of a harlot."

D. SINS AND PUNISHMENT OF TYRE, SIDON, AND PHILISTIA (3:4-8)

These verses are also rhythmic. The long measures are suitable to a solemn indictment.

4. "What is your purpose regarding me?" God asks of the Phoenician cities, **Tyre** and **Sidon,** and of the five **regions** (Josh. 13:2; I Sam. 6:17-18) of the Philistines. These peoples are singled out because of their long-continued hostility toward the Lord's people and so toward the Lord himself. "Is it a recompense you are rendering me, or are you recompensing me?" This interpretation as a double question (LXX, Amer. Trans., Driver, Bewer) is favored by many analogies including 1:2; Job 4:17, and by the poetic parallelism. The second clause could also be taken as a condition (Peshitta, Vulg., KJV, RVS). God's question probably reflects a false claim by the pagans that they are only seeking justice. With grim irony the Lord warns that their so-called "recompense" will be repaid to them (cf. vs. 7; Isa. 59:18; Obad. 15).

---

is of the utmost comfort to men of faith that they have the assurance of God's concern about the wrongs inflicted and endured on earth.

The cruelty (vss. 3, 6) and profanity (vs. 5) of Israel's oppressors are made the subject of special comment in this prophecy. Offense to God and man go hand in hand, and are indeed inseparable. Whoever despises the rights of humanity despises God the creator; and contempt for God leads to contempt for man. This proposition, which has been amply illustrated by various modern totalitarian powers, is the negative side of the ethics of the great commandment (see Matt. 22:36-39). Neither aspect of this twofold sin will be ignored in God's judgment. The earnestness and intensity of the

language of retribution, used so freely in the Scriptures, points again to the Bible's seriousness about historical events. God has an eye to what happens in history, and does not wink at either brutality or blasphemy. At these points the Bible finds it perfectly appropriate to speak of vengeance.

A conspicuous aspect of this passage is summed up in the phrases **my people** and **my heritage Israel** (vs. 2). Joel, like the other scriptural writers, does not speak of cruelty or oppression, or any other kind of wickedness in abstract terms; neither is righteousness treated abstractly. What stands at the center of biblical thought is not vice or virtue abstractly conceived, but God's dealings with his people.

5 Because ye have taken my silver and my gold, and have carried into your temples my goodly pleasant things:

6 The children also of Judah and the children of Jerusalem have ye sold unto the Grecians, that ye might remove them far from their border.

7. Behold, I will rise them out of the place whither ye have sold them, and will return your recompense upon your own head:

8 And I will sell your sons and your daughters into the hand of the children of Judah, and they shall sell them to the Sabeans, to a people far off: for the LORD hath spoken it.

9 ¶ Proclaim ye this among the Gentiles; Prepare war, wake up the mighty men, let all the men of war draw near; let them come up:

---

5 For you have taken my silver and my gold, and have carried my rich treasures into your temples.[e] 6 You have sold the people of Judah and Jerusalem to the Greeks, removing them far from their own border. 7 But now I will stir them up from the place to which you have sold them, and I will requite your deed upon your own head. 8 I will sell your sons and your daughters into the hand of the sons of Judah, and they will sell them to the Sabe′ans, to a nation far off; for the LORD has spoken."

9 Proclaim this among the nations:
Prepare[f] war,
    stir up the mighty men.
Let all the men of war draw near,
    let them come up.

[e] Or palaces
[f] Heb sanctify

---

5. The Lord's **treasures** are not only those of his temple but of his land as a whole. The Philistines had often plundered Israel (Judg. 13:1; I Sam. 5:1; II Chr. 21:17). **Temples** were the usual repositories for foreign booty (I Sam. 5:2; 31:10).

6. Amos also accuses the Philistines and Phoenicians of dealing in Israelite slaves (Amos 1:6, 9). Ezek. 27:13 lists slaves as part of the merchandise between Greece and Tyre. The Phoenicians are also condemned as slave traders in early Greek sources (*Odyssey* XIV. 297; XV. 482-484; Herodotus *History* I. 1; II. 54).

7. God is about to **stir . . . up** the scattered Israelite exiles so that they may return to their land (vs. 1) and take their vengeance and God's vengeance on their enemies. The **recompense** of the pagans will be what they have done to the Israelites. The last clause reiterates the closing words of vs. 4.

8. **Sons** and **daughters** recalls the ill-treatment of the Israelite boys and girls (vs. 3), but could include the whole people (vs. 6). In fulfillment of this warning the Sidonians were sold into slavery by Artaxerxes III in 345 B.C. (Diodorus Siculus XIV. 45), the Tyrians and the people of Gaza in Philistia by Alexander the Great in 332 B.C. (Arrian *Anabasis of Alexander* II. 24, 27). No doubt Jews were among the buyers of these Phoenician and Philistine slaves. The Sabeans were famous as traders (I Kings 10:2; Ezek. 27:22-23). Sheba, their home in southern Arabia, was as **far** (Jer. 6:20) to the southeast as Greece (vs. 6) was to the northwest. **For the LORD has spoken** also follows a divine pronouncement in Obad. 18.

E. The Nations Summoned to the Final Battle (3:9-11)

9. The short, two-stress Hebrew phrases are well suited to the brief commands of this verse. **Proclaim** is probably addressed by God to his heralds, who deliver the following

---

Therefore God is not described as avenging crimes, but as avenging the people against whom the crimes were committed. Here again is a matter of comfort to the Christian. We have to do with One who remembers not just his "principles" but *us*. We have to do with a God who keeps faith with men and fulfills his promises made to people of flesh and blood. God is outraged because his own children are

sold into slavery; and the stress lies more upon his concern for his children than upon his aversion to slavery. Thus throughout the Scriptures God's righteousness is manifested as love.

9-16a. The Valley of Decision.—The significance of this whole passage gathers around the memorable words, **Multitudes, multitudes in the valley of decision** (vs. 14). Tempting as it is to interpret this as referring to the decision

10 Beat your plowshares into swords, and your pruning hooks into spears: let the weak say, I *am* strong.	10 Beat your plowshares into swords, and your pruning hooks into spears; let the weak say, "I am a warrior."
11 Assemble yourselves, and come, all ye heathen, and gather yourselves together round about: thither cause thy mighty ones to come down, O LORD.	11 Hasten and come, all you nations round about, gather yourselves there. Bring down thy warriors, O LORD.
12 Let the heathen be wakened, and come up to the valley of Jehoshaphat: for there will I sit to judge all the heathen round about.	12 Let the nations bestir themselves, and come up to the valley of Jehosh'-aphat; for there I will sit to judge all the nations round about.
13 Put ye in the sickle, for the harvest is ripe: come, get you down; for the press is full, the vats overflow; for their wickedness *is* great.	13 Put in the sickle, for the harvest is ripe. Go in, tread, for the wine press is full. The vats overflow, for their wickedness is great.

summons. **Prepare** [or **sanctify** RSV mg.] **war:** This was done by religious rites (I Sam. 7:8-9); the same verb is used of instituting a national fast (1:14; 2:15). Both **draw near** (Judg. 20:23) and **come up** (1:6 of locusts; I Kings 20:22) are regular terms for an army's approach for battle.

10. This Armageddon demands all possible weapons and warriors. The first part of the verse is almost the exact opposite of the reconversion to peace in the messianic age promised in Isa. 2:4; Mic. 4:3, where the word for **spears** is different. Even the **weak** must volunteer for military service.

11. The first verb, '*ûshû*, occurs only here in the Bible; the related Arabic root has the meaning "help." In English the order of the verbs would be reversed; "come and help." The RSV **hasten** is based on an emendation, *ḥûshû*, and **assemble yourselves** (following LXX) is simply an attempt to suit the context. **All you nations round about** (cf. vs. 12) are not merely those adjoining Palestine, but all nations in every direction. Construing **there** with **gather yourselves** (LXX, Amer. Trans., RSV) makes better rhythm and sense than taking it with the following clause (Masoretic punctuation, Peshitta, Vulg., KJV). To meet this heathen horde an appeal is made to the Lord to **bring down** his angelic hosts, as in Zech. 14:5.

F. THE LAST JUDGMENT (3:12-16a)

12. In answer to this appeal the Lord grimly repeats the verbs which have summoned the pagans to battle (vs. 10), but declares that they come to his judgment seat. **The valley of Jehoshaphat:** See Exeg. on vs. 2. **All the nations round about:** Cf. vs. 11.

13. The accused have been summoned, their crimes have been listed, and their false pleas have been heard (vss. 2-8, 12). The Judge now orders the angels, his "warriors"

which men have to make in time of crisis, such an interpretation is of course unsound exegesis. The reference here is to *God's* decision. What is meant is the situation of God's enemies when they are caught, without possibility of escape, under God's judgment.	tables are often turned, that those who take the sword perish by the sword, that whole nations are destroyed in direct consequence of their iniquity. In such instances we see men trapped **in the valley of decision.** A higher power than their own has overthrown them. An irrevocable decision has been passed, and the decision is against them.
The fate which overtakes the wicked again and again in history points up the meaning of this prophecy. It certainly happens that the	It must, however, be borne in mind that these

14 Multitudes, multitudes in the valley of decision: for the day of the LORD *is* near in the valley of decision.

15 The sun and the moon shall be darkened, and the stars shall withdraw their shining.

---

14 Multitudes, multitudes,
   in the valley of decision!
For the day of the LORD is near
   in the valley of decision.
15 The sun and the moon are darkened,
   and the stars withdraw their shining.

16 And the LORD roars from Zion,
   and utters his voice from Jerusalem,
   and the heavens and the earth shake.

(vs. 11), to execute the sentence. The imagery of the grain **harvest** for judgment is also used in Isa. 17:5 and in Matt. 13:39, where as here the reapers are angels. In Palestine the grain harvest is followed by the vintage, and this too furnishes metaphors of judgment (cf. Isa. 63:1-3). **Go in,** i.e., to the wine presses in order to **tread** the grapes. So **full** are the presses that **the vats overflow,** the same phrase as in 2:24, which in contrast describes God's blessings. The ripeness of the harvest, the fullness of the wine press, and the overflowing of the vats all express metaphorically that the nations' **wickedness is great.** The imagery of this verse colors the picture of the judgment in Rev. 14:14-20.

14. Multitudes, multitudes: The repetition of the plurals emphasizes the great number, as in Exod. 8:14. The meaning of the root indicates that these hordes are murmuring and tumultuous, like the assembled enemies of Israel in Isa. 17:12. What was previously (vss. 2, 12) called "the valley of Jehoshaphat" is here given another symbolic name, **the valley of decision** or "Verdict." The multitudes are assembled for condemnation, **for the day of the LORD is near,** no longer in warning or in part, as in 1:15 or 2:1, but in actuality and finality.

15. With notable restraint the actual destruction of the enemies of God is not described; only the accompanying sights and sounds and sensations are sketched in vss. 15-16. Elements of the Day of Judgment scattered through the book are now brought together for a finale. The darkening of the heavenly bodies in exactly these words is applied by analogy to the locust plague (see 2:10*b*), but now darkness actually veils the sun, the moon, and the stars.

16*a*. The LORD roars from Zion describes a judgment on Israel in Amos 1:2, and the same imagery of a roaring lion is used of God's final judgment of all nations (Jer.

---

historical examples are not equivalent to the actual Last Judgment of which Joel is speaking here. They are only signs or analogies of it. Just as the locust plague was but a foretaste of the day of the Lord, so the many instances of historical nemesis which spring to mind are but warnings of a greater wrath to come. Examination of these verses in Joel discloses a striking fact, viz., that in the battle here depicted the conquering power is not the army of Israel. There is, in fact, no human instrument involved in this final destruction of the foes of God. When the nations have been assembled for the last conflict, the cry goes forth: **Thither cause thy mighty ones to come down, O LORD** (vs. 11). Superhuman powers will do the work of destruction. God will fight the battle without the help of man.

Minds unaccustomed to take angels seriously may stumble at this passage. Yet Joel is here proclaiming a truth of great profundity. Be-

yond all the vicissitudes of history, beyond the ebb and flow of human fortunes, beyond wars and revolutions and world upheavals, there is a more ultimate reckoning that confronts mankind. Man has to stand face to face with God. **The valley of decision** has at last an inescapable finality. There will come a time when there can no longer be any hope or possibility of a kind of moral "muddling through." There is reserved for humankind a final encounter with God, when all the truth shall be told and all accounts reckoned up.

Knowing this certainty, Christians at once hope for the eradication of all evil and the salvation of their own souls. God is not mocked —a fact that confronts us both as a promise and a threat. The promise is that there will be an end of sin. But what of us who are involved in sin? At that point we can but put our trust in **the valley of decision** into which Christ entered at Calvary. God has judged us there,

16 The LORD also shall roar out of Zion, and utter his voice from Jerusalem; and the heavens and the earth shall shake: but the LORD *will be* the hope of his people, and the strength of the children of Israel.

17 So shall ye know that I *am* the LORD your God dwelling in Zion, my holy mountain: then shall Jerusalem be holy, and there shall no strangers pass through her any more.

18 ¶ And it shall come to pass in that day, *that* the mountains shall drop down new wine, and the hills shall flow with milk, and all the rivers of Judah shall flow with waters, and a fountain shall come forth of the house of the LORD, and shall water the valley of Shittim.

But the LORD is a refuge to his people, a stronghold to the people of Israel.

17 "So you shall know that I am the LORD your God,
who dwell in Zion, my holy mountain.
And Jerusalem shall be holy
and strangers shall never again pass through it.

18 "And in that day
the mountains shall drip sweet wine,
and the hills shall flow with milk,
and all the stream beds of Judah
shall flow with water;
and a fountain shall come forth from the house of the LORD
and water the valley of Shittim.

25:30). The parallel, **utters his voice**, is similar to the phrase in 2:11. The shaking of **the heavens and the earth** has already been given as an element of the day of the Lord in 2:11, where the order is earth and heavens.

G. THE BLESSINGS OF JUDAH (3:16b-21)

16b. The description of the judgment is suddenly broken off, and the rest of the chapter, except for vs. 19, pictures God's mercies to his people. To them in the midst of this cataclysm **the LORD is a refuge . . . , a stronghold.** These metaphors of God's protection are often used in the psalms and are also combined in Ps. 61:3.

17. After the judgment of their enemies and their own deliverance Israel will know, with greater assurance than after the destruction of the locusts (2:27), that the Lord is their God. More fully than in 2:27 the Lord will be present to bless in the midst of his people, **dwelling in Zion** (cf. Zech. 8:3; Rev. 21:3). **Jerusalem shall be holy,** set apart for God and his people; no **strangers** or foreign pagans will violate its sanctity again (cf. Isa. 52:1; Zech. 14:21). In Rev. 21:27; 22:14-15 the grounds for inclusion in and exclusion from the Holy City have become purely spiritual and ethical.

18. The mountains shall drip sweet wine: An exaggerated picture of messianic fertility taken from Amos 9:13. **The hills shall flow with milk** is also influenced by Amos 9:13 and by the stock description of the land of promise as "a land flowing with milk" (Exod. 3:8). **The stream beds of Judah,** which dry up during droughts (1:20), **shall flow with water** (cf. Isa. 30:25). Ezek. 47:1-12; Zech. 14:8; and Enoch 26; 28; 30; also speak of life-giving waters flowing from the temple, and the same imagery of a river is carried over into the picture of the New Jerusalem (Rev. 22:1-2). This messianic stream of blessing was probably suggested by the waters of Shiloah (Isa. 8:6; Ps. 46:4), which flow from the spring Gihon under the temple mount and irrigate the Kidron Valley for

and condemned us. Yet in Christ he decided *for* us—that we might live, not die. Therefore as we ponder seriously the decision that we must face, we look to Jesus Christ, praying "that as we joyfully receive him for our Redeemer, so we may with sure confidence behold him when he shall come to be our Judge." [2]

16b-21. Destruction and Reconstruction.— From the formidable prophecy of the day of

[2] Book of Common Prayer.

God's judgment against the wicked, Joel moves at last into the thought of the paradise awaiting Israel when the carnage is over. It is to be noted, however, that even in the midst of these concluding verses he does not hesitate to mention the signs of destruction after the conflict. **Egypt shall be a desolation, and Edom shall be a desolate wilderness** (vs. 19). There is no attempt to gloss over the fact of God's judgment, or to depict a reconstructed world

19 Egypt shall be a desolation, and Edom shall be a desolate wilderness, for the violence *against* the children of Judah, because they have shed innocent blood in their land.

20 But Judah shall dwell for ever, and Jerusalem from generation to generation.

21 For I will cleanse their blood *that* I have not cleansed: for the LORD dwelleth in Zion.

19 "Egypt shall become a desolation
   and Edom a desolate wilderness,
for the violence done to the people of
   Judah,
   because they have shed innocent blood
   in their land.
20 But Judah shall be inhabited for ever,
   and Jerusalem to all generations.
21 I will avenge their blood, and I will not
   clear the guilty,*g*
   for the LORD dwells in Zion."

g Gk Syr: Heb *I will hold innocent their blood which I have not held innocent*

---

a short distance. This is certainly the valley down which Ezekiel's stream was to flow, and Joel's **valley of Shittim,** or "Acacias," is probably the dry lower course of this same valley, Wadi en-Nar, where acacia trees are found to this day.

19. In contrast to Judah's fertility, **Egypt shall become a desolation** [Ezek. 29:9] **and Edom a desolate wilderness** (Ezek. 35:3-4, 7, 14-15). The reason for their punishment is **for violence** [cf. Obad. 11] **done to the people of Judah,** the shedding of **innocent blood** after invading **their land.** This the Egyptians had done on several occasions (I Kings 14:25-26; II Kings 23:29), and the Edomites especially at the fall of Jerusalem in 587 B.C. (Obad. 1-21).

20. "Judah shall remain" or **shall be inhabited. Jerusalem,** the glorified city of God, shall be eternal.

21. This last verse combines punishment and blessing, which are the main themes of the chapter and of the prophecy as a whole. Since the M.T. of vs. 21a is difficult and repetitive, the reading of the LXX and Peshitta followed by the RSV is preferable: "And I will avenge their blood [i.e., of the Judeans, vs. 19], and I will not hold innocent [viz., their oppressors]." Similarly in Rev. 6:10-17 the final judgment avenges the blood of the martyrs. "And the Lord will dwell in Zion": The participle indicates continuity, and the LXX and Vulg. rightly interpreted this as a promise for the future. Thus in closing, Joel characteristically (cf. 1:20; 2:27) repeats one of the main themes of the section, the assurance of the presence of God (vs. 17; 2:27), the vindicator of his people and the source of all their blessings.

---

in such language that one could forget that there had ever been a battle. There has been evil, and it has been overthrown: and part of the grandeur of that new age will lie in the knowledge that the enemy has been routed. We are not allowed to thrust away from us the fact that there is such a thing as hell. The Bible openly exults in the vindication of God's righteousness against those who defied it.

The main thought, however, is of the excellence and beauty of God's kingdom. Once more the imagery reminds us that the Bible does not so "spiritualize" its ideas that the hope of material blessings is denied. As in ch. 2, material plenty and the presence of God are taken together in the prophet's view of the redeemed universe. We dare not so throw the emphasis on either one that the other is ignored. From the biblical standpoint, the comfort of knowing

God is not considered separately from the provisions made for human desires. Nor is this distinctively an O.T. view, as over against N.T. conceptions. The writer of II Pet. 3:13 looked "for new heavens and a new earth, wherein dwelleth righteousness." The reconstructed universe of Christian hope does not fail to do justice to what is of the "earth." The completion and fulfillment of all that legitimately belongs to man will be taken care of. Heaven will not be wholly other than what we know. All that our hearts have rightly cried for will there abound. It will be as Peter Abelard's hymn declares:

Truly Jerusalem name we that shore,
Vision of peace that brings joy evermore;
Wish and fulfillment can sever'd be ne'er,
Nor the thing prayed for come short of the prayer.[3]

[3] "O what their joy and their glory must be."

The Book of

AMOS

Introduction and Exegesis by HUGHELL E. W. FOSBROKE
Exposition by SIDNEY LOVETT

AMOS

INTRODUCTION

Amos is the earliest of the prophets whose utterances have been recorded in books that bear their names. His ministry in the first half of the eighth century B.C. was of epoch-making significance because it was the inauguration of that succession of prophetic ministries through which, in the face of great crises in their history, the people of Israel were to be brought to that deeper and richer knowledge of the being and nature of God which enabled them to survive the tragic ending of their career as a nation, and become the vehicle of God's distinctive revelation of himself to his world.

I. Amos of Tekoa

A. The Shepherd.—The man whose message was to sound as it were the keynote of prophecy was known as Amos of Tekoa. The name of this town now designates a cluster of ruins crowning a hill some six miles south of Bethlehem. These ruins, dating from the Christian Era, are of no great extent, but the statement in II Chr. 11:6, that Rehoboam fortified the town, would indicate that the site had always been of some importance for the defense of the approaches to Jerusalem. So the Chronicler also represents the forces of Judah under the leadership of Jehoshaphat as going out into the wilderness of Tekoa to meet the advance of Moabite and Ammonite invaders (II Chr. 20:20). The word "wilderness" fitly describes the prospect eastward from the summit of the hill across desolate rock-bound heights that fall away sharply to the waters of the Dead Sea. But all the region round about

Tekoa is a welter of limestone hills; on their stony slopes and in the winding valleys that run between them a scanty growth provides but a bare subsistence for flocks of sheep and goats. It was in such surroundings that Amos had his place among the shepherds of Tekoa (1:1). The Hebrew word for "shepherds" is used elsewhere in the Old Testament only of Mesha king of Moab, who is thus described as a "sheepmaster" (II Kings 3:4). For this reason Jewish tradition has thought of Amos as a well-to-do sheep owner, and indeed it is not unlikely that Amos, as other shepherds of Tekoa, tended his own sheep. However, both the character of the region and the necessity of his eking out his living by dressing sycamores (7:14)—the rather insipid fruit of which is the fare of the poor— suggest that such flocks could have been of no great size.

It is the outdoor life of the shepherd that in the first instance provides the imagery on which Amos draws. He had heard the roar of the lion as it leaps upon its prey. He had looked upon the mangled remains of a poor animal that the wild beast had destroyed. Exposure to the burning heat of the sun by day and to the cold winds by night had made him familiar with the sterner aspects that the world of nature can display. But, as the exact and vivid style of his prophecies makes abundantly clear, he was no untutored rustic. Contact with his fellow shepherds, and perhaps with caravans that passed at no great distance from that district, had helped to develop readiness of speech and apt and lucid phrasing in characterization of men and events. William Robertson Smith has rightly insisted that

among the Hebrews, as in the Arabian desert, knowledge and oratory were not affairs of professional education, or dependent for their cultivation on wealth and social status [but] shrewd observation, a memory retentive of traditional lore, and the faculty of original reflection [were] the ground of acknowledged intellectual pre-eminence.[1]

Then, too, Amos' native powers of observation had been brought to bear upon much more than the simple surroundings of the wilderness of Tekoa, for quite evidently he was not dependent on mere hearsay for the surprising range of his knowledge of the great world that lay beyond that region. Obviously the journey he made into the Northern Kingdom to exercise his ministry as a prophet was not the beginning of his travels, for his utterances reveal a familiarity both with conditions in Israel and with the general situation in neighboring countries.

B. The World of His Day.—That world of what we know as the Near East had even then in the eighth century B.C. a long and variegated history behind it. Great empires had waxed and waned, civilizations grown old and perished. Even the little nation of Israel, a comparative newcomer among the peoples of that region, had had a notable history. It had risen to power under David and Solomon but had suffered eclipse with the division into the two kingdoms of Israel and Judah. Under the Omri dynasty and particularly under the notorious Ahab, the Northern Kingdom had become strong and prosperous, and Judah as a subject partner had shared in this prosperity. On the overthrow of this dynasty there had followed another period of decline. The Aramaean kingdom, with its capital at Damascus, had overrun a good part of Israel's territory (II Kings 10:32-33) and pressed to the very gates of Jerusalem, laying that city under tribute (II Kings 12:17-18). But just after the turn of the century the great Assyrian Empire, which had long been threatening to make itself master of western Asia and engulf the little kingdoms in Syria and Palestine, again advanced westward, and in 802 B.C. reduced Damascus and so weakened that state that Israel was once more able to assert itself victoriously (II Kings 13:25). The withdrawal of Assyria from the west because of weakness at home left Israel free to develop its resources; under Jeroboam II the small kingdom enjoyed its third and last period of prosperity. Control of great trade routes of that ancient world was definitely

[1] *The Prophets of Israel* (2nd ed.; London: A. & C. Black, 1897), p. 126.

in its hands, and that meant wealth. Out of its long struggle with its neighbor it had at last emerged victorious. For the time being the threat of the Assyrian Empire had faded into the remote distance. That danger, people felt, could be met when the time came. For the present there was rejoicing over victories won (6:13). These might well be considered the earnest of further triumphs to come. To be sure, the long wars that Israel had undergone had brought about significant changes in the social fabric. The small proprietors had been dispossessed; their property had passed into the hands of those who were engaged in the building of large estates. There was strange and unfamiliar talk of the palaces of the nobility, the winter houses and the summer houses of the well to do. Beneath the surface there was the mutter of discontent, but that was doubtless regarded as the transitory effect of changed conditions. Taken as a whole, the temper of the national life was confident and optimistic.

C. Religious Background in Israel.—To this optimism the religion of the time contributed. Men felt themselves to be the favored worshipers of a very powerful God, able and propitious, and they were zealous in their worship of this obliging deity. They could not overlook so remunerative a duty. At set seasons of the year the countryside gathered at the sanctuaries, and with elaborate round of feast and sacrifice they sang the praises of their God and made him participant in their prosperity. In praising him they praised themselves; in giving him his due of sacrifice they assured themselves the continuance of his services.

As the shepherd of Tekoa moved among these scenes he could not but feel intensely a strange contrast between the conception of a deity with whom men could so easily enter into comfortable partnership and the stern exacting character of the God of Israel as he knew him. For him Yahweh was the great awe-inspiring deity of Israel's desert days who manifested his power again and again in the destructive phenomena of nature. He was the death-dealing storm-god whose might was made known in the tempest that swept resistlessly over the face of the earth, whose voice could be heard in the crashing of the thunder, whose arm was laid bare in the lightning flash. Or again, as the earth shuddered in the terrifying earthquake the presence of Yahweh declared itself. To be sure, this dread God had drawn Israel into an intimate relationship to himself. In battle fury, in surrender to the demonic energy which made itself felt in the tempest, Israel had known what it was to be the instrument of the divine wrath. A little later than the time of Amos, Isaiah gave utterance to an oracle which is of great importance for the light it throws on this experience:

Ho, Assur, rod of mine anger,
Staff of mine indignation!
Against a profane nation do I send him
Against the people of my wrath do I give him a
charge
To take the spoil and to take the prey,
To tread them down like the mire of the streets.
(Isa. 10:5-6.)

Assyria is in this oracle assigned the role that once had been Israel's fearful privilege. Of old, Israel had been chosen not for its own advantage but to be used of God for his purpose.

The work of Moses had indeed made it clear that Yahweh was not simply a God of power but supremely a God of righteousness; however, this righteousness partook of the strange and awful dynamic of the God of storm and battle. It was a righteousness that blazed forth hotly against all iniquity, that turned upon uncleanness all its fierce destructive energy. It demanded the entire surrender of the will bent on its own self-seeking interest to the will of One whose claim on men's obedience was absolute.

D. Preparation for His Ministry.—At home again, as he tended his sheep in the silence of the desolate hills, a silence which seemed to throw into sharp relief man's littleness and helplessness, Amos found himself brooding upon the way in which the temper of the nation, as it had revealed itself in the perversion of justice and the greedy oppression of the poor, in luxurious living and sensual indulgence, constituted a complete reversal of the right relationship between God and his people. In the use of the courts for the ruthless exploitation of the weak, men were manipulating justice—the justice of God—for their own ends. In the use of wealth acquired by violence and oppression for indulgent living they were prostituting to their own sensual satisfaction that good life in the land of the Amorite which God had given them. At the sanctuaries they were following a round of festive observances which in fact represented a comfortable familiarity with God, as if he must gratefully receive the offerings and honors that they liked to bestow upon him. In all this God was in effect made subordinate to human interests. He was treated as existing for man. He was, as it were, enslaved within the circle of selfish human desires.

For Amos the destroying energy of the divine being whom he knew took on new significance against the background of a people's possessive pride that would involve even God himself in its grievous disregard of the elementary principles of justice and its conscienceless satisfaction of its own appetites. The God whose unlimited lordship over nature was revealed in the devastating power of storm and earthquake, whose unfettered lordship over history had been shown not only in the free choice of Israel from among all the families of the earth, but just as manifestly in the overthrow of the Egyptian oppressors and in the destruction of the Amorite, must again give free course to his righteous will even though it was none other than the people of his choice that must be destroyed. The dread reality of the divine being must exercise its inexorable sovereignty by making an end of all human associations that would attempt to subject its power to the furtherance of their own self-seeking ends.

E. The Call.—It was with this conviction dominating his outlook upon life that one day the shepherd's attention was caught by a brood of locusts. It was in the spring of the year, when he and his fellow herdsmen were eagerly awaiting the growth of the fresh grass which was to nourish their flocks. There were vivid memories of the havoc that swarms of these insects had wrought in years gone by. Indeed, this was one of the ways in which Yahweh had now and again visited his people. Could it be that God was now showing him the means he would use for bringing about a complete devastation of the land? In heightened vision Amos saw the countryside stripped bare of herbage and, confronted with concrete calamity, his love for his own folk made itself sharply felt. He found himself pleading that Israel—so great in its own eyes but so little in the sight of God—might be forgiven and the danger averted, and he received assurance that this disaster would not overtake the nation.

Again, in the summer, when the blazing sun was parching the ground, Amos had a vision of a fire fiercely licking up the great deep, the source of all springs and fountains and even of the rain from heaven, a conflagration which must therefore devour the land. It was by fire then that Yahweh would make an end and assert his sovereign freedom. Once more Amos interceded for his people, so frail and helpless in the face of such an overwhelming catastrophe, and again God granted reprieve.

But still the shepherd's consciousness was charged with the sense of impending doom as the inevitable manifestation of the righteous power of God over against a people's efforts to use him for their own ends. For such a consciousness the simplest objects could take on new and strange significance. A plumb line arrested his attention. God had something to say to him in that moment of enhanced perception. A plumb line is for testing and decision. The awful hour of judgment had come, the irrevocable sentence was pronounced, "I will never again pardon them."

This dread certainty was confirmed by a fourth vision. As he looked at a basket of summer fruit he felt again the presence of the something more. The very word "summer fruit" (qáyiç) had for him a knell-like sound in its close resemblance to the sound of the word "end" (qēç). It was God who was saying, "The end is come upon my people Israel." The phrase "my people" adds its own tragic note to the terrible finality of the pronouncement. The decision was taken in full awareness of the past. The divine judgment was to fall upon those whom God had drawn into close relationship to himself. They were to know that it was none other than the God whom they had thought of as their own who would bring about the destruction of the nation.

In thus conveying to the shepherd of Tekoa the dread certainty of his purpose to destroy, God called him to be a prophet. In Amos' own direct statement, "The LORD took me from following the flock, and the LORD said to me, 'Go, prophesy to my people Israel'" (7:15). His preparation had been quite other than that of members of the guilds of prophets who were associated with the local sanctuaries. He had received no training in the technique of music and dance with which ecstasy could be induced. He was not a prophet by profession. He had his own way of supporting himself as shepherd and dresser of sycamores. So he indignantly repudiated the priest Amaziah's injunction that he should use prophecy as a means of earning a living in Judah. Not that Amos meant to cast any slur on the prophets as such. He could speak of them elsewhere as a God-given element in the life of Israel (2:11). It was the verb "to prophesy" that was used in God's commissioning him. His reply to Amaziah (7:14-15) simply insisted on the fact that he had not as a member of a prophetic guild sought the office of a prophet. On the contrary, the initiative had been with God himself. He had felt the wellnigh irresistible pressure of the divine summons. "The Lord GOD hath spoken, who can but prophesy?" (3:8.)

II. Time and Place of Amos' Ministry

A. Reign of Jeroboam II.—The excellent piece of narrative in 7:10-17 definitely places the ministry of Amos in the reign of Jeroboam, who was on the throne from about 783 to about 745 B.C. The datum in the superscription, "two years before the earthquake" (cf. 9:1), is of no assistance in determining the time of his ministry more precisely because, though the earthquake would seem from the reference to it in Zech. 14:5 to have been of exceptional severity, there is no means of fixing its date exactly. That Amos came upon the scene some considerable number of years after Jeroboam's accession is evident from the situation reflected in his oracles. Not only was the nation prosperous; its prosperity was of some standing. The accumulation of wealth in the hands of the upper classes had had time to result in their building palaces and summer houses and in their general indulgence in luxurious living. The early years of Jeroboam's reign were marked by a war which successfully ended the long struggle with Syria and led to the full recovery of Israel's territory (II Kings 14:25), but those to whom Amos spoke were living in proud security. They thought that wars were a thing of the past and they assumed that no further danger threatened them. The time of Amos' ministry has therefore generally been set at about 760 B.C., "probably, between 760 and 759 B.C.";[2] "towards the middle of the eighth century."[3] Some scholars have in recent years assigned Amos a rather later date,[4] but on what would seem insufficient grounds. They base their argument on the fact that during the greater part of Jeroboam's reign Assyrian rulers were unable because of trouble elsewhere to make any sustained effort to advance their power westward. And in fact it was only after the inauguration of a new dynasty with the accession of Tiglath-pileser III in 745 B.C. that Assyria again became a distinct menace to Syria and Palestine. These scholars therefore urge that Amos, with his clear conviction that Assyria was to be the agent of Israel's overthrow, must have delivered his message shortly after 745 B.C. At that time, however, leaders of the people as well as the prophet would have been aware of imminent danger; but of such awareness on the part of the leaders there is no trace in Amos' appraisal of their attitude. The prophet's ability to read the signs of the times was one of the characteristics that distinguished him from his generation. The latent threat of Assyrian power might be ignored by those who were obsessed by pride in their own achievement, but not by an Amos. As John Skinner has put it: "The prophet's mind is the seismograph of providence,

[2] S. R. Driver, *The Books of Joel and Amos* (Cambridge: Cambridge University Press, 1934; "Cambridge Bible"), p. 100.

[3] George Adam Smith, *The Book of the Twelve Prophets* (rev. ed.; New York: Harper & Bros., 1940), I, 67.

[4] Richard S. Cripps, *A Critical and Exegetical Commentary on the Book of Amos* (New York: The Macmillan Co., 1929), pp. 35-41; Norman H. Snaith, *The Book of Amos* (London: Epworth Press, 1946), II, 8-9.

vibrating to the first faint tremors that herald the coming earthquake." [5]

B. The Northern Kingdom.—The scene of Amos' ministry was the Northern Kingdom. It was at the king's sanctuary at Bethel, place of the shrine particularly associated with Jacob, that he came into collision with Amaziah the priest (7:10-14). Amaziah's accusation that the prophet had conspired against Jeroboam in the midst of the house of Israel rested upon misunderstanding or deliberate perversion, but it implies that Amos had not confined his activity to Bethel. His concern in his oracles with Samaria and Gilgal suggests that at these places too he had made himself heard. No doubt at a number of the sanctuaries where at festival time pilgrims and traders came together the prophet's dire message of doom had been pronounced. He does not seem to have prophesied in Judah, but there can be little doubt that his prediction of disaster applied to that kingdom also. One of his greatest utterances, "You only have I known of all the families of the earth: therefore I will punish you for all your iniquities" (3:2), presupposes unequivocally an underlying unity of the two kingdoms grounded in God's choice of his people, even as it speaks of the judgment that was to overtake them both. Indeed, this sense of the oneness of Israel and Judah underneath all political differences had been set forth quite clearly more than a century earlier in the document J, which derived all the tribes from Abraham, called of God to be the father of a chosen people. Necessarily in the political sphere, once the separation into the two kingdoms had been accepted, the relationship between them was generally a close one. Given a strong leadership in Israel, that kingdom with its larger territory and greater resources inevitably kept Judah in a state of dependence. Not long before the time of Amos, Jeroboam's predecessor, Jehoash, had replied with a scornful parable to the effort of Amaziah king of Judah to assert his independence, and had followed this up with an attack on Jerusalem which had reduced the Southern Kingdom to vassalage (II Kings 14:8-14). It was natural therefore that Amos, concerned with the destiny of the chosen people, should deliver his message in the North, where the fortunes of that people were being mainly shaped. It was the North which would first feel the impact of that catastrophic advance of the Assyrian Empire which the prophet had manifestly in mind as God's final visitation of his people. It is true that Assyria is nowhere in Amos' oracles explicitly named as the instrument of the divine judgment, but

the doom that is to overtake Israel and neighboring peoples is unmistakably that of the devastation of war. Almost every utterance centers on "the same outlook of invasion, defeat, or exile." [6] Assyria was the one power that could thus threaten the world of that day. No doubt the possibility of renewed aggression on the part of that empire would be generally recognized, though the optimism of the time regarded the danger as only a remote contingency. That Amos was speaking of Assyria would be abundantly clear; the veiled nature of his reference to that nation was in accord with the touch of mystery that characterized oracular utterance, and with the subordination of the human agent to the sense of the immediacy of the divine activity.

III. Message of Amos

A. Proclamation of Approaching Doom.— The three elements of which the book is composed—vision, oracles, narrative—all agree in placing the prediction of imminent ruin at the heart of Amos' ministry. His message may then be summed up in the simple announcement, "God is about to destroy his people for their sins." That for his hearers was the inconceivable thing. They had no doubt listened with interested approval to the prophet's declaration that their ancient enemy Syria was to go down before the invader. That the same fate was to overtake other neighboring peoples with whom they had been in conflict had seemed to them again a right and proper manifestation of the righteous wrath of the God of Israel. To be sure, the prophet was a solitary and sinister figure. While his fierce energy carried willing conviction to his hearers, as they listened they could not rid themselves of a feeling of uneasiness. His presence as a messenger of the wrath of God was out of keeping with the gay and carefree mood in which they had come together from far and near to keep high festival. Yet theirs, they felt, was after all a privileged position, for it was none other than their own God of whose activity the prophet was speaking. But suddenly Amos turned upon them, and they found themselves involved in the dreadful torrent of destroying energy which he foresaw spreading far and wide. The same irrevocable doom was coming upon them, and the more rightly and reasonably because the sins of ruthless seeking of wealth, of gross injustice, of oppression of the poor, of a lust that knew no bounds, woven into the very fabric of the national life, constituted a continual profanation of the holiness of the God with whom they felt themselves to stand in privileged intimate relationship. This very rela-

---

[5] *Prophecy and Religion* (Cambridge: Cambridge University Press, 1922), p. 38.

[6] Driver, *op. cit.*, p. 103.

tionship, Amos asserted to their astonishment, made all the more inevitable this punishment for their sins. They were no doubt aware that there was much that was wrong in the social order; they could hardly have shut their ears entirely to the anguished protests of those who were being sold into slavery for insignificant debt or could find no just treatment in the courts on account of their poverty. But they had felt that a God who had bestowed upon them the prosperity in which they were rejoicing would be patient with the irregularities that were an almost necessary occurrence in a time of transition. They had forgotten the inexorable character of the divine righteousness, no simple ideal laid up in the heavens to which they might or might not conform, but overwhelming power revealing itself in unceasing energy within the world and in impact upon it. To be drawn into uniquely intimate relationship with such a God was to be uniquely exposed to the devouring fire of that righteousness.

This grievous misconception of the very nature of the divine being was most clearly revealed in the religious practice of the time. The pilgrimage to the shrine was the occasion for pleasurable feasting, with further opportunity for such extraordinary observances as might attest a man's social position. It was their lighthearted familiarity with God, their ease in placing themselves on good terms with Deity, that called forth Amos' contemptuous and scornful denunciation of worship at the sanctuaries. The God of Israel, as he knew him, was not really being venerated there, whatever name of deity might be used. The proceedings at the shrines were substantial apostasy. Yahweh was being treated as if he were one of the gods of the land of Canaan, kindly beings identified with the desires and fortunes of their adherents. Not so could be worshiped the God who through famine, drought, pestilence, earthquake, and like visitations had sought to remind his people of the stern reality of his righteous will and bring them back to a true relationship with himself. They had not heeded, but had persisted in their presumptuous conviction that God belonged to them. They even looked forward to that which they named the day of the Lord, the day of God's final manifestation of power, that would be for them a great time of victory and rejoicing because they identified his interests with theirs. Thus, with startled incredulity, they heard the prophet declare that the day of the Lord would be for them a day of disaster with no faintest gleam of light (5:20).

The distinctive note of Amos' message is to be discerned in the unfaltering prediction that God was about to make an end of the nation. There was most clearly revealed in this an-nouncement of irrevocable doom the tremendous contrast between what God meant to the prophet and what he meant to the Israel of that day.

B. Yahweh, the Lord of Nature.—For the prophet, God was indeed the Lord of nature. All its mysterious forces are in his control. If in the oracles the devastating pestilence and earthquake and like visitations are particularly emphasized as characteristic manifestations of Yahweh's might (4:10-11), it is also clearly implied that the beneficent life-sustaining powers of nature are also at his disposal (4:6-8). But this lordship over nature had long been part of the teaching about God current in Israel. From desert days Yahweh had been the storm-god, and in Canaan much had been learned from the religion of the land about the processes of nature as modes of the divine activity; and thus the conception of the manifoldness of Yahweh's activity had been greatly enriched. There was, however, always the tendency to identify God with these processes, just as earlier he had been identified with the storm. But, as documents extant at the time of Amos clearly show, the actual teaching about God unmistakably placed all these forces under the divine control, and so insisted upon the sovereignty of a God who transcended them all. Thus in the flood story the unfailing alternation of seedtime and harvest, cold and heat, summer and winter, day and night, depends upon the divine decree (Gen. 8:22). The sentence of consecration of Solomon's temple, originally preserved in a very early collection of odes, speaks of the sun, the object of worship among so many peoples, as having been placed in the heavens by God himself (I Kings 8:12 LXX). The cycle of Elijah stories gathering up traditions widely popular in Amos' day conceives of hurricane, earthquake, and fire as forces attendant upon God's manifestation of himself, but expressly asserts that in no one of these is God included (I Kings 19:11-12). The God whose sovereign power was declared upon the lips of Amos was the God whose revelation of himself in the world of nature had long been known to Israel. Only, and here lay the significant contrast between Amos and his hearers, religious leaders and people alike had made central in their thinking and in their practice just those divine activities that obviously ministered to their own welfare. They had thus come to conceive of the Lord of nature as existing for man rather than of man as existing for God. The prophet, on the other hand, was intensely aware of the sovereign power of Yahweh as revealed in every aspect of nature. He knew that such an attempt to subordinate the divine to the human was presumptuous folly.

C. Yahweh, the Lord of History.—Again, for Amos, Yahweh is the Lord of history. If he had brought Israel up out of the land of Egypt, he had also brought the Philistines from Caphtor and the Syrians from Kir (9:7). His judgment fell not only upon Israel but also upon the neighboring peoples. Nor was it only the nations bordering upon Israel whose destinies were in his hands. The great Assyrian Empire was the instrument of his will. It was the whole of the world as Amos knew it that was under the sovereignty of Yahweh. But here too traditional teaching about the range of Yahweh's power in the human story did not really differ from that of the prophet. The account of Israel's origins, with which Amos' contemporaries were familiar, set these in the context of world history. It is against the background of the divinely ordered diversity of peoples as this is accounted for in the Babel story (Gen. 11:1-9) that God called Abraham to be the father of a chosen people. Yahweh had been free to choose among all the families of the earth (3:2). In Egypt it was he who had determined the course of events as he delivered Israel. In one of the Elisha stories a change of dynasty in Syria—a change that spelled disaster for Israel—was brought about at Yahweh's direction (II Kings 8:7-13). It is true that there is no denial of the existence of other gods either in these traditions or in the oracles of Amos. It is, however, significant that just as the prophet makes no mention of the gods of Syria, Ammon, or Moab as involved in the overthrow of these nations, so in the story of the Exodus the helpless king of Egypt is the protagonist as over against Yahweh, and the gods of Egypt make no appearance, although some reference to their powerlessness might well have been thought to magnify the triumph of Israel's God. It would seem that at its best the religious consciousness was so charged with an all-pervading sense of Yahweh's majesty and power as to leave no room for the thought of other divine beings. This is not to forget that the religious outlook of great numbers in Israel would fall far short of this teaching about God. In their concern with their own immediate interests they would conceive of such a concentration of the divine activity in their own particular sphere as to make Yahweh a god of the land, a superior "Baal," rather than God of all the earth. And it would appear that the religious leaders of Amos' day, while retaining their belief in the world-wide sovereignty of Yahweh, had fallen in with this popular misconception to the point of making the very greatness of God simply a national asset. In the face of a people's complacent possession of God Amos declared that Yahweh would vindicate his sovereign freedom through the destruction of the nation which had sought to subject him to its own self-seeking aggrandizement.

D. Yahweh, the God of Righteousness.—For Amos, Yahweh is pre-eminently the god of righteousness. It is for their transgressions that Israel and the peoples round about are to be devastated. There are elementary principles of humanity which have been violated. In Israel particularly there are a day-by-day denial of justice to the poor and helpless and a sensual indulgence that abundantly justify God's dread decision to destroy. The heinousness of sin as rebellion against God stands out with extraordinary vividness in the prophet's utterance. But insistence upon the demand for righteousness was no new teaching in Israel. From obedience to this demand no one, not even the king, was exempt. David fell under the divine condemnation for his sin with Bathsheba and the murder of Uriah the Hittite (II Sam. 11:27). There was vivid memory of the moment at which in the matter of Naboth's vineyard Elijah had confronted Ahab with the ringing challenge, "Thus saith the Lord, Hast thou killed, and also taken possession?" (I Kings 21:19.) Behind all questions concerning the date of the legislation embodied in the Pentateuch there lies the certainty of the persistent remembrance of Moses as the lawgiver who in the name of the dread Sinai God had rendered just judgment in the disputes small and great that had been brought before him, and had thus inaugurated the tradition of the divine concern with rightness in every kind of human relationship, a tradition that was to play so significant a part in Israel's life. The indictment Amos brought against his generation was not that of ignorance but that of the prostitution of knowledge. The very tribunals that were to administer justice had been made the instruments of men's greed and ruthless egoism. Divine sanction was thus claimed for what was really merciless oppression of the poor, and the name of the righteous God was invoked upon crass human selfishness. It was another way in which men were seeking to use God for their own ends, in apparent oblivion of the nature of his devouring righteousness that must flame forth fiercely against all injustice and oppression, and in the end consume these and all responsible for them.

George Adam Smith has well said, "The God who stands behind Amos is indeed the ancient Deity of Israel." [7] The difference between the prophet and his hearers lay in this. For them the doctrine of God as Lord of nature and of history and a righteous being was a set of truths inherited from the past and of course important for their bearing upon life. But these truths were to be held alongside other ideas dealing

[7] *Book of Twelve Prophets,* I, 101.

with man's natural concern with his own interests, and they were of value in so far as they might serve these interests. For Amos these truths were the ways in which the divine reality pressed upon him, laid hold of him, held him in its grasp. They were not simply ideas among others, subject to such adjustment as might seem necessary for practical purposes. They were the truths that dominated his whole outlook upon life. For him life had meaning only as it was the vehicle for the effective manifestation of the sublime and awful majesty of the righteous God. All that was lifted up in senseless, arrogant self-centeredness against that majesty, whether a people's self-sufficiency and pride, or men's manipulation of the law to their own ends, or religious observances that would make use of the divine—all must go down before the irresistible onset of the might of God's righteousness, and in the words of an even greater prophet than Amos, "The Lord alone shall be exalted in that day" (Isa. 2:11).

E. The Finality of Doom.—It is in the light of this God-centered vision of life and its meaning that the further question must be considered as to whether destruction was Amos' last word. At first thought it would seem inconceivable that a man should feel himself called to speak of impending doom unless he hoped that his words would have some effect upon his hearers and bring about a repentance that might avert disaster. One verse (5:15) does indeed speak of the possibility that the Lord may yet be gracious, but it is "the remnant of Joseph" that is to be the object of the divine favor, and the passage is evidently from the hand of one who in later days, after the fall of the Northern Kingdom, felt that what was left of his people was still subject to the judgment of that divine righteousness of which Amos had spoken. But the categorical note of Amos' prediction of doom admits of no qualification. There is about the prophet's own utterance a dreadful consistency. This was in accord with his preparation for his ministry. In the visions that had been so important a part of that preparation there was a sequence leading up to a final and unalterable certainty that the end was come upon Israel. It was this that sent him forth as a prophet. It was not a question of results. The Lord God had spoken; he could not but prophesy (3:8).

Not that Amos was devoid of human sympathy. In the first two visions the prayer that God would forgive Israel came instinctively to his lips (7:1-6). The refrain with which he represents God as pleading with his people through the disasters that had befallen them speaks eloquently of his understanding of God's concern for that people. The austere severity of his utterance and the bitterness of its irony are indicative of one who had cared deeply and had had to overcome a natural reluctance to deliver his message. Only the overwhelming sense of the majesty and splendor of the righteousness of God—a righteousness which must have free course in his world—could sustain the prophet in his harsh and forbidding ministry.

Again, it was because of this sustaining conviction of the sublime reality of God's presence and righteous power that Amos could confine his message to the simple announcement of inevitable doom without any consideration of what might lie beyond the destruction of the nation. For there is quite general agreement that the concluding passage of the book (9:8b-15), which speaks of restoration after judgment, belongs to a later time. Indeed, to accept this as the utterance of Amos himself would be to suppose that at the last moment the prophet suddenly changed the whole character of his message from a sentence of inexorable doom to one of a disciplinary punishment that would simply purge the nation of its evil elements and so clear the way for reconstruction. The qualification in 9:8b introduces such an interpretation of the prophet's message, but it involves an inconsistency between the first and the second half of the verse which suggests that the two passages derive from different writers.[8]

The theory has been advanced that Amos had addressed himself only to the Northern Kingdom and that for him the hope of the future lay with the kingdom of Judah. But this ignores the unity of the chosen people, which is definitely implied in 3:2. Nor is it conceivable that a consciousness so sensitively aware of anything that impugned the majesty of God could be oblivious of the evils in the land of Judah, evils which an Isaiah was within a generation forthrightly to denounce. Indeed, the very passage that speaks of restoration presupposes the fall of the house of David (9:11). It quite evidently comes from one who wrote long after the time of Amos, though his confidence in the future rests upon the prophet's declaration that it was none other than Israel's God who had manifested the power of his righteousness in the destruction of the nation. For Amos himself it was enough that God's righteousness should have its completely triumphant vindication. Beyond that, the future was in the hands of the same God.

IV. The Book of Amos

A. The Record of the Visions.—One of the immediate effects of Amos' ministry is recorded in a narrative (7:10-17) which seems to be an excerpt from an account of the major incident

[8] Cf. Smith, *Book of Twelve Prophets*, I, 190-91.

in the prophet's career. The incorporation of this particular section in the book is apparently due to the desire to represent Amos, even at the moment of his expulsion from Bethel, as proclaiming unfalteringly the divine resolve to make an end of the nation (7:17). None other than this, the writer insists, was the prophet's final word. No doubt the editor had in mind the events of 721 B.C., when Sargon's capture of Samaria and deportation of its inhabitants provided a calamitous vindication of the truth of Amos' prediction. But this took place a generation later than the time of the prophet's ministry. To be sure, as early as 738 B.C. Tiglath-pileser, the Assyrian ruler, had compelled Menahem king of Israel to pay heavy tribute, and in 732 B.C. he had placed his own puppet ruler Hoshea on the throne of the Northern Kingdom. But serious as this decline of Israel's power was, it fell far short of that complete devastation of which the prophet had spoken, and even this partial fulfillment of his prediction did not come until some years after the close of his ministry. Meanwhile in Tekoa, as that fulfillment seemed long delayed, Amos may well have wondered whether his mission had been a failure. He had been silenced, and there had been no immediate ingress of the destroying energy of Yahweh's righteousness, such as the urgency of the pressure upon the prophet had declared imminent. Yet there could be no denying the reality of the revelation of God's power and purpose that had taken possession of his whole being. Delay there might be, but in God's good time his righteous majesty would be made manifest with devastating power. The impact of that power had already made itself felt in his call to be a prophet. So Amos either himself put in writing, or dictated to someone else, an account of the visions which had constituted that call and had then given him the inexorable certainty that the end was come upon Israel. This record could bear its unfailing witness in the days when the words of the Lord should be fulfilled. In like manner, somewhat later, in the crises of his ministry, Isaiah was to "bind up the testimony" as he waited upon the Lord (Isa. 8:16-17) and to "inscribe it in a book" that it might be "for the time to come for ever and ever" (Isa. 30:8).

Only in the account of his visions (7:1-9; 8:1-2; 9:1) did Amos use the first personal pronoun singular with reference to himself, and the autobiographical character of the account sharply distinguishes it from the rest of the book. If, as has been suggested, his purpose in making use of the written word was to provide for a later day of disaster the clear witness that what would then take place was in accordance with the will of God as he had made it known

to his prophet, the simple account of the successive steps by which he had been brought to the dreadful certainty of doom would be sufficient. The specific details of the indictment against Israel, so significant in immediate address to that people in the spoken word, would hardly seem to him to have the same note of elemental permanence as the revelation of the divine being and purpose given him in the visions, and it appears not unlikely that Amos himself was content with recording these alone. On the other hand, the older view has been that the prophecies in chs. 1-6 which contain the indictment of Israel were also put in writing by the prophet, so that the book substantially in its present arrangement is from the hand of Amos himself. But the question at once arises why in that case the account of the visions through which he was called to his ministry was not placed at the beginning of the book instead of toward the end. It is also the apparent intention of the present grouping of the prophecies after the introductory oracles of chs. 1-2 to set forth the utterances of the prophet in three main discourses, each prefaced by "Hear this word" (3:1; 4:1; 5:1).[9] In recent years analysis of these sections into the smaller units of which they are evidently composed has made it seem doubtful that the delivery of sustained discourses was ever a part of the prophet's ministry.

B. Character of the Oracles.—An important factor in this analysis has been the full recognition of what was involved in the fact that the prophet was a poet not only in his use of imagery but in the rhythmic form of his utterance. In the eighteenth century Robert Lowth, professor of poetry at Oxford, pointed out that the same parallelism of thought that is characteristic of the psalms and other Hebrew poems is markedly present in the books of the prophets, and in *Isaiah: A New Translation of Isaiah* (1779) he reproduced the poetical form of the original by dividing the lines on the printed page in accordance with this parallelism of thought. In comparatively recent times a great deal of attention has been given to the study of the metrical scheme that accompanied the sense rhythm. While there is much about Hebrew meter that is still uncertain, it is clear that the determining principle, as in English poetry, is that of accented syllables. For the most part the number of accents in each of the two lines of a couplet is the same; but at times, especially in dirges, a line with three accents is followed by one with two. So, for example, in the distich

Come to Bethel, and transgress;
　to Gilgal, and multiply transgression (4:4),

[9] Driver, *Joel and Amos*, p. 97.

the parallelism of the thought is accompanied by a balance of the rhythm—three accents in each line—while in the prophet's lament in 5:2,

> Fallen, no more to rise,
> is the virgin Israel;
> Forsaken she lies on her land,
> with none to raise her—

in each couplet the first line with three accents is completed by a second line with two accents. The recognition of this sound-rhythm, even though all its principles are not yet fully understood, has greatly helped in distinguishing more clearly the actual spoken words of prophetic utterance. The frequent change both of rhythm and idea, often coinciding with the occurrence of the introductory formula, "Thus saith the LORD," or the concluding, "Saith the LORD," shows that the characteristic form of prophetic utterance was not sustained discourse but the brief pregnant oracle of only a few lines.[10]

C. Collection and Arrangement of the Oracles.

—It is of course possible that the prophet himself was responsible for the ordering of these small units into their present arrangement. But as against this possibility, the fact that they are so often prefaced by an introductory clause suggests that these brief oracles had each had its own independent existence before its incorporation into the longer sections of a book. In some cases this independent existence may have early taken written form, but in view of the limited familiarity with writing in that day it would seem more probable that many of the oracles were simply retained in the memories of the hearers and handed on by word of mouth. At times the oracles clearly bear the marks of oral transmission. For instance, in 3:9-12 there have been brought together three or four separate sayings, fragmentary in substance and of uncertain rhythm. Apparently these particular oracles were only incompletely remembered when they were committed to writing. For the most part, however, the rhythmical form of prophetic utterance did much to ensure an exact repetition of the prophet's actual words.

Those among Amos' hearers who were profoundly impressed by what he had said treasured his utterances in their memory and handed them on to others by word of mouth or by putting them in writing. It would perhaps be too much to call these men disciples, for that would imply a longer association with the prophet than his brief ministry could have made possible; but

[10] Cf. T. H. Robinson, *Prophecy and the Prophets in Ancient Israel* (New York: Charles Scribner's Sons, 1923), pp. 52-53. See also article, "The Prophetic Literature," Vol. I, p. 206.

it was no transitory impression that had been made upon them. Further evidence for the existence of those who had deeply felt that the prophet's ministry was highly significant is furnished by the piece of narrative in 7:10-17. Not only was the writer of this fragment one who had discerned in Amos the greatness of a true prophet of God; he was plainly writing for those who held Amos in like esteem, and for whom an account of the prophet's ministry would therefore have its very real value.

It was in this circle then that these floating oracles had their currency and that presently a first collection of the sayings of Amos was made, both of those which had been written down and of those that were still being handed on by word of mouth. This effort to bring together in written form all the oracles of a prophet was a new departure in the history of prophecy. It sprang from the conviction that not only had God been certainly speaking through the prophet, but the truths which had thus been proclaimed had their meaning for later generations. It may well have been that this committal to writing took place after the substantial fulfillment of Amos' prediction in the fall of Samaria and the collapse of the Northern Kingdom in 721 B.C. In that time of grievous despair the reminder that it was none other than the God of Israel who had manifested his righteous power in the destruction of his people would have had its special significance, as would also the fact that he had declared his purpose beforehand. At any rate, it was at no very long time after his ministry that this first collection of the oracles of Amos was made, for the original superscription to this collection would seem to have been simply "The Words of Amos of Tekoa." The memory of the man was still so vivid as to make "Amos of Tekoa" quite sufficient identification.

It would appear too that in this first assemblage of the sayings there was preserved some memory of the actual course of the prophetic activity. The oracles against the nations, which in all probability marked the beginning of his ministry, were placed first (1:3–2:3), with the like judgment upon Israel immediately following (2:6-16). Next came the great saying of 3:2 that might well be considered the main thesis of Amos' message, as it took Israel's fundamental conviction that she was the people chosen above all others, and made that very choice the ground of her punishment because she had so grievously presumed upon that relationship. It is with a certain fitness that there follows the argument of 3:3-8 with its assertion that the prophet's delivery of the message had all the inevitability which may be observed in the relation of cause and effect in the world of nature. Amos, challenged as to his right to proclaim destruction, declares that he could do no other than prophesy, because God had spoken. The oracles in 3:9–4:3 are concerned with Samaria, while those in 4:4–6:14 seem to center about the cultus at the sanctuaries of which Bethel was the chief. It is reasonable to suppose that the memory of a prophesying that began at Samaria, the capital of the kingdom, and ended at Bethel, the royal sanctuary, was responsible for this arrangement of the oracles, for the narrative of 7:10-17 indicates that at Bethel Amos' ministry came to its close. With the addition of this narrative a fairly complete record of what the prophet had publicly said and done was in the hands of those who were finding in his message power to face and to understand the collapse of the national life.

Even in this first collection of sayings the need of those who must depend upon the written word in contrast with those who had heard the living voice of the prophet was kept clearly in mind. Many of the oracles were already introduced by the formula "Thus saith the LORD," as a reminder that it was indeed the word of God that found utterance on the prophet's lips; but sometimes, as in 3:1, a longer sentence was employed to assist the reader in feeling the full force of the saying that followed. Amos' moving lament over the nation pictured as a young woman in the cold immobility of death (5:2) is explicitly named a dirge in the introductory sentence (5:1), a useful pointer for the reader but not needed by those before whom the prophet had appeared in the guise of a mourner, perhaps with clothes rent and ashes upon his head. Because such introductory sentences are in prose, and thus lack the rhythmic scheme of the oracles, they can easily be distinguished as coming from the collector's hand. At the same time it was this collector's piety that took every care to reproduce the exact wording of the prophecies as they had come to him.

D. Further Growth of the Book.—Meanwhile in the kingdom of Judah those who had received Amos' own account of his visions found a natural interest in the preservation of as many of his utterances as came within their knowledge. In time therefore the vision record was supplemented by a partial representation of his message which is to be found in 8:4-14. In this section there are distinct echoes of the oracles in chs. 1–6. The indictment in 8:4-6 evidently parallels that in 2:6b-7, even to the identity of the phrasing "trample" and "the needy for a pair of shoes." The conjunction of the expressions "the LORD hath sworn" and "the pride of Jacob," both in 8:7 and 6:8, is noteworthy, though the use made of them in the two passages is quite different. In 8:10 there is developed the same theme of a general lamentation as in

5:16-17. It would appear that the sayings of Amos in this addition to the account of the visions represent another stream of tradition than that represented in chs. 1–6, and that they were transmitted in more fragmentary form. The main record of what the prophet had said would naturally be preserved in the North, where the full impact of his ministry had been felt, while only reverberations of his utterances came to those in the South, at a distance from the scene of that ministry, though they were in possession of the record of the strange personal experience that had made Amos a prophet.

It is perhaps a third tradition that is represented by the account of the vision in 9:1-4. This has its points of resemblance to the record of the other visions. In both, Amos speaks in his own person and narrates what took place between God and himself. A marked difference, however, is that in this vision it is Yahweh himself whom the prophet sees, while in the visions of 7:1-8; 8:1-2, Yahweh causes him to see an object that has some deeper meaning. In this vision too the fate of Israel is developed in distinctly rhetorical language in contrast with the trenchant tragic sentence of the others, "I will never again pardon them," or "The end is come upon my people Israel." Here too an earthquake ushers in the destruction of the nation and the part that war was to play seems to come as an afterthought, while in the oracles the devastation that invasion would bring is in the forefront of the prophet's thought. The addition of this passage to the vision-record was probably due to those who felt that an earthquake, which Amos had predicted would demolish the sanctuary at Bethel, had indeed been the first of the series of disasters that had brought the Northern Kingdom to its catastrophic end.

The ministry and message of Amos thus continued to have their own persistent life with varied emphases in different circles. But there came a time when the two main streams of the tradition were blended and the vision-record was added to the oracle-record, to which the narrative section (7:10-17) had already been attached. This union of a section composed of sayings and one made up mainly of visions is perhaps responsible for the present form of the superscription of the book (1:1) in which the somewhat strange phrasing, "words . . . which he saw," may be due to the combining of the title of one section, "The Words of Amos of Tekoa," with the title of the other, "The Visions of Amos, Which He Saw Concerning Israel. . . ."

This bringing together of the oracle-record and the vision-record resulted in the production of a book which was in general identical with the present book of Amos. This process took place at a time subsequent to the fall of the Northern Kingdom, when the center of the life of the people of Israel lay in the South. This is indicated by the way in which the ministry of Amos is dated in the superscription. Uzziah king of Judah is named before Jeroboam son of Joash, king of Israel, although the book itself mentions only Jeroboam. The survival of the Southern Kingdom for more than a century after the kingdom of Israel had come to an end led inevitably to the belief that the kingdom of Judah had always been the more important of the two. But apart from this, the naming of the king of Judah witnesses to the conviction that the preaching of Amos had its significance for the South as well as for the North. It was no doubt to make this clear that the clause "against the whole family which I brought up out of the land of Egypt" was added in 3:1, rightly interpreting the great sentence of 3:2, "You only have I known." If there were many in the South who looked upon the fall of the Northern Kingdom as the just punishment for its sinful schism, there were also those to whom was due the continued life of Amos' message, and they did not hesitate to affirm that Judah too lay under the judgment of the righteous God whose dread reality Amos had so cogently proclaimed. As a matter of fact, the seventh century was the time of Assyrian domination of Judah and of the substantial apostasy of the little kingdom under their King Manasseh. But the persistence of devotion to the teaching of Amos that was to issue in the production of his book bears its testimony, as in the case of the books of the other eighth-century prophets, to the existence of a faithful minority through whom God's further revelation of himself was to be given.

The book, then, was no dead document, no finished monument of the past. Through its medium men felt that the prophet still lived and spoke in the name of the Lord. What he had said had its genuine relevance for the later day but, more than that, the God who had spoken through him was still speaking. This conviction made it possible for those who cherished his message, felt deeply its timeless significance, and saw life always in the light of its teaching about God, to seek to relate it still more closely to the circumstances of their own day. Thus later additions were quite naturally made to the book. In some of these the intention is simply to enable the reader to grasp the implications of the prophetic utterance. For example, to the passionately concentrated saying in 3:8,

The Lord God has spoken;
who can but prophesy?

there has been added in 3:7 the reminder that in the dependence of prophetic utterances upon divine revelation lies the very meaning of prophecy, God's desire to make known his inmost purpose through the agency of those whom he calls to be his prophets.

Surely the Lord God does nothing
without revealing his secret
to his servants the prophets.

In contrast to the poetry of felt experience this generalization with its primary appeal to thought is cast in plain prose.

Additions at greater length are those which express the conviction that the God who had spoken through Amos was still exercising his inexorable judgment and still declaring his righteous will in the disordered conditions that prevailed in Palestine in the times after the fall of Jerusalem in 586 B.C. Tyre and Edom, retaining, as other peoples did not, some freedom of action, made their own contribution to this disorder. So there were added to the oracles against the nations in ch. 1 the judgments on these peoples (1:9-12). There is quite general agreement among scholars that these oracles came from this later date. Amos' authorship of the oracle against the Philistines (1:6) has also been called in question by some commentators on substantial grounds, and nearly all are agreed that the oracle against Judah is from a later hand. This last served to help correct the natural readiness upon the part of great numbers in the South to consider Amos' prophecy as having found complete fulfillment in what had happened to the Northern Kingdom. It is likely that all these added oracles had had independent currency before they were incorporated in the book. However, their use of the form in which Amos cast his prediction indicates that it was their intention to bring their proclamation of judgment into relation to his. It was not, as is sometimes suggested, a question of deliberate misrepresentation of authorship. Their procedure was the equivalent of the way of saying, "If so-and-so were alive now, he would declare"; or better, as these authors would prefer to assert, "God would say this through him." They thus have their place in the living fruitful tradition of Amos' ministry.

E. The Appendix.—Further evidence of the continued life of this tradition of Amos' ministry is to be found in the addition to his book of the oracles in the closing passage (9:11-15). These verses evidently have as their background a time of great desolation, for they speak of the house of David as fallen, of Israel as in exile, of cities that are waste. It is the situation that followed upon the fall of Jerusalem in

586 B.C. when, with the deportation of large numbers to Babylon and the migration of others to Egypt, there was left in the little land of Judah only a broken fragment of a people eking out a poverty-stricken existence. Yet even under these hopeless conditions there persisted the conviction that Israel was the people of God, the God who had indeed visited them for their sins but was nonetheless their God and always supremely lord of history and nature. Voices were heard declaring that in his own good time God would manifest his beneficent creative power by restoring his people. Theirs should be once again the greatness of the glorious days of the reign of David. The land should yield its increase with miraculous fertility, with hardly time between reaping and sowing to gather in the abundant harvest. In all this there is no reference to the stern righteousness of God, with its absolute demand upon human life, of which Amos had spoken. There would even seem to be a persistence of that emphasis upon the material advantages of a privileged relationship to God which had in the prophet's day subordinated God to human interest. But the situation was changed. The excellency of Jacob, the proud self-confidence of a prosperous people, belonged to a remote past. These oracles were addressed to those who were deeply sensible of their own helplessness and of their utter dependence upon God. It was the theocentric note of these promises that made it possible to include them in the book of Amos. To be sure, there was grave difficulty in reconciling his prediction of the complete destruction of Israel with any hope of the future; but in the light of what had actually happened, those who cherished the prophet's message could interpret events as unfolding further the meaning of the divine activity. Judgment had indeed fallen upon Israel; northern and southern kingdoms had both been destroyed. But a remnant of a people was left. God evidently intended his work to go on through them. He had been sifting Israel among the nations and no pebble was to fall to the earth (9:9). This reading of history as the vehicle for the working out of the divine purpose was in complete accord with the teaching of Amos, who had seen God at work even in the fateful rise and advance of the great Assyrian Empire. The passage embodying this conviction of the continued presence and power of God revealed upon the human scene (9:8c-10) gave the ground for the addition to the book of the glowing promises of the future with which it concludes. Nothing is indeed said about repentance as the prelude to restoration, but the fact that these promises were taken up into the Amos tradition and added to his book meant that they were to be understood in the light of the teaching about Yahweh's relationship to man that speaks through the book as a whole. That is to say, they are set against the background of the acknowledgment of the majesty and might of the God whose righteous will ceaselessly governs the course of nature and human history.

The final stage in the growth of the book was the addition of three notable passages (4:13; 5:8-9; 9:5-6), all closely alike in mood and style, while in both these respects markedly different from the rest of the book. They are concerned not with what Yahweh is about to do, but with the continuous manifestation of his power in the creation of the world and in the maintenance of the processes of nature. They make use of participles to set forth the constancy of this sublime revelation of God as creator and sustainer. Their mood is one of awed wonder and adoration, and they have been appropriately called doxologies. They have little connection with the context in which they are set. Therefore it seems not unlikely that they were originally placed on the margin of the manuscript by a devout reader and afterward by some copyist incorporated in the body of the text. However that may be, they bear their valuable testimony to the continued life of Amos' teaching, with its power to center men's thoughts and feelings upon the transcendent majesty of God.

V. Permanent Value of Amos

It is the pervading sense of this transcendent power and majesty of the living God that invests the ministry of Amos with its abiding significance. He sees everything, whether in nature or history, in the light of the divine sovereignty. In the presence of that sovereignty man's aspiration and striving are pathetically weak and helpless; the achievement on which he prides himself, a thing of the moment.

> How can Jacob stand?
> He is so small! (7:2.)

But the transcendent God enters into close and intimate relationship with the human struggle. With divine condescension he places, as it were, something of his own energies and powers at man's disposal. But these are always to be used as coming from him and ministering to the fulfillment of his purpose. Above all, it is his righteous will that is the sustaining bond of human society. The disregard of the principle of justice between man and man is therefore a presumptuous attempt to manipulate divine energy to the advantage of self-seeking pride and greed. The same temper of mind would find in the cultus a comfortable means of making effective a control of the divine which should assure a continuance of its useful subjection to human aggrandizement. All this would prompt the national self-consciousness to identify God with the destiny of the nation. In the face of such arrogant misconception of the true relationship between God and man, the reaffirmation of the divine sovereignty must involve the overthrow of national life: the pride of Jacob must have an end. That is why the prophet as he declares the sublime reality of the sovereign righteousness of God must insist upon its destroying aspect. But in that very declaration he affirms that a transcendent Deity is still at work in his world. God's power upon the human scene is being manifested even in the ruthless advance of the Assyrian Empire. That for the time being is an instrument of his righteous will.

Perhaps even more significantly it was given to Amos to realize, at the cost of tragic experience, that in his own personal life the same dread power of the living God was making itself felt and that he therefore had his part and place in the fulfillment of the divine purpose; he thus humbly knows that human life in its total surrender to God finds its final meaning.

VI. Outline of Contents

I. Oracles against the nations (1:1–2:16)
  A. Superscription and motto (1:1-2)
  B. Oracles against neighboring peoples (1:3–2:3)
    1. Damascus (1:3-5)
    2. The Philistines (1:6-8)
    3. Tyre (1:9-10)
    4. Edom (1:11-12)
    5. Ammon (1:13-15)
    6. Moab (2:1-3)
  C. Oracle against Judah (2:4-5)
  D. Oracles against Israel (2:6-16)
    1. Rebellion in national life (2:6-8)
    2. God's revelation in history (2:9-12)
    3. The coming of judgment (2:13-16)
II. Sermons on the doom of Israel (3:1–6:14)
  A. Amos' interpretation of Israel's relationship to God (3:1-8)
    1. The uniqueness of election (3:1-2)
    2. The prophet's authority (3:3-8)
  B. The corruption of Samaria (3:9–4:3)
    1. A city distinguished for oppression (3:9-10)
    2. Total destruction (3:11-12)
    3. The fate of Bethel (3:13-15)
    4. The selfish greed of the women (4:1-3)
  C. The deep-seatedness of Israel's guilt (4:4–5:3)
    1. The sin of the sanctuaries (4:4-5)
    2. Indifference to chastisement (4:6-12)

3. The first doxology (4:13)
4. The death of a people (5:1-3)
  D. Mingled exhortation and denunciation (5:4-15)
    1. False and true religion (5:4-6)
    2. Brutal treatment of the poor, and a second doxology (5:7-13)
    3. The true seeking of God (5:14-15)
  E. The coming of God (5:16-25)
    1. A day of lamentation (5:16-17)
    2. A day of darkness (5:18-20)
    3. Rejection of the cultus (5:21-25)
  F. Inevitability of invasion and exile (5:26–6:14)
    1. A sad procession (5:26-27)
    2. Blind pride and self-indulgence of the leaders (6:1-7)
    3. The horrors of siege (6:8-11)
    4. The end of a people of unnatural conduct and silly pride (6:12-14)
III. A series of visions, an account of the close of Amos' ministry, and an epilogue (7:1–9:15)
  A. Visions and narrative (7:1–8:3)
    1. The locusts (7:1-3)
    2. The devouring fire (7:4-6)
    3. The plumb line (7:7-9)
    4. Amos and Amaziah (7:10-17)
    5. The basket of summer fruit (8:1-3)
  B. Present iniquity and impending doom (8:4-14)
    1. Oppression of the poor (8:4-7)
    2. Earthquake, darkness, and mourning (8:8-10)
    3. Famine and thirst (8:11-14)
  C. The finality of doom (9:1-7)
    1. A fifth vision and its sequel (9:1-4)
    2. A third doxology (9:5-6)
    3. God's relationship to other peoples (9:7)
  D. An epilogue (9:8-15)
    1. A purging judgment (9:8-10)
    2. Restoration of the Davidic kingdom (9:11-12)
    3. Nature's bounty (9:13)
    4. Return of the exiles (9:14-15)

VII. Selected Bibliography

CRIPPS, RICHARD S. A Critical and Exegetical Commentary on the Book of Amos. New York: The Macmillan Co., 1929.

DRIVER, S. R. The Books of Joel and Amos ("Cambridge Bible"). Cambridge: Cambridge University Press, 1934.

SMITH, GEORGE ADAM. The Book of the Twelve Prophets. Rev. ed. New York: Harper & Bros., 1940. Vol. I.

SNAITH, NORMAN H. The Book of Amos. London: Epworth Press, 1946. Pt. I.

WEISER, ARTUR. Das Buch der zwölf Kleinen Propheten. Göttingen: Vandenhoeck & Ruprecht, 1949. Vol. I.

————. Die Profetie des Amos. Giessen: Alfred Töpelmann, 1929.

WOLFE, ROLLAND E. Meet Amos and Hosea. New York: Harper & Bros., 1945.

AMOS

TEXT, EXEGESIS, AND EXPOSITION

1 The words of Amos, who was among the herdmen of Tekoa, which he saw concerning Israel in the days of Uzziah king of Judah, and in the days of Jeroboam the son of Joash king of Israel, two years before the earthquake.

1 The words of Amos, who was among the shepherds of Teko'a, which he saw concerning Israel in the days of Uzzi'ah king of Judah and in the days of Jerobo'am the son of Jo'ash, king of Israel, two years[a]

[a] Or *during two years*

I. Oracles Against the Nations (1:1–2:16)

A superscription (1:1) intended as a title for the book as a whole is followed by a motto (1:2) characterizing its contents, and this by a series of oracles announcing judgment upon neighboring peoples (1:3–2:3), an oracle against Judah (2:3-5), and an arraignment of Israel with prediction of the overwhelming disaster that was to overtake the nation.

A. Superscription and Motto (1:1-2)

1:1. The words of Amos, who was among the shepherds of Tekoa, which he saw concerning Israel: The two relative clauses, the second of which looks back over the first to the antecedent **words**, form an awkward construction. The phrase **of Tekoa** is more naturally to be taken with **Amos** than with **shepherds.** It is probable therefore that the clause **who was among the shepherds** was introduced by an editor who had 7:14 in mind. The simple expression, "Amos of Tekoa," was a sufficient identification of the prophet while the memory of his ministry was still fresh in men's minds. The Hebrew word here used for shepherd, *nōqēdh*, is not the usual one. Elsewhere in the O.T. it is found only in II Kings 3:4, where it is rendered "sheepmaster." In Arabic the *naqqadh* is a small sheep noted for its abundant wool. It was perhaps for the selling of this commodity that Amos had traveled in the Northern Kingdom and thus became familiar with conditions there. However, it would seem that his flock was of no great size as he derived part of his living from dressing sycamores (7:14).

Tekoa, now Tequ', is today the site of ruins on a hill nearly three thousand feet above sea level, some twelve miles south of Jerusalem. On three sides limestone hills rise above it, but to the east there is a view of the Dead Sea with the mountains of Moab beyond. It is a desolate, rock-bound region affording but scanty pasturage for flocks of sheep and goats. In the second relative clause, **which he saw,** the verb *ḥāzāh*, **saw,** is generally used of heightened vision as of the poet or the seer. Its application to **words** calls for some such rendering as "he received in vision." A like usage is to be found in Isa. 2:1; Mic. 1:1, and the rather strange conjunction of the verb of seeing with "word"

1:1. Amos of Tekoa.—With commendable verbal economy, a nameless editor introduces his readers to "the earliest of the prophets whose utterances have been recorded in books that bear their names" (see Intro., p. 763). **Amos . . . of Tekoa** was a name and an address sufficient to

conjure up in the minds of a succeeding generation the figure of an austere shepherd-prophet who made the oracles and visions of God his familiars. Passage of the centuries has served not only to confirm his identity but to enhance **the words of Amos . . . which he saw concern-**

2 And he said, The Lord will roar from
Zion, and utter his voice from Jerusalem;
and the habitations of the shepherds shall
mourn, and the top of Carmel shall wither.

before the earthquake. 2 And he said:
"The Lord roars from Zion,
    and utters his voice from Jerusalem;
the pastures of the shepherds mourn,
    and the top of Carmel withers."

or "words" may be due to the desire of editors to insist on the connection between
prophetic utterance and prophetic vision. However, in the case of the book of Amos,
chs. 1–6 constitute a collection of oracles, and chs. 7–9 are made up mainly of visions.
It is not unlikely that the editor who brought these together combined the title of the
one, "The Words of Amos of Tekoa," with the title of the other, "The Visions of
Amos, Which He Saw Concerning Israel. . . ."

In the days of Uzziah king of Judah and in the days of Jeroboam the son of
Joash, king of Israel: The excellent piece of narrative in 7:10-17 names Jeroboam king
of Israel as the ruler to whom report was made of Amos' activity. The editor, who in
the superscription is providing information for the readers of a later date, feels it
necessary to speak of him as Jeroboam the son of Joash to distinguish him from the
earlier Jeroboam the son of Nebat, first ruler of the Northern Kingdom. This editor also
reveals his own connection with the South by naming Uzziah king of Judah first,
although Amos' ministry took place in the North, and in his day Israel was much the
more important of the two kingdoms. The contemporary reigns of the two monarchs
marked by a period of great prosperity for both kingdoms covered a good part of the
first half of the eighth century B.C.

Two years before the earthquake: As earthquakes are by no means unusual in
Palestine, the simple reference to the earthquake would indicate that this was one of
exceptional severity. The author of Zech. 14:5 appears to have this same earthquake in
mind. There is, however, no way of determining the exact year in which it occurred.
For the particular period in Jeroboam's reign at which Amos exercised his ministry see
Intro., pp. 766-67.

2. And he said introduces a four-line stanza of balanced rhythm. It is in part
identical with Joel 3:16a and is perhaps an excerpt from a longer poem quoted both
here and in Joel. The divine utterance is as menacing as the roar of the lion and the
crash of the thunder, and its devastating effect is like that of a drought setting its blight
alike on the pastures of the shepherds—habitations (KJV) is here a less satisfactory
rendering of what is a distinctively pastoral term (cf. Ps. 23:2)—and on the top of
Carmel, the heavily wooded slopes of the headland jutting out into the Mediterranean
in the neighborhood of the modern Haifa. The whole of the land would suffer. But
drought is not the natural consequence of thunder or of the roaring of the lion, and
the imagery has a conventional ring, the result of deliberate literary effort rather than
the note of felt experience characteristic of the spoken word of the prophet as, e.g., in 3:8.
Norman H. Snaith (The Book of Amos [London: Epworth Press, 1946], II, 9-11) argues
for Amos' authorship of the verse, but other recent commentators are agreed that it
comes from a later time and was placed here as a kind of motto by way of introduction
to the book. For the editor, as for those whom he addressed, Zion was in a special way
the place of God's manifestation of himself. He would remind readers that it was none

ing Israel. The extravagant figure of a man who
"sees his words" has about it a suggestion of the
eternal. One "measures his words," as we say,
or "weighs his words" to suit the scope and
gravity of a particular occasion. Measures and
weights are prosaic counters; but sight and seeing are poetic terms whose usage involves a sense
of timelessness in one who reads or hears. This

early impression is sustained by a later commentator upon the book of Amos, who said of
the prophet, "He was one of those recruits from
common life, by whom religion and the state
have been reformed." [1]

[1] George Adam Smith, The Book of the Twelve
Prophets (rev. ed.; New York: Harper & Bros., 1928),
I, 83.

3 Thus saith the LORD; For three transgressions of Damascus, and for four, I will not turn away *the punishment* thereof; because they have threshed Gilead with threshing instruments of iron:

4 But I will send a fire into the house of Hazael, which shall devour the palaces of Ben-hadad.

3 Thus says the LORD:
"For three transgressions of Damascus,
 and for four, I will not revoke the punishment;[b]
because they have threshed Gilead
 with threshing sledges of iron.
4 So I will send a fire upon the house of Haz′ael,
 and it shall devour the strongholds of Ben-ha′dad.

[b] Heb *cause it to return*

other than God himself who had spoken through Amos, and that the prophet's utterances still had their meaning as they constituted a particular instance of the dread divine judgment to which human life is constantly subjected.

B. ORACLES AGAINST NEIGHBORING PEOPLES (1:3–2:3)
1. DAMASCUS (1:3-5)

3. Damascus was the capital city of the Aramaean (Syrian) kingdom, with which for a century Israel had been at war the greater part of the time. **For three transgressions . . . and for four:** I.e., for transgressions which one could go on counting indefinitely. "I will not turn it back," such is the literal rendering of the Hebrew. Turn what back? The devastating doom with a foreboding sense of which the prophet's heart is charged. It is as if he had brooded over the question, "Can this doom that obsesses my mind so that I can think of nothing else, can this be averted?" But always there beats in his brain with monotonous insistence the sound of a voice, "I will not turn it back." It is God's unalterable purpose to destroy. Transgression after transgression had made doom inevitable. The essential meaning of the Hebrew word *pésha‘*, "transgression," is revolt or rebellion. The verb from the same root is that used in I Kings 12:19, "Israel rebelled against the house of David." In its conduct the kingdom of Damascus had asserted its independence over against God under whose sovereignty it existed as a people. As a signal illustration of the ways in which it had affronted the divine majesty there is adduced the ruthless barbarity with which, not long before, it had **threshed Gilead with threshing instruments of iron.** Over the prostrate bodies of a conquered foe the cruel victors had dragged the heavy iron-shod sledges, and the jagged teeth meant to cut straw to pieces and thresh out the grain had mangled the quivering flesh of human beings. The reference is to what had taken place during Hazael's conquest of Gilead (II Kings 10:32-33).

4-5. The six lines picture the devastation that is to sweep all before it. The particular names of people and places invest the picture with a concrete realism. **Hazael** had been the founder of the reigning dynasty, his son **Ben-hadad** had carried on his father's conquests (II Kings 13:3, 7). **The Valley of Aven** was probably a broad fertile **plain** (KJV), fairly representative of the rich territory of the Aramaean kingdom; **Beth-eden,** a city of importance as perhaps the seat of an official. Rulers and people, land and towns, are all alike involved in dire disaster. The prophet in his heightened state of consciousness

1:3–2:16. *Rendezvous with Doom.*—Here is set forth a series of oracles delivered by Amos. Scholars are divided in their conjectures as to what portion of these and subsequent pronouncements represent the original message of the prophet and what comprise later additions and embellishments to the text. Another ground for debate is whether Amos delivered his oracles in the form of sustained utterances, or whether we have before us in the book that bears his name random prophecies spoken by the prophet but committed to writing by others who heard and remembered. The Exeg. provides a treatment of these and other critical problems. In the Expos. we shall deliberately substitute the telescope for the microscope and seek to envisage the broad dimensions of the text rather than its nice detail.

5 I will break also the bar of Damascus, and cut off the inhabitant from the plain of Aven, and him that holdeth the sceptre from the house of Eden: and the people of Syria shall go into captivity unto Kir, saith the Lord.

6 ¶ Thus saith the Lord; For three transgressions of Gaza, and for four, I will not turn away *the punishment* thereof; because they carried away captive the whole captivity, to deliver *them* up to Edom:

7 But I will send a fire on the wall of Gaza, which shall devour the palaces thereof:

8 And I will cut off the inhabitant from Ashdod, and him that holdeth the sceptre from Ashkelon, and I will turn mine hand against Ekron: and the remnant of the Philistines shall perish, saith the Lord God.

5 I will break the bar of Damascus,
    and cut off the inhabitants from the
      Valley of Aven,[c]
and him that holds the scepter from Beth-
    eden;
    and the people of Syria shall go into
      exile to Kir,"

                     says the Lord.

6 Thus says the Lord:
"For three transgressions of Gaza,
    and for four, I will not revoke the
      punishment;[d]
because they carried into exile a whole
    people
to deliver them up to Edom.

7 So I will send a fire upon the wall of
    Gaza,
    and it shall devour her strongholds.

8 I will cut off the inhabitants from Ash-
    dod,
    and him that holds the scepter from
      Ash'kelon;
I will turn my hand against Ekron;
    and the remnant of the Philistines
      shall perish,"

                says the Lord God.

[c] Or *On*
[d] Heb *cause it to return*

hears the crackle of the flames, sees the fire leap from building to building. The fortifications of Damascus go down before the irresistible onslaught of the invader. The land is swept bare of the inhabitants who are to be carried into exile in a remote land. **Kir,** named in 9:7 as the region from which the Syrians came, would seem to have lain far to the east (Isa. 22:6). Here is war, ruthless desolating war, and it is the God of Israel who sends it, launching the great armies of the Assyrian Empire against the kingdom of Damascus.

2. The Philistines (1:6-8)

6-8. These verses predict a like destruction which will overtake the Philistines, Israel's rival for the possession of the land from the early days of the settlement in Canaan. The important city of **Gaza** is named first, perhaps because its situation at the point at which a caravan route from Edom joined the highroad between Egypt and Syria made it an important center of the slave traffic, which is singled out for particular denunciation. There had been raids carrying off the total population of villages to be handed over to the Edomites. Of the five Philistine cities, four are named. The omission of any mention of Gath, destroyed by Sargon of Assyria in 711 B.C., may suggest a date for

Early in the book is sounded the awful theme which runs with somber variations through the whole composition. "God is about to destroy his people for their sins" (see Intro., pp. 767-68). Whether we are dealing with the spoken words of Amos, or whether they represent the work of a subsequent editor who has here recorded a

series of Amos' oracles, including several from other and later sources, the arrangement of the material no less than its content attests the forensic skill of speaker or scribe. The reiteration of the note of divine punishment is first employed in condemnation of six of the traditional enemies of Israel. As old as history is the

| 9 ¶ Thus saith the Lord; For three transgressions of Tyrus, and for four, I will not turn away *the punishment* thereof; because they delivered up the whole captivity of Edom, and remembered not the brotherly covenant:

 10 But I will send a fire on the wall of Tyrus, which shall devour the palaces thereof. | 9 Thus says the Lord:
 "For three transgressions of Tyre,
     and for four, I will not revoke the
       punishment;*d*
 because they delivered up a whole people
     to Edom,
     and did not remember the covenant of
       brotherhood.
 10 So I will send a fire upon the wall of
     Tyre,
     and it shall devour her strongholds."

 d Heb *cause it to return* |

the oracle subsequent to the time of Amos. The language of vss. 7-8 echoes that of vss. 4-5. The reference to **the remnant of the Philistines** points to a period at which the land of Palestine had fallen under the domination of the great empires and the little nations had been reduced to mere fragments of peoples. Some commentators therefore would regard this oracle as belonging to the sixth century B.C. This would mean that it expressed the conviction that the God who through Amos had made known his purpose to destroy was still declaring his righteous will and exercising his inexorable judgment.

3. Tyre (1:9-10)

9-10. It is probable that the same conviction was responsible for the oracle against Tyre. That great trading center of the ancient world—see the splendid description of Tyre's commerce in Ezek. 28—had also engaged in the slave trade. The brevity of the announcement of the doom that is to overtake the city, contenting itself with a simple repetition of the phrasing of vs. 4, points to the later hand, but is enough to record the assurance that not even the magnificence of Tyre can escape the judgment of the God whose righteousness Amos had proclaimed.

The clause **not remembering the covenant of brotherhood** (vs. 9) is difficult to interpret. It is hardly possible that anyone could think of a brotherly covenant as existing between Tyre and Israel (yet, cf. I Kings 5:12). It has been suggested that the reference is to the action taken by Tyre in 678-676 B.C. against kindred Phoenicians in aiding Assyria to suppress a revolt. It is more likely, however, that the clause is a gloss on vs. 11, reminding readers of the relation that had once obtained between Edom and Israel. It has been embodied in the text of vs. 9 because of the occurrence there of the name Edom, but was originally intended as comment on the oracle against Edom.

propensity of a clan or tribe or nation to condemn at the bar of high heaven or public opinion the crimes committed by its enemies. Today the issuance of a white paper by a nation's foreign office or department of state serves not only to justify its own conduct of international affairs but to imply, if not to declare, the policies and actions of another nation to be black by comparison. National self-righteousness is one of the marks of chauvinism, whether ancient or modern. It costs nothing for a nation or an individual to bewail another's sins. The Northern Kingdom, under Jeroboam II in the middle of the eighth century B.C., was enjoying a kind of Indian-summer prosperity. The Assyrian menace was, for the moment, abated. There was peace with Judah, and in both kingdoms control of the great trade routes sluiced

moneys into the national coffers. Merchants and landowners were becoming more wealthy, to the consequent distress of the little people. The phrase, "at ease in Zion" (6:1), which we owe to Amos, well expressed the general temper of national complacency. Crowds of people flocking to Bethel to keep festival at the shrines and to make money in the bazaars would have been singularly attracted and attentive to anyone who directed words of divine condemnation upon Syria, Philistia, Phoenicia, Edom, Ammon, or Moab. Against each hostile nation the prophet draws a bill of divine indictment in the recital of some well-remembered act of impiety or inhumanity. This is followed by a prophetic pronouncement of divine punishment, spelled out in terms of defeat, destruction, and exile. The anatomy of war is exposed by Amos with the

11 ¶ Thus saith the LORD; For three transgressions of Edom, and for four, I will not turn away *the punishment* thereof; because he did pursue his brother with the sword, and did cast off all pity, and his anger did tear perpetually, and he kept his wrath for ever:

11 Thus says the LORD:
"For three transgressions of Edom,
     and for four, I will not revoke the punishment;[d]
because he pursued his brother with the sword,
     and cast off all pity,
and his anger tore perpetually,
     and he kept his wrath[e] for ever.

[d] Heb *cause it to return*
[e] Gk Syr Vg: Heb *his wrath kept*

4. EDOM (1:11-12)

The Edomites were of all neighboring peoples the most closely akin to Israel, as is shown by the account of their descent from Esau, Jacob's brother, in Gen. 36. As Gen. 36:31 indicates, they had become an organized kingdom before Israel had attained that standing, and with their advantageous trading position at the head of the Gulf of Aqabah, and their extensive mineral deposits, they had the resources for a rich and prosperous national life. From the time of David on, however, they had been subject to Israel and had nurtured a bitter hostility against those who held them in subjection, the more bitter because of the close kinship of the two peoples. The opportunity for revenge came with the fall of Jerusalem and the dissolution of the kingdom of Judah in 586 B.C. Of this opportunity they took full advantage in aggressive overrunning of the depleted territory, and it is to this exilic or postexilic period that the oracle against Edom may be most appropriately referred (cf. George Adam Smith, *The Book of the Twelve Prophets* [rev. ed.; New York: Harper & Bros., 1940], I, 128-30).

11. The particular charge of the indictment makes much of the fact that the cruelty was directed against those who were their brethren.

**He pursued his brother with the sword,
and cast off all pity.**

The Hebrew of the latter clause is difficult, as is indicated by the alternative rendering in the ASV mg., "corrupted his compassions." In the word for "his compassions," *rahᵃmāw,* there would seem to linger some sense of its association with the word for womb, *réḥem.* It would thus speak of the brotherly feeling that should link those who are born of the same womb. It may well be that it was to help readers grasp this meaning that the gloss **did not remember the covenant of brotherhood** was originally intended. It was perhaps because the author of the oracles did not altogether forget that in days gone by Israel itself had not acted toward Edom in a brotherly way that he went on to single out the insatiability of Edom's lust for revenge as especially heinous.

**And his anger tore perpetually,
and he kept his wrath for ever.**

poetic skill of a Euripides, and the naked prose of an Ernest Hemingway. He catalogues the horrors caused by the devastation of the land, the deportation of whole towns and villages into slavery, the repudiation of treaties, the ravaging of women, and the mutilation of the dead. Modern war includes the same crimes against humanity, compounded by the discoveries of science and the inventions of technology. Modern man, in his preoccupation with total warfare, has lost an earlier sense of revulsion that such things should be. He has, instead, become fatalistic in the face of current wars and rumors of war.

"Peace upon earth!" was said. We sing it,
And pay a million priests to bring it.
After two thousand years of mass
We've got as far as poison-gas.[2]

[2] Thomas Hardy, "Christmas: 1924," from *Winter Words* (London: Macmillan & Co., New York: The Macmillan Co., 1928). Used by permission of the Trustees of the Hardy Estate and the publishers.

12 But I will send a fire upon Teman, which shall devour the palaces of Bozrah.

13 ¶ Thus saith the LORD; For three transgressions of the children of Ammon, and for four, I will not turn away *the punishment* thereof; because they have ripped up the women with child, of Gilead, that they might enlarge their border:

14 But I will kindle a fire in the wall of Rabbah, and it shall devour the palaces thereof, with shouting in the day of battle, with a tempest in the day of the whirlwind:

15 And their king shall go into captivity, he and his princes together, saith the LORD.

12 So I will send a fire upon Teman,
    and it shall devour the strongholds of
    Bozrah."

13 Thus says the LORD:
    "For three transgressions of the Ammon-
    ites,
      and for four, I will not revoke the
      punishment;^d
    because they have ripped up women with
      child in Gilead,
      that they might enlarge their border.
14 So I will kindle a fire in the wall of
    Rabbah,
    and it shall devour her strongholds,
    with shouting in the day of battle,
      with a tempest in the day of the whirl-
      wind;
15 and their king shall go into exile,
    he and his princes together,"
                    says the LORD.

^d Heb *cause it to return*

In the first clause for **tore** many commentators would read, with Syriac and Vulg., "he kept." The change involves only the omission of a single consonant in the Hebrew, ויטר for ויטרף, but the figure in the M.T. of anger ravening as a wild beast is very striking, and **tore** may be the original reading.

12. Both **Teman,** probably a district in the north of Edomite territory, and **Bozrah,** apparently an important city, are elsewhere paralleled with Edom as a whole (Jer. 49:20; Isa. 34:6).

5. AMMON (1:13-15)

13-15. It is in this oracle against the Ammonites that the authentic utterance of Amos can again unquestionably be heard. Their territory lay east of the Jordan, bordering on the Israelite region of Gilead. The specific charge set against the background of repeated transgressions, **they have ripped up women with child in Gilead,** was the more damning because this dreadful brutality had been perpetrated not in defense of their own land but in aggressive warfare **that they might enlarge their border.** The doom pronounced upon them is explicitly that of the same devastation by war that was to overtake Damascus and its ruler and people, and it is set forth with that variation in vivid detail that the poet can command. **Rabbah,** the capital, would be destroyed by fire; the jubilant shout of a victorious enemy would inspire terror while, like a raging

Thomas Hardy composed the cynical lines above as a kind of epitaph on World War I. He was a bit too early to celebrate the A-bomb and the H-bomb! But long ago in Israel Amos spelled out God's pronouncement of doom upon war makers in terms of their ultimate defeat, destruction, and exile.

> Though the mills of God grind slowly,
>   Yet they grind exceeding small.[3]

[3] Longfellow, "Poetic Aphorisms: Retribution." From the *Sinngedichte* of Friedrich von Logau.

The Lord's indictment of Judah, which follows (2:4-5), may be attributed to a later source than Amos. But there is nothing in the total demeanor and temper of the prophet to have prevented him from condemning his native land for its religious apostasy. Only the most sensitive would have been startled by this reference to the Southern Kingdom. The mood of his public was still a complacent, "It can't happen *here.*"

Then with a dramatic suddenness reminiscent of an earlier prophet, Nathan, in conversation

2 Thus saith the Lord; For three transgressions of Moab, and for four, I will not turn away *the punishment* thereof; because he burned the bones of the king of Edom into lime:

2 But I will send a fire upon Moab, and it shall devour the palaces of Kirioth: and Moab shall die with tumult, with shouting, *and* with the sound of the trumpet:

3 And I will cut off the judge from the midst thereof, and will slay all the princes thereof with him, saith the Lord.

4 ¶ Thus saith the Lord; For three transgressions of Judah, and for four, I will not turn away *the punishment* thereof; because they have despised the law of the Lord, and have not kept his commandments, and their lies caused them to err, after the which their fathers have walked:

---

2 Thus says the Lord:
"For three transgressions of Moab,
　　and for four, I will not revoke the
　　　punishment;[d]
because he burned to lime
　　the bones of the king of Edom.
2 So I will send a fire upon Moab,
　　and it shall devour the strongholds of
　　　Ker'ioth,
and Moab shall die amid uproar,
　　amid shouting and the sound of the
　　　trumpet;
3 I will cut off the ruler from its midst,
　　and will slay all its princes with him,"
　　　　　　　　　　　　says the Lord.

4 Thus says the Lord:
"For three transgressions of Judah,
　　and for four, I will not revoke the
　　　punishment;[d]
because they have rejected the law of the
　　Lord,
　　and have not kept his statutes,
but their lies have led them astray,
　　after which their fathers walked.

[d] Heb *cause it to return*

---

tempest laying all low before it, the invader would sweep over the land; the leaders of the nation would be carried into exile.

6. Moab (2:1-3)

The oracle against **Moab** is also beyond doubt an authentic utterance of Amos. The territory of Moab lay to the east of the Dead Sea, and its southern edge bordered on Edom. Inevitably conflict between the two peoples was frequent and the precise occasion of the vindictive desecration of the remains of the king of Edom cannot be determined. It is possible that it took place in connection with the events described in II Kings 3. It is again devastating war that is to make an end of Moab.

2. Kerioth is perhaps to be identified with Ar, elsewhere named as a chief city of Moab (Isa. 15:1). On the Moabite stone (l. 13) it is named as the site of a sanctuary of the Moabite god Chemosh.

C. Oracle Against Judah (2:4-5)

4-5. The oracles against the neighboring peoples prepared the way for the oracles against Israel that were to follow. Perhaps delivered on successive days at the beginning of Amos' ministry, they would awaken in those who heard them a conviction that the

---

with King David (II Sam. 12:7), Amos declares Israel to be the final object of God's wrath and consequent doom.

For three transgressions of Israel,
and for four, I will not revoke the punishment
(2:6*a*).

The oft-used word "transgression," with its implication of rebellion, points up the element of willful disobedience in Israel's guilt. There follows (2:6*b*-8) a specific preferment of charges against the Northern Kingdom. National prosperity had been accompanied by gross perversions of justice as between rich and poor. Wealth was possessed by the few at the cost of impoverishment, even to the point of servitude, of the many. Himself a small farmer on marginal land, Amos had an inbred sense of the relation

5 But I will send a fire upon Judah, and it shall devour the palaces of Jerusalem. | 5 So I will send a fire upon Judah,
    and it shall devour the strongholds of
        Jerusalem."

---

prophet was in touch with reality. Not only did he take account of the menace of Assyrian aggression, for the moment remote but always in the light of the past much more than a possibility; he saw this as bringing about the overthrow of peoples that had never shown proper appreciation of what Israel felt to be its distinctive and superior qualities. What the prophet said would command a sympathetic hearing even if the insistence on God's destroying power struck an ominous note. This enabled Amos to impress effectively upon his hearers truth of fundamental significance. The God to whose rule all peoples are subject, whose will was declared in the movement of the Assyrian Empire, must in his inexorable righteousness destroy nations that set themselves up against him in self-centered disregard of his claim to their obedience. It was truth which would find the readier acceptance among those who heard it because it was none other than their own God who was thus exercising his sovereign power. If, as many commentators hold, some of these oracles belong to a time later than that of Amos, they bear their testimony to the impact that this truth made not only on the prophet's own day but on subsequent generations. It is perhaps worth noting that the three oracles remaining unquestioned, those against Damascus, the Ammonites, and Moab are the ones which most clearly present desolating war as the agency of destruction, with vivid phrases such as "break the bar of Damascus," "shouting in the day of battle," "the blare of trumpets." These are the oracles, too, that are directed against the peoples lying immediately in the path of Assyrian advance, and the naming of these three in direct sequence would give an added touch of realism as the prophet pictured the engulfing tide sweeping in to the very borders of Israel. But before the oracles against Israel there stands in the present order of the book an oracle against Judah.

The authenticity of this passage has long been called in question, and the oracle is now regarded by the great majority of commentators as a later insertion. It is clear that for Amos the peoples of both the Northern and the Southern Kingdoms constituted a single family (3:2), and Judah was therefore included in his denunciation of Israel. It is unlikely therefore that he would have uttered a special oracle against Judah. The fact that God is made to speak of himself in the third person—**I will not revoke the punishment** is followed by **law of the Lord, . . . his statutes**—points to a later formal use of Amos' introductory sentence. The language too reflects the idiom of a later day. Phrases such as **rejected the law, kept his statutes** were commonly used by the Deuteronomic writers who sought to reorganize the national life after the fall of Jerusalem in 586 b.c. In the face of the final overthrow of the little kingdom of Judah, they maintained their faith that God had indeed chosen his people and that a community life which was in accord with his claim on their loving obedience had the promise of the future. Against

---

between scarcity and value. The distortion of this equation in urban centers like Bethel and Gilgal moved him to some of his sternest moral judgments upon the social economy of his own and of all times.

A man and his father go in to the same maiden,
  so that my holy name is profaned;

. . . .

and in the house of their God they drink
  the wine of those who have been fined (2:7b, 8b) .

Long exposure of the Israelites to the seductions of various forms of nature-worship had resulted in a kind of religious syncretism. Yahweh had come to be worshiped as though he were a Baal, to the accompaniment of license and drunkenness. Spiritual obtuseness resulting in an impious ritual kindled the fire of Amos' indignation, in which were forged those molten pronouncements of divine doom and destruction that first and last fell from his lips.

There follows the storm center of Amos' words of divine judgment upon Israel, because of social unrighteousness and spiritual decadence (2:9-11). Just as there is a lull in the midst of a hurricane so the prophet introduces

6 ¶ Thus saith the Lord; For three transgressions of Israel, and for four, I will not turn away *the punishment* thereof; because they sold the righteous for silver, and the poor for a pair of shoes;	6 Thus says the Lord:
	"For three transgressions of Israel,
	  and for four, I will not revoke the punishment;*d*
	because they sell the righteous for silver,
	  and the needy for a pair of shoes —
	
	d Heb *cause it to return*

this background the oracle against Judah represented the conviction that the closeness of its relationship to God did not exempt a people from that stern subjection to his righteous judgment of which Amos had spoken. The clause

But their lies have led them astray,
after which their fathers walked,

reads like a prose gloss by one who wished to insist on the part that the following of falsely imagined gods plays in a people's ruin (cf. S. R. Driver, *The Books of Joel and Amos* [Cambridge: Cambridge University Press, 1934; "Cambridge Bible"], pp. 119-21).

D. Oracles Against Israel (2:6-16)

The oracle against Israel is introduced with the same note of irrevocable doom as that sounded in the oracles against the neighboring peoples. It would be with indignant dismay that those who heard thus found themselves placed on a level with the nations they felt had so rightly fallen under condemnation. But in the indictment that followed they were to learn that theirs remained a special distinction. Instead of naming a single outrage as an instance of repeated transgressions, the prophet went on to enumerate the ways in which rebellion against God was habitually characteristic of the national life (vss. 6-8). These are set against the background of Israel's particular relationship to God as shown in their past history with the greater knowledge of himself that he had thus given them (vss. 9-12). The destruction that was to overtake them is therefore set forth with more vivid detail and invested with even more definite finality than in the preceding oracles (vss. 13-16). Amos' passionate indignation shatters the closely knit form employed in the preceding oracles. Variations in the rhythm do indeed suggest that originally separate oracles have here been combined, but in general the passage sums up the prophet's initial arraignment of Israel.

1. Rebellion in National Life (2:6-8)

6. The first count in the indictment significantly enough is the inhuman treatment of the poor by the well to do: **They sell the righteous for silver.** This has usually been taken to refer to the condemnation of the innocent by judges who take bribes, a procedure widely prevalent and scathingly denounced by eighth-century prophets (Isa. 1:23; Mic. 3:9). But recent commentators (cf. Artur Weiser, *Die Profetie des Amos* [Giessen: Alfred Töpelmann, 1929], pp. 90-91) have pointed out that the verb here employed is most often used of selling into slavery (Gen. 37:27-28; Exod. 21:16), and

into his blast of doom a moving appeal to the memory of his hearers. The great covenanted mercies of God towards Israel are recalled: the deliverance at the Red Sea, the preservation during forty years in the wilderness, the early settlement in the land of promise (vs. 10). In his reference to God's having raised

. . . some of your sons for prophets,
and some of your young men for Nazirites (2:11*a*)

Amos conjures up, in a sentence, God's unique revelation of himself to his people through the discipline of prophecy. Brief suggestion is made of its beginnings in group enthusiasm and ecstasy and its fulfillment in the more austere and unmercenary figure of the solitary spokesman for God. But in her present worldly sophistication, Israel had come to ridicule the simple Nazirites and their strict obedience to an ancient vow. In her complacency and self-right-

7 That pant after the dust of the earth on the head of the poor, and turn aside the way of the meek: and a man and his father will go in unto the *same* maid, to profane my holy name:

7 they that trample the head of the poor
    into the dust of the earth,
  and turn aside the way of the afflicted;
a man and his father go in to the same
    maiden,
  so that my holy name is profaned;

this is its most natural meaning in the clause that follows, **they sell . . . the needy for a pair of shoes.** The creditor would take advantage of a trifling debt to sell his debtor into slavery. The first line must have something of the same meaning; **righteous,** specifically in legal usage "innocent," must here denote one who does not seek to evade his obligations, and Moffatt's translation, "They sell honest folk for money," gives the sense satisfactorily. This employment of due process of law to go to any lengths in the pursuit of their own rights was one of the ways in which the rapacious rich showed their callous disregard of the bitter hardship imposed upon the lives of simple folk by their greed.

7a. **That pant after the dust of the earth on the head of the poor** (KJV) makes the best of the difficult M.T. But **after** is not the natural rendering of the Hebrew preposition, and the suggestion that in their greed the rich crave the very dust that the poor man casts upon his head as a sign of mourning seems too farfetched for Amos' downright manner of utterance. The reading **trample** (RSV) is supported by the LXX and the Vulg. and involves a change only in the vowel pointing. **And turn aside the way of the afflicted: Afflicted** is one meaning of the Hebrew *'anāwîm,* but **meek** (KJV) is a more suitable rendering here, with an emphasis on the uncomplaining acceptance of adverse conditions as contrasted with the brutal self-assertion of their oppressors. There is here an early stage in the development of the use of the word "meek" applied to those who in their looking away from self waited humbly upon divine guidance and care. This meaning of the word is especially frequent in the Psalms (e.g., 25:9) and prepared the way for the great saying of Matt. 5:5.

7b-8. These lines constitute the second count in the indictment of Israel. The behavior at the sanctuaries is further evidence of the arrogant self-centered attitude that would subordinate even the divine to the satisfaction of its own greedy desire. **A man and his father go in to the same maiden.** According to many commentators, they have taken over from the religion of the land the practice of temple prostitution, characteristic of a nature worship that centered about the life process. Hos. 4:14 speaks of the wide prevalence of this practice, so grossly repugnant to the religion of Yahweh, and Deut. 23:17 (Hebrew vs. 18) explicitly repudiates it. Both passages use the technical term *qᵉdhēshāh,* "sacred harlot," while Amos simply says "they resort to the girl," as if the act was just a matter of sensual gratification, stripped of all religious significance. That is perhaps also indicated by the subject **a man and his father.** This can hardly point to incest, for the word **same** is not in the Hebrew. Young and old frequent the shrine together for this purpose, as if taking part in a kind of outing. Both the conduct and the

eousness, the nation was ready to stop the mouths of the successors of Nathan, Elijah, and Elisha who troubled the national conscience. Thus the brief mood of recollection ends; and the gale of Amos' earlier indignation on behalf of God rises to a final fury (2:13-16). He sees and portrays, in words that throb with indubitable meaning, the culmination of Israel's odyssey in approaching disaster and defeat. In a series of short, vivid sentences, Amos pictures her "big battalions" beaten down and routed by the onslaught of an outraged God. Those

that are not crushed in the first onset seek refuge in flight, but for the bowman, however swift of foot, or the horseman, though he is well mounted, there is no covert from the terrible nemesis of God's wrath. It must be said that Amos' stern and narrow theology allows the errant soul little relief from the wrath of God in terms of the mercy of God. We respect the prophet's consistency, but take proper satisfaction in his successor, Hosea, who wove his prophecies with the warp of God's judgment and the woof of his love. Of such ampler mind

8 And they lay *themselves* down upon clothes laid to pledge by every altar, and they drink the wine of the condemned *in* the house of their god.

9 ¶ Yet destroyed I the Amorite before them, whose height *was* like the height of the cedars, and he *was* strong as the oaks; yet I destroyed his fruit from above, and his roots from beneath.

8 they lay themselves down beside every
    altar
upon garments taken in pledge;
and in the house of their God they drink
    the wine of those who have been fined.

9 "Yet I destroyed the Amorite before
    them,
    whose height was like the height of the
      cedars,
    and who was as strong as the oaks;
I destroyed his fruit above,
    and his roots beneath.

---

spirit behind it are such as **to profane my holy name.** The name of God, the manifestation of himself that partakes of the dynamic of his own inmost being, is thus made subservient to the satisfaction of human lust. This consequence is so inevitable that it was as if it were done by deliberate intent. And this pleasure-loving caricature of worship goes hand in hand with the ruthless treatment of the poor.

8. They lay themselves down beside every altar . . . : Commentators generally refer the **garments taken in pledge** to the provision of the ancient law in Exod. 22:26-27 (Hebrew vss. 25-26) that a coat, *ṣalmāh,* taken in pledge, must be returned at sundown because it is the poor man's only covering. But the word used by Amos, *beghādhîm,* would seem to have a wider reference, and the phrase probably means garments pledged and forfeited to creditors quick to take advantage of the debtor's inability to redeem his pledge. Similarly, the obscure Hebrew phrase rendered **wine of those who have been fined** may be interpreted as wine pawned and forfeited to creditors who lose no time in foreclosing (cf. Snaith, *Amos,* II, 44-47). These men whose visits to the shrines are bouts of revelry make both religion and law minister to their sensual indulgence.

2. God's Revelation in History (2:9-12)

Vss. 9-12 set against the background of this subordination of the divine to base human interests a rehearsal of what God had actually done in the past as revelatory of his nature and his power. He had **destroyed the Amorite,** the name used especially in the traditions of the North for the pre-Israelite inhabitants of Canaan; he had brought Israel **up out of the land of Egypt** and led them through the wilderness to their possession of the land of Canaan; he had manifested his further care for his people by raising up prophets and Nazirites as continued evidence of his presence and power among them. As the passage stands, the emphasis falls on the great benefits that God had bestowed upon Israel. But it opens upon an ominous note. **Yet I destroyed.** The pronoun is emphatic. A people of remarkable physical prowess, **whose height was like the height**

---

was the poet Francis Thompson. His "Hound of Heaven" portrays the fugitive soul finding sanctuary at last, not in God's doom but in his grace.

> Now of that long pursuit
> Comes on at hand the bruit;
> That Voice is round me like a bursting sea:
>   "And is thy earth so marred,
>   Shattered in shard on shard?
> Lo, all things fly thee, for thou fliest Me!"
>
> . . . .
>
>   Halts by me that footfall:
>   Is my gloom, after all,

> Shade of His hand, outstretched caressingly?
>   "Ah, fondest, blindest, weakest,
>   I am He Whom thou seekest!
> Thou dravest love from thee, who dravest Me." [4]

The only way to fly *from* God is to fly *to* God. With these words we may round out Amos' rigorous but partial reading of the oracles of God.

In this series of oracles with which the book of Amos opens it is possible to discover a prophetic reading of history which the passage of

[4] From *Collected Works,* ed. Wilfred Meynell. Used by permission of Burns, Oates & Washbourne, Ltd., and Sir Francis Meynell.

10 Also I brought you up from the land of Egypt, and led you forty years through the wilderness, to possess the land of the Amorite.

11 And I raised up of your sons for prophets, and of your young men for Nazarites. *Is it* not even thus, O ye children of Israel? saith the LORD.

12 But ye gave the Nazarites wine to drink; and commanded the prophets, saying, Prophesy not.

10 Also I brought you up out of the land of
 Egypt,
 and led you forty years in the wilderness,
 to possess the land of the Amorite.
11 And I raised up some of your sons for
 prophets,
 and some of your young men for
 Nazirites.
 Is it not indeed so, O people of Israel?"
        says the LORD.

12 "But you made the Nazirites drink wine,
 and commanded the prophets,
 saying, 'You shall not prophesy.'

---

of the cedars—legend spoke of the original inhabitants of the land as men of great stature (Num. 13:32)—**and he was strong as the oaks,** had been wiped out of existence, root and branch, by the divine decree.

Amos identifies himself with the tradition, accepted and rejoiced in by his hearers, in order to draw from it a stern reminder of the pitiful powerlessness of the strength on which men pride themselves when God's destroying energy declares itself. How hopeless then is Israel's position when it is God's purpose to make an end of it. This forms a striking prelude to the announcement of doom in vss. 13-16, when again the sorry frailty of human qualities is portrayed. Weiser (*op. cit.,* pp. 93-96) has therefore argued that vs. 9 alone originally constituted the link between the indictment of vss. 6b-8 and the prediction of punishment in vss. 13-16, and that a compiler, having in mind how the destruction of the Amorite had made possible Israel's possession of the land, added the phrase **before them**—some MSS read "before you"—and then went on to adduce the further instances of God's special care for his people in vss. 10-12. Indeed, the prose of vs. 10 contrasts markedly with the rhythmic form of the preceding verse, and though vs. 11a has the parallelism and the rhythm of poetry, vss. 11b-12 again relapse into prose. However this may be, whether the emphasis on God's goodness to Israel in the past is that of the prophet or of a later teacher, it is significant that the beneficent acts are seen as those of a God who can also utterly destroy, so that the base ingratitude of which Israel has been guilty is more than a failure to observe common decency as between equals. It is the crass folly of those who have forgotten the transcendent majesty and power of the God on whose will their very existence depends.

11. The **Nazirites,** lit., "the separated," "the consecrated ones," in later times took only for a limited period the vow not to cut the hair but to let it grow in its natural state (Num. 6:5), but in earlier times this would seem to have been a life-long commitment. The abstinence from wine required of them is an indication that they had their origin in the desert days before Israel entered Canaan. They were perhaps dedicated warriors. On the other hand, the prophets, subjects of the group ecstasy which expressed itself in dance and excited utterance, were of Canaanite origin. This ecstatic prophetism was taken over by Israel's religion and gradually transformed into a highly significant moral and spiritual force in Israel's history and so in world history. The parallelism of

---

time has served to enhance. Speaking to an informal student discussion at Oxford, William Ralph Inge, then Dean of St. Paul's London, declared, "Civilization is a disease from which nations seldom recover." On first hearing, it sounded like one more of those stunning over-

statements which earned the speaker the sobriquet, "the gloomy Dean"; but as one reflects upon the statement, the more one is convinced that it is the vehicle not of a gratuitous foreboding but of an undeniable fact. Not the predictor but the recorder is speaking, and the

13 Behold, I am pressed under you, as a cart is pressed *that is* full of sheaves.

14 Therefore the flight shall perish from the swift, and the strong shall not strengthen his force, neither shall the mighty deliver himself:

15 Neither shall he stand that handleth the bow; and *he that is* swift of foot shall not deliver *himself:* neither shall he that rideth the horse deliver himself.

16 And *he that is* courageous among the mighty shall flee away naked in that day, saith the LORD.

13 "Behold, I will press you down in your place,
  as a cart full of sheaves presses down.
14 Flight shall perish from the swift,
  and the strong shall not retain his strength,
  nor shall the mighty save his life;
15 he who handles the bow shall not stand,
  and he who is swift of foot shall not save himself,
  nor shall he who rides the horse save his life;
16 and he who is stout of heart among the mighty
  shall flee away naked in that day,"
  says the LORD.

---

prophet and Nazirite reflects the belief that both alike were in a special way vehicles of the divine energy (cf. Article, "The Prophetic Literature," Vol. I, p. 203). It may well be that the adoption of Canaanite prophetism was facilitated by the existence of a similar phenomenon of possession in Israel.

3. THE COMING OF JUDGMENT (2:13-16)

13-16. The full force of homely imagery that Amos used to bring home to his hearers the dread character of the divine visitation is obscured for the modern reader because of the uncertainty as to the exact meaning of the verb עוּק which the KJV and the RSV render **press.**

> **I will press you down in your place,
> as a cart full of sheaves presses down** (RSV)

does justice to the active form of the verb, while **I am pressed . . . as a cart is pressed** (KJV) does not; but both follow commentators who would treat עוּק as the Aramaic form of a Hebrew verb צוק, which in the causative form means "bring into straits," "press upon." Israel is to feel the grinding pressure that the heavily laden cart exerts upon the ground beneath it. Other expositors, by the change of one letter making the verb read פוק, "to reel," "to totter," would translate, "I will make the ground beneath you totter as the cart that is full of sheaves totters" (cf. Driver, *Joel and Amos,* p. 158). Another conjecture is that the verb may be related to an Arabic root meaning "to groan," and that the passage may be translated, "I will make you groan in your place as the cart groans." Whatever the precise meaning of the imagery, it is evidently intended to depict overwhelming disaster. And in lines that follow it is complete and irreversible overthrow in battle that is portrayed. Neither speed of foot, nor strength of body, nor the experience of the warrior, nor skill in handling weapons shall avail in the rout that follows upon calamitous defeat. The word **naked,** on which the description ends, sums up effectively the pitiful helplessness of a man stripped of all the resources on which he counts to maintain himself when he faces the final catastrophe.

---

pith of his testimony is that the odyssey of the human race is littered with the debris of nations and empires in which material prosperity has outstripped spiritual resources. In the oracles of Amos are to be found one of the earliest statements of this sober fact. The prophet's conscience was stirred by the material aggran-dizement of Israel and its consequent spiritual impoverishment. He saw the capacity of religious complacency to dull men's moral sensibilities; human life had become subservient to the tyranny of things. Hence Amos' stern warning of impending national doom, which time was not slow to vindicate.

3 Hear this word that the Lord hath spoken against you, O children of Israel, against the whole family which I brought up from the land of Egypt, saying,

3 Hear this word that the Lord has spoken against you, O people of Israel, against the whole family which I brought up out of the land of Egypt:

The oracles in chs. 1–2 thus represent the opening stage of Amos' ministry and effectively set forth the master theme of that ministry. Along with neighboring peoples, Israel was to be engulfed in the tide of destruction that would mark the advance of the Assyrian Empire. It was none other than the stern inexorable righteousness of the God of Israel which, through the aggression of this overwhelming power, would bring about the overthrow of nations whose deeds clearly showed their refusal to acknowledge the claim of that righteousness upon their obedience. In the case of Israel this refusal so characterized the day-by-day behavior of those who set the note of the national life as to make judicial procedure and the observance of religion, in both of which the divine self-giving was involved, the agencies of their greed and lust. The destruction of such a people must be inevitable and complete.

II. Sermons on the Doom of Israel (3:1–6:14)

In the second section of the book the theme of chs. 1–2 is developed in detail both by particularizing the ways in which this arrogant self-aggrandizement and self-indulgence revealed themselves and by emphasizing the irrevocable finality of impending doom. These oracles, treasured in the memories of those who heard the prophet utter them, have apparently been brought together and put on record for the later reader in the form of three separate addresses, as is suggested by the threefold use of the introductory formula "Hear this word" (3:1; 4:1; 5:1). In their reverent regard for the prophetic utterance the compilers were evidently intent upon gathering up all the oracles in circulation, even to the point of including some that had been preserved only in part. But it is difficult to discern the principle which governed the ordering of the material. The fact that oracles dealing with conditions in Samaria (3:9-12; 4:1-3) precede those that pillory behavior at the sanctuaries—of which Bethel, where the ministry of Amos came to a close, was chief—suggests that some sort of chronological order was attempted.

A. Amos' Interpretation of Israel's Relationship to God (3:1-8)
1. The Uniqueness of Election (3:1-2)

3:1. This verse is in plain prose. The first half, **Hear this word . . . of Israel,** is an introduction provided by the compiler to remind the reader that in the oracles that follow it is none other than God himself who is the speaker. The second half of the verse, **against the whole family,** etc., is from a later hand, as is indicated by the abrupt change of person (**the Lord** in vs. 1a; **I brought up** in vs. 1b), and is perhaps concerned

---

3:1-15. Education for Catastrophe.—In his provocative book, *Christianity and History,* Herbert Butterfield writes:

I think that one of the most significant and revealing chapters in the history of human thought is provided by the ancient Hebrew prophets . . . in their insistence upon this judgment of God, and their vindication of the moral element in history during an age of cataclysm so much like our own. And before the cataclysms occurred it was a remarkable moment . . . when the prophet Amos warned the Jews that "the day of the Lord," which they so eagerly awaited, was to be not a time of triumph and exultation, as they expected, but a dark, terrible day of reckoning.[5]

[5] New York: Charles Scribner's Sons, 1950, p. 57.

Toward this fearful disclosure in 5:20 Amos leads his public by a prophetic procedure which might be designated "Education for Catastrophe." Let us look at this process in more detail, and the steps by which Amos develops the main theme of his prophecy, "God is about to destroy his people for their sins."

First comes a moving invocation of national remembrance of God's ancient deliverance of his people from bondage in Egypt (vs. 1). Memory is alike the glory and bane of our lives. There are those moments when we seek to arrest the fugitive memory of things true and beautiful. And there are, as well, those other moments when it is *we* who are fugitive from memories we would give our right hand to

2 You only have I known of all the families of the earth: therefore I will punish you for all your iniquities.	2 "You only have I known
	    of all the families of the earth;
	therefore I will punish you
	    for all your iniquities.

more particularly with the oracle of vs. 2. **The whole family** made it clear to the writer's contemporaries that the little kingdom of Judah, though it had survived the fall of the Northern Kingdom for more than a century, stood under the same judgment. This indeed is implicit in the oracle itself.

2. The placing of this oracle at the beginning of this collection would seem to support the conjecture of an attempt at chronological arrangement, for it makes pointed and unexpected answer to an objection which must quickly have been raised to Amos' announcement that Israel was to receive the same treatment as neighboring peoples. If, as the prophet had declared, it was none other than Yahweh the God of Israel whose destroying power was revealed in the advance of the Assyrian Empire, was it not reasonable to believe that a people he had drawn into an especially close relationship to himself would be accorded favored treatment, and so at least be spared destruction? To this objection there comes the startling reply, **You only have I known of all the families of the earth: therefore**—not, as might be expected, "I will again forgive your sins," but— **I will punish you for all your iniquities.** Amos accepts the premise but rejects the conclusion that they would draw from it. The verb "to know," as expressing a relationship between persons, is charged with great depth of meaning; e.g., it is frequently used, as in Gen. 4:1, of the intimacy of the marriage tie. It speaks of knowledge based upon immediacy of contact and felt experience. With the phrase that follows, **of all the families of the earth,** it gives vivid expression to Israel's sense of being a chosen people. This cardinal conviction of Israel's history no doubt had its origin in the days of desert warfare when, face to face with the enemy, they had found themselves drawn into union with the fierce energy of the storm-god, and with strangely enhanced power had hurled themselves upon the foe with irresistible onslaught. The teaching of Moses and the life in Canaan had taught them much about the variety of the ways in which the energy of one who was God of righteousness and God of the life-giving powers of nature, as well as God of war, guided and controlled their destiny. In all this, God's choice of Israel had been declaring itself not by some decree of a far-off deity, but in the intimate relationship of the very life of God himself to the life of his people. This conviction meant in the prophet's day that the God of uncompromising righteousness was brought into immediate contact with a greed and self-indulgence that sought to make use of him. How inevitable, then, must be the punishment visited upon their sins,

escape. So often it seems that our capacity to remember is in inverse ratio to our desire to do so; we remember too well what we would forget, and we forget too quickly what we would like to remember. One of the characteristics of our human nature is that we need to be reminded as well as instructed. Many of the O.T. writers appear to have recognized this necessity. In that remarkable collection of books there is much in the way of teaching, yet through all of it runs a call to remembrance that is both clear and continuous. In particular, poets and prophets were given to reminding recalcitrant Israel of the Exodus, by which event in history God had chosen to make known his power. As a result, dispirited tribes were formed into a people and given a law and an

inheritance of land. Israel had been in bondage but was now freed. The sign and seal of this momentous transaction had been the covenant executed at Sinai through the instrumentality of Moses, whose genius it was to realize that "human relations must be regulated by religious principles, and these principles are a manifestation of Yahweh's will." [6]

In vs. 2 Amos equates in a single sentence the recollected concern of God for his people Israel with the impending wrath of God **for all your iniquities.** This juxtaposition of God's love plus God's judgment with respect to his chosen people is born of the prophet's conviction that God's choice of Israel "for his peculiar treasure"

[6] Abram Sacher, *A History of the Jews* (4th ed.; New York: A. A. Knopf, 1953), p. 22.

3 Can two walk together, except they be agreed?
4 Will a lion roar in the forest, when he hath no prey? will a young lion cry out of his den, if he have taken nothing?
	3 "Do two walk together,
	    unless they have made an appointment?
	4 Does a lion roar in the forest,
	    when he has no prey?
	Does a young lion cry out from his den,
	    if he has taken nothing?

as the devouring fire of that righteousness made free course for the sovereign majesty of the God who, of his own free will, had chosen them from among all the peoples of the earth. It is true, as many commentators point out, that the indissoluble connection between privilege and responsibility is here presented; but underlying that, and excluding any possible idea of a give-and-take relationship between God and man, is the insistence upon the dread significance of the divine initiative and upon the sovereign freedom of the righteous God. This oracle, often called the keynote of prophecy, is also typical of prophetic style in its employment of a marked rhythm and in its trenchant brevity.

2. The Prophet's Authority (3:3-8)

This section would seem also to belong to an early stage of Amos' ministry, for apparently it was intended to answer the question: By what authority was the prophet challenging the existing order? Amos adduces instances of the inevitable sequence of cause and effect, to impress upon his hearers that he was speaking under the necessity of the divine compulsion. It is noteworthy that in the main these instances are of disaster overtaking beast or bird or man. In contrast to those who felt themselves at comfortable ease in a self-assured security, the prophet was keenly aware of the presence of forces that make for death and destruction.

3. Do two walk together . . . ? The question does not strike this menacing note, nor does it demand a negative answer as certainly as do the questions that follow. Even in the desert there is the possibility of casual companionship, however infrequent. There is therefore ground for Karl Marti's contention (*Dodekapropheton* [Tübingen: J. C. B. Mohr, 1904; "Kurzer Hand-Commentar zum Alten Testament"], p. 173) that the verse comes from one who wished to establish a connection between vs. 2 and vss. 4-8. For **unless they have made an appointment** the LXX reads "except they know each other." This involves the simple transposition of two letters, נודעו instead of נועדו, and may well have been the original reading. The writer developed in his own way the thought of God's knowledge of Israel. To that must answer Israel's knowledge of God (cf. Hos. 4:2), and failing this there can be no continuance of the relationship between God and his people. (For walking with God cf. Mic. 6:8.)

4. Does a lion . . . : In the first half of the verse the roar of the lion is that with which it leaps upon its prey, while the second half refers to the satisfied growl with

(Ps. 135:4) involved both privilege and responsibility. Where many of his predecessors had stressed the element of privilege inherent in the idea of a chosen people, Amos in the exercise of his prophetic mission and with an eye to the moral element in history accented the imposition of personal and corporate responsibility inherent in God's ancient covenant with his favored Israel. "He that spared not his own Son, but delivered him up for us all" (Rom. 8:32) cannot be expected to deal in a less exacting way with respect to the sons of his adoption. It remained for one of Amos' successors, the poet-prophet of the Exile whom we designate the Second Isaiah, to develop this concept of

the suffering servant into "a new and transformed conception of righteousness, a new posture of human beings under the sun, and a new rôle to be performed by man in the whole human drama." [1] But Amos, in the verse under consideration, gives his public clear intimations of the doom in store for men and nations who accept the privileges but reject the responsibilities implicit in the covenant relationship between a sovereign God and "the people of his pasture, and the sheep of his hand" (Ps. 95:7).

We shall better grasp the dark pronouncements of Amos in the second part of our exposition if we have in mind their relationship to

[1] Butterfield, *op. cit.*, pp. 84-85.

5 Can a bird fall in a snare upon the earth, where no gin *is* for him? shall *one* take up a snare from the earth, and have taken nothing at all?	5 Does a bird fall in a snare on the earth, when there is no trap for it? Does a snare spring up from the ground, when it has taken nothing?
6 Shall a trumpet be blown in the city, and the people not be afraid? shall there be evil in a city, and the LORD hath not done *it?*	6 Is a trumpet blown in a city, and the people are not afraid? Does evil befall a city, unless the LORD has done it?
7 Surely the Lord GOD will do nothing, but he revealeth his secret unto his servants the prophets.	7 Surely the Lord GOD does nothing, without revealing his secret to his servants the prophets.

which it devours what it has taken. The phrase **out of his den,** which overweights the line rhythmically, was probably put in at a later time in order to bring this out more clearly.

5. The first meaning of the word rendered **gin** (KJV) is "bait" or "lure." The picture is of the bird, attracted by the bait, making swift descent to the ground, and the consequent springing of the trap.

6. Is a trumpet blown . . . : As Amos draws to his climax, he brings his illustrations still more closely home to the hearts of his hearers. No one of them but had known the feeling of anxious dread when the trumpet had given notice of approaching marauders, no one of them but had asked in time of disaster, "Why has the Lord sent this upon us?"

7-8. The lion has roared . . . : The force of the immediate appeal to experience might better be conveyed by rendering, "A lion roars; who does not fear, does not feel the shudder that runs through one at the sound that threatens such danger?" Just so, an

the source of life from which he sprang and from which he drew steady sustenance, i.e., the desert. His home town, Tekoa, was a hill village twelve miles south of Jerusalem, situated on the verge of a shelf of stony moorland that falls away in a chaos of barren hills to the coast of the Dead Sea. The Chronicler, in later years, refers to "the wilderness of Tekoa" (II Chr. 20:20), and we may be confident that it was stubborn country in Amos' day. In a rare biographical word, Amos speaks of himself as "a herdsman and a dresser of sycamore trees" (7:14-15a), from which we may conclude that he was one of the shepherds of dwarf sheep who eked a precarious living off marginal land, and who supplemented sheep raising by cultivating sycamore trees, their mean fruit a staple factor in the diet of the poor. The incidence of daily life in the wilderness sharpened a man's powers of natural observation, and this is amply reflected in the figures of speech which Amos employed in his public address. The most cursory reading of his prophecies indicates their origin in the mind of one not city-born and city-bred like the first Isaiah but of one who, in the night watches, has "made the Pleiades and Orion" (5:8a) his familiars, who has heard the **lion roar in the forest** (3:4a) and the **young lion cry out from his den** (3:4b), who has watched not alone the "blight and mildew" (4:9a) laying waste his precious tillage, but also the

"fig trees and olive trees [which] the locust devoured" (4:9b). Every journey to market his produce in the big cities of Judah and Israel induced in Amos a sharp, almost bitter, comparison between the poverty to which he was inured and the idleness and opulence of urban dwellers

. . . who lie upon beds of ivory,
and stretch themselves upon their couches,
and eat lambs from the flock,
and calves from the midst of the stall;
who sing idle songs to the sound of the harp,
. . . .
who drink wine in bowls,
and anoint themselves with the finest oils (6:4-6).

In a series of crisp rhetorical questions he forecasts the catastrophe of God's doom which he sees to be in store (vss. 3-6). All the figures of speech which he employs are chosen to emphasize the inevitability of national disaster. Most of them come out of his own experience in the wilderness and reflect the countryman's powers of observation as well as his acquaintance with the perils of wild beasts and the stern necessity of eking out his limited supply of food by trapping wild birds. The inclusion of the figure of the **trumpet blown in a city** and the consequent panic of the inhabitants makes it clear that Amos, in his seasonal visits to the urban centers of the Northern Kingdom, is not unacquainted

| 8 The lion hath roared, who will not fear? the Lord GOD hath spoken, who can but prophesy? | 8 The lion has roared; who will not fear? The Lord GOD has spoken; who can but prophesy?" |

inner necessity compels a man to utterance when God declares himself. "The Lord GOD speaks; who can help prophesying?" The lines of this verse are shorter than those of the preceding verses, and their conciseness gives striking expression to Amos' sense of the complete mastery of his whole being by the strange and awful power of the righteous God that had laid hold of him. It was perhaps because in later days there was felt the profound significance of this revelation of the inmost secret of the prophet's heart that vs. 7 was added. It is unmistakably prose and interrupts the sequence of the poem in which it is embedded. The phrase **his servants the prophets** is characteristic of the Deuteronomic writers. Many commentators are therefore agreed that it does not come from the prophet himself. A later editor may have found in Amos' utterance an example of the truth that the very existence of prophecy bore witness to God's desire to make known to man his will and his purpose for human life.

with the city's sights and sounds. This suggests a parallel experience in the life of Abraham Lincoln—one of many striking analogies between Amos and the "Great Emancipator." It is recorded that Lincoln as a young man made a trip down the Mississippi River to New Orleans with a cargo of produce. After its disposition Lincoln and a fellow boatman wandered through the city. In so doing they came upon one of the slave marts, where black men and women and children were lined up in rows to be sold into slavery to the highest bidder. The hammer would fall and husbands were separated from wives, children from parents. Lincoln witnessed the scene with inexpressible horror mounting to hot anger. Finally he is reported to have said, more to himself than to his companion, "If I ever get a chance to hit that thing, I'll hit it hard." [1] Out of the chaos of his consciousness a single idea took shape, and when the hour of destiny came Lincoln struck the hated "thing" called chattel slavery a blow so hard that never since has it raised its ugly form in the United States. By an inexorable law, Lincoln's greatest achievement was at first but an idea; entertained in young manhood, it came to full fruition in the subsequent days of his years. There were laid down early in his mind those eternal principles of justice and charity, of righteousness and mercy, to which his later life was as true as the compass needle to the pole. "As [a man] thinketh in his heart, so is he" (Prov. 23:7). So we believe it to have been with Amos at Bethel. His was something more than a countryman's birthright suspicion of the lures and luxuries of the city. Time and experience would have served to allay mere cultural differences, but never

[2] See Benjamin P. Thomas, *Abraham Lincoln* (New York: Alfred A. Knopf, 1952), p. 24.

those stark deviations from justice as between man and man, and from righteousness as between man and God which Amos' visits to the great fairs and shrines of Gilgal and Bethel revealed.

The prophet concludes his series of incisive rhetorical questions, employing vivid figures of speech drawn from both the country and the city, with a final inquiry in which he equates the frightful roar of the lord of the forest with the wrathful voice of the Lord God, evoked by the sins of Israel (vs. 8). In the fear of the Lord were Amos' credentials as a prophet issued. In addition to the cast which so august an authority gave to the prophet's personal ministry, we observe, in his call to prophecy, two important lines of O.T. thought merged in his message and person. In an environment where polytheism was yielding to monolatry, we come in Amos to the exposition of religious monotheism, with its concept of a sovereign God, universal in his power and scope. What to many may well have been the erstwhile desert El and tribal deity is declared by Amos, in the crisis of his time, to be the Lord God of hosts, "in whose hands are all the corners of the earth," and by whose will the destinies of all nations are disposed. Here was knowledge too high for immediate and popular attainment, but Amos, perhaps at the risk of public opprobrium, insisted on proclaiming a God upon whose operation in history the Exile subsequently set the seal of common consent.

The line of development in the role of the prophet comes to an impressive elevation in Amos. From the crude group hysteria which informed a company of prophets whom Saul once met near Gilgal (I Sam. 10:10) through the more restrained office of the seer or foreteller as evinced in Samuel, the prophet comes in

9 ¶ Publish in the palaces at Ashdod, and in the palaces in the land of Egypt, and say, Assemble yourselves upon the mountains of Samaria, and behold the great tumults in the midst thereof, and the oppressed in the midst thereof.

9 Proclaim to the strongholds in Assyria,*
and to the strongholds in the land of Egypt,
and say, "Assemble yourselves upon the mountains of Samar′ia,
and see the great tumults within her,
and the oppressions in her midst."

*Gk: Heb *Ashdod*

B. The Corruption of Samaria (3:9–4:3)

These oracles or parts of oracles, with the exception of 3:13-15, deal with conditions in Samaria, the capital of the Northern Kingdom.

1. A City Distinguished for Oppression (3:9-10)

9. Proclaim to the strongholds . . . : Peoples that had not the standards which were supposed to prevail in Israel are summoned to learn what social disorders and oppression can really be, as they are to be seen in Samaria. The RSV is probably right in following the LXX reading **Assyria,** for this empire affords the best parallel for Egypt, the other great power of that time. באשדוד, **in Ashdod,** is probably a scribal miswriting of באשור, **in Assyria.** This would then be the only place in the book in which Assyria is explicitly

---

Amos to be a man whose function it is to speak on behalf of God. The earlier elements of enthusiasm and prediction were not altogether lost, but rather became subservient to Amos' primary concern to hear for himself and then to declare to his compatriots the word of the Lord. Jeremiah's later cry, "his word was in mine heart as a burning fire shut up in my bones" (Jer. 20:9), is no doubt a more personal but certainly a no more vivid description of the role of the prophet as God's mouthpiece than Amos' own statement:

> **The lion has roared;**
> **who will not fear?**
> **The Lord God has spoken;**
> **who can but prophesy?**

9-15. The New Patriotism.—Many interpreters of O.T. literature claim for the prophet Amos the distinction of being the first internationalist. They rest this conclusion in the main upon the first two chapters of the book that bears his name, in which the prophet recognizes the independent status of other nations besides his own. Similarly Amos has been designated by some biblical commentators as the first pacifist, in part because of his vivid picture (2:14-16) of the futility of Israel's dependence upon military might to avert national disaster. It is not to deny a measure of validity to these claims to say that they are in general subjective rather than objective estimates of Amos' greatness as a prophet. They evidence a concern with the by-products rather than with the hard core of his moral and spiritual preeminence over all God's spokesmen who preceded him. We do better to attribute the prophet's cognizance of Israel's neighbor kingdoms, and his distrust of Israel's military preparedness, to his profound sense of history as a theodicy God-centered and God-controlled.

Irony is one of the weapons of the misunderstood, and Amos, knowing himself early and late to be a solitary critic of the nation's boasting and pride, invites Israel's traditional enemies, Assyria and Egypt, to assemble themselves **upon the mountains of Samaria,** and to behold the cancerous growth of Israel's selfishness and greed manifesting itself in **great tumults . . . and the oppressions in her midst.** To their precarious external position as buffer states, Israel and Judah have added internal perils born of their spiritual impoverishment and their moral degradation in the sight of the Lord God in whose judgment all nations are counted "less than nothing, and vanity" (Isa. 40:17). Aware of that interpretation of history which is today termed "geopolitics," Amos employs a more profound reading of events in his concern with the vagaries of human nature and its timeless propensity to compose individual and national life with man rather than God as its centerpiece. "Theopolitics" might be said to be the center and circumference of the prophet's conception of a new patriotism. In the portion of his prophecy under our immediate consideration, we discover him reminting a noble word and a noble feeling from debasement, and giving it fresh currency in the vocabulary of human history.

10-12. Politics of Time and of Eternity.—At first Israel's patriotism, like that of the Bedouins,

10 For they know not to do right, saith the Lord, who store up violence and robbery in their palaces.

11 Therefore thus saith the Lord God; An adversary *there shall be* even round about the land; and he shall bring down thy strength from thee, and thy palaces shall be spoiled.

10 "They do not know how to do right," says the Lord,
"those who store up violence and robbery in their strongholds."

11 Therefore thus says the Lord God:
"An adversary shall surround the land,
and bring down your defences from you,
and your strongholds shall be plundered."

---

named. Since close scrutiny of conditions in Samaria is invited, it would be better to read with the LXX, "mountain of Samaria," the hill on which the city was built (I Kings 16:24), rather than **mountains** of the Hebrew text, the amphitheater of hills round about. The RSV rightly translates **oppressions** in place of **the oppressed** of the KJV, though the singular "oppression" would be better, for the plural is often used in Hebrew to designate an abstraction.

10. They do not know how to do right . . . : A pregnant sentence of condemnation, pointing to the contrast between the admired magnificence of the possessions that were the proceeds of a ruthless pursuit of gain, and the trail of the devastated lives of the poor and helpless which such greed had left behind it. The word **right** has the primary meaning of "straightforwardness," "honesty." Such people have lost all sense of moral reality.

2. Total Destruction (3:11-12)

11. An adversary shall surround the land . . . : The KJV here makes sense of the awkward Hebrew text by introducing **there shall be** while the RSV accepts a slight emendation—יסבב for וסביב, supported by the Peshitta—which makes a natural Hebrew construction. It might be well to read also with the LXX "thy land." It is the invasion of the enemy that is to make an end of the city with its fortifications and magnificent buildings.

---

was loyalty to the tribe. Into this tribal patriotism Moses injected a sense of nationalism supported by the people's passionate faith in their God Yahweh, the great arbiter of the nation's destiny. In no other people is national pride so inextricably connected with religion. Yahweh's deliverance of his people from the hosts of Pharaoh at the Red Sea was never forgotten. The first man in the biblical records to have questioned this sense of patriotism as consisting of loyalty to one's group or nation, and the assurance that God is partial to them, was the prophet Amos. In some vague way he perceived the dilemma between nature and spirit. In Amos, as in Paul's later conflict between the things of the flesh and the things of the spirit, the issue is not ethical but theological. The contrast between Amos and his contemporaries in regard to God's character arises from this dilemma: Is God chiefly concerned with the things of the flesh, such as group or national interests, or with the things of the spirit, the development of a sense of a common humanity as between men of all tribes and nations, and

their adherence to the right course of action, growing out of the belief in Yahweh, not as the patron and champion of Israel alone, but as a God equally concerned with the Assyrians and the Egyptians. Thus Amos becomes the forerunner of a new kind of patriotism that values the spiritual claims of religion and morality above the material interests of tribe or nation. What we speak of today as the international mind or outlook takes its rise in the great writing prophets of Israel—Amos, Hosea, Isaiah, Jeremiah—who flourished in the eighth and seventh centuries B.C.

On the level of "the politics of time," we have not moved very far from the material conceptions of patriotism—"My country right or wrong," [3] "God is always on the side of the big battalions" [4]—against which Amos inveighed. Selfish pride of class or nation or race hangs as heavy over the land in the twentieth century A.D. as over Israel and Judah in the eighth century B.C. Patriotism is about as limited and provincial

[3] G. K. Chesterton, *The Defendant.*
[4] Voltaire, Letter to M. le Riche, February 6, 1770.

12 Thus saith the Lord; As the shepherd taketh out of the mouth of the lion two legs, or a piece of an ear; so shall the children of Israel be taken out that dwell in Samaria in the corner of a bed, and in Damascus *in* a couch.

13 Hear ye, and testify in the house of Jacob, saith the Lord God, the God of hosts,

12 Thus says the Lord: "As the shepherd rescues from the mouth of the lion two legs, or a piece of an ear, so shall the people of Israel who dwell in Samar′ia be rescued, with the corner of a couch and part*g* of a bed."

13 "Hear, and testify against the house of Jacob,"

　　　says the Lord God, the God of hosts,

g The meaning of the Hebrew word is uncertain

---

12. As the shepherd . . . answers a question, whether actually put to the prophet or felt by him to be in the minds of his hearers. Is the destruction you announce to be complete? Will there not be some at any rate who escape? Yes indeed, Amos replies with bitter irony, so much will be saved as the shepherd saves when he gathers up the remnants of the sheep that the lion has done with, a couple of leg bones or a bit of an ear, remnants that have their value only as proof to the owner that the animal has actually been slain (cf. Exod. 22:13). The reference to **the corner of a couch** sets in striking contrast the luxurious living of the rich city dwellers and the simplicity of the shepherd life from which the illustration of their fate has been taken. As the RSV mg. indicates, the Hebrew word rendered **part** is of uncertain meaning. The consonants are those of the name of the city of **Damascus.** Hence the rendering of KJV, but the Hebrew tradition as represented by the vowel pointing suggests some other word, and indeed the mention of the city of Damascus is hardly relevant at this point. The conjecture "silken cushions" (ASV), resting on a possible association with the word "damask," is as satisfactory as any.

3. The Fate of Bethel (3:13-15)

This oracle announces the doom which is to overtake Bethel, site of the royal sanctuary; it interrupts the sequence of oracles directly concerned with Samaria. The

---

now as then. But there are occasional stirrings in our midst of "the politics of eternity" which the prophets of Israel championed. In World War I it was not given to preacher or politician or publicist to say that one great redeeming word. Rather, a frail slip of an English nurse, Edith Cavell, on the eve of her execution by the enemies of her country, gave voice to a sentiment that gathers up into itself much of the prophet's mind and hope and aspiration: "Patriotism is not enough. I must have no hatred or bitterness towards anyone."[5] Thirteen words which, if the truth they contain could become embodied in our lives as individuals, and through us into the life of the nation, would reshape the world. Then might come to pass the saying that is written, "They shall not hurt nor destroy in all my holy mountain: for the earth shall be full of the knowledge of the Lord, as the waters cover the sea" (Isa. 11:9).

The element of irony with which Amos introduced his dire analysis of Israel's political fortunes and consequent fate comes to a climax

[5] Conversation with the Rev. Mr. Gahan, October 11, 1915, the night before her execution at Brussels by the Germans.

in his expression in vs. 10 of divine judgment upon the nation's sin:

**"They do not know how to do right," says the Lord,
　"those who store up violence and robbery in
　　their strongholds."**

Israel's apostasy is a compounding of spiritual ignorance with social iniquity. Of this evil association come, then as always, those internal corruptions that sicken the soul of a nation, and thus "sell the pass" to the aggressions of its adversary from without. True it is that the prophet in vs. 12 employs a gruesome figure of speech that can be made to anticipate the first Isaiah's doctrine of "the remnant." Yet the more likely suggestion is that as the shepherd salvages nothing of value from the piecemeal destruction of his sheep by a marauding beast, so only a few battered fragments of her material splendor, **the corner of a couch and part of a bed,** will attest the onetime proud and favored Israel, blitzed by God's fiery judgment upon her ignorance and her flouting of his will.

13-15. *The Coming Disaster.*—The chapter ends with as final an utterance of impending

14 That, in the day that I shall visit the transgressions of Israel upon him, I will also visit the altars of Beth-el: and the horns of the altar shall be cut off, and fall to the ground.

14 "that on the day I punished Israel for his transgressions,
I will punish the altars of Bethel,
and the horns of the altar shall be cut off
and fall to the ground.

destruction foretold seems to be that caused by an earthquake rather than by enemy action. The oracle has been provided with an exceptionally elaborate prose introduction. The question may at least be asked whether the presence of this oracle at this point is not due to a later editor who drew upon the stream of the Amos tradition—represented in 9:1—which gave special prominence to Amos' prediction of an earthquake that destroyed the sanctuary at Bethel. Perhaps it was originally intended to be placed with 4:4-5.

13-14a. Hear, and testify . . . for his transgressions. If, as is most probable, the oracle which this sentence introduces is to be taken by itself and has been placed here by a later editor, the appeal would be to those who can of their own knowledge bear their testimony that the disaster foretold actually came to pass. In the concurrence of prediction and event they are summoned to recognize anew the act of God and ponder its meaning. The sublime title, **the Lord God, the God of hosts** is especially appropriate, for if in early use **hosts** meant the armies of Israel, in later time it had come to mean all the forces of heaven and earth. In the earthquake, then, the power of the omnipotent God was at work. It was part of the visitation of Israel for her transgressions. The word **punish** echoes 3:2, and the word **transgressions** looks back to 2:6.

14b-15. I will punish the altars . . . : The divine visitation will demolish both the royal sanctuary with its paraphernalia and the fine houses of the well to do, revealing the

doom upon Israel, church as well as state, as we shall find in the pronouncements of Amos, or of any of the O.T. prophets. Though the Assyrian menace threatened but did not desolate the Northern Kingdom during Amos' prophetic career, time was not slow to vindicate his warnings in the complete dissipation of Israel by the scourge of foreign invasion, concluding with "exile beyond Damascus" (5:25). History may not be said to repeat itself in superficial detail, but there is a kind of moral cause and effect in the grain of history which Amos was the first of God's spokesmen to distinguish and to suggest to his successors.

His conscience stung by the material aggrandizement of the kingdom of Israel and its consequent spiritual impoverishment, the herdsman of Tekoa appears in the city of Bethel with the word of the Lord burning upon his lips.

Woe to those who are at ease in Zion,
and to those who feel secure on the mountain of Samaria (6:1).

**"I will punish the altars of Bethel,
and the horns of the altar shall be cut off . . . ,"
says the Lord.**

His rustic appearance recommended Amos to the prosperous, complacent citizens of Bethel no more than his warning. Unlike him, Isaiah was a man versed in the ways of urban life, a patrician by birth, the friend and counselor of kings. But he saw in the kingdom of Judah the same capacity of material expansion to dull man's moral and spiritual sensibilities as vexed the soul of Amos. And the word of the Lord was not unkindled within him. "Woe to Ariel, to Ariel, the city where David dwelt! . . . For Jerusalem is ruined, and Judah is fallen: because their tongue and their doings are against the Lord, to provoke the eyes of his glory" (Isa. 29:1; 3:8). Whatever heed men gave to Isaiah's declarations was partial and fleeting. Again time set the seal of authority upon his predictions, in the destruction of Jerusalem and the forced migration of her inhabitants to the alleys and ghettos of Babylon.

The writings of the N.T. are unintelligible apart from the climate of the Greco-Roman world. With due respect to the culture of the Greek and to the virtue of the Roman, and in no wise unmindful of the legacy our Western world has received from both, the measured verdict of time upon this ancient civilization declares it to have become progressively hard and inhuman. We speak of "the glory that was Greece . . . the grandeur that was Rome," [6] because in both of these empires the resources of the mind and spirit were become subservient to the tyranny of things.

We may better date Amos' thesis by reference

[6] Edgar Allan Poe, "To Helen."

15 And I will smite the winter house with the summer house; and the houses of ivory shall perish, and the great houses shall have an end, saith the Lord.

15 I will smite the winter house with the summer house;
and the houses of ivory shall perish,
and the great houses[h] shall come to an end,"
says the Lord.

[h] Or many houses

awe-inspiring contrast between God's shattering power and the fragility of human achievement, whether in the realm of the sacred or the secular. The plural **altars** is strange in view of the singular **altar** in the following line. Some commentators would therefore change the plural to the singular. Others would substitute for מזבחות, **altars,** מצבת, "pillar." The sacred stone pillar at Bethel was of special renown, for tradition asserted that it had been set up by Jacob when, fleeing from Esau, he had spent the night at Bethel and the Lord had revealed himself to him with gracious promise (Gen. 28:10-22). **The horns of the altar,** projections from its corners somewhat resembling the horns of an ox, were possessed of special sanctity. It was on these that a man laid hold when he sought refuge from his enemies (I Kings 1:50). The prediction **I will smite**—the verb is that used in 9:1—**the winter house with the summer house** carries with it a touch of contempt for the measures taken to ensure comfort against the forces of nature, while in the reference to **houses of ivory** there is scorn for the elaborate adornment of the homes of the rich.

to a less distant event. In 1876 Thomas Henry Huxley delivered the principal address at the opening of Johns Hopkins University in Baltimore. Prior to this occasion he had traveled extensively through the eastern part of the United States and had paid a succession of visits to some of his scientific friends and correspondents. In his dedicatory address he was moved to assert,

I cannot say that I am in the slightest degree impressed by your bigness, or your material resources, as such. Size is not grandeur, and territory does not make a nation. The great issue, about which hangs a true sublimity, and the terror of overhanging fate, is what are you going to do with all these things? [7]

The years that have passed since this observation have witnessed an amazing development of those material resources which Huxley reckoned to be an inevitable factor in the growth of American civilization. Viewed purely in terms of scientific discovery and mechanical invention there is "a true sublimity" about this period. But anything like a complete appraisal of it would seem to reveal no corresponding increase of those resources of the mind, those amenities of the spirit, which eventuate not in power measured in terms of physical energy, but in power apprehended in terms of moral character. Who can doubt that it is the realization of this discrepancy that invests contemporary life with "the terror of overhanging fate"? Huxley's

[7] *American Addresses* (New York: D. Appleton & Co., 1877), p. 125.

earlier challenge, couched in the general query, "What are you going to do with all these things?" has become today a pertinent and immediate issue in the minds of thoughtful men and women. They are asking one another such questions as these: Is there yet time in which to redress the balance between material expansion and moral insight? Have we access to sources of spiritual power sufficient not only to match but to manipulate the forces represented by scientific discovery and mechanical invention? In short, can we *manage* this machine civilization in which we are set to live and labor, or is it likely to get altogether out of hand and carry us like so many helpless passengers in a runaway car down a steep place to destruction?

It is a fair assumption that as in ancient times there is in our communities no uniform response to the alternative just suggested. There are some who feel modern life to be charged with no sense of imperativeness; dim rumor of conflict between machines and men may have come to their ears, but it is without sufficient impact to arouse them from a state of indifference. There are others quite aware of the struggle that is drawn, who sense its more cosmic aspect, and who have assumed in the face of it an attitude of despair. There are many prompters in the wings who will supply this mood with the proper cues. "Man is only a bundle of cellular matter upon its way to become manure." "Ours is a lost cause and there is no place for us in the natural universe." "Eat, drink, and go a-whoring, for

4 Hear this word, ye kine of Bashan, that *are* in the mountain of Samaria, which oppress the poor, which crush the needy, which say to their masters, Bring, and let us drink.

4 "Hear this word, you cows of Bashan, who are in the mountain of Samar'ia, who oppress the poor, who crush the needy, who say to their husbands, 'Bring, that we may drink!'

4. THE SELFISH GREED OF THE WOMEN (4:1-3)

The women of Samaria, sleek well-fed creatures, who for the satisfaction of their appetite for pleasure made continual demand upon their husbands, and thus have their responsibility for the brutal oppression of the poor, will be pitifully involved in the fate of the doomed city.

4:1. Bashan was the region to the east of the Sea of Galilee, noted for its rich pasturage (cf. Ezek. 39:18). The literal meaning of the verb *shāthāh* is **drink**, but the noun derived from the same root nearly always means "feast," as in Gen. 19:3.

---

today you are defeated and tomorrow you die." There is another group, however, who are fully aware of the varied tempers that confuse the present hour, who are determined in spite of these perilous crosscurrents to keep the shallop of life pointing out toward those beacons which mark deeper water and ample sea room: individuals who are persuaded that out of the confusions of modern civilization intelligence and character may be developed sufficient to ensure its control by spiritual motives and its direction toward ends consonant with creative and abundant living. Such men and women represent, whether in Bethel of old or in the present-day capitals of the world, the hard core of faithful believers in the omnipotent designs of God in history, of which the prophet Amos is the earliest expositor.

4:1-13. A Man Bound Up with God.—"Religion has become so complicated that one hasn't the time or the brains to bother with it." So commented an amiable young student, and he doubtless spoke for many of his own and older generations. Here is something more than a clever rationalization of the individual's religious indifference. There is a ground for complaint that in the Judeo-Christian tradition the basic elemental teachings of the Hebrew prophets and of Jesus have in the course of time and usage been developed into intricate theologies and credos. Certain it is that the synagogue and the church, so informal and so spontaneous in origin, have with the centuries evolved into complex and highly organized institutions. Yet it is not impossible for the ardent spirit and the eager mind to pierce the rind of creedal and ecclesiastical integuments and to discover religion in its essential form, as a conscious, two-way relationship between man and God. "By Religion I mean the knowledge of God, of His will, and of our duties towards Him," declares John

Henry Newman.[1] A more moving, as it is an older, definition of religion is to be found in the words addressed by Abigail to David: "The soul of my lord shall be bound in the bundle of life with the LORD thy God" (I Sam. 25:29).

Truer it would be to level the charge of complexity against the communication of religious insights from person to person, from generation to generation. The common carriers in this transaction are deeds and words, and each should complement the other in the life of the religious person, producing a kind of holy contagion. We know however from experience that this is rarely true of our own spiritual condition. We are seldom as good as our words, and of this discrepancy has come one of the perennial interruptions in the line of religious communication between man and man. In private devotion and corporate worship, which represent the unique, Godward dimensions of religion, the connection is often poor, and that by reason of our own ineptitude. We think, in spite of our Lord's warning, that God will hear us for our much speaking, and our prayers become long and wordy. In the wisdom literature there is a sage rebuke for our facile verbosity in addressing God. "Be not rash with thy mouth, and let not thine heart be hasty to utter any thing before God: for God is in heaven, and thou upon earth: therefore let thy words be few" (Eccl. 5:2). Or it may be we feel prompted in our prayers to give God good advice, to keep him posted as to what goes on in the market place or the political hustings. It is reported of a British parson that when some issue dear to his heart was up for debate in Parliament, he would begin his "long prayer" of a Sunday morning, "Doubtless, O Lord, as Thou hast read in the 'Manchester Guardian,'" and then

[1] *An Essay in Aid of a Grammar of Assent* (new ed.; London: Longmans, Green & Co., 1891), p. 389.

2 The Lord God hath sworn by his holiness, that, lo, the days shall come upon you, that he will take you away with hooks, and your posterity with fishhooks.

2 The Lord God has sworn by his holiness
that, behold, the days are coming upon you,
when they shall take you away with hooks,
even the last of you with fishhooks.

2a. This is an unusual asseveration. **The Lord God has sworn** by himself, for **holiness** is the essential characteristic of deity.

2b-3. The text is in some confusion. The pronominal suffixes in the Hebrew halt inexplicably between the masculine and the feminine, and the abrupt change of imagery from "cows" in vs. 1a to fish in vs. 2b is perplexing. But in spite of uncertainty in detail, the fate in store for the pampered women of Samaria is clear enough. With the siege and capture of the city they will be stripped of their finery and lie dead in the streets, and scavengers will drag their corpses away to the refuse pile. In towns in the East the carcasses of dead animals are still disposed of in this way. **Harmon:** The RSV here simply transliterates a Hebrew word of unknown meaning. Nor can it be identified as a place name. The most likely conjecture would read ערמות, "naked," in place of the present text. Marti, who adopts this suggestion (*Dodekapropheton,* pp. 179-80; cf.

---

go on to inform the Almighty of the rights and wrongs of the matter. This common propensity of ours to "tell God," however subtly we may try to conceal it, comes of our desire to "use God" in the furtherance of our own concerns, which is the hallmark of magic. It would be well for us, before the exercise of God's gift of speech whether in prayer or sermon, to think for a moment to whom we are speaking, and to hearken what the Lord has to say to us.

Amos impresses his later readers, as no doubt he did those who first heard his oracles, as an authentically religious man. His actions and his words indicate that he was bound up with God. We can believe that in his own conduct he had reduced to a minimum the disparity between "mine" and "thine." This herdsman of Tekoa confronts us as a man with firsthand experience of God and with a fresh and vigorous capacity to communicate the word of God to his fellow men through the alembic of his own mind and conscience. J. Seelye Bixler gives us an admirable summary of Amos' religious credentials.

As we examine Amos's teaching we see that what lay back of [his] words was a conviction of the demonstrable rightness of the religious view. The prophet was indeed "taken hold of by God in a forceful way."

And with that is joined this felicitous appraisal of the prophet's form of utterance, so appropriately matched with the substance of his message:

Consider the musical form his words take: "Shall horses run upon the rock? will one plow there with oxen? for ye have turned judgment into gall, and the fruit of righteousness into hemlock." "Hear this, O ye that swallow up the needy, even to make

the poor of the land to fail, saying, When will the new moon be gone, that we may sell corn? and the sabbath, that we may set forth wheat, making the ephah small, and the shekel great, and falsifying the balances by deceit? that we may buy the poor for silver, and the needy for a pair of shoes; yea, and sell the refuse of the wheat?" This, I submit, is the utterance of a musician. For an unlettered herdsman whom God called as he followed the flock, the continuous flow of the patterned and harmonious cadences is remarkable. Amos was primarily a poet, with a poet's sense for balanced form. He could not have prophesied as he did if he had not had an artist's feeling for the demands of rhythm and proportion. . . . Was it not this same feeling for balance in the arrangement of the parts of the social organism that influenced his sensitiveness to the demand of God for justice? [2]

It is in the second part of the book of Amos, now under consideration, that we are impressed by the awesome polarity of his prophecies, revealing their tension between the justice of God and the injustice of men, the righteousness of God and the unrighteousness of his children. The basic threnody of the prophet's message, "God will punish Israel for her sins," rises to a crescendo in a series of particular variations upon this terrible theme.

4:1-3. *The Kine of Bashan.*—This mordant indictment of the women of Samaria, who in their greed for personal luxuries and adornments incite their husbands to extravagant measures at the expense of the poor and disinherited, is one of the most vitriolic of the prophet's utterances. A superficial reading might

[2] Julius Seelye Bixler, *A Faith That Fulfills* (New York: Harper & Bros., 1951), pp. 50-51. Used by permission.

3 And ye shall go out at the breaches, every *cow at that which is* before her; and ye shall cast *them* into the palace, saith the LORD.

3 And you shall go out through the
breaches,
every one straight before her;
and you shall be cast forth into Harmon,"

says the LORD.

Richard S. Cripps, *A Critical and Exegetical Commentary on the Book of Amos* [New York: The Macmillan Co., 1929], p. 167), would also make further plausible changes in the text of vss. 2*b*-3 and translate,

> They will lift your noses with hooks
> And your hinder parts with barbed poles
> As dung and dirt shall ye be dragged away
> And naked shall ye be cast forth.

There is an underlying unity in the oracles that deal with Samaria. It is urban life that is unsparingly condemned for its arrogant display of wealth in costly buildings and lavish luxury, all in shocking contrast to the condition of the poor and oppressed at whose expense the rich prosper. No doubt it was the shepherd who was thus revolted by the degenerate life of the city, but it was a shepherd for whom God in the sovereign majesty of his righteousness was the supreme reality. It was not just the falling away from the simplicity of the pastoral life that he denounced; he saw conditions in Samaria as bringing to a focus the self-sufficiency and self-assertion on the part of man over against God that prevailed in the national life generally. The oppression of the poor and the crushing of the needy were indeed the signs of grave social disorder in hateful contrast with the equality of the desert; but more than that, they represented the presumptuous taking of the God-given processes of life into their own hands for their own ends by those who had forgotten that "power belongs to God" (Ps. 62:11). It is this blind failure to take the reality of God seriously that comes even more clearly to light in their religious practice, and it is with this that the oracles in 4:4–6:13 more specifically deal.

give rise to the notion that Amos is moved, in part if not wholly, by a countryman's native suspicion of cityfolk and their sumptuous scale of living in comparison with the austerities of the desert. We know nothing about the prophet's domestic life in contrast to the insights that his successor, Hosea, gives us about his own unhappy marital experience. We might therefore judge his vulgar expletive, **you cows of Bashan,** to be the carping of a misogynist, directed against women in general, and thus indicative of a blind spot in the prophet's capacity to read the signs of his times. On closer investigation, however, we may discover in this particular pronouncement a clue to understanding many that follow. Amos directs his indignation here as later against those who have mistaken means for ends, whether in the area of personal concerns or in such corporate acts as temple worship. Women are by nature entrusted with a major role in creating and conserving the precious increment of human life. To this end pity and the generosity of strength are their especial endowments. By these and other attributes peculiar to their sex

women are at one and the same time the custodians of the generation already born and a holy link between it and the generation that is yet to come. By means of their God-given offices the end of human life, in terms of its continuity and integrity, is greatly enriched. It was their betrayal of a divine trust by the women of Samaria that brought down upon them the stern rebuke of Amos. He saw them as fouling the springs of being with their poisonous greed for the specious and ephemeral chattels of life. They had forgotten the high purposes for which God created them in a silly, not to say sinful, preoccupation with the tawdry business of personal display and social ambition. They had compounded their own acquisitiveness by such seductive demands upon their husbands' precarious virtues as **Bring, that we may drink!** Thus the ends of womanhood, and of the mutual partnership of husband and wife, became subservient to the selfish accumulation of things, achieved by the exploitation of the many by the few, of the poor by the rich. For their sins Amos spelled out the doom of these gilded creatures in brutal terms suggestive of the disposal of the

4 ¶ Come to Beth-el, and transgress; at Gilgal multiply transgression; and bring your sacrifices every morning, *and* your tithes after three years:

5 And offer a sacrifice of thanksgiving with leaven, and proclaim *and* publish the free offerings: for this liketh you, O ye children of Israel, saith the Lord GOD.

4 "Come to Bethel, and transgress;
  to Gilgal, and multiply transgression;
 bring your sacrifices every morning,
  your tithes every three days;
5 offer a sacrifice of thanksgiving of that
  which is leavened,
 and proclaim freewill offerings, publish
  them;
 for so you love to do, O people of
  Israel!"

says the Lord GOD.

C. THE DEEP-SEATEDNESS OF ISRAEL'S GUILT (4:4–5:3)
1. THE SIN OF THE SANCTUARIES (4:4-5)

Vss. 4-5 are an ironical summons to carry on with the cultus in full realization of the meaning. The poem with its definitely marked rhythm, which in the opening lines especially catches the jaunty spirit of their approach to God, may well have been delivered at Bethel on the occasion of a religious festival.

4a. Come to Bethel, and—not as his hearers would expect, set yourself right with God, but **transgress**, engage in that pleasurable assertion of self which widens the breach between you and him whom you profess to worship. **Gilgal** was evidently a sanctuary of great importance, though not now certainly identified. The word means "The Circle," i.e., of stones, the cromlech, and would therefore be the name of more than one sacred site. Possibly the Gilgal here referred to is the one in the Jordan Valley not far from Jericho, associated with the crossing of the river under Joshua's leadership (Josh. 4:19-20), or more likely the Gilgal mentioned in the Elisha traditions (II Kings 2:1; 4:38), which would seem to have been somewhat north of Bethel.

4b. Sacrifices every morning, . . . tithes every three days would represent what George Adam Smith calls "the caricature of their exaggerated zeal" (*Book of Twelve Prophets*, I, 161). And this is, to be sure, an ordinary translation of the Hebrew, but the phrases **every morning** and **every three days** may also be rendered "in the morning" and "on the third day." Amos was then describing the normal procedure on the occasion of a pilgrimage to the shrine. On the first morning animal sacrifice was offered and on the following day tithes were presented. The sacrifices, *zebhāhîm,* were those in which the ritual slaughter of an animal was followed by a feast in which the flesh was eaten and the god was made participant by being given the blood and the fat of the victim. The presentation of the tithes, as may be inferred from Deut. 14:22-23, offered further opportunity for feasting. On these obligatory sacrifices there would follow perhaps on succeeding days such voluntary offerings as the means of the worshiper would permit.

5. Offer—lit., "burn," "send up in smoke," for the portion given to Yahweh was consumed by fire upon the altar—**a sacrifice of thanksgiving of that which is leavened:** It is a question whether the consumption of leavened cakes upon the altar was in Amos' time forbidden by law, as it was in later times; but in any case it is hardly probable that the prophet would have been greatly concerned with a breach of ritual prescription.

---

diseased and dead corpses from the highways and byways of a polluted city.

4-13. Prepare to Meet Thy God.—In a more inclusive denunciation Amos exposes the hollow pretensions of both men and women who have corrupted the true ends of public worship at the great shrines by means of their vain and vulgar display of the material requirements of ritual, utterly divorced from conduct becoming those who worship the Lord God of righteous-

ness. There is little doubt that his indictment is colored by his native dislike of the elaborate religious cultus which Israel had taken over from the Canaanites. Cultural assimilation inevitably follows political conquest, and the desert tribes of Israel were long since acclimated to the agrarian economy and the political patterns of their erstwhile enemies. What vexed the soul of Amos was the fact that this inevitable process of amalgamation had come to tarnish

| 6 ¶ And I also have given you cleanness of teeth in all your cities, and want of bread in all your places: yet have ye not returned unto me, saith the Lord. | 6 "I gave you cleanness of teeth in all your cities, and lack of bread in all your places, yet you did not return to me," says the Lord. |

Rather, he is contemptuously referring to the practice of making the offering a savory one. **And proclaim freewill offerings . . . :** Make public announcement of further festivities and issue invitations. A large response would be conspicuous evidence of a man's wealth and satisfactory standing. **For so you love to do:** The motive throughout was the satisfaction of their own desires. It all centered about themselves. That was the ground of Amos' scornful repudiation of the worship of the shrines. It is true again that he spoke as the shepherd with a desert background. The round of sacrifice that he condemned was Canaanite in origin. The offerings were those which were associated with agriculture, with the religion of the farmer. But it was not simply because they were Canaanite that Amos condemned them. He saw them as the means through which human beings gave expression to a total attitude toward God, which would to all intents and purposes treat him as one of themselves and draw him into comfortable fellowship so that what they called worship was but subordinating him to the satisfaction of their appetite for pleasure and the exhibition of their own importance. The Amos who spoke was indeed the Amos who bitterly denounced greed, injustice, and oppression; but of these he made here no mention. He was dealing with the temper of mind that produced these evils, for this was clearly revealed where religious practice was concerned. The lighthearted identification of God with self-centered interests was in appalling contrast with the humble acknowledgment of the dread majesty and might of One who made relentless claim on complete surrender to his righteous will. In contrast to the facile assuredness of the divine complaisance, the stern reality of God's way with man is set forth in the following poem.

2. Indifference to Chastisement (4:6-12)

Severe visitations of the past are rehearsed as so many means by which God has striven to bring his people back into right relationship to himself. In this poem the authentic utterance of Amos is clearly heard, but it is placed in its present position perhaps because a compiler had entered into the prophet's mind, felt that this rehearsal of the divine visitation threw light on the deepest meaning of the denunciation of the cultus in vss. 4-5, and so put the two side by side. In this reminder that the disasters which had befallen the nation were from God something more is set forth than the fact that these had been punishment for its sins. Now, it was an established article of belief that wrongdoing provoked the divine anger and brought consequent calamity. So the famine in the days of David was said to be God's visitation of Israel for Saul's slaughter of the Gibeonites (II Sam. 21). But Amos named no specific sins that had been the occasions of the calamities of which he spoke. These had been a revelation of an aspect of the very being of God. He is not only lord of the life-giving powers that manifest themselves in nature and in history; he declares himself also in the forces that make for death and destruction.

the religious insights and aspirations of his countrymen. The Lord God of Abraham and Isaac and Jacob had become just another Baal, to be placated with ritual singsong and prescribed sacrifices offered in a spirit of smug complacency. The stern God of the Promised Land had been forsaken for the fleshpots of a new and more insidious Egypt. The hard terms of the covenant were exchanged for a softer currency of religious accommodation and compromise. If it had been merely a matter of taste Amos might have remained silent in the face of elaborate religious ceremonies at Bethel and Gilgal, however little was their appeal to him. But he was one of the first to see that "the world had got into the church," and he set himself like flint against this immemorial intrusion. Means and ends became confused here, as in

7 And also I have withholden the rain from you, when *there were* yet three months to the harvest: and I caused it to rain upon one city, and caused it not to rain upon another city: one piece was rained upon, and the piece whereupon it rained not withered.

8 So two *or* three cities wandered unto one city, to drink water; but they were not satisfied: yet have ye not returned unto me, saith the Lord.

7 "And I also withheld the rain from you
    when there were yet three months to
      the harvest;
I would send rain upon one city,
    and send no rain upon another city;
one field would be rained upon,
    and the field on which it did not rain
      withered;
8 so two or three cities wandered to one
      city
    to drink water, and were not satisfied;
yet you did not return to me,"
                         says the Lord.

---

6. I gave you . . . : In the Hebrew the emphatic pronoun throws into sharp relief the reminder that it was the power of none other than Yahweh, their own God, that should have been discerned in the onset of famine, drought, etc. Those who were seeking to appropriate to their own use just so much of the divine energy as they felt would minister to their welfare could indeed recognize the necessity of keeping on the right side of God by such propitiatory sacrifices as might avert his occasional bursts of anger. But living in a self-centered world, they could not understand that in the sternness of these visitations God had been summoning them to a deeper knowledge of himself as revealed in every aspect of reality, as One therefore infinitely beyond any easy appropriation for their own ends. Hence the tragic **yet you did not return to me.** The preposition **to** is 'adh, not the more ordinary 'ēl, and it includes the idea of arrival at one's goal, "all the way to me." Amos had found at the heart of that sternness God's demand for a total surrender that had given meaning to his life. And so, far from being the prophet only of inexorable righteousness, he was enabled to give voice to God's concern for his people.

7-8. The drought is described in its twofold effect. **When there were yet three months to the harvest** refers to the premature cessation of the heavy winter rains that generally end in February, the harvest following in April. The resultant crop failure is also in the prophet's mind:

> **One field would be rained upon,
>   and the field on which it did not rain withered.**

On the other hand, the clause

> **I would send rain upon one city,
>   and send no rain upon another city,**

together with **so two or three cities wandered** [lit., "staggered"] **to one city . . . and . . . not satisfied,** depicts the effect of the drought directly upon human beings in quest of water. These two effects are somewhat awkwardly brought together. Because the verses also have not the general rhythmic structure of the other stanzas, various suggestions

---

the fashions and comportment of the women of Samaria. It was this fatal transposition of values that stung him into a vivid rehearsal of God's patient warnings, culminating in a thunderclap of the Lord's personal encounter with his obtuse and recalcitrant people, **prepare to meet your God, O Israel.** This legend, often abbreviated and scrawled by some well-meaning biblicist on a rock dominating a dangerous curve in the

road, to arrest the speed of the motorist, bears only a faint resemblance to the word as it first fell from the lips of Amos. Today's assumption that the phrase is just a quaint, unofficial warning, with even less authority than the customary marker provided by the highway department, is a far cry from the prophet's conviction that the judgment meeting of men and nations with God is the one inevitability in history. We

9 I have smitten you with blasting and mildew: when your gardens and your vineyards and your fig trees and your olive trees increased, the palmerworm devoured *them:* yet have ye not returned unto me, saith the LORD.

10 I have sent among you the pestilence after the manner of Egypt: your young men have I slain with the sword, and have taken away your horses; and I have made the stink of your camps to come up unto your nostrils: yet have ye not returned unto me, saith the LORD.

11 I have overthrown *some* of you, as God overthrew Sodom and Gomorrah, and

9 "I smote you with blight and mildew;
 I laid waste[i] your gardens and your
  vineyards;
 your fig trees and your olive trees the
  locust devoured;
yet you did not return to me,"
       says the LORD.

10 "I sent among you a pestilence after the
  manner of Egypt;
 I slew your young men with the sword;
 I carried away your horses;[j]
  and I made the stench of your camp go
  up into your nostrils;
yet you did not return to me,"
       says the LORD.

11 "I overthrew some of you,
  as when God overthrew Sodom and
  Gomor'rah,
  and you were as a brand plucked out
  of the burning;

[i] Cn: Heb *the multitude of*
[j] Heb *with the captivity of your horses*

have been made as to the original form of this stanza. The most satisfactory is that of Marti (*Dodekapropheton,* 182-83; cf. Weiser, *Profetie des Amos,* p. 168) , who would make it read,

> And I also have withheld the rain from you
> So two or three cities wandered to one city
> To drink water and were not satisfied,
> Yet ye, . . .

To this someone added his own memory of the capricious effects of a drought, as much as to say, "In this too God was at work."

9. Blight describes the devastating effect of the scorching wind from the desert; **mildew,** the premature yellowing of the standing crops; while the havoc wrought by the **locust** could be disastrously complete. **I laid waste** (RSV) in place of "the multitude of" (M.T.) involves the slight change of חרבות to החרבתי and is necessary to make grammatical sense.

10. Pestilence is of frequent occurrence in time of warfare. **After the manner of Egypt:** Such phrases as "evil diseases of Egypt" (Deut. 7:15) and "the boils of Egypt" (Deut. 28.27) indicate the particular malignancy of plagues originating in that country. **I carried away your horses:** As the RSV mg. shows, this is a paraphrase rather than a translation of the Hebrew, and the awkwardness of the construction in the original makes it seem likely that the clause is a later addition (cf. Cripps, *Amos,* pp. 174-75) .

11. I have overthrown some of you: Lit., "I have made an overturning—a devastation—among you." This is generally taken to refer to an earthquake of extreme severity,

hall discover Amos returning to this somber heme in the following chapter, with his terible picture of "the day of the Lord" (5:18-20) . All of which is strongly reminiscent of an incident that occurred in the smoking compartment f a coach, en route from Toronto to Montreal

in the summer of 1940. There was a mixed group of men: farmers, salesmen, a couple of kilted soldiers belonging to the Toronto Scottish. The conversation veered from one topic to another; the heat, the vagaries of women, the war, and would the United States come in. As

ye were as a firebrand plucked out of the
burning: yet have ye not returned unto me,
saith the LORD.

12 Therefore thus will I do unto thee, O
Israel: *and* because I will do this unto thee,
prepare to meet thy God, O Israel.

13 For, lo, he that formeth the mountains, and createth the wind, and declareth
unto man what *is* his thought, that maketh
the morning darkness, and treadeth upon
the high places of the earth, The LORD, The
God of hosts, *is* his name.

yet you did not return to me,"
                                    says the LORD.

12 "Therefore thus I will do to you, O
    Israel;
    because I will do this to you,
    prepare to meet your God, O Israel!"

13 For lo, he who forms the mountains, and
    creates the wind,
    and declares to man what is his
        thought;
    who makes the morning darkness,
        and treads on the heights of the
        earth —
    the LORD, the God of hosts, is his name!

---

although the destruction of **Sodom and Gomorrah** as told in Gen. 19 was by fire. The
point of comparison, however, is the thoroughgoing character of the disaster rather than
the instrumentality. The verb *hāphakh*, "overthrow," is also used of the destruction
wrought by an invader (cf. II Sam. 10:3), and Marti (*op. cit.*, p. 184) may be right in
his contention that the text refers to the critical situation that had come about in the
time of Jehoahaz (II Kings 13:7), when Israel was indeed **as a brand plucked out of
the burning.** However that may be, the account of the calamity, whether of earthquake
or of war, in which the nation had come near to extinction affords a fitting climax in
the rehearsal of God's visitations of his people. These have failed in their purpose;
there remains only final doom.

12. Therefore thus I will do to you . . . ; because I will do this to you: As commentators point out, the very vagueness of the threat leaves the way open for the
imagination to picture with dismay the terrors that were in store for the nation; but since
Amos was generally very concrete in prediction (e.g., in 2:13-16), there is ground for the
belief of some scholars (cf. Cripps, *op. cit.*, p. 184) that **because . . . O Israel** (vs. 12b)
was substituted for the original ending of the poem. This would mean that some later
editor, feeling that such an ending had no particular relevance for his own day, brought
home to the reader the essential teaching of the prophet's message with the simple
admonition, **prepare to meet your God.**

In all the disasters enumerated, God had been seeking to make known to his people
those aspects of his being which they had refused to take into account. In a sense this
persistent refusal was an attempt to avoid admitting the meaning for their lives of the
divine reality. But at last there was to be the inevitable moment when God would come
in final judgment and they who would not return of themselves would find that they had
been brought inescapably face to face with the actuality of God's dread presence.

3. THE FIRST DOXOLOGY (4:13)

13. This doxology as many recent commentators are agreed, along with similar
passages (5:8-9; 9:5-6), was added to the book by a later hand. The style of these passages
differs markedly from that of the oracles. Participles are used to describe the constant

---

the train neared its destination and there was
a general concentration of thought upon lug-
gage in the racks overhead, a tall, angular man,
who had hitherto taken no part in the common
talk, rose up ostensibly to get his bag and, with
a sweeping look at his fellow travelers and
pointing his forefinger upwards, remarked, "God

is giving us all a terrible pounding for our sins.
I think we ought to pay more attention to
Him!" Here spoke an Amos in modern dress and
speech, but with the same imperious accent
upon the need for human penitence in the face
of divine judgment as first was heard in the
market place of ancient Bethel.

5 ¹ Hear ye this word which I take up against you, *even* a lamentation, O house of Israel.

2 The virgin of Israel is fallen; she shall no more rise: she is forsaken upon her land; *there is* none to raise her up.

5 ¹ Hear this word which I take up over you in lamentation, O house of Israel:

2 "Fallen, no more to rise,
is the virgin Israel;
forsaken on her land,
with none to raise her up."

divine activity manifest in the maintenance of the order of nature, while Amos is more concerned with particular acts of God. The verb "create," *bārā'*, which "implies the possession of a sovereign transforming, or productive, energy, altogether transcending what is at the disposal of man" (Driver, *Joel and Amos,* p. 177), is generally characteristic of later writings. This is also true of the solemn formula, **The Lord, the God of hosts, is his name** (cf. George Adam Smith, *Book of Twelve Prophets,* pp. 201-7). The reader is reminded that the forces of nature, not only as they make for destruction but also as in the vastness of the range and sublimity of their power they command wonder and awe, are a revelation of the transcendent majesty of God, the proclamation of which was at the very heart of Amos' ministry.

Mountains and **wind** and the alternation of day and night—the LXX reads, "makes the morning and the darkness"—and the clouds that sweep majestically over the hills are part of a world that seems all oblivious of man's concerns, so that the clause **and declares to man what is his thought** seems something of an intrusion. Nor is its meaning quite clear, for the possessive pronoun **his** may refer either to God or to man, and the word rendered **thought** occurs only in this passage, although the consonants are identical with those of another word translated "musing," "meditation," which is what the Vulg. *eloquium* seems to represent. If, as seems probable, the clause is a gloss upon the doxology, the musing or meditation might well be the doxology itself, and the glossator would be saying that the power—which even in his littleness man possesses—to look out upon the world of nature and give expression to his sense of awe and wonder is itself God-given (cf. Ps. 104:33-34).

4. The Death of a People (5:1-3)

5:1-2. This is an elegy over the fall of the kingdom, for which the compiler has provided a prose introduction. The poem itself is an excellent example of the rhythm ordinarily used for the dirge, three beats followed by two, producing a plaintive cadence

5:1-2. *Lines of Communication.*—We are frequently reminded in the Exeg. that the text before us has evident intrusions from the hand of a later editor. Nevertheless the authentic prophecies of Amos, his variations on the major theme, "God is about to destroy his people for their sins," stand out from the additional material like boulders in a New Hampshire field. Prominent is the elegy over the impending fall of Israel, with which this chapter begins.

**Fallen, no more to rise,
is the virgin Israel;
forsaken on her land,
with none to raise her up** (vs. 2).

Here we are encouraged to believe that Amos may have matched the spoken word with appropriate dramatic action. Presenting himself in the market place in the guise of a mourner, his garments torn and ashes upon his head, the prophet appeared to behold with his own eyes the prostrate form of a young maiden stricken in the bloom of her life. In this posture he both arrested the attention of those who bought and sold and transferred it to his dire theme, the finality of Israel's doom. Thus he may well have introduced the practice of portraying God's message symbolically, a custom which his successors, Isaiah and Jeremiah, adopted with telling results.

The episode opens before us the perennial question confronting ancient prophet and modern preacher, to wit, how to establish and maintain the lines of religious communication between person and person, between one generation and another. The young man mentioned earlier in the Expos. who declared religion to be too complicated to engage his attention would have been on sounder ground had he centered his criticism upon the ways and means of its dissemination. Here is a concern as old as Eden and as new as Hollywood. Modern inventions

3 For thus saith the Lord God; The city that went out *by* a thousand shall leave a hundred, and that which went forth *by* a hundred shall leave ten, to the house of Israel.

4 ¶ For thus saith the Lord unto the house of Israel, Seek ye me, and ye shall live:

3 For thus says the Lord God:
"The city that went forth a thousand
    shall have a hundred left,
and that which went forth a hundred
    shall have ten left
    to the house of Israel."

4 For thus says the Lord to the house of Israel:
"Seek me and live;

---

the effect of which can be felt even in translation. When the prophet appeared upon the scene, probably in the guise of a mourner with garments rent and ashes upon his head, and the first words fell from his lips, **Fallen, no more to rise,** his hearers would at once know that he was lamenting the death of someone. With the words, **the virgin Israel,** to their astonishment and dismay they learn that it is none other than the nation whose end he is mourning and the lines that follow insist upon the finality of its fate. For the prophet himself this was no mere dramatizing of an idea. His heart was torn with the sense of the tragic, untimely end of his people. It is as if he were actually looking upon the inert, prostrate form of one who had died in the prime of youth with the promise of her life unrealized, and all the drear certainty of the doom of Israel had struck in upon him.

Vs. 3 is a separate pronouncement, as is indicated by the new introduction. It is also in the dirge rhythm but it uses more matter-of-fact language to describe the disaster that was to befall the nation in the practical annihilation of its fighting forces. It was probably placed here as an interpretation of vs. 2 for literal-minded readers.

D. Mingled Exhortation and Denunciation (5:4-15)
1. False and True Religion (5:4-6)

Vss. 4-6 are an exhortation contrasting the mere thronging of the sanctuaries with a genuine seeking of God.

4-5. Seek ye me, and ye shall live: but seek not Bethel: This is an effective play upon two distinct meanings of the verb *dārash*, "seek." Originally it was the word used of having recourse to prophet or seer or priest with a view to obtaining through his

---

from the printing press to radio and television provide extraordinary means of spreading the gospel, literally from pole to pole. But in our current preoccupation with inventions and gadgets and their technical manipulation, the end often becomes subservient to the means, if not lost in them, and the genius of the gospel is obscured if not dissipated in meretricious transmission.

Measured by quantitative standards, many preachers today have access of a Sunday morning to more people than ever heard Amos at Bethel or Jesus in Galilee. This fact alone should impose upon them a greater sense of their responsibility to be honest and humble communicators to others of the precious thoughts of God, the bearers of a message and not its authors. Whenever the preacher is tempted—and all are—to lose sight of the chief end of his vocation in some vain obsession with the tricks of the trade, Ezekiel, of old, has

a word of warning. "And, lo, thou art unto them as a very lovely song of one that hath a pleasant voice, and can play well on an instrument: for they hear thy words, but they do them not" (Ezek. 33:32).

The basic components of high religion, whether in Amos' time or in our own, are deeds and words. The communication of religious truth depends, early and late, upon what its disciples do and say. The Word of God becomes primarily flesh, not sight or sound, in those rare persons in every age whose actions and speech are finely joined and by whose example the truth of God is caught rather than taught. The essence of religious communication is contained in a remark once made to Phillips Brooks by one who was greatly moved by his towering appearance and magnificent eloquence in the pulpit. "I like to listen to you, because after a while I forget all about you and think about God." The role of the reformer is thrust by

5 But seek not Beth-el, nor enter into Gilgal, and pass not to Beer-sheba: for Gilgal shall surely go into captivity, and Beth-el shall come to nought.

6 Seek the LORD, and ye shall live; lest he break out like fire in the house of Joseph, and devour *it,* and *there be* none to quench *it* in Beth-el.

5 but do not seek Bethel,
    and do not enter into Gilgal
        or cross over to Beer-sheba;
    for Gilgal shall surely go into exile,
        and Bethel shall come to nought."

6 Seek the LORD and live,
    lest he break out like fire in the house
        of Joseph,
    and it devour, with none to quench it
        for Bethel,

---

agency the divine answer to some question, or the divine decision in some matter of importance (Exod. 18:15; I Sam. 9:9; II Kings 3:11), and so generally of resorting to the sanctuaries where these representatives were ordinarily to be found. But the word came to be used of the turning of desire Godward in a far deeper sense, of a longing for God himself rather than for something he could bestow. So Deut. 4:29 speaks of finding the Lord "if thou seek ["search after" RSV] him with all thy heart and with all thy soul." The word **live** is also here used in a pregnant sense to denote something more than the mere prolongation of existence. It speaks rather of life lived richly in the right relationship to God as in the familiar passage, "Man does not live by bread only" (Deut. 8:3). **Beer-sheba** was the ancient sanctuary particularly associated with the name of Isaac, situated at a crossroads of the desert some fifty miles south-southwest of Jerusalem.

5b. For Gilgal . . . : There is a play upon the sound of the place name, for the repetition of the syllables *gil* and *gal* suggested the like-sounding *gālāh*, "go into exile." **And Bethel . . . :** Here the play is upon the meaning of the name. The place could be referred to contemptuously as not Beth-el, "house of God," but as Beth-aven, "house of idolatry." But the word "aven" (Hebrew *ʾāwen*) seems to have had a root meaning of worthlessness—hence **nought**—"vanity," "misery." The great sanctuary at Bethel would come to be known as the source of grievous disillusionment and trouble. The half verse interrupts the immediate connection between vss. 4*b*-5*a* and vs. 6, and its rhythm differs from that of the context. It is therefore rightly regarded by many commentators as an addition by a later hand.

6. Lest he break out like fire . . . : The description of the divine energy as consuming fire is quite in keeping with Amos' sense of the purging righteousness of God. The **lest,**

---

circumstances on only a few persons in history. No one should act as though he were born to the estate or seek in his own right to achieve it. Most of us have a lifework on our hands to keep ourselves in shape let alone trying to cut other people to some preconceived pattern of righteousness. After all, example is the best discourse of righteousness as witnessed by every genuine reformer from Amos to the present. It is also to be observed that the great bastions of collective evil in human history are not always overthrown by frontal attack on the part of the champions of righteousness. The strongholds of iniquity are often more vulnerable to indirect, oblique movement by quiet folk, who know how to keep their ideals and their tempers as well, how to hate sin yet to cherish and trust human nature, how to speak the truth in love, how to "sing the Lord's song in a strange land" (Ps. 137:4). The times upon which our lives

are cast call for a hallowing of all life, and in particular for a reverent and responsible use of the gift of speech as though it were indeed a precious holding lent to us for high employment. To keep the lines of religious communication clear and open we do well to remember the word of an elder sage: "A wholesome tongue is a tree of life; but perverseness therein is a breach in the spirit" (Prov. 15:4). Also, the humble prayer of an ancient poet, "Let the words of my mouth, and the meditation of my heart, be acceptable in thy sight, O LORD, my strength, and my redeemer" (Ps. 19:14).

5-6, 11-12. *National Apostasy.*—It is reported that in every rope used in the British navy are woven the silken strands of the national ensign. Wherever the rope is cut there are revealed the red, white, and blue threads of the Union Jack. In like fashion the reader of the book of Amos is impressed by the prophet's reiteration of the

| 7 Ye who turn judgment to wormwood, and leave off righteousness in the earth, | 7 O you who turn justice to wormwood, and cast down righteousness to the earth! |

however, raises a question, for along with the hortatory note of vss. 4-6 it assumes the possibility that destruction might be averted. But it was the dread certainty that God was about to destroy his people that set the seal upon Amos' call to his ministry. So in the visions the note of irrevocable doom was sounded (7:8; 8:2) as in the oracles generally. It seems hardly probable therefore that Amos, possessed by the sense of the inevitability of what God was about to do, would have spoken as if for the nation the future was still open. It is more likely that vss. 4-6, along with the companion passage in 5:14-15, are from another hand. The unknown author, on whom Amos' teaching about the inexorable claim of the righteous God had made its profound impression, sought to develop for his own generation the meaning of that claim, that his people were confronted with the necessity of making a momentous life-or-death decision. The depth of this author's spiritual insight derived in no small degree from Amos' fidelity to the forbidding ministry to which he was called.

2. Brutal Treatment of the Poor, and a Second Doxology (5:7-13)

Incisive invective in vs. 7 is followed by a doxology in vss. 8-9, and the invective is resumed in vs. 10. Along with the abrupt change in theme there is a lack of any grammatical connection with vss. 7 and 8. The RSV, partly following the KJV, makes the best of the difficulty by translating the participial noun with which the arraignment opens as a vocative, **O you who turn.** In addition, the KJV introduces at the beginning of vs. 8 the words **Seek him** which are not in the Hebrew text. The doxology is probably an interpolation, like the similar passages in 4:13; 9:5-6. It may be assumed that vs. 7 was originally linked immediately with vs. 10, and the participial noun should be rendered in the third person, "They that turn, . . ." or, with many recent commentators (cf. Snaith, *Book of Amos,* II, 85-86), "woe to those who turn. . . ." Amos denounces those who made the procedure at the tribunals to which the poor might naturally appeal

words "justice" and "judgment." These two terms and the basic idea of "righteousness" which they connote are seen to compose the hard core of the prophet's message.

Seek the Lord and live,

·   ·   ·   ·   ·   ·   ·   ·   ·   ·

O you who turn justice to wormwood, and cast down righteousness to the earth (vss. 6-7).

Hate evil, and love good, and establish justice in the gate (vs. 15).

. . . Let justice roll down like waters, and righteousness like an ever-flowing stream (vs. 24).

In these three excerpts Amos raises before the minds of his hearers the flaming banner of God's covenant with the **house of Joseph,** first unfurled amid the awful fire and cloud of Sinai. He calls attention to the writ of that ancient compact, containing the pledge of God's protection and guidance to an Israel obedient to his claims and commands. "Which my covenant they brake, although I was an husband unto

them" (Jer. 31:32): So spoke a later prophet echoing the charges of Amos against an apostate nation which had acted unilaterally, as we would say today, in repudiating moral obligations undertaken before God in the Sinai wilderness. The stern idea of justice, "the moral attribute which belongs both to God by His nature and to the man who obediently conforms to His will," [3] had become corrupted by Israel's conquest of Canaan and her consequent exposure to the seductions of national and individual prosperity concomitant with the worship of amoral gods and goddesses. It was his anger and disgust at this widespread apostasy of the house of Israel that evoked from Amos his clarion call to national repentance, in terms of a return to the ways of justice and righteousness as embodied in the covenant.

In retrospect we might view the turgid situation that Amos faced as the inevitable pain of change involved in the confluence of cultures. On the economic level the struggle between Hebrew and Canaanite was early drawn between

[3] H. Wheeler Robinson, *Inspiration and Revelation in the Old Testament* (Oxford: Clarendon Press, 1946), p. 84.

8 *Seek him* that maketh the seven stars and Orion, and turneth the shadow of death into the morning, and maketh the day dark with night: that calleth for the waters of the sea, and poureth them out upon the face of the earth: The Lord *is* his name:

9 That strengtheneth the spoiled against the strong, so that the spoiled shall come against the fortress.

8 He who made the Pleiades and Orion,
   and turns deep darkness into the morning,
   and darkens the day into night,
who calls for the waters of the sea,
   and pours them out upon the surface of the earth,
the Lord is his name,
9 who makes destruction flash forth against the strong,
   so that destruction comes upon the fortress.

---

for protection a hateful, bitter thing—**wormwood**, a Palestinian plant always in O.T. standing for something utterly repugnant—so that **righteousness** (civil justice), left lying, as it were, upon the ground, was itself helpless.

8. If, as seems probable, the doxology was originally intended to follow immediately on vs. 6, the KJV's introduction of the words **Seek him** falls in with the intention of those who were responsible for the interpolation, for no doubt they meant to relate it to the exhortation "Seek the Lord," with which vs. 6 begins. He whom the reader is urged to seek is none other than the God whose sublime ordering of the physical world is manifest in the mysterious movement of the stars, in the alternation of day and night, and in the rains that water the earth. **Seven stars** (KJV) is an old English name for **the Pleiades** (RSV). **Shadow of death** is the rendering of the M.T. pointing of a single word which cognate languages show to have simply the root meaning of **deep darkness.**

9. The Lord is also the God whose irresistible might makes havoc of the defenses that human pride considers impregnable. **Who makes destruction flash forth:** The difference between this and the KJV hinges upon the interpretation of the Hebrew *hammabhligh.* The KJV, following Jewish medieval commentators, translates **that**

---

nomadic and agrarian habits and customs. Shepherds were opposed to farmers, a conflict which may be reflected in the story of Cain and Abel (Gen. 4). On the social plane the clash was between clan ethics, with its emphasis upon just dealings between individuals, and the more complicated urban folkways, with property values rather than personal rights the primary consideration. The story of Naboth's vineyard (I Kings 21) is a case in point. As earlier migrants and settlers in the western prong of the Fertile Crescent which extends through the central part of Palestine, the Canaanites were a cut above the Hebrews economically and socially when the latter dispossessed them of their towns and tillage, at the same time absorbing much of their culture. But in the cultural melting pot of Amos' time a third and ultimately decisive ingredient was at work. Less sophisticated than the Canaanites in material accomplishments, the Hebrews were far more mature in their religious insights and nurture. They were bound in a covenant relationship with a living, personal God, pre-eminently a God of history, whose moral power over the gods of Egypt was amply attested by the Exodus. Forty years of divine discipline in the wilderness

had already proved that the worship of Yahweh among the Hebrews was a far stronger integrating factor in their tribal commonwealth than polytheism proved to be in the national fortunes of their enemies. Though Israel in the long period of cultural confusion from the Judges to the Exile was prone to flout God's commandments and to desecrate his worship with the fertility rites of the Baals of Canaan, there was always a minority group faithful to the covenant God of their fathers. Leaders of this remnant arose in such prophets as Elijah and Amos, who rallied the ranks of the loyal by their cries of "No compromise" with Baalism and its idolatries. These two great and courageous "Naysayers" ensured the final precipitate of ethical monotheism from the turbulent caldron of cultural assimilation to become the priceless legacy of Israel to all succeeding ages.

There is a timeless quality inherent in a minority group, implicit in the prophecies of Amos and explicit in Isaiah's doctrine of a "saving remnant," a "holy seed." It appears beyond dispute that everything carries within itself the seeds of its own dissolution. There is some point at which physical deterioration sets in for each one of us. This same principle of

| 10 They hate him that rebuketh in the gate, and they abhor him that speaketh uprightly. | 10 They hate him who reproves in the gate, and they abhor him who speaks the truth. |

strengtheneth, while scholars, in view of the meaning of the corresponding root in the Arabic, render **who makes . . . flash forth.** The word that the KJV translates **the spoiled** is then given its proper meaning, **destruction** (cf. Driver, *Joel and Amos,* pp. 183-84). Ingenious but hardly successful efforts have been made to find the names of stars in what is admittedly an obscure verse (cf. Cripps, *Amos,* pp. 297-99).

10. This continues the denunciation of vs. 7. Any voice that is lifted in protest in the gate, the place of public meeting, or champions the cause of innocence, meets only with hatred and abhorrence on the part of those whose responsibility for the administration of justice should make them eagerly welcome such assistance.

entropy operates in social organizations. Sometimes the recession is rapid, as we hope will be the case with contemporary dictatorships inimical to international sanity and good will. At other times the tide ebbs slowly, as future historians may testify of American democracy. Nor are institutions immune. Very often they have more to fear from their disciples than from their critics. When Catherine Booth, the wife of General William Booth, lay dying, the Salvation Army was already a powerfully established fact, and with its spread there had come the inevitable differences of opinion and the struggle for preferment and power from which even the most single-minded institutions are not exempt. On her deathbed she said to her daughter, "Katie, why is it that God can't keep a thing pure for more than a generation?"[4] Posed with such a poignant question, many would agree with Father George Tyrell and his counsel of despair that the spirit of a founder can be preserved only if his efforts and influence are somehow terminated with his own death. But the prophet Isaiah is nearer to the motions of history as well as to the heart's desire with his more hopeful suggestion of a saving remnant, a holy seed: "Except the LORD of hosts had left unto us a very small remnant, we should have been as Sodom, and we should have been like unto Gomorrah" (Isa. 1:9). Lot and his family, escaped from destruction, are typical of a principle of regeneration that also informs human life. Marcus Aurelius' description of a man as "a little soul carrying a corpse"[5] is suggestive of the undying influence of a good life in spite of all material impediments. No social order is so completely corrupt but there may be found those who have not bowed the knee to Baal and who represent a new planting of the seed of righteousness. Out of the common life in almost every generation comes some individual, an Amos or a Lincoln,

by whom the decadent institution is greatly renewed and refreshed.

With the forces of disintegration abroad in the world, we do well to keep in mind this fact of a saving remnant, a holy seed from which new and fairer ways of life are bound to bloom. Like the inhabitants of ancient Sodom and Gomorrah, we have wearied ourselves in the way of wickedness and destruction. Our collective sins and stupidities have brought us to the brink of universal ruin. Let there be no attempt on our part to blink or palliate this hard fact. "If way to the Better there be, it exacts a full look at the Worst." So Thomas Hardy[6] reminded his sentimental critics who chided him for being a hopeless pessimist. But a full appraisal of our present condition must needs include a recognition of the principle of regeneration that informs human life. It is in the very grain of things that the capacity to create is never wholly outmatched by the power to destroy. It is in the texture of the universe that life is never ultimately at the mercy of death. In deeper sense, this is the witness of the gospel, the good news which Jesus brought for us men and our salvation. To as many as received it and were persuaded by it, to them gave he power to become the creators of better things to come. First, a handful of humble and teachable men and women who overpassed the world's contempt with their faith. Then, in subsequent ages, minority groups who under the yoke of political bondage kept aglow the beacon light of human freedom, who in a complacent church rekindled the altar fires of love and devotion. Of all such is the earth salted that it lose not its savor. By all such is the world lighted that it miss not the way. Out of a hurt so great as in the time of Amos they point our faith to a gain even greater. By their patience we may possess, even in the bleakest days, a measure of sanity and hope.

10. *He Who Gets Slapped.*—Some traveler reported a sign on the wall of a restaurant in

[4] St. John Greer Ervine, *God's Soldier* (New York: The Macmillan Co., 1935), II, 841.

[5] *Meditations* IX. 22.

[6] "In Tenebris, II," st. iv.

11 Forasmuch therefore as your treading *is* upon the poor, and ye take from him burdens of wheat: ye have built houses of hewn stone, but ye shall not dwell in them; ye have planted pleasant vineyards, but ye shall not drink wine of them.

12 For I know your manifold transgressions and your mighty sins: they afflict the just, they take a bribe, and they turn aside the poor in the gate *from their right.*

13 Therefore the prudent shall keep silence in that time; for it *is* an evil time.

14 Seek good, and not evil, that ye may live: and so the LORD, the God of hosts, shall be with you, as ye have spoken.

11 Therefore because you trample upon the poor
and take from him exactions of wheat,
you have built houses of hewn stone,
but you shall not dwell in them;
you have planted pleasant vineyards,
but you shall not drink their wine.

12 For I know how many are your transgressions,
and how great are your sins —
you who afflict the righteous, who take a bribe,
and turn aside the needy in the gate.

13 Therefore he who is prudent will keep silent in such a time;
for it is an evil time.

14 Seek good, and not evil,
that you may live;
and so the LORD, the God of hosts, will be with you,
as you have said.

11. Here is yet another oracle, as is indicated by the change to the second person of direct address, **Therefore because you trample,** and by the wider range of reference, for it indicts all those whose estates have been built up by the exploitation of the poor, particularly by the **exactions of wheat,** the excessive share claimed by the rich landowners from those who tilled the soil. **Houses of hewn stone,** as distinguished from those built of the loose stone lying about, were of special solidity, but the durability of these structures would be of small advantage to those who were shortly to be carried away into captivity.

12. This verse again denounces the corruption of those charged with the administration of justice who treated the innocent with open hostility; the root of the word rendered **afflict** is the same as that of "adversary" in 3:11. Money was accepted as a bribe even where murder had been committed—"ransom" is the actual meaning of the word translated **bribe.** On the other hand, those who had no money were given no chance of a hearing.

13. This verse differs markedly in tone from the rest of the book, for it appears to be more in the nature of an aphorism than an oracle. Taken in immediate connection with vs. 12, it would represent the conviction that in view of the deep-seated corruption of justice, protest would be both unwise and useless. Such an attitude would of course be in complete contrast to Amos' outspoken condemnation of the evils of his day. The exact rendering of the RSV **in such a time** is "at that time," and some commentators regard this as looking forward, so that the verse is a reader's reflection on the total picture and the desolation that must follow as the inevitable result of the divine visitation. The mood would be one of resignation, the verb **keep silence** being used as in Ps. 62:5 (Hebrew vs. 6), "Be thou silent unto God" (ASV mg.).

3. THE TRUE SEEKING OF GOD (5:14-15)

These verses resume and develop the theme of vss. 4-6, the hortatory note being even more pronounced. Commentators therefore have been more ready to regard this passage as added to the book by a later writer (*ibid.,* p. 191 n.). The phrase **the remnant of Joseph** points to this conclusion, for the word "remnant" is frequently used of what was left of a nation after a desolating catastrophe. Addressing himself to such a fragment of a people, the writer sought to put plainly before them the only possible

15 Hate the evil, and love the good, and establish judgment in the gate: it may be that the Lord God of hosts will be gracious unto the remnant of Joseph.

16 Therefore the Lord, the God of hosts, the Lord, saith thus; Wailing *shall be* in all streets; and they shall say in all the highways, Alas! alas! and they shall call the husbandman to mourning, and such as are skilful of lamentation to wailing.

17 And in all vineyards *shall be* wailing: for I will pass through thee, saith the Lord.

15 Hate evil, and love good,
    and establish justice in the gate;
  it may be that the Lord, the God of hosts,
    will be gracious to the remnant of
    Joseph.

16 Therefore thus says the Lord, the God of
    hosts, the Lord:
"In all the squares there shall be wailing;
    and in all the streets they shall say,
    'Alas! alas!'
They shall call the farmers to mourning
    and to wailing those who are skilled in
    lamentation,
17 and in all vineyards there shall be wail-
    ing,
  for I will pass through the midst of
    you,"

                says the Lord.

---

hope for the future. It is as if they had asked what he—or a predecessor—meant by the challenging summons, "Seek the Lord but seek not [the sanctuaries]." The reply reminded them that they knew the difference between good and evil. Let them **Seek good, and not evil,** and their hearts would be turned Godward. That the word **seek** might be understood with its full depth of meaning there was added the injunction **Hate evil, and love good.** Nothing less than the response of the whole of their being was demanded. But the demand remains severely practical. **And establish justice in the gate.** All this insistence upon the elemental principles of morality is set against the background of Amos' proclamation of the inexorable righteousness of the transcendent God. It was the Lord, the God of hosts, who had declared his sovereign power and majesty in the overthrow of the nation and who might again draw his people into life-giving relationship to himself and be gracious unto them if they would order their lives wholeheartedly in accordance with his demand for social justice.

E. The Coming of God (5:16-25)
1. A Day of Lamentation (5:16-17)

These verses picture a people entirely given over to mourning because of the desolation that would attend the coming of God in judgment. In the East the demonstrative expression of grief is carried to great lengths, and mourning even for the death of an individual becomes a public ceremony. Professional mourners, **those who are skilled in lamentation,** rehearse in melancholy chant the virtues of the deceased and lament the untimeliness of his death, while the women relatives break in again with the wailing

---

Wyoming. It bore this homely legend, "If you find your steak tough, walk out quietly. This is no place for weaklings." The motto would do very well to describe the rough and rude times in which Amos lived, and many a day since. It is a tough world, early and late, and in our sober moments we know that we cannot take our hat and stick and walk out of it just because we do not like its fare. Rather we must try, with what help we can muster, to pick our way amid its immediate pitfalls, hoping, in time, to come upon a smoother stretch. Yet with a

kind of prideful perversity we often resent those who raise their voices in continual warning of life's hazards, at the same time offering us guidance in the midst of life's perils. "Let them mind their own business," we say, "and we'll take the risk of fending for ourselves." No prophet is without this kind of cumulative resentment in his own time, and Amos is no exception to the rule. Amaziah, the priest of Bethel, in his report to the king regarding the tone and substance of Amos' preaching, doubtless reflected popular impatience with the

18 Woe unto you that desire the day of the LORD! to what end *is* it for you? the day of the LORD *is* darkness, and not light.

18 Woe to you who desire the day of the LORD! Why would you have the day of the LORD? It is darkness, and not light;

---

refrain, **Alas! alas!** The prolonged syllables *ho-hō* of the Hebrew text echo the cry of despairing grief. Now as God passes through the midst of Israel, as once he passed through the land of Egypt (Exod. 12:12) with the trail of the dead on every hand, these pitiful cries fill the air wherever people congregate, **in all the squares . . . and in all the streets.** On the countryside too the husbandmen will summon the professional mourners to take up their doleful employment, **and in all vineyards,** especially at vintage time places of rejoicing, the note of lamentation will prevail.

2. A DAY OF DARKNESS (5:18-20)

Vss. 18-20 are of great importance as showing the currency of a belief that the day would come when Israel's God would manifest himself in the fullness of his all-conquering might. This day of the expected epiphany was spoken of as **the day of the LORD.** Amos shared in this expectation, but whereas popular opinion held that this final coming of God in power would redound to the advantage of the nation in the overthrow of all its enemies and the decisive establishment of Israel's pre-eminence and privilege, the prophet knew that the vindication of the majesty of the righteous God must mean the destruction of a people who were not only oblivious of the pervasive evil in the national life that cried out for punishment, but in their self-centeredness could conceive of the final manifestation of divine omnipotence in the terms of their own exaltation. For Amos the day of the Lord was indeed God's day; for Israel it was in fact simply their day, so far had they gone in taking God into possession. And the prophet feels the tragedy of this terrible misconception, for the word **woe** is that ordinarily used in lamentation, as in I Kings 13:30; but this in no way blunts the trenchant directness of his utterance. The contrast between Amos and his hearers comes out even more forcibly if, as Marti (*Dodekapropheton*, p. 194) proposed, vs. 20*b* (**even very dark, . . .**) is taken in immediate connection with vs. 18, omitting vs. 20*a* (cf. Smith, *Book of Twelve Prophets,* I, 174) as having been introduced to resume the thought of vs. 18 after vs. 19 had been placed in its present position. The stanza would then read,

> Alas for you who are so eager for the day of the LORD.
> What can it profit you, the day of the LORD?
> It is darkness and not light,
> Even thick darkness with no gleam of light in it.

---

prophet, rising finally to the peak of exasperation. "The land is not able to bear all his words" (7:10). His was probably a correct estimate of public opinion in Bethel, intolerant of Amos and his steady reiteration of the doctrine of divine retribution. We have followed his application of this somber thesis to the international situation, in which the buffer states, Israel and Judah, were threatened with destruction by the Assyrians "for three transgressions . . . , and for four" (1:3) against the God of the covenant and his righteousness. The extravagant women who goad their husbands to provide them new luxuries at the expense of the poor and needy; the venal merchants in the bazaars who think to buy God's favor with

an increase of temple sacrifices and tithes; the corrupt judges in the gates who compound injustice with extortion and bribery; all these in succession have come under the stern denunciation of the shepherd from Tekoa, until even his few loyal followers might have felt that their champion had "poured it on" to the saturation point; but there was more to come.

18-20. *The Day of the Lord.*—The prophet spokesman for God against an apostate Israel draws one more arrow of indictment from his quiver of denunciations. Tipped with the sharp barb of irony, this latest accusation is especially designed to pierce the shallow optimism of his hearers, manifest in their confident expectation of a great day coming, when God will once more

19 As if a man did flee from a lion, and a bear met him; or went into the house, and leaned his hand on the wall, and a serpent bit him.

20 *Shall* not the day of the Lord *be* darkness, and not light? even very dark, and no brightness it it?

21 ¶ I hate, I despise your feast days, and I will not smell in your solemn assemblies.

19 as if a man fled from a lion,
and a bear met him;
or went into the house and leaned with
his hand against the wall,
and a serpent bit him.
20 Is not the day of the Lord darkness, and
not light,
and gloom with no brightness in it?

21 "I hate, I despise your feasts,
and I take no delight in your solemn
assemblies.

This conception of the day of the Lord as the day of God's catastrophic visitation, a *dies irae,* was to find frequent representation on the lips of other prophets (see especially Isa. 2:12-17; Zeph. 1:14-16).

19. It is difficult to know whether in the introduction of this piece of prose someone was drawing upon an actual utterance of Amos or whether, as seems at least possible, he was making use of a proverbial saying that illustrated with homely exaggeration the idea that, for the man whose time is come, escape is impossible. In that case it would be better to read "and" instead of **or.** The interpolator used picturesque language of the people to enforce the truth that the event from which there could be no escape was the coming of the day of the Lord.

3. Rejection of the Cultus (5:21-25)

This is another oracle, for now God himself is the speaker instead of being spoken of. The passionate denunciation of sacrifice and feast is the complement of the ironical invitation of 4:4-5.

21. The verbs sound again and again the note of entire repudiation. **I hate, I despise** —or "reject," "will have nothing to do with"—your festal pilgrimages. The corresponding Arabic word is still used of the great annual Mohammedan pilgrimage to Mecca. **I take no delight** is better than the KJV, **I will not smell,** for no doubt in thoughtful minds the conception of the god's enjoyment of the savor of the sacrifice had been superseded though the language persisted. The old phraseology did, however, bring out vividly

---

show himself as the champion and vindicator of his people against their enemies.

In a book earlier cited, H. Wheeler Robinson devotes a chapter to the consideration of the "Day of Yahweh."

It suggests the twofold character of [human] history as faith interprets it. On the one hand, it is implied that much of the history has been alien or contradictory to the purposes of the God of Israel. On the other, all this history is declared to be but the prelude to the triumphant vindication of God.[7]

Amos is the first to use this phrase, **the day of the Lord;** he announces the occasion to be one of **darkness, and not light.** His description is the complete reversal of the popular credulity and anticipation which, prior to the terrible calamity of the Exile, cherished the conviction that at some fateful point in the national odyssey God would intervene in the course of

[7] *Inspiration and Revelation in the O.T.,* p. 135.

events and vindicate his choice of Israel as "his peculiar treasure" (Ps. 135:4) by taking vengeance on her enemies and exalting his chosen people above all others. Postexilic writers enlarged this basic concept of **the day of the Lord** to include the prediction of a world catastrophe and a world eschatology. But in Amos' time and immediately thereafter the notion of a divine "Der Tag" stood nearer to the tribal spirit of the Song of Deborah, with its picture of Yahweh striding out of his distant abode in Seir to the aid of his people against the hosts of Sisera, than to the more elaborate and sophisticated visions of God's power by Ezekiel and Daniel. We can imagine the public consternation and anger when Amos, like his immediate successors, gave a terrible reverse spin to the popular expectation. The prophet's poetic **gloom with no brightness in it** contained the impending threat of God's punitive judgment upon Israel as well as upon her enemies,

22 Though ye offer me burnt offerings and your meat offerings, I will not accept *them;* neither will I regard the peace offerings of your fat beasts.
 	
23 Take thou away from me the noise of thy songs; for I will not hear the melody of thy viols.
	22 Even though you offer me your burnt offerings and cereal offerings,
	    I will not accept them,
	and the peace offerings of your fatted beasts
	    I will not look upon.
	23 Take away from me the noise of your songs;
	    to the melody of your harps I will not listen.

God's deliberate refusal to participate. It might be paraphrased, "I will have no part in your solemn assemblies," though solemn is not quite the word, for the assemblies were joyous occasions, as vs. 23 makes clear; "ceremonial" might be better.

22. Even though you offer me your burnt offerings: In the Hebrew the possessive pronoun **your** is missing, as in the KJV. This, along with the difficulty of including the clause in the rhythmic structure, provides substantial ground for regarding it as added by someone who wished to make the list of sacrifices complete (cf. Cripps, *Amos,* p. 196). **And cereal offerings**—meat of the KJV is the older use of the word to mean food in general—**I will not accept** is again emphatic refusal, as is also

> the peace offerings of your fatted beasts
> I will not look upon.

The "thank-offerings" of the ASV mg. were a particular class of peace offerings, but in all alike the sacred meal of friendship between God and man was an essential feature.

23. Take away from me—lit., "from upon me"—**the noise . . . :** The Hebrew form of the verb may be taken as an infinitive with the effect of an abrupt exclamation. Moffatt's "No more of your hymns for me!" catches the spirit but fails to suggest something burdensome in the songs which the phrase "from upon me" conveys. The order of the Hebrew in the line following, which puts the verb **I will not listen** at the end, brings the account of festival procedure to a close on a final forcible note of repudiation. And this repudiation meant the unqualified denial of all that the round of feast and sacrifice was intended to accomplish, the establishment and maintenance of an intimacy with God which would involve him in the web of self-seeking human desires. The mood of the worshipers betrayed an easy readiness to treat God as one of themselves and to ignore his sovereign claim to their humble obedience.

the suggestion that the Lord would take a corrective hand in the affairs of history suddenly, and the final prediction that the day of Yahweh's terrible visitation was near at hand. It would be a day of national doom and defeat, and it was just around the corner. Though he may not have lived to see his dark prophecy fulfilled, time put its seal of approval on his words. The Assyrians, on their way to try their strength with the Egyptians, overran the Northern Kingdom, and the proud nation against which Amos inveighed on behalf of God was consigned to oblivion.

Amos' invocation of the **day of the LORD** invites our further consideration of the time factor in both Judaism and Christianity. In his book entitled *Faith and History,* Reinhold Niebuhr reminds us that "time is both the stage and the stuff of history." [8] This correlation has prompted men to speculate upon their own involvement in time and history, with an eye to its significance. The Greeks, who were acutely sensitive to the rhythm of the natural world, the ebb and flow of the tides, the recurrent seasons of the year, conceived of time as cyclical and, as a consequence, of the human odyssey as a changeless recurrence, like a wheel turning on its axis, repeating itself inexorably and endlessly. Though at times tempting, such a view was ultimately unacceptable to the Hebrews. It had been the vocation of Moses to encounter Yahweh and to proclaim him as the God of history, to the accompaniment of the lightning and thunder of Sinai. He was the God who had chosen to enter into a covenant with his people

[8] New York: Charles Scribner's Sons, 1949, p. 35.

| 24 But let judgment run down as waters, and righteousness as a mighty stream. | 24 But let justice roll down like waters, and righteousness like an ever-flowing stream. |

24. Such obedience would issue in the unfailing **justice** as between man and man of which this verse speaks. The **ever-flowing stream** that could be depended upon would be quite unlike the ordinary wadi which in the rainy season is a raging torrent and later dwindles away to a mere trickle or dries up entirely. However, some commentators have felt that the sentence **let justice roll down . . .** is unexpectedly impersonal as a demand following the decisive immediacy of direct address in the preceding verses. They have therefore preferred to translate, "Judgment [i.e., God's judgment] shall roll in as waters and righteousness [God's righteousness sweeping all before it] as an ever-flowing stream" (cf. Weiser, *Profetie des Amos,* pp. 223-24). But the impersonal construction is strange after the emphatically personal repudiation that has gone before, and for Amos God's coming in judgment is a catastrophic event rather than something pervasive and constant. Hermann Guthe (in E. F. Kautzsch and A. Bertholet, eds., *Die Heilige Schrift des Alten Testaments* [4th ed. rev.; Tübingen: J. C. B. Mohr, 1923], II, 40), noting that the rhythmic effect of these two lines is somewhat different from that of the preceding verses, would regard them as placed in their present context by a later editor. The significance of the fundamental contrast between complacent cultus and right conduct, on which commentators rightly insist, would have been developed in line with Amos' teaching by one who had taken to heart the prophet's denunciation of injustice and oppression.

—a covenant, no abstract formula, but a concrete agreement in which were involved the elementary ethical considerations of promise and obedience. So began the divine discipline of Israel, of which the O.T. is the record. One of the results of that discipline was the Hebrew view of human history as linear rather than circular, purposeful rather than repetitious, with a very definite *a quo* in time—the moment of God's act of creation—and an equally definite *ad quem* in the counsels of the Eternal. The Hebrew was persuaded that through all the sins of his people, their breaking of the ancient covenant, and all the calamities that befell them as a result of their apostasy, the sovereign God of holiness and righteousness and grace was working out his purpose. One day history would culminate in the coming of God's kingdom, when "the earth shall be full of the knowledge of the LORD, as the waters cover the sea" (Isa. 11:9). In that future consummation of time and history all God's ways with his people would be fully justified.

From its conception in the matrix of Judaism, Christianity inherited the view of time and history as linear rather than cyclical, as a road stretching out into the unseen distance rather than as a wheel turning forever on its axis. But in its final emancipation from Judaism it made the bold and unique assumption that the great expectations of the Hebrews were fulfilled in the present. The Old Covenant (or O.T.) embodied in the Law was superseded by the N.T.,

revealed in a Life. The Child which the O.T. wistfully anticipates is born! "God, who at sundry times and in divers manners spake in time past . . . , hath in these last days spoken unto us by his Son" (Heb. 1:1-2). The birth and death and resurrection of Jesus are events in time and history that mark the beginning of a divine process of redemption, not of a particular people but of mankind, to be concluded beyond time and history.

In his letter to the Ephesians, Paul writes, "Redeeming the time, because the days are evil" (Eph. 5:16). "Make the very most of your time, for these are evil days," is Moffatt's translation of the text. The words of the apostle are reminiscent of Amos' stern invocation of **the day of the LORD,** but they suggest a more ample appraisal of God and history in terms of both divine judgment and redemption. Paul is aware both of the "politics of time" and of the "politics of eternity," to quote a luminous phrase of the Irish poet, George Russell, better known as "Æ." Not to the exclusion of God's judgment, the great apostle is speaking in concert with the Christian conception of divine redemption as a condition *presently* complete in God through Christ and ultimately to be realized. And this, not through the air, so to speak, by some divine fiat, but the hard way along the ground, by the patient efforts of individual men and women who have become responsible disciples of Jesus Christ. It is to such that Paul is speaking, and in times just as wild and confused

25 Have ye offered unto me sacrifices and offerings in the wilderness forty years, O house of Israel?

26 But ye have borne the tabernacle of your Moloch and Chiun your images, the star of your god, which ye made to yourselves.

25 "Did you bring to me sacrifices and offerings the forty years in the wilderness, O house of Israel? 26 You shall take up Sakkuth your king, and Kaiwan your star-god, your images,[k] which you made for

[k] Heb *your images, your star-god*

25. This verse originally, then, would have followed directly upon vs. 23, appropriately enough, for **sacrifices** is the important word and so is placed at the beginning of the sentence: "Was it sacrifices that you brought me?" **Offerings,** singular in the Hebrew while **sacrifices** is plural, was added later, as **burnt offerings** in vs. 22, for the sake of completeness. The Hebrew word for sacrifices, *zebhāhim,* denotes specifically those sacrifices in which God and man shared together in the consumption of the victim—just those sacrifices emphatically rejected in vss. 21-23. Not in such terms of easy intimacy had the relationship between Israel and the dread storm-god Yahweh found expression in desert days.

F. INEVITABILITY OF INVASION AND EXILE (5:26–6:14)
1. A SAD PROCESSION (5:26-27)

26. This is a difficult verse and the subject of very diverse interpretation. The difficulty was evidently felt very early, for explanatory glosses, **your image** and **star,** have found their way into the text. On two points, however, there is quite general agreement. The verb is future, as in the RSV, **You shall take up,** so that vs. 26 is not the continuation of vs. 25. **Sakkuth** and **Kaiwan,** named as objects of idolatrous worship, are

as our own. The first century was an armed camp, as the twentieth century has come to be. Giant empires in the East and in the West brandished their weapons then as now, seeking to frighten each other. The people caught between were as alternately alarmed or frustrated as are many persons today in the British Isles and western Europe. Neither then nor since have hysteria and despair been known to respect boundaries. In such a crisis the apostle rallied the church at Ephesus, "Make the most of your time. Buy up the opportunity that is yours, to live like heroes. Employ every means available to increase your knowledge of Christ. Use to the utmost the measure of faith in him you already possess. Quit you like men who will need greater invisible means of support than ever before. For these are evil days."

The prophet's concern with **the day of the LORD** as an occurrence within time and history and Paul's anticipation of the ultimate rule of God in the affairs of men, beyond time and history, are both embraced in a word of Father George Tyrell's, "Christianity is an ultimate optimism, founded upon a provisional pessimism."[9] This binocular view of time and eternity should help us rise to the height of the difficult days upon which we have come. Since we are human, we are tormented frequently by

[9] Quoted by Willard L. Sperry, *Sermons Preached at Harvard* (New York: Harper & Bros., 1953), p. 149.

the sense of self-pity to which A. E. Housman gives poignant expression.

> And how am I to face the odds
> Of man's bedevilment and God's?
> I, a stranger and afraid
> In a world I never made.[1]

But in such a momentary dark night of the soul there are, fortunately, more hopeful prompters in the wings. Of such is an inscription to be read by all who visit the chapel at Stanton-Harold, a small village near the center of England. It reads,

> In the year 1653
> When all things sacred were
> throughout the nation
> Either demolished or profaned
> Sir Robert Shirley, Baronet
> founded this church
> Whose singular praise It Is
> To have done the best things
> In the worst times, and
> Hoped them in the most calamitous.

Unknown and unheralded, as the world holds, Sir Robert stands out in the minds of those who read his praise as a man of self-discipline and devotion in the midst of social unrest in the

[1] "The Laws of God, the Laws of Man," from *Last Poems* (London: Jonathan Cape; New York: Henry Holt & Co., 1922). Used by permission of the Society of Authors as the literary representative of the trustees of the estate of A. E. Houseman, and the publishers.

27 Therefore will I cause you to go into captivity beyond Damascus, saith the LORD, whose name *is* The God of hosts.

6 Woe to them *that are* at ease in Zion, and trust in the mountain of Samaria, *which are* named chief of the nations, to whom the house of Israel came!

yourselves; 27 therefore I will take you into exile beyond Damascus," says the LORD, whose name is the God of hosts.

6 "Woe to those who are at ease in Zion, and to those who feel secure on the mountain of Samar'ia, the notable men of the first of the nations, to whom the house of Israel come!

Assyrian gods. In Akkadian texts both of these names are associated with the planet Saturn. The M.T., as often in the case of the names of heathen deities, gave to both words the vowel pointing of '*shiqqûç*, an abominable thing. The KJV follows the LXX in translating the first by **tabernacle,** and simply transliterates the second as **Chiun.** But it was the self-satisfying exaggerations in the worship of Yahweh that Amos denounced, and he would hardly have contented himself with so passing a reference to the apostate worship of foreign deities. In fact, as far as the evidence goes, it would seem that the introduction of Assyrian gods both into the North and into the kingdom of Judah did not take place until a time subsequent to the fall of Samaria. In the face of this later idolatry someone declared that these idolaters should pick up their gods—a contemptuous reference to the powerlessness of these beings—and with them go into exile.

27. This verse, cast also in the future, is the continuation of vs. 26. The solemn formula, **says the LORD, whose name is the God of hosts,** was a striking reminder of the contrast between the Lord of all the powers of heaven and earth and the helpless Assyrian deities. The compiler, who included this oracle in the book, rightly found in it the characteristic note of Amos' utterances.

2. BLIND PRIDE AND SELF-INDULGENCE OF THE LEADERS (6:1-7)

The luxury-loving leaders of the nation, in their pride and self-indulgence blindly unaware of imminent doom, will be carried off into exile.

6:1. Woe to those who are at ease in Zion: Many commentators regard this clause, or at least the words **in Zion,** as a later insertion. Others insist that, inasmuch as Amos took account of Judah as well as of the Northern Kingdom, a reference to Zion was

Cromwellian period, as one who in his way gave the best that he had to the best that he knew, even in the most perilous days of his years. To do the best things in the worst times and hope them in the most calamitous is a song for us to march to when "the days are evil"; for we know and are persuaded that God has his "times" too, and in them even the evil is made to serve the good.

6:1-14. Grieved Over the Ruin of Joseph.—With ch. 6 the second part of the book of Amos comes to a close. The series of stern indictments, "Hear this word that the LORD has spoken against you," and the equally dark pronouncements, "Woe to you," come to a conclusion in the prophet's reiteration of God's doom upon sinful Israel by the invading Assyrians. These fierce instruments of God's wrath will engulf the kingdoms of Israel and Judah **from the entrance of Hamath to the Brook of the Arabah.**

In his *Book of the Twelve Prophets,* George Adam Smith makes a provocative distinction with respect to Amos' condemnation of the evils of his time. In the first part of the book, chs. 1–2, the prophet is moved to excoriate the sins of the heathen nations, wanton war, massacre, and sacrilege, what Smith sums up as the "atrocities of Barbarism." Israel and Judah are not without their share of guilt in this category of evils, wars provoked and treaties broken, in short, the sins of foreign relations. But in the second part of the book, chs. 3–6, Amos sets his prophetic sights upon the internal misdeeds of Israel, "the sins of Civilization, the pressure of the rich upon the poor, the bribery of justice, the seduction of the innocent, impurity, and other evils of luxury." [2]

Partly because Amos knew Israel's civic and religious life to the core, but chiefly because he early grasped the moral equation of privilege

[2] Vol. I, p. 120.

2 Pass ye unto Calneh, and see; and from thence go ye to Hamath the great: then go down to Gath of the Philistines: *be they* better than these kingdoms? or their border greater than your border?

3 Ye that put far away the evil day, and cause the seat of violence to come near;

2 Pass over to Calneh, and see;
  and thence go to Hamath the great;
  then go down to Gath of the Philistines.
Are they better than these kingdoms?
  Or is their territory greater than your territory,
3 O you who put far away the evil day,
  and bring near the seat of violence?

---

natural. It is true that for the prophet North and South constituted a single people (cf. 3:2) but it would seem out of keeping with his habit of concentration upon the immediate situation for him to begin an oracle by a glance at the leaders elsewhere. The phrase or clause is better understood as a later reminder that Amos' message had its terrible relevance for the proud and confident Jerusalem that had witnessed the fall of Samaria. **The notable men of the first of the nations** is Amos' ironical summing up of their opinion of themselves—distinguished leaders of a great people—**to whom the house of Israel come,** supposedly for judgment, but this is not explicitly stated and the exact meaning of the clause is uncertain.

2. According to the KJV reading of the last two lines, **be they better . . . ,** three important cities are named as inferior to Samaria in the size and prosperity of their kingdoms. This would illustrate Israel's conception of itself as "chief of nations" and would be said ironically as preparing the way for the prediction of vs. 7, that it should be among the first to go into captivity (cf. Driver, *Joel and Amos,* pp. 195-96). This is the view taken by some commentators but the majority, noting that the verse interrupts the close connection between vss. 1 and 3, regard it as an interpolation. **Calneh** in northern Syria (probably the Calno of Isa. 10:9), **Hamath the great,** on the Orontes, and the important Philistine city, **Gath,** all fell before the advance of the Assyrian invaders that took place after the time of Amos. The phrase **these kingdoms** refers to Calneh, Hamath, and Gath rather than to Israel and Judah. The warning was perhaps addressed not to Samaria but to the Jerusalem of a later time, in line with the reference to that city added to vs. 1, a warning the more needed because after the fall of the Northern Kingdom there developed in the southern city an overweening sense of its own importance and privileged position.

3. This verse is then the direct continuation of vs. 1, with the same participial construction in the Hebrew. These self-satisfied leaders **put far away the evil day,** brush off disdainfully any suggestion that a day of disaster may be at hand, **bring near the seat of violence,** and foster that oppression which spells ruin. Absorbed in the indulgent enjoyment of the moment, they are oblivious of disruptive forces that threaten both from without and from within the nation.

---

and responsibility—which our Lord later stated for all time, "unto whomsoever much is given, of him shall be much required" (Luke 12:48) — the prophet indicates that in the sight of God the sins of his chosen people are more heinous and thus more deserving of divine punishment than the offenses of nations without the Law. To the "sins of Civilization" Amos devotes nine tenths of his message.

Fixing our attention more particularly on the whole of the second part of the book, we may discover a progressive pattern of prophetic indictment.

(*a*) Here is the picture of the deadly sin of *spiritual ingratitude,* infecting the individual and the nation alike; "Hear this word that the LORD has spoken against you, O people of Israel, against the whole family which I brought up out of the land of Egypt" (3:1). God had delivered his people out of servitude to Pharaoh, and now they have become ungrateful and forgetful of his covenanted mercies. One sees a poor old woman, said Harry Emerson Fosdick long years ago, picking up odds and ends of wood about a building under construction. In her poverty the action is directed by her necessity for fuel, but for most of us, in our superfluity of creature comforts and satisfactions, the scene is symbolic

4 That lie upon beds of ivory, and stretch themselves upon their couches, and eat the lambs out of the flock, and the calves out of the midst of the stall;

5 That chant to the sound of the viol, *and* invent to themselves instruments of music, like David;

6 That drink wine in bowls, and anoint themselves with the chief ointments: but they are not grieved for the affliction of Joseph.

4 "Woe to those who lie upon beds of ivory,
and stretch themselves upon their couches,
and eat lambs from the flock,
and calves from the midst of the stall;
5 who sing idle songs to the sound of the harp,
and like David invent for themselves instruments of music;
6 who drink wine in bowls,
and anoint themselves with the finest oils,
but are not grieved over the ruin of Joseph!

---

4. On divans with framework inlaid with ivory they take their ease and **stretch themselves**—the Hebrew word expresses the shepherd's contempt for the new fashion of reclining at table and might be rendered "sprawl"—**upon their couches** as they feast upon the young of their flocks and herds. From the shepherd's point of view they were thus manifesting a hopelessly improvident lack of concern for the future.

5. Sing idle songs is in the Hebrew a single word which does not occur elsewhere in the O.T. An Arabic equivalent has the meaning of "talk immoderately." "Babble" or "prattle" **to the sound of the harp** would perhaps best convey the note of disdain for their performance. **Invent for themselves instruments of music** is perplexing because reference to the invention of musical instruments seems inappropriate at this point, and indeed hardly a matter for reprobation. In the Hebrew text **like David** comes at the beginning of the line, and the name does not appear at all in the LXX. Weiser (*Profetie des Amos,* pp. 240-41) would read הידד, a word meaning "shouting," for כדויד. With a slight modification of the phrase **instruments of music**—lit., "instruments of song"—reading לשיר for כלי־שיר, he would then translate, "Shouting, they imagine to be singing," a rendering which accords well with the first half of the verse.

6. Who drink wine in bowls: I.e., by the bowlful. **And anoint themselves with the finest oils:** Anointing was a sign of gladness, just as to refrain from it was a sign of mourning. They should be sick at heart **over the ruin of Joseph,** for the coming of that day of disaster, the signs of which they as leaders of the nation should be quick to discern.

---

of our propensity to give to God no more than the fag ends of our time and strength and substance.

(b) Addressed specifically to the women of Israel, Amos' condemnation is inclusive of the whole society that has forsaken the law of God and embraced the licentiousness of the baalim:

"Hear this word, you cows of Bashan,
who are in the mountain of Samaria,
who oppress the poor, who crush the needy,
who say to their husbands, 'Bring, that we may drink!' " (4:1) .

Here is manifest the second deadly sin in the prophet's category, the sin of *moral corruption.* This is the insidious enemy of righteousness, corporate as well as personal, and in every generation. Shortly before World War II broke out, a thoughtful Englishman remarked to an American friend, "The most sobering fact in the

modern world is the general decline of conscience." Even a cursory glance at most aspects of our common life since the war reveals a disturbing degree of moral deterioration. When we are honest with ourselves we are obliged to own an increasing ethical ambiguity in our personal lives, a lowering of standards in our manners and oftentimes in our morals. We suspect a correlation between our condition and the general decline of conscience of which a prophet like Amos was sure. To him and to his successors conscience and history were both witnesses of God. The prophets of Israel would have had little patience with the school of modern sociologists and psychologists who hold that conscience is not something native to the individual, a *capax dei,* but rather a mood acquired from the beliefs and practices, the attitudes and customs, of the group with which the individual happens to be identified. They would have been

7 ¶ Therefore now shall they go captive with the first that go captive, and the banquet of them that stretched themselves shall be removed.

8 The Lord GOD hath sworn by himself, saith the LORD the God of hosts, I abhor the excellency of Jacob, and hate his palaces: therefore will I deliver up the city with all that is therein.

9 And it shall come to pass, if there remain ten men in one house, that they shall die.

7 Therefore they shall now be the first of
 those to go into exile,
 and the revelry of those who stretch
 themselves shall pass away."

8 The Lord GOD has sworn by himself
 (says the LORD, the God of hosts):
"I abhor the pride of Jacob,
 and hate his strongholds;
 and I will deliver up the city and all
 that is in it."

9 And if ten men remain in one house,

---

7. These men who claim pre-eminence and make the most of it for the indulgence of their own appetite for pleasure shall retain a kind of leadership, for they shall head the procession of bewildered captives on their way into exile, and with their departure the government of the nation scornfully described as "sprawlers' revelry" **shall pass away.**

3. THE HORRORS OF SIEGE (6:8-11)

8. The Lord GOD has sworn by himself—as in 4:2 by his holiness—**I abhor the pride of Jacob:** The Hebrew *gā'ôn* generally means "splendor," "majesty"—hence, **excellency** (KJV; cf. Exod. 15:7)—but it is also used in the bad sense of arrogance, self-exaltation, pride (cf. Ezek. 16:49; Prov. 16:18). The parallelism with **palaces** in the following line suggests that Amos had this twofold meaning in mind. That which **Jacob** (Israel) conceived of as witnessing to its greatness as a people was in the sight of God an expression of its arrogant self-sufficiency. He would **deliver up the city,** Samaria, in which this pride in human achievement came as it were to a focus, and all that it contained into the hands of the destroying invader. (The clause, **says the LORD, the God of hosts,** is not in the LXX and would seem therefore to be the note of an editor who may have intended it to refer to vss. 1-7, or on the other hand may have desired to emphasize the especially solemn asseveration of the verse in which it is placed.)

9-10. These verses give a realistic account of the horrors of pestilence attendant on a siege or following upon it. Even where the number of those in a house who have

---

equally shocked by pseudo moralists who go too far in the other direction and confuse opinion and principle. Conscience is one of the words in our lexicon of experience that has become debased. It needs to be reminted and put back into fresh circulation. George Washington's maxim, "labor to keep alive in your breast that little spark of celestial fire, called Conscience," speaks plainly to our condition. There is a sense of "oughtness" about conduct which we believe to be right. Sometimes the spark of conscience in us flickers and all but goes out in the gusts of passion that beat upon our lives. But there are those other moments when the flame burns bright and clear, dissipating the shadows of doubt and the gloom of moral indecision. "Prepare to meet your God" (4:12) was Amos' clear declaration of the nature and function of conscience in the individual or nation that would stem the ravages of moral deterioration and corruption.

(c) Next is introduced the third deadly sin, the sin of *spiritual pride:*

Woe to you who desire the day of the LORD!
 Why would you have the day of the LORD?

Is not the day of the LORD darkness, and not light,
 And gloom with no brightness in it? (5:18, 20).

Reference has been made to the popular belief in Israel that the "day of the LORD" signified the occasion of God's judgment upon the heathen, of his triumph over Israel's enemies. It was to be a final display of divine power over all other nations, save the people of God's choice. Against this popular expression of national and spiritual arrogance Amos set his face like flint. With his belief that God's judgment begins at home, the prophet cries woe upon the unwarranted optimism of his hearers. In figures of speech drawn from his austere and perilous life in the wilderness, he declares the "day of the LORD" to

10 And a man's uncle shall take him up, and he that burneth him, to bring out the bones out of the house, and shall say unto him that *is* by the sides of the house, *Is there yet any* with thee? and he shall say, No. Then shall he say, Hold thy tongue: for we may not make mention of the name of the LORD.

11 For, behold, the LORD commandeth, and he will smite the great house with breaches, and the little house with clefts.

they shall die. 10 And when a man's kinsman, he who burns him,[l] shall take him up to bring the bones out of the house, and shall say to him who is in the innermost parts of the house, "Is there still any one with you?" he shall say, "No"; and he shall say, "Hush! We must not mention the name of the LORD."

11 For behold, the LORD commands,
    and the great house shall be smitten into fragments,
    and the little house into bits.

[l] Or *who makes a burning for him*

---

escaped other dangers is large, no one of them shall escape death. Again, when those who desire to perform the last offices for the dead search the ruins and find a lone survivor, silence is enjoined lest in such desolation someone invoke the name of the Lord and so bring down further manifestation of his wrath. This is the general sense of the passage, but the corruption of the text makes interpretation in detail very uncertain. The verses are evidently prose, as the RSV rightly indicates, and some commentators with good reason regard them as an interpolation. They read as if someone out of his bitter experience of siege and pestilence had added this description to the book as his understanding of the kind of situation in which men find themselves when, as Amos said, God gives up his people.

11. This is a fragment of an oracle preserved in that stream of the Amos tradition which particularly associated him with the prediction of an earthquake of unusual severity. The verb **smite** is that used in 3:15; 9:1.

---

be a day of darkness and not light, of defeat and not victory, for the proud people of the two kingdoms. And events were not slow to vindicate his grim pronouncements.

Amos' ability to call the play correctly is so marked that the modern reader of his book is sometimes tempted to indulge the privilege of historical hindsight and take note of his inability to foresee *all* the twists and turns in the future odyssey of his own people. In this mood, we do well to remember a sober word of the great German historian Ranke, "Every generation is equidistant from eternity"; which saying, interpreted by Herbert Butterfield, demands

that we shall look upon each generation as, so to speak, an end in itself, a world of people existing in their own right. . . . It is always a "Now" that is in direct relation to eternity—not a far future. . . . We envisage our history in the proper light, therefore, if we say that each generation—indeed each individual—exists for the glory of God; [so that] one of the most dangerous things in life is to subordinate human personality to production, to the state, even to civilisation itself, to anything but the glory of God.[3]

[3] *Christianity and History*, pp. 65-67.

Mark then, *sub specie aeternitatis*, the kinship of Amos to such subsequent prophetic persons as Thomas Carlyle and Abraham Lincoln, and in our own times, Norman Thomas in his earlier role as social critic and political educator. The common witness of these four, in their respective centuries, to the glory of God in human affairs both excites our admiration and prevents us from losing sight of the eternal truths they proclaimed in smug side glances at the limitations imposed upon each one of them by the contours of their times.

(*d*) The fourth deadly sin in the prophet's roster of evils was the sin of *ecclesiastical complacency*:

"Woe to those who are at ease in Zion,
    and to those who feel secure on the mountain of Samaria,
. . . .
Therefore they shall now be the first of those to go into exile" (vss. 1*a*, 7*a*) .

From his farm in Tekoa, Amos could see, in clear weather and across the intervening plain, the towers of Jerusalem, the center and symbol of his faith and that of his fathers. "Beautifu

12 ¶ Shall horses run upon the rock? will *one* plow *there* with oxen? for ye have turned judgment into gall, and the fruit of righteousness into hemlock:
 	
13 Ye which rejoice in a thing of nought, which say, Have we not taken to us horns by our own strength?
	12 Do horses run upon rocks?
	    Does one plow the sea with oxen?[m]
	But you have turned justice into poison
	    and the fruit of righteousness into
	        wormwood —
	13 you who rejoice in Lo-debar,[n]
	    who say, "Have we not by our own
	        strength
	    taken Karnaim[o] for ourselves?"

[m] MT *does one plow with oxen?*
[n] Or *a thing of nought*
[o] Or *horns*

4. The End of a People of Unnatural Conduct and Silly Pride (6:12-14)

12. This is another fragment exclaiming over the unnaturalness of the corruption of justice which has turned it into a hateful, poisonous thing (cf. 5:9). Such a perversion is as contrary to the right order of things as it would be for horses to **run upon rocks,** or for a man to **plow the sea with oxen.** The RSV represents the generally accepted reading, which simply makes two words where the pointing of the Hebrew text gives only one (בבקר ים for בבקרים).

13. A further fragment in which Israel's pride in its military power is held up to scorn. **A thing of nought** is the Hebrew *lô' dhābhār,* the consonants of which are the same as those of **Lo-debar,** the name of a town to the east of the Jordan, apparently not far from Mahanaim (II Sam. 17:27). **Karnaim,** which the KJV translates **horns,** is also the name of a town, probably the Ashteroth-karnaim of Gen. 14:5, in the same region. Most scholars are agreed that the reference is to two successes of Israelite arms in the recapture of that region from the Aramaean kingdom of Damascus. The choice of these two comparatively insignificant places was for the sake of the play upon their names. Characteristically, these proud leaders rejoice in a mere nothing—or again make their boast, "Is it not by our own strength that we have got ourselves Karnaim [horns, symbols of power (Deut. 33:17)]?"

for situation, the joy of the whole earth, is Mount Zion, . . . the city of the great King. God is known in her palaces for a refuge." (Ps. 48:2-3.) But the prophet knew from bitter experience how the temple worship had become corrupted by a venal priesthood, and how the fine cutting edge of religious zeal and devotion had been dulled by the indifference and materialism of a complacent people; nor were the conditions any better in the great shrines of the Northern Kingdom, Samaria and Bethel. This widespread popular conception of religious security in God and temple he saw to be the ominous sign and seal of his compatriots' basic moral and spiritual insecurity. Confident as they were in their material prosperity, and lavish in their ritual sacrifices, he was fully aware of their woeful lack of any invisible means of support in terms of the strength and solace that come of a true and humble devotion of the whole man to God and his service. Yet why belabor times gone by? The situation which he confronted and denounced in his day has been disclosed with singular clarity in ours. What Amos meant by "ease in Zion" is manifest still in a smug complacency that turns a Christian church into a kind of museum, where outworn creeds and obsolete methods of education are carefully preserved.

To be **grieved over the ruin of Joseph** (vs. 6) is for the church to shake off its spiritual lethargy and to elect to become a laboratory in Christian living, a fellowship in which men and women exchange ideas and gather new facts with a view to experimenting further with life on a Christian basis. One likes to envision the day when every church has become a workshop in Christian living, every formal service a new attempt to worship God in sincerity and truth, every celebration of holy communion a fresh reminder of the invincible love of God, every gathering of young people a new venture in the development of individual lives of social value in the world, every association with men and women from foreign lands a further extension of world brotherhood and peace. In such

14 But, behold, I will raise up against you a nation, O house of Israel, saith the LORD the God of hosts; and they shall afflict you from the entering in of Hamath unto the river of the wilderness.

14 "For behold, I will raise up against you a nation,
O house of Israel," says the LORD, the God of hosts;
"and they shall oppress you from the entrance of Hamath
to the Brook of the Arabah."

7 Thus hath the Lord GOD showed unto me; and, behold, he formed grasshoppers in the beginning of the shooting up of the latter growth; and, lo, *it was* the latter growth after the king's mowings.

7 Thus the Lord GOD showed me: behold, he was forming locusts in the beginning of the shooting up of the latter growth; and lo, it was the latter growth

14. The main collection of the oracles of Amos embodied in chs. 1–6 is here brought to a close. From the fragmentary character of the sayings in 6:8-13 it may be inferred that the compiler sought to include not only the complete oracles that had come into his possession, but also all the utterances of the prophet that he could glean from others. If, as seems likely, he did his significant work of compilation soon after the fall of the Northern Kingdom in 722 B.C., when Amos' prediction had received its sufficient fulfillment, it was fitting that the final word should be that of vs. 14, with its summary statement of what was in store for Israel. It may even be that the phrasing is in some measure that of the compiler, with his feeling that events had indeed vindicated Amos' ministry. **And they shall oppress you:** The verb *lāḥaç* is frequently used, as in Judg. 4:3, of an invader's prolonged cruel subjugation of a people after attack and conquest. Amos, on the other hand, was concerned with predicting the catastrophic events which would usher in such oppression. **The entrance of Hamath,** whether the pass between Hermon and Lebanon, a little north of Dan, or the beginning of the broad valley somewhat north of Riblah, was conventionally used to denote the farthest boundary of Israel's territory to the north, while the unknown **Brook of the Arabah**—the great trough in which the Dead Sea lies—was evidently the farthest southern boundary. The tyrannous occupation of that whole region, including all the territory that Israel at its greatest had ever held, was the inevitable consequence of the invasion that the prophet had foretold.

III. A SERIES OF VISIONS, AN ACCOUNT OF THE CLOSE OF AMOS' MINISTRY, AND AN EPILOGUE (7:1–9:15)

These chapters form a section distinguished from the rest of the book by the variety of the material it contains: a series of four visions (7:1-8; 8:1-2); a fifth vision with an accompanying oracle (9:1-4); a piece of historical narrative (7:10-17); oracles, for the most part in more fragmentary form than those in chs. 1–6 (chiefly to be found in 8:4-14); and an epilogue announcing a new time of restoration (9:11-15).

an evolution Amos would "see of the travail of his soul, and . . . be satisfied" (Isa. 53:11).

7:1–9:7. *Visions of Judgment.*—Ch. 7 introduces the third and last part of the book of Amos. In this section the authentic text is brought to its conclusion; to it, however, has been appended a kind of postscript (9:8-15) that represents the reflections of a nameless author who lived and wrote some years after Amos. Comment upon this final prophecy and the sharp contrast which it affords to the accepted text of the pre-exilic prophet from Tekoa

is reserved until later. It should be noted here, meanwhile, that the chapter under consideration presents us with a new aspect of the life and message of Amos in what appear to be autobiographical elements which have fortunately been inserted in the hitherto unrelieved transcript of his dark pronouncements of doom and destruction. By inference we have already formed an impression of him as a man, and it is fair to say that the picture we have is one in which the stern features are relatively unrelieved, outlined against a somber background.

The series of four visions forms the nucleus of this section. The account of them is autobiographical in the full sense of the word, for the prophet speaks in the first person of significant events in the shaping of his life, of that which took place between himself and God as he was brought to full recognition of the fact that God was about to make an end of his people. According to some commentators (cf. Cripps, *Amos,* p. 101), the visions should be taken as constituting Amos' call to his ministry and preparation for it. The use of the first person, the carefully worked out symmetry of the narration—the visions are arranged in pairs, each pair with its own distinctive phrasing—and the intimate economy of the style make it almost certain that they were committed to writing by Amos himself, whether by his own hand or by dictation to someone else. As suggested in the Intro. (p. 771), it is not unlikely that it was after his return to Tekoa that he put on record this account of his call. This he did in the face of what may well have seemed a long delay in the fulfillment of his prediction of the destruction of the nation, in the conviction that in due time God's dread purpose to destroy, as it had been made known to him, would be realized. The recital of the visions, which is not so much prophecy as a justification of his appearance as a prophet, is thus parallel to the utterance of 3:4-8 and the statement of his call in 7:14-15.

A. Visions and Narrative (7:1–8:3)
1. The Locusts (7:1-3)

7:1. The Lord God showed me: "Thus the Lord God caused me to see." The initiative was with God. **Behold, he was forming locusts:** It is better to read with many commentators, following the LXX, "Behold, a brood of locusts." This reading requires a change in only the vowel pointing of one word, *yĕçer* for the M.T. *yôçēr.* This last is a participle, the use of which focuses attention on the divine activity. If retained, it should be rendered **was forming** (RSV) rather than **formed** (KJV). The noun "brood" centered on the concrete actuality of the object at which the prophet found himself

---

We are alternately attracted and appalled by the prophet's courage and his apparent lack of charity. But in this particular chapter, with its disclosure of him in a dramatic public appearance and, more especially, in a subsequent mood of private soliloquy with God, the harshness is somewhat abated, and we behold a man still unafraid, yet whose lineaments are softened by a touch of positive love for his errant compatriots. To bring his self-portrait into proper focus, we should read the chapter in reverse. Amos' bold fronting of Amaziah, the priest of Bethel, may well have been the culmination of the prophet's public ministry, and the visions and oracles with which the chapter opens may represent insights discovered in his enforced retirement to the austerities and solitude of his rural home. With this suggestion to the reader, the present order of the chapter will be followed, in deference alike to text and Exeg.

7:1. *Advance and Retreat.*—Before attending to the three visions of Amos set forth in the first part of ch. 7, we are impelled to give consideration to their circumstances. These are quite obviously laid in the prophet's native home of Tekoa, earlier described as to its location in the marginal land of Judea that declines eastward to the desolate wilderness and

the coast of the Dead Sea. It was a place, as George Adam Smith declares, "without sanctity and almost without tradition." [4] One is reminded of the observation of a New Hampshire farmer, when viewing a plot of land purchased by an unwelcome neighbor, "It's all laydge [ledge] and good for nothin', 'cept I suppose it helps to hold the world together." Yet the barrenness of the region, save for small isolated homesteads, and above all its aura of human solitude provide us with an indispensable clue to understanding the austere personality of Amos and the almost unrelieved rigor of his dire prophecies. A. N. Whitehead in his book, *Religion in the Making,* provides an even more exact application of modern wisdom to the character of an ancient prophet. "Religion is what the individual does with his own solitariness. . . . If you are never solitary, you are never religious." [5]

The pattern of advance and retreat suggested by Amos' alternate journeys to the cities of Israel to sell his frugal wares in the bazaars and to declare his burning words in the market place, and his return to the isolation of his farm and quiet seasons of solitary brooding over

[4] *Book of the Twelve Prophets,* I, 72.
[5] New York: The Macmillan Co., 1926, pp. 16, 17.

gazing. With his mind charged with a sense of impending doom for the nation, the sight of a brood of locusts was ominous. It might well portend most disastrous developments, for it was **in the beginning of the shooting up of the latter growth,** just at the time when the spring rains were fostering the final growth of the crops, when locusts would therefore constitute the greatest menace. **And lo, it was the latter growth . . . :** It is generally assumed that this refers to the king's right to a first mowing, before the private owner

---

the ills of his day, in lone communion with God, is suggested by the following quotation:

One of the chief causes of unhappiness in the world is that our mind is preoccupied all the while with its relation with other human minds. Free yourself from this; make the friendliest and kindliest retreat you can into solitude; and in a few moments your nature will have bathed itself so deeply in the cool baths of primordial Being that you will feel yourself able to return to the troubling arena of humanity with an inviolable and a secret strength.[6]

The truth is more economically expressed by our Lord in two well-remembered commands to his disciples: "Go ye therefore, and teach all nations" (Matt. 28:19) and "Come ye yourselves apart into a desert place, and rest a while" (Mark 6:31).

Jesus himself is the greatest teacher and exemplar of the power of solitude to fortify the soul against the recurrent complexities with which life is charged. To a world distracted by manifold appeals to its energy and its credulity, he came preaching the gospel of the unencumbered life, the life that is free from the tyranny of things and therefore more at liberty to undertake the service of God. In view of which may we not better understand some of his sayings that seem to us, at first thought, to be unreasonably hard? For example, Jesus' retort to the man who expressed a desire to follow him, but asked leave first of all to go and bury his father. "Follow me; and let the dead bury their dead" (Matt. 8:22). Or again his declaration, "He that loveth father or mother more than me is not worthy of me" (Matt. 10:37). He is not advocating that the dead should not be decently buried or that a man should not honor his father and mother. He *is* protesting against a social order that drives man to the death of distraction or that lays family life under tribute to the acquisitive instinct. He would make it clear that discipleship involves life become rid of entangling alliances with many or most of the things which the world of men and women has come to hold dear and indispensable. And we know from the records how utterly consistent with these convictions was his own manner of living. The "hidden years" of his young manhood may be best understood as years of prepa-

ration for setting about his Father's business. He was preparing, even then, to rid his life of all that might encumber his whole-souled devotion to the will of God.

His brief public career is no less marked by the extreme simplification of his personal life. He became an itinerant preacher, with no place to lay his head. He never had a family of his own. He never possessed a home. Following his trial, while he was in agony on the cross, his executioners gambled for the only piece of property he had on earth, a seamless robe that would have been ruined by division. The total impression made on us is that of a life that has got itself free from a multitude of distractions and fears, possessions and worldly ambitions, and is in full career to seek and to find itself in God and his service with all the ardor of a runner speeding to the goal, an arrow winging to the mark, or a ship beating into port. And all this in a high mood of joy. "These things I speak in the world, that they might have my joy fulfilled in themselves" (John 17:13). To the accompaniment of that simplicity, he made of solitude his familiar. He dared to live with himself because in close identification with God he created a self clean and true and exciting enough to live with. For Jesus, living *with* himself further meant to live *within* himself. He cultivated those rare moments when he could be alone in spite of crowds and confusion; he conspired to make these occasions more frequent and to discover in them a quality of peace and refreshment which the world could neither give nor destroy. There come to mind words spoken by Joan of Arc to her tormentors in George Bernard Shaw's play, *St. Joan.*

Do not think you can frighten me by telling me that I am alone. France is alone; and God is alone; and what is my loneliness before the loneliness of my country and my God? I see now that the loneliness of God is His strength: what would He be if He listened to your jealous little counsels? Well, my loneliness shall be my strength too: it is better to be alone with God: His friendship will not fail me, nor His counsel, nor His love. In His strength I will dare, and dare, and dare, until I die.[1]

Somehow these words echo from the direction of Judea. "Behold, the hour cometh, yea, is now

---

[6] John Cowper Powys, *A Philosophy of Solitude* (New York: Simon & Schuster, 1933), pp. 113-14.

[1] Scene 5.

2 And it came to pass, *that* when they had made an end of eating the grass of the land, then I said, O Lord God, forgive, I beseech thee: by whom shall Jacob arise? for he *is* small.	after the king's mowings. 2 When they had finished eating the grass of the land, I said, "O Lord God, forgive, I beseech thee! How can Jacob stand? He is so small!"
3 The LORD repented for this: It shall not be, saith the LORD.	3 The LORD repented concerning this; "It shall not be," said the LORD.

was entitled to cut for his own use. But of such tribute in Israel there is no evidence. It is more likely that the clause is a gloss explaining the rare Hebrew word for **latter growth**. "And behold the latter growth is that which comes after the [time of the] king's shearing," for "shearing" is the usual meaning of the word here rendered **mowings** (cf. Snaith, *Book of Amos,* II, 120).

2. When they had finished . . . : The RSV and KJV make the best of a doubtful text, for the sequence of tenses in the Hebrew is difficult. Then, too, it would seem that the intercession which follows comes too late after the work of destruction had been completed. A generally accepted emendation, involving only a slight modification of the C.T., ויהי הא מכלה for והיה אם־כלה, gives, "And as they were about to finish eating the grass"—or better "the herbage," for the Hebrew word covers all kinds of vegetation. Marti (*Dodekapropheton,* p. 208), noting the resemblance of כלה, "make an end," to אכל, "eat," would omit אם כלה, and so arrive at the simple reading, "And as they were about to devour the herbage"; this may well be right. The present text, along with the reading of the participle in vs. 1, is perhaps due to the assumption that the prophet's experience was altogether that of inward vision instead of an ecstatic state associated with the sight of an actual brood of locusts. **O Lord God . . . :** The petition is even more concise in the original. **I beseech thee** is a particle of entreaty, almost the equivalent of a simple "please," but it served to identify the prophet with those for whom he was pleading. At the same time he saw them not as they were in their own eyes, a proud, self-sufficient nation, but as God saw them, a little, helpless people.

How can Jacob stand?
He is so small!

"It was in the experience of prayer for his people that Amos became a prophet" (Gustav Hölscher, *Die Profeten* [Leipzig: J. C. Hinrichs, 1914], p. 195).

3. The LORD repented: God remains always lord of his own purpose and in the laconic **It shall not be** Amos received the assurance that the threatening calamity was averted.

come, that ye shall be scattered, every man to his own, and shall leave me alone: and yet I am not alone, because the Father is with me" (John 16:32). Centuries before our Lord, kindred sentiments stirred in the mind and heart of Amos, brooding over the ills of his own time, in the bleak and solitary region of Tekoa, with God as his sole communicant.

1-9. Locusts, Fire, and Plumb Line.—In his retreat to the stark simplicities and solitude of his home, however, Amos is never withdrawn from his accepted vocation as God's spokesman to a sinful nation. In fact it was here in Tekoa that his sense of mission came to him in the first instance. "The LORD took me from following the flock, and the LORD said to me, 'Go, prophesy to my people Israel'" (vs. 15). In the three

visions now under more detailed review we have undoubted examples of earlier revelations of God that projected a rude farmer into the arena of public life and affairs as the mouthpiece of the Eternal. The imagery of the visions is drawn from rural life. A plague of locusts devastates what is left of the fields for popular consumption **after the king's mowings;** a terrible drought parches the land, and a fire breaks out, drying up even the underground waters; walls and buildings have been twisted out of shape by frequent tremors of the earth and have to be trued up by the help of a plumb line: all these figures we may be sure are drawn from his own experience. Before his call to the prophetic office such disasters would have been held to be the natural accompaniments of the

4 ¶ Thus hath the Lord God showed unto me: and, behold, the Lord God called to contend by fire, and it devoured the great deep, and did eat up a part.

5 Then said I, O Lord God, cease, I beseech thee: by whom shall Jacob arise? for he *is* small.

6 The Lord repented for this: This also shall not be, saith the Lord God.

7 ¶ Thus he showed me: and, behold, the Lord stood upon a wall *made* by a plumb-line, with a plumbline in his hand.

4 Thus the Lord God showed me: behold, the Lord God was calling for a judgment by fire, and it devoured the great deep and was eating up the land. 5 Then I said, "O Lord God, cease, I beseech thee!
How can Jacob stand?
He is so small!"
6 The Lord repented concerning this;
"This also shall not be," said the Lord God.

7 He showed me: behold, the Lord was standing beside a wall built with a plumb

2. THE DEVOURING FIRE (7:4-6)

4. Behold, the Lord God called to contend by fire or, as the participial construction demands, **was calling** (RSV). Again as in the first vision, the present text emphasizes the divine activity. God is summoning fire to be the instrument of his **judgment** upon his people. But the words **the Lord God** stand rather far on in the sentence to be taken as the subject of the participle and appear to have been introduced by a later hand (cf. Snaith, *op. cit.*, II, 122). The phrase **contend by fire** is unusual and many commentators accept a simple emendation of the text, להב אש, "a flaming fire," instead of לרב באש, **to contend by fire**. If then with Weiser (*Profetie des Amos*, p. 13), קרה, "drew near" is read instead of קרא, "called," the simple and direct "flaming fire . . . drawing near" was what the prophet perceived. He saw and felt the fiery heat of the sun as a devouring conflagration. Under the blazing sky it seemed as if the very source of all the life-giving water of spring and fountain and rain from heaven, **the great deep,** the primeval abyss of the creation story (Gen. 1:2) had been devoured. Now it seemed to be **eating up the land** as vegetation withered away before it. **Land** is more exactly "portion"—the territory allotted to Israel (Mic. 2:4).

5-6. Again confronted with the imminence of final disaster, Amos found himself once more pleading for his people, and received the assurance that this peril also would be averted.

3. THE PLUMB LINE (7:7-9)

7. He showed me: "Caused me to see." With the LXX, **the Lord** should be read as the subject of the first clause, not of the second. As in the first two visions, the desire to emphasize further the active presence of God while making the experience wholly one of abnormal vision has led to the overlaying of the original text which recorded the

precarious life of the farmer. But to the farmer become prophet they are events become words, signs, and symbols of God's punishment of his faithless people for their sins. With telling effect Amos translates them into the language of national catastrophe.

There is to be heard, in the first two visions, an impressive note of compassion for his fellow men that is missing in the earlier pronouncements of Amos. It may be that in his retreat to Tekoa, after the explosive events in Bethel (vss. 10-17), the prophet has reason to review his previous words in the comparative tranquillity of solitude. For the moment, at least, his stern cast of countenance and thought are mel-

lowed. For the first time he pleads with the God who confronts him to be merciful to his apostate people:

"O Lord God, forgive, I beseech thee!
How can Jacob stand?
He is so small!" (Vs. 2.)

Hosea and Isaiah, who had experienced the joys and the sorrows of family life, not infrequently introduce into their prophecies references to mother and wife and child, evocative of the element of love and mercy in the nature of God. Amos appears to have been denied the delights and solace of domestic life and this may account, in part, for the almost total ab-

8 And the LORD said unto me, Amos, what seest thou? And I said, A plumbline. Then said the Lord, Behold, I will set a plumbline in the midst of my people Israel: I will not again pass by them any more:

9 And the high places of Isaac shall be desolate, and the sanctuaries of Israel shall be laid waste; and I will rise against the house of Jeroboam with the sword.

line, with a plumb line in his hand. 8 And the LORD said to me, "Amos, what do you see?" And I said, "A plumb line." Then the Lord said,

"Behold, I am setting a plumb line
in the midst of my people Israel;
I will never again pass by them;
9 the high places of Isaac shall be made
desolate,
and the sanctuaries of Israel shall be
laid waste,
and I will rise against the house of
Jerobo'am with the sword."

---

seeing of an actual object—a seeing which, to be sure, Amos himself regarded as directed by God. In the following verse this object is named in a single word, 'anākh. It occurs only in this passage, and the versions were evidently at a loss as to its meaning, the LXX rendering it by "adamant," the Vulg. first by "plaster," then by "trowel." In other Semitic languages the word means "lead," and this fact, together with the association with a wall in vs. 7, is sufficient justification for the rendering **plumb line** of the English versions. In the light of the simple answer of vs. 8, it would seem probable that in vs. 7 the original of **Behold, the Lord was standing beside a wall built with a plumb line** read, "And behold a plumb line set upon a wall" (cf. *ibid.*, pp. 16-17). The additions were due to the introduction into the picture of the Lord as engaged in action, thus anticipating the interpretation that follows.

8. **A plumb line** does not, as in the case of the locusts or the flaming fire, immediately suggest danger, so that in the fixity of his gaze the prophet felt that God was asking him to see something more than what directly met the eye: **Amos, what seest thou?** And as he answered he realized that a plumb line is for testing and decision, and it was borne in upon his consciousness that God was even then testing his people, finding them wanting, and pronouncing the dread sentence, **I will never again pass by them,** the verb **pass by** being used as in Mic. 7:18. With the terrible finality of that sentence ringing in his ears, Amos knew the dread certainty of the doom that was to overtake his people and the pitiful hopelessness of any further intercession. The Lord had spoken; he must prophesy.

9. This is in keeping with other oracles in which Amos predicted destruction by a ruthless invader, but it may be questioned whether this elaboration of the sentence upon Israel was a part of the vision in which the irrevocability of doom rather than the form it would take was the significant note. The style of the language differs, too, from the simple directness of divine utterance in the vision. The overthrow of the nation would indeed involve the demolition of **the high places of Isaac,** the shrines upon the hills, for the most part open to the sky, and of **the sanctuaries of Israel**—perhaps more specifically "buildings"—as well as the downfall of the dynasty of Jeroboam, though the phrasing may reflect the actual course of events. The saying was placed here by the editor who introduced at this point the piece of historical narrative that follows.

---

sence of pity and compassion in his public address. In these two visions is the great exception. Here are words spoken with tears as Amos sees Israel, for all her sins, in the guise of a little child just learning to walk. The effect of his pleading, even as a father pleads before a judge for his wayward child, is reminiscent of a late word in the epistle of James: "The effectual fervent prayer of a righteous man availeth

much" (Jas. 5:16). God's sovereignty is not impaired by the agonizing cry of his servant Amos, neither is it unmoved.

The LORD repented concerning this;
"It shall not be," said the LORD (vs. 3).

Twice Amos pleads, and twice does God intimate that the prophet's pleas are heeded. **"This also shall not be," said the Lord GOD** (vs. 6).

| 10 ¶ Then Amaziah the priest of Beth-el sent to Jeroboam king of Israel, saying, Amos hath conspired against thee in the midst of the house of Israel: the land is not able to bear all his words. | 10 Then Amazi'ah the priest of Bethel sent to Jerobo'am king of Israel, saying, "Amos has conspired against you in the midst of the house of Israel; the land is not |

4. AMOS AND AMAZIAH (7:10-17)

The account of this incident differs from the recital of the visions, for in these Amos speaks in the first person while here someone speaks about him. But the narrator shows a remarkable ability to enter into the mind of the prophet, for he not only reproduces Amos' own language but he catches and conveys the very spirit of the clash between Amaziah and the prophet. The piece of narrative is apparently an excerpt from a longer account of Amos' ministry, for it begins abruptly without any mention of the prophet's arrival at Bethel, and the first naming of Amos in vs. 10 assumes the reader's knowledge of him. For the redactor who placed the passage in its present context, a sufficient background was provided by the visions and the prediction of vs. 9. The section was perhaps originally placed after the account of the fourth vision, with the intention of bringing the book to an end with the unfaltering proclamation of final disaster that marked the close of Amos' public ministry. It is impossible to say what led to the transfer to its present position, but strikingly enough there are now brought together the moment at which Amos came to his realization of the inevitability of God's visitation of his people and the scene in which in fidelity to his vision he carried to its conclusion the ministry entrusted to him.

10. Amaziah's charge of conspiracy rested upon what he felt to be the generally subversive effect of Amos' utterances. Tradition associated the prophets with revolutionary activity, as in Ahijah's role in the first Jeroboam's rebellion (I Kings 11:29-37). It had been the prophet Elisha who had taken a leading part in the revolution that had brought to the throne Jehu, founder of the house of the second Jeroboam (II Kings 9:1-3). But Elisha had worked in association with the prophetic guilds, while Amos was a solitary figure who expressly denied any connection with these professional prophets. Amaziah's

In the last vision, however, as God holds **a plumb line in his hand** and surveys a sagging wall, Amos simply observes the discrepancy and does not speak. Famine and drought are seasonal occurrences and beyond the power of human effort to control. For these reasons one may plead to God for their mitigation. But a wall is the labor of man's hands. If it buckles, for whatever reason, its deviation is inexorably marked by the plumb line. And from the verdict there is no appeal. So are "the judgments of the LORD . . . true and righteous altogether" (Ps. 19:9), and Amos, beholding, bows silently before the impending finality of judgment.

> **"Behold, I am setting a plumb line**
>   **in the midst of my people Israel;**
>   **I will never again pass by them;**
>
> **. . . . .**
>
>   **and I will rise against the house of Jeroboam**
>   **with the sword"** (vss. 8-9).

10-17. Prophet and Priest.—We have come now to a dramatic episode that is packed full of significance both immediate and future. The explosive collision between Amaziah the syco-

phant priest of Bethel and Amos the prophet from Tekoa provides us with one of the most pregnant events in human affairs. In the wings, off stage, is the king, Jeroboam, proud ruler of Israel, whose adroit statecraft has done little more than delay the Assyrian menace to his exposed and decadent kingdom. Here is the inescapable crisis to which the public career of Amos has been moving. Here is the occasion on which his stern, unpalatable prophecies of national doom have come to an inevitable climax in the form of royal rebuke. To grasp the importance of this scene in Bethel is to understand more clearly the general tenor of the prophecies of Amos that precede and the visions and their sober exposition that follow. More than that, the acrid clash of minds on this day in Bethel is a landmark in the great debate between priest and prophet, the fierce conflict between state and church, whose bitter entail infects all subsequent history. Earlier prophets, Elijah and Nathan, had dared to defy the king in person, as representatives of God's righteousness. But there is in this incident not only the stark conflict of personalities but the

11 For thus Amos saith, Jeroboam shall die by the sword, and Israel shall surely be led away captive out of their own land.

12 Also Amaziah said unto Amos, O thou seer, go, flee thee away into the land of Judah, and there eat bread, and prophesy there:

13 But prophesy not again any more at Beth-el: for it *is* the king's chapel, and it *is* the king's court.

14 ¶ Then answered Amos, and said to Amaziah, I *was* no prophet, neither *was* I a prophet's son; but I *was* a herdman, and gatherer of sycamore fruit:

able to bear all his words. 11 For thus Amos has said,

'Jerobo'am shall die by the sword,
and Israel must go into exile
away from his land.' "

12 And Amazi'ah said to Amos, "O seer, go, flee away to the land of Judah, and eat bread there, and prophesy there; 13 but never again prophesy at Bethel, for it is the king's sanctuary, and it is a temple of the kingdom."

14 Then Amos answered Amazi'ah, "I am no prophet, nor a prophet's son;[p] but I am a herdsman, and a dresser of sycamore

[p] Or *one of the sons of the prophets*

language, however, indicates that Amos' ministry had been widely exercised **in the midst of the house of Israel,** and that it was having its effect on considerable numbers of people. The prophet was a man to be feared.

11. Amaziah gives just such a summary of what Amos had predicted as would impress the king with the grave danger of the situation.

12-13. It was perhaps at the king's direction that Amaziah ordered Amos to leave the kingdom, but no doubt the abusive language was the priest's own: **O seer**—with the practical man's contempt for the man of vision—**go, flee away to the land of Judah**—get back where you belong—**and eat bread there**—get your living by your prophesying (cf. Mic. 3:5); and then the peremptory "But here at Bethel no more of your prophesying," **for it is the king's sanctuary.** The reminder that the sanctuary with its precincts was immediately under royal patronage would make it clear that Amaziah had nothing less than the authority of the king behind him.

14. Amos in his reply dealt first of all with the charge that he was a professional prophet. **I am no prophet**—he was not a prophet in that sense—**nor a prophet's son.** The phrase is an exact translation, but the RSV mg., **one of the sons of the prophets,** better brings out its meaning of membership in one of the prophetic guilds. These were

more designed and calculated opposition of vocations and institutions.

The formal charge of treason is preferred against Amos by Amaziah. **Amos has conspired against you** [Jeroboam] **in the midst of the house of Israel** (vs. 10*a*). The vexatious odyssey of that ugly indictment and its counterpart "subversion" runs through all subsequent history to this very moment. For all our current learning and sophistication, we are still without clear knowledge and understanding as to the basic meaning of those two words and the postures of the human mind and conscience which they imply. There follows Amaziah's charge, a brief bill of particulars just one sentence long, which is also an unintended tribute to the power and magnitude of Amos' God-given influence. **The land is not able to bear all his words** (vs. 10*b*). Epitaphs are rarely as enduring as the stones upon which they are impressed. Here is the imprimatur of his own generation upon Amos the prophet, and it

has become timeless in the verity of God, whose servant he was and whose eternal judgments he pronounced.

Not content with his role of priestly prosecutor, Amaziah assumes the responsibility of executor as well. **O seer, go, flee away to the land of Judah, and eat bread there, and prophesy there; but never again prophesy at Bethel, for it is the king's sanctuary, and it is a temple of the kingdom** (vss. 12-13). Observe that to this early decree against freedom of speech is added the venom of personal insult. Amaziah's use of the word "seer" was designed to attach to Amos the stigma of earlier individuals or guilds whose chief claim to prophecy was their fortuitous capacity to tell fortunes, sometimes in a trance, and always for a fee. "Is it a time to receive money, and to receive garments, and oliveyards, and vineyards, and sheep, and oxen, and menservants, and maidservants?" (II Kings 5:26), inquired Elisha of Gehazi, who begged gifts from Naaman. His words marked the

15 And the Lord took me as I followed the flock, and the Lord said unto me, Go, prophesy unto my people Israel.

16 ¶ Now therefore hear thou the word of the Lord: Thou sayest, Prophesy not against Israel, and drop not *thy word* against the house of Isaac.

trees, 15 and the Lord took me from following the flock, and the Lord said to me, 'Go, prophesy to my people Israel.'

16 "Now therefore hear the word of the Lord.

You say, 'Do not prophesy against Israel,
and do not preach against the house of Isaac.'

---

associations of men trained in a technique of dance and response to musical stimulus that could induce a state of ecstasy. As noted above, these groups had under Elisha's leadership played an important part in the overthrow of the house of Omri. Amos' repudiation of membership in any of these guilds was in effect a denial of the charge of conspiracy that Amaziah had brought against him. But, as he went on to say, it was to be a prophet in the truest sense of that office that he had been directly called of God. **I am a herdsman:** The Hebrew word *bôqēr*, found only here, means "a keeper of cattle," and scholars are generally agreed that this is a scribal misreading of an original *nôqēdh*, "shepherd," the word used in 1:1. This is substantiated by the reference to a flock in vs. 15. He had besides been engaged in a seasonal occupation, that of **a dresser of sycamore trees,** bearing a figlike fruit which must be opened in order to get rid of the insects that infest it.

15. The call came to him as he was—a simple shepherd **following the flock,** with none of the professional training that members of prophetic guilds received. **The Lord took me . . . and the Lord said to me:** The emphatic repetition of the name of God is significant. The immediate act of none other than God himself had made him a prophet. The command **Go, prophesy** makes it clear that the disclaimer of the preceding verse implied no disdain for the office in itself.

16-17. Lest Amaziah should suppose that by silencing Amos he could avert the sentence of doom that the prophet had pronounced, Amos declared that the priest himself with his family and his possessions would be involved in the inevitable fate of the nation. **You say . . . :** The pronoun is emphatic, expressing a contrast with the

---

emancipation of the Hebrew prophet from the role of soothsayer, predicting personal fortunes for a price, to the role of incorruptible, unmercenary spokesman of God, represented by Amos and his immediate successors. There is venom in the arbitrary decrees of exile pronounced by Amaziah upon Amos, and this too: a suggestion of the same specious arithmetic of power which was invoked centuries later when priest and prophet were again matched in the persons of Caiaphas and Jesus. "It is expedient for us, that one man should die for the people, and that the whole nation perish not" (John 11:50).

Thus far Amaziah, with no word from the accused prophet until the charge was completed and the sentence pronounced. Then Amos answered Amaziah in words that fairly bleed, so full are they of human vitality and the holy spirit of God that flowed through him. To read the text is sufficient proof of the character and temper of the prophet. His origin as a simple herdsman, his lack of all professional antecedents, a layman whom the Lord took . . .

from following the flock (vs. 15a) and to whom the Lord entrusted a hard, painful commission, **Go, prophesy to my people Israel** (vs. 15b) — all this lies plain for everyone to read. The whole panorama of Amos' life and labors is compressed into a single picture of an utterly disinterested man, fully possessed by the spirit of the Lord and completely fearless as to whither God might lead him or what judgments of men or nations God might put upon his lips. Even the bitter fate Amos predicted would befall Amaziah and his family is not to be considered as a personal taunt, trading exile for exile, but rather as incidental to the fate of a king and nation who had refused to hear and obey the repeated warnings of the Eternal.

The passage opens up several avenues of thought to the present-day reader. The clash between priest and prophet has vexed institutional religion from time immemorial. Two types of religious ministrants, each of which should complement the other, become involved in a struggle for supremacy. To this must be added Amaziah's appeal to the king as indicative

17 Therefore thus saith the Lord; Thy wife shall be a harlot in the city, and thy sons and thy daughters shall fall by the sword, and thy land shall be divided by line; and thou shalt die in a polluted land: and Israel shall surely go into captivity forth of his land.

17 Therefore thus says the Lord:
'Your wife shall be a harlot in the city,
　　and your sons and your daughters shall
　　　fall by the sword,
　　and your land shall be parceled out by
　　　line;
you yourself shall die in an unclean land,
　　and Israel shall surely go into exile
　　　away from its land.' "

---

following **thus saith the Lord. Drop not thy word** or, better, **Do not preach:** The verb does not necessarily express contempt. It seems rather to describe the almost instinctive flow of utterance from the ecstatic.

17. Rape of women, slaying of youth, partition of property among the victors, and exile of the leaders were all part of the ordinary treatment of a conquered people by the victorious invaders. **An unclean land:** A land in which sacrifice could not be offered to Yahweh. The language is that of the popular thought of the time, greatly influenced by the Baal religion that Israel had found in the land of Canaan, a religion which insisted on the identification of the god with a particular piece of territory so that he could not properly be worshiped outside its borders (cf. I Sam. 26:19; II Kings 5:17). For Amaziah the priest this would have special significance. **And Israel shall surely go . . .** repeats Amaziah's language in vs. 11, and was perhaps added by someone who wished to make it clear that what would happen to the priest was only an instance of what was to befall the whole nation.

---

of those conflicting aims and prerogatives of state and church which are still unresolved, especially in times of national crises. Both of these historic areas of opposition are illumined when we see in Amos at Bethel that rare combination of man and moment in which religion is exercising its primary function of protest instead of submitting its basic insights to the trammels of institution or creed. There are those who hold that the primary office of religion is to afford consolation. No sensitive person denies the ministry of comfort and solace which high religion affords to the soul that is bruised. But it cannot be gainsaid that a religion which sets that ministry as its chief aim becomes little more than a comfortable religion. There are others who maintain that the primary office of religion is to provide a bulwark for the existing order of man's life and so to make his immediate lot tolerable. Again no intelligent person will hold that religion does not bear a salutary and necessary part in the preservation of those social relationships and ethical distinctions that are essential to all human progress. Yet it cannot be denied that a religion which is first of all the handmaid of the state and the servant of society soon passes from being of service to being servile. Rather is it the first duty of religion to disturb; its primary function is that of protest. The person who is truly religious is one who has come to be less and less at home in the world

of sense, less and less moved by the things that do appear, less and less confident in the weight and power of sheer material force, and more and more assured of those eternal verities that are hid from the wise and prudent but revealed unto babes; more and more aware of those things which "eye hath not seen, nor ear heard" (I Cor. 2:9), more and more at home in that greater and that better part of life which is out of sight. Of all such, Amos is an early spokesman in his conscientious defiance of priest and king at Bethel. He is the forerunner of another prophetic figure who took his stand centuries later on the primacy of conscience, one man against the world. Fronted with a pile of books of his own writing and asked to retract their contents in whole or in part, what is it that Martin Luther is saying in a voice that is heard in every corner of the council hall at Worms?

Since then Your Majesty and your lordships desire a simple reply, I will answer without horns and without teeth. Unless I am convicted by Scripture and plain reason—I do not accept the authority of popes and councils, for they have contradicted each other—my conscience is captive to the Word of God. I cannot and I will not recant anything, for to go against conscience is neither right nor safe. God help me. Amen.[2]

[2] Roland H. Bainton, *Here I Stand* (New York & Nashville: Abingdon-Cokesbury Press, 1950), p. 185.

8 Thus hath the Lord God showed unto me: and behold a basket of summer fruit.

2 And he said, Amos, what seest thou? And I said, A basket of summer fruit. Then said the Lord unto me, The end is come upon my people of Israel; I will not again pass by them any more.

3 And the songs of the temple shall be howlings in that day, saith the Lord God: *there shall be* many dead bodies in every place; they shall cast *them* forth with silence.

8 Thus the Lord God showed me: behold, a basket of summer fruit.*q* 2 And he said, "Amos, what do you see?" And I said, "A basket of summer fruit."*q* Then the Lord said to me,

"The end*r* has come upon my people Israel;
  I will never again pass by them.
3 The songs of the temple*s* shall become wailings in that day,"
                          says the Lord God;
  "the dead bodies shall be many;
    in every place they shall be cast out in silence."*t*

q qayits
r qets
s Or palace
t Or be silent!

5. The Basket of Summer Fruit (8:1-3)

8:1-2. Again Amos found himself looking fixedly at an object with a strange feeling of the something more. Again he felt the prompting of One who asked, **What seest thou?** As in answer he repeated the word *qáyiç*, **summer fruit,** it became *qēç*, "end," and he knew that God was saying to him, **The end has come upon my people Israel.** In the phrase **my people** there is sounded tragically against the background of the sentence of irrevocable doom the note which was to be struck in the great utterance of 3:2, "You only have I known." God must destroy his own people. And again there follows the dread finality of the declaration **I will never again pass by them.**

Summer fruit is that which ripens during the summer and is gathered in the autumn. The visions seem therefore to have occurred over the course of a year, for that of the locusts was associated with the spring, and that of the flaming fire with the summer heat. They were eventful months in Amos' life which thus brought him the certainty of his call to his austere ministry.

3. Here are described concrete instances of the effect of invasion and conquest by a ruthless enemy. The occurrence of the formula **says the Lord God** suggests that this prediction was not part of the vision but an oracle which once had independent currency. **The songs of the temple shall become wailings:** Since the verb is actually "shall wail," many commentators would, with a slight emendation of the text (*shārôth* for *shîrôth*), read "the singing women" for **the songs.** As the RSV mg. indicates, the

8:1-3. The Basket of Summer Fruit.—With this section (8:1–9:7) we come to the conclusion of the accepted text of the book of Amos. The last eight verses of ch. 9 form a later addition to the book by another than the prophet, and call for special consideration. The vision, however, of the basket of summer fruit would seem to belong to the three similar manifestations of God to Amos described in the preceding chapter. Like the setting of a plumb line against a wall to measure its deviation, there is an element of finality about a basket of summer fruit. Its inevitable end, under a desert sun, is total corruption. This stark interpretation of the parable, for such the four visions are, is further sustained by Amos' deliberate play upon the

words signifying "summer fruit" and "the end," as described in the Exeg., above. The employment of words which sound alike but contain very different meanings is a device which subsequent prophets, notably Jeremiah, invoke with summary effect. Its impact upon those who heard was more profound than upon those who read. Immediately there followed the same devastating rejoinder of God that marked the setting of the plumb line, **I will never again pass by them.**

At the risk of digression, comment should be made upon Amos' effective use of repetition as a means of enhancing the pith of his prophecies. In his earliest utterance, set forth in chs. 1 and 2, we have his reiteration of the divine charge,

4 ¶ Here this, O ye that swallow up the needy, even to make the poor of the land to fail,	4 Hear this, you who trample upon the needy, and bring the poor of the land to an end,

word for temple, *hêkhāl*, may also mean **palace,** and in that case it is the revelry of palace feasting that shall end in woeful cries of distress. In vs. 3*b*, **The dead bodies . . . silence,** the phrasing is abrupt and disjointed with no discernible grammatical construction: "Many the dead bodies—in every place—he hath cast them forth—silence!" The text may be in disorder, but even as it stands it presents effectively the horrors of the aftermath of war or possibly of attendant pestilence: corpses just like refuse—the verb **cast them forth** is that used in 4:3—with the silence of despair brooding over the scene.

B. Present Iniquity and Impending Doom (8:4-14)

A series of statements which in part echoes oracles transmitted in chs. 1–6. It would appear that some sayings of Amos were handed down in another stream of tradition, and fragments of these are now embedded in material which related them to the conditions and outlook of a later day.

1. Oppression of the Poor (8:4-7)

The oppression of the poor is denounced in language reminiscent of Amos' indictment of Israel in 2:6-8. **Trample** (vs. 4) is the verb used in 2:7; **the needy for a pair of shoes** (vs. 7) occurs in 2:6. But those who are now denounced are members of a trading community, and it is in particular the greed and dishonesty of merchants who will stop at nothing in their haste to make money that is here associated with the brutal illtreatment of the weak and helpless.

4. And bring the poor . . . : Lit., "And are for exterminating the poor." Since the construction is unusual, some commentators would prefer the LXX reading, "and oppress the poor," although it demands a radical change in the Hebrew text, העשקות for ולישבית.

"For three transgressions, and for four." The effect is one with the tolling of a bell to signalize the decline and death of a nation. In ch. 4 a more plaintive note is five times sounded, " 'yet you did not return to me,' says the Lord"— each time in response to a statement reminiscent of God's antecedent warning to Israel that her apostasy was wearing his forbearance thin. In the last section of the book occurs the twice repeated phrase, "This also shall not be" (7:3, 6), suggesting a divine reprieve, only to be followed by the reiterated death sentence, "I will never again pass by them" (7:8). "There's a wideness in God's mercy," as the familiar hymn [3] declares, but even as the sea has its limits, so also has the patience of God. Amos' skillful use of the art of repetition, never too much or too often, bespeaks our confidence that the messages are his own and follow a thought pattern construed from his steady pondering of the mind and purpose of God. Like Abraham Lincoln, without benefit of formal education he drew from the breast of nature a sense of her rhythm. When these two come to speak or to write, their style and man-

ner reflect an intimacy with the orbits of stars and the progress of seasons. The conjunction of their powers of outward observation and their profound capacity for inner reflection gives to the speech of both Amos and Lincoln a clarity and cadence as rare as it is impressive to all of us who read.

4-8. *Beyond Humanism.*—The claim often put forward in modern times that Amos represents the earliest and most articulate champion of social justice is amply verified in this particular passage. Earlier in his prophecies he has excoriated the cupidity of Israel's merchant class, who "sell the righteous for silver, and the needy for a pair of shoes" (2:6), "who oppress the poor, who crush the needy" (4:1), who "trample upon the poor and take from him exactions of wheat" (5:11). Here he returns to this theme, spelling out the corrupt practices of the grain tycoons in league with the temple bankers, who tamper with such basic factors in the nation's domestic economy as the standards of weights and measures and the valuation of currency. In doing so he is not taking a new line. In the earlier codes, consonant with the covenant, provisions were made for safeguarding

[3] Frederick W. Faber.

5 Saying, When will the new moon be gone, that we may sell corn? and the sabbath, that we may set forth wheat, making the ephah small, and the shekel great, and falsifying the balances by deceit?

6 That we may buy the poor for silver, and the needy for a pair of shoes; *yea, and* sell the refuse of the wheat?

7 The LORD hath sworn by the excellency of Jacob, Surely I will never forget any of their works.

5 saying, "When will the new moon be over,
　　that we may sell grain?
And the sabbath,
　　that we may offer wheat for sale,
that we may make the ephah small and
　　the shekel great,
　　and deal deceitfully with false balances,
6 that we may buy the poor for silver
　　and the needy for a pair of sandals,
　　and sell the refuse of the wheat?"
7 The LORD has sworn by the pride of
　　Jacob:
"Surely I will never forget any of their
　　deeds.

5. New moon and . . . the sabbath: As II Kings 4:23; Hos. 2:11 (Hebrew vs. 13); Isa. 1:13 indicate, both these were not only days of religious observance but popular holidays when ordinary occupations would be laid aside, days which no doubt were especially prized by working people while the merchants chafed at the interruption of the inflow of their profits. More than that, these men practiced every kind of dishonesty. They cut down the size of **the ephah,** the measure by which they sold, and made heavier **the shekel,** the weight used for measuring the money paid in by the purchasers (cf. Gen. 23:16), thus dealing **deceitfully with false balances** (cf. Deut. 25:13-15). Obviously this account of their business is not what the merchants say of themselves but is the author's description of their procedure. The looseness of the construction is not in the style of Amos, and in part results from the blending of the phraseology of the prophet with the later denunciation.

6. That we may buy the poor . . . differs from 2:6 only in speaking of buying instead of selling. With their ready money these dishonest traders could take every advantage of the bargains in human lives furnished by the situation of distressed debtors, and while they buy slaves for a paltry sum, what they sell for a price is often only **refuse of the wheat.**

7. The LORD has sworn by the pride of Jacob: In 6:8 the Lord swears by himself; in 4:2 by his holiness. Hence some commentators take **the pride of Jacob** as a synonym

the rights of the poor and needy. These humane elements were included and expanded in the Deuteronomic legislation that was enacted subsequent to Amos. Furthermore, there were prophets both before and after him who championed the cause of the impoverished little people of Israel against the ruthless arrogance and aggrandizement of their rich compatriots. Already the unique contribution of the Hebrews to the ethical store of the human race, in terms of the two great commandments enjoining the love of God and the respect for the worth and dignity of the individual, was in process of development. But it was the genius of Amos to accelerate this beneficent growth with his stern insistence upon the radical union of ethics and religion, issuing in his polemics against king and court who based foreign policy upon a "massive retaliation" of military power, against a priest-

hood that elaborated an opulent cultus of ritual and sacrifice in lieu of the true worship of God in terms of right conduct and behavior, and in the passage before us against the custodians of the nation's wealth and resources, against the insidious forms of selfish cupidity to which the rich are ever exposed. Here is one of the earliest variations on a theme given later expression by the poet Goldsmith, in "The Deserted Village,"

Ill fares the land, to hastening ills a prey,
Where wealth accumulates and men decay.

But the accompaniment of a bland humanism to which the poet sets his motif bears little or no resemblance to the dominant chords of a massive theodicy with which Amos sounds the awful note, "God is about to destroy his people for their sins."

8 Shall not the land tremble for this, and every one mourn that dwelleth therein? and it shall rise up wholly as a flood; and it shall be cast out and drowned, as *by* the flood of Egypt.

8 Shall not the land tremble on this account,
and every one mourn who dwells in it,
and all of it rise like the Nile,
and be tossed about and sink again,
like the Nile of Egypt?"

---

of Yahweh himself. In that case **excellency** (KJV) would be a better translation (see Exeg. on 6:8 on the twofold meaning of the word). There would then be ironical reference to the privileged relationship to Yahweh of which 3:2 had spoken. Less probable is the suggestion of other commentators that **pride** taken in the sense of arrogant self-esteem is here regarded as so ingrained and unalterable an element in Israel's character as to constitute that by which an oath could be taken. **Surely I will never forget any of their deeds:** The LXX has "your deeds," which in view of the direct address of **Hear this** (vs. 4) would appear to be the better reading. The threat has its own forcefulness and is in the spirit of Amos' profound insistence on the tremendous fact of the unfaltering scrutiny of the divine righteousness to which human conduct is continually subject. It is, however, unlike the announcement of specific disaster which is characteristic of the oracles of Amos. This and the implied difference in background suggest that a later teacher was applying the prophet's message to the conditions of his own day.

2. Earthquake, Darkness, and Mourning (8:8-10)

8. On this account links rather loosely the denunciation of the greed and dishonesty of the merchants and their devastating effect upon the poor and needy with the threat of earthquake. The land is represented as shuddering at the evil that men do, while everywhere the sound of lamentation is heard. **And all of it rise . . .** is reproduced almost verbatim in 9:5, where the text is better preserved. Along with that passage the RSV rightly reads **like the Nile** in place of the KJV's **as a flood,** and **and sink again** in place of **and drowned.** Also with 9:5 and with the LXX, **and be tossed about** (RSV) should be omitted. The earthquake is described hyperbolically in terms of the inundation of Egypt by the Nile. It is true that the gradual rise and fall of that river have not the suddenness and rapidity of earthquake shock, but the point of comparison is massive and irresistible movement.

Since in 9:5 this description of an earthquake is used in connection with the description of the divine activity on a cosmic scale in 9:6, it is possible that here too there is

---

The prophet gives no comfort to modern conceptions of religion that are marked by a cleavage between ethics and theology. Of this lamentable separation has come, in the contemporary scene, much of the impotence of the church to challenge, let alone to correct, the two great social evils that infest our own times—poverty and war. There are people in the pews who resent the intrusion of the world's ills into the seemly order of corporate worship on a Sunday morning. There are preachers in the pulpit who are reluctant to threaten the institutional fabric of church and synagogue by invoking, except on rare occasions, the disturbing aspects of the prophecies of Amos or the even more shocking qualities inherent in the teachings of Jesus. Ecclesiastical institutions by reason of their present size and intricacy have taken on the protective characteristics of their social environment. So-

ciety which represents the main body of public custom and opinion is notoriously harsh in its treatment of individual members who advance too far ahead of its main body or who lag too far behind—its prophets and its thieves. In ecclesiastical organizations the way of the reformer and the heretic is proverbially hard. On the basis of mere survival there is support for the conservative ideologies with which society is informed. But in essence the Judeo-Christian elements in our culture compose, not a human ideology calculated to maintain a social equilibrium, but a theology that is designed to up-end our human achievements and pretensions into a new accord with "the pattern showed to thee in the mount" (Heb. 8:5*b*).

This whole passage with its reference to Moses is equally relevant to Amos and to Jesus; in fact, to prophetic persons throughout history

9 And it shall come to pass in that day, saith the Lord GOD, that I will cause the sun to go down at noon, and I will darken the earth in the clear day:

10 And I will turn your feasts into mourning, and all your songs into lamentation; and I will bring up sackcloth upon all loins, and baldness upon every head; and I will make it as the mourning of an only *son*, and the end thereof as a bitter day.

9 "And on that day," says the Lord GOD,
　　"I will make the sun go down at noon,
　　and darken the earth in broad daylight.
10 I will turn your feasts into mourning,
　　and all your songs into lamentation;
　I will bring sackcloth upon all loins,
　　and baldness on every head;
　I will make it like the mourning for an
　　only son,
　　and the end of it like a bitter day.

---

the idea of an earthquake of far-reaching effect as one of the woes accompanying the great day of final judgment, about which so much of the apocalyptic thought of a later day entered. In that case *hā'āreç*, **the land**, should be rendered "the earth," as in vs. 9. It is the whole world that is to tremble.

9-10. These verses look in the direction of this interpretation, for the text goes on to speak of a further wonder that **shall come to pass in that day**, an untimely disappearance of the sun plunging the earth in darkness. It is in this setting of unnatural night that everywhere the voice of lamentation is to be heard. Amos' oracle of 5:16-17 had spoken of deep mourning that was to prevail throughout the nation, and in another oracle (5:18, 20), of the day of the Lord as darkness, not light. The judgment upon Israel is now regarded as part of the ultimate manifestation of God's righteous power in the judgment of his world.

I will turn your feasts—festival pilgrimages—**into mourning . . . :** The use of the second person in direct address in the more generalizing context suggests an actual quotation of Amos in the form in which the oracle had come down to the editor. **I will bring sackcloth upon all loins . . .** strikes again the note of universal grief following upon world-wide calamity. The wearing of coarse sackcloth was a customary way of mourning for the dead (cf. II Sam. 3:31), as also the shaving of the forepart of the head to produce artificial baldness. This last, though forbidden in Israel in Deut. 14:1, was a widespread custom among many peoples (cf. Jer. 48:37; Ezek. 27:31). **Mourning for an**

---

whom God has used as levers in the slow but inevitable elevation of his rule into the concern of men. Paul caught the meaning of Jesus' homely references to his disciples as "salt" and "leaven" and "light" in his magnificent charge to a new fellowship, the Christian church, set to do business in an old order of secular affairs, "Be not conformed to this world: but be ye transformed by the renewing of your mind, that ye may prove what is that good, and acceptable, and perfect will of God" (Rom. 12:2). Sometimes in his professional prudence of speech the preacher is transferring his own cautions and fears to his people. There is a word of William Blake's that is appropriate. "Truth can never be told so as to be understood, and not be believ'd." [4] The poet's dictum is reminiscent of the apostle's words about "speaking the truth in love" (Eph. 4:15). There is a "remnant" group in every congregation that is ready to be divinely disturbed of a Sunday

[4] "Proverbs of Hell" from *The Marriage of Heaven & Hell.*

morning, not by the preacher's expression of personal opinions about sex or politics, but by his humble and faithful statement of the great realities of the Christian religion, based upon a theology that posits all our human concerns as so many integral parts of the divine encounter between God and man. The book of Amos is a case in point. The very survival of these divinely disturbing prophecies is a testimony to the existence in Israel of some who heard the prophet's words with solemn attention, and made it their business to transmit them to those who should come after.

9-12. *The Famine of Hearing.*—Following another dark prediction about the anticipated "day of the LORD," in which the prophet disavows completely the popular anticipations that were long attached to this expected theophany, Amos employs another vivid figure of speech to impress the judgments of God upon Israel. Famine was one of the common scourges of the ancient world and is not uncommon today in parts of the globe. From the Joseph saga in

11 ¶ Behold, the days come, saith the Lord GOD, that I will send a famine in the land, not a famine of bread, nor a thirst for water, but of hearing the words of the LORD:

12 And they shall wander from sea to sea, and from the north even to the east, they shall run to and fro to seek the word of the LORD, and shall not find *it*.

13 In that day shall the fair virgins and young men faint for thirst.

11 "Behold, the days are coming," says the Lord GOD,
"when I will send a famine on the land;
not a famine of bread, nor a thirst for water,
but of hearing the words of the LORD.

12 They shall wander from sea to sea,
and from north to east;
they shall run to and fro, to seek the word of the LORD,
but they shall not find it.

13 "In that day the fair virgins and the young men
shall faint for thirst.

only son is described in Jer. 6:26 as "most bitter lamentation," and the closing **I will make . . . the end of it like a bitter day** invests the whole scene with a drear finality.

3. FAMINE AND THIRST (8:11-14)

11-12. The opening clauses, **Behold, the days, . . . says the Lord GOD,** introduce another and separate saying. Commentators, noting that vs. 11*a*, **I will send a famine on the land,** in itself may be taken literally, and that vs. 13 goes on to speak of physical thirst, have tried to distinguish between an authentic utterance of Amos and the later adaptation of that saying. So they would regard vs. 11*b*, **Not a famine of bread . . . ,** and in vs. 12*b*, **To seek the word . . . ,** as additions by another hand (cf. Cripps, *Amos*, pp. 250-51). But as noted below, vss. 13-14 constitute a separate saying, and in vs. 12*a* the phrase **from sea to sea,** though it could conceivably mean from the Mediterranean to the Dead Sea, elsewhere certainly has the meaning "from one end of the world to another" (Zech. 9:10; Ps. 72:8), the earth being thought of as surrounded by water. The vision is therefore again one of world judgment, not simply of the judgment upon Israel of which Amos spoke. Apparently a later teacher, basing upon the tradition that Amos had named famine and drought as ways in which God had visited his people, developed this into a prediction of spiritual famine and drought as part of God's judgment upon mankind. **On the land** (vs. 11) might therefore better be rendered "on the earth." The writer had taken to heart the truth that "man does not live by bread alone" (Deut. 8:3). In the face of God's silence men would realize their desperate need.

13. There is uncertainty on the part of commentators as to whether this is to be taken with vss. 11-12 or with vs. 14. However, the phrase **In that day,** the day of the Lord, points to a new beginning. The word **virgins** and the clause in vs. 14, **They shall fall, and never rise again,** coming together are reminiscent of the language of 5:2. **Young**

Genesis to the apocalyptic visions in the Revelation, the Bible is replete with references to famine and its concomitants of terror and death. Amos, as a dweller on the precarious soil of Tekoa, knew from his own experience the bitter results of a season of bad weather, in terms of ruined crops and hungry people. To his sinister list of God's retributive acts against Israel—foreign invasion, earthquakes, drought, and flood—Amos adds the terrible menace of famine.

But with an adroitness of mind which we have earlier marked, he invests his words with imaginative dimensions.

"Not a famine of bread, nor a thirst for water, but of hearing the words of the LORD."

To the hard, obdurate hearts of his people, God will no more communicate his words, either of mercy or of judgment. The land that once protested a surfeit of divine directives, issued through the mouth of God's spokesman,

14 They that swear by the sin of Samaria, and say, Thy god, O Dan, liveth; and, The manner of Beer-sheba liveth; even they shall fall, and never rise up again.

14 Those who swear by Ash′imah of Samar′ia,
and say, 'As thy god lives, O Dan,'
and, 'As the way of Beer-sheba lives,'
they shall fall, and never rise again.''

---

men are named as suffering because special poignancy attached to their exposure to the severity of God's judgment, and perhaps because in their quest for novelty they were particularly addicted to the idolatrous worship named in vs. 14.

14. This is a verse of obscure meaning. The rendering **Ashimah** is now quite generally accepted, for it involves a change only in the vowel pointing, *'ashîmāh* for *'ashmāh*, "guilt." Ashimah is not only referred to in II Kings 17:30 as worshiped by the men of Hamath, but the name also occurs in the compound Ashem-Bethel in the Elephantine papyri of the fifth to the fourth century B.C. as the name of a god recognized in the Jewish colony on the Egyptian frontier (cf. *ibid.*, pp. 316-17) .

As the way of Beer-sheba lives: Commentators adduce as a parallel the oath that Moslems take by the pilgrim way to Mecca; but in view of the reference to a god in the preceding clause, there is much to be said for the reading adopted by some scholars, "As thy patron deity lives, O Beer-sheba." As far as the consonants are concerned, this involves only the change of one letter, דֹּד for דֶּרֶךְ, and it is supported by the LXX, "thy god." The denunciation of idolatrous worship which became widely prevalent after the collapse of the national life makes it probable that the passage belongs to a time subsequent to that of Amos. It offers another instance of the adaptation of the prophet's message to the conditions of a later day.

---

will have no more. The people of Israel shall suffer a very panic of remorse as the results of this spiritual dearth take hold of them. Like starving men and women they shall frantically attempt to supply their felt needs, to discover new manna from heaven:

"They shall run to and fro, to seek the word of the LORD,
but they shall not find it."

God's forbearance, already frayed, is now finally broken. In an earlier period, when the covenant was forgotten and God's commandments flouted, it is recorded by the commentator that "the word of the LORD was precious in those days; there was no open vision" (I Sam. 3:1). But this partial eclipse of God's providence was in the childhood period of Israel's divine discipline. In Amos' time, and because of a full-grown nation's deliberate refusal to see or to hear God's revelation of his will, there would be a complete blackout of God's self-manifestation in vision, a vast heart hunger, caused by a total cessation of God's bounty.

In his novel, *Contarini Fleming*, Benjamin Disraeli puts a mordant phrase upon the lips of one of his characters. It is the retort of a cynical old statesman to his ardent son, who is eager to get away from words to ideas. "Few ideas are correct ones," declares the father, "and what are correct no one can ascertain; but with words we govern men." [5] It is sometimes the sad fate of religion and its popular expression to fall into the same plight as statecraft. Words come to have an independent existence, like chessmen removed from the board. It is not so much that their intrinsic meaning tends to be debased as that they are often detached from their primary function as pointers of thoughts and ideas. Preachers who must employ words in their professional pursuits may well learn from the Hebrew prophets their sacramental use. Of this sanctity of language Amos is one of the best exemplars. He "saw" his words "concerning Israel" (1:1) . To him they were not mere counters of speech but windows of insight opening upon the eternal acts of God. His grouping of them in figures of speech was born not of idle fancy but of his desire to show his hearers the constellations of God's judgments in the overarching heaven of his power. In the present passage **the words of the LORD** represent the prophet's direct vision of the deeds of God toward his people. That so often the divine judgment was revealed to the apparent exclusion of divine mercy may bespeak the limits of Amos' perception but surely not of God's nature. The prophet's reverent use of the gift of speech to transmit what he saw and what he heard in seasons of profound communion is

[5] Part I, ch. xxi.

9 I saw the Lord standing upon the altar: and he said, Smite the lintel of the door, that the posts may shake: and cut them in the head, all of them; and I will slay the last of them with the sword: he that fleeth of them shall not flee away, and he that escapeth of them shall not be delivered.

9 I saw the LORD standing beside[u] the altar, and he said:
"Smite the capitals until the thresholds shake,
and shatter them on the heads of all the people;[v]
and what are left of them I will slay with the sword;
not one of them shall flee away,
not one of them shall escape.

[u] Or *upon*
[v] Heb *all of them*

C. The Finality of Doom (9:1-7)
1. A Fifth Vision and Its Sequel (9:1-4)

A fifth vision (vs. 1*a*) followed by a poem (vss. 1*b*-4) which depicts the impossibility of escape from the destruction that is to come.

9:1*a*. The sudden demolition of a sanctuary with the consequent death of the worshipers. It is generally assumed that this sanctuary was the one at Bethel, because it is certain that there Amos exercised part of his ministry (7:13). Then, too, the oracle of 3:14 speaks specifically of Bethel as the scene of such a disaster. **I saw the LORD:** Not as in the case of the four other visions, "The Lord GOD caused me to see." Nor does this vision name a specific object in which Amos had come to feel disturbing significance. Attention simply fastened on what the Lord was doing. To be sure, in the present text the Lord is represented as **standing beside the altar** and giving a command, **Smite . . . ;** but the person addressed is not specified and the sentence that follows, **I will slay . . . ,** speaks of God's own activity. It has therefore been proposed (Marti, *Dodekapropheton,* p. 221; Weiser, *Profetie des Amos,* pp. 42-43) to read in place of the imperatives **smite** and **shatter them** the simple statements, "And he smote" and "I will shatter," transferring **and he said** to the position immediately preceding the second of these statements. The verb rendered **shatter,** *bāṣa',* is not found elsewhere in this sense. In Job 27:8 it means "cut off," "make an end of," and that would seem to be its meaning here. But the phrase **on the heads** is difficult. A very slight change, ברעש instead of בראש, would give "by an earthquake." The passage would then read, "And he smote the capitals"—at the top of the columns holding up the roof of the structure—"and the thresholds shook"—the whole building swaying with the shock—"and he said, 'By an earthquake do I make an end of them all.'" The changes that produced the present text would be due to the desire of scribes to mitigate what they felt to be too anthropomorphic an account of the divine activity. However that may be, it is an earthquake of terrible severity that is here regarded as one of the ways in which God will visit his people, and this is followed by a depiction of the finality of the doom that is to overtake the people as a whole, **And what are left of them. . . .** Devastating war is to complete the extinction of the nation.

1*b*. Not one of them . . . , with its insistence on the impossibility of escape, distinctly echoes the thought of 2:14-15; but in the present context the development of the theme

what gives his readers a timeless sense of his wisdom, a wisdom that now belongs to the ages.

9:1-4. The Vision of God.—The O.T. is replete with descriptions of theophanies, occasions in which God manifests himself to an individual or to a particular company of people. Examples will immediately come to mind without specific references. All such phenomena remind us of one aspect of the "many-splendored thing" that we call religion, namely, that its primary inten-

tion is not discovered by believing or doing but by seeing. Isaiah "saw . . . the Lord sitting upon a throne, high and lifted up, and his train filled the temple" (Isa. 6:1), and the result of this holy sight was his acceptance of the arduous career of a prophet. Paul first saw the vision splendid on the Damascus road; then came his response, "Lord, what wilt thou have me to do?" (Acts 9:6). William Booth was first arrested by the presence of God in the flagstoned streets

2 Though they dig into hell, thence shall mine hand take them; though they climb up to heaven, thence will I bring them down:

3 And though they hide themselves in the top of Carmel, I will search and take them out thence; and though they be hid from my sight in the bottom of the sea, thence will I command the serpent, and he shall bite them:

4 And though they go into captivity before their enemies, thence will I command the sword, and it shall slay them: and I will set mine eyes upon them for evil, and not for good.

2 "Though they dig into Sheol,
  from there shall my hand take them;
though they climb up to heaven,
  from there I will bring them down.
3 Though they hide themselves on the top
    of Carmel,
  from there I will search out and take
    them;
and though they hide from my sight at
    the bottom of the sea,
  there I will command the serpent, and
    it shall bite them.
4 And though they go into captivity before
    their enemies,
  there I will command the sword, and
    it shall slay them;
and I will set my eyes upon them
  for evil and not for good."

that follows in vss. 2-4 is quite different. In the earlier passage it is the confused rout of actual warfare that is depicted, with that sense of a concrete situation which characterizes Amos' utterances generally; in vss. 2-4 there is a more deliberately arranged picturing of the futility of any effort to escape, while the actual sense of conflict fades into the background. The oracle is, however, true to Amos' thought, both in its pronouncement of the inevitability of doom and in its awareness of the unlimited range of Yahweh's power.

2. Though in their frenzied flight **they dig into Sheol**—the subterranean world in which the dead carried on a ghostly existence—or **climb up to heaven,** they are always within the menacing reach of the divine grasp.

3. If they seek out a hiding place in the forests and caves on the lofty slopes of Carmel, they cannot escape the divine scrutiny. Even **at the bottom of the sea** they will be subject to the deadly attack of the mythical monster that dwells there obedient to Yahweh's command. These verses with their graphic description of the omnipresence of the divine activity have their later counterpart in Ps. 139, where the note of awed wonder is struck, instead of the fearful realization of impending punishment as in this passage.

4. Not even captivity in a foreign land, which in popular thought might be outside Yahweh's jurisdiction, could exempt them from the pursuing judgment of God—a declaration which would have its particular pertinence at a time when, the blow having fallen

of Nottingham, and then set about the establishment of the Salvation Army. So Amos in the passage before us saw the LORD standing beside the altar, and though the episode comes late in the present text of the book, it should be understood as one of the prophet's rare but impressive references to his initial vocation and seminal to the whole course and content of his prophetic mission. Here is the key that opens the door to our understanding of Amos' public utterances from first to last. His awful conviction of the sovereignty of God, revealed alike in nature and history, is the theme which he felt impelled to elaborate. He saw this majestic truth emblazoned in the sun and moon and the "stars in their courses" (Judg. 5:20). He saw it most starkly displayed in the religious apostasy and moral corruption of his own people. Here was

human rebellion against the most high God that could only lead to human destruction by a series of terrible events in store for both Israel and Judah. "Sinners in the Hands of an Angry God" was a theme ready made for Jonathan Edwards, out of the prophecies of Amos.

What certainty is there that our vaunted civilization is in any better condition Godward than was Israel of old? At the impulse of science and technology, no less than of philosophical rationalism and humanism, we too tend to substitute the sovereignty of man for the rule of God. On occasion Cassandras abound, but in general Coué much more abounds. In any case, these are but human voices, whether for ill or good, and not to be confused with the accents of God, who no more today than in the time of Amos can brook the impairment of his

5 And the Lord God of hosts *is* he that toucheth the land, and it shall melt, and all that dwell therein shall mourn: and it shall rise up wholly like a flood; and shall be drowned, as *by* the flood of Egypt.

6 *It is* he that buildeth his stories in the heaven, and hath founded his troop in the earth; he that calleth for the waters of the sea, and poureth them out upon the face of the earth: The Lord *is* his name.

5 The Lord God of hosts,
  he who touches the earth and it melts,
    and all who dwell in it mourn,
  and all of it rises like the Nile,
    and sinks again, like the Nile of Egypt;
6 who builds his upper chambers in the heavens,
  and founds his vault upon the earth;
who calls for the waters of the sea,
  and pours them out upon the surface
    of the earth —
the Lord is his name.

and the Exile having become an actual experience, there would be many who assumed that they were no longer subject to the divine visitation. Vs. 4*b* brings the poem to a simple but effective climax. **I will set my eyes upon them . . . ,** an expression used elsewhere of watchful care (Jer. 39:12), now carries with it the threat of continued disaster that God's close concern with his people will bring upon them.

2. A Third Doxology (9:5-6)

A third doxology in which, as in the other two (4:13; 5:8-9), it is primarily the transcendent majesty of God as creator and ruler in the world of nature that is set forth, reminding readers that the power of which Amos had spoken as revealed in righteous judgment in the course of human affairs is one with the elemental energy that is manifest in the natural order.

5. This verse, partially repeating 8:8, was perhaps made part of the doxology by an interpolator in order to link it with the book. In 8:8 the earthquake is regarded as punitive; in this context it is simply one instance of Yahweh's sublime power.

6. The **upper chambers in the heaven** rise above the **vault** of the sky, the ends of which rest solidly upon the earth. The picture of the vast structure of the heavens and the earth is that of Gen. 1:6-8, though the word here translated **vault,** *'aghuddāh,* is not the one there used for "firmament." Its root meaning is "bind together"—hence the KJV's **troop** (cf. II Sam. 2:25). The arch of the sky is thus thought of as fitted together or constructed.

sovereignty by the pride of men. The realization of how hard this doctrine is to believe, let alone to declare, should give us more respect for Amos and for the courage born of a great conviction neither then nor now popularly acceptable.

There follows another graphic picture of the doom which is about to descend upon the sinful nation. The cities are like huge anthills overturned. In every direction frantic attempts are made to escape, to the hills, even to **the bottom of the sea.** But there is no hiding place in heaven or hell when the sovereign God decrees the time to be at hand for the exercise of his power. We are used to what is quaintly called "civilian defense" against the uncivilized and brutal explosions of man-made wars, still limited in their scope and impact. Amos has already provided some future reporter, lucky enough to survive a shower of atom and hydrogen bombs, with a grim script depicting the con-

sequent human destruction and panic in New York or Moscow.

5-7. It Cannot Happen Here.—The doxology with which this passage opens, doubtless inserted by another than Amos, celebrating God's sovereignty over nature, is followed by a final invocation of the sovereignty of God in vs. 7 that deserves special comment. Amos has signalized the omnipotent power of God in both nature and history, and in terms as terrible as they are comprehensive. Now in a flash of insight he sees God focusing his whole attention upon the particular pride and folly of a people "who say, 'Evil shall not overtake or meet us'" (vs. 10*b*). Such a hollow hope was, in part, the result of Israel's persistent belief in her preferred position of privilege in the sight of God. The memory of God's deliverance of his people from servitude in Egypt, and their consequent gratitude, is one of the most continuous and moving themes in the O.T. But it was early

7 *Are* ye not as children of the Ethiopians unto me, O children of Israel? saith the LORD. Have not I brought up Israel out of the land of Egypt? and the Philistines from Caphtor, and the Syrians from Kir?

7 "Are you not like the Ethiopians to me,
   O people of Israel?" says the LORD.
"Did I not bring up Israel from the land of Egypt,
   and the Philistines from Caphtor and the Syrians from Kir?

3. GOD'S RELATIONSHIP TO OTHER PEOPLES (9:7)

7. Questions which boldly challenge Israel's conviction that she stood in a privileged relationship to God. The formula, **says the LORD,** again suggests that this saying had independent currency for some time before its incorporation in the book. It appears to have once been the answer to the contention that the favored treatment Israel had received at God's hands in the past made it inconceivable that he would make an end of the nation.

Are you not like the Ethiopians to me? This may be simply saying that because of Israel's sin the intimate relationship to God has been dissolved, and Israel is no more to Yahweh than the far-off Ethiopians inhabiting the region in the Nile Valley south of Syene. It is sometimes also said that because of their dark skin these were a people held in contempt, and Jer. 13:23 is quoted in support of this (cf. Driver, *Joel and Amos,* p. 224). But that passage no more implies disdain for the Ethiopian's skin than it does for the leopard's spots, and in Isa. 18:1-2 the Ethiopians are regarded with something akin to admiration. It would seem probable therefore that the question **Are you not . . .** has not simply a negative intention but enunciates a positive truth. Yahweh is Lord of the whole of human history and all peoples are equal in his sight. At any rate, such positive intention is clearly indicated in the following question, **Did I not bring up . . . ?** The deliverance from Egypt, followed by the entrance into Canaan, was regarded as a signal expression of divine favor, but Yahweh had likewise brought the Philistines into Canaan **from Caphtor**—generally identified with Crete, perhaps the southern coast of Asia Minor—and **the Syrians from Kir,** their home in the distant northeast. With the Philistines Israel had had to contest possession of the land, and for more than a century found it hard to defend her borders against Syrian invasion. But these peoples too had been the objects of the divine interest and their movements directed by God's sovereign will. The universalism thus enunciated, the denial to any one people of an exclusive relationship to God, the equality of them all in his sight, is no mere impartial unconcern with the course of human history but an actual positive control of the destinies of them all. It is a universalism that had learned from the particularism of the past, Israel's sense of all that its unique relationship to God had meant for its history, its realization of the intimacy of his loving care. In the declaration that other peoples too had been guided of God the ground was laid for the belief that the distinctive endowment and history of every people were in like measure bound up with its particular relationship to the one God.

and often corrupted by the human propensity, not yet abated, to exploit a sovereign act of God until it becomes a man's or a nation's selfish assumption of manifest destiny. "My power and the might of mine hand hath gotten me this wealth" (Deut. 8:17). There is a very real sense in which national pride of place is indicative not so much of political ineptitude as of a profound spiritual emptiness. Into such a vacuum flow the demonic corruptions of political power that marked the final course of the kingdoms of Israel and Judah. Into such a vacuum flow policies of isolation and segregation, springing

from dark unconscious fears that can only produce the ugly results of chauvinism and racism.

"Are you not like the Ethiopians to me,
   O people of Israel?" says the LORD.
"Did I not bring up Israel from the land of Egypt,
   and the Philistines from Caphtor and the Syrians from Kir?" (Vs. 7.)

For "Israel" read "the United States" and for "Philistines" and "Syrians" read "Russians" and "Chinese" to get the full implications of Amos' conviction of the sovereignty of God, without limit in time or space.

8 Behold, the eyes of the Lord God *are* upon the sinful kingdom, and I will destroy it from off the face of the earth; saving that I will not utterly destroy the house of Jacob, saith the Lord.

8 Behold, the eyes of the Lord God are
　　upon the sinful kingdom,
　and I will destroy it from the surface
　　of the ground;
　except that I will not utterly destroy
　　the house of Jacob,"
　　　　　　　　　　　　　says the Lord.

This aspect of God's lordship over the whole of human history was indeed implicit elsewhere in the oracles of Amos. Assyria was an instrument of the divine visitation upon Israel, as also upon Syria, Ammon, and Moab. Even in 3:2 God's choice of Israel from all the families of the earth had all the peoples of the world in view. But in none of this is there any suggestion of the divine concern for the welfare of these peoples. It must be admitted too that the general tenor of Amos' utterances centered upon the uniqueness of the intimacy of God's concern for Israel. The "you only have I known" of 3:2, and the "my people" of the dread announcement in 8:2 that the end had come, alike witness to the special significance in Amos' thought of God's choice of Israel. It is argued rightly that Israel's transgressions had rendered inevitable the dissolution of this relationship, and commentators therefore insist that in vs. 7 there is nothing inconsistent with Amos' other utterances. It should be noted, however, that the verse taken as a whole speaks of more than the severance of the bond between Yahweh and Israel; it declares that God had stood and could stand in the same relationship to other peoples as that in which he had stood to Israel. This does not seem to be in accord with Amos' prevailing feeling for the uniqueness of the relationship between Yahweh and his people, a feeling which had no small part in investing his ministry with its heartbreaking urgency. There is the fact too that the position of the saying—the book at one stage in its development perhaps ended with this verse—suggests that it was late in finding a place in the collection of Amos' oracles. It is therefore at least possible that the passage comes from someone who had taken to heart Amos' teaching about God's sovereign control of human history, and so was enabled to draw out the further implications of that teaching and to set forth the conviction that in the fulfillment of his purpose God could and did enter into positive and constructive relation with other peoples in such a way that, whatever might befall Israel, his work would go forward in the world.

D. An Epilogue (9:8-15)

An addition to the book, in which Amos' teaching about God as Lord of history and nature is made the ground of hope for the future.

1. A Purging Judgment (9:8-10)

8-10. Vs. 8a, **Behold, the eyes . . . face of the earth,** repeats the substance of Amos' prediction of the destruction of the nation. With the fall of Samaria in 722 B.C. and that of Jerusalem in 586 B.C., Israel had indeed ceased to exist as a kingdom. This had been as Amos had foretold, the work of none other than Yahweh himself. Therein lay the

---

8-15. Epilogue.—To one without either skill or experience in biblical criticism this passage may well appear on the face of it as an addition. There is evident a complete change of climate from storm to fair weather. Earlier prophecies of unmitigated doom and destruction suddenly give way to an eloquent declaration of God's purpose to reclaim and to **restore the fortunes of my people Israel** (vs. 14). Towns and cities that have been ravaged by the scourge of invasion will be repaired and rebuilt.

Fields and vineyards will be invested with a fertility hitherto unrealized and will yield crops and fruits of unprecedented richness. Best of all, the dwellers in town and country will live and labor in the assurance of stability and permanence, and this from the mouth of none other than **the Lord your God** (vs. 16b). He who promised death and destruction in the main body of the book decrees for his people a renewal of life and prosperity at its close. To God's judgment is added God's forgiveness, and

9 For, lo, I will command, and I will sift the house of Israel among all nations, like as *corn* is sifted in a sieve, yet shall not the least grain fall upon the earth.

10 All the sinners of my people shall die by the sword, which say, The evil shall not overtake nor prevent us.

11 ¶ In that day will I raise up the tabernacle of David that is fallen, and close up the breaches thereof; and I will raise up his ruins, and I will build it as in the days of old:

9 "For lo, I will command,
     and shake the house of Israel among
         all the nations
   as one shakes with a sieve,
     but no pebble shall fall upon the earth.
10 All the sinners of my people shall die by
     the sword,
   who say, 'Evil shall not overtake or
     meet us.'

11 "In that day I will raise up
     the booth of David that is fallen
   and repair its breaches,
     and raise up its ruins,
     and rebuild it as in the days of old;

guarantee that the condition in which the **house of Jacob** found itself scattered in every direction was God's will for his people. He would **not utterly destroy.** Rather, God would toss them about—so the Hebrew word might be rendered, as tossing about is done in a **sieve**—and the result would be that **no pebble shall fall upon the earth.** Faithful servants of God would be preserved from destruction. It was no longer a nation taken as a whole that was in question. The individual was taken into account and a distinction drawn between the evil and the good. This interpretation is borne out by the following verse, which evidently has this distinction in mind with its note of solemn warning that the day of judgment for the evildoer is not, as might be too hastily assumed, a thing of the past.

10. All the sinners . . . : Violent death awaits the sinners who, having escaped so far, in self-sufficient pride go on to say, **Evil shall not overtake or meet us.**

2. Restoration of the Davidic Kingdom (9:11-12)

11. In that day is a phrase which has no immediate connection with the preceding verse and introduces yet another oracle which had had independent currency. The day is still the time of God's special manifestation of power, the day of the Lord, of which Amos had spoken as a day of "darkness, and not light[,] even very dark with no brightness in it" (5:20). But there speaks through this passage not the voice of the prophet who, finding in a people's hopes and aspirations an arrogant self-centeredness which would regard the power of God himself as that which would serve their ends, had unequivocally proclaimed the coming of a dreadful disillusionment. On the contrary, there speaks here the voice of one who identified himself with a people's hope for the future. Deep in

his wrath is ultimately consumed by his love. The whole passage is replete with a divine tolerance that is given pre-exilic expression by Amos' successor, Isaiah, in his doctrine of the righteous remnant within Israel, and, during the subsequent period of national exile in Babylon, comes to a marvelous fruition in the poems of the second Isaiah.

Yet on profounder view, the content of this section is not inherently inconsistent with the preceding pronouncements. This is established by the nameless author's unequivocal confidence that God is the supreme Lord of history as well as of nature. This massive theological conviction

gives an impressive unity to the whole book under our survey. A text to cover all of it, early and late, is the version of the first verse of Psalm 99 in the Book of Common Prayer:

The Lord is King, be the people never so impatient;
   he sitteth between the Cherubim, be the earth
     never so unquiet.

Under the aegis of such a magnificent expression of religious and ethical monotheism, the work and words of Amos are to be appreciated. There is no gainsaying the fact that the prophet from Tekoa portrays the immediate present and future of Israel in the most somber colors.

| 12 That they may possess the remnant of Edom, and of all the heathen, which are called by my name, saith the Lᴏʀᴅ that doeth this. | 12 that they may possess the remnant of Edom and all the nations who are called by my name," says the Lᴏʀᴅ who does this. |

their hearts lingered the memory of the golden age of the reign of David. Then indeed God's blessing had signally rested upon them. The persistence of the hope and belief that there could be a renewal of that wonderful age was possible, even in the days when the **booth of David** was **fallen** and lay in ruins and Israel was but the fragment of a people, only because through the ministry of men like Amos they had been enabled to discern in the overwhelming disaster that had befallen them the hand of their own God and the consequent vindication of his majesty and righteousness. In the very fall of the kingdom Yahweh had been revealed as governing the course of history. He who had smitten could heal.

12. Part of the greatness of the reign of David had been the extent of the territory over which he had ruled, and the renewal of his kingdom must involve a like extent of Israel's domain in the new day. **That they may possess the remnant of Edom:** Edom is perhaps particularly named because of the agelong rivalry with that people (cf. Gen. 27:40) and the hostility with which they had taken advantage of the collapse of the Southern Kingdom. It is called a **remnant** because it too had been reduced to a fragment of a people before the advance of the great empires in the seventh and the sixth centuries B.C.

And all the nations . . . : The nations are those which David had subjugated—the Philistines, Moab, Ammon, Syrian kingdoms. The clause **who are called by my name** signifies simply that these peoples had been conquered by Yahweh and so had passed into his possession. So Joab summoned David to take the final steps himself in the capture of the Ammonite capital Rabbah, "Lest," said Joab, "it be called by my name" (II Sam. 12:28; cf. Isa. 4:1 [Hebrew 3:20]). In Acts 15:16-18 the LXX of vss. 11-12 is quoted freely as showing that the prophets had foretold that God would visit the Gentiles "to take out of them a people for his name." The LXX reading, "that the remnant of men may seek [the Lord]," *yidhreshû she'ērîth 'ādhām*, in place of "that they may possess the remnant of Edom," *yireshû 'ēth she'ērîth 'edhôm*, prepared the way for this interpretation of the passage. Although the Hebrew text falls far short of this spiritual range, it yet regards the conquests which had made Israel great in the past not simply as David's but as Yahweh's, with that constant feeling for the primacy of the activity of God which again finds expression in the clause **who does this** at the end of the verse. The inclusion in the book of Amos of this oracle voicing a people's hope for a renewal of Yahweh's favor would remind readers that it was the same Yahweh of whom Amos had spoken as

| To alter the figure, the primary task of the prophet, confronted with a complacent self-righteous nation, was to sound the tocsin of impending destruction. His main recourse in the face of an apostate people was to proclaim the sin-destroying righteousness of God. There were wounds that must be inflicted by God's truth before they could ever be healed by God's love. Amos was impelled alike by the terms of his divine appointment and by the crisis of his own brief time point in history to accent the retributive power of God rather than his redemptive purpose. Yet a careful review of his messages will reveal the fact that he was not without a | sense of God's mercy toward a truly penitent nation. His dark forebodings of doom are not unrelieved by intimations of divine pity and forgiveness. It is the historian Gilbert Murray, in our own day, who doubts the capacity of a nation to repent, save by the specious device of shifting power from one political party to another. This dictum would seem to warrant an insight of Amos, greatly developed by his prophetic successors: that no nation or society is an impersonal entity abstracted from its human environment; it is instead the corporate expression of the individual men and women who are its |

| 13 Behold, the days come, saith the Lord, that the plowman shall overtake the reaper, and the treader of grapes him that soweth seed; and the mountains shall drop sweet wine, and all the hills shall melt.

14 And I will bring again the captivity of my people of Israel, and they shall build the waste cities, and inhabit *them;* and they shall plant vineyards, and drink the wine thereof; they shall also make gardens, and eat the fruit of them. | 13 "Behold, the days are coming," says the Lord,
"when the plowman shall overtake the reaper
and the treader of grapes him who sows the seed;
the mountains shall drip sweet wine,
and all the hills shall flow with it.
14 I will restore the fortunes of my people Israel,
and they shall rebuild the ruined cities and inhabit them;
they shall plant vineyards and drink their wine,
and they shall make gardens and eat their fruit. |

destroying his people for their sins, and that the hope of the future must rest in obedience to his righteous will.

3. Nature's Bounty (9:13)

13. This concerns the marvelous fertility of the soil in the new age. So abundant would be the grain harvest that it would take all the summer to gather it in, and **the plowman shall overtake the reaper.** The vines would yield so richly that the work of the treader of grapes in the wine press and that of the sower of seed in the fields would overlap (cf. Lev. 26:5). It would seem as if the mountains and hills on the slopes of which the vineyards lay were streaming with the flow of wine. Made part of the book of Amos, this oracle, with its feeling for the unbounded possibilities of divine power manifested in the world of nature bringing wonderful blessing to man, is set against the background of the prophet's rehearsal of the ways in which that same divine power had been made known in famine, drought, blight, mildew, and earthquake, as God summoned his people to repentance (4:6-11). The God who could give corn and wine and other abundance was not as one of the ancient gods of the land, identified with the productive forces of nature, and so more or less at the disposal of man, but supreme Lord of all the forces of nature, using them for the carrying out of his righteous purpose.

4. Return of the Exiles (9:14-15)

14. I will restore the fortunes . . . : The Hebrew phrase in the opinion of most scholars originally meant simply "turn a turning," i.e., "bring about a change in the situation," as in Job 42:10; but the word for turning, *shebhûth,* closely resembles *shebhîth,* captivity, and as for Israel the great change in situation for which they longed was "return from captivity," the phrase came generally as here to have that meaning (cf. Snaith, *Amos,* II, 146-47). **They shall rebuild the ruined cities . . . ,** reflects the longing of those who could not forget the desolation of the land they loved and would find their greatest satisfaction in restoring its ruins and in tilling once again its soil.

living and feeling components. It is this capacity of Amos and the prophets who came after to personify the nation, with a particular eye to the remedial forces inherent in minority groups of humble and penitent men and women, that gives us an impressive reading of history, early and late, in terms of a faithful remnant who are witnesses to the ultimate rule of God, as well before history as in and beyond it. "He which hath begun a good work in you will perform it until the day of Jesus Christ" (Phil. 1:6). We may expand this word of Paul's to the young church at Philippi until it is one with God's sovereign and eternal purpose, both as original Creator and final Perfecter of man whom he has made in his own image.

In that confidence we may take leave of Amos, come at last to retirement from public

15 And I will plant them upon their land, and they shall no more be pulled up out of their land which I have given them, saith the Lord thy God.

15 I will plant them upon their land,
and they shall never again be plucked up
out of the land which I have given them,"
says the Lord your God.

---

15. They shall never again be plucked up . . . : The **again** is eloquent of their present situation. They had been uprooted and, homeless exiles, they knew that the hope of going home again to dwell in quiet security rested on the will of him who in the days of their adversity was still their God.

These verses, as indeed the epilogue as a whole (vss. 8-15), are much more than what has been called a "traditional happy ending" (cf. *ibid.*, II, 146), added as it were to commend the book to readers. Vss. 14-15 in particular take explicit account of the message of the book itself. **They shall plant vineyards and drink their wine** evidently has 5:11 in mind, and the phrase **my people Israel** in this context stands in striking contrast to its use in 8:2, "The end has come upon my people Israel." But those who were responsible for the addition of these verses were not qualifying Amos' utterances. They placed them here because of their profound conviction that Amos had indeed been a true prophet of God, and because they knew that the course of events had vindicated his prediction. Through the ministry which the book represented they felt themselves strengthened in the faith that Yahweh was indeed the living righteous Lord of nature and history. They were convinced that under the changed distressful conditions of their own day the same living Lord would have a further word to say through his prophet. And so the book ends with the significant words **the Lord your God.** The God who in destroying, righteous wrath had visited the nation for its sins had also made known to his people what he was doing, and had proved himself even in judgment, both in his unfailing righteousness and in his continued concern for them, to be in very truth their God.

---

life in the solitude of his home at Tekoa. The passing days served only to authenticate his prophetic word, "God is about to destroy his people for their sins." But we may believe, as well, that time confirmed Amos in his basic conviction that the exile march of humanity will not end in any wilderness of despair and destruction. Rather does it move to the fulfillment of all that is partial, to the completion of all that is fragmentary, to the consummation of all that is temporal—in God, from whom all life comes forth and to whom all life is set to return.

The Book of

OBADIAH

Introduction and Exegesis by JOHN A. THOMPSON
Exposition by NORMAN F. LANGFORD

OBADIAH

INTRODUCTION

About a dozen men of the Old Testament have the name Obadiah, "servant of Yahweh" or "worshiper of Yahweh." Like most Hebrew names this was an expression of the faith of the parents and of their hopes for the child.

I. Author

Presumably Obadiah was the author of the prophecy substantially in its present form, not of the earlier oracle used in vss. 1-9. The political situation implied in the prophecy points to a time after the Exile, probably in the mid-fifth century B.C. No value can be attributed to traditions identifying this prophet with King Ahab's steward (I Kings 18:3-16; so Babylonian Talmud, Sanhedrin 39b) or with King Ahaziah's captain (II Kings 1:13-15; so Pseudo-Epiphanius *The Lives of the Prophets*).

II. Occasion and Summary

The occasion of the prophecy is the expulsion of the Edomites from their land, which the prophet sees as a divine judgment on that nation for its cruelties toward Israel.

The first main division (vss. 1-14) deals with Edom's judgment and the moral reasons therefor. The twofold title (vs. 1a) gives the prophet's name, his inspiration, and the chief subject, Edom. An alliance of surrounding nations is being roused to wage war on Edom (vs. 1b). God's purpose is to humble the Edomites' pride and to rout them out from their supposedly impregnable mountain fortresses (vss. 2-4). The treasures of Edom have been completely ransacked (vss. 5-6). The conquest and expulsion of Edom is the work of her former allies (vs. 7). Edom's vaunted shrewdness will be confounded (vs. 8). Her warriors will be dismayed and, as a result, the nation will be cut off (vs. 9). The reason for these judgments, past and future, is Edom's cruelty to the brother nation, Israel (vs. 10). The Edomites took a willing part in the invasion and plundering of Judah (vss. 11-13) and even cut off those who attempted to escape (vs. 14).

The second main section (vss. 15-21) concerns the day of the Lord, which includes universal judgment, the restoration of Israel, and the establishment of the kingdom of God. All nations and Edom in particular will share in this retribution (vs. 15). Israel also has been punished, but the judgment of the pagan nations will be eternal and complete (vs. 16). A purified remnant of Israel, however, will be saved and will conquer their former conquerors (vs. 17). The reunited northern and southern tribes will absorb Edom (vs. 18), and expand to the south, west, north, and east (vs. 19). Those still remaining in exile from Israel and from Judah will return to complete the reconquest of the land from its northern to its southern limits (vs. 20). Deliverers will arise to lead Israel to victory over Edom (vs. 21a). Thus the kingdom of God will be established (vs. 21b).

III. Style

Several literary features lend animation to this briefest of Old Testament prophetic books. A variety of poetic meters is used, though the pentameter predominates. Much of the prophecy is in the words of the Lord directly addressed to Edom (vss. 2-15). In vs. 2 the perfects are prophetic, describing as completed what is still in process. In vss. 12-14, from a standpoint in the past, for the sake of vividness the Edomites are commanded not to commit crimes which they actually had performed. The list of crimes in vss. 10-14 builds up to a climax: assistance to Judah's enemies, rejoicing in her destruction, plundering, and treacherous slaughter of the refugees. The two main divisions

857

contrast the judgment of Edom with the victory of Israel. The book progresses from the particular to the general: from the judgment of Edom to universal judgment, from the restoration of Israel to the coming of the kingdom of God.

IV. Parallels in Other Old Testament Books

The close verbal parallels between vss. 1-9 and Jer. 49:7-22 can be explained only by some literary relationship between the two passages. The parallels are: vs. 1=Jer. 49:14; vs. 2=Jer. 49:15; vs. 3a=Jer. 49:16a; vs. 4=Jer. 49:16b; vs. 5=Jer. 49:9; vs. 6=Jer. 49:10a; vs. 8, cf. Jer. 49:7; vs. 9a, cf. Jer. 49:22b; vs. 16, cf. Jer. 49:12. The difference in the order of the material makes it likely that both Obadiah and Jeremiah are using an earlier oracle against Edom. Obadiah seems in most instances to be closer to the arrangement and form of this original oracle. The reference to the alliance against Edom is much more natural at the beginning (vs. 2) than in the middle (Jer. 49:14). Furthermore, in several cases Jeremiah expands the material found in Obadiah, and the added words are usually characteristic of Jeremiah. The Jeremiah passage, however, was written earlier, for in it the judgment of Jerusalem is still future (Jer. 49:12), whereas in Obadiah Jerusalem has been captured and plundered (vs. 11).

Several phrases are also common to Obadiah and Joel: "because of the violence" (vs. 10= Joel 3:19); "cast lots" (vs. 11=Joel 3:3); "your deeds shall return on your own head" (vs. 15= Joel 3:4, 7); "for the day of the LORD is near" (vs. 15=Joel 1:15; 2:1; 3:14); "in Mount Zion there shall be those that escape" (vs. 17=Joel 2:32); Zion "shall be holy" (vs. 17=Joel 3:17); "for the LORD has spoken" (vs. 18=Joel 3:8). In 2:32 Joel indicates that he is quoting directly from Obad. 17 by the phrase, "as the LORD has said." Therefore Obadiah must precede Joel, and is probably the source which influenced Joel in some of the other parallels between the two books.

V. Historical Background and Date

Various dates ranging from the ninth to the second centuries B.C. have been proposed for different sections of Obadiah. The literary and historical evidence points to the mid-fifth century as the most likely setting for the prophecy in its present form.

As indicated above, much of vss. 1-9 was adapted from a pre-exilic oracle. The probable historical background for this earlier prophecy is the repeated raids on Edom by the surrounding Arab tribes. Several Arab incursions into Palestine are recorded in the Bible (Judg. 6:1-6;

II Chr. 21:16). According to the records of Ashurbanipal, king of Assyria 669-626 B.C., Arabs were invading the lands west of the north Arabian Desert in the mid-seventh century B.C.[1]

Vs. 7 reflects a later stage in this movement of the Arabs and was probably added by Obadiah, since it has no parallel in Jer. 49. The Arab tribes, formerly Edom's allies, have completely expelled the Edomites from their original land, as is also implied in Mal. 1:3-4, which comes from the mid-fifth century B.C. Inscriptions found at Tell el-Kheleifeh, the biblical Ezion-geber, show that at about 600 B.C. the governor was still an Edomite, but by the fifth century Arab names are found there.[2] The account of the campaigns in 312 B.C. by the armies of Antigonus Cyclops against Petra imply that the Nabataean Arabs had long been established in this former Edomite center.[3] According to these data, the expulsion of the Edomites from their old home must have been in the late sixth or early fifth centuries, shortly after which vs. 7 must have been written.

What then is the geographical and historical background of vss. 8-10, which refer to a still future punishment of the Edomites? Because of the combination of the exile of the Judeans and Arab pressure, the Edomites occupied southern Judea (I Esdras 4:50), which came to be called Idumea.[4] It is on these transplanted Edomites in former Judean territory that Obadiah pronounces doom. Since the judgment is still future, this prophecy must be placed before the absorption of the Edomites by the Jews under John Hyrcanus (134-104 B.C.).

That Jerusalem has already been captured and looted is shown by vss. 10-16. In vss. 12-14 that past conquest is imaginatively relived, and the Edomites are forbidden to perform the cruelties they actually inflicted on their kindred of Judah. The reference is almost certainly to the catastrophe of 587 B.C. This is the only capture of Jerusalem in which it is recorded that the Edomites had a part (Ps. 137:7; I Esdras 4:45).

The historical situation in vss. 17-21 also implies a postexilic date before the Maccabean period. The resettlement of Jews in Judah and Benjamin corresponds to the area occupied in the mid-fifth century B.C. (Neh. 11:25-36).

[1] J. B. Pritchard, ed., *Ancient Near Eastern Texts Relating to the Old Testament* (Princeton: Princeton University Press, 1950), pp. 297-301.

[2] W. F. Albright, "The Old Testament and Archaeology," *Old Testament Commentary*, ed. H. C. Alleman and E. E. Flack (Philadelphia: Muhlenberg Press, 1948), 167.

[3] Diodorus Siculus XIX. 95.

[4] *Ibid.* XIX. 95, 98.

Since the expansion from this nucleus lies still in the future, the prophecy precedes the Jewish conquests in the later second century B.C. An inscription from Sardis or Sepharad (see Exeg. on vs. 20) proves the existence of a Jewish colony there as early as the middle of the fifth century B.C. Vs. 21*a* implies not an exilic setting (contra George Adam Smith), but a re-established Jewish community in Jerusalem to which leaders will come.

The postexilic date for Obadiah demanded by the historical background is further delimited by the parallels in other biblical books. Since Joel 2:32 quotes Obad. 17, Obadiah must precede Joel, whose probable date is about 400 B.C. Mal. 1:3-4, like Obad. 7, reflects the expulsion of the Edomites from their original home, and Obadiah probably comes from the same time, about the middle of the fifth century B.C.

VI. Unity and Critical Analyses

The prophecy of Obadiah, embodying in vss. 1-9 an earlier oracle, is marked by progression and literary unity. The book follows a pattern observable in other prophecies: the first part deals chiefly with the present and judgment, the complementary second part chiefly with the future and Israel's glory. The similar historical background throughout vss. 10-21 is consistent with the literary unity of this section of the book.

Modern analyses (e.g., by T. H. Robinson in 1938) have found various fragments in vss. 10-21 also. The changes in person and time in this section are sudden, but have parallels in other emotional prophetic writings. According to Julius A. Bewer,[5] the references to the end times are from a later writer, but many prophets combine the historical and the eschatological. The hopes of reconquest in vss. 19-21 are just as possible in the fifth-century setting of the rest of the prophecy as in the fourth century proposed by R. H. Pfeiffer.[6]

VII. Leading Ideas

The outstanding thought of this little book is God's moral judgment of nations through history. The chief object of judgment is Edom, and the moral reason for its punishment is its cruel treatment of Israel, the related nation. Israel also has suffered God's judgment through conquest and exile, but victory is promised to the purified remnant. Ultimately not only Edom but all the nations will be judged in the day of the Lord, the final moral reckoning.

Obadiah is sometimes accused of narrow nationalism because he condemns Israel's enemy, Edom, and the other pagan nations, and looks forward to the exaltation of his own people, Israel. He lacks any direct references to the conversion of the nations, such as are common in Second Isaiah (e.g., 42:1, 4, 6). A measure of national and religious particularism was natural for a member of the restored Jewish community, and was even necessary for the preservation of the nation and its faith.

Another abiding positive message of Obadiah is the assurance of the coming of the kingdom of God (vs. 21). That he describes the kingdom in terms of Israel and Palestine is natural in view of his times and circumstances. Two elements of Obadiah's kingdom hope are universalized and spiritualized in the book of Revelation. According to Obadiah, Mount Zion shall be "holy" (vs. 17), reserved for those who have escaped condemnation in the judgment; the new Jerusalem of Revelation is a morally holy city for those whose names are found in the book of life and who are victorious over sin (Rev. 21:7, 27). Obadiah's closing words, "The kingdom shall be the LORD's," are given a higher meaning in the triumphal chorus: "The kingdom of the world has become the kingdom of our Lord and of his Christ" (Rev. 11:15).

VIII. Text

The text of Obadiah is moderately well preserved. Since vss. 7, 19, 21 are difficult to interpret as they now stand, they may have suffered corruption in transmission.

IX. Outline of Contents

I. Edom's judgment and the reasons therefor
  A. Title (vs. 1*a*)
  B. Warning of Edom's fall (vss. 1*b*-4)
  C. Completeness of Edom's destruction (vss. 5-9)
  D. Reasons for Edom's judgment (vss. 10-14)
II. The day of the Lord (vss. 15-21)
  A. The universal judgment (vss. 15-16)
  B. The restoration of Israel (vss. 17-21)

X. Selected Bibliography

BEWER, JULIUS A. *A Critical and Exegetical Commentary on Obadiah and Joel* ("International Critical Commentary"). New York: Charles Scribner's Sons, 1911.

CALKINS, RAYMOND. *The Modern Message of the Minor Prophets.* New York: Harper & Bros., 1947.

LANCHESTER, H. C. O. *Obadiah and Jonah* ("Cambridge Bible"). Cambridge: Cambridge University Press, 1918.

NOWACK, WILHELM. *Die kleinen Propheten* ("Handkommentar zum Alten Testament"). 3rd ed. Göttingen: Vandenhoeck & Ruprecht, 1922.

[5] *A Critical and Exegetical Commentary on Obadiah and Joel* (New York: Charles Scribner's Sons, 1911; "International Critical Commentary").

[6] *Introduction to the Old Testament* (New York: Harper & Bros., 1941), p. 586.

ROBINSON, GEORGE L. *The Sarcophagus of an Ancient Civilization.* New York: The Macmillan Co., 1930.

ROBINSON, T. H. *Die zwölf kleinen Propheten Hosea bis Micha* ("Handbuch zum Alten Testament"). Tübingen: J. C. B. Mohr, 1938.

SELLIN, ERNST. *Das Zwölfprophetenbuch* ("Kommentar zum Alten Testament"). 2nd ed. Leipzig: A. Deichert, 1929. Vol. I.

SMITH, GEORGE ADAM. *The Book of the Twelve Prophets.* Rev. ed. New York: Harper & Bros., 1928. Vol. I.

VAN HOONACKER, ALBIN. *Les douze petits prophètes* ("Études bibliques"). Paris: J. Gabalda, 1908.

WADE, G. W. *The Books of the Prophets,* Micah, Obadiah, Joel, and Jonah ("Westminster Commentaries"). London: Methuen & Co., 1925.

OBADIAH

TEXT, EXEGESIS, AND EXPOSITION

1 The vision of Obadiah. Thus saith the Lord GOD concerning Edom; We have heard a rumor from the LORD, and an ambassador is sent among the heathen, Arise ye, and let us rise up against her in battle.

1 The vision of Obadi'ah.

Thus says the Lord GOD concerning Edom:
We have heard tidings from the LORD,
    and a messenger has been sent among the nations:
"Rise up! let us rise against her for battle!"

I. EDOM'S JUDGMENT AND THE REASONS THEREFOR (vss. 1-14)

A. TITLE (vs. 1a)

1a. The twofold title gives the prophet's name, his divine inspiration, and the subject. A **vision** was originally a scene revealed to a prophet in a trance (as the root is used in Num. 24:4, 16), then any divine communication to a prophet (I Sam. 3:1); in Isa. 1:1; Nah. 1:1, as here, the word is applied to a whole book of prophecy. On **Obadiah,** the author, see Intro., p. 857. **Thus says the LORD** is a common way of claiming divine inspiration (e.g., Amos 1:3). **Edom** is also denounced at some length in other prophecies (cf. Jer. 49:7-22, where the many verbal parallels to Obadiah are noteworthy; Isa. 34; Ezek. 35).

B. WARNING OF EDOM'S FALL (vss. 1b-4)

1b. (Cf. Jer. 49:14.) **We have heard tidings:** In Hebrew two alliterative words from the same root, *shemû'āh shāma'enû.* This report of the rousing of the nations against Edom is communicated to the prophet and his people by the Lord. **A messenger** of God has also carried the same summons to the heathen nations. In **let us rise** the **messenger** includes not only the nations, but also the Lord, his sender, who will lead a war of judgment on Edom (cf. Isa. 14:22, where God rises up to judge Babylon). The historical

---

1-9. The Insecurity of Nations.—Obadiah reminds us that there is no such thing as national security. It is of course the responsibility of statesmen to take thought for the safety of the people whom they serve, and to carry out whatever reasonable projects may help to protect the nation from harm. The idea of invulnerability, however, is a delusion. **Edom**

2 Behold, I have made thee small among the heathen: thou art greatly despised.	2 Behold, I will make you small among the nations,
3 ¶ The pride of thine heart hath deceived thee, thou that dwellest in the clefts of the rock, whose habitation *is* high; that saith in his heart, Who shall bring me down to the ground?	you shall be utterly despised.
	3 The pride of your heart has deceived you, you who live in the clefts of the rock,*a* whose dwelling is high,
4 Though thou exalt *thyself* as the eagle, and though thou set thy nest among the stars, thence will I bring thee down, saith the LORD.	who say in your heart, "Who will bring me down to the ground?"
	4 Though you soar aloft like the eagle, though your nest is set among the stars, thence I will bring you down, says the LORD.

a Or *Sela*

background of the pre-exilic prophecy quoted by Obadiah in vss. 1-9 was probably a coalition of Arab tribes against Edom (see Intro., p. 858).

2. (Cf. Jer. 49:15.) Vividness is gained by the frequent direct addresses to Edom in vss. 2-16. In vss. 2-4 the Lord is the speaker. **I will make you small** is actually a perfect in Hebrew, but a prophetic perfect, referring to something already determined in the counsels of God but still in the human future. That this humiliation of Edom is yet to come is shown by her self-confidence in vs. 3. Moffatt, the Amer. Trans., and Theodore H. Robinson emend *me'ōdh,* **greatly,** to *bā'ādhām,* "among men," according to the reading in Jer. 49:15, a better parallelism, but not a necessary change.

3. (Cf. Jer. 49:16*ab*.) The boastful pride of Edom is also condemned in Ezek. 35:13. The Edomites lived in "retreats of rock" (Song of S. 2:14), hiding places in canyons and caves. The translation **rock** interprets *sela'* as a common noun, alluding to the rugged terrain of the whole region. There is probably also a secondary reference to **Sela** (RSV mg.; II Kings 14:7), the modern Umm el-Bayyârah, the rock citadel of the ancient inhabitants of Teman (vs. 9) and of Petra (G. E. Wright and F. V. Filson, eds., *The Westminster Historical Atlas to the Bible* [Philadelphia: Westminster Press, 1945], p. 66 and Fig. 46). On such an impregnable height the Edomites could well feel secure. The M.T. of the next phrase is, lit., "the height of [*merôm*] his dwelling." The LXX and Vulg. read *mērîm,* and the whole phrase may then be interpreted, "who make high your dwelling" (similarly Moffatt, Amer. Trans., T. H. Robinson), which is better sense and better parallelism. This verse and the following give apt poetic impressions of the crags, fantastic in shape and color, around the Edomite capital, Petra, "A rose-red city—half as old as Time" (J. W. Burgon, "Petra," l. 132).

4. (Cf. Jer. 49:16*c*.) The **eagle** is known for its soaring and high aeries (Job 39:27), and Edom shares the rapacity of this bird. **Though your nest is set** [cf. Num. 24:21]

was so strongly established in her natural fortress that she considered her defenses impregnable (vs. 3). Yet her doom was sealed, and that which she had done to others she herself must now suffer.

It is noteworthy that this fate is not directly ascribed to any supernatural cause. This is not an instance of God's intervening to do miraculously what human power could not perform. It would be by the conspiracy (vs. 1) and treachery (vs. 7) of her neighbors that Edom's downfall would be accomplished. There are

historical forces operative in the world which make the position of any nation, however strong it may appear, actually precarious. Obadiah is therefore peculiarly fitting as a prophetic utterance which every powerful, wealthy, and well-established nation does well to heed.

Although no miracle is in this case involved, Obadiah none the less attributes Edom's doom to God's judgment. It is the Lord who declares that he will **bring** [her] **down** (vs. 4). Thus even within history scripture permits us, and even exhorts us, to see the hand of God be-

5 If thieves came to thee, if robbers by night, (how art thou cut off!) would they not have stolen till they had enough? if the grape gatherers came to thee, would they not leave *some* grapes?

6 How are *the things* of Esau searched out! *how* are his hidden things sought up!

7 All the men of thy confederacy have brought thee *even* to the border: the men that were at peace with thee have deceived thee, *and* prevailed against thee; *they that eat* thy bread have laid a wound under thee: *there is* none understanding in him.

8 Shall I not in that day, saith the LORD, even destroy the wise *men* out of Edom, and understanding out of the mount of Esau?

5 If thieves came to you,
  if plunderers by night —
how you have been destroyed! —
  would they not steal only enough for
    themselves?
If grape gatherers came to you,
  would they not leave gleanings?
6 How Esau has been pillaged,
  his treasures sought out!
7 All your allies have deceived you,
  they have driven you to the border;
your confederates have prevailed against
    you;
  your trusted friends have set a trap
    under you —
there is no understanding of it.
8 Will I not on that day, says the Lord,
  destroy the wise men out of Edom,
  and understanding out of Mount Esau?

---

among the stars is vivid poetic hyperbole. Similarly from starry heights God casts down the king of Babylon (Isa. 14:12-15).

C. COMPLETENESS OF EDOM'S DESTRUCTION (vss. 5-9)

5. (Cf. Jer. 49:9.) **Robbers by night** would "steal only what they could handle" (Amer. Trans.). **Grape gatherers** would leave some **gleanings,** by oversight or to provide for the poor (Lev. 19:9-10). In contrast, the despoilers of Edom have left nothing, so that the prophet is moved to exclaim parenthetically, **How you have been destroyed!**

6. The completeness of this plundering leads to further expressions of astonishment. The stripping of Edom's hidden **treasures** is described in different words in Jer. 49:10*a*. Under the Nabataeans, who supplanted the Edomites, the capital city, Petra, was still known as a trading center where valuable goods were stored (Diodorus Siculus XIX. 95). The most imposing Nabataean temple in Petra is called by the Arabs *el-Khazneh*, "the Treasury" (Wright & Filson, *op. cit.*, Fig. 52).

7. The first clause in the M.T. reads, "Even to the border they have driven you," the subject, **all your allies,** being given in the next clause. The RSV reverses the order of these clauses for greater clarity. Under Arab pressure in the sixth and fifth centuries B.C. the Edomites were finally driven completely out of their original borders and settled in southern Judah. "The men who were at peace with you have overpowered you" (Amer. Trans.; cf. Jer. 38:22). The Arab conquerors had formerly been Edom's allies in raids on Judah (Ps. 83:6). **They that eat thy bread,** or following the preceding parallel "[the men of] your bread," is equivalent to **your confederates** (cf. Ps. 41:9). To this day eating together is a bond of friendship among the Arabs. *Māzôr* usually means **wound,** which does not suit this context; "ambush" (LXX, Peshitta, Vulg.) and **trap** make sense and probably represent an original *māçôdh*. "There is no understanding in him" (ASV; cf. vs. 8), i.e., in Edom, who has lost his discernment and is therefore deceived.

8. This rhetorical question expects an emphatic "Yes." **That day** is the time of Edom's judgment, whose completion is evidently still future. The disappearance of

---

hind the collapse of nations. Our fundamental insecurity lies in the fact that from God there is no escape; and that he is capable of raising up instruments to effect moral retribution. More-

over, this condemnation of the strong nation has a thoroughgoing quality which far exceeds the casual misfortunes that occur in the history of any country (vs. 5). There are such events as

9 And thy mighty *men,* O Teman, shall be dismayed, to the end that every one of the mount of Esau may be cut off by slaughter.	9 And your mighty men shall be dismayed, O Teman, so that every man from Mount Esau will be cut off by slaughter.
10 ¶ For *thy* violence against thy brother Jacob shame shall cover thee, and thou shalt be cut off for ever.	10 For the violence done to your brother Jacob, shame shall cover you, and you shall be cut off for ever.
11 In the day that thou stoodest on the other side, in the day that the strangers carried away captive his forces, and foreigners entered into his gates, and cast lots upon Jerusalem, even thou *wast* as one of them.	11 On the day that you stood aloof, on the day that strangers carried off his wealth, and foreigners entered his gates and cast lots for Jerusalem, you were like one of them.

Edom's vaunted wisdom is also implied in Jer. 49:7. The wisest of Job's friends, Eliphaz, was from Teman (cf. vs. 9), and Temanites are associated with seekers of understanding in Baruch 3:23.

9. The dismay of the "warriors" of Edom is described more fully in Jer. 49:22. **Teman,** one of the chief cities of Edom (Amos 1:12), has recently been identified with the modern Tawîlân, about five miles east of Petra (Nelson Glueck, "Explorations in Eastern Palestine, II," *Annual of the American Schools of Oriental Research,* XV [1935], 82-83). God's purpose in the panic of their army is to judge the Edomites by removing them from their land (cf. Isa. 34:5-8; 63:1-3). **By slaughter** (*miqqáṭel*): The editors of the LXX, Peshitta, and Vulg. transfer this phrase to the following verse, but it disturbs the rhythm in either verse. The root *qāṭal* is more common in postbiblical Hebrew, and this form occurs only here in the Bible. The phrase is probably a later editorial gloss of the following "because of the violence," *mēḥᵃmaṣ* (vs. 10a).

D. REASONS FOR EDOM'S JUDGMENT (vss. 10-14)

The judgment on Edom is only the just retribution for its sins: violence (vs. 10), violation of the ties of kinship (vs. 10), plundering (vss. 11, 13), rejoicing in destruction (vs. 12), and as a climax, the slaughter and enslavement of refugees (vs. 14).

10. From the time of the rivalry between Esau and Jacob, the twin ancestors of the two peoples (Gen. 27:41), Edom's hostility had been manifested in repeated acts of **violence** against Israel (Num. 20:14, 20, 21; II Chr. 28:17; Ezek. 25:12; 35:5-6; Joel 3:19; Amos 1:11). The Israelites, on the other hand, were urged to maintain a friendly attitude toward the Edomites (Deut. 2:4-5; 23:7). **Shame** will replace Edom's former boastfulness (vs. 3), and the Edomite nation will be wiped out. This doom was ultimately fulfilled when the Idumeans (the Grecianized name for this people) were conquered by the Jews under John Hyrcanus (134-104 B.C.) and ceased to have a separate national existence (Josephus *Antiquities* XIII. 9. 1).

11. The context shows that the opening phrase should be translated "On the day that you stood in opposition" (cf. II Sam. 18:13). According to I Esdras 4:45, the

national ruin, the breaking up of empires, the disappearance of one dominant world power and the emergence of another. In such events we are bidden to see the might and justice of God.	**shouldest thou.** Edom dissociated herself from the miseries of her kinfolk in Israel; worse than that, she rejoiced over Israel's suffering and took advantage of it. This is what merits the retribution of God.
10-14. *The Guilty Bystander.*—The prophet drives home the charges against Edom through the repeated formula, so terrible in its literary restraint, **thou shouldest not . . . neither**	Herein lies the painfulness of man's relationship to man. One stands aside and lets another suffer. One takes pleasure in another's distress. One capitalizes on another's misfortunes. De-

12 But thou shouldest not have looked on the day of thy brother in the day that he became a stranger; neither shouldest thou have rejoiced over the children of Judah in the day of their destruction; neither shouldest thou have spoken proudly in the day of distress.

13 Thou shouldest not have entered into the gate of my people in the day of their calamity; yea, thou shouldest not have looked on their affliction in the day of their calamity, nor have laid *hands* on their substance in the day of their calamity;

14 Neither shouldest thou have stood in the crossway, to cut off those of his that did escape; neither shouldest thou have delivered up those of his that did remain in the day of distress.

---

12 But you should not have gloated over the
　　day of your brother
　　in the day of his misfortune;
you should not have rejoiced over the
　　people of Judah
　　in the day of their ruin;
you should not have boasted
　　in the day of distress.
13 You should not have entered the gate of
　　my people
　　in the day of his calamity;
you should not have gloated over his dis-
　　aster
　　in the day of his calamity;
you should not have looted his goods
　　in the day of his calamity.
14 You should not have stood at the parting
　　of the ways
　　to cut off his fugitives;
you should not have delivered up his sur-
　　vivors
　　in the day of distress.

Edomites took an active part with the Chaldeans in the invasion and plundering of Judah, which reached its climax in the destruction of Jerusalem in 587 B.C. The spoil was divided by lot (as in Joel 3:3).

12-14. In these verses the succession of Edom's cruelties is conveyed by the repetition of similar constructions and meters and of the word for **day** with synonyms of **misfortune.** The verbs are all prohibitions, "do not gloat," etc.; for vividness the prophet speaks as if the attack on Jerusalem were present and warns the Edomites against the outrages they actually did perform.

12. The day of your brother is immediately explained as the time of **misfortune** for the kindred nation of Judah (cf. Ps. 137:7). Ezekiel also condemns the Edomites' rejoicing over the desolation of Israel (Ezek. 35:15) and their revilings of their stricken neighbor (Ezek. 35:12).

13. The crimes of invasion, gloating, **and** looting are again mentioned and thereby emphasized. The word *'ēdhām,* **their calamity,** is a play on the word *'edhôm,* Edom.

14. Edomites stationed at the forks of roads could cut off Judeans fleeing southward from their doomed land on either converging route. The last prohibition implies that the Edomites handed over Israelite refugees to the Chaldeans. According to Amos 1:6, 9, this was not the first time Edom had dealt in Israelite slaves.

---

spite all that can be said about the amiability of human nature, this is what happens again and again all down the line of human social life. It is not always so. But we need to be asking ourselves continually about our neutralities, our inward cruelties, our ruthlessness.

Obadiah suggests an application on the national scale of certain parables of Jesus. The parable of the good Samaritan (Luke 10:25-37) finds an analogy in the phrase **in the day that thou stoodest on the other side** (vs. 11). Again, there is the saying: **Thou shouldest not have looked on the day of thy brother in the day that he became a stranger** (vs. 12). There, in principle and anticipation, and applied not only in personal but also in international life, is the parable of the sheep and the goats: "Depart from me, ye cursed . . . . For I was ahungered, and ye gave me no meat, . . . I was a stranger, and ye took me not in" (Matt. 25:41-43). Ruthlessness or heartlessness toward man—even under the guise of national security —is exposed as contempt for our brother; and our brother in the last resort is Christ.

15 For the day of the Lord *is* near upon all the heathen: as thou hast done, it shall be done unto thee: thy reward shall return upon thine own head.

16 For as ye have drunk upon my holy mountain, *so* shall all the heathen drink continually; yea, they shall drink, and they shall swallow down, and they shall be as though they had not been.

17 ¶ But upon mount Zion shall be deliverance, and there shall be holiness; and the house of Jacob shall possess their possessions.

15 For the day of the Lord is near upon all the nations.
As you have done, it shall be done to you,
your deeds shall return on your own head.

16 For as you have drunk upon my holy mountain,
all the nations round about shall drink;
they shall drink, and stagger,*b*
and shall be as though they had not been.

17 But in Mount Zion there shall be those that escape,
and it shall be holy;
and the house of Jacob shall possess their own possessions.

b Cn: Heb *swallow*

II. The Day of the Lord (vss. 15-21)
A. The Universal Judgment (vss. 15-16)

15. For the day of the Lord is near: Cf. Joel 1:15; 3:14; Zeph. 1:7. The above warnings to Edom are based upon the assurance of the coming of God's judgment. **The day of the Lord** is the time when God punishes the wicked among Israel and the pagans and when he exalts his faithful people (Joel 3; Zeph. 1–3). This time of judgment is **near,** i.e., certainly approaching. The second half of the verse refers to Edom, which will be judged by the law of retribution (cf. Ezek. 35:11 for an expansion of the idea and Joel 3:4, 8 for verbal parallels to the last clause).

16. Parallels such as Jer. 49:12; Isa. 51:22-23 indicate that probably the Judeans are addressed in the first part of this verse. Edom is generally referred to in the singular, not the plural as here, and is one of, not distinguished from, the pagan **nations.** The imagery of drinking the cup of God's wrath is most fully developed in Jer. 25:15-28, where the figure is explained as God's judgment, first on Judah and then on the pagans. **My holy mountain,** as in Isa. 11:9; Joel 2:1; 3:17, is Mount Zion, the site of the Lord's temple. **Continually,** *tāmîdh* (most Hebrew MSS, Peshitta, Vulg.), refers to the perpetuity of God's punishment of the pagans (cf. Isa. 66:24). **Round about,** *ṣābhîbh,* is the reading of a few Hebrew MSS. **Swallow down** adds the idea of completeness to the previous **drink.** By this judgment the pagan nations will be destroyed without a remaining trace.

B. The Restoration of Israel (vss. 17-21)

17. But in Mount Zion there shall be those that escape: Expressly quoted and elaborated in Joel 2:32. Evidently some Israelites also will fall under judgment, but a purified remnant in Jerusalem will be saved. **It** [i.e., **Mount Zion**] **shall be holy** is explained in Joel 3:17 as meaning that Jerusalem will be safe from heathen profanation. **The house of Jacob** here stands for Judah, as in vs. 18; Isa. 46:3; Nah. 2:2. Instead of

15-21. *Whose Kingdom?*—The last clause of all—the kingdom shall be the Lord's—determines the direction of this whole passage. For without this it could be understood merely as wishful thinking about the fulfillment of Israel's national ambitions, grandiose dreams inspired by patriotism and bitterness. Edom will fall,

Israel will rise. That indeed is part of the picture. But what is referred to is not the conquest of other nations by God's people. It is the conquest of the **heathen** by the Lord; and the end is man's salvation.

Such is human sin that even this final declaration can be perverted; i.e., it can be used to

18 And the house of Jacob shall be a fire, and the house of Joseph a flame, and the house of Esau for stubble, and they shall kindle in them, and devour them; and there shall not be *any* remaining of the house of Esau; for the LORD hath spoken *it.*

19 And *they of* the south shall possess the mount of Esau; and *they of* the plain, the Philistines: and they shall possess the fields of Ephraim, and the fields of Samaria: and Benjamin *shall possess* Gilead.

20 And the captivity of this host of the children of Israel *shall possess* that of the

---

18 The house of Jacob shall be a fire,
  and the house of Joseph a flame,
  and the house of Esau stubble;
they shall burn them and consume them,
  and there shall be no survivor to the
  house of Esau;
              for the LORD has spoken.
19 Those of the Negeb shall possess Mount
  Esau,
  and those of the Shephe'lah the land of
  the Philistines;
they shall possess the land of E'phraim
  and the land of Samar'ia
  and Benjamin shall possess Gilead.
20 The exiles in Halah[c] who are of the people of Israel
  shall possess[d] Phoenicia as far as Zar'-
  ephath;

c Cn: Heb *this army*
d Cn: Heb *which*

---

the M.T. *môrāshêhem,* **their possessions,** the LXX, Peshitta, Vulg., Targ. read *môrîshêhem,* "their dispossessors," which agrees better with the following verses.

18. According to previous prophecies (Hos. 1:11; Ezek. 37:16-22), **the house of Jacob,** i.e., the tribes of the kingdom of Judah, and **the house of Joseph,** i.e., the tribes of the kingdom of Israel, will be reunited and will conquer their surrounding enemies (cf. Isa. 11:13-14). The vivid imagery of **fire** is also used to describe Israel's destruction of its foes in Num. 21:28, and the wicked are often compared to **stubble,** which is burned quickly and completely (cf. Mal. 4:1). For the historical realization of this doom see vs. 10. **For the LORD has spoken:** Guaranteeing the fulfillment of the prophecy.

19. During the Exile Edomites occupied towns of **the south** or **the Negeb,** the southern portion of Judah (I Esdras 4:50). **They of the south,** i.e., the Israelites in this area, will turn the tables and occupy Edom's territory. Similarly, "they of the lowland" (ASV) or **Shephelah,** the low hill country to the west of Judah, will drive out the **Philistines** and conquer Philistia itself (cf. Zeph. 2:4-7). The Israelites also **shall possess the fields** [i.e., as in Gen. 32:3, the territory] **of Ephraim,** here a general term for central Palestine from the name of the leading tribe (cf. Josh. 17:15), a district also called **Samaria** from the name of the chief city (cf. I Kings 13:32). **Gilead** lay to the east of **Benjamin,** beyond the Jordan. The directions in which the expansion would take place are thus south, west, north, and east. These conquests were accomplished in the second century B.C., when northern Judah and Benjamin were the nucleus from which the Jews under the Maccabees pressed out into the areas indicated in this verse.

20. Appropriately **the captivity of this host,** viz., the exiles from the Northern Kingdom, shall occupy "the territory of the Canaanites" as far north as **Zarephath**

---

sanctify any kind of military or national triumph, identifying the cause of the nation with the cause of God. It therefore behooves us to take seriously what is expressed in the clause. Where the Lord rules, man serves him, and does not reign sovereignly in his own right. There cannot be two kings. Where God triumphs, we cannot rightly call the triumph ours. What is permitted us is to enjoy the fruits of

God's word, to gather under his shadow in gratitude and humility. There will be many blessings here and hereafter for the people of God. That is not denied but affirmed in the N.T. But the giver of the blessings is God. All that we have is his gift.

By God's prowess the victory is won. We enjoy the spoils of battle. But what from the Christian standpoint is the battle? It is not the

Canaanites, *even* unto Zarephath; and the captivity of Jerusalem, which *is* in Sepharad, shall possess the cities of the south.
 	
21 And saviours shall come up on mount Zion to judge the mount of Esau; and the kingdom shall be the LORD's.
	and the exiles of Jerusalem who are in Sephar'ad
	  shall possess the cities of the Negeb.
	21 Saviors shall go up to Mount Zion
	  to rule Mount Esau;
	  and the kingdom shall be the LORD's.

(I Kings 17:9), a city between Tyre and Sidon. The RSV follows the Amer. Trans. and Moffatt in the conjectural emendation of *haḥēl-hazzeh,* **this host,** to *ḥalaḥ,* **Halah,** a district in northern Mesopotamia (II Kings 17:6). The exiles from Jerusalem, on the other hand, **shall possess the cities of the south** or the **Negeb** (cf. vs. 19). Thus the Promised Land shall be regained from north to south. **Sepharad** is Sardis, *Çparda* in Persian monuments, the capital of Lydia in Asia Minor. An Aramaic inscription with a parallel Lydian text, found at Sardis, calls this city *sprd,* the same consonants as here, and proves the existence of a Jewish colony there as early as the tenth year of Artaxerxes, probably Artaxerxes I Longimanus, king of Persia (465-424 B.C.; C. C. Torrey, "The Bilingual Inscription from Sardis," *American Journal of Semitic Languages and Literatures,* XXXIV [1917-18], 185-98). The Peshitta and Targ. misinterpreted this name as Spain, and consequently Spanish and Portuguese Jews are called Sephardim.

21. These reconquests will be led by **saviors** who, like the judges of old (Judg. 2:16; 3:9, 15), will deliver the Israelites from their oppressors. From **Mount Zion** as a center they will extend their rule over **Mount Esau.** The use of **mount** with both names sharpens the contrast between these two nations, the one holy, the other profane; the one destined to triumph, the other to destruction. Obadiah's hope transcends mere nationalism, for he sees in Israel's victory the establishment of the kingdom of God (cf. Ps. 22:28; Zech. 14:9; Rev. 11:15).

battle between nations, not even the battle between bad and better ideologies. It is the battle of Good Friday and Easter. **The kingdom is the LORD's** means the kingdom of our Lord and Savior Jesus Christ; and this is not to be confused or identified with any temporal dominion exercised by earthly powers. Scripture points on beyond all our conflicts, all our revolutions, all our wars, to **the kingdom** where God reigns by the power of grace.

The Book of

JONAH

Introduction and Exegesis by JAMES D. SMART
Exposition by WILLIAM SCARLETT

JONAH

INTRODUCTION

The book of Jonah stands fifth among the books of the twelve minor prophets, but it is quickly apparent to the reader that it is of a nature very different from the other eleven. These contain chiefly the messages delivered by the prophets to their people, while in the book of Jonah the only record of the prophet's preaching consists of eight words: "Yet forty days, and Nineveh shall be overthrown!" (3:4.) The eleven also contain few references to the personal history of the prophets concerned (e.g., Amos 7:10-17) while the book of Jonah from beginning to end narrates the prophet's adventures. In all other books of the prophets we encounter men whose one care was to proclaim faithfully, first to Israel but sometimes also to the nations, the judgment of God which turns men to repentance; but in this book there is no mention of Jonah preaching to Israel. Moreover, he was unwilling to proclaim God's judgment upon the people of Nineveh because of his fear that they might repent and thereby be saved from destruction. Such comparisons and contrasts are sufficient to show that this brief book must be set in a different classification from other books of the prophets and that it is likely to speak most plainly to us if we respect this uniqueness of its form.

1. History or Parable?

Before a reader can rightly understand the book he must make up his mind what kind of literature he has before him. Is it history or is it a great parable such as the prophets, and later Jesus, used so cunningly? There is no reason to prejudice the issue on dogmatic grounds as though some dishonor would be done to Scripture if the decision should be that the book is parable, not history. The Scriptures contain many different kinds of literature—psalms, proverbs, histories, sagas, sermons, parables, letters, apocalypses—and it is important for any sound interpretation that a book or a portion of a book be placed in its proper category. Only when this is done can it be read as it was originally intended to be read.

The impression that the book of Jonah is to be considered history is based partly on its narrative form and partly upon the reference to a prophet Jonah in II Kings 14:25. All that is recorded of this prophet who lived in Israel about 785 B.C. is that he foretold the great expansion of Israel's territory under Jeroboam II. The fact that he is called "the son of Amittai," like the prophet in the book of Jonah (1:1), seems to identify the two as being the same person. Therefore, since the main character of the book of Jonah is clearly known in Israelite history, the conclusion is drawn that the book as a whole must be history. This is further reinforced by the way in which Jesus is known to have referred to Jonah (Matt. 12:39-41; Luke 11:29-30). He spoke of Jonah's being three days and three nights in the whale's belly, and of the men of Nineveh repenting at the preaching of Jonah. The former of these references Jesus used as a symbol of his own death and resurrection, and the latter as a means of reproaching the Jews of his time for their unwillingness to repent. To advocates of the view that the book of Jonah is history it has always seemed to bring discredit upon Jesus to suggest that the events to which he refers never really took place. Some even allege that to challenge the historicity of Jonah is to set in question the resurrection of our Lord.

The chief difficulty with this view is that it obscures the message of the book as a whole. To an interpreter who felt called upon to prove that Jesus' story of the prodigal son is history we would answer that his hypothesis fails to do justice to the plain meaning of the story. As history, the book of Jonah becomes the account of an eccentric prophet who shows his utter unfitness for his office by running away from his assigned task, who is returned to his task only by the miraculous interposition of a great fish, and who stupidly mourns his success when the people of Nineveh repent at his preaching. If it is history, then it is exceedingly curious history, without a parallel elsewhere in the Old Testament, and it is hard to see much reason for its preservation.

The theory that it is history creates still other serious problems. A storm is raised at sea in order to plague the boat which carries the disobedient prophet, but it is changed to a calm when the offender is pitched overboard. The prophet spends three days and three nights in the interior of a whale without any ill effects. A gourd large enough to give shade to a man grows up in a single day. The city of Nineveh is of vast size, at least sixty miles in diameter, many times the actual size of Nineveh as determined by archaeological examination of the ancient ruins. The entire population of the pagan city of Nineveh repents at the preaching of Jonah, an event of such vast significance that it would be likely to have left behind some perceptible results. All these elements in the story suggest that it is something other than history that we are reading.

The connection with the prophet Jonah in II Kings 14:25 may be nothing more than the consequence of a later writer building his story around an obscure figure of earlier times, on the strength of some tradition concerning the eighth-century prophet that made him an appropriate character for the story. Jesus' references to Jonah do not commit us to a historical theory of the book. Jesus merely used certain details of a well-known story to drive his teaching home in the minds of his hearers. This no more determines the character of the earlier book than a reference by a modern preacher to Macbeth in Shakespeare's play suggests that the preacher regards the play as history.

The form of literature into which the book of Jonah fits most naturally is that of parable. The parables in both the Old Testament and the New Testament are misunderstood when they are interpreted merely as illustrations of spiritual truths. Often they are a device designed by the prophets by means of which men are led to pronounce judgment upon themselves. The prophet tells a story which to the hearer seems to present an objective case for his judgment (II Sam. 12:1 ff.; cf. Luke 7:41-43). But the hearer is being trapped, for it is his own case upon which he is deciding. Once the judgment is given there is no turning back; the prophet strips away the concealment and lets the man before him know that he has condemned himself. Isaiah uses this device in his parable of the vineyard (Isa. 5). Perhaps the clearest use of it in the New Testament is the parable of the good Samaritan (Luke 10:25-37), which Jesus used in an attempt to pierce the shell of a self-assured religious lawyer.

The book of Jonah may well be a parable of this kind. This would explain many of its characteristics and would also justify its place among the twelve minor prophets. The prophet Jonah may be an absurd character, but the unknown prophet who drew his portrait and set him in this parable stands with the greatest of them all, a prophet worthy by the breadth of his vision and the incisiveness of his speech to be ranked with Second Isaiah and Jeremiah.

II. Object of the Parable

In the years after the Exile there grew up in Israel a spirit of bitterness and vengefulness toward other lands. The nation had endured so much at the hands of enemies that there was little inclination to keep alive the vision of Israel as God's servant through whom redemptive truth would one day reach all men (Isa. 42:1, 6). The most passionate desire was that God's wrath should utterly consume all of Israel's enemies. The problem of the prophet in such a time was how to reawaken in the nation a sense of the missionary destiny to which, as God's people, it had been called. No better weapon for this task could be found than the parable.

A prophet who, when ordered to preach to the people of Nineveh, took ship in the opposite direction, would capture at once the interest and sympathy of people to whom the very thought of salvation for the Gentiles was abhorrent. He was doing just what they would do. As the story continued and Jonah nobly offered to sacrifice his own life that the others in the boat might be saved from the storm, they would not notice the inconsistency of Jonah—giving his life to save Gentile sailors but unable to bear the thought that God should save the Gentiles in Nineveh. Even the most vengeful Jews would commend Jonah for his self-sacrifice, for their faith had taught them to be considerate of others. Jonah could have mercy on the Gentiles in this one particular instance; individual Jews could have mercy upon individual Gentiles when occasion arose; but God must not have mercy upon them. No. God must have only wrath for the Gentiles.

Thus the writer of the book gently but sharply exposed in the person of Jonah the absurdity of the attitude which prevailed among so many of his countrymen. It is as though he were drawing a caricature of them and holding it up so that they might recognize themselves as in a mirror. The theme of the parable is really complete in ch. 1; chs. 2–4 repeat the theme and make crystal clear the absurdity, one might almost say the idiocy, of the attitude which is represented by Jonah. A grim humor should be recognized in the unfolding of the story, very like the humor of Jesus with which he unmasked men's hypocrisies and follies.

The picture of Jonah in chs. 3–4 is ludicrous in the extreme. The prophet finally did as God commanded him and pronounced the word of impending judgment upon the city of Nineveh. But when the whole population, with the king at its head, repented and humbled itself, Jonah did not behave as one would expect a prophet to behave, rejoicing in the success of his preaching. Instead he conducted himself like a sulky child. God was moved to compassion by the response of the Ninevites, but not Jonah. Jonah was angry; more than that, he was heartbroken, so that he wanted to die when he saw that the people of Nineveh were to be saved from destruction.

It is important to see clearly what Jonah in 4:2 states to be the point of his rebellion. He is not willing that God should be gracious, merciful, slow to anger, and of great kindness. In short, he is repudiating the God of Abraham, of Isaac, and of Jacob, the God of the covenant, whom Israel had served all the years. Here the parable is becoming transparent. There can be no longer any secret as to who is meant to be the butt of the parable. The nation, insofar as it rejects its commission to be a light to the Gentiles, is identical with Jonah. The nation is being warned, therefore, that at the root of its narrow and bitter attitude there is a rejection of the God of their fathers.

The final incident sets Jonah in a still more unfavorable light. Sitting down outside the city to await the outcome of events, he was comforted in his silly grief by the pleasant shade of a gourd that grew up in a day to protect him from the sun. But the next morning when the gourd faded away as quickly as it had come, Jonah was as angry at the destruction of the gourd as he had been at the deliverance of the Ninevites from destruction. Here Jonah's attitude, and with it the attitude of the postexilic Israelites, was reduced to a complete absurdity. Jonah could have pity upon a gourd that grew up in a day and vanished in a day, but he was unwilling that God should have pity upon more than a million helpless folk in a Gentile city.

Some commentators have felt that the book ends abruptly. They have failed to see the consummate artistry of its ending. The sharpest blow is struck; the deepest point of contradiction in Jonah's attitude is exposed, and with that the parable breaks off. When the knife has been driven in to the hilt, what more remains to be done? It was unnecessary for the prophetic writer to add any explanation pointing out who was represented by Jonah, just as it would have been superfluous for Jesus to have pointed out to the lawyer that in his judgment upon the characters in the parable of the good Samaritan he had condemned himself.

III. Date and Authorship

Those who identify Jonah with the prophet mentioned in II Kings 14:25 and assume that the book was written by him, place its date in the early years of the eighth century B.C. There is no evidence in the book, however, to support this theory of authorship, and there are many signs of a much later date. It is significant that in 3:3 Nineveh is spoken of as a city of the distant past. The author is so far away from it in time that he greatly magnifies the size of it. It is also unlikely that a contemporary of the king of Assyria would call him "the king of Nineveh" (3:6) and would fail to give him his proper name and title.

There are a number of words used in the book which are found only in late Hebrew literature. There are also a number of Aramaisms: יִתְעַשֵּׁת (1:6); טַעַם used with the meaning "command" (3:7); the use of שֶׁ for אֲשֶׁר (1:7, 12; 4:10b). The practice of calling Yahweh the "God of heaven" (1:9) belongs also in general to the postexilic period, occurring only in a single story in pre-exilic literature.

It seems clear therefore that the book was written in the period after the Exile. The influence of Isa. 40–66 upon the author, inspiring him with his vision of a world upon which God might yet have compassion through Israel's ministry, points to a date in the fifth century or later. It could not have been later than the third century B.C., since Jonah's name has been included by Jesus ben Sirach as one of the twelve (Ecclus. 49:10). The narrowness of the nation's sympathies as reflected in Jonah suggests a time when the exclusiveness engendered by Ezra's reforms in 444 B.C. had long been at work in the life of the community. The closest therefore that we can fix the date is somewhere between 400 and 200 B.C.

The identity of the author is unknown. It is one of the glories of Israel's faith that a man saturated with the teachings of the great prophets could create a parable as perfect as this, could let it speak its message in his time, and could leave it to posterity without recording his own name.

IV. Unity of the Book

Questions regarding the unity of the book of Jonah have come from two directions. Kaufman Kohler in 1870 and Wilhelm Böhme in 1887, followed by other scholars in later years, found a variety of sources in the book. The chief impetus in this direction was given by the fact that both Yahweh and Elohim occur as names for God. Böhme found four writers at work as well as glossators, but the distinctions upon which he built his argument are such as may be discovered in almost any unit of literature.

The second reason for questioning the unity arises from the presence of the psalm in ch. 2. It is evident at a glance that 2:10 continues directly the narrative of 2:1, so that 2:2-9 has the appearance of an interpolation. Also, the content of the psalm is not wholly appropriate to the situation in which Jonah finds himself. The speaker is plunged in the depths of the sea (2:3) so that the weeds are wrapped about his head (2:5). He is so far down that he is at the bottoms of the mountains (2:6). He gives us to understand, however, that these depths of the sea are figurative, representing how far he has been cast away from God. He is in the "belly of hell" because of his sore affliction (2:2); his life is in a state of corruption (2:6); he is cast out of God's sight and removed far from the temple where he was accustomed to worship God (2:4, 7). Nowhere is there any suggestion that he is praying from the belly of a fish.

It is also noteworthy that the psalm has a number of parallels with other psalms (vs. 3a, cf. Ps. 18:4-5; vs. 3d, cf. Ps. 42:7; vs. 4b, cf. Pss. 5:7; 43:4; vs. 5, cf. Ps. 18:5, 16; vs. 6, cf. Ps. 30:3; vs. 7, cf. Ps. 142:3; vs. 7b, cf. Ps. 18:6). These parallels do not detract from the forcefulness of the psalm in Jonah but rather show only the manner in which the writer was familiar with earlier psalms. A number of the phrases used in the psalm in Jonah have a definitely figurative use in the other psalms (e.g., with 2:3d, "all thy billows and thy waves have passed over me," cf. Ps. 42:7).

The evidence seems to indicate that the psalm was not originally composed to express Jonah's plight as he lay in the belly of the great fish. The question that remains is whether it was placed in its present position by the original author or by a later hand. The fact that it interrupts the parable, leaving no gap when it is removed, suggests that it was not a part of the original composition.

V. The Great Fish

Three of the forty-eight verses of the book of Jonah relate to the incident of the great fish. Unfortunately in the minds of many people these three verses have been seized upon as though they were of greater importance than all else. As a result, the book is widely remembered not for its unique message but as though it were chiefly a curious story about a man being swallowed by a fish and coming forth alive after three days.

This incident has been variously interpreted. Those who insist that the book is history seek to find instances in modern times of persons being swallowed by whales and yet surviving. Eduard König professed to have found an authentic instance of this in the story of the whale fisher, James Bartley, but investigation showed the story to have no ground in fact. It can be said that there is no known instance of a man being swallowed by a fish and being later cast forth alive.

It is significant that stories have been told among many peoples of men being swallowed by monsters, remaining for a time inside them, and later coming forth unharmed. Among maritime peoples the story features a sea monster, but in inland countries a wolf, bear, or some other animal serves as well. Well known in the Semitic world were stories of the great dragon which fought even with the gods of heaven; and Leviathan, the monster of the deep, appears in scripture as a symbolic representation of the vast power of evil that stands against God (Isa. 27:1; 51:9; Ps. 74:13-14).

There is one specific instance, however, where the dragon is identified with Israel's enemies and the Exile is represented as a swallowing up of the nation by the dragon. This occurs in Jer. 51:34: "Nebuchadrezzar, the king of Babylon hath devoured me, he hath crushed me, he hath made me an empty vessel, he hath swallowed me up like a dragon." In Jer. 51:44 God says: "I will punish Bel in Babylon, and I will bring forth out of his mouth that which he hath swallowed up." Here quite clearly the Exile and the return are meant. We may assume that the author of the book of Jonah was familiar both with these passages in Jeremiah and with the imagery of the all-consuming dragon that was so widely current in his world. When to this is added the fact that the author saw in Jonah the whole nation of Israel, the conclusion seems inescapable that the incident of the great fish is a symbolic representation of the Exile and the return.

VI. Outline of Contents

I. A prophet fleeing from his God (1:1-17)
II. A psalm of thanksgiving for deliverance (2:1-10)
III. The reluctant missionary (3:1-10)
IV. The absurdity of limiting God's mercy (4:1-11)

VII. Selected Bibliography

HORTON, R. F., ed. The Minor Prophets ("Century Bible"). Edinbugh: T. C. & E. C. Jack, n.d.
LANCHESTER, H. C. O. Obadiah and Jonah ("Cam-

bridge Bible"). Cambridge: Cambridge University Press, 1918.

MITCHELL, H. G., SMITH, J. M. POWIS, and BEWER, JULIUS A. *A Critical and Exegetical Commentary on Haggai, Zechariah, Malachi, and Jonah* ("International Critical Commentary"). New York: Charles Scribner's Sons, 1912.

SCHMIDT, HANS. *Jona. Eine Untersuchung zur vergleichenden Religionsgeschichte.* Göttingen: Vandenhoeck & Ruprecht, 1907.

SELLIN, ERNST. *Das Zwölfprophetenbuch* ("Kommentar zum Alten Testament"). Leipzig: A. Deichert, 1922.

SMITH, GEORGE ADAM. *The Book of the Twelve Prophets.* Rev. ed. New York: Harper & Bros., 1928.

WADE, G. W. *The Books of the Prophets* ("Westminster Commentaries"). London: Methuen & Co., 1925.

JONAH

TEXT, EXEGESIS, AND EXPOSITION

1 Now the word of the LORD came unto Jonah the son of Amittai, saying,

1 Now the word of the LORD came to Jonah the son of Amit'tai, saying,

I. A PROPHET FLEEING FROM HIS GOD (1:1-17)

1:1. The intention of this verse is to fix in the mind of the reader that Jonah is a regularly commissioned prophet like other prophets of the past. **The word of the LORD came.** This phrase through long use by the prophets had become the mark of their calling (Hos. 1:1; Joel 1:1; Mic. 1:1; Zeph. 1:1; Hag. 1:1; Zech. 1:1). The prophet was constituted a prophet not by any human ordination or by membership in a human institution (cf. Amos 7:14), but by God himself speaking to him and commissioning him for his task. The basis of the prophet's life is the confidence that God is able to communicate with man, making known to him his will. Without a revelation of God there can be no prophet. **Jonah:** The name means "dove" and has an appropriateness

---

1:1. Introduction.—This amazing little book, so full of spiritual insight and beauty, is one of the noblest in the O.T. One cannot read it without experiencing some of the glowing contagion of the author's dream. And he cannot put it down without wistfully saying to himself, "If men only would, if men only could, 'Earth [might] be fair, and all her people one.' "[1] C. H. Cornill said that he had read this little book at least a hundred times, and he would publicly avow, since he was not ashamed of his weakness, that even then he could not read it or even speak of it without tears rising to his eyes and his pulse beating faster; because this book is one of the deepest and grandest ever written, and he would say to anyone approaching it, "Take off your shoes, for the ground whereon thou standest is holy ground."

It is a vast pity that in the past and even today the value and beauty of this book has been obscured by the fish story which was swal-

[1] Clifford Bax, "Turn back, O man."

lowed whole by so many people. It has given rise to much controversy: how was it possible for a fish to swallow a man? And even Phillips Brooks's playful rejoinder, that this posed no particular problem seeing that Jonah was only one of the *minor* prophets, did not alleviate the tension.

But it is quite apparent that the book is not history, and obviously it was never intended to be read as history; the author of this magnificent document would turn over in his grave at the thought of such literalism. He was on fire with a great message. He would teach his people a great truth:

the love of God is broader
Than the measure of man's mind,[2]

and it is a constant rebuke to our pretensions, our narrow judgments, and our divisions. He would set the meanness and foolishness of man

[2] Frederick W. Faber, "There's a wideness in God's mercy."

2 Arise, go to Nineveh, that great city, and cry against it; for their wickedness is come up before me.

2 "Arise, go to Nin'eveh, that great city, and cry against it; for their wickedness has

---

in the parable since the dove was a symbol of Israel. **Son of Amittai:** These words identify Jonah with the prophet in II Kings 14:25; no further mark of identity is to be found.

2. Nineveh: A city on the east bank of the Tigris River near the modern Mosul, founded most likely by the Babylonians but rebuilt and fortified by Sennacherib as the capital of Assyria (*ca.* 705 B.C.). In 612 B.C. it was destroyed by the Medes, but its fame was legendary in the ancient world for centuries. That it no longer existed at the time the book of Jonah was written is clear from 3:3, where it is spoken of in the past tense. The Assyrians were responsible for a number of Israel's greatest disasters. In the eighth and seventh centuries B.C. they invaded Palestine again and again, burning and looting cities, laying waste the countryside and deporting the inhabitants. The Northern Kingdom of Israel passed out of existence as a result of Assyrian conquest in 722-721 B.C. The author of the book of Jonah chose Nineveh to be the object of God's mercy in his parable for the definite reason that its inhabitants would be more hated by Israelites than the people of any other city. **Cry:** The word may be translated "call"

---

against the background of the greatness and goodness and love of God. And against the background of the great dream of universal human brotherhood, solidly grounded in the fatherhood of God, he would place his present world, torn asunder by antagonisms. But how best could he drive home the lesson? That was his problem. How could he put it so that people would most easily grasp his message? He would adopt the rememberable method of the parable, the story. It was a technique which Jesus employed constantly. "A certain man had two sons: and the younger of them said to his father, Father, give me the portion of goods that falleth to me . . ." (Luke 15:11 ff.). Obviously that was not history nor was it intended to be interpreted as history. But the figure of that father bending in pity over his returned and repentant son has moved through the ages and through men's hearts as a great and beckoning light. In Jean Forain's etching of the prodigal son is not the line of the father's back as he stoops in love over his kneeling son as pitying a line as ever was drawn?

This, then, would be the author's method. He would take a historical figure, one Jonah, who had been prophet and adviser to King Jeroboam II, possibly the author of the national expansionist program of that day—and no doubt revered by national expansionists ever since. (It should be noted, however, that not all the Jewish people of that day felt as did the central figure in this drama. One cannot indict a whole people. And many had caught the largehearted catholicity and vision of the prophets.) But the author would take as a type that narrow little man, that first-class national

expansionist ("Israel First"), who hated all foreigners, and then he would send him on an errand of warning and mercy to—of all places in the world—Nineveh, the capital of the dread Assyrian Empire, the most hated and feared of Israel's oppressors. Then, in contrast to Jonah and his point of view, he would portray the love and unpredictable mercy of God. Here is all the material necessary for high drama, so that the reader puts the book down feeling as did the converted prize fighter in John Masefield's *Everlasting Mercy,*

> I knew that Christ had given me birth
> To brother all the souls on earth.[3]

2. The Call.—How came the call to one who was "eyeless with hate," so blinded by prejudice that he could not see? Whence came the impulse to carry this message of warning to their most hated foe? How could a fresh revelation of God's mercy, and his justice too, penetrate such spiritual opaqueness? For Jonah recognized from the beginning with what kind of God he was dealing: "I knew that thou art a gracious God, and merciful, slow to anger, and of great kindness, and repentest thee of the evil" (4:2).

We are only told that "the word of the LORD came to Jonah the son of Amittai." "The wind bloweth where it listeth, and thou hearest the sound thereof, but canst not tell whence it cometh, and whither it goeth: so is every one that is born of the Spirit" (John 3:8). The word of the Lord came to Amos, a simple herdsman, watching his flock by night, under the Palestinian sky with the Milky Way trailing

[3] Copyright 1911. Used by permission of The Macmillan Co., Society of Authors, and Dr. John Masefield, O.M.

or "preach." What Jonah was to preach is found in 3:4. That it was to be a message of judgment is clear from the fact that it is the wickedness of Nineveh which actuates God to send a prophet to that city. **Is come up before me:** Behind this phrase lies the conviction that what happens among men is made known before the presence of God. Because heaven, God's dwelling place, is conceived as distant from the earth, the report has by some means to go up from the one region to the other (cf. Gen. 4:10; I Sam. 5:12,

---

clouds of glory overhead. It came to young Isaiah (6:1-8), praying in the temple and suddenly realizing he was not alone. It came to Jeremiah, "Ah, Lord God! behold, I cannot speak: for I am a child" (Jer. 1:6). Each one for different reasons at first recoiled. But in the end their common response was, "Here am I; send me."

The word of the Lord came also to Jonah. We all have our "moments," momentous experiences on which a whole life and its destiny may turn. For we cannot easily escape our "nature," which at its best touches the divine. We cannot escape the pressure of the mind of God on our dim minds. Just as a scientist in his pursuit of truth, guided by his reason, his experiment and observation, comes into contact with a truth which is objective to himself, which he does not create but discovers, so the human spirit, seeking the satisfaction of its deep desires, also makes a discovery, comes into contact with Something which it does not create but discerns, which is there, objective to one's self, the Without, which is also the Within. For God is the ground of all existence. "In him we live, and move, and have our being" (Acts 17:28). It is the pressure of his mind on ours which is the source of all our seeking after him. It is the pressure of his mind on ours which is the source of all our seeking after good. A Scots preacher once told the story of a blind boy flying a kite in a park in Edinburgh. His pastor came along and watched him, and after a while he said, "Jimmy, what fun do you get out of kite flying? I thought the only fun was to see it climbing higher and higher in the sky until it is but a speck against the blue dome of heaven. But you with your blind eyes cannot see it." The boy replied, "No, I cannot see it. But I can feel the tug of it." We all have our "moments." Toward the end of his life, in his private diary Cosmo Gordon Lang set down an illuminating entry. Early in life he had suddenly turned to the Christian ministry. At the time he was not even confirmed. But there had been experiences from which he could not escape. He wrote as follows:

I have tried hard to *rationalise* those early experiences. . . . But it won't do, unless the whole of one's inner life and the highest and truest part of the life of man is a delusion and a mockery. No: if I am called to swear my conviction of the truth of anything, I will swear that behind these experiences there is a Reality—God in Christ. I must stake my life on that truth. Else indeed it is "a tale told by an idiot . . . signifying nothing." [4]

Jonah had his "moment." Perhaps for an instant he took fire. His prejudices were softened. And then the old reasoning, the old habits of thought, the ingrained prejudices and hostilities, swept over and captured him. And he knew what he would do. (Contrast the rich young man and the great refusal with Paul's "I was not disobedient to the heavenly vision.")

2. God's Concern for His World.—The idea here is that God is at work in human history, deeply concerned in human affairs, now and then taking a hand in them. **Their wickedness has come up before me.** There is a similar idea in Mic. 6:2, representing God as having a controversy with his people and about to contend with Israel. So God will plead through the prophet with the people of Nineveh to turn from their wickedness and live.

If God has a controversy with his people today, it is because we are all selfish men; because our main preoccupation is with ourselves; because our reaction to every new proposal is a personal one, "How will this affect me, my wealth, my position, my future?" rather than "How will it further the general good of men?" We forget that once it was said, "Whoever would save his life will lose it, and whoever loses his life for my sake will find it" (Matt. 16:25).

If God has a controversy with his people, it is because there has been in our world too little concern for our brother, too little recognition that his fate is bound up in ours, and ours in his, even unto the least, too much forgetting that word of old, "We are members one of another" (Eph. 4:25), and if one member suffers, "all the members suffer with it" (I Cor. 12:26). A plain fact of the nineteen-thirties is that Hitler climbed to power on the backs of the unemployed in Germany, and it was this frustration, this sense of uselessness, in millions of lives which made his way easy.

If God has a controversy with his people, it is because there has been in our world too little corporate sense, too little conviction of human

[4] J. G. Lockhart, *Cosmo Gordon Lang* (London: Hodder & Stoughton, 1949), p. 189.

3 But Jonah rose up to flee unto Tarshish from the presence of the LORD, and went down to Joppa; and he found a ship going to Tarshish: so he paid the fare

come up before me." 3 But Jonah rose to flee to Tarshish from the presence of the LORD. He went down to Joppa and found a ship going to Tarshish; so he paid the fare,

---

and particularly the messengers in Job 1–2). Not until the kingdom of heaven was established in the midst of men through the coming of Jesus Christ did confidence in the omniscience and omnipresence of God overcome this dualism in men's thinking concerning the relationship of God to events upon earth. There is nothing new in the conception of God as maintaining a watchfulness over the conduct of Nineveh. The God of the prophets had long been recognized as Lord of the whole earth (Isa. 6:3), who claimed sovereignty over the nations (Jer. 1:10) and punished severely the wickedness of other nations than Israel (Amos 1:3, 6, 9, 11, 13).

3. At this early point the perverse conduct of the prophet begins and continues to the end of the book. At no time does Jonah conduct himself as one would expect a

---

solidarity and interdependence, too little conviction that the world has now become one, for better or for worse, that whatever happens anywhere now in the end, if not in the beginning, happens to us; and that we must therefore organize our world accordingly. Are we not all one family; have we not all one Father?

If God has a controversy with his people, it is because there has been too little recognition of our common humanity, and of our common destiny with the peoples of the earth—the people of Ethiopia, of India, of China and Japan, of Thailand and Burma, our own Negroes; too convenient an assumption that we are not our brother's keeper, no matter what suffering and death are visited upon other peoples. "We are only a small race," said the daughter of the emperor of Ethiopia as the Italians were marching in, "but I am seventeen and its leading daughter, and I know, as you know, that if mankind lets armies and gas destroy my country and people, civilization will be destroyed too. We have common cause, you and I." [5] It is said of one of the foremost world leaders that he has a curious blind spot: when he speaks of humanity, what he really means is the white race, forgetting that it has been said, "You are all brethren" (Matt. 23:8).

If God has a controversy with his people, it is because the present crisis is deeper still and touches the loss even of faith itself. In much modern thought and teaching man has lost his former spiritual grandeur and significance, and history is deprived of its spiritual meaning; so that many people, especially among the young, having been deprived of any conviction that there is profound and abiding meaning in life, became easy prey to the new barbarian.

And now history has again reached one of its great moments. We have to choose, and the

[5] Hans Kohn, World Order in Historical Perspective (Cambridge: Harvard University Press, 1942), p. 148.

choice is quite explicit. The Russian philosopher Nicholas Berdyaev has said:

The hour has struck when, after terrible struggle, after an unprecedented de-Christianization of the world and its passage through all the results of that process, . . . it will be clear what Christianity stands for and what it stands against. . . . Christianity stands for man and for humanity, for the value and dignity of personality, for freedom, for social justice, for the brotherhood of man and nations, for enlightenment, for the creation of a new life. And it will be clear that only Christianity stands for these things.[6]

3. A Conflict of Wills.—Jonah fled not because he was afraid or because of the hardships involved or because of the personal danger in approaching Nineveh with a message of doom. Jonah was anything but a coward. Later, when the lot fell against him, he suggested to the sailors, "Throw me into the sea; then the sea will quiet down for you" (1:12).

Rather he runs from his office as a prophet of God. A word has come to him which he cannot deliver and he flees as a servant from his Lord. But not because he is afraid. Rather because there had arisen a conflict of wills and purposes. What he wanted and what God intended were entirely different. Jonah would see Nineveh destroyed and all the enemies of his people within it. But he feared that God might repent and checkmate him (4:2). He doubted that God could be bent to Jonah's will, but would fulfill his own purposes. He put the word of God which came to him over against the background of God's character as revealed by Amos, Isaiah, Jeremiah, and the psalmists, by his own deepest insight. And he foresaw the frustration of his own intentions. He knew that God's warning to Nineveh was preliminary to

[6] The Fate of Man in the Modern World, tr. Donald A. Lowrie (London: Student Christian Movement Press, 1935), p. 130.

| thereof, and went down into it, to go with them unto Tarshish from the presence of the LORD. | and went on board, to go with them to Tarshish, away from the presence of the LORD. |

faithful Israelite prophet to do. The story from beginning to end is that of a man called to be a prophet but stubbornly refusing to accept his commission. Even the partial acceptance of it in ch. 3 is so vitiated by the spirit of vengefulness that it can hardly be counted an acceptance at all. **Tarshish:** A city most likely to be identified with Greek Tartessos in the south of Spain, probably a Phoenician colony (Isa. 23:1, 6, 10), maintaining a vigorous trade with Tyre (Ezek. 27:12). It was as far west as ships were likely to sail from Palestine. **From the presence of the LORD:** Jonah is represented as thinking that by flight from the territory of Israel he will be able to escape from the presence of Israel's God. The idea was common in the ancient Near East that the power and presence of a god was localized in the territory inhabited by his worshipers (I Sam. 26:19; II Kings 5:17). Jonah does not know that all lands belong to God. **Joppa:** The modern Jaffa, the one usable seaport on the unbroken Palestinian seacoast below Mount Carmel. **From the presence:** The repetition of this phrase at the end of the

an endeavor to save Nineveh if he could. That was God's nature—"Whose property is always to have mercy."[7] He remembered Jeremiah's vivid figure of the potter marring a vessel as he turned it on the wheel but, instead of flinging it away as useless, putting it on the wheel again, giving it a second chance (Jer. 18:1-10). God would redeem; Jonah would destroy without mercy. Jonah was willing to be the prophet of doom to Nineveh; he would not be the agent of God's redemption. God was not on his side, therefore he arose to flee. He feared the everlasting mercy which might follow in the wake of the warning of doom.

We think of another man, a lone man in the White House during a nation's mortal crisis, not caring whether God was on his side, but only striving to know what the will of God might be in order that he might be found on God's side. He too was sure of God's character, sure of God's justice. "The Almighty has His own purposes." Lincoln would strive to discern these purposes that he might further them. In *John Brown's Body* Stephen Vincent Benét recounts Lincoln's struggle to know the will of God. At one point he recalls a friend who had some hunting dogs, young, sleek, alert. But there was an old deaf dog which had only one virtue: he never lost the scent. And Lincoln lifts his eyes on high and says,

I am that old, deaf hunting dog, O Lord
. . . .
Therefore I utterly lift up my hands
To You, and here and now beseech Your aid.
I have held back when others tugged me on,
I have gone on when others pulled me back,
Striving to read Your will, striving to find
The justice and expedience of this case,
Hunting an arrow down the chilly airs

[7] Book of Common Prayer, Holy Communion Service.

Until my eyes are blind with the great wind
And my heart sick with running after peace.
And now, I stand and tremble on the last
Edge of the last blue cliff, a hound beat out,
Tail down and belly flattened to the ground,
My lungs are breathless and my legs are whipped.
Everything in me's whipped except my will.
I can't go on. And yet, I must go on.
. . . .
So much for my will. Show me what is Yours.[8]

There was no such struggle in Jonah's mind. He asked only that God should be on his side. When he recognized the incongruity of this, he rose to flee. One man sought to know the will of God that he might do it; the other knew the will of God but, swept away by his prejudices, turned his back upon it. Many people today will not see the hand of God in the events of our generation because the moving finger of God points forward to a more equal world, whereas they would return to the days of special privilege—"the good old days."

3. *Whither Shall I Go?*—It was not that Jonah localized God in Palestine alone. The thought of the day had passed far beyond this. "The whole earth is full of his glory," said Isaiah (6:3). Second Isaiah extended the idea of God's sovereignty throughout the earth. And the writer of Ps. 139 said: "If I take the wings of the morning, and dwell in the uttermost parts of the sea; even there shall thy hand lead me and thy right hand shall hold me." Jonah himself said (vs. 9), "I fear the LORD, the God of heaven, which hath made the sea and the dry land." And yet he would put distance between him and his own land. For with his point of view, his belief in the peculiar destiny of his own people, and his contempt for all foreigners,

[8] Copyright, 1927, 1928, by Stephen Vincent Benét. Used by permission.

4 ¶ But the LORD sent out a great wind into the sea, and there was a mighty tempest in the sea, so that the ship was like to be broken.

5 Then the mariners were afraid, and cried every man unto his god, and cast forth

4 But the LORD hurled a great wind upon the sea, and there was a mighty tempest on the sea, so that the ship threatened to break up. 5 Then the mariners were afraid,

---

verse drives home upon the mind of the reader that it is from **the LORD** that Jonah wants to get away. The presence of God is intolerable to him because it demands of him the renunciation of his prejudices and of his lust for a divine vengeance upon Israel's enemies. Rather than let his own mind and will be shaped in accordance with God's, Jonah seeks to separate himself entirely from God. The significance of this point in the parable is that behind Israel's narrow and vengeful attitude toward its enemies lay actually a flight from God, a repudiation of God.

4. God is inescapable (cf. Ps. 139:7-12). The ship had set sail from Joppa with Jonah, confident and secure, fast asleep in the hold (vs. 5), but suddenly it was met by a storm so fierce that it seemed impossible for the ship to come through. This storm was the direct action of God in order to block the rebellious flight of Jonah. That God is Lord of nature and can effect his purpose through its operations belongs to the divine character throughout the O.T. He is creator and sovereign of the whole created world. Therefore it is fantastic for Jonah to think that he can escape from him. **Threatened:** Lit., "thought that it would," an idiom that represents the ship itself as reacting to the storm in fear.

5. **Mariners:** Not Hebrews but worshipers of foreign gods. They seem to have been from different lands, since in their fear **each cried to his god.** Some would undoubtedly

---

he must have believed that Palestine was God's special dwelling place and his people God's special care. So he went to Joppa and took ship to flee to Tarshish at the other end of the world, as far away as he could possibly get. But he was on a hopeless quest unless he could translate into reality the lovely lines of Aeschylus:

> Whither can I fly?
> In all this Apian land is there no lair
>   Hid deep from every eye?
> I'd be a wisp of smoke, up-curled
> To the soft clouds above the world,
>   Up, without wings, in the bright day,
> Like dust, in dying streamers whirled
>   To pass in nothingness away.[1]

For he was trying to escape; but that from which he was trying to escape was within him. No change of environment, not the mountains, not sea air, not the desert, not altitude or latitude or longitude, could help him to escape if what he was trying to escape was there compelling him. And God was there—not in Palestine, not in Tarshish, but besieging Jonah.[2] In Laurence Housman's *The Burden of Nineveh* a friend says to Jonah, "So you're going down to Joppa—and from there to Tarshish, eh? Yes.

[1] *The Suppliant Women*, tr. Gilbert Murray, p. 73. Copyright, 1930, by Oxford University Press, Inc., and George Allen & Unwin, Ltd., publishers. Used by permission.

[2] See Francis Thompson, "The Hound of Heaven."

Tarshish is a long way, isn't it?—takes you further from Nineveh; so you think Tarshish is a safer place for you. But you'll hear the cry of Nineveh even in Tarshish, Jonah." [3]

Man has always entertained the sublime assumption that interfusing the physical force and structure of the universe there is ethical spirit, ultimately controlling physical force for ethical ends. And so in this parable inanimate nature becomes an instrument of God's purpose. God's wind sweeps down from the hills of Palestine; God's storm rages across the sea; God's sea becomes magnificent in its fury; the lots fall as God wills; the fish is an instrument of his will, and the heat and the gourd and the worm—all are instruments of his purpose. "All things betray thee, who betrayest Me." [4]

Jonah fled God's presence because it was too uncomfortable. He was exposed to God's searching judgments, and his littleness and his sin, his prejudices and hypocrisies, stood revealed for what they were. Yet in God's presence he would have been a changed man. In God's presence his prides and his hatreds could have been transcended. In God's presence only would he have found inner healing.

5. *Blindness.*—Worn out by his inner turmoil and the hardships of his hasty journey of escape

[3] Scene 1. See *Palestine Plays* (New York: Charles Scribner's Sons, 1943), p. 130.

[4] Thompson, *loc. cit.*

the wares that *were* in the ship into the sea, to lighten *it* of them. But Jonah was gone down into the sides of the ship; and he lay, and was fast asleep.

6 So the shipmaster came to him, and said unto him, What meanest thou, O sleeper? arise, call upon thy God, if so be that God will think upon us, that we perish not.

7 And they said every one to his fellow, Come, and let us cast lots, that we may know for whose cause this evil *is* upon us. So they cast lots, and the lot fell upon Jonah.

and each cried to his god; and they threw the wares that were in the ship into the sea, to lighten it for them. But Jonah had gone down into the inner part of the ship and had lain down, and was fast asleep. 6 So the captain came and said to him, "What do you mean, you sleeper? Arise, call upon your god! Perhaps the god will give a thought to us, that we do not perish."

7 And they said to one another, "Come, let us cast lots, that we may know on whose account this evil has come upon us." So they cast lots, and the lot fell upon Jonah.

---

be Phoenicians. Their first impulse when they saw their danger was to pray. Though unenlightened with true faith, they had a right sense of their dependence upon an unseen power. **Wares:** Tackle and equipment, but they may also include the cargo of the ship. Being lightened, the vessel would ride higher in the water and be in less danger of capsizing. **Had gone down:** Not during, but before, the storm. The contrast is between the frantic sailors and the quietly sleeping Jonah. The man who is trying to escape God lies down and sleeps peacefully under the delusion that his flight is successful. But all the time the forces are swirling round him which will frustrate his plan.

6. The captain shows no awareness of any difference between Jonah's god and the gods of the other men. His concern is simply that no possibility of getting help should be neglected. He is astonished that one passenger should have failed to pray to his god. His may be the very god who needs to be placated. The background of the captain's conduct is the polytheistic world in which life was continually at the mercy of the whims of various deities: unless a man knew which god was causing his misfortune, he could do nothing to ward it off. **Perhaps the god:** Not the Lord, the sovereign of nature and history, but, in the captain's mind, the one deity among many who happened to be Jonah's. The author may intend some irony in the picture of a heathen sailor pleading with the Hebrew prophet to pray to his god. Israel, in the peril that it has brought upon itself by its repudiation of God, does not know even as well as the heathen that it should pray to God for deliverance; instead it slumbers on in false security.

7. The scene shifts abruptly forward. The persistence of the storm has convinced the sailors that someone is on board the ship who has offended one of the gods, and that the offended god is responsible for the storm. This kind of thinking was common in ancient times and was perfectly in keeping with the polytheism of the sailors (cf. I Sam. 14:36-42). **Cast lots:** The lot was used in Israel, as in other ancient countries, to decide issues of various kinds: in criminal cases to discover the culprit (Josh. 7:14), in political affairs to choose a king (I Sam. 10:20-21; cf. Acts 1:26), in distribution of property (Num. 26:55). The supposition was that divine influence would determine the way in

---

to the coast, Jonah went down into the hold of the ship and promptly fell **fast asleep.** Mighty forces were stirring about him. A storm was sweeping across the sea which would imperil his ship, his companions, and him. But Jonah was fast asleep. He was as fast asleep as were, in general, the more comfortably situated classes of England at the beginning of the Industrial Revolution, when the introduction of the power machine was making life intolerable for the workers and their children. They

were fast asleep to what it was doing to human beings, fast asleep to all but their own interests, and oblivious of the incipient human tempest gathering about them. He was as fast asleep as we have been for generations. It was years ago that one of our modern prophets said that the heart of the world's crisis is to be found in the fact of the "stagnation of the masses" [5] of the world. In other words, for the masses life

[5] Arnold J. Toynbee, *A Study of History* (2nd ed.; London: Oxford University Press, 1935), III, 242.

8 Then said they unto him, Tell us, we pray thee, for whose cause this evil *is* upon us; What *is* thine occupation? and whence comest thou? what *is* thy country? and of what people *art* thou?

9 And he said unto them, I *am* a Hebrew; and I fear the LORD, the God of heaven, which hath made the sea and the dry *land*.

8 Then they said to him, "Tell us, on whose account this evil has come upon us? What is your occupation? And whence do you come? What is your country? And of what people are you?" 9 And he said to them, "I am a Hebrew; and I fear the LORD, the God of heaven, who made the sea and the

---

which the lots fell, so that the decision would actually be made by God himself. To the author of the parable, the lot, like the storm, was merely an instrument in the hand of God whereby he relentlessly pursued Jonah and set his hand upon him. It is futile for a man to try to escape from God.

8. **On whose account this evil has come upon us:** The sailors have no reason to ask this question since the casting of lots has already given them the answer. Several Hebrew MSS and the LXXBℵ omit the phrase. There is general agreement among scholars that it is a gloss that has crept into the text. The sailors, having found Jonah the guilty party, are anxious to know what it is in his place of origin or his occupation that has made him the unhappy object of divine anger.

9. **A Hebrew:** Israelites in describing themselves to foreigners call themselves Hebrews (Gen. 40:15; Exod. 2:7; 3:18). **I fear the LORD:** The sailors did not ask Jonah concerning his God, but he was impelled to confess freely to them who his God was, for in that alone lay the explanation of the storm. Jonah's confession sets the contradiction of his faith in sharp focus. The "fear of the Lord" signified an unconditional trust in God, with reverent and humble obedience to his every command. The shocking hypocrisy of Jonah is that he can glibly use this term at a time when he is in full flight from God and a rebel against his will. Jonah, like the Israel he represents, thinks that one can turn a deaf ear to all God's bidding and yet count oneself a true believer. In Jonah's confession there is a note of pride in the evident superiority of his God to the gods of the heathen sailors. Some commentators emend **fear** to "am fleeing from," but there is no basis for the change in any existing texts. **The God of heaven:** A common postexilic title for Yahweh; cf. its wide use in the book of Ezra and in the Elephantine papyri of the fifth century B.C. **Who made the sea and the dry land:** That God is the creator establishes his present authority and power over all created things. To the sailors it

---

was one grim struggle for sheer survival. And there is a revolt in our world against this fact, in the name of human dignity. This is the ground swell underlying two world wars which have already been fought; it is the ground swell underlying much of the postwar discontent. George C. Marshall, speaking in Honolulu, said:

There is no doubt in my mind that we are in the middle of a world revolution—and I don't mean communism. They, the Communists, are like your surf riders here; they're just riding on the crest of a wave. The revolution I'm talking about is that of the little people all over the world. They're beginning to learn what there is in life, and what they're missing.[6]

Jonah was as fast asleep as we Christian people have been, professing maximum Christian ideals but being content with a minimum

[6] *St. Louis Post-Dispatch*, Feb. 26, 1950.

of social action to achieve them. Two thousand years of preaching the brotherhood of man, and our world trapped in a barbed-wire entanglement. Two thousand years of preaching the dignity and sacredness of every individual, and racialism still lifting its ugly head. And since the ideals we profess no longer protect these people, it is not to be wondered at if they rebel even against the ideals themselves. The law seems to be, "If you will have it so, then you will even have it so." William James once said that the more ideals a man has, the more contemptible is he if the matter ends there; if there is no courage shown, no privations undergone, no risks incurred to get the ideals realized.

And now we have to choose. We no longer can act as though Christianity were something irrelevant to life, something which touches only the fringes of life, something which is relatively

10 Then were the men exceedingly afraid, and said unto him, Why hast thou done this? For the men knew that he fled from the presence of the Lord, because he had told them.

11 ¶ Then said they unto him, What shall we do unto thee, that the sea may be calm unto us? for the sea wrought, and was tempestuous.

12 And he said unto them, Take me up, and cast me forth into the sea; so shall the sea be calm unto you: for I know that for my sake this great tempest *is* upon you.

dry land." **10** Then the men were exceedingly afraid, and said to him, "What is this that you have done!" For the men knew that he was fleeing from the presence of the Lord, because he had told them.

11 Then they said to him, "What shall we do to you, that the sea may quiet down for us?" For the sea grew more and more tempestuous. **12** He said to them, "Take me up and throw me into the sea; then the sea will quiet down for you; for I know it is because of me that this great tempest has

---

makes clear whence the storm has come. They begin to see also that Jonah's God is not the deity of some one nation and land but the Ruler of heaven and earth. This explains the increase in their fear which now takes place, for it terrifies them to think that they are the objects of the wrath of so mighty a God.

10. What is this that you have done! As in the RSV this should be understood as an exclamation, not as a question. The sailors are in terror that Jonah should have offended the God who possesses such power. Reading this as a question (as in KJV) led to misunderstanding, for it was evident to readers that Jonah had not yet told the sailors what he had done or that he was fleeing from God's presence. Therefore it may be that a scribe, thinking to supply the deficiency added, **For the men knew that he was fleeing from the presence of the Lord.** This still left the question open how they knew it, so someone else added the note **because he had told them.** Both phrases interrupt the natural flow of the story.

11. The considerateness of the heathen sailors is marked. They do not immediately rid themselves of Jonah but inquire of him, as one who knows the laws of his God, what must be done to appease the anger of this God. The increasing fury of the sea makes plain that something must be done immediately. The humanity of the sailors' conduct toward Jonah was intended by the author of the parable to stand out; the sailors are specimens of the heathen world which men like Jonah are eager to exclude from the mercy of God.

12. In order to save the lives of the heathen sailors and passengers on board the ship, Jonah commanded them to throw him overboard. This act was the natural consequence of all that Jonah had learned from the prophetic faith; both justice and mercy demanded

---

of little importance so that we can take it or leave it as we like. Rather, Christianity is the truth about man, about man's relationship to God and his relationship to his fellow men, about God's relationship to his world. We shall have to take our stand at this center, make our decisions from it, act from it, draw our strength from this center which is Christ; and then tolerate nothing, accept nothing as final in our human situation which cuts across these principles. Stephen Spender urges

the peoples and nations who love liberty to lead a movement throughout the world to improve the conditions of the millions of people who care more for bread than for freedom; thus raising them to a level of existence where they can care for freedom. The interests of the very few people in the world who care for the values of freedom must

be identified with those of the many who need bread, or freedom will be lost.[7]

12. *A Moment of Insight.*—Jonah's willing sacrifice of himself was the result of his personal contact with "foreigners" whom previously he had hated en masse. The nobility of their conduct, their consideration for him, their prayers, each to a different god, "each going to a different address," their heroic efforts to save him, had changed somewhat his point of view. He found it difficult to hate them as individuals. **Throw me into the sea; then the sea will quiet down for you.**

Like many others, he had hated en masse. He hated Gentiles, Assyrians, Nineveh. He is the

[7] Richard H. Crossman, ed., *The God that Failed* (New York: Harper & Bros., 1949), pp. 272-73.

13 Nevertheless the men rowed hard to bring *it* to the land; but they could not: for the sea wrought, and was tempestuous against them.

14 Wherefore they cried unto the Lord, and said, We beseech thee, O Lord, we beseech thee, let us not perish for this man's life, and lay not upon us innocent blood: for thou, O Lord, hast done as it pleased thee.

15 So they took up Jonah, and cast him forth into the sea: and the sea ceased from her raging.

come upon you." 13 Nevertheless the men rowed hard to bring the ship back to land, but they could not, for the sea grew more and more tempestuous against them. 14 Therefore they cried to the Lord, "We beseech thee, O Lord, let us not perish for this man's life, and lay not on us innocent blood; for thou, O Lord, hast done as it pleased thee." 15 So they took up Jonah and threw him into the sea; and the sea ceased

---

of him this sacrifice of himself. Rare would be the Israelite who would not commend him for what he did. And yet these Israelites, like Jonah, were unwilling that God should have mercy upon millions of heathen no different from the sailors in the ship. **Throw me into the sea:** There was a widespread ancient belief that a storm at sea could be allayed by throwing overboard or casting adrift in a boat the person whose guilt was causing the deity to vent his anger on the ship. In the Buddhist story of Mittapindaka, which parallels the chapter in a number of ways, the guilty man was set adrift on a raft of reeds. **It is because of me:** Jonah recognizes God's hand in the story, but there is no indication of any repentance for his disobedience. He is sorry to have involved the ship in trouble and to have endangered the men's lives, sorry also that his flight has been unsuccessful, but his heart and mind are not softened in the least into a responsiveness to the mind of God.

13. Rowed hard: Again the humanity of the heathen sailors is evident. They shrink from so harsh a step as Jonah has proposed. They try their utmost to reach the shore. The reefs on the Palestinian coastline made this a dangerous procedure, sailors usually preferring to ride out a storm at sea rather than to risk having their ship dashed on the reefs in an attempt to make shore. Soon the still increasing ferocity of the storm made plain to them that their plan could not succeed.

14. They cried unto the Lord: The heathen sailors pray to Jonah's God before following Jonah's advice. They are certain that they will be sending Jonah to his death, and they fear that his God may hold them responsible for what they are about to do. **Innocent:** They are not declaring Jonah innocent before God, but only that he has done nothing to merit death at their hands. **Thou, O Lord, hast done as it pleased thee:** The decision to destroy Jonah is God's, not any man's; in pursuing the ship, in having the lot fall upon Jonah, in preventing the ship from reaching land, God himself has determined Jonah's fate. Therefore no punishment should fall upon those who cast him overboard.

---

type who would hate Russians, Germans, Negroes, Jews, en masse. He would indict a whole people. In his hatred he is like Harry A. Overstreet's "gentle people of prejudice," who are courteous, kindly, but who draw a line against a whole class of their fellow citizens. It is this spirit that gives rise to anti-Semitism and racialism. It often stems from ordinary, kindly people, with their seemingly harmless streak of racial prejudice, who permit the unmoral principle of condemning people in the mass to take root. Stephen Spender notes that it was this same principle which drove out of

communism several of the writers who had embraced it. It was the fact that the Communists viewed human beings as abstractions:

> Thus, when men have decided to pursue a course of action, everything which serves to support this seems vivid and real; everything which stands against it becomes abstraction. Your friends are allies and therefore real human beings. . . . Your opponents are just tiresome, unreasonable, unnecessary theses, . . . which you would like to strike out with a lead bullet as you would put a stroke of a lead pencil through a bungled paragraph.[8]

[8] *Ibid.,* p. 253.

16 Then the men feared the Lord exceedingly, and offered a sacrifice unto the Lord, and made vows.

17 ¶ Now the Lord had prepared a great fish to swallow up Jonah. And Jonah was in the belly of the fish three days and three nights.

from its raging. 16 Then the men feared the Lord exceedingly, and they offered a sacrifice to the Lord and made vows.

17[a] And the Lord appointed a great fish to swallow up Jonah; and Jonah was in the belly of the fish three days and three nights.

[a] Heb Ch 2. 1

---

16. The sailors, impressed by the power of Jonah's God when the sea becomes calm, worship him, offer **a sacrifice** and make **vows.** There is no suggestion that they are converted from the worship of other gods or that they learn anything of what it means to serve the God of Israel. They merely own that such a God is to be reckoned with seriously and placated with sacrifices and vows. The author undoubtedly means to suggest, however, in closing the incident in this way, how heathens might be led to become worshipers of the one true God. The sailors show a responsiveness that might be found in many other quarters if Israelites would believe that others than themselves are capable of responding to the God who made all lands and the nations that inhabit them.

17. The Lord appointed: Each event in the story takes place at God's direct command (cf. vss. 2, 4; 2:10; 3:1-2; 4:6, 8). Behind this lies a belief in God's sovereignty over the events of life so that each one is related definitely to his purpose. God's word and act are the primary determining factors in life. There is a danger, however, which becomes evident here, that God's relationship to events may be conceived in a mechanical fashion. The KJV translation, **the Lord prepared,** is unfortunate, giving the impression that the fish was specially made ready for the occasion. **A great fish:** There is no mention of a whale such as popular comment attributes to the book of Jonah (see Intro., p. 874, on the meaning of the great fish). **Three days and three nights:** If the swallowing of Jonah is meant to represent the swallowing up of Israel in the Exile, the three days and three nights suggest the extended period of the Exile. The sojourn in the bowels of the monster was not quickly over.

But on shipboard Jonah saw the hated "foreigners" as persons. He felt their common humanity, and compared to this capital and overwhelming fact the differences between them became of secondary importance. It was an experience similar to that of Ezekiel, who was ordered to visit a group of his people who had been sent into captivity. He rebelled against it. Nevertheless he went and reported, "I sat where they sat, and remained there astonished" (Ezek. 3:15). Why was he astonished? Because what had been to him a problem en masse had suddenly become personalized, and he saw the problem not abstractly but in terms of men and women and little children, and so saw it truly. This is what great art does for us; it takes a problem out of the air and personalizes it. So Euripides in his *Trojan Women* makes one see war through the eyes of a few noble women who had lost everything. John Steinbeck in *The Grapes of Wrath* makes one look at the problem of the Okie through the eyes of a noble mother tortured by what was happening to those she loved. Thus we may become aware of the abrupt failure of our own imaginations. These problems of real people too often are just problems to us. They are depersonalized. We need to make our imaginations force us to sit where they sit and see the problems in their true lines. Walt Whitman said: "I do not ask the wounded person how he feels, I myself become the wounded person." [9] And when we ourselves become "the wounded person," then we see the problem clearly and the gates of the pool of human compassion are unloosed and water begins to flood a thirsty land.

For a moment Jonah felt his kinship with these "foreigners." The scales fell from his eyes. He saw the sailors as persons like him. He sacrificed himself for them. "Throw me into the sea; then the sea will quiet down for you."

17. *An Old Story.*—The idea of the **great fish** was an old one even in Jonah's day. It runs through all the folk tales of Greece, Rome, Persia, India, Palestine (cf. Exeg.). A common form of the tale is that of a great fish lying motionless on the surface of the water, which a sailor mistakes for an island, puts on shore, builds a fire to cook his meal, whereupon the

[9] "Song of Myself."

2 Then Jonah prayed unto the Lord his
God out of the fish's belly,

2 And said, I cried by reason of mine
affliction unto the Lord, and he heard me;
out of the belly of hell cried I, *and* thou
heardest my voice.

3 For thou hadst cast me into the deep,
in the midst of the seas; and the floods compassed me about: all thy billows and thy
waves passed over me.

4 Then I said, I am cast out of thy sight;
yet I will look again toward thy holy
temple.

5 The waters compassed me about, *even*
to the soul: the depth closed me round
about, the weeds were wrapped about my
head.

6 I went down to the bottoms of the
mountains; the earth with her bars *was*

---

2 Then Jonah prayed to the Lord his
God from the belly of the fish, 2 saying,
"I called to the Lord, out of my distress,
    and he answered me;
out of the belly of Sheol I cried,
    and thou didst hear my voice.

3 For thou didst cast me into the deep,
    into the heart of the seas,
    and the flood was round about me;
all thy waves and thy billows
    passed over me.

4 Then I said, 'I am cast out
    from thy presence;
how shall I again look
    upon thy holy temple?'

5 The waters closed in over me,
    the deep was round about me;
weeds were wrapped about my head

6   at the roots of the mountains.
I went down to the land
    whose bars closed upon me for ever;

II. A PSALM OF THANKSGIVING FOR DELIVERANCE (2:1-10)

2:1. Jonah prayed . . . from the belly of the fish: This would be a prayer for
deliverance which in vs. 10 has its answer. But the prayer in vss. 2-9 is one of thanksgiving
after deliverance (see Intro., p. 874, for a detailed examination of the psalm). Since
the psalm is clearly a later interpolation, the original text did not contain the words of
Jonah's prayer.

2. In its first half this verse is almost identical with Ps. 120:1 and similar to Ps. 18:6.
Distress: The exact nature of the psalmist's distress is not at once clear. He uses figures of
speech for it: he is in **the belly of Sheol**; he is like a man drowning in the farthest depths
of the sea; he is shut out from God's presence. The indication in vs. 4*b* that he is far
removed from the temple suggests that his predicament is that of exile. This throws
light upon the question why the psalm was introduced in the chapter. If the great fish
in vs. 1 is understood as representing the Exile, which for a time swallowed up Israel,
a psalm celebrating deliverance from the distress of the Exile would seem appropriate.

3. Heart of the seas: This phrase is often used figuratively in scripture. In Mic. 7:19
it describes merely a region in which men's sins will be swallowed up out of sight.
Flood: The same word occurs in Ps. 24:2, where it denotes the waters beneath the earth.
In vs. 5 **the deep** is used with the same meaning (cf. Gen. 1:2). It thus begins to be plain
that the author is not thinking of some sea such as the Mediterranean but of the
monstrous deep, which in ancient legend was sometimes conceived as an all-consuming
dragon, Tiamat, and so became a symbol of the most extreme distresses that threatened
the human soul. **All thy waves and thy billows:** This line is an exact reproduction of a
line in Ps. 42:7, where it definitely has a figurative sense. It is significant that the psalmist
in the book of Jonah had Ps. 42 in mind, for it is the outcry of Israel in exile.

4. The two halves of this verse explain each other. Banishment from the **temple**
means to the speaker banishment from God's **presence.** He is perhaps still thinking of
Ps. 42, which is the passionate outcry of a man who feels shut out from the joy of God's
worship because he is far from the temple, among a foreign people who do not share
his faith.

5-6. Waters . . . deep: See Exeg. on vs. 3; cf. Ps. 69:2, where similar imagery denotes
the spiritual distress of a man who in a time when he is hard pressed by his enemies
does not yet feel that God has come to his help. **At the roots of the mountains:** The

about me for ever: yet hast thou brought up my life from corruption, O Lord my God.

7 When my soul fainted within me I remembered the Lord: and my prayer came in unto thee, into thine holy temple.

8 They that observe lying vanities forsake their own mercy.

9 But I will sacrifice unto thee with the voice of thanksgiving; I will pay *that* that I have vowed. Salvation *is* of the Lord.

yet thou didst bring up my life from the
　Pit,
　O Lord my God.
7 When my soul fainted within me,
　I remembered the Lord;
and my prayer came to thee,
　into thy holy temple.
8 Those who pay regard to vain idols
　forsake their true loyalty.
9 But I with the voice of thanksgiving
　will sacrifice to thee;
what I have vowed I will pay.
　Deliverance belongs to the Lord!"

Hebrews conceived of the earth as floating upon the great deep of waters (Ps. 24:2). Therefore one who was plunged to the very bottom of the great deep would find himself below the foundations of the mountains.

The land whose bars closed upon me for ever: Sheol, as in vs. 2. The Hebrews thought of the land of the dead as lying beneath the great deep. Sheol, however, like the deep waters, was often used as a likeness of spiritual distress (Pss. 18:5; 30:3; 116:3), just as a man in modern times will say, "I was in the torments of hell." Julius A. Bewer ("Jonah," in H. G. Mitchell, J. M. Powis Smith, and Julius A. Bewer, *A Critical and Exegetical Commentary on Haggai, Zechariah, Malachi, and Jonah* [New York: Charles Scribner's Sons, 1912; "International Critical Commentary"], p. 46), by a slight emendation reads, "the land whose gate-bars are eternal bolts," and assumes that the psalmist thinks of himself as only at Sheol's gates, Sheol being the land from which there is no return. This ignores vs. 2, where the psalmist is in **the belly of Sheol,** and also fails to recognize that the imagery is metaphorical throughout. **Yet thou didst bring up my life:** The deliverance has already taken place. **From the pit:** From Sheol (cf. Ps. 30:3).

7. My soul fainted: Lit., "was overwhelmed" (cf. Pss. 142:3; 143:4, where the same verb is used). **My prayer came to thee:** Again an echo of Pss. 42; 43, where the psalmist finally breaks through his sense of isolation from God and becomes confident that God hears and answers his prayer. **Into thy holy temple:** Physical separation from the temple does not prevent the prayer that is offered from reaching God in his holy temple. Nothing is said concerning how God answered the prayer, but only that he heard and brought deliverance.

8. The psalmist contrasts himself in his reliance upon God with those who in the distress of their souls have turned to idols for help. **Forsake their own mercy:** In abandoning their God, they give up the love and mercy that they would have received at his hand had they persevered.

9. The psalm ends on the note of joyful thanksgiving. **Sacrifice:** Not to gain God's favor, but to express gratitude for the favor that has been shown. **What I have vowed:** There has been no mention of vows before. The reference here seems to be to vows made in the extremity of distress which now the psalmist is glad to fulfill. **Salvation:** Rather, **deliverance.** It is to God alone that man should look for deliverance.

---

monster, feeling the discomfort of the fire on his back, turns over to cool off. Another form of this story is that of a whale so large that it swallows a ship and all its crew. In the vast interior of the fish there is an extensive island made of the mud which the fish has swallowed. The men try to chop their way out of the fish, but to no avail. They build a fire and the fish vomits them forth. The natives on the north

coast of Dutch New Guinea tell a story of five men in a canoe, swallowed by a great fish. As they sat in his belly they cut strips of liver and made fires to roast the meat. The injury to the vitals of the fish caused its death and it drifted ashore, where they pried open its mouth and escaped. In the Middle Ages the great fish was still popular, and even as late as the sixteenth century the whale-island story was repeated

10 ¶ And the LORD spake unto the fish, and it vomited out Jonah upon the dry land.

3 And the word of the LORD came unto Jonah the second time, saying,

2 Arise, go unto Nineveh, that great city, and preach unto it the preaching that I bid thee.

3 So Jonah arose, and went unto Nineveh, according to the word of the LORD. Now Nineveh was an exceeding great city of three days' journey.

10 And the LORD spoke to the fish, and it vomited out Jonah upon the dry land.

3 Then the word of the LORD came to Jonah the second time, saying, 2 "Arise, go to Nin'eveh, that great city, and proclaim to it the message that I tell you." 3 So Jonah arose and went to Nin'eveh, according to the word of the LORD. Now Nin'eveh was an exceedingly great city, three days'

10. This verse follows logically upon vs. 1 rather than upon vs. 9, which presupposes that a deliverance has already taken place. **Vomited out:** In Jer. 51:44, the Babylonians who, like a monster (Jer. 51:34) had swallowed up Israel and other nations, are forced to vomit them forth again. **Dry land:** No identification is made of what land. It may be assumed that it was the coast of Palestine.

III. THE RELUCTANT MISSIONARY (3:1-10)

3:1. Again the story shifts abruptly forward. God's original command to Jonah is repeated. There is no mention of Jonah's unfaithfulness or of any change in his attitude as a result of his harrowing experience. At no point is there an acknowledgment of disobedience or an expression of repentance. The only indication that God's severe pursuit of Jonah has had an effect is when Jonah obeys God's command and goes to Nineveh. It soon becomes evident that the obedience is not a willing one but rather a temporary forced compliance.

If in this parable Jonah represents Israel and the incident of the great fish represents the Exile, the question arises whether ch. 1 is meant to refer to the pre-exilic period and chs. 3-4 to the postexilic. The inference then would be that whereas in the former period Israel refused entirely its commission to be a missionary to the Gentiles, in the latter period, chastened by exile, it took up the commission grudgingly. This may be straining too far the details of the parable but it is at least possible.

3. Nineveh was: The past tense shows that the writing belongs to a period after the destruction of Nineveh in 612 B.C. **Three days' journey in breadth:** This would be sixty to seventy-five miles, since a day's journey would be twenty to twenty-five miles. A city of such vast extent is unknown in ancient or modern times. A survey of ancient Nineveh published in 1855 by F. Jones ("Topography of Nineveh," *Journal of the Royal Asiatic Society,* XV, 324) showed the city at its greatest length to be sixteen thousand feet, and at its greatest width seven thousand feet. One mile and a half, therefore, would be the farthest Jonah had to travel to reach the center of the city. Later centuries magnified the extent of the city until it was thought to have taken in a huge area between the Tigris and Euphrates rivers.

without change, surviving several centuries more in literary allusions.[1]

3:1. Second Chance.—It was the same **Lord,** the same **word,** the same purpose. It was the revelation of God's character which Jonah had feared; he would save Nineveh; he would also save Jonah (cf. Ps. 103). Said Arnold J. Toynbee: "The society of which man is a part in-

cludes God as well as human personalities, and therefore includes also an unbending righteous Judgment, and a universal redemptive Will, set above all action, both social and personal."[2]

Jonah had felt now the outreaching presence of God from which there is no escape, without or within. He had sensed the nobility of these "foreigners," finding in them a common humanity transcending all their differences. An-

[1] Cornelia Catlin Coulter, "The 'Great Fish' in Ancient and Medieval Story," *Transactions of the American Philological Association,* LVII (1926), 32-50.

[2] David Wesley Soper, "A Second Look at Toynbee," *Religion in Life,* XIX (1950), 201.

4 And Jonah began to enter into the city a day's journey, and he cried, and said, Yet forty days, and Nineveh shall be overthrown.

5 ¶ So the people of Nineveh believed God, and proclaimed a fast, and put on sackcloth, from the greatest of them even to the least of them.

journey in breadth. 4 Jonah began to go into the city, going a day's journey. And he cried, "Yet forty days, and Nin'eveh shall be overthrown!" 5 And the people of Nin'eveh believed God; they proclaimed a fast, and put on sackcloth, from the greatest of them to the least of them.

---

4. **Cried:** The impression is that Jonah proclaimed his message of judgment all day long as he traveled into the city. He had gone only one third of the way through the city when his words took startling effect upon the population. **Yet forty days:** The LXX reads "three days," which fits better the swift movement of the story. Thus Jonah sits down to wait not forty but only three days to see what will happen.

5. **Believed:** The construction אמן with the preposition ב is used in Gen. 15:6 to signify Abraham's trust and reliance upon God. The Ninevites did not merely believe Jonah's prediction to be true and repent in fear; they responded in faith to Israel's God. The question how Assyrians would understand Jonah has sometimes been answered by referring to Isa. 36:11, where it is evident that Aramaic was a lingua franca for the educated classes; it is assumed then that Jonah spoke Aramaic. The impression one receives from the story, however, is that educated and uneducated alike—**the greatest . . . to the least**—understood the proclamation of doom. It is more likely that the author of the parable did not concern himself about the detail of language. **Fast . . . sackcloth:** Signs of profound repentance. The lack of repentance on the part of Jonah himself throughout the book stands in striking contrast to the universal repentance and humiliation of the Assyrians. Jonah is singularly unmoved by his sins against God, while the heathen repent at the first word of judgment. This is surely intended to indicate how hardened against God Israel had become in its proud self-assurance, and how wrong

---

toine de Saint Exupéry, in *Wind, Sand and Stars,* writes of gallant French airmen who, when forced to land in the desert after wandering for days and at the end of their strength, were found by a Bedouin. Of the Bedouin he says,

You, Bedouin of Libya who saved lives, though you will dwell for ever in my memory yet I shall never be able to recapture your features. You are Humanity and your face comes into my mind simply as man incarnate. You, our beloved fellowman, did not know who we might be, and yet you recognized us without fail. And I, in my turn, shall recognize you in the faces of all mankind. You came towards me in an aureole of charity and magnanimity bearing the gift of water. All my friends and all my enemies marched towards me in your person. It did not seem to me that you were rescuing me: rather did it seem that you were forgiving me. And I felt I had no enemy left in all the world.[3]

Jonah has risen to heights in his confession of guilt and in his sacrifice of himself. And even there the hand of God had found him, the

"Hound of Heaven" had pursued him for a purpose. And now **the word of the LORD came to Jonah the second time;** he is given a second chance. Surely he will go forward. Who can refuse so gracious a God?

But it is also the same Jonah who emerges from these experiences. There is no real change of heart. Still he is a first-class nationalist, exalting his own country, his own people, his own God. He has not learned by suffering.[4] He will give reluctant obedience, though he cannot rise even to the level of Cleanthes, who prays for grace to follow God's lead of his own will: "For if I quail and rebel I shall have to follow just the same." Jonah had learned nothing from his experiences, like so many today who have learned little from the sufferings of our generations, tending to confirm Heine's bitter words that we "learn from history that we do not learn from history."

Jonah arose and went. But there was no mercy in his heart. God's graciousness to him had not kindled mercy in him toward others.

[3] Tr. Lewis Galantiere (New York: Harcourt, Brace, & Co.; London: William Heinemann, 1939), p. 235. Used by permission.

[4] See the Greek classics, especially the Gilbert Murray translations of Aeschylus, *Eumenides* (New York: Oxford University Press, 1925), p. viii, and *Prometheus Bound* (New York: Oxford University Press, 1931), p. 11.

6 For word came unto the king of Nineveh, and he arose from his throne, and he laid his robe from him, and covered *him* with sackcloth, and sat in ashes.

7 And he caused *it* to be proclaimed and published through Nineveh by the decree of the king and his nobles, saying, Let neither man nor beast, herd nor flock, taste any thing: let them not feed, nor drink water:

8 But let man and beast be covered with sackcloth, and cry mightily unto God: yea, let them turn every one from his evil way, and from the violence that *is* in their hands.

9 Who can tell *if* God will turn and repent, and turn away from his fierce anger, that we perish not?

10 ¶ And God saw their works, that they turned from their evil way; and God re-

6 Then tidings reached the king of Nin'eveh, and he arose from his throne, removed his robe, and covered himself with sackcloth, and sat in ashes. 7 And he made proclamation and published through Nin'eveh, "By the decree of the king and his nobles: Let neither man nor beast, herd nor flock, taste anything; let them not feed, or drink water, 8 but let man and beast be covered with sackcloth, and let them cry mightily to God; yea, let every one turn from his evil way and from the violence which is in his hands. 9 Who knows, God may yet repent and turn from his fierce anger, so that we perish not?"

10 When God saw what they did, how they turned from their evil way, God re-

---

the Israelites were to think that they stood in a relationship to God of which the heathen were incapable.

6. The climax of Nineveh's humiliation before God is reached when the great **king** himself comes down from the throne, removes the symbols of his royal authority, dons sackcloth like his subjects, and sits in ashes. The king has thus acknowledged his subjection to the King of kings. **King of Nineveh:** It is another indication of the author's remoteness from an actual historical situation that he uses this title instead of king of Assyria, and gives to the king no proper name.

7. Made proclamation: The repentance which had been spontaneous now becomes obligatory upon every citizen, and even the animals are to share the fasting and the sackcloth. This was in keeping with ancient custom. Herodotus reports that in Persia animals were given a part in some ceremonies of mourning, and Judith 4:10 shows the existence of the custom among the Jews.

8. Man and beast: This phrase creates a difficulty since it makes the command to cry to God and to amend their ways of life apply to the beasts as well as to the men. It is perhaps an addition. **Let them turn:** The national humiliation is not to expend its energy in fasting and donning of sackcloth but is to result in a moral transformation of the life of the people.

9. The decree ends with the expression of a humble hope that God may forgive them and spare them from destruction. The whole is a model of how men should respond to God's word of judgment upon them. It is as though the author were saying to Israel: When have you responded like this to a prophet's proclamation of God's judgment upon you?

10. What they did: Their deeds. It is the change in the moral life of the Ninevites that moves God to compassion. Repentance issuing in reformation of conduct brings

---

"Forty days, and Nineveh shall be overthrown" was his message. There was only judgment in it, no hope. In spite of the warning of the storm, the nobility of the sailors, his rescue from the fish, his knowledge of God's mercy! With such intractable human material God has to work, and work through. No wonder the going is rough at times.

But to the people of Nineveh there came an-

other message. Plotinus maintained that God was gotten and holden by love; by thought never. God has not left himself without witnesses in us; and saving common sense often runs counter to the dictates of the priest. It was as though the people had said, "If we repent, who can tell if God will not relent?"

10. The Everlasting Mercy.—The people of Nineveh in their repentance had appealed not

pented of the evil, that he had said that he would do unto them; and he did *it* not.

4 But it displeased Jonah exceedingly, and he was very angry.

2 And he prayed unto the Lord, and said, I pray thee, O Lord, *was* not this my saying, when I was yet in my country? Therefore I fled before unto Tarshish: for I knew that thou *art* a gracious God, and merciful, slow to anger, and of great kindness, and repentest thee of the evil.

pented of the evil which he had said he would do to them; and he did not do it.

4 But it displeased Jonah exceedingly, and he was angry. 2 And he prayed to the Lord and said, "I pray thee, Lord, is not this what I said when I was yet in my country? That is why I made haste to flee to Tarshish; for I knew that thou art a gracious God and merciful, slow to anger, and abounding in steadfast love, and re-

---

a lifting of the sentence of doom. **God repented:** Cf. Exod. 32:14; II Sam. 24:16; Amos 7:3, 6. The O.T. has no embarrassment in saying that God changes his mind. He does not change his nature, but as the responses of men to him change, it becomes necessary for him to follow a different line of action in order to be true to his nature.

IV. The Absurdity of Limiting God's Mercy (4:1-11)

4:1. It displeased Jonah: The whole of ch. 4 is the account of Jonah's displeasure. His anger was as much a repudiation of God as was his flight in ch. 1. It was an anger that could not tolerate the thought of God having compassion upon the heathen. The character of Jonah here again stands in direct contrast to the general expectation concerning a prophet. At the point where a prophet might be expected to rejoice, Jonah is consumed by disappointment and anger. The sight of thousands of Assyrians repenting and turning to God enrages him. Every Israelite must condemn such conduct in a prophet; but having passed that judgment upon Jonah, the Israelite would soon learn that he had pronounced judgment upon himself.

2. And he prayed: As in 1:9, Jonah conducts himself as though he were a faithful believer, not a rebel against God. This is true to life in every age, for the most thoroughgoing rejection of God's will often takes place in persons who observe the forms of piety and in their own minds count themselves believers. **What I said:** Lit., "my word." Jonah's word stands over against God's which has been first one of judgment, then one of pardon; Jonah's has in it judgment alone. In his prayer Jonah's concern is to justify himself and his word. To him it is perfectly clear that he has been right from the beginning; everything has worked out just as he foresaw. So intent is he upon his own rightness that he is quite unable to understand what God is doing. **A gracious God and**

---

to a law but to a Person. A law is inexorable; a person may change his mind. Consequently, as Jonah recognized from the beginning, prophecy always has an element of uncertainty attached to it. It is always possible for God to change his mind. As Joel (2:13-14) had said: "Rend your heart, and not your garments, and turn unto the Lord your God. . . . Who knoweth if he will return and repent, and leave a blessing behind him?" So also Jeremiah (18:8) had said: "If that nation, against whom I have pronounced, turn from their evil, I will repent of the evil that I thought to do unto them." So one thesis of this little book of Jonah is a declaration of the universality of God's love and of his willingness to receive and bless all who turn to him in humble repentance and obedience, no matter what their race or condition of life.

God changes his mind as man changes his conduct. When man repents of his wickedness and does that which is right in God's sight, the ground of the divine judgment ceases to exist. Always possible is the escape to the Everlasting Mercy. "In the same place in which you find God's omnipotence you will find his humility." [5]

4:1-14. *Jonah's Anger.*—It was the same Jonah, still the narrow little nationalist, despising others, hoping for the doom of his enemies, catching none of the vision of human brotherhood which God was trying to teach him. Yet he had expected that the Everlasting Mercy would have the last word. **I knew that thou art a gracious God, and merciful, slow to anger, and of great kindness, and repentest thee of the evil.** To ascribe such qualities to God and then turn **angry** because these qualities mani-

[5] Rabbi Johanan.

3 Therefore now, O Lord, take, I beseech thee, my life from me; for *it is* better for me to die than to live.

4 ¶ Then said the Lord, Doest thou well to be angry?

5 So Jonah went out of the city, and sat on the east side of the city, and there made him a booth, and sat under it in the shadow, till he might see what would become of the city.

pentest of evil. 3 Therefore now, O Lord, take my life from me, I beseech thee, for it is better for me to die than to live." 4 And the Lord said, "Do you do well to be angry?" 5 Then Jonah went out of the city and sat to the east of the city, and made a booth for himself there. He sat under it in the shade, till he should see what would become of the city.

merciful: Here it is revealed fully what Jonah is rejecting. The words would carry every Israelite mind back to Exod. 34:6-7, where Yahweh reveals himself to Moses as the God that he is. "Jehovah, Jehovah, a God merciful and gracious, slow to anger, and abundant in lovingkindness and truth; keeping lovingkindness for thousands, forgiving iniquity and transgression and sin" (ASV). Jonah has known all along that it is the nature of God to have compassion on the Assyrians if they should repent of their sin. It was because he knew the nature of God so well that he refused to go as a prophet to the hated Assyrians.

3. Take my life from me: So central was hatred of the Assyrians in Jonah's existence that when they escaped from the threatened destruction he seemed to have nothing left for which to live. This was a sharp accusation against Israel, that they had let hatred of the heathen become so dominant in their thoughts that to be frustrated in the desire for vengeance robbed life of all meaning.

4. Do you do well to be angry? may also be translated, "Are you very angry?" suggesting a gentleness and pity on the part of God toward Jonah, as a parent might speak to a sulking child. The RSV represents God as pressing home upon Jonah the question of the rightfulness of his anger. Some commentators regard this verse as an intrusion, since the question receives no answer from Jonah, as it does when repeated in vs. 9. The question, however, is most appropriate as God's response to Jonah's prayer and does not require an answer.

5. Sat on the east side: Jonah has passed through the whole city to reach the east side, three days' journey. It is therefore two days since he first saw the repentance of the people. If the LXX reading of 3:4 is correct, only one of the three days' intermission before the threatened judgment would remain. **Made a booth** seems to render the gourd of vs. 6 unnecessary. The phrase may have been added as a consequence of the reading "forty days" in 3:4. An Oriental would be conscious of the severity of the ordeal of sitting thirty-eight days unprotected in the hot sun outside the city. **Till he might see:** Some commentators think this clause also has been added, since Jonah already knew the fate of the city. Its force, however, may be to show Jonah clinging still to the hope that destruction may come upon Nineveh.

fested themselves is irony but not history. So Jonah sulks outside the city wall.

Plato contended that the divine agency is always a persuasive agency, trying to win men through the persuasion of ideals. And there follows the story of the gourd vine protecting Jonah from the blistering heat of the desert sun, stirring him to gratitude for its shade; and then of its destruction and Jonah's anger. Then come the great words: **Thou hast had pity on the gourd, . . . which came up in a night, and perished in a night: and should not I spare Nineveh, that great city, wherein are more** than sixscore thousand persons that cannot discern between their right hand and their left hand; and also much cattle? So we are left with this moving plea to Jonah to recognize his kinship, his common humanity with these "foreigners"—this vision of the universal love of God brooding over the wayward race of men, seeking to bind up its wounds and its divisions, this dawning dream of human brotherhood comprising all races and peoples, set on the only indestructible base, the love of universal fatherhood of God in whom all men live, and move, and have their being.

6 And the Lord God prepared a gourd, and made *it* to come up over Jonah, that it might be a shadow over his head, to deliver him from his grief. So Jonah was exceeding glad of the gourd.

7 But God prepared a worm when the morning rose the next day, and it smote the gourd that it withered.

8 And it came to pass, when the sun did arise, that God prepared a vehement east wind; and the sun beat upon the head of Jonah, that he fainted, and wished in himself to die, and said, *It is* better for me to die than to live.

6 And the Lord God appointed a plant,[b] and made it come up over Jonah, that it might be a shade over his head, to save him from his discomfort. So Jonah was exceedingly glad because of the plant.[b] 7 But when dawn came up the next day, God appointed a worm which attacked the plant,[b] so that it withered. 8 When the sun rose, God appointed a sultry east wind, and the sun beat upon the head of Jonah so that he was faint; and he asked that he might die, and said, "It is better for me to die than to

[b] Heb *qiqayon,* probably *the castor oil plant*

---

6. **Gourd:** Probably the ricinus or **castor oil plant,** which with its large leaves would supply the needful shade. The attempt to find a plant which would grow high enough in a single day to give shade to Jonah is beside the point. The plant grows suddenly at God's command, just as the great fish swallowed Jonah at God's command. The author does not mean to describe natural happenings. **Was exceedingly glad:** The anger of Jonah disappears and in its place is delight in the gourd that shades him.

7. God permits the gourd only a very short life. At dawn the next day it is destroyed by a **worm.** Destruction thus comes not upon Nineveh, as Jonah desires, but upon an object which has become precious to Jonah. He is given a taste of what destruction is like. He finds the taste bitter, but he does not draw the conclusion how bitter to the inhabitants of Nineveh would be the destruction that he hoped might overtake them.

8. **A sultry east wind:** The scorching sirocco, which with its intense heat and its dust makes life intolerable even indoors. Jonah, sitting unprotected under the sun, would suffer severely. **Asked that he might die:** Lit., "asked his soul to die." He does not ask God that he may die, as in vs. 3, but in his grief communes within himself. What Jonah does not see is that the judgment of God is resting upon him rather than upon Nineveh. The heathen rejoice in their salvation while the prophet of God is crushed under the hand of God. This scene, as well as the one in vs. 3, is like an echo of Elijah's hour of despair in I Kings 19:4. But Jonah and Elijah stand in sharp contrast:

The brotherhood of Man presupposes the fatherhood of God—a truth which involves the converse proposition that, if the divine father of the human family is ever left out of the reckoning, there is no possibility of forging any alternative bond of purely human texture which will avail by itself to hold Mankind together.[6]

This is the reason for the fact that the Jewish church reads this little book of Jonah on its day of Atonement. For here is atonement, at-one-ment, drawing men closer to God and closer to their fellow men.

What became of Jonah? Could he resist this so gracious God? Was he touched by the divine compassion, so that compassion was kindled in his own heart and he became in fact a prophet of God? For pity is no meek, mild emotion. It is a "rebel passion. Its hand is against the strong, against the organized force of society, against conventional sanctions and accepted

[6] Toynbee, *Study of History,* VI, 9.

Gods. It is the Kingdom of Heaven within us fighting against the brute powers of the world."[7] Is Jonah's depression an indication of something more profound:

Is my gloom, after all,
Shade of His hand, outstretched caressingly?
"Ah, fondest, blindest, weakest,
I am He Whom thou seekest!
Thou dravest love from thee, who dravest Me."[8]

But we are not told what happened to Jonah. The author is not concerned with him, but with his readers. He is asking: What does this mean to you in your day of hatreds, prejudices, and fears? Can any one of us resist this brooding, loving gracious God? Especially, can we

[7] Euripides, *The Trojan Women,* tr. Gilbert Murray (4th ed.; London: George Allen & Unwin, 1904), p. 7.
[8] Francis Thompson, "The Hound of Heaven." From *Collected Works,* ed. Wilfred Meynell. Used by permission of Burns, Oates & Washbourne, Ltd., and Sir Francis Meynell

9 And God said to Jonah, Doest thou well to be angry for the gourd? And he said, I do well to be angry, *even* unto death.

10 Then said the LORD, Thou hast had pity on the gourd, for the which thou hast not labored, neither madest it grow; which came up in a night, and perished in a night:

11 And should not I spare Nineveh, that great city, wherein are more than sixscore thousand persons that cannot discern between their right hand and their left hand; and *also* much cattle?

live." 9 But God said to Jonah, "Do you do well to be angry for the plant?"[b] And he said, "I do well to be angry, angry enough to die." 10 And the LORD said, "You pity the plant,[b] for which you did not labor, nor did you make it grow, which came into being in a night, and perished in a night. 11 And should not I pity Nin'eveh, that great city, in which there are more than a hundred and twenty thousand persons who do not know their right hand from their left, and also much cattle?"

[b] Heb *qiqayon*, probably *the castor oil plant*

Elijah wanting to die because so few would heed his word of judgment; Jonah wanting to die because so many have repented at his word.

9. God chides Jonah again as he did in vs. 4. **To be angry:** So far in this incident Jonah has shown not anger but grief. God's question and Jonah's answer reveal, however, that he has been angry with God for destroying the gourd. Jonah is capable of compassion, great compassion—for a plant that lasts only for a day and has no further life.

10. Jonah's unreasonableness stands fully unmasked. He can be merciful, yet he is unwilling that God should be merciful. The theme which came to expression in ch. 1 is driven home in the concluding verses of the parable, and then the parable in characteristic fashion breaks off abruptly. The Israelite who did not get the point of God's unanswered question would have to be stupid indeed. An Israel without compassion would be unthinkable, yet Israel rebels at the thought of God's looking with compassion upon the heathen and having a care for their salvation. **For which you did not labor:** Jonah did nothing to create the gourd, but, by contrast, the Ninevites are God's creation and naturally belong under his care. His sending of Jonah to them was one evidence of his care. All lands and nations belong to God and must be the objects of his compassion.

11. Persons who do not know their right hand from their left: Children who are not yet old enough to distinguish right from left, and who therefore like **cattle** cannot be held responsible before God for the city's sins. Could any Israelite fail to be moved by this final appeal and still demand the unrelenting destruction of the heathen, innocent and guilty, repentant and unrepentant alike? The God who makes this appeal to Israel is the Lord of the whole earth, whose compassion reaches to all peoples, and the destiny that he has for Israel is to be his prophet to the nations, proclaiming judgment to them that they may repent and live.

---

resist the God who has revealed himself, on the highest level possible for our poor minds, in Christ? The handle of the door of a church in Sweden is a great bronze ring, enclosing a crucifix. But the ring itself is held by a great hand protruding from the door, the hand of God; and a finger extends from the hand, pointing directly at anyone who would open that door, as though to say: "What does this mean to you, this cross, this sacrifice? And what are you doing about it?" This in our day is what the author of the book of Jonah would ask us. We have our own problems, we "gentle people of

prejudice." The neo-isolationist, the racist, the detractor of foreign people, the resister of human brotherhood—are they not with us still, blocking constructive action, facing toward the past and hoping for the return of the society they once knew and knew how to manipulate to their own advantage? They have not learned, as Jonah did not learn, as we all are slow to learn, that we now face ruin unless we change our ways; that we live in a world where if we would save ourselves, we must also save others, and if we will not save others, ourselves we cannot save.

The Book of

MICAH

Introduction and Exegesis by Rolland E. Wolfe
Exposition by Harold A. Bosley

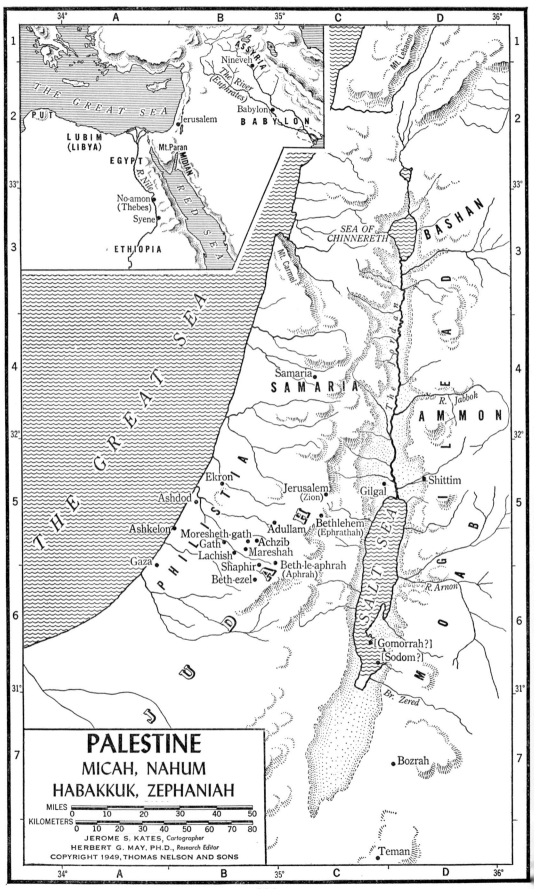

PALESTINE
MICAH, NAHUM
HABAKKUK, ZEPHANIAH

MILES
0   10   20   30   40   50

KILOMETERS
0 10 20 30 40 50 60 70 80

JEROME S. KATES, *Cartographer*
HERBERT G. MAY, PH.D., *Research Editor*
COPYRIGHT 1949, THOMAS NELSON AND SONS

MICAH

INTRODUCTION

Of all the prophets, Micah is perhaps the one whose contributions have been most habitually underestimated. Rather than being judged by the quality of their poetic utterances, the hitherto prevalent rating of the prophets has been based largely on the number of written pages that has happened to survive from each of them. By this standard Micah has not fared well. This common depreciation of him is assisted by the situation that, with regard to biographical data, only a few facts can be ascertained regarding him. These two circumstances have conspired to make Micah one of the least adequately appreciated among the company of the prophets.

In these days, when the relative significance of the various prophets is being reappraised, the prestige of Micah is rising in the estimation of biblical scholars. Because of this trend, we may approach the study of Micah with new expectation, realizing that we are not dealing with a second-rate individual but with an important link in the great prophetic succession.

I. Home

One of the few facts that has survived with regard to Micah concerns his home, which was at Mareshah, sometimes written Moresheth or Morasheth (1:1, 14-15; Jer. 26:18). The place survives today as Marissa, the Arabized form of the name. From the time of Micah to the present this small town has remained much the same. It was an insignificant location, mentioned otherwise in the Bible only in routine lists of places (Josh. 15:44; II Chr. 11:8) as the location of a battle (II Chr. 14:9-10) and as the home of a certain Eliezer (II Chr. 20:37). If it had not been for Micah this village would never have been more than a mere name.

Mareshah was located in the southwest part of Palestine in the region called the Shephelah, a foothill area between the coastal plain and the central highlands. On the border line between Judah and the Philistine country, as well as an outpost in the direction of Egypt, this was a frontier village in a dual sense. It was one of the first objectives for attack in case of a military campaign against Palestine from either south or west. The prophet accordingly displayed that international concern, and fear of invasion, which always has been typical of seacoast and borderline people. He was deeply concerned for the peace and welfare of his home town and its neighboring communities.

II. Prophetic Relationships

Nothing is known concerning the "call" of Micah. The remote inspiration for taking up his prophetic task may have come from the example of "Eliezer the son of Dodavahu of Mareshah," who lived almost two centuries earlier, and "prophesied against Jehoshaphat," asserting that the destruction of the Judean navy was God's punishment upon him for making an alliance with King Ahaziah of Israel (II Chr. 20:37). Micah may well have been a lineal descendant of this prophet Eliezer. In this case Micah would have been reactivating an old family prophetic tradition. The more immediate stimulus was provided by the continuing influence of his late neighbor Amos, who had lived only twenty miles from Mareshah, for Micah was most profoundly moved by the spirit of Amos.

Micah was fourth in the line of those great prophets which we call the prophetic succession. He was the second important prophet in the southern kingdom of Judah. With Amos, Hosea, and Isaiah, he formed a quartet of major characters who produced the golden age of Hebrew prophecy during the latter half of the eighth century B.C.

In social status Micah differed from the other

three. Amos was a shepherd from the mountain wastes; Hosea, a prosperous farmer from north Israel; and Isaiah, an aristocrat reared at court in the capital city of Jerusalem. By contrast, Micah apparently was a small town artisan. In present-day terminology he would be called a proletarian. His prophecies indicate deep sympathy for the poor. In our age he probably would feel more at home in a labor hall than in a cathedral.

His addresses were delivered for the most part not in his home town of Mareshah, but on trips to Jerusalem. In that metropolis Isaiah was presumably delivering prophetic utterances at the same time. Yet there is no evidence to indicate they ever met, for Micah was only remotely influenced by Isaiah, his older contemporary. Perhaps they were kept apart by the different social grooves into which they were born. Their messages, however, were in complete harmony.

III. International Setting

The initial factors which called forth both Isaiah and Micah were mainly political and international. Assyria had embarked on an era of military activity, menacing the West with her tyranny. Syria, with her capital at Damascus, had been conquered in 732 B.C., and many of her people were carried into exile. Israel suffered the same fate ten years later. This left Judah in a precarious position as the first line of defense against Assyria in the regions of Palestine. By the time of Micah, Judah had become merely a small surviving buffer between Assyria and the eventual realization of her dreams in Egypt. Since the beginning of Assyria's aggressiveness there had been thirteen major campaigns toward Palestine and Egypt. There was every indication that these would be accelerated rather than diminished until the imperialistic aspirations of Assyria in the West would be accomplished. It therefore seemed evident to Micah that unless she should be very scrupulous with regard to her internal life and foreign relationships, Judah was destined sooner or later for annihilation. Micah knew he was living in a time when it was a question of life or death for his nation, and how could anyone who had power of discernment remain silent?

IV. Date

The exact date of Micah's activity is uncertain. The opening verse states that his work was contemporary with the three kings of Judah, Jotham, Ahaz, and Hezekiah. This would make 737 to 686 B.C. the maximum period for his prophetic teaching. He would then have been contemporary with Isaiah almost throughout his ministry. This has been the older view among scholars and commentators. However,

introductory verses which were prefixed to the various prophetic collections, presumably by a late editor in the third century B.C., are frequently inaccurate. The verse introducing the book of Micah seems to offer one of these instances.

Internal evidence in the prophecies themselves gives little indication that any of them were produced during the reigns of Jotham or Ahaz. C. H. Cornill was one of the first to point out that the names of these two kings are out of place in vs. 1. Most significant is the statement in the book of Jeremiah that the prophetic work of Micah occurred during the reign of King Hezekiah (Jer. 26:18-19). Jeremiah lived sufficiently near in time to Micah to have retained proper historical perspectives. This statement of the prophet Jeremiah, combined with the internal evidence within the book of Micah, indicates this prophet's work was not so early as Jotham and Ahaz but was confined to the reign of King Hezekiah, which gives the maximum range of 715-686 B.C.

By careful examination of the book it becomes evident that even this possible latitude is to be further reduced. There is no reason to believe that Micah began his public work immediately at the king's accession. Internal evidence suggests that he did so at approximately 714 B.C., only shortly before the great Assyrian western campaign to Palestine in 711 B.C. He proclaimed that Judah would be annihilated, but this did not come true. So it seems Micah was discredited and passed from public view for perhaps half a decade.

His closing work was connected with the crisis of 701 B.C., when an Assyrian attack was materializing and the armies of Sennacherib seemed destined to conquer all of Judah. Although almost destroyed by the Assyrians, Jerusalem's eventual survival again discredited Micah, for he had predicted that city's utter downfall (3:12; Jer. 26:18). Inasmuch as only several prophecies seem to be later than that crisis, 700 B.C. would be the approximate *terminus ad quem* of his work.

Although nothing can be "proved" for any specific dating of Micah's mission, the aforementioned indications point to the years 714-700 B.C. for the period of his public activity. Most of his speaking was done immediately before the dates 711 and 701 B.C., when the national situations were critical. These two "prophetic campaigns" were likely separated by five or six years of relative inactivity.

V. Domestic Situation

The other major factor which commanded attention from Micah was corruption within Judah. Morals were appallingly low. Governmental officials were dishonest. A low ethical tone prevailed in most areas of life. Because the nation had lost her moral integrity, she had become sinful, soft, and ripe for conquest. Faced with this situation, Micah was willing to give his life to the task of strengthening the moral fiber of his people as their only sure defense.

As kings of Judah went, Hezekiah was one of the best, especially with regard to religious matters. He was favorably inclined toward the prophetic ideals. It is not known whether he was naturally so or became this way under the prodding of Isaiah and Micah. The latter, however, seems probable. It is notable that in the days of Jeremiah the "elders of the land" gave Micah credit for having caused King Hezekiah to "fear the LORD and entreat the favor of the LORD" (Jer. 26:17-19). They also went on to indicate that the sparing of Jerusalem in the crisis of 701 B.C. was attributable to the prophetic work of Micah.

King Hezekiah instituted a sweeping reform in which he destroyed the semipagan "high places" and demolished the images worshiped by both the believers in Yahweh and the adherents of non-Yahweh cults. This foretaste of the later Deuteronomic reformation was probably executed as an expression of royal action resulting from the vigorous demands in the preaching of Isaiah and Micah. It may well be regarded as a monument to their prophetic accomplishments when the Deuteronomic editor of the book of Kings states in his epitaph to King Hezekiah: "He trusted in the LORD the God of Israel; so that there was none like him. . . . For he held fast to the LORD; he did not depart from following him, but kept the commandments which the LORD commanded Moses. And the LORD was with him; wherever he went forth he prospered" (II Kings 18:5-7).

This ultraeulogistic appraisal of Hezekiah ignores the tragedies precipitated upon the period of his kingship by his unwise international policies. Also, even though Hezekiah was "good" and carried out a reformation, he seemed relatively powerless to do much in a fundamental way toward raising the low morality, ethical practices, and religious perspectives of his time.

VI. Literary Factors

Like most of the prophets, Micah was a poet and expressed his thoughts in rhythmic verse. His writings therefore must be interpreted from poetic rather than prosaic standards. With respect to literary ability, it has been customary to underestimate him. Admittedly, Micah was not a master such as Amos or Isaiah, but he appears much superior to Ezekiel and those who rank in that class. In these days, when Micah is being rediscovered and the poetic significance of his productions is becoming better understood, there is developing a new appreciation for the way in which the power and zeal behind his utterances have been given literary expression.

The text of Micah is in a good state of preservation, which indicates it was in possession of people who gave it good care during the precanonical period. Contrasting with the extreme corruptness in the prophecies of Hosea, the book of Micah is in the best condition of any of the eighth-century prophetic texts. The exegesis therefore presents relatively few problems.

By contrast with the three large prophetic collections which bear the names of Isaiah, Jeremiah, and Ezekiel, the book of Micah is found in the collection designated in the Hebrew canon as "The Book of the Twelve." In Hebrew and English Bibles it occupies sixth place among the twelve. In the Greek canon it is in third position.

VII. Unity

The chief problem concerns the question as to how much of the content is by the prophet and how much consists of supplements added by later generations. The older view accepted without question the entire collection as the work of Micah. Since 1850 there has been a tendency to challenge this assumption. Bernhard Stade, in his epoch-making articles in the *Zeitschrift für die alttestamentliche Wissenschaft* from 1881 to 1884, concluded that no part of chs. 4–7 should be ascribed to the prophet Micah, and his view has been adopted by many since that time. The fact that the ending of ch. 3 is quoted in Jer. 26:18 has been held to indicate that this was the conclusion of Micah's book in the days of Jeremiah. It is considered likely that the elders, whom the prophet Jeremiah was describing, quoted the final words of Micah in the light of their observation that no violent action was taken against him. In recent times there has developed a tendency to regard chs. 4–5 and 6–7 as two miscellaneous collections which have been added to the book as later supplements, coming for the most part from postexilic times.

More considered opinion regards the findings of the Stade school too radical. Although there may be no material by Micah in the first appendix (chs. 4–5) or the latter part of the second (7:5-20), there is a strong likelihood that the concluding utterances of this prophet are found in a detached position in 6:1–7:4. Even within chs. 1–3, secondary portions have apparently been inserted in 1:2-4 and 2:12-13. Thus it may be said that of the seven chapters in the book, an approximate total of four are in all likelihood by Micah. The remainder, which would amount to a total of three, may be ascribed to secondary writers.

It is gradually coming to be realized that in those days commentators did not make separate books of their productions but that a manuscript, such as the present text of Micah, consisted of the basic document plus the comments which accrued to it during the time it circulated as a living growing book. In the case of Micah this period of growth lasted almost five centuries, from the time some collector edited what was available of the addresses into a manuscript shortly after 700 B.C. until the collection became regarded as sacred scripture at approximately 200 B.C. Thereafter it was an unalterable text, and no further additions were permissible. One must be prepared therefore to find in this collection not only the writings of Micah but also selected manuscripts and comments from the various ages in that five-hundred-year period. In a sense Micah is a source book for observing the development of Hebrew thought from 714 B.C. to approximately 200 B.C.

VIII. The Prophet's Significance

As it becomes realized that the division between so-called "major" and "minor" prophets is based solely on the criterion of volume rather than quality, there is renewed hope for the rating of Micah. He was not a "minor" prophet. None of the four eighth-century prophets were minor characters. It has already been noted that Jer. 26:19 credits Micah with having brought about a major repentance among the people of Judah. It might be said that the whole proletarian movement of modern times is indebted to Amos and Micah as the first individuals in the Judeo-Christian tradition to espouse in an especially active way the cause of the oppressed. Their influence in championing the welfare of the poor and needy was to become perpetuated in Zephaniah, the psalmists, John the Baptist, Jesus, Francis of Assisi, and John Wesley, to mention only a few subsequent figures who have stood in the special succession of these two prophets.

Jeremiah told how "your own sword hath devoured your prophets, like a destroying lion" (Jer. 2:30). He went on, however, to say (26:18-19) that when Micah "prophesied . . . to all the people of Judah," he was not dealt with in this manner but was allowed to speak his message and live. This was in contrast with his contemporary Isaiah who, according to tradition, was put into a hollow log, which then was sawed in two. It may therefore be assumed that Micah died a natural death and is not to be reckoned among the prophet-martyrs.

IX. Outline of Contents

I. Background to Micah's prophecies (1:1-4)
  A. Introductory heading (1:1)
  B. An eschatological psalm (1:2-4)
II. Discourses on the Assyrian crisis (1:5-16)
  A. The wailing prophet (1:5-9)
  B. The alarm (1:10-16)
III. Prophecies of ethical concern (2:1–3:12)
  A. The Jerusalem men of wealth (2:1-10)
  B. Love for false prophets (2:11)
  C. Dreams of restoration (2:12-13)
  D. Appeal to the leaders of Judah (3:1-12)
IV. Visions of a glorious future (4:1–5:15)
  A. Universal religion and perpetual peace (4:1-8)
  B. The way of monarchy, militarism, and vengeance (4:9–5:6)
  C. A world of purity, blessing, and benediction (5:7-15)
V. Adversity that triumphs in hope (6:1–7:20)
  A. God's controversy with his wayward people (6:1-5)
  B. Incidentals or fundamentals in religion (6:6-8)
  C. The Deity's final plea to Jerusalem (6:9-16)
  D. The pessimism of despair (7:1-6)
  E. The invincible triumph of faith (7:7-20)

X. Selected Bibliography

HAUPT, PAUL. "The Book of Micah" and "Notes on Micah," *American Journal of Semitic Languages and Literatures*, XXVII (1910), 1-63.

LINDBLOM, JOHANNES. *Micha literarisch untersucht* ("Acta Academiae Aboensis"). Åbo: Åbo Akademi, 1929.

SMITH, J. M. P. "The Strophic Structure of the Book of Micah," in R. F. Harper, *et al.*, eds., *Old Testament and Semitic Studies in Memory of W. R. Harper*. Chicago: University of Chicago Press, 1908. Vol. II, pp. 415-38.

STADE, BERNHARD. "Bemerkungen über das Buch Micha," *u.s.w.*, *Zeitschrift für die alttestamentliche Wissenschaft*, I (1881), 161-72; III (1883), 1-16; IV (1884), 291-97; VI (1886), 122-23; XXIII (1903), 163-71.

TAIT, ARTHUR J. *The Prophecy of Micah.* New York: Charles Scribner's Sons, 1917.

MICAH

TEXT, EXEGESIS, AND EXPOSITION

1 The word of the Lord that came to Micah the Morasthite in the days of Jotham, Ahaz, *and* Hezekiah, kings of Judah, which he saw concerning Samaria and Jerusalem.

1 The word of the Lord that came to Micah of Mo′resheth in the days of Jotham, Ahaz, and Hezeki′ah, kings of Judah, which he saw concerning Samar′ia and Jerusalem.

I. Background to Micah's Prophecies (1:1-4)
A. Introductory Heading (1:1)

1:1. This verse was apparently prefixed to the collection by the compiler of the Book of the Twelve. It asserts that Micah's messages are **the word of the Lord,** and that they **came to Micah** presumably by way of revelation. The last clause places Micah in the variant role of a "seer," for it says **he saw** (חזה) these messages, apparently in the form of visions.

The Mission of the Prophet.—The book of Micah is a lesson in how to take God seriously. It is instructive of the tremendous difference religious faith makes in the way one looks at life, particularly the life of one's own time. Micah was not the only religious man in Israel —he would have been the first to deny that claim. There were priests, prophets, and multitudes of worshipers in the temples and before the altars of Israel. Yet the difference between their faith and that of Micah is the difference between a static and a living personal faith.

A dynamic prophetic faith is not so much a possession of man as the possessor of man. Micah's faith literally hurls him at the great issues of the day. It will not let him smile tolerantly at the spiritual complacency of formalism in religion; it drives him into a heated— and frequently unfair—attack upon it. It will not let him accept comfortable convictions about the eternal security of even the holy cities of Samaria and Zion: they are corrupt and therefore doomed, his faith forces him to cry. Nor can he cry out this judgment in the solitariness of his rural home; he must needs go to the cities themselves and to all surrounding cities with his far from pleasant message.

Yet faith in God does not conclude on a note of despair. Hope is the last word, then as now. But the hope which prophetic religion exalts is born of faith in God and in his love

of man. Micah sees that more clearly than some of his famous prophetic predecessors, and this explains why he comes closer than they to the beating heart of the N.T. conception of the proper relationship between God and man.

One thing is clear from a study of this book: the way of prophetic religion is as hard as it is holy. Only one who feels compelled by God will dare to start, and one who feels this compulsion dare not tarry.

1:1. *The Word of the Lord.*—On the face of it the calm claim that **the word of the Lord . . . came to Micah** is either the most important or the most impertinent assertion imaginable. Yet Micah is but one among the company of the prophets of Israel who claim to have had some such theophany. The details of Micah's great experience are unknown—quite unlike the experiences of Moses on Mount Sinai or Isaiah in the temple. We can safely say, however, that like those others it was rooted in this fact: God confronts man with a new experience of, new insight into, his holy will. Social insight and tremendous ethical preachments come later as the blade follows the planting of the seed.

We do well to emphasize the objective nature of **the word of the Lord.** For whatever else this experience is, it is not an adventure in autosuggestion; it is man the creature in conscious and vital relationship with God the creator. But there is no reason for theologians to make

901

| 2 Hear, all ye people; hearken, O earth, and all that therein is: and let the Lord God be witness against you, the Lord from his holy temple. | 2 Hear, you peoples, all of you; hearken, O earth, and all that is in it; and let the Lord God be a witness against you, the Lord from his holy temple. |

B. An Eschatological Psalm (1:2-4)

This fragment of excellent poetry seems dependent on Second Isaiah (Isa. 40:3-5), and probably was not written until at least a century and a half later than Micah. It does not purport to be the word of God, for the Deity is spoken of in the third person. The style and apparent date suggest its non-Micah character. By contrast with Micah, who proclaimed the impending destruction of Judah by the Assyrians, this eschatological psalm envisions the redeeming and reconditioning of the whole world at the hand of God. The editor may have prefixed these five couplets to the prophecies to create an atmosphere for the book. The psalm is incomplete, for it describes only the anticipated coming of God to earth and breaks off before his dealings with mankind are described.

2-3a. Proclamation concerning God's coming is made to all the world. As in post-exilic expectations, the Deity **cometh forth** from his abode, i.e., **from his holy temple** in

a fetish of objectivity. Equal emphasis must fall upon the words **came to Micah.** The word of God seems never to be like Longfellow's arrow —shot "into the air." It is always aimed at someone in particular, and unless it finds effective lodgment in that person's mind and life, we know nothing of it.

The word of the Lord . . . came to Micah, yes, and to other prophets, to Paul, to Wesley; it comes to all who are willing to hear and heed the will of God. We are dealing in the Bible with more than the record of what God said in some particular instance—though this is priceless; we are always dealing too with the conviction that such experiences continue to happen, that they can happen to anyone.

Yet a warning, well founded in experience, should be lifted: without exception, the word of God has proved to be a stern master. Our greatest religious spirits have quailed before its clear meaning and, like Jeremiah, have sought "an inn" in the wilderness where they might rest from its hard demands. One reason for this sternness is that God speaks in, through, and about the great issues of life. His voice is never a summons to ignore or to abandon the world but is an imperative to reclaim and to reform it. If the world at any given time honestly desired reformation, the way of the prophet would be less difficult. But usually the world is either quite content with itself as it is, or it is sure it can figure out how to become contented by some less drastic means than that proposed by the prophet.

2. God Calls His People.—As by Isaiah and by later prophets, God is pictured here as calling all peoples and the entire earth to hear what he is about to say. The urgency of the

message strikes us at once. It says in effect: "Give attention! Stop what you are doing and listen!" This is one of the hardest requests for men to hear and to obey. It is almost impossible to believe that something else—anything else— is more important than what we are doing at any given moment. It is ever so much easier to keep on as we are, where we are, and doing what we are doing. Jesus sensed this same weakness when he urged his disciples to "seek ye first the kingdom of God." Ivan Turgenev once wrote that the most important problem in life is to know what to put first. Here is given the answer to that: put the word of God first.

Notwithstanding the obvious urgency of their message, the prophets had to work hard for a hearing. Most of them never got the kind they wanted—the kind their message deserved. One reason seems to be that people gave them only casual notice—a moment of attention, then indifference. It is impossible to excuse such negligence either then or now on the part of ordinary people. The minimum obligation of an intelligent man is to listen, to heed, to learn. William James was the despair of his more fastidious and punctual friends because, when late for an engagement, he was frequently found in deep conversation with some laboring man he had encountered along the way. Phillips Brooks had the same sensitive regard for the fact that anyone might become his teacher if he would but give that one a hearing.

The universality of the message is as apparent as its urgency: **All ye people, . . . earth, and all that therein is.** But how can anyone get and keep the whole of humanity in the focus of attention and concern? Try to think about it and at once you find racial or national groups floa

3 For, behold, the LORD cometh forth out of his place, and will come down, and tread upon the high places of the earth.	**3** For behold, the LORD is coming forth out of his place, and will come down and tread upon the high places of the earth.
4 And the mountains shall be molten under him, and the valleys shall be cleft, as wax before the fire, *and* as the waters *that are* poured down a steep place.	**4** And the mountains will melt under him and the valleys will be cleft, like wax before the fire, like waters poured down a steep place.

heaven. He descends to earth, probably not so much a **witness against** all mankind as a "witness among all mankind." The idea of judgment is probably not present here.

3b-4. God strides over the earth, using the mountaintops as his steppingstones. At the touch of his feet the mountains and hills melt **as wax before the fire,** and flow into the valleys as waters rush down a hillside. The earth thus becomes a level plain, as in Second Isaiah. Vs. 4 is a quatrain in which the third clause repeats the thought of the first, and the fourth repeats the second. This symmetry and excellent imagery is spoiled by general mistranslation of the second clause, usually rendering it **the valleys shall** [or **will**] **be cleft.** Instead of taking the word **valleys** as subject, one should see in it the locative object. **The mountains** remains the subject of the second clause as well as the first. The translation would then be: "Even the mountains shall be melted under him, and they shall flow down [be cleft] into the valleys; as wax before the fire, as torrents rushing down a steep slope."

ing before your mind in rapid succession. Usually you individualize or personalize the concept still further and think of persons you know, accepting them as suitable symbols of mankind. Yet in spite of the human difficulty of trying to grasp all of mankind in one act of attention and concern, the prophets both made the effort and were strikingly successful in it. Prophetic religion now as then must be able honestly to universalize its message. Yet even the prophets had their difficulties now and then. There is some comfort for us in the fact that even the greatest of them had lapses into a provincialism which proclaimed that God was more interested in some people than in others.

One dearly bought fact of human experience is this: only as faith casts or is able to cast its message in universal terms has it a message for mankind. Never has this fact needed to be more centrally placed in our thinking than now. Arnold J. Toynbee has given it as his judgment that one of the sources of greatest strength for Christianity has been her universal message and her conception of world mission. A parochial faith, a provincial world view, and special pleading for some group or other, for whatever reason—these are not "shadows" cast by the good of sincere conviction, but active evils seeking nothing less than the soul of mankind.

This no doubt requires more of us than we are prepared to give. It is not hard to pay heed when we think our own welfare is at stake. We can and will listen when someone wants to tell us how to benefit ourselves. But it is not so easy to give heed to someone who speaks of another's welfare. "Bear ye one another's burdens" is not an easy injunction to obey. "Give heed to the welfare of all mankind" is no easier. The very fact that every development in foreign policy must be presented to the nation under the guise of "self-interest" illustrates the weakness of nationalism everywhere. When we are asked to give aid to needy peoples we must be shown how in the end we will be benefited by it. Self-interest, whether "enlightened" or simply crass, is the permanent foe of biblical faith, which insists that our judgments must be actuated by the God whose prime motive is the furthering of the welfare of all mankind. Until and unless that victory is achieved, the world will go on its warring way—and "religion" will be an all-too-fit citizen of it.

3-4. *When God Draws Near.*—This is poetic and prophetic imagery in the grand style. Intensely personal and plainly anthropomorphic, it depicts the God of the universe emerging from his abode in mystery and majesty and coming down to earth, treading only on the mountaintops. At his touch these great symbols of eternity—the mountains—melt, and all earth changes her appearance.

How better could there have been expressed the conviction that when God enters a situation it undergoes a radical alteration of form and must be completely reorganized around his meaning and will? That, it was perceived, was what God was doing in the life of Israel and Judah. The prophet was trying to get his hear-

5 For the transgression of Jacob *is* all this, and for the sins of the house of Israel. What *is* the transgression of Jacob? *is it* not Samaria? and what *are* the high places of Judah? *are they* not Jerusalem?

6 Therefore I will make Samaria as a heap of the field, *and* as plantings of a vine-

5 All this is for the transgression of Jacob
and for the sins of the house of Israel.
What is the transgression of Jacob?
Is it not Samar'ia?
And what is the sin of the house[a] of
Judah?
Is it not Jerusalem?
6 Therefore I will make Samar'ia a heap
in the open country,
a place for planting vineyards;

[a] Gk Tg Compare Syr: Heb *what are the high places*

II. Discourses on the Assyrian Crisis (1:5-16)
A. The Wailing Prophet (1:5-9)

This was presumably Micah's first address, probably delivered in Jerusalem (vss. 5, 9). To accentuate his message he went about **stripped and naked** (vs. 8) as a parable of the way all the people of Judah soon would be. He probably walked from street to street and square to square, all over the city, wailing this song of lament wherever he went. Perhaps he did this in outlying towns and villages also. This wailing campaign of Micah may have been an important factor in causing King Hezekiah to make a sweeping reformation in the early part of his reign.

5. Jacob refers to the ten northern tribes by contrast with **Judah,** the common designation for the southern kingdom. Micah regarded **Samaria** as the starting place of the moral infection which had spread as a plague over Palestine. The last couplet implies that Jerusalem had now become as bad as Samaria before her fall. Instead of Samaria and Jerusalem dispensing law, order, and wholesome influences upon their respective nations, these two capitals had become centers of corruption. The second and fourth questions suggest a decisive "Yes" for their answer. **High places of** (as in KJV and M.T.) apparently came into the text as a gloss replacing an original **sin of the house of** (as M.T. is emended in RSV). By making this marginal note the glossator meant to indicate that the **high places** (semipagan hilltop shrines) constituted the **sin** of Jerusalem. The dual restoration in the RSV, done partially by using more original readings preserved in non-Hebrew versions, makes it much superior to the KJV by bringing vs. 5b and vs. 5e into harmony with each other.

6. Traditionally this verse was regarded as written before the fall of Samaria, predicting that event which occurred in 722 B.C. Today it seems doubtful if Micah began

---

ers to be prepared for the vast and almost unbearable alterations that God's will was going to make in their history.

It is of utmost importance that we should not lose sight of the enduring meaning of these passages in our admiration for their matchless imagery. For Micah and his stern comrades in prophecy were not out to enthrall their hearers with forewarnings of doom, they were trying to stab them wide awake to the full meaning for Israel's life and history of coming under the judgment of the living God.

Ralph Waldo Emerson somewhere asks, "What is so odious as polite bows to God?" Micah's prophecy exhibits similar scorn and recommends complete prostration of person and people before the onrushing judgment of the God of Israel. For if the very mountains are

consumed at his touch, what will happen to men and nations when he lays his hand on them?

5-9. *The Wages of Sin Is Death.*—Micah wastes no words in accounting for the judgment of God which is about to strike. The words **transgression** and **sin** tell the story; and it is a story which loses none of its sting for having been told so many times before. The prophet is nothing if not exact in indicating the nature of the sin to be punished. It is the worship of false gods being conducted in the capital cities of the two kingdoms, Samaria and Jerusalem. These cities are to be destroyed, the offending images are to be pulverized, and everything connected with their worship is to be utterly scattered.

The simple declarative statement, **for her wound is incurable,** must have been a shock to

yard: and I will pour down the stones
thereof into the valley, and I will discover
the foundations thereof.

7 And all the graven images thereof shall
be beaten to pieces, and all the hires thereof
shall be burned with the fire, and all the
idols thereof will I lay desolate: for she
gathered *it* of the hire of a harlot, and they
shall return to the hire of a harlot.

and I will pour down her stones into the
 valley,
and uncover her foundations.

7 All her images shall be beaten to pieces,
 all her hires shall be burned with fire,
 and all her idols I will lay waste;
for from the hire of a harlot she gathered
 them,
 and to the hire of a harlot they shall
 return.

---

prophesying so early (see Intro., p. 898). This verse probably was spoken in 714 B.C.
at the beginning of Micah's ministry. Then the verbs would be translated in the present
tense. This is equally permissible, for there is no distinction between present and future
in the Hebrew imperfect. The verse has perhaps even more significance as a description of
the devastation to be witnessed around the site of Samaria at the moment Micah was
speaking. Such a translation would read: "So I make Samaria as a deserted mound in a
field, as planting sites for vineyards; I even wash down her stones into the valley, and lay
bare the foundations thereof." Samaria was a hill fortress which had been able to hold
out against the mightiest (Assyrian) armies of that day for a siege of three years (II
Kings 17:5; 18:10). Only ten years later Micah beheld the ruined site of that once-proud
city, almost a forgotten memory, eroding disastrously away. The implication is that Judah
would soon suffer the same fate.

7. Those scholars who regard this verse as an interpolation on idolatry from postexilic times are probably correct (Karl Marti, *Das Dodekapropheton* [Tübingen: J. C. B.
Mohr, 1904; "Kurzer Hand-Commentar zum Alten Testament"], p. 268; J. M. P. Smith,
A Critical and Exegetical Commentary on Micah [New York: Charles Scribner's Sons,
1911; "International Critical Commentary"], p. 37; W. Nowack, *Micha,* in Rudolf Kittel,
ed., *Biblia Hebraica* [2nd ed.; Leipzig: J. C. B. Mohr, 1913], p. 866; Ernst Sellin, *Das
Zwölfprophetenbuch* [Leipzig: A. Deichert, 1922; "Kommentar zum Alten Testament"],
p. 265; R. H. Pfeiffer, *Introduction to the Old Testament* [New York: Harper & Bros.,
1941], p. 590; "The Polemic Against Idolatry in the Old Testament," *Journal of Biblical
Literature,* XLIII [1924], 233, 240). Echoing the polemic against idolatry, now thought

---

many hearers who had been brought up in the
fond belief that however much God might
punish Israel for her sins, he would never
actually permit her destruction, much less bring
it about himself. Micah cherishes and encourages no such hope. He announces the full end
of the two kingdoms and the complete destruction of their capital cities.

Even today his words make grim reading We
have been so accustomed to "a happy ending"
that we are reluctant to accept anything else
or less. Our scientists and generals tell us that
we must not have another war because our
weapons are so deadly that civilization will be
destroyed—yet we go right on muddling in the
same old ways, thinking, like Micah's contemporaries, that the forecast is unnecessarily gloomy.
Lewis Mumford in his sharp essay, "Gentlemen,
You Are Mad!"[1] put into words the reaction
of thoughtful men to this refusal to face facts.
But, mad or not, most people refuse to believe

that our civilization is in so desperate a plight
as that pictured by many of our prophets.
Arnold J. Toynbee can point to twenty-one
civilizations, and call attention to the fact that,
among those which we should have to account
as living, ours is clearly suffering from most of
the ailments that proved fatal to those now
dead; yet many of us wait impatiently for him
to speak some pleasant word of reassurance
about our prospects of survival. Paul Hutchinson of the *Christian Century,* as well as others
who stand in the tradition of Micah, has been
writing and lecturing in the same troubled vein.
Yet it is a frequent comment on Hutchinson's
work that "he is so pessimistic!" Let these men
warily suggest that a spiritual revolution might
conceivably alter our fate, and we want them
to give us some more "practical" hope. No
more than the contemporaries of Micah can we
grasp the idea that our **wound is incurable.**

This attitude, of course, is part and parcel of
the ordinary human way of facing bitter and

[1] *Saturday Review of Literature,* XXIX (1946), 9.

8 Therefore I will wail and howl, I will go stripped and naked: I will make a wailing like the dragons, and mourning as the owls.

9 For her wound *is* incurable; for it is come unto Judah; he is come unto the gate of my people, *even* to Jerusalem.

8 For this I will lament and wail;
  I will go stripped and naked;
  I will make lamentation like the jackals,
    and mourning like the ostriches.
9 For her wound[b] is incurable;
  and it has come to Judah,
  it has reached to the gate of my people,
    to Jerusalem.

[b] Gk Syr Vg: Heb *wounds*

---

to have been first enunciated in a classic way by Second Isaiah, this verse probably illustrates the rising resentment of Judeans against image worship as practiced in the Samaria region during the times after Ezra, when hatred between Jews and Samaritans was intense. Because the image cults themselves were spoken of as religious harlotry, the word **hires** has a cult meaning, designating the gifts presented to the images. In the last couplet **hire** has its literal meaning, i.e., the pay given to a prostitute. Reference is to the gain achieved through practice of "sacred prostitution" at these holy places. The author foresaw that both the cults and their immoral rites would pass into oblivion.

8. For this refers to what is described in vss. 5-6. This is an added reason why vs. 7 is secondary, for Micah would not have lamented over its content. Micah went about wailing because Samaria's fate (vs. 6) was about to overtake Jerusalem. As in vs. 6, the tenses throughout vs. 8 should be rendered consistently in the present, for the prophet described what he was actually doing, not what he intended to do. Those who have heard the terrifying night calls of **jackals** know how Micah must have felt when he compared his lament over Jerusalem's impending destruction to their fearful cries. The sound of the **ostriches** is mournful, representing this phase of the prophet's feeling. The KJV translation **dragons** and **owls** has no justification. Micah probably did not go about absolutely naked, but clad with only a loincloth. This dramatized his message, impressing indelibly on all who saw him that they would soon be as destitute as he.

9. Her refers to Jerusalem. The wickedness of Israel had swept down over Palestine. Micah described it under the figure of a flood of corruption and destruction which was already at the gates of the capital, about to engulf Judah and Jerusalem. Micah had deep feeling for his country. He called the citizens **my people.** He was overcome

---

unpleasant facts over which we have little or no control. Death is one such fact. A malignant disease which is certain to prove fatal is another. When subjects of this sort are brought up, a noticeable depression descends upon the spirits of all present. The kindlier part of the reaction is due to genuine sympathy for those who suffer. But much of it is due to our chronic aversion to facing such facts. They leave us weaponless; they are so decisive, final, unarguable, and uncontrollable.

But they must be faced sooner or later, and they are better faced sooner than later. The concealment of truths which if known would have a serious effect, however wise it may be thought to be in exceptional cases, is much more widely practiced than any attempted rationalization of it would seem able to justify. One especially trying situation may be cited. A woman was seriously ill of cancer. The doctor told her husband; together they agreed not to tell her or the two children, who were in their

early maturity. The special nurse as well as the family belonged to a local church, and it was not long before the minister discovered the true nature of the ailment. When the husband found out that someone else knew, he was obviously relieved to be able to share the burden of it. Before long it was apparent that the patient herself suspected the truth about the situation. One day she asked the minister point-blank if he could tell her what was wrong. He parried the question by repeating the vague phrases of the doctor. Meanwhile the children were making the same kind of guess, and their anxiety was heightened by their inability to believe what anyone was telling them. Finally, in an effort to bring some sort of community into the life of the home, they were brought into a family council and told the truth. After an initial period of heartbreak each found strength in the others for their common grief, and within a few days were of the opinion that the wife and mother knew what the trouble

10 ¶ Declare ye *it* not at Gath, weep ye not at all: in the house of Aphrah roll thyself in the dust.	10 Tell it not in Gath,
	    weep not at all;
	in Beth-le-aph'rah
	    roll yourselves in the dust.

with pathos as he was forced to announce that his nation's **wounds** were **incurable.** In the actual wording of his first message there is no hope. However, Micah would hardly have spent the energy and subjected himself to ridicule if he had not had some expectation that his people might change their ways and avoid the doom which seemed imminent. His was a desperate attempt to bring a nation to her senses.

B. The Alarm (1:10-16)

Micah presumably was in Jerusalem in 711 B.C. when he heard that the Assyrians were advancing upon Palestine. He proceeded toward home at once, spreading the news along the roadway. As Paul Revere and his two companions rode by night, awakened the countryside, and informed the people of Lexington and Concord that the British were coming, Micah went from town to town warning the cities and villages of southwestern Palestine concerning the enemy's approach. As he passed through each settlement he gave a distinctive couplet alarm, especially applicable to it. Inasmuch as he apparently prefaced his unique call to each locality by repeating the ejaculatory warnings he had given in the preceding cities and villages, this production increased in length the farther Micah continued his march. By the time he arrived at his home town of Mareshah, this accumulated complex of terse warnings had come to approximate a poem of considerable length, an urgent call of alarm to the people of all southwestern Palestine.

Presumably in each instance the special couplet alarm contained a play on words in which the meaning of the respective town's name was utilized. Apparently scribes and copyists, failing to see significance in these forms, tried to make them more intelligible by altering them. However, they did the exact reverse, so that in a number of instances the wordplays have become blurred and in several cases hopelessly obscured. Also, some verbs in this passage became changed in form during the course of transmission. Apparently most of them were originally in the imperative, as preserved in some Greek MSS and as suggested by the context. All this alteration has resulted in making this poem one of the most confused passages in the Bible.

Translations are usually not presented so as to make the plays on words, and their significance, apparent to the English reader. If one were to get the full purport of this passage the names of the towns should be translated rather than transliterated. By using a combination of translation, transliteration, and verb restoration, it is possible to give the English reader some comprehension of these plays on words. However, because this passage carries little religious significance, it is not necessary here to go into the grammatical and philological minutiae of such a restored translation.

10. The opening clause is taken from David's classic lament over the death of Saul and Jonathan (II Sam. 1:20), when the Israelite territory was overrun and the Philistines

was and would welcome knowing that they too understood. Soon the family was knit tightly together, facing as a unit the fact of incurable disease and early death. There is good reason to believe that the grief occasioned by this method is more easily and healthfully managed than that incidental to the method of deception.

10-16. What We Expect and What We Get.— Here the prophet is calling the roll of neighboring cities and peoples, some of whom will rejoice and some grieve over the catastrophe soon to sweep over Samaria and Jerusalem. He bids

them proceed with care in their judgments on the erring cities and peoples. And well they might, because the wrathful judgment of God was not going to miss them completely. They too were to feel the full force of it. One such is the village of **Maroth,** a city preserved to us in name only, but apparently located on the road which ran from Jerusalem to the coastal plain up and down which the commerce of antiquity moved, and armies often enough fought their way. Maroth derived her livelihood from the trade going to and from Jerusalem. Yet her

11 Pass ye away, thou inhabitant of Saphir, having thy shame naked: the inhabitant of Zaanan came not forth in the mourning of Beth-ezel; he shall receive of you his standing.

12 For the inhabitant of Maroth waited carefully for good: but evil came down from the LORD unto the gate of Jerusalem.

13 O thou inhabitant of Lachish, bind

---

11 Pass on your way,
    inhabitants of Shaphir,
    in nakedness and shame;
the inhabitants of Za'anan
    do not come forth;
the wailing of Beth-e'zel
    shall take away from you its standing
    place.
12 For the inhabitants of Maroth
    wait anxiously for good,
because evil has come down from the
    LORD
    to the gate of Jerusalem.
13 Harness the steeds to the chariots,
    inhabitants of Lachish;

---

could have eliminated Israel, if they had only known. Choice of the opening words indicates that Micah felt the tragedy impending in 711 B.C. carried potentialities as catastrophic as the crisis of Gilboa might have been if the Philistines had pressed their gains.

12. רע here carries the sense of calamity, rather than **evil,** for God does not bring evil upon people.

13. Here the prophet's attention was centered on the city of Lachish in the remote southwest Shephelah country, thirty miles from Jerusalem and only four miles from

---

location had its great disadvantages, and Micah is but pointing them out when he says of her that **Maroth waited carefully for good: but evil came down from the LORD unto the gate of Jerusalem.**

What a parable Maroth provides for much that happens in life! The many half-cynical definitions of friendship are illustrations of the same point. The real difference between an acquaintance and a friend is this: an acquaintance will want to share your prosperity; a friend will insist upon sharing your adversity. For true friendship is a sharing of dark days as well as of light ones. It will not seek merely the good things that come along the roadway of human relationships; it will be ready and braced for the hard and bitter ones as well.

When Mussolini and Hitler marched to power in the lives of their ill-starred nations, business, labor, education, and most other groups, including many churches, joined in the parade, being eager to share in the good that might come. They gathered round their "iron men" with monotonous chants of "Duce!" and "Heil!" until the manacles of fascism had been securely welded on the spirit of freedom in those countries. Little did they realize what a tempest of evil was going to come down that road sweeping all before it! When Dwight L. Morrow was asked to comment on the Republican campaign of 1928 in the United States, a campaign in which prosperity was decked out

as a purely party achievement, he replied, "Whoever takes the credit for the sunshine must be prepared to be blamed for the rain." The parable of Maroth makes much the same point. No position in life is so protected that good may be enjoyed with complete immunity from evil. To put one's self in the position of being able to experience good is to be in a position which is exposed to evil as well. The two go hand in hand in human history, not because they are so much alike, but because both grow out of human relationships that can be either good or evil, and can be changed from one to the other all too easily.

Marriage furnishes an example. It is a relationship that can be good or evil, depending upon the attitude, ideals, and efforts of the parties to it. But to seek the good of marriage is to be exposed to the evil of it as well. The same thing is true of patriotism, church loyalty, or any other great relationship. They can all be perverted, and only the utmost vigilance can prevent it. Yet the good they introduce into human life can be known only by those who are both willing to run the risk of the evil implicit in them and able to manage it.

If Maroth had served no other purpose than to remind us of this probing fact about life, it would have earned our enduring gratitude.

13. The Power of Recall.—The city or section of Lachish is charged with another sort of transgression: **She is the beginning of the sin**

the chariot to the swift beast: she *is* the beginning of the sin to the daughter of Zion:
for the transgressions of Israel were found
in thee.

14 Therefore shalt thou give presents to
Moresheth-gath: the houses of Achzib *shall
be* a lie to the kings of Israel.

15 Yet will I bring an heir unto thee, O
inhabitant of Mareshah: he shall come unto
Adullam the glory of Israel.

you were[c] the beginning of sin
    to the daughter of Zion,
for in you were found
    the transgressions of Israel.

14 Therefore you shall give parting gifts
    to Mo′resheth-gath;
the houses of Achzib shall be a deceitful
        thing
    to the kings of Israel.

15 I will again bring a conqueror upon you,
    inhabitants of Mare′shah;
the glory of Israel
    shall come to Adullam.

[c] Cn: Heb *it was*

Mareshah. Micah described how the corruption, which had started in the northern tribes of Israel, gained its first foothold in the south at Lachish. She in turn mediated this moral contamination to Jerusalem, where the infestation had now come to lodge with all its deadliness. **Daughter of Zion** is simply a poetic variant for Jerusalem.

14-15. Israel is used here not in the narrow sense of the ten northern tribes but as a general designation of the Hebrew people. The first couplet in each verse deals with Micah's home town, and the second couplets with **Achzib** (eight miles northeast of Mareshah) and its nearby cave of **Adullam**. Reference seems to be to the time David fled from King Saul and in desperation sought refuge in this cave (I Sam. 22:1-2; II Sam. 23:13). Micah saw the people of Judah facing their Adullam in 711 B.C., but for them he anticipated no escape. In the coming tragedy the institution of the kingship and the

---

to the daughter of Zion: for the transgressions of Israel were found in thee. It is not possible to know precisely what this means, but every indication points to the sin of idolatry. There can be no question that the Hebrew historians found in the current practices of other religions the reason for the presence of idolatry in Israel's life. Since the wrath of Micah is poured upon image worship, there is reason to think that he is here echoing the now familiar charge of the prophets that Israel has adopted the nature cults of her neighbors. Consider, however, his pathetic and eloquent backward look to the day when Israel was innocent of the sin that was to prove her undoing; he speaks of **the beginning of the sin.**

The power of recall is fundamental to the human mind. Without it reason, culture, art, science, ethics, and religion would be impossible. It can be the source of the keenest kind of joy in life. Parents like to recall events in the lives of their children. Family gatherings are made hilarious by the recollection of one thing after another. Couples celebrating their golden wedding anniversary recall with tenderness the days of their young love. The power of recall can lead us through "the valley of the shadow" in which we have lost a loved one. It can re-animate the sympathy of friends, neighbors, and family. It can conjure up the dear days when life seemed so good, so whole, so utterly

creative. It can remind us of the hard struggle we had as we sought to find a firmer foundation for life and faith (yet cf. Expos. on 7:14-15).

But Micah is using the power of recall to remind Israel that she was not always guilty of idolatry and apostasy. He centers attention upon that far-off day when she learned from her neighbors the practice of idol worship. At first it did not seem a serious threat to the ancestral, nomadic faith, the sheer monotheism which the prophets believed sustained her in the wilderness and brought her into the Promised Land. But as desert life faded into the background, the faith of her fathers lost its luster and the faith of her neighbors grew stronger in her life. Idol worship increased its hold on her religious rites and thought. Soon images were brought out of their fugitive niches and altars and placed in the temples and homes of the people. The sin which had had its beginning in the life of her neighbors now dominated the life of Israel. Hence the inevitability of the judgment of God coming as destruction upon Zion.

It is impossible to study this panorama of one phase of Israel's life without echoing the universal human lament, "Oh, that I had another chance!" But Micah rarely if ever approaches the greater insight of Hosea that Israel can and will have another chance. Later writers who contributed to the present book of Micah

16 Make thee bald, and poll thee for thy delicate children; enlarge thy baldness as the eagle; for they are gone into captivity from thee.

16 Make yourselves bald and cut off your hair,
  for the children of your delight;
make yourselves as bald as the eagle,
  for they shall go from you in exile.

2 Woe to them that devise iniquity, and work evil upon their beds! when the morning is light, they practise it, because it is in the power of their hand.

2 Woe to those who devise wickedness
  and work evil upon their beds!
When the morning dawns, they perform it,
  because it is in the power of their hand.

---

glory of what was once the twelve tribes **of Israel** would vanish in a new Adullam of despair. Thus the last couplet of vs. 15 summarizes the accumulated tragedy described in its anticipated details in vss. 10-15*b*.

16. Micah's Paul Revere cry to the people of southwest Palestine came to an end, in his home town of Mareshah, with an appeal to parents, calling them to mourn over the impending loss of their **children.** He told them to shave their heads and shear off their beards because these young ones in whom they took such delight soon would be herded together by the enemy and carried into exile as slaves. The past tenses (Hebrew and KJV) indicate that this eventuality seemed so certain to Micah that he regarded these children already as good as **gone into captivity from thee.** Shaving the head was the sign of great mourning (Amos 8:10; Isa. 22:12; Jer. 16:6). In presenting his premonitions of impending calamity (vss. 10-16), Micah was apparently so wrought up that the dwellers in those villages and cities where his doleful voice was heard could hardly have escaped catching some of his anxiety over the corruption which would inevitably result, according to his belief, in the destruction of his nation.

III. Prophecies of Ethical Concern (2:1–3:12)

A. The Jerusalem Men of Wealth (2:1-10)

Micah's expectations in his second prophecy (1:10-16) were not fulfilled. In the Assyrian campaign of 711 B.C. the Philistine territory, particularly Ashdod, suffered the brunt of attack. The Hebrew portion of Palestine was almost untouched. This may have discredited Micah as a prophet in the eyes of the people, and it appears he went into a rather prolonged period of inactivity. Perhaps at least five or six years elapsed between chs. 1 and 2. Micah resumed his activity (ch. 2) apparently between 705 and 701 B.C., when he was aroused over the corruption and exploitation of that day. Here Micah appears as the friend of the poor and oppressed. The opening blast in the second phase of his public work seems to have been delivered on the "Wall Street" of Jerusalem, perhaps near the "Palestine Stock Exchange."

2:1. The wealthy were so interested in exploiting that they were unable to sleep at night. They spent these wakeful hours devising schemes to defraud and dispossess

---

have supplied this element of hope (e.g., 2:12-13), probably under the influence of other prophets who counted heavily on the mercy of God. Micah is like the judge who summarizes the crime of the accused before pronouncing sentence. Thus has he read the meaning of God in Israel's history.

2:1-3. *The Evil that Kills.*—Here is an ideal depiction of premeditated evil; the kind of evil which is deliberate, intentional, fathered by a conscious purpose and a full awareness of both the pleasurable consequences to the doer and

the painful consequences to the victim. There is another kind of evil—that which is born of blind, uncritical, irrational anger or greed or lust. When a man acts under it, we say he "runs amuck" or "goes beserk." Common sense, conscience, and the dictates of law agree that these two kinds of evil dwell in different moral worlds, and must be treated accordingly. Even though the deed done by two men, one under the guidance of purpose, the other of impulse, is the same, the offenders must be treated differently. Each is held morally liable for what he

2 And they covet fields, and take *them* by violence; and houses, and take *them* away: so they oppress a man and his house, even a man and his heritage.

3 Therefore thus saith the LORD; Behold, against this family do I devise an evil, from which ye shall not remove your necks; neither shall ye go haughtily: for this time *is* evil.

2 They covet fields, and seize them;
and houses, and take them away;
they oppress a man and his house,
a man and his inheritance.

3 Therefore thus says the LORD:
Behold, against this family I am devising evil,
from which you cannot remove your necks;
and you shall not walk haughtily,
for it will be an evil time.

---

their fellow countrymen. When daylight came they proceeded to execute their plots. These "men of the day" had such power that they could do almost anything they wished. The last clause indicates there was no one, either in government or the courts, who would call them to account, for the authorities were in league with them. This was a free enterprise society in which the men of affairs could do what they wished, and there was no reckoning.

2. In a day when wealth consisted largely of real estate these unscrupulous people had a mania for acquiring houses and lands. This was accomplished by resort to seizure, theft, and violence. The specific methods used to obtain these possessions are not stated. Perhaps the offenders may have followed occasionally in the traditions of Jezebel, trumping up false charges of subversiveness, including atheism and treason (I Kings 21), and then stoning the victims to death. Usually there were less brutal ways of foreclosing on properties or otherwise appropriating them. As the poor and middle classes of Palestine had their inherited estates taken from them these dispossessed people and their families were reduced to a practical and often actual condition of slavery. **A man and his house** means "a man and his family," i.e., "household." **His heritage** or **inheritance** refers to his inherited property, a sacred material trust to be passed on unsquandered to his progeny.

3. In vss. 1-2 Micah stated his charges against these unprincipled people. In vss. 3-5 he announced God's judgment upon them. **This family** refers to the exploiting classes of Jerusalem who were glorying in their day of opportunity. Micah proclaimed to them that

---

has done; but the schemer so much more so that he must face the full wrath of society, while the other is likely to have justice with a liberal tempering of mercy—because, we reason, "He did not know what he was doing." If the deed is serious enough, the former can suffer death while the latter is imprisoned for life.

One phrase etches itself in the memory: they practice evil **because it is in the power of their hand.** Not only do **they covet fields,** they **take them by violence.** Nor do they stop with fields: they covet **houses, and take them away.** Thus they strip their victims of every sort of security; not simply because they want to do it, but also because they can do it. While what we plan and what we do may be two quite different things, each one, could we but know it, furnishes ground for a fairly accurate measurement of the moral make-up of a man. Leslie Stephens once wrote that Jesus' greatest contribution to morality was his discovery of "the inner pole of

ethics." It is true that Jesus did pay great attention to motive and purpose. He sought to enlarge our moral judgments until they linked motive and deed. But he nowhere lost sight of the deed as being an essential factor in the judgment. "By their fruits" would have precious little meaning if he had gone to this extreme.

It is a searching question to ask what we would do if we were given, with the desire, the power to bring it to pass. Aladdin's plight would be easier to understand in that case. It is all well and good to say, "I would like to have this, or do this, or be this"; but if granted the power to bring the wish to fulfillment, would we continue to want those ends? Is it not true that one of the greatest incentives to daydreaming is the deep and firm awareness of the fact that we do not have the power to translate the daydream into the real world? The famous cure for the radical, "give him responsibility," suggests itself with real force. The desire for power is deep-seated in human

4 ¶ In that day shall *one* take up a parable against you, and lament with a doleful lamentation, *and* say, We be utterly spoiled: he hath changed the portion of my people: how hath he removed *it* from me! turning away he hath divided our fields.

4 In that day they shall take up a taunt song against you,
and wail with bitter lamentation,
and say, "We are utterly ruined;
he changes the portion of my people;
how he removes it from me!
Among our captors[d] he divides our fields."

[d] Cn: Heb *the rebellious*

---

they were due for **an evil time.** He beheld a day about to arrive when those who had been accustomed to **walk haughtily** would find the tables turned. Using the figure of a yoked ox, Micah told how these corrupt people would soon find themselves under a yoke of bondage, and there would be no escape: **you cannot remove your necks.** In the impending slavery of exile they would be little better off than oxen bound to their burdens.

4. Both translations miss the point in the couplet which introduces the body of the verse. The word מָשָׁל refers neither to a **taunt song** nor to a **parable**, but it has here the sense of "byword" or "word of reproach." In addition, the word עַל does not mean **against** but "on behalf of." Proper translation therefore would be: "In that day one (of your number) shall take up a word of reproach on your behalf, and wail with a doleful lamentation, saying. . . ." The quatrain dirge which forms the body of the verse (the last four lines) gives the wailing of the Jerusalem monopolists as they in turn become dispossessed by the Assyrian invaders. They had gleefully brought ruin upon others. Micah shows how they themselves would soon be subjected to the same fate, and it would be anything but pleasant. These who had once despoiled Palestine to their own selfish advantage would soon mourn because they would be **utterly ruined.** They would not be able to understand why God had taken away their acquisitions from them: **How hath he removed it from me!** i.e., "How can God do such a thing?" It would seem to them inconceivable that God could allow their properties to be divided among rebel revolutionaries. So they would stand aghast as **he divides** their **fields** to their **captors.** In addition to the exchange populations with which Assyria was accustomed to resettle conquered territories whose people had been partially exiled, there were also the poor who were not usually considered worth taking into exile. It would be a painful experience for the property barons to see their lands divided up among these two types of good-for-nothing people.

---

nature. As an ambition, willing to prepare for and assume responsibility, it can be an ingredient of good; as the sheer impulse to dominate others, it is evil both to subject and object. Many a generation has demonstrated the eternal truth in Lord Acton's famous dictum: "Power tends to corrupt and absolute power corrupts absolutely." [2]

Micah might well have stopped at this point, as do the secularists and pagans of today; but he would have been less the prophet of the living God had he done so. For him God is not standing idly by, observing these evil deeds with Olympian calm; rather does his sense of outraged justice mount until he himself proposes to take a hand and see that the wrongdoer is not only thwarted but punished. That, says Micah, is why we confront an inescapable evil,

[2] *Essays on Freedom and Power* (Boston: Beacon Press, 1948), p. 364.

one so dire as to make the entire period an evil time. Yet underlying the imminent catastrophe which is to level cities and decimate peoples is the purpose of God, who is determined to uphold the way of righteousness even against the princes and the priests of Israel.

4-6. God and Public Morale.—Micah knew the sting of public criticism and disapproval. He had felt it from the beginning of his work. These verses make it clear that he expected it to increase as times became more desperate. Finally, when confusion had reached the point that no one knew where the boundaries of their lands were (the height of confusion in an agrarian economy), the prophet would not be permitted even to wail over the plight of the people, let alone draw the prophetic lesson, "our sins have found us out."

It should not be hard for anyone who lived through World War II to understand the pro-

5 Therefore thou shalt have none that shall cast a cord by lot in the congregation of the LORD.

6 Prophesy ye not, *say they to them that* prophesy: they shall not prophesy to them, *that* they shall not take shame.

7 ¶ O *thou that art* named the house of Jacob, is the Spirit of the LORD straitened? *are* these his doings? do not my words do good to him that walketh uprightly?

5 Therefore you will have none to cast the line by lot
in the assembly of the LORD.

6 "Do not preach" — thus they preach —
"one should not preach of such things;
disgrace will not overtake us."

7 Should this be said, O house of Jacob?
Is the Spirit of the LORD impatient?
Are these his doings?
Do not my words do good
to him who walks uprightly?

---

5. Amplifying the fate of these oppressors, Micah stated that they would have no inheritance in Israel. The use of term קהל יהוה (**the assembly [congregation] of the LORD**) may indicate these people would be cut off not only from their political and economic advantages but also would be removed from having any part in the religious community, presumably by reason of being exiled to a foreign land. This was somewhat of a proletarian revolution when those who had been up would go down, and those who had been down would come up. In the redistribution of land, when the remnant poor and the imported Assyrians would **cast a cord** [**the line**] **by lot,** the once wealthy would have no part.

6. Apparently after Micah had spoken his biting words in vss. 1-5 many in his audience were indignant at his exposing their crimes before the public and resolved such words could not be tolerated any longer. It seems most likely that the verse is made up of two of these outcries from the audience, in which they tried to silence him, followed in each instance by a quick rejoinder from the prophet. One enraged member of the audience shouted at him, **Prophesy ye not.** We would phrase it, "Stop your prophesying." Instantly Micah fired back, "They shall prophesy" (see T. H. Robinson, *Die zwölf kleinen Propheten Hosea bis Micha* [Tübingen: J. C. B. Mohr, 1938; "Handbuch zum Alten Testament"], p. 135), in the sense that the right to prophesy, for people moved by the spirit of God, must be maintained. Immediately another disgruntled listener interrupted, blasting forth in an even more disdainful tone, **They shall not prophesy to them.** This is equivalent to: "We can't let prophets continue to put such ideas in the minds of these contented masses. If they want to preach, let them preach the simple gospel." Micah snapped back immediately, saying, "One must not refrain from reproaches," i.e., "A prophet must speak without fear or favor, and must not pull his punches."

7. House of Jacob refers here to the whole Hebrew people. Micah propounded four questions (RSV) to the citizens of his nation. (*a*) **Should** such things not **be said, O house of Jacob?** (*b*) "Is the Spirit of the LORD to be restricted?" seems to give the proper rendering of the verb קצר ("to be short"). (*c*) **Are these his doings?** suggests that simply

---

hibition which civil leaders sought to place upon the prophet in this case. We recall how the great word was "morale." It became the standard by which we were asked to measure everything we said or did. The ultimate question to be put was not "Is it true or false?" but "Will it weaken or strengthen our morale?" Anything which strengthened morale was good and true; anything that weakened it was evil and false.

Here the prophet was but anticipating the fact that he would have to live through some such period in the near future. He must not

lead the people in lamentation—it would weaken their morale. He must not lead them to shame and penitence—it would weaken their morale. The true prophet of God must give way to the false prophets of men, prophets who would say what men wanted them to say.

7-11. *The Faith that Leads to Impotence.*— Micah reacts with characteristic vigor. Since when, he wants to know, has the word of God become weakness rather than strength for one who seeks to live righteously? If God bids a man speak words of lamentation and condemnation, are they not to be spoken and heard as

8 Even of late my people is risen up as an enemy: ye pull off the robe with the garment from them that pass by securely as men averse from war.

9 The women of my people have ye cast out from their pleasant houses; from their children have ye taken away my glory for ever.

10 Arise ye, and depart; for this *is* not *your* rest: because it is polluted, it shall destroy *you,* even with a sore destruction.

8 But you rise against my people[e] as an enemy;
  you strip the robe from the peaceful,[f]
from those who pass by trustingly
  with no thought of war.
9 The women of my people you drive out
  from their pleasant houses;
from their young children you take away
  my glory for ever.
10 Arise and go,
  for this is no place to rest;
because of uncleanness that destroys
  with a grievous destruction.

[e] Cn: Heb *yesterday my people rose*
[f] Cn: Heb *from before a garment*

because God has allowed these deplorable conditions to go on so long is no indication that he looks approvingly upon them. (*d*) This question implies the answer that the prophetic message held good news for those who were good, but was ominous only for those who had not been walking uprightly. The righteous had nothing to fear from him. Those who interrupted did so, Micah reminded them, only because the shoe had pinched.

8. After the interruptions from his audience (vss. 6*a,c*) and the prophet's quick rejoinders (vss. 6*b,d,* 7), Micah resumed in vs. 8 the thread of his discourse where it had been interrupted at the end of vs. 5. In a fresh attack he described the gangsterism which was prevalent in Judah. Lawless people were wreaking almost as great disaster upon the country as if it had been looted by an enemy army, i.e., **as an enemy.** Robber gangs, perhaps thugs hired by the wealthy, stripped unsuspecting people who, thinking themselves secure, were going peaceably about their ways with no designs for harm against anyone. A more literal translation of the last phrase would be, "even those returning from war." Instead of being given pensions, the returning veteran of those days seems to have been robbed of even those few articles he brought with him from the front.

9. For the widow and her children, home (**their pleasant houses**) was the last remaining joy of life. Nevertheless, greedy and inconsiderate creditors foreclosed on these homes, ruthlessly turning widows and children out into the streets. Micah regarded the welfare of the rising generation as the greatest wealth asset of a country and the key to its future. It seemed tragic that a whole generation of children should be exploited into want and misery. By this shortsighted policy Israel was forfeiting the possibility of a glorious future (**take away my glory for ever**). One such lost generation could bring permanent blight upon a nation's hopes.

10. This is the terse conclusion to the address in vss. 1-9. **Arise and go,** in the sense of "attention" and "march," are commands the invading soldiers would give while

tokens of his love for his people? Micah's confidence in God, in his holy will, in his righteousness, gives him a trust that transcends the tumult of the day. The sun did not have to be shining for him to believe in the goodness of God.

He then proceeds to do the very thing he was warned not to do: to bring Israel under judgment. Has Israel treated God as a father and friend? Rather, he has been treated as an enemy! His word and will have not so much been ignored as they have been violated. The leaders of the people have so managed affairs that no one is safe anywhere in the land. Justice is perverted, families are dispossessed of their homes and heritage, children are robbed not only of food now but also of their heritage which would be the foundation of their homes in the future. Then comes the hammerlike judgment of destruction: **Arise ye, and depart; for this is not your rest: because it is polluted, it shall destroy you, even with a sore destruction.**

This is the final answer that the religious spirit must give to anyone who wants us to "let well enough alone." It is the one irrefutable answer that all proponents of compromises who counsel contentment in spite of admitted evils

11 If a man walking in the spirit and falsehood do lie, *saying*, I will prophesy unto thee of wine and of strong drink; he shall even be the prophet of this people.

12 ¶ I will surely assemble, O Jacob, all of thee; I will surely gather the remnant of Israel; I will put them together as the sheep of Bozrah, as the flock in the midst of their fold: they shall make great noise by reason of *the multitude of* men.

11 If a man should go about and utter wind and lies,
  saying, "I will preach to you of wine and strong drink,"
he would be the preacher for this people!

12 I will surely gather all of you, O Jacob,
  I will gather the remnant of Israel;
I will set them together
  like sheep in a fold,
like a flock in its pasture,
  a noisy multitude of men.

---

marshaling their victims into captive bands to be taken into the slavery of exile. **This is no place to rest** means that Palestine would no longer remain the heritage of the Israelites. Inasmuch as they had misused it, this Promised Land would be taken from them. Because of their ethical **uncleanness,** they had forfeited all right to further possession of the Holy Land. Since "the wages of sin is death," for nations as for individuals, Micah could behold only annihilation for his people. Because their sins were so great, he foresaw that there must be **a grievous destruction.**

B. LOVE FOR FALSE PROPHETS (2:11)

11. This seems to be a fragment from one of Micah's lost addresses. It cites the example of the lying impostor **(and falsehood do lie)** who offered to prophesy "for [as it probably should be translated] wine and for strong drink." If people would supply him with the liquor he desired, he in turn would preach what they wanted to hear. Such a drunken scoundrel, without moral scruples, would be taken in with open arms as **the prophet of this people,** while a man of integrity, such as Micah, was not wanted. This was one of those days when the pew ruled the pulpit, and the chief criterion in choosing a prophet or minister was that he should say what pleased people's ears, dispensing cheerful lies rather than the ofttimes bitter truth.

C. DREAMS OF RESTORATION (2:12-13)

This is presumably a late exilic interpolation, inserted to nullify Micah's biting utterances. By contrast with the prophet's threatening words, this offers only invincible optimism. This portion may have been written shortly after 540 B.C. It seems also to be an adaptation of the writings of Second Isaiah and was probably inserted by the same author who prefixed 1:2-4 to the book of Micah.

12. Jacob and **Israel** refer to the twelve tribes. This writer of hope envisioned that the **remnant** of these twelve tribes would be brought from the places of their scatterment to be reunited once more in Palestine. These dispersed remnants would again become one **flock,** as in the days of Saul, David, and Solomon. The children of Israel would

---

must face. In a world that is rooted in righteousness there is no rest in halfway measures. Even though they are better than what went before, they are not good enough to enable a man to quit with them.

There are two ways of evaluating the present stage in the development of a person or an institution. We can survey the distance already covered, and we can survey the distance yet to be traveled. The former standard is conducive to contentment, the latter to unrest. If we survey the progress made by the American Negro people since their emancipation, there is reason for real rejoicing. But if we survey the distance yet to be traveled before they exercise full equality of opportunity and life in this country, who among us can be content?

Thus we find prophetic religion siring this paradox: it counsels complete trust in God yet gives rise to a holy impatience when asked to dwell in the halfway houses of history.

12-13. See Expos. on 4:12, 6, 9-10.

13 The breaker is come up before them:
they have broken up, and have passed
through the gate, and are gone out by it;
and their king shall pass before them, and
the LORD on the head of them.

13 He who opens the breach will go up be-
    fore them;
    they will break through and pass the
      gate,
    going out by it.
  Their king will pass on before them,
    the LORD at their head.

3 And I said, Hear, I pray you, O heads
of Jacob, and ye princes of the house of
Israel; *Is it* not for you to know judgment?
2 Who hate the good, and love the evil;
who pluck off their skin from off them, and
their flesh from off their bones;

3 And I said:
  Hear, you heads of Jacob
    and rulers of the house of Israel!
  Is it not for you to know justice? —
2   you who hate the good and love the
    evil
  who tear the skin from off my people,
    and their flesh from off their bones;

then grow multitudinous, as promised to their ancestor Abraham (Gen. 15:5, 18; 17:1-8, 19; 22:17-18). Except perhaps in the last clause, the RSV is much the better translation here.

13. God is **the breaker** who will open **the breach** in the prison of exile and allow the captives to **break through** and escape, presumably after the Persian conquest of Babylon in 538 B.C. **The gate** is the "gate of exile" or "gate of Babylon," through which they would pass in returning to Palestine. **Their king** and **the LORD** are synonymous, as in Isa. 33:22; 40:10; 41:21; 43:15; 44:6. Consequently, the last connective should be translated "even" rather than **and** (KJV). This verse follows the expectation of Second Isaiah (Isa. 40:3-5, 10-11; 52:12; etc.), with God himself leading the exiles back to Palestine.

D. APPEAL TO THE LEADERS OF JUDAH (3:1-12)

This address probably was delivered at some gathering of prominent individuals in Jerusalem. It is the most powerful of Micah's presentations. He pointed out how the supposed leaders of Judah had become misleaders of the people, dragging their nation to ruin.

3:1. Heads of Jacob were those prominent in the civil life of that day. **Rulers of the house of Israel** refers to governmental personnel. These people had been ignoring the demands of righteousness. Micah reminded them that **justice** in administration was an obligation upon their positions of leadership. In this strong call for justice we hear echoes of Amos, who had lived less than half a century earlier and only about twenty miles away (Amos 2:6-7; 5:7, 10-12, 15, 24; 8:4-7).

2. The only thing on which the elite of that day seemed agreed was in their common predilection to **hate the good and love the evil** (cf. Amos 5:14-15). In reinforcing this affirmation Micah used two illustrations. One was the figure of a butcher who, after killing an animal, proceeded with callous ruthlessness to skin it. To Micah the leaders

---

3:1-4. When Trust Is Betrayed.—This is the language of revolution. For sheer vividness it has few equals in Scripture or anywhere else. No pictorial artist is needed to dramatize Micah's point; in fact, any such efforts would be anticlimactic. In a few over one hundred words he does what Dickens and Dostoevski devote an entire book to: he gives the "feel" of the social situation in which revolutions are born. You are let down, as it were, into the very depths of human agony, despair, and burning hatred, where the waters of bitter, bloody, and uncontrollably violent revolutions are heated to the point of erupting like social geysers.

But Micah is not trying to write a literary classic; he is trying to interpret to his contemporaries the reasons why the wrath of God is about to strike and utterly destroy the house of Israel. The situation depicted in these verses

3 Who also eat the flesh of my people,
and flay their skin from off them; and they
break their bones, and chop them in pieces,
as for the pot, and as flesh within the
caldron.

4 Then shall they cry unto the LORD, but
he will not hear them: he will even hide
his face from them at that time, as they have
behaved themselves ill in their doings.

3 who eat the flesh of my people,
    and flay their skin from off them,
  and break their bones in pieces,
    and chop them up like meat*s* in a
      kettle,
    like flesh in a caldron.

4 Then they will cry to the LORD,
    but he will not answer them;
  he will hide his face from them at that
    time,
    because they have made their deeds
      evil.

g Gk: Heb *as*

of Judah seemed even more inconsiderate, for they, as it were, skinned their helpless fellow countrymen alive. The last clause apparently refers to the wild beast tearing flesh from the bones of its victims. To the masses of the people in Micah's time the upper classes had become both butchers and beasts.

3. The first clause continues the wild beast figure, with reference to devouring the flesh of its victims. Micah said the leaders of his day were equally bestial, devouring the common people. The remainder of the verse elaborates the other figure of vs. 2, telling how a butcher chops a beef in pieces, cuts the bones with his cleaver, and casually throws the chunks of flesh into a caldron to be boiled in preparation for eating. Micah felt that the upper segments of society had no more consideration for their human victims than a butcher had for his carcasses.

4. Cry to the LORD means "pray to God." These unscrupulous exploiters regarded themselves as religious. They probably were effusive to God in their prayers. After they had devoured a man and his household (2:2), they praised the Lord for their system of free enterprise and thanked him for his bounty. Micah reminded his audience that God does not listen to prayers from pseudoreligious individuals of this sort. When they pray to him, **he will hide his face.** He cannot bear to look on people who have reduced religion to such mockery. Their religion was operative while worshiping and while praying, but did not carry over into the week's activities. The last clause points out that, to the degree that people do wickedly, they isolate themselves from God, for he is accessible only to those who try to do right.

reeks with the hypocritical piety and savage arbitrary barbarisms so characteristic of despots then and now.

If one of the ruling class of that day could have heard Micah's opening remark, he would have accepted its humble tone and gracious meaning with a pleasant smile. For, addressing himself directly to the rulers, Micah asked the rhetorical question, **Is it not for you to know judgment?** "Is it not your province to know righteousness, to serve justice, and to guide the life of your people into the paths of security and peace?" Even Oriental despots accepted, at least in principle, such responsibility for the public welfare of their country. But the hypothetical smile would certainly have vanished at the rush of superheated denunciations which tumbled from Micah's lips in the next breath.

With this phrase he etches upon the rulers of Israel the sin of ethical betrayal of trust: **Who hate the good, and love the evil.** Nor is the charge left in the area of an ethical abstraction. Choosing the figure of preparation for a great feast, he describes the rulers as the economical cooks who go over the carcass of the slain animal and make good use of every part: skin, bones, and meat. The rulers have done just this to the people of Israel, Micah charges, and behind his indictment you hear the roll of the thunder of an approaching social cataclysm. When the day of retribution comes, it will do the leaders no good to turn to God. Their hardest punishment is not going to be the roaring wrath of a mistreated people or even the strident shouts of victorious foes but the impenetrable silence of an outraged God.

5 ¶ Thus saith the LORD concerning the prophets that make my people err, that bite with their teeth, and cry, Peace; and he that putteth not into their mouths, they even prepare war against him:	5 Thus says the LORD concerning the prophets
	  who lead my people astray,
	who cry "Peace"
	  when they have something to eat,
	but declare war against him
	  who puts nothing into their mouths.

6 Therefore night *shall be* unto you, that ye shall not have a vision; and it shall be dark unto you, that ye shall not divine; and the sun shall go down over the prophets, and the day shall be dark over them.	6 Therefore it shall be night to you, without vision,
	  and darkness to you, without divination.
	The sun shall go down upon the prophets,
	  and the day shall be black over them;

5. The RSV is superior here. By contrast with vss. 1-4, in which the secular leaders of the nation were dealt with, the second stanza of this poem (vss. 5-8) is devoted to the **prophets,** i.e., men of the prophetic guilds. These might be called "majority prophets" and were usually individuals without much integrity, simply yes men. Apparently Micah regarded these **prophets who lead my people astray** as one of the chief causes of corruption. To those who satisfied their exploiting demands the prophets were genial and could **cry "Peace."** But against any who did not comply (**puts nothing into their mouths**), either by reason of principle or financial inability, these false prophets were accustomed to declare a holy inquisition (**declare war against**), in an attempt to impoverish and exterminate all such. Instead of an agency of human uplift, religion in Micah's day was becoming a system of racketeering carried on by unscrupulous prophetic professionals for personal profit.

6. The word חָזוֹן refers to a **vision** in which the individual beheld supernatural things which gave him information about the future. Such a person was called a "beholder of visions," or simply "seer" as in vs. 7. By contrast, **divination** was a more primitive art of foretelling the future by resorting usually to material means such as casting lots, observing flights of birds, etc. Micah, however, challenged the validity of these visions and divinations. By a succession of four synonymous and forceful statements (the four lines in RSV), he made certain to impress upon the two types of prophets that they were at the point of being discredited, for the people were about to see that their supposed ability at making predictions was but a form of quackery.

5-7. The Prophets that Make My People Err. —Having paid his respects to the princes, Micah has something equally unpleasant to say to the spiritual leaders: priests, prophets, and other diviners. He accuses them of putting on a good show of piety, but of being as savagely avaricious as the princes themselves. Do these servants of God try to find a remedy for the abuses which pound the meaning out of the lives of ordinary people? Do they intercede with the princes in the name of justice and brotherhood? Do they share the privations of their people in the hour of desperate need?

The answer is "No" all along the line. They, the spiritual leaders, counsel "peace" and quiescence. They demand a good living lest they grow angry and call down the wrath of God upon niggardly givers. In disgust Micah pro-

nounces the total loss of the glory of prophecy to them. Their visions will fade, their light will become darkness, and they will be overtaken by total shame because no longer will they receive an answer from God.

Micah is not the last layman to be thoroughly disgusted with the contradictions in which religious leaders frequently become involved, and for which they seek pious explanations that are little more than moral evasions. A servant of God either serves God or he does not. He either gets his directive for living from God, or he gets it from some other source. Micah charges his contemporary religious leaders with getting their orders from the princes while pretending to get them from God. To him a priest and prophet should be a humble spokesman for the living God, and for no one else. In this capacity

7 Then shall the seers be ashamed, and the diviners confounded: yea, they shall all cover their lips; for *there is* no answer of God.

8 ¶ But truly I am full of power by the Spirit of the LORD, and of judgment, and of might, to declare unto Jacob his transgression, and to Israel his sin.

9 Hear this, I pray you, ye heads of the house of Jacob, and princes of the house of Israel, that abhor judgment, and pervert all equity.

7 the seers shall be disgraced,
and the diviners put to shame;
they shall all cover their lips,
for there is no answer from God.
8 But as for me, I am filled with power,
with the Spirit of the LORD,
and with justice and might,
to declare to Jacob his transgression
and to Israel his sin.

9 Hear this, you heads of the house of
Jacob
and rulers of the house of Israel,
who abhor justice
and pervert all equity,

7. For **seers** and **diviners** see Exeg. on vs. 6. Micah proclaimed that they would speedily be put to shame. He saw them deserted by God, with no valid message coming henceforth from that source (vs. 7d). Although they had an opportunity to mediate high ideals, they had so abused their positions of leadership for selfish ends that the whole institution of prophecy was falling into disrepute. **They shall all cover their lips** refers to putting their beards up over their heads to hide their faces because of shame in their approaching time of disgrace. In exposing the baselessness of their supposed art before their clientele, Micah must have incurred the wrath of these unworthy prophets, for he was undermining their lucrative profession.

8. Micah contrasted himself with the unworthy characters he had been vilifying (vss. 5-7). He felt the divine **Spirit** surging through him in a way that presumably was not true of the other prophets. **Judgment** means judging rightly. Micah never allowed personal advantage to take precedence over the demands of **justice**. The majority prophets could not approach his high standards in these matters. This gave him an invincible **power** and **might** (moral courage) in exposing the **transgression** and **sin** of his people. **Jacob** and **Israel** are used here (and in vs. 9) as synonyms, designating presumably what was left of the Hebrew people (mostly in Judah) after the ten northern tribes had been carried into exile.

9. In this third and summarizing stanza (vss. 9-12) Micah allowed his prophetic X ray to fall in panoramic manner on governmental officials, judges, priests, and prophets. The chief failing of all was that they had lost their sense of fair dealing (**equity**) and had become patrons of injustice. The very idea of **justice** had become abhorrent, for it was incompatible with their mania for exploitation and greed.

a spiritual leader would be an avowed champion of the welfare of God's children. He would seek those policies and ends for their common life which would correct inequities and heal divisions. He would have as the goal of his endeavors the achievement of a family relationship among men—the kingdom of God in which God reigns supreme.

8-12. *Foundations of Confidence.*—Now that he has dissociated himself from the professional religious leaders, Micah proceeds to claim for himself the relationship with God which they have lost. There is something awesome about his towering claim, **But truly I am full of power by the Spirit of the LORD, and of judg-**

ment, and of might, to declare unto Jacob his transgression, and to Israel his sin. This is the great tradition of prophecy: confident, assured, humble, alert, deadly in earnest, born of complete commitment to the will and the way of Almighty God. Prophecy so conceived and experienced is both a way of life and the power to follow it. Consider the claim which Micah makes with such matter-of-factness: he has the power and the charge to bring Jacob and Israel under the judgment of God for their sins. Note: Not under the judgment of Micah, but under the judgment of God.

Against the background of this tremendous claim he proceeds in forthright fashion to do

10 They build up Zion with blood, and Jerusalem with iniquity.	10 who build Zion with blood and Jerusalem with wrong.

11 The heads thereof judge for reward, and the priests thereof teach for hire, and the prophets thereof divine for money: yet will they lean upon the LORD, and say, *Is* not the LORD among us? none evil can come upon us.	11 Its heads give judgment for a bribe,
	   its priests teach for hire,
	   its prophets divine for money;
	yet they lean upon the LORD and say,
	   "Is not the LORD in the midst of us?
	   No evil shall come upon us."

10. Zion is a poetic variant for **Jerusalem**. The sentence **build . . . with blood and . . . with wrong** refers to the civil violence, corruption, and crime which had become the basis on which Jerusalem, and the nation of which it was the nucleus, was being built. Micah warned that this made a very insecure foundation for the future of any city or nation.

11. Money, rather than principle, guided the various types of national leaders in most of their dealings. The **heads** were the old men of the community who served as judges. In most ages they could be trusted implicitly. However, this judiciary had degenerated until now decisions were being determined no longer by legal principles but by the influence of those who could pay the highest bribe (שׁחֹר). The **priests** were equally unprincipled. They also had their price. This commercialized priesthood had become the tool of the rich rather than a worthy spiritual service to all people. The **prophets** also caught the spirit of the age and prostituted their callings to the service of mammon. Yet all these influential groups pretended to **lean upon the LORD,** thus giving an air of sanctimoniousness to their evil designs. Micah ended his list of accusations against the leaders of his country (vss. 1-11) by quoting two of their typical statements, samples of their soothing words, phrased so as not even to ripple the consciences of wrongdoers. Instead of **evil,** "misfortune" would be a better translation in this context.

just that. Summoning the **heads of the house of Jacob** and the **princes of the house of Israel,** he arraigns them for abhorring judgment, perverting equity, and for building their cities on blood and sin. He summons the judges and arraigns them for accepting bribes. The priests are called and charged with being paid to teach what they teach, and the prophets are stamped as wholly mercenary, despite their pious pretensions and complacent assurances. Confronting this array of leaders—princes, rulers, judges, priests, and prophets—Micah hammers out the simple sweeping judgment on them and on all their works: **Therefore shall Zion for your sake be plowed as a field, and Jerusalem shall become heaps, and the mountain of the house as the high places of the forest.** This of course was rankest heresy. One of the oft-repeated assurances of the priesthood and of the earlier prophets guaranteed the sanctity of Zion. God might bring grievous punishment on his people for their sins, and there was no telling what form the punishment might take. God had afflicted them with drought, diseases of men and animals, war, defeat in war, darkness, and earthquake. Such calamities were not easily borne or contemplated with anything less than grave alarm. But the religious leaders of Israel

almost to a man had been sure that no punishment of God, however serious, would involve the destruction of Jerusalem. For Jerusalem was God's city; the temple was his dwelling place. He could be counted on to defend it himself, no matter how angry he might be with its citizens. Micah did not share this feeling about the security of Jerusalem. In fact, he believed it to be wholly false. He could not see the judgment of God upon Israel fairly executed without razing the iniquitous cities whence evil radiated out to the farthest corners of the land.

It is impossible to believe that the rulers and spiritual leaders of Israel took Micah's judgment seriously. They were not bereft of the kind of evasions which men in similar situations had used before and have used since. Just as Amaziah, the royal priest, had attributed Amos' denunciations to the fact that he was a farmer from another country, so the denounced leaders of Israel could dismiss Micah with the claim that he was merely working off a countryman's jealousy and envy of the city and its enlightened leadership. The religious leaders would inquire loftily whether the word of this irresponsible ranter from the "provinces" was preferable to the solemn assurances of the duly elected and established priesthood of the temple in the holy

12 Therefore shall Zion for your sake be plowed *as* a field, and Jerusalem shall become heaps, and the mountain of the house as the high places of the forest.

4 But in the last days it shall come to pass, *that* the mountain of the house of the LORD shall be established in the top of

12 Therefore because of you
    Zion shall be plowed as a field;
Jerusalem shall become a heap of ruins,
    and the mountain of the house a
        wooded height.

4 It shall come to pass in the latter days
    that the mountain of the house of the
        LORD
    shall be established as the highest of the
        mountains,

---

12. Eleven verses were used to describe the liabilities in the contemporary situation. The twelfth was devoted to Micah's anticipations with regard to the future. He could behold only one thing for such a corrupt country, and that was destruction—spell it however one wished. **Because of you:** The corruption of the national leaders would be to blame for the calamity that was about to descend upon the kingdom. In Micah's vision of the future the city of Jerusalem was no more. The lands thereabouts were but fields, plowed by the few farmers who chanced to occupy those regions. He beheld the once-populous city of David as **a heap of ruins,** speaking mute evidence as to the glory that once was the pride of Israel. The most sacred site in Palestine, that of Solomon's temple, looked as but a bare deserted hilltop in the midst of woodland thickets. This would be the end of the nation which, forgetting God and standards of right conduct, had become a land of iniquity.

IV. VISIONS OF A GLORIOUS FUTURE (4:1–5:15)

According to best scholarly opinion chs. 4–5 contain no material by the prophet, but constitute a collection of fragments which had their origins several centuries or more after the time of Micah. Closer examination of the material reveals that most of it consists of two documents intertwined.

The earlier of these (4:1-4, 6-8; 5:7, 10-14) records a voice from the closing days of the Exile. This document reflects the spirit of Second Isaiah (*ca.* 540 B.C.), and is therefore later than that date. It is almost a review of Isa. 40–44, beginning with preparation of the way for the full return, and ending with the elimination of all idolatries and unworthy worship. It is probably by the same author who wrote and inserted 1:2-4; 2:12-13, for these are parallel treatments, and all three are based especially

---

city. And there, in the way, was only this defenseless confidence: **I am full of power by the Spirit of the LORD.**

12. *For Your Sake.*—But supposing for a moment that Micah's indictment might have stung the culprits into an attack of conscience, how unbearably heavy it would have been for them! That phrase **for your sake** strikes to the very heart of life. **Because of you,** Jerusalem is to be destroyed, reduced to ruin. **Because of you** this must and will come to pass. Think of walking even in a moment of imagination down the streets of the city and into the temple with courts and altars hallowed by memory and tradition, saying to yourself, "For my sake all this is going to be reduced to a pile of rubble!" Could anyone bear that burden?

Man is not noticeably strong when he faces the consequences of his own guilt, as we have

seen when careless drivers are forced to view their victims, or when the survivor in a fight is forced to see the dead enemy. Even the aviators who dropped the bomb on Hiroshima turned away with the pilot's words ringing in their ears, "Let's get out of here. It smells of death." It takes more strength than most of us have to accept full, open responsibility for our evil deeds. We protect ourselves by rationalizations which may deflect the blows of outraged conscience but cannot wholly ward them off.

4:1-2. *In the Last Days.*—In this chapter other hands and hearts than those of Micah are clearly discernible. At least two—some scholars think four—are mirrored in the various sections.

The writer of vss. 1-2 and the editor who inserts them at this point in the MS of an ancient prophecy (if writer and editor are two different persons) feel that Micah closes on the

the mountains, and it shall be exalted above the hills; and people shall flow unto it.	and shall be raised up above the hills; and peoples shall flow to it,

on Isa. 40:1-11. The same person who wrote and appended this basic document in chs. 4–5 presumably also wrote and inserted a similar production among the prophecies of Isaiah (2:2-18). The first three verses of each are almost identical. Then they diverge, but not far, for they consider the same subjects and eventually both end with a climax in the abolishing of idolatry. By contrast with the doleful outlook of Micah and other pre-exilic prophets, these four secondary passages, three in Micah and one in Isaiah, reveal that invincible hope with regard to the future which prevailed as the Exile was coming to its close.

Most of the remaining verses in these two chapters (4:5, 9-13; 5:1-5a, 8-9, 15) comprise another document which came from a period in postexilic times at least a century later than the intermeshed late exilic material. This deals with the restoration of Israel by resorting to militaristic means. By contrast with the benevolent feeling toward all peoples which prevailed among the Hebrew remnant at the close of the Exile, and which is expressed in the basic document in these chapters, this production takes the opposite view and breathes vengeance upon other nations.

A. Universal Religion and Perpetual Peace (4:1-8)

This passage expresses the unclouded optimism of late exilic times, with its hope for restoration of the Israelite nation from exile, the rebuilding of Jerusalem, establishment of a world theocracy on Zion, and an era of universal peace. This prophetic vision was one of mankind's first glimpses of one world of justice, law, and peace.

4:1. In the latter days or **last days** must not be construed as referring to the end time or an eschatological age in the distant future. This באחרית הימים was a technical term for the end of the Exile. The **days** therefore were the days of exile. Here, as in 1:2-4 and Isa. 40, the expectation was that miraculous geologic and cosmic changes would accompany the restoration of the Hebrew people to Palestine. The earth would become leveled into a great plain (1:4; Isa. 40:4). The only exception would be Mount Zion, where the reverse would happen. It, accompanied by the immediately surrounding hills, would be raised high into the air so as to be visible over all the earth. This exalted sacred mount would be the focal point of interest to all humanity, presumably the center of the earth.

---

wrong note when he depicts the utter ruin of Jerusalem. They prefer the earlier dream of **Zion** as the City of God, the symbol of honor, security, and power. Consequently they call up the ancient vision of Zion as the spiritual, cultural, economic, and political center of the earth. Like Second Isaiah, they spread on the bruised consciousness of the badly mauled Hebrew people the balm of glorious anticipation, rousing visions of the day when the very peoples who have been so cruel and superior to Israel will come to her humbly admitting her greatness and asking only for the right to serve her and her God.

In so far as it is the human cry of a defeated Israel, it is not easy to know what to make of this kind of thinking and feeling. It may be an inevitable expression of human nature in the presence of defeat and adversity. It refuses to accept disaster as ultimate by insisting that **in the last days** the victors will be the vanquished

and vice versa. As a strong vote of continuing confidence in the validity of "a lost cause" this sort of expression commands admiration. But it scarcely merits a respect born of an awareness of facts. In other words, it is a poor way to deal with the realities of history. For in that arena defeats are as real as victories and tragedy is at least as strong as triumph. It simply is not true to say that "everything will finally come out just as we had planned and believed." Too many dead and dying civilizations dot the roadway of history to give even a semblance of comfort to this dangerous illusion.

But we must admit that the catch is in the phrase **in the last days**. As every beleaguered fundamentalist and biblical literalist knows, this phrase is his ever-present escape hatch when facts sink his prophecies. Both fanatic and prophet can appeal to **the last days** for vindication—and no one can say them nay at the time they make the appeal, because the last days have

2 And many nations shall come, and say, Come, and let us go up to the mountain of the LORD, and to the house of the God of Jacob; and he will teach us of his ways, and we will walk in his paths: for the law shall go forth of Zion, and the word of the LORD from Jerusalem.

3 ¶ And he shall judge among many people, and rebuke strong nations afar off; and

2 and many nations shall come, and say:
"Come, let us go up to the mountain of the LORD,
to the house of the God of Jacob;
that he may teach us his ways
and we may walk in his paths."
For out of Zion shall go forth the law,
and the word of the LORD from Jerusalem.
3 He shall judge between many peoples,
and shall decide for strong nations afar off;
and they shall beat their swords into plowshares,

---

2. The anticipation in the last clause of vs. 1 and in vs. 2 was that all peoples would embrace the religion of Israel and come to the temple mount as their place of worship. As in Isa. 53, the nations are speaking in the body of vs. 2, in a four-line stanza of excellent poetry. In the first couplet they exhort each other to make the pilgrimage to Palestine and worship the supreme God, newly adopted from the Hebrews. The expression **God of Jacob** is equivalent to "God of the Hebrew people." This picture of Jerusalem as the city of God is diametrically opposite to that of Jerusalem the apostate in 3:12. In the second couplet the nations tell how Jerusalem would become a center of divine teaching, and that all people would follow in the ways of the Lord as there taught, in an era of universal and united religion among mankind. In the third couplet the author seems to be continuing from where the nations left off, glorying concerning the law and the way it would flow forth from the holy mount of Zion as a benediction to all the world. **The law** and **the word of the LORD** are synonymous terms, as also **Zion** and **Jerusalem.** Similar passages, possibly from approximately the same late exilic time, are found in Isa. 11:10; 60:1-14; Jer. 3:17; 31:12; Zech. 2:11; 8:22-23; 14:9, 16.

3. As presumably in 1:2-4 (if it had been carried further), in the references cited above (end of vs. 2), and in Isa. 40:9-11, a theocracy was anticipated in which there

---

yet to come. There is, however, this one great difference between fanatic and prophet: the latter has an enormous respect for the activity of God in history; the former has a bland contempt for—and usually immeasurable ignorance of—history.

No one knows what historical facts or clues prompted the writer of these verses to the superlative hope which animates them. There seems to be no period in the history of Israel after the days of Micah (with the possible exception of the Maccabean period) that gave the slightest foundation for them. Yet it would be folly for us to ignore or underrate the plain fact that this sort of utterance may be one of the strongest ways man has of facing adversity under the guidance of religious faith. Deeper than the all too human need to which it ministered in the life of downtrodden Israel is the realization that God, not man, is the Lord of history. If, or to the extent that, Israel is the "chosen people" of God, then God can be depended upon to overthrow the human oppressors of Israel.

Let us then not lose sight of the strong theocratic emphasis of the writer. Israel is not to rise in her own might and work the subjugation of the world to her will. God shall do this and shall subdue the world to his will. Clearly this faith in the ultimate vindication of God's historic purpose is more than fantasy thinking; it is the kind of faith that can face historic reverses, even calamities, with an even gaze and be unafraid. For in its eyes **the last days** will be "the day of the Lord," the Day of Judgment, when all the earth shall stand before God for the final winnowing. Then truly the whole world will honor Israel, and seek to learn from her that way of life in which she has found her mission and strength. The nations must either do that or perish—this is the faith of the prophetic spirit clearly discernible in this section of the book.

3-4. The Day of the Lord Is Peace.—No word of scripture is quoted more frequently and with greater longing than this passage which depicts the world at peace. Truly it is to be "the day

they shall beat their swords into plowshares, and their spears into pruning hooks: nation shall not lift up a sword against nation, neither shall they learn war any more.

4 But they shall sit every man under his vine and under his fig tree; and none shall make *them* afraid: for the mouth of the Lord of hosts hath spoken *it*.

and their spears into pruning hooks;
nation shall not lift up sword against nation,
neither shall they learn war any more;
4 but they shall sit every man under his vine and under his fig tree,
and none shall make them afraid;
for the mouth of the Lord of hosts has spoken.

---

would be no earthly ruler in the one world that was anticipated, but God himself would reign. Apparently all nations would be merged into a world commonwealth under this divine rule. Here there are three couplets, as in vs. 2. The first tells how God, as part of his rule, would be **judge** among the nations, executing justice between them as he would come to **rebuke** or **decide** concerning (not **for** RSV) even the **strong nations**, i.e., he would bring into subjection the major powers which in their wantonness have always been the cause of mankind's troubles. The second couplet is the first brilliant call for disarmament in the history of the world's thought. It remains the classic of all time, for nothing has been uttered since to surpass it in effectiveness. This gives a vision of the parasitical and nonproductive implements of war giving way to the tools of well-being and construction. The third couplet is devoted to the reign of peace which will follow. War will be no more. Even the arts of war shall no longer be taught to the rising generations. This dream of a world at peace is one of the most powerful concepts ever to find its way into the perspective of man.

4. This four-verse poem ends with a picture of the personal peace and security which this new era will bring to the individual. Each person will be able to dwell in his humble home with freedom from fear and molestation. The phraseology is adapted from the description of the era of peace in Solomon's time (I Kings 4:25). The special divine attestation at the end seems to be taken from Isa. 40:5. This poem (vss. 1-4), about the

---

of the Lord," since through his judgment strong nations will be curbed and the occasions for war removed. This done, a world at peace will use its precious metals for implements of agriculture rather than for weapons. War and the preparation for it will no longer obsess the mind and engage the energies of men.

In that glorious day what will be the lot of "the common man"? The well-worn words of almost holy longing for security come welling up as the writer answers this question: **They shall sit every man under his vine and under his fig tree; and none shall make them afraid: for the mouth of the Lord of hosts hath spoken it.** When the writer of the book of Kings wants to bring his depiction of the glories of the reign of Solomon to a climax, he does not talk of the trappings of royalty or enumerate material and geographical possessions; he writes, "And Judah and Israel dwelt safely, every man under his vine and under his fig tree, from Dan even to Beer-sheba, all the days of Solomon" (I Kings 4:25). Isaiah gives a touch of added color to this picture by including, "and drink ye every one the waters of his own cistern" (Isa. 36:16).

War may once have been compared to "the

sport of kings," [3] but it always has been the scourge of those whom we all too readily call ordinary men and women. The literature of every people is filled with longings for peace and security. The symbols of security and peace for Israel were the **vine**, the **fig tree**, and the cistern, with none to **make them afraid**. It is frequently objected that this condition would not long satisfy man's restless, activistic nature. We want to do something more than **sit** under a vine or a fig tree. Such objections, interestingly enough, always come from city dwellers. Every farmer knows that if all you propose to do is to sit under a vine or a fig tree, you will not long have either a vine or a fig tree to sit under. Most of us cast our thought of peace in terms of the ability to pursue the ordinary rounds of life without interruption and without anxiety. One of the most poignant passages in all scripture is this: **and none shall make them afraid.** It is comparable with only one other—the passage in Revelation outlining the way of life in the new Jerusalem: "And God shall wipe away all tears from their eyes; and there shall be no more death, neither sorrow, nor crying,

[3] See William Somerville, *The Chase*, Bk. I.

5 For all people will walk every one in the name of his god, and we will walk in the name of the LORD our God for ever and ever.

5 For all the peoples walk
each in the name of its god,
but we will walk in the name of the LORD
our God
for ever and ever.

conversion of the nations to the ways of godliness, is one of the most challenging passages in the Bible.

5. There is some basis for the contention that this verse was inserted as a refutation by some individual who believed the content of vss. 1-4, 6-8 expressed only an idle dream. To bring out this contrast כי (**For**) at the beginning might better be translated "But." This verse is exclusive in its emphasis by contrast with vss. 1-4, 6-8 where there is religious universalism. The expression **all the peoples** refers to the Gentiles. This verse implies that only the Hebrews had the true religion, and it was to remain an eternal monopoly with them. It expresses the anticipation that the nations would not embrace a common world faith but would continue indefinitely to worship their distinctive national gods. By contrast, as the last clause implies, the Hebrews always had worshiped Yahweh and always would continue to do so.

neither shall there be any more pain" (Rev. 21:4). While it is not easy for us to foresee a day in history when fears and sorrows will be removed from the lot of human life, no vision of the world in which God's will is perfectly realized could conceivably be formulated without it.

5. Real Tolerance—Too Good to Be True.— Easily the most extraordinary verse in this section of Micah is the one which reads: **For all people will walk every one in the name of his god, and we will walk in the name of the LORD our God for ever and ever.** This would seem to be a generous sentiment—one not shared by the writer of vs. 1, or by many other writers of biblical books. Could there be for Israel such a recognition of many gods, coupled with the worship of one? Under the fierce poundings of the prophets she had been forced to desert that view for the sharp unity of monotheism, which is the recognition and the worship of but one God. At first glance it seems that only bigotry and dogmatism would insist on any such thing. On the face of it such "catholicity" seems close to the principle of freedom which we prize so highly—and so rightly. This probably explains why there is so much talk of what goes by the name of "tolerance"—though it goes by other names too, and incorporates its credo in other language. There are the moral relativists who say, "What you think is right, is right for you; what I think is right, is right for me." They are obviously ethical blood brothers to those who would say, "You worship your God, and I'll worship mine." What is wrong with it, the contemporary world asks?

By way of answer, what would you think of the physicist who would say to a colleague: "Well, we disagree on the validity of this experiment. What you think is true, is true for you; what I think is true, is true for me"? We do not live in the kind of moral world that will support the line of reasoning of the moral relativist any more than we live in the kind of world that would support the attitude of such a physicist. This world is one world in basic structure and design, as truly in the area of religion and morals as in physics and chemistry.

Consequently, when the ancient Hebrew chanted his Shema, "Hear, O Israel, the LORD thy God is one God," he was giving true religion's final answer to all forms of relativism, whether religious or moral. There is a unitive power, principle, and structure in the world, and we cannot rest with our fragmentary insights into its nature. Neither dare we absolutize those insights. That is the only and the permanent danger of dogmatism and intolerance.

But we must not let our judgment that the writer of this passage is moving in the wrong direction keep us from appreciating the fact that he could not see a real peace for his time which did not bring some sort of truce amid the warring religions of the day. In this he was and is exactly right. The spirit of freedom and tolerance must find some kind of creative approach to the fact of religious differences. No one of us is in a position to blueprint a final answer in this difficult and controversial matter, but the search for it constitutes one of our primary obligations. Until and unless this problem is attacked and solved with some degree of mutual satisfaction, the idea that "religion" can furnish the spiritual basis of one world politically and economically is little more than a futile dream. Farseeing church leaders sense as

6 In that day, saith the Lord, will I assemble her that halteth, and I will gather her that is driven out, and her that I have afflicted;

7 And I will make her that halted a remnant, and her that was cast far off a strong nation: and the Lord shall reign over them in mount Zion from henceforth, even for ever.

8 ¶ And thou, O tower of the flock, the stronghold of the daughter of Zion, unto thee shall it come, even the first dominion; the kingdom shall come to the daughter of Jerusalem.

6 In that day, says the Lord,
    I will assemble the lame
and gather those who have been driven
        away,
    and those whom I have afflicted;
7 and the lame I will make the remnant;
    and those who were cast off, a strong
        nation;
and the Lord will reign over them in
        Mount Zion
    from this time forth and for evermore.

8 And you, O tower of the flock,
    hill of the daughter of Zion,
to you shall it come,
    the former dominion shall come,
        the kingdom of the daughter of Jerusalem.

---

6. This resumes the thought of vs. 4. **In that day** (cf. the beginning of vs. 1) was a reference to the time when the Exile would be at an end. **Lame, driven away,** and **afflicted** are adjectives describing the situation of the Hebrew people during the Exile in Mesopotamia. God himself had lamed, driven away, and afflicted them, as the end of the verse implies, but now he was about to make amends, as in Isa. 40:2 ff. From their various places of exile the people would return. They believed that God was about to **assemble** and **gather** them from the far regions of the earth. This seems to be the figure of the good shepherd, reassembling his mutilated and scattered flock. It probably has as its background inspiration the figure of God as the good shepherd in Isa. 40:11.

7. This writer, in the late years of exile, had faith to believe that out of this **remnant** that was **lame** and **cast off**, God was about to build **a strong nation.** In this restored Israel there would be no mortal king, for as in Isa. 24:23; 40:9-11; 52:7, they anticipated that God himself would rule in Zion over the restored nation. This rule was to be permanent, enduring throughout all future time.

8. **Zion** (also in vs. 7) was an alternate name for **Jerusalem. Daughter of Zion** and **daughter of Jerusalem** were simply further poetic variants. The dual address to Jerusalem seems inspired by the same literary technique in Isa. 40:9. **Hill of the daughter of Zion** refers to the miraculously exalted temple mount, as described in vss. 1-2. **Tower of the flock** continues the shepherd figure, indicating that this holy mountain was to be God's watchtower from which he would guard and tend (Isa. 40:11) his flock of humanity which would extend over all the earth. **The former dominion** refers to the glorious days of the Israelite monarchy under David and Solomon, when the temple existed in its

---

much, and are throwing the total weight of their ecclesiastical and personal influence behind a strengthening of the World Council of Churches, and a building of bridges of understanding and intercommunication between and among the religions of the world. In no other way can an honest beginning be made toward realizing Jesus' hope for his followers, "That they all may be one" (John 17:21).

6. *Glorious Reunion.*—No Hebrew writer could envisage "the last days" without a gathering together of the scattered portions of the people of Israel from the ends of the earth.

After the Exile had wounded Israel to the point of death, the writer there too anticipates the renewal of the unity and well-being of his people. This is but another expression of the almost incredible social solidarity of the Hebrew consciousness—a solidarity deeper than the many differences which have always separated any given generation of Hebrews into quarreling factions. When the Jewish faith had at a later date accepted from outside sources the ideas of bodily resurrection and immortality, it phrased them in such a way as to preserve the ancient consciousness of being "the chosen

9 Now why dost thou cry out aloud? *is there* no king in thee? is thy counselor perished? for pangs have taken thee as a woman in travail.	9 Now why do you cry aloud?
	  Is there no king in you?
	Has your counselor perished,
	  that pangs have seized you like a
	  woman in travail?

magnificence and the twelve tribes were joined in a unity which was transformed by those two kings into one of the major nations of the world. In those days Solomon ruled, at least by league and marriage alliances, practically from the Euphrates to the Nile. Now this was about to be equaled. Although not stated in so many words, the context implies the anticipation that this new **kingdom of the daughter of Jerusalem** would immeasurably outshine the splendors of Israel's most glorious past.

B. The Way of Monarchy, Militarism, and Vengeance (4:9–5:6)

This passage presumably reflects a period in mid-postexilic times, after Jerusalem had been destroyed on several occasions by neighbor nations and international complications had placed repeated impediments in the way of restoring Judah and Zion. These Palestinians now determined to supplement their exilic trust in God by resort to political and military might. By contrast with the basic document in chs. 4–5, which abounds in love and good feeling toward all people, this rises to a climax of hate and vindictiveness against other nations, calling for their annihilation.

9. This apparently describes the desperate plight of the Jews as they struggled for existence in Jerusalem during the first century after their return to Palestine. **Cry aloud** refers to the weeping of this saddened community. The questions imply that the returned

people." In similar manner, the notion that the eternal destiny of Israel is somehow bound up with the Holy Land finds expression both in Micah and in contemporary Zionism. As a noted rabbi once put it, "The Torah, the Promised Land, the Chosen People—this is the trinity of Israel's faith and history." The writer of this portion of Micah would add a fervent "Amen" to such a sentiment.

9-10. Strength for Tragedy.—Once again the mood of the prophecy swings from future triumph to present tragedy. The city is leaderless; no trusted person is at the center of the life of the people; chaos reigns. And it will get worse—much worse—before it gets better. Captivity and exile loom beyond the defeat of Israel and the destruction of the city. But beyond these lies the certainty of divine redemption and restoration. The much-used metaphor of biblical writers (**a woman in travail**) is again invoked—with its usual dramatic effectiveness.

Pointless pain is the most inexplicable form of evil. Almost any amount of pain can be borne if it seems to be making toward some good end. During World War II the mother of a son lost at sea said: "If any good can come of it, we can bear the loss." In contrast, and with a bitterness that is beyond description, a father said of his son's death: "And for what? Nothing! Absolutely nothing!" Every person in pain becomes a theologian of some sort since he seeks some ultimate explanation of the suffering he

endures. When he finds, or thinks he finds, an adequate one, he is spiritually "braced" for the next onslaught of pain. He has the strength, the heart, the will, to wrestle with it. If he is unable to find this internal strength, he pulls down the flag of spiritual understanding, abandons the wheel of the ship of faith, and goes below, resigning the entire life enterprise to the storm. Physicians lay great stress on a patient's "will to live" in certain kinds of illness. This is so important that some do not hesitate to mix a few "illusions" with their medicine.

Social and political leaders have always laid great stress on the "morale" of their group or people. A foreman on a railroad crew once explained why he kept a lazy, inefficient workman on the job: "He keeps the men in good spirits with his jokes." A cheerful radiant person is always a most acceptable addition to an office force, faculty, church, or any other co-operative undertaking.

One of the most important ingredients in the morale of a people facing great suffering is the belief that some great and good end can and will be served by a courageous facing of the ordeal. The glowing promises of a "free world" which came from the radio, the press, and the lips of public officials in World War II are a case in point. The Atlantic Charter, signed and presented with great fanfare five months before the United States entered the war, was at the time hailed as a statement of "war aims";

10 Be in pain, and labor to bring forth, O daughter of Zion, like a woman in travail: for now shalt thou go forth out of the city, and thou shalt dwell in the field, and thou shalt go *even* to Babylon; there shalt thou be delivered; there the Lord shall redeem thee from the hand of thine enemies.

10 Writhe and groan,[h] O daughter of Zion,
like a woman in travail;
for now you shall go forth from the city
and dwell in the open country;
you shall go to Babylon.
There you shall be rescued,
there the Lord will redeem you
from the hand of your enemies.

[h] Heb uncertain

ones had settled into a mood of despair. At the time of this verse they had neither **king** nor **counselor. Pangs have seized you like a woman in travail** probably refers to the early postexilic ill-fated attempts at re-establishing the Hebrew kingship under Zerubbabel in 516 B.C., and still later under Menahem, *ca.* 485 B.C. At each of these times, and perhaps others of which we have no record, Jerusalem was **in travail**, trying to bring forth. But in each instance nothing came of it, for the Persians and neighbors heard of the plans and dealt violently with the returned exiles, presumably killing the aspirants to the kingship and devastating Jerusalem and its environs. That is why this section begins with the loud crying of the returned community in its increasing despair.

10. In the introductory couplet, as in vs. 9*b*, the attempt of Israel to restore the kingship is spoken of under the figure of a woman striving to give birth to a child. The call comes to Jerusalem to make one more attempt at bringing forth. The major part of the verse (three couplets) gives a review of the past, as if it were future. God is represented as speaking to Israel in prophetic address (using future tenses) before the days of her decline.

**Shall go forth from the city
and dwell in the open country**

as such it gave public morale a great lift. Yet as the war ground on, pushing the possibility of fulfilling the Charter farther and farther away, one of its chief signatories, Franklin D. Roosevelt, felt called upon publicly to disown it as a definitive document. The superb speeches of Winston Churchill were valuable as recitals of fact by a man with a keen sense of history; but they were immeasurably more important at the time of their delivery because of their effect on public morale in the British Empire as well as in the United States. Churchill never closed one of his major utterances on a depressed or depressing note. Always he pointed to the dawn that was about to break beyond the ordeal of bitter struggle. Londoners, crouched in bomb shelters, took heart even as did the weary armies in the field.

At an earlier day Second Isaiah, the unknown prophet of the Exile, literally sang heart and will back into the exiles in Babylon with his "songs of the servant." When Jeremiah wrote to the exiles, his letter radiated confidence in an early and complete vindication and restoration. The whole point of apocalyptical literature was to persuade men going through the fiery furnaces of history that God would be with them as companion and savior.

So the writer of Micah stands in a modern as well as in an ancient tradition when he assures his contemporaries that new life will come from the agony of their ordeal. But what about the ethics of offering that kind of assurance—save on the basis of the faith which found expression in the prophet (see Expos. on vss. 1-2)? White lies have a way of turning black. The ordinary propagandist has no difficulty with the question. "The end justifies the means," he answers, and proceeds to "tell people" what they need to hear in order to keep up their morale. As has been noted, this may be good politics, but it is bad religion. And it may be doubted whether anything that is indubitably bad religion can long endure as good politics. It is bad religion to say something you know to be untrue, or something for which you have only the flimsiest sort of evidence. To say that "people need to hear it" is sheer evasion. People need to hear one thing—the truth, as clearly as we know it and can speak it. Sooner or later they must live in accordance with it, and the earlier they know it the more quickly they will face it. The whole sickening story of facts and information withheld from the public during World War II came in the years that followed. An inevitable revulsion against the integrity of the

11 ¶ Now also many nations are gathered against thee, that say, Let her be defiled, and let our eye look upon Zion.	11 Now many nations
	    are assembled against you,
	  saying, "Let her be profaned,
	    and let our eyes gaze upon Zion."

12 But they know not the thoughts of the LORD, neither understand they his coun-	12 But they do not know
	    the thoughts of the LORD,
	  they do not understand his plan,

refers to the final years before the Exile, when the refugees fled from the few remaining cities into the country districts where they tried to hide from the enemy. **Go to Babylon** refers to the exiles of 597 and 586 B.C. The last three clauses tell of the rescue by God's help from the Exile. With the return under Cyrus in 538 B.C., and smaller ones which followed, it seemed the Israelite dreams had at last been fulfilled, for God had chosen to **redeem** them from their enemies. This is the taproot of the redemption idea, which plays an increasingly important role in the latter part of the O.T. and in the N.T. **From the hand of** means "from the power of."

11. This verse describes the aftermath, during 516-445 B.C. Julian Morgenstern has worked out carefully the history of those tragic years, showing that many descriptions of devastated Jerusalem in various parts of the Bible (e.g., in Lamentations, certain psalms, etc.) belong in this period and describe the destruction of Jerusalem in 485 B.C. The Persians had been firm in their resolve that there should be no restoration of the Hebrew monarchy in Palestine. The neighboring nations also were determined there should be no substantial Jewish settlement there. So they harassed the struggling Jerusalem community in every way possible, destroying time after time what fortifying of the city had been accomplished. When Nehemiah came from Babylon *ca.* 445 B.C., he found the community in "great affliction and reproach" with "the wall of Jerusalem . . . broken down, and the gates thereof . . . burned with fire" (Neh. 1:3). The residents were so harassed by their neighbors that workmen were forced to hold their weapons in readiness with one hand while working on the walls with the other (Neh. 4:16-20). In light of all this vs. 11 has significant meaning. It comes from Israel's dark hour, in postexilic times, when these neighboring nations had conspired in assault upon her and were trying to bring about the destruction of the Jewish people. The last half of the verse quotes two of these calls to war given by the enemy neighbors as they proceeded about their task of destroying the returned community on Mount Zion. **Be defiled** means "devastated by war." In the last clause **gaze upon** has the sense of "see our vengeance upon."

12. In their reckonings there was one factor of which the enemy nations were unaware—God was to have something to say about this matter too. The last clause

---

word of even the President of the United States set in and moved to great height. A further undermining of public confidence in the spoken word of elected officials was inescapable.

This sort of calculated deception is not a new thing in human affairs, or in the history of any country. But it is especially serious now because of the speed of communications. Formerly people expected news to come trickling in finally and slowly. Days, even weeks, would elapse before it was possible for corrections to be made in case of original error. Now some sort of information is demanded immediately about almost every major event. Popular judgments are frequently arrived at on the basis of initial releases that themselves are shot through with falsehood and misinterpretation. When

the true statement of fact emerges, it must fight for a hearing with minds and spirits already schooled in misrepresentation. The answer is obviously not to be found in the kind of secret diplomacy which was practiced with such grim results for so many years, nor in any effort to slow down the speed with which news reaches the people who have to do their thinking in terms of it. Rather it must be found in a heightening of the sense of integrity on the part of persons engaged in the gathering and dissemination of information, whether they are employed by radio, press, or are public officials.

11-13. The Savage in All of Us.—Once more the mood changes and the songs of vengeance burst out. Anyone who has either had a hand in the destruction of Zion or has gloried in her

sel: for he shall gather them as the sheaves into the floor.

13 Arise and thresh, O daughter of Zion; for I will make thine horn iron, and I will make thy hoofs brass: and thou shalt beat in pieces many people: and I will consecrate their gain unto the LORD, and their substance unto the Lord of the whole earth.

that he has gathered them as sheaves to the threshing floor.

13 Arise and thresh,
   O daughter of Zion,
for I will make your horn iron
   and your hoofs bronze;
you shall beat in pieces many peoples,
   and shall[i] devote their gain to the
      LORD,
   their wealth to the Lord of the whole
      earth.

5 Now gather thyself in troops, O daughter of troops: he hath laid siege against us: they shall smite the judge of Israel with a rod upon the cheek.

5 [j] Now you are walled about with a
      wall;[k]
   siege is laid against us;
with a rod they strike upon the cheek
   the ruler of Israel.

i Gk Syr Tg: Heb *I will*
j Heb Ch 4. 14
k Cn Compare Gk: Heb obscure

---

expresses what the writer regarded as the real purpose of God in all this. This gathering together of the heathen nations against the struggling community on Zion was part of the divine plan to seal their guilt and bring them together into one location in order that God might more easily annihilate them, as in Joel 3:9-17 (4:9-17 in Hebrew). The nations are described under the figure of **sheaves** about to be trampled into chaff on the **threshing floor.** They were now being assembled, and the threshing was about to begin.

13. Using three phases of the figure, God gave the people of Israel their call to battle. (*a*) Taking the imagery as a whole, God's people were called upon to get into action and thresh their enemies. (*b*) Israel was likened to a goring bull, except that the horns, with which she would gore the nations to death, would be made of iron. This refers to the way a spirited bull gores the sheaves as he treads them on the threshing floor. (*c*) Israel would have hoofs of brass with which her victims would be trampled to death and ground, as it were, into chaff. So the Gentile nations would be beaten **in pieces.** This seems dependent on Isa. 41:11-16 (especially vs. 15). **Their gain** and **their wealth** refer to the loot God's people would take from the annihilated nations. Instead of destroying all booty, as in the days of Joshua, it was to be consecrated to God and his service (as in Isa. 60:11-12).

5:1. In the first clause the unemended Hebrew text (as in KJV) seems preferable. The first verb, translated **gather thyself in troops,** might better be rendered by our expression "mobilize yourselves." The noun גדוד, **troops,** is the equivalent of our

---

trouble is going to be destroyed. God purposes it and will bring it to pass. He will gather the enemies of Israel together as grain on a threshing floor and will invite Israel to beat them to pieces, to take away their possessions and to **consecrate their gain unto the LORD.**

No defense or justification of this kind of reaction can be made or given. It is the ethic of a conscience untutored in Christ. It is the negation of every lofty ethical and spiritual insight of the Christian faith. To call it "eschatological" describes but does not justify it.

5:1-15. *Scripture Betrayed by Its Friends.*— No other chapter in Scripture has been more

abused by its friends than this. It is one of the scriptural sources of the messianic hope that was to loom so large in postexilic Judaism. The tradition that Jesus came in fulfillment of this and other prophecies was so early and so deep a part of the Christian apologetic that it wrote itself into the Gospels, notably into Matthew, Luke, and John. It is hard to believe that anyone who had actually read this chapter carefully could think that it had any reference at all to the coming of Jesus Christ. There is little or nothing in common between its central theme and anything he did or said. Actually the gospel records claim only that Bethlehem was the

2 But thou, Beth-lehem Ephratah, *though* thou be little among the thousands of Judah, *yet* out of thee shall he come forth unto me *that is* to be ruler in Israel; whose goings forth *have been* from of old, from everlasting.

3 Therefore will he give them up, until

2[1] But you, O Bethlehem Eph'rathah,
  who are little to be among the clans of
  Judah,
from you shall come forth for me
  one who is to be ruler in Israel,
whose origin is from of old,
  from ancient days.

3 Therefore he shall give them up until
  the time

[1] Heb Ch 5. 1

"divisions." The people of Jerusalem and its environs were called upon to mobilize themselves at once (**Now**), according to their divisions, into an army which would execute the designs as outlined in 4:13. The remainder of the verse tells why this proposed action was so urgent. The last two verbs should probably both be plural (as in Syriac, Targ., and Vulg.) and in the present tense (as in RSV), describing the desperateness of the situation which at the moment was menacing the Jerusalem community (for further treatment of this plight see Exeg. on 4:9, 11). In those times, as in the chaotic days before the monarchy, judges served as the last stand of civil authority. Yet enemies proceeded to smite even these judges **of Israel with a rod upon the cheek,** i.e., the neighbor nations proposed to obliterate all that remained of civil government among the Jewish communities and thus bring about their elimination as separate entities.

2. As in 4:10, the author here takes another panoramic view in retrospect over the history of the Hebrew monarchy, going back this time to the period of its origins. Much as in 4:10, future tenses are used here because the author is incorporating the prophetic address (in the future tense) of God to **Bethlehem** at the time David was being called to the kingship. The first four lines must therefore be understood as God's address at that ancient time to Bethlehem regarding her future destiny. This village was five miles southwest of Jerusalem. **Ephrathah** refers to the specific region in which it was located. The combined designation distinguished this from other villages by the name Bethlehem in various parts of Palestine. **The thousands of Judah** (not **clans of**), is equivalent to "the villages of Judah," for the average village consisted roughly of a thousand people. In the days of David, when Palestine was well populated, this particular Bethlehem was insignificant among the villages of Judah. Yet out of this undistinguished place (I Sam. 17:12) came David the son of Jesse, who was to establish the Hebrew monarchy on a solid basis and become the founder of a dynasty of kings who were to rule Judah for almost half a millennium, until the Exile of 586 B.C. The author marvels at what a great movement came from such a little place. The **me** refers to God, for David and the kings following him were thought of as God's anointed agents in ruling Israel. The last couplet stresses the remoteness of those origins of the Hebrew kingship, back in the time of David, **from of old, from ancient days.**

3. Here the panoramic spotlight swings on from the time of David (vs. 2) to the period of the Exile. Carrying further God's prophetic foretelling to Israel of her coming vicissitudes and destiny, the future tenses (as in vs. 2) are continued. The first part of

ordained birthplace of the one who was to be the **ruler in Israel.** Once they have "established" that by reference to vs. 2, they walk straight away from everything else in the chapter.

The sentiments expressed here can be easily understood as the normal reaction of one who has seen his country defeated, her cities destroyed, her farms devastated, and her leaders sent into exile. The writer, confronted by what appeared to be a complete end, refused to be-

lieve it. As a man of faith in God he anticipates the day when the tables will be turned. His mind dwells, sometimes almost serenely and sometimes with actual savagery, upon the details of the revolution in events.

1-4. *The Religious Approach to Disaster.*— The writer accepts, as he must, the defeat of Israel. Her troops have been beaten, her cities besieged, her government overthrown. But that is far from the end. Her revival and triumph

the time *that* she which travaileth hath brought forth: then the remnant of his brethren shall return unto the children of Israel.

4 ¶ And he shall stand and feed in the strength of the LORD, in the majesty of the name of the LORD his God; and they shall abide: for now shall he be great unto the ends of the earth.

5 And this *man* shall be the peace, when the Assyrian shall come into our land: and when he shall tread in our palaces, then shall we raise against him seven shepherds, and eight principal men.

when she who is in travail has brought forth;
then the rest of his brethren shall return to the people of Israel.

4 And he shall stand and feed his flock in the strength of the LORD,
in the majesty of the name of the LORD his God.
And they shall dwell secure, for now he shall be great
to the ends of the earth.

5 And this shall be peace,
when the Assyrian comes into our land and treads upon our soil,[m]
that we will raise against him seven shepherds
and eight princes of men;

[m] Gk: Heb *in our palaces*

vs. 3 gives a philosophy of the Exile. The Hebrews would be given into the hands of the nations by God himself, and would be subjected to terrifying experiences until such a time as the Deity chose to bring forth a new king and re-establish the monarchy, i.e., **the time when she who is in travail has brought forth.** The woman here is Israel, as in 4:9-10. By contrast with previous unsuccessful attempts (4:9-10), this time Mother Israel, by God's help, would be successful in giving birth to a king who would restore the nation and the monarchy. As vs. 3 follows vs. 2, the implication is that something equally significant to the exaltation of David was about to take place again. With this restoration of the kingship the Jews who were scattered in exile among the nations (**the rest of his brethren**) would be brought back to Palestine **to the people of Israel** who had already returned to the Holy Land, thus bringing about a spectacular reunification of the Hebrew people.

4. This verse tells the manner of the new king's rule. By contrast with late exilic expectation (Isa. 40:10-11), where God himself was to rule as a good shepherd, here the Deity was expected to delegate his power to the coming king who would care for and **feed his flock** as God would do if he had chosen to assume the rulership himself. Thus the dream of a theocracy gave way to the hope for a monarchy in which the divine right of the ruler was to be an important consideration. The new monarch was to be characterized by **strength** and **majesty. They shall dwell secure** indicates this restored kingship would not come to a tragic end, as in pre-exilic days, but would endure through all time. The last clause reflects the expectation that this would be a world empire in which everyone on the face of the globe would give allegiance to the divinely instituted kingship. This was another of those frequent times when ancient people felt they were on the verge of the dawning of one world.

5. The coming king (**this man**) would inaugurate an era of perpetual **peace**. The remainder of vs. 5, and all of vs. 6, as indicated by the arrangement in the RSV, is a separate fragment. It seems to be an interpolated comment, inserted some time later, after the

will begin in a small way and place and proceed apace. The new leader will come from **Bethlehem**—a small town hallowed by shrine and story. He is to be the long-awaited deliverer of Israel, **whose goings forth have been from of old, from everlasting.** Hence he is to be no temporary leader blessed with evanescent tri-

umphs. He will re-establish the Davidic kingdom and it will last forever.

4-6. *The New Leader.*—The clue to the new leader's power is this: **He shall stand and feed in the strength of the LORD, in the majesty of the name of the LORD his God: and they shall abide.** He will be strong enough to beat off the

6 And they shall waste the land of Assyria with the sword, and the land of Nimrod in the entrances thereof: thus shall he deliver *us* from the Assyrian, when he cometh into our land, and when he treadeth within our borders.

7 And the remnant of Jacob shall be in the midst of many people as a dew from the LORD, as the showers upon the grass, that

6 they shall rule the land of Assyria with
    the sword,
  and the land of Nimrod with the drawn
    sword;[n]
and they[o] shall deliver us from the Assyrian
  when he comes into our land
  and treads within our border.
7 Then the remnant of Jacob shall be
  in the midst of many peoples
like dew from the LORD,
  like showers upon the grass,

[n] Cn: Heb *in its entrances*
[o] Heb *he*

expectations expressed in the document 4:9–5:5*a* had failed of realization. In this interpolation, which may come from as late as Maccabean times, no king is mentioned, for by that time the Judean community apparently had come to despair concerning the possibility of establishing a kingship. In this section the terms **Assyria** and **land of Nimrod** (vs. 6) seem to be used with reference to Syria (north and northeast of Palestine) and her Seleucid kings. This interpolation therefore must have come from some time between 312 and 65 B.C. The writer implies that these rulers had been causing depredations by coming into the land of Palestine and wreaking destruction upon it. This may suggest some otherwise unrecorded episodes in the reigns of earlier Seleucid kings. Probably it refers to the conquest of Palestine by Antiochus III which was in progress from 218 to 198 B.C. The raising up against him of **seven shepherds** or (as it probably should be translated) **eight princes of men** may refer to the coalition of leaders who rallied the Jews to the defense of Palestine in that crisis. Karl Marti, Paul Haupt, and Hermann Guthe assume it is still later and refers to the Maccabean coalition which, after the plundering of the temple in 170 B.C., joined together in trying to redeem Israel's former defeat and meet the new blows leveled against the Jewish community by Antiochus Epiphanes and his successors. This verse indicates that at a time of national emergency, during that series of Seleucidan crises, the people placed their faith for deliverance in this coalition of seven or eight revolutionaries and prominent people who had taken it upon themselves to organize the defenses of their country.

6. After clearing Palestine of invading armies, the coalition would carry its war to the enemy country and would **rule** their land **with the sword**. The RSV is the better translation. The last half of the verse expresses the assurance that if the Seleucids (see vs. 5) should ever regain their strength and choose to invade Palestine again, the coalition (**they**) would bring about the liberation of the Holy Land once more.

C. A WORLD OF PURITY, BLESSING, AND BENEDICTION (5:7-15)

After the intervening section 4:9–5:6, breathing hate and vindictiveness against the nations, the basic portion in 5:7-15 resumes the late exilic strand 4:1-4, 6-8, which is diametrically opposite, displaying good will toward all peoples. Vs. 7 may originally have followed directly after 4:8. Vss. 10-14 parallel closely Isa. 2:6-8, as Mic. 4:1-8 and 5:7 parallel Isa. 2:1-5.

7. Here the Jews are presented with a high sense of mission. As the **dew** refreshes the morning landscape, and as **showers** cause the **grass** to grow, so Israel (**the remnant of**

most powerful of enemies when they come. He will call into existence a mighty army and carry the fight to Assyria herself, defeating her and laying her lands waste even as she has destroyed Israel.

7. *A Dew from the Lord.*—Whether this verse is an interpolation is for the exegetes to determine, but the idea obviously interrupts a train of vengeful thought. It is a eulogy, couched in pastoral terms, of how much the captive Israel-

tarrieth not for man, nor waiteth for the sons of men.

8 ¶ And the remnant of Jacob shall be among the Gentiles in the midst of many people, as a lion among the beasts of the forest, as a young lion among the flocks of sheep: who, if he go through, both treadeth down, and teareth in pieces, and none can deliver.

9 Thine hand shall be lifted up upon thine adversaries, and all thine enemies shall be cut off.

10 And it shall come to pass in that day, saith the LORD, that I will cut off thy horses out of the midst of thee, and I will destroy thy chariots:

which tarry not for men
nor wait for the sons of men.

8 And the remnant of Jacob shall be among the nations,
in the midst of many peoples,
like a lion among the beasts of the forest,
like a young lion among the flocks of sheep,
which, when it goes through, treads down
and tears in pieces, and there is none to deliver.

9 Your hand shall be lifted up over your adversaries,
and all your enemies shall be cut off.

10 And in that day, says the LORD,
I will cut off your horses from among you
and will destroy your chariots;

Jacob) would be a blessing and benediction to all humanity. The last couplet indicates this was not to come about by human effort, for it was in the purposes of God and as inevitable as the coming of the rains in springtime. **Sons of men** is but a poetic variant for **men**.

8. Vss. 8-9 are decidedly out of harmony with the section (vss. 7-15). Vs. 8 is a direct refutation of vs. 7. Throughout chs. 4–5 there is a fundamental conflict between the pacifist and militarist concepts. This opposition comes to its most pointed focus in the antithesis between these two verses. Both express hope for peace. The author of 4:1-4, 6-8; 5:7 hoped to achieve peace through peace. The authors of 4:9–5:6; 5:8-9 proposed to obtain peace through war. The antithesis is accentuated by the fact that the author of vs. 8 began his verse with virtually the same couplet used by the writer of vs. 7. After the first couplets, however, they branch off in opposite directions. The body of vs. 8 is devoted to the **lion** motif. The first figure is of the lion as it devours other wild animals in the forest. Then the imagery is changed slightly, and Israel is represented as a lion in the sheepfold of the world. The other nations are the **sheep.** Soon the lion of Judah would descend upon them and the nations would be torn to shreds. The author of vs. 7 felt assured that his peaceful expectations regarding the future were inevitable; likewise the author of vs. 8—as indicated by the last clause—cherished his bloodcurdling prospect with equal earnestness.

9. Continuing vs. 8, but changing the figure again, the destroying nation of Israel is pictured here as a warrior with weaponed **hand** raised high over his **enemies** (the other nations), ready to smite them into oblivion. Soon this end would be achieved.

10. Vss. 10-14 seem to resume the thought of vs. 7, and may originally have followed directly thereafter. Vs. 10 amplifies a further phase of the late exilic pacifist concept of peace and security. **In that day** (as in 4:6) refers to "in the latter days" of 4:1, i.e., the closing days of the Exile. **Says the LORD** follows out the previous usage in this late exilic

---

ites are going to mean to their captors. Since these captives were the best of Israel's leaders, they would gain central respect wherever they were and would be a blessing to all peoples. This thought is akin to Jesus' conception of his disciples as "leaven," as "salt." The faithful doers of the will of God are going to be characterized by the grace of God wherever they go.

8-15. Vengeance Enthroned.—The thought now is of the **remnant** in possession of power and bent on full revenge. Not meekness and humility, but power—the power of the **lion** who is lord over all beasts; the power of the young lion that savagely destroys a flock of sheep—this is the token of the **remnant.** Every enemy is to be confronted and destroyed. The

11 And I will cut off the cities of thy land, and throw down all thy strongholds:	11 and I will cut off the cities of your land and throw down all your strongholds;
12 And I will cut off witchcrafts out of thine hand; and thou shalt have no *more* soothsayers:	12 and I will cut off sorceries from your hand, and you shall have no more soothsayers;
13 Thy graven images also will I cut off, and thy standing images out of the midst of thee; and thou shalt no more worship the work of thine hands.	13 and I will cut off your images and your pillars from among you, and you shall bow down no more to the work of your hands;

document as observed in 4:4, 6. Vs. 10 elaborates the thought partially developed in the second couplet of 4:3. There it was told how swords and spears would be banished in the new era of peace. In vs. 10 this is supplemented by asserting that also **horses** and **chariots** would be eliminated from the earth in a disarmament program in which all tools of war would be outlawed. In the Palestine of those days there was no realization that the horse had any value except for military purposes. The donkey was the animal of peace. The horse was equivalent in significance to poison gas in the first world war and the atomic bomb in the second. In all three instances the peace-loving people called for outlawry of the new devastating weapon.

11. This verse deals with military installations. They also were to go. Cities were walled **strongholds** or fortresses. Because of their association with war, it appears that cities themselves were construed as wrong, and were to be banished with the other military **strongholds** in a great decentralization program. This verse anticipated a time of security when every farmer would live on the land he tilled, and it would no longer be necessary to be huddled in villages and cities for purposes of mutual protection.

12. This verse goes on to deal with the cult of magic and divination. These were the forerunners of religion as alchemy was the forerunner of chemistry. **Sorceries** or **witchcrafts** connoted the arts by which primitive people believed they could gain miraculous power over other people or things. We call these arts a phase of magic. **Soothsayers** refer to the complementary quest of gaining in a miraculous way extraordinary information about people or things. This we call divination. The time had come when all things which retarded human progress were to be eliminated. So both magic and divination, with their primitivisms, were due to be discarded, to clear the way for an era of more constructive and exalted spiritual religion.

13-14. Continuing the trend (started in vs. 12) of banishing the primitive from the earth, these two verses call for elimination of idol cults in the interests of establishing an imageless worship. Four types of these cult objects are specifically mentioned. **Graven images** were tooled or carved images. The word translated **pillars** or **standing images** refers to uncarved tree trunks or stones in which some deity was supposed to reside. Such objects were brought to the sacred places and formed pantheons of worship. **Asherim** were images of the mother goddess, the consort of the male god Baal. This was a sex worship which had sacred prostitution as one of its integral parts. Evidently the word

destruction is to be complete: armies, cities, forts, and shrines. The tolerance expressed in 4:5 is explicitly repudiated. What we have here is not "eye for eye, tooth for tooth." We have here, to use a modern statement of it, "ten bombs for one, ten cities for one." And the writer is not alone among the prophets in this matter. The "songs of vengeance" in Isaiah, to which allusion has already been made, belong to the same school of emotion and ethics.	Such a cry for unlimited vengeance is the natural reaction to defeat. We love what we have and hate whoever destroys it. In our hatred we want to make him suffer. Believing ourselves to be innocent and undeserving of disaster, we feel that he ought to suffer even more than we do—as much more as possible. Sentiments like this write the "songs of vengeance" of every generation of men. What an irony of fate and history it is that Jesus of Nazareth should be

14 And I will pluck up thy groves out of the midst of thee: so will I destroy thy cities.

15 And I will execute vengeance in anger and fury upon the heathen, such as they have not heard.

6 Hear ye now what the LORD saith; Arise, contend thou before the mountains, and let the hills hear thy voice.

---

14 and I will root out your Ashe′rim from among you
and destroy your cities.

15 And in anger and wrath I will execute vengeance
upon the nations that did not obey.

6 Hear what the LORD says:
Arise, plead your case before the mountains,
and let the hills hear your voice.

---

cities does not belong in this list. It seems to be a corruption of the similar Hebrew word עצביך, "your idols," an inclusive term to cover all forms of images, even those types not specifically mentioned in this verse. Asherim and idols occur together in II Chr. 24:18, which may show dependence on this passage as it was before the corruption occurred. It is rather significant that, in eliminating all things primitive and destructive, the author should have ended his list in discarding the less worthy types of religion. Second Isaiah seems to have begun the classic polemic against idolatry in 40:18-20; 41:6-7; 44:9-20; etc. Here again it appears that our author is dependent upon the pioneering work of Second Isaiah, as has been pointed out at every stage in the progress of this basic late exilic document 4:1-4, 6-8; 5:7, 10-14. As presumably the same author's work in Isa. 2:2-18, this document comes to an abrupt ending, for neither seems completed.

15. Here transition is suddenly made back to the antiforeign document 4:5, 9-13; 5:1-5a, 8-9. This verse probably forms its displaced conclusion. The KJV is much the better translation here. God himself, **in anger and wrath,** is about to wreak vengeance upon the other nations of the world. **Such as they have not heard** implies that the destruction of these nations at the hands of God and his people would be so terrible that nothing comparable to it had ever been heard before.

V. Adversity that Triumphs in Hope (6:1–7:20)

By contrast with chs. 4–5, where none of the material was by Micah and the content consisted almost entirely of two intermingled documents, the major part of the last two chapters (6:1–7:4) may well have come from the lips of the prophet Micah. This is supplemented at the end by a minor comment (7:5-6) and by a late exilic psalm (7:7-20). Chs. 6–7 may therefore be regarded as the misplaced ending of the book, split away from chs. 1–3 by the later insertion of chs. 4–5.

A. God's Controversy with His Wayward People (6:1-5)

6:1-2. These verses call upon God to **arise** and **plead.** This is legal terminology. God was about to bring suit (ריב, **controversy**) against **Israel.** This was a cosmically

---

even remotely related to this of all sections of prophetic literature! There is literally nothing in common between it and the Sermon on the Mount. If this is an accurate prophecy of messianic acts, then his teachings on forgiveness are a delusion and his dying for even his enemies (instead of killing them) was an unforgivable betrayal of his trust. Christian ethics is indebted to it for one thing only: a clear description of a thoroughly unchristian attitude toward an enemy.

6:1-8. Scaling the Heights.—This entire chapter is written in a quite different vein from that

which precedes it. Whereas ch. 5 is jubilant over the destruction which is to be visited upon the enemies of Israel, ch. 6 examines the reasons for Israel's punishment, the meaning of "true religion," and the ways in which Israel has forsaken God's will. There is real humility in the search. Here the book once more swings into line with the great tradition of prophecy. It ceases to be an almost hysterical oscillation from utopian hopes to screams for vengeance and becomes the heart-searching record of what happens when sinful man confronts the claims of the God whom he has forsaken. It is no wonder

2 Hear ye, O mountains, the Lord's controversy, and ye strong foundations of the earth: for the Lord hath a controversy with his people, and he will plead with Israel.

3 O my people, what have I done unto thee? and wherein have I wearied thee? testify against me.

4 For I brought thee up out of the land of Egypt, and redeemed thee out of the house of servants; and I sent before thee Moses, Aaron, and Miriam.

2 Hear, you mountains, the controversy of the Lord,
  and you enduring foundations of the earth;
for the Lord has a controversy with his people,
  and he will contend with Israel.

3 "O my people, what have I done to you?
  In what have I wearied you? Answer me!
4 For I brought you up from the land of Egypt,
  and redeemed you from the house of bondage;
and I sent before you Moses,
  Aaron, and Miriam.

---

constituted court, for **the hills, mountains,** and even the **foundations of the earth** were the jury in this case of world significance. God was about to assume also the role of prosecutor **(will contend).** Israel, the offender, was in the witness box. The trial was ready to start.

3. Here begin the words of God to the court. At the trial's opening the Deity gave Israel the first opportunity to speak, inviting the nation to testify against him. In a tone of pathos he inquired whether he had done anything to make them so bad. Apparently even they recognized that God had done his part faithfully. So there was presumably no response.

4-5. In the absence of any defense on the part of Israel, God resumed by giving a history of the case, recounting how he had **redeemed** these people from **Egypt** by working through **Moses, Aaron, and Miriam,** whom he raised up as leaders in the crisis of history recorded in Exodus. **House of bondage** is a synonym for **Egypt.** The first part of vs. 5 refers to the Balaam story in Num. 22–24. **Shittim** was the place where the Israelites tarried after the close of the Balaam episode (Num. 25:1; Josh. 2:1; 3:1). After crossing the Jordan successfully, they made **Gilgal,** the stone circle around which they encamped

---

that the supreme expression of ethical religion in the O.T. is reached in this mood.

1-5. The Challenge of God.—This section obeys the pattern of prophecy already embraced in ch. 1. God is demanding a hearing with his people. He summons them to give account of themselves, not merely in the presence of each other, but in the presence of the loftiest, most permanent realities of the physical world—the mountains. God's **controversy with his people** does not lie simply on the surface; it plumbs to the very foundations of the world.

This simile better than any other illustrates the fundamental nature of the will of God as visualized by the prophets: that will is more impressive than the mountains, it is deeper than the foundations of the earth. God calls these indubitably impressive realities to witness to the serious nature of his lament against his people. He frames his lament in human terms: Israel has tired of him, but why? He has delivered them from their oppressors, raised up

mighty leaders, and brought them to a full awareness of his righteousness. Yet withal they have forsaken him. This he is unable to understand. In a very real sense this burden of God is the permanent theme of revelation. Anthropomorphic? Yes, in a limited way, but inevitable if God is regarded as a loving father. When the love of God incarnate in the Christ considers Jerusalem, the same divine incredulity at the blindness of man breaks forth: "O Jerusalem, Jerusalem, thou that killest the prophets, and stonest them which are sent unto thee, how often would I have gathered thy children together, even as a hen gathereth her chickens under her wings, and ye would not!" (Matt. 23:37.) Prophetic religion through the ages has stressed as one of its central themes the spiritual blindness of men to the glorious works of God in nature, in history, and in the immediate present. How to account for this failing has provided theologians, ancient and modern, with one of their most difficult problems—one we are

5 O my people, remember now what Balak king of Moab consulted, and what Balaam the son of Beor answered him from Shittim unto Gilgal; that ye may know the righteousness of the LORD.

6 ¶ Wherewith shall I come before the LORD, *and* bow myself before the high God? shall I come before him with burnt offerings, with calves of a year old?

5 O my people, remember what Balak king
　of Moab devised,
　　and what Balaam the son of Be′or
　　answered him,
　and what happened from Shittim to Gil-
　gal,
　　that you may know the saving acts of
　　the LORD."

6 "With what shall I come before the LORD,
　and bow myself before God on high?
　Shall I come before him with burnt offer-
　ings,
　　with calves a year old?

(Josh. 4:19–5:12) while waiting to attack Jericho. The description of this trial begins in a magnificent manner in vss. 1-4, but dwindles out in vs. 5. The trial never advances beyond giving the history of the case, and even this is hardly completed, for no **saving acts of the LORD** are listed after **Gilgal.** The record of the trial never advances to the point of God's making his accusations against Israel. The person who recorded it apparently remembered only the first part of the proceedings. This passage (vss. 1-5) seems dependent upon the beginning of Samuel's speech to the Israelites in I Sam. 12:6-8.

B. INCIDENTALS OR FUNDAMENTALS IN RELIGION (6:6-8)

This passage, which might be described as "The Five Questions," presents a call to higher religion. It deals with the basic problem of the validity of sacrifice. These three verses gather up the power of the classic antiritual passages in Amos 5:21-24 and Isa. 1:10-17, and seem related to Second Isaiah (40:16) and Ps. 51:16-17. Although traditionally ascribed to Micah, modern opinion has tended to regard this portion as postexilic. Recently the pendulum has begun to swing back once more, and many scholars ascribe these verses to Micah. The name of the specific individual who brought this amazing prophetic insight is of relatively slight concern. Whether pre-exilic or postexilic, whether by Micah or some later sage, this is perhaps the greatest passage in the Bible on the futility of ritualistic worship which assumes that divine favor can be obtained by presenting

---

no nearer solving now than were Isaiah and Jeremiah. Yet—explain it as best we can—the fact remains: We live and die immersed in the love of God; yet we are blind to much if not most of it. This glory and tragedy of human life is close to the heart of biblical faith.

6-9. Wherewith?—God singles out for rejection not only **burnt offerings,** though they are **with thousands of rams;** not only libations, though **with thousands of rivers of oil;** not even the **firstborn** fruit of the body—reminiscent of Abraham—for the sin of the soul. The passage reflects the persistence of human sacrifice in Israel's religion; but it does more, it also points out in dramatic ways that there is literally no objective rite or ritual act that can be taken as the will of God for man. God wants none of these. He wants what he has already showed man to be good: justice, mercy, humility.

What a comedown (or comeup) this is from the tedious passages in the Pentateuch which

specify the rules of propriety and ritual worship! With one magnificent stroke of the hand the prophet brushes them off the table of careful spiritual consideration. He substitutes a trilogy of spiritual qualities that are as social as they are personal in nature. Each one roots in a personal conviction and attitude, yet it indicates a certain kind of relationship with others. The proper relationship has nothing whatever to do with ritual worship. Its foundation is the righteous will of God which demands a sensitive, sincere righteousness throughout the whole range of life. Nor is God content to be the passive custodian of this righteousness. He cries aloud in the city, calling for men to hear. And the man of wisdom does hear, and knowing that God will back up his will with the **rod,** seeks to be guided by it.

6. The Proper Approach to God.—Here, unhesitatingly, the author plunges into one of the most widely discussed and hotly disputed ques-

7 Will the LORD be pleased with thousands of rams, *or* with ten thousands of rivers of oil? shall I give my firstborn *for* my transgression, the fruit of my body *for* the sin of my soul?	7 Will the LORD be pleased with thousands of rams, with ten thousands of rivers of oil? Shall I give my first-born for my transgression, the fruit of my body for the sin of my soul?"

sacrifices to the Deity. These thoughts mark one of the highest points of religious attainment in the Bible.

6-7b. The first three questions deal with animal or inanimate sacrifices. Traditionally it was thought, as vs. 6*a,b* implies, that one could not worship God unless he came with some material offerings to present as a burnt sacrifice to the Deity, a modified form of feeding by causing the essence of the food to rise to him. Vs. 6*a,b* seems to suggest the plight of the person who could not afford such material offerings. Was he cut off from all worship and contact with God? Vs. 6*c,d* deals with the wealthy who could afford to offer such delicacies as **calves a year old.** Did such offerings make these people religious and acceptable to God? Vs. 7*a,b* refers to those of extreme wealth who could supply myriads of offerings. This seems to contain a gentle rebuke by the prophet to his monarch, King Hezekiah, who was especially zealous in presenting unspeakable quantities of offerings (II Chr. 30:24; cf. also Solomon in I Kings 8:63 and Josiah in II Chr. 35:7). Did these demonstrations make those kings acceptable to God? The implied answer in each of these three cases is a decisive "No." One does not achieve purity of life and secure the favor of God in such ways.

7c,d. By contrast with the first three questions (vss. 6-7*b*), which dealt with sacrificial products from farm, barn, and orchard, in vs. 7*c,d* the concern is with human sacrifice. Immemorial custom in the Near East required that the first-born son should be sacrificed to God in order that the Deity would give the couple more children and grant the family prosperity. As expressed in the early law of Exod. 22:29, people felt that all the first fruits

---

tions in historical religion. On one extreme are those professing theists—classical Epicureans are an example—who feel that God, or the gods, are real but too remote and actually unconcerned to be approached by man at all. For such, the proper approach to God is no approach. At the other point of the pendulum are those for whom God is "closer . . . than breathing, and nearer than hands and feet." [4] He is so much a part of their total life that it is pointless to talk in any realistic fashion about "approaching him." As soon talk about "approaching" the air or the germ plasm or the cultural milieu of one's own family! One has no describable or even discernible reality apart from them. How, except in a purely figurative sense, could he "approach" them? In similar manner, God is so integral a fact and factor in all life and reality that any thought of approaching him is sheer metaphor. He is to be worshiped, adored, studied, served, but never as One outside the worshiper or the student; rather is he the definitive Fact in, the true Source of, all life—thus concludes another group of believers.

[4] Tennyson, "The Higher Pantheism."

Somewhere between these two poles of thought are two other positions, partaking of some essential emphases of each. Most worshipers find themselves in one or the other of these two mediating positions. One holds steadily to the objectivity of God, calling him "Wholly Other," in order to separate him as much as possible from man and all his works. While God is essentially different from man, he nonetheless is creator, sustainer, and redeemer of man through Jesus Christ. This thought of God is admittedly a paradox, and can be entertained only by the mind of faith. Reason objects to it, but faith embraces it—and approaches God in love and trust. The other mediating position rejects the paradox as a distortion of facts and reason, and holds that God is both within and beyond any given event or individual. The proper approach to him is therefore both a look within and a look beyond. It is penitence and adoration. It is the offering of one's whole self on the altar of complete commitment to God. How else would one dare approach "the God of heaven"?

7-8. *What Does God Want of Man?*—This is the most important question man can raise.

8 He hath showed thee, O man, what *is* good; and what doth the Lord require of thee, but to do justly, and to love mercy, and to walk humbly with thy God?	8 He has showed you, O man, what is good; and what does the Lord require of you but to do justice, and to love kindness,*p* and to walk humbly with your God?
	p Or *Steadfast love*

were required by God, including the first fruits of their own bodies. Archaeologists find the ashes and remaining bones of sacrificed children deposited in urns at the corners of houses—the origin of laying the cornerstone. Even though the story in Gen. 22:1-19 and the later law in Exod. 34:20 should have put an end to this custom, its continuance is reflected in Josh. 6:26; Judg. 11:30-40; I Kings 16:34. This practice of human sacrifice was even accelerated during the latter days of the monarchy when it became popular to "pass their children through the fire" as observed in II Kings 16:3; 17:17, 31; 21:2-6; 23:10; II Chr. 28:3; 33:6; Jer. 7:31; Ezek. 16:20. In later times this "abomination" of human sacrifice was generally regarded as having had an important part in bringing about the downfall of the Hebrew monarchy. The question in vs. 7c,d implies another decisive "No" as its answer. It was absurd to think of trying to remove one's **sin,** or make amends for **transgression,** by burning one's child as an offering to God. This was murder and only added to the individual's sins. It also must have been extremely offensive to the Deity.

8. This verse suggests that religious acceptability is not to be found along any of the proposals suggested in vss. 6-7. The first line of vs. 8 says that God has shown man **what is good,** i.e., he has shown "a better way" of religious achievement than by offering material or personal sacrifices. This "better way" is a threefold way, consisting of **justice** in the daily relationships of life, **kindness** to one's fellows, and walking **humbly** before God. It is worthy of notice that in this formula for acceptable religion two parts deal with man and only one is concerned with God. This is because it is rather futile to talk about God unless we first come to respect the god-images about us, i.e., man. We are not likely to love God whom we have not seen unless we first come to love man whom we can see (I John 4:20). The religion of this verse is a religion that is geared to everyday life. Whatever theologies or incidentals may be mixed with religion, a person cannot go far wrong, either among men or in the sight of God, if these three fundamentals are observed. The fifth and last question in this series asks if the pursuing of these three quests is sufficient to develop an ample religion. The implied answer is an emphatic, "Nothing more is needful." This passage is one of perhaps four mountain peaks of spiritual attainment in the O.T., the others being Deut. 6:4-5 plus Lev. 19:18b; Amos 5:24; and Jonah 4:2. By no means least of these in its potentialities is this classic statement in Micah, with its simple but profound threefold guide to religious development.

On his answer—or answers—to it, his life and work hinge. The writer of Micah is keenly aware of its crucial nature and presents in vivid contrast two answers. The earlier and more popular answer can be reduced to two words: blood sacrifice. The blood of the best that man has is required, whether of the first-lings of the flock or of his own firstborn son. It is not difficult to reconstruct the scene of the sacrifice here described. The altar on a high place, the chanting priests and people, the precious blood and oil poured on the fire, the sense of deliverance which sweeps over the worshipers: even at this distance it is easy to understand the power of so concrete a ceremonial and experience. But this sort of ceremonial is not enough; it is basically not so much wrong as irrelevant, argues Micah. The real demands of God on man are moral and spiritual, and the proper worship of God is a life obedient to them. Apart from this, the altar ceremonial is an actual affront to God, an attempt to bargain him into taking something less than he actually wants of man.

Yet it is difficult to see why people then or now seem to breathe easier when the prophetic conception of true sacrifice is announced: **To do justly, and to love mercy, and to walk humbly with thy God.** Or as Moffatt has translated it, "To be just and kind and live in quiet fellowship with your God." This may sound comforting and comfortable to the man who

9 The Lord's voice crieth unto the city, and *the man of* wisdom shall see thy name: hear ye the rod, and who hath appointed it.
 	
10 ¶ Are there yet the treasures of wickedness in the house of the wicked, and the scant measure *that is* abominable?
 	
11 Shall I count *them* pure with the wicked balances, and with the bag of deceitful weights?
	9 The voice of the Lord cries to the city —
	    and it is sound wisdom to fear thy
	      name:
	    "Hear, O tribe and assembly of the city!*q*
	10 Can I forget*r* the treasures of wickedness in the house of the wicked,
	  and the scant measure that is accursed?
	11 Shall I acquit the man with wicked scales
	    and with a bag of deceitful weights?

q Cn Compare Gk: Heb *and who has appointed it yet*
r Cn: Heb uncertain

C. The Deity's Final Plea to Jerusalem (6:9-16)

Although there may be small interpolations found here, this section seems indisputably the work of Micah. It may have been delivered to the people of Jerusalem sometime after the almost disastrous siege by Sennacherib in 701 B.C., when most of Judah was laid waste and Jerusalem itself had almost been conquered before the attacking Assyrian troops were mysteriously called away. The utterance was prompted by the continuing wickedness in this metropolis, even in those days of almost complete tragedy, when it would seem the people should have been renewed in their devotion to righteousness. It is significant that Isa. 1:2-9, which presumably contains the last utterance by that prophet, is contemporary in time and similar in thought to the section here, which may have been also the last prophecy of Micah.

9. These are the words of the prophet introducing God, who speaks in vss. 10-16. The first clause simply points out that the utterance of the Deity is to follow. The expression **cries to the city** signifies alarm in the face of impending disaster. Since the warnings sounded repeatedly by the prophets had not been heeded, God himself was about to issue this one. If they were people of **wisdom,** they would stand in **fear** before the Lord and his final ultimatum. Instead of **see** (KJV), the verb should be **fear,** as in the LXX, Vulg., and Syriac, and in the identical phrase in Ps. 86:11. In the last line the Hebrew text (followed by KJV) is presumably corrupt, for it has the ambiguity of asking the reader to listen both to the **rod** and to the one **who hath appointed it.** Even the idea of listening to a rod seems strange. The Syriac and Targ. apparently preserve an older and more correct text (only slightly different consonantally) and the RSV has done wisely to follow these versions. The latter part of the verse then is an appeal to the people of Jerusalem to listen to the divine message which is about to follow.

10-11. These words begin the speech (vss. 10-16) of the Deity to Jerusalem, and concern the corrupt mercantile practices which prevailed there. Special attention is given to four items: the loot of the racketeers and the use of scant measures, balances that did not weigh properly, and weights that were not up to standard. People who engaged in these practices were obliged to accept the consequences and could not hope to be accepted by God. Each of these two questions implies a decisive "No" for its answer. The Deity could not be expected to **forget** such abominations.

has never tried it, but the unanimous verdict of prophetic spirits through the ages underscores its costliness. Every student of law knows how necessary yet how difficult the quest for justice has been and continues to be. Mercy and humility are surely two of the highest and holiest of virtues—and no others are more difficult of the kind of achievement God requires, i.e., incarnation. Yet Micah joins the prophetic succession of Amos, Hosea, and Isaiah in demanding just this.	**10-16. *The Treasures of Wickedness.***—The evils of Israel are now indicated with as much vigor as in chs. 2–3. The statement of them reflects an agrarian background. Great houses are suspect as containing **treasures of wickedness** accumulated by using false weights and measures in the purchase and sale of goods. Such sin is an affront to God himself. This judgment may well have startled the businessmen of the time. It has startled a good many of their counterparts in today's world. When con-

12 For the rich men thereof are full of violence, and the inhabitants thereof have spoken lies, and their tongue *is* deceitful in their mouth.

13 Therefore also will I make *thee* sick in smiting thee, in making *thee* desolate because of thy sins.

14 Thou shalt eat, but not be satisfied; and thy casting down *shall be* in the midst of thee; and thou shalt take hold, but shalt not deliver; and *that* which thou deliverest will I give up to the sword.

15 Thou shalt sow, but thou shalt not reap; thou shalt tread the olives, but thou shalt not anoint thee with oil; and sweet wine, but shalt not drink wine.

12 Your[s] rich men are full of violence;
　　your[s] inhabitants speak lies,
　　and their tongue is deceitful in their
　　　mouth.
13 Therefore I have begun[t] to smite you,
　　making you desolate because of your
　　　sins.
14 You shall eat, but not be satisfied,
　　and there shall be hunger in your in-
　　　ward parts;
　you shall put away, but not save,
　　and what you save I will give to the
　　　sword.
15 You shall sow, but not reap;
　　you shall tread olives, but not anoint
　　　yourselves with oil;
　　you shall tread grapes, but not drink
　　　wine.

[s] Heb *whose*
[t] Gk Syr Vg: Heb *have made sick*

12. The civil **violence**, practiced particularly by the **rich** and described previously by Micah in greater detail (3:1-3), was presumably still continuing. Complaint is made also concerning the **lies** and **deceitful** actions that had come to characterize the average resident of Jerusalem. This was a society in which unreliability in speech shattered all good relationships and led to mutual distrust.

13. The RSV is wise in following the LXX, Aquila, Theod., Syriac, and Vulg. The Hebrew verbs החלותי (**begun**) and החליתי (**make sick**) are almost identical and so have apparently been confused by some copyist. This presumably refers to the narrow escape of Jerusalem when, as Isaiah pointed out, the capital was left as a shack in a deserted vineyard, or as a shelter in what was once a garden of cucumbers (Isa. 1:8). The verse here implies that this near tragedy of 701 B.C. was not likely to be the end of the story. Unless an ethical revolution in the manner of living should be forthcoming, even greater disaster might soon be expected. The catastrophe of 701 B.C. was only a beginning.

14-15. The already desolate picture in the post-701 B.C. Jerusalem community was about to be made infinitely worse when the Assyrians would strike their all-out blow. Micah anticipated that this would be in perhaps not more than a year from the time these words were uttered. On their way to exile (vs. 14a) the Hebrews would receive some food, but never enough to make them **satisfied**. There always would be that gnawing **hunger** within. The second couplet tells how the material things they treasured and their financial savings would all be taken by their captors. In vs. 15, God announces that the grain they were about to sow would be reaped by the enemy. The olive oil they were about to extract would be used by the Assyrians. The wine they were about to press would be drunk by their conquerors who would appropriate all the material wealth of Palestine for their own uses. Here Micah was indebted for his imagery and even phrase-

fronted by the social claims of the gospel, they have tried to draw a sharp line between the spiritual and material realms, holding that religion must keep to the latter, while in the former, "business is business." Any serious attempt to point out the inseparability of the two, let alone to find a creative partnership for them in human affairs, is treated as a sin against God and the dictates of pure religion.

The writer of these verses is sure that all such reasoning is false. He brings a divine indictment against it to the effect that these very sins will be the actual destruction of Israel. For the sinner will be involved in perpetual frustration; the ends he seeks—happiness, security, power— will always elude him because the means by which he seeks them are not congruent with the end. Nor is this judgment left dangling in

16 ¶ For the statutes of Omri are kept, and all the works of the house of Ahab, and ye walk in their counsels; that I should make thee a desolation, and the inhabitants thereof a hissing: therefore ye shall bear the reproach of my people.

7 Woe is me! for I am as when they have gathered the summer fruits, as the grape gleanings of the vintage: *there is* no cluster to eat: my soul desired the first ripe fruit.

2 The good *man* is perished out of the earth; and *there is* none upright among

16 For you have kept the statutes of Omri,[u] and all the works of the house of Ahab; and you have walked in their counsels; that I may make you a desolation, and your[v] inhabitants a hissing; so you shall bear the scorn of the peoples."[w]

7 Woe is me! For I have become
    as when the summer fruit has been gathered,
as when the vintage has been gleaned:
there is no cluster to eat,
    no first-ripe fig which my soul desires.
2 The godly man has perished from the earth,
    and there is none upright among men;

[u] Gk Syr Vg Tg: *the statutes of Omri are kept*
[v] Heb *its*
[w] Gk: Heb *my people*

ology, which he elaborated somewhat, to the prophet Amos (5:11). It is a vivid description of the doom that was overshadowing Jerusalem.

16. Here the people of Judah were reminded that they had degenerated religiously and morally until they had become as bad as that notorious dynasty, headed by **Omri** and his son **Ahab** (who married the wicked Jezebel), against which the prophet Elijah had battled almost two centuries earlier (I Kings 16–22, especially 16:21-34; 18:1-18; 21:1-26). Inasmuch as the people of the southern kingdom had again returned to the depraved traditions of Omri and Ahab, there seemed little hope for Judah. This address ends with the implication that, unless there should be rapid repentance, there could be only the prospect of catastrophe, with **desolation, hissing,** and **scorn** at the hands of other nations, i.e., **the peoples** (as in LXX and Ezek. 34:29; 36:6). This would be the lot of unrepentant Israel.

D. The Pessimism of Despair (7:1-6)

It is possible that this is not a separate section, but in reality the conclusion to Micah's final prophecy, whose main part is found in 6:9-16. In vss. 1-4 Micah cast a final survey over the society of his day, looking for an upright person, but he was disappointed. His example was to be followed later by Jeremiah, hunting through the streets and squares of Jerusalem in search of a righteous man (Jer. 5:1), and by Diogenes, who went about Athens with a lantern, trying to find an honest man.

7:1-2b. Here the figure is of an individual who went out into the vineyard and orchards after the season of fruitage was over, hoping he might still find some fresh fruit. However, he was forced to return disappointed. His search was in vain. Not even one

vagueness. It is nothing if not precise: **Thou shalt eat, but not be satisfied. . . . Thou shalt sow, but thou shalt not reap.**

16. The Crowning Sin.—The prophetic protest against idolatry finds expression in this verse. The crowning sin of the rulers of Israel is their apostasy from the true God and their worship of the false gods introduced into the life of Israel from neighboring cultures. The house of Ahab (and Jezebel) has become the

symbol of sin in high places and is regarded as the fountainhead of apostasy (see Expos. on 1:13).

7:1-20. After the Deluge.—No one sentiment or concern runs through this chapter. Rather it is a collection of diverse reactions to the desolation of Israel following defeat in war.

1-4. Every Man for Himself.—Here is the picture of a land without law and order, a land bereft of great leaders in whose word it

men: they all lie in wait for blood; they hunt every man his brother with a net.	they all lie in wait for blood, and each hunts his brother with a net.
3 ¶ That they may do evil with both hands earnestly, the prince asketh, and the judge *asketh* for a reward; and the great *man,* he uttereth his mischievous desire: so they wrap it up.	3 Their hands are upon what is evil, to do it diligently; the prince and the judge ask for a bribe, and the great man utters the evil desire of his soul; thus they weave it together.
4 The best of them *is* as a brier: the most upright *is sharper* than a thorn hedge: the day of thy watchmen *and* thy visitation cometh; now shall be their perplexity.	4 The best of them is like a brier, the most upright of them a thorn hedge. The day of their[x] watchmen, of their[x] punishment, has come; now their confusion is at hand.
5 ¶ Trust ye not in a friend, put ye not confidence in a guide: keep the doors of thy mouth from her that lieth in thy bosom.	5 Put no trust in a neighbor, have no confidence in a friend; guard the doors of your mouth from her who lies in your bosom;

[x] Heb your

ripe fig or small surviving cluster of grapes could be found. Similarly, Micah was looking about among the men of affairs in Judah for a good person, and he was completely disappointed. He could not find a single **godly man** or one who was **upright.** The season of Israel's moral and spiritual fruitage was apparently over. Micah found in this a portent of **woe** for the future of his people. "Land" (in the sense of "the whole country") would seem to be a better translation than **earth,** for the prophet probably was not thinking of the earth as we conceive it. The Hebrew ארץ was made to serve both purposes.

2c-4b. These four couplets describe the web of iniquity (**they weave it together**) that had been spread over Palestine at that time by the amalgamated forces of evil. "Every man for himself, and the devil take the hindmost" seemed the motto of this ruthless society in which murder (**blood**) was blinked at when it served selfish ends, and the exploitation of one's fellows seemed the rule of the day. Politicians, judges, and prominent leaders were in collusion. The receiving of **a bribe** and graft (**the evil desire of his soul**) seemed their chief concern. It was a day when the **best** and **most upright** were presumably living on a lower level than what would have been the lowest in most ages. God pity such a country!

4c,d. This is the conclusion of the whole matter. "The wages of sin is death" is as true for nations as for individuals. Using only one couplet, the hour of Judah's annihilation at the hands of her enemies is so suggestively described as to leave readers imagining the details. There are three phases to the action. (*a*) The **watchmen** on the walls of Jerusalem would announce the enemy's approach. (*b*) The siege (**their punishment**) would take place. (*c*) Finally there would be the **confusion** of the defeated people. Such would be the end of this nation which had forsaken its spiritual heritage.

5-6. These verses can hardly be ascribed to this prophet. Although it is not always specifically stated, there were optimisms which Micah retained; e.g., he did not despair of the humble poor, but seems to have pinned his faith for the future on them. If vss. 5-6

has confidence. It is every man for himself now. Princes, judges, famous men—all seek to feather their own nests rather than to perform their duties with honor. When the common man can say, **The best of them is as a brier: the most upright is sharper than a thorn hedge,** one senses the complete loss of the kind of confidence	which is the cement of a society and the strong stay of personal integrity. There can be no escape from the simple judgment that **now shall be their perplexity.** **5-6. *A People in Ruin.*—**This is complete disintegration; it is defeat in the spiritual as well as in the military and material realm.

6 For the son dishonoreth the father, the daughter riseth up against her mother, the daughter-in-law against her mother-in-law; a man's enemies *are* the men of his own house.

7 Therefore I will look unto the Lord; I will wait for the God of my salvation: my God will hear me.

8 ¶ Rejoice not against me, O mine enemy: when I fall, I shall arise; when I sit in darkness, the Lord *shall be* a light unto me.

6 for the son treats the father with contempt,
  the daughter rises up against her mother,
  the daughter-in-law against her mother-in-law;
  a man's enemies are the men of his own house.

7 But as for me, I will look to the Lord,
  I will wait for the God of my salvation;
  my God will hear me.

8 Rejoice not over me, O my enemy;
  when I fall, I shall rise;
  when I sit in darkness,
  the Lord will be a light to me.

were by Micah, it would be necessary to assume he finally slipped into an abnormally depressed mood, for the author of these verses was afflicted with a psychopathic pessimism, despairing of everyone in the world except himself. He had lost regard even for the members of his own family and his relatives. His condition must have been the personification of misery. When any individual gets the idea that he is the only good person remaining alive he drifts into a detachment from his fellows and thereby forfeits all possibility of rendering further usefulness.

E. The Invincible Triumph of Faith (7:7-20)

This is a psalm which apparently was appended to the book of Micah by a later editor. Inasmuch as it is dependent on both Second Isaiah and Ps. 137, it seems likely that it should be dated *ca.* 539 or 538 b.c., when it began to appear that the day of return to Palestine was imminent. Although not quite so exultant as Second Isaiah, this writer looked forward to the return with eager expectation.

7. The background of this psalm of exilic review was that mood of utter despondency which was fairly dominant among the early exiles. They blamed God for forsaking them and causing their terrible plight. Many of them became atheists or adopted one of the religions of Mesopotamia. The **But as for me** indicates this individual was one of those minority persons who retained his faith in God **(will look to the Lord)** even in the bitterness of exile. Although it seemed interminably delayed, he was resigned to **wait for** the day of **salvation,** i.e., the day when God would at last **hear** prayers and save the people out of their captivity.

8. This writer in exile spoke rhetorically to his Babylonian captors **(O my enemy),** warning them not to be so exultant **(rejoice not)** over possession of their Hebrew slaves. Beginning with this verse, the individual "I" is lost in the collective "I" of Israel. In this context "though" would be a better translation for כי than **when.** Also, **fall** should probably be translated in the past tense, "Though I have fallen, I shall rise." Israel may have had a tragic **fall,** but the author had faith to believe she would **rise** once more.

Friends, guides, wife, children, other relatives— none can be trusted. In fact, **a man's enemies are the men of his own house.** Here is the negation of life itself, since man cannot live in isolation from family, friends, and comrades. It is the doom of every effort of man to live unto himself alone.

7. But What About God?—Small wonder the writer casts in his lot with God! Man cannot be trusted, he says, but God can. This echoes the strong faith, "When my father and my mother forsake me, then the Lord will take me up" (Ps. 27:10).

8-12. Patience Before God.—All that has happened is accepted as **the indignation of the Lord,** and it must be endured with patience, penitence, and real hope for the day when God will bring an end to punishment. Man cannot

9 I will bear the indignation of the LORD, because I have sinned against him, until he plead my cause, and execute judgment for me: he will bring me forth to the light, *and* I shall behold his righteousness.

10 Then *she that is* mine enemy shall see *it,* and shame shall cover her which said unto me, Where is the LORD thy God? mine eyes shall behold her: now shall she be trodden down as the mire of the streets.

11 *In* the day that thy walls are to be built, *in* that day shall the decree be far removed.

9 I will bear the indignation of the LORD
    because I have sinned against him,
until he pleads my cause
    and executes judgment for me.
He will bring me forth to the light;
    I shall behold his deliverance.

10 Then my enemy will see,
    and shame will cover her who said to me,
"Where is the LORD your God?"
My eyes will gloat over her;
    now she will be trodden down
    like the mire of the streets.

11 A day for the building of your walls!
    In that day the boundary shall be far extended.

The nation may have been forced for the moment to **sit in** the **darkness** of exile, but the **light** of a new day was about to dawn.

9. In a mood of confession the author realized that the Israelites were being made to **bear the indignation of the LORD** because they **have sinned against him.** Their fate was deserved. They must be contrite and repentant over it. The author was certain that, after this disciplinary period, God would yet **plead** the **cause** of Israel and **execute judgment** for them. He could see clearly the time when God would again **bring** them **forth to the light,** i.e., deliver them from their exile and return them to their country once more. The last clause (KJV is the better translation) indicates he was certain of this because he was sure of the **righteousness** of God, and felt confident he would soon behold it. Vss. 7-9 are like three bouncings of a ball. At the beginning of each it is down, but at the end of each there is a rebound, the rebound of faith.

10. This describes the anticipated astonishment of Babylon **(my enemy)** in the day of God's redeeming his people from exile and restoring them in Palestine as a world power. **Where is the LORD your God?** had been the classic gibe of their Babylonian persecutors (Pss. 42:3; 79:10; 115:2; Joel 2:17). They insinuated that the Hebrew God was a nonentity or he would not have allowed his people to be taken into exile. Now **shame** was about to **cover** Babylon because of the indignities heaped upon captive Israel and her God. Babylon would awake to a realization of what a terrible thing she had done to Israel. This seems influenced by the account of the repentant nations in Isa. 52:13–53:12. But it would be too late, because God had already marked Babylon for destruction. She who had leveled Jerusalem was to be treated similarly in turn (Ps. 137:8-9), and **be trodden down like the mire of the streets.** God's mills may have been slow in grinding, but they were about to grind, and "grind exceeding small."

11. This is a forward look through the clouds of exile to the day when devastated Jerusalem and her walls would be rebuilt. In the second line the RSV has the better

lighten or set aside the judgment of God. It must be borne until in God's own time it is fulfilled. Something of the same attitude runs through the theology found in one of the most unusual state papers ever produced in the United States—Lincoln's Second Inaugural Address. This attitude of accepting judgment is one of the most difficult for us to achieve. Like Paul, we find it much easier to "kick against the pricks" or to bewail our fate.

The writer steadily rejects "the cup of vinegar" which many take so eagerly when caught up in agony, i.e., the idea that there is no purpose at all in events, that in brief there is no God. Not only is there a God, but in some mysterious way his will is to be found in events. In present events it may mean suffering and punishment; in future events it will mean release and victory. For light will break on darkness, walls will be rebuilt, and exiled captives will

12 *In* that day *also* he shall come even to thee from Assyria, and *from* the fortified cities, and from the fortress even to the river, and from sea to sea, and *from* mountain to mountain.

13 Notwithstanding, the land shall be desolate because of them that dwell therein, for the fruit of their doings.

14 ¶ Feed thy people with thy rod, the flock of thine heritage, which dwell solitarily *in* the wood, in the midst of Carmel: let them feed *in* Bashan and Gilead, as in the days of old.

12 In that day they will come to you,
    from Assyria to*y* Egypt,
  and from Egypt to the River,
    from sea to sea and from mountain to
    mountain.

13 But the earth will be desolate
    because of its inhabitants,
    for the fruit of their doings.

14 Shepherd thy people with thy staff,
    the flock of thy inheritance,
  who dwell alone in a forest
    in the midst of a garden land;
  let them feed in Bashan and Gilead
    as in the days of old.

y Cn: Heb *and cities of*

translation. **The boundary shall be far extended** indicates the reconstructed postexilic Jerusalem would be much grander and vaster in scope than the pre-exilic city—another daring venture of faith.

12. This describes the anticipated triumphal return of the dispersed Jews from all countries to which they had fled or were carried as exiles. **The River** refers to the Euphrates. The KJV translation is particularly bad in this verse. The last three lines (RSV), using four parallel expressions, give multiple stress to the belief that the dispersed of Israel shall return "from all lands."

13. The land (not **the earth**) probably refers to the territory from the Nile to the Euphrates (vs. 12), the total world comprehended by the Hebrews in that day. The anticipation was that after the return of the Jews to Palestine devastation would overtake these lands of the Near East which had mistreated the dispersed of Judah who had been exiled or had sought refuge in their midst. The chief reference is undoubtedly to Babylonia.

14. By contrast with the desolation that was to overtake the nations (vs. 13), the returned Israel in Palestine was to enter upon a new era of prosperity. The first part of the verse is addressed to God, inviting him to come and take possession of his **inheritance** (Israel) and rule over them. **With thy staff:** This is the figure of God the good **shepherd,**

return to their homeland. **When I fall, I shall arise** in the power of God—this is the final posture of faith.

13. *Reaping the Whirlwind.*—Lest some reader should draw an easy conclusion that the indignation of the Lord was soon to pass away, the writer keeps the hopeful future tightly tied to the realities of the present. Not all prophetic and apocalyptical writers are this realistic. They are frequently so intoxicated with their vision of the new day that they have little or no interest in the day that now is. Consequently their vision tends to lose its relevance to the actual situation, becoming in fact an escape from it instead of a way of meeting and managing it.

14-15. *The Never-Never World.*—The clue to these verses lies in the phrase **as in the days of old.** Some people find relief from present adversity by a flight to the past when things were thought to be better. They single out as symbols

of that era of security certain events and use them as food for their spirits. Yet this desire always rather idealizes than remembers the past. Take the famous flight from Egypt with Moses as leader and God as protector. Later generations looked back to it as the supreme example of how God would intervene to save them; it became a most impressive symbol of the power of God. Consequently men in need recalled it with longing, implying that they wished God would intervene once more **as in the days of old.** But in that early day the very Israelites who were being benefited by God's mighty act were a most reluctant, ungrateful, and rebellious people. This grim fact tends to drop out of the meaning of the symbol, "deliverance from Egypt," and all that remains is the activity of God and the devout thanksgiving of his people.

History idealized is a dangerous fiction; history recalled and used fairly is a most helpful

15 According to the days of thy coming out of the land of Egypt will I show unto him marvelous *things.*

16 ¶ The nations shall see and be confounded at all their might: they shall lay *their* hand upon *their* mouth, their ears shall be deaf.

17 They shall lick the dust like a serpent, they shall move out of their holes like worms of the earth: they shall be afraid of the Lord our God, and shall fear because of thee.

15 As in the days when you came out of the land of Egypt
I will show them^z marvelous things.

16 The nations shall see and be ashamed
of all their might;
they shall lay their hands on their mouths;
their ears shall be deaf;
17 they shall lick the dust like a serpent,
like the crawling things of the earth;
they shall come trembling out of their strongholds,
they shall turn in dread to the Lord our God,
and they shall fear because of thee.

^z Heb *him*

---

as in Pss. 23; 95:7; Isa. 40:11; 49:10. **Alone** or **solitarily** here has the sense of "unmolested," i.e, God's flock would be unmolested. After the return, Palestine would again be a land of **forest, garden land,** and rich pasture, such as were found in **Bashan and Gilead.** The most nostalgic idealizations of Israel's past glory would soon be immeasurably surpassed.

15. With the restoration of Israel, miracles (**marvelous things**) would again abound, as they did centuries earlier at the Red Sea, Mount Sinai, and other points along the route of the Exodus from Egypt to Palestine.

16. Before the miraculous power (**all their might**) of God's restored people in Palestine, the other nations would stand **ashamed.** They would **lay their hands on their mouths,** i.e., they would stand speechless before the wonder of a restored Israel. **Their ears** would be deafened by the tales they would hear of Israel's glory. This verse (as vs. 10) seems dependent on Isa. 52:13-15.

17. The first part describes the anticipated humbling of the nations, even into **the dust;** and the second, their ensuing conversion as they come in **trembling, dread,** and **fear** to the Lord our God.

---

fact. Yet the idealization of the past is one of the commonest habits of mankind. Legends from the folklore of all peoples bear testimony to this fact. The Hebrew story of the Garden of Eden has its counterpart in every known literature. The Greek tale of the various ages of man, beginning with the Golden Age and descending to the Iron Age, has many parallels in other cultures. This tendency to idealize the past manifests itself in many other ways, notably in the glorification of great men. The process by which historical persons become epic heroes like Gilgamesh, Moses, Ulysses, Siegfried, to name but a few, is well known to any student of human origins. They are finally thought to have possessed special means of communication with deity, to have lived incredibly long lives, and to have endured insufferable tribulations for their faith or country or people.

When men so idealize the past, most of them take one more step and seek to recapture its essential glory. It is at this point that the

historical idealization becomes the gravest kind of ethical and social menace. For whatever the glories of the past, they cannot be recaptured except in imagination. They can be celebrated —and it is proper that they should be—but they cannot be relived. The God of the past is God of the present and future as well. **The days of old** can make an invaluable contribution to any contemporary age that will not seek in them a substitute for living in its own day and time. Religion, because of its all too frequent preoccupation with the backward look, has much to answer for in this regard. It can easily, and with more than a measure of truth, be accused of being the "opium of the people," or an attempt to live in a never-never world instead of in the world of present facts.

16-20. *A Psalm of Hope.*—These verses appear to be an attempt to recapitulate some of the main emphases of the book: (a) Israel will become powerful again, and nations that now tread on her will be humble in her presence;

18 Who *is* a God like unto thee, that pardoneth iniquity, and passeth by the transgression of the remnant of his heritage? he retaineth not his anger for ever, because he delighteth *in* mercy.

19 He will turn again, he will have compassion upon us; he will subdue our iniquities; and thou wilt cast all their sins into the depths of the sea.

20 Thou wilt perform the truth to Jacob, *and* the mercy to Abraham, which thou hast sworn unto our fathers from the days of old.

18 Who is a God like thee, pardoning iniquity
and passing over transgression
for the remnant of his inheritance?
He does not retain his anger for ever
because he delights in steadfast love.

19 He will again have compassion upon us,
he will tread our iniquities under foot.
Thou wilt cast all our[a] sins
into the depths of the sea.

20 Thou wilt show faithfulness to Jacob
and steadfast love to Abraham,
as thou hast sworn to our fathers
from the days of old.

a Gk Syr Vg Tg: Heb *their*

18. The summarizing remarks (vss. 18-20) at this psalm's conclusion are devoted to praising Yahweh, the Hebrew Deity. Here there is a trace or echo of polytheism, for it is implied that no other deity is comparable to the God of Israel. These people, on the brink of return from exile, believed the attitude of their God was about to change from one of **anger** and punishment to a mood of **pardoning iniquity, passing over transgression,** and **not** retaining **his anger,** but becoming a Deity who **delighteth in mercy.** There is no indication that these qualities were to be manifested by him to all the world, but rather to **the remnant of his inheritance,** i.e., to what was left of his chosen people. This would renew their confidence that they were his favorites among the nations.

19. Inasmuch as Israel had been punished "double for all her sins" (Isa. 40:2), this matter would receive no more attention from the Deity. He would banish into oblivion even his recollection of the pre-exilic **sins** and **iniquities** of the Hebrew people, treading **under foot** or casting **into the depths of the sea** the very memory of them. The postexilic mood of God, as in vs. 18, would be characterized by **compassion** to his people.

20. This psalm of hope for the return from exile (vss. 7-20) closes with a reminder that by rescuing his much-punished people from exile, and providing them a glorious future, God would be respecting his oath and fulfilling his promises made centuries before **(from the days of old)** to **Abraham** (Gen. 12:1-3; 13:14-17; 15:18; 17:1-21; 22:15-18; 26:3-4, 24) and **Jacob** (Gen. 28:13-17). Return from exile would not only benefit Israel but would vindicate the **faithfulness** of God in fulfilling those promises made to Abraham and Jacob. The attitude of **steadfast love** shown to those remote ancestors was now about to be manifested to all Israel.

With this late exilic psalm the book which bears the name of Micah comes to a conclusion by stressing the faithfulness and goodness of God.

(*b*) God in his greatness and mercy will forgive her when his judgment on her has been fulfilled; and (*c*) in that day he will fulfill to her his richest promises. The final editor of Micah brings the multiple strains in the book into a profound spiritual unity of hope and faith.

He has not resolved the conflicting judgments and hostile attitudes of the preceding pages by argument but by a simple statement of faith in the ultimate justice and goodness of God. Less than this prophetic faith dare not do; more it cannot do.

The Book of

NAHUM

Introduction and Exegesis by Charles L. Taylor, Jr.
Exposition by James T. Cleland

NAHUM

INTRODUCTION

The section of the Book of the Twelve ascribed to Nahum of Elkosh appears at first sight to be one of the least valuable parts of the Old Testament. It consists of two poems, both of which breathe hatred and vengeance. Neither is written in the spirit of Amos, Hosea, Micah, Isaiah, or Jeremiah. Neither declares God's moral judgment upon Israel or Judah. Neither, in fact, intimates that Judah need repent of its sins. Although the second and longer poem was composed probably within a decade of the appearance of Deuteronomy, no mention is made of that document; no hint is given of the reform to which Deuteronomy led.[1]

But if Nahum does not upbraid, neither does he comfort (yet cf. 1:7). So far from proclaiming God's mercy, the author of this poem gloats over the fall of the Assyrian capital, Nineveh. The God of Judah is pictured as one who wreaks vengeance on his adversaries and counters with violence those who are so foolhardy as to plot evil against him. This is not the teaching of Isa. 40–55 nor of Jonah, certainly not of the Christian cross.

Both ethically and theologically, therefore, Nahum is deficient. It seems to be a reversion to that nationalistic, chauvinistic type of prophecy represented by the four hundred with whom Micaiah ben Imlah contended (I Kings 22), and from which Amos dissociated himself to the great, lasting benefit of mankind (Amos 7:14). This book consorts strangely with much of the Bible. Yet despite its deficiencies, Nahum is one of the outstanding literary masterpieces of the Bible, and even religiously, as will appear shortly, should by no means be ignored.

I. Composition

A. The Long Poem.—The work of Nahum the poet of Elkosh, the basis of these three chapters, is an oracle, more than one hundred lines in length, depicting the sack of Nineveh. Of

[1] For the historical background see Intro. to Zephaniah, pp. 1007-9.

this extraordinary poem the first couplet is found in 1:11,

> Did one not come out from you,
>   who plotted evil against the LORD?

Probably five or six more of its lines are now contained in 1:11, 14; but the greater part is preserved nearly intact and relatively free from additions in chs. 2–3. Both of these chapters deal not only with the attack upon Nineveh and its capture, but also with its crimes; a change of order in this subject matter in ch. 3 heightens the dramatic effect. Thus, 2:1-5 describes the attack, 2:6-10 the flight and capture, and 2:11-12 the reason for destruction—Nineveh's cruel oppression. In ch. 3, vss. 1-3 resume the picture of confusion as Nineveh totters, vs. 4 returns to her wickedness, and the remaining verses paint a striking word picture of the plight of the city on the day of its fall.

Although there are scholars who believe this poem to have been written *post eventum*, it is more likely to be a genuine prediction (cf., e.g., 2:13; 3:5-7, 11, 15) written just before a coalition of Medes and Chaldeans overthrew Nineveh in 612 B.C. In either case the author is inflamed to a white heat over this event, so stirred that he strikes off poetry which for vividness and force is perhaps unmatched in the Bible or even in all literature. His work ranks with the other classics of early Hebrew, with the Song of Deborah in Judg. 5 and the lament of David for Saul and Jonathan in II Sam. 1:17-27. For conciseness, vigor, concreteness, and fervor it holds a place all its own. Picture upon picture flashes before the reader's eye with the swiftness with which

> The chariots rage in the streets,
>   they rush to and fro through the squares (2:4),

until the story is fully told—the tyrant Nineveh has received the just recompense for its crimes and is no more.

B. The Alphabetic Psalm of Chapter 1.—In order to provide a suitable introduction to this remarkable long poem the editor of the Book of the Twelve recalled and used a shorter work on a similar theme, the wrathful vengeance of the Lord. There are indications that an acrostic underlies the present confusion. Thus 1:2 begins with the first letter of the alphabet (א), vs. 3b ("in whirlwind") with the second letter (ב), vs. 4 with the third (ג), and so on until from ten to sixteen of the twenty-two letters have appeared. In places the scheme breaks down; probably the redactor did not know the original poem very well, and became confused to the point of substituting lines from other poems in the place of what he had forgotten. At least it may be said that in the process of transmission what was once an alphabetic poem has now been seriously corrupted, rearranged, and supplemented.

The literary quality of this acrostic, although decidedly inferior when compared with the long masterpiece of chs. 2–3, is higher than that of most such artificially constructed verse. (For other examples cf. Lam. 1; 2; 3; 4; Prov. 31:10-31; Pss. 9–10; 25; 34; 37; 111; 112; 119; 145.) When it was composed cannot be exactly determined. The probabilities are that it belongs to the third or second century B.C.[2]

II. Religious Value

Although all three chapters fall below the standards set by the developed Judaeo-Christian tradition concerning the nature of God and man's relation with his brother man, so that Nahum is not highly regarded as a source of inspiration or ethical nourishment, it is not without a significant religious message to its own time, the present, and every age. For, first, it is one of the world's classic rebukes of militarism, "They that take the sword shall perish with the sword" (Matt. 26:52). Of all the peoples of antiquity, the Assyrians had been among the most ruthless, as their inscriptions abundantly testify. But such a policy is self-destructive. In the end payment will be made. The proud city is no more able to withstand its inevitable destiny than Thebes, which had fallen fifty-one years earlier. All tyrants are doomed. They make enemies of those whom they attack and oppress; they become corrupt, dissolute, drunken, effeminate; they are lulled into false security. The day comes when the world rejoices that the depredations of the liar and the wiles of the mistress of sorceries suffer the fate of all such wickedness.

But even more important is Nahum's declaration that the Lord, or Yahweh, the God of little Judah, is in control and is responsible for Nineveh's overthrow. An obscure poet of an obscure part of a mighty empire proclaims as he foresees the crumbling of the great capital, "Our God is doing that." To be sure, the poet asks no reform, no repentance. He declares only one small part of the truth about God. Yet that fraction is of untold importance, for it reminds him who will heed that there is no withstanding the Lord who maintains justice and answers human need. "Did one not come out from you, who plotted evil against the LORD? . . . I will break his yoke" (1:11, 13). "Behold I am against you, says the LORD, . . . and I will burn your chariots, . . . and I will cut off your prey from the earth" (2:13). "For upon whom has not come your unceasing evil?" (3:19.) The Lord is exalted over the nations. "The stars in their courses" fight against Sisera or whoever opposes him (Judg. 5:20). "The world fighteth for the righteous" (Wisd. Sol. 16:17).

The injustices of Nineveh stirred Nahum to the highest degree of moral indignation. They burned within him to the point where he could utter truth in language so plain, so unvarnished, and so memorable that it has survived as the classic description of the tyrant's fate. Perhaps one of the faults of current preaching is that it lacks Nahum's concern over entrenched wrong.

III. Meter and Text

The long poem, without doubt, originally was read with two accents in each half line. Sometimes there are two accents on one word, and throughout there are many more stresses than would be given a similar amount of prose. By this rapid, staccato meter the dramatic effect is greatly enhanced, especially in such passages as 3:2 or 2:2, where the poet does not stop to form complete sentences, but hurls pictures in breath-taking succession. The lines in 2:13e and 3:19c may have an extra accent in each half.

In the shorter introductory poem there were probably four accents balanced by four in each line, although some scholars see a 3+3 arrangement. Unfortunately, as mentioned above, this poem has been partly lost, partly disarranged, and partly interwoven with the poem which follows. The result is a seriously corrupt text in ch. 1; but for chs. 2–3, although editors have made some twenty minor additions, and although in the course of the centuries numerous mistakes in copying have occurred, fortunately the original poem in the

---

[2] On the problems of this chapter cf. William R. Arnold, "The Composition of Nahum 1–2:3," *Zeitschrift für die alttestamentliche Wissenschaft*, XXI (1901), 225-65.

main is recoverable. Some half dozen textual problems still await solution.

IV. The Proposed Translation

I. THE ACROSTIC POEM (1:1-10)

1:1. The Oracle on Nineveh

The Book of the Vision of Nahum the Elkoshite

2. א The LORD is an ardent and vengeful God;
the LORD is vengeful and full of wrath;
[the LORD is vengeful toward his adversaries
and watchful is he of his enemies.

3. The LORD is long suffering and of great might,
but the LORD by no means fails to punish.]

ב In storm and tempest is his path,
and cloud is the dust of his feet.

4. ג He rebukes the sea and makes it dry,
and parches all the rivers.

(ד) Bashan and Carmel are crushed,
and the bloom of Lebanon fades.

5. ה The mountains tremble because of him
and the hills quake;

ו and the earth heaves before him,
the world and all that dwell therein.

6. ז Who can stand before his anger
and who can endure the heat of his wrath?

ח His indignation seethes like fire,
and the rocks are shattered by him.

7. ט The LORD is good for a stronghold [in the day of trouble],
and acknowledges those who trust in him.

8. [But with an overwhelming flood]

כ he brings about the end of his adversaries [1]
and drives his enemies into darkness.

9. מ What do you plot against the LORD?
He brings about the end.

(ל) Not twice does hostility appear. . . .

10. [Like entangled thorns, drunken as with their drink,
they are consumed like dry stubble.]

II. THE LONG POEM (1:11–3:19)

A. THE VISION OF NAHUM THE ELKOSHITE (1:11-15)

11. Did he not come forth from you,
who plotted evil against the LORD,
counseling villainy?

12. [Thus says the LORD,
though they be intact and so numerous
yet they are cut off when he passes over.
And though I have afflicted you
I will afflict you no longer.

13. And now I will break his yoke from off you
and will shatter your bonds.]

14. The LORD has commanded concerning you,
no longer shall your name be sown,
From the house of your gods I will cut off
graven image and molten image;
I will make your grave a stench.[2]

15. [Behold, on the mountains
the feet of him who brings good tidings,
who proclaims peace!
Keep your feasts, O Judah,
fulfill your vows,

for never again shall the wicked pass over you,
he is utterly cut off.]

B. THE ATTACK (2:1-5)

2:1. He that puts to rout [3] has come up against you.
"Defenses manned!
Road watched! Loins girded!
Strength mustered to the utmost!"

2. [For the LORD is restoring the pride of Jacob as the pride of Israel,
for plunderers have plundered them and have stripped their branches.]

3. The shield of his warriors is colored red,[4]
the mighty men are gleaming,[4]
the squadrons of chariots are spread like the sea,[4]
and the chargers [5] are arrayed.

4. In the streets the chariots rage,
they rush to and fro through the squares.
Their appearance is like torches,
like lightning do they dart.

5. His nobles [6] are felling the timbers,
they hasten with their blows,[7]
against the wall is set up [8] the shield.

C. FLIGHT AND CAPTURE (2:6-10)

6. The river gates are thrown open,
and the palace surges with terror.

7. In a litter [9] departs her majesty
and her maidens are driven along [like the sound of doves]
beating upon their breasts.

8. And Nineveh is like a pool of water.
Water is she, while they flee.
"Halt! halt!"
but no one turns.

9. "'Plunder silver!
plunder gold!"
There is no end to the treasures,
wealth of all desirable things.

10. Empty! emptied out and devastated!
Fainting heart and tottering knees!
and anguish on all loins,
and the faces of all increasingly livid!

D. NINEVEH'S CRIMES (2:11-13)

11. Where is the den of the lions
and the field for the whelps,
whither the lion hastened to come,
where dwelt the lion whom none dismayed?

12. The lion tore in pieces for his whelps
and strangled for his lionesses,
and filled with prey his dens
and his habitations with plunder.

13. Behold I have caught you,[10] says the LORD [of hosts],
and I will burn in smoke your horde,[11]

---

[1] Hebrew, *her place.*
[2] Hebrew, *for you are vile.*
[3] Or, by a different vocalization, *the bludgeon.*
[4] By a slight change.
[5] Hebrew, *cypresses.*
[6] Hebrew, *he remembers his nobles, they stumble.*
[7] Hebrew, *as they go.*
[8] Hebrew, *and is set up.*
[9] By a slight change.
[10] Hebrew, *I am unto you.*
[11] By transposing two Hebrew letters; Hebrew, *your chariots.*

and your whelps shall the sword devour;
and I will cut off your depredations from the
earth
and the voice of your envoys shall no more
be heard.

E. Woe to the Bloody City (3:1-4)

3:1. Woe to the bloody city,
completely false, full of booty!
no limit to the plunder there!
2. Crack of whip, [and sound of] rattle of wheel,
rearing steed, somersaulting horse.[12]
and jolting chariot!
3. and flashing sword and glittering spear,
heaps of slain, and no end to the corpses!
[They stumble over their corpses.]
4. For the countless harlotries of the harlot,
fair and graceful, bewitchingly charming,
who betrays nations with her harlotries
and peoples with her charms.

F. The Fall (3:5-19)

5. Behold I have caught you, says the Lord [of
hosts],
and I will throw your skirts upon your face,
and I will show nations your nakedness
and kingdoms your shame.
6. And I will cast upon you filth,
and I will insult you and make you a sight.
7. [And it will come to pass, all who look on you
will shrink from you and say,
Nineveh is desolate: Who will mourn for her?
Whence shall I seek comforters for you?]
8. Are you better than Thebes [13]
situated by the Nile,
surrounded by water,
as for whose rampart, the sea [water] her
wall?
9. Ethiopia and Egypt were her strength
and there was no end to her helpers;
Put and the Libyans were on her side.
10. Even she [into exile] went into captivity
even her children were dashed in pieces [at
the head of every street]
and for her nobility men cast lots,
and all her dignities were bound in chains.
11. You also will be drunken,
you also will be frenzied,
you will seek refuge from the enemy.
12. [All your fortresses are fig trees with first ripe
figs,
if shaken they fall into the mouth of the
eater.]
13. Behold your people are a pack of women,
the gates of your land lie wide open [to
your foes];
fire has devoured your bars.
14. Draw you water for the siege,
strengthen your fortresses, go to the clay pit,

[12] Two words transposed from vs. 3.
[13] Hebrew, No-Amon.

tread the mortar, take hold of the brick
mold.
15. There fire will devour you,
sword will cut you [will devour you like the
locust].
Increase like the locust!
Increase like the grasshopper!
16. Your merchants are more
than the stars of heaven. [The locust spreads
its wings and flies away.]
17. Your princes are like grasshoppers
and your scribes like a swarm [swarm]
that perch on fences [on a cold day]—
when the sun rises, then fly away,
and their place is not known [where they
are].
18. Your shepherds sleep [O king of Assyria],
your nobles slumber.
Your people are scattered [on the mountains]
with none to gather them.
19. Your hurt will not heal,
your wound is festered.
All who hear the news of you
clap their hands over you,
for over whom has not passed
your evil continually?

V. Outline of Contents

I. The acrostic poem (1:1-9)
II. A series of marginal notes (1:10, 12, 13, 15; 2:2)
III. The long poem (1:11–3:19)
A. Nineveh's crime and punishment (1:11, 14)
B. The attack (2:1-5)
C. Flight and capture (2:6-10)
D. Nineveh's crimes (2:11-13)
E. Woe to the bloody city (3:1-4)
F. The fall (3:5-19)

VI. Selected Bibliography

Arnold, William R. "The Composition of Nahum
1–2:3," *Zeitschrift für die alttestamentliche Wissenschaft*, XXI (1901), 225-65.

Davidson, A. B. *The Books of Nahum, Habakkuk
and Zephaniah* ("Cambridge Bible"). Cambridge:
Cambridge University Press, 1920.

Driver, S. R., ed. *The Minor Prophets* ("New Century Bible"). New York: Oxford University Press,
1906. Vol. II.

Haldar, Alfred O. *Studies in the Book of Nahum.*
Uppsala: Lundequistska Bokhandeln, 1947.

Pilcher, C. V. *Three Hebrew Prophets and the
Passing of Empires.* London: Religious Tract Society, 1931.

Smith, George Adam. *The Book of the Twelve
Prophets.* Rev. ed. New York: Harper & Bros.,
1928. Vol. II.

Smith, J. M. P., Ward, W. H., and Bewer, Julius A.
*A Critical and Exegetical Commentary on Micah,
Zephaniah, Nahum, Habakkuk, Obadiah and Joel*
("International Critical Commentary"). New
York: Charles Scribner's Sons, 1911.

NAHUM

TEXT, EXEGESIS, AND EXPOSITION

1 The burden of Nineveh. The book of the vision of Nahum the Elkoshite.

1 An oracle concerning Nin'eveh. The book of the vision of Nahum of Elkosh.

I. THE ACROSTIC POEM (1:1-9)

1:1. The title of the long poem was probably **the vision of Nahum of Elkosh. Vision,** a technical term, might well be rendered "prophecy." When the acrostic was prefaced and both were incorporated into the Book of the Twelve to form the section called Nahum, the editors added "The Oracle [or "message," lit., **burden**] on Nineveh," and supplied **the book** as a connective. Although for centuries legend has associated the grave of Nahum with a place called Elkosh, near Nineveh, and some scholars have thought that Nahum was a descendant of Israelites deported to Mesopo-

---

1:1. Nahum's Message and Its Limitations.— Here, at the beginning, one must attempt to understand, appreciate, and, if necessary, modify the **oracle concerning Nineveh. The book of the vision of Nahum of Elkosh.** There are three things to be noted:

First, Nahum was right. There is a spiritual strength here, because there is expressed a point of view that is at rock-bottom biblical: God is Lord of history. The book expresses the conception that there is a moral law which undergirds the world, and though it may be ignored, slighted, or deliberately broken, it crushes the moral criminal in the end. Here are the mills of God grinding slowly, exceeding slowly perhaps, but also grinding exceeding small. When a nation exalts itself above measure, God moves into action. "Behold I am against you, says the LORD of hosts" (2:13; 3:5).

Second, Nahum was wrong. There is spiritual weakness here too. Nahum gives no conscious recognition of the fact that the sins of the Assyrians were also the sins of the Judeans. The other prophets were always aware of that, even the earliest of them (Amos 2:6-8). Nahum cannot keep step with Amos, Hosca, Isaiah, and Jeremiah. His God is a throwback to the Yahweh of battles of the early days of the kingdom.[1] He is a militant nationalist as he infers that Judah is not as other nations, espe-

cially Assyria. But it is hardly for us to fling the first stone.[2] Nationalism with a Christian tinge is our subconscious religion, and at times of crisis it is apt to take control.

Third, Nahum may be redeemed. Nahum need not be the norm; Jesus may be. The remedy for Nahum is a simple and drastic one. It is nothing more or less than a change of heart, a fundamental conversion in terms of Jesus' view of God and man. It happened to another Nahum. In 1897, when the British Empire was at the height of its power, the diamond jubilee of Queen Victoria was observed. The obvious man was chosen to write a poem of celebration, Rudyard Kipling, the jingoist poet of the imperial mood, the "Nahum of the empire." After days of futility, in desperation he composed a poem that baffled and angered many of his countrymen—"Recessional":

> Lo, all our pomp of yesterday
> Is one with Nineveh and Tyre!
> Judge of the Nations, spare us yet,
> Lest we forget—lest we forget![3]

[2] For a shrewd comment on Nahum and Rev. 18 see Harry Emerson Fosdick, *A Guide to Understanding the Bible* (New York: Harper & Bros., 1938), pp. 138-39.

[3] Rudyard Kipling, "Recessional," from *The Five Nations.* Copyright 1903, 1931 by Rudyard Kipling. Used by permission of Mrs. George Bambridge; Methuen & Co.; The Macmillan Co., Canada; and Doubleday & Co. For Kipling's own comments on the writing of the poem see R. G. McCutchan, *Our Hymnody* (New York: The Methodist Book Concern, 1937), p. 480.

[1] For a vivid description of a warrior-god and his worshiper see the early stanzas of Stephen Vincent Benét's *King David* (New York: Henry Holt & Co., 1923).

2 God *is* jealous, and the LORD revengeth; the LORD revengeth, and *is* furious; the LORD will take vengeance on his adversaries, and he reserveth *wrath* for his enemies.

3 The LORD *is* slow to anger, and great in power, and will not at all acquit *the wicked:* the LORD *hath* his way in the whirlwind and in the storm, and the clouds *are* the dust of his feet.

4 He rebuketh the sea, and maketh it dry, and drieth up all the rivers: Bashan languisheth, and Carmel, and the flower of Lebanon languisheth.

2 The LORD is a jealous God and avenging,
  the LORD is avenging and wrathful;
the LORD takes vengeance on his adversaries
  and keeps wrath for his enemies.
3 The LORD is slow to anger and of great might,
  and the LORD will by no means clear the guilty.

His way is in whirlwind and storm,
  and the clouds are the dust of his feet.
4 He rebukes the sea and makes it dry,
  he dries up all the rivers;
Bashan and Carmel wither,
  the bloom of Lebanon fades.

---

tamia after the fall of Samaria in 722 B.C., the location of Elkosh is unknown. Jerome placed it in the northern part of Galilee, others in Judah.

2-9. Despite the difficulties that beset reconstruction of the introductory acrostic, its main purport is clear: the Lord is a God who is not to be trifled with. He is both powerful and active on behalf of his friends against his enemies. He is **jealous** in the sense of being ardent or fervent or hot. His power may be seen in the storm, in drought, in earthquakes, and in the destruction caused by lava (cf. Amos 1:14; Hos. 13:15; Jer. 23:19; I Kings 19:11; II Kings 2:1; Job 9:17; 38:1; 40:6; Exod. 19:18; Judg. 5:4; Hab. 3:6; Ps. 97:4). But there is a purpose in all these portents: the protection of those who trust in him and the overthrow—in fact the annihilation—of all opposition.

2. Wrathful: Lit., "master," "possessor," "baal" of wrath. The second half of this verse may possibly be a line of the acrostic poem now misplaced; if so, it belongs after vs. 9a. Or it may be an editorial comment on vs. 2a. **Keeps wrath:** Better, "watchful." The picture, as in Ps. 103:9, is of an intense stare, or frown, or scowl.

3. Vs. 3a may be the lost *yôdh* line which should follow vs. 7, but it seems more likely to be an editorial addition. With vs. 3b cf. the words of the hymn "O worship the King, all glorious above"; "And dark is his path on the wings of the storm."

4. The verb translated **fades** in the Hebrew appears in both halves of the second line of this verse; probably in the first half it takes the place of a forgotten word beginning with *dáleth*, the fourth letter of the Hebrew alphabet, *Dukke'û*, "are crushed" (cf. **wither**), is here substituted.

Under God Kipling was not proud but humble. When one really stands under the eye of the God revealed in our Lord Jesus Christ, boasting and arrogance disappear. The horizontal effect of that vertical relationship is good will in one's dealings with his neighbor. It is then recognized that God uses history for his purposes, not ours. In the light of that revelation it behooves a man to come into line with God's purposes. That is not the religion of the ordinary man, but of the redeemed man.

Nahum has a valid place in the canon because he is superbly right in considering history as the expression of a God who is creator, sustainer, and redeemer. He is in harmony with the dominant note of biblical theology both in the O.T. and the N.T. Even the foolishness of Nahum expresses the wisdom of God. But he falls below, far below, the best interpreters of that *Weltanschauung*, who refuse to apportion God's condemnation to this state and his saving grace to that nation. All stand under his judgment, which can both condemn and save, because both are the result of his active love. That is the sermon from Nahum when the book is considered not in isolation, but within the biblical philosophy of history.

1:2-10. *The Attributes of God.*—Such is the theme that may be suggested by these verses, an addition of the redactor. God is **of great might**, as can be seen by the revelations of himself in nature (vss. 3-6); but there are better passages

5 The mountains quake at him, and the hills melt, and the earth is burned at his presence, yea, the world, and all that dwell therein.

6 Who can stand before his indignation? and who can abide in the fierceness of his anger? his fury is poured out like fire, and the rocks are thrown down by him.

7 The LORD *is* good, a stronghold in the day of trouble; and he knoweth them that trust in him.

8 But with an overrunning flood he will

5 The mountains quake before him,
    the hills melt;
the earth is laid waste before him,
    the world and all that dwell therein.

6 Who can stand before his indignation?
    Who can endure the heat of his anger?
His wrath is poured out like fire,
    and the rocks are broken asunder by
    him.

7 The LORD is good,
    a stronghold in the day of trouble;
he knows those who take refuge in him.

8 But with an overflowing flood
    he will make a full end of his adver-
    saries,[a]

[a] Gk: Heb *her place*

Bashan, in the northeastern part of Palestine, watered by the river Yarmuk, and Mount **Carmel,** which by jutting out into the Mediterranean attracts moisture, are among the most fruitful sections of the country. **Lebanon,** farther north in Syria, famous for its cedars, would again be one of the last nearby regions to be affected by drought.

5. Quake (vs. 5*a*) is more likely than **melt** (vs. 5*b*). The verb in the next line (vs. 5*c*) is dubious; as it stands it means "to heave" or "to lift up," but may be a corruption of an original form meaning "to crash in ruins." Note that natural portents are considered to be the product of the direct action of the Lord.

6. Cf. Ps. 24:3. **His indignation,** which continues the acrostic, should stand at the beginning of the line. "His indignation—who can stand before it?" The picture in the second half of the verse is that of seething molten metal or lava.

7. Stronghold denotes here a place of refuge or means of protection, figuratively used of God in Pss. 27:1; 31:4; 37:39; 52:7, and in the LXX of Ps. 90:1, which underlies the version of the Book of Common Prayer. **In the day of trouble,** outside the metrical scheme, is probably a gloss. The Lord **knows,** recognizes, and takes care of those who **trust** or **take refuge in him,** an expression which occurs more than a dozen times in the Psalter, e.g., Pss. 11:1; 16:1; 36:7; 91:4. As noted above, vs. 3*a* may belong at this point.

"Another side of the divine nature is now emphasized. The wrath of Yahweh is vented upon those who hate him; but for those who put their trust in him he has loving kindness (Dt. 5⁹ f.). The whole history of Israel from the Assyrian period to the end was one long agony of waiting. . . . Disappointed in one expectation, Israel did but transform it into another and continue to 'expect great things from God.'" (J. M. P. Smith, W. H. Ward, and Julius A. Bewer, *A Critical and Exegetical Commentary on Micah, Zephaniah, Nahum, Habakkuk, Obadiah and Joel* [New York: Charles Scribner's Sons, 1911; "International Critical Commentary"], p. 291.)

8. The LXX, Aramaic, and Targ. are clearly right in reading **adversaries** for **her place.** But **with an overflowing flood** is more likely to be a marginal note like **in the**

than this elsewhere to describe the God who creates and sustains the world (e.g., Job 38–39; Pss. 93; 97; 104; 139). He is also a God of moral worth.

  The LORD takes vengeance on his adversaries
    and keeps wrath for his enemies. . . .
  The LORD will by no means clear the guilty.

The poet is probably here thinking of Assyria's international behavior, which he considers an affront to the Lord. Therefore he **will pursue his enemies into darkness.** Perhaps to answer the unspoken questions of those who wonder why the Lord did not bestir himself sooner, he is described as **slow to anger.** All of this need not worry the reader. To such a one

make an utter end of the place thereof, and darkness shall pursue his enemies.

9 What do ye imagine against the Lord? he will make an utter end: affliction shall not rise up the second time.

10 For while *they be* folden together *as* thorns, and while they are drunken *as* drunkards, they shall be devoured as stubble fully dry.

11 There is *one* come out of thee, that imagineth evil against the Lord, a wicked counselor.

12 Thus saith the Lord; Though *they be* quiet, and likewise many, yet thus shall

and will pursue his enemies into darkness.

9 What do you plot against the Lord?
He will make a full end;
he will not take vengeance[b] twice on his foes.[c]

10 Like entangled thorns they are consumed,[d]
like dry stubble.

11 Did one not[e] come out from you,
who plotted evil against the Lord,
and counseled villainy?

12 Thus says the Lord,
"Though they be strong and many,[f]

[b] Gk: Heb *rise up*
[c] Cn: Heb *distress*
[d] Heb *are consumed, drunken as with their drink*
[e] Cn: Heb *fully*
[f] Heb uncertain

day of trouble in vs. 7 than part of a line from which a word or words have been lost. **Full end** or **utter end** is a characteristic expression of the book of Jeremiah, where it is asserted frequently that the Lord will not make a full end of Judah, but will leave a remnant.

9. At this point the breakdown of the acrostic arrangement makes further reconstruction of the introductory poem very difficult, if not hopeless. The first half of the *lāmedh* line appears to be given in vs. 9*b*, which, although variously read in Greek and Hebrew, indicates either way that the Lord needs no second chance to deal with opposition. Another rendering of the line, with slight changes, gives "Not twice do his foes arise." The LXX reads, **He will not take vengeance twice.**

II. A Series of Marginal Notes (1:10, 12, 13, 15; 2:2)

10. Three Hebrew words look very much alike; dittography is probable. The sense may be that however drenched the thickets, they are consumed like dry stubble when the Lord acts. J. M. P. Smith (*ibid.,* p. 294) conjectures: "Thorns cut down and dried out—they will be devoured like dry stubble." The last word in the verse (**fully**) should be emended and taken with the first line of the long poem which begins in vs. 11, **Did one not . . . ,** as in the RSV.

12. Vs. 12*ab*, which may have been the line of the acrostic beginning with the letter *shin,* is similar to vs. 10; although the opponents are "intact" and **many**, they will be **cut off** as sheep are sheared when the Lord "passes over." Or perhaps read, **they will be cut off and pass away.** In vs. 12*c* begin supplementary promises of balm to the people of Judah, i.e., vaguely remembered quotations from I Kings 11:39; Jer. 30:8; Isa. 52:7, which now appear as vss. 12*c*, 13, 15*a*. Further encouragement is added in vs. 15*b*—Judah is to keep its feast days unmolested, and in 2:2, where, as in Ezek. 37, the kingdom of Israel, long plundered and stripped, shall be restored.

the Lord is good, a stronghold in the day of trouble; and he knoweth them that trust in him. That is consoling, though it is not borne out in a material sense by history.

1:11, 12*a*, 14; 2:1, 3–3:19. *The Judgment of God.*—That Nahum is a glorious piece of impetuous poetry is obvious from the RSV and

the Moffatt translations. For R. H. Pfeiffer, the book is one of three great masterpieces of classical Hebrew poetry, ranking with the Song of Deborah (Judg. 5) and David's lament over Saul and Jonathan (II Sam. 1:19-27).[4] But it

[4] *Introduction to the Old Testament* (New York: Harper & Bros., 1941), pp. 594-97.

they be cut down, when he shall pass through. Though I have afflicted thee, I will afflict thee no more.

13 For now will I break his yoke from off thee, and will burst thy bonds in sunder.

14 And the Lord hath given a commandment concerning thee, *that* no more of thy name be sown: out of the house of thy gods will I cut off the graven image and the molten image: I will make thy grave; for thou art vile.

15 Behold upon the mountains the feet

they will be cut off and pass away.
  Though I have afflicted you,
    I will afflict you no more.

13 And now I will break his yoke from off
    you
  and will burst your bonds asunder."

14 The Lord has given commandment
    about you:
  "No more shall your name be perpetu-
    ated;
  from the house of your gods I will cut off
    the graven image and the molten
    image.
  I will make your grave, for you are vile."

15ɡ Behold, on the mountains the feet of
    him
  who brings good tidings,
  who proclaims peace!

ɡ Heb Ch 2.1

---

15. Wicked, Hebrew "Belial," is an ancient word, possibly the name of an evil spirit. It may mean "without worth" or may be derived from a root meaning "to decay," "to rot." Sons of Belial are both mentally and morally depraved. Shimei calls David "a man of blood and man of Belial" (II Sam. 16:7), i.e., a cruel, depraved murderer.

III. The Long Poem (1:11–3:19)
A. Nineveh's Crime and Punishment (1:11, 14)

11, 14. The long poem opens with a rhetorical question: Is not Nineveh responsible for opposition to the Lord's will? **Who plotted evil against the Lord** is a stronger expression than **counseled villainy,** which seems to be a variant of it. Just

is an exercise fraught with considerable risk to seek to discover religious themes in the sections of Nahum which may with certainty be ascribed to the original prophet. Some O.T. scholars are not enthusiastic about ascribing the name "prophet" to the author of these passages. And unless one plans to allegorize mercilessly, or to be guilty of the most flagrant eisegesis, then one had better use this original poem as support material either for passages from the genuine prophets (e.g., Jer. 50:18; Zeph. 2:13), or for the thesis of the redactor who penned Nah. 1:2-10.

However, there are two passages (2:13; 3:5, 6) which may be treated as one for purposes of exposition, which offer some substance. In these verses a judgment in the name of the Lord is passed on Nineveh. It is perhaps too naïve to look upon this merely as the outburst of a nationalist who gloats because an ancient enemy is finally receiving measure for measure, pressed down and running over. He does point out the

fact that the cause of this devastating attack by the Lord is the harlotry of Nineveh, **the bloody city** (3:1), **full of lies** (3:4), and perpetrator of **unceasing evil** (3:19). His faith in both the power and the holiness of God has been restored. The Lord has moved slowly, very slowly, but now that he is on the move, he is being thorough, as befits the Lord of hosts. There is no hope for Assyria (3:18-19a). The poet's ethical sensitivity has been aroused because of the lusty wickedness and beguiling sorcery of Nineveh. And he confronts her with the holy anger of an all-powerful Deity who does not forever suffer iniquity to go unpunished. This is a vindication of the Deuteronomic interpretation of history, in accordance with which goodness brings success, and evil invites and receives disaster (cf. Deut. 28). Yet it must be recognized that one might find it difficult to make this consistent with an interpretation of the attitude of God toward Nineveh in Jonah.

1:12b, 13, 15; 2:2. *A Message of Hope.*—Here are prophecies (echoes of I Kings 11:39; Jer.

of him that bringeth good tidings, that publisheth peace! O Judah, keep thy solemn feasts, perform thy vows: for the wicked shall no more pass through thee; he is utterly cut off.

2 He that dasheth in pieces is come up before thy face: keep the munition, watch the way, make *thy* loins strong, fortify *thy* power mightily.

2 For the LORD hath turned away the excellency of Jacob, as the excellency of Israel: for the emptiers have emptied them out, and marred their vine branches.

3 The shield of his mighty men is made red, the valiant men *are* in scarlet: the chariots *shall be* with flaming torches in the

Keep your feasts, O Judah,
    fulfill your vows,
for never again shall the wicked come
        against you,
    he is utterly cut off.

2 The shatterer has come up against you.
    Man the ramparts;
    watch the road;
gird your loins;
    collect all your strength.

2 (For the LORD is restoring the majesty of
        Jacob
    as the majesty of Israel,
for plunderers have stripped them
    and ruined their branches.)

3 The shield of his mighty men is red,
    his soldiers are clothed in scarlet.
The chariots flash like flame[h]

[h] Cn: The meaning of the Heb word is uncertain

possibly both could be original. **Villainy** represents an attempt to translate the word "Belial," rendered **wicked** in vs. 15 (see Exeg. below). But the Lord does not remain idle; he has ordered that no longer shall Nineveh's name be **sown** or **perpetuated** or, by a change commonly but needlessly made, "remembered." Its deities, made of carved wood and poured metal, are powerless when he acts. For the classic expression of scorn against idols made out of scraps of wood in scraps of the workmen's time, see Isa. 44:9-20. Throughout vs. 14 the masculine suffixes should be read as feminines, and at the end, for the words **for you are vile**, read "as a stench."

B. THE ATTACK (2:1-5)

The description of the attack begins. The disperser has arrived, i.e., the coalition of Babylonians and Medes is about to take Nineveh. In Hebrew the following verbs in vs. 1 are not ordinary imperatives, but so-called infinitive absolutes, by which the force of the verb is expressed with maximum emphasis: "Defenses manned! Road watched! Loins girded! Strength mustered to the utmost!" No definite article appears with the four nouns. The naked ideas are presented with all possible force and biting irony.

Herodotus pictures part of the army of Xerxes as wearing brightly colored clothing. Some "painted their bodies, half with chalk, and half with vermillion" (*History* VII. 61, 69).

2:3. This verse needs slight emendation: either "like the fire of torches are the chariots," which is freely rendered **the chariots flash like flame**, or, omitting the word "fire," "the squadrons of cavalry are spread like the sea" (*kayyām* for *beyôm*). The

30:8; Isa. 52:7) expressive of the perennial and pathetic optimism of man. This recurring expression of faith is both heroic (because he who cries out thus looks to God to vindicate the good) and distressing (in that he assumes the vindication will occur in his lifetime); it is at one and the same time a deeper and a shallower estimate of human existence than history gives

man any warrant for holding. Yet at its best i[t] created in the believer a spiritual tenacity; a[t] its worst it led to a superficial identification o[f] spiritual goodness with material prosperity.

2:1. See Expos. on 1:11, 12*a*, 14; 2:1, 3–3:19.
2. See Expos. on 1:12*b*, 13, 15; 2:2.
2:3–3:19. See Expos. on 1:11, 12*a*, 14; 2:1 3–3:19.

day of his preparation, and the fir trees shall be terribly shaken.

4 The chariots shall rage in the streets, they shall justle one against another in the broad ways: they shall seem like torches, they shall run like the lightnings.

5 He shall recount his worthies: they shall stumble in their walk; they shall make haste to the wall thereof, and the defense shall be prepared.

6 The gates of the rivers shall be opened, and the palace shall be dissolved.

7 And Huzzab shall be led away captive, she shall be brought up, and her maids shall lead *her* as with the voice of doves, taboring upon their breasts.

8 But Nineveh *is* of old like a pool of water: yet they shall flee away. Stand, stand, *shall they cry;* but none shall look back.

when mustered in array;
the chargers[i] prance.
4 The chariots rage in the streets,
they rush to and fro through the squares;
they gleam like torches,
they dart like lightning.
5 The officers are summoned,
they stumble as they go,
they hasten to the wall,
the mantelet is set up.
6 The river gates are opened,
the palace is in dismay;
7 its mistress[j] is stripped, she is carried off,
her maidens lamenting,
moaning like doves,
and beating their breasts.
8 Nin'eveh is like a pool
whose waters[k] run away.
"Halt! Halt!" they cry;
but none turns back.

[i] Cn Compare Gk Syr: Heb *cypresses*
[j] The meaning of the Hebrew is uncertain
[k] Cn Compare Gk: Heb *from the days that she has become, and they*

former is less likely because **torches** are mentioned in vs. 4. In the next line the LXX and Syriac rightly read **chargers** for **cypresses** (i.e., "spear shafts"?) ; an Arabic root gives the clue to the meaning of the following verb: **mustered in array.**

4. It is possible to regard this scene as outside the walled city proper, and preferable to understand it as referring to the attackers rather than to the defenders. The attack on the walls and gates now follows.

5. The text is clearly corrupt: "He remembers his nobles; they stumble" cannot be right. For the verb "he remembers" (**summoned** is an *ad hoc* translation) should be read a noun such as 'ēçîm, "logs," "timbers," and the following verb should be pointed as Piel: **His nobles** or axmen are felling the timbers with which to batter down the gates, to which they now charge or hasten with their blows, under the protection afforded by the **mantelet** (testudo) or shield, a well-recognized part of the equipment of such an attack. The translation "blows" for **as they go** involves a slight change in Hebrew.

C. Flight and Capture (2:6-10)

6. Now the attack is successful. The gates are opened, whether for the besiegers to enter or for the besieged to flee is uncertain. **River gates** and the lines following suggest the latter, but the word for **rivers** may be incorrect and may be a corruption of a word such as "bronze." **The palace** heaves: Cf. 1:5; everything is in confusion and terror.

7. Huzzab is meaningless, but a change of the first letter gives an excellent sense: "in a litter departs" (probably reading Qal) or possibly, "is carried off her eminence [or "her majesty"] the queen," representative of the flight which is now more fully described. **Lamenting** is another *ad hoc* translation, but the normal rendering "are driven along beating their breasts" makes excellent sense if the intrusive gloss **moaning like doves** is removed.

8. The difficulty of this verse is easily solved by comparing the Hebrew with the LXX and Vulg., dropping one letter (') and allowing the forceful comparison of Nineveh with water to be repeated. She is **like a pool of water;** nay, she is water while

9 Take ye the spoil of silver, take the spoil of gold: for *there is* none end of the store *and* glory out of all the pleasant furniture.

10 She is empty, and void, and waste: and the heart melteth, and the knees smite together, and much pain *is* in all loins, and the faces of them all gather blackness.

11 Where *is* the dwelling of the lions, and the feeding place of the young lions, where the lion, *even* the old lion, walked, *and* the lion's whelp, and none made *them* afraid?

12 The lion did tear in pieces enough for his whelps, and strangled for his lionesses, and filled his holes with prey, and his dens with ravin.

13 Behold, I *am* against thee, saith the Lord of hosts, and I will burn her chariots in the smoke, and the sword shall devour thy young lions: and I will cut off thy prey from the earth, and the voice of thy messengers shall no more be heard.

9 Plunder the silver,
    plunder the gold!
There is no end of treasure,
    or wealth of every precious thing.

10 Desolate! Desolation and ruin!
    Hearts faint and knees tremble,
anguish is on all loins,
    all faces grow pale!

11 Where is the lions' den
    the cave[l] of the young lions,
where the lion brought his prey,
    where his cubs were, with none to disturb?

12 The lion tore enough for his whelps
    and strangled prey for his lionesses;
he filled his caves with prey
    and his dens with torn flesh.

13 Behold I am against you, says the Lord of hosts, and I will burn your[m] chariots in smoke, and the sword shall devour your young lions; I will cut off your prey from the earth, and the voice of your messengers shall no more be heard.

[l] Cn: Heb *pasture*
[m] Heb *her*

they (her people) **flee** so headlong that when one attempts to rally them, **Halt! Halt!** or Make a stand, make a stand, nobody turns.

9. As Nineveh had despoiled her captives, so she has become rich spoil for her captors. **Silver** and **gold** have no articles; the bare picture is presented without adornment, but with maximum vividness. The word translated in older versions **furniture** means "articles," "things." It is almost a pity that accuracy and clarity demand the sacrifice of the phrase, **glory out of all the pleasant furniture.** The annals of Nabopolassar describe the capture of the city by a coalition of Medes and Babylonians thus: "By the bank of the Tigris they marched against Nineveh: a mighty assualt they made upon the city, and in the month of Ab . . . a great havoc of the chief men was made. . . . The spoil of the city, a quantity beyond counting, they plundered, and turned the city into a mound and a ruin" (cf. J. B. Pritchard, ed., *Ancient Near Eastern Texts Relating to the Old Testament* [Princeton: Princeton University Press, 1950], p. 304).

10. In contrast to the abundance of everything Nineveh could desire, she is now completely "cleaned out." The words of the first line, sounding somewhat alike and giving a picture of complete desolation, are followed by a brief description of the appearance of the once proud Ninevites. The last clause of the verse is not quite clear: **the faces of them** gather either a glow or pallor, but which? Fear is usually but not necessarily thought of as causing faces to be **pale** rather than livid.

D. Nineveh's Crimes (2:11-13)

11-13. Lions figure prominently in Assyrian inscriptions. Very appropriately, therefore, the poet calls Assyria itself a lion and asks what has become of his **den.** It seems scarcely necessary to emend **pasture** to **cave.** What, in other words, has become of Nineveh, whither the lion, i.e., the Assyrian army, hastened back where he dwelt without fear, unmolested? The picture is that of the lion hurrying home after a raid. Vs. 12 describes the ferocity, the enormity of Nineveh's depredations—the lion tore and strangled

<table>
<tr><td>

3 Woe to the bloody city! it *is* all full of lies *and* robbery; the prey departeth not;

2 The noise of a whip, and the noise of the rattling of the wheels, and of the prancing horses, and of the jumping chariots.

3 The horseman lifteth up both the bright sword and the glittering spear: and *there is* a multitude of slain, and a great number of carcasses; and *there is* none end of *their* corpses; they stumble upon their corpses:

4 Because of the multitude of the whoredoms of the well-favored harlot, the mistress of witchcrafts, that selleth nations through her whoredoms, and families through her witchcrafts.

</td><td>

3 Woe to the bloody city, all full of lies and booty — no end to the plunder!

2 The crack of whip, and rumble of wheel, galloping horse and bounding chariot!

3 Horsemen charging, flashing sword and glittering spear, hosts of slain, heaps of corpses, dead bodies without end — they stumble over the bodies!

4 And all for the countless harlotries of the harlot, graceful and of deadly charms, who betrays nations with her harlotries, and people with her charms

</td></tr>
</table>

and heaped up his spoils, but now (vs. 13) comes the inevitable end. For "I have caught you," lit., **I am against you** or "I am unto you," might be read "I am thy God." Omit **of hosts,** and in the next line transpose two letters and translate "your horde" (Hebrew **your chariots**). The lion is smoked out. The Lord is offended; he is in control. No longer will Nineveh plunder, no longer will it bear rule. Its population will be burned and put to the sword. Thus the first half of the poem closes, not in prose nor in meter that is rough, but with possibly an extra accent in each half of the last line to round off this particular picture.

E. Woe to the Bloody City (3:1-4)

3:1, 4. The second half of the poem, like the first, depicts in the most vivid terms conditions in Nineveh on the day of her impending fall. But in this chapter the reasons are given at the beginning, vss. 1, 4. She has been ruthlessly oppressive and cruel, and she has shown herself dishonest, unreliable, treacherous, and deceitful. Nineveh, for all her wealth, is rotten at the core; her charms, like those of a harlot, are ephemeral, and the day of her exposure has come. **Mistress of witchcrafts:** "Bewitchingly charming," lit., "mistress of charms," with an evil implication. The metaphor must not be pushed too far. The essential point is that nations and their rulers, like Ahaz in the days of Isaiah, are easily deceived, and come to rue it. There is no necessity for altering the verb **betrays** (lit., "sells") to another such as "warns." **People:** Lit., **families** (cf. Gen. 12:3, "In thee shall all the families [i.e., peoples] of the earth be blessed"; Amos 3:1; *et al.*). Jeremiah's indictment, not of Nineveh, but of Jerusalem (Jer. 5:1-3, 26-29), includes these two basic evils of cruelty and dishonesty. Most of the prophets, in fact, express the Lord's indignation over cruelty (e.g., Amos 1:3, 13; 4:1; 5:11; Hos. 4:2; 6:9; Isa. 5:8; 14:4 ff.; 58:1-14; Ezek. 22:23 ff.; Mic. 2:1-5, 9; *et al.*). And cruelty's handmaid is falsehood (cf. Hos. 4:1 ff.; 7:3; Isa. 10:1; 47:1-15; Mic. 2:11). Oppression earns the enmity of all who have suffered the tyrant's heel. Broken promises destroy the trust which is essential to enduring peace. Those who fail to keep faith with minorities betray an inner weakness which must inevitably be fatal. Logically, then, the description of the attack on Nineveh which results in her utter destruction is resumed in vs. 2.

2-3. The first words of vs. 3, "somersaulting horse," are read more easily before rather than after the last phrase of vs. 2, **and bounding chariot.** The topsy-turvy confusion of the battle is not unlike that described in another classic of Hebrew poetry, the Song of Deborah (Judg. 5:20-22), although here given in greater detail. By the absence of verbs and juxtaposition of generic nouns the poet paints with maximum effectiveness the strokes of the picture. For this brilliant effect the staccato of the rhythm, two accents balanced by two in each half line, is perfect. **Flashing** [or "flaming"]

5 Behold, I *am* against thee, saith the Lord of hosts; and I will discover thy skirts upon thy face, and I will show the nations thy nakedness, and the kingdoms thy shame.

6 And I will cast abominable filth upon thee, and make thee vile, and will set thee as a gazingstock.

7 And it shall come to pass, *that* all they that look upon thee shall flee from thee, and say, Nineveh is laid waste: who will bemoan her? whence shall I seek comforters for thee?

8 Art thou better than populous No, that was situate among the rivers, *that had* the waters round about it, whose rampart *was* the sea, *and* her wall *was* from the sea?

5 Behold I am against you,
  says the Lord of hosts,
  and will lift up your skirts over your
    face;
and I will let nations look on your naked-
    ness
  and kingdoms on your shame.
6 I will throw filth at you
  and treat you with contempt,
  and make you a gazingstock.
7 And all who look on you will shrink from
    you and say,
  Wasted is Nin'eveh; who will bemoan
    her?
  whence shall I seek comforters for her?[n]

8 Are you better than Thebes[o]
  that sat by the Nile,
with water around her,
  her rampart a sea,
  and water her wall?

[n] Gk: Heb *you*
[o] Heb *No-amon*

---

sword: Cf. Gen. 3:24. "Bleeding": Lit., "pierced." Though the word sometimes means dead, here there are two other words to describe the **slain** and **corpses.** In the Kentucky mountains the "killed" are not always "killed dead." A scribe has added a prosy note to the effect that **they** [without antecedent] **stumble upon their** [also grammatically unconnected] **corpses.**

F. The Fall (3:5-19)

5-6. Behold I: The end result of the harlotry is not, however, that the victims revolt, but that the Lord brings judgment. **Am against you:** Lit., "am unto you" (cf. 2:13 and Exeg.). The very fact that the Lord is so sparingly introduced as the speaker in this poem (1:14; 2:13; and here) produces all the greater effect. As in chs. 1–2, so in ch. 3, the statement of what this Deity does is poles removed from the N.T. account of God's character, e.g., in I John. He is represented as throwing the **skirts** of the harlot around her face, exposing her nakedness, casting **filth** at her, and making of her a horrible sight. The brutality of the ancient world (and the modern also?) colored its theology. But the Lord does not literally do these things, even if men do; here is the strongest kind of metaphor to describe the punishment of the wicked city. The language used should not obscure the essential point: the Lord is offended by the crimes of Nineveh, or any city, and brings about the judgment.

7. The note of pity for Nineveh is out of place. A scribe's hand is further betrayed by the introduction, **and it shall come to pass.** It is not strange that an early editor felt the language of vss. 5 ff. needed tempering.

8. In 663 B.C. Ashurbanipal had extended the Assyrian power to its farthest southern limit by the capture of Thebes, the Egyptian capital, about 140 miles north of the first cataract of the Nile and 440 miles from Memphis. Thebes is the Greek name for the Egyptian *Weset* or *Newt,* "the city." Hence **No** in Jer. 46:25; Ezek. 30:14-16, and **No-amon,** "city of Amun," here. For over fourteen hundred years it had been one of the world's leading cities, as modern excavations at Luxor and Karnak abundantly testify. There is a special barb to this question: "Are you, Nineveh, better than this Egyptian capital which your own king took?" It is true that the Nile today does not seem to afford much protection. But allowance must be made for Nahum's poetic

9 Ethiopia and Egypt *were* her strength, and *it was* infinite; Put and Lubim were thy helpers.

10 Yet *was* she carried away, she went into captivity: her young children also were dashed in pieces at the top of all the streets: and they cast lots for her honorable men, and all her great men were bound in chains.

11 Thou also shalt be drunken: thou shalt be hid, thou also shalt seek strength because of the enemy.

12 All thy strongholds *shall be like* fig trees with the first ripe figs: if they be shaken, they shall even fall into the mouth of the eater.

13 Behold, thy people in the midst of

9 Ethiopia was her strength,
　　Egypt too, and that without limit;
　　Put and the Libyans were her*p* helpers.

10 Yet she was carried away,
　　she went into captivity;
　　her little ones were dashed in pieces
　　　at the head of every street;
　　for her honored men lots were cast,
　　　and all her great men were bound in
　　　　chains.

11 You also will be drunken
　　you will be dazed;
　　you will seek
　　　a refuge from the enemy.

12 All your fortresses are like fig trees
　　with first-ripe figs —
　　if shaken they fall
　　　into the mouth of the eater.

13 Behold your troops
　　are women in your midst.

p Gk: Heb *your*

---

license, for the fact that there may have been far more extensive moats and canals guarding Thebes than we know of, and for the general similarity in the situation of the two cities. No other could offer such excellent comparison. The reference to this historical event gives a date after which the poem must have been written.

9. Some slight rearrangement is desirable here. There are three lines in the verse, of which the first is plain: **Ethiopia and Egypt were her strength.** To round out the second, which begins **and that without limit** and there stops in mid-air, move the last word of the verse to this position, read ל for ב, "to her help" (**helpers**); at the end of the third line supply *lāh:* "Put and Lubim were hers" or "on her side."

"Cush" is the term regularly used for Ethiopia, which ruled Egypt at the time Ashurbanipal took Thebes. Help was therefore available from this large country to the south, and from the Libyans on the west. In Gen. 10:6 **Put** is associated with Cush, like Egypt one of the sons of Ham (Canaan is there wrongly joined with these three), and may refer to Somaliland on the Red Sea.

10. Despite all her strength, Thebes **went into captivity,** as Ashurbanipal's account of his campaigns testifies. A Jewish scribe is responsible for the added word "into exile" and for the precise location of the cruelty to the children, **at the head of every street.** The **children** are young, **little ones** (cf. Ps. 8:2). The practices mentioned in this verse were unhappily not uncommon in ancient times, nor was Israel without spot in regard to them.

11. Now comes the *tu quoque.* The parallelism would be improved if the second **thou also** were moved to a point earlier in the verse than the Hebrew has it: "you also will be frenzied," not faint, nor hid, nor dispersed, but out of your senses, beside yourself, like a **drunken** man. For the metaphor of a drunken man to describe one who has drunk of the Lord's punishment cf. Ps. 60:3; Jer. 25:16, 27.

12. Contrast the short, swift phrases of the long poem with this prose of a scribe who writes his leisurely general proposition as a comment on the following verses, which suggested the idea of eating. Nahum does not stop for conditional propositions.

13. The fact that Nineveh's defenders actually put up a good fight, and were not at all like a "pack of women," is evidence that this poem was not written *post eventum.* The second line is overlong: **to your foes** may be an addition.

thee *are* women: the gates of thy land shall be set wide open unto thine enemies: the fire shall devour thy bars.

14 Draw thee waters for the siege, fortify thy strongholds: go into clay, and tread the mortar, make strong the brickkiln.

15 There shall the fire devour thee; the sword shall cut thee off, it shall eat thee up like the cankerworm: make thyself many as the cankerworm, make thyself many as the locusts.

16 Thou hast multiplied thy merchants above the stars of heaven: the cankerworm spoileth, and fleeth away.

17 Thy crowned *are* as the locusts, and thy captains as the great grasshoppers, which camp in the hedges in the cold day, *but* when the sun ariseth they flee away, and their place is not known where they *are*.

18 Thy shepherds slumber, O king of

The gates of your land
   are wide open to your foes;
   fire has devoured your bars.

14 Draw water for the siege,
   strengthen your forts;
go into the clay,
   tread the mortar,
   take hold of the brick mold!
15 There will the fire devour you,
   the sword will cut you off.
   It will devour you like the locust.

Multiply yourselves like the locust,
   multiply like the grasshopper!
16 You increased your merchants
   more than the stars of the heavens.
   The locust spreads its wings and flies
     away.
17 Your princes are like grasshoppers,
   your scribes[q] like clouds of locusts
settling on the fences
   in a day of cold —
when the sun rises, they fly away;
   no one knows where they are.

18 Your shepherds are asleep,
   O king of Assyria;
   your nobles slumber.

[q] Or *marshals*

14. Now begin again the ironical imperatives: Be sure to have enough water for drinking, or possibly, to fill the moats; strengthen the fortifications; many bricks will be necessary; see to the clay; go to all the work of preparing it by trampling, and either **make strong the brickkiln** or **take hold of the brick mold;** all this effort will be of no avail.

15. **Fire** and **sword** will do their work. No matter how numerous the people of Nineveh, though the ruling classes, merchants, princes, and scribes are as plentiful as stars and grasshoppers, the leaders will die (**slumber**) and the people be **scattered.** There are a number of brief additions here: **will devour you like the locust,** perhaps due to dittography. The sense is awkward, for the sword does not cut as the locust devours, subjects are mixed, and there is ungainly repetition.

16. **The locust spreads its wings and flies away** interrupts the good connection between what precedes and what follows with a commonplace remark which anticipates the better-expressed thought of the last line of vs. 17.

17. "Swarm" (**locusts**) is repeated, probably by accident. **In a day of cold** adds a detail to the picture of the scattering of the locusts at sunrise but is not easily fitted into the metrical structure. **Where they are** should probably be combined with the preceding word, **their place.**

18. **King of Assyria** has long been recognized as a gloss; the king is himself a shepherd. **Your,** in the phrase **your shepherds,** refers to the nation, as elsewhere throughout the poem. Under the influence of this gloss the suffixes in vss. 18-19 have been changed from feminine to masculine. **On the mountains** is of a piece with **in a day of cold** in vs. 17.

Assyria: thy nobles shall dwell *in the dust:* thy people is scattered upon the mountains, and no man gathereth *them.*

19 *There is* no healing of thy bruise; thy wound is grievous: all that hear the bruit of thee shall clap the hands over thee: for upon whom hath not thy wickedness passed continually?

Your people are scattered on the mountains
   with none to gather them.
19 There is no assuaging your hurt,
   your wound is grievous.
All who hear the news of you
   clap their hands over you.
For upon whom has not come
   your unceasing evil?

---

19. As in 2:13, there may be here a supplementary accent in each half line to enhance the closing effect. "Festered" is better than **grievous;** the wound is gangrenous, a reason why **there is no healing,** rather than a mere repetition of the statement. The poet here at the end, after foreseeing the death of the leaders of Nineveh and the dispersion of the people, speaks of the sound of joy and relief that will echo through the world, for all nations have been the tyrant's victims.

So closes the long poem, the meter of which, with the two exceptions just mentioned, is regular throughout. We cannot assert that we possess now the work as it left Nahum's pen. But we can be grateful that despite the difficulties due to the addition of the acrostic and other extraneous material at the beginning, the poem has been so wonderfully preserved. It stands as one of the great landmarks of Hebrew literature, and its message is all the clearer for its simplicity: the Lord avenges the ruthlessness of those who put their trust in the sword.

The Book of

HABAKKUK

Introduction and Exegesis by CHARLES L. TAYLOR, JR.

Exposition by HOWARD THURMAN

HABAKKUK

INTRODUCTION

Those chapters in the Book of the Twelve Prophets which are ascribed to Habakkuk give a unified and artistic impression. Ch. 1 asks why God governs the world in such a way as to permit violence, oppression, and other forms of wrong to swallow up the righteous. Ch. 2 offers an answer to that question. Ch. 3, in one of the highest flights of Old Testament poetry, declares that even in adversity the author finds the ready help and strength of God. Fidelity to him brings its own reward. Let material goods vanish: "Yet"—one of the most eloquent conjunctions in all literature—"I will rejoice in the LORD" (3:18).

I. The Diversity of Material

To one who looks beneath the surface, however, there are at least four different kinds of material in this book, sufficiently diverse in character to raise the question whether all of them are the work of the same hand. These are:

(a) The complaint of one representing either Israel or its righteous core who asks God, as many of the psalmists implore him, why the God of right permits the rule of wrong, why there should be such a gulf between faith and fact, and how long the wicked must prevail.

(b) A divine oracle, which declares that a "bitter and hasty" nation, raised up by God, will come with speed and power to overrun the peoples of the earth and plunder them as he pleases.

(c) A series of five woes or threats against this or some other robber, "greedy as hell, insatiable as death," who is guilty of (i) the plunder of many nations, (ii) unscrupulous and selfish building (either in a literal or figurative sense), (iii) sanguinary and unjust oppression, (iv) insulting behavior, and (v) idolatry.

(d) A psalm with attached liturgical notes, similar to hymns of the book of Psalms, in which God comes from beyond the borders of Israel to make himself known, to shake heaven and earth with his portents, to help his people and deliver his "anointed." At the end of this poem is found the rapturous statement, to which reference has been made above, that the man who has found God, even when all that the world commonly calls "goods" are wanting, has found his sufficient strength and joy.

The materials of the last two groups are not difficult to recognize. The woes, though not without their problems, are easily found in 2:5-20, or, strictly speaking, begin at 2:6b. The psalm with the liturgical notes comprises ch. 3. But in 1:2–2:4 there is a confusing alternation of subject matter. Putting the verses together that are alike in content and form, one may divide the psalm that wrestles with God's justice and the prophecy that deals with the robber nations thus:

(A) THE COMPLAINT AND ANSWER

1:2. How long, O LORD, shall I call
    and thou not heed?
  Shall I cry to thee, "Violence!"
    and thou not help?

3. Why dost thou make me see injustice
    and suffer wrong,
  While destruction and violence are before me
    and strife and contention arise?

4. So the law is ineffective
    and justice never comes out,
  For the wicked surround the righteous,
    and so justice comes out distorted.

12a. Art thou not from everlasting, O LORD,
    my holy, immortal God?

13. Thou who hast eyes too pure to see evil
    and canst not tolerate wrong,
  Why dost thou tolerate the treacherous,
    keep still when the wicked swallow the righteous?

2:1. Upon my watch tower I take my stand
    and station myself on my lookout,

And watch to see what he will say to me
and what he will answer to my plea.

2. Then the LORD answered me and said,
"Write the vision
And inscribe it upon tablets
that one may read it at a glance.[1]

3. For the vision is still maturing till its time,
it hastens to its inevitable fulfillment;
If it seem slow, wait for it,
for it surely comes, it will not be late:

4. The unrighteous—his soul swoons within him,
but the righteous shall live by his faithfulness."

(B) THE ORACLE ON THE ROBBER NATION

1:5. Look, you treacherous, and pay heed,
be astounded and dumbfounded,
For I am doing something right now,
you would not believe if told.

6. I am raising up the Chaldeans,
a bitter and hasty nation,
That marches through the breadth of the earth,
to seize dwellings that are not his.

7. Dreadful and terrible is he,
his justice is all his own,

8. And his horses are swifter than leopards,
and fiercer than evening wolves.
His cavalry gallop,
and his cavalry come from afar,
They fly like a vulture swift to devour,

9. all of them come for violence,
The set of their faces is eastward,
and he collects captives like the sand.

10. He it is who derides kings,
and princes are his laughingstock,
He laughs at every fortress
and heaps up dust and takes it.

11. Then he sweeps on like the wind and is gone,
and he makes his strength his god.

12b. O Lord, for judgment thou hast ordained him,
O Rock, for chastisement thou hast established him.

14. And thou makest men like the fish of the sea,
like reptiles without any ruler.

15. He brings them all up on his hook,
he drags them away in his net,
And gathers them in his seine,
and so he laughs and is glad.

16. And so he sacrifices to his net
and burns incense to his seine,
Because by them his ration is fat
and his food is rich.

17. Therefore he draws his sword continually,
to slay nations without mercy.

For justification regarding omissions, alterations in the text, and departure from customary
translations see the Exegesis on these passages.

II. The Scroll from 'Ain Feshkha

Further light has been shed on Habakkuk
by the discovery in 1947-48, in a cave near the
Dead Sea, of a manuscript containing the text
of chs. 1–2, together with a commentary upon

[1] Colloquially, "on the run."

these chapters "which employs midrashic principles of exegesis," that is, attempts to apply
the text to the reader's own time in an edifying
way.[2] While scholars are still debating the age
of this document,[3] the evidence from comparison with other ancient manuscripts, corrobo-
rated by that from the pottery in the cave
where the manuscript was found, points toward a date in the first century B.C. Even if
those scholars are right who think that the
document was written considerably later, it is
still likely to be our oldest witness to the text
of Habakkuk, perhaps by many centuries. Very
significantly, it does not contain ch. 3, and because the end of the scroll was wound inside,
there is no possibility that ch. 3 could have
been accidentally torn off. The view long held
by many students of Habakkuk that ch. 3 was
not a part of the original work thus receives
noteworthy support.

Apparently the manuscript was the property
of a sect centering in the desert country west of
the Dead Sea, which was organized in a manner
not unlike the earliest Christian monastic
orders. In its use of Habakkuk it quoted the
Hebrew text of chs. 1–2, a verse or two at a
time, then appended a word or phrase such as
"its meaning" or "its meaning concerning," following which it made the application to the
contemporary situation. To cite but two examples, the midrash on 1:10 (col. 4, ll. 5-9)
reads: "Its meaning concerns the Chittiim who
scorn the fortresses of the people and with
ridicule laugh at them" and on 1:17 (col. 6,
l. 10), "Its meaning concerns the Chittiim who
destroy many with the sword." These two illustrations indicate part of the importance of this
scroll. From I Macc. 1:1 ("Philip, . . . who came
out of the land of Chittim") and 8:5 ("Philip,
and Perseus, king of Chittim"), it appears that
the Jews of the Greek period called the Mace-

[2] William H. Brownlee, "Further Light on Habakkuk,"
Bulletin of the American Schools of Oriental Research,
No. 114 (Apr., 1949), pp. 9-10. The details of this
extraordinary find and discussion of its importance may
be studied in the bulletins of the American Schools of
Oriental Research, beginning with that for October,
1948 (No. 111), and in the *Biblical Archaeologist*, XI
(1948), 45-61; XII (1949), 26-46, 54-68. See especially
Brownlee, "The Jerusalem Habakkuk Scroll," *Bulletin
of the American Schools of Oriental Research*, No. 112
(Dec., 1948), pp. 8-18.

[3] E.g., cf. E. R. Lacheman, "A Matter of Method in
Hebrew Paleography," *Jewish Quarterly Review*, XL
(1949-50), 15-39; W. F. Albright, "Are the 'Ain Feshkha
Scrolls a Hoax?" *ibid.*, pp. 41-49; Millar Burrows, "A
Note on the Recently Discovered Manuscripts," *ibid.*,
pp. 51-56; S. Zeitlin, "The Alleged Antiquity of the
Scrolls," *ibid.*, pp. 57-78. See also Zeitlin, "'A Commen-
tary on the Book of Habakkuk' Important Discovery or
Hoax?" *ibid.*, XXXIX (1948-49), 235-47, and S. A.
Birnbaum, "The Date of the Habakkuk Cave Scroll,"
Journal of Biblical Literature, LXVIII (1949), 161-68.

donians Chittim or Chittiim (Chittites). Another scroll, found in the same cave with the Habakkuk manuscript, speaks of the Chittites of Assyria and the Chittites of Egypt, by which it designates the Seleucids and Ptolemies.[4] At an early time therefore, probably in the century before the Christian Era, Jews interpreted Habakkuk to refer to the Greeks; nevertheless the text on which the comment is made bears valuable witness to the reading "Chaldeans" in 1:6, where some modern scholars have wished to substitute Chittim. On the other hand, the second example cited justifies the scholars who, following the Coptic version and one Greek manuscript, have conjectured "sword" for "net" in 1:17. Further divergences from the standard Hebrew text will appear in the Exegesis. Many of them are of minor significance, such as the inclusion or omission of a conjunction or preposition, an article or an interrogatory particle, a pronoun or sometimes even a verb or noun. Here it will be sufficient to call attention to one or two additional important variants. In 2:5, for "wine is treacherous," the 'Ain Feshkha manuscript reads "wealth is treacherous" (hôn for hayyáyin), and in 1:11, where commentators have long suspected the word "and be guilty," this document gives "this man makes [wayyāsem for we'āshēm] his strength his god." At the same time, very curiously, it refers in the comment on that verse to "the house of guilt." Was the author of the commentary aware of another text besides the one before him?[5] Perhaps enough has been said to indicate the interest and value of this new spur to the study of Habakkuk.

III. Origin, Integrity, and Date

Certain questions require an answer before any understanding of this book is possible. Who is responsible for the destruction and violence alluded to in chs. 1–2? Is the trouble internal or external; does the prophet complain in 1:2-4, 13 of evils caused by oppressors within his own nation or without? Is this a party matter or an international problem? Are the righteous the same in 1:4 and 1:13, and are the treacherous the same in 1:13; 2:5, and (if the Hebrew is changed as it was above) in 1:5? If this treacherous dealer is a nation other than Israel, which is it?

Assuming that the reading "Chaldeans" in

1:6 is right, whom are they to punish? Judah or another? Why does God raise them up? "For violence"? In order to catch men "in his net"? Will the Chaldeans then worship a material object instead of the God who empowered them? In other words, do those who are called to take vengeance on the tyrant themselves become the tyrant? Does the hammer become the anvil? Against whom are the woes of 2:5-20 directed? Are there any indications of date for the whole of chs. 1–2, or at least for various parts?

While the solutions to these problems are almost as numerous as the scholars who write about them, they may for convenience be grouped into five main types.[6]

(a) Chs. 1–2 constitute a unified dialogue, the work of one man, although he may have spaced his utterances over a period of a dozen years. In 1:2-4, his first complaint, written in the early part of Jehoiakim's reign (i.e., ca. 608-605 B.C.), Habakkuk speaks not of Judah's suffering under a foreign power but of its own corrupt morals. In 1:5-11 comes God's first response, written soon after the Battle of Carchemish[7] in 605; God is rousing the Chaldeans to punish the evil in Judah. But these Chaldeans create more problems than they solve. Their dealings with the nations they conquer lead the prophet to renew his complaint in 1:12-17, a passage which does not continue 1:2-4 but deals with a different topic—the danger which impends because of Chaldean cruelty. To this second complaint 2:1-4 is God's new response—this time not "I will raise up the Chaldeans," but "The just shall live by his faithfulness." Finally, shortly after 597, when this new overlord has taken Jerusalem and deported its leading classes, the prophet delivers against him the woes of 2:5-20, although he cannot mention the Chaldeans by name because they are in power in his land.[8]

(b) Other scholars consider that the strictures of 1:14-17; 2:5-20 do not suit the Chal-

---

[4] This terminology is derived from an interpretation of Num. 24:24. Cf. H. L. Ginsberg, "The Hebrew University Scrolls from the Sectarian Cache," *Bulletin of the American Schools of Oriental Research*, No. 112 (Dec., 1948), pp. 19-23.

[5] Similarly in 2:16 the 'Ain Feshkha reading agrees with the Greek against the Hebrew, but the commentary is based upon the latter!

[6] For other views, not to be considered here, see Otto Happel, *Das Buch des Propheten Habakuk* (Würzberg: Andreas Göbel, 1900), who dates the prophet about 170; Willy Staerk, "Zu Habakuk 1:5-11," *Zeitschrift für die alttestamentliche Wissenschaft*, LI (1933), 1-28, who regards the invaders as apocalyptic horsemen; and E. Balla, in *Die Religion in Geschichte und Gegenwart* (2nd ed.; Tübingen: J. C. B. Mohr, 1928), II, 1556-57, who finds in Habakkuk a prophetic liturgy.

[7] For the historical background of this period see Intro. to Zephaniah.

[8] This is the argument of W. W. Cannon, "The Integrity of Habakkuk," *Zeitschrift für die alttestamentliche Wissenschaft*, XLIII (1925), 62-90. Cf. S. R. Driver, *An Introduction to the Literature of the Old Testament* (rev. ed.; New York: Charles Scribner's Sons, 1913), pp. 337-40. Driver calls this the "usual" explanation of the book.

deans, but the Assyrians. The law that is ineffective (1:4) is the Deuteronomic Code. The time is about 615 B.C. Judah has not yet had time to know the Chaldean cruelty. It was Assyria that "fished up" various nations (1:14-16) to build its empire, to which the Chaldeans became with a minimum of struggle the "smiling heir." Hence the treacherous (1:13, 2:5) are the Assyrians, and 1:2-4 refers to an external enemy, not to a party within righteous Judah. It is even possible that in 1:11 the original reading of the word translated by the RSV "guilty men," for which the 'Ain Feshkha Scroll reads "and he makes," was not we'āshēm or wayyāsem but 'ashshûr, Assyria. Habakkuk, then, deals with two nations beyond the borders of Judah. The key to the problem of the book is to recognize that 1:12 follows 1:4, and that 1:5-11 has been displaced from its proper position after 2:4. Otherwise the oracle which finally follows the extended introduction (2:1-3) is the very meager one verse, 2:4. The displacement of 1:5-11 from its position after 2:4 was due to the fact that the Chaldeans failed to live up to expectations, and turned out to be tyrants themselves. An editor revised this passage about the nation whose role was to have been that of redeemer into condemnation of the oppressor, soon to be destroyed.[9]

(c) Another solution is to recognize two stages in the composition of these chapters. Hab. 1:5-10 and perhaps 1:14-17 in an earlier form are an anonymous prophecy from about 603 B.C. The Chaldeans at that time were expected to be the Lord's agents to restore law and order in Judah. But Habakkuk (or the author given this nickname) lived and wrote about 555-549, just before the coming of Cyrus and the Persians, while there was still hope of a general revolt against the Chaldean power. He quoted the earlier oracle, adapted it to the needs of his own situation, and used it "as the theme of his mournful reflections on the triumph of proud nations."[10]

(d) Still another group of scholars regards Habakkuk as a "meditation on the conquests of Alexander the Great and his armies in Asia"[11] between 334 and 331, before the Battle of Arbela in the latter year but after Alexander's appearance in Palestine. The book is "manifestly a unit and a carefully construed composition from beginning to end."[12] In support of this theory, which at first sight may seem startling, it is urged that Habakkuk presupposes well-established Judaism. The terms "law," "justice," "my Holy One" applied to God (1:12; 3:3), for example, point toward the fourth or third century, when much of the prophetic literature was collected and redacted. The Chaldeans came slowly, not as a surprise, not as furious riders, not as ruthless destroyers, whereas the descriptions of the insatiable marauder fit the Macedonians exactly. Why should the faces of any great power save Alexander's be set "eastward," or "toward the east" (1:9)? One proposal goes so far as to read in this verse, "From Gomer [that is, Cappadocia,] they marched toward the east." The heaping up of dust to take the fortress refers to the siege of Tyre (1:10). Who is the proud warrior who does not keep at home (2:5) if not Alexander? Who came to possess dwelling places not his (1:6; 2:6)? The plunder of Palestine was an old story to Mesopotamian powers. Therefore in 1:6 one should read "Chittim," a term for the Macedonians, rather than "Chaldeans," and in 2:5, for "wine" (hayyáyin), substitute the regular word for "the Greeks" (hayyewāni) or "Greece" (yāwān).[13]

(e) Is there still another way of regarding Habakkuk that will take into account the evidence that has led each of the four groups of scholars just described to conclusions that differ so radically? There are a few previously formed judgments which receive confirmation from the 'Ain Feshkha scroll. (i) Ch. 3 is not a part of the original work, but must be considered separately. While there is no positive evidence that another than Habakkuk was the author of that chapter, the theory that Habakkuk was a temple prophet and poet is seriously weakened.[14] Similarly, there is little warrant for

Das Buch Habakuk (Tübingen: J. C. B. Mohr, 1906), and The Twelve Prophets (tr. Archibald Duff; London: A. & C. Black, 1912), pp. 221-32.

[12] Torrey, "Alexander the Great in the Old Testament Prophecies," in Karl Budde, ed., Karl Marti zum siebsten Geburtstage (Giessen: A. Töpelmann, 1925; "Beihefte zur Zeitschrift für die alttestamentliche Wissenschaft"), p. 283.

[13] Cf. Duhm, Habakuk and The Twelve Prophets; Torrey, "Alexander the Great in O.T. Prophecies," p. 283.

[14] It is unnecessary to collect here the evidence by which scholars arrived at this previous judgment. The picture of a world judgment (3:12) and the reference to a Messiah (3:13), among other indications, fit a time much later than 600 B.C.

[9] For this view cf. Karl Budde, article "Habakkuk," in Encyclopedia Biblica, ed. T. K. Cheyne and J. Sutherland Black (New York: The Macmillan Co., 1901), II, 1921-28, and "Problems of the Prophetic Literature, II, Habakkuk," The Expositor, Ser. 5, I (1895), 372-85; also George Adam Smith, The Book of the Twelve Prophets (rev. ed.; New York: Harper & Bros., 1928), II, 117-26.

[10] So Adolphe Lods, The Prophets and the Rise of Judaism (tr. S. H. Hooke; New York: E. P. Dutton & Co., 1937), p. 165.

[11] C. C. Torrey, The Second Isaiah (New York: Charles Scribner's Sons, 1928), p. 96; cf. Bernhard Duhm,

putting ch. 3 between ch. 1 and ch. 2.[15] (ii) The reading Chaldeans in 1:6 seems genuine. If Chittim had been the original reading, then it was changed to Chaldeans and interpreted as Chittim. But it is more likely that the authors of the 'Ain Feshkha commentary were simply trying to interpret an ancient text in terms of their own day, as doubtless the Jews did earlier in the Greek period and Jews and Christians have done ever since. (iii) The text of Habakkuk was more or less fluid even up to the time the 'Ain Feshkha scroll was written, and additions, subtractions, and alterations were possible from the time of composition for several centuries; thus 2:14 is a quotation from Isa. 11:9, while 2:13 is similar to Jer. 51:58, and 2:12 seems to know Mic. 3:10. There are other verses in the series of woes, 2:5-20, which can hardly have been written in the seventh or sixth centuries B.C., for example, vss. 18-20. The words "how much more" which introduce 2:5 may mean in effect, "How much worse is the oppressing nation in our day than the Chaldeans ever were," and "the Greeks" or "Greece" may be the word for which both "wine" and "wealth" ('Ain Feshkha) are substitutes; "oppressor" is a modern guess. It would appear that 2:5 and 2:6a, up to the word "woe," are an editor's introduction to the material he has compiled, for the word "taunt" (2:6) suggests that the tyrant has fallen, while the content of the woes makes clear that the retribution is still to come. In 2:6a prose takes the place of poetry. Moreover, these woes imply that the tyrant has been in power for a long time, in contrast to 1:6, which depicts the Chaldeans as rising to prominence. A long process of compilation is discernible in many of the books of the Old Testament; so also it is probable here in Habakkuk.

The following, then, is an outline of the development of the book in four principal stages:

(a) About 600 B.C. a prophet called Habakkuk delivered an oracle on the Chaldeans' rise to power (1:6-11, 14-17), much as Isaiah had interpreted the Assyrian advance as God's judgment on Judah (Isa. 5:26-29; 10:5-9).[16]

(b) An editor of the period 500-200 B.C. incorporated with this oracle a psalm (1:2-4, 12a, 13; 2:1-4) which he thought appropriate.

The psalm deals not with foreign oppression, or at least not with external pressure alone, but with internal strife, disregard of the developed Jewish law, and injustice. It seems at one time to have stood on the margin of the oracle, and then to have been copied before, in the middle, and after that work. To the question "Why take these verses from the Habakkuk of 600 B.C.?" the answer, in the words of so conservative a scholar as A. B. Davidson, is: "If the date of Habakkuk had to be fixed from the circle of his ideas alone, he might be assigned to the end of the Exile or later."[17] The problem of theodicy, the traitors surrounding the righteous, the vision hastening to its appointed time, the term "my Holy One," are a few of the evidences which Davidson may have had in mind.

(c) Very likely in the Greek period another or possibly the same editor added the woes of 2:6b-20, to which he prefixed 2:5-6a. It is possible that in part he used earlier writings of which we are not aware, although we do see how he quoted from Isaiah, Jeremiah, and Micah to build 2:12-14. The verses dealing with idols, 2:18-19, indicate familiarity with the ideas of such late passages as Isa. 44:9-20 and Jer. 10:1-16. The introduction of the five sections (2:6-19) with the word "woe" is patterned after Isa. 5:8-23; 10:1-4.

(d) Finally, the "prayer" or psalm (ch. 3) was added as a further answer to the problem posed in ch. 1. This position is essentially that of Karl Marti,[18] except that he dates the woes around 540 B.C. If it is objected that such a view leaves too little to Habakkuk, the point is not whether that prophet wrote much or not so much, but what from the evidence appears to account best for the book as we now have it. A few matters remain to be clarified, e.g., why "the set of their faces is eastward." If the text was not fixed until toward the end of the pre-Christian era, minor changes could occur and probably did alter the book in the direction of the new interpretations of it (see Exeg., ad loc.).

IV. Religious Teaching

While Habakkuk is chiefly remembered for a few oft-quoted verses such as "the just shall live by his faith" (2:4) and "the LORD is in his holy temple: let all the earth keep silence before him" (2:20), there is a wealth of religious nourishment in this brief book.[19]

---

[15] Julius A. Bewer, *The Literature of the Old Testament in Its Historical Development* (rev. ed.; New York: Columbia University Press, 1933), p. 142.

[16] Hab. 1:5 is probably an introductory verse supplied by an editor to make a good joint. Just as later hands have touched up Isa. 10, where, e.g., vss. 10-12, 15b, are editorial, so it is possible that later animus against the Chaldeans has crept into Hab. 1, e.g., vss. 5, 17 (see Exeg. on vs. 15).

[17] *The Books of Nahum, Habakkuk and Zephaniah* (Cambridge: Cambridge University Press, 1920; "Cambridge Bible"), p. 63.

[18] *Das Dodekapropheton* (Tübingen: J. C. B. Mohr, 1904; "Kurzer Hand-Commentar zum Alten Testament").

[19] For a valuable brief discussion of this subject see Raymond Calkins, *The Modern Message of the Minor Prophets* (New York: Harper & Bros., 1947).

The teaching of the prophetic oracle on the Chaldeans is not unlike that of Isa. 10:5. The mighty nation which seems to wreak such havoc in the world is the scourge of God. Thus the sting is drawn from the disaster which overtakes Judah, when men realize that the power which seems so evil is an instrument by which the divine will to good is being accomplished.

In the psalmlike material of chs. 1–2 the fairness of God's government of the world is questioned in words which have become classic (1:13). Technically this problem is known as the problem of theodicy. Throughout the ages man ponders why a good God, who also controls the world, should allow the righteous to suffer and the evil to prosper. Another expression of similar complaint appears in Jer. 12:1, although there the question is couched in more personal and less general terms. The poem of Job as well as various psalms deal with the subject, among them Pss. 37; 49, and best of all, Ps. 73. All these writings indicate a capacity for reflection and speculation which is not characteristic of early Israel. The genius of Israel, and of Christianity too, is practical rather than philosophical. The Christian finds the supreme answer to the problem in the Cross. There the cry is still "My God, my God, why hast thou forsaken me?" In the outcome God turned the worst that man could do to a good end. Similarly, the sufferings of the Jews, so great beyond all calculation, have been inseparable from the contribution which that nation, alone surviving while great powers that oppressed it have waxed and waned, has made to mankind. Why? The answer is only dimly seen even after a score of centuries. At the end of Job, it would seem that God is more willing to support the sufferer in his honest questioning against the friends who would silence him than to countenance their arguments. The faith that emerges from a struggle with doubt rests on firmer foundations than blind acceptance.

The answer given in Hab. 2:4 is that the just shall live by being faithful. This does not solve the problem, but it clearly is a part of the right response to it. Hold steady! Maintain integrity! Remember that the vision is hastening to its inevitable fulfillment and will not be late. In God's good time, not man's, all is well and will be well. Therefore be ready, be attentive, be on the watch for whatever the Lord chooses to reveal. Fidelity through good or ill until that time shall fully come is the mark of every "just" man.

The author of the woes declares a truth of permanent importance—that evil carries in it the seeds of its own destruction. Greed and pride will make "the stone . . . cry out from the wall" (2:11); the cup that the tyrant made quaff, he too shall drink. There is justice even among nations, for the ruler who prides himself on his nest perched high above the reach of harm is in special danger. Moreover, "The earth, the woods, and the beasts, no less than man, have rights; there is nothing that exists which is not moral; wanton excess . . . recoils on the head of the perpetrator." [20]

Finally, the poem of ch. 3 concludes this little book with its expression of thanksgiving, joy, faith, and trust. What William Temple wrote of the author of Ps. 73 applies also to him who gave the world the concluding verses of Hab. 3:

In his fellowship with God he has found that nothing matters in comparison with that fellowship. He had been perplexed that the ungodly should prosper, and almost thought of throwing in his lot with them. But now he knows that, however great their possessions, they are truly destitute, while the man who has found fellowship with God is rich though he possesses nothing. That is the real solution—not an answer to the riddle, but the attainment of a state of mind in which there is no desire to ask it.[21]

V. Outline of Contents

I. Why does God permit tyrannical injustice? (1:1-17)
  A. Title (1:1)
  B. First series of questions (1:2-4)
  C. The bitter and hasty nation (1:5-11)
  D. Second series of questions (1:12-17)
II. The righteous shall live by his faithfulness (2:1-20)
  A. The answer from the tower (2:1-4)
  B. Introduction to the woes (2:5-6a)
  C. The self-destructiveness of tyranny (2:6b-20)
    1. First woe (2:6b-8)
    2. Second woe (2:9-11)
    3. Third woe (2:12-14, 17)
    4. Fourth woe (2:15-16)
    5. Fifth woe (2:18-20)
III. A psalm of praise (3:1-15)
  A. Title (3:1)
  B. Introduction (3:2)
  C. Theophany (3:3-15)
  D. Joy despite adversity (3:16-19)

VI. Selected Bibliography

ALBRIGHT, W. F. "The Psalm of Habakkuk," in Rowley, H. H., ed. *Studies in Old Testament Prophecy*. New York: Charles Scribner's Sons, 1950. Pp. 1-18.

DAVIDSON, A. B. *The Books of Nahum, Habakkuk and Zephaniah* ("Cambridge Bible"). Cambridge: Cambridge University Press, 1920.

[20] Davidson, *op. cit.*, p. 83.
[21] *Nature, Man and God* (London: Macmillan & Co., 1934), p. 43.

DRIVER, S. R., ed. *The Minor Prophets* ("New Century Bible"). New York: Oxford University Press, 1906. Vol. II.

HORST, FRIEDRICH. *Die zwölf kleinen Propheten Nahum bis Maleachi* ("Handbuch zum Alten Testament"). Tübingen: J. C. B. Mohr, 1938.

HUMBERT, PAUL. *Problèmes du livre d'Habacuc.* Neuchâtel: Secrétariat de l'Université, 1944.

IRWIN, W. A. "The Psalm of Habakkuk," *Journal of Near Eastern Studies,* I (1942), 10-40.

ROWLEY, H. H. *The Zadokite Fragments and the Dead Sea Scrolls.* Oxford: Blackwell, 1952.

SMITH, GEORGE ADAM. *The Book of the Twelve Prophets.* Rev. ed. New York: Harper & Bros., 1928. Vol. II.

SMITH, J. M. P., WARD, W. H., and BEWER, JULIUS A., *A Critical and Exegetical Commentary on Micah, Zephaniah, Nahum, Habakkuk, Obadiah and Joel* ("International Critical Commentary"). New York: Charles Scribner's Sons, 1911.

HABAKKUK

TEXT, EXEGESIS, AND EXPOSITION

1 The burden which Habakkuk the prophet did see.

2 O LORD, how long shall I cry, and thou will not hear! *even* cry out unto thee *of* violence, and thou wilt not save!

1 The oracle of God which Habak'kuk the prophet saw.

2 O LORD, how long shall I cry for help,
and thou wilt not hear?
Or cry to thee "Violence!"
and thou wilt not save?

I. WHY DOES GOD PERMIT TYRANNICAL INJUSTICE? (1:1-17)

1:1. Except for what may be deduced from this book and for late legends, nothing is known of **Habakkuk.** In Assyrian the word is the name of a plant. It may be only a nickname. Typical of the legendary material is the story found in Bel and the Dragon, vss. 33-39, where the angel of the Lord bids Habakkuk carry his dinner to Daniel in Babylon in the lion's den. When Habakkuk replies that he never saw Babylon and does not know where the den is, the angel lifts him by his hair, carries him thither, and returns him to his place.

The title is the work of an editor. **Burden** is a technical term for an **oracle** or prophecy, here almost the equivalent of vision or divine revelation. **The prophet** is added not so much to distinguish this Habakkuk from another, for the name is not otherwise known, as to honor him, in the way in which editors add "the prophet" to Jeremiah's name over and over again.

B. FIRST SERIES OF QUESTIONS (1:2-4)

2-4. Although these verses are considered by some scholars as an editor's preface, they are here regarded as the first part of a psalmlike appeal to God for an explanation of his apparent injustice. The problem receives its fullest treatment in the O.T. in

---

1:2a. None to Help.—Habakkuk opens with a cry which reveals the prophet's mood of despair. The prayer experience must ever take into account the times of dryness, of denials, of emptiness. The reasons for this are numerous. It may be due to scattered thoughts or attachment to plans, ideas, or experiences that break the divine accord; or to bad timing, when the mood of prayer is strangely alien to the spirit; or

to the movement of the spirit of God in a manner unpredictable and strange. It is instructive that the mystics, despite their insistence upon the necessity of spiritual disciplines or exercises, are careful to point out that the exercises themselves do not guarantee the "coming of the spirit" or an awareness of the Presence. Always undergirding prayer there must be an attitude of trust and confidence that

3 Why dost thou show me iniquity, and cause *me* to behold grievance? for spoiling and violence *are* before me: and there are *that* raise up strife and contention.

4 Therefore the law is slacked, and judg-

3 Why dost thou make me see wrongs
    and look upon trouble?
Destruction and violence are before me;
    strife and contention arise.
4 So the law is slacked
    and justice never goes forth.

---

the book of Job, but is also raised in Jeremiah (e.g., 12:1) and in a number of psalms (e.g., Ps. 73; cf. Intro., p. 978). **How long** is the cry of the psalmist in Pss. 13:1; 74:10; 79:5; 89:46; 94:3; the souls "slain for the word of God" repeat it in Rev. 6:9-10. Several of these psalms are among the latest in the Psalter, reflecting the struggles of the Hellenistic age between the pious who were jealous for the law and the backsliders who, siding with the Hellenizing rulers, threatened the very existence of Judaism. **Destruction and violence, strife and contention,** while not confined to one period of Jewish history, point on the whole to the Greek period (333-63 B.C.), especially because **the law is slacked** and **the wicked surround the righteous.** It is doubtful whether the righteous and wicked would be spoken of in this way (and **the law** also) in the period *ca.* 600 B.C.

3. There is disagreement among the versions as to the identity of him who is to **look upon trouble** (better than "perverseness"), God (Hebrew) or the writer (Syriac and Aramaic Targ.). The former is the more likely reading (cf. vs. 13, where the word here translated **trouble** is rendered "wrong"). In the last line of this verse, **strife and contention arise,** the Hebrew has a second verb, "and there is," but metrically it is superfluous, and the other verb, **arise,** may also be an addition.

4. **The law** is probably not merely the content of the divine revelation, but that revelation embodied in statutory form in the Pentateuch. **Justice** (*mishpāṭ*), originally

---

submits one's total enterprise to the will and the mind of God. But sometimes the urgency is so great, the pain growing out of the need so overwhelming, that the anguish and frustration spill over into a cry which in itself becomes a judgment and a startled accusation! **How long shall I cry, and thou wilt not hear?**

2b. Finding Words for It.—Often there is great relief in being able to put into words the quality or the very nuance of need and suffering. To suffer in dumb silence, to be able to find no word capable of voicing what is being experienced, seems degrading to the self because it pushes the individual back into a vast feeling continuum from which he has emerged into a personality, self-conscious and self-aware. Man was a feeling creature long before he was a thinking creature. The mind is younger than the body and younger than the emotions. When we are able to be articulate it means that detachment from immediate experience, however great, has been achieved. A context of objectivity has been established, from within which the individual is able to look on his experience and name it. This seems to characterize the divine act always. When the individual is thus able to voice his profoundest feelings, he sees himself quite unconsciously presenting God with a compulsion on his behalf. There is added challenge in the words if they name what is happening.

3. The Divine Context.—The idea that God is responsible for ills in life is a great safety valve for the spirit of man. And yet it is much more. It springs out of a deeper insight: at long last there must be no distinction between the God of life and the God of religion. All events in life take place somehow within the divine context. The tendency to fix responsibility is inescapable. If responsibility for ills can be pinned down, then the possibility of attacking and uprooting them is very real. This possibility is grounded in the profound confidence that a structure of moral integrity bottoms all of life, that such a structure is basic in the totality of all experience. Things do not merely happen; they are a part of some kind of rationale. If the rationale can be tracked down and understood, then the living experience, however terrible, makes sense. Yet even when that is not possible, one cannot down the confidence that the logic of all ills is knowable. A man traces them as far as he can, until at last he seeks no longer to understand the ills but rather to understand God's understanding. Lacking this, he rests himself in the assurance of God's presence and sovereignty in him and in life about him. He sees the travail of his own soul and is satisfied (cf. 2:20).

4. What Is the Matter?—The plaint of the prophet that **the law is slacked** has a familiar ring. The lines have an undertone of self-pity,

ment doth never go forth: for the wicked doth compass about the righteous; therefore wrong judgment proceedeth.

5 ¶ Behold ye among the heathen, and regard, and wonder marvelously: for I will work a work in your days, *which* ye will not believe, though it be told *you*.

For the wicked surround the righteous,
  so justice goes forth perverted.

5 Look among the nations, and see;
  wonder and be astounded.
For I am doing a work in your days
  that you would not believe if told.

---

established practice or custom, here as in Ps. 119 is another word for that law which is slacked, i.e., numb, frozen, ineffectual, and **never goes forth,** does not "come out"— "nothing comes out right"; or when a semblance of justice is practiced, it is **perverted,** twisted, distorted. The commandments of the Pentateuch, in other words, are not kept, because **the wicked surround** [or "circumvent"] **the righteous.** There is obviously a close connection between vs. 4 and vs. 13. For **surround** the LXX has "overpower." It is possible that the last two lines of vs. 4, or even the whole verse, are an embellishment to the preceding by a later hand. Not infrequently glosses use *'al-kēn,* **so,** "therefore" (e.g., Isa. 5:13, 14, 24, 25).

C. The Bitter and Hasty Nation (1:5-11)

The first part of the prophetic oracle. Some scholars would begin the book with it, others transpose it to a point after 2:4. Vs. 5, however, may not be the original introduction, but a verse supplied by the editor who combined the psalmlike material with vss. 6-11 in order to form a suitable transition.

5-6. For בגוים, **among the nations,** the LXX reads בוגדים, "despisers," "treacherous ones," "traitors," the equivalent of the word for "faithless men" used in vs. 13; 2:5.

---

which is one of the most natural reactions of those subjected to injustice. The orderly process seems to be ever at the mercy of the disorderly. Weeds do not have to be cultivated, but vegetables must be. Those things in life which make for disintegration seem ever alert, taking advantage of every situation to turn it to their account.

The wicked do prosper. A casual observation suggests that this is true because of sin in human life. But the basic problem remains untouched, for the crux of the issue is not merely the fact of wickedness and injustice in life, rather the supervitality which they always seem to possess. The "evilness" of evil seems to be more dynamic and energizing than the "goodness" of good. When we are ill with tonsillitis we seek to amuse ourselves by trying to remember how we felt when we did not have tonsillitis; but we cannot do it.

The behavior of the wicked discloses an intensity of loyalty which is indeed striking. One seems to discover among them the general recognition that the stakes are very high and nothing less than a binding devotion will suffice. There is an efficiency and an intelligence about deliberate injustice that yields power even though it may be short lived. Whereas the behavior of the righteous often appears to be weak, indecisive, and uncertain. They seem to find it very difficult to make up their minds and

to define their terms. The assumption that there is something about goodness that is so inherently superior to evil that it is not necessary to "work at" goodness is thoroughly gratuitous.

Note, however, that the ground rules for righteousness and for unrighteousness are the same. Whatever it is that causes strawberries to grow causes poison ivy to grow, and for exactly the same reasons. When the conditions for growth have been met, then growth follows automatically. The fact that the former is a delight and the latter is a disorder is beside the point. But this is not the whole story. If both are sustained by the same energies and guaranteed by the same vitality, then we are faced with a problem that cuts deeper than the conflict between righteousness and unrighteousness. There must be a unity deeper than the area of conflict. This unity is in God, so that back of all the outcrying against evil, back of all protests, lies the conviction that rejects evil as ultimate. This assumption is present all through the utterances of Habakkuk. The deep confidence that life will not finally sustain evil is a part of the distilled wisdom of the race, and the door of hope through which the generations have passed into the city of God.

5-17. *The Dimensions of Moral Behavior.*— This entire section calls attention to a very important insight concerning human history.

6 For, lo, I raise up the Chaldeans, *that* bitter and hasty nation, which shall march through the breadth of the land, to possess the dwelling places *that are* not theirs.

7 They *are* terrible and dreadful: their judgment and their dignity shall proceed of themselves.

8 Their horses also are swifter than the leopards, and are more fierce than the evening wolves: and their horsemen shall spread themselves, and their horsemen shall come from far; they shall fly as the eagle *that* hasteth to eat.

6 For lo, I am rousing the Chalde'ans,
    that bitter and hasty nation,
who march through the breadth of the
    earth,
    to seize habitations not their own.
7 Dread and terrible are they;
    their justice and dignity proceed from
    themselves.
8 Their horses are swifter than leopards,
    more fierce than the evening wolves;
    their horsemen press proudly on.
Yea, their horsemen come from afar;
    they fly like an eagle swift to devour.

Wonder and be astounded: In Hebrew two forms of the same verb; similarity in sound may be reproduced in English by "shudder and be shocked." The Hebrew lacks the pronoun **I** with **am doing** or "on the point of doing." As has been noted above (see Intro., pp. 974-75), the scroll from the 'Ain Feshkha cave supports the reading **Chaldeans** in vs. 6. Some Greek MSS have not only **Chaldeans** but "warriors," for which several explanations may be given. (*a*) Was **Chaldeans** objectionable, giving rise to a substitute now found together with it? (*b*) Was "warriors" too general a reading, needing to be defined by Chaldeans—but what motive would there be for using the particular word **Chaldeans?** (*c*) Are both **Chaldeans** and "warriors" substitutes for some other word? Or (*d*), because the line could be read in good metrical form without **Chaldeans,** are we dealing here with a word originally on the margin? The first of these four views governs the account given in the Intro. of the composition of this book. For **bitter and hasty** one is tempted to translate "rough and ready." Despite the assertion that these terms fit the armies of Alexander better than the Chaldeans, and that the Greeks especially marched **through the breadth of the earth,** and seized **habitations not their own,** the Chaldeans could well be so described. **Not their own:** Hebrew, "not his"; the singular pronoun is used also in vss. 7, 8, 10, 11, 12*b*. The verbs in vs. 9, **come** and **gather,** are also singular. The ideas of this verse are reproduced in 2:5-6.

7-8. Their . . . dignity is a free translation of "his lifting up" (or read "destruction"?). The half line is metrically too long; "lifting up" may be omitted without violence to the sense, which is that the subject is a law unto himself, his justice is all his own—i.e., he acknowledges no higher law, or as vs. 11 says, makes his might his god. The **evening wolves** of vs. 8 become in Greek "Arabian wolves"; the two words look alike in Hebrew. Jeremiah also expects whirlwind chariots and "horses . . . swifter than eagles" (Jer. 4:13). The **eagle** is, strictly speaking, a vulture. There is manifest confusion in this verse; the repetition of **horsemen** (cavalry) is ungainly, and the text of the 'Ain Feshkha scroll differs somewhat without giving sufficient help to determine what the

---

It was clear to the prophets of Israel that God was the creator of life, the world, and all mankind. God was also righteous will, who had expressed himself through a series of mighty acts. One of the mighty acts was the creation of a community so sensitive to his will and purpose that they were a peculiar and special people. It was a faith that recognized the fact that God was at work in all of human history, even in those aspects of human history which seemed most negative. All movements among the nations, whether they acknowledged God or not,

had to be regarded as a part of the divine process. His was a sovereignty intent on making even the selfish and most antisocial ends of all the peoples of the earth serve his holy purpose.

Such a position raises a profoundly significant moral question: If the behavior of **the Chaldeans** is the result of a movement of God in their midst, and not due to acts initiated by themselves for ends which they have determined, how can moral responsibility be fixed? If a nation acts as an agent of the divine purpose, the judgment of its acts belongs only to

9 They shall come all for violence: their faces shall sup up *as* the east wind, and they shall gather the captivity as the sand.

10 And they shall scoff at the kings, and the princes shall be a scorn unto them: they shall deride every stronghold; for they shall heap dust, and take it.

11 Then shall *his* mind change, and he shall pass over, and offend, *imputing* this his power unto his god.

9 They all come for violence;
    terror[a] of them goes before them.
  They gather captives like sand.
10 At kings they scoff,
    and of rulers they make sport.
  They laugh at every fortress,
    for they heap up earth and take it.
11 Then they sweep by like the wind and go
    on,
    guilty men, whose own might is their
    god!

a Cn: Heb uncertain

original reading was. **Press proudly on:** Perhaps "prance" or "gallop." The colorless **come** is lacking in the 'Ain Feshkha MS, which Brownlee ("The Jerusalem Habakkuk Scroll," *Bulletin of the American Schools of Oriental Research*, No. 112 [Dec., 1948], p. 10) translates:

> Stretching forth and spreading out,
> His horsemen from afar
> Fly as a vulture. . . .

9-10. The first clause of vs. 9, **they all come for violence,** seems to be the second half of the Hebrew line which begins **they fly.** The rest of the verse, however, is notoriously difficult. **Terror of them goes before them** is perhaps as good a way as any to emend the text if one wishes to change it. Duhm's "from Gomer [Cappadocia] they marched toward the east" has already been mentioned (see Intro., p. 976). The ERV has "Their faces are set eagerly as the east wind"; or read "toward the east," or "forward." But **as the east wind** is a highly questionable translation; and to say that they look forward is commonplace between the violence of the first clause and the gathering of captives like sand in the last. Why **their faces** (plural) between singular verbs? Unfortunately the meaning of the word translated "eagerness" or "set" or "gathering" is not clear. The KJV reads **Their faces shall sup up as the east wind.** The 'Ain Feshkha MS does not help to establish the difficult text: "the set of their faces eastward." Is this a place where an editor, possibly he who was responsible for 2:5-20, has intentionally introduced or altered a passage to make a reference to the Greeks? In vs. 10 the subject is emphatic, "and he is one who derides kings" or "it is he who scoffs at kings," and "princes" or "rulers are his laughingstock." The root used in the word "laughingstock" is repeated, **they laugh at every fortress,** and **heap up earth and take it.** Those who favor a date between 334 and 331 B.C. see in this verse a reference to the mole which Alexander built in order to capture Tyre.

11. Like vs. 9, this verse is one of the most puzzling of the book. The 'Ain Feshkha MS reads here וישם, "and he makes," for ואשם, "and be guilty" (ASV) or **guilty men** (RSV), although that same MS in the commentary oddly refers to a "house of guilt." Did the author know one text that read "and he makes" but another that had the word for **guilty** at this point? Budde conjectures "Assyria." But the difficulties extend further. **Then they** [or "he"] **sweep by like the wind and go on** gives a good meaning but lacks

God. But does this mean that the normal operation of moral law described in terms of reaping and sowing is suspended? In the text, it is true, the Chaldeans are characterized as **that bitter and hasty nation;** further, they are **dread and terrible. They all come for violence** . . . . **They**

gather captives like sand. And finally, they are called men of guilt, **whose own might is their god!**

It seems clear that the prophet is recognizing two distinct dimensions of moral behavior and ethical responsibility. One dimension involves

12 ¶ *Art* thou not from everlasting, O LORD my God, mine Holy One? We shall not die. O LORD, thou hast ordained them for judgment; and, O mighty God, thou hast established them for correction.

13 *Thou art* of purer eyes than to behold evil, and canst not look on iniquity: wherefore lookest thou upon them that deal treacherously, *and* holdest thy tongue when the wicked devoureth *the man that is* more righteous than he?

12 Art thou not from everlasting,
    O LORD my God, my Holy One?
    We shall not die.
 O LORD, thou hast ordained them as a
    judgment;
    and thou, O Rock, hast established
    them for chastisement.
13 Thou who art of purer eyes than to be-
    hold evil
    and canst not look on wrong,
 why dost thou look on faithless men,
    and art silent when the wicked swal-
    lows up
    the man more righteous than he?

the letter which normally indicates comparison. On the other hand, "then the wind changes and removes" makes little sense in this connection. The Syriac has "his wind"; hence it is possible to render "his spirit changes," i.e., his purpose alters, and he goes on. Moreover, the expression **whose own might is their god** does not represent ordinary Hebrew; there the Greek has "my God." Marti regards this verse as secondary; Adolphe Lods (*The Prophets and the Rise of Judaism* [tr. S. H. Hooke; New York: E. P. Dutton & Co., 1937], p. 234) couples it with the following rather than the preceding, and reconstructs: "Then was my spirit heavy and I uttered my complaint, I laid my complaint . . . before my God." On the whole it seems best to take vs. 11 with vs. 10: as a climax to this part of the description, the conqueror swiftly goes on, relying on his own power.

D. Second Series of Questions (1:12-17)

12. The first half of this verse returns to the questioning of vss. 2-3. In the midst of injustice, **art thou not from everlasting?** Does not God reign over the vicissitudes of time? Is there not eternal holiness above passing wrongs? (Cf. Pss. 90:2; 93:2; Deut. 33:27.) **We shall not die** represents the Hebrew text, followed by the LXX, but at this point occurs one of the eighteen "emendations of the scribes" (*Tiqqûnê Şôpherîm*): the margin bids one read "Thou shalt not die" parallel to **from everlasting.** This is preferable. If **we shall not die** is the true reading, it is hard to understand its presence here unless it is a gloss. **Holy One,** implying God's separation from man's sin and frailty, is a term used for the most part in late books, notably Leviticus. The second half of the verse again belongs to the prophetic oracle, although George Adam Smith (*The Book of the Twelve Prophets* [rev. ed.; New York: Harper & Bros., 1928], II, 134) declares it is "rightly regarded by most moderns as an intrusion." Rather it gives the clue as to why God has raised the "bitter and hasty nation"—for judgment and chastisement. Without this half verse the oracle would leave God's reason unexplained. **Rock** is a term for God; cf. Deut. 32 (six times) ; Pss. 18:2, 31; 95:1; Isa. 30:29.

13. Here follows the classic question: "Thou whose eyes are too pure to behold evil, and cannot tolerate [i.e., look with equanimity upon] wrong, why dost thou tolerate

the private end and the personal good of a nation. These may arise out of concerns and desires which are selfish and antisocial in character. The means used to fulfill such ends are determined by the ends themselves. The moral judgment of such means and ends may be measured in terms of the effect on the nation and of the suffering such behavior inflicts upon

others. But there is a still wider and more comprehensive sense in which the behavior may be interpreted. The private life of a nation takes place on a world stage, and the nation itself is involved in a vast historic movement, the total significance of which can be understood only by one who sees all of life as a whole or as a single unit. In the light of this dimension

14 And makest men as the fishes of the sea, as the creeping things, *that have* no ruler over them?

15 They take up all of them with the angle, they catch them in their net, and gather them in their drag: therefore they rejoice and are glad.

16 Therefore they sacrifice unto their net, and burn incense unto their drag; because by them their portion *is* fat, and their meat plenteous.

17 Shall they therefore empty their net, and not spare continually to slay the nations?

14 For thou makest men like the fish of the sea,
    like crawling things that have no ruler.
15 He brings all of them up with a hook,
    he drags them out with his net,
  he gathers them in his seine;
    so he rejoices and exults.
16 Therefore he sacrifices to his net
    and burns incense to his seine;
  for by them he lives in luxury,[b]
    and his food is rich.
17 Is he then to keep on emptying his net,
    and mercilessly slaying nations for ever?

[b] Heb *his portion is fat*

[the same verb repeated] the treacherous, keep silent when the wicked swallows the righteous?" The additional words **than he** are not in the LXX or Syriac and overload the line. Jeremiah's complaint (Jer. 12:1) is that God treats him as he does; the Habakkuk query is why God governs the world in this way. But the question fundamentally concerns not so much the world as God himself. Why is God this kind of a God? Here is one of the most important steps in the history of Jewish speculation.

14-17. The picture of the marauding power is resumed, though as the text stands the subject of **makest** in vs. 14 is **thou**, the God of vs. 12*b*. He has caused men to become like disorganized **fish** or **crawling things;** the latter term George Adam Smith translates as "vermin." **That have no ruler:** By a curious omission of one letter, the 'Ain Feshkha MS lacks the negative and reads "over which to rule." The **hook** of vs. 15 is derived from the word for the roof of the mouth into which it is fastened. Some scholars consider this clause **He brings all of them up with a hook** secondary for three reasons: (*a*) the tense differs from that of the surrounding verbs; (*b*) vs. 16 resumes mention of the **net** and **seine** but not the hook; and especially (*c*) the Chaldeans were not of a kind to linger long trying to catch one fish at a time. By **net** and **seine** (KJV **drag**) the fish are taken rapidly in quantity. The last line of the verse, **so he rejoices and exults,** is also under suspicion, for some MSS omit it, the succession of the word **so** or **therefore** is not felicitous (there is a third occurrence in vs. 17 represented by **then**), and the 'Ain Feshkha MS, though wordy and confused at this place, shows **therefore he sacrifices** immediately after **he gathers them in his seine.** Though there is no record of Chaldean sacrifice to nets, there is a statement in Herodotus (*History* IV. 62) of a yearly Scythian

not only will the Chaldeans be involved in moral judgment because of responsibility for their own actions, but they will also become, at one and the same time, instrumental in a wider moral judgment. God relates the totality of their own situation to the fate of Judah and makes them instruments in his hands to measure his judgment upon Judah for its apostasy. The struggle of the prophet is seen most accurately in the assertion:

Art thou not from everlasting,
  O LORD my God, my Holy One?
. . . .
O LORD, thou hast ordained them as a judgment;
  and thou, O Rock, hast established them for
    chastisement.

The prophet closes the chapter with a vivid picture of life as comparable to a **sea,** and men are thought of as **fish** and **crawling things that have no ruler.** They are caught ruthlessly and indiscriminately to be destroyed. The method by which such destruction takes place guarantees the economic security of the destroyer and becomes the object of his devotion and worship. There is a wide and sweeping note of contemporaneity in all of this. Men worship the symbols of their economic security and the guarantors of their standard of life. Consequently they tend to be moral and religious as they move away from the areas of their security, and immoral and irreligious as they move toward the centers of their security. So overwhelming is the

<table>
<tr><td>

2 I will stand upon my watch, and set me upon the tower, and will watch to see what he will say unto me, and what I shall answer when I am reproved.

</td><td>

2 I will take my stand to watch,
   and station myself on the tower,
and look forth to see what he will say to me,
      and what I will answer concerning my complaint.

</td></tr>
</table>

offering to a sword. Alexander also is reported by Arrian (*Anabasis* II. 24. 6) to have put the siege machine with which he captured Tyre into the Temple of Melkart. The plunder of other nations keeps the fisherman **fat** and **rich.**

In vs. 17 the 'Ain Feshkha MS confirms the judgment of scholars who omitted the interrogative particle, dropped the conjunction **and,** which in Hebrew is joined with **for ever,** and read "sword" for **net:** "Therefore he draws his sword continually, to slay nations without mercy." Again there are those who question whether this verse was part of the original description. The whole chapter may have undergone a development very similar to that of Isa. 10, in which the nation that was first called the rod of the Lord's anger (Isa. 10:5) comes to be spoken of in less and less flattering terms. But if its literary history is long, its religious meaning is not diminished. The light may come from several reflectors rather than one, but by them the Holy One imparts as much light—or more—as if he had used one alone.

II. The Righteous Shall Live by His Faithfulness (2:1-20)
A. The Answer from the Tower (2:1-4)

2:1. To the questions of 1:2-4, 12*a*, 13, there is now an answer. Here is the revelation for which ch. 1 was the preparation. But first the poet takes his **stand to watch,** or, better than **to watch,** "upon my watchtower," for the word is a noun, derived from the same root as that of Samaria, "the watchtower." The 'Ain Feshkha MS confirms the conjecture of scholars who have read **my** with the parallel word for **tower** in the second line. Probably the use of a tower here is only figurative, but an important truth is represented

prophet's reaction to his observation that he forgets, for one breathless moment, that all human history is in God's hand, and cries out in bewilderment and confusion:

> **Is he then to keep on emptying his net,**
>   **and mercilessly slaying nations for ever?**

How hard it is to remember that under God life is its own restraint!

2:1. Man Challenges God.—There is something authentic and dignified about standing one's ground. This can be done in various ways. Sometimes it is the result of being directly challenged by another, whereupon the ground of one's position has to be stated. When this is done, one's own convictions become clarified and defined. What we defend, we possess—though indeed we may possess it from either the inside or the outside.

But there is another way of taking a stand. It is to wager one's own integrity on the rightness of an issue. This is to be reckoned with. The prophet sees the destruction, the evil that has befallen his people, and he refuses to accept at its face value what he sees. He recognizes the

evil; but there must be a deeper meaning, some hidden clue which, if he could understand it, would fit the terrible events into a perspective that would justify his faith in God. Fundamental to the prophet's insistence is the assumption that there is a structure of dependability undergirding the universe and informing all events. There is nothing that can exist outside the divine contingency. Against the darkness of the period something wars, something struggles to break through that will give meaning and significance to all experience. The basis of such confidence may be merely the result of a steady observation of events over a time interval of sufficient duration to give an objective basis for hope. It may go deeper, and be the result of an inner testimony of the soul which informs the interpretation of experiences.

One cannot overlook the element of arrogance implicit in the demand that God answer to man for his behavior. Here is a recognition, as we would phrase it, of that autonomy in personality which must ever be respected by God, the creator of life. The audacity of the implication is as startling as the insight is

2 And the LORD answered me, and said,
Write the vision, and make *it* plain upon
tables, that he may run that readeth it.

2 And the LORD answered me:
"Write the vision;
    make it plain upon tablets,
    so he may run who reads it.

---

by it: the vision comes to one whose feet are on the firm foundation of confident
expectation, and who rises even a little above the toil and moil to take a look about him.
God's revelation, though available for all, is not actually received by all; man must
look forth or be on the alert as a watchman stands attentive. The language here is not
unlike that of Ps. 130. Despite the agreement of the 'Ain Feshkha MS with the M.T.,
"what I will reply," the reading of the Syriac, **what he will say,** is clearly better.

2. Once he has taken his stand, the poet is instructed to **write the vision** so plainly,
perhaps in such large letters, that "he who runs may read," or **so he may run who reads
it.** The point is that anyone passing by "on the run" may see it plainly and read it at a
glance. **Tablets** and "ships' planks" are the same word in Hebrew, but chiefly it is used
of the stones on which the Decalogue was written. The tablets might be of wood or stone
or other material. "The vision bears upon the future and must be preserved; also, it is
of common interest to all, learned or unlearned, and the speedy understanding of it
will quiet minds that are perplexed" (A. B. Davidson, *The Books of Nahum, Habakkuk
and Zephaniah* [Cambridge: Cambridge University Press, 1920; "Cambridge Bible"],
p. 76).

---

exhilarating. The prophet is declaring that
what we call personality must be taken into
account in the far-reaching plans of the divine
order. Even though he may admit his powerlessness to change circumstances, he knows that evil
can be overcome as long as its center does not
shift from circumstances to God, from conditions to the springs of the inner life. To say
"Yes" to evil, as if it were ultimate, is to be
overcome by evil. It is the recognition of this
fact that underwrites the integrity of the
prophet's challenge.

There is also a significant suggestion of detachment in these opening words of challenge.
From the watchtower it is possible to have a
sense of objectivity with reference to the crucial
events of the common life. It makes it possible
for one to seem to be outside of, or above, the
struggle; one is aware of, but not involved in,
what is going on. The detachment which fulfills itself in a thoroughgoing asceticism issues
too often in avoidance; but this in no way
lessens the importance of detachment. We are
all activated in small or great degree by what
W. E. Hocking has called the principle of
alternation. Involvement and withdrawal, taking up our burdens and putting them down,
working and resting—all are a part of the central rhythm of existence. The prophet uses the
principle as a tool by which he is enabled to
lift his sight above the movement of the Chaldeans and the cry of the stricken, to glimpse the
design of which all these things are but for
instances.

God is not only in history; he is above history.
We are in history, involved in the necessity of
time-space relationships, and therefore, to say
no more, often find it difficult to decipher the
meaning of our personal struggles, of the struggles of our times. If, however, we could be lifted
out of that context even for one swirling moment of profound perspective, then we might
see the whole through the eyes of God; then
with quiet courage and confidence we might
walk on the earth by the light in the sky. This
the prophet seeks for his times.

2. *The Moving Finger Writes.*—It is a matter
of more than passing significance that the
prophet is urged to **write the vision,** to put it
down. This gives to the vision more than a
temporary character, the result of the prophet's
response to a temporary stimulus. It will serve
also as a check against being carried away by
sheer drama and emotion. *Scripta littera manet.*
The written word establishes a point of authentic response against which unfolding events may
be checked. It is in this instance a commitment,
even a covenant, giving the declared counsels
of God. Moreover, it is an objective manifestation, that divine and righteous intent which
places the covenant out of bounds as far as
rumor or denial is concerned. It is as if God
were saying to the prophet, "This is my deliberate purpose backed by my own integrity.
Write it out that all may know what it is that
I will do, to the end that you yourself may be
protected when it seems as if my promises are
not being fulfilled."

3 For the vision *is* yet for an appointed time, but at the end it shall speak, and not lie: though it tarry, wait for it; because it will surely come, it will not tarry.

4 Behold, his soul *which* is lifted up is not upright in him: but the just shall live by his faith.

3 For still the vision awaits its time;
　　it hastens to the end — it will not lie.
If it seems slow, wait for it;
　　it will surely come, it will not delay.
4 Behold, he whose soul is not upright in
　　him shall fail,[c]
　　but the righteous shall live by his
　　faith.[d]

[c] Cn: Heb *is puffed up*
[d] Or *faithfulness*

---

3. In Moffatt's translation, this verse reads:

　　The vision has its own appointed hour;
　　it ripens, it will flower;
　　if it be long, then wait,
　　for it is sure, and it will not be late.

While the direct reply to the question of ch. 1 appears only in vs. 4, here is a preliminary caution to exercise patience. The **vision** or revelation is still maturing or building up to **its time,** its appointed time, the hour, not far away, which has been surely fixed; for **it hastens,** "pants," hurries **to the end,** i.e., to the fulfillment which "will not fail," and is inevitable. The exact force of the next verb is well brought out by the translation, **if it seem slow.** This vision is coming on God's time, which can neither be delayed nor rushed, but like the "Hound of Heaven," has swift, inexorable feet. So **wait,** for there will be no postponement; no cajoling will put it off; no delusion or self-deception will alter its schedule one moment. All this language suggests late Judaism, when speculation was rife as to when God would intervene in men's sadly troubled affairs.

4. Now, at the climax of the book, the long-awaited answer is transmitted to us in a corrupted text. What does God say when the vision is actually given? What is on the tablet? For the first half of the verse the Hebrew reads, lit., "Behold, it [feminine] is puffed up, not right is his soul in him"; the Greek, "If he draw back, my soul is not well pleased with him" (cf. Heb. 10:38); Aq., "Behold, the lazy, my soul is not straight with him." The 'Ain Feshkha MS bears witness to **is puffed up** and "not made straight," but much of the line in this MS has been destroyed. Probably because the meter is strained by too many words, "puffed up" and "not right" are variant expressions, the latter very likely an explanation of the former. But a noun form is expected as a counterpart to **righteous,** which occurs in the second half of the verse; "the wicked"

---

3. Wait for It.—The reason for this necessity is made obvious in the opening words of the verse. The **vision** may not come to pass as quickly as is expected. Here we are face to face with the ever-present problem of timing in relation to ends. The acuteness of human need at any moment may cry out for immediate release, immediate action at the point of urgency. Because the help does not come in accordance with our own timetables, we seem driven to conclude that it will not come at all—or if it does, that it will be too late. The assumption is that our own problems are completely unique and isolated from other considerations. The assurance here is that even though the vision seems **slow,** it will come; **wait for it.** Life is so interwoven, so deeply unified, that there are no solitary, isolated events. Unless we can stand outside of process, outside of all time-space operations, it is impossible to know what the particular experience which is ours means in the divine schedule. And since we can never quite do that, we must be willing to wait, informing our waiting with the assurance of faith.

There are several ways by which men **wait.** There is the waiting in rebellion. It means bringing the judgment of a great impatience upon the waiting experience. There is the waiting in resignation. All the life is given out and nothing remains but a dull listlessness. There is the waiting in anticipation. Such is the waiting of the righteous, so the prophet insists. It is alert, charged with expectation. It is on tiptoe.

4. Timetables.—Here is a radical contrast. The just, the righteous man waits in anticipation. He is active, but his activity is from within

5 ¶ Yea also, because he transgresseth by wine, *he is* a proud man, neither keepeth at home, who enlargeth his desire as hell, and *is* as death, and cannot be satisfied, but gathereth unto him all nations, and heapeth unto him all people:

5 Moreover, wine is treacherous;
    the arrogant man shall not abide.[e]
His greed is as wide as Sheol;
    like death he has never enough.
He gathers for himself all nations,
    and collects as his own all peoples."

[e] The Hebrew of these two lines is obscure

---

would be normal, and is found in the Aramaic paraphrase (Targ.). Is the sense that the wicked's soul is puffed with pride or (changing '*upp*ᵉ*lāh* to '*ullephāh*) that it swoons (Isa. 51:20), by which is meant that it dies? Is the Greek, "my soul is not well pleased with him," simply an attempt to supply something for a text too difficult to be translated? The best contrast would be given in some such way as this: "As for the wicked, his life [soul] fails within him, but the righteous lives by his faithfulness." Unfortunately there is no guarantee that this is what the author wrote. **Faithfulness** is a more accurate translation than **faith** for the Hebrew word '*emûnāh,* from the root of which is derived "Amen." In Exod. 17:12 the word is used of the steadiness of Moses' arms when supported on either side by Aaron and Hur. In Jer. 5:3; 7:28 it is fidelity as opposed to falsehood. In Isa. 11:5 it is used as a parallel to righteousness. It means moral steadfastness. Paul (Rom. 1:17; Gal. 3:11), using the Greek word πίστις, which, though representing '*emûnāh* here, had different connotations, built his doctrine of justification by faith with the help of this text, and Luther followed. In Habakkuk the words mean "the righteous survives if he is faithful," or we might say, "if he maintains his integrity." **Shall live** perhaps implies that on the day of judgment, when the wicked perish, the righteous who trust God will, in the words of Isa. 7:9, be established. Here, unless those scholars are right who transpose 1:5-11 to this point, the vision ends. But it is not perhaps so "meager" as some have found it. It is one of the important biblical statements of the truth elsewhere notably expressed by Socrates, "No evil can happen to a good man, either in life or after death" (*Apology* 23, tr. Benjamin Jowett). Why do the wicked swallow the righteous? In the end they do not; the righteous who trusts in God is vindicated. Faithfulness, according to George Adam Smith, is the motto and fame of Judaism, and the first commandment for nascent skepticism.

B. Introduction to the Woes (2:5-6*a*)

5. If vs. 4 is perplexing to scholars, vs. 5 is doubly so. "The text is manifestly at fault" (Davidson, *op. cit.,* p. 77). The difficulty is plainly with the word **wine.** The LXX lacks it: "But the arrogant man and the scorner, the boastful man, shall not finish anything." The KJV denies it its place as the subject. The 'Ain Feshkha MS has still another word for it: "Yea, wealth [*hôn*] indeed is treacherous." And the ERV, trying to translate it as it stands, becomes almost unintelligible: "Yea, moreover, wine is a treacherous dealer, a haughty man, and that keepeth not at home." Some scholars would

---

the timetable of God's plan. Not so with the faithless oppressor, the impious man. He is arrogant, full of idle boasting, ever trying to bolster up a sagging self-respect. That he can never do by the methods he is using; but a part of his sickness is his inability to realize this fact. It is not an accident that Christianity never tires of warning against the sin of pride and inculcating the virtue of humility. Pride is never possible when a man measures his life and deeds by God's demands held steadily before him. It can be maintained only when a man measures his life and deeds by his own egocentric impulses, or the life and deeds of others seen

always from the outside. Therefore the arrogant man is never satisfied; how can he be when he is both judge and juror for his own case? There is no other-than-self reference. He is God; he can do no wrong, for who is there to make it clear? On penalty of death he may conquer others; but he cannot cope with their spirits—they always elude him. This only increases his arrogance, because it eats away at his self-respect. Only **the righteous shall live**; and he shall live **by his faith,** by his patient trust and obedience (cf. Paul's use of this text in Gal. 3:11).

5-20. *The Cup in the Lord's Right Hand.*—The resistance against oppression often height-

6 Shall not all these take up a parable against him, and a taunting proverb against him, and say, Woe to him that increaseth

6 Shall not all these take up their taunt against him, in scoffing derision of him, and say,

> "Woe to him who heaps up what is not his own —

make the series of woes start here, and see in the word for wine the first *hôy*, "woe." Some would eliminate **Moreover** at the beginning. Some would change **neither keepeth at home** or **not abide** to "is not satisfied." Clearly there is corruption in the text; clearly a proper noun in place of **wine** is the easiest and best solution. Will "oppressor" (היונה) do? **Wine** in Hebrew is *hayyáyin;* the word "the Greek" is very similar (*hayyᵉwānî*). Thus:

> How much more treacherous is the Greek,
>   the arrogant one, who stays not at home!
> Greedy as hell,
>   insatiable as death,
> Who gathers to himself all nations
>   and collects to himself all peoples.

There at least is meaning, with a minimum alteration of the text. So read, this verse does not prove that chs. 1–3 were written in the Greek period. Indeed, it indicates the opposite, for "how much more" implies that a previous oracle has dealt with another nation. Vs. 5 does not even prove that all of vss. 5-20 is of that late date. But there is every likelihood that an editor, or perhaps an author, writing in the Greek period, set down this verse and the first half of vs. 6 as a transition from the materials of 1:2–2:4 to the "woes" which are to follow, some of which may be old, some new. For the other **treacherous** party cf. 1:13 and 1:5 emended (see Exeg.). For **the arrogant man** cf. Prov. 21:24. The meaning "does not stay at home," **not abide,** though the verb is unique, seems to be clear. For the picture of a greedy underworld, **Sheol,** the place where one is conscious only that all the good of life has departed, cf. Isa. 5:14, the same chapter in which there are "woes" similar to those in Hab. 2; cf. also Prov. 27:20. For

> **His greed is as wide as Sheol;**
>   **like death he has never enough,**

a literal rendering would demand, "who has broadened his soul [i.e., desire] like Sheol, and he is like death and is not satisfied."

6a. On several grounds this verse up to and including the words **and say** may be ascribed to an editor. It is prose. The word order is poor, and the change in it made by the 'Ain Feshkha MS, though an improvement, does not create a smooth line. One word, **scoffing,** seems to be a variant of another, **derision.** A taunt—a song with hidden and provocative allusions—does not really fit the denunciations following. Moreover, although **all these**—the nations who have suffered from the tyrant's greed—are to **take up their taunt,** soon the author speaks in his own right, not through the nations.

C. The Self-Destructiveness of Tyranny (2:6b-20)

This passage consists of a series of five woes, after the manner of Isa. 5:8-22. Some scholars have held that they refer to Jehoiakim king of Judah (608-597 B.C.), some to

ens perception and yields an uncanny insight into the weakness of the oppressor. The prophet spells this out by voicing the thoughts of the oppressed. They whisper among themselves words, the basic import of which is to stabilize their own morale. Since morale springs largely

from belief in one's own cause, the words provide a judgment upon the life and deeds of the oppressor.

Here the prophet discusses five great woes. These woes are the judgment of God; and that judgment is in a very real sense, from our point

that which is not his! how long? and to him
that ladeth himself with thick clay!

7 Shall they not rise up suddenly that
shall bite thee, and awake that shall vex
thee, and thou shalt be for booties unto
them?

8 Because thou hast spoiled many nations, all the remnant of the people shall
spoil thee; because of men's blood, and *for*
the violence of the land, of the city, and of
all that dwell therein.

for how long? —
and loads himself with pledges!"

7 Will not your debtors suddenly arise,
and those awake who will make you
tremble?
Then you will be booty for them.

8 Because you have plundered many nations,
all the remnant of the peoples shall
plunder you,
for the blood of men and violence to the
earth,
to cities and all who dwell therein.

Assyria, some to the Chaldeans, and some to the Greeks. If taken as a unit, in their
present form they must almost certainly be late. But the possibility is not precluded
that parts, particularly vss. 6-7, 9-11, may first have been directed to a tyrant earlier
than Alexander. More likely not; but the evidence does not permit a decisive answer.

1. First Woe (2:6b-8)

6b-8. Oppression breeds insurrection. For this form of address see Isa. 5:8-22. For
what is not his own cf. Hab. 1:6. **Heaps up: Increaseth,** multiplies, amasses. **For how
long?** is intrusive, probably inserted from the margin. The **pledges** are extorted, the
heavy debts and taxation that the tyrant inflicts. (The KJV renders curiously **thick clay,**
dividing the word into two.) Will not those who suffer under this burden revolt? The
word translated **debtors** could also mean "biters"; there may be a play on it. The 'Ain
Feshkha MS varies slightly: "Will not they suddenly arise and exact from you?" **Who
will make you tremble:** Your tormentors, your torturers, those who violently shake
you (cf. Eccl. 12:3; Esth. 5:9) —will they not **awake** and turn the tables? The last line
of vs. 7, **Then you will be booty for them,** does not fit metrically, and while correct
enough, adds nothing of value to the thought of vs. 8. It is a gloss. In vs. 8 **all the
remnant of the peoples,** if the point made in vs. 7 is continued, means not the nations
which have hitherto escaped but the survivors among those plundered, or everyone
except the oppressor. "The Chittiim," says the midrash of the 'Ain Feshkha MS, "are
the remnant of the peoples," which is not easy to understand. The last two lines of vs. 8
are repeated in vs. 17. **Men** and **cities** are generic; more than one "city" (ERV) is
meant. Because the description here fits many an oppressor, it is difficult to say when
and to whom these lines were first directed, but their message is clear: sure retribution!

---

of view, inherent in the moral structure of life.
Men who act in certain ways—so we should be
inclined to say—encounter them automatically.
To the prophet there was nothing automatic
about it. Such men encountered God (vs. 16b).

The first woe has to do with plundering,
taking by violence what does not belong to one
(see Exeg. on vs. 5). Those who suffer such
deprivations tend to be supported by an inner
assurance that retribution will redeem their
losses. The very plundering itself seems to
solidify the sufferers and becomes a curious
confirmation of the brotherhood of man, until
at length the power of the plunderer is undermined by his own voracity, and the victims seek
to get back their own. When this happens,
there is all too often no mercy for the plun-

derer, and all ethical considerations are waived.
The assumption seems to be that the act of the
plunderer places the whole relationship of man
to man in an amoral dimension. May it not be,
however, that this is an illusion? When the
victims seek to overcome the oppressor and get
back what was taken from them, are they not
bound by the same moral law that binds the
oppressor? It is an unresolved dilemma for
which there is no solution. The victims become
the agents of retribution; but as such, are they
not also morally responsible?

The second woe has to do with another kind
of dishonesty. This woe deals with economic
exploitation. When a person or a nation exploits the needs of others at a price which
brings **evil gain for his house** (vs. 9), he inspires

9 ¶ Woe to him that coveteth an evil covetousness to his house, that he may set his nest on high, that he may be delivered from the power of evil!

10 Thou hast consulted shame to thy house by cutting off many people, and hast sinned *against* thy soul.

11 For the stone shall cry out of the wall, and the beam out of the timber shall answer it.

12 ¶ Woe to him that buildeth a town with blood, and establisheth a city by iniquity!

9 Woe to him who gets evil gain for his house,
   to set his nest on high,
   to be safe from the reach of harm!

10 You have devised shame to your house
   by cutting off many peoples;
   you have forfeited your life.

11 For the stone will cry out from the wall,
   and the beam from the woodwork respond.

12 Woe to him who builds a town with blood,
   and founds a city on iniquity!

2. SECOND WOE (2:9-11)

9-11. Rapacity is no security. Many see in these verses a reference to Jehoiakim's building projects, especially since Jer. 22:13 also condemns that king in similar terms:

> Woe to him that builds his house by unrighteousness,
>   and his chambers by injustice;
> That uses his neighbor's service without wages,
>   and gives him not his hire.

To get **evil gain** is to "obtain by violence." But the **house** does not necessarily refer to a building; rather it means "family," "dynasty," or a monarch's "people." **To set his nest on high:** Cf. Isa. 14:13, "And you said to yourself, I will ascend into heaven, I will exalt my throne above the stars of God." Cf. also Jer. 49:16; Obad. 4. But it is impossible so **to be safe from the reach of harm.** The moment of proud security is the moment of greatest danger. Readers of Arnold J. Toynbee will recall his exposition of this theme with particular reference to Goliath (*A Study of History*, Abridgement of Volumes I-VI by D. C. Somervell [New York: Oxford University Press, 1947], p. 331), and readers of Reinhold Niebuhr, his sermon on Ezek. 31 (*Discerning the Signs of the Times* [New York: Charles Scribner's Sons, 1946], pp. 57-72). **You have devised** [lit., "You have planned"] **shame to your house:** I.e., the net result will be the opposite of what you think. As this verse is metrically too long, some would move **you have forfeited your life** to a point after **for his house** in vs. 9, the first line of which is metrically short; but it is better to keep it where it is as the parallel to **you have devised shame to your house.** Then **by cutting off many peoples** is a marginal explanation of the plans, perhaps influenced by Isa. 10:7. Possibly, but less likely, the word **cutting** should be read with the last clause, "you have cut off sin for your soul," i.e., "have brought sin on your own life" (cf. Prov. 8:36). The very ingredients of ill-gotten power will be the source of the downfall. Vs. 11 is sometimes compared with Luke 19:40, in which the stones cry out; but perhaps a more genuine parallel to this second woe is "All they that take the sword shall perish with the sword" (Matt. 26:52).

3. THIRD WOE (2:12-14, 17)

12-13. Cruelty's violent wave rolls back again. Vs. 12 is a reminiscence of Mic. 3:10; vs. 13, a loose remembrance of Jer. 51:58. The thought is not unlike that of the preceding

bitterness and contempt. For it means that gain has been got out of the helplessness and desperation of others. The fact that this is done in an effort to guarantee one's self against the same kind of desperation is beside the point. The problem is not simple in a complex society,

because so many operations for gain are impersonal and ethically mindless. It is natural to seek to make one's family safe from the plight of those whose predicament is exploited. Such behavior, says the prophet, actually defeats the end one seeks, for it corrodes the very fiber of

13 Behold, *is it* not of the Lord of hosts that the people shall labor in the very fire, and the people shall weary themselves for very vanity?

14 For the earth shall be filled with the knowledge of the glory of the Lord, as the waters cover the sea.

15 ¶ Woe unto him that giveth his neighbor drink, that puttest thy bottle to *him,* and makest *him* drunken also, that thou mayest look on their nakedness!

13 Behold, is it not from the Lord of hosts
   that peoples labor only for fire,
   and nations weary themselves for
      naught?

14 For the earth will be filled
   with the knowledge of the glory of the
      Lord,
   as the waters cover the sea.

15 Woe to him who makes his neighbors
      drink
   of the cup of his wrath,*f* and makes
      them drunk,
   to gaze on their shame!

f Cn: Heb *joining to your wrath*

---

sections: Woe to him who builds his city on bloodshed and crime! Not forever will the peoples see their labor go up in smoke and weary themselves for nothing—for emptiness, in vain. The KJV reads **labor in the very fire,** but the sense is rather, in twentieth-century terms, that nations will not endure forever that their efforts be sacrificed on the altar of pride and greed, only to be wiped out in a moment by a bomb.

14. This verse, which quotes Isa. 11:9 not quite exactly (adding **glory** and altering several forms), does not fit the context according to modern notions of suitability. Its meaning seems to be that when the earth is filled with the knowledge of God's **glory,** when the kingdom comes, it is God's purpose to do away with all human achievement. No man's effort will be of any avail. In order, then, to make a proper connection with vs. 13, the words **Behold, is it not from the Lord of hosts** were inserted there. A better conclusion to vss. 12-13 is to be found in vs. 17, which is more suitable here than after vs. 16.

17. The Chaldeans had apparently been ruthless in their stripping of Lebanon (Isa. 14:8), and Jehoiakim may have been equally guilty (cf. Jer. 22:15, 20-23). **The destruction of the beasts will terrify you,** not **them.** For **terrify** some would read "snatch away"; so the 'Ain Feshkha MS. The last two lines of vs. 17 have already appeared in vs. 8; here they are less closely related to their context. Even the violence done to trees and animals must have its recompense (for Davidson's comment on this see Intro., p. 978).

4. Fourth Woe (2:15-16)

15-16. He who degrades another is himself degraded. In vs. 15 the line originally seems to have read: **Woe to him who makes his neighbours drink** [i.e., drunk] **to gaze on their shame** [i.e., their nakedness, pudenda; cf. Nah. 3:5]. **Of the cup of** [your] **wrath** [yca] **and makes . . . drunk** was a marginal note anticipating vs. 16, but this note was wrongly copied, **joining to your wrath,** etc. Alexander is known for his drunken brawls. The 'Ain Feshkha MS reads "festivals" for nakedness, then in vs. 16 follows the LXX in reading **stagger,** but comments as if the word there were as it is in Hebrew,

---

those who enter into such a heritage. **The stone will cry out from the wall** (vs. 11).

The third woe is still another facet of the same issue. Here the figure is one of a nation that is built upon blood, whose cities are founded upon crime. The judgment cuts deeply into the whole basis upon which men give effect to the political, social, and economic agreements by which they live. Violence and bloodshed are the means by which civilizations

are built. In one sense they are a part of the procedures of cultural and economic expansion. In the long march toward orderly social living, violence has been the mentor of man. There is no civilization that has appeared in human history that does not rest upon some form of conquest. Not only is this true, but it is also true that civilizations have found it expedient to maintain themselves in the same way. As their position became more secure, they have been

16 Thou art filled with shame for glory: drink thou also, and let thy foreskin be uncovered: the cup of the Lord's right hand shall be turned unto thee, and shameful spewing *shall be* on thy glory.

17 For the violence of Lebanon shall cover thee, and the spoil of beasts, *which* made them afraid, because of men's blood, and for the violence of the land, of the city, and of all that dwell therein.

18 ¶ What profiteth the graven image that the maker thereof hath graven it; the molten image, and a teacher of lies, that the maker of his work trusteth therein, to make dumb idols?

16 You will be sated with contempt instead
    of glory.
  Drink, yourself, and stagger!*g*
  The cup in the Lord's right hand
    will come around to you,
    and shame will come upon your glory!

17 The violence done to Lebanon will overwhelm you;
    the destruction of the beasts will terrify
    you,*h*
  for the blood of men and violence to the
    earth,
    to cities and all who dwell therein.

18 What profit is an idol
    when its maker has shaped it,
    a metal image, a teacher of lies?
  For the workman trusts in his own creation
    when he makes dumb idols!

g Cn Compare Gk Syr: Heb *be uncircumcised*
h Gk Syr: Heb *them*

be uncircumcised. The Hebrew is stronger and offers better parallelism; cf. Exeg. on 1:11 for the curious reading of the 'Ain Feshkha MS. **Thou art filled, sated,** not **will be;** already this is shame to you rather than honor. **It will come around to you,** i.e., **the cup in the Lord's right hand.** The line has one word too many, possibly **right hand.** The KJV wrongly makes two words out of one: **and shameful spewing**—an intensive form of **shame,** "foul shame," "disgrace." If vs. 17 is coupled with vs. 13, each of the three preceding woes contained four lines; this fourth has only three.

17. See Exeg. on p. 993.

5. Fifth Woe (2:18-20)

18-20. Idols are worthless. Because the word **woe** introduces four out of the five sections into which vss. 6*b*-20 are divided, one expects it also at the beginning of vs. 18. Either vs. 18 belongs after vs. 19 or, more likely, it is a scribe's comment, for it is prosy and redundant. An **idol** (*péṣel*) is carved out of wood or stone, but the word in apposition with it, **a metal image** (*maṣṣēkāh*) is poured. Notice that the idol itself is **a teacher of lies.** Yet idols are **dumb.** The 'Ain Feshkha MS for **teacher** has "bitterness."

content to protect themselves by the threat of violence. The prophet urges that nations are bound by the same morals as individuals. Perhaps this is the reason why the seeds of decay seem ever inherent in civilizations. They rise, they fall. Always the judgment of God is upon them (vs. 13) because they make impossible the realization of God's plan for men. And what is that plan? That the **knowledge** of him shall **cover the earth as the waters cover the sea** (vs. 14). It is a dreadful judgment. The prophet implies that until nations are built in a manner that makes a climate for an immediate awareness of the knowledge of God, they cannot survive.

The fourth woe shifts the ground somewhat.

It has to do with another kind of exploitation, the exploitation of the person. It is an attack upon the individual's self-estimate. Here is a picture which is strangely moving: a man is goaded by the oppressor until at last he strikes out in a kind of behavior that denies the orderly ground of his own living. He is driven to act in a way that disgraces himself. He is stripped of all dignity and sees himself as one who has been laid bare by his own rage. The feeling is that he has been tricked; as indeed, the prophet suggests, was the intent of the evildoer. When he has been thus exposed, his taunter gloats over his shame. But beware! It shall surely be repaid. The "cup of God's fury" shall the oppressor himself be forced to drink and his share

19 Woe unto him that saith to the wood, Awake; to the dumb stone, Arise, it shall teach! Behold, it *is* laid over with gold and silver, and *there is* no breath at all in the midst of it.	19 Woe to him who says to a wooden thing, Awake; to a dumb stone, Arise! Can this give revelation? Behold, it is overlaid with gold and silver, and there is no breath at all in it.
20 But the LORD *is* in his holy temple: let all the earth keep silence before him.	20 But the LORD is in his holy temple; let all the earth keep silence before him.
3 A prayer of Habakkuk the prophet upon Shigionoth.	3 A prayer of Habak'kuk the prophet, according to Shigion'oth.

Vs. 19 suggests Elijah's taunt to his opponents on Mount Carmel (I Kings 18:26-27). How foolish to expect response from **wood** or **stone!** (Cf. Pss. 115:4-8; 135:15-18.) The 'Ain Feshkha MS, confusing the letters *dáleth* and *rēsh,* reads "to a lofty stone" for **dumb stone. Can this give revelation?** Lit., "It teaches" (cf. KJV), undoubtedly a marginal comment, which may be true also of **and silver,** although one does not expect great poetry or even regular meter in idol passages (cf. Isa. 44:9-20; 46:1-2; Jer. 10:1-14; *et al.*). **Breath:** Or "spirit." In contrast to the impotence of the idols, **the LORD is in his holy temple** in heaven (cf. Ps. 11:4). "Hush" **before him, all the earth** (cf. Zeph. 1:7; Zech. 2:13; Ps. 46:10). So at the end the chapter returns to the thought of its opening verses, that man is to wait upon the Lord (vs. 3).

III. A PSALM OF PRAISE (3:1-15)

Because chs. 1–2 deal with the problem of suffering, it seemed to an editor fitting that he should append to them this hymn of praise to God for his aid to his people in their oppression, especially since also it expresses thanksgiving and trust in a time of

shall be double. He will experience the shame of his victim as well as his own (vs. 15). He will say to himself: "Woe is me! What my victim experienced was wrapped in his innocence; but what I am going through is cradled in my guilt."

The fifth and final woe has to do with idolatry, which is the source of all the woes. The essence of idolatry may perhaps be said to consist in calling a good thing bad or a bad thing good. It is the delusion which causes one to impute the prerogatives and the power of God to a no-God. This is what happens when a man makes the demand of an idol that should be made only of God. Who is being fooled? The man knows that he has fashioned the idol; he knows that it is his conception and creation. Does the fact that he made it give it certain powers that are unique? This is the ultimate arrogance. One is reminded here of the words with which Jesus spelled out the meaning of the sin that shall not be forgiven. A man who calls a bad thing good, or a good thing bad, over a time interval of sufficient duration, will arrive irrevocably at the point of no-discrimination in values. He becomes a person without moral judgment. No idol can act like God.

Such behavior as is set forth in the five woes

presupposes the assumption on the part of men that they are outside the divine scrutiny. They suppose that they are here

as on a darkling plain
Swept with confused alarms of struggle and flight,
Where ignorant armies clash by night.[1]

But this is not so. **The LORD is in his holy temple,** which is the whole earth. Therefore all of life must be lived within the context of that knowledge. It is with reference to God finally that we are to live out our days, deep within the stillness of our spirit to carry with us the constant awareness of his presence. Out of that reverence let the deeds of a man's life pour forth.

3:1-7. *The Judgment Implicit in Events.*—I have heard . . . . I saw. Here we come upon the empirical basis for moral judgment. Even the prophet cannot escape the necessity for seeking such a basis. There is a sense, however, in which for him moral judgments and religious experience are absolute, carrying their own sure integrity, needing no ground for validation other than in God. They are therefore on one aspect not contingent upon any data beyond them-

[1] Matthew Arnold, "Dover Beach."

want. Doubtless at one period this poem stood in a collection of psalms. The title, the note that it is suitable for an accompaniment of strings (vs. 19), the use of the Selahs, and its similarity in form and content with other psalms identify it. Just as in the LXX, Pss. 146–148 were ascribed to Haggai and Zechariah (cf. Pss. 138 [Hebrew 139]), so this was probably called Habakkuk's and then lifted out of its psalm book to stand with the prophecy.

The poem is thirty lines long (like Pss. 42–43), but because the last five or six of these are not closely connected with the theophany which precedes, many scholars see in them a later addition. Nevertheless, S. R. Driver (*An Introduction to the Literature of the Old Testament* [rev. ed.; New York: Charles Scribner's Sons, 1913], p. 339) could say of the total product that "for sublimity of poetic conception and splendour of diction, [it] ranks with the finest which Hebrew poetry has produced." Unfortunately there are serious corruptions in the text. Its date is probably in the fourth or third century B.C., or possibly later, if the **anointed** in vs. 13 should refer to a Maccabean ruler rather than to the whole nation. Ps. 77:17-19 seems to depend on this theophany, but as those verses fit loosely in their context there, they do not offer appreciable help to the problem of time of origin. Other related poems are Judg. 5; Deut. 33; Ps. 18 (II Sam. 22). The Lord's coming to battle to destroy the godless reminds students of Babylonian literature of the creation myth in which the ruler of the storm, Marduk, fighting against Chaos, slays the primeval monster Tiamat (cf. G. A. Barton, *Archaeology and the Bible* [7th ed. rev.; Philadelphia: American Sunday School Union, 1937], pp. 279-302). Tiamat's cognate word in Hebrew is *tehôm*, **the deep**, used in vs. 10, **the deep gave forth its voice.** In an older form of this poem, therefore, the deity whose **glory covered the heavens** (vs. 3), and whose **brightness was like the light** (vs. 4), may have been the Babylonian god. The related Phoenician solar deity carried fire bolts and spread plagues (cf. vss. 4-6, 14). As the chapter now stands, however, mythological elements have been tamed to liturgical use. The theophany in vss. 3-15, which may have been a psalm for wheat harvest (Pentecost), possibly picked up other material (vss. 17-19) used at the festival when the crops were poor (cf. H. St. John Thackeray, *The Septuagint and Jewish Worship* [London: British Academy, 1921], 47-55). However this may be, the chapter now makes an impressive and powerful whole. It has been much used in Jewish and Christian worship.

A. Title (3:1)

3:1. A prayer of Habakkuk the prophet: Various psalms are also called prayers: Pss. 17; 86; 90; 102; 142 (cf. Ps. 72:20). Except for a questionable reading of vs. 2, however, this chapter can hardly be accurately so described. **The prophet:** Cf. Exeg. on

---

selves. It is ever so with the prophet. "Thus saith the LORD" puts for him the final stamp upon the act, the word, the deed. Standing within the enclosure of such assurance he is protected from the invasion of the urgency to prove that what he says is true.

The peril of this kind of authority is of course that there is provided no means by which the individual can be protected from the ever-present possibility of self-deception. At some point error may have entered into his judgment, error that may not be related to the judgment itself, but error which may have crept into his interpretation. That contingency never disappears from the horizon of human activity and thought. That it does not is one of the high tributes which God pays to personality. Personality is dynamic, characterized by growth,

by change, by elasticity. Man is not an automaton, thanks be to God. But this very fact makes it possible for all calculations and judgments to go awry.

Suppose then that the moral judgment and the empirical experience seem to be irrelevant or contradictory. It may be that the individual is looking in the wrong places for verification. It may be that the time interval at his immediate disposal is too short. Here again we pick up the earlier note of the prophet—we must wait, we must not be hasty in our judgment. We may be overlooking the whole matter of timing and of process. It may be with the events of human history as it is with seeds. Some seeds grow, blossom, and fulfill themselves in a single short season; others take many months, or even years, before they realize

2 O Lord, I have heard thy speech, *and* was afraid: O Lord, revive thy work in the midst of the years, in the midst of the years make known; in wrath remember mercy.

3 God came from Teman, and the Holy One from mount Paran. Selah. His glory covered the heavens, and the earth was full of his praise.

---

2 O Lord, I have heard the report of thee,
    and thy work, O Lord, do I fear.
In the midst of the years renew it;
    in the midst of the years make it
      known;
    in wrath remember mercy.
3 God came from Teman,
    and the Holy One from Mount Paran.
His glory covered the heavens,
    and the earth was full of his praise.
                      Selah

1:1. The rest of this verse reads, lit., "set to Shigionoth" (cf. Ps. 7, superscription), but the M.T. is doubtful, and it is better to follow the LXX and to combine the notes of vs. 1 and vs. 19—"suitable for one who performs on stringed instruments." The "chief musician" or **choirmaster** is likely to have been an accompanist. The corresponding verb in I Chr. 15:21 parallels another verb "to sound aloud on brass" in I Chr. 15:19, and seems to mean to play on strings, and so to lead.

B. Introduction (3:2)

2 O Lord, I have heard the report of thee,
    I have seen thy work, O Lord . . . .
In the midst of hard years thou revealest thyself,
    in time of wrath rememberest mercy.

2. The poet appeals to God's action reported from of old as a ground for present help. Although in vs. 16, after the story has been heard, he is afraid, here in vs. 2 the Greek **I have heard** is clearly superior to the Hebrew, "I am afraid." The next clause in the text, **in the midst of the years renew it,** lit., "keep him alive," is probably a gloss, which may first have read **make known** (from *ḥāwāh* not *ḥāyāh*). The imperative is followed by two declarations, that **in the midst of the years** God reveals himself, following the LXX again, and that **in wrath,** or turmoil, trouble, he remembers to be merciful (cf. Ps. 77:9). **The years** means the difficult times. The night is darkest before the dawn.

C. Theophany (3:3-15)

3 God came from Teman
    and the Holy One from Mount Paran. Selah.
His glory covered the heavens,
    and the earth was full of his praise.

---

themselves. The law of growth, the schedule of each, is its own secret disclosure. Thus it may be with the events of human history. But in the last analysis the imperious demand of the moral judgment is inescapable, even though we are unable to decipher its empirical involvement. Yet the attempt has to be made. Inherent in the experience of moral judgment is the insistence to establish its validity outside of one's private relationship with the judgment itself. Its relevancy must ever be sought, even though it may always escape detection. Paradox of paradoxes.

The prophet, however, is speaking from within an inclusive perspective. He is not confronted with the customary dilemma. For him the moral judgment is implicit in the event.

Of this he is sure because of what he has seen and heard. On the basis of such data he confidently asks and expects God to *be* God. In this divine movement, however, despite his confidence, he wants to be sure that there will be no wide sweep of divine judgment which will include the innocent as well as the guilty. He wants God to **remember mercy.** Is there a place for mercy in the concept of retributive justice? Can there be reaping and sowing without the innocent being involved? The prayer of the prophet is that God's judgment will be a discriminatory one within the context of the divine morality. And with that he leaves the final issue to God.

3-16. *The God Above History.*—In these verses the prophet reviews what he has seen

4 And *his* brightness was as the light; he had horns *coming* out of his hand: and there *was* the hiding of his power.	4 His brightness was like the light, rays flashed from his hand; and there he veiled his power.

4 And *his* brightness was as the light; he had horns *coming* out of his hand: and there *was* the hiding of his power.

5 Before him went the pestilence, and burning coals went forth at his feet.

6 He stood, and measured the earth: he beheld, and drove asunder the nations; and the everlasting mountains were scattered, the perpetual hills did bow: his ways *are* everlasting.

7 I saw the tents of Cushan in affliction: *and* the curtains of the land of Midian did tremble.

4 His brightness was like the light,
rays flashed from his hand;
and there he veiled his power.

5 Before him went pestilence,
and plague followed close behind.

6 He stood and measured the earth;
he looked and shook the nations;
then the eternal mountains were scattered,
the everlasting hills sank low.
His ways were as of old.

7 I saw the tents of Cushan in affliction;
the curtains of the land of Mid'ian did tremble.

---

3. Teman is another name for Edom, properly a district of Edom, to the south and east of Judah. **Paran** is the hill country along the Gulf of Aqabah between Edom and Sinai. In the Song of Deborah also (Judg. 5:4), God comes to help his people from this region. To it Elijah went for divine aid, for here was the cradle of Israel's religion (cf. Deut. 33:2). The word used for **God** is *'elôah*, a sign of late date, as is **Holy One. Selah** is a liturgical note, the force of which in this place nobody knows. It appears also in vss. 9, 13.

4 When he gleamed, it was as the daylight . . . .
Rays flashed from his hand,
and there was the hiding place of his power.
5 Before him marched pestilence,
and at his heels stalked plague.

4-5. Vs. 4 bristles with difficulties, the most probable solutions to which are indicated in the translation. A half line is missing. William R. Arnold ("The Interpretation of קרנים מידו לו, Hab. 3:4," *American Journal of Semitic Languages and Literatures,* XXI [1905], 171-72) translates: "He hath horns that reach below his hand," i.e., long braids of hair, which, like Samson's, are "the depository of his strength." The word translated **rays** or **horns** is dual, not plural. But the study of archaeology and of the religion of Israel's neighbors points to a deity who wields the thunderbolt and spreads diseases.

6 When he stopped, he measured the earth,
when he looked, he spied out the nations.
Then the eternal mountains were scattered,
the everlasting hills sank low.
7 The tents of Cushan were shattered,
the curtains of . . . Midian trembled.

6-7. Again difficulties abound. Another possibility is to read:

When he stopped [lit., "stood"] he shook the earth,
when he looked, he made nations [or "rocks"] quake.

But the former does less violence to the text. Thus interpreted, God so to speak takes aim before he releases the thunder and lightning. At the end of vs. 6, after **the everlasting**

---

and heard, the mighty manifestation which he prays may take place again: "In the midst of the years make [thyself] known" (vs. 2b). God is the creator of the world and all of life, and the proper response of the earth to his **glory** is to give him praise (vs. 3b). But be not mistaken by this glory; it is the light behind which his **power** rests (vs. 4). It is awful majesty, and when it operates among the works of creation, it moves in as a mighty force on the rampage

8 Was the Lᴏʀᴅ displeased against the rivers? *was* thine anger against the rivers? *was* thy wrath against the sea, that thou didst ride upon thine horses *and* thy chariots of salvation?	**8** Was thy wrath against the rivers, O Lᴏʀᴅ? Was thy anger against the rivers, or thy indignation against the sea, when thou didst ride upon thy horses, upon thy chariot of victory?
9 Thy bow was made quite naked, *according* to the oaths of the tribes, *even thy* word. Selah. Thou didst cleave the earth with rivers.	**9** Thou didst strip the sheath from thy bow, and put the arrows to the string.*i* *Selah* Thou didst cleave the earth with rivers.

i Cn: Heb obscure

---

hills sank low, there is a gloss: **his ways were as of old**—"his are everlasting ways." G. R. Driver ("Critical Note on Habakkuk 3₇," *Journal of Biblical Literature,* LXII [1943], 121), putting together parts of vss. 4 and 7, obtains: "And the heavens are the hiding place of His strength, and the everlasting ways are for His swooping." But this is not likely to have been the ancient reading. **Cushan** is not Cush (Ethiopia) but refers to the Bedouin tribes near Edom, as does **Midian. I saw the tents of Cushan in affliction** is not a true translation of the Hebrew, which has become corrupted. Better: "The tents of Cushan were torn to shreds and the curtains of Midian fluttered wildly." Omit **I saw** and in the next half line **the land of.** So ends the first third of the poem. W. F. Albright ("Two Letters from Ugarit [Ras Shamrah]," *Bulletin of the American Schools of Oriental Research,* No. 82 [Apr., 1941], pp. 46-49), appealing to a Canaanite letter from Ugarit, obtains for **his ways were as of old,** "the everlasting roads [of the stars] were destroyed."

> 8 Was thy wrath hot against the rivers . . .
> or thy indignation against the sea,
> When thou didst ride upon thy horses,
> thy chariots of victory?

8. The second section of ten lines begins with a rhetorical question: What was the occasion for all these manifestations of God's power? In ll. 19-20 (vs. 13) the answer appears: he came out to save his people. In vs. 8 repetition has occurred. One instance of **was thy wrath against the rivers** and probably **O Lᴏʀᴅ** should be omitted. Popular mythology puts God on horseback and pictures him as a warrior. With vss. 8-13 cf. Ps. 77:16-20; see also Ps. 114:5-8.

> 9 Thou didst strip thy bow stark bare, . . .
> thou didst split the earth with rivers.

9. For the splitting of **the earth with rivers** see Ps. 78:15-16. In the middle of this verse are three perplexing words, **oaths, tribes** or "rods," and **word,** which are said to have evoked over one hundred different translations. Thackeray finds in them liturgical references to the lections for Pentecost, **oaths** to Deut. 16:9-12, **tribes** or "rods" to the lesson beginning at Num. 17:1, and **word** the catchword for the lesson commencing with Gen. 12:1 (see *op. cit.,* and "Primitive Lectionary Notes in the Psalm of Habakkuk," *Journal of Theological Studies,* XII [1910-11], 191-213). A Selah follows these three words.

(vs. 5), inspiring a deep fear where once was praise. Now the God above history, the God above nature, is on the march. And terrible things follow in his wake.	the mind of God, but all of nature as well. The moral judgment of God is inherent in the whole process of creation. There is nothing that is not included in the divine movement. "The Lᴏʀᴅ is in his holy temple," and his holy temple is "all the earth" (2:20).
In a single question, **was thy wrath against the rivers?** the prophet raises the whole problem of the involvement of creation in the judgments of God. Not only man is responsive to	Note that it is the moral judgment of God expressed in his concern for his people that

10 The mountains saw thee, *and* they trembled: the overflowing of the water passed by: the deep uttered his voice, *and* lifted up his hands on high.

11 The sun *and* moon stood still in their habitation: at the light of thine arrows they went, *and* at the shining of thy glittering spear.

12 Thou didst march through the land in indignation, thou didst thresh the heathen in anger.

13 Thou wentest forth for the salvation of thy people, *even* for salvation with thine anointed; thou woundedst the head out of the house of the wicked, by discovering the foundation unto the neck. Selah.

10 The mountains saw thee, and writhed;
   the raging waters swept on;
the deep gave forth its voice,
   it lifted its hands on high.

11 The sun and moon stood still in their habitation[j]
  at the light of thine arrows as they sped,
  at the flash of thy glittering spear.

12 Thou didst bestride the earth in fury,
   thou didst trample the nations in anger.

13 Thou wentest forth for the salvation of thy people,
  for the salvation of thy anointed.
Thou didst crush the head of the wicked,[k]
  laying him bare from thigh to neck.[l]
          Selah

[j] Heb uncertain
[k] Cn: Heb *head from the house of the wicked*
[l] Heb obscure

10 When they saw thee, the mountains writhed,
   the clouds poured out water;
The deep put forth its voice,
   it lifted its hands on high.

10. Ps. 77:17 has the better text here, reading "the clouds poured out water" for **the raging waters swept on. The deep,** as has been noted above, is *tehôm*, the Hebrew equivalent of the mythological Tiamat, the primeval monster whom Marduk split in two like a great fish at the creation. For **it lifted its hands on high** one is tempted to read "the height lifted up its hands." Another proposal is to combine the last clause of vs. 10 with the first word (**sun**) of vs. 11, to obtain "the sun lifted up its light." But it is more probable that two words have dropped out of vs. 11, as the LXX suggests (cf. Judg. 5:4, 5).

11 The sun withheld its light,
   the moon stood in its lofty abode,
For light thine arrows ran abroad,
   for brightness the glittering of thy spear.

11. Possibly the sun and moon are eclipsed; at any rate, the normal course of nature is suspended while the lightning flashes. Another possible rendering is: "The sun forgot its rising."

12 In fury thou didst stamp the earth,
   in wrath thou didst trample nations.
13 Thou didst go forth to the help of thy people,
   to save thine anointed.
Thou didst shatter the house of the wicked,
   laying bare foundations even to the rock. Selah.

12-13. The purpose of the storm is now clarified: the overthrow of the enemy nations and the rescue of God's people. Who are **the wicked** and the **anointed?** A Seleucid and a priest-king, one of the Maccabees? Or is the "Messiah" ("anointed") the Jewish people as a whole? In vs. 13 the LXX varies widely, and the last half is overlong. Hence omit "the top of," lit., "head from" and read "rock" for the impossible Hebrew, **neck. Head** or "top" has crept up from vs. 14.

14 Thou didst strike through with his staves the head of his villages: they came out as a whirlwind to scatter me: their rejoicing *was* as to devour the poor secretly.

15 Thou didst walk through the sea with thine horses, *through* the heap of great waters.

16 When I heard, my belly trembled; my lips quivered at the voice: rottenness entered into my bones, and I trembled in myself, that I might rest in the day of trouble: when he cometh up unto the people, he will invade them with his troops.

14 Thou didst pierce with thy[m] shafts the
  head of his warriors,[n]
who came like a whirlwind to scatter
  me,
rejoicing as if to devour the poor in
  secret.
15 Thou didst trample the sea with thy
  horses,
  the surging of mighty waters.

16 I hear, and my body trembles,
  my lips quiver at the sound;
rottenness enters into my bones,
  my steps totter[o] beneath me.
I will quietly wait for the day of trouble
  to come upon people who invade us.

[m] Heb *his*
[n] Vg Compare Gk Syr: Heb uncertain
[o] Cn Compare Gk: Heb *I tremble because*

14 Thou didst pierce his head with thy shafts,
    his leaders are driven by the storm . . . .
15 Thou didst trample the sea with thy horses,
    the mighty waters foamed.

14-15. Vs. 14 is one of the most difficult of all. Read **thy shafts** or "arrows" for **his shafts,** and add "his" to **head.** The LXX gives the clue to the unusual word translated "leaders," possibly **warriors;** the verb with that noun means "to drive," like a tempest, "storm along," drive as chaff is driven before the wind. The next words read, lit., "To scatter me is their exultation, as to devour the poor in ambush." But this makes no appropriate sense in the context, and the line is either hopelessly corrupt or has come from the margin, or both. In vs. 15, for **surging,** or **heap,** read a verb, "foam." Some would transpose this verse to a point after vs. 7 or after vs. 11; if any move is made, the former seems less objectionable. Ps. 77:19 speaks of God's "way . . . in the sea" and "path in the great waters."

D. Joy Despite Adversity (3:16-19)

16 When I hear, my body trembles,
    my lips quiver at the sound.
Decay enters into my bones,
    and my footsteps tremble beneath me.
I await the day of trouble
    to arise for the people who assail us.

16. As vs. 2 is the introduction to the theophany, vs. 16 is its conclusion, and takes the reader back to the words, "I have heard the report of thee." **My body:** Lit., **My belly.** Slight changes must be made in the Hebrew forms in this verse, and the sense is not quite certain: "Though I am thoroughly awed and frightened by the account of what

initiates the movement in which all creation is involved. God as righteous will expressed himself in a series of mighty events of which the creation of the world was one. But another of his works was the creation of a people peculiarly responsive to his will. On their behalf he sweeps through all time and space.

We may quarrel with the way in which the prophet seems to establish squatters' rights over the divine prerogative. We may find it difficult to accept the validity of the ancient insistence of Israel that they are a peculiar people. But the fact remains that the influence of Israel on human history, growing out of that presupposi-

17 ¶ Although the fig tree shall not blossom, neither *shall* fruit *be* in the vines; the labor of the olive shall fail, and the fields shall yield no meat; the flock shall be cut off from the fold, and *there shall be* no herd in the stalls:

18 Yet I will rejoice in the LORD, I will joy in the God of my salvation.

19 The LORD God *is* my strength, and he will make my feet like hinds' *feet,* and he will make me to walk upon mine high places. To the chief singer on my stringed instruments.

17 Though the fig tree do not blossom,
  nor fruit be on the vines,
 the produce of the olive fail
  and the fields yield no food,
 the flock be cut off from the fold
  and there be no herd in the stalls,

18 yet I will rejoice in the LORD,
  I will joy in the God of my salvation.

19 GOD, the Lord, is my strength;
  he makes my feet like hinds' feet,
  he makes me tread upon my high
   places.

To the choirmaster: with stringed[p] instruments.

[p] Heb *my stringed*

God has done and will presumably do again, I wait [rest or wait quietly] for the day of judgment to fall upon the enemy." Or, removing one letter, "I wait unperturbed for the day of trouble to come upon me, when our assailants arise" (for the rising of the people who assail us). The latter would perhaps form a better link with what follows.

> 17 For though the fig tree bear no fruit,
>   and there be no grapes on the vines,
> The produce of the olive fail,
>   and the fields yield no food,
> The sheep be cut off from the fold,
>   and there be no ox in the stalls,
> 18 Yet will I exult in the Lord,
>   I will joy in the God who saves me . . .
> 19 Who makes my feet like hind's feet,
>   and lets me tread upon my high places.

17-19. Strange as it may appear, the psalm literature—outside the canonical Psalter—reaches one of its topmost peaks in these five lines. The author's religion does not defer its dividends. In the very midst of his destitution he finds reason to exult and rejoice; living by his faithfulness, he finds life's supreme good that lifts him to high places above material calamities. For **blossom** read "bear fruit," as does the Greek. **Fruit:** Better, "grapes"; lit., "increase" or "produce." **God of my salvation:** "The God who saves me," "helps me," or "gives me victory." After this line a scribe is responsible for

---

tion, has moved through the centuries like the Gulf Stream in the Atlantic. Why this is true remains to this day a baffling enigma. The miracle of Israel provides at least one empirical basis for the moral judgment of God on human history. So convinced is the prophet of this that with confidence he can say:

> **I will quietly wait for the day of trouble**
> **to come upon people who invade us.**

17-19. What Are the Odds?—These verses are an idyl of hope and confidence. The conclusion

is that paradox itself may be the ultimate validation of the moral judgment. The final resting place of the religious spirit is that the basis of hope is never ultimately to be found in the course of events. Man is not required to wait until the stubborn and unyielding facts of life justify his faith in life. The testimony of the spirit of God in man is the final testimony, the ultimate truth by which his steps must be guided. His assurance must never be at the mercy of the movement of life about him; he must find the witness of God in his own heart or he will never find it.

GOD, the Lord, is my strength (cf. Ps. 18:32-33; II Sam. 22:33-34). For walking on **high places** cf. Deut. 33:29; 32:13; Mic. 1:3; Amos 4:13; II Sam. 1:19, 25. For the musical notations at the end cf. Exeg. on vs. 1.

Commenting on vss. 3-15, W. A. Irwin in his revision of J. M. P. Smith, *The Prophets and Their Times* [2nd ed., rev.; Chicago: University of Chicago Press, 1941], pp. 162-63; see also J. M. P. Smith, *The Religion of the Psalms* [Chicago: University of Chicago Press, 1922], pp. 93-95), speaks of this poem as

but an adaptation to Yahweh of the incidents of the Babylonian "Creation Epic"; step by step we can follow precisely the movements and adventures ascribed to Marduk in that most famous and most influential liturgy of the ancient world. . . . The enemy of the Lord was the primeval foe, chaos and darkness; but he was also the ever recurring persecutor and oppressor of the Lord's people. Pharaoh, Amalek, Edom, or Nebuchadrezzar, and far down the centuries, Antiochus Epiphanes or even Adolph Hitler—all alike were but the demon of the primeval deep over whom the Lord triumphed at the beginning, over whom he is perennially and eternally triumphant.

The Book of

ZEPHANIAH

Introduction and Exegesis by CHARLES L. TAYLOR, JR.
Exposition by HOWARD THURMAN

ZEPHANIAH

INTRODUCTION

According to the title, the word of the Lord came to Zephaniah "in the days of Josiah the son of Amon, king of Judah" (1:1). The editor who incorporated his writings into the Book of the Twelve, in other words, believed that he preached within the period 638-609 b.c. Is this tradition sound? If so, at what point in that quarter century is he most likely to have been active?

I. Historical Background and Date

As in the eighth century b.c., so in the seventh, the history of Judah can be understood only against the background of events in Assyria, the dominant power. Under Esarhaddon (681-669) and Ashurbanipal (669-626) Assyrian fortunes were at their zenith (see articles "The Old Testament World" and "The History of Israel," Vol. I, pp. 233-71, 272-91). Even Thebes, the Egyptian capital far up the distant Nile, had fallen to the latter king (663), an event of such importance that Nahum recalled it a half century later (Nah. 3:8-10). Although within two decades Egypt had recovered her independence, the Pharaoh Psamtik I (663-609) was not unfriendly to Ashurbanipal, under whose rule Assyrian power began to totter but maintained itself until 626.[1]

Manasseh, king of Judah (687-642), ruled by permission of his Assyrian masters and for their benefit. To later tradition his name stands as a symbol of evil. According to II Kings 21, it was Manasseh who seduced his people to greater crimes than those of the ancient nations whose territory the Lord had given Israel. Syncretism is the word that sums up his religion and his fault. To please the Assyrians he adopted and spread Assyrian customs. Nor was he alone in this; in a time of Assyrian power,

what more natural than that her vassals worship Assyrian gods? The account in Kings suggests child sacrifice ("He made his son pass through the fire," II Kings 21:6). He revived the local divinities of Canaan (II Kings 21:3, 7). He supported witchcraft and the cult of the dead (II Kings 21:6), and practiced the worship of the astral deities of the Assyrians (II Kings 21:5). Many of these departures from the purer practice of Israel of course were old; now, however, they were no longer naïve but conscious apostasy. "Moreover Manasseh shed very much innocent blood, till he had filled Jerusalem from one end to another" (II Kings 21:16). Precisely who his victims were nobody can say. But since politics and religion were inextricably and wholly intertwined, presumably he attacked those who opposed his pre-Assyrian policy, or who withstood Assyrian customs and championed the worship of Yahweh alone. Manasseh found room in his pantheon for Israel's traditional deity as one among many gods. Those who heeded the teaching of the eighth-century prophets, on the other hand, could brook no confusion between Yahweh and the baals, and paid for their convictions with their lives, or went into hiding, biding their time.

The brief reign of Amon, the successor of Manasseh, ended abruptly in less than two years with his murder. But the reformers had their day under the next king, Josiah, who was brought up by tutors, presumably of the prophets' party. This ruler, unequaled for his piety in all the history of Judah, later generations remembered as the king "that turned to the Lord with all his heart, and with all his soul, and with all his might" (II Kings 23:25). Under him came the publication in 621 of the book of Deuteronomy and the enforcement of its provisions upon the state of Judah. Syncretism, apostasy from the Lord, worship of astral

---

[1] Cf. J. B. Bury, S. A. Cook, and F. E. Adcock, eds., *The Cambridge Ancient History* (New York: The Macmillan Co., 1923), III, 294-95, 146.

deities, adoption of foreign customs, indifference to the Lord's demands—such are the evils attacked in Deuteronomy and in Josiah's reform program, and such might be expected to be the concern of a prophet of this period.

Upon the death of Ashurbanipal, about 626, the political situation changed rapidly. Weakened by overexpansion and by civil wars, Assyria had no strength to withstand the revolts against the flabby rulers who followed Ashurbanipal. To be sure, in 626 a Babylonian uprising against Assyria was suppressed, at which time Assyria seems to have been aided by Scythian raids upon her enemies. But war broke out between Babylonians and Assyrians again in 616. In the following year Nabopolassar of Babylon found an ally in Cyaxares, king of the Medes, in 614 Tarbiz and Asshur fell, and two years later the capital, Nineveh, lay in ruins. Although Assyria maintained another capital at Harran for two years longer, Babylonia was to be the dominant power from 612 until the rise of Cyrus in the middle of the sixth century. An Egyptian expedition in 609 to help the lost Assyrian cause succeeded only in killing Josiah of Judah, and in 605 the battle of Carchemish definitely established Babylonian supremacy over Egypt. The books of Kings and Jeremiah bear witness to the struggle in Jerusalem between pro-Assyrian and pro-Egyptian parties of this period, and to the futile intrigues and revolts which brought about the fall of Jerusalem to Nebuchadrezzar in 586.

Herodotus reports that when the Medes under Cyaxares were on the point of conquering the Assyrians and had already defeated them in one battle, a numerous band of Scyths burst into Asia, "were opposed by the Medes, who gave them battle, but, being defeated, lost their empire," whereupon "the Scythians became masters of Asia." Then follows a passage important for the interpretation of Zephaniah: "After this they marched forward with the design of invading Egypt. When they had reached Palestine, however, Psammetichus the Egyptian king met them with gifts and prayers, and prevailed on them to advance no further." [2]

Herodotus goes on to say that on their return some stragglers pillaged the temple of Celestial Venus at Ashkelon, that the dominion of the Scythians over Asia lasted twenty-eight years, that they were cruelly insolent and oppressive, and that finally Cyaxares and the Medes made the greater part of them drunk, massacred them, and so recovered their empire. Does Zeph. 1:18 refer to the Egyptian bribery of the Scythians? Does 2:4-15 predict disaster upon the nations through the activity of the Scythians? Herodotus is sometimes untrustworthy. Was there a Scyth-

ian invasion of the Philistine plain between 630 and 624 B.C., and did it prompt Zephaniah (and Jeremiah) to speak the Lord's judgments?

So far, then, two related problems have emerged. Assuming that the title is correct, did Zephaniah preach before or after the Deuteronomic reform of 621, and did Scythian raids prompt his message? Sure answers to both of these questions are impossible. But at least the evil with which Zephaniah is concerned are those likely to have been rife in the decade before the reform and reported to have existed in II Kings 21–23: foreign customs, worship of astral bodies, syncretism, apostasy, and practical skepticism (cf. Zeph. 1:4-5, 8-9, 12; II Kings 21:3-7). Again the reference in Zephaniah to the wearing of foreign clothes reflects the political connection between Judah and Assyria which the reform, with its important political as well as religious consequences, severed.[3] A date around 626 fits such evidence as we possess reasonably well, and until better reasons can be given for placing the prophet at another time, here he remains, a witness to the days shortly before the Deuteronomic Code was found.

Our knowledge of the Scythians is meager. The arguments against the identification of the foe from the north in Jeremiah with the Scythians have considerable strength. If Assyria and the Scythians were both fighting against the Medes about 625, would Zephaniah consider the Scythians the agent of the Lord to bring about the destruction of the Assyrians (2:13)? Perhaps there was no alliance between them. Perhaps it was too loose to concern or even be known to a prophet of Judah. It seems very unlikely that the Scythians exercised dominion over Asia, as Herodotus says they did, for twenty-eight years. In point of fact, they did not destroy Assyria or Egypt or Judah, and perhaps not Philistia. Was Zephaniah only frightened by their irruption into thinking that they would? [4] Or was the breakdown of Assyrian power sufficient to account for the expectation of judgment that pervades this book? Again no facile answer will suffice. If Zephaniah

[3] No stress should be put upon the fact that the punishing agent of the Lord is expected to march on Jerusalem from the north (1:10) and that actually the Scythian invasion of the coastal plain (not Jerusalem) came from that quarter. Nor should much be made of the point that the royal family is denounced but not the king. These considerations give the flimsiest sort of evidence as to when Zephaniah preached, and no help as to whether before or after 621. Moreover, no weight can be given to the phrase "remnant of Baal" (1:4) as indicative of a time after the reform. For the Greek text at this point reads "the names of Baal" and the Hebrew may be translated "last vestige of Baal" without any implication that Baal in part has already been cut off.

[4] Does the name Scythopolis (Beth-shean) which occurs on an inscription in 218 B.C., go back to the raids of this time?

[2] *History* I. 104-5.

preached about 625, and the Scythians were active in that decade, they may have stimulated his preaching. But two further problems also related to these must now be considered.

II. *The Prophet's Lineage*

The first of these is simply stated. Does the title mean that Zephaniah is the grandson of the grandson of King Hezekiah of Judah (715-687), and if so, could he have delivered these oracles by 626? Very likely Hezekiah is none other than the king, for otherwise the editor would scarcely have bothered to give Zephaniah's ancestry, in this highly unusual fashion, for four previous generations. Zephaniah is almost certainly of royal lineage, a second cousin once removed of Josiah the king, who is still in his early twenties before the reform. Zephaniah is known to have been a citizen of Jerusalem (1:4); he shows little knowledge of or sympathy with the poor; he does not hesitate to denounce the royal family or royal household, although he spares the king himself. All this offers no difficulty to the hypothesis that Zephaniah may have been trained by the same teachers who influenced Josiah, and in fact may have been Josiah's close contemporary. The objection is offered that in one branch of the family there are five generations in a century, in the other only four, and that five are too many. Yet five are surely possible, and the long reign of Manasseh would give ample opportunity for his nephew and grandnephew to have grown to maturity by the time of the accession of Amon.[5]

To summarize, shortly before 621 a cousin of Josiah could have learned his lessons out of the recorded words of Amos and Isaiah, as his preaching indicates that he did, and could have said something worthy of preservation, possibly under the stimulus of Scythian marauders in the offing. But how much? This leads to a consideration of the fourth problem, the integrity of the book.

III. *Composition*

Nowhere better than in Zephaniah appears the pattern of the editors of the prophetic books, the three parts of which are (*a*) woe to Judah, (*b*) an extension of judgment to other nations, and (*c*) comfort to Judah after the

[5] It is true that whereas elsewhere the name Cushi is generic (=Ethiopian), its use in this genealogy invites questions. Was Cushi born some twenty years before Zephaniah, and was Zephaniah about twenty around 626? Then did the war between Assyria and Egypt, which at that time was ruled by an Ethiopian dynasty, prompt a member of the royal family in Judah to name his son Cushi out of love for Egypt at the time (663) when Thebes fell? Or is the text which gives "Cushi" correct?

world catastrophe. In Isaiah, Jeremiah, and Ezekiel the pattern is present but to some extent obscured by the bulk of the material (Isa. 1–12; 23–27; 34–35; 40–66; Jer. 1–25; 46–51 [which in the Septuagint came after 25:13]; 30–33; Ezek. 1–24; 25–32; 33–48). When the editors felt that the message of the Lord to their day was not condemnation but comfort, they fortunately did not destroy the threats of the early prophets, but supplemented them first by broadening the scope of God's wrath and then by promising that a righteous remnant of Judah would escape from the universal assize. Against the background of this editorial method Zephaniah's work is to be studied.

A. Chapter 1.—The difficulties of ch. 1 are perhaps insoluble. Nevertheless a right judgment may be approximated if several important points are remembered.

First, as the editorial hand is clearly active in other chapters of Zephaniah, so it may be detected also in ch. 1. An obvious instance is vs. 13*b*, quoted loosely from Amos 5:11.

Second, late editors had a tendency to forget the historical agencies with which prophecy was concerned while they drew vague and general pictures of the end of the age. The book of Zephaniah, says George Adam Smith, "is the first tinging of prophecy with apocalypse: that is the moment which it supplies in the history of Israel's religion."[6] But there is always the possibility that these eschatological ideas, which are characteristic of writers several centuries later, may have been imported into Zephaniah. The prophet may have proclaimed judgment upon the leading classes of Jerusalem, and upon Assyrians and Philistines; another may have transformed this material into predictions of a world catastrophe. Adolphe Lods[7] finds that Zephaniah is dealing with an enemy invasion in vss. 10-12, 16-17, not a cosmic upheaval, and he acknowledges some editing. "Even so," he says, "it is obvious that the catastrophe envisaged by Zephaniah was a 'world' catastrophe." But will that estimate stand?

Third, ordinarily where the phrase "in that day" appears, eschatologists are at work. There are references to "the day," of course, in the early prophets. The day of the Lord in Amos is a day close at hand, not at the end of history. But "The Day of the Lord tends to become the Last Day."[8] The question here is whether the day of Zeph. 1 means essentially the same as the day in Amos 5:18-20, or the final Judgment Day, or possibly a mixture of both.

[6] *The Book of the Twelve Prophets* (rev. ed.; New York: Harper & Bros., 1928), II, 48.
[7] *The Prophets and the Rise of Judaism* (tr. S. H. Hooke; New York: E. P. Dutton & Co., 1937), p. 133.
[8] George Adam Smith, *loc. cit.*

Fourth, while it is generally agreed that the prophets speak in the name of the Lord, using the first person, there can be little doubt that editors have used this form freely. A good example is Amos 3:1, where the clause "against the whole family which I brought up out of the land of Egypt" appears in the Lord's mouth before "this word that the LORD has spoken" is fully introduced by the participle "saying." There is no guarantee, in other words, that either first-person passages or third-person passages stem from the early period of Hebrew prophecy. The relation between first- and third-person passages needs much further study, which may prove inconclusive, but at least sudden shifts from one to the other should be examined for what light they may shed on editorial activity.

Led by these considerations we can ascribe 1:2, 3 to an eschatological writer whom nothing less than universal destruction would satisfy. A similar catalogue appears in the secondary Hos. 4:3. Similarly, Zeph. 1:17, if the reading "I will bring distress on men" is right, suggests the extension of the judgment to all mankind, and most of vs. 18 (at least from "all the earth shall be consumed" to the end) is clearly another addition of this kind. Vs. 6 seems to be a reference to apostates of Judaism who do not perform their religious duties.

There remain: (a) Eleven lines descriptive of the Lord's punishment on Jerusalem for religious disloyalty and moral offenses, written in the first person: vss. 4-5 (overloaded by "with the priests" and "those who swear"—still another clause must be deleted to produce regular meter); vss. 8-9 (introduced by "and on the day of the LORD's sacrifice," which stands outside the metrical structure; "on that day" in vs. 9 may also be a marginal note); and vs. 12 (again introduced by a note outside the meter, "At that time it will come to pass"). The meter of these lines, though somewhat dubious, is apparently meant to be catalectic, four accents followed by three in each line. (b) The balance of the chapter (vss. 7, 10 [omit "on that day, says the LORD"], 11, 13a, 14, 15, 16) consists of twelve lines written in the third person, in regular catalectic meter (like the material which can be ascribed to Zephaniah in ch. 2; see below), describing the day of the Lord, a day which is not distant but near. Like the poems in Isa. 5:26-29 and 10:28-32, they have little or no reference to the morals of those about to suffer on the day. The overwhelming fact is presented without reasons. It is possible that vss. 17b and 18a (as far as "to deliver them") are a part of this poem, though they would follow better vs. 11 than vs. 16.

If this analysis is correct, then the two poems have been interwoven, four lines from the first, two from the second, four more from the first, three (or five) from the second, three from the first, and seven from the second. It is possible that a line or more assigned to the second poem may properly belong to the first (e.g., vs. 13a). No finality should be attached to this suggestion, but if two poems written in the same meter were thus combined, it is easy to see how glosses crept in, for example, vss. 8a, 9 ("on that day"), vs. 10 ("'on that day,' says the LORD"), vs. 12 ("At that time it will come to pass"), and how ample opportunity was afforded for the introduction of material quoted from other books (vs. 13b) or designed to make the catastrophe universal (vss. 2-3, 17a, 18b). There seems to be no sufficient reason to deny to Zephaniah authorship of either of these poems. Both of them, especially the first, appear to be truncated portions of larger works. There remains the possibility, however, that the first poem is the ad hoc effort of a later writer who, building on II Kings 23, reconstructed what Zephaniah—or a prophet of 630-620 B.C.—might be expected to have said. Nor can it be denied that the "day of the LORD" material, which has many affinities with late literature, may have developed out of a smaller nucleus than has been here presented.[9]

B. Chapter 2.—This chapter affords several illustrations of editorial work. Vss. 13-14 are a prediction that "he," presumably the Lord, will make Nineveh a desert waste. But vs. 15 is not prediction; it is written *post eventum* and makes ample use of Isa. 47:8; Jer. 19:8. Vss. 10-11 (third person) are an expansion and in part a repetition of vss. 8-9 (first person). Because vss. 8-9 reflect the attitude of Moab and the Ammonites in the sixth century, most scholars ascribe them to an editor rather than to Zephaniah. In vs. 7a,c another editor full of comfort for Judah has inserted the promise that Philistine territory will become the property of the Jewish remnant (cf. 2:9). In vs. 2 there are apparently two variants, both of which have become a part of the text, and it is likely that vs. 3 is a late effort to modify vss. 1-2. These first two verses of the chapter are not really a call to repentance, as is often supposed, but an ironical exhortation to keep on in shameless ways and be destroyed. Vs. 3 is an invitation to the humble who keep the law (both "the humble" and "the law" are late concepts) to become a righteous remnant. In this chapter, therefore, vss. 1, 2a, 4-6, 7b, 12-14 may be from Zephaniah. Vs. 12, nevertheless, is short and fragmentary, and it is perhaps sig-

⁹ Cf. Rolland E. Wolfe, "The Editing of the Book of the Twelve," *Zeitschrift für die alttestamentliche Wissenschaft*, LIII (1935), 104.

nificant that in this material the Lord speaks in the first person only in vs. 12 and in what may be an added line, vs. 5c, which stands outside the metrical scheme.

C. Chapter 3.—Vss. 14-20 are generally recognized as late. Judah has been scattered but will be gathered home again. Disaster is past; victory, peace, and rejoicing lie ahead. The Lord is wholly favorable toward Judah, with scarcely a hint of displeasure. In short, the whole tone of this passage is like that of Isa. 40–66 rather than Zeph. 1. Prophecy has passed over into eschatological prediction. Concern with historical events has vanished into the generalities of the golden age.

Similarly, many scholars regard vss. 8-13 as the work of writers long after Zephaniah. After the failure of Judah to accept correction in vs. 7, one expects a sentence of doom. Instead the thought abruptly changes: it is the nations, not Judah, who are to feel the heat of the divine anger (vs. 8). Apparently a substitution has been made for the threat that originally may have followed vs. 7. The phrase "on that day" (vs. 11) is characteristic of editors (e.g., Isa. 19:16-24). The doctrine of the remnant (vss. 12-13) was developed and popularized by the experience of the nation in the sixth century B.C. The concept of "a people humble and lowly" (vs. 12) is characteristic of the later psalms and the piety of Judaism. Although A. B. Davidson called vss. 11-13 "the most beautiful thing in the book," [10] these verses make a distinction between Judah and the heathen very different from the inclusive condemnation of ch. 1. In fact ch. 3 within itself shows the editorial pattern: condemnation of Judah (vss. 1-7); extension of judgment to the heathen (vs. 8); who shall be converted (vss. 9-10; vss. 8 and 9 are not wholly consistent); the balm for the remnant (vss. 11-13) and for all dispersed Israel (vss. 14-20).

As Mic. 6:1–7:6 threatens punishment but was written by another than Micah, probably some centuries later, so Zeph. 3:1-7 may not be Zephaniah's work. Its accusations are vague and general, "but a pale reflection of the fierce indignation of ch. 1"; [11] its reference to the law (vs. 4) suggests a later time; and the vocabulary has late affinities. Vss. 6-7 are apparently a fragment originally unconnected with vs. 5. But on vss. 1-7 judgment may be left suspended, with the caution that it is unsafe to lean upon them, especially vss. 6-7, in a summary of Zephaniah's teaching.

[10] *The Books of Nahum, Habakkuk and Zephaniah* (Cambridge: Cambridge University Press, 1920; "Cambridge Bible"), pp. 114-15.

[11] Raymond Calkins, *The Modern Message of the Minor Prophets* (New York: Harper & Bros., 1947), p. 67.

One may rearrange the material of ch. 3 as follows:

THREATS AGAINST THE OBSTINATE CITY

1. Woe to her that is rebellious and defiled,
   the oppressing city!
2. She listens to no voice,
   she accepts no correction.
   In the Lord she does not trust,
   to her God she does not draw near.

THE RULING CLASSES

3. Her princes within her
   are roaring lions;
   Her judges are evening wolves
   that leave nothing till morning.
4. Her prophets are wanton,
   faithless men;
   Her priests profane what is sacred,
   violate the law.

THE RIGHTEOUSNESS OF THE LORD

5. The Lord within her is righteous,
   he does no wrong;
   Morning by morning he shows his justice,
   like the light he does not fail.
   But the unjust knows no shame.

THE PAST JUDGMENTS OF THE LORD

6. "I have cut off nations,
   their battlements are ruined;
   I have emptied their streets
   so that none walks in them;
   Their cities have been laid waste
   without a man, without inhabitant.
7. I said, 'Surely she will fear me,
   she will accept correction;
   She will not lose sight
   of all my injunctions upon her.'
   But all the more they were eager
   to make all their deeds corrupt.

THE DAY OF THE LORD

8. "Therefore wait for me," says the Lord,
   "For the day when I arise as a witness.
   For my decision is to gather nations,
   to assemble kingdoms,
   To pour out upon them my indignation,
   all the heat of my anger;
   For in the fire of my jealous wrath,
   all the earth shall be consumed.

THE CONVERSION OF THE PEOPLES

9. "For then
   I will change the speech of the peoples
   to a pure speech,
   That all of them may call on my name
   and serve me with one accord.
10. From beyond the rivers of Ethiopia to the
    distant north
    they shall bring my offering.

THE SECURITY OF THE REMNANT

11. "On that day
    You shall not be put to shame for all the deeds
    by which you rebelled against me;

For then I will remove from your midst
  your proudly exultant ones,
And you shall no longer be haughty
  on my holy mountain.
12. And I will leave in your midst
    a people humble and lowly.
  And they shall seek refuge in the name of the
    Lord,
13. a remnant of Israel.
  They shall do no wrong
    and utter no lies
  Nor shall there be found in their mouth
    a deceitful tongue.
  And they shall pasture and lie down
    with none to frighten them."

Invitation to Rejoice

14. Sing aloud, O daughter of Zion;
    shout, O Israel!
  Rejoice and exult with all your heart,
    O daughter of Jerusalem.
15. The Lord has removed your opponents
    and turned away your enemies.
  The king of Israel, the Lord, is in your midst,
    you shall see trouble no more.
16. On that day it shall be said to Jerusalem:
  "Do not fear, O Zion,
    let not your hands droop.
17. The Lord your God is in your midst,
    a victorious warrior,
  He will rejoice over you with gladness,
    he will renew you in his love,
  He will exult over you with loud singing
18a. as on a day of festival.

The Promises of the Lord

18b. "I have gathered your wounded
    and will take away your reproach.

19. "Behold I am about to make an end
    of all your oppressors at that time
  And I will save the lame
    and gather the outcast,
  And I will make them praised and renowned
    throughout all the earth their shame.

20. "At that time I will bring you home
    and at that time I will gather you together;
  For I will make you renowned and praised
    among all the peoples of the earth,
  When I restore your fortunes
    before your eyes," says the Lord.

IV. Religious Teaching

From what has already been said five summary statements may be made about Zephaniah's teaching:

(a) He took over from Amos and Isaiah the concept of a day near at hand on which his nation would suffer invasion and dire calamity, and in turn inspired the medieval hymn attributed to Thomas of Celano, "Dies Irae," of which the beginning reads:

Day of wrath! O day of mourning!
See fulfilled the prophets' warning,
Heav'n and earth in ashes burning!

O what fear man's bosom rendeth
When from heav'n the Judge descendeth,
On whose sentence all dependeth!

Wondrous sound the trumpet flingeth;
Through earth's sepulchers it ringeth;
All before the throne it bringeth.

Death is struck, and nature quaking,
All creation is awaking,
To its Judge an answer making.[12]

(b) He received also from the eighth-century prophets the concept that God has a conscience and is offended by the moral and religious sins of his people. It is often said that Zephaniah was unoriginal, lacking in imagination, understanding, and an appreciation of beauty. His role was a difficult one. It was his part to point out the specific ills of his own time, similar to those which his predecessors had denounced, and to apply their judgments, namely, upon syncretism (1:4); foreign worship (1:5); adoption of foreign ways (1:8-9); oppression and deceit (1:9); indifference (1:12); and practical skepticism (1:12). If Zeph. 3:1-5 is derived from the prophet, oppression is stressed again (3:1, 3), and other wrongs are added: obstinacy (3:2); lack of trust (3:2, 4); rebellion (3:1); and profanation (3:4). In other words, the collaborationists, the tyrannical, the degraded and corrupt, and those who prostitute and neglect their religion encounter Zephaniah's special scorn. Of all the expressions in the book, perhaps the most striking is "the men who are thickening upon their lees" (1:12) which called forth from George Adam Smith the classic comment: "The great causes of God and Humanity are not defeated by the hot assaults of the Devil, but by the slow, crushing, glacier-like mass of thousands and thousands of indifferent nobodies. God's causes are never destroyed by being blown up, but by being sat upon."[13] In the same verse with this memorable word to describe the indifferent appears the picture of the Lord searching Jerusalem with lamps (1:12), which has led to the representation of Zephaniah in art with a lamp in his hand.

(c) It seems unlikely, however, that Zephaniah is "the first of our Old Testament writers whose mind is dominated entirely by eschatological ideas."[14] He does not flee altogether from the realm of practical ethics to speculation about the distant future.

(d) Nor may we attribute to him the prom-

---

[12] Tr. William J. Irons.
[13] Book of the Twelve Prophets, II, 52.
[14] W. O. E. Oesterley and T. H. Robinson, An Introduction to the Books of the Old Testament (New York: The Macmillan Co., 1934), p. 403.

ises of the golden age, in one of which (3:9) there is a hint of the conversion of all peoples to "serve [the Lord] with one accord."

(e) If parts of ch. 2 are derived from Zephaniah, vss. 1-2 and the oracles on the Philistines (vss. 4-7) and the Assyrians (vss. 13-14) are the most likely, but none of these make important contributions to the history of religious thought or to an understanding of the divine will. It is the editor of this chapter who skillfully arranged the material to enforce the lesson that the Lord resists the proud and rewards the humble.

V. Outline of Contents

VI. Selected Bibliography

DAVIDSON, A. B. The Books of Nahum, Habakkuk and Zephaniah ("Combridge Bible"). Cambridge: Cambridge University Press, 1920.

DRIVER, S. R., ed. The Minor Prophets ("New Century Bible"). New York: Oxford University Press, 1906. Vol. II.

ELLIGER, KARL. Das Buch der zwölf kleinen Propheten: Nahum, Habakuk, Zephanja, Haggai, Sacharja, Maleachi ("Das Alte Testament Deutsch"). Göttingen: Vandenhoeck & Ruprecht, 1950.

GERLEMAN, GILLIS. Zephanja. Lund: C. W. K. Gleerup, 1942.

HORST, FRIEDRICH. Die zwölf kleinen Propheten Nahum bis Maleachi ("Handbuch zum Alten Testament"). Tübingen: J. C. B. Mohr, 1938.

HYATT, J. PHILIP. "The Date and Background of Zephaniah," Journal of Near Eastern Studies, VII (1948), 25-29.

SMITH, GEORGE ADAM. The Book of the Twelve Prophets. Rev. ed. New York: Harper & Bros., 1928. Vol. II.

SMITH, J. M. P., WARD, W. H., and BEWER, JULIUS A. A Critical and Exegetical Commentary on Micah, Zephaniah, Nahum, Habakkuk, Obadiah and Joel ("International Critical Commentary"). New York: Charles Scribner's Sons, 1911.

ZEPHANIAH

TEXT, EXEGESIS, AND EXPOSITION

1 The word of the LORD which came unto Zephaniah the son of Cushi, the son of

1 The word of the LORD which came to Zephani'ah the son of Cushi, son of Gedali'ah, son of Amari'ah, son of Heze-

---

I. JUDGMENT ON JERUSALEM (1:1-18)

A. TITLE (1:1)

1:1. In Zephaniah only does the editor who prefixes the titles to the prophetic books carry the ancestry of the prophet back four generations. The reason undoubtedly

---

1:1-18. The Day of the Lord.—Zephaniah is dealing with mighty words of judgment. It is the judgment of God upon Jerusalem and Judah. The mood is that of the sensitive reli- gious spirit so outraged by the collective un- righteousness of an age or a people or a civiliza- tion that all of life seems to be stained, to be unholy. It can find rest only in the thought of

Gedaliah, the son of Amariah, the son of Hizkiah, in the days of Josiah the son of Amon, king of Judah.

2 I will utterly consume all *things* from off the land, saith the Lord.

3 I will consume man and beast; I will consume the fowls of the heaven, and the fishes of the sea, and the stumblingblocks with the wicked; and I will cut off man from off the land, saith the Lord.

4 I will also stretch out mine hand upon Judah, and upon all the inhabitants of Jerusalem; and I will cut off the remnant of Baal from this place, *and* the name of the Chemarim with the priests;

ki'ah, in the days of Josi'ah the son of Amon, king of Judah.

2 "I will utterly sweep away everything
　　from the face of the earth," says the
　　Lord.
3 "I will sweep away man and beast;
　　I will sweep away the birds of the air
　　and the fish of the sea.
　I will overthrow*a* the wicked;
　　I will cut off mankind
　　from the face of the earth," says the
　　Lord.
4 "I will stretch out my hand against Ju-
　　dah,
　　and against all the inhabitants of Jeru-
　　salem;
　and I will cut off from this place of the
　　remnant of Ba'al
　and the name of the idolatrous priests;*b*

a Cn: Heb *the stumbling blocks*
b Compare Gk: Heb *idolatrous priests with the priests*

is that the **Hezekiah** mentioned is the king of that name, who ruled Judah in 715-687 B.C. On the problem of the date of Zephaniah's ministry cf. the Intro., pp. 1007-9. **Word of the Lord:** In a technical sense the equivalent of prophecy or oracle. **Cushi:** Elsewhere generic; an Ethiopian or Cushite (cf. Intro., p. 1009).

B. Threat of Destruction (1:2-6)

As has already been mentioned, vss. 2, 3, and 6 are likely to be secondary expansions of vss. 4-5. After the total annihilation of vss. 2-3, the limited destruction of vss. 4-5 falls a bit flat. Rolland E. Wolfe ("The Editing of the Book of the Twelve," *Zeitschrift für die alttestamentliche Wissenschaft*, LIII [1935], 104) solves this problem by translating vs. 2, "I will indeed gather all together" to witness the execution of judgment on those mentioned in vss. 4-5. But such an explanation is forced.

2-3. Sweep away: Consume, "remove," "make an end of" (cf. Hos. 4:3). This kind of catalogue is generally scribal. The **wicked** are not a special class prior to Ezekiel. **Overthrow:** Hebrew, **the stumbling blocks,** which cannot be right. A slight change gives the verb parallel to **cut off.**

4. On the theory that the words of Zephaniah begin at this verse, an introduction has been lost, or more probably vss. 4-5, 8-9, 12 are only part of a longer work. Vss. 4-5 do not list all the evils mentioned in II Kings 23:10-15. **From this place** can only be Jerusalem. But since Jerusalem has just been mentioned, and the line is impossible metrically, perhaps **from this place** is a correct gloss. **Remnant of Baal:** LXX, "the names of Baal." **Remnant** can be translated "last trace," but this is not the ordinary meaning (cf. Amos 4:2; Isa. 14:22; 17:3). **Idolatrous priests:** Cf. Hos. 10:5; II Kings 23:5. The Hebrew adds "with the priests," but this phrase is lacking in the LXX and seems to be

some kind of complete and final decimation. And such a decimation bears most heavily upon those whose iniquity is deliberate, who have put aside the knowledge of a better way. It is one thing to run afoul of righteousness in a mindless, amoral manner. Under such circumstances the penalty is nevertheless exacting, but

somehow it seems to be softened by the fact of innocence.

There is a sense of justice which ultimately takes into account the fact that the offender against God was not quite aware of the awful import of his deeds. It is revealed in one's innate reaction in the presence of death caused

5 And them that worship the host of heaven upon the housetops; and them that worship *and* that swear by the Lord, and that swear by Malcham;

6 And them that are turned back from the Lord; and *those* that have not sought the Lord, nor inquired for him.

5 those who bow down on the roofs
to the host of the heavens;
those who bow down and swear to the Lord
and yet swear by Milcom;
6 those who have turned back from following the Lord,
who do not seek the Lord or inquire of him."

---

merely an explanation of the unusual word. Vs. 4 has obviously suffered much in transmission.

5. Worship **on the roofs** was practiced by offerings of incense and libations (cf. Jer. 19:13; 32:29; II Kings 23:5, 12). The influence of Assyrian (or Babylonian, Akkadian) practices in Judah in Manasseh's time and for some years later may have been more extensive than the O.T. cares to admit (cf. II Kings 21:3, 5; 23:4, 5, 11-12; Jer. 8:2; 19:13; Deut. 4:19; 17:3). The struggle of the prophetic party is not only with foreign cults, but also against practices that perhaps had long been a part of the religion of Canaan, though disapproved by strict Yahwists. Double allegiance is the root evil here, as each line of this verse shows. **Who bow down . . . to the Lord:** The phrase is interrupted in the Hebrew by "those who swear," apparently a gloss inserted under the influence of the same word in the second half line. Notice the change here to the Lord in the third person, where "those who bow down to me" might be expected. **Milcom** is undoubtedly the correct vocalization (so the ancient versions). As Judah in vassalage to Assyria worshiped the gods of Assyria, so, when friendly with the Ammonites, it worshiped the Ammonites' god. Solomon long before had set a precedent (I Kings 11:5, 33; II Kings 23:13).

6. Those who have turned back are the apostates or backsliders prominent in the Psalms, Proverbs, and other late literature (e.g., Pss. 53:3; 80:18; Prov. 14:14; Isa. 59:13). To **inquire** almost comes to mean "to worship at the temple" or "to attend the synagogue." In early times men sought the will of the Lord through priests who manipulated lots in an oracle box or ark (e.g., I Sam. 14:17-19; 30:7-8). Later the interpretation of the divine will was taken over more and more by the prophets (I Kings 22:8; Jer. 37:7; cf. William R. Arnold, *Ephod and Ark* [Cambridge: Harvard University Press, 1917], p. 138). But in Judaism the older purpose for visiting the shrine is virtually forgotten, and **inquire** becomes a technical term. Ps. 10:4, e.g., might well be paraphrased, "The wicked in the pride of his countenance does not go to church." Vs. 6 is repetitious, metrically impossible; it is not likely to have been written by Zephaniah.

---

by nature as over against death caused by a deliberate act of violence on the part of human beings. When we are faced with death by what may be called "an act of God," there is something clean and unfouled about it, despite the fact itself. We may be filled with awe or overwhelmed by a profound sense of mystery or even helplessness. But when we are faced with death by another human being, there is something nasty and foul about it. It depresses, humiliates, and degrades; it is an attack upon the very grounds of the integrity of the race. The same qualitative difference appears in the reaction to the innocent man or nation who runs afoul of God's law. Jerusalem and Judah know

what the law of God is; he has planted it in their hearts. The judgment of God against them has to do therefore not only with the external aspects of their situation; in their inward parts there is a laying waste. This the prophet sees with deep clarity.

The conception of human history as being a climactic movement is most significant. It occurs many times in the thought of Israel. It points up the basic difference between a philosophy of history and a theology of history. Both of these get their meaning from the theory of time upon which they are projected.

There are at least two important theories of time that have influenced the thought and

7 Hold thy peace at the presence of the Lord G<small>OD</small>: for the day of the L<small>ORD</small> is at hand: for the L<small>ORD</small> hath prepared a sacrifice, he hath bid his guests.

8 And it shall come to pass in the day of the L<small>ORD</small>'s sacrifice, that I will punish the princes, and the king's children, and all such as are clothed with strange apparel.

9 In the same day also will I punish all those that leap on the threshold, which fill their masters' houses with violence and deceit.

7 Be silent before the Lord G<small>OD</small>!
  For the day of the L<small>ORD</small> is at hand;
the L<small>ORD</small> has prepared a sacrifice
  and consecrated his guests.

8 And on the day of the L<small>ORD</small>'s sacrifice —
  "I will punish the officials and the king's sons
  and all who array themselves in foreign attire.

9 On that day I will punish
  every one who leaps over the threshold,
  and those who fill their master's house
    with violence and fraud."

C. The Lord's Sacrifice (1:7)

7. Now begins the poem, written in the third person, dealing with **the day of the L<small>ORD</small>.** In the presence of Yahweh it is best to keep silence (cf. Ps. 46:10; Hab. 2:20; Zech. 2:13) for the day is imminent. On it the Lord is depicted as performing a sacrifice. Judah is the victim, and the enemy armies are the invited guests who take a part in the feast (cf. I Sam. 9:13, 22; II Sam. 6:19; 15:11; I Kings 1:9). Before any religious act, including war, cleansing was required (cf. I Sam. 16:5; Isa. 13:3), but it is not necessary to think of the invaders of Judah as particularly holy. The point is that the Lord is ready. The guests are added to complete a picture, details of which need not be taken literally. Proposals to change the position of this verse either to a point before vs. 2 or before vs. 14 raise as many problems as they solve. It is true, however, that the subject matter which it best introduces does not immediately follow. Is there sufficient evidence for the assumption that vss. 7, 10-11, 14-16 refer to the day at the end of the world rather than to a day of defeat for Judah soon to develop out of the historical circumstances of Zephaniah's day? (Cf. Intro., p. 1010; Wolfe, *loc. cit.*) At least in vs. 7 the judgment is not as yet universal, for guests are bidden to watch the sacrifice.

D. Punishment of the Princes (1:8-9)

8-9. After the first clause, which is an editorial patch, the poem in the first person is resumed. The abuses here mentioned are four: (*a*) **foreign attire,** (*b*) leaping over the **threshold,** (*c*) **violence,** and (*d*) **fraud.** The foreign clothes are a sign of political and religious disloyalty, with a hint of softness (cf. Matt. 11:8). Leaping over the threshold is best explained by I Sam. 5:5; it is Philistine practice, not Judahite. The LXX reads, "all who fill the house of the Lord their God with violence and fraud," but it is better to understand **house** to mean not the temple but the palace. Zephaniah, like his eighth-century predecessors, denounces those in high position who lead in

behavior of the race. One is what may be regarded as circular. All creation is involved in an endless series of repetitive events, occurrences, or even existences. All creatures are time bound and cannot escape the time-space necessity of their existence. No margins of reality can be experienced outside this necessity. It is important to make clear that this conception of time is in some sense transcendent, as far as any particular time-space event is concerned. All events are conceived as taking place in time, even though time itself is not an event. Even dramatic events such as birth and death

are seen as taking place in time: thus time becomes coterminous with existence itself. Outside time there is no existence, because there can be no frame of reference for awareness. Such a view really means that time itself is a perpetually revolving image of eternity, if eternity is regarded as an awareness without differentiation.

Given the fact of existence as the beginning of the time process, continuity is made possible by it, and the only relief from that continuity must mean release from time. The interpretation of history (time-space events of long or

10 And it shall come to pass in that day, saith the LORD, *that there shall be* the noise of a cry from the fish gate, and a howling from the second, and a great crashing from the hills.

11 Howl, ye inhabitants of Maktesh, for all the merchant people are cut down; all they that bear silver are cut off.

12 And it shall come to pass at that time, *that* I will search Jerusalem with candles, and punish the men that are settled on their lees: that say in their heart, The LORD will not do good, neither will he do evil.

10 "On that day," says the LORD,
  "a cry will be heard from the Fish Gate,
  a wail from the Second Quarter,
  a loud crash from the hills.
11 Wail, O inhabitants of the Mortar!
  For all the traders are no more;
  all who weigh out silver are cut off.
12 At that time I will search Jerusalem with lamps,
  and I will punish the men
who are thickening upon their lees,
  those who say in their hearts,
'The LORD will not do good,
  nor will he do ill.'

vice rather than virtue. The **officials** (*sārîm*) are the princes (Sarah, a feminine form of the word used, means "princess"). For **king's sons** the LXX has "the house of the king," or "household," which is approximately equivalent. Josiah's sons would hardly be old enough for serious criticism by 625. The king himself is not mentioned, perhaps because he was innocent. The verb translated **punish** means first of all to "turn one's attention to" or "upon." From the same root is derived the term for the Persian "overseer." When God notices sin he frequently punishes, but the attention can be favorable, as in 2:7 or Ps. 8:4 ("or the son of man, that thou shouldest notice him"). In vs. 9 omit **on that day.**

E. The Effect of the Day in Jerusalem (1:10-11)

10-11. After another line of editorial piecing, **And it shall come to pass in that day, saith the LORD,** the description of the day, from the second poem, is resumed. The places mentioned seem in part at least to be on the north side of Jerusalem, from which direction the attack will come. There is probably no animus against the **traders** or merchants as such; it is their misfortune that they live in the exposed part of the city. The **Fish Gate** is mentioned in Neh. 12:39 as between the Old Gate and the Sheep Gate near the tower of Hananel; it was one of the north entrances (cf. Neh. 3:1-6). Was it nearest to the fish market? **The Second Quarter** may refer to a relatively vulnerable addition to the city on the only side where expansion was feasible, the north. Huldah lived there (II Kings 22:14). **The hills** are probably not hills in general around Jerusalem, but a section of the city called by that name. **The Mortar (Maktesh)** is elsewhere unmentioned; one can only guess at its location. For the verb **wail** (vs. 11) a noun parallel to **cry, wail,** and **crash** is expected. **The traders:** Lit., all the people of Canaan who gave their name to their principal occupation. While they may be foreign, the likelihood is that they are Judeans here. Vs. 13*a* would fit well at this point. **Weigh out silver:** In the absence of coined money, weighing was necessary.

F. Fate of the Indifferent (1:12-13)

12. Again there is an editorial half line, **It shall come to pass at that time,** following which appears the continuation of vs. 9. It is this verse which gives rise to the representation of Zephaniah in art with a lamp. The LXX has the singular "lamp"; the Hebrew

short duration) growing out of such a theory must result in a long-drawn-out or endless futility unless there is some device for breaking the perpetual rotation. The meaning of history must be very narrowly circumscribed in terms of a sheer antecedent and consequence relation, with ample provision made for the swift judg-ment of the act; or the meaning of history must be determined by the possibility that certain events will break the cycle of repetition and make possible the escape from the time-space predicament. The bearing of all events upon this possibility becomes at once the basis of the philosophy of history.

13 Therefore, their goods shall become a booty, and their houses a desolation: they shall also build houses, but not inhabit *them;* and they shall plant vineyards, but not drink the wine thereof.	13 Their goods shall be plundered, and their houses laid waste. Though they build houses, they shall not inhabit them; though they plant vineyards, they shall not drink wine from them."
14 The great day of the Lord *is* near, *it is* near, and hasteth greatly, *even* the voice of the day of the Lord: the mighty man shall cry there bitterly.	14 The great day of the Lord is near, near and hastening fast; the sound of the day of the Lord is bitter, the mighty man cries aloud there.

has **lamps;** the singular seems sufficient. No one can escape the eye of the Lord (cf. Amos 9:2-3; Jonah; Ps. 139:7-12; and for the searching of dark corners with the aid of a lamp cf. Luke 15:8). **Punish:** Cf. Exeg. on vs. 8. **Men** is a bit pale, leading to suggested emendations, such as "those who are at ease" (cf. Amos 6:1). **Who are thickening upon their lees,** on the other hand, is perhaps the most vivid figure in Zephaniah (cf. Intro., p. 1012, and George Adam Smith's comment upon it cited there). The wine needs to be stirred up, poured from vat to vat; otherwise it **thickens** and lacks strength. So "Moab hath been at ease from his youth, and hath settled on his lees, and hath not been emptied from vessel to vessel, neither hath he gone into captivity; therefore his taste remains in him, and his scent is not changed" (Jer. 48:11). **Say in their hearts:** To themselves, i.e., think (cf. 3:7). **Good** and **ill** refer here not to moral quality, but to help or hindrance in the physical world. These skeptics deny the Lord's participation in such events as the crossing of the Red Sea (Exod. 14) or the downfall of the Northern Kingdom.

13. The first line would fit well after vs. 11. It may also belong with vs. 12; in that case it could be the twelfth line of the poem which for the most part consists of speeches of the Lord in the first person. But the rest of vs. 13 is almost certainly derived from neither poem of Zephaniah, but from Amos 5:11. Similar expressions are to be found in Mic. 6:15; Deut. 28:30, 39. In Amos the punishment is appropriate and the time of it soon enough, but here vs. 13 accords very ill with vs. 14, where the day is advancing so rapidly that there is scarcely time to build houses and plant vineyards. The meter is also askew.

G. Dies Irae (1:14-16)

14-16. This is the classic description of **the great day of the Lord,** on which Thomas of Celano is said to have based his thirteenth-century hymn (cf. Intro., p. 1012). The force of the passage lies in the brevity and clarity of the elements that compose the picture. The day is imminent, painful, devastating, gloomy, martial. Vs. 7 stressed its near approach, and under the figure of sacrifice told of death for the people addressed. Vss. 10-11 indicated the path of the disaster and consequent cries from the northern and perhaps other parts of Jerusalem. Now vs. 14 returns to the thought of vs. 7, the immediacy of the day. But there are difficulties with the text, for the Hebrew in the

The other theory is one which regards time as an irreversible process moving in a definite direction. In this theory time has a beginning and an ending. The beginning and ending are not involved in the fateful resultants of events, but rather in the quality of time-space experience. It suggests that within the time band the event may take on the character of the timeless, the finite may become involved in the infinite while it remains finite. It was this manner of apprehending time that claimed the mind and the thought of the prophet.

But to return to the distinction between a philosophy of history and a theology of history. A philosophy of history seeks to make an end of historic process. If there is a goal in history, it is thought of in terms of process itself. Such a goal is the product of historical evolution and can have meaning only in direct relation to the facts of history. In no sense can such a goal

15 That day *is* a day of wrath, a day of trouble and distress, a day of wasteness and desolation, a day of darkness and gloominess, a day of clouds and thick darkness,
 	
16 A day of the trumpet and alarm against the fenced cities, and against the high towers.
	15 A day of wrath is that day,
	    a day of distress and anguish,
	  a day of ruin and devastation,
	    a day of darkness and gloom,
	  a day of clouds and thick darkness,
	16 a day of trumpet blast and battle cry
	    against the fortified cities
	      and against the lofty battlements.

second line is, lit., "The sound of the day of the Lord is bitter; a warrior is crying there." The **there** is without a proper antecedent, and the order of words is unusual, not to say wrong. For **sound** read "swifter," by simple omission of only one letter; and by transposing one letter from **cries** to the preceding word, obtain "than a runner." The last letter of **cries** and the first of **there** make "speedier," and the final letter of **there** is the particle used in comparison, "than." This is such an excellent illustration of how rearrangement of the letters of a line can yield vastly improved sense that it seems worth while to put the two texts together:

> M.T.:
> קול יום יהוה מר צרח שם גבור
> Reconstructed:
> קל יום יהוה מרץ וחש מגבור

> M.T.:
> The sound of the day of the Lord bitter cries there a warrior.
> Reconstructed:
> Swifter than a runner the day of the Lord and speedier than a warrior.

In ancient MSS the words were run together without space between. As has often been pointed out, there is a big difference when one reads GODISNOWHERE as "God is now here" or as "God is nowhere."

For the day as a day of wrath cf. Isa. 13:9-10 (where also the day produces desolation and darkness); Joel 1:15 (where the day is at hand, coming as destruction from the Almighty); and Ezek. 7:19 (where the day of wrath is one on which neither silver nor gold will be able to save; cf. Zeph. 1:18). For other descriptions of the day cf. Amos 5:18, 20; 8:9 (darkness, not light); and Joel 2:1-2 (darkness and gloom, cloud and murk). Amos accepted the popular notion that there would be a day of the Lord, but completely reversed the expectation of its nature. It would be a day not of victory but of defeat; not of light but of darkness. It would be a day on which the conquering righteousness of the Lord would express itself in the punishment of his unrighteous people (cf. J. M. P. Smith, "The Day of Yahweh," *American Journal of Theology,* V [1901], 505-33). **Distress and anguish:** The words sound alike in Hebrew; for a parallel in English, one might suggest "stress and distress." So also **ruin and devastation,** *shô'āh ûmeshô'āh* (cf. Job 30:3; 38:27). **Darkness and gloom, . . . clouds and thick darkness:** It

be regarded as transcendent or having a meaning beyond and perhaps outside history. A theology of history, however, views history as a process in time moving always toward a definite goal. The total process is relevant to a wider plan that includes but is not derived from human history. Such is the conception of the **day of the LORD** (vs. 7) of which the prophet speaks. It is the moment when the true meaning of life, of event, of history, of creation itself will be made clear. There is no escape from it. God will search Jerusalem with lamps (vs. 12). From the divine scrutiny there is no hiding place. Of this the prophet is so sure that he calls the roll of those who seem to think that God has been unmindful of their deeds because they are the prestige-bearing members of society (vss. 4-6).

The sweeping character of the divine accounting is completely devastating. It falls upon those in authority as well as upon the less responsible. For **the day of the LORD** is the ulti-

17 And I will bring distress upon men, that they shall walk like blind men, because they have sinned against the LORD: and their blood shall be poured out as dust, and their flesh as the dung.

18 Neither their silver nor their gold shall be able to deliver them in the day of the LORD's wrath; but the whole land shall be devoured by the fire of his jealousy: for he shall make even a speedy riddance of all them that dwell in the land.

17 I will bring distress on men,
    so that they shall walk like the blind,
      because they have sinned against the
        LORD;
  their blood shall be poured out like dust,
    and their flesh like dung.
18 Neither their silver nor their gold
    shall be able to deliver them
      on the day of the wrath of the LORD.
  In the fire of his jealous wrath,
    all the earth shall be consumed;
  for a full, yea, sudden end
    he will make of all the inhabitants of
      the earth.

should be remembered that for half the year there is scarcely a cloud in the Palestinian sky. The **trumpet** is the shophar or ram's horn, blown in time of war. According to Amos 2:2, Moab "shall die . . . amid shouting and the sound of the trumpet" (cf. also Josh. 6:5). The **battlements**: Lit., "corners" (cf. 3:6).

H. UNIVERSAL JUDGMENT (1:17-18)

17-18. Again the Lord speaks in the first line of vs. 17, but almost at once the first person is abandoned for the third. If by **men** are meant the people of Judah, the latter are poorly defined. **Men** is more naturally understood as referring to mankind. **Bring distress on:** Lit., "squeeze," "bring into straits," from which, **like the blind,** they shall try vainly to grope their way out. The next clause, **because they have sinned against the LORD,** is generally regarded as a gloss. It does not fit the meter and the change to the third person is awkward; it gives a reason for vs. 17a. As previously noted, the last line of vs. 17 (beginning with **their blood**) and the first line of vs. 18 might be read after vs. 12 (or vs. 13). **Their flesh:** So the LXX. The word is highly uncertain, used only here and in Job 20:23. Some would read *lēḥām,* "their moisture" or *ḥēlām,* "their strength." It may be a euphemism for "bowels."

Bribery will be of no avail. Is there a reference here to the fact—if it is a fact—mentioned by Herodotus that the Egyptians paid the Scythians not to invade their border? The next line is probably scribal:

> **on the day of the wrath of the LORD.**
> **In the fire of his jealous wrath,**
> **all the earth shall be consumed.**

It is deficient in metrical form, it seems to be taken from 3:8, and it adds nothing to the thought beyond what is said in the next line. The last line too is not from Zephaniah,

mate guarantor of the equality of man. It is a grand and noble affirmation. Soon or late, one by one, each must account for his deeds.

The same conception appears in the thought of Jesus concerning the Last Judgment. Here is the climax of human history and before God all peoples of the earth appear (Matt. 25:31-46). They are divided into two groups: the sheep on the right, the goats on the left. But unlike most of the picture that Zephaniah draws for us, it is a time of reward as well as of punishment. The thing that determines whether a man goes to the left or to the right is not the

arbitrary will of the judge but the deeds of the man himself. In the thought of Jesus the moral judgment does have an empirical basis in history.

Near the end of the chapter the prophet draws a most striking picture of the distress of those upon whom **the day of the LORD** makes its sudden appearance. They are dazed. **They shall walk like the blind** (vs. 17). All the grounds of their security have given way; the evil in which they have been engaged has moved from outside them in their deeds and actions, and now has taken over the deep center of their

2 Gather yourselves together, yea, gather together, O nation not desired;

2 Before the decree bring forth, *before* the day pass as the chaff, before the fierce anger of the LORD come upon you, before the day of the LORD's anger come upon you.

2 Come together and hold assembly,
     O shameless nation,
2 before you are driven away
     like the drifting chaff,c
before there comes upon you
     the fierce anger of the LORD,
before there comes upon you
     the day of the wrath of the LORD.

c Cn Compare Gk Syr: Heb *before a decree is born; like chaff a day has passed away*

but from one interested in eschatology. **A full . . . end** is a phrase characteristic of the book of Jeremiah, although not necessarily of Jeremiah himself. **Sudden, speedy,** is a late connotation for the word which earlier meant "terrible," "fearful." **Inhabitants of the earth** could be rendered "inhabitants of the land," but in the light of the previous line and other expressions in the chapter (e.g., vs. 2) the former is preferable. A long and perhaps unfathomable literary history lies behind this chapter in its present form. Yet its two major religious contributions ring out with the clarity of great bells: (*a*) the Lord requires undivided allegiance, and (*b*) his day is near.

II. JUDGMENTS ON THE NATIONS (2:1-15)
A. SUMMONS TO GATHER AND BE PUNISHED (2:1-2)

2:1. The difficulties of this corrupt text are considerable. Who is the **shameless nation** addressed? Because of what has gone before in ch. 1, the reader would suppose it to be Judah. Jerusalem has heard the warning but rejects it (cf. 1:12). She is shameless (cf. 3:5). She is shortly to be cut off (cf. 1:4). But if, as seems probable, the last four lines of vs. 2 and the whole of vs. 3 are secondary, then there is a close connection between vss. 1, 2*a*, and 4-6, in which case the **shameless nation** may well be the Philistines. Were it not that the present text lacks an indication of the nation's identity, this latter interpretation would seem preferable. But that is only one of the difficulties. The first verb in vs. 1 ordinarily means "to gather sticks" or "stubble." Its form here is unique. Should one letter be changed in it and in the next word to read, "Be ashamed together and feel shame" (cf. Gen. 2:25)? The suggestion "sanctify yourselves and be holy" is less probable. The ordinary meaning of the word translated **shameless** is "to long for," as in Ps. 84:2; it may be connected with an Arabic root that means "to be obscure" or "eclipsed" or an Aramaic root, "colorless," hence "pale" or "white." The nation does not "turn pale," hence is not ashamed. But great uncertainty remains.

2. Here the text is even more difficult. The M.T. reads, "Before a decree is born, like chaff a day has passed away," which is senseless. Fortunately there is help from the

souls. For the first time in their lives they cannot pay their bills. All of the accumulated security which they have built up is completely worthless. At last here is something from which their gold and silver cannot deliver them. They are stripped to the literal substance of themselves, face to face with God; and there is nothing they can say to him.

There is nothing they can say to him because already in their hearts they have said that God is completely without moral character. The prophet states that they say in their hearts, **The LORD will not do good, neither will he do evil** (vs. 12*c*). This is the final atheism, because it reduces all values to zero and strips life of its moral significance. It is a form of moral

nihilism in which the point of reference for value-judgment is locked within the confines of ends that do not extend beyond the individual. The behavior pattern resulting from such amorality finds its dynamic in the temporary success it may achieve in fulfilling itself. If it is true that the God worshiped is the God with whom we must deal at last, then to such as worship a God to whom moral values have no significance there can be no alternative but an end that is like the life, barren and meaningless.

2:1-7. *The Way of Escape.*—There is but one way to escape the wrath of God—that is to change one's direction. The judgment of God may be averted by Judah if she stops and considers. If she will **hold assembly,** surely there

3 Seek ye the Lord, all ye meek of the earth, which have wrought his judgment; seek righteousness, seek meekness: it may be ye shall be hid in the day of the Lord's anger.	3 Seek the Lord, all you humble of the land, who do his commands; seek righteousness, seek humility; perhaps you may be hidden on the day of the wrath of the Lord.

LXX ("Before you become like drifting chaff") and Syriac. For the familiar metaphor of the **chaff**, scattered to the winds, cf. Ps. 1:4; Isa. 17:13; Hos. 13:3; Job 21:18. Though the LXX lacks the verb **driven away**, which can be formed by the transposition of the letters of "a decree is born," clearly it is on the right track. The nation addressed is about to be thoroughly dispersed. The next four lines are probably two variants of a marginal comment, both of which have crept into the text. **Anger** and **wrath** are the same word in Hebrew. The phrase in the first of the two versions, **the fierce anger of the Lord**, lit., "the heat of the Lord's anger," occurs thirty-three times in the O.T. (cf. vs. 3). He is no God to trifle with. The variant, **day of the Lord's anger**, like the addition of **day** in the first line of this verse (in Hebrew), shows that someone was working over this text with the day very much in mind.

B. Invitation to the Humble to Seek the Lord (2:3)

3. The different spirit of this verse is matched by a different meter. The vocabulary also suggests the work of an editor who wished to mitigate the severity of the threats and provide a means of escape for the remnant. The **humble of the land**, the **meek of the earth**, are a class that developed in persecuted Judaism and eventually became the Hasidim of Daniel and the Maccabean struggle. References to them are in late literature (e.g., Pss. 76:9; 147:6; 149:4; Isa. 11:4; Job 24:4).

Those **who do his commands** and **seek righteousness** are likewise a clearly defined group: those who keep the law and for whom **righteousness** means the observance of God's revealed will. Hence seeking the Lord and seeking righteousness are equated in

will be opportunity under God for the distilled wisdom of the race to come to the fore, reminding all of the meaning of the life that is being lived. There is a chance that disaster may be averted if action is taken before **the wrath of the Lord** is unleashed. In the general assembly there will be a chance for the simple of heart and the humble to be heard. It is they who are not smart enough to go against the divine will.

Here is something that men often overlook. The strong, the powerful, those who carry great authority and upon whose decision turns the destiny of the body politic, are apt ever to ignore the humble and the simple man. The responsibility of the ordinary, garden-variety individual must never be forgotten. In one of Petrarch's *Letters of Old Age* appear these words:

When a word must be spoken to further a good cause, and those whom it behooves to speak remain silent, anybody ought to raise his voice, and break a silence which may be fraught with evil. . . . Many a time a few simple words have helped further the welfare of the nation, no matter who uttered them; the voice itself displaying the latent powers, sufficed to move the hearts of men.

It is so easy to underestimate the potential power of one word spoken at the critical moment! We say to ourselves sometimes that because we are not famous or learned or rich or powerful or gifted, our word means nothing in the presence of a great injustice or a great iniquity. Who would pay attention to us? Many good causes are hindered, often nameless persons are brought to untimely ends, because "those whom it behooves to speak remain silent"; and because they do not speak, we do not speak. It is important to remember that there is no limit to the power of any single life or any single voice when it is the only outlet, the only channel for righteousness in a fateful situation. The silence of the high and mighty sometimes gives greater power to the simple voice of the solitary individual.

There is still another aspect to be noted here. The perspective from which even the prophet looks at human history can become distorted due to the despair growing out of the hopelessness of the situation. The more closely he is associated wtih the life of his times the more clearly he may see the starkness of the depravity of his people. The surer he is of the judgment

4 ¶ For Gaza shall be forsaken, and Ashkelon a desolation: they shall drive out Ashdod at the noonday, and Ekron shall be rooted up.

4 For Gaza shall be deserted,
  and Ash'kelon shall become a desolation;
Ashdod's people shall be driven out at noon,
  and Ekron shall be uprooted.

this verse. The Jewish community had hardened by the time it was written; some are clearly within the pale; not all fall under the judgment (contrast 1:4). Theologians may value the word **perhaps**. Whatever man can do will not necessarily win salvation, for salvation is of God only. But for the faithful there is a possibility of being hidden **on the day of the wrath of the LORD.**

C. ORACLE AGAINST PHILISTIA (2:4-7)

4. It is possible, as has been pointed out, that vss. 1-2a are part of this oracle. Of the five principal Philistine cities Gath is not mentioned because it no longer existed. According to II Chr. 26:6, it had been destroyed by Uzziah ca. 760 B.C. Gaza, in Jer. 47:1, is said to have been smitten by Pharaoh. There is considerable doubt as to the value of either of these statements. Gaza may be referred to by Herodotus (*History* II. 159), who says that Pharaoh Neco "took Kadytis, which is a great city of Syria." But Kadesh on the Orontes is more likely (cf. M. A. Meyer, *History of the City of Gaza from the Earliest Times to the Present Day* [New York: Columbia University Press, 1907], pp. 37-38). **Ashdod** had been taken by Sargon when an "Ionian" (probably Greek) led a revolt (713-711 B.C.; cf. Isa. 20:1; see D. D. Luckenbill, *Ancient Records of Assyria and Babylonia* [Chicago: University of Chicago Press, 1927], II, 51-52) and **Ekron** and **Ashkelon** by Sennacherib a decade later. If Herodotus (*op. cit.* II. 157) can be trusted, Ashdod had again suffered siege and capture at the hands of the Egyptian Psamtik I (640-611?). Jer. 25:20 distinguishes between Ashkelon, Gaza, Ekron, and "the remnant of Ashdod." An Aramaic papyrus found in 1942 at Saqqara (Memphis), requesting aid from Egypt against the forces of the king of Babylon who had advanced as far as Aphek, may be an appeal from Ashkelon from ca. 603-602 B.C. (cf. John Bright, "A New Letter in Aramaic, Written to a Pharaoh of Egypt," *Biblical Archaeologist,* XII [1949], 46-52). There is warrant, therefore, in Philistine history for these predictions of scattered populations and devastated cities. Like Judah, the Philistine plain lay between the great powers of Mesopotamia and the Nile.

In Hebrew the words **Gaza** and **deserted** sound alike, and there is a similar play on the sound of **Ekron** and **uprooted** (cf. Mic. 1:10-12; Ezek. 25:16). The meaning of the phrase **at noon** may be that during the siesta the city will be off guard, as Rechab and

of God the more convinced he may become that in its clear sweep all will be carried away. That any may escape because they have sought righteousness is a rare but highly precarious prospect. What saves him from complete despair is the recollection that God will somehow be mindful of a **remnant of the house of Judah** (vs. 7).

No situation is ever completely without hope as far as the divine option is concerned. God is never without a redemptive alternative. This is the meaning of the remnant. And that meaning becomes clear the moment we apply the insight in terms of personal behavior. Despite a man's pretensions, as long as he has a fair degree of mental health he does not give up his sense of self. True, he may not be as good as

his admirers think he is, or as good as his mother thinks he is, but he does not give himself up. On the contrary, he clings to himself with an abiding enthusiasm. Somewhere deep within him is the assurance that he can and will be a better man. Something seems ever to be arguing on the side of the wisdom of a better alternative. The margin favoring the seed of the remnant concept is resident in the life of every man.

But this is not all. The psychology of the remnant is manifest in every situation where love abounds. Where there is love between human beings the allowance, the exception, is always made. Somehow the blow is softened and the harsh judgment mellowed into something

5 Woe unto the inhabitants of the seacoast, the nation of the Cherethites! the
word of the LORD *is* against you; O Canaan,
the land of the Philistines, I will even destroy thee, that there shall be no inhabitant.
6 And the seacoast shall be dwellings *and*
cottages for shepherds, and folds for flocks.
7 And the coast shall be for the remnant
of the house of Judah; they shall feed thereupon: in the houses of Ashkelon shall they
lie down in the evening: for the LORD their
God shall visit them, and turn away their
captivity.

5 Woe to you inhabitants of the seacoast,
  you nation of the Cher'ethites!
The word of the LORD is against you,
  O Canaan, land of the Philistines;
  and I will destroy you till no inhab-
    itant is left.
6 And you, O seacoast, shall be pastures,
  meadows for shepherds
  and folds for flocks.
7 The seacoast shall become the possession
  of the remnant of the house of Judah,
  on which they shall pasture,
and in the houses of Ash'kelon
  they shall lie down at evening.
For the LORD their God will be mindful
  of them
  and restore their fortunes.

Baanah were caught (II Sam. 4:5; cf. Jer. 15:8). But better light may be shed upon
this expression from the Moabite stone (ll. 15-16), "And I fought against it from the
break of dawn until noon, and I took it," or the Zenjirli inscription, "Memphis, his
capital, I took by midday." In other words, only a brief half day will be required.

5. The **inhabitants of the seacoast** are of course the Philistines, who had settled
there soon after 1200 B.C. as part of a migration from Asia Minor and the Mediterranean
islands, including Crete, with which Herodotus (*op. cit.* I. 173) links them, as does
Amos 9:7, "Have not I brought up . . . the Philistines from Caphtor?" (Cf. Deut. 2:23;
Jer. 47:4.) The Cherethites and Pelethites, who together play an important part in
the story of David, are his Philistine bodyguard. Here **Cherethites** is another name
for Philistines.

The word of the LORD is against you is a gloss intended to explain what follows
in the first person. But the next word, **Canaan**, has also probably been misread or
intentionally altered in transmission. Better, "I will humble you," the letters of which
are similar, and which gives an excellent parallel with **I will destroy you**. If under
the influence of **Cherethites**, the word before **land of the Philistines** was mistakenly
read **Canaan**, it is easy to see how the gloss **the word of the LORD is against you** became
necessary.

6. The text offers further difficulties here: "And the seacoast shall be pastures,
with cottages ["caves"] for shepherds and folds for flocks." The LXX reads, "And Crete,
the border of the sea, will become pastures." It is best to consider **seacoast** as having
moved up into this verse by mistake from vs. 7, and to omit **cottages** or "caves" as the
Vulg. does. Its presence is probably due to dittography. Read, therefore, restoring the
second person address as in vs. 5, "And you shall become pastures for shepherds and
folds for flocks." The thought is clear enough. Nothing will be left of the Philistine
territory except pasture land.

7. This verse clearly shows an annotator's hand. His gloss has been divided and
inserted into the text both before and after the original line, which, continuing vs. 6,
reads approximately, "They will graze in the houses of Ashkelon, they will lie down in

which redeems. We are never quite willing to
say that the bad deed done by the beloved is
quite what it appears to be. If we can get the
true story, the accurate account, there will appear sufficient reason to make forgiveness a
mutually shared experience. Always this is implicit in Yahweh's relationship with Israel. The

judgment of the prophet bears down mercilessly
in the fulfillment of the task appointed him by
God, but running through it all is another
note, full of the warm overtones of lovingkindness. This total tendency becomes articulate at
the place of the remnant in the stormy experiences of God with his people.

8 ¶ I have heard the reproach of Moab, and the revilings of the children of Ammon, whereby they have reproached my people, and magnified *themselves* against their border.

9 Therefore, *as* I live, saith the LORD of hosts, the God of Israel, Surely Moab shall be as Sodom, and the children of Ammon as Gomorrah, *even* the breeding of nettles, and saltpits, and a perpetual desolation: the residue of my people shall spoil them, and the remnant of my people shall possess them.

8 "I have heard the taunts of Moab
    and the revilings of the Ammonites,
how they have taunted my people
    and made boasts against their territory.
9 Therefore, as I live," says the LORD of
    hosts,
    the God of Israel,
"Moab shall become like Sodom,
    and the Ammonites like Gomor′rah,
a land possessed by nettles and salt pits,
    and a waste for ever.
The remnant of my people shall plunder
    them,
    and the survivors of my nation shall
    possess them."

Ekron." "In Ekron" is obtained by a slight change from **at evening**, which, though appropriate enough, is weak. **The seacoast:** Hebrew, "by them," a word supplied to connect the gloss with the text. "Them" (masculine) refers to **meadows** or **folds** (vs. 6), both of which are feminine. Hence the usual change. But **the seacoast** has already been mentioned in vs. 5; furthermore, the word "them" in vs. 7 would be metrically superfluous.

The gloss, the balance of the verse except for this line, held out a promise to Judah, not woe to the Philistines. For a similar case in which a note originally on the margin has found its way into the text only by being divided, cf. Judg. 5:19, "The kings came and fought, . . . but took no gain of money." **Will be mindful of them:** The verb is the same as that translated **punish** in 1:8 (cf. Exeg., *ad loc.*). **Restore their fortunes:** The Hebrew may mean "turn their fortune" or **turn away their captivity.** The annotator may have the Exile in mind; in that case he has gone beyond the possibility of hiding from God's wrath mentioned in vs. 3. But in Job 42:10, where there is also a difference between the spoken and written text, the meaning is clearly **restore the fortunes** (cf. 3:20; Amos 9:14; Hos. 6:11; Ps. 126:1, 4).

D. ORACLES AGAINST MOAB, THE AMMONITES, AND THE ETHIOPIANS (2:8-12)

8-9. Because of the pride and taunts of these neighbors of Judah to the east, their land, like that of the Philistines to the west, will be both devastated and plundered. But it is very unlikely that either vss. 8-9, in the first person, or vss. 10-11, in the third person, come from the seventh century. They reflect the attitude of the Moabites and Ammonites in the sixth century, when these people made capital of Judah's misfortune. For the pride of Moab cf. Isa. 16:6; Jer. 48:29. It is true that Amos also declares punishment on both countries (Amos 2:1-3; 1:13-15), but for a totally different reason. In Amos the punishment of the Lord extends to those who offend his righteous will by their outrageous and cruel behavior, desecrating the bones of the dead and showing merciless savagery toward the women of Gilead in order to enlarge their territory; here the charge is a boastful spirit toward Judah. **Made boasts:** Lit., "enlarged," which may mean that the enemy enlarged their territory at the expense of Judah, or be taken

---

8-15. *The Enemies of Judah.*—The rest of the chapter deals with the judgment of God against the enemies of Judah. The proof offered as justification of the judgment is the fact that they needled and taunted God's people and **made boasts against their territory** (vs. 8). For this they will be punished by a complete destruction of their cities and their civilization. Even

their gods will be destroyed. When this is accomplished,

    . . . to him [the LORD of hosts] shall bow down,
    each in its place,
    all the lands of the nations.

The tendency on the part of the prophet to regard the enemies of his people as also the enemies of God is a very human one. The de-

10 This shall they have for their pride, because they have reproached and magnified *themselves* against the people of the LORD of hosts.
 	
11 The LORD *will be* terrible unto them: for he will famish all the gods of the earth; and *men* shall worship him, every one from his place, *even* all the isles of the heathen.
	10 This shall be their lot in return for their
	    pride,
	  because they scoffed and boasted
	    against the people of the LORD of hosts.
	11 The LORD will be terrible against them;
	  yea, he will famish all the gods of the
	    earth,
	  and to him shall bow down,
	    each in its place,
	  all the lands of the nations.

as here, "enlarged their mouths" (cf. the modern expression, "a swelled head"). The first person is introduced very suddenly, but as vs. 9 shows, the speaker must be the Lord. For **their territory** the LXX has "my territory," which may well be right. In vs. 9 the Lord swears by himself that

> Moab shall become like Sodom,
> and the Ammonites like Gomorrah.

The reference to the Pentateuch (Gen. 19:24-28) is another sign of late date. **The LORD of hosts, the God of Israel** is an expanded title, too long for a line of poetry after the preceding **Therefore as I live, says . . . . Of hosts,** "Sabaoth," has probably been added (cf. Arnold, *Ephod and Ark*, pp. 142-48) .

The words translated **possessed by nettles and salt pits** are difficult; it is necessary to guess at the first word. But the general sense is plain. There is no serious discrepancy between the statements that Moab and the Ammonite territory will be desolate and that the **remnant of my people shall plunder them.** The loss to Moab and the Ammonites is complete, which is the point, and the two forms of loss, desolate land and plundered land, occur together.

While the picture of vengeance given here is not particularly edifying, the passage may suggest the fate of pride as depicted elsewhere in the O.T., e.g., in Isa. 47:1-15 (Babylon) ; 14:4-6 (Babylon) ; Ezek. 27:1-36 (Tyre) ; Daniel 5:22-24 (Belshazzar) ; Esth. 5:1–8:7, and may serve as a reminder that this sin is among those particularly denounced by Jesus.

10-12. Although these verses contain a hint of the conversion of the Gentiles, they are stylistically an inferior comment on vss. 8-9, written in prose in the third person. They repeat a number of words from the preceding lines. The LXX lacks **people;** the taunt and boast in vs. 10 is directly against the Lord of hosts. For **will be terrible** the LXX has "will appear"; the words in Hebrew are very similar. The verb **famish** is in the perfect tense—he has "made thin," in contrast to the enlarging boasts of vs. 8. **All the gods of the earth:** Lit., "in order that all the coastlands of the nations, each in its place, may worship him." "Coastlands" is the word common in Isa. 40–42; it is often rendered **isles.** So the largehearted spirit of Second Isaiah, who seeks to convert rather than to destroy, slips into the threats of destruction in which Zephaniah abounds.

struction which is to be meted out is all-inclusive—those who are responsible for policies and those who are not, the guilty and the innocent. At best, in retrospect, it is a curious kind of ethical behavior. There is to be no discrimination in judgment. The assumption is that even the alien nations are responsible to God. This is equivalent to saying that even though the other nations worship other gods, the fact of their being regarded as morally responsible to

God means that they are in candidacy to worship the true God. An attitude of exclusive relationship to the one true God leads inevitably to the conclusion that the borders of such exclusiveness must be widened until all are included.

Of course there can be no universal worship of the true God unless all people are one. The idea of monotheism leads irrevocably to the idea of one people—one family inclusive of all

12 ¶ Ye Ethiopians also, ye *shall be* slain by my sword.

13 And he will stretch out his hand against the north, and destroy Assyria; and will make Nineveh a desolation, *and* dry like a wilderness.

14 And flocks shall lie down in the midst of her, all the beasts of the nations: both the cormorant and the bittern shall lodge in the upper lintels of it; *their* voice shall sing in the windows; desolation *shall be* in the thresholds: for he shall uncover the cedar work.

15 This *is* the rejoicing city that dwelt carelessly, that said in her heart, I *am,* and *there is* none besides me: how is she become

---

12 You also, O Ethiopians,
    shall be slain by my sword.

13 And he will stretch out his hand against
        the north,
    and destroy Assyria;
  and he will make Nin'eveh a desolation,
    a dry waste like the desert.

14 Herds shall lie down in the midst of her,
    all the beasts of the field;[d]
  the vulture[e] and the hedgehog
    shall lodge in her capitals;
  the owl[f] shall hoot in the window,
    the raven[g] croak on the threshold;
  for her cedar work will be laid bare.

15 This is the exultant city
      that dwelt secure,
    that said to herself,
    "I am and there is none else."
  What a desolation she has become,
    a lair for wild beasts!

[d] Tg Compare Gk: Heb *nation*
[e] The meaning of the Hebrew word is uncertain
[f] Cn: Heb *a voice*
[g] Gk Vg: Heb *desolation*

---

12. This verse is a fragment of an oracle on Ethiopia (Cush) or else a brief note by an editor who felt a word about this nation on the south was needed. The Hebrew is awkward, "You, too, Cushites are the slain of my sword." Why **my sword**, in the first person again? To read "the slain of the sword of the Lord" would ease the line somewhat, but the note is still too fragmentary to give much clue as to its origin and place. It neither presupposes nor continues vs. 11; a better connection is with vs. 7.

E. Warning to Assyria (2:13-14)

13-14. A proclamation of desolation against Assyria, the foe on the north, completes the compass. Its terms are similar to those used for the Philistines. **Nineveh**, like Ashkelon (vs. 4), will become a **desolation**. Unless the threat is taken at other than its face value, Nineveh has not yet been destroyed. But when **he will stretch out his hand,** it will be. **He** has no closer antecedent than vs. 11, unless "sword of the Lord" is read in vs. 12. With vs. 14, cf. vss. 6-7. The Hebrew in vs. 14 reads, **all the beasts of the nations,** which cannot be right. The LXX has "of the earth," but read "valley" or **field.** Again, as in vss. 6-7, wild creatures will make the destroyed city their home. Not only **herds,** but the **vulture,** or pelican or jackdaw (the meaning is unknown), and the **hedgehog,** or porcupine, will make their home in the cornices or **capitals** of the ruined pillars (cf. Amos 9:1). Some ignorant scribe probably has miscopied the names of the birds in the next line, writing **voice** or "sound" for **owl** and **desolation** for **raven.** The LXX has "wild beasts" for **owl. For her cedar work will be laid bare,** outside the meter, is probably a dittograph of the first three words of vs. 15, garbled and then arranged to give a reasonably intelligible meaning.

F. Editorial Addition (2:15)

15. Nineveh here is already destroyed, a **desolation** and **lair for wild beasts.** The words

that dwelt secure,
that said to herself,
"I am and there is none else"

a desolation, a place for beasts to lie down in! every one that passeth by her shall hiss, *and* wag his hand.

3 Woe to her that is filthy and polluted, to the oppressing city!

2 She obeyed not the voice; she received not correction; she trusted not in the LORD; she drew not near to her God.

3 Her princes within her *are* roaring lions; her judges *are* evening wolves; they gnaw not the bones till the morrow.

Every one who passes by her
    hisses and shakes his fist.

3 Woe to her that is rebellious and defiled,
    the oppressing city!
2 She listens to no voice,
    she accepts no correction.
She does not trust in the LORD,
    she does not draw near to her God.

3 Her officials within her
    are roaring lions;
her judges are evening wolves
    that leave nothing till the morning.

---

are copied verbatim from Isa. 47:8. The rest is similar to Jer. 19:8. In this way the editor drives home what he wishes to say in this chapter: "Pride goeth before destruction, and a haughty spirit before a fall" (Prov. 16:18), or perhaps, "He hath put down the mighty from their seats and exalted them of low degree" (Luke 1:52).

III. Threats and Promises (3:1-20)
A. Charges Against Jerusalem (3:1-5)

1-5. Ch. 3 opens with further denunciation of those who refuse correction and break the law. Their home is the rebellious city, Jerusalem, the ruling classes of which are guilty both of indifference toward God and oppression of their fellows. The specific charges are (a) rebellion, (b) pollution, (c) oppression, (d) obstinacy, (e) lack of trust, and (f) irreligion. The indictment against the city on the ground of oppression (vs. 1) is then expanded. Her officials and judges prey like animals, her prophets are extravagant and treacherous, and her priests are guilty of profanation and lawlessness (vss. 1-4). In contrast, the Lord is perfectly righteous (vs. 5). Except for the last clause of vs. 5, the meter is regular, the text relatively free from corruptions, and there are no sudden shifts of speaker.

As has already been stated in the Intro., vss. 8-20 are very likely to have originated long after the time of Zephaniah, and there are strong grounds for suspecting also that vss. 1-5 are not his. The concern shown in vs. 4 for **the law** and what is sacred is characteristic of developed Judaism. The charges are not so specific as in ch. 1. Contrast the men who are thickening upon their lees with those who listen **to no voice,** a difference not unlike that between the specific accusation of Israel in Amos 2:6 and the general condemnation of Judah in Amos 2:4, where the latter verse is clearly secondary. The righteousness of the Lord is first stressed in Isa. 41:10; 42:21; 45:19, 21. The words translated **defiled** and **oppressing** (vs. 1) appear almost wholly in late passages. In vs. 2 the nouns lack the definite article. While the evidence is not great, such as there

---

peoples—under God. This is just the reverse of the modern tendency. The unity of the peoples of the earth is manifest in a wide variety of interdependencies made possible by the annihilation of space and time. This has been achieved by the application of scientific method to the world of nature. Given the facts making for one world, they lead irrevocably to one faith as the logic of the modern experience. The demand for one faith to match one world means that the concept of monotheism is the only one that provides a religious basis for modern life.

The insight of the prophet becomes the necessitous affirmation for modern man.

3:1-20. Beyond Judgment.—Jerusalem has betrayed the Eternal. The proof of her apostasy is the fact that

> **her prophets are wanton,
> faithless men.**

Even her priests do violence to God's law. This has happened even though it is clear that it is not the Lord by whom they are guided in this disgraceful behavior. These men are acquainted

4 Her prophets *are* light *and* treacherous persons: her priests have polluted the sanctuary, they have done violence to the law.

5 The just LORD *is* in the midst thereof; he will not do iniquity: every morning doth he bring his judgment to light, he faileth not; but the unjust knoweth no shame.

6 I have cut off the nations: their towers are desolate; I made their streets waste, that none passeth by: their cities are destroyed, so that there is no man, that there is none inhabitant.

4 Her prophets are wanton,
   faithless men;
her priests profane what is sacred,
   they do violence to the law.
5 The LORD within her is righteous,
   he does no wrong;
every morning he shows forth his justice,
   each dawn he does not fail;
   but the unjust knows no shame.

6 "I have cut off nations;
   their battlements are in ruins;
I have laid waste their streets
   so that none walks in them;
their cities have been made desolate,
   without a man, without an inhabitant.

---

is points to an editor's hand. In Mic. 6:1–7:6 there is a similar proclamation of woe, from another than the Micah of chs. 1–3, before the final promises of 7:7-20. It is probable, then, that all of Zeph. 3:1-20 is from other hands than Zephaniah's.

A similar combination of pollution and oppression may be found in Jer. 6:7, and obstinacy (vs. 2) is the complaint of Jer. 7:28, couched in very similar language. For failure to trust in the Lord and to perform religious duties cf. Zeph. 1:5-6. Officials, priests, and prophets are coupled together in the scathing rebuke of Mic. 3 (cf. especially vs. 11) and in Jer. 2:8. For a charge against rulers and prophets, like that of vss. 3-4, cf. also Isa. 56:9-11, and for priests who make no distinction between sacred and profane, and violate the law, see Ezek. 22:26. Similarly this Ezekiel passage attacks the ravenous officials (Ezek. 22:27) and untrustworthy and greedy prophets (Ezek. 22:28, 25). In it, as in Zephaniah, the prophets are likened to **lions** and the princes to **wolves.** Because the Hebrew words are similar, the LXX renders, instead of **evening wolves** in vs. 3, "wolves of Arabia." The consonants of the verb in the final half line of this verse usually mean to break **bones, gnaw,** or crunch, but the LXX renders **leave** or "leave over." This sense is good; the wolves are so greedy that they devour at once everything they can catch, with no remainder overnight. The prophets are wanton or extravagant, lacking in all decent restraint, and men of treachery, while the priests fail in their chief business of preserving the holy and maintaining the law. **Law** is here a technical term for the corpus of God's revelation in statute form. Some disorder exists in vs. 5. The last clause, **but the unjust knows no shame,** is possibly a variant. At any rate, it is outside the meter and repeats the charge of shamelessness made in 2:1. On the other hand, the Lord in his righteousness **does no wrong. Every morning** the rising of the sun shows his control over the natural order (cf. Ps. 19:1-2). And as he is dependable in the realm of nature, so is he in his dealings with men. The time when justice is done is in the **morning** (Jer. 21:12). **Each dawn he does not fail,** however, is a free translation; lit., "with respect to the light [or, "like the light"] he does not fail [or, "is not found wanting"]."

B. FAILURE OF DISCIPLINE (3:6-7)

6-7. A new section begins here, expanding the thought of vs. 2 that Judah has refused to receive correction. This had been the complaint of Amos 4:6-11; Israel had been

---

with the righteousness of the Lord. They know what his record is; it is its own witness. Surrounded by the evidence of his righteousness and his wrath, they have not taken it into account. They have gone on their relentless way,

unmindful of what their eyes have seen and their hearts have felt.

It is important to note the crucial problem ever present for the man whose daily work involves him in the use of the holy materials of

7 I said, Surely, thou wilt fear me, thou wilt receive instruction; so their dwelling should not be cut off, howsoever I punished them: but they rose early, *and* corrupted all their doings.

8 ¶ Therefore wait ye upon me, saith the LORD, until the day that I rise up to the prey: for my determination *is* to gather the nations, that I may assemble the kingdoms, to pour upon them mine indignation, *even* all my fierce anger: for all the earth shall be devoured with the fire of my jealousy.

7 I said, 'Surely she will fear me,
    she will accept correction;
she will not lose sight[h]
    of all that I have enjoined upon her.'
But all the more they were eager
    to make all their deeds corrupt."

8 "Therefore wait for me," says the LORD,
    "for the day when I arise as a witness.
For my decision is to gather nations,
    to assemble kingdoms,
to pour out upon them my indignation,
    all the heat of my anger;
for in the fire of my jealous wrath
    all the earth shall be consumed.

[h] Gk Syr: Heb *and her dwelling will not be cut off*

repeatedly chastised but had learned nothing. In Zeph. 3:6 other nations have been devastated. Judah might have learned from them. In vs. 7 Judah herself had received many injunctions which the Lord thought she would keep, but instead of that, her deeds became worse. Notice that the Lord speaks abruptly in the first person without introduction. Again the vocabulary suggests a late period of composition. **Battlements** are "corners," the same word used in 1:16. The desolation is so complete that not only is there no inhabitant of the ruined cities (cf. 2:5) but not even a passer-by (cf. Zech. 7:14; 9:8). **I said:** In the sense "I thought" (cf. 1:12). It is better to read the verbs of vs. 7 (**fear** and **accept**) as third person feminine rather than second person masculine, although the forms permit either. In Hebrew **her dwelling** and **will not lose sight** are similar. The LXX and Syriac are clearly right against the Hebrew: **And her dwelling will not be cut off. Enjoined** is the same word as that translated "punish" in 1:9 (cf. Exeg. there and on 2:7; cf. also Job 36:23; II Chr. 36:23; Ezra 1:2). **They were eager: They rose early** in the morning, an expression used eleven times in Jeremiah; lit., "made shoulder move" for foul purposes. While **deeds** may be good or bad (cf. Ps. 103:7), very frequently there is a connotation of evil in the word, which occurs eight times in this sense in Ezekiel (cf. also Zeph. 3:11).

C. PROCLAMATION OF UNIVERSAL PUNISHMENT (3:8)

8. There is only a rough connection between vs. 7 and vs. 8. After vs. 7 one expects a declaration of the punishment due the "rebellious and defiled, the oppressing city" (vs. 1), which has become adamant to correction and increasingly corrupt. Instead, the people addressed, who now appear to be the pious in Jerusalem, not the shameless, are bidden to await the universal judgment day on which the Lord's **wrath** will be poured not on Jerusalem, but on all the nations and kingdoms. Logically **therefore** does not follow. **Wait,** in the Hebrew, is plural; in the LXX, singular (cf. Ps. 37:7, "Rest in the LORD, and wait patiently for him" [a different verb]; Ps. 33:20; Isa. 8:17, "I will wait for the LORD"; and Hab. 2:3). **As a witness:** So the LXX and Syriac, but the Hebrew reads **to the prey.** The Lord appears as a witness in Jer. 29:23; Mal. 3:5; Mic. 1:2. But the thought of his spoiling the nations is not inconsistent with the wrath of the last two lines of this verse. **Decision: Determination,** "judgment." The witness

religious worship and dedication. First, such a man tends to develop a veneer of professionalism. He is a prophet, not a religious man; he is a priest, not a religious man. This professionalism becomes a part of the etiquette of his calling. Second, there is an increasing immunity

to the personal moral demands of his work. It is true that no man can handle the holy materials of worship as a part of vocation without either becoming more holy thereby or developing an immunity so that he will not be affected by his function. The rationalization is that what

9 For then will I turn to the people a pure language, that they may all call upon the name of the Lord, to serve him with one consent.

10 From beyond the rivers of Ethiopia my suppliants, *even* the daughter of my dispersed, shall bring mine offering.

9 "Yea, at that time I will change the
    speech of the peoples
    to a pure speech,
that all of them may call on the name of
    the Lord
    and serve him with one accord.

10 From beyond the rivers of Ethiopia
    my suppliants, the daughter of my dispersed ones,
    shall bring my offering.

---

is also the judge. For the gathering of the peoples to judgment cf. Joel 3:2; Zech. 14:2. **Assemble:** So the LXX; the Hebrew adds a suffix, **that I may assemble.** For the rest of the verse cf. 1:18. A similar expression of the divine anger appears in Isa. 42:25, and prayers for its operation in Jer. 10:25; Pss. 69:24; 79:6. In this verse prophecy has clearly become apocalyptic.

D. Conversion of the Nations (3:9-10)

9. Another spirit, more kindly and less grim, breathes through these two verses. **Yea, at that time** (Hebrew, "For then, I will change"): Lit., "I will turn over [as a cake is turned to be baked on the other side] for peoples a pure lip." It is possible also to translate, "I will restore to the peoples a pure speech." Isaiah lamented (6:5) that he was a man of unclean lips and that he dwelt among a people of unclean lips. The fault is not that there are different languages, but that gods other than the Lord are invoked and served. God can make the unclean into clean. Here the hope of a universal language antedates modern times and even the experience of Pentecost. Isa. 19:18 expects five Egyptian cities to speak Hebrew, the language of Canaan. In Zephaniah the conversion to the one language is universal. The purpose of this change is that **all of them may call on the name of the Lord** in harmony. They will cease to invoke other deities (cf. 1:4-5) and worship the Lord alone. For the ancients the **name** was of great importance. To call a deity by name, as in the story of Elijah on Mount Carmel (I Kings 18), was believed in itself to exercise some hold upon him. In Zephaniah, as in the Psalms, the stage of magic has been passed, but the phrase survives as a synonym for **serve** or worship, and in Judaism, as in the Lord's Prayer, the hallowing of the name is of primary importance. **With one accord:** Lit., "with one shoulder." It is a pity that this image cannot be brought over into English more readily, for it suggests a degree of effort which the phrases **with one accord,** "with one mind," "with one mouth," or "with one spirit" do not. The LXX is equally striking, "under one yoke." The first person lapses into the third. Perhaps **the Lord** was expanded out of the suffix "my," and in consequence "me" changed to **him** in the second half line. The universalism of this passage is not common in the O.T., but neither is it absent (cf. Isa. 40–66, *passim,* especially 49:5-6; also Isa. 2:2-4=Mic. 4:1-4; Isa. 11:9; 19:23-25; Pss. 67; 87; 95–100).

10. The meaning of this verse as it stands is by no means clear and the probability of corruption is high. For the words **my suppliants, the daughter of my dispersed ones,** read with some rearrangement but essentially the same letters, "to the sides of the north," i.e., to the distant north. For the phrase cf. Isa. 14:13 ("uttermost parts of the north"); Ezek. 38:6, 15; 39:2; also Ps. 48:2. This reading gives excellent sense, relieves the grammatical difficulties, and continues the thought of vs. 9; from all over the world, the peoples worshiping together in one language **shall bring my offering.** The **rivers of**

God requires of the average layman is not required of the priest: "Become more holy and genuine or less holy and unreal." The handling of the rites of the office turns into a substitute for becoming one with one's function.

The time will come, so the chapter declares, when God will be his own **witness.** He will gather together all peoples and enter into judgment against them. At such a time he will change the speech and give to all a common

11 In that day shalt thou not be ashamed for all thy doings, wherein thou hast transgressed against me: for then I will take away out of the midst of thee them that rejoice in thy pride, and thou shalt no more be haughty because of my holy mountain.

12 I will also leave in the midst of thee an afflicted and poor people, and they shall trust in the name of the LORD.

13 The remnant of Israel shall not do iniquity, nor speak lies; neither shall a deceitful tongue be found in their mouth: for they shall feed and lie down, and none shall make *them* afraid.

14 ¶ Sing, O daughter of Zion; shout, O Israel; be glad and rejoice with all the heart, O daughter of Jerusalem.

---

11 "On that day you shall not be put to shame
  because of the deeds by which you have rebelled against me;
for then I will remove from your midst
  your proudly exultant ones,
and you shall no longer be haughty
  in my holy mountain.
12 For I will leave in the midst of you
  a people humble and lowly.
They shall seek refuge in the name of the LORD,
13   those who are left in Israel;
they shall do no wrong
  and utter no lies,
nor shall there be found in their mouth
  a deceitful tongue.
For they shall pasture and lie down,
  and none shall make them afraid."
14 Sing aloud, O daughter of Zion;
  shout, O Israel!
Rejoice and exult with all your heart,
  O daughter of Jerusalem!

Ethiopia are just short of the southern limits of the known world. One clause in this verse may be an addition; the line is too long.

E. SECURITY OF THE REMNANT (3:11-13)

11-13. A new section begins, introduced by an editor with the familiar formula found again in vs. 16, **on that day.** The thought of these three verses, which is often praised as the best in the book, is that instead of the proud and rebellious who are described in vss. 1-5, Jerusalem shall be filled with a humble, trustful, upright and honest **remnant** who will have nothing to fear. As in ch. 2 (e.g., vss. 3, 10), this contrast between the proud and the humble is stressed. Pride, the root sin, causes those who exult in it to be **put to shame,** while humility is rewarded. These are concepts prominent in the literature of developed Judaism. The passage may well be coupled with vs. 8, but also harks back to vss. 1-4. As the Lord does no wrong (vs. 5), so it is with the purified remnant (vs. 13). Whereas the haughty did not trust in the Lord (vs. 2), the humble do (vs. 12). The language here lacks originality; most of the phrases are paralleled elsewhere, and the section could have been built up by one familiar with scripture. Cf. Isa. 54:4; Ezek. 39:26; Isa. 13:3; Ps. 120:3; Zeph. 2:7.

Notice in vs. 12 a change from the first to the third person. Possibly the last clause of vs. 12 and the first of vs. 13, **the remnant of Israel** (cf. 2:7) are a marginal note on the **humble and lowly.** As this passage is memorable for its rebuke of the proud and its promise for the humble, so it reminds the reader that God alone can provide security. It holds out the promise of a day when Jerusalem is purged of the haughty and the lowly worship on Zion in peace. God only is strong; he alone controls the world.

F. FINAL PICTURE OF THE GOLDEN AGE (3:14-20)

14-15. Israel is bidden to celebrate the absence of enemies and the presence of the Lord. A vast difference between these lines and the strictures of ch. 1 is evident. There is no need for a change of Israel's ways; the time of trial is past, and now come the fruits of victory and peace. In spirit this is close to Isa. 40–66 (e.g., Isa. 54:1) and some of the psalms of praise (e.g., Pss. 96; 98; cf. Zech. 2:10; 9:9). The **daughter** is first a

15 The LORD hath taken away thy judgments, he hath cast out thine enemy: the King of Israel, *even* the LORD, *is* in the midst of thee: thou shalt not see evil any more.

16 In that day it shall be said to Jerusalem, Fear thou not: *and to* Zion, Let not thine hands be slack.

17 The LORD thy God in the midst of thee *is* mighty; he will save, he will rejoice over thee with joy; he will rest in his love, he will joy over thee with singing.

15 The LORD has taken away the judgments
     against you,
  he has cast out your enemies.
The King of Israel, the LORD, is in your
     midst;
  you shall fear evil no more.
16 On that day it shall be said to Jerusalem:
  "Do not fear, O Zion;
  let not your hands grow weak.
17 The LORD, your God, is in your midst,
  a warrior who gives victory;
he will rejoice over you with gladness,
  he will renew you[i] in his love;
he will exult over you with loud singing

[i] Gk Syr: Heb *he will be silent*

subsidiary town under the protection of the walled city (cf. e.g., Judg. 1:27); then the town comes to stand for the community as a whole, the equivalent of Israel. For **Israel** the LXX has "daughter of Jerusalem." **With all your heart:** The heart is primarily the seat of the intellect, but more, here the entire being.

The text of vs. 15 has suffered some corruption. The versions read the plural **enemies** against the singular of the Hebrew. **Judgments** may mean "the sentences" or "decisions of judgment passed upon you," but ordinarily a word parallel to **enemies** would be expected here. Perhaps, therefore, one should vocalize the same consonants differently and read "opponents" (cf. Job 9:15; Ps. 109:31): "The Lord has removed your opponents and turned away your enemies." **Taken away** is the word from which the translation "prepared" is derived in the story of Isaac's servant at Laban's house (Gen. 24:31). A house "prepared" for hospitality is one in which things scattered about have been put in order, cleared away. So also the verb is used in Isa. 40:3, "prepare the way," i.e., "clear away the debris," "free the ground from obstacles." In the next line the meter is strained by too many words. A so-called *pāsēq* line calls attention to a faulty text (cf. E. F. Kautzsch, *Gesenius' Hebrew Grammar,* tr. A. E. Cowley [2nd Eng. ed.; Oxford: Clarendon Press, 1910], p. 59, n. 2). Either omit **the LORD** or follow some Greek MSS in reading, "The Lord reigns in your midst." **Fear:** The LXX has **see.** The two words in Hebrew are very similar and each gives excellent sense, for **evil** means "disaster," "trouble," "adversity." The point is very similar to that of Ps. 46:5, security in the presence of the Lord.

16-18. The appearance of a new start in vs. 16 may be due to an editor's hand; he may also be the author of the last line of vs. 17, of vs. 18, and of vs. 20. **Do not fear, O Zion** follows well if read directly after vs. 15, especially if the LXX is followed in that verse. **Let not your hands grow weak:** Lit., **slack,** "drop," "sink," or "droop." There is no reason to be **slack** when the Lord is present. Vs. 17 repeats the point: the Lord is not only **in your midst,** but he is a **warrior who gives victory,** who brings deliverance, who conquers. The phraseology is similar to that of Zech. 9:9, where Zion's king, described as just or righteous (cf. Zeph. 3:5), comes "having salvation," i.e., victorious. So the Amer. Trans. renders "vindicated and victorious." And in Zech. 9:9, as here, Zion is summoned to be comforted in the presence of the conquering king. Vs. 17*a* adds that the Lord also rejoices. Then the Hebrew in vs. 17*b* says, **He will be silent**

tongue, the purpose of which will be to enable all to worship God and serve him with one accord. The dream of seer and prophet finally comes to the same resting place. There is one God, one family, and one habitation. God is

the creator of life and all that therein is. The mark of the creator is on every forehead and his signature is in every living thing. What is inherent in life will become manifest in deed. This is the destiny of man, this is the destiny of

18 I will gather *them that are* sorrowful for the solemn assembly, *who* are of thee, *to whom* the reproach of it *was* a burden.

19 Behold, at that time I will undo all that afflict thee: and I will save her that halteth, and gather her that was driven out; and I will get them praise and fame in every land where they have been put to shame.

20 At that time will I bring you *again*, even in the time that I gather you: for I will make you a name and a praise among all people of the earth, when I turn back your captivity before your eyes, saith the LORD.

---

18   as on a day of festival.*j*
"I will remove disaster*k* from you,
   so that you will not bear reproach for
     it.

19 Behold, at that time I will deal
   with all your oppressors.
And I will save the lame
   and gather the outcast,
and I will change their shame into praise
   and renown in all the earth.

20 At that time I will bring you home,
   at the time when I gather you together;
yea, I will make you renowned and
     praised
   among all the peoples of the earth,
when I restore your fortunes
   before your eyes," says the LORD.

j Gk Syr: Heb obscure
k Cn: Heb *they were*

---

in his love, the LXX, **he will renew you in his love.** But better parallelism is secured if **he will exult over you with loud singing** is taken as the other member of the line which begins **he will rejoice over you with gladness.** In that case, **he will be silent in his love** should be regarded as having come in from the margin. One is tempted to see in these words the comment of a scribe who realized that God's love is not always manifested in the sounds of loud singing.

The text of vss. 18-20 bears signs of more serious corruption. The first two words of vs. 18 in the Hebrew are rendered by the KJV, **them that are sorrowful for the solemn assembly,** and are connected with the verb which follows, translated **gather** in the KJV and **remove** in the RSV. But the two words are in an awkward position, and are better emended in accordance with the LXX and regarded as the conclusion of vs. 17 or as a note upon it: **as on a day of festival** (cf. Hos. 12:9). The LXX continues: "And I will gather your wounded; alas! who love reproach for her," which, though difficult, is not so unintelligible as the Hebrew: "I gather, they were from you. The burden upon her was a reproach." As an alternative to the RSV read: "I have gathered your wounded, and I will take away your reproach." This is similar to the thought of vs. 19, and the verse may be a corrupt comment upon it. The oppressed Jews will be rescued, and their oppressors destroyed.

19-20. In vs. 19 a word such as "end" seems to have dropped out after the verb "make," translated by the RSV as **deal. At that time,** on the other hand, has been inserted. The thought of the previous verse continues. The Lord will overthrow the oppressors and rescue his lame and scattered people. The same idea is found in Mic. 4:6-10. A third promise is made: the lowly will be honored, praised, and renowned throughout all the earth (cf. Jer. 3:9). **Their shame** is probably the result of dittography; the suffix "them" is already attached to the verb "make," rendered **change** by the RSV.

Vs. 20 is a weak variant or repetitious expansion of vs. 19, with the further note:

       when I restore your fortunes
       before your eyes, says the LORD.

Cf. 2:7 and Exeg. These promises will be fulfilled in your lifetime. The time is at hand.

---

all of life. The homing instinct is given, and the time shall come when there shall be no alien lands, no strange peoples, and no expression of life outside the divine accord. Every knee

shall bow and every living thing and all creation shall join in the grand paean of praise and worship of the God of life who is at once the God of faith.

The Book of

HAGGAI

Introduction and Exegesis by D. Winton Thomas
Exposition by Willard L. Sperry

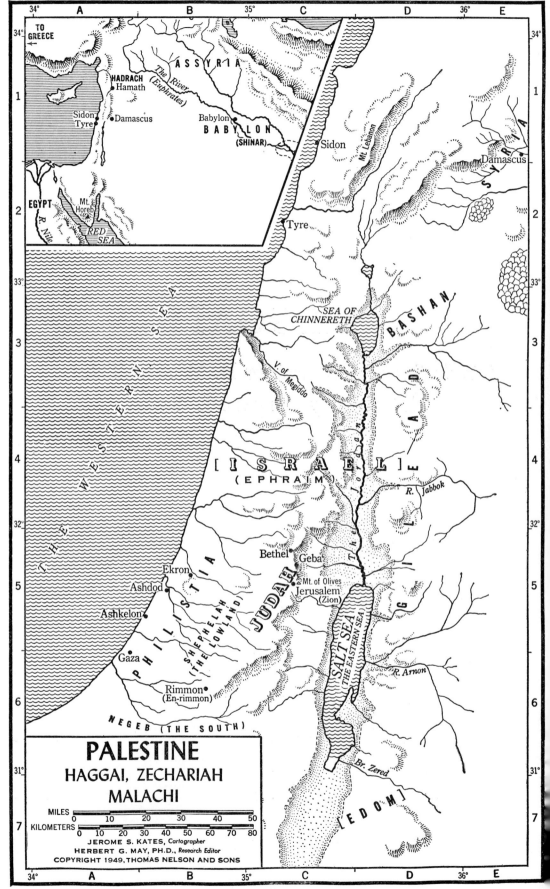

TO
GREECE

ASSYRIA

HADRACH
Hamath

Sidon
Tyre
Damascus

The River (Euphrates)

BABYLON
(SHINAR)

Babylon

EGYPT

Mt. Horeb

RED SEA

R. Nile

Sidon

Tyre

Mt. Lebanon

SYRIA

Damascus

SEA OF CHINNERETH

BASHAN

[I S R A E L]
(EPHRAIM)

THE WESTERN SEA

V. of Megiddo

R. Jabbok

The Jordan

G I L E A D

Ekron
Ashdod

Bethel
Geba

Ashkelon

P H I L I S T I A

SHEPHELAH (THE LOWLAND)

J U D A H

Mt. of Olives
Jerusalem
(Zion)

SALT SEA
THE EASTERN SEA

R. Arnon

Gaza

Rimmon
(En-rimmon)

N E G E B   (T H E   S O U T H)

Br. Zered

[E D O M]

PALESTINE
HAGGAI, ZECHARIAH
MALACHI

MILES 0   10   20   30   40   50
KILOMETERS 0 10 20 30 40 50 60 70 80

JEROME S. KATES, *Cartographer*
HERBERT G. MAY, PH.D., *Research Editor*
COPYRIGHT 1949, THOMAS NELSON AND SONS

HAGGAI

INTRODUCTION

Haggai is mentioned in the Old Testament only in this book and in Ezra 5:1; 6:14. Personal details about him are entirely lacking. No information is given, for example, as to his parentage (contrast Isa. 1:1; Jer. 1:1) or as to where he lived (contrast Amos 1:1; Jer. 1:1). It has indeed been inferred from 2:3 that he was an old man at the time of his preaching, and from 2:10-14 that he was a priest. Such inferences are, however, hazardous. The fact is that nothing at all is known about the prophet's personality, either from the Old Testament or from other sources.

I. Name

The name "Haggai," which means "festal," was probably given to him by his parents because he was born on a feast day; the birth of a child on such a day was thought to be a favorable omen which deserved to be preserved in the name of the child. A name of the same class is Shabbethai (Ezra 10:15; et al.), meaning "born on the sabbath." Related names in the Old Testament are Haggi (Gen. 46:16); Haggiah (I Chr. 6:30); and Haggith (II Sam. 3:4); and similar names are known outside the Old Testament from Phoenician and Aramaic sources.[1]

Haggai's activity as a prophet was of short duration, all his utterances having been delivered in the course of four months in the second year of Darius I Hystaspis (522-486 B.C.), that is, in the year 520 B.C.

II. Composition

Haggai differs from most other prophetical books in the Old Testament in that while the others are mainly collections of prophetical utterances, Haggai is more in the nature of a report on the prophet's utterances and on the effect they produced upon his hearers. Thus

it may be noted that Haggai is frequently referred to in the third person (1:1, 3, 12, et al.). This would suggest that the prophet himself is not the author of the book in its present form. Other features of the book point in the same direction. For example, the addition of the title "the prophet" to the name of Haggai (1:1, 3, 12, et al.) is more easily explicable on the supposition that the prophet himself was not responsible for it. Though Haggai thus cannot be regarded as the author of the book in its present form, there can be no doubt that the book contains genuine utterances of the prophet. It may well be that the editor who drew up the report had in his possession some of the prophet's personal notes. From these he may have obtained his information as to the dates on which Haggai's utterances were delivered. Who the editor was is not known, nor can it be said with any certainty when he did his work. In all probability it was not long after Haggai's prophetic activity was past. His work was in turn revised by later editors.

The book falls into five main sections which follow one upon the other in chronological order: (a) 1:1-14; (b) 1:15a; 2:15-19; (c) 1:15b; 2:1-9; (d) 2:10-14; (e) 2:20-23.[2] These sections are exactly dated according to the day and month of the second year of Darius I—in 520 B.C. The last two sections are dated on the same day.

The Hebrew text, though on the whole well preserved, has suffered in the process of transmission. For example, the text has not always been preserved in its original order; compare sections (b) and (c) in the preceding paragraph. Furthermore, a number of corruptions have crept in (e.g., in 1:2, 10; 2:17) and glosses too have found their way into the text (e.g., in 1:13; 2:5, 18). The Septuagint is fre-

---

[1] See Martin Noth, *Die israelitischen Personennamen im Rahmen der gemeinsemitischen Namengebung* (Stuttgart: W. Kohlhammer, 1928; "Beiträge zur Wissenschaft vom Alten und Neuen Testament"), pp. 222, 242.

[2] The arrangement of sections here adopted is from Friedrich Horst, *Die zwölf kleinen Propheten Nahum bis Maleachi* (Tübingen: J. C. B. Mohr, 1954; "Handbuch zum Alten Testament"), pp. 201-9.

quently of much value for the light it throws on the original Hebrew text. This may be seen not only in most of the passages just cited, but also in 2:7, 16, 19. In two passages—at the end of 2:9 and of 2:14—the Septuagint has noteworthy additions. But in neither case is it likely that the additions formed part of the original text.

III. Historical Background

The entry of Cyrus into Babylon in 539 B.C. was an event which was to have important consequences for the political and religious life of the Jews. For nearly fifty years, from 586 B.C. onward, Palestine had formed part of the Babylonian Empire; and for this same period the Jews who had been taken into exile by Nebuchadrezzar had lived in Babylon, exiled from their native land. The conquest of Babylon by Cyrus brought the Babylonian Empire to an end, and its incorporation into the Persian Empire resulted in Palestine's becoming a province of that empire. It is clear from the Cyrus Cylinder that it was his policy to conciliate the peoples he had conquered, to encourage them to pursue their traditional way of worship, and to allow exiles to return home from the lands to which they had been taken. In accordance with this policy Cyrus may well have issued some such decree as is to be found in Ezra 1:2-4, permitting the Jewish exiles in Babylon to return to Palestine. According to Ezra 1:5-11 a certain number of exiles took advantage of the Cyrus decree and at once returned to Jerusalem under the leadership of Sheshbazzar, a Babylonian, who was thus to become the first Persian governor of Judah; and according to Ezra 3:8-13 the foundation of the second temple was laid by these returning exiles in 537 B.C. This evidence from the book of Ezra, however, not only belongs to a period some two hundred years and more after the events recorded, but originates from the Chronicler, whose main aim was to show that the exiles in Babylon were so enthusiastic for their religion that they lost no time in leaving the land of their captivity and returning to rebuild the temple in Jerusalem. By reason of its lateness and of its idealization of the past, the evidence of the book of Ezra has not the same value that attaches to the contemporary evidence of Haggai and Zechariah, whose testimony is to be preferred. Neither Haggai nor Zechariah has any knowledge of an attempt to rebuild the temple in 537. The writings of these two prophets make it certain that the rebuilding was only begun in 520.

The successful career of Cyrus had filled Second Isaiah, the great prophet of the Exile, with the highest hopes for the future of his people (cf. Isa. 40:1-2; 44:28–45:3). Of Jerusalem he had said that it should be built, and of the temple that its foundation should be laid (44:28). Yet almost twenty years after Cyrus' conquest of Babylon had brought liberation to the exiled Jews and given them the opportunity to return home and fulfill the hopes of Second Isaiah, no attempt had been made to rebuild the temple. How is this fact to be explained? Several answers may be given. First, though the temple had been burned out by Nebuchadrezzar's men in 586 (II Kings 25:9; Jer. 52:13), its stone foundations remained, if in a damaged condition. Jer. 41:4-5 tells how, soon after the fall of Jerusalem, pilgrims from the north presented offerings there. The people of the south too, it may safely be assumed, will likewise have made use of the old place of worship in the years following 586. Thus in the course of a fairly long period the people had grown accustomed to the sight of the old temple, in a sorry state though it was. There they worshiped, and they felt no need to rebuild. The burned-out shrine had come to be accepted. Again, the invasion of Egypt by Cambyses in 525 brought the Persian armies to Palestine, and their passage through the country on their way westward doubtless brought distress and suffering to the people of Palestine. There was, however, another and more compelling reason, which is revealed very clearly in the book of Haggai. It was the wretched condition of the people generally. The provision of a roof over their heads was a prime object of their existence (1:4); harvests had been bad, food and drink were in short supply, warm clothes were scarce, and money had little value (1:6, 9-10; 2:16-17, 19). All the people's energy went to supply their daily physical needs. They were in no mood to undertake a religious duty. It mattered not at all to them that Yahweh's house had no roof on it so long as theirs had. So had faded the bright hopes of Second Isaiah. Life, physical and spiritual, was indeed at a low ebb.

It was to such a people and at such a time that Haggai came forward as a prophet—soon to be joined by Zechariah—with the divine command laid upon him to urge the people to rebuild the temple. His task was not an easy one. The time had not yet come to build, so the people in their disappointment and apathy excused their indifference (1:2). Admittedly times were hard. But whereas the people found in the difficult conditions of life a good reason for indifference, Haggai saw in these same conditions a consequence of it. They were the result, he argued, of the prevailing indifference to the claims of religion, and so long as these claims remained unhonored, so long would their misfortunes continue. If only they will shake off their indifference and build—the prophet is firm in his assurance—there will be an end of the hard life. Instead, the people will know what it is to be blessed of Yahweh. Haggai's words were addressed in the first place to Zerubbabel, the civil head of the community, and to Joshua, the religious head. They had their effect, and under the leadership of these two men the rebuilding of the temple was begun. In 516, four years after Haggai first made his appeal, it was completed (Ezra 6:14-15).

There can be little doubt that in Haggai's intervention in the religious life of the struggling community of Judah two historical events played an important part. The first was the widespread revolts which broke out in the Persian Empire when Darius I succeeded Cambyses on the throne of Persia in 522. These revolts, which were for the most part suppressed by the late summer of 520, seem to have been associated in the prophet's mind with the final world catastrophe which, as earlier Hebrew thought supposed, was to precede the coming of the messianic age (2:6-9, 20-23). The other event was the appointment by Darius of the Babylonian Jew, Zerubbabel, of the royal house of David, as governor of Judah (I Esdras 4:47-57). In him Haggai saw the long-expected Messiah. Yahweh was, so he thought, preparing to restore the Davidic kingdom, and would himself quite soon—for Haggai believed the messianic age to be imminent—return to Jerusalem. Yahweh's home must therefore be ready for his coming. This is at once the motive for Haggai's insistence on the necessity of rebuilding the temple and the ground for his confidence that, with Yahweh home again in his temple—which the world's offerings have rendered more glorious than its predecessor (2:7-9) —and with Zerubbabel, the servant of Yahweh and his signet ring (2:23), installed in Jerusalem, the curse which had for so long lain upon the land would be removed and give place to perpetual blessing. As a matter of history, Zerubbabel never became king of Judah, as Haggai hoped and believed he would. He disappears quite suddenly from the scene. We can only guess at the reason. Perhaps the Persian authorities, hearing of the kingly role for which he was cast (cf. Neh. 6:7) and of his plan to rebuild the walls of Jerusalem (cf. Zech. 2:1-5), became suspicious of his loyalty and removed him quietly to another post—or to his death.

IV. Significance

Haggai has no claim to be ranked with his great predecessors in the prophetic office. It is true that he was powerfully animated by some themes which animated them, for example, the conception of a world destruction and the hope of a king-messiah sprung from the house of David. But "there is no longer a really spiritual message. Even the denunciations of sin and corruption which had marked the utterances of the pre-exilic Prophets are wanting, and the Prophet seems to have included stone and timber amongst the essentials of his spiritual and religious ideal." [3] Haggai is indeed a minor prophet. Yet he has an importance all his own for the history of postexilic Judaism. In fact, he is no less than a decisive figure in this history. This is evident in two respects. First, in the postexilic age the temple became the very center of the religious life of the community. For the fact that there was a restored temple at all at which Jews of this age could worship the chief credit must go to Haggai, who persuaded his fellow countrymen—some of whom were inclined to make light of his efforts (2:3) —to take in hand the work of rebuilding. Second, in Haggai's opposition to the Samaritans (2:10-14) —an opposition which was shared by Zechariah (cf. chs. 7–8) —may be seen the beginning of that rigid exclusiveness which was to become so essential a characteristic of the postexilic community in Judah.

V. Outline of Contents

VI. Selected Bibliography

BARNES, W. E. Haggai and Zechariah ("Cambridge Bible"). Cambridge: Cambridge University Press, 1917.

BROWNE, LAURENCE E. Early Judaism. Cambridge: Cambridge University Press, 1920.

DRIVER, S. R., ed. The Minor Prophets ("New Century Bible"). New York: Oxford University Press, 1906. Vol. II.

HORST, FRIEDRICH. Die zwölf kleinen Propheten Nahum bis Maleachi ("Handbuch zum Alten Testament"). Tübingen: J. C. B. Mohr, 1954.

MITCHELL, H. G., SMITH, J. M. P., and BEWER, JULIUS A. A Critical and Exegetical Commentary on Haggai, Zechariah, Malachi, and Jonah ("International Critical Commentary"). New York: Charles Scribner's Sons, 1912.

SELLIN, ERNST. Das Zwölfprophetenbuch ("Kommentar zum Alten Testament"). 2nd & 3rd ed. Leipzig: A. Deichert, 1929-30.

[3] T. H. Robinson, Prophecy and the Prophets in Ancient Israel (New York: Charles Scribner's Sons, 1923), p. 177.

HAGGAI

TEXT, EXEGESIS, AND EXPOSITION

1 In the second year of Darius the king, in the sixth month, in the first day of the month, came the word of the LORD by Haggai the prophet unto Zerubbabel the son of Shealtiel, governor of Judah, and to Joshua the son of Josedech, the high priest, saying,

1 In the second year of Darius the king, in the sixth month, on the first day of the month, the word of the LORD came by Haggai the prophet to Zerub'babel the son of She-al'ti-el, governor of Judah, and to Joshua the son of Jehoz'adak, the high

I. APPEAL TO REBUILD THE TEMPLE (1:1-14)

A. OBJECTIONS AND REPLY (1:1-11)

In the second year of Darius, on the first day of the sixth month, Haggai appeals to the people to begin the rebuilding of the temple. The people show no willingness to respond to his appeal, objecting that the time has not yet come to rebuild. Haggai, knowing that their objection is but a cloak for their selfishness and indifference to Yahweh, points out that their preoccupation with the building of houses for themselves, while Yahweh's house lies neglected, has resulted in failure of crops and drought, and in other misfortunes which Yahweh in his displeasure has brought upon them.

1:1. The **second year of Darius** was 520 B.C. The **sixth month,** corresponding to our August-September, was later called Elul (cf. Neh. 6:15). In pre-exilic days the Hebrew year was reckoned from autumn to autumn. During the Exile, however, the Jews adopted the Babylonian calendar, according to which the year began in the spring. They dropped the old Hebrew names of the months, and in early postexilic days the months were known by numbers. This is normally the case in the books of Haggai and Zechariah. Later on the Babylonian names of the months were introduced (Neh. 1:1; 2:1; Ezra 6:15). The occurrences of such names in Zechariah (1:7; 7:1) are probably later additions to the text. **Zerubbabel** was a Babylonian Jew of the royal house of David, being the grandson of Jehoiachin, who was taken into exile by Nebuchadrezzar in 597 (II Kings 24:15; I Chr. 3:17). His name is a Hebraized modification of the Babylonian name *Zēr-Bābili,* "seed of Babylon" (Martin Noth, *Die israelitischen Personennamen im Rahmen der gemeinsemitischen Namengebung* [Stuttgart: W. Kohlhammer, 1928; "Beiträge zur Wissenschaft vom Alten und Neuen Testament"], p. 63). **Shealtiel:** This

---

1:1–2:23. *The Message of Haggai.*—In his poem *Paracelsus* Browning says:

> If some mortal, born too soon,
> Were laid away in some great trance—the ages
> Coming and going all the while—till dawned
> His true time's advent . . . .[1]

There are certain books of the Bible, relevant enough in the days when they were written, which seem to lose their relevance in later times,

[1] Part I.

not because they were not true in the first instance, but because the times have changed. They lie, on the pages of the Bible, neglected and unread "in some great trance," until the cycling of history brings the wheel back full circle to the state of affairs at the date of their composition. Then their "true time's advent" comes again.

The prophecy of Haggai is such a book. It could have meant little or nothing to our world fifty or a hundred years ago. Those were the

1040

2 Thus speaketh the LORD of hosts, saying, This people say, The time is not come, the time that the LORD's house should be built.

3 Then came the word of the LORD by Haggai the prophet, saying,

4 *Is it* time for you, O ye, to dwell in your ceiled houses, and this house *lie* waste?

5 Now therefore thus saith the LORD of hosts; Consider your ways.

6 Ye have sown much, and bring in little; ye eat, but ye have not enough; ye drink, but ye are not filled with drink; ye clothe you, but there is none warm; and he that earneth wages, earneth wages *to put it* into a bag with holes.

7 ¶ Thus saith the LORD of hosts; Consider your ways.

8 Go up to the mountain, and bring wood, and build the house; and I will take

priest, 2 "Thus says the LORD of hosts: This people say the time has not yet come to rebuild the house of the LORD." 3 Then the word of the LORD came by Haggai the prophet, 4 "Is it a time for you yourselves to dwell in your paneled houses, while this house lies in ruins? 5 Now therefore thus says the LORD of hosts: Consider how you have fared. 6 You have sown much, and harvested little; you eat, but you never have enough; you drink, but you never have your fill; you clothe yourselves, but no one is warm; and he who earns wages earns wages to put them into a bag with holes.

7 "Thus says the LORD of hosts: Consider how you have fared. 8 Go up to the hills

form of the name occurs again in 2:23; Ezra 3:2, 8; Neh. 12:1. The form Shaltiel, found in 1:12, 14; 2:2 (M.T.), is, however, probably more original (*ibid.*, n. 7). The title **governor** designates Zerubbabel as the civil head of the community. **Joshua** was the grandson of Seraiah (I Chr. 6:14), who was chief priest in 586, when Nebuchadrezzar took Jerusalem (II Kings 25:18; Jer. 52:24). His father Jehozadak was taken into captivity in that year (I Chr. 6:15). Joshua, therefore, like Zerubbabel, came to Palestine from Babylon. As high priest he was the religious head of the community.

2. The time has not yet come to rebuild: The Hebrew text is corrupt here. The first '*ēth*, **time**, should either be deleted—it is not in the LXX—or should be vocalized '*attāh*, "now"; and *bā*', **has come** (so LXX ἥκει), should be read for *bō*', "to come." The seventy years which Jeremiah (25:11) had said would be the period of the Exile were not yet over. The people, in a mood to seize upon any excuse for postponing the rebuilding of the temple, sheltered behind Jeremiah's forecast.

4. The word ceiled is sometimes taken to mean **paneled.** The interpretation would then be that the people are concerned only about lining their own houses with timber (cf. Jer. 22:14; I Kings 7:7) instead of being concerned about renewing the woodwork of the temple (cf. I Kings 6:9), which was destroyed in the flames of 586. It is more likely, however, that Haggai is here contrasting the people's houses which have roofs—the Hebrew word used (*sephûnîm*) means, lit., "covered"—with the temple, which was still without a roof.

5. Consider how you have fared: A characteristic phrase of Haggai (cf. vs. 7; 2:15, 18).

6. Bad harvests, insufficient to eat and drink, inadequate clothing, money that has no value—in all these things Haggai sees the curse of Yahweh upon his people.

8. The hills: The hilly country to the south of Jerusalem, which was at that time well wooded (cf. Neh. 2:8; 8:15). There was no need to tell the people to go and bring

days of what seemed to be peaceful expansion. Haggai's message about the reconstruction of the temple did not fit the facts. All that began to change in early August, 1914, with the beginning of World War I. On August 8, 1914, the London *Nation* carried an editorial which said: "The society of hope and ideas lies in

ruins; in months or years to come our enfeebled hands must collect its broken stones and try to rebuild it." [2] Those prophetic words, far more true today than their author could have realized when he wrote them, mark the rebirth of the prophecy of Haggai in our world, or, more

[2] Vol. XV, p. 692.

pleasure in it, and I will be glorified, saith the LORD.

9 Ye looked for much, and, lo, *it came* to little; and when ye brought *it* home, I did blow upon it. Why? saith the LORD of hosts. Because of mine house that *is* waste, and ye run every man unto his own house.

10 Therefore the heaven over you is stayed from dew, and the earth is stayed *from* her fruit.

11 And I called for a drought upon the land, and upon the mountains, and upon the corn, and upon the new wine, and upon the oil, and upon *that* which the ground bringeth forth, and upon men, and upon cattle, and upon all the labor of the hands.

12 ¶ Then Zerubbabel the son of Shealtiel, and Joshua the son of Josedech, the high priest, with all the remnant of the

and bring wood and build the house, that I may take pleasure in it and that I may appear in my glory, says the LORD. 9 You have looked for much, and, lo, it came to little; and when you brought it home, I blew it away. Why? says the LORD of hosts. Because of my house that lies in ruins, while you busy yourselves each with his own house. 10 Therefore the heavens above you have withheld the dew, and the earth has withheld its produce. 11 And I have called for a drought upon the land and the hills, upon the grain, the new wine, the oil, upon what the ground brings forth, upon men and cattle, and upon all their labors."

12 Then Zerub'babel the son of She-al'ti-el, and Joshua the son of Jehoz'adak, the

stone—there was plenty of it at hand in the ruins of the city. **Appear in my glory:** When the messianic age dawns, Yahweh will return to his temple in Jerusalem. Earlier Ezekiel had seen the glory of Yahweh depart (10:18) and return (43:4).

9. When you brought . . . home the produce of the fields, **I blew it away.** In ancient thought breath could have a salutary or a harmful effect (for the former cf. Ezek. 37:9-10; for the latter cf. Isa. 11:4; 40:24). The effect here is of course harmful. This superstition still lives on in the Semitic East: "It is in the highest degree disagreeable to Moslems if any one whistles over a threshing-floor heaped with grain. Then comes the devil, they say, in the night and takes a part of the harvest." (L. Bauer, quoted in H. G. Mitchell, J. M. P. Smith, and Julius A. Bewer, *A Critical and Exegetical Commentary on Haggai, Zechariah, Malachi, and Jonah* [New York: Charles Scribner's Sons, 1912; "International Critical Commentary"], p. 48).

10. For **dew** the original text may have had "their dew" (טלם for מטל; cf. Zech. 8:12). A slight emendation (מטר for מטל) would give the meaning "rain" (so Targ.; cf. Deut. 11:17; I Kings 8:35; Amos 4:7).

11. The Hebrew word for **drought** is *ḥōrebh*. In vs. 9 the temple is described as *ḥārēbh*, **in ruins.** Evidently a play upon words is intended. **The grain, the new wine, the oil:** These three staple products of Palestine are frequently mentioned together in the O.T. (e.g., Hos. 2:8; Deut. 11:14). **All the labor of the hands:** The produce of the fields (cf. Ps. 128:2). **Labor** is sometimes used by itself, without **hands** (cf. RSV), in the same sense (e.g., Deut. 28:33; Ps. 78:46).

B. THE PEOPLE'S RESPONSE (1:12-14)

Haggai's words have their effect. Work on the rebuilding of the temple is begun under the leadership of Zerubbabel and Joshua.

12. The phrase **the remnant of the people,** as used in Haggai (cf. vs. 14; 2:2) and Zechariah (8:6, 11, 12), always means the returned exiles.

exactly perhaps, the sober return of our world to the circumstances of his world. For our enfeebled hands are now concerned to gather together the broken stones of the society of hope and ideas and to try to put them in place again. There are few books in the Bible more timely

today, or likely to be more timely for many years to come, than this brief, earnest, austere book of Haggai.

The book brings us far nearer to total truth of the Bible than once it did. The Bible is the record of God's acts of creation and redemption.

people, obeyed the voice of the Lord their God, and the words of Haggai the prophet, as the Lord their God had sent him, and the people did fear before the Lord.

13 Then spake Haggai the Lord's messenger in the Lord's message unto the people, saying, I *am* with you, saith the Lord.

14 And the Lord stirred up the spirit of Zerubbabel the son of Shealtiel, governor of Judah, and the spirit of Joshua the son of Josedech, the high priest, and the spirit of all the remnant of the people; and they came and did work in the house of the Lord of hosts, their God,

15 In the four and twentieth day of the sixth month, in the second year of Darius the king.

high priest, with all the remnant of the people, obeyed the voice of the Lord their God, and the words of Haggai the prophet, as the Lord their God had sent him; and the people feared before the Lord. 13 Then Haggai, the messenger of the Lord, spoke to the people with the Lord's message, "I am with you, says the Lord." 14 And the Lord stirred up the spirit of Zerub′babel the son of She-al′ti-el, governor of Judah, and the spirit of Joshua the son of Jehoz′-adak, the high priest, and the spirit of all the remnant of the people; and they came and worked on the house of the Lord of hosts, their God, 15 on the twenty-fourth day of the month, in the sixth month.

---

13. This verse is probably a later addition. The use of **the Lord's messenger** in place of the more usual "the prophet" (as in 1:1, 12; 2:1, 10) is noteworthy.

II. A Promise of Better Times (1:15a; 2:15-19)

The thought of the opening section (1:1-11) recurs here. The people's misfortunes—failure of crops, drought, etc.—originate from their neglect of Yahweh's house. But an end of all this is promised. The laying of the foundation stone of the temple will bring with it a change in their fortunes. Instead of being victims of Yahweh's curse they will enjoy his blessing.

15a. The date, **the twenty-fourth day** of the sixth month—three weeks after Haggai's first appeal—probably refers not to the day on which work was begun on the temple (so KJV and RSV), but to the day on which the foundation stone of the temple was laid; and 2:15-19 should probably follow immediately after it. This last section has no connection, so far as subject matter is concerned, with 2:10-14, and is better explained as a pronouncement made on the day when the foundation stone was laid—the gloss in vs. 18 **since the day that the foundation of the Lord's temple was laid** gives a hint of this—than one made on the twenty-fourth day of the ninth month (vs. 18), by which time the work on the rebuilding had already been in progress for three months. The date in vs. 18 is probably a gloss, having come in from vs. 10.

1:15b–2:14. See Exeg. on pp. 1044-47.

2:15. How did you fare? This translation is based upon the LXX rendering of the Hebrew מהיותם (vs. 16)—which the KJV translates "Since those days were"—by τίνες ἦτε, "what sort of men you were." The LXX rendering points to a reading מי הייתם.

17. Yet you did not return to me: The Hebrew text (ואין אתכם אלי) is untranslatable as it stands. The best solution is to emend it on the basis of the final words of Amos 4:9 and read ולא שבתם אלי, and translate as in the RSV. Another possibility would be to read ואין אתכם אני (*'ittekhem* instead of M.T.'s *'ethekhem*), "and I was not with you" (cf. 1:13; 2:4).

18. Everything in this verse after **Consider from this day onward** is a gloss except the last word, **consider,** with which vs. 19 should begin (cf. LXX). The two verses are

---

In other days we felt ourselves challenged to try to share with God in his still unfinished creation of the world. The ideal of a "creative life" was held before us as valid interpretation of our religion. "Creativity" was to be a major virtue.

But today, and because of stern necessity, we are far more concerned with the reconstruction of our world than with its further creation. To this extent the prophecy of Haggai takes its proper place in a fully biblical view of life, for

2 In the seventh *month,* in the one and twentieth *day* of the month, came the word of the LORD by the prophet Haggai, saying,

2 Speak now to Zerubbabel the son of Shealtiel, governor of Judah, and to Joshua the son of Josedech, the high priest, and to the residue of the people, saying,

3 Who *is* left among you that saw this house in her first glory? and how do ye see it now? *is it* not in your eyes in comparison of it as nothing?

4 Yet now be strong, O Zerubbabel, saith the LORD; and be strong, O Joshua, son of Josedech, the high priest; and be strong, all ye people of the land, saith the LORD, and work: for I *am* with you, saith the LORD of hosts:

2 In the second year of Darius the king,
1 in the seventh month, on the twenty-first day of the month, the word of the LORD came by Haggai the prophet, 2 "Speak now to Zerub'babel the son of She-al'ti-el, governor of Judah, and to Joshua the son of Jehoz'adak, the high priest, and to all the remnant of the people, and say, 3 'Who is left among you that saw this house in its former glory? How do you see it now? Is it not in your sight as nothing? 4 Yet now take courage, O Joshua, son of Jehoz'adak, the high priest; take courage, all you people of the land, says the LORD; work, for I am with you, says the LORD of hosts,

best rendered: "Consider from this day onward, whether the seed is still diminishing in the granary, and whether the vine, the fig tree, the pomegranate, and the olive tree still continue not to bear. From this day on I will bless." The prophet bids his hearers consider whether their agricultural pursuits will be as unrewarding as they have been hitherto while they have been living under Yahweh's curse (cf. 1:9; 2:16). He assures them that they will not be. From the time when the foundation stone of the temple is laid, Yahweh will bless "the fruits of the field" (not **you**). The translation given above requires the supplying of נגרע, "is diminishing"—it could easily have fallen out after הזרע, **the seed**—and the reading *we'ôdh,* "still" (with LXX καὶ εἰ ἔτι), for *we'adh,* "even."

III. THE GLORY OF THE TEMPLE (1:15b–2:9)

On the twenty-first day of the seventh month Haggai encourages those who might have seen the temple of Solomon which was burned in 586, and who were inclined to be contemptuous of the temple now going up when they compared it with its predecessor. Haggai tells them that the future glory of the temple will be greater than its past glory, for the treasures of all the nations will flow to Jerusalem. While the whole world will be convulsed, Jerusalem will enjoy peace, so that the rebuilding can proceed undisturbed.

2:1. The **seventh month,** which corresponded to our September-October, was later, in postbiblical times, called Tishri. See Exeg. on 1:1.

3. Saw this house in its former glory: The number of those old enough to remember the temple of Solomon will have been small (cf. Ezra 3:12). The second half of the verse indicates that these older men were inclined to scoff at the attempt to rebuild the temple.

4. In place of **all you people of the land,** "all the remnant of the people" is rather to be expected, as in vs. 2.

the Bible, after its serene beginnings, has much to say of the reconstruction of the shattered fabric of society, and even more to say of the redemption of man himself. When Paul says that we are "workers together" with Christ (II Cor. 6:1), he means that we share with Christ his ministry of reconciliation and redemption. All this is intimated and symbolized in Haggai's concern for the rebuilding of the temple.

Scholars stress the blunt prose style of the book, whether in the original or in translation.

It is markedly wanting in the more romantic and poetic passages which we find in some of the other prophecies. But the book cannot be dismissed on that account. Life is a compound of poetry and prose. At this point Haggai is at one with the saints and mystics, who were only too familiar with long periods of "dryness." The religious life is a matter of negotiating its desert traverses as well as of repose in its oases. When Albert Schweitzer went back to Lambaréné after his first furlough, he found the buildings

5 *According to* the word that I covenanted with you when ye came out of
Egypt, so my Spirit remaineth among you:
fear ye not.

6 For thus saith the LORD of hosts; Yet
once, it *is* a little while, and I will shake
the heavens, and the earth, and the sea, and
the dry *land;*

7 And I will shake all nations, and the
Desire of all nations shall come: and I will
fill this house with glory, saith the LORD of
hosts.

8 The silver *is* mine, and the gold *is*
mine, saith the LORD of hosts.

9 The glory of this latter house shall be
greater than of the former, saith the LORD
of hosts: and in this place will I give peace,
saith the LORD of hosts.

5 according to the promise that I made
you when you came out of Egypt. My
Spirit abides among you; fear not. 6 For
thus says the LORD of hosts: Once again,
in a little while, I will shake the heavens
and the earth and the sea and the dry
land; 7 and I will shake all nations, so
that the treasures of all nations shall come
in, and I will fill this house with splendor,
says the LORD of hosts. 8 The silver is mine,
and the gold is mine, says the LORD of hosts.
9 The latter splendor of this house shall be
greater than the former, says the LORD of
hosts; and in this place I will give prosperity, says the LORD of hosts.' "

5. The words **according to the word that I covenanted with you when ye came
out of Egypt** are difficult of translation in the Hebrew, and they are not in the LXX.
They are probably a gloss, introduced by someone to whom vs. 4*b* recalled the Exodus
from Egypt. Perhaps the glossator had in mind some such passage as Exod. 19:5 or 33:14.

6. **Shake the heavens and the earth:** Haggai here proclaims, in terms reminiscent
of those used by the earlier prophets (cf. Hos. 10:8; Isa. 13:13; Mic. 1:4), the world
cataclysm which is to be the prelude to the coming of the messianic age. For the association
of this world cataclysm in the prophet's mind with the revolts that accompanied Darius'
accession to the throne of Persia, see Intro., p. 1039.

7. **The treasures of all nations:** As the Hebrew text stands, the verb באו, **come in,**
is in the plural, while the subject (*ḥemdath*) is in the singular—hence, **the Desire of
all nations.** The plural subject that is required (cf. LXX τὰ ἐκλεκτὰ, "the choice things")
can be most easily obtained if instead of *ḥemdath* is read *ḥamûdhôth,* "delightful, desired
things" (cf. Gen. 27:15). The messianic interpretation of these words (cf. Vulg. *veniet
desideratus cunctis gentibus*) has long been abandoned. Vs. 8, with its reference to
silver and **gold,** clearly shows what is meant by **treasures** in this verse (for the thought
cf. Isa. 60:5, 9, 11). **Fill this house with glory:** As once the glory of Yahweh filled the
temple of Solomon (cf. I Kings 8:11).

8. All the **silver** and **gold** the world over belongs to Yahweh, the God of the small,
weak Jewish community—a daring thought which reveals the strength of Haggai's
belief in the power of his God.

9. **The latter splendor of this house:** Haggai's firm assurance to the scoffers (cf.
vs. 3). The building that is going up will be more than a worthy successor to the first

of his little hospital in tumbled-down disrepair.
He set about rebuilding them with his own
hands. As he soberly said, he realized that the
poetry of his African adventure was over, he
had entered on its prose period.[3] But he was a
mature soul, equal to that occasion.

The prose periods of the religious life are our
opportunity to make good the truth of their
initial poetry. Without them our insights, inspirations, and visions lack substantial and en-

during reality. The prophet Haggai challenged
his contemporaries to make good the glory of
the first temple in the terms of the reconstructed
temple. He refused to be deterred by the wistful
and reminiscent mood of those who still remembered the first temple and compared the
reconstructed temple unfavorably. The moral
earnestness of the man prevailed over the sentimental inertia of his fellows. He "kept the
faith" in a tedious time.

We may no longer share his simple attribu-
tion of the sufferings of his time at the hand of

[3] See *Out of My Life and Thought,* tr. C. T. Campion
(New York: Henry Holt & Co., 1933), pp. 204 ff.

10 ¶ In the four and twentieth *day* of the ninth *month,* in the second year of Darius, came the word of the LORD by Haggai the prophet, saying,

10 On the twenty-fourth day of the ninth month, in the second year of Darius, the word of the LORD came by Haggai the

---

temple. **This place** signifies Jerusalem, not the temple. There is perhaps a play on words here between *shālôm* (**prosperity**) and Jeru*salem*. At the end of this verse the LXX adds: καὶ εἰρήνην ψυχῆς εἰς περιποίησιν παντὶ τῷ κτίζοντι τοῦ ἀναστῆσαι τὸν ναὸν τοῦτον, "even peace of soul for a possession [salvation ?] to every one that builds, to raise up this temple." These words probably did not form part of the original text.

IV. HOLINESS AND UNCLEANNESS (2:10-14)

On the twenty-fourth day of the ninth month Haggai addresses to the priests two questions concerning the effect if, on the one hand, that which is holy and, on the other hand, that which is unclean, are brought into contact with certain objects. The priests reply that the objects are not in the first case thereby made holy; but that they are in the second case made unclean; i.e., uncleanness is more far-reaching in its effect than holiness.

Haggai's argument in these verses is generally taken to be that the people, by their neglect of the rebuilding of the temple, and by this neglect failing to prepare for the coming of Yahweh and the messianic age, have defiled themselves, and that they have communicated their uncleanness to their agricultural pursuits, and to the offerings therefrom which they present at the temple. It is difficult to believe, however, that **this people** (vs. 14) —the people whom the prophet dubs as unclean—refers to those same persons who, according to 1:12, 14, listened to Haggai's appeal and set to work on the temple, and to whom a time of future blessing had so recently been promised (2:1-9). To whom then does **this people** refer? Probably to the Samaritans. Read in conjunction with Ezra 4:1-5, these verses would seem to indicate Haggai's unfriendly attitude to the Samaritan offer to share in the rebuilding of the temple. Whereas, Haggai argues, the sacred Jewish community of the returned exiles cannot communicate its holiness to others, it can quite easily contract uncleanness from them. The Samaritan offer must therefore be rejected.

The Samaritans were not at this time regarded by the Jews, as they were by the time of Nehemiah, as suspect on religious grounds. When Haggai imputes uncleanness to them, therefore, the reason must be sought elsewhere than in the sphere of religion. It should be looked for most probably in the sphere of politics. "It was true enough that, according to the recognized ritual, uncleanness could be communicated by touch; but it was mere assumption that the Samaritans were unclean. One can only conjecture the reason for this assumption, but it may well be that some spark of the old tribal jealousy between the North and South Kingdoms had survived through all the political changes, and that the inhabitants of Judah did not love their northern neighbours." (Laurence E. Browne, *Early Judaism* [Cambridge: Cambridge University Press, 1920], pp. 61-62; also cf. Zech. 8:10.) With this decision of Haggai to rebuff the Samaritans we are at the beginning of that process which led later, in the days of Nehemiah and Ezra, to the erection of a wall of separation between the Jewish community and the outside world.

10. The **ninth month,** which corresponded to our November-December, was later called Kislev (cf. Zech. 7:1; Hag. 1:1).

---

the natural order—droughts, famines, pestilences, etc.—with the delay of his people at the task of temple rebuilding. But we can share his conviction that the well-being of a society rests upon its concern for spiritual values and its fidelity to the moral order. The temple was to be the "outward and visible symbol" of such devotion. It was for him the test case. His brief urgent message is as timely in these days of reconstruction as it was when first uttered. He has only one thing to say, but he has said it for all time, and with renewed validity for our times.

11 Thus saith the LORD of hosts; Ask now the priests *concerning* the law, saying,

12 If one bear holy flesh in the skirt of his garment, and with his skirt do touch bread, or pottage, or wine, or oil, or any meat, shall it be holy? And the priests answered and said, No.

13 Then said Haggai, If *one that is* unclean by a dead body touch any of these, shall it be unclean? And the priests answered and said, It shall be unclean.

14 Then answered Haggai, and said, So *is* this people, and so *is* this nation before me, saith the LORD; and so *is* every work of their hands; and that which they offer there *is* unclean.

15 And now, I pray you, consider from this day and upward, from before a stone was laid upon a stone in the temple of the LORD:

16 Since those *days* were, when *one* came to a heap of twenty *measures,* there were *but* ten: when *one* came to the pressvat for to draw out fifty *vessels* out of the press, there were *but* twenty.

prophet, 11 "Thus says the LORD of hosts: Ask the priests to decide this question, 12 'If one carries holy flesh in the skirt of his garment, and touches with his skirt bread, or pottage, or wine, or oil, or any kind of food, does it become holy?'" The priests answered, "No." 13 Then said Haggai, "If one who is unclean by contact with a dead body touches any of these, does it become unclean?" The priests answered, "It does become unclean." 14 Then Haggai said, "So is it with this people, and with this nation before me, says the LORD; and so with every work of their hands; and what they offer there is unclean. 15 Pray now, consider what will come to pass from this day onward. Before a stone was placed upon a stone in the temple of the LORD, how did you fare?[a] 16 When one came to a heap of twenty measures, there were but ten; when one came to the winevat to draw fifty meas-

[a] Gk: Heb *since they were*

11. The Hebrew word *tôrāh* signifies an authoritative decision given by word of mouth (cf. Mal. 2:7; and Zech. 7:2-3, where a deputation from Bethel comes to Jerusalem seeking an official decision from the priests and prophets there on a point of religious observance). The oral teaching of the priests was eventually incorporated in the Torah (the Pentateuch). Nothing can be proved from Haggai's words as to the existence in his day of a written code of laws. No exact parallel to the torah here given is to be found in the Pentateuch. Lev. 6:27-28 provides the closest parallel to it.

12. **Holy flesh:** Flesh of a sacred animal slain for an offering.

13. **Unclean by contact with a dead body:** Cf. Lev. 21:11; Num. 9:6-7; 19:11-13.

14. **This people** refers to the Samaritans, and **every work of their hands** refers to their participation in the rebuilding of the temple. **That which they offer there:** I.e., at the temple. At the end of the verse the LXX adds: ἕνεκεν τῶν λημμάτων αὐτῶν τῶν ὀρθρινῶν, ὀδυνηθήσονται ἀπὸ προσώπου πόνων αὐτῶν· καὶ ἐμισεῖτε ἐν πύλαις ἐλέγχοντας, "because of their early burdens; they shall be pained because of their toils; and you have hated them that reprove in the gates." It is improbable that these words formed part of the original text.

15-19. See Exeg. on 1:15a; 2:15-19.

We have said that the prophecy of Haggai is a work of prose rather than of poetry. That fact may be verified by any reader who will turn from the KJV to one of the modern translations in which poetic passages are set as such, clearly distinct from the framework of prose. There is not a line of poetry in Haggai. But the book is not, however, without those pictorial and parabolic figures of speech by which the Hebrew writer habitually illustrates his idea. These metaphors save the style from lifeless abstraction.

One of the most familiar problems of the world is that of fluctuating costs, inflation, and shrunken values. Arbitrary changes in the standards of a currency can wipe out the hard-earned savings of a lifetime. Haggai understood what such a situation is, and stated the case in words so apposite that they are almost classic. **He that earneth wages earneth wages to put it into a bag with holes** (1:6). Again, **When one came to a heap of twenty measures, there were but ten: when one came to the pressvat for to draw**

17 I smote you with blasting and with mildew and with hail in all the labors of your hands; yet ye *turned* not to me, saith the Lord.

18 Consider now from this day and upward, from the four and twentieth day of the ninth *month, even* from the day that the foundation of the Lord's temple was laid, consider *it.*

19 Is the seed yet in the barn? yea, as yet the vine, and the fig tree, and the pomegranate, and the olive tree, hath not brought forth: from this day will I bless *you.*

20 ¶ And again the word of the Lord came unto Haggai in the four and twentieth *day* of the month, saying,

21 Speak to Zerubbabel, governor of Judah, saying, I will shake the heavens and the earth;

22 And I will overthrow the throne of kingdoms, and I will destroy the strength of the kingdoms of the heathen; and I will overthrow the chariots, and those that ride in them; and the horses and their riders shall come down, every one by the sword of his brother.

ures, there were but twenty. 17 I smote you and all the products of your toil with blight and mildew and hail; yet you did not return to me, says the Lord. 18 Consider from this day onward, from the twenty-fourth day of the ninth month. Since the day that the foundation of the Lord's temple was laid, consider: 19 Is the seed yet in the barn? Do the vine, the fig tree, the pomegranate, and the olive tree still yield nothing? From this day on I will bless you."

20 The word of the Lord came a second time to Haggai on the twenty-fourth day of the month, 21 "Speak to Zerub'babel, governor of Judah, saying, I am about to shake the heavens and the earth, 22 and to overthrow the throne of kingdoms; I am about to destroy the strength of the kingdoms of the nations, and overthrow the chariots and their riders; and the horses and their riders shall go down, every one by the sword of his

---

V. Zerubbabel as Yahweh's Servant (2:20-23)

On the twenty-fourth day of the ninth month, the day on which the previous prophecy was uttered, Haggai speaks in encouraging terms to Zerubbabel. The heathen kingdoms will be overthrown, and Zerubbabel will be the recipient of Yahweh's special favor. He will be Yahweh's servant and his signet ring, the chosen one of the Lord of hosts.

21. **I am about to shake:** The words "the sea and the dry land" should probably be inserted (cf. LXX; 2:6).

22. **The kingdoms of the nations:** Rhythmical considerations suggest that **the kingdoms** should be omitted. **Go down:** To Sheol. For ירד, in the sense of going down to the underworld without the destination being expressed, cf. Ezek. 32:19. **Every one**

---

out fifty vessels out of the press, there were but twenty (2:16). The case may be stated differently; it cannot be stated more vividly.

Once again, the prophet appeals to that resolute mood which in another book the Preacher proposes to us: "He that observeth the wind shall not sow; and he that regardeth the clouds shall not reap. . . . In the morning sow thy seed, and in the evening withhold not thine hand" (Eccl. 11:4, 6). Every genuine act of faith must have precisely this element of adventure and of trust, if not of actual risk. Haggai makes the same demand of his fellow workers on the temple. They were not to delude themselves into thinking that, once begun, the work was as good as ended. They would have

to be content to wait as well as work for its fulfillment. The metaphor of Ecclesiastes is paralleled in Haggai's words: **Is the seed yet in the barn? yea, as yet the vine, and the fig tree, and the pomegranate, and the olive tree, hath not brought forth** (2:19). The builders of the City of God must often be warned against their own holy but hasty impatience. Jesus reiterated this truth in his matchless little parable about the seed growing secretly (Mark 4:26-29).

And finally, the builders of the temple were encouraged to identify their seemingly meager and local labors with the vast plan of God. The heavens and the earth were to be shaken, and Zerubbabel was to be a divinely appointed

23 In that day, saith the Lord of hosts, will I take thee, O Zerubbabel, my servant, the son of Shealtiel, saith the Lord, and will make thee as a signet: for I have chosen thee, saith the Lord of hosts.

fellow. 23 On that day, says the Lord of hosts, I will take you, O Zerub'babel my servant, the son of She-al'ti-el, says the Lord, and make you like a signet ring; for I have chosen you, says the Lord of hosts."

by the sword of his fellow: These words are probably an addition. If they are retained, some verb like "shall fall" needs to be supplied.

23. Many persons are called **my servant** in the O.T., e.g., Abraham (Gen. 26:24), Jacob (Ezek. 28:25), Moses (Num. 12:7), Job (1:8), and David (II Sam. 3:18). The application of the term by Haggai (cf. Zech. 3:8) to **Zerubbabel,** of the house of David, links up with the promises of future kingship made to David by Ezekiel (e.g., 34:23-24; 37:24). The long-expected son of David, who is to be king, has come at last. He is to be Yahweh's **signet ring**—the heir of the honorable position which King Jehoiachin enjoyed and of which he was deprived (Jer. 22:24-30). As Yahweh's vice-regent on earth (cf. Zech. 3:8; 6:12-13) he is to bear the stamp of divine authority (cf. Esth. 3:10; 8:2, 10). It is "as a signet on the right hand" that Zerubbabel is remembered by Ben Sirach (Ecclus. 49:11).

signet (2:23). In Hebrew prophecy the ideas of nationalism and particularism on the one hand, and of universalism on the other, are always found side by side, almost in a state of tension. The paradox is never logically resolved; in the nature of the case it cannot be resolved. For all religion is a matter of living in two worlds at the same time. In days when we feel with fresh force the valid religious claims of both nationalism and internationalism, it is well to try to recover the faith of Haggai, that our local loyalties and our universal loyalties ought not to be incompatible, since they are two faces of the same shield.

The Book of

ZECHARIAH

Chapters 1–8

Introduction and Exegesis by D. WINTON THOMAS
Exposition by THEODORE CUYLER SPEERS

Chapters 9–14

Introduction and Exegesis by ROBERT C. DENTAN
Exposition by JAMES T. CLELAND

ZECHARIAH

INTRODUCTION, CHS. 1-8

According to 1:1 the prophet was the son of Berechiah and the grandson of Iddo. According to Ezra 5:1; 6:14, however, he was the son of Iddo (cf. Neh. 12:16), no mention being made of Berechiah. This discrepancy is best explained on the supposition that the words "the son of Berechiah" did not form part of the original text of 1:1—had they done so, it is very improbable that they would have been omitted in the Ezra passages—but that they are an insertion on the part of someone who identified the prophet Zechariah with Zechariah the son of Jeberechiah, who is mentioned in Isa. 8:2, Berechiah in Zech. 1:1 being a corruption of Jeberechiah. By the removal of the words "the son of Berechiah," Zech. 1:1 is thus brought into harmony with the other Old Testament passages where Zechariah is said to be the son of Iddo.

I. The Prophet's Career

Zechariah's prophetic career began in the eighth month of the second year of Darius I Hystaspis (1:1), that is, in 520 B.C., and ceased in the ninth month of the fourth year of the king's reign, that is, in 518 (7:1). His career therefore was a short one, but considerably longer than that of his contemporary Haggai. He came on the scene a month before Haggai delivered his final utterances (Hag. 2:10-14, 20-23) so, for the most part, his career fell after Haggai's activity as a prophet was over.

Iddo, Zechariah's father, was, according to Neh. 12:4, the head of a priestly family which returned from exile. From this it is commonly inferred that Zechariah was a priest as well as a prophet. This inference may well be a correct one. But his book provides no decisive evidence either in favor of it or against it. On the one hand, he does sometimes appear to evince a special interest in the temple and the priesthood (e.g., 3:7; 6:14). On the other hand, he

seems sometimes to speak of the priesthood in a way which suggests that he thought of it as something quite apart from himself (e.g., 7:5). His book does not mention animal sacrifice; and in place of fasting he lays emphasis on the need of right living (7:5-6, 9-10; 8:19).

II. The Book

It is generally agreed that of the fourteen chapters of the book of Zechariah, only chs. 1-8 are to be attributed to the son of Iddo. That they are the genuine work of the prophet is indisputable. But as in the case of Haggai's prophecies, those of Zechariah have been edited. Thus Zechariah, like Haggai, is referred to in the third person (1:1, 7; 7:1, 8); and in 1:1, 7, he is, again like Haggai, given the title "the prophet," which it is unlikely he would have applied to himself. Although the book, like the book of Haggai, is in the nature of a report on the prophet's utterances, it is less markedly so than Haggai. For while in the latter the prophet never speaks of himself in the first person, Zechariah does so speak of himself (1:8; 4:6; 6:9; etc.), a personal note being thereby introduced which is absent in Haggai. The editor who put the book of Zechariah into substantially its present form probably did so shortly after Zechariah had ceased to be active as a prophet in 518.

Chs. 1-8 fall into three main sections.

First section: 1:1-6, dated in the eighth month of the year 520; the day of the month is not given. This part is of an introductory character, being a call to the people to repent and to return to Yahweh.

Second section: 1:7-6:15, dated the twenty-fourth day of the eleventh month, 520. The passage 1:7-6:8 consists in the main of a series of eight visions, together with their interpretations: (a) 1:7-17, the four horsemen; (b) 1:18-21 (Hebrew 2:1-4), the four horns and the four smiths; (c) 2:1-5 (Hebrew 2:5-9), the angel with the measuring line; 2:6-13 (Hebrew 2:10-17), a call to the exiles in Babylon to return home, intervenes between the third and fourth visions; (d) 3:1-10, the accusation laid against Joshua, the high priest, and his acquittal; (e) 4:1-6a, 10b-14, the seven-branched lampstand and the two olive trees; 4:6b-10a, which probably belongs after this vision, reflects current doubts as to the successful completion of the rebuilding of the temple by Zerubbabel; (f) 5:1-4, the flying scroll; (g) 5:5-11, the woman in the ephah measure; (h) 6:1-8, the four chariots; 6:9-15 is a historical appendix whose theme is the symbolic crowning of Zerubbabel as king-messiah.

Third section: 7:1–8:28, dated the fourth day of the ninth month of 518. In ch. 7 the prophet, in response to an inquiry put to him by a deputation from Bethel concerning the keeping of the fast of the fifth month, replies that their fasting has little spiritual value, and that they must learn to practice the moral virtues. In 8:1-17, which is the second part of Zechariah's reply to his questioners, he declares that when the messianic age dawns Zion and Judah will be greatly blessed. In 8:18-23, the third part of his reply, he proclaims that Judah will in the future celebrate the fast days as joyful seasons, and that the heathen peoples will join the Jews in seeking Yahweh, and so obtain a share in the blessings that are to come.

The Hebrew text of Zechariah, like that of Haggai, has not been preserved intact. Corruptions in the text are numerous (e.g., in 1:6; 2:3 [Hebrew 2:7]; 2:6 [Hebrew 2:10]; 3:4-5; 5:6; 6:13; 7:2). In all these cases, and in others, the Septuagint affords great help in arriving at the true text. Glosses too are frequent (e.g., in 1:7, 11, 19 [Hebrew 2:2]; 6:3; 7:1, 8; 8:13). Two very noteworthy features of the text are (a) the displacement of 4:6b-10a from its original position after 4:1-6a, 10b-14 to its present position; and (b) the deliberate alteration of the name Zerubbabel, which stood originally in 6:11, to Joshua.

III. Historical Background

Since Zechariah was a contemporary of Haggai, the historical background of his book is for the most part the same as that of the book of Haggai. The rebuilding of the temple is with him, as with Haggai, a main theme. That it was not yet completed is shown by 4:9; 6:13. The hard conditions of life to which Haggai testifies are met with again in Zech. 8:10. The peace and quiet which settled on the Persian Empire after Darius had successfully quelled the revolts which accompanied his accession to the throne (cf. Hag. 2:6-9, 20-23) are reflected in Zech. 1:11. The high hopes which Haggai had reposed in Zerubbabel as the long-awaited king-messiah find expression again in Zechariah. Indeed, it emerges more clearly in this book (3:8; 4:14; 6:12) than in Haggai that Zerubbabel was the "branch of David" promised in earlier prophecy (e.g., Isa. 11:1; Jer. 23:5). Zechariah, moreover, provides some further information concerning him which is not to be found in the book of Haggai, for example, his attempt to rebuild the walls of Jerusalem (2:1-5 [Hebrew 2:5-9]). Whatever may have been the motive behind this attempt (see Exeg., ad loc.), Zechariah discouraged it. Not only Zerubbabel but Joshua, the high priest, the religious head of the community, is more prominent in Zechariah than in Haggai (cf. Zech. 3:1-10; 4:14; 6:13). A hint that the relationship between Haggai and Zerubbabel had not been altogether happy may perhaps be seen in 6:13. Zechariah here appears as a conciliator. Each of the two leaders has a necessary function to perform in the new community. Between the two anointed of Yahweh (cf. 4:14), harmony, not rivalry, should obtain.

IV. Zechariah's Place in Old Testament Religion

A. Zechariah as a Founder of Judaism.— Haggai was one of the chief founders of Judaism. So too was Zechariah. Like Haggai, he played a significant part in the rebuilding of the temple; again like Haggai, he was no friend of the Samaritans. The first impulse to rebuild the temple had been provided by Haggai, who saw in the revolts that shook the Persian Empire when Darius came to the throne the prelude to the advent of the messianic age. Yahweh's house must be prepared for him. And so he urged upon his fellow countrymen the necessity for the rebuilding of the temple, and work was started upon it. But soon the revolts were put down, and Darius was firmly established on his throne. It is not surprising that the enthusiasm which the revolts had kindled among the Jews began to wane. The news from the east was disappointing. It looked as if there was to be no messianic crisis after all (1:11). Zechariah, however, believed as firmly as did Haggai in the near advent of the messianic age. Yahweh was already on the move (1:13-17), and Zerubbabel and Joshua, his instruments for the bringing in of the messianic kingdom, were in Jerusalem (3:7-8; 4:14; 6:13). Zechariah, therefore, with energy hardly less than that displayed by Haggai, continued to urge the people to proceed with the rebuilding. In his message of encouragement to the people he was at one with Haggai. And when the postexilic Jew worshiped at the restored temple, it was to Zechariah, as well as to Haggai, that he with good reason looked back with gratitude. As for Zechariah's hostility to the Samaritans, more than once does he imply that the blessings of the messianic age are to be enjoyed by Judah only, not by the people of the north (8:13, where "house of Israel" is probably a gloss, 15, 19; cf. 7:1-14). He should therefore be regarded as sharing with Haggai the responsibility for taking a decisive step in the direction of that narrow exclusiveness which was typical of postexilic Judaism.

B. Divine Revelation.—Certain passages in Zechariah (e.g., 4:8; 7:4; 8:18) indicate that the prophet could still feel, as did the preexilic prophets, that Yahweh revealed himself directly to him. At the same time he appears to be conscious that he is not quite of their company, and that their authority derives more directly from Yahweh than does his own (1:4; 7:7, 12). Yahweh is indeed thought of as far off from man, and revelation of himself is conceived of as less direct than it was. Revelation has now to be mediated (contrast Isa. 6). Prophets before Zechariah had experienced visions, but only comparatively rarely. In the case of Zechariah the vision has become the normal vehicle of revelation. The direct revelation which the older prophets enjoyed has now given place to this indirect method of revelation. Moreover, the visions which the older prophets saw were interpreted for them by Yahweh himself, again speaking directly to them (cf., e.g., Amos 7:8; Jer. 1:13-14). Zechariah's visions, however, have to be interpreted for him by a mediating angel (1:9; *et al.*; cf. Ezek. 40:3-4). Visions and a mediating angel who acts as interpreter—so great is the distance that now separates Yahweh from man, and so indistinct has the divine voice become. Yahweh has been enthroned high beyond the reach of man. He sits above the heavens, remotely transcendent. Not even prophets now have direct access to him.

C. Angelology.—The emphasis upon the transcendental character of Yahweh is accompanied in the book of Zechariah by a prominence accorded to angelic figures which is quite remarkable: "Not even in the book of Daniel are these celestial beings so constantly in evidence." [1] Reference has already been made to the angel who interprets Zechariah's visions to him. In 1:11; 3:1; *et al.,* "the angel of the LORD" appears. Opinions differ as to his identity, but most probably he and the interpreting angel are one and the same person. Other

angelic beings meet us in 1:11, where they appear as horsemen; in 2:1 (Hebrew 2:5), where an angel sets out to measure Jerusalem; in 2:3 (Hebrew 2:7), where "another angel" goes forth to meet the interpreting angel; and in 3:4, where angels who attend upon "the angel of the LORD" carry out his behest. Of special interest and importance is the fact that in the book of Zechariah (3:1-2) there occurs for the first time in the Old Testament a reference to "The Satan," the superhuman adversary (cf. ERV mg.). His function here is to accuse Joshua, the high priest. "The Satan" is next mentioned in the book of Job, where his function is twofold. First, as in the book of Zechariah, he accuses a man—Job—before Yahweh (Job 1:6-11); and second, he tests the strength and genuineness of Job's faith in Yahweh (Job 1:12; 2:6). The latest mention in the Old Testament of Satan, now no longer, as in the books of Zechariah and Job, a title, but a proper name—the definite article of the earlier passages has been dropped—is to be found in I Chr. 21:1, where later religious scruples have attributed to him the responsibility for provoking David to sin, which in the earlier literature (II Sam. 24:1) was attributed to Yahweh. The book of Zechariah is thus of very special importance for the study of Old Testament angelology in general, and of the Satan idea in particular.

D. The Messianic Age.—In Zechariah some features of the messianic age which, it is expected, is soon to arrive, appear with greater clarity than in Haggai. The greater prominence which Zechariah gives to Zerubbabel and Joshua has already been mentioned. Joshua is, like Zerubbabel, anointed of Yahweh (4:14). In the new age that is to be born he, as the religious head of the community, is to stand in the place of honor at the right hand of the throne which Zerubbabel, as king-messiah, is to occupy; and priest and king are to work in close and friendly association for the well-being of the community, of which they are the divinely appointed leaders (6:13). Zechariah too has more to say than Haggai concerning the participation by the heathen in the blessings of the messianic age (cf. Hag. 2:7 with Zech. 8:20-23). In this last passage is clearly seen the universalistic outlook which Zechariah inherited from Second Isaiah (cf., e.g., Isa. 42:1-7; 49:6), though he could also believe that Judah was destined to hold a privileged position to which the people of the north could not attain (see paragraph A, above; Exeg. on 1:12). Again, Haggai had seen that no uncleanness should be allowed to taint the Jewish community on the eve of the messianic age. This theme is carried further by Zechariah, two of

[1] H. G. Mitchell, J. M. P. Smith, and Julius A. Bewer, *A Critical and Exegetical Commentary on Haggai, Zechariah, Malachi, and Jonah* (New York: Charles Scribner's Sons, 1912; "International Critical Commentary"), p. 103.

his visions (5:1-4, 5-11; cf. 3:9) being concerned with the removal of all sin from Judah. A new feature in Zechariah's conception of the messianic age, not found in the book of Haggai, is the demand that in the new world the claims of morality shall not be forgotten (7:5-10; 8:19).

V. Interpretation of the Visions

It may be supposed that the interpretation of Zechariah's visions presented little difficulty to his contemporaries, who would have interpreted them against the background of current events and expectations of the time with which they had a close familiarity. We today who would attempt to interpret them must inevitably find the details of contemporary life and thought obscured by the distance in time which separates us from the prophet's own time. The most that we can expect to achieve in the matter of interpretation is therefore a fairly clear idea of their general import. And this it is possible to achieve. The visions have received a great deal of attention from scholars, and widely differing interpretations have been advanced. The Exegesis presents the interpretation which appears to be the most probable.

VI. Outline of Contents

VII. Selected Bibliography

BARNES, W. E. Haggai and Zechariah ("Cambridge Bible"). Cambridge: Cambridge University Press, 1917.

BROWNE, LAURENCE E. Early Judaism. Cambridge: Cambridge University Press, 1920.

DRIVER, S. R., ed. The Minor Prophets ("New Century Bible"). New York: Oxford University Press, 1906. Vol. II.

HORST, FRIEDRICH. Die zwölf kleinen Propheten Nahum bis Maleachi ("Handbuch zum Alten Testament"). Tübingen: J. C. B. Mohr, 1954.

MITCHELL, H. G., SMITH, J. M. P., and BEWER, JULIUS A. A Critical and Exegetical Commentary on Haggai, Zechariah, Malachi, and Jonah ("International Critical Commentary"). New York: Charles Scribner's Sons, 1912.

SELLIN, ERNST. Das Zwölfprophetenbuch ("Kommentar zum Alten Testament"). 2nd and 3rd ed. Leipzig: A. Deichert, 1929-30.

ZECHARIAH

TEXT, EXEGESIS, AND EXPOSITION, CHS. 1-8

The Prophet of Unrealized Hopes.—Zechariah was a prophet called to give his message to a people whose hearts and minds were heavy and sluggish with discouragement. These he must move and incite to action. The Exile had lasted about seventy years. Cyrus king of Persia had conquered Babylon in 539 B.C. and shortly set into operation a policy of permitting displaced persons to return to their homelands. Zechariah, born into a priestly family, had been taken from Babylon to Jerusalem as a child, in

Pp. 1056-57 include the expositor's introduction. Text and Exegesis begin on p. 1058. Editors.

one of the first groups to return to the beloved city in 537 B.C. Seventeen years later, in 520, he began to prophesy. He was summoned to this task because the burning hopes which had been set on fire by the ascendancy of Darius, successor to Cyrus, had not materialized. The community at Jerusalem was still small and weak, consisting mainly of a few young men and a few men in middle life who had seized the opportunity to return from the captivity. They were finding it no easy task to live happily and to carry on the work of reconstruction with the lineal descendants of those who had been left behind as not worth deportation at the time of the Exile. The work of rebuilding the city and reconstructing the ruined temple seemed slow and inconsequential, despite the able leadership of Zerubbabel the king, and Joshua the high priest, both repatriates from Babylon. Multitudes of Jews still remained in Babylon, and gave no evidence of interest and enthusiasm for the return to Jerusalem. The first-century historian Josephus wrote of this period: "Many abode in Babylon because they did not wish to leave their possessions." [1]

Disillusionment had gripped the little company in Jerusalem. In the face of this mood, George Adam Smith says, "The prophet's duty is to quiet the people's apprehensions about the state of the world, to provoke their zeal, give them confidence in their great men, and, above all, assure them that God is returned to them and their sin pardoned." [2]

A graph of world history shows humanity rising to heights of enthusiasm and confidence, then dipping to depths of fear, discouragement, and despair. Since the sickening discovery spread over the world, at the conclusion of World War I, that the hopes poured into that conflict for the achievement of peace and justice were not to be realized, the mood of the world has been one of discouragement and near-despair. The kingdom of peace, justice, and freedom seems far beyond our reach despite the enormous sacrifices of recent years. In fact, many people have adopted the hopeless conclusion that it is never destined to be established in this world. Side by side with these unrealized hopes we all have to wrestle with a vast host of expectations and desires concerning the church, the nation, and our own lives, which at any given moment seem far beyond realization.

There are only two possible reactions to hopes delayed in fulfillment. The easy and popular one is to surrender to cynicism and despair, to believe that we have been led into chasing will-o'-the-wisps which have no counterpart in reality. Many times the truth of the old biblical proverb has been burned into our minds by the white heat of experience: "Hope deferred maketh the heart sick" (Prov. 13:12). The more difficult reaction, and few there are who find it, is to cling to what we believe until the power of unrealized hopes is discovered. The unknown author of the Epistle to the Hebrews, in kinship of spirit with Zechariah, wrote to encourage the early church at a time when courage and hope were at a new low, to remind the church of the gallant spirit of its forebears: "These all died in faith, not having received the promises, but having seen them afar off, and were persuaded of them, and embraced them, and confessed that they were strangers and pilgrims on the earth" (Heb. 11:13). The power of unrealized hopes is revealed to those who believe that their hopes are somehow linked to the ultimates of life, to the unchanging, unchangeable certainties of human experience. These hopes serve as stars to steer by when the night is dark and we are far from home.

It is one of the grave problems of our times that so many are so uncertain of the ultimates. Sir Richard W. Livingstone, president of Corpus Christi College, Oxford, thus diagnoses the dilemma of modern man:

He has no ruling principle, no clear end, no standard by which he approves or rejects except the impulse of the moment; and his disease is that he does not know what goodness is, has no real hold on it and so drifts to and fro. . . . If you want a description of our age, here is one. The civilisation of means without ends; rich in means beyond any other epoch, and almost beyond human needs; squandering and misusing them, because it has no overruling ideal; an ample body with a meager soul. [3]

In the same vein, probing for the cause of the peculiar lethargy of our times, C. E. M. Joad has written a book [4] describing our decadence as "the dropping of the object," by which he means that we are busy, fruitlessly busy, about many things, because we have lost the supreme end in every field of endeavor.

The rediscovery of creative power lies in the rediscovery of supreme ends and those subsidiary ends which lead directly to the ultimate goal. Zechariah achieved the power of unrealized hopes by his profound belief that the reconstruction of Jerusalem and the rebuilding of the temple would usher in the messianic age, the ultimate goal of all hopes. Even his name, which means "God remembers," was a symbol of his undaunted faith. His contemporaries at Jerusalem had sunk under the weight of difficulty and discouragement to the belief that they were the "forgotten people." It was Zechariah's task to rekindle the flame on the cold altars of their hearts with his burning conviction that they were God's "chosen people." He would have appreciated the old Buddhist scripture which reads: "Struggle on, always remembering God is not dead."

[1] *Antiquities* XI. 1. 3.
[2] George Adam Smith, *The Book of the Twelve Prophets* (rev. ed.; New York: Harper & Bros., 1928), II, 258.
[3] *On Education* (New York: The Macmillan Co., 1944), pp. 111, 118.
[4] *Decadence* (New York: Philosophical Library, 1949), pp. 108-27.

1 In the eighth month, in the second year of Darius, came the word of the LORD unto Zechariah, the son of Berechiah, the son of Iddo the prophet, saying,

2 The LORD hath been sore displeased with your fathers.

3 Therefore say thou unto them, Thus

1 In the eighth month, in the second **year** of Darius, the word of the LORD came to Zechari'ah the son of Berechi'ah, son of Iddo, the prophet, saying, 2 "The LORD was very angry with your fathers. 3 There-

---

I. A CALL TO THE PEOPLE TO REPENT (1:1-6)

In the eighth month of the year 520 B.C. Yahweh bids the prophet to call upon the people to return to him, and to assure them that if they will do so, he will return to them. Their ancestors had neglected the warnings of the pre-exilic prophets who had called upon them to repent, with dire consequences to themselves. Their ancestors and the prophets are no more. But the effective power of Yahweh's words remains, as the people whom the prophet is addressing have good reason to know, for it has overtaken them.

This introductory section falls between the dates given in Hag. 2:1-9 (the seventh month) and Hag. 2:10 (the ninth month).

1. The old Hebrew name of the **eighth month** was Bul, which corresponded to our October-November (cf. I Kings 6:38; see Exeg. on Hag. 1:1). In contrast to 1:7; 7:1, and to the general practice in the book of Haggai, the day of the month is not given here. Very probably a day originally appeared in the text but fell out in the course of transmission. The Syriac has "the first day." **Second year of Darius:** Cf. Hag. 1:1. In Hag. 1:1, 15; Zech. 7:1, Darius is called "the king." The title is lacking here, as in Hag. 2:10. **Zechariah the son of Berechiah, son of Iddo:** See Intro., p. 1053.

3. Return to me: Already at the beginning of his prophecies Zechariah's demand for the exercise of the moral virtues is evident. More than the rebuilding of the temple

---

1:1. The Priest and the Prophet.—Zechariah combined the priestly and prophetic functions. By family background and tradition he was a priest. His father and grandfather before him had served as priests to the exiled Jews in Babylon. By conviction arising from the conditions at hand in Jerusalem he became a prophet. Perhaps it would have been easier for him if he could have performed a single function, either as a priest or as a prophet. One of his difficulties, and yet one which makes him particularly appealing to us, lay in the fact that he felt impelled to fulfill both functions.

While there are men and women who are definitely cut out to fulfill one function or the other, most of us, like Zechariah, feel impelled to do both. Much of the time, week by week, year in and year out, those of us who are engaged in religious work are endeavoring to meet the current personal needs of individuals who are thwarted, puzzled, broken, and confused by the experiences of life. Like the Red Cross, it is one of our essential tasks to follow in the wake of the conflict of life and minister to the wounded, restore the broken, and succor the needy.

But there are times when we must lift up our eyes from the immediate and see the direction in which we are being carried by the currents

of life. Our business is to discern whether or not those currents are carrying us toward or away from the ultimate goals which constitute the supreme meaning and purpose of life. It is our privilege and responsibility to be interpreters of the meaning of the suffering, the tragedy, the disillusionment that afflict us. Like the mariner of a ship far out on the trackless wastes of the ocean, we are to study our position by the unchanging, unchangeable lights of heaven; so that we may know and declare how far we are on or off the course that leads to "the haven of our [and God's] desires." The exact length of Zechariah's ministry at Jerusalem we do not know. We do know that his recorded prophecies were made within the compass of only two years. Our prophetic function may be small compared with our priestly function, but we prove false to God's faith in us and his summons to us if we do not strive to fulfill it. Let it be said of us as George Adam Smith wrote of Zechariah, that there was in him "the absence of all ambition to be original or anything but the clear voice of the lessons of the past and of the conscience of to-day." [5]

3. A Constructive Historic Sense.—The real foundation for the work of reconstruction that

[5] *Op. cit.*, II, 267.

saith the LORD of hosts; Turn ye unto me, saith the LORD of hosts, and I will turn unto you, saith the LORD of hosts.

4 Be ye not as your fathers, unto whom the former prophets have cried, saying, Thus saith the LORD of hosts; Turn ye now from your evil ways, and *from* your evildoings: but they did not hear, nor hearken unto me, saith the LORD.

5 Your fathers, where *are* they? and the prophets, do they live for ever?

6 But my words and my statutes, which I commanded my servants the prophets, did they not take hold of your fathers? and they returned and said, Like as the LORD of hosts thought to do unto us, according to our

fore say to them, Thus says the LORD of hosts: Return to me, says the LORD of hosts, and I will return to you, says the LORD of hosts. 4 Be not like your fathers, to whom the former prophets cried out, 'Thus says the LORD of hosts, Return from your evil ways and from your evil deeds.' But they did not hear or heed me, says the LORD. 5 Your fathers, where are they? And the prophets, do they live for ever? 6 But my words and my statutes, which I commanded my servants the prophets, did they not overtake your fathers? So they repented and said, As the LORD of hosts purposed to deal

---

is required. Society itself needs to be built on firm moral foundations (cf. vss. 4; 7:8-10; 8:16-17, 19).

4. The former prophets are those of the pre-exilic period. Zechariah's appeal to these earlier prophets (cf. 7:7, 12) reveals his consciousness of the significance of the Exile, which, like a great gulf, separated him from them (see Intro., p. 1055).

5-6. Your ancestors and the earlier prophets, says Zechariah, are of the past, but Yahweh's words, which have been revealed through the mouth of these prophets, and whose effect has been clearly seen in your past history, have still an effective power which reaches right up to the present time, for they have overtaken you. This interpretation of these two difficult verses requires the reading in vs. 6 אתכם, "you," for אבתיכם, **your fathers.** The M.T. reading could easily have come in through a copyist's error

---

was to be done at Jerusalem in Zechariah's time was not that of brick, mortar, and stone, but that of the moral obedience of the heart to the commandments of God: **Return to me, says the LORD of hosts.** In this Zechariah was what Paul would have called "a wise master builder." Paul was saying as much for his day when he declared: "For no other foundation can any one lay than that which is laid, which is Jesus Christ" (I Cor. 3:11). Both men turned to the past, not in the spirit of rigid and sterile devotion to the forms and ceremonies of an earlier day, but to profit by the experience of the past, the wisdom, dearly bought through suffering, failure, chastisement, and insight.

Tennyson wrote:

> I held it truth, with him who sings
> To one clear harp in divers tones,
> That men may rise on stepping-stones
> Of their dead selves to higher things.[6]

Both Zechariah and Paul looked to the past as to an incentive for higher achievement. All history so conceived is not "bunk" but consists of enormously helpful steppingstones on which men may rise to higher things.

[6] *In Memoriam,* Part I, st. i.

4. *Outreaching the Past.*—Sometimes the present is inclined to look upon the past with too much deference. Sometimes we see the people of an earlier generation through rose-colored glasses. Perspective is needed for judgment; as we look back we are inclined to discard or discount the errors and weaknesses of an earlier generation, and join harmoniously in the anthem "Let Us Now Praise Famous Men." There is often justification for this attitude, but many times it is a substitute for the high expectations which we ought to be focusing upon ourselves. Elijah, overwhelmed by what he mistakenly thought to be his failure, prayed: "O LORD, take away my life; for I am not better than my fathers" (I Kings 19:4). On every count we ought to be better than our fathers, not because we are better people, but because their wisdom, accumulated both from success and failure, has been made available to us. In fact, we might say that if we are not better than they, we fall far short of their achievements.

5-6. *Truth and Consequences.*—Everything on earth is transient and perishable save the vitality of the will and purpose of God. Writes Raymond Calkins: "God's Word and Will are not dead but live right on. The bodies of the

ways, and according to our doings, so hath he dealt with us.

7 ¶ Upon the four and twentieth day of the eleventh month, which is the month Sebat, in the second year of Darius, came the word of the LORD unto Zechariah, the son of Berechiah, the son of Iddo the prophet, saying,

8 I saw by night, and behold a man riding upon a red horse, and he stood among the myrtle trees that were in the bottom;

with us for our ways and deeds, so has he dealt with us."

7 On the twenty-fourth day of the eleventh month which is the month of Shebat, in the second year of Darius, the word of the LORD came to Zechari'ah the son of Berechi'ah, son of Iddo, the prophet; and Zechari'ah said, 8 "I saw in the night, and behold, a man riding upon a red horse!

---

from vs. 5. The second half of vs. 6, which refers to the people's ancestors, thus becomes meaningless. Note that it contradicts what is said at the end of vs. 4. It is probably a later editorial interpolation. For the idea of the effective power of Yahweh's words cf. Isa. 40:8; 55:11.

II. THE VISIONS OF ZECHARIAH (1:7–6:8)

7. This verse is an editorial introduction to the whole series of visions. The date, **the twenty-fourth day of the eleventh month,** is to be understood as that on which Zechariah saw all his visions. It is three months later than the date given in 1:1, and two months after the final utterances of Haggai were delivered (Hag. 2:10, 20). **Which is the month of Shebat** is probably a gloss (see Exeg. on Hag. 1:1).

A. THE FOUR HORSEMEN (1:8-17)

The four horsemen whom Yahweh has sent to patrol the earth and to obtain information about world events report that all is quiet on earth. The break-up of the world, which was to herald the coming of the messianic age, is not yet. Yahweh's indignation, which has burned against Jerusalem for the last seventy years, burns still, and release from it is still delayed. But it will not be delayed indefinitely. Yahweh has a message of comfort for his people. The heathen powers will not forever escape his anger, and with the rebuilding of the temple, a prosperous new era will dawn for Judah. With this first vision the last (6:1-8) should be compared.

8. The **man** is sometimes thought to be identical with Yahweh. More probably, however, he is an angelic figure, like "the man" in 2:1, and is to be identified with the

---

fathers may lie moldering in the grave but God's truth has gone marching on. All through the life and death of men, running like a golden thread through the ebb and flow of human effort and failure, there is the Will of God." [7] "The grass withereth, the flower fadeth: but the word of our God shall stand for ever" (Isa. 40:8). Man's one chance to secure continuing vitality for those things which mean most to him on earth lies in being linked with the will and purpose of God. The tomb of Lenin in Moscow is symbolic of the fruitless effort of our age to preserve what is obviously dead. Ideas and ideals alone may live, and then only if they can meet the searching test of "the refiner's fire."

The moral order of the universe is no less indestructible than the physical order. One is

as binding as the other. Soon or late God's will and purpose overtake us, to confound or confirm what we have done. "God," Mohammed once said, "is good at accounts." William Temple rightly interpreted the Hound of Heaven in these forthright words: "While we deliberate, He reigns; when we decide wisely, He reigns; when we decide foolishly, He reigns; when we serve Him in humble loyalty, He reigns; when we serve Him self-assertively, He reigns; when we rebel and seek to withhold our service, He reigns—the Alpha and Omega, which is and which was and which is to come, the Almighty." [8]

8. *The Religion for Midnight.*—When the world is floundering in the darkness, it is the unerring mark of a prophet that he is able to see by night. Again and again the world has

---

[7] *The Modern Message of the Minor Prophets* (New York: Harper & Bros., 1947), p. 117.

[8] Quoted in H. R. L. Sheppard, *Some of My Religion* (New York: Harper & Bros., 1936), p. 64.

and behind him *were there* red horses, speckled, and white.

9 Then said I, O my lord, what *are* these? And the angel that talked with me said unto me, I will show thee what these *be*.

10 And the man that stood among the myrtle trees answered and said, These *are they* whom the LORD hath sent to walk to and fro through the earth.

11 And they answered the angel of the LORD that stood among the myrtle trees, and said, We have walked to and fro through the earth, and, behold, all the earth sitteth still, and is at rest.

He was standing among the myrtle trees in the glen; and behind him were red, sorrel, and white horses. 9 Then I said, 'What are these, my lord?' The angel who talked with me said to me, 'I will show you what they are.' 10 So the man who was standing among the myrtle trees answered, 'These are they whom the LORD has sent to patrol the earth.' 11 And they answered the angel of the LORD who was standing among the myrtle trees, 'We have patrolled the earth, and behold, all the earth remains at rest.'

---

interpreting angel (1:9; *et al.*), and with "the angel of the LORD" (3:1; *et al.*). Instead of **myrtle trees,** the LXX here and in vs. 10, has, perhaps correctly, "mountains" (ὀρέων, i.e., הרים for M.T. הדסים). **Glen:** The Hebrew word *meçulāh* is of uncertain meaning. If it means "basin," "hollow," it might refer to some locality in the neighborhood of Jerusalem. The LXX has κατασκίων, "shady," an epithet of the "mountains," which may point to a reading *meçillāh,* "shade," "shadow" (cf. ERV mg.). **Red:** If the colors of the **horses** have any symbolic significance, the clue to it eludes us.

9. **My lord:** The person addressed is the interpreting angel.

11. The subject of **they answered** is the horsemen. **The angel of the LORD who was standing among the myrtle trees** is a gloss. Someone rightly identified "the man" of vss. 8, 10 with "the angel of the LORD." **At rest:** The hopes for the messianic age which the Jews saw in the revolts against Persia were disappointed (see Intro. to Haggai, p. 1039).

---

been saved from self-destruction by the God-given capacity of those whose eyes are not blinded by the density of the moral night. "Human progress," writes Sir Richard Livingstone, "depends chiefly on what men see in life and how they interpret it; and the ages in which the world has moved forward are those rare ages when men of religious or poetic or intellectual genius have caught sight of levels higher than those in which the world is moving." [9]

On the darkest nights there is always light for those who have the capacity to see. The author of the Fourth Gospel reports the advent of Christ as the shining of a great light in the darkness, which the darkness was not able to overwhelm. A small company of far-seeing men and women did discern his light in the darkness, and the whole direction of our civilization was turned as a result of their discernment. Raymond Calkins graphically describes Christianity as

the religion for midnight. It was then that it was born, and in the darkness before dawn in Joseph's tomb it won its final victory. If in the darkness of our night we can see what Zechariah saw, then, though terror succeed terror, and woe follow woe, the conviction that God is, that God reigns, and that events are not left to work them-

selves out as chance or accident or lawless force may decree, will bring the assurance of an eternal Hope into every human heart.[1]

Christendom's increasing capacity to lift up its eyes in the darkness and discern the Light that was in him is attested in one of our best-loved hymns:

Thee would I sing: Thy truth is still the light
Which guides the nations groping on their way,
Stumbling and falling in disastrous night,
Yet hoping ever for the perfect day.[2]

11. *God Moves in a Mysterious Way.*—Some months previously Haggai, Zechariah's contemporary, had prophesied that with the advent of Darius in succession to Cyrus there would be uprisings and rebellions throughout the world, which would usher in the fulfillment of the messianic hope for Zion. Like so many others, this prophecy had failed of fulfillment; and the flame of expectation which Haggai's prophecy had kindled had dwindled to a mere spark. In the first of his eight visions Zechariah envisages the heavenly horsemen searching the earth and returning to report, **We have patrolled the earth, and behold, all the earth remains at rest.**

[9] *On Education,* p. 84.

[1] *Op. cit.,* p. 124.
[2] Theodore Parker, "O thou great Friend to all the sons of men."

12 ¶ Then the angel of the Lord answered and said, O Lord of hosts, how long wilt thou not have mercy on Jerusalem and on the cities of Judah, against which thou hast had indignation these threescore and ten years?

13 And the Lord answered the angel that talked with me *with* good words *and* comfortable words.

14 So the angel that communed with me said unto me, Cry thou, saying, Thus saith the Lord of hosts; I am jealous for Jerusalem and for Zion with a great jealousy.

15 And I am very sore displeased with the heathen *that are* at ease: for I was but a little displeased, and they helped forward the affliction.

16 Therefore thus saith the Lord; I am returned to Jerusalem with mercies: my house shall be built in it, saith the Lord of hosts, and a line shall be stretched upon Jerusalem.

17 Cry yet, saying, Thus saith the Lord of hosts; My cities through prosperity shall yet be spread abroad; and the Lord shall yet comfort Zion, and shall yet choose Jerusalem.

12 Then the angel of the Lord said, 'O Lord of hosts, how long wilt thou have no mercy on Jerusalem and the cities of Judah, against which thou hast had indignation these seventy years?' 13 And the Lord answered gracious and comforting words to the angel who talked with me. 14 So the angel who talked with me said to me, 'Cry out, Thus says the Lord of hosts: I am exceedingly jealous for Jerusalem and for Zion. 15 And I am very angry with the nations that are at ease; for while I was angry but a little they furthered the disaster. 16 Therefore, thus says the Lord, I have returned to Jerusalem with compassion; my house shall be built in it, says the Lord of hosts, and the measuring line shall be stretched out over Jerusalem. 17 Cry again, Thus says the Lord of hosts: My cities shall again overflow with prosperity, and the Lord will again comfort Zion and again choose Jerusalem.' "

---

12. Instead of **the angel of the Lord** should probably be read "the angel who talked with me" (cf. vs. 13) . **Jerusalem and the cities of Judah:** Zechariah exhibits throughout a special concern for the pre-eminence and welfare of the south (cf. vss. 17, 19, 21; 2:12; 8:3, 15, 19, 23) . **These seventy years:** The years 586-520—not quite seventy years. This phrase reveals the hopes that rested on the words of Jeremiah (25:12; cf. Hag. 1:2) .

15. The expression **at ease** embraces the ideas of carelessness and arrogance (cf. Amos 6:1; Isa. 32:9, 11) . **They furthered the disaster:** This is the probable meaning of a difficult Hebrew phrase. Though the nations were destined to oppress Judah by way of chastisement, they have gone beyond the limits of their divinely appointed task, and so have increased Judah's misfortunes (cf. Isa. 10:5-7; Mic. 7:8; Obad. 12) .

16. Measuring line: From Hag. 1:4, 9 it is clear that Jerusalem was partly settled, but for the most part it was still in ruins.

17. Cities: I.e., of Judah (cf. vs. 12) .

Zechariah was disturbed but not defeated by the report of the angelic hosts that there were no signs of the anticipated tumult in the earth. What man in his insensitive inaction could not or would not do, God would bring to pass in his own way and time. The frustrations of human endeavor which were visited upon the Jews in exile brought into being a new vision of God, not as the companion of man but as a transcendent Being who rules the universe. The prophets then became the mouthpiece of a new revelation of a God not to be frustrated in his purposes by the failure of man to perform his

will. Such was Second Isaiah, who wrote: "For my thoughts are not your thoughts, neither are your ways my ways, saith the Lord. For as the heavens are higher than the earth, so are my ways higher than your ways, and my thoughts than your thoughts" (Isa. 55:8-9) . It was this character of vision which accounted for the apocalyptic strain in Ezekiel and his young admirer, Zechariah. They stoutly contended that man's failure was God's opportunity.

These writings hold encouragement for us who live in a time when the forces of materialism and tyranny seem to have taken much of

18 ¶ Then lifted I up mine eyes, and saw, and behold four horns.

19 And I said unto the angel that talked with me, What *be* these? And he answered me, Thesc *are* the horns which have scattered Judah, Israel, and Jerusalem.

20 And the LORD showed me four carpenters.

18*a* And I lifted my eyes and saw, and behold, four horns! 19 And I said to the angel who talked with me, "What are these?" And he answered me, "These are the horns which have scattered Judah, Israel, and Jerusalem." 20 Then the LORD

a Heb Ch 2. 1

B. THE FOUR HORNS AND THE FOUR SMITHS (1:18-21 = Hebrew 2:1-4)

The four horns represent the powerful nations hostile to Judah, while the four smiths represent the divine punishment which will fall upon these nations. Their task is to destroy the horns—the destruction of the hostile nations is the prelude to the coming of the messianic age.

18. **Horns** are frequently used figuratively of strength in the O.T. (e.g., Amos 6:13; Jer. 48:25). The number **four** probably corresponds to the four points of the compass; cf. the four horsemen in the first vision (1:7-17), and the four chariots in the last (6:1-8). Zechariah is thinking here of the whole heathen world (cf. 2:6).

19. In vs. 21 **Israel** is not mentioned, only Judah. In this verse it is probably a gloss, as it is also in 8:13 (cf. 1:12).

20. For **smiths** as agents of divine destruction cf. Ezek. 21:31, where "skilful to destroy" means, lit., "smiths of destruction." The word used for **smiths** here and in Ezekiel is the same—חרשׁ.

---

the best of man's achievements into exile. Many hopes and dreams of a better world are fenced in with frustration and despair. In such a time we do well to grasp a fuller vision of the divine nature, the God who gives significance to the moral struggles of the earth with his ways and means which are often above and beyond our human grasp and understanding.

18. *God Giveth the Victory.*—A prophet is one who does not fail to take into account all that upon which the average man bases his judgments, but who also, by the lifting of his eyes from the immediate, discerns as well the eternal forces that are at work in and through the present moment, driving for ultimate ends. The so-called "practical man" makes his contribution, but it is to the seer, who cannot at once back up his diagnosis with facts and figures, that we look to find the final solution to our woes.

In this second vision the prophet Zechariah symbolizes the enemies of Israel as **horns** that hem his people in on every side and make resistance seem futile. This was the popular view. But the prophet also sees, and in this he must have been one of a small minority, the gathering accumulation of God's power that is to break those horns and bring release.

Harry Emerson Fosdick reported this tribute paid by one of our leading doctors to a friend who had been a pioneer in medical research: "He was wrong for so long, and then he turned

out to be right." For years his fellows had not been able to see what he saw, and then suddenly it dawned on them that he had been right all the time. That is an accurate description of all who have stood in the royal succession of the prophets. For so long it seemed that they were wrong, and then came the day when it dawned on even the less discerning that they were right.

For long centuries, though man has not often dared to say so, he has thought Jesus was wrong in much that he taught, in more that he required. Slowly, a little here and a little there, it has begun to dawn on us that he was terribly and inevitably right. We have grown to witness the wisdom of his words: "Heaven and earth shall pass away, but my words shall not pass away" (Matt. 24:35).

The irresistible forces of righteousness and truth often do not appear in the obvious and seemingly strong. Abraham Lincoln was thought to be dead at birth. The advent of the one whose glory was "as of the only begotten of the Father, full of grace and truth" (John 1:14) came to pass in a peasant family, in the days of Herod the king, when Caesar Augustus stood astride the world in apparently unconquerable fashion. For so long they seemed inconsequential, these instruments of God's truth, and then they were unconquerable because they were right.

Those who would understand the prophets and in even a small way perform the prophet's

21 Then said I, What come these to do? And he spake, saying, These *are* the horns which have scattered Judah, so that no man did lift up his head: but these are come to fray them, to cast out the horns of the Gentiles, which lifted up *their* horn over the land of Judah to scatter it.

2 I lifted up mine eyes again, and looked, and behold a man with a measuring line in his hand.

2 Then said I, Whither goest thou? And he said unto me, To measure Jerusalem, to see what *is* the breadth thereof, and what *is* the length thereof.

3 And, behold, the angel that talked with me went forth, and another angel went out to meet him,

4 And said unto him, Run, speak to this young man, saying, Jerusalem shall be in-

---

showed me four smiths. 21 And I said, "What are these coming to do?" He answered, "These are the horns which scattered Judah, so that no man raised his head; and these have come to terrify them, to cast down the horns of the nations who lifted up their horns against the land of Judah to scatter it."

2 b And I lifted my eyes and saw, and behold, a man with a measuring line in his hand! 2 Then I said, "Where are you going?" And he said to me, "To measure Jerusalem, to see what is its breadth and what is its length." 3 And behold, the angel who talked with me came forward, and another angel came forward to meet him, 4 and said to him, "Run, say to that young

b Heb Ch 2. 5

---

21. Judah: Cf. 1:12. To terrify them. The LXX τοῦ ὀξῦναι points to a reading להחד (or possibly להחדיד), "to sharpen."

C. The Angel with the Measuring Line (2:1-5=Hebrew 2:5-9)

An angel carrying a measuring line is seen going forth to measure Jerusalem. He is told, however, that Jerusalem will not again need walls, for Yahweh himself will be a protecting wall of fire round about her.

This vision probably relates to an attempt by Zerubbabel to rebuild the walls of Jerusalem as a defense against unfriendly neighbors, more especially perhaps the Samaritans (cf. Ezra 4:4-5). Zechariah opposed any such attempt for two reasons. First, it would have given the Samaritans grounds for accusing the Jews of disloyalty to the Persian authorities (cf. Neh. 6:5-7); and second, the people should put their trust not in walls but in Yahweh.

2:1. The man is an angelic figure as in 1:8.

3. For went forth read "was standing still" (so LXX, εἰστήκει, which represents עמד; M.T., יצא; cf. 3:5).

4-5. The subject of said is the interpreting angel. The pronoun him refers to the other angel mentioned in vs. 3. The young man is the man (angel) of vs. 1. Villages:

---

function would do well to meditate on these words of William James:

I am against bigness and greatness in all their forms, and with the invisible molecular moral forces that work from individual to individual, stealing in through the crannies of the world like so many soft rootlets, or like the capillary oozing of water, and yet rending the hardest monuments of man's pride, if you give them time. . . . So I am . . . in favor of the eternal forces of truth which always work in the individual and immediately unsuccessful way, under-dogs always, till history comes, after they are long dead, and puts them on top.[3]

[3] *The Letters of William James*, ed. Henry James (Boston: Atlantic Monthly Press, 1920), II, 90.

2:1-5. *A City Without Walls.*—In the third vision a young man is about to survey the limits whereon the walls are to rise for the defense of the newly constructed Jerusalem, when one angel bids another, Run, say to that young man, "Jerusalem shall be inhabited as villages without walls, because of the multitude of men and cattle in it. For I will be to her a wall of fire round about, says the LORD, and I will be the glory within her."

Naturally if there was to be any enthusiasm and confidence in rebuilding a city completely leveled by the enemy a generation before, the matter of defense was of primary concern to everyone engaged in the project. Newer and

habited *as* towns without walls for the multitude of men and cattle therein:

5 For I, saith the Lord, will be unto her a wall of fire round about, and will be the glory in the midst of her.

6 ¶ Ho, ho, *come forth,* and flee from the land of the north, saith the Lord: for I have spread you abroad as the four winds of the heaven, saith the Lord.

7 Deliver thyself, O Zion, that dwellest *with* the daughter of Babylon.

man, 'Jerusalem shall be inhabited as villages without walls, because of the multitude of men and cattle in it. 5 For I will be to her a wall of fire round about, says the Lord, and I will be the glory within her.' "

6 Ho! ho! Flee from the land of the north, says the Lord; for I have spread you abroad as the four winds of the heavens, says the Lord. 7 Ho! Escape to Zion, you who dwell with the daughter of Babylon.

Jerusalem, dense in population and **without walls,** will become like open, undefended hamlets (cf. Ezek. 38:11). But she need have no fear, for Yahweh will **be to her a wall of fire round about,** which will consume all enemies who may approach (cf. Isa. 26:1). **Glory:** Cf. Hag. 1:8.

D. Call to the Exiles in Babylon (2:6-13=Hebrew 2:10-17)

The prophet addresses an excited call to the Jews still in Babylon to leave and return to Palestine, for the divine punishment is soon to fall in all its weight upon the nations which have been hostile to Judah. Zion is bidden to rejoice; for Yahweh will return to dwell there. Many nations will thereafter attach themselves to Yahweh, and will be reckoned as his people. Yet Judah and its capital city Jerusalem will be the objects of Yahweh's special choice and care.

6. The land of the north is Babylon; but it lies east, not north, of Palestine (cf. 6:6, 8; for the thought cf. Jer. 51:6, 45). "From the four winds of the heavens I will gather you" is the rendering of the LXX (ἐκ τῶν τεσσάρων ἀνέμων τοῦ οὐρανοῦ συνάξω ὑμᾶς); it implies the reading מארבע רוחות, "from the four winds," for the M.T. כארבע רוחות, "as the four winds," and אספתי (or קבצתי), "I will gather," for M.T. פרשתי, **I have spread abroad.** The LXX rendering is more in accord with the context, where the prophet is thinking of the gathering in of the Jews still outside Palestine, than is the M.T., which refers to the spreading abroad of the Jews all over the world. The **four winds** refer to the four points of the compass (cf. 6:5; Ezek. 37:9).

7. Zion is correctly treated in the RSV as an accusative of direction (so LXX, εἰς Σειὼν). The KJV and the ERV wrongly treat it as a vocative.

---

stronger walls than those destroyed by the Babylonians were in the blueprint stage. This time Jerusalem was to be made really impregnable. But in Zechariah's vision the instruments for sighting the position of the projected defenses had scarcely been set up when the startling declaration came from heaven that the city was to be rebuilt without walls. This was partly because no one was to be shut out, and so many people would wish to live in the community which was to be "the apple of God's eye" that no limits could be set; but also because God himself was to be "their rock, their fortress, and their might."

Here is a conception of the church which after all these centuries is still beyond our reach. As churches we are concerned to protect the truth we presume ourselves to possess by setting up restrictive defenses about it. There are not as many divisions, nor is there as much isolation-

ism, among the nations of the world as are to be found within the church. Men and women are not free to come within the walls which each sect creates unless their passports have received the official stamp of approval by the ecclesiastical authorities of that church body. Whatever makes us think we can fit God into the strait jacket of our narrow ecclesiastical concepts? The suspicion will not down that our man-made walls close God out, not in.

Zechariah advances the still novel idea that the defense of God's truth is God's business, not ours. We seem more concerned to defend the sacred than to present it. We are more worried and anxious lest the truth be desecrated than revealed. The result is that we are busy keeping people out, whereas God's whole concern is to bring people in to his fellowship and ours. We emphasize the things that divide. He emphasizes the things that unite. In the hubbub

8 For thus saith the Lord of hosts; After the glory hath he sent me unto the nations which spoiled you: for he that toucheth you, toucheth the apple of his eye.

9 For, behold, I will shake mine hand upon them, and they shall be a spoil to their servants: and ye shall know that the Lord of hosts hath sent me.

10 ¶ Sing and rejoice, O daughter of Zion: for, lo, I come, and I will dwell in the midst of thee, saith the Lord.

11 And many nations shall be joined to the Lord in that day, and shall be my people: and I will dwell in the midst of thee,

8 For thus said the Lord of hosts, after his glory sent me to the nations who plundered you, for he who touches you touches the apple of his eye: **9** "Behold, I will shake my hand over them, and they shall become plunder for those who served them. Then you will know that the Lord of hosts has sent me. **10** Sing and rejoice, O daughter of Zion; for lo, I come and I will dwell in the midst of you, says the Lord. **11** And many

---

8. After his glory sent me: Probably the best translation of the Hebrew text, which is very difficult, is "whose glory has sent me," reading אשר כבודו, "whose glory," for the M.T., אחר כבוד, "after glory." **The apple of his eye:** The word *bâbhâh*, **apple,** occurs only here, and means probably "pupil" (of the eye), conceived of either as the "gate," "door" of the eye (cf. Arabic *bâb* and the Akkadian *bâbu,* both meaning "gate," "door"), or as the "baby" of the eye, i.e., the tiny image reflected in the eye (see Edward Robertson, "The Apple of the Eye in the Masoretic Text," *Journal of Theological Studies,* XXXVIII [1937], 57-59). The pupil of the eye is sensitive and vulnerable, and is therefore highly prized by its owner. Who touches Judah, so highly prized by Yahweh, touches him at a sensitive point. **His eye** (Hebrew עינו) was, in the original text, "my eye" (עיני). This is one of the recognized "corrections of the scribes." The correction was made through motives of reverence, the original "my eye" being thought by later generations to be altogether too anthropomorphic an expression to be applied by Yahweh to himself (see C. D. Ginsburg, *Introduction to the Massoretico-Critical Edition of the Hebrew Bible* [London: Trinitarian Bible Society, 1897], pp. 347-63, especially p. 359).

11. For the thought of the first half of the verse cf. Isa. 2:2-4 (=Mic. 4:1-3); 19:18-25; 42:6; 49:6; 56:3, 6; Hag. 2:7. For **my people** (Hebrew לי לעם) read "his people" (לו לעם;

---

and confusion of our petty ecclesiastical debates we fail to hear his continual command: "Let my people come—together!"

If we were more concerned to reveal the truth we see, we would not need to defend it. Any so-called "truth" that man can destroy should be destroyed; for it is obviously not the truth at all. We can no more destroy God's truth than we can destroy God's stars. We are not equipped to defend God's truth; we are only equipped—and this is a very great capacity—to reveal it.

How can the church, now so miserably divided, minister to a world that is doomed unless it can manifest the spirit of unity in itself and help to level the political, economic, and ideological walls that spell death, not life; conflict, not peace; defeat, not victory for the world?

How futile for the establishment of lasting peace are man-made walls, whether built of stone, as in China long, long ago; or of steel and reinforced concrete sunk deep in the ground, as in the Maginot Line; or even of

planes and ships and tanks and factories capable of producing atomic bombs! The walls of Jericho, archaeologists tell us, tumbled and fell at least twenty-three times before Joshua came in the fourteenth century B.C. and tumbled them again.

> Something there is that doesn't love a wall,
> That wants it down![4]

The newest wall is a survival of the past. The oldest bridge is part of the prophecy of tomorrow. It is a mark of hope that we are becoming increasingly skilled in building bridges.

American history reminds us that following the War of 1812 the border between the United States and Canada was heavily fortified. American and British fleets patrolled the Great Lakes

[4] "Mending Wall" from *Complete Poems of Robert Frost.* Copyright, 1930, 1949, by Henry Holt and Co., New York. Copyright, 1936, 1948, by Robert Frost. Reprinted by permission of the publishers.

and thou shalt know that the Lord of hosts hath sent me unto thee.

12 And the Lord shall inherit Judah his portion in the holy land, and shall choose Jerusalem again.

13 Be silent, O all flesh, before the Lord: for he is raised up out of his holy habitation.

3 And he showed me Joshua the high priest standing before the angel of the Lord, and Satan standing at his right hand to resist him.

nations shall join themselves to the Lord in that day, and shall be my people; and I will dwell in the midst of you, **12** and you shall know that the Lord of hosts has sent me to you. And the Lord will inherit Judah as his portion in the holy land, and will again choose Jerusalem."

13 Be silent, all flesh, before the Lord; for he has roused himself from his holy dwelling.

3 Then he showed me Joshua the high priest standing before the angel of the Lord, and Satan standing at his right hand

cf. LXX αὐτῷ εἰς λαόν) ; and for **I will dwell** read either "they will dwell" (cf. LXX κατασκηνώσουσιν) , or "he will dwell" (cf. Peshitta *neshrē*) .

12. Judah . . . Jerusalem: Cf. 1:12. **The holy land.** This is the oldest occurrence of this designation of Palestine and the only instance of it in the O.T. Examples of its use in the Apoc. may be found in Wisd. Sol. 12:3; II Macc. 1:7.

13. Roused himself from his holy dwelling: Yahweh is issuing forth from his dwelling in heaven (cf. Deut. 26:15; Jer. 25:30; Isa. 63:15) to take his place in the sanctuary prepared for him. With this verse cf. Zeph. 1:7; Hab. 2:20. It may be that there is here a relic of an ancient liturgical formula.

E. Joshua Accused and Acquitted (3:1-10)

In this and the next vision the divinely appointed leaders of the people, Joshua and Zerubbabel, are in the forefront. Here Joshua, clothed in filthy garments, symbolic of guilt, is accused at the heavenly court by the Satan. He is acquitted, the filthy garments being replaced by clean ones in token of his acquittal. He is then given jurisdiction over the temple and its precincts, and the right of direct access to Yahweh, on condition that he pays due regard to the observance of the moral life and priestly duties. He and his fellow priests are a guarantee of the blessed days to be. The Messiah is on the way; a stone with seven facets, to be engraved by Yahweh himself, is prepared, and is to be worn by Joshua; sin is to be removed from the land; and an idyllic state of existence will follow.

What was the nature of the accusation laid against Joshua, and who were his accusers? Joshua, it seems, is accused of being unfit for the high priestly office because of some uncleanness. His accusers very probably were to be found among those who had not gone into exile, who had been ministered to all these years in Palestine by their own priests, and who regarded as unclean men like Joshua and his fellow priests: were not these polluted by heathen Babylon? Through their residence in Babylon, Joshua and his fellow priests had, so his accusers argued, contracted a religious taint. Before he could be regarded as eligible to assume the high priestly office, therefore, Joshua

and eyed one another with suspicion and disdain. On both sides of the border an armament race appeared to be in the making. At this crucial point in history Richard Rush, American Secretary of State, consulted with Sir Charles Bagot, British minister in Washington. Largely as a result of their patient labors, a wholly original and daring policy was promulgated, of dismantling all the fleets on the Great Lakes and the fortifications along the border. There

and then was established the first unarmed boundary between two nations in all history. At that point two countries advanced to a new social view and they have never retreated from it. What human misery and economic waste was saved thereby is beyond our imagination to compute.

3:1-10. Personality Problems Are Primary.— The fourth vision deals with the selection and the preparation of **Joshua** for the high priest-

2 And the LORD said unto Satan, The LORD rebuke thee, O Satan; even the LORD that hath chosen Jerusalem rebuke thee: *is* not this a brand plucked out of the fire?

3 Now Joshua was clothed with filthy garments, and stood before the angel.

4 And he answered and spake unto those that stood before him, saying, Take away the filthy garments from him. And unto him he said, Behold, I have caused thine iniquity to pass from thee, and I will clothe thee with change of raiment.

to accuse him. 2 And the LORD said to Satan, "The LORD rebuke you, O Satan! The LORD who has chosen Jerusalem rebuke you! Is not this a brand plucked from the fire?" 3 Now Joshua was standing before the angel, clothed with filthy garments.

4 And the angel said to those who were standing before him, "Remove the filthy garments from him." And to him he said, "Behold, I have taken your iniquity away from you, and I will clothe you with rich

---

stood in need of purification. The filthy garments, the symbol of his uncleanness, are removed from him, and clean garments, the symbol of his purification, are put on him. His eligibility for the high priestly office has received divine sanction. This **brand plucked out of the fire** (vs. 2) —this priest saved out of the fire of the Exile—is shown to be Yahweh's chosen one as the religious head of the community.

3:1. The subject of **he showed me** is Yahweh. **The angel of the LORD** is preferable (so Peshitta) to the "Yahweh" of the M.T. (cf. also 1:8). For **Satan** see Intro., p. 1055; for the scene in heaven cf. Job 1:6-12.

2. Has chosen Jerusalem: I.e., as his dwelling (cf. 1:14; 2:12). **A brand plucked out of the fire** may be an old proverbial expression (cf. Amos 4:11).

4. The angel is not in the M.T., but the Peshitta has it. **Those who were standing before him** are angelic beings. "Stand before" is equivalent to "serve" (cf. Gen. 41:46). "Clothe him" is preferable (cf. LXX ἐνδύσατε αὐτὸν) to the M.T. **clothe you. Rich**

---

hood of the new temple under construction in Jerusalem. This vision mirrors several problems of prime importance for us, as contemporaneous and more fundamental than the morning newspaper.

First consider what was involved in the selection of Joshua for this high office. There were present at the time in Jerusalem two groups, from either of which the candidate might properly be selected. There were a few people who had remained at Jerusalem throughout the seventy years of the Exile. They had reverently observed the ordinances of their faith and had kept up some semblance of worship amid the rubble of the temple ruins throughout all those weary years. Now that the new temple was under construction, why should not one of their number be selected for the post of high priest? They had never deserted God's chosen holy place.

The other group, by far the larger in point of numbers, consisted of those who had undergone the rigorous and heart-rending experiences of deportation to a foreign country, where they and their forebears had striven through all those long years to remain faithful to the faith of their fathers, and through homesickness and heartache to continue to "sing the Lord's song in a strange land" (Ps. 137:4). Perhaps because they were more in numbers, and in some ways

represented a more talented group, one of them, Joshua, was selected for the sacred office.

The problem then remained how to induce both groups, whose experiences had been so totally different, to accept Joshua as their common representative before the Lord. The tension between these two groups represents one of our most common problems. The failure to fuse together people of wholly different backgrounds is the rock on which many creative projects in church and community founder. We see this problem reflected in the chasm which yawns between creeds and classes and races; between the generations wherein youth and maturity each claim sole possession of the cream of wisdom. It is reflected in the friction between those who have had the privilege of formal education and those who have been brought up in "the University of Hard Knocks"; in the lack of sympathy and understanding between veterans and noncombatants in war, and even between those who served overseas and those who were kept for service in homelands; between those in the United States whose ancestors came on the "Mayflower" or fought in the Revolutionary War, and those whose forebears were among the later arrivals on American shores; between those who were brought up in a given church, whose families were "pillars of the church" before them, and those who moved into

5 And I said, Let them set a fair mitre upon his head. So they set a fair mitre upon his head, and clothed him with garments. And the angel of the LORD stood by.

6 And the angel of the LORD protested unto Joshua, saying,

7 Thus saith the LORD of hosts; If thou wilt walk in my ways, and if thou wilt keep my charge, then thou shalt also judge my house, and shalt also keep my courts, and I will give thee places to walk among these that stand by.

apparel." **5** And I said, "Let them put a clean turban on his head." So they put a clean turban on his head and clothed him with garments; and the angel of the LORD was standing by.

6 And the angel of the LORD enjoined Joshua, **7** "Thus says the LORD of hosts: If you will walk in my ways and keep my charge, then you shall rule my house and have charge of my courts, and I will give you the right of access among those who are

---

apparel: Better, "clean garments." The word מחלצות, which occurs only here and in Isa. 3:22, is usually explained as meaning either a **change of raiment** or **rich apparel.** The context here, however, requires the meaning "clean garments" (cf. vs. 5), and there are good philological grounds for believing that this is what the Hebrew word in fact means (see D. Winton Thomas, "A Note on מחלצות in Zechariah iii 4," *Journal of Theological Studies,* XXXIII [1932], 279-80; "A Note on חליצותם in Judges xiv 19," *ibid.,* XXXIV [1933], 165).

5. And I said, "Let them put": The words **and I said** are not represented in the LXX and should be deleted. The imperative **put** (reading שימו for the M.T. ישימו) finds support in the LXX ἐπίθετε. **Turban:** Cf. Exod. 28:4. The word "clean" before **garments** is not in the M.T. but should be supplied.

7. Walk in my ways and **keep my charge** are expressions signifying respectively the moral life (cf. Deut. 8:6; 10:12; Ps. 128:1) and the cultic life (cf. Ezek. 44:15-16; Lev.

---

town and became identified with the church more recently.

Experience tends to nullify its creative function by isolating people in unrelated segments. If the wholly different organs of the body failed to work together in a comparable fashion, it would spell death. Something akin to that may happen, and often does, in many a community and many a church, as a result of the separatism of experience. Paul graphically depicts the interdependence and interrelation of the gifts of experience in I Cor. 12. There is no background out of which people come, no experience through which they have passed or are passing, which does not have its own peculiar contribution for the enrichment of our common life and understanding.

In the opening words of his address to the 1948 assembly of the representatives of the Protestant churches in Amsterdam, John Foster Dulles declared that great diversity and great unity would both be needed if the world is to be saved from disaster. Those sage words have their obvious application to the churches, but also to the nations and the community. Unity in diversity is the keynote of God's creative function in nature. It is only too evident that he has been striving against certain recalcitrant tendencies on the part of his children to produce the same in humanity. We are not told,

but one would hope, that the minority who remained at Jerusalem were not "frozen out" by the more numerous repatriates from Babylon when Joshua ascended to the high priesthood. The community and the church would have been far, far poorer without the contribution of both.

Next, consider two instructive points in the ordination of Joshua as high priest, which are reflected in Zechariah's vision.

First, there was his need for purification: **Now Joshua was standing before the angel, clothed with filthy garments. . . . And to him he said, "Behold, I have taken your iniquity away from you."**

We would miss the full depth of the prophet's penetrating insight if we assumed from his words that the right to represent the people before God was a simple matter of putting on the proper vestments. The young prophet clearly understands that to lift people into the presence of the highest not only requires personal confession and cleansing—"For their sakes I sanctify myself, that they also might be sanctified through the truth" (John 17:19) —but the willingness to take upon one's self the burden of those whom one would lift.

This is one of the oldest insights having to do with the history of religion. Its truth is confirmed by the fact that it has cropped up in the

8 Hear now, O Joshua the high priest, thou, and thy fellows that sit before thee: for they *are* men wondered at: for, behold, I will bring forth my servant the BRANCH.

9 For behold the stone that I have laid before Joshua; upon one stone *shall be* seven eyes: behold, I will engrave the graving thereof, saith the LORD of hosts, and I will remove the iniquity of that land in one day.

standing here. **8** Hear now, O Joshua the high priest, you and your friends who sit before you, for they are men of good omen: behold, I will bring my servant the Branch.

9 For behold, upon the stone which I have set before Joshua, upon a single stone with seven facets, I will engrave its inscription, says the LORD of hosts, and I will remove

---

8:35). **Rule my house and have charge of my courts:** The whole temple area is to come under Joshua's control. In pre-exilic days the king had jurisdiction over the temple and the cult, and had complete control in matters of religion (cf. I Kings 2:27; II Kings 16:10-18). **Right of access:** Joshua can now feel sure that his prayers will reach Yahweh (cf. 4:14). **Who are standing here:** The attendant angels.

8. Thy fellows: Joshua's fellow priests. The words **for they** are best omitted. Joshua and his fellow priests are **men of good omen,** i.e., they serve as a symbol (cf. ERV) that the future will be a happy one. **The Branch,** lit., shoot, is a messianic term, the reference being, of course, to Zerubbabel (cf. 6:12; Isa. 11:1; Jer. 23:5-6; 33:14-16). Joshua, the now-legitimate high priest, is joined by the true king (cf. 4:14).

9. Many suggestions have been made as to the significance of **the stone.** Some have thought, for example, that it may have been a jewel intended for Zerubbabel's crown (cf. 6:10-15), perhaps inscribed with his name. But the stone is set before Joshua, not Zerubbabel. Others have suggested that it may have been the final stone which was to be laid on the temple (cf. 4:7, 10), appropriately inscribed or decorated with ornamental carving. Such a stone, however, would more properly have been laid before Zerubbabel,

---

most diverse and widely separated places and people. Long centuries before the Christian Era, long, long before the spiritual pilgrimage of the Jews, the Chinese emperor was wont, once a year, to take upon himself before God the sins of the people and bespeak God's favor on their behalf. Much the same idea has been manifest in many of the great men and women of our nation who have sought to release some segment of humanity from its burdens. In each instance they took upon themselves the burdens of those they would set free. The fact is, one wonders if personal cleansing can be had apart from this sort of self-forgetfulness.

Eugene V. Debs was convinced that he was not free so long as any man was shackled in body, mind, or spirit. Jacob Riis assumed the burden of the city's poor in New York, as Jane Addams assumed the burden of the foreign-born in Chicago, in order to set them free from ignorance, poverty, and exploitation. Horace Mann, first secretary of the Massachusetts Board of Education, took upon himself the difficulties and failures of public-school education at a time when the people of the state were largely indifferent, and to an amazing degree he opened the doors of understanding to all the children of the commonwealth. Booker T. Washington and Walter White,

though both might have gained prestige, power, and wealth by the exercise of their own considerable talents for personal aggrandizement, preferred to throw in their lot with the Negro and to assume the curse of color for the sake of enriching and fulfilling the lives of their oppressed brethren.

Something akin to the tribute paid by the author of Hebrews to Moses could be paid to these and other able, selfless people who have taken upon themselves the burdens of the needy for the sake of lifting them. "Moses, when he was grown up, refused to be called the son of Pharaoh's daughter, choosing rather to share ill-treatment with the people of God" (Heb. 11:24-25).

The penitent thief, as his lifeblood ebbed out on the cross, knew where to turn for the release he needed: " 'We are receiving the due reward of our deeds, but this man has done nothing wrong.' And he said, 'Jesus, remember me when you come in your kingly power.' " (Luke 23:41-42).

Along with the difficult task of assuming the burdens of others for the sake of lifting them into the presence of God, there must go simultaneously the act of pouring one's own strength into the weak so that they may rise. Every good physician does this daily. He takes upon himself

10 In that day, saith the LORD of hosts, shall ye call every man his neighbor under the vine and under the fig tree.

4 And the angel that talked with me came again, and waked me, as a man that is wakened out of his sleep,

the guilt of this land in a single day. 10 In that day, says the LORD of hosts, every one of you will invite his neighbor under his vine and under his fig tree."

4 And the angel who talked with me came again, and waked me, like a man

---

who was engaged with the rebuilding of the temple, rather than before Joshua. It is best perhaps to see in the stone a precious gem which was to be worn by Joshua on the breast or forehead (cf. Exod. 28:11-12, 36-38). **Facets:** Lit., **eyes.** For **eye** used for "surface" cf. Exod. 10:15; Num. 22:5, 11. The reference to the removal of the **iniquity** of the land anticipates the theme of the sixth and seventh visions (5:1-4, 5-11).

10. In the messianic age which is coming men will again, as in the glorious days of Solomon (I Kings 4:25), entertain their friends in peace and security under the vine and under the fig tree (cf. Mic. 4:4).

F. THE SEVEN-BRANCHED LAMPSTAND AND THE TWO OLIVE TREES (4:1-6a, 10b-14)

This vision, in which the prophet sees a seven-branched lampstand of gold, with a bowl at the top from which run seven pipes to feed the seven lamps, and flanked on either side by an olive tree, is perhaps the most obscure of all the visions. Vs. 12 has suggested to some commentators that the lampstand is a symbol of the Jewish community, and that the olive trees, which are thought to supply the lamps with oil, represent Zerubbabel and Joshua as channels of divine grace. There is reason, however, for believing that vs. 12 is not part of the original text (see below). If it is omitted, there is no suggestion in the text that the olive trees supply the lamp with oil. They merely stand one on each side of the lampstand (vss. 3, 11).

What, then, does the lampstand symbolize? The answer is provided by the statement in vs. 10b that the seven lamps are **the eyes of the LORD, which range through the whole earth.** The lampstand with its seven lamps is therefore a symbol of Yahweh, watchful

---

the burdens of the diseased in order, through his skill and understanding, to bring them health and well-being.

During World War II many donated blood again and again through the Red Cross for the sake of the wounded on fields of combat in all parts of the world. Men and women never knew for whom their blood was given or to what race or creed or color the one who would receive it belonged. They knew only that their healthy blood, transfused into the veins of the needy, would give to them the strength to fight for life. Something like this, and yet something far more significant and more difficult to bring about than physical well-being, was in our Lord's mind when in the upper room, he handed the cup to the disciples and said: "This is my blood . . . which is poured out for many for the forgiveness of sins" (Matt. 26:28).

Zechariah perhaps dimly understood what has come to be increasingly clear to us with the passage of the centuries, "Under the law almost everything is purified with blood, and without the shedding of blood there is no forgiveness of sins" (Heb. 9:22). When all this is done,

forgiveness and healing are not to be had as the achievement of man but as the gift of God through man's obedience and response (see vss. 6, 7, 9b).

4:1-14. An Early Concept of Church and State.—The fifth vision portrays the character of government to be enjoyed by Israel after its return from exile. Zechariah, **as a man that is wakened out of his sleep,** sees a lampstand with seven lamps, flanked by two olive trees. The lamps are **the eyes of the LORD, which range through the whole earth.** The trees are **the two anointed who stand by the LORD of the whole earth.** The Lord is to be the direct inspiration of both the secular and the religious arms of the government. Zerubbabel the king and Joshua the high priest are to carry jointly the responsibilities of rule. Zechariah is here proposing something new to his day but familiar to ours—the separation of church and state.

The idea is not now nor ever has been a panacea for all the problems of government. It is a satisfactory means of governing which, in the long view of history, has avoided some of the ill effects of theocracy, the rule of the

2 And said unto me, What seest thou? And I said, I have looked, and behold a candlestick all *of* gold, with a bowl upon the top of it, and his seven lamps thereon, and seven pipes to the seven lamps, which *are* upon the top thereof:

3 And two olive trees by it, one upon the right *side* of the bowl, and the other upon the left *side* thereof.

4 So I answered and spake to the angel that talked with me, saying, What *are* these, my lord?

5 Then the angel that talked with me answered and said unto me, Knowest thou not what these be? And I said, No, my lord.

6 Then he answered and spake unto me, saying, This *is* the word of the Lord unto Zerubbabel, saying, Not by might, nor by

that is wakened out of his sleep. 2 And he said to me, "What do you see?" I said, "I see, and behold, a lampstand all of gold, with a bowl on the top of it, and seven lamps on it, with seven lips on each of the lamps which are on the top of it. 3 And there are two olive trees by it, one on the right of the bowl and the other on its left." 4 And I said to the angel who talked with me, "What are these, my lord?" 5 Then the angel who talked with me answered me, "Do you not know what these are?" I said, "No, my lord." 6 Then he said to me,

---

over all the earth. The two olive trees then represent Zerubbabel and Joshua, the **two anointed ones,** who stand under Yahweh's protection and are filled with his spirit (vs. 14; cf. Isa. 61:1) .

4:3. **Right side** is preferable to the M.T., **right side of the bowl.**
6b-10a. See Exeg. below.

---

church, or of any form of government in which the church was enslaved or dominated by the state. In the early centuries of the Christian Era the church existed on sufferance by the Roman state without any voice in the government. Following the break-up of the Roman Empire and the barbarian invasions in the west, there came a period in which the church gradually became the master of the state. So far as the Roman Catholic Church was concerned, the power of church over state was broken in central and northern Europe and Britain by the impact of the sixteenth-century Reformation.

The central problem of every form of government has always been the use and misuse of power. The idea that the church alone was fit to rule grew out of the assumption that religious men were necessarily good men who could be trusted to handle power and yet escape the taint of corruption. Sad to say, this has not proved to be the case. Into whatever hands absolute power has been put, corruption has followed. In the United States the separation of church and state was established by the founding fathers in the hope that thereby the people might avoid the unhappy results of the domination of the government by the church or of the church by the government, which their forebears had fled from Europe and Britain to escape.

Nothing was further from the minds of the men who framed the Bill of Rights in the

United States Constitution than that the government could or would try to function without the guidance, restraint, and inspiration of religion. It was in the midst of one of the crucial debates of the Constitutional Convention that Benjamin Franklin rose to say:

I have lived, Sir, a long time, and the longer I live, the more convincing proofs I see of this truth— *that God governs in the affairs of men.* And if a sparrow cannot fall to the ground without his notice, is it probable that an empire can raise without his aid? We have been assured, Sir, that "except the Lord build the House, they labour in vain that build it." I firmly believe this; and I also believe that without his concurring aid we shall succeed in this political building no better than the Builders of Babel: We shall be divided by our little partial local interests; our projects will be confounded, and we ourselves shall become a reproach and byword down to future ages.[4]

Neither was it anticipated that churches, privileged to work and worship freely within the framework of government, would manifest no interest in, or accept no responsibility for, the affairs and problems of state.

It is conceivable that the phrase "separation of church and state" is misleading, suggesting two institutions operating along parallel lines, failing to touch at any point. The "interdependence of church and state," or the "co-opera-

[4] Carl Van Doren, *The Great Rehearsal* (New York: Viking Press, 1948), p. 101.

power, but by my Spirit, saith the LORD of hosts.

7 Who *art* thou, O great mountain? before Zerubbabel *thou shalt become* a plain: and he shall bring forth the headstone *thereof with* shoutings, *crying*, Grace, grace unto it.

8 Moreover the word of the LORD came unto me, saying,

9 The hands of Zerubbabel have laid the foundation of this house; his hands shall also finish it; and thou shalt know that the LORD of hosts hath sent me unto you.

10 For who hath despised the day of small things? for they shall rejoice, and shall see the plummet in the hand of Zerubbabel *with* those seven; they *are* the eyes of the LORD, which run to and fro through the whole earth.

11 ¶ Then answered I, and said unto him, What *are* these two olive trees upon the right *side* of the candlestick and upon the left *side* thereof?

12 And I answered again, and said unto him, What *be these* two olive branches,

"This is the word of the LORD to Zerub'-babel: Not by might, nor by power, but by my Spirit, says the LORD of hosts. 7 What are you, O great mountain? Before Zerub'-babel you shall become a plain; and he shall bring forward the top stone amid shouts of 'Grace, grace to it!' " 8 Moreover the word of the LORD came to me, saying, 9 "The hands of Zerub'babel have laid the foundation of this house; his hands shall also complete it. Then you will know that the LORD of hosts has sent me to you. 10 For whoever has despised the day of small things shall rejoice, and shall see the plummet in the hand of Zerub'babel.

"These seven are the eyes of the LORD, which range through the whole earth." 11 Then I said to him, "What are these two olive trees on the right and the left of the lampstand?" 12 And a second time I said to him, "What are these two branches of the

---

12. The whole verse is probably a gloss. Note that whereas in vss. 3, 11 "olive trees" are mentioned, in this verse **branches of the olive trees** are referred to. In this verse too mention is made of **two golden pipes**, to which no reference has been made previously.

---

tion of church and state," puts into more realistic language what is sought to be accomplished. The church is and must ever be the conscience of the nation, supplying public servants who are experienced in and concerned for the pre-eminence of religious values and truths. The church completely divorced from the state is in dire danger of becoming irrelevant. The state divorced from religion falls easy prey to the idolatry of man. H. G. Wells once observed that as soon as man thinks he is god, he begins to act like the devil.

The separation of church and state can function for the well-being of all only if we conceive it as Zechariah presented it in his vision—the heads of both acknowledging that God is the sole source and final arbiter of all power, the representatives of government and religion remaining mindful that they are trustees of that power on God's behalf for the welfare of *his* children.

One of the truest and most profound expressions in all our religious heritage is to be found in the words which the angel in Zechariah's vision directed to the head of the state: **This is the word of the LORD to Zerubbabel: Not by**

might, nor by power, but by my Spirit, says the LORD of hosts (vs. 6). These words must be engraved in the hearts of statesmen and churchmen alike if people are to continue to enjoy the real blessings of freedom. It was William Penn who said: "Those people who are not governed by God will be ruled by tyrants." [5]

Zechariah rightly prophesies that if and when the leaders of church and state acknowledge their responsibility to God and their dependence on him as the supreme power of the universe, all manner of mountainous difficulties, which tower above men and forbid their progress, will flatten out like a plain (vs. 7) Does not this at once link up in our minds with the statement of Jesus: "If you have faith as a grain of mustard seed, you will say to this mountain, 'Move hence to yonder place,' and it will move; and nothing will be impossible to you" (Matt. 17:20) ?

10. *The Day of Small Things.*—The erroneous impression lives on to plague us that real progress awaits the discovery of something akin to the proverbial "seven-league boots." In the

[5] Quoted in James Keller, *You Can Change the World* (New York: Longmans, Green & Co., 1948), p. 21.

which through the two golden pipes empty
the golden *oil* out of themselves?

13 And he answered me and said, Knowest thou not what these *be?* And I said, No,
my lord.

14 Then said he, These *are* the two
anointed ones, that stand by the Lord of the
whole earth.

olive trees, which are beside the two golden
pipes from which the oil[c] is poured out?"
13 He said to me, "Do you not know what
these are?" I said, "No, my lord." 14 Then
he said, "These are the two anointed who
stand by the LORD of the whole earth."

[c] Cn: Heb *gold*

The twofold **golden** may also be suspect. The verse may be a doublet of vs. 11, or it may
be part of another vision with similar imagery which has been accidentally incorporated
into this one.

14. Anointed: Lit., "sons of oil." Zerubbabel and Joshua are not mentioned by
name but they are intended; cf. 3:8, where Zerubbabel is not mentioned but is clearly
intended.

G. ZERUBBABEL AND THE TEMPLE (4:6*b*-10*a*)

6*b*-10*a*. It is generally agreed that this section, beginning with the words **This is
the word of the LORD** (vs. 6*b*), and ending with the words **in the hand of Zerubbabel**
(vs. 10*a*), is out of place where it now stands, for it interrupts the connection between
vs. 6*a* and vs. 10*b*. Commentators, however, do not agree as to its original position.
Some would place it after 3:10; others would take it in conjunction with 6:15; while
still others believe it belongs after 4:1-6*a*, 10*b*-14. The last view is followed here.

In this section are reflected the doubts of those who were skeptical about the
successful completion of the rebuilding of the temple by Zerubbabel. These doubts
Zechariah silences. Zerubbabel will indeed carry through the rebuilding to a successful
conclusion. Human strength and energy alone, however, will not be enough; only
through divine power can its completion be brought about. The difficulties and trials
that face Zerubbabel in his task will be cleared from his path, and the laying of the
final stone of the new temple by him will be greeted with enthusiastic shouts. The
people will see that the new temple is a worthy successor to the old one, and the doubts
which some of them have entertained will give place to joy when they see Zerubbabel
laying the last stone straight and true.

The difficulties with which Zerubbabel has to contend, but which are soon to
disappear, are likened to a **great mountain** which no longer bars the way of a traveler
but becomes a **plain** for his easier journeying (cf. Isa. 40:4; 49:11). **Grace, grace unto it!**
Perhaps better, "Beauty, beauty to it!" i.e., "How beautiful it is!"—the people's cry that
greets the laying of the last stone.

10*a*. The day of small things: Cf. Hag. 2:3.

10*b*-14. See Exeg. on 4:1-6*a*, 10*b*-14, above.

---

meantime we indulge in the easy but fruitless
pastime of heaping scorn on those who would
take the small steps that can be taken.

Zechariah notes that the gigantic task of raising Jerusalem from the rubble and rebuilding
the temple required great patience and confidence in performing a host of seemingly little
tasks. Many people not so endowed were content, as always, to "sit in the seat of the scornful," and to scoff at such small beginnings. In
contrast, Zechariah's faith was so dynamic that
he confidently anticipated the day when even
these scoffers would rejoice, seeing **the plummet
in the hands of the king** at the temple. This was

the traditional symbolic ceremony which accompanied the placing of the topstone and
indicated that the building had been completed.

A group of friends were spending a summer's
day rummaging through the barn of an old New
England farm. There they found the stratified
dust-covered discardings of generations of
Yankees, the candle mold, the cutter, the old
bureaus and beds, and in a far corner a motto
that had once hung in the parlor, on which
were printed the words, "Honesty, Industry,
Sobriety." One of the group was heard to observe, "Too bad they didn't keep that in the
house." Far, far too many things have been

5 Then I turned, and lifted up mine eyes, and looked, and behold a flying roll.

2 And he said unto me, What seest thou? And I answered, I see a flying roll; the length thereof *is* twenty cubits, and the breadth thereof ten cubits.

3 Then said he unto me, This *is* the curse that goeth forth over the face of the whole earth: for every one that stealeth shall be cut off *as* on this side according to it; and every one that sweareth shall be cut off *as* on that side according to it.

5 Again I lifted my eyes and saw, and behold, a flying scroll! 2 And he said to me, "What do you see?" I answered, "I see a flying scroll; its length is twenty cubits, and its breadth ten cubits." 3 Then he said to me, "This is the curse that goes out over the face of the whole land; for every one who steals shall be cut off henceforth according to it, and every one who swears falsely shall be cut off henceforth according

---

H. The Flying Scroll (5:1-4)

In this and the next vision (5:5-11) Zechariah returns to a theme which he touched upon in 3:9, viz., the removal of sin from the land as a necessary prelude to the coming of the messianic age. He sees an immense scroll, on which is inscribed a curse, flying over the land of Palestine. It is a symbol of Yahweh's curse which will light upon the houses of thieves and perjurers.

5:2. According to the measurements given, the scroll was approximately thirty by fifteen feet.

3. Cut off: The word נקה used here could mean "purged out," "cleansed" (cf. Isa. 3:26). **Henceforth according to it:** The Hebrew could possibly be rendered "according to the wording on one of its sides." **Swears falsely:** The word **falsely**, which is not in the

---

discarded by recent generations as commonplace or trifling, without which the building of our hopes into substantial reality is impossible.

Was it a group of scoffers, noting the contrast between seemingly small things that Jesus did and said compared with the vastness of the hopes he outlined, who provoked Jesus' parable of the tiny mustard seed springing up to a growth so great that "the birds of the air can make nests in its shade" (Mark 4:30-32)?

5:1-4. *A Curse upon Evildoers.*—This chapter of the prophecy portrays two methods of getting rid of evil in order to prepare Jerusalem for the coming of the messianic age. First, the prophet proposes a curse upon it. He sees a gigantic scroll, listing the names and crimes of evildoers, flying over the land, plainly revealing their iniquity and showering the curse of the Almighty upon them.

Rudolph Smend says that in ancient times curses were written on slips of paper and sent down the wind into the houses of those against whom they were directed.[6] We see here the forerunner of a familiar technique often resorted to in modern times—the black list. Our belief seems to be that if we show up those of whom we disapprove, they will be so cursed by the revelation of their iniquity that they will

---

6 Cited in George Adam Smith, *Book of the Twelve Prophets*, II, 302.

be rendered impotent. Mark Twain had the delightful and, for him, satisfying custom of writing letters to people of whom he disapproved, telling them exactly what he thought of them, "calling a spade a spade," in no uncertain terms. But he never mailed the letters. He placed them in his desk drawer, and from time to time his wife went through the drawer and destroyed these highly explosive missives. That was his way of raining down curses upon those whom he regarded as malicious.

But if and when we set out to wipe out evil by publicly blacklisting evildoers, we are more than apt to compound the very influence we would destroy. We further complicate the problem, instead of solving it. For one thing, we open ourselves to the subtle attack of self-righteousness, the most vicious influence with which religious folk have to struggle. For the blacklisting method implies that we who emblazon the scroll with names and deeds are pure. We are white; they are black. We are good; they are evil. In this procedure we happily concentrate on the faults and failures of others, thereby escaping the unhappy necessity to look deep within our own hearts and acknowledge our own shortcomings. Nobody ever got rid of evil that way. If we insist on listing evildoers, we must needs provide an even longer scroll and place our own names at the top. Then our

4 I will bring it forth, saith the Lord of hosts, and it shall enter into the house of the thief, and into the house of him that sweareth falsely by my name: and it shall remain in the midst of his house, and shall consume it with the timber thereof and the stones thereof.

5 ¶ Then the angel that talked with me went forth, and said unto me, Lift up now thine eyes, and see what is this that goeth forth.

6 And I said, What is it? And he said, This is an ephah that goeth forth. He said moreover, This is their resemblance through all the earth.

to it. 4 I will send it forth, says the Lord of hosts, and it shall enter the house of the thief, and the house of him who swears falsely by my name; and it shall abide in his house and consume it, both timber and stones."

5 Then the angel who talked with me came forward and said to me, "Lift your eyes, and see what this is that goes forth." 6 And I said, "What is it?" He said, "This is the ephah that goes forth." And he said, "This is the iniquity[d] in all the land."

[d] Gk Compare Syr: Heb eye

M.T., should certainly be supplied, and probably also "by my name" (cf. vs. 4). Zechariah singles out one moral and one religious sin as typical of sin generally.

4. **Consume it:** For the idea of the curse of God resting upon ruined cities and houses cf. Job 15:28.

J. The Woman in the Ephah Measure (5:5-11)

This vision continues the theme of the last one. The prophet sees all the sin of the community, personified as a woman, gathered up and put into an ephah measure. The heavy leaden cover is placed upon it, and it is carried through the air by two women with storklike wings, to Babylon, the home of wickedness, where a temple is to be built for it.

5-6. The word 'ēphāh is used both of a grain measure (cf. Deut. 25:14; Ezek. 45:11) and of a vessel of the capacity to hold such a measure. Here it is used in the latter sense. **And he said, This is an ephah that goeth forth:** These words should probably be deleted. **Iniquity:** Read עֲוֺנָם (so LXX ἡ ἀδικία αὐτῶν; cf. 3:9) for the M.T. עֵינָם eye ("appearance"; RSV mg.).

chosen method might have some effect. "If we say we have no sin, we deceive ourselves, and the truth is not in us. If we confess our sins, he is faithful and just, and will forgive our sins and cleanse us from all unrighteousness." (I John 1:8-9.)

Furthermore, the whole purpose of religion is not to "show people up" but to lift them up. The prophet's vision of the curse descending upon evildoers pictures their damnation but not their salvation. Religion has suffered immeasurably from the "big stick" technique, of which this is a typical example. The modern counterpart of the method is the roadside sign reading, "Be Sure Your Sins Will Find You Out." Of course they will, but so far as we know nobody was ever hounded or harassed into the kingdom of God by fear. Men are won into it by love—which means understanding and forgiveness of the kind that is productive of self-condemnation, humility, contrition, and penitence. Our Lord did not refer to evildoers as black sheep but as lost sheep who were to be

found and brought back. It is easy to call people names. It is something else again to win them for him "whose name is above every name."

5-11. *A Woman as the Scapegoat.*—In the seventh vision the prophet sees a huge barrel. When the lid is removed, a woman is to be found sitting inside. She is **Wickedness** personified. When the lid is replaced, two flying angels carry the barrel to Babylon, where a temple is made to receive it and worship is offered to it.

This is a curious description of the manner in which Israel is to be rid of evil. It does not fit easily into the framework of our thinking. We understand and also believe that without God's power we cannot hope to rid the world, or be rid ourselves, of evil. It is all too obvious from experience that a more than human wisdom and strength is needed to win even partial victories in the continuing struggle against that curious bent in human nature which so often makes the worse appear the better part.

But the prophet's description of the solution does not even suggest that man has any respon-

7 And, behold, there was lifted up a talent of lead: and this *is* a woman that sitteth in the midst of the ephah.

8 And he said, This *is* wickedness. And he cast it into the midst of the ephah; and he cast the weight of lead upon the mouth thereof.

9 Then lifted I up mine eyes, and looked, and, behold, there came out two women, and the wind *was* in their wings; for they had wings like the wings of a stork: and they lifted up the ephah between the earth and the heaven.

10 Then said I to the angel that talked with me, Whither do these bear the ephah?

11 And he said unto me, To build it a house in the land of Shinar: and it shall be established, and set there upon her own base.

7 And behold, the leaden cover was lifted, and there was a woman sitting in the ephah! 8 And he said, "This is Wickedness." And he thrust her back into the ephah, and thrust down the leaden weight upon its mouth. 9 Then I lifted my eyes and saw, and behold, two women coming forward! The wind was in their wings; they had wings like the wings of a stork, and they lifted up the ephah between earth and heaven. 10 Then I said to the angel who talked with me, "Where are they taking the ephah?" 11 He said to me, "To the land of Shinar, to build a house for it; and when this is prepared, they will set the ephah down there on its base."

---

7. A woman: The M.T. reads, **and this** [זאת] **is a woman. Behold** (הנה) is the reading of the LXX (ἰδού).

8. Wickedness in Hebrew is feminine (רשעה). Hence it is symbolized by a woman.

11. The use of **Shinar** for Babylon is perhaps an intentional archaism (cf. Gen 11:2). Babylon, the deadly enemy of the Jews, is the appropriate place in Zechariah's view for the dumping of Palestine's concentrated sin. But more than this. A **house**, i.e., a temple (cf. 1:16), is to be built for the ephah measure, which is to be set upon its **base**, as an image. The word מכונה, **base**, is likewise used in a cultic connection wherever it occurs in the O.T. (e.g., I Kings 7:27; Jer. 27:19; 52:17; Ezra 3:3). Sin thus not only finds its natural home in Babylon, but worship is to be paid to it! Zechariah here is grandly ironical.

---

sibility for the struggle and the release that is to come. To us our Lord's parable of the tares (Matt. 13:24-30) seems more inclusive of all the elements involved in the struggle. Here is displayed that amazing fashion in which goodness and evil are inextricably intertwined so that it is hard to know where one ends and the other begins. It is one of our most puzzling problems that often no sharp line of cleavage can be drawn between good and bad, right and wrong. Our destiny seems to be to struggle all our life long, to fight a good fight, to finish our course and to keep the faith against all the adversaries that are arrayed against us. Along the way we harvest considerable fruits from this endless struggle, but the final reckoning and the final harvest are in God's hands and beyond the limitations of our human vision. Who is to say? It may be as the prophet declares, "Thus says the LORD of hosts, . . . I will remove the guilt of this land in a single day" (3:7, 9). We can safely leave the ultimate outcome with God. Our daily job is to buckle on "the whole armor of God," that we "may be able to withstand in

the evil day, and having done all to stand" (Eph. 6:13).

The prophet is here resorting to the ancient Hebrew philosophy of the scapegoat. As the final act in the drama of the day of Atonement, the high priest placed both hands on the head of a goat allotted to Azazel, prince of fallen angels. Thus the people of Israel believed that he actually transferred the nation's sins to the head of the goat. The ancient practice has contributed a most graphic term to our vocabulary.

Still more curious and distasteful to us is the prophet's use of woman as the personification of evil. It may be, as the Exeg. notes, that he was only following the implication of the Hebrew language, in which wickedness is feminine and is symbolized by a woman.

In the ever-fascinating story of the Creation in Genesis, when Adam is faced with his disobedience, he evades responsibility and passes the buck, as we would say, to the woman. "The woman whom thou gavest to be with me, she gave me of the tree, and I did eat. And the LORD God said unto the woman, What is this

6 And I turned, and lifted up mine eyes, and looked, and, behold, there came four chariots out from between two mountains; and the mountains *were* mountains of brass.

2 In the first chariot *were* red horses; and in the second chariot black horses;

3 And in the third chariot white horses; and in the fourth chariot grizzled and bay horses.

4 Then I answered and said unto the angel that talked with me, What *are* these, my lord?

5 And the angel answered and said unto me, These *are* the four spirits of the heavens, which go forth from standing before the Lord of all the earth.

6 The black horses which *are* therein go forth into the north country; and the white go forth after them; and the grizzled go forth toward the south country.

6 And again I lifted my eyes and saw, and behold, four chariots came out from between two mountains; and the mountains were mountains of bronze. 2 The first chariot had red horses, the second black horses, 3 the third white horses, and the fourth chariot dappled gray[e] horses. 4 Then I said to the angel who talked with me, "What are these, my lord?" 5 And the angel answered me, "These are going forth to the four winds of heaven, after presenting themselves before the Lord of all the earth. 6 The chariot with the black horses goes toward the north country, the white ones go toward the west country,[f] and the dappled ones go toward the south country."

[e] Compare Gk: The meaning of the Hebrew word is uncertain

[f] Cn: Heb *after them*

K. The Four Chariots (6:1-8)

In this last vision Zechariah sees four chariots, drawn by horses of different colors, coming out from between two mountains of bronze. The chariots go forth to the four points of the compass. Those that go to the north country—to Babylon—have the special task of executing Yahweh's anger upon this enemy par excellence of the Jews.

With this last vision the first (1:8-17) should be compared.

6:1. Mountains: Cf. 1:8, 11.

2. For the colors cf. 1:8.

3. White horses: The word אמצים does not signify a color (as in KJV), but means "strong." It is probably a gloss from vs. 7, where it was taken to be a color, and was thought in consequence to belong also in this verse.

5. The four winds of heaven: Cf. 2:6.

6. The west country: Read ארץ הים or אחרי הים in place of the M.T. אחריהם, **after them.** Only three points of the compass are referred to in this verse as it stands, no mention being made of the east. Nor are the red horses (cf. vs. 2) mentioned here.

---

that thou hast done? And the woman said, The serpent beguiled me, and I did eat." (Gen. 3:12-13.) Here plainly the woman, so far as human beings are concerned, is made to bear the onus of evil.

With us neither sex seems to have any corner on the capacity to instigate evil. In our time woman is far more often the personification of the best rather than the worst. This view of womanhood has come about in part because of the mystery and the majesty of childbearing and child rearing. But there is another reason. It has been our experience that there is a type of deep spiritual insight and spiritual sensitiveness more often to be found in women than in men. The first person to be made aware of the miracle of the Resurrection was a woman.

Very human is the thought of the prophet that woman, as the personification of wickedness, is transported to the land of the former enemy and there is worshiped. That is a typical line of reasoning, even in our time, on the part of those whose thinking has been warped by bitterness and hatred. What we abominate, we say our enemies worship; what we revere, we say they hate. Babylon not only worshiped idols, which were anathema to the Hebrews, but idolized evil. An unprejudiced appraisal would scarcely go to such lengths to blacken an enemy.

6:1-15. The Double Victory.—The final vision describes the impact of God's power on two fronts. In the external world the enemies of Israel are overwhelmed. In the realm of the spirit the sin of Israel is pardoned and a re-

7 And the bay went forth, and sought to go that they might walk to and fro through the earth: and he said, Get you hence, walk to and fro through the earth. So they walked to and fro through the earth.

8 Then cried he upon me, and spake unto me, saying, Behold, these that go toward the north country have quieted my spirit in the north country.

9 ¶ And the word of the LORD came unto me, saying,

10 Take of *them of* the captivity, *even* of Heldai, of Tobijah, and of Jedaiah, which are come from Babylon, and come thou the same day, and go into the house of Josiah the son of Zephaniah;

7 When the steeds came out, they were impatient to get off and patrol the earth. And he said, "Go, patrol the earth." So they patrolled the earth. 8 Then he cried to me, "Behold, those who go toward the north country have set my Spirit at rest in the north country."

9 And the word of the LORD came to me: 10 "Take from the exiles Heldai, Tobi'jah, and Jedai'ah, who have arrived from Babylon; and go the same day to the house of

Perhaps some words like "the red [horses] were going out to the land of the east and," האדמים יצאים אל ארץ הקדם ו', should be read at the beginning of this verse.

7. The steeds: Lit., "the strong" (Hebrew אמצים; cf. vs. 3), a general term descriptive of the horses. Horses are called "mighty, strong ones" (Hebrew אבירים) in Judg. 5:22; Jer. 8:16; 47:3. The subject of **he said,** as of "he cried" in vs. 8, is the interpreting angel.

8. By the north country is meant Babylon; cf. 2:6. **My spirit:** Here **spirit** means "anger," as frequently in the O.T. (e.g., Judg. 8:3; Prov. 16:32). The chariots go forth to execute Yahweh's anger on Babylon for the injury she has done to his people.

III. SYMBOLIC CROWNING OF ZERUBBABEL AS KING-MESSIAH (6:9-15)

This section, which is in the nature of a historical appendix, deals with the symbolic crowning of Zerubbabel as king-messiah. Zechariah is told to take of the silver and gold which some Jewish exiles had brought with them from Babylon to Jerusalem—no doubt as offerings for the temple—and to make from them a crown which he is to place upon the head of Zerubbabel. Joshua, the high priest, will be at his side, and harmonious co-operation will exist between them. The crown itself is to be preserved in the temple as a memorial to the Babylonian Jews who presented the silver and gold from which it was made. The section ends with the prophet looking forward to a return to Jerusalem of the scattered Jews who will help in the completion of the temple.

10. This verse should probably be translated, "Take the gifts of the exiles, from Heldai, from Tobijah, and from Jedaiah, and from the house of Josiah, the son of Zephaniah, who have come from Babylon." This translation involves reading משאת, "gifts," "contributions" (cf. II Chr. 24:6, 9), for the first מאת, translated **from** in the RSV; the omission of **come thou the same day;** and reading ומאת, "and from," in place of the second ובאת, **and go into.** Three points of interest concerning the names mentioned in this verse may be noted. First, whereas here the name **Heldai** appears, in vs. 14 the name given is "Helem." Second, only the name **Josiah, the son of Zephaniah,** is

newed spirit of devotion to, and zeal for, the God of their fathers is awakened in the Jews, both in those still in Babylon and in those who have returned to Jerusalem. As a result, Zerubbabel is crowned king-messiah as the messianic age begins. Even military victory is not ensured by man's strength alone but by the loosing of God's "terrible swift sword." A still more compelling victory occurs simultaneously in the hearts and minds of God's children, manifesting

itself in a spirit of penitence, confession, and renewed devotion to the faith of the fathers.

Zerubbabel's **crown** is to be made from gold sent as a gift to the temple at Jerusalem by members of the Jewish community still remaining in Babylon. Following the coronation the crown is to be kept in the temple as a memorial to the experience and the men of the Exile. So often the crowning events of our lives arise from our struggles with untoward, unhappy experiences

11 Then take silver and gold, and make crowns, and set *them* upon the head of Joshua the son of Josedech, the high priest;

12 And speak unto him, saying, Thus speaketh the Lord of hosts, saying, Behold the man whose name *is* The BRANCH; and he shall grow up out of his place, and he shall build the temple of the Lord:

13 Even he shall build the temple of the Lord; and he shall bear the glory, and shall sit and rule upon his throne; and he shall be a priest upon his throne: and the counsel of peace shall be between them both.

Josi'ah, the son of Zephani'ah. 11 Take from them silver and gold, and make a crown,ᵍ and set it upon the head of Joshua, the son of Jehoz'adak, the high priest; 12 and say to him, 'Thus says the Lord of hosts, "Behold, the man whose name is the Branch: for he shall grow up in his place, and he shall build the temple of the Lord. 13 It is he who shall build the temple of the Lord, and shall bear royal honor, and shall sit and rule upon his throne. And there shall be a priest by his throne, and peaceful understanding shall be between them

ᵍ Gk Mss: Heb *crowns*

considered a proper name by the LXX, the others being treated as appellatives and translated as such, e.g., **Heldai** is translated by τῶν ἀρχόντων, "the chief men," "rulers." And third, only in the case of Josiah is the father's name given—rather strikingly both here and in vs. 14. Perhaps the party which **arrived from Babylon** was composed of returning exiles who came to Jerusalem with the intention of settling there. Or again, they may have been sent by their fellow exiles in Babylon for some purpose, perhaps in connection with the difficulties which were being experienced in Jerusalem, more especially, it may be guessed, in the matter of the rebuilding of the temple.

11. A crown: The M.T. has **crowns.** In vs. 14 the Hebrew verb is in the singular, while in the LXX both the subject and the verb are in the singular (ὁ δὲ στέφανος ἔσται). It seems clearly intended that there shall be one crown only, and that Zerubbabel shall wear it. **Joshua:** Vss. 12-13 show that not this name, but Zerubbabel's, originally stood here. It has been suggested that both names stood in the text originally. But the singular "to him" (vs. 12 M.T.), which refers to Zerubbabel, as well as the fact that only one crown is intended, argues against this suggestion. Most probably the name Zerubbabel was altered later to Joshua by someone who, when the hopes that were centered in Zerubbabel were disappointed, transferred the prophecy relating to the Messiah to the high priest who, as time went on, became the civil, as well as the religious, head of the community. In this way Zechariah's prophecy was brought by a reviser into harmony with later history.

12. The Branch: Cf. 3:8. **Build** is here used (as in 1:16; 6:15) in the sense of completing the building. Work on the temple had by this time been in progress for some five months.

13. The priest is Joshua. **By his throne:** Better, "at his right hand," reading מימינו for על־כסאו (so LXX, ἐκ δεξιῶν αὐτοῦ). For the position of honor at a king's right hand cf. I Kings 2:19. **Peaceful understanding:** I.e., harmonious co-operation for the welfare of Judah. The words may possibly suggest that there had been some friction between

that are forced upon us. Sickness, death, and misfortune are the common adversaries of the race which carry us away from the vision of life that we desire. At the time of their occurrence they seem to mark the end of all our hopes. But in time, through the victory of faith, we learn to rise above them. Though they are still undesired, through our struggle to stand up to what they mean, in God's power they may become the crowning events of our lives. But always there has to be that victory of the spirit before the harsh events of the external world make their lasting contribution to our lives.

The prophet's final vision is an ideal picture of the consummation of the human struggle under the guidance of the divine Spirit. But is it not more realistic than many of the current thoughts of our world concerning the final outcome of its hopes? Within our memory and experience there have been victories in the conflicts between nations which seemed to portend great things that failed of realization. The cause of this bitter disappointment and disillusionment is the failure to recognize the need for the simultaneous victory in the realm of character. Man himself must change before his

14 And the crowns shall be to Helem, and to Tobijah, and to Jedaiah, and to Hen the son of Zephaniah, for a memorial in the temple of the LORD.

15 And they *that are* far off shall come and build in the temple of the LORD, and ye shall know that the LORD of hosts hath sent me unto you. And *this* shall come to pass, if ye will diligently obey the voice of the LORD your God.

7 And it came to pass in the fourth year of king Darius, *that* the word of the LORD came unto Zechariah in the fourth *day* of the ninth month, *even* in Chisleu;

both."' 14 And the crown*h* shall be in the temple of the LORD as a reminder to Heldai,*i* Tobi'jah, Jedai'ah, and Josi'ah*j* the son of Zephani'ah.

15 "And those who are far off shall come and help to build the temple of the LORD; and you shall know that the LORD of hosts has sent me to you. And this shall come to pass, if you will diligently obey the voice of the LORD your God."

7 In the fourth year of King Darius, the word of the LORD came to Zechari'ah in the fourth day of the ninth month, which

h Gk: Heb *crowns*
i With verse 10: Heb *Helm*
j With verse 10: Heb *Hen*

Zerubbabel and Joshua. If so, Zechariah makes it clear that there is no room for it, both the civil and religious heads of the community being Yahweh's accredited representatives (4:14).

14. This verse should be translated: "And the crown shall be for Heldai, and for Tobijah, and for Jedaiah, and for Josiah the son of Zephaniah, for a memorial and for a sign of favor in the temple of the LORD." **Crown:** Cf. vs. 11. **Heldai:** The M.T. has **Helem** (חלם), a name which does not occur elsewhere in the O.T. The Peshitta here has **Heldai,** and this name should be read, as in vs. 10. The LXX, as in the case of the other names mentioned in this section (cf. vs. 10), treats **Helem** as an appellative, not as a proper name. The name **Josiah** is not mentioned in this verse in the M.T., as it is in vs. 10. The Peshitta, however, reads his name here, no doubt correctly, for the four names in vs. 10 and in this verse should clearly be the same. Before **the son of Zephaniah,** where the name Josiah is to be expected, the M.T. has חן. The word חן should not be regarded as a proper name (as in KJV **Hen**), but as a noun meaning "a sign of favor" (so LXX χάριτα; cf. ERV mg.), and it should stand after the words **for a memorial.** For this kind of memorial cf. Num. 31:54.

15. **Those who are far off:** Not the heathen but the scattered Jews (cf. Isa. 60:4, 9). The second half of this verse should be translated, "and it shall come to pass, if you will diligently obey the voice of the LORD your God . . . ." The sentence is thus left unfinished. It could be completed from Deut. 28:1.

IV. A DEPUTATION FROM BETHEL (7:1–8:23)
A. THE INQUIRY (7:1-3)

The people of Bethel send a deputation to Jerusalem, first **to entreat the favor of the LORD** by the bringing of offerings to the temple, and second to inquire whether they

---

world can manifest any permanent change for the better. Paul recognized the fundamental nature of this battle of the soul when he wrote to the church at Ephesus: "We are not contending against flesh and blood, but against the principalities, against the powers, against the world rulers of this present darkness, against the spiritual hosts of wickedness in the heavenly places" (Eph. 6:12). Anyone who overlooks the significant nature and necessity of this inner victory is no realist.

John Mason Brown concluded his play-by-play account of all that went into the prodigious

effort to establish the Normandy beachheads in 1944 with this wise observation concerning the imperative nature of the inner battle that must take place if such sacrifices are to pay dividends in terms of lasting peace: "If only men could realize that the maintenance of a proud peace requires more vigilance than the prosecution of a just war. Yes, and equal courage. And greater characters and character." [7]

7:1-14. When Ye Fast.—The prophet utters an enlightening word on the use and abuse of

[7] *Many a Watchful Night* (New York: Whittlesey House, 1944), p. 218.

2 When they had sent unto the house of God Sherezer and Regem-melech, and their men, to pray before the LORD,

3 *And* to speak unto the priests which *were* in the house of the LORD of hosts, and to the prophets, saying, Should I weep in the fifth month, separating myself, as I have done these so many years?

is Chislev. 2 Now the people of Bethel had sent Share'zer and Reg'em-mel'ech and their men, to entreat the favor of the LORD, 3 and to ask the priests of the house of the LORD of hosts and the prophets, "Should I mourn and fast in the fifth month, as I

should continue to observe the fast of the fifth month, as they had observed it during the period of the Exile. Zechariah's reply to their inquiry is to declare that their fasting and mourning have had little spiritual value, and that what Yahweh requires primarily is not the keeping of fasts, but the observance of those moral demands which he had made of their ancestors, who, however, to their cost, had paid no heed to them.

7:1. The fourth year is 518 B.C. The date in this verse should be understood as the date also of ch. 8. **Chislev** corresponded to our November-December. The name of the month is probably a later addition (cf. 1:7; Hag. 1:1).

2. The Hebrew text of the first half of this verse is in a bad state of preservation. Of the many translations which have been offered, perhaps the most satisfactory reads: "Now Bethel sent [El]sharezer, the chief officer of the king, and his men . . . ." This translation requires the insertion of a name of a god before **Sharezer** so as to form a proper name comparable in form with the Babylonian name Nergal-sharezer—"may Nergal protect the king" (Jer. 39:3). The name of the god may have been El or Bel (cf. Dan. 5:1) or Bethel, the latter being the name of an ancient Canaanite deity (cf. Gen. 31:13, and names such as Bethelnathan and Bethelakab, which are found in the fifth-century Aramaic papyri from Elephantine in Egypt). Any one of these names could easily have fallen out after the place name Bethel. It is further necessary to read רב מג המלך (with support from the Peshitta) in place of the M.T. ורגם מלך (and **Regem-melech**), which is a corruption of it. The proposed reading *rabh māgh* means "the chief officer of the king," and is perhaps identical with the Assyrian *rab mugi*, a title of a high officer. This title is found in Jer. 39:3, 13, where it is applied to Nergal-sharezer. Here it is probably a gloss, due to someone who, missing the mention of a title in the case of (El)sharezer, introduced here the one he found applied to Nergal-sharezer in Jer. 39.

3. Both the **priests** and the **prophets** were regarded by the deputation from Bethel as revealers of the divine will on a question of ritual. In Hag. 2:11 only the priests were consulted. **Should I weep:** The northern community is here personified. **Separating myself:** In a ceremonial sense, equivalent to "consecrating myself" (by fasting). In the **fifth month** the temple was burned out by the Babylonians (II Kings 25:8-9). **So many years** refers to the period since 586 (cf. vs. 5).

ceremonial practices in the institution of religion. When the work of rebuilding the temple had gone forward for several years and some of the services had been resumed, there came a deputation from **Bethel,** twelve miles to the north of Jerusalem, in the land of the Samaritans. They claimed to have come **to entreat the favor of the LORD** and to inquire as to the advisability of continuing the great fasts instituted in the days of the Exile.

One wonders if they were entirely sincere in their expressed purpose, for Bethel was the seat of a rival shrine, established by the Northern Kingdom; and the people of Bethel not

infrequently endeavored to cast the shadow of doubt on the claims of Jerusalem to be the one shrine for the correct worship of the God of the Hebrews.

At any rate, Zechariah made the question they raised an opportunity to point out in no uncertain terms that the ceremonial system was no adequate substitute for obedience to the ethical demands of the God of their fathers. He speaks in God's name, as a prophet, not as a priest, to these visitors from the north (vss. 5-6).

It is a relevant question in any age how much of the ceremony practiced in the name of God

4 ¶ Then came the word of the Lord of hosts unto me, saying,

5 Speak unto all the people of the land, and to the priests, saying, When ye fasted and mourned in the fifth and seventh *month,* even those seventy years, did ye at all fast unto me, *even* to me?

6 And when ye did eat, and when ye did drink, did not ye eat *for yourselves,* and drink *for yourselves?*

7 *Should* ye not *hear* the words which the Lord hath cried by the former prophets, when Jerusalem was inhabited and in pros-

have done for so many years?" 4 Then the word of the Lord of hosts came to me; 5 "Say to all the people of the land and the priests, When you fasted and mourned in the fifth month and in the seventh, for these seventy years, was it for me that you fasted? 6 And when you eat and when you drink, do you not eat for yourselves and drink for yourselves? 7 When Jerusalem was inhabited and in prosperity, with her cities round about her, and the South and the lowland

---

What the object of the deputation was in inquiring whether the people of Bethel should continue to observe the fast of the fifth month is obscure. Perhaps the Bethelites may have argued that since the rebuilding of the temple was now so far advanced, there was little point in their continuing the fast in commemoration of its destruction by the Babylonians. Yet it would be well, before deciding to discontinue the fast, to seek an official ruling from the authorities in Jerusalem. So the deputation was sent. It returned to Bethel rebuffed. Zechariah tells them in reply to their inquiry that their fasts have no value, and that they should rather live the good life which Yahweh had demanded of men through the earlier prophets. Zechariah here follows in the footsteps of Haggai, exhibiting the same unfriendly attitude to the northern—Samaritan—population which his predecessor had adopted on another occasion (see Exeg. on Hag. 2:10-14).

B. Zechariah's Reply (7:4–8:23)

4-14. These verses contain the first part of Zechariah's reply to the inquiry put to him by the deputation from Bethel. Yahweh demands not fasts, but morality.

5. In the **seventh month** Gedaliah, whom the Babylonians had made governor of Judah, was murdered (II Kings 25:25; Jer. 41:1-2).

6. The kind of fast which is acceptable to Yahweh finds expression in Isa. 58:6-10.

7. Former prophets: Cf. 1:4. In the reference to the populous and prosperous south of the pre-exilic times is an implied comparison with the still sparse population and dreary mode of life in Zechariah's own day (cf. 8:10).

---

is in actuality performed for human satisfaction. That does not mean that ceremonials do not have their value, but we sometimes get confused and suppose that God requires them, when all the time they may be of man's creation, for the purpose of meeting man's need.

Zechariah bluntly states that as his people eat and drink to satisfy their own needs, so they created the great fasts for the meeting of their own needs. The fasts of the Exile were instituted as a means of mourning for the destruction of Jerusalem and the temple, for the carrying off of the people from their homeland, and for the failures of their fathers which had caused all these calamities to descend upon them. But a fast is a means to an end, and sometimes the end is not so pure. Jesus said, "When you fast, do not look dismal, like the hypocrites, for they disfigure their faces that their fasting may be seen by men. Truly, I say to you, they

have their reward. But when you fast, anoint your head and wash your face, that your fasting may not be seen by men but by your Father who is in secret; and your Father who sees in secret will reward you." (Matt. 6:16-18.)

A fast is a means to an end, and if the end is mediocre, as in the case of the hypocrite, it has no place in religion. One fears sometimes that there exists in churches, especially in the Lenten season, a temptation to indulge in a sort of professional mourning which is productive of spiritual pride. This obviously defeats the very end for which religion strives. Religion and all religious practices exist for the sole purpose of establishing a closer, more meaningful relationship between people and God. All means used must be focused on that supreme end and must bring us closer to that end; else they are futile, nay more, inimical, to the best interests of religious faith.

perity, and the cities thereof round about her, when *men* inhabited the south and the plain?

8 ¶ And the word of the LORD came unto Zechariah, saying,

9 Thus speaketh the LORD of hosts, saying, Execute true judgment, and show mercy and compassions every man to his brother:

10 And oppress not the widow, nor the fatherless, the stranger, nor the poor; and let none of you imagine evil against his brother in your heart.

11 But they refused to hearken, and pulled away the shoulder, and stopped their ears, that they should not hear.

12 Yea, they made their hearts *as* an adamant stone, lest they should hear the law, and the words which the LORD of hosts hath sent in his Spirit by the former prophets: therefore came a great wrath from the LORD of hosts.

13 Therefore it is come to pass, *that* as he cried, and they would not hear; so they cried, and I would not hear, saith the LORD of hosts:

14 But I scattered them with a whirlwind among all the nations whom they knew not. Thus the land was desolate after them, that no man passed through nor returned: for they laid the pleasant land desolate.

were inhabited, were not these the words which the LORD proclaimed by the former prophets?"

8 And the word of the LORD came to Zechari'ah, saying, 9 "Thus says the LORD of hosts, Render true judgments, show kindness and mercy each to his brother, 10 do not oppress the widow, the fatherless, the sojourner, or the poor; and let none of you devise evil against his brother in your heart." 11 But they refused to hearken, and turned a stubborn shoulder, and stopped their ears that they might not hear. 12 They made their hearts like adamant lest they should hear the law and the words which the LORD of hosts had sent by his Spirit through the former prophets. Therefore great wrath came from the LORD of hosts. 13 As I called, and they would not hear, so they called, and I would not hear," says the LORD of hosts, 14 "and I scattered them with a whirlwind among all the nations which they had not known. Thus the land they left was desolate, so that no one went to and fro, and the pleasant land was made desolate."

8. This verse breaks the connection between vs. 7 and vs. 9 and should be deleted.

9. **True judgment:** There is to be no favoritism in the giving of decisions in the law courts (cf. 8:16). Many parallels to the moral teaching here and in vs. 10 are to be found in the utterances of the pre-exilic prophets (e.g., Amos 5:14-15; Hos. 6:6; Isa. 1:17; 10:2).

11. The pre-exilic prophets themselves testify that this was the reception which was given to their words (cf. Hos. 4:16; Isa. 6:10; Jer. 5:23).

12. **The law:** Cf. Hag. 2:11.

14. **Was desolate after them:** The implied subject is **the nations,** not the ancestors of the people.

This discussion impinges on the whole question of the sacramental view of life, far too large a question to discuss adequately here. The supreme purpose of regarding life or any part of the life experience as a sacrament is to instill reverence and, through reverence, insight into the deep realities that lie hidden within those things which come within the reach of the five senses. A sacrament is a means by which to apprehend the presence and purpose of God. It is never an end in itself.

Zechariah soundly observes that in former times, before the Exile, the words of the Lord to their forefathers were couched in ethical, not ceremonial, terms. They commanded justice, kindness, and the care of the helpless and the poor. It was in consequence of the disobedience of the people to these commands that grievous misfortune befell them, resulting in the annual periods of mourning and fasting. Now that the temple was being restored and the people were free to come back, let them cease to observe the fasts and observe rather the ethical commandments of the Lord.

8 Again the word of the LORD of hosts came *to me,* saying,

2 Thus saith the LORD of hosts; I was jealous for Zion with great jealousy, and I was jealous for her with great fury.

3 Thus saith the LORD; I am returned unto Zion, and will dwell in the midst of Jerusalem: and Jerusalem shall be called A city of truth; and the mountain of the LORD of hosts, The holy mountain.

4 Thus saith the LORD of hosts; There shall yet old men and old women dwell in the streets of Jerusalem, and every man with his staff in his hand for very age.

5 And the streets of the city shall be full of boys and girls playing in the streets thereof.

6 Thus saith the LORD of hosts; If it be marvelous in the eyes of the remnant of this people in these days, should it also be marvelous in mine eyes? saith the LORD of hosts.

8 And the word of the LORD of hosts came to me, saying, **2** "Thus says the LORD of hosts: I am jealous for Zion with great jealousy, and I am jealous for her with great wrath. **3** Thus says the LORD: I will return to Zion, and will dwell in the midst of Jerusalem, and Jerusalem shall be called the faithful city, and the mountain of the LORD of hosts, the holy mountain. **4** Thus says the LORD of hosts: Old men and old women shall again sit in the streets of Jerusalem, each with staff in hand for very age. **5** And the streets of the city shall be full of boys and girls playing in its streets. **6** Thus says the LORD of hosts: If it is marvelous in the sight of the remnant of this people in these days, should it also be marvelous in my sight, says the LORD of

8:1-17. The second part of Zechariah's reply consists of seven sayings, all introduced by "Thus says the LORD of hosts," except in the case of the second saying in vs. 3, where the words **of hosts** are not found. The sayings are concerned with the promise of future happiness to Jerusalem and Judah.

2. The first saying. Cf. 1:14.

3. The second saying. Cf. 1:16; 2:10. The terms which Zechariah uses to describe the new Jerusalem re-echo the language of Isaiah (e.g., 1:21; 2:3; 11:9).

4-5. The third saying. **For very age:** Cf. Isa. 65:20. Old age was regarded in O.T. times as a supreme blessing (cf. Exod. 20:12; Prov. 3:2; *et al.*) because, so long as there was no firm belief in an afterlife which was within the sphere of Yahweh's activity, communion with Yahweh was possible only on this earth. The O.T. blessing of long life was thus no mere gift of longevity, but an extended opportunity for the exercise of the spiritual life.

6. The fourth saying. This verse reflects further the doubts which were current among a certain section of the community concerning Zerubbabel's ability to complete

8:1-19. *The Picture of a Restored Society.*— Here the prophet gives the deputation from Bethel a vivid portrayal of what Jerusalem will be like when city and temple are restored and the exiles have returned. It shall come to pass that, if the ethical commands are observed, God's favor will be manifest in their midst, and **seasons of joy and gladness, and cheerful feasts** (vs. 19) will be the common lot.

Two details in this picture are most intriguing. The prophet establishes (vss. 4-6) a novel criterion for an ideal city which brings us up short. It is one in which old people and children are obviously happy and contented. Too often men are apt to measure a city's significance by its business, professions, and industry, its buildings, its wealth, its art and culture.

Zechariah suggests that we measure the significance of our cities by their effect upon two groups easily overlooked—the old and the young.

There was a practical reason for this observation in his thought of Jerusalem after the Exile. The Babylonians had all but swept the city clean of people when they conquered it seventy years before. The first to return would necessarily come from that age group which could stand the strain of primitive conditions devoid of all comforts and would be capable of long hours of hard manual labor. This meant that the old and the very young would be among the last to return, when the work of reconstruction had progressed to the point where they could enjoy some safety and comfort.

7 Thus saith the LORD of hosts; Behold, I will save my people from the east country, and from the west country;

8 And I will bring them, and they shall dwell in the midst of Jerusalem: and they shall be my people, and I will be their God, in truth and in righteousness.

9 ¶ Thus saith the LORD of hosts; Let your hands be strong, ye that hear in these days these words by the mouth of the prophets, which *were* in the day *that* the foundation of the house of the LORD of hosts was laid, that the temple might be built.

10 For before these days there was no hire for man, nor any hire for beast; neither *was there any* peace to him that went out or came in because of the affliction: for I set all men every one against his neighbor.

11 But now I *will* not *be* unto the residue of this people as in the former days, saith the LORD of hosts.

12 For the seed *shall be* prosperous; the vine shall give her fruit, and the ground shall give her increase, and the heavens shall give their dew; and I will cause the remnant of this people to possess all these *things.*

hosts? 7 Thus says the LORD of hosts: Behold, I will save my people from the east country and from the west country; 8 and I will bring them to dwell in the midst of Jerusalem; and they shall be my people and I will be their God, in faithfulness and in righteousness."

9 Thus says the LORD of hosts: "Let your hands be strong, you who in these days have been hearing these words from the mouth of the prophets, since the day that the foundation of the house of the LORD of hosts was laid, that the temple might be built. 10 For before those days there was no wage for man or any wage for beast, neither was there any safety from the foe for him who went out or came in; for I set every man against his fellow. 11 But now I will not deal with the remnant of this people as in the former days, says the LORD of hosts. 12 For there shall be a sowing of peace and prosperity; the vine shall yield its fruit, and the ground shall give its increase, and the heavens shall give their dew; and I will cause the remnant of this people to possess

---

the rebuilding of the temple, and concerning the realization of the happy times that had been promised (cf. 4:10; Hag. 2:3). **The remnant:** Cf. Hag. 1:12.

7-8. The fifth saying. By the **east country** is meant Babylon, which in 2:6 (cf. 6:8) is located in the north. By the **west country** is meant probably Egypt (cf. Jer. 43:1-7). For the general thought cf. Isa. 43:5-6; Jer. 30:10. In vs. 8b Zechariah reiterates an ancient formula (cf. Hos. 2:23; Jer. 11:4; *et al.*).

9-13. The sixth saying. Cf. Hag. 1:6-11; 2:15-19. **The foe:** The end of the verse shows that it was not only trouble from hostile neighbors that the Jewish community had to fear (cf. Neh. 4:7-8), but also civil strife among its own members. **The seed shall be prosperous:** Cf. Hag. 2:19. **House of Israel** is probably an addition (cf. 1:12, 19).

Nevertheless the prophet establishes the welfare and contentment of old people and children as the mark of a city functioning as a city is meant to function. There is something excitingly contemporaneous in this observation of the ancient prophet. In the hurry and bustle of city life the very old and the very young, who cannot look out for themselves and who serve no productive social or economic function, are too apt to be considered a nuisance, to be brushed out of the way. This is particularly true of those who by dint of age have been "shelved" from those pursuits which make life creative in our urban communities.

It is to be assumed that the church would not share this feeling but would reverence the

value of all personalities regardless of age. Regretfully it must be admitted that such an assumption cannot always be made. Not all churches gauge their programs to meet the needs and make use of the particular talents of older people. The increasing size of the group of older people in modern communities must rectify this stupid error, sooner rather than later, one would hope. Not because the group is growing, not because the members are old, but because they are people, unique personalities, children of God, it is the privilege of the church to serve them and, more important still, to make use of the service which they can render.

More attention in recent years has been given to the needs of children in our cities. Yet even

13 And it shall come to pass, *that* as ye were a curse among the heathen, O house of Judah, and house of Israel; so will I save you, and ye shall be a blessing: fear not, *but* let your hands be strong.

14 For thus saith the LORD of hosts; As I thought to punish you, when your fathers provoked me to wrath, saith the LORD of hosts, and I repented not:

15 So again have I thought in these days to do well unto Jerusalem and to the house of Judah: fear ye not.

16 ¶ These *are* the things that ye shall do; Speak ye every man the truth to his neighbor; execute the judgment of truth and peace in your gates:

17 And let none of you imagine evil in your hearts against his neighbor; and love no false oath: for all these *are things* that I hate, saith the LORD.

18 ¶ And the word of the LORD of hosts came unto me, saying,

19 Thus saith the LORD of hosts; The fast of the fourth *month,* and the fast of the fifth, and the fast of the seventh, and the fast of the tenth, shall be to the house of Judah joy and gladness, and cheerful feasts; therefore love the truth and peace.

all these things. 13 And as you have been a byword of cursing among the nations, O house of Judah and house of Israel, so will I save you and you shall be a blessing. Fear not, but let your hands be strong."

14 For thus says the LORD of hosts: "As I purposed to do evil to you, when your fathers provoked me to wrath, and I did not relent, says the LORD of hosts, 15 so again have I purposed in these days to do good to Jerusalem and to the house of Judah; fear not. 16 These are the things that you shall do: Speak the truth to one another, render in your gates judgments that are true and make for peace, 17 do not devise evil in your hearts against one another, and love no false oath, for all these things I hate, says the LORD."

18 And the word of the LORD of hosts came to me, saying, 19 "Thus says the LORD of hosts: The fast of the fourth month, and the fast of the fifth, and the fast of the seventh, and the fast of the tenth, shall be to the house of Judah seasons of joy and gladness, and cheerful feasts; therefore love truth and peace.

14-17. The seventh saying. In the happy days to be, the moral demands of Yahweh are not to be neglected as they have been in the past. **Jerusalem . . . Judah:** Zechariah's emphasis on the south appears to exclude the north from the sphere of Yahweh's benevolent acts (cf. 1:12). **Judgments that are true:** Cf. 7:9. **Judgments that . . . make for peace** are judicial decisions which lead to the reconciliation of the contending parties. **False oath:** Cf. 5:4.

18-23. The third part of Zechariah's reply consists of three sayings introduced by "Thus says the LORD of hosts," which declare that fast days will become for Judah seasons of joy, and that the heathen nations will join with the Jews in seeking Yahweh, and so share in the blessings which they are to enjoy.

19. The first saying. Neither the **fourth month** nor the **tenth** is mentioned in 7:3, 5. It was in the former that the Babylonians entered Jerusalem (II Kings 25:3-4; Jer. 39:2); in the latter they began the siege of Jerusalem (II Kings 25:1). **House of Judah:** Cf. vs. 15.

here the church in too many city communities is organized around adults, with the interests, needs, and the very great potential contributions of children lost to view. The prophet's ideal of a city **full of boys and girls playing in its streets** seems appalling to us. That is the only way perhaps in which our present cities bear any resemblance to the prophet's vision of a city "wherein dwelleth righteousness." To be sure, the Jerusalem of his day or even of his dreams anticipated no traffic problem, streets

crowded with cars and trucks, a menace to old and young alike, such as we experience. But can we not see what he is driving at? He has a very sound point. What makes the streets of our cities so much of a menace to the young is the indifference and neglect of the citizenry to their needs and welfare. If we were looking for the presence of God as the chief end of life we would be made aware, more aware by far than we now are, of his presence in "even the least of these." Placing that high value on them, we

20 Thus saith the Lord of hosts; *It shall yet come to pass,* that there shall come people, and the inhabitants of many cities:

21 And the inhabitants of one *city* shall go to another, saying, Let us go speedily to pray before the Lord, and to seek the Lord of hosts: I will go also.

22 Yea, many people and strong nations shall come to seek the Lord of hosts in Jerusalem, and to pray before the Lord.

23 Thus saith the Lord of hosts; In those days *it shall come to pass,* that ten men shall take hold out of all languages of the nations, even shall take hold of the skirt of him that is a Jew, saying, We will go with you: for we have heard *that* God *is* with you.

20 "Thus says the Lord of hosts: Peoples shall yet come, even the inhabitants of many cities; 21 the inhabitants of one city shall go to another, saying, 'Let us go at once to entreat the favor of the Lord, and to seek the Lord of hosts; I am going.' 22 Many peoples and strong nations shall come to seek the Lord of hosts in Jerusalem, and to entreat the favor of the Lord. 23 Thus says the Lord of hosts: In those days ten men from the nations of every tongue shall take hold of the robe of a Jew, saying, 'Let us go with you, for we have heard that God is with you.' "

20-22. The second saying. Cf. Isa. 2:2-4=Mic. 4:1-3. **At once:** Better, "most certainly," "by all means." **I will go also:** The Hebrew is much stronger, "Let me go; yes, me too." These words are probably not part of the speech, but are interjected by an enthusiastic member of the prophet's audience.

23. The third saying. **A Jew:** Cf. vs. 15. **God is with you:** An echo of the Immanuel ("With us is God") prophecy of Isa. 7:14 (cf. 45:14) .

---

would want to serve them and be served by them. We would not deal with them as a problem or a nuisance, but as an opportunity to be developed for the enrichment of all of us.

20-23. *Me Too.*—The final verses picture the inhabitants of many cities converging on Jerusalem, **to entreat the favor of the Lord, and to seek the Lord of hosts.** All want to share in the ecstatic joy of the messianic age. **In those days ten men from the nations of every tongue shall take hold of the robe of a Jew, saying, "Let us go with you, for we have heard that God is with you."**

So ends the prophecy on the threshold of the vision of Immanuel, "God with us." Considering that Zechariah lived five centuries before the time of Christ, none can deny that his vision was far reaching. The strange mingling of the universal with the national at the close of so great a vision will perplex some. To others it will seem but natural. "Every man," wrote Schopenhauer, "takes the limits of his own field of vision for the limits of the world." [8] And beyond that, no vision of life is sufficient to engage a man's heart and mind and soul unless he sees in it what is universally true and universally applicable.

But what shall we say to the fact that Zechariah's prophecy was not fulfilled then, nor ever has been completely fulfilled? Does that cast the

shadow of doubt over its validity? Or does it point to a conviction of overwhelming dimensions, discerned by the author of the Epistle to the Hebrews and shared in by all the succeeding generations? Concerning the great men of faith he wrote: "These all, having received a good report through faith, received not the promise: God having provided some better thing for us, that they without us should not be made perfect" (Heb. 11:39-40) .

We all have a part to play in the fulfillment of the great prophecies of the past, even as they of the past must play as large a part in the fulfillment of our hopes for the future. Said President Lowell of Harvard in a sermon at the university: "We are single links in a long chain of which we cannot see the end. On the monument to the Wesley brothers in Westminster Abbey are inscribed Wesley's own words, 'God buries his workmen, but carries on his work.' " [9]

"Let your hands be strong, you who in these days have been hearing these words from the mouth of the prophets" (vs. 9) .

So, let him wait God's instant men call years;
Meantime hold hard by truth and his great soul,
Do out the duty! Through such souls alone
God stooping shows sufficient of his light
For us i' the dark to rise by. [1]

[8] *Studies in Pessimism,* tr. Thomas Bailey Saunders (New York: The Macmillan Co., 1908), p. 69.

[9] H. A. Yeomans, *Abbott Lawrence Lowell* (Cambridge: Harvard University Press, 1948), p. 520.

[1] Browning, *The Ring and the Book,* "Pompilia," concluding lines.

INTRODUCTION, CHS. 9-14

The latest prophecies in the Old Testament are all anonymous. The natural conservatism which is always one side of conventional religious thought eventually led to the belief that the only true prophets were the old prophets. Consequently a writer of the late postexilic age who desired to get a hearing for his message either had to attach the name of some ancient worthy to his oracle or to write anonymously. To have signed his own name would have been to guarantee that he would have no audience. The low estate to which public oral prophecy had fallen is painfully clear from the chapters which lie before us (see 13:3-5). The Book of the Twelve Prophets has three collections of such anonymous prophecies as its concluding appendix (Zech. 9-11; 12-14; Mal. 1-4). These are clearly marked off from each other and from the preceding material by separate titles, each of which begins with the elsewhere unparalleled expression, "The burden of the word of the LORD." In order to make up the sacred number twelve for the books of the minor prophets, the third of these collections eventually became the book of Malachi. The other two collections (Zech. 9-11; 12-14) were simply treated as a part of the preceding book of Zechariah, although every test, linguistic, historical, and ideological, shows that they have no real connection with it.

Second Zechariah, as chs. 9-11 are often called—the name Third Zechariah being sometimes given to chs. 12-14—contains some of the most obscure and difficult material in the entire corpus of Old Testament literature. There is no general agreement on such basic questions as the date, authorship, and occasion of the prophecies, and consequently no common ground for the interpretation of their meaning. To these difficulties must be added the offensiveness of certain passages to the religious sensibilities of Christian readers: for example, the savage inhumanity of 9:15 and 14:12; the narrow nationalism of 14:14-19; the legalism of 9:7; and the purely physical conception of holiness in 14:20-21. Over against such difficulties, however, must be set the fact that these chapters had an extraordinary significance for the early

Christian community and are frequently quoted by New Testament writers, especially in connection with the narrative of the passion (e.g., Matt. 21:5; John 12:15; Matt. 26:15; 27:9; John 19:37; Rev. 1:7; Matt. 26:31; Mark 14:27). Some scholars believe that the influence of this material upon the formation of the gospel tradition was even more pervasive than a mere list of quotations would indicate. This fact alone would justify a careful study of this extremely enigmatic part of the Old Testament. It may also be said, by way of anticipation, that careful study will remove most of the moral difficulties and will reveal a depth of spiritual perceptiveness which is not apparent to the merely casual reader.

I. Authorship

Because attached to the book of the sixth-century prophet Zechariah, these chapters were for a long time regarded as a part of his work and interpreted in that light. The discovery that they were not of his authorship came about in the following fashion: Critics attempted to vindicate the credibility of Matt. 27:9, where Zech. 11:12-13 is quoted verbatim, but attributed to Jeremiah. Joseph Mede in the mid-seventeeth century asserted that the apparent misquotation was actually due to the influence of the Holy Spirit, who wished to show who the true author was. Mede went on to say that many things in these chapters applied far better to the time of Jeremiah than to that of Zechariah. Though ignored for several decades, the opinion of Mede eventually gained credence and down nearly to the end of the nineteenth century Zech. 9-14 was commonly regarded by critical scholars as a collection of pre-exilic prophecies attached by accident to the post-exilic book of Zechariah. Because of the political situation which seemed to be envisaged— the prominence of Egypt and Assyria and the frequent mention of the Northern Kingdom (Ephraim) as still existing—the general tendency was to date them in the latter half of the eighth century. However, J. G. Eichhorn in his epoch-making *Introduction to the Old Testament* (1824), suggested that 9:1-8 might refer to the conquests of Alexander the Great, and that parts of the rest of the collection might also be later than Zechariah. This suggestion of a postexilic date, though reasonable, was not generally accepted until after 1881, when Bernard Stade published an article [1] in which he demonstrated conclusively, by a study of the literary relationships and historical allusions, that the material could not be earlier than Ezekiel. With a few exceptions [2] modern critical scholarship is generally agreed that Zech. 9–14 is not by the author of chs. 1–8 and is considerably later in date.

Within this broad area of agreement there is, however, a great variety of opinion as to the particular period within the postexilic age to which it should be referred. There is also no general agreement as to whether it is by one author, by two, or by several. Stade attempted to prove the literary unity of the whole section, but the evidence he adduced for this has not proved as convincing as that for a postexilic date. In the nature of things it is extremely difficult to prove the literary unity or disunity of a body of writing as small as this and one which contains oracles of such varied type. It is only fair to the general reader to state that any decision with regard either to unity of authorship or date within the broad limits of the postexilic age is based in large measure upon subjective considerations. However, the general tendency of present-day scholarship is to regard Zech. 9–14 as a collection of oracles by two or more different writers and to connect these oracles with different situations in the life of the nation during the late Persian or Greek periods.

There are five periods which, it has been suggested, offer a suitable background for some of the oracles:

1. The period of Alexander the Great (i.e., the period immediately following the Battle of the Issus in 333 B.C.).

2. The wars of the Diadochi (the successors of Alexander who fought for control of his empire after his death) 323–ca. 278 B.C.

3. The period from 311 to 198 B.C., when Palestine was a province of the Ptolemaic Egyptian Empire.

4. The period of the invasion of Palestine by Antiochus III (218-217 B.C.) and its conquest by the same ruler in 198 B.C.

5. The age of the Maccabean Wars (beginning in 165 B.C.).

Although the Maccabean date has been widely accepted and is supported by several

important and justly popular works on the Old Testament—such as Julius A. Bewer, *The Literature of the Old Testament in Its Historical Development* [3] and W. O. E. Oesterley and T. H. Robinson, *A History of Israel* [4]—yet it must almost certainly be ruled out. Ben Sirach, author of the apocryphal book of Ecclesiasticus, writing about 190 B.C., testifies to the existence in his day of the Book of the Twelve (Ecclus. 49:10). It is hardly possible that any extensive additions could have been made to this collection after the book had attained what was evidently canonical status, although minor alterations and glosses of not more than a verse may well have been added. It would also seem unlikely that any considerable amount of the material is as late as the reign of Antiochus III. Unfortunately the preceding period (from 333 to 218 B.C.) is almost a complete blank in Jewish history, and, while the oracles with which we are dealing almost certainly fall within this age, the attempt to connect them with particular events or situations must be regarded as conjectural and tentative.

In this Commentary the following has been adopted as the most convincing interpretation of the evidence.

(a) An oracle (9:1-12) composed during the siege of Tyre by Alexander the Great in 332 B.C. As C. C. Torrey has pointed out, it would be strange if so momentous an event as Alexander's conquest of the Oriental world had not left some impression upon the contemporary literature of the Old Testament. This passage seems to be an eyewitness account of his southward march through Syria following the Battle of the Issus. Certain apparent anachronisms in the text are due to the kind of conscious archaizing which is frequently found in late postexilic prophecy. The prophet sees in the triumphant advance of the Greek armies the beginnings of the messianic age.

(b) An appendix (9:13-17) to the preceding oracle written sometime later, perhaps during the wars of the Diadochi or the period of Ptolemaic rule, when it became evident that the Greeks would be as ruthless and oppressive as their predecessors and that another great act of God on behalf of his people would be necessary.

(c) A brief oracle (10:1-2) coming from a time when the country was suffering a drought. In the present arrangement of the book it is connected with the following oracle because both contain the key word "shepherd."

(d) An oracle (10:3-12) from the period of Ptolemaic domination in Palestine prophesying the overthrow of foreign rule by the vic-

---

[1] "Deuterozacharja," *Zeitschrift für die alttestamentliche Wissenschaft*, I (1881), 1-96.

[2] Most notable are E. G. Kraeling and Friedrich Horst, both of whom regard some of the material as pre-exilic.

[3] Rev. ed.; New York: Columbia University Press, 1933.

[4] Oxford: Clarendon Press, 1932.

torious people of God and the return of the Diaspora.

(e) From the same period, a call (11:1-3) to lament over the fall of the world rulers, who are represented under the familiar image of great trees in a forest.

(f) An allegory (11:4-14) from the Ptolemaic period—the most enigmatic part of the book—which represents the distress of the people under foreign rule as being the result of their own faithlessness.

(g) An appendix (11:15-17) containing a threat against some particularly vicious governor.

(h) A brief apocalypse (12:1–13:6) describing the last great attempt of heathen powers to destroy the people of God and how it is to be frustrated by the intervention of God himself.

(j) A brief oracle (13:7-9) which describes the purification of the nation by a period of anarchy and suffering, a familiar apocalyptic theme.

(k) A parallel account (14:1-20) of the apocalyptic siege of Jerusalem described in 12:1–13:6, but in very different terms.

It seems doubtful that one author could have produced such a diversity of material. Linguistic tests are indecisive, since the units are so brief, but it may be said with confidence that ch. 14 cannot be from the same hand as 12:1–13:6. It also seems improbable that the apocalypse of ch. 12 is from the same source as the more conventional prophetic oracles in chs. 9–11. Whether the oracles in chs. 9–11 are all from the same hand cannot be determined with any certainty, but diversity of authorship is at least as probable as unity. Zech. 9–14 is then the work of at least three different writers, possibly more.

II. Significance

These chapters not only give us a valuable glimpse into the mind of the Jewish community in Palestine during the Greek period, but they also have permanent religious value because of their strong emphasis upon the ultimate establishment of God's kingdom and its extension to all the peoples of the earth. Not only are the Philistines to be incorporated as equals into the Jewish community (9:7) but all nations will find their true spiritual home in the Holy City (14:16). The beauty of this conception is unfortunately partly obscured by the conventional apocalyptic language in which it is contained, especially in chs. 12–14,

and by the concern with ceremonial and legalistic ideas. Both apocalyptic and legalism are characteristic of Jewish religion in this period and demand upon the part of the modern reader an unusual effort at sympathy. It should be remembered that the language of apocalyptic is a borrowed and conventional language, which is not to be taken at its face value since it is partly derived from primitive mythological conceptions, and that legalism is an attempt to express in terms of visible and material symbols ideas which are ultimately of profound spiritual meaning. If we approach the writings before us with a genuine attempt at understanding them in the light of the situations out of which they arose, we shall find ourselves able not only to share in the travail of a great people at an important period in its history, but we shall also find here a faith which is permanently valid and which justifies the importance which these strange chapters assumed in the eyes of the early church.

III. Outline of Contents

IV. Selected Bibliography

CANNON, WILLIAM W. "Some Notes on Zechariah c. 11," *Archiv für Orientforschung*, IV (1927), 139-46.

HORST, FRIEDRICH. *Die zwölf kleinen Propheten Nahum bis Maleachi* ("Handbuch zum Alten Testament"). Tübingen: J. C. B. Mohr, 1938.

KRAELING, EMIL G. "The Historical Situation in Zech. 9:1-10," *American Journal of Semitic Languages and Literatures*, XLI (1924-25), 24-33.

KREMER, JOSEF. *Die Hirtenallegorie im Buche Zacharias* ("Alttestamentliche Abhandlungen"). Münster i.W.: Aschendorff, 1930.

MITCHELL, H. G., SMITH, J. M. P., and BEWER, JULIUS A. *A Critical and Exegetical Commentary on Haggai, Zechariah, Malachi, and Jonah* ("International Critical Commentary"). New York: Charles Scribner's Sons, 1912.

SMITH, GEORGE ADAM. *The Book of the Twelve Prophets*. Rev. ed. New York: Harper & Bros., 1928. Vol. II.

9 The burden of the word of the Lord
in the land of Hadrach, and Damascus

9 An Oracle

The word of the Lord is against the land
of Hadrach
and will rest upon Damascus.

I. Triumph of the Messianic King (9:1-12)

9:1. Great movements among the nations have always provided the chief occasions for prophecy. The great age of the Hebrew prophets began during the triumphant westward advance of the Assyrian armies in the mid-eighth century B.C. The second flowering of prophecy was closely connected with the spread of Babylonian supremacy and reached its climax in the writings of Second Isaiah, when the Babylonian Empire was being overthrown by the Persian. The present oracle was probably inspired by the fall of Persia before the advancing armies of Alexander the Great. Alexander had administered a decisive defeat to Darius, the Persian emperor, at the Battle of the Issus in southeastern Asia Minor in October, 333 B.C. Instead of immediately pursuing Darius toward the east, the conqueror moved south through Syria, with the aim of first seizing Egypt from the Persians. Within the year all Syria was in his hands and shortly afterward Egypt fell without a struggle. These are among the most important events in world history, and the little Jewish community in Jerusalem, located in the hills a few miles

On Zechariah 9-14.—The exposition of these chapters is no easy task for the minister who refuses to preach on abbreviated texts totally detached from the context. He is immediately faced with three primary problems: (*a*) Scholars do not agree on the division of the passage or on the dating of the divisions.[1] (*b*) They are likewise in lack of accord with respect to the number of authors whose work is included in these chapters.[2] (*c*) But these are only minor matters compared with the problem of what the twentieth-century teacher is to do with the whole matter of the apocalyptic interpretation of history, which intensifies the faith of the believer and yet misinterprets the outcome of history in terms of time and space. This second half of Zechariah is one which most expositors side-step, and such a ca' canny policy is not entirely blameworthy.

The following guiding principles may help in an attempt to understand apocalyptic as a philosophy of history: (*a*) There is a sharp distinction between the present wicked age and the future age which will be one of glory for the believer. (*b*) There is a foreshortening of the future in that the intervention of God is looked upon as immediate and catastrophic. (*c*) There is an overemphasis on the fantastic aspects of the supernatural. (*d*) There is utter assurance of the victory of God, though this triumph is only after conflict in which the faithful undergo suffering.[3]

Appreciating the difficulties and showing patience toward thought forms that may be strange to him, the Christian reader must not forget that verses from these chapters are quoted by N.T. writers; e.g., Zech. 9:9=Matt. 21:5 and John 12:15; Zech. 11:12=Matt. 26:15 and 27:9; Zech. 12:10=John 19:37 and Rev. 1:7; Zech. 13:7=Matt. 26:31 and Mark 14:27. These references are intimately connected with the last week of our Lord's life and suggest that, whatever disuse Zech. 9-14 has fallen into today, it had a vital meaning for N.T. interpreters of the life of Jesus.

9:1. *The Word of the Lord.*—Our message is God's *word*; but it is God's word as interpreted

[1] See Intro., pp. 1089-91.
[2] *Ibid.*

[3] For a good discussion of apocalyptic see R. H. Charles, *A Critical History of the Doctrine of a Future Life* (2nd ed.; London: A. & C. Black, 1913).

shall be the rest thereof: when the eyes of man, as of all the tribes of Israel, *shall be* toward the LORD.

2 And Hamath also shall border thereby; Tyrus, and Zidon, though it be very wise.

3 And Tyrus did build herself a stronghold, and heaped up silver as the dust, and fine gold as the mire of the streets.

For to the LORD belong the cities of Aram,[k]
even as all the tribes of Israel;
2 Hamath also, which borders thereon,
Tyre and Sidon, though they are very wise.
3 Tyre has built herself a rampart,
and heaped up silver like dust,
and gold like the dirt of the streets.

[k] Cn: Heb *the eye of Adam* (or *man*)

east of Alexander's line of march, saw in them the working of the mighty hand of God. The first words, **The burden of the word of the LORD,** are the superscription for the whole collection of prophecies in chs. 9–11. Original in this place, the same words were later copied in 12:1 and Mal. 1:1 to distinguish these as separate collections. The expression is found nowhere else in the Bible and is almost certainly the result of some kind of textual corruption. The reading of the RSV is possible, but the corruption is even deeper than this would indicate. The original reading of vs. 1a, following the title, was probably "The Lord is in the land of Hadrach, and in Damascus is his dwelling place." The confusion between the common noun for "man" (אדם) and **Aram** (ארם), the proper name for "Syria," is a familiar one, and the emendation of the RSV is undoubtedly correct. The emendation of **eye** (עין) to **cities of** (ערי), though generally accepted, is less convincing. "The eye of Syria" has an original ring and may well have been a popular name for Damascus. **Hadrach** is mentioned in Assyrian documents as a city of Syria, north of Damascus and Hamath. While the name does not occur in postexilic times, its appearance here may be an example of popular survival or of conscious archaism. **Damascus** is the greatest city of Syria.

2. Hamath: The modern Ḥamā, is another important Syrian city, north of Damascus. The phrase **shall border thereby** is probably corrupt, the word for **border** (*gābhal*) concealing the name of the Syrian coastal city of Gebal. **Tyre and Sidon** were the great seacoast cities of the Phoenicians. The siege of Tyre, Alexander's most brilliant military exploit, lasted seven months, ending successfully in July, 332 B.C. Ezek. 28:1-23 (which some believe to be another prophecy inspired by Alexander's siege) also makes a great point of the alleged "wisdom" of Tyre.

3. The position of Tyre on an island off the coast had proved impregnable before Alexander's time. Her wealth as the greatest commercial nation of the ancient world was proverbial. The word for **stronghold** (*māçôr*) is a pun upon the name **Tyre** (*çôr*).

by man. Therefore there is always room for both truth and error. There runs through the Bible a *Weltanschauung*, a view of the world, a philosophy of history, which is God's revelation of his will for man. Before one interprets any passage, one must know that. Therefore the expositor must be steeped in biblical theology. But as soon as that is recognized, it must also be acknowledged that man, in his fallibility or sin, may misinterpret that word; e.g., Nahum was right in believing that God intervened in history; he was wrong in limiting the judgment of God to Assyria alone.

1-4. The Disapproval of God.—This word may be a word of disapproval. God is universal; therefore he cannot overlook the iniquity of

Aram any more than he can ignore the sin of Israel. It is also not **wise** for **Tyre and Sidon** to be so very "clever" that they think wealth will give them protection. Great possessions tend to make a nation foolish as they may make a man a fool (cf. Luke 12:16-21). The reason for God's censure is not given—it may be enough for the writer that the old nationalistic foes of Syria and Phoenicia should be doomed—but the cause seems to be the materialism which dominated their everyday living. If so, it anticipates our Lord's "It is easier for a camel to go through the eye of a needle, than for a rich man to enter into the kingdom of God" (Mark 10:25). There is a change in emphasis from the corporate-individual sin of the O.T. to the individual-corporate sin of the N.T. It is wise to keep both

4 Behold, the Lord will cast her out, and he will smite her power in the sea; and she shall be devoured with fire.

5 Ashkelon shall see *it,* and fear; Gaza also *shall see it,* and be very sorrowful, and Ekron; for her expectation shall be ashamed; and the king shall perish from Gaza, and Ashkelon shall not be inhabited.

6 And a bastard shall dwell in Ashdod, and I will cut off the pride of the Philistines.

7 And I will take away his blood out of his mouth, and his abominations from between his teeth: but he that remaineth,

4 But lo, the Lord will strip her of her possessions
and hurl her wealth into the sea,
and she shall be devoured by fire.

5 Ash'kelon shall see it, and be afraid;
Gaza too, and shall writhe in anguish;
Ekron also, because its hopes are confounded.
The king shall perish from Gaza;
Ash'kelon shall be uninhabited;
6 a mongrel people shall dwell in Ashdod;
and I will make an end of the pride of Philistia.
7 I will take away its blood from its mouth,
and its abominations from between its teeth;

---

4. Although the Hebrew verb tenses are notoriously ambiguous, it seems most probable from this verse that the fall of Tyre, though imminent, had not yet occurred. The fact of the siege would be quickly known in Jerusalem, as commercial relations with Tyre were close in the postexilic world (Ezra 3:7; Neh. 13:16), and the prophecy was probably uttered while it was still taking place.

5-6. Ashkelon . . . Gaza . . . Ekron . . . Ashdod (plus Gath, which is not mentioned here) were the five cities of the Philistine confederation in the southern coastal plain of Palestine, traditional enemies of Israel. Gaza had no **king** at this period, being a subject city of the Persian Empire with a military governor, but the language is merely conventional. These cities were obviously next on Alexander's line of march. The phrase **a mongrel people** is a contemptuous name for the foreigners who would now rule the city and exploit its resources.

7. I will take away his blood . . . from between his teeth: The prophet does not look forward to the extermination of the Philistines, but to their conversion. The result of God's victory, achieved by the hand of Alexander, will be that the Philistines will henceforth observe the dietary laws, which forbade the eating of blood (Gen. 9:4) and of certain kinds of animals (Deut. 14:3-20; Lev. 11:2-23), and will become a **remnant**

---

in mind in a day when sin is both retail and wholesale in its practice.[4]

5-6. *On Failing to Learn from Others.*—What would happen to Tyre is for others to see and apply to themselves, specifically the cities of Philistia. Evidently their fear was not yet unto salvation, because the passage goes on to describe one city **in anguish,** another **confounded,** another without its **king** and a fourth **uninhabited.** It is difficult to learn from the experience of others—even in the twentieth century. The biblical writer does not mince words; he

[4] My former colleague Franklin W. Young has pointed out that vss. 1-4 are a good example of the Hebrew predilection for seeing the judgment of God wherever and whenever there was strife on earth. Moreover, it is a judgment that is always transcending the individual judgments of men, as later ages, reinterpreting the events, may be able to see the workings of God as those embroiled in the events often cannot, because of the emotional turmoil caused by their participation.

talks of a **mongrel people** in Ashdod. But it is hardly for Jerusalem to point the finger of scorn; Nehemiah (13:23-27) and Ezra (9:1–10:44) had both to deal with the fact of **a bastard** in Judah. They forgot what the author of Ruth remembered, that David, the great king (to look back), and the ancestor of the Messiah (to look forward), had Moabite blood in his veins (Ruth 4:13-22).

7. *The Mercy of God.*—God is universal, not only in disapproval but in mercy. His favor, like his wrath, may extend beyond Israel. Here is an echo of the late prophets, of Jonah and Ruth. Some of the Philistines will be **like a clan in Judah.** The author is either not as bigoted as we made him out to be in previous verses, or else he is, like Yahweh, "full of unexpected moments," a phrase reminiscent of James Bridie, the Scots playwright. This is the type of surprise of which the Bible is full,

even he, *shall be* for our God, and he shall be as a governor in Judah, and Ekron as a Jebusite.	it too shall be a remnant for our God; it shall be like a clan in Judah, and Ekron shall be like the Jeb'usites.
8 And I will encamp about mine house because of the army, because of him that passeth by, and because of him that returneth: and no oppressor shall pass through them any more: for now have I seen with mine eyes.	8 Then I will encamp at my house as a guard, so that none shall march to and fro; no oppressor shall again overrun them, for now I see with my own eyes.
9 ¶ Rejoice greatly, O daughter of Zion;	9 Rejoice greatly, O daughter of Zion! Shout aloud, O daughter of Jerusalem!

for God like the faithful remnant of Israel of which the book of Isaiah speaks (10:20-22). Just as the Jebusites, the original Canaanite inhabitants of Jerusalem (II Sam. 5:6), were assimilated into the Hebrew population (II Sam. 24:18), so the Philistines will become a part of the people of God under conditions of full equality. The RSV correctly emends to read *'eleph,* **clan,** instead of *'allûph,* "chieftain."

8. Though surrounding nations are overrun by the conqueror, God will protect his temple and his people. The RSV reading **as a guard** is a conjectural translation supported by the LXX and Syriac. The KJV represents what seems to be the meaning of the Hebrew text, which, though peculiar, is not impossible and fits the context more closely.

9. The climax of the oracle pictures the coming of the messianic king. The prophet sees the army of Alexander as only a tool in the hand of God. Riding invisibly with

but which continues to catch the reader off-guard, even to shock him. The two aspects of the universality of God here mentioned, condemnation and mercy, are subsumed in the N.T. conception of *agapē,* the love which tests everything by love and therefore punishes and/or blesses. Thus far the author would seem to anticipate the N.T. good news and to be in line with the world view enunciated by Jesus. But his human frailty interferes and narrows the universal mercy of God. Granted that some Philistines become Jews, they must become legalistic Jews. They must observe the dietary laws. Moffatt translates vs. 7:

> so I stop them from drinking blood,
> from eating food detestable.

But before a too quick protest, recall Acts 15 and Gal. 2:11-14. The difference in a man's outlook is not made by B.C. or A.D.; chronological lateness is no guarantee of superior religious insight. Wherein are we today legalistic, in a manner worthy of the Christ's condemnation? In our denominational requirements that hamper ecumenicity? In our insistence on our polity and observances? In our preference for tradition even where it conflicts with truth? But on the other hand, how far are we antinomian, in our sentimental good will toward all kinds and conditions of men? Maybe the author had a point in insisting on the acceptance of a symbolism which stood for "holiness unto God." Is our ecumenicity just a general carelessness? Is our ignoring of tradition a misunderstanding of history?

8. The House of God.—A priestly emphasis is found here, in that the religious importance of the temple for God is recognized. Before we use as a rebuttal the prophetic protest of a Jeremiah (7:1-15) or Christ's words to the woman of Samaria (John 4:19-24), it will be well for us to recall just where we shall be preaching a sermon on this verse. The setting aside of a special place for the worship of God is the dedication of a part of space to him, as the observance of the sabbath or the Lord's Day is the dedication of a portion of time. That may be theoretically unsound in that he is Lord of all space and time, but it is practically useful and symbolically wise. (We must be careful not to confuse the theoretical and the practical, or to shift ground unobtrusively from the one to the other in developing the thesis of an exposition.) It is not unnatural for a religious man to believe that God watches his **house**—in the twofold sense of protection and judgment, which modify each other.

9-10. The Victory of God.—These verses are so inextricably interwoven with the entry of our Lord into Jerusalem (Matt. 21:1-11; Mark 11:1-11; Luke 19:29-44; John 12:12-15) that it is difficult to disentangle them entirely from that setting. Yet exposition in terms of the gospel story is for the N.T. commentators. We must

shout, O daughter of Jerusalem: behold, thy King cometh unto thee: he *is* just, and having salvation; lowly, and riding upon an ass, and upon a colt the foal of an ass.

10 And I will cut off the chariot from Ephraim, and the horse from Jerusalem, and the battle bow shall be cut off: and he shall speak peace unto the heathen: and his dominion *shall be* from sea *even* to sea, and from the river *even* to the ends of the earth.

11 As for thee also, by the blood of thy covenant I have sent forth thy prisoners out of the pit wherein *is* no water.

Lo, your king comes to you;
 triumphant and victorious is he,
humble and riding on an ass,
 on a colt the foal of an ass.

10 I will cut off the chariot from E'phraim
 and the war horse from Jerusalem;
and the battle bow shall be cut off,
 and he shall command peace to the nations;
his dominion shall be from sea to sea,
 and from the River to the ends of the earth.

11 As for you also, because of the blood of my covenant with you,
 I will set your captives free from the waterless pit.

---

it is the God of Israel and the long-expected Prince of Peace, who is about to enter Jerusalem and re-establish both the geographical borders and the spiritual glories of the ancient kingdom of David. The victory is his, even though he is no warrior and comes riding not upon a war horse, but upon a beast which symbolizes a nation at peace. The portrait of the messianic ruler is no doubt modeled in part on the mysterious figure pictured in Gen. 49:10-11.

10. Peace will rule over all the earth; **Ephraim** and Judah (**Jerusalem**) will be once more a united nation and will no longer have need of armaments. Although **Ephraim** (the Northern Kingdom of Israel) had been destroyed nearly four hundred years previously (721 B.C.; II Kings 17), yet ideally she had always been considered as still existing and as ultimately to be reunited with Judah (Ezek. 37:15-23).

11-12. Vs. 12 is usually taken as the beginning of the following section. However, its picture of the return of the dispersed Jews to their Palestinian fatherland provides a fitting and beautiful conclusion to the picture of the glories of the messianic kingdom. The ground for the hopefulness of the **prisoners,** now about to be justified, is the covenant God made with his people at Sinai, sealed by the sprinkling of blood (Exod. 24:7-8).

---

consider them in the O.T. context. (Note carefully the historical background as sketched in the Exeg.)

There are several points worthy of observance: (*a*) The unexpected linking of humility and victory which is a mark of God's way of thinking rather than man's. (*b*) The reuniting of the destroyed Northern Kingdom (**Ephraim**) and the remnant that was Judah (**Jerusalem**). Truly God is he who "gathers the outcasts of Israel" (Ps. 147:2; Isa. 11:12; 56:8). (*c*) The juxtaposition of **command** and **peace.** The point is not a choice between power and peace, but the relationship of both in the combined fact of the use of power for peace. Only God knows how to combine them, but man must seek to know the mind of God, always realizing that man may twist that knowledge to his own sinful ends. (*d*) The kingdom which will be set up is a universal one. Even though there is a stress on Jewish exclusiveness, yet there is a

more than national note in the hoped-for triumph. This is to be expected in a prophet like Second Isaiah; it is interesting to find it in a prophetic book with legalistic leanings.

In so far as these emphases are focused and realized in Jesus, it is important to notice that in him there is an earnest of fulfillment rather than complete victory. He won a peaceful battle, but the war goes on. Yet in his tragic triumph there is the promise of ultimate success because of what God did to him and for him in the Resurrection.

11-12. *The Hope in the Covenant.*—These verses are the climax of the messianic victory. God cannot forget his covenant promises, but man must give him time. The concept of the covenant relationship between God and his people as a corporate entity (the nation in the O.T.; the church in the N.T.), between God and the individual (Jer. 31:31-34), and between God and the individual within a brotherhood

12 ¶ Turn you to the stronghold, ye prisoners of hope: even to-day do I declare *that* I will render double unto thee;

13 When I have bent Judah for me, filled the bow with Ephraim, and raised up thy sons, O Zion, against thy sons, O Greece, and made thee as the sword of a mighty man.

14 And the LORD shall be seen over them, and his arrow shall go forth as the lightning: and the Lord GOD shall blow the trumpet, and shall go with whirlwinds of the south.

15 The LORD of hosts shall defend them; and they shall devour, and subdue with sling stones; and they shall drink, *and* make

12 Return to your stronghold, O prisoners
    of hope;
today I declare that I will restore to you
    double.

13 For I have bent Judah as my bow;
    I have made E′phraim its arrow.
I will brandish your sons, O Zion,
    over your sons, O Greece,
    and wield you like a warrior's sword.

14 Then the LORD will appear over them,
    and his arrow go forth like lightning;
the Lord GOD will sound the trumpet,
    and march forth in the whirlwinds of
    the south.

15 The LORD of hosts will protect them,
    and they shall devour and tread down
    the slinger;[l]
and they shall drink their blood[m] like
    wine,

[l] Cn: Heb *the slingstones*
[m] Gk: Heb *be turbulent*

II. VICTORIOUS WAR AGAINST THE TYRANTS (9:13-17)

13. The rest of the chapter seems to be an appendix added to the preceding oracle when its prophecies were not fulfilled and the Greeks had become the world power from whom deliverance was to be expected. Its warlike spirit contrasts sharply with the peaceful temper of the preceding section, and suggests at least the possibility that it may stem from a different hand. Here Judah and Ephraim play an active role as warriors against the enemy. The phrase **against thy sons, O Greece,** which provides the chief clue for dating the passage, has been regarded by a number of commentators as a gloss; this conclusion, however, is extremely improbable. The passage requires the mention of a definite enemy.

14. Although Judah and Ephraim play an active role, the victory is God's, who rides to battle with them. In Assyrian and Babylonian art the god is sometimes pictured as riding, bow in hand, above his armies.

15. This verse and the two following are very corrupt; the RSV represents a plausible attempt to recapture the original meaning. The ferocity of vs. 15*b* is almost unparalleled and is perhaps due to a corruption of sense which is even deeper than the versions would

(I Cor. 12, 14) must ever be in the foreground of our exposition. It is the key to an understanding of the religious-ethical content of our religion. **Prisoners of hope** is an interesting linking of words. Both nouns are true. They are almost the key words in the O.T. for an understanding of the Jewish race. Battered, beaten, despised, it keeps coming back, "the granite symbol of unquenchable hope," as a colleague commented. The best commentator on this paradox is Paul, with his realization that we are still in bondage to the flesh (Rom. 7), yet stressing hope as one of his trilogy of virtues (I Cor. 13:13; Col. 1:4-5; I Thess. 1:3). An understanding of the relationship of the new Israel, the church, to the historic Jewish kingdom will keep us from

focusing our attention only on the individualistic aspect of this hope.

13-17. *On Misunderstanding the Will of God.* —Here is a difficult passage for the follower of the Prince of Peace to expound. It is not enough to say that it is the wishful thinking of a disappointed man of religion whose sensitivity has been turned to vengeful anger by the facts of history. There is real religion here. God is central; he is in charge; he will not allow goodness always to be worsted by evil. The Lord reigns, and when one day he decides to act, then woe betide those who are against him. The book of Revelation is a N.T. counterpart of this passage. But man must be careful not to read his worried, angry thoughts into the mind

a noise as through wine; and they shall be filled like bowls, *and* as the corners of the altar.

16 And the Lord their God shall save them in that day as the flock of his people: for *they shall be as* the stones of a crown, lifted up as an ensign upon his land.

17 For how great *is* his goodness, and how great *is* his beauty! corn shall make the young men cheerful, and new wine the maids.

10 Ask ye of the Lord rain in the time of the latter rain; *so* the Lord shall make bright clouds, and give them showers of rain, to every one grass in the field.

and be full like a bowl,
　　drenched like the corners of the altar.

16 On that day the Lord their God will save them
　　for they are the flock of his people;
　for like the jewels of a crown
　　they shall shine on his land.
17 Yea, how good and how fair it shall be!
　　Grain shall make the young men flourish,
　　and new wine the maidens.

10 Ask rain from the Lord
　　in the season of the spring rain,
　from the Lord who makes the storm clouds,
　　who gives men showers of rain,
　to every one the vegetation in the field.

---

indicate. The phrase translated **slingstones** (אבני קלע) may conceal another attempt to represent the name of the enemy.

16-17. Difficult as these verses are in Hebrew, the thought is clear. God will make his people glorious and give supernatural fertility to their land. The kingdom of God, which did not arrive with Alexander, is still to be realized. The belief in the coming kingdom, constantly disappointed in particular secular situations, remains an indestructible element in biblical faith.

III. God Alone Gives the Rain (10:1-2)

10:1. While in ancient times religion always had an important part in securing each year an adequate supply of rain, yet it seems to have been a special matter of concern in postexilic Judaism. One whole tractate of the Talmud (*Taanith*) is chiefly concerned with this matter. This brief oracle, consisting of two verses unrelated to the context in which they are now found, was no doubt composed in some time of drought when the people, despairing of help from God, were turning to superstitious means of controlling the forces of nature.

---

of God—a natural but a dangerous piece of theological eisegesis. A kingdom that is not of this world is hardly likely to be set up in this world. The church may well be "a colony of heaven," but the conclusion to that is not that the world will be the kingdom, but that "we wait for the Saviour who comes from heaven" (Phil. 3:20 Moffatt). It is better to recognize that we are God's but that here

　　　all our joy
　　Is touched with pain.[5]

However, even the mistaken insights of man may redound to the glory of God, and there is truth in the idea that to effect his purposes God makes use of men and nations. Yet there is sufficient warning in Jewish history that man must not take the bit between his own teeth

[5] Adelaide A. Procter, "My God, I thank thee, who hast made the earth so bright."

and assume that his runaway stampede is God's will for the world (see Isa. 10). This is a word to any great and victorious nation in any time. The passage ends with a wistful picture of the triumph of God, with his people protected as sheep by a good shepherd, shining as **jewels of a crown,** and sustained by a bountiful harvest. The understandable exuberance excuses the mixture of metaphors. One of the secrets of the appeal of apocalyptic was that it bolstered hope despite the facts of history.

10:1-2. *The God of Nature.*—There is an appreciation here of God's control over nature. It is the belief of the man of deep spiritual sensitivity that God and nature must not be separated. How can they be when one of his attributes is that of creation? Thus the psalmist sings of the praise of God in nature (Ps. 148); Jesus saw God revealed in the birds and flowers and grass (Matt. 6:25-34); Paul believed that

2 For the idols have spoken vanity, and the diviners have seen a lie, and have told false dreams; they comfort in vain: therefore they went their way as a flock, they were troubled, because *there was* no shepherd.

3 Mine anger was kindled against the shepherds, and I punished the goats: for the LORD of hosts hath visited his flock the house of Judah, and hath made them as his goodly horse in the battle.

4 Out of him came forth the corner, out of him the nail, out of him the battle bow, out of him every oppressor together.

5 ¶ And they shall be as mighty *men,* which tread down *their enemies* in the mire

2 For the teraphim utter nonsense,
    and the diviners see lies;
  the dreamers tell false dreams,
    and give empty consolation.
  Therefore the people wander like sheep;
    they are afflicted for want of a shepherd.

3 "My anger is hot against the shepherds,
    and I will punish the leaders;[n]
  for the LORD of hosts cares for his flock,
    the house of Judah,
  and will make them like his proud steed in battle.
4 Out of them shall come the cornerstone,
    out of them the tent peg,
  out of them the battle bow,
    out of them every ruler.
5 Together they shall be like mighty men in battle,
    trampling the foe in the mud of the streets;
  they shall fight because the LORD is with them,

[n] Or he-goats

2. Adopting a consciously archaic style, the prophet calls the unclean powers of magic **teraphim,** the name of the little household gods who were worshiped in ancient Israel (Gen. 31:19). Because the people had deserted the worship of God for magical practices, they were as confused as a shepherdless flock. The mention of the **shepherd** in the following verse provided the editor with a peg to which he could attach this oracle.

IV. GOD'S ANGER AGAINST HIS PEOPLE'S OPPRESSORS (10:3-12)

3. This oracle is closely parallel to 9:13-17. Once again there is a prediction of war against the tyrants in which Ephraim and Judah will play an active role and ultimately be secure under God's rule. The time is obviously that of Ptolemaic rule in Palestine. The **Egypt** and **Assyria** of vs. 10 are the Ptolemaic and Seleucid empires. On the whole the Jews were not badly treated by the Ptolemies, but there were recurring periods of persecution (as illustrated by the story told in III Maccabees), and in any case Ptolemaic rule was rule by foreigners. **The shepherds** and **the leaders** of this verse are foreign rulers—specifically the Ptolemies and their agents.

4. If the reading of the RSV **Out of them** is correct, the verse means that in the future the leaders and governors of Israel will be natives instead of foreigners. The Targ. understands this verse to refer to the Messiah.

5-6. Once again the victory of Judah and Ephraim (here called **Joseph**) is attributed to God's support of their armies. The Diaspora, which had begun with the deportation

the natural order would have a part in the final redemption (Rom. 8:18-21; cf. Eph. 1:8-12). Therefore there was no sense in the Jew's turning to soothsayers and idols when he desired rain. For us there is no place for magic and astrology. But it is well to notice the intimation in this passage that times of stress may drive a person away from God as well as to him. The

church must emphasize the right source of knowledge in the face of false religions and wavering believers. As vs. 2 points out, when one deserts the flock of God, he finds that he is without a real **shepherd.**

3-12. *The God of Nationalism.*—As in 9:13-17, there is here a description of the religion of theocratic nationalism, an ever-present modifica-

of the streets in the battle: and they shall fight, because the Lord *is* with them, and the riders on horses shall be confounded.

6 And I will strengthen the house of Judah, and I will save the house of Joseph, and I will bring them again to place them; for I have mercy upon them: and they shall be as though I had not cast them off: for I *am* the Lord their God, and will hear them.

7 And *they of* Ephraim shall be like a mighty *man,* and their heart shall rejoice as through wine: yea, their children shall see *it,* and be glad; their heart shall rejoice in the Lord.

8 I will hiss for them, and gather them; for I have redeemed them: and they shall increase as they have increased.

9 And I will sow them among the people: and they shall remember me in far countries; and they shall live with their children, and turn again.

---

and they shall confound the riders on horses.

6 "I will strengthen the house of Judah,
and I will save the house of Joseph.
I will bring them back because I have
compassion on them,
and they shall be as though I had not
rejected them;
for I am the Lord their God and I will
answer them.
7 Then E'phraim shall become like a
mighty warrior,
and their hearts shall be glad as with
wine.
Their children shall see it and rejoice,
their hearts shall exult in the Lord.

8 "I will signal for them and gather them
in,
for I have redeemed them,
and they shall be as many as of old.
9 Though I scattered them among the nations,
yet in far countries they shall remember me,
and with their children they shall live
and return.

---

of the ten tribes in 721 b.c. and was regarded as punishment for the long-continued disloyalty of the nation, is at last to be brought to an end. The thought of the mercy and compassion of God, in contrast to his anger and justice, is one of the great notes of postexilic prophecy (e.g., Isa. 49:14-15).

7. It is possible that the plain sense of this verse may provide a hint as to the original sense of 9:15c, which is so repulsive in its present form.

8. I will hiss: The reading of the RSV follows the LXX in giving a weakened sense to the verb *shāraq,* which the KJV translates literally as **hiss** (or better, "whistle"). The vigorous anthropomorphism of the KJV is to be preferred. The picture is imitated from Isa. 5:26; 7:18, where it is used with reference to the Assyrians. Here of course it refers to the Jews of the Dispersion.

9. The past tense used by the RSV is based upon a slight and obviously correct emendation. The RSV **scattered** for the KJV **sow** is also the result of a slight emendation (זרה for זרע). Among the ancient versions this reading is supported only by the Targ.

---

tion of the conception of the universal reign of God. This is a constant struggle in the O.T. as can be seen by comparing Nahum with Jonah and Ezra with Ruth. It is the more serious for us in that it is contrary to the revelation of the truth in Jesus Christ, and it must be kept in mind when we too naïvely stress a Christian United States as contrasted with some of the other countries of the earth. There is but little need for an expository development of the ideas in this passage (see Expos. on 9:13-17). In

outline they are: (*a*) God cares for his people (vs. 3). (*b*) God uses his people to carry out his will for the world; mercy and castigation are both part of his love (vss. 4-5). (*c*) God restores all his people; his righteousness is his saving power and is operative socially; the deliverance is of such magnitude that it is another Exodus (vss. 6-12).

An appreciation of this section will give one some sympathy for Zionism and an understanding of why on the Sunday morning after Dun-

10 I will bring them again also out of the land of Egypt, and gather them out of Assyria; and I will bring them into the land of Gilead and Lebanon; and *place* shall not be found for them.

11 And he shall pass through the sea with affliction, and shall smite the waves in the sea, and all the deeps of the river shall dry up: and the pride of Assyria shall be brought down, and the sceptre of Egypt shall depart away.

12 And I will strengthen them in the LORD; and they shall walk up and down in his name, saith the LORD.

11 Open thy doors, O Lebanon, that the fire may devour thy cedars.

---

10 I will bring them home from the land of Egypt,
and gather them from Assyria;
and I will bring them to the land of Gilead and to Lebanon,
till there is no room for them.

11 They shall pass through the sea of Egypt,[o]
and the waves of the sea shall be smitten,
and all the depths of the Nile dried up.
The pride of Assyria shall be laid low,
and the scepter of Egypt shall depart.

12 I will make them strong in the LORD
and they shall glory[p] in his name,"
says the LORD.

11 Open your doors, O Lebanon,
that the fire may devour your cedars!

[o] Cn: Heb *distress*
[p] Gk: Heb *walk*

---

and, while an acceptable paraphrase, is less pregnant than the Hebrew text. **Scattered** suggests the idea of a loss, whereas **sow** implies the thought of a harvest to come.

10. The Dispersion will return especially from Ptolemaic **Egypt** and Seleucid Syria (**Assyria**). These two Greek kingdoms which had grown out of the shattered remnants of Alexander's empire both contained large colonies of Jews, some of whom had been taken as slaves while others, the majority, had emigrated as the result of hard times in Palestine (Josephus *Antiquities* XII. 1). The greatest of these colonies was that at Alexandria. The returning Jews, says the prophet, will fill to the limit of its capacity the area once occupied by the kingdom of David, including especially the east Jordan district of **Gilead**, the first to be lost to the Assyrians (II Kings 15:29), and the **Lebanon** district in southern Syria, which represented the extreme north of David's conquests (II Sam. 8:6).

11. So great will be the return that it will seem like another Exodus and similar wonders will accompany it. The reading **of Egypt** (*miçráyim*) in the RSV is based upon a conjectural and probably correct emendation of the Hebrew word *çārā,* translated in the KJV by the meaningless phrase **with affliction.**

V. FALL OF THE TYRANTS (11:1-3)

11:1. The brief oracle formed by vss. 1-3 presumably refers to the same situation as 10:3-12. In anticipation of the fall of the tyrants, the prophet utters a mock lamentation for their fate. Following an example at least as old as Isaiah (2:13; cf. Ezek. 31:1-18), he pictures them under the image of the great cedars of **Lebanon,** the mightiest trees known to the Hebrews. A forest fire is about to destroy them.

---

kirk (1940) Ps. 124 was sung in the churches of Scotland. There seems to be an almost inevitable conflict between religious emotionalism and theological intellectualism. Moreover, it looks as if it were an impossible task to separate religion and politics, whatever one's views on the relationship of church and state.

11:1-3. *An Allegorical Interpretation of History.*—Again there is repetition of the thought

of the passage immediately preceding. It is well to remember that destruction goes hand in hand with reconstruction, that if one is building a highway, a bulldozer is as necessary a piece of equipment as a concrete paver. If—to change the metaphor—the enemies of God are as great as cedars, then the friends of God may be as "a tender plant" and as "a root out of a dry ground" (Isa. 53:2). There is also the picture of

2 Howl, fir tree; for the cedar is fallen; because the mighty are spoiled: howl, O ye oaks of Bashan; for the forest of the vintage is come down.

3 ¶ *There is* a voice of the howling of the shepherds; for their glory is spoiled: a voice of the roaring of young lions; for the pride of Jordan is spoiled.

4 Thus saith the Lord my God; Feed the flock of the slaughter;

2 Wail, O cypress, for the cedar has fallen,
   for the glorious trees are ruined!
Wail, oaks of Bashan,
   for the thick forest has been felled!
3 Hark, the wail of the shepherds,
   for their glory is despoiled!
Hark, the roar of the lions,
   for the jungle of the Jordan is laid waste!

4 Thus said the Lord my God: "Become shepherd of the flock doomed to slaughter."

---

2. Bashan is the region immediately bordering upon the Lebanon to the southeast. Its oak trees and its cattle were famous. **Thick forest** is a translation of the *Kethîbh* (C.T.); **forest of the vintage** represents the *Qerê* (vowel text). The former certainly gives the better sense.

3. Hark, the wail is a more idiomatic rendering of the same Hebrew text as the KJV. With characteristic Hebrew disregard for consistency, the **cedars** now suddenly become **shepherds** (in the O.T. normally a designation for rulers) and, in the second half of the verse, **lions** from the jungle which borders the Jordan River, roaring because their hiding place is destroyed (for a description of this jungle see Nelson Glueck, *The River Jordan* [Philadelphia: Westminster Press, 1946], pp. 63, 68. For a typical cedar of Lebanon see G. E. Wright and Floyd V. Filson, eds., *The Westminster Historical Atlas to the Bible* [Philadelphia: Westminster Press, 1946], p. 13).

VI. God's Judgment upon an Ungrateful People (11:4-14)

4. There is no more enigmatic section in the Bible than the one which follows, and none which has given rise to a greater variety of interpretations. The complexity of the problem is indicated by the fact that Josef Kremer (*Die Hirtenallegorie im Buche Zacharias* [Münster i.W.: Aschendorff, 1930; "Alttestamentliche Abhandlungen"] pp. 83-85), lists no less than thirty proposed identifications of the **three shepherds** in vs. 8, and declares that even this enumeration is by no means exhaustive. Similar difficulties cling to almost every detail of the narrative. However, the majority of commentators today are agreed that the passage is not messianic (though it is taken as such in the N.T.), nor eschatological, but is a description in allegorical form of a historical situation. It is tempting to follow many commentators in referring the allegory to the time of the Maccabean wars, but it is hardly likely that the passage can be so late in date. It is more probable that the situation is that of the Ptolemaic period. The oracle takes the form

---

the vine (John 15:1-6), if one must interpret allegorically. But be warned by the metamorphosis of **trees** into **shepherds** in vs. 3 that it is difficult to be allegorical and consistent, to say nothing of being intelligible.

4-14. On the Covenant Relationship.—As can be seen from the Exeg., this passage is full of trouble for the expositor. Perhaps the wisest thing to do is to read it appreciatively and pass quietly on to the next section. If the passage is neither messianic nor eschatological but an allegorical description of a historical situation which is unknown, it is difficult to discover what the expositor can do with it in honesty. Basically these verses are a reminder that there are two parties to a covenant. If one party

violates his part of the bargain, then the other is released from his. God breaks off relations officially after the people have broken them off actually. When God is thus released from the compact, two things happen: the **Grace** of God is withdrawn, that which makes life bearable is taken away (vs. 10); and the sense of community—**Union**—is destroyed, strife and struggle taking its place (vs. 14). There is a clue here to the continual disorder upon earth, with the promise in Christ that God is ever ready to renew the covenant if man will but turn and in repentance ask forgiveness.

4. The Foreknowledge of God.—The problem of predestination may be inherent in this verse. But inasmuch as it is the behavior of men

5 Whose possessors slay them, and hold themselves not guilty: and they that sell them say, Blessed *be* the LORD; for I am rich: and their own shepherds pity them not.

6 For I will no more pity the inhabitants of the land, saith the LORD: but, lo, I will deliver the men every one into his neighbor's hand, and into the hand of his king: and they shall smite the land, and out of their hand I will not deliver *them*.

7 And I will feed the flock of slaughter, *even* you, O poor of the flock. And I took unto me two staves; the one I called Beauty, and the other I called Bands; and I fed the flock.

5 Those who buy them slay them and go unpunished; and those who sell them say, 'Blessed be the LORD, I have become rich'; and their own shepherds have no pity on them. 6 For I will no longer have pity on the inhabitants of this land, says the LORD. Lo, I will cause men to fall each into the hand of his shepherd, and each into the hand of his king; and they shall crush the earth, and I will deliver none from their hand."

7 So I became the shepherd of the flock doomed to be slain for those who trafficked in the sheep. And I took two staffs; one I named Grace, the other I named Union.

of a parable acted out in imitation of the dramatic parables of older prophets (e.g., Isa. 20; Jer. 19). However, it is clear that this form is merely a literary device, since the actions could not possibly have been performed. The prophet is pictured as having been summoned by God to act as the **shepherd** of his people, who are called **the flock doomed to slaughter** because their foreign owners (presumably the Ptolemies) are concerned only to exploit them for what they will bring in the market and at the slaughterhouse. But who is the **shepherd?** This is the crucial question. He is unfortunately a somewhat Protean figure and the allegory is obviously confused, but the facts that only God can be speaking in vs. 10, and that it is difficult to see who other than God can be speaking in vs. 14, lead to the belief that the shepherd represents primarily God's governance of his people. It is not impossible that the prophet who speaks these words may himself have once occupied for a brief period the position of governor under the Ptolemies. If this is so, it would account for those passages in which the shepherd appears to be an individual speaking in his own name (cf. vss. 11-13). Whether it is so or not, the primary sovereignty in any case is God's. It is God whom the people reject and who therefore rejects them (vs. 8*b*), and it is God who breaks the staffs and delivers the people over to external enemies (vs. 10) and internal strife (vs. 14). The whole is an allegory of God's attempt to rule an oppressed but still refractory people.

5. The foreign rulers are represented as absentee owners (buyers and sellers), whereas the native governors are the **shepherds.** Both are harsh and selfish.

6. Although rejected as a gloss by most commentators, this verse fits perfectly well into the thought of the oracle and may well be original. It anticipates the threat implicit in the concluding verse of the oracle (vs. 14). **Land** is quite as legitimate a translation of ארץ as **earth,** and fits the context better.

7. The prophet begins to play the part of a shepherd in the employ of the owners of the flock—a picture of God's rule of his people under the conditions of Ptolemaic overlordship. The imagery is derived from the fact that local government even under foreign suzerainty was in the hands of native governors (vs. 5). The change of the meaningless **even you, O poor of the flock** to **those who trafficked in the sheep** is based on the LXX, and involves only a slight change in the C.T. of the Hebrew. The **two**

which causes the judgment of God to fall so blisteringly, we may be more accurate to consider the verse as an illustration of his foreknowledge.

5. The Third Commandment.—Here is a very practical example of a breach of the Third Commandment. It is akin to blasphemy to

thank God for that which he cannot bless because of the attitude of mind of the man who prays. It is the prostitution of religion in a manner in which the rich fool was guilty even though not vocally guilty (Luke 12:16-21).

6. The Wrath of God.—It may seem on the surface that this verse is contrary to N.T. teach-

8 Three shepherds also I cut off in one month; and my soul loathed them, and their soul also abhorred me.

9 Then said I, I will not feed you: that that dieth, let it die; and that that is to be cut off, let it be cut off; and let the rest eat every one the flesh of another.

10 ¶ And I took my staff, *even* Beauty, and cut it asunder, that I might break my covenant which I had made with all the people.

11 And it was broken in that day: and so the poor of the flock that waited upon me knew that it *was* the word of the LORD.

12 And I said unto them, If ye think good, give *me* my price; and if not, forbear. So they weighed for my price thirty *pieces* of silver.

And I tended the sheep. 8 In one month I destroyed the three shepherds. But I became impatient with them, and they also detested me. 9 So I said, "I will not be your shepherd. What is to die, let it die; what is to be destroyed, let it be destroyed; and let those that are left devour the flesh of one another." 10 And I took my staff Grace, and I broke it, annulling the covenant which I had made with all the peoples. 11 So it was annulled on that day, and the traffickers in the sheep, who were watching me, knew that it was the word of the LORD. 12 Then I said to them, "If it seems right to you, give me my wages; but if not, keep them." And they weighed out as my wages

---

staffs taken by the prophet symbolize the nature of the rule of the divine shepherd. God's government is based upon gracious persuasion and the promotion of brotherhood within the community. The allegorical use of two sticks is borrowed from Ezek. 37:16. The image is a very old one, since in ancient Canaanite literature Baal is also represented as furnished with two sticks which have proper names (Cyrus H. Gordon, *The Loves and Wars of Baal and Anat* [Princeton: Princeton University Press, 1943], p. xii).

8. The part of this verse which deals with **the three shepherds** is enigmatic and should probably be omitted as an interpolation by an editor who desired to give the passage a contemporary relevance. The RSV is right in reading **the** three shepherds. The persons referred to by the editor were well known to his contemporaries (of Maccabean times?) but can no longer be identified with certainty. The second half of the verse, taken with vs. 9, shows that God's attempt to govern his people favorably and graciously met with an ungrateful response which led him to abandon the nation to its fate.

10. The prophet therefore breaks the rod which symbolizes God's kindly and protective rule and gives Israel over to be despoiled by **all the** [surrounding] **peoples** who had previously been restrained by means of a covenant which God had imposed upon them.

11. The troubles which immediately followed are evidence, even to the owners of the flock, who are watching curiously, that the prophet's interpretation of God's will is correct.

12. Having given up his hopeless and ungrateful job of exercising sovereignty on God's behalf, the shepherd asks the owners for his wages, and is paid **thirty shekels of silver.** The underlying irony of the situation is shown by the fact that the wage, though not inconsiderable, equals the value of a Hebrew slave (Exod. 21:32).

---

ing. But there was no doubt in either Jesus or Paul that the wrath of God is a real and awesome fact; cf., e.g., Matt. 22:13; 25:10-13, 30, 41-46; Rom. 1:18; 2:1-9. As a fellow student years ago remarked: "The fatherhood of God must not be confused with the daddyhood of God."

11. *The Knowledge of God.*—Even the "world" can recognize the will of God in action, though it does nothing to conform to it. That

is a salutary warning to religious people who are too hesitant about noting God at work in history.

12-13. *On Hidden Meanings.*—Since these verses are referred to in the Judas episode (Matt. 26:15; 27:9), it would be of interest to make something of them. But the thought appears to be confusion worse confounded, especially in the KJV. Even Matthew has trouble with them, quoting them as from Jeremiah. The

13 And the Lord said unto me, Cast it unto the potter: a goodly price that I was prized at of them. And I took the thirty *pieces* of silver, and cast them to the potter in the house of the Lord.

14 Then I cut asunder mine other staff, *even* Bands, that I might break the brotherhood between Judah and Israel.

15 ¶ And the Lord said unto me, Take unto thee yet the instruments of a foolish shepherd.

16 For, lo, I will raise up a shepherd in the land, *which* shall not visit those that be cut off, neither shall seek the young one, nor heal that that is broken, nor feed that that standeth still: but he shall eat the flesh of the fat, and tear their claws in pieces.

17 Woe to the idol shepherd that leaveth the flock! the sword *shall be* upon his arm, and upon his right eye: his arm shall be clean dried up, and his right eye shall be utterly darkened.

thirty shekels of silver. **13** Then the Lord said to me, "Cast it into the treasury"*q* — the lordly price at which I was paid off by them. So I took the thirty shekels of silver and cast them into the treasury*q* in the house of the Lord. **14** Then I broke my second staff Union, annulling the brotherhood between Judah and Israel.

15 Then the Lord said to me, "Take once more the implements of a worthless shepherd. **16** For lo, I am raising up in the land a shepherd who does not care for the perishing, or seek the wandering,*r* or heal the maimed, or nourish the sound, but devours the flesh of the fat ones, tearing off even their hoofs.

17 Woe to my worthless shepherd,
 who deserts the flock!
May the sword smite his arm
 and his right eye!
Let his arm be wholly withered,
 his right eye utterly blinded!"

q Syr: Heb *the potter*
r Syr Compare Gk Vg: Heb *the youth*

---

13. Since it is not himself, but God, who has been so ignominiously treated by the people and their foreign rulers, the prophet symbolically deposits the wages in the temple **treasury**. The translation **potter** is based upon an ancient corruption of the text (יוצר for אוצר).

14. He breaks the **second staff**, thereby delivering the nation over to civil strife and confusion. **Judah and Israel** means merely "the whole nation." With this verse the point of the satire becomes clear. The prevalent disharmony in the nation and its troubles with its neighbors (vs. 10) the prophet believed to be the result of a disloyalty to God (vs. 8) which was no less insulting toward him than the contemptuous attitude of Israel's pagan overlords.

VII. Doom of a Wicked Governor (11:15-17)

15. This oracle is an appendix to the above, added in a later situation when the Jews were being exploited by a particularly worthless native governor.

16-17. Even though God has placed him in power in order to punish an ungrateful people, yet he will meet the fate which he deserves. As is appropriate, the oracle of doom in vs. 17 is in poetic form (RSV).

---

easiest way to handle them is to follow the advice of the Scots layman who counseled a budding clergyman: "Ye micht wi' advantage find out a hidden meaning in your text. It will, maybe, be easier for ye to do that than to find out the real one."

15-17. On Judgment.—It is of interest to note the allegorical marks of a good governor from the negative résumé in vs. 16. (*a*) He cares for the **perishing**; (*b*) seeks the **wandering**; (*c*) heals the **maimed**; (*d*) nourishes the **sound**; (*e*) deals honestly with the flock. But

one can do better with Ps. 23 or John 10:1-18 if he wishes to interpret life in terms of a **shepherd.**

In vss. 16-17 the problem is again raised—and left unanswered—of the relationship between foreordination and moral responsibility. Before these verses are used in exposition, one had better understand the theological outlook of the period that produced them. When God is considered as the prime and direct author of all events and man is regarded as morally competent there is apt to be theological confusion.

12 The burden of the word of the LORD for Israel, saith the LORD, which stretcheth forth the heavens, and layeth the foundation of the earth, and formeth the spirit of man within him.

2 Behold, I will make Jerusalem a cup of trembling unto all the people round about, when they shall be in the siege both against Judah *and* against Jerusalem.

3 ¶ And in that day will I make Jerusalem a burdensome stone for all people: all that burden themselves with it shall be cut in pieces, though all the people of the earth be gathered together against it.

4 In that day, saith the LORD, I will smite every horse with astonishment, and his rider with madness: and I will open mine eyes upon the house of Judah, and will smite every horse of the people with blindness.

5 And the governors of Judah shall say in their heart, The inhabitants of Jerusalem

12   An Oracle

The word of the LORD concerning Israel: Thus says the LORD, who stretched out the heavens and founded the earth and formed the spirit of man within him: 2 "Lo I am about to make Jerusalem a cup of reeling to all the peoples round about; it will be against Judah also in the siege against Jerusalem. 3 On that day I will make Jerusalem a heavy stone for all the peoples; all who lift it shall grievously hurt themselves. And all the nations of the earth will come together against it. 4 On that day, says the LORD, I will strike every horse with panic, and its rider with madness. But upon the house of Judah I will open my eyes, when I strike every horse of the peoples with blindness. 5 Then the clans of Judah shall say to themselves, 'The inhabitants of Jeru-

---

VIII. VICTORY OF GOD'S PEOPLE OVER THE HEATHEN (12:1–13:6)

1. In chs. 12–14 the spirit of apocalyptic becomes dominant. The concern is no longer with contemporary events, but with "the last days" when the armies of the heathen world will unite in a final great effort to crush the people of God. The model upon which the present section (and also ch. 14) is based is Ezek. 38–39 (the Gog sections). This part of the book opens with a superscription copied from 9:1, which is then followed by a brief hymn in liturgical style similar to the nature passages in II Isaiah (e.g., 42:5) and in the book of Amos (e.g., 4:13).

2. The oracle begins with an assertion of the inviolability of Jerusalem. Using a familiar image (Jer. 25:15; 51:7; Ps. 75:8), the prophet pictures all the nations who attack her as being made to reel like drunkards. The awkward clause **it will be against Judah also** seems to be an interpolation.

3-4. The phrase **in that day** is typically eschatological and occurs repeatedly in chs. 12–14. With a sudden change of imagery, the prophet pictures Jerusalem as a **stone** such as was used in weight-lifting contests. Those who try to lift her will do so to their own injury. Now there begins a description of the battle (RSV). The heathen world unites in an effort to destroy the people of God, but God himself confounds their armies by supernatural means. The passage seems to reflect a time when there was tension between Jerusalem and the countryside round about. At first the countrymen (**Judah**), offended by the arrogant pretensions of the city folk, stand by and watch the siege from a distance, but when supernatural panic falls upon the armies of the heathen, God directs his attention toward the country people.

5. Their indifference falls from them and they see that God is truly on the side of Jerusalem. The text of the verse is corrupt, but the RSV is probably right in reading *le yôshebhêy* (**the inhabitants of [Jerusalem] have**) instead of *li yôshebhêy* (**the inhabitants**

12:1–13:6. *On Apocalyptic Preaching.*—In chs. 12-14—sometimes referred to as Third Zechariah—the note of apocalyptic is dominant (see Exeg.). Therefore we are in the realm of the phantasmagoria of religious hope based upon a fighting faith. The content of the vision is a combination of current events, unfulfilled prophecies, and enthusiastic imaginings. It is a "pep talk" to the faithful and a nightmare to the sober expositor.

shall be my strength in the LORD of hosts their God.

6 ¶ In that day will I make the governors of Judah like a hearth of fire among the wood, and like a torch of fire in a sheaf; and they shall devour all the people round about, on the right hand and on the left: and Jerusalem shall be inhabited again in her own place, even in Jerusalem.

7 The LORD also shall save the tents of Judah first, that the glory of the house of David and the glory of the inhabitants of Jerusalem do not magnify themselves against Judah.

8 In that day shall the LORD defend the inhabitants of Jerusalem; and he that is feeble among them at that day shall be as David; and the house of David shall be as God, as the angel of the LORD before them.

9 ¶ And it shall come to pass in that day, that I will seek to destroy all the nations that come against Jerusalem.

10 And I will pour upon the house of David, and upon the inhabitants of Jerusalem, the spirit of grace and of supplications: and they shall look upon me whom they have pierced, and they shall mourn for him, as one mourneth for his only son, and shall be in bitterness for him, as one that is in bitterness for his firstborn.

salem have strength through the LORD of hosts, their God.'

6 "On that day I will make the clans of Judah like a blazing pot in the midst of wood, like a flaming torch among sheaves; and they shall devour to the right and to the left all the peoples round about, while Jerusalem shall still be inhabited in its place, in Jerusalem.

7 "And the LORD will give victory to the tents of Judah first, that the glory of the house of David and the glory of the inhabitants of Jerusalem may not be exalted over that of Judah. 8 On that day the LORD will put a shield about the inhabitants of Jerusalem so that the feeblest among them on that day shall be like David, and the house of David shall be like God, like the angel of the LORD, at their head. 9 And on that day I will seek to destroy all the nations that come against Jerusalem.

10 "And I will pour out on the house of David and the inhabitants of Jerusalem a spirit of compassion and supplication, so that, when they look on him[s] whom they have pierced, they shall mourn for him, as one mourns for an only child, and weep bitterly over him, as one weeps over a first-

[s] Theodotion: Heb me

of [Jerusalem] shall be my). As in 9:7, 'éleph (clans) is preferable to 'allûph (chieftains or governors).

6-7. The country people, once aroused, advance to the attack with the utmost ferocity and play a larger part in the defeat of the heathen than the inhabitants of Jerusalem themselves. This is represented as in accord with the divine will, to rebuke the arrogance of Jerusalem and the members of the one-time royal family, who evidently still occupied positions of importance.

8-9. The humiliation of Jerusalem was intended to be only temporary and to restore to the people a lost sense of proportion. Under a messianic ruler the nation will become strong and glorious. The phrase like the angel of the LORD is an explanatory gloss intended to weaken the bold expression which precedes it.

10. This verse introduces an element not previously met in the story. Some person of great spiritual dignity has met a martyr's death, apparently with the connivance of the authorities of the city. After the victory over the heathen is complete, remorse lays hold upon those who were responsible for his murder and a solemn public lamentation takes place. Innumerable attempts have been made to identify this figure with various historical personages, but it is more likely that we have here a reference to some well-known

There may be an outline for a course of studies in the idea of God which is sketched here: (a) Creator of the world and the spirit in man (12:1); (b) Lord of history (12:2-6); (c) Author of victory for his people (12:7-9);

(d) God of compassion (12:10); (e) God of cleansing and redemption (13:1); (f) Universal God (13:2). The God of apocalyptic is not fundamentally different from the God of the law and the prophets.

11 In that day shall there be a great mourning in Jerusalem, as the mourning of Hadadrimmon in the valley of Megiddon.

12 And the land shall mourn, every family apart; the family of the house of David apart, and their wives apart; the family of the house of Nathan apart, and their wives apart;

13 The family of the house of Levi apart, and their wives apart; the family of Shimei apart, and their wives apart;

14 All the families that remain, every family apart, and their wives apart.

13 In that day there shall be a fountain opened to the house of David and to the inhabitants of Jerusalem for sin and for uncleanness.

2 ¶ And it shall come to pass in that day, saith the LORD of hosts, *that* I will cut off the names of the idols out of the land, and

---

born. 11 On that day the mourning in Jerusalem will be as great as the mourning for Hadadrim'mon in the plain of Megid'do.

12 The land shall mourn, each family by itself; the family of the house of David by itself, and their wives by themselves; the family of the house of Nathan by itself, and their wives by themselves; 13 the family of the house of Levi by itself, and their wives by themselves; the family of the Shim'e-ites by itself, and their wives by themselves; 14 and all the families that are left, each by itself, and their wives by themselves.

13 "On that day there shall be a fountain opened for the house of David and the inhabitants of Jerusalem to cleanse them from sin and uncleanness.

2 "And on that day, says the LORD of hosts, I will cut off the names of the idols

---

eschatological legend, and that the one **whom they have pierced** is a martyred prophet of the future or even a martyred messiah. Brief as the picture is, the points of contact with Isa. 53 are obvious. C. C. Torrey ("The Messiah, Son of Ephraim," *Journal of Biblical Literature,* LXVI [1947], 253-77) adduces Jewish evidence to support his view that this is the martyr messiah, son of Joseph, who plays a part in later Jewish tradition alongside the triumphant Messiah, son of David.

11. So great will be the mourning that it can be compared only with the annual ritual mourning of the heathen for the dying gods of vegetation (Ezek. 8:14). Why such mourning should be especially associated with **the plain of Megiddo** is uncertain.

12-14. The monotonous repetition, as well as the Hebrew meter, helps to create the atmosphere and reproduce the movement of a lament. The four names mentioned seem to cover only two clans. **Nathan** apparently represents a subordinate branch of the Davidic line (II Sam. 5:14) and **Shimei** a subordinate branch of the Levitical line (Num. 3:18). The picture is that of a nation mourning by orders: aristocracy, clergy, and people.

13:1. In what seems to be a continuation of the preceding account, the prophet describes the positive results of God's great act of deliverance. The nation having been aroused to sincere repentance, a supernatural means is provided for purifying community life from its corruptions, especially from the worship of false gods and—most remarkable of all—from the institution of prophecy. The passage is clearly dependent upon Ezekiel. The use of the word **uncleanness** (*niddāh,* which often means menstrual uncleanness) for idolatry is reminiscent of Ezek. 36:17; the water of purification of Ezek. 36:25 (cf. Num. 19:9); the **fountain** of waters of Ezek. 47:1. The result is a kind of midrash upon this last passage.

2. The unhappy estate to which oral public prophecy had fallen is strikingly shown by the inclusion of **prophets** with idolatry and **the unclean spirit** as corrupting influences

---

13:1-5. *The Passing of Prophecy.*—The most surprising element in this section is the condemnation of prophecy. In the victorious day of the Lord idols will be removed, and also **prophets and the unclean spirit.** It could be

concluded that there would be no need of prophets in that day because God himself would speak to men. But that is not the point. This is a text for the pulpit rather than the pew. Interpreters almost deserve death if they (in-

they shall no more be remembered: and also I will cause the prophets and the unclean spirit to pass out of the land.

3 And it shall come to pass, *that* when any shall yet prophesy, then his father and his mother that begat him shall say unto him, Thou shalt not live; for thou speakest lies in the name of the Lord: and his father and his mother that begat him shall thrust him through when he prophesieth.

4 And it shall come to pass in that day, *that* the prophets shall be ashamed every one of his vision, when he hath prophesied; neither shall they wear a rough garment to deceive:

5 But he shall say, I *am* no prophet, I *am* a husbandman; for man taught me to keep cattle from my youth.

6 And *one* shall say unto him, What *are* these wounds in thine hands? Then he shall answer, *Those* with which I was wounded *in* the house of my friends.

7 ¶ Awake, O sword, against my shepherd, and against the man *that is* my fellow, saith the Lord of hosts: smite the shepherd,

from the land, so that they shall be remembered no more; and also I will remove from the land the prophets and the unclean spirit. 3 And if any one again appears as a prophet, his father and mother who bore him will say to him, 'You shall not live, for you speak lies in the name of the Lord'; and his father and mother who bore him shall pierce him through when he prophesies. 4 On that day every prophet will be ashamed of his vision when he prophesies; he will not put on a hairy mantle in order to deceive, 5 but he will say, 'I am no prophet, I am a tiller of the soil; for the land has been my possession[t] since my youth.' 6 And if one asks him, 'What are these wounds on your back?' He will say, 'The wounds I received in the house of my friends.' "

7 "Awake, O sword, against my shepherd,
  against the man who stands next to me,"
                              says the Lord of hosts.
"Strike the shepherd, that the sheep may be scattered;

[t] Cn: Heb *for man has caused me to possess*

which are to be rooted out of the land. Ecstatic prophecy had always been easily subject to perversion by the fanatic or charlatan, and, while capable of being used for higher ends, had in these times become an object of universal contempt. Neh. 6:12-14 illustrates the kind of activities which prompted this feeling. Our author clearly does not regard himself as a prophet in this sense of the term. While he imitates the style of the great prophets of former days, he is not an ecstatic, or a speaker, but a writer and a self-conscious literary artist.

4. Those who formerly practiced the profession of prophecy will at last repudiate it and refuse to wear the uniform (cf. II Kings 1:8; Matt. 3:4).

5. Like Amos (7:14), the first of the great prophets, they will deny that they have ever been members of the prophetic profession. The reading of the RSV, which is based upon a slight change in the division of letters in the C.T., is certainly correct.

6. The **wounds on your back** are presumably the scars of incisions made during the prophetic ecstasy (I Kings 18:28). The one-time prophet attempts to explain them as caused by blows during a drunken revel.

IX. National Purification (13:7-9)

7. **My shepherd** in this oracle has no connection with the shepherd of 11:15-17. He is not an evil shepherd but **the man that is my fellow,** and the smiting is not a punishment but a means of scattering the sheep and purifying them by suffering. The

tentionally) **speak lies in the name of the Lord** —the uttermost blasphemy. They should forsake such false prophecy and take up a trade (cf. Amos 7:14). The passage in all probability expresses the view of a priestly scribe who saw no

need for prophets now that the law had been given in its entirety.

6. For the meaning of this verse see Exeg.

7-9. *The Remnant of Israel.*—Here is a doctrine of the remnant with a vengeance. The

and the sheep shall be scattered: and I will turn mine hand upon the little ones.

8 And it shall come to pass, *that* in all the land, saith the LORD, two parts therein shall be cut off *and* die; but the third shall be left therein.

9 And I will bring the third part through the fire, and will refine them as silver is refined, and will try them as gold is tried: they shall call on my name, and I will hear them: I will say, It *is* my people: and they shall say, The LORD *is* my God.

I will turn my hand against the little ones.

8 In the whole land, says the LORD,
two thirds shall be cut off and perish,
and one third shall be left alive.
9 And I will put this third into the fire,
and refine them as one refines silver,
and test them as gold is tested.
They will call on my name,
and I will answer them.
I will say, 'They are my people';
and they will say, 'The LORD is my God.' "

14 Behold, the day of the LORD cometh, and thy spoil shall be divided in the midst of thee.

2 For I will gather all nations against Jerusalem to battle; and the city shall be taken, and the houses rifled, and the women ravished; and half of the city shall go forth into captivity, and the residue of the people shall not be cut off from the city.

3 Then shall the LORD go forth, and fight against those nations, as when he fought in the day of battle.

14 Behold, a day of the LORD is coming, when the spoil taken from you will be divided in the midst of you. **2** For I will gather all the nations against Jerusalem to battle, and the city shall be taken and the houses plundered and the women ravished; half of the city shall go into exile, but the rest of the people shall not be cut off from the city. **3** Then the LORD will go forth and fight against those nations as

---

setting is eschatological and the picture is that of "the messianic woes," the "wars and rumors of wars" which, in the dramatic scheme of late Jewish eschatology, would precede the last days (Mark 13:7-8).

8-9. Only a **third** of the nation will survive the testing of that time, but it will be the remnant out of which God will forge a community of men conformed to his own will.

X. THE LAST DAYS (14:1-21)

14:1. This chapter contains another account of the last great siege of Jerusalem by the forces of heathenism. It is parallel to that in 12:1–13:6, but entirely different in detail and much more saturated with the supernatural atmosphere of apocalyptic. The differences both of detail and spirit are so great that it is hardly possible to conceive of it as being by the same author as the previous account.

2-3. In this version Jerusalem is taken and **half** its population made subject to deportation. However, when the fortunes of the nation have touched bottom, God himself will intervene and alter the result of the battle, as he had done so often in battles of the past (e.g., Judg. 5:4-5; I Sam. 7:10; II Kings 19:35).

---

whole nation is reduced to **one third,** then that fraction is further reduced by being refined as **silver** and tested as **gold** with **fire.** It is no easy testing, but the validity of the conception is supported by Mark 13:7-31. What is left is good—God's people acknowledging God. That testing may seem to have been enacted in countries harrowed by world wars. It is an idea not easily grasped by a country which has escaped invasion for over a hundred years, unless one's imagination is spiritually hypersensitive. Never-

theless it is salutary warning to those who sit at ease in any land. It can happen here.

14:1-21. *The New Earth.*—This is the quintessence of apocalyptic: A last tremendous battle for Jerusalem (vss. 1-2); the intervention of God with the heavenly hosts (vss. 3-5); the redemption of nature (vss. 6-8); the universal reign of God (vs. 9); the revival of Palestine with Jerusalem secure (vss. 10-11); the punishment of God's foes (vss. 12-15); the re-creation of Jerusalem as an international holy city

4 ¶ And his feet shall stand in that day upon the mount of Olives, which *is* before Jerusalem on the east, and the mount of Olives shall cleave in the midst thereof toward the east and toward the west, *and there shall be* a very great valley; and half of the mountain shall remove toward the north, and half of it toward the south.

5 And ye shall flee *to* the valley of the mountains; for the valley of the mountains shall reach unto Azal: yea, ye shall flee, like as ye fled from before the earthquake in the days of Uzziah king of Judah: and the LORD my God shall come, *and* all the saints with thee.

6 And it shall come to pass in that day, *that* the light shall not be clear, *nor* dark:

7 But it shall be one day which shall be known to the LORD, not day, nor night: but it shall come to pass, *that* at evening time it shall be light.

8 And it shall be in that day, *that* living waters shall go out from Jerusalem; half of them toward the former sea, and half of them toward the hinder sea: in summer and in winter shall it be.

when he fights on a day of battle. 4 On that day his feet shall stand on the Mount of Olives which lies before Jerusalem on the east; and the Mount of Olives shall be split in two from east to west by a very wide valley; so that one half of the Mount shall withdraw northward, and the other half southward. 5 And the valley of my mountains shall be stopped up, for the valley of the mountains shall touch the side of it; and you shall flee as you fled from the earthquake in the days of Uzzi'ah king of Judah. Then the LORD your[u] God will come, and all the holy ones with him.[v]

6 On that day there shall be neither cold nor frost.[w] 7 And there shall be continuous day (it is known to the LORD), not day and not night, for at evening time there shall be light.

8 On that day living waters shall flow out from Jerusalem, half of them to the eastern sea and half of them to the western sea; it shall continue in summer as in winter.

[u] Heb *my*
[v] Gk Syr Vg Tg: Heb *you*
[w] Compare Gk Syr Vg Tg: Heb uncertain

---

4. Gigantic in stature, God will appear eastward of the city on the summit of **the mount of Olives** and the mountain will be suddenly split by an earthquake which will produce a valley cutting through it from east to west (cf. Judg. 5:5; Pss. 18:7; 114:4).

5. This verse is extremely corrupt. **The valley of my mountains** (*gē'hāray*) should probably be "Gehinnom" (*gê Hinnôm*), the valley which borders Jerusalem to the south and west. The RSV, following the LXX and Targ., is undoubtedly correct in reading *niṣtam* (**be stopped up**) instead of *naṣtem* (**ye shall flee**) and probably correct in taking אצל as a preposition (*'ēçel*) rather than a proper name (*'āçal*), thereby obtaining the sense [to] **the side of it**, viz., the Mount of Olives. The second half of the verse **and you shall flee . . . king of Judah** is a learned note by some editor who not only misunderstood the general situation, but already misunderstood the verb form **be stopped up** to mean **ye shall flee.** The **earthquake** he refers to is that mentioned in Amos 1:1.

6-7. God's victory over the heathen will be the prelude to a general transformation of nature. Winter and night will be abolished; the world will bask in perpetual springtime and in the unfailing light of day (cf. Rev. 21:25). The words in parentheses (RSV) are the wistful sigh of a reader or copyist who acknowledges that only God knows when this wonderful time will come.

8. The perpetual fountain, which in 13:1 has a religious function, here has the same purpose as in Ezek. 47:1—the provision of an adequate supply of water for a land in which the water supply was a chief problem. The prophet improves on Ezekiel by

---

(vss. 16-19); the transformation of the secular into the sacred (vss. 20-21). This is a formidable picture, more easily depicted on a mural than in print. The "new earth" is conceived of as the realization of what was longed for and lacking on the earth as it is.

There are aspects of this picture that pique the mind: (*a*) the universality of a redeeming God, territorially and creedally (vs. 10); (*b*) the international worship of God (vs. 16); (*c*) the sanctification of common, everyday life, with the breakdown of the barrier between the

9 And the LORD shall be King over all the earth: in that day shall there be one LORD, and his name one.

10 All the land shall be turned as a plain from Geba to Rimmon south of Jerusalem: and it shall be lifted up, and inhabited in her place, from Benjamin's gate unto the place of the first gate, unto the corner gate, and *from* the tower of Hananeel unto the king's winepresses.

11 And *men* shall dwell in it, and there shall be no more utter destruction; but Jerusalem shall be safely inhabited.

12 ¶ And this shall be the plague wherewith the LORD will smite all the people that have fought against Jerusalem; Their flesh shall consume away while they stand upon their feet, and their eyes shall consume away in their holes, and their tongue shall consume away in their mouth.

13 And it shall come to pass in that day, *that* a great tumult from the LORD shall be among them; and they shall lay hold every one on the hand of his neighbor, and his hand shall rise up against the hand of his neighbor.

9 And the LORD will become king over all the earth; on that day the LORD will be one and his name one.

10 The whole land shall be turned into a plain from Geba to Rimmon south of Jerusalem. But Jerusalem shall remain aloft upon its site from the Gate of Benjamin to the place of the former gate, to the Corner Gate, and from the Tower of Hanan'el to the king's wine presses. 11 And it shall be inhabited, for there shall be no more curse;[x] Jerusalem shall dwell in security.

12 And this shall be the plague with which the LORD will smite all the peoples that wage war against Jerusalem: their flesh shall rot while they are still on their feet, their eyes shall rot in their sockets, and their tongues shall rot in their mouths. 13 And on that day a great panic from the LORD shall fall on them, so that each will lay hold on the hand of his fellow, and the hand of the one will be raised against the

[x] Or *ban of utter destruction*

picturing the waters of the spring flowing west into the Mediterranean as well as east into the Dead Sea.

9. The kingdom of God will be established over all the earth and the Jewish confession of faith—the Shema (Deut. 6:4)—will become the universal creed.

10. The rest of the land will sink to the level of the Jordan Valley, while Jerusalem will be exalted on a high hill above it (Isa. 2:2). **Geba to Rimmon** represents the approximate limits of the pre-exilic kingdom of Judah (II Kings 23:8). Geba is about ten miles north of Jerusalem; Rimmon about ten miles north of Beer-sheba. The city of Jerusalem is also to be rebuilt to her pre-exilic dimensions (Jer. 31:38).

11. Jerusalem's exaltation will not only increase her glory, but ensure her against attack. The **curse** (*ḥērem*) was the ban which was sometimes placed upon a captured city, whereby all that was in it was offered as a holocaust to the god of the conqueror (Josh. 6:17-19, 24).

12. The details of this horrifying verse are typical of the savagery which is part of the literary stock of apocalyptic, and which is found even in the N.T. apocalypse (e.g., Rev. 19:17-18; cf. Ezek. 39:17). It must be remembered that the language is conventional, and that in the mind of the writer the foes are not simply enemy nations, but the embodiment of demonic forces. The continuation of this verse is in vs. 15.

13-14. These verses are an interpolation which suggest a different means for securing the defeat of the enemy. A supernatural panic, which was so contagious as to affect in

sacred and the secular (vss. 20-21). It is a consummation devoutly to be wished.

Let the last word be the caveat with which this exposition opened. It is dangerous to the integrity of the expositor and unfair to the credence of the listener to shake verses out of

the context of Zech. 9–14 and treat them in the usual fashion of much "textual" interpretation. That type of treatment is always worthy of reprimand, but it is particularly so when "based" upon a book whose environment is not well known and whose *Weltanschauung* is not well

14 And Judah also shall fight at Jerusalem; and the wealth of all the heathen round about shall be gathered together, gold, and silver, and apparel, in great abundance.

15 And so shall be the plague of the horse, of the mule, of the camel, and of the ass, and of all the beasts that shall be in these tents, as this plague.

16 ¶ And it shall come to pass, *that* every one that is left of all the nations which came against Jerusalem, shall even go up from year to year to worship the King, the LORD of hosts, and to keep the feast of tabernacles.

17 And it shall be, *that* whoso will not come up of *all* the families of the earth unto Jerusalem to worship the King, the LORD of hosts, even upon them shall be no rain.

18 And if the family of Egypt go not up, and come not, that *have* no *rain;* there shall be the plague, wherewith the LORD will smite the heathen that come not up to keep the feast of tabernacles.

19 This shall be the punishment of Egypt, and the punishment of all nations that come not up to keep the feast of tabernacles.

hand of the other; 14 even Judah will fight against Jerusalem. And the wealth of all the nations round about shall be collected, gold, silver, and garments in great abundance. 15 And a plague like this plague shall fall on the horses, the mules, the camels, the asses, and whatever beasts may be in those camps.

16 Then every one that survives of all the nations that have come against Jerusalem shall go up year after year to worship the King, the LORD of hosts, and to keep the feast of booths. 17 And if any of the families of the earth do not go up to Jerusalem to worship the King, the LORD of hosts, there will be no rain upon them. 18 And if the family of Egypt do not go up and present themselves, then upon them shall*y* come the plague with which the LORD afflicts the nations that do not go up to keep the feast of booths. 19 This shall be the punishment to Egypt and the punishment to all the nations that do not go up to keep the feast of booths.

y Gk Syr: Heb *shall not*

---

part even the Jewish armies, will cause the enemy soldiers to begin fighting among themselves. This conception obviously cannot be harmonized with that in vss. 12, 15.

15. This verse continues the picture of vs. 12. The animals in the enemy camp will also rot away with the **plague.**

16. The result of the final annihilation of the forces of evil will be the conversion of the rest of the world to the worship of the one God whose shrine is in Jerusalem. The somewhat objective and exterior way in which this conversion is described should not blind one to the sublimity of the idea. It is the same hope which is expressed in more appealing terms in such passages as 8:20-23; Isa. 2:2-4. The external bond of unity among the nations is to be the celebration of **the feast of tabernacles,** which formed a part of the old Jewish New Year celebration. It was originally the principal feast of the whole year, and the thought of Yahweh's enthronement as king of the universe was one of the leading ideas associated with it.

17. One of the great matters of concern in the celebration at the beginning of each new year was to make sure that there would be an adequate rainfall during the growing season, and specific ceremonies were enacted with this in view. Even in late times a libation of water, obviously an act of sympathetic magic, formed part of the ceremonies of the feast of tabernacles (Mishnah: Sukkah 4:9). Those nations, says the prophet, which fail to perform their annual pilgrimage will be deprived of the blessing which the feast secures.

18-19. Rather pedantically the prophet makes special provision for Egyptians, who, he remembers, are not dependent on rainfall for the growth of their crops. Some special form of punishment will be reserved for them, perhaps the one already mentioned in vss. 12, 15.

20 ¶ In that day shall there be upon the bells of the horses, HOLINESS UNTO THE LORD; and the pots in the LORD'S house shall be like the bowls before the altar.

21 Yea, every pot in Jerusalem and in Judah shall be holiness unto the LORD of hosts: and all they that sacrifice shall come and take of them, and seethe therein: and in that day there shall be no more the Canaanite in the house of the LORD of hosts.

20 And on that day there shall be inscribed on the bells of the horses, "Holy to the LORD." And the pots in the house of the LORD shall be as the bowls before the altar; 21 and every pot in Jerusalem and Judah shall be sacred to the LORD of hosts, so that all who sacrifice may come and take of them and boil the flesh of the sacrifice in them. And there shall no longer be a trader in the house of the LORD of hosts on that day.

---

20. The late priestly point of view of the writer is especially evident in these concluding verses in which he describes how **holiness,** conceived as a physical rather than a moral quality, is to become an attribute of the whole city of Jerusalem, extending even to the **horses** and the **pots** and **bowls.** Horses, regarded by the old prophets as an offense to God (Hos. 14:3), will now be consecrated to his service and will wear upon the bells of their harness the same inscription as is found on the breastplate of the high priest (Exod. 39:30). So great will be the number of pilgrims that ordinary cooking pots will not be sufficient for the sacrificial meat. They will have to be made as large as the great ceremonial **bowls** which were used for dashing the blood of the sacrificial victim upon the altar.

21. There will be no need to provide special vessels for the service of the temple, since every vessel in Jerusalem will be sacred because of its surroundings. Therefore there will no longer be need for merchants to sit in the temple for the purpose of changing secular utensils, brought by the pilgrims, for utensils specially consecrated to the service of God. The RSV correctly follows the lead of the Vulg. and Targ. in understanding **Canaanite** to mean **trader** (as in 11:7, 11, "those who trafficked"). If the conception of **holiness** in these verses seems crudely materialistic, it should be remembered that the essential point is that in a renovated world—in the kingdom of God—the artificial distinction commonly made between the secular and the sacred will be abolished. Everything **shall be sacred.**

---

understood. It may be advisable in an era married to atomic energy—for better or for worse, until death them do part—for the expositor to know a thought form which runs counter to the evolutionary philosophy that dominated most

of our thinking until World War II. But until it is known and understood, and accepted or rejected, he would be well advised to deal warily, if at all, with these chapters so dominated by a vigorous apocalyptic outlook.

The Book of

MALACHI

Introduction and Exegesis by Robert C. Dentan
Exposition by Willard L. Sperry

MALACHI

INTRODUCTION

The book of Malachi is one of three collections of anonymous oracles which originally made up the concluding appendix to the Book of the Twelve (see Intro. to Zech. 9–14, p. 1089). The prophecies in this third collection possess a unity which sets them apart from the preceding oracles, now attached to the book of Zechariah, and in time they came to be regarded as a separate book. This treatment, eminently reasonable in itself, was assisted by the error of an editor who believed he had discovered the name of the author at the beginning of ch. 3 in the word *mal'ākhi* translated by the English phrase, "my messenger." This, of course, was not the name of the prophet, but by such a literary accident a significant body of late Hebrew prophecy was given an independence and dignity which its intrinsic importance amply justifies.

I. Unity

There can be little question that these prophecies as a whole are the product of the activity of a single mind. The unity of the collection, which has only occasionally been brought into question, covers not only such items as vocabulary and general point of view, but also the historical background implied in the various sections, and the literary mannerism of using rhetorical questions and answers which occurs in each of the oracles. The only verses which stand clearly outside the general scheme are 4:4-6, which are no part of the book, but are rather a kind of colophon added to the Book of the Twelve by one of its editors. The only other section which has aroused any considerable amount of suspicion is 2:11-12, which seems to some commentators to introduce an irrelevant discussion of marriage to foreign women into a context which originally dealt only with the question of divorce. However, the apparent confusion is probably the result of the prophet's attempt to deal with a complex social situation rather than the consequence of any interpolation into the text.

II. Date and Authorship

The question as to the identity of the prophet is raised only to be immediately dismissed since the explanation given above of the name of "Malachi" is almost certainly correct. If the prophet's name was not Malachi, then we have no idea what it was, and any reconstruction of his character and the role he played will be dependent on determining the date of his ministry and the historical circumstances under which these prophecies were published.

Fortunately there is very wide agreement with regard to these matters. There have been occasional efforts to place the prophecies in the Greek period, but these attempts involve an unnecessarily subtle interpretation of such evidence as we possess. The indications of date are provided by quite clear historical allusions: Judah is under the rule of a governor (1:8). The general spiritual condition of the nation is at a low ebb, and although the worship of the temple is being formally carried on, the priests are so slovenly in the exercise of their office that they are a standing disgrace to the community and an offense to God (1:6–2:9). The people, on their part, are careless about the payment of tithes and the appointed offerings (3:8). The disrespect which the Jews show toward the worship of the one true God, who is in a special sense their God, stands in marked contrast, says the prophet, to the attitude of the "heathen," who are reaching out after true monotheism and whose worship is far more acceptable to him (1:11). The spiritual depression which prevails generally is reflected also in a declining respect for marriage. Divorce is prevalent, and frequent marriages with women of other nations and religious backgrounds are corrupting the purity and integrity of community life (2:11-16). Further evidence of date

1117

is provided by the fact that the laws of the Priestly Code have not yet been introduced and life in Judah is still regulated by the laws of Deuteronomy, as is shown, for example, by the terminology used for the sacrificing priests, who are called sons of "Levi," as in Deuteronomy, rather than sons of "Aaron," as in the Priestly Code (cf. Deut. 18:1 with Lev. 1:5 and Num. 18:2-3, both P).

All of these indications point unmistakably to the time immediately preceding the activity of the reforming governor Nehemiah, and the abuses mentioned are exactly those which occupied his attention (Neh. 13:10-29). Nehemiah became governor for the first time in 444 B.C. and then had a second administration which began in 433. It was during his second term that Nehemiah dealt with mixed marriages and the abuses of the cult, but it would be precarious to date the prophecies between his two terms as has commonly been done. Since Nehemiah, whose whole program would certainly have been viewed with great sympathy by the prophet, is nowhere mentioned in the course of the book, it is perhaps more likely that the prophecies, which contain no hint of any constructive force at work in the community, antedate by a few years the beginning of his first governorship. The date would therefore be about 450 B.C.

The book contains one other explicit historical allusion—the reference in 1:2-5 to a calamity which has recently befallen the Edomites, a nation closely related to the Jews by blood, but in recent years their bitterest enemies. There is no doubt that the event referred to is the conquest of Edom and the expulsion of the Edomites by the Nabataean Arabs, an event well known to secular history. Unfortunately, however, the date of this is quite uncertain and provides little assistance in dating the prophecy.

III. The Situation

The bitter frustrations of the postexilic age made their mark upon the soul of Israel. To many devout persons the end of the Babylonian captivity had seemed a promise that the glorious messianic age was just at hand. One has only to read the prophecies of Second Isaiah (e.g., 49:8-26) to see the tremendous enthusiasm generated by the permission to re-establish once more a dignified and honorable Jewish national life in Palestine. The nation, it was believed, was about to recover the vanished glory of the days when David ruled in righteousness and power (Jer. 23:5-6). The land would become miraculously fruitful and the rain would never fail to come when needed (Ezek. 34:26-30; Isa. 41:18-19). The population would increase until the land would not be able to hold it (Isa. 54:1-3) and all nations would come and serve them (Isa. 49:22-23).

The realities were very different. It was only a small portion of the nation which returned, and those who did found that life was just as hard as it had ever been. The new Jewish community was only a tiny district in the vast Persian Empire, its area scarcely more than the city of Jerusalem and its immediate environs. Such land as it possessed was rocky and unproductive. From the book of Haggai we learn that the effort merely to keep body and soul together required so much energy that none was left for such an important project as rebuilding the temple. If the traditional interpretation of the evidence in the book of Nehemiah is correct, even the city walls of Jerusalem were not restored until the days of Nehemiah, more than ninety years after the return from Babylon. Periodically the rains would fail to come when expected, and drought and famine would follow (Hag. 1:10-11; Mal. 3:10). As these conditions persisted year after year and the fabulous dreams of earlier times were not realized, it is no wonder that a spirit of dull depression settled over the community and that cynicism and impiety gained ground. Even those who tried to remain faithful to the religion of their fathers began to ask the question, "Why?" "What is the good of our keeping his charge or of walking as in mourning before the LORD of hosts?" (3:14.) "Where is the God of justice?" (2:17.) "What evidence is there that God loves us?" (1:2 paraphrase.) The appointed spiritual leaders of the people, the priests, who should have contributed most to the maintenance of the nation's morale, were affected by the general atmosphere of discouragement in which they lived. They conducted the appointed services of worship with indifference (1:12-13) and neglected their responsibility for giving proper religious instruction to the people (2:7-8).

Such was the background against which the prophecies of Malachi must be understood. It was a kind of situation which the preacher frequently has to meet, for even in the modern world such periods of spiritual depression are not unknown. The book of Malachi might be subtitled "A Message for an Age of Discouragement," and as such it may reasonably be expected that it will have something to say of abiding worth.

IV. Message

Whoever Malachi may have been—and we shall continue to call him by that name for want of a better—he was no cloistered soul but a man of great spiritual force who felt himself obliged to go out into the market place and on the street corner to contend actively for what he believed to be the truth. The unique form in which the material is presented in the book—the dialogue of question and answer—is no doubt a literary device consciously adopted by the author, but it also reflects the actual situation in which he found himself and the frequent verbal conflicts in which he publicly defended the honor and justice of God against the attacks of skeptical opponents. In Malachi's day the lot of the prophet was not an easy one. The institution of oral prophecy was rapidly falling into disrepute and was on the verge of disappearing (Zech. 13:2-5; Ps. 74:9). It was no longer possible for a prophet to gain a hearing simply by saying, "Thus saith the Lord." There was a spirit of rationalism in the air which required a logical and reasoned argument. Assertions must be justified and objections met. Malachi's message was not the product of sudden inspiration or quiet introspection, but was hammered out in the actual discipline of public debate.

The basic query which he attempted to answer was that concerning the justice of God. The people said, "If God loves us, why does he not show it? If he is good and righteous, why are not the rewards of life more equitably distributed?" To this Malachi gives a threefold answer: First of all (i.e., logically, not in the present order of the book), the hard conditions of the times are largely justified by the people's disloyalty to God and the prevalent neglect of his service (2:17 plus 3:7-12 and 1:6–2:9). This is essentially the old orthodox answer to the problem of retribution which is stated so clearly in Deuteronomy, Proverbs, Ps. 37, and the friends' speeches in the book of Job. Suffering is the consequence of sin. This is of course an oversimplified answer to a difficult and complex question. Because for the modern mind, as for the author of Job, this answer seems to raise as many questions as it solves, we are perhaps today inclined to disregard the truth which it contains. Much of the suffering in life is as a matter of fact quite clearly the result of sin—the obvious consequence of self-indulgence and self-centeredness in thought and behavior. It is also true that even where misfortune cannot be directly traced to sin, suffering is greatly increased by the fretfulness of mind which arises when the heart is estranged from God. So far, then, there is a large measure of truth in Malachi's teaching—although we should certainly not be prepared to agree with him that, once sin is removed, the rains might be expected to fall (3:10). The thing which most disturbs the modern reader about Malachi's position is the disproportionate attention

he seems to give to cultic sins, such as the offering of inferior animals in sacrifice and the nonpayment of tithes (1:8, 14; 3:8), as contrasted with sins against social morality (3:5). This is partly to be excused by considering the time in which he lived—a time in which the legal system of postexilic Judaism was effectively taking shape—but in fairness to Malachi it should be noted that in his mind disrespect toward the cult is not important for its own sake but because it is a symbol of a general indifference toward God. It is an outward and visible sign of an inward and spiritual *dis*-grace, since a man who will deliberately offer the worst animal in his flock on God's altar is obviously not right with God in his heart.

Malachi's second answer to the people's question is that in spite of the general hardness of the times, there is at least one contemporary event which shows that God is in control of things and still loves his people. The Edomites, blood brothers of the Hebrews, had expressed their delight at the sack of Jerusalem by the Babylonians in 586 B.C. (Ps. 137:7), and presumably in later years had continued to be hostile to the almost defenseless Jewish community. The fate which they had recently suffered was for the prophet evidence that God does not permit faithlessness and cruelty to go unpunished (1:2-5). Although the example may not seem to us an altogether happy one, and was perhaps used merely because it was the only one immediately available, yet the principle which underlies it is sound. Far more clearly than in the case of individuals, one can see the operation of a moral law in the history of nations. Many persons in our own day, though they would express themselves in more sophisticated language than Malachi, would see in the final collapse of Nazi Germany, as in the disappearance of other great nations of the past whose power was built upon fraud and injustice, an objective vindication of the moral order of the universe.

The third argument is that the day of God's judgment is not far distant and, when it comes, rewards and punishments will be measured out and all men will see that loyalty and justice are not forgotten in the record books of God (3:16-18). The conviction that God will one day place the whole of the secular order under judgment, and create a new order of things in which justice and righteousness will prevail, is one which Malachi shares with most of the Old Testament. The eschatological element, never entirely absent in Hebrew thought, increases rapidly after the Exile and provides the immediate background for the proclamation in the New Testament that "the kingdom of God is at hand." One of the fundamental articles of biblical religion is that there is a divine purpose which runs through history, and that in the end God's purpose will be completely realized.

In these direct answers to the great question of the day Malachi merely repeats in his own words certain basic ideas of prophetic religion. The true originality and greatness of the man appear, however, in things which are almost incidental to his principal theme. They are bright flashes of insight thrown off almost casually in the course of the discussion. First of all, there is his magnificent and unparalleled assertion that all true worship, even that of the heathen, who think they are worshiping other gods, is really offered to Yahweh, who is the God not only of Israel but of all the earth. "For among the nations, from east to west, my name is great, and in every sacred place incense is offered to my name, and a pure offering; for among the nations my name is great, says the LORD of hosts" (1:11). Although we must be careful not to press this too far—it is of course a homiletic device to put his own people to shame for their neglect of God's worship—yet there is no reason to suppose that the prophet would not have agreed with the plain meaning of his words. He thus gives expression to a universalistic monotheism which is more far-reaching than that of any other passage in the Old Testament. The Exegesis will show that this breadth of outlook is in no way inconsistent with the apparent narrowness of his attitude toward Edom or his opposition to mixed marriages. The second point in which this book is unique—if the Hebrew text is correct—is in its denunciation of divorce. Divorce, which was of course the privilege of the husband alone, is rather lightly regarded throughout most of the Old Testament, although the practice was for the most part undoubtedly far stricter than the law (Deut. 24:1-4) would seem to imply. That it might at times become a source of grave scandal, however, is shown by the opinion of some of the later rabbis that a man might put away his wife if she spoiled his dinner or even if he found a more beautiful woman (Gittin 9:10). Malachi will have nothing to do with such inhumanity of view and practice. He is aware of the cruelty and treachery which is almost inseparable from the institution of divorce as it then existed, and declares that it is hateful to God (2:16). Thus Malachi seems to anticipate by nearly five hundred years the position which would one day be taken by Jesus (Mark 10:2-12). As a final point we may note with some reserve that Malachi comes very close to expressing the conception of the brotherhood of man under the common father-hood of God: "Have we not all one father?

hath not one God created us? why do we deal treacherously every man against his brother?" (2:10; cf. 1:6; 3:17.) It is true that the prophet is here speaking only of Jews, but the thought once spoken is not subject to any such limitations, and it contains in germinal form a view of men's relationship to God and their ethical obligations to each other which agrees with the noblest religious and moral insights which we know.

The book of Malachi stands at the end of the books of prophetic canon, and appropriately so. As we read it we feel that the age of the prophets is drawing to a close. The classical period of Hebrew prophecy extended from the eighth century to the end of the Babylonian exile; the prophets of the postexilic age were men of lesser stature. In this book a new spirit is plainly evident—the spirit of the scribe and the casuist. Instruction by lecture and classroom disputation is preparing to take the place of the fiery oracles of the older prophets. There is an interest in the details of ritual which would have provoked the angry impatience of an Amos or a Jeremiah. Nevertheless we also notice with gratitude that under new forms the old spirit still could live. There is in this book a passion for God and a sympathy with man which is not unworthy of the great prophets of older days and which justifies the importance which seems to attach to it as the last book of the English Old Testament.

V. Outline of Contents

VI. Selected Bibliography

BULMERINCQ, ALEXANDER VON. Einleitung in das Buch des Propheten Maleachi. Tartu: Acta et Commentationes Universitatis Tartuensis, 1922, 1932.

HORST, FRIEDRICH. Die zwölf kleinen Propheten Nahum bis Maleachi ("Handbuch zum Alten Testament"). Tübingen: J. C. B. Mohr, 1938.

LATTEY, CUTHBERT. The Book of Malachy ("Westminster Version of the Sacred Scriptures"). London: Longmans, Green & Co., 1934.

MITCHELL, H. G., SMITH, J. M. P., and BEWER, JULIUS A. A Critical and Exegetical Commentary on Haggai, Zechariah, Malachi, and Jonah ("International Critical Commentary"). New York: Charles Scribner's Sons, 1912.

SMITH, GEORGE ADAM. The Book of the Twelve Prophets. Rev. ed. New York: Harper & Bros., 1928. Vol. II.

MALACHI

TEXT, EXEGESIS, AND EXPOSITION

1 The burden of the word of the Lord to Israel by Malachi.

1 The oracle of the word of the Lord to Israel by Mal'achi.[a]

[a] Or *my messenger*

I. Superscription (1:1)

1:1. The first part of this title is copied from Zech. 9:1 (see Exeg., *ad loc.*, pp. 1092-93). The word מַשָּׂא, translated, lit., **burden,** and idiomatically, **oracle,** is derived from the Hebrew verb נשא, "to lift up." The expression goes back ultimately to the phrase "to lift up the voice"; then by a natural extension of meaning it comes to refer to the words which the voice utters—the message of the speaker. The **oracle** of a prophet

---

1:1–4:6. *Malachi Among the Prophets.*—Most readers of the Bible are familiar with John Sargent's frieze of the prophets, either in the original or in reproduction, which is the most famous of his series of mural paintings in the Boston Public Library. Sargent must have pondered the Bible long and to good purpose before he took his brush in hand. He has caught each of his subjects in what may well have been a characteristic pose and in what is for us a faithfully representative attitude.

The figures, as the painter has portrayed them, suggest the difficulty of the times in which they lived, the complexity of their characters, and the alternating moods of despair and hope which were written into their works. They manifest resolute courage, an agonized conscience, and an indomitable spirit. Occasionally, as in the familiar figure of Hosea, clothed and cowled in his white robe, the face shows a tranquil serenity beyond all pain and sorrow. Here is "central peace subsisting at the heart of endless agitation." But for the most part the painter's subjects suggest the travail of soul which the true prophet must expect and endure.

As a matter of actual chronology, Malachi was not the latest of the prophets. Sargent, however, follows the order of the canon of the O.T. in placing him at the end of the line on the extreme right. Both his pose and his expression reflect the character of the book itself. The face is not tortured, but neither is it wholly untroubled. It has been said that our religion is a matter of ultimate optimism, but that this optimism rests upon a provisional pessimism,

and that the maturest religions are therefore those in which the pessimistic elements are most fully developed. The prophecy of Malachi reflects this duality of mood and manner.

American Protestantism has suffered in the past from a premature optimism. The difficult period of world history in which we are now involved has done much to cure us of our too-facile faith. We have had to make our reckoning with hard and unlovely facts which previously we had preferred to ignore. This latest discipline in sobriety is greatly fortified by an honest study of the Hebrew prophets. They were at once stern moral realists and passionate believers in the ultimate triumph of righteousness.

The prophecy of Malachi serves us well in this connection. The man was under no illusions as to the degeneracy of institutional religion in his own day and the moral laxity which was abroad among his people. He was pitiless in the indictment of the evils of the day, while at the same time he held out the challenge of a great hope for the future. His literary skill is that of an artist who works in chiaroscuro, with light and shade as in a Rembrandt portrait. The passages which stand in the foreground are the more bright precisely because of the dark gloom of the background. The book is therefore religiously mature and fitted to serve our time as it served the prophet's own time.

In particular, Sargent has turned Malachi's face away from the past and directed it toward the future. Christians have always felt that Malachi seemed to foreshadow the N.T., to

2 I have loved you, saith the LORD. Yet ye say, Wherein hast thou loved us? *Was* not Esau Jacob's brother? saith the LORD: yet I loved Jacob,

2 "I have loved you," says the LORD. But you say, "How hast thou loved us?" "Is not Esau Jacob's brother?" says the

---

can therefore be appropriately described as his **burden** (lit., "that which is lifted up"). Although the editor of the book seems to believe that the name of the prophet was **Malachi,** there can scarcely be any doubt that the word is not a proper name, but merely the word translated "my messenger" in 3:1. The LXX so understands it, though reading it with a different suffix, and translates "by his messenger." The Targ. also understands that the word is not a proper name and identifies the author—implausibly—as "Ezra the scribe."

II. God's Love for Israel Proved by the Fate of Edom (1:2-5)

2. The dialectical style which is so distinctive of this book appears here. Malachi (we shall call him by that name for the sake of convenience), unlike the prophets of the eighth century who could speak in God's name without apology, had to argue his points with an audience which was at least critical and in part hostile. He here asserts the truth of the view, at least as old as the prophet Hosea (e.g., 11:1) and strongly

---

which we pass on in the pages of our Bible. Malachi does not part with the beloved community of memory to which he belonged, but he anticipates for us the beloved community of hope which we find beyond his pages in the distinctively Christian record.

The place which the book occupies in the canon of the O.T. has been conventionally accepted as marking the end of prophecy in Judaism. Prophecy can never be guaranteed at any given time. The prophet is a man who is immediately inspired by the spirit of God and who speaks for God. The authentic prophetic experience cannot be manipulated or self-induced by any known regimen. The O.T. has much to say of false prophets, whose claim to this gift was little more than a matter of professional autointoxication. The true prophet was always warning the world against false prophets, a warning which is repeated in the N.T. in the sober injunction that we must "prove the spirits." The truth of this whole matter has been spoken once for all in that memorable saying: "The wind bloweth where it listeth, and thou hearest the sound thereof, but canst not tell whence it cometh, and whither it goeth: so is every one that is born of the Spirit" (John 3:8). It is precisely because man can never control the winds of the Spirit that we find, early in the record, the statement: "The word of the LORD was precious [i.e., rare] in those days; there was no open vision" (I Sam. 3:1). The prophets themselves were aware that at times inspiration was denied them: "Shut thou up the vision; for it shall be for many days" (Dan. 8:26). The periods when prophecy was in abeyance called for fidelity to

insights already given: "The vision is yet for an appointed time, but at the end it shall speak, and not lie: though it tarry, wait for it; because it will surely come" (Hab. 2:3). Such is the ebb and flow of the tides of the Spirit. Their times and seasons are determined by God, not by ourselves. This dual mood of sure insight and of patient waiting through the uninspired times is written into the book of Malachi.

A late psalm (74:9) says, "There is no more any prophet." Tradition had it, according to Josephus, that after Haggai, Zechariah, and Malachi, there were no more prophets in Israel. The books of the Apocrypha, which lie between the O.T. and the N.T., yield us much stirring history during the Maccabean period, many picturesque and suggestive allegories, certain romantic folk tales, considerable poetry, and in particular a wealth of mature wisdom literature. But the Apocrypha lays no claim to prophecy. Malachi therefore may be said to stand looking across the unprophetic years which lie between the two testaments, to the rebirth of prophecy in the ministry of Jesus and in the gifts of the Spirit to the early church. Despite the pitiless moral realism which prompted Malachi's indictment of his own age, and the preliminary pessimism of his appraisal of his own times, he remains a classic exemplar of the thesis that the messianic hope of Israel burned brightest just when the world seemed darkest. He validates George Meredith's saying, "Who can think and not think hopefully?"

1:2. Man's Ingratitude.—"Man's inhumanity to man" [1] is always prefaced by man's ingratitude to God. It is commonly said that of all the

[1] Robert Burns, "Man Was Made to Mourn."

3 And I hated Esau, and laid his mountains and his heritage waste for the dragons
of the wilderness.

LORD. "Yet I have loved Jacob 3 but I have
hated Esau; I have laid waste his hill country and left his heritage to jackals of the

---

emphasized in Deuteronomy (e.g., 7:8), that God chose Israel because he loved her
above all the other nations of the earth. The people of Malachi's day were skeptical
of this alleged love of God, because the glowing promises of Deuteronomy (7:12-15)
and such prophets as Second Isaiah (54:1-17) and Haggai (2:6-9) had not been fulfilled,
and the nation was reduced to a state of unprecedented poverty. The tiny postexilic
community hardly extended beyond the outlying suburbs of Jerusalem, and the barren
soil, which scarcely produced an adequate living at best, was periodically desiccated
by long sieges of drought. These conditions, the people said with understandable skepticism, were hardly evidence of God's love for Israel. The prophet's reply was that, if
things were bad in Israel, they were infinitely worse in Edom. The close racial affinity
between Edom and Israel was expressed in Israelite tradition by making Esau, the
supposed ancestor of the Edomites, a twin brother of Jacob, the ancestor of Israel (Gen.
25:21-26). Since the two nations were so closely related, and their lands bordered
directly upon each other, they might have been expected to share the same fate. Yet God
had clearly given the advantage to Israel, as anyone could see who would consider the
unhappy recent history of Edom.

3. This verse by itself does not indicate that God's "hatred" of Esau, i.e., the
Edomites, was based upon anything more intelligible than arbitrary choice. It was this
apparent element of irrationality which led Paul to use these words as a proof text for
his doctrine of free election (Rom. 9:14). However, we know from other passages in
postexilic literature that the Jews had a real reason to hate the Edomites, if such hatred
can ever be justified. Edom had not only failed to come to the help of their Jewish
brothers during the siege of Jerusalem by the Babylonians in 586 B.C., but may actually
have participated in the sack of the city. There is no doubt at least that they rejoiced
in its fall (Lam. 4:21-22; Ps. 137:7). As a result, the old antagonism between the two
nations (Amos 1:11-12) rose to the bitterest possible heights in the postexilic period,
and Edom became a living symbol of cruelty and faithlessness, ripe for destruction
(Ezek. 25:12; Isa. 63:1-6; Obad. 1-21). Therefore it seemed to Malachi, as no doubt to
many others of his day, that the expulsion of the Edomites from their old territory

---

problems with which religion is confronted, the
problem of evil is the most serious. That problem, a modern philosopher tells us, is the
sunken rock on which all immature religions
suffer shipwreck. No single theoretical solution
which can satisfy all minds has ever been found.
Each of us has to achieve his own best working
answer to the problem of evil as he meets it in
immediate experience.

When the problem presses hard on us, usually
in the form of what seems to be undeserved
suffering or poverty or sorrow, it is well to
remember how much undeserved happiness has
fallen to our lot. For, if the problem of evil
seems to suggest an irrationality in the scheme
of things, so also does the problem of good.
When the world is viewed dispassionately, the
inequity of the goodness that we have enjoyed
is as inexplicable as the evil we have suffered.
No one of us in his honest moments can equate
his measure of life's creature blessings with his
character. We are all of us recipients of the

grace of God mediated to us by others, for grace
is the name we give to a goodness we have not
earned and perhaps do not even morally deserve.

The very fact that we think of evil as a
problem, but of good as no problem, is proof
of the fact that we start with the premise that
life and the world are and ought to be good.
It is to some such reappraisal of our total lot
that Malachi summons us in this verse. Our
insensitiveness to the goodness we have known
and our forgetfulness of it is a sorry commentary on our fair-mindedness. One of the most
common sins, even among supposedly devout
persons, is this sin of taking goodness for
granted. It was pilloried once for all in those
words of Jesus: "Were there not ten cleansed?
but where are the nine?" (Luke 17:17.)

3. *The Peril of Imputing Our Feelings to
God.*—There was no doubt that the Jews hated
the Edomites. That ancient feud was part of
their inheritance. Here in this verse they impute

4 Whereas Edom saith, We are impoverished, but we will return and build the desolate places; thus saith the LORD of hosts, They shall build, but I will throw down; and they shall call them, The border of wickedness, and, The people against whom the LORD hath indignation for ever.

5 And your eyes shall see, and ye shall say, The LORD will be magnified from the border of Israel.

desert." 4 If Edom says, "We are shattered but we will rebuild the ruins," the LORD of hosts says, "They may build, but I will tear down, till they are called the wicked country, the people with whom the LORD is angry for ever." 5 Your own eyes shall see this, and you shall say, "Great is the LORD, beyond the border of Israel!"

---

southeast of the Dead Sea by the Nabataean Arabs was an act of divine vengeance for their unbrotherly and inhuman conduct. It is not known exactly when the Nabataean invasion took place, but the Edomites were settled in southern Judah (Idumaea as it came to be called) by 312 B.C. (Diodorus Siculus XIX. 94-100). Presumably, though, if our dating of Malachi is correct, this happened before 450 B.C. The prophecy seems to point to it as something which had occurred fairly recently.

4. The Edomites regarded the disaster which had befallen them as only a temporary setback, and looked forward hopefully to re-establishing their life in the old environment and under the old conditions. Their optimism was similar to that of the people of the northern kingdom of Israel in its last days, as reported by Isaiah (9:9-10). Malachi's message is much the same as Isaiah's had been. The end has really come, he says, and the ruin is permanent, so permanent that it will provide incontrovertible evidence for future generations of the wickedness of Edom and—by implication—of the justice of God. Malachi's prophecy proved correct, and Edom never returned to her former lands. The Edomites (Idumaeans) remained settled in southern Palestine with their capital at Hebron (I Macc. 5:3, 65), and were eventually incorporated by force into the renascent Jewish commonwealth in the time of John Hyrcanus (135-104 B.C.; Josephus *Antiquities* XIII. 9). By a curious irony of history it was from these same Idumaeans that the family of the Herods came. **The LORD of hosts** recurs like a refrain twenty-four times in this little book. The **hosts** are in this late literature the heavenly bodies, and the phrase is monotheistic and universalistic in its connotations. It is perhaps significant that the term "God of Israel" occurs only once in Malachi (2:16).

5. Malachi's concern was not of course chiefly with the fate of Edom in itself, but as an illustration of God's love for his people and of his concern for moral values. While

---

their hatred to God as well. Were they warranted in doing so?

One of the most common charges brought against theology is that of anthropomorphism, i.e., thinking of God in terms of human nature and character. The ancient philosophers were well aware of this trait in the mind. Five hundred years before Christ, Zenophanes said:

Mortals fancy gods are born, and wear clothes, and have voice and form like themselves. . . . If oxen and lions had hands, and could paint with their hands, and fashion images, as men do, they would make the pictures and images of their gods in their own likeness; horses would make them like horses, oxen like oxen. . . . Æthiopians make their gods black and snub-nosed; Thracians give theirs blue eyes and red hair.[2]

[2] Fragments 5-6. Quoted in Charles M. Bakewell, *Source Book in Ancient Philosophy* (New York: Charles Scribner's Sons, 1907), p. 8.

The prophets at their best were always aware of this tendency and constantly reminded us that God's thoughts are not our thoughts, nor his ways our ways.

Should it be said that perhaps we have here an instance of anthropomorphism carried too far? It may be well to set over against this verse a later passage from the wisdom literature of Israel: "Thou lovest all the things that are, and abhorrest nothing which thou hast made: for never wouldest thou have made any thing, if thou hadst hated it. . . . But thou sparest all: for they are thine, O Lord, thou lover of souls" (Wisd. Sol. 11:24, 26). If it is said that one should hate the sin, but love the sinner, one might add that this may be a divine prerogative, but that it is only too easy for human beings to identify the sinner with the sin, and turn what should be an impersonal love of the sinner into a personal hatred of him.

6 ¶ A son honoreth *his* father, and a servant his master: if then I *be* a father, where *is* mine honor? and if I *be* a master, where *is* my fear? saith the LORD of hosts unto you, O priests, that despise my name. And ye say, Wherein have we despised thy name?	6 "A son honors his father, and a servant his master. If then I am a father, where is my honor? And if I am a master, where is my fear? says the LORD of hosts to you, O priests, who despise my name. You say,

Malachi was interested principally in Israel and was indignant over Edom's treatment of her, yet we must not suppose that he was concerned only with the indignity done to his own people. He would undoubtedly have agreed with Amos that nations will be punished, not just for their attitude toward Israel, but for their inhumanity to each other (Amos 2:1-3). Edom was not punished merely for what she had done to the chosen people, but for her brutal violation of the moral law. The prophet predicts that when the Jews see the finality of God's judgment upon their treacherous enemies, they will realize that God does indeed reign, and that in spite of all appearances to the contrary the love which he once manifested toward Israel cannot have changed. God is too great for his actions to be judged upon the narrow stage of Israel's contemporary life; if the people will only lift up their eyes to look beyond their own immediate difficulties and observe what is taking place upon the great stage of world history, they will know that **Great is the LORD, beyond the border of Israel!**

III. The Sins of the Ministry (1:6–2:9)

6. The full force of the prophet's indictment of the clergy is seen in the concluding verses of this section. Their sins are so great because their calling is so high. They were appointed to give spiritual leadership (2:7). If they had done their task well and given

6. *The Fatherhood of God.*—The doctrine of the fatherhood of God is the major premise of our religion. We need to remember that the word is not an exhaustive definition; it is at the best a suggestive metaphor. It is intended to intimate that which can never be defined. Calvin was right when he said that the essence of God is incomprehensible by us. Nevertheless we stand by Phillips Brooks's simple statement: "In all its human uses, the idea of fatherhood comes nearer to being a religious idea than that of any other human relationship." [3] It avoids the rather cold connotations of the idea of God as king or master, and of man as subject and slave. It avoids also the perils of sentimentalism which attend the very common use of the experiences of sex as suggestive for religion, in which the soul is thought of as the bride of a divine lover.

But given the pattern of fatherhood as we commonly know it in our modern homes, the metaphor too often fails of its proper religious significance. For in our day the father is thought of mainly as a provider for his children, and—when occasion arises—their pardoner. He is the breadwinner, and in emergency he is the one who rescues his children from the consequences of their own mistakes. In many homes there is

[3] *The Influence of Jesus* (New York: E. P. Dutton & Co., 1879), p. 17.

little feeling of filial respect for the father, of deference to him and devotion to him. He is there to be freely used, rather than to be honored and enjoyed. All this is a perversion of the basic biblical idea of fatherhood and sonship. The doctrine of the fatherhood of God is found in both the O.T. and the N.T. It was not an innovation which Jesus introduced into Jewish thought. True, in the older tradition God was most often conceived of as the father of the people as a whole. Jesus gave to the metaphor the directness and intimacy of a more individual relationship.

Someone has said that the O.T. conceives of men as "the guests of God." They accept gladly and gratefully his bounteous provision for their needs. This mood of creaturely dependence upon God carries over into the N.T. Its most conspicuous and unequivocal statement is found in the familiar words of Jesus: "Your heavenly Father knoweth that ye have need of all these things" (Matt. 6:32). Jesus is not laboring a disputed article of faith; he is simply stating one of its major axioms which may be taken for granted.

Whether in the O.T. or in the N.T., moral stress is laid not upon God's paternal duties toward man, but upon man's filial duty toward God. The metaphor of God's fatherhood presupposes a family life in which the father is

7 Ye offer polluted bread upon mine altar; and ye say, Wherein have we polluted thee? In that ye say, The table of the LORD *is* contemptible.

'How have we despised thy name?' 7 By offering polluted food upon my altar. And you say, 'How have we polluted it?'[b] By thinking that the LORD's table may be despised.

[b] Gk: Heb *thee*

the people the teaching which was needed, this time of spiritual discouragement need never have come. But because they failed and themselves set a vicious example of indifferent and indolent professionalism, they made God contemptible in the eyes of the nation and became contemptible themselves (2:9). Once again an oracle of Malachi begins with the statement of a general proposition, followed by a question—this time asked by the querulous voice of the priests. In stating his proposition the prophet makes use of two of the characteristic images under which the relationship of God to Israel was conceived. On the one hand God was like a **master** (*'ādhôn*) and Israel like a **servant** (*'ébhedh*)—the same image which Paul uses frequently to describe the relationship of the Christian to Christ (e.g., I Cor. 7:22); on the other hand, God is like a **father** and Israel a **son** (cf. Hos. 11:1; Jer. 3:19). The priests no doubt frequently gave lip service to these ideas, but they failed to exhibit in their conduct any sense of the reality beneath the figure of speech. The priests did not of course consciously **despise** [God's] **name;** the prophet's words are only a very strong statement of the impression which their behavior created. At the end of the verse the priests, who are unconscious of acting irreverently, demand evidence of their misconduct. God's **name** is a pious surrogate for God himself.

7. The priests do not of course actually say, **The table of the LORD is contemptible.** The RSV renders more idiomatically **thinking. Say** in Hebrew not infrequently has the sense "say to oneself." In the present case one is not to suppose that they had come to the deliberate and reasoned conclusion that the worship of God was unimportant. The prophet means merely that their attitude shows that unconsciously they really feel the performance of the ritual to be a secondary matter which requires no particular care on their part. They see nothing irreverent in bringing food of inferior quality to God's altar. Affected by the rationalism of the times, they may have felt that a sacrifice was only a symbol anyway, and that one kind of food was as good as another. The word **table** here means **altar,** and is reminiscent of a more primitive time when God was actually believed to partake of the sacred banquet which was spread for him. As the rest of the chapter makes evident, the word **polluted** is simply a very strong expression for "blemished," "imperfect."

the center of values. The fifth of the Ten Commandments prescribed the honor due to a father. The homely counsels of the wisdom literature reiterate the commandment: "The Lord hath given the father honor over the children" (Ecclus. 3:2). When the family relationship provides a religious metaphor, the obedience and respect which the human son pays his father matures as the reverence which man owes to God. The moral stress falls on our reverence for God, rather than on his providence for us. Thus in the Lord's Prayer we are bidden to pray first for the things that are God's before we go on to the things that are our own. Much of our modern theology inclines us in our thought of God to be too self-centered. God is to be valued because he can be used by us for our own ends. The older Protestant theology, running true to biblical form, said

that the chief end of man is to glorify God, and thus to enjoy him rather than to use him. Most of us, in faith and practice, need to correct our too self-centered interest in religion by the thought of God as the center of all the values of our life. We must learn to pray that his will may be done, rather than our will. For God still says to us: **If then I be a father, where is mine honor?**

7-8. The Lowering of Moral Standards.—This is a charge leveled at a morally degenerate priesthood. The verses which follow elaborate the charge, and the first part of ch. 2 voices God's judgment which is to be meted out to those who are guilty of ceremonial sharp practices. Levi, the founding father of the priesthood, had been granted a covenant of peace and life; in turn, he had walked honestly and uprightly before God. But by the time of Mala-

8 And if ye offer the blind for sacrifice, *is it* not evil? and if ye offer the lame and sick, *is it* not evil? offer it now unto thy governor; will he be pleased with thee, or accept thy person? saith the LORD of hosts.

9 And now, I pray you, beseech God that he will be gracious unto us: this hath been by your means: will he regard your persons? saith the LORD of hosts.

8 When you offer blind animals in sacrifice, is that no evil? And when you offer those that are lame or sick, is that no evil? Present that to your governor; will he be pleased with you or show you favor? says the LORD of hosts. 9 And now entreat the favor of God, that he may be gracious to us. With such a gift from your hand, will he show favor to any of you? says the LORD of hosts.

---

8. The prophet now becomes quite specific in his charges. Ancient law, of which the priests were the chief guardians (2:7), required that only animals which were perfect in every particular should be offered as sacrificial victims (Deut. 15:21), but there would be a tendency, especially with increasing sophistication and in difficult times, to feel that less valuable animals might just as well be substituted. This subverted the whole principle of sacrifice, which in its purest form meant the offering to God of something as valuable as possible, to be a symbol of the offerer's willing consecration of himself. The priests had yielded to this tendency and were accepting inferior offerings which made a blasphemous mockery of the whole procedure. Malachi challenges them vigorously to treat their governor as they are now treating their God. The mention of the **governor** points unmistakably to the Persian period, when Judah was ruled by appointees of the great king. The word *peḥāh* is the same as that used in connection with the governorships of Zerubbabel (Hag. 1:1) and Nehemiah (Neh. 5:14).

9. The first part of the verse is the ironical conclusion to the argument in vs. 8. Assuming a negative answer to have been given to his question, the prophet dares the priests to ask for God's favor in return for offering to him the lame and the blind. The words **With such a gift from your hand** are better omitted as a gloss. They are syntactically awkward in Hebrew, stand outside the metrical scheme, and the verse reads more smoothly without them.

---

chi the breed had degenerated. The priests of that day had probably been able to deceive themselves as to the quality of their sacrifices; Malachi warns them that they cannot deceive God. The moldy bread and the imperfect animal may have seemed to them to meet the requirements of the ceremonial act, but they were not acceptable to God because of the inherent dishonesty of the transaction.

Throughout the O.T. we find recurring emphasis upon the need for sincerity and purity in sacrificial acts. Araunah the Jebusite offered to give David oxen and firewood for the proposed sacrifice on his threshing floor, but David said: "Nay; but I will surely buy it of thee at a price: neither will I offer burnt offerings unto the LORD my God of that which doth cost me nothing" (II Sam. 24:24).

The sin of the idolater was the more flagrantly grievous because he made his idol not of the best of his wood, but of "the residue" which was left over when he had satisfied his own personal needs (Isa. 44:9-17). This satire upon idolatry is stated in even more pungent terms in Wisd. Sol. 13. In that passage the carpenter, having made vessels for his use and having cooked his meal and eaten to repletion, turns to the task of whittling out a god, "taking the very refuse among those which served to no use, being a crooked piece of wood, and full of knots, hath carved it diligently, when he had nothing else to do" (Wisd. Sol. 13:13). A religion fashioned out of second-rate material in our idle time hardly deserves the name; it is indeed idolatry.

Meanwhile, it is a sad fact that as religion becomes institutionalized and thus standardized it is apt to lose its primitive purity. Toward the end of General William Booth's life, the Salvation Army, into which he had poured the wealth of his single-minded devotion, began to be torn by rivalries which sprang up between his possible successors. As his wife, whose heart was saddened by these dissensions, lay dying, she said to her daughter: "Katie, why is it that God can't keep a thing pure for more than a generation?"[4] A whole series of studies in church history could be written around that one question; e.g., witness the story of Francis of Assisi and the degeneration of the Franciscan

[4] St. John Greer Ervine, *God's Soldier* (New York: The Macmillan Co., 1935), II, 841.

10 Who *is there* even among you that would shut the doors *for nought?* neither do ye kindle *fire* on mine altar for nought. I have no pleasure in you, saith the Lord of hosts, neither will I accept an offering at your hand.

11 For, from the rising of the sun even unto the going down of the same, my name *shall be* great among the Gentiles; and in every place incense *shall be* offered unto my name, and a pure offering: for my name *shall be* great among the heathen, saith the Lord of hosts.

10 Oh, that there were one among you who would shut the doors, that you might not kindle fire upon my altar in vain! I have no pleasure in you, says the Lord of hosts, and I will not accept an offering from your hand. 11 For from the rising of the sun to its setting my name is great among the nations, and in every place incense is offered to my name, and a pure offering; for my name is great among the nations, says the

---

10. The first half of this verse is very difficult in the Hebrew, as a comparison of the two versions indicates. The RSV, however, contains the more plausible reading. The **doors** are, in all probability, those of the temple. According to this interpretation God, by the mouth of his prophet, declares that it would be better if the doors to the temple court were closed and the sacrifices should cease altogether than that the priests should continue to perform services which were only an insulting parody of genuine worship.

11. Ancient commentators used to take this verse as a prophecy of the world-wide worship of the Christian church, and even, at times, as a specific prediction of the Christian Eucharist (see Cuthbert Lattey, *The Book of Malachy* [London: Longmans, Green & Co., 1934; "Westminster Version of the Sacred Scriptures"], pp. xix-xxxiv). The text, however, certainly refers to a contemporary situation. Two interpretations are possible. The prophet may be referring to the worship of the Diaspora in foreign lands, or he refers actually to the worship of the heathen. The former interpretation is improbable, because the picture of the vast extent of this worship (**from the rising of the sun even unto the going down of the same**) would be a gross and inappropriate exaggeration, and also because the terms plainly point to sacrificial worship, which was permitted only in Jerusalem (and exceptionally in such a place as Elephantine in Egypt). The picture exactly describes the elaborate and universal worship of the heathen, whose sincerity and meticulousness in carrying on the cult of their gods is contrasted

---

Order, which set in even before the saint's death. We shall do well in our churches to be aware of the peril of lowered moral standards to which institutional religion is always open.

11. *Other Sheep Not of This Fold.*—This bold statement must have seemed to contemporaries little short of treason and heresy. The history of Judaism has been that of a struggle between two ideas, particularism and universalism. Theoretically, these ideas are complementary; practically, they tend to be at any given moment antithetical, if not mutually exclusive. There is on the one hand the basic idea of Israel as a chosen and specially privileged people, with peculiar rights. But since there is no such thing as a right without its correlative duty, Judaism at its best conceived of itself as "a light of the Gentiles" (Isa. 42:6). This sense of a universal mission reached its height and received its most classic statement in the latter half of the prophecy of Isaiah: "For, behold, the darkness shall cover the earth, and gross

darkness the people: but the Lord shall arise upon thee, and his glory shall be seen upon thee. And the Gentiles shall come to thy light, and kings to the brightness of thy rising" (Isa. 60:2-3).

Judaism had at the time those words were written the high and holy prospect of becoming a universal religion. Why it failed to realize that hope and that mission, and turned inward to a particularist emphasis, is one of the riddles of history. Perhaps anti-Semitism, ancient and modern, is to blame for this introversion. But it can have been only in a moment of moral despair that Malachi faced the prospect that the glory of God, which he saw departing from the temple and its priesthood, should remove from Israel altogether, and rest over the Gentiles. No church today should refuse to face, in the terms of its present life, that same somber prospect. Jesus may well have been reminding his own generation of Malachi's sobering prophecy when he said: "The kingdom of God shall be taken

12 ¶ But ye have profaned it, in that ye say, The table of the LORD *is* polluted; and the fruit thereof, *even* his meat, *is* contemptible.

13 Ye said also, Behold, what a weariness *is it!* and ye have snuffed at it, saith the LORD of hosts; and ye brought *that which was* torn, and the lame, and the sick; thus ye brought an offering: should I accept this of your hand? saith the LORD.

LORD of hosts. 12 But you profane it when you say that the LORD's table is polluted, and the food for it*c* may be despised. 13 'What a weariness this is,' you say, and you sniff at me,*d* says the LORD of hosts. You bring what has been taken by violence or is lame or sick, and this you bring as your offering! Shall I accept that from your

c Heb *its fruit, its food*
d Another reading is *it*

---

with the Jews' slovenly indifference to the worship of the only God. The monotheism which had characterized Jewish thought at least since the days of Second Isaiah finds expression, surprisingly but not illogically, in the assertion that all honest worship, to whatever divinity it may ostensibly be offered, is really worship of the one true God. There is no contradiction between these words and the thought that God hates Edom (1:3). The Edomites were hated not because they were heathen, but because they were cruel and treacherous. The atmosphere of the Persian Empire, with its high religion and tolerant policies, was conducive to the growth of a more magnanimous attitude toward paganism, and while the "liberalism" of Malachi must not be exaggerated (see Intro., p. 1120), he should not be denied the credit of having given the most generous estimate of foreign religion to be found in the O.T.

12. The prophet's purpose is of course not to praise the heathen, but to shame the Jews. The heathen by their carefulness and munificence are honoring God, while the Jews by their indifference are dishonoring him.

13. The boredom of the merely professional priest, when required to carry out the routine of his office, is beautifully caricatured in this verse. The reading of the RSV, **you sniff at me,** is based upon a Jewish tradition that the original reading was changed to **at it** in order to avoid the appearance of irreverence. Either rendering of course makes good sense. It was a great temptation to the people not to bring for sacrifice the best of their flocks and herds, but rather that which was unfit for the market. Modern religion is not unfamiliar with the idea that what is useless for other purposes may still be good enough for the church. The present verse has the priests chiefly in mind, since they actually carry out the most important part of the ritual of sacrifice, but, as the

---

from you, and given to a nation bringing forth the fruits thereof" (Matt. 21:43). He was speaking to his fellow Jews, but his words are as pertinent for twentieth-century Christians and their churches as they were for those to whom they were first addressed. A secularized and worldly church may well see its spiritual heritage taken from it and vested in some alien society. Meanwhile, even if a church keeps something of its original purity and sense of vocation, it should never forget or ignore those gracious and catholic words about the world's spiritual sheepfolds: "And other sheep I have, which are not of this fold" (John 10:16). Failure to concede that fact is the source of all our tragic denominational rivalries and our unhappy divisions.

13. Religious Boredom.—These are the words of the degenerate priesthood, going mechanically about their holy offices. Yet one does not have to be a degenerate priest to know the

promptings of such a mood. For the best of men have confessed to the same humiliating lassitude. The Christian mystics were only too familiar with the stubborn problem of spiritual and moral "dryness." So Thomas à Kempis says:

I never found any so religious and devout, that he had not sometimes a withdrawing of grace, or felt not some decrease of zeal. . . . When I call to mind some devout persons, who approach to Thy Sacrament, O Lord, with the greatest devotion and affection, I am oftentimes confounded and blush within myself, that I am come with such lukewarmness, yea coldness, to Thy Altar and the Table of sacred Communion. I grieve to think that I remain so dry, without affection of heart.[5]

There is perhaps this important difference between Thomas à Kempis and the priests whom Malachi pilloried: they had unashamedly made their peace with the boredom of their

[5] *The Imitation of Christ,* II. 9. 7; IV. 14. 1.

14 But cursed *be* the deceiver, which hath in his flock a male, and voweth, and sacrificeth unto the Lord a corrupt thing: for I *am* a great King, saith the Lord of hosts, and my name *is* dreadful among the heathen.

2 And now, O ye priests, this commandment *is* for you.

2 If ye will not hear, and if ye will not lay *it* to heart, to give glory unto my name, saith the Lord of hosts, I will even send a curse upon you, and I will curse your blessings: yea, I have cursed them already, because ye do not lay *it* to heart.

hand? says the Lord. 14 Cursed be the cheat who has a male in his flock, and vows it, and yet sacrifices to the Lord what is blemished; for I am a great King, says the Lord of hosts, and my name is feared among the nations.

2 "And now, O priests, this command is for you. 2 If you will not listen, if you will not lay it to heart to give glory to my name, says the Lord of hosts, then I will send the curse upon you and I will curse your blessings; indeed I have already cursed them, because you do not lay it to heart.

---

following verse makes clear, the laity who bring such offerings to the priests are also condemned.

14. The curse here is explicitly directed toward the layman. In some time of distress, perhaps of illness, a man prays to God for deliverance and vows a male from his flock. But when all is well with him again and the time comes to fulfill the vow, his native parsimony comes to the fore and he decides to offer some imperfect animal which will cause him little actual loss. The sin is aggravated by the fact that the offering was a purely voluntary one to begin with, not one of the obligatory sacrifices. To the people who do them, these things seem to be matters of minor importance; they are not consciously irreverent, but feel that even in religion one should be "practical." They fail to realize that it is more irreverent to serve God with only half one's heart than not to serve him at all. It is more devout to ignore him altogether than to suppose one can trifle with him, for he is **a great King,** a fact to which even the heathen bear witness by the magnificence of their temples and the costliness of their worship.

2:1. The preceding verses contain the essence of the prophet's indictment of the priests. He now proceeds in God's name to pronounce judgment upon them.

2. Like all the prophetic messages of doom, the judgment which Malachi pronounces is conditional. Even when such messages are stated in the most absolute form, it is always to be understood that change of heart would effect a change of fate. As in 1:6, **my name** means "me." If the priests continue their present course and fail to take their responsibilities seriously, God will send his curse upon them. The form of expression illustrates the tendency of the Hebrew mind to objectify concepts which to us are merely subjective. **The curse** (the Hebrew also has the definite article) is represented as not merely an expression of ill-will, but as a missile which can be sent out and will damage the thing which it strikes (for a similar view of a blessing see Matt. 10:12-13). The nature of the curse is specified in the words **I will curse your blessings. Blessings** here does not refer to the priestly benedictions, but to the benefits which the priests enjoyed (in the sense of the evangelical hymn, "Count Your Blessings"; cf. Gen. 49:25). The priestly office had

---

perfunctory offices; the medieval saint, like all the mystics, was perplexed and saddened by his "dryness." The experience was common to both, but the connotations differed radically. The religious man must learn to expect seasons of weariness in the practice of his religion; but he must also know how to interpret them and make proper use of them.

William Sanday used to tell his classes at Christ Church, Oxford, that three quarters of all the honest intellectual work of the world is

unrelieved drudgery. Such drudgery is our moral opportunity to consolidate in achieved character the inspiration we have already had, and then it is the price we pay for inspiration yet to come. The same is true of the familiar and constantly repeated offices of religion, our familiar hymns and formal prayers and well-known passages of the Bible. True, they are often so well known that they lack novelty, but constant repetition and return to them in the services of the church implants them so deeply

3 Behold, I will corrupt your seed, and spread dung upon your faces, *even* the dung of your solemn feasts; and *one* shall take you away with it.

4 And ye shall know that I have sent this commandment unto you, that my covenant might be with Levi, saith the LORD of hosts.

5 My covenant was with him of life and peace; and I gave them to him *for* the fear wherewith he feared me, and was afraid before my name.

3 Behold, I will rebuke your offspring, and spread dung upon your faces, the dung of your offerings, and I will put you out of my presence.[e] 4 So shall you know that I have sent this command to you, that my covenant with Levi may hold, says the LORD of hosts. 5 My covenant with him was a covenant of life and peace, and I gave them to him, that he might fear; and he feared me,

[e] Cn Compare Gk Syr: Heb *and he shall bear you to it*

certain perquisites attached to it (cf. Num. 18:8-19), and the priests enjoyed many privileges. It is this "benefit of clergy" which is to be cursed. The concluding words, **yea, I have cursed . . . lay it to heart,** constitute a note added by a scribe to record his own observation that in some respects at least the prophecy was being fulfilled. The LXX takes the words **lay it to heart,** here awkwardly repeated from the first part of the verse, and adds them to the superscription in 1:1 as a suitable motto for the whole book.

3. The first and last clauses of this verse are difficult. The KJV (in agreement with the Targ. and Syriac) gives a literal translation of the Hebrew of the first clause. The sense of this would be that the curse is to affect the productiveness of the land so that the revenues of the priests would be reduced. The RSV takes "seed" in the metaphorical sense of **offspring** and thus gives a more natural sense to the preceding Hebrew verb. **The dung of your offerings** is undoubtedly a scribal note to connect the word **dung** in the preceding clause with the technical terminology of sacrifice. In this connection (cf. Lev. 4:11) **dung** does not mean excrement, but the contents of the bowels of the slain sacrificial animals. The figure is intended to express as forcibly as possible the complete degradation which will be inflicted upon the priests. The difficult last clause is rendered literally by the KJV, and may mean that the priests are to be removed from the city just like the dung of the sacrifice (Lev. 4:12). The RSV is an interesting conjectural reading which is partly supported by the LXX and the Syriac. Whatever the words mean, they are almost certainly no part of the original prophecy.

4. The RSV accurately gives the sense of the words which are translated literally but without meaning in the KJV. The reference to **Levi** as the ancestor of the priestly order gives one of the chief clues to the date of the book, since the Priestly Code—which seems to have come into effect in the latter part of the fifth century B.C.—regards only the descendants of Aaron as priests (Lev. 1:5), the Levites being a subordinate order who merely assisted the priests (Num. 18:2-4). In Deuteronomy, however—the law which was in effect from *ca.* 621 B.C. until the acceptance of the Priestly Code—no distinction is made between priests and Levites (cf. Deut. 17:9). Malachi must then come from the period between Deuteronomy and the time when the Priestly Code became the law of the land.

5. Nowhere else in the O.T. is the arrangement whereby the tribe of Levi became the priestly order explicitly called a **covenant.** However, a story now contained in a document later than the time of Malachi speaks, in language which suggests the present

in our mind that they finally become second mental nature. In times of crisis, when we are put to the proof, it is this deeper level of the mind, rather than its surface rationalizations, which determines our action. Therefore our habitual religious practices cannot be safely discarded. They are the drill ground where char-

acter is trained against the day of spiritual battle and moral proving. If Malachi's priests had ever known this, they had forgotten it.

Meanwhile, the candor of Thomas à Kempis encourages us to be equally candid. There is in religious circles unfortunately a vast amount of pious pretense; persons professing a warmth

6 The law of truth was in his mouth, and iniquity was not found in his lips: he walked with me in peace and equity, and did turn many away from iniquity.

7 For the priest's lips should keep knowledge, and they should seek the law at his

he stood in awe of my name. 6 True instruction/ was in his mouth, and no wrong was found on his lips. He walked with me in peace and uprightness, and he turned many from iniquity. 7 For the lips of a priest

---

passage, of a priestly covenant with Phinehas the grandson of Aaron (Num. 25:12-13 [P]). However, the idea of covenant is much less technical than we might suppose, and any special arrangement between two parties might be called by that name. The background of this verse is found in the ancient Hebrew poem now contained in Deut. 33:8-11. Like all God's covenants, that which he made with Levi was not merely an arbitrary imposition, but was intended for the benefit of those who received it. The RSV, translating freely, renders the noun "fear" as a purpose clause, **that he might fear.** This was the human side of the covenant. God promised **life and peace;** the priests were expected to perform their duties with reverence and awe, and in former times had done so.

6. All through this section the name "Levi" is to be understood as a vivid personification of the priestly order, not as a reference to the Hebrew patriarch. The point of the verse is that in times past the priests had faithfully discharged their duties. It is significant for the point of view of Malachi and for absolving him of the charge of being unduly preoccupied with ritual that the particular duty which is mentioned is not that of performing the ritual of sacrifice, but rather that of giving **true instruction.** As a matter of historical fact, the original function of the priest among the Hebrews had been to determine the will of God by casting the sacred lots (I Sam. 22:9-10) and to preserve the sacred traditions rather than to offer sacrifice. The Hebrew word *tôrāh,* **law,** really means oral "direction" or "instruction" such as the priests were accustomed to give. Originally this torah would largely have had to do with what we should consider superstitious matters—taboo, omens, correct ritual procedures, etc.—although ethical matters were not excluded. Malachi revitalizes this whole conception of the priest as teacher by relating it to religious and ethical attitudes rather than to the minutiae of liturgical practice. Idealizing the past in typical homiletic fashion, he pictures the priests of former days as animated wholly by a spirit of true devotion and as powerful influences for sustaining the moral life of the community.

7. The function of the priest is primarily that of a teacher. This verse contains both the noblest statement of the function of priesthood to be found in the O.T. and the

---

which they do not at the moment actually feel. The honesty of Thomas à Kempis may well be preferable to the great "devotion and affection" of those whom he professes to envy. His sane and wholesome words in a later passage have a salty moral flavor which should save us from sentimental affectation:

Thou art a man, and not God; thou art flesh, not an Angel. How canst thou look to continue alway in the same state of virtue: when an Angel in Heaven hath fallen, as also the first man in Paradise? . . . Thinkest thou that thou shalt always have spiritual consolations at thine own will? My saints had not such always, but they had many afflictions. . . . Nevertheless in all these they bore themselves up patiently, and trusted rather in God than in themselves. . . . Wait for the Lord, behave thyself manfully, and be of good courage.[6]

[6] *Ibid.,* III. 62. 3; 35. 3.

The mystic has but one golden rule for negotiating the sandy stretches of dryness which so often seem to lie between life's spiritual oases: carry on faithfully with a good conscience and leave the issue to God.

2:7. Keeping Sound Knowledge.—Both Judaism and Christianity are numbered among the world's learned religions. The Bible concedes the limitations of the human mind, but it never disparages that mind. What Wordsworth calls "an eternity of thought" broods over its pages, and we are invited into that eternal thoughtfulness.

Christianity needs to be constantly on its guard against the cult of irrationality, which century after century has been a recurring menace to a reasonable faith. This cult is practiced by two quite distinct types of persons. There is, on the one hand, the unlettered and

mouth: for he *is* the messenger of the LORD of hosts.

8 But ye are departed out of the way; ye have caused many to stumble at the law; ye have corrupted the covenant of Levi, saith the LORD of hosts.

9 Therefore have I also made you contemptible and base before all the people, according as ye have not kept my ways, but have been partial in the law.

should guard knowledge, and men should seek instruction*ƒ* from his mouth, for he is the messenger of the LORD of hosts. 8 But you have turned aside from the way; you have caused many to stumble by your instruction;*ƒ* you have corrupted the covenant of Levi, says the LORD of hosts, 9 and so I make you despised and abased before all the people, inasmuch as you have not kept my ways but have shown partiality in your instruction."*ƒ*

ƒ Or *law*

---

highest estimate of its dignity. The priest is **the messenger of the LORD of hosts** and thus takes over the office formerly filled by the prophets. When the charismatic age of prophecy began to pass away the work of religious and moral instruction inevitably passed to men whose authority did not rest on their claim to a special personal kind of inspiration, but on some kind of objective commission. Malachi had visions of the priests becoming the religious teachers of the new age; actually, however, this function came to be performed by the "scribes." The danger of substituting authorized teachers for inspired prophets is that the teachers may succumb to a spirit of mere professionalism. Malachi insists that the acceptance of the office of priest is not a matter of privilege, but involves the most serious kind of responsibility. The word *mal'ākh*, translated **messenger**, is the same as that translated "angel" in the phrase "the angel of the LORD" in such passages as Gen. 22:15; Exod. 3:2; Judg. 6:11. The **knowledge** of which the prophet speaks is not primarily "book learning" but rather "the knowledge of God" (Hos. 4:1; 6:6).

8-9. In shocking contrast with the faithfulness of former generations of priests (vss. 5-6) and with the true ideal of the priesthood (vs. 7), the priests of Malachi's day have proved recreant to their high calling and, so far from being a counterweight to the natural evil of the human heart, have actually contributed to the spiritual depression and moral weakness of the community. Since a covenant must be maintained by both parties, the covenant which should have brought happiness and blessing (vs. 5) upon them has been annulled, and they are despised by the very people who should have respected them and sought instruction from their lips (vs. 7). In the concluding clause the priests are accused of being **partial** toward the rich and powerful, a vice not unknown among clergy of other lands and times. Perhaps *tôrāh* would here be better translated **law** (KJV) than **instruction** (RSV) since it almost certainly includes the adjudication of disputes brought before the priest for his decision.

---

poorly educated man who uses the cult of irrationality as a kind of fig leaf to hide his own pathetic ignorance. So employed, this deliberate disparagement of the mind and of sober knowledge is merely a defense mechanism. At the other end of the scale is the overintellectual man who has reached the point of sophistication, if not of disillusionment. He is so depressed by the limits of his intelligence that he deliberately affects irrationality as his only solace. In so far as he still professes to be a believer, he believes precisely because faith is both absurd and impossible. (*Credo quia absurdam est . . . Credo quia impossibile est.*) Much of the newer theology of our own day rests upon this premise. Kierkegaard is quoted

as saying that "God is the most ridiculous being that ever existed."

Religion has no quarrel with a devout agnosticism. But it can never make its peace with a complacent agnosticism. Job came to the time when he was willing to concede his own ignorance and to capitulate to a mood of mental indifference to the riddle of existence. "I will lay mine hand upon my mouth. Once have I spoken; but I will not answer: yea, twice; but I will proceed no further" (Job 40:4-5). But it was precisely this studied indifferentism which was denied him. "Then answered the LORD unto Job out of the whirlwind, and said, Gird up thy loins now like a man: I will demand of thee, and declare thou unto me" (Job 40:6-7). The

10 Have we not all one father? hath not one God created us? why do we deal treacherously every man against his brother, by profaning the covenant of our fathers?

11 ¶ Judah hath dealt treacherously, and an abomination is committed in Israel and in Jerusalem; for Judah hath profaned the holiness of the LORD which he loved, and hath married the daughter of a strange god.

10 Have we not all one father? Has not one God created us? Why then are we faithless to one another, profaning the covenant of our fathers? 11 Judah has been faithless, and abomination has been committed in Israel and in Jerusalem; for Judah has profaned the sanctuary of the LORD, which he loves, and has married the daughter of a

IV. The Degradation of Marriage (2:10-16)

10. Malachi begins his argument by stating a general principle of far-reaching importance. Every Jew would proudly have claimed that God was his **father.** This meant primarily that God was the father of the nation (Jer. 3:19; Isa. 63:16), but the thought of God as the father of pious individuals was not entirely absent (Ps. 103:13), and was probably much more prevalent than the biblical record would seem to indicate. It should of course be remembered that both in the O.T. and the N.T. the idea of God's fatherhood connotes progenitorship and authority quite as much as affection. In this passage the thought of God as father is based, as the parallel shows, on the fact that God is the creator. The context seems to show that Malachi is thinking more of God as the creator of the Jewish nation than of individual men (notice the reference to **the covenant of our fathers,** and in vs. 11, to a Gentile woman as **the daughter of a foreign god**). Yet the prophet gave utterance to words which are capable of conveying a greater measure of truth than he dreamed of. The ideal of common brotherhood under a common fatherhood, which Malachi sets forth as the true pattern of life for the Jewish community, is capable, under the presuppositions of the prophetic faith itself, of being extended to the whole of humankind. From the acknowledged fact of God's common fatherhood, Malachi draws the conclusion that his children should behave like members of a family. And yet how different is the reality! So far from the Jews behaving like brothers, the prophet sees on every hand violations of the common decencies which were long ago accepted by the ancestors of the people as part of the basic law of their common life. He is obviously thinking of the general moral law as well as of the Deuteronomic prohibition against marriage with the heathen (Deut. 7:3).

11. The first charge, that marriages with heathen women are tolerated and have apparently become commonplace, is not inconsistent with the rhetorical universalism of 1:11. It was one thing to feel sympathy, and even affection for the heathen; it was quite a different thing to allow the purity of Israel's religion, already corrupted by the indifference and neglect of the people and their leaders, to be further diluted by introducing into Jewish families wives and mothers who had no knowledge or understanding of Israel's God. There is abundant evidence in our own day that mixed marriages on the whole tend to undermine religious loyalties. The RSV is undoubtedly right in understanding *qōdhesh* to mean concretely **the sanctuary.** Since it was believed that in some

---

cult of irrationality always invites the imperative voice out of the whirlwind. The priest of God must get and keep sound knowledge. The cult of irrationality may satisfy and thus serve the two extremes of pathetic ignorance and sophisticated disillusionment. It can mean little or nothing to the great mass of sober Christians between these extremes.

10. The Basis of Brotherhood.—Philosophers have always said that, however important it may be to find someone who knows the answer to a question, it is even more important in the

first instance to find someone who knows what the question is. This verse is an instance of that proposition. The questions which Malachi asks are not rhetorical, they are real and supremely important.

Many, if not most, of the tragedies in human interrelationships arise from the failure to ask Malachi's questions at the outset. Enduring human relationships always presuppose a common interest and a common reality shared by those concerned. Thus Browning says of his two lovers that behind them was "a shadowy

12 The LORD will cut off the man that doeth this, the master and the scholar, out of the tabernacles of Jacob, and him that offereth an offering unto the LORD of hosts.

13 And this have ye done again, covering the altar of the LORD with tears, with weeping, and with crying out, insomuch that he regardeth not the offering any more, or receiveth *it* with good will at your hand.

14 ¶ Yet ye say, Wherefore? Because the LORD hath been witness between thee and the wife of thy youth, against whom thou hast dealt treacherously: yet *is* she thy companion, and the wife of thy covenant.

foreign god. **12** May the LORD cut off from the tents of Jacob, for the man who does this, any to witness[g] or answer, or to bring offering to the LORD of hosts!

13 And this again you do. You cover the LORD's altar with tears, with weeping and groaning because he no longer regards the offering or accepts it with favor at your hand. **14** You ask, "Why does he not?" Because the LORD was witness to the covenant between you and the wife of your youth, to whom you have been faithless, though she is your companion and your wife by cove-

g Cn Compare Gk: Heb *arouse*

way God actually dwelt in the temple, the presence in its vicinity of anyone or anything unconsecrated to him, such as a woman of heathen religion, **the daughter of a foreign god,** could be regarded as a profanation. The prevalence of mixed marriages is an important clue to the date of the book (see Intro., p. 1117; cf. Neh. 13:23-28; Ezra 9–10).

12. The prophet announces a curse upon those who have so slight a sense of communal loyalty as to contract mixed marriages. They are to be solemnly **excommunicated** from Israel. By a slight emendation (עֵד for עֵר) the RSV gets the meaning **any to witness** from the mysterious word which the KJV (following the tradition preserved in the Vulg.) translates **the master** (the Hebrew means, literally, "one who arouses"). This is the most plausible rendering of a difficult passage although it is not supported by the ancient versions. The excommunicated person is to be deprived of access to the law courts and to the temple.

13. As noted in the Intro. (p. 1117), some scholars regard this verse as the continuation of vs. 10, vss. 11-12 being an interpolation. However, it is more probable that the present order is original and this verse marks the beginning of a second item or second stage in the indictment. In vss. 11-12 the charge is faithlessness toward God and the community; in the following verses, the charge is faithlessness toward wives. The precise meaning of vs. 13 is uncertain because the Hebrew is ambiguous. The translation of the RSV is attractive and helps to connect the whole passage with the general message of the book. If this interpretation is correct, the people are represented as complaining of the hardness of the times and lamenting that God no longer answers their prayers.

14. The prophet is quite sure that the distress of the times is in large measure due to the general contempt for the solemn obligations of marriage. The special mention of **the wife of thy youth** seems to show that elderly Jewish wives were being put aside so that husbands might marry young and attractive girls from the neighboring nations. Note that, if the usual interpretation is correct, monogamy is apparently assumed as the normal practice. Marriage, says the prophet, is not a matter of private arrangement or personal convenience, but a solemn **covenant** entered into before God (marriage seems to be called a covenant also in Ezek. 16:8; Prov. 2:17), and its obligations may not be disregarded for frivolous reasons.

third." [7] No two human beings can be all in all to each other. The basis of their affection is a fund of common concerns, ultimately none other than a mutual devotion to God.

So with rival classes in society and anti-

[7] "By the Fireside," st. xlvi.

pathetic states or races. They will never achieve permanent peace on the ground of direct human relationships alone. They must acknowledge and rest upon a brotherhood which derives from the fatherhood of God. Someone has said that the broken link between classes in the

15 And did not he make one? Yet had he the residue of the Spirit. And wherefore one? That he might seek a godly seed. Therefore take heed to your spirit, and let none deal treacherously against the wife of his youth.

16 For the LORD, the God of Israel, saith that he hateth putting away: for *one* covereth violence with his garment, saith the LORD of hosts: therefore take heed to your spirit, that ye deal not treacherously.

17 ¶ Ye have wearied the LORD with your words. Yet ye say, Wherein have we wearied *him?* When ye say, Every one that doeth evil *is* good in the sight of the LORD, and he delighteth in them; or, Where *is* the God of judgment?

nant. **15** Has not the one God made[h] and sustained for us the spirit of life?[i] And what does he desire? Godly offspring. So take heed to yourselves, and let none be faithless to the wife of his youth. **16** "For I hate[j] divorce, says the LORD the God of Israel, and covering one's garment with violence, says the LORD of hosts. So take heed to yourselves and do not be faithless."

17 You have wearied the LORD with your words. Yet you say, "How have we wearied him?" By saying, "Every one who does evil is good in the sight of the LORD, and he delights in them." Or by asking, "Where is the God of justice?"

[h] Or *has he not made one?*
[i] Cn: Heb *and a remnant of spirit was his*
[j] Cn: Heb *he hates*

15. In the Hebrew this is one of the most obscure verses in the entire O.T. Almost every word raises a question. The reading of the RSV is a reasonable conjecture and may be accepted provisionally. The point seems to be that the purpose of marriage is the strengthening of God's chosen people by the rearing of children who will hold fast to the ancient traditions (**Godly offspring**), a purpose which is defeated when wives and mothers in Israel are daughters "of a foreign god" (vs. 11).

16. The particular situation in his day leads the prophet to announce (if the text is correct) a general truth which is found nowhere else in the O.T.—that God is opposed to divorce. This verse also is corrupt in the Hebrew and the versions render it very differently. The difficulties may result in part from the fact that ancient Jewish tradition did not accept Malachi's general condemnation of divorce (see Intro., p. 1120). The Targ. (with which the LXX and Vulg. closely agree) paraphrases, "If thou hate her, divorce her." Von Bulmerincq finds in the verse an explicit command to put away the foreign wife whom God hates. It seems better, however, to hold to the plain general sense of the Hebrew, while recognizing that the evidence is not unambiguous. There are parallels in Arabic literature (Koran 2:183) to the figurative use of **garment** in the sense of "wife." That the prophet is no mere ritualist or fanatical nationalist, but a man of deep human sympathies, is shown by his perception that the divorce of a faithful wife is an act of cruelty toward her as a person as well as an act of disloyalty to God.

V. WHERE IS THE GOD OF JUSTICE? (2:17–3:5)

17. The prophet again returns to the problem of theodicy. The ills of the time, he says, are due in part to the fact that God has become tired of hearing the people complain of his injustice. With the growing sophistication of the postexilic age and the growth of rationalism, a skeptical spirit threatened to undermine the prophetic faith in a righteous God who rewards the good and punishes the evil. Sin seems to prosper (cf. Ps. 73:3-12) and righteousness seems to be useless (3:14; Eccl. 9:13-15). Many passages in the later literature are concerned with the problem of reconciling

modern world is a fundamental defect of the imagination. That statement is true as far as it goes. One must make, by acts of imagination, a deliberate effort to enter into, to understand, and thus to share, the lives of others. But even this act—and it is the most mature form of unselfishness in that it is an unselfishness of

mind and heart rather than of the purse—remains imperfect unless it presupposes the thought of God as the ground and warrant for our human interdependence.

It is one of the tragedies of our time that nations which still acknowledge God are faced with other nations which are professedly athe-

3 Behold, I will send my messenger, and he shall prepare the way before me: and the Lord, whom ye seek, shall suddenly come to his temple, even the messenger of the covenant, whom ye delight in: behold, he shall come, saith the LORD of hosts.

2 But who may abide the day of his coming? and who shall stand when he appeareth? for he *is* like a refiner's fire, and like fullers' soap:

3 "Behold, I send my messenger to prepare the way before me, and the Lord whom you seek will suddenly come to his temple; the messenger of the covenant in whom you delight, behold, he is coming, says the LORD of hosts. 2 But who can endure the day of his coming, and who can stand when he appears?

"For he is like a refiner's fire and like

God's supposed justice with the evident inequalities of life (Eccl. 9:2-3, 11; Pss. 37; 73; Hab. 1:13).

3:1. Malachi answers that, evil as the present time may seem, God is coming soon to correct its inequities. The distinctive feature of Malachi's eschatology is that it involves two acts: first, the coming of the **messenger,** to purify the temple cult and the priesthood (vs. 3) and, second, the coming of the Lord himself to his purified **temple** to judge his people according to their deserts. The clause **whom you seek** refers to the question at the end of 2:17. The editor who wrote the superscription to the book understood **my messenger** (*mal'ākhî*) to be the prophet; the editor who added 4:5-6 thought it was Elijah. The prophet himself was not thinking in such definite terms. The messenger is simply a divine being whose prototype is "the angel of the LORD" who appears in the early legends of Israel (e.g., Judg. 13:3). The words **the messenger of the covenant . . . he is coming,** which somewhat confuse the picture, are probably the parenthetical note of a commentator who wished to explain that even at this second stage it would not be the transcendent God in the fullness of his being (the tendency of priestly theology was to remove God as far as possible from direct contact with men), but his angel or messenger—a special revelational manifestation of God—who would finally appear in the temple.

2-4. The purpose of the preliminary coming of the messenger is to purify the temple and its ministers in preparation for the full advent of God the judge. Quite in accordance with the ancient view, God is conceived of as a king and the temple is his palace (I Kings 8:13). He cannot come until his house is set in order. His messenger

---

istic. Thus prayer is prohibited at some international conferences, and exception is taken even to a moment of silence before a session opens, lest believers in God make use of that silence for an act of devotion which those who deny God disapprove of. This situation is a poor basis for peacemaking.

The answer to Malachi's questions are to be found in Augustine's matchless passage, which is fully biblical in its spirit and content: "Blessed is he who loves Thee, and his friend in Thee, and his enemy for Thee. For he alone loses no one dear to him, to whom all are dear in Him who never can be lost." [8]

3:1. *The Need of the Forerunner.*—The doctrine of the forerunner became a fixed item in the messianic hope of Israel. At a later time the ministry of Jesus was prefaced by that of John the Baptist, and the ministry of the Baptist was construed both as a preparation for the

ministry of Jesus and indeed a portent of the messiahship itself.

Whether as a part of the prophetic expectation or as a recorded fact in the Gospels, the place of the forerunner in religious history is one which is well recognized. Many a reformer and pioneer has failed in his would-be mission to his age, not because he was mistaken or lacking in integrity, but rather because the soil of the common mind was not yet ready to receive his message. Thus Ezekiel, after having prophesied to the people whose ears were deaf to his words, cried out: "Ah Lord GOD! they say of me, Doth he not speak parables? . . . The vision that he seeth is for many days to come, and he prophesieth of the times that are far off" (Ezek. 20:49; 12:27).

The Protestant Reformation did not begin with the nailing of Luther's theses on the church door at Wittenberg in 1517. That act and the events which followed in swift succession were the consummation of processes which had been

[8] *Confessions* IV. 9. 14.

3 And he shall sit *as* a refiner and purifier of silver: and he shall purify the sons of Levi, and purge them as gold and silver, that they may offer unto the LORD an offering in righteousness.

4 Then shall the offering of Judah and Jerusalem be pleasant unto the LORD, as in the days of old, and as in former years.

5 And I will come near to you to judgment; and I will be a swift witness against the sorcerers, and against the adulterers, and against false swearers, and against those that oppress the hireling in *his* wages, the widow, and the fatherless, and that turn aside the stranger *from his right,* and fear not me, saith the LORD of hosts.

fullers' soap; 3 he will sit as a refiner and purifier of silver, and he will purify the sons of Levi and refine them like gold and silver, till they present right offerings to the LORD.

4 Then the offering of Judah and Jerusalem will be pleasing to the LORD as in the days of old and as in former years.

5 "Then I will draw near to you for judgment; I will be a swift witness against the sorcerers, against the adulterers, against those who swear falsely, against those who oppress the hireling in his wages, the widow and the orphan, against those who thrust aside the sojourner, and do not fear me, says the LORD of hosts.

will straighten out the abuses described in 1:6–2:9, and will restore the golden days of old, when worship was offered to God with dignity and in sincerity of heart (2:6) .

5. When the temple has been cleansed and the house prepared for its Master, then God will come to set right the injustices which make men doubt his goodness. Here one sees that Malachi is no mere ritualist, in the sense of being preoccupied with cultic sins to the exclusion of sins against humanity. Looking more deeply into the human heart than some of his predecessors, he saw that contempt for the symbols of religion may be not a sign of spiritual emancipation, but the symptom of a profound contempt for religion and morality itself. But like the greatest of his predecessors, he regards sins against the social order as the sins with which God is most particularly concerned. In this list only sorcery might be classed as a "religious" sin (in the narrow sense) ; all the others are social, and the prophet lays chief emphasis upon the wickedness of those who exploit the weak and helpless. In the court which will be set up God will be both the judge and the principal witness, and the swiftness of his procedure then will make it plain that his apparent failure to act previously was not the result of impotence or indifference.

going on for at least two hundred years prior to that time. So construed, the Reformation was the culmination of a long period of preparation at the hands of the predecessors of Luther, Calvin, and Zwingli. These pre-Reformers, Wycliff, Huss, *et al.,* were forerunners of the finally fulfilled movement.

These facts are not without their suggestion for us today. It was much the fashion in the years before World War I to assume that the social gospel was so far advanced in its victories that our Western world was in sight of the utopian order which was its goal. In an eager and holy impatience we were like those impetuous first disciples who "thought that the kingdom should immediately appear" (Luke 19:11) . This expectation rested upon a superficial appraisal of our culture, and failed to reckon with the deeper and underlying causes for moral disquiet. This hope was, however, none the less widely held, and the disillusionment of the intervening years has been to no small de-

gree responsible for that loss of religion which many one-time optimists now confess. Plainly there was need of far more preliminary spade work by forerunners of a Christian society than was at hand a generation ago.

The experience of these years should have persuaded us that the postponement of the realization of our "messianic" hopes is in itself an indication of our proper part and place in the longer reaches of Christian history. There is little to hope for from persons who suffer from premature "messianic delusions," however sincere they may be. But there is much needful work to be done in prophetic service of the Christian cause by those who construe their discipleship as the task of the forerunner, and can say with good confidence: "He it is, who coming after me is preferred before me. . . . He must increase, but I must decrease" (John 1:27; 3:30) .

3. The Refining of Our Lives.—George La Piana, the Harvard church historian, has said

6 For I *am* the Lord, I change not; therefore ye sons of Jacob are not consumed.

7 ¶ Even from the days of your fathers ye are gone away from mine ordinances, and have not kept *them*. Return unto me, and I will return unto you, saith the Lord of hosts. But ye said, Wherein shall we return?

8 ¶ Will a man rob God? Yet ye have robbed me. But ye say, Wherein have we robbed thee? In tithes and offerings.

9 Ye *are* cursed with a curse: for ye have robbed me, *even* this whole nation.

10 Bring ye all the tithes into the storehouse, that there may be meat in mine house, and prove me now herewith, saith the Lord of hosts, if I will not open you the windows of heaven, and pour you out a blessing, that *there shall* not *be room* enough *to receive it.*

6 "For I the Lord do not change; therefore you, O sons of Jacob, are not consumed.

7 From the days of your fathers you have turned aside from my statutes and have not kept them. Return to me, and I will return to you, says the Lord of hosts. But you say, 'How shall we return?' **8** Will man rob God? Yet you are robbing me. But you say, 'How are we robbing thee?' In your tithes and offerings. **9** You are cursed with a curse, for you are robbing me; the whole nation of you. **10** Bring the full tithes into the storehouse, that there may be food in my house; and thereby put me to the test, says the Lord of hosts, if I will not open the windows of heaven for you and pour

---

VI. The Sins of the Common People (3:6-12)

6. Even when one omits, with almost all commentators, the word **for** as an artificial connective introduced by an editor, the verse still remains difficult. The KJV and the RSV give a literal translation of the second half, but the sense is not clear.

7. God is faithful (vs. 6), but Israel is faithless and has always been so. This is the reason for the recurrent failure of the crops (vss. 10-11), which has caused the people to complain that God has deserted them. If they return to God, God will return to them. The thought is not that merely of turning in a particular direction, but of retracing one's steps. The people of Israel must return to the road from which they have wandered. While repentance must of course involve a basic change of attitude, yet to the Hebrew mind such a change must necessarily manifest itself in action. But what action? As in previous instances (1:6; 2:17), the prophet's interlocutors demand that he shall be more specific in his charges. "In what respect have we gone astray and therefore must return?"

8. The prophet quickly descends from the general charge of infidelity to the specific one of "robbing God." The word קבע, **rob,** is a rare one, occurring elsewhere only in Prov. 22:23. The imaginary audience presses the prophet still further and demands that he itemize his charges. He replies that they have been disregarding the statutes which ordered the giving of a tithe and other specified offerings for the support of the temple. No doubt they pleaded the hardness of the times.

9. As vs. 10 shows, the **curse** with which they are cursed is the failure of their crops and the suffering which necessarily follows. The prophet intentionally here applies to the people a word for **nation** (*gôy*) which is ordinarily used only of the heathen.

10-12. If only they will fulfill the law and pay their debt to God in full, he will give them a prosperous season. Malachi is here merely repeating the dogma of retribution,

---

that every religious movement passes through three stages: the ethical, the theological, the aesthetic. It begins as an instinctive moral reform; it goes on to the reflective formulation of its faith and practice; finally it elaborates in terms of beauty its buildings and the apparatus of its worship. The last of these stages marks a

point of intellectual arrest and often of incipient moral decay. The movement must then be born again in a fresh reformation, primarily moral in its intention.

There is every reason why we should give hard thought to the substance of our theology, and added reason for enriching our worship;

11 And I will rebuke the devourer for your sakes, and he shall not destroy the fruits of your ground; neither shall your vine cast her fruit before the time in the field, saith the LORD of hosts.

12 And all nations shall call you blessed: for ye shall be a delightsome land, saith the LORD of hosts.

13 ¶ Your words have been stout against me, saith the LORD. Yet ye say, What have we spoken *so much* against thee?

14 Ye have said, It *is* vain to serve God: and what profit *is it* that we have kept his ordinance, and that we have walked mournfully before the LORD of hosts?

down for you an overflowing blessing. 11 I will rebuke the devourer[k] for you, so that it will not destroy the fruits of your soil; and your vine in the field shall not fail to bear, says the LORD of hosts. 12 Then all nations will call you blessed, for you will be a land of delight, says the LORD of hosts.

13 "Your words have been stout against me, says the LORD. Yet you say, 'How have we spoken against thee?' 14 You have said, 'It is vain to serve God. What is the good of our keeping his charge or of walking as in mourning before the LORD of hosts?

[k] Or *devouring locust*

to which Deuteronomy gives classical expression (Deut. 28:15; cf. 28:1-2, 12). It has often been noticed that the law to which Malachi apparently refers is that of the Priestly Code, which required the entire tithe to be paid to the temple (Lev. 27:30; Num. 18:21), rather than that of Deuteronomy (14:22-28; 26:12), which ordered it to be used ordinarily to provide a ceremonial feast for the giver and his friends and every third year to be set aside for charity. This does not mean that Malachi is later than P, but merely that the change in the law of the tithe which P embodies had already come into effect. As is the case with all codes of law, the Priestly Code crystallized the final result of a long period of development. When the people show their inner devotion to God by faithfully obeying his laws, the prophet says, and by contributing as they should to his worship, the rains will fall, the locusts will not come, the fields will bring forth their crops abundantly and without fail (Deut. 11:13-15). Then all the surrounding peoples will look at their prosperity and know that God is truly with them.

VII. WHAT IS THE GOOD OF SERVING GOD? (3:13–4:3)

13. The insistent question which Malachi hears his stubborn audience repeating to him over and over again is treated once more in this last oracle. The people say, "Why is God treating us so badly?" The prophet answers, "Your hearts are alienated and you have been saying harsh things against him. If you have no faith in him, how can you expect him to bless you?" The people then demand a more specific answer.

14. While there were always a few bold cynics who openly scoffed at religious beliefs and practice (cf. Pss. 14:1; 42:3; 73:11), the prophet is not here concerned with them.

but if these preoccupations mark a decline in moral earnestness, they are not of themselves guarantees of the survival of religion. The burden of the prophets and the teaching of Jesus were often aimed at theological sophistication and ceremonial elaboration. The alloy of pedantry and aestheticism needs constantly to be refined out of what should be the pure metal of a morally earnest faith.

14. *The Doctrine of Rewards.*—When Satan stood before the Lord he asked, "Doth Job fear God for nought?" (Job 1:9.) Satan, the prover of men's integrity, was apparently unable to believe that any man serves God for nought.

Our religious faith and practice have their consequences in our character and often in our

circumstance. No one will deny the sequence of cause and effect in the religious life. There are rewards and punishments, which can be identified in retrospect. Jesus seems to have recognized this sequence in the reiterated statement in the Sermon on the Mount: "Verily I say unto you, They have their reward" (Matt. 6:2 ff.). They got what they deserved; they were paid in kind, and in the terms of their original investment. They wanted to be seen of men, and they were seen of men. The transaction began and ended there. Conversely, the pure in heart were also paid in kind; they saw God.

But recognition of this reliability in the moral and spiritual order was not, and is not, a

15 And now we call the proud happy; yea, they that work wickedness are set up; yea, *they that* tempt God are even delivered.

16 ¶ Then they that feared the LORD spake often one to another: and the LORD hearkened, and heard *it,* and a book of remembrance was written before him for them that feared the LORD, and that thought upon his name.

15 Henceforth we deem the arrogant blessed; evildoers not only prosper but when they put God to the test they escape.' "

16 Then those who feared the LORD spoke with one another; the LORD heeded and heard them, and a book of remembrance was written before him of those who feared the LORD and thought on his name.

He is speaking rather of the genuinely pious members of the community who are disturbed by the first stirring of doubt in their own minds. In view of the unrelieved hardships of the time, they were beginning to question the value of piety and the efficacy of the practices of religion. God seemed to pay no attention to their prayers, fasts, and sacrifices.

15. The only people who seemed to prosper were the rugged individualists who had no regard either for God or their neighbors and who regarded religion as a refuge for incompetent weaklings. To raise questions is never of course a sign of an essentially irreligious spirit, but may be quite the contrary. As in the cases of Jeremiah (12:1-2), Habakkuk (1:13), and the author of the book of Job, such doubts may be an indication of growing sensitivity and thoughtfulness. Malachi treats it as such and in the following verses deals very gently with these people.

16. It is best to follow the LXX and Syriac and read "thus" instead of **then.** These were things which the pious were beginning to say. However, God is aware of their difficulties. Even if he does not act immediately to answer prayer and correct injustice, yet he keeps a careful record in heaven of those who reverently serve him. One day he will reward them according to the faithfulness which they have shown. This belief in the heavenly **book of remembrance** contains the germ out of which would one day develop the doctrine of eternal life for the righteous. (Oskar Holtzmann, "Der Prophet Maleachi und der Ursprung des Pharisäerbundes," *Archiv für Religionswissenschaft,* XXIX [1931], 1-21, dates Malachi in the high priesthood of Simon [142-135 B.C.], and argues that this verse gives an account of the founding of the Pharisaic party. While the date is impossible, the article is valuable as indicating the spiritual affinities of

---

warrant for making the hope of reward and the fear of punishment a motive for action in the first instance. Religion as it matures moves away from magic toward mysticism. The essence of magic is the attempt to manipulate God in one's own behalf and the hope of rewards which will follow the use of the correct formula. Mysticism aims at the selfless love of God for his own sake, thus letting the consequences of that love take care of themselves.

The great Christian mystics have always preached the doctrine of "the unmercenary love of God," i.e., a love apart from the hope of rewards or the fear of punishments. The unknown author of the *Theologia Germanica,* anonymous because he was so sincerely selfless, says that the most fully religious persons are "those who are enlightened with the True Light, who do not practice things for reward, for they neither look nor desire to get anything thereby, but all that they do is from love alone. . . . A lover of God is better and dearer to him than a

hundred thousand hirelings [who obey for the sake of reward]." [9]

This is an austere ideal, but it should remain our ideal. There is such a thing as art for art's sake, duty for duty's sake, service of one's country for the country's sake, devotion to a profession like medicine for its own sake. Such indeed is the genius of the professions as against the trades which are based on the premise of profit. Our religion ought not to fall below these levels of the secular life round about. Indeed, it should interpret and inspire all selfless motives for conduct. In so far as our Christianity is a profession rather than a trade, it moves away from the mercenary to "the unmercenary love of God."

16. *Speaking Out.*—It was said of the poet Thomas Gray that "he never spoke out." Perhaps he was right. There is an ugly vice which is known as exhibitionism. It has its unpleasant counterpart in the religious life, as a

[9] Boston: J. P. Jewett & Co., 1856, pp. 127-28.

17 And they shall be mine, saith the Lord of hosts, in that day when I make up my jewels; and I will spare them, as a man spareth his own son that serveth him.

18 Then shall ye return, and discern between the righteous and the wicked, between him that serveth God and him that serveth him not.

4 For, behold, the day cometh, that shall burn as an oven; and all the proud, yea, and all that do wickedly, shall be stubble: and the day that cometh shall burn them up, saith the Lord of hosts, that it shall leave them neither root nor branch.

2 ¶ But unto you that fear my name shall the Sun of righteousness arise with healing in his wings; and ye shall go forth, and grow up as calves of the stall.

---

17 "They shall be mine, says the Lord of hosts, my special possession on the day when I act, and I will spare them as a man spares his son who serves him. 18 Then once more you shall distinguish between the righteous and the wicked, between one who serves God and one who does not serve him.

4¹ "For behold, the day comes, burning like an oven, when all the arrogant and all evildoers will be stubble; the day that comes shall burn them up, says the Lord of hosts, so that it will leave them neither root nor branch. 2 But for you who fear my name the sun of righteousness shall rise, with healing in its wings. You shall go forth leaping like calves from the stall.

¹ Ch 4. 1-6 are Ch 3. 19-24 in the Hebrew

Malachi and its relation to later partisan movements. This verse illustrates the disintegration of a sense of national solidarity and the rise of a separate group of "the pious.")

17. The answer which the prophet gives to the doubts of the pious is essentially the same answer as that which he gave in 2:17–3:6. It is the eschatological answer. Very soon the day of the Lord is coming, and when that day of wrath and mourning (Zeph. 1:14-18) comes, God will not destroy the righteous with the wicked—as some of the older prophets had implied—but will set apart the faithful among his people and make them his special treasure. To the wicked he will come as a judge; but to the righteous he will be as a father (cf. 1:6; 2:10).

18. If the RSV is right in taking the Hebrew idiom to mean **once more,** the thought is that in the day of judgment God's justice will become as evident as in the idyllic days of the distant past.

4:1. The oracle concludes with a hymn like the *Dies Irae,* a vivid description of the coming of the day of judgment. As in many of the later apocalypses (e.g., Matt. 3:10-12), its coming is pictured as like a destructive and purifying fire which will consume the wicked, who now seem so strong and firmly rooted, as quickly as a flame consumes a handful of straw. The **oven** is a small portable fire pot, used for baking.

2. Unlike most such eschatological hymns, the purpose of this one is not to inspire terror in the hearts of the wicked, but rather to comfort the devout, who had been tempted to doubt the value of religion (3:14) and to speak bitterly of God's justice (3:13). When the day comes, they will enter into their reward. To **fear my name** means "to practice reverently my religion." The beautiful image of **the sun of righteousness** is derived from the symbolism of Egyptian religion—a symbolism also found elsewhere in the ancient Near East—in which the winged disk of the sun is often represented as

---

matter of wearing one's heart on one's sleeve, of exposing to the curious crowd one's most intimate and sacred things. Religion should always preserve a certain sensitive reticence. To exhibit one's soul too freely and too often is to run the risk of losing the sense of one's sanctities. In a moment of indiscretion Hezekiah showed the king of Babylon's envoys all his treasures. Isaiah asked him: "What have they seen in thine house? And Hezekiah answered, All that is in mine house have they seen: there

is nothing among my treasures that I have not showed them" (Isa. 39:4). But that indiscretion, as the prophet went on to say, was to cost Hezekiah those treasures. So it is with the inner sanctities of our life.

Most of us, however, err in the other direction. Our reticences become studied silences. We become too self-conscious, too shy to speak freely about religion, particularly to those closest to us. It is hard to learn to speak simply, naturally, directly, and without affectation about

3 And ye shall tread down the wicked; for they shall be ashes under the soles of your feet in the day that I shall do *this,* saith the LORD of hosts.

4 ¶ Remember ye the law of Moses my servant, which I commanded unto him in Horeb for all Israel, *with* the statutes and judgments.

5 ¶ Behold, I will send you Elijah the prophet before the coming of the great and dreadful day of the LORD:

6 And he shall turn the heart of the fathers to the children, and the heart of the

3 And you shall tread down the wicked, for they will be ashes under the soles of your feet, on the day when I act, says the LORD of hosts.

4 "Remember the law of my servant Moses, the statutes and ordinances that I commanded him at Horeb for all Israel.

5 "Behold, I will send you Eli'jah the prophet before the great and terrible day of the LORD comes. **6** And he will turn the hearts of fathers to their children and the

---

a source of protection and blessing (see J. H. Breasted, *The Dawn of Conscience* [New York: Charles Scribner's Sons, 1933], Fig. 3; cf. Figs. 16, 19). The joy which will then drive out all present gloom is compared to the healthy exuberance of a calf when released from the confinement of its stall.

3. The imagery of this verse is not attractive to the Christian, but is intended merely to picture as vividly as possible the complete triumph of the good and the defeat of the wicked. Oriental kings sometimes actually trod upon the necks of their defeated foes (cf. Josh. 10:24).

VIII. CONCLUSION TO THE BOOK OF THE TWELVE (4:4-6)

4. At some time during the process of arranging the material in its present canonical form, a scribal editor appended to the whole collection of the Book of the Twelve this brief summary of what he regarded as the main burden of its teaching (cf. the editorial note in Eccl. 12:13-14). His point of view is legalistic rather than prophetic.

5-6. These verses are a later exegetical note intended to supplement the eschatology of 3:13–4:3 by a reference to the more elaborate eschatological scheme of 3:1-5, where the coming of the Lord is preceded by the coming of his messenger, and also to identify the mysterious "messenger" with **Elijah the prophet.** The commentator presumably picked on Elijah because of the latter's ascension into heaven (II Kings 2:1-11), which would seem to make him available for this kind of mission. As a result of this bit of

---

religion to those whom one knows best; but we should discipline ourselves in this delicate art. Particularly in these troubled times of the world's history we should keep in unaffected touch with our fellow Christians. Too studied a silence is as grave a mistake as too indiscreet self-exhibition in speech. This ought to be a time when "they that love the Lord speak often one to another."

4:6. *The Link Between the Generations.*— The link between the generations often wears very thin and sometimes breaks. Misunderstanding between parents and children, between the older and the younger generation, is a commonplace in our homes and in our wider societies. In a sense this ought always to be so. For unless the oncoming generation deserves and achieves its own independent life, there can be no such thing as progress in history. Were it not for that breakaway of eternal youth, we should still be gnawing bones in the caves of prehis-

toric man, living after the pattern of life observed by our distant forebears.

The break, however, ought not to be final. It is, or should be, the prelude to a mature relationship in which parent and child come to a new understanding and reaffirm their interdependence. Thus the grown-up son makes a deeper peace with his father than he ever could have had in childhood, the grown-up daughter with her mother. All the preliminary discipline in the earlier relationship looks to this later welding of the links between the generations into a stronger tie than existed at the first. This should be as true in our churches as in our homes. Whatever the immediate misunderstanding between the generations, which so often seems to involve rebellious youth in controversy with unyielding age, both old and young should keep always in mind the ultimate meaning of these clashes of temperament, which is finally discovered in the day when the hearts

children to their fathers, lest I come and smite the earth with a curse.

hearts of children to their fathers, lest I come and smite the land with a curse."*m*

m Or ban of utter destruction

speculative exegesis, the figure of Elijah came to have a considerable role to play in later apocalyptic thought (cf. Ecclus. 48:10; Mark 6:15; 9:4, 11) and in rabbinical literature (Mishnah, Baba Metzia 1:8; 2:8; 3:4-5; Eduyoth 8:7). The commentator has changed the messenger's task somewhat from that which Malachi assigned in 3:3. He is not to prepare the temple for the Lord's coming but to restore peace and social well-being to the community so as to avert God's wrath in the day of judgment. Jewish tradition (the Massorah) requires vs. 5 to be repeated after vs. 6 in public reading, so that the Book of the Twelve will not end with a threat.

of the father shall be turned to the children and the hearts of the children to the fathers.

This is the secret of the unbroken continuity of our religion in history as it is shared by the successive generations. What Edmund Burke in his *Reflections on the Revolution in France* said of politics and the state may be said with even greater truth of Christian homes and the Christian church:

As the ends of such a partnership cannot be obtained in many generations, it becomes a partnership not only between those who are living, but between those who are living, those who are dead, and those who are to be born. Each contract . . . is but a clause in the great primaeval contract of eternal society, . . . connecting the visible and invisible world.[1]

[1] *The Works of the Right Honourable Edmund Burke* (London: F. & C. Rivington, 1803), V, 184.

COMMITTEE FOR
TECHNICAL EDUCATION

• Gaza

PLAIN OF SHAR

• Beer-sheba

Samaria •

• Hebron

Mt. Gerizim   Mt. Ebal

• Jerusalem

• Jericho   Jordan Riv

SALT SEA

Mt. Nebo

• Rabbath- ammon

PALESTINE
in Old Testament Times